מחזור קורן ליום הכיפורים • נוסח אשכנז

The Koren Yom Kippur Mahzor • Nusah Ashkenaz

THE ROHR FAMILY EDITION

מחזור קורן ליום הכיפורים

THE KOREN YOM KIPPUR MAḤZOR

WITH INTRODUCTION, TRANSLATION AND COMMENTARY BY

Chief Rabbi Lord Jonathan Sacks שליט״א

•

KOREN PUBLISHERS JERUSALEM

The Koren Yom Kippur Maḥzor
The Rohr Family Edition
Second North American Hebrew/English Edition, 2013

Koren Publishers Jerusalem Ltd.
POB 4044, Jerusalem 91040, ISRAEL
POB 8531, New Milford, CT 06776, USA

www.korenpub.com

The creation of this Maḥzor was made possible through the generous support of Torah Education in Israel.

Standard Size, Hardcover, ISBN 978 965 301 345 2
Compact Size, Hardcover, ISBN 978 965 301 358 2

YKUSA20

דּוֹר לְדוֹר יְשַׁבַּח מַעֲשֶׂיךָ...

The Rohr Family Edition of
The Koren Yom Kippur Maḥzor
pays tribute to the memory of

Mrs. Charlotte Rohr (née Kastner) ע״ה
שרה בת ר׳ יקותיאל יהודה ע״ה

Born in Mukachevo, Czechoslovakia
to an illustrious Hasidic family,
she survived the fires of the *Shoah*
to become the elegant and gracious matriarch,
first in Colombia and later in the United States,
of a family nurtured by her love and unstinting devotion.
She found grace in the eyes of all whose lives she touched,
and merited to see all her children build lives
enriched by faithful commitment
to the spreading of Torah and *Ahavat Yisrael.*

Dedicated with love by

The Rohr Family

NEW YORK & MIAMI, USA

CONTENTS

PREFACE

You have given us one day in the year,
a great and holy day, this Day of Atonement…

From the opening haunting melody of *Kol Nidrei* to the closing shofar blasts of *Ne'ila*, the prayers of Yom Kippur carry us on a journey of self-reflection, confession, and contrition – and ultimately, we hope, a rededication of our covenant with God. The ancient words of *tefilla* and the heartfelt poetry of *piyut* are our roadmap to *teshuva*, our path back home to the One who gifted us with this one day in the year on which the way is clear and open to all who seek to return. It is with hope and humility that we have created the *Koren Yom Kippur Maḥzor* to aid, support, and guide us on this long road home to God.

Once again, a project of this scope would have been virtually impossible without the partnership of the Rohr family, in memory of whose matriarch, Mrs. Charlotte Rohr ע״ה, it is dedicated. The Rohr family's passions for *Avodat HaShem* and for books come together in their support for the creation of this Maḥzor. On behalf of the scholars, editors and designers of this volume, we again thank you; on behalf of the users and readers of this Maḥzor, we are forever in your debt.

We could not have embarked on this project without the moral leadership and intellectual spark of Rabbi Lord Jonathan Sacks. Rabbi Sacks provides an invaluable guide to the liturgy through his remarkable introduction, translation, and commentary. His work not only clarifies the text and explains the teachings of our sages, but uniquely and seamlessly weaves profound concepts of Judaism into the reality of contemporary life. It was our distinct privilege to work with Rabbi Sacks to create a Maḥzor that we believe appropriately reflects the complexity and depth of Jewish prayer.

We only hope that Rabbi Sacks' contribution is matched by the scholarship, design and typography that have been hallmarks of Koren Publishers Jerusalem for more than fifty years. Raphaël Freeman led Koren's small but highly professional team of scholars, editors and artists. Rabbi David Fuchs supervised the textual aspects of the work. Rachel Meghnagi edited the English texts. Efrat Gross edited the Hebrew texts, and these were ably proofread by Baruch Braner and Yisrael Elizur.

Jessica Sacks supplied the superb translation to *Mishnayot Yoma* and Rabbi David Fuchs elucidated the *Mishnayot* commentary. We thank Dena Landowne Bailey and Chaya Mendelson for their invaluable assistance in assembling and typesetting the text. Rabbi Eli Clark contributed the informative and useful Halakha Guide, and we are grateful to Jessica Sacks and Adina Luber for their translation of the *piyutim*.

This new edition of the Koren Maḥzor continues the Koren tradition of making the language of prayer more accessible, thus enhancing the prayer experience. One of the unique features of the Maḥzor is the use of typesetting to break up a prayer phrase-by-phrase – rather than using a block paragraph format – so that the reader will naturally pause at the correct places. No commas appear in the Hebrew text at the end of lines, but in the English translation, where linguistic clarity requires, we have retained the use of commas at the end of lines. Unlike other Hebrew/English maḥzorim, the Hebrew text is on the left-hand page and the English on the right. This arrangement preserves the distinctive "fanning out" effect of the Koren text and the beauty of the Koren layout.

We hope and pray that this Maḥzor, like all our publications, extends the vision of Koren's founder, Eliyahu Koren, to a new generation to further *Avodat HaShem* for Jews everywhere.

Matthew Miller, Publisher
Jerusalem 5772 (2012)

INTRODUCTION

Ideas and Insights for Yom Kippur

by

CHIEF RABBI LORD

JONATHAN SACKS

INTRODUCTION

Yom Kippur is the holy of holies of Jewish time. Observed with immense ceremony in the Temple, almost miraculously rescued after the Temple was destroyed, sustained ever since with unparalleled awe, it is Judaism's answer to one of the most haunting of human questions: How is it possible to live the ethical life without an overwhelming sense of guilt, inadequacy and failure?

The distance between who we are and who we ought to be is, for most of us, vast. We fail. We fall. We give in to temptation. We drift into bad habits. We say or do things in anger we later deeply regret. We disappoint those who had faith in us. We betray those who trusted us. We lose friends. Sometimes our deepest relationships can fall apart. We experience frustration, shame, humiliation, remorse. We let others down. We let ourselves down. These things are not rare. They happen to all of us, even the greatest. One of the most powerful features of biblical narrative is that its portraits are not idealized. Its heroes are human. They too have their moments of self-doubt. They too sin.

Judaism sets the bar high, expecting great things of us in word and deed. So demanding are the Torah's commandments that we cannot but fall short some, even much, of the time. God asks us in some sense to be like Him ("Be holy for I, the Lord your God, am holy" [Lev. 19:2]). Yet how can we be equal to such a challenge when we are, and know we are, human, all too human? How can we fail to disappoint Him? Better surely to accept what we are than aspire to be better than we are. Yet this is a recipe for faint hearts and small spirits, and it is a route Judaism never took. Better to fail while striving greatly than not to strive at all.

Judaism's resolution to this tension is so radical that it transformed the moral horizons of humankind. It says that the God of love and forgiveness created us in love and forgiveness, asking that we love and forgive others. God does not ask us not to fail. Rather, He asks us to acknowledge our failures, repair what we have harmed, and move on, learning from our errors and growing thereby. Human life, thus conceived, is neither tragic nor mired in sin. But it is demanding, intensely so. Therefore at its heart there had to be an institution capable of transmuting guilt into moral growth, and estrangement from God or our fellow humans into reconciliation. That institution is Yom Kippur, when in total honesty we fast and afflict ourselves, confessing our failures and immersing ourselves, mystically and metaphorically, in the purifying waters of God's forgiving love.

I want in this introduction to tell the story of the day and the ideas it embodies, for it is one of the most fascinating narratives in the history of ethics and spirituality. In ancient times the day was celebrated in the form of a massive public ceremony set in the Temple in Jerusalem. The holiest man in Israel, the High Priest, entered the most sacred space, the Holy of Holies, confessed the sins of the nation using the holiest name of God, and secured atonement for all Israel. It was a moment of intense drama in the life of a people who believed, however fitfully, that their fate depended on their relationship with God, who knew that there is no life, let alone a nation, without sin, and who knew from their history that sin could be punished by catastrophe.

Crowds of people thronged the Temple in Jerusalem, hoping to catch a glimpse of the High Priest as he fulfilled his ministrations. We have eyewitness testimony of a Roman consul, Marcus, who served in Jerusalem at the time of the Second Temple. This is how he describes the procession that made its way to the Temple Mount:

> And this I have seen with my own eyes: first to go before [the High Priest] would be all those who were of the seed of the kings of Israel… A herald would go before them, crying, "Give honor to the house of David." After them came the house of Levi, and a herald crying, "Give honor to the house of Levi." There were thirty-six thousand of them, and all the prefects wore clothing of blue silk; and the priests, of whom there were twenty-four thousand, wore clothing of white silk.
>
> After them came the singers, and after them, the instrumentalists, then the trumpeters, then the guards of the gate, then the incense-makers, then the curtain-makers, then the watchmen and the treasurers, then a class called *chartophylax,* then all the workingmen who worked in the Sanctuary, then the seventy of the Sanhedrin, then a hundred priests with silver rods in their hands to clear the way. Then came the High Priest, and after him all the elders of the priesthood,

> two by two. And the heads of the academies stood at vantage points and cried, "Lord High Priest, may you come in peace! Pray to our Maker to grant us long life that we may engage in His Torah."*

It was a glittering spectacle, the closest of encounters between man and God at the supreme intersection of sacred time and space. The service itself was long and elaborate. The High Priest would be rehearsed in his rituals for seven days beforehand. Five times on the day itself he would have to immerse himself in a *mikveh* and change his robes: gold for his public appearances, plain white for his ministrations within the Holy of Holies. Three times he would make confession, first for himself and his family, then for his fellow priests, and finally for the people as a whole. Each time he used the holy name of God, the watching crowd would prostrate themselves, falling on their faces.

The confession involved a strange and unique ceremony. Two goats, identical in size, height and appearance, would be brought before the High Priest, and with them a box containing two plaques, one inscribed, "To the Lord," the other "To Azazel." Over the goat on which the lot "To Azazel" had fallen, he would confess the sins of the nation, and the goat would then be led by a special person selected for the task into the desert hills outside Jerusalem where it would plunge to its death from a steep precipice. If the confession had been effective, so an ancient tradition states, the red thread it carried would turn white.**

After the destruction of the Second Temple there would be no more such scenes. Now there was no High Priest, no sacrifice, no divine fire, no Levites singing praises or crowds thronging the precincts of Jerusalem and filling the Temple Mount. Above all there was no Yom Kippur ritual through which the people could find forgiveness.

It was then that a transformation took place that must constitute one of the great creative responses to tragedy in history. Tradition has cast Rabbi Akiva in the role of the savior of hope. The Mishna in *Yoma*, the tractate dedicated to Yom Kippur, tells us in effect that Rabbi Akiva could see a new possibility of atonement even in the absence of a High Priest

* Solomon ibn Verga, *Shevet Yehuda* (c. 1550), cited in Shmuel Yosef Agnon, *Days of Awe*. New York: Schocken, 1948, 255–258.

** Mishna, *Yoma*, ch. 1–7.

and a Temple. God Himself would purify His people without the need for an intermediary.* Even ordinary Jews could, as it were, come face to face with the *Shekhina*, the Divine Presence. They needed no one else to apologize for them. The drama that once took place in the Temple could now take place in the human heart. Yom Kippur was saved. It is not too much to say that Jewish faith was saved.

Every synagogue became a fragment of the Temple. Every prayer became a sacrifice. Every Jew became a kind of priest, offering God not an animal but instead the gathered shards of a broken heart. For if God was the God of everywhere, He could be encountered anywhere. And if there were places from which He seemed distant, then time could substitute for place. "Seek God where He is to be found, call on Him where He is close" (Is. 55:6) – this, said the sages, refers to the Ten Days of Repentance from Rosh HaShana to Yom Kippur (*Yevamot* 105a). Holy days became the surrogate for holy spaces. Yom Kippur became the Jerusalem of time, the holy city of the Jewish soul.

Thereafter it never lost its hold on the Jewish imagination. There is a tradition that during the Middle Ages, when Jews were being pressured under threat of expulsion or death to convert to Christianity or Islam, many who did so – the *anusim* or, as they were contemptuously called by the Spanish, *marranos* (swine) – often remained Jews in secret. Some scholars assert that once a year they would make their way to the synagogue on the night of Yom Kippur to reaffirm their Jewish identity.

More recently the story of Franz Rosenzweig (1886–1929) became emblematic. This young German-Jewish intellectual from a highly assimilated family had been persuaded by a friend to convert to Christianity. Insisting on entering the Church not as a pagan but as a Jew, he decided that his last Jewish act would be to go to synagogue. He traveled to Berlin in 1913 to spend Yom Kippur in a small orthodox synagogue as his last Jewish act.

The experience changed his life. A few days later he wrote that "Leaving Judaism no longer seems necessary to me and ... no longer possible." He became a *ba'al teshuva*, one of the greatest in the pre-war years. On postcards in the trenches of the First World War he wrote one of

* Mishna, *Yoma* 8:9.

the masterpieces of Jewish theology in the twentieth century, *The Star of Redemption*. He became a friend of Martin Buber and founded the *Judisches Lehrhaus*, the House of Jewish Learning, in Frankfurt.* For the secular *marranos* of the twentieth century as for their medieval forerunners, Yom Kippur was the day that touched the heart even of those who were otherwise estranged from their faith. It was the day of "coming home," one of the root meanings of the word *teshuva*.

And so it is for us. What has given Yom Kippur its unique place on the map of the Jewish heart is that it is the most intensely personal of all the festivals. Pesaḥ, Shavuot and Sukkot are celebrations of Jewish memory and history. They remind us of what it means to be a member of the Jewish people, sharing its past, its present and its hopes. Rosh HaShana, the anniversary of creation, is about what it means to be human under the sovereignty of God. But Yom Kippur is about what it means to be me, this unique person that I am. It makes us ask, What have I done with my life? Whom have I hurt or harmed? How have I behaved? What have I done with God's greatest gift, life itself? What have I lived for and what will I be remembered for? To be sure, we ask these questions in the company of others. Ours is a communal faith. We pray together, confess together and throw ourselves on God's mercy together. But Yom Kippur remains an intensely personal day of conscience and self-reckoning.

It is the day on which, as the Torah says five times, we are commanded to "afflict" ourselves.** Hence: no eating or drinking, no bathing, no anointing, no sexual relations, no leather shoes. It is customary for men to wear a *kittel*, a white garment reminiscent, some say, of the white tunic the High Priest wore when he entered the Holy of Holies (*Mateh Efrayim* 610:11). Others say it is like a burial shroud (Rema, ibid. 3). Either way, it reminds us of the truths we must face alone. The Torah says that "No man shall be in the Tent of Meeting when [Aaron] comes to make atonement in the holiest place, until he leaves" (Lev. 16:17). Like the High Priest on this holy day, we face God alone. We confront our mortality alone. Outwardly we are in the company of others, but inwardly we are giving a reckoning for our individual life, singular and unique. The fact that everyone else around us is doing likewise makes it bearable.

* Nahum N. Glatzer, *Franz Rosenzweig: His Life and Thought*. New York: Schocken, 1961.
** Leviticus 16:29, 31; 23:27, 32; Numbers 29:7.

◂ Fasting

Fasting and repenting, I stand between two selves, as the High Priest once stood facing two goats, symbolic of the duality of human nature. There is the self I see in the mirror and know in my darkest hours. I know how short life is and how little I have achieved. I remember, with a shame undiminished by the passing of time, the people I offended, wounded, disappointed; the promises I made but did not fulfill; the harsh words I said and the healing words I left unsaid. I know how insignificant I am in the scheme of things, one among billions who will live, die, and eventually vanish from living memory. I am next-to-nothing, a fleeting breath, a driven leaf: "dust you are and to dust you will return" (Gen. 3:19).

Yet there is a second self, the one I see in the reflection of God's love. It is not always easy to feel God's love but it is there, holding us gently, telling us that every wrong we repent of is forgiven, every act of kindness we perform is unforgotten, that we are here because God wants us to be and because there is work He needs us to do. He loves us as a parent loves a child and has a faith in us that never wavers however many times we fail. In Isaiah's words, "Though the mountains be shaken and the hills be removed, yet My unfailing love for you will not be shaken nor My covenant of peace be removed" (Is. 54:10). God, who "counts the number of the stars and calls each of them by name" (Ps. 147:4), knows each of us by name, and by that knowledge confers on us inalienable dignity and unconditional love. *Teshuva* means "coming home" to this second self and to the better angels of our nature.

The history of Yom Kippur stands in sharp contrast to that of Rosh HaShana. About the New Year, the biblical sources are sparse and enigmatic, but to the Day of Atonement the Torah devotes an entire and detailed chapter, Leviticus 16. On the face of it there is little left unsaid. This introduction will, however, argue otherwise. The intellectual history of Yom Kippur is still too little understood. Tracing it will take us through a dispute between two of the greatest rabbis of the Middle Ages, a study of the difference between the way priests and prophets understood the moral life, the power of the rabbinic mind to unite two institutions that had remained distinct throughout the whole of the biblical era, and much else besides. First, however, we begin with one of Judaism's greatest innovations, the idea of forgiveness itself.

A Brief History of Forgiveness

There are rare moments when the world changes and a new possibility is born: when the Wright brothers achieved the first man-made flight in 1903; or in 1969 when Neil Armstrong became the first man to set foot on the moon; or when five thousand years ago someone discovered that marks made in clay with a stick could, when the clay dried, become permanent signs, and thus writing and civilization were born.

The birth of forgiveness is one such moment. It is one of the most radical ideas ever to have been introduced into the moral imagination of humankind. Forgiveness is an action that is not a reaction. It breaks the cycle of stimulus-response, harm and retaliation, wrong and revenge, which has led whole cultures to their destruction and still threatens the future of the world. It frees individuals from the burden of their past, and humanity from the irreversibility of history. It tells us that enemies can become friends.

Forgiveness, writes David Konstan in an important philosophical study (*Before Forgiveness: The Origins of a Moral Idea*), did not exist before Judaism.* It is, on the face of it, an odd claim to make. Surely every culture has a need to avoid the sheer destructiveness of anger and vengeance that arises in every society when one person wrongs another. That is true, but not every society develops the idea of forgiveness. The ancient Greeks, for example, did not. Instead they had something else often mistaken for forgiveness, namely the *appeasement of anger.*

When someone harms someone else, the victim is angry and seeks revenge. This is clearly dangerous for the perpetrator who will then seek to calm the victim and move on. They may make excuses: It wasn't me, it was someone else. Or, it was me but I couldn't help it. Or, it was me but it was a small wrong, and I have done you much good in the past, so that on balance you should let it pass.

Alternatively, or in conjunction with these other strategies, the perpetrator may beg, plead, and perform some ritual of abasement or humiliation. This is a way of saying to the victim, "I am not really a threat." The Greek word *sungnome*, sometimes translated as forgiveness, really means, says Konstan, *exculpation* or *absolution*. It is not that I forgive you for what

* David Konstan, *Before Forgiveness: The Origins of a Moral Idea*. Cambridge: Cambridge University Press, 2010.

◂ you did

you did, but that I understand why you did it – you were caught up in circumstances beyond your control – or, alternatively, I do not need to take revenge because you have now shown by your deference to me that you hold me in proper respect. My dignity has been restored. The result of excuse or self-abasement is that, in the phrase of the book of Esther, "the anger of the king abated" (7:10). Appeasement is a way of defusing anger but it is not repentance and it does not lead to forgiveness.

There is a classic example of this in the Torah itself. In Genesis 32–33, Jacob is terrified at the prospect of his meeting with Esau. Twenty-two years earlier Jacob had fled into exile after taking Esau's blessing and hearing that his brother had vowed to kill him as soon as their father was dead. Now they are about to meet. Jacob hears that Esau is coming with a force of four hundred men. His response is a paradigm case of appeasement. He sends Esau gifts, accompanied by messengers. When Esau finally appears he abases himself, prostrating himself seven times to the ground. Repeatedly he calls Esau, "my lord" and himself, "your servant." Esau is placated. The two brothers embrace, weep and go their separate ways. Anger has been averted. But between them there has been appeasement, not forgiveness. Forgiveness plays no part in the story.

THE IDEA OF FREEDOM

Before forgiveness can enter the world, another world-changing idea had to appear: the idea of human freedom. Despite its centrality to Western thought, freedom – the ability to choose between alternatives and act in accordance with one's choices – is anything but self-evident and has been challenged in most cultures and ages.

The ancients did not think about it much, and when they did they were more inclined to deny it than affirm it. The human person was a boat adrift on the waves of an ocean, chaff blown by the wind, a plaything of the gods, a pawn moved by other hands, a slave, not the master, of his fate. We are what we are and we cannot change what we are.

Once our fate has been decided, there is nothing we can do to avoid it. Laius was told by the Delphic oracle that his son would kill him and take his place. Laius tried every way to ensure this did not come about. So did his son, Oedipus. Yet each plan they made to avoid the outcome helped make it happen. This – the idea of *moira*, inevitability, or *ananke*, blind fate – is at the heart of Greek tragedy and is central to its bleak view of the human situation.

Freewill has been denied many times in history. Spinoza did so in the name of natural necessity: our acts are the result of causes beyond our control. For Marx, the shaper of human behavior was economics; for Freud, the play of unconscious drives; for the neo-Darwinians, our genetically encoded instincts. Science has never given a compelling account of freewill. For if there can be a complete scientific account of human behavior, it would tell us that our acts have causes such that we could not have acted other than we did.

Radical unconditioned freedom enters Western civilization in the first chapter of Genesis when the free God freely creates the universe, saying "Let there be." Making humankind in His image, after His likeness (see Genesis 1:26–27), He endowed us too with freedom. We may be dust of the earth but there is within us the breath of God. The human person is, as Pico Della Mirandola put it in his *Oration on the Dignity of Man*, the one being in creation that is neither angel nor beast but can be either depending on his choice. To be human, said Jean-Paul Sartre, is to know that our existence precedes our essence. We have no essence. All we have is choice.

All life was created. Humans alone are creative. Every life-form has drives, inherent instincts of survival. Humans alone are capable of what philosophers call second-order evaluations, deciding which drives to pursue and which not. Other animals act. We alone bear responsibility for our acts because we could have chosen to act otherwise. Freedom is God's greatest gift to humankind but it is also the most fateful and terrifying. For it means that we alone have the power to destroy the work of God.

Genesis tells a troubled story. Gifted with freedom, almost immediately humans betray that gift. Adam and Eve sin. Cain, the first human child, murders Abel his brother. By Genesis 6, the world has become a place of violence and random cruelty, and God regrets He created man. The modern world with its extermination camps and gulags, its oppression and terror, seems hardly to have advanced at all. Technically humans have excelled. Morally they have failed and continue to fail. For freedom is a double-edged sword. The freedom to do good is inseparable from the freedom to do harm, to commit sin, to practice evil. The problem of evil is *the* problem of humanity.

◂ Yom Kippur

Yom Kippur is the answer.

For if freedom means that humans will sin, then God must have accepted in advance that they would sin, which means that He provided a mechanism for their forgiveness – a mechanism that, without releasing people from moral responsibility, acknowledges that they can recognize that they did wrong, express remorse for the past and dedicate themselves to learning from it and growing thereby, in short, that they can do *teshuva*. They can repent. This is the meaning of the following remarkable midrash:

> Rabbi Yannai said: from the beginning of creation God foresaw the deeds of the righteous and wicked. *The earth was void* – this refers to the deeds of the wicked. *And God said, Let there be light* – this refers to the deeds of the righteous. *And God separated the light from the darkness* – this means, the deeds of the righteous from the deeds of the wicked. *God called the light "day,"* – this refers to the deeds of the righteous. *The darkness He called night* – this refers to the deeds of the wicked. *And there was evening* – the deeds of the wicked. *And there was morning* – the deeds of the righteous. *One day* – this means that God gave them [both] a single day. Which was it? Yom Kippur. (*Bereshit Raba* 3:8)

The midrash is based on the observation that the Hebrew text of Genesis calls the first day of creation, *yom eḥad*, literally "one day," when it should have said, *yom rishon*, "the first day" (see *Bemidbar Raba* 13:6). Evidently, then, the Torah does not mean "the first day." It means the singular, unique day of days, which in Jewish terms means Yom Kippur.

But the midrash is clearly saying something deeper. It is asserting that *divine forgiveness preceded the creation of the first humans* for without a mechanism for repentance, the creation of Homo sapiens does not make sense. Without it, our guilt would accumulate, as it did in the generation of the Flood. There would be no way of mending the past or moving on from it. The human condition would be tragic. We would live weighed down by the burden of remorse, or worse we would seek to liberate ourselves from the voice of conscience altogether, and we would then become lower than the beasts.

Repentance and atonement alone redeem the human situation, telling us that though "There is no one on earth who is righteous, does only good, and never sins" (Eccl. 7:20), still God accepts our fallibility and failures so long as we acknowledge them as such. Indeed, when we grow through our failures, we become greater than those who never failed. "Where penitents stand," said the sages, "even the perfectly righteous cannot stand" (*Berakhot* 34b).

God gave us freedom, knowing the risks. Because we are free, we bear responsibility for our deeds: we *need* to repent. But because we are free, we can change, so we are *able* to repent. This Jewish insistence on freedom – that morally, we become what we choose to be – is one of its greatest contributions to the ethical imagination. Economics may make us rich or poor. Genetics may make us tall or short. But it is our freely made choices that make us good or bad, honest or deceptive, generous or mean-spirited, altruistic or self-centered, patient or irascible, courageous or cowardly, responsible or feckless. Judaism is the world's great ethic of responsibility, born in the vision of the free God seeking the free worship of free human beings honoring the freedom and dignity of others.

God, who made us in love, forgives. Only on this assumption does the creation of humanity make any sense at all.

BEFORE GOD FORGIVES, MAN MUST FORGIVE

Oddly enough, though, it takes time for forgiveness to make its appearance in the Torah. This is strange. If, as the Midrash states and logic dictates, God created forgiveness before He made man, why does it play no obvious part in the early stories of Genesis? Did God forgive Adam and Eve? Did God forgive Cain after he had murdered Abel? Not explicitly. He may have mitigated their punishment. Adam and Eve did not immediately die after eating the forbidden fruit. God placed a mark on Cain's forehead to protect him from being killed by someone else. But mitigation is not the same as forgiveness.

God does not forgive the generation of the Flood, or the builders of Babel, or the sinners of Sodom. Significantly, when Abraham prayed for the people of Sodom he did not ask God to forgive them. His argument was markedly different. He said, "Perhaps there are innocent people there," maybe fifty, perhaps no more than ten. Their merit should, he implied, save the others, but that is quite different from asking God to forgive the others (Gen.18).

The first time we encounter a clear instance of forgiveness is when Joseph, by now viceroy of Egypt, finally reveals his identity to his brothers. Years earlier, they had contemplated killing him and eventually sold him as a slave. They have come before him in Egypt twice without recognizing who he was. Now he discloses his identity and, while they are silent and in a state of shock, goes on to say these words:

> I am your brother Joseph, whom you sold into Egypt! And now, do not be distressed and do not be angry with yourselves for selling me here, because it was to save lives that God sent me ahead of you. For two years now there has been famine in the land, and for the next five years there will be no plowing and reaping. But God sent me ahead of you to preserve for you a remnant on earth and to save your lives by a great deliverance. So then, it was not you who sent me here, but God. (Genesis 45:4–8)

This is *the first recorded moment in history in which one human being forgives another.*

So astonishing is this forgiveness that the brothers cannot entirely believe it. Years later, after their father Jacob has died, the brothers come to Joseph fearing that he will now take revenge. They concoct a story:

> They sent word to Joseph, saying, "Your father left these instructions before he died: 'This is what you are to say to Joseph: I ask you to forgive your brothers for the sins and the wrongs they committed in treating you so badly.' Now please forgive the sins of the servants of the God of your father." When their message came to him, Joseph wept. (Genesis 50:16–18)

The brothers understand the word "forgive" – they use it in their speech – but they are uneasy about it. Did Joseph really mean it? Does someone really forgive those who sold him into slavery? Joseph weeps that his brothers haven't really understood that he meant it when he said it. But he did, then and now.

◂ David

David Konstan, in *Before Forgiveness*, identifies this as the first recorded instance of forgiving in history. What he does not make clear is *why* Joseph forgives. There is nothing accidental about Joseph's behavior. In fact the whole sequence of events, from the moment the brothers appear before him in Egypt for the first time to the moment when he announces his identity and forgives them, is an intricately detailed account of *teshuva*, repentance, the key act of Yom Kippur itself.

Recall what happens. Joseph, having been sold into Egypt as a slave, then thrown into prison on a false charge, eventually rises to become second-in-command in Egypt, having successfully interpreted Pharaoh's dreams. As he predicted, there are seven years of plenty followed by seven years of famine and drought. Lacking food, Jacob sends his sons to Egypt to buy grain, and there they meet the viceroy, not recognizing him as their brother. He is, after all, dressed as an Egyptian ruler and goes by the name Tzafenat-Pane'aḥ. Coming before him, they "bowed down to him with their faces to the ground" (Gen. 42:6).

At this point, by the logic of the story, something should happen. As a young man Joseph had dreamed that one day his brothers would bow down to him. They have just done so. We now expect him to announce his identity and tell the brothers to bring Jacob and the rest of the family to Egypt. His dreams would be fulfilled and the story would reach closure.

Eventually this happens, but not without the longest detour in any narrative in the Torah. Seemingly without reason, Joseph embarks on an elaborate and convoluted stratagem whose purpose is initially far from clear. He keeps his identity secret. He accuses the brothers of a crime they have not committed. He says they are spies. He has them imprisoned for three days. Then, holding Simeon as a hostage, he tells them that they must now return home and bring back their youngest brother, Benjamin.

Slowly as the plot unfolds we begin to get a glimpse of what Joseph is doing. He is forcing the brothers to reenact the earlier occasion when they came back to their father with one of their number, Joseph, missing. Note what happens next:

> They said to one another, "Truly we are guilty [*aval ashemim anaḥnu*] because of our brother. We saw how distressed he was when he pleaded with us for his life, but we would not listen; that's why this distress

◂ has come

> has come on us"… They did not realize that Joseph could understand them, since he was using an interpreter. (Genesis 42:21–23)

An echo of those words, *Aval ashemim anaḥnu*, "truly we are guilty," will reverberate throughout our prayers on Yom Kippur. They represent the first stage of repentance. The brothers *admit they have done wrong and demonstrate remorse.*

The brothers duly return with Benjamin. Joseph receives them warmly and has them served with a meal. The food comes from Joseph's own table, a sign of royal favor. There is only one discrepant note. The text says that Benjamin, the youngest, is served with a portion that is "five times the size" of that of the other brothers (Gen. 43:34). At this stage we do not know why.

The next morning, the brothers are on their way home when an Egyptian officer pursues them, accusing them of stealing a precious silver cup. It has been planted deliberately in Benjamin's sack. The cup is found and the brothers are brought back. Benjamin has been found with stolen property in his possession. Judah then says this:

> What can we say to my lord? What can we say? How can we prove our innocence? God has uncovered your servants' guilt. We are now my lord's slaves – we ourselves and the one who was found to have the cup. (Genesis 44:16)

This is the second stage of repentance: *confession*. Judah does more. He speaks of collective responsibility. This is important. When the brothers sold Joseph into slavery it was Judah who proposed the crime (Gen. 37:26–27) but they were all (except Reuben) complicit in it.

Joseph dismisses Judah's words: "Only the man who was found to have the cup will become my slave. The rest of you, go back to your father in peace" (42:17). He gives the brothers the opportunity to walk away, leaving Benjamin a slave as they once left Joseph. But Judah, undeterred, mounts a passionate plea to be allowed to take the guilt on himself so that Benjamin can be reunited with his father: "So now let me remain as your slave in place of the lad. Let the lad go back with his brothers!" (42:33). It is at this point that Joseph breaks down, discloses his identity, and forgives his brothers.

◂ The reason

The reason is clear. Judah, who had many years earlier sold Joseph as a slave, is now willing to become a slave so that his brother Benjamin can go free. He has just demonstrated what the Talmud and Maimonides define as *complete repentance*, namely *when circumstances repeat themselves and you have an opportunity to commit the same offense again, but you refrain from doing so because you have changed* (*Yoma* 86b; Maimonides, Laws of Repentance 2:1).

We now, in retrospect, understand Joseph's entire strategy. With great care and precision he has set up a controlled experiment to see whether the brothers have changed. Will they abandon Benjamin as they once abandoned Joseph? Like Joseph, Benjamin is a son of Jacob's beloved wife Rachel who died young. The brothers – sons of the less-loved Leah or the handmaids – might be expected to be jealous of Benjamin as they were of Joseph. And just as Joseph had his "many-colored coat" (37:3), so Benjamin at the feast is given five times as much as the others. Will they be provoked by envy yet again?

The parallel is complete. The brothers are free to repeat their crime and no one would blame them. It was, after all, the Egyptian ruler who seized Benjamin through no fault of their own. But they do not repeat the crime. Judah ensures that they do not. He offers to sacrifice his freedom for the sake of Benjamin's. The villain has become a hero. Judah is the first *ba'al teshuva*, the first penitent, the first morally transformed individual in history. Joseph's behavior has had nothing to do with his dreams, or revenge, and everything to do with repentance. Where there is repentance there is forgiveness. The brothers, led by Judah, have gone through all three stages of repentance: (1) admission and remorse (*ḥarata*), (2) confession (*viduy*) and (3) behavioral change (*shinui ma'aseh*).

Forgiveness only exists in a culture in which repentance exists. Repentance presupposes that we are free and morally responsible agents who are capable of change, specifically the change that comes about when we recognize that what we have done is wrong and we are responsible for it and must never do it again. The possibility of that kind of moral transformation simply did not exist in ancient Greece or any other pagan culture. Greece was a culture of character and fate. Judaism is a culture of will and choice, the first of its kind in the world.

Forgiveness is not just one idea among many. It transformed the human

◂ situation

situation. For the first time it established the possibility that we are not condemned endlessly to repeat the past. When I repent, I show I can change. The future is not predestined. I can make it different from what it might have been. And when I forgive, I show that my action is not mere reaction, the way revenge would be. *Forgiveness breaks the irreversibility of the past.* It is the undoing of what has been done. Repentance and forgiveness – the two great gifts of human freedom – redeem the human condition from tragedy.

Now we can return to our original question. If God created forgiveness before He made man, why does it play no part in the stories of Genesis from Adam and Eve to the patriarchs? We cannot be sure of the answer. The Torah is a cryptic work. It leaves much unsaid. It has, as the sages said, "seventy faces" (*Bemidbar Raba* 13:15). More than one interpretation is possible. But one suggests itself overwhelmingly: *God does not forgive human beings until human beings learn to forgive one another.*

Consider the alternative. What would happen if God forgave but humans did not? Then history would be an endless story of retaliation, vendetta, vindictiveness and rancor, violence begetting violence and evil engendering new evil – in short, the world before the Flood, the world that still exists today in the form of tribal warfare and ethnic conflict, the world of Bosnia, Rwanda, Kosovo and Darfur, a world of victims seeking vengeance thereby creating new victims and new vengeance in a process that, without forgiveness, never ends.

The first act of forgiveness in the Torah is Joseph forgiving his brothers, to teach us that only when we forgive one another does God forgive us. Only when we confess our wrongs to one another does God hear our confession to Him. Only when we repent and show we are worthy of being forgiven, do we show that we have learned the responsibility that goes with freedom, without which "mere anarchy is loosed upon the world."

Humanity changed the day Joseph forgave his brothers. Only when the book of Genesis reaches this note of forgiveness and reconciliation can the drama of Exodus and the first Yom Kippur begin.

Two Types of Atonement

It was the most shocking, unexpected sin in history. The Israelites were encamped near Mount Sinai. They had just been liberated from slavery. No exiled people had ever been freed this way before. The supreme Power

◂ had intervened

had intervened in history to rescue the supremely powerless. The rescue had been accompanied throughout by signs and wonders. Ten plagues had struck the Egyptians until Pharaoh let the people go.

Even then the wonders did not cease. When the people were thirsty on their journey through the desert, God sent them water from a rock. When they were hungry, he gave them manna from heaven. When they came up against the impassable barrier of the Sea of Reeds, God divided the waters so that they could cross on dry land. More than three thousand years later we have not stopped telling the story, the greatest narrative of hope the world has ever known.

Then, at Mount Sinai, the people had experienced the greatest revelation in history, when God spoke to an entire nation and made a covenant with them, promising to be their Sovereign and Protector, inviting them to become a kingdom of priests and a holy nation, a nation unlike any other, constituted by its faith.

Now, forty days later, after the memory of that moment had receded, the people wondered what had become of their leader. Moses had climbed the mountain to receive a record of the covenant on tablets of stone, and had not returned. The people panicked. What were they to do in the absence of the man who led them out of Egypt and communicated with God on their behalf? They felt the need for a substitute. They clamored around Aaron. They made a golden calf. Even today, reading the story, it remains a shocking moment. From the heights they had descended to the depths. God, aware of what was happening, told Moses: "Go down, because your people, whom you brought up out of Egypt, have become corrupt" (Ex. 32:7).

Moses prays. Never had there been a prayer as long, protracted, passionate, as this. "I fell prostrate before the Lord for forty days and forty nights; I ate no bread and drank no water, because of all the sin you had committed, doing what was evil in the Lord's sight and so arousing His anger" (Deut. 9:18). In the end God relented. He agreed to forgive the people, and promised Moses a new set of tablets to replace those he had broken in his anger and now lay in fragments beyond repair.

The new tablets symbolized a new beginning. For another forty days Moses was with God. He then descended the mountain, holding the tablets. The people saw him and what he was carrying and knew that they

◂ had been

had been forgiven. That day, when Moses came down the mountain with the second tablets, became the enduring image of forgiveness. Moses descended on the tenth of Tishrei, and thereafter, the anniversary of that day would become established as a time of forgiveness for all generations.

There is a daring midrash on this, taking as its point of departure the line from Psalm 61, "Hear my cry, O God; listen to my prayer." The psalm, like many others, begins with the word *Lamenatze'aḥ*, literally, "For the conductor, the director of music." The word could be read, however, as "For the victor," and with a truly remarkable inversion, the midrash interprets this as: "For the victor who sought to be defeated":

> For the victor who sought to be defeated, as it is said [Is. 57:16], *I will not accuse them forever, nor will I always be angry, for then they would faint away because of Me – the very people I have created.* Do not read it thus, but, *I will accuse in order to be defeated.* How so? Thus said the Holy One, blessed be He, "When I win, I lose; and when I lose, I win. I defeated the generation of the Flood, but I lost thereby, for I destroyed My own creation, as it says [Gen. 7: 23], *Every living thing on the face of the earth was wiped out.* The same happened with the generation of the Tower of Babel and the people of Sodom. But in the days of Moses who defeated Me [by persuading Me to forgive the Israelites whom I had sworn to destroy], I gained for I did not destroy Israel. (*Pesikta Rabati*, 9)

Moses is the hero who defeated God – which turned out to be God's own deepest victory. That day, when Moses came down with the symbol of the power of penitential prayer, became the first Yom Kippur.

THE AFTERMATH OF SINAI: PENITENTIAL PRAYER

That is not the only legacy of that moment, however. Something else happened that has had a decisive impact on Jewish prayer. To understand it we must turn to the great scene when Moses, having secured the people's forgiveness, asks God to show him His glory (Ex. 33:18). God tells Moses to stand in the crevice of a rock. There God will cause His glory to pass by. Moses will not be able to see God directly, "for no one may see Me and live," but he will come as close as is possible for a human being:

◂ And the LORD

> And the LORD descended in the cloud and stood with him there, and proclaimed in the name of the LORD. And the LORD passed by before him and proclaimed: "The LORD, the LORD, compassionate and gracious God, slow to anger, abounding in loving-kindness and truth, extending loving-kindness to a thousand generations, forgiving iniquity, rebellion and sin, and absolving [the guilty who repent]..." (Exodus 34:5–7)

Note that God speaks these words, which became known as the Thirteen Attributes of Mercy, not Moses. What is God doing at this point? God Himself says, "I am making a covenant with you" (Ex. 34:10). But it is not yet clear what this means. After all, God had just made a covenant with the people. They had endangered it by their sin, but Moses had prayed for and achieved their pardon. What then is this new covenant with Moses? The answer to all these questions becomes clear only two books later, in the book of Numbers.

It is then that the people commit another sin as grievous as the making of the golden calf. Moses had sent spies to look at the land. They had come back with a demoralizing report. The land is indeed good, they said, flowing with milk and honey. But the people are strong. Their cities are highly fortified. We will not be able to defeat them. They are giants. We are grasshoppers (Num. 13).

At this point the people, despondent and hopeless, say, "Let's choose a leader and go back to Egypt" (Num. 14:4). As He did at the time of the golden calf, God threatens to destroy the people and begin a nation anew with Moses. Again Moses prays to God to forgive the people, for His sake if not for theirs. Then he adds a new element to his prayer:

> Now may the LORD's strength be displayed, just as You have declared: "The LORD is slow to anger, abounding in loving-kindness, forgiving iniquity and rebellion." Yet he does not leave the guilty unpunished; he punishes the children for the sin of the parents to the third and fourth generation. In accordance with Your great love, forgive the sin of these people, just as You have pardoned them from the time they left Egypt until now. (Numbers 14:17–19)

◀ Moses

Moses is doing something he has not done before. Previously he has prayed on the basis of how God's acts will look to the world, and on the basis of His covenant with the patriarchs. Now he is praying on the basis of God's own nature. He is, as it were, recalling God to Himself. Essentially he is repeating what God Himself had said at Mount Sinai. He says so. He says, "as You have declared," as if to say, "These are Your words not mine."

Only now do we fully understand what God was doing on that previous occasion. *He was teaching Moses how to pray*. This is how the sages put it, with their characteristic daring:

> Were it not written in the Torah it would be impossible to say it, but this teaches that God wrapped Himself in a tallit like a leader of prayer and taught Moses the order of prayer. He said: whenever Israel sin, say these words and I will forgive them. (*Rosh HaShana* 17b)

That is what Moses inferred, and what he did during the episode of the spies. We now understand what God meant earlier when He said, "I am making a covenant with you." This was a covenant specifically about the Thirteen Attributes of Mercy. God was saying that when Israel said these words, He would relent and forgive. As for the anthropomorphic idea that God "wrapped Himself" in a tallit, the sages are translating the words *vaya'avor… al panav* (Ex. 34:6) not as "God passed before him [Moses]" but rather, "God passed [a cloak, a cloud] over His face" so that Moses would not see His face (Malbim). The tallit is the screen separating us from God – the distance that allows God to be God and humans to be human.

No sooner does Moses pray this prayer, than God says two momentous words that will be repeated time and again during Yom Kippur: *Salaḥti kidvarekha,* "I have forgiven, as you asked" (Num. 14:20). So forgiveness for the sin of the golden calf was more than a one-time event. It gave Moses and his successors the words needed to secure divine forgiveness on other occasions also. The Thirteen Attributes of Mercy are the prayer God taught humanity, the prayer Moses used successfully after the episode of the spies.

◂ The dual

The dual episode of the calf and the spies became an essential element of our devotions on Yom Kippur and other penitential days, the prayers we know as *Seliḥot*. Every time we say them we reenact the drama of Moses pleading for his people. *Seliḥot* take us back to the scene of Moses in the crevice of a rock at Mount Sinai as God's glory passed by. It was one of the great moments in the history of the prophets.

THE SECOND YOM KIPPUR

But prophets are not the only type of religious leader in Judaism, and for a compelling reason. There was only one Moses. Not every generation produces a prophet. We have not had them in Judaism since Malachi two and half millennia ago.

Judaism begins in a series of transfiguring moments of epiphany. Something momentous happens. The world seems lit as if by a heavenly light. God has entered the human arena. People glimpse new possibilities. The world will never be quite the same again. So it was when Abraham first heard the call of God, when Moses encountered God in the burning bush, when the Israelites left Egypt on their way to freedom, and when the sea divided and they passed through on dry land. But how do you turn unique moments into ongoing continuity? How do you translate them into the biorhythms of succeeding generations? How do you prevent epoch-making moments fading into the distant past?

That is when we need memory and ritual. You take a unique event and turn it into a recurring ceremony. You turn linear time into cyclical time. You reenact history by writing it into the calendar. The Hebrew word for calendar, *luaḥ*, also means "a tablet." The tablets of stone are written onto the tablet of the year and thus into the tablet of the heart. The descent of Moses from the mountain in a blaze of divine light was to become not a once-only event but a regularly repeated one. Thus Yom Kippur as an annual event, the Sabbath of Sabbaths of the Jewish year, was born.

But that required someone other than a prophet. The prophet lives in the immediacy of the moment, not in the endlessly reiterated cycles of time. This required religious leadership of a different order, namely, the priest. The priest represents order, structure, continuity, the precisely formulated ritual followed in strict, meticulous obedience. Max Weber called

◂ this the

this the routinization of charisma. The first Day of Atonement needed the intercession of a Moses, but the second and subsequent occasions required the agency of an Aaron, a High Priest. That is indeed how the Torah describes it in Leviticus 16.

The service of the High Priest on Yom Kippur was high drama. It was an event like no other. It involved strange rituals performed at no other time, such as the casting of lots on two animals, one of which was offered as a sacrifice to God, the other of which was led, bearing the sins of the people, "to Azazel." There is nothing remotely comparable in any of the other Temple rituals.

This was the moment of supreme solemnity when, each year, the High Priest atoned for the sins of the entire nation. He prepared for it for seven days in advance. Elaborate contingency measures were taken in case at the last moment he was unable to officiate. It involved an elaborate choreography of ritual and changes of garments. There were public moments when the High Priest appeared before the people robed in gold and splendor. There were also intensely private ones, as when he entered the Holy of Holies alone, dressed in a simple white tunic, and communed with God.

The transition from the first to the second Yom Kippur involved a move from prophet to priest. This is a huge difference. Prophets and priests were different kinds of people who served God in different ways. What was appropriate to one was inappropriate, even forbidden, to the other. Judaism is a religion of distinctions and differences. Only thus do we bring order to the world. Judaism radically distinguishes between priestly and prophetic sensibilities. Each has its place in the religious life. Each receives eloquent expression on Yom Kippur. But they are different, especially when it comes to atonement and sin.

PRIESTS AND ATONEMENT

Some of the differences between priests and prophets are obvious. Priesthood was dynastic. It passed from father to son, from Aaron to his descendants. Prophecy was not. Moses' children did not succeed him. The son of a prophet is not necessarily a prophet. In general, the prophets were drawn from no particular tribe, class, region or occupational group. Prophecy is a uniquely individual gift that you do not inherit.

◂ The priesthood

The priesthood was exclusively masculine, whereas there were women prophets as well as men. Tradition counts seven: Sarah, Miriam, Deborah, Hannah, Abigail, Ḥuldah and Esther. Priests wore robes of office; prophets had none. Priests functioned within the precincts of the Temple; prophets lived among the people.

The authority of the priest was official, while that of the prophet was personal. That is why the prophets were so distinctive. Their personalities shaped their perception and message. Hosea was not Amos. Isaiah was not Jeremiah. Prophet and priest exemplified Max Weber's famous distinction between charismatic and traditional-legal authority.

What I want to explore here, though, is the difference between *Torat Kohanim* and *Torat Nevi'im* – the codes that guided priestly and prophetic sensibilities – in their response to the religious life, obedience and sin, atonement and repentance. We are used to thinking about these things as if they all belonged to a single system. They do now, but they did not always. When prophets and priests were the active Jewish religious leaders, they had different ways of thinking about the life of faith, so far apart that they hardly overlapped at all.

For the priest, the key words of the religious life are *kadosh*, holy, and *tahor*, pure. To be a Jew is to be *set apart*: that is what the word *kadosh*, holy, actually means. This in turn has to do with the special closeness the Jewish people have to God. Because of this we are bound to a special code of conduct that gives expression to this singularity. It means, for example, eating only certain kinds of food and being bound to a strict discipline of sexual ethics. In *Torat Kohanim*, the priestly law, there are statutes, *ḥukkim*, that do not seem to make obvious sense in terms of conventional ethics, such as not eating meat and milk together, or wearing clothes of mixed wool and linen, or not sowing fields with mixed seeds. All these laws have to do with the special perspective of *Torat Kohanim*.

They have to do with order. The priestly mind sees the universe in terms of distinctions, boundaries and domains, in which each object or act has its proper place and they must not be mixed. The Kohen's task is to maintain boundaries and respect limits. For the Kohen, goodness equals order. We learn this from the way God created the world. He took chaos – *tohu vavohu* – and turned it into a finely tuned universe with its myriad life-forms, each with its ecological niche, its place in the scheme of things. A world that is ordered is good. One that is chaotic is bad and unsustainable.

So Jews are charged to respect and honor boundaries and differences by obeying the will of God, Creator of the world and Architect of its order. Priests see the world in terms of strictly defined categories: *kodesh* and *ḥol,* holy and profane, *tahor* and *tameh,* pure and impure. The key priestly verbs are *lehavdil,* "to distinguish, separate, demarcate," and *lehorot,* "to teach" in the sense of giving halakhic rulings.

Priests have a strong moral sense. The commands to love your neighbor and the stranger as yourself occur, in the Torah, in the most priestly of the books, Leviticus, and are taught alongside the *ḥukkim,* the statutes, that have no apparent moral content. The highest virtue for the priest is obedience: doing exactly as God told us to do. Prophets often acted on the spur of the moment. That is what Moses did when he smashed the tablets on seeing the golden calf. But there is absolutely no place for spontaneity in the world of the priest.

Nadav and Avihu, two of Aaron's sons, spontaneously made a fire offering at the consecration of the Tabernacle and died as a result. When priests, charged with maintaining order, act spontaneously, it is like mixing milk and meat, or matter and anti-matter. It creates disorder, and disorder in the moral universe is like entropy in the physical universe. It means a loss of energy, a diminution of the presence of God. So when people sin, they have to restore order through the appropriate ritual.

When the Temple stood, this involved purification if you had become defiled, or the bringing of a sacrifice if you had done wrong. You had to come to the Temple because that, in the world of the priest, is where humans meet God. God is everywhere, but we meet Him only in special places at special times. Each time has its appropriate sacrifice and service, just as each prayer has its appropriate words. It is through acting exactly as God has prescribed that we restore the order we have damaged through our sins.

Listening carefully to how the Torah describes the ritual of the High Priest on Yom Kippur, we hear the key terms of the priestly sensibility:

> When he finishes bringing atonement for the holiest place and the Tent of Meeting and the altar, he shall offer up the living goat. Aaron

◂ shall

> shall press his hands onto the head of the living goat and confess all the guilt of Israel, and all of their rebellions, all of their sins … For you will be atoned on this day and made pure; of all your sins before the LORD you shall be purified. (Leviticus 16:20–21, 30)

The key themes are confession, purification, and atonement, the last of which occurs a sizeable twenty-three times in the space of a single chapter. The day itself, the tenth of Tishrei, is described three times in the Torah as *Yom* [*Ha*]*Kippurim*, the "Day of Atonements."

The root *k-p-r*, "atone," has a variety of meanings. It means "to cover over": Noah was told to cover [*vekhafarta*, Gen. 6:14] the ark with pitch. The gold covering of the Ark in the Tabernacle was called a *kaporet*. A *kofer* was also a ransom, a sum paid to redeem a debt or avoid a hazard (see Exodus 21:30).

Guilt, therefore, is seen as a kind of debt incurred by the sinner to God and must be redeemed by the performance of a ritual, confession, and the payment of a ransom, the sin-offering. This "covers over" or obliterates the sin. It also cleanses the sinner since sin leaves a mark on the soul. It is a kind of defilement (see Nahmanides to Leviticus 4:2).

Sin, for the Kohen, is the transgression of a boundary, and there are specific names for the different kinds of sin: *ḥet*, for an unintentional sin, *avon* for a deliberate sin, and *pesha* for a sin committed as a rebellion. All sin threatens the Divine–human harmony on which the universe depends. Confession accompanied by sacrifice restores that harmony, and the ritual itself must follow a highly structured procedure. Structure is of the essence, for the priest is the guardian of order, and only by obediently following divine instructions do we honor the order God made in creating the universe. Note that the fundamental concern of the priest is the relationship between the people and God.

Note also what is missing from the priestly account. There is nothing here about the relationship of human beings with one another. The verb *shuv*, to "return" or "repent," does not appear at all. The priest is engaged in *kapara* and *tahara*, atonement and purification, not with *teshuva*, repentance and return.

◂ Prophets

PROPHETS AND REPENTANCE

The prophets are quite different. They use different words. They think in different ways. Here, for example, are Isaiah, Jeremiah, Hosea and Joel on the subject of repentance:

> Wash and make yourselves clean. Take your evil deeds out of My sight; stop doing wrong. Learn to do right; seek justice. Defend the oppressed. Take up the cause of the fatherless; plead the case of the widow. Come now, let us reason together, says the LORD: If your sins are like scarlet, they shall be whitened like snow; should they be as red as crimson, they shall become like wool. (Isaiah 1:16–18)

> Now reform your ways and your actions and obey the LORD your God. Then the LORD will relent and not bring the disaster He has pronounced against you. (Jeremiah 26:13)

> Return, Israel, to the LORD your God. Your sins have been your downfall! Take words with you and return to the LORD. Say to Him: "Forgive all our sins and receive us graciously, that we may offer the fruit of our lips." (Hosea 14:2–3)

> Rend your heart and not your garments. Return to the LORD your God, for He is gracious and compassionate, slow to anger and abounding in loving-kindness, and He relents from sending calamity. (Joel 2:13)

This is a completely different way of thinking. The prophets are intensely concerned with social morality. They regard injustice, corruption, the neglect of the poor and the oppression of the weak as national catastrophes. They are not indifferent to the relationship between the people and God: far from it. They constantly castigate idolatry. But they see this in moral terms. It is an act of betrayal, disloyalty, faithlessness. Also they are concerned less with outward ritual than with inner remorse: "Rend your heart and not your garments." They are not opposed to ritual and sacrifice, but they are outraged when it is used as an attempt, as it were, to bribe God to avert His eyes from evil and injustice.

Note also that the prophets speak from and in the midst of history. Sin is not something that has consequences only for the spiritual relationship between the people and God. It damages the nation's fate. It threatens its future. When drought, famine, war and defeat happen it is because the people have sinned, and if they continue to do so, worse will follow.

The language the prophets use is quite different from that of the priests. Time and again they use the word the priests never use, namely "return," *shuv*, from which we get the word *teshuva*. Return to God, they say, and He will return to You. The priestly word *k-p-r*, "atone," plays almost no role whatsoever in the prophetic literature. Isaiah uses it rarely, Jeremiah only once and negatively ("Do not forgive their crimes or blot out their sins from your sight" [18:23]). The twelve minor prophets do not use it at all (Amos uses it once [5:12] to mean a bribe). This is particularly noticeable in the book of Jonah whose entire theme is repentance.

There is one other difference between the language of priests and prophets. They both make use of the verb *s-l-ḥ*, to forgive. But the prophets use it always and only in the active form: God forgives. Priests use it exclusively in the passive form: *venislaḥ*, "it will be forgiven."

So we have two types of religious leader, the priest and the prophet, both of whom serve the same God as part of the same faith and the same people, whose visions of the spiritual-moral life are quite different. The priest thinks of sin primarily in terms of the relationship between humans and God. The prophet sees the effects of sin on society. He or she knows that if you dishonor God you will eventually dishonor human beings.

What angers the prophet is seeing people trying to have it both ways – honoring God by bringing sacrifices at the Temple while exploiting or oppressing their fellow humans. Don't think you can fool God, the prophet says. You cannot ignore Him and survive as a nation. The prophet speaks not in the language of holy and profane, pure and defiled, commandment and sin, but in terms of the great covenantal virtues: *tzedek*, righteousness, *mishpat*, justice, *ḥesed*, love and *raḥamim*, compassion.

The prophet does not speak about putting things right by sacrifice and confession but by a change of heart and deed, abandoning evil and returning to God. The one exception was Ezekiel, the only person to use both a prophetic and a priestly vocabulary. The reason is simple: Ezekiel was that rare phenomenon, a prophet who was also a priest (unlike Jeremiah, both roles are evident in the language of Ezekiel).

Priests and prophets belong to different worlds. The only reason we think of them together is because of the history of Yom Kippur. The first

Yom Kippur was brought about by Moses, the greatest of the prophets. The second and subsequent Days of Atonement belonged to Aaron and his descendants, the High Priests.

It took historical catastrophe and a religious genius to bring the two worlds together. The catastrophe was the destruction of the Second Temple. The genius was Rabbi Akiva.

The Two Hemispheres United

It was one of the most turbulent periods in history. An ancient order was coming to an end, and almost everyone knew it. With the death of Herod in 4 BCE, Israel came under direct Roman rule. There was unrest throughout the land. Jews and Greeks vied for influence, and conflict often flared into violence. There were Jewish uprisings, brutally suppressed. Throughout Israel there were sects convinced they were living through the end of days. In Qumran on the shores of the Dead Sea a group of religious pietists were living in expectation of the final confrontation between the sons of light and the sons of darkness. A whole series of messianic figures emerged, each the harbinger of a new "kingdom of heaven." All were killed.

In the year 66 CE the tension erupted. Provoked by persecution, buoyed by messianic hope, Jews rose in rebellion. A heavy contingent of Roman troops under Vespasian and Titus was sent to crush the uprising. It took seven years. In 70 CE the Temple was destroyed. Three years later the last remaining outpost of zealots in the mountain fastness of Masada committed suicide rather than allow themselves to be taken captive by the Romans. Some contemporary estimates put the number of Jewish casualties during this period at over a million. It was a devastating blow.

In 132 there was another uprising, this time under Shimon bar Kosiva, known as Bar Kokhba and considered by some of the rabbis to be the messiah. For a while it was a success. For two years Jews regained a fragile independence. The Roman reprisal, when it came, was merciless. The Roman historian Dio estimated that in the course of the campaign, 580,000 Jews were killed and 985 Jewish settlements destroyed. Almost an entire generation of Jewish leaders and teachers, sages and scholars, was put to death. Hadrian had Jerusalem leveled, then rebuilt as the Roman city Aelia Capitolina. Jews were forbidden entry on pain of death. It was the end of resistance and the beginning of what would eventually become the longest exile ever suffered by a people. Within a century the center of Jewish life had moved to Babylon.

All the institutions of national Jewish life were now gone. There was no Temple, no sacrificial order, no priests, no kings, no prophets, no land, no independence, and no expectation that they might soon return. With the possible exception of the Holocaust it was the most traumatic period in Jewish history. A passage in the Talmud records that at the height of the Hadrianic persecutions there were rabbis who taught that "By rights we should issue a decree that Jews should not marry and have children, so that the seed of Abraham comes to an end of its own accord."* To many it seemed as if the Jewish journey had reached its close. Where in the despair was there a route to hope?

In the encompassing turmoil one problem was acute for those whose religious imagination was most sensitive. What, in the absence of a Temple and its sacrifices, would now lift the burden of sin and guilt? Judaism is a system of high moral and spiritual demands. Without some way of resolving the tension between the ideal of perfection and the all-too-imperfect nature of human conduct, the weight of undischarged guilt would be immense.

So long as the Temple stood, the service of the High Priest on Yom Kippur was designed to secure atonement for all Israel.** Already, though, even before the destruction of the Temple, the priesthood no longer commanded the respect of all sections of the population. For several generations it had become enmeshed in politics. Some Hasmonean kings had served as High Priests, transgressing against the principled separation of powers in Judaism. There were times under Greek and Roman rule when the office went to the highest bidder. There were other times when the priesthood was caught up in the conflict between Pharisees and Sadducees, a serious rift in late Second Temple times. All too often the office of High Priest became a pawn in a game of power.

Many sages wrestled with this problem. One in particular, though,

* Babylonian Talmud, *Bava Batra* 60b.

** Leviticus 16:2–34.

is associated with the conceptual revolution that occurred in the post-Temple age. Rabbi Akiva had an almost legendary life. He had grown up as an illiterate shepherd with a violent dislike of rabbis and their culture. At the insistence of his wife, he undertook a course of study and eventually became prodigiously learned, a leader of Jewish scholarship and one of its most heroic figures. Amid the despair at the destruction of the Temple, his was one of the great voices of hope. In old age he gave his support to the Bar Kokhba rebellion, and was put to a cruel death by the Romans. He remains a symbol of Jewish martyrdom.

His response to the end of the Temple and its Day of Atonement rites was not one of mourning, but a paradoxical sense of uplift. Tragedy had not defeated hope. It could even be used to bring about a spiritual advance. The Temple rites might be lost, but in their place would come something even deeper and more democratic. Far from being separated from God, the sinner was now able to come closer to the Divine Presence. His words were these: "Happy are you, Israel: before whom do you purify yourselves, and who purifies you? – Your Father in heaven."*

He meant this: Now that there was no Temple and no High Priest, atonement need no longer be vicarious. The sinner could obtain forgiveness directly. All he or she needed to do was confess the sin, express remorse and resolve not to repeat it in the future. Atonement was no longer mediated by a third party. It needed no High Priest, no sacrifice and no Temple ritual. It was a direct relationship between the individual and God. This was one of rabbinic Judaism's most magnificent ideas. Jews continue to mourn the loss of the Temple and pray for its restoration, but their ability to transform grief into growth, defeat into spiritual victory, remains awe-inspiring.

UNITING PRIEST AND PROPHET

Essentially what Rabbi Akiva and the sages did was to bring together the priestly and prophetic ideas of atonement and return. They took from *Torat Kohanim*, the law of the priests, the idea of Yom Kippur itself – a special day in the Jewish calendar dedicated to fasting, self-affliction and the rectification of sin. The prophets never thought in terms of specific

* Mishna, *Yoma* 8:9.

succeeded in uniting two religious mindsets, that of the priest and the prophet, that had been distinct and separate for more than a thousand years. It was an immense achievement.

MAIMONIDES ON REPENTANCE

We can gain a deeper insight into this synthesis by looking closely at a major disagreement between two of the greatest rabbis of the Middle Ages, Maimonides and Nahmanides.

Maimonides was one of the most polymathic minds the Jewish people has ever produced. Born in Spain (c. 1135) to Rabbi Maimon, a rabbi and religious judge, he spent his childhood in Cordoba, then enjoying the brief period of relative tolerance known as the *Convivencia* when Muslims, Christians and Jews lived together in relative harmony. In 1148 a radical Islamic sect, the Almohads, came to power, instituting religious persecution and forcing the Maimon family into flight. Originally they went to Fez in Morocco, then to Israel, but the Jewish community, devastated by the Crusades, offered no possibility of a livelihood, and the family eventually settled in Fustat, near Cairo, where Maimonides was to live out the rest of his days until his death in 1204. There he wrote some of the greatest works of Jewish scholarship, including the unsurpassed code of law, the *Mishneh Torah*, and the sublime if enigmatic philosophical masterpiece, *The Guide for the Perplexed*.

Nahmanides, born in Gerona, Catalonia, in 1194, was, like Maimonides, a physician as well as the greatest rabbi of his time, equally adept at Jewish law and biblical interpretation. In 1263 in Barcelona he was enlisted into one of the great confrontations between Judaism and Christianity: the public disputation, in the presence of King James I of Aragon, with Pablo Christiani, a Jewish convert to Christianity. Nahmanides spoke brilliantly, but was forced into exile in 1265 when the king was put under pressure by the Christian authorities. He traveled to Israel and set about strengthening the Jewish community in Jerusalem, establishing a yeshiva and a synagogue. It was the beginning of the recovery of a Jewish presence in the holy city.

Both men were concerned to find the source of the command at the heart of Yom Kippur, namely *teshuva*, the duty to repent one's sins

◀ and "return"

and "return" to God, but they differed utterly in their analyses. Here is Maimonides' account:

> In respect of all the commands of the Torah, positive or negative, if a person transgressed any of them, deliberately or in error, and repents and turns away from his sins, he is under a duty to confess before God, blessed be He, as it is said, "If a man or a woman sins against his fellow man, thus being untrue to God, and becoming guilty of a crime, he must confess the sin he has committed" [Num. 5:6–7]. This means verbal confession, and this confession is a positive command.
>
> How does one confess? The penitent says, "I beg of You, O Lord, I have sinned, I have acted perversely, I have transgressed before You and have done such and such; and behold, I repent and am ashamed of my deeds and I will never do this again." This constitutes the essence of confession. The fuller and more detailed the confession one makes, the more praiseworthy he is. (Laws of Repentance 1:1)

Note how circuitous Maimonides' prose is: *If* one commits a sin, and *if* one then repents, *then* one must confess. It sounds as if the command is the confession, not the repentance that precedes it. In the superscription to the Laws of Repentance he puts it slightly differently. There he says that the command is "that the sinner repent of his sin before God and confess," as if the mitzva were *both* the repentance and the confession.

What Maimonides is saying is that the actual command is the confession, a verbal declaration. But confession must be sincere in order to count, and a sincere confession presupposes that you repent of the sin, meaning, (1) you know it was a sin, (2) you feel remorse that you committed it, and (3) you are now formally declaring your guilt and your determination not to repeat the offense. Repentance, for Maimonides, is not directly commanded in the Torah. It is commanded obliquely. You have to have it in order to fulfill the command of confession. Confession is the *ma'aseh mitzva,* the physical act, while *teshuva* is the *kiyum mitzva,* the mental component necessary to make the act the fulfillment of a command.

Note that Maimonides locates the mitzva in the world of the Temple and its sacrifices. It was there that individuals confessed when they

◂ brought

brought sin or guilt offerings. It was there that the High Priest confessed his and the people's sins on Yom Kippur. We might have thought that, since confession was an accompaniment of sacrifices, when the sacrifices ceased, so too did confession itself. However, elsewhere (*Sefer HaMitzvot,* positive command 73) Maimonides cites the *Sifri,* an authoritative halakhic midrash, to prove that the command of confession still holds, even though we lack the sacrifices that accompanied it in Temple times.

In short, for Maimonides, repentance belongs to *Torat Kohanim,* the law of the priests. It derives, ultimately, from the Sanctuary and its rituals, the world over which Aaron and his descendants officiated. It is what we have left from the Temple.

NAHMANIDES ON REPENTANCE

The view of Nahmanides could not be more different. Searching for the basis of the command of *teshuva,* he turns to one of the great prophetic visions Moses outlined at the end of his life:

> When all these blessings and curses I have set before you come upon you and you take them to heart wherever the LORD your God disperses you among the nations, and when you and your children return to the LORD your God and obey Him with all your heart and with all your soul according to everything I command you today, then the LORD your God will restore your fortunes and have compassion on you and gather you again from all the nations where He scattered you. Even if you have been banished to the most distant land under the heavens, from there the LORD your God will gather you and bring you back… The LORD will again delight in you and make you prosperous, just as He delighted in your ancestors, if you obey the LORD your God and keep His commands and decrees that are written in this Book of the Law and turn to the LORD your God with all your heart and with all your soul. (Deuteronomy 30:1–10)

This is the passage in which Moses, lifting his eyes to the furthermost horizon of prophecy, foresees a time when the Israelites will be defeated and forced into exile. There they will come to the conclusion that this was no mere happenstance. It occurred because they had sinned and forsaken

◂ God

God and He in return had forsaken them. They would then return to God. He would return to them and they would return to their land.

Note that the entire passage does not mention sin or transgression, confession or sacrifice. It makes no mention of any ritual or verbal declaration. Nor does it mention the key word, *k-p-r,* "atonement," in any of its forms or inflections. There is not a single hint of *Torat Kohanim,* the world and mindset of the priest. It is a vast conspectus of history, a portrait of national decline and restoration, exile and a new beginning.

What is missed in almost every English translation is the fact that the key word in the passage is the verb *shuv,* "to return," from which the word *teshuva,* repentance, is derived. It appears no less than eight times in ten verses. This was clearly the decisive consideration as far as Nahmanides was concerned. If we are looking for a source of the command of *teshuva,* then we must seek a passage in which the verb occurs. Nahmanides then notes that immediately after this vision Moses adds:

> *This command* I am prescribing to you today is not too difficult for you or beyond your reach. It is not in heaven, so [that you should] say, "Who shall go up to heaven and bring it to us so that we can hear it and keep it?" It is not over the sea so [that you should] say, "Who will cross the sea and get if for us, so that we will be able to hear it and keep it?" It is something that is very close to you. It is in your mouth and in your heart, so that you can keep it. (Deuteronomy 30:11–14)

Which is "This command"? asks Nahmanides, and answers: "This is the command of *teshuva,* repentance."

Note how very different Nahmanides' view of repentance is from that of Maimonides. For him repentance is part of the historical drama of the Jewish people. The punishment for sin is exile. Adam and Eve were exiled from the Garden of Eden. Cain was condemned to permanent exile ("You shall be a restless wanderer" [Gen. 4:12]) after murdering his brother Abel. So would the Israelites, if they sinned, suffer defeat and displacement. Hence the rich double meaning of the word *teshuva,* signifying both spiritual and physical return. If they came home spiritually to God He would bring them home physically to their land.

It would be hard to find a wider disagreement not only on the source but also the nature of the command. For Nahmanides repentance is not about a ritual of atonement but about the complete reorientation of an individual, or the people as a whole, from estrangement from God to rededication and return. Nahmanides' account locates repentance not in *Torat Kohanim*, the law of the priests, but in *Torat Nevi'im*, the world of the prophet. It is the prophet who relates spirituality to history, the state of a nation's soul to its fate in the vicissitudes of time. Where Maimonides finds *teshuva* in the world of Aaron and the priests, Nahmanides locates it in the mind of Moses and the prophets.

In the light of all we have said, we can see that Maimonides and Nahmanides were both right because they were speaking about different things. Maimonides tells us that the origin of *kapara*, atonement, is priestly. Nahmanides tells us that the basis of *teshuva*, repentance-and-return, is prophetic. It was the genius of the sages to bring these two processes together, strengthening the connection between honoring God and honoring the image of God that is our fellow human.

That, then, is Yom Kippur, a day of restoring our relationship with God, with our fellows and with the better angels of our nature. Rabbinical Judaism integrated the twin hemispheres of the Jewish brain, the priestly and prophetic mindsets. Yom Kippur still bears traces of its dual origin in the prophetic moment of the first year when Moses achieved divine forgiveness for the Israelites' sin, and the priestly nature of the second, when Aaron secured atonement for the people by his service in the Sanctuary.

A REPUBLIC OF FREE AND EQUAL CITIZENS

The following speech, adapted from Ansky's play *The Dybbuk*, expresses beautifully the revolution wrought by rabbinic Judaism:

> At a certain hour, on a certain day of the year, the four supreme sanctities met together. On the Day of Atonement, the holiest day of the year, the holiest person, the High Priest, entered the holiest place, the Holy of Holies in Jerusalem, and there pronounced the holiest word, the Divine Name. Now that there is no Temple, wherever a person stands to lift his eyes to heaven becomes a Holy of Holies. Every human being created by God in His own likeness is a High Priest. Each

◂ day of

day of a person's life is the Day of Atonement. Every word he speaks from the heart is the name of God.

At Mount Sinai in the days of Moses, God invited the Israelites to become "a kingdom of priests and a holy nation" (Ex. 19:6). All would be priests. The nation as a whole would be holy. Under the sovereignty of God, there would be a republic of free and equal citizens held together not by hierarchy or power but by the moral bond of covenant.

It did not happen, at least not literally. Throughout the biblical era there were hierarchies. There were kings, prophets and priests. Yet ideals, repeatedly invoked, do not die. They lie like seeds in parched earth waiting for the rain. It was precisely at Israel's bleakest moment that something like the biblical vision did emerge. Monarchy, priesthood and prophecy ceased, and were succeeded by more egalitarian institutions. Prayer took the place of sacrifice. The synagogue replaced the Temple. Repentance substituted for the rites of the High Priest.

Judaism, no longer a religion of land and state, kings and armies, became a faith built around homes, schools and communities. For eighteen hundred years without a state Jews were a nation linked not by relationships of power but by a common commitment to the covenant. Jewry, no longer a sovereign nation, became a global people. From that point onward every Jew in politics became a king, in study a prophet, and in prayer, especially on Yom Kippur, a priest.

Out of catastrophe, the Jewish people, inspired by sages like Rabbi Akiva, brought about a revolution in the life of the spirit, foreshadowed at Mount Sinai but not fully realized until more than a thousand years later, and perhaps not fully appreciated even now. The Judaism of the sages – a Judaism without the revelatory events or manifest miracles of the Bible – achieved what no other religion has ever done, sustaining the identity of a people, dispersed, stateless and largely powerless, everywhere a minority and often a despised one, for two millennia, leading it in generation after generation to heights of scholarship and piety that transfigured lives and lit them with an inner fire of love and longing and religious passion that turned pain into poetry and transformed Yom Kippur from a day on which one man atoned for all, into one on which all atoned for each in a covenant of human solidarity in the direct unmediated presence of God.

◂ New Insights

New Insights into Ancient Texts

Three passages in the Yom Kippur prayers have occasioned much speculation, and in this chapter I offer a new interpretation of each. First is *Kol Nidrei,* the prayer-that-is-not-a-prayer with which Yom Kippur begins. Second is the service of the High Priest, in the Tabernacle and later the Temple, especially the rite of the goat sent to Azazel, the original "scapegoat." What was the meaning of this strange procedure? Third is the poem said on *Kol Nidrei* night, "Like clay in the potter's hands" misunderstood by many commentators and translators.

KOL NIDREI

Kol Nidrei is an enigma wrapped in a mystery, the strangest prayer ever to capture the religious imagination. First, it is not a prayer at all. It is not even a confession. It is a dry legal formula for the annulment of vows. It is written in Aramaic. It does not mention God. It is not part of the service. It does not require a synagogue. And it was disapproved of, or at least questioned, by generations of halakhic authorities.

The first time we hear of *Kol Nidrei,* in the ninth century, it is already being opposed by Rav Natronai Gaon (Responsa 1:185), the first of many sages through the centuries who found it problematic. In their view, one cannot annul the vows of an entire congregation this way. Even if one could, one should not, since it may lead people to treat vows lightly. Besides which, there has already been an annulment of vows ten days earlier, on the morning before Rosh HaShana. This is mentioned explicitly in the Talmud (*Nedarim* 23b). There is no mention of an annulment on Yom Kippur.

Rabbeinu Tam, Rashi's grandson, was particularly insistent in arguing that the kind of annulment *Kol Nidrei* represents cannot be retroactive. It cannot apply to vows already taken. It can only be a preemptive qualification of vows in the future. Accordingly, he insisted on changing its wording so that *Kol Nidrei* refers not to vows from last year to this, but from this year to next (*Sefer HaYashar* 100). However, the custom developed to say both – a compromise at the cost of coherence. It is one thing to seek to undo vows we have already made, quite another to preclude vows we might make in the future.

◂ Disturbingly

Disturbingly, *Kol Nidrei* created hostility on the part of non-Jews, who said it showed that Jews did not feel bound to honor their promises since they vitiated them on the holiest night of the year. In vain it was repeatedly emphasized that *Kol Nidrei* applies only to vows between us and God, not those between us and our fellow humans. Throughout the Middle Ages, and in some places until the eighteenth century, in lawsuits with non-Jews, Jews were forced to take a special oath *More Judaica*, because of this concern.

So there were communal and halakhic reasons not to say *Kol Nidrei*, yet it survived all the doubts and misgivings. It remains the quintessential expression of the awe and solemnity of the day. Its undiminished power defies all obvious explanations. Somehow it seems to point to something larger than itself, whether in Jewish history or the inner heartbeat of the Jewish soul.

Several historians have argued that it acquired its pathos from the phenomenon of forced conversions, whether to Christianity or Islam, that occurred in several places in the Middle Ages, most notably Spain and Portugal in the fourteenth and fifteenth century. Jews would be offered the choice: convert or suffer persecution. Sometimes it was: convert or be expelled. At times it was even: convert or die. Some Jews did convert. They were known in Hebrew as *anusim* (people who acted under coercion). In Spanish they were known as *conversos*, or contemptuously as *marranos* (swine).

Many of them remained Jews in secret, and once a year on the night of Yom Kippur they would make their way in secret to the synagogue to seek release from the vows they had taken to adopt another faith, on the compelling grounds that they had no other choice. For them, coming to the synagogue was like *coming home*, the root meaning of *teshuva*.

There are obvious problems with this hypothesis. Firstly, *Kol Nidrei* was in existence several centuries *before* the era of forced conversions. So historian Joseph S. Bloch suggested that *Kol Nidrei* may have originated in the much earlier Christian persecution of Jews in Visigoth Spain, when in 613 Sisebur issued a decree that all Jews should either convert or be expelled, anticipating the Spanish expulsion of 1492. Even so, it is unlikely that *conversos* would have taken the risk of being discovered practicing

Judaism. Had they done so during the centuries in which the Inquisition was in force, they would have risked torture, trial and death.

Yet the connection between *Kol Nidrei* and Jews estranged from the community continues to tantalize, and may be the explanation for the preceding passage introduced by Rabbi Meir of Rothenburg in the thirteenth century: "By the authority of the heavenly and earthly court we grant permission to pray with the transgressors." This constitutes the formal lifting of a ban of excommunication and was a way of welcoming outcasts back into the community. The fact remains, though, that the text of *Kol Nidrei* makes no reference to conversion, return, identity, or atonement. It is what it is: simply an annulment of vows.

Others have suggested that it is not the words of *Kol Nidrei* that have ensured its survival, but the music, the ancient, moving melody that immediately evokes a mood of drama and expectancy as the leader of prayer turns toward heaven, pleading on behalf of the congregation. The tune of *Kol Nidrei* is one of those known as *miSinai*, "from Sinai," meaning in this context, of great antiquity, though probably it was composed in Rhineland Germany in the age of the Crusades. The music is indeed uniquely soulful. Beethoven chose the same opening sequence of notes for the sixth movement of his *String Quartet in* C *sharp minor, opus 131*, one of his most sublime compositions. Already in the fifteenth century we read of rabbis who sought to rectify the text of *Kol Nidrei*, only to find their suggestions rejected on the grounds that they would interfere with the melodic phrasing.

The Ashkenazi melody, rising from diminuendo to fortissimo in the course of its threefold repetition, has intense power. Music, since the Israelites sang a song to God at the Reed Sea, has been the language of the soul as it reaches out toward the unsayable. Yet rather than solve the problem, this suggestion only deepens it. Why chant a melody at all to a text that is not a prayer but a legal process?

So the theories as they stand do not satisfy.

To understand *Kol Nidrei* we need to go back to a unique feature of Tanakh, without counterpart in any other religion. Time and again we find that the dialogue between God and the prophets takes the form of a legal challenge. Sometimes, especially in the books of Hosea and Micah, the plaintiff is God and the accused, the children of Israel. At other times,

◂ as when

as when Abraham argues with God over the fate of Sodom, or Jeremiah or Habakkuk or Job protest the sufferings of the innocent, the roles are reversed. Always the subject is justice, and the context, the covenant between God and Israel. This genre – the dialogue between God and humanity structured as a courtroom drama – is known as the *riv* ("contention, dispute, accusation") pattern, and it is central to Judaism.

It emerges from the logic of *covenant*, Judaism's fundamental idea. A covenant is an agreement between two or more parties who, each respecting the dignity and freedom of the other, come together to pledge their mutual loyalty. In human terms the closest analogy is a marriage. In political terms it is a treaty between two nations. Only in Judaism is the idea given religious dignity (Christianity borrowed the idea of covenant from Judaism but gave it a somewhat different interpretation). It means that God, having liberated the Israelites from slavery in Egypt, adopts them as His *am segula*, His specially cherished nation, while the Israelites accept God as their Sovereign, the Torah as their written constitution, and their mission as "a kingdom of priests and a holy nation" (Ex. 19:6) or, as Isaiah puts it, God's "witnesses" in the world (Is. ch. 43–44).

The covenant bestows an unrivaled dignity on humans. Judaism acknowledges, as do most faiths, that God is infinite and we infinitesimal, God is eternal and we ephemeral, God is everything and we next-to-nothing. But Judaism makes the momentous claim in the opposite direction, that we are "God's partners in the work of creation" (*Shabbat* 10a and 119b). We are not tainted by original sin; we are not incapable of greatness; we are God's stake in the world. Tanakh tells an astonishing love story: about the love of God for a people to whom He binds Himself in covenant, a covenant He never breaks, rescinds or changes however many times we betray it and Him. The covenant is law as love and loyalty.

Hence the model of the courtroom drama when either partner feels that the other has not honored the terms of the agreement. Before the impersonal bar of justice, God may accuse Israel of abandoning Him, or sometimes the roles are reversed and the prophets challenge God on what they perceive as a lack of justice in the world. This is a consistent theme in both Tanakh and the rabbinic literature. It also had a major practical influence on synagogue life.

Any Jew who felt he or she had suffered an injustice could interrupt the reading of the Torah in synagogue (*ikuv keria*) and present their case before the congregation. The plaintiff would mount the *bima*, bang three times on the table and say, "I am delaying the Torah reading." He would explain why he had chosen to present his case directly to the community instead of a court or Beit Din. He would then tell the members of the community that he was depending on them for truth and justice, and one of the leaders of the congregation would accept the responsibility.

The case would be discussed, the *gabbai* would mount the *bima* and announce the names of three arbitrators (*borerim*) who had been chosen to hear the case, and the deadline for settling the disagreement. Usually this was accepted, but if the plaintiff still felt unfairly treated, he could continue to delay the Torah reading. Yaffa Eliach, who describes how this worked in Poland in the interwar years, says that it "proved a potent social weapon, quite often providing the community with a satisfactory and speedy resolution to extremely knotty problems."*

The synagogue, in other words, could be turned into a court of law. That is the function of *Kol Nidrei*. Precisely because it is not a prayer but a legal process, it signals that for the next twenty-five hours what is about to happen is something more and other than prayer in the conventional sense.

The prayers of Yom Kippur are different from those of any other festival. They include a legal act, confession, a plea of guilt that rightly belongs in a court of law. Physically, the synagogue looks like it does the rest of the year, but functionally it has changed. The Beit Knesset has become a Beit Din. The synagogue is now a court of law. Sitting on the Throne of Justice is God Himself and we are the prisoners at the bar. The trial that began on Rosh HaShana has reached its last day. We are the accused, and we are about to be judged on the evidence of our lives. So *Kol Nidrei*, the prayer-that-is-not-a-prayer, transforms the house of prayer into a law-court, providing the setting and mood for the unique drama that will reach its climax at Ne'ila when the court rises, the Judge is ready to leave, and the verdict, written, is about to be sealed.

That is the first dimension of *Kol Nidrei*, but we can go a level deeper.

How, after all, does *teshuva* work? We confess our wrongs, express remorse, and resolve not to repeat, but how can we undo the past? Surely,

* Yaffa Eliach, *There Once Was a World*. New York: Little, Brown and Company, 1998, 84–87.

what's done is done. The asymmetry of time means that we can affect the future but not the past. However, it is not quite so. *The release of vows that takes place through Kol Nidrei constitutes a legal precedent – the only one – for what we seek, through teshuva, to achieve for our sins.* The ground on which we seek annulment of vows is *ḥarata,* "remorse." The fact that we now regret having taken the vow is the reason the sages were able to say that full intent – an essential element of a valid vow – was lacking from the outset.

But this is precisely what we do when we confess our sins and express our remorse for them. We thereby signal retroactively that full intent was lacking from our sins. Had we known then what we know now, we would not have acted as we did. Therefore we did not really mean to do what we did. This is what Resh Lakish meant when he said that *teshuva* has the power retroactively to turn deliberate sins into inadvertent ones (*Yoma* 86b), and inadvertent sins can be forgiven. In fact this is why, immediately after *Kol Nidrei,* we recite the biblical verse that says: "All the congregation of Israel will be forgiven ... for they sinned without intent [*bishgaga*]" (Num. 15:26). So both the annulment of vows and *teshuva* share the power of remorse to change or mitigate the past and liberate us from its bonds.

But there is a third level of significance to *Kol Nidrei* that is deeper still. Recall that Yom Kippur only exists in virtue of the fact that Moses secured God's forgiveness of the Israelites after the sin of the golden calf, descending from the mountain on the tenth of Tishrei with a new set of tablets to replace those he had smashed in anger at their sin.

How did Moses secure God's forgiveness of the people? The text introducing Moses' prayer begins with the Hebrew words, *Vayeḥal Moshe.* Normally these are translated as "Moses besought, implored, entreated, pleaded, or attempted to pacify" God (Ex. 32:11). However, *the same verb is used in the context of annulling or breaking a vow* (Num. 30:3). On this basis the sages advanced a truly remarkable interpretation:

> [*Vayeḥal Moshe* means] "Moses *absolved God of His vow.*" When the Israelites made the golden calf, Moses sought to persuade God to forgive them, but God said, "I have already taken an oath that *Whoever sacrifices to any god other than the* Lord *must be punished* [Ex. 22:19]. I cannot retract what I have said." Moses replied, "Lord of the universe,

> You have given me the power to annul oaths, for You taught me that one who takes an oath cannot break his word but a scholar can absolve him. I hereby absolve You of Your vow." (Abridged from *Shemot Raba* 43:4)

According to the sages, *the original act of divine forgiveness on which Yom Kippur is based came about through the annulment of a vow,* when Moses annulled the vow of God.

If this is so, we understand precisely why *Kol Nidrei* was chosen to introduce the prayers of Yom Kippur:

1. It transforms the synagogue into a courtroom, and prayer into a trial.
2. It establishes the logic of atonement through the power of *ḥarata,* "remorse," retroactively to vitiate the intention behind the deed, thus rendering our sins unwitting (*beshogeg*) and hence forgivable.
3. An act of annulment of a vow – the sages' interpretation of Moses' daring plea to God after the sin of the golden calf – constitutes the historical precedent for Yom Kippur.

Judaism has been accused over the centuries of being a religion of law, not love. This is precisely untrue. Judaism is a religion of law *and* love, for without law there is no justice, and even with law (indeed, *only* with law) there is still mercy, compassion and forgiveness. God's great gift of love *was* law: the law that establishes human rights and responsibilities, that treats rich and poor alike, that allows God to challenge humans but also humans to challenge God, the law studied by every Jewish child, the law written in letters of black fire on white fire that burns in our hearts, making Jews among the most passionate fighters for justice the world has ever known.

Law without love is harsh, but love without law is anarchy and eventually turns to hate. So in the name of the love-of-law and the law-of-love, we ask God to release us from our vows and from our sins, for the same reason: that we regret and have remorse for both. The power of *Kol Nidrei* has less to do with forced conversions, or even music, than with the courtroom drama, unique to Judaism, in which we stand, giving an account of our lives, our fate poised between God's justice and compassion.

◂ The Scapegoat

THE SCAPEGOAT

The strangest element of the service on Yom Kippur in Temple times was the ritual of the two goats, one offered as a sacrifice, the other sent away into the desert "to Azazel." They were brought before the High Priest, to all intents and purposes indistinguishable from one another: they were chosen to be as similar as possible to one another in size and appearance. Lots were drawn, one bearing the words "To the LORD," the other, "To Azazel." The one on which the lot "To the LORD" fell was offered as a sacrifice. Over the other the high priest confessed the sins of the nation and it was then taken away into the desert hills outside Jerusalem where it plunged to its death. Tradition tells us that a red thread would be attached to its horns, half of which was removed before the animal was sent away. If the rite had been effective, the red thread would turn to white.

Sin and guilt offerings were common in ancient Israel, but this ceremony was unique. Normally confession was made over the animal to be offered as a sacrifice. In this case confession was made over the goat *not* offered as a sacrifice. Why the division of the offering into two? Why two identical animals whose fate, so different, was decided by the drawing of a lot? And who or what was Azazel?

The word Azazel appears nowhere else in Scripture, and three major theories emerged as to its meaning. According to the sages and Rashi it meant "a steep, rocky or hard place," in other words a description of its destination. According to Ibn Ezra (cryptically) and Nahmanides (explicitly), Azazel was the name of a spirit or demon, one of the fallen angels referred to in Genesis 6:2. The third interpretation is that the word simply means "the goat [*ez*] that was sent away [*azal*]." Hence the English word "(e)scapegoat" coined by William Tyndale in his 1530 English translation of the Bible.

Maimonides offers the most compelling explanation, that the ritual was intended as a symbolic drama: "There is no doubt that sins cannot be carried like a burden, and taken off the shoulder of one being to be laid on that of another being. But these ceremonies are of a symbolic character, and serve to impress men with a certain idea, and to induce them to repent; as if to say, we have freed ourselves of our previous deeds, have cast them behind our backs, and removed them from us as far as possible" (*Guide for the Perplexed*, 3:46). This makes sense, but the question

◂ remains

remains. Why was this ritual different from all other sin or guilt offerings? Why two goats rather than one?

The simplest answer is that the High Priest's service on Yom Kippur was intended to achieve something other and more than ordinary sacrifices occasioned by sin. The Torah specifies two objectives, not one: "For on this day you will be atoned and made pure; of all your sins before the LORD you shall be purified" (Lev. 16:30). Normally all that was aimed at was atonement, *kapara*. On Yom Kippur something else was aimed at: cleansing, purification, *tahara*. Atonement is for acts. Purification is for persons. Sins leave stains on the character of those who commit them, and these need to be cleansed before we can undergo catharsis and begin anew.

Sin defiles. King David felt stained after his adultery with Bathsheba: "Wash me thoroughly of my iniquity and cleanse me of my sin" (Ps. 51:4). Shakespeare has Macbeth say, after his crime, "Will these hands ne'er be clean?" The ceremony closest to the rite of the scapegoat – where an animal was let loose rather than sacrificed – was the ritual for someone who was being cleansed of a skin disease:

> If they have been healed of their defiling skin disease, the priest shall order that *two live clean birds* and some cedar wood, scarlet yarn, and hyssop be brought for the person to be cleansed. Then the priest shall order that *one of the birds be sacrificed* over fresh water in a clay pot. He is then to take the live bird... And he is *to release the live bird in the open fields*. (Leviticus 14:4–7)

The released bird, like the scapegoat, was sent away carrying the impurity, the stain. Clearly this is psychological. A moral stain is not something physical. It exists in the mind, the emotions, the soul. It is hard to rid oneself of the feeling of defilement when you have committed a wrong, even when you know it has been forgiven. Some symbolic action seems necessary. The survival of such rites as *Tashlikh*, the "casting away" of sins on Rosh HaShana, and *Kaparot*, "atonements, expiations" on the eve of Yom Kippur – the first involving crumbs, the second a live chicken – is evidence of this. Both practices were criticized by leading halakhic authorities yet both survived for the reason Maimonides gives.

◂ It is easier

It is easier to feel that defilement has gone if we have had some visible representation of its departure. We feel cleansed once we see it go somewhere, carried by something. This may not be rational, but then neither are we, much of the time.

That is the simplest explanation. The sacrificed goat represented *kapara,* atonement. The goat sent away symbolized *tahara,* cleansing of the moral stain. There is however an additional suggestion made by the Midrash, the *Zohar,* and the fifteenth-century Spanish commentator Abarbanel that takes us to an altogether deeper level of symbolism. All three note a series of connections, verbal or visual, between the two goats and the sibling rivalry between Jacob and Esau.

Two identical goats suggest twins, and Jacob and Esau are the Torah's most notable (if non-identical) twins. Two goats also play a part in their story. When Rebecca hears that Isaac is about to bless Esau, she tells Jacob, "Go out to the flock and bring me *two choice young goats,* so I can prepare some tasty food for your father, such as he likes" (Gen. 27:9).

The Hebrew word used for "goat" in Leviticus 16 is *se'ir,* which also means "hairy." This is the word used to describe Esau at birth ("His whole body was like a hairy garment" [Gen. 25:25]) and later when Jacob was about to take Esau's blessing ("But my brother Esau is a hairy man" [Gen. 27:11]). Esau's territory throughout the Bible is Mount Seir. The red thread attached to the goat also has Esau connections. His alternative name, Edom, means "red," either because his hair was red at birth (Gen. 25:25) or because of the red lentil soup for which he traded his birthright (25:30).

The keyword of Leviticus 16 is *k-p-r,* "atone." It appears twenty-three times in this one chapter. Significantly, the only time it appears in the sense of "atone" in Genesis is when Jacob, about to meet Esau after an absence of twenty-two years, sends messengers with gifts, saying, "I will pacify him [*akhapra panav*] with these gifts I am sending on ahead; later, when I see him, perhaps he will receive me" (32:20).

If there *is* a connection between the scapegoat and the rivalry between Jacob and Esau, what is it? A clue is offered by the analysis of sacrificial rites by the French scholar Rene Girard in his classic work, *Violence and the Sacred.* Girard argues (1) that the primary religious act is sacrifice; (2) sacrifice is always an attempt to curb violence within society; and (3) the primary source of violence is sibling rivalry.

◂ Girard

Girard takes issue with Freud who argued that violence is born in the tension between fathers and sons: the Oedipus and Laius complexes. Genesis supports Girard. One of its key themes is sibling rivalry – between Cain and Abel, Isaac and Ishmael, Jacob and Esau and Joseph and his brothers. In at least three of these cases, violence is waiting in the wings and in one, Cain and Abel, there is actual fratricide.

Girard suggests that the origin of violence is "mimetic desire," that is, *the desire to be someone else, to have what they have*. The classic instances of this in literature usually have to do with twins. Non-biblical examples are, in Greek myth, Oedipus' sons Eteocles and Polynices, and in Roman folklore, Romulus and Remus. Girard states that "The proliferation of enemy brothers in Greek myth and in dramatic adaptations of myth implies the continual presence of a sacrificial crisis" – that is, without sacrifice there is violence between siblings, at least one of whom wants what the other has.

Turning to Esau and Jacob, this is the dominant theme of their early life. Jacob buys Esau's birthright, takes Esau's blessing, and when asked by his blind father Isaac, "Who are you, my son?" replies, "I am Esau your firstborn" (Gen. 27:18–19). Even when the twins were born, Jacob was clinging to Esau's heel. Jacob is the supreme instance in the Torah of mimetic desire.

It can be hard for us today to realize that there was once a time when Jacob and Esau were not seen in black-and-white terms. Rabbinic tradition tends to give Jacob all the virtues, Esau all the vices (except in honoring his father, where all agree that he was exemplary). Already in Tanakh we find this contrast in the statement of Malachi (1:2–3) that God loves Jacob and hates Esau. But Malachi was the last of the prophets, and two earlier prophets, Hosea and Jeremiah, saw matters in a very different light.

Hosea says: "The Lord has a charge to bring against Judah; He will punish Jacob according to his ways and repay him according to his deeds. In the womb he grasped his brother's heel" (Hos. 12:3–4). Jeremiah says, in a passage laden with echoes of the Jacob story, "Beware of your friends; do not trust your brothers, for every brother behaves like Jacob [*kol aḥ akov Yaakov*]" (Jer. 9:3). Hosea and Jeremiah are criticizing Jacob for his behavior toward Esau. Both are speaking about sin and the need for repentance. The Jeremiah passage is the haftara for Tisha B'Av, the saddest day of the year.

In the haunting passage (Gen. 32:24–32) in which Jacob wrestles, alone at night, with an unnamed adversary, he finally throws off his mimetic desire to be like Esau. The stranger, who refuses to be named, was identified by the sages as "the guardian angel of Esau" ("*saro shel Esav*," *Bereshit Raba* 77:3, 78:3). He asks Jacob to let him go. Jacob says, "I will not let you go until you bless me." The stranger then gives him a new name, Israel. A new name in this context means a new identity. Jacob will no longer be *Yaakov*, the child who would not let go of his brother's heel (Gen. 25:26). He will be content to be himself, "the man who wrestles with [or, who has become great before] man and God" (Gen. 32:28). At that point, Jacob lets go. It is the turning point in his life.

The next morning he meets Esau after their long separation. He bows down to him seven times, calls him "my lord," and himself "your servant," and says about the huge gift of cattle which Esau is reluctant to accept, "Please *take my blessing* that is brought to you, for God has shown me favor and I have everything" (33:11). The reference is to the blessing Jacob took pretending to be Esau, in which Isaac said, "May nations serve you and peoples *bow down to you*. Be *lord over your brothers*, and may the sons of your mother bow down to you" (Gen. 27:29). By bowing down to Esau and calling him "my lord," Jacob is showing that he no longer wants his brother's blessing and is content with his own ("I have everything").

Putting all this together we arrive at a dramatic conclusion. (1) *The worst sin – it caused the Flood – is violence*; (2) *the greatest source of violence in Genesis is sibling rivalry, one person wanting the blessing that rightly belongs to another*; (3) *the antidote to violence is to stop wanting to be someone else and to be content to be yourself.* Jacob and Esau were able to meet, embrace, and peaceably go their separate ways as soon as Jacob was content to be himself and no longer wanted Esau's blessings. So it is with us. We can live at peace with the world when we are at peace with ourselves. If we seek to cure ourselves of the will to sin, we must let go of the desire to have someone else's blessings.

The ritual of the two identical goats, one of which was sent away bearing with it our sins, can then be seen to symbolize the two identities that live in every troubled heart: the one that is myself and the one that is not-myself. *When I learn to let the "not-myself" go, as the goat was let go on Yom Kippur, I find inner peace and can live at peace with the world.* The goat

◂ sent away

sent away is the Esau that lived in Jacob's mind until, one night wrestling with a stranger, Jacob learned to let go, and in that act became Israel, the father of the Jewish people, content to be itself, no longer seeking the identity or the blessings of others.

OF POTTERS AND CLAY

One poem said on *Kol Nidrei* night has long confused commentators and translators, the one beginning, "Like clay in the potter's hands" (page 151). What has puzzled them is the refrain, "Look to the covenant and disregard our inclination." Many have understood "the covenant" to be a reference to the Thirteen Attributes of Mercy, about which the Talmud says that God made a covenant that this prayer would not go unanswered (*Rosh HaShana* 17b). They have interpreted *Yetzer* as "the Accuser," that is, the angel, Satan, who is prosecuting counsel on the Day of Judgment.

However the poem is in fact about an earlier covenant, and the word *yetzer* means "inclination," not "Accuser." The refrain is based on a remarkable midrash that weaves together four biblical verses – two from the story of Noah and the Flood, and two from the prophets Isaiah and Jeremiah – to provide a stunning account of the human condition and a powerful plea for the defense of those who sin.

The story begins with the moment in the book of Genesis when God decided to bring a Flood:

> God saw that man's wickedness on earth was increasing. Every inclination [*yetzer*] of his innermost thought was only for evil, all day long. God regretted that He had made man on earth, and He was pained to His very core. (Genesis 6:5–6)

> God then brought a flood that wiped out everything He had made other than Noah, his family and the animals he brought with him into the ark. Eventually the flood ended, the waters receded, and Noah and his entourage set foot on dry land to begin the story again. Noah made an offering to God, which moved God to vow that never again would He punish humanity in this wholesale way:

> God said to Himself, "Never again will I curse the soil because of man, for the inclination [*yetzer*] of man's heart is evil from his youth. I will never again strike down all life as I have just done." (Genesis 8:21)

◂ The contradiction

The contradiction between the two passages is glaring. In Genesis 6 man's inclination was a reason for God to bring a flood. In Genesis 8 it has become a reason for God *not* to bring another flood. How are we to understand this?

The sages made an intuitive connection between the word *yetzer*, "inclination," and *yotzer*, "creator, former, molder, shaper." The verb *y-tz-r* is the one used in Genesis 2:7 to describe the creation of the first man: "Then the LORD God formed [*vayitzer*] the man from the dust of the earth and breathed into his nostrils the breath of life." More specifically, *yotzer* also means "potter," and this led the sages to two other biblical verses. One appears in the book of Jeremiah. The prophet has been told by God to go the house of the local potter and watch him as he shapes the clay. Then Jeremiah hears God saying:

> "Can I not do with you, Israel, as this potter does?" declares the LORD. "Like clay in the hand of the potter [*yotzer*], so are you in My hand, Israel. (Jeremiah 18:6)

Jeremiah heard this as a warning of imminent catastrophe. The people were sinning and they were about to suffer defeat and exile at the hands of the Babylonians. Israel could do nothing to avoid this fate except to repent. Without God, all attempts to defeat their enemy would fail. They were in God's hands, like the clay on the potter's wheel.

Isaiah, however, took the same image and gave it a quite different slant:

> Yet You, LORD, are our Father.
> We are the clay, You are our Potter [*Yotzrenu*];
> we are all the work of Your hand.
> Do not be angry beyond measure, LORD;
> do not remember our sins forever. (Isaiah 64:7–8)

Forgive us, says Isaiah, for we are what You made us. If we do wrong, it is because You gave us the freedom to do wrong. If we disappoint You, remember it is You who shaped us, formed us, made us what we are. You are the Potter, we merely the clay in Your hands.

Out of this array of verses spanning the centuries, and playing on the

◂ connection

connection between *yetzer* and *yotzer*, "inclination" and "potter," the sages constructed the following remarkable midrash:

> What is the meaning of *We are the clay, You are our Potter*? Israel said: "Master of the universe, You have caused it to be written about us, *Like clay in the hand of the potter, so are you in My hand, Israel.* Therefore do not leave us even though we sin and provoke You, for we are merely the clay and You are the Potter. Consider: if a potter makes a jar and leaves a pebble in it, when it comes out of the furnace it will leak from the hole left by the pebble and lose the liquid poured into it. Who caused the jar to leak and lose its liquid? The potter who left the pebble in the jar as it was being made." This is how Israel pleaded before God: "Master of the universe, You created in us an evil inclination from our youth, as it says, *for the inclination of man's heart is evil from his youth*, and it is this that has caused us to sin, since You have not removed from us the inclination that instigates us to sin." (*Shemot Raba* 46:4)

We now see how the sages understood the change in God's relation to the world before and after the Flood. Before the Flood, God was exasperated at the human capacity for evil, the *yetzer*. After the Flood, however, seeing Noah's devotion, God realizes that it is not the human capacity for evil that is remarkable. It is our capacity for good. We do evil because we are flesh and blood. We are physical. We have instinctual drives. We are clay not fire, mortals not angels. God formed us from the dust of the earth. Dust we are, and to dust we return.

"How then can I punish them for their *yetzer* if I am their *Yotzer*?" That is the thought God had after the Flood. It was then that He made a covenant with Noah that He would never again destroy humanity. Many centuries later the same dialectic occurs in the prophecies of Jeremiah and Isaiah. He reminds Jeremiah of His total power over the fate of nations. But the powerlessness of humanity in the face of God serves Isaiah as the great plea for the defense: How can You blame us for what we are if You made us what we are?

Isaiah's prayer serves as the basis for the poet to say we are "like clay in the potter's hands… look to the covenant, and disregard our inclination." We have a *yetzer* because God is the *Yotzer*. We have instinctual drives that

◂ lead us

lead us to sin because that is how we were made, creatures of earth with earthly passions, physical beings imprisoned in our physicality. We are, said Hamlet, the "quintessence of dust." The poet throws himself on the mercy of God expressed in the covenant He made with Noah after the Flood when He said, "Never again will I curse the soil because of man, for the inclination of man's heart is evil from his youth."

Is this, considered impartially, an adequate defense? Can we blame our sins on God who made us? In general terms, No. For God gave us the power to defeat the inclination. That is what He said to Cain at the dawn of the human story: "Sin is crouching at your door; it desires to have you, but you can master it" (Gen. 4:7).

Nonetheless, tonight we are on trial, and the poet is concerned less to state a metaphysical truth than to throw himself on the mercy of the Judge, reminding Him of the time when He first made a covenant of compassion and forbearance with humankind. This is, in short, a plea in the great Judaic tradition of audacity in prayer, about which the Talmud says, "*Ḥutzpa* even toward Heaven, helps" (*Sanhedrin* 105a).

As with *Kol Nidrei* so with "Like clay in the potter's hands," this is less a conventional prayer than a judicial hearing in which counsel for the defense pleads with every argument at his disposal, from confession to self-abasement, to the annulment of vows, to a reminder of the great moment of divine compassion after the Flood when God forgave humanity for merely being human. An ultimate truth? No. Rather a prayer said in the confidence borne of the love God has for us, His human children, the work of His hands.

Yom Kippur – How It Changes Us

To those who fully open themselves to it, Yom Kippur is a life-transforming experience. It tells us that God, who created the universe in love and forgiveness, reaches out to us in love and forgiveness, asking us to love and forgive others. God never asked us not to make mistakes. All He asks is that we acknowledge our mistakes, learn from them, grow through them, and make amends where we can.

No religion has held such a high view of human possibility. The God who created us in His image, gave us freedom. We are not tainted by original sin, destined to fail, caught in the grip of an evil only divine grace

◂ can defeat

can defeat. To the contrary we have within us the power to choose life. Together we have the power to change the world.

Nor are we, as some scientific materialists claim, mere concatenations of chemicals, a bundle of selfish genes blindly replicating themselves into the future. Our souls are more than our minds, our minds are more than our brains, and our brains are more than mere chemical impulses responding to stimuli. Human freedom – the freedom to choose to be better than we were – remains a mystery but it is not a mere given. Freedom is like a muscle and the more we exercise it, the stronger and healthier it becomes.

Judaism constantly asks us to exercise our freedom. To be a Jew is not to go with the flow, to be like everyone else, to follow the path of least resistance, to worship the conventional wisdom of the age. To the contrary, to be a Jew is to have the courage to live in a way that is not the way of everyone. Each time we eat, drink, pray or go to work, we are conscious of the demands our faith makes on us, to live God's will and be one of His ambassadors to the world. Judaism always has been, perhaps always will be, counter-cultural.

In ages of collectivism, Jews emphasized the value of the individual. In ages of individualism, Jews built strong communities. When most of humanity was consigned to ignorance, Jews were highly literate. When others were building monuments and amphitheaters, Jews were building schools. In materialistic times they kept faith with the spiritual. In ages of poverty they practiced *tzedaka* so that none would lack the essentials of a dignified life. The sages said that Abraham was called *haIvri*, "the Hebrew," because all the world was on one side (*ever eḥad*) and Abraham on the other (*Bereshit Raba* 42:8). To be a Jew is to swim against the current, challenging the idols of the age whatever the idol, whatever the age.

So, as our ancestors used to say, "*S'iz schver tzu zein a Yid*," It is not easy to be a Jew. But if Jews have contributed to the human heritage out of all proportion to our numbers, the explanation lies here. Those of whom great things are asked, become great – not because they are inherently better or more gifted than others but because they feel themselves challenged, summoned, to greatness.

Few religions have asked more of their followers. There are 613 commandments in the Torah. Jewish law applies to every aspect of our being,

◂ from

from the highest aspirations to the most prosaic details of quotidian life. Our library of sacred texts – Tanakh, Mishna, Gemara, Midrash, codes and commentaries – is so vast that no lifetime is long enough to master it. Theophrastus, a pupil of Aristotle, sought for a description that would explain to his fellow Greeks what Jews are. The answer he came up with was, "a nation of philosophers."

So high does Judaism set the bar that it is inevitable that we should fall short time and again. This means that forgiveness was written into the script from the beginning. God, said the sages, sought to create the world under the attribute of strict justice but He saw that it could not stand. What did He do? He added mercy to justice, compassion to retribution, forbearance to the strict rule of law. God forgives. Judaism is a religion, the world's first, of forgiveness.

Not every civilization is as forgiving as Judaism. There were religions that never forgave Jews for refusing to convert. Many of the greatest European intellectuals – among them Voltaire, Fichte, Kant, Hegel, Schopenhauer, Nietzsche, Frege and Heidegger – never quite forgave Jews for staying Jews, different, angular, countercultural, iconoclastic. Yet despite the tragedies of more than twenty centuries, Jews and Judaism still flourish, refusing to grant victory to cultures of contempt or the angel of death.

The majesty and mystery of Judaism is that though at best Jews were a small people in a small land, no match for the circumambient empires that periodically assaulted them, Jews did not give way to self-hate, self-disesteem or despair. Beneath the awe and solemnity of Yom Kippur one fact shines radiant throughout: that God loves us more than we love ourselves. He believes in us more than we believe in ourselves. He never gives up on us, however many times we slip and fall. The story of Judaism from beginning to end is the tale of a love of God for a people who rarely fully reciprocated that love, yet never altogether failed to be moved by it.

Rabbi Akiva put it best in a mere two words: *Avinu Malkenu* (*Ta'anit* 25b). Yes, You are our Sovereign, God Almighty, Maker of the cosmos, King of kings. But You are also our Father. You told Moses to say to Pharaoh in Your name: "My child, My firstborn, Israel" (Ex. 4:22). That love continues to make Jews a symbol of hope to humanity, testifying that a nation does not need to be large to be great, nor powerful to have influence. Each of us can, by a single act of kindness or generosity of spirit, cause a ray of the divine light to shine in the human darkness, allowing the *Shekhina*, at least for a moment, to be at home in our world.

More than Yom Kippur expresses our faith in God, it is the expression of God's faith in us.

SHAME AND GUILT

Judaism is the world's greatest example of a guilt-and-repentance culture as opposed to the shame-and-honor culture of the ancient Greeks.

In a shame culture such as that of Greek tragedy, evil attaches to the person. It is a kind of indelible stain. There is no way back for one who has done a shameful deed. He is a pariah and the best he can hope for is to die in a noble cause. In a guilt culture like that of Judaism, evil is an attribute of the act not the agent. Even one who has done wrong has a sacred self that remains intact. He may have to undergo punishment. He certainly has to make amends. But there remains a core of worth that can never be lost. A guilt culture hates the sin, not the sinner. Repentance, rehabilitation and return are always possible.

A guilt culture is a culture of responsibility. We do not blame anyone else for the wrong we do. It is always tempting to blame others – it wasn't me, it was my parents, my upbringing, my friends, my genes, my social class, the media, the system, "them." That was what the first two humans did in the Garden of Eden. When challenged by God for eating the forbidden fruit, the man blamed the woman. The woman blamed the serpent. The result was paradise lost.

Blaming others for our failings is as old as humanity, but it is disastrous. It means that we define ourselves as victims. A culture of victimhood wins the compassion of others but at too high a cost. It incubates feelings of resentment, humiliation, grievance and grudge. It leads people to rage against the world instead of taking steps to mend it. Jews have suffered much, but Yom Kippur prevents us from ever defining ourselves as victims. As we confess our sins, we blame no one but ourselves.

That is demanding, psychologically and spiritually. Yet it is the price we must pay for freedom. Other ancient literatures record the successes of rulers and empires. The Hebrew Bible is a unique chronicle of failures. No one in its pages is perfect, not the patriarchs and matriarchs, not

◂ priests

priests or prophets, not kings or the ruling elite. No history is as painfully honest as that of Tanakh, and it was possible only on the deep belief that God forgives. God pardons; God atones; God is holding out His hand, calling us back with unextinguishable love. That allows us to be honest with ourselves.

THE GROWTH MINDSET

It also allows us to grow. We owe a debt to cognitive behavioral therapy for reminding us of a classic element of Jewish faith, that when we change the way we think, we change the way we feel. And when we feel differently, we live differently. What we believe shapes what we become.

At the heart of *teshuva* is the belief that we can change. We are not destined to be forever what we were. In the Torah we see Judah grow from an envious brother prepared to sell Joseph as a slave, to a man with the conscience and courage to offer himself as a slave so that his brother Benjamin can go free.

We see Moses grow from a man lacking the confidence to lead – "Who am I?" (Ex. 3:11), "They will not believe in me" (Ex. 4:1) – to become the greatest leader of all time. The man who once stammered and said of himself "I am not a man of words" (Ex. 4:10), becomes by the end of his life the most eloquent and visionary of all the prophets.

We see remarkable women transcend their social situation. Tamar, the woman Judah mistakes for a prostitute, eventually teaches him to have the courage to admit he was wrong, reinforcing his role as the first *ba'al teshuva* in history. Ruth, the woman from Moab, Israel's enemy, displays such growth through her loyalty to Naomi that she becomes the great-grandmother of David, Israel's greatest king.

We see Hosea, Jeremiah, Jonah and Job wrestle with themselves and with God. That, after all, is what the name Israel means: one who wrestles, not one who accepts the status quo. The figures of the Hebrew Bible are not two-dimensional figures who remain at the end of their lives what they were at the beginning. Theirs may be a painful, but not a tragic, fate.

We know that some people relish a challenge and take risks, while others, no less gifted, play it safe and ultimately underachieve. Psychologists tell us that the crucial difference lies in whether you think of your ability as a fixed quantum or as something developed through effort and experience. *Teshuva* is essentially about effort and experience. It assumes we can grow.

Teshuva means I can take risks, knowing that I may fail but knowing that failure is not final. Time and again Moses failed to engender in his people a clear sense of history and destiny, even a basic gratitude for what God had done for them. But failing a hundred times does not make a failure. Indeed in God's eyes none of us is a failure so long as we still have breath to breathe and a life to live.

Teshuva means that if I get it wrong and make mistakes, God does not lose faith in me even though I may lose faith in myself. "Were my father and my mother to forsake me, the Lord would take me in" (Ps. 27:10). Some of the greatest heroes in the Bible did not believe in themselves. Isaiah said, "I am a man of unclean lips" (Is. 6:5). Jeremiah said, "I cannot speak for I am a child" (Jer. 1:6). Jonah, given a mission by God, ran away. God believes in us, even if we do not. That alone is a life-changing fact if we fully open ourselves to its implications.

Teshuva means that the past is not irredeemable. Through *teshuva* undertaken in love, said Resh Lakish, "even deliberate sins may be transformed into merits" (*Yoma* 86b). Resh Lakish himself was a *ba'al teshuva,* a reformed bandit who used the strength he had once devoted to robbery to save people held hostage. King David, another *ba'al teshuva,* drew some of his deepest poetry from the pain of his personal abyss.

Teshuva means that from every mistake, I grow. There is no failure I experience that does not make me a deeper human being; no challenge I accept, however much I fall short, that does not develop in me strengths I would not otherwise have had.

That is the first transformation of Yom Kippur: a renewed relationship with myself.

OUR RELATIONSHIPS WITH OTHERS

The second is a renewed relationship with others. We know that Yom Kippur atones only for sins between us and God, but that does not mean that these are the only sins for which we need to seek atonement. To the contrary: many, even most, of the sins we confess on Yom Kippur are about our relationships with others. Rabbi Ḥanina ben Dosa taught: "In one whom people delight, God delights" (*Avot* 3:13). Throughout the

◂ prophetic

prophetic and rabbinic literature it is assumed that as we act to others so God acts to us. Those who forgive are forgiven. Those who condemn are condemned.

The days from Rosh HaShana to Yom Kippur are a time when we try to mend relationships that have broken. It takes one kind of moral courage to apologize, another to forgive, but both may be necessary. Failure to heal relationships can split families, destroy marriages, ruin friendships and divide communities. That is not where God wants us to be. As the sages pointed out, God allowed his own name to be blotted out to make peace between husband and wife. They also said that after Sarah died, Abraham took back Hagar and Ishmael into his family, mending the rift that had occurred many years before. Aaron, according to tradition, was loved by all the people because he was able to mend fractured friendships.

Writing as a self-confessed secular Jew, the philosopher Alain de Botton says that Yom Kippur is "one of the most psychologically effective mechanisms ever devised for the resolution of social conflict." He explains:

> The Day of Atonement has the immense advantage of making the idea of saying sorry look like it came from somewhere else, the initiative of neither the perpetrator nor the victim. It is the day itself that is making us sit here and talk about the peculiar incident six months ago when you lied and I blustered and you accused me of insincerity and I made you cry, an incident that neither of us can quite forget but that we can't quite mention either and which has slowly been corroding the trust and love we once had for each other.*

Without a designated day, would we ever get around to mending our broken relationships? Often we do not tell people how they have hurt us because we do not want to look vulnerable and small-minded. In the opposite direction, sometimes we are reluctant to apologize because we feel so guilty that we do not want to expose our guilt. As De Botton puts it: "We can be so sorry that we find ourselves incapable of saying sorry."

* Alain de Botton, *Religion for Atheists: A Non-Believer's Guide to the Uses of Religion*. London: Hamish Hamilton, 2012.

◂ He adds

He adds: "So cathartic is the Day of Atonement, it seems a pity that there should be only one of them a year."

That is the second transformation of Yom Kippur: a renewed relationship with others.

COMING HOME

The third is a renewed relationship with God.

On Yom Kippur, God is close. Admittedly in Judaism we prefer to talk *to* God than *about* God. Hence we have relatively little theology. We know that God is beyond our understanding. If I could know God, said one Jewish philosopher, I would be God. Yet Jewish life is full of signals of transcendence, intimations of eternity. We encounter God in three ways: through creation, revelation and redemption.

Through creation: the more we understand of cosmology, the more we realize how improbable the universe is. According to Lord Rees, former President of the Royal Society and Britain's most distinguished scientist, the margin of error in the six mathematical constants that determine the shape of the physical universe is almost infinitesimally small. The universe is too finely tuned for the emergence of stars, planets and life to have come into existence by chance. The only alternative hypothesis is that there is an infinity of parallel universes of which we happen to inhabit the one congenial to the emergence of life. That raises as many questions as it solves, if indeed it solves any. The more we understand of the sheer improbability of the existence of the universe, the emergence of life from inanimate matter, and the equally mysterious appearance of Homo sapiens, the only life-form capable of asking the question "Why?" the more the line from Psalms rings true: "How numerous are Your works, LORD; You made them all in wisdom" (Ps. 104:24).

Through revelation: the words of God as recorded in the Torah. There is nothing in history to compare to the fact that Jews spent a thousand years (from Moses to the last of the prophets) compiling a commentary to the Torah in the form of the prophetic, historical and wisdom books of Tanakh, then another thousand years (from Malachi to the Babylonian Talmud) compiling a commentary to the commentary in the form of the vast literature of the Oral Torah (Midrash, Mishna and Gemara), then another thousand years (from the Geonim to the *Aḥaronim*, the

◂ later

later authorities) writing commentaries to the commentary to the commentary.

No people has so loved a book, declaring that its study is a higher religious experience than prayer. In the land of Israel it was their written constitution as a nation. In the Diaspora it was, as Heine put it, the "portable homeland" of the Jews. It remains the source and wellspring from which the West has drawn its great ideals of the sanctity of life, the twin imperatives of justice and love, personal and social responsibility, peace as an ideal, *tzedaka* as an imperative, the importance of equal access to knowledge and dignity, our duties as guardians of the natural world and many other ideals without which the West would not be what it is. If we search anywhere for the voice of God, it is here, in the Book of books.

And through history: many great thinkers, including Blaise Pascal and Leo Tolstoy, believed that Jewish history was the most compelling evidence of the existence of God. Nikolai Berdyaev (1874–1948) was a former professor of philosophy at the University of Moscow who eventually rejected Marxism and devoted the rest of his life to religion. In *The Meaning of History* he explains why:

> I remember how the materialist interpretation of history, when I attempted in my youth to verify it by applying it to the destinies of peoples, broke down in the case of the Jews, where destiny seemed absolutely inexplicable from the materialistic standpoint… Its survival is a mysterious and wonderful phenomenon demonstrating that the life of this people is governed by a special predetermination, transcending the processes of adaptation expounded by the materialistic interpretation of history. The survival of the Jews, their resistance to destruction, their endurance under absolutely peculiar conditions and the fateful role played by them in history: all these point to the particular and mysterious foundations of their destiny.*

But perhaps such reflections are beside the point. For it can sometimes be that God comes to us not as the conclusion of a line of reasoning but as a feeling, an intuition, a sensed presence, as we stand in the synagogue on this holy day – listening to our people's melodies, saying

* Nikolai Berdyaev, *The Meaning of History*. New Brunswick, NJ: Transaction, 2009, 86–87.

◂ the words

the words Jews have said from Barcelona to Bergen-Belsen to Benei Berak, from Toledo to Treblinka to Tel Aviv – knowing that we are part of an immense story that has played itself out through the centuries and continents, the tempestuous yet ultimately hope-inspiring love story of a people in search of God and God in search of a people.

There has never been a drama remotely like this in its ups and downs, triumphs and tragedies, its songs of praise and lamentation, and we are part of it. For most of us it is not something we chose but a fate we were born in to. But as Winston Churchill put it, "Some people like the Jews, and some do not. But no thoughtful man can deny the fact that they are beyond question the most formidable and the most remarkable race which has ever appeared in the world." Or as the Oxford literary scholar A.L. Rowse wrote toward the end of his life, "If there is one honor in the world I should like, it would be to be an honorary member of the Jewish people."

WHAT CHAPTER WILL WE WRITE IN THE BOOK OF LIFE?

In 1888, Alfred Nobel, the man who invented dynamite, was reading his morning papers when, with a shock, he found himself reading his own obituary. It turned out that a journalist had made a simple mistake. It was Nobel's *brother* who had died.

What horrified Nobel was what he read. It spoke about "the dynamite king" who had made a fortune from explosives. Nobel suddenly realized that if he did not change his life, that was all he would be remembered for. At that moment he decided to dedicate his fortune to creating five annual prizes for those who'd made outstanding contributions in physics, chemistry, medicine, literature and peace. Nobel chose to be remembered not for selling weapons of destruction but for honoring contributions to human knowledge. The question Yom Kippur forces on us is not so much "Will we live?" but "*How* will we live?" For what would we wish to be remembered?

On this day of days we are brutally candid: "before I was formed I was unworthy, and now that I have been formed it is as if I had not been formed. I am dust while alive, how much more so when I am dead" (page 119). Yet the same faith that inspired those words also declared that we should see ourselves and the world as if equally poised between merit

◂ and guilt

and guilt, and that our next act could tilt the balance, for my life and for the world (Maimonides, Laws of Repentance 3:4). Judaism lives in this dialect between our smallness and our potential greatness. We may be dust, but within us are immortal longings.

Yom Kippur invites us to become better than we were in the knowledge that we can be better than we are. That knowledge comes from God. I remember as a student hearing a witty put-down of a brash business tycoon: "He is a self-made man, thereby relieving God of a great responsibility." If we are only self-made, we live within the prison of our own limitations. The truly great human beings are those who have opened themselves to the inspiration of something greater than themselves.

"Wherever you find the greatness of God," said Rabbi Yoḥanan, "there you find His humility" (*Megilla* 31a). Yom Kippur is about the humility that leads to greatness: our ability to say, over and over again, "We have sinned," and yet know that this is not a maudlin self-abasement, but rather, the prelude to greater achievement in the future, the way a champion in any sport, a maestro in any field, reviews his or her past mistakes as part of their preparation for the next challenge, the next rung to climb.

Jews had a genius for spiritual greatness. Even Sigmund Freud, hostile as he was to religion in general, could not but express admiration in the last book he wrote, *Moses and Monotheism*, for the way Judaism produced not one charismatic figure but generation after generation of them. The philosopher Ludwig Wittgenstein, even more ambivalent about his Jewish ancestry, wrote in his notebook in 1931, "Amongst Jews 'genius' is found only in the holy man."* Jews had this genius not because they are better than others – often, reading the prophets, you get the impression that the opposite was sometimes true – but because they worked harder at it. The Hebrew word for serving God, *avoda*, also means "hard work."

Judaism takes the simple things of life and makes them holy. *Kashrut* makes eating holy. *Kiddush* makes drinking holy. The laws of family purity make the physical relationship between husband and wife holy. Study sanctifies the intellect. Prayer reconfigures the mind. Constant acts of generosity and care sharpen our emotional intelligence, honing our skills

* Ludwig Wittgenstein, *Culture and Value*. Chicago: University of Chicago Press, 1980, 18e.

◂ of empathy

of empathy. Judaism, as Rabbi Joseph Soloveitchik put it, sees creativity as the essence of humanity, and our greatest creation is our self. We forge our life in the fire of love: love of God, the neighbor and the stranger. And by sanctifying family and community, Judaism sacralizes the bonds of belonging that make us who we are.

The power of Yom Kippur is that it brings us face to face with these truths. Through its words, music and devotions, through the way it focuses energies by depriving us of all the physical pleasures we normally associate with a Jewish festival, through the sheer driving passion of the liturgy with its hundred ways of saying sorry, it confronts us with the ultimate question: How will we live? Will we live a life that explores to the full the capacity of the human mind to reach out to that which lies beyond it? Will we grow emotionally? Will we learn the arts of loyalty and love? Will we train our inner ear to hear the cry of the lonely and the poor? Will we live a life that makes a difference, bringing the world-that-is a little closer to being the world-that-ought-to-be? Will we open our hearts and minds to God?

It is possible to live a lifetime without asking any of these questions. It is the genius of Judaism that it makes us do so once a year, when God is close to us because we are close to Him. Yom Kippur retains the traces of those two great figures, Moses the prophet and Aaron the priest, who between them created a tension between spontaneity and structure, passion and order, which continues to vitalize the Jewish spirit, giving it the blessings of both restlessness and rest. Alone with God, together with our people, singing the songs and praying the prayers they said in every age under the most diverse circumstances, we find ourselves questioned, challenged, summoned, inspired.

Like Moses on the mountain, like Aaron in the Holy of Holies, we come as near as we can to being face-to-face with God, and after it we are not the same as we were before. That personal transformation, the ability to make our tomorrow greater than our yesterday, is the essence of *teshuva* and of Yom Kippur.

The most demanding day of the Jewish year, a day without food and drink, a day of prayer and penitence, confession and pleading, in which we accuse ourselves of every conceivable sin, still calls to Jews, touching us at the deepest level of our being. It is a day in which we run toward the open arms of God, weeping because we may have disappointed Him, or because sometimes we feel He has disappointed us, yet knowing that we need one another, for though God can create universes, He cannot live within the human heart unless we let Him in.

It is a day not just of confession and forgiveness but of a profound liberation. Atonement means that we can begin again. We are not held captive by the past, by our failures. The book is open and God invites us – His hand guiding us the way a scribe guides the hand of those who write a letter in a Torah scroll – to write a new chapter in the story of our people, a chapter uniquely our own yet one that we cannot write on our own without being open to something vaster than we will ever fully understand. It is a day on which God invites us to greatness.

May He forgive us. May we, lifted by His love, rise to meet His call.

Chief Rabbi Jonathan Sacks
London, 5772 (2012)

מחזור קורן ליום הכיפורים
THE KOREN YOM KIPPUR MAḤZOR

KAPAROT

Taking a rooster (men), or a hen (women) in the right hand (alternatively one may use money), say the following paragraph three times:

בְּנֵי אָדָם Children of men,
those who sat in darkness and the shadow of death, *Ps. 107*
cruelly bound in iron chains –
He brought them out from darkness
and the shadow of death and broke open their chains.
Some were fools with sinful ways,
and suffered affliction because of their iniquities.
They found all food repulsive,
and came close to the gates of death.
Then they cried to the LORD in their trouble,
and He saved them from their distress.
He sent His word and healed them;
He rescued them from their destruction.
Let them thank the LORD for his loving-kindness
and His wondrous deeds for humankind.
If there is one angel out of a thousand in his defense, *Job 33*
to declare his righteousness on his behalf,
He will be gracious to him
and say,
"Spare him from going down to the pit;
I have found atonement."

---

induce them to repent, as if to say: we have freed ourselves of our previous deeds, have cast them behind our backs, and removed them from us as far as possible" (*The Guide for the Perplexed* 3:46). It is difficult to experience the absolution of sin without some physical ceremony. Therefore symbolic action has often been felt to be helpful.

Nowadays most people use money instead, distributing it to charity since, "Charity delivers from death." Maimonides states that it is the custom to increase one's charitable giving at this time of the year (Laws of Repentance 3:4).

סדר כפרות

Taking a rooster (men), or a hen (women) in the right hand (alternatively one may use money), say the following paragraph three times:

תהלים קז בְּנֵי אָדָם, יֹשְׁבֵי חֹשֶׁךְ וְצַלְמָוֶת, אֲסִירֵי עֳנִי וּבַרְזֶל:
יוֹצִיאֵם מֵחֹשֶׁךְ וְצַלְמָוֶת, וּמוֹסְרוֹתֵיהֶם יְנַתֵּק:
אֱוִלִים מִדֶּרֶךְ פִּשְׁעָם, וּמֵעֲוֹנוֹתֵיהֶם יִתְעַנּוּ:
כׇּל־אֹכֶל תְּתַעֵב נַפְשָׁם, וַיַּגִּיעוּ עַד־שַׁעֲרֵי מָוֶת:
וַיִּזְעֲקוּ אֶל־יהוה בַּצַּר לָהֶם, מִמְּצֻקוֹתֵיהֶם יוֹשִׁיעֵם:
יִשְׁלַח דְּבָרוֹ וְיִרְפָּאֵם, וִימַלֵּט מִשְּׁחִיתוֹתָם:
יוֹדוּ לַיהוה חַסְדּוֹ, וְנִפְלְאוֹתָיו לִבְנֵי אָדָם:
איוב לג אִם־יֵשׁ עָלָיו מַלְאָךְ מֵלִיץ אֶחָד מִנִּי־אָלֶף
לְהַגִּיד לְאָדָם יׇשְׁרוֹ:
וַיְחֻנֶּנּוּ, וַיֹּאמֶר פְּדָעֵהוּ מֵרֶדֶת שַׁחַת, מָצָאתִי כֹפֶר:

KAPAROT

Kaparot, meaning "atonements," or "expiations," is the name of a custom that originally involved taking a chicken, circling it round the head three times, and saying over it, "Let this be my exchange, let this be my substitute, let this be my atonement…" The chicken was then slaughtered, and it or an equivalent sum of money given to the poor. A chicken was used rather than any animal that might in Temple times have been offered as a sacrifice, so as not to confuse the custom with a sacrificial rite.

Not mentioned in the Talmud, it is first referred to in Geonic times. Strong objections were raised against the practice by, among others, Rabbi Solomon ibn Adret, Nahmanides and Joseph Karo, who believed it was an imitation of non-Jewish customs and a superstitious practice with no basis in Judaism. Others, notably the mystics Isaac Luria and Isaiah Horowitz as well as Moses Isserles, defended it.

The psychological force of *Kaparot* was similar to that of the scapegoat in Temple times, about which Maimonides writes: "These ceremonies are of a symbolic character, serving to impress people with a certain idea, and to

A man revolves the rooster around his head and says:

זֶה חֲלִיפָתִי Let this be my exchange, let this be my substitute,
let this be my atonement. Let this rooster go to death
while I go and enter a good, long life and peace.

A woman revolves the hen around her head and says:

זֹאת חֲלִיפָתִי Let this be my exchange, let this be my substitute,
let this be my atonement. Let this hen go to death
while I go and enter a good, long life and peace.

If money is used, then revolve the money around the head and say:

אֵלּוּ חֲלִיפָתִי Let this be my exchange, let this be my substitute,
let this be my atonement. Let this money go to charity
while I go and enter a good, long life and peace.

---

or unintentionally. If the other person is unwilling to forgive, we should ask those close to him or her to intercede on our behalf. If this too fails, we should try again a second and third time. If forgiveness is still not forthcoming, we have fulfilled our duty, and it is now the other who is at fault (Maimonides, Laws of Repentance 2:9).

If others apologize to us, we should forgive. We should be hard to provoke, easy to placate. In any case, it is forbidden to take vengeance or harbor a grudge (ibid. 2:10). When others offend us, we should say so rather than storing up silent resentment (Maimonides, Laws of Ethical Character 6:6). However, if this would not make things better because the other is unwilling or unable to accept the reprimand, it is permitted to forgive silently even those who have not apologized to us (ibid. 6:9).

As we behave toward others, so does God behave toward us (*Mekhilta, Beshallaḥ*). Those who forgive are forgiven. Those who are loved by their fellows are loved by God (*Avot* 3:13), while those who judge others harshly are themselves harshly judged. Therefore, as Yom Kippur draws near, when we and the Jewish people stand before God in judgment, we should make every effort to restore peace where we can, apologizing, forgiving, placating, reconciling and mending fractured relationships, for where there is peace, there the Divine Presence finds its home in our midst.

A man revolves the rooster around his head and says:

זֶה חֲלִיפָתִי, זֶה תְּמוּרָתִי, זֶה כַּפָּרָתִי.
זֶה הַתַּרְנְגוֹל יֵלֵךְ לְמִיתָה
וַאֲנִי אֵלֵךְ וְאֶכָּנֵס לְחַיִּים טוֹבִים אֲרֻכִּים וּלְשָׁלוֹם.

A woman revolves the hen around her head and says:

זֹאת חֲלִיפָתִי, זֹאת תְּמוּרָתִי, זֹאת כַּפָּרָתִי.
זֹאת הַתַּרְנְגֹלֶת תֵּלֵךְ לְמִיתָה
וַאֲנִי אֵלֵךְ וְאֶכָּנֵס לְחַיִּים טוֹבִים אֲרֻכִּים וּלְשָׁלוֹם.

If money is used, then revolve the money around the head and says:

אֵלּוּ חֲלִיפָתִי, אֵלּוּ תְּמוּרָתִי, אֵלּוּ כַּפָּרָתִי.
אֵלּוּ הַמָּעוֹת יֵלְכוּ לִצְדָקָה
וַאֲנִי אֵלֵךְ וְאֶכָּנֵס לְחַיִּים טוֹבִים אֲרֻכִּים וּלְשָׁלוֹם.

THE FIVE AFFLICTIONS

Five times in the Torah we are commanded to "afflict your souls" on Yom Kippur (Lev. 16:29, 31; 23:27, 32; Num. 29:7). The sages inferred from this that there are five forms of affliction: refraining from (1) eating and drinking, (2) washing, (3) anointing, (4) wearing leather shoes, and (5) sexual relations (Mishna *Yoma* 8:1).

Some say the reason we do not wear leather shoes on Yom Kippur is because on this day all the world is holy, and we stand on holy ground. Therefore we are like Moses to whom God said: "Take off your sandals, for the place where you are standing is holy ground" (Ex. 3:5).

APOLOGY AND FORGIVENESS

The eve of Yom Kippur is a time for mending broken relationships. Yom Kippur itself atones only for sins between us and God. For sins between us and others, there is atonement only when we have been forgiven by those we have offended or harmed (Mishna, *Yoma* 8:9). Therefore we should make every effort to apologize to those we have wronged in word or deed, intentionally

Minḥa for Erev Yom Kippur

אַשְׁרֵי Happy are those who dwell in Your House; Ps. 84
they shall continue to praise You, Selah!
Happy are the people for whom this is so; Ps. 144
happy are the people whose God is the LORD.
A song of praise by David. Ps. 145

I will exalt You, my God, the King, and bless Your name for ever and all time. Every day I will bless You, and praise Your name for ever and all time. Great is the LORD and greatly to be praised; His greatness is unfathomable. One generation will praise Your works to the next, and tell of Your mighty deeds. On the glorious splendor of Your majesty I will meditate, and on the acts of Your wonders. They shall talk of the power of Your awesome deeds, and I will tell of Your greatness. They shall recite the record of Your great goodness, and sing with joy of Your righteousness. The LORD is gracious and compassionate, slow to anger and great in loving-kindness. The LORD is good to all, and His compassion extends to all His works. All Your works shall thank You, LORD, and Your devoted ones shall bless You. They shall talk of the glory of Your kingship, and speak of Your might. To make known to mankind His mighty deeds and the glorious majesty of His kingship. Your kingdom is an everlasting kingdom, and Your reign is for all generations. The LORD supports all who fall, and raises all who are bowed down. All raise their eyes to You in hope, and You give them their food in due season. You open Your hand, and satisfy every living thing with favor. The LORD is righteous in all His ways, and kind in all He does. The LORD is close to all who call on Him, to all who call on Him in truth. He fulfills the will of those who revere Him; He hears their cry and saves them. The LORD guards all who love Him,

מנחה לערב יום הכיפורים

אַשְׁרֵי יוֹשְׁבֵי בֵיתֶךָ, עוֹד יְהַלְלוּךָ סֶּלָה: תהלים פד
אַשְׁרֵי הָעָם שֶׁכָּכָה לּוֹ, אַשְׁרֵי הָעָם שֶׁיהוה אֱלֹהָיו: תהלים קמד
תְּהִלָּה לְדָוִד תהלים קמה

אֲרוֹמִמְךָ אֱלוֹהַי הַמֶּלֶךְ, וַאֲבָרְכָה שִׁמְךָ לְעוֹלָם וָעֶד:
בְּכָל־יוֹם אֲבָרְכֶךָּ, וַאֲהַלְלָה שִׁמְךָ לְעוֹלָם וָעֶד:
גָּדוֹל יהוה וּמְהֻלָּל מְאֹד, וְלִגְדֻלָּתוֹ אֵין חֵקֶר:
דּוֹר לְדוֹר יְשַׁבַּח מַעֲשֶׂיךָ, וּגְבוּרֹתֶיךָ יַגִּידוּ:
הֲדַר כְּבוֹד הוֹדֶךָ, וְדִבְרֵי נִפְלְאֹתֶיךָ אָשִׂיחָה:
וֶעֱזוּז נוֹרְאֹתֶיךָ יֹאמֵרוּ, וּגְדוּלָּתְךָ אֲסַפְּרֶנָּה:
זֵכֶר רַב־טוּבְךָ יַבִּיעוּ, וְצִדְקָתְךָ יְרַנֵּנוּ:
חַנּוּן וְרַחוּם יהוה, אֶרֶךְ אַפַּיִם וּגְדָל־חָסֶד:
טוֹב־יהוה לַכֹּל, וְרַחֲמָיו עַל־כָּל־מַעֲשָׂיו:
יוֹדוּךָ יהוה כָּל־מַעֲשֶׂיךָ, וַחֲסִידֶיךָ יְבָרְכוּכָה:
כְּבוֹד מַלְכוּתְךָ יֹאמֵרוּ, וּגְבוּרָתְךָ יְדַבֵּרוּ:
לְהוֹדִיעַ לִבְנֵי הָאָדָם גְּבוּרֹתָיו, וּכְבוֹד הֲדַר מַלְכוּתוֹ:
מַלְכוּתְךָ מַלְכוּת כָּל־עֹלָמִים, וּמֶמְשַׁלְתְּךָ בְּכָל־דּוֹר וָדֹר:
סוֹמֵךְ יהוה לְכָל־הַנֹּפְלִים, וְזוֹקֵף לְכָל־הַכְּפוּפִים:
עֵינֵי־כֹל אֵלֶיךָ יְשַׂבֵּרוּ, וְאַתָּה נוֹתֵן־לָהֶם אֶת־אָכְלָם בְּעִתּוֹ:
פּוֹתֵחַ אֶת־יָדֶךָ, וּמַשְׂבִּיעַ לְכָל־חַי רָצוֹן:
צַדִּיק יהוה בְּכָל־דְּרָכָיו, וְחָסִיד בְּכָל־מַעֲשָׂיו:
קָרוֹב יהוה לְכָל־קֹרְאָיו, לְכֹל אֲשֶׁר יִקְרָאֻהוּ בֶאֱמֶת:

but all the wicked He will destroy. ▸ My mouth shall speak the praise of the LORD, and all creatures shall bless His holy name for ever and all time.

We will bless the LORD now and for ever. Halleluya! *Ps. 115*

HALF KADDISH

Leader: יִתְגַּדַּל Magnified and sanctified
may His great name be,
in the world He created by His will.
May He establish His kingdom
in your lifetime and in your days,
and in the lifetime of all the house of Israel,
swiftly and soon –
and say: Amen.

All: May His great name be blessed for ever and all time.

Leader: Blessed and praised,
glorified and exalted,
raised and honored,
uplifted and lauded
be the name of the Holy One, blessed be He,
above and beyond any blessing, song,
praise and consolation
uttered in the world –
and say: Amen.

רְצוֹן־יְרֵאָיו יַעֲשֶׂה, וְאֶת־שַׁוְעָתָם יִשְׁמַע, וְיוֹשִׁיעֵם:
שׁוֹמֵר יהוה אֶת־כָּל־אֹהֲבָיו, וְאֵת כָּל־הָרְשָׁעִים יַשְׁמִיד:
› תְּהִלַּת יהוה יְדַבֶּר פִּי, וִיבָרֵךְ כָּל־בָּשָׂר שֵׁם קָדְשׁוֹ לְעוֹלָם וָעֶד:
וַאֲנַחְנוּ נְבָרֵךְ יָהּ מֵעַתָּה וְעַד־עוֹלָם, הַלְלוּיָהּ: תהלים קטו

חצי קדיש

ש״ץ: יִתְגַּדַּל וְיִתְקַדַּשׁ שְׁמֵהּ רַבָּא (קהל: אָמֵן)
בְּעָלְמָא דִּי בְרָא כִרְעוּתֵהּ
וְיַמְלִיךְ מַלְכוּתֵהּ
בְּחַיֵּיכוֹן וּבְיוֹמֵיכוֹן וּבְחַיֵּי דְכָל בֵּית יִשְׂרָאֵל
בַּעֲגָלָא וּבִזְמַן קָרִיב
וְאִמְרוּ אָמֵן. (קהל: אָמֵן)

קהל וש״ץ: יְהֵא שְׁמֵהּ רַבָּא מְבָרַךְ לְעָלַם וּלְעָלְמֵי עָלְמַיָּא.

ש״ץ: יִתְבָּרַךְ וְיִשְׁתַּבַּח וְיִתְפָּאַר וְיִתְרוֹמַם וְיִתְנַשֵּׂא
וְיִתְהַדָּר וְיִתְעַלֶּה וְיִתְהַלָּל
שְׁמֵהּ דְּקֻדְשָׁא בְּרִיךְ הוּא (קהל: בְּרִיךְ הוּא)
לְעֵלָּא לְעֵלָּא מִכָּל בִּרְכָתָא וְשִׁירָתָא, תֻּשְׁבְּחָתָא וְנֶחֱמָתָא
דַּאֲמִירָן בְּעָלְמָא
וְאִמְרוּ אָמֵן. (קהל: אָמֵן)

THE AMIDA

The following prayer, until "in former years" on page 34, is said silently, standing with feet together. If there is a minyan, the Amida is repeated aloud by the Leader. Take three steps forward and at the points indicated by ▾, bend the knees at the first word, bow at the second, and stand straight before saying God's name.

When I proclaim the LORD's name, give glory to our God. *Deut. 32*
O LORD, open my lips, so that my mouth may declare Your praise. *Ps. 51*

PATRIARCHS

▾בָּרוּךְ Blessed are You, LORD our God and God of our fathers,
God of Abraham, God of Isaac and God of Jacob;
the great, mighty and awesome God, God Most High,
who bestows acts of loving-kindness and creates all,
who remembers the loving-kindness of the fathers
and will bring a Redeemer to their children's children
for the sake of His name, in love.

זָכְרֵנוּ לְחַיִּים Remember us for life, O King who desires life,
and write us in the book of life –
for Your sake, O God of life.

If forgotten, the Amida is not repeated.

King, Helper, Savior, Shield:
▾Blessed are You, LORD, Shield of Abraham.

DIVINE MIGHT

אַתָּה גִּבּוֹר You are eternally mighty, LORD.
You give life to the dead and have great power to save.

In Israel: He causes the dew to fall.

He sustains the living with loving-kindness,
and with great compassion revives the dead.
He supports the fallen,
heals the sick,
sets captives free,
and keeps His faith with those who sleep in the dust.

עמידה

The following prayer, until קַדְמֹנִיּוֹת *on page 35, is said silently, standing with feet together. If there is a* מנין, *the* עמידה *is repeated aloud by the* שליח ציבור. *Take three steps forward and at the points indicated by* ˺, *bend the knees at the first word, bow at the second, and stand straight before saying God's name.*

דברים לב כִּי שֵׁם יהוה אֶקְרָא, הָבוּ גֹדֶל לֵאלֹהֵינוּ:

תהלים נא אֲדֹנָי, שְׂפָתַי תִּפְתָּח, וּפִי יַגִּיד תְּהִלָּתֶךָ:

אבות

˺בָּרוּךְ אַתָּה יהוה, אֱלֹהֵינוּ וֵאלֹהֵי אֲבוֹתֵינוּ
אֱלֹהֵי אַבְרָהָם, אֱלֹהֵי יִצְחָק, וֵאלֹהֵי יַעֲקֹב
הָאֵל הַגָּדוֹל הַגִּבּוֹר וְהַנּוֹרָא, אֵל עֶלְיוֹן
גּוֹמֵל חֲסָדִים טוֹבִים, וְקוֹנֵה הַכֹּל
וְזוֹכֵר חַסְדֵי אָבוֹת
וּמֵבִיא גוֹאֵל לִבְנֵי בְנֵיהֶם לְמַעַן שְׁמוֹ בְּאַהֲבָה.

זָכְרֵנוּ לְחַיִּים, מֶלֶךְ חָפֵץ בַּחַיִּים
וְכָתְבֵנוּ בְּסֵפֶר הַחַיִּים, לְמַעַנְךָ אֱלֹהִים חַיִּים.

If forgotten, the עמידה *is not repeated.*

מֶלֶךְ עוֹזֵר וּמוֹשִׁיעַ וּמָגֵן.
˺בָּרוּךְ אַתָּה יהוה, מָגֵן אַבְרָהָם.

גבורות

אַתָּה גִּבּוֹר לְעוֹלָם, אֲדֹנָי
מְחַיֵּה מֵתִים אַתָּה, רַב לְהוֹשִׁיעַ

בארץ ישראל: מוֹרִיד הַטָּל

מְכַלְכֵּל חַיִּים בְּחֶסֶד, מְחַיֵּה מֵתִים בְּרַחֲמִים רַבִּים
סוֹמֵךְ נוֹפְלִים, וְרוֹפֵא חוֹלִים, וּמַתִּיר אֲסוּרִים
וּמְקַיֵּם אֱמוּנָתוֹ לִישֵׁנֵי עָפָר.

Who is like You, Master of might,
and to whom can You be compared,
O King who brings death and gives life,
and makes salvation grow?

מִי כָמְוֹךָ Who is like You, compassionate Father,
who remembers His creatures in compassion, for life?
If forgotten, the Amida is not repeated.

Faithful are You to revive the dead.
Blessed are You, Lord, who revives the dead.

When saying the Amida silently, continue with "You are holy" on the next page.

KEDUSHA

During the Leader's Repetition, the following is said standing with feet together, rising on the toes at the words indicated by ▴.

Cong. then Leader: נְקַדֵּשׁ We will sanctify Your name on earth,
as they sanctify it in the highest heavens,
as is written by Your prophet,
"And they [the angels] call to one another saying: *Is. 6*

Cong. then Leader: ▴Holy, ▴holy, ▴holy is the Lord of hosts;
the whole world is filled with His glory."
Those facing them say "Blessed –"

Cong. then Leader: ▴"Blessed is the Lord's glory from His place." *Ezek. 3*
And in Your holy Writings it is written thus:

Cong. then Leader: ▴"The Lord shall reign for ever. He is your God, Zion, *Ps. 146*
from generation to generation, Halleluya!"

Leader: From generation to generation
we will declare Your greatness,
and we will proclaim Your holiness for evermore.
Your praise, our God, shall not leave our mouth forever,
for You, God, are a great and holy King.
Blessed are You, Lord, the holy King.

The Leader continues with "You grace humanity" on the next page.

מִי כָמְוֹךָ, בַּעַל גְּבוּרוֹת, וּמִי דְּוֹמֶה לָּךְ
מֶלֶךְ, מֵמִית וּמְחַיֶּה וּמַצְמִיחַ יְשׁוּעָה.

מִי כָמְוֹךָ אַב הָרַחֲמִים
זוֹכֵר יְצוּרָיו לְחַיִּים בְּרַחֲמִים.

If forgotten, the עמידה *is not repeated.*

וְנֶאֱמָן אַתָּה לְהַחֲיוֹת מֵתִים.
בָּרוּךְ אַתָּה יהוה, מְחַיֵּה הַמֵּתִים.

When saying the עמידה *silently, continue with* אַתָּה קָדוֹשׁ *on the next page.*

קדושה

During the חזרת הש״ץ, *the following is said standing with feet together, rising on the toes at the words indicated by* ^.

קהל *then* ש״ץ: נְקַדֵּשׁ אֶת שִׁמְךָ בָּעוֹלָם,
כְּשֵׁם שֶׁמַּקְדִּישִׁים אוֹתוֹ בִּשְׁמֵי מָרוֹם
כַּכָּתוּב עַל יַד נְבִיאֶךָ: וְקָרָא זֶה אֶל־זֶה וְאָמַר ישעיה ו

קהל *then* ש״ץ: ^קָדוֹשׁ, ^קָדוֹשׁ, ^קָדוֹשׁ, יהוה צְבָאוֹת
מְלֹא כָל־הָאָרֶץ כְּבוֹדוֹ:
לְעֻמָּתָם בָּרוּךְ יֹאמֵרוּ

קהל *then* ש״ץ: ^בָּרוּךְ כְּבוֹד־יהוה מִמְּקוֹמוֹ: יחזקאל ג
וּבְדִבְרֵי קָדְשְׁךָ כָּתוּב לֵאמֹר

קהל *then* ש״ץ: ^יִמְלֹךְ יהוה לְעוֹלָם, אֱלֹהַיִךְ צִיּוֹן לְדֹר וָדֹר, הַלְלוּיָהּ: תהלים קמו

ש״ץ: לְדוֹר וָדוֹר נַגִּיד גָּדְלֶךָ, וּלְנֵצַח נְצָחִים קְדֻשָּׁתְךָ נַקְדִּישׁ
וְשִׁבְחֲךָ אֱלֹהֵינוּ מִפִּינוּ לֹא יָמוּשׁ לְעוֹלָם וָעֶד
כִּי אֵל מֶלֶךְ גָּדוֹל וְקָדוֹשׁ אָתָּה.
בָּרוּךְ אַתָּה יהוה, הַמֶּלֶךְ הַקָּדוֹשׁ.

The שליח ציבור *continues with* אַתָּה חוֹנֵן *on the next page.*

HOLINESS

אַתָּה קָדוֹשׁ You are holy and Your name is holy,
and holy ones praise You daily, Selah!
Blessed are You, LORD, the holy King.

If "holy God" is said, then the Amida is repeated.

KNOWLEDGE

אַתָּה חוֹנֵן You grace humanity with knowledge
and teach mortals understanding.
Grace us with the knowledge, understanding
and discernment that come from You.
Blessed are You, LORD, who graciously grants knowledge.

REPENTANCE

הֲשִׁיבֵנוּ Bring us back, our Father, to Your Torah.
Draw us near, our King, to Your service.
Lead us back to You in perfect repentance.
Blessed are You, LORD, who desires repentance.

FORGIVENESS

Strike the left side of the chest at °.

סְלַח לָנוּ Forgive us, our Father, for we have °sinned.
Pardon us, our King, for we have °transgressed;
for You pardon and forgive.
Blessed are You, LORD, the gracious One who repeatedly forgives.

REDEMPTION

רְאֵה Look on our affliction, plead our cause,
and redeem us soon for Your name's sake,
for You are a powerful Redeemer.
Blessed are You, LORD, the Redeemer of Israel.

הַמֶּלֶךְ הַקָּדוֹשׁ *The holy King:* During the Ten Days of Repentance we substitute this phrase for "the holy God," to emphasize that these are days of judgment in which we are especially conscious of divine sovereignty over all humanity. For this reason too, in the eleventh paragraph we substitute "the King of justice" for the usual ending.

קדושת השם

אַתָּה קָדוֹשׁ וְשִׁמְךָ קָדוֹשׁ
וּקְדוֹשִׁים בְּכָל יוֹם יְהַלְלוּךָ סֶּלָה.
בָּרוּךְ אַתָּה יהוה, הַמֶּלֶךְ הַקָּדוֹשׁ.

If הָאֵל הַקָּדוֹשׁ *is said, then the* עמידה *is repeated.*

דעת

אַתָּה חוֹנֵן לְאָדָם דַּעַת, וּמְלַמֵּד לֶאֱנוֹשׁ בִּינָה.
חָנֵּנוּ מֵאִתְּךָ דֵּעָה בִּינָה וְהַשְׂכֵּל.
בָּרוּךְ אַתָּה יהוה, חוֹנֵן הַדָּעַת.

תשובה

הֲשִׁיבֵנוּ אָבִינוּ לְתוֹרָתֶךָ
וְקָרְבֵנוּ מַלְכֵּנוּ לַעֲבוֹדָתֶךָ
וְהַחֲזִירֵנוּ בִּתְשׁוּבָה שְׁלֵמָה לְפָנֶיךָ.
בָּרוּךְ אַתָּה יהוה, הָרוֹצֶה בִּתְשׁוּבָה.

סליחה

Strike the left side of the chest at °.

סְלַח לָנוּ אָבִינוּ כִּי °חָטָאנוּ
מְחַל לָנוּ מַלְכֵּנוּ כִּי °פָשָׁעְנוּ
כִּי מוֹחֵל וְסוֹלֵחַ אָתָּה.
בָּרוּךְ אַתָּה יהוה, חַנּוּן הַמַּרְבֶּה לִסְלֹחַ.

גאולה

רְאֵה בְעָנְיֵנוּ, וְרִיבָה רִיבֵנוּ
וּגְאָלֵנוּ מְהֵרָה לְמַעַן שְׁמֶךָ
כִּי גּוֹאֵל חָזָק אָתָּה.
בָּרוּךְ אַתָּה יהוה, גּוֹאֵל יִשְׂרָאֵל.

HEALING

רְפָאֵנוּ Heal us, Lord, and we shall be healed.
Save us and we shall be saved,
for You are our praise.
Bring complete recovery for all our ailments,

The following prayer for a sick person may be said here:
May it be Your will, O Lord my God and God of my ancestors, that You speedily send a complete recovery from heaven, a healing of both soul and body, to the patient (*name*), son/daughter of (*mother's name*) among the other afflicted of Israel.

---

for You, God, King,
are a faithful and compassionate Healer.
Blessed are You, Lord,
Healer of the sick of His people Israel.

PROSPERITY

בָּרֵךְ Bless this year for us, Lord our God,
and all its types of produce for good.
Grant blessing on the face of the earth,
and from its goodness satisfy us,
blessing our year as the best of years.
Blessed are You, Lord,
who blesses the years.

INGATHERING OF EXILES

תְּקַע Sound the great shofar for our freedom,
raise high the banner to gather our exiles,
and gather us together
from the four quarters of the earth.
Blessed are You, Lord,
who gathers the dispersed of His people Israel.

רפואה

רְפָאֵנוּ יהוה וְנֵרָפֵא
הוֹשִׁיעֵנוּ וְנִוָּשֵׁעָה
כִּי תְהִלָּתֵנוּ אָתָּה
וְהַעֲלֵה רְפוּאָה שְׁלֵמָה לְכָל מַכּוֹתֵינוּ

The following prayer for a sick person may be said here:

יְהִי רָצוֹן מִלְּפָנֶיךָ יהוה אֱלֹהַי וֵאלֹהֵי אֲבוֹתַי, שֶׁתִּשְׁלַח מְהֵרָה רְפוּאָה שְׁלֵמָה מִן הַשָּׁמַיִם רְפוּאַת הַנֶּפֶשׁ וּרְפוּאַת הַגּוּף לַחוֹלֶה/לַחוֹלָה *name of patient* בֶּן/בַּת *mother's name* בְּתוֹךְ שְׁאָר חוֹלֵי יִשְׂרָאֵל.

כִּי אֵל מֶלֶךְ רוֹפֵא נֶאֱמָן וְרַחֲמָן אָתָּה.
בָּרוּךְ אַתָּה יהוה, רוֹפֵא חוֹלֵי עַמּוֹ יִשְׂרָאֵל.

ברכת השנים

בָּרֵךְ עָלֵינוּ יהוה אֱלֹהֵינוּ אֶת הַשָּׁנָה הַזֹּאת
וְאֶת כָּל מִינֵי תְבוּאָתָהּ, לְטוֹבָה
וְתֵן בְּרָכָה עַל פְּנֵי הָאֲדָמָה, וְשַׂבְּעֵנוּ מִטּוּבָהּ
וּבָרֵךְ שְׁנָתֵנוּ כַּשָּׁנִים הַטּוֹבוֹת.
בָּרוּךְ אַתָּה יהוה, מְבָרֵךְ הַשָּׁנִים.

קבוץ גלויות

תְּקַע בְּשׁוֹפָר גָּדוֹל לְחֵרוּתֵנוּ
וְשָׂא נֵס לְקַבֵּץ גָּלֻיּוֹתֵינוּ
וְקַבְּצֵנוּ יַחַד מֵאַרְבַּע כַּנְפוֹת הָאָרֶץ.
בָּרוּךְ אַתָּה יהוה, מְקַבֵּץ נִדְחֵי עַמּוֹ יִשְׂרָאֵל.

JUSTICE

הָשִׁיבָה Restore our judges as at first,
and our counselors as at the beginning,
and remove from us sorrow and sighing.
May You alone, Lord,
reign over us with loving-kindness and compassion,
and vindicate us in justice.
Blessed are You, Lord,
the King of justice.

If "the King who loves righteousness and justice" is said, then the Amida is not repeated.

AGAINST INFORMERS

וְלַמַּלְשִׁינִים For the slanderers let there be no hope,
and may all wickedness perish in an instant.
May all Your people's enemies swiftly be cut down.
May You swiftly uproot, crush, cast down
and humble the arrogant swiftly in our days.
Blessed are You, Lord,
who destroys enemies and humbles the arrogant.

THE RIGHTEOUS

עַל הַצַּדִּיקִים To the righteous, the pious,
the elders of Your people the house of Israel,
the remnant of their scholars,
the righteous converts, and to us,
may Your compassion be aroused, Lord our God.
Grant a good reward
to all who sincerely trust in Your name.
Set our lot with them,
so that we may never be ashamed,
for in You we trust.
Blessed are You, Lord,
who is the support and trust of the righteous.

השבת המשפט

הָשִׁיבָה שׁוֹפְטֵינוּ כְּבָרִאשׁוֹנָה וְיוֹעֲצֵינוּ כְּבַתְּחִלָּה
וְהָסֵר מִמֶּנּוּ יָגוֹן וַאֲנָחָה
וּמְלֹךְ עָלֵינוּ אַתָּה יהוה לְבַדְּךָ בְּחֶסֶד וּבְרַחֲמִים
וְצַדְּקֵנוּ בַּמִּשְׁפָּט.
בָּרוּךְ אַתָּה יהוה, הַמֶּלֶךְ הַמִּשְׁפָּט.

If מֶלֶךְ אוֹהֵב צְדָקָה וּמִשְׁפָּט *is said, then the* עמידה *is not repeated.*

ברכת המינים

וְלַמַּלְשִׁינִים אַל תְּהִי תִקְוָה
וְכָל הָרִשְׁעָה כְּרֶגַע תֹּאבֵד
וְכָל אוֹיְבֵי עַמְּךָ מְהֵרָה יִכָּרֵתוּ
וְהַזֵּדִים מְהֵרָה תְעַקֵּר וּתְשַׁבֵּר וּתְמַגֵּר וְתַכְנִיעַ בִּמְהֵרָה בְיָמֵינוּ.
בָּרוּךְ אַתָּה יהוה, שׁוֹבֵר אוֹיְבִים וּמַכְנִיעַ זֵדִים.

על הצדיקים

עַל הַצַּדִּיקִים וְעַל הַחֲסִידִים
וְעַל זִקְנֵי עַמְּךָ בֵּית יִשְׂרָאֵל
וְעַל פְּלֵיטַת סוֹפְרֵיהֶם
וְעַל גֵּרֵי הַצֶּדֶק, וְעָלֵינוּ
יֶהֱמוּ רַחֲמֶיךָ יהוה אֱלֹהֵינוּ
וְתֵן שָׂכָר טוֹב לְכָל הַבּוֹטְחִים בְּשִׁמְךָ בֶּאֱמֶת
וְשִׂים חֶלְקֵנוּ עִמָּהֶם
וּלְעוֹלָם לֹא נֵבוֹשׁ כִּי בְךָ בָּטָחְנוּ.
בָּרוּךְ אַתָּה יהוה, מִשְׁעָן וּמִבְטָח לַצַּדִּיקִים.

REBUILDING JERUSALEM

וְלִירוּשָׁלַיִם To Jerusalem, Your city, may You return in compassion,
and may You dwell in it as You promised.
May You rebuild it rapidly in our days
as an everlasting structure,
and install within it soon the throne of David.
Blessed are You, Lord, who builds Jerusalem.

KINGDOM OF DAVID

אֶת צֶמַח May the offshoot of Your servant David soon flower,
and may his pride be raised high by Your salvation,
for we wait for Your salvation all day.
Blessed are You, Lord, who makes the glory of salvation flourish.

RESPONSE TO PRAYER

שְׁמַע קוֹלֵנוּ Listen to our voice, Lord our God.
Spare us and have compassion on us,
and in compassion and favor accept our prayer,
for You, God, listen to prayers and pleas.
Do not turn us away, O our King,
empty-handed from Your presence,
for You listen with compassion
to the prayer of Your people Israel.
Blessed are You, Lord, who listens to prayer.

TEMPLE SERVICE

רְצֵה Find favor, Lord our God,
in Your people Israel and their prayer.
Restore the service to Your most holy House,
and accept in love and favor
the fire-offerings of Israel and their prayer.
May the service of Your people Israel always find favor with You.
And may our eyes witness Your return to Zion in compassion.
Blessed are You, Lord,
who restores His Presence to Zion.

בניין ירושלים

וְלִירוּשָׁלַיִם עִירְךָ בְּרַחֲמִים תָּשׁוּב
וְתִשְׁכֹּן בְּתוֹכָהּ כַּאֲשֶׁר דִּבַּרְתָּ
וּבְנֵה אוֹתָהּ בְּקָרוֹב בְּיָמֵינוּ בִּנְיַן עוֹלָם
וְכִסֵּא דָוִד מְהֵרָה לְתוֹכָהּ תָּכִין.
בָּרוּךְ אַתָּה יהוה, בּוֹנֵה יְרוּשָׁלָיִם.

משיח בן דוד

אֶת צֶמַח דָּוִד עַבְדְּךָ מְהֵרָה תַצְמִיחַ
וְקַרְנוֹ תָּרוּם בִּישׁוּעָתֶךָ, כִּי לִישׁוּעָתְךָ קִוִּינוּ כָּל הַיּוֹם.
בָּרוּךְ אַתָּה יהוה, מַצְמִיחַ קֶרֶן יְשׁוּעָה.

שומע תפלה

שְׁמַע קוֹלֵנוּ יהוה אֱלֹהֵינוּ
חוּס וְרַחֵם עָלֵינוּ, וְקַבֵּל בְּרַחֲמִים וּבְרָצוֹן אֶת תְּפִלָּתֵנוּ
כִּי אֵל שׁוֹמֵעַ תְּפִלּוֹת וְתַחֲנוּנִים אָתָּה
וּמִלְּפָנֶיךָ מַלְכֵּנוּ רֵיקָם אַל תְּשִׁיבֵנוּ
כִּי אַתָּה שׁוֹמֵעַ תְּפִלַּת עַמְּךָ יִשְׂרָאֵל בְּרַחֲמִים.
בָּרוּךְ אַתָּה יהוה, שׁוֹמֵעַ תְּפִלָּה.

עבודה

רְצֵה יהוה אֱלֹהֵינוּ בְּעַמְּךָ יִשְׂרָאֵל, וּבִתְפִלָּתָם
וְהָשֵׁב אֶת הָעֲבוֹדָה לִדְבִיר בֵּיתֶךָ
וְאִשֵּׁי יִשְׂרָאֵל וּתְפִלָּתָם בְּאַהֲבָה תְקַבֵּל בְּרָצוֹן
וּתְהִי לְרָצוֹן תָּמִיד עֲבוֹדַת יִשְׂרָאֵל עַמֶּךָ.
וְתֶחֱזֶינָה עֵינֵינוּ בְּשׁוּבְךָ לְצִיּוֹן בְּרַחֲמִים.
בָּרוּךְ אַתָּה יהוה, הַמַּחֲזִיר שְׁכִינָתוֹ לְצִיּוֹן.

THANKSGIVING

Bow at the first nine words.

ᵛמוֹדִים We give thanks to You,
for You are the LORD our God
and God of our ancestors
for ever and all time.
You are the Rock of our lives,
Shield of our salvation
from generation to generation.
We will thank You and
declare Your praise for our lives,
which are entrusted into Your hand;
for our souls,
which are placed in Your charge;
for Your miracles
which are with us every day;
and for Your wonders and favors
at all times, evening, morning and midday.
You are good –
for Your compassion never fails.
You are compassionate –
for Your loving-kindnesses never cease.
We have always placed our hope in You.

During the Leader's Repetition, the congregation says quietly:

ᵛמוֹדִים We give thanks to You,
for You are the LORD our God
and God of our ancestors,
God of all flesh,
who formed us
and formed the universe.
Blessings and thanks
are due to Your great
and holy name for giving us
life and sustaining us.
May You continue
to give us life and sustain us;
and may You gather our
exiles to Your holy courts,
to keep Your decrees,
do Your will and serve You
with a perfect heart,
for it is for us
to give You thanks.
Blessed be God to whom
thanksgiving is due.

וְעַל כֻּלָּם For all these things may Your name be blessed and exalted,
our King, continually, for ever and all time.

וּכְתֹב And write, for a good life,
all the children of Your covenant.
If forgotten, the Amida is not repeated.

Let all that lives thank You, Selah!
and praise Your name in truth,
God, our Savior and Help, Selah!
ᵛBlessed are You, LORD, whose name is "the Good"
and to whom thanks are due.

הודאה

Bow at the first five words.

מוֹדִים אֲנַחְנוּ לָךְ
שָׁאַתָּה הוּא יהוה אֱלֹהֵינוּ
וֵאלֹהֵי אֲבוֹתֵינוּ לְעוֹלָם וָעֶד.
צוּר חַיֵּינוּ, מָגֵן יִשְׁעֵנוּ
אַתָּה הוּא לְדוֹר וָדוֹר.
נוֹדֶה לְּךָ וּנְסַפֵּר תְּהִלָּתֶךָ
עַל חַיֵּינוּ הַמְּסוּרִים בְּיָדֶךָ
וְעַל נִשְׁמוֹתֵינוּ הַפְּקוּדוֹת לָךְ
וְעַל נִסֶּיךָ שֶׁבְּכָל יוֹם עִמָּנוּ
וְעַל נִפְלְאוֹתֶיךָ וְטוֹבוֹתֶיךָ
שֶׁבְּכָל עֵת, עֶרֶב וָבֹקֶר וְצָהֳרָיִם.
הַטּוֹב, כִּי לֹא כָלוּ רַחֲמֶיךָ
וְהַמְרַחֵם, כִּי לֹא תַמּוּ חֲסָדֶיךָ
מֵעוֹלָם קִוִּינוּ לָךְ.

During the חזרת הש״ץ, the קהל says quietly:

מוֹדִים אֲנַחְנוּ לָךְ
שָׁאַתָּה הוּא יהוה אֱלֹהֵינוּ
וֵאלֹהֵי אֲבוֹתֵינוּ
אֱלֹהֵי כָל בָּשָׂר
יוֹצְרֵנוּ, יוֹצֵר בְּרֵאשִׁית.
בְּרָכוֹת וְהוֹדָאוֹת
לְשִׁמְךָ הַגָּדוֹל וְהַקָּדוֹשׁ
עַל שֶׁהֶחֱיִיתָנוּ וְקִיַּמְתָּנוּ.
כֵּן תְּחַיֵּנוּ וּתְקַיְּמֵנוּ
וְתֶאֱסֹף גָּלֻיּוֹתֵינוּ
לְחַצְרוֹת קָדְשֶׁךָ
לִשְׁמֹר חֻקֶּיךָ וְלַעֲשׂוֹת רְצוֹנֶךָ
וּלְעָבְדְּךָ בְּלֵבָב שָׁלֵם
עַל שֶׁאֲנַחְנוּ מוֹדִים לָךְ.
בָּרוּךְ אֵל הַהוֹדָאוֹת.

וְעַל כֻּלָּם יִתְבָּרַךְ וְיִתְרוֹמַם שִׁמְךָ מַלְכֵּנוּ תָּמִיד לְעוֹלָם וָעֶד.

וּכְתֹב לְחַיִּים טוֹבִים כָּל בְּנֵי בְרִיתֶךָ.

If forgotten, the עמידה is not repeated.

וְכֹל הַחַיִּים יוֹדוּךָ סֶּלָה, וִיהַלְלוּ אֶת שִׁמְךָ בֶּאֱמֶת
הָאֵל יְשׁוּעָתֵנוּ וְעֶזְרָתֵנוּ סֶלָה.
בָּרוּךְ אַתָּה יהוה, הַטּוֹב שִׁמְךָ וּלְךָ נָאֶה לְהוֹדוֹת.

PEACE

שָׁלוֹם רָב Grant great peace to Your people Israel for ever,
for You are the sovereign LORD of all peace;
and may it be good in Your eyes
to bless Your people Israel
at every time, at every hour, with Your peace.

בְּסֵפֶר חַיִּים In the book of life, blessing, peace and prosperity,
may we and all Your people the house of Israel be remembered
and written before You for a good life, and for peace.*

If forgotten, the Amida is not repeated.

Blessed are You, LORD, who makes peace.

**In Israel, end the blessing:*

Blessed are You, LORD, who blesses His people Israel with peace.

The following verse concludes the Leader's Repetition of the Amida.
Some also say it here as part of the silent Amida.

May the words of my mouth and the meditation of my heart *Ps. 19*
find favor before You, LORD, my Rock and Redeemer.

VIDUY

For linear translation and commentary, see page 1353.

אֱלֹהֵינוּ Our God and God of our fathers,
let our prayer come before You,
and do not hide Yourself from our plea,
for we are not so arrogant or obstinate as to say before You,
LORD, our God and God of our fathers,
we are righteous and have not sinned,
for in truth, we and our fathers have sinned.

Tishrei already partakes of some of the holiness of Yom Kippur itself, as it says: "From the evening of the ninth day of the month until the following evening you are to observe your Sabbath" (Lev. 23:32).

ברכת שלום

שָׁלוֹם רָב עַל יִשְׂרָאֵל עַמְּךָ תָּשִׂים לְעוֹלָם
כִּי אַתָּה הוּא מֶלֶךְ אָדוֹן לְכָל הַשָּׁלוֹם.
וְטוֹב בְּעֵינֶיךָ לְבָרֵךְ אֶת עַמְּךָ יִשְׂרָאֵל
בְּכָל עֵת וּבְכָל שָׁעָה בִּשְׁלוֹמֶךָ.

בְּסֵפֶר חַיִּים, בְּרָכָה וְשָׁלוֹם, וּפַרְנָסָה טוֹבָה
נִזָּכֵר וְנִכָּתֵב לְפָנֶיךָ, אֲנַחְנוּ וְכָל עַמְּךָ בֵּית יִשְׂרָאֵל
לְחַיִּים טוֹבִים וּלְשָׁלוֹם.*

If forgotten, the עמידה *is not repeated.*

בָּרוּךְ אַתָּה יהוה, עוֹשֶׂה הַשָּׁלוֹם.

**In* ארץ ישראל*, end the blessing:*

בָּרוּךְ אַתָּה יהוה, הַמְבָרֵךְ אֶת עַמּוֹ יִשְׂרָאֵל בַּשָּׁלוֹם.

The following verse concludes the חזרת הש״ץ.
Some also say it here as part of the silent עמידה.

יִהְיוּ לְרָצוֹן אִמְרֵי־פִי וְהֶגְיוֹן לִבִּי לְפָנֶיךָ, יהוה צוּרִי וְגֹאֲלִי: תהלים יט

וידוי

For linear translation and commentary, see page 1353.

אֱלֹהֵינוּ וֵאלֹהֵי אֲבוֹתֵינוּ
תָּבוֹא לְפָנֶיךָ תְּפִלָּתֵנוּ, וְאַל תִּתְעַלַּם מִתְּחִנָּתֵנוּ.
שֶׁאֵין אֲנַחְנוּ עַזֵּי פָנִים וּקְשֵׁי עֹרֶף לוֹמַר לְפָנֶיךָ
יהוה אֱלֹהֵינוּ וֵאלֹהֵי אֲבוֹתֵינוּ
צַדִּיקִים אֲנַחְנוּ וְלֹא חָטָאנוּ.
אֲבָל אֲנַחְנוּ וַאֲבוֹתֵינוּ חָטָאנוּ.

AFTERNOON SERVICE

One of the reasons it is our custom to say the confession during Minḥa on the afternoon prior to Yom Kippur, is because the afternoon of the ninth of

Strike the left side of the chest with the right fist while saying each of the sins.

אָשַׁמְנוּ We have sinned, we have acted treacherously,
we have robbed, we have spoken slander.
We have acted perversely, we have acted wickedly,
we have acted presumptuously, we have been violent,
we have framed lies.
We have given bad advice, we have deceived, we have scorned,
we have rebelled, we have provoked, we have turned away,
we have committed iniquity, we have transgressed,
we have persecuted, we have been obstinate.
We have acted wickedly, we have corrupted,
we have acted abominably, we have strayed, we have led others astray.

סַרְנוּ We have turned away from Your commandments and good laws,
to no avail, for You are just in all that has befallen us, *Neh. 9*
for You have acted faithfully while we have done wickedly.

מַה נֹּאמַר What can we say before You, You who dwell on high?
What can we declare before You, You who abide in heaven?
Do You not know all, the hidden and revealed alike?

אַתָּה יוֹדֵעַ You know every secret since the world began,
and what is hidden deep inside every living thing.
You search each person's inner chambers,
examining conscience and mind.
Nothing is shrouded from You, and nothing is hidden before Your eyes.
And so, may it be Your will, LORD our God and God of our ancestors,
that You forgive us all our sins, pardon all our iniquities,
and grant us atonement for all of our transgressions.

Strike the left side of the chest with the right fist while saying each of the sins.

עַל חֵטְא For the sin we have sinned before You under duress or freewill,
and for the sin we have sinned before You in hardness of heart.

For the sin we have sinned before You unwittingly,
and for the sin we have sinned before You by an utterance of our lips.

For the sin we have sinned before You by unchastity,
and for the sin we have sinned before You openly or secretly.

Strike the left side of the chest with the right fist while saying each of the sins.

אָשַׁמְנוּ, בָּגַדְנוּ, גָּזַלְנוּ, דִּבַּרְנוּ דֹפִי
הֶעֱוִינוּ, וְהִרְשַׁעְנוּ, זַדְנוּ, חָמַסְנוּ, טָפַלְנוּ שֶׁקֶר
יָעַצְנוּ רָע, כִּזַּבְנוּ, לַצְנוּ, מָרַדְנוּ, נִאַצְנוּ, סָרַרְנוּ
עָוִינוּ, פָּשַׁעְנוּ, צָרַרְנוּ, קִשִּׁינוּ עֹרֶף
רָשַׁעְנוּ, שִׁחַתְנוּ, תִּעַבְנוּ, תָּעִינוּ, תִּעְתָּעְנוּ.

סַרְנוּ מִמִּצְוֹתֶיךָ וּמִמִּשְׁפָּטֶיךָ הַטּוֹבִים, וְלֹא שָׁוָה לָנוּ.
וְאַתָּה צַדִּיק עַל כָּל־הַבָּא עָלֵינוּ נחמיה ט
כִּי־אֱמֶת עָשִׂיתָ, וַאֲנַחְנוּ הִרְשָׁעְנוּ:

מַה נֹּאמַר לְפָנֶיךָ יוֹשֵׁב מָרוֹם, וּמַה נְּסַפֵּר לְפָנֶיךָ שׁוֹכֵן שְׁחָקִים
הֲלֹא כָּל הַנִּסְתָּרוֹת וְהַנִּגְלוֹת אַתָּה יוֹדֵעַ.

אַתָּה יוֹדֵעַ רָזֵי עוֹלָם וְתַעֲלוּמוֹת סִתְרֵי כָּל חָי.
אַתָּה חוֹפֵשׂ כָּל חַדְרֵי בָטֶן וּבוֹחֵן כְּלָיוֹת וָלֵב.
אֵין דָּבָר נֶעְלָם מִמֶּךָּ וְאֵין נִסְתָּר מִנֶּגֶד עֵינֶיךָ.
וּבְכֵן, יְהִי רָצוֹן מִלְּפָנֶיךָ, יהוה אֱלֹהֵינוּ וֵאלֹהֵי אֲבוֹתֵינוּ
שֶׁתִּסְלַח לָנוּ עַל כָּל חַטֹּאתֵינוּ
וְתִמְחַל לָנוּ עַל כָּל עֲוֹנוֹתֵינוּ
וּתְכַפֵּר לָנוּ עַל כָּל פְּשָׁעֵינוּ.

Strike the left side of the chest with the right fist while saying each of the sins.

עַל חֵטְא שֶׁחָטָאנוּ לְפָנֶיךָ בְּאֹנֶס וּבְרָצוֹן
וְעַל חֵטְא שֶׁחָטָאנוּ לְפָנֶיךָ בְּאִמּוּץ הַלֵּב
עַל חֵטְא שֶׁחָטָאנוּ לְפָנֶיךָ בִּבְלִי דָעַת
וְעַל חֵטְא שֶׁחָטָאנוּ לְפָנֶיךָ בְּבִטּוּי שְׂפָתָיִם
עַל חֵטְא שֶׁחָטָאנוּ לְפָנֶיךָ בְּגִלּוּי עֲרָיוֹת
וְעַל חֵטְא שֶׁחָטָאנוּ לְפָנֶיךָ בְּגָלוּי וּבַסָּתֶר

For the sin we have sinned before You knowingly and deceitfully,
and for the sin we have sinned before You in speech.

For the sin we have sinned before You by wronging a neighbor,
and for the sin we have sinned before You by thoughts of the heart.

For the sin we have sinned before You in a gathering for immorality,
and for the sin we have sinned before You by insincere confession.

For the sin we have sinned before You by contempt for parents and teachers,
and for the sin we have sinned before You willfully or in error.

For the sin we have sinned before You by force,
and for the sin we have sinned before You by desecrating Your name.

For the sin we have sinned before You by impure lips,
and for the sin we have sinned before You by foolish speech.

For the sin we have sinned before You by the evil inclination,
and for the sin we have sinned before You knowingly or unwittingly.

FOR ALL THESE, GOD OF FORGIVENESS,
FORGIVE US, PARDON US, GRANT US ATONEMENT.

For the sin we have sinned before You by deceit and lies,
and for the sin we have sinned before You by bribery.

For the sin we have sinned before You by scorn,
and for the sin we have sinned before You by evil speech.

For the sin we have sinned before You in business,
and for the sin we have sinned before You with food and drink.

For the sin we have sinned before You by interest and extortion,
and for the sin we have sinned before You by being haughty.

For the sin we have sinned before You by the idle chatter of our lips,
and for the sin we have sinned before You by prying eyes.

עַל חֵטְא שֶׁחָטָאנוּ לְפָנֶיךָ בְּדַעַת וּבְמִרְמָה
וְעַל חֵטְא שֶׁחָטָאנוּ לְפָנֶיךָ בְּדִבּוּר פֶּה
עַל חֵטְא שֶׁחָטָאנוּ לְפָנֶיךָ בְּהוֹנָאַת רֵעַ
וְעַל חֵטְא שֶׁחָטָאנוּ לְפָנֶיךָ בְּהַרְהוֹר הַלֵּב
עַל חֵטְא שֶׁחָטָאנוּ לְפָנֶיךָ בִּוְעִידַת זְנוּת
וְעַל חֵטְא שֶׁחָטָאנוּ לְפָנֶיךָ בְּוִדּוּי פֶּה
עַל חֵטְא שֶׁחָטָאנוּ לְפָנֶיךָ בְּזִלְזוּל הוֹרִים וּמוֹרִים
וְעַל חֵטְא שֶׁחָטָאנוּ לְפָנֶיךָ בְּזָדוֹן וּבִשְׁגָגָה
עַל חֵטְא שֶׁחָטָאנוּ לְפָנֶיךָ בְּחֹזֶק יָד
וְעַל חֵטְא שֶׁחָטָאנוּ לְפָנֶיךָ בְּחִלּוּל הַשֵּׁם
עַל חֵטְא שֶׁחָטָאנוּ לְפָנֶיךָ בְּטֻמְאַת שְׂפָתָיִם
וְעַל חֵטְא שֶׁחָטָאנוּ לְפָנֶיךָ בְּטִפְּשׁוּת פֶּה
עַל חֵטְא שֶׁחָטָאנוּ לְפָנֶיךָ בְּיֵצֶר הָרָע
וְעַל חֵטְא שֶׁחָטָאנוּ לְפָנֶיךָ בְּיוֹדְעִים וּבְלֹא יוֹדְעִים

וְעַל כֻּלָּם אֱלוֹהַּ סְלִיחוֹת סְלַח לָנוּ, מְחַל לָנוּ, כַּפֶּר לָנוּ.

עַל חֵטְא שֶׁחָטָאנוּ לְפָנֶיךָ בְּכַחַשׁ וּבְכָזָב
וְעַל חֵטְא שֶׁחָטָאנוּ לְפָנֶיךָ בְּכַפַּת שֹׁחַד
עַל חֵטְא שֶׁחָטָאנוּ לְפָנֶיךָ בְּלָצוֹן
וְעַל חֵטְא שֶׁחָטָאנוּ לְפָנֶיךָ בְּלָשׁוֹן הָרָע
עַל חֵטְא שֶׁחָטָאנוּ לְפָנֶיךָ בְּמַשָּׂא וּבְמַתָּן
וְעַל חֵטְא שֶׁחָטָאנוּ לְפָנֶיךָ בְּמַאֲכָל וּבְמִשְׁתֶּה
עַל חֵטְא שֶׁחָטָאנוּ לְפָנֶיךָ בְּנֶשֶׁךְ וּבְמַרְבִּית
וְעַל חֵטְא שֶׁחָטָאנוּ לְפָנֶיךָ בִּנְטִיַּת גָּרוֹן
עַל חֵטְא שֶׁחָטָאנוּ לְפָנֶיךָ בְּשִׂיחַ שִׂפְתוֹתֵינוּ
וְעַל חֵטְא שֶׁחָטָאנוּ לְפָנֶיךָ בְּשִׂקּוּר עָיִן

For the sin we have sinned before You by arrogance,
and for the sin we have sinned before You by insolence.

FOR ALL THESE, GOD OF FORGIVENESS,
FORGIVE US, PARDON US, GRANT US ATONEMENT.

For the sin we have sinned before You by casting off the yoke,
and for the sin we have sinned before You by perverting judgment.

For the sin we have sinned before You by entrapping a neighbor,
and for the sin we have sinned before You by envy.

For the sin we have sinned before You by lack of seriousness,
and for the sin we have sinned before You by obstinacy.

For the sin we have sinned before You by running to do evil,
and for the sin we have sinned before You by gossip.

For the sin we have sinned before You by vain oath,
and for the sin we have sinned before You by baseless hatred.

For the sin we have sinned before You by breach of trust,
and for the sin we have sinned before You by confusion of heart.

FOR ALL THESE, GOD OF FORGIVENESS,
FORGIVE US, PARDON US, GRANT US ATONEMENT.

וְעַל חֲטָאִים And for the sins for which we are liable to bring a burnt-offering,
and for the sins for which we are liable to bring a sin-offering,
and for the sins for which we are liable to bring an offering according to our means,
and for the sins for which we are liable to bring a guilt-offering for certain or possible sin,
and for the sins for which we are liable to lashes for rebellion,
and for the sins for which we are liable to forty lashes,
and for the sins for which we are liable to death by the hands of Heaven,
and for the sins for which we are liable to be cut off and childless,
and for the sins for which we are liable to the four death penalties
inflicted by the court: stoning, burning, beheading and strangling.

עַל חֵטְא שֶׁחָטָאנוּ לְפָנֶיךָ בְּעֵינַיִם רָמוֹת
וְעַל חֵטְא שֶׁחָטָאנוּ לְפָנֶיךָ בְּעַזּוּת מֵצַח

וְעַל כֻּלָּם אֱלוֹהַּ סְלִיחוֹת סְלַח לָנוּ, מְחַל לָנוּ, כַּפֶּר לָנוּ.

עַל חֵטְא שֶׁחָטָאנוּ לְפָנֶיךָ בִּפְרִיקַת עֹל
וְעַל חֵטְא שֶׁחָטָאנוּ לְפָנֶיךָ בִּפְלִילוּת
עַל חֵטְא שֶׁחָטָאנוּ לְפָנֶיךָ בִּצְדִיַּת רֵעַ
וְעַל חֵטְא שֶׁחָטָאנוּ לְפָנֶיךָ בְּצָרוּת עָיִן
עַל חֵטְא שֶׁחָטָאנוּ לְפָנֶיךָ בְּקַלּוּת רֹאשׁ
וְעַל חֵטְא שֶׁחָטָאנוּ לְפָנֶיךָ בְּקַשְׁיוּת עֹרֶף
עַל חֵטְא שֶׁחָטָאנוּ לְפָנֶיךָ בְּרִיצַת רַגְלַיִם לְהָרַע
וְעַל חֵטְא שֶׁחָטָאנוּ לְפָנֶיךָ בִּרְכִילוּת
עַל חֵטְא שֶׁחָטָאנוּ לְפָנֶיךָ בִּשְׁבוּעַת שָׁוְא
וְעַל חֵטְא שֶׁחָטָאנוּ לְפָנֶיךָ בְּשִׂנְאַת חִנָּם
עַל חֵטְא שֶׁחָטָאנוּ לְפָנֶיךָ בִּתְשׂוּמֶת יָד
וְעַל חֵטְא שֶׁחָטָאנוּ לְפָנֶיךָ בְּתִמְהוֹן לֵבָב

וְעַל כֻּלָּם אֱלוֹהַּ סְלִיחוֹת סְלַח לָנוּ, מְחַל לָנוּ, כַּפֶּר לָנוּ.

וְעַל חֲטָאִים שֶׁאָנוּ חַיָּבִים עֲלֵיהֶם עוֹלָה
וְעַל חֲטָאִים שֶׁאָנוּ חַיָּבִים עֲלֵיהֶם חַטָּאת
וְעַל חֲטָאִים שֶׁאָנוּ חַיָּבִים עֲלֵיהֶם קָרְבָּן עוֹלֶה וְיוֹרֵד
וְעַל חֲטָאִים שֶׁאָנוּ חַיָּבִים עֲלֵיהֶם אָשָׁם וַדַּאי וְתָלוּי
וְעַל חֲטָאִים שֶׁאָנוּ חַיָּבִים עֲלֵיהֶם מַכַּת מַרְדּוּת
וְעַל חֲטָאִים שֶׁאָנוּ חַיָּבִים עֲלֵיהֶם מַלְקוּת אַרְבָּעִים
וְעַל חֲטָאִים שֶׁאָנוּ חַיָּבִים עֲלֵיהֶם מִיתָה בִּידֵי שָׁמַיִם
וְעַל חֲטָאִים שֶׁאָנוּ חַיָּבִים עֲלֵיהֶם כָּרֵת וַעֲרִירִי
וְעַל חֲטָאִים שֶׁאָנוּ חַיָּבִים עֲלֵיהֶם אַרְבַּע מִיתוֹת בֵּית דִּין
סְקִילָה, שְׂרֵפָה, הֶרֶג, וְחֶנֶק.

For positive and negative commandments,
whether they can be remedied by an act or not,
for sins known to us and for those that are unknown –
for those that are known,
we have already declared them before You and confessed them to You;
and for those that are unknown,
before You they are revealed and known,
as it is said,
"The secret things belong to the LORD our God, *Deut. 29*
but the things that are revealed are for us and our children for ever,
that we may fulfill all the words of this Torah."
For You are the Forgiver of Israel
and the Pardoner of the tribes of Yeshurun in every generation,
and without You we have no king who pardons and forgives,
none but You.

אֱלֹהַי My God,
before I was formed I was unworthy,
and now that I have been formed it is as if I had not been formed.
I am dust while alive,
how much more so when I am dead.
See, I am before You like a vessel filled with shame and disgrace.
May it be Your will, LORD my God and God of my fathers,
that I may sin no more,
and as for the sins I have committed before You,
erase them in Your great compassion,
but not by suffering or severe illness.

אֱלֹהַי My God, *Berakhot 17a*
guard my tongue from evil
and my lips from deceitful speech.
To those who curse me, let my soul be silent;
may my soul be to all like the dust.
Open my heart to Your Torah
and let my soul pursue Your commandments.
As for all who plan evil against me,
swiftly thwart their counsel and frustrate their plans.

עַל מִצְוַת עֲשֵׂה וְעַל מִצְוַת לֹא תַעֲשֶׂה.
בֵּין שֶׁיֵּשׁ בָּהּ קוּם עֲשֵׂה וּבֵין שֶׁאֵין בָּהּ קוּם עֲשֵׂה.
אֶת הַגְּלוּיִים לָנוּ וְאֶת שֶׁאֵינָם גְּלוּיִים לָנוּ
אֶת הַגְּלוּיִים לָנוּ, כְּבָר אֲמַרְנוּם לְפָנֶיךָ, וְהוֹדִינוּ לְךָ עֲלֵיהֶם
וְאֶת שֶׁאֵינָם גְּלוּיִים לָנוּ, לְפָנֶיךָ הֵם גְּלוּיִים וִידוּעִים
כַּדָּבָר שֶׁנֶּאֱמַר
הַנִּסְתָּרֹת לַיהוה אֱלֹהֵינוּ דברים כט
וְהַנִּגְלֹת לָנוּ וּלְבָנֵינוּ עַד־עוֹלָם
לַעֲשׂוֹת אֶת־כָּל־דִּבְרֵי הַתּוֹרָה הַזֹּאת:

כִּי אַתָּה סָלְחָן לְיִשְׂרָאֵל וּמָחֳלָן לְשִׁבְטֵי יְשֻׁרוּן בְּכָל דּוֹר וָדוֹר
וּמִבַּלְעָדֶיךָ אֵין לָנוּ מֶלֶךְ מוֹחֵל וְסוֹלֵחַ אֶלָּא אָתָּה.

אֱלֹהַי
עַד שֶׁלֹּא נוֹצַרְתִּי אֵינִי כְדַאי
וְעַכְשָׁיו שֶׁנּוֹצַרְתִּי, כְּאִלּוּ לֹא נוֹצַרְתִּי
עָפָר אֲנִי בְּחַיָּי, קַל וָחֹמֶר בְּמִיתָתִי.
הֲרֵי אֲנִי לְפָנֶיךָ כִּכְלִי מָלֵא בוּשָׁה וּכְלִמָּה.
יְהִי רָצוֹן מִלְּפָנֶיךָ, יהוה אֱלֹהַי וֵאלֹהֵי אֲבוֹתַי, שֶׁלֹּא אֶחֱטָא עוֹד.
וּמַה שֶּׁחָטָאתִי לְפָנֶיךָ, מְחֹק בְּרַחֲמֶיךָ הָרַבִּים
אֲבָל לֹא עַל יְדֵי יִסּוּרִים וָחֳלָיִם רָעִים.

אֱלֹהַי ברכות יז.
נְצֹר לְשׁוֹנִי מֵרָע וּשְׂפָתַי מִדַּבֵּר מִרְמָה
וְלִמְקַלְלַי נַפְשִׁי תִדֹּם, וְנַפְשִׁי כֶּעָפָר לַכֹּל תִּהְיֶה.
פְּתַח לִבִּי בְּתוֹרָתֶךָ, וּבְמִצְוֹתֶיךָ תִּרְדֹּף נַפְשִׁי.
וְכָל הַחוֹשְׁבִים עָלַי רָעָה
מְהֵרָה הָפֵר עֲצָתָם וְקַלְקֵל מַחֲשַׁבְתָּם.

Act for the sake of Your name; act for the sake of Your right hand;
act for the sake of Your holiness; act for the sake of Your Torah.

That Your beloved ones may be delivered, *Ps. 60*
save with Your right hand and answer me.

May the words of my mouth and the meditation of my heart *Ps. 19*
find favor before You, LORD, my Rock and Redeemer.

Bow, take three steps back, then bow, first left, then right, then center, while saying:

May He who makes peace in His high places,
make peace for us and all Israel – and say: Amen.

יְהִי רָצוֹן May it be Your will, LORD our God and God of our ancestors,
that the Temple be rebuilt speedily in our days, and grant us a share in Your Torah.
And there we will serve You with reverence,
as in the days of old and as in former years.
Then the offering of Judah and Jerusalem *Mal. 3*
will be pleasing to the LORD as in the days of old and as in former years.

FULL KADDISH

Leader: יִתְגַּדַּל Magnified and sanctified may His great name be,
in the world He created by His will.
May He establish His kingdom
in your lifetime and in your days,
and in the lifetime of all the house of Israel,
swiftly and soon –
and say: Amen.

All: May His great name be blessed for ever and all time.

Leader: Blessed and praised,
glorified and exalted,
raised and honored,
uplifted and lauded be
the name of the Holy One, blessed be He,
above and beyond any blessing, song,
praise and consolation
uttered in the world –
and say: Amen.

עֲשֵׂה לְמַעַן שְׁמֶךָ, עֲשֵׂה לְמַעַן יְמִינֶךָ

עֲשֵׂה לְמַעַן קְדֻשָּׁתֶךָ, עֲשֵׂה לְמַעַן תּוֹרָתֶךָ.

לְמַעַן יֵחָלְצוּן יְדִידֶיךָ, הוֹשִׁיעָה יְמִינְךָ וַעֲנֵנִי: תהלים ס

יִהְיוּ לְרָצוֹן אִמְרֵי פִי וְהֶגְיוֹן לִבִּי לְפָנֶיךָ, יהוה צוּרִי וְגוֹאֲלִי: תהלים יט

Bow, take three steps back, then bow, first left, then right, then center, while saying:

עֹשֶׂה הַשָּׁלוֹם בִּמְרוֹמָיו

הוּא יַעֲשֶׂה שָׁלוֹם עָלֵינוּ וְעַל כָּל יִשְׂרָאֵל וְאִמְרוּ אָמֵן.

יְהִי רָצוֹן מִלְּפָנֶיךָ יהוה אֱלֹהֵינוּ וֵאלֹהֵי אֲבוֹתֵינוּ

שֶׁיִּבָּנֶה בֵּית הַמִּקְדָּשׁ בִּמְהֵרָה בְיָמֵינוּ, וְתֵן חֶלְקֵנוּ בְּתוֹרָתֶךָ

וְשָׁם נַעֲבָדְךָ בְּיִרְאָה כִּימֵי עוֹלָם וּכְשָׁנִים קַדְמֹנִיּוֹת.

וְעָרְבָה לַיהוה מִנְחַת יְהוּדָה וִירוּשָׁלָםִ כִּימֵי עוֹלָם וּכְשָׁנִים קַדְמֹנִיּוֹת: מלאכי ג

קדיש שלם

ש״ץ: יִתְגַּדַּל וְיִתְקַדַּשׁ שְׁמֵהּ רַבָּא (קהל: אָמֵן)

בְּעָלְמָא דִּי בְרָא כִרְעוּתֵהּ

וְיַמְלִיךְ מַלְכוּתֵהּ

בְּחַיֵּיכוֹן וּבְיוֹמֵיכוֹן וּבְחַיֵּי דְכָל בֵּית יִשְׂרָאֵל

בַּעֲגָלָא וּבִזְמַן קָרִיב, וְאִמְרוּ אָמֵן. (קהל: אָמֵן)

קהל וש״ץ: יְהֵא שְׁמֵהּ רַבָּא מְבָרַךְ לְעָלַם וּלְעָלְמֵי עָלְמַיָּא.

ש״ץ: יִתְבָּרַךְ וְיִשְׁתַּבַּח וְיִתְפָּאַר וְיִתְרוֹמַם וְיִתְנַשֵּׂא

וְיִתְהַדָּר וְיִתְעַלֶּה וְיִתְהַלָּל

שְׁמֵהּ דְּקֻדְשָׁא בְּרִיךְ הוּא (קהל: בְּרִיךְ הוּא)

לְעֵלָּא לְעֵלָּא מִכָּל בִּרְכָתָא וְשִׁירָתָא, תֻּשְׁבְּחָתָא וְנֶחֱמָתָא

דַּאֲמִירָן בְּעָלְמָא, וְאִמְרוּ אָמֵן. (קהל: אָמֵן)

May the prayers and pleas of all Israel
be accepted by their Father in heaven –
and say: Amen.

May there be great peace from heaven,
and life for us and all Israel –
and say: Amen.

Bow, take three steps back, as if taking leave of the Divine Presence, then bow, first left, then right, then center, while saying:

May He who makes peace in His high places,
make peace for us and all Israel –
and say: Amen.

Stand while saying Aleinu. Bow at ▾.

עָלֵינוּ It is our duty to praise the Master of all,
and ascribe greatness
to the Author of creation,
who has not made us
like the nations of the lands,
nor placed us
like the families of the earth;
who has not made our portion like theirs,
nor our destiny like all their multitudes.
(For they worship vanity and emptiness,
and pray to a god who cannot save.)
▾But we bow in worship
and thank the Supreme King of kings,
the Holy One, blessed be He,
who extends the heavens and establishes the earth,
whose throne of glory is in the heavens above,
and whose power's Presence
is in the highest of heights.

תִּתְקַבַּל צְלוֹתְהוֹן וּבָעוּתְהוֹן דְּכָל יִשְׂרָאֵל
קֳדָם אֲבוּהוֹן דִּי בִשְׁמַיָּא, וְאִמְרוּ אָמֵן. (קהל: אָמֵן)

יְהֵא שְׁלָמָא רַבָּא מִן שְׁמַיָּא
וְחַיִּים, עָלֵינוּ וְעַל כָּל יִשְׂרָאֵל
וְאִמְרוּ אָמֵן. (קהל: אָמֵן)

Bow, take three steps back, as if taking leave of the Divine Presence, then bow, first left, then right, then center, while saying:

עֹשֶׂה הַשָּׁלוֹם בִּמְרוֹמָיו
הוּא יַעֲשֶׂה שָׁלוֹם עָלֵינוּ וְעַל כָּל יִשְׂרָאֵל
וְאִמְרוּ אָמֵן. (קהל: אָמֵן)

Stand while saying עָלֵינוּ. Bow at ▾.

עָלֵינוּ לְשַׁבֵּחַ לַאֲדוֹן הַכֹּל
לָתֵת גְּדֻלָּה לְיוֹצֵר בְּרֵאשִׁית
שֶׁלֹּא עָשָׂנוּ כְּגוֹיֵי הָאֲרָצוֹת
וְלֹא שָׂמָנוּ כְּמִשְׁפְּחוֹת הָאֲדָמָה
שֶׁלֹּא שָׂם חֶלְקֵנוּ כָּהֶם וְגוֹרָלֵנוּ כְּכָל הֲמוֹנָם.
(שֶׁהֵם מִשְׁתַּחֲוִים לְהֶבֶל וָרִיק וּמִתְפַּלְלִים אֶל אֵל לֹא יוֹשִׁיעַ.)
▾וַאֲנַחְנוּ כּוֹרְעִים וּמִשְׁתַּחֲוִים וּמוֹדִים
לִפְנֵי מֶלֶךְ מַלְכֵי הַמְּלָכִים, הַקָּדוֹשׁ בָּרוּךְ הוּא
שֶׁהוּא נוֹטֶה שָׁמַיִם וְיוֹסֵד אָרֶץ
וּמוֹשַׁב יְקָרוֹ בַּשָּׁמַיִם מִמַּעַל
וּשְׁכִינַת עֻזּוֹ בְּגָבְהֵי מְרוֹמִים.

He is our God; there is no other.
Truly He is our King; there is none else,
as it is written in His Torah:
"You shall know and take to heart this day *Deut. 4*
that the Lord is God,
in the heavens above and on the earth below.
There is no other."

Therefore, we place our hope in You, Lord our God,
that we may soon see the glory of Your power,
when You will remove abominations from the earth,
and idols will be utterly destroyed,
when the world will be perfected
under the sovereignty of the Almighty,
when all humanity will call on Your name,
to turn all the earth's wicked toward You.
All the world's inhabitants will realize
and know that to You
every knee must bow
and every tongue swear loyalty.
Before You, Lord our God,
they will kneel and bow down
and give honor to Your glorious name.
They will all accept the yoke of Your kingdom,
and You will reign over them
soon and for ever.
For the kingdom is Yours,
and to all eternity You will reign in glory,
as it is written in Your Torah:
"The Lord will reign for ever and ever." *Ex. 15*
▸ And it is said:
"Then the Lord shall be King over all the earth; *Zech. 14*
on that day the Lord shall be One and His name One."

הוּא אֱלֹהֵינוּ, אֵין עוֹד.
אֱמֶת מַלְכֵּנוּ, אֶפֶס זוּלָתוֹ
כַּכָּתוּב בְּתוֹרָתוֹ
וְיָדַעְתָּ הַיּוֹם וַהֲשֵׁבֹתָ אֶל־לְבָבֶךָ דברים ד
כִּי יהוה הוּא הָאֱלֹהִים בַּשָּׁמַיִם מִמַּעַל וְעַל־הָאָרֶץ מִתָּחַת
אֵין עוֹד:

עַל כֵּן נְקַוֶּה לְּךָ יהוה אֱלֹהֵינוּ
לִרְאוֹת מְהֵרָה בְּתִפְאֶרֶת עֻזֶּךָ
לְהַעֲבִיר גִּלּוּלִים מִן הָאָרֶץ
וְהָאֱלִילִים כָּרוֹת יִכָּרֵתוּן
לְתַקֵּן עוֹלָם בְּמַלְכוּת שַׁדַּי.
וְכָל בְּנֵי בָשָׂר יִקְרְאוּ בִשְׁמֶךָ
לְהַפְנוֹת אֵלֶיךָ כָּל רִשְׁעֵי אָרֶץ.
יַכִּירוּ וְיֵדְעוּ כָּל יוֹשְׁבֵי תֵבֵל
כִּי לְךָ תִּכְרַע כָּל בֶּרֶךְ, תִּשָּׁבַע כָּל לָשׁוֹן.
לְפָנֶיךָ יהוה אֱלֹהֵינוּ יִכְרְעוּ וְיִפֹּלוּ
וְלִכְבוֹד שִׁמְךָ יְקָר יִתֵּנוּ
וִיקַבְּלוּ כֻלָּם אֶת עֹל מַלְכוּתֶךָ
וְתִמְלֹךְ עֲלֵיהֶם מְהֵרָה לְעוֹלָם וָעֶד.
כִּי הַמַּלְכוּת שֶׁלְּךָ הִיא וּלְעוֹלְמֵי עַד תִּמְלֹךְ בְּכָבוֹד
כַּכָּתוּב בְּתוֹרָתֶךָ, יהוה יִמְלֹךְ לְעֹלָם וָעֶד: שמות טו
◂ וְנֶאֱמַר, וְהָיָה יהוה לְמֶלֶךְ עַל־כָּל־הָאָרֶץ זכריה יד
בַּיּוֹם הַהוּא יִהְיֶה יהוה אֶחָד וּשְׁמוֹ אֶחָד:

Some add:

Have no fear of sudden terror or of the ruin when it overtakes the wicked. *Prov. 3*
Devise your strategy, but it will be thwarted; propose your plan, *Is. 8*
but it will not stand, for God is with us.
When you grow old, I will still be the same. *Is. 46*
When your hair turns gray, I will still carry you.
I made you, I will bear you, I will carry you, and I will rescue you.

MOURNER'S KADDISH

The following prayer requires the presence of a minyan.
A transliteration can be found on page 1375.

Mourner: יִתְגַּדַּל Magnified and sanctified
may His great name be,
in the world He created by His will.
May He establish His kingdom
in your lifetime and in your days,
and in the lifetime
of all the house of Israel,
swiftly and soon – and say: Amen.

All: May His great name be blessed for ever and all time.

Mourner: Blessed and praised, glorified and exalted,
raised and honored, uplifted and lauded
be the name of the Holy One, blessed be He,
above and beyond any blessing, song,
praise and consolation
uttered in the world – and say: Amen.

May there be great peace from heaven,
and life for us and all Israel – and say: Amen.

Bow, take three steps back, as if taking leave of the Divine Presence, then bow, first left, then right, then center, while saying:

May He who makes peace in His high places,
make peace for us and all Israel – and say: Amen.

Some add:

אַל־תִּירָא מִפַּחַד פִּתְאֹם וּמִשֹּׁאַת רְשָׁעִים כִּי תָבֹא: משלי ג

עֻצוּ עֵצָה וְתֻפָר, דַּבְּרוּ דָבָר וְלֹא יָקוּם, כִּי עִמָּנוּ אֵל: ישעיה ח

וְעַד־זִקְנָה אֲנִי הוּא, וְעַד־שֵׂיבָה אֲנִי אֶסְבֹּל ישעיה מו

אֲנִי עָשִׂיתִי וַאֲנִי אֶשָּׂא וַאֲנִי אֶסְבֹּל וַאֲמַלֵּט:

קדיש יתום

The following prayer requires the presence of a מנין.
A transliteration can be found on page 1375.

אבל: יִתְגַּדַּל וְיִתְקַדַּשׁ שְׁמֵהּ רַבָּא (קהל: אָמֵן)
בְּעָלְמָא דִּי בְרָא כִרְעוּתֵהּ
וְיַמְלִיךְ מַלְכוּתֵהּ
בְּחַיֵּיכוֹן וּבְיוֹמֵיכוֹן וּבְחַיֵּי דְכָל בֵּית יִשְׂרָאֵל
בַּעֲגָלָא וּבִזְמַן קָרִיב, וְאִמְרוּ אָמֵן. (קהל: אָמֵן)

קהל ואבל: יְהֵא שְׁמֵהּ רַבָּא מְבָרַךְ לְעָלַם וּלְעָלְמֵי עָלְמַיָּא.

אבל: יִתְבָּרַךְ וְיִשְׁתַּבַּח וְיִתְפָּאַר וְיִתְרוֹמַם וְיִתְנַשֵּׂא
וְיִתְהַדָּר וְיִתְעַלֶּה וְיִתְהַלָּל
שְׁמֵהּ דְּקֻדְשָׁא בְּרִיךְ הוּא (קהל: בְּרִיךְ הוּא)
לְעֵלָּא לְעֵלָּא מִכָּל בִּרְכָתָא וְשִׁירָתָא, תֻּשְׁבְּחָתָא וְנֶחֱמָתָא
דַּאֲמִירָן בְּעָלְמָא, וְאִמְרוּ אָמֵן. (קהל: אָמֵן)

יְהֵא שְׁלָמָא רַבָּא מִן שְׁמַיָּא
וְחַיִּים, עָלֵינוּ וְעַל כָּל יִשְׂרָאֵל, וְאִמְרוּ אָמֵן. (קהל: אָמֵן)

Bow, take three steps back, as if taking leave of the Divine Presence, then bow, first left, then right, then center, while saying:

עֹשֶׂה הַשָּׁלוֹם בִּמְרוֹמָיו
הוּא יַעֲשֶׂה שָׁלוֹם עָלֵינוּ וְעַל כָּל יִשְׂרָאֵל, וְאִמְרוּ אָמֵן. (קהל: אָמֵן)

Erev Yom Kippur

EIRUV TEḤUMIN

On Yom Kippur, as on Shabbat, it is forbidden to walk more than 2000 cubits (about 3000 feet) beyond the boundary (teḥum) of the town where you live or are staying when the day begins. By placing food sufficient for two meals, before nightfall, at a point within 2000 cubits from the town limits, you confer on that place the status of a dwelling for the next day, and are then permitted to walk 2000 cubits from there.

בָּרוּךְ Blessed are You, Lord our God, King of the Universe,
who has made us holy through His commandments,
and has commanded us about the mitzva of Eiruv.

By this Eiruv may we be permitted to walk from this place, two thousand cubits in any direction.

EIRUV ḤATZEROT

On Yom Kippur, as on Shabbat, it is forbidden to carry objects from one private domain to another, or from a private domain into space shared by others, such as a communal staircase, corridor or courtyard. An Eiruv Ḥatzerot is created when each of the Jewish households in a court or apartment block, before Yom Kippur or Shabbat, places a loaf of bread or matza in one of the homes. The entire court or block then becomes a single private domain within which it is permitted to carry.

בָּרוּךְ Blessed are You, Lord our God, King of the Universe,
who has made us holy through His commandments,
and has commanded us about the mitzva of Eiruv.

By this Eiruv may we be permitted to move, carry out and carry in from the houses to the courtyard, or from the courtyard to the houses, or from house to house, for all the houses within the courtyard.

---

festivals by eating and drinking. This is impossible on Yom Kippur itself, which is a fast, so the Torah ordained that we should celebrate the festival before the fast (*Beit Yosef*, OḤ 604). Others say it was to preclude the interpretation of the Sadducees, who understood the Torah to be saying that we should fast for two days, the ninth and tenth (*Shibolei HaLeket*, 307). Yet others say that our ability to eat a festive meal on the eve of the day of judgment it is an expression of our faith in God's forgiveness (*Or Yesharim*).

ערב יום הכיפורים

עירוב תחומין

On יום כיפור, as on שבת, it is forbidden to walk more than 2000 cubits (about 3000 feet) beyond the boundary (תחום) of the town where you live or are staying when the day begins. By placing food sufficient for two meals, before nightfall, at a point within 2000 cubits from the town limits, you confer on that place the status of a dwelling for the next day, and are then permitted to walk 2000 cubits from there.

בָּרוּךְ אַתָּה יהוה אֱלֹהֵינוּ מֶלֶךְ הָעוֹלָם
אֲשֶׁר קִדְּשָׁנוּ בְּמִצְוֹתָיו וְצִוָּנוּ עַל מִצְוַת עֵרוּב.
בְּדֵין עֵרוּבָא יְהֵא שְׁרֵא לִי לְמֵיזַל מֵאַתְרָא הָדֵין תְּרֵין אַלְפִּין אַמִּין לְכָל רוּחָא.

עירוב חצרות

On יום כיפור, as on שבת, it is forbidden to carry objects from one private domain to another, or from a private domain into space shared by others, such as a communal staircase, corridor or courtyard. An עירוב חצרות is created when each of the Jewish households in a court or apartment block, before יום כיפור or שבת, places a loaf of bread or matza in one of the homes. The entire court or block then becomes a single private domain within which it is permitted to carry.

בָּרוּךְ אַתָּה יהוה אֱלֹהֵינוּ מֶלֶךְ הָעוֹלָם
אֲשֶׁר קִדְּשָׁנוּ בְּמִצְוֹתָיו וְצִוָּנוּ עַל מִצְוַת עֵרוּב.
בְּדֵין עֵרוּבָא יְהֵא שְׁרֵא לַנָא לְטַלְטוּלֵי וּלְאַפּוּקֵי וּלְעַיּוּלֵי מִן הַבָּתִּים לֶחָצֵר וּמִן הֶחָצֵר לַבָּתִּים וּמִבַּיִת לְבַיִת לְכָל הַבָּתִּים שֶׁבֶּחָצֵר.

SE'UDA HAMAFSEKET

The meal before the fast has a special sanctity. The Torah states, "You shall afflict yourselves on the ninth day of the month in the evening, from evening to evening" (Lev. 23:32). On this the Talmud says, "Do we indeed afflict ourselves on the ninth? Do we not fast on the tenth? Rather, the verse is telling us that one who eats and drinks on the ninth is considered as if he had fasted on both the ninth and tenth" (*Rosh HaShana* 9a–b; *Yoma* 81b). So this meal is part of the service of Yom Kippur itself.

Some say it was ordained because Yom Kippur is a festival, and we honor

CANDLE LIGHTING

On Erev Yom Kippur, cover the eyes with the hands after lighting the candles, and say (on Shabbat add the words in parentheses):

בָּרוּךְ Blessed are You, Lord our God, King of the Universe, who has made us holy through His commandments, and has commanded us to light (the Sabbath light and) the light of the Day of Atonement.

בָּרוּךְ Blessed are You, Lord our God, King of the Universe, who has given us life, sustained us, and brought us to this time.

Prayer after candlelighting (add the words in parentheses as appropriate):

יְהִי May it be Your will, Lord my God and God of my forebears, that You give me grace – me (and my husband/and my father/and my mother/and my sons and my daughters) and all those close to me, and give us and all Israel good and long lives. And remember us with a memory that brings goodness and blessing; come to us with compassion and bless us with great blessings. Build our homes until they are complete, and allow Your Presence to live among us. And may I merit to raise children and grandchildren, each one wise and understanding, loving the Lord and in awe of God, people of truth, holy children, who will cling on to the Lord and light up the world with Torah and with good actions, and with all the kinds of work that serve the Creator. Please, hear my pleading at this time, by the merit of Sarah and Rebecca, Rachel and Leah our mothers, and light our candle that it should never go out, and light up Your face, so that we shall be saved, Amen.

Normally we make a blessing over a commandment *before* performing it. In this case, however, the blessing is made afterward, so that the lighting precedes mental acceptance of the day and its prohibitions. The blessing is made while covering one's eyes, so that the blessing follows the act but precedes its benefit (Rema, *OḤ* 263:10).

הדלקת נרות

On ערב יום כיפור*, cover the eyes with the hands after lighting the candles, and say (on* שבת *add the words in parentheses):*

בָּרוּךְ אַתָּה יהוה אֱלֹהֵינוּ מֶלֶךְ הָעוֹלָם
אֲשֶׁר קִדְּשָׁנוּ בְּמִצְוֹתָיו
וְצִוָּנוּ לְהַדְלִיק נֵר שֶׁל (שַׁבָּת וְשֶׁל) יוֹם הַכִּפּוּרִים.

בָּרוּךְ אַתָּה יהוה אֱלֹהֵינוּ מֶלֶךְ הָעוֹלָם
שֶׁהֶחֱיָנוּ וְקִיְּמָנוּ, וְהִגִּיעָנוּ לַזְּמַן הַזֶּה.

Prayer after candlelighting (add the words in parentheses as appropriate):

יְהִי רָצוֹן מִלְּפָנֶיךָ יהוה אֱלֹהַי וֵאלֹהֵי אֲבוֹתַי, שֶׁתְּחוֹנֵן אוֹתִי (וְאֶת אִישִׁי / וְאֶת אָבִי / וְאֶת אִמִּי / וְאֶת בָּנַי וְאֶת בְּנוֹתַי) וְאֶת כָּל קְרוֹבַי, וְתִתֶּן לָנוּ וּלְכָל יִשְׂרָאֵל חַיִּים טוֹבִים וַאֲרֻכִּים, וְתִזְכְּרֵנוּ בְּזִכְרוֹן טוֹבָה וּבְרָכָה, וְתִפְקְדֵנוּ בִּפְקֻדַּת יְשׁוּעָה וְרַחֲמִים, וּתְבָרְכֵנוּ בְּרָכוֹת גְּדוֹלוֹת, וְתַשְׁלִים בָּתֵּינוּ וְתַשְׁכֵּן שְׁכִינָתְךָ בֵּינֵינוּ. וְזַכֵּנִי לְגַדֵּל בָּנִים וּבְנֵי בָנִים חֲכָמִים וּנְבוֹנִים, אוֹהֲבֵי יהוה יִרְאֵי אֱלֹהִים, אַנְשֵׁי אֱמֶת זֶרַע קֹדֶשׁ, בַּיהוה דְּבֵקִים וּמְאִירִים אֶת הָעוֹלָם בַּתּוֹרָה וּבְמַעֲשִׂים טוֹבִים וּבְכָל מְלֶאכֶת עֲבוֹדַת הַבּוֹרֵא. אָנָּא שְׁמַע אֶת תְּחִנָּתִי בָּעֵת הַזֹּאת בִּזְכוּת שָׂרָה וְרִבְקָה וְרָחֵל וְלֵאָה אִמּוֹתֵינוּ, וְהָאֵר נֵרֵנוּ שֶׁלֹּא יִכְבֶּה לְעוֹלָם וָעֶד, וְהָאֵר פָּנֶיךָ וְנִוָּשֵׁעָה. אָמֵן.

CANDLE LIGHTING

Lighting candles is a positive rabbinic commandment, symbolizing *shalom bayit*, domestic peace. By creating peace in the home, we are helping to make peace in the world.

The ancient custom is for women to perform this commandment since they are the primary guardians of the home.

BLESSING THE CHILDREN

On the evening of Yom Kippur, many have the custom to bless their children.

To sons, say:

יְשִׂמְךָ May God make you like Ephraim and Manasseh.

To daughters, say:

יְשִׂימֵךְ May God make you like Sarah, Rebecca, Rachel and Leah. *Gen. 48*

יְבָרֶכְךָ May the Lord bless you and protect you. *Num. 6*
May the Lord make His face shine on you and be gracious to you.
May the Lord turn His face toward you
and grant you peace.

וִיהִי May it be the will of our Father in heaven, that He place the love and awe of Him into your heart, and that the awe of the Lord be with you throughout your days, that you do not sin. That your ardor be all for the Torah and the commandments, that your eyes gaze straight before you, your mouth speak wisdom and your heart ponder what it holds in awe; may your hands be busy with the commandments, and your legs run to do the will of Your Father in heaven. And may He grant you sons and daughters, each one righteous and engaged with the Torah and commandments all their days. May your wellspring be blessed. And may God bring you your sustenance in lawful ways, coming easily and liberally and from His broad hand, and not from the hands of human beings; so that you may be free to serve the Lord. And may you be written and sealed for a good, long life, together with all the righteous of Israel. Amen.

---

be tension. Between grandparents and grandchildren the tension is absent and the blessing is given with a full heart (Lord Jakobovits).

וִיהִי רָצוֹן *May it be the will.* This lovely blessing expresses the hopes of Jewish parents for their children throughout the ages. Note that it does not speak of success, fame, wealth, power, or worldly achievement. It is a simple prayer that our children should grow up to fear and love God, walking in His ways, using their body and strengths to His service. The blessing for livelihood, too, is a modest one: that one's children should be able to support themselves without dependence on charity and with sufficient time to devote to Torah study and the life of the mitzvot. Children grow to the size of the ideals they see their parents live by, and the greatest gift we can give our children is high ideals: love of God and of humankind, loyalty to one's people and dedication to the service of God.

ברכת הבנים

On the evening of יום כיפור*, many have the custom to bless their children.*

To sons, say:

יְשִׂמְךָ אֱלֹהִים
כְּאֶפְרַיִם וְכִמְנַשֶּׁה:

To daughters, say:

בראשית מח
יְשִׂימֵךְ אֱלֹהִים
כְּשָׂרָה רִבְקָה רָחֵל וְלֵאָה.

במדבר ו
יְבָרֶכְךָ יהוה וְיִשְׁמְרֶךָ:
יָאֵר יהוה פָּנָיו אֵלֶיךָ וִיחֻנֶּךָּ:
יִשָּׂא יהוה פָּנָיו אֵלֶיךָ וְיָשֵׂם לְךָ שָׁלוֹם:

To sons, say:

וִיהִי רָצוֹן מִלִּפְנֵי אָבִינוּ שֶׁבַּשָּׁמַיִם, שֶׁיִּתֵּן בְּלִבְּךָ אַהֲבָתוֹ וְיִרְאָתוֹ, וְתִהְיֶה יִרְאַת יהוה עַל פָּנֶיךָ כָּל יָמֶיךָ שֶׁלֹּא תֶחֱטָא, וּתְהִי חֶשְׁקְךָ בַּתּוֹרָה וּבַמִּצְוֹת, עֵינֶיךָ לְנֹכַח יַבִּיטוּ, פִּיךָ יְדַבֵּר חָכְמוֹת וְלִבְּךָ יֶהְגֶּה אֵימוֹת, יָדֶיךָ יַעַסְקוּ בְּמִצְוֹת, רַגְלֶיךָ יָרוּצוּ לַעֲשׂוֹת רְצוֹן אָבִיךָ שֶׁבַּשָּׁמַיִם. יִתֵּן לְךָ בָּנִים וּבָנוֹת צַדִּיקִים וְצִדְקָנִיּוֹת, עוֹסְקִים בַּתּוֹרָה וּבַמִּצְוֹת כָּל יְמֵיהֶם, וִיהִי מְקוֹרְךָ בָּרוּךְ, וְיַזְמִין לְךָ פַּרְנָסָתְךָ בְּהֶתֵּר בְּנַחַת וּבְרֶוַח מִתַּחַת יָדוֹ הָרְחָבָה וְלֹא עַל יְדֵי מַתְּנַת בָּשָׂר וָדָם כְּדֵי שֶׁתִּהְיֶה פָּנוּי לַעֲבוֹדַת יהוה, וְתִכָּתֵב וְתֵחָתֵם לְחַיִּים טוֹבִים וַאֲרֻכִּים בְּתוֹךְ כָּל צַדִּיקֵי יִשְׂרָאֵל, אָמֵן.

To daughters, say:

וִיהִי רָצוֹן מִלִּפְנֵי אָבִינוּ שֶׁבַּשָּׁמַיִם, שֶׁיִּתֵּן בְּלִבֵּךְ אַהֲבָתוֹ וְיִרְאָתוֹ, וְתִהְיֶה יִרְאַת יהוה עַל פָּנַיִךְ כָּל יָמַיִךְ שֶׁלֹּא תֶחֶטְאִי, וּתְהִי חֶשְׁקֵךְ בַּתּוֹרָה וּבַמִּצְוֹת, עֵינַיִךְ לְנֹכַח יַבִּיטוּ, פִּיךְ יְדַבֵּר חָכְמוֹת וְלִבֵּךְ יֶהְגֶּה אֵימוֹת, יָדַיִךְ יַעַסְקוּ בְּמִצְוֹת, רַגְלַיִךְ יָרוּצוּ לַעֲשׂוֹת רְצוֹן אָבִיךְ שֶׁבַּשָּׁמַיִם. יִתֵּן לָךְ בָּנִים וּבָנוֹת צַדִּיקִים וְצִדְקָנִיּוֹת, עוֹסְקִים בַּתּוֹרָה וּבַמִּצְוֹת כָּל יְמֵיהֶם, וִיהִי מְקוֹרֵךְ בָּרוּךְ, וְיַזְמִין לָךְ פַּרְנָסָתֵךְ בְּהֶתֵּר, בְּנַחַת וּבְרֶוַח מִתַּחַת יָדוֹ הָרְחָבָה וְלֹא עַל יְדֵי מַתְּנַת בָּשָׂר וָדָם כְּדֵי שֶׁתִּהְיִי פְּנוּיָה לַעֲבוֹדַת יהוה, וְתִכָּתְבִי וְתֵחָתְמִי לְחַיִּים טוֹבִים וַאֲרֻכִּים בְּתוֹךְ כָּל צַדִּיקֵי יִשְׂרָאֵל, אָמֵן.

יְשִׂמְךָ אֱלֹהִים כְּאֶפְרַיִם וְכִמְנַשֶּׁה *May God make you like Ephraim and Manasseh.* This blessing was chosen, rather than any other parental blessing in the Torah because this – given by Jacob to Joseph's children – is the only case where a grandparent blesses a grandchild. Between parents and children there may

TALLIT

Say the following meditation before putting on the tallit. Meditations before the fulfillment of mitzvot are to ensure that we do so with the requisite intention (kavana). This particularly applies to mitzvot whose purpose is to induce in us certain states of mind, as is the case with tallit and tefillin, both of which are external symbols of inward commitment to the life of observance of the mitzvot.

בָּרְכִי נַפְשִׁי Bless the LORD, my soul. LORD, my God, You are very great, *Ps. 104*
clothed in majesty and splendor, wrapped in a robe of light, spreading out the heavens like a tent.

Some say:

For the sake of the unification of the Holy One, blessed be He, and His Divine Presence, in reverence and love, to unify the name *Yod-Heh* with *Vav-Heh* in perfect unity in the name of all Israel.

I am about to wrap myself in this tasseled garment (tallit). So may my soul, my 248 limbs and 365 sinews be wrapped in the light of the tassel (*hatzitzit*) which amounts to 613 [commandments]. And just as I cover myself with a tasseled garment in this world, so may I be worthy of rabbinical dress and a fine garment in the World to Come in the Garden of Eden. Through the commandment of tassels may my life's-breath, spirit, soul and prayer be delivered from external impediments, and may the tallit spread its wings over them like an eagle stirring up its nest, hovering over its young. May the *Deut. 32*
commandment of the tasseled garment be considered before the Holy One, blessed be He, as if I had fulfilled it in all its specifics, details and intentions, as well as the 613 commandments dependent on it, Amen, Selah.

Before wrapping oneself in the tallit, say:

בָּרוּךְ Blessed are You, LORD our God, King of the Universe,
who has made us holy through His commandments,
and has commanded us to wrap ourselves in the tasseled garment.

According to the Shela (Rabbi Isaiah Horowitz), one should say these verses after wrapping oneself in the tallit:

מַה־יָּקָר How precious is Your loving-kindness, O God, and the children of *Ps. 36*
men find refuge under the shadow of Your wings. They are filled with the rich plenty of Your House. You give them drink from Your river of delights. For with You is the fountain of life; in Your light, we see light. Continue Your loving-kindness to those who know You, and Your righteousness to the upright in heart.

---

to pray (*Rosh HaShana* 17b), and it is on this that the institution of *Seliḥot* is based. Originally only the leader of prayer wore a tallit, but eventually the custom developed that all should do so, since the service of Yom Kippur – repentance – falls on each of us equally. The blessing over the tallit should be said before sunset.

עטיפת טלית

Say the following meditation before putting on the טלית. *Meditations before the fulfillment of* מצוות *are to ensure that we do so with the requisite intention* (כוונה). *This particularly applies to* מצוות *whose purpose is to induce in us certain states of mind, as is the case with* טלית *and* תפילין, *both of which are external symbols of inward commitment to the life of observance of the* מצוות.

בָּרְכִי נַפְשִׁי אֶת־יהוה, יהוה אֱלֹהַי גָּדַלְתָּ מְּאֹד, הוֹד וְהָדָר לָבָשְׁתָּ: תהלים קד
עֹטֶה־אוֹר כַּשַּׂלְמָה, נוֹטֶה שָׁמַיִם כַּיְרִיעָה:

Some say:

לְשֵׁם יִחוּד קֻדְשָׁא בְּרִיךְ הוּא וּשְׁכִינְתֵּהּ בִּדְחִילוּ וּרְחִימוּ, לְיַחֵד שֵׁם י״ה בו״ה בְּיִחוּדָא שְׁלִים בְּשֵׁם כָּל יִשְׂרָאֵל.

הֲרֵינִי מִתְעַטֵּף בַּצִּיצִית. כֵּן תִּתְעַטֵּף נִשְׁמָתִי וּרְמַ״ח אֵבָרַי וּשְׁסָ״ה גִידַי בְּאוֹר הַצִּיצִית הָעוֹלָה תַּרְיַ״ג. וּכְשֵׁם שֶׁאֲנִי מִתְכַּסֶּה בְּטַלִּית בָּעוֹלָם הַזֶּה, כָּךְ אֶזְכֶּה לַחֲלוּקָא דְרַבָּנָן וּלְטַלִּית נָאָה לָעוֹלָם הַבָּא בְּגַן עֵדֶן. וְעַל יְדֵי מִצְוַת צִיצִית תִּנָּצֵל נַפְשִׁי רוּחִי
וְנִשְׁמָתִי וּתְפִלָּתִי מִן הַחִיצוֹנִים. וְהַטַּלִּית תִּפְרֹשׂ כְּנָפֶיהָ עֲלֵיהֶם וְתַצִּילֵם, כְּנֶשֶׁר יָעִיר דברים לב
קִנּוֹ עַל גּוֹזָלָיו יְרַחֵף. וּתְהֵא חֲשׁוּבָה מִצְוַת צִיצִית לִפְנֵי הַקָּדוֹשׁ בָּרוּךְ הוּא, כְּאִלּוּ קִיַּמְתִּיהָ בְּכָל פְּרָטֶיהָ וְדִקְדּוּקֶיהָ וְכַוָּנוֹתֶיהָ וְתַרְיַ״ג מִצְוֹת הַתְּלוּיוֹת בָּהּ, אָמֵן סֶלָה.

Before wrapping oneself in the טלית, *say:*

בָּרוּךְ אַתָּה יהוה אֱלֹהֵינוּ מֶלֶךְ הָעוֹלָם
אֲשֶׁר קִדְּשָׁנוּ בְּמִצְוֹתָיו וְצִוָּנוּ לְהִתְעַטֵּף בַּצִּיצִית.

According to the Shela (Rabbi Isaiah Horowitz), one should say these verses after wrapping oneself in the טלית:

מַה־יָּקָר חַסְדְּךָ אֱלֹהִים, וּבְנֵי אָדָם בְּצֵל כְּנָפֶיךָ יֶחֱסָיוּן: יִרְוְיֻן מִדֶּשֶׁן תהלים לו
בֵּיתֶךָ, וְנַחַל עֲדָנֶיךָ תַשְׁקֵם: כִּי־עִמְּךָ מְקוֹר חַיִּים, בְּאוֹרְךָ נִרְאֶה־אוֹר:
מְשֹׁךְ חַסְדְּךָ לְיֹדְעֶיךָ, וְצִדְקָתְךָ לְיִשְׁרֵי־לֵב:

WEARING THE TALLIT

Yom Kippur is the only time we wear a tallit at night since the command of tzitzit only applies during the day. The custom began with Rabbi Meir of Rothenburg (thirteenth century) and is based on the fact that tonight we say *Seliḥot*, penitential prayers, as part of the evening service. *Seliḥot* are associated in the Talmud specifically with the wearing of a tallit. When Moses prayed to God to forgive the Israelites after the sin of the golden calf, according to the Talmud God "wrapped Himself in a tallit" and showed Moses how

וּבֶעָשׂוֹר לַחֹדֶשׁ הַשְּׁבִיעִי הַזֶּה
מִקְרָא־קֹדֶשׁ יִהְיֶה לָכֶם

במדבר כט

כִּי
יוֹם כִּפֻּרִים
הוּא
לְכַפֵּר עֲלֵיכֶם
לִפְנֵי ה׳ אֱלֹהֵיכֶם:

ויקרא כג

TEFILLA ZAKA – A PURE PRAYER

Before Kol Nidrei, it is customary to say this prayer, taken from the Ḥayyei Adam (Rabbi Avraham Danzig, Lithuania, nineteenth century). It includes three major themes: a detailed confession, an undertaking of the five afflictions of Yom Kippur, and forgiveness for the sins of others against oneself. In recent editions, the third part is often said before the second.

Women omit the words in parentheses.

רִבּוֹן כָּל הָעוֹלָמִים Master of all worlds, compassionate, forgiving Father, You whose right hand is stretched out to bring in penitents, and who created man, intending to do good for him at his life's end; You created him with two impulses, one urging him to good, the other goading him to evil, so that the choice between good and evil would remain in his hands, and to give him good reward when he chooses the good, for so Your wisdom decreed, as it is written: "See that I have given you today life and goodness; death and evil… *Deut. 30*
Now, choose life."

And now, my God, I have failed to listen to Your voice, and have allowed my evil impulse and the course of my own heart to guide me; I have scorned goodness and chosen evil; and not only have I failed to sanctify my limbs – I have defiled them.

You made within me a brain and heart, and with them the power of thought, with which I may develop good intentions and good reflections; and a heart to understand Your words of holiness, to pray and to recite every blessing with pure intentions – and I have made these impure with forbidden reveries and distractions. (Not only this, but through such forbidden musings I have come to emit semen wastefully, sometimes willfully, and sometimes against my will, with the impurity of proscribed emissions, which makes the whole body impure; and on these occasions I have created adversaries and destroyers, which are known as the afflictions of men). Alas – for with better intentions I could have created holy angels, which would be defenders and champions for me; and in place of these I have formed destroyers to damage my own self, as it is written: "I shall punish him with the rod of people, and *II Sam. 7*
with the afflictions of men."

You made me eyes, and in them the sense of sight by which we may see what You have written in the Torah, and which I am to make holy by looking at what is holy. You warned us in Your Torah: "Do not stray after your heart or *Num. 15*
after your eyes." Alas, I have strayed after my eyes and made them impure, by looking at impure things of all kinds.

תפילה זכה

Before כל נדרי*, it is customary to say this prayer, taken from the* חיי אדם *(Rabbi Avraham Danzig, Lithuania, nineteenth century). It includes three major themes: a detailed confession, an undertaking of the five afflictions of* יום כיפור*, and forgiveness for the sins of others against oneself. In recent editions, the third part is often said before the second. Women omit the words in parentheses.*

רִבּוֹן כָּל הָעוֹלָמִים, אַב הָרַחֲמִים וְהַסְּלִיחוֹת, אֲשֶׁר יְמִינְךָ פְּשׁוּטָה לְקַבֵּל שָׁבִים, וְאַתָּה בָּרָאתָ אֶת הָאָדָם לְהֵיטִיב לוֹ בְּאַחֲרִיתוֹ, וּבָרָאתָ לוֹ שְׁנֵי יְצָרִים, יֵצֶר טוֹב וְיֵצֶר רָע, כְּדֵי שֶׁתִּהְיֶה הַבְּחִירָה בְּיָדוֹ לִבְחֹר בַּטּוֹב אוֹ בָּרָע וּכְדֵי לִתֵּן לוֹ שְׂכַר טוֹב עַל טוּב בְּחִירָתוֹ, כִּי כֵן גָּזְרָה חָכְמָתֶךָ, כְּמוֹ
שֶׁכָּתוּב: רְאֵה נָתַתִּי לְפָנֶיךָ הַיּוֹם אֶת־הַחַיִּים וְאֶת־הַטּוֹב, וְאֶת־הַמָּוֶת דברים ל
וְאֶת־הָרָע: וּבָחַרְתָּ בַּחַיִּים:

וְעַתָּה, אֱלֹהַי, לֹא שָׁמַעְתִּי לְקוֹלֶךָ, וְהָלַכְתִּי בַּעֲצַת יֵצֶר הָרָע וּבְדַרְכֵי לִבִּי, וּמָאַסְתִּי בְּטוֹב וּבָחַרְתִּי בְּרָע, וְלֹא דַי לִי שֶׁלֹּא קִדַּשְׁתִּי אֶת אֵבָרַי אֶלָּא טִמֵּאתִי אוֹתָם.

בָּרָאתָ בִּי מֹחַ וָלֵב וּבָהֶם חוּשׁ הַמַּחֲשָׁבָה לַחְשֹׁב מַחֲשָׁבוֹת טוֹבוֹת וְהִרְהוּרִים טוֹבִים, וְלֵב לְהָבִין דִּבְרֵי קָדְשֶׁךָ, וּלְהִתְפַּלֵּל וּלְבָרֵךְ כָּל הַבְּרָכוֹת בְּמַחֲשָׁבָה טְהוֹרָה, וַאֲנִי טִמֵּאתִי אוֹתָם בְּהִרְהוּרִים רָעִים וּמַחֲשָׁבוֹת זָרוֹת. (וְלֹא דַי בָּזֶה, אֶלָּא שֶׁעַל יְדֵי הִרְהוּרִים רָעִים בָּאתִי לִידֵי הוֹצָאוֹת זֶרַע לְבַטָּלָה, פַּעַם בְּרָצוֹן וּפַעַם בְּאֹנֶס, בְּטֻמְאַת קֶרִי הַמְטַמֵּא אֶת כָּל הַגּוּף, וּמֵהֶם בָּרָאתִי מַשְׁחִיתִים וּמְחַבְּלִים הַנִּקְרָאִים נִגְעֵי בְּנֵי אָדָם.) אוֹי לִי כִּי תַּחַת מַחֲשָׁבוֹת טוֹבוֹת שֶׁיָּכֹלְתִּי לִבְרֹא עַל יְדֵיהֶן מַלְאָכִים קְדוֹשִׁים, שֶׁיִּהְיוּ סַנֵּגוֹרִים וּפְרַקְלִיטִים טוֹבִים עָלַי, תַּחְתֵּיהֶם בָּרָאתִי מַשְׁחִיתִים
לְחַבֵּל בְּעַצְמִי, כְּמוֹ שֶׁכָּתוּב: וְהֹכַחְתִּיו בְּשֵׁבֶט אֲנָשִׁים וּבְנִגְעֵי בְּנֵי אָדָם: שמואל ב׳ ז

בָּרָאתָ בִּי עֵינַיִם וּבָהֶן חוּשׁ הָרְאוּת לִרְאוֹת בָּהֶן מַה שֶּׁכָּתוּב בַּתּוֹרָה,
וּלְקַדֵּשׁ אוֹתָן בִּרְאִיַּת כָּל דָּבָר שֶׁבִּקְדֻשָּׁה. הִזְהַרְתָּ בְּתוֹרָתֶךָ: וְלֹא תָתֻרוּ במדבר טו
אַחֲרֵי לְבַבְכֶם וְאַחֲרֵי עֵינֵיכֶם: אוֹי לִי כִּי הָלַכְתִּי אַחֲרֵי עֵינַי וְטִמֵּאתִי אוֹתָן לְהִסְתַּכֵּל בְּכָל דְּבַר טֻמְאָה.

You made me ears, to hear words of holiness and words of Torah; alas, I have made them impure by listening to disgraceful and slanderous words and forbidden speech. Alas to any ear that hears such words.

You made me a mouth and tongue and teeth and a palate and throat, and You gave these, the five articulators, the ability to speak the holy letters of the alef-beit, with which You created heaven and earth and all that fills them, and from which You wove Your holy Torah. In the power of speech You have separated man from the animals – and I have not been even as good as an animal, for I have made my mouth impure with disgraceful speech, with slander, lies, sneering, gossip, conflict, by humiliating others and cursing them, by taking pride in another's disgrace, speaking of business on the Sabbath and the festivals, and by swearing oaths and vows.

You made me hands and the sense of touch, through which to engage with the commandments, and I have made them impure with forbidden touch, with the blows of a vicious fist, by raising my hand to strike another, and by moving set-aside objects on the Sabbath and on festivals.

You made me feet to carry me to all that I am commanded to do – and I have made them impure by hurrying, running toward evil.

I feel all my limbs and I find each one flawed; from the soles of my feet to my head, there is no place without blemish. I am too humiliated and ashamed to raise my face toward You, my God, for I have used these limbs and senses with which You have graced me, and the life force You have always emanated to them, to do what is evil in Your eyes and to act against Your will. Alas; and alas for my soul.

I know that there is almost no righteous man on this earth, who does not sin against his fellow man, against his property or person, in actions or in speech, and over this my very heart ails me within, for Yom Kippur does not atone for what one person does to another, until he has appeased him. And for this my heart is broken within me, and my bones shake, for even the day of one's death cannot atone for such things. And so I lay my plea before You, that You have compassion for me and let me find grace and kindness and compassion in Your eyes, and in the eyes of all my fellow men. I hereby forgive completely and absolutely, anyone who may have sinned against me, by his person or his property, who has spoken slander about me, even one who may have discredited my name, and anyone who has damaged my body or property, and

בָּרָאתָ בִּי אָזְנַיִם לִשְׁמֹעַ דִּבְרֵי קְדֻשָּׁה וְדִבְרֵי תּוֹרָה, אוֹי לִי כִּי טִמֵּאתִי אוֹתָן לִשְׁמֹעַ דִּבְרֵי נְבָלָה וְלָשׁוֹן הָרָע וּדְבָרִים אֲסוּרִים. אוֹי לְאָזְנַיִם שֶׁכָּךְ שׁוֹמְעוֹת.

בָּרָאתָ בִּי פֶּה וְלָשׁוֹן וְשִׁנַּיִם וְחֵיךְ וְגָרוֹן, וְנָתַתָּ בָּהֶם כֹּחַ לְדַבֵּר בָּהֶם חָמֵשׁ מוֹצָאוֹת הָאוֹתִיּוֹת הַקְּדוֹשׁוֹת שֶׁל אָלֶף בֵּית, אֲשֶׁר בָּהֶן בָּרָאתָ שָׁמַיִם וָאָרֶץ וּמְלוֹאָם, וּבָהֶן אָרַגְתָּ תּוֹרָתְךָ הַקְּדוֹשָׁה, וּבְכֹחַ הַדִּבּוּר הִבְדַּלְתָּ אֶת הָאָדָם מִן הַבְּהֵמָה, וַאֲפִלּוּ כִּבְהֵמָה לֹא הָיִיתִי, כִּי טִמֵּאתִי פִּי בְּדִבְרֵי נְבָלָה, בְּלָשׁוֹן הָרָע, בִּשְׁקָרִים, לֵיצָנוּת, רְכִילוּת, מַחֲלֹקֶת, מַלְבִּין פְּנֵי חֲבֵרוֹ, מְקַלֵּל אֶת חֲבֵרוֹ, מִתְכַּבֵּד בִּקְלוֹן חֲבֵרוֹ, דִּבְרֵי מַשָּׂא וּמַתָּן בְּשַׁבָּת וְיוֹם טוֹב, בִּשְׁבוּעוֹת וּנְדָרִים.

בָּרָאתָ בִּי יָדַיִם וְחוּשׁ הַמִּשּׁוּשׁ לַעֲסֹק בָּהֶן בְּמִצְוֹת, וַאֲנִי טִמֵּאתִי אוֹתָן בְּמִשְׁמוּשִׁין שֶׁל אִסּוּר, לְהַכּוֹת בְּאֶגְרוֹף רֶשַׁע וּלְהָרִים יָד לְהַכּוֹת בֶּן אָדָם וּלְטַלְטֵל דְּבָרִים הַמֻּקְצִים בְּשַׁבָּת וְיוֹם טוֹב.

בָּרָאתָ בִּי רַגְלַיִם לַהֲלֹךְ לְכָל דְּבַר מִצְוָה, וַאֲנִי טִמֵּאתִי אוֹתָן בְּרַגְלַיִם מְמַהֲרוֹת לָרוּץ לָרָעָה.

מִשַּׁשְׁתִּי אֶת כָּל אֵבָרַי וּמָצָאתִי אוֹתָם בַּעֲלֵי מוּמִין, מִכַּף רַגְלִי וְעַד רֹאשִׁי אֵין בִּי מְתֹם. בֹּשְׁתִּי וְנִכְלַמְתִּי לְהָרִים אֱלֹהַי פָּנַי אֵלֶיךָ, כִּי בְּאֵלֶּה הָאֵבָרִים וְהַחוּשִׁים שֶׁחֲנַנְתַּנִי בָּהֶם, וּבְכֹחַ הַחַיִּים שֶׁהִשְׁפַּעְתָּ עֲלֵיהֶם תָּמִיד, בָּהֶם נִשְׁתַּמַּשְׁתִּי לַעֲשׂוֹת הָרַע בְּעֵינֶיךָ וְלַעֲבֹר עַל רְצוֹנֶךָ. אוֹי לִי וְאוֹי לְנַפְשִׁי.

וְלִהְיוֹת שֶׁיָּדַעְתִּי שֶׁכִּמְעַט אֵין צַדִּיק בָּאָרֶץ אֲשֶׁר לֹא יֶחֱטָא בֵּין אָדָם לַחֲבֵרוֹ בְּמָמוֹן אוֹ בְּגוּפוֹ, בְּמַעֲשֶׂה אוֹ בְּדִבּוּר פֶּה, וְעַל זֶה דָּוֶה לִבִּי בְּקִרְבִּי, כִּי עַל חֵטְא שֶׁבֵּין אָדָם לַחֲבֵרוֹ אֵין יוֹם הַכִּפּוּרִים מְכַפֵּר עַד שֶׁיְּרַצֶּה אֶת חֲבֵרוֹ, וְעַל זֶה נִשְׁבַּר לִבִּי בְּקִרְבִּי וְרָחֲפוּ עַצְמוֹתַי, כִּי אֲפִלּוּ יוֹם הַמִּיתָה אֵינוֹ מְכַפֵּר. לָכֵן אֲנִי מַפִּיל תְּחִנָּתִי לְפָנֶיךָ שֶׁתְּרַחֵם עָלַי, וְתִתְּנֵנִי לְחֵן וּלְחֶסֶד וּלְרַחֲמִים בְּעֵינֶיךָ וּבְעֵינֵי כָל בְּנֵי אָדָם. וְהִנְנִי מוֹחֵל בִּמְחִילָה גְּמוּרָה לְכָל

for all the sins that one person commits against another – though without relinquishing my claim to any money I could legally recover, and excluding anyone who has sinned against me saying "I shall sin against him and he will surely forgive me." With these exceptions, I forgive completely and utterly; let no man be punished for my sake. And just as I forgive every other person, so make me gracious in the eyes of every other, so that they forgive me completely and absolutely.

And now, LORD my God, it is revealed and known before You, that through all my sins and injustices I never intended to anger You or to rebel against You; I simply allowed my evil impulse to guide me, the impulse which always, every day, spreads a net at my feet to trap me. And I am poor and destitute, more a worm than a human being; my strength to stand up to this impulse fails me, and the labor of earning a living, of sustaining my family, and the worries of the time and its events have plagued me. And as all this is revealed and known before You, for there is no righteous person on all this earth who *Eccl. 7* does only what is good and does not sin, so, with Your great compassion, You have given us one day in the year, a great and holy day, this Day of Atonement – may it come to us for the good – to let us repent in Your presence, to atone for all our sins, and be purified of what taints us, as it is written: "For *Lev. 16* on this day you will be atoned and made pure; of all your sins before the LORD you shall be purified."

And now, look upon Your nation Israel, the one You have taken as Your own nation; who is like Your nation Israel, who are pure and holy and who long for and wait for Your pardon? We have come before You broken and oppressed at heart, a poor and needy and destitute people, to ask Your pardon, forgiveness and atonement, for all the sins, the wrongs and the rebellions that we have committed before You. We know, LORD, our own evil, and the iniquities of our ancestors. We are too humiliated and ashamed to raise our faces toward You, like the shame of a thief discovered in the act. How then can we open *Jer. 2* our mouths and lift our heads? In our many injustices we have taken off the holy image that clothed us, and which no demon or accuser can even look upon, as it is written: "All the nations of the earth will see that you are called *Deut. 28* by the LORD's name, and they will fear you." We have exchanged all this for an impure image, we have dressed ourselves in filthy clothes, and now how can we come to the gate of the King, dressed in sackcloth, dirtied with our own filth? We are astonished at our own souls; how can we have done this abhorrent thing? We have taken our own souls and spirits out of the world of holiness and run away to a desert place of thirst and the shadow of death, to a place of the impurity of the broken shells.

מִי שֶׁחָטָא נֶגְדִּי, בֵּין בְּגוּפוֹ וּבֵין בְּמָמוֹנוֹ אוֹ שֶׁדִּבֵּר עָלַי לָשׁוֹן הָרָע, וַאֲפִלּוּ הוֹצָאַת שֵׁם רָע, וְכֵן לְכָל מִי שֶׁהִזִּיק לִי בְּגוּפִי אוֹ בְּמָמוֹנִי, וּלְכָל חַטֹּאת הָאָדָם אֲשֶׁר בֵּין אָדָם לַחֲבֵרוֹ, חוּץ מִמָּמוֹן אֲשֶׁר אוּכַל לְהוֹצִיא עַל פִּי דִין, וְחוּץ מִמִּי שֶׁחָטָא כְּנֶגְדִּי וְאָמַר: אֶחֱטָא לוֹ וְהוּא יִמְחַל לִי. חוּץ מֵאֵלּוּ, אֲנִי מוֹחֵל בִּמְחִילָה גְּמוּרָה, וְלֹא יֵעָנֵשׁ שׁוּם אָדָם בְּסִבָּתִי. וּכְשֵׁם שֶׁאֲנִי מוֹחֵל לְכָל אָדָם, כֵּן תִּתֵּן אֶת חִנִּי בְּעֵינֵי כָּל אָדָם, שֶׁיִּמְחֲלוּ לִי בִּמְחִילָה גְּמוּרָה.

וְעַתָּה יהוה אֱלֹהַי, גָּלוּי וְיָדוּעַ לְפָנֶיךָ, שֶׁלֹּא נִתְכַּוַּנְתִּי בְּכָל הַחֲטָאִים וְהָעֲוֹנוֹת לְהַכְעִיסְךָ וְלִמְרֹד כְּנֶגְדְּךָ, אַךְ הָלַכְתִּי בַּעֲצַת יִצְרִי הָרָע, אֲשֶׁר תָּמִיד בְּכָל יוֹם פּוֹרֵשׂ רֶשֶׁת לְרַגְלַי לְלָכְדֵנִי. וַאֲנִי עָנִי וְאֶבְיוֹן תּוֹלַעַת וְלֹא אִישׁ, כָּשַׁל כֹּחִי לַעֲמֹד כְּנֶגְדּוֹ, וַעֲמַל הַפַּרְנָסָה לְפַרְנֵס אֶת בְּנֵי בֵיתִי וְטִרְדַּת הַזְּמַן וּמִקְרָיו הֵם הָיוּ בְּעוֹכְרָי. וּלְפִי שֶׁכָּל זֶה גָּלוּי וְיָדוּעַ לְפָנֶיךָ, כִּי אָדָם קהלת ז
אֵין צַדִּיק בָּאָרֶץ, אֲשֶׁר יַעֲשֶׂה־טּוֹב וְלֹא יֶחֱטָא: לָכֵן בְּרַחֲמֶיךָ הָרַבִּים נָתַתָּ לָנוּ יוֹם אֶחָד בַּשָּׁנָה, יוֹם אַדִּיר וְקָדוֹשׁ, יוֹם הַכִּפּוּרִים הַזֶּה הַבָּא עָלֵינוּ לְטוֹבָה, לָשׁוּב לְפָנֶיךָ וּלְכַפֵּר אֶת כָּל עֲוֹנוֹתֵינוּ וּלְטַהֵר אוֹתָנוּ מִטֻּמְאוֹתֵינוּ,
כְּמוֹ שֶׁכָּתוּב: כִּי־בַיּוֹם הַזֶּה יְכַפֵּר עֲלֵיכֶם לְטַהֵר אֶתְכֶם, מִכֹּל חַטֹּאתֵיכֶם, ויקרא טז
לִפְנֵי יהוה תִּטְהָרוּ:

וְעַתָּה רְאֵה עַמְּךָ יִשְׂרָאֵל אֲשֶׁר לָקַחְתָּ אוֹתָם לְךָ לְעָם, מִי כְּעַמְּךָ יִשְׂרָאֵל טְהוֹרִים וּקְדוֹשִׁים הַמְיַחֲלִים וּמְצַפִּים לִמְחִילָתֶךָ. בָּאנוּ בְּלֵב נִשְׁבָּר וְנִדְכֶּה, כַּעֲנִיִּים וְדַלִּים וָרָשִׁים, לְבַקֵּשׁ מִמְּךָ מְחִילָה וּסְלִיחָה וְכַפָּרָה עַל כָּל מַה שֶּׁחָטָאנוּ וְעָוִינוּ וּפָשַׁעְנוּ לְפָנֶיךָ. יָדַעְנוּ יהוה רִשְׁעֵנוּ עֲוֹן אֲבוֹתֵינוּ. בֹּשְׁנוּ
וְנִכְלַמְנוּ לְהָרִים פָּנֵינוּ אֵלֶיךָ, כְּבֹשֶׁת גַּנָּב כִּי יִמָּצֵא: וְאֵיךְ נִפְתַּח פֶּה וְנָרִים ירמיה ב
רֹאשׁ, כִּי בְּרֹב עֲוֹנֵינוּ הֶעֱבַרְנוּ מֵעָלֵינוּ הַצֶּלֶם הַקָּדוֹשׁ אֲשֶׁר הוּא מַלְבִּישׁ אוֹתָנוּ, אֲשֶׁר כָּל הַמַּזִּיקִים וְהַמְקַטְרְגִים אֵינָם יְכוֹלִים לְהַבִּיט בְּפָנָיו, כְּמָה
שֶׁכָּתוּב: וְרָאוּ כָּל־עַמֵּי הָאָרֶץ, כִּי שֵׁם יהוה נִקְרָא עָלֶיךָ, וְיָרְאוּ מִמֶּךָּ: דברים כח
וְהֶחֱלַפְנוּ אוֹתוֹ בְּצֶלֶם טָמֵא, וְלָבַשְׁנוּ בְּגָדִים צוֹאִים, וְאֵיךְ נָבוֹא בְּשַׁעַר הַמֶּלֶךְ בִּלְבוּשׁ שַׂק מְלֻכְלָךְ בְּצוֹאָה. מִתְמִיהִים אֲנַחְנוּ עַל נַפְשֵׁנוּ אֵיךְ נֶעֶשְׂתָה הַתּוֹעֵבָה הַזֹּאת, כִּי הוֹצֵאנוּ נַפְשֵׁנוּ וְרוּחֵנוּ מֵהָעוֹלָם הַקָּדוֹשׁ וּבְרַחְנוּ לִמְקוֹם מִדְבַּר צִיָּה וְצַלְמָוֶת, לִמְקוֹם טֻמְאַת הַקְּלִפּוֹת.

And You, Lord our God, who desire the repentance of the wicked, as it is written: "Repent, repent your evil ways; why should you die, O house of Israel?" *Ezek. 33* And as it is said: "Do I desire the wicked man's death? – so says the Lord God – *Ezek. 18* Do I not desire him to come back from his ways and live?" Now we have taken to heart the wish to repent and to come before You, shamefaced. Our Father, our King, have compassion for us, as a father has compassion for a son who has rebelled against him, who has left his house – and when that son returns shamefaced to his father, weeping and calling out, throwing himself at his feet, it is in a father's nature to have compassion for him. And if we are slaves, slaves beaten by their master for rebelling against him – behold: we have already been stricken, through our subjugation by governments, bodily sufferings, or with poverty and the distresses of raising children, and other forms of pain. Punish us, Lord, but with judgment; not in Your fury, lest You reduce us to nothing. Have compassion for us and command those of Your holy angels who are responsible for purity, to strip our filthy clothes from us and to purify us of all our sins, as it is written: "Take his filthy clothes from him –" and dress us too in *Zech. 3* clean garments. And, in the prayer of King David, peace be upon him: "Bring *Ps. 51* back the joy of Your salvation to me, and support me with a willing spirit." Create a pure heart in us, God, and place a steadfast spirit within us. And if we have transgressed and rebelled, as is the way of flesh and blood, then follow Your own way – to pardon and forgive. Do not let our sins prevent us returning to You: it is Your way to welcome in those who return. Strengthen our hearts in Your Torah and in awe of You, that Your awe may always be fixed in our hearts. And make our ideas and thoughts pure in readiness for Your service. Witness my heartbreak, for I regret the bad actions I have done thus far, and weep and lament and confess them, and say: I have sinned, I have done wrong, I have rebelled before You. Accept my repentance among that of all Your nation Israel, who return to You with all their hearts, for I too am among the children of Abraham, Isaac and Jacob. Do not let my many sins prevent me from returning wholeheartedly to You. Grant me the merit of returning to You with a perfect heart, regretting all my sins utterly and completely, and leaving all my bad practices behind me eternally. Have compassion for me and save me forever from every sin and iniquity; for were it not for Your compassion and kindness there would be no way to stand up to the evil impulse that burns like fire in my bones. And so, have compassion for me and give me the strength to stand up to my own impulse, as the sages and righteous ones said among their holy words: "One who comes to purify himself is helped along his way."

I hereby accept the holiness of the Day of Atonement, and take upon myself its five forms of abstinence, as You commanded us at the hand of Moses Your

וְאַתָּה יהוה אֱלֹהֵינוּ, הָרוֹצֶה בִּתְשׁוּבַת רְשָׁעִים, כְּמָה שֶׁכָּתוּב: שׁוּבוּ שׁוּבוּ יחזקאל לג
מִדַּרְכֵיכֶם הָרָעִים, וְלָמָּה תָמוּתוּ בֵּית יִשְׂרָאֵל: וְנֶאֱמַר: הֶחָפֹץ אֶחְפֹּץ מוֹת יחזקאל יח
רָשָׁע, נְאֻם אֲדֹנָי יֱהוִה, הֲלוֹא בְּשׁוּבוֹ מִדְּרָכָיו וְחָיָה: עַתָּה שַׂמְנוּ אֶל לִבֵּנוּ
לָשׁוּב, וְלָבוֹא לְפָנֶיךָ בְּבֹשֶׁת פָּנִים. אָבִינוּ מַלְכֵּנוּ, רַחֵם עָלֵינוּ כְּרַחֵם אָב
עַל בְּנוֹ שֶׁמָּרַד בְּאָבִיו וְיָצָא מִבֵּיתוֹ, וּבְשׁוּבוֹ אֶל אָבִיו בְּבֹשֶׁת פָּנִים וּבְכִי
וּצְעָקָה וּמִתְנַפֵּל לְפָנָיו, מִדֶּרֶךְ הָאָב לְרַחֵם עַל בְּנוֹ. וְאִם עֲבָדִים אֲנַחְנוּ,
הַמַּכֶּה אֶת עַבְדּוֹ בְּיִסּוּרִים כְּשֶׁמָּרַד בּוֹ, הִנֵּה כְּבָר לָקִינוּ בְּשִׁעְבּוּד מַלְכֻיּוֹת
וְיִסּוּרִין שֶׁבְּגוּף, אוֹ עֲנִיּוּת וְצַעַר גִּדּוּל בָּנִים וּשְׁאָר מַכְאוֹבִים. יַסְּרֵנוּ יהוה
אַךְ בְּמִשְׁפָּט, אַל בְּאַפְּךָ פֶּן תַּמְעִטֵנוּ. רַחֵם עָלֵינוּ וְצַוֵּה לְמַלְאָכֶיךָ הַקְּדוֹשִׁים
הַמְמֻנִּים עַל הַטָּהֳרָה, לְהַפְשִׁיט אֶת הַבְּגָדִים הַצּוֹאִים מֵעָלֵינוּ וּלְטַהֲרֵנוּ
מִכָּל חַטֹּאתֵינוּ, כְּמָה שֶׁכָּתוּב: הָסִירוּ הַבְּגָדִים הַצֹּאִים מֵעָלָיו: וְהַלְבֵּשׁ זכריה ג
אוֹתָנוּ מַחֲלָצוֹת. וְכִתְפִלַּת דָּוִד הַמֶּלֶךְ עָלָיו הַשָּׁלוֹם: הָשִׁיבָה לִּי שְׂשׂוֹן תהלים נא
יִשְׁעֶךָ, וְרוּחַ נְדִיבָה תִסְמְכֵנִי: לֵב טָהוֹר בְּרָא לָנוּ אֱלֹהִים, וְרוּחַ חֲדָשָׁה
תִּתֵּן בְּקִרְבֵּנוּ. וְאִם פָּשַׁעְנוּ וּמָרַדְנוּ כְּמִדַּת בָּשָׂר וָדָם, אַתָּה עֲשֵׂה כְּמִדָּתְךָ
לִמְחֹל וְלִסְלֹחַ. וְאַל יְעַכְּבוּ עֲוֹנוֹתֵינוּ מִלָּשׁוּב לְפָנֶיךָ, כְּמִדָּתְךָ לְקַבֵּל שָׁבִים.
וְחַזֵּק לִבֵּנוּ בְּתוֹרָתְךָ וּבְיִרְאָתֶךָ, שֶׁתִּהְיֶה יִרְאָתְךָ תָּמִיד קְבוּעָה בְּלִבֵּנוּ. וְטַהֵר
רַעְיוֹנֵינוּ וּמַחְשְׁבוֹתֵינוּ לַעֲבוֹדָתֶךָ. וּרְאֵה בְּשִׁבְרוֹן לִבִּי, כִּי מִתְנַחֵם אֲנִי עַל
מַעֲשַׂי הָרָעִים שֶׁעָשִׂיתִי עַד הַיּוֹם הַזֶּה, וּבוֹכֶה וּמִתְאוֹנֵן וּמִתְוַדֶּה עֲלֵיהֶם,
וְאוֹמֵר: חָטָאתִי עָוִיתִי פָּשַׁעְתִּי לְפָנֶיךָ. וְקַבֵּל תְּשׁוּבָתִי בְּתוֹךְ תְּשׁוּבַת כָּל
עַמְּךָ יִשְׂרָאֵל הַשָּׁבִים לְפָנֶיךָ בְּכָל לִבָּם, כִּי גַם אֲנִי מִבְּנֵי אַבְרָהָם יִצְחָק
וְיַעֲקֹב. וְאַל יְעַכְּבוּ עֲוֹנוֹתַי הָרַבִּים מִלָּשׁוּב לְפָנֶיךָ בְּכָל לֵב. וְזַכֵּנִי שֶׁאָשׁוּב
לְפָנֶיךָ בְּלֵב שָׁלֵם וּלְהִתְחָרֵט עַל עֲוֹנוֹתַי חֲרָטָה גְמוּרָה, וְלַעֲזֹב מַעֲשַׂי הָרָעִים
עֲזִיבָה עוֹלָמִית. וְרַחֵם עָלַי וְהַצִּילֵנִי עַד עוֹלָם מִכָּל חֵטְא וְעָוֹן, כִּי לוּלֵא
רַחֲמֶיךָ וַחֲסָדֶיךָ אִי אֶפְשָׁר לַעֲמֹד נֶגֶד הַיֵּצֶר הָרָע, אֲשֶׁר הוּא בּוֹעֵר כָּאֵשׁ
בְּעַצְמוֹתַי, וְלָכֵן רַחֵם עָלַי וְתֵן בִּי כֹּחַ לַעֲמֹד כְּנֶגְדּוֹ. כְּמוֹ שֶׁאָמְרוּ הַחֲכָמִים
וְהַצַּדִּיקִים בְּדִבְרֵי קָדְשָׁם, הַבָּא לְטַהֵר מְסַיְּעִין אוֹתוֹ.

וְהִנֵּה אֲנִי מְקַבֵּל עָלַי קְדֻשַּׁת יוֹם הַכִּפּוּרִים, וּלְהִתְעַנּוֹת בּוֹ בַּחֲמִשָּׁה עִנּוּיִים
שֶׁצִּוִּיתָ לָנוּ עַל יְדֵי מֹשֶׁה עַבְדֶּךָ בְּתוֹרָתְךָ הַקְּדוֹשָׁה: אֲכִילָה וּשְׁתִיָּה,

servant in Your holy Torah: abstinence from eating and drinking, washing, anointing, wearing shoes and having marital relations – as well as the obligation to rest from all work on this holy day. Through our abstinence from eating and drinking, atone for us all that we have sinned through forbidden eating and drinking. And through our abstinence from washing and anointing, atone for us all that we have sinned through indulging ourselves on weekdays, and particularly for the forbidden indulgences. And through our abstinence from shoes, atone for us all that we have sinned with these feet that have hurried, running toward evil, and for infringing the twenty-four laws for which a court rules banishment from the community, making us liable to go barefoot like one who has been banished. And through our abstinence from sexual relations, atone for us our sins (and the damage we have done to the holy covenant through the impurity of forbidden emissions and through emitting semen wastefully and for forbidden sexual relations). And through the five prayer services and the supplications and prayers, may we repair the damage we have done with the five articulators of our mouths – the palate, throat, tongue, teeth and lips – from which speech comes, and which I have made impure with forbidden speech and with vows and oaths. And as we embrace and kiss the Torah scroll, and by merit of the prayers that we shall pray on this holy day, may all the prayers that we have prayed this year without full concentration, rise and come and reach and join with them; may they all be included with the prayers of this day, and arrive at Your head to become a crown upon it, with all the other prayers of Israel. And may the tears in my eyes repair all that we have damaged through seeing impure things. And as our bodies burn with the fast and with the prayers, may we repair the burning of our two hundred and forty-eight bones and three hundred and sixty-five sinews in the fire of the evil impulse. And may the depletion of our fat and blood by the fast, atone for all that we have sinned, done wrong and rebelled before You. May this fast be regarded as if it were the offering up of our own bodies upon the altar, and be accepted for a pleasant scent before You, like a sacrifice, an offering.

We know that, according to the [kabbalistic] order of repentance, we are required to afflict ourselves for every single sin, and to torment our bodies in direct balance with the pleasure we enjoyed as we transgressed. But it is revealed and known before You that we have not the strength to torment ourselves even for one sin, to say nothing of every single one, for our sins are too many to count, and our strength fails us. And so may it be Your will, Lord our God, that this fast we perform on this holy day, the Day of Atonement – may it come to us for the good – may be atonement for all our sins.

רְחִיצָה, סִיכָה, נְעִילַת הַסַּנְדָּל, תַּשְׁמִישׁ הַמִּטָּה, וְלִשְׁבֹּת בַּיּוֹם הַקָּדוֹשׁ הַזֶּה מִכָּל מְלָאכָה. וְעַל יְדֵי עִנּוּי מֵאֲכִילָה וּשְׁתִיָּה, תְּכַפֵּר לָנוּ מַה שֶּׁחָטָאנוּ בַּאֲכִילוֹת וּשְׁתִיּוֹת אֲסוּרוֹת. וְעַל יְדֵי עִנּוּי מֵרְחִיצָה וְסִיכָה, תְּכַפֵּר לָנוּ מַה שֶּׁחָטָאנוּ בְּתַעֲנוּגִים בִּימֵי הַחֹל, וּבִפְרָט תַּעֲנוּגִים הָאֲסוּרִים. וְעַל יְדֵי עִנּוּי מִנְּעִילַת הַסַּנְדָּל, תְּכַפֵּר לָנוּ מַה שֶּׁחָטָאנוּ בְּרַגְלַיִם הַמְמַהֲרוֹת לָרוּץ לָרַע, וְאֵת אֲשֶׁר עָבַרְנוּ עַל עֶשְׂרִים וְאַרְבָּעָה דְּבָרִים שֶׁבֵּית דִּין מְנַדִּין עֲלֵיהֶם, וְנִתְחַיַּבְנוּ לִהְיוֹת יְחֵפֵי רַגְלַיִם כִּמְנֻדִּים. וְעַל יְדֵי עִנּוּי מִתַּשְׁמִישׁ הַמִּטָּה, תְּכַפֵּר לָנוּ מַה שֶּׁחָטָאנוּ (וּפָגַמְנוּ בִּבְרִית קֹדֶשׁ בְּטֻמְאַת קֶרִי וּבְהוֹצָאַת זֶרַע לְבַטָּלָה וּמַה שֶּׁבָּעַלְנוּ בְּעִילוֹת אֲסוּרוֹת). וְעַל יְדֵי חָמֵשׁ תְּפִלּוֹת וּתְחִנּוֹת וּבַקָּשׁוֹת, יְתֻקַּן מַה שֶּׁפָּגַמְנוּ בְּחָמֵשׁ מוֹצָאוֹת הַפֶּה: הַחֵיךְ, וְהַגָּרוֹן, וְהַלָּשׁוֹן, וְהַשִּׁנַּיִם, וְהַשְּׂפָתַיִם, שֶׁמֵּהֶם יוֹצֵא הַדִּבּוּר, וְטִמֵּאתִי אוֹתָם בְּכָל הַדְּבָרִים הָאֲסוּרִים וּנְדָרִים וּשְׁבוּעוֹת. וְעַל יְדֵי חִבּוּק וְנִשּׁוּק סֵפֶר הַתּוֹרָה, וְעַל יְדֵי זְכוּת הַתְּפִלּוֹת שֶׁנִּתְפַּלֵּל בַּיּוֹם הַקָּדוֹשׁ הַזֶּה, יַעֲלוּ וְיָבוֹאוּ וְיַגִּיעוּ וְיִצְטָרְפוּ עִמָּהֶן כָּל הַתְּפִלּוֹת שֶׁהִתְפַּלַּלְנוּ בְּכָל הַשָּׁנָה בְּלֹא כַוָּנָה, וְיִהְיוּ כֻּלָּן נִכְלָלוֹת בִּתְפִלּוֹת הַיּוֹם הַזֶּה, וְיַגִּיעוּ לְרֹאשְׁךָ לִהְיוֹת עֲטָרָה לְרֹאשְׁךָ בִּכְלַל תְּפִלּוֹת יִשְׂרָאֵל. וְעַל יְדֵי דִּמְעוֹת עֵינַי, יְתֻקַּן מַה שֶּׁפָּגַמְנוּ בִּרְאִיַּת עֵינַיִם בְּכָל דָּבָר טָמֵא. וְעַל יְדֵי רְתִיחַת גּוּפֵנוּ עַל יְדֵי הַתַּעֲנִית וְהַתְּפִלּוֹת, יְתֻקַּן מַה שֶּׁהִרְתַּחְנוּ רַמַ״ח אֵבָרֵינוּ וּשְׁסָ״ה גִּידֵינוּ בָּאֵשׁ שֶׁל יֵצֶר הָרָע. וּבְמִעוּט חֶלְבֵּנוּ וְדָמֵנוּ עַל יְדֵי הַתַּעֲנִית, יְכֻפַּר כָּל מַה שֶּׁחָטָאנוּ וְשֶׁעָוִינוּ וְשֶׁפָּשַׁעְנוּ לְפָנֶיךָ, וּתְהֵא נֶחְשֶׁבֶת לְפָנֶיךָ הַתַּעֲנִית כְּאִלּוּ הִקְרַבְנוּ אֶת גּוּפֵנוּ עַל גַּבֵּי הַמִּזְבֵּחַ, וּתְקַבֵּל לְפָנֶיךָ לְרֵיחַ נִיחוֹחַ כְּקָרְבָּן וּכְעוֹלָה.

וְהִנֵּה יָדַעְנוּ כִּי אֲנַחְנוּ מְחֻיָּבִים לְהִתְעַנּוֹת עַל פִּי תִּקּוּנֵי הַתְּשׁוּבָה עַל כָּל חֵטְא, וּלְסַגֵּף אֶת גּוּפֵנוּ בִּתְשׁוּבַת הַמִּשְׁקָל נֶגֶד מַה שֶּׁהִתְעַנַּגְנוּ בַּעֲבֵרוֹת. אַךְ גָּלוּי וְיָדוּעַ לְפָנֶיךָ, שֶׁאֵין בָּנוּ כֹּחַ לְהִתְעַנּוֹת אֲפִלּוּ עַל חֵטְא אֶחָד וּמִכָּל שֶׁכֵּן עַל כָּל עָוֹן וְעָוֹן, כִּי רַבּוּ עֲוֹנוֹתֵינוּ מִלִּסְפֹּר וְכָשַׁל כֹּחֵנוּ. וְלָכֵן יְהִי רָצוֹן מִלְּפָנֶיךָ יהוה אֱלֹהֵינוּ, שֶׁיִּהְיֶה צוֹם הַתַּעֲנִית בַּיּוֹם הַקָּדוֹשׁ הַזֶּה, יוֹם הַכִּפּוּרִים הַבָּא עָלֵינוּ לְטוֹבָה, כַּפָּרָה עַל כָּל עֲוֹנוֹתֵינוּ.

May it be Your will, God, King who sits upon a throne of compassion, who desires the repentance of the wicked, that You place the love and awe of You into our hearts, and into the hearts of all Your people, the house of Israel, that we may be in awe of You always. And among us, have compassion for the transgressors of Your people, the house of Israel, and place the fear of Your glorious might into their hearts – make their stone hearts humble and let them return to You wholeheartedly, as You promised at the hands of Your prophets, that no outcast would be banished. Though they have done many culpable acts before You, to such a degree that the ways of repentance must surely be locked in their faces – still, in Your great compassion, dig them a tunnel beneath the walls, through to the throne of Your glory, and accept them back in repentance. Have compassion for us, and place within us the strength to serve You always. And remove all the obstacles and constraints that prevent us serving You; for You have formed us, and You know all that is lacking in human beings and their nature, which bewilders them away from Your service; and it is in Your power to remove and to block these things. Do not confound the hour for us – not until we have returned to You wholeheartedly; and let us spend all our days in repentance and good deeds, until the end of the very last moment, when the desire will arise before You to collect our souls in to You. And at that moment, may all our thoughts be bound to Your name, so that our souls will leave us in a state of holiness and purity, and let us then merit to rise from here below, up to the heights, and to emanate plenty to all the worlds, from the heights above to here below. And give us the strength to complete the rites of the fast on this holy day, to perform the fast with all its five forms of abstinence, without our deeds bringing us to fail, Heaven forbid, in any of these five – for all of us are children of Abraham, Isaac and Jacob, Your beloved ones. May we merit to raise our children to Torah and to good actions, and let them not be caught and punished, Heaven forbid, for our sins. And seal us in the book of good lives: lives in awe of Your name; lives in which we will serve You wholeheartedly; lives in which we will not stumble, Heaven forbid, into any sin or iniquity or guilt; lives of sustenance that comes calmly, with dignity, and in lawful ways; and do not let the demands of our livelihoods harry our time, and give us our sustenance in quiet and tranquility, so that our hearts may be free to serve You. Purify our thinking and intentions, so that we may cling to You always.

And so let our prayers rise, come, reach, appear, be favored and heard before You. Accept Your people's prayer. Strengthen us, purify us, You who are revered. And bring out all those holy sparks that have fallen away into the shell by means of our sins. And through the holiness of this Day of Atonement,

יְהִי רָצוֹן מִלְּפָנֶיךָ, אֵל מֶלֶךְ יוֹשֵׁב עַל כִּסֵּא רַחֲמִים, הָרוֹצֶה בִּתְשׁוּבַת רְשָׁעִים, שֶׁתִּתֵּן בְּלִבֵּנוּ וּבְלֵב כָּל עַמְּךָ בֵּית יִשְׂרָאֵל אַהֲבָתְךָ וְיִרְאָתְךָ לִירְאָה אוֹתְךָ כָּל הַיָּמִים. וּבְתוֹכָם תְּרַחֵם עַל פּוֹשְׁעֵי עַמְּךָ בֵּית יִשְׂרָאֵל, וְתֵן בְּלִבָּם פַּחַד הֲדַר גְּאוֹנְךָ, וְהַכְנַע לִבָּם הָאֶבֶן וְיָשׁוּבוּ לְפָנֶיךָ בְּלֵב שָׁלֵם, כְּמוֹ שֶׁהִבְטַחְתָּ עַל יְדֵי נְבִיאֶיךָ, לְבַל יִדַּח מִמֶּנּוּ נִדָּח. גַּם כִּי הִרְבּוּ אַשְׁמָה לְפָנֶיךָ עַד שֶׁנִּנְעֲלוּ בִּפְנֵיהֶם דַּרְכֵי תְּשׁוּבָה, אַתָּה בְּרַחֲמֶיךָ הָרַבִּים חֲתֹר לָהֶם חֲתִירָה מִתַּחַת כִּסֵּא כְבוֹדֶךָ וְקַבְּלֵם בִּתְשׁוּבָה. וְרַחֵם עָלֵינוּ וְתֵן בָּנוּ כֹּחַ לַעֲבֹד אוֹתְךָ כָּל הַיָּמִים, וְהָסֵר מִמֶּנּוּ כָּל הַמְּנִיעוֹת וְהַסִּבּוֹת הַמּוֹנְעוֹת אוֹתָנוּ מִלַּעֲבֹד אוֹתְךָ, כִּי אַתָּה יְצַרְתָּנוּ וְתֵדַע כָּל מַחְסוֹרֵי בְּנֵי אָדָם וְטִבְעָם הַמְבַלְבְּלִים אוֹתָם מֵעֲבוֹדָתֶךָ, וּבְיָדְךָ לַהֲסִירָם וּלְמָנְעָם. וְלֹא תִטְרֹף עָלֵינוּ אֶת הַשָּׁעָה עַד שֶׁנָּשׁוּב לְפָנֶיךָ בְּלֵב שָׁלֵם, וְנִהְיֶה כָּל יָמֵינוּ בִּתְשׁוּבָה וּמַעֲשִׂים טוֹבִים, עַד סוֹף הָרֶגַע הָאַחֲרוֹן, אֲשֶׁר יִהְיֶה לְרָצוֹן לְפָנֶיךָ לֶאֱסֹף אֶת נִשְׁמוֹתֵינוּ אֵלֶיךָ, אָז יִהְיוּ כָּל מַחְשְׁבוֹתֵינוּ דְּבוּקוֹת בַּשֵּׁם, וְאָז תֵּצֵא נִשְׁמָתֵנוּ בִּקְדֻשָּׁה וּבְטָהֳרָה, וְאָז נִזְכֶּה לַעֲלוֹת מִמַּטָּה לְמַעְלָה וּלְהַשְׁפִּיעַ שֶׁפַע בְּכָל הָעוֹלָמוֹת מִמַּעְלָה לְמַטָּה. וְתֵן בָּנוּ כֹּחַ לְהִתְעַנּוֹת בַּיּוֹם הַקָּדוֹשׁ הַזֶּה, וּלְהַשְׁלִים הַתַּעֲנִית בְּכָל חֲמֵשֶׁת הָעִנּוּיִים, וְשֶׁלֹּא יִגְרְמוּ מַעֲשֵׂינוּ לִהְיוֹת נִכְשָׁלִים חַס וְשָׁלוֹם בְּשׁוּם אֶחָד מִן חֲמֵשֶׁת הָעִנּוּיִים, כִּי כֻלָּנוּ בְּנֵי אַבְרָהָם יִצְחָק וְיַעֲקֹב יְדִידֶיךָ. וְזַכֵּנוּ לְגַדֵּל בָּנֵינוּ לַתּוֹרָה וּלְמַעֲשִׂים טוֹבִים, וְלֹא יִתָּפְסוּ חַס וְשָׁלוֹם בַּעֲוֹנוֹתֵינוּ. וְחָתְמֵנוּ בְּסֵפֶר חַיִּים טוֹבִים שֶׁל יִרְאֵי שְׁמֶךָ, חַיִּים שֶׁנַּעֲבֹד אוֹתְךָ בְּלֵב שָׁלֵם, חַיִּים שֶׁלֹּא נִכָּשֵׁל חַס וְשָׁלוֹם בְּשׁוּם חֵטְא וְעָוֹן וְאַשְׁמָה, חַיִּים שֶׁל פַּרְנָסָה בְּנַחַת וּבְכָבוֹד וּבְהֶתֵּר, וְלֹא תַטְרִידֵנוּ הַפַּרְנָסָה בְּטִרְדַּת הַזְּמַן, וְתֵן לָנוּ פַּרְנָסָה בְּהַשְׁקֵט וְשַׁלְוָה, כְּדֵי שֶׁיִּהְיֶה לִבֵּנוּ פָּנוּי לַעֲבוֹדָתֶךָ. וְטַהֵר רַעְיוֹנֵינוּ וּמַחְשְׁבוֹתֵינוּ כְּדֵי שֶׁנִּהְיֶה דְּבוּקִים בְּךָ תָּמִיד.

וּבְכֵן יַעֲלוּ וְיָבוֹאוּ וְיַגִּיעוּ וְיֵרָאוּ וְיֵרָצוּ וְיִשָּׁמְעוּ תְּפִלּוֹתֵינוּ. קַבֵּל רִנַּת עַמְּךָ, שַׂגְּבֵנוּ טַהֲרֵנוּ נוֹרָא. וְתוֹצִיא כָּל הַנִּיצוֹצוֹת הַקְּדוֹשִׁים שֶׁנָּפְלוּ לַקְּלִפָּה עַל יְדֵי חַטֹּאתֵינוּ. וְעַל יְדֵי קְדֻשַּׁת יוֹם הַכִּפּוּרִים יִתְעוֹרְרוּ מִדּוֹתֶיךָ, הַגְּדֻלָּה דברי הימים א׳ כט

may Your attributes be awakened, Your greatness and power and glory and *1 Chr. 29*
majesty and splendor, for everything in heaven and earth is Yours. Yours,
Lord is the kingdom. "Light is sown for the righteous, and for the noble *Ps. 97*
hearted, joy." Let the holiness of the Day of Atonement be spread out over
them, and atone for our actions, as is written in the Torah of Moses Your
servant: "For on this day you will be atoned and made pure; of all your sins *Lev. 16*
before the Lord you shall be purified." "May the pleasantness of the Lord *Ps. 90*
our God be upon us. Establish for us the work of our hands, O establish the
work of our hands." Sweep the rule of arrogance from the earth; rule over all
the world in Your honor, and be raised above all the earth in Your glory, and
bring gladness to Your land and joy to Your city, and the flourishing of pride
to David Your servant.

May the words of my mouth and the meditation of my heart *Ps. 19*
find favor before You, Lord, my Rock and Redeemer.
Amen – so may it be Your will.

Some have the custom to say the "Confession of Rabbeinu Nissim" (attributed to Rabbi Nisi Naharwani, Babylonia, late ninth to early tenth century).

Master of the Universe, before anything else be said – I have no mouth to reply, I have not the boldness to raise my head, for my iniquities are too many to count, my sins are more than can be told, and the burden they form is too much for me to bear. I confess before You, Lord my God – with my head bowed, my body bowed, my strength quelled, my power dulled, my spirit laid low, bowing, prostrate, throwing myself down before You, in fear and in terror, trembling and perspiring, shaking, fearful, awed. I will tell You, Lord my God, only some of my evil actions, my ugly habitual ways, my shameful practices. It is impossible to speak them all, and I have no strength to explain them, I do not command the strength to reveal them, I do not know how to speak them out, I am not worthy to tell them. And to ask forgiveness and pardon and atonement for all these things – who am I? What is my life? I am vanity and emptiness; I am a maggot, a worm; I am dust and ashes. I am ashamed of my sins, humiliated by my transgressions. I have no voice even to confess before You; my iniquity is too great to bear; my transgressions are too heinous to be told; I am ashamed and humiliated, like a thief caught in the act of breaking in.

Master of the Universe, if I were to come forward to lay out all my sins and to explain them – my time would come to an end and the list would not have ended. For which of them should I beg mercy? From which of them should I ask relief? Which ones should I confess? General categories or individual deeds? The hidden sins or those in the open? The earliest or the last? New ones or old? Hidden ones or known? Those that I remember, or those I have forgotten? I myself know that I have no learning and no wisdom, no knowledge or understanding, no righteousness, no nobility and no acts of kindness to my name. I am a fool and know nothing; I am ignorant and

וְהַגְּבוּרָה וְהַתִּפְאֶרֶת וְהַנֵּצַח וְהַהוֹד כִּי־כֹל בַּשָּׁמַיִם וּבָאָרֶץ, לְךָ יהוה
הַמַּמְלָכָה: אוֹר זָרֻעַ לַצַּדִּיק וּלְיִשְׁרֵי־לֵב שִׂמְחָה: וְתִתְפַּשֵּׁט עֲלֵיהֶם קְדֻשַּׁת תהלים צז
יוֹם הַכִּפּוּרִים לְכַפֵּר עָלֵינוּ, כְּמָה שֶׁכָּתוּב בְּתוֹרַת מֹשֶׁה עַבְדְּךָ: כִּי־בַיּוֹם ויקרא טז
הַזֶּה יְכַפֵּר עֲלֵיכֶם לְטַהֵר אֶתְכֶם, מִכֹּל חַטֹּאתֵיכֶם, לִפְנֵי יהוה תִּטְהָרוּ:
וִיהִי נֹעַם אֲדֹנָי אֱלֹהֵינוּ עָלֵינוּ, וּמַעֲשֵׂה יָדֵינוּ כּוֹנְנָה עָלֵינוּ, וּמַעֲשֵׂה יָדֵינוּ תהלים צ
כּוֹנְנֵהוּ: וְתַעֲבִיר מֶמְשֶׁלֶת זָדוֹן מִן הָאָרֶץ, וּמְלֹךְ עַל כָּל הָעוֹלָם כֻּלּוֹ בִּכְבוֹדֶךָ
וְהִנָּשֵׂא עַל כָּל הָאָרֶץ בִּיקָרֶךָ, וְתֵן שִׂמְחָה לְאַרְצֶךָ וְשָׂשׂוֹן לְעִירֶךָ וּצְמִיחַת
קֶרֶן לְדָוִד עַבְדֶּךָ.

יִהְיוּ לְרָצוֹן אִמְרֵי־פִי וְהֶגְיוֹן לִבִּי לְפָנֶיךָ, יהוה צוּרִי וְגֹאֲלִי: תהלים יט
אָמֵן, כֵּן יְהִי רָצוֹן.

Some have the custom to say the וידוי של רבינו נסים
(attributed to Rabbi Nisi Naharwani, Babylonia, late ninth to early tenth century).

רִבּוֹנוֹ שֶׁל עוֹלָם, קֹדֶם כָּל דָּבָר, אֵין לִי פֶּה לְהָשִׁיב וְלֹא מֵצַח לְהָרִים רֹאשׁ. כִּי מִפְּנֵי שֶׁעֲוֹנוֹתַי רַבּוּ מִלִּמְנוֹת, וְחַטֹּאתַי עָצְמוּ מִסַּפֵּר, וּכְמַשָּׂא כָבֵד יִכְבְּדוּ מִמֶּנִּי, מִתְוַדֶּה אֲנִי לְפָנֶיךָ יהוה אֱלֹהַי בִּכְפִיפַת רֹאשׁ, בִּכְפִיפַת קוֹמָה, בִּכְנִיעַת חַיִל, בַּחֲלִישׁוּת כֹּחַ, בִּשְׁבִירוּת לֵב, בִּנְמִיכוּת רוּחַ, בְּקִדָּה, בִּכְרִיעָה, בְּהִשְׁתַּחֲוָיָה, בְּאֵימָה, בִּבְעָתָה, בְּרֶתֶת, בְּזִיעַ, בְּחַלְחוּל, בְּיִרְאָה, בְּמוֹרָא. אוֹמֵר אֲנִי לְפָנֶיךָ יהוה אֱלֹהַי מִקְצָת מַעֲשַׂי הָרָעִים, וּמִדְּרָכַי הַמְכֹעָרִים וּמִמַּעֲלָלַי הַמְקֻלְקָלִים. לְאָמְרָם אִי אֶפְשָׁר, לְבָרְרָם אֵין בִּי כֹּחַ, לְגַלּוֹתָם לֹא אֶעֱצָר חַיִל, לְדַבְּרָם לֹא אֵדָעֵם, לְהַגִּידָם אֵינִי כְּדַאי, וְלִתְבֹּעַ עֲלֵיהֶם סְלִיחָה וּמְחִילָה וְכַפָּרָה. מָה אֲנִי מֶה חַיַּי, אֲנִי הֶבֶל וָרִיק, אֲנִי רִמָּה וְתוֹלֵעָה, אֲנִי עָפָר וָאֵפֶר. בּוֹשׁ אֲנִי מֵחֲטָאַי, וּמִכֻּלָּם אֲנִי מִפְּשָׁעַי. אֵין לִי פִּתְחוֹן פֶּה לְהִתְוַדּוֹת לְפָנֶיךָ, גָּדוֹל עֲוֹנִי מִנְּשֹׂא, עָצְמוּ פְּשָׁעַי מִסַּפֵּר. בֹּשְׁתִּי וְגַם נִכְלַמְתִּי, כְּגַנָּב הַנִּמְצָא בַּמַּחְתֶּרֶת.

רִבּוֹנוֹ שֶׁל עוֹלָם, אִם עָמַדְתִּי לְפָרֵשׁ אֶת חֲטָאַי וּלְבָאֲרָם, יִכְלֶה הַזְּמַן וְהֵם לֹא יִכְלוּ. עַל אֵיזֶה מֵהֶם אֶתְבַּע, וְעַל אֵיזֶה מֵהֶם אֲבַקֵּשׁ, וְעַל אֵיזֶה מֵהֶם אֶתְוַדֶּה. עַל הַכְּלָל אוֹ עַל הַפְּרָט, עַל הַנִּסְתָּרוֹת אוֹ עַל הַנִּגְלוֹת, עַל הָרִאשׁוֹנוֹת אוֹ עַל הָאַחֲרוֹנוֹת, עַל הַחֲדָשׁוֹת אוֹ עַל הַיְשָׁנוֹת, עַל הַטְּמוּנוֹת אוֹ עַל הַנּוֹדָעוֹת, עַל הַנִּזְכָּרוֹת אוֹ עַל הַנִּשְׁכָּחוֹת מִמֶּנִּי. יוֹדֵעַ אֲנִי בְּעַצְמִי שֶׁאֵין בִּי לֹא תוֹרָה וְלֹא חָכְמָה, לֹא דַעַת וְלֹא תְבוּנָה, לֹא צְדָקָה וְלֹא יַשְׁרוּת וְלֹא גְמִילוּת חֲסָדִים. אֲבָל אֲנִי

do not understand; a thief, not to be trusted, guilty and with no merit, wicked and not righteous, evil and not good. I have performed every kind of vile deed, and have committed vilest iniquities. And were You to judge me as befits my actions – alas, oh, and woe on me, alas to my soul. And were You to seek to cleanse me, as a silversmith purifies and refines silver – then nothing would remain of me at all. For I am like straw before the fire, like dry wood before the furnace – like silver alloy only thinly plating clay; I am empty, utterly empty, without substance.

How should I begin? What healing can I look for? I have been like a stubborn and rebellious son, like a slave rebelling against his master, like a student disputing with his own teacher. I have declared impure the things that You hold pure, and declared pure the things You hold impure. I have prohibited what You allow and allowed what You prohibit. I have hated that which You love, and loved that which You hate. I have been stringent where You are lenient, and lenient where You are stringent. I have distanced what You draw close, and drawn close what You have distanced. But my intention was not to provoke Your anger – and in my brazenness I am coming now to ask for forgiveness before You. My demeanor has been as shameless as a dog's – I was brazen as a whore – and I come before You now full of shame. It was as it is written: You had the brazen face of a whore, and refused to feel your humiliation. *Jer. 3*

Master of the Universe, it is not only for myself that I pray and confess, but for myself and for Your congregation who stand before You. And even though I am not worthy and do not merit to confess, even on my own behalf, and certainly not for others – yet, it is Your way to be patient, Your trait to overlook Your fury, Your custom to have compassion for Your creations, and most of all for those who return to You and confess before You, who desert and regret their transgressions and do not hide them. For so it is written: One who hides his transgressions will never succeed, but *Prov. 28* one who confesses and leaves them will find compassion – and he will save his spirit from the judgment of Gehinnom.

Master of the Universe, the custom of Your righteous court is not the custom of the courts of men. For the way of a person is to bring a claim for payment against his fellow to a court or to a judge – and if that other then denies the claim he is spared the payment, while if he confesses, he is obliged to pay. But Your righteous law court is not so, for there if one denies – alas to him, and alas to his soul. But if he confesses and leaves his sin behind – then You will show him compassion.

Master of the Universe, were it not for our sins and our transgressions we would feel no shame or humiliation, and what, then, would we confess? No one can ask for forgiveness for sin, if he has not sinned. And the power of Your compassion would never be known were it not through Your forgiveness of the sins of those who hold You in awe. And now it is not only for myself that I confess, but for myself and for all Your congregation.

May it be Your will, Lord, our God and God of our ancestors, that You forgive and pardon us for all our iniquities and transgressions, and grant us atonement for all our sins.

סָכָל וְלֹא יוֹדֵעַ, בַּעַר וְלֹא מֵבִין, גַּזְלָן וְלֹא נֶאֱמָן, חַיָּב וְלֹא זַכַּאי, רָשָׁע וְלֹא צַדִּיק, רַע וְלֹא טוֹב. וְכָל מַעֲשִׂים רָעִים עָשִׂיתִי, וְגַם עֲבֵרוֹת רָעוֹת עָשִׂיתִי. וְאִם אַתָּה דָּן אוֹתִי כְּמַעֲשַׂי, אוֹי לִי, וַי לִי, אֲהָהּ עָלַי, אוֹיָה עַל נַפְשִׁי. וְאִם תְּבַקֵּשׁ לְנַקּוֹתִי כִּמְטַהֵר וְכִמְצָרֵף כֶּסֶף, לֹא יִשָּׁאֵר מִמֶּנִּי מְאוּמָה. כִּי אֲנִי כְּקַשׁ לִפְנֵי אֵשׁ, וּכְעֵצִים יְבֵשִׁים לִפְנֵי הָאוּר, כֶּסֶף סִיגִים מְצֻפֶּה עַל חֶרֶשׂ, הֲבֵל הֲבָלִים אֵין בּוֹ מַמָּשׁ.

בַּמָּה אֲקַדֵּם, אוֹ מָה רְפוּאָה אֲבַקֵּשׁ. כְּבֵן סוֹרֵר וּמוֹרֶה הָיִיתִי, כְּעֶבֶד מוֹרֵד עַל אֲדוֹנָיו, כְּתַלְמִיד חוֹלֵק עַל רַבּוֹ. אֶת אֲשֶׁר טִהַרְתָּ טִמֵּאתִי וַאֲשֶׁר טִמֵּאתָ טִהַרְתִּי, אֶת אֲשֶׁר הִתַּרְתָּ אָסַרְתִּי וַאֲשֶׁר אָסַרְתָּ הִתַּרְתִּי, אֶת אֲשֶׁר אָהַבְתָּ שָׂנֵאתִי וַאֲשֶׁר שָׂנֵאתָ אָהַבְתִּי, אֶת אֲשֶׁר הֵקַלְתָּ הֶחֱמַרְתִּי וַאֲשֶׁר הֶחֱמַרְתָּ הֵקַלְתִּי, אֶת אֲשֶׁר קֵרַבְתָּ רִחַקְתִּי וַאֲשֶׁר רִחַקְתָּ קֵרַבְתִּי. אַךְ לֹא לְהַכְעִיסְךָ נִתְכַּוַּנְתִּי, וּבְעַזּוּת מֵצַח בָּאתִי לְבַקֵּשׁ סְלִיחָה מִלְּפָנֶיךָ. שַׂמְתִּי פָּנַי כַּכֶּלֶב, הֵעַזְתִּי מֵצַח כַּזּוֹנָה, וְנִגַּשְׁתִּי לְפָנֶיךָ בְּבֹשֶׁת פָּנִים. וְכֵן כָּתוּב: וּמֵצַח אִשָּׁה זוֹנָה הָיָה לָךְ, מֵאַנְתְּ הִכָּלֵם: ירמיה ג

רִבּוֹנוֹ שֶׁל עוֹלָם, לֹא עַל עַצְמִי בִּלְבַד אֲנִי מִתְפַּלֵּל וּמִתְוַדֶּה, כִּי אִם בַּעֲדִי וּבְעַד
קְהָלֶיךָ הָעוֹמְדִים לְפָנֶיךָ, וְאַף עַל פִּי שֶׁאֵינִי רָאוּי וְלֹא זַכַּאי לְהִתְוַדּוֹת עַל עַצְמִי,
וְכָל שֶׁכֵּן עַל אֲחֵרִים. אֲבָל כִּי דַרְכְּךָ לְהַאֲרִיךְ אַפֶּךָ, וּמִדָּתְךָ לְהַעֲבִיר קִצְפֶּךָ,
וּמִנְהָגְךָ לְרַחֵם עַל בְּרִיּוֹתֶיךָ, וּבְיוֹתֵר לַשָּׁבִים אֵלֶיךָ וּמוֹדִים לְפָנֶיךָ, וְעוֹזְבִים
וּמִתְנַחֲמִים עַל פִּשְׁעֵיהֶם, וְלֹא מְכַסִּים אוֹתָם. שֶׁכֵּן כָּתוּב: מְכַסֶּה פְשָׁעָיו לֹא משלי כח
יַצְלִיחַ, וּמוֹדֶה וְעֹזֵב יְרֻחָם: וּמַצִּיל אֶת נַפְשׁוֹ מִדִּינָהּ שֶׁל גֵּיהִנֹּם.

רִבּוֹנוֹ שֶׁל עוֹלָם, מִנְהַג בֵּית דִּינְךָ הַצֶּדֶק לֹא כְּמִנְהַג בָּתֵּי דִינִין שֶׁל בְּנֵי אָדָם. שֶׁמִּדַּת בְּנֵי אָדָם, כְּשֶׁהוּא תּוֹבֵעַ אֶת חֲבֵרוֹ בְּמָמוֹן אֶל הַבֵּית דִּין אוֹ אֶל הַשּׁוֹפֵט, אִם יִכְפּוֹר יִנָּצֵל מִן הַמָּמוֹן, וְאִם יוֹדֶה מִתְחַיֵּב לִתֵּן. וּבֵית דִּינְךָ הַצֶּדֶק לֹא כֵן הוּא, אֶלָּא אִם יִכְפּוֹר אָדָם אוֹי לוֹ וְאוֹי לְנַפְשׁוֹ, וְאִם מוֹדֶה וְעוֹזֵב אַתָּה מְרַחֲמֵהוּ.

רִבּוֹנוֹ שֶׁל עוֹלָם, לוּלֵי חֲטָאֵינוּ וּפְשָׁעֵינוּ, לֹא הָיִינוּ בּוֹשִׁים וְנִכְלָמִים, וְעַל מָה הָיִינוּ מִתְוַדִּים, כִּי אִי אֶפְשָׁר לוֹ לְאָדָם לְבַקֵּשׁ עַל חֵטְא וְהוּא לֹא חָטָא, וְלֹא יָדַע עֹז רַחֲמֶיךָ אֶלָּא בְּהַעֲבִירְךָ חַטֹּאת יְרֵאֶיךָ. וְלֹא עַל עַצְמִי בִּלְבַד אֲנִי מִתְוַדֶּה, כִּי אִם בַּעֲדִי וּבְעַד כָּל קְהָלֶיךָ.

יְהִי רָצוֹן מִלְּפָנֶיךָ, יהוה אֱלֹהֵינוּ וֵאלֹהֵי אֲבוֹתֵינוּ, שֶׁתִּסְלַח וְתִמְחַל לָנוּ עַל כָּל עֲוֹנוֹתֵינוּ וּפְשָׁעֵינוּ, וּתְכַפֵּר לָנוּ עַל כָּל חַטֹּאתֵינוּ.

KOL NIDREI

Two Torah scrolls are removed from the Ark and passed to two honorees who stand on either side of the Leader.

The Leader recites the following several times:

LIGHT HAS BEEN SOWN FOR THE RIGHTEOUS, *Ps. 97*

AND FOR THE NOBLE HEARTED, JOY.

Some have the custom to recite "Kam Rabbi Shimon" (facing page).

---

of taking scrolls around at the start of the service is to highlight its solemnity, and to give the congregation a chance to kiss the scrolls prior to repenting of their sins. The scroll reminds us of the commandments and of our failure to observe them in the past year.

Of the beginning of creation it is written, "It was evening and it was morning, one day" (Gen. 1:5), *not* "the first day." On this the sages said: "What is the meaning of 'one day'? This is Yom Kippur" (*Bereshit Raba* 3:8). So on this night of nights we sense ourselves in the presence of the light of the first day of creation – not physical light, for the sun and stars were not created until the fourth day, but a spiritual light that God reserved for the righteous in generations to come.

The sun is setting. Outside there is darkness. But in the synagogue there is spiritual light: the light of Eden before there was sin, the light of God's love through which we learn to love, the light of God's forgiveness through which we learn to forgive.

Arnold Schoenberg, the great composer, abandoned Judaism as a young man. But as anti-Semitism grew, in 1933 he decided to take his stand as a Jew, formally seeking readmission into his ancestral faith at a ceremony in the rue Copernic Synagogue in Paris. The painter Marc Chagall was a witness. Schoenberg subsequently composed a piece of music called *Kol Nidrei* to express the power he sensed in this moment. A narrator begins with these words:

> The Kabbala relates a legend. In the beginning, God said, "Let there be light." From infinite space a flame sprang up. God scattered this light into atoms. Myriad sparks were hidden in the universe but not all of us can perceive them. The vain man who walks proudly will never notice them, but the modest and humble man whose eyes are lowered is able to see them. *A light has been sown for the righteous.* (Andre Neher, *They Made Their Souls Anew*)

כל נדרי

Two ספרי תורה *are removed from the* ארון קודש *and passed to two honorees who stand on either side of the* שליח ציבור.

The שליח ציבור *recites the following several times:*

אוֹר זָרֻעַ לַצַּדִּיק וּלְיִשְׁרֵי־לֵב שִׂמְחָה: תהלים צז

Some have the custom to recite the following:

קָם רַבִּי שִׁמְעוֹן, סָלִיק יְדוֹי לְגַבֵּי עֵלָּא וְשַׁבַּח לְמָארֵי עָלְמָא, וְאָמַר: רִבּוֹן עָלְמִין, עֲבִיד בְּגִין שְׁכִינְתָּא דְּאִיהִי בְּגָלוּתָא. וְאִם אִיהִי בְּאוּמָאָה, הָא אַבָּא וְאִמָּא דְּאִינוּן חָכְמָה וּבִינָה, יָכְלִין לְמֶעְבַּד הַתָּרָה. הָדָא הוּא דִכְתִיב: יהוה צְבָאוֹת יָעָץ, וּמִי יָפֵר: אִם הַתַּלְמִיד אוּמֵי, הָרַב יָכִיל לְמֶעְבַּד הַתָּרָה. וְאִם נָדַר אוֹ נִשְׁבַּע בֵּן, דְּאִיהוּ ו׳, דְּלָא יִפְרֹק לַהּ אֶלָּא דִתְהֵא בְּגָלוּתָא עַד זִמְנָא יְדִיעָא, וְנֶדֶר אוֹ שְׁבוּעָה אִיהוּ בְּי״ה, דְּאִינוּן חָכְמָה וּבִינָה, וְאִיהוּ אִתְחָרֵט, הָא תְּלַת בְּנֵי נָשָׁא יְכִילִין לְמִפְטַר לֵהּ, וְאִינוּן תְּלַת אֲבָהָן לְעֵלָּא לְקַבְּלֵיהוּ. וְאִם לָא תִתְחָרֵט, אֲנָא בְעֵינָא מִנָּךְ וּמִכָּל אִינוּן דִּמְתִיבְתָּא דִלְעֵלָּא וְתַתָּא, דְּתַעֲבֵד בְּגִין רַעְיָא מְהֵימְנָא דְּלָא זָז מִשְּׁכִינְתָּא בְּכָל אֲתַר, וְאִיהוּ עָאל שְׁלָם בֵּינָךְ וּבֵינָהּ זִמְנִין סַגִּיאִין, וּמָסַר גַּרְמֵיהּ לְמִיתָה בְּגִינָהּ וּבְגִין בְּנָהָא. הָדָא הוּא דִכְתִיב: וְאִם־אַיִן מְחֵנִי נָא מִסִּפְרְךָ אֲשֶׁר כָּתָבְתָּ: תיקוני זוהר, קמג · ישעיה יד · שמות לב

וְאִם הוּא נֶדֶר מִסִּטְרָא דְּאַבָּא וְאִמָּא וְלָא בָעֵי, אֲנָא סָלִיק לְגַבֵּי הַהוּא דְּאִתְּמַר בֵּיהּ: כִּי יִפָּלֵא מִמְּךָ דָבָר: דְּאִתְּמַר בֵּיהּ, בְּמֻפְלָא מִמְּךָ אַל תִּדְרֹשׁ, דְּיִפְטֹר נֶדֶר. דברים יז

וְאַף עַל גַּב דִּשְׁכִינְתָּא אִיהִי בְגָלוּתָא לְגַבֵּי בַּעְלָהּ כְּנִדָּה, דְּאִיהוּ יַפְרִישׁ בֵּין דָּם לְדָם, וְאִתְפַּתַּח מְקוֹרָא דִילָהּ לְדַכָּאָה לַהּ בְּמַיִם דְּאוֹרַיְתָא, מַיִם חַיִּים דְּלָא פָּסְקִין. וְאַפְרֵישׁ מִנָּהּ דַּם נִדָּה, דְּאִיהִי לִילִית דְּלָא אִתְקְרִיבַת בַּהֲדָהּ, דְּאִיהוּ חוֹבָא דְנִשְׁמְתָא דְּסָאִיבַת לַהּ, וְלֵית לַהּ רְשׁוּ לְסַלְּקָא נִשְׁמְתָא לְגַבֵּי בַּעְלָהּ, לְהַהוּא אֲתַר דְּאִתְיְהִיבַת מִתַּמָּן. וְאִתְדָּנַת בֵּין דִּין לְדִין, בֵּין דִּינֵי נְפָשׁוֹת לְדִינֵי מָמוֹנוֹת, דְּאִית מַאן דְּפָרַע בְּמָמוֹנֵיהּ וְאִית מַאן דְּפָרַע בְּנַפְשֵׁיהּ.

וּבֵין נֶגַע לָנֶגַע, כְּמָה דְאוּקְמוּהוּ: אֵיכָה יָשְׁבָה בָדָד: דְּאִיהִי חֲשִׁיבָא שְׁכִינְתָּא בְּגָלוּתָא כִּמְצוֹרָע, דְּאִתְּמַר בָּהּ: בָּדָד יֵשֵׁב מִחוּץ לַמַּחֲנֶה: מִחוּץ וַדַּאי דָא גָלוּתָא, דְּאִיהִי לְבַר מֵאַרְעָא דְיִשְׂרָאֵל, דְּאִיהִי מוֹתְבָא דְאָת (ה׳). איכה א · ויקרא יג

וְאִי מְקוֹרָא לָא יָכִיל לְמִפְתַּח, עַד דְּיִפְתַּח לַהּ הַהוּא דְּסָגִיר לַהּ, אֲנָא מְפַיְּסְנָא לֵהּ בְּגִין (יו״ד ה״א וא״ו ה״א) דְּאִיהוּ יִחוּדָא דְיִחוּדֵיהּ תַּמָּן, וּבְגִין לְבוּשִׁין דְּאִתְלַבַּשׁ. מִיַּד אִתְפַּתְּחַת מְקוֹרָא וְאִתְדַּכִּיאַת שְׁכִינְתָּא. וְרָזָא דְמִלָּה: מִקְוֵה יִשְׂרָאֵל יהוה, מוֹשִׁיעוֹ בְּעֵת צָרָה. מוֹשִׁיעוֹ וַדַּאי, הַהוּא דִמְקוֹרָא דְמִקְוֵה בִּידֵיהּ. אָמֵן.

אוֹר זָרֻעַ לַצַּדִּיק *Light has been sown for the righteous.* This line from Psalm 97 is said while the Torah scrolls are carried around the congregation. The custom

The Leader recites the following three times:

עַל דַּעַת הַמָּקוֹם With the agreement of God
and of the community,
in the heavenly council,
and in the council of man,
we give leave to pray
with the transgressors among us.

---

ments. The rabbis ruled explicitly that when an evildoer who sinned by choice comes to the synagogue, he is to be welcomed, not insulted. In this ruling they relied on Solomon's advice: "Do not despise a thief when he steals to appease his hunger" [Prov. 6:30]. This means: do not despise the wrongdoer in Israel when he comes secretly to "steal" some observance.

Maimonides' generosity of spirit should be our guide. How can we ask God to forgive us if we fail to forgive our fellow Jews?

The three people who stand on the *bima* – the leader of prayer flanked by two others – form a Beit Din, or court of three, since what they are now engaged in (annulling vows) is a legal act and requires a court of law. Their presence has also been compared to Aaron and Ḥur who stood, one on each side of Moses, supporting his arms as he raised them to inspire Israel to victory against the Amalekites (Ex. 17:12), and to the Deputy High Priest and the head of the officiating priestly family who stood on either side of the High Priest on Yom Kippur as he drew lots over the two goats (Mishna *Yoma* 4:1).

KOL NIDREI

For an essay on *Kol Nidrei*, see the Introduction, page xlviii.

Kol Nidrei, a prayer first mentioned in the ninth century, has been, more than almost any other prayer, the subject of controversy, historical speculation and religious passion. Ironically it is not a prayer at all but a legal formula for the annulment of vows to God. For many centuries it faced opposition. Some argued that vows could not be annulled, collectively and *en masse*, in this way. Others pointed to the fact that it created a negative impression among gentiles, despite the fact that, as was regularly explained, *Kol Nidrei* does not apply at all to vows made to another human being, only to God. Yet it survived all its critics and continues to intrigue those who have sought to explain its popularity.

Some attribute it to the fact that this holy night became the time when Jews estranged from the community – some having undergone forced conversion,

The שליח ציבור *recites the following three times:*

עַל דַּעַת הַמָּקוֹם, וְעַל דַּעַת הַקָּהָל
בִּישִׁיבָה שֶׁל מַעְלָה וּבִישִׁיבָה שֶׁל מַטָּה
אָנוּ מַתִּירִין לְהִתְפַּלֵּל עִם הָעֲבַרְיָנִים.

עַל דַּעַת הַמָּקוֹם *With the agreement of God. HaMakom,* literally "the Place," is one of the names of God, meaning, God who is in every place. Rabbi Joseph Soloveitchik said that we use this name specifically on occasions when we might feel as if God were absent. So we comfort mourners by saying "May *HaMakom* comfort you," since bereavement can isolate us from God. We use it at the Seder service because our ancestors, enslaved in Egypt, may have felt the remoteness of God. We use it on *Kol Nidrei* night because now, more than at other times of the year, we are conscious of how our sins separate us from God. The word *HaMakom* reminds us that God is never far from us however far we may feel ourselves to be from Him.

אָנוּ מַתִּירִין לְהִתְפַּלֵּל עִם הָעֲבַרְיָנִים *We give leave to pray with the transgressors.* A formal lifting of the ban against those who had been excommunicated in the course of the year, instituted in the thirteenth century by Rabbi Meir of Rothenburg. The sages said that "Any fast that does not include the transgressors of Israel is not a fast" (*Keritot* 6b). Judaism is the faith of an entire nation, righteous and not-yet-righteous alike.

In the twelfth century, Moses Maimonides was asked the following question: Some Jews, under threat of death, had converted to Islam. Were they permitted to carry on practicing Judaism in secret? Could they be allowed to attend synagogue? One rabbi had given a ruling, replying to both questions in the negative. They had abandoned Judaism. Therefore every Jewish act they did was a further sin and they had no place in a Jewish house of prayer. Maimonides was horrified by this answer. The converts had acted under duress, and Jewish law does not condemn someone under such circumstances. Besides, both they and their oppressors knew that the conversion was a sham. No one means what they say under threat of death. Such people should be welcomed, not shunned; forgiven, not condemned.

At the end of his reply, known as *Iggeret HaShemad,* The Epistle on Martyrdom, Maimonides writes:

> It is not right to alienate, scorn, and hate people who desecrate the Sabbath. It is our duty to befriend them, and encourage them to fulfil the command-

The Leader recites Kol Nidrei three times, each time progressively louder. The congregation recites quietly along with him.

EVERY VOW

and bind, oath, ban, restriction, penalty,
and every term that sets things out of bounds;
all that we vow or swear, ban or bar from ourselves,
(from last Yom Kippur to this, and)
from this Yom Kippur
until that which is to come – let it be for the good –
each one, we regret. Let each be released,
forgotten, halted, null and void,
without power and without hold.
What we vow is not vowed,
what we bind is not bound,
and what we swear is not sworn.

---

ings and vows. If we honor our commitments, there is trust, cooperation and graciousness in human relations. If we fail to do so, trust wanes and the social fabric begins to unravel. So when we ask God to release us from promises we made to Him that we now regret, we are signaling the intense seriousness with which we regard verbal undertakings.

כָּל נִדְרֵי *Every vow… etc.* Different kinds of vows, oaths, voluntary undertakings, self-imposed prohibitions, dedications and penalties. The basis on which they are annulled is that had we been aware at the time of all the facts and circumstances, we would not have made them. Verbal undertakings are sacred. Therefore, "It is better not to make a vow than to make one and not fulfill it" (Eccl. 5:5). *From this Yom Kippur until that which is to come:* This reflects the view of Rabbeinu Tam (France, twelfth century) that *Kol Nidrei* does not apply to vows we have made in the past but is a pre-emptive proviso against vows we may rashly take in the future.

PRIVATE MEDITATION

Master of the universe, who created the world with words, help me to understand and respect the seriousness of words, for words are no less serious than deeds and may do much harm. Release me from those words in which

The שליח ציבור *recites* כָּל נִדְרֵי *three times, each time progressively louder. The* קהל *recites quietly along with him.*

כָּל נִדְרֵי

וֶאֱסָרֵי וּשְׁבוּעֵי וַחֲרָמֵי וְקוֹנָמֵי וְקִנּוּסֵי וְכִנּוּיֵי
דְּאִנְדַּרְנָא, וּדְאִשְׁתַּבַּעְנָא, וּדְאַחֲרִימְנָא וּדְאָסַרְנָא עַל נַפְשָׁתָנָא
(מִיּוֹם כִּפּוּרִים שֶׁעָבַר עַד יוֹם כִּפּוּרִים זֶה וּ)
מִיּוֹם כִּפּוּרִים זֶה עַד יוֹם כִּפּוּרִים הַבָּא עָלֵינוּ לְטוֹבָה.
בְּכֻלְּהוֹן אִחֲרַטְנָא בְהוֹן, כֻּלְּהוֹן יְהוֹן שָׁרָן.
שְׁבִיקִין, שְׁבִיתִין, בְּטֵלִין וּמְבֻטָּלִין
לָא שְׁרִירִין, וְלָא קַיָּמִין.
נִדְרָנָא לָא נִדְרֵי
וֶאֱסָרָנָא לָא אֱסָרֵי
וּשְׁבוּעָתָנָא לָא שְׁבוּעוֹת.

---

others having been excommunicated – returned and rejoined their people and their God. Yom Kippur has long been a time of "coming home," the original meaning of the word *teshuva*. Others point to the powerful, plaintive melody: the lonely pleading of the leader of prayer with God. Some say that we need look no further than the fact that, regardless of *Kol Nidrei*, this is the start of the holiest day of the year when, more palpably and emotively than at any other time, we stand in the presence of God, answerable to Him for our lives.

At the simplest level, *Kol Nidrei* testifies to the unique sanctity Judaism attaches to words and speech. God created the cosmos with words: "And God said, Let there be… and there was." God, invisible, revealed Himself to the prophets in words. Our entire relationship with God is based on words: the covenant our ancestors made with Him at Mount Sinai and by which we are still bound. And just as God made the natural universe with words, so we make or unmake the social universe with words: promises, verbal undertak-

The Leader recites three times, then the congregation repeats three times:

וְנִסְלַח And all the congregation of Israel are forgiven, Num. 15
along with the strangers living in their midst;
for they acted without knowing what they did.

The Leader continues:

סְלַח־נָא Please, forgive this people's iniquity Num. 14
in the abundance of Your kindness,
as You have forgiven this people
from the time of Egypt until now,
and there it is said:

The congregation recites three times, then the Leader repeats three times:

וַיֹּאמֶר And the LORD said, I have forgiven as you asked. Ibid.

The Leader recites the following blessing and the congregation (except those who have already recited it at candle lighting) recite it quietly along with him.

בָּרוּךְ Blessed are You, LORD our God, King of the Universe,
who has given us life, sustained us, and brought us to this time.

The Torah scrolls are returned to the Ark.

---

forgiveness, and (2) that through repentance, even deliberate sins come to be regarded as unintentional ones and can thus be forgiven. The importance of the first is that we should never rely on our own merits. Judaism is the faith of a people and its communities, not just of individuals in their private lives. The second reminds us that by expressing remorse for the past, we may not cancel the wrong we have done but we revoke the intention with which we did it.

סְלַח־נָא *Please, forgive.* Moses' prayer and God's pardon after the sin of the spies, whose report – the land is good but we cannot conquer it – demoralized the people to the point that they proposed going back to Egypt. God threatened to destroy the people and begin again with Moses. Moses prayed on the people's behalf and God relented: "I have forgiven, as you asked" (Num. 14:19–20). This became a paradigm for future prayers for forgiveness.

שֶׁהֶחֱיָנוּ *Who has given us life.* Yom Kippur is a festival as well as a fast, and the fast itself is not an act of mourning but of penitence and rededication. Therefore, as on other festivals, we say *Sheheḥeyanu*. Normally it is said over *Kiddush*, but since there is no *Kiddush* on Yom Kippur it is said here, after *Kol Nidrei*, immediately prior to the evening prayers.

The שליח ציבור *recites three times, then the* קהל *repeats three times:*

במדבר טו

וְנִסְלַח לְכָל־עֲדַת בְּנֵי יִשְׂרָאֵל
וְלַגֵּר הַגָּר בְּתוֹכָם, כִּי לְכָל־הָעָם בִּשְׁגָגָה:

The שליח ציבור *continues:*

במדבר יד

סְלַח־נָא לַעֲוֹן הָעָם הַזֶּה כְּגֹדֶל חַסְדֶּךָ
וְכַאֲשֶׁר נָשָׂאתָה לָעָם הַזֶּה מִמִּצְרַיִם וְעַד־הֵנָּה:
וְשָׁם נֶאֱמַר

The קהל *recites three times, then the* שליח ציבור *repeats three times:*

שם

וַיֹּאמֶר יהוה, סָלַחְתִּי כִּדְבָרֶךָ:

The שליח ציבור *recites the following blessing and the* קהל
(except those who have already recited it at הדלקת נרות*) recite it quietly along with him.*

בָּרוּךְ אַתָּה יהוה אֱלֹהֵינוּ מֶלֶךְ הָעוֹלָם
שֶׁהֶחֱיָנוּ וְקִיְּמָנוּ, וְהִגִּיעָנוּ לַזְּמַן הַזֶּה.

The ספרי תורה *are returned to the* ארון קודש.

I made a promise to You that I did not or cannot keep, and help me not make such vows in the future. Help me honor all the promises I made to others. Keep me from words I should not say, rash or thoughtless or hurtful words, or words that create expectations I cannot meet. Grant me the strength to apologize for the words I said that injured others, whether in their presence or their absence, whether I meant to or not. Help me weigh everything I say before I say it and teach me the importance of self-restraint in speech as well as in deed. May the words of my mouth and the meditation of my heart find favor before You, Lord, my Rock and Redeemer.

Once on *Kol Nidrei* night Rabbi Zusya of Hanipol heard the cantor chanting the words in most beautiful tones. He turned his eyes to heaven and said, "Master of the universe, had Israel not sinned, how could such a song have been intoned before You?"

וְנִסְלַח לְכָל־עֲדַת בְּנֵי יִשְׂרָאֵל *And all the congregation of Israel are forgiven.* This is taken from the passage in Numbers (15:26) dealing with a case in which the whole community sins unintentionally. The verse, in its context here, signals two things: (1) that tonight we have come together *as a community* to seek

On a weekday, Ma'ariv begins on page 80. On Shabbat begin here:

מִזְמוֹר A psalm. A song for the Sabbath day. It is good to thank the LORD and sing psalms to Your name, Most High – to tell of Your loving-kindness in the morning and Your faithfulness at night, to the music of the ten-stringed lyre and the melody of the harp. For You have made me rejoice by Your work, O LORD; I sing for joy at the deeds of Your hands. How great are Your deeds, LORD, and how very deep Your thoughts. A boor cannot know, nor can a fool understand, that though the wicked spring up like grass and all evildoers flourish, it is only that they may be destroyed for ever. But You, LORD, are eternally exalted. For behold Your enemies, LORD, behold Your enemies will perish; all evildoers will be scattered. You have raised my pride like that of a wild ox; I am anointed with fresh oil. My eyes shall look in triumph on my adversaries, my ears shall hear the downfall of the wicked who rise against me. ▸ The righteous will flourish like a palm tree and grow tall like a cedar in Lebanon. Planted in the LORD's House, blossoming in our God's courtyards, they will still bear fruit in old age, and stay vigorous and fresh, proclaiming that the LORD is upright: He is my Rock, in whom there is no wrong. *Ps. 92*

יהוה מָלָךְ The LORD reigns. He is robed in majesty. The LORD is robed, girded with strength. The world is firmly established; it cannot be moved. Your throne stands firm as of old; You are eternal. Rivers lift up, LORD, rivers lift up their voice, rivers lift up their crashing waves. ▸ Mightier than the noise of many waters, than the mighty waves of the sea is the LORD on high. Your testimonies are very sure; holiness adorns Your House, LORD, for evermore. *Ps. 93*

---

will be seen that evil – though it seems to grow like grass – may win the battle but not the war. Evil is shortsighted and short lived. In the long run, tyrants are defeated and totalitarian regimes fall. Human dignity – the fact that we are all in God's image – cannot be forever denied. In the end, justice rules.

On a weekday, מעריב *begins on page 81. On* שבת *begin here:*

תהלים צב

מִזְמוֹר שִׁיר לְיוֹם הַשַּׁבָּת: טוֹב לְהֹדוֹת לַיהוה, וּלְזַמֵּר לְשִׁמְךָ עֶלְיוֹן: לְהַגִּיד בַּבֹּקֶר חַסְדֶּךָ, וֶאֱמוּנָתְךָ בַּלֵּילוֹת: עֲלֵי־עָשׂוֹר וַעֲלֵי־נָבֶל, עֲלֵי הִגָּיוֹן בְּכִנּוֹר: כִּי שִׂמַּחְתַּנִי יהוה בְּפָעֳלֶךָ, בְּמַעֲשֵׂי יָדֶיךָ אֲרַנֵּן: מַה־גָּדְלוּ מַעֲשֶׂיךָ יהוה, מְאֹד עָמְקוּ מַחְשְׁבֹתֶיךָ: אִישׁ־בַּעַר לֹא יֵדָע, וּכְסִיל לֹא־יָבִין אֶת־זֹאת: בִּפְרֹחַ רְשָׁעִים כְּמוֹ עֵשֶׂב, וַיָּצִיצוּ כָּל־פֹּעֲלֵי אָוֶן, לְהִשָּׁמְדָם עֲדֵי־עַד: וְאַתָּה מָרוֹם לְעֹלָם יהוה: כִּי הִנֵּה אֹיְבֶיךָ יהוה, כִּי־הִנֵּה אֹיְבֶיךָ יֹאבֵדוּ, יִתְפָּרְדוּ כָּל־פֹּעֲלֵי אָוֶן: וַתָּרֶם כִּרְאֵים קַרְנִי, בַּלֹּתִי בְּשֶׁמֶן רַעֲנָן: וַתַּבֵּט עֵינִי בְּשׁוּרָי, בַּקָּמִים עָלַי מְרֵעִים תִּשְׁמַעְנָה אָזְנָי: ‹ צַדִּיק כַּתָּמָר יִפְרָח, כְּאֶרֶז בַּלְּבָנוֹן יִשְׂגֶּה: שְׁתוּלִים בְּבֵית יהוה, בְּחַצְרוֹת אֱלֹהֵינוּ יַפְרִיחוּ: עוֹד יְנוּבוּן בְּשֵׂיבָה, דְּשֵׁנִים וְרַעֲנַנִּים יִהְיוּ: לְהַגִּיד כִּי־יָשָׁר יהוה, צוּרִי, וְלֹא־עַוְלָתָה בּוֹ:

תהלים צג

יהוה מָלָךְ, גֵּאוּת לָבֵשׁ, לָבֵשׁ יהוה עֹז הִתְאַזָּר, אַף־תִּכּוֹן תֵּבֵל בַּל־תִּמּוֹט: נָכוֹן כִּסְאֲךָ מֵאָז, מֵעוֹלָם אָתָּה: נָשְׂאוּ נְהָרוֹת יהוה, נָשְׂאוּ נְהָרוֹת קוֹלָם, יִשְׂאוּ נְהָרוֹת דָּכְיָם: ‹ מִקֹּלוֹת מַיִם רַבִּים, אַדִּירִים מִשְׁבְּרֵי־יָם, אַדִּיר בַּמָּרוֹם יהוה: עֵדֹתֶיךָ נֶאֶמְנוּ מְאֹד, לְבֵיתְךָ נַאֲוָה־קֹדֶשׁ, יהוה לְאֹרֶךְ יָמִים:

KABBALAT SHABBAT

On festivals, the full *Kabbalat Shabbat* service, with its first six psalms and *Lekha Dodi*, is not said. Only Psalms 92 and 93 are said since they relate directly to the day. *A psalm. A song for the Sabbath day* refers, according to the sages, to the Sabbath at the end of days, when the world will be at peace and there will be neither strife nor war. At that time, in the full perspective of history, it

MOURNER'S KADDISH

The following prayer requires the presence of a minyan.
A transliteration can be found on page 1375.

Mourner: יִתְגַּדַּל Magnified and sanctified
may His great name be,
in the world He created by His will.
May He establish His kingdom
in your lifetime and in your days,
and in the lifetime of all the house of Israel,
swiftly and soon – and say: Amen.

All: May His great name
be blessed for ever and all time.

Mourner: Blessed and praised,
glorified and exalted,
raised and honored,
uplifted and lauded
be the name of the Holy One,
blessed be He,
above and beyond any blessing, song,
praise and consolation
uttered in the world – and say: Amen.

May there be great peace from heaven,
and life for us and all Israel – and say: Amen.

Bow, take three steps back, as if taking leave of the Divine Presence, then bow, first left, then right, then center, while saying:

May He who makes peace in His high places,
make peace for us and all Israel – and say: Amen.

לְעֵלָּא לְעֵלָּא *Above and beyond.* The widespread Ashkenazi custom since the fifteenth century is to double the word לְעֵלָּא, "above," during the Ten Days of Repentance. At this time God's justice is beyond praise, and His compassion is above His justice.

קדיש יתום

The following prayer requires the presence of a מנין.
A transliteration can be found on page 1375.

אבל: יִתְגַּדַּל וְיִתְקַדַּשׁ שְׁמֵהּ רַבָּא (קהל: אָמֵן)
בְּעָלְמָא דִּי בְרָא כִרְעוּתֵהּ
וְיַמְלִיךְ מַלְכוּתֵהּ
בְּחַיֵּיכוֹן וּבְיוֹמֵיכוֹן וּבְחַיֵּי דְכָל בֵּית יִשְׂרָאֵל
בַּעֲגָלָא וּבִזְמַן קָרִיב
וְאִמְרוּ אָמֵן. (קהל: אָמֵן)

קהל ואבל: יְהֵא שְׁמֵהּ רַבָּא מְבָרַךְ לְעָלַם וּלְעָלְמֵי עָלְמַיָּא.

אבל: יִתְבָּרַךְ וְיִשְׁתַּבַּח וְיִתְפָּאַר וְיִתְרוֹמַם וְיִתְנַשֵּׂא
וְיִתְהַדָּר וְיִתְעַלֶּה וְיִתְהַלָּל
שְׁמֵהּ דְּקֻדְשָׁא בְּרִיךְ הוּא (קהל: בְּרִיךְ הוּא)
לְעֵלָּא לְעֵלָּא מִכָּל בִּרְכָתָא וְשִׁירָתָא, תֻּשְׁבְּחָתָא וְנֶחֱמָתָא
דַּאֲמִירָן בְּעָלְמָא
וְאִמְרוּ אָמֵן. (קהל: אָמֵן)

יְהֵא שְׁלָמָא רַבָּא מִן שְׁמַיָּא
וְחַיִּים, עָלֵינוּ וְעַל כָּל יִשְׂרָאֵל
וְאִמְרוּ אָמֵן. (קהל: אָמֵן)

Bow, take three steps back, as if taking leave of the Divine Presence, then bow, first left, then right, then center, while saying:

עֹשֶׂה הַשָּׁלוֹם בִּמְרוֹמָיו
הוּא יַעֲשֶׂה שָׁלוֹם עָלֵינוּ וְעַל כָּל יִשְׂרָאֵל
וְאִמְרוּ אָמֵן. (קהל: אָמֵן)

Ma'ariv for Yom Kippur

BLESSINGS OF THE SHEMA

The Leader says the following, bowing at "Bless," standing straight at "the Lord." The congregation, followed by the Leader, responds, bowing at "Bless," standing straight at "the Lord."

Leader: **BLESS**
the Lord, the blessed One.

Congregation: Bless the Lord, the blessed One,
for ever and all time.

Leader: Bless the Lord, the blessed One,
for ever and all time.

בָּרוּךְ Blessed are You, Lord our God, King of the Universe,
who by His word brings on evenings,
by His wisdom opens the gates of heaven,
with understanding makes time change and the seasons rotate,
and by His will orders the stars in their constellations in the sky.
He creates day and night,
rolling away the light before the darkness,
and darkness before the light.
▸ He makes the day pass and brings on night,
distinguishing day from night:
the Lord of hosts is His name.
May the living and forever enduring God rule over us for all time.
Blessed are You, Lord, who brings on evenings.

THE BLESSINGS OF THE SHEMA
Morning and evening, the Shema is surrounded by three blessings, two before, one afterward (plus a supplementary blessing in the evening, a prayer for safety). Together they articulate the three fundamental principles of Jewish

מעריב ליום הכיפורים

קריאת שמע וברכותיה

The שליח ציבור *says the following, bowing at* בָּרְכוּ, *standing straight at* ה׳.
The קהל, *followed by the* שליח ציבור, *responds, bowing at* בָּרוּךְ, *standing straight at* ה׳.

ש״ץ: 

אֶת יהוה הַמְבֹרָךְ.

קהל: בָּרוּךְ יהוה הַמְבֹרָךְ לְעוֹלָם וָעֶד.

ש״ץ: בָּרוּךְ יהוה הַמְבֹרָךְ לְעוֹלָם וָעֶד.

בָּרוּךְ אַתָּה יהוה אֱלֹהֵינוּ מֶלֶךְ הָעוֹלָם
אֲשֶׁר בִּדְבָרוֹ מַעֲרִיב עֲרָבִים
בְּחָכְמָה פּוֹתֵחַ שְׁעָרִים
וּבִתְבוּנָה מְשַׁנֶּה עִתִּים וּמַחֲלִיף אֶת הַזְּמַנִּים
וּמְסַדֵּר אֶת הַכּוֹכָבִים בְּמִשְׁמְרוֹתֵיהֶם בָּרָקִיעַ כִּרְצוֹנוֹ.
בּוֹרֵא יוֹם וָלָיְלָה
גּוֹלֵל אוֹר מִפְּנֵי חֹשֶׁךְ וְחֹשֶׁךְ מִפְּנֵי אוֹר
◂ וּמַעֲבִיר יוֹם וּמֵבִיא לָיְלָה, וּמַבְדִּיל בֵּין יוֹם וּבֵין לָיְלָה
יהוה צְבָאוֹת שְׁמוֹ.
אֵל חַי וְקַיָּם תָּמִיד, יִמְלֹךְ עָלֵינוּ לְעוֹלָם וָעֶד.
בָּרוּךְ אַתָּה יהוה, הַמַּעֲרִיב עֲרָבִים.

אַהֲבַת עוֹלָם With everlasting love
have You loved Your people, the house of Israel.
You have taught us Torah and commandments,
decrees and laws of justice.
Therefore, LORD our God, when we lie down and when we rise up
we will speak of Your decrees, rejoicing in the words of Your Torah
and Your commandments for ever.
▸ For they are our life and the length of our days;
on them will we meditate day and night.
May You never take away Your love from us.
Blessed are You, LORD, who loves His people Israel.

The Shema must be said with intense concentration. See laws 17–20.
When not with a מנין*, say:*

God, faithful King!

The following verse should be said aloud, while covering the eyes with the right hand:

Listen, Israel: the LORD is our God, the LORD is One. *Deut. 6*

Aloud: Blessed be the name of His glorious kingdom for ever and all time.

שְׁמַע יִשְׂרָאֵל, יהוה אֱלֹהֵינוּ, יהוה אֶחָד *Listen, Israel: the LORD is our God, the LORD is One.* This, the single most famous declaration of faith, has many dimensions of meaning. (1) There is ultimately only one creative force that brought the universe into being. Conflict is not written into the fabric of reality. At the heart of all is the One. (2) All life has a single source, an idea given new resonance since the discovery and decoding of DNA. Diversity on earth points to unity in heaven. (3) God alone is our ultimate sovereign and our sole object of worship. (4) The love of God and God's creations leads to unity, within and between ourselves.

בָּרוּךְ שֵׁם *Blessed be the name.* Yom Kippur is the only time we say this sentence aloud. Normally it is said silently because it is not part of the biblical text of the Shema (Deut. 6:4–9). Three reasons are given for saying it aloud tonight: one midrashic, another mystical, the third historical. The midrashic reason is

אַהֲבַת עוֹלָם בֵּית יִשְׂרָאֵל עַמְּךָ אָהָבְתָּ
תּוֹרָה וּמִצְוֹת, חֻקִּים וּמִשְׁפָּטִים, אוֹתָנוּ לִמַּדְתָּ
עַל כֵּן יהוה אֱלֹהֵינוּ בְּשָׁכְבֵנוּ וּבְקוּמֵנוּ נָשִׂיחַ בְּחֻקֶּיךָ
וְנִשְׂמַח בְּדִבְרֵי תוֹרָתֶךָ וּבְמִצְוֹתֶיךָ לְעוֹלָם וָעֶד
◂ כִּי הֵם חַיֵּינוּ וְאֹרֶךְ יָמֵינוּ, וּבָהֶם נֶהְגֶּה יוֹמָם וָלָיְלָה.
וְאַהֲבָתְךָ אַל תָּסִיר מִמֶּנּוּ לְעוֹלָמִים.
בָּרוּךְ אַתָּה יהוה, אוֹהֵב עַמּוֹ יִשְׂרָאֵל.

The שמע *must be said with intense concentration. See laws 17–20.*
When not with a מנין*, say:*

אֵל מֶלֶךְ נֶאֱמָן

The following verse should be said aloud, while covering the eyes with the right hand:

שְׁמַע יִשְׂרָאֵל, יהוה אֱלֹהֵינוּ, יהוה ׀ אֶחָד׃ דברים ו

Aloud בָּרוּךְ שֵׁם כְּבוֹד מַלְכוּתוֹ לְעוֹלָם וָעֶד.

---

faith: creation, revelation and redemption. Creation: God is the Author of the universe. Revelation: God has revealed Himself to us in the form of His word, the Torah, the text of our covenant with Him and the code of our existence as a holy nation. Redemption: God brought our ancestors from slavery to freedom, leading them out of Egypt, dividing the Reed Sea for them, protecting and sustaining them for forty years in the wilderness. These paragraphs are precisely directed to these three ways through which we come to know God: through the wonders of the natural universe, the teachings of the Torah, and the miracles of Jewish history.

אַהֲבַת עוֹלָם *With everlasting love.* Of all the ways in which God has made Himself known to us, the one that is central is revelation: God's word as recorded in Torah. The history of the Jewish mind is in effect the story of an extended love affair between a people and a book. Heinrich Heine called the Torah "the portable homeland of the Jew." Wherever Jews went they took Torah with them. Where Torah study was strong, Jewish life was strong. This paragraph expresses that love.

וְאָהַבְתָּ Love the LORD your God with all your heart, with all your soul, and with all your might. These words which I command you today shall be on your heart. Teach them repeatedly to your children, speaking of them when you sit at home and when you travel on the way, when you lie down and when you rise. Bind them as a sign on your hand, and they shall be an emblem between your eyes. Write them on the doorposts of your house and gates. *Deut. 6*

וְהָיָה If you indeed heed My commandments with which I charge you today, to love the LORD your God and worship Him with all your heart and with all your soul, I will give rain in your land in its season, the early and late rain; and you shall gather in your grain, wine and oil. I will give grass in your field for your cattle, and you shall eat and be satisfied. Be careful lest your heart be tempted and you go astray and worship other gods, bowing down to them. Then the LORD's *Deut. 11*

---

should be "on" your heart, not "in" your heart? Because the heart is not always open. Therefore the Torah commands us to lay these words "on" our heart so that when the heart opens, they are there, ready to enter."

וְשִׁנַּנְתָּם לְבָנֶיךָ *Teach them repeatedly to your children.* In Judaism, education as the conversation between the generations is a sacred task, the sole guarantor of Jewish continuity.

> Civilization hangs suspended, from generation to generation, by the gossamer strand of memory. If only one cohort of mothers and fathers fails to convey to its children what it has learned from its parents, then the great chain of learning and wisdom snaps. If the guardians of human knowledge stumble only one time, in their fall collapses the entire edifice of knowledge and understanding. (Jacob Neusner)

וְנָתַתִּי מְטַר־אַרְצְכֶם בְּעִתּוֹ *I will give rain in your land in its season.* At the end of his life, Moses told the next generation, who would enter the land, that they would find it "not like the land of Egypt, from which you have come, where you planted your seed and irrigated it by foot as in a vegetable garden. But the land you are crossing the Jordan to take possession of is a land of mountains and valleys that drinks rain from heaven" (Deut. 11:10–11). Unlike the Nile Valley and Delta, it did not have a constant, regular supply of water. In Egypt, the natural instinct is to look down for sustenance to the river. In Israel, dependent on rain, the natural instinct is to look up to heaven.

הִשָּׁמְרוּ לָכֶם פֶּן־יִפְתֶּה לְבַבְכֶם *Be careful lest your heart be tempted.* Throughout the book of Deuteronomy, from which this paragraph is taken, Moses warns the

דברים ו וְאָהַבְתָּ אֵת יהוה אֱלֹהֶיךָ, בְּכָל־לְבָבְךָ וּבְכָל־נַפְשְׁךָ וּבְכָל־מְאֹדֶךָ:
וְהָיוּ הַדְּבָרִים הָאֵלֶּה, אֲשֶׁר אָנֹכִי מְצַוְּךָ הַיּוֹם, עַל־לְבָבֶךָ: וְשִׁנַּנְתָּם
לְבָנֶיךָ וְדִבַּרְתָּ בָּם, בְּשִׁבְתְּךָ בְּבֵיתֶךָ וּבְלֶכְתְּךָ בַדֶּרֶךְ, וּבְשָׁכְבְּךָ
וּבְקוּמֶךָ: וּקְשַׁרְתָּם לְאוֹת עַל־יָדֶךָ וְהָיוּ לְטֹטָפֹת בֵּין עֵינֶיךָ:
וּכְתַבְתָּם עַל־מְזֻזוֹת בֵּיתֶךָ וּבִשְׁעָרֶיךָ:

דברים יא וְהָיָה אִם־שָׁמֹעַ תִּשְׁמְעוּ אֶל־מִצְוֹתַי אֲשֶׁר אָנֹכִי מְצַוֶּה אֶתְכֶם
הַיּוֹם, לְאַהֲבָה אֶת־יהוה אֱלֹהֵיכֶם וּלְעָבְדוֹ, בְּכָל־לְבַבְכֶם וּבְכָל־
נַפְשְׁכֶם: וְנָתַתִּי מְטַר־אַרְצְכֶם בְּעִתּוֹ, יוֹרֶה וּמַלְקוֹשׁ, וְאָסַפְתָּ דְגָנֶךָ
וְתִירֹשְׁךָ וְיִצְהָרֶךָ: וְנָתַתִּי עֵשֶׂב בְּשָׂדְךָ לִבְהֶמְתֶּךָ, וְאָכַלְתָּ וְשָׂבָעְתָּ:
הִשָּׁמְרוּ לָכֶם פֶּן־יִפְתֶּה לְבַבְכֶם, וְסַרְתֶּם וַעֲבַדְתֶּם אֱלֹהִים אֲחֵרִים

---

that, on his deathbed, Jacob worried that one or other of his children might have doubts about their faith. They reassured him: "Listen, Israel [Jacob's other name], the Lord is our God, the Lord alone." In thanks Jacob replied, "Blessed be the name" (*Pesaḥim* 56a). Tonight the synagogue is full of Jacob's children, and like him we give thanks.

The mystical reason is that according to the sages, Moses heard the angels saying these words when he went to heaven to receive the Torah, but he was not commanded to make them part of the Torah, so he taught future generations to say them silently (*Devarim Raba* 2:36). Today however, having foresworn food and drink and other pleasures, we are like the angels, and like them we can say the words aloud.

The historical reason is that this was the congregational response said in the Temple instead of the word Amen. Throughout the year we say it silently as a reminder of the Temple. On Yom Kippur, when we collectively re-create the service of the High Priest in ancient times, it is as if we *were* in the Temple. Therefore we say it aloud as those present at the Temple service said it aloud.

Rabbi Joseph Soloveitchik added a fourth reason: On Yom Kippur the reading of the Shema is a *davar shebikedusha,* a holy act requiring a *minyan* since, when the Temple stood, the High Priest said the first line using the most sacred name of God. A *davar shebikedusha* always involves a public invitation by the Leader and a public response by the congregation.

וְהָיוּ הַדְּבָרִים הָאֵלֶּה...עַל־לְבָבֶךָ *These words… shall be on your heart.* Said Rabbi Menaḥem Mendel of Kotzk: "Why does the Torah say that these words

anger will flare against you and He will close the heavens so that there will be no rain. The land will not yield its crops, and you will perish swiftly from the good land that the LORD is giving you. Therefore, set these, My words, on your heart and soul. Bind them as a sign on your hand, and they shall be an emblem between your eyes. Teach them to your children, speaking of them when you sit at home and when you travel on the way, when you lie down and when you rise. Write them on the doorposts of your house and gates, so that you and your children may live long in the land that the LORD swore to your ancestors to give them, for as long as the heavens are above the earth.

וַיֹּאמֶר The LORD spoke to Moses, saying: Speak to the Israelites and tell them to make tassels on the corners of their garments for all generations. They shall attach to the tassel at each corner a thread of blue. This shall be your tassel, and you shall see it and remember all of the LORD's commandments and keep them, not straying after your heart and after your eyes, following your own sinful desires. Thus you will be reminded to keep all My commandments, and be holy to your God. I am the LORD your God, who brought you out of the land of Egypt to be your God. I am the LORD your God. *Num. 15*

True –

The Leader repeats:

▸ The LORD your God is true –

צִיצִת *Tassels.* The command of tzitzit appears in the Torah after the episode of the spies (Num. 13–14). The connection between the two has to do with seeing. The spies saw, but fear distorted what they saw, so they concluded that the land was unconquerable, its cities invincible, its population giants. The tzitzit, whose blue thread is a reminder of heaven, were intended to ensure that we should not "stray after your heart and after your eyes." Faith allows us to see what is really there, not what we fear.

אֱמֶת *True.* The Hebrew word *Emet* means more than "truth" in the conventional Western sense of fact as opposed to falsehood. *Emet* also means

וְהִשְׁתַּחֲוִיתֶם לָהֶם: וְחָרָה אַף־יהוה בָּכֶם, וְעָצַר אֶת־הַשָּׁמַיִם
וְלֹא־יִהְיֶה מָטָר, וְהָאֲדָמָה לֹא תִתֵּן אֶת־יְבוּלָהּ, וַאֲבַדְתֶּם מְהֵרָה
מֵעַל הָאָרֶץ הַטֹּבָה אֲשֶׁר יהוה נֹתֵן לָכֶם: וְשַׂמְתֶּם אֶת־דְּבָרַי
אֵלֶּה עַל־לְבַבְכֶם וְעַל־נַפְשְׁכֶם, וּקְשַׁרְתֶּם אֹתָם לְאוֹת עַל־יֶדְכֶם,
וְהָיוּ לְטוֹטָפֹת בֵּין עֵינֵיכֶם: וְלִמַּדְתֶּם אֹתָם אֶת־בְּנֵיכֶם לְדַבֵּר בָּם,
בְּשִׁבְתְּךָ בְּבֵיתֶךָ, וּבְלֶכְתְּךָ בַדֶּרֶךְ, וּבְשָׁכְבְּךָ וּבְקוּמֶךָ: וּכְתַבְתָּם
עַל־מְזוּזוֹת בֵּיתֶךָ וּבִשְׁעָרֶיךָ: לְמַעַן יִרְבּוּ יְמֵיכֶם וִימֵי בְנֵיכֶם עַל
הָאֲדָמָה אֲשֶׁר נִשְׁבַּע יהוה לַאֲבֹתֵיכֶם לָתֵת לָהֶם, כִּימֵי הַשָּׁמַיִם
עַל־הָאָרֶץ:

וַיֹּאמֶר יהוה אֶל־מֹשֶׁה לֵּאמֹר: דַּבֵּר אֶל־בְּנֵי יִשְׂרָאֵל וְאָמַרְתָּ במדבר טו
אֲלֵהֶם, וְעָשׂוּ לָהֶם צִיצִת עַל־כַּנְפֵי בִגְדֵיהֶם לְדֹרֹתָם, וְנָתְנוּ עַל־
צִיצִת הַכָּנָף פְּתִיל תְּכֵלֶת: וְהָיָה לָכֶם לְצִיצִת, וּרְאִיתֶם אֹתוֹ,
וּזְכַרְתֶּם אֶת־כָּל־מִצְוֹת יהוה וַעֲשִׂיתֶם אֹתָם, וְלֹא תָתוּרוּ אַחֲרֵי
לְבַבְכֶם וְאַחֲרֵי עֵינֵיכֶם, אֲשֶׁר־אַתֶּם זֹנִים אַחֲרֵיהֶם: לְמַעַן תִּזְכְּרוּ
וַעֲשִׂיתֶם אֶת־כָּל־מִצְוֹתָי, וִהְיִיתֶם קְדֹשִׁים לֵאלֹהֵיכֶם: אֲנִי יהוה
אֱלֹהֵיכֶם, אֲשֶׁר הוֹצֵאתִי אֶתְכֶם מֵאֶרֶץ מִצְרַיִם, לִהְיוֹת לָכֶם
לֵאלֹהִים, אֲנִי יהוה אֱלֹהֵיכֶם:

אֱמֶת

The שליח ציבור *repeats:*

› יהוה אֱלֹהֵיכֶם אֱמֶת

---

people that their greatest trial was not the wilderness years when they wandered without a home. It would be when they entered the land and became prosperous. The greatest challenge to faith is not poverty but affluence. It is then we are in danger of becoming complacent, forgetting why we are here.

וֶאֱמוּנָה – and faithful is all this,
and firmly established for us
that He is the LORD our God,
and there is none besides Him,
and that we, Israel, are His people.
He is our King, who redeems us
from the hand of kings
and delivers us from the grasp of all tyrants.
He is our God, who on our behalf repays our foes
and brings just retribution on our mortal enemies;
who performs great deeds beyond understanding
and wonders beyond number;
who kept us alive, not letting our foot slip;
who led us on the high places of our enemies,
raising our pride above all our foes;
who did miracles for us
and brought vengeance against Pharaoh;
who performed signs and wonders
in the land of Ham's children;

who smote in His wrath all the firstborn of Egypt,
and brought out His people Israel from their midst
into everlasting freedom;
who led His children through the divided Reed Sea,
plunging their pursuers and enemies
into the depths.
When His children saw His might,
they gave praise and thanks to His name,
▸ and willingly accepted His Sovereignty.
Moses and the children of Israel
then sang a song to You with great joy, and they all exclaimed:

---

future redemption on the basis of the history of the past when He brought us out of Egypt as He said He would. God honors His word. His truth is the basis of our hope.

וֶאֱמוּנָה כָּל זֹאת וְקַיָּם עָלֵינוּ
כִּי הוּא יהוה אֱלֹהֵינוּ וְאֵין זוּלָתוֹ
וַאֲנַחְנוּ יִשְׂרָאֵל עַמּוֹ.
הַפּוֹדֵנוּ מִיַּד מְלָכִים
מַלְכֵּנוּ הַגּוֹאֲלֵנוּ מִכַּף כָּל הֶעָרִיצִים.
הָאֵל הַנִּפְרָע לָנוּ מִצָּרֵינוּ
וְהַמְשַׁלֵּם גְּמוּל לְכָל אוֹיְבֵי נַפְשֵׁנוּ.
הָעוֹשֶׂה גְדוֹלוֹת עַד אֵין חֵקֶר, וְנִפְלָאוֹת עַד אֵין מִסְפָּר
הַשָּׂם נַפְשֵׁנוּ בַּחַיִּים, וְלֹא נָתַן לַמּוֹט רַגְלֵנוּ
הַמַּדְרִיכֵנוּ עַל בָּמוֹת אוֹיְבֵינוּ
וַיָּרֶם קַרְנֵנוּ עַל כָּל שׂוֹנְאֵינוּ.
הָעוֹשֶׂה לָּנוּ נִסִּים וּנְקָמָה בְּפַרְעֹה
אוֹתוֹת וּמוֹפְתִים בְּאַדְמַת בְּנֵי חָם.

הַמַּכֶּה בְעֶבְרָתוֹ כָּל בְּכוֹרֵי מִצְרָיִם
וַיּוֹצֵא אֶת עַמּוֹ יִשְׂרָאֵל מִתּוֹכָם לְחֵרוּת עוֹלָם.
הַמַּעֲבִיר בָּנָיו בֵּין גִּזְרֵי יַם סוּף
אֶת רוֹדְפֵיהֶם וְאֶת שׂוֹנְאֵיהֶם בִּתְהוֹמוֹת טִבַּע
וְרָאוּ בָנָיו גְּבוּרָתוֹ, שִׁבְּחוּ וְהוֹדוּ לִשְׁמוֹ
◂ וּמַלְכוּתוֹ בְּרָצוֹן קִבְּלוּ עֲלֵיהֶם.
מֹשֶׁה וּבְנֵי יִשְׂרָאֵל, לְךָ עָנוּ שִׁירָה בְּשִׂמְחָה רַבָּה
וְאָמְרוּ כֻלָּם

"being truthful," keeping your word, honoring your commitments. Hence the importance here of connecting past redemption to future deliverance. As the Shema segues into the blessing of redemption, we base our faith in God's

"Who is like You, LORD, among the mighty? *Ex. 15*
Who is like You, majestic in holiness,
awesome in praises, doing wonders?"

▸ Your children beheld Your majesty
as You parted the sea before Moses.
"This is my God!" they responded, and then said:

"The LORD shall reign for ever and ever." *Ibid.*

▸ And it is said,
"For the LORD has redeemed Jacob *Jer. 31*
and rescued him
from a power stronger than his own."
Blessed are You, LORD
who redeemed Israel.

הַשְׁכִּיבֵנוּ Help us lie down,
O LORD our God, in peace,
and rise up, O our King, to life.
Spread over us Your canopy of peace.
Direct us with Your good counsel,
and save us for the sake of Your name.
Shield us and remove from us every enemy,
plague, sword, famine and sorrow.
Remove the adversary from before and behind us.
Shelter us in the shadow of Your wings,
for You, God, are our Guardian and Deliverer;
You, God, are a gracious and compassionate King.
▸ Guard our going out and our coming in,
for life and peace, from now and for ever.
Spread over us Your canopy of peace.
Blessed are You, LORD,
who spreads a canopy of peace over us,
over all His people Israel, and over Jerusalem.

מִי־כָמֹכָה בָּאֵלִם יהוה שמות טו
מִי כָּמֹכָה נֶאְדָּר בַּקֹּדֶשׁ
נוֹרָא תְהִלֹּת עֹשֵׂה פֶלֶא:

› מַלְכוּתְךָ רָאוּ בָנֶיךָ, בּוֹקֵעַ יָם לִפְנֵי מֹשֶׁה
זֶה אֵלִי עָנוּ, וְאָמְרוּ
יהוה יִמְלֹךְ לְעֹלָם וָעֶד: שם

› וְנֶאֱמַר
כִּי־פָדָה יהוה אֶת־יַעֲקֹב ירמיה לא
וּגְאָלוֹ מִיַּד חָזָק מִמֶּנּוּ:
בָּרוּךְ אַתָּה יהוה, גָּאַל יִשְׂרָאֵל.

הַשְׁכִּיבֵנוּ יהוה אֱלֹהֵינוּ לְשָׁלוֹם
וְהַעֲמִידֵנוּ מַלְכֵּנוּ לְחַיִּים
וּפְרֹשׂ עָלֵינוּ סֻכַּת שְׁלוֹמֶךָ, וְתַקְּנֵנוּ בְּעֵצָה טוֹבָה מִלְּפָנֶיךָ
וְהוֹשִׁיעֵנוּ לְמַעַן שְׁמֶךָ.
וְהָגֵן בַּעֲדֵנוּ
וְהָסֵר מֵעָלֵינוּ אוֹיֵב, דֶּבֶר וְחֶרֶב וְרָעָב וְיָגוֹן
וְהָסֵר שָׂטָן מִלְּפָנֵינוּ וּמֵאַחֲרֵינוּ, וּבְצֵל כְּנָפֶיךָ תַּסְתִּירֵנוּ
כִּי אֵל שׁוֹמְרֵנוּ וּמַצִּילֵנוּ אָתָּה
כִּי אֵל מֶלֶךְ חַנּוּן וְרַחוּם אָתָּה.
› וּשְׁמֹר צֵאתֵנוּ וּבוֹאֵנוּ לְחַיִּים וּלְשָׁלוֹם מֵעַתָּה וְעַד עוֹלָם.
וּפְרֹשׂ עָלֵינוּ סֻכַּת שְׁלוֹמֶךָ.
בָּרוּךְ אַתָּה יהוה
הַפּוֹרֵשׂ סֻכַּת שָׁלוֹם עָלֵינוּ וְעַל כָּל עַמּוֹ יִשְׂרָאֵל וְעַל יְרוּשָׁלָיִם.

The congregation stands.

On Shabbat, the congregation, together with the Leader, adds:

וְשָׁמְרוּ The children of Israel must keep the Sabbath, *Ex. 31*
observing the Sabbath in every generation
as an everlasting covenant.
It is a sign between Me and the children of Israel for ever,
for in six days the LORD made the heavens and the earth,
but on the seventh day He ceased work and refreshed Himself.

The congregation, then the Leader:

כִּי־בַיּוֹם For on this day you will be atoned and made pure; *Lev. 16*
of all your sins before the LORD you shall be purified.

HALF KADDISH

Leader: יִתְגַּדַּל Magnified and sanctified may His great name be,
in the world He created by His will.
May He establish His kingdom
in your lifetime and in your days,
and in the lifetime of all the house of Israel,
swiftly and soon –
and say: Amen.

All: May His great name be blessed for ever and all time.

Leader: Blessed and praised,
glorified and exalted,
raised and honored,
uplifted and lauded
be the name of the Holy One, blessed be He,
above and beyond any blessing, song,
praise and consolation
uttered in the world –
and say: Amen.

The קהל *stands.*

On שבת*, the* קהל*, together with the* שליח ציבור*, adds:*

וְשָׁמְרוּ בְנֵי־יִשְׂרָאֵל אֶת־הַשַּׁבָּת שמות לא
לַעֲשׂוֹת אֶת־הַשַּׁבָּת לְדֹרֹתָם בְּרִית עוֹלָם:
בֵּינִי וּבֵין בְּנֵי יִשְׂרָאֵל, אוֹת הִוא לְעֹלָם
כִּי־שֵׁשֶׁת יָמִים עָשָׂה יהוה אֶת־הַשָּׁמַיִם וְאֶת־הָאָרֶץ
וּבַיּוֹם הַשְּׁבִיעִי שָׁבַת וַיִּנָּפַשׁ:

The קהל*, then the* שליח ציבור*:*

כִּי־בַיּוֹם הַזֶּה יְכַפֵּר עֲלֵיכֶם לְטַהֵר אֶתְכֶם ויקרא טז
מִכֹּל חַטֹּאתֵיכֶם, לִפְנֵי יהוה תִּטְהָרוּ:

חצי קדיש

ש״ץ: יִתְגַּדַּל וְיִתְקַדַּשׁ שְׁמֵהּ רַבָּא (קהל: אָמֵן)
בְּעָלְמָא דִּי בְרָא כִרְעוּתֵהּ
וְיַמְלִיךְ מַלְכוּתֵהּ
בְּחַיֵּיכוֹן וּבְיוֹמֵיכוֹן וּבְחַיֵּי דְכָל בֵּית יִשְׂרָאֵל
בַּעֲגָלָא וּבִזְמַן קָרִיב, וְאִמְרוּ אָמֵן. (קהל: אָמֵן)

קהל וש״ץ: יְהֵא שְׁמֵהּ רַבָּא מְבָרַךְ לְעָלַם וּלְעָלְמֵי עָלְמַיָּא.

ש״ץ: יִתְבָּרַךְ וְיִשְׁתַּבַּח וְיִתְפָּאַר וְיִתְרוֹמַם וְיִתְנַשֵּׂא
וְיִתְהַדָּר וְיִתְעַלֶּה וְיִתְהַלָּל
שְׁמֵהּ דְּקֻדְשָׁא בְּרִיךְ הוּא (קהל: בְּרִיךְ הוּא)
לְעֵלָּא לְעֵלָּא מִכָּל בִּרְכָתָא וְשִׁירָתָא, תֻּשְׁבְּחָתָא וְנֶחֱמָתָא
דַּאֲמִירָן בְּעָלְמָא, וְאִמְרוּ אָמֵן. (קהל: אָמֵן)

THE AMIDA

The following prayer, until "in former years" on page 118, is said silently, standing with feet together. Take three steps forward and at the points indicated by ▾, bend the knees at the first word, bow at the second, and stand straight before saying God's name.

O Lord, open my lips, Ps. 51
so that my mouth may declare Your praise.

PATRIARCHS

▾בָּרוּךְ▾ Blessed are You, Lord our God and God of our fathers,
God of Abraham, God of Isaac and God of Jacob;
the great, mighty and awesome God, God Most High,
who bestows acts of loving-kindness and creates all,
who remembers the loving-kindness of the fathers
and will bring a Redeemer to their children's children
for the sake of His name, in love.

זָכְרֵנוּ לְחַיִּים Remember us for life, O King who desires life,
and write us in the book of life –
for Your sake, O God of life.
King, Helper, Savior, Shield:
▾Blessed are You, Lord, Shield of Abraham.

DIVINE MIGHT

אַתָּה גִּבּוֹר You are eternally mighty, Lord.
You give life to the dead and have great power to save.

In Israel: He causes the dew to fall.

He sustains the living with loving-kindness,
and with great compassion revives the dead.
He supports the fallen, heals the sick, sets captives free,
and keeps His faith with those who sleep in the dust.

Supreme King of kings. Tongue-tied, we ask God to open our lips. We stand, head bowed in the face of majesty. We explain by what right we claim the attention of the King: we are the children of Abraham, Isaac and Jacob, the first to heed God's call and make His name known in the world. Next, in the second paragraph, we explain why we have come before Him: because He is no earthly king, merely exercising power. He is the Giver of life itself.

עמידה

The following prayer, until קַדְמֹנִיּוֹת *on page 119, is said silently, standing with feet together. Take three steps forward and at the points indicated by* ˺*, bend the knees at the first word, bow at the second, and stand straight before saying God's name.*

תהלים נא

אֲדֹנָי, שְׂפָתַי תִּפְתָּח, וּפִי יַגִּיד תְּהִלָּתֶךָ:

אבות

˺בָּרוּךְ ˺אַתָּה יהוה, אֱלֹהֵינוּ וֵאלֹהֵי אֲבוֹתֵינוּ
אֱלֹהֵי אַבְרָהָם, אֱלֹהֵי יִצְחָק, וֵאלֹהֵי יַעֲקֹב
הָאֵל הַגָּדוֹל הַגִּבּוֹר וְהַנּוֹרָא, אֵל עֶלְיוֹן
גּוֹמֵל חֲסָדִים טוֹבִים, וְקוֹנֵה הַכֹּל
וְזוֹכֵר חַסְדֵי אָבוֹת
וּמֵבִיא גוֹאֵל לִבְנֵי בְנֵיהֶם לְמַעַן שְׁמוֹ בְּאַהֲבָה.

זָכְרֵנוּ לְחַיִּים, מֶלֶךְ חָפֵץ בַּחַיִּים
וְכָתְבֵנוּ בְּסֵפֶר הַחַיִּים, לְמַעַנְךָ אֱלֹהִים חַיִּים.

מֶלֶךְ עוֹזֵר וּמוֹשִׁיעַ וּמָגֵן.
˺בָּרוּךְ ˺אַתָּה יהוה, מָגֵן אַבְרָהָם.

גבורות

אַתָּה גִּבּוֹר לְעוֹלָם, אֲדֹנָי
מְחַיֵּה מֵתִים אַתָּה, רַב לְהוֹשִׁיעַ

בארץ ישראל: מוֹרִיד הַטָּל

מְכַלְכֵּל חַיִּים בְּחֶסֶד, מְחַיֵּה מֵתִים בְּרַחֲמִים רַבִּים
סוֹמֵךְ נוֹפְלִים, וְרוֹפֵא חוֹלִים, וּמַתִּיר אֲסוּרִים
וּמְקַיֵּם אֱמוּנָתוֹ לִישֵׁנֵי עָפָר.

THE AMIDA

The Amida, the "Standing Prayer," is the prayer par excellence. We take three steps forward and bow, for we are entering the presence of a king, the

Who is like You, Master of might,
and to whom can You be compared,
O King who brings death and gives life,
and makes salvation grow?

מִי כָמְוֹךָ Who is like You, compassionate Father,
who remembers His creatures in compassion, for life?
Faithful are You to revive the dead.
Blessed are You, Lord, who revives the dead.

HOLINESS

אַתָּה קָדוֹשׁ You are holy and Your name is holy,
and holy ones praise You daily, Selah!

וּבְכֵן תֵּן פַּחְדְּךָ And so place the fear of You, Lord our God,
over all that You have made,
and the terror of You over all You have created,
and all who were made will stand in awe of You,
and all of creation will worship You,
and they will be bound all together as one
to carry out Your will with an undivided heart;
for we know, Lord our God,
that all dominion is laid out before You,
strength is in Your palm,
and might in Your right hand,
Your name spreading awe over all You have created.

---

trepidation that leads people to sin. Hubris leads to nemesis. When humans aspire to be more than human they become less than human. Evil happens when people see themselves as the measure of all things.

פַּחְדְּךָ, וְאֵימָתְךָ, וְיִרְאָתְךָ *Fear, terror, awe.* A progression from inarticulate fear to reflective awe in the presence of the Infinite.

וְיֵעָשׂוּ כֻלָּם אֲגֻדָּה אֶחָת *And they will be bound all together as one.* The ultimate hope of the prophets, that by recognizing that "we have one Father" in heaven (see Malachi 2:10) we will become one family on earth.

מִי כָמְוֹךָ, בַּעַל גְּבוּרוֹת, וּמִי דְּוֹמֶה לָּךְ
מֶלֶךְ, מֵמִית וּמְחַיֶּה וּמַצְמִיחַ יְשׁוּעָה.

מִי כָמְוֹךָ אַב הָרַחֲמִים
זוֹכֵר יְצוּרָיו לְחַיִּים בְּרַחֲמִים.
וְנֶאֱמָן אַתָּה לְהַחֲיוֹת מֵתִים.
בָּרוּךְ אַתָּה יהוה, מְחַיֵּה הַמֵּתִים.

קדושת השם

אַתָּה קָדוֹשׁ וְשִׁמְךָ קָדוֹשׁ
וּקְדוֹשִׁים בְּכָל יוֹם יְהַלְלְוּךָ סֶּלָה.

וּבְכֵן תֵּן פַּחְדְּךָ יהוה אֱלֹהֵינוּ עַל כָּל מַעֲשֶׂיךָ
וְאֵימָתְךָ עַל כָּל מַה שֶּׁבָּרָאתָ
וְיִירָאְוּךָ כָּל הַמַּעֲשִׂים, וְיִשְׁתַּחֲווּ לְפָנֶיךָ כָּל הַבְּרוּאִים
וְיֵעָשׂוּ כֻלָּם אֲגֻדָּה אַחַת לַעֲשׂוֹת רְצוֹנְךָ בְּלֵבָב שָׁלֵם
כְּמוֹ שֶׁיָּדַעְנוּ יהוה אֱלֹהֵינוּ שֶׁהַשָּׁלְטָן לְפָנֶיךָ
עֹז בְּיָדְךָ וּגְבוּרָה בִּימִינֶךָ
וְשִׁמְךָ נוֹרָא עַל כָּל מַה שֶּׁבָּרָאתָ.

וּבְכֵן תֵּן פַּחְדְּךָ *And so place the fear of You.* A three-paragraph insertion into the Amida specifically on Rosh HaShana and Yom Kippur. It begins with a note of universality not found in the prayers of Pesaḥ, Shavuot and Sukkot, which emphasize Jewish differentness. The latter are festivals of history, and Jewish history is unique. Rosh HaShana and Yom Kippur are about the human condition as such under the sovereignty of God, Creator and Judge of the universe and all humanity. So we speak of "all Your works" and "all You have created" before we turn to the specific fate and destiny of the Jewish people.

We begin by asking God to inspire us all in awe and fear, for it is lack of

וּבְכֵן תֵּן כָּבוֹד And so place honor, Lord, upon Your people,
praise on those who fear You and hope into those who seek You,
the confidence to speak into all who long for You,
gladness to Your land and joy to Your city,
the flourishing of pride to David Your servant,
and a lamp laid out for his descendant, Your anointed, soon, in our days.

וּבְכֵן צַדִּיקִים And then righteous people will see and rejoice,
and the upright will exult, and the pious revel in joy,
and injustice will have nothing more to say,
and all wickedness will fade away like smoke
as You sweep the rule of arrogance from the earth.

וְתִמְלֹךְ אַתָּה And You, Lord, will rule alone over those You have made,
in Mount Zion, the dwelling of Your glory,
and in Jerusalem, Your holy city, as it is written in Your holy Writings:
"The Lord shall reign for ever. *Ps. 146*
He is your God, Zion, from generation to generation, Halleluya!"

קָדוֹשׁ אַתָּה You are holy, Your name is awesome,
and there is no god but You, as it is written,
"The Lord of hosts shall be raised up through His judgment, *Is. 5*
the holy God, made holy in righteousness."
Blessed are You, Lord, the holy King.

---

people, to the righteous and pious. Unlike Greek thought, the Jewish mind moves from the universal to the particular.

וְכָל הָרִשְׁעָה כֻּלָּהּ כְּעָשָׁן תִּכְלֶה *And all wickedness will fade away like smoke.* Wickedness rather than the wicked: we pray for the disappearance of the sin not the sinner (*Berakhot* 10a).

נִקְדָּשׁ בִּצְדָקָה *Made holy in righteousness.* This phrase, from Isaiah 5:16, is a rare juxtaposition of two concepts from different spheres of thought. "Holy" is a religious idea meaning, "set apart." "Righteousness" is an ethical idea meaning, giving everything its due. By joining these two words, Isaiah summarizes the essential prophetic message that religious faith is inseparable from ethical conduct, and that we learn this from God Himself.

הַמֶּלֶךְ הַקָּדוֹשׁ *The holy King.* A phrase specific to the Ten Days of Repentance, when we focus not simply on God as the force that sustains the universe, but on *Melekh*: God as the supreme Sovereign who is now sitting in judgment on our lives.

וּבְכֵן תֵּן כָּבוֹד יהוה לְעַמֶּךָ
תְּהִלָּה לִירֵאֶיךָ, וְתִקְוָה טוֹבָה לְדוֹרְשֶׁיךָ
וּפִתְחוֹן פֶּה לַמְיַחֲלִים לָךְ
שִׂמְחָה לְאַרְצֶךָ, וְשָׂשׂוֹן לְעִירֶךָ
וּצְמִיחַת קֶרֶן לְדָוִד עַבְדֶּךָ
וַעֲרִיכַת נֵר לְבֶן יִשַׁי מְשִׁיחֶךָ
בִּמְהֵרָה בְיָמֵינוּ.

וּבְכֵן צַדִּיקִים יִרְאוּ וְיִשְׂמָחוּ, וִישָׁרִים יַעֲלֹזוּ
וַחֲסִידִים בְּרִנָּה יָגִילוּ, וְעוֹלָתָה תִּקְפָּץ פִּיהָ
וְכָל הָרִשְׁעָה כֻּלָּהּ כְּעָשָׁן תִּכְלֶה
כִּי תַעֲבִיר מֶמְשֶׁלֶת זָדוֹן מִן הָאָרֶץ.

וְתִמְלֹךְ אַתָּה יהוה לְבַדֶּךָ עַל כָּל מַעֲשֶׂיךָ
בְּהַר צִיּוֹן מִשְׁכַּן כְּבוֹדֶךָ, וּבִירוּשָׁלַיִם עִיר קָדְשֶׁךָ
כַּכָּתוּב בְּדִבְרֵי קָדְשֶׁךָ
תהלים קמו יִמְלֹךְ יהוה לְעוֹלָם, אֱלֹהַיִךְ צִיּוֹן לְדֹר וָדֹר, הַלְלוּיָהּ:
קָדוֹשׁ אַתָּה וְנוֹרָא שְׁמֶךָ, וְאֵין אֱלוֹהַּ מִבַּלְעָדֶיךָ
ישעיה ה כַּכָּתוּב, וַיִּגְבַּהּ יהוה צְבָאוֹת בַּמִּשְׁפָּט
וְהָאֵל הַקָּדוֹשׁ נִקְדַּשׁ בִּצְדָקָה:
בָּרוּךְ אַתָּה יהוה, הַמֶּלֶךְ הַקָּדוֹשׁ.

כָּבוֹד...לְעַמֶּךָ *Honor… upon Your people.* Honor *because* they are Your people. We seek no honor other than to serve as Your witnesses, Your covenant-partners, Your ambassadors.

וַעֲרִיכַת נֵר לְבֶן יִשַׁי *A lamp laid out for his descendant.* This means the Messiah, who will be a light to his people (see Psalms 132:17).

צַדִּיקִים, וִישָׁרִים, וַחֲסִידִים *Righteous, upright, pious.* Righteous in what they do, upright in what they are, pious in going beyond the requirements of the law. Note the progression in these three paragraphs: from all humanity, to Your

HOLINESS OF THE DAY

אַתָּה בְחַרְתָּנוּ You have chosen us
from among all peoples.
You have loved and favored us.
You have raised us above all tongues.
You have made us holy
through Your commandments.
You have brought us near, our King,
to Your service,
and have called us by Your great and holy name.

On Shabbat, add the words in parentheses:

וַתִּתֶּן לָנוּ And You, Lord our God, have given us in love
(this Sabbath day for holiness and rest, and)
this Day of Atonement
for pardon and forgiveness and atonement,
to pardon all our iniquities,
(with love,) a holy assembly
in memory of the exodus from Egypt.

---

atonements of the High Priest on this day (for himself and his family, his fellow priests, and the nation as a whole), as well as the two dimensions of the day itself, atoning as it does for individuals as individuals, and for the community as a collective entity (see Maimonides, Laws of Repentance, 2:7).

לִמְחִילָה וְלִסְלִיחָה וּלְכַפָּרָה *For pardon and forgiveness and atonement.* These are three different acts. Pardon, *meḥila*, means that though wrong has been done, punishment is withheld. It is a judicial act of clemency. Forgiveness, *seliḥa*, means that the injured party feels no ill will. It belongs to the domain of I–Thou relationship. A judge may pardon but a judge cannot forgive: only the offended party can do so. Atonement, *kapara*, means that the offense is stricken from the record. It is "covered over, erased," the root meaning of *k-p-r*. We pray for God to pardon in His role as Judge, forgive in His role as Father, and atone by allowing us to begin again, freed from the burden of an unredeemed past.

קדושת היום

אַתָּה בְחַרְתָּנוּ מִכָּל הָעַמִּים
אָהַבְתָּ אוֹתָנוּ וְרָצִיתָ בָּנוּ
וְרוֹמַמְתָּנוּ מִכָּל הַלְּשׁוֹנוֹת
וְקִדַּשְׁתָּנוּ בְּמִצְוֹתֶיךָ
וְקֵרַבְתָּנוּ מַלְכֵּנוּ לַעֲבוֹדָתֶךָ
וְשִׁמְךָ הַגָּדוֹל וְהַקָּדוֹשׁ עָלֵינוּ קָרָאתָ.

On שבת*, add the words in parentheses:*

וַתִּתֶּן לָנוּ יהוה אֱלֹהֵינוּ בְּאַהֲבָה אֶת
(יוֹם הַשַּׁבָּת הַזֶּה לִקְדֻשָּׁה וְלִמְנוּחָה, וְאֶת)
יוֹם הַכִּפּוּרִים הַזֶּה, לִמְחִילָה וְלִסְלִיחָה וּלְכַפָּרָה
וְלִמְחָל בּוֹ אֶת כָּל עֲוֹנוֹתֵינוּ
(בְּאַהֲבָה) מִקְרָא קֹדֶשׁ
זֵכֶר לִיצִיאַת מִצְרָיִם.

אַתָּה בְחַרְתָּנוּ *You have chosen us.* This is the beginning of the central blessing of the Amida, dedicated to the specific sanctity of the day. Note the definition here and throughout Judaism of what it is to be a chosen people. It means to live the life of the commandments, to serve God, and to carry His name. There is nothing here about ethnicity or superiority. What makes us chosen is not what we are but what we are called on to be.

מִכָּל הַלְּשׁוֹנוֹת *Above all tongues.* Not everything is translatable from one language to another. Robert Frost said: "Poetry is what is lost in translation." The holiness of Hebrew as the language of revelation is not fully reproducible in other tongues, and the long history of misunderstanding of Judaism has often been the result of the untranslatability of its most distinctive concepts.

יוֹם הַכִּפּוּרִים הַזֶּה *This Day of Atonement.* Literally, "Day of Atonements" in the plural. This is the biblical name of the day, the plural referring to the multiple

אֱלֹהֵינוּ Our God and God of our ancestors,
may there rise, come, reach, appear, be favored, heard,
regarded and remembered before You,
our recollection and remembrance,
as well as the remembrance of our ancestors,
and of the Messiah, son of David Your servant,
and of Jerusalem Your holy city,
and of all Your people the house of Israel –
for deliverance and well-being,
grace, loving-kindness and compassion,
life and peace, on this Day of Atonement.
On it remember us, LORD our God, for good;
recollect us for blessing, and deliver us for life.
In accord with Your promise of salvation and compassion,
spare us and be gracious to us;
have compassion on us and deliver us,
for our eyes are turned to You
because You, God, are a gracious and compassionate King.

On Shabbat, add the words in parentheses:

אֱלֹהֵינוּ Our God and God of our ancestors,
pardon our iniquities on (this Sabbath day, and on)
this Day of Atonement;
wipe away and remove all our transgressions and sins
from before Your eyes, as it is said:
"I, I am the One who shall wipe out your transgressions for My sake, *Is. 43*
and I shall not recall your sins."
And it is said:
"I have wiped out your transgressions like a cloud, *Is. 44*
and as a haze your sins;
come back to Me for I have redeemed you."

---

wipe this away, says God, for My sake not yours, for such sins do not deserve to be forgiven (Rashi).

כָּעָב *Like a cloud.* Just as a cloud separates us from the light of the sun so sin separates us from the light of the Divine Presence, but God, like a wind, will disperse the clouds (Malbim).

אֱלֹהֵֽינוּ וֵאלֹהֵי אֲבוֹתֵֽינוּ
יַעֲלֶה וְיָבוֹא וְיַגִּֽיעַ, וְיֵרָאֶה וְיֵרָצֶה וְיִשָּׁמַע
וְיִפָּקֵד וְיִזָּכֵר זִכְרוֹנֵֽנוּ וּפִקְדּוֹנֵֽנוּ וְזִכְרוֹן אֲבוֹתֵֽינוּ
וְזִכְרוֹן מָשִֽׁיחַ בֶּן דָּוִד עַבְדֶּֽךָ, וְזִכְרוֹן יְרוּשָׁלַֽיִם עִיר קָדְשֶֽׁךָ
וְזִכְרוֹן כָּל עַמְּךָ בֵּית יִשְׂרָאֵל, לְפָנֶֽיךָ
לִפְלֵיטָה לְטוֹבָה, לְחֵן וּלְחֶֽסֶד וּלְרַחֲמִים, לְחַיִּים וּלְשָׁלוֹם
בְּיוֹם הַכִּפּוּרִים הַזֶּה.
זָכְרֵֽנוּ יהוה אֱלֹהֵֽינוּ בּוֹ לְטוֹבָה
וּפָקְדֵֽנוּ בוֹ לִבְרָכָה וְהוֹשִׁיעֵֽנוּ בוֹ לְחַיִּים.
וּבִדְבַר יְשׁוּעָה וְרַחֲמִים חוּס וְחָנֵּֽנוּ, וְרַחֵם עָלֵֽינוּ וְהוֹשִׁיעֵֽנוּ
כִּי אֵלֶֽיךָ עֵינֵֽינוּ, כִּי אֵל מֶֽלֶךְ חַנּוּן וְרַחוּם אָֽתָּה.

On שבת, add the words in parentheses:

אֱלֹהֵֽינוּ וֵאלֹהֵי אֲבוֹתֵֽינוּ
מְחַל לַעֲוֹנוֹתֵֽינוּ בְּיוֹם (הַשַּׁבָּת הַזֶּה וּבְיוֹם) הַכִּפּוּרִים הַזֶּה
מְחֵה וְהַעֲבֵר פְּשָׁעֵֽינוּ וְחַטֹּאתֵֽינוּ מִנֶּֽגֶד עֵינֶֽיךָ
כָּאָמוּר
ישעיה מג אָנֹכִי אָנֹכִי הוּא מֹחֶה פְשָׁעֶֽיךָ לְמַעֲנִי
וְחַטֹּאתֶֽיךָ לֹא אֶזְכֹּר:
וְנֶאֱמַר
ישעיה מד מָחִֽיתִי כָעָב פְּשָׁעֶֽיךָ וְכֶעָנָן חַטֹּאותֶֽיךָ
שׁוּבָה אֵלַי כִּי גְאַלְתִּֽיךָ:

יַעֲלֶה וְיָבוֹא וְיַגִּֽיעַ *Rise, come, reach…* A crescendo of eight verbs, signifying the seven heavenly realms, with God above them all – a spatial metaphor meaning, may our prayers reach the innermost heart of God.

אָנֹכִי אָנֹכִי הוּא מֹחֶה פְשָׁעֶֽיךָ לְמַעֲנִי *I, I am the One who shall wipe out your transgressions for My sake. Pesha* signifies a sin committed knowingly and rebelliously. I

And it is said:

"For on this day you will be atoned and made pure; *Lev. 16*
of all your sins before the LORD you shall be purified."

(Our God and God of our ancestors,
may You find favor in our rest.)
Make us holy through Your commandments
and grant us our share in Your Torah.
Satisfy us with Your goodness,
grant us joy in Your salvation
(in love and favor, LORD our God,
grant us as our heritage Your holy Sabbath,
so that Israel, who sanctify Your name,
may find rest on it),
and purify our hearts to serve You in truth.
For You are the Forgiver of Israel
and the Pardoner of the tribes of Yeshurun in every generation,
and without You we have no king who pardons and forgives,
none but You.
Blessed are You, LORD,
King who pardons and forgives our iniquities
and those of all His people the house of Israel,
and makes our guilt pass away, every single year,
King of all the earth, who sanctifies (the Sabbath,)
Israel and the Day of Atonement.

---

and *mikveh* (ritual bath). God, he intimates, is not just the hope of Israel but the purifying waters in which we immerse ourselves and thereby become cleansed.

סָלְחָן, מָחֳלָן *The Forgiver, the Pardoner.* By turning verbs (forgive, pardon) into nouns, the prayer suggests that forgiving and pardoning are not simply what God does; they are part of what He is. They are constant rather than occasional features of His dealings with us.

יְשֻׁרוּן *Yeshurun.* An alternative biblical name for Israel, signifying *yashar*, "upright" (Ibn Ezra, Deut. 32:15).

וְנֶאֱמַר
כִּי־בַיּוֹם הַזֶּה יְכַפֵּר עֲלֵיכֶם לְטַהֵר אֶתְכֶם ויקרא טז
מִכֹּל חַטֹּאתֵיכֶם, לִפְנֵי יהוה תִּטְהָרוּ:
(אֱלֹהֵינוּ וֵאלֹהֵי אֲבוֹתֵינוּ, רְצֵה בִמְנוּחָתֵנוּ)
קַדְּשֵׁנוּ בְּמִצְוֹתֶיךָ וְתֵן חֶלְקֵנוּ בְּתוֹרָתֶךָ
שַׂבְּעֵנוּ מִטּוּבֶךָ וְשַׂמְּחֵנוּ בִּישׁוּעָתֶךָ
(וְהַנְחִילֵנוּ יהוה אֱלֹהֵינוּ בְּאַהֲבָה וּבְרָצוֹן שַׁבַּת קָדְשֶׁךָ
וְיָנוּחוּ בָהּ יִשְׂרָאֵל מְקַדְּשֵׁי שְׁמֶךָ)
וְטַהֵר לִבֵּנוּ לְעָבְדְּךָ בֶּאֱמֶת
כִּי אַתָּה סָלְחָן לְיִשְׂרָאֵל
וּמָחֳלָן לְשִׁבְטֵי יְשֻׁרוּן בְּכָל דּוֹר וָדוֹר
וּמִבַּלְעָדֶיךָ אֵין לָנוּ מֶלֶךְ מוֹחֵל וְסוֹלֵחַ אֶלָּא אָתָּה.
בָּרוּךְ אַתָּה יהוה
מֶלֶךְ מוֹחֵל וְסוֹלֵחַ לַעֲוֹנוֹתֵינוּ, וְלַעֲוֹנוֹת עַמּוֹ בֵּית יִשְׂרָאֵל
וּמַעֲבִיר אַשְׁמוֹתֵינוּ בְּכָל שָׁנָה וְשָׁנָה
מֶלֶךְ עַל כָּל הָאָרֶץ
מְקַדֵּשׁ (הַשַּׁבָּת וְ) יִשְׂרָאֵל וְיוֹם הַכִּפּוּרִים.

כִּי־בַיּוֹם הַזֶּה יְכַפֵּר עֲלֵיכֶם לְטַהֵר אֶתְכֶם *For on this day you will be atoned and made pure.* Sin has two aspects. First is the act itself, the deed that should not have been done. Second is the trace it leaves in the sinner. It defiles, degrades, demeans; it leaves a blemish on the soul. The first needs *atonement*, the second needs *purifying*. God does both. The Mishna teaches in the name of Rabbi Akiva: "Happy are you, Israel: before whom do you purify yourselves, and who purifies you? – Your Father in heaven, as it is said, 'I will sprinkle clean water on you, and you will be clean,' [Ezek. 36:25] and 'God is the hope of Israel' [Jeremiah 17:13]" (Mishna *Yoma* 8:9). Quoting Jeremiah, Rabbi Akiva is making a daring play on the similar sounding words *mikvei* (hope)

TEMPLE SERVICE

רְצֵה Find favor, LORD our God,
in Your people Israel and their prayer.
Restore the service to Your most holy House,
and accept in love and favor
the fire-offerings of Israel and their prayer.
May the service of Your people Israel
always find favor with You.
And may our eyes witness Your return to Zion in compassion.
Blessed are You, LORD,
who restores His Presence to Zion.

THANKSGIVING

Bow at the first nine words.

מוֹדִים We give thanks to You,
for You are the LORD our God and God of our ancestors
for ever and all time.
You are the Rock of our lives,
Shield of our salvation from generation to generation.
We will thank You and declare Your praise for our lives,
which are entrusted into Your hand;
for our souls, which are placed in Your charge;
for Your miracles which are with us every day;
and for Your wonders and favors
at all times, evening, morning and midday.
You are good –
for Your compassion never fails.
You are compassionate –
for Your loving-kindnesses never cease.
We have always placed our hope in You.

Yom Kippur the second comes to dominate, for it will be at the end of these three blessings that we will perform *Viduy*, admitting and confessing our sins.

עבודה

רְצֵה יהוה אֱלֹהֵינוּ בְּעַמְּךָ יִשְׂרָאֵל, וּבִתְפִלָּתָם
וְהָשֵׁב אֶת הָעֲבוֹדָה לִדְבִיר בֵּיתֶךָ
וְאִשֵּׁי יִשְׂרָאֵל וּתְפִלָּתָם בְּאַהֲבָה תְקַבֵּל בְּרָצוֹן
וּתְהִי לְרָצוֹן תָּמִיד עֲבוֹדַת יִשְׂרָאֵל עַמֶּךָ.
וְתֶחֱזֶינָה עֵינֵינוּ בְּשׁוּבְךָ לְצִיּוֹן בְּרַחֲמִים.
בָּרוּךְ אַתָּה יהוה
הַמַּחֲזִיר שְׁכִינָתוֹ לְצִיּוֹן.

הודאה

Bow at the first five words.

מוֹדִים אֲנַחְנוּ לָךְ
שָׁאַתָּה הוּא יהוה אֱלֹהֵינוּ וֵאלֹהֵי אֲבוֹתֵינוּ לְעוֹלָם וָעֶד.
צוּר חַיֵּינוּ, מָגֵן יִשְׁעֵנוּ, אַתָּה הוּא לְדוֹר וָדוֹר.
נוֹדֶה לְּךָ וּנְסַפֵּר תְּהִלָּתֶךָ
עַל חַיֵּינוּ הַמְּסוּרִים בְּיָדֶךָ
וְעַל נִשְׁמוֹתֵינוּ הַפְּקוּדוֹת לָךְ
וְעַל נִסֶּיךָ שֶׁבְּכָל יוֹם עִמָּנוּ
וְעַל נִפְלְאוֹתֶיךָ וְטוֹבוֹתֶיךָ שֶׁבְּכָל עֵת, עֶרֶב וָבֹקֶר וְצָהֳרָיִם.
הַטּוֹב, כִּי לֹא כָלוּ רַחֲמֶיךָ
וְהַמְרַחֵם, כִּי לֹא תַמּוּ חֲסָדֶיךָ
מֵעוֹלָם קִוִּינוּ לָךְ.

מוֹדִים *We give thanks.* The start of the last three blessings of the Amida, known collectively as *Hoda'a*. This word has two meanings, (1) thanks, and (2) admission, confession. On other days of the year the first is to the fore, but on

וְעַל כֻּלָּם For all these things
may Your name be blessed and exalted, our King,
continually, for ever and all time.

וּכְתֹב And write, for a good life, all the children of Your covenant.

Let all that lives thank You, Selah!
and praise Your name in truth,
God, our Savior and Help, Selah!
▾Blessed are You, LORD,
whose name is "the Good"
and to whom thanks are due.

PEACE

שָׁלוֹם רָב Grant great peace to Your people Israel for ever,
for You are the sovereign LORD of all peace;
and may it be good in Your eyes
to bless Your people Israel
at every time, at every hour,
with Your peace.

בְּסֵפֶר חַיִּים In the book of life, blessing, peace and prosperity,
may we and all Your people the house of Israel
be remembered and written before You
for a good life, and for peace.*

Blessed are You, LORD,
who blesses His people Israel with peace.

**Outside Israel, many end the blessing:*
Blessed are You, LORD, who makes peace.

Some say the following verse:
May the words of my mouth and the meditation of my heart *Ps. 19*
find favor before You, LORD, my Rock and Redeemer.

---

itself, for life filled with the energy of the Divine, for life in harmony with other lives, and for sustenance, the ability to earn a dignified living.

וְעַל כֻּלָּם יִתְבָּרַךְ וְיִתְרוֹמַם שִׁמְךָ מַלְכֵּנוּ תָּמִיד לְעוֹלָם וָעֶד.

וּכְתֹב לְחַיִּים טוֹבִים כָּל בְּנֵי בְרִיתֶךָ.

וְכֹל הַחַיִּים יוֹדְוּךָ סֶּלָה, וִיהַלְלוּ אֶת שִׁמְךָ בֶּאֱמֶת
הָאֵל יְשׁוּעָתֵנוּ וְעֶזְרָתֵנוּ סֶלָה.
ּבָּרוּךְ אַתָּה יהוה
הַטּוֹב שִׁמְךָ וּלְךָ נָאֶה לְהוֹדוֹת.

ברכת שלום

שָׁלוֹם רָב עַל יִשְׂרָאֵל עַמְּךָ תָּשִׂים לְעוֹלָם
כִּי אַתָּה הוּא מֶלֶךְ אָדוֹן לְכָל הַשָּׁלוֹם.
וְטוֹב בְּעֵינֶיךָ לְבָרֵךְ אֶת עַמְּךָ יִשְׂרָאֵל
בְּכָל עֵת וּבְכָל שָׁעָה בִּשְׁלוֹמֶךָ.

בְּסֵפֶר חַיִּים, בְּרָכָה וְשָׁלוֹם, וּפַרְנָסָה טוֹבָה
נִזָּכֵר וְנִכָּתֵב לְפָנֶיךָ, אֲנַחְנוּ וְכָל עַמְּךָ בֵּית יִשְׂרָאֵל
לְחַיִּים טוֹבִים וּלְשָׁלוֹם.*

בָּרוּךְ אַתָּה יהוה, הַמְבָרֵךְ אֶת עַמּוֹ יִשְׂרָאֵל בַּשָּׁלוֹם.

In חוץ לארץ, many end the blessing:

בָּרוּךְ אַתָּה יהוה, עוֹשֵׂה הַשָּׁלוֹם.

Some say the following verse:

יִהְיוּ לְרָצוֹן אִמְרֵי־פִי וְהֶגְיוֹן לִבִּי לְפָנֶיךָ, יהוה צוּרִי וְגֹאֲלִי: תהלים יט

בְּסֵפֶר חַיִּים, בְּרָכָה וְשָׁלוֹם, וּפַרְנָסָה טוֹבָה *In the book of life, blessing, peace and prosperity.* The last of the four special insertions for the Ten Days of Repentance. Hence the four requests, three of which we have saved to this point: for life

VIDUY

For linear translation and commentary, see page 1353.

אֱלֹהֵינוּ Our God and God of our fathers,
let our prayer come before You, and do not hide Yourself from our plea,
for we are not so arrogant or obstinate as to say before You,
Lord, our God and God of our fathers,
we are righteous and have not sinned,
for in truth, we and our fathers have sinned.

Strike the left side of the chest with the right fist while saying each of the sins.

אָשַׁמְנוּ We have sinned, we have acted treacherously,
we have robbed, we have spoken slander.
We have acted perversely, we have acted wickedly,
we have acted presumptuously, we have been violent,
we have framed lies.
We have given bad advice, we have deceived, we have scorned,
we have rebelled, we have provoked, we have turned away,
we have committed iniquity, we have transgressed,
we have persecuted, we have been obstinate.
We have acted wickedly, we have corrupted,
we have acted abominably, we have strayed, we have led others astray.

סַרְנוּ We have turned away from Your commandments and good laws,
to no avail, for You are just in all that has befallen us, *Neh. 9*
for You have acted faithfully while we have done wickedly.

מַה נֹּאמַר What can we say before You, You who dwell on high?
What can we declare before You, You who abide in heaven?
Do You not know all, the hidden and revealed alike?

אַתָּה יוֹדֵעַ You know every secret since the world began,
and what is hidden deep inside every living thing.
You search each person's inner chambers,
examining conscience and mind.
Nothing is shrouded from You,
and nothing is hidden before Your eyes.
And so, may it be Your will, Lord our God and God of our ancestors,
that You forgive us all our sins, pardon all our iniquities,
and grant us atonement for all of our transgressions.

וידוי

For linear translation and commentary, see page 1353.

אֱלֹהֵינוּ וֵאלֹהֵי אֲבוֹתֵינוּ
תָּבוֹא לְפָנֶיךָ תְּפִלָּתֵנוּ, וְאַל תִּתְעַלַּם מִתְּחִנָּתֵנוּ.
שֶׁאֵין אֲנַחְנוּ עַזֵּי פָנִים וּקְשֵׁי עֹרֶף לוֹמַר לְפָנֶיךָ
יהוה אֱלֹהֵינוּ וֵאלֹהֵי אֲבוֹתֵינוּ
צַדִּיקִים אֲנַחְנוּ וְלֹא חָטָאנוּ.
אֲבָל אֲנַחְנוּ וַאֲבוֹתֵינוּ חָטָאנוּ.

Strike the left side of the chest with the right fist while saying each of the sins.

אָשַׁמְנוּ, בָּגַדְנוּ, גָּזַלְנוּ, דִּבַּרְנוּ דֹפִי
הֶעֱוִינוּ, וְהִרְשַׁעְנוּ, זַדְנוּ, חָמַסְנוּ, טָפַלְנוּ שֶׁקֶר
יָעַצְנוּ רָע, כִּזַּבְנוּ, לַצְנוּ, מָרַדְנוּ, נִאַצְנוּ, סָרַרְנוּ
עָוִינוּ, פָּשַׁעְנוּ, צָרַרְנוּ, קִשִּׁינוּ עֹרֶף
רָשַׁעְנוּ, שִׁחַתְנוּ, תִּעַבְנוּ, תָּעִינוּ, תִּעְתָּעְנוּ.

סַרְנוּ מִמִּצְוֹתֶיךָ וּמִמִּשְׁפָּטֶיךָ הַטּוֹבִים, וְלֹא שָׁוָה לָנוּ.
וְאַתָּה צַדִּיק עַל כָּל־הַבָּא עָלֵינוּ נחמיה ט
כִּי־אֱמֶת עָשִׂיתָ, וַאֲנַחְנוּ הִרְשָׁעְנוּ:

מַה נֹּאמַר לְפָנֶיךָ יוֹשֵׁב מָרוֹם, וּמַה נְּסַפֵּר לְפָנֶיךָ שׁוֹכֵן שְׁחָקִים
הֲלֹא כָּל הַנִּסְתָּרוֹת וְהַנִּגְלוֹת אַתָּה יוֹדֵעַ.

אַתָּה יוֹדֵעַ רָזֵי עוֹלָם וְתַעֲלוּמוֹת סִתְרֵי כָּל חָי.
אַתָּה חוֹפֵשׂ כָּל חַדְרֵי בָטֶן וּבוֹחֵן כְּלָיוֹת וָלֵב.
אֵין דָּבָר נֶעְלָם מִמָּךְ וְאֵין נִסְתָּר מִנֶּגֶד עֵינֶיךָ.
וּבְכֵן, יְהִי רָצוֹן מִלְּפָנֶיךָ, יהוה אֱלֹהֵינוּ וֵאלֹהֵי אֲבוֹתֵינוּ
שֶׁתִּסְלַח לָנוּ עַל כָּל חַטֹּאתֵינוּ
וְתִמְחַל לָנוּ עַל כָּל עֲוֹנוֹתֵינוּ
וּתְכַפֵּר לָנוּ עַל כָּל פְּשָׁעֵינוּ.

Strike the left side of the chest with the right fist while saying each of the sins.

עַל חֵטְא For the sin we have sinned before You under duress or freewill,
and for the sin we have sinned before You in hardness of heart.

For the sin we have sinned before You unwittingly,
and for the sin we have sinned before You by an utterance of our lips.

For the sin we have sinned before You by unchastity,
and for the sin we have sinned before You openly or secretly.

For the sin we have sinned before You knowingly and deceitfully,
and for the sin we have sinned before You in speech.

For the sin we have sinned before You by wronging a neighbor,
and for the sin we have sinned before You by thoughts of the heart.

For the sin we have sinned before You in a gathering for immorality,
and for the sin we have sinned before You by insincere confession.

For the sin we have sinned before You by contempt for parents and teachers,
and for the sin we have sinned before You willfully or in error.

For the sin we have sinned before You by force,
and for the sin we have sinned before You by desecrating Your name.

For the sin we have sinned before You by impure lips,
and for the sin we have sinned before You by foolish speech.

For the sin we have sinned before You by the evil inclination,
and for the sin we have sinned before You knowingly or unwittingly.

FOR ALL THESE, GOD OF FORGIVENESS,
FORGIVE US, PARDON US, GRANT US ATONEMENT.

Strike the left side of the chest with the right fist while saying each of the sins.

עַל חֵטְא שֶׁחָטָאנוּ לְפָנֶיךָ בְּאֹנֶס וּבְרָצוֹן
וְעַל חֵטְא שֶׁחָטָאנוּ לְפָנֶיךָ בְּאִמּוּץ הַלֵּב

עַל חֵטְא שֶׁחָטָאנוּ לְפָנֶיךָ בִּבְלִי דָעַת
וְעַל חֵטְא שֶׁחָטָאנוּ לְפָנֶיךָ בְּבִטּוּי שְׂפָתָיִם

עַל חֵטְא שֶׁחָטָאנוּ לְפָנֶיךָ בְּגִלּוּי עֲרָיוֹת
וְעַל חֵטְא שֶׁחָטָאנוּ לְפָנֶיךָ בְּגָלוּי וּבַסָּתֶר

עַל חֵטְא שֶׁחָטָאנוּ לְפָנֶיךָ בְּדַעַת וּבְמִרְמָה
וְעַל חֵטְא שֶׁחָטָאנוּ לְפָנֶיךָ בְּדִבּוּר פֶּה

עַל חֵטְא שֶׁחָטָאנוּ לְפָנֶיךָ בְּהוֹנָאַת רֵעַ
וְעַל חֵטְא שֶׁחָטָאנוּ לְפָנֶיךָ בְּהַרְהוֹר הַלֵּב

עַל חֵטְא שֶׁחָטָאנוּ לְפָנֶיךָ בִּוְעִידַת זְנוּת
וְעַל חֵטְא שֶׁחָטָאנוּ לְפָנֶיךָ בְּוִדּוּי פֶּה

עַל חֵטְא שֶׁחָטָאנוּ לְפָנֶיךָ בְּזִלְזוּל הוֹרִים וּמוֹרִים
וְעַל חֵטְא שֶׁחָטָאנוּ לְפָנֶיךָ בְּזָדוֹן וּבִשְׁגָגָה

עַל חֵטְא שֶׁחָטָאנוּ לְפָנֶיךָ בְּחֹזֶק יָד
וְעַל חֵטְא שֶׁחָטָאנוּ לְפָנֶיךָ בְּחִלּוּל הַשֵּׁם

עַל חֵטְא שֶׁחָטָאנוּ לְפָנֶיךָ בְּטֻמְאַת שְׂפָתָיִם
וְעַל חֵטְא שֶׁחָטָאנוּ לְפָנֶיךָ בְּטִפְשׁוּת פֶּה

עַל חֵטְא שֶׁחָטָאנוּ לְפָנֶיךָ בְּיֵצֶר הָרָע
וְעַל חֵטְא שֶׁחָטָאנוּ לְפָנֶיךָ בְּיוֹדְעִים וּבְלֹא יוֹדְעִים

וְעַל כֻּלָּם אֱלוֹהַּ סְלִיחוֹת סְלַח לָנוּ, מְחַל לָנוּ, כַּפֶּר לָנוּ.

For the sin we have sinned before You by deceit and lies,
and for the sin we have sinned before You by bribery.

For the sin we have sinned before You by scorn,
and for the sin we have sinned before You by evil speech.

For the sin we have sinned before You in business,
and for the sin we have sinned before You with food and drink.

For the sin we have sinned before You by interest and extortion,
and for the sin we have sinned before You by being haughty.

For the sin we have sinned before You by the idle chatter of our lips,
and for the sin we have sinned before You by prying eyes.

For the sin we have sinned before You by arrogance,
and for the sin we have sinned before You by insolence.

FOR ALL THESE, GOD OF FORGIVENESS,
FORGIVE US, PARDON US, GRANT US ATONEMENT.

For the sin we have sinned before You by casting off the yoke,
and for the sin we have sinned before You by perverting judgment.

For the sin we have sinned before You by entrapping a neighbor,
and for the sin we have sinned before You by envy.

For the sin we have sinned before You by lack of seriousness,
and for the sin we have sinned before You by obstinacy.

For the sin we have sinned before You by running to do evil,
and for the sin we have sinned before You by gossip.

For the sin we have sinned before You by vain oath,
and for the sin we have sinned before You by baseless hatred.

For the sin we have sinned before You by breach of trust,
and for the sin we have sinned before You by confusion of heart.

FOR ALL THESE, GOD OF FORGIVENESS,
FORGIVE US, PARDON US, GRANT US ATONEMENT.

עַל חֵטְא שֶׁחָטָאנוּ לְפָנֶיךָ בְּכַחַשׁ וּבְכָזָב
וְעַל חֵטְא שֶׁחָטָאנוּ לְפָנֶיךָ בְּכַפַּת שֹׁחַד
עַל חֵטְא שֶׁחָטָאנוּ לְפָנֶיךָ בְּלָצוֹן
וְעַל חֵטְא שֶׁחָטָאנוּ לְפָנֶיךָ בְּלָשׁוֹן הָרָע
עַל חֵטְא שֶׁחָטָאנוּ לְפָנֶיךָ בְּמַשָּׂא וּבְמַתָּן
וְעַל חֵטְא שֶׁחָטָאנוּ לְפָנֶיךָ בְּמַאֲכָל וּבְמִשְׁתֶּה
עַל חֵטְא שֶׁחָטָאנוּ לְפָנֶיךָ בְּנֶשֶׁךְ וּבְמַרְבִּית
וְעַל חֵטְא שֶׁחָטָאנוּ לְפָנֶיךָ בִּנְטִיַּת גָּרוֹן
עַל חֵטְא שֶׁחָטָאנוּ לְפָנֶיךָ בְּשִׂיחַ שִׂפְתוֹתֵינוּ
וְעַל חֵטְא שֶׁחָטָאנוּ לְפָנֶיךָ בְּשִׂקּוּר עָיִן
עַל חֵטְא שֶׁחָטָאנוּ לְפָנֶיךָ בְּעֵינַיִם רָמוֹת
וְעַל חֵטְא שֶׁחָטָאנוּ לְפָנֶיךָ בְּעַזּוּת מֵצַח

וְעַל כֻּלָּם אֱלוֹהַּ סְלִיחוֹת סְלַח לָנוּ, מְחַל לָנוּ, כַּפֶּר לָנוּ.

עַל חֵטְא שֶׁחָטָאנוּ לְפָנֶיךָ בִּפְרִיקַת עֹל
וְעַל חֵטְא שֶׁחָטָאנוּ לְפָנֶיךָ בִּפְלִילוּת
עַל חֵטְא שֶׁחָטָאנוּ לְפָנֶיךָ בִּצְדִיַּת רֵעַ
וְעַל חֵטְא שֶׁחָטָאנוּ לְפָנֶיךָ בְּצָרוּת עָיִן
עַל חֵטְא שֶׁחָטָאנוּ לְפָנֶיךָ בְּקַלּוּת רֹאשׁ
וְעַל חֵטְא שֶׁחָטָאנוּ לְפָנֶיךָ בְּקַשְׁיוּת עֹרֶף
עַל חֵטְא שֶׁחָטָאנוּ לְפָנֶיךָ בְּרִיצַת רַגְלַיִם לְהָרַע
וְעַל חֵטְא שֶׁחָטָאנוּ לְפָנֶיךָ בִּרְכִילוּת
עַל חֵטְא שֶׁחָטָאנוּ לְפָנֶיךָ בִּשְׁבוּעַת שָׁוְא
וְעַל חֵטְא שֶׁחָטָאנוּ לְפָנֶיךָ בְּשִׂנְאַת חִנָּם
עַל חֵטְא שֶׁחָטָאנוּ לְפָנֶיךָ בִּתְשׂוּמֶת יָד
וְעַל חֵטְא שֶׁחָטָאנוּ לְפָנֶיךָ בְּתִמְהוֹן לֵבָב

וְעַל כֻּלָּם אֱלוֹהַּ סְלִיחוֹת סְלַח לָנוּ, מְחַל לָנוּ, כַּפֶּר לָנוּ.

וְעַל חֲטָאִים and for the sins for which we are liable to bring a burnt-offering,

and for the sins for which we are liable to bring a sin-offering,

and for the sins for which we are liable to bring an offering according to our means,

and for the sins for which we are liable to bring a guilt-offering for certain or possible sin,

and for the sins for which we are liable to lashes for rebellion,

and for the sins for which we are liable to forty lashes,

and for the sins for which we are liable to death by the hands of Heaven,

and for the sins for which we are liable to be cut off and childless,

and for the sins for which we are liable to the four death penalties inflicted by the court: stoning, burning, beheading and strangling.

For positive and negative commandments,
whether they can be remedied by an act or not,
for sins known to us and for those that are unknown –
for those that are known,
we have already declared them before You
and confessed them to You;
and for those that are unknown,
before You they are revealed and known,
as it is said,
"The secret things belong to the LORD our God, *Deut. 29*
but the things that are revealed are for us and our children for ever,
that we may fulfill all the words of this Torah."

For You are the Forgiver of Israel
and the Pardoner of the tribes of Yeshurun in every generation,
and without You we have no king who pardons and forgives,
none but You.

וְעַל חֲטָאִים שֶׁאָנוּ חַיָּבִים עֲלֵיהֶם עוֹלָה

וְעַל חֲטָאִים שֶׁאָנוּ חַיָּבִים עֲלֵיהֶם חַטָּאת

וְעַל חֲטָאִים שֶׁאָנוּ חַיָּבִים עֲלֵיהֶם קָרְבָּן עוֹלֶה וְיוֹרֵד

וְעַל חֲטָאִים שֶׁאָנוּ חַיָּבִים עֲלֵיהֶם אָשָׁם וַדַּאי וְתָלוּי

וְעַל חֲטָאִים שֶׁאָנוּ חַיָּבִים עֲלֵיהֶם מַכַּת מַרְדּוּת

וְעַל חֲטָאִים שֶׁאָנוּ חַיָּבִים עֲלֵיהֶם מַלְקוּת אַרְבָּעִים

וְעַל חֲטָאִים שֶׁאָנוּ חַיָּבִים עֲלֵיהֶם מִיתָה בִּידֵי שָׁמָיִם

וְעַל חֲטָאִים שֶׁאָנוּ חַיָּבִים עֲלֵיהֶם כָּרֵת וַעֲרִירִי

וְעַל חֲטָאִים שֶׁאָנוּ חַיָּבִים עֲלֵיהֶם אַרְבַּע מִיתוֹת בֵּית דִּין
סְקִילָה, שְׂרֵפָה, הֶרֶג, וְחֶנֶק.

עַל מִצְוַת עֲשֵׂה וְעַל מִצְוַת לֹא תַעֲשֶׂה.
בֵּין שֶׁיֵּשׁ בָּהּ קוּם עֲשֵׂה וּבֵין שֶׁאֵין בָּהּ קוּם עֲשֵׂה.
אֶת הַגְּלוּיִים לָנוּ וְאֶת שֶׁאֵינָם גְּלוּיִים לָנוּ
אֶת הַגְּלוּיִים לָנוּ, כְּבָר אֲמַרְנוּם לְפָנֶיךָ, וְהוֹדִינוּ לְךָ עֲלֵיהֶם
וְאֶת שֶׁאֵינָם גְּלוּיִים לָנוּ, לְפָנֶיךָ הֵם גְּלוּיִים וִידוּעִים
כַּדָּבָר שֶׁנֶּאֱמַר
הַנִּסְתָּרֹת לַיהוה אֱלֹהֵינוּ — דברים כט
וְהַנִּגְלֹת לָנוּ וּלְבָנֵינוּ עַד־עוֹלָם
לַעֲשׂוֹת אֶת־כָּל־דִּבְרֵי הַתּוֹרָה הַזֹּאת:

כִּי אַתָּה סָלְחָן לְיִשְׂרָאֵל
וּמָחֳלָן לְשִׁבְטֵי יְשֻׁרוּן בְּכָל דּוֹר וָדוֹר
וּמִבַּלְעָדֶיךָ אֵין לָנוּ מֶלֶךְ מוֹחֵל וְסוֹלֵחַ אֶלָּא אָתָּה.

אֱלֹהַי My God,
before I was formed I was unworthy,
and now that I have been formed it is as if I had not been formed.
I am dust while alive,
how much more so when I am dead.
See, I am before You like a vessel filled with shame and disgrace.
May it be Your will, Lord my God and God of my fathers,
that I may sin no more,
and as for the sins I have committed before You,
erase them in Your great compassion,
but not by suffering or severe illness.

אֱלֹהַי My God, *Berakhot 17a*
guard my tongue from evil
and my lips from deceitful speech.
To those who curse me, let my soul be silent;
may my soul be to all like the dust.
Open my heart to Your Torah
and let my soul pursue Your commandments.
As for all who plan evil against me,
swiftly thwart their counsel and frustrate their plans.
Act for the sake of Your name; act for the sake of Your right hand;
act for the sake of Your holiness; act for the sake of Your Torah.
That Your beloved ones may be delivered, *Ps. 60*
save with Your right hand and answer me.
May the words of my mouth and the meditation of my heart *Ps. 19*
find favor before You, Lord, my Rock and Redeemer.

Bow, take three steps back, then bow, first left, then right, then center, while saying:
May He who makes peace in His high places,
make peace for us and all Israel – and say: Amen.

יְהִי רָצוֹן May it be Your will, Lord our God and God of our ancestors,
that the Temple be rebuilt speedily in our days, and grant us a share in Your Torah.
And there we will serve You with reverence,
as in the days of old and as in former years.
Then the offering of Judah and Jerusalem *Mal. 3*
will be pleasing to the Lord as in the days of old and as in former years.

אֱלֹהַי
עַד שֶׁלֹּא נוֹצַרְתִּי אֵינִי כְדַאי
וְעַכְשָׁיו שֶׁנּוֹצַרְתִּי, כְּאִלּוּ לֹא נוֹצַרְתִּי
עָפָר אֲנִי בְּחַיַּי, קַל וָחֹמֶר בְּמִיתָתִי.
הֲרֵי אֲנִי לְפָנֶיךָ כִּכְלִי מָלֵא בּוּשָׁה וּכְלִמָּה.
יְהִי רָצוֹן מִלְּפָנֶיךָ, יהוה אֱלֹהַי וֵאלֹהֵי אֲבוֹתַי שֶׁלֹּא אֶחֱטָא עוֹד.
וּמַה שֶּׁחָטָאתִי לְפָנֶיךָ, מְחֹק בְּרַחֲמֶיךָ הָרַבִּים
אֲבָל לֹא עַל יְדֵי יִסּוּרִים וָחֳלָיִם רָעִים.

אֱלֹהַי ברכות יז.
נְצֹר לְשׁוֹנִי מֵרָע וּשְׂפָתַי מִדַּבֵּר מִרְמָה
וְלִמְקַלְלַי נַפְשִׁי תִדֹּם, וְנַפְשִׁי כֶּעָפָר לַכֹּל תִּהְיֶה.
פְּתַח לִבִּי בְּתוֹרָתֶךָ, וּבְמִצְוֹתֶיךָ תִּרְדֹּף נַפְשִׁי.
וְכָל הַחוֹשְׁבִים עָלַי רָעָה
מְהֵרָה הָפֵר עֲצָתָם וְקַלְקֵל מַחֲשַׁבְתָּם.
עֲשֵׂה לְמַעַן שְׁמֶךָ, עֲשֵׂה לְמַעַן יְמִינֶךָ
עֲשֵׂה לְמַעַן קְדֻשָּׁתֶךָ, עֲשֵׂה לְמַעַן תּוֹרָתֶךָ.
לְמַעַן יֵחָלְצוּן יְדִידֶיךָ, הוֹשִׁיעָה יְמִינְךָ וַעֲנֵנִי: תהלים ס
יִהְיוּ לְרָצוֹן אִמְרֵי פִי וְהֶגְיוֹן לִבִּי לְפָנֶיךָ, יהוה צוּרִי וְגֹאֲלִי: תהלים יט

Bow, take three steps back, then bow, first left, then right, then center, while saying:

עֹשֶׂה הַשָּׁלוֹם בִּמְרוֹמָיו
הוּא יַעֲשֶׂה שָׁלוֹם עָלֵינוּ וְעַל כָּל יִשְׂרָאֵל וְאִמְרוּ אָמֵן.

יְהִי רָצוֹן מִלְּפָנֶיךָ יהוה אֱלֹהֵינוּ וֵאלֹהֵי אֲבוֹתֵינוּ
שֶׁיִּבָּנֶה בֵּית הַמִּקְדָּשׁ בִּמְהֵרָה בְיָמֵינוּ, וְתֵן חֶלְקֵנוּ בְּתוֹרָתֶךָ
וְשָׁם נַעֲבָדְךָ בְּיִרְאָה כִּימֵי עוֹלָם וּכְשָׁנִים קַדְמוֹנִיּוֹת.
וְעָרְבָה לַיהוה מִנְחַת יְהוּדָה וִירוּשָׁלָםִ כִּימֵי עוֹלָם וּכְשָׁנִים קַדְמֹנִיּוֹת: מלאכי ג

When Yom Kippur falls on a weekday, continue with Seliḥot on page 124.

On Shabbat, all stand and say:

וַיְכֻלּוּ Then the heavens and the earth were completed, Gen. 2
and all their array.
With the seventh day, God completed the work He had done.
He ceased on the seventh day from all the work He had done.
God blessed the seventh day and declared it holy,
because on it He ceased from all His work He had created to do.

ME'EIN SHEVA

The Leader continues:

בָּרוּךְ Blessed are You, Lord our God and God of our fathers,
God of Abraham, God of Isaac and God of Jacob,
the great, mighty and awesome God,
God Most High, Creator of heaven and earth.

The congregation then the Leader:

מָגֵן אָבוֹת By His word, He was the Shield of our ancestors.
By His promise, He will revive the dead.
There is none like the holy King
who gives rest to His people on His holy Sabbath day,
for He found them worthy of His favor to give them rest.
Before Him we will come in worship
with reverence and awe,
giving thanks to His name daily,
continually, with due blessings.
He is God to whom thanks are due, the Lord of peace
who sanctifies the Sabbath and blesses the seventh day,
and in holiness gives rest to a people filled with delight,
in remembrance of the work of creation.

---

other nights of the week, so it was important to make provision for latecomers so that they would not have to walk home alone.

מָגֵן אָבוֹת *Shield of our ancestors.* A one-paragraph summary of the entire Friday night Amida, using single phrases in place of complete blessings.

When יום כיפור *falls on a weekday, continue with* סליחות *on page 125.*

On שבת*, all stand and say:*

בראשית ב

וַיְכֻלּוּ הַשָּׁמַיִם וְהָאָרֶץ וְכׇל־צְבָאָם:
וַיְכַל אֱלֹהִים בַּיּוֹם הַשְּׁבִיעִי מְלַאכְתּוֹ אֲשֶׁר עָשָׂה
וַיִּשְׁבֹּת בַּיּוֹם הַשְּׁבִיעִי מִכׇּל־מְלַאכְתּוֹ אֲשֶׁר עָשָׂה:
וַיְבָרֶךְ אֱלֹהִים אֶת־יוֹם הַשְּׁבִיעִי, וַיְקַדֵּשׁ אֹתוֹ
כִּי בוֹ שָׁבַת מִכׇּל־מְלַאכְתּוֹ, אֲשֶׁר־בָּרָא אֱלֹהִים, לַעֲשׂוֹת:

ברכה מעין שבע

The שליח ציבור *continues:*

בָּרוּךְ אַתָּה יהוה, אֱלֹהֵינוּ וֵאלֹהֵי אֲבוֹתֵינוּ
אֱלֹהֵי אַבְרָהָם, אֱלֹהֵי יִצְחָק, וֵאלֹהֵי יַעֲקֹב
הָאֵל הַגָּדוֹל הַגִּבּוֹר וְהַנּוֹרָא, אֵל עֶלְיוֹן, קֹנֵה שָׁמַיִם וָאָרֶץ.

The קהל *then the* שליח ציבור*:*

מָגֵן אָבוֹת בִּדְבָרוֹ, מְחַיֵּה מֵתִים בְּמַאֲמָרוֹ
הַמֶּלֶךְ הַקָּדוֹשׁ שֶׁאֵין כָּמוֹהוּ
הַמֵּנִיחַ לְעַמּוֹ בְּיוֹם שַׁבַּת קָדְשׁוֹ, כִּי בָם רָצָה לְהָנִיחַ לָהֶם
לְפָנָיו נַעֲבֹד בְּיִרְאָה וָפַחַד
וְנוֹדֶה לִשְׁמוֹ בְּכׇל יוֹם תָּמִיד, מֵעֵין הַבְּרָכוֹת
אֵל הַהוֹדָאוֹת, אֲדוֹן הַשָּׁלוֹם
מְקַדֵּשׁ הַשַּׁבָּת וּמְבָרֵךְ שְׁבִיעִי
וּמֵנִיחַ בִּקְדֻשָּׁה לְעַם מְדֻשְּׁנֵי עֹנֶג
זֵכֶר לְמַעֲשֵׂה בְרֵאשִׁית.

BERAKHA ME'EIN SHEVA – THE SEVENFOLD BLESSING

The practice of saying these extra blessings on Friday evening was for the sake of latecomers, and to ensure that everyone was able to leave the synagogue together (Tur, *OḤ* 268). Traveling to and from the synagogue at night was often dangerous, and more people came on Friday nights than during the

The Leader continues:

אֱלֹהֵינוּ Our God and God of our ancestors,
may You find favor in our rest.
Make us holy through Your commandments
and grant us our share in Your Torah.
Satisfy us with Your goodness, grant us joy in Your salvation,
and purify our hearts to serve You in truth.
In love and favor, Lord our God,
grant us as our heritage Your holy Sabbath,
so that Israel who sanctify Your name may find rest on it.
Blessed are You, Lord, who sanctifies the Sabbath.

---

the people, in a state of fear at the non-appearance of Moses, made a golden calf. Moses, descending the mountain, smashed the tablets of the law, brought order to the camp, and then prayed to God for forty days and forty nights to forgive the people. At the height of this encounter God appeared to him: "And He passed before Moses, proclaiming, 'The Lord, the Lord, compassionate and gracious God, slow to anger, abounding in loving-kindness and truth, extending loving-kindness to a thousand generations, forgiving iniquity, rebellion and sin…'" (Ex. 34:6–7). Note that it is God speaking, not Moses.

Some time later a second crisis occurred. Ten of the spies sent by Moses to see the land came back with a demoralizing report, saying that though the land was good it was unconquerable: The inhabitants were too strong. The people lost faith and said that they wanted to return to Egypt. God threatened to destroy the people. Moses then prayed in these words:

> Now may the Lord's strength be displayed, just as You have declared: "The Lord is slow to anger, abounding in loving-kindness, forgiving iniquity and rebellion…" In accordance with Your great love, forgive the sin of these people, just as You have pardoned them from the time they left Egypt until now.
>
> The Lord replied, "I have forgiven them, as you asked." (Num. 14:17–20)

When Moses prays on this second occasion, he is paraphrasing back to God the words (known as The Thirteen Attributes of Mercy) that God had said to him on Mount Sinai. From this the rabbis inferred: "This teaches us that God, as it were, robed Himself as if He were a leader of prayer, and said to Moses: Whenever Israel sins, let them perform this rite before Me and I shall forgive them… Rabbi Judah said: There is a covenant that the Thirteen Attributes do not return unanswered" (*Rosh HaShana* 17b). God taught Moses how to pray, and this became the model for *Seliḥot*.

The שליח ציבור *continues:*

אֱלֹהֵינוּ וֵאלֹהֵי אֲבוֹתֵינוּ, רְצֵה בִמְנוּחָתֵנוּ.
קַדְּשֵׁנוּ בְּמִצְוֹתֶיךָ וְתֵן חֶלְקֵנוּ בְּתוֹרָתֶךָ
שַׂבְּעֵנוּ מִטּוּבֶךָ וְשַׂמְּחֵנוּ בִּישׁוּעָתֶךָ
וְטַהֵר לִבֵּנוּ לְעָבְדְּךָ בֶּאֱמֶת.
וְהַנְחִילֵנוּ יהוה אֱלֹהֵינוּ בְּאַהֲבָה וּבְרָצוֹן שַׁבַּת קָדְשֶׁךָ
וְיָנוּחוּ בָהּ יִשְׂרָאֵל מְקַדְּשֵׁי שְׁמֶךָ.
בָּרוּךְ אַתָּה יהוה, מְקַדֵּשׁ הַשַּׁבָּת.

SELIḤOT – PENITENTIAL PRAYERS

We now begin the *Seliḥot*, penitential prayers, that form an essential part of the service of Yom Kippur (Rabbi Amram Gaon). *Seliḥot* are ways of asking God to forgive us for our sins, individual or collective, known and unknown, intentional or unintentional.

We have records of such pleas long before Jewish prayer was formalized. One, moving and eloquent, was said by Daniel in exile: "Lord, the great and awesome God, who keeps His covenant of love with those who love Him and keep His commandments: we have sinned and done wrong. We have been wicked and have rebelled; we have turned away from Your commands and laws" (Daniel 9:4–5).

Another was said by Ezra: "But now, our God, what can we say after this? For we have forsaken the commands You gave through Your servants the prophets... Here we are before You in our guilt, though because of it not one of us can stand in Your presence" (Ezra 9:10–11, 15). A third was said by Nehemiah: "I confess the sins we Israelites, including myself and my father's family, have committed against You. We have acted very wickedly toward You. We have not obeyed the commands, decrees and laws You gave Your servant Moses" (Neh. 1:6–7).

All three prayers were said in the aftermath of the Babylonian exile and the later return of Jews to a devastated Israel, and represent the authentic Jewish response to calamity: "When sufferings come, search your deeds and return in repentance" (*Berakhot* 5a). All renewal, whether in the life of an individual or a nation, begins with spiritual and moral renewal, and this in turn begins with *Seliḥa*, the act of saying sorry to God.

The institution of *Seliḥot* draws its inspiration from an earlier episode in the lifetime of Moses. Some forty days after the revelation at Mount Sinai,

SELIḤOT

The Seliḥot section of the service opens with a prefatory piyut (liturgical poem) followed by a selection of verses describing the greatness of God. This opening is followed by several Seliḥot – piyutim of repentance, punctuated with the communal recitation of the Thirteen Attributes of Mercy – and concludes with closing piyutim. Traditionally, Seliḥot were said in all five services of Yom Kippur, but in the last 150 years they have come to be said in their complete form only in Ma'ariv and Ne'ila; in Shaḥarit, Musaf and Minḥa the prevailing custom is to begin directly with "Remember, Lord, Your compassion" and Viduy. In Ma'ariv, the Seliḥot are said after the Amida, with the closing piyutim leading up to Avinu Malkenu and Kaddish; in the daytime services, they are said in the fourth blessing of the Leader's Repetition.

The Ark is opened and the congregation stands.

The Leader recites the first verse and the congregation repeats. The subsequent verses are each recited first by the congregation, then repeated by the Leader.

יַעֲלֶה Let our plea rise from evening,
let our cry come [to You] from morning,
and let our song appear by evening.

Let our voice rise from evening,
let our righteousness come [to You] from morning,
and let our [plea for] redemption appear by evening.

Let our suffering rise from evening,
let our [plea for] forgiveness come [to You], from morning,
and let our groans appear by evening.

Let our refuge [through prayer] rise from evening,
let it, for Your sake, come [to You] from morning,
and let our atonement appear by evening.

Let our [plea for] salvation rise from evening,
let our purification come [to You] from morning,
and let our pardon appear by evening.

---

pear" – recall three stages in the story of the Israelites in Egypt before the exodus. The cry of the Israelites in Egypt "*rose* to God" (Ex. 2:23). God told Moses at the burning bush: "Now, behold, the cry of the sons of Israel has *come* before Me" (Ex. 3:9). We are also told that "God *saw* the children of Israel, and God took notice of them" (Ex. 2:25). Jewish prayer constantly invokes the past for the sake of the future, as if to say, "As it was then, so may it be now."

סליחות

The סליחות *section of the service opens with a prefatory piyut (liturgical poem) followed by a selection of verses describing the greatness of God. This opening is followed by several* סליחות *– piyutim of repentance, punctuated with the communal recitation of the* י״ג מידות הרחמים *– and concludes with closing piyutim.*

Traditionally, סליחות *were said in all five services of* יום כיפור*, but in the last 150 years they have come to be said in their complete form only in* מעריב *and* נעילה*; in* שחרית*,* מוסף *and* מנחה *the prevailing custom is to begin directly with* זְכֹר־רַחֲמֶיךָ *and* וידוי*. In* מעריב*, the* סליחות *are said after the* עמידה*, with the closing piyutim leading up to* אבינו מלכנו *and* קדיש*; in the daytime services, they are said in the fourth blessing of the* חזרת הש״ץ*.*

The ארון קודש *is opened and the* קהל *stands.*

The שליח ציבור *recites the first verse and the* קהל *repeats. The subsequent verses are each recited first by the* קהל*, then repeated by the* שליח ציבור*.*

יַעֲלֶה תַחֲנוּנֵנוּ מֵעֶרֶב / וְיָבֹא שַׁוְעָתֵנוּ מִבֹּקֶר
וְיֵרָאֶה רִנּוּנֵנוּ עַד עָרֶב.

יַעֲלֶה קוֹלֵנוּ מֵעֶרֶב / וְיָבֹא צִדְקָתֵנוּ מִבֹּקֶר
וְיֵרָאֶה פִּדְיוֹנֵנוּ עַד עָרֶב.

יַעֲלֶה עִנּוּיֵנוּ מֵעֶרֶב / וְיָבֹא סְלִיחָתֵנוּ מִבֹּקֶר
וְיֵרָאֶה נַאֲקָתֵנוּ עַד עָרֶב.

יַעֲלֶה מְנוּסֵנוּ מֵעֶרֶב / וְיָבֹא לְמַעֲנוֹ מִבֹּקֶר
וְיֵרָאֶה כִּפּוּרֵנוּ עַד עָרֶב.

יַעֲלֶה יִשְׁעֵנוּ מֵעֶרֶב / וְיָבֹא טָהֳרֵנוּ מִבֹּקֶר
וְיֵרָאֶה חִנּוּנֵנוּ עַד עָרֶב.

SELIḤOT (*see previous page for introductory commentary*)

יַעֲלֶה תַחֲנוּנֵנוּ *Let our plea rise.* A poetic prelude to *Seliḥot,* author unknown. The poem is written in eight three-line verses, each line opening with one of the three verbs from the start of the special prayer for festivals: יַעֲלֶה, וְיָבוֹא, וְיֵרָאֶה, "May there rise, come and appear," and ending with the words "from evening," "from morning," and "by evening," a reference to a biblical verse about Yom Kippur: "It is a Sabbath of utter rest to you, and you shall afflict your souls: on the ninth day of the month at evening, *from evening to evening* shall you keep your Sabbath" (Lev. 23:32). The three verbs – "rise, come, ap-

Let remembrance of us rise from evening,
let our gathering for prayer come [to You], from morning,
and let our splendor appear by evening.

Let our knocking [at Your gate] rise from evening,
let our joyousness come [to You] from morning,
and let our appeal appear by evening.

Let our distressed cries rise from evening,
let them come to You from morning,
and let [Your answer] appear to us by evening.

The Ark is closed.

Before the first recitation of the Thirteen Attributes, the following verses are said. These are arranged according to subject matter, alternately addressing the congregants and God Himself. The overarching theme is the greatness and majesty of God, which, in the context of most of the verses, precedes a supplication (see especially Psalms 74 and 89). The order and arrangement of verses varies between different communities. The sequence below was practiced in Poland, and is now accepted by most Ashkenazi congregations; the sequence according to Lithuanian custom is on page 1277.

All:

שֹׁמֵעַ תְּפִלָּה You who listen to prayer – all creatures of flesh will come to You. *Ps. 65*
All creatures of flesh will come and bow down before You, O LORD.
They will come and bow down before You, LORD, and give honor to Your name. *Ps. 86*
Come, let us bow in worship, bend our knees before the LORD our Maker. *Ps. 95*
Come in at His gates with thanksgiving; come to His courts with praise. Thank Him and bless His name. *Ps. 100*
Come, bless the LORD, all you servants of the LORD, who nightly stand in the House of the LORD. *Ps. 134*
Lift up your hands toward the Sanctuary and bless the LORD.
Come, let us enter His dwelling, bow before His footstool. *Ps. 132*
Exalt the LORD our God, and bow before His footstool – He is holy. *Ps. 99*

---

ninth century onward these poems began to be added to the *Seliḥot* verses and prayers. The basic structure of all Jewish prayer is first *shevaḥ*, praise; then *bakasha*, request; then *hoda'a*, acknowledgment and thanks (Maimonides, Laws of Prayer, 1:2). So the whole of this introductory passage is dedicated to the first: praise.

שֹׁמֵעַ *You who listen.* A phrase from Psalm 65:3, the verb *sh-m-a* means more than simply "to listen." It means, among other things, to internalize, to be

יַעֲלֶה זִכְרוֹנֵנוּ מֵעֶרֶב / וְיָבֹא וְעוּדֵנוּ מִבֹּקֶר
וְיֵרָאֶה הֲדָרָתֵנוּ עַד עָרֶב.
יַעֲלֶה דָּפְקֵנוּ מֵעֶרֶב / וְיָבֹא גִּילֵנוּ מִבֹּקֶר
וְיֵרָאֶה בַּקָּשָׁתֵנוּ עַד עָרֶב.
יַעֲלֶה אֶנְקָתֵנוּ מֵעֶרֶב / וְיָבֹא אֵלֶיךָ מִבֹּקֶר
וְיֵרָאֶה אֵלֵינוּ עַד עָרֶב.

The ארון קודש *is closed.*

Before the first recitation of the י״ג מידות*, the following verses are said. These are arranged according to subject matter, alternately addressing the congregants and God Himself. The overarching theme is the greatness and majesty of God, which, in the context of most of the verses, precedes a supplication (see especially Psalms 74 and 89). The order and arrangement of verses varies between different communities. The sequence below was practiced in Poland, and is now accepted by most Ashkenazi congregations; the sequence according to Lithuanian custom is on page 1277.*

All:

שְׁמֵעַ תְּפִלָּה, עָדֶיךָ כָּל־בָּשָׂר יָבֹאוּ: תהלים סה
יָבוֹא כָל בָּשָׂר לְהִשְׁתַּחֲוֹת לְפָנֶיךָ יהוה.
יָבוֹאוּ וְיִשְׁתַּחֲווּ לְפָנֶיךָ אֲדֹנָי, וִיכַבְּדוּ לִשְׁמֶךָ: תהלים פו
בֹּאוּ נִשְׁתַּחֲוֶה וְנִכְרָעָה, נִבְרְכָה לִפְנֵי־יהוה עֹשֵׂנוּ: תהלים צה
בֹּאוּ שְׁעָרָיו בְּתוֹדָה, חֲצֵרֹתָיו בִּתְהִלָּה הוֹדוּ לוֹ בָּרְכוּ שְׁמוֹ: תהלים ק
הִנֵּה בָּרְכוּ אֶת־יהוה כָּל־עַבְדֵי יהוה, הָעֹמְדִים בְּבֵית־יהוה בַּלֵּילוֹת: תהלים קלד
שְׂאוּ־יְדֵכֶם קֹדֶשׁ, וּבָרְכוּ אֶת־יהוה:
נָבוֹאָה לְמִשְׁכְּנוֹתָיו, נִשְׁתַּחֲוֶה לַהֲדֹם רַגְלָיו: תהלים קלב
רוֹמְמוּ יהוה אֱלֹהֵינוּ וְהִשְׁתַּחֲווּ לַהֲדֹם רַגְלָיו, קָדוֹשׁ הוּא: תהלים צט

שְׁמֵעַ תְּפִלָּה *You who listen to prayer.* An ancient introduction to *Seliḥot*: a selection of verses, mainly from Psalms, but also from Deuteronomy, Isaiah, Jeremiah, Job and Chronicles, linked by certain thematic words like "come," "bow," "bless," and "great." The effect of these repeated words is to weave the verses together to form a coherent and powerful hymn of praise to God. This is how *Seliḥot* were composed before the emergence, in the third or fourth century CE, of a literature of specially written liturgical poetry. From the

Exalt the LORD our God, and bow at His holy mountain, for holy is the LORD our God. *Ibid.*

Bow down to the LORD in the splendor of holiness; tremble before Him, all the earth. *Ps. 96*

As for us, in Your great loving-kindness we will come into Your House; we will bow down to Your holy Temple in awe of You.

We will bow down to Your holy Temple and give thanks to Your name for Your loving-kindness and truth, for You have magnified Your name and Your word above all else.

LORD, God of hosts, who is like You – Mighty One, LORD, with Your faithfulness all round You? *Ps. 89*

For who in the heavens may be compared to the LORD; who is like the LORD among the angels? *Ibid.*

For You are great, and You do wonders, You are God alone. *Ps. 86*

For Your loving-kindness reaches over heaven itself, and Your truth as high as the skies. *Ps. 108*

Great is the LORD and greatly to be praised; His greatness cannot be fathomed. *Ps. 145*

For great is the LORD and greatly to be praised; He is awesome beyond all heavenly powers. *1 Chr. 16*

For the LORD is the great God, the King great above all heavenly powers. *Ps. 95*

Who is the god, in heaven or on earth, who can perform works and mighty acts like Yours? *Deut. 3*

Who would not hold You in awe, King of the nations, for that befits You, *Jer. 10*

for among all the wise people of nations, in all their realms, there is none like You.

There is none like You, LORD; You are great, and Your name is great in its might.

Your arm is mighty; Your hand holds its power, Your right hand raised. *Ps. 89*

The day is Yours, and Yours is the night; You established light and the sun. *Ps. 74*

In His hands are the depths of the earth, and the mountain peaks are His. *Ps. 95*

Who can tell of the LORD's mighty acts and make all His praises heard? *Ps. 106*

Yours, LORD, are the greatness and the power, the glory and the majesty and splendor, for everything in heaven and earth is Yours. *1 Chr. 29*

Yours, LORD, is the kingdom; You are exalted as Head over all.

The heavens are Yours, and Yours is the earth; the world and all that is in it – it is You who founded them. *Ps. 89*

רוֹמְמוּ יהוה אֱלֹהֵינוּ וְהִשְׁתַּחֲווּ לְהַר קָדְשׁוֹ, כִּי־קָדוֹשׁ יהוה אֱלֹהֵינוּ: שם
הִשְׁתַּחֲווּ לַיהוה בְּהַדְרַת־קֹדֶשׁ, חִילוּ מִפָּנָיו כָּל־הָאָרֶץ: תהלים צו
וַאֲנַחְנוּ בְּרֹב חַסְדְּךָ נָבוֹא בֵיתֶךָ, נִשְׁתַּחֲוֶה אֶל הֵיכַל קָדְשְׁךָ בְּיִרְאָתֶךָ.
נִשְׁתַּחֲוֶה אֶל הֵיכַל קָדְשְׁךָ, וְנוֹדֶה אֶת שְׁמֶךָ עַל חַסְדְּךָ וְעַל אֲמִתֶּךָ
כִּי הִגְדַּלְתָּ עַל כָּל שִׁמְךָ אִמְרָתֶךָ.
יהוה אֱלֹהֵי צְבָאוֹת מִי־כָמוֹךָ חֲסִין יָהּ, וֶאֱמוּנָתְךָ סְבִיבוֹתֶיךָ: תהלים פט
כִּי מִי בַשַּׁחַק יַעֲרֹךְ לַיהוה, יִדְמֶה לַיהוה בִּבְנֵי אֵלִים: שם
כִּי־גָדוֹל אַתָּה וְעֹשֵׂה נִפְלָאוֹת, אַתָּה אֱלֹהִים לְבַדֶּךָ: תהלים פו
כִּי־גָדוֹל מֵעַל־שָׁמַיִם חַסְדֶּךָ, וְעַד־שְׁחָקִים אֲמִתֶּךָ: תהלים קח
גָּדוֹל יהוה וּמְהֻלָּל מְאֹד, וְלִגְדֻלָּתוֹ אֵין חֵקֶר: תהלים קמה
כִּי גָדוֹל יהוה וּמְהֻלָּל מְאֹד, וְנוֹרָא הוּא עַל־כָּל־אֱלֹהִים: דברי הימים א׳ טז
כִּי אֵל גָּדוֹל יהוה, וּמֶלֶךְ גָּדוֹל עַל־כָּל־אֱלֹהִים: תהלים צה
אֲשֶׁר מִי־אֵל בַּשָּׁמַיִם וּבָאָרֶץ אֲשֶׁר־יַעֲשֶׂה כְמַעֲשֶׂיךָ וְכִגְבוּרֹתֶךָ: דברים ג
מִי לֹא יִרָאֲךָ מֶלֶךְ הַגּוֹיִם, כִּי לְךָ יָאָתָה ירמיה י
כִּי בְכָל־חַכְמֵי הַגּוֹיִם וּבְכָל־מַלְכוּתָם מֵאֵין כָּמוֹךָ:
מֵאֵין כָּמוֹךָ יהוה, גָּדוֹל אַתָּה וְגָדוֹל שִׁמְךָ בִּגְבוּרָה:
לְךָ זְרוֹעַ עִם־גְּבוּרָה, תָּעֹז יָדְךָ תָּרוּם יְמִינֶךָ: תהלים פט
לְךָ יוֹם אַף־לְךָ לָיְלָה, אַתָּה הֲכִינוֹתָ מָאוֹר וָשָׁמֶשׁ: תהלים עד
אֲשֶׁר בְּיָדוֹ מֶחְקְרֵי־אָרֶץ, וְתוֹעֲפוֹת הָרִים לוֹ: תהלים צה
מִי יְמַלֵּל גְּבוּרוֹת יהוה, יַשְׁמִיעַ כָּל־תְּהִלָּתוֹ: תהלים קו
לְךָ יהוה הַגְּדֻלָּה וְהַגְּבוּרָה וְהַתִּפְאֶרֶת וְהַנֵּצַח וְהַהוֹד דברי הימים א׳ כט
כִּי־כֹל בַּשָּׁמַיִם וּבָאָרֶץ, לְךָ יהוה הַמַּמְלָכָה וְהַמִּתְנַשֵּׂא לְכֹל לְרֹאשׁ:
לְךָ שָׁמַיִם אַף־לְךָ אָרֶץ, תֵּבֵל וּמְלֹאָהּ אַתָּה יְסַדְתָּם: תהלים פט

---

moved to compassion, to respond. The idea that God hears prayer is central to Jewish faith. Ultimate reality is not blind to our existence, indifferent to our fate, deaf to our prayers. At the heart of being is One who created us in love, who knows us, cares for us, hears our prayers, and responds "to all who call on Him in truth."

You laid out the boundaries of the earth; summer and winter – it is You who formed them. *Ps. 74*
You shattered the Leviathan's heads; You turned him into food for desert creatures.
You split the channels of spring and stream, You dried up mighty rivers.
You shattered the sea with Your might; You broke the sea-monsters' heads on the water.
You rule over the surge of the sea; as its waves swell, it is You who still them. *Ps. 89*
Great is the LORD and greatly to be praised in the city of God, on His holy mountain. *Ps. 48*
LORD of hosts, the God of Israel, enthroned above the Cherubim, You are God alone. *Is. 37*
God who is revered in a company of many holy ones, awesome over all that surrounds Him. *Ps. 89*
The heavens will declare Your wonders, LORD, and Your faithfulness, in the assembly of holy ones.
Come, let us sing for joy to the LORD; let us shout aloud to the Rock of our salvation. *Ps. 95*
Let us greet Him with thanksgiving, shout aloud to Him in songs of praise.
Righteousness and justice are the foundation of Your throne; kindness and truth come out to greet You. *Ps. 89*
Together we made sweet company; in a great crowd we came to the House of God. *Ps. 55*
The sea is His, He made it; the dry land too, for His hands formed it. *Ps. 95*
In His hand is every living soul, the breath of all mankind. *Job 12*

▸ The spirit is Yours, and the body Your creation; spare those You have formed.
The spirit is Yours, and the body is Yours; LORD, act for the sake of Your name.
We have come because of Your name, LORD; act for the sake of Your name.
For the glory of Your name, for Your name is Gracious and Compassionate God.
For the sake of Your name, LORD, forgive our iniquity, though it is great.

---

is a subtle allusion here, in the verb חוּסָה, "spare, take pity," to the last two verses of the book of Jonah that we will read tomorrow afternoon, when God criticizes Jonah for taking pity on a plant he did not labor to make grow while complaining about God taking pity on the inhabitants of Nineveh.

Rabbi Levi Yitzḥak of Berditchev once prayed: "Master of the universe, if a Jew were to see tefillin lying in the street, would he not bend down to pick them up? We are Your tefillin, and we are lying in the street, ignored or trodden upon by passersby. How, then, can You not pick us up?"

אַתָּה הִצַּבְתָּ כָּל־גְּבוּלוֹת אָרֶץ, קַיִץ וָחֹרֶף אַתָּה יְצַרְתָּם: תהלים עד
אַתָּה רִצַּצְתָּ רָאשֵׁי לִוְיָתָן, תִּתְּנֶנּוּ מַאֲכָל לְעָם לְצִיִּים:
אַתָּה בָקַעְתָּ מַעְיָן וָנָחַל, אַתָּה הוֹבַשְׁתָּ נַהֲרוֹת אֵיתָן:
אַתָּה פוֹרַרְתָּ בְעָזְּךָ יָם, שִׁבַּרְתָּ רָאשֵׁי תַנִּינִים עַל־הַמָּיִם:
אַתָּה מוֹשֵׁל בְּגֵאוּת הַיָּם, בְּשׂוֹא גַלָּיו אַתָּה תְשַׁבְּחֵם: תהלים פט
גָּדוֹל יהוה וּמְהֻלָּל מְאֹד, בְּעִיר אֱלֹהֵינוּ הַר־קָדְשׁוֹ: תהלים מח
יהוה צְבָאוֹת אֱלֹהֵי יִשְׂרָאֵל יֹשֵׁב הַכְּרֻבִים אַתָּה־הוּא הָאֱלֹהִים לְבַדֶּךָ: ישעיה לז
אֵל נַעֲרָץ בְּסוֹד־קְדֹשִׁים רַבָּה, וְנוֹרָא עַל־כָּל־סְבִיבָיו: תהלים פט
וְיוֹדוּ שָׁמַיִם פִּלְאֲךָ יהוה, אַף־אֱמוּנָתְךָ בִּקְהַל קְדֹשִׁים:
לְכוּ נְרַנְּנָה לַיהוה, נָרִיעָה לְצוּר יִשְׁעֵנוּ: תהלים צה
נְקַדְּמָה פָנָיו בְּתוֹדָה, בִּזְמִרוֹת נָרִיעַ לוֹ:
צֶדֶק וּמִשְׁפָּט מְכוֹן כִּסְאֶךָ, חֶסֶד וֶאֱמֶת יְקַדְּמוּ פָנֶיךָ: תהלים פט
אֲשֶׁר יַחְדָּו נַמְתִּיק סוֹד, בְּבֵית אֱלֹהִים נְהַלֵּךְ בְּרָגֶשׁ: תהלים נה
אֲשֶׁר־לוֹ הַיָּם וְהוּא עָשָׂהוּ, וְיַבֶּשֶׁת יָדָיו יָצָרוּ: תהלים צה
אֲשֶׁר בְּיָדוֹ נֶפֶשׁ כָּל־חָי, וְרוּחַ כָּל־בְּשַׂר־אִישׁ: איוב יב

◂ הַנְּשָׁמָה לָךְ וְהַגּוּף פָּעֳלָךְ, חוּסָה עַל עֲמָלָךְ.
הַנְּשָׁמָה לָךְ וְהַגּוּף שֶׁלָּךְ, יהוה עֲשֵׂה לְמַעַן שְׁמֶךָ.
אָתָאנוּ עַל שִׁמְךָ, יהוה עֲשֵׂה לְמַעַן שְׁמֶךָ
בַּעֲבוּר כְּבוֹד שִׁמְךָ, כִּי אֵל חַנּוּן וְרַחוּם שְׁמֶךָ.
לְמַעַן שִׁמְךָ יהוה, וְסָלַחְתָּ לַעֲוֹנֵנוּ כִּי רַב הוּא.

צֶדֶק וּמִשְׁפָּט...חֶסֶד וֶאֱמֶת *Righteousness and justice... kindness and truth.* These are the four bases of the moral life according to Judaism. They represent two kinds of justice and two kinds of love. *Tzedek* is distributive justice – justice as fairness. *Mishpat* is retributive justice – justice as law. *Ḥesed* is love as kindness, emotion translated into deed. *Emet,* "truth," here means love as loyalty and fidelity (Ibn Ezra to Gen. 24:49).

הַנְּשָׁמָה לָךְ וְהַגּוּף פָּעֳלָךְ, חוּסָה עַל עֲמָלָךְ *The spirit is Yours, and the body Your creation; spare those You have formed.* A liturgical poem, not a biblical verse, beautiful in its simplicity and brevity. We are what You made us. Therefore, were You to destroy us You would be destroying Your own handiwork. There

Traditionally, the piyut "Surely, our guilty actions" (page 1279) was said at this point. Nowadays, most congregations say only the two lines of the original alternating refrains, and the last stanza, beginning with "Heal the wound."

The Leader recites each verse and the congregation repeats.

דַּרְכְּךָ Your way, our God, is to be slow to anger,
with both sinners and the righteous – this is Your praise.

לְמַעַנְךָ Act for Your sake, our God, and not for ours –
see how we stand before You, inadequate and empty.

The Leader then the congregation:

תַּעֲלָה אֲרוּכָה Heal the wound of this driven leaf;
relent for the sake of dust and ashes.
Cast away our sins and pardon Your handiwork;
behold, there is no one worthy among us:
act righteously with us.

Jews were dispersed, and each community developed its own customs. Hence the variations from place to place, particularly noticeable on Yom Kippur when many of the prayers and most of the liturgical poems are non-statutory.

The following are some of the principles governing custom in prayer: (1) With rare exceptions, each custom has its own logic and halakhic integrity, and should be respected. (2) Communities are bound to follow their own customs, for they are bound by those who came before them. (3) Individuals who move from one community to another are bound by the customs of the place where they now belong, rather than the place from which they came. (4) Individuals who are visiting a community rather than staying there as permanent residents are bound in their public behavior to follow local custom; in private they should observe the stringencies of the community from which they came and to which they intend to return. The overarching principle is: *Minhag Yisrael Torah hi*, "Jewish custom is also part of Torah."

Explaining the different customs of prayer among different groups of Jews, the Maggid of Mezeritch said: "Just as there were thirteen gates in the Temple (*Shekalim* 6:2), so there are thirteen gates of prayer: one for each of the twelve tribes and the thirteenth for the individual who does not know from which tribe he comes."

Traditionally, the piyut אָמְנָם אֲשָׁמֵינוּ *(page 1279) was said at this point. Nowadays, most congregations say only the two lines of the original alternating refrains, and the last stanza, beginning with* תַּעֲלֶה אֲרוּכָה.
The שליח ציבור *recites each verse and the* קהל *repeats.*

דַּרְכְּךָ אֱלֹהֵינוּ לְהַאֲרִיךְ אַפֶּךָ, לָרָעִים וְלַטּוֹבִים, וְהִיא תְהִלָּתֶךָ.
לְמַעַנְךָ אֱלֹהֵינוּ עֲשֵׂה, וְלֹא לָנוּ, רְאֵה עֲמִידָתֵנוּ דַּלִּים וְרֵיקִים.

The שליח ציבור *then the* קהל*:*

תַּעֲלֶה אֲרוּכָה לְעָלֶה נִדָּף / תְּנַחֵם עַל עָפָר וָאֵפֶר
תַּשְׁלִיךְ חֲטָאֵינוּ, וְתָחֹן מַעֲשֶׂיךָ
תֵּרֶא כִּי אֵין אִישׁ, עֲשֵׂה עִמָּנוּ צְדָקָה.

דַּרְכְּךָ *Your way.* These two lines are the opening and refrain of a poem beginning *Omnam Ashameinu,* said in full in some rites, in part in others, while some say only the first two lines and the last verse, "Heal the wound." The poem is the work of the earliest liturgical poet we know by name, Yose ben Yose, who lived and worked in Israel in the fourth or fifth century. He was a pioneer of the highly-structured alphabetical acrostic style of poetry that plays so large a part in the prayers of Rosh HaShana and Yom Kippur. *Slow to anger with both sinners and the righteous:* One of the Thirteen Attributes of Mercy is *erekh apayim,* "slow to anger" (Ex. 34:6). The Talmud asks why the phrase is in the plural, and answers: God is slow to anger both to the righteous and to the wicked (*Eiruvin* 22a).

ON DIFFERENCES OF CUSTOM

The "Thirteen Attributes of Mercy," prefaced by the paragraph beginning "God, King who sits," is the epicenter of *Seliḥot,* the basis of our plea for forgiveness. There are significantly different customs as to how many times this is said during the evening service: some say it seven times, others four, yet others once. The reason is that the basic structures of Jewish prayer were established long ago, in Second Temple times and their immediate aftermath, when there was a single center of Jewish life in the land of Israel. The principles established then, apply to all Jewish communities. Thereafter, however,

THE THIRTEEN ATTRIBUTES OF MERCY

All, while standing:

אֵל מֶלֶךְ God, King who sits upon a throne of compassion, who acts with loving-kindness, who pardons the iniquities of His people, passing them before Him in order; who forgives sinners and pardons transgressors; who performs righteousness with all flesh and spirit, do not repay their bad actions in kind. ▸ God, You taught us to speak thirteen attributes: recall for us today the covenant of the thirteen attributes, as You in ancient times showed the humble one [Moses], as is written: The LORD descended in the cloud and stood with him there, and proclaimed in the name of the LORD: *Ex. 34*

The congregation then Leader:

וַיַּעֲבֹר And the LORD passed by before him and proclaimed: *Ibid.*

All say aloud:

יהוה The LORD, the LORD, compassionate and gracious God, slow to anger, abounding in loving-kindness and truth, extending loving-kindness to a thousand generations, forgiving iniquity, rebellion and sin, and absolving [the guilty who repent].

All continue:

Forgive us our iniquity and our sin, and take us as Your inheritance.

הוֹרֵיתָ לָּנוּ *You taught us.* A reference to the idea stated in the Talmud that when God appeared to Moses on Mount Sinai in answer to his prayer for forgiveness for the people, He taught him and all future generations how to pray by invoking the "Thirteen Attributes of Mercy" (*Rosh HaShana* 17b).

בְּרִית שְׁלֹשׁ עֶשְׂרֵה *The covenant of the thirteen attributes.* The covenant God made with Moses at that time that no prayer that invoked the Thirteen Attributes would go unanswered (*ibid.*).

THE THIRTEEN ATTRIBUTES OF MERCY

The "Thirteen Attributes of Mercy," the name given by the sages to God's declaration to Moses when he prayed on behalf of the people after the sin of the golden calf, are the basis of all *seliḥot*, prayers for forgiveness, for they are God's Self-definition as the source of compassion and pardon that frames

י״ג מידות הרחמים

All, while standing:

אֵל מֶלֶךְ יוֹשֵׁב עַל כִּסֵּא רַחֲמִים, מִתְנַהֵג בַּחֲסִידוּת.
מוֹחֵל עֲוֹנוֹת עַמּוֹ, מַעֲבִיר רִאשׁוֹן רִאשׁוֹן.
מַרְבֶּה מְחִילָה לְחַטָּאִים, וּסְלִיחָה לְפוֹשְׁעִים.
עֹשֶׂה צְדָקוֹת עִם כָּל בָּשָׂר וָרוּחַ, לֹא כְרָעָתָם תִּגְמֹל.
‹ אֵל, הוֹרֵיתָ לָּנוּ לוֹמַר שְׁלֹשׁ עֶשְׂרֵה
וּזְכָר לָנוּ הַיּוֹם בְּרִית שְׁלֹשׁ עֶשְׂרֵה
כְּמוֹ שֶׁהוֹדַעְתָּ לֶעָנָו מִקֶּדֶם, כְּמוֹ שֶׁכָּתוּב:
שמות לד וַיֵּרֶד יהוה בֶּעָנָן, וַיִּתְיַצֵּב עִמּוֹ שָׁם
וַיִּקְרָא בְשֵׁם, יהוה:

The קהל *then* שליח ציבור*:*

שם וַיַּעֲבֹר יהוה עַל־פָּנָיו וַיִּקְרָא

All say aloud:

יהוה, יהוה, אֵל רַחוּם וְחַנּוּן, אֶרֶךְ אַפַּיִם, וְרַב־חֶסֶד וֶאֱמֶת:
נֹצֵר חֶסֶד לָאֲלָפִים, נֹשֵׂא עָוֹן וָפֶשַׁע וְחַטָּאָה, וְנַקֵּה:

All continue:

וְסָלַחְתָּ לַעֲוֹנֵנוּ וּלְחַטָּאתֵנוּ, וּנְחַלְתָּנוּ:

אֵל מֶלֶךְ יוֹשֵׁב *God, King who sits.* Though at the beginning of Rosh HaShana God takes His seat on the Throne of Justice, He is moved by the sound of the shofar to sit instead on the Throne of Compassion (*Vayikra Raba* 29:9).

מִתְנַהֵג בַּחֲסִידוּת *Who acts with loving-kindness.* Based on the phrase (II Samuel 22:26; Ps. 18:26), "With the kind, You are kind." God's kindness to us has its origins in the kindness of our ancestors, which God never forgets.

מַעֲבִיר רִאשׁוֹן רִאשׁוֹן *Passing them before Him in order.* God forgives our first sin if we do not repeat it; or, if our sins are equal to our merits, He removes a sin from the scale so as to tilt it in our favor (Alfassi, Rashi to *Rosh HaShana* 17a).

סְלַח לָנוּ Forgive us, our Father, for we have sinned. Pardon us, our King, for we have transgressed. For You, LORD, are good and forgiving, *Ps. 86*
abounding in loving-kindness to all who call on You.

הַאֲזִינָה Give ear, LORD, to our prayer, and listen to the voice of our pleading. Listen to the sound of our pleading, our King and our God, for it is to You we pray. Let Your ears be intent and Your eyes be open to hear the prayer of Your servants, the people of Israel. And from heaven, *1 Kings 8*
the sanctuary of Your dwelling, hear their prayer and their plea, and do justice for them. Forgive Your people who have sinned against You.

כְּרַחֵם As a father has compassion for his children,
so, LORD, have compassion for us.
Salvation belongs to the LORD; *Ps. 3*
may Your blessing rest upon Your people, Selah!
The LORD of hosts is with us, *Ps. 46*
the God of Jacob is our stronghold, Selah!
LORD of hosts: happy is the one who trusts in You. *Ps. 84*
LORD, save! May the King answer us on the day we call. *Ps. 20*

---

osity of the one who does it, not the merits of the one to whom, or for whom, it is done.

6. *Slow to anger:* Thus giving time for wrongdoers to repent.
7. *Abounding in loving-kindness:* According to a person's needs, not their deserts.
8. *And truth:* Giving a just reward to those who do His will.
9. *Extending loving-kindness to a thousand generations.* God remembers through the ages the kindness of the patriarchs and the merits of our ancestors.
10. *Forgiving iniquity:* Sins committed knowingly.
11. *Rebellion:* Sins committed in a spirit of defiance.
12. *And sin:* Sins committed unwittingly, either because we did not know what we were doing or did not know that it was forbidden.
13. *And absolving*: Literally "cleansing" those who repent.

סְלַח לָנוּ אָבִינוּ כִּי חָטָאנוּ, מְחַל לָנוּ מַלְכֵּנוּ כִּי פָשָׁעְנוּ.
כִּי־אַתָּה אֲדֹנָי טוֹב וְסַלָּח, וְרַב־חֶסֶד לְכָל־קֹרְאֶיךָ׃ תהלים פו

הַאֲזִינָה יהוה תְּפִלָּתֵנוּ, וְהַקְשִׁיבָה בְּקוֹל תַּחֲנוּנוֹתֵינוּ. הַקְשִׁיבָה
לְקוֹל שַׁוְעֵנוּ מַלְכֵּנוּ וֵאלֹהֵינוּ כִּי אֵלֶיךָ נִתְפַּלָּל. תְּהִי נָא אָזְנְךָ
קַשֶּׁבֶת וְעֵינֶיךָ פְּתוּחוֹת לִשְׁמֹעַ אֶל תְּפִלַּת עֲבָדֶיךָ עַמְּךָ יִשְׂרָאֵל.
וְשָׁמַעְתָּ הַשָּׁמַיִם מְכוֹן שִׁבְתֶּךָ אֶת־תְּפִלָּתָם וְאֶת־תְּחִנָּתָם וְעָשִׂיתָ מלכים א׳ ח
מִשְׁפָּטָם׃ וְסָלַחְתָּ לְעַמְּךָ אֲשֶׁר חָטְאוּ־לָךְ׃

כְּרַחֵם אָב עַל בָּנִים, כֵּן תְּרַחֵם יהוה עָלֵינוּ.
לַיהוה הַיְשׁוּעָה, עַל־עַמְּךָ בִרְכָתֶךָ סֶּלָה׃ תהלים ג
יהוה צְבָאוֹת עִמָּנוּ, מִשְׂגָּב לָנוּ אֱלֹהֵי יַעֲקֹב סֶלָה׃ תהלים מו
יהוה צְבָאוֹת, אַשְׁרֵי אָדָם בֹּטֵחַ בָּךְ׃ תהלים פד
יהוה הוֹשִׁיעָה, הַמֶּלֶךְ יַעֲנֵנוּ בְיוֹם־קָרְאֵנוּ׃ תהלים כ

---

the moral life. They tell us that God "does not desire the death of the wicked, but rather that they turn from their ways and live" (Ezek. 33:11). When we repent and make good the harm we have done, God forgives. The Thirteen Attributes are as follows:

1. *The Lord:* The name that signifies God's attribute of compassion as opposed to strict justice.
2. *The Lord:* God retains the same compassion even after we have sinned, thus making repentance possible.
3. *God:* The power and force through which God sustains the universe and all that lives.
4. *Compassionate:* The root *r-ḥ-m* is the same as "womb." Hence, it means the kind of compassion a mother has for a child.
5. *Gracious:* The root *ḥ-n-n* refers to behavior that comes from the gener-

▸ סְלַח־נָא Forgive, please, this people's iniquity, *Num. 14*
in the abundance of Your kindness,
and as You have forgiven this people
from the time of Egypt until now,
and there it is said:

Congregation then Leader:

And the LORD said, I have forgiven as you asked.

All continue:

הַטֵּה Give ear, my God and hear; open Your eyes and see our desolation, and the city that bears Your name, for it is not on the strength of our righteousness that we throw down our pleadings before You, but on the strength of Your great compassion. LORD, hear me; LORD, forgive; LORD, listen and act and do not delay – for Your sake, my God; for Your city and Your people bear Your name. *Dan. 9*

The Ark is opened.

Our God and God of our fathers,

The Leader recites the first verse and the congregation repeats.
The subsequent verses are each recited first by the congregation, then repeated by the Leader.

סְלַח נָא Forgive, please,
the faults and transgressions of Your nation;
at the iniquity of Your children, may Your anger not flare.
Forgive, please, what is repulsive in them, and they will draw life
from the wellspring that is with You;
the iniquity of Your tribes tolerate, and relent as You have promised.
Forgive, please, those who confess and forsake their folly, as You
have written;
iniquity and transgression forgive, for the sake of Your name.

---

prayers. Written as an alphabetical acrostic in the third word of the first line and the second of the second in each couplet, its author is unknown.

מוֹדִים וְעוֹזְבִים *Those who confess and forsake their sinful ways.* Two of the essential ingredients of repentance, the phrase is a reference to Proverbs 28:13, "Whoever conceals their sins does not prosper, but one who confesses and renounces them finds mercy."

› סְלַח־נָא לַעֲוֹן הָעָם הַזֶּה כְּגֹדֶל חַסְדֶּךָ במדבר יד
וְכַאֲשֶׁר נָשָׂאתָה לָעָם הַזֶּה מִמִּצְרַיִם וְעַד־הֵנָּה:
וְשָׁם נֶאֱמַר

קהל then שליח ציבור:

וַיֹּאמֶר יהוה, סָלַחְתִּי כִּדְבָרֶךָ:

All continue:

דניאל ט הַטֵּה אֱלֹהַי אָזְנְךָ וּשְׁמָע, פְּקַח עֵינֶיךָ וּרְאֵה שֹׁמְמֹתֵינוּ וְהָעִיר אֲשֶׁר־נִקְרָא שִׁמְךָ עָלֶיהָ, כִּי לֹא עַל־צִדְקֹתֵינוּ אֲנַחְנוּ מַפִּילִים תַּחֲנוּנֵינוּ לְפָנֶיךָ, כִּי עַל־רַחֲמֶיךָ הָרַבִּים: אֲדֹנָי שְׁמָעָה, אֲדֹנָי סְלָחָה, אֲדֹנָי הַקְשִׁיבָה וַעֲשֵׂה אַל־תְּאַחַר, לְמַעַנְךָ אֱלֹהַי, כִּי־שִׁמְךָ נִקְרָא עַל־עִירְךָ וְעַל־עַמֶּךָ:

The ארון קודש is opened.

אֱלֹהֵינוּ וֵאלֹהֵי אֲבוֹתֵינוּ

The שליח ציבור recites the first verse and the קהל repeats.
The subsequent verses are each recited first by the קהל, then repeated by the שליח ציבור.

סְלַח נָא אֲשָׁמוֹת וּפְשָׁעֵי לְאֻמֶּךָ
לַעֲוֹן בָּנֶיךָ בַּל יֶחֱרֶה זַעְמֶךָ.

סְלַח נָא גְּעוּלָם וְיִחְיוּ מִמְּקוֹר עִמֶּךָ
לַעֲוֹן דְּגָלֶיךָ שָׂא וְתִנָּחֵם כִּנְאֻמֶּךָ.

סְלַח נָא הֶבֶל מוֹדִים וְעוֹזְבִים כְּרִשּׁוּמֶךָ
לַעֲוֹן וָפֶשַׁע מְחַל לְמַעַן שְׁמֶךָ.

סְלַח נָא אֲשָׁמוֹת *Forgive, please, the faults.* A poem based on the plea of Moses after the sin of the spies: "Forgive, please [*selaḥ na*] this people's iniquity [*avon*], in the abundance of Your kindness, and as You have forgiven this people from the time of Egypt until now" (Num. 14:19). This, as noted above, was one of the two great occasions when the prayers of Moses secured forgiveness for the people, thus becoming a basis for all future penitential

Forgive, please, the evil and error of those created to glorify Your name;
the iniquity of their sins, cleanse in Your bounteous rain.

Forgive, please, the petty foolishness of the wicked of Your nation;
let the iniquity of Your beloved ones be sought and not be there – as You promised.

Forgive, please, the deceit of those who bow and prostrate themselves before You;
the iniquity of Your chosen ones, atone with the good of Your discernment.

Forgive, please, the rebellion of those who seek You and proclaim Your unity in Your world;
the iniquity of the dispersed erase, and rebuild Your Temple.

Forgive, please, their perversity and shelter them under Your canopy of peace;
the iniquity of Your servants overlook, and tread it down into Your hiddenness.

Forgive, please, lest they be punished from Your lofty realm;
let the iniquity of Your flock be forgotten, for this is Your praise and exaltation.

Forgive, please, their shameful acts, take pity on them from Your lofty realm;
the iniquity of those You love, forgive; let them not become ensnared in Your nets.

Forgive, please, the stain of the abominable straying of Your beloved ones;
let the iniquity of Your pure ones pass, in the greatness of Your compassion.

The Ark is closed.

---

love for Israel. The poet, acknowledging the sins of the people, appeals in the end not to justice but to love.

סְלַח נָא זְדוֹנוֹת וּשְׁגָגוֹת לְבָרוּאֵי לִשְׁמֶךָ
לַעֲוֹן חֲטָאֵימוֹ חַטֵּא בִּנְדִיבַת גִּשְׁמֶךָ.

סְלַח נָא טֶפֶשׂ טִפְלוּת רִשְׁעֵי אֻמֶּךָ
לַעֲוֹן יְדִידֶיךָ יְבֻקַּשׁ וְאֵינֶנּוּ כִּנְאֻמֶךָ.

סְלַח נָא כַּחַשׁ כּוֹרְעִים וּמִשְׁתַּחֲוִים לְעֻמֶּךָ
לַעֲוֹן לְקוֹחֶיךָ כַּפֵּר בְּטוּב טַעְמֶךָ.

סְלַח נָא מְרִי מְיַחֲלֶיךָ וּמְיַחֲדֶיךָ בְּעוֹלָמֶךָ
לַעֲוֹן נִדָּחִים מְחֵה וּבְנֵה אוּלַמֶּךָ.

סְלַח נָא סִלּוּפָם וְגוֹנְנֵם בְּסֻכַּת שְׁלוֹמֶךָ
לַעֲוֹן עֲבָדֶיךָ עַלֵּם וּכְבֹשׁ בְּעִלּוּמֶךָ.

סְלַח נָא פֶּן יֵעָנְשׁוּ מִמְּרוֹמֶךָ
לַעֲוֹן צֹאנְךָ שַׁכַּח וְהִיא תְּהִלָּתְךָ וְרוֹמְמֶךָ.

סְלַח נָא קְלוֹנָם וַחֲמֹל עָלֵימוֹ מִמְּרוֹמֶךָ
לַעֲוֹן רְחוּמֶיךָ תִּשָּׂא מִלְּצוּדָם בְּחֶרְמֶךָ.

סְלַח נָא שֶׁמֶץ תַּעְתּוּעַ תִּעוּב רְחוּמֶיךָ
לַעֲוֹן תְּמִימֶיךָ הַעֲבֵר כְּגֹדֶל רַחֲמֶיךָ.

The ארון קודש *is closed.*

יְבֻקַּשׁ וְאֵינֶנּוּ כִּנְאֻמֶךָ *Be sought and not be there – as You promised.* A reference to Jeremiah 50:20: "In those days, at that time, says the Lord, they will search for Israel's iniquity and it will not be there, they will seek the sins of Judah and they will be nowhere to be found, for I shall forgive those I leave behind."

לַעֲוֹן רְחוּמֶיךָ תִּשָּׂא *The iniquity of those You love, forgive.* Note the threefold reference, in the last three lines, to *raḥamim* (ר-ח-מ), God's compassionate

All, while standing:

אֵל מֶלֶךְ God, King who sits upon a throne of compassion, who acts with loving-kindness, who pardons the iniquities of His people, passing them before Him in order; who forgives sinners and pardons transgressors; who performs righteousness with all flesh and spirit, do not repay their bad actions in kind. ▸ God, You taught us to speak thirteen attributes: recall for us today the covenant of the thirteen attributes, as You in ancient times showed the humble one [Moses], as is written: The LORD descended in the cloud and stood with him *Ex. 34*
there, and proclaimed in the name of the LORD:

The congregation then Leader:

And the LORD passed by before him and proclaimed: *Ibid.*

All say aloud:

יהוה The LORD, the LORD, compassionate and gracious God, slow to anger, abounding in loving-kindness and truth, extending loving-kindness to a thousand generations, forgiving iniquity, rebellion and sin, and absolving [the guilty who repent].

All continue:

Forgive us our iniquity and our sin, and take us as Your inheritance.

סְלַח לָנוּ Forgive us, our Father, for we have sinned. Pardon us, our
King, for we have transgressed. For You, LORD, are good and forgiving, *Ps. 86*
abounding in loving-kindness to all who call on You.

אַל תָּבוֹא Do not come into judgment with us, for no living being can vindicate itself before You. What can we say in Your presence, LORD our God? What can we plead? How can we justify ourselves? Our God, we are humiliated by our actions, ashamed of our sins. Our God, we are too humiliated and ashamed to raise our faces to You, our God. We know we have sinned and that there is no one to stand up for us. Let Your great name stand up for us in time of trouble.

כְּרַחֵם As a father has compassion for his children, so, LORD, have
compassion for us. Salvation belongs to the LORD; may Your blessing *Ps. 3*
rest upon Your people, Selah! The LORD of hosts is with us, the God of *Ps. 46*
Jacob is our stronghold, Selah! LORD of hosts: happy is the one who *Ps. 84*
trusts in You. LORD, save! May the King answer us on the day we call. *Ps. 20*

All, while standing:

אֵל מֶלֶךְ יוֹשֵׁב עַל כִּסֵּא רַחֲמִים, מִתְנַהֵג בַּחֲסִידוּת.
מוֹחֵל עֲוֹנוֹת עַמּוֹ, מַעֲבִיר רִאשׁוֹן רִאשׁוֹן.
מַרְבֶּה מְחִילָה לְחַטָּאִים, וּסְלִיחָה לְפוֹשְׁעִים.
עֹשֶׂה צְדָקוֹת עִם כָּל בָּשָׂר וָרוּחַ, לֹא כְרָעָתָם תִּגְמֹל.
◂ אֵל, הוֹרֵיתָ לָּנוּ לוֹמַר שְׁלֹשׁ עֶשְׂרֵה
וּזְכָר לָנוּ הַיּוֹם בְּרִית שְׁלֹשׁ עֶשְׂרֵה
כְּמוֹ שֶׁהוֹדַעְתָּ לֶעָנָו מִקֶּדֶם, כְּמוֹ שֶׁכָּתוּב:
וַיֵּרֶד יהוה בֶּעָנָן, וַיִּתְיַצֵּב עִמּוֹ שָׁם שמות לד
וַיִּקְרָא בְשֵׁם, יהוה:

The שליח ציבור *then* קהל*:*

וַיַּעֲבֹר יהוה עַל־פָּנָיו וַיִּקְרָא שם

All say aloud:

יהוה, יהוה, אֵל רַחוּם וְחַנּוּן, אֶרֶךְ אַפַּיִם, וְרַב־חֶסֶד וֶאֱמֶת:
נֹצֵר חֶסֶד לָאֲלָפִים, נֹשֵׂא עָוֹן וָפֶשַׁע וְחַטָּאָה, וְנַקֵּה:

All continue:

וְסָלַחְתָּ לַעֲוֹנֵנוּ וּלְחַטָּאתֵנוּ, וּנְחַלְתָּנוּ:

סְלַח לָנוּ אָבִינוּ כִּי חָטָאנוּ, מְחַל לָנוּ מַלְכֵּנוּ כִּי פָשָׁעְנוּ.
כִּי־אַתָּה אֲדֹנָי טוֹב וְסַלָּח, וְרַב־חֶסֶד לְכָל־קֹרְאֶיךָ: תהלים פו

אַל תָּבוֹא בְמִשְׁפָּט עִמָּנוּ, כִּי לֹא יִצְדַּק לְפָנֶיךָ כָל חָי. מַה נֹּאמַר לְפָנֶיךָ יהוה אֱלֹהֵינוּ, מַה נְּדַבֵּר וּמַה נִּצְטַדָּק. אֱלֹהֵינוּ, בּוֹשְׁנוּ בְּמַעֲשֵׂינוּ וְנִכְלַמְנוּ בַּעֲוֹנֵינוּ. אֱלֹהֵינוּ, בֹּשְׁנוּ וְנִכְלַמְנוּ, לְהָרִים אֱלֹהֵינוּ פָּנֵינוּ אֵלֶיךָ. יָדַעְנוּ כִּי חָטָאנוּ וְאֵין מִי יַעֲמֹד בַּעֲדֵנוּ שִׁמְךָ הַגָּדוֹל יַעֲמָד לָנוּ בְּעֵת צָרָה.

תהלים ג כְּרַחֵם אָב עַל בָּנִים, כֵּן תְּרַחֵם יהוה עָלֵינוּ. לַיהוה הַיְשׁוּעָה, עַל־עַמְּךָ
תהלים מו בִרְכָתֶךָ סֶּלָה: יהוה צְבָאוֹת עִמָּנוּ, מִשְׂגָּב לָנוּ אֱלֹהֵי יַעֲקֹב סֶלָה:
תהלים פד תהלים כ יהוה צְבָאוֹת, אַשְׁרֵי אָדָם בֹּטֵחַ בָּךְ: יהוה הוֹשִׁיעָה, הַמֶּלֶךְ יַעֲנֵנוּ
בְיוֹם־קָרְאֵנוּ:

Some say "Forgive, please" at this point; however, the prevailing custom is to continue with "Our God and God of our fathers" below.

▸ Forgive, please, this people's iniquity, in the abundance of Your kindness, and as You have forgiven this people from the time of Egypt until now, and there it is said: *Num. 14*

Congregation then Leader:

And the LORD said, I have forgiven as you asked.

All continue:

הַטֵּה Give ear, my God and hear; open Your eyes and see our desolation, and the city that bears Your name, for it is not on the strength of our righteousness that we throw down our pleadings before You, but on the strength of Your great compassion. LORD, hear me; LORD, forgive; LORD, listen and act and do not delay – for Your sake, my God; for Your city and Your people bear Your name. *Dan. 9*

The following verse is a prelude to the subsequent piyut, "It is surely true." Nowadays, most congregations omit it.

Day by day / they seek / You;
the good Stronghold – / may the mighty strength / of Your speech be in saying:
"I have forgiven."

The Ark is opened.

Our God and God of our fathers,

In many congregations, the Leader recites the first verse and the congregation repeats. The subsequent verses are each recited first by the congregation, then repeated by the Leader. In others, the Leader and the congregation recite them alternately.

אָמְנָם כֵּן It is surely true / that our impulse controls / us;
You alone can clear us, / abundantly righteous One, / answer us:
"I have forgiven."

Despise the informer/ and invalidate / his indictment;
let our Beloved roar out, / and give voice / to His word:
"I have forgiven."

---

law – his decisions are cited by the halakhic sages of the time – as well as a liturgical poet who had written an elegy on the Blois martyrs of 1171. He himself died as a martyr during the anti-Jewish riots on *Shabbat HaGadol*, 16–17 March, 1190. Fearing an attack, the Jews obtained permission from the sheriff of York to take refuge in Clifford's Tower in the royal castle, but a violent mob gathered below, and the Jews realized they would not escape

Some say סְלַח־נָא at this point; however, the prevailing custom is to continue with אֱלֹהֵינוּ וֵאלֹהֵי אֲבוֹתֵינוּ below.

במדבר יד ‹ סְלַח־נָא לַעֲוֹן הָעָם הַזֶּה כְּגֹדֶל חַסְדֶּךָ
וְכַאֲשֶׁר נָשָׂאתָה לָעָם הַזֶּה מִמִּצְרַיִם וְעַד־הֵנָּה:
וְשָׁם נֶאֱמַר

שליח ציבור then קהל:

וַיֹּאמֶר יהוה, סָלַחְתִּי כִּדְבָרֶךָ:

All continue:

דניאל ט הַטֵּה אֱלֹהַי אָזְנְךָ וּשְׁמָע, פְּקַח עֵינֶיךָ וּרְאֵה שֹׁמְמֹתֵינוּ וְהָעִיר אֲשֶׁר־נִקְרָא שִׁמְךָ עָלֶיהָ, כִּי לֹא עַל־צִדְקֹתֵינוּ אֲנַחְנוּ מַפִּילִים תַּחֲנוּנֵינוּ לְפָנֶיךָ, כִּי עַל־רַחֲמֶיךָ הָרַבִּים: אֲדֹנָי שְׁמָעָה, אֲדֹנָי סְלָחָה, אֲדֹנָי הַקְשִׁיבָה וַעֲשֵׂה אַל־תְּאַחַר, לְמַעַנְךָ אֱלֹהַי, כִּי־שִׁמְךָ נִקְרָא עַל־עִירְךָ וְעַל־עַמֶּךָ:

The following verse is a prelude to the subsequent piyut, אָמְנָם כֵּן. Nowadays, most congregations omit it.

יוֹם יוֹם / יִדְרֹשׁוּן / לָךְ / טוֹב לְמָעוֹז / יְהִי עֹז / מִלּוּלָךְ סָלַחְתִּי.

The ארון קודש is opened.

אֱלֹהֵינוּ וֵאלֹהֵי אֲבוֹתֵינוּ

In many congregations, the שליח ציבור recites the first verse and the קהל repeats. The subsequent verses are each recited first by the קהל, then repeated by the שליח ציבור. In others, the שליח ציבור and the קהל recite them alternately.

אָמְנָם כֵּן / יֵצֶר סוֹכֵן / בָּנוּ
בְּךָ לְהַצְדִּיק / רַב צֶדֶק / וַעֲנֵנוּ סָלַחְתִּי.
גְּעֹל מְרַגֵּל / וְגַם פִּגֵּל / סִפְּרוּ
דּוֹד שׁוֹאֵג בְּקוֹל / יִתֵּן קוֹל / דַּבְּרוּ סָלַחְתִּי.

אָמְנָם כֵּן *It is surely true.* One of the rare contributions of medieval English Jewry to the prayer book, the poem "*Omnam Ken*" is the work of the twelfth-century scholar and poet, Rabbi Yom Tov of Joigny. In around 1180 he settled in York, in the north of England. He was a respected authority on Jewish

Silence the Accuser / and let the Defender / take his place,
and let the LORD be his support, / so that He may / say:
"I have forgiven."

Let the merits of [Abraham] the Easterner / blossom also / for [the nation called] the lily;
remove all sin / and raise Your voice / from Your dwelling place:
"I have forgiven."

Beneficent and forgiving One, / pardon and forgive / our faults;
O LORD, listen / and respond / from on high: "I have forgiven."

Heal my pain, / and into the depths submerge / my iniquity;
praise shall be Yours / when You speak these words / for my sake:
"I have forgiven."

Wipe away the transgressions / and wickedness / of the children of Your covenant;
apply Your loving-kindness / and place Your glory / upon the remnant: "I have forgiven."

Hear the stirrings of my heart, / and my whispered prayer / accept.
Forgiver of sins, / act for Your own sake / and speak:
"I have forgiven."

Turn to our shame, / let it take the place / of iniquity;
remove the stench [of sin] / and bring tidings / to all who seek shelter in You: "I have forgiven."

Omnam Ken is based on Moses' plea to God after the sin of the spies, as a result of which God declared, "I have forgiven (as you asked)." This forms the refrain of the poem, which is composed as an alphabetical acrostic. The poet urges God to ignore and disdain the Accuser (Satan, as he appears at the beginning of the book of Job) and listen instead to the Defender who appeals to God's mercy and compassion. *The Easterner:* Abraham who came from Mesopotamia in the East (see Psalm 89:1).

פְּנֵה לְעֶלְבּוֹן *Turn to our shame.* A reference to exile generally, specifically the pitiful condition of Jews in the age of the Crusades.

הַס קָטֵגוֹר / וְקַח סָנֵגוֹר / מְקוֹמוֹ
וִיהִי יהוה לְמִשְׁעָן / לוֹ, לְמַעַן / נְאֻמוֹ סָלַחְתִּי.
זְכוּת אֶזְרָח / גַּם יִפְרַח / לְשׁוֹשַׁנָּה
חֵטְא הָעֵבֶר / וְקוֹל הַגֶּבֶר / מִמְּעוֹנָה סָלַחְתִּי.
טוֹב וְסַלָּח / מְחַל וּסְלַח / אֲשָׁמִים
יָהּ הַקְשֵׁב / וְגַם הָשֵׁב / מִמְּרוֹמִים סָלַחְתִּי.
כְּאָב תַּחֲבֹשׁ / וּבְצוּל תִּכְבֹּשׁ / עֲוֹנִי
לְךָ תְהִלָּה / אֱמֹר מִלָּה / לְמַעֲנִי סָלַחְתִּי.
מְחֵה פֶּשַׁע / וְגַם רֶשַׁע / בְּנֵי בְרִית
נְהֹג חַסְדְּךָ / וְתֵן הוֹדְךָ / לִשְׁאֵרִית סָלַחְתִּי.
סְכֹת רַחֲשִׁי / וְגַם לַחֲשִׁי / תִּרְצֶה
עָוֹן נוֹשֵׂא / לְמַעַנְךָ עֲשֵׂה / וְתִפְצֶה סָלַחְתִּי.
פְּנֵה לְעֶלְבּוֹן / מְקוֹם עָוֹן / לְהָשִׂים
צַחַן הָסֵר / וְגַם תְּבַשֵּׂר / לְבָךְ חוֹסִים סָלַחְתִּי.

---

alive. Many of them, inspired by Yom Tov, committed suicide. Those who surrendered were massacred.

> Crusaders preparing to follow their king against the Saracens, burgesses envious of Jewish wealth, barons indebted to the Jews, the fanatical clergy, all conspired to exterminate the Jews… The alarmed Jews, with their leader Joseph [Josce of York], sought shelter in the royal castle… Richard Malebys, a noble deeply in debt to the Jews, commanded the siege…
>
> The hapless Jews were short of rations; surrender spelled baptism or death by torture. In obedience to the exhortations of their religious leader, Yom Tob of Joigny, they chose to lay hands on themselves… When, at daybreak, the [burning] citadel was captured, those who were still alive were put to death. Altogether some five hundred Jews perished. (Margolis and Marx, *A History of the Jewish People*, p. 387)

Hear my voice / and see the tears / in my eye;
plead my cause, / heed my words / and answer me: "I have forgiven."

Wipe out our transgressions / like a passing cloud, swiftly, / as it is said,
wipe away the transgression / of Your delivered people / and say: "I have forgiven."

The Ark is closed.

All, while standing:

אֵל מֶלֶךְ God, King who sits upon a throne of compassion, who acts with loving-kindness, who pardons the iniquities of His people, passing them before Him in order; who forgives sinners and pardons transgressors; who performs righteousness with all flesh and spirit, do not repay their bad actions in kind. ‣ God, You taught us to speak thirteen attributes: recall for us today the covenant of the thirteen attributes, as You in ancient times showed the humble one [Moses], as is written: The LORD descended in the cloud and stood with him *Ex. 34*
there, and proclaimed in the name of the LORD:

Congregation then Leader:

And the LORD passed by before him and proclaimed: *Ibid.*

All say aloud:

יהוה The LORD, the LORD, compassionate and gracious God, slow to anger, abounding in loving-kindness and truth, extending loving-kindness to a thousand generations, forgiving iniquity, rebellion and sin, and absolving [the guilty who repent].

All continue:

Forgive us our iniquity and our sin, and take us as Your inheritance.

סְלַח לָנוּ Forgive us, our Father, for we have sinned. Pardon us, our King, for we have transgressed. For You, LORD, are good and forgiving, *Ps. 86*
abounding in loving-kindness to all who call on You.

רִיב רִיבִי *Plead my cause.* This is the language of legal pleading in a court of law, used often by the prophets as a metaphor (see Jeremiah 50:34, Hosea 4:1, Micah 6:2), and a dominant image on Yom Kippur.

קוֹלִי שְׁמַע / וּרְאֵה דֶּמַע / עֵינִי
רִיב רִיבִי / שְׁעֵה נִיבִי / וַהֲשִׁיבֵנִי סָלַחְתִּי.

שֶׁמֶץ טַהֵר / כְּעָב מַהֵר / כְּנֶאֱמַר
תִּמְחֶה פֶּשַׁע / לְעַם נוֹשַׁע / וְתֹאמַר סָלַחְתִּי.

The ארון קודש *is closed.*

All, while standing:

אֵל מֶלֶךְ יוֹשֵׁב עַל כִּסֵּא רַחֲמִים, מִתְנַהֵג בַּחֲסִידוּת.
מוֹחֵל עֲוֹנוֹת עַמּוֹ, מַעֲבִיר רִאשׁוֹן רִאשׁוֹן.
מַרְבֶּה מְחִילָה לְחַטָּאִים, וּסְלִיחָה לְפוֹשְׁעִים.
עֹשֶׂה צְדָקוֹת עִם כָּל בָּשָׂר וָרוּחַ, לֹא כְרָעָתָם תִּגְמֹל.
◄ אֵל, הוֹרֵיתָ לָּנוּ לוֹמַר שְׁלֹשׁ עֶשְׂרֵה
וּזְכָר לָנוּ הַיּוֹם בְּרִית שְׁלֹשׁ עֶשְׂרֵה
כְּמוֹ שֶׁהוֹדַעְתָּ לֶעָנָו מִקֶּדֶם, כְּמוֹ שֶׁכָּתוּב:
וַיֵּרֶד יהוה בֶּעָנָן, וַיִּתְיַצֵּב עִמּוֹ שָׁם שמות לד
וַיִּקְרָא בְשֵׁם, יהוה:

שליח ציבור *then* קהל*:*

וַיַּעֲבֹר יהוה עַל־פָּנָיו וַיִּקְרָא שם

All say aloud:

יהוה, יהוה, אֵל רַחוּם וְחַנּוּן, אֶרֶךְ אַפַּיִם, וְרַב־חֶסֶד וֶאֱמֶת:
נֹצֵר חֶסֶד לָאֲלָפִים, נֹשֵׂא עָוֹן וָפֶשַׁע וְחַטָּאָה, וְנַקֵּה:

All continue:

וְסָלַחְתָּ לַעֲוֹנֵנוּ וּלְחַטָּאתֵנוּ, וּנְחַלְתָּנוּ:

סְלַח לָנוּ אָבִינוּ כִּי חָטָאנוּ, מְחַל לָנוּ מַלְכֵּנוּ כִּי פָשָׁעְנוּ.
כִּי־אַתָּה אֲדֹנָי טוֹב וְסַלָּח, וְרַב־חֶסֶד לְכָל־קֹרְאֶיךָ: תהלים פו

The piyut preceding the last Thirteen Attributes of the evening is a "pizmon" (refrain) with a clearly discernible structure. Traditionally, the Leader said the verses and the congregation only the refrains. Nowadays, in many congregations, the Leader and the congregation recite it stanza by stanza, as in the two preceding piyutim; in others, the entire piyut is sung by all.

The Ark is opened.

כִּי הִנֵּה Like clay in the potter's hands –
expanded or contracted at will –
so are we in Your hand, Guardian of loving-kindness;
look to the covenant, and disregard our inclination.

Like a stone in the stonecutter's hands –
held fast or smashed at will –
so are we in Your hand, Source of life and death;
look to the covenant, and disregard our inclination.

Like an ax-head in the blacksmith's hands –
held to the flame or distanced from it at will –
so are we in Your hand, Supporter of the poor and destitute;
look to the covenant, and disregard our inclination.

Like the helm in the sea captain's hands –
held fast or released at will –
so are we in Your hand, beneficent and forgiving God;
look to the covenant, and disregard our inclination.

Like glass in the glassblower's hands –
shaped or dissolved at will –
so are we in Your hand, Forgiver of willful and inadvertent sins;
look to the covenant, and disregard our inclination.

Like cloth in the weaver's hands –
straightened or twisted at will –
so are we in Your hand, jealous and avenging God;
look to the covenant, and disregard our inclination.

Like silver in the silversmith's hands –
adulterated or purified at will –
so are we in Your hand, Provider of healing to the sick;
look to the covenant, and disregard our inclination.

The Ark is closed.

---

not told them to take it with them when they left Egypt (*Berakhot* 32a). So too here: We are God's creations. Let not the Potter blame the pot He has made.

לַבְּרִית הַבֵּט *Look to the covenant.* This refers to the covenant with Noah (see Introduction, page lx).

The piyut preceding the last י״ג מידות *of the evening is a* פזמון *(refrain) with a clearly discernible structure. Traditionally, the* שליח ציבור *said the verses and the* קהל *only the refrains. Nowadays, in many congregations, the* שליח ציבור *and the* קהל *recite it stanza by stanza, as in the two preceding piyutim; in others, the entire piyut is sung by all.*

The ארון קודש *is opened.*

כִּי הִנֵּה כַּחֹמֶר בְּיַד הַיּוֹצֵר / בִּרְצוֹתוֹ מַרְחִיב וּבִרְצוֹתוֹ מְקַצֵּר
כֵּן אֲנַחְנוּ בְּיָדְךָ, חֶסֶד נוֹצֵר לַבְּרִית הַבֵּט, וְאַל תֵּפֶן לַיֵּצֶר.

כִּי הִנֵּה כָּאֶבֶן בְּיַד הַמְסַתֵּת / בִּרְצוֹתוֹ אוֹחֵז וּבִרְצוֹתוֹ מְכַתֵּת
כֵּן אֲנַחְנוּ בְּיָדְךָ, מְחַיֶּה וּמְמוֹתֵת לַבְּרִית הַבֵּט, וְאַל תֵּפֶן לַיֵּצֶר.

כִּי הִנֵּה כַּגַּרְזֶן בְּיַד הֶחָרָשׁ / בִּרְצוֹתוֹ דִּבֵּק לָאוּר וּבִרְצוֹתוֹ פֵּרַשׁ
כֵּן אֲנַחְנוּ בְּיָדְךָ, תּוֹמֵךְ עָנִי וָרָשׁ לַבְּרִית הַבֵּט, וְאַל תֵּפֶן לַיֵּצֶר.

כִּי הִנֵּה כַּהֶגֶה בְּיַד הַמַּלָּח / בִּרְצוֹתוֹ אוֹחֵז וּבִרְצוֹתוֹ שִׁלַּח
כֵּן אֲנַחְנוּ בְּיָדְךָ, אֵל טוֹב וְסַלָּח לַבְּרִית הַבֵּט, וְאַל תֵּפֶן לַיֵּצֶר.

כִּי הִנֵּה כִּזְכוּכִית בְּיַד הַמְזַגֵּג / בִּרְצוֹתוֹ חוֹגֵג וּבִרְצוֹתוֹ מְמוֹגֵג
כֵּן אֲנַחְנוּ בְּיָדְךָ, מַעֲבִיר זָדוֹן וָשֶׁגֶג לַבְּרִית הַבֵּט, וְאַל תֵּפֶן לַיֵּצֶר.

כִּי הִנֵּה כַּיְרִיעָה בְּיַד הָרוֹקֵם / בִּרְצוֹתוֹ מְיַשֵּׁר וּבִרְצוֹתוֹ מְעַקֵּם
כֵּן אֲנַחְנוּ בְּיָדְךָ, אֵל קַנֹּא וְנוֹקֵם לַבְּרִית הַבֵּט, וְאַל תֵּפֶן לַיֵּצֶר.

כִּי הִנֵּה כַּכֶּסֶף בְּיַד הַצּוֹרֵף / בִּרְצוֹתוֹ מְסַגְסֵג וּבִרְצוֹתוֹ מְצָרֵף
כֵּן אֲנַחְנוּ בְּיָדְךָ, מַמְצִיא לְמָזוֹר תֶּרֶף לַבְּרִית הַבֵּט וְאַל תֵּפֶן לַיֵּצֶר.

The ארון קודש *is closed.*

כִּי הִנֵּה כַּחֹמֶר *Like clay in the potter's hands.* For an essay on this *piyut*, see Introduction, page lx.

This poem is a daring plea for the defense: Forgive us for we are what You made us. We sin because You gave us both the ability and inclination. Had You made us like angels we would have been like angels.

Based on ideas in Isaiah (64:7) and Jeremiah (18:6), the poem belongs to a radical tradition, in prophetic and rabbinic literature, of audacity in prayer. One example is Moses' prayer to God to forgive the Israelites for the sin of the golden calf on the grounds that they would not have had the gold, had God

All:

אֵל מֶלֶךְ God, King who sits upon a throne of compassion, who acts with loving-kindness, who pardons the iniquities of His people, passing them before Him in order; who forgives sinners and pardons transgressors; who performs righteousness with all flesh and spirit, do not repay their bad actions in kind. ▸ God, You taught us to speak thirteen attributes: recall for us today the covenant of the thirteen attributes, as You in ancient times showed the humble one [Moses], as is written: The LORD descended in the cloud and stood with him there, and proclaimed in the name of the LORD: *Ex. 34*

The congregation then Leader:

And the LORD passed by before him and proclaimed: *Ibid.*

All say aloud:

יהוה The LORD, the LORD, compassionate and gracious God, slow to anger, abounding in loving-kindness and truth, extending loving-kindness to a thousand generations, forgiving iniquity, rebellion and sin, and absolving [the guilty who repent].

All continue:

Forgive us our iniquity and our sin, and take us as Your inheritance.

סְלַח לָנוּ Forgive us, our Father, for we have sinned. Pardon us, our King, for we have transgressed. For You, LORD, are good and forgiving, abounding in loving-kindness to all who call on You. *Ps. 86*

After invoking the Thirteen Attributes of Mercy, two sets of biblical verses, pleading with God to remember us with favor, are recited by all:

זְכֹר Remember, LORD, Your compassion and loving-kindness, *Ps. 25*
for they are everlasting.
Do not hold against us the sins of those who came before us. *Ps. 79*
May Your mercies meet us swiftly, for we have been brought very low.
Remember us, LORD, in favoring Your people;
redeem us with Your salvation.

---

particular collection is "Remember." We normally think of memory in terms of the past. Yet the three occasions in which the word *Vayizkor,* "and He remembered," appears in connection with God in Genesis all have to do with the future. God remembered Noah and brought him out on dry land (8:1). God remembered Abraham, and so brought Lot to safety (19:29). God remembered Rachel and gave her a child (30:22). In Judaism memory is future-oriented. We ask God to remember the past in order to grant us a future.

All:

אֵל מֶלֶךְ יוֹשֵׁב עַל כִּסֵּא רַחֲמִים, מִתְנַהֵג בַּחֲסִידוּת.
מוֹחֵל עֲוֹנוֹת עַמּוֹ, מַעֲבִיר רִאשׁוֹן רִאשׁוֹן.
מַרְבֶּה מְחִילָה לְחַטָּאִים, וּסְלִיחָה לְפוֹשְׁעִים.
עֹשֶׂה צְדָקוֹת עִם כָּל בָּשָׂר וָרוּחַ, לֹא כְרָעָתָם תִּגְמֹל.
▸ אֵל, הוֹרֵיתָ לָּנוּ לוֹמַר שְׁלֹשׁ עֶשְׂרֵה
וּזְכָר לָנוּ הַיּוֹם בְּרִית שְׁלֹשׁ עֶשְׂרֵה
כְּמוֹ שֶׁהוֹדַעְתָּ לֶעָנָו מִקֶּדֶם, כְּמוֹ שֶׁכָּתוּב:
וַיֵּרֶד יהוה בֶּעָנָן, וַיִּתְיַצֵּב עִמּוֹ שָׁם שמות לד
וַיִּקְרָא בְשֵׁם, יהוה:

The קהל *then* שליח ציבור*:*

וַיַּעֲבֹר יהוה עַל־פָּנָיו וַיִּקְרָא שם

All say aloud:

יהוה, יהוה, אֵל רַחוּם וְחַנּוּן, אֶרֶךְ אַפַּיִם, וְרַב־חֶסֶד וֶאֱמֶת:
נֹצֵר חֶסֶד לָאֲלָפִים, נֹשֵׂא עָוֹן וָפֶשַׁע וְחַטָּאָה, וְנַקֵּה:

All continue:

וְסָלַחְתָּ לַעֲוֹנֵנוּ וּלְחַטָּאתֵנוּ, וּנְחַלְתָּנוּ:

סְלַח לָנוּ אָבִינוּ כִּי חָטָאנוּ, מְחַל לָנוּ מַלְכֵּנוּ כִּי פָשָׁעְנוּ.
כִּי־אַתָּה אֲדֹנָי טוֹב וְסַלָּח, וְרַב־חֶסֶד לְכָל־קֹרְאֶיךָ: תהלים פו

After invoking the Thirteen Attributes of Mercy, two sets of biblical verses, pleading with God to remember us with favor, are recited by all:

זְכֹר־רַחֲמֶיךָ יהוה וַחֲסָדֶיךָ, כִּי מֵעוֹלָם הֵמָּה: תהלים כה
אַל־תִּזְכָּר־לָנוּ עֲוֹנֹת רִאשֹׁנִים תהלים עט
מַהֵר יְקַדְּמוּנוּ רַחֲמֶיךָ כִּי דַלּוֹנוּ מְאֹד:
זָכְרֵנוּ יהוה בִּרְצוֹן עַמֶּךָ, פָּקְדֵנוּ בִּישׁוּעָתֶךָ.

זְכֹר־רַחֲמֶיךָ יהוה *Remember, Lord, Your compassion.* This is part of the earliest stratum of *seliḥot* prayers, compiled in the days of the Geonim. It consists, as did most of their prayers, of a collection of biblical verses. The theme of this

זְכֹר Remember Your congregation, the one that You acquired long ago, *Ps. 74*
the tribe of Your inheritance that You redeemed,
this Mount Zion that You have dwelt in.
זְכֹר Remember, LORD, the fondness of Jerusalem;
do not forever forget the love of Zion.
You shall rise up and have compassion for Zion, *Ps. 102*
for now it is right to be gracious, for the time has come.
זְכֹר Remember, LORD, what the Edomites did on the day Jerusalem fell. *Ps. 137*
They said, "Tear it down, tear it down to its very foundations!"
זְכֹר Remember Abraham, Isaac and Yisrael, Your servants, *Ex. 32*
to whom You swore by Your own Self, when You said to them,
"I shall make your descendants as numerous as the stars in the sky,
and I shall give all this land that I spoke of to your descendants,
and they shall inherit it forever."
זְכֹר Remember Your servants, Abraham, Isaac and Jacob; do not attend to *Deut. 9*
the stubbornness of this people, to their wickedness or sinfulness.

Each of the following verses is said by the Leader, then the congregation:

אַל־נָא Please, do not hold against us the sin *Num. 12*
that we committed so foolishly, that we have sinned.
We have sinned, our Rock; forgive us, our Creator.

Traditionally, a piyut of confession was inserted between the two sets of remembrance verses. The piyut for the evening was "You I will seek" (page 1282). Nowadays, most congregations say only the last line, the Leader followed by the congregation:

He transforms willful sin into error,
for the nation acted without knowing what they did. *Num. 15*

Some say (the Leader then the congregation):

We have sinned, our Rock; forgive us, our Creator.

All:

זְכָר Remember the covenant of our fathers, as You have said,
"I will remember My covenant with Jacob, and also My covenant *Lev. 26*
with Isaac, and also My covenant with Abraham I will remember,
and the land I will remember."

---

powerful effects of *teshuva* is that it allows us retroactively to remove the element of sinful intent from our acts in virtue of the fact that we now have, and declare, remorse for what we have done.

זְכֹר עֲדָתְךָ קָנִיתָ קֶּדֶם, גָּאַלְתָּ שֵׁבֶט נַחֲלָתֶךָ, הַר־צִיּוֹן זֶה שָׁכַנְתָּ בּוֹ: תהלים עד
זְכֹר יהוה חִבַּת יְרוּשָׁלָיִם, אַהֲבַת צִיּוֹן אַל תִּשְׁכַּח לָנֶצַח.
אַתָּה תָקוּם תְּרַחֵם צִיּוֹן, כִּי־עֵת לְחֶנְנָהּ, כִּי־בָא מוֹעֵד: תהלים קב
זְכֹר יהוה לִבְנֵי אֱדוֹם אֵת יוֹם יְרוּשָׁלָיִם תהלים קלז
הָאֹמְרִים עָרוּ עָרוּ, עַד הַיְסוֹד בָּהּ:
זְכֹר לְאַבְרָהָם לְיִצְחָק וּלְיִשְׂרָאֵל עֲבָדֶיךָ, אֲשֶׁר נִשְׁבַּעְתָּ לָהֶם בָּךְ
וַתְּדַבֵּר אֲלֵהֶם: אַרְבֶּה אֶת־זַרְעֲכֶם כְּכוֹכְבֵי הַשָּׁמָיִם שמות לב
וְכָל־הָאָרֶץ הַזֹּאת אֲשֶׁר אָמַרְתִּי אֶתֵּן לְזַרְעֲכֶם, וְנָחֲלוּ לְעֹלָם:
זְכֹר לַעֲבָדֶיךָ לְאַבְרָהָם לְיִצְחָק וּלְיַעֲקֹב דברים ט
אַל־תֵּפֶן אֶל־קְשִׁי הָעָם הַזֶּה וְאֶל־רִשְׁעוֹ וְאֶל־חַטָּאתוֹ:

Each of the following verses is said by the שליח ציבור*, then the* קהל*:*

אַל־נָא תָשֵׁת עָלֵינוּ חַטָּאת אֲשֶׁר נוֹאַלְנוּ וַאֲשֶׁר חָטָאנוּ: במדבר יב
חָטָאנוּ צוּרֵנוּ, סְלַח לָנוּ יוֹצְרֵנוּ

Traditionally, a piyut of confession was inserted between the two sets of remembrance verses. The piyut for the evening was אוֹדְךָ אֶדְרֹשׁ *(page 1282). Nowadays, most congregations say only the last line, the* שליח ציבור *followed by the* קהל*:*

הֵן יַעֲבִיר זָדוֹן לִמְשׁוּגָה / כִּי לְכָל־הָעָם בִּשְׁגָגָה: במדבר טו

Some say (the שליח ציבור *then the* קהל*):*

חָטָאנוּ צוּרֵנוּ, סְלַח לָנוּ יוֹצְרֵנוּ

All:

זְכָר לָנוּ בְּרִית אָבוֹת כַּאֲשֶׁר אָמַרְתָּ:
וְזָכַרְתִּי אֶת־בְּרִיתִי יַעֲקוֹב ויקרא כו
וְאַף אֶת־בְּרִיתִי יִצְחָק וְאַף אֶת־בְּרִיתִי אַבְרָהָם אֶזְכֹּר
וְהָאָרֶץ אֶזְכֹּר:

הֵן יַעֲבִיר זָדוֹן לִמְשׁוּגָה *He transforms willful sin into error.* This is based on the statement of Reish Lakish (Israel, third century CE) that through repentance, willful sins are turned into inadvertent ones (*Yoma* 86b). One of the most

Remember the covenant of the early ones, as You have said,
"I shall remember for them the covenant of the early ones, *Lev. 26*
whom I brought out of the land of Egypt
before the eyes of the nations,
in order to be their God: I am the LORD."

Deal kindly with us as You have promised,
"Even so, when they are in the land of their enemies *Ibid.*
I shall not reject them
and shall not detest them to the point of destruction,
to the point of breaking My covenant with them,
for I am the LORD their God."

Have compassion for us and do not destroy us, as it is written:
"For the LORD your God is a compassionate God; *Deut. 4*
He will not forsake you, He will not destroy you,
and He will not forget the covenant of your fathers,
that He pledged to them."

Circumcise our hearts to love Your name, as it is written:
"And the LORD your God will circumcise your heart *Deut. 30*
and the heart of your descendants
to love the LORD your God with all your heart
and with all your soul,
so that you shall live."

Restore our fortunes and have compassion for us, as it is written:
"And the LORD your God shall restore your fortunes *Ibid.*
and have compassion for you,
and shall return and gather you in from all the nations
among whom the LORD your God has scattered you."

Gather those of us who have been distanced, as is written,
"If your distanced ones are at the very ends of the heavens, *Ibid.*
from there shall the LORD your God gather you;
from there shall He bring you."

זְכֹר לָנוּ בְּרִית רִאשׁוֹנִים. כַּאֲשֶׁר אָמַרְתָּ:
וְזָכַרְתִּי לָהֶם בְּרִית רִאשֹׁנִים ויקרא כו
אֲשֶׁר הוֹצֵאתִי־אֹתָם מֵאֶרֶץ מִצְרַיִם לְעֵינֵי הַגּוֹיִם
לִהְיוֹת לָהֶם לֵאלֹהִים, אֲנִי יהוה:

עֲשֵׂה עִמָּנוּ כְּמָה שֶׁהִבְטַחְתָּנוּ:
וְאַף גַּם־זֹאת בִּהְיוֹתָם בְּאֶרֶץ אֹיְבֵיהֶם שם
לֹא־מְאַסְתִּים וְלֹא־גְעַלְתִּים לְכַלֹּתָם
לְהָפֵר בְּרִיתִי אִתָּם
כִּי אֲנִי יהוה אֱלֹהֵיהֶם:

רַחֵם עָלֵינוּ וְאַל תַּשְׁחִיתֵנוּ, כְּמָה שֶׁכָּתוּב:
כִּי אֵל רַחוּם יהוה אֱלֹהֶיךָ, לֹא יַרְפְּךָ וְלֹא יַשְׁחִיתֶךָ דברים ד
וְלֹא יִשְׁכַּח אֶת־בְּרִית אֲבוֹתֶיךָ אֲשֶׁר נִשְׁבַּע לָהֶם:

מוֹל אֶת לְבָבֵנוּ לְאַהֲבָה אֶת שְׁמֶךָ, כְּמָה שֶׁכָּתוּב:
וּמָל יהוה אֱלֹהֶיךָ אֶת־לְבָבְךָ וְאֶת־לְבַב זַרְעֶךָ דברים ל
לְאַהֲבָה אֶת־יהוה אֱלֹהֶיךָ בְּכָל־לְבָבְךָ וּבְכָל־נַפְשְׁךָ
לְמַעַן חַיֶּיךָ:

הָשֵׁב שְׁבוּתֵנוּ וְרַחֲמֵנוּ, כְּמָה שֶׁכָּתוּב:
וְשָׁב יהוה אֱלֹהֶיךָ אֶת־שְׁבוּתְךָ וְרִחֲמֶךָ שם
וְשָׁב וְקִבֶּצְךָ מִכָּל־הָעַמִּים אֲשֶׁר הֱפִיצְךָ יהוה אֱלֹהֶיךָ שָׁמָּה:

קַבֵּץ נִדָּחֵינוּ כְּמָה שֶׁכָּתוּב:
אִם־יִהְיֶה נִדַּחֲךָ בִּקְצֵה הַשָּׁמָיִם שם
מִשָּׁם יְקַבֶּצְךָ יהוה אֱלֹהֶיךָ, וּמִשָּׁם יִקָּחֶךָ:

Let us find You when we seek You, as it is written:
"And if from there you seek the LORD your God, *Deut. 4*
you shall find Him,
when you seek Him out with all your heart
and with all your soul."

Wipe out our transgressions for Your sake, as You have said:
"I, I am the One who shall wipe out your transgressions for My sake, *Is. 43*
and I shall not recall your sins."

Wipe out our transgressions as if they were a cloud,
as if they were a haze,
as is written,
"I have wiped out your transgressions like a cloud, *Is. 44*
and as a haze your sins;
come back to Me for I have redeemed you."

Whiten our sins as snow and as wool, as is written,
"Come now, let us reason together, says the LORD: *Is. 1*
If your sins are like scarlet, they shall be whitened like snow;
should they be as red as crimson, they shall become like wool."

Throw over us pure waters and purify us, as is written,
"I shall throw pure waters over you and you shall be pure. *Ezek. 36*
I shall purify you of all your impurities and of all your idolatry."

Atone our sins on this day and purify us, as it is written,
"For on this day you will be atoned and made pure; *Lev. 16*
of all your sins before the LORD you shall be purified."

▸ Bring us to Your holy mountain,
and let us rejoice in Your House of prayer,
as is written,
"I shall bring them to My holy mountain, *Is. 56*
and I shall make them rejoice in My House of prayer;
their offerings and their sacrifices will be accepted,
desired on My altar,
for My House will be called a house of prayer for all peoples."

הַמָּצֵא לָנוּ בְּבַקָּשָׁתֵנוּ, כְּמָה שֶׁכָּתוּב:
וּבִקַּשְׁתֶּם מִשָּׁם אֶת־יהוה אֱלֹהֶיךָ, וּמָצָאתָ ‏ דברים ד
כִּי תִדְרְשֶׁנּוּ בְּכָל־לְבָבְךָ וּבְכָל־נַפְשֶׁךָ:

מְחֵה פְשָׁעֵינוּ לְמַעַנְךָ, כַּאֲשֶׁר אָמַרְתָּ:
אָנֹכִי אָנֹכִי הוּא מֹחֶה פְשָׁעֶיךָ לְמַעֲנִי, וְחַטֹּאתֶיךָ לֹא אֶזְכֹּר: ‏ ישעיה מג

מְחֵה פְשָׁעֵינוּ כָּעָב וְכֶעָנָן, כְּמָה שֶׁכָּתוּב:
מָחִיתִי כָעָב פְּשָׁעֶיךָ וְכֶעָנָן חַטֹּאותֶיךָ ‏ ישעיה מד
שׁוּבָה אֵלַי כִּי גְאַלְתִּיךָ:

הַלְבֵּן חֲטָאֵינוּ כַּשֶּׁלֶג וְכַצֶּמֶר, כְּמָה שֶׁכָּתוּב:
לְכוּ־נָא וְנִוָּכְחָה, יֹאמַר יהוה ‏ ישעיה א
אִם־יִהְיוּ חֲטָאֵיכֶם כַּשָּׁנִים, כַּשֶּׁלֶג יַלְבִּינוּ
אִם־יַאְדִּימוּ כַתּוֹלָע, כַּצֶּמֶר יִהְיוּ:

זְרֹק עָלֵינוּ מַיִם טְהוֹרִים וְטַהֲרֵנוּ, כְּמָה שֶׁכָּתוּב:
וְזָרַקְתִּי עֲלֵיכֶם מַיִם טְהוֹרִים, וּטְהַרְתֶּם ‏ יחזקאל לו
מִכֹּל טֻמְאוֹתֵיכֶם וּמִכָּל־גִּלּוּלֵיכֶם אֲטַהֵר אֶתְכֶם:

כַּפֵּר חֲטָאֵינוּ בַּיּוֹם הַזֶּה וְטַהֲרֵנוּ, כְּמָה שֶׁכָּתוּב:
כִּי־בַיּוֹם הַזֶּה יְכַפֵּר עֲלֵיכֶם לְטַהֵר אֶתְכֶם ‏ ויקרא טז
מִכֹּל חַטֹּאתֵיכֶם, לִפְנֵי יהוה תִּטְהָרוּ:

◂ תְּבִיאֵנוּ אֶל הַר קָדְשֶׁךָ, וְשַׂמְּחֵנוּ בְּבֵית תְּפִלָּתֶךָ
כְּמָה שֶׁכָּתוּב:
וַהֲבִיאוֹתִים אֶל־הַר קָדְשִׁי, וְשִׂמַּחְתִּים בְּבֵית תְּפִלָּתִי ‏ ישעיה נו
עוֹלֹתֵיהֶם וְזִבְחֵיהֶם לְרָצוֹן עַל־מִזְבְּחִי
כִּי בֵיתִי בֵּית־תְּפִלָּה יִקָּרֵא לְכָל־הָעַמִּים:

The Ark is opened.

The following is said responsively, verse by verse.

שְׁמַע קוֹלֵנוּ Listen to our voice, LORD our God.
Spare us and have compassion on us,
and in compassion and favor accept our prayer.
Turn us back, O LORD, to You, and we will return. *Lam. 5*
Renew our days as of old.
Do not cast us away from You, and do not take Your holy spirit from us.
Do not cast us away in our old age;
when our strength is gone do not desert us.

End of responsive reading.

Do not desert us, LORD; our God, do not be distant from us.
Give us a sign of good things,
and those who hate us shall see it and be ashamed,
for You, LORD, will help us and console us.
Hear our speech, LORD, consider our thoughts.
May the words of our mouths and the meditations of our hearts
find favor before You, LORD, our Rock and Redeemer.
For it is You, LORD, that we have longed for;
You shall answer us, LORD our God.

The Ark is closed.

---

to us and who listens when we call to Him. It is not intellect and rationality alone that join us to God, but also emotion, sympathy, empathy, and compassion. These are part of the divine reality we inhabit when we live the life of faith. An impersonal force cannot hear prayer. An "It" cannot forgive. Only One to whom we can say "You" can do these things. The more we know of neuroscience and emotional intelligence, the more we come to understand the limits of rationalism alone in explaining human behavior, and the more we come to appreciate the role of emotion in shaping what we do and who we are. The faith of Judaism is that this is no mere accident or random evolution, but part of what makes us human in the image of God. God does more than create. God loves. And because God loves, we can approach Him in prayer.

אַל תַּשְׁלִיכֵנוּ לְעֵת זִקְנָה *Do not cast us away in our old age.* One of the most poignant lines of all. Every civilization has valued the vigorous, the strong, those

The ארון קודש *is opened.*

The following is said responsively, verse by verse.

שְׁמַע קוֹלֵנוּ, יהוה אֱלֹהֵינוּ, חוּס וְרַחֵם עָלֵינוּ
וְקַבֵּל בְּרַחֲמִים וּבְרָצוֹן אֶת תְּפִלָּתֵנוּ.

הֲשִׁיבֵנוּ יהוה אֵלֶיךָ וְנָשׁוּבָה, חַדֵּשׁ יָמֵינוּ כְּקֶדֶם: איכה ה

אַל תַּשְׁלִיכֵנוּ מִלְּפָנֶיךָ, וְרוּחַ קָדְשְׁךָ אַל תִּקַּח מִמֶּנּוּ.

אַל תַּשְׁלִיכֵנוּ לְעֵת זִקְנָה, כִּכְלוֹת כֹּחֵנוּ אַל תַּעַזְבֵנוּ.

End of responsive reading.

אַל תַּעַזְבֵנוּ יהוה, אֱלֹהֵינוּ אַל תִּרְחַק מִמֶּנּוּ.

עֲשֵׂה עִמָּנוּ אוֹת לְטוֹבָה, וְיִרְאוּ שׂוֹנְאֵינוּ וְיֵבֹשׁוּ
כִּי אַתָּה יהוה עֲזַרְתָּנוּ וְנִחַמְתָּנוּ.

אֲמָרֵינוּ הַאֲזִינָה יהוה, בִּינָה הֲגִיגֵנוּ.

יִהְיוּ לְרָצוֹן אִמְרֵי פִינוּ וְהֶגְיוֹן לִבֵּנוּ לְפָנֶיךָ, יהוה צוּרֵנוּ וְגוֹאֲלֵנוּ.

כִּי לְךָ יהוה הוֹחָלְנוּ, אַתָּה תַעֲנֶה אֲדֹנָי אֱלֹהֵינוּ.

The ארון קודש *is closed.*

SHEMA KOLENU – LISTEN TO OUR VOICE

A prayer, opening with a line from the weekday Amida, followed by a verse from Lamentations, and a series of sentences based on verses from the book of Psalms. It is said with great intensity, the Ark opened to enhance the drama of the moment.

שְׁמַע קוֹלֵנוּ *Listen to our voice.* The core of our faith on which the whole life of prayer is predicated. Judaism is not mere abstract monotheism, the idea that there is One God, Architect and Creator of all. God is also a "personal" God, that is to say, one who loves, cares, forgives, and relates to us as persons with our own fears and loves. God is more than an impersonal concept, entity or force, the God acknowledged by philosophers and scientists through the ages, the source of order in the universe. Judah HaLevi called this "the God of Aristotle" (*Kuzari* 4:16). For us He is also "the God of Abraham," who calls

The Leader continues:

אֱלֹהֵינוּ Our God and God of our ancestors,
do not abandon us and do not desert us,
do not shame us and do not abandon Your covenant with us;
bring us close to Your Torah, teach us Your commandments,
show us Your ways, and turn our hearts toward the awe of Your name.
Circumcise our hearts to love You,
so that we return to You in truth, wholeheartedly.
For the sake of Your great name, pardon and forgive our iniquities,
as it is written in Your holy Writings:
"For the sake of Your name, Lord, forgive my iniquity, though it is great." *Ps. 25*

Our God and God of our ancestors,
forgive us, pardon us, grant us atonement.

In many congregations, the Leader and the congregation recite the following piyut responsively, couplet by couplet, until and "You give us Yours"; in others, it is sung collectively.

כִּי אָנוּ For we are Your people and You are our God;
we are Your children and You are our Father;
we are Your servants and You are our Master;
we are Your gathering and You are our Place;
we are Your legacy and You are our Land;
we are Your flock and You are our Shepherd;
we are Your vineyard and You are our Keeper;
we are Your work and You are our Maker;
we are Your bride and You are our Lover;
we are Your treasure and You are our God;
we are Your people and You are our King;
we give You our word and You give us Yours.

---

they have experience; they are our living connection with the past. And they are human; they remain the image and likeness of God; they deserve dignity and we, like God, must grant it to them. "The [whole] tablets and the broken tablets lay in the Ark," said the sages, referring to the Ark of the Covenant that traveled with the Israelites in the wilderness as well as in the Holy Land. The "broken tablets," they said, refer to the elderly who have forgotten what once they knew (*Berakhot* 8b). They too were given a place of honor.

כִּי אָנוּ עַמֶּךָ *For we are Your people.* An introduction to the Confession that is about to follow, based on a midrashic interpretation of the line from the Song of Songs, "My Beloved is mine and I am His" (Song. 2:16, *Shir HaShirim Raba*

The שליח ציבור *continues:*

אֱלֹהֵינוּ וֵאלֹהֵי אֲבוֹתֵינוּ
אַל תַּעַזְבֵנוּ, וְאַל תִּטְּשֵׁנוּ, וְאַל תַּכְלִימֵנוּ, וְאַל תָּפֵר בְּרִיתְךָ אִתָּנוּ
קָרְבֵנוּ לְתוֹרָתֶךָ, לַמְּדֵנוּ מִצְוֹתֶיךָ
הוֹרֵנוּ דְרָכֶיךָ, הַט לִבֵּנוּ לְיִרְאָה אֶת שְׁמֶךָ
וּמוֹל אֶת לְבָבֵנוּ לְאַהֲבָתֶךָ, וְנָשׁוּב אֵלֶיךָ בֶּאֱמֶת וּבְלֵב שָׁלֵם
וּלְמַעַן שִׁמְךָ הַגָּדוֹל תִּמְחֹל וְתִסְלַח לַעֲוֹנֵינוּ
כַּכָּתוּב בְּדִבְרֵי קָדְשֶׁךָ
תהלים כה לְמַעַן־שִׁמְךָ יהוה, וְסָלַחְתָּ לַעֲוֹנִי כִּי רַב־הוּא:

אֱלֹהֵינוּ וֵאלֹהֵי אֲבוֹתֵינוּ
סְלַח לָנוּ, מְחַל לָנוּ, כַּפֶּר לָנוּ.

In many congregations, the שליח ציבור *and the* קהל *recite the following piyut responsively, couplet by couplet, until* וְאַתָּה מַאֲמִירֵנוּ*; in others, it is sung collectively.*

כִּי אָנוּ עַמֶּךָ וְאַתָּה אֱלֹהֵינוּ אָנוּ בָנֶיךָ וְאַתָּה אָבִינוּ
אָנוּ עֲבָדֶיךָ וְאַתָּה אֲדוֹנֵנוּ אָנוּ קְהָלֶךָ וְאַתָּה חֶלְקֵנוּ
אָנוּ נַחֲלָתֶךָ וְאַתָּה גוֹרָלֵנוּ אָנוּ צֹאנֶךָ וְאַתָּה רוֹעֵנוּ
אָנוּ כַרְמֶךָ וְאַתָּה נוֹטְרֵנוּ אָנוּ פְעֻלָּתֶךָ וְאַתָּה יוֹצְרֵנוּ
אָנוּ רַעְיָתֶךָ וְאַתָּה דוֹדֵנוּ אָנוּ סְגֻלָּתֶךָ וְאַתָּה אֱלֹהֵינוּ
אָנוּ עַמֶּךָ וְאַתָּה מַלְכֵּנוּ אָנוּ מַאֲמִירֶיךָ וְאַתָּה מַאֲמִירֵנוּ.

---

who can fight battles, win wars, farm fields and work. Judaism, however, believes that the test of a civilization is how it treats the very young and the very old. "Who do you wish to take with you?" asked Pharaoh of Moses when he asked to be allowed to leave Egypt. "We will go with our young and our old," Moses replied (Ex. 10:9). It was an answer Pharaoh could not understand.

The paradox of history is that a civilization is tested not by its strength but how it values the weak; nor by its wealth but how it treats the poor. A nation becomes invulnerable when it cares for the vulnerable: the orphan, the widow, the stranger, and the old. "Stand before a hoary head and honor the presence of the old," says the Torah (Lev. 19:32). For the old have wisdom;

The congregation then the Leader:

We are brazen and You are compassionate, gracious.
We are stubborn and You are long forbearing.
We are as full of iniquity as You are full of compassion.
Our days are like a fleeting shadow. Ps. 102
But You are here, and Your years will not end.

VIDUY

For linear translation and commentary, see page 1353.

The Leader continues, with the congregation following him in an undertone:

אֱלֹהֵינוּ Our God and God of our fathers,
let our prayer come before You,
and do not hide Yourself from our plea,
for we are not so arrogant or obstinate as to say before You,
Lord, our God and God of our fathers,
we are righteous and have not sinned,
for in truth, we and our fathers have sinned.

---

shame there is no way back. People who were shamed either committed suicide, died in a noble cause, or went into voluntary exile. From guilt there is a way back, namely repentance and forgiveness. For shame is something that touches the essence of a person. It is a stain that cannot be removed. Guilt, however, makes a principled distinction between the person and the act. The act may have been wrong. But the person is never beyond the reach of salvation. God forgives those who truly confess their guilt.

Therefore, it is God's forgiveness that empowers us to admit we did wrong, that gives us the strength to say with every letter of the alphabet and every fiber of our being: "We are guilty, we have betrayed, we have robbed, we have spoken slander." In a shame culture the primary imperative is, "Thou shalt not be found out." In a guilt culture, we know that we are found out, even if no other human being knows what we have done. In that ruthless honesty of guilt lies our salvation, our hope, our forgiveness, our ability to make amends and start again, rebuilding a new life out of the fragments of the old.

VIDUY – CONFESSION

Confession is the hardest act in the moral life, since Homo sapiens has been endowed with an inexhaustible capacity for self-justification and self-deception. Only the knowledge that God loves, forgives and never gives up on us, makes it possible.

The confession as we have it today is the result of a long process of development, with its roots in the Torah, many elements from Mishnaic and

The קהל *then the* שליח ציבור*:*

אָנוּ עַזֵּי פָנִים וְאַתָּה רַחוּם וְחַנּוּן
אָנוּ קְשֵׁי עֹרֶף וְאַתָּה אֶרֶךְ אַפַּיִם
אָנוּ מְלֵאֵי עָוֹן וְאַתָּה מָלֵא רַחֲמִים
אָנוּ יָמֵינוּ כְּצֵל עוֹבֵר וְאַתָּה־הוּא וּשְׁנוֹתֶיךָ לֹא יִתָּמּוּ: תהלים קב

וידוי

For linear translation and commentary, see page 1353.

The שליח ציבור *continues, with the* קהל *following him in an undertone:*

אֱלֹהֵינוּ וֵאלֹהֵי אֲבוֹתֵינוּ
תָּבוֹא לְפָנֶיךָ תְּפִלָּתֵנוּ, וְאַל תִּתְעַלַּם מִתְּחִנָּתֵנוּ.
שֶׁאֵין אֲנַחְנוּ עַזֵּי פָנִים וּקְשֵׁי עֹרֶף לוֹמַר לְפָנֶיךָ
יהוה אֱלֹהֵינוּ וֵאלֹהֵי אֲבוֹתֵינוּ
צַדִּיקִים אֲנַחְנוּ וְלֹא חָטָאנוּ.
אֲבָל אֲנַחְנוּ וַאֲבוֹתֵינוּ חָטָאנוּ.

---

ad loc.). The poet enumerates the many facets of the relationship between God and His people: He is our God, Father, Master, Shepherd, the Keeper of our vineyard and so on through multiple metaphors.

אָנוּ עַזֵּי פָנִים, וְאַתָּה רַחוּם וְחַנּוּן *We are brazen and You are compassionate, gracious.* The poem then shifts in mood, from God's love for us to our disobedience to Him. Only the certainty that God forgives lends us the courage and honesty to admit that we need forgiveness.

There are shame cultures and there are guilt cultures. To be sure, most actual societies are a mix of both. But as ideal types they are profoundly different. Shame is an emotion we feel when we think of ourselves as being seen by others. Our deepest desire when we feel shame is the wish to be invisible. Adam and Eve felt shame after they had eaten the fruit of the Tree of Knowledge and tried to hide. The feeling of guilt is altogether different and deeper. We know we would still feel it even if we were invisible. Guilt is the voice within that tells us, regardless of anyone else knowing about it, that we have done wrong. The opposite of shame is honor. The opposite of guilt is righteousness.

Ancient Greece was predominantly a shame culture. Ancient Israel was a guilt culture. In Greece what mattered was your reputation in the eyes of others. In Israel what mattered was your innocence in the sight of God. From

Strike the left side of the chest with the right fist while saying each of the sins:

אָשַׁמְנוּ We have sinned, we have acted treacherously,
we have robbed, we have spoken slander.
We have acted perversely, we have acted wickedly,
we have acted presumptuously, we have been violent, we have framed lies.
We have given bad advice, we have deceived, we have scorned,
we have rebelled, we have provoked, we have turned away,
we have committed iniquity, we have transgressed,
we have persecuted, we have been obstinate.
We have acted wickedly, we have corrupted,
we have acted abominably, we have strayed, we have led others astray.

All:

סַרְנוּ We have turned away from Your commandments and good laws,
to no avail, for You are just in all that has befallen us, *Neh. 9*
for You have acted faithfully while we have done wickedly.

We have been wicked and we have transgressed,
and so we have not been saved.
Place it in our hearts to abandon the way of wickedness,
and hasten our salvation,
as it is written by Your prophet:
"Let each wicked person abandon his ways, *Is. 55*
each man of iniquity his thoughts,
and let him come back to the LORD
and He will have compassion for him,
back to our God for He will forgive abundantly."

---

so to God. The true confession is the one engaged in silently by each of us within the soul. Confession as mere ritual without remorse is, said the sages, like trying to purify yourself by immersing yourself in a *mikveh* while still holding in your hand the source of the impurity.

No sin is too great for God to pardon. No wrong is too small for habit to magnify. (Rabbi Baḥya ibn Pakuda)

To sin against a fellow human is worse than to sin against God. The person you harmed may have gone to an unknown place and you may lose the opportunity to beg his forgiveness. God, however, is everywhere and you can always find Him when you seek Him. (Rabbi Yaakov David Kalish, the Amshinover Rebbe)

/ continued on page 171

Strike the left side of the chest with the right fist while saying each of the sins.

אָשַׁמְנוּ, בָּגַדְנוּ, גָּזַלְנוּ, דִּבַּרְנוּ דֹפִי
הֶעֱוִינוּ, וְהִרְשַׁעְנוּ, זַדְנוּ, חָמַסְנוּ, טָפַלְנוּ שֶׁקֶר
יָעַצְנוּ רָע, כִּזַּבְנוּ, לַצְנוּ, מָרַדְנוּ, נִאַצְנוּ, סָרַרְנוּ
עָוִינוּ, פָּשַׁעְנוּ, צָרַרְנוּ, קִשִּׁינוּ עֹרֶף
רָשַׁעְנוּ, שִׁחַתְנוּ, תִּעַבְנוּ, תָּעִינוּ, תִּעְתָּעְנוּ.

All:

סַרְנוּ מִמִּצְוֹתֶיךָ וּמִמִּשְׁפָּטֶיךָ הַטּוֹבִים, וְלֹא שָׁוָה לָנוּ.
נחמיה ט וְאַתָּה צַדִּיק עַל כָּל־הַבָּא עָלֵינוּ
כִּי־אֱמֶת עָשִׂיתָ, וַאֲנַחְנוּ הִרְשָׁעְנוּ:

הִרְשַׁעְנוּ וּפָשַׁעְנוּ, לָכֵן לֹא נוֹשָׁעְנוּ
וְתֵן בְּלִבֵּנוּ לַעֲזֹב דֶּרֶךְ רֶשַׁע, וְחִישׁ לָנוּ יֶשַׁע
כַּכָּתוּב עַל יַד נְבִיאֶךָ
ישעיה נה יַעֲזֹב רָשָׁע דַּרְכּוֹ, וְאִישׁ אָוֶן מַחְשְׁבֹתָיו
וְיָשֹׁב אֶל־יהוה וִירַחֲמֵהוּ, וְאֶל־אֱלֹהֵינוּ כִּי־יַרְבֶּה לִסְלוֹחַ:

Talmudic times, and further elaborations over the centuries. It resolves a series of tensions between conflicting considerations. It is powerful to declare our sins in public but it can also seem shameless, almost like bragging. It is good to confess our sins in the first person plural – "We" rather than "I" – since "All Israel are responsible for one another" (*Shevuot* 39a); we are responsible not only for our own sins but for those of others that we might have prevented (*Shabbat* 54b–55a). But it is also important to confess in the singular, since *teshuva* requires that I put right what I have done wrong.

So we confess publicly and collectively, while also admitting our wrongs individually and privately. The public confession includes two alphabetical lists of sins, one short, the other long. But this is only the outer form of an act (the *ma'aseh mitzva*) whose inner fulfillment (*kiyum*) requires that *I acknowledge the specific sins and wrongs I committed, resolving not to repeat them.* So while reciting the public confession along with the community, I must constantly be asking myself in detail what I have done wrong, and saying

The Leader continues:

אֱלֹהֵינוּ Our God, and God of our ancestors,
forgive and pardon our iniquities
on (*on Shabbat:* this Sabbath day, and on) this Day of Atonement;
be responsive to us as we pray,
wipe away and remove all our transgressions and sins
from before Your eyes,
subdue our urges, that they be submitted to You,
and temper our obstinacy, that we may return to You truly;
renew our conscience that it may guard all Your commands,
and circumcise our hearts that we may love and revere Your name,
as it is written in Your Torah:
"And the LORD your God will circumcise your heart *Deut. 30*
and the heart of your descendants
to love the LORD your God with all your heart and with all your
soul, so that you shall live."
The deliberate and the unwitting sins you recognize;
the willful and the compelled, the open deeds and the hidden –
before You they are all revealed and known.
What are we? What are our lives?
What is our loving-kindness? What is our righteousness?
What is our salvation? What is our strength? What is our might?
What shall we say before You,
LORD our God and God of our ancestors?
Are not all the mighty like nothing before You,
the men of renown as if they had never been,
the wise as if they know nothing,
and the understanding as if they lack intelligence?
For their many works are in vain,
and the days of their lives like a fleeting breath before You.
The pre-eminence of man over the animals is nothing, *Eccl. 3*
for all is but a fleeting breath.

▸ What can we say before You, You who dwell on high?
What can we declare before You, You who abide in heaven?
Do You not know all, the hidden and revealed alike?

The שליח ציבור *continues:*

אֱלֹהֵינוּ וֵאלֹהֵי אֲבוֹתֵינוּ
סְלַח וּמְחַל לַעֲוֹנוֹתֵינוּ
בְּיוֹם (בשבת: הַשַּׁבָּת הַזֶּה וּבְיוֹם) הַכִּפּוּרִים הַזֶּה
וְהֵעָתֵר לָנוּ בִּתְפִלָּתֵנוּ
מְחֵה וְהַעֲבֵר פְּשָׁעֵינוּ וְחַטֹּאתֵינוּ מִנֶּגֶד עֵינֶיךָ
וְכֹף אֶת יִצְרֵנוּ לְהִשְׁתַּעְבֶּד לָךְ
וְהַכְנַע עָרְפֵּנוּ לָשׁוּב אֵלֶיךָ בֶּאֱמֶת
וְחַדֵּשׁ כִּלְיוֹתֵינוּ לִשְׁמֹר פִּקּוּדֶיךָ
וּמוֹל אֶת לְבָבֵנוּ לְאַהֲבָה וּלְיִרְאָה אֶת שְׁמֶךָ
כַּכָּתוּב בְּתוֹרָתֶךָ
וּמָל יהוה אֱלֹהֶיךָ אֶת־לְבָבְךָ וְאֶת־לְבַב זַרְעֶךָ דברים ל
לְאַהֲבָה אֶת־יהוה אֱלֹהֶיךָ בְּכָל־לְבָבְךָ וּבְכָל־נַפְשְׁךָ, לְמַעַן חַיֶּיךָ:
הַזְּדוֹנוֹת וְהַשְּׁגָגוֹת אַתָּה מַכִּיר
הָרָצוֹן וְהָאֹנֶס, הַגְּלוּיִים וְהַנִּסְתָּרִים
לְפָנֶיךָ הֵם גְּלוּיִים וִידוּעִים.
מָה אָנוּ, מֶה חַיֵּינוּ
מֶה חַסְדֵּנוּ, מַה צִּדְקוֹתֵינוּ
מַה יְּשׁוּעָתֵנוּ, מַה כֹּחֵנוּ, מַה גְּבוּרָתֵנוּ
מַה נֹּאמַר לְפָנֶיךָ, יהוה אֱלֹהֵינוּ וֵאלֹהֵי אֲבוֹתֵינוּ
הֲלֹא כָל הַגִּבּוֹרִים כְּאַיִן לְפָנֶיךָ, וְאַנְשֵׁי הַשֵּׁם כְּלֹא הָיוּ
וַחֲכָמִים כִּבְלִי מַדָּע, וּנְבוֹנִים כִּבְלִי הַשְׂכֵּל
כִּי רֹב מַעֲשֵׂיהֶם תֹּהוּ, וִימֵי חַיֵּיהֶם הֶבֶל לְפָנֶיךָ
וּמוֹתַר הָאָדָם מִן־הַבְּהֵמָה אָיִן, כִּי הַכֹּל הָבֶל: קהלת ג

◂ מַה נֹּאמַר לְפָנֶיךָ יוֹשֵׁב מָרוֹם, וּמַה נְּסַפֵּר לְפָנֶיךָ שׁוֹכֵן שְׁחָקִים
הֲלֹא כָּל הַנִּסְתָּרוֹת וְהַנִּגְלוֹת אַתָּה יוֹדֵעַ.

In Western Europe, the stanza "You know every secret" was said here, followed by the piyut "You understand" (page 1285). Nowadays, most congregations follow the Eastern European custom, according to which only the last two stanzas of the piyut are said (below), followed by "You know every secret."

The Leader then the congregation:

שִׁמְךָ Your name has always been the Forgiver of Sins.
Listen to our pleading as we stand before You in prayer.

Overlook sin, for this people returning from sin,
and wipe our transgressions away before Your eyes.

The Leader continues, with the congregation following him in an undertone:

אַתָּה יוֹדֵעַ You know every secret since the world began,
and what is hidden deep inside every living thing.
You search each person's inner chambers,
examining conscience and mind.
Nothing is shrouded from You,
and nothing is hidden before Your eyes.
And so, may it be Your will,
LORD our God and God of our ancestors,
that You forgive us all our sins,
pardon all our iniquities,
and grant us atonement for all of our transgressions.

Those who want the world to share their own high opinion of themselves are destined to a life of self-deception.

The irrationality of envy is that it allows someone else's happiness to poison mine. The two have nothing to do with one another. That someone else has much does not mean that I have little; that someone else is great does not mean that I am small. No one found happiness by "desiring this man's art or that man's scope." Who is rich? One who rejoices in what he has (Mishna, *Avot* 4:1), that is, unaffected by what anyone else has.

Anger is a failure of self control, allowing the amygdala, the seat of reactive emotion, to bypass the prefrontal cortex, the part of the brain that allows us to reflect on our actions and their likely consequences. Anger injures others and ultimately ourselves. The sages said: "When a person becomes angry, if he is a sage, his wisdom departs from him; if he is a prophet, his prophecy departs from him… Even if greatness has been decreed for him, he forfeits greatness" (*Pesaḥim* 66b). "The life of an angry person is not a life" (*ibid.* 113b).

In Western Europe, the stanza אַתָּה יוֹדֵעַ רָזֵי עוֹלָם *was said here, followed by the piyut* אַתָּה מֵבִין *(page 1285). Nowadays, most congregations follow the Eastern European custom, according to which only the last two stanzas of the piyut are said (below), followed by* אַתָּה יוֹדֵעַ רָזֵי עוֹלָם.

The שליח ציבור *then the* קהל:

שִׁמְךָ מֵעוֹלָם עוֹבֵר עַל פֶּשַׁע
שַׁוְעָתֵנוּ תַּאֲזִין, בְּעָמְדֵנוּ לְפָנֶיךָ בִּתְפִלָּה

תַּעֲבֹר עַל פֶּשַׁע לְעַם שָׁבֵי פֶשַׁע
תִּמְחֶה פְשָׁעֵינוּ מִנֶּגֶד עֵינֶיךָ.

The שליח ציבור *continues, with the* קהל *following him in an undertone:*

אַתָּה יוֹדֵעַ רָזֵי עוֹלָם וְתַעֲלוּמוֹת סִתְרֵי כָּל חָי.
אַתָּה חוֹפֵשׂ כָּל חַדְרֵי בָטֶן וּבוֹחֵן כְּלָיוֹת וָלֵב.
אֵין דָּבָר נֶעְלָם מִמֶּךָּ וְאֵין נִסְתָּר מִנֶּגֶד עֵינֶיךָ.
וּבְכֵן, יְהִי רָצוֹן מִלְּפָנֶיךָ, יהוה אֱלֹהֵינוּ וֵאלֹהֵי אֲבוֹתֵינוּ
שֶׁתִּסְלַח לָנוּ עַל כָּל חַטֹּאתֵינוּ
וְתִמְחַל לָנוּ עַל כָּל עֲוֹנוֹתֵינוּ
וּתְכַפֵּר לָנוּ עַל כָּל פְּשָׁעֵינוּ.

If you have done someone a small wrong, let it be in your eyes great. If you have done someone a great good, let it be in your eyes small. If someone has done you a small good, let it be in your eyes great. If someone has done you a great wrong, let it be in your eyes small. (*Avot deRabbi Natan* 41:11)

Whether we choose to or not, we are an influence on those around us. If we are cynical they will become cynical; if we are dishonest they will become dishonest; if we exploit others they will feel free to do likewise. Do this and we will eventually lose the friendship of the genuinely good people in our lives.

One of the ways we become trapped in bad habits is that we find ourselves surrounded by friends who have the same bad habits. This allows us to believe that they are not bad habits at all.

Those driven by envy, animosity, resentment or a sense of grievance are not only unhappy; they are a cause of unhappiness in others. Worst of all are those who combine these faults with a sense of self-righteousness.

Strike the left side of the chest with the right fist while saying each of the sins.

עַל חֵטְא For the sin we have sinned before You under duress or freewill, and for the sin we have sinned before You in hardness of heart.

For the sin we have sinned before You unwittingly,
and for the sin we have sinned before You by an utterance of our lips.

For the sin we have sinned before You by unchastity,
and for the sin we have sinned before You openly or secretly.

For the sin we have sinned before You knowingly and deceitfully,
and for the sin we have sinned before You in speech.

For the sin we have sinned before You by wronging a neighbor,
and for the sin we have sinned before You by thoughts of the heart.

For the sin we have sinned before You in a gathering for immorality,
and for the sin we have sinned before You by insincere confession.

For the sin we have sinned before You by contempt for parents and teachers,
and for the sin we have sinned before You willfully or in error.

---

practitioners tell themselves they have done no harm: they did no more than tell the truth, and people ought to know the faults of others. The sages said that in biblical times leprosy was the punishment for evil speech (ibid.). The act done in private was thus exposed in public, and those guilty of it were shamed and forced temporarily to live outside the camp as pariahs.

Once, a man went about speaking derogatorily about the rabbi. Later, realizing the wrong he had done, he felt remorse, and went to the rabbi to beg forgiveness, saying he would do all he could to make amends. The rabbi told him, "Take a feather pillow, cut it open, and scatter the feathers to the winds." The man did not understand why, but did so. Returning to tell the rabbi that he had done as he requested, the rabbi then said, "Now, go and collect the feathers." "I can't," said the man. "They have been carried far and wide by the wind." "So it is with evil speech," said the rabbi. "You cannot undo the harm it does, for you do not know where it has gone and where it has spread."

Strike the left side of the chest with the right fist while saying each of the sins.

עַל חֵטְא שֶׁחָטָאנוּ לְפָנֶיךָ בְּאֹנֶס וּבְרָצוֹן
וְעַל חֵטְא שֶׁחָטָאנוּ לְפָנֶיךָ בְּאִמּוּץ הַלֵּב

עַל חֵטְא שֶׁחָטָאנוּ לְפָנֶיךָ בִּבְלִי דָעַת
וְעַל חֵטְא שֶׁחָטָאנוּ לְפָנֶיךָ בְּבִטּוּי שְׂפָתָיִם

עַל חֵטְא שֶׁחָטָאנוּ לְפָנֶיךָ בְּגִלּוּי עֲרָיוֹת
וְעַל חֵטְא שֶׁחָטָאנוּ לְפָנֶיךָ בְּגָלוּי וּבַסָּתֶר

עַל חֵטְא שֶׁחָטָאנוּ לְפָנֶיךָ בְּדַעַת וּבְמִרְמָה
וְעַל חֵטְא שֶׁחָטָאנוּ לְפָנֶיךָ בְּדִבּוּר פֶּה

עַל חֵטְא שֶׁחָטָאנוּ לְפָנֶיךָ בְּהוֹנָאַת רֵעַ
וְעַל חֵטְא שֶׁחָטָאנוּ לְפָנֶיךָ בְּהַרְהוֹר הַלֵּב

עַל חֵטְא שֶׁחָטָאנוּ לְפָנֶיךָ בִּוְעִידַת זְנוּת
וְעַל חֵטְא שֶׁחָטָאנוּ לְפָנֶיךָ בְּוִדּוּי פֶה

עַל חֵטְא שֶׁחָטָאנוּ לְפָנֶיךָ בְּזִלְזוּל הוֹרִים וּמוֹרִים
וְעַל חֵטְא שֶׁחָטָאנוּ לְפָנֶיךָ בְּזָדוֹן וּבִשְׁגָגָה

בְּבִטּוּי שְׂפָתָיִם *By an utterance of our lips.* Note how many of the sins enumerated here have to do with speech (eleven out of the forty-four). The sages took "evil speech" with utmost seriousness. They said it is as bad as the three cardinal sins – murder, forbidden sex, and idolatry – combined (*Arakhin* 15b). It kills three people: the one who says it, the one who listens to it, and the one about whom it is said. Speech may be evil even when it is true. Character assassination, insinuation, the spreading of suspicion, the sowing of unrest, derogatory talk, depreciation, back-biting and bad-mouthing are subtle ways in which the trust on which human relations depend is undermined. It is all the more dangerous since it is often done in private and denied in public. Its

For the sin we have sinned before You by force,
and for the sin we have sinned before You by desecrating Your name.

For the sin we have sinned before You by impure lips,
and for the sin we have sinned before You by foolish speech.

For the sin we have sinned before You by the evil inclination,
and for the sin we have sinned before You knowingly or unwittingly.

The congregation aloud, followed by the Leader:

FOR ALL THESE, GOD OF FORGIVENESS,
FORGIVE US, PARDON US, GRANT US ATONEMENT.

All continue in an undertone. Strike the left side of the chest with the right fist while saying each of the sins.

For the sin we have sinned before You by deceit and lies,
and for the sin we have sinned before You by bribery.

For the sin we have sinned before You by scorn,
and for the sin we have sinned before You by evil speech.

For the sin we have sinned before You in business,
and for the sin we have sinned before You with food and drink.

For the sin we have sinned before You by interest and extortion,
and for the sin we have sinned before You by being haughty.

For the sin we have sinned before You by the idle chatter of our lips,
and for the sin we have sinned before You by prying eyes.

For the sin we have sinned before You by arrogance,
and for the sin we have sinned before You by insolence.

The congregation aloud, followed by the Leader:

FOR ALL THESE, GOD OF FORGIVENESS,
FORGIVE US, PARDON US, GRANT US ATONEMENT.

עַל חֵטְא שֶׁחָטָאנוּ לְפָנֶיךָ בְּחֹזֶק יָד
וְעַל חֵטְא שֶׁחָטָאנוּ לְפָנֶיךָ בְּחִלּוּל הַשֵּׁם

עַל חֵטְא שֶׁחָטָאנוּ לְפָנֶיךָ בְּטֻמְאַת שְׂפָתָיִם
וְעַל חֵטְא שֶׁחָטָאנוּ לְפָנֶיךָ בְּטִפְּשׁוּת פֶּה

עַל חֵטְא שֶׁחָטָאנוּ לְפָנֶיךָ בְּיֵצֶר הָרָע
וְעַל חֵטְא שֶׁחָטָאנוּ לְפָנֶיךָ בְּיוֹדְעִים וּבְלֹא יוֹדְעִים

The קהל *aloud, followed by the* שליח ציבור:

וְעַל כֻּלָּם אֱלוֹהַּ סְלִיחוֹת סְלַח לָנוּ, מְחַל לָנוּ, כַּפֶּר לָנוּ.

All continue in an undertone. Strike the left side of the chest with the right fist while saying each of the sins.

עַל חֵטְא שֶׁחָטָאנוּ לְפָנֶיךָ בְּכַחַשׁ וּבְכָזָב
וְעַל חֵטְא שֶׁחָטָאנוּ לְפָנֶיךָ בְּכַפַּת שֹׁחַד

עַל חֵטְא שֶׁחָטָאנוּ לְפָנֶיךָ בְּלָצוֹן
וְעַל חֵטְא שֶׁחָטָאנוּ לְפָנֶיךָ בְּלָשׁוֹן הָרָע

עַל חֵטְא שֶׁחָטָאנוּ לְפָנֶיךָ בְּמַשָּׂא וּבְמַתָּן
וְעַל חֵטְא שֶׁחָטָאנוּ לְפָנֶיךָ בְּמַאֲכָל וּבְמִשְׁתֶּה

עַל חֵטְא שֶׁחָטָאנוּ לְפָנֶיךָ בְּנֶשֶׁךְ וּבְמַרְבִּית
וְעַל חֵטְא שֶׁחָטָאנוּ לְפָנֶיךָ בִּנְטִיַּת גָּרוֹן

עַל חֵטְא שֶׁחָטָאנוּ לְפָנֶיךָ בְּשִׂיחַ שִׂפְתוֹתֵינוּ
וְעַל חֵטְא שֶׁחָטָאנוּ לְפָנֶיךָ בְּשִׂקּוּר עָיִן

עַל חֵטְא שֶׁחָטָאנוּ לְפָנֶיךָ בְּעֵינַיִם רָמוֹת
וְעַל חֵטְא שֶׁחָטָאנוּ לְפָנֶיךָ בְּעַזּוּת מֵצַח

The קהל *aloud, followed by the* שליח ציבור:

וְעַל כֻּלָּם אֱלוֹהַּ סְלִיחוֹת סְלַח לָנוּ, מְחַל לָנוּ, כַּפֶּר לָנוּ.

All continue in an undertone. Strike the left side of the chest with the right fist while saying each of the sins.

For the sin we have sinned before You by casting off the yoke,
and for the sin we have sinned before You by perverting judgment.

For the sin we have sinned before You by entrapping a neighbor,
and for the sin we have sinned before You by envy.

For the sin we have sinned before You by lack of seriousness,
and for the sin we have sinned before You by obstinacy.

For the sin we have sinned before You by running to do evil,
and for the sin we have sinned before You by gossip.

For the sin we have sinned before You by vain oath,
and for the sin we have sinned before You by baseless hatred.

For the sin we have sinned before You by breach of trust,
and for the sin we have sinned before You by confusion of heart.

The congregation aloud, followed by the Leader:

FOR ALL THESE, GOD OF FORGIVENESS,
FORGIVE US, PARDON US, GRANT US ATONEMENT.

All:

וְעַל חֲטָאִים And for the sins for which we are liable to bring a burnt-offering,
and for the sins for which we are liable to bring a sin-offering,
and for the sins for which we are liable to bring an offering according to our means,
and for the sins for which we are liable to bring a guilt-offering for certain or possible sin,
and for the sins for which we are liable to lashes for rebellion,
and for the sins for which we are liable to forty lashes,
and for the sins for which we are liable to death by the hands of Heaven,
and for the sins for which we are liable to be cut off and childless,
and for the sins for which we are liable to the four death penalties inflicted by the court: stoning, burning, beheading and strangling.

All continue in an undertone. Strike the left side of the chest with the right fist while saying each of the sins.

עַל חֵטְא שֶׁחָטָאנוּ לְפָנֶיךָ בִּפְרִיקַת עֹל
וְעַל חֵטְא שֶׁחָטָאנוּ לְפָנֶיךָ בִּפְלִילוּת

עַל חֵטְא שֶׁחָטָאנוּ לְפָנֶיךָ בִּצְדִיַּת רֵעַ
וְעַל חֵטְא שֶׁחָטָאנוּ לְפָנֶיךָ בְּצָרוּת עָיִן

עַל חֵטְא שֶׁחָטָאנוּ לְפָנֶיךָ בְּקַלּוּת רֹאשׁ
וְעַל חֵטְא שֶׁחָטָאנוּ לְפָנֶיךָ בְּקַשְׁיוּת עֹרֶף

עַל חֵטְא שֶׁחָטָאנוּ לְפָנֶיךָ בְּרִיצַת רַגְלַיִם לְהָרַע
וְעַל חֵטְא שֶׁחָטָאנוּ לְפָנֶיךָ בִּרְכִילוּת

עַל חֵטְא שֶׁחָטָאנוּ לְפָנֶיךָ בִּשְׁבוּעַת שָׁוְא
וְעַל חֵטְא שֶׁחָטָאנוּ לְפָנֶיךָ בְּשִׂנְאַת חִנָּם

עַל חֵטְא שֶׁחָטָאנוּ לְפָנֶיךָ בִּתְשׂוּמֶת יָד
וְעַל חֵטְא שֶׁחָטָאנוּ לְפָנֶיךָ בְּתִמְהוֹן לֵבָב

The קהל *aloud, followed by the* שליח ציבור*:*

וְעַל כֻּלָּם אֱלוֹהַ סְלִיחוֹת סְלַח לָנוּ, מְחַל לָנוּ, כַּפֶּר לָנוּ.

All:

וְעַל חֲטָאִים שֶׁאָנוּ חַיָּבִים עֲלֵיהֶם עוֹלָה
וְעַל חֲטָאִים שֶׁאָנוּ חַיָּבִים עֲלֵיהֶם חַטָּאת
וְעַל חֲטָאִים שֶׁאָנוּ חַיָּבִים עֲלֵיהֶם קָרְבָּן עוֹלֶה וְיוֹרֵד
וְעַל חֲטָאִים שֶׁאָנוּ חַיָּבִים עֲלֵיהֶם אָשָׁם וַדַּאי וְתָלוּי
וְעַל חֲטָאִים שֶׁאָנוּ חַיָּבִים עֲלֵיהֶם מַכַּת מַרְדּוּת
וְעַל חֲטָאִים שֶׁאָנוּ חַיָּבִים עֲלֵיהֶם מַלְקוּת אַרְבָּעִים
וְעַל חֲטָאִים שֶׁאָנוּ חַיָּבִים עֲלֵיהֶם מִיתָה בִּידֵי שָׁמָיִם
וְעַל חֲטָאִים שֶׁאָנוּ חַיָּבִים עֲלֵיהֶם כָּרֵת וַעֲרִירִי
וְעַל חֲטָאִים שֶׁאָנוּ חַיָּבִים עֲלֵיהֶם אַרְבַּע מִיתוֹת בֵּית דִּין
סְקִילָה, שְׂרֵפָה, הֶרֶג, וְחֶנֶק.

עַל מִצְוֹת For positive and negative commandments,
whether they can be remedied by an act or not,
for sins known to us and for those that are unknown –
for those that are known,
we have already declared them before You and confessed them to You;
and for those that are unknown, before You they are revealed and known,
as it is said,
"The secret things belong to the LORD our God, *Deut. 29*
but the things that are revealed are for us and our children for ever,
that we may fulfill all the words of this Torah."

וְאַתָּה And You are compassionate, receiving those who return;
You promised us repentance before the world began,
and it is for repentance that our eyes turn longingly to You.

וְדָוִד David Your servant said before You:
"Who can discern his own mistakes? Cleanse me of my hidden faults." *Ps. 19*
Cleanse us, LORD our God,
of all our transgressions, and purify us of all our impurities,
and throw clear waters over us to purify us,
as was written by Your prophet:
"I shall throw clear waters over you and you shall be pure. *Ezek. 36*
I shall purify you of all your impurities and of all your idolatry."

מִיכָה Micah Your servant said before You:
"Who is a God like You, who pardons iniquity *Mic. 7*
and forgives the transgression of the remnant of His heritage?
He does not stay angry forever, but delights in loving-kindness.
He will again have compassion on us, suppress our iniquities,
and cast into the depths of the sea all their sins."
Cast all the sins of Your people, the house of Israel,
to a place where they will not be remembered and will not be recalled,
and will not ever come to mind again.
Grant truth to Jacob, loving-kindness to Abraham,
as You promised our ancestors in ancient times.

דָּוִד, מִיכָה, דָּנִיאֵל, עֶזְרָא *David, Micah, Daniel, Ezra.* Having invoked the prophetic precedent of Moses' prayer after the sin of the golden calf, and the

עַל מִצְוַת עֲשֵׂה וְעַל מִצְוַת לֹא תַעֲשֶׂה.
בֵּין שֶׁיֵּשׁ בָּהּ קוּם עֲשֵׂה וּבֵין שֶׁאֵין בָּהּ קוּם עֲשֵׂה.
אֶת הַגְּלוּיִים לָנוּ וְאֶת שֶׁאֵינָם גְּלוּיִים לָנוּ
אֶת הַגְּלוּיִים לָנוּ, כְּבָר אֲמַרְנוּם לְפָנֶיךָ, וְהוֹדִינוּ לְךָ עֲלֵיהֶם
וְאֶת שֶׁאֵינָם גְּלוּיִים לָנוּ, לְפָנֶיךָ הֵם גְּלוּיִים וִידוּעִים
כַּדָּבָר שֶׁנֶּאֱמַר
דברים כט הַנִּסְתָּרֹת לַיהוה אֱלֹהֵינוּ, וְהַנִּגְלֹת לָנוּ וּלְבָנֵינוּ עַד־עוֹלָם
לַעֲשׂוֹת אֶת־כָּל־דִּבְרֵי הַתּוֹרָה הַזֹּאת:

וְאַתָּה רַחוּם מְקַבֵּל שָׁבִים
עַל הַתְּשׁוּבָה מֵרֹאשׁ הִבְטַחְתָּנוּ, וְעַל הַתְּשׁוּבָה עֵינֵינוּ מְיַחֲלוֹת לָךְ.

וְדָוִד עַבְדְּךָ אָמַר לְפָנֶיךָ
תהלים יט שְׁגִיאוֹת מִי־יָבִין, מִנִּסְתָּרוֹת נַקֵּנִי:
נַקֵּנוּ יהוה אֱלֹהֵינוּ מִכָּל פְּשָׁעֵינוּ, וְטַהֲרֵנוּ מִכָּל טֻמְאוֹתֵינוּ
וּזְרֹק עָלֵינוּ מַיִם טְהוֹרִים וְטַהֲרֵנוּ
כַּכָּתוּב עַל יַד נְבִיאֶךָ
יחזקאל לו וְזָרַקְתִּי עֲלֵיכֶם מַיִם טְהוֹרִים, וּטְהַרְתֶּם
מִכֹּל טֻמְאוֹתֵיכֶם וּמִכָּל־גִּלּוּלֵיכֶם אֲטַהֵר אֶתְכֶם:

מִיכָה עַבְדְּךָ אָמַר לְפָנֶיךָ
מיכה ז מִי־אֵל כָּמוֹךָ, נֹשֵׂא עָוֹן וְעֹבֵר עַל־פֶּשַׁע לִשְׁאֵרִית נַחֲלָתוֹ
לֹא־הֶחֱזִיק לָעַד אַפּוֹ כִּי־חָפֵץ חֶסֶד הוּא:
יָשׁוּב יְרַחֲמֵנוּ, יִכְבֹּשׁ עֲוֹנֹתֵינוּ, וְתַשְׁלִיךְ בִּמְצֻלוֹת יָם כָּל־חַטֹּאתָם:
וְכָל חַטֹּאת עַמְּךָ בֵּית יִשְׂרָאֵל תַּשְׁלִיךְ
בִּמְקוֹם אֲשֶׁר לֹא יִזָּכְרוּ וְלֹא יִפָּקְדוּ, וְלֹא יַעֲלוּ עַל לֵב לְעוֹלָם.
תִּתֵּן אֱמֶת לְיַעֲקֹב, חֶסֶד לְאַבְרָהָם
אֲשֶׁר־נִשְׁבַּעְתָּ לַאֲבֹתֵינוּ מִימֵי קֶדֶם:

דָּנִיֵּאל Daniel, the beloved man, pleaded before You:
Incline Your ear, my God, and hear. *Dan. 9*
Open Your eyes and see our desolation
and that of the city called by Your name.
For not because of our righteousness do we lay our pleas before You,
but because of Your great compassion.
LORD, hear! LORD, forgive! LORD, listen and act! Do not delay –
for Your sake, my God, because Your city and Your people
are called by Your name.

עֶזְרָא Ezra the scribe said before You:
"My God, I am too humiliated and ashamed *Ezra 9*
to raise my face toward You, my God.
For our iniquities have multiplied over our very heads,
and our guilt has grown as high as the heavens."
And You are the God of forgiveness, gracious and compassionate,
slow to anger and abounding in loving-kindness,
and have not abandoned us.

אַל תַּעַזְבֵנוּ Do not abandon us, our Father,
and do not desert us, our Creator.
Do not leave us, our Maker,
and do not destroy us as befits our sins.
Fulfill in us, LORD our God, the promise You passed down to us
at the hand of Your seer Jeremiah, as it is said:
"In those days, at that time, says the LORD, *Jer. 50*
they will search for Israel's iniquity and it will not be there,
they will seek the sins of Judah and they will be nowhere to be found,
for I shall forgive those I leave behind."

עַמְּךָ וְנַחֲלָתְךָ Your people and Your inheritance, famished of Your good,
thirsting for Your loving-kindness, craving Your salvation –
they will recognize and know that compassion and forgiveness
belong to the LORD our God.

---

prophet Micah; Daniel, adviser to the royal court in Babylon; and Ezra, the priest and scribe.

דָּנִיֵּאל אִישׁ חֲמוּדוֹת שִׁוַּע לְפָנֶיךָ
הַטֵּה אֱלֹהַי אָזְנְךָ וּשְׁמָע דניאל ט
פְּקַח עֵינֶיךָ וּרְאֵה שֹׁמְמֹתֵינוּ, וְהָעִיר אֲשֶׁר־נִקְרָא שִׁמְךָ עָלֶיהָ
כִּי לֹא עַל־צִדְקֹתֵינוּ אֲנַחְנוּ מַפִּילִים תַּחֲנוּנֵינוּ לְפָנֶיךָ
כִּי עַל־רַחֲמֶיךָ הָרַבִּים:
אֲדֹנָי שְׁמָעָה, אֲדֹנָי סְלָחָה
אֲדֹנָי הַקְשִׁיבָה וַעֲשֵׂה אַל־תְּאַחַר
לְמַעַנְךָ אֱלֹהַי, כִּי־שִׁמְךָ נִקְרָא עַל־עִירְךָ וְעַל־עַמֶּךָ:

עֶזְרָא הַסּוֹפֵר אָמַר לְפָנֶיךָ
אֱלֹהַי, בֹּשְׁתִּי וְנִכְלַמְתִּי לְהָרִים אֱלֹהַי פָּנַי אֵלֶיךָ עזרא ט
כִּי עֲוֹנֹתֵינוּ רָבוּ לְמַעְלָה רֹּאשׁ, וְאַשְׁמָתֵנוּ גָדְלָה עַד לַשָּׁמָיִם:
וְאַתָּה אֱלוֹהַּ סְלִיחוֹת חַנּוּן וְרַחוּם
אֶרֶךְ אַפַּיִם וְרַב חֶסֶד, וְלֹא עֲזַבְתָּנוּ.

אַל תַּעַזְבֵנוּ אָבִינוּ, וְאַל תִּטְּשֵׁנוּ בּוֹרְאֵנוּ, וְאַל תַּזְנִיחֵנוּ יוֹצְרֵנוּ
וְאַל תַּעַשׂ עִמָּנוּ כָּלָה כְּחַטֹּאתֵינוּ
וְקַיֶּם לָנוּ יהוה אֱלֹהֵינוּ אֶת הַדָּבָר שֶׁהִבְטַחְתָּנוּ בְּקַבָּלָה
עַל יְדֵי יִרְמְיָהוּ חוֹזָךְ, כָּאָמוּר
בַּיָּמִים הָהֵם וּבָעֵת הַהִיא נְאֻם־יהוה יְבֻקַּשׁ אֶת־עֲוֹן יִשְׂרָאֵל, וְאֵינֶנּוּ ירמיה נ
וְאֶת־חַטֹּאת יְהוּדָה, וְלֹא תִמָּצֶאינָה
כִּי אֶסְלַח לַאֲשֶׁר אַשְׁאִיר:

עַמְּךָ וְנַחֲלָתְךָ, רְעֵבֵי טוּבְךָ, צְמֵאֵי חַסְדְּךָ, תְּאֵבֵי יִשְׁעֲךָ
יַכִּירוּ וְיֵדְעוּ, כִּי לַיהוה אֱלֹהֵינוּ הָרַחֲמִים וְהַסְּלִיחוֹת.

---

priestly ritual of confession, we now turn to other historic precedents of biblical figures who prayed for forgiveness, among them King David; the

When Yom Kippur falls on Shabbat, some congregations omit the following and continue with Psalm 24 on on page 194.

אֵל רַחוּם Compassionate God is Your name.
Gracious God is Your name.
We are called by Your name.
LORD, act for the sake of Your name.

Act for the sake of Your truth. Act for the sake of Your covenant.
Act for the sake of Your greatness and glory. Act for the sake of Your Law.
Act for the sake of Your majesty. Act for the sake of Your promise.
Act for the sake of Your remembrance. Act for the sake of Your loving-kindness.
Act for the sake of Your goodness. Act for the sake of Your Oneness.
Act for the sake of Your honor. Act for the sake of Your wisdom.
Act for the sake of Your kingship. Act for the sake of Your eternity.
Act for the sake of Your mystery. Act for the sake of Your might.
Act for the sake of Your splendor. Act for the sake of Your righteousness.
Act for the sake of Your holiness. Act for the sake of Your great compassion.
Act for the sake of Your Presence. Act for the sake of Your praise.

Act for the sake of those who loved You,
who now dwell in the dust.
Act for the sake of Abraham, Isaac and Jacob.
Act for the sake of Moses and Aaron.
Act for the sake of David and Solomon.
Act for the sake of Jerusalem, Your holy city.
Act for the sake of Zion, the dwelling place of Your glory.
Act for the sake of the desolate site of Your Temple.
Act for the sake of the ruins of Your altar.

אֵל רַחוּם שְׁמֶךָ *Compassionate God is Your name.* This and the following prayers have the basic structure of a litany or a chant. Chants derive their power from rhythm and repetition. They consist of short, repetitive lines, and are often structured alphabetically. Among the most famous in Jewish prayer are the *Hoshanot* said on Sukkot. Chants are mood-inducing rather than the expression of a structured supplication.

When יום כיפור falls on שבת, some congregations omit the following and continue with לדוד מזמור *on page 195.*

אֵל רַחוּם שְׁמֶךָ.
אֵל חַנּוּן שְׁמֶךָ.
בָּנוּ נִקְרָא שְׁמֶךָ.
יהוה עֲשֵׂה לְמַעַן שְׁמֶךָ.

עֲשֵׂה לְמַעַן אֲמִתָּךְ. עֲשֵׂה לְמַעַן בְּרִיתָךְ.
עֲשֵׂה לְמַעַן גָּדְלָךְ וְתִפְאַרְתָּךְ. עֲשֵׂה לְמַעַן דָּתָךְ.
עֲשֵׂה לְמַעַן הוֹדָךְ. עֲשֵׂה לְמַעַן וִעוּדָךְ.
עֲשֵׂה לְמַעַן זִכְרָךְ. עֲשֵׂה לְמַעַן חַסְדָּךְ.
עֲשֵׂה לְמַעַן טוּבָךְ. עֲשֵׂה לְמַעַן יִחוּדָךְ.
עֲשֵׂה לְמַעַן כְּבוֹדָךְ. עֲשֵׂה לְמַעַן לִמּוּדָךְ.
עֲשֵׂה לְמַעַן מַלְכוּתָךְ. עֲשֵׂה לְמַעַן נִצְחָךְ.
עֲשֵׂה לְמַעַן סוֹדָךְ. עֲשֵׂה לְמַעַן עֻזָּךְ.
עֲשֵׂה לְמַעַן פְּאֵרָךְ. עֲשֵׂה לְמַעַן צִדְקָתָךְ.
עֲשֵׂה לְמַעַן קְדֻשָּׁתָךְ. עֲשֵׂה לְמַעַן רַחֲמֶיךָ הָרַבִּים.
עֲשֵׂה לְמַעַן שְׁכִינָתָךְ. עֲשֵׂה לְמַעַן תְּהִלָּתָךְ.

עֲשֵׂה לְמַעַן אוֹהֲבֶיךָ שׁוֹכְנֵי עָפָר.
עֲשֵׂה לְמַעַן אַבְרָהָם יִצְחָק וְיַעֲקֹב.
עֲשֵׂה לְמַעַן מֹשֶׁה וְאַהֲרֹן.
עֲשֵׂה לְמַעַן דָּוִד וּשְׁלֹמֹה.
עֲשֵׂה לְמַעַן יְרוּשָׁלַיִם עִיר קָדְשֶׁךָ.
עֲשֵׂה לְמַעַן צִיּוֹן מִשְׁכַּן כְּבוֹדֶךָ.
עֲשֵׂה לְמַעַן שִׁמְמוֹת הֵיכָלֶךָ.
עֲשֵׂה לְמַעַן הֲרִיסוּת מִזְבְּחֶךָ.

Act for the sake of those killed in sanctification of Your name.

Act for the sake of those slaughtered over Your unity.

Act for the sake of those who have gone through fire and water in sanctification of Your name.

Act for the sake of suckling infants who have not sinned.

Act for the sake of little ones just weaned who have done no wrong.

Act for the sake of schoolchildren.

Act for Your own sake if not for ours.

Act for Your own sake, and save us.

עֲנֵנוּ Answer us, LORD, answer us. Answer us, our God, answer us. Answer us, our Father, answer us. Answer us, our Creator, answer us. Answer us, our Redeemer, answer us. Answer us, You who seek us, answer us. Answer us, God who is faithful, answer us. Answer us, You who are ancient and kind, answer us. Answer us, You who are pure and upright, answer us. Answer us, You who are alive and remain, answer us. Answer us, You who are good and do good, answer us. Answer us, You who know our impulses, answer us. Answer us, You who conquer rage, answer us. Answer us, You who clothe Yourself in righteousness, answer us. Answer us, Supreme King of kings, answer us. Answer us, You who are awesome and elevated, answer us. Answer us, You who forgive and pardon, answer us. Answer us, You who answer in times of trouble, answer us. Answer us, You who redeem and save, answer us. Answer us, You who are righteous and straightforward, answer us. Answer us, You who are close to those who call, answer us. Answer us, You who are compassionate and gracious, answer us. Answer us, You who listen to the destitute, answer us. Answer us, You who support the innocent, answer us. Answer us, God of our fathers, answer us. Answer us, God of Abraham, answer us. Answer us, Terror of Isaac, answer us. Answer us, Champion of Jacob, answer us. Answer us, Help of the tribes, answer us. Answer us, Stronghold of the mothers, answer us. Answer us, You who are slow to anger, answer us. Answer us, You who are lightly appeased, answer us. Answer us, You who answer at times of favor, answer us. Answer us, Father of orphans, answer us.

Answer us, Justice of widows, answer us.

עֲשֵׂה לְמַעַן הֲרוּגִים עַל שֵׁם קָדְשֶׁךָ.
עֲשֵׂה לְמַעַן טְבוּחִים עַל יִחוּדֶךָ.
עֲשֵׂה לְמַעַן בָּאֵי בָאֵשׁ וּבַמַּיִם עַל קִדּוּשׁ שְׁמֶךָ.
עֲשֵׂה לְמַעַן יוֹנְקֵי שָׁדַיִם שֶׁלֹּא חָטְאוּ.
עֲשֵׂה לְמַעַן גְּמוּלֵי חָלָב שֶׁלֹּא פָשְׁעוּ.
עֲשֵׂה לְמַעַן תִּינוֹקוֹת שֶׁל בֵּית רַבָּן.
עֲשֵׂה לְמַעַנְךָ אִם לֹא לְמַעֲנֵנוּ.
עֲשֵׂה לְמַעַנְךָ וְהוֹשִׁיעֵנוּ.

עֲנֵנוּ יהוה עֲנֵנוּ. עֲנֵנוּ אֱלֹהֵינוּ עֲנֵנוּ.

עֲנֵנוּ אָבִינוּ עֲנֵנוּ. עֲנֵנוּ בּוֹרְאֵנוּ עֲנֵנוּ.
עֲנֵנוּ גּוֹאֲלֵנוּ עֲנֵנוּ. עֲנֵנוּ דּוֹרְשֵׁנוּ עֲנֵנוּ.
עֲנֵנוּ הָאֵל הַנֶּאֱמָן עֲנֵנוּ. עֲנֵנוּ וָתִיק וְחָסִיד עֲנֵנוּ.
עֲנֵנוּ זַךְ וְיָשָׁר עֲנֵנוּ. עֲנֵנוּ חַי וְקַיָּם עֲנֵנוּ.
עֲנֵנוּ טוֹב וּמֵטִיב עֲנֵנוּ. עֲנֵנוּ יוֹדֵעַ יֵצֶר עֲנֵנוּ.
עֲנֵנוּ כּוֹבֵשׁ כְּעָסִים עֲנֵנוּ. עֲנֵנוּ לוֹבֵשׁ צְדָקוֹת עֲנֵנוּ.
עֲנֵנוּ מֶלֶךְ מַלְכֵי הַמְּלָכִים עֲנֵנוּ. עֲנֵנוּ נוֹרָא וְנִשְׂגָּב עֲנֵנוּ.
עֲנֵנוּ סוֹלֵחַ וּמוֹחֵל עֲנֵנוּ. עֲנֵנוּ עוֹנֶה בְּעֵת צָרָה עֲנֵנוּ.
עֲנֵנוּ פּוֹדֶה וּמַצִּיל עֲנֵנוּ. עֲנֵנוּ צַדִּיק וְיָשָׁר עֲנֵנוּ.
עֲנֵנוּ קָרוֹב לְקוֹרְאָיו עֲנֵנוּ. עֲנֵנוּ רַחוּם וְחַנּוּן עֲנֵנוּ.
עֲנֵנוּ שׁוֹמֵעַ אֶל אֶבְיוֹנִים עֲנֵנוּ. עֲנֵנוּ תּוֹמֵךְ תְּמִימִים עֲנֵנוּ.
עֲנֵנוּ אֱלֹהֵי אֲבוֹתֵינוּ עֲנֵנוּ. עֲנֵנוּ אֱלֹהֵי אַבְרָהָם עֲנֵנוּ.
עֲנֵנוּ פַּחַד יִצְחָק עֲנֵנוּ. עֲנֵנוּ אֲבִיר יַעֲקֹב עֲנֵנוּ.
עֲנֵנוּ עֶזְרַת הַשְּׁבָטִים עֲנֵנוּ. עֲנֵנוּ מִשְׂגַּב אִמָּהוֹת עֲנֵנוּ.
עֲנֵנוּ קָשֶׁה לִכְעֹס עֲנֵנוּ. עֲנֵנוּ רַךְ לִרְצוֹת עֲנֵנוּ.
עֲנֵנוּ עוֹנֶה בְּעֵת רָצוֹן עֲנֵנוּ. עֲנֵנוּ אֲבִי יְתוֹמִים עֲנֵנוּ.
עֲנֵנוּ דַּיַּן אַלְמָנוֹת עֲנֵנוּ.

מִי שֶׁעָנָה The One who answered Abraham our father on Mount Moriah – answer us.
The One who answered Isaac his son, when he was bound upon the altar – answer us.
The One who answered Jacob in Beth-El – answer us.
The One who answered Joseph in prison – answer us.
The One who answered our fathers at the Reed Sea – answer us.
The One who answered Moses at Horeb – answer us.
The One who answered Aaron over his firepan – answer us.
The One who answered Pinehas when he stood up from among the congregation – answer us.
The One who answered Joshua at Gilgal – answer us.
The One who answered Samuel at Mitzpah – answer us.
The One who answered David and Solomon his son in Jerusalem – answer us.
The One who answered Elijah on Mount Carmel – answer us.
The One who answered Elisha at Jericho – answer us.
The One who answered Jonah in the belly of the fish – answer us.
The One who answered Hezekiah the king of Judah in his illness – answer us.
The One who answered Hananiah, Mishael and Azariah in the furnace of fire – answer us.
The One who answered Daniel in the lions' den – answer us.
The One who answered Mordekhai and Esther in Shushan the capital city – answer us.
The One who answered Ezra in his exile – answer us.
The One who answered so many righteous, devoted, innocent and upright people – answer us.

---

pened; memory is our attempt to discover meaning in what happened. History focuses on the uniqueness of events; memory on their repeated patterns, the structure visible through the details, the music beneath the noise. Judaism is a religion of memory, not just history, and this prayer is a key example. It takes events from different eras and links them as instances of a single pattern. People – our ancestors – prayed and God answered. We are not wanderers in the void, alone in a universe bereft of moral form. We pray not out of wishful thinking but out of the concrete experience of our people's past. Prayer made a difference to them; it will make a difference to us. This we believe, not blindly, but in the full consciousness of memory as it educates and gives substance to our hopes.

מִי שֶׁעָנָה לְאַבְרָהָם אָבִינוּ בְּהַר הַמּוֹרִיָּה, הוּא יַעֲנֵנוּ.
מִי שֶׁעָנָה לְיִצְחָק בְּנוֹ כְּשֶׁנֶּעֱקַד עַל גַּבֵּי הַמִּזְבֵּחַ, הוּא יַעֲנֵנוּ.
מִי שֶׁעָנָה לְיַעֲקֹב בְּבֵית אֵל, הוּא יַעֲנֵנוּ.
מִי שֶׁעָנָה לְיוֹסֵף בְּבֵית הָאֲסוּרִים, הוּא יַעֲנֵנוּ.
מִי שֶׁעָנָה לַאֲבוֹתֵינוּ עַל יַם סוּף, הוּא יַעֲנֵנוּ.
מִי שֶׁעָנָה לְמֹשֶׁה בְּחוֹרֵב, הוּא יַעֲנֵנוּ.
מִי שֶׁעָנָה לְאַהֲרֹן בַּמַּחְתָּה, הוּא יַעֲנֵנוּ.
מִי שֶׁעָנָה לְפִינְחָס בְּקוּמוֹ מִתּוֹךְ הָעֵדָה, הוּא יַעֲנֵנוּ.
מִי שֶׁעָנָה לִיהוֹשֻׁעַ בַּגִּלְגָּל, הוּא יַעֲנֵנוּ.
מִי שֶׁעָנָה לִשְׁמוּאֵל בַּמִּצְפָּה, הוּא יַעֲנֵנוּ.
מִי שֶׁעָנָה לְדָוִד וּשְׁלֹמֹה בְנוֹ בִּירוּשָׁלָיִם, הוּא יַעֲנֵנוּ.
מִי שֶׁעָנָה לְאֵלִיָּהוּ בְּהַר הַכַּרְמֶל, הוּא יַעֲנֵנוּ.
מִי שֶׁעָנָה לֶאֱלִישָׁע בִּירִיחוֹ, הוּא יַעֲנֵנוּ.
מִי שֶׁעָנָה לְיוֹנָה בִּמְעֵי הַדָּגָה, הוּא יַעֲנֵנוּ.
מִי שֶׁעָנָה לְחִזְקִיָּהוּ מֶלֶךְ יְהוּדָה בְּחָלְיוֹ, הוּא יַעֲנֵנוּ.
מִי שֶׁעָנָה לַחֲנַנְיָה מִישָׁאֵל וַעֲזַרְיָה בְּתוֹךְ כִּבְשַׁן הָאֵשׁ, הוּא יַעֲנֵנוּ.
מִי שֶׁעָנָה לְדָנִיֵּאל בְּגוֹב הָאֲרָיוֹת, הוּא יַעֲנֵנוּ.
מִי שֶׁעָנָה לְמָרְדְּכַי וְאֶסְתֵּר בְּשׁוּשַׁן הַבִּירָה, הוּא יַעֲנֵנוּ.
מִי שֶׁעָנָה לְעֶזְרָא בַּגּוֹלָה, הוּא יַעֲנֵנוּ.
מִי שֶׁעָנָה לְכָל הַצַּדִּיקִים וְהַחֲסִידִים וְהַתְּמִימִים וְהַיְשָׁרִים, הוּא יַעֲנֵנוּ.

מִי שֶׁעָנָה *The One who answered.* This prayer derives its basic form from the special Amida said in Israel on public fasts proclaimed at times of national emergency, especially during prolonged drought. In its original form it mentioned seven great occasions when prayer was answered: Abraham in Nimrod's furnace, the Israelites at the Reed Sea, Joshua at Gilgal during his campaign against Jericho, Samuel in his battle against the Philistines at Mitzpah, Elijah in his confrontation with the false prophets at Mount Carmel, Jonah in the belly of the fish, and David and Solomon when they faced famine (Mishna *Ta'anit* 15a). It is considerably expanded in its present form.

There is a difference between history and memory. History is what hap-

רַחֲמָנָא Loving God, who answers the oppressed: answer us.
Loving God, who answers the broken hearted: answer us.
Loving God, who answers those of humbled spirit: answer us.
Loving God, answer us.
Loving God, spare; Loving God, release; Loving God, save us.
Loving God, have compassion for us now, swiftly,
at a time soon coming.

AVINU MALKENU

On Shabbat, "Avinu Malkenu" is not said,
and the service continues with Psalm 24 on page 194.

The Ark is opened.

אָבִינוּ מַלְכֵּנוּ Our Father, our King, we have sinned before You.
Our Father, our King, we have no king but You.
Our Father, our King, deal kindly with us for the sake of Your name.
Our Father our King, renew for us a good year.

Rabbi Akiva's genius to place these two words next to one another, giving primacy to the first, to God's love over and above His justice.

The Nobel Prize–winning physicist Niels Bohr is said to have arrived at his Complementarity Theory – his explanation of the fact that we perceive light both as waves and as particles but not at the same time – when his son committed a minor crime. He found himself able to think of his son in two ways: as a judge in court passing judgment on his act, and as a father with compassion for his child, but not both at the same time. It is some such perception that lies behind Rabbi Akiva's formulation. We are, he says to God, Your subjects, and we understand that You are judging us. But we are also Your children, therefore do not judge us: give us help instead. At that moment, rain fell.

The idea that God loves us as a parent loves a child sounds obvious. Did God not tell Moses to say to Pharaoh: "My child, My firstborn, Israel" (Ex. 4:22)? Yet it was revolutionary in the ancient world and remains challenging in an age of scientific rationalism. Love – the concrete love of a parent for a child, as opposed to *agape*, the generalized love of all things, or *eros*, physical desire, – defines Judaism and is one of its greatest contributions to the imaginative horizons of humankind.

רַחֲמָנָא דְּעָנֵי לַעֲנִיֵּי עֲנֵינָן.
רַחֲמָנָא דְּעָנֵי לִתְבִירֵי לִבָּא עֲנֵינָן.
רַחֲמָנָא דְּעָנֵי לְמַכִּיכֵי רוּחָא עֲנֵינָן.
רַחֲמָנָא עֲנֵינָן.
רַחֲמָנָא חוּס, רַחֲמָנָא פְּרֹק, רַחֲמָנָא שֵׁיזִב.
רַחֲמָנָא רְחֵם עֲלָן
הַשְׁתָּא בַּעֲגָלָא וּבִזְמַן קָרִיב.

אבינו מלכנו

On שבת, אָבִינוּ מַלְכֵּנוּ *is not said,*
and the service continues with לְדָוִד מִזְמוֹר *on page 195.*
The ארון קודש *is opened.*

אָבִינוּ מַלְכֵּנוּ, חָטָאנוּ לְפָנֶיךָ.
אָבִינוּ מַלְכֵּנוּ, אֵין לָנוּ מֶלֶךְ אֶלָּא אָתָּה.
אָבִינוּ מַלְכֵּנוּ, עֲשֵׂה עִמָּנוּ לְמַעַן שְׁמֶךָ.
אָבִינוּ מַלְכֵּנוּ, חַדֵּשׁ עָלֵינוּ שָׁנָה טוֹבָה.

רַחֲמָנָא *Loving God.* A short, moving plea, written in Aramaic and in part based on the previous prayer. It appeared for the first time in the siddur of Rabbi Amram Gaon (821–875), the first Jewish prayer book.

AVINU MALKENU – OUR FATHER, OUR KING
The Talmud tells us that once a series of fasts was ordained after a prolonged drought. On the last of these, Rabbi Eliezer prayed twenty-four prayers and was not answered. Rabbi Akiva prayed a short prayer, beginning with the words "Our Father, our King," and was answered (*Ta'anit* 25b). That was the origin of this prayer.

Its power consists of the juxtaposition of the two phrases, "our Father" and "our King." We are related to God in two primary ways. He is our Father and we are His children. He is our King and we are His subjects. The first bespeaks a relationship of love and compassion, the second of law and justice. It was

Our Father, our King, nullify all harsh decrees against us.
Our Father, our King, nullify the plans of those who hate us.
Our Father, our King, thwart the counsel of our enemies.
Our Father, our King, rid us of every oppressor and adversary.
Our Father, our King, close the mouths of our adversaries and accusers.
Our Father, our King, eradicate pestilence, sword, famine, captivity and destruction, iniquity and eradication from the people of Your covenant.
Our Father, our King, withhold the plague from Your heritage.
Our Father, our King, forgive and pardon all our iniquities.
Our Father, our King, wipe away and remove our transgressions and sins from Your sight.
Our Father, our King, erase in Your abundant mercy all records of our sins.

The following nine verses are said responsively, first by the Leader, then by the congregation:

Our Father, our King, bring us back to You in perfect repentance.
Our Father, our King, send a complete healing to the sick of Your people.
Our Father, our King, tear up the evil decree against us.
Our Father, our King, remember us with a memory of favorable deeds before You.
Our Father, our King, write us in the book of good life.
Our Father, our King, write us in the book of redemption and salvation.
Our Father, our King, write us in the book of livelihood and sustenance.
Our Father, our King, write us in the book of merit.
Our Father, our King, write us in the book of pardon and forgiveness.

End of responsive reading.

גְּזֵרוֹת קָשׁוֹת *Harsh decrees.* Jews have often suffered harsh decrees, from Haman to Hitler. Those who sought to deny God have focused their attack on the people of God.

שׂוֹנְאֵינוּ...אוֹיְבֵינוּ *Those who hate us... our enemies.* Jews have been attacked sometimes for religious reasons ("those who hate us"), sometimes for political and economic reasons ("our enemies").

סְתֹם פִּיּוֹת *Close the mouths.* Assaults on Jews have almost invariably been preceded by false accusations.

אָבִינוּ מַלְכֵּנוּ, בַּטֵּל מֵעָלֵינוּ כָּל גְּזֵרוֹת קָשׁוֹת.
אָבִינוּ מַלְכֵּנוּ, בַּטֵּל מַחְשְׁבוֹת שׂוֹנְאֵינוּ.
אָבִינוּ מַלְכֵּנוּ, הָפֵר עֲצַת אוֹיְבֵינוּ.
אָבִינוּ מַלְכֵּנוּ, כַּלֵּה כָּל צַר וּמַשְׂטִין מֵעָלֵינוּ.
אָבִינוּ מַלְכֵּנוּ, סְתֹם פִּיּוֹת מַשְׂטִינֵנוּ וּמְקַטְרְגֵינוּ.
אָבִינוּ מַלְכֵּנוּ, כַּלֵּה דֶּבֶר וְחֶרֶב וְרָעָב וּשְׁבִי וּמַשְׁחִית וְעָוֹן וּשְׁמַד מִבְּנֵי בְרִיתֶךָ.
אָבִינוּ מַלְכֵּנוּ, מְנַע מַגֵּפָה מִנַּחֲלָתֶךָ.
אָבִינוּ מַלְכֵּנוּ, סְלַח וּמְחַל לְכָל עֲוֹנוֹתֵינוּ.
אָבִינוּ מַלְכֵּנוּ, מְחֵה וְהַעֲבֵר פְּשָׁעֵינוּ וְחַטֹּאתֵינוּ מִנֶּגֶד עֵינֶיךָ.
אָבִינוּ מַלְכֵּנוּ, מְחֹק בְּרַחֲמֶיךָ הָרַבִּים כָּל שִׁטְרֵי חוֹבוֹתֵינוּ.

The following nine verses are said responsively, first by the שליח ציבור*, then by the* קהל*:*

אָבִינוּ מַלְכֵּנוּ, הַחֲזִירֵנוּ בִּתְשׁוּבָה שְׁלֵמָה לְפָנֶיךָ.
אָבִינוּ מַלְכֵּנוּ, שְׁלַח רְפוּאָה שְׁלֵמָה לְחוֹלֵי עַמֶּךָ.
אָבִינוּ מַלְכֵּנוּ, קְרַע רֹעַ גְּזַר דִּינֵנוּ.
אָבִינוּ מַלְכֵּנוּ, זָכְרֵנוּ בְּזִכָּרוֹן טוֹב לְפָנֶיךָ.
אָבִינוּ מַלְכֵּנוּ, כָּתְבֵנוּ בְּסֵפֶר חַיִּים טוֹבִים.
אָבִינוּ מַלְכֵּנוּ, כָּתְבֵנוּ בְּסֵפֶר גְּאֻלָּה וִישׁוּעָה.
אָבִינוּ מַלְכֵּנוּ, כָּתְבֵנוּ בְּסֵפֶר פַּרְנָסָה וְכַלְכָּלָה.
אָבִינוּ מַלְכֵּנוּ, כָּתְבֵנוּ בְּסֵפֶר זְכֻיּוֹת.
אָבִינוּ מַלְכֵּנוּ, כָּתְבֵנוּ בְּסֵפֶר סְלִיחָה וּמְחִילָה.

End of responsive reading.

Avinu Malkenu had its origins in public fasts for lack of rain. Therefore it is not said on Shabbat, even on Yom Kippur, since on Shabbat we do not pray for specific needs, nor do we give expression to distress.

Our Father, our King, let salvation soon flourish for us.

Our Father, our King, raise the honor of Your people Israel.

Our Father, our King, raise the honor of Your anointed.

Our Father, our King, fill our hands with Your blessings.

Our Father, our King, fill our storehouses with abundance.

Our Father, our King, hear our voice, pity and be compassionate to us.

Our Father, our King, accept, with compassion and favor, our prayer.

Our Father, our King, open the gates of heaven to our prayer.

Our Father, our King, remember that we are dust.

Our Father, our King, please do not turn us away from You empty-handed.

Our Father, our King, may this moment be a moment of compassion
and a time of favor before You.

Our Father, our King, have pity on us, our children and our infants.

Our Father, our King, act for the sake of those who were killed
for Your holy name.

Our Father, our King, act for the sake of those who were slaughtered
for proclaiming Your Unity.

Our Father, our King, act for the sake of those
who went through fire and water
to sanctify Your name.

Our Father, our King, avenge before our eyes
the spilt blood of Your servants.

Our Father, our King, act for Your sake, if not for ours.

Our Father, our King, act for Your sake, and save us.

Our Father, our King, act for the sake of Your abundant compassion.

Our Father, our King, act for the sake of Your great, mighty and awesome
name by which we are called.

▸ Our Father, our King, be gracious to us and answer us, though we have
no worthy deeds; act with us in charity and
loving-kindness and save us.

In some congregations, the Ark is closed.
Others keep the Ark open until after Psalm 24 on the next page.

כִּי אֵין בָּנוּ מַעֲשִׂים *Though we have no worthy deeds.* This last line is paradoxically often sung to a joyous tune. The Ba'al Shem Tov said: The servant who sweeps the courtyard of the king sings a cheerful song. So we, when we sweep

אָבִינוּ מַלְכֵּנוּ, הַצְמַח לָנוּ יְשׁוּעָה בְּקָרוֹב.
אָבִינוּ מַלְכֵּנוּ, הָרֵם קֶרֶן יִשְׂרָאֵל עַמֶּךָ.
אָבִינוּ מַלְכֵּנוּ, הָרֵם קֶרֶן מְשִׁיחֶךָ.
אָבִינוּ מַלְכֵּנוּ, מַלֵּא יָדֵינוּ מִבִּרְכוֹתֶיךָ.
אָבִינוּ מַלְכֵּנוּ, מַלֵּא אֲסָמֵינוּ שָׂבָע.
אָבִינוּ מַלְכֵּנוּ, שְׁמַע קוֹלֵנוּ, חוּס וְרַחֵם עָלֵינוּ.
אָבִינוּ מַלְכֵּנוּ, קַבֵּל בְּרַחֲמִים וּבְרָצוֹן אֶת תְּפִלָּתֵנוּ.
אָבִינוּ מַלְכֵּנוּ, פְּתַח שַׁעֲרֵי שָׁמַיִם לִתְפִלָּתֵנוּ.
אָבִינוּ מַלְכֵּנוּ, זְכֹר כִּי עָפָר אֲנָחְנוּ.
אָבִינוּ מַלְכֵּנוּ, נָא אַל תְּשִׁיבֵנוּ רֵיקָם מִלְּפָנֶיךָ.
אָבִינוּ מַלְכֵּנוּ, תְּהֵא הַשָּׁעָה הַזֹּאת שְׁעַת רַחֲמִים וְעֵת רָצוֹן מִלְּפָנֶיךָ.
אָבִינוּ מַלְכֵּנוּ, חֲמֹל עָלֵינוּ וְעַל עוֹלָלֵינוּ וְטַפֵּנוּ.
אָבִינוּ מַלְכֵּנוּ, עֲשֵׂה לְמַעַן הֲרוּגִים עַל שֵׁם קָדְשֶׁךָ.
אָבִינוּ מַלְכֵּנוּ, עֲשֵׂה לְמַעַן טְבוּחִים עַל יִחוּדֶךָ.
אָבִינוּ מַלְכֵּנוּ, עֲשֵׂה לְמַעַן בָּאֵי בָאֵשׁ וּבַמַּיִם עַל קִדּוּשׁ שְׁמֶךָ.
אָבִינוּ מַלְכֵּנוּ, נְקֹם לְעֵינֵינוּ נִקְמַת דַּם עֲבָדֶיךָ הַשָּׁפוּךְ.
אָבִינוּ מַלְכֵּנוּ, עֲשֵׂה לְמַעַנְךָ אִם לֹא לְמַעֲנֵנוּ.
אָבִינוּ מַלְכֵּנוּ, עֲשֵׂה לְמַעַנְךָ וְהוֹשִׁיעֵנוּ.
אָבִינוּ מַלְכֵּנוּ, עֲשֵׂה לְמַעַן רַחֲמֶיךָ הָרַבִּים.
אָבִינוּ מַלְכֵּנוּ, עֲשֵׂה לְמַעַן שִׁמְךָ הַגָּדוֹל הַגִּבּוֹר וְהַנּוֹרָא, שֶׁנִּקְרָא עָלֵינוּ.
◂ אָבִינוּ מַלְכֵּנוּ, חָנֵּנוּ וַעֲנֵנוּ, כִּי אֵין בָּנוּ מַעֲשִׂים
עֲשֵׂה עִמָּנוּ צְדָקָה וָחֶסֶד וְהוֹשִׁיעֵנוּ.

In some congregations, the ארון קודש *is closed.*
Others keep the ארון קודש *open until after* לְדָוִד מִזְמוֹר *on the next page.*

לְמַעַן הֲרוּגִים *For the sake of those who were killed.* This and the following lines are the mark left on our prayers by the many Jews who went to their deaths rather than renounce their faith.

In most congregations, the Ark remains open and the following psalm is said responsively:

לְדָוִד מִזְמוֹר A psalm of David. The earth is the LORD's and all it contains, *Ps. 24*
the world and all who live in it. For He founded it on the seas and established it on the streams. Who may climb the mountain of the LORD? Who may stand in His holy place? He who has clean hands and a pure heart, who has not taken My name in vain, or sworn deceitfully. He shall receive blessing from the LORD, and just reward from God, his salvation. This is a generation of those who seek Him, the descendants of Jacob who seek Your presence, Selah! Lift up your heads, O gates; be uplifted, eternal doors, so that the King of glory may enter. Who is the King of glory? It is the LORD, strong and mighty, the LORD mighty in battle. Lift up your heads, O gates; lift them up, eternal doors, so that the King of glory may enter. Who is He, the King of glory? The LORD of hosts, He is the King of glory, Selah!

PRAYER FOR SUSTENANCE

Some add silently the following Kabbalistic prayer.

May it be Your will, LORD our God, the great, mighty and awesome God, that You be filled with compassion, and are gracious to us, for Your own sake and for the holiness of this psalm [we have said], and the holy names mentioned in it, and for the holiness of its verses and words and letters and notes, and its secrets, and
the holiness of the Holy Name (דיקרנוסא) that arises from the verse "I shall rain *Mal. 3*
down upon you blessing without bounds" – and from the verse "Turn the light *Ps. 4*
of Your face toward us, LORD." And write us in the book of good sustenance, this year and for every year after – write us there, and all the people of our households, all the days of our lives, [that we may sustain ourselves] fully, with all that is needed and more, in permitted ways and not forbidden ones, in serenity, without suffering, and without hard labor and struggle, in tranquility and peace and security, with no evil eye upon us. Allow us the merit of carrying out our holy service untroubled. And sustain us with a living that comes without any shame or humiliation; let us never be dependent on the gifts of other people, but always receive from Your full, broad hand. Let us be successful, let us profit from all our study and in all the works of our hands and our dealings. May our houses be full of the LORD's blessing, and let us have bread enough to satisfy us, let us be well. Compassionate and Gracious One, Protector, Supporter, Savior, Upright One, Redeemer (רח״ש תמי״ך), have compassion for us and listen to our prayer, for You listen to the prayers that each mouth speaks. Blessed is the One who listens to prayers (אוכ״ף אראריתי״א כוז״ו אזבוגא).

The Ark is closed.

In most congregations, the ארון קודש *remains open and the following psalm is said responsively:*

תהלים כד לְדָוִד מִזְמוֹר, לַיהוה הָאָרֶץ וּמְלוֹאָהּ, תֵּבֵל וְיֹשְׁבֵי בָהּ: כִּי־הוּא עַל־יַמִּים יְסָדָהּ, וְעַל־נְהָרוֹת יְכוֹנְנֶהָ: מִי־יַעֲלֶה בְהַר־יהוה, וּמִי־יָקוּם בִּמְקוֹם קָדְשׁוֹ: נְקִי כַפַּיִם וּבַר־לֵבָב, אֲשֶׁר לֹא־נָשָׂא לַשָּׁוְא נַפְשִׁי, וְלֹא נִשְׁבַּע לְמִרְמָה: יִשָּׂא בְרָכָה מֵאֵת יהוה, וּצְדָקָה מֵאֱלֹהֵי יִשְׁעוֹ: זֶה דּוֹר דֹּרְשָׁו, מְבַקְשֵׁי פָנֶיךָ יַעֲקֹב סֶלָה: שְׂאוּ שְׁעָרִים רָאשֵׁיכֶם, וְהִנָּשְׂאוּ פִּתְחֵי עוֹלָם, וְיָבוֹא מֶלֶךְ הַכָּבוֹד: מִי זֶה מֶלֶךְ הַכָּבוֹד, יהוה עִזּוּז וְגִבּוֹר, יהוה גִּבּוֹר מִלְחָמָה: שְׂאוּ שְׁעָרִים רָאשֵׁיכֶם, וּשְׂאוּ פִּתְחֵי עוֹלָם, וְיָבֹא מֶלֶךְ הַכָּבוֹד: מִי הוּא זֶה מֶלֶךְ הַכָּבוֹד, יהוה צְבָאוֹת הוּא מֶלֶךְ הַכָּבוֹד סֶלָה:

תפילה לפרנסה

Some add silently the following Kabbalistic prayer.

יְהִי רָצוֹן מִלְּפָנֶיךָ, יהוה אֱלֹהֵינוּ, הָאֵל הַגָּדוֹל הַגִּבּוֹר וְהַנּוֹרָא, שֶׁתִּתְמַלֵּא רַחֲמִים,
וְתָחֹן עָלֵינוּ לְמַעַנְךָ וּלְמַעַן קְדֻשַּׁת הַמִּזְמוֹר הַזֶּה, וְהַשֵּׁמוֹת הַקְּדוֹשִׁים הַנִּזְכָּרִים
בּוֹ, וּקְדֻשַּׁת פְּסוּקָיו וְתֵבוֹתָיו וְאוֹתִיּוֹתָיו וּטְעָמָיו וְסוֹדוֹתָיו, וּקְדֻשַּׁת הַשֵּׁם הַקָּדוֹשׁ
מלאכי ג (דיקרנוסא) הַיּוֹצֵא מִפָּסוּק: וַהֲרִיקֹתִי לָכֶם בְּרָכָה עַד־בְּלִי־דָי: וּמִפָּסוּק: נְסָה־עָלֵינוּ
תהלים ד אוֹר פָּנֶיךָ יהוה: וְכָתְבֵנוּ בְּסֵפֶר פַּרְנָסָה טוֹבָה וְכַלְכָּלָה שָׁנָה זוֹ וְכָל שָׁנָה וְשָׁנָה, לָנוּ
וּלְכָל בְּנֵי בֵיתֵנוּ כָּל יְמֵי חַיֵּינוּ, בִּמְלוּי וּבְרֶוַח, בְּהֶתֵּר וְלֹא בְאִסּוּר, בְּנַחַת וְלֹא בְצַעַר,
וְלֹא בְעָמָל וָטֹרַח, בְּשַׁלְוָה וְהַשְׁקֵט וָבֶטַח, בְּלִי שׁוּם עַיִן הָרָע. וּתְזַכֵּנוּ לַעֲבֹד עֲבוֹדַת
הַקֹּדֶשׁ בְּלִי שׁוּם טִרְדָּה. וּתְפַרְנְסֵנוּ פַּרְנָסָה שֶׁלֹּא יִהְיֶה בָהּ שׁוּם בּוּשָׁה וּכְלִמָּה. וְלֹא
נִצְטָרֵךְ לְמַתְּנַת בָּשָׂר וָדָם, כִּי אִם מִיָּדְךָ הַמְּלֵאָה וְהָרְחָבָה. וְתַצְלִיחֵנוּ וְתַרְוִיחֵנוּ
בְּכָל לִמּוּדֵנוּ וּבְכָל מַעֲשֵׂה יָדֵינוּ וַעֲסָקֵינוּ. וִיהִי בֵיתֵנוּ מָלֵא בִּרְכַּת יהוה. וְנִשְׂבַּע
לֶחֶם וְנִהְיֶה טוֹבִים. רַחוּם חַנּוּן שׁוֹמֵר תּוֹמֵךְ מַצִּיל יָשָׁר פּוֹדֶה (רח״ש תמי״ף) רַחֵם
עָלֵינוּ וּשְׁמַע תְּפִלָּתֵנוּ, כִּי אַתָּה שׁוֹמֵעַ תְּפִלַּת כָּל פֶּה. בָּרוּךְ שׁוֹמֵעַ תְּפִלָּה (אוכ״ף
אראריתא כוז״ו אזבוגא).

The ארון קודש *is closed.*

---

the courtyard of our deeds, sing a song, for we too are in the courtyard of the King.

What is the worst thing the evil inclination can do? Make us forget that we are a child of the King. (Rabbi Shlomo of Karlin)

FULL KADDISH

Leader: יִתְגַּדַּל Magnified and sanctified
may His great name be,
in the world He created by His will.
May He establish His kingdom
in your lifetime and in your days,
and in the lifetime of all the house of Israel,
swiftly and soon – and say: Amen.

All: May His great name be blessed for ever and all time.

Leader: Blessed and praised, glorified and exalted,
raised and honored, uplifted and lauded be
the name of the Holy One, blessed be He,
above and beyond any blessing, song,
praise and consolation
uttered in the world – and say: Amen.

May the prayers and pleas of all Israel
be accepted by their Father in heaven – and say: Amen.

May there be great peace from heaven,
and life for us and all Israel – and say: Amen.

Bow, take three steps back, as if taking leave of the Divine Presence, then bow, first left, then right, then center, while saying:

May He who makes peace in His high places,
make peace for us and all Israel – and say: Amen.

---

an act of religious devotion that it entered the synagogue as a way of marking the conclusion of an act of prayer.

Kaddish exists in a variety of forms: (1) the Full Kaddish said at the end of the Leader's Repetition of the Amida, (2) Half Kaddish said at the end of a subsection of prayer, (3) the Mourner's Kaddish, said by those observing a period of mourning, (4) the Rabbis' Kaddish, said after an act of study, and (5) the Kaddish of Renewal, said only at the conclusion of a tractate of the Talmud or by a child at the funeral of a parent.

This, the Full Kaddish, is marked by the line "May the prayers… be accepted" a prayer after prayer for the reception of our prayers, a final footnote to our devotions.

קדיש שלם

ש״ץ: יִתְגַּדַּל וְיִתְקַדַּשׁ שְׁמֵהּ רַבָּא (קהל: אָמֵן)
בְּעָלְמָא דִּי בְרָא כִרְעוּתֵהּ
וְיַמְלִיךְ מַלְכוּתֵהּ
בְּחַיֵּיכוֹן וּבְיוֹמֵיכוֹן וּבְחַיֵּי דְכָל בֵּית יִשְׂרָאֵל
בַּעֲגָלָא וּבִזְמַן קָרִיב, וְאִמְרוּ אָמֵן. (קהל: אָמֵן)

קהל וש״ץ: יְהֵא שְׁמֵהּ רַבָּא מְבָרַךְ לְעָלַם וּלְעָלְמֵי עָלְמַיָּא.

ש״ץ: יִתְבָּרַךְ וְיִשְׁתַּבַּח וְיִתְפָּאַר וְיִתְרוֹמַם וְיִתְנַשֵּׂא
וְיִתְהַדָּר וְיִתְעַלֶּה וְיִתְהַלָּל
שְׁמֵהּ דְּקֻדְשָׁא בְּרִיךְ הוּא (קהל: בְּרִיךְ הוּא)
לְעֵלָּא לְעֵלָּא מִכָּל בִּרְכָתָא וְשִׁירָתָא, תֻּשְׁבְּחָתָא וְנֶחֱמָתָא
דַּאֲמִירָן בְּעָלְמָא, וְאִמְרוּ אָמֵן. (קהל: אָמֵן)

תִּתְקַבַּל צְלוֹתְהוֹן וּבָעוּתְהוֹן דְּכָל יִשְׂרָאֵל
קֳדָם אֲבוּהוֹן דִּי בִשְׁמַיָּא, וְאִמְרוּ אָמֵן. (קהל: אָמֵן)

יְהֵא שְׁלָמָא רַבָּא מִן שְׁמַיָּא
וְחַיִּים, עָלֵינוּ וְעַל כָּל יִשְׂרָאֵל, וְאִמְרוּ אָמֵן. (קהל: אָמֵן)

Bow, take three steps back, as if taking leave of the Divine Presence, then bow, first left, then right, then center, while saying:

עֹשֶׂה הַשָּׁלוֹם בִּמְרוֹמָיו
הוּא יַעֲשֶׂה שָׁלוֹם עָלֵינוּ וְעַל כָּל יִשְׂרָאֵל, וְאִמְרוּ אָמֵן. (קהל: אָמֵן)

FULL KADDISH

Kaddish has its origins in the *Beit Midrash*, the House of Study. Originally it served as the conclusion to a sermon or exposition, with its prayer for the establishment of the Kingdom of God – that is, His manifest sovereignty in the world – "in your lifetime." It is written for the most part in Aramaic since that was the vernacular of the Jews of Israel in Second Temple times and immediately thereafter. So powerful was its language and so fitting an ending to

Stand while saying Aleinu. Bow at ▾.

עָלֵינוּ It is our duty to praise the Master of all,
and ascribe greatness to the Author of creation,
who has not made us like the nations of the lands,
nor placed us like the families of the earth;
who has not made our portion like theirs,
nor our destiny like all their multitudes.
(For they worship vanity and emptiness,
and pray to a god who cannot save.)
▾But we bow in worship
and thank the Supreme King of kings, the Holy One, blessed be He,
who extends the heavens and establishes the earth,
whose throne of glory is in the heavens above,
and whose power's Presence is in the highest of heights.
He is our God; there is no other.
Truly He is our King; there is none else,
as it is written in His Torah:
"You shall know and take to heart this day *Deut. 4*
that the LORD is God, in the heavens above and on the earth below.
There is no other."

Therefore, we place our hope in You, LORD our God,
that we may soon see the glory of Your power,
when You will remove abominations from the earth,
and idols will be utterly destroyed,
when the world will be perfected
under the sovereignty of the Almighty,
when all humanity will call on Your name,
to turn all the earth's wicked toward You.
All the world's inhabitants will realize and know
that to You every knee must bow and every tongue swear loyalty.

Rav. Originally it served as the prelude to *Malkhiyot,* the Kingship section of the Musaf Amida of Rosh HaShana, where it still appears. Around the twelfth or thirteenth century it was adopted as a conclusion to the daily prayers as well.

Stand while saying עָלֵינוּ*. Bow at* ▼.

עָלֵינוּ לְשַׁבֵּחַ לַאֲדוֹן הַכֹּל, לָתֵת גְּדֻלָּה לְיוֹצֵר בְּרֵאשִׁית
שֶׁלֹּא עָשָׂנוּ כְּגוֹיֵי הָאֲרָצוֹת, וְלֹא שָׂמָנוּ כְּמִשְׁפְּחוֹת הָאֲדָמָה
שֶׁלֹּא שָׂם חֶלְקֵנוּ כָּהֶם וְגוֹרָלֵנוּ כְּכָל הֲמוֹנָם.
(שֶׁהֵם מִשְׁתַּחֲוִים לְהֶבֶל וָרִיק וּמִתְפַּלְּלִים אֶל אֵל לֹא יוֹשִׁיעַ.)
▼וַאֲנַחְנוּ כּוֹרְעִים וּמִשְׁתַּחֲוִים וּמוֹדִים
לִפְנֵי מֶלֶךְ מַלְכֵי הַמְּלָכִים, הַקָּדוֹשׁ בָּרוּךְ הוּא
שֶׁהוּא נוֹטֶה שָׁמַיִם וְיוֹסֵד אָרֶץ
וּמוֹשַׁב יְקָרוֹ בַּשָּׁמַיִם מִמַּעַל
וּשְׁכִינַת עֻזּוֹ בְּגָבְהֵי מְרוֹמִים.
הוּא אֱלֹהֵינוּ, אֵין עוֹד.
אֱמֶת מַלְכֵּנוּ, אֶפֶס זוּלָתוֹ
כַּכָּתוּב בְּתוֹרָתוֹ, וְיָדַעְתָּ הַיּוֹם וַהֲשֵׁבֹתָ אֶל־לְבָבֶךָ דברים ד
כִּי יהוה הוּא הָאֱלֹהִים בַּשָּׁמַיִם מִמַּעַל וְעַל־הָאָרֶץ מִתָּחַת
אֵין עוֹד:

עַל כֵּן נְקַוֶּה לְּךָ יהוה אֱלֹהֵינוּ, לִרְאוֹת מְהֵרָה בְּתִפְאֶרֶת עֻזֶּךָ
לְהַעֲבִיר גִּלּוּלִים מִן הָאָרֶץ, וְהָאֱלִילִים כָּרוֹת יִכָּרֵתוּן
לְתַקֵּן עוֹלָם בְּמַלְכוּת שַׁדַּי.
וְכָל בְּנֵי בָשָׂר יִקְרְאוּ בִשְׁמֶךָ לְהַפְנוֹת אֵלֶיךָ כָּל רִשְׁעֵי אָרֶץ.
יַכִּירוּ וְיֵדְעוּ כָּל יוֹשְׁבֵי תֵבֵל
כִּי לְךָ תִּכְרַע כָּל בֶּרֶךְ, תִּשָּׁבַע כָּל לָשׁוֹן.

ALEINU – IT IS OUR DUTY

An ancient prayer, ascribed by some to the biblical Joshua, by others to the Men of the Great Assembly, and others to the third-century Talmudic sage

Before You, LORD our God, they will kneel and bow down
and give honor to Your glorious name.
They will all accept the yoke of Your kingdom,
and You will reign over them soon and for ever.
For the kingdom is Yours,
and to all eternity You will reign in glory,
as it is written in Your Torah:
"The LORD will reign for ever and ever." *Ex. 15*
▸ And it is said: "Then the LORD shall be King over all the earth; *Zech. 14*
on that day the LORD shall be One and His name One."

Some add:

Have no fear of sudden terror or of the ruin when it overtakes the wicked. *Prov. 3*
Devise your strategy, but it will be thwarted; *Is. 8*
propose your plan, but it will not stand, for God is with us.
When you grow old, I will still be the same. *Is. 46*
When your hair turns gray, I will still carry you.
I made you, I will bear you, I will carry you, and I will rescue you.

That is the Jewish vocation. At times of paganism it involved the fight against myth and the idea that the universe was the arena of a cosmic struggle of heavenly powers, played out on earth in the form of wars, battles and a hierarchy of power. At times of secularism it means insisting that the material universe is not the only, or even the most important, dimension in which we live; ultimate reality is not blind to our existence, deaf to our prayers, and indifferent to our fate; and morality is not simply what we choose it to be. To insist otherwise, that there is only one God and we are each in His image, has often meant shouldering a heavy burden, attracting the scorn, sometimes the violence, of others. Yet this is the message we are called on to bear witness to, and *Aleinu* expresses it with great power.

Given this background we can understand why it became associated with martyrdom. It was, according to eyewitnesses, the last prayer uttered by the Jews of Blois in 1171 when they went to their deaths because of their faith. Despite the many centuries of persecution, *Aleinu*, in its strategic position at the culmination of the service, continues to testify to our sacred vocation as living witnesses to the living God.

לְפָנֶיךָ יהוה אֱלֹהֵינוּ יִכְרְעוּ וְיִפֹּלוּ
וְלִכְבוֹד שִׁמְךָ יְקָר יִתֵּנוּ
וִיקַבְּלוּ כֻלָּם אֶת עֹל מַלְכוּתֶךָ
וְתִמְלֹךְ עֲלֵיהֶם מְהֵרָה לְעוֹלָם וָעֶד.
כִּי הַמַּלְכוּת שֶׁלְּךָ הִיא וּלְעוֹלְמֵי עַד תִּמְלֹךְ בְּכָבוֹד
שמות טו כַּכָּתוּב בְּתוֹרָתֶךָ, יהוה יִמְלֹךְ לְעֹלָם וָעֶד:
זכריה יד ◂ וְנֶאֱמַר, וְהָיָה יהוה לְמֶלֶךְ עַל־כָּל־הָאָרֶץ
בַּיּוֹם הַהוּא יִהְיֶה יהוה אֶחָד וּשְׁמוֹ אֶחָד:

Some add:

משלי ג אַל־תִּירָא מִפַּחַד פִּתְאֹם וּמִשֹּׁאַת רְשָׁעִים כִּי תָבֹא:
ישעיה ח עֻצוּ עֵצָה וְתֻפָר, דַּבְּרוּ דָבָר וְלֹא יָקוּם, כִּי עִמָּנוּ אֵל:
ישעיה מו וְעַד־זִקְנָה אֲנִי הוּא, וְעַד־שֵׂיבָה אֲנִי אֶסְבֹּל
אֲנִי עָשִׂיתִי וַאֲנִי אֶשָּׂא וַאֲנִי אֶסְבֹּל וַאֲמַלֵּט:

Essentially it is a testimony of monotheistic faith against idolatry – hence its antiquity. It belongs to an age in which Jews were the sole monotheists, a lonely island in a pagan sea. The first paragraph is an affirmation of that faith and the singularity of the Jewish people in holding and proclaiming it. The second is a prayer that one day all humankind will share our belief in the oneness of God.

In the first line of the Shema, the last letter of the first and last words – in a Torah scroll, written larger than the other letters – spell out the word *"ed"* (עד), meaning "witness." The first and last letters of the *Aleinu* prayer spell out the same word. This recalls the great passage in Isaiah in which God declares "You are My witnesses ... and My servant whom I have chosen ... You are my witnesses – declares the Lord – that I am God" (Is. 43:10–12), which the sages interpreted as meaning: "If you are My witnesses, then I am God, but if you are not My witnesses it is as if I were not God" (*Midrash Tanna'im; Pesikta deRav Kahana*). It is our task to bear witness to God on earth, to be His ambassadors to humanity.

MOURNER'S KADDISH

The following prayer requires the presence of a minyan.
A transliteration can be found on page 1375.

Mourner: יִתְגַּדַּל Magnified and sanctified
may His great name be,
in the world He created by His will.
May He establish His kingdom
in your lifetime and in your days,
and in the lifetime of all the house of Israel,
swiftly and soon –
and say: Amen.

All: May His great name be blessed for ever and all time.

Mourner: Blessed and praised,
glorified and exalted,
raised and honored,
uplifted and lauded
be the name of the Holy One, blessed be He,
above and beyond any blessing, song,
praise and consolation
uttered in the world –
and say: Amen.

May there be great peace from heaven,
and life for us and all Israel –
and say: Amen.

Bow, take three steps back, as if taking leave of the Divine Presence,
then bow, first left, then right, then center, while saying:

May He who makes peace in His high places,
make peace for us and all Israel –
and say: Amen.

קדיש יתום

The following prayer requires the presence of a מנין.
A transliteration can be found on page 1375.

אבל: יִתְגַּדַּל וְיִתְקַדַּשׁ שְׁמֵהּ רַבָּא (קהל: אָמֵן)
בְּעָלְמָא דִּי בְרָא כִרְעוּתֵהּ
וְיַמְלִיךְ מַלְכוּתֵהּ
בְּחַיֵּיכוֹן וּבְיוֹמֵיכוֹן וּבְחַיֵּי דְכָל בֵּית יִשְׂרָאֵל
בַּעֲגָלָא וּבִזְמַן קָרִיב
וְאִמְרוּ אָמֵן. (קהל: אָמֵן)

קהל ואבל: יְהֵא שְׁמֵהּ רַבָּא מְבָרַךְ לְעָלַם וּלְעָלְמֵי עָלְמַיָּא.

אבל: יִתְבָּרַךְ וְיִשְׁתַּבַּח וְיִתְפָּאַר וְיִתְרוֹמַם וְיִתְנַשֵּׂא
וְיִתְהַדָּר וְיִתְעַלֶּה וְיִתְהַלָּל
שְׁמֵהּ דְּקֻדְשָׁא בְּרִיךְ הוּא (קהל: בְּרִיךְ הוּא)
לְעֵלָּא לְעֵלָּא מִכָּל בִּרְכָתָא וְשִׁירָתָא, תֻּשְׁבְּחָתָא וְנֶחֱמָתָא
דַּאֲמִירָן בְּעָלְמָא
וְאִמְרוּ אָמֵן. (קהל: אָמֵן)

יְהֵא שְׁלָמָא רַבָּא מִן שְׁמַיָּא
וְחַיִּים, עָלֵינוּ וְעַל כָּל יִשְׂרָאֵל
וְאִמְרוּ אָמֵן. (קהל: אָמֵן)

Bow, take three steps back, as if taking leave of the Divine Presence, then bow, first left, then right, then center, while saying:

עֹשֶׂה הַשָּׁלוֹם בִּמְרוֹמָיו
הוּא יַעֲשֶׂה שָׁלוֹם עָלֵינוּ וְעַל כָּל יִשְׂרָאֵל
וְאִמְרוּ אָמֵן. (קהל: אָמֵן)

לְדָוִד A psalm of David. The Lord is my light and my salvation – Ps. 27
whom then shall I fear? The Lord is the stronghold of my life – of whom shall I be afraid? When evil men close in on me to devour my flesh, it is they, my enemies and foes, who stumble and fall. Should an army besiege me, my heart would not fear. Should war break out against me, still I would be confident. One thing I ask of the Lord, only this do I seek: to live in the House of the Lord all the days of my life, to gaze on the beauty of the Lord and worship in His Temple. For He will keep me safe in His pavilion on the day of trouble. He will hide me under the cover of His tent. He will set me high upon a rock. Now my head is high above my enemies who surround me. I will sacrifice in His tent with shouts of joy. I will sing and chant praises to the Lord. Lord, hear my voice when I call. Be gracious to me and answer me. On Your behalf my heart says, "Seek My face." Your face, Lord, will I seek. Do not hide Your face from me. Do not turn Your servant away in anger. You have been my help. Do not reject or forsake me, God, my Savior. Were my father and my mother to forsake me, the Lord would take me in. Teach me Your way, Lord, and lead me on a level path, because of my oppressors. Do not abandon me to the will of my foes, for false witnesses have risen against me, breathing violence. ▸ Were it not for my faith that I shall see the Lord's goodness in the land of the living. Hope in the Lord. Be strong and of good courage, and hope in the Lord!

Mourner's Kaddish (on previous page)

כִּי־אָבִי וְאִמִּי עֲזָבוּנִי *Were my father and my mother to forsake me:* were they to die (Ibn Ezra), or, when I leave home (Radak).

לוּלֵא הֶאֱמַנְתִּי *Were it not for my faith.* Some commentators link this to the previous verse – my foes and false witnesses might have prevailed had it not been for my faith.

וְקַוֵּה אֶל־יהוה *Hope in the Lord.* Judaism is the voice of hope in the conversation of humankind. Because we are not alone, because there is a God, and because He cares, we have hope. The Jewish people kept hope alive, and hope kept the Jewish people alive.

תהלים כז

לְדָוִד, יהוה אוֹרִי וְיִשְׁעִי, מִמִּי אִירָא, יהוה מָעוֹז־חַיַּי, מִמִּי אֶפְחָד: בִּקְרֹב עָלַי מְרֵעִים לֶאֱכֹל אֶת־בְּשָׂרִי, צָרַי וְאֹיְבַי לִי, הֵמָּה כָשְׁלוּ וְנָפָלוּ: אִם־תַּחֲנֶה עָלַי מַחֲנֶה, לֹא־יִירָא לִבִּי, אִם־תָּקוּם עָלַי, מִלְחָמָה, בְּזֹאת אֲנִי בוֹטֵחַ: אַחַת שָׁאַלְתִּי מֵאֵת־יהוה, אוֹתָהּ אֲבַקֵּשׁ, שִׁבְתִּי בְּבֵית־יהוה כָּל־יְמֵי חַיַּי, לַחֲזוֹת בְּנֹעַם־יהוה, וּלְבַקֵּר בְּהֵיכָלוֹ: כִּי יִצְפְּנֵנִי בְּסֻכֹּה בְּיוֹם רָעָה, יַסְתִּרֵנִי בְּסֵתֶר אָהֳלוֹ, בְּצוּר יְרוֹמְמֵנִי: וְעַתָּה יָרוּם רֹאשִׁי עַל אֹיְבַי סְבִיבוֹתַי, וְאֶזְבְּחָה בְאָהֳלוֹ זִבְחֵי תְרוּעָה, אָשִׁירָה וַאֲזַמְּרָה לַיהוה: שְׁמַע־יהוה קוֹלִי אֶקְרָא, וְחָנֵּנִי וַעֲנֵנִי: לְךָ אָמַר לִבִּי בַּקְּשׁוּ פָנָי, אֶת־פָּנֶיךָ יהוה אֲבַקֵּשׁ: אַל־תַּסְתֵּר פָּנֶיךָ מִמֶּנִּי, אַל תַּט־בְּאַף עַבְדֶּךָ, עֶזְרָתִי הָיִיתָ, אַל־תִּטְּשֵׁנִי וְאַל־תַּעַזְבֵנִי, אֱלֹהֵי יִשְׁעִי: כִּי־אָבִי וְאִמִּי עֲזָבוּנִי, וַיהוה יַאַסְפֵנִי: הוֹרֵנִי יהוה דַּרְכֶּךָ, וּנְחֵנִי בְּאֹרַח מִישׁוֹר, לְמַעַן שׁוֹרְרָי: אַל־תִּתְּנֵנִי בְּנֶפֶשׁ צָרָי, כִּי קָמוּ־בִי עֵדֵי־שֶׁקֶר, וִיפֵחַ חָמָס: ▸ לוּלֵא הֶאֱמַנְתִּי לִרְאוֹת בְּטוּב־יהוה בְּאֶרֶץ חַיִּים: קַוֵּה אֶל־יהוה, חֲזַק וְיַאֲמֵץ לִבֶּךָ, וְקַוֵּה אֶל־יהוה:

קדיש יתום (*on previous page*)

לְדָוִד, יהוה אוֹרִי וְיִשְׁעִי *Psalm 27.* A psalm of surpassing beauty expressing our faith that those who place their trust in God need fear no enemy. This does not mean that life is free of risk, nor that we have no enemies. It means that those for whom God is a living presence in their lives have access to a source of strength greater than themselves, that faith is the antidote to fear. It is said during the month of Elul and up to the end of Sukkot because of an interpretation given by the sages: "The Lord is my light" on Rosh HaShana, "and my salvation" on Yom Kippur. "He will keep me safe in His pavilion (*besukko*)" refers to Sukkot (*Mateh Efrayim* 581:6).

לְךָ אָמַר לִבִּי *On Your behalf my heart says.* This is the voice of God within the human heart.

Most congregations recite Adon Olam or Yigdal, or both.

LORD OF THE UNIVERSE,
who reigned before the birth of any thing –

When by His will all things were made
then was His name proclaimed King.

And when all things shall cease to be
He alone will reign in awe.

He was, He is, and He shall be
glorious for evermore.

He is One, there is none else,
alone, unique, beyond compare;

Without beginning, without end,
His might, His rule are everywhere.

He is my God; my Redeemer lives.
He is the Rock on whom I rely –

My banner and my safe retreat,
my cup, my portion when I cry.

Into His hand my soul I place,
when I awake and when I sleep.

The LORD is with me, I shall not fear;
body and soul from harm will He keep.

Mekor Ḥayyim (in Latin, *Fons Vitae*), and was one of the first since Philo ten centuries earlier, to synthesize Judaism with Greek philosophy. Apart from the limpid simplicity, what gives *Adon Olam* its power and enduring popularity is the way it moves seamlessly from God, Creator of the universe, beyond time and space, to God who is close and ever-comforting, each day as I sleep and awake.

Most congregations recite אדון עולם *or* יגדל*, or both.*

אֲדוֹן עוֹלָם

אֲשֶׁר מָלַךְ בְּטֶרֶם כָּל־יְצִיר נִבְרָא.
לְעֵת נַעֲשָׂה בְחֶפְצוֹ כֹּל אֲזַי מֶלֶךְ שְׁמוֹ נִקְרָא.
וְאַחֲרֵי כִּכְלוֹת הַכֹּל לְבַדּוֹ יִמְלֹךְ נוֹרָא.
וְהוּא הָיָה וְהוּא הֹוֶה וְהוּא יִהְיֶה בְּתִפְאָרָה.
וְהוּא אֶחָד וְאֵין שֵׁנִי לְהַמְשִׁיל לוֹ לְהַחְבִּירָה.
בְּלִי רֵאשִׁית בְּלִי תַכְלִית וְלוֹ הָעֹז וְהַמִּשְׂרָה.
וְהוּא אֵלִי וְחַי גּוֹאֲלִי וְצוּר חֶבְלִי בְּעֵת צָרָה.
וְהוּא נִסִּי וּמָנוֹס לִי מְנָת כּוֹסִי בְּיוֹם אֶקְרָא.
בְּיָדוֹ אַפְקִיד רוּחִי בְּעֵת אִישַׁן וְאָעִירָה.
וְעִם רוּחִי גְּוִיָּתִי יהוה לִי וְלֹא אִירָא.

אֲדוֹן עוֹלָם LORD *of the Universe.* One of the simplest and most beautiful hymn-like celebrations of Jewish faith. It has been attributed to several possible authors, among them Rabbi Sherira Gaon and Rabbi Hai Gaon in the tenth century. Most scholars, however, believe it was written by the poet and philosopher Rabbi Solomon ibn Gabirol (born Malaga, Spain, c.1021; died Valencia, c.1058). Little is known about Ibn Gabirol's life or death, except that he spent several unsettled years wandering from town to town and that he died comparatively young. He was the author of a philosophical work,

GREAT
is the living God and praised.
He exists, and His existence is beyond time.
He is One, and there is no unity like His.
Unfathomable, His Oneness is infinite.
He has neither bodily form nor substance;
His holiness is beyond compare.
He preceded all that was created.
He was first: there was no beginning to His beginning.
Behold He is Master of the Universe; every creature
shows His greatness and majesty.
The rich flow of His prophecy He gave
to His treasured people in whom He gloried.
Never in Israel has there arisen another like Moses,
a prophet who beheld God's image.
God gave His people a Torah of truth
by the hand of His prophet, most faithful of His House.
God will not alter or change His law
for any other, for eternity.
He sees and knows our secret thoughts;
as soon as something is begun, He foresees its end.
He rewards people with loving-kindness according to their deeds;
He punishes the wicked according to his wickedness.
At the end of days He will send our Messiah,
to redeem those who await His final salvation.
God will revive the dead in His great loving-kindness.
Blessed for evermore is His glorious name!

---

perfect faith" (אֲנִי מַאֲמִין בֶּאֱמוּנָה שְׁלֵמָה), is printed in most prayer books. The poetic form is *Yigdal.* The first five principles have to do with the unity, eternity and non-physicality of God; principles 6–9 are about revelation; principles 10–13 are about divine providence, reward and punishment, and end with faith in the messianic age and the end of days when those who have died will live again.

יִגְדַּל

אֱלֹהִים חַי וְיִשְׁתַּבַּח, נִמְצָא וְאֵין עֵת אֶל מְצִיאוּתוֹ.
אֶחָד וְאֵין יָחִיד כְּיִחוּדוֹ, נֶעְלָם וְגַם אֵין סוֹף לְאַחְדוּתוֹ.
אֵין לוֹ דְּמוּת הַגּוּף וְאֵינוֹ גוּף, לֹא נַעֲרֹךְ אֵלָיו קְדֻשָּׁתוֹ.
קַדְמוֹן לְכָל דָּבָר אֲשֶׁר נִבְרָא, רִאשׁוֹן וְאֵין רֵאשִׁית לְרֵאשִׁיתוֹ.
הִנּוֹ אֲדוֹן עוֹלָם, וְכָל נוֹצָר יוֹרֶה גְדֻלָּתוֹ וּמַלְכוּתוֹ.
שֶׁפַע נְבוּאָתוֹ נְתָנוֹ אֶל־אַנְשֵׁי סְגֻלָּתוֹ וְתִפְאַרְתּוֹ.
לֹא קָם בְּיִשְׂרָאֵל כְּמֹשֶׁה עוֹד נָבִיא וּמַבִּיט אֶת תְּמוּנָתוֹ.
תּוֹרַת אֱמֶת נָתַן לְעַמּוֹ אֵל עַל יַד נְבִיאוֹ נֶאֱמַן בֵּיתוֹ.
לֹא יַחֲלִיף הָאֵל וְלֹא יָמִיר דָּתוֹ לְעוֹלָמִים לְזוּלָתוֹ.
צוֹפֶה וְיוֹדֵעַ סְתָרֵינוּ, מַבִּיט לְסוֹף דָּבָר בְּקַדְמָתוֹ.
גּוֹמֵל לְאִישׁ חֶסֶד כְּמִפְעָלוֹ, נוֹתֵן לְרָשָׁע רָע כְּרִשְׁעָתוֹ.
יִשְׁלַח לְקֵץ יָמִין מְשִׁיחֵנוּ לִפְדּוֹת מְחַכֵּי קֵץ יְשׁוּעָתוֹ.
מֵתִים יְחַיֶּה אֵל בְּרֹב חַסְדּוֹ, בָּרוּךְ עֲדֵי עַד שֵׁם תְּהִלָּתוֹ.

יִגְדַּל *Great.* A poetic setting of the most famous "creed" in Judaism: Moses Maimonides' Thirteen Principles of Jewish Faith. Before the twelfth century there had been few attempts at summarizing Jewish faith, not because Judaism has no fundamental beliefs – it does – but because these only tended to come to the fore at times of controversy; at other times they were taken for granted. The Mishna (*Sanhedrin* 90a) lists several such beliefs, including the Resurrection of the Dead, since this was a point of controversy between Pharisees and Sadducees. In general, the sages tended to use the prayer book as the place where they gave expression to the fundamentals of faith. Faced, however, with a philosophically sophisticated, contemporary Islamic culture, Maimonides felt the need to set out the principles of faith in a structured way, which he did in his *Commentary to the Mishna* to *Sanhedrin* 10. So influential was this account that it was summarized, after his death, in both prose and poetry. The prose form, thirteen paragraphs each beginning, "I believe with

Some have the custom of reciting the following four psalms after Ma'ariv.

אַשְׁרֵי־הָאִישׁ Happy is the man who does not walk in the counsel of the wicked, who does not stand on the path of sinners, who does not sit among the jeering cynics. Instead, the LORD's teaching is all his desire, and he ponders that Torah by day and night. He will become like a tree planted on streams of water, yielding fruit in its season, with leaves that will not dry, and all that he produces will succeed. Not so the wicked – they are like chaff blown away by the wind. Therefore, they will not survive the judgment, nor shall sinners be acquitted in a court of the righteous. For the way of the righteous is known to the LORD, and that of the wicked shall come to an end. *Ps. 1*

לָמָּה Why do the nations clamor, why are the peoples speaking futilities? The kings of this earth have assembled; the leaders have bonded together, against the LORD and His anointed. "Let us cut their bonds," they have said, "and cast from us their cords." The One who presides in heaven shall laugh; the LORD will jeer at them. He will speak to them in His fury; He will fill them with terror in His rage: "I have anointed My king over Zion My holy mountain." I shall tell the LORD's ruling: He told me, "You are My son; this very day I gave you life. Ask anything of Me, I shall give you nations for your inheritance, I shall give you your estate to the ends of the earth. You will shatter [those enemies] with an iron rod, you will break them into pieces like pottery." And now, kings, be wiser, take counsel, judges of the world. Serve the LORD with awe, and tremble as you rejoice. Adore God with a pure heart, lest He grow furious, and your way be lost forever. For His fury flares up in a moment; and happy are those who seek refuge in Him. *Ps. 2*

מִזְמוֹר לְדָוִד A psalm of David, when he fled his son Avshalom. LORD, how many are my enemies – so many rise up against me! So many say of me, "He has no salvation with God" – Selah! But You, LORD, are the shield that protects me; my honor; the One who raises my head. My voice, it cries out to the LORD, and He answers from His holy mountain – Selah! I will lie down to sleep; I shall wake again, for the LORD sustains me always. I have no fear of the myriads of men encamped all around me. Rise up, LORD; save me, my God! You have struck all my enemies on the cheek, You have broken the teeth of the wicked. Salvation belongs to the LORD; Your blessing is over Your people – Selah! *Ps. 3*

לַמְנַצֵּחַ For the conductor of music. A psalm of David. When I cry out, answer me, my righteous God; in my straits You have broadened out my spaces – show me grace, and listen to my prayer. All you people, how long will my honor be disgraced, how long will you love emptiness, will you seek after illusions? Selah! Know that the LORD singles out those who are faithful to Him; when I cry out to the LORD, He will hear. Tremble and do not sin. Contemplate as you lie awake, and stay silent – Selah! Offer righteous offerings, and place Your trust in the LORD. So many say, "Who will show me goodness?" Make the light of Your face shine upon us, LORD. You have placed joy in my heart, more than others have from all their abundance of grain and grape-juice at harvest time. In peace I shall lie down and shall sleep, for You, LORD, allow me to abide alone in safety. *Ps. 4*

Some have the custom of reciting the following four psalms after מעריב.

תהלים א אַשְׁרֵי־הָאִישׁ אֲשֶׁר לֹא הָלַךְ בַּעֲצַת רְשָׁעִים, וּבְדֶרֶךְ חַטָּאִים לֹא עָמָד, וּבְמוֹשַׁב לֵצִים לֹא יָשָׁב: כִּי אִם בְּתוֹרַת יהוה חֶפְצוֹ, וּבְתוֹרָתוֹ יֶהְגֶּה יוֹמָם וָלָיְלָה: וְהָיָה כְּעֵץ שָׁתוּל עַל־פַּלְגֵי מָיִם, אֲשֶׁר פִּרְיוֹ יִתֵּן בְּעִתּוֹ וְעָלֵהוּ לֹא־יִבּוֹל, וְכֹל אֲשֶׁר־יַעֲשֶׂה יַצְלִיחַ: לֹא־כֵן הָרְשָׁעִים, כִּי אִם־כַּמֹּץ אֲשֶׁר־תִּדְּפֶנּוּ רוּחַ: עַל־כֵּן לֹא־יָקֻמוּ רְשָׁעִים בַּמִּשְׁפָּט, וְחַטָּאִים בַּעֲדַת צַדִּיקִים: כִּי־יוֹדֵעַ יהוה דֶּרֶךְ צַדִּיקִים, וְדֶרֶךְ רְשָׁעִים תֹּאבֵד:

תהלים ב לָמָּה רָגְשׁוּ גוֹיִם, וּלְאֻמִּים יֶהְגּוּ־רִיק: יִתְיַצְּבוּ מַלְכֵי־אֶרֶץ, וְרוֹזְנִים נוֹסְדוּ־יָחַד, עַל־יהוה וְעַל־מְשִׁיחוֹ: נְנַתְּקָה אֶת־מוֹסְרוֹתֵימוֹ, וְנַשְׁלִיכָה מִמֶּנּוּ עֲבֹתֵימוֹ: יוֹשֵׁב בַּשָּׁמַיִם יִשְׂחָק, אֲדֹנָי יִלְעַג־לָמוֹ: אָז יְדַבֵּר אֵלֵימוֹ בְאַפּוֹ, וּבַחֲרוֹנוֹ יְבַהֲלֵמוֹ: וַאֲנִי נָסַכְתִּי מַלְכִּי, עַל־צִיּוֹן הַר־קָדְשִׁי: אֲסַפְּרָה אֶל חֹק, יהוה אָמַר אֵלַי בְּנִי־אַתָּה, אֲנִי הַיּוֹם יְלִדְתִּיךָ: שְׁאַל מִמֶּנִּי, וְאֶתְּנָה גוֹיִם נַחֲלָתֶךָ, וַאֲחֻזָּתְךָ אַפְסֵי־אָרֶץ: תְּרֹעֵם בְּשֵׁבֶט בַּרְזֶל, כִּכְלִי יוֹצֵר תְּנַפְּצֵם: וְעַתָּה מְלָכִים הַשְׂכִּילוּ, הִוָּסְרוּ שֹׁפְטֵי אָרֶץ: עִבְדוּ אֶת־יהוה בְּיִרְאָה, וְגִילוּ בִּרְעָדָה: נַשְּׁקוּ־בַר פֶּן־יֶאֱנַף וְתֹאבְדוּ דֶרֶךְ כִּי־יִבְעַר כִּמְעַט אַפּוֹ, אַשְׁרֵי כָּל־חוֹסֵי בוֹ:

תהלים ג מִזְמוֹר לְדָוִד, בְּבָרְחוֹ מִפְּנֵי ׀ אַבְשָׁלוֹם בְּנוֹ: יהוה מָה־רַבּוּ צָרָי, רַבִּים קָמִים עָלָי: רַבִּים אֹמְרִים לְנַפְשִׁי, אֵין יְשׁוּעָתָה לּוֹ בֵאלֹהִים סֶלָה: וְאַתָּה יהוה מָגֵן בַּעֲדִי, כְּבוֹדִי וּמֵרִים רֹאשִׁי: קוֹלִי אֶל־יהוה אֶקְרָא, וַיַּעֲנֵנִי מֵהַר קָדְשׁוֹ סֶלָה: אֲנִי שָׁכַבְתִּי וָאִישָׁנָה, הֱקִיצוֹתִי כִּי יהוה יִסְמְכֵנִי: לֹא־אִירָא מֵרִבְבוֹת עָם, אֲשֶׁר סָבִיב שָׁתוּ עָלָי: קוּמָה יהוה, הוֹשִׁיעֵנִי אֱלֹהַי, כִּי־הִכִּיתָ אֶת־כָּל־אֹיְבַי לֶחִי, שִׁנֵּי רְשָׁעִים שִׁבַּרְתָּ: לַיהוה הַיְשׁוּעָה, עַל־עַמְּךָ בִרְכָתֶךָ סֶּלָה:

תהלים ד לַמְנַצֵּחַ בִּנְגִינוֹת מִזְמוֹר לְדָוִד: בְּקָרְאִי עֲנֵנִי אֱלֹהֵי צִדְקִי, בַּצָּר הִרְחַבְתָּ לִּי, חָנֵּנִי וּשְׁמַע תְּפִלָּתִי: בְּנֵי־אִישׁ עַד־מֶה כְבוֹדִי לִכְלִמָּה תֶּאֱהָבוּן רִיק, תְּבַקְשׁוּ כָזָב סֶלָה: וּדְעוּ כִּי־הִפְלָה יהוה חָסִיד לוֹ, יהוה יִשְׁמַע בְּקָרְאִי אֵלָיו: רִגְזוּ וְאַל־תֶּחֱטָאוּ, אִמְרוּ בִלְבַבְכֶם עַל־מִשְׁכַּבְכֶם וְדֹמּוּ סֶלָה: זִבְחוּ זִבְחֵי־צֶדֶק וּבִטְחוּ אֶל־יהוה: רַבִּים אֹמְרִים מִי־יַרְאֵנוּ טוֹב, נְסָה־עָלֵינוּ אוֹר פָּנֶיךָ יהוה: נָתַתָּה שִׂמְחָה בְלִבִּי, מֵעֵת דְּגָנָם וְתִירוֹשָׁם רָבּוּ: בְּשָׁלוֹם יַחְדָּו אֶשְׁכְּבָה וְאִישָׁן, כִּי־אַתָּה יהוה לְבָדָד, לָבֶטַח תּוֹשִׁיבֵנִי:

SONGS OF GOD'S ONENESS

Sunday:

Leader: I shall sing and make music for my God as long as I live, / the God who has guided me ever since my creation. *Ps. 104* *Gen. 48*

Cong: To this very day You have held on to my hand; / You have given me life and kindness. *Job 10*

Leader: Blessed be the LORD, blessed be His glorious name, / for He has bestowed wondrous kindness upon His servant.

Cong: With what shall I come before the God on high; / how shall I bow to this everlasting God?

Leader: Even if the mountains were the array of wood on the altar, / all the wood of Lebanon spread upon it;

Cong: And all cattle and beasts slaughtered, / their pieces laid above the wood-pile;

Leader: Even if the altar corners were to wallow / in their blood, as the waters cover the sea, *Is. 11*

Cong: And the lush, rich meal offerings were as abundant as the sand, / mingled with myriads of rivers of oil; *Mic. 6*

Leader: And frankincense and fragrant spices were to be offered as a memorial-offering / of incense, along with the choicest of balsams;

Cong: And even if the lamps of the Menora / were to shine as bright as the two great lights in the sky,

Leader: And the showbread were to be as high as the majestic mountains, / set out upon tables in the inner sanctuary,

Cong: With wine like the rain from heaven, / and intoxicating wine for libations as springs of water;

---

which emphasizes "humility for the sake of Heaven" and an elevated life in search of spiritual perfection.

In some communities the Song faced opposition because of its dense imagery and daring anthropomorphisms, most notably on the part of Rabbi Shlomo Luria in sixteenth-century Poland. Many communities recited it in its entirety only on *Kol Nidrei* night. Others, dividing it into seven, said a section each day, completing it in the course of a week. Many communities, however, say the appropriate daily section in the morning services of the High Holy Days.

אָשִׁירָה וַאֲזַמְּרָה *I shall sing and make music.* A lyrical poem on the inadequacy of any offering to express thanks for the wonder of our existence as finite creatures of the Infinite God. Besides, we have no Temple any more. The priests, the sacrifices, the daily worship of the Sanctuary in Jerusalem, are gone. All each of us can do is to "build an altar out of my shattered heart."

שיר היחוד

Sunday:

ש״ץ: אָשִׁירָה וַאֲזַמְּרָה לֵאלֹהַי בְּעוֹדִי / הָאֱלֹהִים הָרֹעֶה אֹתִי מֵעוֹדִי: תהלים קד בראשית מח

קהל: עַד הַיּוֹם הַזֶּה הֶחֱזַקְתָּ בְּיָדִי / חַיִּים וָחֶסֶד עָשִׂיתָ עִמָּדִי: איוב י

ש״ץ: בָּרוּךְ יהוה וּבָרוּךְ שֵׁם כְּבוֹדוֹ / כִּי עַל עַבְדּוֹ הִפְלִיא חַסְדּוֹ.

קהל: אֱלֹהֵי מָרוֹם בַּמָּה אֲקַדֵּם / וּבַמָּה אִכַּף לֵאלֹהֵי קֶדֶם.

ש״ץ: אִלּוּ הָרִים הֵם לְמַעֲרָכָה / וְכָל עֲצֵי לְבָנוֹן, בְּכֹל עֲרוּכָה.

קהל: וְאִם כָּל בְּהֵמוֹת וְחַיּוֹת קְרוּצִים / נְתָחִים עֲרוּכִים עַל הָעֵצִים.

ש״ץ: וְאַף זָוִיּוֹת מִזְבֵּחַ מְבוּסִים / דָּם, כַּמַּיִם לַיָּם מְכַסִּים: ישעיה יא

קהל: וְכַחוֹל סֹלֶת דָּשֵׁן וְשָׁמֵן / בָּלוּל בְּרִבְבוֹת נַחֲלֵי שָׁמֶן: מיכה ו

ש״ץ: וּלְאַזְכָּרָה לְבוֹנָה וְסַמִּים / לִקְטֹרֶת וְכָל רָאשֵׁי בְשָׂמִים.

קהל: וְאִלּוּ נֵרוֹת עַל הַמְּנוֹרוֹת / יִהְיוּ מְאִירוֹת כִּשְׁנֵי הַמְּאוֹרוֹת.

ש״ץ: וּכְהַרְרֵי אֵל, לֶחֶם הַפָּנִים / עַל שֻׁלְחָנוֹת עֲרוּכִים בִּפְנִים.

קהל: וְיַיִן כְּמוֹ מְטַר הַשָּׁמַיִם / וְשֵׁכָר לְנֶסֶךְ כְּעֵינוֹת מָיִם.

SHIR HAYIḤUD – SONGS OF GOD'S ONENESS

Originally a single song, now divided into seven, known as the Song of Oneness because of its dominant theme, the unity of God through all manifestations, revelations and intimations. Attributed to Rabbi Samuel the Pious, whose son, Rabbi Judah, composed the Hymn of Glory, *Anim Zemirot*. It is one of the great creations of the *Ḥasidei Ashkenaz*, the pietistic and mystical movement that flourished in northern Germany in the twelfth and thirteenth centuries in such centers as Regensburg, Speyer, Worms and Mainz.

These were communities that suffered persecution and massacres during the Crusades. The concept of *Kiddush HaShem*, martyrdom, giving one's life for God, played an important part in their experience and thought. Their religious experience, as evidenced by their writings, was intense, shot through with yearning for God and for the life of holiness. Their ethical teachings are contained in *Sefer Ḥasidim, The Book of the Pious*, composed by Rabbi Judah,

Leader: And even if all men were priests / and Levites who sang like a joyful angelic songbird,

Cong: And all the trees of Eden, and trees of all forests / were fashioned into lyres and harps for the Levite singers,

Leader: And all of God's angels joined in with the sound of their shouts, / along with the stars from their courses above –

Cong: All of the trees of Lebanon and all animals / could never suffice as kindling and burnt offerings for Him.

Leader: Behold, none of these would suffice to worship Him; / nothing is adequate to approach the God of glory.

Cong: For You are greatly honored, our King, / and how shall we bow before our Master?

Leader: Indeed, none can glorify You, / no living creature, including myself, Your servant.

Cong: And I am a despicable man, forsaken by men, / spurned in my own eyes and lowly among men.

Leader: And Your servant has nothing with which to honor You, / to repay You for Your kindnesses;

Cong: For You have heaped good upon me, / and Your kindness to me has been great.

Leader: And many a debt have I incurred toward You, / for You have done good with me;

Cong: Yet You do not ask me to repay my debt to You, / all Your goodness to me is due to Your benevolence alone.

Leader: I have not sufficiently worshiped You for all of this good; / I have not repaid You even one part of ten thousand.

Cong: If I tried to count the good You have done, / I would not know how to learn its number.

Leader: And what shall I give back to You? All is Yours! / The heavens are Yours as well as the earth.

Cong: The seas and all that is within are in Your hands; / all receive nourishment from Your hand.

Leader: And we are Your nation, Your flock, / who desire to perform Your will!

Cong: And how shall we worship when we lack strength, / and our holy Temple has been consumed by fire?

Leader: And how shall we worship now that peace-offerings and meal-offerings are no more – / for we have not yet come to that restful place [Jerusalem].

Cong: And there is no water to wash away impurity; / and we are situated in an impure land.

Leader: Your words render me joyous; / I have now come before You to follow Your utterances.

Cong: For it is said: Not concerning your peace-offerings / and burnt-offerings will I rebuke you. *Ps. 50*

Leader: Concerning peace-offerings and burnt-offerings, / I did not command your ancestors.

Cong: What have I asked and what have I required / of you? – only to fear Me!

ש״ץ: וְאִלּוּ כָּל בְּנֵי אָדָם כֹּהֲנִים / לְוִיִּם מְשׁוֹרְרִים כִּכְנַף רְנָנִים.
קהל: וְכָל עֲצֵי עֵדֶן, וְכָל עֲצֵי יְעָרִים / כִּנּוֹרוֹת וּנְבָלִים לְשָׁרִים.

ש״ץ: וְכָל בְּנֵי אֱלֹהִים בְּקוֹל תְּרוּעָתָם / וְהַכּוֹכָבִים מִמְּסִלּוֹתָם.
קהל: וְכָל הַלְּבָנוֹן וְחַיָּה כֻּלָּהּ / אֵין דֵּי בָעֵר, וְאֵין דֵּי עוֹלָה.

ש״ץ: הֵן בְּכָל אֵלֶּה אֵין דֵּי לַעֲבוֹד / וְאֵין דֵּי לְקַדֵּם אֵל הַכָּבוֹד.
קהל: כִּי נִכְבַּדְתָּ מְאֹד מַלְכֵּנוּ / וּבַמֶּה נִכַּף לַאֲדוֹנֵנוּ.

ש״ץ: אָמְנָם לֹא יוּכְלוּ כַּבְּדֶךָ / כָּל חַי, אַף כִּי אֲנִי עַבְדֶּךָ.
קהל: וַאֲנִי נִבְזֶה וַחֲדַל אִישִׁים / נִמְאָס בְּעֵינַי וּשְׁפַל אֲנָשִׁים.

ש״ץ: וְאֵין לְעַבְדְּךָ כֹּל לְכַבְּדֶךָ / לְהָשִׁיב לְךָ גְּמוּל עַל חֲסָדֶיךָ.
קהל: כִּי הִרְבֵּיתָ טוֹבוֹת אֵלַי / כִּי הִגְדַּלְתָּ חַסְדְּךָ עָלַי.

ש״ץ: וְרַב שִׁלּוּמִים, לְךָ חִיַּבְתִּי / כִּי עָשִׂיתָ טוֹבוֹת אִתִּי.
קהל: וְלֹא חִיַּבְתָּ לִי גְּמוּלֶיךָ / כָּל טוֹבָתִי בַּל עָלֶיךָ.

ש״ץ: עַל הַטּוֹבוֹת לֹא עֲבַדְתִּיךָ / אַחַת לְרִבּוֹא לֹא גְמַלְתִּיךָ.
קהל: אִם אָמַרְתִּי אֲסַפְּרָה נָא, כְּמוֹ / לֹא יָדַעְתִּי סְפֹרוֹת לָמוֹ.

ש״ץ: וּמָה אָשִׁיב לְךָ, וְהַכֹּל שֶׁלָּךְ / לְךָ שָׁמַיִם, אַף אֶרֶץ לָךְ.
קהל: יַמִּים וְכָל אֲשֶׁר בָּם, בְּיָדֶךָ / וְכֻלָּם יִשְׂבְּעוּן מִיָּדֶךָ.

ש״ץ: וַאֲנַחְנוּ עַמְּךָ וְצֹאנֶךָ / וַחֲפֵצִים לַעֲשׂוֹת רְצוֹנֶךָ.
קהל: וְאֵיךְ נַעֲבֹד וְאֵין לְאֵל יָדֵנוּ / וְלִשְׂרֵפַת אֵשׁ, בֵּית קָדְשֵׁנוּ.

ש״ץ: וְאֵיךְ נַעֲבֹד, וְאֵין זֶבַח וּמִנְחָה / כִּי לֹא בָאנוּ אֶל הַמְּנוּחָה.
קהל: וּמַיִם אַיִן לְהַעֲבִיר טֻמְאָה / וַאֲנַחְנוּ עַל אֲדָמָה טְמֵאָה.

ש״ץ: שָׂשׂ אָנֹכִי עַל אֲמָרֶיךָ / וַאֲנִי בָאתִי בִּדְבָרֶיךָ.
קהל: כִּי כָתוּב, לֹא עַל זְבָחֶיךָ / וְעוֹלֹתֶיךָ אוֹכִיחֶךָ. תהלים נ

ש״ץ: עַל דְּבַר זֶבַח, וְעוֹלוֹתֵיכֶם / לֹא צִוִּיתִי אֶת אֲבוֹתֵיכֶם.
קהל: מָה שָּׁאַלְתִּי וּמָה דָּרַשְׁתִּי / מִמְּךָ, כִּי אִם לְיִרְאָה אוֹתִי.

Leader: To worship Me with joy and a glad heart –
"For heeding Me is better than a choice sacrifice." *1 Sam. 15*

Cong: And a broken heart is better than a pure meal-offering; / a broken spirit is equivalent to a sacrifice to God. *Ps. 51*

Leader: You do not desire peace-offerings and meal-offerings, / You did not request sin-offerings or burnt-offerings. *Ps. 40*

Cong: I shall build an altar out of my shattered heart, / and I shall break and humble my spirit within me.

Leader: I shall bring low my haughty heart and lower my haughty eyes; / I shall rend my heart for the sake of my Lord.

Cong: The fragments of my spirit shall be Your offerings; / may they rise up to You upon Your altar and be willingly accepted.

Leader: And I shall loudly sound out Your praise, / and recount of all Your wonders.

Cong: For that which my soul has known – I shall compose words, / I shall speak profusely of Your mighty deeds.

Leader: And what shall I formulate when I do not know what to say? / Indeed, is there anything I can say? *Num. 22*

Cong: For His greatness cannot be understood, / His insight cannot be measured.

Leader: He is wise of heart – who is like Him? / We shall never fully perceive the greatness of His strength. *Job 37*

Cong: The doer of great works; chief of awesome acts – / You are great, and You work wonders. *Ps. 86*

Leader: Innumerable, inscrutable – / their number shall never be known, for none shall succeed to discover their scope.

Cong: What eye can witness having seen You; / what mouth might tell of You?

Leader: No living being has seen You, nor has their heart known You; / what praise shall suffice for You?

Cong: Even Your servants have not seen You, / nor have the wise of heart discovered You.

Leader: You alone know Your praise; / no one but You knows Your true strength.

Cong: And no one but You knows / which praises befit Your glory.

Leader: Therefore, may You be blessed as befits You, / according to Your holiness, glory and greatness.

Cong: And so all shall bless You with their fullest strength, / according to the knowledge You have granted them.

Leader: The heavens shall laud Your wonders, / and the sounds of water shall exalt You.

Cong: And all the earth's inhabitants shall shout out to You, / all earthly kings shall laud You.

Leader: All nations shall give thanks to You, / and all peoples shall praise You.

Cong: As will all of the descendants of Jacob, Your servant, / for Your kindnesses have overwhelmed them.

Leader: The name of the Lord shall be praised by them all: / The true Lord God and King of the Universe.

Cong: Blessed are You, unique and singular One – / "The Lord is One and His name is One"! *Zech. 14*

ש״ץ: לַעֲבוֹד בְּשִׂמְחָה וּבְלֵבָב טוֹב / הִנֵּה שְׁמֹעַ מִזֶּבַח טוֹב: שמואל א׳ טו

קהל: וְלֵב נִשְׁבָּר, מִמִּנְחָה טְהוֹרָה / זִבְחֵי אֱלֹהִים רוּחַ נִשְׁבָּרָה: תהלים נא

ש״ץ: זֶבַח וּמִנְחָה לֹא־חָפַצְתָּ: / חַטָּאת וְעוֹלָה לֹא שָׁאָלְתָּ. תהלים מ

קהל: מִזְבֵּחַ אֶבְנֶה בְּשִׁבְרוֹן לִבִּי / וַאֲשַׁבְּרָה אַף רוּחִי בְּקִרְבִּי.

ש״ץ: רוּם לֵב אַשְׁפִּיל, וְאֶת רוּם עֵינַי / וְאֶקְרַע לְבָבִי לְמַעַן אֲדֹנָי.

קהל: שִׁבְרֵי רוּחִי הֵם זְבָחֶיךָ / יַעֲלוּ לְרָצוֹן עַל מִזְבְּחֶךָ.

ש״ץ: וְאַשְׁמִיעַ בְּקוֹל הוֹדְיוֹתֶיךָ / וַאֲסַפְּרָה כָּל נִפְלְאוֹתֶיךָ.

קהל: אֲשֶׁר יָדְעָה נַפְשִׁי אַחְבִּירָה / אֲמַלֵּל גְּבוּרוֹת וַאֲדַבֵּרָה.

ש״ץ: וּמָה אֶעֱרוֹךְ, וְלֹא יָדַעְתִּי מָה / הֲיָכֹל אוּכַל דַּבֵּר מְאוּמָה: במדבר כב

קהל: כִּי אֵין חֵקֶר לִגְדֻלָּתוֹ / וְגַם אֵין מִסְפָּר לִתְבוּנָתוֹ.

ש״ץ: חֲכַם לֵבָב הוּא, מִי כָמְוֹהוּ / שַׂגִּיא כֹחַ, לֹא מְצָאנֻהוּ. איוב לז

קהל: עוֹשֶׂה גְדוֹלוֹת וְרַב נוֹרָאוֹת / גָּדוֹל אַתָּה וְעֹשֵׂה נִפְלָאוֹת: תהלים פו

ש״ץ: עַד אֵין מִסְפָּר וְעַד אֵין חֵקֶר / וְלֹא נוֹדַע כִּי לֹא יֵחָקֵר.

קהל: אֵיזוֹ עַיִן אֲשֶׁר תְּעִידֶךָ / וְאֵיזֶה פֶּה אֲשֶׁר יַגִּידֶךָ.

ש״ץ: חַי לֹא רָאֲךָ וְלֵב לֹא יְדָעֲךָ / וְאֵיזֶה שֶׁבַח אֲשֶׁר יַגִּיעֲךָ.

קהל: גַּם מְשָׁרְתֶיךָ לֹא רָאוּךָ / וְכָל חַכְמֵי לֵב לֹא מְצָאוּךָ.

ש״ץ: אַתָּה לְבַדְּךָ מַכִּיר שִׁבְחֲךָ / וְאֵין זוּלָתְךָ יוֹדֵעַ כֹּחֲךָ.

קהל: וְאֵין יוֹדֵעַ בִּלְעָדֶיךָ / שְׁבָחוֹת רְאוּיוֹת לִכְבוֹדֶךָ.

ש״ץ: עַל כֵּן תְּבֹרַךְ כָּרָאוּי לָךְ / כְּפִי קָדְשְׁךָ, כְּבוֹדְךָ וְגָדְלָךְ.

קהל: וּמִפִּי הַכֹּל, בְּכָל אֱיָלוּתָם / כְּפִי מַדָּע אֲשֶׁר אַתָּה חֲנַנְתָּם.

ש״ץ: יוֹדוּ פִלְאֲךָ הַשָּׁמַיִם / וִיאַדְּרוּךָ קוֹלוֹת מַיִם.

קהל: וְיָרִיעוּ לְךָ כָּל הָאָרֶץ / יוֹדוּךָ כָּל מַלְכֵי אָרֶץ.

ש״ץ: אַף יוֹדוּךָ כָּל הָעַמִּים / וִישַׁבְּחוּךָ כָּל הָאֻמִּים.

קהל: כָּל זֶרַע יַעֲקֹב עֲבָדֶיךָ / כִּי עֲלֵיהֶם גָּבְרוּ חֲסָדֶיךָ.

ש״ץ: אֶת שֵׁם יהוה יְהַלְלוּ כֻלָּם / אֵל אֱלֹהִים אֱמֶת, וּמֶלֶךְ עוֹלָם.

קהל: בָּרוּךְ אַתָּה יָחִיד וּמְיֻחָד / יהוה אֶחָד וּשְׁמוֹ אֶחָד: זכריה יד

Monday:

Leader: And I, Your servant, the son of Your maidservant, / I shall speak at length of Your mighty wonders.

Cong: I shall recount only a few of Your praiseworthy ways, / I shall say of Your deeds: how awesome are they!

Leader: No one greater than You can be told of; / Your wonders are far too numerous to recount.

Cong: The deep thoughts of God can never be uncovered; / the perfection of the Almighty is endless.

Leader: Indeed, His insight may not be perceived, / the number of His years cannot be found.

Cong: Your troops are also too numerous to be counted, / Your glory is a sign among Your hosts.

Leader: Whose eye can testify to having seen You, / when no living being has ever seen Your glorious presence?

Cong: The wise and insightful do not know You; / how then shall I formulate words for the unknown?

Leader: If a man dares to say: "To God's limits / I shall measure; I shall arrive at His true form;

Cong: I shall proceed to discover the end of His praiseworthiness" – / such a man's spirit is unfaithful to God! *Ps. 78*

Leader: He shall be destroyed, for he knows not His worth; / for even if he were to tell of God's greatness until the end of his life, it would be only the beginning.

Cong: And I, this shall not be my path; / I shall not allow my mouth or palate to sin!

Leader: I shall recount to my brethren just a few of God's ways, / and tell Israel what God has done. *Num. 23*

Cong: As it is said: "Say to God: / How awesome are Your works, O God!" *Ps. 66*

Leader: And You have said: "This is the nation I have created for My sake, / that they might tell all of My name and My glory; *Is. 43*

Cong: I displayed My works in Egypt, / that you might tell of My miracles."

Leader: And I am Your servant, so I shall tell, / as I orate from a book.

Cong: My soul shall laud the power of Your deeds, / and all my body shall praise Your holy name.

Leader: And I shall bless You through all of my tasks; / I shall thank the LORD with all of my heart.

Cong: High songs to You shall be in my throat, / and my mouth I shall fill with Your praise.

Leader: For my mouth shall relate Your glory, / I shall recount Your splendor always.

Cong: And I shall indeed speak of the might of Your awesome works; / I shall tell of Your wonders.

Leader: And I will recall Your goodness and righteous deeds, / Your kindnesses and Your mighty works.

Cong: I have known that You are great, / You are exalted above all gods.

Monday:

ש״ץ: וַאֲנִי עַבְדְּךָ בֶּן אֲמָתֶךָ / אֲדַבֵּר, אֲמַלֵּל גְּבוּרוֹתֶיךָ.
קהל: דַּרְכֵי שִׁבְחֲךָ, קְצָתָם אֲסַפְּרָה / מַעֲשֶׂיךָ מַה נּוֹרָא, אוֹמְרָה.
ש״ץ: אֵין אֵלֶיךָ עֲרוֹךְ בְּסֵפֶר / אַגִּידָה, עָצְמוּ מִסַּפֵּר.
קהל: חֵקֶר אֱלוֹהַּ לֹא יִמָּצֵא / וְתַכְלִית שַׁדַּי לֹא תִקָּצֶה.
ש״ץ: וְלִתְבוּנָתוֹ הֲלֹא אֵין חֵקֶר / וּמִסְפַּר שָׁנָיו לֹא יֵחָקֵר.
קהל: וְגַם אֵין מִסְפָּר לִגְדוּדֶיךָ / בְּצִבְאוֹתֶיךָ, אוֹת כְּבוֹדֶךָ.
ש״ץ: אֵיזוֹ עַיִן אֲשֶׁר תְּעִידֶךָ / וְחַי לֹא רָאָה פְּנֵי כְבוֹדֶךָ.
קהל: נָבוֹן וְחָכָם הֵן לֹא יָדַע / וְאֵיךְ אֶעֱרוֹךְ, עַל אֲשֶׁר לֹא אֵדַע.
ש״ץ: וְאִם יֹאמַר אִישׁ, עַד תַּכְלִיתוֹ / אֶעֱרוֹךְ אֵלָיו, וּבְמַתְכֻּנְתּוֹ.
תהלים עח קהל: אָבֹא וְאֶמְצָא תַּכְלִית שִׁבְחוֹ / לֹא־נֶאֶמְנָה אֶת־אֵל רוּחוֹ:
ש״ץ: יְבֻלַּע כִּי לֹא יֵדַע עֶרְכּוֹ / אַחֲרִית פִּיהוּ רֵאשִׁית דַּרְכּוֹ.
קהל: וְעִמָּדִי לֹא כֵן אָנֹכִי / וּפִי לֹא אֶתֵּן לַחֲטוֹא, וְחִכִּי.
במדבר כג ש״ץ: אֲסַפְּרָה לְאֶחָי קְצוֹת דַּרְכֵי אֵל / וּלְיִשְׂרָאֵל מַה־פָּעַל אֵל:
תהלים סו קהל: כַּכָּתוּב, אִמְרוּ לֵאלֹהִים / מַה־נּוֹרָא מַעֲשֶׂיךָ: אֱלֹהִים.
ישעיה מג ש״ץ: וְאָמַרְתָּ, עַם־זוּ יָצַרְתִּי לִי: / יְסַפְּרוּ שְׁמִי וּתְהִלָּתִי.
קהל: בְּמִצְרַיִם שַׂמְתִּי עֲלִילוֹתַי / לְמַעַן תְּסַפֵּר אֶת אוֹתוֹתַי.
ש״ץ: וַאֲנִי עַבְדְּךָ, עַל כֵּן אֲסַפֵּר / כַּאֲשֶׁר אֶדְרוֹשׁ מֵעַל סֵפֶר.
קהל: תְּהַלֵּל נַפְשִׁי כֹּחַ מַעֲשֶׂיךָ / וְכָל קְרָבַי אֶת שֵׁם קָדְשֶׁךָ.
ש״ץ: וַאֲבָרְכְכָה בְּכָל עִנְיָנַי / וּבְכָל לִבִּי אוֹדֶה אֶת אֲדֹנָי.
קהל: גַּם בִּגְרוֹנִי רוֹמְמוֹתֶיךָ / וְאֶת פִּי אֲמַלֵּא תְּהִלָּתֶךָ.
ש״ץ: כִּי פִי יַגִּיד תְּהִלָּתֶךָ / כָּל הַיּוֹם אֶת תִּפְאַרְתֶּךָ.
קהל: וְאֹמְרָה נָּא עֱזוּז נוֹרְאוֹתֶיךָ / וְאָשִׂיחָה דִּבְרֵי נִפְלְאֹתֶיךָ.
ש״ץ: וְאַזְכִּיר טוּבְךָ וְצִדְקוֹתֶיךָ / חֲסָדֶיךָ וּגְבוּרוֹתֶיךָ.
קהל: יָדַעְתִּי כִּי גָדוֹל אַתָּה / עַל כָּל אֱלֹהִים, מְאֹד גָּדַלְתָּ.

וַאֲנִי עַבְדְּךָ *And I am Your servant.* No words can do justice to God's greatness as Architect of the universe and Shaper of history. We are Your people, Your children, Your witnesses.

Leader: For all the gods of the nations are / mute, worthless gods, devoid of all spirit.

Cong: For they do not provide recompense to their worshipers; / why then should the worshipers treat them so well?

Leader: And in times of distress they pray, / but they do not answer them because they are futile.

Cong: With all their heart, they seek out that which has no spirit, / while the LORD is close to His closest nation.

Leader: The Creator of all is our God; / He made us and we are His alone.

Cong: We are His nation, His flock, the sheep He tends; / we shall bless His name, for His kindness endures forever.

Leader: You were at hand when we were in great distress, / for You have not forsaken those who seek You.

Cong: Your praise is always upon our lips; / we shall forever sing praise to Your glorious name. *1 Chr. 29*

Leader: You serve as testimony to Your own glory; / as do Your angelic attendants, and Your servants [Israel].

Cong: For Your glory fills all the world; / Your glory rests upon all the world.

Leader: Our ancestors chose You / alone to worship, without linking strange gods to You.

Cong: We too – You alone / shall we worship; we shall honor You as a son honors his father.

Leader: Behold, of Your Oneness, / we shall testify day and night,

Cong: Declaring with our lips and hearts / that You alone are our God.

Leader: Our God, of Your Oneness / we are witnesses, and we are Your servants.

Cong: There was no prelude to Your beginning; / there is no end to Your eternal existence.

Leader: The first and last without beginning / or end; no one's heart can grasp this concept.

Cong: There is no end to Your loftiness, / and Your qualities run endlessly deep.

Leader: You have no perimeter and no corners, / and so, no living being has seen You.

Cong: No side or edge limits You; / You are not split by width or length.

Leader: No corners surround You, / no center splits You.

Cong: No wisdom shall ever truly know You; / no knowledge can ever reach understanding of You.

Leader: No knowledge can grasp You; / no mind can comprehend and know You.

Cong: All is from You, yet where are You? / How is it that You created all from nothing?

ש״ץ: כִּי כָל אֱלֹהֵי הָעַמִּים הֵם / אֱלִילִים אִלְּמִים, רוּחַ אֵין בָּהֶם.

קהל: הֵן לְעוֹבְדֵיהֶם גְּמוּל אֵין מְשִׁיבִים / וְלָמָּה לָהֶם, הֵמָּה מֵיטִיבִים.

ש״ץ: וּבְעֵת צָרָה אָז יִתְפַּלְּלוּ / וְלֹא יַעֲנוּם, כִּי לֹא יוֹעִילוּ.

קהל: דּוֹרְשִׁים בְּכָל לֵב לְרוּחַ אֵין בּוֹ / וְקָרוֹב יהוה אֶל עַם קְרוֹבוֹ.

ש״ץ: הַיּוֹצֵר כֹּל הוּא אֱלֹהֵינוּ / הוּא עָשָׂנוּ, וְלוֹ לְבַד אֲנָחְנוּ.

קהל: עַם מַרְעִיתוֹ וְצֹאן יָדוֹ / נְבָרֵךְ שְׁמוֹ כִּי לְעוֹלָם חַסְדּוֹ.

ש״ץ: בַּצַּר לָנוּ מְאֹד נִמְצֵאתָ / כִּי דֹרְשֶׁיךָ לֹא עָזָבְתָּ.

קהל: וְתָמִיד בְּפִינוּ תְּהִלָּתֶךָ / וּמְהַלְלִים לְשֵׁם תִּפְאַרְתֶּךָ: דברי הימים א׳ כט

ש״ץ: עַד אַתָּה בְּךָ וּבִכְבוֹדֶךָ / וּמְשָׁרְתֶיךָ אַף עֲבָדֶיךָ.

קהל: אֲשֶׁר כְּבוֹדְךָ מְלֹא כָל הָאָרֶץ / וּכְבוֹדְךָ עַל כָּל הָאָרֶץ.

ש״ץ: וַאֲבוֹתֵינוּ בָּחֲרוּ אוֹתְךָ / לְבַדְּךָ לַעֲבוֹד, וְאֵין לְזָר אִתָּךְ.

קהל: גַּם אֲנַחְנוּ אוֹתְךָ לְבַדֶּךָ / נַעֲבוֹד, כְּבֵן אֶת אָב נְכַבְּדֶךָ.

ש״ץ: וְהִנְנוּ עַל יִחוּדֶךָ / יוֹמָם וָלַיְלָה עֵדֶיךָ.

קהל: בְּפִי כֻלָּנוּ וּבִלְבָבֵנוּ / שֶׁאַתָּה לְבַדְּךָ אֱלֹהֵינוּ.

ש״ץ: אֱלֹהֵינוּ עַל יִחוּדֶךָ / עֵדִים אֲנַחְנוּ וַעֲבָדֶיךָ.

קהל: אֵין תְּחִלָּה אֶל רֵאשִׁיתֶךָ / וְאֵין קֵץ וְתִכְלָה לְאַחֲרִיתֶךָ.

ש״ץ: רִאשׁוֹן וְאַחֲרוֹן מִבְּלִי רֵאשִׁית / וּמִבְּלִי אַחֲרִית, וְאֵין לֵב לְהָשִׁית.

קהל: אֵין קְצָה אֶל גַּבְהוּתֶךָ / וְאֵין סוֹף לְעֹמֶק מִדּוֹתֶיךָ.

ש״ץ: אֵין לְךָ סוֹבֵב וְאֵין לְךָ פֵּאָה / עַל כֵּן אוֹתְךָ, חַי לֹא רָאָה.

קהל: אֵין צַד וְצֵלָע יַצְלִיעוּךָ / וְרֹחַב וְאֹרֶךְ לֹא יְמַצְּעוּךָ.

ש״ץ: אֵין פֵּאָה לִסְבִיבוֹתֶיךָ / וְאֵין תּוֹךְ מַבְדִּיל בֵּינוֹתֶיךָ.

קהל: אֵין חָכְמָה אֲשֶׁר תֵּדָעֶךָ / וְאֵין מַדָּע אֲשֶׁר יַגִּיעֶךָ.

ש״ץ: וְלֹא יַשִּׂיג אוֹתְךָ כָּל מַדָּע / וְאֵין שֵׂכֶל אֲשֶׁר יָבִין וְיֵדָע.

קהל: מִמְּךָ מְאוּמָה וְאֵיכָה אַתָּה / וְאֵיךְ בְּלִי מְאוּמָה כֹּל בָּרָאתָ.

Tuesday:

Leader: Indeed, I know that You, / the God of Jacob, created all things.

Cong: You are Creator but were not created; / You form every creature but You were not formed.

Leader: You bring death and shall consume all away; / You bring down to the grave and shall also bring out of it.

Cong: Faithful are You to revive the dead; / You have indeed made this known through Your prophets.

Leader: And You, O living God, shall not die, nor have You died; / You exist forever and ever.

Cong: You bring babies to breach and give life, but You were not born; / You crush and heal but You have never been afflicted.

Leader: You know no death or pain; / Your eyes know not sleep or slumber.

Cong: For from the earliest days, You have been a living God; / You have not changed from what You have always been.

Leader: And You shall never change; / You shall never be degraded from Your divinity.

Cong: The terms "new" and "old" do not apply to You; / You initiated all but You were not initiated.

Leader: Old age and youth cannot be ascribed / to You; neither can hoariness or childhood.

Cong: Joy and sadness cannot be ascribed to You; / nor can the form of any creature or finite being.

Leader: For no material matter affects You; / You are unlike any creature or soul.

Cong: You surrounded each of Your creatures with boundaries; / their beginnings and ends are defined.

Leader: For You have placed boundaries for Your creatures; / You have surrounded the cycle of their lives with limits.

Cong: But You have no boundaries; neither do Your days, / Your years or Your great power.

Leader: Therefore, You need no one; / yet all beings need Your hand and Your kindness.

Cong: All require Your acts of righteousness, / yet You do not require Your creatures.

Leader: For before any creature, You existed / alone; You were in need of nothing.

Cong: All their beginnings and ends are arranged by Your hand; / You are within them and they are bound up with You.

Leader: All that was at the beginning, / and all that will be in later years;

Cong: All creatures and all their deeds, / their speech and all their thoughts;

Leader: From beginning to end You know all / and shall never forget; for You are near them.

Cong: You created them and Your heart arranged them; / You alone know their place and their path.

---

the inner secrets of all. Because You exist beyond all boundaries, we, bounded in space and time, can never fully fathom Your greatness or power.

Tuesday:

ש״ץ: אָמְנָם יָדַעְתִּי, כִּי אַתָּה / אֱלֹהֵי יַעֲקֹב, כֹּל יָצַרְתָּ.

קהל: אַתָּה בוֹרֵא וְלֹא נִבְרֵאתָ / אַתָּה יוֹצֵר וְלֹא נוֹצַרְתָּ.

ש״ץ: אַתָּה מֵמִית, וְאֶת כֹּל תְּבַלֶּה / אַתָּה מוֹרִיד שְׁאוֹל וְאַף תַּעֲלֶה.

קהל: וְנֶאֱמָן לְהַחֲיוֹת מֵתִים אָתָּה / וְעַל יְדֵי נְבִיאֶךָ כֵּן הוֹדַעְתָּ.

ש״ץ: וְלֹא תָמוּת אֵל חַי, וְלֹא מֵתָה / מֵעוֹלָם וְעַד עוֹלָם אָתָּה.

קהל: מַשְׁבִּיר וּמוֹלִיד וְלֹא נוֹלַדְתָּ / מוֹחֵץ וְרוֹפֵא וְלֹא חָלִיתָ.

ש״ץ: מָוֶת וּמַדְוֶה אֵין לְפָנֶיךָ / תְּנוּמָה וְשֵׁנָה אֵין לְעֵינֶיךָ.

קהל: הֲלֹא מִקֶּדֶם, אֵל חַי אַתָּה / מֵאֲשֶׁר בְּךָ לֹא נִשְׁתַּנֵּיתָ.

ש״ץ: וְעַד הָעוֹלָם לֹא תִשְׁתַּנֶּה / מֵאֱלָהוּתְךָ לֹא תִתְגַּנֶּה.

קהל: חָדָשׁ וְנוֹשָׁן לֹא נִמְצֵאתָ / חִדַּשְׁתָּ כֹּל וְלֹא חֻדַּשְׁתָּ.

ש״ץ: לֹא יָחְולוּ זִקְנָה וּבַחֲרוּת / עָלֶיךָ, גַּם שֵׂיבָה וְשַׁחֲרוּת.

קהל: וְלֹא חָלוּ בְךָ שִׂמְחָה וְעֶצֶב / וְדִמְיוֹן נוֹצָר, וְכָל דְּבַר קֶצֶב.

ש״ץ: כִּי לֹא יְסוֹבֵב אוֹתְךָ גֶּשֶׁם / אַף לֹא תִדְמֶה אֶל כָּל נֶשֶׁם.

קהל: כָּל הַיְצוּרִים גְּבוּל סִבָּתָם / אֶל רֵאשִׁיתָם וּלְאַחֲרִיתָם.

ש״ץ: כִּי הַבְּרוּאִים בִּגְבוּל שַׁמְתָּם / וְלִימֵי צְבָאָם, גְּבוּל הִקַּפְתָּם.

קהל: וּלְךָ אֵין גְּבוּל וְלְיָמֶיךָ / וְלִשְׁנוֹתֶיךָ וּלְעָצְמֶךָ.

ש״ץ: עַל כֵּן אֵינְךָ צָרִיךְ לַכֹּל / לְיָדְךָ וּלְחַסְדְּךָ צְרִיכִים הַכֹּל.

קהל: הַכֹּל צְרִיכִים לְצִדְקוֹתֶיךָ / וְאֵינְךָ צָרִיךְ לִבְרִיּוֹתֶיךָ.

ש״ץ: כִּי טֶרֶם כָּל יְצִיר הָיִיתָ / לְבַדְּךָ, מְאוּמָה לֹא נִצְרַכְתָּ.

קהל: רֵאשִׁית וְאַחֲרִית, בְּיָדְךָ עֲרוּכִים / אַתָּה בָם, וְהֵם בְּרוּחֲךָ שְׂרוּכִים.

ש״ץ: כֹּל אֲשֶׁר הָיָה בָּרִאשׁוֹנָה / וַאֲשֶׁר יִהְיֶה בָּאַחֲרוֹנָה.

קהל: כָּל הַיְצוּרִים וְכָל מַעֲשֵׂיהֶם / וְכָל דִּבְרֵיהֶם וּמַחְשְׁבוֹתֵיהֶם.

ש״ץ: מֵרֹאשׁ וְעַד סוֹף תֵּדַע כֻּלָּם / וְלֹא תִשְׁכַּח, כִּי אַתָּה אֶצְלָם.

קהל: אַתָּה בְּרָאתָם וְלִבְּךָ עֲרָכָם / לְבַדְּךָ תֵּדַע מְקוֹמָם וְדַרְכָּם.

אָמְנָם יָדַעְתִּי *Indeed, I know.* You, God of eternal life, give life to all, and know

Leader: For nothing is concealed from You; / for all of them stand before You.

Cong: There is no darkness or refuge or concealed place / to which one can flee and hide.

Leader: You shall find what You seek / without inclining toward them, whenever You so desire.

Cong: For You see all in one sweeping glance; / You act alone and do not become weary.

Leader: For You can speak of a nation, or of all mankind, / of all there is, in a single moment.

Cong: You can hear all voices at the very same moment, / cries, whispers, and all prayers.

Leader: You also discern all of their deeds; / You seek out the inner workings of their hearts in an instant.

Cong: You do not prolong Your thoughts; / You do not hesitate upon Your counsel.

Leader: Your counsel and decrees are one and the same; / they shall be carried out at the time You determine.

Cong: All of them are true, complete and upright, / with no excess or deficiency.

Leader: Nothing shall ever be lost from You; / nothing is too burdensome for You.

Cong: You are able to do all that You desire, / and no one can overrule You.

Leader: The ability of the LORD is inseparable from His will; / when the LORD so desires, it will not be delayed.

Cong: No secret is hidden from You; / for You, future and past events are one and the same.

Leader: From end to end of eternity, / all are within You and You are within all.

Cong: You tell of Your innovations and Your secret ways / to Your servants and Your angels.

Leader: Yet You do not need to be informed / or told of any secret, hidden matter.

Cong: For every secret is revealed to You / even before it enters the mind of any creature.

Leader: No creature's heart can discover You; / no haughty words shall flow out of our mouths.

Cong: Because He has no bounds and cannot be divided, / no heart can explore His existence and no mouth shall dare to open.

Leader: He does not have sides or borders; / no words could ever rebuke Him.

Cong: It is beyond any being to obtain His knowledge; / to grasp its beginning or end.

Leader: His beginning, middle and end are unified and bound up together; / I shall prevent all mouths and hearts from seeking and exploring it.

Cong: His height and depth are attached like a circle's ends; / even the wise of heart and discerning shall not fathom it.

Leader: His glory permeates all and fills the world entire; / since You are all, You are within all.

Cong: No one is above or under You; / no one outside You and no one in between.

Leader: No image, front or back, can be ascribed to Your unity; / the power of Your Oneness has no form.

Cong: No one in the midst is separated from You; / not even the narrowest place exists, that is empty of You.

ש״ץ: הֵן אֵין דָּבָר מִמְּךָ נֶעְלָם / כִּי לְפָנֶיךָ נְכוֹנִים כֻּלָּם.
קהל: אֵין חֹשֶׁךְ וְאֵין מָנוֹס וְסֵתֶר / לָנוּס שָׁמָּה וּלְהִסָּתֵר.

ש״ץ: אֵת אֲשֶׁר תְּבַקֵּשׁ אַתָּה מוֹצֵא / בְּלִי נְטוֹת אֲלֵיהֶם בְּעֵת שֶׁתִּרְצֶה.
קהל: כִּי אֶת הַכֹּל כְּאַחַת תִּרְאֶה / לְבַדְּךָ תַּעֲשֶׂה וְאֵינְךָ נִלְאֶה.

ש״ץ: כִּי עַל גּוֹי וְעַל אָדָם יַחַד / עַל כֹּל תְּדַבֵּר בְּרֶגַע אֶחָד.
קהל: תִּשְׁמַע בְּרֶגַע כָּל הַקּוֹלוֹת / זַעַק וְלַחַשׁ וְכָל הַתְּפִלּוֹת.

ש״ץ: אַף תָּבִין אֶל כָּל מַעֲשֵׂיהֶם / בְּרֶגַע תַּחְקוֹר כָּל לְבָבֵיהֶם.
קהל: וְלֹא תַאֲרִיךְ עַל מַחְשְׁבוֹתֶיךָ / וְלֹא תִתְמַהְמַהּ עַל עֲצָתֶךָ.

ש״ץ: אֵצֶל עֲצָתְךָ גְּזֵרָתֶךָ / לְקֵץ וּלְמוֹעֵד קְרִיאָתֶךָ.
קהל: וְכֻלָּם בֶּאֱמֶת בְּתֹם וּבְיֹשֶׁר / מִבְּלִי עֹדֶף וּמִבְּלִי חֹסֶר.

ש״ץ: מִמְּךָ דָּבָר לֹא יֹאבַד / וְדָבָר מִמְּךָ לֹא יִכָּבֵד.
קהל: כֹּל אֲשֶׁר תַּחְפּוֹץ תּוּכַל לַעֲשׂוֹת / וְאֵין מִי מוֹחֶה בְּיָדְךָ מֵעֲשׂוֹת.

ש״ץ: יְכֹלֶת יהוה בְּחֶפְצוֹ קְשׁוּרָה / וּבִרְצוֹת יהוה לֹא אִחֲרָה.
קהל: אֵין דְּבַר סֵתֶר מִמְּךָ נִכְחָד / עֲתִידוֹת וְעוֹבְרוֹת לְךָ הֵם יַחַד.

ש״ץ: אֲשֶׁר מֵעוֹלָם וְעַד הָעוֹלָם / הֵם כֻּלָּם בְּךָ, וְאַתָּה בְּכֻלָּם.
קהל: חֲדָשׁוֹת תַּגִּיד וְסוֹד דְּרָכֶיךָ / אֶל עֲבָדֶיךָ וּמַלְאָכֶיךָ.

ש״ץ: וְאֵינְךָ צָרִיךְ לְהַשְׁמִיעֶךָ / דְּבַר סוֹד וְסֵתֶר לְהוֹדִיעֶךָ.
קהל: כִּי מִמְּךָ כָּל סוֹד יִגָּלֶה / בְּטֶרֶם עַל לֵב כָּל יְצִיר יַעֲלֶה.

ש״ץ: בְּלֵב כָּל נִבְרָא לֹא תִמָּצֵא / מִפִּינוּ עָתָק לֹא יֵצֵא.
קהל: בְּאֵין לוֹ קָצֶה וְלֹא יֵחָצֶה / לֵב לֹא יָתוּר וְאֵין פֶּה פוֹצֶה.

ש״ץ: בְּאֵין לוֹ רוּחוֹת וְאֵין בּוֹ רְוָחוֹת / אֵין לוֹ שִׂיחוֹת, בּוֹ מוֹכִיחוֹת.
קהל: לְמֵרָחוֹק מִי יִשָּׂא דֵעוֹ / לְלֹא תְחִלָּה וְלֹא סוֹף לְהַגִּיעוֹ.

ש״ץ: אֲגוּדִים אֲחוּדִים תּוֹךְ וָסוֹף וָרֹאשׁ / פֶּה וָלֵב אֶבְלֹם מִדְּרֹשׁ וּמֵחֲרֹשׁ.
קהל: גֹּבַהּ וְעֹמֶק נְעוּצִים כְּסוֹבֵב / חֲכַם לֵב וְנָבוֹן לֹא יִלָּבֵב.

ש״ץ: סוֹבֵב הַכֹּל וּמָלֵא אֶת כֹּל / וּבִהְיוֹת הַכֹּל אַתָּה בַכֹּל.
קהל: אֵין עָלֶיךָ וְאֵין תַּחְתֶּיךָ / אֵין חוּץ וְאֵין בֵּינוֹתֶיךָ.

ש״ץ: אֵין מַרְאֶה וְגַב לְאִחוּדֶךָ / וְאֵין גּוּף לְעֹצֶם יִחוּדֶךָ.
קהל: וְאֵין בַּתָּוֶךְ מִמְּךָ נִבְדָּל / וְאֵין מָקוֹם דַּק, מִמְּךָ נֶחְדָּל.

Leader: Yet You are not set aside or secluded from all; / no area is devoid of Your presence.

Cong: Chance and change do not exist for You; / neither do time, transience or inadequacy.

Leader: You establish every time and season; / You arrange them and change them.

Cong: No wisdom can grasp You; / no mind can attain You.

Leader: Your wisdom is as great as Your stature; / Your insight is as great as Your majesty.

Cong: Your wisdom is Yours alone; / Your vitality comes from within Yourself and no one is like You.

Leader: No wisdom exists aside from Yours; / no plan holds true without Your insight.

Cong: You have provided the hearts of the wise with intelligence; / it is Your spirit that fills them and renders their minds wise.

Leader: Without Your power there is no might; / without Your strength there is no succor.

Cong: No one is honored unless You provide him with honor; / no one is great unless You render him great.

Leader: All value and goodness shall come from Your hand / to whomever You desire to show Your kindness.

Cong: Your greatness can never be uncovered; / Your insight has no limit.

Leader: If not for Your existence none could exist; / You are alive, omnipotent, and there is none but You.

Cong: And You existed before all; / since the world was created, You have permeated it all.

Leader: You were not pressed or swayed by / Your creatures; neither did they diminish You in any way.

Cong: Although You created all You did not separate Yourself; / You did not cease to exist within Your works.

Leader: In Your creation of the heavens, / the land and water,

Cong: Creating them did not cause You to become closer or more distant, / for You know no limits.

Leader: No flood of water can wash You away; / no mighty wind can blow You asunder.

Cong: No filth can contaminate You; / Your divine fire cannot consume You.

Leader: Your existence lacks nothing; / Your Oneness has no excess.

Cong: Just as You have always been – You shall always be; / You know no want or surplus.

Leader: Your own name testifies that You have always existed in all, / You exist now and shall forever be.

Cong: You forever exist and have always been renowned; / we shall testify to this and You are Your own witness –

Leader: That You exist in all; / all is Yours and all comes from You.

Cong: Your honorable names shall declare and testify – / testify to the power of Your honor.

ש״ץ: וְאֵינְךָ נֶאֱצָל מִכֹּל וְנִבְדָּל / וְאֵין מָקוֹם רֵיק מִמְּךָ וְנֶחְדָּל.
קהל: מִקְרֶה וְשִׁנּוּי אֵין בְּךָ נִמְצָא / וְלֹא זְמַן וְעַרְעַר, וְלֹא כָּל שִׁמְצָה.
ש״ץ: כָּל זְמַן וְכָל עֵת אַתָּה מְכִינָם / אַתָּה עוֹרְכָם וְאַתָּה מְשַׁנָּם.
קהל: כָּל מַדָּע לֹא יַשִּׂיג אוֹתָךְ / אֵין שֵׂכֶל אֲשֶׁר יִמְצָא אוֹתָךְ.
ש״ץ: כְּמִדָּתְךָ כֵּן חָכְמָתֶךָ / כִּגְדֻלָּתְךָ תְּבוּנָתֶךָ.
קהל: חָכָם אַתָּה מֵאֵלֶיךָ / חַי מֵעַצְמְךָ, וְאֵין כְּגִילֶךָ.
ש״ץ: זוּלַת חָכְמָתְךָ אֵין חָכְמָה / בִּלְתִּי בִינָתְךָ אֵין מְזִמָּה.
קהל: חָלַקְתָּ בְּלֵב חֲכָמִים שֵׂכֶל / וְרוּחֲךָ תְּמַלְּאֵם וְדַעְתָּם תַּשְׂכֵּל.
ש״ץ: מִבַּלְעֲדֵי כֹחֲךָ אֵין גְּבוּרָה / וּמִבַּלְעֲדֵי עֻזְּךָ אֵין עֶזְרָה.
קהל: אֵין נִכְבָּד כִּי אִם כִּבַּדְתּוֹ / וְאֵין גָּדוֹל כִּי אִם גִּדַּלְתּוֹ.
ש״ץ: כָּל יְקָר וְכָל טוּב מִיָּדֶךָ / לַאֲשֶׁר תַּחְפּוֹץ לַעֲשׂוֹת חֲסָדֶיךָ.
קהל: אֵין חֵקֶר לִגְדֻלָּתֶךָ / וְאֵין מִסְפָּר לִתְבוּנָתֶךָ.
ש״ץ: אֵין עוֹד זוּלַת הֲוָיוֹתֶיךָ / חַי וְכֹל תּוּכַל, וְאֵין בִּלְתֶּךָ.
קהל: וְלִפְנֵי הַכֹּל כֹּל הָיִיתָ / וּבִהְיוֹת הַכֹּל, כֹּל מִלֵּאתָ.
ש״ץ: לֹא לְחָצוּךָ וְלֹא הִטּוּךָ / יְצוּרֶיךָ, אַף לֹא מִעֲטוּךָ.
קהל: בַּעֲשׂוֹתְךָ כֹּל לֹא נִבְדַּלְתָּ / מִתּוֹךְ מְלַאכְתְּךָ לֹא נֶחְדַּלְתָּ.
ש״ץ: בַּעֲשׂוֹתְךָ אֶת הַשָּׁמַיִם / וְאֶת הָאָרֶץ וְאֶת הַמַּיִם.
קהל: לֹא קֵרְבוּךָ וְלֹא רִחֲקוּךָ / כִּי כָל קִירוֹת לֹא יְחַלְּקוּךָ.
ש״ץ: זֶרֶם מַיִם לֹא יִשְׁטְפֶךָ / וְרוּחַ כַּבִּיר לֹא יֶהְדְּפֶךָ.
קהל: אַף כָּל טִנֹּפֶת לֹא תְטַנְּפֶךָ / אֵשׁ אֹכְלָה, אֵשׁ לֹא תִשְׂרְפֶךָ.
ש״ץ: לַהֲוָיָתְךָ אֵין חִסָּרוֹן / וּלְיִחוּדְךָ אֵין יִתָּרוֹן.
קהל: כְּמוֹ הָיִיתָ לְעוֹלָם תִּהְיֶה / חָסֵר וְעֹדֵף בְּךָ לֹא יִהְיֶה.
ש״ץ: וְשִׁמְךָ מְעִידְךָ כִּי הָיִיתָ / וְהֹוֶה וְתִהְיֶה וּבַכֹּל אָתָּה.
קהל: הֹוֶה לְעוֹלָם וְכֵן נוֹדַעְתָּ / נְעִידְךָ וְכֵן בְּךָ הַעִידוֹתָ.
ש״ץ: שֶׁאַתָּה הוּא, וְהֹוֶה בַּכֹּל / שֶׁלְּךָ הַכֹּל וּמִמְּךָ הַכֹּל.
קהל: שְׁמוֹת יְקָרְךָ יַעֲנוּ וְיָעִידוּ / בְּתֹקֶף יְקָרְךָ בְּךָ יַסְהִידוּ.

Wednesday:

Leader: I shall exalt the God of my father, my God; / I shall beautify my God, my Rock and Redeemer.

Cong: I shall declare the Oneness of the God of heaven / and earth, twice each day.

Leader: One living God created us, / the Mighty One of Israel, Father to us all.

Cong: Our Master, Master of all the earth – / Your name is great throughout the earth! *Ps. 8*

Leader: There is none like the jealous God of consuming fire; / the LORD is forever truth, a faithful God.

Cong: My Light and Salvation, the Fortress of my life; / all my aspirations are cast upon Him.

Leader: The God of truth is a living God; / nations shall not contain His wrath.

Cong: Mighty, of valiant power, abundantly strong; / He is the God of gods and Master of masters. *Deut. 10*

Leader: The God who created me; my Husband and Master; / the Champion of my youth, my Protector and Shelter.

Cong: The Creator of all and Redeemer of Israel; / blessed be God, the God of Israel. *Ps. 72*

Leader: Maker of wind, Creator of mountains; / no device can be hidden from You.

Cong: Majestic One, You repay the haughty, / the lofty and the proud.

Leader: He is mighty when He rises up in His anger to strike with awe; / who does not fear the splendor of His majesty?

Cong: Lofty One, He bears all that is below Him; / the powerful One works wonders.

Leader: He is great and His name bears His strength; / if a lion roars, who shall not be afraid? *Amos 3*

Cong: My Beloved is encircled by myriads; / a God revered in the vast counsel of holy angels. *Song. 5* *Ps. 89*

Leader: He sits in judgment as One who has always existed; / His hosts stand on His left and right.

Cong: His splendor and glory rest upon the descendants of His servants, our ancestors; / He is glorified as the glory of all His devoted ones.

Leader: He is the LORD, the God whose spirit dwells in all / flesh; He hears the prayers of all.

Cong: He is affirmed, diligent, knowing, a witness; / the LORD shall reign forever and ever. *Ex. 15*

Leader: He is the Sword of our pride, / our Helper and Protector.

Cong: He recalls the covenant with the early ones forever; / to Him, a thousand years seem as recent as yesterday.

Shelter, Creator, Redeemer, Judge and Warrior. He is like an eagle, a leopard, a lion, a gazelle, a hart, a bird sheltering its young; like a tall cedar, an apple tree, myrrh and henna. The poet pours out his love for God, "my Promise, my Hope…, my Praise, my Glory, my Strength."

Wednesday:

ש״ץ: אֲרוֹמֵם אֱלֹהֵי אָבִי, וְאֵלִי / אַנְוֶה אֱלֹהַי, צוּרִי וְגֹאֲלִי.

קהל: אֲיַחֵד אֱלֹהֵי הַשָּׁמַיִם / וְהָאָרֶץ, בְּכָל יוֹם פַּעֲמַיִם.

ש״ץ: אֵל חַי אֶחָד הוּא בְּרָאָנוּ / אֲבִיר יִשְׂרָאֵל אָב לְכֻלָּנוּ.

קהל: אֲדוֹנֵינוּ, אֲדוֹן כָּל הָאָרֶץ / אַדִּיר שִׁמְךָ בְּכָל־הָאָרֶץ: תהלים ח

ש״ץ: אֵין כָּאֵל אֵשׁ אֹכְלָה וְקַנָּא / לְעוֹלָם יהוה אֱמֶת, אֵל אֱמוּנָה.

קהל: אוֹרִי וְיִשְׁעִי, מָעוֹז חַיַּי / עָלָיו תְּלוּיִים כָּל מַאֲוַיַּי.

ש״ץ: אֱלֹהִים אֱמֶת הוּא, אֱלֹהִים חַיִּים / לֹא יָכִילוּ זַעְמוֹ גּוֹיִם.

קהל: אַדִּיר וְאַמִּיץ כֹּחַ וְרַב אוֹנִים / אֱלֹהֵי הָאֱלֹהִים וַאֲדֹנֵי הָאֲדֹנִים: דברים י

ש״ץ: אֱלוֹהַּ עוֹשִׂי, אִישִׁי וּבוֹעֲלִי / אַלּוּף נְעוּרַי, שׁוֹמְרִי וְצִלִּי.

קהל: בּוֹרֵא כֹל, וְיִשְׂרָאֵל גּוֹאֵל / בָּרוּךְ אֱלֹהִים אֱלֹהֵי יִשְׂרָאֵל: תהלים עב

ש״ץ: בּוֹרֵא רוּחַ, הָרִים יוֹצֵר / מִמְּךָ מְזִמָּה לֹא יִבָּצֵר.

קהל: גֵּאֶה, מֵשִׁיב גְּמוּל עַל גֵּאִים / עַל הָרָמִים וְעַל הַנִּשָּׂאִים.

ש״ץ: גִּבּוֹר בְּקוּמוֹ לַעֲרוֹץ בְּעֶבְרָה / מֵהֲדַר גְּאוֹנוֹ, מִי לֹא יִירָא.

קהל: גָּבֹהַּ, כָּל אֲשֶׁר תַּחְתָּיו נוֹשֵׂא / וּגְדָל כֹּחַ, גְּדוֹלוֹת עוֹשֶׂה.

ש״ץ: גָּדוֹל הוּא וּשְׁמוֹ בִּגְבוּרָה / אַרְיֵה שָׁאָג, מִי לֹא יִירָא: עמוס ג

קהל: דּוֹדִי, דָּגוּל הוּא מֵרְבָבָה / אֵל נַעֲרָץ בְּסוֹד־קְדֹשִׁים רַבָּה: שיר השירים ה תהלים פט

ש״ץ: דַּיָּן, יָתִיב כְּעַתִּיק יוֹמִין / וּצְבָאוֹ עַל שְׂמֹאל וְעַל יָמִין.

קהל: הֲדָרוֹ וְהוֹדוֹ עַל בְּנֵי עֲבָדָיו / הָדוּר, הָדָר הוּא לְכָל חֲסִידָיו.

ש״ץ: הוּא אֵל אֱלֹהֵי הָרוּחֹת לְכָל / בָּשָׂר, שׁוֹמֵעַ תְּפִלָּה מִכֹּל.

קהל: וַדַּאי, וָתִיק, יוֹדֵעַ וָעֵד / יהוה יִמְלֹךְ לְעֹלָם וָעֶד: שמות טו

ש״ץ: וַאֲשֶׁר חֶרֶב גַּאֲוָתֵנוּ / עֶזְרֵנוּ וּמָגִנֵּנוּ.

קהל: זוֹכֵר לְעוֹלָם בְּרִית רִאשׁוֹנִים / כְּיוֹם אֶתְמוֹל לוֹ, אֶלֶף שָׁנִים.

אֲרוֹמֵם *I shall exalt.* The poet evokes God's protective power using a series of vivid images drawn from Tanakh: God is Husband, Master, Champion,

Leader: This is our God; we await Him eagerly, / and the song of the LORD shall be our salvation.

Cong: He is the inheritance of Jacob, the Creator of all; / the LORD is gracious and kind in all He does.

Leader: The LORD who lives forever shall be my lot; / the LORD who knows all secrets is my strength.

Cong: He is good and does good, He teaches knowledge; / too pure of eye to behold evil.

Leader: The LORD is upright and His words upright; / He favors His close ones, the angels, who dwell in His Temple.

Cong: He designs and decrees – who can annul His decision? / He strikes and acts – who can hinder Him?

Leader: My Beloved is beautiful, both His beauty and goodness / are evident. All shall witness His return to Zion.

Cong: Like a hero He shall go forth like a man of war; / His jealousy shall be aroused to perform vengeance.

Leader: Like an eagle upon eagles' wings, / He has carried His servants and straightened crooked paths.

Cong: Like a bereaved bear and a mighty leopard, / He shall reduce them to rottenness and moths; His spirit shall engulf them like an overflowing stream.

Leader: He is like a bereaved bear and a diligent leopard, / carrying out His word like an almond branch quick to blossom.

Cong: Mighty of heart like a lion, / like a lion and a lioness, His spirit shall engulf them like an overflowing stream.

Leader: His greatness is as robust as a cedar tree; / His humility is likened to a flourishing cypress.

Cong: The boldness of His love is like a fragrant apple tree; / His glory is upon His people, Israel.

Leader: As an apple tree among the trees of the forest, / so is my Beloved among the judges who sit at their gates. *Song. 2*

Cong: Might and strength are displayed to those who anger the God / of vengeance; while He is as gentle as dew to His people, Israel.

Leader: He is my cup of blessing, the portion of my inheritance, my lot; / I am my Beloved's inheritance and He is mine.

Cong: LORD, I shall never relinquish my honor; / we have avowed ourselves to Him and He to us.

Leader: He shall roar and growl like a lion; / He will not be as a stranger, or a man astounded.

Cong: He is not like a valiant shepherd unable / to rescue His flock, leaving it to be consumed.

Leader: Not like a powerless man of valor or a passing wayfarer, / who flees and runs while screaming bitterly.

Cong: He is like a destructive young lion to those who forsake Him; / reducing His enemies to rottenness and moths.

ש״ץ: זֶה אֱלֹהֵינוּ וְלוֹ קִוִּינוּ / וְזִמְרָת יָהּ, הוּא יוֹשִׁיעֵנוּ.

קהל: חֵלֶק יַעֲקֹב, יוֹצֵר הַכֹּל / חַנּוּן יהוה וְחָסִיד בַּכֹּל.

ש״ץ: חֵי הָעוֹלָם יהוה חֶלְקִי / חֲכַם הָרָזִים יהוה חִזְקִי.

קהל: טוֹב וּמֵטִיב, הַמְלַמֵּד דֵּעָה / טְהוֹר עֵינַיִם מֵרְאוֹת בְּרָעָה.

ש״ץ: יָשָׁר יהוה וְיָשָׁר דְּבָרוֹ / יְדִידֵי יְדִידוּת, מִשְׁכְּנוֹת דְּבִירוֹ.

קהל: יוֹעֵץ וְגוֹזֵר, מִי יְפִירֶנָּה / וְיַחְתֹּף וְיִפְעַל, מִי יְשִׁיבֶנָּה.

ש״ץ: יָפֶה דוֹדִי, יָפְיוֹ וְטוּבוֹ / יִרְאוּ, וְיֶחֱזוּ צִיּוֹן בְּשׁוּבוֹ.

קהל: כַּגִּבּוֹר יֵצֵא כְּאִישׁ מִלְחָמוֹת / יָעִיר קִנְאָה לַעֲשׂוֹת נְקָמוֹת.

ש״ץ: כְּנֶשֶׁר, עַל כַּנְפֵי נְשָׁרִים / נָשָׂא עֲבָדָיו, וְיִשֵּׁר הֲדוּרִים.

קהל: כְּדֹב שַׁכּוּל וּכְנָמֵר שַׁחַל / כְּרָקָב וּכְעָשׁ, וְרוּחוֹ כְּנַחַל.

ש״ץ: כְּדֹב שַׁכּוּל וּכְנָמֵר שׁוֹקֵד / דְּבָרוֹ לַעֲשׂוֹת כְּמַקֵּל שָׁקֵד.

קהל: כַּבִּיר כֹּחַ, לֵב כְּמוֹ שָׁחַל / כְּלָבִיא וְכַאֲרִי, וְרוּחוֹ כְּנָחַל.

ש״ץ: כְּאֶרֶז בָּחוּר בְּגָדְלָתוֹ / כִּבְרוֹשׁ רַעֲנָן עֲנֻותָנוּתוֹ.

קהל: כְּתַפּוּחַ בְּרֵיחוֹ, עֹז אַהֲבָתוֹ / עַל עַם יִשְׂרָאֵל גַּאֲוָתוֹ.

ש״ץ: כְּתַפּוּחַ בַּעֲצֵי הַיַּעַר / כֵּן דּוֹדִי עִם יוֹשְׁבֵי שָׂעַר. שיר השירים ב

קהל: כַּבִּיר כֹּחַ, לְמַרְגִּיזֵי אֵל / נוֹקֵם, וְכַטַּל הוּא לְיִשְׂרָאֵל.

ש״ץ: כּוֹסִי, מְנָת חֶלְקִי וְגוֹרָלִי / אֲנִי לְדוֹדִי נַחֲלָה וְדוֹדִי לִי.

קהל: כְּבוֹדִי יהוה לֹא אֲמִירֶנּוּ / הֶאֱמַרְנוּהוּ וְהֶאֱמִירָנוּ.

ש״ץ: כְּאַרְיֵה יִשְׁאַג וְכַכְּפִיר יִנְהַם / אַל יִהְיֶה כְּגֵר, וּכְאִישׁ נִדְהָם.

קהל: כְּרוֹעֶה גִּבּוֹר, אֲשֶׁר לֹא יוּכַל / צֹאנוֹ לְהַצִּיל, וְהָיָה לְמַאֲכָל.

ש״ץ: כְּגִבּוֹר אֵין אֱיָל, וּכְאוֹרֵחַ / נָס וּבוֹרֵחַ, מַר צוֹרֵחַ.

קהל: כְּאַרְיֵה מַשְׁחִית וְכַכְּפִיר לְעֹזְבָיו / כְּרָקָב גַּם כָּעָשׁ לְאוֹיְבָיו.

Leader: Of mighty power, He will reduce them to thorns on thorn bushes; / not a single shake of an olive tree shall remain of them.

Cong: Like thorns on thorn bushes He shall deliver His foes to destruction; / He shall protect His city like birds hovering above.

Leader: He shall appear to us like generous rains; / He will be like the spring rain and the dew to those who cleave to Him.

Cong: He shall hover above His young like an eagle; / those who await Him shall seek refuge beneath the shadow of His wings.

Leader: He shall protect His city like birds hovering above, / and in the shadow of His wings we shall play joyful songs.

Cong: He is One alone and great wonders / He performs – God of awesome works.

Leader: My Beloved is like a gazelle and young hart; / My God of kindness hastens to receive me.

Cong: He shall straighten crooked paths for His people, / and will lift them up upon eagles' wings.

Leader: He shall always be my lot, the rock of my heart; / my heart and flesh long for You.

Cong: Our LORD is alone; / He works great wonders and does many awesome things.

Leader: Your world has a place and dwelling, / yet no one knows Your dwelling place.

Cong: My Awesome One – God my Shepherd, my Creator, / the Rock who birthed me, my Creator and my Rock.

Leader: He is my exalted One, my Fortress and Shelter; / the name of the LORD, my Redeemer, is a tower of strength.

Cong: The King of Jacob is our Stronghold; / He is the Prescriber of our laws and our Savior.

Leader: The tower of salvation shall be my support and confidence; / the LORD God, is my strength.

Cong: Ruler of the world, Your kingdom / and reign are for all generations.

Leader: O that You were my Brother in times of distress; / save me, for Your hand lacks no strength.

Cong: The Source of life, the Hope of Israel; / I shall not leave Him for God is my Fortress.

Leader: The shield of my salvation, sword of pride; / our souls desire Your name and memory.

Cong: He is a shield for all who take shelter in Him; / happy is the man who takes strength in Him. *Ps. 18*

Leader: Clear, pleasant, enveloped in light, awesome; / His name is glorious and girded with might.

Cong: The Everlasting One of Israel and its Redeemer is faithful, / He never speaks falsehood; happy are those who await Him. *Is. 30*

Leader: The Everlasting God of Yeshurun, the faithful God; / Judah has not been forsaken by its God.

Cong: More wondrous than all wonders; / loftier than all lofty beings.

ש״ץ: כַּבִּיר כֹּחַ כְּשָׁמִיר וָשַׁיִת / וְלֹא יַשְׁאִיר כְּנֹקֶף זָיִת.

קהל: כְּשָׁמִיר וָשַׁיִת, צָרִים יְמַגֵּן / כְּצִפֳּרִים עָפוֹת לְעִירוֹ יָגֵן.

ש״ץ: כְּגִשְׁמֵי נְדָבָה לָנוּ יָבֹא / כְּמַלְקוֹשׁ וְכַטַּל לַדְּבֵקִים בּוֹ.

קהל: כְּנֶשֶׁר יְרַחֵף עַל גּוֹזָלָיו / וּבְצֵל כְּנָפָיו יֶחֱסוּ מְיַחֲלָיו.

ש״ץ: כְּצִפֳּרִים, עַל עִירוֹ יָגֵן / וּבְצֵל כְּנָפָיו רְנָנוֹת נְנַגֵּן.

קהל: לְבַדּוֹ הוּא, וְנִפְלָאוֹת גְּדוֹלוֹת / עוֹשֶׂה אֵל נוֹרָא עֲלִילוֹת.

ש״ץ: לִצְבִי וְעֹפֶר דּוֹמֶה דוֹדִי / כִּי יְקַדְּמֵנִי אֱלֹהֵי חַסְדִּי.

קהל: לִפְנֵי עַמּוֹ יְיַשֵּׁר הֲדוּרִים / וַיִּנַשְּׂאֵם עַל כַּנְפֵי נְשָׁרִים.

ש״ץ: לְעוֹלָם חֶלְקִי הוּא, וְצוּר לְבָבִי / כָּלָה שְׁאֵרִי לְךָ וּלְבָבִי.

קהל: לְבַדּוֹ יהוה הוּא, וְנִפְלָאוֹת / גְּדוֹלוֹת עוֹשֶׂה, וְרַב נוֹרָאוֹת.

ש״ץ: מָקוֹם וּמָעוֹן לְעוֹלָמֶךָ / וְאֵין יוֹדֵעַ אֶת מְקוֹמֶךָ.

קהל: מוֹרָאִי, אֵל רוֹעִי וְיוֹצְרִי / צוּר יְלָדַנִי, מְחוֹלְלִי וְצוּרִי.

ש״ץ: מָרוֹם וּמָעוֹז הוּא לִי, וּמַחְסִי / מִגְדַּל עֹז שֵׁם יהוה, מְנוּסִי.

קהל: מֶלֶךְ יַעֲקֹב, מִשְׂגָּב לָנוּ / הוּא מְחוֹקְקֵנוּ וּמוֹשִׁיעֵנוּ.

ש״ץ: מִגְדּוֹל יְשׁוּעוֹת, מִשְׁעָן יְהִי לִי / מִבְטָח, אֱלֹהִים יהוה חֵילִי.

קהל: מוֹשֵׁל עוֹלָם מַלְכוּתֶךָ / בְּכָל דּוֹר וָדוֹר מֶמְשַׁלְתֶּךָ.

ש״ץ: מִי יִתֶּנְךָ כְּאָח לִי, לְצָרָה / הוֹשַׁע, כִּי יָדְךָ לֹא קָצְרָה.

קהל: מְקוֹר חַיִּים, מִקְוֵה יִשְׂרָאֵל / לֹא אֶעֱזֹב כִּי מָעֻזִּי אֵל.

ש״ץ: מָגֵן יִשְׁעִי, וְחֶרֶב גַּאֲוָה / לְשִׁמְךָ וּלְזִכְרְךָ נֶפֶשׁ תַּאֲוָה.

קהל: מָגֵן הוּא לְכֹל הַחוֹסִים בּוֹ: / אַשְׁרֵי אָדָם אֲשֶׁר עוֹז לוֹ בוֹ. תהלים יח

ש״ץ: נָבָר וְנָעִים, נָאוֹר וְנוֹרָא / נֶאְדָּר וְנֶאְזָר שְׁמוֹ בִּגְבוּרָה.

קהל: נֶאֱמָן, נֵצַח יִשְׂרָאֵל וְגוֹאֲלוֹ / לֹא יְשַׁקֵּר, אַשְׁרֵי כָּל־חוֹכֵי לוֹ: ישעיה ל

ש״ץ: נֵצַח יְשֻׁרוּן, הָאֵל הַנֶּאֱמָן / מֵאֱלֹהָיו יְהוּדָה לֹא אַלְמָן.

קהל: נִפְלָא עַל כָּל הַנִּפְלָאִים / וּמִתְנַשֵּׂא לְכָל הַנְּשָׂאִים.

Leader: Sanctified and revered is my Holy One; / firmly established and exalted is my LORD, my Standard.

Cong: God of vengeance, He maintains His anger / toward His foes; He treats His enemies like a warrior.

Leader: The LORD is my lamp when He illuminates His lamp / above my head; His word serves as a candle for my path.

Cong: My LORD, my Rock, supports and sustains; / He is patient and forgiving, He bears my sins.

Leader: God is my Witness, my Rock and my Shelter; / He forgives and bears; He sustains me; He is my Hope.

Cong: Our Rock and our Fortress; / our Succor and Rescuer.

Leader: He is mighty and strong, my Strength and my Help; / the One On High is my strength; may He not be my enemy.

Cong: He placed angels around His concealed presence; / indeed, You are a concealed God. *Is. 45*

Leader: He is a swift witness when visiting punishment upon His enemies; / He safeguards His covenant and kindness for His beloved.

Cong: He redeemed His beloved Abraham; / He shall redeem Israel His servant.

Leader: The One feared by Isaac shall cast His fear / upon the foes of the children of His servant Jacob.

Cong: My Creator seeks out and examines / all hearts; I shall show Him righteousness.

Leader: He is like a parcel of myrrh, a cluster of henna; / He offers His nation redemption from sin.

Cong: The Beloved One is bright and ruddy; He is the Master of His hosts; / therefore He is called the LORD of hosts.

Leader: The LORD is righteous, the perfect Rock; / I shall eternally trust the Rock of worlds.

Cong: The hosts of heaven bow to Him; / Seraphim stand beside Him. *Is. 6*

Leader: He is sanctified by a variety of holy declarations; / three bands of angels recite the threefold Kedusha.

Cong: The living God exists forever; / the Master of the earth and the heavens.

Leader: My Creator is merciful yet He is zealous toward His foes; / my Deliverer is close to those who call out to Him.

Cong: He is distant from all, yet He sees all; / the LORD is lofty, yet He sees the lowly.

Leader: The LORD is my Shepherd, I shall not want; / He possesses great strength and does much kindness with all.

Cong: The LORD is merciful: He heals and binds up the wounds / of the brokenhearted and suppresses sin.

Leader: My Friend is wholly desirable; / His laws are true, sweet and precious.

Cong: The first and the last from now until / eternity, You are God who abides forever.

ש״ץ: נִקְדָּשׁ וְנַעֲרָץ, אֱלֹהֵי קְדוֹשִׁי / נָכוֹן וְנִשְׂגָּב, יהוה נִסִּי.

קהל: נוֹקֵם וְנוֹטֵר וּבַעַל חֵמָה / לְצָרָיו, לְאוֹיְבָיו אִישׁ מִלְחָמָה.

ש״ץ: נֵרִי יהוה, בְּהִלּוֹ נֵרוֹ / עֲלֵי רֹאשִׁי, וְנֵר לְרַגְלִי דְּבָרוֹ.

קהל: סוֹמֵךְ וְסוֹעֵד, יהוה סַלְעִי / סוֹבֵל וְסוֹלֵחַ וְנוֹשֵׂא פִשְׁעִי.

ש״ץ: סַהֲדִי יהוה, סַלְעִי וְסִתְרִי / סוֹלֵחַ וְסוֹבֵל, סַעֲדִי וְסִבְרִי.

קהל: סַלְעֵנוּ וּמְצוּדָתֵנוּ / עֶזְרָתֵנוּ וּמְפַלְטֵנוּ.

ש״ץ: עִזּוּז וְגִבּוֹר, עֻזִּי וְעֶזְרִי / עֶלְיוֹן, עֹז לִי, אַל יְהִי עָרִי.

קהל: עִיר וְקַדִּישׁ שָׁת סְבִיבָיו סֵתֶר / אָכֵן אַתָּה אֵל מִסְתַּתֵּר: ישעיה מה

ש״ץ: עֵד מְמַהֵר לְשַׁלֵּם גְּמוּל לְאוֹיְבָיו / שֹׁמֵר הַבְּרִית וְחֶסֶד לְאֹהֲבָיו.

קהל: פָּדָה אֶת אַבְרָהָם יְדִידוֹ / הוּא יִפְדֶּה יִשְׂרָאֵל עַבְדּוֹ.

ש״ץ: פַּחַד יִצְחָק יִתֵּן פַּחְדּוֹ / עַל צָרֵי בְּנֵי יַעֲקֹב עַבְדּוֹ.

קהל: פּוֹעֲלִי חוֹקֵר וְדוֹרֵשׁ וּבוֹדֵק / כָּל לְבָבוֹת, לוֹ אֶתֵּן צֶדֶק.

ש״ץ: צְרוֹר הַמֹּר, אֶשְׁכּוֹל הַכֹּפֶר / נוֹתֵן לְעַמּוֹ צָרָיו כֹּפֶר.

קהל: צַח וְאָדוֹם, דּוֹד בִּצְבָאָיו אוֹת / עַל כֵּן נִקְרָא יהוה צְבָאוֹת.

ש״ץ: צַדִּיק יהוה הַצּוּר תָּמִים / אֶבְטַח עֲדֵי עַד בְּצוּר עוֹלָמִים.

קהל: צְבָא הַשָּׁמַיִם מִשְׁתַּחֲוִים לוֹ / שְׂרָפִים עֹמְדִים מִמַּעַל לוֹ: ישעיה ו

ש״ץ: קָדוֹשׁ הוּא בְּכָל מִינֵי קְדֻשּׁוֹת / כִּתּוֹת שָׁלֹשׁ, קָדוֹשׁ מְשַׁלְּשׁוֹת.

קהל: קַיָּם לְעָלְמִין אֱלָהָא חַיָּא / מָרֵא דִי אַרְעָא וְדִי שְׁמַיָּא.

ש״ץ: קוֹנִי מְרַחֵם, מְקַנֵּא לְשׂוֹנְאָיו / קֶרֶן יִשְׁעִי, קָרוֹב לְקוֹרְאָיו.

קהל: רָחוֹק מִכֹּל, וְאֶת כֹּל רוֹאֶה / כִּי רָם יהוה וְשָׁפָל יִרְאֶה.

ש״ץ: רוֹעִי יהוה, לֹא אֶחְסַר כֹּל / וְרַב כֹּחַ וְרַב חֶסֶד לַכֹּל.

קהל: רַחוּם יהוה, רוֹפֵא וּמְחַבֵּשׁ / לִשְׁבוּרֵי לֵב, וְעָוֹן כּוֹבֵשׁ.

ש״ץ: רֵעִי כֻּלּוֹ הוּא מַחֲמַדִּים / מִשְׁפָּטָיו אֱמֶת, מְתוּקִים וַחֲמוּדִים.

קהל: רִאשׁוֹן וְאַחֲרוֹן, מֵעוֹלָם וְעַד / עוֹלָם, אַתָּה אֵל שׁוֹכֵן עַד.

Leader: The King of the heavens shall reign for all generations; / it is He that I praise, exalt and glorify.

Cong: A Sun and a Shield is our LORD God; / a righteous Judge who lays the haughty low. *Ps. 84*

Leader: A Stronghold of strength – we cannot reveal Him; / He is exalted in His might – who is like Him?

Cong: His name is Solomon for peace (Shalom) is His alone; / He shall speak peace unto His devoted ones.

Leader: The name of the LORD is "I will be what I shall be"; / He is like the lofty horns of the wild ox to His people; He is like a lion.

Cong: The Almighty, my Light, my King and God; / Halleluya! My soul shall praise His name.

Leader: You act uprightly with the righteous who dwell among Your plantations; / the tendrils are the three shepherds [our forefathers].

Cong: You act kindly, purely, with their descendants; / while the twisted are dealt with tortuously until they are overwhelmed.

Leader: Your path is perfect, O mightiest One; / You alone are capable of doing everything.

Cong: You are my Expectation, my Promise, my Hope; / subject of my soul's desire and longing.

Leader: My Praise, my Glory, my Strength; the One who brought me out of my mother's womb.

Cong: His knowledge is perfect; the knowing God is One; / He seeks out all hearts as one.

Thursday:

Leader: Who is like You, O Teacher of knowledge? / You create the speech of all lips.

Cong: Your thoughts are deep and lofty, / Your years of existence shall never end. *Ps. 102*

Leader: No one taught You Your wisdom, / and no one granted You Your insight.

Cong: You did not receive Your reign from others, / and did not inherit Your dominion.

Leader: Forever Yours alone / and never shared by others, shall be Your majestic glory.

Cong: And You will never grant to foreign gods / Your glory, nor to idols or strange deities.

Leader: All glory and honor is from You; / Your honor shall never belong to other gods.

Cong: You shall testify to Your own Oneness, / and so shall Your Torah and Your servants.

Leader: Our God, to Your Oneness / You are true Witness, and we are Your servants.

Cong: No god preceded You, / and in Your creation, no stranger collaborated with You.

מִי כָמְוֹךָ *Who is like You?* A hymn to the intricate wisdom with which God created and sustains the world. God transcends all categories of space and time. All things fade; God alone is eternal, transcendent, undiminished, everlasting.

ש״ץ: שַׁלִּיט, מֶלֶךְ שְׁמַיָּא, בְּכָל דָּר וְדָר / לֵהּ אֲנָא מְשַׁבַּח, מְרוֹמֵם וּמְהַדַּר.

קהל: שֶׁמֶשׁ וּמָגֵן יהוה אֱלֹהִים: / שׁוֹפֵט צֶדֶק וּמַשְׁפִּיל גְּבוֹהִים. תהלים פד

ש״ץ: שַׂגִּיא כֹחַ, לֹא מְצָאנֻהוּ / יַשְׂגִּיב בְּכֹחוֹ, וּמִי כָמוֹהוּ.

קהל: שְׁלֹמֹה שְׁמוֹ, כִּי שֶׁלּוֹ שָׁלוֹם / כִּי יְדַבֵּר אֶל חֲסִידָיו שָׁלוֹם.

ש״ץ: שֵׁם יהוה אֶהְיֶה אֲשֶׁר אֶהְיֶה / כְּתוֹעֲפֹת רְאֵם לוֹ, כַּכְּפִיר וּכְאַרְיֵה.

קהל: שַׁדַּי מְאוֹרִי, מַלְכִּי וְאֵלִי / הַלְלוּיָהּ שְׁמוֹ נַפְשִׁי הַלְלִי.

ש״ץ: תִּתַּמָּם עִם יוֹשְׁבֵי נְטָעִים / הַשָּׂרִיגִים שְׁלֹשֶׁת הָרוֹעִים.

קהל: תִּתְחַסָּד, תִּתָּבַר עִמָּם / וְעִם עִקְּשִׁים תִּתְפַּל לְהָמָם.

ש״ץ: תָּמִים דַּרְכְּךָ, תַּקִּיף מִכֹּל / תּוּכַל לְבַדְּךָ לַעֲשׂוֹת אֶת כֹּל.

קהל: תּוֹחַלְתִּי וְסִבְרִי וְתִקְוָתִי / תַּאֲוַת נַפְשִׁי וּתְשׁוּקָתִי.

ש״ץ: תְּהִלָּתִי וְתִפְאַרְתִּי וְעֻזִּי / מִמְּעֵי אִמִּי גּוֹחִי וְגוֹזִי.

קהל: תְּמִים דֵּעִים, אֵל דֵּעוֹת אֶחָד / כָּל הַלְּבָבוֹת דּוֹרֵשׁ יָחַד.

Thursday:

ש״ץ: מִי כָמוֹךָ, דֵּעָה מוֹרֶה / נִיב שְׂפָתַיִם אַתָּה בוֹרֵא.

קהל: מַחְשְׁבֹתֶיךָ עָמְקוּ וָרָמוּ / וּשְׁנוֹתֶיךָ לֹא יִתָּמּוּ: תהלים קב

ש״ץ: לֹא לִמְּדוּךָ חָכְמָתֶךָ / וְלֹא הֱבִינוּךָ תְּבוּנָתֶךָ.

קהל: לֹא קִבַּלְתָּ מַלְכוּתְךָ / וְלֹא יָרַשְׁתָּ מֶמְשַׁלְתֶּךָ.

ש״ץ: לְעוֹלָם יְהִי לְךָ לְבַדֶּךָ / וְלֹא לַאֲחֵרִים, כְּבוֹד הוֹדֶךָ.

קהל: וְלֹא תִתֵּן לֵאלֹהִים אֲחֵרִים / תְּהִלָּתְךָ, לַפְּסִילִים וְזָרִים.

ש״ץ: וְכָבוֹד וְגַם כָּל יְקָר מֵאִתָּךְ / וּכְבוֹדְךָ לֹא לְזָרִים אִתָּךְ.

קהל: אַתָּה תָעִיד בְּיִחוּדֶךָ / וְתוֹרָתְךָ וַעֲבָדֶיךָ.

ש״ץ: אֱלֹהֵינוּ, עַל יִחוּדֶךָ / אַתָּה עֵד אֱמֶת, וַאֲנַחְנוּ עֲבָדֶיךָ.

קהל: לְפָנֶיךָ, לֹא אֵל הִקְדִּימְךָ / וּבִמְלַאכְתְּךָ אֵין זָר עִמָּךְ.

Leader: You did not receive counsel and were not instructed / when, in Your own great insight, You invented creatures.

Cong: From within the depths of Your thoughts / and heart, came all Your actions.

Leader: We have come to know but some of Your ways; / we have recognized You through some of Your deeds.

Cong: For You are the God who created all / alone, yet nothing was diminished from Your greatness.

Leader: You were not pressed to perform Your work; / neither did You require the help of others.

Cong: For You existed before all, / and even then You needed nothing.

Leader: For out of love for Your servants, / You created all for Your glory.

Cong: And no God but You exists; / none is like You and there is none but You.

Leader: No other has been heard of from that time onwards; none has risen or existed nor been seen.

Cong: And after You, there will be no other god – / the God of Israel is both first and last!

Leader: Blessed are You, unique and singular One; / The LORD is One and His name is One. *Zech. 14*

Cong: For who can perform works, / deeds and mighty miracles such as Yours?

Leader: No creation exists but Yours, / and no work exists but Yours alone.

Cong: You do whatever You desire with regard to all, / for You are exalted above all.

Leader: There is none like You and none other than You, / for there is no God but You.

Cong: You, God, work wonders; / nothing is beyond You. *Ps. 77*

Leader: Who is like You, awesome in praises? / You alone, God, perform great miracles.

Cong: There are no miracles like Your miracles, / no wonders like Your wonders.

Leader: There is no insight like Your insight, / no greatness like Your greatness.

Cong: For Your thoughts are very deep; / the ways of Your conduct are lofty.

Leader: There is no majesty like Your majesty, / no humility like Your humility.

Cong: There is no holiness like Your holiness, / no nearness like Your nearness.

Leader: There is no righteousness like Your righteousness, / no salvation like Your salvation.

Cong: There is no strong arm like Your strong arm, / no sound as loud as Your mighty thunder.

Leader: There is no mercy like Your mercy, / no compassion like Your compassion.

Cong: There is no divinity like Your divinity; / none can do wonders as can Your glorious name.

ש״ץ: לֹא נוֹעַצְתָּ וְלֹא לָמַדְתָּ / בְּחַדֶּשְׁךָ בְּרִיּוֹת, כִּי נְבוֹנוֹתָ.

קהל: מִמַּעֲמַקֵּי מַחְשְׁבוֹתֶיךָ / וּמִלִּבְּךָ, כָּל פְּעֻלּוֹתֶיךָ.

ש״ץ: קְצוֹת דְּרָכֶיךָ הֲלֹא הִכַּרְנוּ / וּמִמַּעֲשֶׂיךָ הֵן יָדַעְנוּ.

קהל: שֶׁאַתָּה אֵל, כֹּל יָצַרְתָּ / לְבַדְּךָ, מְאוּמָה לֹא נִגְרַעְתָּ.

ש״ץ: לַעֲשׂוֹת מְלַאכְתְּךָ, לֹא לְחַצְתָּ / וְגַם לְעֵזֶר לֹא נִצְרַכְתָּ.

קהל: כִּי הָיִיתָ לִפְנֵי הַכֹּל / וְאָז בְּאֵין כֹּל, לֹא נִצְרַכְתָּ כֹּל.

ש״ץ: כִּי מֵאַהֲבָתְךָ עֲבָדֶיךָ / כֹּל בָּרָאתָ לִכְבוֹדֶךָ.

קהל: וְלֹא נוֹדַע אֵל זוּלָתֶךָ / וְאֵין כָּמוֹךָ וְאֵין בִּלְתֶּךָ.

ש״ץ: וְלֹא נִשְׁמַע מִן אָז וְהָלְאָה / וְלֹא קָם וְלֹא נִהְיָה וְלֹא נִרְאָה.

קהל: וְגַם אַחֲרֶיךָ לֹא יִהְיֶה אֵל / רִאשׁוֹן וְאַחֲרוֹן, אֵל יִשְׂרָאֵל.

ש״ץ: בָּרוּךְ אַתָּה, יָחִיד וּמְיֻחָד / יהוה אֶחָד וּשְׁמוֹ אֶחָד: זכריה יד

קהל: אֲשֶׁר מִי יַעֲשֶׂה כְּמְלַאכְתֶּךָ / כְּמַעֲשֶׂיךָ וְכִגְבוּרֹתֶךָ.

ש״ץ: אֵין יְצִיר זוּלַת יְצִירָתֶךָ / וְאֵין בְּרִיאָה כִּי אִם בְּרִיאָתֶךָ.

קהל: כָּל אֲשֶׁר תַּחְפּוֹץ, תַּעֲשֶׂה בַכֹּל / כִּי אַתָּה נַעֲלֵיתָ עַל כֹּל.

ש״ץ: אֵין כָּמוֹךָ וְאֵין בִּלְתֶּךָ / כִּי אֵין אֱלֹהִים זוּלָתֶךָ.

קהל: אַתָּה הָאֵל עֹשֵׂה פֶלֶא: / וְדָבָר מִמְּךָ לֹא יִפָּלֵא. תהלים עז

ש״ץ: מִי כָמוֹךָ נוֹרָא תְהִלּוֹת / אֱלֹהִים לְבַדְּךָ עוֹשֶׂה גְדוֹלוֹת.

קהל: אֵין אוֹתוֹת כְּמוֹ אוֹתוֹתֶיךָ / אַף אֵין מוֹפֵת כְּמוֹ מוֹפְתֶיךָ.

ש״ץ: אֵין תְּבוּנָה כִּתְבוּנָתֶךָ / אֵין גְּדֻלָּה כִּגְדֻלָּתֶךָ.

קהל: כִּי מְאֹד עָמְקוּ מַחְשְׁבוֹתֶיךָ / וְגָבְהוּ דַּרְכֵי אָרְחוֹתֶיךָ.

ש״ץ: אֵין גַּאֲוָה כְּמוֹ גַאֲוָתֶךָ / אַף אֵין עֲנָוָה כְּעַנְוָתֶךָ.

קהל: אֵין קְדֻשָּׁה כִּקְדֻשָּׁתֶךָ / אֵין קְרֵבוּת כְּמוֹ קְרֵבוּתֶךָ.

ש״ץ: אֵין צְדָקָה כְּמוֹ צִדְקָתֶךָ / אֵין תְּשׁוּעָה כִּתְשׁוּעָתֶךָ.

קהל: אֵין זְרוֹעַ כִּזְרוֹעוֹתֶיךָ / אֵין קוֹל כְּרַעַם גְּבוּרוֹתֶיךָ.

ש״ץ: אֵין רַחֲמִים כְּרַחֲמָנוּתֶךָ / אֵין חֲנִינוּת כַּחֲנִינוּתֶךָ.

קהל: אֵין אֱלָהוּת כֶּאֱלָהוּתֶךָ / וְאֵין מַפְלִיא כְּשֵׁם תִּפְאַרְתֶּךָ.

Leader: For in Your name the angels make haste, / to work wonders for Your oppressed people when You remember them.

Cong: Enchanters and sorcerers do not press You; / no spell or enchantment can defeat You.

Leader: Even all shrewd men could never defeat You, / nor magicians and sorcerers.

Cong: You leave wise men dumbfounded; / crafty men and magicians could never overpower You.

Leader: None could reverse Your plans / or void the counsel of Your concealed decrees.

Cong: You shall never be swayed from Your will; / none can cause You to hasten or delay it.

Leader: Your counsel shall void the counsel of all advisers; / Your might weakens the hearts of brave men.

Cong: You alone command all; Your dread straightens the paths of men; / no one gives You orders or commands You.

Leader: You are the hope of all – but You do not hope; / You satiate all souls who await You.

Cong: And all creatures and all that is theirs – / Your honor cannot be fathomed.

Leader: Your thoughts are not like their thoughts, / for there is no creator but You alone.

Cong: Our God is extraordinary and cannot be compared; / no one can grasp our Master's loftiness.

Leader: He is the most hidden of all hidden, concealed / of all concealed, and of all enshrouded.

Cong: More veiled than anything veiled; more deeply encrypted than anything encrypted; more powerful than any powerful being.

Leader: Exalted above all that is exalted; more mysterious / than any mysterious thing; His name is everlasting.

Cong: Higher than the highest being, loftier / than all lofty and all unknowable.

Leader: Concealed, deeper than the deepest; / His knowledge shall evade the heart of he who attempts to know Him.

Cong: For intellect, knowledge and wisdom / lack the power to attribute anything to Him.

Leader: They are incapable of grasping His quality and quantity; / they cannot find any semblance of Him.

Cong: Nor can they attribute to Him chance or temporality; change or subordinacy, / attachment to another or dependence, physical light or darkness.

Leader: They cannot attach to Him an appearance or color; nor any natural thing that is six [like the movements] or seven [like the physical quantities].

Cong: Therefore, all human thought is confused, / all calculations disturbed.

Leader: All thoughts and reflections / are powerless to apply measurements to Him.

Cong: And cannot assess or apply limits to Him, / nor describe Him or expose Him.

ש״ץ: כִּי שְׁמוּעֹתֶיךָ אֵלִים מְרוּצִים / בְּזָכְרְךָ לְחוּצִים, לְהַפְלִיא נְחוּצִים.

קהל: וְאַשָּׁף וְחַרְטֹם לֹא יְלַחֲצוּךָ / וְכָל שֵׁם וְלַהַט לֹא יְנַצְּחוּךָ.

ש״ץ: לֹא יְנַצְּחוּךָ כָּל הַחֲכָמִים / כָּל הַקּוֹסְמִים וְהַחַרְטֻמִּים.

קהל: אַתָּה מֵשִׁיב לְאָחוֹר חֲכָמִים / לֹא יוּכְלוּ לְךָ עֲרוּמִים וְקוֹסְמִים.

ש״ץ: לְהָשִׁיב לְאָחוֹר מְזִמּוֹתֶיךָ / לְהָפֵר עֲצַת סוֹד גְּזֵרָתֶךָ.

קהל: מֵרְצוֹנְךָ לֹא יַעֲבִירוּךָ / לֹא יְמַהֲרוּךָ וְלֹא יְאַחֲרוּךָ.

ש״ץ: עֲצָתְךָ תָּפֵר עֲצַת כָּל יוֹעֲצִים / וְעֻזְּךָ מַחֲלִישׁ לֵב אַמִּיצִים.

קהל: אַתָּה מְצַוֶּה, וּפַחְדְּךָ מַשְׁוֶה / וְאֵין עָלֶיךָ פָּקִיד וּמְצַוֶּה.

ש״ץ: אַתָּה מִקְוֶה וְאֵינְךָ מְקַוֶּה / לְךָ כָּל מְקַוֶּה נֶפֶשׁ תִּרְוֶה.

קהל: וְכָל הַיְצוּרִים וְכָל עִנְיָנָם / וְכָל יְקָר אֲשֶׁר בְּךָ, אֵין דִּמְיוֹנָם.

ש״ץ: לֹא מַחְשְׁבוֹתָם מַחְשְׁבוֹתֶיךָ / כִּי אֵין בּוֹרֵא זוּלָתֶךָ.

קהל: לְאֵין דִּמְיוֹן, נִפְלָא אֱלֹהֵינוּ / לְאֵין חֵקֶר, נִשְׂגָּב אֲדוֹנֵנוּ.

ש״ץ: סָתוּר מִכָּל סָתוּר, וְעָמוּס / מִכָּל עָמוּס, וּמִכָּל כָּמוּס.

קהל: דַּק מִכָּל דַּק, וְצָפוּן מִכָּל / צָפוּן, וְיָכוֹל מִכָּל יָכוֹל.

ש״ץ: נִשְׂגָּב מִכָּל נִשְׂגָּב, וְנֶעְלָם / מִכָּל נֶעְלָם, וּשְׁמוֹ לְעוֹלָם.

קהל: גָּבֹהַּ מִכָּל גָּבֹהַּ, וְעֶלְיוֹן / מִכָּל עֶלְיוֹן וּמִכָּל חֶבְיוֹן.

ש״ץ: חָבוּי וְעָמוֹק מִכָּל עָמוֹק / לֵב כָּל דַּעַת עָלָיו חָמוֹק.

קהל: שֶׁאֵין שֵׂכֶל וּמַדָּע וְחָכְמָה / יְכוֹלִים לְהַשְׁווֹת לוֹ כָּל מְאוּמָה.

ש״ץ: לֹא מַשִּׂיגִים לוֹ אֵיךְ וְכַמָּה / לֹא מוֹצְאִים לוֹ דָּבָר דּוֹמֶה.

קהל: מִקְרֶה וְעַרְעֵר וְשִׁנּוּי וְטָפֵל / וְחֵבֶר וּמִסְמַךְ, אוֹר וְגַם אֹפֶל.

ש״ץ: וְלֹא מוֹצְאִים לוֹ מַרְאֶה וְצֶבַע / וְלֹא כָל טֶבַע אֲשֶׁר שֵׁשׁ וָשֶׁבַע.

קהל: לָכֵן נְבוּכוֹת כָּל עֶשְׁתּוֹנוֹת / וְנִבְהָלוֹת כָּל הַחֶשְׁבּוֹנוֹת.

ש״ץ: וְכָל שַׂרְעַפִּים וְכָל הַרְהוּרִים / נִלְאִים לָשׂוּם בּוֹ שִׁעוּרִים.

קהל: מִלְּשַׁעֲרֵהוּ וּמִלְּהַגְבִּילֵהוּ / מִלְּתָאֲרֵהוּ וּמִלְּפַרְסְמֵהוּ.

Leader: With all our intellect we have searched for Him, / trying with our knowledge to discover what He is.

Cong: We have not discovered His nature nor have we become familiar with Him, / but we have recognized Him from His deeds.

Leader: For He alone is the sole Creator, / a living, omnipotent Being, uniquely wise.

Cong: For He existed before all, / therefore He is called the ancient God.

Leader: He created all from nothingness; / we know that He is omnipotent.

Cong: All His works are performed with wisdom; / we know they are a result of insight.

Leader: When He renews creation each and every day, / we know that He is the God of the universe.

Cong: Since He preceded all, / we know that He is everlasting.

Leader: We must not have doubts about our Creator, / neither in our hearts nor in our words.

Cong: We shall not attribute physicality to Him; / we shall not ascribe to Him subordinacy or form.

Leader: We shall not consider Him to be in a sitting or standing position, / nor a natural species or defined power or limited being.

Cong: He is not like any of the visible beings who were granted intellect / and knowledge in the ten statements of creation.

Leader: Nor can He be defined within the seven physical quantities or six movements, / nor the three decreed characteristics, nor the times or measurements.

Cong: For the Creator has none of these, / since He created them all as one.

Leader: All will shrivel and pass; / they shall perish and come to an end.

Cong: But You shall rise up and waste them away, / for You are forever alive and shall endure.

Friday:

Leader: You alone are the Creator of all things; / Your works cannot be like their Maker.

Cong: All lands cannot contain You, / nor can the heavens sustain You.

Leader: The living waters then whirled about / in fear of You, O living God.

Cong: The earth quaked and the waters took flight; / even the sky dropped water from above.

Leader: You alone spread out the heavens, / extended the earth above the waters. *Ps. 136*

Cong: You created all You desired alone; / You did not need a helpmate.

אַתָּה לְבַדְּךָ *You alone.* A creation hymn, which evokes the language and imagery of Psalm 104 and other biblical passages describing God's wisdom and greatness as evident in nature.

ש״ץ: בְּכָל שִׂכְלֵנוּ חִפַּשְׂנוּהוּ / בְּמַדָּעֵנוּ, לִמְצוֹא מַה הוּא.
קהל: לֹא מְצָאנוּהוּ וְלֹא יְדַעְנוּהוּ / אַךְ מִמַּעֲשָׂיו הִכַּרְנוּהוּ.
ש״ץ: שֶׁהוּא לְבַדּוֹ יוֹצֵר אֶחָד / חַי וְכֹל יוּכַל וְחָכָם מְיֻחָד.
קהל: כִּי הוּא הָיָה לַכֹּל קֹדֶם / עַל כֵּן נִקְרָא אֱלֹהֵי קֶדֶם.
ש״ץ: בַּעֲשׂוֹתוֹ בְּלִי כֹל אֶת הַכֹּל / יָדַעְנוּ כִּי הוּא כֹּל יָכוֹל.
קהל: בַּאֲשֶׁר מַעֲשָׂיו, בְּחָכְמָה כֻּלָּם / יָדַעְנוּ כִּי בְּבִינָה פְעָלָם.
ש״ץ: בְּכָל יוֹם וָיוֹם, בְּחַדְּשׁוֹ כֻלָּם / יָדַעְנוּ כִּי הוּא אֱלֹהֵי עוֹלָם.
קהל: בַּאֲשֶׁר הָיָה קֹדֶם לְכֻלָּם / יָדַעְנוּ כִּי הוּא חַי לְעוֹלָם.
ש״ץ: וְאֵין לְהַרְהֵר אַחַר יוֹצְרֵנוּ / בְּלִבֵּנוּ, וְלֹא בְּסִפּוּרֵנוּ.
קהל: לְמֶמֶשׁ וְגֹדֶשׁ לֹא נְשַׁעֲרֵהוּ / לְטֶפֶל וְתֹאַר לֹא נְדַמֵּהוּ.
ש״ץ: וְלֹא נַחְשְׁבֵהוּ לְעִקָּר וְנִצָּב / וְלֹא לְמִין וְכָל אוֹן, וּלְכָל נִקְצָב.
קהל: כָּל הַנִּרְאִים וְהַנִּשְׂכָּלִים / וְהַמַּדָּעִים בְּעֶשֶׂר כְּלוּלִים.
ש״ץ: וְשֶׁבַע כַּמָּיוֹת וְשֵׁשֶׁת נִדּוֹת / וְשָׁלֹשׁ גְּזֵרוֹת וְעִתּוֹת וּמִדּוֹת.
קהל: הֵן בַּבּוֹרֵא אֵין גַּם אֶחָד / כִּי הוּא בְרָאָם כֻּלָּם יָחַד.
ש״ץ: כֻּלָּם יִבְלוּ, אַף יַחֲלוֹפוּ / הֵם יֹאבֵדוּ וְאַף יָסוּפוּ.
קהל: וְאַתָּה תַעֲמֹד וּתְבַלֶּה כֻּלָּם / כִּי חַי וְקַיָּם אַתָּה לְעוֹלָם.

Friday:

ש״ץ: אַתָּה לְבַדְּךָ, יוֹצֵר כֹּל הוּא / וְלֹא יִדְמֶה מַעֲשֶׂה לְעוֹשֵׂהוּ.
קהל: כָּל הָאֲרָצוֹת לֹא יְכִילוּךָ / וְאַף שָׁמַיִם לֹא יְכַלְכְּלוּךָ.
ש״ץ: אָז יָחִילוּ מַיִם חַיִּים / מִפָּנֶיךָ אֱלֹהִים חַיִּים.
קהל: רָעֲשָׁה אֶרֶץ, וְנָסוּ מַיִם / וְנָטְפוּ מַיִם אַף שָׁמָיִם.
ש״ץ: נוֹטֶה לְבַדְּךָ הַשָּׁמַיִם / רֹקַע הָאָרֶץ עַל־הַמָּיִם: תהלים קלו
קהל: עָשִׂיתָ כָל חֶפְצְךָ לְבַדֶּךָ / וְלֹא נִצְרַכְתָּ עֵזֶר כְּנֶגְדֶּךָ.

Leader: Provider, no one can provide for You; / all is from You, and from Your own hand.

Cong: Your strength and knowledge now is the same as it was then; / Your glory is always with You.

Leader: And You were never tired or weary, / for You did not toil in Your work.

Cong: For all creatures were formed by Your speech; / all You desired was made by Your word.

Leader: And You did not delay nor hasten a thing; / You created everything beautifully in its proper time.

Cong: Without anything You renewed all; / You formed everything without tools.

Leader: You established everything without foundations; / You suspended everything with the will of Your spirit.

Cong: Your arms carry the entire universe / from beginning to end; they never tire.

Leader: In Your eyes, nothing is too difficult; / anything You desire, Your spirit performs.

Cong: You are unlike Your creation; / You cannot be compared to any kind of form.

Leader: No work preceded Yours; / Your wisdom arranged it all.

Cong: Nothing was before or after Your will; / nothing was added to or omitted from what You desired.

Leader: Of all You desired, You forgot nothing; / You did not omit a single thing.

Cong: You neither omitted nor exceeded; / You did not create anything useless.

Leader: You praised Your creations Yourself – who shall degrade them? / No inadequacy can be found among them.

Cong: You began to make them with wisdom; / You completed them with insight and knowledge.

Leader: They are completely formed from beginning to end, / created with befitting truth, uprightness and goodness.

Cong: You preceded Your handiwork / with great compassion and kindness.

Leader: For Your compassion and kindness / have always been upon Your servants.

Cong: And before You even created living beings, You created their sustenance; / before there was one who consumes, You provided nourishment.

Leader: You prepare food for all mouths; / You satisfy the needs of everything according to each being.

Cong: During the first three days of creation / You prepared all the needs of those who were to be created.

Leader: You then robed Yourself in light like a garment, / the splendor of the luminaries opposite Your garment.

Cong: You were very great before any creature existed; / and after creation You became greater still.

Leader: Before garments existed, He donned splendor and honor; / before weavers came to be, He donned majesty.

Cong: Like a robe or a cloak He dons light; / He spreads out the skies like a tent.

ש״ץ: סוֹעֵד, אֵין מִי יְסַעֲדֶךָ / הַכֹּל מִמְּךָ וּמִיָּדֶךָ.

קהל: כְּכֹחֲךָ אָז כֵּן עַתָּה, וְדַעְתְּךָ / וּלְעוֹלָם כָּל כְּבוֹדְךָ אִתָּךְ.

ש״ץ: וְלֹא יָעַפְתָּ וְלֹא יָגַעְתָּ / כִּי בִמְלַאכְתְּךָ לֹא עָמָלְתָּ.

קהל: כִּי בִדְבָרְךָ כָּל יְצוּרֶיךָ / וּמַעֲשֵׂה חֶפְצְךָ בְּמַאֲמָרֶיךָ.

ש״ץ: וְלֹא אִחַרְתּוֹ וְלֹא מִהַרְתּוֹ / הַכֹּל עֲשִׂיתוֹ יָפֶה בְעִתּוֹ.

קהל: מִבְּלִי מְאוּמָה כֹּל חִדַּשְׁתָּ / וְאֶת הַכֹּל בְּלִי כְלִי פָּעָלְתָּ.

ש״ץ: וְעַל לֹא יְסוֹד, הַכֹּל יָסַדְתָּ / בִּרְצוֹן רוּחֲךָ כֹּל תָּלִיתָ.

קהל: זְרוֹעוֹת עוֹלָם אֶת כֹּל נוֹשְׂאוֹת / מֵרֹאשׁ וְעַד סוֹף וְאֵינָם נִלְאוֹת.

ש״ץ: בְּעֵינֶיךָ לֹא דָבָר הִקְשָׁה / רְצוֹנְךָ כָּל דָּבָר, רוּחֲךָ עוֹשָׂה.

קהל: לִפְעֻלָּתְךָ לֹא דָמִיתָ / אֶל כָּל תֹּאַר לֹא שָׁוִיתָ.

ש״ץ: וְלֹא קָדְמָה לִמְלַאכְתְּךָ מְלָאכָה / חָכְמָתְךָ הִיא הַכֹּל עָרְכָה.

קהל: לִרְצוֹנְךָ לֹא קִדְּמוּ וְאִחֲרוּ / וְעַל חֶפְצְךָ לֹא נוֹסְפוּ וְחָסְרוּ.

ש״ץ: מִכָּל חֶפְצְךָ לֹא שָׁכַחְתָּ / וְדָבָר אֶחָד לֹא חִסַּרְתָּ.

קהל: לֹא הֶחְסַרְתָּ וְלֹא הֶעְדַּפְתָּ / וְדָבָר רֵיק בָּם לֹא פָעָלְתָּ.

ש״ץ: אַתָּה תְשַׁבְּחֵם וּמִי הִתְעִיבָם / וְשֶׁמֶץ דָּבָר לֹא נִמְצָא בָם.

קהל: הַחִלּוֹתָ בְּחָכְמָה, עֲשִׂיתָם / בִּתְבוּנָה, וּבְדַעַת כִּלִּיתָם.

ש״ץ: מֵרֵאשִׁית וְעַד אַחֲרִית עֲשׂוּיִים / בֶּאֱמֶת וּבְיֹשֶׁר, וְטוֹב רְאוּיִים.

קהל: הִקְדַּמְתָּ בְּמַעֲשֵׂי יָדֶיךָ / רֹב רַחֲמֶיךָ וַחֲסָדֶיךָ.

ש״ץ: כִּי רַחֲמֶיךָ וַחֲסָדֶיךָ / הֲלֹא מֵעוֹלָם עַל עֲבָדֶיךָ.

קהל: וְעַד לֹא כָּל חַי הוּכַן לְכַלְכֵּל / לִפְנֵי אוֹכֵל תִּתֵּן אֹכֶל.

ש״ץ: וּמָזוֹן וּמָכוֹן תַּעֲשֶׂה בְּפִי כֹל / צָרְכֵי הַכֹּל, כַּאֲשֶׁר לַכֹּל.

קהל: שְׁלֹשֶׁת יָמִים הָרִאשׁוֹנִים / אָז הֱכִינוֹתָם לָאַחֲרוֹנִים.

ש״ץ: אָז עָטִיתָ אוֹר כַּשַּׂלְמָה / אֶדֶר מְאוֹרוֹת מִמּוּל שַׂלְמָה.

קהל: בְּטֶרֶם כָּל יְצוּר, מְאֹד גָּדַלְתָּ / וְאַחַר כֹּל, מְאֹד נִתְגַּדַּלְתָּ.

ש״ץ: אָז בְּאֵין לְבוּשׁ, הוֹד וְהָדָר לוֹבֵשׁ / עַד לֹא אֹרַג, גֵּאוּת לָבֵשׁ.

קהל: אוֹר כַּשַּׂלְמָה וְכִמְעִיל עֹטֶה / שָׁמַיִם כַּיְרִיעָה נוֹטֶה.

Leader: You created pathways for the luminaries, / and they move back and forth pleasantly.

Cong: You separated water from water / when You stretched out the firmament of the sky.

Leader: You created both nourishment and habitat for the swarming creatures of the water, / and birds that fly in the sky.

Cong: The earth became clothed in herbage and grass; / nourishment for wild animals and cattle.

Leader: You planted a garden in a lush corner / for the man You created.

Cong: You made for him a helpmate, / thus fulfilling all that he lacked.

Leader: You handed him domination over all Your creatures; / You placed him above all of them.

Cong: From them to offer up cattle and sheep / which were to be accepted by You on Your altar.

Leader: You made a cloak [of light] for him, to serve You; / thereby granting him holy glory and majesty.

Cong: You placed the wisdom of God inside him, / for You created him for Yourself in the image of God.

Leader: You did not omit from the face of the earth any of man's needs; / all were created with wisdom.

Cong: Your works have greatly increased and proliferated; / Your name, LORD, all shall praise.

Leader: Your works have greatly increased and proliferated; LORD, all Your creatures shall thank You. *Ps. 145*

Cong: You created everything for Your own sake; / all You formed was for Your glory.

Shabbat:

Leader: Long ago, You rested on the seventh day; / therefore, You blessed the Sabbath day.

Cong: Praise is set forth for Your creation entire; / Your devoted ones shall bless You at all times.

Leader: Blessed is the LORD, Creator of all, / the living God, eternal King. *Jer. 10*

Cong: For always upon Your servants / is Your great compassion and kindness.

Leader: In Egypt You began / to make it known that You are exalted

Cong: above all gods, by working / great acts of judgment upon them and their gods.

Leader: When You split the Sea of Reeds, Your nation saw / Your great hand and they were awed.

Cong: You led Your nation so as to create for Yourself / a glorious name, displaying Your greatness.

אָז בַּיּוֹם *Long ago.* A summary of God's kindness to the Israelites, expressing the hope for redemption, the ingathering of exiles and the restoration of the Temple service.

ש״ץ: עָשִׂיתָ בָּם לְאוֹרִים דְּרָכִים / וְרָצוֹא וָשׁוֹב בְּנַחַת מְהַלְּכִים.

קהל: הִבְדַּלְתָּ בֵּין מַיִם לְמָיִם / בְּמְתִיחַת רְקִיעַ הַשָּׁמַיִם.

ש״ץ: מְזוֹנוֹת מְעוֹנוֹת לְשֶׁרֶץ מַיִם / וְעוֹף יְעוֹפֵף עַל הַשָּׁמַיִם.

קהל: עֵשֶׂב וְחָצִיר לְבִשָׁה אֲדָמָה / מַאֲכָל לְחַיָּה וּלְכָל בְּהֵמָה.

ש״ץ: בְּקֶרֶן שֶׁמֶן גַּן נָטַעְתָּ / אֶל הָאָדָם אֲשֶׁר עָשִׂיתָ.

קהל: עֵזֶר כְּנֶגְדּוֹ עָשִׂיתָ לוֹ / דֵּי מַחְסוֹרוֹ אֲשֶׁר יֶחְסַר לוֹ.

ש״ץ: כָּל מַעֲשֶׂיךָ, בְּיָדוֹ תַּתָּה / וְתַחַת רַגְלָיו הַכֹּל שַׁתָּה.

קהל: לְהַעֲלוֹת מֵהֶם בָּקָר וָצֹאן / עַל מִזְבַּחֲךָ יַעֲלוּ לְרָצוֹן.

ש״ץ: עָשִׂיתָ לוֹ כְּתֹנֶת לְשָׁרֵת / לְהַדְרַת קֹדֶשׁ וּלְתִפְאֶרֶת.

קהל: שַׂמְתָּ בְּקִרְבּוֹ חָכְמַת אֱלֹהִים / כִּי יְצַרְתּוֹ לְךָ בְּצֶלֶם אֱלֹהִים.

ש״ץ: לֹא מָנַעְתָּ עַל פְּנֵי אֲדָמָה / צָרְכֵי אָדָם, וְכֻלָּם בְּחָכְמָה.

קהל: מַעֲשֶׂיךָ מְאֹד רַבּוּ וְגָדְלוּ / וְשִׁמְךָ יהוה, כֻּלָּם יְהַלְלוּ.

ש״ץ: רַבּוּ וְגָדְלוּ מְאֹד מַעֲשֶׂיךָ / יוֹדוּךָ יהוה כָּל־מַעֲשֶׂיךָ: תהלים קמה

קהל: כֹּל פָּעַלְתָּ לְמַעַנְךָ / וְלִכְבוֹדְךָ כָּל קִנְיָנְךָ.

שבת:

ש״ץ: אָז בַּיּוֹם הַשְּׁבִיעִי נַחְתָּ / יוֹם הַשַּׁבָּת, עַל כֵּן בֵּרַכְתָּ.

קהל: וְעַל כָּל פֹּעַל תְּהִלָּה עֲרוּכָה / חֲסִידֶיךָ בְּכָל עֵת יְבָרְכוּכָה.

ש״ץ: בָּרוּךְ יהוה יוֹצֵר כֻּלָּם / אֱלֹהִים חַיִּים וּמֶלֶךְ עוֹלָם: ירמיה י

קהל: כִּי מֵעוֹלָם עַל עֲבָדֶיךָ / רֹב רַחֲמֶיךָ וַחֲסָדֶיךָ.

ש״ץ: וּבְמִצְרַיִם הַחִלּוֹתָ / לְהוֹדִיעַ, כִּי מְאֹד נַעֲלֵיתָ.

קהל: עַל כָּל אֱלֹהִים, בַּעֲשׂוֹת בָּהֶם / שְׁפָטִים גְּדֹלִים, וּבֵאלֹהֵיהֶם.

ש״ץ: בְּבָקְעֲךָ יַם סוּף, עַמְּךָ רָאוּ / הַיָּד הַגְּדוֹלָה, וַיִּירָאוּ.

קהל: נִהַגְתָּ עַמְּךָ, לַעֲשׂוֹת לְךָ / שֵׁם תִּפְאֶרֶת, לְהַרְאוֹת גָּדְלָךְ.

Leader: And You spoke to them from the heavens [at Mount Sinai]; / the clouds dropped water.

Cong: You knew their wanderings in the desert, / in a parched land not traversed by any man.

Leader: You gave Your people grain from heaven, / meat as plentiful as dust, and water from the rock.

Cong: You banished many nations and peoples, / that Israel might inherit their land and the toil of nations.

Leader: That they might safeguard the laws and teachings; / the LORD's utterances are all holy. *Ps. 12*

Cong: They luxuriated in fat pastures, / with streams of oil from flint rock.

Leader: When they found rest, they built up Your holy city / and glorified Your holy Temple.

Cong: And You said: I shall dwell here for evermore, / I will surely bless its livelihood. *Ps. 132*

Leader: For there, they shall offer up righteous offerings; / Your priests shall also be clothed in righteousness.

Cong: And the house of Levi shall chant pleasant songs; / they shall ring out cries of joy and sing to You.

Leader: The house of Israel and those who fear the LORD / shall glorify and offer thanks to Your name, O LORD.

Cong: You dealt very kindly with the ancients of our nation; / deal kindly also with their descendants.

Leader: O LORD, please rejoice over us / just as You rejoiced over our ancestors.

Cong: Do good for us and let us multiply, / and for this we shall forever thank You.

Leader: O LORD, build Your city speedily, / for it carries Your name.

Cong: Raise up a ruler from the house of David in Your city; / O LORD, dwell in it forever.

Leader: There, we shall offer up righteous offerings; / our meal-offerings shall be as pleasing to You as in days of old.

Cong: Bless Your people with the light of Your countenance, / for we desire to perform Your will.

Leader: May it be Your will to fulfill our desire; / please, look upon us, for we are Your nation! *Is. 64*

Cong: You have chosen us to be Your treasured nation; / Your blessing is upon Your people, Selah! *Ps. 3*

Leader: And we shall always recount Your praise / and laud Your glorious name.

Cong: May Your nation be blessed from Your own blessing, / for all whom You bless shall be blessed.

Leader: As for me, I shall praise my Creator as long as I live; / I shall bless Him all the days I am allotted in this world.

Cong: Blessed is the name of the LORD forever, / from eternity to eternity. *Ps. 106*

ש״ץ: וְדִבַּרְתָּ עִמָּם מִן הַשָּׁמַיִם / וְגַם הֶעָבִים נָטְפוּ מָיִם.

קהל: יָדַעְתָּ לֶכְתָּם הַמִּדְבָּר / בְּאֶרֶץ צִיָּה, אִישׁ לֹא עָבַר.

ש״ץ: תַּתָּה לְעַמְּךָ דְּגַן שָׁמַיִם / וְכֶעָפָר שְׁאֵר, וּמִצּוּר מָיִם.

קהל: תְּגָרֵשׁ גּוֹיִם רַבִּים, עַמִּים / יִירְשׁוּ אֲרָצָם, וַעֲמַל לְאֻמִּים.

ש״ץ: בַּעֲבוּר יִשְׁמְרוּ חֻקִּים וְתוֹרוֹת / אִמְרוֹת יהוה אֲמָרוֹת טְהֹרוֹת: תהלים יב

קהל: וַיִּתְעַדְּנוּ בְּמִרְעֶה שָׁמֵן / וּמֵחַלָּמִישׁ צוּר פַּלְגֵי שָׁמֶן.

ש״ץ: בְּנוּחָם בָּנוּ עִיר קָדְשֶׁךָ / וַיְפָאֲרוּ בֵּית מִקְדָּשֶׁךָ.

קהל: וַתֹּאמֶר, פֹּה אֵשֵׁב לְאֹרֶךְ / יָמִים, צֵידָהּ בָּרֵךְ אֲבָרֵךְ: תהלים קלב

ש״ץ: כִּי שָׁם יִזְבְּחוּ זִבְחֵי צֶדֶק / אַף כֹּהֲנֶיךָ יִלְבְּשׁוּ צֶדֶק.

קהל: וּבֵית הַלֵּוִי נְעִימוֹת יְזַמְּרוּ / לְךָ יִתְרוֹעֲעוּ אַף יָשִׁירוּ.

ש״ץ: בֵּית יִשְׂרָאֵל וְיִרְאֵי יהוה / יְכַבְּדוּ וְיוֹדוּ שִׁמְךָ יהוה.

קהל: הֲטִיבוֹתָ מְאֹד לָרִאשׁוֹנִים / כֵּן תֵּיטִיב גַּם לָאַחֲרוֹנִים.

ש״ץ: יהוה תָּשִׂישׂ נָא עָלֵינוּ / כַּאֲשֶׁר שַׂשְׂתָּ עַל אֲבוֹתֵינוּ.

קהל: אוֹתָנוּ לְהַרְבּוֹת וּלְהֵיטִיב / וְנוֹדֶה לְךָ לְעוֹלָם כִּי תֵיטִיב.

ש״ץ: יהוה תִּבְנֶה עִירְךָ מְהֵרָה / כִּי עָלֶיהָ שִׁמְךָ נִקְרָא.

קהל: וְקֶרֶן דָּוִד תַּצְמִיחַ בָּהּ / וְתִשְׁכּוֹן לְעוֹלָם יהוה בְּקִרְבָּהּ.

ש״ץ: זִבְחֵי צֶדֶק שָׁמָּה נִזְבְּחָה / וְכִימֵי קֶדֶם תֶּעֱרַב מִנְחָה.

קהל: וּבָרֵךְ עַמְּךָ בְּאוֹר פָּנֶיךָ / כִּי חֲפֵצִים לַעֲשׂוֹת רְצוֹנֶךָ.

ש״ץ: וּבִרְצוֹנְךָ תַּעֲשֶׂה חֶפְצֵנוּ / הַבֶּט־נָא עַמְּךָ כֻלָּנוּ: ישעיה סד

קהל: בְּחַרְתָּנוּ הֱיוֹת לְךָ לְעַם סְגֻלָּה / עַל־עַמְּךָ בִרְכָתֶךָ סֶּלָה: תהלים ג

ש״ץ: וְתָמִיד נְסַפֵּר תְּהִלָּתֶךָ / וּנְהַלֵּל לְשֵׁם תִּפְאַרְתֶּךָ.

קהל: וּמִבִּרְכָתְךָ עַמְּךָ יְבֹרַךְ / כִּי אֵת כֹּל אֲשֶׁר תְּבָרֵךְ מְבֹרָךְ.

ש״ץ: וַאֲנִי בְּעוֹדִי אֲהַלְלָה בּוֹרְאִי / וַאֲבָרְכֵהוּ כָּל יְמֵי צְבָאִי.

קהל: יְהִי שֵׁם יהוה מְבֹרָךְ לְעוֹלָם / מִן־הָעוֹלָם וְעַד הָעוֹלָם: תהלים קו

As it is written: Blessed is the Lord, God of Israel, from this world to eternity. *1 Chr. 16*
And let all the people say "Amen" and "Praise the Lord." Daniel said, "Blessed be *Dan. 2*
the name of the Lord from this world to eternity, for wisdom and might belong
to Him." And it is said: The Levites – Yeshua and Kadmiel, Bani, Ḥashavneya, *Neh. 9*
Sherevia, Hodia, Shevania and Petaḥia – said, "Rise up and bless the Lord your
God, from this world to eternity; may they bless Your glorious name, exalted
above all blessing and praise." And it is said, Blessed is the Lord, God of Israel, *Ps. 106*
from this world to eternity. And all the people said, "Amen, Halleluya." And it is
said, David blessed the Lord in front of the entire assembley. David said, "Blessed *1 Chr. 29*
are You, Lord, God of our father Yisrael, from this world to eternity."

MOURNER'S KADDISH

The following prayer requires the presence of a minyan.
A transliteration can be found on page 1375.

Mourner: יִתְגַּדַּל Magnified and sanctified
may His great name be,
in the world He created by His will.
May He establish His kingdom
in your lifetime and in your days,
and in the lifetime of all the house of Israel,
swiftly and soon – and say: Amen.

All: May His great name be blessed for ever and all time.

Mourner: Blessed and praised,
glorified and exalted,
raised and honored,
uplifted and lauded
be the name of the Holy One, blessed be He,
above and beyond any blessing, song,
praise and consolation
uttered in the world – and say: Amen.

May there be great peace from heaven,
and life for us and all Israel – and say: Amen.

Bow, take three steps back, as if taking leave of the Divine Presence,
then bow, first left, then right, then center, while saying:

May He who makes peace in His high places,
make peace for us and all Israel – and say: Amen.

כַּכָּתוּב: בָּרוּךְ יהוה אֱלֹהֵי יִשְׂרָאֵל מִן־הָעוֹלָם וְעַד־הָעֹלָם, וַיֹּאמְרוּ כָל־הָעָם דברי הימים א׳ טז
אָמֵן, וְהַלֵּל לַיהוה: עָנֵה דָנִיֵּאל וְאָמַר: לֶהֱוֵא שְׁמֵהּ דִּי־אֱלָהָא מְבָרַךְ מִן־עָלְמָא דניאל ב
וְעַד־עָלְמָא, דִּי חָכְמְתָא וּגְבוּרְתָא דִּי־לֵהּ הִיא: וְנֶאֱמַר: וַיֹּאמְרוּ הַלְוִיִּם, יֵשׁוּעַ נחמיה ט
וְקַדְמִיאֵל בָּנִי חֲשַׁבְנְיָה שֵׁרֵבְיָה הוֹדִיָּה שְׁבַנְיָה פְתַחְיָה, קוּמוּ בָּרְכוּ אֶת־יהוה
אֱלֹהֵיכֶם מִן־הָעוֹלָם עַד־הָעוֹלָם, וִיבָרְכוּ שֵׁם כְּבֹדֶךָ, וּמְרוֹמַם עַל־כָּל־בְּרָכָה
וּתְהִלָּה: וְנֶאֱמַר: בָּרוּךְ יהוה אֱלֹהֵי יִשְׂרָאֵל מִן־הָעוֹלָם וְעַד הָעוֹלָם, וְאָמַר תהלים קו
כָּל־הָעָם אָמֵן, הַלְלוּיָהּ: וְנֶאֱמַר: וַיְבָרֶךְ דָּוִיד אֶת־יהוה לְעֵינֵי כָּל־הַקָּהָל, דברי הימים א׳ כט
וַיֹּאמֶר דָּוִיד, בָּרוּךְ אַתָּה יהוה אֱלֹהֵי יִשְׂרָאֵל אָבִינוּ, מֵעוֹלָם וְעַד־עוֹלָם:

קדיש יתום

The following prayer requires the presence of a מנין.
A transliteration can be found on page 1375.

אבל: יִתְגַּדַּל וְיִתְקַדַּשׁ שְׁמֵהּ רַבָּא (קהל: אָמֵן)
בְּעָלְמָא דִּי בְרָא כִרְעוּתֵהּ
וְיַמְלִיךְ מַלְכוּתֵהּ
בְּחַיֵּיכוֹן וּבְיוֹמֵיכוֹן וּבְחַיֵּי דְכָל בֵּית יִשְׂרָאֵל
בַּעֲגָלָא וּבִזְמַן קָרִיב, וְאִמְרוּ אָמֵן. (קהל: אָמֵן)

קהל ואבל: יְהֵא שְׁמֵהּ רַבָּא מְבָרַךְ לְעָלַם וּלְעָלְמֵי עָלְמַיָּא.

אבל: יִתְבָּרַךְ וְיִשְׁתַּבַּח וְיִתְפָּאַר וְיִתְרוֹמַם וְיִתְנַשֵּׂא
וְיִתְהַדָּר וְיִתְעַלֶּה וְיִתְהַלָּל
שְׁמֵהּ דְּקֻדְשָׁא בְּרִיךְ הוּא (קהל: בְּרִיךְ הוּא)
לְעֵלָּא לְעֵלָּא מִכָּל בִּרְכָתָא וְשִׁירָתָא, תֻּשְׁבְּחָתָא וְנֶחֱמָתָא
דַּאֲמִירָן בְּעָלְמָא, וְאִמְרוּ אָמֵן. (קהל: אָמֵן)
יְהֵא שְׁלָמָא רַבָּא מִן שְׁמַיָּא
וְחַיִּים, עָלֵינוּ וְעַל כָּל יִשְׂרָאֵל, וְאִמְרוּ אָמֵן. (קהל: אָמֵן)

Bow, take three steps back, as if taking leave of the Divine Presence, then bow, first left, then right, then center, while saying:

עֹשֶׂה הַשָּׁלוֹם בִּמְרוֹמָיו
הוּא יַעֲשֶׂה שָׁלוֹם עָלֵינוּ וְעַל כָּל יִשְׂרָאֵל, וְאִמְרוּ אָמֵן. (קהל: אָמֵן)

SONG OF GLORY

The Ark is opened and all stand.

Leader: I will sing sweet psalms and I will weave songs,
to You for whom my soul longs.

Cong: My soul yearns for the shelter of Your hand,
that all Your mystic secrets I might understand.

Leader: Whenever I speak of Your glory above,
my heart is yearning for Your love.

Cong: So Your glories I will proclaim,
and in songs of love give honor to Your name.

Leader: I will tell of Your glory though I have not seen You;
imagine and describe You, though I have not known You.

Cong: By the hand of Your prophets, through Your servants' mystery,
You gave a glimpse of Your wondrous majesty.

Leader: Recounting Your grandeur and Your glory,
of Your great deeds they told the story.

Cong: They depicted You, though not as You are,
but as You do: Your acts, Your power.

Leader: They represented You in many visions;
through them all You are One without divisions.

Cong: They saw You, now old, then young,
Your head with gray, with black hair hung.

Leader: Aged on the day of judgment, yet on the day of war,
a young warrior with mighty hands they saw.

Cong: Triumph like a helmet He wore on His head;
His right hand and holy arm to victory have led.

Leader: His curls are filled with dew drops of light,
His locks with fragments of the night.

Cong: He will glory in me, for He delights in me;
My diadem of beauty He shall be.

Leader: His head is like pure beaten gold;
Engraved on His brow, His sacred name behold.

Cong: For grace and glory, beauty and renown,
His people have adorned Him with a crown.

שיר הכבוד

The ארון קודש *is opened and all stand.*

ש״ץ: אַנְעִים זְמִירוֹת וְשִׁירִים אֶאֱרֹג, כִּי אֵלֶיךָ נַפְשִׁי תַעֲרֹג.
קהל: נַפְשִׁי חִמְּדָה בְּצֵל יָדֶךָ, לָדַעַת כָּל רָז סוֹדֶךָ.
ש״ץ: מִדֵּי דַבְּרִי בִּכְבוֹדֶךָ, הוֹמֶה לִבִּי אֶל דּוֹדֶיךָ.
קהל: עַל כֵּן אֲדַבֵּר בְּךָ נִכְבָּדוֹת, וְשִׁמְךָ אֲכַבֵּד בְּשִׁירֵי יְדִידוֹת.
ש״ץ: אֲסַפְּרָה כְבוֹדְךָ וְלֹא רְאִיתִיךָ, אֲדַמְּךָ אֲכַנְּךָ וְלֹא יְדַעְתִּיךָ.
קהל: בְּיַד נְבִיאֶיךָ בְּסוֹד עֲבָדֶיךָ, דִּמִּיתָ הֲדַר כְּבוֹד הוֹדֶךָ.
ש״ץ: גְּדֻלָּתְךָ וּגְבוּרָתֶךָ, כִּנּוּ לְתֹקֶף פְּעֻלָּתֶךָ.
קהל: דִּמּוּ אוֹתְךָ וְלֹא כְּפִי יֶשְׁךָ, וַיְשַׁוּוּךָ לְפִי מַעֲשֶׂיךָ.
ש״ץ: הִמְשִׁילוּךָ בְּרֹב חֶזְיוֹנוֹת, הִנְּךָ אֶחָד בְּכָל דִּמְיוֹנוֹת.
קהל: וַיֶּחֱזוּ בְךָ זִקְנָה וּבַחֲרוּת, וּשְׂעַר רֹאשְׁךָ בְּשֵׂיבָה וְשַׁחֲרוּת.
ש״ץ: זִקְנָה בְּיוֹם דִּין וּבַחֲרוּת בְּיוֹם קְרָב, כְּאִישׁ מִלְחָמוֹת יָדָיו לוֹ רָב.
קהל: חָבַשׁ כּוֹבַע יְשׁוּעָה בְּרֹאשׁוֹ, הוֹשִׁיעָה לּוֹ יְמִינוֹ וּזְרוֹעַ קָדְשׁוֹ.
ש״ץ: טַלְלֵי אוֹרוֹת רֹאשׁוֹ נִמְלָא, קְוֻצּוֹתָיו רְסִיסֵי לָיְלָה.
קהל: יִתְפָּאֵר בִּי כִּי חָפֵץ בִּי, וְהוּא יִהְיֶה לִּי לַעֲטֶרֶת צְבִי.
ש״ץ: כֶּתֶם טָהוֹר פָּז דְּמוּת רֹאשׁוֹ, וְחַק עַל מֵצַח כְּבוֹד שֵׁם קָדְשׁוֹ.
קהל: לְחֵן וּלְכָבוֹד צְבִי תִפְאָרָה, אֻמָּתוֹ לוֹ עִטְּרָה עֲטָרָה.

ANIM ZEMIROT – SONG OF GLORY

A mystical poem, attributed to Rabbi Judah the Pious (Germany, 1150–1217). Its theme is that God appears in many forms – the poet weaves together a long list of the metaphors and metonyms by which He is described by the prophets and poets of Tanakh – yet He remains One. Beyond the diversity of creation is the unity of the Creator. Beneath the noise of events is the music of Being. Behind the many ways in which we experience God – as Warrior,

Leader: Like a youth's, His hair in locks unfurls;
Its black tresses flowing in curls.

Cong: Jerusalem, His splendor, is the dwelling place of right;
may He prize it as His highest delight.

Leader: Like a crown in His hand may His treasured people be,
a turban of beauty and of majesty.

Cong: He bore them, carried them, with a crown He adorned them.
They were precious in His sight, and He honored them.

Leader: His glory is on me; my glory is on Him.
He is near to me when I call to Him.

Cong: He is bright and rosy; red will be His dress,
when He comes from Edom, treading the winepress.

Leader: He showed the tefillin-knot to Moses, humble, wise,
when the LORD's likeness was before his eyes.

Cong: He delights in His people; the humble He does raise –
He glories in them; He sits enthroned upon their praise.

Leader: Your first word, Your call to every age, is true:
O seek the people who seek You.

Cong: My many songs please take and hear
and may my hymn of joy to You come near.

Leader: May my praise be a crown for Your head,
and like incense before You, the prayers I have said.

Cong: May a poor man's song be precious in Your eyes,
like a song sung over sacrifice.

Leader: To the One who sustains all, may my blessing take flight:
Creator, Life-Giver, God of right and might.

Cong: And when I offer blessing, to me Your head incline:
accepting it as spice, fragrant and fine.

Leader: May my prayer be to You sweet song.
For You my soul will always long.

The Ark is closed.

Yours, LORD, are the greatness and the power, the glory, the majesty and *1 Chr. 29*
splendor, for everything in heaven and earth is Yours. Yours, LORD, is the
kingdom; You are exalted as Head over all. ▸ Who can tell of the mighty *Ps. 106*
acts of the LORD and make all His praise be heard?

ש״ץ: מַחְלְפוֹת רֹאשׁוֹ כְּבִימֵי בְחוּרוֹת, קְוֻצּוֹתָיו תַּלְתַּלִּים שְׁחוֹרוֹת.
קהל: נְוֵה הַצֶּדֶק צְבִי תִפְאַרְתּוֹ, יַעֲלֶה נָּא עַל רֹאשׁ שִׂמְחָתוֹ.
ש״ץ: סְגֻלָּתוֹ תְּהִי בְיָדוֹ עֲטֶרֶת, וּצְנִיף מְלוּכָה צְבִי תִפְאֶרֶת.
קהל: עֲמוּסִים נְשָׂאָם, עֲטֶרֶת עִנְּדָם, מֵאֲשֶׁר יָקְרוּ בְעֵינָיו כִּבְּדָם.
ש״ץ: פְּאֵרוֹ עָלַי וּפְאֵרִי עָלָיו, וְקָרוֹב אֵלַי בְּקָרְאִי אֵלָיו.
קהל: צַח וְאָדֹם לִלְבוּשׁוֹ אָדֹם, פּוּרָה בְדָרְכוֹ בְּבוֹאוֹ מֵאֱדוֹם.
ש״ץ: קֶשֶׁר תְּפִלִּין הֶרְאָה לֶעָנָו, תְּמוּנַת יהוה לְנֶגֶד עֵינָיו.
קהל: רוֹצֶה בְעַמּוֹ עֲנָוִים יְפָאֵר, יוֹשֵׁב תְּהִלּוֹת בָּם לְהִתְפָּאֵר.
ש״ץ: רֹאשׁ דְּבָרְךָ אֱמֶת קוֹרֵא מֵרֹאשׁ, דּוֹר וָדוֹר עַם דּוֹרֶשְׁךָ דְּרשׁ.
קהל: שִׁית הֲמוֹן שִׁירַי נָא עָלֶיךָ, וְרִנָּתִי תִּקְרַב אֵלֶיךָ.
ש״ץ: תְּהִלָּתִי תְּהִי לְרֹאשְׁךָ עֲטֶרֶת, וּתְפִלָּתִי תִּכּוֹן קְטֹרֶת.
קהל: תִּיקַר שִׁירַת רָשׁ בְּעֵינֶיךָ, כַּשִּׁיר יוּשַׁר עַל קָרְבָּנֶיךָ.
ש״ץ: בִּרְכָתִי תַעֲלֶה לְרֹאשׁ מַשְׁבִּיר, מְחוֹלֵל וּמוֹלִיד, צַדִּיק כַּבִּיר.
קהל: וּבְבִרְכָתִי תְנַעֲנַע לִי רֹאשׁ, וְאוֹתָהּ קַח לְךָ כִּבְשָׂמִים רֹאשׁ.
ש״ץ: יֶעֱרַב נָא שִׂיחִי עָלֶיךָ, כִּי נַפְשִׁי תַעֲרֹג אֵלֶיךָ.

The ארון קודש *is closed.*

לְךָ יהוה הַגְּדֻלָּה וְהַגְּבוּרָה וְהַתִּפְאֶרֶת וְהַנֵּצַח וְהַהוֹד, כִּי־כֹל בַּשָּׁמַיִם (דברי הימים א׳ כט)
וּבָאָרֶץ, לְךָ יהוה הַמַּמְלָכָה וְהַמִּתְנַשֵּׂא לְכֹל לְרֹאשׁ: › מִי יְמַלֵּל גְּבוּרוֹת (תהלים קו)
יהוה, יַשְׁמִיעַ כָּל־תְּהִלָּתוֹ:

King, Father, Judge, in joy and grief, closeness and distance, intimacy and awe, penitence and praise – there is unity. Hence conflict is not written into the script of existence. As science is beginning to discover, the natural universe exhibits a precisely calibrated harmony of forces. Humans too will one day live in harmony when, together, they acknowledge the unity of God. This lovely poem with its daring imagery was considered by many to be too holy to be said daily. To mark its sanctity, the Ark is opened.

MOURNER'S KADDISH

The following prayer requires the presence of a minyan.
A transliteration can be found on page 1375.

Mourner: יִתְגַּדַּל Magnified and sanctified
may His great name be,
in the world He created by His will.
May He establish His kingdom
in your lifetime and in your days,
and in the lifetime of all the house of Israel,
swiftly and soon –
and say: Amen.

All: May His great name be blessed for ever and all time.

Mourner: Blessed and praised,
glorified and exalted,
raised and honored,
uplifted and lauded
be the name of the Holy One, blessed be He,
above and beyond any blessing, song,
praise and consolation
uttered in the world –
and say: Amen.

May there be great peace from heaven,
and life for us and all Israel –
and say: Amen.

Bow, take three steps back, as if taking leave of the Divine Presence, then bow, first left, then right, then center, while saying:

May He who makes peace in His high places,
make peace for us and all Israel –
and say: Amen.

קדיש יתום

The following prayer requires the presence of a מנין.
A transliteration can be found on page 1375.

אבל: יִתְגַּדַּל וְיִתְקַדַּשׁ שְׁמֵהּ רַבָּא (קהל: אָמֵן)
בְּעָלְמָא דִּי בְרָא כִרְעוּתֵהּ
וְיַמְלִיךְ מַלְכוּתֵהּ
בְּחַיֵּיכוֹן וּבְיוֹמֵיכוֹן וּבְחַיֵּי דְכָל בֵּית יִשְׂרָאֵל
בַּעֲגָלָא וּבִזְמַן קָרִיב
וְאִמְרוּ אָמֵן. (קהל: אָמֵן)

קהל ואבל: יְהֵא שְׁמֵהּ רַבָּא מְבָרַךְ לְעָלַם וּלְעָלְמֵי עָלְמַיָּא.

אבל: יִתְבָּרַךְ וְיִשְׁתַּבַּח וְיִתְפָּאַר וְיִתְרוֹמַם וְיִתְנַשֵּׂא
וְיִתְהַדָּר וְיִתְעַלֶּה וְיִתְהַלָּל
שְׁמֵהּ דְּקֻדְשָׁא בְּרִיךְ הוּא (קהל: בְּרִיךְ הוּא)
לְעֵלָּא לְעֵלָּא מִכָּל בִּרְכָתָא וְשִׁירָתָא, תֻּשְׁבְּחָתָא וְנֶחֱמָתָא
דַּאֲמִירָן בְּעָלְמָא
וְאִמְרוּ אָמֵן. (קהל: אָמֵן)

יְהֵא שְׁלָמָא רַבָּא מִן שְׁמַיָּא
וְחַיִּים, עָלֵינוּ וְעַל כָּל יִשְׂרָאֵל
וְאִמְרוּ אָמֵן. (קהל: אָמֵן)

Bow, take three steps back, as if taking leave of the Divine Presence, then bow, first left, then right, then center, while saying:

עֹשֶׂה הַשָּׁלוֹם בִּמְרוֹמָיו
הוּא יַעֲשֶׂה שָׁלוֹם עָלֵינוּ וְעַל כָּל יִשְׂרָאֵל
וְאִמְרוּ אָמֵן. (קהל: אָמֵן)

מסכת יומא
MASSEKHET YOMA

NOTE TO COMMENTARY ON THE MISHNAYOT

References to the Mishna are often confusing, as the division of each chapter into individual mishnayot changes from edition to edition. Therefore, we have reluctantly adopted the policy of referencing mishnayot according to the page number of the Babylonian Talmud where the mishna appears, such as: Mishna, *Menaḥot* 65a. Mishnayot which have no Talmud tractate are also referenced according to the Vilna edition, such as: Mishna, *Bikkurim* 1:10. The exceptions are the references within *Yoma, Rosh HaShana* and *Avot*, where cross-references to the mishna, translation, and notes appear according to the order we have followed here, in the Koren Rosh HaShana Maḥzor and the Koren Siddur.

Likewise, references to the *Tosefta* are according to the Vilna edition. (Despite some other editions being considered more reliable, the Vilna Talmud edition is still more accessible, and in none of the references does the edition make any substantial difference.)

References to the Jerusalem Talmud have the chapter and mishna according to the Venice 1523 edition, which is the cornerstone for most printed editions. We have used the Hebrew name Yerushalmi.

Unless otherwise specified, a citation of the Talmud refers to the Babylonian Talmud, and a citation of a page or a commentary refers to *Massekhet Yoma*.

Citations of the Rif and his commentators are according to the pages of *Hilkhot Rav Alfas* printed at the back of the Vilna edition. An unspecified reference to Rambam refers to his commentary on the Mishna; an unspecified reference to Rosh refers to his "order of the Yom Kippur service" which is printed before his rulings on chapter eight. Rav Soloveitchik is cited from his *Kuntras Avodat Yom HaKippurim*, second edition, Jerusalem 2005.

In the commentary to the Maḥzor, the names Maimonides and Nahmanides are used; in these notes, we have used the Hebrew acronyms Rambam and Ramban.

The *Tur, Shulḥan Arukh* and commentaries around them are written in longhand; however, we have abbreviated the names of their components: OḤ for *Oraḥ Ḥayyim*, and YD for *Yoreh De'ah* (*Ḥoshen Mishpat* and *Even HaEzer* are not referred to in these notes). Some commentaries only wrote on one of the components, and those we have left unspecified.

Rabbi David Fuchs

Massekhet Yoma

CHAPTER ONE

1 Seven days before the Day of Atonement,
the High Priest is brought away from his house
and taken to the Chamber of Palhedrin,

The Netziv (*Haamek Davar,* Lev. 8:35) makes a further suggestion. The Yom Kippur Temple service is difficult and complex; these seven preparatory days, then, are an opportunity to train the High Priest in all of its details. This first chapter of our tractate, indeed, describes the High Priest practicing the Yom Kippur rituals in these days, (mishna 2), studying the relevant laws (mishna 3), swearing to observe them correctly (mishna 5), and becoming fully ready to perform them when the day arrives. Avoiding defilement is part of this preparation process; avoiding sleep on the night of Yom Kippur is one of the precautions taken (mishna 4, 6, 7).

לְשְׁכַּת פַּלְהֶדְרִין *Chamber of Palhedrin.* In the context of the Temple, the word לִשְׁכָּה refers to any one of a number of chambers within its grounds, used for a variety of functions. The Sanhedrin held court in the לִשְׁכַּת הַגָּזִית, the Chamber of Hewn Stone; another chamber was designated to store the salt for the offerings; the לִשְׁכַּת חֲשָׁאִין, Chamber of the Discreet, enabled people to donate and receive charity in an inconspicuous way. The Mishna (*Midot* 5:4) enumerates six chambers in the Temple courtyard itself, though the Talmud lists many more.

The Chamber of Palhedrin was noteworthy as the only chamber to serve as living quarters (and consequently the only chamber in the Temple with a *mezuza* at its opening: see *Yoma* 10a). The Talmud (19a) debates whether it was on the north side of the courtyard or the south; most commentators agree that it was to the south (see figure 1, page 444).

The word "Parhedrin," as it appears in the Talmud, is borrowed from the Greek meaning "clerks." Specifically, it refers to the subordinate clerks of Roman procurators, who were recruited annually. Rabbi Yehuda (8b–9a) remarks that this was not the chamber's official name; "the Chamber of Balvatei" (the Ministers' Chamber) was given this derogatory label, expressing – as Rashi suggests – disapproval of the political selection of High Priests "in accordance with the 'priesthood money' they paid to the king."

מסכת יומא

פרק ראשון

א שִׁבְעַת יָמִים קֹדֶם יוֹם הַכִּפּוּרִים
מַפְרִישִׁין כֹּהֵן גָּדוֹל מִבֵּיתוֹ לְלִשְׁכַּת פַּלְהֶדְרִין

CHAPTER ONE

After the description of the Tabernacle's construction in the book of Leviticus, we are told of the ceremony that inaugurates Aaron and his sons into the priesthood (chapter eight). Moses dresses them in the priestly vestments and anoints them with the sacred oil, after which they bring special inaugural offerings. They are then secluded inside the Tabernacle for a period of seven days. According to the Talmud Yerushalmi, these seven days parallel the week of Moses' ascent to Mount Sinai, as described in the book of Exodus (24:16).

To this description of the inauguration the Torah appends the words, "As was done on this day, so the Lord has commanded to be done, to make atonement for you" (Lev. 8:34). The *Sifra* (cited by Rashi) derives from this verse that there are two other situations in which these seven days of seclusion are to continue to be observed: the week leading up to Yom Kippur (see אַמִּיץ כֹּחַ, page 881), and the days prior to the burning of the red heifer, which purifies one who has become ritually impure though contact with a dead body.

The Mishna (*Para* 3:1; *Yoma* 8a–b; see also the *Seder HaAvoda piyutim*, pages 881 and 1263) states that during the week leading up to Yom Kippur, the High Priest is purified using the ashes of the red heifer, a process that takes seven days to complete. This may suggest that, besides evoking the inauguration days, this period also serves to shore against the risk that contact with a corpse may have rendered the High Priest impure, and therefore unfit for service. Should this have happened, perhaps without his knowledge, the week of separation and the ritual of the red heifer would be enough to purify him again.

Rabbi Yehuda ben Beteira (*Yoma* 3b, Rambam 1:3) suggests another possible reason for the seven days' separation. Impurity caused by relations with a menstrually impure woman lasts for seven days (Lev. 15:24). A week's separation, then, from his wife, ensures that no mistake or misjudgment will render him invalid for service.

and another priest is appointed as his substitute,
in case something should happen to disqualify him.
Rabbi Yehuda says:
Another wife is appointed to him also,
in case his wife should die –
for it is written, "He shall make atonement for himself and for his house": Lev. 16
his house means "his wife."
The sages say:
But if so, there would be no end to it.

בֵּיתוֹ – זוֹ אִשְׁתּוֹ *His house means "his wife."* The phrase "He shall make atonement for himself and for his house" is taken from the Yom Kippur service described in Leviticus (our translation there, page 728, is slightly different in its context). The phrase appears twice in this passage (verses 6 and 11), and the rabbis understand the first to refer to the High Priest's personal household – his family – and the second, to his tribal house, the entire priesthood. The High Priest is required to offer an independent confession for each of these two "houses."

Rabbi Yehuda understands "his house" in the specific sense of "his wife," in line with Rabbi Yose's saying "I have never called my wife, 'my wife'; I call her 'my house'" (*Shabbat* 118b). Rabbi Yehuda further rules that the High Priest's confession for his household is an essential part of the Yom Kippur service, without which he is unable to atone for the rest of the people. Therefore, another woman is designated to take the place of his wife, in the event of his current wife dying suddenly.

This ruling is reflected in the custom, first mentioned in the *Kol Bo* (65), always to select a married man to lead the prayers on the High Holidays, and the *Seliḥot* on the preceding days (Rema, *OḤ* 581:1). Later authorities, however, stress that the leader's moral goodness and acceptance by the community are more important selection criteria than his marital status (*Mishna Berura* ibid. 13).

אֵין לַדָּבָר סוֹף *There would be no end to it.* The Talmud in *Yevamot* 26a–b discusses at length the extent to which one may legally presume that a person will continue to live; in certain situations one is required to take precautions for the eventuality of a person dying without warning. The passage discusses these circumstances and concludes that while one must take precautions

וּמַתְקִינִין לוֹ כֹּהֵן אַחֵר תַּחְתָּיו
שֶׁמָּא יֶאֱרַע בּוֹ פְּסוּל.
רַבִּי יְהוּדָה אוֹמֵר:
אַף אִשָּׁה אַחֶרֶת מַתְקִינִין לוֹ
שֶׁמָּא תָמוּת אִשְׁתּוֹ
שֶׁנֶּאֱמַר: וְכִפֶּר בַּעֲדוֹ וּבְעַד בֵּיתוֹ: ויקרא טז
בֵּיתוֹ – זוֹ אִשְׁתּוֹ.
אָמְרוּ לוֹ:
אִם כֵּן, אֵין לַדָּבָר סוֹף.

וּמַתְקִינִין לוֹ כֹּהֵן אַחֵר תַּחְתָּיו *And another priest is appointed as his substitute.* The appointment of a substitute High Priest to be on standby from this early stage seems to be a precaution, aimed to avoid delays in the event that a replacement should be needed at the last minute. *Tosafot Yeshanim* (2a) note that an entirely new set of the priestly garments would have to be tailored for the substitute – a lengthy and expensive process (see mishna 3:7). The Talmud (13a) highlights a psychological advantage of the preemptive appointment; conscious that a substitute is readily available to replace him, the High Priest would be likely to be extra vigilant, to avoid any mistakes that might disqualify him.

יֶאֱרַע בּוֹ פְּסוּל *Disqualify him.* The mishna in *Avot* (5:5) lists ten miracles that happened in the Temple; one of them is the fact that no High Priest was ever defiled by a nocturnal emission on Yom Kippur. The Yerushalmi, however, does record one such case (*Yoma* 1:1), and names Yosef ben Ilem as the replacement. Significantly, though both the *Tosefta* (1:4) and the Talmud Bavli (12b) do cite the case of Yosef ben Ilem's appointment, neither mention why the original High Priest was disqualified.

The Talmud tells us of Yosef ben Ilem's ardent hope that his appointment would be permanent. After being purified, however, the original High Priest was restored to office. This left Yosef ben Ilem in a legal limbo. No longer a High Priest, he was also unable to return to his previous status, as this would have been considered a degradation of the level of sanctity he had obtained in his short term of office (an application of the principle of מַעֲלִין בַּקֹּדֶשׁ וְאֵין מוֹרִידִין, "One may raise a thing in sanctity, but may not lower it").

2 All the seven days beforehand,
he throws the blood [of the daily sacrifices],
burns the incense,
tends the lamps,
and offers up the head and the right hind leg [of the daily sacrifice].

---

remain from the previous day and cleans the lamps out, while the lighting itself takes place only in the evening. Support for this position is found in the words that describe these duties in the Torah: "And Aaron burned the fragrant incense in the morning, as he would improve the lights [...] and when Aaron would raise up the lights in the evening..." (Ex. 30:7–8). "Raise up" suggests the lighting of the lamps, and is distinguished from "improving the lamps" which clearly happens at an earlier stage.

In the mishna's description of the Temple service, the lamps are tended after the throwing of the blood. In Abaye's tradition, however, the tending of the lamps occurs in two stages; five are tended before the blood is thrown, and the other two after. Only when these tasks are complete is the incense burned and then the limbs offered up (page 497). The Talmud (14b, 34b), in line with the mishna, insists that the blood is thrown first. Accepting Abaye's tradition that the lamps were tended in sets of five and two, this account suggests that the task was performed on either side of the burning of the incense. (For the difference between the sets of five and two lamps, see *Tamid* 33a.)

Tosafot (14a) claim that only the last two lamps are tended by the High Priest. Although the Temple rites must be performed by a priest, any priest would be qualified. Similarly, on Yom Kippur, when the High Priest performs all the rites, he need not carry them out from beginning to end, as long as it is he who completes them.

וּמַקְרִיב *Offers up.* The literal meaning of מַקְרִיב is "to bring close." The word is generally used, as here, to denote the actual burning of an offering on the altar. Sometimes, however, it appears in a broader usage, to describe the bringing of an offering to the altar and the placing of its limbs on the ramp (see mishna 2:6).

אֶת הָרֹאשׁ וְאֶת הָרֶגֶל *The head and the right hind leg.* Although all the organs are offered up (see mishna 2:3), the Meiri suggests that during the week prior to Yom Kippur the High Priest only offers up the head and the right hind

ב כָּל שִׁבְעַת הַיָּמִים
הוּא זוֹרֵק אֶת הַדָּם
וּמַקְטִיר אֶת הַקְּטֹרֶת
וּמֵטִיב אֶת הַנֵּרוֹת
וּמַקְרִיב אֶת הָרֹאשׁ וְאֶת הָרֶגֶל;

against the death of one person, there is no need to be concerned about the (smaller) risk of two people dying in close succession.

Although this seems to be in line with Rabbi Yehuda's position in our mishna, the Talmud explains that neither Rabbi Yehuda nor the rabbis there in fact agree with the conclusion of the discussion in *Yevamot* (see *Sukka* 24a). Both, rather, hold that even the risk of one person dying need not concern us under most circumstances. It is because of the gravity and importance of the High Priest's service on Yom Kippur that Rabbi Yehuda asserts the need for extra concern in this case, with preparations being made not only for the High Priest's possible defilement, but also for his possible widowerhood. Even Rabbi Yehuda, however, concedes that there is no need to prepare a third woman for fear that the replacement may also die (13a). He also does not require a second wife to be prepared for the replacement High Priest (*Tosafot Yeshanim*).

The rabbis reject Rabbi Yehuda's heightened concern. Their claim, "אֵין לַדָּבָר סוֹף, There would be no end to it," is used in the mishna (here and in *Pesaḥim* 9a) to reject the compulsion to consider possibilities which would normally not concern us. If we begin to overstep the boundaries of reasonable caution, there is no longer any logical place to stop.

הוּא זוֹרֵק אֶת הַדָּם *He throws the blood.* Rashi (14a) explains that although the High Priest does not normally perform these tasks, he is assigned them now in order to become proficient by Yom Kippur (see the Netziv's comments in the introduction to this chapter).

וּמֵטִיב אֶת הַנֵּרוֹת *Tends the lamps.* The phrase "מֵטִיב אֶת הַנֵּרוֹת" literally means "to improve the lamps." Rambam (*Hilkhot Temidim UMusafim* 3:12) understands this to mean that the High Priest would actually light the lamps. Rashi (*Yoma* 14a) reads it to refer only to the preparation of the lamps. In his understanding, the priest tending the lamps in the morning removes the wicks and oil that

On other days [of the year],
if he wants to perform any offering, he does,
for the High Priest always has first choice to make the offering,
and the first choice of portion to take [from the offering].

3 And elders of the court would be sent to him
and would read him the Order of the Day,
and they would say, "My honored High Priest, you read this out,
in case you have forgotten,
in case you have not learned."

---

the original High Priest – on equal footing with the collective group of all his sons – the lay priests. This privilege, however, is limited to the inner world of the Temple. With regard to tithes and other consecrated items, which need not be brought to the Temple, all priests, including the High Priest, share equal rights (*Tosefta* ibid; Rambam, *Hilkhot Klei HaMikdash* 5:12).

וְקוֹרִין לְפָנָיו בְּסֵדֶר הַיּוֹם *Would read him the Order of the Day.* Most commentaries follow Rashi, who interprets this as a reference to the section of the Torah that deals with the laws of Yom Kippur (Lev. 16). Rambam adds: "They would read before him, and teach him the order of the day," implying this was not just a formal reading, but an active and in-depth study (Rambam appears to be based upon a variant version of the mishna text, as it appears in the Munich manuscript, see *Dikdukei Sofrim* 14a).

אִישִׁי כֹּהֵן גָּדוֹל *My honored High Priest.* Literally, "My man, the High Priest." In the Bible the word אִישִׁי is used by a wife to refer to her husband with a connotation of partnership or love (Rashi, Gen. 4:1 and Hos. 2:18 – and see Rekanati, Gen. 29:32 who associates the term with the word אֵשׁ, "fire"), rather than of legal status. In mishnaic Hebrew, it is used as a respectful term for the High Priest (see *Tamid* 6:3; *Para* 3:8). We have chosen "my honored" to maintain the personal "my" while carrying the deferent tone that an appellation reserved for the High Priest would bear.

שֶׁמָּא לֹא לָמַדְתָּ *In case you have not learned.* There is a stated requirement for the High Priest to be more learned than his brethren (see *Horayot* 9a; *Ḥullin* 134b). This being so, it is surprising that the elders would suspect he may not know the laws of the day. The Talmud (18a) notes, however, that there was

וּשְׁאָר כָּל הַיָּמִים
אִם רָצָה לְהַקְרִיב - מַקְרִיב
שֶׁכֹּהֵן גָּדוֹל מַקְרִיב חֵלֶק בָּרֹאשׁ
וְנוֹטֵל חֵלֶק בָּרֹאשׁ.

ג מָסְרוּ לוֹ זְקֵנִים מִזִּקְנֵי בֵית דִּין
וְקוֹרִין לְפָנָיו בְּסֵדֶר הַיּוֹם
וְאוֹמְרִים לוֹ: אִישִׁי כֹּהֵן גָּדוֹל, קְרָא אַתָּה בְּפִיךָ
שֶׁמָּא שָׁכַחְתָּ אוֹ שֶׁמָּא לֹא לָמַדְתָּ.

---

leg (and so only these are mentioned in the mishna); the rest of the limbs are brought by the other priests. Since the High Priest's involvement is only needed now in order to train him, it is unnecessary for him to offer all parts of the sacrificial animal himself. Rambam, however, rules that "All those seven days, he practices the rites … and burns the limbs of the daily offering upon the altar" (*Hilkhot Avodat Yom HaKippurim* 1:5). In his reading, then, our mishna is only citing examples, and in fact the High Priest offers up all the organs himself (see *Tosafot Yom Tov*, and *Smag*, 209).

וְנוֹטֵל חֵלֶק בָּרֹאשׁ *The first choice of portion to take.* The Torah's instructions concerning the role of a priest conclude with the words, addressed to the people at large, "and you shall hold him sacred" (Lev. 21:8). Rabbi Yishmael explains this to mean that priests must be given honor and precedence over others (*Horayot* 12b); this idea forms the basis for honoring a priest with the first *aliya* to the Torah in the synagogue (*Megilla* 28a, although see also *Gittin* 59a–b), and for inviting him to lead *Birkat HaMazon* (*Shulḥan Arukh* OḤ 201:2, *Mishna Berura* ibid. 12, and *Shakh* YD 246:14).

The Talmud (*Horayot* 12b) applies this rule more broadly, wherever people are differently ranked in sanctity. Thus, the High Priest, who has a higher level of sanctity than a regular priest, is accorded precedence over his fellows. He may therefore choose his portion of an offering even before the priest who brought it (Rashi, *Horayot* 12b).

An extreme example of the High Priest's privilege is in the division of the showbread; he automatically receives half of the bread, while the other half is divided up among the other priests. The *Tosefta* (1:5) derives this practice from the verse (Lev. 2:10) "for Aaron and his sons" which presents Aaron –

On the eve of the Day of Atonement in the morning,
they would stand him at the Eastern Gate
and pass bulls and rams and sheep before him –
so that he would learn to know them well
and be accustomed to the Service.

4 All the seven days beforehand
they would not limit his food or drink;
but on the eve of the Day of Atonement, before dark fell,
they would not let him eat much,
because food brings on sleep.

5 The elders of the court would bring him to the elders of the priesthood,
who would take him up to the Avtinas Upper Chamber
and have him take his oath,
and then would part from him and leave.

The Yerushalmi follows the first of these views; however, Rambam omits any mention of the goats, suggesting that he takes the second view.

מִפְּנֵי שֶׁהַמַּאֲכָל מֵבִיא אֶת הַשֵּׁנָה *Because food brings on sleep.* "Whoever eats and drinks on the ninth [of Tishrei] is considered as if he had fasted both on the ninth and on the tenth" (81b et al.). The Rosh (8:22) understands this to mean that eating and drinking on the day before Yom Kippur is a positive mitzva, aimed at helping people to fast well on the day itself. In the case of the High Priest, however, there is another concern that overrides this. Food brings on sleep, and sleep would carry the risk of the High Priest becoming impure though a nocturnal emission. In spite of the general prescription to eat and drink, then, the High Priest's consumption is limited (see אַמִּיץ כֹּחַ, page 883). The Talmud also provides a list of specific foods he is denied, for fear that they will make him more sleepy (18a).

לַעֲלִיַּת בֵּית אַבְטִינָס *The Avtinas Upper Chamber.* The name בֵּית אַבְטִינָס, "the House of Avtinas," is used to refer both to the priestly family who prepared the incense (see below, 3:11) and to the chamber in the Temple in which they prepared it.

This chamber is named as one of the two chambers of the High Priest (*Yoma* 19a), the other being the Chamber of Palhedrin mentioned in the first

עֶרֶב יוֹם הַכִּפּוּרִים שַׁחֲרִית
מַעֲמִידִין אוֹתוֹ בְּשַׁעַר הַמִּזְרָח
וּמַעֲבִירִין לְפָנָיו פָּרִים וְאֵילִים וּכְבָשִׂים
כְּדֵי שֶׁיְּהֵא מַכִּיר וְרָגִיל בָּעֲבוֹדָה.

ד כָּל שִׁבְעַת הַיָּמִים
לֹא הָיוּ מוֹנְעִין מִמֶּנּוּ מַאֲכָל וּמִשְׁתֶּה.
עֶרֶב יוֹם הַכִּפּוּרִים עִם חֲשֵׁכָה
לֹא הָיוּ מַנִּיחִים אוֹתוֹ לֶאֱכוֹל הַרְבֵּה
מִפְּנֵי שֶׁהַמַּאֲכָל מֵבִיא אֶת הַשֵּׁנָה.

ה מְסָרוּהוּ זִקְנֵי בֵית דִּין לְזִקְנֵי כְהֻנָּה
וְהֶעֱלוּהוּ לַעֲלִיַּת בֵּית אַבְטִינָס
וְהִשְׁבִּיעוּהוּ, וְנִפְטְרוּ וְהָלְכוּ לָהֶם.

---

a marked difference between the standards expected of High Priests in the First Temple, and those actually upheld in the Second Temple. At this time the position was usually not inherited, but purchased from the ruling kings, with the result that many incumbents were not worthy of the role.

פָּרִים וְאֵילִים וּכְבָשִׂים *Bulls and rams and sheep.* The full tally of offerings brought on Yom Kippur is as follows: two bulls (one to atone for the priesthood and one as a part of the Musaf offering); two rams (one as the High Priest's burnt offering, and one as a part of the Musaf offering); three goats (a pair, one of which was to be used as an offering and the other sent to Azazel; and a third as the sin-offering accompanying the Musaf offering); and nine sheep (two for the daily offering, seven as a part of the Musaf offering, and, on Shabbat, two more sheep for the Musaf offering of Shabbat).

The Talmud (18a) notes the omission of the goats from the list in this mishna, and offers two explanations for it. Either the mishna is speaking in general terms, and, although not specified, goats were also passed in front of the High Priest; or else, because the goats were to be used for the sin-offering and so symbolized the sins of the people, it was considered tactless to put them on display before it was absolutely necessary.

This is what they would say:
"My honored High Priest, we are the emissaries of the court
and you are our emissary and an emissary of the court;
we have you swear
by the One who has made His name dwell in this House,
that you will not depart in any detail from what we have taught you."
And he would turn away and weep,
and they would turn away and weep.

---

be disrespectful to enter when not explicitly instructed to do so. The sages (also mentioned by Rashi) understand the verse to explain not the reason for the High Priest's limited access to the Holy of Holies, but the condition under which he is able to enter at all. The "cloud," in their understanding, is the cloud of incense which the High Priest must offer when he approaches.

This part of the Yom Kippur service was the center of a bitter dispute between the sages and the Sadducee dissenters. The Sadducees claimed that if the incense is what affords the High Priest permission to enter the Holy of Holies, it should certainly be offered *before* he enters. The sages, on the other hand, held that as the incense must be offered "in the presence of the Lord" (Lev. 16:13) – that is, inside the Holy of Holies – it should only be burnt after the High Priest has entered.

During the Second Temple period many of the High Priests were Sadducees (see note to 1:3 on the appointment of the High Priest). Since no other person may be in the Temple when the High Priest enters the Holy of Holies (Lev. 16:17), the elders would adjure the High Priest beforehand with a solemn oath to follow the rabbinic practice (19b; and see אַמִּיץ כֹּחַ, page 883).

The *Tosefta* (quoted in 19b, expanded in the Yerushalmi ad loc.) tells of a High Priest who broke his vow and followed the Sadducean teaching regarding the incense; in this narrative the priest is severely punished by God for his brazenness.

פּוֹרְשִׁין וּבוֹכִין *Turn away and weep.* The High Priest wept because he was suspected, and the elders wept, according to the Talmud, because they may have suspected an innocent person, itself a very grave offense (19b). The Yerushalmi suggests, perhaps more simply, that the elders lamented the need they felt to resort to such methods.

The *piyut* אַתָּה כּוֹנַנְתָּ (page 1263) implies that the oath was sworn daily during the week leading up to Yom Kippur.

וְאָמְרוּ לוֹ: אִישִׁי כֹּהֵן גָּדוֹל
אָנוּ שְׁלוּחֵי בֵית דִּין
וְאַתָּה שְׁלוּחֵנוּ וּשְׁלִיחַ בֵּית דִּין;
מַשְׁבִּיעִין אָנוּ עָלֶיךָ בְּמִי שֶׁשִּׁכֵּן שְׁמוֹ בַּבַּיִת הַזֶּה
שֶׁלֹּא תְשַׁנֶּה דָבָר מִכָּל מַה שֶּׁאָמַרְנוּ לָךְ.
הוּא פּוֹרֵשׁ וּבוֹכֶה
וְהֵן פּוֹרְשִׁין וּבוֹכִין.

---

mishna. (See figure 1, page 444 for its location.) According to the mishna in *Tamid* 1:1, בֵּית אַבְטִינָס was one of the two chambers which had upper floors, and one of the three chambers in which young priests would stand guard at night (see also *Midot* 1:1).

Rashi explains that the High Priest is taken there to practice חֲפִינָה, the taking of a handful of incense (see 5:1). The Talmud (47b) lists this as one of the three most difficult rites performed in the Temple. The skill is naturally practiced in the place where the incense is prepared (Meiri). The *Smag* (209) seems to differ with Rashi and states that the High Priest is taken to the chamber only to take his oath, discussed in this chamber because it concerns the rite of burning the incense (see note to 5:1).

שְׁלוּחֵי בֵית דִּין *Emissaries of the court.* The Talmud (*Nedarim* 35b) discusses whether priests are primarily emissaries of God, receiving the offerings from the people as God's representatives, or emissaries of the people, representing the public and their offerings before God. The *Rishonim* (Rashi, *Kiddushin* 23b; Rambam, *Hilkhot Nedarim* 6:5) conclude that they are emissaries of God (see *Keren Ora* in *Nedarim*). With this view in mind, the Talmud (19b) explains that the phrase "our emissary" here refers to a responsibility to study from the elders, and their authority to define the content of the oath, rather than implying a deeper statement of the High Priest's function.

שֶׁלֹּא תְשַׁנֶּה דָבָר מִכָּל מַה שֶּׁאָמַרְנוּ לָךְ *You will not depart in any detail from what we have taught you.* The Torah warns Aaron (and by implication, all future High Priests) not to enter the Holy of Holies except on Yom Kippur, "for I shall be revealed in the cloud" (Lev. 16:2; see Introduction to chapter 5 for a discussion of this). Rashi explains the "cloud" as referring to the Divine Presence. As God's Presence is openly manifest inside the Holy of Holies, it would

6 Then, if he were a scholar, he would interpret Torah;
if not, then scholars would interpret it for him.
If he were accustomed to reading, he would read;
if not, then they would read to him.
What would they read to him?
They read from Job
and from Ezra
and from the books of Chronicles.
Zekharya ben Kevutal says:
I read to him many times
from the book of Daniel.

7 If he began to fall asleep,
then young priests would snap their fingers before him;

בְּדָנִיֵּאל *The book of Daniel.* Zekharya ben Kevutal was one of the priests who stayed up through the night with the High Priest and was, apparently, a distinguished scholar.

The book of Daniel is the only bilingual book in the Bible – half of it (chapters two to seven) is written in Aramaic. Rabbi Isser Yehuda Unterman (Chief Rabbi of Israel 1964–1972; quoted in the commentary of Kehati) explains Zekhariya ben Kevutal's practice as a sad comment on the less educated generation he lived in, that even the High Priest's attention could only be engaged by a text in his vernacular Aramaic. A more charitable explanation is brought by the Meiri, who adds Daniel to the books of special interest (Meiri). This is borne out by the intensive study the book enjoyed in later ages – no less than ten full commentaries by the *Rishonim* are known today. Perhaps the High Priest, before entering the Holy of Holies, needed to reflect upon eschatology, or to fortify himself with the promise of redemption, which is nowhere more explicit than in the book of Daniel.

פִּרְחֵי כְהֻנָּה *Young priests.* Literally, "the flowers of the priesthood," Bartenura explains this term as referring to their newly sprouting beards. Rambam (1:8) and Meiri call them "flowers of Levites," but the term פִּרְחֵי כְהֻנָּה appears in the Mishna and Talmud nearly twenty more times.

בְּאֶצְבַּע צְרְדָה *Would snap their fingers.* The Yerushalmi understands that the young priests would make sounds with their hands and mouths. Most commentaries, however, suggest that they would snap their fingers against

ו אִם הָיָה חָכָם – דּוֹרֵשׁ
וְאִם לָאו – תַּלְמִידֵי חֲכָמִים דּוֹרְשִׁין לְפָנָיו;
וְאִם רָגִיל לִקְרוֹת – קוֹרֵא
וְאִם לָאו – קוֹרִין לְפָנָיו.
וּבַמֶּה קוֹרִין לְפָנָיו?
בְּאִיּוֹב וּבְעֶזְרָא וּבְדִבְרֵי הַיָּמִים.
זְכַרְיָה בֶּן קְבוּטָל אוֹמֵר:
פְּעָמִים הַרְבֵּה קָרִיתִי לְפָנָיו בְּדָנִיֵּאל.

ז בִּקֵּשׁ לְהִתְנַמְנֵם
פִּרְחֵי כְהֻנָּה מַכִּין לְפָנָיו בְּאֶצְבַּע צְרָדָה

דּוֹרֵשׁ *He would interpret Torah.* The Hebrew "דּוֹרֵשׁ" implies not just a recital of the text, but an active study, elucidation and exegeses. The introduction to the *Sifra* includes Rabbi Yishmael's Thirteen Interpretative Principles, which are used to expound (לִדְרוֹשׁ) the Torah (see page 503). This list, however, is not exhaustive; the obscure midrash *Mishnat Rabbi Eliezer* (mentioned by Rashi in II Chronicles 30:19) lists thirty-two additional principles which were used by Rabbi Eliezer the son of Rabbi Yose HaGlili. Rabbi Shimshon of Chinon (France, circa 1300) devotes a section of his *Sefer HaKritot* to explaining these thirty-two principles, (a version of his essay is printed at the back of tractate *Berakhot* in the Vilna Talmud).

These interpretative techniques belong to an oral and social tradition of textual study. The expounding of the High Priest described here is not only an elucidation of the text, but also a public discourse which the other priests could hear and learn from.

Although the High Priest was halakhically required to be a scholar, this was not always the case. Other people, then, were often needed to interpret the Torah for him. In some cases he was not even able to read the Bible to himself, so others would have to read it to him.

בְּאִיּוֹב וּבְעֶזְרָא וּבְדִבְרֵי הַיָּמִים *From Job… Ezra, and… Chronicles.* These books, Rashi explains, are especially interesting, providing extra stimulation to ward off sleep (see *Tiferet Yisrael* which explains why these three books specifically are of particular interest). The Yerushalmi also includes Proverbs and Psalms in the list.

they would say,
"My honored High Priest, rise up, banish sleep, once and for all, against the floor."
And they would keep him occupied
until the time of the slaughtering arrived.

8 On all other days,
the ashes on the altar were taken up at cock's crow or thereabouts,
a little before or after;

---

after the Exile. The practice was not constructive, however, and ultimately led to sin (19b).

תּוֹרְמִין אֶת הַמִּזְבֵּחַ *Ashes... were taken up.* One of the daily services in the Temple was תְּרוּמַת הַדֶּשֶׁן, the removal of ashes from the altar. The altar represents the connection between God and Israel (Rashi, Ex. 20:21) and resting upon it is the נֵר תָּמִיד, the deeply symbolic "eternal flame," which is never to be extinguished (Lev. 6:6). The ashes are removed to ensure that it continues to burn well.

תְּרוּמָה, however, does not literally mean "remove," but rather "lift"; the form evolved in rabbinic Hebrew from the biblical verb הֵרִים, see Leviticus 6:3. (A תְּרוּמָה in the biblical usage of the form is a thing "raised" in status from profane to holy; a gift offered to God.) The term, then, hints at a significance to the lifting of the ashes in itself, beyond the functionality of removing them; the ashes, which are the residue of the offerings brought to God, retain some worth of their own. This perspective is supported by Rashi's view that the *lifting* of the ashes (from their place on the altar to the floor beside it) is performed daily, while their *removal* from the premises is only carried out as required (Lev. 6:4; *Ḥullin* 90a; for an opposing view see Ra'avad on Rambam's *Hilkhot Temidim UMusafim* 2:7 and *Mishneh LaMelekh* ad loc. 2:13). In any case, while the removal of the ashes is performed in ordinary garments, suggesting that it is not a ceremonial service but simply a functional task, the lifting of the ashes is performed in the priestly garments, though only in two of the usual four, suggesting a service which is partly functional and partly ceremonial in its own right.

בִּקְרִיאַת הַגֶּבֶר *At cock's crow.* Literally, "the man's call." The Talmud (20b–21a) debates whether this was the call of a specific man (such as Gevini the crier,

וְאוֹמְרִים לוֹ:
אִישִׁי כֹּהֵן גָּדוֹל, עֲמֹד וְהָפֵג אַחַת עַל הָרִצְפָּה!
וּמַעֲסִיקִין אוֹתוֹ עַד שֶׁיַּגִּיעַ זְמַן הַשְּׁחִיטָה.

ח בְּכָל יוֹם
תּוֹרְמִין אֶת הַמִּזְבֵּחַ בִּקְרִיאַת הַגֶּבֶר אוֹ סָמוּךְ לוֹ
בֵּין לְפָנָיו בֵּין לְאַחֲרָיו;

---

their thumbs (see *Tosafot Yeshanim* 19b for a fuller discussion of the term אֶצְבַּע צְרָדָה).

The *Terumat HaDeshen* (62), a leading halakhic authority in the fifteenth century, uses this mishna to prove that snapping fingers is permitted on Shabbat. The *Shulḥan Arukh*, however, rules otherwise (*OḤ* 339:2), though the *Magen Avraham* permits snapping one's fingers on Shabbat if one's aim is to wake a person up.

וְהָפֵג אַחַת עַל הָרִצְפָּה *Banish sleep... against the floor.* The Talmud (19b) suggests that the High Priest's companions would urge him to practice prostrating himself, which involved lying down on the floor (*Megilla* 22b, based upon I Kings 1:31); the exhilaration of this physical activity and the coolness of the floor would refresh him and restore his alertness. Rambam writes that the High Priest was simply asked to stand on the cool floor, tacitly assuming that the High Priest was barefoot even while waiting in the Avtinas Chamber, as he would have to be while performing the Yom Kippur service. This, however, was certainly not a requirement – wearing shoes is only forbidden in the courtyard (*Zevaḥim* 24a).

The Hebrew phrase הָפֵג אַחַת literally means "banish one." The *Tiferet Yisrael* reads this as a shorthand notation of what they actually said: "Banish sleep, just this once!" Alternatively, it could be understood to refer to the Talmudic proverb, "Sleep is *one* part in sixty of death" (*Berakhot* 57b).

וּמַעֲסִיקִין אוֹתוֹ *Keep him occupied.* The Talmud describes the people of Jerusalem staying up all night, so that the High Priest would hear their bustle outside and feel less inclined to fall asleep. It goes on to relate that this custom was practiced in other places also, even by Diaspora communities

but on the Day of Atonement
they were taken up at midnight –
and on Festivals,
at the first watch –
and by the time the cock would crow,
the courtyard would be crowded with [the people of] Israel.

---

schedule demands that the process begin during the night. Rashi assumes that the *terumat hadeshen* is performed by the High Priest himself. Tosafot disagree, claiming that *terumat hadeshen* is not an integral rite of the day (see above) and so may be performed by a lay priest. As the task is a physically demanding one, however, and the strain of fasting causes weakness, the rite is brought forward to midnight to allow more time for its completion. The Yerushalmi cites Rabbi Mana, who explains that the *terumat hadeshen*, which required the officiating priest to run up and down the altar ramp, close to the burning fire, was so demanding that the rite needed to begin even earlier, as early as the first watch. He suggests emending the mishna accordingly.

עַד שֶׁהָיְתָה הָעֲזָרָה מְלֵאָה *The courtyard would be crowded.* "Festivals" certainly refers to the three pilgrimage festivals, when the pilgrims would arrive early, eager to bring their offerings. The *Tiferet Yisrael* suggests that Yom Kippur may also be included in this statement, bringing, as it did, crowds of people to witness the day's service (see mishna 3:4 and 7:2).

בְּיוֹם הַכִּפּוּרִים מֵחֲצוֹת,
וּבָרְגָלִים מֵאַשְׁמוּרָה הָרִאשׁוֹנָה;
וְלֹא הָיְתָה קְרִיאַת הַגֶּבֶר מַגַּעַת
עַד שֶׁהָיְתָה הָעֲזָרָה מְלֵאָה מִיִּשְׂרָאֵל.

---

who is mentioned in *Shekalim* 5:1) or whether the word גֶּבֶר refers figuratively to the rooster; this is clearly the meaning of the phrase in other places, where it is used, similarly, to describe the beginning of the day. Rambam (*Hilkhot Temidim UMusafim* 2:11) skirts the issue, simply stating that the service begins at dawn.

מֵאַשְׁמוּרָה הָרִאשׁוֹנָה *At the first watch.* The *Tosefta* (cited in *Berakhot* 3b) records a dispute as to whether the night is divided into three or four "watches." Both Rashi (*Yoma* 20a) and Rambam (*Hilkhot Temidim UMusafim* 2:11) take the view that there are only three. On the festivals, then, the ashes are lifted at the very beginning of the second watch.

During the festivals, in order to cope with the large volume of offerings brought by the festival pilgrims, the preparations for each coming day (including the removal of ashes) must begin earlier in the night (20b). On Yom Kippur as well, there is a need to begin preparations early. Rashi explains that since the entire service falls to the High Priest's responsibility, his busy

CHAPTER TWO

1 At first, whoever wished to take up the ashes on the altar
would take them;
and when there were several [priests] who wished to,
they would run up the ramp of the altar,
and the one who was first to reach the upper four cubits,
gained the privilege.

בָּרִאשׁוֹנָה *At first.* The rite of *terumat hadeshen*, the removal of the ashes from the altar, was performed before dawn. It was not a fundamental part of the daily service (see note to 1:8), and it was originally assumed that the priests would not be overly enthusiastic to undertake it, especially at the expense of sleep (Yerushalmi). The low demand for this privilege made it possible to select between the few volunteers by means of a race up the altar ramp. Experience, however, proved the priests' enthusiasm to be more potent than predicted, and the chances of having a clear victor (see mishna 2) were diminished (Rabbeinu Ḥananel). The use of a lottery was therefore extended to this ritual as well. The change proved counterproductive however; with the selection process being founded on chance rather than prowess, the priests' enthusiasm for the privilege waned. To provide the priests with extra incentive to get up in the night, the sages then enacted that the priests who won this lottery would also gain the privileges of setting the piles of wood upon the altar and of bringing up the two logs of kindling wood; the one who removed the ashes, then, essentially became the caretaker of the fire for the day (see note to 2:5) (Rav Ashi in *Yoma* 22a).

בַּכֶּבֶשׁ *The ramp of the altar.* The Torah (Ex. 20:23) forbids the use of stairs to ascend the altar; raising one's legs at each step would breach the high standards of modesty required in the Temple. Therefore, a ramp, thirty two cubits long, was constructed on the altar's southern side (see 4:5). This rose at a gentle gradient to the surrounding ledge, which was just less than nine cubits high.

בְּאַרְבַּע אַמּוֹת *The upper four cubits.* The idea of using a race to select a priest for this privilege perhaps helped to determine which volunteer was most alert and capable of the task in the early pre-dawn. If the race failed to produce an outright winner, a lottery would be held among all the volunteers, not only among those who succeeded in reaching the top of the ramp (Rashi).

פרק שני

א בָּרִאשׁוֹנָה
כָּל מִי שֶׁרוֹצֶה לִתְרוֹם אֶת הַמִּזְבֵּחַ, תּוֹרֵם;
וּבִזְמַן שֶׁהֵן מְרֻבִּין, רָצִין וְעוֹלִין בַּכֶּבֶשׁ
וְכָל הַקּוֹדֵם אֶת חֲבֵרוֹ בְּאַרְבַּע אַמּוֹת – זָכָה.

CHAPTER TWO

This chapter provides an overview of the order of the daily Temple service as it was performed throughout the year. This is presented more fully in *Tamid*, the tractate devoted specifically to this topic. The Yom Kippur service follows the same general structure as the Temple routine of other days, with the significant difference that on the Day of Atonement, the entire service is undertaken by the High Priest (*Horayot* 12b).

The first four *mishnayot* of our chapter describe the lotteries used to allocate the various ceremonial tasks to the priests who would perform them; according to the narrative we know from the *piyut* אַמִּיץ כֹּחַ (see page 883), these lotteries were performed on Yom Kippur as on every other day. Rabbi Zeraḥya HaLevi (*Sefer HaMa'or*, 1a) takes issue with this. He takes the rule that the Yom Kippur service should be performed by the High Priest alone as an absolute one. If this is so, then the details of the role-allocations are listed here without specific relevance to Yom Kippur. In defense of the *piyutim*, Ramban (ibid.) suggests that different rules apply to different parts of the Yom Kippur service; only those rites which are fundamental to Yom Kippur itself require the High Priest; other, more everyday elements of the ceremony may be performed by regular priests. He goes on to demonstrate that all the usual task-lotteries are held on Yom Kippur as on other days. (See note to 1:8 for a parallel dispute between Rashi and Tosafot as to whether the High Priest performs the rite of *terumat hadeshen* on Yom Kippur, which would otherwise be the subject of the first lottery of the day.) Rambam (*Hilkhot Avodat Yom HaKippurim* 4:1) appears to rule that the lottery which allocates the *terumat hadeshen* is held on this day too, while the other lotteries, of which he makes no mention, are omitted.

After narrating the ritual of the lotteries, our chapter goes on to describe how the various offerings were brought, beginning with the daily offering (the *Tamid*), and then moving on to other categories of sacrifice.

If two of them [ran] alike,
the one who gave their appointment would say:
"Put out fingers!"
And what would they hold out?
Any one finger or two;
but one does not hold out a thumb in the Temple.

2 Once, two were alike
and when they had run up the ramp of the altar
one pushed the other and he fell,
and his leg was broken.
When the court saw that they were coming into danger,

---

by actual lots (see note on 3:1). This may be linked to the etymology of the word פְּיָסוֹת; see note on 4:2.

אַחַת אוֹ שְׁתַּיִם *One finger or two.* The *Tosefta* explains that each priest would extend one finger, though a priest who was unable to extend one finger individually was allowed to extend two. In this case, it is noted in the Talmud (23a), his two fingers would be counted as one. Rambam rules, however, that the fingers are indeed each counted separately (*Hilkhot Temidim UMusafim* 4:3; see Rambam's *Responsa,* no. 126). It would appear that he had a variant text of the Talmud; Rabbeinu Ḥananel seemingly shares such a version and explains that only those who were known as *talmidei ḥakhamim* were permitted to extend two fingers, as only they were fully trusted not to cheat (see next note).

וְאֵין מוֹצִיאִין אֲגוּדָל *Does not hold out a thumb.* If a dishonest priest saw that the count was coming to an end, he might extend his thumb, far from his extended finger, to create the illusion that they belonged to two different people, and increase the chances that the count would end with him.

שֶׁבָּאִין לִידֵי סַכָּנָה *Coming into danger.* The Talmud (23a) relates an incident in which the rivalry of the race led one priest to assault his colleague to prevent him reaching the top of the ramp. Although this case was indeed shocking, it was considered exceptional and the races continued. When the sages saw, however, that even under ordinary circumstances priests would push one another accidentally – which could be very dangerous – they abolished the practice, and established the selection lottery, as described in the mishna here.

וְאִם הָיוּ שְׁנֵיהֶם שָׁוִין
הַמְמֻנֶּה אוֹמֵר לָהֶם: הַצְבִּיעוּ;
וּמָה הֵן מוֹצִיאִין?
אַחַת אוֹ שְׁתַּיִם
וְאֵין מוֹצִיאִין אֲגוּדָל בַּמִּקְדָּשׁ.

ב מַעֲשֶׂה שֶׁהָיוּ שְׁנֵיהֶם שָׁוִין וְרָצִין וְעוֹלִין בַּכֶּבֶשׁ
וְדָחַף אֶחָד מֵהֶן אֶת חֲבֵרוֹ
וְנָפַל וְנִשְׁבְּרָה רַגְלוֹ.
וְכֵיוָן שֶׁרָאוּ בֵּית דִּין שֶׁבָּאִין לִידֵי סַכָּנָה

A literal translation of the phrase, כָּל הַקּוֹדֵם אֶת חֲבֵרוֹ בְּאַרְבַּע אַמּוֹת implies that a *lead* of four cubits was required in order to gain the privilege. According to Rashi (22a), however, the rule is that the first to arrive *within* four cubits of the top was selected. (See Maharam di Lunzano, quoted by *Melekhet Shlomo*, who suggests that according to Rashi's explanation, the text of our mishna should be emended; and, indeed, in several manuscripts a slightly different wording is found.)

הַצְבִּיעוּ *Put out fingers.* Rashi (following the *Tosefta* and *Yoma* 22b) describes this method in more detail. Each priest would extend one finger. The administrator would then decide upon a large number, remove the miter of one of the priests and, beginning with him, count the outstretched fingers until he reached the chosen number. According to Ritva, a different priest would choose the number, to prevent the administrator from pre-calculating the result.

The *Tosefta* records that this lottery was held in the Chamber of Hewn Stone (לְשִׁכַּת הַגָּזִית). Rabbeinu Tam (*Tosafot*, 25a s.v. וְהָא) explains that this was necessary because it is forbidden to be bareheaded in the main courtyard of the Temple. Rambam (*Hilkhot Temidim UMusafim* 4:1) writes that even in the Chamber of Hewn Stone, the miter would be returned immediately after the selection; even there, bareheadedness was inappropriate.

Rambam (*Hilkhot Temidim UMusafim* 4:3) rules that all the פַּיָּסוֹת were carried out using this elaborate system of counting fingers. According to Rabbi Yehuda bar Binyamin, however, the subsequent lotteries were determined

they instituted that taking up the ashes on the altar
would only be assigned by lots.
Four sets of lots were cast,
and this was the first.

3 The second set of lots:
who was to slaughter the daily offering,
who was to throw its blood,
who was to clear the ashes from the Inner Altar,
who was to clear the ashes from the Menora,
and who was to place the limbs of the offering on the ramp of the altar:

---

given to the priest who stands immediately next to him; the actual slaughtering of the animal is considered a lesser honor than the throwing of its blood, being valid even when performed by a non-priest (Mishna, *Zevaḥim* 31b). In his *Mishneh Torah*, however, Rambam rules that the first priest selected would indeed perform the slaughtering, as an intuitive reading of our mishna would suggest (*Hilkhot Temidim UMusafim* 4:3).

Ramban, who holds, as discussed in the introduction to this chapter, that the four lotteries were also held on Yom Kippur, suggests that on this day the second lottery only allocated the task of removing the ashes, which need not be carried out by the High Priest.

מִזְבֵּחַ הַפְּנִימִי *The Inner Altar.* There were two altars in the Temple. The Great Altar, in the courtyard, was used for burning offerings, and the Golden Altar (here referred to as the Inner Altar) for burning incense inside the Sanctuary. These parallel the two altars of the original Tabernacle. There, one altar, a copper-plated wooden structure filled with earth, was placed in the courtyard, while another, gold-plated and used for the twice-daily burning of incense, was positioned inside the Curtain (Ex. 20:21, 27:1–8, 40:6; Ex. 30:1–10). In אַמִּיץ כֹּחַ (page 893) the altar is said to be of זָהָב סָגוּר, "high-quality gold" (see Rashi to 1 Kings 6:20 and 1 Kings 10:21). Purifying the Golden Altar was one of the central rites of Yom Kippur (see mishna 5:7).

לַכֶּבֶשׁ *The ramp of the altar.* The mishna in *Shekalim* (8:8) describes where on the ramp the limbs of the different offerings were positioned: "The limbs of the Daily Offering were placed on the lower half of the ramp on the eastern

הִתְקִינוּ שֶׁלֹּא יְהוּ תוֹרְמִין אֶת הַמִּזְבֵּחַ אֶלָּא בַּפַּיִס.
אַרְבָּעָה פְּיָסוֹת הָיוּ שָׁם
וְזֶה הַפַּיִס הָרִאשׁוֹן.

ג הַפַּיִס הַשֵּׁנִי
מִי שׁוֹחֵט
מִי זוֹרֵק
מִי מְדַשֵּׁן מִזְבֵּחַ הַפְּנִימִי
וּמִי מְדַשֵּׁן אֶת הַמְּנוֹרָה
וּמִי מַעֲלֶה אֵבָרִים לַכֶּבֶשׁ:

בַּפַּיִס *By lots.* פַּיִס is usually translated "lottery" (see its usage in *Shabbat* 148b). The *Arukh* suggests that the word literally refers to a fragment of earth or wood (see *Sanhedrin* 64a and *Makkot* 8a), which would often be used for casting lots. Rashi (*Yoma* 14b) suggests that the word is related to אֲסִיפָה, "assembly," as the participants gather together to take part. The *Melekhet Shlomo* offers a third suggestion. פַּיִס, he suggests, is related to פִּיּוּס, "appeasement" or "pacifying"; the lottery, an impartial method of selecting, can help to avoid and resolve conflicts.

הַפַּיִס הַשֵּׁנִי *The second set of lots.* The second lottery distributes thirteen separate privileges; the priest to whom the lot falls receives the main privilege of slaughtering the daily offering, while the other twelve appointments are given to the priests standing next to him (25b).

Bringing the daily offering is considered a more important role than clearing the ashes from the altar, even though, chronologically, it is performed second. The right to bring the offering is therefore awarded first, and so is also listed first in the mishna (*Tosafot Yeshanim*). There is still some question, however, as to how to read this first list of allocations. The slaughtering of the daily offering incorporates four stages known as the "blood rites" – slaughtering the animal, receiving its blood in a bowl, carrying the blood to the altar, and, finally, throwing the blood against its sides. *Tamid* 30b indicates that the three latter tasks are all performed by a single priest. In his Commentary on the Mishna, Rambam writes that the priest to whom the lot falls is allocated these three rites, but he does not slaughter the offering, that privilege being

the head and right hind leg;
the two forelegs;
the rump and the left hind leg;
the breast and the neck;
the two sides;
the intestines;
the meal;
the pan cakes;
and the wine.

Thirteen priests were given these privileges.

Ben Azai said before Rabbi Akiva, in the name of Rabbi Yehoshua:
They would offer up the [parts of the] sheep
in the order in which it walked while alive.

Leviticus 6 requires each priest to bring an inaugural meal-offering, a מִנְחַת חִינּוּךְ, when he first comes to serve in the Tabernacle. The High Priest has to bring a parallel meal-offering called a מִנְחַת חֲבִתִּין, though in his case a new one must be brought every day (see *Menaḥot* 78a and Rashi ad loc., for a discussion as to whether the two offerings were the same). The מִנְחַת חֲבִתִּין is fried in a pan; hence our translation of חֲבִתִּין as "pan cake." This is not an integral part of the daily offering (indeed, Rambam in *Hilkhot Ma'aseh HaKorbanot* 6:16 omits the item from his list of those who carry the daily offering to the altar). One could argue that the mishna includes it here with the daily offering because it serves a parallel function, inaugurating, together with it, the daily service in the Temple. One indication of this is that it must be brought even in the High Priest's absence, for example in the event of his death. In *Menaḥot* 51b, Rabbi Shimon rules that the meal is purchased using public funds. His opinion was rejected, in favor of the view that it was purchased from the deceased High Priest's estate; however, all agree that this offering was an integral part of the daily service.

דֶּרֶךְ הִלּוּכוֹ הָיָה קָרֵב *The order in which it walked while alive.* The Talmud (25b) records other views as to the correct order of the organs. The listing of privileges in the mishna suggests that the better quality meat is brought first. Ben Azai, on the other hand, follows the order in which "the animal walks when alive" – the head, right leg, neck and breast, forelegs, sides, left leg and rump. Rabbi Akiva suggests that as the limbs become available as the animal is carved they are taken directly to the altar. Rabbi Yose proposes the order of

הָרֹאשׁ וְהָרֶגֶל
וּשְׁתֵּי הַיָּדַיִם
הָעֹקֶץ וְהָרֶגֶל
הֶחָזֶה וְהַגֵּרָה
וּשְׁתֵּי הַדְּפָנוֹת
וְהַקְּרָבַיִם
וְהַסֹּלֶת
וְהַחֲבִתִּין
וְהַיַּיִן.
שְׁלֹשָׁה עָשָׂר כֹּהֲנִים זָכוּ בוֹ.
אָמַר בֶּן עַזַּאי לִפְנֵי רַבִּי עֲקִיבָא מִשּׁוּם רַבִּי יְהוֹשֻׁעַ:
דֶּרֶךְ הִלּוּכוֹ הָיָה קָרֵב.

---

side. Those of the Additional offerings, on the lower half on the western side. Those of the New Moon Additional Offering were placed atop the 'rim.'" (The Talmud, *Zevaḥim* 62a, explains that "rim" refers to the area parallel to the ledge, surrounding the altar, on which the priests would walk; see figure 11, page 446.)

וְהַגֵּרָה *The neck.* One of the conditions for an animal to be kosher is that it be מַעֲלֵה גֵרָה, a ruminant (an animal that chews the cud). גֵּרָה, then, clearly refers to part of the animal associated with this particular quality. Ibn Ezra (Lev. 11:3) identifies it as the neck. Rashi understands it to be the esophagus. Commentating on the mishna here, however, even Rashi interprets גֵּרָה as referring to the neck.

The mishna in *Tamid* 4:3 adds that in addition to carrying the neck, this priest would also bring the esophagus, the heart and the lungs, all of which remained attached to it. Indeed, all the entrails were brought to the altar attached to a major organ; the priest carrying the sides would bring the spine, liver and spleen with them; the intestines would be carried together with the haunches.

וְהַחֲבִתִּין *The pan cakes.* The meal and the wine constitute the meal-offering and libations which are brought as part of the daily offering (see page 497).

4 The third set of lots:
"New priests to the incense,
come and cast lots!"

And the fourth:
New priests and experienced,
who will lift the organs from the ramp onto the altar.

5 The daily sacrifice is offered up
by nine, by ten, by eleven and by twelve –
never by less or by more.
How so?
[The offering] itself by nine,
and on Sukkot, one man holds a bowl of water;
this, then, makes ten.

מִי מַעֲלֶה...לַמִּזְבֵּחַ *Who will lift... onto the altar.* Most commentaries (Rashi; Tosafot; Rambam in *Hilkhot Temidim UMusafim* 4:8 and 6:5) understand that only one priest would be selected to lift the organs, here the limbs, to the altar; the burning of the limbs being a functional necessity rather than a fully independent rite (this parallels many opinions regarding the removal of the ashes from the Temple – see note to 1:8). *Tosafot Yeshanim* and Ritva contend that a full set of priests was selected.

Ramban holds with the majority, that it was the High Priest who lifted the limbs onto the altar on Yom Kippur. He explains that a fourth lottery was held to determine who would carry the fats left from the previous day to burn on the fire prepared for them (see 4:6).

Rabbi Eliezer ben Ya'akov (26b) disputes our mishna. He claims the limbs were lifted onto the altar by the same priests who carried them to the ramp. According to him, the fourth lottery was held only to select a priest to bring the coals for the burning of the incense.

לֹא פָּחוּת וְלֹא יוֹתֵר *Never by less or by more.* This style of counting is common in rabbinic literature (see for example *Shabbat* 137a, *Megilla* 2a).

The nine priests mentioned here are the last nine of the thirteen assigned by the second lottery.

בֶּחָג *And on Sukkot.* The generic term חַג, "the Festival" is used by the sages to refer specifically to Sukkot, a time of heightened celebration and rejoicing

ד הַפַּיִס הַשְּׁלִישִׁי
חֲדָשִׁים לַקְּטֹרֶת בּוֹאוּ וְהָפִיסוּ.
וְהָרְבִיעִי
חֲדָשִׁים עִם יְשָׁנִים
מִי מַעֲלֶה אֵבָרִים מִן הַכֶּבֶשׁ לַמִּזְבֵּחַ.

ה תָּמִיד קָרֵב בְּתִשְׁעָה, בַּעֲשָׂרָה, בְּאַחַד עָשָׂר, בִּשְׁנֵים עָשָׂר
לֹא פָּחוֹת וְלֹא יוֹתֵר.
כֵּיצַד?
עַצְמוֹ בְּתִשְׁעָה
בֶּחָג – בְּיַד אֶחָד צְלוֹחִית שֶׁל מַיִם
הֲרֵי כָּאן עֲשָׂרָה;

---

the flaying, beginning with the legs which are skinned first and concluding with the neck and breast. Rabbi Yose HaGlili holds that the fattest meat should be brought first (see Rashi and *Baḥ* note a).

חֲדָשִׁים לַקְּטֹרֶת...וְהָפִיסוּ *New priests… cast lots.* In Deuteronomy (33:10–11), Moses blesses the tribe of Levi, "They shall bring You the scent of incense, and burnt offerings upon Your altar. Bless, O Lord, their possessions…" This last phrase is understood to imply that God will increase the wealth of those who bring the incense (see *Yoma* 26a and *Tosafot Yeshanim*; also Ramban on the verse). Consequently, this task was very popular, and a rule was established that each priest should only once have the opportunity to do it. Hence the announcement: "*New* priests, come and cast lots."

The Yerushalmi explains that two priests were chosen in this lottery. The priest to whom the lot fell would offer the incense; the priest standing next to him would fetch the coals with which to burn it, from the fire on the Great Altar (Rabbi Eliezer ben Ya'akov argues that this role was allocated by a separate lottery – see next note).

On Yom Kippur, the incense is offered by the High Priest. According to Ramban, however, a lottery was held to determine who would bring the coals, even on Yom Kippur, as this role could be fulfilled by a regular priest (see the introduction to this chapter).

The afternoon sacrifice is offered by eleven:
[the offering] itself by nine,
and two men carry kindling wood.
On Shabbat, by eleven:
[the offering] itself by nine,
and two men carry censers of incense for the showbread.
And on the Shabbat of Sukkot –
one man holds a bowl of water.

6 A ram is offered up by eleven:
the meat by five,
the intestines and the meal and the wine – each by two.

---

as part of the morning lottery (Tosafot), or fall to the responsibility of the priests selected to clear the Inner Altar and the Menora in the morning (Rid).

בָּזִכֵּי לְבוֹנָה שֶׁלְּלֶחֶם הַפָּנִים *Incense for the showbread.* Every Shabbat, twelve loaves of showbread would be arranged in two rows on the Table in the Sanctuary, and two censers of frankincense would be placed between them. The bread from the previous week would be removed and divided amongst the priests to be eaten (see Lev. 24 and Mishna, *Menaḥot* 96a) and the old frankincense would be brought to the altar.

Exactly when the frankincense was offered up is a matter of debate. The Talmud (33a) records Abba Shaul's description of the Order of the Day (see page 497) which states that it is offered after the additional offering (the *Musaf*); Rabbi Akiva contends that it is brought before (*Pesaḥim* 58a). The Rid points out that our mishna here supports a third possibility: that the frankincense is brought together with the daily offering. Tosafot rule in accordance with Rabbi Akiva, while Rambam (*Hilkhot Temidim UMusafim* 4:11, 6:11) sides with Abba Shaul.

בְּאַחַד עָשָׂר...בַּחֲמִשָּׁה...בִּשְׁנַיִם שְׁנַיִם *By eleven… by five… each by two.* Because of its size and accompanying offerings, a ram requires more priests to offer it than a goat; even more are needed for a bull. The meal offering brought with a ram is double the volume brought with a goat; for a bull it is triple. The wine libation brought with a goat is a quarter of a hin (approximately one liter, according to Rabbi A.H. Naeh); for a ram it is a third of a hin, and for a bull, a half (Num. 15:4–7).

בֵּין הָעַרְבַּיִם – בְּאַחַד עָשָׂר:
הוּא עַצְמוֹ בְּתִשְׁעָה
וּשְׁנַיִם בְּיָדָם שְׁנֵי גִזְרֵי עֵצִים;
וּבַשַּׁבָּת – בְּאַחַד עָשָׂר:
הוּא עַצְמוֹ בְּתִשְׁעָה
וּשְׁנַיִם בְּיָדָם שְׁנֵי בָזִכֵּי לְבוֹנָה שֶׁלְּלֶחֶם הַפָּנִים;
וּבַשַּׁבָּת שֶׁבְּתוֹךְ הֶחָג
בְּיַד אֶחָד צְלוֹחִית שֶׁלְּמַיִם.

ו אַיִל קָרֵב בְּאַחַד עָשָׂר:
הַבָּשָׂר – בַּחֲמִשָּׁה
הַקְּרָבַיִם וְהַסֹּלֶת וְהַיַּיִן – בִּשְׁנַיִם שְׁנַיִם.

(see Mishna *Rosh HaShana* 1:2, and the commentary in the Koren Rosh HaShana Maḥzor). The Sukkot festivities reach a climax at the Water Drawing ceremony, as water collected from the Shiloaḥ spring is poured out onto the altar (see *Sukka* chapter five).

וּשְׁנַיִם בְּיָדָם שְׁנֵי גִזְרֵי עֵצִים *Two men carry kindling wood.* There are two separate commands in Leviticus concerning the tending of the fire on the altar. The first (1:7) addresses "the sons of Aaron" in the plural, while the second (6:5) is worded in terms of an individual priest. The second of these verses refers explicitly to the morning; the sages, then, understand that a single priest is required for this service – the same priest who lifted the ashes (see commentary to 1:8) – while the earlier verse must refer to the tending of the fire in the afternoon. At that stage in the daily ritual, two priests perform the rite, each carrying a single log (*Yoma* 26b).

The four lotteries listed here all serve to select priests for the morning service. Rabbi Yoḥanan states (*Yoma* 26a) that there was no additional lottery for the service of the afternoon; the same priests who performed the service in the morning gain the privilege to repeat it later in the day. The tending of the fire in the afternoon, then, must either be allotted to additional priests

7 A bull is offered up by twenty-four:
the head and the right hind leg –
the head by one, the leg by two;
the rump and the left hind leg –
the rump by two and the leg by two;
the breast and neck –
the breast by one, the neck by three;
the two forelegs by two;
the two sides by two;
the intestines and the meal and the wine –
each by three.
When is this the case?
For communal offerings.
In the case of individual offerings,
if one priest wishes to offer up [everything], he does.
With regard to their flaying and carving, however,
the two kinds of offering are alike.

---

to the meal offerings and wine libations; they are not divided up into smaller vessels but rather carried to the altar in large vessels by a number of priests.

אִם רָצָה לְהַקְרִיב – מַקְרִיב *If one priest wishes... he does.* The *Mishneh LaMelekh* (*Hilkhot Temidim UMusafim* 4:9) suggests that any priest could choose independently to bring the whole offering. In direct contrast, Rashi explains that priests were still selected for the various tasks, but that the owner of the offering had the right to make the selection (*Temura* 32a).

ז פַּר קָרֵב בְּעֶשְׂרִים וְאַרְבָּעָה:
הָרֹאשׁ וְהָרֶגֶל – הָרֹאשׁ בְּאֶחָד, וְהָרֶגֶל בִּשְׁנַיִם
הָעֹקֶץ וְהָרֶגֶל – הָעֹקֶץ בִּשְׁנַיִם, וְהָרֶגֶל בִּשְׁנַיִם
הֶחָזֶה וְהַגֵּרָה – הֶחָזֶה בְּאֶחָד, וְהַגֵּרָה בִּשְׁלֹשָׁה
שְׁתֵּי הַיָּדַיִם בִּשְׁנַיִם
שְׁתֵּי הַדְּפָנוֹת בִּשְׁנַיִם
הַקְּרָבַיִם וְהַסֹּלֶת וְהַיַּיִן – בִּשְׁלֹשָׁה שְׁלֹשָׁה.
בַּמֶּה דְבָרִים אֲמוּרִים? בְּקָרְבְּנוֹת הַצִּבּוּר.
אֲבָל בְּקָרְבַּן הַיָּחִיד
אִם רָצָה לְהַקְרִיב – מַקְרִיב.
הֶפְשֵׁטָן וְנִתּוּחָן שֶׁלָּאֵלּוּ וָאֵלּוּ שָׁוִין.

וְהָרֶגֶל בִּשְׁנַיִם *The leg by two.* A bull's leg is too large for one priest to carry it alone. Rabbeinu Elyakim and Ra'avad (on the *Sifra*, Dibura DeNedava 5) claim that the leg is divided into two, each half carried by a different priest. Rid (26b) strongly objects to this suggestion. He argues it is forbidden to dissect an offering any more than the Torah explicitly directs (see Lev. 1:6). He suggests instead that the leg is left undivided, and that the two priests carry it together. The *Tiferet Yisrael* assumes that this principle also applies

CHAPTER THREE

1 The appointed [priest] would say,
"Go out and see if the time for slaughtering has come."
If it had come, the one who saw it would say,
"Light!"
Mattitya ben Shmuel would say,

הַמְּמֻנֶּה *The appointed priest.* Tosafot (*Menaḥot* 100a) identify this priest as the administrator of the lotteries described in the previous chapter, a claim supported by the phrasing of the parallel mishnayot in *Tamid,* chapter three. Rashi, however, suggests this was the סְגָן, the Deputy High Priest (see mishna 9). This is in line with the Talmud in *Sanhedrin* 19a where the "the appointed priest" is explicitly equated, albeit in a different context, with the Deputy. It seems unlikely, however, that someone in such a high position would perform such a technical daily duty. The Meiri suggests there were several deputies with different responsibilities; another possibility is that there was no single appointment, but rather that every day the officiating priest was granted the elevated status of Deputy (see Rosh, *Tamid* 5:1; for the view that there was one permanent Deputy see Rambam, *Hilkhot Klei HaMikdash* 5:12). Many commentators argue that the Deputy here was the priest appointed to replace the High Priest, should he be disqualified (see mishna 1:1).

מַתִּתְיָא בֶּן שְׁמוּאֵל *Mattitya ben Shmuel.* Rabbeinu Gershom (*Menaḥot* 100a) and Rambam understand that Mattitya ben Shmuel disagrees with the first opinion in the mishna: light having appeared at one point (עַמּוּד הַשַּׁחַר), he argues, is not enough, but rather the entire eastern horizon must be lit. Rashi and Tosafot differ: Mattitya ben Shmuel does not appear anywhere as a halakhic authority, but in Mishna *Shekalim* 5:1 he is named as the administrator of the lotteries. His words in our mishna, then, should not be read as a dissenting opinion, but as another voice within the narrative. In his time in the Temple, the watcher would announce the morning light, and Mattitya ben Shmuel would then ask whether the entire eastern horizon was lit up (this view is reflected in our translation).

Understanding these words to be the words of Mattitya ben Shmuel may make it less likely that he is also the "appointed priest" at the beginning of the mishna. This would be at odds with Tosafot's claim (cited in the previous note) that the "appointed priest" was also the administrator of the lotteries,

פרק שלישי

א אָמַר לָהֶם הַמְמֻנֶּה:
צְאוּ וּרְאוּ, אִם הִגִּיעַ זְמַן הַשְּׁחִיטָה.
אִם הִגִּיעַ
הָרוֹאֶה אוֹמֵר: בַּרְקַאי!
מַתִּתְיָא בֶּן שְׁמוּאֵל אוֹמֵר:

CHAPTER THREE

The Mishna now focuses its attention on the day of Yom Kippur itself. Nonetheless, details relevant to the rest of the year continue to be woven in among those specific to the day. The first three mishnayot of the chapter describe both the sanctifications necessary for priests working in the Temple throughout the year, and the five immersions specific to the High Priest on Yom Kippur. The majority of the chapter (mishnayot 4–9) is then devoted to a discussion of the rites of the morning, leading up to, but not including, the casting of the lots on the two goats. The chapter concludes with a record of people remembered for their personal contributions to the Temple, as well as of those who gained infamy by refusing to share the secrets of their skills. The *Tosefta* expands on this section, providing many stories of the individuals mentioned, as well as of others and of the marks they made upon the Temple and its traditions. The Mishna, as ever, discusses the Temple service with an attitude of both halakhic inquiry and historical interest. Technical details of the rituals are debated with the same immediate involvement, in the same present tense, as are devoted to every other field of practical law; and this is woven in among passages of descriptive narrative about the Temple, which move seamlessly among past tense and present, oral tradition, personal memory and legal deduction. At times the impression that arises from this is of deep-rooted grief for a lost time and lost ideal; at other times – or simultaneously – the close engagement with the subject-matter transcends the loss and becomes an expression of hope. Here, the memories of some of those who left their imprints on the life of the Temple remind us that, within the broad sweep of history, of Temple and Exile, an individual person can have his or her lasting personal impact, for good or for bad.

"Has all the eastern horizon lit up as far as Hebron?"
and the other would answer him "Yes!"

2 Why was this found necessary?
For once the light of the moon came up
and it looked as if the east were alight,
and they slaughtered the daily sacrifice
and had to take it out to the place of burning.

They would take the High Priest down to the ritual bath.
This was the rule in the Temple:

וְלָמָּה הֻצְרְכוּ לְכָךְ *Why was this found necessary?* Waiting for so much light (Meiri); or climbing up to a high vantage point to make sure (Rashi).

וְדִמּוּ שֶׁהֵאִיר הַמִּזְרָח *It looked as if the east were alight.* The Talmud (29a) notes this could not have happened on Yom Kippur, as the moon sets early at that time of the month. This episode must, rather, have taken place toward the end of the month, when the moon might not be expected to rise at all.

וְהוֹצִיאוּהוּ לְבֵית הַשְּׂרֵפָה *Take it out to the place of burning.* An offering becomes disqualified when either the body of the animal or its blood becomes ritually contaminated (for instance by coming into contact with ritual impurity, Lev. 7:19, or by being left standing for too long, Lev. 7:17). Where the body is affected, the offering is burned immediately in the Temple's courtyard; if the blood is affected, the offering is removed from the Temple and burned outside (*Pesaḥim* 73b). Offerings may only be brought in the daytime (29b); in the case brought in the mishna, the offering's blood is disqualified by the slaughtering having occurred too early. The whole animal is therefore taken out of the Temple to be burned.

זֶה הַכְּלָל הָיָה *This was the rule.* Before entering the Temple, a priest is required to sanctify himself by washing his hands and feet from the Basin (Ex. 30:17–21) and immersing in a *mikveh* (see next mishna). This sanctification only remains valid while the priest is entirely focused on the Temple service. Relieving himself is considered a lapse of concentration and thus a new washing is required – not, as one might suppose, because bodily functions entail impurity. A minor lapse requires that he rewash his hands and feet; a total lapse requires him to immerse again. Thus, the *Tosefta* similarly rules that if a priest speaks to a friend or goes to sleep he is required to immerse himself, while if he only exchanges a few words or dozes, he is only required to wash his hands (1:14).

הֵאִיר פְּנֵי כָל הַמִּזְרָח עַד שֶׁבְּחֶבְרוֹן?
וְהוּא אוֹמֵר: הֵן.

ב וְלָמָּה הֻצְרְכוּ לְכָךְ?
שֶׁפַּעַם אַחַת עָלָה מְאוֹר הַלְּבָנָה
וְדִמּוּ שֶׁהֵאִיר הַמִּזְרָח
וְשָׁחֲטוּ אֶת הַתָּמִיד
וְהוֹצִיאוּהוּ לְבֵית הַשְּׂרֵפָה.
הוֹרִידוּ כֹּהֵן גָּדוֹל לְבֵית הַטְּבִילָה.
זֶה הַכְּלָל הָיָה בַמִּקְדָּשׁ:

---

a role which in Mishna *Shekalim* 5:1, as mentioned above, is identified with Mattitya ben Shmuel. A resolution of this tension may arise from the commentary of Rabbi Yehuda bar Binyamin (Italy, twelfth century, the first to write a commentary on tractate *Shekalim*). He suggests that Mattitya ben Shmuel was responsible for the lots themselves, and for teaching the officiating priests to use them (although see note to 2:1 – in Rambam's view the lotteries were conducted using finger counting, not lots). If so, it would seem there were two administrators: the one who conducted the lottery – and also instructed the watchman to look for the first light; and the one who took care of the lots but did not cast them – and it was he who asked the watchman how far the light had spread.

הֵאִיר פְּנֵי כָל הַמִּזְרָח עַד שֶׁבְּחֶבְרוֹן *Has all the eastern horizon lit up.* We follow Rashi (as do most of the commentators) in translating the question "Has all the eastern horizon lit up as far as Hebron?" Ra'avad, on the other hand – interpreting פְּנֵי הַמִּזְרָח "the land in the east" rather than the eastern horizon – understands the question to mean "Could you recognize the silhouettes of those standing in Hebron?" (Mishna *Tamid* 3:2). The Yerushalmi reads the mention of Hebron here as a conscious allusion to the patriarchs buried there, intended to invoke their merit. In the recently published *Mishnat Aryeh*, Rabbi Aryeh Levin suggests that the reference is specifically to Abraham and his eagerness to serve God from the earliest moment in the day (see Gen. 22:3).

one who sits to relieve himself
requires immersion,
and one who passes water
requires sanctification of the hands and feet.

3 But no one enters the courtyard for service,
even if he is pure,
until he has immersed himself.
On that day the High Priest
would immerse himself five times
and sanctify himself ten times.

---

the priest to focus his mind on his state of purity, and to jog his memory of any forgotten event that may have made him impure. Should this happen, he will be able to focus his attention on correcting this impurity through his immersion (assuming it was of a type for which immersion could be effective).

בּוֹ בַּיּוֹם *On that day.* The High Priest had two sets of garments. The בִּגְדֵי זָהָב, "the golden vestments" consisted of eight separate, colorful garments, four of which contained gold. These are described in Exodus twenty-eight, and were used throughout the year. The second set of garments, "the white vestments," includes four white linen garments (see Lev. 16:4) which were worn only on Yom Kippur, and only for certain parts of the Service (see mishna 7:5).

The Torah (Lev. 16) instructs the High Priest to immerse in a ritual bath before donning the white vestments, and again between removing them and putting on the golden vestments. The Talmud counts five immersions required of the High Priest on this day: (1) before entering the Temple (wearing the golden vestments) to bring the daily offering; (2) before entering the Holy of Holies (in white) to purify it, and the Golden Altar; (3) before bringing the burnt offering (in golden vestments; regarding the Musaf offering, see 7:3 and commentary there); (4) before re-entering the Holy of Holies (again in white) to take out the censer and the coal pan; (5) before bringing the afternoon daily offering (in golden vestments; see Appendix 1, page 436).

The Talmud (31b) also uses the wording of the Yom Kippur service in Leviticus chapter sixteen to deduce that before removing and after donning either set of vestments, the High Priest was required to wash his hands and feet; requiring ten "sanctifications of the hands and feet" in total (see note to 3:6).

כָּל הַמֵּסִיךְ אֶת רַגְלָיו
טָעוּן טְבִילָה
וְכָל הַמֵּטִיל מַיִם
טָעוּן קִדּוּשׁ יָדַיִם וְרַגְלַיִם.

ג אֵין אָדָם נִכְנָס לָעֲזָרָה לַעֲבוֹדָה
אֲפִלּוּ טָהוֹר
עַד שֶׁיִּטְבֹּל.
חָמֵשׁ טְבִילוֹת וַעֲשָׂרָה קִדּוּשִׁין
טוֹבֵל כֹּהֵן גָּדוֹל וּמְקַדֵּשׁ בּוֹ בַּיּוֹם

אֵין אָדָם נִכְנָס לָעֲזָרָה לַעֲבוֹדָה *But no one enters the courtyard for service.* A literal reading of the mishna implies that only someone who enters the courtyard for the sake of the service is required to immerse. *Tosafot Yeshanim* add that one who is not actually performing the offering, but is otherwise involved – for instance the owner of the offering – is also required to immerse; spectators, however (such as those who appear in mishna 1:8), are exempt. Rashi rejects the notion that anyone may be allowed into the courtyard without immersion, and indeed several manuscripts omit the word לַעֲבוֹדָה from their texts of the mishna; this appears to be also the version used by Rash of Sens (*Kelim* 1:8). The Rid suggests that the mishna should read אוֹ לַעֲבוֹדָה, "*or* for service," indicating two reasons for immersion: either entering the courtyard or, once inside, beginning a new service (a priest who sleeps overnight in the courtyard, for instance, must immerse himself in the morning). This reading is endorsed by the Yerushalmi (see *Dikdukei Sofrim*).

The requirement to immerse is derived from the High Priest's requirement to immerse before entering the Holy of Holies; if going from a holy to a holier place requires immersion, then certainly entering the courtyard from the mundane world outside must require it also. This is the view of Ben Zoma; his logic would suggest that the obligation to immerse is a biblical one. Rabbi Yehuda, however, argues that there is no true obligation for one who is ritually pure to immerse – following this view, Rabbeinu Ḥananel names the practice "a custom." The immersion, in this view, was prescribed to help

And each of these purifications were performed in the Holy Place,
above the Parva Chamber,
except for this one.

4 A sheet of linen would be stretched out between him and the people.
And he would undress and go down and immerse himself,
come up and dry himself.
They would bring him [his] golden vestments,
and he would dress and sanctify his hands and feet.

(31a) who, in contrast to Rashi, insist that all five immersions are an integral part of the Order of the Service.

וְנִסְתַּפֵּג *And dry himself.* Literally: "and absorbed the water from himself." The Mishna (*Shabbat* 143a) prohibits wiping with a sponge on Shabbat and festivals, because it inevitably squeezes some liquid out of the sponge (which is analogous to squeezing juice from a fruit, and forbidden on Shabbat). Therefore, Rashi holds that the High Priest did not wipe himself dry, but merely draped the towel over himself, allowing it to absorb the water from him.

Because of this concern regarding water squeezed from a towel, the *Magen Avraham* and Vilna Gaon (OḤ 326:8) forbid any immersing which is not halakhically mandated on Shabbat. The *Mishna Berura*, however, concludes that one who has the custom regularly to immerse may do so, as long as he or she is careful not to wring water from the towel (ibid. 24, and see *Bi'ur Halakha* ad loc.).

The *piyut* אַתָּה כּוֹנַנְתָּ (page 1263) implies that the High Priest does indeed wipe himself dry in a normal manner, and that this is considered part of the Order of the Day. The *Mishneh LaMelekh* (*Hilkhot Avodat Yom HaKippurim* 2:2) suggests this is also the opinion of the Rambam, who rules that he must wipe himself dry, as any water that remained on his skin would be considered a חֲצִיצָה – an obstruction – between the priest's body and his vestments, invalidating his service (see *Zevaḥim* 19a). This position would have implications for other areas of halakha in which חֲצִיצָה poses a problem – may a man, for example, wear *tefillin* when his arm or head is wet? Although some later authorities prohibit this (see, for instance, *Birkei Yosef*, OḤ 27:1), most do not raise the issue at all.

וְקִדֵּשׁ יָדָיו וְרַגְלָיו *And sanctify his hands and feet.* Rashi understands that his hands and feet are washed from the Basin. The *Smag* (209) and Rosh argue

וְכֻלָּן בַּקֹּדֶשׁ עַל בֵּית הַפַּרְוָה
חוּץ מִזּוֹ בִּלְבַד.

ד פֵּרְסוּ סָדִין שֶׁלְּבוּץ בֵּינוֹ לְבֵין הָעָם.
פָּשַׁט יָרַד וְטָבַל, עָלָה וְנִסְתַּפֵּג.
הֵבִיאוּ לוֹ בִגְדֵי זָהָב
וְלָבַשׁ וְקִדֵּשׁ יָדָיו וְרַגְלָיו.

עַל בֵּית הַפַּרְוָה *Above the Parva Chamber.* The Talmud (35a) records that Parva was the name of an אַמְגּוּשׁ, a Zoroastrian Priest (*Magus* in Latin). Rashi understands that he built the chamber and lent it his name. The *Arukh* (cited by Tosafot) records a tradition that Parva tunneled under the Temple in hope of seeing the High Priest inside the Holy of Holies; he was discovered in the act, however, and the tunnel was transformed into a chamber. The minor tractate *Mezuza* equates this chamber with the Palhedrin chamber, where the High Priest would reside during the week before Yom Kippur (1:1; *Mezuza* 1:8). The chamber was normally used for preparing animal hides (*Midot* 5:3). In Hebrew as used today, פַּרְוָה is the word for "fur."

חוּץ מִזּוֹ בִּלְבַד *Except for this one.* This immersion was performed, not above the Parva Chamber but above the Water Gate. This gate is mentioned several times in the book of Nehemiah. The Mishna (in *Shekalim* 6:2 and *Midot* 2:6) suggests two possible reasons for its name: water was carried through the gate from the Shiloaḥ spring, to be poured upon the altar during the Water Drawing Ceremony on Sukkot; and Ezekiel prophesies that, in the future, water will flow though this gate to heal the Dead Sea (47:1–12).

The High Priest has to immerse before entering the courtyard, and so the first immersion of the day takes place at the Water Gate. Rashi (32b) suggests that this immersion is not an integral part of the day's service, but simply the immersion required of any priest before entering the courtyard (three notes above). Rambam explains the need for the immersion with reference to Rabbi Yehuda's reasoning (ibid.) that it served to remind him of any impurity he may carry (*Hilkhot Avodat Yom HaKippurim* 2:3). The *Arukh HaShulḥan HaAtid* (159:17) understands this to mean that it is only a rabbinic safeguard, but Rav Soloveitchik submits that it is a biblical requirement, carried out with special intention to prepare for the day. This is in line with *Tosafot Yeshanim*

Then they would bring him the daily offering.
He would make the first cut,
and another priest would complete the slaughtering;
he would receive the blood and throw it.
And he would enter [the Sanctuary] to burn the morning incense,
and tend the lamps.
And he would offer up the head and the organs,
the pan cakes and the wine.

5 The morning incense was offered
between [throwing the] blood and [offering the] organs.
That of the afternoon –
between the organs and the libations.

Rabbeinu Yehonatan points out that receiving the blood of the offering in a sacred bowl must certainly be performed by the High Priest on this day, and, as the blood begins to flow as soon as the first cut is made, he cannot possibly complete the slaughtering by himself.

נִכְנָס *And he would enter.* Only the burning of the incense and the tending of the lamps were performed inside the Sanctuary. Sacrificial animals were offered up at the altar in the courtyard. For a discussion of the tending of the lamps, see commentary to mishna 1:2.

Tosafot Yom Tov note that the mishna neglects to mention the meal-offering that was always brought with the daily offering. *Tosafot Yeshanim* suggest that it is implied together with the pan cakes, which constitute the High Priest's personal offering (see also *Melekhet Shlomo*).

שֶׁלְּבֵין הָעַרְבַּיִם *That of the afternoon.* In אַתָּה כוֹנַנְתָּ, if Yom Kippur falls on Shabbat, some add "וּבְיוֹם הַשַּׁבָּת מַקְרִיב שְׁנֵי כִבְשֵׂי מוּסַף שַׁבָּת וּמִנְחָתָם..." (page 1264) – this accords with Rambam's ruling that the Musaf offerings of Shabbat were also slaughtered on Yom Kippur, and their blood was thrown by the High Priest himself (*Hilkhot Avodat Yom HaKippurim* 2:1). The *Or Same'aḥ* (ibid. 4:1) explains that when Yom Kippur falls on Shabbat, their two respective Musaf offerings are not seen as two separate entities, but combine to be considered one double sacrifice. The High Priest, then, must clearly bring them both. Tosafot and Ramban disagree with Rambam (see note to mishna 4). They maintain that a lay priest can bring the additional offerings of Shabbat; in the Ashkenazi *piyut* אַמִּיץ כֹּחַ, there is no mention at all of the Shabbat

הֵבִיאוּ לוֹ אֶת הַתָּמִיד.
קְרָצוֹ, וּמֵרֵק אַחֵר שְׁחִיטָה עַל יָדוֹ
קִבֵּל אֶת הַדָּם וּזְרָקוֹ.
נִכְנַס לְהַקְטִיר קְטֹרֶת שֶׁלַּשַּׁחַר
וּלְהֵטִיב אֶת הַנֵּרוֹת
וּלְהַקְרִיב אֶת הָרֹאשׁ וְאֶת הָאֵבָרִים
וְאֶת הַחֲבִתִּין וְאֶת הַיַּיִן.

ה קְטֹרֶת שֶׁלַּשַּׁחַר
הָיְתָה קְרֵבָה בֵּין הַדָּם לָאֵבָרִים
שֶׁלְּבֵין הָעַרְבַּיִם
בֵּין אֵבָרִים לַנְּסָכִים.

---

that the golden jug was used, as it was for all the washings of the day (see mishna 4:5). Our version of אַתָּה כּוֹנַנְתָּ (page 1263) is in line with the *Smag* and Rosh, though the Sephardi version of the piyut leaves out any details of how he washes. The Yerushalmi (4:5) records a debate over this issue but leaves it unresolved.

וּמֵרֵק אַחֵר שְׁחִיטָה עַל יָדוֹ *Another priest would complete the slaughtering.* A valid *sheḥita,* or ritual slaughter, requires that the two סִימָנִים, the esophagus and trachea, are slit. Although the *sheḥita* is valid even if only the greater part of their girth is cut, ideally the סִימָנִים should cut through entirely (*Ḥullin* 27a). Some discussion, then, is devoted to the question of why the High Priest is not required to complete the action, but may delegate part of it, on this solemnest of days, to a lay priest. The Meiri (*Yoma* 32b) suggests that the requirement to complete the *sheḥita* is only rabbinic. Under the extreme time-pressure of the day, then, it is acceptable for the completion of the action to be performed by somebody else. Furthermore, as Tosafot note, the slaughter of an offering is valid even when performed by a non-priest (*Zevaḥim* 14b). If so, even if the High Priest performs none of the *sheḥita,* it should, after the event, be considered valid. Ramban, cited by Ritva, (12b) accepts this conclusion, although Tosafot themselves suggest that the offerings of Yom Kippur are an exception to the rule and must be slaughtered by the High Priest. In any case,

If the High Priest were elderly or delicate,
they would heat water and pour it into the cold,
so that the chill would pass off it.

6 They would bring him to the Parva chamber;
this was in the Holy Place.
A sheet of linen would be stretched out between him and the people,
and he would sanctify his hands and feet, and undress.
Rabbi Meir says,
he would undress and then sanctify his hands and feet.

---

able; some authorities consider it a violation of the rabbinic prohibition against tempering metals on Shabbat. All the same, rabbinic prohibitions are waived inside the Temple (אֵין שְׁבוּת בַּמִּקְדָּשׁ – see *Pesaḥim* 65a) and the solution was permissible (see Tosafot and Rid for a full discussion). The fact that this detail is withheld until now, though the issue of the High Priest's immersion arises in mishna 2, may have something to do with this (see *Melekhet Shlomo*). Rabbi Ḥizkiya de Silva (author of *Pri Ḥadash*) suggests that as the first immersion of the day takes place outside the Temple, all rabbinic prohibitions remain in force; only later, inside the Temple, does heating the water become possible (*Mayim Ḥayyim, Hilkhot Avodat Yom HaKippurim* 2:4; but note that Rosh brings his discussion of heating the *mikveh* alongside his discussion of the first immersion). Despite the Yerushalmi's objections to adding warm water, Rambam (ibid. 2:2), Rosh and the Meiri cite both methods of heating the water as equally valid, though the Meiri claims that Rabbi Yehuda's method was the one followed in the Temple.

Authorities through the ages have debated the validity of heated *mikvaot* – even for use on weekdays. Some argue that heated water is no longer in its natural state, and is therefore no longer valid (see *Or Zarua* 1:366). This mishna constitutes an important precedent for leniency on this question. Most authorities permit the use of heated *mikvaot* as long as they do not reach the temperature at which "the hand is repelled" – יָד סוֹלֶדֶת בּוֹ – estimated variously as somewhere between 40°C and 52°C; hotter than this the water is considered to be "cooked" and so no longer in its natural state.

רַבִּי מֵאִיר אוֹמֵר *Rabbi Meir says.* The Talmud (31b) deduces from the choice of words in Leviticus chapter sixteen that every time the High Priest undresses, and again after he puts on either of his sets of vestments, he is required

אִם הָיָה כֹּהֵן גָּדוֹל זָקֵן אוֹ אִסְטְנִיס
מְחַמִּין לוֹ חַמִּין
וּמַטִּילִין לְתוֹךְ הַצּוֹנִין
כְּדֵי שֶׁתָּפוּג צִנָּתָן.

ו הֱבִיאוּהוּ לְבֵית הַפַּרְוָה
וּבַקֹּדֶשׁ הָיְתָה.
פֵּרְסוּ סָדִין שֶׁל בּוּץ בֵּינוֹ לְבֵין הָעָם.
קִדֵּשׁ יָדָיו וְרַגְלָיו, וּפָשַׁט.
רַבִּי מֵאִיר אוֹמֵר:
פָּשַׁט, קִדֵּשׁ יָדָיו וְרַגְלָיו.

---

additional offering, and Rabbi Moishe Sternbuch (*Moadim UZemanim* 1:61) suggests that this reflects the view that it is performed in the background by a lay priest.

זָקֵן אוֹ אִסְטְנִיס *Elderly or delicate.* The word אִסְטְנִיס (translated here as "delicate") is neither a particularly complementary term (see for instance *Bava Batra* 145a), nor an insulting one; Rabban Gamliel refers to himself in the Mishna as an אִסְטְנִיס (see *Berakhot* 16b). The word likely derives from the Greek *asthenos,* "lacking in strength" and carries the double-edged connotations of over-sensitivity and delicate refinement.

מְחַמִּין לוֹ חַמִּין *They would heat water.* A *mikveh* must be a natural body of water; drawn water is invalid for this purpose. The warm water, then, cannot be poured directly into the *mikveh,* but is instead directed through a conduit that still carries mostly rain or spring water into the pool (*Shulḥan Arukh,* YD 201:44, following Rashi, *Yoma* 31b; see *Temura* 12a; *Beit Yosef* ibid). Technically, such a solution would be quite legitimate, but the Yerushalmi raises the concern that people may misunderstand the arrangement and think, mistakenly, that the High Priest is bathing in warm, drawn water. Rabbi Yehuda is cited there suggesting that instead of pouring in warmed water, the priests should heat lumps of iron the previous day and throw them into the *mikveh* to heat the water on Yom Kippur. Even this method is halakhically question-

He would go down and immerse himself,
come up and dry himself.
They would bring him white vestments,
and he would dress and sanctify his hands and feet.

7 In the morning he would wear Pelusium linen
worth twelve manehs,
and in the afternoon, Indian linen
worth eight hundred zuz:
thus says Rabbi Meir.

---

here, however, the count of ten washings must presumably be completed at the end of the day's service (*Yoma* 32a); see the Order of the Service *piyutim*, pages 895 and 1273.

פְּלוּסִין *Pelusium linen.* פְּלוּסִין and הִנְדְּוִין are the Greek or Arabic names of the fabrics (Rabbeinu Ḥananel, but see *Tosafot Yeshanim*). פְּלוּסִין may refer to Pylos in Greece, where the earliest manufacture of linen is recorded, but more likely relates to Pelusium in Egypt, where fine linen was widely used ("linum pelusiacum" is attested in Roman sources). Some have identified this city with the biblical Pithom (Ex. 1:11); the *Targum Yerushalmi* identifies it as Raamses, mentioned in the same verse.

הִנְדְּוִין is naturally assumed to refer to India (see Ritva, for example), and indeed the Cochin region, which had extensive commercial relations with the Middle East at the time, is today a center of flax-based fabrics exports. The *Targum Yonatan* on Jer. 13:23 (quoted by Rashi, *Yoma* 34b) translates the designation כּוּשִׁי as הִינְדְּוָאָה; but it is unclear whether כּוּשׁ refers to India or to Sudan. Rav Shrira Gaon (in the Harkabi collection of Geonic Responsa, 362) attributes to the הִנְדְּוִין the *K'tab Kalila wa Dimna*, a collection of parables in Arabic.

שֶׁל שְׁנֵים עָשָׂר מָנֶה *Worth twelve manehs.* A maneh is a hundred zuz; the sages add fifty percent to the value suggested by Rabbi Meir. In all views, this is a lavish sum. Rashi and most commentators assume the values to represent the full set of four white vestments. Rambam suggests that the sums are each ascribed to the tunic alone (*Hilkhot Klei HaMikdash* 8:3).

וּבֵין הָעַרְבַּיִם *And in the afternoon.* However they are priced, there is a 60:40 ratio between the morning and afternoon vestments. Rabbeinu Yehonatan

יָרַד וְטָבַל, עָלָה וְנִסְתַּפֵּג.
הֵבִיאוּ לוֹ בִּגְדֵי לָבָן
לָבַשׁ וְקִדֵּשׁ יָדָיו וְרַגְלָיו.

ז בַּשַּׁחַר
הָיָה לוֹבֵשׁ פִּלוּסִין שֶׁלִּשְׁנֵים עָשָׂר מָנֶה
וּבֵין הָעַרְבַּיִם
הִנְדְּוִין שֶׁלִּשְׁמוֹנֶה מֵאוֹת זוּז
דִּבְרֵי רַבִּי מֵאִיר.

---

to wash his hands and feet. In our mishna the rabbis (the first, unnamed opinion) and Rabbi Meir debate whether the washing corresponding to the removal of his clothes should take place before or after he removes them. The two Talmuds approach the dispute very differently. In the Yerushalmi the basic assumption is that washing takes place after a stage of the service is completed – Abarbanel is later to describe the washing of hands and feet as a gesture of homage performed as a servant leaves the presence of his master. With this assumption in mind, the debate is framed as a question of whether or not the act of undressing is an independent ritual of the service; Rabbi Meir argues that it is, while the rabbis consider it a functional stage, and assume that the High Priest would wash before it.

In the Bavli, on the other hand, the debate pivots on the purpose of the washing. The rabbis understand it to be an act of respect due to the vestments being taken off; the High Priest must then wash his hands before undressing. For Rabbi Meir, washing is understood as part of the sanctification process, something to be done in immediate preparation for the new vestments he is about to put on. A third opinion in the Bavli takes Rabbi Meir's understanding to its logical conclusion – that both washings of the hands should be performed while undressed. This view is rejected, however, as one washing must take place immediately before the actual service (32b).

In mishna 4, at the first immersion of the day, no washing of the hands and feet is mentioned; at this point the High Priest is removing his own, ordinary clothes, and need not wash before immersing, according to the rabbis, or to Rabbi Meir as he appears in the Yerushalmi. If he does not wash his hands

The sages say:
In the morning he would wear vestments
worth eighteen manehs,
and in the afternoon,
worth twelve manehs –
thirty manehs altogether.
This is what the public provided –
and if he wished to add on to this,
he would add from his own pocket.

8 He would come to his bull;
the bull would be standing between the Antechamber and the altar,
its head to the south, its face turned to the west;
the priest stood to its eastern side
facing west,
and he would press his two hands down upon the bull and confess.

The bull is placed between the Antechamber and the altar, to the west of the northern side. It is positioned in a north-south alignment, with his rump toward the north, away from the altar, so that if it defecates it will not desecrate the altar. Its face is then turned toward the Sanctuary. (The Ritva records a tradition that the bull never defecated; but concludes that we cannot rely on miracles.) The High Priest stands alongside the bull, positioning himself behind the bull's head, facing the Sanctuary and with his back toward the people watching from the east.

וְסוֹמֵךְ שְׁתֵּי יָדָיו *He would press his two hands down.* Before any private offering is slaughtered, the owner is required to perform סְמִיכָה by laying his hands down, and resting his full weight, upon its head; the High Priest, then, is required to perform סְמִיכָה on the bull, which is considered his private sin-offering. The ritual has been understood in a number of different ways. According to the Rekanati (Italy, thirteenth century) this was a way of transferring one's sins onto the animal. The *Kli Yakar* (Prague, seventeenth century) sees it as forging a bond between the owner and the animal that is to provide his atonement. Rabbi Moshe Alsheikh (Safed, sixteenth century) saw the animal's head as representing the penitent's mind, in which the sin was first conceived; סְמִיכָה was a demonstration of this idea.

וַחֲכָמִים אוֹמְרִים:
בַּשַּׁחַר הָיָה לוֹבֵשׁ שֶׁלִּשְׁמוֹנָה עָשָׂר מָנֶה
וּבֵין הָעַרְבַּיִם שֶׁלִּשְׁנֵים עָשָׂר מָנֶה
הַכֹּל שְׁלֹשִׁים מָנֶה.
אֵלּוּ מִשֶּׁלַּצִּבּוּר
וְאִם רָצָה לְהוֹסִיף, מוֹסִיף מִשֶּׁלּוֹ.

ח בָּא לוֹ אֵצֶל פָּרוֹ
וּפָרוֹ הָיָה עוֹמֵד בֵּין הָאוּלָם וְלַמִּזְבֵּחַ
רֹאשׁוֹ לַדָּרוֹם וּפָנָיו לַמַּעֲרָב
וְהַכֹּהֵן עוֹמֵד בַּמִּזְרָח וּפָנָיו לַמַּעֲרָב
וְסוֹמֵךְ שְׁתֵּי יָדָיו עָלָיו וּמִתְוַדֶּה.

---

explains that in contrast to the service of the morning, the afternoon service, which only involves retrieving the incense censers and the coal pan from the Holy of Holies, is viewed more as an act of restoring the Temple to order than as an independent act of service. Greater emphasis, therefore, is placed on the vestments worn in the morning. The Talmud (35a) suggests that the High Priest was given the thirty manehs to purchase to the vestments, but was not bound to retain the exact 60:40 ratio between their values, as long as the morning vestments were more expensive that the afternoon ones.

בָּא לוֹ אֵצֶל פָּרוֹ *He would come to his bull.* The bull is designated to be a sin-offering for the High Priest himself; it must therefore be purchased with his own money (Lev. 16:3, Rashi). This is in contradistinction to the two goats, which atone for the whole Jewish people and are bought from public funds (ibid. 5). See אַמִּיץ כֹּחַ (page 887).

וְהַכֹּהֵן עוֹמֵד בַּמִּזְרָח *The priest stood to its eastern side.* Offerings are ranked in two levels of holiness: *kodashim kalim,* offerings of lesser sanctity, and *kodshei kodashim,* offerings of high sanctity. The former may be slaughtered anywhere in the courtyard; the latter are slaughtered only on the northern side (see mishna *Zevaḥim* 5:1, page 499). See figure 1 (page 444) for the parameters of the "northern side."

And this is what he would say:
"Please, [LORD] –
I have done wrong,
I have rebelled,
I have sinned before You –
I and my family.
Please, by the Name,
make atonement, please,
for the wrongs
and the rebellions
and sins
that I have done wrong,
I have rebelled,
that I have sinned before You –
I and my family,

עָוִיתִי, פָּשַׁעְתִּי, חָטָאתִי *I have done wrong.* Rabbi Meir and the rabbis debate the correct sequence for mentioning the different categories of sin (36b, *Tosefta* 2:1). Rabbi Meir argues that as the sequence עָוֹן, פֶּשַׁע, חֵטְא – "wrongdoing, rebellion, sin" – appears twice in the Torah (Ex. 34:7 and Lev. 16:21), it is appropriate to maintain that order here. The mishna here follows his view. The rabbis, however, argue that one should progress from lesser to more serious sins, as it is illogical to ask for forgiveness for small sins when one has already sought forgiveness for the grave ones. They understand חֵטְא to describe an inadvertent sin, עָוֹן a willful sin and פֶּשַׁע a rebellious one. Thus, the order should be חָטָאתִי, עָוִיתִי, פָּשַׁעְתִּי. They draw support for their view from sources later in the Bible where חָטָאתִי precedes the admission of more severe sins (see Ps. 106:6; 1 Kings 8:47; Daniel 9:5).

אָנָּא הַשֵּׁם *Please, by the Name.* In *piyut* narratives of the day's rituals, this second addressing of God begins not אָנָּא הַשֵּׁם, but אָנָּא בַּשֵּׁם "Please, *by* the Name," a version which is supported by Rabbi Ḥaggai in the Yerushalmi. The Geonim did not accept this version (Rabbeinu Ḥananel explicitly rejects it), but Ra'aviya (Cologne, early thirteenth century) argues that the tradition of the *paytanim* and of the Yerushalmi should be considered definitive, and his opinion is accepted by the Rosh (*Yoma* 8:19) and *Tur* (OḤ 621). Our translation reflects the mishna text we have received.

וְכָךְ הָיָה אוֹמֵר:
אָנָּא הַשֵּׁם
עָוִיתִי, פָּשַׁעְתִּי, חָטָאתִי לְפָנֶיךָ
אֲנִי וּבֵיתִי.
אָנָּא הַשֵּׁם
כַּפֶּר נָא לָעֲוֹנוֹת וְלַפְּשָׁעִים וְלַחֲטָאִים
שֶׁעָוִיתִי וְשֶׁפָּשַׁעְתִּי וְשֶׁחָטָאתִי לְפָנֶיךָ
אֲנִי וּבֵיתִי

אָנָּא הַשֵּׁם *Please, [Lord].* The Mishna uses the word הַשֵּׁם, "the Name," to represent the ineffable name of God, which may not be voiced or written in vain. The idea that the name of God is more than simply a way of addressing Him is at least as old as the Bible. "Let them praise the name of the Lord, for His name alone is sublime" (Psalms 148:13); the name is a symbol that contains something of the divinity it represents. The name the High Priest articulates in this prayer is perceived as carrying, not only divine sanctity, but also great power, not to be entrusted to the hands of those who may misuse it. As the name was uttered in the Temple on Yom Kippur, "those close by would fall on their faces, and those further off would say 'Blessed be the name of His glorious kingdom for ever and all time' – and none of them would move from there until the name had eluded them again. 'This is My name forever [*le'olam*]' [Ex. 3:15] means 'this is My name – to be hidden [*le'alem*]'" (Yerushalmi 3:7). The phrase from Exodus, which is interpreted here to express hiddenness, is from the speech in which God first introduces Himself with a form of the Tetragrammaton – "I shall be what I shall be" (Ex. 3:14) – a phrase that both reveals and hides God from the people. The Taz (*OḤ* 621:2) states that "the Name" referred to here is the Tetragrammaton (rather than any other secret name), which, as this is the appellation used to reflect God's attribute of Mercy (see Rashi, Gen. 8:1 and Ex. 34:6), is apt in this context.

Our translation convention is to use "Lord" to translate all forms of God's name which in Hebrew speech are substituted with הַשֵּׁם. Here we have placed the name in square brackets, to indicate that, in the Hebrew text also, the name written is not the name uttered.

as it is written in the Torah of Moses Your servant,
"For you will be atoned on this day..." *Lev. 16*
And they would respond,
"Blessed be the name of His glorious kingdom for ever and all time."

9 He would come to the eastern part of the courtyard,
north of the altar,
with the Deputy High Priest to his right
and the Head of the [officiating] house to his left.
And there two goats would be standing,
and a ballot would be there,
and in it there would be two lots.

---

on this midrash, a tradition developed in medieval Europe that on Yom Kippur, when the Jewish people are compared to angels, they too say the verse aloud. This was initially practiced only when the words are proclaimed at the conclusion of Ne'ila; (*Maḥzor Vitry* 356; see commentary on page 1197) later the custom was introduced to speak the words aloud as part of the Shema as well (*Shibolei HaLeket* 15).

וְראשׁ בֵּית אָב *The Head of the [officiating] house.* The Priesthood was divided into various בתי אבות, patrilineal houses, which were referred to as משמרות, "watches." The watches rotated throughout the year, each watch serving in the Temple for one week at a time. On festivals, all the priests came together to serve (*Sukka* 55b–56b).

King David created twenty-four בתי אבות (see 1 Chron. 24–26). The Talmud asserts that this was not the first organization of houses, but was built upon a pre-existing division from the time of Moses. After the first exile, only four of the priestly houses returned to the Land (Ezra 2:36–39). These four were then subdivided to form, again, twenty-four different houses (*Ta'anit* 27a).

The twenty-four priestly houses were a favorite theme of the early *paytanim*, especially Rabbi Elazar HaKalir. See his elegy for Tisha B'Av אֵיכָה יָשְׁבָה חֲבַצֶּלֶת הַשָּׁרוֹן, "How the Rose of Sharon sat alone," which laments their loss.

כַּכָּתוּב בְּתוֹרַת מֹשֶׁה עַבְדֶּךָ:

כִּי־בַיּוֹם הַזֶּה יְכַפֵּר עֲלֵיכֶם: וגו׳. ויקרא טז

וְהֵן עוֹנִין אַחֲרָיו:

׳בָּרוּךְ שֵׁם כְּבוֹד מַלְכוּתוֹ לְעוֹלָם וָעֶד׳.

ט בָּא לוֹ לְמִזְרַח הָעֲזָרָה, לִצְפוֹן הַמִּזְבֵּחַ

הַסְּגָן מִימִינוֹ וְרֹאשׁ בֵּית אָב מִשְּׂמֹאלוֹ.

וְשָׁם שְׁנֵי שְׂעִירִים

וְקַלְפִּי הָיְתָה שָׁם

וּבָהּ שְׁנֵי גוֹרָלוֹת.

בָּרוּךְ שֵׁם *Blessed be the name.* The *Tosefta* (quoted in *Ta'anit* 16b) explains this was the usual response to blessings used in the Temple, paralleling the use of "Amen" outside the Temple. On Yom Kippur, the High Priest mentions the Holy Name ten times, each time evoking this response – three times in each confession, the third time as part of the verse לִפְנֵי ה׳ תִּטְהָרוּ, "Before the Lord you shall be purified" – and once again after casting lots on the goats (see mishna 4:1) (39b).

The Talmud (*Pesaḥim* 56a) relates that as Jacob lay on his deathbed he wished to reveal to his children his prophetic knowledge of the End of Days. But the Divine Presence eluded him. He feared that one of his children may be unworthy; they reassured him: שְׁמַע יִשְׂרָאֵל ה׳ אֱלֹהֵינוּ ה׳ אֶחָד, "Listen, Israel: the Lord is our God, the Lord is One." Reassured that all his children were faithful, Jacob gratefully responded: בָּרוּךְ שֵׁם כְּבוֹד מַלְכוּתוֹ לְעוֹלָם וָעֶד, "Blessed be the name of His glorious kingdom for ever and all time." The sages wished to insert Jacob's words into the daily Shema, but as it does not appear in the passage from Deuteronomy (six) from which the first paragraph of the Shema is taken, it was decided that it should not be recited aloud, but only said quietly to oneself.

A different reference to this response formula appears in the Midrash (*Bereshit Raba* 65:21): "When the children of Israel say '*Shema Yisrael*...' the angels are silent... and then... they respond, 'Blessed be the name...'" Based

These were made of boxwood,
but Ben Gamla made them out of gold,
and he was spoken of afterwards in praise.

10 Ben Katin made twelve taps for the basin,
which had not had more than two;
he also made a pulley for the basin,
so that its waters would not become invalid by standing overnight.

בֶּן קָטִין עָשָׂה שְׁנֵים עָשָׂר *Ben Katin made twelve taps.* Ben Katin is not mentioned elsewhere. The donation of taps was to enable all the twelve priests bringing the daily offering (on the Shabbat of Sukkot – see mishna 2:5) to wash themselves simultaneously (37a).

מוּכְנִי לַכִּיּוֹר *A pulley for the basin.* The word מוּכְנִי is probably derived from the same Greek and Roman origins as the word "machine." Abaye describes it as a wheel (and pulley system – see below), which is consistent with the other appearances of the word in the Mishna (see *Kelim* 18:2; *Oholot* 4:3).

Ben Katin's system came to counter two problems. Consecrated items, once received into sacred vessels, are sanctified further. This sanctity must be realized on the same day; if the item – a meal-offering or libation, for instance – is left to stand overnight, it becomes invalid and cannot be used (Mishna, *Menaḥot* 79a). This rule applies, likewise, to water once gathered in the Basin; but while it was inevitable that at the end of each day there would be water left over, its disqualification was considered a disgrace to its sanctity. Another challenge was posed by the necessity to fill the basin – like a *mikveh* (see 3:5 and commentary there) – directly from a fresh water source, without drawing the water.

Ben Katin's system consisted of a wheel and pulley system that lowered the basin every evening into the בּוֹר הַגּוֹלָה, the Well of Returning Exiles (see *Eiruvin* 104a and *Yoma* 19a), so that its waters would join the natural water table and not be disqualified overnight. In the morning, the full Basin was pulled out of the well, with care taken not to let it lose contact with the ground so the water would not be considered to have been drawn (*Zevaḥim* 21a–b). Rabbeinu Ḥananel and Rashi write that it was lowered into the יָם שֶׁל שְׁלֹמֹה, the Sea of Solomon, a large vat-like structure built by King Solomon which was used as a *mikveh* (II Kings 8:23–26). *Tosafot Rosh* notes that this could

שֶׁלְּאֶשְׁכְּרוֹעַ הָיוּ
וַעֲשָׂאָן בֶּן גַּמְלָא שֶׁלְּזָהָב
וְהָיוּ מַזְכִּירִין אוֹתוֹ לְשֶׁבַח.

י בֶּן קָטִין עָשָׂה שְׁנֵים עָשָׂר דַּד לַכִּיּוֹר
שֶׁלֹּא הָיוּ לוֹ אֶלָּא שְׁנַיִם;
וְאַף הוּא עָשָׂה מוּכְנִי לַכִּיּוֹר
שֶׁלֹּא יִהְיוּ מֵימָיו נִפְסָלִין בְּלִינָה.

שֶׁלְּאֶשְׁכְּרוֹעַ *Boxwood.* Rashi and Meiri identify the tree as a בְּרוֹשׁ; in modern Hebrew this denotes a cypress, but it is likely that Rashi and Meiri were referring to the list of seven trees in Isaiah 41:19 which the Talmud in *Bava Batra* 80b expanded to a list of "ten types of cedar" (the cedar itself being the first). Rashbam (ad loc.) and Rambam (on our mishna) identify אֶשְׁכְּרוֹעַ with the boxwood. This is a relatively small tree with wood of high density and fine grain, ideal for carving; today it is used to make chess pieces and musical instruments.

וַעֲשָׂאָן בֶּן גַּמְלָא שֶׁלְּזָהָב *Ben Gamla made them out of gold.* The *Sifra* deduces from the wording of Leviticus 16:8 that the two lots must be identical (*Aḥarei Mot*, 2:3); Rambam adds that, provided they are so, it does not matter what they are made of (*Hilkhot Avodat Yom HaKippurim* 3:1). The golden lots donated by Yehoshua ben Gamla form the beginning of a list of exceptional private donations made to the Temple.

Yehoshua ben Gamla appears twice in the Mishna – here, and in *Yevamot* 61a, which mentions his marriage to Martha bat Baitos. Ben Gamla was a High Priest, and Martha bat Baitos, a widow. Although a High Priest is not allowed to marry a widow (Lev. 21:14) he had married her before receiving his appointment and was not required to divorce her. The Talmud (ibid. and in *Yoma* 18a) accuses Martha bat Baitos of purchasing the High Priesthood for her husband. This notoriety, however, did not prevent him from being spoken of with praise, both for this donation, and, even more especially, for instituting an education system that made literacy available to children in all sectors of the population (*Bava Batra* 21a).

King Monobaz
made the handles of all the vessels of the Day of Atonement of gold.
His mother Helene
made a lamp of gold for the opening of the Sanctuary;
she also made a tablet of gold,
with the Sota declaration written on it.

---

to mean "chandelier." The נִבְרֶשֶׁת donated by Queen Helene was placed on the Sanctuary's threshold. The Talmud (37b) narrates that as the sun would rise each day, the נִבְרֶשֶׁת would reflect the light so that it could be seen by all that the time for reading the Shema had arrived. This is likely the basis for Rambam's translation, though in truth a lamp could reflect the light in a similar way.

Interestingly, Rabbeinu Tam derives from this remark in the Talmud that the time in which one may read the Shema begins only at sunrise. This leads him to the surprising position that the much praised practice of the *vatikin*, who read the Shema in the moments leading up to sunrise, timing their prayers such that they will open their Amida prayer straight after the sun's first appearance – is in fact incorrect. His nephew, Rabbeinu Yitzḥak (known as the Ri), however, strongly defended their practice as the ideal (see Tosafot *Berakhot* 9b; *Smag*, 18); and his position is accepted as authoritative (*Shulḥan Arukh* OḤ 58:1).

The first book to include a comprehensive discussion of halakhic hours and how they are calculated, the *Tevuot Shemesh*, was written by Rabbi Yehosef Schwarz (Hungary; emigrated to Israel in 1833). His pupil, Rabbi Ḥiyya Spitzer, ascended Mount Scopus daily for several years to record the time of sunrise, and the results of his observations were published in a book named סֵפֶר הַנִּבְרֶשֶׁת.

שֶׁפָּרָשַׁת סוֹטָה *The Sota declaration.* In Numbers chapter five, the Torah describes the proper procedure in the case of a woman whose husband suspects her of infidelity (a *sota*). The procedure in the Temple includes writing out the curses specified in the Torah – including God's holy name – and washing the text away in a cup of water for the woman to drink. The tablet Queen Heleni donated served as a source for the priest transcribing the verses.

מֻנְבַּז הַמֶּלֶךְ
הָיָה עוֹשֶׂה כָּל יְדוֹת הַכֵּלִים שֶׁלְּיוֹם הַכִּפּוּרִים שֶׁלְּזָהָב
הִילְנִי אִמּוֹ
עָשְׂתָה נִבְרֶשֶׁת שֶׁלְּזָהָב עַל פִּתְחוֹ שֶׁלַּהֵיכָל;
וְאַף הִיא עָשְׂתָה טַבְלָא שֶׁלְּזָהָב
שֶׁפָּרָשַׁת סוֹטָה כְּתוּבָה עָלֶיהָ.

---

only be true in the First Temple, as the Sea was no longer extant during the Second Temple period (see II Kings 25:13).

מֻנְבַּז הַמֶּלֶךְ *King Monobaz.* Monobaz II (first century) was king of Adiabene, a small independent kingdom in present day Armenia or Iraq. He, his elder brother Izates, and their mother Queen Heleni all converted to Judaism (see *Bereshit Raba, Lekh Lekha* 46:10). Their palaces were quite prominent on the Jerusalem landscape, very close to the Temple. Monobaz supported the Judean settlement in the Galil and ordered the building of the royal tomb in Jerusalem, in which he had his mother's and brother's bodies buried (Josephus, *The Wars of the Jews*, book v).

In *Bava Batra* 11a, a man by the similar name of Munbaz is mentioned as a philanthropist on an immense scale, which would be consistent with the mishna here. In *Shabbat* 68b and *Shevuot* 26b a *Tana* named Munbaz disputes with Rabbi Akiva regarding a gentile who converted to Judaism but remained living among the nations and, as a consequence, continued violating the Torah. The subject matter of the dispute is certainly suggestive of Monobaz's situation. Munbaz, however, is also mentioned in a seemingly unconnected context in the *Sifra, Metzora* 1:4 where he discusses the laws of purifying lepers.

יְדוֹת הַכֵּלִים *The handles of all the vessels.* The blades of the knives could not be of gold (a soft and malleable metal); so only the handles were fashioned from gold (*Yoma* 37b).

נִבְרֶשֶׁת *A lamp of gold.* The word נִבְרֶשֶׁת first appears (in an Aramaic form) in Daniel 5:5, indicating an object close to which the mysterious finger wrote upon the wall in Balthazar's court. Rashi and Ibn Ezra understand this to be a lamp. Rambam translates it as "mirror." In modern Hebrew, the term has come

Miracles happened for the doors of Nikanor,
and he was spoken of afterwards in praise.

11 And these were spoken of for shame:
Those of the house of Garmu
chose not to teach others the art of the showbread.
Those of the house of Avtinas
chose not to teach others the art of the incense.

---

are mentioned in the mishna in *Shekalim* which names the skilled people of the Temple (5:1).

The twelve loaves of the Showbread (see 2:6 and commentary there) were placed on the Table in the Sanctuary on Shabbat and were needed to remain fresh for a full week until they were replaced. To prevent mold and staleness, they were baked into a special structure, which the Talmud compares to a lidless box, or a ship on the high seas (*Menaḥot* 94a–b). This was a special art, which the Garmu family guarded jealously for themselves. The Talmud (*Yoma* 38a; Yerushalmi, *Shekalim* 5:1) relates how, exasperated by the Garmu family's refusal to divulge the secrets of their trade, the sages brought bakers from Alexandria to bake the bread instead of them, but they failed.

שֶׁלְּבֵית אַבְטִינָס *Those of the house of Avtinas.* The house of Avtinas prepared the incense (see 1:5 and commentary there). Among the other ingredients used, they included one named מַעֲלֶה עָשָׁן – "what makes smoke rise" – which caused the incense to form a perfectly straight column of smoke. They refused to disclose what this substance was, and their secret died with them. The Talmud does record a story of one of the surviving members of the Avtinas family who tries to divulge the secret, but dies before he can do so. In modern Hebrew, the broom-brush (*Leptadenia pyrotechnica*) which grows in the Judean desert, is named after this mysterious herb.

נִיקָנוֹר
נַעֲשׂוּ נִסִּים לְדַלְתוֹתָיו
וְהָיוּ מַזְכִּירִין אוֹתוֹ לְשֶׁבַח.

יא וְאֵלּוּ לִגְנַאי:
שֶׁלְּבֵית גַּרְמוּ
לֹא רָצוּ לְלַמֵּד עַל מַעֲשֵׂה לֶחֶם הַפָּנִים
שֶׁלְּבֵית אַבְטִינָס
לֹא רָצוּ לְלַמֵּד עַל מַעֲשֵׂה הַקְּטֹרֶת

נִיקָנוֹר *The doors of Nikanor.* Nikanor brought the huge, magnificent doors from Alexandria. On his way back, his ship was caught in a storm. The sailors tried to save the vessel by lightening it, and cast one of the heavy doors into the sea, but to no avail. As they were about to throw the second door overboard also, Nikanor took hold of it in an embrace, refusing to let it be thrown in unless he be thrown in with it. The sea calmed, and he arrived safely to land, lamenting the loss of the discarded door. After alighting from the ship, however, he saw the door in the shallow water near the beach – clearly by a miracle; such a heavy object would never normally be washed so far (38a, based on the *Tosefta*). When Herod rebuilt the Temple, he replaced all the doors leading into the Temple with golden ones (*Bava Batra* 4a). The original gate of Nikanor, however, was left unchanged, in honor of the miracle and because its copper plating anyway provided a golden sheen (according to the Talmud they were actually plated with renowned Corinthian bronze, mentioned in Ezra 8:27 as "precious as gold") (Mishna *Middot* 2:3).

Interestingly, Ze'ev Safrai (מִשְׁנַת אֶרֶץ יִשְׂרָאֵל [Jerusalem: Mikhlelet Lifshits, 2010], p. 135) notes that archaeologists have found an inscription in a grave cut into Jerusalem rock, referring to "Nikanor of the Doors."

וְאֵלּוּ לִגְנַאי *And these were spoken of for shame.* Those listed here for their disgraced are all criticized for refusing to share their unique skills. The first three

Hugras ben Levi knew a lesson in the art of song
and chose not to teach it to others.
Ben Kamtzar
chose not to teach others the art of penmanship.
Of those mentioned first it is said,
"A righteous man's memory is a blessing…" Prov. 10
and of the others,
"… and the name of the wicked will rot."

וְשֵׁם רְשָׁעִים יִרְקָב *The name of the wicked will rot.* The *Tosefta* relates that the sages ask each family why they have been so protective of their secret skills. The houses of Garmu and Avtinas and Hugras ben Levi each reply, "Father's family always knew that one day the Temple would be destroyed – and they did not want to teach their secrets, lest they be used to do for idols as was done before God." (2:5) Only Ben Kamtzar does not answer the question. After quoting this *Tosefta*, the Talmud cites the verse brought in the mishna, this time applying "the name of the wicked will rot" to "Ben Kamtzar and his friends." Rambam assumes that the others' excuses were not accepted as valid and that "his friends" refers to the other three in the list. The Rid and Rabbeinu Yehonatan, however, understand this as an amendment to the Mishna's original formulation, accepting that the first three's intentions were indeed noble, and deeming only Ben Kamtzar to have acted wrongly. The Talmud and *Tosefta*, indeed, bear witness to the fact that the houses of Garmu and Avtinas were meticulously careful not to use their skills for mundane purposes and praises them for this; the Garmu family never ate white bread, and the Avtinas family never used perfume, "that it should not be said" that they made private use of their sacred arts.

הֻגְרַס בֶּן לֵוִי
הָיָה יוֹדֵעַ פֶּרֶק בַּשִּׁיר
וְלֹא רָצָה לְלַמֵּד
בֶּן קַמְצָר
לֹא רָצָה לְלַמֵּד עַל מַעֲשֵׂה הַכְּתָב.
עַל הָרִאשׁוֹנִים נֶאֱמַר:
זֵכֶר צַדִּיק לִבְרָכָה משלי י
וְעַל אֵלּוּ נֶאֱמַר:
וְשֵׁם רְשָׁעִים יִרְקָב:

הֻגְרַס בֶּן לֵוִי...בֶּן קַמְצָר *Hugras ben Levi… Ben Kamtzar.* The Talmud expands upon this, explaining that Hugras ben Levi knew how to project his voice in a uniquely powerful way, while Ben Kamtzar was able to hold four pens between his fingers and write four letters simultaneously (38b).

זֵכֶר צַדִּיק לִבְרָכָה *A righteous man's memory is a blessing.* The Talmud point out that as soon as He mentions Abraham's name, God blesses him (*Yoma* 38b on Gen. 18:18; cited by Rashi there). The verse in Proverbs is then taken as a prescription for any time in which a righteous person's name is mentioned. The Talmud and Midrash (*Bereshit Raba* 49:1) assume that the second half of the verse, "the name of the wicked will rot," mirrors the first half, also comprising an instruction. Rashi explains the verse in its context in Proverbs not as a directive, but simply as an expression of the reality that the name of a wicked person fades away over time until it is forgotten. The deeds and inspiration of the righteous are of eternal value and create a living, self-perpetuating legacy. The acts of the wicked, by way of contrast, are based on their indulgence in things of fleeting value and do not withstand the passing of time (see Eccl. 9:3–6; Responsa of the Rashba 4:30; the Vilna Gaon to Proverbs).

CHAPTER FOUR

1 The High Priest shook the box,
and drew out each of the two lots.
One of them had written on it "To [the LORD]";
and the other, "To Azazel."
The Prefect of the priests would be standing to his right,
and the Head of the ministering house to his left.
If the lot to [the LORD] came up in his right hand,
the Prefect would say to him,
"My honored High Priest, raise your right hand!"

טָרַף בַּקַּלְפִּי *The High Priest shook the box.* The right hand is a symbol of strength (see, for instance, Ex. 15:6). It is therefore considered a good omen if the lot "for the LORD" arises in the High Priest's right hand. The Talmud (39a) explains the High Priest "shook the box" (our translation) to prevent him manipulating the result. The *Arukh* translates the verb טָרַף as "mixed," and on the basis of this understanding, Rabbeinu Ḥananel (39a) and Rashbam (*Bava Batra* 122a) explain he shook the box containing the ballots in order to mix them up; we have translated in accordance with this reading. Rashi interprets טָרַף as "snatched," closer to the biblical sense of the word, "to tear apart prey." Although the lots were both alike (see below), it might still be possible to distinguish between them from the engraving of the words. Snatching at them quickly precludes this possibility. The public nature of the ceremony also counters any suspicion (*Mishnat Aryeh*).

הַגְבֵּה יְמִינְךָ *"Raise your right hand!"* The Talmud (39a) relates that this happened every year throughout Shimon HaTzaddik's forty-year tenure as High Priest, a testimony to the righteousness of his generation.

The mishna follows the rabbis' view that both lots are drawn out by the High Priest. Rabbi Yehuda, it is noted in the Talmud, disagrees, maintaining that the High Priest only draws the first lot, while the second is drawn by the Deputy. The dispute, it is suggested, hinges on whether the Deputy's right hand or the High Priest's left is deemed more fitting. The commentators consider that the issue is, again, whether the casting of the lots is a ritual of the day in its own right, to be performed exclusively by the High Priest, or merely a way to fairly allocate the roles of the two goats (see Rav Soloveitchik ad loc.) in preparation for the rituals proper. Alongside the preferred status

פרק רביעי

א טָרַף בַּקַּלְפִּי
וְהֶעֱלָה שְׁנֵי גוֹרָלוֹת.
אֶחָד כָּתוּב עָלָיו: לַשֵּׁם
וְאֶחָד כָּתוּב עָלָיו: לַעֲזָאזֵל.
הַסְּגַן מִימִינוֹ, וְרֹאשׁ בֵּית אָב מִשְּׂמֹאלוֹ.
אִם שֶׁלַּשֵּׁם עָלָה בִימִינוֹ
הַסְּגַן אוֹמֵר לוֹ:
אִישִׁי כֹהֵן גָּדוֹל, הַגְבֵּה יְמִינְךָ!

CHAPTER FOUR

The description of the Order of the Day in chapter three has brought us to the point at which the two goats are positioned near the altar (3:9). Continuing from this place, chapter four will now describe how the two goats are designated to their respective roles; one as a sin-offering, the other to be sent to Azazel. The chapter then continues with the confession over, and subsequent slaughter of the bull.

Before the High Priest can enter the Holy of Holies, the climax of the day's service, he must complete his own atonement. This is realized through the two confessions he makes over the bull; one for his personal household and one for the Priesthood (see note to 1:1). The first of these confessions appears in chapter three, and the second will be discussed in this chapter. A third confession, for all the people, will be made over the sin-offering goat in chapter six. All confessions consist of the admission of a sin, (Talmud 87b), and a supplication for forgiveness (Rabbeinu Yona's *Sha'arei Teshuva,* chapter four). Both elements are included in the High Priest's confessions.

The other condition for entering the Holy of Holies is the burning of the incense (see note to 4:2). In this chapter, the High Priest sets aside the coals for this purpose. The mishna notes that a different coal pan is used on Yom Kippur than on other days; this signals the beginning of a digression in which the mishna lists other differences between the service of Yom Kippur and those of the rest of the year.

And if the lot to [the LORD] came up in his left hand,
the Head of the ministering house would say,
"My honored High Priest, raise your left!"
He would place the lots upon the two goats and say,
"A sin-offering to [the LORD]."
Rabbi Yishmael says:
There was no need to say "a sin-offering" –
only "to [the LORD]."
And they would respond,
"Blessed be the name of His glorious kingdom for ever and all time."

---

621) objects to such a notion and rules that this line should be removed from the *piyut*; today it is absent in most Sephardi *maḥzorim*. Maharam Nigrin (a contemporary of the *Beit Yosef*) suggests interpreting the line not as a conditional statement but as an expression of hope that the lot for the LORD would indeed be drawn by the Priest's right hand. Following this suggestion, many Ashkenazi *maḥzorim* retain the line (see Appendix II, page 439). In אַמִּיץ כֹּחַ, the point is not mentioned.

חַטָּאת *A sin-offering.* "And Aaron shall offer up the goat whose lot falls to the LORD, and make it a sin-offering" (Lev. 16:9). *Tosafot Yeshanim* explain that the rabbis understand the conclusion, "and make it a sin-offering," as the final step required to sanctify the goat as a sin-offering, by verbally designating it as such. According to Rabbi Yishmael, on the other hand, the end of the verse is descriptive, not prescriptive; the drawing of the lots mentioned in the first half of the verse is enough to define its status without verbal confirmation.

The *Tosefta* (2:9) words the disagreement differently; there the rabbis have the High Priest declare, "For the LORD!" and the Deputy continuing, "A sin-offering." Rabbi Yishmael, then, disputes the need for the Deputy's participation.

Rashi (Lev. 16:9) and Rambam (*Hilkhot Avodat Yom HaKippurim* 2:6) state that the High Priest would say the whole sentence, and this is also how the scene is narrated in the Order of the Service *piyutim*. *Smag* (209) and Ritva (39a) follow the *Tosefta*'s description.

וְהֵן עוֹנִין *And they would respond.* We have translated this line as an independent clause, continuing the mishna's account, and not as the conclusion of Rabbi Yishmael's dissenting view. In this we follow the ruling of Rambam (ibid.),

וְאִם שֶׁל־שֵׁם עָלָה בִשְׂמֹאלוֹ
רֹאשׁ בֵּית אָב אוֹמֵר לוֹ:
אִישִׁי כֹהֵן גָּדוֹל, הַגְבֵּהַּ שְׂמֹאלְךָ!
נְתָנָן עַל שְׁנֵי הַשְּׂעִירִים
וְאוֹמֵר: ׳לַה׳ חַטָּאת׳.
רַבִּי יִשְׁמָעֵאל אוֹמֵר:
לֹא הָיָה צָרִיךְ לוֹמַר ׳חַטָּאת׳
אֶלָּא ׳לַה׳׳.
וְהֵן עוֹנִין אַחֲרָיו:
׳בָּרוּךְ שֵׁם כְּבוֹד מַלְכוּתוֹ לְעוֹלָם וָעֶד׳.

---

of the High Priest, however, all Temple rites are to be performed with the right hand; Rambam (*Hilkhot Avodat Yom HaKippurim* 3:3) writes explicitly that although the drawing of the lots is an essential rite of the day, it is not an "act of service," so can be partly held by the High Priest's left hand. The Meiri insists that it must be considered a full part of the service, as it is clearly mandated in the Torah and the High Priest performs it in his white vestments. He therefore interprets Rambam's statement to mean only that the designation of the lots should not to be considered an act of service in the same way as an offering.

נְתָנָן עַל שְׁנֵי הַשְּׂעִירִים *He would place the lots upon the two goats.* The phrase אֲשֶׁר עָלָה עָלָיו הַגּוֹרָל (Lev. 16:9), literally, "[the goat] that the lot comes up upon," is somewhat ambiguous. According to Rabbi Yoḥanan it suggests that the lots must literally be placed upon the goats, this being an indispensable stage in designating one goat as the sin-offering. Rabbi Yanai argues that it is simply an idiomatic way of referring to the result of the lottery, and not a directive. Rambam (3:3) rules in accordance with Rabbi Yanai. He therefore permits the placing of the lots by a non-priest, while insisting that the actual drawing of the lots, which is an essential part of the ritual, only be done by the High Priest.

אַתָּה כּוֹנַנְתָּ oddly states גּוֹרָל יָמִין כְּשֶׁהוּא שֶׁל שֵׁם / יִתְּנֵהוּ עַל הַשָּׂעִיר "If the lot to the Lord was in his right, he would place it upon the goat" (page 1265), seeming to imply that if it came up in his left hand, he would not. The *Beit Yosef* (OḤ

2 He would tie a strip of scarlet wool
to the head of the goat that was to be sent away,
and stand it by the place from which it would be sent.
And to the one which would be slaughtered
[he would tie one] at the place where it would be slaughtered.
The High Priest would come to his bull a second time,
and would press his two hands down upon it and confess.
And this is what he would say:

לָשׁוֹן שֶׁלְּזְהוֹרִית *A strip of scarlet wool.* According to the Talmud this weighed two *selaim,* approximately 38 grams (42a). Rashi explains that it had to be relatively large because it would be redivided later on (see mishna 6:6).

בֵּית שִׁלּוּחוֹ *The place from which it would be sent.* "And the goat whose lot falls to Azazel shall be left to stand alive before the LORD, to be an atonement – to be sent away to Azazel, into the wastelands" (Lev. 16:10). Once there, it is led to the crag and cast to its death. The Talmud (40b) discusses the timing of this, based on a reading of the word לְכַפֵּר in the verse quoted – translated here "to be an atonement" but read exegetically to describe the process through which the goat must "be left to stand alive before the LORD"; it is not sent to its death until its "twin" goat, designated for the LORD, has completed its atonement (v. 20). Rabbi Yehuda understands this atonement to be the purification of the Temple realized though the sprinkling of that goat's blood. According to Rabbi Shimon the essential "atonement" they are waiting for is the verbal confession of the High Priest over the Azazel goat.

Ritva suggests that the dispute reflects a fundamental disagreement about the importance of the Azazel goat. According to Rabbi Yehuda, it is only essential that the Azazel goat survives until the sprinkling of its twin's blood. If it dies after this point and its rite is never performed, while certainly a cause for dismay, it would not prevent the people's atonement (see Rashi 40b). Rabbi Shimon disagrees. He holds that the confession over the Azazel goat, and the "atonement of words" that it achieves, are critical to the atonement of the day. The goat must survive until that point. Even Rabbi Shimon, however, concedes that if the goat dies after the confession but before being sent away, the day's atonement has still been accomplished.

בֵּית שְׁחִיטָתוֹ *At the place where it would be slaughtered.* This line is ambiguous; it is unclear whether the "house of slaughter" referred to is the goat's throat

ב קָשַׁר לָשׁוֹן שֶׁל זְהוֹרִית בְּרֹאשׁ שָׂעִיר הַמִּשְׁתַּלֵּחַ
וְהֶעֱמִידוֹ כְּנֶגֶד בֵּית שִׁלּוּחוֹ
וְלַנִּשְׁחָט
כְּנֶגֶד בֵּית שְׁחִיטָתוֹ.
בָּא לוֹ אֵצֶל פָּרוֹ שְׁנִיָּה
וְסוֹמֵךְ שְׁתֵּי יָדָיו עָלָיו
וּמִתְוַדֶּה.
וְכָךְ הָיָה אוֹמֵר:

---

also reflected in the Order of the Service *piyutim* (see below). However, the earliest *piyutim* (up to the period of Rav Sa'adia Gaon) make no mention of this line, suggesting that they indeed understand it as part of Rabbi Yishmael's account, and, as his opinion is not accepted as authoritative, omit it.

In אַמִּיץ כֹּחַ (page 887) this response is mentioned without any addition; but in אַתָּה כּוֹנַנְתָּ (according to our version) a passage beginning with "וְהַכֹּהֲנִים" is added, describing the people kneeling in prostration upon the mention of the Holy Name (page 1265). Rabbi Moishe Sternbuch (*Mo'adim UZemanim* 1:61) suggests that a halakhic obligation to kneel exists only when the Holy Name is formally mentioned in a prayer or a blessing. The response here should therefore be understood as a spontaneous demonstration of praise and submission. Indeed, God's name is mentioned three times in each confession, but the people kneel only after the third, responding to the prayer as a whole.

In truth, even in אַתָּה כּוֹנַנְתָּ, the passage beginning with "וְהַכֹּהֲנִים" is not a part of the original *piyut*, but an addition based on the Abudraham. Rabbi Yosef Karo supports this addition (*Beit Yosef*, OḤ 621; Responsum *Avkat Rokhel* 27–28), but as late as the eighteenth century it was not accepted by all Sephardi congregations (it does not appear, for instance, in *Shifat Revivim*). The early Hasidic *Maḥzorim* (those of Rabbi Shabtai of Rashkov and of Shneur Zalman of Liadi), which were the first to introduce אַתָּה כּוֹנַנְתָּ to the European (*Nusaḥ Sepharad*) liturgy, specify that the congregation should not kneel at this point. In recent generations, some have added it (see Rav Soloveitchik on 37a), and this is the practice most common in Sephardi congregations today.

Please, [Lord],
I have done wrong,
I have rebelled,
I have sinned before You –
I and my family
and the descendants of Aaron, Your holy people.
Please, [Lord],
make atonement, please, for the wrongs
and the rebellions
and sins
that I have done wrong,
I have rebelled,
that I have sinned before You –
I and my family
and the descendants of Aaron, Your holy people.
As it is written in the Torah of Moses Your servant,
"For you will be atoned on this day..." *Lev. 16*
And they would respond,
"Blessed be the name of His glorious kingdom forever."

3 He would slaughter it
and gather its blood in a bowl,

---

hood. Any other sins committed by the priests are included in the general confession for all Israel, which is made over the goat (Mishna, *Shevuot* 2b). For commentary on the confession, see 3:8.

שְׁחָטוֹ *He would slaughter it.* The *Tosafot Yom Tov* suggest that the bull is slaughtered in the same way as the daily offering, the High Priest making the first incision and a different priest finishing the slaughtering (see 3:4). This fits well with the rationale presented there by Rashi and Rabbeinu Yehonatan (see commentary there) and is reflected in the Ashkenazi version of אַתָּה כּוֹנַנְתָּ (page 1266; the Sephardi version omits it). The *Tiferet Yisrael* disagrees. He understands the slaughter of the bull to be a special rite of Yom Kippur, which must be performed by the High Priest alone. He cites in his support *Yoma* 70b, which describes the meticulous care the High Priest takes throughout the day, which would ensure that no blood is spilt.

אָנָּא הַשֵּׁם
עָוִיתִי פָּשַׁעְתִּי חָטָאתִי לְפָנֶיךָ
אֲנִי וּבֵיתִי וּבְנֵי אַהֲרֹן עַם קְדוֹשֶׁךָ.
אָנָּא הַשֵּׁם
כַּפֶּר נָא לָעֲוֹנוֹת וְלַפְּשָׁעִים וְלַחֲטָאִים
שֶׁעָוִיתִי וְשֶׁפָּשַׁעְתִּי וְשֶׁחָטָאתִי לְפָנֶיךָ
אֲנִי וּבֵיתִי וּבְנֵי אַהֲרֹן עַם קְדוֹשֶׁךָ
כַּכָּתוּב בְּתוֹרַת מֹשֶׁה עַבְדֶּךָ:
כִּי־בַיּוֹם הַזֶּה יְכַפֵּר עֲלֵיכֶם לְטַהֵר אֶתְכֶם ויקרא טז
מִכֹּל חַטֹּאתֵיכֶם, לִפְנֵי ה׳ תִּטְהָרוּ:
וְהֵן עוֹנִין אַחֲרָיו:
׳בָּרוּךְ שֵׁם כְּבוֹד מַלְכוּתוֹ לְעוֹלָם וָעֶד׳.

ג שְׁחָטוֹ
וְקִבֵּל בַּמִּזְרָק אֶת דָּמוֹ

(such a usage is attested in *Tosefta Ḥullin* 9:11), or simply the place in the Temple where it will be slaughtered. The mishna clearly parallels the two goats, its language reflecting the fact (6:1) that the goats themselves must be alike, though their destinies are different. The "place" referred to here may parallel the "head" of the other goat, or "the place from which it would be sent" – either of the two parts of the description of what is done to it. The Talmud (41b) asks which is intended and concludes that the comparison relates to the scarlet wool. The wool is attached to the goat for the Lord to make it clearly identifiable, although it is tied in a different place to that of its twin to distinguish the two from one another. Since the purpose of this wool is only practical, there are no formal requirements as to its size or shape; it is valid as long as it fulfills its purpose (Tosafot).

וּבְנֵי אַהֲרֹן *The descendants of Aaron.* The confession over the bull is only for sins of desecration to the Temple, the sin specifically associated with the Priest-

and give it to the one who would keep it stirring
on the fourth tile of the Sanctuary,
so that it would not congeal.
He would take the coal pan
and go up to the head of the altar,
and clear the spent coals this way and that,
and lift out the inner, live ones,
and then go down and lay the pan on the fourth tile of the courtyard.

4 On all other days,
he would lift out the coals with a silver pan
and empty them into a golden one.
But today he would lift them out with a golden pan,
and with that pan he would bring the coals in.

Rama of Fano provides an original explanation. There are twelve steps connecting the courtyard to the Sanctuary. After every third step there is a plateau, which he identifies as the רוֹבֶד the mishna refers to. The fourth רוֹבֶד was thus the top step which lay on the border between the courtyard and the Sanctuary (res. 11). A similar interpretation is suggested by Ḥanoch Albeck in his edition of the Mishna, with corroborating Geonic sources.

וְחוֹתֶה מִן הַמְעֻכָּלוֹת הַפְּנִימִיּוֹת *And lift out the inner, live ones.* The Talmud (*Keritot* 20a–b) argues the possibility that moving coals around on Shabbat, as opposed to adding them to a fire, is only a rabbinic prohibition. If so, it would certainly be permitted inside the Temple (where many rabbinic prohibitions are waived). Even if it is a biblical prohibition (it being inevitable that some coals will either flair up or be extinguished in the process), as the Torah specifies the need for live coals in this case (Lev. 16:12) the prohibition is suspended, as with any other labor required for the Temple offerings (*Pesaḥim* 66a).

בְּשֶׁל זָהָב *With a golden pan.* Placing the golden pan directly into the fire can damage it. On other days, therefore, a silver pan is used in the fire and then the coals are transferred to the gold one (Rabbeinu Yehonatan). On Yom Kippur,

וּנְתָנוֹ לְמִי שֶׁהוּא מְמָרֵס בּוֹ
עַל הָרוֹבֵד הָרְבִיעִי שֶׁבַּהֵיכָל
כְּדֵי שֶׁלֹּא יִקְרֹשׁ.
נָטַל אֶת הַמַּחְתָּה
וְעָלָה לְרֹאשׁ הַמִּזְבֵּחַ
וּפִנָּה גֶחָלִים אֵילָךְ וְאֵילָךְ
וְחוֹתֶה מִן הַמְעֻכָּלוֹת הַפְּנִימִיּוֹת
וְיָרַד
וְהִנִּיחָהּ עַל הָרוֹבֵד הָרְבִיעִי שֶׁבָּעֲזָרָה.

ד בְּכָל יוֹם
הָיָה חוֹתֶה בְשֶׁל־כֶּסֶף
וּמְעָרֶה בְתוֹךְ שֶׁל־זָהָב
וְהַיּוֹם
חוֹתֶה בְשֶׁל־זָהָב
וּבָהּ הָיָה מַכְנִיס.

עַל הָרוֹבֵד הָרְבִיעִי *On the fourth tile.* The term רוֹבֵד in the mishna is used to refer to two entirely different places: (1) The mishna in *Tamid* (1:1) mentions the רוֹבְדִים as the place where the elder priests would sleep; the younger priests slept on the floor. Rabbeinu Gershom understands these רוֹבְדִים to be marble chairs. Rosh describes them as benches protruding from the wall (but see Rambam, *Hilkhot Beit HaBeḥira* 8:5). (2) Rashi on this mishna explains רוֹבְדִים to be large marble floor tiles. The "fourth one" means the fourth one in from the door of the Sanctuary. The blood would be stirred by a man standing on this tile. The Talmud (43b), however, points out that as no one is permitted to be inside the Sanctuary while the High Priest is in the Holy of Holies, the mishna should be read as referring to a tile outside the Sanctuary, the fourth one from its opening in the other direction.

On all other days
he would lift them with a pan of four kabs
and empty the coals into one of three kabs.
But today
he would lift them with a pan of three kabs,
and with that pan he would bring the coals in.
Rabbi Yose says:
On all other days he would lift them with a pan of a se'ah
and empty the coals into one of three kabs;
but today he would lift them with a pan of three kabs,
and with that pan he would bring the coals in.

---

distinction may lie in the source of the funds: while the public purse should not be overburdened, donations from wealthy individuals are encouraged, as demonstrated in the cases specified in chapter three. The donations of the Jewish people toward the construction of the Tabernacle may be the model here; the pillars and public offerings were purchased using the small half-shekel donation taken from rich and poor alike. The expensive materials needed for the curtains and other vessels, however, were provided through larger, voluntary donations (Rashi, Ex. 25:2). This preserves a basic level of maintenance in which all are equal partners, while still providing opportunity for those who can to contribute more.

שֶׁלִּשְׁלֹשֶׁת קַבִּין *A pan of three kabs.* A *kab* is a unit of volume equivalent to approximately 1.4 liters (according to Rabbi Ḥayyim Naeh). A *se'ah* is six kabs.

During the year, more coals than needed are initially taken. The Yerushalmi explains that usually, the extra coals are swept into the אַמָּה, the conduit leading from the courtyard to the Kidron valley. On Shabbat, they are covered over with a brass container instead.

Rav Nissim Gaon (in his *Megillat Setarim*) uses this procedure to demonstrate that the coal pan does not have the status of a כְּלִי שָׁרֵת, sacred vessel. Had it been one, anything placed into it would become consecrated and could not be simply swept away. Rabbeinu Tam rejects this proof, claiming that as there is never any intention to consecrate more than three kabs, the vessel does not have the power to consecrate more (Tosafot, *Yoma* 46b; see also Rashi on Num. 17:2). However, all agree that on Yom Kippur, when all the coals collected are used, the pan is certainly a sacred vessel.

בְּכָל יוֹם
חוֹתֶה בְּשֶׁלְּאַרְבַּעַת קַבִּין
וּמְעָרֶה בְּתוֹךְ שֶׁלִּשְׁלֹשֶׁת קַבִּין
וְהַיּוֹם
חוֹתֶה בְּשֶׁלִּשְׁלֹשֶׁת קַבִּין
וּבָהּ הָיָה מַכְנִיס.
רַבִּי יוֹסֵי אוֹמֵר:
בְּכָל יוֹם חוֹתֶה בְּשֶׁלִּסְאָה
וּמְעָרֶה בְּתוֹךְ שֶׁלִּשְׁלֹשֶׁת קַבִּין;
וְהַיּוֹם חוֹתֶה בְּשֶׁלִּשְׁלֹשֶׁת קַבִּין
וּבָהּ הָיָה מַכְנִיס.

---

however, to avoid overtaxing the fasting High Priest's strength, the golden pan is used throughout (44b).

The Talmud (ibid.) justifies the use of silver for the standard coal pan, and also the original use of wood for the ballot boxes, with the saying: הַתּוֹרָה חָסָה עַל מָמוֹנָן שֶׁל יִשְׂרָאֵל, "The Torah has mercy on the money of Israel." This principle directs that in certain cases, where a more exacting attitude would entail great expense, a more lenient approach should be taken. It is derived from the biblical case of a *tzara'at*-infected house: the Torah instructs the house to be cleared of its contents before the priest formally declares it and anything inside it to be impure, thus saving the contents from impurity (Rashi). In our case, this principle would seem to conflict with another one: אֵין עֲנִיּוּת בִּמְקוֹם עֲשִׁירוּת, "In a place of wealth [the Temple] there is no poverty." Compromising on costs in the Temple is seen as a belittling of its status (see *Shabbat* 102b, *Tamid* 29a). Indeed, the Talmud in *Menaḥot* 89a pits these two principles directly against one another.

Many different guidelines have been suggested for balancing these two values. Maharam ibn Ḥaviv (*Rosh HaShana* 27a) suggests that the boundaries are left to the decisions of the sages in each generation. Others (see for example Ritva, *Yoma* 39a) apply the price respectively to different cases (see both principles in the *Talmudic Encyclopedia* for a full discussion). Perhaps a

On all other days it would be heavy,
    but today it was light.
On all other days its handle would be short,
    but today it was long.
On all other days would be of yellow gold,
    but today of red gold;
    thus says Rabbi Menaḥem.
On all other days he would offer up half a maneh in the morning
    and half a maneh in the evening,
    but today he would add a handful of incense.

---

cover for the handle to protect his arm (Riva, cited in *Tosafot Yeshanim*, 45a), or a cover to protect his face, since his left hand, which held the censer, was not free to protect it (Ritva). Meiri suggests a third option: the pan was made with a base which it could stand on without risk of the coals being scattered.

זְהָבָה יָרֹק *Yellow gold.* In the Talmud (44b–45a), Rav Ḥisda counts seven grades of quality for gold, while Rav Ashi argues that these constitute are only five distinct types. Red gold, the זְהַב פַּרְוָיִם (II Chron. 3:6), is considered the most prized.

In modern Hebrew, יָרֹק means green; but in Talmudic literature, it signifies yellow (see mishna in *Ḥullin* 47b and *Nidda* 19a). The Baḥ, YD 188 discusses which shades of yellow are called יָרֹק. See *Arukh HaShulḥan* YD 38:9–11 for a general discussion of names for colors.

פְּרַס *Half a maneh.* In rabbinic Hebrew, the word פְּרַס usually signifies "one half" (*Bekhorot* 58a), although it has many derivate meanings: it is also used to refer to daily bread (which may have been half a loaf) and it was likely adapted from this usage to come to refer to daily wages (*Ta'anit* 25b). It is probably in this sense that it is used in the Mishna in *Avot* (1:3), "Do not be like a servant who serves his master only to receive a *pras.*" In Modern Hebrew it has developed further to mean "prize."

מְלֹא חָפְנָיו *A handful of incense.* This is the same as is used on other days (see page 495) (Yerushalmi).

בְּכָל יוֹם הָיְתָה כְּבֵדָה
וְהַיּוֹם קַלָּה.
בְּכָל יוֹם הָיְתָה יָדָהּ קְצָרָה
וְהַיּוֹם אֲרֻכָּה.
בְּכָל יוֹם הָיָה זְהָבָהּ יָרֹק
וְהַיּוֹם אָדֹם
דִּבְרֵי רַבִּי מְנַחֵם.
בְּכָל יוֹם
מַקְרִיב פְּרַס בְּשַׁחֲרִית וּפְרַס בֵּין הָעַרְבַּיִם
וְהַיּוֹם
מוֹסִיף מְלֹא חָפְנָיו.

וְהַיּוֹם אֲרֻכָּה *But today it was long.* The smaller pan, much lighter that its everyday counterpart, was used on Yom Kippur to conserve the High Priest's energy (Yerushalmi). The regular coal pan was not only larger, but also thicker and more durable. The longer handle on the pan of Yom Kippur gave the High Priest greater leverage by allowing him to hold it underneath his arm, thus making it easier to carry (*Yoma* 44b, Rashi and Meiri).

The Talmud states that the pan for Yom Kippur was also made with a נְיָאשְׁתִּיק. Rashi suggests that this was a ring, loosely attached to the pan, which would make a noise when moved. The High Priest's entrance to the Sanctuary must be marked by a sound (Ex. 28:35). This is usually accomplished by the bells attached to his robe (ibid. 33). On Yom Kippur, however, when he comes to burn the incense, he wears the white vestments which do not have bells attached; the ring on the pan, therefore, is aimed to achieve the same effect. The Yerushalmi and Geonim understand the נְיָאשְׁתִּיק to be a cover to protect the High Priest from being scorched by the burning coals. This was either a

On all other days it would be fine –
but today it was finer than fine.

5 On all other days the priests would ascend the eastern side of the ramp to the altar,
and descend at the western side.
But today the High Priest would ascend its center
and descend at its center.
Rabbi Yehuda says:
The High Priest would always ascend its center
and descend at its center.
On all other days the High Priest would sanctify his hands and feet from the basin,
but today he would use the golden jug.

---

ascend the minor ramp, turn east to the ledge, circle the altar and descend by the main ramp (see page 499). They begin turning east because it is their right, in accordance with the principle that כׇּל פְּנִיּוֹת שֶׁאַתָּה פּוֹנֶה לֹא יְהִיוּ אֶלָּא דֶּרֶךְ יָמִין, "At all junctions one should turn right" (cf. note to 4:1). Likewise, a priest who had to ascend to the top of the altar would do so on the eastern side, which is to the left of the ramp, so that he could turn right upon reaching the top.

כֹּהֵן גָּדוֹל עוֹלֶה בָאֶמְצַע *The High Priest would ascend its center.* In a show of God's affection for the Jewish people, whom the High Priest represents, he is given license to ascend the center of the ramp, without the need to take any unnecessary steps (45a; Rashi 43b, s.v. וְהַיּוֹם). Rambam has a different version of the mishna, which states that on Yom Kippur the other priests also ascend the middle of the ramp. Since their presence is only required to support the High Priest, it is included within his honor that they too should be given this license, so that he will not be made to wait for them (*Tosafot Yom Tov, Melekhet Shlomo*).

לְעוֹלָם כֹּהֵן גָּדוֹל *The High Priest would always.* In this mishna, two disputes are recorded: in both, Rabbi Yehuda holds that the distinctions granted to

בְּכָל יוֹם הָיְתָה דַקָּה
וְהַיּוֹם דַּקָּה מִן הַדַּקָּה.

ה בְּכָל יוֹם
כֹּהֲנִים עוֹלִין בְּמִזְרָחוֹ שֶׁלַּכֶּבֶשׁ
וְיוֹרְדִין בְּמַעֲרָבוֹ
וְהַיּוֹם
כֹּהֵן גָּדוֹל עוֹלֶה בָאֶמְצַע וְיוֹרֵד בָּאֶמְצַע.
רַבִּי יְהוּדָה אוֹמֵר:
לְעוֹלָם כֹּהֵן גָּדוֹל עוֹלֶה בָאֶמְצַע וְיוֹרֵד בָּאֶמְצַע.
בְּכָל יוֹם
כֹּהֵן גָּדוֹל מְקַדֵּשׁ יָדָיו וְרַגְלָיו מִן הַכִּיּוֹר
וְהַיּוֹם
מִן הַקִּיתוֹן שֶׁלַּזָּהָב.

דַּקָּה מִן הַדַּקָּה *Finer than fine.* Concerning the incense brought throughout the year, the Torah instructs "Grind it finely" (Ex. 30:36). The incense on Yom Kippur is also described as "finely ground" (Lev. 16:12). The Talmud derives from this reiteration of the need for it to be fine, that on Yom Kippur it was to be even finer than usual. Meiri claims that the extra grinding is a special mitzva. His opinion is also reflected in the version of "Order of the Incense" which Sephardim recite as part of the Order of the Offerings during Shaḥarit.

כֹּהֲנִים עוֹלִין בְּמִזְרָחוֹ שֶׁלַּכֶּבֶשׁ *The priests would ascend the eastern side of the ramp.* The ramp was on the south side of the altar (62b), with two smaller ramps dividing off from it – the left one leading down to the base and the right one to the surrounding ledge (Rashi, ibid. 64a; Rambam, *Hilkhot Beit HaBeḥira* 2:14; however, Tosafot on 64a state that both smaller ramps led to the ledge). Priests coming to throw the blood of sacrifices against the walls of the altar

Rabbi Yehuda says:
The High Priest would always sanctify his hands and feet
using the golden jug.

6 On all other days,
four fires would be prepared there.
But today there were five;
thus says Rabbi Meir.
Rabbi Yose says:
On all other days there would be three,
but today there were four.
Rabbi Yehuda says:
On all other days there would be two,
and today there were three.

---

coals with which to burn the incense (see page 497). Rabbi Yose requires a third to provide extra burning wood for the large pyre, in case it begins to diminish. Rabbi Meir adds a fourth for the burning fats and limbs which were not sufficiently burnt on the previous day, rather than having them returned to the main fire.

The Talmud does not clarify why there is need for an extra fire on Yom Kippur. Rambam (*Hilkhot Avodat Yom HaKippurim* 2:5) suggests that it is added simply to beautify the altar on this auspicious and ceremonial day. Rashi, however, suggests that it is there to provide the coals with which the incense will be burnt in the Holy of Holies. These coals must come from a source separate from the coals used to burn the incense throughout the year (a similar view is presented in the Yerushalmi). Rambam rules in accordance with Rabbi Yose, while Rabbeinu Yehonatan (in the next chapter) sides with Rabbi Meir.

רַבִּי יְהוּדָה אוֹמֵר:
לְעוֹלָם כֹּהֵן גָּדוֹל מְקַדֵּשׁ יָדָיו וְרַגְלָיו מִן הַקִּיתוֹן שֶׁלַּזָּהָב.

ו בְּכָל יוֹם הָיוּ שָׁם אַרְבַּע מַעֲרָכוֹת
וְהַיּוֹם חָמֵשׁ;
דִּבְרֵי רַבִּי מֵאִיר.
רַבִּי יוֹסֵי אוֹמֵר:
בְּכָל יוֹם שָׁלֹשׁ
וְהַיּוֹם אַרְבַּע.
רַבִּי יְהוּדָה אוֹמֵר:
בְּכָל יוֹם שְׁתַּיִם
וְהַיּוֹם שָׁלֹשׁ.

---

the High Priest were not specific to Yom Kippur, but were his privileges all year round. In the commentary to 3:3 we cited a dispute between Rashi and Rosh as to when the High Priest sanctifies his hands and feet for the first time before entering the Temple. According to Rashi, this sanctification is not particular to Yom Kippur or to the High Priest, but is a fulfillment of the standard obligation upon any priest entering the temple. Therefore, Rashi claims he washes his hands from the Basin (see there). This diametrically opposes Rabbi Yehuda's approach.

מַעֲרָכוֹת *Fires.* In its narrowest sense, מַעֲרָכָה, "arrangement," refers to the bundles of wood that are set on fire on the altar. The word is used to refer (by extension) to the fires themselves (see *Tamid* 1:1).

בְּכָל יוֹם *On all other days.* The Talmud (45a) delineates the purposes of each of these pyres. Rabbi Yehuda holds that two fires are burnt: a large one to burn the sacrificial parts of the offerings and a smaller one to provide the

to retrieve the incense and coal pan that remain there throughout. Thus he enters the Holy of Holies four times in total. The fourth entry, in contrast to the first three, does not involve a positive act of service. It is therefore further postponed to the afternoon, after the offering of the rams (mishna 7:3) (see Rabbi Mordekhai Breuer in *Pirkei Mikra'ot* p. 290).

Generally, it is assumed that no one may enter the Holy of Holies except for the High Priest, and that even he only enters on Yom Kippur. This is indeed the opinion of Rashi (Lev. 16:3) and Ramban (ibid, 2). However, the beginning of Leviticus chapter sixteen, which discusses the license to enter the Holy of Holies, does not explicitly limit it to Yom Kippur. The Vilna Gaon is cited (at the end of *Ḥokhmat Adam*) as explaining that Aaron himself had the privilege of entering the Holy of Holies at any time, as long as he followed the incense procedure outlined. The restriction of the license to Yom Kippur was applied only in future generations. This may already be hinted at in the *Sifra* (cited by Rashi on v. 34) which praises Aaron for not wearing the garments for his own magnificence, but only "as one fulfilling the decree of a king." Perhaps this is to be understood as praise for relinquishing his personal privilege to enter at any time, entering only when commanded to on Yom Kippur.

If Yom Kippur was the high point of the Temple year, the climax of the day is described in this chapter. It begins with the taking of the incense and its burning inside the Holy of Holies (mishnayot 1–2), the offering of the blood of the bull (3), and the slaughter of the goat and offering of its blood (4). After sprinkling the blood of both offerings at the covering of the Ark (or in the Second Temple, toward the place where the Ark used to stand), the High Priest sprinkles it again at the Curtain of the Holy of Holies, thus completing the purification of the Temple (4). At this point, the second chapter of the *Tosefta* (which may be considered to parallel the Mishna here) ends, emphasizing that this is the culmination of the day's main rite. Our chapter continues with the second act of purification, that of the Golden Altar (5–6) and ends by reiterating the importance of following the exact Order of the Service as laid out in the Bible (7).

CHAPTER FIVE:

On the first Yom Kippur, as the Talmud calculates the date, Moses descends from Mount Sinai with the Second Tablets, restoring the relationship between the Jewish people and God in the wake of the sin of the Golden Calf (*Ta'anit* 30b). Later in history, on another momentous Yom Kippur, God reveals to the prophet Ezekiel a vision of the future Redemption and rebuilding of the Temple (Ezek. 40:1; see *Arakhin* 12a). Yom Kippur is referred to there as רֹאשׁ הַשָּׁנָה, New Year, the only use of that term in the Bible.

Even when the Temple stood, Yom Kippur was the climax of the year's worship; twice the Torah emphasizes the rites of Yom Kippur are but אַחַת בַּשָּׁנָה, "once a year" (see Ex. 30:10 and Lev. 16:34).

Only on this day is the High Priest enjoined to enter the Holy of Holies. On other days he may not enter at will: "And the LORD said to Moses: speak to Aaron your brother, that he come not at any time to the holiest place – behind the curtain, to the presence of the *kaporet* that covers the Ark – so that he does not die; for I shall be revealed in the cloud above the *kaporet*. This is how Aaron shall come to the holiest place..." (Lev. 16:2–3). This would seem to indicate that entry is dependent on God revealing Himself in a "cloud." However, from verse 13 it is apparent that the "cloud" which permits entry is in fact the cloud of smoke rising from the incense. This is likely the rationale behind the Sadducees' insistence that the incense should be burned *before* entering the Holy of Holies. If the incense serves as a license to enter, it surely should be kindled first. The sages, however, insist that on Yom Kippur the High Priest was not entering in order to bask in the Divine Presence; he was summoned to serve. Just as a servant begs permission to serve only once he is in the presence of his master, so too the High Priest offers the incense only once already inside the Holy of Holies.

The entrance to the Holy of Holies is only permitted with this attitude of humility. Indeed, one of the first commands to Aaron in the passage is that his entry to the Holy of Holies is only to be made in the modest attire of an ordinary priest (the four white vestments) and not in the spectacular and honorific golden vestments normally worn by the High Priest.

The atonement of Yom Kippur is achieved in just two entrances of the High Priest into the Holy of Holies: offering the blood of the bull to atone for himself, and offering the blood of the goat to atone for the whole of Israel. However, the burning of the incense in order to permit entry necessitates that he also enter before these two atonement ceremonies, in order to create the incense cloud, and then again once more, after the atonements,

CHAPTER FIVE

1 They would bring him out the censer and the pan [of incense],
and he would fill his hands [with incense]
and place it in the censer –
as much or little as would fill his hands,
large or small.
He would take the coal pan in his right hand
and the censer in his left.
And he would walk across the Sanctuary
until he reached the place between the two curtains
that divide the Holy from the Holy of Holies

---

important item is held in the right hand (see 4:5). The coal pan, however, is very hot and much heavier than the incense, and so, for practical reasons, the pans are switched around (47a).

הָיָה מְהַלֵּךְ בַּהֵיכָל *And he would walk across the Sanctuary.* The Sanctuary contains the Golden Altar, Table and Menora (see figure 1, page 444). According to Rabbi Yehuda, the High Priest proceeds to walk directly down the center of the Sanctuary, bearing left to pass the Golden Altar on its southern side, and then returning to his course to pass between the Table and Menora. Rabbi Meir describes a similar path, but suggests that the Priest passes the altar on its northern side. A third opinion explains that he does not walk in between any of the vessels, but rather walks along the northern side of the Sanctuary, passing everything on his left-hand side. The Talmud explains that this third opinion is based on the assumption, held by Rabbi Yose in the mishna here, that the Holy of Holies has only one curtain, which opens at its northern end, making the quickest approach to it a straight path along the northern end of the room. Although this route would require the High Priest to take a left turn into the Holy of Holies (see commentary to 4:5), with all of Israel anxiously awaiting the news of their atonement, the desire for speed outweighs other concerns (51b).

לְבֵין שְׁתֵּי הַפָּרֹכוֹת *The place between the two curtains.* In the Tabernacle, a curtain separated the Holy of Holies from the rest of the Tent of Meeting (Ex. 26:34). In the First Temple, King Solomon constructed a דְּבִיר, a solid "partition" (translation follows Rashi, see also Radak) to divide the Holy of Holies from the Sanctuary, and he hung the curtain upon it (1 Kings ch. 6 and

פרק חמישי

א הוֹצִיאוּ לוֹ אֶת הַכַּף וְאֶת הַמַּחְתָּה
וְחָפַן מְלֹא חָפְנָיו
וְנָתַן לְתוֹךְ הַכַּף:
הַגָּדוֹל לְפִי גָדְלוֹ, וְהַקָּטָן לְפִי קָטְנוֹ;
וְכָךְ הָיְתָה מִדָּתָהּ.
נָטַל אֶת הַמַּחְתָּה בִּימִינוֹ
וְאֶת הַכַּף בִּשְׂמֹאלוֹ.
הָיָה מְהַלֵּךְ בַּהֵיכָל
עַד שֶׁמַּגִּיעַ לְבֵין שְׁתֵּי הַפָּרֹכוֹת
הַמַּבְדִּילוֹת בֵּין הַקֹּדֶשׁ וּבֵין קֹדֶשׁ הַקֳּדָשִׁים

אֶת הַכַּף וְאֶת הַמַּחְתָּה *The censer and the pan.* This is not the coal pan mentioned in the previous chapter, but a different pan filled with incense brought from the Avtinas Chamber (47a). The High Priest then performs the חֲפִינָה, "taking a handful," from the incense in this pan, using both hands cupped together. This is somewhat less challenging than קְמִיצָה, "taking a handful of flour" for the meal offering, as in our case he is not required to take a precise amount (*Yoma* 48a; see *Tosafot Rosh* ad loc.). The Yerushalmi questions whether this חֲפִינָה carries the full status of one of the rites of the day, or whether it simply serves the practical purpose of measuring out a quantity of incense. Assuming that it only serves a practical purpose, the procedure would be valid even if the rite were not performed correctly; for instance if a different priest measured the incense into the High Priest's hands. The Yerushalmi does not resolve this question, leading Rambam to rule that ideally in such a situation the חֲפִינָה should be performed again, but that if the incense has already been offered, it is acceptable (*Hilkhot Avodat Yom HaKippurim* 5:28).

וְאֶת הַכַּף בִּשְׂמֹאלוֹ *And the censer in his left.* It is not feasible for him to hold the fine incense in his hands for an extended period, and in any case, he also needs to carry the coal pan to the Holy of Holies (see Lev. 16:12). The only option available, then, is to place the incense into a censer which he holds with one hand, while carrying the coal pan in the other. Usually the more

There was a cubit between them.
Rabbi Yose says: There was only one curtain there, as is said:
"The curtain shall make a division for you Ex. 26
between the Holy and the Holy of Holies."
The outer one was [loosely] tied at the southern end,
and the inner one at the northern.
He would walk between the two
until he reached the northern end.
When he reached the north
he would turn his face to the south
and walk with the curtain to his left
until he had come to the Ark.
When he came to the Ark
he would set down the coal pan between its two staves.
He would pile the incense on the coals,

Rabbi Yose, who maintains there was only one curtain, relates to the status of the sanctity of the space taken by the original solid partition.

הָיְתָה פְרוּפָה [*Loosely*] *tied.* Most commentators follow Rashi, who suggests that the curtain was folded on the outside and caught in a single hook to create an opening for entry. Meiri suggests there were several such hooks, to stabilize the curtain. A dissenting opinion is that of Rabbeinu Yeroḥam (7:3), who holds that the curtain remained connected to the wall, and that the High Priest would detach it himself to gain entry. These last two opinions are combined by Rid: usually the curtain would be attached to the wall of the Sanctuary by several hooks, but before Yom Kippur it would be almost fully detached, to make it easier for the High Priest to enter.

מְהַלֵּךְ בֵּינֵיהֶן *He would walk between the two.* To avoid setting the curtain alight with the burning coals that he was carrying, the High Priest would use his shoulders and elbows to push the curtains away from him (Yerushalmi).

צָבַר אֶת הַקְּטֹרֶת *He would pile the incense.* The Talmud (47b) lists קְמִיצָה, taking a handful of flour for a meal offering, מְלִיקָה, slaughtering a bird with the priest's fingernail, and חֲפִינָה, taking the handful of incense, as the three most difficult rituals in the Temple. For this reason, the High Priest spends some time on the night of Yom Kippur practicing the חֲפִינָה (Rashi, see note on 1:7).

The difficulty of חֲפִינָה lies not in the initial taking of the handful in the

וּבֵינֵיהֶן אַמָּה.
רַבִּי יוֹסֵי אוֹמֵר:
לֹא הָיְתָה שָׁם אֶלָּא פָּרֹכֶת אַחַת בִּלְבַד
שֶׁנֶּאֱמַר: וְהִבְדִּילָה הַפָּרֹכֶת לָכֶם בֵּין הַקֹּדֶשׁ שמות כו
וּבֵין קֹדֶשׁ הַקֳּדָשִׁים:
הַחִיצוֹנָה הָיְתָה פְּרוּפָה מִן הַדָּרוֹם
וְהַפְּנִימִית מִן הַצָּפוֹן.
מְהַלֵּךְ בֵּינֵיהֶן, עַד שֶׁמַּגִּיעַ לַצָּפוֹן.
הִגִּיעַ לַצָּפוֹן, הוֹפֵךְ פָּנָיו לַדָּרוֹם
מְהַלֵּךְ לִשְׂמֹאלוֹ עִם הַפָּרֹכֶת
עַד שֶׁהוּא מַגִּיעַ לָאָרוֹן.
הִגִּיעַ לָאָרוֹן
נוֹתֵן אֶת הַמַּחְתָּה בֵּין שְׁנֵי הַבַּדִּים.
צָבַר אֶת הַקְּטֹרֶת עַל גַּבֵּי הַגֶּחָלִים

Ralbag ibid. 8:8). In the Second Temple there was no partition. The Talmud (52b) explains that the walls of the Holy of Holies in the Second Temple were extremely high – a hundred cubits – so that it was not feasible to build so high a partition of only a cubit thickness; to do so would require the construction of buttresses which would encroach upon the space of the Sanctuary. It was also disputed whether the space occupied by the partition had the sanctity of the Sanctuary or of the Holy of Holies.

To avoid all doubts, two curtains were erected, one on either side of the one cubit space the wall would have occupied, known as the אַמָּה טְרַקְסִין, the "one-cubit partition." According to the Yerushalmi (*Kilayim* 8:4) the word טְרַקְסִין is an elision of the Greek words for "inside" and "outside," suggesting that the partition was named after doubt concerning the space was raised. Rabbeinu Tam suggests a different etymology, deriving the name from the Aramaic טְרוֹק, "to close," in which case the word refers to the whole enclosure around the Holy of Holies (Tosafot, *Bava Batra* 3a). It remains unclear how

and the whole house would be filled with [its] smoke.
Then he would go out
by way of his entrance
and pray a short prayer, in the outer Sanctuary,
but he would not spend too long in his prayer,
not to terrify the people.

2 After the Ark was taken away –
there was a stone there ever since the days of the early Prophets,

---

however, suggests that it is an intrinsic part of the ceremony of entry into the Holy of Holies: although the sages rule that the "incense cloud" does not need to be formed *before* the High Priest enters, they accept that without it, his entry is not fully valid.

בֵּית כְּנִיסָתוֹ *By way of his entrance.* Literally retracing his steps, he walks backwards, with his face toward the Holy of Holies (53a).

תְּפִלָּה קְצָרָה *A short prayer.* There was no standard text for this prayer, although, as the mishna indicates, it was expected that it be brief. The Talmud records one occasion on which a High Priest did prolong his prayer and was reproached for doing so (53b). The people were concerned that he may have died while inside the Holy of Holies. Rambam reports that several did indeed die. The *Tiferet Yisrael* suggests that if he were a Sadducee and incorrectly performed the rites, he might be punished. However, the *Tashbetz* (3:37) asserts that most of the High Priests were above this suspicion. The *Zohar* (*Emor*, 102a; *Aḥarei Mot* 67a) relates that a rope was tied to the High Priest's leg so that, in the event that he did die, he could be pulled away from the Holy of Holies. However, there is no mention of this in the *Rishonim*, and the cases related in the Talmud imply that, at least during that period, there was nothing with which to pull the Priest out (see *Yoma* 53b; Rabbeinu Ḥananel on 19b).

מִשֶּׁנִּטַּל הָאָרוֹן *After the Ark was taken away.* The Tanakh (II Chron. 36) tells of three separate occasions on which the Temple was plundered. When King Yehoyakhin surrenders to the Babylonians, the "treasured vessels of the House of the LORD" (v. 10) were taken to Babylonia. The Talmud sees these "treasured vessels" as an allusion to the Holy Ark.

If the Ark was indeed stolen, this would well explain the frustration and

וְנִתְמַלֵּא כָּל הַבַּיִת כֻּלּוֹ עָשָׁן.
יָצָא וּבָא לוֹ בְּדֶרֶךְ בֵּית כְּנִיסָתוֹ
וּמִתְפַּלֵּל תְּפִלָּה קְצָרָה בַּבַּיִת הַחִיצוֹן
וְלֹא הָיָה מַאֲרִיךְ בִּתְפִלָּתוֹ
שֶׁלֹּא לְהַבְעִית אֶת יִשְׂרָאֵל.

ב מִשֶּׁנִּטַּל הָאָרוֹן
אֶבֶן הָיְתָה שָׁם מִימוֹת הַנְּבִיאִים הָרִאשׁוֹנִים

---

courtyard, but in returning the incense back to his hands when he arrives inside the Holy of Holies. First he must place the coal pan on the ground to free his hands (Rashi). He then grasps the censer of incense with the tips of his fingers, or with his teeth, and empties its entire contents into his cupped hands. He must do this without spilling even a single granule; if this happens, in the view of Rabbeinu Yehonatan, the measurement of his handful would be considered lacking. He then places the incense onto the coals, starting with the further side in order not to be scorched (52b).

The Talmud records a debate as to how the piling of the incense should be done. Some suggest that the incense should be spread thinly, allowing it to burn quickly and rapidly fill the room with smoke. This will prevent the High Priest seeing the Holy of Holies. Others suggest he should heap the incense in a pile such that it will not burn too quickly, which might startle or even choke him (Meiri).

וְנִתְמַלֵּא כָּל הַבַּיִת כֻּלּוֹ *The whole house would be filled.* This smoke is a fulfillment of the verse "for I shall be revealed in the cloud" (Lev. 16:2), which the sages explain to stipulate the formation of an "incense cloud" as a precondition for entry (see introduction to this chapter). Depending on which method he uses (see previous note), this will either be immediate, or take some time. In either case, Rambam (*Hilkhot Avodat Yom HaKippurim* 5:28) rules that the High Priest must remain in the Holy of Holies until the entire chamber fills with smoke. Rabbi Yitzḥak Ze'ev Soloveitchik (the "Brisker Rav") explains that this is just an application of the general requirement for a priest to see the whole rite though to its fruition. His nephew, Rabbi Yosef Dov Soloveitchik,

its name was *Shetiya*,
and it rose three fingers high above the earth –
and he would set [the firepan] down upon that.

3 He would take the blood
from the one who was keeping it stirring,
and enter the place he had entered
and stand in the place where he had stood,
and he would sprinkle of that blood,
once upward and seven times downward,
not aiming to sprinkle either upward or down,
but as if he were administering lashes.

---

doing. In the Second Temple, with no Ark, the whole rite was conducted in the dark. The possibility that the High Priest might trip on the אֶבֶן הַשְּׁתִיָּה (especially as it was low and small) was then a real fear. Even putting aside the fear, then, of any Divine Retribution, the ceremony had its own dangers. All this would have increased the suspense of the people mentioned at the end of the previous mishna.

אַחַת לְמַעְלָה וְשֶׁבַע לְמַטָּה *Once upward and seven times downward.* To sprinkle "upward" the High Priest first dips his fingertips in blood and then turns his hand palm upward, with the fingertips pointing upward. He then flicks his finger in an upward motion to cast the blood in the desired direction. To sprinkle downward, he raises his hand to above the point he needs to sprinkle to. With his palm facing the floor and the tips of his fingers bent and pointing downward, he flicks the blood in a downward motion.

כְּמַצְלִיף *Administering lashes.* Rashi depicts the image of a law court official administering lashes to a criminal's back such that each blow (here, each blood drop) will fall a little lower than the one before. Other *Rishonim* (Rabbeinu Ḥananel; Tosafot, *Zevaḥim* 38a) suggest that the simile refers to the way the High Priest holds his hands during the sprinkling, each time raising his hands and then lowering them. If so, there is no requirement to aim at any specific point (Meiri).

וּשְׁתִיָּה הָיְתָה נִקְרֵאת
גְּבוֹהָה מִן הָאָרֶץ שָׁלֹשׁ אֶצְבָּעוֹת
וְעָלֶיהָ הָיָה נוֹתֵן.

ג נָטַל אֶת הַדָּם מִמִּי שֶׁהָיָה מְמָרֵס בּוֹ
נִכְנַס לְמָקוֹם שֶׁנִּכְנַס
וְעָמַד בְּמָקוֹם שֶׁעָמַד
וְהִזָּה מִמֶּנּוּ אַחַת לְמַעְלָה וְשֶׁבַע לְמַטָּה
וְלֹא הָיָה מִתְכַּוֵּן לְהַזּוֹת לֹא לְמַעְלָה וְלֹא לְמַטָּה
אֶלָּא כְּמַצְלִיף.

---

anger, as well as the yearning desire for revenge and restoration, in the background of Hananiah's prophecy and Jeremiah's rebuke to him (Jer. 27:16–28:11). In the Mishna (*Shekalim* 6:2) a different tradition is recorded: aware that the destruction of the Temple is near, King Josiah hid the Ark in order to protect it (*Yoma* 52a, 53b–54a).

וּשְׁתִיָּה הָיְתָה נִקְרֵאת *Its name was Shetiya.* The Talmud (54b) explains that this stone is called אֶבֶן הַשְּׁתִיָּה, "The Foundation Rock," שֶׁמִּמֶּנָּה הוּשְׁתַּת הָעוֹלָם, "because from it the world was founded." It proceeds to explain that this was the first piece God created and that from it the world was expanded until it was complete. In the First Temple, the Ark was placed upon this stone (Rambam, *Hilkhot Beit HaBeḥira* 4:1, based on *Beraita DiMelekhet HaMishkan*).

Radbaz (2:691) identifies אֶבֶן הַשְּׁתִיָּה as el-Sakhra, the Rock of the Dome of the Rock. Other authorities dispute this, both citing Talmudic discussions to the contrary (Maharsha, *Makkot* 24b) and observing that el-Sakhra is both very large, and rises much higher than three fingerbreadths above the surrounding area. This last objection has been rebutted by Rabbi Yeḥiel Mikhel Tukichinsky, who suggests that following Muslim excavation, the floor level of the current Dome is lower than ground level at the time of the Temple (*Ir HaKodesh VeHaMikdash*, 4:1:5).

The Yerushalmi (5:3) tells that in the First Temple light emanated from the Ark, illuminating the room so that the High Priest could see what he was

And he would count thus:
One
one and one
one and two
one and three
one and four
one and five
one and six
one and seven.
Then he would go out and lay [the bowl] down
on the golden stand in the Sanctuary.

4 They would bring him the goat,
and he would slaughter it
and receive its blood in a bowl.
He would enter the place he had entered,
and stand in the place where he had stood,
and he would sprinkle of that blood,
once upward and seven times downward,
not aiming to sprinkle either upward or down,
but as if he were administering lashes.

---

method of counting was used both to avoid confusion, and in order to count all of the eight sprinklings together, while maintaining the one-seven split described in the verse.

וְהִנִּיחוֹ *Lay the [bowl] down.* He needs both hands to slaughter the goat (Rabbeinu Yehonatan). The golden stand was probably placed between the curtain and the altar – see commentary to the next mishna.

הֵבִיאוּ לוֹ אֶת הַשָּׂעִיר *They would bring him the goat.* The service involving the goat parallels that of the bull, except that no confession is made over this goat; it will be made instead over the goat for Azazel (see 6:2 below). The

וְכָךְ הָיָה מוֹנֶה:
אַחַת
אַחַת וְאַחַת
אַחַת וּשְׁתַּיִם
אַחַת וְשָׁלֹשׁ
אַחַת וְאַרְבַּע
אַחַת וְחָמֵשׁ
אַחַת וָשֵׁשׁ
אַחַת וָשֶׁבַע.
יָצָא
וְהִנִּיחוֹ עַל כַּן הַזָּהָב שֶׁבַּהֵיכָל.

ד הֵבִיאוּ לוֹ אֶת הַשָּׂעִיר
שְׁחָטוֹ, וְקִבֵּל בַּמִּזְרָק אֶת דָּמוֹ.
נִכְנַס לְמָקוֹם שֶׁנִּכְנַס
וְעָמַד בְּמָקוֹם שֶׁעָמַד
וְהִזָּה מִמֶּנּוּ אַחַת לְמַעְלָה וְשֶׁבַע לְמַטָּה
וְלֹא הָיָה מִתְכַּוֵּן לְהַזּוֹת לֹא לְמַעְלָה וְלֹא לְמַטָּה
אֶלָּא כְּמַצְלִיף.

The Hebrew word מַצְלִיף is onomatopoeic; Rashi (15a) admits that he does not know its etymological derivation.

אַחַת וְאַחַת *One and one…* "He shall take of the bull's blood and sprinkle with his finger onto the *kaporet* before him – and in front of the *kaporet*, he shall sprinkle seven times from the blood with his finger" (Lev. 16:14). This

And he would count thus:
One
one and one
one and two [etc.].
Then he would go out and lay [the bowl] down
on the second golden stand in the Sanctuary.
Rabbi Yehuda says:
There was only one stand.
He would take up the blood of the bull,
and lay down the blood of the goat,
and sprinkle of that blood toward the curtain,
at the place behind which the ark stood, on the outside,
once upward and seven times downward,
not aiming [etc.].

Sa'adia Gaon, pages 264–275; 280–288). In אַמִּיץ כֹּחַ the first two countings appear in full, while the other two are referred to by the short רִקְמֵי פָּרֹכֶת...מִדַּם שָׂעִיר "He would sprinkle the embroidered curtain as he had with the curtain within, / stir up the blood again and sprinkle with the blood of the goat." (page 893). This distinction between the first and last two is also paralleled in the first printed full edition of the Mishna (Naples, 1492). The *Nishmat Adam* (145:3) strongly criticizes the practice of omitting the second two countings, and cites *Maharil* (*Musaf on Yom Kippur*, 19) who was scrupulous in reciting them in full.

לֹא הָיָה שָׁם אֶלָּא כֵן אֶחָד בִּלְבַד *There was only one stand.* The Talmud explains that Rabbi Yehuda was concerned that if there were two stands, the High Priest might confuse them; simply labeling each stand before Yom Kippur would not avert the risk, as with a combination of hunger, tiredness and excitement he may not remember to check the writing (55a–56b). This concern for a remote possibility may seem excessive, but it is in line with Rabbi Yehuda's concern with regard to the High Priest's wife (1:1).

Most *Rishonim* (Rambam, *Smag*, Rosh) rule in accordance with the rabbis that there were two stands. אַתָּה כּוֹנַנְתָּ (page 1269) also follows this view. Rashi, however, notes that the continuation of the mishna seems to agree with Rabbi Yehuda (53b).

וְכָךְ הָיָה מוֹנֶה:
אַחַת
אַחַת וְאַחַת
אַחַת וּשְׁתַּיִם וְכוּ'.
יָצָא
וְהִנִּיחוֹ עַל כַּן הַשֵּׁנִי, שֶׁהָיָה בַּהֵיכָל.
רַבִּי יְהוּדָה אוֹמֵר:
לֹא הָיָה שָׁם אֶלָּא כַּן אֶחָד בִּלְבַד.
נָטַל דַּם הַפָּר
וְהִנִּיחַ דַּם הַשָּׂעִיר
וְהִזָּה מִמֶּנּוּ עַל הַפָּרֹכֶת שֶׁכְּנֶגֶד הָאָרוֹן מִבַּחוּץ
אַחַת לְמַעְלָה וְשֶׁבַע לְמַטָּה
וְלֹא הָיָה מִתְכַּוֵּן וְכוּ'.

---

goat's blood is used immediately after slaughter, so there is no need for it to be given to another priest for stirring.

אַחַת אַחַת וְאַחַת *One, one and one…* The rite of the eight sprinklings of blood is performed four times; the blood of the bull and the blood of the goat are each sprinkled, separately, once inside the Holy of Holies and once again on the outside curtain. In ancient manuscripts of the Mishna, the description of how the high priest would sprinkle is indeed repeated four times, although the actual counting (one, one and one…) only appears in full the first time around. Some manuscripts also include the introductory phrase וְכָךְ הָיָה מוֹנֶה, "counting thus," familiar to us from the Order of the Service *piyut* in Musaf. The text used here follows the first complete edition of Talmud (Venice, 1520–1523), which was followed by the Vilna edition.

These counts form one of the high points of the סֵדֶר הָעֲבוֹדָה recited in Musaf. In אַתָּה כּוֹנַנְתָּ the count is repeated each time in full (page 1269). In several ancient *piyutim* the counts were not recited at all (see *Seder Rav*

And he would count thus: [etc.].
He would take up the blood of the goat
and lay down the blood of the bull,
and sprinkle of that blood toward the curtain,
at the place behind which the ark stood, on the outside,
once upward and seven times downward [etc.].
And then he would pour the blood of the bull
into the blood of the goat
and drain the full bowl back into the empty one.

5 "He shall go out to the altar, which stands in the presence of the LORD": *Lev. 16*
This refers to the Golden Altar.

---

would first lay down the blood of the bull and then take up the blood of the goat.

עֵרָה דַם *And then he would pour the blood.* "[He takes] of the blood of the bullock and of the goat and [applies] it to the horns around the altar" (Lev. 16:18). The mishna follows the view of Rabbi Yoshiya that this verse requires the blood of the two animals to be mixed and then applied to the altar together. The blood is poured from one bowl to the other and back again, in order for them to be fully mixed (58a). Rabbi Yonatan disagrees, arguing that the blood of each animal is applied to the altar separately (*Yoma* 57b–58a). *Tosafot Yeshanim* (58b) cite Riva, who claims that for the last sprinkling, upon the top of the altar (see mishna 6), even Rabbi Yonatan concedes that the blood should be mixed together.

וְיָצָא *"He shall go out."* By this stage, the High Priest has already left the Holy of Holies. "He shall go out" cannot therefore be understood as an instruction to leave. Rabbi Neḥemia suggests that as the High Priest's last action was to sprinkle the blood of the bull against the Curtain, he must be standing in the area between it and the Golden Altar. He is now instructed to leave that area in order to begin the sprinkling. For this reason, he does not begin sprinkling blood on the Golden Altar at the first point at which he encounters it, but rather continues to the next corner, so that he should have fully "gone out" of the space he was in before (*Yoma* 58b).

וְכָךְ הָיָה מוֹנֶה, וְכוּ׳.
נָטַל דַּם הַשָּׂעִיר
וְהִנִּיחַ דַּם הַפָּר
וְהִזָּה מִמֶּנּוּ עַל הַפָּרֹכֶת שֶׁכְּנֶגֶד הָאָרוֹן מִבַּחוּץ
אַחַת לְמַעְלָה וְשֶׁבַע לְמַטָּה, וְכוּ׳.
עֵרָה דַּם הַפָּר לְתוֹךְ דַּם הַשָּׂעִיר
וְנָתַן אֶת הַמָּלֵא בָּרֵיקָן.
ה וְיָצָא אֶל־הַמִּזְבֵּחַ אֲשֶׁר לִפְנֵי־ה׳: ויקרא טז
זֶה מִזְבַּח הַזָּהָב.

וְהִזָּה מִמֶּנּוּ *And sprinkle of that blood.* Following the description of the sprinklings outside the Holy of Holies, the Torah states "And so shall he do also for the Tent of Meeting" (Lev. 16:16). This is understood to mandate an additional sprinkling to atone for the Holy of Holies (*Sifra Aḥarei Mot* 4:5; *Yoma* 56b).

The Talmud (57a) suggests that the sprinkling should be done toward the curtain, with no need for the blood to actually touch it. It then, however, cites Rabbi Elazar ben Yose who testifies to having seen the curtain in Rome, after the Temple's destruction, with drops of sprinkled blood marking it. It is argued, nonetheless, that one cannot conclude from this that the blood of Yom Kippur was specifically required to reach the curtain, as there were other offerings – the bull brought to atone a communal error, for instance (see Lev. 4:17), which also involved sprinkling and could also account for the blood on the curtain.

Rabbi Elazar ben Yose's remarks on the curtain are part of the testimony he bears to several of the sacred vessels taken by the Romans, which, it is told, he was given access to after being sent to treat the daughter of the Emperor, who was stricken with madness (*Me'ila* 17b; see *Shabbat* 63b and *Sukka* 5a for other testimonies, and *Tosefta Kifshuta* pp. 775–776).

נָטַל דַּם הַשָּׂעִיר *He would take up the blood of the goat.* As Rashi notes, this follows the view of Rabbi Yehuda. According to the rabbis, the High Priest

He would begin to purify it, [sprinkling] downward –
where would he begin?
He would begin at the north-eastern corner,
then move to the north-western,
the south-western,
the south-eastern.
In the position where he began sprinkling the sin-offering blood on the Outer Altar,
there he would finish at the Inner Altar.

High Priest begin this ritual at the south-eastern corner and then circle the altar clockwise. Rabbi Akiva must accept the importance of turning to the right, but here he apparently gives priority to another principle: אֵין מַעֲבִירִין עַל הַמִּצְוֹת, "Do not pass by the opportunity to fulfill a mitzva." Rabbi Akiva explains that the High Priest has already walked past the south-western corner on his way to the Holy of Holies (see mishna 1), and so must return to it to perform its sprinkling of blood at the first opportunity. He cannot begin his sprinkling from that corner because, as discussed above, he must walk on to the second (for Rabbi Akiva, south-eastern) corner to begin.

Rashi explains this disagreement as a playing-out of the disagreement between Rabbi Yose HaGlili (who should not be confused with the Rabbi Yose in the mishna, who is Rabbi Yose bar Ḥalafta) and the other sages in mishna 1. Rabbi Yose HaGlili assumes, like Rabbi Yose there, that only one curtain separated the Sanctuary from the Holy of Holies, with its opening at the northern end. Thus, as the High Priest exits, he first approaches the altar from its north-western corner. He walks past this corner, to fulfill "He shall go out…" and so begins at the north-eastern corner. From here the two principles of אֵין מַעֲבִירִין and כָּל פְּנִיּוֹת coincide, and he moves around the altar in an anti-clockwise direction. Rabbi Akiva, on the other hand, takes the majority opinion that there are two curtains, the outer one opening at the southern end. In this case, the High Priest would reach the south-western corner of the altar first, and would begin the ritual from the south-east. In this case, there would be a conflict between the two principles for movement, and preference is given to אֵין מַעֲבִירִין. Since, according to Rashi, the dispute between Rabbi Akiva and Rabbi Yose HaGlili is entirely a derivative of the dispute in mishna 1, if we rule in accordance with the rabbis there, we should follow the view of Rabbi Akiva here, and reject the ruling of this mishna; Rosh, indeed, does so.

הִתְחִיל מְחַטֵּא וְיוֹרֵד.
מֵהֵיכָן הוּא מַתְחִיל?
מִקֶּרֶן מִזְרָחִית־צְפוֹנִית
צְפוֹנִית־מַעֲרָבִית
מַעֲרָבִית־דְּרוֹמִית
דְּרוֹמִית־מִזְרָחִית.
מְקוֹם שֶׁהוּא מַתְחִיל בַּחַטָּאת עַל מִזְבֵּחַ הַחִיצוֹן
מִשָּׁם הָיָה גוֹמֵר עַל מִזְבֵּחַ הַפְּנִימִי.

וְיוֹרֵד [*Sprinkling*] *downward.* Applications of blood to the altars is usually referred to in the Torah with the verb הִזָּה, "to sprinkle" (e.g. Lev. 16:14, 19). This describes the act of a priest dipping his finger in the blood and then flicking it onto the altar. The applications of blood to the Golden Altar on Yom Kippur are referred to, exceptionally, with the verb נָתַן, most simply translated "he puts" (Lev. 16:18). This distinction is also preserved in the language of the mishna here. This may suggest that rather than sprinkling the blood toward the altar from a distance, the High Priest here daubs it directly on to the altar's surface. The *Ḥazon Ish* (OḤ 126:38) suggests this may be Rashi's understanding. However, many *Rishonim* clearly reject this distinction, assuming that the applications here are also achieved through sprinkling (see Rambam, *Hilkhot Avodat Yom HaKippurim* 4:2; Rosh; Ritva, *Yoma* 58b; see also Rashi *Zevaḥim* 53a s.v. וּמְחַטֵּא, where this is made explicit). In our translation and commentary we follow this view.

מִקֶּרֶן מִזְרָחִית־צְפוֹנִית *He would begin at the north-eastern corner.* According to this description, the High Priest walks to the north-eastern corner of the Golden Altar, and there makes the first application. He then moves around the altar in an anti-clockwise direction applying the rest of the blood to the three remaining corners. The Talmud (58b) identifies this view with the opinion of Rabbi Yose HaGlili. The anti-clockwise movement, during which the Priest continues to face the altar and steps sideways, fulfills the dictum, mentioned above in note to 4:5, that in the context of Temple service, all turns should be made to the right – כׇּל פְּנִיּוֹת שֶׁאַתָּה פּוֹנֶה לֹא יְהִיוּ אֶלָּא דֶּרֶךְ יָמִין. The Talmud also cites the opposing view of Rabbi Akiva, who would have the

Rabbi Eliezer says:
He would stand in one place and purify it all.
He would sprinkle upward toward each corner,
except for the one in front of him:
there he would [sprinkle] downward.

---

of the First Temple, one of whom testifies to circling the altar, and the other to remaining standing in one place (see Rabbeinu Ḥananel). The Yerushalmi relates a similar story of two High Priests who fled at the time of the Great Revolt. Rabbi Yudan concludes there that both ways are halakhically legitimate (which would support Rabbeinu Yehonatan's understanding of Rabbi Eliezer's opinion).

אַתָּה כּוֹנַנְתָּ (page 1270) describes the Service in line with Rabbi Eliezer's opinion. The *Rishonim*, on the other hand, rule in accordance with the rabbis.

בִּמְקוֹמוֹ הָיָה עוֹמֵד *He would stand in one place.* The Golden Altar was only one cubit square and three cubits high, making it possible for the High Priest to stretch above and around it to reach all four corners without moving from where he stood. The Talmud (59a) brings two traditions of Rabbi Eliezer's method: Rabbi Yehuda (the view expressed in our mishna) maintains that the application to the corner immediately in front of him must be done downward. With the altar directly in front of the High Priest, his arm has little room to maneuver, and he is restricted to raising and lowering his forearm at the elbow. To sprinkle the blood onto the corners of the altar, therefore, he must raise his hand with his arm in an upward slant. If he points his fingers upward to sprinkle in that direction (see note to 5:3), the blood is liable to drip down his fingers and over his palm and wrist to soil the sleeves of his vestments. To avoid this, he applies the blood in a downward motion. Since the tips of his fingers face downward in this motion, the blood will not drip onto his hands and soil his sleeve. This concern does not exist for the other corners, since his distance from them allows him to maneuver his hand and raise his arm in such a way to avoid the blood dripping onto his vestments; the High Priest, then, sprinkles once downward and three times upward.

The second tradition, not represented in our mishna, is that of Rabbi Meir. Principally he believes that since the first sprinkling was done downward (albeit out of practical necessity), the subsequent sprinklings should also be done downward. However, he concedes that for the corner furthest from

רַבִּי אֱלִיעֶזֶר אוֹמֵר:
בִּמְקוֹמוֹ הָיָה עוֹמֵד וּמְחַטֵּא.
וְעַל כֻּלָּן הָיָה נוֹתֵן מִלְּמַטָּה לְמַעְלָה
חוּץ מִזּוֹ שֶׁהָיְתָה לְפָנָיו
שֶׁעָלֶיהָ הָיָה נוֹתֵן מִלְמַעְלָה לְמַטָּה.

Tosafot Yeshanim, however, argue that both Rabbi Yose HaGlili and Rabbi Akiva hold, with the rabbis in mishna 1, that there were two curtains, and that the High Priest leaves the Holy of Holies by the southern wall. They understand the dispute between Rabbi Yose HaGlili and Rabbi Akiva as a disagreement over which of the two principles we have mentioned takes precedence: Rabbi Akiva maintains that אֵין מַעֲבִירִין עַל הַמִּצְוֹת prevails, while Rabbi Yose HaGlili considers turning to one's right more important. This leaves open the possibility of ruling in accordance with Rabbi Yose HaGlili, whose view is presented in the mishna as though uncontested, suggesting that is was accepted as authoritative, while still maintaining the majority view that there were two curtains. Rambam and *Smag*, indeed, do so (*Hilkhot Avodat Yom HaKippurim* 4:2; *Hilkhot Ma'aseh HaKorbanot* 5:14; *Smag* 209).

The Hebrew formulation of the compass-points is based here on the direction from which the High Priest makes his approach. Thus the first corner is מִזְרָחִית צְפוֹנִית, east-north, not צְפוֹנִית מִזְרָחִית, north-east (compare to mishna *Zevaḥim* 8:3, page 499).

רַבִּי אֱלִיעֶזֶר אוֹמֵר *Rabbi Eliezer says.* In the Talmud (59a), the dispute between the rabbis and Rabbi Eliezer is understood to hinge upon the fact that the Outer Altar, which is very large, must of necessity be walked around for the blood to be applied to each corner. The rabbis argue that, as the laws of the Inner Altar are in many ways consistent with those of the Outer Altar, this detail, too, should be kept consistent between them. Rabbi Eliezer is not concerned by this point. Rabbeinu Yehonatan suggests that Rabbi Eliezer holds there to be no specific requirement either way, the choice of whether to walk around the Inner Altar or to stand still being left to the High Priest. Rashi, on the other hand, implies that Rabbi Eliezer views his method as compulsory.

The Talmud (ibid.) tells of two High Priests who survived the destruction

6 Then, seven times, he would sprinkle blood onto the clear space on the altar,
and then he would pour out what was left
against the western base of the Outer Altar;
and that of [the offerings on] the Outer Altar
he would pour against the southern base.
These and those would mingle in the duct
and flow out into the Kidron Valley.

---

is cited, according to which the base did surround the altar on all four sides except for the southeastern corner (see figure 11, page 446).

After sprinkling the blood of a sin-offering, the remaining blood is poured out onto this base. This practice is mentioned with reference to the various different sin-offerings in Leviticus chapter four. There the Torah instructs that the blood should be poured "onto the base of the altar which stands at the entrance to the Tent of Meeting" (verses 7 and 18). The question of which side is considered to face the entrance rests on a debate concerning the positioning of the altar itself; if the altar is located on the northern side of the courtyard, then the southern ledge most prominently faces the entrance to the Sanctuary (the Sanctuary in the Temple paralleling the Tent of Meeting in the Tabernacle). If, however, the altar is situated in the middle of the courtyard, then only the western side of the base faces the entrance, and the blood is poured on that side (*Zevaḥim* 58a; see *Shita Mekubetzet*, ibid. 53a no. 13).

Although Leviticus chapter four mentions the requirement to pour the blood onto the base in four separate verses (7, 18, 25 and 30), the specification of the side "at the entrance to the Tent" is mentioned only in the cases of the two "inner sin-offerings" (those in which the blood is sprinkled inside the Sanctuary toward the Curtain – verses 7 and 18). This being so, the Mishna in *Zevaḥim* (53a) mandates the blood of "outer sin-offerings" to be poured out on the southern side. This distinction also makes practical sense: After sprinkling the blood on the Outer Altar, the priest descends the ramp, coming down on the southern side where he can immediately pour out the blood. A priest exiting the Sanctuary, having sprinkled the blood of an inner sin-offering there, comes first to the western side, making it the natural place to pour out the blood.

בָּאַמָּה *The duct.* The duct carried water to and from the Temple. It was called אַמָּה – "cubit" – because it was a cubit wide (Rashbam, *Pesaḥim* 109b). When

ו הִזָּה עַל טָהֳרוֹ שֶׁלַּמִּזְבֵּחַ שֶׁבַע פְּעָמִים
וּשְׁיָרֵי הַדָּם הָיָה שׁוֹפֵךְ עַל יְסוֹד מַעֲרָבִי שֶׁלַּמִּזְבֵּחַ הַחִיצוֹן
וְשֶׁלַּמִּזְבֵּחַ הַחִיצוֹן הָיָה שׁוֹפֵךְ עַל יְסוֹד דְּרוֹמִי.
אֵלּוּ וָאֵלּוּ
מִתְעָרְבִין בָּאַמָּה וְיוֹצְאִין לְנַחַל קִדְרוֹן

---

him, he applies the blood in an upward motion as this is much easier for him (Rashi). In light of the above, it is understandable why the rabbis (the first, anonymous opinion mentioned) hold that all the applications were done downward. If the High Priest circles the altar, he will always be in direct proximity to each corner as he applies the blood to it, making a downward movement much more practical.

עַל טָהֳרוֹ שֶׁלַּמִּזְבֵּחַ *Onto the clear space on the altar.* The Talmud (59a) debates the meaning of the word טָהֳרוֹ. It may derive from the Aramaic word טִיהֲרָא, *noon,* corresponding to the Hebrew צָהֳרַיִם (see Rashi, Gen. 43:16; "ט" in Aramaic sometimes interchanges with "צ" in Hebrew). If so, the intention is to the midpoint of the altar, halfway up its wall (parallel to noon, the midpoint of the day). Alternatively, it may derive from the more obvious Hebrew root ט-ה-ר and mean "purity" or "cleanliness" (see *Berakhot* 2b in which the two etymologies are connected). If so, the intention is that the High Priest should clear an area on the top of the altar of the ashes remaining from the daily burning of the incense and sprinkle the blood on that exposed, *clean,* area. Indeed, the *Tosefta* (3:2) states explicitly that the High Priest is required to rake the altar to prepare a place to sprinkle onto; on the basis of this source, the Talmud favors the second understanding of the word.

In אַמִּיץ כֹּחַ (page 893) the description of this rite is very concise and somewhat misleading (see *Nishmat Adam,* 145:3), probably simply because of the demands of the acrostic.

יְסוֹד מַעֲרָבִי שֶׁלַּמִּזְבֵּחַ הַחִיצוֹן *The western base of the Outer Altar.* At the bottom of the altar there is a ledge, called the יְסוֹד, the "base," a cubit high and a cubit wide. This does not surround the altar on all four sides; it runs along the northern and western sides, turning to extend just a cubit into the eastern and southern sides (Mishna *Middot* 3:1). In *Zevaḥim* 53b a dissenting opinion

They would be sold to smallholders for fertilizer,
and [one who took them without payment]
had trespassed on the sacred.

7 All the service of the Day of Atonement,
stated in its order –
if [the priest] performed one part before the part before –
nothing was achieved.

---

to atone once a year – the "inside," understood by Rashi to mean the Holy of Holies. This then includes the various blood applications and the burning of the incense, but not the rituals performed in the courtyard or Sanctuary.

Rambam (*Hilkhot Avodat Yom HaKippurim* 5:4) rules that not only the rites performed inside the Holy of Holies but also the sprinkling of the blood upon the Curtain must be performed in the correct sequence, even though this is actually performed in the Sanctuary. This ruling was the subject of some debate, as it seems to accord with neither of the opinions in the Talmud. The *Leḥem Mishneh* suggests that Rambam follows Rabbi Yehuda's opinion, but, unlike Rashi, understands "inside" to include rites performed inside the Sanctuary, as well as in the "innermost place," the Holy of Holies. This does not explain, however, why Rambam does not include in his list the sprinkling of blood on the Golden Altar, which is also inside the Sanctuary. Rav Ḥayyim Soloveitchik (cited by his grandson Rav Yosef Dov Soloveitchik, 40a) suggests that Rambam does indeed rule in accordance with Rabbi Yehuda, and, like Rashi, understands his "inside" to denote the Holy of Holies only; he understands the principle, however, to extend to rites performed outside the Holy of Holies but associated with it. The sprinkling of blood on the Curtain is part of the purification of the Holy of Holies, which is performed both from within and from without. The sprinkling on the Golden Altar, on the other hand, is a ritual of its own, not part of the atonement of the Holy of Holies. This might be supported in the biblical text by the slightly unexpected position of verse 17, "No man shall be in the Tent of Meeting when [Aaron] comes to make atonement…" – which interrupts the sequence of events between the ritual of the Curtain and that of the Golden Altar, as if to suggest that the ritual of the Curtain completes one stage of the Service.

The *Tosefta* (3:4) states that the retrieving of the coal pan and censer is

וְנִמְכָּרִין לַגַּנָּנִין לְזֶבֶל
וּמוֹעֲלִין בָּהֶן.

ז כָּל מַעֲשֵׂה יוֹם הַכִּפּוּרִים הָאָמוּר עַל הַסֵּדֶר
אִם הִקְדִּים מַעֲשֶׂה לַחֲבֵרוֹ
לֹא עָשָׂה כְלוּם;

---

the priests wanted to clean the courtyard, they would dam the duct, so that the overflowing water would wash the floor (Rashi, *Pesaḥim* 64a).

וּמוֹעֲלִין בָּהֶן *Trespassed on the sacred.* It is forbidden to derive private benefit from consecrated items. Doing so, even inadvertently, is considered מְעִילָה – misappropriation of sacred property. In modern Hebrew, this term is used to denote embezzlement, which is not entirely dissimilar. The violation only exists where the consecrated item's sacred purpose has not been realized. Therefore, once the blood has been sprinkled and poured out onto the base, benefit from it is no longer considered to be מְעִילָה. It may therefore be bought by laymen for their own benefit (*Yoma* 59b; see *Pesaḥim* 22a for a derivation of this from the Torah).

The מְעִילָה mentioned in the mishna here, then, is only so by rabbinic decree. One who takes this blood without payment is required to return its value to the Temple purse, but is exempt from both the extra one-fifth fine and the guilt-offering that are normally required for the biblical violation (Lev. 5:15–16).

הָאָמוּר עַל הַסֵּדֶר *Stated in its order.* The Torah concludes its discussion of the Yom Kippur service with the declaration, "This shall be an everlasting law [חֻקַּת עוֹלָם] for you, to make atonement … once a year" (Lev. 16:34). The word חוקה implies a law that is fixed and unchanging. The word is interpreted to indicate that the specific order of the rites performed "once a year" is essential. Rabbi Neḥemia understands the reference to be to any rite performed just once a year, that is, to all those rites unique to the day of Yom Kippur and thus performed in the white vestments, irrespective of where they take place. He therefore includes the confessions, the casting of lots upon the goats and the sprinkling of blood upon the Curtain and Golden Altar. Rabbi Yehuda maintains, on the other hand, that the reference is to the rites of a *place* used

If he puts the blood of the goat before the blood of the bull
he had to go back and sprinkle of the blood of the goat again
after the blood of the bull.
If the blood were spilled
before he finished sprinkling it in the inner place,
he must bring more blood
and go back to sprinkle from the beginning in the inner place.
So also in the Sanctuary,
and so at the Golden Altar;
each made a separate atonement in itself.
Rabbi Elazar and Rabbi Shimon say:
From the place where he leaves off,
there he starts again.

---

one set of sprinklings, then, has no implications for a previous set already completed (61a). This is true even of the sprinkling of the bull and goat bloods inside the Holy of Holies: if the bull's blood has been sprinkled but the blood of the goat spills during its sprinkling, the High Priest only returns to the beginning of the set of the goat's blood (Ri Korkus, *Hilkhot Avodat Yom HaKippurim* 5:5).

רַבִּי אֶלְעָזָר וְרַבִּי שִׁמְעוֹן אוֹמְרִים *Rabbi Elazar and Rabbi Shimon say.* Rabbi Elazar and Rabbi Shimon hold that even if some of the droplets have been sprinkled when the blood spills, the High Priest continues sprinkling the blood of the newly slaughtered animal beginning from the number where he left off, as each droplet constitutes a mitzva in its own right, and repeating the sprinkling is forbidden (Rabbeinu Ḥananel, 61a). The principle here is similar to that applied to the blood of the goat and the blood of the bull in the previous note; what there asserted the independence of one set of sprinklings from another is understood by Rabbi Elazar and Rabbi Shimon to apply to the independent status of each individual sprinkling. They do agree, however, that a new animal must be slaughtered to complete the set of eight sprinklings.

הִקְדִּים דַּם הַשָּׂעִיר לְדַם הַפָּר
יַחֲזוֹר וְיַזֶּה מִדַּם הַשָּׂעִיר לְאַחַר דַּם הַפָּר.
וְאִם עַד שֶׁלֹּא גָמַר אֶת הַמַּתָּנוֹת שֶׁבִּפְנִים, נִשְׁפַּךְ הַדָּם
יָבִיא דָם אַחֵר
וְיַחֲזוֹר וְיַזֶּה בַּתְּחִלָּה בִּפְנִים.
וְכֵן בַּהֵיכָל
וְכֵן בְּמִזְבַּח הַזָּהָב
שֶׁכֻּלָּן כַּפָּרָה בִּפְנֵי עַצְמָן.
רַבִּי אֶלְעָזָר וְרַבִּי שִׁמְעוֹן אוֹמְרִים:
מִמָּקוֹם שֶׁפָּסַק, מִשָּׁם הוּא מַתְחִיל.

---

not included in the "statute," and that its placement in the Order of the Day is not essential – despite the rite certainly being performed in the Holy of Holies. Even if these are retrieved out of sequence, before offering the rams (see chapter seven), the rite is still considered to have been performed properly. *Tosafot Yeshanim* (61a–b) suggest that this is because the retrieving of the coal pan and censer is not considered a positive act of service, but a technical necessity to clear the Holy of Holies. The *Mikdash David* (24:7) suggests a simpler distinction: the assertion that "nothing was achieved" is only applicable to cases where the rite could conceivably be required to be performed again, which is clearly not the case here.

יָבִיא דָם אַחֵר *He must bring more blood.* The few sprinklings that he may already have performed are now invalidated and he must start all eight sprinklings again. The reason for this is that each set of sprinklings must be performed from the blood of a single animal. If the blood spills, then a new animal must be slaughtered and the sprinklings must be repeated from the beginning (Rashi, 61a). Each set of sprinklings is independent, and there is no requirement that each of them use the blood of the same animal; interruption of

longer challenge the domain of Holiness. His idea, indeed, is not a new one; the Midrash hears it resonate in the verse: וְנָשָׂא הַשָּׂעִיר עָלָיו אֶת כָּל עֲוֹנֹתָם, "That goat shall bear upon itself all [the people's] guilt." The word שָׂעִיר, *goat*, links associatively with Esau, אִישׁ שָׂעִר, "a hairy man" (Gen. 27:11; this characteristic becomes emblematic of him in the language of the Midrash; see *Shemot Raba* 42:7). הַר שֵׂעִיר, Mount Se'ir, is Esau's eventual home (Gen. 32:3). The word עֲוֹנֹתָם, literally "their iniquities," is split in two, a common technique in midrashic exegesis, to read עֲוֹנוֹת תָּם, "the sins of the pure one." תָּם is the defining characteristic of Jacob – אִישׁ תָּם יֹשֵׁב אֹהָלִים (Gen. 25:27), "A pure man, dwelling in tents." In this midrash, then, the verse is read "The hairy one – Esau – shall carry away all the iniquities of the pure one – Jacob." This is also a common motif in the Yom Kippur *piyutim*; Esau is often cast as the קָטֵגוֹר, the accuser, ever eager to point out Israel's fatal flaws. The descent of the goat to Azazel – carrying their confessed guilt with it – represents the silencing of his claims (see for instance page 147).

The typology of Jacob and Esau represents not only the Jewish people's struggle with external enemies, but more particularly, in our context, its internal struggle with the sinful elements of their own nature. A person holds two opposing forces inside; usually these are inseparable, and on Yom Kippur they are broken apart. The good is revealed as the true, essential quality; the bad is banished to the abyss (see *Or HaḤayyim*, Lev. 16:7).

Drawing upon ideas expressed in the *Zohar* (the most direct expression is in *Raya Meheimana, Naso* 123b), Ramban offers the disquieting suggestion that the goat sent to Azazel is being offered to the "force of destruction" as a "bribe" not to interfere on this momentous day. He takes great pains to emphasize that this should not be understood as an "offering" from the Jewish people; it could only be done under God's direct instructions and is in fact considered to come from Him. Therefore, explains Ramban, it is critical that the selection is made through a lottery, and not by human decision. Using a lottery makes it clear that both goats are ultimately given to God, and that it is He who makes the choice to give one to Azazel.

Rabbi Tzvi Elimelekh of Dinov (*Bnei Yissakhar,* Yom Kippur) refers as a parallel to the two bulls Elijah offers on Mount Carmel as he adjures the people to renew their covenant with God. One of these bulls is indeed offered to God; the other is offered to Ba'al, the pagan god, by the priests that serve him (1 Kings 18:23–26). The Midrash (*Bereshit Raba* 23:9) narrates that the bull to be offered to Ba'al tries to escape, not wishing to suffer this degradation. Elijah, however, tells him that he too is to take his part in sanctifying God's name –

CHAPTER SIX:

Chapter five described the High Priest's entrance into the Holy of Holies, the highest point of the year's worship. Despite the great public importance of this ceremony, it is also an essentially private moment; no one is permitted to be in the Sanctuary while the High Priest performs these rituals (Lev. 16:17), and the other priests and the assembled crowds wait outside in anxious anticipation for the High Priest's reappearance at the end of the Service. Chapter six, by way of contrast, discusses the very public rite of sending away the goat to Azazel. It is this ceremony that brings us to the emotional climax of the day.

The Torah explains the purpose of this ceremony by the words: וְנָשָׂא הַשָּׂעִיר עָלָיו אֶת כָּל עֲוֹנֹתָם, "That goat shall bear upon itself all the people's guilt" (Lev. 16:22). The Mishna (*Shevuot* 2b) explains that Azazel atones for all the sins of the Jewish people; sins of all degrees of seriousness, whether willful or inadvertent, known or unknown. Seforno (verse 5) submits that it is for this reason that it must be cast away. The great burden of sin the goat carries makes it unfit to be brought before God. And for the very same reason it engenders impurity in anyone involved with it (see mishna 6). Instead of being offered up, then, it is removed from the Temple, the city and all habitation to be cast to the abyss. According to Seforno, then, the only reason to send the goat to Azazel is because it cannot be brought to the Temple. Other commentaries, however, understand the sending away of the goat as part of a much greater scheme.

The Midrash (*Bereshit Raba* 65:14) sees the rite of the goats already foreshadowed in the actions of Jacob. When Isaac wishes to give his patriarchal blessing to Esau, he asks Esau to prepare him a meal of good meat. Rebecca, however, understanding Jacob to be the true spiritual heir, instructs him to prepare the foods Isaac desires, so that he may take Esau's place and gain the blessing, saying, "Bring me two good kids of the flock" (Gen. 27:9). The Midrash sees new layers of meaning in this pair of young goats: "*Good* – good for yourself, as through them you will receive the blessing; and good for your descendants, as through them they will be atoned for on Yom Kippur."

Abarbanel (Lev. 16:5) develops this idea further and suggests that the two goats represent the continuing struggle between Jacob and Esau. These twins are born identical (Rashi, Gen. 25:27), yet one chooses eternal life while the other rejects it. The two goats play out this elemental conflict to its conclusion; although seemingly identical, one goat is brought to the altar of God, its blood sprinkled in the innermost sanctum of the Temple, while the other is cast out, banished to a desolate place, far removed, where it can no

CHAPTER SIX

1 The two goats for the Day of Atonement are to be alike
in appearance,
in height
and in value,
and to be bought together as one.
But if they are not alike,
they are still valid.

---

the time at which impurity of clothes occurs. The mishna does, however, also contribute to a sense of the suspense and apprehension that the people in the courtyard must have felt waiting to hear that the goat had reached the desert and that the sins of Israel had been atoned.

שְׁנֵיהֶן שָׁוִין *To be alike.* The two goats should be similar. This does not, however, mean that they must be indistinguishable. As long as they share the same basic qualities listed in the mishna, they are considered sufficiently alike. This is acceptable, as people do not usually focus on the finer characteristics of livestock (*Tosafot Yeshanim*, 62b).

שֶׁאֵינָן שָׁוִין *But if they are not alike.* The Talmud derives from the verses in Leviticus 16:5–10 that the two goats should be similar, while also demonstrating that if this guideline is not met, they are still valid (62b). The same logic is also applied to the verses regarding the two birds used for purifying a person with *tzara'at* (Lev. 14:4–7). The Mishna, indeed, provides an identical list of requirements for the two birds, and the same caveat allowing for differences (*Nega'im* 14:4). The two lists are clearly written in deliberate parallel; the Mishna there states that the birds should be equal in height, a feature not usually considered relevant in birds.

This parallel reflects on the rite of the two goats. Whenever birds are sacrificed, it is always a pair of them together (Lev. 1:14–17, 5:7, 12:8, 14:21–22); therefore, if one of the *metzora* birds is offered to God, it is likely that both are components of one offering. The same idea might be suggested here – that the two goats are one single offering, a part of which is brought into the Holy of Holies to atone for Israel and the other sent away to the desert (an idea developed by Rabbi Zalman Sorotzkin, *Oznayim LaTorah*, Lev. 16:5).

פרק שישי

א שְׁנֵי שְׂעִירֵי יוֹם הַכִּפּוּרִים
מִצְוָתָן שֶׁיִּהְיוּ שְׁנֵיהֶן שָׁוִין
בְּמַרְאֶה, וּבְקוֹמָה, וּבְדָמִים
וּבִלְקִיחָתָן כְּאֶחָד.
וְאַף עַל פִּי שֶׁאֵינָן שָׁוִין, כְּשֵׁרִין.

---

as proves, indeed, to be the case, when the priests of Ba'al fail to bring down fire to burn the offering. The event – with its double, similar-but-opposite offering – brings the people, at least briefly, back to their covenant with God.

Choice, then, is a major theme here; man's choice of good over evil, God's choice of Jacob over Esau, and His choice determining the respective fate of the two goats. Rabbi Samson Raphael Hirsch, commenting on Leviticus 16:10, develops at length the idea that choice is the central motif of the day. He suggests that the lottery of the goats is also a moment of choice for each individual: whether to yield to temptation and follow the path of sin to the desert, or whether to assert one's freedom and control over one's needs and desires (Gen. 4:7), and to offer oneself to the service of God. On first inspection it is difficult to distinguish between these two goats, these two facets of our personalities, two possible projections of our selves into the future; but all the same, one leads to God, and the other to the abyss.

Our chapter opens with the laws governing this rite; the selection criteria for the goats and the questions that arise if one of them dies (mishna 1). The chapter continues with details specific to the goat that is sent away: the confession upon it (2), how it is led out into the desert (3–6), and the method of informing the High Priest that the rite has been completed (8). While the goat is being led into the desert, the High Priest himself, who remains in the Temple, prepares the dead bull and goat, and sends their organs outside to be burnt (7).

Mishna 7 is out of place thematically, and according to some commentaries, chronologically as well (see the commentary there). It may have been placed here because of the Mishna's tendency to group together similar disputes – both in mishna 6 and there, Rabbi Shimon disagrees with the sages about

If he buys one on one day and the other on the next,
they are valid.
If one of them dies –
if it happens before the drawing of the lots,
[the High Priest] must take a new partner for the other;
and if one dies after the lots have been drawn,
he must bring another pair
and draw lots over them from the beginning.
And he says, if the one for the LORD has died,
"The one whose lot comes up for the LORD shall take its place;"
and if the one for Azazel has died,
"The one whose lot comes up for Azazel shall take its place."
The other goat is put to pasture until it becomes unfit for sacrifice,
and is sold, and its money is used for a free-will offering;
for a public sin-offering is not left to die.
Rabbi Yehuda says:
It is left to die.

---

are cast a second time in order to designate a goat to replace the one that died, and the declaration made by the High Priest proclaims the substitution.

The Hebrew text of this declaration can be read in more than one way. Before the scarlet strip is attached to the Azazel goat (see mishna 4:2), the identities of the two goats could be confused, so that it would not be certain which of the two goats had actually died. This being so, what we have read as two possible speeches introduced by conditional clauses could be one long speech with a double clause: "If the one for the LORD has died, let the one whose lot comes up for the LORD take its place, and if…" Assuming, however, that there was no room for confusion, the mishna should be punctuated as we have translated – two separate declarations for two different events (Bartenura following Rambam).

תָּמוּת *It is left to die.* There is a הֲלָכָה לְמֹשֶׁה מִסִּינַי, (literally: "a law given to Moses on Sinai") – an oral tradition not explicit in the biblical text – that certain sin-offerings, when they lose their designation, are left to die (see Mishna, *Me'ila* 10b). The Mishna (*Temura* 21b) lists four such cases: the offspring of an animal set aside for a sin-offering; an animal the owners of which

לָקַח אֶחָד הַיּוֹם וְאֶחָד לְמָחָר, כְּשֵׁרִין.
מֵת אֶחָד מֵהֶן
אִם עַד שֶׁלֹּא הִגְרִיל מֵת
יִקַּח זוּג לַשֵּׁנִי;
וְאִם מִשֶּׁהִגְרִיל מֵת
יָבִיא זוּג אַחֵר וְיַגְרִיל עֲלֵיהֶם בַּתְּחִלָּה
וְיֹאמַר, אִם שֶׁלַּשֵּׁם מֵת:
זֶה שֶׁעָלָה עָלָיו הַגּוֹרָל ׳לַשֵּׁם׳ יִתְקַיֵּם תַּחְתָּיו;
וְאִם שֶׁלַּעֲזָאזֵל מֵת:
זֶה שֶׁעָלָה עָלָיו הַגּוֹרָל ׳לַעֲזָאזֵל׳ יִתְקַיֵּם תַּחְתָּיו.
וְהַשֵּׁנִי יִרְעֶה עַד שֶׁיִּסְתָּאֵב
וְיִמָּכֵר, וְיִפְּלוּ דָמָיו לִנְדָבָה
שֶׁאֵין חַטַּאת צִבּוּר מֵתָה.
רַבִּי יְהוּדָה אוֹמֵר: תָּמוּת.

אִם עַד שֶׁלֹּא הִגְרִיל מֵת *If it happens before the drawing of the lots.* Purchasing the two goats together increases the likelihood that they will be similar; but they are not considered formally to be a pair until the lots are drawn. After this, the two goats are bound as a formal pair and disqualification of one invalidates the other, requiring two new goats to be purchased and the lots to be drawn again (Rabbeinu Yehonatan).

For the two birds of the *metzora,* there is no defining moment parallel to the drawing of lots which could define them as a pair. The disqualification of one, therefore, does not invalidate the other, unless it happens after the rite has begun, the first bird having been successfully offered to the Lord (Rosh ibid).

וְאִם מִשֶּׁהִגְרִיל מֵת *If one dies after the lots have been drawn.* According to the majority view, against which Rabbi Yehuda argues, a goat that remains after its "partner" has died can – and thus should – still be used (see below). It is the corresponding goat from the second pair that is sent to graze. The lots

Rabbi Yehuda also says:
If the blood of the one is spilled [before its sprinkling],
the one to be sent away [to Azazel] is left to die;
and if the goat to be sent away dies,
the blood of the other is poured out [without sprinkling].

---

will never give birth. Rabbi Yehuda disagrees and maintains that in the one situation when the rule can apply to a public sin-offering, it does.

וְעוֹד אָמַר רַבִּי יְהוּדָה *Rabbi Yehuda also says.* A case where one goat is invalidated and the other survives, but a complete new pair must be found to repeat the lottery, creates a situation of redundancy; the surviving goat and the new pair now make three. The rabbis maintain that as the surviving goat of the original pair is still valid, it should still be used, while its parallel from the second pair is left to graze; Rabbi Yehuda argues that the loss of its "twin" disqualifies the surviving goat, so that both goats of the new pair should be used. The Talmud (64b–65a) locates the root of the dispute in the more general question of whether to endorse the principle: בַּעֲלֵי חַיִּים נִדְחִין, "living animals can be permanently disqualified" – meaning that if the reason for an offering's invalidation itself becomes irrelevant, the animal nonetheless remains disqualified. In our case, one goat is rendered unfit by a problem that arises with the other. Even if the problem with the other is "mended" by its replacement, the principle would imply that the surviving goat is still invalid, and must also be replaced, as held by Rabbi Yehuda. The majority view here would seem, in this perspective, to reject the בַּעֲלֵי חַיִּים נִדְחִין principle.

יִשָּׁפֵךְ הַדָּם *The blood of the other is poured out.* If the blood of the goat for the LORD is spilled, the purpose of the goats cannot be fulfilled, so it follows that the Azazel goat is also disqualified. The reverse case is less clear-cut: the sending of the goat to Azazel, while very important in its own right, is not a precondition for the atonement achieved by its "twin" goat in the Holy of Holies. The fact that the premature death of the Azazel goat does, nonetheless, have implications for the goat for the LORD is explained in the Talmud (65a) through a midrashic reading of Leviticus 16:10. The statement that the Azazel goat shall "stand alive before the LORD, to atone" is understood to indicate that the sprinkling of the blood in the Sanctuary must take place while the Azazel goat is still alive.

The principle בַּעֲלֵי חַיִּים נִדְחִין (see previous note), if it does hold true, only

וְעוֹד אָמַר רַבִּי יְהוּדָה:
נִשְׁפַּךְ הַדָּם, יָמוּת הַמִּשְׁתַּלֵּחַ
מֵת הַמִּשְׁתַּלֵּחַ, יִשָּׁפֵךְ הַדָּם.

---

have tried, inappropriately, to substitute for a sin-offering (see Lev. 27:33); a sin-offering whose owner has died; and a sin-offering whose owner has meanwhile achieved atonement by offering a different animal. In these four cases, the animal is already invested with the sanctity by being designated as a sin-offering, but there is no sin for it to atone for. Rabbi Shimon adds a fifth case: a sin-offering more than a year old; but the rabbis reject this.

The Talmud (*Temura* 18a) states that: כָּל שֶׁבְּחַטָּאת מֵתָה בְּאָשָׁם רוֹעָה: "a disqualification which would require a sin-offering to be left to die – [when it occurs] in a guilt-offering, the animal is sent to pasture." An invalidated guilt-offering – while it cannot be offered up – is not left to die like an invalidated sin-offering, but instead is left to pasture until it develops a permanent blemish which invalidates it to an extent that allows it to be sold for secular use (with certain limitations). Its purchase value is then reinvested into the Temple service (Mishna *Shekalim* 6:5 states that these monies were used for the קֵיץ הַמִּזְבֵּחַ offerings, communal offerings brought in times when the altar stood idle).

The distinction between a sin- and a guilt-offering in this regard may be understood in light of the distinction offered by Ramban (Lev. 5:15). A sin-offering, he suggests, atones by "neutralizing" the *sin*, while a guilt-offering protects the *person* from the effects of his sin. If there is no sin to atone for, a sin-offering is meaningless, as there is nothing to achieve. There is always, however, significance to the guilt-offering, as the person can always benefit from its merit. Therefore even if the current animal is invalidated, its value can be donated to the Temple, and still, to some extent, fulfill its goal.

The implied question behind our mishna is why, when the goat bereft of its partner and replaced by another is apparently an invalidated sin-offering (see Lev. 16:5), it is not treated as such and left to die. The answer given is that this הֲלָכָה לְמֹשֶׁה מִסִּינַי does not apply to public sin-offerings such as the goats, which are paid for out of the communal purse. These surely fall into a separate category of offering; indeed, three of the four reasons for being left to die can never apply to a public offering. It is not subject to substitution; its owners (the people as a whole) can never "die"; and, being male, the offering

2 The High Priest would come to the goat that is to be sent away
and press his two hands down upon it and confess.
And this is what he would say:
Please, [Lord],
Your people Israel
have done wrong,
have rebelled,
have sinned before You –
Please, by the Name,
make atonement, please,
for the wrongs
and the rebellions
and sins
that Your people Israel
have done wrong,
have rebelled,
and have sinned before You –
as it is written in the Torah of Moses Your servant,
"For you will be atoned on this day and made pure; *Lev. 16*
of all your sins before the Lord you shall be purified."
And the priests and all the people who were standing in the courtyard,
when they heard the Name
spoken out loud by the High Priest,
would bow down in worship;
would fall upon their faces and say –
"Blessed be the name of His glorious kingdom forever."

---

hand, atones for the sins of the people, and although the High Priest speaks personally in that confession too, he does so as one of his people.

וְהַכֹּהֲנִים וְהָעָם *And the priests and all the people...* These lines are missing here in most manuscripts of the mishna, and in ours they appear only in this third confession. The Meiri's version of the mishna has them in each of the three confessions, and they appear in most of the Order of the Service *piyutim*. But

ב בָּא לוֹ אֵצֶל שְׂעִיר הַמִּשְׁתַּלֵּחַ
וְסוֹמֵךְ שְׁתֵּי יָדָיו עָלָיו, וּמִתְוַדֶּה.
וְכָךְ הָיָה אוֹמֵר:
אָנָּא הַשֵּׁם
עָווּ פָּשְׁעוּ חָטְאוּ לְפָנֶיךָ
עַמְּךָ בֵּית יִשְׂרָאֵל.
אָנָּא בַּשֵּׁם
כַּפֶּר נָא לָעֲוֹנוֹת וְלַפְּשָׁעִים וְלַחֲטָאִים
שֶׁעָווּ וְשֶׁפָּשְׁעוּ וְשֶׁחָטְאוּ לְפָנֶיךָ
עַמְּךָ בֵּית יִשְׂרָאֵל
כַּכָּתוּב בְּתוֹרַת מֹשֶׁה עַבְדֶּךָ, לֵאמֹר:
ויקרא טז כִּי־בַיּוֹם הַזֶּה יְכַפֵּר עֲלֵיכֶם לְטַהֵר אֶתְכֶם
מִכֹּל חַטֹּאתֵיכֶם לִפְנֵי ה׳ תִּטְהָרוּ:
וְהַכֹּהֲנִים וְהָעָם הָעוֹמְדִים בָּעֲזָרָה
כְּשֶׁהָיוּ שׁוֹמְעִים שֵׁם הַמְּפֹרָשׁ
שֶׁהוּא יוֹצֵא מִפִּי כֹהֵן גָּדוֹל
הָיוּ כּוֹרְעִים וּמִשְׁתַּחֲוִים וְנוֹפְלִים עַל פְּנֵיהֶם
וְאוֹמְרִים: ׳בָּרוּךְ שֵׁם כְּבוֹד מַלְכוּתוֹ לְעוֹלָם וָעֶד׳.

---

applies to living animals; all agree that when other objects are rendered unfit, their disqualification is permanent. Thus, even the rabbis agree that if the Azazel goat dies, the blood of the other, already slaughtered goat, is permanently disqualified (Rashi).

עַמְּךָ בֵּית יִשְׂרָאֵל *Your people Israel.* The offering of the bull atones for the sins of the High Priest, his family and tribe; it must be offered before he can enter the Holy of Holies (see introduction to chapter 5). The goat, on the other

3 The goat would be given to the one who would lead it.
Everyone is valid to lead it,
but the High Priests made it their custom
not to allow a lay Israelite to lead it.
Rabbi Yose said:
Once Arsela led it,
and he was of Israel.

4 They built a ramp for these,
because of the Babylonians who used to pull at their hair saying,
"Take it, go on, take it and go!"

---

previous day; *Targum Yerushalmi* on Lev. 16:21: the previous year), and that his appointment must be fulfilled whenever its time falls, even on Shabbat, and even if he chances to be impure and would not usually be allowed to enter the Temple courtyard.

Rashbam (Lev. 16:21) offers an alternative suggestion. The man should be an expert guide, familiar with the paths in the wilderness, so that he will be ready to leave at any time. The *Ḥizkuni* cites a midrash stating that the appointment is given to "a man whose time has come" – who is to die in the coming year. The *Zohar* (*Raya Meheimana, Pineḥas* 248a) tells that the person chosen was one who had his own burden of sin to bear to Azazel.

עַרְסְלָא *Arsela.* The version of the mishna in the Yerushalmi has "Arsela of Tzipori." If this represents him rightly, Rabbi Yose, who resided in Tzipori two generations after the Destruction (*Shabbat* 33b; *Sanhedrin* 32b), may be reporting a local tradition.

The Talmud derives from the term אִישׁ in אִישׁ עִתִּי that the appointed man did not have to be a priest. Both אַתָּה כּוֹנַנְתָּ (page 1272) and Rambam (*Hilkhot Avodat Yom HaKippurim* 3:7), however, indicate that one of the priests would take the goat. The *Mayim Ḥayyim* proposes that the priests saw themselves as responsible for purifying Israel and therefore took on this responsibility as well. Rabbi Aryeh Levin suggests that the priests wished to show that they too were included in the atonement of the Azazel goat (*Mishnat Aryeh*).

מִפְּנֵי הַבַּבְלִיִּים *Because of the Babylonians.* The "Babylonians" would jostle the appointed man roughly, pulling at his hair, and hassling him to begin the journey without delay. To protect him from the crowd, an elevated walkway was

ג מְסָרוֹ לְמִי שֶׁהָיָה מוֹלִיכוֹ.
הַכֹּל כְּשֵׁרִין לְהוֹלִיכוֹ
אֶלָּא שֶׁעָשׂוּ כֹהֲנִים גְּדוֹלִים קֶבַע
וְלֹא הָיוּ מַנִּיחִין אֶת יִשְׂרָאֵל לְהוֹלִיכוֹ.
אָמַר רַבִּי יוֹסֵי:
מַעֲשֶׂה וְהוֹלִיכוֹ עַרְסְלָא
וְיִשְׂרָאֵל הָיָה.

ד וְכֶבֶשׁ עָשׂוּ לוֹ
מִפְּנֵי הַבַּבְלִיִּים שֶׁהָיוּ מְתַלְּשִׁים בִּשְׂעָרוֹ
וְאוֹמְרִים לוֹ:
טֹל וָצֵא, טֹל וָצֵא!

---

as late as the early sixteenth century, Radbaz (2:810) writes: "this does not appear in the Talmud at all" (see also Tosafot, *Sota* 40b and *Or Zarua* 2:281).

Tosafot Yom Tov suggests that they appear in all three confessions, but in the Mishna are abbreviated out of the first two for the sake of conciseness. *Tiferet Yisrael* suggests that in the first two times, when the High Priest is confessing for himself and his tribe, only those standing close to him hear him quietly mentioning God's name and bow down (see Yerushalmi 3:7). In the third confession, however, made for all Israel, the crowds gathered to listen and participate in his confession (through the principle of שׁוֹמֵעַ כְּעוֹנֶה, "through listening, it is considered as if he had spoken the words," see *Sukka* 38b). Only during this confession would the High Priest mention God's name out loud and evoke a sonorous public response.

מְסָרוֹ *The goat would be given.* "[Aaron shall] send it away at the hand of an appointed man (אִישׁ עִתִּי), into the wastelands" (Lev. 16:21). Rambam rules that the High Priest himself must give it to the appointed man (*Hilkhot Avodat Yom HaKippurim* 2:2; see also *Baḥ, Yoma* 66b, 5).

The word עִתִּי, translated here "appointed," derives from עֵת, "time," suggesting perhaps that the appointment is time-dependent. The Talmud (66a–b) understands both that the man must be appointed in good time, (Rashi: the

The honored of Jerusalem used to accompany him
as far as the first hut;
there were ten huts between Jerusalem and the crag.
It was a distance of ninety riss,
and there are seven and a half riss in a mil.

5 At every hut they would say to him
"Here is food and here is water,"

---

of the place; *Tosafot Yom Tov* suggests that it was to realize the term אֶרֶץ גְּזֵרָה, "a desolate land" (Lev. 16:22), that the place was preserved as one near which no one had ever set up any kind of dwelling.

Rashash argues that sending the goat to the Azazel should not be reason enough to permit the attendant to violate biblical law by walking so far outside of the settlement. Among the *Rishonim* there are three approaches to the status of the rule of תְּחוּם שַׁבָּת: 1. Rav Aḥai Gaon (*She'ilta* 48) maintains that the "Shabbat limit" constitutes a biblical prohibition. 2. Most *Rishonim* consider it an entirely rabbinic decree (see Tosafot, *Eiruvin* 17b and *Beit Yosef*, OḤ 397). 3. Rif (*Eiruvin* 5a) and Rambam (*Hilkhot Shabbat* 27:1) draw a distinction: the two-thousand cubit limit is of rabbinic origin; biblically the limit is twelve mil. According to Rashash, choosing a crag no more than twelve mil outside the city – according to the opinion of Rif and Rambam – is what makes the ritual permissible.

הֲרֵי מָזוֹן וַהֲרֵי מַיִם *"Here is food and here is water."* It is noted in the Talmud (67a) that never once did the attendant partake of the food or drink available; however, "one who has bread in his basket is not like one who does not have bread in his basket." This proverb is invoked in a number of places – most often in the context of sexual desire – to describe the psychological truth that a hunger is generally much easier to bear if it will be, or can be, satisfied soon. Another slant on this phenomenon appears elsewhere in this tractate; invoking Moses' words in Deut. 8:16, "[God] fed you in the wilderness with manna…to afflict you," it is asked how manna could be experienced as an affliction. The answer is found in the principle of "bread in the basket" (74a) – manna is certainly good, but the psychological insecurity of being unable to store food for the future, to plan and control and to feel independent, is a constant challenge in itself.

מִיקִּירֵי יְרוּשָׁלַיִם הָיוּ מְלַוִּין אוֹתוֹ עַד סֻכָּה הָרִאשׁוֹנָה.
עֶשֶׂר סֻכּוֹת מִירוּשָׁלַיִם וְעַד צוּק
תִּשְׁעִים רִיס
שִׁבְעָה וּמֶחֱצָה לְכָל מִיל.

ה עַל כָּל סֻכָּה וְסֻכָּה
אוֹמְרִים לוֹ: הֲרֵי מָזוֹן וַהֲרֵי מַיִם

---

built, leading from the courtyard outside the city (Rashi). Rabbeinu Elyakim considers that they pulled, not at the attendant's hair, but at the goat's. *Piskei HaRid* adds they would even detach some of the goat's fur in the process, a *melakha* prohibited on Yom Kippur.

In the *Tosefta*'s version (3:8) the offenders are identified not as Babylonians but as Alexandrians. The Talmud (66b) remarks that the people of *Eretz Yisrael* disliked the Babylonian Jews and referred to anyone whom they disapproved of as Babylonians. This seems harsh. Tosafot (*Menaḥot* 100a) associate it with the criticism the *Eretz Yisrael* Jews felt toward those who did not return to reestablish the homeland and build the Second Temple when the opportunity arose in the days of Ezra (*Yoma* 9b). If so, "Babylonians" may be understood as a general, disparaging term for all Diaspora Jews.

תִּשְׁעִים רִיס *It was a distance of ninety riss.* The total distance from Jerusalem to the crag, then, was twelve mil (11–14 kilometers). The mishnaic "mil" is equal to two-thousand cubits and is equivalent neither to the Roman nor to the modern mile. It corresponds to the תְּחוּם שַׁבָּת, the "Shabbat limit"; this is the distance one is permitted to walk out of the city on Shabbat, or to stray from the place or settlement one has established as one's dwelling for that day (*Eiruvin* 51a). The huts here, placed at a one mil distance from each other, serve as temporary dwellings for the groups accompanying the attendant, allowing each group to walk on one mil with him, as far as the next hut, but no further. Only the attendant himself had a mission which transcended the prohibition of travel on Yom Kippur. There were only ten huts, but twelve mil, so the last leg of the journey was two mil, and the people accompanying the attendant had to stop half way, and leave him to complete his journey alone (see next mishna). This would have the effect of accentuating the desolation

and they would walk with him from one hut to the next,
except for the last;
[the man in the last hut] would not come with him to the crag,
but would stand at a distance and see what he did.

6 And what would he do?
He would divide the scarlet strip in two,
tie half to the rock and half between the goat's two horns,
and he would push the goat backwards,
it would roll down and down,
and it would not fall halfway down the mountain
before it was torn limb from limb.
The man would go and sit in the last hut until dark.

וּדְחָפוֹ *And he would push the goat.* According to *Zohar* (*Aḥarei Mot*, 63b) and the description in אַתָּה כּוֹנַנְתָּ (page 1272), as he cast down the goat, the man would say "Thus may all the sins of Israel Your people be wiped away."

The Netziv (*Ha'amek Davar*, Lev. 16:21) notes that the Torah does not state explicitly that the goat is to be cast down a crag, but only that it should be sent הַמִּדְבָּרָה – "into the wastelands." He therefore claims that the casting of the goat into the crag was only a לְכַתְּחִלָּה, *ab initio*, requirement, and the rite would still be valid if it did not fall. In support of this, he cites the Yerushalmi, which lists six signs of God's favor that ceased to be manifest after the death of Shimon HaTzaddik (6:3). One of these is that the Azazel goat always descended into the crag; but after that High Priest's death there were years in which it would escape and run off into the desert, and be caught and eaten by outlaws. The implication is not that this invalidated the ritual, but only that it showed a diminishing of divine favor.

בָּא וְיָשַׁב לוֹ *The man would go and sit.* Although the rite was now over, and the last hut was two mil away, which is outside the תְּחוּם שַׁבָּת limit, the sages nevertheless permitted him to return to the last hut to rest until nightfall. Rashi suggests that they feared that in his weakened state it would be harmful for him to remain in the sun. Furthermore, he would be afraid to wait in the wilderness alone, and in the hut he was awaited by others.

וּמְלַוִּין אוֹתוֹ מִסֻּכָּה לְסֻכָּה
חוּץ מֵאַחֲרוֹנָה שֶׁבָּהֶן
שֶׁאֵינוֹ מַגִּיעַ עִמּוֹ לַצּוּק
אֶלָּא עוֹמֵד מֵרָחוֹק וְרוֹאֶה אֶת מַעֲשָׂיו.

ו מֶה הָיָה עוֹשֶׂה?
חוֹלֵק לָשׁוֹן שֶׁל זְהוֹרִית
חֶצְיוֹ קָשַׁר בַּסֶּלַע
וְחֶצְיוֹ קָשַׁר בֵּין שְׁתֵּי קַרְנָיו
וּדְחָפוֹ לַאֲחוֹרָיו
וְהוּא מִתְגַּלְגֵּל וְיוֹרֵד
וְלֹא הָיָה מַגִּיעַ לַחֲצִי הָהָר, עַד שֶׁנַּעֲשָׂה אֵבָרִים אֵבָרִים.
בָּא וְיָשַׁב לוֹ תַּחַת סֻכָּה הָאַחֲרוֹנָה
עַד שֶׁתֶּחְשַׁךְ.

חוֹלֵק לָשׁוֹן שֶׁל זְהוֹרִית *He would divide the scarlet strip in two.* Originally the strip would be tied to the doorway of the Antechamber. If it turned white, there would be public rejoicing; and if it remained red, public dismay. The sages then instituted that it should be tied on the inside of the door, not in full view. All the same, the people would contrive to peek inside. The rabbis therefore instituted that, instead, half the strip should be tied between the goat's horns and the other half on a rock near the crag. In this way it was kept entirely out of view (*Yoma* 67a). Rabbi Moshe ibn Ḥaviv (the Chief Rabbi of Jerusalem in the seventeenth century) suggests that the cause of concern was that, seeing the strip turn white, the people's joy would stop them fully repenting; while if it did not change, their worry would also cause them to falter (*Yom Terua, Rosh HaShana* 31b; see also *Arukh LeNer, Rosh HaShana* 31b).

And from what moment do his clothes become impure?
From the moment they pass across the wall of Jerusalem.
Rabbi Shimon says:
From the moment it is pushed from the cliff.

7 The High Priest would come to the bull and the goat to be burnt.
He would cut them open and take out the sacrificial parts,
place them in a basin
and burn them like incense on the altar.
Then he would braid the limbs together

---

its destination, the desolate desert (Rabbeinu Yehonatan; compare to the comments of the Netziv, above).

וְהִקְטִירָן *And burn them.* The Talmud (67b) states that this line is not to be understood literally, because the entrails are in fact not burned at this point, but only much later, after the High Priest has changed into the golden vestments (see note to 7:4). It therefore emends the mishna to say they were only placed in a basin in order to be burned at a later point. It would seem that the reason the mishna mentions the burning of the entrails at this stage is because of the subsequent mention of the impurity engendered in doing so, paralleling the impurity mentioned above, which is caused by accompanying the Azazel goat.

קְלָעָן *Then he would braid.* Rabbeinu Ḥananel and Rashi describe how the braiding is achieved. The limbs of the slaughtered bull and goat are intertwined; they are then strung onto two poles and carried by four people, each supporting one end of a pole. According to them, at this point the animals are still intact, except for their entrails, which have been removed. Their limbs are only fully detached after they leave the Temple and reach the place to be burnt. Taking a slightly different approach, Rambam (*Hilkhot Avodat Yom HaKippurim* 3:7) rules that they are already partially dismembered inside the Temple, but are only fully separated when they arrive at the place where they will be burned.

The dismembering of these animals was done differently from usual. Normally, a burnt offering is dismembered in two stages (see Lev. 1:6): first it is flayed, and then, with the hide removed, the limbs are cut up. The Talmud (67b) explains that in the case of the goat and the bull, the carcasses are carved up into pieces directly without being flayed.

וּמֵאֵימָתַי מְטַמֵּא בְגָדִים?
מִשֶּׁיֵּצֵא חוּץ לְחוֹמַת יְרוּשָׁלַיִם.
רַבִּי שִׁמְעוֹן אוֹמֵר:
מִשְּׁעַת דְּחִיָּתוֹ לַצּוּק.

ז בָּא לוֹ אֵצֶל הַפָּר וְאֵצֶל הַשָּׂעִיר הַנִּשְׂרָפִין.
קְרָעָן
וְהוֹצִיא אֶת אֵמוּרֵיהֶן
נְתָנָן בְּמָגִיס
וְהִקְטִירָן עַל גַּבֵּי הַמִּזְבֵּחַ.
קְלָעָן בְּמִקְלָעוֹת

וּמֵאֵימָתַי *And from what moment..?* Among the many causes of *tuma*, ritual impurity, some are considered severe enough to make not only a person's body, but also his clothes, impure (see Rambam, *Hilkhot She'ar Avot HaTumot* 6:11–15). Included in this group is involvement in certain rites associated with atonement and purification – preparing the ashes of the Red Heifer, for instance (see Num. 19:8, 21; Mishna *Kelim* 1:2). The burning of the entrails of the goat "for the Lord" also engenders impurity, as discussed in the following mishna (see Lev. 16:28). Escorting the Azazel goat, then, is another example: "The one who sends the goat away to Azazel shall clean his clothes" (Lev. 16:26).

The mishna debates at which point the impurity is engendered. The anonymous first opinion in our mishna, which the Talmud (67b) identifies with Rabbi Yehuda, maintains that as soon as he leaves the city walls, he becomes impure. According to Rabbi Shimon, he does not become impure until he actually pushes the goat into the crag. The Talmud also cites the opinion of Rabbi Yose that he becomes impure on reaching the crag even without pushing the goat in. Their debate pivots on how to interpret the word הַמְשַׁלֵּחַ, "the one who sends": Rabbi Yehuda assumes that the goat is "sent away" as soon as it leaves the city; Rabbi Shimon, that it is to be "sent" to its death. Rabbi Yose, presumably, understands the man's role as sending the goat to

and send them out to the place of burning.
And from what moment do [the bearers'] clothes become impure?
From the moment they leave the courtyard walls.
Rabbi Shimon says:
From the moment the fire has taken hold of the greater part [of the limbs].

8 They would say to the High Priest,
"The goat has reached the desert."
How would they know when the goat had reached the desert?
They would form look-out posts,
and wave sheets of cloth
to let them know the goat had reached the desert.
Rabbi Yehuda said:

The Tosefta cites the third position of Rabbi Yehuda: the bearer of the organs becomes impure as he casts them into the fire, before they begin to burn.

אָמְרוּ *They would say.* It is understood from the ordering of the biblical text that each phase of the service is not to be performed until the previous one has been completed (see Lev. 16:22–15 and mishna 5:7 above). The High Priest therefore needs to be informed that the Azazel goat has reached the desert before he may continue (Rashi). Rabbeinu Yehonatan suggests that the Torah reading described in 7:1 serves primarily to fill in this time gap. Rambam (*Hilkhot Avodat Yom HaKippurim* 3:7) differs, ruling that the reading is only held after the news has arrived (see also Rashi s.v. נַעֲשֵׂית מִצְוָתוֹ).

אָמַר רַבִּי יְהוּדָה *Rabbi Yehuda said.* The Talmud adds that Rabbi Yehuda and the rabbis also disagree about the stage at which the mitzva of sending the goat away is considered officially fulfilled (68b). There are twelve mil from Jerusalem to the crag (see 6:4), yet Rabbi Yehuda's method suggests that as soon as the goat reaches the desert, only three mil away, he considers the mitzva to be complete and allows the High Priest to proceed to the next phase of the service. The rabbis, on the other hand, might not consider the

וְהוֹצִיאָן לְבֵית הַשְּׂרֵפָה.
וּמֵאֵימָתַי מְטַמְּאִין בְּגָדִים?
מִשֶּׁיֵּצְאוּ חוּץ לְחוֹמַת הָעֲזָרָה.
רַבִּי שִׁמְעוֹן אוֹמֵר:
מִשֶּׁיִּצַּת הָאוּר בְּרֻבָּן.

ח אָמְרוּ לוֹ לְכֹהֵן גָּדוֹל:
הִגִּיעַ שָׂעִיר לַמִּדְבָּר.
וּמִנַּיִן הָיוּ יוֹדְעִין שֶׁהִגִּיעַ שָׂעִיר לַמִּדְבָּר?
דַּרְכִּיּוֹת הָיוּ עוֹשִׂין
וּמְנִיפִין בְּסוּדָרִין
וְיוֹדְעִין שֶׁהִגִּיעַ שָׂעִיר לַמִּדְבָּר.
אָמַר רַבִּי יְהוּדָה:

לְבֵית הַשְּׂרֵפָה *The place of burning.* The bull and goat would be burned in a designated place north of Jerusalem, outside the city limits. This rite was apparently a popular spectacle which many people thronged to see. To ensure the safety of the crowds, the priests formed a circle around the bonfire, so that no one should come too close and be jostled into the blaze (*Tosefta* 3:12).

וּמֵאֵימָתַי *From what moment…?* Here, as in the parallel case of the man who leads the Azazel goat, there are three views on the question of when the completed ritual engenders impurity for the one who has performed it. According to the rabbis (the first opinion in the mishna, which the Tosefta (3:11) identifies with Rabbi Meir), a person carrying the organs becomes impure as soon as he has conveyed them out of the courtyard. This parallels the majority view in the previous case; as soon as the initial stage of the mitzva is complete, the one responsible for it becomes impure. Rabbi Shimon is also consistent here with his opinion above: in his view impurity is only imparted after the mitzva has been completed, in this case, once the limbs have been set ablaze.

Was there not a better sign than this!
From Jerusalem to Beit Ḥidudo was three mils.
They would walk a mil,
walk back a mil,
then wait the time it takes to walk a mil,
and know that the goat had reached the desert.
Rabbi Yishmael says:
Was there not another sign as well?
A strip of scarlet wool was tied at the Sanctuary doors,
and when the goat reached the desert, the wool would turn white,
as it is said:
"If Your sins are like scarlet, *Is. 1*
they shall be whitened like snow."

---

expressed. Nevertheless, its inclusion closes off the chapter, with the all the anxiety in its background, in an apt and powerful image.

The joy and relief of the moment when the crowds would observe the scarlet strip turn white is captured poetically toward the end of אַמִּיץ כֹּחַ (page 897). This recalls the mishna in *Ta'anit* 26b, which relates "Israel had no days as joyous as the fifteenth of Av and Yom Kippur… and the daughters of Jerusalem would go out and dance in the vineyards…" This, we may guess, followed this moment of transformation; a spontaneous outpouring of the exhilarated joy of Israel.

וַהֲלֹא סִימָן גָּדוֹל הָיָה לָהֶם!
מִירוּשָׁלַיִם וְעַד בֵּית חִדּוּדוֹ שְׁלֹשָׁה מִילִין;
הוֹלְכִין מִיל
וְחוֹזְרִין מִיל
וְשׁוֹהִין כְּדֵי מִיל
וְיוֹדְעִין שֶׁהִגִּיעַ שָׂעִיר לַמִּדְבָּר.
רַבִּי יִשְׁמָעֵאל אוֹמֵר:
וַהֲלֹא סִימָן אַחֵר הָיָה לָהֶם!
לָשׁוֹן שֶׁלִּזְהוֹרִית הָיָה קָשׁוּר עַל פִּתְחוֹ שֶׁלַּהֵיכָל
וּכְשֶׁהִגִּיעַ שָׂעִיר לַמִּדְבָּר הָיָה הַלָּשׁוֹן מַלְבִּין
שֶׁנֶּאֱמַר: אִם־יִהְיוּ חֲטָאֵיכֶם כַּשָּׁנִים, כַּשֶּׁלֶג יַלְבִּינוּ: ישעיה א

mitzva complete until the goat has arrived at the crag. The quickest way to relay that moment is through their system of flag signaling.

Tosafot Yom Tov suggest that these methods were only necessary in the period when the scarlet strip was no longer tied on the Sanctuary doors (see note on 6:6). When it still was, its miraculous changing of color could be relied upon to indicate that the mitzva had been completed.

כַּשָּׁנִים *Like scarlet.* The opinion of Rabbi Yishmael does not appear in most manuscripts, and both the *Baḥ* and Vilna Gaon argue that it should be deleted from the text of the mishna. According to the *Tosafot Yom Tov* cited in the previous note, it refers to a different historical period than the other views

CHAPTER SEVEN

1 The High Priest then came to read out from the Scriptures.
If he wished to read wearing linen vestments,
he would read in them,
and if not
he would read wearing his own robe of white.

---

is not an essential part of the Service (the opposing view, among others, is cited in the Meiri).

The Yerushalmi founds the obligation on the verse which concludes the Yom Kippur proceedings in the Torah: "And just as the LORD commanded Moses, so it was done" (Lev. 16:34). It may be that the public reading, quite simply, was aimed at inspiring the people to repentance, as was the seven-yearly הַקְהֵל – Assembly – at which the people gather at the Temple to hear the king's public reading of the Torah (Deut. 31:12; see *Kli Yakar* ad loc.).

As mentioned above (6:8), Rabbeinu Yehonatan suggests that the Torah reading was held to fill the time while waiting for the goat to make its way to the wilderness. Most commentaries, however, reject this, holding that the Torah reading was held only after the goat had arrived, this chapter continuing on in chronological sequence from the one before.

אִם רָצָה *If he wished*… The latitude granted here is somewhat surprising, on a day in which so much emphasis is placed on the exact execution of each rite in its finest details. The Torah reading, however, is not an essential part of the service (*Yoma* 68b), so this is understandable. The *piyutim* commonly said today indicate that the High Priest did not change out of his vestments (pages 895 and 1272), while the *piyutim* composed by Yose ben Yose state that he did. The *Rishonim* all rule that the choice lies with the High Priest; possibly this choice depended on practical considerations, such as whether his vestments became soiled in the previous rites (see note to 5:5).

The Talmud is concerned, not by his freedom to choose, but by the fact that he is permitted to continue wearing the white vestments even though the Torah reading is not really considered part of the day's service. Therefore, the Talmud revokes its initial assumption that it is forbidden to wear the vestments after the Service has finished (see also *Kiddushin* 54a and Rosh, *Tamid* 27a).

פרק שביעי

א בָּא לוֹ כֹּהֵן גָּדוֹל לִקְרוֹת.
אִם רָצָה לִקְרוֹת בְּבִגְדֵי בוּץ – קוֹרֵא
וְאִם לֹא – קוֹרֵא בְּאִצְטְלִית לָבָן מִשֶּׁלּוֹ.

CHAPTER SEVEN:

The central rites of the day have now all been completed. This chapter now, more briefly, describes the concluding stages of the day, and with it the Mishna's dealings with the Yom Kippur service is complete. We begin, then, with the reading of the Torah (1), continue with the sending of the remains of the bull and goat to be burned (2), the offering of the two rams (3), and then the High Priest's final entry into the Holy of Holies, this time to retrieve the coal pan and censer. He then offers the afternoon daily-offering to conclude the day. The chapter then describes his return home, accompanied by joyous crowds of the people celebrating the successful atonement (4). The last mishna is a description of the priestly vestments. The description of the vestments that express the "honor and splendor" of the Priesthood (see Ex. 28:2, 40; see also *Yoma* 69a) conjures up the majesty of the Temple service. The chapter ends with the Urim and Tumim, the central item of the High Priest's apparel, through which God communicates with the Jewish people. These, we are told, were only used "for one to whom the public looks for its need," reasserting that all this opulence was not created for its own sake, but as a means to attain the good of Israel.

בָּא לוֹ כֹּהֵן גָּדוֹל *The High Priest then came.* The reading is held in the עֶזְרַת נָשִׁים, The Women's Courtyard, where the people visiting the Temple, both men and women, are gathered (69b). No reason is given in the Mishna for holding a ceremonial Torah reading at this point; this was not a feature of other Temple services. Rashi refers back to the parallels we discussed in the introduction to chapter one, between the Yom Kippur service and the Inauguration of the Tabernacle, and suggests that here too, the ceremony recalls the daily Torah readings during those days of inauguration. The *Gevurat Ari* (ad loc.) considers this unconvincing; the Talmud never suggests that the comparison between the days is far-reaching. What is more, most opinions hold that the Torah reading on Yom Kippur, unlike that of the Inauguration,

The Shamash of the synagogue takes the Torah scroll
and gives it to the synagogue leader,
and the leader of the synagogue gives it to the Deputy,
and the Deputy gives it to the High Priest,
and the High Priest stands and receives it and reads
[the passage beginning] "After the death…" *Lev. 16*
and [the passage beginning] "On the tenth…" *Lev. 23*

---

taking the scroll out to the courtyard was considered disrespectful may also have considered it preferable not to take out more scrolls than necessary.

The single scroll, then, would have to be scrolled from one place to the next for the two readings, the third being recited from memory. Scrolling while the congregation waits is usually considered disrespectful to the community, but in this case would not have kept them waiting too long, as the two readings appear close to one another. In Temple times, a translator ("*meturgeman*") would be employed to translate each passage into the vernacular Aramaic as it was read (compare with the note on 1:6); this would take enough time to perform the scrolling without causing much delay. It is noted in the Talmud that the small delay would not be permissible either, were it not that the two readings deal with the same topic; otherwise the two readings from one scroll would be difficult to follow (69b–70a with Rashi).

The custom of employing a translator for public Torah readings dates to Nehemiah 8:8 (see *Megilla* 3a; *Nedarim* 37b); the Mishna mentions the translating as a routine practice (*Megilla* 25a). Rav Natronai Gaon ruled that translating is an indispensible component of the reading (resp. 45); but in the Middle Ages, the custom was discontinued (Tosafot, *Megilla* 23b; see *Tur*, OḤ 144), and today is preserved only in Yemenite communities.

When reading *haftarot* from the prophets it is acceptable to skip from one passage to another, likewise, only when the two readings appear is the same book. However, in the case of the twelve Minor Prophets, which are short and in some ways considered a single volume, it is permissible to roll between books. In current practice this usually happens twice a year: On *Shabbat Shuva* (between Rosh HaShana and Yom Kippur) the haftara contains portions of Hosea and Joel, and in Minḥa of Yom Kippur, the book of Jonah is read and the haftara then concludes with verses from Micah.

חַזַּן הַכְּנֶסֶת נוֹטֵל סֵפֶר תּוֹרָה וְנוֹתְנוֹ לְרֹאשׁ הַכְּנֶסֶת
וְרֹאשׁ הַכְּנֶסֶת נוֹתְנוֹ לַסְּגַן
וְהַסְּגַן נוֹתְנוֹ לְכֹהֵן גָּדוֹל
וְכֹהֵן גָּדוֹל עוֹמֵד וּמְקַבֵּל וְקוֹרֵא (עוֹמֵד, וְקוֹרֵא)
'אַחֲרֵי מוֹת' וְ'אַךְ בֶּעָשׂוֹר'.

חַזַּן הַכְּנֶסֶת *The Shamash of the synagogue*... The synagogue was on the Temple Mount, just outside the courtyard (Rashi). The Yerushalmi notes that in general it is considered respectful for people to come to where the Torah is stored, rather than the Torah being brought to them; on this mass public occasion, however, this could not be feasible.

The word חַזָּן today means "cantor," based on the definition of the *Arukh*. In rabbinic Hebrew, however, is it used for any attendant; *ḥazanim* typically maintained the synagogue building, led services, read from the Torah and taught children (see, for instance, Tosafot, *Menaḥot* 44b; Mordekhai, *Megilla* 817). The *ḥazanim* of the Temple would assist the priests in dressing (Rosh, *Tamid* 32b). We have used the Hebrew term *Shamash*, which is how Rashi translates the word, as this is probably the closest job title in contemporary synagogue terminology (*Shabbat* 35b; *Sukka* 51b).

The other synagogue functionary, the רֹאשׁ הַכְּנֶסֶת, is explained by Rashi to have a similar administrative role to a modern *gabbai*; we have translated the term more literally, however, to reflect the dignity attached to his office in this case.

וְכֹהֵן גָּדוֹל עוֹמֵד *The High Priest stands*... The Talmud (69a–b) uses the word "stands" to deduce that the ceremony takes place in the Women's Courtyard. The High Priest has clearly been sitting until now, and this would not be permitted (except to a Davidic king) in the main courtyard.

וְקוֹרֵא *And reads*... The High Priest recites three passages (today only the first and third are read). Although the three passages come from different books of the Torah, only one scroll is used. This may be to prevent the suspicion among the crowd that the first scroll was incomplete (70a), or because using a different scroll would necessitate the reciting of additional, and so superfluous, blessings (Rosh, *Ḥullin* 6:6). The view mentioned above (note 191) that

And then he rolls up the scroll
and places it in his breast,
and says,
"More than I have read to you is written here."
And [the passage beginning] "On the tenth..." from the book of Numbers, Num. 29
he recites from memory;
over this he makes eight blessings:
for the Torah,
and for the Service
and for Thanksgiving

עַל הַתּוֹרָה *For the Torah.* The blessing recited (still today) after all public readings from the Torah, ... אֲשֶׁר נָתַן לָנוּ תּוֹרַת אֱמֶת "who has given us the Torah of truth..." (70a). Meiri notes that before reading from the Torah he will also have recited the blessing, ... אֲשֶׁר בָּחַר בָּנוּ, "who has chosen us..."

וְעַל הָעֲבוֹדָה *The Service.* The next two blessings correspond to the blessings of the weekday Amida (Yerushalmi, *Sota* 7:6). "Thanksgiving" is the מוֹדִים blessing. "the Service" is רְצֵה, although the conclusion of the version used in the Temple differs from our current liturgy. In the Temple, the blessing ended either שֶׁאוֹתְךָ לְבַדְּךָ בְּיִרְאָה נַעֲבֹד, "for You alone do we serve with reverence" or הַמְקַבֵּל עֲבוֹדַת עַמּוֹ יִשְׂרָאֵל בְּרָצוֹן, "who accepts the service of His people Israel with favor" (Rashi, *Berakhot* 11b). Our current ending, הַמַּחֲזִיר שְׁכִינָתוֹ לְצִיּוֹן, "who returns His presence to Zion" was introduced after the destruction of the Temple as a prayer for its restoration.

In Ashkenazi communities, the conclusion שֶׁאוֹתְךָ לְבַדְּךָ בְּיִרְאָה נַעֲבֹד is retained for use during *Birkat Kohanim* (the priestly blessing) in the Musaf of festivals (see page 969), this being a vestige of the Temple service (*Maḥzor Vitry*, 347). The Vilna Gaon (cited in *Pe'at HaShulḥan* 2:17) objected to this practice, insisting that the conclusion should be reserved for use in the Temple only. Some congregations follow this view, re-arranging the paragraph וְתֶעֱרַב "May our entreaty..." to accommodate it; in Israel this practice is common.

וְגוֹלֵל אֶת הַתּוֹרָה
וּמַנִּיחָהּ בְּחֵיקוֹ
וְאוֹמֵר: יוֹתֵר מִמַּה שֶׁקָּרָאתִי לִפְנֵיכֶם כָּתוּב כָּאן.
'וּבֶעָשׂוֹר' שֶׁבְּחוּמַשׁ הַפְּקוּדִים
קוֹרֵא עַל פֶּה.
וּמְבָרֵךְ עָלֶיהָ שְׁמוֹנֶה בְּרָכוֹת:
עַל הַתּוֹרָה
וְעַל הָעֲבוֹדָה
וְעַל הַהוֹדָאָה

קוֹרֵא עַל פֶּה *He recites from memory.* The third passage is taken from the book of Numbers, distant in the scroll from the two previous readings, and so, rather than causing a long delay by scrolling to it (see previous note), the High Priest recites it from memory. He announces, "More than I have read to you is written here," to assuage any suggestion that he is reciting the passage because it does not actually appear in the text (70b).

Tosafot Yeshanim note that the Talmud rules it is prohibited to recite the written Torah by heart (*Gittin* 60b). To square the High Priest's oral recitation with this prohibition, they cite Riva who makes a distinction between reciting the Torah as an act of public learning, in which case it must be read from a scroll, and the case here, when the recitation is largely an announcement of the Order of the Service. They also refer to Ri, who restricts the prohibition to recitations that are required to fulfill a community's obligation.

It is noteworthy that, even though the mishna describes a situation in which some High Priests were unaccustomed to reading from the Tanakh (1:6), it is still expected of them to perform this reading in public. Perhaps the reading skills needed for studying during a long vigil were rare, whereas these passages could be learnt by rote, as is done today.

and for the Forgiveness of Iniquity;
for the Temple its own blessing,
for Israel their own,
(for Jerusalem her own,)
for the Priests their own –
and for all the rest of the prayers.

2 One who sees the High Priest as he reads
does not see the bull and the goat being burned,
and one who sees the bull and the goat being burned
does not see the High Priest as he reads.
Not because it is not allowed,

---

another prayer for the Temple service, but concludes "who has sanctified the priests."

In the *Tosefta* and Yerushalmi, the blessing for Jerusalem is omitted; this is followed by most of the *Rishonim*. The Meiri argues for its inclusion, also noting that it is better placed after the blessing for the priests, as the version in *Sota* 40b. It also appeared in the original version of אַתָּה כּוֹנַנְתָּ, but was removed at the behest of the *Beit Yosef* (OḤ 621). According to the Meiri, it ends "who chooses Jerusalem."

The Talmud (*Yoma* 70a and *Sota* 41a) expands "for the rest of the prayers" to read: "[May all] song, supplication and pleas come before You, for Israel, Your people, who are in need of salvation. Blessed be He... who listens to prayer."

וְעַל שְׁאָר *And for all the rest...* The *Tosefta* (3:13, brought in *Yoma* 70a) describes how, after these prayers, everyone would produce their own scrolls (brought to the Temple the day before – Rashi) and read from them together. Yom Kippur thus became a day of public study, appropriately, perhaps, for the day when Moses descended from Mount Sinai with the second Tablets of the Law (*Ta'anit* 30b).

וְלֹא מִפְּנֵי שֶׁאֵינוֹ רַשַּׁאי *Not because it is not allowed.* Watching the performance of these rites is considered to be a mitzva, fulfilling the principle of בְּרָב עָם הַדְרַת מֶלֶךְ, "The king's glory is [most felt] in the multitude of people" (Prov. 14:28). Normally it is forbidden to abandon one mitzva in favor of another. Here, however, where the people's involvement is only passive, it would be permissible – were it possible. Another concern is the prohibition to leave

וְעַל מְחִילַת הֶעָוֹן
וְעַל הַמִּקְדָּשׁ בִּפְנֵי עַצְמוֹ
וְעַל יִשְׂרָאֵל בִּפְנֵי עַצְמָן
(וְעַל יְרוּשָׁלַיִם בִּפְנֵי עַצְמָהּ)
וְעַל הַכֹּהֲנִים בִּפְנֵי עַצְמָן
וְעַל שְׁאָר הַתְּפִלָּה.

ב הָרוֹאֶה כֹּהֵן גָּדוֹל כְּשֶׁהוּא קוֹרֵא
אֵינוֹ רוֹאֶה פַּר וְשָׂעִיר הַנִּשְׂרָפִים
וְהָרוֹאֶה פַּר וְשָׂעִיר הַנִּשְׂרָפִים
אֵינוֹ רוֹאֶה כֹּהֵן גָּדוֹל כְּשֶׁהוּא קוֹרֵא.
וְלֹא מִפְּנֵי שֶׁאֵינוֹ רַשַּׁאי

וְעַל מְחִילַת הֶעָוֹן *And for the Forgiveness of Iniquity.* Rambam (*Hilkhot Avodat Yom HaKippurim* 3:11) identifies this as the סְלַח לָנוּ blessing from the regular weekday Amida, with a specially extended ending מוֹחֵל עֲוֹנוֹת עַמּוֹ יִשְׂרָאֵל בְּרַחֲמִים, "who mercifully forgives the iniquities of His people Israel" (based on Yerushalmi *Sota* 7:7). Rashi suggests that it is the last paragraph of the fourth blessing of the Yom Kippur Amida, מְחַל לַעֲוֹנוֹתֵינוּ בְּיוֹם הַכִּפּוּרִים הַזֶּה... מֶלֶךְ מוֹחֵל וְסוֹלֵחַ... מְקַדֵּשׁ יִשְׂרָאֵל וְיוֹם הַכִּפּוּרִים (page 105).

בִּפְנֵי עַצְמוֹ *Its own blessing.* The Yerushalmi in *Sota* discusses these blessings but only provides the endings for each. Regarding the blessing for the Temple, the Yerushalmi cites two possible endings, "who chooses the Temple," or Rabbi Idi's view, "who resides in Zion." The dispute reflects two different possible emphases – God's original selection of the place, or His continuing presence there. Rashi (*Yoma* 68b) favors the first opinion, although he makes a noteworthy change; he records the ending as "who has chosen the Temple." Rambam rules in accordance with Rav Idi.

The Yerushalmi reads the blessing for Israel and the Priests, too, as praising God for choosing them: "who chooses Israel" and "who chooses the priests." Again, Rashi's version has them in the past tense. According to Rambam, the blessing for Israel is for the kings of Israel, and that for the priests is in fact

but because the way between is long,
and they happen together, alike as one.

3 If [the High Priest] read in [the priestly] linen vestments,
he would sanctify his hands and feet,
undress and go down and immerse himself,
come up and dry himself.
They would bring him his golden vestments,
and he would put them on
and sanctify his hands and feet,
and go out and perform the offering of his ram
and of the ram of the people,
and the seven unblemished yearling lambs;
thus says Rabbi Eliezer.
Rabbi Akiva says:
With the regular morning offering
these too would be offered.

Malbim, Gen. 4:7). The exception to this rule would appear to be the pair of sin and burnt offerings brought following childbirth. However, the Talmud (*Zevaḥim* 90a) explains that the sin-offering there is not actually brought to atone for any iniquity, and so this is not really an infraction of the rule.

רַבִּי עֲקִיבָא אוֹמֵר *Rabbi Akiva says.* On every festival, aside from the offerings of the day (in our case, those discussed in Leviticus 16), additional – Musaf – offerings are brought, as discussed in Numbers 29. On Yom Kippur, the additional offerings consist of seven sheep and a bull, all brought as burnt-offerings (v. 8; the phrasing of the mishna here is based on that verse) and a goat brought as a sin-offering (verse 11). A bull burnt-offering is mentioned both in Leviticus (16:5) and Numbers (29:8), and Rabbi Elazar ben Shimon understands these to be two distinct sacrifices, one of the Order of the Day and the other to the Musaf offering. Rabbi Yehuda HaNasi holds there was only one burnt bull offering, and the Mishna clearly takes this view.

The dispute in our mishna revolves around the timing of these offerings; Rabbi Eliezer would have the additional offerings made after the atoning service, while Rabbi Akiva sees them as an extension of the morning's daily offering, to be brought immediately after it (based on his reading of Numbers 28:23).

The *Tosefta* (3:14, quoted partially in *Yoma* 70b) records a different version of the dispute, in which all agree that the additional offerings are divided;

אֶלָּא שֶׁהָיְתָה דֶרֶךְ רְחוֹקָה
וּמְלֶאכֶת שְׁנֵיהֶן שָׁוָה כְּאַחַת.

ג אִם בְּבִגְדֵי בוּץ קוֹרֵא
קִדֵּשׁ יָדָיו וְרַגְלָיו
פָּשַׁט יָרַד וְטָבַל, עָלָה וְנִסְתַּפַּג.
הֵבִיאוּ לוֹ בִּגְדֵי זָהָב
וְלָבַשׁ וְקִדֵּשׁ יָדָיו וְרַגְלָיו
וְיָצָא וְעָשָׂה אֶת אֵילוֹ וְאֶת אֵיל הָעָם
וְאֶת שִׁבְעַת כְּבָשִׂים תְּמִימִים בְּנֵי שָׁנָה;
דִּבְרֵי רַבִּי אֱלִיעֶזֶר.
רַבִּי עֲקִיבָא אוֹמֵר:
עִם תָּמִיד שֶׁלַּשַּׁחַר הָיוּ קְרֵבִין.

---

the synagogue in the middle of the Torah reading (see *Berakhot* 8a). This, however, could be avoided by leaving during the time when the Torah was being rolled from one passage to the other (*Tosafot Yeshanim*).

אִם בְּבִגְדֵי בוּץ קוֹרֵא *If... in [the priestly] linen vestments.* If he reads in his own clothes, then he will already have sanctified his hands and feet before undressing (Rosh).

וְעָשָׂה אֶת אֵילוֹ *The offering of his ram.* The offering of these two rams, brought as burnt offerings, is commanded in Leviticus 16:24 as the service following the sending of the goat to the Azazel. They are considered the counterparts of the sin-offerings of the High Priest's bull (Lev. 16:3) and of the people's two goats (16:5).

The *Sifra* ("Dibura DeḤova," 18:5) derives from Leviticus chapter five that whenever a sin-offering and a burnt-offering are brought together, the sin-offering is brought first; the timing of the offerings here is an application of this rule.

The Talmud (*Zevaḥim* 7b) elaborates that while a sin-offering atones, a burnt offering is perceived as a gift; it is only appropriate to seek favor by offering a gift if one is no longer burdened by sin (see Rekanati, Lev. 5:8;

The bull of the burnt offering
and the goat, offered outside
would be sacrificed with the daily offering of the afternoon.

4 [The High Priest] would sanctify his hands and feet,
undress and go down and immerse himself,
come up and dry himself.
They would bring him white vestments
and he would put them on,
and sanctify his hands and feet.
He would enter within
to retrieve the censer and the firepan.

---

vestments. The rites of the day and the regular Temple rights are performed in alternation; hence the frequent changes of clothes. Each change is accompanied by the required sanctifications of hands-and-feet washing and immersions (see Appendix 11).

נִכְנַס *He would enter within.* Four rites now remain to be performed: the outstanding additional offerings (see mishna 3); the retrieval of coal pan and censer from the Holy of Holies; the burning of the fats of the bull and goat on the altar; and the afternoon daily offerings.

Mishna 3 seems to imply that all remaining additional offerings are brought immediately after the two rams. Most *Rishonim* and the *piyutim* follow this view; Rambam essentially agrees, although he intersperses the burning of the fats here (see below).

As for the retrieval of the coal pan and censer – most commentators assume that this was delayed to the end of the day, either directly before or directly after the afternoon daily offering (before: the *piyutim*, Rashi and Tosafot; after: Rambam). The notable exception to this is Rabbeinu Ḥananel, who holds that the coal pan and censer should be retrieved as early as possible, so as not to leave extraneous items in the Holy of Holies. In his view, then, the retrieval immediately follows the offering of the two rams. Taken to its logical end (which Rabbeinu Ḥananel does not explicitly do), the same reason would mandate delaying the additional offerings until after the High Priest has left the Holy of Holies.

The placing of the other two rites, the burning of the fats and the afternoon daily offering, is not mentioned in the Mishna, although mishna 6:7 suggests that the fats were burnt much earlier on, after dispatching the goat to Azazel.

וּפַר הָעוֹלָה וְשָׂעִיר הַנַּעֲשֶׂה בַחוּץ
הָיוּ קְרֵבִין עִם תָּמִיד שֶׁלְּבֵין הָעַרְבַּיִם.

ד קִדֵּשׁ יָדָיו וְרַגְלָיו
וּפָשַׁט וְיָרַד וְטָבַל וְעָלָה וְנִסְתַּפַּג.
הֵבִיאוּ לוֹ בִּגְדֵי לָבָן וְלָבַשׁ
וְקִדֵּשׁ יָדָיו וְרַגְלָיו.
נִכְנַס לְהוֹצִיא אֶת הַכַּף וְאֶת הַמַּחְתָּה.

---

some are offered in the morning, others at the end of the day. Rabbi Eliezer states that the bull and goat are offered after the daily offering and the seven sheep postponed; Rabbi Akiva maintains that all the burnt-offerings (the sheep and bull) are offered in the morning, with the sin-offering (the goat) later. The *Tosefta* then quotes two more opinions, according to which the sheep are divided, so that the additional offering "frames" the Order of the Day (see *Yoma* 70b for the derivation of this). Rabbi Yehuda suggests that only one sheep need be offered with the daily offering. This is a concession to the High Priest's limited strength; while some of the additional offerings must be brought together with the daily offering, it is important to preserve the High Priest's strength for the day's service, so his morning's burden is minimized. Rabbi Elazar ben Shimon judges that the High Priest is bound to be able to muster extra energy for such a hugely important occasion. He would therefore have him offer six sheep in the morning, and only one postponed until later.

Rambam (*Hilkhot Avodat Yom HaKippurim* 4:2) and *Smag* (209) rule in accordance with Rabbi Akiva as quoted in the *Tosefta*. The Rosh suggests the halakha should follow either Rabbi Yehuda or Rabbi Elazar ben Shimon, following Rashi's understanding of their opinions being modifications of Rabbi Akiva's opinion. The old *piyutim*, however, followed Rabbi Eliezer's opinion (see אַמִּיץ כֹּחַ, page 895). The printed version of אַתָּה כּוֹנַנְתָּ follows Rabbi Akiva (page 1263), but this is an emendation by the *Beit Yosef* (OḤ 621). *Nishmat Adam* 145:3 suggests that אַמִּיץ כֹּחַ should likewise be changed.

קִדֵּשׁ [*The High Priest*] *would sanctify*... The mishna now describes the three final changes of vestments and the accompanying two immersions. As explained previously, only those rites that form part of the special Yom Kippur service require the white vestments; others are performed in the gold

Then he would sanctify his hands and feet,
undress and go down and immerse himself,
come up and dry himself.
They would bring him his golden vestments
and he would put them on,
sanctify his hands and feet,
enter within to burn the incense of the afternoon,
and tend to the lights,
and sanctify his hands and feet
and undress.
Then they would bring him his own clothes,
and he would put them on.
And they would accompany him to his house,

וְנִכְנַס *Enter within…* These two rites within the Sanctuary – the burning of the afternoon incense and the lighting of the lamps (see note to 1:2) – belong to the daily order of the Temple service. The Torah states that these two rites are performed together (Ex. 30:8; see also *Yoma* 14b–15a and *Zevaḥim* 11b–12a). Mishna 3:5, however, instructs that the incense be burnt between offering the organs of the daily offering and pouring the libations upon the altar in the courtyard, the implication being that the tending of the lamps does not happen immediately after the incense burning begins.

Rid (*Yoma* 34a) explains the Mishna to mean that the libations follow the combined rites of the incense and the lamps. This is how the Service is described in the version of אַתָּה כּוֹנַנְתָּ said in Ashkenazi congregations (page 1273). On the other hand, *Smag* (192) and Ramban (quoted by Rabbi Menaḥem di Lunzano, *Shtei Yadot* 56a) take the Mishna on face value, and rule the order to be incense – libations – lamps, despite this requiring the High Priest to enter the Sanctuary twice. *Shifat Revivim* emends his version of אַתָּה כּוֹנַנְתָּ to follow the Ramban, and this is read by most Sephardi congregations today.

Rambam (*Hilkhot Temidin UMusafin* 6:11) writes that the evening order followed exactly that of the morning. If so the order was libations – incense – lamps. This accords well with Exodus 30, but seems to contradict mishna 3:5. The commentators struggle with this, but the Meiri (*Yoma* 34a) notes that mishna 3:5 presents only one view; an opposing view, in which the libations are brought before the incense, is recorded in *Pesaḥim* 59a. Apparently, Rambam rules in accordance with the Talmud in *Pesaḥim*.

קִדֵּשׁ יָדָיו וְרַגְלָיו
וּפָשַׁט וְיָרַד וְטָבַל, עָלָה וְנִסְתַּפֵּג.
הֵבִיאוּ לוֹ בִּגְדֵי זָהָב וְלָבַשׁ
וְקִדֵּשׁ יָדָיו וְרַגְלָיו
וְנִכְנַס לְהַקְטִיר אֶת הַקְּטֹרֶת שֶׁלְּבֵין הָעַרְבַּיִם
וּלְהֵטִיב אֶת הַנֵּרוֹת
וְקִדֵּשׁ יָדָיו וְרַגְלָיו, וּפָשַׁט.
הֵבִיאוּ לוֹ בִּגְדֵי עַצְמוֹ, וְלָבַשׁ.
וּמְלַוִּין אוֹתוֹ עַד בֵּיתוֹ.

The Yerushalmi does not challenge this, and the early *piyutim*, notably those by Yose ben Yose and Ibn Avitur, have the fats burned as soon as they are removed from the animals. The Talmud Bavli, on the other hand, emends the mishna to say that at that point they are only prepared for their burning, which was carried out later (see note to 6:7). אַמִּיץ כֹּחַ reconciles the Talmud with the competing tradition by having the fats burnt not *immediately* after their removal but very soon after, only interrupted by the reading of the Torah (see page 895). The *Rishonim*, however, all assume that the fats were burned only after the two rams were offered. Rambam rules that they were burnt immediately after the rams, Rashi assumes that the additional offerings were brought first. Rabbeinu Ḥananel and Tosafot understand that the burning of the fats was delayed until much later, just before the afternoon daily offering.

With regard to the afternoon daily offering, the Yerushalmi cites Rabbi Yoḥanan who states that this too was brought after the rams. Rambam (*Hilkhot Avodat Yom HaKippurim* 4:2) and *Smag* (209) accept both these placings as authoritative, explaining that the fats were burnt first, followed immediately by the afternoon daily offering. Ramban (70a) himself agrees to this but cites "all the early Spanish sages" as well as all the *paytanim*, as holding otherwise (with the exception of אַתָּה כּוֹנַנְתָּ, see page 1273). They place the Daily Offering only after the retrieval of censer and coal pan from the Holy of Holies, as do Rabbeinu Ḥananel, Rashi, and most of the *Rishonim*. This opinion has an even earlier source in the *Sifra* (*Aḥarei Mot* 6:5).

and he would make a celebration for his friends,
when he left the Holy Place in peace.

5 The High Priest serves wearing eight garments
and the lay priests in four:
in the tunic,
the breeches,
the miter,

(*Zevaḥim* 18b; Rashi, Ex. 28:43; Rambam, *Hilkhot Klei HaMikdash* 10:4–5; however, see Tosafot cited two notes below). In *Arakhin* 16a, the Talmud suggests that each of the priestly vestments atones for a different type of sin, and elaborates.

בְּכֻתֹּנֶת *The tunic.* This is the most visible of the four linen vestments. Individually fitted for each priest, it covers his body as far as his ankles, with the sleeves covering his arms down to his wrists (Rambam, *Hilkhot Klei HaMikdash* 8:17). It is woven in three pieces: The main body of the garment is fashioned in one piece, and then each sleeve is formed as a single piece and attached to the body (*Yoma* 72b).

וּבְמִכְנָסַיִם *The breeches.* These serve a functional role, "to cover their nakedness" (Ex. 28:42). They cover the priest's legs from the hips down to his knees (ibid), and are the first of the vestments to be put on (*Yoma* 25a). Rabbi Ya'akov of Orleans holds that it is only the absence of this garment, essential to the priest's modesty, that is punishable by death at the hand of heaven (Tosafot, *Sanhedrin* 83b, following Ex. 28:43; also Ramban, ibid. 35); this is, however, a minority view, see two notes above.

וּבְמִצְנֶפֶת *The miter.* The Torah uses different terms for the headgear of a High Priest and that of a lay priest; the lay priests' is referred to as a מִגְבַּעַת (Ex. 28:40), the High Priest's as a מִצְנֶפֶת (Ex. 28:4). The term מִצְנֶפֶת is used even when referring to the headgear the High Priest wears on Yom Kippur as one of his white vestments (Lev. 16:4). In mishnaic Hebrew, both are always termed מִצְנֶפֶת.

Whether or not there was any distinction between the two is a matter of debate. This mishna implies that the same headdress is worn by the lay and High Priest. Rashi (Ex. 28:4) also implies this, explaining that Onkelos' translation

וְיוֹם טוֹב הָיָה עוֹשֶׂה לְאוֹהֲבָיו
בְּשָׁעָה שֶׁיָּצָא בְשָׁלוֹם מִן הַקֹּדֶשׁ.

ה כֹּהֵן גָּדוֹל מְשַׁמֵּשׁ בִּשְׁמוֹנָה כֵלִים
וְהַהֶדְיוֹט בְּאַרְבָּעָה:
בְּכֻתֹּנֶת
וּבְמִכְנָסַיִם
וּבְמִצְנֶפֶת

בְּשָׁעָה שֶׁיָּצָא בְשָׁלוֹם מִן הַקֹּדֶשׁ *When he left the Holy Place in peace.* This emerging unscathed from the most holy place is celebrated in the *piyut* מַרְאֵה כֹהֵן, (page 901), which opens a series of *piyutim* leading from the recital of the Order of the Day to the *Seliḥot* of Musaf (today the *Seliḥot* are usually omitted, with the congregation proceeding directly to (זְכֹר רַחֲמֶיךָ). In some North African traditions, the day following Yom Kippur is called יוֹם שִׂמְחַת כֹּהֵן, "the day of the Priest's celebration," and kohanim mark it with a festive meal.

כֹּהֵן גָּדוֹל מְשַׁמֵּשׁ *The High Priest serves… During the Second Temple period, the donning of the priestly garments served to consecrate the High Priest for his service.* In the first Temple this was achieved through the anointing oil, which was then still in use (Mishna, *Megilla* 9b and *Horayot* 11b).

בִּשְׁמוֹנָה כֵלִים *Wearing eight garments.* The mishna here enumerates the eight priestly vestments. The first four are made entirely from white linen and are worn by each lay priest whenever he serves. These also constitute the "white vestments" worn by the High Priest when he enters the Holy of Holies on Yom Kippur, and to perform the rite of the red heifer (Mishna *Para* 4:1). The additional four vestments worn by the High Priest also contain other materials, are colored, and all contain gold (hence the phrase "gold vestments").

The vestments are each woven in one piece, without seams (*Yoma* 72b), and are individually fitted for each priest (*Zevaḥim* 18b). A priest who serves without wearing all his priestly vestments, or wearing an additional vestment, invalidates his service, and is punishable by death at the hands of Heaven

and the sash;
along with these the High Priest wears
the breastplate,
the Ephod,

---

or not the sash, with its *sha'atnez*, is included in this. Rambam (*Hilkhot Klei HaMikdash* 8:12) rules that the prohibition of *sha'atnez* is only waived while performing the service, and that the sash must be removed immediately afterwards. Ra'avad (ad loc.) and Rabbeinu Tam (Tosafot, *Menaḥot* 41a) are more lenient and permit the sash to be worn as long as the priest remains in the Temple precinct.

חֹשֶׁן *The breastplate.* The Torah instructs Moses to use five different fibers for the priestly vestments (Ex. 28:5): wool died in three different colors – sky-blue, purple and scarlet; finely-twisted linen (see Rashi, Ex. 25:4; this, then, is another use of *sha'atnez*, see Tosafot, *Yoma* 6a); and gold thread. Six threads of each of the four fibers were spun together with a single gold thread to create one yarn. This composite yarn was then further spun to produce a yarn of twenty-eight threads from which the Ephod and breastplate were then woven (*Yoma* 72a).

The חֹשֶׁן – the breastplate – is a piece of fabric woven of this yarn and then folded over with the Urim and Tumim (see below) placed inside. On its front, twelve precious stones, bearing the names of the twelve tribes, are attached in a golden setting. (See Rambam, *Hilkhot Klei HaMikdash* 9:7 and Radbaz ad loc.; *Ḥizkuni*, Ex. 28:21 for different suggestions regarding the sequence in which these are engraved.) Four rings of gold are attached to its corners; through the upper two, chains of wreathed gold are threaded, connecting it to the fixtures of the Ephod's shoulder-pieces; from the other two, laces of sky-blue wool are tied, connecting it to similar rings on the Ephod's girdle. These serve to fasten the breastplate tightly to the Ephod, in keeping with the Torah warning that "the breastplate shall not be detached from Ephod" (Ex. 28:28).

וְאֵפוֹד *The Ephod.* Aside from stating that it is woven from the same fiber as the breastplate (see previous note), the Torah's only description of the Ephod is a mention of its shoulder straps and girdle. The ends of the shoulder straps are fastened to the breastplate with golden chains. On the shoulders, two golden fixtures (resembling epaulettes) containing the two "Shoham" stones (usually identified as onyx) are attached, with the names of the twelve tribes

וּבְאַבְנֵט.
מוֹסִיף עָלָיו כֹּהֵן גָּדוֹל:
חֹשֶׁן
וְאֵפוֹד

---

of מִגְבַּעַת as "hat" should equally be applied to a מִצְנֶפֶת. Rambam (*Hilkhot Klei HaMikdash* 8:2) and Ramban (Ex. 28:31) describe both as made from identical scarves, sixteen cubits long, wrapped around the head, but wrapped differently. The lay priests' is wrapped to form a conical, hat-like shape – in line with Onkelos' translation of "hat," while the High Priest's is wrapped around the head like a bandage. Following this description, many artists draw the מִצְנֶפֶת as a turban. Ra'avad (*Hilkhot Klei HaMikdash* 8:2), however, argues that the two miters are completely distinct. He describes the High Priest's מִצְנֶפֶת in line with Rambam, but suggests that the lay priests' מִגְבָּעוֹת was not a scarf at all, but a fully constructed hat. Riva (cited in Tosafot, 25a) highlights a different distinction; each miter must leave enough room to allow space for the tefillin, but the High Priest's must allow additional space for the צִיץ, the frontlet. It is unclear whether Riva imagines the two headgears to be otherwise similar, or assumes them to be completely different garments, in line with Ra'avad. (The first view is reflected in *Tosafot Yeshanim, Yoma* 71b; the other in *Tosafot Yom Tov*, following *Talmidei Rabbeinu Yona, Berakhot* 21b, and probably Tosafot, *Yoma* 25a.)

וּבְאַבְנֵט *The sash.* The sash is thirty-two cubits (approximately fifteen meters) long, and three fingers wide. It is wound around the priest's body on a level with his heart (Rambam, *Hilkhot Klei HaMikdash* 8:19; see also *Zevaḥim* 18b). Like the other white vestments, it is woven from linen. However, there is a distinction (the only one) among the sashes of the lay priests' vestments, of the High Priest's gold vestments and of his white vestments. The Torah states that the sash of the High Priest's white vestments is made of pure white linen (Lev. 16:4; see also *Yoma* 12a–b). The sash of the golden vestments also includes wools of different colors (Ex. 39:29). The lay priests' sash also contains wool (according to Ramban, colored wool; according to Rambam 8:1, white wool).

The inclusion of wool in the linen sash is an exception to the prohibition of *sha'atnez* (wearing clothes including wool and linen fibers mixed together). As mentioned above (note to 7:1), the Talmud allows a priest to continue wearing his vestments even when not on duty. The *Rishonim* debate whether

the robe,
and the frontlet.

---

similar to a skirt; he also argues that the straps were wide enough to cover most of the Priest's chest.

The *piyutim* of Yose ben Yose (the earliest extant description of the vestments) describe the Ephod very differently. He suggests that the main part of the Ephod lay over the High Priest's chest, like a cuirass, and was held in place by the girdle (tied behind the back) and shoulder straps. A similar description, possibly influenced by these piyutim, is that of *Ḥizkuni* (Ex. 28:27), who envisions the Ephod as a full sleeveless upper garment. According to either description, the breastplate was placed directly onto the Ephod.

וּמְעִיל *The robe.* The robe is made entirely from תְּכֵלֶת, sky-blue wool. It is also known as מְעִיל הָאֵפוֹד, "the robe of the Ephod," because it is belted with the Ephod's girdle (Rashi, Ex. 28:31). Its hem is also woven with scarlet and purple, with small decorative pomegranates and golden bells attached, which would sound whenever the High Priest would enter the Sanctuary or leave it (Ex. 28:35; see commentary to 5:1). According to Rashi, the bells and pomegranates were alternatingly placed. According to Ramban, the pomegranates were hollow with the bells inside them.

Rambam (*Hilkhot Klei HaMikdash* 9:3) describes the robe as a long sleeveless cape draped over the High Priest's body, open in the front and fastened around the neck. Ra'avad twice protests וְזוֹ מִנַּיִן לוֹ? ("where does he get this from?"), but Ramban (Ex. 28:31) founds Rambam's reading on lexicographic arguments. Ralbag assumes Rambam actually to be suggesting a garment similar to our *tallit katan.* This is disputed by Radbaz, but accepted by many *Aḥaronim*; the *Minḥat Ḥinukh* (99:1) takes pains to explain why it is exempt from the requirement of *tzitzit.*

Most commentaries, however, follow Rashi (Ex. 28:4), who explains the robe to be a cloak, attached around the sides, and with sleeves, similar to the tunic. Indeed, the Talmud (*Yoma* 72b) indicates that two of the priestly vestments had sleeves; presumably the tunic and the robe (*Torah Shelema*, vol. 23 p. 176).

וְצִיץ *The frontlet.* This is a gold plate worn by the High Priest across his forehead, extending from one ear to the other (*Shabbat* 63b), and held in place

וּמְעִיל
וָצִיץ.

inscribed upon them. The girdle is wrapped around the High Priest's body and tied at the front with the bottom of the breastplate fastened to it with two laces of sky-blue wool.

From the limited description in the Torah, one could imagine the Ephod to be little more than an accessory for supporting the breastplate. In II Samuel, indeed, David is described as being "girded with an Ephod," which suggests that it is a type of belt (6:14). Rashi, however, insists that the Ephod must be more than simply a girdle, since in the description of the Inaugural Ceremony for the Tabernacle, the Torah states "the Ephod was placed upon him and then he was girded with the girdle of the Ephod" (Lev. 8:7, see Onkelos). Having a girdle of its own, the Ephod itself must be something more. Rashi, then, suggests that the Ephod is a significant ornamental vestment. With this in mind, he derives the word אֵפוֹד from the verb א-פ-ד, "to beautify" (see Ex. 28:8 with Rashi and Lev. 8:7). This being so, a description of the Ephod is striking in its absence. This, combined with the very limited Tannaitic and Talmudic source material regarding it (there is no *Mekhilta*, for instance, on *parashat Tetzaveh*), leads to a diversity of opinions on its appearance and positioning, among the various *Rishonim*. Rashi himself, noting the lack of available information, opens his description with the words, וְלִבִּי אוֹמֵר לִי, "my heart tells me" (Ex. 28:4).

According to Rambam (*Hilkhot Klei HaMikdash* 9:9–11) the main piece of the Ephod was worn on the High Priest's back, a kind of counter-piece to the breastplate, extending from beneath his armpits to his legs (likely meaning the hips, as in Meiri, *Yoma* 72a). The girdle was attached to the middle of the Ephod and was tied underneath the breastplate, on a level with his heart. Ra'avad appears to agree with this general description but holds that the girdle was tied beneath the stomach.

Rashi compares the Ephod to the horse-riding habit worn by the French noblewomen of his time. The supercommentaries explain that this was a garment that covered the back and legs, wrapping round to the front on either side, but there left open to allow the legs freedom of movement.

Rashbam writes that the Ephod was closed at the front, making it more

By means of these [vestments], the Urim and Tumim are
enquired of;
but enquired of only for the sake of the king or the Court
or for one to whom the public looks for its need.

---

translated to be a piece of parchment with God's Ineffable Name written on it. Others understand them to be the precious stones set into the breastplate (Ibn Ezra; see *Kesef Mishneh, Hilkhot Beit HaBeḥira* 4:1 who understands this also to be the view of Rambam, and of Tosafot cited below). The Talmud interprets the words to indicate that they relay divine messages to provide enlightened (מְאִירִים) and complete (תַּמִּים) answers (*Yoma* 73a; see Yerushalmi ad loc.).

In the Second Temple, according to the Talmud, the High Priest had no Urim and Tumim, as the Divine Presence was absent at that time (*Yoma* 21b, based on Ezra 2:63 and Nehemiah 7:65). Tosafot (ad loc.) hold that the absence of the Urim and Tumim disqualifies the breastplate. They therefore explain that they were still present, but no longer functioned as an oracle.

בְּאֵלּוּ נִשְׁאָלִין בְּאוּרִים וְתֻמִּים;
וְאֵין נִשְׁאָלִין אֶלָּא לַמֶּלֶךְ
וּלְבֵית דִּין
וּלְמִי שֶׁהַצִּבּוּר צָרִיךְ בּוֹ.

---

by threads of sky-blue wool (Exodus 28:37; see Ramban). On the plate is written: "Holy to the Lord." The Talmud reports that these words were not engraved, but written in relief (*Gittin* 20a, and Rashi there). The *Rishonim* differ regarding the technique used to attain this effect (see Rambam and Ra'avad, *Hilkhot Klei HaMikdash* 9:2). When it was placed on his forehead, a space remained between the frontlet and the miter, to leave room for the head *tefillin* (*Zevaḥim* 19a).

בְּאֵלּוּ נִשְׁאָלִין *By means of these…* "And into the breastplate of judgment you shall place the Urim and Tumim; and they shall be on Aaron's heart when he goes in before the Lord, and Aaron shall bear the judgment of the children of Israel on his heart, before the Lord, continuously" (Ex. 28:30). Most commentaries follow *Targum Yonatan,* in which the "Urim and Tumim" are

CHAPTER EIGHT

1 On the Day of Atonement it is prohibited

---

neglecting the obligations of the day (see Maharal, *Netiv HaTeshuva* chapter seven), which at first glance seems somewhat harsh. The only other two positive commandments punishable by *karet* if neglected are circumcision and the Paschal offering (see Rabbi Yeruḥam Perla on Rav Sa'adia Gaon's *Sefer HaMitzvot*, Negative Commandment 264, s.v. "וְלָכֵן נִרְאֶה לוֹמַר"). Yom Kippur, it seems, enters the same category – that of circumcision, the Abrahamic covenant, and of the Paschal offering, which reconfirms the covenant made between God and the people He redeemed from slavery (*Pirkei DeRabbi Eliezer*, 28; see *Sefat Emet*, *Bo* 654). This day too is an annual opportunity to reconvene with God; rejecting the opportunity is deemed an active separation from Him, a person's initiation of what will then be framed as a two-way "cutting off" from the covenant.

"You, Lord our God, have given us in love this Day of Atonement, to be the end, the pardon and forgiveness of all our iniquities, that we may end the oppression that is in our hands, and return to You" (Ne'ila, page 1131). Repentance – literally "return" – is seen as a mutual movement-toward of man and of God; "How exalted is repentance! Yesterday, the [transgressor] was separated from God ... He would call out without being answered ... fulfill mitzvot, only to have them crushed before him ... But today, he clings to the Divine Presence ... is immediately answered ... and his mitzvot are accepted with pleasure and joy" (Rambam, *Hilkhot Teshuva* 7:7).

Most of our tractate has recalled the long lost atonement rituals of the Temple; the deepest emotional and spiritual elements of the Day as we still live it were played out there with a kind of resolution and clarity that are lost to us now. The theme of Return, then – the personal and, in parallel, collective and national, opportunity to renew our covenant with God – draws the tractate together, in the present tense and with an eye to the future. In Jeremiah 4:1, the prophet calls: "If you will return, Israel, says the Lord, return to Me." God beckons us to Him. Dare we approach?

יוֹם הַכִּפּוּרִים *On the Day of Atonement*... The mishna lists the חֲמִשָּׁה עִנּוּיִם, literally, the five afflictions, of Yom Kippur. In the Torah itself there is no direct reference to any of the five; the command simply reads, "On the tenth of the month, you shall afflict yourselves" (Lev. 16:29). The Talmud uses various biblical proof-texts to identify the five restrictions listed here as expressions of this affliction.

פרק שמיני

א יוֹם הַכִּפּוּרִים אָסוּר

CHAPTER EIGHT:

The seven chapters of our tractate have described the Yom Kippur Service performed in the Temple by the High Priest. This closing chapter now turns to the laws of the day as they apply to every Jew at every time (Tosafot, *Yoma* 73b), concluding with a more metaphysical discussion of atonement itself. The laws of the fast open with the five restrictions of the day (1–3) and those exempted from them, including cases of *pikuaḥ nefesh*, life and death (4–6). The mishna then digresses to a more general discussion of *pikuaḥ nefesh* situations (7). The last two *mishnayot* enlarge upon the day's main theme – that of atonement – the focus now being not on the public atonement of the High Priest's service, but on the private atonement of individual sins (8–9).

The restrictions that apply to Yom Kippur have two aspects; this is at once both שַׁבַּת שַׁבָּתוֹן, "a Sabbath of utter rest," and a day on which we are commanded, וְעִנִּיתֶם אֶת נַפְשֹׁתֵיכֶם, "afflict yourselves" – abstaining from food and drink and a number of other comforts (see mishna 1). These two models seem quite distinct from one another; cessation from work creates a day free from the everyday distractions of engagement with the world, creating a more contemplative or spiritual space. The "afflictions," on the other hand, break a person's sense of certainty and sufficiency, bringing him to a fragile state of mind in which he can truly submit himself to God. However, these two concepts might be united if we consider the five forms of abstinence as additional areas in which, as in the world of work, the Day brings respite from the preoccupations of the everyday. This might be indicated by Rambam's entitling the section of his work that deals with Yom Kippur *Hilkhot Shevitat Asor*, "Laws of the Cessation of the Tenth Day."

The ultimate, double purpose of all the aspects of service that the tractate has discussed – the Temple service, the study, the prayer, the fasting – is the repentance of man, and atonement from God.

The Mishna elsewhere enumerates thirty-six sins which bring about a punishment of *karet* – spiritual excision; literally, becoming "cut off from one's people" (*Keritot* 2a). Eating and working on Yom Kippur are two of the sins listed; and there is a difference between the two. Work is presented as a prohibition of the day, while fasting, perhaps counterintuitively, is a positive command: "and you shall afflict yourselves" (Lev. 16:31). *Karet*, then, is the punishment not only for infringing the prohibitions, but even simply for

to eat or drink,
to wash,

Jewish people, and the custom that developed for the more minor fasts was only to refrain from eating and drinking.

בַּאֲכִילָה וּבִשְׁתִיָּה *To eat or drink.* The *Sifra* (*Parasha* 5) and Talmud (74b) provide various possible Torah derivations for eating and drinking as Yom Kippur "afflictions." The first suggestion in the *Sifra* uses the original commandment itself; translated literally – "You shall afflict your spirits." This last word, נַפְשֹׁתֵיכֶם, refers to the animal soul with its physical needs (cf. Is. 58:10). The Talmud turns to the verse describing the *karet* punishment: וְהַאֲבַדְתִּי אֶת הַנֶּפֶשׁ, "I will destroy that spirit" (Lev. 23:29–30); affliction of that spirit, then, is read to indicate "affliction which destroys the spirit." Rabbi Yishmael derives a similar idea from the verse in Deuteronomy 8:3: "He afflicted you, and starved you…" Here causing hunger is presented as the paradigmatic affliction.

וּבִרְחִיצָה *To wash.* "I ate no pleasant bread; no meat or wine came into my mouth, and I did not anoint myself" (Daniel 10:3). Although this verse describes mourning rather than fasting, the Talmud (76b) derives from it that avoiding washing and anointing is also considered an affliction. Another proof text proposed (although ultimately rejected) is Proverbs 25:25: "As cold water upon a weary soul…" – the parched body's desire for water on the skin is read as an example of affliction (77a). The Talmud (*Pesaḥim* 54b) states that even pouring water over a single finger is forbidden on Yom Kippur.

There are, however, many exceptions and qualifications to this. The mishna itself continues by permitting a bride or king to wash. The Talmud (77b) states that a person actually sullied by dirt may wash it off. This includes washing after using the lavatory (Ra'avan, codified in *Shulḥan Arukh* ibid. 3) and upon waking up (Rabbeinu Tam, Tosafot, *Yoma* 77b) – but only as far as the knuckles (*Shulḥan Arukh* ibid. 2 following Rosh; see law 33).

As mentioned above, the *Yere'im* understands all the restrictions to be biblical. He suggests, however, that the biblical prohibition only applies to washing the majority of the body for comfort; washing part of the body is only rabbinically prohibited. The rabbis, then, may waive the prohibition where they deem it necessary.

The Talmud (88a) allows a person who is impure to purify him- or herself through immersion in a *mikveh* on Yom Kippur. As immersing at the first

בַּאֲכִילָה וּבִשְׁתִיָּה וּבְרְחִיצָה

Rav Ḥisda (76a) derives the number five from the number of times the mitzva of Yom Kippur is mentioned in the Torah. This would seem to imply that all five afflictions have biblical status, as is indeed the opinion of the Geonim (She'ilta 167; Behag) and the *Yere'im* (420). Ran (1a) explains this to be an example of the principle of מְסָרָן הַכָּתוּב לַחֲכָמִים; "the verse is given to the sages." This principle, used in a number of contexts, suggests that while the Torah has commanded a certain effect, it is left to the sages to determine the means of achieving it; specifically, which particular prohibitions must be enforced to achieve the goal. These are then considered subcategories of the more overarching biblical prohibition, and the power to waive them when circumstances allow is left in the hands of the rabbis.

A distinction is made between the prohibition on eating and drinking on the one hand, and the other restrictions on the other. *Tosafot Yeshanim* (73b) and Rabbeinu Tam (Tosafot, 77a) claim that only fasting is a biblical "affliction," while the other restrictions are rabbinic. The proof-texts provided by the Talmud (see below in each case) are thus to be understood to be no more than אַסְמַכְתּוֹת – scriptural supports, for rabbinic enactments.

The Talmud (74a) states clearly that the *karet* punishment for violating the restrictions only applies to eating and drinking, the most blatant infringement of the fast. The nature of *karet* is much debated. The Talmud suggests that a *karet* liability leads a person to die young (either under the age of fifty or under the age of sixty; *Mo'ed Katan* 28a). Elsewhere there is a suggestion that the punishment causes a person to remain childless or to lose the children he has (*Yevamot* 55a). Many of the *Rishonim*, however, understand it as a spiritual punishment (based on *Sanhedrin* 90b). Rambam defines it as losing one's share in the World to Come (Introduction to *Perek Ḥelek*). For a fuller analysis of the punishment and the different forms it is conceived in, see Ramban to Leviticus 18:29 and Abarbanel to Numbers 15:22.

The five forms of abstinence are common both to Yom Kippur and to Tisha B'Av; on other fast days only eating and drinking are prohibited (Tosafot, *Ta'anit* 13a; Ra'aviya 3:854). Ramban (*Rosh HaShana* 18b) claims that theoretically, all fast days should include all the restrictions. However, he says that the rules of non-biblical fast days are defined by the practice accepted by the

to anoint oneself,
to wear shoes

וּבִנְעִילַת הַסַּנְדָּל *To wear shoes.* The prohibition on wearing shoes is restricted to ones made of leather, considered the standard material for them. The Talmud in *Yoma* 78b asks whether on Yom Kippur a shoe made of cloth or שַׁעַם (cork in modern Hebrew; Rashi interprets it to be a kind of rubber) or other materials may be worn, and then attests that many *Amoraim* did indeed wear such shoes. Similarly, in *Yevamot* 102b, the Talmud allows the use of cloth slippers at home, but not leather ones.

Rambam (*Hilkhot Shevitat Asor* 3:7) explains that it is permitted to wear non-leather shoes because one can still then feel the harsh ground underfoot; he understands the essence of the prohibition to be in the pain caused by walking barefoot. Rabbi Zeraḥya HaLevi, on the other hand, rules that the conclusion to the Talmudic discussion is that the practice of the *Amoraim* is not to be followed by others. In his view, no shoes may be worn on Yom Kippur (*HaMa'or, Yoma* 2a). The Talmud also discusses the permissibility of wearing wooden shoes; Rashi rules that these too are forbidden (*Yoma* 78b). This would be consistent with Rambam's reasoning. Ramban, however, rules that wood is permitted, and only leather shoes – including ones that are only leather covered – are forbidden. The *Shulḥan Arukh* (OḤ 614:2) rules in accordance with the Ramban. This ruling suggests an understanding that it is not the discomfort that lies at the root of the prohibition, but the specific status of a leather shoe. During the biblical *ḥalitza* ceremony, performed when a brother chooses not to enter a levirate marriage with his deceased brother's wife (Deut. 25:7–10), a shoe is removed from his foot as a mark of dishonor; the Talmud rules that a leather shoe is required for this, suggesting that these, specifically, convey a certain respectability (*Yevamot* 102b drawing from Ezek. 16:10, see also *Shemot Raba* 25:6). Walking barefoot appears in the Bible several times as an embodiment of degradation (see, for instance, Is. 20:2–4). A similar attitude to this "affliction" is expressed in תְּפִלָּה זַכָּה, said before the *Kol Nidrei* service (page 61), in which we are said to walk "barefoot like one who has been banished."

Behag (*Hilkhot Yom HaKippurim*) allows shoes to be worn only to fulfill a mitzva (such as walking to the synagogue), or in a case of danger. Ra'aviya (2:531) understands that all (even leather) shoes are allowed in such cases, but the *Tur* (OḤ 614) understands that the ruling is in fact a stringency, implying that only cloth shoes are allowed in these circumstances, while in regular

וּבְסִיכָה
וּבִנְעִילַת הַסַּנְדָּל

---

opportunity is considered a mitzva in such a situation (8a), the prohibition against washing for comfort does not apply here. Rambam and Ra'aviya accept this as halakha (*Hilkhot Shevitat Asor* 3:2; Ra'aviya 2:531). In the Yerushalmi, however, it is argued that all immersions are forbidden (*Beitza* 2:2). The *Teruma* (108) cites this and adds that even according to the Talmud Bavli the only sufficient justification for immersing is it being a mitzva. Today, the laws of ritual purity are no longer observed, it being assumed that everyone is טְמֵא מֵת – impure through contact with dead bodies – an impurity which immersion alone cannot purify (see Rabbeinu Tam, Tosafot, *Yoma* 8a). Sexual relations are forbidden on Yom Kippur, so there is no need for a woman to immerse in order to permit contact between her and her husband. Therefore, concludes the *Teruma*, there are no longer any cases for which immersion would be considered a mitzva on this day, and so neither Talmud would permit it. His opinion is codified in the *Shulḥan Arukh* (OḤ 613:11–12).

וּבְסִיכָה *To anoint oneself.* The source for the prohibition on anointing is debated in the Talmud (76b); the first verse cited is the one from Daniel, discussed above in the context of washing, in which anointing is listed as one of the things Daniel avoids while grieving (10:3). Later the Talmud suggests that anointing is avoided because of the principle סִיכָה כִּשְׁתִיָּה – "anointing is considered like drinking." This principle in turn is derived from the verse "it came into his innards like water – like oil, into his bones" (Ps. 109:18). In *Nidda* 32a, the Talmud uses the same verse to compare anointing oneself with *Teruma* oil to drinking *Teruma* wine (Rashi ad loc.); the Bible apparently views the two acts as equivalent.

The Yerushalmi, however, implies that the principle is a rabbinic enactment (*Yoma* 8:1, compare Mishna *Terumot* 6:1). Based on this, *Smag* (Positive Commandment 32) limits the comparison between *teruma* oil and wine, ruling that they are equivalent only in the fines they incur with misuse, not in the punishments.

The Talmud (77b) mentions one exception to the prohibition of anointing on Yom Kippur: one is allowed to apply an ointment to a wound or scab, or to treat an illness.

or to have marital relations.
But a king and a bride may wash their faces,
and a woman after childbirth may wear shoes:
thus says Rabbi Eliezer.
The sages say these too are forbidden.

2 One who eats something the size of a coarse date with its pit,

---

In Exodus 1:15–21, Onkelos translates מְיַלְּדוֹת, midwives, as חַיָּתָא, and this meaning is also used by the Mishna in *Ḥullin* 71a. Here, however, the word seems to refer to the mother herself (see Rashi, Ex. 1:19).

אוֹסְרִין *These too are forbidden.* Rabbi Yitzḥak ibn Gi'at (*Hilkhot Yom HaKippurim*) and *Smag* (Negative Commandment 68) rule according to the sages, but most of the *Rishonim* cite Rabbi Eliezer, which the *Tur* understands to indicate that they accept his position as authoritative (OḤ 614); and so is codified in the *Shulḥan Arukh* (ibid. 10; 615:3). *Ḥayyei Adam* and *Mishna Berura* rule that today a bride cannot be lenient; couples now generally know one another before getting married, and, in any case, at least the husband will generally be in the synagogue all day; therefore there is no additional need to wash (614:26). With regard to a woman just after childbirth, these authorities too continue to be lenient. However, see *Shemirat Shabbat KeHilkhata* (note 113 to chapter 39), for a discussion regarding whether today, when comfortable non-leather shoes are readily available, this leniency still applies.

כְּכוֹתֶבֶת הַגַּסָּה *The size of a coarse date.* In *Yoma* 79a, Rav Papa asks whether the date-quantity includes its pit. The commentators puzzle over this question, as it is answered in the mishna itself (see Tosafot; *Tosafot Yeshanim*). Some scholars suggest that Rav Papa may have had a different version of the mishna (see Albeck), and this might be supported by Rambam's phrasing in his commentary on *Me'ila* 17b and in *Hilkhot Shevitat Asor* 2:1.

The fact that the measure includes the pit, which is inedible, suggests that a date is selected, not as an example of a small meal, but simply because it is a measure of quantity. A date is the chosen example because it is one of the fruits by which the land of Israel is praised (Deut. 8:8); Rav Ḥanan, indeed, derives a different unit of measurement, for a different area of *halakha*, from each of the seven species (*Berakhot* 41a–b).

The Talmud (79b) states that the size of date is somewhere between that of

וּבְתַשְׁמִישׁ הַמִּטָּה.
וְהַמֶּלֶךְ וְהַכַּלָּה יִרְחֲצוּ אֶת פְּנֵיהֶם
וְהֶחָיָה תִּנְעֹל אֶת הַסַּנְדָּל
דִּבְרֵי רַבִּי אֱלִיעֶזֶר
וַחֲכָמִים אוֹסְרִין.

ב הָאוֹכֵל כְּכוֹתֶבֶת הַגַּסָּה
כָּמוֹהָ וּכְגַרְעִינָתָהּ

---

circumstances even those are forbidden. He rules, however, in accordance with the majority of the *Rishonim*, allowing leather shoes in cases of imminent danger, and non-leather shoes in other circumstances. Based on this ruling, contemporary rabbis allow soldiers and policemen to wear their uniform boots while on duty, in an extension of the category of "imminent danger."

In rabbinic Hebrew, סַנְדָּל usually refers to a closed shoe, and נַעַל to an open one (Rashi, *Yevamot* 102a; Rashbam, *Bava Batra* 58a). In modern Hebrew this is reversed. On Yom Kippur, in any case, both types are prohibited.

וּבְתַשְׁמִישׁ הַמִּטָּה *Marital relations.* The *Shulḥan Arukh* rules that all restrictions that apply to a couple when the wife is *Nidda* (menstrually impure) are also observed on Yom Kippur (OḤ 615:1 following the *Aguda*).

וְהַמֶּלֶךְ וְהַכַּלָּה *A king and a bride.* These people wash not for their own pleasure, but to make sure that their appearance is pleasing. The Talmud (78b) remarks that a new bride (for the first thirty days of her marriage – see *Ketubot* 4a) takes particular care of her appearance in order to be beautiful in her new husband's eyes, until the two begin to feel more at home with one another. A king has to be particular about his appearance in order to maintain the prestige of his office (derived from Is. 33:17).

וְהֶחָיָה *A woman after childbirth.* The Talmud (73b) explains that in the time after labor, a mother is dangerously sensitive to the cold and is therefore permitted to wear shoes. The Talmud in *Shabbat* 129a notes that this sensitivity can last up to thirty days after the birth. Rambam (*Hilkhot Shevitat Asor* 3:8) therefore rules that she is permitted to wear shoes on Yom Kippur during that period.

or one who drinks his mouth's full,
is liable.
Any foods he eats count together for the date measure,
and anything he drinks counts together for the mouthful;
but food and drink are not counted with each other.

3 If one eats and drinks in one oversight,
he is only liable for one sin-offering.

---

offering, if eaten inadvertently. Rabbi Shimon ben Lakish argues that the biblical prohibition is not violated at all unless one consumes a full measure. However, he concedes there is a rabbinic prohibition regarding even tinier amounts. Rabbi Yoḥanan's opinion is accepted as authoritative.

All agree that one is only liable to *karet* for eating a complete measure. Moreover, this measure must be eaten within a certain span of time to be defined as a single act of eating. This time-frame is determined as כְּדֵי אֲכִילַת פְּרָס, "the time it takes to eat half a loaf of bread" (*Tosefta* 4:4; see commentary on mishna 4:4). This rule has applications for those who are medically unable to fast; even though they are permitted to eat, they should still try to avoid eating in a way that would avoid full liability. They are instructed, then, to eat less than a full measure at one time and then wait the span of כְּדֵי אֲכִילַת פְּרָס before eating again (Rosh, *Yoma* 8:13). This time has been estimated differently by different authorities; the *Ḥatam Sofer* (cited in *Mishna Berura*, OḤ 618:20) rules one should wait nine minutes between mouthfuls; *Arukh HaShulḥan* (ibid. 14) is more lenient, allowing for gaps of only six minutes.

This way of avoiding liability is only necessary, according to many authorities, in the case of biblical prohibitions; on Tisha B'Av they allow an ill person to eat and drink normally (*Avnei Nezer* 540; *Arukh HaShulḥan*, OḤ 554:7; however, *Bi'ur Halakha* ibid., rules that even on Tisha B'Av the same strictures apply).

בְּהֶעְלֵם אֶחָד *In one oversight.* One who inadvertently violates a prohibition, either being ignorant of the law or not knowing that it applies to his action (in our case, not realizing the day to be Yom Kippur), is required to bring a sin-offering to atone for it. This only applies to sins of such gravity that their willful transgression is punishable by *karet*, as is the case with eating, drinking and doing forbidden work on Yom Kippur. A sin-offering is only atonement enough in a case where the lack of awareness that causes the transgression

וְהַשּׁוֹתֶה מְלֹא לֻגְמָיו
חַיָּב.
כָּל הָאֳכָלִין מִצְטָרְפִין לְכַכּוֹתֶבֶת
וְכָל הַמַּשְׁקִין מִצְטָרְפִין לִמְלֹא לֻגְמָיו.
הָאוֹכֵל וְהַשּׁוֹתֶה אֵין מִצְטָרְפִין.

ג אָכַל וְשָׁתָה בְּהֶעְלֵם אֶחָד
אֵינוֹ חַיָּב אֶלָּא חַטָּאת אַחַת.

---

an olive and that of an egg, but does not provide a more precise ratio. The Ran (3a) estimates that it is two thirds the size of an egg. The Ashkenazi custom is to measure according to volume (taken when the food is tightly packed, *Ḥazon Ish*, *OḤ* 39:17, following Rema, *OḤ* 486:1). This comes to at least 30 cc. (based on the more stringent estimation; see *Ḥatam Sofer*, Responsa, *OḤ* 127). The Sephardi custom is to estimate by weight (*Kaf HaḤayyim* 168:45–46; 486:1), coming to around 30 grams.

The Talmud (79b) notes that the date measure is more lenient than the usual measure for the violation of an eating prohibition, which is an olive-sized amount. This is because with less than a date measure, a fasting person would not be able to regain his composure, and his affliction would not be fully compromised (cf. note to 8:3).

מְלֹא לֻגְמָיו *His mouth's full.* The Talmud (80a) defines this more precisely as a cheekful. Unlike the unit used for solid food, this one is subjective, measured in proportion to the individual (Mishna *Kelim* 17:11).

הָאוֹכֵל וְהַשּׁוֹתֶה אֵין מִצְטָרְפִין *But food and drink are not counted...* Although abstention from food and drink is categorized as a single restriction (*Yoma* 76a), hunger and thirst are still two distinct needs (81a). Food and drink, then, do not combine to complete a measure. If a food has a sauce or seasoning, however, they are included in the measure as they do enhance the food, although they would not count as food if consumed by themselves.

The Talmud (73b) records a dispute regarding the permissibility of eating less than a complete measure. Rabbi Yoḥanan maintains that this is biblically forbidden; the measure of a date only marks liability for the most stringent punishment, *karet* ("cutting off" of the soul), if eaten knowingly, or a sin-

If he eats and does work,
he is liable for two sin-offerings.
If he eats foods that are not fit for eating
or drinks liquids that are not fit for drinking,
or brine, or the juice of pickled fish,
he is not liable.

4 One does not make children fast on the Day of Atonement,
but one has them practice a year or two years before,
so that they become accustomed to the mitzvot.

---

same principle applies here. While explaining the exemption on Yom Kippur, however, Rashi comments, "these foods do not give יִשּׁוּב הַדַּעַת – restore composure – because they are not normal acts of eating." Rashi implies that the abnormality of an act of eating is not enough to exempt it from prohibition on Yom Kippur; the relevant factor is that, failing to set one's mind at ease, these foods do not mitigate one's "affliction." This may suggest that "affliction" is determined not only by the physical state of hunger, but also by the emotional desire to eat. A support for Rashi's contention may be found in the Talmud's discussion of whether liability would be entailed for drinking vinegar. Although this is not a normal act of drinking, it is considered מֵשִׁיב אֶת הַנֶּפֶשׁ – restoring the spirit.

The Talmud records that there were people who would drink vinegar on Yom Kippur, and that they were rebuked for it. Conflicting traditions are represented there, as to whether they were rebuked for breaking the fast by diluting the vinegar with water – which would imply that eating truly inedible food is actually permitted – or whether such eating is merely exempt from *karet*, but still forbidden. Rambam rules according to the more stringent view (*Hilkhot Shevitat Asor* 2:5).

הַתִּינוֹקוֹת אֵין מְעַנִּין אוֹתָן *One does not make children fast.* According to the Talmud (82a), one begins training children when they turn nine. This is done by gradually postponing their meals, an extra hour at a time. By the time they turn eleven (or twelve, if they are sickly) they are rabbinically obliged to complete the fast. Rabbeinu Ḥananel assumes the ages stated in the Talmud refer to boys, relative to the age they attain majority (thirteen); the age of girls should thus be shifted one year earlier. However Rif (3b), followed by

אָכַל וְעָשָׂה מְלָאכָה
חַיָּב שְׁתֵּי חַטָּאוֹת.
אָכַל אֳכָלִין שֶׁאֵינָן רְאוּיִין לַאֲכִילָה
וְשָׁתָה מַשְׁקִין שֶׁאֵינָן רְאוּיִין לִשְׁתִיָּה
וְשָׁתָה צִיר אוֹ מֻרְיָס
פָּטוּר.

ד הַתִּינוֹקוֹת
אֵין מְעַנִּין אוֹתָן בְּיוֹם הַכִּפּוּרִים
אֲבָל מְחַנְּכִין אוֹתָם לִפְנֵי שָׁנָה וְלִפְנֵי שְׁנָתַיִם
בִּשְׁבִיל שֶׁיִּהְיוּ רְגִילִין בַּמִּצְוֹת.

---

is present throughout. The actual obligation to bring a sin-offering only devolves onto the person when he realizes his mistake. As such, if a person transgresses multiple times during a single period of unawareness, he is only obliged to bring one sin-offering (Mishna, *Shabbat* 67b with Rashi). This is the meaning of the first clause in the mishna; the rule, however, only applies to repetitions of the same violation. If he violates more than one prohibition during a single period of unawareness, he becomes liable to bring one sin-offering for each kind of transgression; the mishna gives the example of eating and working. Eating and drinking, as already noted, are considered part of the same prohibition (they are listed together as one of the five afflictions; see also the mishna in *Keritot* 2a); so a meal consisting of food and drink will only make one liable to a single sin-offering.

אֳכָלִין שֶׁאֵינָן רְאוּיִין לַאֲכִילָה *Foods that are not fit for eating.* The Talmud (81b) adds to this list other foods which are considered inedible. In general, complete liability for eating forbidden foods is only incurred when they are eaten in what falls into the category of normal eating. Eating inedible foods is considered abnormal, and does not constitute an infringement of the biblical law. Similarly, in *Berakhot* 36a–b, the Talmud debates whether inedible foods require a blessing; Tosafot (ibid. 36b) and Rambam (*Hilkhot Berakhot* 8:7) conclude that such foods are exempt. The Talmud compares the exemption on Yom Kippur to the laws of blessings, suggesting that the

5 If a pregnant woman is [overcome] by the smell [of food] –
she is allowed to eat until her spirit returns.
A person who is ill
is fed according to the instructions of experts,

---

forbidden, and one who does is "held guilty of his own blood." This approach, apart from emphasizing the immense value of life, also did much to comfort the people of his generation, many of whom could not withstand the tribulations of their tumultuous times and made significant compromises in their observance of mitzvot. The *Rishonim* of France and Ashkenaz built a dramatically different ethos of "*Kiddush HaShem*" ("sanctifying God's name") around the many Ashkenazi communities of the Middle Ages who readily gave up their lives rather than compromising their religious principles (Tosafot, *Avoda Zara* 27b; *Smak*, 44).

Our mishna permits a pregnant woman to break the fast if she is overcome by hunger. Her distress is considered life threatening, both to her and to her unborn child. It is permitted, therefore, to feed her until "her spirit returns" and she feels calm again. The danger is perceived as being posed specifically by her distress and not by the lack of food per se; in the mishna she is overcome by a smell, rather than by hunger itself. For that reason, even before she is offered food, she should be reminded that it is Yom Kippur, in case this should in some way ease her. Even if this fails, she is only allowed to eat partial measures at a time (see note to mishna 2) as a small amount of food may well suffice to set her mind at ease. In ordinary circumstances, she is required to fast (*Pesaḥim* 54b).

Some contemporary authorities rule that today, even healthy pregnant women should eat "partial measures" rather than fast fully. This is based on the notion that people today are weaker than in the Talmudic period, such that it has since become more dangerous for a pregnant woman to fast. This leniency is often extended to nursing mothers as well, on the basis of the *Ḥazon Ish*'s ruling that premature weaning is considered life-endangering for the baby (*OḤ* 59:3–4). The majority of contemporary authorities, however, reject the general claim and rule that a pregnant woman should fast as normal, unless she suffers from a medical condition that makes this dangerous, or has a history of miscarriage (*Tzitz Eliezer* 17:20:4).

חוֹלֶה *A person who is ill*... The mishna mentions two cases in which a person who is ill may eat – where experts assess the patient's condition to require it,

ה עֻבָּרָה שֶׁהֵרִיחָה
מַאֲכִילִין אוֹתָהּ עַד שֶׁתָּשׁוּב נַפְשָׁהּ.
חוֹלֶה
מַאֲכִילִין אוֹתוֹ עַל פִּי בְקִיאִין

---

the *Shulḥan Arukh* (OḤ 616:1) makes no distinction between boys and girls, implying that the same rules apply to both.

Rashi notes that the mishna's formulation, "One does not *make* children fast," implies that until a certain age one does not impose fasting on a child, but if a child wished to do so, he or she may fast before the prescribed age. Rambam (*Hilkhot Shevitat Asor* 2:11) takes issue with this, asserting that fasting from a younger age is dangerous to a child's heath, and should be not be allowed. The *Shulḥan Arukh* (OḤ 616:1) rules in accordance with the Rambam.

These rules regarding age apply to all the other restrictions, except for the prohibition on wearing shoes (Rama ibid). Although a child is still not obligated in mitzvot, it is forbidden for an adult to actively engage him or her in a forbidden activity. Allowing a child to wear shoes, even if he puts them on himself, may give the impression that an adult has put them on him, which would be forbidden. This concern should, in theory, apply to the other restrictions as well, but it is made clear in the Talmud, that as fasting would be harmful for children, it is fully allowed to feed them (78b).

עֻבָּרָה שֶׁהֵרִיחָה *If a pregnant woman is [overcome]*. The following three *mishnayot* discuss cases of פִּקּוּחַ נֶפֶשׁ, life-or-death (literally "uncovering a person"). The preservation of life is such a central value in Jewish law that it is prioritized over all biblical prohibitions, including violation of Shabbat. This is derived from Leviticus 18:5: "Keep My precepts and My laws; one who practices them, shall live by them" to which the Talmud (85b) appends: "*shall live by them* – and not die by them." The three cardinal sins of murder, idolatry and adultery-incest are the only exceptions to this rule, considered too grave to be transgressed even at the expense of one's life; a person forced to transgress one of the cardinal sins on pain of death is required to give up his life "in sanctification of God's name," rather than transgress (*Sanhedrin* 74b).

Whether one is permitted to choose to give up one's life to avoid transgressing others sins, for which there is no requirement to do so, is strongly debated. Rambam (*Hilkhot Yesodei HaTorah* 5:4) rules that doing so is strictly

or, if there are no experts there,
then according to his own instructions,
until he says "Enough."

6 A person overcome with *bulmus*
is fed, even with impure things,
until his vision is restored.
One who has been bitten by a mad dog
is not fed of the appendage of its liver;
Rabbi Matia ben Ḥarash permits this.

מִי שֶׁאֲחָזוֹ בֻלְמוּס *A person overcome with bulmus. Bulmus* is apparently a disease characterized by a ravenous hunger. One of its symptoms is a loss of vision. Hence, the license to feed him holds only until his vision is restored. The Talmud (83b) recommends feeding the patient honey and sweet fruits. This suggests that *bulmus* may be a form of hypoglycemia, an attack of which often carries symptoms of hunger and blurred vision, and which should be treated by immediately restoring sugar to the patient's bloodstream.

Permission to eat non-kosher food applies to the treatment of any life-threatening illness. In the case of *bulmus* the patient must be fed immediately, time being of the essence, so that non-kosher food is used if kosher food is not immediately to hand, even if it could be produced at a delay (Rambam, *Hilkhot Shevitat Asor* 2:8). A person suffering from such an attack is not fed in "partial measures" as with other illnesses (see note to mishna 2), but with as much as he needs, immediately (*Shulḥan Arukh* OḤ 618:7–9; *Mishna Berura* 26 suggests that this is implicit in the mishna's stipulation that he must be fed "until the light returns to his eyes"). Rosh (8:13, following *Ketubot* 61b) rules that any sick person whose face suddenly loses its color should be treated in a similar way.

The name *bulmus* is taken from the Greek: *bous*, intense (literally, an ox) and *limos* hunger. The Latin form "bulimia" now lends its name to an (unrelated) eating disorder. In rabbinic literature, the term *bulmus* is borrowed to refer to any overpowering desire (see *Bereshit Raba* 51:9, cited in Rashi, Gen. 19:33). The use of מִי שֶׁאֲחָזוֹ, "one who is possessed by" [bulmus] is also typical in rabbinic literature (see Mishna, *Gittin* 67b and Rashi).

מִי שֶׁנְּשָׁכוֹ כֶּלֶב שׁוֹטֶה *One who has been bitten by a mad dog.* The dispute does not hinge upon the laws of Yom Kippur but on a medical disagreement as to

וְאִם אֵין שָׁם בְּקִיאִין
מַאֲכִילִין אוֹתוֹ עַל פִּי עַצְמוֹ
עַד שֶׁיֹּאמַר דַּי.

ו מִי שֶׁאֲחָזוֹ בֻּלְמוּס
מַאֲכִילִין אוֹתוֹ אֲפִלּוּ דְּבָרִים טְמֵאִים
עַד שֶׁיֵּאוֹרוּ עֵינָיו.
מִי שֶׁנְּשָׁכוֹ כֶּלֶב שׁוֹטֶה
אֵין מַאֲכִילִין אוֹתוֹ מֵחֲצַר הַכָּבֵד שֶׁלּוֹ
וְרַבִּי מַתְיָא בֶּן חָרָשׁ מַתִּיר.

---

and where the patient himself insists that it is necessary. The mishna does not, however, mention cases in which the two conditions clash. The Talmud (83a) considers the case of a patient who asserts that he needs to eat, despite the contrary advice of doctors. It concludes "The heart knows its own bitterness" (Prov. 14:10); the law trusts the patient's understanding of his own condition and allows him to eat if he feels the need acutely. The opposite case, in which experts insist that he needs to eat, but the patient disagrees, is not mentioned. This is considered to be an obvious application of the first clause in the mishna: if experts say that a person needs to eat, their advice is followed. Rabbi Ovadia Yosef (*Yeḥaveh Da'at* 1:61) adds that in such a case it is strictly forbidden to fast.

The *Rishonim* debate the case in which two or more doctors disagree on a person's need to eat. Rav Aḥai Gaon (*She'iltot*, 38) rules that the majority opinion should be followed. Rambam (*Hilkhot Shevitat Asor* 2:8) accepts this rule but adds that it only applies where the experts are of the same caliber; if one with greater expertise permits him to eat, his opinion is followed even where he is outnumbered. Ran (4b) suggests this is indicated by the mishna's use of the term "experts" rather than "doctors." Ramban (*Torat HaAdam*) disagrees. He insists that in matters of life and death, we rule on the basis of a minority opinion even if the opposing experts are better qualified, and take the more lenient and cautious course of action. Even he, however, limits this to a case in which at least two experts agree that the patient should eat. The *Shulḥan Arukh* (OḤ 618:4) rules in accordance with this view.

Rabbi Matia ben Ḥarash also said this:
If a person has pain in his throat,
one may put medicine into his mouth on Shabbat,
because it may be a life-saving treatment,
and any doubtful case of life and death
is enough to suspend the Shabbat prohibition.

7 If debris falls on a person,
and it is not clear whether he is still there or not,
or not clear whether he is alive or dead,
or whether he is Jewish or gentile –

וְכָל סְפֵק נְפָשׁוֹת *Any doubtful case of life and death.* The principle that פִּקּוּחַ נֶפֶשׁ, saving a life, overrides the prohibitions of Shabbat and Yom Kippur, is not disputed, even if Rabbi Matia ben Ḥarash's medical claims are contested. The Talmud (*Shabbat* 129a) adds that even an uncertain danger is given precedence over the regulations of the day. The Talmud (*Yoma* 84b) states that when necessary, Shabbat is violated by גְּדוֹלֵי יִשְׂרָאֵל, Jewish adults, and not by gentiles or children, despite their exemption from halakhic obligations. *Behag* (*Hilkhot Shabbat*) understands this as stating a leniency; if no gentiles or children are available, Shabbat may be violated even by a Jewish adult. However, most *Rishonim* take it to be a directive; even when it is possible to rely on a gentile or child, the action should still be performed by an adult Jew. Rambam (*Hilkhot Shabbat* 2:3) suggests that this stems from a concern that encouraging people to violate Shabbat via those who are not bound by it may lead them to treat the laws of Shabbat lightly even where there is no danger. Tosafot (ad loc.) suggest that the concern is that a gentile or child might be lax in performing the required procedures; the one commanded with *pikuaḥ nefesh* must take full responsibility for carrying it out. Rabbeinu Yeroḥam (12:9) suggests that if a gentile or child is specifically asked to perform the life-saving action, people may mistakenly think that it is not permissible for a Jewish adult to act in such circumstances. This could lead to delays on other occasions when a gentile or child is not present. In a similar vein, *Or Zarua* (2:38) relates that when people asked him how to atone for violating Shabbat in a case of *pikuaḥ nefesh*, he forbade them to repent it at all, so that they will not hesitate the next time such a situation arises.

מִי שֶׁנָּפְלָה עָלָיו מַפֹּלֶת *If debris falls.* This is often used as the archetypal case of *pikuaḥ nefesh* on Shabbat, and may be the source of the phrase itself. The

וְעוֹד אָמַר רַבִּי מַתְיָא בֶּן חָרָשׁ:
הַחוֹשֵׁשׁ בִּגְרוֹנוֹ
מַטִּילִין לוֹ סַם בְּתוֹךְ פִּיו בַּשַּׁבָּת
מִפְּנֵי שֶׁהוּא סְפֵק נְפָשׁוֹת
וְכָל סְפֵק נְפָשׁוֹת דּוֹחֶה אֶת הַשַּׁבָּת.

ז מִי שֶׁנָּפְלָה עָלָיו מַפֹּלֶת
סָפֵק הוּא שָׁם סָפֵק אֵינוֹ שָׁם
סָפֵק חַי סָפֵק מֵת
סָפֵק נָכְרִי סָפֵק יִשְׂרָאֵל

---

whether this part of the liver of an infected dog, which would be used by doctors as a cure for rabies, is really an effective treatment (Rashi, 83a). If it is, then it is certainly permitted for treatment on Yom Kippur, despite not being kosher.

חֲצַרָא דְּכַבְדָּא is the Aramaic translation of the יוֹתֶרֶת הַכָּבֵד, "the appendage of the liver," mentioned many times in the Torah (see for example, Ex. 29:13 with Onkelos). Rashi identifies it with the diaphragm.

This cure for rabies was practiced in the ancient world (see, for instance, Pliny the Elder's *Naturalis Historia*). The vaccine introduced by Louis Pasteur is founded on the same principle of using (extracts from) dead infected animals to treat the diseases they carry. Rabbi Matia was the leading rabbi of Rome (*Sanhedrin* 32b), the hub of the scientific world of his time. He must have been aware of this method, and presumably considered it potentially effective. The other sages, however, disagree with him (Rashi, 83a).

This case raises the issue of the status of questionable and unproven medical practices in halakha. For example, *Shevet HaLevi* 5:55 cites this mishna in his discussion of homeopathic and similar cures. Rabbi Yitzḥak Nunes (Italy, eighteenth century, in *Siaḥ Yitzḥak* ad loc.) adds a significant factor to the debate. He claims that Rabbi Matia ben Ḥarash realized that the חֲצַר הַכָּבֵד bore no concrete medical benefit. He permitted it, then, because of its placebo effect on much of the population, who believed it to be effective. The importance of calming a patient's mind is clearly established in halakhic theory as a significant factor in treatment, to be fully considered in rulings (see Rambam, *Hilkhot Avodat Kokhavim* 11:11 for another use of this principle).

one must remove the rocks from him.
If he is found alive,
one removes them from him,
and if he is dead,
one leaves him.

8 A sin-offering, and the guilt-offering for a certain sin
make atonement;
death and the Day of Atonement
make atonement where there is repentance.
Repentance makes atonement for small sins,

---

but only *suspending* it until such a time as it will become clear to the one who brings the offering whether he has sinned or not. If he finds out he has, he must then bring a sin-offering.

Both types of guilt-offerings provide atonement of a kind. The Talmud (85b) asks, then, why our mishna only mentions the guilt-offering for a certain sin. Two possible reasons are suggested. The atonement of a suspending guilt-offering is incomplete, being effective only until the transgressor assuages his doubt. What is more, Yom Kippur atones even for sins the transgressor is not certain about. Therefore, if a person has neglected to bring a suspending guilt-offering before Yom Kippur, he does not need to bring it afterwards. The obligation to bring a definite guilt-offering or a sin-offering, however, is considered to be a debt to the Temple and must be fulfilled even when atonement has already been effected by Yom Kippur (Mishna, *Keritot* 25a). The mishna lists here only forms of atonement that cannot be substituted by other means.

עִם הַתְּשׁוּבָה *Where there is repentance.* Repentance is critical; without it, atonement cannot be achieved even for very minor sins, because one sin leads to another (עֲבֵירָה גּוֹרֶרֶת עֲבֵירָה), unless the sinner makes a firm resolve to change. Even death does not atone for extremely serious, unrepented sins (*Sifrei, Shelaḥ* 112).

הַתְּשׁוּבָה מְכַפֶּרֶת *Repentance makes atonement…* The mishna lists three basic categories of sin: (1) Sins that may be atoned for through repentance alone. (2) Sins that require the atoning qualities of Yom Kippur or death. (3) Sins that require the transgressor to bring an offering. As mentioned above, a

מְפַקְּחִין עָלָיו אֶת הַגַּל.
מְצָאוּהוּ חַי – מְפַקְּחִין עָלָיו
וְאִם מֵת – יַנִּיחוּהוּ.

ח חַטָּאת וְאָשָׁם וַדַּאי מְכַפְּרִין
מִיתָה וְיוֹם הַכִּפּוּרִים מְכַפְּרִין עִם הַתְּשׁוּבָה.
הַתְּשׁוּבָה מְכַפֶּרֶת עַל עֲבֵרוֹת הַקַּלּוֹת

Talmud (85a) points out that the end of the mishna is also significant: people are likely to become so involved in a rescue operation that they forget that the laws of Shabbat still apply. The Mishna reiterates that one may not desecrate Shabbat to remove dead bodies.

חַטָּאת וְאָשָׁם *A sin-offering etc.* This mishna discusses various paths to the atonement of different kinds of sin. In its very narrow sense, atonement can refer simply to the suspension of punishment for a sin. The goal, however, is a higher degree of atonement in which God cleanses man of his guilt, wiping it away with complete forgiveness as if it had never been. Indeed, the word כַּפָּרָה may derive from the sense of "covering" over the sin (the כַּפֹּרֶת, for instance, covers the Ark; see Malbim, *Yair Or*); or from the root's other meaning, "wipe," implying that the sin is wiped away in atonement, and ceases to exist (see *Arukh* for examples, specifically *Menaḥot* 7b, Deut. 21:8, Is. 6:7).

חַטָּאת *A sin-offering.* Although both a sin-offering and a guilt-offering are brought to atone for sins, they are two distinct categories of offerings, and are brought under different circumstances. A guilt-offering is held to be of lesser sanctity; this is expressed in the way its blood is sprinkled (Mishna, *Zevaḥim* 89a), in the leniency of the rules when it is performed with incorrect intention (Mishna, *Zevaḥim* 2a), and in the rules governing an offering brought when its owners have already been atoned (see note to 6:1).

There are two basic categories of guilt-offerings: אָשָׁם וַדַּאי, "a guilt-offering for certain sin," is brought for a clear and willful violation of five very specific sins (see page 501); and אָשָׁם תָּלוּי, "a suspending guilt-offering," brought only where a person is unsure if he has violated a prohibition which would require the bringing of a sin-offering. When a suspending guilt-offering is brought, the offering only provides a partial atonement, not preventing punishment

whether of deed or of omission;
over serious sins, repentance holds [the judgment] over,
until the Day of Atonement comes, and atones.

9 One who says
"I shall sin and then repent, I shall sin and then repent" –
he is not given the chance to repent.
If he says "I shall sin and the Day of Atonement will atone" –
the Day of Atonement will not make him atonement.

---

ing Maharshal, Responsum 64) recommends reciting the passages from the Torah detailing the offerings one would have been required to bring had the Temple remained, and appending a short prayer asking God to consider this a substitute for actually bringing the offering. The idea echoes Hosea's words, as read by Rashi "Let us offer [the words of] our lips [in place of] bulls" (14:3).

אין מַסְפִּיקִין בְּיָדוֹ *He is not given the chance.* Even if one does rely upon repentance to atone, it is still possible and effective to do *teshuva*; in practice, however, in Rambam's view, God does not assist one's attempts to repent (*Hilkhot Teshuva* 4:1). The *Orḥot Tzaddikim* (*Sha'ar HaTeshuva*) sees the awareness that repentance is readily in reach as a barrier to achieving it; assurance of atonement in the future can weaken a person's resolve to avoid sin, and impede his inner work. In a similar vein, Rav Sa'adia Gaon states that "if one says 'I shall sin and the Day of Atonement will atone,' the Day of Atonement will not make him atonement – without *teshuva*;" true repentance is always possible, regardless of past cynicism, but one may not rely on the day to grant atonement in itself, without true renouncement the sin (*The Book of Beliefs and Opinions*, chapter five).

Rambam regards a person to have forfeited the possibility of atonement even if he only abuses his confidence in it once. The mishna, however, implies a situation in which the sinner repeats his folly more than once. The Talmud remarks that in such a case there is an added psychological reason for the difficulty of repenting: "If a person sins and then repeats his sin, he begins to regard the sin as something permitted" (87a); the very repetition of the act makes it habitual, erodes the sinner's inhibitions, and changes his perception of the sin and its gravity. This will make it much harder for him to repent with sincerity (Rashi; see also *Sha'arei Teshuva* 1:2).

עַל עֲשֵׂה וְעַל לֹא תַעֲשֶׂה
וְעַל הַחֲמוּרוֹת הִיא תוֹלָה
עַד שֶׁיָּבֹא יוֹם הַכִּפּוּרִים וִיכַפֵּר.

ט הָאוֹמֵר:
אֶחֱטָא וְאָשׁוּב, אֶחֱטָא וְאָשׁוּב
אֵין מַסְפִּיקִין בְּיָדוֹ לַעֲשׂוֹת תְּשׁוּבָה
אֶחֱטָא, וְיוֹם הַכִּפּוּרִים מְכַפֵּר
אֵין יוֹם הַכִּפּוּרִים מְכַפֵּר.

---

sin-offering is only required for inadvertent transgressions; a willful sin is too grave to be atoned for through a sin-offering, and most fall into one of the first two categories. A definite guilt-offering however, is also brought for willful sins.

The Talmud (86a) records a different formulation, Rabbi Yishmael's, in which sins divide into four groups, different types of sin being atoned for in different ways. (1) Neglect of a positive mitzva is considered less severe than violating a prohibition; repentance alone is enough to atone for this. (2) Violation of a prohibition is more heinous and so repentance can only suspend punishment for this, until full atonement is achieved on Yom Kippur (this would appear to contradict the mishna, which implies that some violations can be atoned for by repentance alone – see 85b for a reconciliation of these two statements). (3) The willful violation of a grave sin, punishable either by death through a court of law or *karet* at the hands of Heaven, is only fully atoned for when, after passing through repentance and Yom Kippur, the sinner is also purged by suffering. (4) The most severe category of sin is the desecration of God's name. Such a sin is not fully atoned for until death.

Clearly, the Temple service provided a fundamental element of the atonement process in its time. The atonement of Yom Kippur is primarily achieved though the Temple service of the day (Mishna, *Shevuot* 2b). Similarly, certain sins require a sin or guilt-offering to achieve atonement. Nevertheless, Rambam writes that since the destruction of the Temple, the day itself provides atonement for all penitents (*Hilkhot Teshuva* 1:3). *Shelah* (*Ta'anit* 37; follow-

For sins between a man and his God,
the Day of Atonement makes atonement;
for sins between a man and his fellow,
the Day of Atonement does not make atonement,
until he makes peace with his fellow.
Rabbi Elazar ben Azaria interpreted this verse:
"Of all your *sins before the Lord* you shall be purified." *Lev. 16*
for sins that are between a man and his God,
the Day of Atonement makes atonement;
for sins between a man and his fellow,
the Day of Atonement does not make atonement,
until he makes peace with his fellow.

---

extent that even after the death of a person one has wronged, it is said that one should gather ten people at his grave and ask for forgiveness. The wronged party is also enjoined not to be cruel, but to forgive when asked (Rema, *OḤ* 606:1, following Mahari Weil). The notable exception to this is slander – for this offense there is no requirement that the victim forgive (Ra'aviya 531, based on the Yerushalmi, *Bava Kama* 8:7). Asking for forgiveness is only permitted where doing so will not cause further damage or pain. Therefore, Rabbi Israel Salanter expressly prohibits asking forgiveness for slandering someone, if that person is still unaware of the offense (cited in *Paḥad Yitzḥak*, Yom Kippur 2:8).

It has become the custom for people to ask one another for forgiveness on Yom Kippur Eve, for any offenses committed throughout the year (Mordekhai, *Yoma* 723). Some Sephardi congregations follow the recommendation of the *Ben Ish Ḥai* (*Vayelekh*, 5), and announce before *Kol Nidrei* that all are enjoined to forgive each other; in the Ashkenazi tradition, this is included in תְּפִלָּה זַכָּה, "A Pure Prayer" (page 55).

עֲבֵרוֹת שֶׁבֵּין אָדָם לַמָּקוֹם
יוֹם הַכִּפּוּרִים מְכַפֵּר
עֲבֵרוֹת שֶׁבֵּין אָדָם לַחֲבֵרוֹ
אֵין יוֹם הַכִּפּוּרִים מְכַפֵּר
עַד שֶׁיְּרַצֶּה אֶת חֲבֵרוֹ.
אֶת זוֹ דָּרַשׁ רַבִּי אֶלְעָזָר בֶּן עֲזַרְיָה:
ויקרא טז מִכֹּל חַטֹּאתֵיכֶם לִפְנֵי ה׳ תִּטְהָרוּ:
עֲבֵרוֹת שֶׁבֵּין אָדָם לַמָּקוֹם
יוֹם הַכִּפּוּרִים מְכַפֵּר
עֲבֵרוֹת שֶׁבֵּין אָדָם לַחֲבֵרוֹ
אֵין יוֹם הַכִּפּוּרִים מְכַפֵּר, עַד שֶׁיְּרַצֶּה אֶת חֲבֵרוֹ.

The Yerushalmi (ad loc.) applies to a person like this the words, "As a dog returns to his vomit, so a fool returns to his folly" (Prov. 26:11). This proverb is also used to describe one who, despite having fully repented for a certain sin, never accepts its closure and continues to confess. When a person repents fully, this is accepted by God and is enough to atone for the transgression. While one should certainly remain alert to past pitfalls (Ps. 51:4), it is incorrect to feel that guilt continues to hang over one indefinitely. For this reason Rabbi Yitzḥak Luria (the Ar"i) instituted that *viduy* – confession – should only be recited once on each day of *Seliḥot* (*Sha'ar HaKavanot, Drush Nusaḥ HaTefilla*). The practice was accepted by the Vilna Gaon (*Ma'aseh Rav* 202) and his pupils. Most Ashkenazi congregations, however, continue in the tradition of Rabbi Yitzḥak Tirna (whose fifteenth-century compilation of customs forms the basis to the Ashkenazi *minhag*), and repeat *viduy* three times in each *Seliḥot* service.

עַד שֶׁיְּרַצֶּה אֶת חֲבֵרוֹ *Until he makes peace.* The Talmud (87a–b) places great emphasis on the need to ask forgiveness of those one has wronged, to the

Rabbi Akiva said:
Happy are you, Israel:
before whom do you purify yourselves,
and who purifies you –
Your Father in heaven,
as it is said "I shall throw pure waters over you Ez. 36
and you shall be pure."
And say, "Israel's hope [*mikveh*] is the LORD" – Jer. 17
as a ritual bath [*mikveh*] makes those who were impure, pure –
so the Holy One, blessed be He, purifies Israel.

In the Prophets, however, the word is also used to describe the gathering together of people (Jer. 3:17; I Kings 10:28 according to Rashi; though Radak disagrees), and more commonly, as a term for hope (from the root "ק-ו-ה"). A typical usage is in Jeremiah 14:8: מִקְוֵה יִשְׂרָאֵל, מוֹשִׁיעוֹ בְּעֵת צָרָה, "[God,] Hope of Israel, their Savior in times of trouble!" In this prayer in a time of drought, the double meaning of hope and of a reservoir of water is poignant and apt. Similarly in Jeremiah 17:13: מִקְוֵה יִשְׂרָאֵל ה׳, כָּל עֹזְבֶיךָ יֵבֹשׁוּ...כִּי עָזְבוּ מְקוֹר מַיִם חַיִּים, אֶת ה׳, "Hope [*Mikveh*] of Israel, all that forsake You shall be ashamed… for they have forsaken the LORD, the Spring of living waters." The term *mikveh* usually refers specifically to a standing body of rainwater. In the continuation of this verse, however, the image is refined to mean a body of "living waters," welling from deep below the ground, the archetypal purifier (Mishna *Mikvaot* 1:8). A spring of living waters welling from Jerusalem (according to Ezekiel 47:1 from the threshold of the Temple itself) is in the future to heal the land and herald the Redemption (Zech. 14:8). Rabbi Akiva, then, closes the tractate of Atonement by invoking God as Israel's ultimate Bearer both of purification and of hope.

אָמַר רַבִּי עֲקִיבָא:
אַשְׁרֵיכֶם יִשְׂרָאֵל!
לִפְנֵי מִי אַתֶּם מִטַּהֲרִין?
מִי מְטַהֵר אֶתְכֶם?
אֲבִיכֶם שֶׁבַּשָּׁמַיִם
שֶׁנֶּאֱמַר: וְזָרַקְתִּי עֲלֵיכֶם מַיִם טְהוֹרִים, וּטְהַרְתֶּם: יחזקאל לו
וְאוֹמֵר: מִקְוֵה יִשְׂרָאֵל ה׳: ירמיה יז
מָה הַמִּקְוֶה מְטַהֵר אֶת הַטְּמֵאִים
אַף הַקָּדוֹשׁ בָּרוּךְ הוּא מְטַהֵר אֶת יִשְׂרָאֵל.

אֲבִיכֶם שֶׁבַּשָּׁמַיִם *Your Father in heaven.* "They asked Wisdom, 'How is the sinner punished?' Wisdom replied: 'Evil pursues sinners' [Prov. 13:21]. They asked Prophecy: 'How is the sinner punished?' Prophecy replied: 'The soul that sins shall die' [Ezek. 18:4]. Then they asked of the Holy One: 'How is the sinner punished?' He replied: 'Let him repent and he will find atonement'" (Yerushalmi *Makkot* 2:6). If the repercussions of a sin are followed to their logical conclusion, there is no escape from it; it will lead the sinner to his grave. But repentance breaks the boundaries of logic and destiny. God raises the sinner above the fetters of causality and allows him to restore himself to his original standing and relationship with God (Maharal, *Netiv HaTeshuva* ch. 1).

מִקְוֵה יִשְׂרָאֵל *Israel's hope.* On the third day of Creation, God decrees: יִקָּווּ הַמַּיִם מִתַּחַת הַשָּׁמַיִם אֶל מָקוֹם אֶחָד, "Let all the waters beneath the sky be gathered together to one place"; after this: וּלְמִקְוֵה הַמַּיִם קָרָא יַמִּים – "and He named this gathering of the waters, seas (Gen. 1:9–10). In the Torah, the root "ק-ו-ה" is used only to refer to the gathering together of water.

Appendix 1: A Summary of the Order of the Day according to the Different Views Represented in the Mishna and Commentary

BEFORE THE FIRST IMMERSION:

Lotteries to allocate duties to the various lay priests (2:1):

- Rabbi Zerahya HaLevi (1:8): On Yom Kippur everything is done by High Priest; lotteries are redundant.
- Rambam: Only the first lottery is held, for the taking up of the ashes.
- Ramban: Four lotteries are held; the first for the taking of the ashes, the others to determine who will assist the High Priest.

Lifting of the ashes (1:8):

- Ra'avad: The ashes are also removed from the premises.
- Rashi: The ashes are only removed when necessary (presumably this was not done on Yom Kippur).

THE FIRST IMMERSION: THE HIGH PRIEST DONS THE GOLDEN VESTMENTS.

Each immersion is preceded and followed by washing of the hands and feet (3:6):

- Rabbi Meir: This includes the first.
- The sages: The first immersion is only followed by washing.

The rite of the daily offering:

- The High Priest performs the morning's daily offering, with all its accompanying rituals (3:5).

The additional offering (7:3):

- Rabbi Eliezer: None of the additional offering is brought at this point (most *piyutim* represent this view).
- The sages: At least part is brought immediately:
  Rabbi Akiva: The seven yearling sheep and the bull (accepted by Rambam).
  Rabbi Yehuda and Rabbi Elazar ben Shimon: Some of the sheep only (accepted by Rosh).

THE SECOND IMMERSION: THE HIGH PRIEST DONS THE WHITE VESTMENTS.

The rites of sprinkling the blood of the bull and the goat:

- The High Priest confesses over the bull (3:8).
- He draws the lots for the two goats (4:1).
- He makes a second confession over the bull (4:2).
- He slaughters the bull (4:3).

- He enters the Holy of Holies and burns the incense (5:1).
- He leaves to retrieve the blood of the bull from the priest stirring it in the courtyard.
- He re-enters to sprinkle the blood toward the Ark
  (in the Second Temple, toward the place where it used to stand) (5:3).
- He leaves again to slaughter the goat "for the LORD."
- He returns to the Holy of Holies to sprinkle the goat's blood in the same manner as the bull's (5:4).
- He then leaves the Holy of Holies.
- He sprinkles the blood (first the bull's, then the goat's) toward the curtain (5:4).
- He mixes the blood of both animals and sprinkles it upon the corners and top of the Golden Altar (5:5–6).
- He confesses over the scapegoat and sends it away (6:2).
- He cuts up the slaughtered bull and goat.
- He prepares their fats to be offered on the altar.
  (Some *piyutim* narrate that he offers them at this point; the Talmud rejects this view.)
- He sends the carcasses to be burned outside the Temple (6:7).

THE TORAH READING:

- The High Priest reads from three passages in the Torah that relate to Yom Kippur (two from a scroll, the third by heart). He may continue wearing white vestments, or use a white robe of his own (7:1).
  Rabbeinu Yehonatan: This is done while he waits for news that the scapegoat has reached the desert.
  Most *Rishonim*: The reading begins after the news arrives.

THE THIRD IMMERSION: THE HIGH PRIEST DONS THE GOLDEN VESTMENTS.

- He offers the two rams: his own and the people's (6:3).
- He offers whatever remains of the Additional Offering (see above, after first immersion).
- Burning of the fats of the bull and goats:
  Most *Rishonim*: Now.
  Rabbeinu Ḥananel and Tosafot: Only later, after fifth immersion (7:4).

- Afternoon daily offering:
  Rambam: Offered at this point, without meal-offering and libations.
  Most *Rishonim*: not offered at this point (7:4).

THE FOURTH IMMERSION: THE HIGH PRIEST DONS A SECOND PAIR OF WHITE VESTMENTS.

- He re-enters the Holy of Holies to retrieve the coal pan and censer (7:4).

THE FIFTH IMMERSION: THE HIGH PRIEST DONS THE GOLDEN VESTMENTS.

- Burning of the fats of the bull and goats:
  Rabbeinu Ḥananel and Tosafot: Now.
  Most *Rishonim*: Already burned (see above).
- Afternoon daily offering:
  Most *Rishonim*: Offered at this point.
  Meiri: including meal-offering and libations.
  Rambam: Daily offering already offered (see above).
- He enters the Sanctuary to burn the incense and tend the lamps.
- Meal-offering and libations:
  Meiri: Already brought
  Ramban and *Smag*: The High Priest briefly leaves the Sanctuary for the courtyard to offer them between incense and tending the lamps.
  Rid: Offered after completing both the incense and tending the lamps (7:4).

CLOSE OF THE DAY: HIGH PRIEST REMOVES HIS PRIESTLY VESTMENTS, AND PUTS ON HIS OWN CLOTHES.

- He sanctifies his hands for the tenth time (according to the accepted opinion, see 3:6).
- He leaves the Temple Precinct in a public procession and returns home (7:4).

Appendix II: The Order of the Temple Service Piyutim

THE CUSTOMS OF LEARNING THE MISHNAYOT OF YOMA AND RECITING THE AVODA

The custom to recite the סֵדֶר הָעֲבוֹדָה, *Order of the Service*, has its earliest roots in the Temple Torah reading described in our Mishna. Following the rites inside the Holy of Holies, the High Priest would enter the Women's Courtyard and read the biblical passages that delineated the day's service (mishna 7:1). *Tosafot Yeshanim* (*Yoma* 70a) note that this Temple ritual was not a parallel to the regular reading of the Torah performed in the synagogue on Shabbatot and Festivals. The High Priest, indeed, would recite one of the passages from memory, something that would normally be forbidden in a public Torah reading. The *Tosefta* (3:13) adds that the gathered public, who had come to the Women's Courtyard to witness the events of the day, would produce their own scrolls and recite the Order of the Service together with the High Priest. This, then, is not a regular Torah reading, but a ritual recitation of the Service that has just been performed.

The Talmud records the practice of reciting the Order of Service during prayers (*Yoma* 36b and 56b). The specific case mentioned there is that of a prayer leader who recited the Order in Rabba's community (Babylonia, c. 300 AD) and made an error in his description, which Rabba then corrected. Rashi (36b) comments that since the Destruction, the recital of the Order of the Service also constitutes a fulfillment of the verse, וּנְשַׁלְּמָה פָרִים שְׂפָתֵינוּ, "Let us offer [the words of] our lips [in place of] bulls" (Hosea 14:3). Studying the laws of offerings and reliving them in words is considered a kind of substitute, in a time when it is no longer possible to bring them in practice (see *Midrash Tanḥuma, Tzav* 14; *Megilla* 31b).

It is unclear which text was used to recite the Order of the Service in Talmudic times. The small fragments cited in the story of Rabba's community are almost direct quotations from the Mishna. The *Ittur* suggests that the leader of the service used the "language of the mishna" and compares this to the style of the *piyut* אַתָּה כּוֹנַנְתָּ (not the one said today, but another poem of the same title, see below), written in a clear and terse Hebrew similar to that of the Mishna (*Hilkhot Yom HaKippurim* 108a). The *Ittur*, it seems, does not think that the exact text of the Mishna was used; but *Shibolei HaLeket* (320) does record such a practice, and *Yoma* is, indeed, eminently suited to the purpose. As Rashi phrases it, "the tractate is like a single extended mishna dealing entirely with the Order [of the Service] as it is, in the order of the text [of the Torah]" (15a).

The *Mishna Berura* (619:16) records a practice to learn *Mishna Yoma* on Yom Kippur night. This derives from the recommendation of the *Shelah* (*Yoma, Amud HaTeshuva*), aimed to encourage repentance; a similar recommendation is mentioned by the *Or Tzaddikim* (cited in *Mateh Efrayim* 619:24), who refers to the Kabbalistic significance of the tractate. The custom is also a fulfillment of the charge to study the laws of each festival as it arises (*Megilla* 4a).

THE ORDER OF SERVICE PIYUTIM

Our knowledge of the details of the service on Yom Kippur comes primarily from Talmudic material: the *Tannaitic* sources – Mishna, *Tosefta* and Midrash Halakha – and later discussions in the Talmud Bavli and Yerushalmi. In most areas, these and the developing chains of commentaries and halakhic writings that follow them are our main aids to understanding, but in this case another invaluable source is available in the genre of poetry known as Order of the Service *piyut*. The earliest authors of these *piyutim* were considered bearers of a tradition grounded on the reports of eyewitnesses, and the descriptions of the day that they provided were taken very seriously by the *Rishonim* (see for example Ramban cited in the introduction to chapter two). Despite this, however, the *Rishonim* and *Aḥaronim* were quite ready to amend the *piyutim* where they believed them to veer from accepted halakha (see below), and any discussion of the Service of the Day must necessarily draw both from Talmudic material and from *piyut*.

The Order of the Service was perhaps the most popular theme among *paytanim* (liturgical poets); we know of some eighty *piyutim*, some surviving in full, some only as fragments. Such luminaries as Elazar HaKalir, Rabbi Shlomo HaBavli, Solomon ibn Gabirol, Ibn Ezra and the Meiri all contributed to the genre, as have many others, known and anonymous. Especially noteworthy is the *paytan* Yose ben Yose. He was the first of the *paytanim* in *Eretz Yisrael* of the Byzantine period to be known by name, a great and highly innovative poet, and composer of at least three Order of the Service *piyutim*. One of these, אַזְכִּיר גְּבוּרוֹת, is recommended by Rav Sa'adia Gaon as the *piyut* to be recited at Shaḥarit.

The question of when the Order of the Service should be recited unfolded into a number of different traditions. Both siddurim of the Geonic period include *piyutim* in the Yom Kippur liturgy: Rav Amram Gaon has one for Musaf and Rav Sa'adia Gaon has for both Shaḥarit and Musaf. Ra'aviya (2:530) reports a custom of reciting *piyutim* three times on Yom Kippur, although he ultimately concludes that one should be recited only with Musaf, as is the accepted practice today. The desire to recite different Orders throughout the day is a testimony to the beloved status of these verses in the Jewish community throughout the ages. Indeed, Rav Hai Gaon (*Otzar HaGeonim, Yoma* 121) attests that he tried to influence his community in Baghdad to recite the *piyut* only at Musaf, but the people insisted on reciting it at Shaḥarit also, and he was unable to sway them. This love for the genre doubtless contributed to the tremendous proliferation of these *piyutim*. A notable departure from all this is Rambam's view, or lack thereof. He makes no mention at all of any recital of the Order of the Service. This may be a reflection of his general condemnation of *piyutim* (Responsum 207).

The earliest known Order of the Service *piyut* is known by its opening words, שִׁבְעַת יָמִים. It is little more than a rhythmic rephrasing of tractate *Yoma* (parts of it are published in Rabbi Yissakhar Yakobson's *Netiv Bina* p. 247–248). Later poets began composing far more complex *piyutim*, giving step-by-step accounts of the Service. אַתָּה כּוֹנַנְתָּ, an early example of the genre, already shows the format which was to become standard, including a lengthy prologue which fills in the historical background of the service, beginning with Creation, and then narrowing to the selection of the Jewish people, and finally to the appointment of Aaron and the Priesthood, who are charged with the Service then laid out in detail. These *piyutim* usually concluded the recitation with a jubilant description of the High Priest celebrating his safe return home.

THE PIYUTIM SAID TODAY

Different communities down the generations have selected from a huge variety of Order of the Service poems. Two are commonly recited today; אַתָּה כּוֹנַנְתָּ by Sephardi and most Hasidic communities, and אַמִּיץ כֹּחַ by Ashkenazim.

The *piyut* beginning אַתָּה כּוֹנַנְתָּ עוֹלָם מֵרֹאשׁ is among the earliest of the genre and is cited in the works of the Geonim. Fragments of it appear in many *geniza* documents; using them, Dr. Daniel Goldschmidt reconstructed a version which is probably very close to the original; this has been published in the introduction to the *maḥzor* he edited (Jerusalem, 1970). The poem is already mentioned in the Geonic siddurim, and became the standard *piyut* used across the communities of North Africa and Asia.

Ramban, writing in thirteenth-century Spain, twice refers to an Order of the Service *piyut* (see introduction to chapter two, and note to 7:4). In both cases his references accord with one authored by Rabbi Yosef ibn Avitur entitled אֵל אֱלֹהִים, but contradict the contents of אַתָּה כּוֹנַנְתָּ, suggesting that its use had not yet spread to Europe. Two generations later, אַתָּה כּוֹנַנְתָּ is mentioned by the *Rishonim* of Spain as the standard *piyut*, despite their reservations concerning its halakhic accuracy (Rosh, "וּבָא"; Ran, *Yoma* 6a). *Seder Rav Sa'adia Gaon* already has a much changed version of אַתָּה כּוֹנַנְתָּ, attributing it לְכָל חַכְמֵי יִשְׂרָאֵל – to all the wise men of Israel – seeming to indicate that many had already made amendments to it. Nonetheless, he also suggests an alternative of his own composition, בַּאדֹנָי יִצְדְּקוּ וְיוֹדוּהוּ. It seems fair to suppose he was not entirely satisfied with אַתָּה כּוֹנַנְתָּ as he knew it. Rabbi David Abudraham offered a further amended version of אַתָּה כּוֹנַנְתָּ, adjusting it to align with the accepted halakhic conclusions of the *Rishonim*. This process of emending the *piyut* continued yet further, most significantly at the hands of Rabbi Yosef Karo (*Beit Yosef*, OḤ 621), Rabbi Moshe Nigrin (*Melekhet Avodat HaKodesh*, Salonika 1568), and Rabbi David Pardo (Livorno 1788). The version included by the latter in *Shifat Revivim*, is the cornerstone of the present Sephardi custom, though slight variations remain among different communities.

Another *piyut*, composed by Yose ben Yose, bears an almost identical heading: אַתָּה כּוֹנַנְתָּ עוֹלָם בְּרֹב חֶסֶד, and was widespread in the communities of France (*Maḥzor Vitry*, 354; in *Yoma* 68b, *Tosafot Yeshanim* record a gloss made for it by Rabbeinu Tam). Both the *piyut* and its attribution to Yose ben Yose are mentioned by the *Ittur* (ibid.) and Abudraham cites this in his discussion of the piyut אַתָּה כּוֹנַנְתָּ עוֹלָם מֵרֹאשׁ, assuming the reference to be to the same *piyut*. He therefore names Yose ben Yose as the composer of the אַתָּה כּוֹנַנְתָּ recited in Spain, adding a tradition that he was one of the High Priests from the period of the Second Temple (or at least a direct descendant). This attribution was even accepted by the *Beit Yosef*, despite the evidence to the contrary in *Seder Rav Sa'adia Gaon*.

The *piyut* אַמִּיץ כֹּחַ, composed by Rabbi Meshulam ben Kalonymus (Lucca-Mainz, c. 1000) was widely used in Germany (Ra'aviya 2:529) and was to become standard among Ashkenazi communities. Its superior halakhic accuracy was celebrated by several prominent authorities (see *Magen Avraham* 621:4), although some note that it also contains some divergences from the halakhic norm (*Nishmat Adam*, the author's notes to *Ḥayyei Adam*, 145:3). An extensive commentary on the *piyut* was written by Rabbi Issachar Yakobson (*Netiv Bina* p. 251–285).

From the eighteenth century onwards, many Hasidic congregations adopted the Sephardi custom of reciting אַתָּה כּוֹנַנְתָּ (following Rabbi Shabtai of Rashkov, Moldova). This was a part of their much broader tendency to embrace elements of Sephardic custom and liturgy, with its heavy influences from Lurianic Kabbala; a likely source is Rabbi Raphael Kimḥi's *Avodat Yisrael* (Izmir, 1739) reportedly written on Mount Meron. A significant part of the *piyut*'s resurging popularity in Ashkenaz was probably due to its simpler language: while אַמִּיץ כֹּחַ interweaves many midrashic references and complex phrases, אַתָּה כּוֹנַנְתָּ is clear and terse. For this reason, Rabbi Alexander Ziskind (*Yesod VeShoresh HaAvoda,* 11:9, Lithuania, eighteenth century) recommends that even Ashkenazim who retain the custom to recite אַמִּיץ כֹּחַ should first read אַתָּה כּוֹנַנְתָּ in preparation. However, the differences in detail should be taken into account: in general, אַתָּה כּוֹנַנְתָּ describes the rite in accordance with the rulings of Rambam, while אַמִּיץ כֹּחַ is more consistent with Rashi's readings.

There is a subtle difference in tone between these two *piyutim*: where it describes the Service itself, אַמִּיץ כֹּחַ is usually briefer and more succinct than אַתָּה כּוֹנַנְתָּ, describing the rites in less detail and omitting some of the stages of the process. The High Priest's counting alongside the sprinkling of blood is only mentioned twice, for instance; the purification upon the Golden Altar is dealt with very briefly, and the blessings following the Torah reading and actions accompanying the goat's casting from the crag are omitted entirely. Most of the missing details, interestingly, are those performed by individuals away from the public eye. The ordering of events is also less precise; the High Priest's prayer, for instance, is mentioned only at the very end, while in אַתָּה כּוֹנַנְתָּ it appears in its chronological position (5:1; but see commentary there). The prologue to אַמִּיץ כֹּחַ, on the other hand, is longer, including in its gentle movement from Creation several incidents from the book of Genesis which are brought to demonstrate God's compassion. It also includes in its narrative the night vigil on Yom Kippur eve and a description of the people's joy on achieving atonement. All this seems to suggest that while the poet of אַתָּה כּוֹנַנְתָּ aims to provide a poetic but succinct survey of the rites of the day and to impart knowledge to the reader, that of אַמִּיץ כֹּחַ is more concerned with recreating the experience of the people gathered in the Temple.

Appendix III: Diagrams of the Temple and the Altar

FIG. I: THE TEMPLE

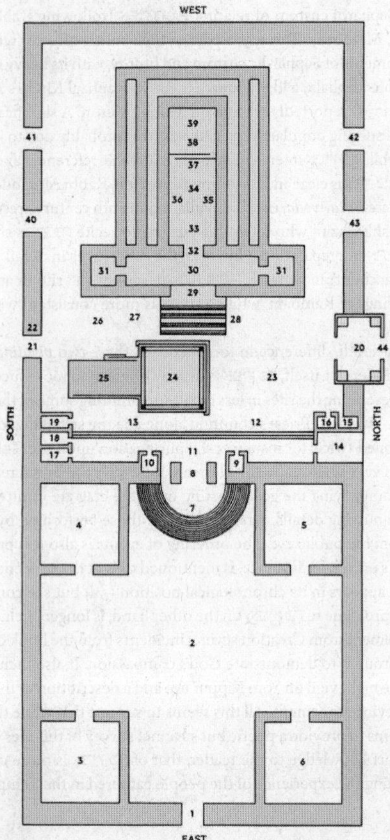

1. The Eastern Gate (1:3)
2. Women's Courtyard (7:1)
3. Chamber of Nazirites
4. Chamber of Oils
5. Chamber of Lepers
6. Chamber of Wood
7. Stairs leading to the Israelites' Courtyard
8. Doors of Nikanor (3:10)
9. Chamber of Pineḥas, keeper of vestments
10. Chamber of Pan Cakes
11. Israelites' Courtyard (1:8)
12. The Platform
13. The Temple's Courtyard/ Priests' Courtyard (3:3)
14. Chamber of Hewn Stone (1:1)
15. Chamber of Palhedrin (1:1)
16. The Returning Exiles Chamber
17. Salt Chamber (1:1)
18. Parva Chamber (3:3; but see Commentary there)
19. Rinsing Chamber
20. Chamber of the Hearth
21. The Water Gate (3:3)
22. Chamber of the House of Avtinas (1:5)
23. The place the rites of the two goats is held (3:9)
24. The altar
25. The Ramp
26. The Basin (3:10)
27. The place the High Priest's bull is slaughtered (3:8)
28. Steps leading to the Sanctuary (4:3)
29. The Sanctuary doors (6:8)
30. The Antechamber
31. Chamber of Knives
32. Gate of the Sanctuary (3:10)
33. The (outer) Sanctuary (5:1)
34. The Golden (incense) Altar (5:5)
35. Table of the Showbread (2:5)
36. Candelabrum/Menora (2:3)
37. Curtains (one-cubit partition) (5:1)
38. Holy of Holies (5:1)

39. Ark of the Covenant (5:2)
40. The Gate of the Firstborn
41. The Gate of Kindling
42. The Gate of the Flame
43. The Gate of the Offerings
44. The Gate of the Chamber of the Hearth

FIG. II: THE ALTAR

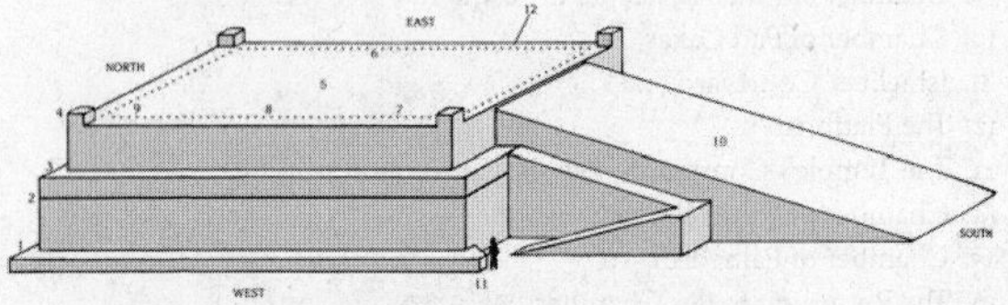

1. The base of the altar (4:5)
2. The red line separating the upper and lower parts of the altar
3. The surrounding ledge (4:5)
4. The altar's horns (see commentary on 5:6)
5. The pile of ashes (1:8)
6. The large arrangement of wood (4:6)
7. The arrangement for the incense (4:6)
8. The arrangement for Yom Kippur (4:6)
9. The Eternal Flame
10. The ramp (2:1)
11. The drain pipes (5:6)
12. The rim (2:3)

Shaḥarit

The following order of prayers and blessings, which departs from that of most prayer books, is based on the consensus of recent halakhic authorities. See laws 35–38.

ON WAKING

On waking, our first thought should be that we are in the presence of God. Since we are forbidden to speak God's name until we have washed our hands, the following prayer is said, which, without mentioning God's name, acknowledges His presence and gives thanks for a new day and for the gift of life. See law 29.

מוֹדֶה I thank You, living and eternal King,
for giving me back my soul in mercy.
Great is Your faithfulness.

Wash fingers up to the knuckles (see law 33) and say the following blessings. Some have the custom to say "Wisdom begins" on page 454 at this point.

בָּרוּךְ Blessed are You, LORD our God, King of the Universe,
who has made us holy through His commandments,
and has commanded us about washing hands.

בָּרוּךְ Blessed are You, LORD our God, King of the Universe,
who formed man in wisdom
and created in him many orifices and cavities.
It is revealed and known before the throne of Your glory
that were one of them to be ruptured or blocked,
it would be impossible to survive and stand before You.
Blessed are You, LORD,
Healer of all flesh who does wondrous deeds.

---

about the human body the more wondrous we discover it is. There are a hundred trillion cells in the human body. Within each cell is a nucleus and within each nucleus a double copy of the human genome. Each genome consists of 3.1 billion letters of genetic code, sufficient if transcribed to fill a library of five thousand volumes. Nor is the development of the body a matter of simple genetic determinism. It is an elaborate process of interaction between genes and environment, nature *and* nurture. Natural science is a way

שחרית

The following order of prayers and blessings, which departs from that of most prayer books, is based on the consensus of recent halakhic authorities. See laws 35–38.

השכמת הבוקר

On waking, our first thought should be that we are in the presence of God. Since we are forbidden to speak God's name until we have washed our hands, the following prayer is said, which, without mentioning God's name, acknowledges His presence and gives thanks for a new day and for the gift of life. See law 29.

מוֹדֶה/*women* מוֹדָה/ אֲנִי לְפָנֶיךָ מֶלֶךְ חַי וְקַיָּם
שֶׁהֶחֱזַרְתָּ בִּי נִשְׁמָתִי בְּחֶמְלָה
רַבָּה אֱמוּנָתֶךָ.

Wash fingers up to the knuckles (see law 33) and say the following blessings. Some have the custom to say רֵאשִׁית חָכְמָה *on page 455 at this point.*

בָּרוּךְ אַתָּה יהוה אֱלֹהֵינוּ מֶלֶךְ הָעוֹלָם
אֲשֶׁר קִדְּשָׁנוּ בְּמִצְוֹתָיו וְצִוָּנוּ עַל נְטִילַת יָדָיִם.

בָּרוּךְ אַתָּה יהוה אֱלֹהֵינוּ מֶלֶךְ הָעוֹלָם
אֲשֶׁר יָצַר אֶת הָאָדָם בְּחָכְמָה
וּבָרָא בוֹ נְקָבִים נְקָבִים, חֲלוּלִים חֲלוּלִים.
גָּלוּי וְיָדוּעַ לִפְנֵי כִסֵּא כְבוֹדֶךָ
שֶׁאִם יִפָּתֵחַ אֶחָד מֵהֶם אוֹ יִסָּתֵם אֶחָד מֵהֶם
אִי אֶפְשַׁר לְהִתְקַיֵּם וְלַעֲמֹד לְפָנֶיךָ.
בָּרוּךְ אַתָּה יהוה, רוֹפֵא כָל בָּשָׂר וּמַפְלִיא לַעֲשׂוֹת.

MORNING PRAYERS

מוֹדֶה אֲנִי *I thank you.* Sleep, said the sages, is a sixtieth, a foretaste, of death. Waking each morning is like a resurrection. In this simple prayer we say thank you to God for giving us back our life.

אֲשֶׁר יָצַר אֶת הָאָדָם בְּחָכְמָה *Who formed man in wisdom.* The more we know

אֱלֹהַי My God,
the soul You placed within me is pure.
You created it, You formed it, You breathed it into me,
and You guard it while it is within me.
One day You will take it from me,
and restore it to me in the time to come.
As long as the soul is within me,
I will thank You, LORD my God and God of my ancestors,
Master of all works, LORD of all souls.
Blessed are You, LORD, who restores souls to lifeless bodies.

TZITZIT

The following blessing is said before putting on tzitzit. Neither it nor the subsequent prayer is said by those who wear a tallit. The blessing over the latter exempts the former. See law 41.

בָּרוּךְ Blessed are You, LORD our God, King of the Universe,
who has made us holy through His commandments,
and has commanded us
about the command of tasseled garments.

After putting on tzitzit, say:

יְהִי רָצוֹן May it be Your will, LORD my God and God of my ancestors,
that the commandment of the tasseled garment be considered before You
as if I had fulfilled it in all its specifics, details and intentions,
as well as the 613 commandments dependent on it, Amen, Selah.

נְשָׁמָה שֶׁנָּתַתָּ בִּי טְהוֹרָה הִיא *The soul You placed within me is pure.* Despite the fact that we have genetically encoded instincts and desires, there is nothing predetermined about whether we use them for good or bad.

הַמַּחֲזִיר נְשָׁמוֹת לִפְגָרִים מֵתִים *Who restores souls to lifeless bodies.* Since waking each morning is like a resurrection, it is an intimation of the fact that the dead can be restored to life, as we believe they will be at the end of days. This prayer is a simple, subtle way of making us daily aware of the interplay between mortality and immortality in the human condition. It opens our eyes to the wonder of being, the miracle that we are here at all.

אֱלֹהַי
נְשָׁמָה שֶׁנָּתַתָּ בִּי טְהוֹרָה הִיא.
אַתָּה בְרָאתָהּ, אַתָּה יְצַרְתָּהּ, אַתָּה נְפַחְתָּהּ בִּי
וְאַתָּה מְשַׁמְּרָהּ בְּקִרְבִּי
וְאַתָּה עָתִיד לִטְּלָהּ מִמֶּנִּי
וּלְהַחֲזִירָהּ בִּי לֶעָתִיד לָבוֹא.
כָּל זְמַן שֶׁהַנְּשָׁמָה בְקִרְבִּי, מוֹדֶה/*women* מוֹדָה/ אֲנִי לְפָנֶיךָ
יהוה אֱלֹהַי וֵאלֹהֵי אֲבוֹתַי
רִבּוֹן כָּל הַמַּעֲשִׂים, אֲדוֹן כָּל הַנְּשָׁמוֹת.
בָּרוּךְ אַתָּה יהוה, הַמַּחֲזִיר נְשָׁמוֹת לִפְגָרִים מֵתִים.

לבישת ציצית

The following blessing is said before putting on a טלית קטן*. Neither it nor* יְהִי רָצוֹן *is said by those who wear a* טלית*. The blessing over the latter exempts the former. See law 41.*

בָּרוּךְ אַתָּה יהוה אֱלֹהֵינוּ מֶלֶךְ הָעוֹלָם
אֲשֶׁר קִדְּשָׁנוּ בְּמִצְוֹתָיו וְצִוָּנוּ עַל מִצְוַת צִיצִת.

After putting on the טלית קטן*, say:*

יְהִי רָצוֹן מִלְּפָנֶיךָ, יהוה אֱלֹהַי וֵאלֹהֵי אֲבוֹתַי
שֶׁתְּהֵא חֲשׁוּבָה מִצְוַת צִיצִית לְפָנֶיךָ
כְּאִלּוּ קִיַּמְתִּיהָ בְּכָל פְּרָטֶיהָ וְדִקְדּוּקֶיהָ וְכַוָּנוֹתֶיהָ
וְתַרְיַ״ג מִצְוֹת הַתְּלוּיוֹת בָּהּ, אָמֵן סֶלָה.

---

to the love and awe of God, as we realize the vastness of the universe and the complexity of life (Maimonides, Laws of the Foundations of the Torah 2:2). Each new scientific discovery gives new resonance to the words of the psalm: "How numerous are Your works, LORD; You made them all in wisdom; the earth is full of Your creations" (Ps. 104:24).

BLESSINGS OVER THE TORAH

In Judaism, study is greater even than prayer. So, before beginning to pray, we engage in a miniature act of study, preceded by the appropriate blessings. The blessings are followed by brief selections from Scripture, Mishna and Gemara, the three foundational texts of Judaism.

בָּרוּךְ Blessed are You, LORD our God, King of the Universe,
who has made us holy through His commandments,
and has commanded us to engage in study of the words of Torah.

וְהַעֲרֶב נָא Please, LORD our God, make the words of Your Torah
sweet in our mouths and in the mouths of Your people,
the house of Israel,
so that we, our descendants (and their descendants)
and the descendants of Your people, the house of Israel,
may all know Your name and study Your Torah for its own sake.
Blessed are You, LORD, who teaches Torah to His people Israel.

בָּרוּךְ Blessed are You, LORD our God, King of the Universe,
who has chosen us from all the peoples and given us His Torah.
Blessed are You, LORD, Giver of the Torah.

We become holy by what we do. The word *kadosh*, "holy," means distinctive, set apart. Just as God is holy because He transcends the physical universe, so we become holy by transcending natural impulses and instincts.

בְּמִצְוֹתָיו *Through His commandments.* This blessing, said over commands between us and God, represents the intention to fulfill an act as a command, thus endowing it with holiness. Only commands between us and God require a blessing beforehand. Commands between us and our fellow humans – such as giving charity, visiting the sick, comforting mourners and so on – do not require a blessing beforehand, since in these cases the command has to do with its effect (*nifal*), rather than the act itself (*pe'ula*) or its agent (*po'el*). Since the effect of acts of kindness is independent of the intention of the agent, no preliminary declaration of intent, that is, a blessing, is necessary.

בָּרוּךְ אַתָּה...אֲשֶׁר בָּחַר בָּנוּ *Blessed are You... who has chosen us.* Unlike the previous blessing, which is one of the *birkot hamitzvot*, blessings over a command, this is a *birkat hoda'a*, a blessing of thanks and acknowledgment.

ברכות התורה

In Judaism, study is greater even than prayer. So, before beginning to pray, we engage in a miniature act of study, preceded by the appropriate blessings. The blessings are followed by brief selections from תנ״ך, משנה and גמרא, the three foundational texts of Judaism.

בָּרוּךְ אַתָּה יהוה אֱלֹהֵינוּ מֶלֶךְ הָעוֹלָם
אֲשֶׁר קִדְּשָׁנוּ בְּמִצְוֹתָיו
וְצִוָּנוּ לַעֲסֹק בְּדִבְרֵי תוֹרָה.

וְהַעֲרֶב נָא יהוה אֱלֹהֵינוּ אֶת דִּבְרֵי תוֹרָתְךָ
בְּפִינוּ וּבְפִי עַמְּךָ בֵּית יִשְׂרָאֵל
וְנִהְיֶה אֲנַחְנוּ וְצֶאֱצָאֵינוּ (וְצֶאֱצָאֵי צֶאֱצָאֵינוּ)
וְצֶאֱצָאֵי עַמְּךָ בֵּית יִשְׂרָאֵל
כֻּלָּנוּ יוֹדְעֵי שְׁמֶךָ וְלוֹמְדֵי תוֹרָתְךָ לִשְׁמָהּ.
בָּרוּךְ אַתָּה יהוה, הַמְלַמֵּד תּוֹרָה לְעַמּוֹ יִשְׂרָאֵל.

בָּרוּךְ אַתָּה יהוה אֱלֹהֵינוּ מֶלֶךְ הָעוֹלָם
אֲשֶׁר בָּחַר בָּנוּ מִכָּל הָעַמִּים וְנָתַן לָנוּ אֶת תּוֹרָתוֹ.
בָּרוּךְ אַתָּה יהוה, נוֹתֵן הַתּוֹרָה.

BLESSINGS OVER THE TORAH

In Judaism, Torah study is the highest of all spiritual engagements, higher even than prayer (*Shabbat* 10a), for in prayer we speak to God but in Torah study we listen to God speaking to us, through the sacred texts of our tradition. Judaism is supremely a religion of study. Hence we preface prayer with an act of Torah study.

There are three types of Torah study: (1) study in order to know what to do, (2) study as a substitute for rituals that we are unable to perform, most notably the sacrifices, and (3) study as a religious act for its own sake, an aligning of our intellect with the mind of God.

אֲשֶׁר קִדְּשָׁנוּ *Who has made us holy.* Holiness is not a given of birth, a genetic endowment. It is what we become when we submit our will to that of God.

יְבָרֶכְךָ May the LORD bless you and protect you. *Num. 6*
May the LORD make His face shine on you and be gracious to you.
May the LORD turn His face toward you and grant you peace.

אֵלּוּ These are the things for which there is no fixed measure: *Mishna Pe'ah 1:1*
the corner of the field, first-fruits,
appearances before the LORD [on festivals, with offerings],
acts of kindness and the study of Torah.

אֵלּוּ These are the things whose fruits we eat in this world *Shabbat 127a*
but whose full reward awaits us in the World to Come:
honoring parents; acts of kindness;
arriving early at the house of study morning and evening;
hospitality to strangers; visiting the sick;
helping the needy bride; attending to the dead;
devotion in prayer; and bringing peace between people –
but the study of Torah is equal to them all.

Some say:

רֵאשִׁית חָכְמָה Wisdom begins in awe of the LORD; *Ps. 111*
all who fulfill [His commandments] gain good understanding;
His praise is ever-lasting.
The Torah Moses commanded us is the heritage of the congregation of Jacob. *Deut. 33*
Listen, my son, to your father's instruction, *Prov. 1*
and do not forsake your mother's teaching.
May the Torah be my faith and Almighty God my help.
Blessed be the name of His glorious kingdom for ever and all time.

Torah; (2) *Mishna*, study of the Oral Torah; (3) *Talmud*, that is, the logic of the Oral Law (Maimonides, Laws of Torah Study 1:11).

So here, "May the LORD bless you" is a passage from the Torah (Num. 6:24–26); אֵלּוּ דְבָרִים שֶׁאֵין לָהֶם שִׁעוּר, "These are the things for which there is no fixed measure," is a passage from the Mishna (*Pe'ah* 1:1); and אֵלּוּ דְבָרִים שֶׁאָדָם אוֹכֵל פֵּרוֹתֵיהֶם בָּעוֹלָם הַזֶּה, "These are the things of which a man enjoys the fruits in this life" is a teaching from the Talmud (*Shabbat* 127a).

וְתַלְמוּד תּוֹרָה כְּנֶגֶד כֻּלָּם *The study of Torah is equal to them all.* There was a debate among the sages as to which is greater, learning or doing? The conclusion was that "Great is learning, for it leads to doing" (*Kiddushin* 40b).

יְבָרֶכְךָ יהוה וְיִשְׁמְרֶךָ: במדבר ו
יָאֵר יהוה פָּנָיו אֵלֶיךָ וִיחֻנֶּךָּ:
יִשָּׂא יהוה פָּנָיו אֵלֶיךָ וְיָשֵׂם לְךָ שָׁלוֹם:

אֵלּוּ דְבָרִים שֶׁאֵין לָהֶם שִׁעוּר משנה פאה א:א
הַפֵּאָה וְהַבִּכּוּרִים וְהָרֵאָיוֹן
וּגְמִילוּת חֲסָדִים וְתַלְמוּד תּוֹרָה.

אֵלּוּ דְבָרִים שֶׁאָדָם אוֹכֵל פֵּרוֹתֵיהֶם בָּעוֹלָם הַזֶּה שבת קכז.
וְהַקֶּרֶן קַיֶּמֶת לוֹ לָעוֹלָם הַבָּא
וְאֵלּוּ הֵן
כִּבּוּד אָב וָאֵם, וּגְמִילוּת חֲסָדִים
וְהַשְׁכָּמַת בֵּית הַמִּדְרָשׁ שַׁחֲרִית וְעַרְבִית
וְהַכְנָסַת אוֹרְחִים, וּבִקּוּר חוֹלִים
וְהַכְנָסַת כַּלָּה, וּלְוָיַת הַמֵּת
וְעִיּוּן תְּפִלָּה
וַהֲבָאַת שָׁלוֹם בֵּין אָדָם לַחֲבֵרוֹ
וְתַלְמוּד תּוֹרָה כְּנֶגֶד כֻּלָּם.

Some say:

רֵאשִׁית חָכְמָה יִרְאַת יהוה, שֵׂכֶל טוֹב לְכָל־עֹשֵׂיהֶם, תְּהִלָּתוֹ עֹמֶדֶת לָעַד: תהלים קיא
תּוֹרָה צִוָּה־לָנוּ מֹשֶׁה, מוֹרָשָׁה קְהִלַּת יַעֲקֹב: דברים לג
שְׁמַע בְּנִי מוּסַר אָבִיךָ וְאַל־תִּטֹּשׁ תּוֹרַת אִמֶּךָ: משלי א
תּוֹרָה תְּהֵא אֱמוּנָתִי, וְאֵל שַׁדַּי בְּעֶזְרָתִי.
בָּרוּךְ שֵׁם כְּבוֹד מַלְכוּתוֹ לְעוֹלָם וָעֶד.

יְבָרֶכְךָ יהוה *May the* Lord *bless you.* According to the sages (*Kiddushin* 30a), one should divide one's study time into three: (1) *Mikra*, study of the written

TALLIT

Say the following meditation before putting on the tallit. Meditations before the fulfillment of mitzvot are to ensure that we do so with the requisite intention (kavana). This particularly applies to mitzvot whose purpose is to induce in us certain states of mind, as is the case with tallit and tefillin, both of which are external symbols of inward commitment to the life of observance of the mitzvot.

בָּרְכִי נַפְשִׁי Bless the Lord, my soul. Lord, my God, You are very great, clothed in majesty and splendor, wrapped in a robe of light, spreading out the heavens like a tent. *Ps. 104*

Some say:

For the sake of the unification of the Holy One, blessed be He, and His Divine Presence, in reverence and love, to unify the name *Yod-Heh* with *Vav-Heh* in perfect unity in the name of all Israel.

I am about to wrap myself in this tasseled garment (tallit). So may my soul, my 248 limbs and 365 sinews be wrapped in the light of the tassel (*hatzitzit*) which amounts to 613 [commandments]. And just as I cover myself with a tasseled garment in this world, so may I be worthy of rabbinical dress and a fine garment in the World to Come in the Garden of Eden. Through the commandment of tassels may my life's-breath, spirit, soul and prayer be delivered from external impediments, and may the tallit spread its wings over them like an eagle stirring up its nest, hovering over its young. May the commandment of the tasseled garment be considered before the Holy One, blessed be He, as if I had fulfilled it in all its specifics, details and intentions, as well as the 613 commandments dependent on it, Amen, Selah. *Deut. 32*

Before wrapping oneself in the tallit, say:

בָּרוּךְ Blessed are You, Lord our God, King of the Universe,
who has made us holy through His commandments,
and has commanded us to wrap ourselves in the tasseled garment.

According to the Shela (Rabbi Isaiah Horowitz), one should say these verses after wrapping oneself in the tallit:

מַה־יָּקָר How precious is Your loving-kindness, O God, *Ps. 36*
and the children of men find refuge under the shadow of Your wings.
They are filled with the rich plenty of Your House.
You give them drink from Your river of delights.
For with You is the fountain of life; in Your light, we see light.
Continue Your loving-kindness to those who know You,
and Your righteousness to the upright in heart.

עטיפת טלית

Say the following meditation before putting on the טלית. Meditations before the fulfillment of מצוות are to ensure that we do so with the requisite intention (כוונה). This particularly applies to מצוות whose purpose is to induce in us certain states of mind, as is the case with טלית and תפילין, both of which are external symbols of inward commitment to the life of observance of the מצוות.

בָּרְכִי נַפְשִׁי אֶת־יהוה, יהוה אֱלֹהַי גָּדַלְתָּ מְאֹד, הוֹד וְהָדָר לָבָשְׁתָּ: תהלים קד
עֹטֶה־אוֹר כַּשַּׂלְמָה, נוֹטֶה שָׁמַיִם כַּיְרִיעָה:

Some say:

לְשֵׁם יִחוּד קֻדְשָׁא בְּרִיךְ הוּא וּשְׁכִינְתֵּהּ בִּדְחִילוּ וּרְחִימוּ, לְיַחֵד שֵׁם י״ה בו״ה בְּיִחוּדָא שְׁלִים בְּשֵׁם כָּל יִשְׂרָאֵל.

הֲרֵינִי מִתְעַטֵּף בְּצִיצִית. כֵּן תִּתְעַטֵּף נִשְׁמָתִי וּרְמַ״ח אֵבָרַי וּשְׁסַ״ה גִידַי בְּאוֹר הַצִּיצִית הָעוֹלֶה תַּרְיַ״ג. וּכְשֵׁם שֶׁאֲנִי מִתְכַּסֶּה בְּטַלִּית בָּעוֹלָם הַזֶּה, כָּךְ אֶזְכֶּה לַחֲלוּקָא דְרַבָּנָן וּלְטַלִּית נָאָה לָעוֹלָם הַבָּא בְּגַן עֵדֶן. וְעַל יְדֵי מִצְוַת צִיצִית תִּנָּצֵל נַפְשִׁי רוּחִי וְנִשְׁמָתִי וּתְפִלָּתִי מִן הַחִיצוֹנִים. וְהַטַּלִּית תִּפְרֹשׂ כְּנָפֶיהָ עֲלֵיהֶם וְתַצִּילֵם, כְּנֶשֶׁר יָעִיר קִנּוֹ עַל גּוֹזָלָיו יְרַחֵף. וּתְהֵא חֲשׁוּבָה מִצְוַת צִיצִית לִפְנֵי הַקָּדוֹשׁ בָּרוּךְ הוּא, כְּאִלּוּ קִיַּמְתִּיהָ בְּכָל פְּרָטֶיהָ וְדִקְדּוּקֶיהָ וְכַוָּנוֹתֶיהָ וְתַרְיַ״ג מִצְוֹת הַתְּלוּיוֹת בָּהּ, אָמֵן סֶלָה. (דברים לב)

Before wrapping oneself in the טלית, say:

בָּרוּךְ אַתָּה יהוה אֱלֹהֵינוּ מֶלֶךְ הָעוֹלָם
אֲשֶׁר קִדְּשָׁנוּ בְּמִצְוֹתָיו וְצִוָּנוּ לְהִתְעַטֵּף בַּצִּיצִית.

According to the Shela (Rabbi Isaiah Horowitz), one should say these verses after wrapping oneself in the טלית:

מַה־יָּקָר חַסְדְּךָ אֱלֹהִים, וּבְנֵי אָדָם בְּצֵל כְּנָפֶיךָ יֶחֱסָיוּן: תהלים לו
יִרְוְיֻן מִדֶּשֶׁן בֵּיתֶךָ, וְנַחַל עֲדָנֶיךָ תַשְׁקֵם:
כִּי־עִמְּךָ מְקוֹר חַיִּים, בְּאוֹרְךָ נִרְאֶה־אוֹר:
מְשֹׁךְ חַסְדְּךָ לְיֹדְעֶיךָ, וְצִדְקָתְךָ לְיִשְׁרֵי־לֵב:

PREPARATION FOR PRAYER

On entering the synagogue:

HOW GOODLY

Num. 24

are your tents, Jacob, your dwelling places, Israel.
As for me, *Ps. 5*
in Your great loving-kindness,
I will come into Your House.
I will bow down to Your holy Temple
in awe of You.
Lord, I love the habitation of Your House, *Ps. 26*
the place where Your glory dwells.

As for me,
I will bow in worship;

I will bend the knee
before the Lord my Maker.

As for me, *Ps. 69*
may my prayer come to You, Lord,

at a time of favor.
God, in Your great loving-kindness,
answer me with Your faithful salvation.

הכנה לתפילה

On entering the בית כנסת:

מַה־טֹּבוּ במדבר כד
אֹהָלֶיךָ יַעֲקֹב, מִשְׁכְּנֹתֶיךָ יִשְׂרָאֵל:
וַאֲנִי בְּרֹב חַסְדְּךָ אָבוֹא בֵיתֶךָ תהלים ה
אֶשְׁתַּחֲוֶה אֶל־הֵיכַל־קָדְשְׁךָ
בְּיִרְאָתֶךָ:
יהוה אָהַבְתִּי מְעוֹן בֵּיתֶךָ תהלים כו
וּמְקוֹם מִשְׁכַּן כְּבוֹדֶךָ:

וַאֲנִי אֶשְׁתַּחֲוֶה
וְאֶכְרָעָה
אֶבְרְכָה לִפְנֵי יהוה עֹשִׂי.

וַאֲנִי תְפִלָּתִי־לְךָ יהוה תהלים סט
עֵת רָצוֹן
אֱלֹהִים בְּרָב־חַסְדֶּךָ
עֲנֵנִי בֶּאֱמֶת יִשְׁעֶךָ:

THE DAILY PSALM

Some congregations recite Shir HaYiḥud and Anim Zemirot at this point, followed by Mourners Kaddish (pages 212–256).

Most recite the Daily Psalm and Psalm 27 (below) at this point. In some congregations, they are said before Removing the Torah from the Ark on page 719.

One of the following psalms is said on the appropriate day of the week as indicated.

Monday: Today is the second day of the week,
on which the Levites used to say this psalm in the Temple:

שִׁיר מִזְמוֹר A song. A psalm of the sons of Koraḥ. Great is the Lord and *Ps. 48*
greatly to be praised in the city of God, on His holy mountain – beautiful in its heights, joy of all the earth, Mount Zion on its northern side, city of the great King. In its citadels God is known as a stronghold. See how the kings joined forces, advancing together. They saw, they were astounded, they panicked, they fled. There fear seized them, like the pains of a woman giving birth, like ships of Tarshish wrecked by an eastern wind. What we had heard, now we have seen, in the city of the Lord of hosts, in the city of our God. May God preserve it for ever, Selah! In the midst of Your Temple, God, we meditate on Your love. As is Your name, God, so is Your praise: it reaches to the ends of the earth. Your right hand is filled with righteousness. Let Mount Zion rejoice, let the towns of Judah be glad, because of Your judgments. Walk around Zion and encircle it. Count its towers, note its strong walls, view its citadels, so that you may tell a future generation ▸ that this is God, our God, for ever and ever. He will guide us for evermore.

Mourner's Kaddish (page 468)

Wednesday: Today is the fourth day of the week,
on which the Levites used to say this psalm in the Temple:

אֵל־נְקָמוֹת God of retribution, Lord, God of retribution, appear! Rise up, *Ps. 94*
Judge of the earth. Repay to the arrogant what they deserve. How long shall the wicked, Lord, how long shall the wicked triumph? They pour out insolent words. All the evildoers are full of boasting. They crush Your people, Lord, and oppress Your inheritance. They kill the widow and the stranger. They murder the orphaned. They say, "The Lord does not see. The God of Jacob pays no heed." Take heed, you most brutish people. You fools, when will you grow wise? Will He who implants the ear not hear? Will He

שיר של יום

Some congregations recite שיר הכבוד *and* שיר היחוד *at this point,*
followed by קדיש יתום *(pages 213–257).*

Most recite שיר של יום *and* לְדָוִד, יהוה אוֹרִי *(below) at this point.*
In some congregations, they are said before הוצאת ספר תורה *on page 719.*

One of the following psalms is said on the appropriate day of the week as indicated.

Monday הַיּוֹם יוֹם שֵׁנִי בְּשַׁבָּת, שֶׁבּוֹ הָיוּ הַלְוִיִּם אוֹמְרִים בְּבֵית הַמִּקְדָּשׁ:

שִׁיר מִזְמוֹר לִבְנֵי־קֹֽרַח: גָּדוֹל יהוה וּמְהֻלָּל מְאֹד, בְּעִיר אֱלֹהֵֽינוּ, הַר־ תהלים מח
קָדְשׁוֹ: יְפֵה נוֹף מְשׂוֹשׂ כָּל־הָאָֽרֶץ, הַר־צִיּוֹן יַרְכְּתֵי צָפוֹן, קִרְיַת מֶֽלֶךְ
רָב: אֱלֹהִים בְּאַרְמְנוֹתֶֽיהָ נוֹדַע לְמִשְׂגָּב: כִּי־הִנֵּה הַמְּלָכִים נוֹעֲדוּ,
עָבְרוּ יַחְדָּו: הֵֽמָּה רָאוּ כֵּן תָּמָֽהוּ, נִבְהֲלוּ נֶחְפָּֽזוּ: רְעָדָה אֲחָזָֽתַם שָׁם,
חִיל כַּיּוֹלֵדָה: בְּרֽוּחַ קָדִים תְּשַׁבֵּר אֳנִיּוֹת תַּרְשִׁישׁ: כַּאֲשֶׁר שָׁמַֽעְנוּ
כֵּן רָאִֽינוּ, בְּעִיר־יהוה צְבָאוֹת, בְּעִיר אֱלֹהֵֽינוּ, אֱלֹהִים יְכוֹנְנֶֽהָ עַד־
עוֹלָם סֶֽלָה: דִּמִּֽינוּ אֱלֹהִים חַסְדֶּֽךָ, בְּקֶֽרֶב הֵיכָלֶֽךָ: כְּשִׁמְךָ אֱלֹהִים
כֵּן תְּהִלָּתְךָ עַל־קַצְוֵי־אֶֽרֶץ, צֶֽדֶק מָלְאָה יְמִינֶֽךָ: יִשְׂמַח הַר־צִיּוֹן,
תָּגֵֽלְנָה בְּנוֹת יְהוּדָה, לְמַֽעַן מִשְׁפָּטֶֽיךָ: סֹֽבּוּ צִיּוֹן וְהַקִּיפֽוּהָ, סִפְרוּ
מִגְדָּלֶֽיהָ: שִֽׁיתוּ לִבְּכֶם לְחֵילָה, פַּסְּגוּ אַרְמְנוֹתֶֽיהָ, לְמַֽעַן תְּסַפְּרוּ לְדוֹר
אַחֲרוֹן: ‹ כִּי זֶה אֱלֹהִים אֱלֹהֵֽינוּ עוֹלָם וָעֶד, הוּא יְנַהֲגֵֽנוּ עַל־מוּת:

קדיש יתום *(page 469)*

Wednesday הַיּוֹם יוֹם רְבִיעִי בְּשַׁבָּת, שֶׁבּוֹ הָיוּ הַלְוִיִּם אוֹמְרִים בְּבֵית הַמִּקְדָּשׁ:

אֵל־נְקָמוֹת יהוה, אֵל נְקָמוֹת הוֹפִֽיעַ: הִנָּשֵׂא שֹׁפֵט הָאָֽרֶץ, הָשֵׁב תהלים צד
גְּמוּל עַל־גֵּאִים: עַד־מָתַי רְשָׁעִים, יהוה, עַד־מָתַי רְשָׁעִים יַעֲלֹֽזוּ:
יַבִּֽיעוּ יְדַבְּרוּ עָתָק, יִתְאַמְּרוּ כָּל־פֹּֽעֲלֵי אָֽוֶן: עַמְּךָ יהוה יְדַכְּאוּ,
וְנַחֲלָתְךָ יְעַנּוּ: אַלְמָנָה וְגֵר יַהֲרֹֽגוּ, וִיתוֹמִים יְרַצֵּֽחוּ: וַיֹּאמְרוּ לֹא
יִרְאֶה־יָּהּ, וְלֹא־יָבִין אֱלֹהֵי יַעֲקֹב: בִּֽינוּ בֹּעֲרִים בָּעָם, וּכְסִילִים מָתַי

who formed the eye not see? Will He who disciplines nations – He who teaches man knowledge – not punish? The LORD knows that the thoughts of man are a mere fleeting breath. Happy is the man whom You discipline, LORD, the one You instruct in Your Torah, giving him tranquility in days of trouble, until a pit is dug for the wicked. For the LORD will not forsake His people, nor abandon His heritage. Judgment shall again accord with justice, and all the upright in heart will follow it. Who will rise up for me against the wicked? Who will stand up for me against wrongdoers? Had the LORD not been my help, I would soon have dwelt in death's silence. When I thought my foot was slipping, Your loving-kindness, LORD, gave me support. When I was filled with anxiety, Your consolations soothed my soul. Can a corrupt throne be allied with You? Can injustice be framed into law? They join forces against the life of the righteous, and condemn the innocent to death. But the LORD is my stronghold, my God is the Rock of my refuge. He will bring back on them their wickedness, and destroy them for their evil deeds. The LORD our God will destroy them.

▸ Come, let us sing for joy to the LORD; let us shout aloud to the Rock of our salvation. Let us greet Him with thanksgiving, shout aloud to Him with songs of praise. For the LORD is the great God, the King great above all powers. *Ps. 95*

Mourner's Kaddish (page 468)

Thursday: Today is the fifth day of the week,
on which the Levites used to say this psalm in the Temple:

לַמְנַצֵּחַ For the conductor of music. On the Gittit. By Asaph. Sing for joy to God, our strength. Shout aloud to the God of Jacob. Raise a song, beat the drum, play the sweet harp and lyre. Sound the shofar on the new moon, on our feast day when the moon is hidden. For it is a statute for Israel, an ordinance of the God of Jacob. He established it as a testimony for Joseph when He went forth against the land of Egypt, where I heard a language that I did not know. I relieved his shoulder of the burden. His hands were freed from the builder's basket. In distress you called and I rescued you. I answered you from the secret place of thunder; I tested you at the waters of Meribah, Selah! Hear, My people, and I will warn you. Israel, if you would only listen to Me! Let there be no strange god among you. Do not bow down to an alien god. I am the LORD your God who brought you out of the land of Egypt. Open your mouth wide and I will fill it. But My people would not listen to Me. Israel would have none of Me. So I left them to their stubborn *Ps. 81*

תַשְׂכִּילוּ: הֲנֹטַע אֹזֶן הֲלֹא יִשְׁמָע, אִם־יֹצֵר עַיִן הֲלֹא יַבִּיט: הֲיֹסֵר גּוֹיִם הֲלֹא יוֹכִיחַ, הַמְלַמֵּד אָדָם דָּעַת: יהוה יֹדֵעַ מַחְשְׁבוֹת אָדָם, כִּי־הֵמָּה הָבֶל: אַשְׁרֵי הַגֶּבֶר אֲשֶׁר־תְּיַסְּרֶנּוּ יָּהּ, וּמִתּוֹרָתְךָ תְלַמְּדֶנּוּ: לְהַשְׁקִיט לוֹ מִימֵי רָע, עַד יִכָּרֶה לָרָשָׁע שָׁחַת: כִּי לֹא־יִטֹּשׁ יהוה עַמּוֹ, וְנַחֲלָתוֹ לֹא יַעֲזֹב: כִּי־עַד־צֶדֶק יָשׁוּב מִשְׁפָּט, וְאַחֲרָיו כָּל־יִשְׁרֵי־לֵב: מִי־יָקוּם לִי עִם־מְרֵעִים, מִי־יִתְיַצֵּב לִי עִם־פֹּעֲלֵי אָוֶן: לוּלֵי יהוה עֶזְרָתָה לִּי, כִּמְעַט שָׁכְנָה דוּמָה נַפְשִׁי: אִם־אָמַרְתִּי מָטָה רַגְלִי, חַסְדְּךָ יהוה יִסְעָדֵנִי: בְּרֹב שַׂרְעַפַּי בְּקִרְבִּי, תַּנְחוּמֶיךָ יְשַׁעַשְׁעוּ נַפְשִׁי: הַיְחָבְרְךָ כִּסֵּא הַוּוֹת, יֹצֵר עָמָל עֲלֵי־חֹק: יָגוֹדּוּ עַל־נֶפֶשׁ צַדִּיק, וְדָם נָקִי יַרְשִׁיעוּ: וַיְהִי יהוה לִי לְמִשְׂגָּב, וֵאלֹהַי לְצוּר מַחְסִי: וַיָּשֶׁב עֲלֵיהֶם אֶת־אוֹנָם, וּבְרָעָתָם יַצְמִיתֵם, יַצְמִיתֵם יהוה אֱלֹהֵינוּ:
תהלים צה ‹ לְכוּ נְרַנְּנָה לַיהוה, נָרִיעָה לְצוּר יִשְׁעֵנוּ: נְקַדְּמָה פָנָיו בְּתוֹדָה, בִּזְמִרוֹת נָרִיעַ לוֹ: כִּי אֵל גָּדוֹל יהוה, וּמֶלֶךְ גָּדוֹל עַל־כָּל־אֱלֹהִים:

קדיש יתום (*page 469*)

Thursday הַיּוֹם יוֹם חֲמִישִׁי בְּשַׁבָּת, שֶׁבּוֹ הָיוּ הַלְוִיִּם אוֹמְרִים בְּבֵית הַמִּקְדָּשׁ:

תהלים פא לַמְנַצֵּחַ עַל־הַגִּתִּית לְאָסָף: הַרְנִינוּ לֵאלֹהִים עוּזֵּנוּ, הָרִיעוּ לֵאלֹהֵי יַעֲקֹב: שְׂאוּ־זִמְרָה וּתְנוּ־תֹף, כִּנּוֹר נָעִים עִם־נָבֶל: תִּקְעוּ בַחֹדֶשׁ שׁוֹפָר, בַּכֵּסֶה לְיוֹם חַגֵּנוּ: כִּי חֹק לְיִשְׂרָאֵל הוּא, מִשְׁפָּט לֵאלֹהֵי יַעֲקֹב: עֵדוּת בִּיהוֹסֵף שָׂמוֹ, בְּצֵאתוֹ עַל־אֶרֶץ מִצְרָיִם, שְׂפַת לֹא־יָדַעְתִּי אֶשְׁמָע: הֲסִירוֹתִי מִסֵּבֶל שִׁכְמוֹ, כַּפָּיו מִדּוּד תַּעֲבֹרְנָה: בַּצָּרָה קָרָאתָ וָאֲחַלְּצֶךָּ, אֶעֶנְךָ בְּסֵתֶר רַעַם, אֶבְחָנְךָ עַל־מֵי מְרִיבָה סֶלָה: שְׁמַע עַמִּי וְאָעִידָה בָּךְ, יִשְׂרָאֵל אִם־תִּשְׁמַע־לִי: לֹא־יִהְיֶה בְךָ אֵל זָר, וְלֹא תִשְׁתַּחֲוֶה לְאֵל נֵכָר: אָנֹכִי יהוה אֱלֹהֶיךָ, הַמַּעַלְךָ מֵאֶרֶץ מִצְרָיִם, הַרְחֶב־פִּיךָ וַאֲמַלְאֵהוּ: וְלֹא־שָׁמַע עַמִּי לְקוֹלִי, וְיִשְׂרָאֵל

hearts, letting them follow their own devices. If only My people would listen to Me, if Israel would walk in My ways, I would soon subdue their enemies, and turn My hand against their foes. Those who hate the LORD would cower before Him and their doom would last for ever. ▸ He would feed Israel with the finest wheat – with honey from the rock I would satisfy you.

Mourner's Kaddish (page 468)

Shabbat: Today is the holy Sabbath,
on which the Levites used to say this psalm in the Temple:

מִזְמוֹר A psalm. A song for the Sabbath day. It is good to thank the LORD and sing psalms to Your name, Most High – to tell of Your loving-kindness in the morning and Your faithfulness at night, to the music of the ten-stringed lyre and the melody of the harp. For You have made me rejoice by Your work, O LORD; I sing for joy at the deeds of Your hands. How great are Your deeds, LORD, and how very deep Your thoughts. A boor cannot know, nor can a fool understand, that though the wicked spring up like grass and all evildoers flourish, it is only that they may be destroyed for ever. But You, LORD, are eternally exalted. For behold Your enemies, LORD, behold Your enemies will perish; all evildoers will be scattered. You have raised my pride like that of a wild ox; I am anointed with fresh oil. My eyes shall look in triumph on my adversaries; my ears shall hear the downfall of the wicked who rise against me. The righteous will flourish like a palm tree and grow tall like a cedar in Lebanon. Planted in the LORD's House, blossoming in our God's courtyards, ▸ they will still bear fruit in old age, and stay vigorous and fresh, proclaiming that the LORD is upright: He is my Rock, in whom there is no wrong. *Ps. 92*

Mourner's Kaddish (page 468)

The following is said by some congregations in addition to the Daily Psalm, except on Shabbat.

לְדָוִד מַשְׂכִּיל A psalm of David. Happy is one whose burden of iniquity is lightened, whose sin is covered over; happy is one whom the LORD does not hold guilty, who has no deception within him. My very bones rotted – as I sat silent and as I roared out, always. For day and night Your hand lay heavy on me, turning my marrow to a summer desert – Selah! I confessed my sins to You, I concealed no iniquity; I said, "I will tell the LORD of my transgressions," and You forgave my iniquity and sin, Selah! Every faithful man shall *Ps. 32*

לֹא־אָבָה לִי: וָאֲשַׁלְּחֵהוּ בִּשְׁרִירוּת לִבָּם, יֵלְכוּ בְּמוֹעֲצוֹתֵיהֶם: לוּ
עַמִּי שֹׁמֵעַ לִי, יִשְׂרָאֵל בִּדְרָכַי יְהַלֵּכוּ: כִּמְעַט אוֹיְבֵיהֶם אַכְנִיעַ,
וְעַל־צָרֵיהֶם אָשִׁיב יָדִי: מְשַׂנְאֵי יהוה יְכַחֲשׁוּ־לוֹ, וִיהִי עִתָּם לְעוֹלָם:
› וַיַּאֲכִילֵהוּ מֵחֵלֶב חִטָּה, וּמִצּוּר, דְּבַשׁ אַשְׂבִּיעֶךָ:

קדיש יתום (*page 469*)

שבת הַיּוֹם יוֹם שַׁבַּת קֹדֶשׁ, שֶׁבּוֹ הָיוּ הַלְוִיִּם אוֹמְרִים בְּבֵית הַמִּקְדָּשׁ:

מִזְמוֹר שִׁיר לְיוֹם הַשַּׁבָּת: טוֹב לְהֹדוֹת לַיהוה, וּלְזַמֵּר לְשִׁמְךָ עֶלְיוֹן: תהלים צב
לְהַגִּיד בַּבֹּקֶר חַסְדֶּךָ, וֶאֱמוּנָתְךָ בַּלֵּילוֹת: עֲלֵי־עָשׂוֹר וַעֲלֵי־נָבֶל, עֲלֵי
הִגָּיוֹן בְּכִנּוֹר: כִּי שִׂמַּחְתַּנִי יהוה בְּפָעֳלֶךָ, בְּמַעֲשֵׂי יָדֶיךָ אֲרַנֵּן: מַה־
גָּדְלוּ מַעֲשֶׂיךָ יהוה, מְאֹד עָמְקוּ מַחְשְׁבֹתֶיךָ: אִישׁ־בַּעַר לֹא יֵדָע,
וּכְסִיל לֹא־יָבִין אֶת־זֹאת: בִּפְרֹחַ רְשָׁעִים כְּמוֹ־עֵשֶׂב, וַיָּצִיצוּ כָּל־פֹּעֲלֵי
אָוֶן, לְהִשָּׁמְדָם עֲדֵי־עַד: וְאַתָּה מָרוֹם לְעֹלָם יהוה: כִּי הִנֵּה אֹיְבֶיךָ
יהוה, כִּי־הִנֵּה אֹיְבֶיךָ יֹאבֵדוּ, יִתְפָּרְדוּ כָּל־פֹּעֲלֵי אָוֶן: וַתָּרֶם כִּרְאֵים
קַרְנִי, בַּלֹּתִי בְּשֶׁמֶן רַעֲנָן: וַתַּבֵּט עֵינִי בְּשׁוּרָי, בַּקָּמִים עָלַי מְרֵעִים
תִּשְׁמַעְנָה אָזְנָי: צַדִּיק כַּתָּמָר יִפְרָח, כְּאֶרֶז בַּלְּבָנוֹן יִשְׂגֶּה: שְׁתוּלִים
בְּבֵית יהוה, בְּחַצְרוֹת אֱלֹהֵינוּ יַפְרִיחוּ: › עוֹד יְנוּבוּן בְּשֵׂיבָה, דְּשֵׁנִים
וְרַעֲנַנִּים יִהְיוּ: לְהַגִּיד כִּי־יָשָׁר יהוה, צוּרִי, וְלֹא־עַוְלָתָה בּוֹ:

קדיש יתום (*page 469*)

The following is said by some congregations in addition to the שיר של יום*, except on* שבת*.*

לְדָוִד מַשְׂכִּיל אַשְׁרֵי נְשׂוּי־פֶּשַׁע כְּסוּי חֲטָאָה: אַשְׁרֵי־אָדָם לֹא יַחְשֹׁב תהלים לב
יהוה לוֹ עָוֹן וְאֵין בְּרוּחוֹ רְמִיָּה: כִּי־הֶחֱרַשְׁתִּי בָּלוּ עֲצָמָי בְּשַׁאֲגָתִי
כָּל־הַיּוֹם: כִּי ׀ יוֹמָם וָלַיְלָה תִּכְבַּד עָלַי יָדֶךָ נֶהְפַּךְ לְשַׁדִּי בְּחַרְבֹנֵי
קַיִץ סֶלָה: חַטָּאתִי אוֹדִיעֲךָ וַעֲוֺנִי לֹא־כִסִּיתִי אָמַרְתִּי אוֹדֶה עֲלֵי
פְשָׁעַי לַיהוה וְאַתָּה נָשָׂאתָ עֲוֺן חַטָּאתִי סֶלָה: עַל־זֹאת יִתְפַּלֵּל

pray to You for this, whenever distress finds him: only that this great flood of waters should not reach him. You are my refuge, rescuing me from the enemy. With songs of deliverance You surround me – Selah! "I shall grant you knowledge, shall teach you the path to follow; I shall keep My eye upon you as you go." Do not be like a horse, like a mule without thought, whose bit and straps, his ornament, restrain him; let this pain never come close to you. The sufferings of sinners are great indeed, but one who trusts the LORD – He will surround him with loving-kindness. Be happy and find joy in the LORD, righteous ones; sing out in celebration, all you noble-hearted.

Mourner's Kaddish (next page)

The following psalm is said on all days after the Daily Psalm. Some congregations recite the Daily Psalm and Psalm 27 before Removing the Torah from the Ark on page 718.

לְדָוִד By David. The LORD is my light and my salvation – whom then shall I fear? The LORD is the stronghold of my life – of whom shall I be afraid? When evil men close in on me to devour my flesh, it is they, my enemies and foes, who stumble and fall. Should an army besiege me, my heart would not fear. Should war break out against me, still I would be confident. One thing I ask of the LORD, only this do I seek: to live in the House of the LORD all the days of my life, to gaze on the beauty of the LORD and worship in His Temple. For He will keep me safe in His pavilion on the day of trouble. He will hide me under the cover of His tent. He will set me high upon a rock. Now my head is high above my enemies who surround me. I will sacrifice in His tent with shouts of joy. I will sing and chant praises to the LORD. LORD, hear my voice when I call. Be gracious to me and answer me. On Your behalf my heart says, "Seek My face." Your face, LORD, will I seek. Do not hide Your face from me. Do not turn Your servant away in anger. You have been my help. Do not reject or forsake me, God, my Savior. Were my father and my mother to forsake me, the LORD would take me in. Teach me Your way, LORD, and lead me on a level path, because of my oppressors. Do not abandon me to the will of my foes, for false witnesses have risen against me, breathing violence. ▸ Were it not for my faith that I shall see the LORD's goodness in the land of the living. Hope in the LORD. Be strong and of good courage, and hope in the LORD! *Ps. 27*

Mourner's Kaddish (next page)

כָּל־חָסִיד | אֵלֶיךָ לְעֵת מְצֹא רַק לְשֵׁטֶף מַיִם רַבִּים אֵלָיו לֹא יַגִּיעוּ: אַתָּה | סֵתֶר לִי מִצַּר תִּצְּרֵנִי רָנֵּי פַלֵּט תְּסוֹבְבֵנִי סֶלָה: אַשְׂכִּילְךָ | וְאוֹרְךָ בְּדֶרֶךְ־זוּ תֵלֵךְ אִיעֲצָה עָלֶיךָ עֵינִי: אַל־תִּהְיוּ | כְּסוּס כְּפֶרֶד אֵין הָבִין בְּמֶתֶג־וָרֶסֶן עֶדְיוֹ לִבְלוֹם בַּל קְרֹב אֵלֶיךָ: רַבִּים מַכְאוֹבִים לָרָשָׁע וְהַבּוֹטֵחַ בַּיהוה חֶסֶד יְסוֹבְבֶנּוּ: שִׂמְחוּ בַיהוה וְגִילוּ צַדִּיקִים וְהַרְנִינוּ כָּל־יִשְׁרֵי־לֵב:

קדיש יתום (*next page*)

The following psalm is said on all days after the שיר של יום*. Some congregations recite the* שיר של יום *and* לְדָוִד, יהוה אוֹרִי *before* הוצאת ספר תורה *on page 719.*

תהלים כז

לְדָוִד, יהוה אוֹרִי וְיִשְׁעִי, מִמִּי אִירָא, יהוה מָעוֹז־חַיַּי, מִמִּי אֶפְחָד: בִּקְרֹב עָלַי מְרֵעִים לֶאֱכֹל אֶת־בְּשָׂרִי, צָרַי וְאֹיְבַי לִי, הֵמָּה כָשְׁלוּ וְנָפָלוּ: אִם־תַּחֲנֶה עָלַי מַחֲנֶה, לֹא־יִירָא לִבִּי, אִם־תָּקוּם עָלַי מִלְחָמָה, בְּזֹאת אֲנִי בוֹטֵחַ: אַחַת שָׁאַלְתִּי מֵאֵת־יהוה, אוֹתָהּ אֲבַקֵּשׁ, שִׁבְתִּי בְּבֵית־יהוה כָּל־יְמֵי חַיַּי, לַחֲזוֹת בְּנֹעַם־יהוה, וּלְבַקֵּר בְּהֵיכָלוֹ: כִּי יִצְפְּנֵנִי בְּסֻכֹּה בְּיוֹם רָעָה, יַסְתִּרֵנִי בְּסֵתֶר אָהֳלוֹ, בְּצוּר יְרוֹמְמֵנִי: וְעַתָּה יָרוּם רֹאשִׁי עַל אֹיְבַי סְבִיבוֹתַי, וְאֶזְבְּחָה בְאָהֳלוֹ זִבְחֵי תְרוּעָה, אָשִׁירָה וַאֲזַמְּרָה לַיהוה: שְׁמַע־יהוה קוֹלִי אֶקְרָא, וְחָנֵּנִי וַעֲנֵנִי: לְךָ אָמַר לִבִּי בַּקְּשׁוּ פָנָי, אֶת־פָּנֶיךָ יהוה אֲבַקֵּשׁ: אַל־תַּסְתֵּר פָּנֶיךָ מִמֶּנִּי, אַל תַּט־בְּאַף עַבְדֶּךָ, עֶזְרָתִי הָיִיתָ, אַל־תִּטְּשֵׁנִי וְאַל־תַּעַזְבֵנִי, אֱלֹהֵי יִשְׁעִי: כִּי־אָבִי וְאִמִּי עֲזָבוּנִי, וַיהוה יַאַסְפֵנִי: הוֹרֵנִי יהוה דַּרְכֶּךָ, וּנְחֵנִי בְּאֹרַח מִישׁוֹר, לְמַעַן שׁוֹרְרָי: אַל־תִּתְּנֵנִי בְּנֶפֶשׁ צָרָי, כִּי קָמוּ־בִי עֵדֵי־שֶׁקֶר, וִיפֵחַ חָמָס: ‹ לוּלֵא הֶאֱמַנְתִּי לִרְאוֹת בְּטוּב־יהוה בְּאֶרֶץ חַיִּים: קַוֵּה אֶל־יהוה, חֲזַק וְיַאֲמֵץ לִבֶּךָ, וְקַוֵּה אֶל־יהוה:

קדיש יתום (*next page*)

MOURNER'S KADDISH

The following prayer requires the presence of a minyan.
A transliteration can be found on page 1375.

Mourner: יִתְגַּדַּל Magnified and sanctified
may His great name be,
in the world He created by His will.
May He establish His kingdom
in your lifetime and in your days,
and in the lifetime of all the house of Israel,
swiftly and soon –
and say: Amen.

All: May His great name be blessed for ever and all time.

Mourner: Blessed and praised,
glorified and exalted,
raised and honored,
uplifted and lauded
be the name of the Holy One, blessed be He,
above and beyond any blessing, song,
praise and consolation
uttered in the world –
and say: Amen.

May there be great peace from heaven,
and life for us and all Israel –
and say: Amen.

Bow, take three steps back, as if taking leave of the Divine Presence,
then bow, first left, then right, then center, while saying:

May He who makes peace in His high places,
make peace for us and all Israel –
and say: Amen.

קדיש יתום

The following prayer requires the presence of a מנין.
A transliteration can be found on page 1375.

אבל: יִתְגַּדַּל וְיִתְקַדַּשׁ שְׁמֵהּ רַבָּא (קהל: אָמֵן)
בְּעָלְמָא דִּי בְרָא כִרְעוּתֵהּ
וְיַמְלִיךְ מַלְכוּתֵהּ
בְּחַיֵּיכוֹן וּבְיוֹמֵיכוֹן וּבְחַיֵּי דְכָל בֵּית יִשְׂרָאֵל
בַּעֲגָלָא וּבִזְמַן קָרִיב
וְאִמְרוּ אָמֵן. (קהל: אָמֵן)

קהל ואבל: יְהֵא שְׁמֵהּ רַבָּא מְבָרַךְ לְעָלַם וּלְעָלְמֵי עָלְמַיָּא.

אבל: יִתְבָּרַךְ וְיִשְׁתַּבַּח וְיִתְפָּאַר וְיִתְרוֹמַם וְיִתְנַשֵּׂא
וְיִתְהַדָּר וְיִתְעַלֶּה וְיִתְהַלָּל
שְׁמֵהּ דְּקֻדְשָׁא בְּרִיךְ הוּא (קהל: בְּרִיךְ הוּא)
לְעֵלָּא לְעֵלָּא מִכָּל בִּרְכָתָא וְשִׁירָתָא, תֻּשְׁבְּחָתָא וְנֶחֱמָתָא
דַּאֲמִירָן בְּעָלְמָא
וְאִמְרוּ אָמֵן. (קהל: אָמֵן)

יְהֵא שְׁלָמָא רַבָּא מִן שְׁמַיָּא
וְחַיִּים, עָלֵינוּ וְעַל כָּל יִשְׂרָאֵל
וְאִמְרוּ אָמֵן. (קהל: אָמֵן)

Bow, take three steps back, as if taking leave of the Divine Presence, then bow, first left, then right, then center, while saying:

עֹשֶׂה הַשָּׁלוֹם בִּמְרוֹמָיו
הוּא יַעֲשֶׂה שָׁלוֹם עָלֵינוּ וְעַל כָּל יִשְׂרָאֵל
וְאִמְרוּ אָמֵן. (קהל: אָמֵן)

The following poems, on this page and the next, both from the Middle Ages, are summary statements of Jewish faith, orienting us to the spiritual contours of the world that we actualize in the mind by the act of prayer.

Lord of the universe,
who reigned before the birth of any thing –

When by His will all things were made
then was His name proclaimed King.

And when all things shall cease to be
He alone will reign in awe.

He was, He is, and He shall be
glorious for evermore.

He is One, there is none else,
alone, unique, beyond compare;

Without beginning, without end,
His might, His rule are everywhere.

He is my God; my Redeemer lives.
He is the Rock on whom I rely –

My banner and my safe retreat,
my cup, my portion when I cry.

Into His hand my soul I place,
when I awake and when I sleep.

The Lord is with me, I shall not fear;
body and soul from harm will He keep.

The following poems, on this page and the next, both from the Middle Ages, are summary statements of Jewish faith, orienting us to the spiritual contours of the world that we actualize in the mind by the act of prayer.

אֲדוֹן עוֹלָם

אֲשֶׁר מָלַךְ בְּטֶרֶם כָּל־יְצִיר נִבְרָא.
לְעֵת נַעֲשָׂה בְחֶפְצוֹ כֹּל אֲזַי מֶלֶךְ שְׁמוֹ נִקְרָא.
וְאַחֲרֵי כִּכְלוֹת הַכֹּל לְבַדּוֹ יִמְלֹךְ נוֹרָא.
וְהוּא הָיָה וְהוּא הֹוֶה וְהוּא יִהְיֶה בְּתִפְאָרָה.
וְהוּא אֶחָד וְאֵין שֵׁנִי לְהַמְשִׁיל לוֹ לְהַחְבִּירָה.
בְּלִי רֵאשִׁית בְּלִי תַכְלִית וְלוֹ הָעֹז וְהַמִּשְׂרָה.
וְהוּא אֵלִי וְחַי גּוֹאֲלִי וְצוּר חֶבְלִי בְּעֵת צָרָה.
וְהוּא נִסִּי וּמָנוֹס לִי מְנָת כּוֹסִי בְּיוֹם אֶקְרָא.
בְּיָדוֹ אַפְקִיד רוּחִי בְּעֵת אִישַׁן וְאָעִירָה.
וְעִם רוּחִי גְּוִיָּתִי יהוה לִי וְלֹא אִירָא.

GREAT

is the living God and praised.
He exists, and His existence is beyond time.

He is One, and there is no unity like His.
Unfathomable, His Oneness is infinite.

He has neither bodily form nor substance;
His holiness is beyond compare.

He preceded all that was created.
He was first: there was no beginning to His beginning.

Behold He is Master of the Universe; and every creature
shows His greatness and majesty.

The rich flow of His prophecy He gave
to His treasured people in whom He gloried.

Never in Israel has there arisen another like Moses,
a prophet who beheld God's image.

God gave His people a Torah of truth
by the hand of His prophet, most faithful of His House.

God will not alter or change His law
for any other, for eternity.

He sees and knows our secret thoughts;
as soon as something is begun, He foresees its end.

He rewards people with loving-kindness according to their deeds;
He punishes the wicked according to his wickedness.

At the end of days He will send our Messiah
to redeem those who await His final salvation.

God will revive the dead in His great loving-kindness.
Blessed for evermore is His glorious name!

יִגְדַּל

אֱלֹהִים חַי וְיִשְׁתַּבַּח, נִמְצָא וְאֵין עֵת אֶל מְצִיאוּתוֹ.

אֶחָד וְאֵין יָחִיד כְּיִחוּדוֹ, נֶעְלָם וְגַם אֵין סוֹף לְאַחְדוּתוֹ.

אֵין לוֹ דְּמוּת הַגּוּף וְאֵינוֹ גוּף, לֹא נַעֲרֹךְ אֵלָיו קְדֻשָּׁתוֹ.

קַדְמוֹן לְכָל דָּבָר אֲשֶׁר נִבְרָא, רִאשׁוֹן וְאֵין רֵאשִׁית לְרֵאשִׁיתוֹ.

הִנּוֹ אֲדוֹן עוֹלָם, וְכָל נוֹצָר יוֹרֶה גְדֻלָּתוֹ וּמַלְכוּתוֹ.

שֶׁפַע נְבוּאָתוֹ נְתָנוֹ אֶל־אַנְשֵׁי סְגֻלָּתוֹ וְתִפְאַרְתּוֹ.

לֹא קָם בְּיִשְׂרָאֵל כְּמֹשֶׁה עוֹד נָבִיא וּמַבִּיט אֶת תְּמוּנָתוֹ.

תּוֹרַת אֱמֶת נָתַן לְעַמּוֹ אֵל עַל יַד נְבִיאוֹ נֶאֱמַן בֵּיתוֹ.

לֹא יַחֲלִיף הָאֵל וְלֹא יָמִיר דָּתוֹ לְעוֹלָמִים לְזוּלָתוֹ.

צוֹפֶה וְיוֹדֵעַ סְתָרֵינוּ, מַבִּיט לְסוֹף דָּבָר בְּקַדְמָתוֹ.

גּוֹמֵל לְאִישׁ חֶסֶד כְּמִפְעָלוֹ, נוֹתֵן לְרָשָׁע רָע כְּרִשְׁעָתוֹ.

יִשְׁלַח לְקֵץ יָמִין מְשִׁיחֵנוּ לִפְדּוֹת מְחַכֵּי קֵץ יְשׁוּעָתוֹ.

מֵתִים יְחַיֶּה אֵל בְּרֹב חַסְדּוֹ, בָּרוּךְ עֲדֵי עַד שֵׁם תְּהִלָּתוֹ.

MORNING BLESSINGS

The following blessings are said aloud by the Leader, but each individual should say them quietly as well. It is our custom to say them standing.

בָּרוּךְ Blessed are You, LORD our God, King of the Universe,
who gives the heart understanding
to distinguish day from night.

Blessed are You, LORD our God, King of the Universe,
who has not made me a heathen.

Blessed are You, LORD our God, King of the Universe,
who has not made me a slave.

Blessed are You, LORD our God, King of the Universe,
men: who has not made me a woman.
women: who has made me according to His will.

Blessed are You, LORD our God, King of the Universe,
who gives sight to the blind.

Blessed are You, LORD our God, King of the Universe,
who clothes the naked.

Blessed are You, LORD our God, King of the Universe,
who sets captives free.

Blessed are You, LORD our God, King of the Universe,
who raises those bowed down.

---

understanding begins in the ability to make distinctions, refers to the first distinction mentioned in the Torah, when God divided darkness from light, creating night and day.

שֶׁלֹּא עָשַׂנִי גּוֹי...עָבֶד *Who has not made me a heathen… a slave.* We each have our part to play in the divine economy. We thank God for ours, for the privilege of being part of "a kingdom of priests and a holy nation."

פּוֹקֵחַ עִוְרִים *Gives sight to the blind… etc.* A series of blessings originally said at home, later made part of the synagogue service. They were initially said to accompany the various actions involved in waking and getting up – opening our eyes, putting on clothes, stretching our limbs, setting foot on the ground and so on. Descartes said: I *think* therefore I am. A Jew says: I *thank* therefore I am. To stand consciously in the presence of God involves an attitude of gratitude.

ברכות השחר

The following blessings are said aloud by the שליח ציבור*, but each individual should say them quietly as well. It is our custom to say them standing.*

בָּרוּךְ אַתָּה יהוה אֱלֹהֵינוּ מֶלֶךְ הָעוֹלָם
אֲשֶׁר נָתַן לַשֶּׂכְוִי בִינָה
לְהַבְחִין בֵּין יוֹם וּבֵין לָיְלָה.
בָּרוּךְ אַתָּה יהוה אֱלֹהֵינוּ מֶלֶךְ הָעוֹלָם
שֶׁלֹּא עָשַׂנִי גּוֹי.
בָּרוּךְ אַתָּה יהוה אֱלֹהֵינוּ מֶלֶךְ הָעוֹלָם
שֶׁלֹּא עָשַׂנִי עָבֶד.
בָּרוּךְ אַתָּה יהוה אֱלֹהֵינוּ מֶלֶךְ הָעוֹלָם
men שֶׁלֹּא עָשַׂנִי אִשָּׁה. / *women* שֶׁעָשַׂנִי כִּרְצוֹנוֹ.
בָּרוּךְ אַתָּה יהוה אֱלֹהֵינוּ מֶלֶךְ הָעוֹלָם
פּוֹקֵחַ עִוְרִים.
בָּרוּךְ אַתָּה יהוה אֱלֹהֵינוּ מֶלֶךְ הָעוֹלָם
מַלְבִּישׁ עֲרֻמִּים.
בָּרוּךְ אַתָּה יהוה אֱלֹהֵינוּ מֶלֶךְ הָעוֹלָם
מַתִּיר אֲסוּרִים.
בָּרוּךְ אַתָּה יהוה אֱלֹהֵינוּ מֶלֶךְ הָעוֹלָם
זוֹקֵף כְּפוּפִים.

MORNING BLESSINGS

A series of thanksgivings, designed to open our eyes to the wonders of the world and of existence. The religious sense is not so much a matter of seeing new things but of seeing things anew.

אֲשֶׁר נָתַן לַשֶּׂכְוִי בִינָה *Who gives the heart understanding.* The translation follows the view of Rabbeinu Asher (Rosh). Rashi and Abudarham translate it as "Who gives the cockerel understanding." The blessing, which tells us that

Blessed are You, Lord our God, King of the Universe,
who spreads the earth above the waters.
Blessed are You, Lord our God, King of the Universe,
who has provided me with all I need.
Blessed are You, Lord our God, King of the Universe,
who makes firm the steps of man.
Blessed are You, Lord our God, King of the Universe,
who girds Israel with strength.
Blessed are You, Lord our God, King of the Universe,
who crowns Israel with glory.
Blessed are You, Lord our God, King of the Universe,
who gives strength to the weary.

בָּרוּךְ Blessed are You, Lord our God, King of the Universe, who removes sleep from my eyes and slumber from my eyelids. And may it be Your will, Lord our God and God of our ancestors, to accustom us to Your Torah, and make us attached to Your commandments. Lead us not into error, transgression, iniquity, temptation or disgrace. Do not let the evil instinct dominate us. Keep us far from a bad man and a bad companion. Help us attach ourselves to the good instinct and to good deeds and bend our instincts to be subservient to You. Grant us, this day and every day, grace, loving-kindness and compassion in Your eyes and in the eyes of all who see us, and bestow loving-kindness upon us. Blessed are You, Lord, who bestows loving-kindness on His people Israel.

יְהִי רָצוֹן May it be Your will, Lord my God and God of my ancestors, to save me today and every day, from the arrogant and from arrogance itself, from a bad man, a bad friend, a bad neighbor, a bad mishap, a destructive adversary, a harsh trial and a harsh opponent, whether or not he is a son of the covenant. *Berakhot 16b*

יְהִי רָצוֹן *May it be Your will.* We ask for God's help in leading a holy and moral life. We need that help. We have primal instincts that can lead us to act badly if we do so without deliberation and foresight, in the heat of the moment. We are also social animals. Therefore we are influenced by our environment. So we pray to be protected from bad social influences: not only from bad companions but also, today, the media and the ambient culture.

בָּרוּךְ אַתָּה יהוה אֱלֹהֵינוּ מֶלֶךְ הָעוֹלָם
רוֹקַע הָאָרֶץ עַל הַמָּיִם.
בָּרוּךְ אַתָּה יהוה אֱלֹהֵינוּ מֶלֶךְ הָעוֹלָם
שֶׁעָשָׂה לִי כָּל צָרְכִּי.
בָּרוּךְ אַתָּה יהוה אֱלֹהֵינוּ מֶלֶךְ הָעוֹלָם
הַמֵּכִין מִצְעֲדֵי גָבֶר.
בָּרוּךְ אַתָּה יהוה אֱלֹהֵינוּ מֶלֶךְ הָעוֹלָם
אוֹזֵר יִשְׂרָאֵל בִּגְבוּרָה.
בָּרוּךְ אַתָּה יהוה אֱלֹהֵינוּ מֶלֶךְ הָעוֹלָם
עוֹטֵר יִשְׂרָאֵל בְּתִפְאָרָה.
בָּרוּךְ אַתָּה יהוה אֱלֹהֵינוּ מֶלֶךְ הָעוֹלָם
הַנּוֹתֵן לַיָּעֵף כֹּחַ.

בָּרוּךְ אַתָּה יהוה אֱלֹהֵינוּ מֶלֶךְ הָעוֹלָם, הַמַּעֲבִיר שֵׁנָה מֵעֵינַי וּתְנוּמָה מֵעַפְעַפָּי, וִיהִי רָצוֹן מִלְּפָנֶיךָ יהוה אֱלֹהֵינוּ וֵאלֹהֵי אֲבוֹתֵינוּ שֶׁתַּרְגִּילֵנוּ בְּתוֹרָתֶךָ, וְדַבְּקֵנוּ בְּמִצְוֹתֶיךָ, וְאַל תְּבִיאֵנוּ לֹא לִידֵי חֵטְא, וְלֹא לִידֵי עֲבֵרָה וְעָוֹן, וְלֹא לִידֵי נִסָּיוֹן וְלֹא לִידֵי בִזָּיוֹן, וְאַל תַּשְׁלֶט בָּנוּ יֵצֶר הָרָע, וְהַרְחִיקֵנוּ מֵאָדָם רָע וּמֵחָבֵר רָע, וְדַבְּקֵנוּ בְּיֵצֶר הַטּוֹב וּבְמַעֲשִׂים טוֹבִים, וְכֹף אֶת יִצְרֵנוּ לְהִשְׁתַּעְבֶּד לָךְ, וּתְנֵנוּ הַיּוֹם וּבְכָל יוֹם לְחֵן וּלְחֶסֶד וּלְרַחֲמִים, בְּעֵינֶיךָ, וּבְעֵינֵי כָל רוֹאֵינוּ, וְתִגְמְלֵנוּ חֲסָדִים טוֹבִים, בָּרוּךְ אַתָּה יהוה, גּוֹמֵל חֲסָדִים טוֹבִים לְעַמּוֹ יִשְׂרָאֵל.

יְהִי רָצוֹן מִלְּפָנֶיךָ יהוה אֱלֹהַי וֵאלֹהֵי אֲבוֹתַי, שֶׁתַּצִּילֵנִי הַיּוֹם וּבְכָל יוֹם ברכות טז:
מֵעַזֵּי פָנִים וּמֵעַזּוּת פָּנִים, מֵאָדָם רָע, וּמֵחָבֵר רָע, וּמִשָּׁכֵן רָע, וּמִפֶּגַע רָע, וּמִשָּׂטָן הַמַּשְׁחִית, מִדִּין קָשֶׁה, וּמִבַּעַל דִּין קָשֶׁה בֵּין שֶׁהוּא בֶן בְּרִית וּבֵין שֶׁאֵינוֹ בֶן בְּרִית.

THE BINDING OF ISAAC

On the basis of Jewish mystical tradition, some have the custom of saying daily the biblical passage recounting the Binding of Isaac, the supreme trial of faith in which Abraham demonstrated his love of God above all other loves. Most omit the introductory and concluding prayers, "Our God and God of our ancestors" and "Master of the Universe." Others continue with "A person should" on page 482.

Our God and God of our ancestors, remember us with a favorable memory, and recall us with a remembrance of salvation and compassion from the highest of high heavens. Remember, LORD our God, on our behalf, the love of the ancients, Abraham, Isaac and Yisrael Your servants; the covenant, the loving-kindness, and the oath You swore to Abraham our father on Mount Moriah, and the Binding, when he bound Isaac his son on the altar, as is written in Your Torah:

It happened after these things that God tested Abraham. He said to him, "Abraham!" "Here I am," he replied. He said, "Take your son, your only son, Isaac, whom you love, and go to the land of Moriah and offer him there as a burnt-offering on one of the mountains which I shall say to you." Early the next morning Abraham rose and saddled his donkey and took his two lads with him, and Isaac his son, and he cut wood for the burnt-offering, and he set out for the place of which God had told him. On the third day Abraham looked up and saw the place from afar. Abraham said to his lads, "Stay here with the donkey while I and the boy go on ahead. We will worship and we will return to you." Abraham took the wood for the burnt-offering and placed it on Isaac his son, and he took in his hand the fire and the knife, and the two of them went together. Isaac said to Abraham his father, "Father?" and he said "Here I am, my son." And he said, "Here are the fire and the wood, but where is the sheep for *Gen. 22*

Isaac's children through whom the covenant would continue and become eternal (Gen. 17:19). On the other, God had now commanded him to take Isaac and offer him as a sacrifice (Gen. 22:3). It was Abraham's willingness, not merely to sacrifice that which was most precious to him, but to live with the contradiction, in the faith that God would resolve it in the course of time, that made him the hero of faith and its role model through the centuries.

פרשת העקדה

On the basis of Jewish mystical tradition, some have the custom of saying daily the biblical passage recounting the Binding of Isaac, the supreme trial of faith in which Abraham demonstrated his love of God above all other loves. Most omit the introductory and concluding prayers, אֱלֹהֵינוּ וֵאלֹהֵי אֲבוֹתֵינוּ *and* רִבּוֹנוֹ שֶׁל עוֹלָם. *Others continue with* לְעוֹלָם יְהֵא אָדָם *on page 483.*

אֱלֹהֵינוּ וֵאלֹהֵי אֲבוֹתֵינוּ, זׇכְרֵנוּ בְּזִכְרוֹן טוֹב לְפָנֶיךָ, וּפׇקְדֵנוּ בִּפְקֻדַּת יְשׁוּעָה וְרַחֲמִים מִשְּׁמֵי שְׁמֵי קֶדֶם, וּזְכׇר לָנוּ יהוה אֱלֹהֵינוּ, אַהֲבַת הַקַּדְמוֹנִים אַבְרָהָם יִצְחָק וְיִשְׂרָאֵל עֲבָדֶיךָ, אֶת הַבְּרִית וְאֶת הַחֶסֶד וְאֶת הַשְּׁבוּעָה שֶׁנִּשְׁבַּעְתָּ לְאַבְרָהָם אָבִינוּ בְּהַר הַמּוֹרִיָּה, וְאֶת הָעֲקֵדָה שֶׁעָקַד אֶת יִצְחָק בְּנוֹ עַל גַּבֵּי הַמִּזְבֵּחַ, כַּכָּתוּב בְּתוֹרָתֶךָ:

בראשית כב וַיְהִי אַחַר הַדְּבָרִים הָאֵלֶּה, וְהָאֱלֹהִים נִסָּה אֶת־אַבְרָהָם, וַיֹּאמֶר אֵלָיו אַבְרָהָם, וַיֹּאמֶר הִנֵּנִי: וַיֹּאמֶר קַח־נָא אֶת־בִּנְךָ אֶת־יְחִידְךָ אֲשֶׁר־אָהַבְתָּ, אֶת־יִצְחָק, וְלֶךְ־לְךָ אֶל־אֶרֶץ הַמֹּרִיָּה, וְהַעֲלֵהוּ שָׁם לְעֹלָה עַל אַחַד הֶהָרִים אֲשֶׁר אֹמַר אֵלֶיךָ: וַיַּשְׁכֵּם אַבְרָהָם בַּבֹּקֶר, וַיַּחֲבֹשׁ אֶת־חֲמֹרוֹ, וַיִּקַּח אֶת־שְׁנֵי נְעָרָיו אִתּוֹ וְאֵת יִצְחָק בְּנוֹ, וַיְבַקַּע עֲצֵי עֹלָה, וַיָּקָם וַיֵּלֶךְ אֶל־הַמָּקוֹם אֲשֶׁר־אָמַר־לוֹ הָאֱלֹהִים: בַּיּוֹם הַשְּׁלִישִׁי וַיִּשָּׂא אַבְרָהָם אֶת־עֵינָיו וַיַּרְא אֶת־הַמָּקוֹם מֵרָחֹק: וַיֹּאמֶר אַבְרָהָם אֶל־נְעָרָיו, שְׁבוּ־לָכֶם פֹּה עִם־הַחֲמוֹר, וַאֲנִי וְהַנַּעַר נֵלְכָה עַד־כֹּה, וְנִשְׁתַּחֲוֶה וְנָשׁוּבָה אֲלֵיכֶם: וַיִּקַּח אַבְרָהָם אֶת־עֲצֵי הָעֹלָה וַיָּשֶׂם עַל־יִצְחָק בְּנוֹ, וַיִּקַּח בְּיָדוֹ אֶת־הָאֵשׁ וְאֶת־הַמַּאֲכֶלֶת, וַיֵּלְכוּ שְׁנֵיהֶם יַחְדָּו: וַיֹּאמֶר יִצְחָק אֶל־אַבְרָהָם אָבִיו, וַיֹּאמֶר אָבִי, וַיֹּאמֶר הִנֶּנִּי בְנִי, וַיֹּאמֶר, הִנֵּה הָאֵשׁ וְהָעֵצִים, וְאַיֵּה הַשֶּׂה לְעֹלָה:

THE BINDING OF ISAAC

This passage, said daily by those whose liturgy follows the Jewish mystical tradition, evokes the supreme moment of sacrifice by the grandfather of Jewish faith, Abraham. Abraham found himself caught within a seeming contradiction. On the one hand God had told him that it would be Isaac and

the burnt-offering?" Abraham said, "God will see to the sheep for the burnt-offering, my son." And the two of them went together. They came to the place God had told him about, and Abraham built there an altar and arranged the wood and bound Isaac his son and laid him on the altar on top of the wood. He reached out his hand and took the knife to slay his son. Then an angel of the Lord called out to him from heaven, "Abraham! Abraham!" He said, "Here I am." He said, "Do not reach out your hand against the boy; do not do anything to him, for now I know that you fear God, because you have not held back your son, your only son, from Me." Abraham looked up and there he saw a ram caught in a thicket by its horns, and Abraham went and took the ram and offered it as a burnt-offering instead of his son. Abraham called that place "The Lord will see," as is said to this day, "On the mountain of the Lord He will be seen." The angel of the Lord called to Abraham a second time from heaven, and said, "By Myself I swear, declares the Lord, that because you have done this and have not held back your son, your only son, I will greatly bless you and greatly multiply your descendants, as the stars of heaven and the sand of the seashore, and your descendants shall take possession of the gates of their enemies. Through your descendants, all the nations of the earth will be blessed, because you have heeded My voice." Then Abraham returned to his lads, and they rose and went together to Beersheba, and Abraham stayed in Beersheba.

Most omit:

Master of the Universe, just as Abraham our father suppressed his compassion to do Your will wholeheartedly, so may Your compassion suppress Your anger from us and may Your compassion prevail over Your other attributes. Deal with us, Lord our God, with the attributes of loving-kindness and compassion, and in Your great goodness may Your anger be turned away from Your people, Your city, Your land and Your inheritance. Fulfill in us, Lord our God, the promise You made in Your Torah through the hand of Moses Your servant, as it is said: "I will remember My covenant with Jacob, and also My covenant with Isaac, and also My covenant with Abraham I will remember, and the land I will remember." *Lev. 26*

וַיֹּאמֶר אַבְרָהָם, אֱלֹהִים יִרְאֶה־לּוֹ הַשֶּׂה לְעֹלָה, בְּנִי, וַיֵּלְכוּ שְׁנֵיהֶם
יַחְדָּו: וַיָּבֹאוּ אֶל־הַמָּקוֹם אֲשֶׁר אָמַר־לוֹ הָאֱלֹהִים, וַיִּבֶן שָׁם אַבְרָהָם
אֶת־הַמִּזְבֵּחַ וַיַּעֲרֹךְ אֶת־הָעֵצִים, וַיַּעֲקֹד אֶת־יִצְחָק בְּנוֹ, וַיָּשֶׂם אֹתוֹ
עַל־הַמִּזְבֵּחַ מִמַּעַל לָעֵצִים: וַיִּשְׁלַח אַבְרָהָם אֶת־יָדוֹ, וַיִּקַּח אֶת־
הַמַּאֲכֶלֶת, לִשְׁחֹט אֶת־בְּנוֹ: וַיִּקְרָא אֵלָיו מַלְאַךְ יהוה מִן־הַשָּׁמַיִם,
וַיֹּאמֶר אַבְרָהָם אַבְרָהָם, וַיֹּאמֶר הִנֵּנִי: וַיֹּאמֶר אַל־תִּשְׁלַח יָדְךָ אֶל־
הַנַּעַר, וְאַל־תַּעַשׂ לוֹ מְאוּמָה, כִּי עַתָּה יָדַעְתִּי כִּי־יְרֵא אֱלֹהִים אַתָּה,
וְלֹא חָשַׂכְתָּ אֶת־בִּנְךָ אֶת־יְחִידְךָ מִמֶּנִּי: וַיִּשָּׂא אַבְרָהָם אֶת־עֵינָיו,
וַיַּרְא וְהִנֵּה־אַיִל, אַחַר נֶאֱחַז בַּסְּבַךְ בְּקַרְנָיו, וַיֵּלֶךְ אַבְרָהָם וַיִּקַּח אֶת־
הָאַיִל, וַיַּעֲלֵהוּ לְעֹלָה תַּחַת בְּנוֹ: וַיִּקְרָא אַבְרָהָם שֵׁם־הַמָּקוֹם הַהוּא
יהוה יִרְאֶה, אֲשֶׁר יֵאָמֵר הַיּוֹם בְּהַר יהוה יֵרָאֶה: וַיִּקְרָא מַלְאַךְ יהוה
אֶל־אַבְרָהָם שֵׁנִית מִן־הַשָּׁמָיִם: וַיֹּאמֶר, בִּי נִשְׁבַּעְתִּי נְאֻם־יהוה, כִּי
יַעַן אֲשֶׁר עָשִׂיתָ אֶת־הַדָּבָר הַזֶּה, וְלֹא חָשַׂכְתָּ אֶת־בִּנְךָ אֶת־יְחִידֶךָ:
כִּי־בָרֵךְ אֲבָרֶכְךָ, וְהַרְבָּה אַרְבֶּה אֶת־זַרְעֲךָ כְּכוֹכְבֵי הַשָּׁמַיִם, וְכַחוֹל
אֲשֶׁר עַל־שְׂפַת הַיָּם, וְיִרַשׁ זַרְעֲךָ אֵת שַׁעַר אֹיְבָיו: וְהִתְבָּרְכוּ בְזַרְעֲךָ
כֹּל גּוֹיֵי הָאָרֶץ, עֵקֶב אֲשֶׁר שָׁמַעְתָּ בְּקֹלִי: וַיָּשָׁב אַבְרָהָם אֶל־נְעָרָיו,
וַיָּקֻמוּ וַיֵּלְכוּ יַחְדָּו אֶל־בְּאֵר שָׁבַע, וַיֵּשֶׁב אַבְרָהָם בִּבְאֵר שָׁבַע:

Most omit:

רִבּוֹנוֹ שֶׁל עוֹלָם, כְּמוֹ שֶׁכָּבַשׁ אַבְרָהָם אָבִינוּ אֶת רַחֲמָיו לַעֲשׂוֹת רְצוֹנְךָ
בְּלֵבָב שָׁלֵם, כֵּן יִכְבְּשׁוּ רַחֲמֶיךָ אֶת כַּעַסְךָ מֵעָלֵינוּ וְיִגֹּלּוּ רַחֲמֶיךָ עַל
מִדּוֹתֶיךָ. וְתִתְנַהֵג עִמָּנוּ יהוה אֱלֹהֵינוּ בְּמִדַּת הַחֶסֶד וּבְמִדַּת הָרַחֲמִים,
וּבְטוּבְךָ הַגָּדוֹל יָשׁוּב חֲרוֹן אַפְּךָ מֵעַמְּךָ וּמֵעִירְךָ וּמֵאַרְצְךָ וּמִנַּחֲלָתֶךָ. וְקַיֶּם
לָנוּ יהוה אֱלֹהֵינוּ אֶת הַדָּבָר שֶׁהִבְטַחְתָּנוּ בְּתוֹרָתֶךָ עַל יְדֵי מֹשֶׁה עַבְדֶּךָ,
כָּאָמוּר: וְזָכַרְתִּי אֶת־בְּרִיתִי יַעֲקוֹב וְאַף אֶת־בְּרִיתִי יִצְחָק, וְאַף אֶת־בְּרִיתִי ויקרא כו
אַבְרָהָם אֶזְכֹּר, וְהָאָרֶץ אֶזְכֹּר:

ACCEPTING THE SOVEREIGNTY OF HEAVEN

לְעוֹלָם A person should always be God-fearing, privately and publicly, acknowledging the truth and speaking it in his heart. He should rise early and say: *Tanna DeVei Eliyahu, ch. 21*

Master of all worlds,
not because of our righteousness *Dan. 9*
do we lay our pleas before You,
but because of Your great compassion.

What are we? What are our lives?
What is our loving-kindness? What is our righteousness?
What is our salvation? What is our strength?
What is our might? What shall we say before You,
LORD our God and God of our ancestors?
Are not all the mighty like nothing before You,
the men of renown as if they had never been,
the wise as if they know nothing,
and the understanding as if they lack intelligence?
For their many works are in vain,
and the days of their lives like a fleeting breath before You.
The pre-eminence of man over the animals is nothing, *Eccl. 3*
for all is but a fleeting breath.

---

could not be said at the normal time. The final blessing, "Who sanctifies His name among the multitudes," refers to the martyrdom of those who went to their deaths rather than renounce their faith. Martyrdom is called *Kiddush HaShem,* "sanctifying [God's] name."

רִבּוֹן כָּל הָעוֹלָמִים *Master of all worlds.* This passage expresses the paradox of the human condition in the presence of God. We know how small we are and how brief our lives.

הֶבֶל *Fleeting breath.* The Hebrew word *hevel* – the key word of the opening chapters of Ecclesiastes, from which this line is taken – has been translated as "vain, meaningless, empty, futile." However, it literally means "a short breath."

קבלת עול מלכות שמים

לְעוֹלָם יְהֵא אָדָם יְרֵא שָׁמַיִם בְּסֵתֶר וּבְגָלוּי
וּמוֹדֶה עַל הָאֱמֶת, וְדוֹבֵר אֱמֶת בִּלְבָבוֹ
וְיַשְׁכֵּם וְיֹאמַר
רִבּוֹן כָּל הָעוֹלָמִים
לֹא עַל־צִדְקוֹתֵינוּ אֲנַחְנוּ מַפִּילִים תַּחֲנוּנֵינוּ לְפָנֶיךָ
כִּי עַל־רַחֲמֶיךָ הָרַבִּים:

תנא דבי אליהו, פרק כא
דניאל ט

מָה אָנוּ, מֶה חַיֵּינוּ, מֶה חַסְדֵּנוּ, מַה צִּדְקוֹתֵינוּ
מַה יְּשׁוּעָתֵנוּ, מַה כֹּחֵנוּ, מַה גְּבוּרָתֵנוּ
מַה נֹּאמַר לְפָנֶיךָ, יהוה אֱלֹהֵינוּ וֵאלֹהֵי אֲבוֹתֵינוּ
הֲלֹא כָּל הַגִּבּוֹרִים כְּאַיִן לְפָנֶיךָ
וְאַנְשֵׁי הַשֵּׁם כְּלֹא הָיוּ
וַחֲכָמִים כִּבְלִי מַדָּע, וּנְבוֹנִים כִּבְלִי הַשְׂכֵּל
כִּי רֹב מַעֲשֵׂיהֶם תֹּהוּ, וִימֵי חַיֵּיהֶם הֶבֶל לְפָנֶיךָ
וּמוֹתַר הָאָדָם מִן־הַבְּהֵמָה אָיִן
כִּי הַכֹּל הָבֶל:

קהלת ג

ACCEPTING THE SOVEREIGNTY OF HEAVEN

לְעוֹלָם יְהֵא אָדָם *A person should always.* This whole section until "Who sanctifies His name among the multitudes" appears in the tenth-century Midrash, *Tanna DeVei Eliyahu* (ch. 21). Some believe that it dates from a period of persecution under the Persian ruler Yazdegerd II who, in 456 CE, forbade the observance of Shabbat and the reading of the Torah. Jews continued to practice their faith in secret, saying prayers at times and in ways that would not be detected by their persecutors. This explains the reference to fearing God "privately" and "speaking truth in the heart" (that is, the secret practice of Judaism) and the recitation here of the first lines of the Shema, which

אֲבָל Yet we are Your people, the children of Your covenant,
the children of Abraham, Your beloved,
to whom You made a promise on Mount Moriah;
the offspring of Isaac his only one who was bound on the altar;
the congregation of Jacob Your firstborn son
whom – because of the love with which You loved him
and the joy with which You rejoiced in him –
You called Yisrael and Yeshurun.

לְפִיכָךְ Therefore it is our duty
to thank You, and to praise, glorify, bless, sanctify
and give praise and thanks to Your name.
Happy are we, how good is our portion,
how lovely our fate, how beautiful our heritage.

▸ Happy are we who, early and late, evening and morning,
say twice each day –

Listen, Israel: the LORD is our God, the LORD is One. *Deut. 6*

Aloud: Blessed be the name of His glorious kingdom
for ever and all time.

Some congregations say the entire first paragraph of the Shema (below) at this point. If there is a concern that the Shema will not be recited within the prescribed time, then all three paragraphs should be said. See law 49.

Love the LORD your God with all your heart, with all your soul, and with all your might. These words which I command you today shall be on your heart. Teach them repeatedly to your children, speaking of them when you sit at home and when you travel on the way, when you lie down and when you rise. Bind them as a sign on your hand, and they shall be an emblem between your eyes. Write them on the doorposts of your house and gates.

---

something momentous, for "we are Your people, the children of Your covenant," descendants of those You singled out to be witnesses to the world of Your existence and majesty.

יַעֲקֹב בִּנְךָ בְּכוֹרֶךָ *Jacob your firstborn son.* Though Jacob was not the biological firstborn of Isaac and Rebecca, God subsequently declared, "My child, My firstborn, Israel" (Ex. 4:22).

אֲבָל אֲנַחְנוּ עַמְּךָ בְּנֵי בְרִיתֶךָ
בְּנֵי אַבְרָהָם אֹהַבְךָ שֶׁנִּשְׁבַּעְתָּ לּוֹ בְּהַר הַמּוֹרִיָּה
זֶרַע יִצְחָק יְחִידוֹ שֶׁנֶּעֱקַד עַל גַּבֵּי הַמִּזְבֵּחַ
עֲדַת יַעֲקֹב בִּנְךָ בְּכוֹרֶךָ
שֶׁמֵּאַהֲבָתְךָ שֶׁאָהַבְתָּ אוֹתוֹ, וּמִשִּׂמְחָתְךָ שֶׁשָּׂמַחְתָּ בּוֹ
קָרָאתָ אֶת שְׁמוֹ יִשְׂרָאֵל וִישֻׁרוּן.

לְפִיכָךְ אֲנַחְנוּ חַיָּבִים
לְהוֹדוֹת לְךָ וּלְשַׁבֵּחֲךָ וּלְפָאֶרְךָ
וּלְבָרֵךְ וּלְקַדֵּשׁ וְלָתֵת שֶׁבַח וְהוֹדָיָה לִשְׁמֶךָ.
אַשְׁרֵינוּ, מַה טּוֹב חֶלְקֵנוּ
וּמַה נָּעִים גּוֹרָלֵנוּ, וּמַה יָּפָה יְרֻשָּׁתֵנוּ.

◂ אַשְׁרֵינוּ, שֶׁאֲנַחְנוּ מַשְׁכִּימִים וּמַעֲרִיבִים עֶרֶב וָבֹקֶר
וְאוֹמְרִים פַּעֲמַיִם בְּכָל יוֹם

שְׁמַע יִשְׂרָאֵל, יהוה אֱלֹהֵינוּ, יהוה אֶחָד: דברים ו

Aloud בָּרוּךְ שֵׁם כְּבוֹד מַלְכוּתוֹ לְעוֹלָם וָעֶד.

Some congregations say the entire first paragraph of the שמע *(below) at this point. If there is a concern that the* שמע *will not be recited within the prescribed time, then all three paragraphs should be said. See law 49.*

וְאָהַבְתָּ אֵת יהוה אֱלֹהֶיךָ, בְּכָל־לְבָבְךָ, וּבְכָל־נַפְשְׁךָ, וּבְכָל־מְאֹדֶךָ: וְהָיוּ הַדְּבָרִים הָאֵלֶּה, אֲשֶׁר אָנֹכִי מְצַוְּךָ הַיּוֹם, עַל־לְבָבֶךָ: וְשִׁנַּנְתָּם לְבָנֶיךָ, וְדִבַּרְתָּ בָּם, בְּשִׁבְתְּךָ בְּבֵיתֶךָ, וּבְלֶכְתְּךָ בַדֶּרֶךְ, וּבְשָׁכְבְּךָ וּבְקוּמֶךָ: וּקְשַׁרְתָּם לְאוֹת עַל־יָדֶךָ וְהָיוּ לְטֹטָפֹת בֵּין עֵינֶיךָ: וּכְתַבְתָּם עַל־מְזֻזוֹת בֵּיתֶךָ וּבִשְׁעָרֶיךָ:

It conveys a sense of the brevity and insubstantiality of life as a physical phenomenon. All that lives soon dies, and is as if it had never been.

אֲבָל *Yet.* Though we may be insignificant as individuals, we are part of

אַתָּה הוּא It was You who existed
before the world was created,
it is You now that the world has been created.
It is You in this world and You in the World to Come.
▸ Sanctify Your name through those who sanctify Your name,
and sanctify Your name throughout Your world.
By Your salvation may our pride be exalted;
raise high our pride.
Blessed are You, LORD,
who sanctifies His name among the multitudes.

אַתָּה הוּא You are the LORD our God
in heaven and on earth,
and in the highest heaven of heavens.
Truly, You are the first
and You are the last,
and besides You there is no god.
Gather those who hope in You
from the four quarters of the earth.
May all mankind recognize and know
that You alone are God
over all the kingdoms on earth.

You made the heavens and the earth,
the sea and all they contain.
Who among all the works of Your hands, above and below,
can tell You what to do?

His covenant; therefore, we may not renounce our religion or identity: "I, God, do not change; so you, children of Jacob, are not destroyed" (Mal. 3:6).

אַתָּה הוּא יהוה אֱלֹהֵינוּ *You are the LORD our God.* A prayer for the end of exile, culminating with the verse from Zephaniah (3:20) which speaks of the ingathering of Jews and of a time when "I will give you renown and praise among all the peoples of the earth." This entire sequence of prayers is eloquent testimony to how Jews sustained faith and hope, dignity and pride, during some of the most prolonged periods of persecution in history.

אַתָּה הוּא עַד שֶׁלֹּא נִבְרָא הָעוֹלָם
אַתָּה הוּא מִשֶּׁנִּבְרָא הָעוֹלָם.
אַתָּה הוּא בָּעוֹלָם הַזֶּה
וְאַתָּה הוּא לָעוֹלָם הַבָּא.
◂ קַדֵּשׁ אֶת שִׁמְךָ עַל מַקְדִּישֵׁי שְׁמֶךָ
וְקַדֵּשׁ אֶת שִׁמְךָ בְּעוֹלָמֶךָ
וּבִישׁוּעָתְךָ תָּרוּם וְתַגְבִּיהַּ קַרְנֵנוּ.
בָּרוּךְ אַתָּה יהוה, הַמְקַדֵּשׁ אֶת שְׁמוֹ בָּרַבִּים.

אַתָּה הוּא יהוה אֱלֹהֵינוּ
בַּשָּׁמַיִם וּבָאָרֶץ
וּבִשְׁמֵי הַשָּׁמַיִם הָעֶלְיוֹנִים.
אֱמֶת, אַתָּה הוּא רִאשׁוֹן
וְאַתָּה הוּא אַחֲרוֹן
וּמִבַּלְעָדֶיךָ אֵין אֱלֹהִים.
קַבֵּץ קֹוֶיךָ מֵאַרְבַּע כַּנְפוֹת הָאָרֶץ.
יַכִּירוּ וְיֵדְעוּ כָּל בָּאֵי עוֹלָם
כִּי אַתָּה הוּא הָאֱלֹהִים לְבַדְּךָ לְכֹל מַמְלְכוֹת הָאָרֶץ.

אַתָּה עָשִׂיתָ אֶת הַשָּׁמַיִם וְאֶת הָאָרֶץ
אֶת הַיָּם וְאֶת כָּל אֲשֶׁר בָּם
וּמִי בְּכָל מַעֲשֵׂי יָדֶיךָ בָּעֶלְיוֹנִים אוֹ בַתַּחְתּוֹנִים
שֶׁיֹּאמַר לְךָ מַה תַּעֲשֶׂה.

אַתָּה הוּא *It was You who existed.* This prayer, with its emphasis on the changelessness of God, may have been incorporated at a time of persecution, expressing the refusal of Jews to abandon their faith. God does not alter or revoke

Heavenly Father,
deal kindly with us for the sake of Your great name
by which we are called,
and fulfill for us, LORD our God,
that which is written:

"At that time I will bring you home, and at that time I will gather you, for I will give you renown and praise among all the peoples of the earth when I bring back your exiles before your eyes, says the LORD." *Zeph. 3*

---

we alone. We are here because someone willed us into being, who wanted us to be, who knows our innermost thoughts, who values us in our uniqueness, whose breath we breathe, and in whose arms we rest; someone in and through whom we are connected to all that is.

That discovery – that we are the image of, the trace left by God – was utterly explosive in its implications. It meant that the key to interpreting the universe is not force or power, but the personal; and the personal is anything but blind. Everything else in the Torah flows from the attempt to make this fact the foundation of a new social order. The question becomes: What relationships and what kind of society honor the dignity of the person – of all persons in their dependence and independence? We redeem the world to the degree that we personalize it, taming the great forces so that they serve rather than dominate humanity. That was and remains a marvelous vision. It changed and still changes the world.

Finding God, our ancestors discovered something new about themselves. Hearing God reaching out to us, they began to understand the significance of human beings reaching out to one another. They began, haltingly at first, to realize that God is not about power but relationship; that religion is not about control but about freedom; and that God is found, less in nature than in society, in the structures we make to honor His presence by honoring His image in other human beings.

This much can never be made redundant by science. For God is dispensable only if humanity is. God is reality with a loving face, the mirror without which we cannot see ourselves.

אָבִינוּ שֶׁבַּשָּׁמַיִם
עֲשֵׂה עִמָּנוּ חֶסֶד
בַּעֲבוּר שִׁמְךָ הַגָּדוֹל שֶׁנִּקְרָא עָלֵינוּ
וְקַיֶּם לָנוּ יהוה אֱלֹהֵינוּ
מַה שֶּׁכָּתוּב:
בָּעֵת הַהִיא אָבִיא אֶתְכֶם, וּבָעֵת קַבְּצִי אֶתְכֶם, צפניה ג
כִּי־אֶתֵּן אֶתְכֶם לְשֵׁם וְלִתְהִלָּה בְּכֹל עַמֵּי הָאָרֶץ,
בְּשׁוּבִי אֶת־שְׁבוּתֵיכֶם לְעֵינֵיכֶם, אָמַר יהוה:

From the dawn of civilization to today, mankind has reflected on its place in the universe. Compared to all there is, each of us is infinitesimally small. We are born, we live, we act, we die. At any given moment our deeds are at best a hand waving in the crowd, a ripple in the ocean, a grain of sand on the human beach. The world long preceded us, and it will survive long after we die. How is our life related to the totality of things? To this, there have always been two answers, fundamentally opposed.

There have been cultures, ancient and modern, that saw the world in terms of vast impersonal forces. For the ancients they were earthquakes, floods, famines, droughts, together with the processes of nature: birth, growth, decline and death. Today, we are more likely to identify those forces with the world economy, international politics, the environment and global media. What is common to them is that they are impersonal. They are indifferent to us, just as a tidal wave is indifferent to what it sweeps away.

Seen in this perspective the forces that govern the world are essentially blind. They are not addressed to us. We may stand in their path; we may step out of the way. But they are unmoved by our existence. They don't relate to us as persons. In such a world, hubris (the idea that we can change things) is punished by nemesis. Human hope is a prelude to tragedy. The best we can aim for is to seize what pleasure comes our way and make ourselves stoically indifferent to our fate. This is a coherent vision, but a bleak one.

In ancient Israel, a different vision was born, one that saw in the cosmos the face of the personal: God who brought the universe into being as parents conceive a child, not blindly but in love. We are not insignificant, nor are

OFFERINGS

The sages held that, in the absence of the Temple, studying the laws of sacrifices is the equivalent of offering them. Hence the following texts. There are different customs as to how many passages are to be said, and one should follow the custom of one's congregation. The minimum requirement is to say the verses relating to The Daily Sacrifice on the next page.

THE BASIN

The LORD spoke to Moses, saying: Make a bronze basin, with its bronze stand for washing, and place it between the Tent of Meeting and the altar, and put water in it. From it, Aaron and his sons are to wash their hands and feet. When they enter the Tent of Meeting, they shall wash with water so that they will not die; likewise when they approach the altar to minister, presenting a fire-offering to the LORD. They must wash their hands and feet so that they will not die. This shall be an everlasting ordinance for Aaron and his descendants throughout their generations. *Ex. 30*

TAKING OF THE ASHES

The LORD spoke to Moses, saying: Instruct Aaron and his sons, saying, This is the law of the burnt-offering. The burnt-offering shall remain on the altar hearth throughout the night until morning, and the altar fire shall be kept burning on it. The priest shall then put on his linen garments, and linen breeches next to his body, and shall remove the ashes of the burnt-offering that the fire has consumed on the altar and place them beside the altar. Then he shall take off these clothes and put on others, and carry the ashes outside the camp to a clean place. The fire on the altar must be kept burning; it must not go out. Each morning the priest shall burn wood on it, and prepare on it the burnt-offering and burn the fat of the peace-offerings. A perpetual fire must be kept burning on the altar; it must not go out. *Lev. 6*

May it be Your will, LORD our God and God of our ancestors, that You have compassion on us and pardon us all our sins, grant atonement for all our iniquities and forgive all our transgressions. May You rebuild the Temple swiftly in our days so that we may offer You the continual-offering that it may atone for us as You have prescribed for us in Your Torah through Moses Your servant, from the mouthpiece of Your glory, as it is said:

---

the laws about sacrifice was a substitute for sacrifice itself (*Ta'anit* 27b). The passage from the Mishna (*Zevaḥim* 5) is also about sacrifices, and was chosen because it does not contain any disagreement between the sages, and thus accords with the rule that one should pray "after a decided halakha," that is, an item of Jewish law about which there is no debate.

סדר הקרבנות

חז״ל held that, in the absence of the Temple, studying the laws of sacrifices is the equivalent of offering them. Hence the following texts. There are different customs as to how many passages are to be said, and one should follow the custom of one's congregation. The minimum requirement is to say the verses relating to the קרבן תמיד *on the next page.*

פרשת הכיור

וַיְדַבֵּר יהוה אֶל־מֹשֶׁה לֵּאמֹר: וְעָשִׂיתָ כִּיּוֹר נְחֹשֶׁת וְכַנּוֹ נְחֹשֶׁת לְרָחְצָה, שמות ל
וְנָתַתָּ אֹתוֹ בֵּין־אֹהֶל מוֹעֵד וּבֵין הַמִּזְבֵּחַ, וְנָתַתָּ שָׁמָּה מָיִם: וְרָחֲצוּ אַהֲרֹן
וּבָנָיו מִמֶּנּוּ אֶת־יְדֵיהֶם וְאֶת־רַגְלֵיהֶם: בְּבֹאָם אֶל־אֹהֶל מוֹעֵד יִרְחֲצוּ־מַיִם,
וְלֹא יָמֻתוּ, אוֹ בְגִשְׁתָּם אֶל־הַמִּזְבֵּחַ לְשָׁרֵת, לְהַקְטִיר אִשֶּׁה לַיהוה: וְרָחֲצוּ
יְדֵיהֶם וְרַגְלֵיהֶם וְלֹא יָמֻתוּ, וְהָיְתָה לָהֶם חָק־עוֹלָם, לוֹ וּלְזַרְעוֹ לְדֹרֹתָם:

פרשת תרומת הדשן

וַיְדַבֵּר יהוה אֶל־מֹשֶׁה לֵּאמֹר: צַו אֶת־אַהֲרֹן וְאֶת־בָּנָיו לֵאמֹר, זֹאת תּוֹרַת ויקרא ו
הָעֹלָה, הִוא הָעֹלָה עַל מוֹקְדָה עַל־הַמִּזְבֵּחַ כָּל־הַלַּיְלָה עַד־הַבֹּקֶר, וְאֵשׁ
הַמִּזְבֵּחַ תּוּקַד בּוֹ: וְלָבַשׁ הַכֹּהֵן מִדּוֹ בַד, וּמִכְנְסֵי־בַד יִלְבַּשׁ עַל־בְּשָׂרוֹ,
וְהֵרִים אֶת־הַדֶּשֶׁן אֲשֶׁר תֹּאכַל הָאֵשׁ אֶת־הָעֹלָה, עַל־הַמִּזְבֵּחַ, וְשָׂמוֹ אֵצֶל
הַמִּזְבֵּחַ: וּפָשַׁט אֶת־בְּגָדָיו, וְלָבַשׁ בְּגָדִים אֲחֵרִים, וְהוֹצִיא אֶת־הַדֶּשֶׁן אֶל־
מִחוּץ לַמַּחֲנֶה, אֶל־מָקוֹם טָהוֹר: וְהָאֵשׁ עַל־הַמִּזְבֵּחַ תּוּקַד־בּוֹ, לֹא תִכְבֶּה,
וּבִעֵר עָלֶיהָ הַכֹּהֵן עֵצִים בַּבֹּקֶר בַּבֹּקֶר, וְעָרַךְ עָלֶיהָ הָעֹלָה, וְהִקְטִיר עָלֶיהָ
חֶלְבֵי הַשְּׁלָמִים: אֵשׁ, תָּמִיד תּוּקַד עַל־הַמִּזְבֵּחַ, לֹא תִכְבֶּה:

יְהִי רָצוֹן מִלְּפָנֶיךָ יהוה אֱלֹהֵינוּ וֵאלֹהֵי אֲבוֹתֵינוּ, שֶׁתְּרַחֵם עָלֵינוּ, וְתִמְחֹל לָנוּ עַל כָּל חַטֹּאתֵינוּ וּתְכַפֵּר לָנוּ עַל כָּל עֲוֹנוֹתֵינוּ וְתִסְלַח לָנוּ עַל כָּל פְּשָׁעֵינוּ, וְתִבְנֶה בֵּית הַמִּקְדָּשׁ בִּמְהֵרָה בְיָמֵינוּ, וְנַקְרִיב לְפָנֶיךָ קָרְבַּן הַתָּמִיד שֶׁיְּכַפֵּר בַּעֲדֵנוּ, כְּמוֹ שֶׁכָּתַבְתָּ עָלֵינוּ בְּתוֹרָתֶךָ עַל יְדֵי מֹשֶׁה עַבְדֶּךָ מִפִּי כְבוֹדֶךָ, כָּאָמוּר

OFFERINGS

There now follows a second cycle of study, with the same structure as the first, with passages from: (1) the Torah, (2) the Mishna, and (3) the Talmud (see below). The passages from the Torah relate to the daily, weekly and monthly sacrifices because, in the absence of the Temple, the sages held that study of

THE DAILY SACRIFICE

וַיְדַבֵּר The Lord said to Moses, "Command the Israelites and tell them: 'Be careful to offer to Me at the appointed time My food-offering consumed by fire, as an aroma pleasing to Me.' Tell them: 'This is the fire-offering you shall offer to the Lord – two lambs a year old without blemish, as a regular burnt-offering each day. Prepare one lamb in the morning and the other toward evening, together with a meal-offering of a tenth of an ephah of fine flour mixed with a quarter of a hin of oil from pressed olives. This is the regular burnt-offering instituted at Mount Sinai as a pleasing aroma, a fire-offering made to the Lord. Its libation is to be a quarter of a hin [of wine] with each lamb, poured in the Sanctuary as a libation of strong drink to the Lord. Prepare the second lamb in the afternoon, along with the same meal-offering and libation as in the morning. This is a fire-offering, an aroma pleasing to the Lord.'" *Num. 28*

וְשָׁחַט He shall slaughter it at the north side of the altar before the Lord, and Aaron's sons the priests shall sprinkle its blood against the altar on all sides. *Lev. 1*

May it be Your will, Lord our God and God of our ancestors,
that this recitation be considered accepted and favored before You
as if we had offered the daily sacrifice at its appointed time and place, according to its laws.

It is You, Lord our God, to whom our ancestors offered fragrant incense when the Temple stood, as You commanded them through Moses Your prophet, as is written in Your Torah:

THE INCENSE

The Lord said to Moses: Take fragrant spices – balsam, onycha, galbanum and pure frankincense, all in equal amounts – and make a fragrant blend of incense, the work of a perfumer, well mixed, pure and holy. Grind it very finely and place it in front of the [Ark of] Testimony in the Tent of Meeting, where I will meet with you. It shall be most holy to you. *Ex. 30*

There are different customs about how many and which passages are to be said. The passages in large type represent the text as it exists in the earliest siddurim, those of Rabbi Amram Gaon and Rabbi Sa'adia Gaon.

פרשת קרבן התמיד

במדבר כח וַיְדַבֵּר יהוה אֶל־מֹשֶׁה לֵּאמֹר: צַו אֶת־בְּנֵי יִשְׂרָאֵל
וְאָמַרְתָּ אֲלֵהֶם, אֶת־קָרְבָּנִי לַחְמִי לְאִשַּׁי, רֵיחַ נִיחֹחִי,
תִּשְׁמְרוּ לְהַקְרִיב לִי בְּמוֹעֲדוֹ: וְאָמַרְתָּ לָהֶם, זֶה הָאִשֶּׁה
אֲשֶׁר תַּקְרִיבוּ לַיהוה, כְּבָשִׂים בְּנֵי־שָׁנָה תְמִימִם שְׁנַיִם
לַיּוֹם, עֹלָה תָמִיד: אֶת־הַכֶּבֶשׂ אֶחָד תַּעֲשֶׂה בַבֹּקֶר, וְאֵת
הַכֶּבֶשׂ הַשֵּׁנִי תַּעֲשֶׂה בֵּין הָעַרְבָּיִם: וַעֲשִׂירִית הָאֵיפָה
סֹלֶת לְמִנְחָה, בְּלוּלָה בְּשֶׁמֶן כָּתִית רְבִיעִת הַהִין: עֹלַת
תָּמִיד, הָעֲשֻׂיָה בְּהַר סִינַי, לְרֵיחַ נִיחֹחַ אִשֶּׁה לַיהוה:
וְנִסְכּוֹ רְבִיעִת הַהִין לַכֶּבֶשׂ הָאֶחָד, בַּקֹּדֶשׁ הַסֵּךְ נֶסֶךְ שֵׁכָר
לַיהוה: וְאֵת הַכֶּבֶשׂ הַשֵּׁנִי תַּעֲשֶׂה בֵּין הָעַרְבָּיִם, כְּמִנְחַת
הַבֹּקֶר וּכְנִסְכּוֹ תַּעֲשֶׂה, אִשֵּׁה רֵיחַ נִיחֹחַ לַיהוה:

ויקרא א וְשָׁחַט אֹתוֹ עַל יֶרֶךְ הַמִּזְבֵּחַ צָפֹנָה לִפְנֵי יהוה, וְזָרְקוּ בְּנֵי
אַהֲרֹן הַכֹּהֲנִים אֶת־דָּמוֹ עַל־הַמִּזְבֵּחַ, סָבִיב:

יְהִי רָצוֹן מִלְּפָנֶיךָ, יהוה אֱלֹהֵינוּ וֵאלֹהֵי אֲבוֹתֵינוּ
שֶׁתְּהֵא אֲמִירָה זוֹ חֲשׁוּבָה וּמְקֻבֶּלֶת וּמְרֻצָּה לְפָנֶיךָ
כְּאִלּוּ הִקְרַבְנוּ קָרְבַּן הַתָּמִיד בְּמוֹעֲדוֹ וּבִמְקוֹמוֹ וּכְהִלְכָתוֹ.

אַתָּה הוּא יהוה אֱלֹהֵינוּ שֶׁהִקְטִירוּ אֲבוֹתֵינוּ לְפָנֶיךָ אֶת קְטֹרֶת הַסַּמִּים בִּזְמַן שֶׁבֵּית הַמִּקְדָּשׁ הָיָה קַיָּם, כַּאֲשֶׁר צִוִּיתָ אוֹתָם עַל יְדֵי מֹשֶׁה נְבִיאֶךָ, כַּכָּתוּב בְּתוֹרָתֶךָ:

פרשת הקטורת

שמות ל וַיֹּאמֶר יהוה אֶל־מֹשֶׁה, קַח־לְךָ סַמִּים נָטָף וּשְׁחֵלֶת וְחֶלְבְּנָה, סַמִּים וּלְבֹנָה
זַכָּה, בַּד בְּבַד יִהְיֶה: וְעָשִׂיתָ אֹתָהּ קְטֹרֶת, רֹקַח מַעֲשֵׂה רוֹקֵחַ, מְמֻלָּח, טָהוֹר
קֹדֶשׁ: וְשָׁחַקְתָּ מִמֶּנָּה הָדֵק, וְנָתַתָּה מִמֶּנָּה לִפְנֵי הָעֵדֻת בְּאֹהֶל מוֹעֵד אֲשֶׁר
אִוָּעֵד לְךָ שָׁמָּה, קֹדֶשׁ קָדָשִׁים תִּהְיֶה לָכֶם:

And it is said:

> Aaron shall burn fragrant incense on the altar every morning when he cleans the lamps. He shall burn incense again when he lights the lamps toward evening so that there will be incense before the LORD at all times, throughout your generations.

The rabbis taught: How was the incense prepared? It weighed 368 manehs, 365 corresponding to the number of days in a solar year, a maneh for each day, half to be offered in the morning and half in the afternoon, and three additional manehs from which the High Priest took two handfuls on Yom Kippur. These were put back into the mortar on the day before Yom Kippur and ground again very thoroughly so as to be extremely fine. The incense contained eleven kinds of spices: balsam, onycha, galbanum and frankincense, each weighing seventy manehs; myrrh, cassia, spikenard and saffron, each weighing sixteen manehs; twelve manehs of costus, three of aromatic bark; nine of cinnamon; nine kabs of Carsina lye; three seahs and three kabs of Cyprus wine. If Cyprus wine was not available, old white wine might be used. A quarter of a kab of Sodom salt, and a minute amount of a smoke-raising herb. Rabbi Nathan the Babylonian says: also a minute amount of Jordan amber. If one added honey to the mixture, he rendered it unfit for sacred use. If he omitted any one of its ingredients, he is guilty of a capital offense. *Keritot 6a*

Rabban Simeon ben Gamliel says: "Balsam" refers to the sap that drips from the balsam tree. The Carsina lye was used for bleaching the onycha to improve it. The Cyprus wine was used to soak the onycha in it to make it pungent. Though urine is suitable for this purpose, it is not brought into the Temple out of respect.

It was taught, Rabbi Nathan says: While it was being ground, another would say, "Grind well, well grind," because the [rhythmic] sound is good for spices. If it was mixed in half-quantities, it is fit for use, but we have not heard whether this applies to a third or a quarter. Rabbi Judah said: The general rule is that if it was made in the correct proportions, it is fit for use even if made in half-quantity, but if he omitted any one of its ingredients, he is guilty of a capital offense.

It was taught, Bar Kapara says: Once every sixty or seventy years, the accumulated surpluses amounted to half the yearly quantity. Bar Kapara also taught: If a minute quantity of honey had been mixed into the incense, no one could have resisted the scent. Why did they not put honey into it? Because the Torah says, "For you are not to burn any leaven or honey in a fire-offering made to the LORD." *JT Yoma 4:5* *Lev. 2*

The following three verses are each said three times:

The LORD of hosts is with us; the God of Jacob is our stronghold, Selah. *Ps. 46*
LORD of hosts, happy is the one who trusts in You. *Ps. 84*
LORD, save! May the King answer us on the day we call. *Ps. 20*

וְנֶאֱמַר
וְהִקְטִיר עָלָיו אַהֲרֹן קְטֹֽרֶת סַמִּים, בַּבֹּֽקֶר בַּבֹּֽקֶר בְּהֵיטִיבוֹ אֶת־הַנֵּרֹת יַקְטִירֶֽנָּה:
וּבְהַעֲלֹת אַהֲרֹן אֶת־הַנֵּרֹת בֵּין הָעַרְבַּֽיִם יַקְטִירֶֽנָּה, קְטֹֽרֶת תָּמִיד לִפְנֵי יהוה
לְדֹרֹתֵיכֶם:

תָּנוּ רַבָּנָן: פִּטּוּם הַקְּטֹֽרֶת כֵּיצַד, שְׁלֹשׁ מֵאוֹת וְשִׁשִּׁים וּשְׁמוֹנָה מָנִים הָיוּ בָהּ. שְׁלֹשׁ כריתות ו.
מֵאוֹת וְשִׁשִּׁים וַחֲמִשָּׁה כְּמִנְיַן יְמוֹת הַחַמָּה, מָנֶה לְכָל יוֹם, פְּרַס בְּשַׁחֲרִית וּפְרַס
בֵּין הָעַרְבַּֽיִם, וּשְׁלֹשָׁה מָנִים יְתֵרִים שֶׁמֵּהֶם מַכְנִיס כֹּהֵן גָּדוֹל מְלֹא חָפְנָיו בְּיוֹם
הַכִּפּוּרִים, וּמַחֲזִירָן לְמַכְתֶּשֶׁת בְּעֶרֶב יוֹם הַכִּפּוּרִים וְשׁוֹחֲקָן יָפֶה יָפֶה, כְּדֵי שֶׁתְּהֵא
דַקָּה מִן הַדַּקָּה. וְאַחַד עָשָׂר סַמָּנִים הָיוּ בָהּ, וְאֵלּוּ הֵן: הַצֳּרִי, וְהַצִּפֹּֽרֶן, וְהַחֶלְבְּנָה,
וְהַלְּבוֹנָה מִשְׁקַל שִׁבְעִים שִׁבְעִים מָנֶה, מוֹר, וּקְצִיעָה, שִׁבֹּֽלֶת נֵרְדְּ, וְכַרְכֹּם מִשְׁקַל
שִׁשָּׁה עָשָׂר שִׁשָּׁה עָשָׂר מָנֶה, הַקֹּשְׁטְ שְׁנֵים עָשָׂר, קִלּוּפָה שְׁלֹשָׁה, קִנָּמוֹן תִּשְׁעָה,
בֹּרִית כַּרְשִׁינָה תִּשְׁעָה קַבִּין, יֵין קַפְרִיסִין סְאִין תְּלָת וְקַבִּין תְּלָתָא, וְאִם לֹא מָצָא
יֵין קַפְרִיסִין, מֵבִיא חֲמַר חִוַּרְיָן עַתִּיק. מֶֽלַח סְדוֹמִית רֹֽבַע, מַעֲלֶה עָשָׁן כָּל שֶׁהוּא.
רַבִּי נָתָן הַבַּבְלִי אוֹמֵר: אַף כִּפַּת הַיַּרְדֵּן כָּל שֶׁהוּא, וְאִם נָתַן בָּהּ דְּבַשׁ פְּסָלָהּ, וְאִם
חִסֵּר אֶחָד מִכָּל סַמָּנֶֽיהָ, חַיָּב מִיתָה.

רַבָּן שִׁמְעוֹן בֶּן גַּמְלִיאֵל אוֹמֵר: הַצֳּרִי אֵינוֹ אֶלָּא שְׂרָף הַנּוֹטֵף מֵעֲצֵי הַקְּטָף. בֹּרִית
כַּרְשִׁינָה שֶׁשָּׁפִין בָּהּ אֶת הַצִּפֹּֽרֶן כְּדֵי שֶׁתְּהֵא נָאָה, יֵין קַפְרִיסִין שֶׁשּׁוֹרִין בּוֹ אֶת
הַצִּפֹּֽרֶן כְּדֵי שֶׁתְּהֵא עַזָּה, וַהֲלֹא מֵי רַגְלַֽיִם יָפִין לָהּ, אֶלָּא שֶׁאֵין מַכְנִיסִין מֵי רַגְלַֽיִם
בַּמִּקְדָּשׁ מִפְּנֵי הַכָּבוֹד.

תַּנְיָא, רַבִּי נָתָן אוֹמֵר: כְּשֶׁהוּא שׁוֹחֵק אוֹמֵר, הָדֵק הֵיטֵב הֵיטֵב הָדֵק, מִפְּנֵי שֶׁהַקּוֹל
יָפֶה לַבְּשָׂמִים. פִּטְּמָהּ לַחֲצָאִין כְּשֵׁרָה, לִשְׁלִישׁ וְלִרְבִֽיעַ לֹא שָׁמַֽעְנוּ. אָמַר רַבִּי יְהוּדָה:
זֶה הַכְּלָל, אִם כְּמִדָּתָהּ כְּשֵׁרָה לַחֲצָאִין, וְאִם חִסֵּר אֶחָד מִכָּל סַמָּנֶֽיהָ חַיָּב מִיתָה.

תַּנְיָא, בַּר קַפָּרָא אוֹמֵר: אַחַת לְשִׁשִּׁים אוֹ לְשִׁבְעִים שָׁנָה הָיְתָה בָאָה שֶׁל שִׁירַֽיִם ירושלמי
לַחֲצָאִין. וְעוֹד תָּנֵי בַּר קַפָּרָא: אִלּוּ הָיָה נוֹתֵן בָּהּ קוֹרְטוֹב שֶׁל דְּבַשׁ אֵין אָדָם יָכוֹל יומא ד, הלכה ה
לַעֲמֹד מִפְּנֵי רֵיחָהּ, וְלָמָּה אֵין מְעָרְבִין בָּהּ דְּבַשׁ, מִפְּנֵי שֶׁהַתּוֹרָה אָמְרָה: כִּי כָל־שְׂאֹר ויקרא ב
וְכָל־דְּבַשׁ לֹא־תַקְטִֽירוּ מִמֶּֽנּוּ אִשֶּׁה לַיהוה:

The following three verses are each said three times:

יהוה צְבָאוֹת עִמָּֽנוּ, מִשְׂגָּב לָֽנוּ אֱלֹהֵי יַעֲקֹב סֶֽלָה: תהלים מו
יהוה צְבָאוֹת, אַשְׁרֵי אָדָם בֹּטֵֽחַ בָּךְ: תהלים פד
יהוה הוֹשִֽׁיעָה, הַמֶּֽלֶךְ יַעֲנֵֽנוּ בְיוֹם־קָרְאֵֽנוּ: תהלים כ

You are my hiding place; You will protect me from distress *Ps. 32*
and surround me with songs of salvation, Selah.
Then the offering of Judah and Jerusalem will be pleasing to the LORD *Mal. 3*
as in the days of old and as in former years.

THE ORDER OF THE PRIESTLY FUNCTIONS

Yoma 33a Abaye related the order of the daily priestly functions in the name of tradition and in accordance with Abba Shaul: The large pile [of wood] comes before the second pile for the incense; the second pile for the incense precedes the laying in order of the two logs of wood; the laying in order of the two logs of wood comes before the removing of ashes from the inner altar; the removing of ashes from the inner altar precedes the cleaning of the five lamps; the cleaning of the five lamps comes before the blood of the daily offering; the blood of the daily offering precedes the cleaning of the [other] two lamps; the cleaning of the two lamps comes before the incense-offering; the incense-offering precedes the burning of the limbs; the burning of the limbs comes before the meal-offering; the meal-offering precedes the pancakes; the pancakes come before the wine-libations; the wine-libations precede the additional offerings; the additional offerings come before the [frankincense] censers; the censers precede the daily afternoon offering; as it is said, "On it he shall arrange burnt-offerings, and on it he shall burn the fat of the peace-offerings" – "on it" [the daily offering] all the offerings were completed. *Lev. 6*

Please, by the power of Your great right hand, set the captive nation free.
Accept Your people's prayer. Strengthen us, purify us, You who are revered.
Please, Mighty One, guard like the pupil of the eye those who seek Your unity.
Bless them, cleanse them, have compassion on them, grant them Your righteousness always.
Mighty One, Holy One, in Your great goodness guide Your congregation.
Only One, Exalted One, turn to Your people, who proclaim Your holiness.
Accept our plea and heed our cry, You who know all secret thoughts.
Blessed be the name of His glorious kingdom for ever and all time.

Some omit:

Master of the Universe, You have commanded us to offer the daily sacrifice at its appointed time with the priests at their service, the Levites on their platform, and the Israelites at their post. Now, because of our sins, the Temple is destroyed and the daily sacrifice discontinued, and we have no priest at his service, no Levite on his platform, no Israelite at his post. But You said: "We will offer in place of bullocks [the prayer of] our lips." *Hos. 14* Therefore may it be Your will, LORD our God and God of our ancestors, that the prayer of our lips be considered, accepted and favored before You as if we had offered the daily sacrifice at its appointed time and place, according to its laws.

On Shabbat:

וּבְיוֹם הַשַּׁבָּת On the Shabbat day, make an offering of two lambs a year old, without blemish, together with two-tenths of an ephah of fine flour mixed with oil as a meal-offering, and its appropriate libation. This is the burnt-offering for every Shabbat, in addition to the regular daily burnt-offering and its libation. *Num. 28*

אַתָּה סֵתֶר לִי, מִצַּר תִּצְּרֵנִי, רָנֵּי פַלֵּט תְּסוֹבְבֵנִי סֶלָה: תהלים לב
וְעָרְבָה לַיהוה מִנְחַת יְהוּדָה וִירוּשָׁלָםִ מלאכי ג
כִּימֵי עוֹלָם וּכְשָׁנִים קַדְמֹנִיּוֹת:

סדר המערכה

אַבַּיֵּי הֲוָה מְסַדֵּר סֵדֶר הַמַּעֲרָכָה מִשְּׁמָא דִּגְמָרָא, וְאַלִּבָּא דְאַבָּא שָׁאוּל: יומא לג.
מַעֲרָכָה גְדוֹלָה קוֹדֶמֶת לְמַעֲרָכָה שְׁנִיָּה שֶׁל קְטֹרֶת, וּמַעֲרָכָה שְׁנִיָּה שֶׁל
קְטֹרֶת קוֹדֶמֶת לְסִדּוּר שְׁנֵי גִזְרֵי עֵצִים, וְסִדּוּר שְׁנֵי גִזְרֵי עֵצִים קוֹדֵם לְדִשּׁוּן
מִזְבֵּחַ הַפְּנִימִי, וְדִשּׁוּן מִזְבֵּחַ הַפְּנִימִי קוֹדֵם לַהֲטָבַת חָמֵשׁ נֵרוֹת, וַהֲטָבַת
חָמֵשׁ נֵרוֹת קוֹדֶמֶת לְדַם הַתָּמִיד, וְדַם הַתָּמִיד קוֹדֵם לַהֲטָבַת שְׁתֵּי נֵרוֹת,
וַהֲטָבַת שְׁתֵּי נֵרוֹת קוֹדֶמֶת לִקְטֹרֶת, וּקְטֹרֶת קוֹדֶמֶת לְאֵבָרִים, וְאֵבָרִים
לְמִנְחָה, וּמִנְחָה לַחֲבִתִּין, וַחֲבִתִּין לִנְסָכִין, וּנְסָכִין לְמוּסָפִין, וּמוּסָפִין
לְבָזִיכִין, וּבָזִיכִין קוֹדְמִין לְתָמִיד שֶׁל בֵּין הָעַרְבָּיִם. שֶׁנֶּאֱמַר: וְעָרַךְ עָלֶיהָ ויקרא ו
הָעֹלָה, וְהִקְטִיר עָלֶיהָ חֶלְבֵי הַשְּׁלָמִים: עָלֶיהָ הַשְׁלֵם כָּל הַקָּרְבָּנוֹת כֻּלָּם.

אָנָּא, בְּכֹחַ גְּדֻלַּת יְמִינְךָ, תַּתִּיר צְרוּרָה.
קַבֵּל רִנַּת עַמְּךָ, שַׂגְּבֵנוּ, טַהֲרֵנוּ, נוֹרָא.
נָא גִבּוֹר, דּוֹרְשֵׁי יִחוּדְךָ כְּבָבַת שָׁמְרֵם.
בָּרְכֵם, טַהֲרֵם, רַחֲמֵם, צִדְקָתְךָ תָּמִיד גָּמְלֵם.
חֲסִין קָדוֹשׁ, בְּרֹב טוּבְךָ נַהֵל עֲדָתֶךָ.
יָחִיד גֵּאֶה, לְעַמְּךָ פְּנֵה, זוֹכְרֵי קְדֻשָּׁתֶךָ.
שַׁוְעָתֵנוּ קַבֵּל וּשְׁמַע צַעֲקָתֵנוּ, יוֹדֵעַ תַּעֲלוּמוֹת.
בָּרוּךְ שֵׁם כְּבוֹד מַלְכוּתוֹ לְעוֹלָם וָעֶד.

Some omit:

רִבּוֹן הָעוֹלָמִים, אַתָּה צִוִּיתָנוּ לְהַקְרִיב קָרְבַּן הַתָּמִיד בְּמוֹעֲדוֹ וְלִהְיוֹת כֹּהֲנִים
בַּעֲבוֹדָתָם וּלְוִיִּם בְּדוּכָנָם וְיִשְׂרָאֵל בְּמַעֲמָדָם, וְעַתָּה בַּעֲוֺנוֹתֵינוּ חָרַב בֵּית הַמִּקְדָּשׁ
וּבָטַל הַתָּמִיד וְאֵין לָנוּ לֹא כֹהֵן בַּעֲבוֹדָתוֹ וְלֹא לֵוִי בְּדוּכָנוֹ וְלֹא יִשְׂרָאֵל בְּמַעֲמָדוֹ,
וְאַתָּה אָמַרְתָּ: וּנְשַׁלְּמָה פָרִים שְׂפָתֵינוּ: לָכֵן יְהִי רָצוֹן מִלְּפָנֶיךָ יהוה אֱלֹהֵינוּ וֵאלֹהֵי הושע יד
אֲבוֹתֵינוּ, שֶׁיְּהֵא שִׂיחַ שִׂפְתוֹתֵינוּ חָשׁוּב וּמְקֻבָּל וּמְרֻצֶּה לְפָנֶיךָ, כְּאִלּוּ הִקְרַבְנוּ קָרְבַּן
הַתָּמִיד בְּמוֹעֲדוֹ וּבִמְקוֹמוֹ וּכְהִלְכָתוֹ.

בשבת:

וּבְיוֹם הַשַּׁבָּת שְׁנֵי־כְבָשִׂים בְּנֵי־שָׁנָה תְּמִימִם, וּשְׁנֵי עֶשְׂרֹנִים סֹלֶת מִנְחָה במדבר כח
בְּלוּלָה בַשֶּׁמֶן, וְנִסְכּוֹ: עֹלַת שַׁבַּת בְּשַׁבַּתּוֹ, עַל־עֹלַת הַתָּמִיד וְנִסְכָּהּ:

LAWS OF OFFERINGS, MISHNA ZEVAḤIM

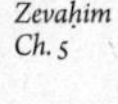
Zevaḥim Ch. 5

אֵיזֶהוּ מְקוֹמָן What is the location for sacrifices? The holiest offerings were slaughtered on the north side. The bull and he-goat of Yom Kippur were slaughtered on the north side. Their blood was received in a sacred vessel on the north side, and had to be sprinkled between the poles [of the Ark], toward the veil [screening the Holy of Holies], and on the golden altar. [The omission of] one of these sprinklings invalidated [the atonement ceremony]. The leftover blood was to be poured onto the western base of the outer altar. If this was not done, however, the omission did not invalidate [the ceremony].

The bulls and he-goats that were completely burnt were slaughtered on the north side, their blood was received in a sacred vessel on the north side, and had to be sprinkled toward the veil and on the golden altar. [The omission of] one of these sprinklings invalidated [the ceremony]. The leftover blood was to be poured onto the western base of the outer altar. If this was not done, however, the omission did not invalidate [the ceremony]. All these offerings were burnt where the altar ashes were deposited.

The communal and individual sin-offerings – these are the communal sin-offerings: the he-goats offered on Rosh Ḥodesh and Festivals were slaughtered on the north side, their blood was received in a sacred vessel on the north side, and required four sprinklings, one on each of the four corners of the altar. How was this done? The priest ascended the ramp and turned [right] onto the surrounding ledge. He came to the southeast corner, then went to the northeast, then to the northwest, then to the southwest. The leftover blood he poured onto the southern base. [The meat of these offerings], prepared in any manner, was eaten within the [courtyard] curtains, by males of the priest-hood, on that day and the following night, until midnight.

The burnt-offering was among the holiest of sacrifices. It was slaughtered on the north side, its blood was received in a sacred vessel on the north side, and required two sprinklings [at opposite corners of the altar], making four in all. The offering had to be flayed, dismembered and wholly consumed by fire.

דיני זבחים

אֵיזֶהוּ מְקוֹמָן שֶׁל זְבָחִים. קָדְשֵׁי קָדָשִׁים שְׁחִיטָתָן בַּצָּפוֹן. זבחים פרק ה
פַּר וְשָׂעִיר שֶׁל יוֹם הַכִּפּוּרִים, שְׁחִיטָתָן בַּצָּפוֹן, וְקִבּוּל דָּמָן בִּכְלִי שָׁרֵת בַּצָּפוֹן, וְדָמָן טָעוּן הַזָּיָה עַל בֵּין הַבַּדִּים, וְעַל הַפָּרֹכֶת, וְעַל מִזְבַּח הַזָּהָב. מַתָּנָה אַחַת מֵהֶן מְעַכֶּבֶת. שְׁיָרֵי הַדָּם הָיָה שׁוֹפֵךְ עַל יְסוֹד מַעֲרָבִי שֶׁל מִזְבֵּחַ הַחִיצוֹן, אִם לֹא נָתַן לֹא עִכֵּב.

פָּרִים הַנִּשְׂרָפִים וּשְׂעִירִים הַנִּשְׂרָפִים, שְׁחִיטָתָן בַּצָּפוֹן, וְקִבּוּל דָּמָן בִּכְלִי שָׁרֵת בַּצָּפוֹן, וְדָמָן טָעוּן הַזָּיָה עַל הַפָּרֹכֶת וְעַל מִזְבַּח הַזָּהָב. מַתָּנָה אַחַת מֵהֶן מְעַכֶּבֶת. שְׁיָרֵי הַדָּם הָיָה שׁוֹפֵךְ עַל יְסוֹד מַעֲרָבִי שֶׁל מִזְבֵּחַ הַחִיצוֹן, אִם לֹא נָתַן לֹא עִכֵּב. אֵלּוּ וָאֵלּוּ נִשְׂרָפִין בְּבֵית הַדֶּשֶׁן.

חַטֹּאת הַצִּבּוּר וְהַיָּחִיד. אֵלּוּ הֵן חַטֹּאת הַצִּבּוּר: שְׂעִירֵי רָאשֵׁי חֳדָשִׁים וְשֶׁל מוֹעֲדוֹת. שְׁחִיטָתָן בַּצָּפוֹן, וְקִבּוּל דָּמָן בִּכְלִי שָׁרֵת בַּצָּפוֹן, וְדָמָן טָעוּן אַרְבַּע מַתָּנוֹת עַל אַרְבַּע קְרָנוֹת. כֵּיצַד, עָלָה בַכֶּבֶשׁ, וּפָנָה לַסּוֹבֵב, וּבָא לוֹ לְקֶרֶן דְּרוֹמִית מִזְרָחִית, מִזְרָחִית צְפוֹנִית, צְפוֹנִית מַעֲרָבִית, מַעֲרָבִית דְּרוֹמִית. שְׁיָרֵי הַדָּם הָיָה שׁוֹפֵךְ עַל יְסוֹד דְּרוֹמִי. וְנֶאֱכָלִין לִפְנִים מִן הַקְּלָעִים, לְזִכְרֵי כְהֻנָּה, בְּכָל מַאֲכָל, לְיוֹם וָלַיְלָה עַד חֲצוֹת.

הָעוֹלָה קֹדֶשׁ קָדָשִׁים. שְׁחִיטָתָהּ בַּצָּפוֹן, וְקִבּוּל דָּמָהּ בִּכְלִי שָׁרֵת בַּצָּפוֹן, וְדָמָהּ טָעוּן שְׁתֵּי מַתָּנוֹת שֶׁהֵן אַרְבַּע, וּטְעוּנָה הֶפְשֵׁט וְנִתּוּחַ, וְכָלִיל לָאִשִּׁים.

The communal peace-offerings and the guilt-offerings – these are the guilt-offerings: the guilt-offering for robbery; the guilt-offering for profane use of a sacred object; the guilt-offering [for violating] a betrothed maidservant; the guilt-offering of a Nazirite [who had become defiled by a corpse]; the guilt-offering of a leper [at his cleansing]; and the guilt-offering in case of doubt. All these were slaughtered on the north side, their blood was received in a sacred vessel on the north side, and required two sprinklings [at opposite corners of the altar], making four in all. [The meat of these offerings], prepared in any manner, was eaten within the [courtyard] curtains, by males of the priesthood, on that day and the following night, until midnight.

The thanksgiving-offering and the ram of a Nazirite were offerings of lesser holiness. They could be slaughtered anywhere in the Temple court, and their blood required two sprinklings [at opposite corners of the altar], making four in all. The meat of these offerings, prepared in any manner, was eaten anywhere within the city [Jerusalem], by anyone during that day and the following night until midnight. This also applied to the portion of these sacrifices [given to the priests], except that the priests' portion was only to be eaten by the priests, their wives, children and servants.

Peace-offerings were [also] of lesser holiness. They could be slaughtered anywhere in the Temple court, and their blood required two sprinklings [at opposite corners of the altar], making four in all. The meat of these offerings, prepared in any manner, was eaten anywhere within the city [Jerusalem], by anyone, for two days and one night. This also applied to the portion of these sacrifices [given to the priests], except that the priests' portion was only to be eaten by the priests, their wives, children and servants.

The firstborn and tithe of cattle and the Pesaḥ lamb were sacrifices of lesser holiness. They could be slaughtered anywhere in the Temple court, and their blood required only one sprinkling, which had to be done at the base of the altar. They differed in their consumption: the firstborn was eaten only by priests, while the tithe could be eaten by anyone. Both could be eaten anywhere within the city, prepared in any manner, during two days and one night. The Pesaḥ lamb had to be eaten that night until midnight. It could only be eaten by those who had been numbered for it, and eaten only roasted.

זִבְחֵי שַׁלְמֵי צִבּוּר וַאֲשָׁמוֹת. אֵלּוּ הֵן אֲשָׁמוֹת: אֲשַׁם גְּזֵלוֹת, אֲשַׁם מְעִילוֹת, אֲשַׁם שִׁפְחָה חֲרוּפָה, אֲשַׁם נָזִיר, אֲשַׁם מְצֹרָע, אָשָׁם תָּלוּי. שְׁחִיטָתָן בַּצָּפוֹן, וְקִבּוּל דָּמָן בִּכְלִי שָׁרֵת בַּצָּפוֹן, וְדָמָן טָעוּן שְׁתֵּי מַתָּנוֹת שֶׁהֵן אַרְבַּע. וְנֶאֱכָלִין לִפְנִים מִן הַקְּלָעִים, לְזִכְרֵי כְהֻנָּה, בְּכָל מַאֲכָל, לְיוֹם וָלַיְלָה עַד חֲצוֹת.

הַתּוֹדָה וְאֵיל נָזִיר קָדָשִׁים קַלִּים. שְׁחִיטָתָן בְּכָל מָקוֹם בָּעֲזָרָה, וְדָמָן טָעוּן שְׁתֵּי מַתָּנוֹת שֶׁהֵן אַרְבַּע, וְנֶאֱכָלִין בְּכָל הָעִיר, לְכָל אָדָם, בְּכָל מַאֲכָל, לְיוֹם וָלַיְלָה עַד חֲצוֹת. הַמּוּרָם מֵהֶם כַּיּוֹצֵא בָהֶם, אֶלָּא שֶׁהַמּוּרָם נֶאֱכָל לַכֹּהֲנִים, לִנְשֵׁיהֶם, וְלִבְנֵיהֶם וּלְעַבְדֵיהֶם.

שְׁלָמִים קָדָשִׁים קַלִּים. שְׁחִיטָתָן בְּכָל מָקוֹם בָּעֲזָרָה, וְדָמָן טָעוּן שְׁתֵּי מַתָּנוֹת שֶׁהֵן אַרְבַּע, וְנֶאֱכָלִין בְּכָל הָעִיר, לְכָל אָדָם, בְּכָל מַאֲכָל, לִשְׁנֵי יָמִים וְלַיְלָה אֶחָד. הַמּוּרָם מֵהֶם כַּיּוֹצֵא בָהֶם, אֶלָּא שֶׁהַמּוּרָם נֶאֱכָל לַכֹּהֲנִים, לִנְשֵׁיהֶם, וְלִבְנֵיהֶם וּלְעַבְדֵיהֶם.

הַבְּכוֹר וְהַמַּעֲשֵׂר וְהַפֶּסַח קָדָשִׁים קַלִּים. שְׁחִיטָתָן בְּכָל מָקוֹם בָּעֲזָרָה, וְדָמָן טָעוּן מַתָּנָה אֶחָת, וּבִלְבָד שֶׁיִּתֵּן כְּנֶגֶד הַיְסוֹד. שִׁנָּה בַאֲכִילָתָן, הַבְּכוֹר נֶאֱכָל לַכֹּהֲנִים וְהַמַּעֲשֵׂר לְכָל אָדָם, וְנֶאֱכָלִין בְּכָל הָעִיר, בְּכָל מַאֲכָל, לִשְׁנֵי יָמִים וְלַיְלָה אֶחָד. הַפֶּסַח אֵינוֹ נֶאֱכָל אֶלָּא בַלַּיְלָה, וְאֵינוֹ נֶאֱכָל אֶלָּא עַד חֲצוֹת, וְאֵינוֹ נֶאֱכָל אֶלָּא לִמְנוּיָו, וְאֵינוֹ נֶאֱכָל אֶלָּא צָלִי.

THE INTERPRETIVE PRINCIPLES OF RABBI YISHMAEL

רַבִּי יִשְׁמָעֵאל Rabbi Yishma'el says:

The Torah is expounded by thirteen principles:

1. An inference from a lenient law to a strict one, and vice versa.
2. An inference drawn from identical words in two passages.
3. A general principle derived from one text or two related texts.
4. A general law followed by specific examples
   [where the law applies exclusively to those examples].
5. A specific example followed by a general law
   [where the law applies to everything implied in the general statement].
6. A general law followed by specific examples and concluding with a general law: here you may infer only cases similar to the examples.
7. When a general statement requires clarification by a specific example,
   or a specific example requires clarification by a general statement
   [then rules 4 and 5 do not apply].
8. When a particular case, already included in the general statement,
   is expressly mentioned to teach something new, that special provision applies
   to all other cases included in the general statement.
9. When a particular case, though included in the general statement,
   is expressly mentioned with a provision similar to the general law,
   such a case is singled out to lessen the severity of the law, not to increase it.
10. When a particular case, though included in the general statement,
    is explicitly mentioned with a provision differing from the general law,
    it is singled out to lessen in some respects, and in others to increase,
    the severity of the law.
11. When a particular case, though included in the general statement, is explicitly mentioned with a new provision, the terms of the general statement no longer apply to it, unless Scripture indicates explicitly that they do apply.
12. A matter elucidated from its context, or from the following passage.
13. Also, when two passages [seem to] contradict each other,
    [they are to be elucidated by] a third passage that reconciles them.

May it be Your will, LORD our God and God of our ancestors, that the Temple be speedily rebuilt in our days, and grant us our share in Your Torah. And may we serve You there in reverence, as in the days of old and as in former years.

Torah is interpreted" (Maimonides, Laws of Torah Study 1:11). It was chosen because it appears at the beginning of the *Sifra*, the halakhic commentary to Leviticus, which is the source of most of the laws of offerings. It also reminds us of the indissoluble connection between the Written Law (the Mosaic books) and the Oral Law (Mishna, Midrash and Talmud). Rabbi Yishmael's principles show how the latter can be derived from the former.

ברייתא דרבי ישמעאל

רַבִּי יִשְׁמָעֵאל אוֹמֵר: בִּשְׁלֹשׁ עֶשְׂרֵה מִדּוֹת הַתּוֹרָה נִדְרֶשֶׁת

א מִקַּל וָחֹמֶר

ב וּמִגְּזֵרָה שָׁוָה

ג מִבִּנְיַן אָב מִכָּתוּב אֶחָד, וּמִבִּנְיַן אָב מִשְּׁנֵי כְתוּבִים

ד מִכְּלָל וּפְרָט

ה מִפְּרָט וּכְלָל

ו כְּלָל וּפְרָט וּכְלָל, אִי אַתָּה דָן אֶלָּא כְּעֵין הַפְּרָט

ז מִכְּלָל שֶׁהוּא צָרִיךְ לִפְרָט, וּמִפְּרָט שֶׁהוּא צָרִיךְ לִכְלָל

ח כָּל דָּבָר שֶׁהָיָה בִּכְלָל, וְיָצָא מִן הַכְּלָל לְלַמֵּד
לֹא לְלַמֵּד עַל עַצְמוֹ יָצָא, אֶלָּא לְלַמֵּד עַל הַכְּלָל כֻּלּוֹ יָצָא

ט כָּל דָּבָר שֶׁהָיָה בִּכְלָל, וְיָצָא לִטְעֹן טֹעַן אֶחָד שֶׁהוּא כְעִנְיָנוֹ
יָצָא לְהָקֵל וְלֹא לְהַחֲמִיר

י כָּל דָּבָר שֶׁהָיָה בִּכְלָל, וְיָצָא לִטְעֹן טֹעַן אַחֵר שֶׁלֹּא כְעִנְיָנוֹ
יָצָא לְהָקֵל וּלְהַחֲמִיר

יא כָּל דָּבָר שֶׁהָיָה בִּכְלָל, וְיָצָא לִדּוֹן בַּדָּבָר הֶחָדָשׁ
אִי אַתָּה יָכוֹל לְהַחֲזִירוֹ לִכְלָלוֹ
עַד שֶׁיַּחֲזִירֶנּוּ הַכָּתוּב לִכְלָלוֹ בְּפֵרוּשׁ

יב דָּבָר הַלָּמֵד מֵעִנְיָנוֹ, וְדָבָר הַלָּמֵד מִסּוֹפוֹ

יג וְכֵן שְׁנֵי כְתוּבִים הַמַּכְחִישִׁים זֶה אֶת זֶה
עַד שֶׁיָּבוֹא הַכָּתוּב הַשְּׁלִישִׁי וְיַכְרִיעַ בֵּינֵיהֶם.

יְהִי רָצוֹן מִלְּפָנֶיךָ, יהוה אֱלֹהֵינוּ וֵאלֹהֵי אֲבוֹתֵינוּ, שֶׁיִּבָּנֶה בֵּית הַמִּקְדָּשׁ בִּמְהֵרָה בְיָמֵינוּ, וְתֵן חֶלְקֵנוּ בְּתוֹרָתֶךָ, וְשָׁם נַעֲבָדְךָ בְּיִרְאָה כִּימֵי עוֹלָם וּכְשָׁנִים קַדְמוֹנִיּוֹת.

THE INTERPRETIVE PRINCIPLES OF RABBI YISHMAEL
This passage is included as an item of Talmud, defined in its broadest sense as "deducing conclusions from premises, developing implications of statements, comparing dicta, and studying the hermeneutical principles by which the

THE RABBIS' KADDISH

The following prayer requires the presence of a minyan.
A transliteration can be found on page 1374.

Mourner: יִתְגַּדַּל Magnified and sanctified
may His great name be,
in the world He created by His will.
May He establish His kingdom in your lifetime
and in your days,
and in the lifetime of all the house of Israel,
swiftly and soon –
and say: Amen.

All: May His great name be blessed for ever and all time.

Mourner: Blessed and praised,
glorified and exalted,
raised and honored,
uplifted and lauded
be the name of the Holy One, blessed be He,
above and beyond any blessing, song,
praise and consolation
uttered in the world –
and say: Amen.

To Israel, to the teachers,
their disciples and their disciples' disciples,
and to all who engage in the study of Torah,
in this (*in Israel:* holy) place or elsewhere,
may there come to them and you great peace,
grace, kindness and compassion,
long life, ample sustenance and deliverance,
from their Father in Heaven –
and say: Amen.

קדיש דרבנן

The following prayer requires the presence of a מנין*.*
A transliteration can be found on *page 1374.*

אבל: יִתְגַּדַּל וְיִתְקַדַּשׁ שְׁמֵהּ רַבָּא (קהל: אָמֵן)
בְּעָלְמָא דִּי בְרָא כִרְעוּתֵהּ
וְיַמְלִיךְ מַלְכוּתֵהּ
בְּחַיֵּיכוֹן וּבְיוֹמֵיכוֹן וּבְחַיֵּי דְכָל בֵּית יִשְׂרָאֵל
בַּעֲגָלָא וּבִזְמַן קָרִיב
וְאִמְרוּ אָמֵן. (קהל: אָמֵן)

קהל ואבל: יְהֵא שְׁמֵהּ רַבָּא מְבָרַךְ לְעָלַם וּלְעָלְמֵי עָלְמַיָּא.

אבל: יִתְבָּרַךְ וְיִשְׁתַּבַּח וְיִתְפָּאַר וְיִתְרוֹמַם וְיִתְנַשֵּׂא
וְיִתְהַדָּר וְיִתְעַלֶּה וְיִתְהַלָּל
שְׁמֵהּ דְּקֻדְשָׁא בְּרִיךְ הוּא (קהל: בְּרִיךְ הוּא)
לְעֵלָּא לְעֵלָּא מִכָּל בִּרְכָתָא וְשִׁירָתָא, תֻּשְׁבְּחָתָא וְנֶחֱמָתָא
דַּאֲמִירָן בְּעָלְמָא
וְאִמְרוּ אָמֵן. (קהל: אָמֵן)

עַל יִשְׂרָאֵל וְעַל רַבָּנָן
וְעַל תַּלְמִידֵיהוֹן וְעַל כָּל תַּלְמִידֵי תַלְמִידֵיהוֹן
וְעַל כָּל מָאן דְּעָסְקִין בְּאוֹרַיְתָא
דִּי בְּאַתְרָא (בארץ ישראל: קַדִּישָׁא) הָדֵין, וְדִי בְּכָל אֲתַר וַאֲתַר
יְהֵא לְהוֹן וּלְכוֹן שְׁלָמָא רַבָּא
חִנָּא וְחִסְדָּא, וְרַחֲמֵי, וְחַיֵּי אֲרִיכֵי, וּמְזוֹנֵי רְוִיחֵי
וּפֻרְקָנָא מִן קֳדָם אֲבוּהוֹן דִּי בִשְׁמַיָּא
וְאִמְרוּ אָמֵן. (קהל: אָמֵן)

May there be great peace from heaven,
and (good) life for us and all Israel –
and say: Amen.

Bow, take three steps back, as if taking leave of the Divine Presence, then bow, first left, then right, then center, while saying:

May He who makes peace in His high places,
in His compassion make peace for us and all Israel –
and say: Amen.

A PSALM BEFORE VERSES OF PRAISE

מִזְמוֹר שִׁיר A psalm of David. A song for the dedication of the House. I will exalt You, LORD, for You have lifted me up, and not let my enemies rejoice over me. LORD, my God, I cried to You for help and You healed me. LORD, You lifted my soul from the grave; You spared me from going down to the pit. Sing to the LORD, you His devoted ones, and give thanks to His holy name. For His anger is for a moment, but His favor for a lifetime. At night there may be weeping, but in the morning there is joy. When I felt secure, I said, "I shall never be shaken." LORD, when You favored me, You made me stand firm as a mountain, but when You hid Your face, I was terrified. To You, LORD, I called; I pleaded with my LORD: "What gain would there be if I died and went down to the grave? Can dust thank You? Can it declare Your truth? Hear, LORD, and be gracious to me; LORD, be my help." ▸ You have turned my sorrow into dancing. You have removed my sackcloth and clothed me with joy, so that my soul may sing to You and not be silent. LORD my God, for ever will I thank You. *Ps. 30*

---

conceived the plan to build the Temple, he wrote this psalm to be sung on that occasion (Rashi). In it David relates how, when his life was in danger, God delivered him to safety. Set here, it beautifully connects the dawn blessings (waking from sleep as a miniature experience of being saved from death to life) with the Verses of Praise that are about to follow ("So that my soul may sing to You").

יְהֵא שְׁלָמָא רַבָּא מִן שְׁמַיָּא
וְחַיִּים (טוֹבִים) עָלֵינוּ וְעַל כָּל יִשְׂרָאֵל
וְאִמְרוּ אָמֵן. (קהל: אָמֵן)

Bow, take three steps back, as if taking leave of the Divine Presence, then bow, first left, then right, then center, while saying:

עֹשֶׂה הַשָּׁלוֹם בִּמְרוֹמָיו
הוּא יַעֲשֶׂה בְרַחֲמָיו שָׁלוֹם, עָלֵינוּ וְעַל כָּל יִשְׂרָאֵל
וְאִמְרוּ אָמֵן. (קהל: אָמֵן)

מזמור לפני פסוקי דזמרה

תהלים ל מִזְמוֹר שִׁיר־חֲנֻכַּת הַבַּיִת לְדָוִד: אֲרוֹמִמְךָ יהוה כִּי דִלִּיתָנִי, וְלֹא־
שִׂמַּחְתָּ אֹיְבַי לִי: יהוה אֱלֹהָי, שִׁוַּעְתִּי אֵלֶיךָ וַתִּרְפָּאֵנִי: יהוה,
הֶעֱלִיתָ מִן־שְׁאוֹל נַפְשִׁי, חִיִּיתַנִי מִיָּרְדִי־בוֹר: זַמְּרוּ לַיהוה חֲסִידָיו,
וְהוֹדוּ לְזֵכֶר קָדְשׁוֹ: כִּי רֶגַע בְּאַפּוֹ, חַיִּים בִּרְצוֹנוֹ, בָּעֶרֶב יָלִין בֶּכִי
וְלַבֹּקֶר רִנָּה: וַאֲנִי אָמַרְתִּי בְשַׁלְוִי, בַּל־אֶמּוֹט לְעוֹלָם: יהוה, בִּרְצוֹנְךָ
הֶעֱמַדְתָּה לְהַרְרִי עֹז, הִסְתַּרְתָּ פָנֶיךָ הָיִיתִי נִבְהָל: אֵלֶיךָ יהוה
אֶקְרָא, וְאֶל־אֲדֹנָי אֶתְחַנָּן: מַה־בֶּצַע בְּדָמִי, בְּרִדְתִּי אֶל שָׁחַת,
הֲיוֹדְךָ עָפָר, הֲיַגִּיד אֲמִתֶּךָ: שְׁמַע־יהוה וְחָנֵּנִי, יהוה הֱיֵה־עֹזֵר לִי:
‹ הָפַכְתָּ מִסְפְּדִי לְמָחוֹל לִי, פִּתַּחְתָּ שַׂקִּי, וַתְּאַזְּרֵנִי שִׂמְחָה: לְמַעַן
יְזַמֶּרְךָ כָבוֹד וְלֹא יִדֹּם, יהוה אֱלֹהַי, לְעוֹלָם אוֹדֶךָּ:

מִזְמוֹר שִׁיר *Psalm 30.* This psalm was a late addition to the morning prayers, appearing for the first time in the seventeenth century. Although entitled "A psalm of David. A song for the Dedication of the House," we know that the Temple was not built in his lifetime. As a soldier and military leader he was deemed not to be privileged to build a Temple that symbolized peace (1 Chr. 22:8). Hence it was built by his son King Solomon, whose name means peace and whose reign was marked by peace. Nonetheless, since it was David who

MOURNER'S KADDISH

The following prayer requires the presence of a minyan.
A transliteration can be found on page 1375.

Mourner: יִתְגַּדַּל Magnified and sanctified
may His great name be,
in the world He created by His will.
May He establish His kingdom
in your lifetime and in your days,
and in the lifetime of all the house of Israel,
swiftly and soon –
and say: Amen.

All: May His great name be blessed for ever and all time.

Mourner: Blessed and praised,
glorified and exalted,
raised and honored,
uplifted and lauded
be the name of the Holy One, blessed be He,
above and beyond any blessing, song,
praise and consolation
uttered in the world –
and say: Amen.

May there be great peace from heaven,
and life for us and all Israel –
and say: Amen.

Bow, take three steps back, as if taking leave of the Divine Presence,
then bow, first left, then right, then center, while saying:

May He who makes peace in His high places,
make peace for us and all Israel –
and say: Amen.

קדיש יתום

The following prayer requires the presence of a מנין.
A transliteration can be found on page 1375.

אבל: יִתְגַּדַּל וְיִתְקַדַּשׁ שְׁמֵהּ רַבָּא (קהל: אָמֵן)
בְּעָלְמָא דִּי בְרָא כִרְעוּתֵהּ
וְיַמְלִיךְ מַלְכוּתֵהּ
בְּחַיֵּיכוֹן וּבְיוֹמֵיכוֹן וּבְחַיֵּי דְכָל בֵּית יִשְׂרָאֵל
בַּעֲגָלָא וּבִזְמַן קָרִיב
וְאִמְרוּ אָמֵן. (קהל: אָמֵן)

קהל ואבל: יְהֵא שְׁמֵהּ רַבָּא מְבָרַךְ לְעָלַם וּלְעָלְמֵי עָלְמַיָּא.

אבל: יִתְבָּרַךְ וְיִשְׁתַּבַּח וְיִתְפָּאַר וְיִתְרוֹמַם וְיִתְנַשֵּׂא
וְיִתְהַדָּר וְיִתְעַלֶּה וְיִתְהַלָּל
שְׁמֵהּ דְּקֻדְשָׁא בְּרִיךְ הוּא (קהל: בְּרִיךְ הוּא)
לְעֵלָּא לְעֵלָּא מִכָּל בִּרְכָתָא וְשִׁירָתָא, תֻּשְׁבְּחָתָא וְנֶחֱמָתָא
דַּאֲמִירָן בְּעָלְמָא
וְאִמְרוּ אָמֵן. (קהל: אָמֵן)

יְהֵא שְׁלָמָא רַבָּא מִן שְׁמַיָּא
וְחַיִּים, עָלֵינוּ וְעַל כָּל יִשְׂרָאֵל
וְאִמְרוּ אָמֵן. (קהל: אָמֵן)

Bow, take three steps back, as if taking leave of the Divine Presence, then bow, first left, then right, then center, while saying:

עֹשֶׂה הַשָּׁלוֹם בִּמְרוֹמָיו
הוּא יַעֲשֶׂה שָׁלוֹם עָלֵינוּ וְעַל כָּל יִשְׂרָאֵל
וְאִמְרוּ אָמֵן. (קהל: אָמֵן)

PESUKEI DEZIMRA

The following introductory blessing to the Pesukei DeZimra (Verses of Praise) is said standing, while holding the two front tzitziot of the tallit. They are kissed and released at the end of the blessing at "songs of praise" (on the next page). From the beginning of this prayer to the end of the Amida, conversation is forbidden.

Some say:

I hereby prepare my mouth to thank, praise and laud my Creator, for the sake of the unification of the Holy One, blessed be He, and His Divine Presence, through that which is hidden and concealed, in the name of all Israel.

BLESSED IS HE WHO SPOKE

and the world came into being, blessed is He.
Blessed is He who creates the universe.
Blessed is He who speaks and acts.
Blessed is He who decrees and fulfills.
Blessed is He who shows compassion to the earth.
Blessed is He who shows compassion to all creatures.
Blessed is He who gives a good reward
to those who fear Him.
Blessed is He who lives for ever and exists to eternity.
Blessed is He who redeems and saves.
Blessed is His name.

בָּרוּךְ שֶׁאָמַר וְהָיָה הָעוֹלָם *Blessed is He who spoke and the world came into being.* In the sharpest possible contrast to the mythology of the pagan world, creation unfolds in Genesis 1 without clash or conflict between the elements. God said, "Let there be" and there was. There is an essential underlying harmony in the universe. All that exists is the result of a single creative will. The world is fundamentally good – the word "good" appears seven times in the opening chapter. The opening section of this two-part blessing is a ten-line litany of blessings, corresponding to the ten times in Genesis 1 in which the phrase, "And God said" appears: the "ten utterances" by which the world was made (*Avot* 5:1).

פסוקי דזמרה

The following introductory blessing to the פסוקי דזמרה *is said standing, while holding the two front* ציציות *of the* טלית*. They are kissed and released at the end of the blessing at* בַּתִּשְׁבָּחוֹת *(on the next page). From the beginning of this prayer to the end of the* עמידה*, conversation is forbidden.*

Some say:

הֲרֵינִי מְזַמֵּן אֶת פִּי לְהוֹדוֹת וּלְהַלֵּל וּלְשַׁבֵּחַ אֶת בּוֹרְאִי, לְשֵׁם יִחוּד קֻדְשָׁא בְּרִיךְ הוּא וּשְׁכִינְתֵּהּ עַל יְדֵי הַהוּא טָמִיר וְנֶעְלָם בְּשֵׁם כָּל יִשְׂרָאֵל.

בָּרוּךְ שֶׁאָמַר וְהָיָה הָעוֹלָם, בָּרוּךְ הוּא.

בָּרוּךְ עוֹשֶׂה בְרֵאשִׁית

בָּרוּךְ אוֹמֵר וְעוֹשֶׂה

בָּרוּךְ גּוֹזֵר וּמְקַיֵּם

בָּרוּךְ מְרַחֵם עַל הָאָרֶץ

בָּרוּךְ מְרַחֵם עַל הַבְּרִיּוֹת

בָּרוּךְ מְשַׁלֵּם שָׂכָר טוֹב לִירֵאָיו

בָּרוּךְ חַי לָעַד וְקַיָּם לָנֶצַח

בָּרוּךְ פּוֹדֶה וּמַצִּיל

בָּרוּךְ שְׁמוֹ

בָּרוּךְ שֶׁאָמַר *Blessed is He who spoke.* An introductory blessing to the Verses of Praise that follow, mainly taken from the Psalms. Their essential theme is God as He exists in Creation, designing and sustaining the universe in wisdom, justice and compassion. At their core are six psalms, 145–150, the last in the book of Psalms, which correspond to the six days of creation in Genesis 1.

Blessed are You, LORD our God, King of the Universe,
God, compassionate Father,
extolled by the mouth of His people,
praised and glorified by the tongue of His devoted ones
and those who serve Him.
With the songs of Your servant David
we will praise You, O LORD our God.
With praises and psalms
we will magnify and praise You, glorify You,
Speak Your name and proclaim Your kingship,
our King, our God, ‣ the only One, Giver of life to the worlds,
the King whose great name is praised
and glorified to all eternity.
Blessed are You, LORD, the King extolled with songs of praise.

הוֹדוּ Thank the LORD, call on His name, make His acts known among *1 Chr. 16* the peoples. Sing to Him, make music to Him, tell of all His wonders. Glory in His holy name; let the hearts of those who seek the LORD rejoice. Search out the LORD and His strength; seek His presence at all times. Remember the wonders He has done, His miracles, and the judgments He pronounced. Descendants of Yisrael His servant, sons of Jacob His chosen ones: He is the LORD our God. His judgments are throughout the earth. Remember His covenant for ever, the word He commanded for a thousand generations. He made it with Abraham,

---

to Radak this is a reference to the miraculous afflictions that struck the Philistines when they captured the Ark (1 Sam. 5).

מְבַקְשֵׁי יהוה *Those who seek the LORD:* including those of other nations (Radak).

בַּקְּשׁוּ פָנָיו *Seek His presence:* in prayer (Radak), or contemplation (Malbim).

וּמִשְׁפְּטֵי־פִיהוּ *The judgments He pronounced:* the warnings God sends in advance through His prophets, as Moses warned Pharaoh of the impending plagues (Radak).

לְאֶלֶף דּוֹר *For a thousand generations:* a poetic way of saying "forever."

אַבְרָהָם, יִצְחָק, יַעֲקֹב *Abraham, Isaac, Jacob.* God made a promise to each of the three patriarchs that their descendants would inherit the land.

בָּרוּךְ אַתָּה יהוה אֱלֹהֵינוּ מֶלֶךְ הָעוֹלָם
הָאֵל הָאָב הָרַחֲמָן הַמְהֻלָּל בְּפִי עַמּוֹ
מְשֻׁבָּח וּמְפֹאָר בִּלְשׁוֹן חֲסִידָיו וַעֲבָדָיו
וּבְשִׁירֵי דָוִד עַבְדֶּךָ
נְהַלֶּלְךָ יהוה אֱלֹהֵינוּ.
בִּשְׁבָחוֹת וּבִזְמִירוֹת
נְגַדֶּלְךָ וּנְשַׁבֵּחֲךָ וּנְפָאֶרְךָ
וְנַזְכִּיר שִׁמְךָ וְנַמְלִיכְךָ
מַלְכֵּנוּ אֱלֹהֵינוּ, ‹ יָחִיד חֵי הָעוֹלָמִים
מֶלֶךְ, מְשֻׁבָּח וּמְפֹאָר עֲדֵי עַד שְׁמוֹ הַגָּדוֹל
בָּרוּךְ אַתָּה יהוה, מֶלֶךְ מְהֻלָּל בַּתִּשְׁבָּחוֹת.

הוֹדוּ לַיהוה קִרְאוּ בִשְׁמוֹ, הוֹדִיעוּ בָעַמִּים עֲלִילֹתָיו: שִׁירוּ לוֹ, דברי הימים א׳ טז
זַמְּרוּ־לוֹ, שִׂיחוּ בְּכָל־נִפְלְאוֹתָיו: הִתְהַלְלוּ בְּשֵׁם קָדְשׁוֹ, יִשְׂמַח לֵב
מְבַקְשֵׁי יהוה: דִּרְשׁוּ יהוה וְעֻזּוֹ, בַּקְּשׁוּ פָנָיו תָּמִיד: זִכְרוּ נִפְלְאֹתָיו
אֲשֶׁר עָשָׂה, מֹפְתָיו וּמִשְׁפְּטֵי־פִיהוּ: זֶרַע יִשְׂרָאֵל עַבְדּוֹ, בְּנֵי יַעֲקֹב
בְּחִירָיו: הוּא יהוה אֱלֹהֵינוּ בְּכָל־הָאָרֶץ מִשְׁפָּטָיו: זִכְרוּ לְעוֹלָם
בְּרִיתוֹ, דָּבָר צִוָּה לְאֶלֶף דּוֹר: אֲשֶׁר כָּרַת אֶת־אַבְרָהָם, וּשְׁבוּעָתוֹ

בָּרוּךְ אַתָּה *Blessed are You.* The second part of this two-part blessing is an introduction to the biblical passages that follow.

וּבְשִׁירֵי דָוִד עַבְדֶּךָ *With the songs of Your servant David.* A reference to the psalms that form the core of the Verses of Praise.

הוֹדוּ לַיהוה *Thank the Lord.* A joyous celebration of Jewish history, this is the song David composed for the day the Ark was brought, in joy and dance, to Jerusalem.

הוֹדִיעוּ בָעַמִּים עֲלִילֹתָיו *Make His acts known among the peoples.* According

vowed it to Isaac, and confirmed it to Jacob as a statute and to Israel as an everlasting covenant, saying, "To you I will give the land of Canaan as your allotted heritage." You were then small in number, few, strangers there, wandering from nation to nation, from one kingdom to another, but He let no man oppress them, and for their sake He rebuked kings: "Do not touch My anointed ones, and do My prophets no harm." Sing to the LORD, all the earth; proclaim His salvation daily. Declare His glory among the nations, His marvels among all the peoples. For great is the LORD and greatly to be praised; He is awesome beyond all heavenly powers. ▸ For all the gods of the peoples are mere idols; it was the LORD who made the heavens.

Before Him are majesty and splendor; there is strength and beauty in His holy place. Render to the LORD, families of the peoples, render to the LORD honor and might. Render to the LORD the glory due to His name; bring an offering and come before Him; bow down to the LORD in the splendor of holiness. Tremble before Him, all the earth; the world stands firm, it will not be shaken. Let the heavens rejoice and the earth be glad; let them declare among the nations, "The LORD is King." Let the sea roar, and all that is in it; let the fields be jubilant, and all they contain. Then the trees of the forest will sing for joy before the LORD, for He is coming to judge the earth. Thank the LORD for He is good; His loving-kindness is for ever. Say: "Save us, God of our salvation; gather us and rescue us from the nations, to acknowledge Your holy name and glory in Your praise. Blessed is the LORD, God of Israel, from this world to eternity." And let all the people say "Amen" and "Praise the LORD."

---

pagans worshiped the sun, moon and stars as gods, not realizing that none was an independent power. Each had been made by the One God.

יִשְׂמְחוּ הַשָּׁמַיִם *Let the heavens rejoice.* A sentiment typical of the radiant vision of the Psalms: the universe moves in accordance with both the natural and moral laws that ensure its order and stability. Nature is not something to fear, but to celebrate.

וַיֹּאמְרוּ כָל־הָעָם *And let all the people say.* This was their response to the song sung the day the Ark was brought to Jerusalem (Ralbag).

לְיִצְחָק: וַיַּעֲמִידֶהָ לְיַעֲקֹב לְחֹק, לְיִשְׂרָאֵל בְּרִית עוֹלָם: לֵאמֹר, לְךָ אֶתֵּן אֶרֶץ־כְּנָעַן, חֶבֶל נַחֲלַתְכֶם: בִּהְיוֹתְכֶם מְתֵי מִסְפָּר, כִּמְעַט וְגָרִים בָּהּ: וַיִּתְהַלְּכוּ מִגּוֹי אֶל־גּוֹי, וּמִמַּמְלָכָה אֶל־עַם אַחֵר: לֹא־הִנִּיחַ לְאִישׁ לְעָשְׁקָם, וַיּוֹכַח עֲלֵיהֶם מְלָכִים: אַל־תִּגְּעוּ בִּמְשִׁיחָי, וּבִנְבִיאַי אַל־תָּרֵעוּ: שִׁירוּ לַיהוה כָּל־הָאָרֶץ, בַּשְּׂרוּ מִיּוֹם־אֶל־יוֹם יְשׁוּעָתוֹ: סַפְּרוּ בַגּוֹיִם אֶת־כְּבוֹדוֹ, בְּכָל־הָעַמִּים נִפְלְאֹתָיו: כִּי גָדוֹל יהוה וּמְהֻלָּל מְאֹד, וְנוֹרָא הוּא עַל־כָּל־אֱלֹהִים: › כִּי כָּל־אֱלֹהֵי הָעַמִּים אֱלִילִים, וַיהוה שָׁמַיִם עָשָׂה:

הוֹד וְהָדָר לְפָנָיו, עֹז וְחֶדְוָה בִּמְקֹמוֹ: הָבוּ לַיהוה מִשְׁפְּחוֹת עַמִּים, הָבוּ לַיהוה כָּבוֹד וָעֹז: הָבוּ לַיהוה כְּבוֹד שְׁמוֹ, שְׂאוּ מִנְחָה וּבֹאוּ לְפָנָיו, הִשְׁתַּחֲווּ לַיהוה בְּהַדְרַת־קֹדֶשׁ: חִילוּ מִלְּפָנָיו כָּל־הָאָרֶץ, אַף־תִּכּוֹן תֵּבֵל בַּל־תִּמּוֹט: יִשְׂמְחוּ הַשָּׁמַיִם וְתָגֵל הָאָרֶץ, וְיֹאמְרוּ בַגּוֹיִם יהוה מָלָךְ: יִרְעַם הַיָּם וּמְלוֹאוֹ, יַעֲלֹץ הַשָּׂדֶה וְכָל־אֲשֶׁר־בּוֹ: אָז יְרַנְּנוּ עֲצֵי הַיָּעַר, מִלִּפְנֵי יהוה, כִּי־בָא לִשְׁפּוֹט אֶת־הָאָרֶץ: הוֹדוּ לַיהוה כִּי טוֹב, כִּי לְעוֹלָם חַסְדּוֹ: וְאִמְרוּ, הוֹשִׁיעֵנוּ אֱלֹהֵי יִשְׁעֵנוּ, וְקַבְּצֵנוּ וְהַצִּילֵנוּ מִן־הַגּוֹיִם, לְהֹדוֹת לְשֵׁם קָדְשֶׁךָ, לְהִשְׁתַּבֵּחַ בִּתְהִלָּתֶךָ: בָּרוּךְ יהוה אֱלֹהֵי יִשְׂרָאֵל מִן־הָעוֹלָם וְעַד־הָעֹלָם, וַיֹּאמְרוּ כָל־הָעָם אָמֵן, וְהַלֵּל לַיהוה:

וַיִּתְהַלְּכוּ *Wandering.* Each of the patriarchs was forced to leave the land because of famine.

וַיּוֹכַח עֲלֵיהֶם מְלָכִים *For their sake He rebuked kings.* A reference to God's affliction of Pharaoh (Gen. 12:17) and Abimelech, King of Gerar (Gen. 20:18) for taking Sarah; and Laban when he was pursuing Jacob (Gen. 31:24, 29).

מְשִׁיחָי *My anointed ones.* Although only kings and priests were anointed, here the phrase is used as a metaphor meaning "chosen ones."

אֱלִילִים, וַיהוה שָׁמַיִם עָשָׂה *Mere idols; it was the Lord who made the heavens.* The

▸ Exalt the LORD our God and bow before His footstool: He is *Ps. 99*
holy. Exalt the LORD our God and bow at His holy mountain; for
holy is the LORD our God.

He is compassionate. He forgives iniquity and does not destroy. *Ps. 78*
Repeatedly He suppresses His anger, not rousing His full wrath.
You, LORD: do not withhold Your compassion from me. May Your *Ps. 40*
loving-kindness and truth always guard me. Remember, LORD, Your *Ps. 25*
acts of compassion and love, for they have existed for ever. Ascribe *Ps. 68*
power to God, whose majesty is over Israel and whose might is in
the skies. You are awesome, God, in Your holy places. It is the God
of Israel who gives might and strength to the people, may God
be blessed. God of retribution, LORD, God of retribution, appear. *Ps. 94*
Arise, Judge of the earth, to repay the arrogant their just deserts.
Salvation belongs to the LORD; may Your blessing rest upon Your *Ps. 3*
people, Selah! ▸ The LORD of hosts is with us, the God of Jacob is *Ps. 46*
our stronghold, Selah! LORD of hosts, happy is the one who trusts *Ps. 84*
in You. LORD, save! May the King answer us on the day we call. *Ps. 20*

Save Your people and bless Your heritage; tend them and carry *Ps. 28*
them for ever. Our soul longs for the LORD; He is our Help and *Ps. 33*
Shield. For in Him our hearts rejoice, for in His holy name we have
trusted. May Your loving-kindness, LORD, be upon us, as we have
put our hope in You. Show us, LORD, Your loving-kindness and *Ps. 85*
grant us Your salvation. Arise, help us and redeem us for the sake *Ps. 44*
of Your love. I am the LORD your God who brought you up from *Ps. 81*
the land of Egypt: open your mouth wide and I will fill it. Happy *Ps. 144*
is the people for whom this is so; happy is the people whose God
the LORD. ▸ As for me, I trust in Your loving-kindness; my heart *Ps. 13*
rejoices in Your salvation. I will sing to the LORD for He has been
good to me.

---

divine justice and compassion, moving seamlessly from national to individual thanksgiving.

‹ רוֹמְמוּ יהוה אֱלֹהֵינוּ וְהִשְׁתַּחֲווּ לַהֲדֹם רַגְלָיו, קָדוֹשׁ הוּא: תהלים צט
רוֹמְמוּ יהוה אֱלֹהֵינוּ וְהִשְׁתַּחֲווּ לְהַר קָדְשׁוֹ, כִּי־קָדוֹשׁ יהוה
אֱלֹהֵינוּ:
וְהוּא רַחוּם, יְכַפֵּר עָוֹן וְלֹא־יַשְׁחִית, וְהִרְבָּה לְהָשִׁיב אַפּוֹ, תהלים עח
וְלֹא־יָעִיר כָּל־חֲמָתוֹ: אַתָּה יהוה לֹא־תִכְלָא רַחֲמֶיךָ מִמֶּנִּי, חַסְדְּךָ תהלים מ
וַאֲמִתְּךָ תָּמִיד יִצְּרוּנִי: זְכֹר־רַחֲמֶיךָ יהוה וַחֲסָדֶיךָ, כִּי מֵעוֹלָם תהלים כה
הֵמָּה: תְּנוּ עֹז לֵאלֹהִים, עַל־יִשְׂרָאֵל גַּאֲוָתוֹ, וְעֻזּוֹ בַּשְּׁחָקִים: תהלים סח
נוֹרָא אֱלֹהִים מִמִּקְדָּשֶׁיךָ, אֵל יִשְׂרָאֵל הוּא נֹתֵן עֹז וְתַעֲצֻמוֹת
לָעָם, בָּרוּךְ אֱלֹהִים: אֵל־נְקָמוֹת יהוה, אֵל נְקָמוֹת הוֹפִיעַ: הִנָּשֵׂא תהלים צד
שֹׁפֵט הָאָרֶץ, הָשֵׁב גְּמוּל עַל־גֵּאִים: לַיהוה הַיְשׁוּעָה, עַל־עַמְּךָ תהלים ג
בִרְכָתֶךָ סֶּלָה: ‹ יהוה צְבָאוֹת עִמָּנוּ, מִשְׂגָּב לָנוּ אֱלֹהֵי יַעֲקֹב תהלים מו
סֶלָה: יהוה צְבָאוֹת, אַשְׁרֵי אָדָם בֹּטֵחַ בָּךְ: יהוה הוֹשִׁיעָה, תהלים פד תהלים כ
הַמֶּלֶךְ יַעֲנֵנוּ בְיוֹם־קָרְאֵנוּ:
הוֹשִׁיעָה אֶת־עַמֶּךָ, וּבָרֵךְ אֶת־נַחֲלָתֶךָ, וּרְעֵם וְנַשְּׂאֵם עַד־ תהלים כח
הָעוֹלָם: נַפְשֵׁנוּ חִכְּתָה לַיהוה, עֶזְרֵנוּ וּמָגִנֵּנוּ הוּא: כִּי־בוֹ יִשְׂמַח תהלים לג
לִבֵּנוּ, כִּי בְשֵׁם קָדְשׁוֹ בָטָחְנוּ: יְהִי־חַסְדְּךָ יהוה עָלֵינוּ, כַּאֲשֶׁר
יִחַלְנוּ לָךְ: הַרְאֵנוּ יהוה חַסְדֶּךָ, וְיֶשְׁעֲךָ תִּתֶּן־לָנוּ: קוּמָה עֶזְרָתָה תהלים פה תהלים מד
לָּנוּ, וּפְדֵנוּ לְמַעַן חַסְדֶּךָ: אָנֹכִי יהוה אֱלֹהֶיךָ הַמַּעַלְךָ מֵאֶרֶץ תהלים פא
מִצְרָיִם, הַרְחֶב־פִּיךָ וַאֲמַלְאֵהוּ: אַשְׁרֵי הָעָם שֶׁכָּכָה לּוֹ, אַשְׁרֵי תהלים קמד
הָעָם שֶׁיהוה אֱלֹהָיו: ‹ וַאֲנִי בְּחַסְדְּךָ בָטַחְתִּי, יָגֵל לִבִּי בִּישׁוּעָתֶךָ, תהלים יג
אָשִׁירָה לַיהוה, כִּי גָמַל עָלָי:

רוֹמְמוּ *Exalt.* A selection of verses from the book of Psalms, on the themes of

לַמְנַצֵּחַ For the conductor of music. A psalm of David. *Ps. 19*
The heavens declare the glory of God;
the skies proclaim the work of His hands.
Day to day they pour forth speech;
night to night they communicate knowledge.
There is no speech, there are no words,
their voice is not heard.
Yet their music carries throughout the earth,
their words to the end of the world.
In them He has set a tent for the sun.
It emerges like a groom from his marriage chamber,
rejoicing like a champion about to run a race.
It rises at one end of the heaven
and makes its circuit to the other:
nothing is hidden from its heat.
The Lord's Torah is perfect, refreshing the soul.
The Lord's testimony is faithful, making the simple wise.
The Lord's precepts are just, gladdening the heart.
The Lord's commandment is radiant, giving light to the eyes.
The fear of the Lord is pure, enduring for ever.
The Lord's judgments are true, altogether righteous.
More precious than gold, than much fine gold.
They are sweeter than honey, than honey from the comb.
Your servant, too, is careful of them,
for in observing them there is great reward.

---

will in the form of the Torah. The Psalmist speaks ecstatically about the power of Torah to transform those who open themselves to its radiance. In Creation we encounter the world that is, but in Revelation we catch a glimpse of the world that ought to be, and will come to be when we align our will with the will of God. Finally comes the speech of humanity to God ("the words of my mouth and the meditation of my heart") in the form of prayer.

לַמְנַצֵּחַ מִזְמוֹר לְדָוִד: תהלים יט

הַשָּׁמַיִם מְסַפְּרִים כְּבוֹד־אֵל, וּמַעֲשֵׂה יָדָיו מַגִּיד הָרָקִיעַ:

יוֹם לְיוֹם יַבִּיעַ אֹמֶר, וְלַיְלָה לְּלַיְלָה יְחַוֶּה־דָּעַת:

אֵין־אֹמֶר וְאֵין דְּבָרִים, בְּלִי נִשְׁמָע קוֹלָם:

בְּכָל־הָאָרֶץ יָצָא קַוָּם, וּבִקְצֵה תֵבֵל מִלֵּיהֶם
 לַשֶּׁמֶשׁ שָׂם־אֹהֶל בָּהֶם:

וְהוּא כְּחָתָן יֹצֵא מֵחֻפָּתוֹ, יָשִׂישׂ כְּגִבּוֹר לָרוּץ אֹרַח:

מִקְצֵה הַשָּׁמַיִם מוֹצָאוֹ, וּתְקוּפָתוֹ עַל־קְצוֹתָם
 וְאֵין נִסְתָּר מֵחַמָּתוֹ:

תּוֹרַת יהוה תְּמִימָה, מְשִׁיבַת נָפֶשׁ
 עֵדוּת יהוה נֶאֱמָנָה, מַחְכִּימַת פֶּתִי:

פִּקּוּדֵי יהוה יְשָׁרִים, מְשַׂמְּחֵי־לֵב
 מִצְוַת יהוה בָּרָה, מְאִירַת עֵינָיִם:

יִרְאַת יהוה טְהוֹרָה, עוֹמֶדֶת לָעַד
 מִשְׁפְּטֵי־יהוה אֱמֶת, צָדְקוּ יַחְדָּו:

הַנֶּחֱמָדִים מִזָּהָב וּמִפַּז רָב, וּמְתוּקִים מִדְּבַשׁ וְנֹפֶת צוּפִים:

גַּם־עַבְדְּךָ נִזְהָר בָּהֶם, בְּשָׁמְרָם עֵקֶב רָב:

לַמְנַצֵּחַ *Psalm 19.* A magnificent psalm in three parts, corresponding to the basic tripartite structure of Jewish belief: Creation, Revelation, and Redemption. The first seven verses are a hymn about Creation as God's work. The second section (verses 8–11) is about Revelation – Torah – as God's word. The third is a prayer for forgiveness, ending with the word "Redeemer." What connects them is the idea of speech. First is the silent speech of the universe, the "music of the spheres," that the universe continually utters to its Creator. Then comes the audible speech of God to humankind, the revelation of His

Yet who can discern his errors?
  Cleanse me of hidden faults.
Keep Your servant also from willful sins;
  let them not have dominion over me.
Then shall I be blameless,
  and innocent of grave sin.
▸ May the words of my mouth and the meditation of my heart
find favor before You, LORD, my Rock and my Redeemer.

לְדָוִד Of David. When he pretended to be insane before Abimelech, *Ps. 34*
who drove him away, and he left.
I will bless the LORD at all times;
  His praise will be always on my lips.
My soul will glory in the LORD;
  let the lowly hear this and rejoice.
Magnify the LORD with me;
  let us exalt His name together.
I sought the LORD, and He answered me;
  He saved me from all my fears.
Those who look to Him are radiant;
  their faces are never downcast.
This poor man called, and the LORD heard;
  He saved him from all his troubles.
The LORD's angel encamps around those who fear Him,
  and He rescues them.
Taste and see that the LORD is good;
  happy is the man who takes refuge in Him.
Fear the LORD, you His holy ones,
  for those who fear Him lack nothing.

---

thanksgiving: "This poor man called, and the LORD heard… None who take refuge in Him shall be condemned." God is not on the side of those who embody the arrogance of power: "The LORD is close to the brokenhearted, and saves those who are crushed in spirit."

שְׁגִיאוֹת מִי־יָבִין, מִנִּסְתָּרוֹת נַקֵּנִי:
גַּם מִזֵּדִים חֲשֹׂךְ עַבְדֶּךָ, אַל־יִמְשְׁלוּ־בִי אָז אֵיתָם
וְנִקֵּיתִי מִפֶּשַׁע רָב:
◂ יִהְיוּ לְרָצוֹן אִמְרֵי־פִי וְהֶגְיוֹן לִבִּי לְפָנֶיךָ, יהוה, צוּרִי וְגֹאֲלִי:

תהלים לד
לְדָוִד, בְּשַׁנּוֹתוֹ אֶת־טַעְמוֹ לִפְנֵי אֲבִימֶלֶךְ, וַיְגָרְשֵׁהוּ וַיֵּלַךְ:
אֲבָרְכָה אֶת־יהוה בְּכָל־עֵת, תָּמִיד תְּהִלָּתוֹ בְּפִי:
בַּיהוה תִּתְהַלֵּל נַפְשִׁי, יִשְׁמְעוּ עֲנָוִים וְיִשְׂמָחוּ:
גַּדְּלוּ לַיהוה אִתִּי, וּנְרוֹמְמָה שְׁמוֹ יַחְדָּו:
דָּרַשְׁתִּי אֶת־יהוה וְעָנָנִי, וּמִכָּל־מְגוּרוֹתַי הִצִּילָנִי:
הִבִּיטוּ אֵלָיו וְנָהָרוּ, וּפְנֵיהֶם אַל־יֶחְפָּרוּ:
זֶה עָנִי קָרָא, וַיהוה שָׁמֵעַ, וּמִכָּל־צָרוֹתָיו הוֹשִׁיעוֹ:
חֹנֶה מַלְאַךְ־יהוה סָבִיב לִירֵאָיו, וַיְחַלְּצֵם:
טַעֲמוּ וּרְאוּ כִּי־טוֹב יהוה, אַשְׁרֵי הַגֶּבֶר יֶחֱסֶה־בּוֹ:
יְראוּ אֶת־יהוה קְדֹשָׁיו, כִּי־אֵין מַחְסוֹר לִירֵאָיו:

שְׁגִיאוֹת מִי־יָבִין *Yet who can discern his errors?* The Psalmist notes the fundamental difference between humans and inanimate nature: the latter automatically conforms to the will of its Creator, but mankind does not. He therefore prays to be protected from sin, deliberate or unwitting.

יִהְיוּ לְרָצוֹן אִמְרֵי־פִי *May the words of my mouth.* A beautiful prayer we say at the end of every Amida.

לְדָוִד *Psalm 34.* David, fleeing from Saul, took refuge in the Philistine city of Gath. There he was recognized, and knew that his life was in danger. He decided to pretend to be insane, "making marks on the doors of the gate and letting saliva run down his beard." The Philistine king, dismissing him as a madman, told his servants to remove him. Thus David was able to make good his escape (1 Sam. 21:11–16). He composed this psalm as a song of

Young lions may grow weak and hungry,
but those who seek the LORD lack no good thing.
Come, my children, listen to me;
I will teach you the fear of the LORD.
Who desires life,
loving each day to see good?
Then guard your tongue from evil
and your lips from speaking deceit.
Turn from evil and do good;
seek peace and pursue it.
The eyes of the LORD are on the righteous
and His ears attentive to their cry;
The LORD's face is set against those who do evil,
to erase their memory from the earth.
The righteous cry out, and the LORD hears them;
delivering them from all their troubles.
The LORD is close to the brokenhearted,
and saves those who are crushed in spirit.
Many troubles may befall the righteous,
but the LORD delivers him from them all;
He protects all his bones,
so that none of them will be broken.
Evil will slay the wicked;
the enemies of the righteous will be condemned.
▸ The LORD redeems His servants;
none who take refuge in Him shall be condemned.

תְּפִלָּה לְמֹשֶׁה A prayer of Moses, the man of God. LORD, You have *Ps. 90*
been our shelter in every generation. Before the mountains were born, before You brought forth the earth and the world, from everlasting to everlasting You are God. You turn men back to dust, saying, "Return, you children of men." For a thousand years in Your sight

כְּפִירִים רָשׁוּ וְרָעֵבוּ, וְדֹרְשֵׁי יהוה לֹא־יַחְסְרוּ כָל־טוֹב:
לְכוּ־בָנִים שִׁמְעוּ־לִי, יִרְאַת יהוה אֲלַמֶּדְכֶם:
מִי־הָאִישׁ הֶחָפֵץ חַיִּים, אֹהֵב יָמִים לִרְאוֹת טוֹב:
נְצֹר לְשׁוֹנְךָ מֵרָע, וּשְׂפָתֶיךָ מִדַּבֵּר מִרְמָה:
סוּר מֵרָע וַעֲשֵׂה־טוֹב, בַּקֵּשׁ שָׁלוֹם וְרָדְפֵהוּ:
עֵינֵי יהוה אֶל־צַדִּיקִים, וְאָזְנָיו אֶל־שַׁוְעָתָם:
פְּנֵי יהוה בְּעֹשֵׂי רָע, לְהַכְרִית מֵאֶרֶץ זִכְרָם:
צָעֲקוּ וַיהוה שָׁמֵעַ, וּמִכָּל־צָרוֹתָם הִצִּילָם:
קָרוֹב יהוה לְנִשְׁבְּרֵי־לֵב, וְאֶת־דַּכְּאֵי־רוּחַ יוֹשִׁיעַ:
רַבּוֹת רָעוֹת צַדִּיק, וּמִכֻּלָּם יַצִּילֶנּוּ יהוה:
שֹׁמֵר כָּל־עַצְמֹתָיו, אַחַת מֵהֵנָּה לֹא נִשְׁבָּרָה:
תְּמוֹתֵת רָשָׁע רָעָה, וְשֹׂנְאֵי צַדִּיק יֶאְשָׁמוּ:
◂ פּוֹדֶה יהוה נֶפֶשׁ עֲבָדָיו, וְלֹא יֶאְשְׁמוּ כָּל־הַחֹסִים בּוֹ:

תהלים צ
תְּפִלָּה לְמֹשֶׁה אִישׁ־הָאֱלֹהִים, אֲדֹנָי, מָעוֹן אַתָּה הָיִיתָ לָּנוּ בְּדֹר
וָדֹר: בְּטֶרֶם הָרִים יֻלָּדוּ, וַתְּחוֹלֵל אֶרֶץ וְתֵבֵל, וּמֵעוֹלָם עַד־עוֹלָם
אַתָּה אֵל: תָּשֵׁב אֱנוֹשׁ עַד־דַּכָּא, וַתֹּאמֶר שׁוּבוּ בְנֵי־אָדָם: כִּי

תְּפִלָּה לְמֹשֶׁה *Psalm 90.* A magnificent poem, the only psalm attributed to Moses, on God's eternity and our mortality. However long we live, our lives are a mere microsecond in the history of the cosmos. Wisdom consists in knowing how brief is our stay on earth, and in the determination to use every day in service of the right, the just and the holy. The good we do lives after us; the rest is oft interred with our bones.

אִישׁ־הָאֱלֹהִים *The man of God.* This description also occurs in Deuteronomy 33:1, prefacing Moses' final blessing to the people.

are like yesterday when it has passed, like a watch in the night. You sweep men away; they sleep. In the morning they are like grass newly grown: in the morning it flourishes and is new, but by evening it withers and dries up. For we are consumed by Your anger, terrified by Your fury. You have set our iniquities before You, our secret sins in the light of Your presence. All our days pass away in Your wrath, we spend our years like a sigh. The span of our life is seventy years, or if we are strong, eighty years; but the best of them is trouble and sorrow, for they quickly pass, and we fly away. Who can know the force of Your anger? Your wrath matches the fear due to You. Teach us rightly to number our days, that we may gain a heart of wisdom. Relent, O Lord! How much longer? Be sorry for Your servants. Satisfy us in the morning with Your loving-kindness, that we may sing and rejoice all our days. Grant us joy for as many days as You have afflicted us, for as many years as we saw trouble. Let Your deeds be seen by Your servants, and Your glory by their children. ▸ May the pleasantness of the Lord our God be upon us. Establish for us the work of our hands, O establish the work of our hands.

יֹשֵׁב בְּסֵתֶר He who lives in the shelter of the Most High dwells in *Ps. 91*
the shadow of the Almighty. I say of the Lord, my Refuge and Stronghold, my God in whom I trust, that He will save you from the fowler's snare and the deadly pestilence. With His pinions He will cover you, and beneath His wings you will find shelter; His faithfulness is an encircling shield. You need not fear terror by night, nor the arrow that flies by day; not the pestilence that stalks in darkness, nor the plague that ravages at noon. A thousand may fall at your side, ten thousand at your right hand, but it will not come near you. You will only look with your eyes and see the punishment of the wicked.

יֹשֵׁב בְּסֵתֶר *Psalm 91.* A psalm for protection at a time of danger. There is no life without risk, and courage does not mean having no fear; it means feeling it, yet overcoming it in the knowledge that we are not alone. "We have nothing to fear but fear itself," and faith is the antidote to fear. The psalm radiates a sense of confidence and trust even in a world full of hazards.

אֶלֶף שָׁנִים בְּעֵינֶיךָ, כְּיוֹם אֶתְמוֹל כִּי יַעֲבֹר, וְאַשְׁמוּרָה בַלָּיְלָה:
זְרַמְתָּם, שֵׁנָה יִהְיוּ, בַּבֹּקֶר כֶּחָצִיר יַחֲלֹף: בַּבֹּקֶר יָצִיץ וְחָלָף, לָעֶרֶב
יְמוֹלֵל וְיָבֵשׁ: כִּי־כָלִינוּ בְאַפֶּךָ, וּבַחֲמָתְךָ נִבְהָלְנוּ: שַׁתָּ עֲוֹנֹתֵינוּ,
לְנֶגְדֶּךָ, עֲלֻמֵנוּ לִמְאוֹר פָּנֶיךָ: כִּי כָל־יָמֵינוּ פָּנוּ בְעֶבְרָתֶךָ, כִּלִּינוּ
שָׁנֵינוּ כְמוֹ־הֶגֶה: יְמֵי־שְׁנוֹתֵינוּ בָהֶם שִׁבְעִים שָׁנָה, וְאִם בִּגְבוּרֹת
שְׁמוֹנִים שָׁנָה, וְרָהְבָּם עָמָל וָאָוֶן, כִּי־גָז חִישׁ וַנָּעֻפָה: מִי־יוֹדֵעַ
עֹז אַפֶּךָ, וּכְיִרְאָתְךָ עֶבְרָתֶךָ, לִמְנוֹת יָמֵינוּ כֵּן הוֹדַע, וְנָבִא לְבַב
חָכְמָה: שׁוּבָה יהוה עַד־מָתָי, וְהִנָּחֵם עַל־עֲבָדֶיךָ: שַׂבְּעֵנוּ בַבֹּקֶר
חַסְדֶּךָ, וּנְרַנְּנָה וְנִשְׂמְחָה בְּכָל־יָמֵינוּ: שַׂמְּחֵנוּ כִּימוֹת עִנִּיתָנוּ,
שְׁנוֹת רָאִינוּ רָעָה: יֵרָאֶה אֶל־עֲבָדֶיךָ פָעֳלֶךָ, וַהֲדָרְךָ עַל־בְּנֵיהֶם:
◂ וִיהִי נֹעַם אֲדֹנָי אֱלֹהֵינוּ עָלֵינוּ, וּמַעֲשֵׂה יָדֵינוּ כּוֹנְנָה עָלֵינוּ,
וּמַעֲשֵׂה יָדֵינוּ כּוֹנְנֵהוּ:

יֹשֵׁב בְּסֵתֶר עֶלְיוֹן, בְּצֵל שַׁדַּי יִתְלוֹנָן: אֹמַר לַיהוה מַחְסִי וּמְצוּדָתִי, תהלים צא
אֱלֹהַי אֶבְטַח־בּוֹ: כִּי הוּא יַצִּילְךָ מִפַּח יָקוּשׁ, מִדֶּבֶר הַוּוֹת:
בְּאֶבְרָתוֹ יָסֶךְ לָךְ, וְתַחַת־כְּנָפָיו תֶּחְסֶה, צִנָּה וְסֹחֵרָה אֲמִתּוֹ:
לֹא־תִירָא מִפַּחַד לָיְלָה, מֵחֵץ יָעוּף יוֹמָם: מִדֶּבֶר בָּאֹפֶל יַהֲלֹךְ,
מִקֶּטֶב יָשׁוּד צָהֳרָיִם: יִפֹּל מִצִּדְּךָ אֶלֶף, וּרְבָבָה מִימִינֶךָ, אֵלֶיךָ
לֹא יִגָּשׁ: רַק בְּעֵינֶיךָ תַבִּיט, וְשִׁלֻּמַת רְשָׁעִים תִּרְאֶה: כִּי־אַתָּה

אֶלֶף שָׁנִים...וְאַשְׁמוּרָה בַלָּיְלָה *A thousand years… a watch in the night.* A dramatic contrast between God's time-scale and ours. Note the succession of poetic images conveying the brevity of human life: it flows as fast as a swollen river, as quickly as a sleep or a dream, it is like grass in a parched land that soon withers, it is like a sigh, a mere breath, like a bird that briefly lands then flies away.

וּמַעֲשֵׂה יָדֵינוּ כּוֹנְנָה עָלֵינוּ *Establish for us the work of our hands.* Help us create achievements that last. According to the sages, this is the blessing Moses gave the Israelites when they completed the building of the Tabernacle.

Because you said "The LORD is my Refuge," taking the Most High as your shelter, no harm will befall you, no plague will come near your tent, for He will command His angels about you, to guard you in all your ways. They will lift you in their hands, lest your foot stumble on a stone. You will tread on lions and vipers, you will trample on young lions and snakes. [God says] "Because he loves Me, I will rescue him; I will protect him, because he acknowledges My name. When he calls on Me, I will answer him, I will be with him in distress, I will deliver him and bring him honor. ▸ With long life I will satisfy him, and show him My salvation. With long life I will satisfy him, and show him My salvation."

הַלְלוּיָהּ Halleluya! Praise the name of the LORD. Praise Him, you servants of the LORD who stand in the LORD's House, in the courtyards of the House of our God. Praise the LORD, for the LORD is good; sing praises to His name, for it is lovely. For the LORD has chosen Jacob as His own, Israel as His treasure. For I know that the LORD is great, that our LORD is above all heavenly powers. Whatever pleases the LORD, He does, in heaven and on earth, in the seas and all the depths. He raises clouds from the ends of the earth; He sends lightning with the rain; He brings out the wind from His storehouses. He struck down the firstborn of Egypt, of both man and animals. He sent signs and wonders into your midst, Egypt – against Pharaoh and all his servants. He struck down many nations and slew mighty kings: Siḥon, King of the Amorites, Og, King of Bashan, and all the kingdoms of Canaan, giving their land as a heritage, a heritage for His people Israel. Your name, LORD, endures for ever; Your renown, LORD, for all generations. For the LORD will bring justice to His people, and have compassion on His servants. The idols of the nations are silver and gold, the work of human hands. They have mouths, but cannot speak; eyes, but cannot see; ears, but cannot *Ps. 135*

פֶּה־לָהֶם וְלֹא יְדַבֵּרוּ *They have mouths but cannot speak.* Those who put their faith in forces that are less than human, themselves become less than human. Many have been the idols of history: power, wealth, status, the nation, the race, the state, the ideology, the system. None has lasted, for each has crushed the human spirit. None has given rise to stable systems of liberty and dignity.

יהוה מַחְסִי, עֶלְיוֹן שַׂמְתָּ מְעוֹנֶךָ: לֹא־תְאֻנֶּה אֵלֶיךָ רָעָה, וְנֶגַע
לֹא־יִקְרַב בְּאָהֳלֶךָ: כִּי מַלְאָכָיו יְצַוֶּה־לָּךְ, לִשְׁמָרְךָ בְּכָל־דְּרָכֶיךָ:
עַל־כַּפַּיִם יִשָּׂאוּנְךָ, פֶּן־תִּגֹּף בָּאֶבֶן רַגְלֶךָ: עַל־שַׁחַל וָפֶתֶן תִּדְרֹךְ,
תִּרְמֹס כְּפִיר וְתַנִּין: כִּי בִי חָשַׁק וַאֲפַלְּטֵהוּ, אֲשַׂגְּבֵהוּ כִּי־יָדַע
שְׁמִי: יִקְרָאֵנִי וְאֶעֱנֵהוּ, עִמּוֹ אָנֹכִי בְצָרָה, אֲחַלְּצֵהוּ וַאֲכַבְּדֵהוּ:
‹ אֹרֶךְ יָמִים אַשְׂבִּיעֵהוּ, וְאַרְאֵהוּ בִּישׁוּעָתִי:
אֹרֶךְ יָמִים אַשְׂבִּיעֵהוּ, וְאַרְאֵהוּ בִּישׁוּעָתִי:

הַלְלוּיָהּ, הַלְלוּ אֶת־שֵׁם יהוה, הַלְלוּ עַבְדֵי יהוה: שֶׁעֹמְדִים בְּבֵית תהלים קלה
יהוה, בְּחַצְרוֹת בֵּית אֱלֹהֵינוּ: הַלְלוּיָהּ כִּי־טוֹב יהוה, זַמְּרוּ לִשְׁמוֹ
כִּי נָעִים: כִּי־יַעֲקֹב בָּחַר לוֹ יָהּ, יִשְׂרָאֵל לִסְגֻלָּתוֹ: כִּי אֲנִי יָדַעְתִּי
כִּי־גָדוֹל יהוה, וַאֲדֹנֵינוּ מִכָּל־אֱלֹהִים: כֹּל אֲשֶׁר־חָפֵץ יהוה עָשָׂה,
בַּשָּׁמַיִם וּבָאָרֶץ, בַּיַּמִּים וְכָל־תְּהֹמוֹת: מַעֲלֶה נְשִׂאִים מִקְצֵה
הָאָרֶץ, בְּרָקִים לַמָּטָר עָשָׂה, מוֹצֵא־רוּחַ מֵאוֹצְרוֹתָיו: שֶׁהִכָּה
בְּכוֹרֵי מִצְרָיִם, מֵאָדָם עַד־בְּהֵמָה: שָׁלַח אוֹתֹת וּמֹפְתִים בְּתוֹכֵכִי
מִצְרָיִם, בְּפַרְעֹה וּבְכָל־עֲבָדָיו: שֶׁהִכָּה גּוֹיִם רַבִּים, וְהָרַג מְלָכִים
עֲצוּמִים: לְסִיחוֹן מֶלֶךְ הָאֱמֹרִי, וּלְעוֹג מֶלֶךְ הַבָּשָׁן, וּלְכֹל מַמְלְכוֹת
כְּנָעַן: וְנָתַן אַרְצָם נַחֲלָה, נַחֲלָה לְיִשְׂרָאֵל עַמּוֹ: יהוה שִׁמְךָ
לְעוֹלָם, יהוה זִכְרְךָ לְדֹר־וָדֹר: כִּי־יָדִין יהוה עַמּוֹ, וְעַל־עֲבָדָיו
יִתְנֶחָם: עֲצַבֵּי הַגּוֹיִם כֶּסֶף וְזָהָב, מַעֲשֵׂה יְדֵי אָדָם: פֶּה־לָהֶם
וְלֹא יְדַבֵּרוּ, עֵינַיִם לָהֶם וְלֹא יִרְאוּ: אָזְנַיִם לָהֶם וְלֹא יַאֲזִינוּ, אַף

הַלְלוּיָהּ *Psalm 135.* Psalms 135 and 136 are a matched pair, describing the same events: the exodus from Egypt and the battles prior to the Israelites' entry into the Promised Land. What Psalm 135 says in prose, Psalm 136 says in poetry. Both are joyous celebrations of the redeeming power of God in history. Blaise Pascal thought that the history of the Jews was proof of the existence of God. Israel are the people who, in themselves, testify to something greater than themselves. Their miraculous survival is a signal of transcendence.

hear; there is no breath in their mouths. Those who make them will become like them: so will all who trust in them. ▸ House of Israel, bless the LORD. House of Aaron, bless the LORD. House of Levi, bless the LORD. You who fear the LORD, bless the LORD. Blessed is the LORD from Zion, He who dwells in Jerusalem. Halleluya!

The custom is to stand for the following psalm.

הודו Thank the LORD for He is good; His loving-kindness is for ever. *Ps. 136*
Thank the God of gods, His loving-kindness is for ever.
Thank the LORD of lords, His loving-kindness is for ever.
To the One who alone
works great wonders, His loving-kindness is for ever.
Who made the heavens with wisdom, His loving-kindness is for ever.
Who spread the earth upon the waters, His loving-kindness is for ever.
Who made the great lights, His loving-kindness is for ever.
The sun to rule by day, His loving-kindness is for ever.
The moon and the stars to rule by night, His loving-kindness is for ever.
Who struck Egypt
through their firstborn, His loving-kindness is for ever.
And brought out Israel from their midst, His loving-kindness is for ever.
With a strong hand
and outstretched arm, His loving-kindness is for ever.
Who split the Reed Sea into parts, His loving-kindness is for ever.
And made Israel pass through it, His loving-kindness is for ever.

כִּי־טוֹב *For He is good.* The phrase *ki tov* occurs repeatedly in Genesis 1: "And God said, Let there be… and there was… and God saw that it was good [*ki tov*]." Rabbi Jacob Zvi Mecklenburg (Germany, nineteenth century) suggested that the phrase be translated, as here, "and God saw, *for* He is good." The phrase does not mean merely that what God created was good. It means that He created because of His goodness. One who is good seeks to share good with others. It was God's desire to share the blessing of existence with others that led Him to create the universe.

אֵין־יֶשׁ־רְוּחַ בְּפִיהֶם: כְּמוֹהֶם יִהְיוּ עֹשֵׂיהֶם, כֹּל אֲשֶׁר־בֹּטֵחַ בָּהֶם:
‹ בֵּית יִשְׂרָאֵל בָּרְכוּ אֶת־יהוה, בֵּית אַהֲרֹן בָּרְכוּ אֶת־יהוה: בֵּית
הַלֵּוִי בָּרְכוּ אֶת־יהוה, יִרְאֵי יהוה בָּרְכוּ אֶת־יהוה: בָּרוּךְ יהוה
מִצִּיּוֹן, שֹׁכֵן יְרוּשָׁלָםִ, הַלְלוּיָהּ:

The custom is to stand for the following psalm.

הוֹדוּ לַיהוה כִּי־טוֹב כִּי לְעוֹלָם חַסְדּוֹ: תהלים קלו
הוֹדוּ לֵאלֹהֵי הָאֱלֹהִים כִּי לְעוֹלָם חַסְדּוֹ:
הוֹדוּ לַאֲדֹנֵי הָאֲדֹנִים כִּי לְעוֹלָם חַסְדּוֹ:
לְעֹשֵׂה נִפְלָאוֹת גְּדֹלוֹת לְבַדּוֹ כִּי לְעוֹלָם חַסְדּוֹ:
לְעֹשֵׂה הַשָּׁמַיִם בִּתְבוּנָה כִּי לְעוֹלָם חַסְדּוֹ:
לְרֹקַע הָאָרֶץ עַל־הַמָּיִם כִּי לְעוֹלָם חַסְדּוֹ:
לְעֹשֵׂה אוֹרִים גְּדֹלִים כִּי לְעוֹלָם חַסְדּוֹ:
אֶת־הַשֶּׁמֶשׁ לְמֶמְשֶׁלֶת בַּיּוֹם כִּי לְעוֹלָם חַסְדּוֹ:
אֶת־הַיָּרֵחַ וְכוֹכָבִים לְמֶמְשְׁלוֹת בַּלָּיְלָה כִּי לְעוֹלָם חַסְדּוֹ:
לְמַכֵּה מִצְרַיִם בִּבְכוֹרֵיהֶם כִּי לְעוֹלָם חַסְדּוֹ:
וַיּוֹצֵא יִשְׂרָאֵל מִתּוֹכָם כִּי לְעוֹלָם חַסְדּוֹ:
בְּיָד חֲזָקָה וּבִזְרוֹעַ נְטוּיָה כִּי לְעוֹלָם חַסְדּוֹ:
לְגֹזֵר יַם־סוּף לִגְזָרִים כִּי לְעוֹלָם חַסְדּוֹ:
וְהֶעֱבִיר יִשְׂרָאֵל בְּתוֹכוֹ כִּי לְעוֹלָם חַסְדּוֹ:

הודו *Psalm 136.* This psalm, known as *Hallel HaGadol,* "the Great Hallel," is one of the earliest forms of a litany, a prayer in which the leader utters a series of praises to which the congregation responds with a set reply. Jewish prayer contains many litanies, most notably during *Seliḥot,* the penitential prayers prior to and during Yom Kippur, and the *Hoshanot* said on Sukkot and Hoshana Raba.

Casting Pharaoh and his army
into the Reed Sea; His loving-kindness is for ever.
Who led His people
through the wilderness; His loving-kindness is for ever.
Who struck down great kings, His loving-kindness is for ever.
And slew mighty kings, His loving-kindness is for ever.
Siḥon, King of the Amorites, His loving-kindness is for ever.
And Og, King of Bashan, His loving-kindness is for ever.
And gave their land as a heritage, His loving-kindness is for ever.
A heritage for His servant Israel; His loving-kindness is for ever.
Who remembered us in our lowly state, His loving-kindness is for ever.
And rescued us from our tormentors, His loving-kindness is for ever.
▸ Who gives food to all flesh, His loving-kindness is for ever.
Give thanks to the God of heaven. His loving-kindness is for ever.

רַנְּנוּ Sing joyfully to the Lord, you righteous, for praise from the upright is seemly. Give thanks to the Lord with the harp; make music to Him on the ten-stringed lute. Sing Him a new song, play skillfully with shouts of joy. For the Lord's word is right, and all His deeds are done in faith. He loves righteousness and justice; the earth is full of the Lord's loving-kindness. By the Lord's word the heavens were made, and all their starry host by the breath of His mouth. He gathers the sea waters as a heap, and places the deep in storehouses. Let all the earth fear the Lord, and all the world's inhabitants stand in awe of Him. For He spoke, and it was; He commanded, and it stood firm. The Lord foils the plans of nations; He thwarts the intentions of peoples. The Lord's plans stand for ever, His heart's intents for all generations. Happy is the nation whose God is the Lord, the people He has chosen as His own. From heaven the Lord looks down and sees all mankind; from Ps. 33

---

earth He created and in the midst of the history He guides. To the Psalmist the universe has a moral as well as physical beauty: "The earth is full of the Lord's loving-kindness."

וְנִעֵר פַּרְעֹה וְחֵילוֹ בְיַם־סוּף	כִּי לְעוֹלָם חַסְדּוֹ:
לְמוֹלִיךְ עַמּוֹ בַּמִּדְבָּר	כִּי לְעוֹלָם חַסְדּוֹ:
לְמַכֵּה מְלָכִים גְּדֹלִים	כִּי לְעוֹלָם חַסְדּוֹ:
וַיַּהֲרֹג מְלָכִים אַדִּירִים	כִּי לְעוֹלָם חַסְדּוֹ:
לְסִיחוֹן מֶלֶךְ הָאֱמֹרִי	כִּי לְעוֹלָם חַסְדּוֹ:
וּלְעוֹג מֶלֶךְ הַבָּשָׁן	כִּי לְעוֹלָם חַסְדּוֹ:
וְנָתַן אַרְצָם לְנַחֲלָה	כִּי לְעוֹלָם חַסְדּוֹ:
נַחֲלָה לְיִשְׂרָאֵל עַבְדּוֹ	כִּי לְעוֹלָם חַסְדּוֹ:
שֶׁבְּשִׁפְלֵנוּ זָכַר לָנוּ	כִּי לְעוֹלָם חַסְדּוֹ:
וַיִּפְרְקֵנוּ מִצָּרֵינוּ	כִּי לְעוֹלָם חַסְדּוֹ:
◄ נֹתֵן לֶחֶם לְכָל־בָּשָׂר	כִּי לְעוֹלָם חַסְדּוֹ:
הוֹדוּ לְאֵל הַשָּׁמָיִם	כִּי לְעוֹלָם חַסְדּוֹ:

רַנְּנוּ צַדִּיקִים בַּיהוה, לַיְשָׁרִים נָאוָה תְהִלָּה: הוֹדוּ לַיהוה בְּכִנּוֹר, תהלים לג
בְּנֵבֶל עָשׂוֹר זַמְּרוּ־לוֹ: שִׁירוּ־לוֹ שִׁיר חָדָשׁ, הֵיטִיבוּ נַגֵּן בִּתְרוּעָה:
כִּי־יָשָׁר דְּבַר־יהוה, וְכָל־מַעֲשֵׂהוּ בֶּאֱמוּנָה: אֹהֵב צְדָקָה וּמִשְׁפָּט,
חֶסֶד יהוה מָלְאָה הָאָרֶץ: בִּדְבַר יהוה שָׁמַיִם נַעֲשׂוּ, וּבְרוּחַ פִּיו
כָּל־צְבָאָם: כֹּנֵס כַּנֵּד מֵי הַיָּם, נֹתֵן בְּאֹצָרוֹת תְּהוֹמוֹת: יִירְאוּ
מֵיהוה כָּל־הָאָרֶץ, מִמֶּנּוּ יָגוּרוּ כָּל־יֹשְׁבֵי תֵבֵל: כִּי הוּא אָמַר
וַיֶּהִי, הוּא־צִוָּה וַיַּעֲמֹד: יהוה הֵפִיר עֲצַת־גּוֹיִם, הֵנִיא מַחְשְׁבוֹת
עַמִּים: עֲצַת יהוה לְעוֹלָם תַּעֲמֹד, מַחְשְׁבוֹת לִבּוֹ לְדֹר וָדֹר:
אַשְׁרֵי הַגּוֹי אֲשֶׁר־יהוה אֱלֹהָיו, הָעָם בָּחַר לְנַחֲלָה לוֹ: מִשָּׁמַיִם
הִבִּיט יהוה, רָאָה אֶת־כָּל־בְּנֵי הָאָדָם: מִמְּכוֹן־שִׁבְתּוֹ הִשְׁגִּיחַ,

רַנְּנוּ *Psalm* 33. A joyous creation psalm inviting us to sing God's praises on the

His dwelling place He oversees all who live on earth. He forms the hearts of all, and discerns all their deeds. No king is saved by the size of his army; no warrior is delivered by great strength. A horse is a vain hope for deliverance; despite its great strength, it cannot save. The eye of the LORD is on those who fear Him, on those who place their hope in His unfailing love, to rescue their soul from death, and keep them alive in famine. Our soul waits for the LORD; He is our Help and Shield. ▸ In Him our hearts rejoice, for we trust in His holy name. Let Your unfailing love be upon us, LORD, as we have put our hope in You.

מִזְמוֹר שִׁיר A psalm. A song for the Sabbath day. It is good to thank *Ps. 92*
the LORD and sing psalms to Your name, Most High – to tell of Your loving-kindness in the morning and Your faithfulness at night, to the music of the ten-stringed lyre and the melody of the harp. For You have made me rejoice by Your work, O LORD; I sing for joy at the deeds of Your hands. How great are Your deeds, LORD, and how very deep Your thoughts. A boor cannot know, nor can a fool understand, that though the wicked spring up like grass and all evildoers flourish, it is only that they may be destroyed for ever. But You, LORD, are eternally exalted. For behold Your enemies, LORD, behold Your enemies will perish; all evildoers will be scattered. You have raised my pride like that of a wild ox; I am anointed with fresh oil. My eyes shall look in triumph on my adversaries, my ears shall hear the downfall of the wicked who rise against me. ▸ The righteous will flourish like a palm tree and grow tall like a cedar in Lebanon. Planted in the LORD's House, blossoming in our God's courtyards, they will still bear fruit in old age, and stay vigorous and fresh, proclaiming that the LORD is upright: He is my Rock, in whom there is no wrong.

Yet the psalm speaks not about creation but about justice. The universe is not simply matter and anti-matter governed by certain scientific laws. It is also – as Genesis 1 tells us seven times – "good." But how can we consider it

אֶל כׇּל־יֹשְׁבֵי הָאָֽרֶץ: הַיֹּצֵר יַֽחַד לִבָּם, הַמֵּבִין אֶל־כׇּל־מַעֲשֵׂיהֶם:
אֵין־הַמֶּֽלֶךְ נוֹשָׁע בְּרׇב־חָֽיִל, גִּבּוֹר לֹא־יִנָּצֵל בְּרׇב־כֹּֽחַ: שֶֽׁקֶר
הַסּוּס לִתְשׁוּעָה, וּבְרֹב חֵילוֹ לֹא יְמַלֵּט: הִנֵּה עֵין יהוה אֶל־יְרֵאָיו,
לַמְיַחֲלִים לְחַסְדּוֹ: לְהַצִּיל מִמָּֽוֶת נַפְשָׁם, וּלְחַיּוֹתָם בָּרָעָב: נַפְשֵֽׁנוּ
חִכְּתָה לַיהוה, עֶזְרֵֽנוּ וּמָגִנֵּֽנוּ הוּא: › כִּי־בוֹ יִשְׂמַח לִבֵּֽנוּ, כִּי בְשֵׁם
קׇדְשׁוֹ בָטָֽחְנוּ: יְהִי־חַסְדְּךָ יהוה עָלֵֽינוּ, כַּאֲשֶׁר יִחַֽלְנוּ לָךְ:

תהלים צב
מִזְמוֹר שִׁיר לְיוֹם הַשַּׁבָּת: טוֹב לְהֹדוֹת לַיהוה, וּלְזַמֵּר לְשִׁמְךָ
עֶלְיוֹן: לְהַגִּיד בַּבֹּֽקֶר חַסְדֶּֽךָ, וֶאֱמוּנָתְךָ בַּלֵּילוֹת: עֲלֵי־עָשׂוֹר
וַעֲלֵי־נָֽבֶל, עֲלֵי הִגָּיוֹן בְּכִנּוֹר: כִּי שִׂמַּחְתַּֽנִי יהוה בְּפׇעֳלֶֽךָ, בְּמַעֲשֵׂי
יָדֶֽיךָ אֲרַנֵּן: מַה־גָּדְלוּ מַעֲשֶֽׂיךָ יהוה, מְאֹד עָמְקוּ מַחְשְׁבֹתֶֽיךָ:
אִישׁ־בַּֽעַר לֹא יֵדָע, וּכְסִיל לֹא־יָבִין אֶת־זֹאת: בִּפְרֹֽחַ רְשָׁעִים
כְּמוֹ עֵֽשֶׂב, וַיָּצִֽיצוּ כׇּל־פֹּֽעֲלֵי אָֽוֶן, לְהִשָּׁמְדָם עֲדֵי־עַד: וְאַתָּה
מָרוֹם לְעֹלָם יהוה: כִּי הִנֵּה אֹיְבֶֽיךָ יהוה, כִּי־הִנֵּה אֹיְבֶֽיךָ יֹאבֵֽדוּ,
יִתְפָּרְדוּ כׇּל־פֹּֽעֲלֵי אָֽוֶן: וַתָּֽרֶם כִּרְאֵים קַרְנִי, בַּלֹּתִי בְּשֶֽׁמֶן רַעֲנָן:
וַתַּבֵּט עֵינִי בְּשׁוּרָי, בַּקָּמִים עָלַי מְרֵעִים תִּשְׁמַֽעְנָה אׇזְנָי: › צַדִּיק
כַּתָּמָר יִפְרָח, כְּאֶֽרֶז בַּלְּבָנוֹן יִשְׂגֶּה: שְׁתוּלִים בְּבֵית יהוה, בְּחַצְרוֹת
אֱלֹהֵֽינוּ יַפְרִֽיחוּ: עוֹד יְנוּבוּן בְּשֵׂיבָה, דְּשֵׁנִים וְרַעֲנַנִּים יִהְיוּ: לְהַגִּיד
כִּי־יָשָׁר יהוה, צוּרִי, וְלֹא־עַוְלָֽתָה בּוֹ:

מִזְמוֹר שִׁיר *Psalm 92.* The sages interpreted the opening of this psalm as meaning not just "a song *for* the Sabbath day" but also "a song sung *by* the Sabbath day," as if the day itself gave testimony to the Creator, which in effect it does. By being the day on which we do no creative work, time itself makes us aware that we are not just creators; we are also creations. The more we understand about the nature of the universe, its vast complexity, and the way it is finely tuned for the emergence of life, the more we sense a vast intelligence at work, framing its "fearful symmetry."

יהוה מָלָךְ The Lord reigns. He is robed in majesty. The Lord is Ps. 93
robed, girded with strength. The world is firmly established; it cannot be moved. Your throne stands firm as of old; You are eternal.
Rivers lift up, Lord, rivers lift up their voice, rivers lift up their
crashing waves. ▸ Mightier than the noise of many waters, than the
mighty waves of the sea is the Lord on high. Your testimonies are
very sure; holiness adorns Your House, Lord, for evermore.

יְהִי כְבוֹד May the Lord's glory be for ever; may the Lord rejoice Ps. 104
in His works. May the Lord's name be blessed, now and for ever. Ps. 113
From the rising of the sun to its setting, may the Lord's name be
praised. The Lord is high above all nations; His glory is above the
heavens. Lord, Your name is for ever. Your renown, Lord, is for all Ps. 135
generations. The Lord has established His throne in heaven; His Ps. 103
kingdom rules all. Let the heavens rejoice and the earth be glad. Let 1 Chr. 16
them say among the nations, "The Lord is King." The Lord is King,
the Lord was King, the Lord will be King for ever and all time.
The Lord is King for ever and all time; nations will perish from Ps. 10
His land. The Lord foils the plans of nations; He frustrates the Ps. 33
intentions of peoples. Many are the intentions in a person's mind, Prov. 19

---

creative power, that the universe is fundamentally good, and that chaos is merely order of a complexity we can neither understand nor predict. This is beautifully expressed in this psalm which sees the roar of the oceans as part of creation paying homage to its Creator. God is beyond – not within – nature, time and space.

יְהִי כְבוֹד *May the Lord's glory.* An anthology of verses, mainly from the books of Psalms, Proverbs, and Chronicles. God created the universe; therefore He is sole Sovereign of the universe, ruling nature through scientific law, and history through the moral law. Those who pit themselves against God are destined to fail: "Many are the intentions in a person's mind, but the Lord's plan prevails." Israel, as the people of the eternal God, is itself eternal, and though it often suffers persecution, it will never be destroyed, for divine compassion ultimately prevails over divine anger: "The Lord will not abandon His people."

יהוה מָלָךְ, גֵּאוּת לָבֵשׁ, לָבֵשׁ יהוה עֹז הִתְאַזָּר, אַף־תִּכּוֹן תֵּבֵל תהלים צג
בַּל־תִּמּוֹט: נָכוֹן כִּסְאֲךָ מֵאָז, מֵעוֹלָם אָתָּה: נָשְׂאוּ נְהָרוֹת יהוה,
נָשְׂאוּ נְהָרוֹת קוֹלָם, יִשְׂאוּ נְהָרוֹת דָּכְיָם: ‹ מִקֹּלוֹת מַיִם רַבִּים,
אַדִּירִים מִשְׁבְּרֵי־יָם, אַדִּיר בַּמָּרוֹם יהוה: עֵדֹתֶיךָ נֶאֶמְנוּ מְאֹד
לְבֵיתְךָ נַאֲוָה־קֹדֶשׁ, יהוה לְאֹרֶךְ יָמִים:

יְהִי כְבוֹד יהוה לְעוֹלָם, יִשְׂמַח יהוה בְּמַעֲשָׂיו: יְהִי שֵׁם יהוה מְבֹרָךְ, תהלים קד תהלים קיג
מֵעַתָּה וְעַד־עוֹלָם: מִמִּזְרַח־שֶׁמֶשׁ עַד־מְבוֹאוֹ, מְהֻלָּל שֵׁם יהוה:
רָם עַל־כָּל־גּוֹיִם יהוה, עַל הַשָּׁמַיִם כְּבוֹדוֹ: יהוה שִׁמְךָ לְעוֹלָם, תהלים קלה
יהוה זִכְרְךָ לְדֹר־וָדֹר: יהוה בַּשָּׁמַיִם הֵכִין כִּסְאוֹ, וּמַלְכוּתוֹ בַּכֹּל תהלים קג
מָשָׁלָה: יִשְׂמְחוּ הַשָּׁמַיִם וְתָגֵל הָאָרֶץ, וְיֹאמְרוּ בַגּוֹיִם יהוה מָלָךְ: דברי הימים א׳ טז
יהוה מֶלֶךְ, יהוה מָלָךְ, יהוה יִמְלֹךְ לְעוֹלָם וָעֶד. יהוה מֶלֶךְ עוֹלָם תהלים י
וָעֶד, אָבְדוּ גוֹיִם מֵאַרְצוֹ: יהוה הֵפִיר עֲצַת־גּוֹיִם, הֵנִיא מַחְשְׁבוֹת תהלים לג
עַמִּים: רַבּוֹת מַחֲשָׁבוֹת בְּלֶב־אִישׁ, וַעֲצַת יהוה הִיא תָקוּם: עֲצַת משלי יט תהלים לג

---

good if, all too often, evildoers seize power, injustice prevails, the innocent suffer and the guilty escape punishment? The psalm tells us that our time-horizon is too constricted. We look at the short term, not the long. Evil may win temporary victories but in the long run, right, justice and liberty prevail. Tyrants may seem impregnable in their day, but evil empires crumble, and are condemned by the full perspective of history. That is what "a fool cannot understand" but the wise know. The Sabbath of the psalm is thus not the Sabbath of past or present but of the future, the Messianic age, the "day that is entirely Shabbat," when there will be neither master nor slave, oppressor and oppressed, when hierarchies of power are abandoned and humanity finally recognizes the universe as God's work, and the human person as God's image. That is the ultimate Shabbat to which all our current Sabbaths are a prelude and preparation.

יהוה מָלָךְ *Psalm 93.* Almost all ancient polytheistic myths saw the sea as an independent force of chaos against which the gods were forced to do battle. The great revolution of monotheism was to insist that there is only one

but the LORD's plan prevails. The LORD's plan shall stand for ever, *Ps. 33*
His mind's intent for all generations. For He spoke and it was; He
commanded and it stood firm. For the LORD has chosen Zion; He *Ps. 132*
desired it for His dwelling. For the LORD has chosen Jacob, Israel *Ps. 135*
as His special treasure. For the LORD will not abandon His people; *Ps. 94*
nor will He forsake His heritage. ▸ He is compassionate. He forgives *Ps. 78*
iniquity and does not destroy. Repeatedly He suppresses His anger,
not rousing His full wrath. LORD, save! May the King answer us on *Ps. 20*
the day we call.

The line beginning with "You open Your hand" should be said with special concentration, representing as it does the key idea of this psalm, and of Pesukei DeZimra as a whole, that God is the creator and sustainer of all.

אַשְׁרֵי Happy are those who dwell in Your House; *Ps. 84*
they shall continue to praise You, Selah!
Happy are the people for whom this is so; *Ps. 144*
happy are the people whose God is the LORD.
A song of praise by David. *Ps. 145*

I will exalt You, my God, the King, and bless Your name for ever and all time. Every day I will bless You, and praise Your name for ever and all time. Great is the LORD and greatly to be praised; His greatness is unfathomable. One generation will praise Your works to the next, and tell of Your mighty deeds. On the glorious splendor of Your majesty I will meditate, and on the acts of Your wonders. They shall talk of the power of Your awesome deeds, and I will tell of Your greatness. They shall recite the record of Your great goodness, and sing with joy of Your righteousness. The LORD is gracious and compassionate, slow to anger and great in loving-kindness. The LORD is good to all, and His compassion

---

Added to the psalm are verses from other psalms: two at the beginning, which include the word *Ashrei* (happy) three times; and one at the end, which ends with *Halleluya*. It thus epitomizes the book of Psalms as a whole, which begins with the word *Ashrei* and ends with the word *Halleluya*.

יהוה לְעוֹלָם תַּעֲמֹד, מַחְשְׁבוֹת לִבּוֹ לְדֹר וָדֹר: כִּי הוּא אָמַר וַיֶּהִי,
הוּא־צִוָּה וַיַּעֲמֹד: כִּי־בָחַר יהוה בְּצִיּוֹן, אִוָּהּ לְמוֹשָׁב לוֹ: כִּי־יַעֲקֹב תהלים קלב / תהלים קלה
בָּחַר לוֹ יָהּ, יִשְׂרָאֵל לִסְגֻלָּתוֹ: כִּי לֹא־יִטֹּשׁ יהוה עַמּוֹ, וְנַחֲלָתוֹ לֹא תהלים צד
יַעֲזֹב: ◂ וְהוּא רַחוּם, יְכַפֵּר עָוֹן וְלֹא־יַשְׁחִית, וְהִרְבָּה לְהָשִׁיב אַפּוֹ, תהלים עח
וְלֹא־יָעִיר כָּל־חֲמָתוֹ: יהוה הוֹשִׁיעָה, הַמֶּלֶךְ יַעֲנֵנוּ בְיוֹם־קָרְאֵנוּ: תהלים כ

The line beginning with פּוֹתֵחַ אֶת יָדֶךָ *should be said with special concentration, representing as it does the key idea of this psalm, and of* פסוקי דזמרה *as a whole, that God is the creator and sustainer of all.*

אַשְׁרֵי יוֹשְׁבֵי בֵיתֶךָ, עוֹד יְהַלְלוּךָ סֶּלָה: תהלים פד
אַשְׁרֵי הָעָם שֶׁכָּכָה לּוֹ, אַשְׁרֵי הָעָם שֶׁיהוה אֱלֹהָיו: תהלים קמד
תְּהִלָּה לְדָוִד תהלים קמה
אֲרוֹמִמְךָ אֱלוֹהַי הַמֶּלֶךְ, וַאֲבָרְכָה שִׁמְךָ לְעוֹלָם וָעֶד:
בְּכָל־יוֹם אֲבָרְכֶךָּ, וַאֲהַלְלָה שִׁמְךָ לְעוֹלָם וָעֶד:
גָּדוֹל יהוה וּמְהֻלָּל מְאֹד, וְלִגְדֻלָּתוֹ אֵין חֵקֶר:
דּוֹר לְדוֹר יְשַׁבַּח מַעֲשֶׂיךָ, וּגְבוּרֹתֶיךָ יַגִּידוּ:
הֲדַר כְּבוֹד הוֹדֶךָ, וְדִבְרֵי נִפְלְאֹתֶיךָ אָשִׂיחָה:
וֶעֱזוּז נוֹרְאֹתֶיךָ יֹאמֵרוּ, וּגְדוּלָּתְךָ אֲסַפְּרֶנָּה:
זֵכֶר רַב־טוּבְךָ יַבִּיעוּ, וְצִדְקָתְךָ יְרַנֵּנוּ:
חַנּוּן וְרַחוּם יהוה, אֶרֶךְ אַפַּיִם וּגְדָל־חָסֶד:
טוֹב־יהוה לַכֹּל, וְרַחֲמָיו עַל־כָּל־מַעֲשָׂיו:

אַשְׁרֵי *Happy are those.* Psalm 145 was seen by the sages as the quintessential expression of the book of Psalms, especially the creation psalms that dominate the Verses of Praise, because (a) it is an alphabetic acrostic, praising God with each letter of the alphabet (with the exception of *nun,* a letter omitted lest it recall *nefila,* the fall of ancient Israel), and (b) because it contains the line, "You open Your hand, and satisfy every living thing with favor." It is also (c) the only poem to be explicitly called *tehilla,* "a psalm" (the book of Psalms is called, in Hebrew, *Sefer Tehillim*).

extends to all His works. All Your works shall thank You, Lord, and Your devoted ones shall bless You. They shall talk of the glory of Your kingship, and speak of Your might. To make known to mankind His mighty deeds and the glorious majesty of His kingship. Your kingdom is an everlasting kingdom, and Your reign is for all generations. The Lord supports all who fall, and raises all who are bowed down. All raise their eyes to You in hope, and You give them their food in due season. You open Your hand, and satisfy every living thing with favor. The Lord is righteous in all His ways, and kind in all He does. The Lord is close to all who call on Him, to all who call on Him in truth. He fulfills the will of those who revere Him; He hears their cry and saves them. The Lord guards all who love Him, but all the wicked He will destroy. ▸ My mouth shall speak the praise of the Lord, and all creatures shall bless His holy name for ever and all time.

We will bless the Lord now and for ever. Halleluya! *Ps. 115*

הַלְלוּיָהּ Halleluya! Praise the Lord, my soul. I will praise the Lord *Ps. 146* all my life; I will sing to my God as long as I live. Put not your trust in princes, or in mortal man who cannot save. His breath expires, he returns to the earth; on that day his plans come to an end. Happy is he whose help is the God of Jacob, whose hope is in the Lord his God who made heaven and earth, the sea and all they contain; He who keeps faith for ever. He secures justice for the oppressed. He gives food to the hungry. The Lord sets captives free. The Lord gives sight to the blind. The Lord raises those bowed down. The Lord loves the righteous. The Lord protects the stranger. He gives courage to the orphan and widow. He thwarts the way of the wicked. ▸ The Lord shall reign for ever. He is your God, Zion, for all generations. Halleluya!

---

your faith in mortals but in God, who cares for the oppressed, the hungry, the victims of injustice, and those who have no one else to care for them. The supreme Power supremely cares for the powerless.

יוֹדוּךָ יהוה כָּל־מַעֲשֶׂיךָ, וַחֲסִידֶיךָ יְבָרְכוּכָה:
כְּבוֹד מַלְכוּתְךָ יֹאמֵרוּ, וּגְבוּרָתְךָ יְדַבֵּרוּ:
לְהוֹדִיעַ לִבְנֵי הָאָדָם גְּבוּרֹתָיו, וּכְבוֹד הֲדַר מַלְכוּתוֹ:
מַלְכוּתְךָ מַלְכוּת כָּל־עֹלָמִים, וּמֶמְשַׁלְתְּךָ בְּכָל־דּוֹר וָדֹר:
סוֹמֵךְ יהוה לְכָל־הַנֹּפְלִים, וְזוֹקֵף לְכָל־הַכְּפוּפִים:
עֵינֵי־כֹל אֵלֶיךָ יְשַׂבֵּרוּ, וְאַתָּה נוֹתֵן־לָהֶם אֶת־אָכְלָם בְּעִתּוֹ:
פּוֹתֵחַ אֶת־יָדֶךָ, וּמַשְׂבִּיעַ לְכָל־חַי רָצוֹן:
צַדִּיק יהוה בְּכָל־דְּרָכָיו, וְחָסִיד בְּכָל־מַעֲשָׂיו:
קָרוֹב יהוה לְכָל־קֹרְאָיו, לְכֹל אֲשֶׁר יִקְרָאֻהוּ בֶאֱמֶת:
רְצוֹן־יְרֵאָיו יַעֲשֶׂה, וְאֶת־שַׁוְעָתָם יִשְׁמַע, וְיוֹשִׁיעֵם:
שׁוֹמֵר יהוה אֶת־כָּל־אֹהֲבָיו, וְאֵת כָּל־הָרְשָׁעִים יַשְׁמִיד:
◂ תְּהִלַּת יהוה יְדַבֶּר פִּי, וִיבָרֵךְ כָּל־בָּשָׂר שֵׁם קָדְשׁוֹ לְעוֹלָם וָעֶד:
וַאֲנַחְנוּ נְבָרֵךְ יָהּ מֵעַתָּה וְעַד־עוֹלָם, הַלְלוּיָהּ: תהלים קטו

הַלְלוּיָהּ, הַלְלִי נַפְשִׁי אֶת־יהוה: אֲהַלְלָה יהוה בְּחַיָּי, אֲזַמְּרָה תהלים קמו
לֵאלֹהַי בְּעוֹדִי: אַל־תִּבְטְחוּ בִנְדִיבִים, בְּבֶן־אָדָם שֶׁאֵין לוֹ
תְשׁוּעָה: תֵּצֵא רוּחוֹ, יָשֻׁב לְאַדְמָתוֹ, בַּיּוֹם הַהוּא אָבְדוּ עֶשְׁתֹּנֹתָיו:
אַשְׁרֵי שֶׁאֵל יַעֲקֹב בְּעֶזְרוֹ, שִׂבְרוֹ עַל־יהוה אֱלֹהָיו: עֹשֶׂה שָׁמַיִם
וָאָרֶץ, אֶת־הַיָּם וְאֶת־כָּל־אֲשֶׁר־בָּם, הַשֹּׁמֵר אֱמֶת לְעוֹלָם: עֹשֶׂה
מִשְׁפָּט לַעֲשׁוּקִים, נֹתֵן לֶחֶם לָרְעֵבִים, יהוה מַתִּיר אֲסוּרִים:
יהוה פֹּקֵחַ עִוְרִים, יהוה זֹקֵף כְּפוּפִים, יהוה אֹהֵב צַדִּיקִים: יהוה
שֹׁמֵר אֶת־גֵּרִים, יָתוֹם וְאַלְמָנָה יְעוֹדֵד, וְדֶרֶךְ רְשָׁעִים יְעַוֵּת:
◂ יִמְלֹךְ יהוה לְעוֹלָם, אֱלֹהַיִךְ צִיּוֹן לְדֹר וָדֹר, הַלְלוּיָהּ:

הַלְלוּיָהּ *Psalm 146.* A hymn of praise to God's justice and compassion. Put not

הַלְלוּיָהּ Halleluya! How good it is to sing songs to our God; how pleasant and fitting to praise Him. The LORD rebuilds Jerusalem. He gathers the scattered exiles of Israel. He heals the brokenhearted and binds up their wounds. He counts the number of the stars, calling each by name. Great is our LORD and mighty in power; His understanding has no limit. The LORD gives courage to the humble, but casts the wicked to the ground. Sing to the LORD in thanks; make music to our God on the harp. He covers the sky with clouds. He provides the earth with rain and makes grass grow on the hills. He gives food to the cattle and to the ravens when they cry. He does not take delight in the strength of horses nor pleasure in the fleetness of man. The LORD takes pleasure in those who fear Him, who put their hope in His loving care. Praise the LORD, Jerusalem; sing to your God, Zion, for He has strengthened the bars of your gates and blessed your children in your midst. He has brought peace to your borders, and satisfied you with the finest wheat. He sends His commandment to earth; swiftly runs His word. He spreads snow like fleece, sprinkles frost like ashes, scatters hail like crumbs. Who can stand His cold? He sends His word and melts them; He makes the wind blow and the waters flow. ▸ He has declared His words to Jacob, His statutes and laws to Israel. He has done this for no other nation; such laws they do not know. Halleluya! *Ps. 147*

הַלְלוּיָהּ Halleluya! Praise the LORD from the heavens, praise Him in the heights. Praise Him, all His angels; praise Him, all His hosts. Praise Him, sun and moon; praise Him, all shining stars. Praise Him, highest heavens and the waters above the heavens. Let them praise the name of the LORD, for He commanded and they were created. He established them for ever and all time, issuing a decree that will never change. Praise the LORD from the earth: sea monsters and all the deep seas; fire and hail, snow and mist, storm winds that obey His word; *Ps. 148*

לֹא עָשָׂה כֵן לְכָל־גּוֹי *He has done this for no other nation.* Although there has been a covenant between God and all humanity since the days of Noah, only to Israel did He reveal an entire body of laws, the detailed architectonics of a society under the sovereignty of God, dedicated to justice, holiness and respect for human dignity.

תהלים קמז הַלְלוּיָהּ, כִּי־טוֹב זַמְּרָה אֱלֹהֵינוּ, כִּי־נָעִים נָאוָה תְהִלָּה: בּוֹנֵה
יְרוּשָׁלַםִ יהוה, נִדְחֵי יִשְׂרָאֵל יְכַנֵּס: הָרֹפֵא לִשְׁבוּרֵי לֵב, וּמְחַבֵּשׁ
לְעַצְּבוֹתָם: מוֹנֶה מִסְפָּר לַכּוֹכָבִים, לְכֻלָּם שֵׁמוֹת יִקְרָא: גָּדוֹל
אֲדוֹנֵינוּ וְרַב־כֹּחַ, לִתְבוּנָתוֹ אֵין מִסְפָּר: מְעוֹדֵד עֲנָוִים יהוה,
מַשְׁפִּיל רְשָׁעִים עֲדֵי־אָרֶץ: עֱנוּ לַיהוה בְּתוֹדָה, זַמְּרוּ לֵאלֹהֵינוּ
בְכִנּוֹר: הַמְכַסֶּה שָׁמַיִם בְּעָבִים, הַמֵּכִין לָאָרֶץ מָטָר, הַמַּצְמִיחַ
הָרִים חָצִיר: נוֹתֵן לִבְהֵמָה לַחְמָהּ, לִבְנֵי עֹרֵב אֲשֶׁר יִקְרָאוּ: לֹא
בִגְבוּרַת הַסּוּס יֶחְפָּץ, לֹא־בְשׁוֹקֵי הָאִישׁ יִרְצֶה: רוֹצֶה יהוה אֶת־
יְרֵאָיו, אֶת־הַמְיַחֲלִים לְחַסְדּוֹ: שַׁבְּחִי יְרוּשָׁלַםִ אֶת־יהוה, הַלְלִי
אֱלֹהַיִךְ צִיּוֹן: כִּי־חִזַּק בְּרִיחֵי שְׁעָרָיִךְ, בֵּרַךְ בָּנַיִךְ בְּקִרְבֵּךְ: הַשָּׂם־
גְּבוּלֵךְ שָׁלוֹם, חֵלֶב חִטִּים יַשְׂבִּיעֵךְ: הַשֹּׁלֵחַ אִמְרָתוֹ אָרֶץ, עַד־
מְהֵרָה יָרוּץ דְּבָרוֹ: הַנֹּתֵן שֶׁלֶג כַּצָּמֶר, כְּפוֹר כָּאֵפֶר יְפַזֵּר: מַשְׁלִיךְ
קַרְחוֹ כְפִתִּים, לִפְנֵי קָרָתוֹ מִי יַעֲמֹד: יִשְׁלַח דְּבָרוֹ וְיַמְסֵם, יַשֵּׁב
רוּחוֹ יִזְּלוּ־מָיִם: › מַגִּיד דְּבָרָו לְיַעֲקֹב, חֻקָּיו וּמִשְׁפָּטָיו לְיִשְׂרָאֵל:
לֹא עָשָׂה כֵן לְכָל־גּוֹי, וּמִשְׁפָּטִים בַּל־יְדָעוּם, הַלְלוּיָהּ:

תהלים קמח הַלְלוּיָהּ, הַלְלוּ אֶת־יהוה מִן־הַשָּׁמַיִם, הַלְלוּהוּ בַּמְּרוֹמִים: הַלְלוּהוּ
כָל־מַלְאָכָיו, הַלְלוּהוּ כָּל־צְבָאָו: הַלְלוּהוּ שֶׁמֶשׁ וְיָרֵחַ, הַלְלוּהוּ כָּל־
כּוֹכְבֵי אוֹר: הַלְלוּהוּ שְׁמֵי הַשָּׁמָיִם, וְהַמַּיִם אֲשֶׁר מֵעַל הַשָּׁמָיִם:
יְהַלְלוּ אֶת־שֵׁם יהוה, כִּי הוּא צִוָּה וְנִבְרָאוּ: וַיַּעֲמִידֵם לָעַד לְעוֹלָם,
חָק־נָתַן וְלֹא יַעֲבוֹר: הַלְלוּ אֶת־יהוה מִן־הָאָרֶץ, תַּנִּינִים וְכָל־
תְּהֹמוֹת: אֵשׁ וּבָרָד שֶׁלֶג וְקִיטוֹר, רוּחַ סְעָרָה עֹשָׂה דְבָרוֹ: הֶהָרִים

הַלְלוּיָהּ *Psalm 147.* God, the Shaper of history ("gathers the scattered exiles") and Architect of the cosmos ("counts the number of the stars"), is nonetheless close to us, healing the broken heart and ministering to our emotional wounds.

mountains and all hills, fruit trees and all cedars; wild animals and all cattle, creeping things and winged birds; kings of the earth and all nations, princes and all judges on earth; youths and maidens, old and young. ▸ Let them praise the name of the LORD, for His name alone is sublime; His majesty is above earth and heaven. He has raised the pride of His people, for the glory of all His devoted ones, the children of Israel, the people close to Him. Halleluya!

הַלְלוּיָהּ Halleluya! Sing to the LORD a new song, His praise in the Ps. 149
assembly of the devoted. Let Israel rejoice in its Maker; let the children of Zion exult in their King. Let them praise His name with dancing; sing praises to Him with timbrel and harp. For the LORD delights in His people; He adorns the humble with salvation. Let the devoted revel in glory; let them sing for joy on their beds. Let high praises of God be in their throats, and a two-edged sword in their hand: to impose retribution on the nations, punishment on the peoples, ▸ binding their kings with chains, their nobles with iron fetters, carrying out the judgment written against them. This is the glory of all His devoted ones. Halleluya!

הַלְלוּיָהּ Halleluya! Praise God in His holy place; praise Him in the Ps. 150
heavens of His power. Praise Him for His mighty deeds; praise Him for His surpassing greatness. Praise Him with blasts of the shofar; praise Him with the harp and lyre. Praise Him with timbrel and dance; praise Him with strings and flute. ▸ Praise Him with clashing cymbals; praise Him with resounding cymbals. Let all that breathes praise the LORD. Halleluya! Let all that breathes praise the LORD. Halleluya!

---

of mouths" echoes the previous phrase, "praises of God be in their throats" (*Or Penei Moshe*).

הַלְלוּיָהּ *Psalm 150.* The last psalm in the book of Psalms, gathering all previous praise into a majestic choral finale. More than a third of the words consist of various forms of the verb "to praise."

כֹּל הַנְּשָׁמָה *Let all that breathes.* Note the universalism of this closing verse, one reason why "the book of Psalms has spoken to people through the ages across the borders of nations, languages, and sectarian divisions" (Robert Alter).

וְכׇל־גְּבָעוֹת, עֵץ פְּרִי וְכׇל־אֲרָזִים: הַחַיָּה וְכׇל־בְּהֵמָה, רֶמֶשׂ וְצִפּוֹר
כָּנָף: מַלְכֵי־אֶרֶץ וְכׇל־לְאֻמִּים, שָׂרִים וְכׇל־שֹׁפְטֵי אָרֶץ: בַּחוּרִים
וְגַם־בְּתוּלוֹת, זְקֵנִים עִם־נְעָרִים: › יְהַלְלוּ אֶת־שֵׁם יהוה, כִּי־נִשְׂגָּב
שְׁמוֹ לְבַדּוֹ, הוֹדוֹ עַל־אֶרֶץ וְשָׁמָיִם: וַיָּרֶם קֶרֶן לְעַמּוֹ, תְּהִלָּה לְכׇל־
חֲסִידָיו, לִבְנֵי יִשְׂרָאֵל עַם קְרֹבוֹ, הַלְלוּיָהּ:

תהלים קמט הַלְלוּיָהּ, שִׁירוּ לַיהוה שִׁיר חָדָשׁ, תְּהִלָּתוֹ בִּקְהַל חֲסִידִים:
יִשְׂמַח יִשְׂרָאֵל בְּעֹשָׂיו, בְּנֵי־צִיּוֹן יָגִילוּ בְמַלְכָּם: יְהַלְלוּ שְׁמוֹ
בְמָחוֹל, בְּתֹף וְכִנּוֹר יְזַמְּרוּ־לוֹ: כִּי־רוֹצֶה יהוה בְּעַמּוֹ, יְפָאֵר
עֲנָוִים בִּישׁוּעָה: יַעְלְזוּ חֲסִידִים בְּכָבוֹד, יְרַנְּנוּ עַל־מִשְׁכְּבוֹתָם:
רוֹמְמוֹת אֵל בִּגְרוֹנָם, וְחֶרֶב פִּיפִיּוֹת בְּיָדָם: לַעֲשׂוֹת נְקָמָה בַּגּוֹיִם,
תּוֹכֵחוֹת בַּלְאֻמִּים: › לֶאְסֹר מַלְכֵיהֶם בְּזִקִּים, וְנִכְבְּדֵיהֶם בְּכַבְלֵי
בַרְזֶל: לַעֲשׂוֹת בָּהֶם מִשְׁפָּט כָּתוּב, הָדָר הוּא לְכׇל־חֲסִידָיו,
הַלְלוּיָהּ:

תהלים קנ הַלְלוּיָהּ, הַלְלוּ־אֵל בְּקׇדְשׁוֹ, הַלְלוּהוּ בִּרְקִיעַ עֻזּוֹ: הַלְלוּהוּ
בִגְבוּרֹתָיו, הַלְלוּהוּ כְּרֹב גֻּדְלוֹ: הַלְלוּהוּ בְּתֵקַע שׁוֹפָר, הַלְלוּהוּ
בְּנֵבֶל וְכִנּוֹר: הַלְלוּהוּ בְתֹף וּמָחוֹל, הַלְלוּהוּ בְּמִנִּים וְעֻגָב:
› הַלְלוּהוּ בְצִלְצְלֵי־שָׁמַע, הַלְלוּהוּ בְּצִלְצְלֵי תְרוּעָה: כֹּל הַנְּשָׁמָה
תְּהַלֵּל יָהּ, הַלְלוּיָהּ: כֹּל הַנְּשָׁמָה תְּהַלֵּל יָהּ, הַלְלוּיָהּ:

הַלְלוּיָהּ *Psalm 148* (*previous page*). A cosmic psalm of praise, beginning with the heavens, sun, moon, and stars; then moving to earth and all living things, culminating with humanity.

הַלְלוּיָהּ *Psalm 149*. A song of victory. Israel emerges triumphant over those who seek to destroy it, not because of its strength but because of its faith.

חֶרֶב פִּיפִיּוֹת *A two-edged sword*. Literally, "a sword of mouths." Israel does not live by the physical sword but by words: the power of prayer. Thus the "sword

בָּרוּךְ Blessed be the LORD for ever. Amen and Amen. *Ps. 89*
Blessed from Zion be the LORD who dwells in Jerusalem. Halleluya! *Ps. 135*
Blessed be the LORD, God of Israel, who alone does wonders. *Ps. 72*
▸ Blessed be His glorious name for ever,
and may all the earth be filled with His glory. Amen and Amen.

Stand until "The soul" on page 550.

וַיְבָרֶךְ David blessed the LORD in front of the entire assembly. David said, *1 Chr. 29* "Blessed are You, LORD, God of our father Yisrael, for ever and ever. Yours, LORD, are the greatness and the power, the glory, majesty and splendor, for everything in heaven and earth is Yours. Yours, LORD, is the kingdom; You are exalted as Head over all. Both riches and honor are in Your gift and You reign over all things. In Your hand are strength and might. It is in Your power to make great and give strength to all. Therefore, our God, we thank You and praise Your glorious name." You alone *Neh. 9* are the LORD. You made the heavens, even the highest heavens, and all their hosts, the earth and all that is on it, the seas and all they contain. You give life to them all, and the hosts of heaven worship You. ▸ You are the LORD God who chose Abram and brought him out of Ur of the Chaldees, changing his name to Abraham. You found his heart faithful toward You, ◂ and You made a covenant with him to give to his descendants the land of the Canaanites, Hittites, Amorites, Perizzites, Jebusites and Girgashites. You fulfilled Your promise for You are righteous. You saw the suffering of our ancestors in Egypt. You heard their cry at the Sea

---

None of the following passages belongs to either category. They are (1) the national assembly convened by David shortly before his death to initiate the building of the Temple under the aegis of his son and successor Solomon; (2) the national assembly gathered by Ezra and Nehemiah to renew the covenant between Israel and God; and (3) the song sung by the Israelites after they had crossed the Reed Sea and become "the people You acquired." These were key historic moments when the Jewish people came together as a collective body to praise God and pledge their loyalty to Him. Their presence here marks the transition from private to public prayer, which is about to begin.

A *tzibbur*, a public, is more than a mere assemblage of individuals, just as the human body is more than a collection of cells. It is an emergent phenomenon, a higher order of being. At this moment of transition, therefore, we undergo a metamorphosis, and we do so by a historical reenactment, retracing the steps of our ancestors as they cast off their private concerns

בָּרוּךְ יהוה לְעוֹלָם, אָמֵן וְאָמֵן: תהלים פט

בָּרוּךְ יהוה מִצִּיּוֹן, שֹׁכֵן יְרוּשָׁלָֽםִ, הַלְלוּיָהּ: תהלים קלה

בָּרוּךְ יהוה אֱלֹהִים אֱלֹהֵי יִשְׂרָאֵל, עֹשֵׂה נִפְלָאוֹת לְבַדּוֹ: תהלים עב

◂ וּבָרוּךְ שֵׁם כְּבוֹדוֹ לְעוֹלָם

וְיִמָּלֵא כְבוֹדוֹ אֶת־כָּל־הָאָֽרֶץ, אָמֵן וְאָמֵן:

Stand until נִשְׁמַת *on page 551.*

וַיְבָֽרֶךְ דָּוִיד אֶת־יהוה לְעֵינֵי כָּל־הַקָּהָל, וַיֹּֽאמֶר דָּוִיד, בָּרוּךְ דברי הימים א׳ כט
אַתָּה יהוה, אֱלֹהֵי יִשְׂרָאֵל אָבִֽינוּ, מֵעוֹלָם וְעַד־עוֹלָם: לְךָ יהוה
הַגְּדֻלָּה וְהַגְּבוּרָה וְהַתִּפְאֶֽרֶת וְהַנֵּֽצַח וְהַהוֹד, כִּי־כֹל בַּשָּׁמַֽיִם
וּבָאָֽרֶץ, לְךָ יהוה הַמַּמְלָכָה וְהַמִּתְנַשֵּׂא לְכֹל לְרֹאשׁ: וְהָעֹֽשֶׁר
וְהַכָּבוֹד מִלְּפָנֶֽיךָ, וְאַתָּה מוֹשֵׁל בַּכֹּל, וּבְיָדְךָ כֹּֽחַ וּגְבוּרָה, וּבְיָדְךָ
לְגַדֵּל וּלְחַזֵּק לַכֹּל: וְעַתָּה אֱלֹהֵֽינוּ מוֹדִים אֲנַֽחְנוּ לָךְ, וּמְהַלְלִים
לְשֵׁם תִּפְאַרְתֶּֽךָ: אַתָּה־הוּא יהוה לְבַדֶּֽךָ, אַתָּ עָשִֽׂיתָ נחמיה ט
אֶת־הַשָּׁמַֽיִם, שְׁמֵי הַשָּׁמַֽיִם וְכָל־צְבָאָם, הָאָֽרֶץ וְכָל־אֲשֶׁר עָלֶֽיהָ,
הַיַּמִּים וְכָל־אֲשֶׁר בָּהֶם, וְאַתָּה מְחַיֶּה אֶת־כֻּלָּם, וּצְבָא הַשָּׁמַֽיִם לְךָ
מִשְׁתַּחֲוִים: ◂ אַתָּה הוּא יהוה הָאֱלֹהִים אֲשֶׁר בָּחַֽרְתָּ בְּאַבְרָם,
וְהוֹצֵאתוֹ מֵאוּר כַּשְׂדִּים, וְשַֽׂמְתָּ שְּׁמוֹ אַבְרָהָם: וּמָצָֽאתָ אֶת־לְבָבוֹ
נֶאֱמָן לְפָנֶֽיךָ, ◂ וְכָרוֹת עִמּוֹ הַבְּרִית לָתֵת אֶת־אֶֽרֶץ הַכְּנַעֲנִי הַחִתִּי
הָאֱמֹרִי וְהַפְּרִזִּי וְהַיְבוּסִי וְהַגִּרְגָּשִׁי, לָתֵת לְזַרְעוֹ, וַתָּֽקֶם אֶת־דְּבָרֶֽיךָ,
כִּי צַדִּיק אָֽתָּה: וַתֵּֽרֶא אֶת־עֳנִי אֲבֹתֵֽינוּ בְּמִצְרָֽיִם, וְאֶת־זַעֲקָתָם

בָּרוּךְ יהוה לְעוֹלָם *Blessed be the* Lord *for ever.* A passage marking the end of the Verses of Praise, consisting of four verses from Psalms, each opening with the word "Blessed," thus echoing the opening paragraph, "Blessed is He who spoke."

וַיְבָֽרֶךְ דָּוִיד *David blessed.* There now follow three biblical passages that strictly speaking do not belong to the Verses of Praise, either in source or subject matter. The Verses of Praise are "songs of Your servant David" – that is, passages from the book of Psalms – and they are about "He who spoke and the world came into being," about God as Creator and Sovereign of the universe.

of Reeds. You sent signs and wonders against Pharaoh, all his servants and all the people of his land, because You knew how arrogantly the Egyptians treated them. You created for Yourself renown that remains to this day. ▸ You divided the sea before them, so that they passed through the sea on dry land, but You cast their pursuers into the depths, like a stone into mighty waters.

וַיּוֹשַׁע That day the Lord saved Israel from the hands of the Egyp- *Ex. 14*
tians, and Israel saw the Egyptians lying dead on the seashore.
▸ When Israel saw the great power the Lord had displayed against the Egyptians, the people feared the Lord, and believed in the Lord and in His servant, Moses.

אָז יָשִׁיר־מֹשֶׁה Then Moses and the Israelites *Ex. 15*
sang this song to the Lord, saying:
I will sing to the Lord, for He has triumphed gloriously;
horse and rider He has hurled into the sea.
The Lord is my strength and song; He has become my salvation.
This is my God, and I will beautify Him,
my father's God, and I will exalt Him.
The Lord is a Master of war; Lord is His name.
Pharaoh's chariots and army He cast into the sea;
the best of his officers drowned in the Sea of Reeds.
The deep waters covered them;
they went down to the depths like a stone.
Your right hand, Lord, is majestic in power.
Your right hand, Lord, shatters the enemy.
In the greatness of Your majesty,
You overthrew those who rose against You.
You sent out Your fury; it consumed them like stubble.
By the blast of Your nostrils the waters piled up.
The surging waters stood straight like a wall;
the deeps congealed in the heart of the sea.
The enemy said, "I will pursue. I will overtake. I will divide the spoil.
My desire shall have its fill of them.
I will draw my sword. My hand will destroy them."
You blew with Your wind; the sea covered them.
They sank in the mighty waters like lead.

שָׁמְעַתְּ עַל־יַם־סוּף: וַתִּתֵּן אֹתֹת וּמֹפְתִים בְּפַרְעֹה וּבְכָל־עֲבָדָיו
וּבְכָל־עַם אַרְצוֹ, כִּי יָדַעְתָּ כִּי הֵזִידוּ עֲלֵיהֶם, וַתַּעַשׂ־לְךָ שֵׁם כְּהַיּוֹם
הַזֶּה: › וְהַיָּם בָּקַעְתָּ לִפְנֵיהֶם, וַיַּעַבְרוּ בְתוֹךְ־הַיָּם בַּיַּבָּשָׁה, וְאֶת־
רֹדְפֵיהֶם הִשְׁלַכְתָּ בִמְצוֹלֹת כְּמוֹ־אֶבֶן, בְּמַיִם עַזִּים:

וַיּוֹשַׁע יהוה בַּיּוֹם הַהוּא אֶת־יִשְׂרָאֵל מִיַּד מִצְרָיִם, וַיַּרְא יִשְׂרָאֵל שמות יד
אֶת־מִצְרַיִם מֵת עַל־שְׂפַת הַיָּם: › וַיַּרְא יִשְׂרָאֵל אֶת־הַיָּד הַגְּדֹלָה
אֲשֶׁר עָשָׂה יהוה בְּמִצְרַיִם, וַיִּירְאוּ הָעָם אֶת־יהוה, וַיַּאֲמִינוּ בַּיהוה
וּבְמשֶׁה עַבְדּוֹ:

אָז יָשִׁיר־מֹשֶׁה וּבְנֵי יִשְׂרָאֵל אֶת־הַשִּׁירָה הַזֹּאת לַיהוה, וַיֹּאמְרוּ שמות טו
לֵאמֹר, אָשִׁירָה לַיהוה כִּי־גָאֹה גָּאָה, סוּס
וְרֹכְבוֹ רָמָה בַיָּם: עָזִּי וְזִמְרָת יָהּ וַיְהִי־לִי
לִישׁוּעָה, זֶה אֵלִי וְאַנְוֵהוּ, אֱלֹהֵי
אָבִי וַאֲרֹמְמֶנְהוּ: יהוה אִישׁ מִלְחָמָה, יהוה
שְׁמוֹ: מַרְכְּבֹת פַּרְעֹה וְחֵילוֹ יָרָה בַיָּם, וּמִבְחַר
שָׁלִשָׁיו טֻבְּעוּ בְיַם־סוּף: תְּהֹמֹת יְכַסְיֻמוּ, יָרְדוּ בִמְצוֹלֹת כְּמוֹ־
אָבֶן: יְמִינְךָ יהוה נֶאְדָּרִי בַּכֹּחַ, יְמִינְךָ
יהוה תִּרְעַץ אוֹיֵב: וּבְרֹב גְּאוֹנְךָ תַּהֲרֹס
קָמֶיךָ, תְּשַׁלַּח חֲרֹנְךָ יֹאכְלֵמוֹ כַּקַּשׁ: וּבְרוּחַ
אַפֶּיךָ נֶעֶרְמוּ מַיִם, נִצְּבוּ כְמוֹ־נֵד
נֹזְלִים, קָפְאוּ תְהֹמֹת בְּלֶב־יָם: אָמַר
אוֹיֵב אֶרְדֹּף, אַשִּׂיג, אֲחַלֵּק שָׁלָל, תִּמְלָאֵמוֹ
נַפְשִׁי, אָרִיק חַרְבִּי תּוֹרִישֵׁמוֹ יָדִי: נָשַׁפְתָּ
בְרוּחֲךָ כִּסָּמוֹ יָם, צָלְלוּ כַּעוֹפֶרֶת בְּמַיִם

---

as individuals to become a community of faith dedicated to the collective worship of God.

Who is like You, LORD, among the mighty?
Who is like You – majestic in holiness, awesome in glory, working wonders?
You stretched out Your right hand,
the earth swallowed them.
In Your loving-kindness, You led the people You redeemed.
In Your strength, You guided them to Your holy abode.
Nations heard and trembled;
terror gripped Philistia's inhabitants.
The chiefs of Edom were dismayed,
Moab's leaders were seized with trembling,
the people of Canaan melted away.
Fear and dread fell upon them.
By the power of Your arm, they were still as stone –
until Your people crossed, LORD,
until the people You acquired crossed over.
You will bring them and plant them on the mountain of Your heritage –
the place, LORD, You made for Your dwelling,
the Sanctuary, LORD, Your hands established.
The LORD will reign for ever and all time.

The LORD will reign for ever and all time.
The LORD's kingship is established for ever and to all eternity.

When Pharaoh's horses, chariots and riders went into the sea,
the LORD brought the waters of the sea back over them, but the Israelites walked on dry land through the sea.

▸ For kingship is the LORD's and He rules over the nations. *Ps. 22*
Saviors shall go up to Mount Zion *Ob. 1*
to judge Mount Esau,
and the LORD's shall be the kingdom.

Then the LORD shall be King over all the earth; *Zech. 14*
on that day the LORD shall be One and His name One,

(as it is written in Your Torah, saying:
Listen, Israel: the LORD is our God, the LORD is One.) *Deut. 6*

אַדִּירִים: מִי־כָמֹכָה בָּאֵלִם יהוה, מִי
כָּמֹכָה נֶאְדָּר בַּקֹּדֶשׁ, נוֹרָא תְהִלֹּת עֹשֵׂה
פֶלֶא: נָטִיתָ יְמִינְךָ תִּבְלָעֵמוֹ אָרֶץ: נָחִיתָ
בְחַסְדְּךָ עַם־זוּ גָּאָלְתָּ, נֵהַלְתָּ בְעָזְּךָ אֶל־נְוֵה
קָדְשֶׁךָ: שָׁמְעוּ עַמִּים יִרְגָּזוּן, חִיל
אָחַז יֹשְׁבֵי פְּלָשֶׁת: אָז נִבְהֲלוּ אַלּוּפֵי
אֱדוֹם, אֵילֵי מוֹאָב יֹאחֲזֵמוֹ רָעַד, נָמֹגוּ
כֹּל יֹשְׁבֵי כְנָעַן: תִּפֹּל עֲלֵיהֶם אֵימָתָה
וָפַחַד, בִּגְדֹל זְרוֹעֲךָ יִדְּמוּ כָּאָבֶן, עַד־
יַעֲבֹר עַמְּךָ יהוה, עַד־יַעֲבֹר עַם־זוּ
קָנִיתָ: תְּבִאֵמוֹ וְתִטָּעֵמוֹ בְּהַר נַחֲלָתְךָ, מָכוֹן
לְשִׁבְתְּךָ פָּעַלְתָּ יהוה, מִקְּדָשׁ אֲדֹנָי כּוֹנְנוּ
יָדֶיךָ: יהוה יִמְלֹךְ לְעֹלָם וָעֶד:

יהוה יִמְלֹךְ לְעֹלָם וָעֶד.
יהוה מַלְכוּתֵהּ קָאֵם לְעָלַם וּלְעָלְמֵי עָלְמַיָּא.

כִּי
בָא סוּס פַּרְעֹה בְּרִכְבּוֹ וּבְפָרָשָׁיו בַּיָּם, וַיָּשֶׁב יהוה עֲלֵהֶם אֶת־מֵי
הַיָּם, וּבְנֵי יִשְׂרָאֵל הָלְכוּ בַיַּבָּשָׁה בְּתוֹךְ הַיָּם:

▸ כִּי לַיהוה הַמְּלוּכָה וּמֹשֵׁל בַּגּוֹיִם: תהלים כב
וְעָלוּ מוֹשִׁעִים בְּהַר צִיּוֹן לִשְׁפֹּט אֶת־הַר עֵשָׂו עובדיה א
וְהָיְתָה לַיהוה הַמְּלוּכָה:
וְהָיָה יהוה לְמֶלֶךְ עַל־כָּל־הָאָרֶץ זכריה יד
בַּיּוֹם הַהוּא יִהְיֶה יהוה אֶחָד וּשְׁמוֹ אֶחָד:
(וּבְתוֹרָתְךָ כָּתוּב לֵאמֹר, שְׁמַע יִשְׂרָאֵל, יהוה אֱלֹהֵינוּ יהוה אֶחָד:) דברים ו

THE SOUL

of all that lives shall bless Your name, LORD our God,
and the spirit of all flesh shall always glorify
and exalt Your remembrance, our King.
From eternity to eternity You are God.
Without You, we have no King, Redeemer or Savior,
who liberates, rescues, sustains
and shows compassion in every time of trouble and distress.
We have no King but You, God of the first and last,
God of all creatures, Master of all ages,
extolled by a multitude of praises,
who guides His world with loving-kindness
and His creatures with compassion.
The LORD neither slumbers nor sleeps.
He rouses the sleepers and wakens the slumberers.
He makes the dumb speak, sets the bound free,
supports the fallen, and raises those bowed down.
To You alone we give thanks:
If our mouths were as full of song as the sea,
and our tongue with jubilation as its myriad waves,
if our lips were full of praise like the spacious heavens,
and our eyes shone like the sun and moon,
if our hands were outstretched like eagles of the sky,
and our feet as swift as hinds – still we could not thank You enough,
LORD our God and God of our ancestors, or bless Your name
for even one of the thousand thousands and myriad myriads of favors
You did for our ancestors and for us.

HaShir, "the blessing of the song" (*Pesaḥim* 118a). It artfully weaves together many of the themes of the Verses of Praise, taking its cue from the last verse of Psalms, "Let all that breathes [*kol haneshama*] praise the LORD" – the words *neshama* and *nishmat* ("the soul of") come from the same root. It also elaborates on the phrase, "All my bones shall say" (Ps. 35:10), describing how each part of the body seeks to praise God – an ancient prefiguration of the idea of "body language."

נִשְׁמַת

כָּל חַי תְּבָרֵךְ אֶת שִׁמְךָ, יהוה אֱלֹהֵינוּ
וְרוּחַ כָּל בָּשָׂר תְּפָאֵר וּתְרוֹמֵם זִכְרְךָ מַלְכֵּנוּ תָּמִיד.
מִן הָעוֹלָם וְעַד הָעוֹלָם אַתָּה אֵל
וּמִבַּלְעָדֶיךָ אֵין לָנוּ מֶלֶךְ גּוֹאֵל וּמוֹשִׁיעַ
פּוֹדֶה וּמַצִּיל וּמְפַרְנֵס וּמְרַחֵם
בְּכָל עֵת צָרָה וְצוּקָה אֵין לָנוּ מֶלֶךְ אֶלָּא אָתָּה.
אֱלֹהֵי הָרִאשׁוֹנִים וְהָאַחֲרוֹנִים, אֱלוֹהַּ כָּל בְּרִיּוֹת
אֲדוֹן כָּל תּוֹלָדוֹת, הַמְהֻלָּל בְּרֹב הַתִּשְׁבָּחוֹת
הַמְנַהֵג עוֹלָמוֹ בְּחֶסֶד וּבְרִיּוֹתָיו בְּרַחֲמִים.
וַיהוה לֹא יָנוּם וְלֹא יִישָׁן
הַמְעוֹרֵר יְשֵׁנִים וְהַמֵּקִיץ נִרְדָּמִים וְהַמֵּשִׂיחַ אִלְּמִים
וְהַמַּתִּיר אֲסוּרִים וְהַסּוֹמֵךְ נוֹפְלִים וְהַזּוֹקֵף כְּפוּפִים.
לְךָ לְבַדְּךָ אֲנַחְנוּ מוֹדִים.
אִלּוּ פִינוּ מָלֵא שִׁירָה כַּיָּם, וּלְשׁוֹנֵנוּ רִנָּה כַּהֲמוֹן גַּלָּיו
וְשִׂפְתוֹתֵינוּ שֶׁבַח כְּמֶרְחֲבֵי רָקִיעַ, וְעֵינֵינוּ מְאִירוֹת כַּשֶּׁמֶשׁ וְכַיָּרֵחַ
וְיָדֵינוּ פְרוּשׂוֹת כְּנִשְׁרֵי שָׁמָיִם, וְרַגְלֵינוּ קַלּוֹת כָּאַיָּלוֹת
אֵין אֲנַחְנוּ מַסְפִּיקִים לְהוֹדוֹת לְךָ, יהוה אֱלֹהֵינוּ וֵאלֹהֵי אֲבוֹתֵינוּ
וּלְבָרֵךְ אֶת שְׁמֶךָ
עַל אַחַת מֵאֶלֶף אֶלֶף אַלְפֵי אֲלָפִים, וְרִבֵּי רְבָבוֹת פְּעָמִים הַטּוֹבוֹת
שֶׁעָשִׂיתָ עִם אֲבוֹתֵינוּ וְעִמָּנוּ.

נִשְׁמַת *The soul.* An ancient poem, elements of which are cited in the Talmud, where it is referred to as a prayer of thanksgiving for rain after prolonged drought and as part of the Seder service on Pesaḥ. It is also known as *Birkat*

You redeemed us from Egypt, LORD our God,
and freed us from the house of bondage.
In famine You nourished us;
in times of plenty You sustained us.
You delivered us from the sword,
saved us from the plague,
and spared us from serious and lasting illness.
Until now Your mercies have helped us.
Your love has not forsaken us.
May You, LORD our God, never abandon us.
Therefore the limbs You formed within us,
the spirit and soul You breathed into our nostrils,
and the tongue You placed in our mouth –
they will thank and bless, praise and glorify, exalt and esteem,
hallow and do homage to Your name, O our King.
For every mouth shall give thanks to You,
every tongue vow allegiance to You,
every knee shall bend to You,
every upright body shall bow to You,
all hearts shall fear You, and our innermost being
sing praises to Your name, as is written:

"All my bones shall say: LORD, who is like You? *Ps. 35*
You save the poor from one stronger than him,
the poor and needy from one who would rob him."

Who is like You? Who is equal to You? Who can be compared to You?
O great, mighty and awesome God, God Most High,
Maker of heaven and earth.
▸ We will laud, praise and glorify You and bless Your holy name,
as it is said:

"Of David. Bless the LORD, O my soul, *Ps. 103*
and all that is within me bless His holy name."

הָאֵל God – in Your absolute power,
Great – in the glory of Your name,
Mighty – for ever,
Awesome – in Your awe-inspiring deeds,

מִמִּצְרַיִם גְּאַלְתָּנוּ, יהוה אֱלֹהֵינוּ
וּמִבֵּית עֲבָדִים פְּדִיתָנוּ
בְּרָעָב זַנְתָּנוּ וּבְשָׂבָע כִּלְכַּלְתָּנוּ
מֵחֶרֶב הִצַּלְתָּנוּ וּמִדֶּבֶר מִלַּטְתָּנוּ
וּמֵחֳלָיִים רָעִים וְנֶאֱמָנִים דִּלִּיתָנוּ.
עַד הֵנָּה עֲזָרוּנוּ רַחֲמֶיךָ, וְלֹא עֲזָבוּנוּ חֲסָדֶיךָ
וְאַל תִּטְּשֵׁנוּ, יהוה אֱלֹהֵינוּ, לָנֶצַח.
עַל כֵּן אֵבָרִים שֶׁפִּלַּגְתָּ בָּנוּ
וְרוּחַ וּנְשָׁמָה שֶׁנָּפַחְתָּ בְּאַפֵּינוּ, וְלָשׁוֹן אֲשֶׁר שַׂמְתָּ בְּפִינוּ
הֵן הֵם יוֹדוּ וִיבָרְכוּ וִישַׁבְּחוּ וִיפָאֲרוּ
וִירוֹמְמוּ וְיַעֲרִיצוּ וְיַקְדִּישׁוּ וְיַמְלִיכוּ אֶת שִׁמְךָ מַלְכֵּנוּ
כִּי כָל פֶּה לְךָ יוֹדֶה וְכָל לָשׁוֹן לְךָ תִשָּׁבַע
וְכָל בֶּרֶךְ לְךָ תִכְרַע וְכָל קוֹמָה לְפָנֶיךָ תִשְׁתַּחֲוֶה
וְכָל לְבָבוֹת יִירָאוּךָ וְכָל קֶרֶב וּכְלָיוֹת יְזַמְּרוּ לִשְׁמֶךָ
כַּדָּבָר שֶׁכָּתוּב
כָּל עַצְמֹתַי תֹּאמַרְנָה יהוה מִי כָמוֹךָ תהלים לה
מַצִּיל עָנִי מֵחָזָק מִמֶּנּוּ, וְעָנִי וְאֶבְיוֹן מִגֹּזְלוֹ:
מִי יִדְמֶה לָּךְ וּמִי יִשְׁוֶה לָּךְ וּמִי יַעֲרָךְ לָךְ
הָאֵל הַגָּדוֹל, הַגִּבּוֹר וְהַנּוֹרָא, אֵל עֶלְיוֹן, קוֹנֵה שָׁמַיִם וָאָרֶץ.
◂ נְהַלֶּלְךָ וּנְשַׁבֵּחֲךָ וּנְפָאֶרְךָ וּנְבָרֵךְ אֶת שֵׁם קָדְשֶׁךָ
כָּאָמוּר
לְדָוִד, בָּרְכִי נַפְשִׁי אֶת־יהוה, וְכָל־קְרָבַי אֶת־שֵׁם קָדְשׁוֹ: תהלים קג

הָאֵל בְּתַעֲצֻמוֹת עֻזֶּךָ
הַגָּדוֹל בִּכְבוֹד שְׁמֶךָ
הַגִּבּוֹר לָנֶצַח וְהַנּוֹרָא בְּנוֹרְאוֹתֶיךָ

The Leader for Shaḥarit begins here:

THE KING –

who sits on a throne, high and lofty.
He inhabits eternity;
exalted and holy is His name.
And it is written:
"Sing joyfully to the Lord, you righteous, *Ps. 33*
for praise from the upright is seemly."

▸ By the mouth	of the upright	You shall be praised;
by the words	of the righteous	You shall be blessed;
by the tongue	of the devout	You shall be extolled;
and in the midst	of the holy	You shall be sanctified.

וּבְמַקְהֲלוֹת And in the assemblies
of tens of thousands of Your people, the house of Israel,
with joyous song shall Your name, our King,
be glorified in every generation.
▸ For this is the duty of all creatures before You,
Lord our God and God of our ancestors:
to thank, praise, laud, glorify, exalt,
honor, bless, raise high and acclaim –
even beyond all the words of song and praise
of David, son of Jesse, Your servant, Your anointed.

---

over at this point, singing the word as he ascends the *bima*, and by the music itself which begins softly in a minor key and rises to triumphant major, a practice dating back to Rabbi Meir of Rothenburg in the thirteenth century.

וּבְמַקְהֲלוֹת *And in the assemblies.* The word "assemblies" refers to the large congregations present in synagogues on holy days, reminding us of the Temple, full at such times.

לְהוֹדוֹת, לְהַלֵּל... *To thank, praise, etc.* The nine infinitives of praise correspond to the nine additional psalms we say on Sabbaths and festivals.

The שליח ציבור *for* שחרית *begins here:*

יוֹשֵׁב עַל כִּסֵּא, רָם וְנִשָּׂא

שׁוֹכֵן עַד, מָרוֹם וְקָדוֹשׁ שְׁמוֹ

וְכָתוּב

רַנְּנוּ צַדִּיקִים בַּיהוה, לַיְשָׁרִים נָאוָה תְהִלָּה: תהלים לג

◂ בְּפִי יְשָׁרִים תִּתְהַלָּל

וּבְדִבְרֵי צַדִּיקִים תִּתְבָּרַךְ

וּבִלְשׁוֹן חֲסִידִים תִּתְרוֹמָם

וּבְקֶרֶב קְדוֹשִׁים תִּתְקַדָּשׁ

וּבְמַקְהֲלוֹת רִבְבוֹת עַמְּךָ בֵּית יִשְׂרָאֵל

בְּרִנָּה יִתְפָּאַר שִׁמְךָ מַלְכֵּנוּ בְּכָל דּוֹר וָדוֹר

◂ שֶׁכֵּן חוֹבַת כָּל הַיְצוּרִים

לְפָנֶיךָ יהוה אֱלֹהֵינוּ וֵאלֹהֵי אֲבוֹתֵינוּ

לְהוֹדוֹת, לְהַלֵּל, לְשַׁבֵּחַ, לְפָאֵר, לְרוֹמֵם

לְהַדֵּר, לְבָרֵךְ, לְעַלֵּה וּלְקַלֵּס

עַל כָּל דִּבְרֵי שִׁירוֹת וְתִשְׁבְּחוֹת

דָּוִד בֶּן יִשַׁי, עַבְדְּךָ מְשִׁיחֶךָ.

הַמֶּלֶךְ *The King.* Without changing the words of the usual Shabbat and festival prayers, the overarching theme of the Days of Awe – God's kingship – is signaled at this point by the emphasis placed on one word, *HaMelekh,* "the King." This is amplified by the custom for the main leader of prayer to take

Stand until after "Barekhu" on page 560.

יִשְׁתַּבַּח May Your name be praised for ever, our King,
the great and holy God, King in heaven and on earth.
For to You, LORD our God and God of our ancestors,
it is right to offer song and praise, hymn and psalm,
strength and dominion, eternity, greatness and power,
song of praise and glory, holiness and kingship,
▸ blessings and thanks, from now and for ever.
Blessed are You, LORD, God and King, exalted in praises,
God of thanksgivings, Master of wonders,
who delights in hymns of song,
King, God, Giver of life to the worlds.

Most congregations open the Ark and say this psalm responsively, verse by verse.

שִׁיר הַמַּעֲלוֹת A song of ascents. *Ps. 130*
From the depths I have called to You, LORD.
LORD, hear my voice; let Your ears be attentive to my plea.
If You, LORD, should keep account of sins, O LORD, who could stand?
But with You there is forgiveness, that You may be held in awe.
I wait for the LORD, my soul waits, and in His word I put my hope.
My soul waits for the LORD more than watchmen wait for the morning,
more than watchmen wait for the morning.
Israel, put your hope in the LORD,
for with the LORD there is loving-kindness,
and great is His power to redeem.
It is He who will redeem Israel from all their sins.

The Ark is closed.

שִׁיר הַמַּעֲלוֹת *Psalm 130.* One of the supreme *cris de coeur* in literature, a prayer from the abyss. Judaism is a faith some of whose deepest moments come in the midst of defeat, dejection, and the sense that, were it not for God, we would be utterly alone. Jacob, fleeing and far from home, encounters angels. David wrote some of his most powerful psalms on the brink of despair. Yet it is precisely our ability to speak to God that redeems us from solitude, God's forgiveness that allows us to live with our failures, God's love that gives us strength, and God's radiance that lights the heart of darkness.

Stand until after בָּרְכוּ *on page 561.*

יִשְׁתַּבַּח שִׁמְךָ לָעַד, מַלְכֵּנוּ
הָאֵל הַמֶּלֶךְ הַגָּדוֹל וְהַקָּדוֹשׁ בַּשָּׁמַיִם וּבָאָרֶץ
כִּי לְךָ נָאֶה, יהוה אֱלֹהֵינוּ וֵאלֹהֵי אֲבוֹתֵינוּ
שִׁיר וּשְׁבָחָה, הַלֵּל וְזִמְרָה
עֹז וּמֶמְשָׁלָה, נֶצַח, גְּדֻלָּה וּגְבוּרָה
תְּהִלָּה וְתִפְאֶרֶת, קְדֻשָּׁה וּמַלְכוּת
◂ בְּרָכוֹת וְהוֹדָאוֹת, מֵעַתָּה וְעַד עוֹלָם.
בָּרוּךְ אַתָּה יהוה, אֵל מֶלֶךְ גָּדוֹל בַּתִּשְׁבָּחוֹת
אֵל הַהוֹדָאוֹת, אֲדוֹן הַנִּפְלָאוֹת, הַבּוֹחֵר בְּשִׁירֵי זִמְרָה
מֶלֶךְ, אֵל, חֵי הָעוֹלָמִים.

Most congregations open the ארון קודש *and say this psalm responsively, verse by verse.*

שִׁיר הַמַּעֲלוֹת, מִמַּעֲמַקִּים קְרָאתִיךָ יהוה: תהלים קל
אֲדֹנָי שִׁמְעָה בְקוֹלִי, תִּהְיֶינָה אָזְנֶיךָ קַשֻּׁבוֹת לְקוֹל תַּחֲנוּנָי:
אִם־עֲוֹנוֹת תִּשְׁמָר־יָהּ, אֲדֹנָי מִי יַעֲמֹד:
כִּי־עִמְּךָ הַסְּלִיחָה, לְמַעַן תִּוָּרֵא:
קִוִּיתִי יהוה קִוְּתָה נַפְשִׁי, וְלִדְבָרוֹ הוֹחָלְתִּי:
נַפְשִׁי לַאדֹנָי, מִשֹּׁמְרִים לַבֹּקֶר, שֹׁמְרִים לַבֹּקֶר:
יַחֵל יִשְׂרָאֵל אֶל יהוה, כִּי־עִם־יהוה הַחֶסֶד, וְהַרְבֵּה עִמּוֹ פְדוּת:
וְהוּא יִפְדֶּה אֶת־יִשְׂרָאֵל, מִכֹּל עֲוֹנֹתָיו:

The ארון קודש *is closed.*

יִשְׁתַּבַּח שִׁמְךָ לָעַד *May Your name be praised forever.* The concluding blessing over the Verses of Praise which, like the introductory blessing, is said standing. The fifteen terms of glorification equal the number of psalms in the Verses of Praise on Sabbaths and festivals, as well as the number of "Songs of Ascents."

HALF KADDISH

Leader: יִתְגַּדַּל Magnified and sanctified
may His great name be,
in the world He created by His will.
May He establish His kingdom
in your lifetime and in your days,
and in the lifetime of all the house of Israel,
swiftly and soon –
and say: Amen.

All: May His great name be blessed for ever and all time.

Leader: Blessed and praised, glorified and exalted,
raised and honored, uplifted and lauded
be the name of the Holy One, blessed be He,
above and beyond any blessing, song,
praise and consolation uttered in the world –
and say: Amen.

---

but internal guilt. "If You, Lord, should keep account of sins, O Lord, who could stand?" Then the poet states the paradox: what is awesome about God is precisely His forgiveness. He never gives up on us; He refuses to let go. We may lose faith in Him; He never loses faith in us.

מִשֹּׁמְרִים לַבֹּקֶר *More than watchmen wait for the morning* (*previous page*). The Psalmist compares his longing for God's light in the dark night of the soul to that of the watchmen waiting for the first light of dawn.

HALF KADDISH

This, the shortest of the five forms of Kaddish, marks the end of one section of the prayers. More like a semicolon than a period, or a pause between the different movements of a symphony rather than the beginning of a new piece, the Half Kaddish denotes an internal break between two connected sections of prayer. Like all other versions of Kaddish it requires a quorum of ten men, the smallest number that constitutes a community as opposed to a group of individuals.

חצי קדיש

ש״ץ: יִתְגַּדַּל וְיִתְקַדַּשׁ שְׁמֵהּ רַבָּא (קהל: אָמֵן)
בְּעָלְמָא דִּי בְרָא כִרְעוּתֵהּ
וְיַמְלִיךְ מַלְכוּתֵהּ
בְּחַיֵּיכוֹן וּבְיוֹמֵיכוֹן וּבְחַיֵּי דְכָל בֵּית יִשְׂרָאֵל
בַּעֲגָלָא וּבִזְמַן קָרִיב, וְאִמְרוּ אָמֵן. (קהל: אָמֵן)

קהל וש״ץ: יְהֵא שְׁמֵהּ רַבָּא מְבָרַךְ לְעָלַם וּלְעָלְמֵי עָלְמַיָּא.

ש״ץ: יִתְבָּרַךְ וְיִשְׁתַּבַּח וְיִתְפָּאַר וְיִתְרוֹמַם וְיִתְנַשֵּׂא
וְיִתְהַדָּר וְיִתְעַלֶּה וְיִתְהַלָּל
שְׁמֵהּ דְּקֻדְשָׁא בְּרִיךְ הוּא (קהל: בְּרִיךְ הוּא)
לְעֵלָּא לְעֵלָּא מִכָּל בִּרְכָתָא וְשִׁירָתָא, תֻּשְׁבְּחָתָא וְנֶחֱמָתָא
דַּאֲמִירָן בְּעָלְמָא, וְאִמְרוּ אָמֵן. (קהל: אָמֵן)

Rabbi Yitzḥak Hutner (1906–1980), one of the great yeshiva teachers of the twentieth century, wrote to a disciple who was wrestling with disappointment and depression:

> Certainly you have stumbled and will stumble again, and in many battles you will fall lame. I promise you, though, that after those losing campaigns you will emerge from the war with laurels of victory on your head… The wisest of men said, "A righteous man falls seven times, but rises again" [Proverbs 24:16]. Fools believe the intent of the verse is to teach us something remarkable – that the righteous man falls seven times and, despite this, he rises. But the knowledgable are aware that the essence of the righteous man's rising again is *because of* his seven falls. (*Paḥad Yitzḥak, Letters,* 128)

This is a penitential psalm: hence its inclusion here on the Days of Awe and the days between. What troubles the Psalmist is not external enemies

BLESSINGS OF THE SHEMA

The following blessing and response are said only in the presence of a minyan. They represent a formal summons to the congregation to engage in an act of collective prayer. The custom of bowing at this point is based on 1 Chronicles 29:20, "David said to the whole assembly, 'Now bless the Lord your God.' All the assembly blessed the Lord God of their fathers and bowed their heads low to the Lord and the King." The Leader says the following, bowing at "Bless," standing straight at "the Lord." The congregation, followed by the Leader, responds, bowing at "Bless," standing straight at "the Lord."

Leader: **BLESS**
the Lord, the blessed One.

Congregation: Bless the Lord, the blessed One,
for ever and all time.

Leader: Bless the Lord, the blessed One,
for ever and all time.

The custom is to sit from this point until the Amida (except when the Ark is open), since the predominant emotion of this section of the prayers is love rather than awe. Conversation is forbidden until after the Amida.

The Ark is opened.

בָּרוּךְ Blessed are You, Lord our God, King of the Universe,
who opens for us the gates of compassion
and brings light to the eyes of those who await His forgiveness,
who forms light and creates darkness, makes peace and creates all.

הַפּוֹתֵחַ לָנוּ שַׁעֲרֵי רַחֲמִים *Who opens for us the gates of compassion.* Already at the beginning of the service, there is a hint that at the end of the day we will be praying Ne'ila, meaning "the closing" of the gates of prayer.

וּמֵאִיר עֵינֵי הַמְחַכִּים *Brings light to the eyes of those who await.* A subtle inflection of the normal prayer which speaks of physical light. The poet wants us to know that on the Days of Awe we encounter a spiritual light.

יוֹצֵר אוֹר וּבוֹרֵא חֹשֶׁךְ *Who forms light and creates darkness.* This affirmation,

קריאת שמע וברכותיה

The following blessing and response are said only in the presence of a מנין.
They represent a formal summons to the קהל *to engage in an act of collective prayer.*
The custom of bowing at this point is based on דברי הימים א׳ כט, כ, *"David said to the whole assembly, 'Now bless the Lord your God.' All the assembly blessed the Lord God of their fathers and bowed their heads low to the Lord and the King."*
The שליח ציבור *says the following, bowing at* בָּרְכוּ, *standing straight at* ה׳.
The קהל, *followed by the* שליח ציבור, *responds, bowing at* בָּרוּךְ, *standing straight at* ה׳.

ש״ץ: 

אֶת יהוה הַמְבֹרָךְ.

קהל: בָּרוּךְ יהוה הַמְבֹרָךְ לְעוֹלָם וָעֶד.

ש״ץ: בָּרוּךְ יהוה הַמְבֹרָךְ לְעוֹלָם וָעֶד.

The custom is to sit from this point until the עמידה *(except when the* ארון קודש *is open), since the predominant emotion of this section of the prayers is love rather than awe. Conversation is forbidden until after the* עמידה.

The ארון קודש *is opened.*

בָּרוּךְ אַתָּה יהוה אֱלֹהֵינוּ מֶלֶךְ הָעוֹלָם
הַפּוֹתֵחַ לָנוּ שַׁעֲרֵי רַחֲמִים
וּמֵאִיר עֵינֵי הַמְחַכִּים לִסְלִיחָתוֹ
יוֹצֵר אוֹר וּבוֹרֵא חֹשֶׁךְ
עֹשֶׂה שָׁלוֹם וּבוֹרֵא אֶת הַכֹּל.

בָּרְכוּ אֶת יהוה *Bless the Lord.* The formal start of communal prayer, to which the Verses of Praise have been a prelude and preparation. *Barekhu*, like the *zimmun* said before the Grace after Meals, is an invitation to others to join in an act of praise, based on the verse, "Magnify the Lord with me, let us exalt His name together" (Ps. 34:4).

אוֹר עוֹלָם Endless light in a treasure-house of life.
Lights from obscurity – He spoke and they became.

The Ark is closed.

Traditionally, the piyut אָז בְּיוֹם כִּפּוּר (page 1287) *was said at this point. Today, most congregations say only the two lines of the original alternating refrains.*

The Leader recites each verse and the congregation repeats.

סְלַח Forgive Your holy nation / on this holy day, /
O Exalted and Holy One.
We have sinned, our Rock; / forgive us, our Creator.

On Shabbat continue with "All will thank You" on page 566.
On a weekday continue here:

הַמֵּאִיר In compassion He gives light to the earth
and its inhabitants,
and in His goodness continually renews the work of creation,
day after day.

Hebrew Bible with several chapters of the book of Lamentations structured in this way, as well as the last section of the book of Proverbs ("A woman of worth"), and several of the Psalms (most notably Psalm 119, with eight verses for each letter of the alphabet). There may be mystical reasons for such compositions, but the practical reason is that they were easier to remember at a time, long before the invention of printing, when manuscripts were scarce and prayer books for personal use rare.

סְלַח לְגוֹי קָדוֹשׁ בְּיוֹם קָדוֹשׁ מָרוֹם וְקָדוֹשׁ *Holy nation… holy day… Holy One.* Isaiah heard the angels singing a threefold praise: "Holy, holy, holy." The poet interprets this to refer to three forms of holinesses: (1) Israel the holy nation, (2) Yom Kippur the holy day, and (3) God the Holy One. Heaven and earth meet at this sacred point in time where our consciousness of fallibility seeks healing in God's forgiving love.

וּבְטוּבוֹ מְחַדֵּשׁ...מַעֲשֵׂה בְרֵאשִׁית *In His goodness… renews the work of creation.* Judah HaLevi explains that the difference between creation from something

אוֹר עוֹלָם בְּאוֹצַר חַיִּים, אוֹרוֹת מֵאֹפֶל אָמַר וַיֶּהִי.

The ארון קודש *is closed.*

Traditionally, the piyut אָז בְּיוֹם כִּפּוּר (page 1287) *was said at this point. Today, most congregations say only the two lines of the original alternating refrains.*

The שליח ציבור *recites each verse and the* קהל *repeats.*

סְלַח לְגוֹי קָדוֹשׁ / בְּיוֹם קָדוֹשׁ / מָרוֹם וְקָדוֹשׁ.
חָטָאנוּ צוּרֵנוּ / סְלַח לָנוּ יוֹצְרֵנוּ.

On שבת *continue with* הַכֹּל יוֹדְוּךָ *on page 567.*
On a weekday continue here:

הַמֵּאִיר לָאָרֶץ וְלַדָּרִים עָלֶיהָ בְּרַחֲמִים
וּבְטוּבוֹ מְחַדֵּשׁ בְּכָל יוֹם תָּמִיד מַעֲשֵׂה בְרֵאשִׁית.

---

based on a verse in Isaiah (45:7), is an emphatic denial of dualism, the idea, whose origin lay in Greek Gnosticism, that there are two supreme and contending forces at work in the universe, one of good, the other of evil – known variously as the demiurge, the devil, Satan, Belial, Lucifer or the prince of darkness. Dualism arises as an attempt to explain the prevalence of evil in the world by attributing it to a malign power, the enemy of God and the good. Such a view is radically incompatible with monotheism. It is also exceptionally dangerous: it has led some groups to see others as the personification of evil. Nonetheless, there is evidence that such views were held by some sectarian groups of Jews in the late Second Temple period; hence the need to discountenance it at the very start of communal prayer.

אוֹר עוֹלָם *Endless light.* A fragment of a prayer composed by the earliest known composer of *piyut* (liturgical poetry), Yose ben Yose, who lived in the land of Israel, probably in the fifth century. It refers to the light of the first day of creation – not physical light, since the sun was not created until the fourth day, but spiritual light.

סְלַח לְגוֹי קָדוֹשׁ *Forgive Your holy nation.* This poem, author unknown, is constructed as a double alphabetical acrostic. Alphabetical acrostics appear in the

How numerous are Your works, Lord; *Ps. 104*
You made them all in wisdom;
the earth is full of Your creations.
He is the King exalted alone since the beginning of time –
praised, glorified and elevated since the world began.
Eternal God,
in Your great compassion, have compassion on us,
Lord of our strength, Rock of our refuge,
Shield of our salvation, Stronghold of our safety.
The blessed God, great in knowledge,
prepared and made the rays of the sun.
He who is good formed glory for His name,
surrounding His power with radiant stars.
The leaders of His hosts,
the holy ones, exalt the Almighty,
constantly proclaiming God's glory and holiness.
▸ Be blessed, Lord our God,
for the magnificence of Your handiwork
and for the radiant lights You have made.
May they glorify You, Selah!

"I do not know what I may appear to the world, but to myself I seem to have been only like a boy playing on the sea-shore, and diverting myself in now and then finding a smoother pebble or a prettier shell than ordinary, whilst the great ocean of truth lay all undiscovered before me." The more we discover about the universe, the greater its mystery and majesty inspire awe.

אֵל בָּרוּךְ *The blessed God.* An alphabetical acrostic of twenty-two words. Although this, the first blessing before the Shema, is about creation as a whole, the morning prayer emphasizes the element of which we are most conscious at the start of the day: the creation of light. Of this, there are two forms: the physical light of the sun, moon and stars, made on the fourth day of creation, and the spiritual light created on the first day ("Let there be light"). The prayer modulates from the first to the second, from the universe as we see it, to the mystical vision of God enthroned in glory, surrounded by angels.

מָה רַבּוּ מַעֲשֶׂיךָ יהוה, כֻּלָּם בְּחָכְמָה עָשִׂיתָ תהלים קד
מָלְאָה הָאָרֶץ קִנְיָנֶךָ:
הַמֶּלֶךְ הַמְרוֹמָם לְבַדּוֹ מֵאָז
הַמְשֻׁבָּח וְהַמְפֹאָר וְהַמִּתְנַשֵּׂא מִימוֹת עוֹלָם.
אֱלֹהֵי עוֹלָם
בְּרַחֲמֶיךָ הָרַבִּים רַחֵם עָלֵינוּ
אֲדוֹן עֻזֵּנוּ, צוּר מִשְׂגַּבֵּנוּ
מָגֵן יִשְׁעֵנוּ, מִשְׂגָּב בַּעֲדֵנוּ.
אֵל בָּרוּךְ גְּדוֹל דֵּעָה
הֵכִין וּפָעַל זָהֳרֵי חַמָּה
טוֹב יָצַר כָּבוֹד לִשְׁמוֹ
מְאוֹרוֹת נָתַן סְבִיבוֹת עֻזּוֹ
פִּנּוֹת צְבָאָיו קְדוֹשִׁים, רוֹמְמֵי שַׁדַּי
תָּמִיד מְסַפְּרִים כְּבוֹד אֵל וּקְדֻשָּׁתוֹ.
◂ תִּתְבָּרַךְ יהוה אֱלֹהֵינוּ
עַל שֶׁבַח מַעֲשֵׂה יָדֶיךָ
וְעַל מְאוֹרֵי אוֹר שֶׁעָשִׂיתָ
יְפָאֲרוּךָ סֶּלָה.

---

and creation from nothing is that in the former, when the act of creation stops, the object continues to exist. When a carpenter finishes a cabinet from wood, it continues to be without further effort from its maker. But when something is created from nothing, the act of creation must continue, for were it to cease the object would cease to be. Thus God, who made the universe from nothing, must re-create it at every moment. Every day the world is new, and prayer, like art, helps us see its newness.

Isaac Newton, the greatest scientist of the seventeenth century, once said:

On a weekday continue with "May You be blessed" on page 570. On Shabbat continue here:

On a weekday continue with "May You be blessed" on page 570.

All will thank You. All will praise You.
All will declare: Nothing is as holy as the LORD.
All will exalt You, Selah, You who form all –
the God who daily opens the doors of the gates of the East
and cleaves the windows of the sky,
who brings out the sun from its place and the moon from its abode,
giving light to the whole world and its inhabitants
whom He created by the attribute of compassion.
In compassion He gives light to the earth and its inhabitants,
and in His goodness daily, continually, renews the work of creation.
He is the King who alone was exalted since time began,
praised, glorified and raised high from days of old.
Eternal God, in Your great compassion, have compassion on us,
LORD of our strength, Rock of our refuge,
Shield of our salvation, Stronghold of our safety.

אֵין כְּעֶרְכְּךָ None can be compared to You, there is none besides You;
None without You. Who is like You?

▸ None can be compared to You, LORD our God –
in this world.
There is none besides You, our King –
in the life of the World to Come.
There is none but You, our Redeemer –
in the days of the Messiah.
There is none like You, our Savior –
at the resurrection of the dead.

שֶׁבָּרָא בְּמִדַּת הָרַחֲמִים *Whom He created by the attribute of compassion.* According to tradition, God initially sought to create the world under the attribute of strict justice, but saw that it could not survive. What did He do? To justice He joined the attribute of compassion (*Bereshit Raba* 8:5). One of the supreme ironies of literature is that Portia's speech in Shakespeare's *The Merchant of Venice*, framed in opposition to Jewish ethics, is in fact a precise statement of it:

The quality of mercy is not strained.
It droppeth as the gentle rain from heaven

On a weekday continue with תִּתְבָּרַךְ, צוּרֵנוּ *on page 571. On* שבת *continue here:*

הַכֹּל יוֹדְוּךָ וְהַכֹּל יְשַׁבְּחְוּךָ
וְהַכֹּל יֹאמְרוּ אֵין קָדוֹשׁ כַּיהוה
הַכֹּל יְרוֹמְמְוּךָ סֶּלָה, יוֹצֵר הַכֹּל.
הָאֵל הַפּוֹתֵחַ בְּכָל יוֹם דַּלְתוֹת שַׁעֲרֵי מִזְרָח
וּבוֹקֵעַ חַלּוֹנֵי רָקִיעַ
מוֹצִיא חַמָּה מִמְּקוֹמָהּ וּלְבָנָה מִמְּכוֹן שִׁבְתָּהּ
וּמֵאִיר לָעוֹלָם כֻּלּוֹ וּלְיוֹשְׁבָיו
שֶׁבָּרָא בְּמִדַּת הָרַחֲמִים.
הַמֵּאִיר לָאָרֶץ וְלַדָּרִים עָלֶיהָ בְּרַחֲמִים
וּבְטוּבוֹ מְחַדֵּשׁ בְּכָל יוֹם תָּמִיד מַעֲשֵׂה בְרֵאשִׁית.
הַמֶּלֶךְ הַמְרוֹמָם לְבַדּוֹ מֵאָז
הַמְשֻׁבָּח וְהַמְפֹאָר וְהַמִּתְנַשֵּׂא מִימוֹת עוֹלָם.
אֱלֹהֵי עוֹלָם, בְּרַחֲמֶיךָ הָרַבִּים רַחֵם עָלֵינוּ
אֲדוֹן עֻזֵּנוּ, צוּר מִשְׂגַּבֵּנוּ, מָגֵן יִשְׁעֵנוּ, מִשְׂגָּב בַּעֲדֵנוּ.

אֵין כְּעֶרְכֶּךָ
וְאֵין זוּלָתֶךָ
אֶפֶס בִּלְתֶּךָ
וּמִי דּוֹמֶה לָּךְ.

◂ אֵין כְּעֶרְכְּךָ, יהוה אֱלֹהֵינוּ, בָּעוֹלָם הַזֶּה
וְאֵין זוּלָתְךָ, מַלְכֵּנוּ, לְחַיֵּי הָעוֹלָם הַבָּא
אֶפֶס בִּלְתְּךָ, גּוֹאֲלֵנוּ, לִימוֹת הַמָּשִׁיחַ
וְאֵין דּוֹמֶה לְּךָ, מוֹשִׁיעֵנוּ, לִתְחִיַּת הַמֵּתִים.

הַכֹּל יוֹדְוּךָ *All will thank You.* This passage, said on Shabbat, is longer than its weekday equivalent since Shabbat is a memorial of creation (Roke'aḥ).

אֵל אָדוֹן God, Lord of all creation,
the Blessed, is blessed by every soul.
His greatness and goodness fill the world;
knowledge and wisdom surround Him.

Exalted above the holy Ḥayyot,
adorned in glory on the Chariot;
merit and right are before His throne,
kindness and compassion before His glory.

Good are the radiant stars our God created;
He formed them with knowledge,
understanding and deliberation.
He gave them strength and might
to rule throughout the world.

Full of splendor, radiating light,
beautiful is their splendor throughout the world.
Glad as they go forth, joyous as they return,
they fulfill with awe their Creator's will.

Glory and honor they give to His name,
jubilation and song at the mention of His majesty.
He called the sun into being and it shone with light.
He looked and fashioned the form of the moon.

All the hosts on high give Him praise;
the Seraphim, Ophanim and holy Ḥayyot
ascribe glory and greatness –

אֵל אָדוֹן עַל כָּל הַמַּעֲשִׂים *God, Lord of all creation.* An ancient prayer, influenced by *Merkava* mysticism, envisioning God surrounded by the angels and the myriad stars. *Merkava* or "Chariot" mysticism was based on the vision seen by Ezekiel and described by him in the first chapter of the book that bears his name.

כָּל צְבָא מָרוֹם *All the hosts on high.* Having mentioned the sun and moon, the Hebrew hints at the other planets of the Ptolemaic system: שֶׁבַח נוֹתְנִים לוֹ כָּל צְבָא מָרוֹם – the ש of *shevaḥ* signaling Saturn (*Shabbetai*), and so on for Venus (נ for *Noga*), Mercury (כ for *Kokhav*), Jupiter (צ for *Tzedek*), and Mars (מ for *Maadim*).

אֵל אָדוֹן עַל כָּל הַמַּעֲשִׂים
בָּרוּךְ וּמְבֹרָךְ בְּפִי כָּל נְשָׁמָה
גָּדְלוֹ וְטוּבוֹ מָלֵא עוֹלָם
דַּעַת וּתְבוּנָה סוֹבְבִים אוֹתוֹ.

הַמִּתְגָּאֶה עַל חַיּוֹת הַקֹּדֶשׁ
וְנֶהְדָּר בְּכָבוֹד עַל הַמֶּרְכָּבָה
זְכוּת וּמִישׁוֹר לִפְנֵי כִסְאוֹ
חֶסֶד וְרַחֲמִים לִפְנֵי כְבוֹדוֹ.

טוֹבִים מְאוֹרוֹת שֶׁבָּרָא אֱלֹהֵינוּ
יְצָרָם בְּדַעַת בְּבִינָה וּבְהַשְׂכֵּל
כֹּחַ וּגְבוּרָה נָתַן בָּהֶם
לִהְיוֹת מוֹשְׁלִים בְּקֶרֶב תֵּבֵל.

מְלֵאִים זִיו וּמְפִיקִים נֹגַהּ
נָאֶה זִיוָם בְּכָל הָעוֹלָם
שְׂמֵחִים בְּצֵאתָם וְשָׂשִׂים בְּבוֹאָם
עוֹשִׂים בְּאֵימָה רְצוֹן קוֹנָם.

פְּאֵר וְכָבוֹד נוֹתְנִים לִשְׁמוֹ
צָהֳלָה וְרִנָּה לְזֵכֶר מַלְכוּתוֹ
קָרָא לַשֶּׁמֶשׁ וַיִּזְרַח אוֹר
רָאָה וְהִתְקִין צוּרַת הַלְּבָנָה.

שֶׁבַח נוֹתְנִים לוֹ כָּל צְבָא מָרוֹם
תִּפְאֶרֶת וּגְדֻלָּה, שְׂרָפִים וְאוֹפַנִּים וְחַיּוֹת הַקֹּדֶשׁ.

Upon the place beneath […] / It is an attribute to God himself
And earthly power doth then show likest God's
Where mercy seasons justice. (IV, i)

לָאֵל To God who rested from all works, and on the seventh day
ascended and sat on His throne of glory.
He robed the day of rest in glory and called the Sabbath day a delight.
This is the praise of the seventh day,
that on it God rested from all His work.
The seventh day itself gives praise, saying,
"A psalm, a song for the Sabbath day. *Ps. 92*
It is good to give thanks to the LORD."
Therefore let all He has formed glorify and bless God.
Let them give praise, honor and grandeur to God,
the King, who formed all things,
and in His holiness gave a heritage of rest
to His people Israel on the holy Sabbath day.
May Your name, O LORD our God, be sanctified,
and Your renown, O our King, be glorified
in the heavens above and on the earth below.
May You be blessed, our Deliverer, by the praises of Your handiwork,
and by the radiant lights You have made: may they glorify You. Selah!

On all days continue here:

תִּתְבָּרַךְ May You be blessed,
our Rock, King and Redeemer,
Creator of holy beings.
May Your name be praised for ever,
our King, Creator of the ministering angels,
all of whom stand in the universe's heights,
proclaiming together,
in awe, aloud,
the words of the living God,
the eternal King.

---

understood not as a song *for* the Sabbath, but *by* the Sabbath. It is as if, in the silence of Shabbat, we hear the song creation sings to its Creator, the "music of the spheres."

תִּתְבָּרַךְ *May You be blessed.* Two prophets, Isaiah and Ezekiel, saw mystical visions of God enthroned among His heavenly host, the choir of angels.

לָאֵל אֲשֶׁר שָׁבַת מִכָּל הַמַּעֲשִׂים
בַּיּוֹם הַשְּׁבִיעִי נִתְעַלָּה וְיָשַׁב עַל כִּסֵּא כְבוֹדוֹ.
תִּפְאֶרֶת עָטָה לְיוֹם הַמְּנוּחָה
עֹנֶג קָרָא לְיוֹם הַשַּׁבָּת.
זֶה שֶׁבַח שֶׁלַּיּוֹם הַשְּׁבִיעִי
שֶׁבּוֹ שָׁבַת אֵל מִכָּל מְלַאכְתּוֹ
וְיוֹם הַשְּׁבִיעִי מְשַׁבֵּחַ וְאוֹמֵר
מִזְמוֹר שִׁיר לְיוֹם הַשַּׁבָּת, טוֹב לְהֹדוֹת לַיהוה: תהלים צב
לְפִיכָךְ יְפָאֲרוּ וִיבָרְכוּ לָאֵל כָּל יְצוּרָיו
שֶׁבַח יְקָר וּגְדֻלָּה יִתְּנוּ לָאֵל מֶלֶךְ יוֹצֵר כֹּל
הַמַּנְחִיל מְנוּחָה לְעַמּוֹ יִשְׂרָאֵל בִּקְדֻשָּׁתוֹ בְּיוֹם שַׁבַּת קֹדֶשׁ.
שִׁמְךָ יהוה אֱלֹהֵינוּ יִתְקַדַּשׁ, וְזִכְרְךָ מַלְכֵּנוּ יִתְפָּאַר
בַּשָּׁמַיִם מִמַּעַל וְעַל הָאָרֶץ מִתָּחַת.
תִּתְבָּרַךְ מוֹשִׁיעֵנוּ עַל שֶׁבַח מַעֲשֵׂה יָדֶיךָ
וְעַל מְאוֹרֵי אוֹר שֶׁעָשִׂיתָ, יְפָאֲרוּךָ סֶּלָה.

On all days continue here:

תִּתְבָּרַךְ
צוּרֵנוּ מַלְכֵּנוּ וְגוֹאֲלֵנוּ, בּוֹרֵא קְדוֹשִׁים
יִשְׁתַּבַּח שִׁמְךָ לָעַד
מַלְכֵּנוּ, יוֹצֵר מְשָׁרְתִים
וַאֲשֶׁר מְשָׁרְתָיו כֻּלָּם עוֹמְדִים בְּרוּם עוֹלָם
וּמַשְׁמִיעִים בְּיִרְאָה יַחַד בְּקוֹל
דִּבְרֵי אֱלֹהִים חַיִּים וּמֶלֶךְ עוֹלָם.

וְיוֹם הַשְּׁבִיעִי מְשַׁבֵּחַ *The seventh day itself gives praise.* A midrashic idea, based on the phrase that opens Psalm 92: "A psalm, a song of the Sabbath day," here

They are all beloved,
all pure,
all mighty,
and all perform in awe and reverence
the will of their Maker.
▸ All open their mouths
in holiness and purity,
with song and psalm,
and bless, praise, glorify,
revere, sanctify and declare the sovereignty of – ◂
the name of the great, mighty
and awesome God and King,
holy is He.
▸ All accept on themselves, one from another,
the yoke of the kingdom of heaven,
granting permission to one another
to sanctify the One who formed them, in serene spirit,
pure speech and sweet melody.
All, as one, proclaim His holiness,
saying in reverence:

All say aloud:

Holy, holy, holy is the LORD of hosts: *Is. 6*
the whole world is filled with His glory.

---

the Leader's Repetition of the Amida, and (3) toward the end of prayer, except on Shabbat and festivals, when the third is transferred to the afternoon.

This section of the prayers – the vision of the heavenly throne and the angels – is part of the mystical tradition in Judaism. Prayer is Jacob's ladder, stretching from earth to heaven, with "angels of the LORD" ascending and descending (*Zohar*). The three *kedushot* represent, respectively, the ascent, the summit, and the descent: the journey of the soul from earth to heaven and back again, transformed by our experience of the Divine.

כֻּלָּם אֲהוּבִים
כֻּלָּם בְּרוּרִים
כֻּלָּם גִּבּוֹרִים
וְכֻלָּם עוֹשִׂים בְּאֵימָה וּבְיִרְאָה רְצוֹן קוֹנָם
► וְכֻלָּם פּוֹתְחִים אֶת פִּיהֶם
בִּקְדֻשָּׁה וּבְטָהֳרָה
בְּשִׁירָה וּבְזִמְרָה
וּמְבָרְכִים וּמְשַׁבְּחִים וּמְפָאֲרִים
► וּמַעֲרִיצִים וּמַקְדִּישִׁים וּמַמְלִיכִים
אֶת שֵׁם הָאֵל הַמֶּלֶךְ הַגָּדוֹל, הַגִּבּוֹר וְהַנּוֹרָא
קָדוֹשׁ הוּא.
► וְכֻלָּם מְקַבְּלִים עֲלֵיהֶם עֹל מַלְכוּת שָׁמַיִם זֶה מִזֶּה
וְנוֹתְנִים רְשׁוּת זֶה לָזֶה
לְהַקְדִּישׁ לְיוֹצְרָם בְּנַחַת רוּחַ
בְּשָׂפָה בְרוּרָה וּבִנְעִימָה
קְדֻשָּׁה כֻּלָּם כְּאֶחָד
עוֹנִים וְאוֹמְרִים בְּיִרְאָה

All say aloud:

קָדוֹשׁ, קָדוֹשׁ, קָדוֹשׁ יהוה צְבָאוֹת ישעיה ו
מְלֹא כָל־הָאָרֶץ כְּבוֹדוֹ:

These visions, together with the words the prophets heard the angels sing ("Holy, holy, holy" in Isaiah's vision; "Blessed is the Lord's glory from His place" in Ezekiel's), form the heart of *Kedusha*, the "Holiness" prayer. This is recited three times in the morning prayers: (1) before the Shema, (2) during

Some congregations say the piyut מַלְכוּתוֹ בִּקְהַל עֲדָתִי *(page 1288) at this point.*

The congregation, followed by the Leader, recites one of the following versions according to their custom. Some hold that a congregation which doesn't say Yotzerot (the piyutim added to the blessing of Yotzer) should say "Then the Ophanim."

The Ḥayyot sing out, / and the Cherubim glorify, / and the Seraphim pray, / and the Erelim bless, / with the face of each Ḥayya and Ophan and Cherub / turned towards the Seraphim. / Facing these, they give praise, saying:

Then the Ophanim and the Holy Ḥayyot, / with a roar of noise, / raise themselves toward the Seraphim and, / facing them, give praise, saying:

All say aloud:

Blessed is the LORD's glory from His place. *Ezek. 3*

לְאֵל To the blessed God they offer melodies.
To the King, living and eternal God,
they say psalms and proclaim praises.
For it is He alone who does mighty deeds
and creates new things,
who is Master of battles and sows righteousness,
who makes salvation grow and creates cures,
who is is revered in praises, the LORD of wonders,
who in His goodness,
continually renews the work of creation, day after day,
as it is said,
"[Praise] Him who made the great lights, *Ps. 136*
for His love endures for ever."
▸ May You make a new light shine over Zion,
and may we all soon be worthy of its light.
Blessed are You, LORD, who forms the radiant lights.

Representations of them were above the Ark in the Tabernacle and later the Temple. Seraphim are angels of fire. Erelim are described by Isaiah (33:7) as angels of peace. Ophanim are angels described as "wheels within wheels." Together they form a heavenly retinue surrounding the divine throne, an angelic choir singing God's praises. Angels appear in Tanakh as divine emissaries, but in prayer we focus on their role, in mystic visions, as singers of God's song in heaven.

Some congregations say the piyut מַלְכוּתוֹ בִּקְהַל עֲדָתִי *(page 1288) at this point.*

The קהל*, followed by the* שליח ציבור*, recites one of the following versions according to their custom.*
Some hold that a congregation which doesn't say יוצרות *should say* וְהָאוֹפַנִּים.

וְהַחַיּוֹת יְשׁוֹרֵרוּ / וּכְרוּבִים יְפָאֵרוּ
וּשְׂרָפִים יָרֹנּוּ / וְאֶרְאֶלִּים יְבָרֵכוּ
פְּנֵי כָל חַיָּה וְאוֹפָן וּכְרוּב לְעֻמַּת שְׂרָפִים
לְעֻמָּתָם מְשַׁבְּחִים וְאוֹמְרִים

וְהָאוֹפַנִּים וְחַיּוֹת הַקֹּדֶשׁ
בְּרַעַשׁ גָּדוֹל
מִתְנַשְּׂאִים לְעֻמַּת שְׂרָפִים
לְעֻמָּתָם מְשַׁבְּחִים וְאוֹמְרִים

All say aloud:

בָּרוּךְ כְּבוֹד־יהוה מִמְּקוֹמוֹ: יחזקאל ג

לָאֵל בָּרוּךְ נְעִימוֹת יִתֵּנוּ
לַמֶּלֶךְ אֵל חַי וְקַיָּם
זְמִירוֹת יֹאמֵרוּ וְתִשְׁבָּחוֹת יַשְׁמִיעוּ
כִּי הוּא לְבַדּוֹ
פּוֹעֵל גְּבוּרוֹת, עוֹשֶׂה חֲדָשׁוֹת
בַּעַל מִלְחָמוֹת, זוֹרֵעַ צְדָקוֹת
מַצְמִיחַ יְשׁוּעוֹת, בּוֹרֵא רְפוּאוֹת
נוֹרָא תְהִלּוֹת, אֲדוֹן הַנִּפְלָאוֹת
הַמְחַדֵּשׁ בְּטוּבוֹ בְּכָל יוֹם תָּמִיד מַעֲשֵׂה בְרֵאשִׁית
כָּאָמוּר
לְעֹשֵׂה אוֹרִים גְּדֹלִים, כִּי לְעוֹלָם חַסְדּוֹ: תהלים קלו
◄ אוֹר חָדָשׁ עַל צִיּוֹן תָּאִיר
וְנִזְכֶּה כֻלָּנוּ מְהֵרָה לְאוֹרוֹ.
בָּרוּךְ אַתָּה יהוה, יוֹצֵר הַמְּאוֹרוֹת.

וְהַחַיּוֹת...וּכְרוּבִים...וּשְׂרָפִים...וְאֶרְאֶלִּים...וְאוֹפָן *Ḥayyot… Cherubim… Seraphim… Erelim…* [*each*] *Ophan.* Five kinds of angels seen by Isaiah and Ezekiel in their visions. Ḥayyot are "living beings" surrounded by fire. Cherubim are guardian angels, mentioned in the story of the Garden of Eden (Gen. 3:24).

אַהֲבָה You have loved us with great love, LORD our God,
and with surpassing compassion have You had compassion on us.
Our Father, our King,
for the sake of our ancestors who trusted in You,
and to whom You taught the laws of life,
be gracious also to us and teach us.
Our Father, compassionate Father, ever compassionate,
have compassion on us.
Instill in our hearts the desire to understand and discern,
to listen, learn and teach, to observe, perform and fulfill
all the teachings of Your Torah in love.
Enlighten our eyes in Your Torah
and let our hearts cling to Your commandments.
Unite our hearts to love and revere Your name,
so that we may never be ashamed.
And because we have trusted in Your holy, great and revered name,
may we be glad and rejoice in Your salvation.

At this point, gather the four tzitziot of the tallit, holding them in the left hand.

Bring us back in peace from the four quarters of the earth
and lead us upright to our land.
▸ For You are a God who performs acts of salvation,
and You chose us from all peoples and tongues,
bringing us close to Your great name for ever in truth,
that we may thank You and proclaim Your Oneness in love.
Blessed are You, LORD, who chooses His people Israel in love.

---

life." Christianity at times contrasted law and love as if they were opposed. In Judaism law *is* love: the expression of God's love for us and ours for Him.

Franz Rosenzweig criticized Martin Buber for failing to understand the centrality of law in Judaism: "...the law of millennia, studied and lived, analyzed and rhapsodized, the law of everyday and of the day of death, petty and yet sublime, sober and yet woven in legend; a law which knows both the fire of the Sabbath candle and that of the martyr's stake" (Franz Rosenzweig, *On Jewish Learning*, 77). The law, through which Israel is charged with bringing the Divine Presence into the shared spaces of our common life, is itself based on a threefold love: for God, the neighbor, and the stranger. Through

אַהֲבָה רַבָּה אֲהַבְתָּנוּ, יהוה אֱלֹהֵינוּ
חֶמְלָה גְדוֹלָה וִיתֵרָה חָמַלְתָּ עָלֵינוּ.
אָבִינוּ מַלְכֵּנוּ
בַּעֲבוּר אֲבוֹתֵינוּ שֶׁבָּטְחוּ בְךָ, וַתְּלַמְּדֵם חֻקֵּי חַיִּים
כֵּן תְּחָנֵּנוּ וּתְלַמְּדֵנוּ.
אָבִינוּ, הָאָב הָרַחֲמָן, הַמְרַחֵם
רַחֵם עָלֵינוּ
וְתֵן בְּלִבֵּנוּ לְהָבִין וּלְהַשְׂכִּיל
לִשְׁמֹעַ, לִלְמֹד וּלְלַמֵּד, לִשְׁמֹר וְלַעֲשׂוֹת, וּלְקַיֵּם
אֶת כָּל דִּבְרֵי תַלְמוּד תּוֹרָתֶךָ בְּאַהֲבָה.
וְהָאֵר עֵינֵינוּ בְּתוֹרָתֶךָ, וְדַבֵּק לִבֵּנוּ בְּמִצְוֹתֶיךָ
וְיַחֵד לְבָבֵנוּ לְאַהֲבָה וּלְיִרְאָה אֶת שְׁמֶךָ
וְלֹא נֵבוֹשׁ לְעוֹלָם וָעֶד.
כִּי בְשֵׁם קָדְשְׁךָ הַגָּדוֹל וְהַנּוֹרָא בָּטָחְנוּ
נָגִילָה וְנִשְׂמְחָה בִּישׁוּעָתֶךָ.

At this point, gather the four ציציות *of the* טלית*, holding them in the left hand.*

וַהֲבִיאֵנוּ לְשָׁלוֹם מֵאַרְבַּע כַּנְפוֹת הָאָרֶץ
וְתוֹלִיכֵנוּ קוֹמְמִיּוּת לְאַרְצֵנוּ.
◂ כִּי אֵל פּוֹעֵל יְשׁוּעוֹת אָתָּה, וּבָנוּ בָחַרְתָּ מִכָּל עַם וְלָשׁוֹן
וְקֵרַבְתָּנוּ לְשִׁמְךָ הַגָּדוֹל סֶלָה, בֶּאֱמֶת
לְהוֹדוֹת לְךָ וּלְיַחֶדְךָ בְּאַהֲבָה.
בָּרוּךְ אַתָּה יהוה, הַבּוֹחֵר בְּעַמּוֹ יִשְׂרָאֵל בְּאַהֲבָה.

אַהֲבָה רַבָּה אֲהַבְתָּנוּ *You have loved us with great love.* Even before reciting the Shema with its command, "Love the Lord your God with all your heart, with all your soul, and with all your might," we speak of God's love for us. Note how that love is expressed: in the fact that God taught us "the laws of

The Shema must be said with intense concentration. In the first paragraph one should accept, with love, the sovereignty of God; in the second, the mitzvot as the will of God. The end of the third paragraph constitutes fulfillment of the mitzva to remember, morning and evening, the exodus from Egypt. See laws 17–20.

When not praying with a minyan, say:

God, faithful King!

The following verse should be said aloud, while covering the eyes with the right hand:

Listen, Israel: the LORD is our God, the LORD is One. *Deut. 6*

Aloud: Blessed be the name of His glorious kingdom for ever and all time.

וְאָהַבְתָּ Love the LORD your God with all your heart, with all your soul, and with all your might. These words which I command you today shall be on your heart. Teach them repeatedly to your children, speaking of them when you sit at home and when you travel on the way, when you lie down and when you rise. Bind them as a sign on your hand, and they shall be an emblem between your eyes. Write them on the doorposts of your house and gates. *Deut. 6*

וְהָיָה If you indeed heed My commandments with which I charge you today, to love the LORD your God and worship Him with all your heart and with all your soul, I will give rain in your land in its season, the early and late rain; and you shall gather in your grain, wine and oil. I will give grass in your field for your cattle, and you shall eat and be satisfied. Be careful lest your heart be tempted and you go astray and worship other gods, bowing down to them. Then *Deut. 11*

---

our eyes, shutting out the visible world to concentrate on the commanding Voice.

וְאָהַבְתָּ אֵת יהוה אֱלֹהֶיךָ *Love the LORD your God.* What is the love of God that is befitting? It is to love God with a great and exceeding love, so strong that one's soul shall be knit up with the love of God, such that it is continually enraptured by it, like a lovesick individual whose mind is at no time free from passion for a particular woman and is enraptured by her at all times… Even more intense should be the love of God in the hearts of those who love Him;

The שמע *must be said with intense concentration. In the first paragraph one should accept, with love, the sovereignty of God; in the second, the* מצוות *as the will of God. The end of the third paragraph constitutes fulfillment of the* מצווה *to remember, morning and evening, the exodus from Egypt. See laws 17–20.*

When not praying with a מנין*, say:*

אֵל מֶלֶךְ נֶאֱמָן

The following verse should be said aloud, while covering the eyes with the right hand:

דברים ו **שְׁמַע יִשְׂרָאֵל, יהוה אֱלֹהֵינוּ, יהוה ׀ אֶחָד:**

Aloud בָּרוּךְ שֵׁם כְּבוֹד מַלְכוּתוֹ לְעוֹלָם וָעֶד.

דברים ו וְאָהַבְתָּ אֵת יהוה אֱלֹהֶיךָ, בְּכָל־לְבָבְךָ וּבְכָל־נַפְשְׁךָ וּבְכָל־
מְאֹדֶךָ: וְהָיוּ הַדְּבָרִים הָאֵלֶּה, אֲשֶׁר אָנֹכִי מְצַוְּךָ הַיּוֹם, עַל־לְבָבֶךָ:
וְשִׁנַּנְתָּם לְבָנֶיךָ וְדִבַּרְתָּ בָּם, בְּשִׁבְתְּךָ בְּבֵיתֶךָ וּבְלֶכְתְּךָ בַדֶּרֶךְ,
וּבְשָׁכְבְּךָ וּבְקוּמֶךָ: וּקְשַׁרְתָּם לְאוֹת עַל־יָדֶךָ וְהָיוּ לְטֹטָפֹת בֵּין
עֵינֶיךָ: וּכְתַבְתָּם עַל־מְזֻזוֹת בֵּיתֶךָ וּבִשְׁעָרֶיךָ:

דברים יא וְהָיָה אִם־שָׁמֹעַ תִּשְׁמְעוּ אֶל־מִצְוֺתַי אֲשֶׁר אָנֹכִי מְצַוֶּה אֶתְכֶם
הַיּוֹם, לְאַהֲבָה אֶת־יהוה אֱלֹהֵיכֶם וּלְעָבְדוֹ, בְּכָל־לְבַבְכֶם וּבְכָל־
נַפְשְׁכֶם: וְנָתַתִּי מְטַר־אַרְצְכֶם בְּעִתּוֹ, יוֹרֶה וּמַלְקוֹשׁ, וְאָסַפְתָּ
דְגָנֶךָ וְתִירֹשְׁךָ וְיִצְהָרֶךָ: וְנָתַתִּי עֵשֶׂב בְּשָׂדְךָ לִבְהֶמְתֶּךָ, וְאָכַלְתָּ
וְשָׂבָעְתָּ: הִשָּׁמְרוּ לָכֶם פֶּן־יִפְתֶּה לְבַבְכֶם, וְסַרְתֶּם וַעֲבַדְתֶּם

---

law – the choreography of grace in relationship – we redeem our finitude, turning the prose of daily life into religious poetry and making gentle the life of this world.

שְׁמַע יִשְׂרָאֵל *Listen, Israel.* Most of the ancient civilizations, from Mesopotamia and Egypt to Greece and Rome, were predominantly visual, with monumental architecture and iconic use of art. Judaism, with its faith in the invisible God, emphasized hearing over seeing, and listening over looking. Hence the verb "Listen" in this key text, as well as our custom, when saying it, to cover

the LORD's anger will flare against you and He will close the heavens so that there will be no rain. The land will not yield its crops, and you will perish swiftly from the good land that the LORD is giving you. Therefore, set these, My words, on your heart and soul. Bind them as a sign on your hand, and they shall be an emblem between your eyes. Teach them to your children, speaking of them when you sit at home and when you travel on the way, when you lie down and when you rise. Write them on the doorposts of your house and gates, so that you and your children may live long in the land that the LORD swore to your ancestors to give them, for as long as the heavens are above the earth.

Transfer the tzitziot to the right hand, kissing them at °.

וַיֹּאמֶר The LORD spoke to Moses, saying: Speak to the Israelites and tell them to make °tassels on the corners of their garments for all generations. They shall attach to the °tassel at each corner a thread of blue. This shall be your °tassel, and you shall see it and remember all of the LORD's commandments and keep them, not straying after your heart and after your eyes, following your own sinful desires. Thus you will be reminded to keep all My commandments, and be holy to your God. I am the LORD your God, who brought you out of the land of Egypt to be your God. I am the LORD your God. *Num. 15*

°True –

The Leader repeats:

▸ The LORD your God is true –

וְלִמַּדְתֶּם אֹתָם אֶת־בְּנֵיכֶם...לְמַעַן יִרְבּוּ יְמֵיכֶם *Teach them to your children… so that you… may live long.* Jews are the only people to have predicated their very survival on education. The Mesopotamians built ziggurats, the Egyptians built pyramids, the Athenians the Parthenon and the Romans the Colosseum. Jews built schools and houses of study. Those other civilizations died and disappeared; Jews and Judaism survived.

אֱמֶת *True.* The word *emet* does not just mean "true" in the narrow Western

אֱלֹהִים אֲחֵרִים וְהִשְׁתַּחֲוִיתֶם לָהֶם: וְחָרָה אַף־יהוה בָּכֶם, וְעָצַר אֶת־הַשָּׁמַיִם וְלֹא־יִהְיֶה מָטָר, וְהָאֲדָמָה לֹא תִתֵּן אֶת־יְבוּלָהּ, וַאֲבַדְתֶּם מְהֵרָה מֵעַל הָאָרֶץ הַטֹּבָה אֲשֶׁר יהוה נֹתֵן לָכֶם: וְשַׂמְתֶּם אֶת־דְּבָרַי אֵלֶּה עַל־לְבַבְכֶם וְעַל־נַפְשְׁכֶם, וּקְשַׁרְתֶּם אֹתָם לְאוֹת עַל־יֶדְכֶם, וְהָיוּ לְטוֹטָפֹת בֵּין עֵינֵיכֶם: וְלִמַּדְתֶּם אֹתָם אֶת־בְּנֵיכֶם לְדַבֵּר בָּם, בְּשִׁבְתְּךָ בְּבֵיתֶךָ, וּבְלֶכְתְּךָ בַדֶּרֶךְ, וּבְשָׁכְבְּךָ וּבְקוּמֶךָ: וּכְתַבְתָּם עַל־מְזוּזוֹת בֵּיתֶךָ וּבִשְׁעָרֶיךָ: לְמַעַן יִרְבּוּ יְמֵיכֶם וִימֵי בְנֵיכֶם עַל הָאֲדָמָה אֲשֶׁר נִשְׁבַּע יהוה לַאֲבֹתֵיכֶם לָתֵת לָהֶם, כִּימֵי הַשָּׁמַיִם עַל־הָאָרֶץ:

Transfer the ציציות *to the right hand, kissing them at* °.

במדבר טו וַיֹּאמֶר יהוה אֶל־מֹשֶׁה לֵּאמֹר: דַּבֵּר אֶל־בְּנֵי יִשְׂרָאֵל וְאָמַרְתָּ אֲלֵהֶם, וְעָשׂוּ לָהֶם °צִיצִת עַל־כַּנְפֵי בִגְדֵיהֶם לְדֹרֹתָם, וְנָתְנוּ °עַל־צִיצִת הַכָּנָף פְּתִיל תְּכֵלֶת: וְהָיָה לָכֶם °לְצִיצִת, וּרְאִיתֶם אֹתוֹ, וּזְכַרְתֶּם אֶת־כָּל־מִצְוֺת יהוה וַעֲשִׂיתֶם אֹתָם, וְלֹא תָתֻרוּ אַחֲרֵי לְבַבְכֶם וְאַחֲרֵי עֵינֵיכֶם, אֲשֶׁר־אַתֶּם זֹנִים אַחֲרֵיהֶם: לְמַעַן תִּזְכְּרוּ וַעֲשִׂיתֶם אֶת־כָּל־מִצְוֺתָי, וִהְיִיתֶם קְדֹשִׁים לֵאלֹהֵיכֶם: אֲנִי יהוה אֱלֹהֵיכֶם, אֲשֶׁר הוֹצֵאתִי אֶתְכֶם מֵאֶרֶץ מִצְרַיִם, לִהְיוֹת לָכֶם לֵאלֹהִים, אֲנִי יהוה אֱלֹהֵיכֶם:

°אֱמֶת

The שליח ציבור *repeats:*

◂ יהוה אֱלֹהֵיכֶם אֱמֶת

---

they should be enraptured by this love at all times. (Maimonides, Laws of Repentance 10:3)

If love in the Western world has a founding text, that text is Hebrew. (Simon May, *Love: A History*)

וְיַצִּיב And firm, established and enduring,
right, faithful,
beloved, cherished, delightful, pleasant,
awesome, mighty, perfect, accepted,
good and beautiful
is this faith for us for ever.

True is the eternal God, our King,
Rock of Jacob,
Shield of our salvation.
He exists and His name exists through all generations.
His throne is established,
His kingship and faithfulness endure for ever.

At °, kiss the tzitziot and release them.

His words live and persist, faithful and desirable
°for ever and all time.
▸ So they were for our ancestors, so they are for us,
and so they will be for our children
and all our generations and for all future generations
of the seed of Israel, Your servants. ◂
For the early and the later generations
this faith has proved good and enduring for ever –
True and faithful, an irrevocable law.

---

in the future. Just as God was true to His word then, so we pray He will be now. The sixfold repetition of *emet* acts as a reminder of the six steps we have taken – the three blessings surrounding the Shema and the three paragraphs of the Shema itself – toward the ultimate destination of prayer, the act of standing directly before God in the Amida. This is the seventh step, and in Judaism seven is the sign of the Holy.

The three steps back that we take when approaching the Amida are done in order to take three steps forward at the beginning of the prayer, a physical movement to signal that we are entering the presence of the King.

וְיַצִּיב, וְנָכוֹן וְקַיָּם, וְיָשָׁר וְנֶאֱמָן
וְאָהוּב וְחָבִיב, וְנֶחְמָד וְנָעִים
וְנוֹרָא וְאַדִּיר, וּמְתֻקָּן וּמְקֻבָּל, וְטוֹב וְיָפֶה
הַדָּבָר הַזֶּה עָלֵינוּ לְעוֹלָם וָעֶד.

אֱמֶת אֱלֹהֵי עוֹלָם מַלְכֵּנוּ
צוּר יַעֲקֹב מָגֵן יִשְׁעֵנוּ
לְדוֹר וָדוֹר הוּא קַיָּם וּשְׁמוֹ קַיָּם
וְכִסְאוֹ נָכוֹן
וּמַלְכוּתוֹ וֶאֱמוּנָתוֹ לָעַד קַיֶּמֶת.

At °, kiss the ציציות *and release them.*

וּדְבָרָיו חָיִים וְקַיָּמִים
נֶאֱמָנִים וְנֶחֱמָדִים
°לָעַד וּלְעוֹלְמֵי עוֹלָמִים
◂ עַל אֲבוֹתֵינוּ וְעָלֵינוּ, עַל בָּנֵינוּ וְעַל דּוֹרוֹתֵינוּ
וְעַל כָּל דּוֹרוֹת זֶרַע יִשְׂרָאֵל עֲבָדֶיךָ. ◂
עַל הָרִאשׁוֹנִים וְעַל הָאַחֲרוֹנִים
דָּבָר טוֹב וְקַיָּם לְעוֹלָם וָעֶד
אֱמֶת וֶאֱמוּנָה, חֹק וְלֹא יַעֲבֹר.

sense of something that corresponds to reality. In Hebrew it means honoring your promises, being true to your word, doing what you said you would do. According to Rashi (to Exodus 6:3), the holiest name of God means "the One who is true to His word." This concept of truth serves as the bridge between the end of the Shema, with its reference to the exodus from Egypt, and the quintessential prayer, the Amida, that we are now approaching. The fact that God redeemed His people in the past is the basis of our prayer for redemption

True You are the LORD:
our God and God of our ancestors,
▸ our King and King of our ancestors,
our Redeemer and Redeemer of our ancestors,
our Maker, Rock of our salvation.
Our Deliverer and Rescuer:
this has ever been Your name.
There is no God but You.

עֶזְרַת You have always been the help of our ancestors,
Shield and Savior of their children
after them in every generation.
Your dwelling is in the heights of the universe,
and Your judgments and righteousness
reach to the ends of the earth.
Happy is the one
who obeys Your commandments
and takes to heart Your teaching
and Your word.
True You are the Master of Your people
and a mighty King who pleads their cause.
True You are the first and You are the last.
Besides You, we have no king, redeemer or savior.
From Egypt You redeemed us, LORD our God,
and from the slave-house
You delivered us.
All their firstborn You killed,
but Your firstborn You redeemed.
You split the Sea of Reeds
and drowned the arrogant.
You brought Your beloved ones across.
The water covered their foes; *Ps. 106*
not one of them was left.

אֱמֶת שָׁאַתָּה הוּא יהוה אֱלֹהֵינוּ וֵאלֹהֵי אֲבוֹתֵינוּ
‹ מַלְכֵּנוּ מֶלֶךְ אֲבוֹתֵינוּ
גּוֹאֲלֵנוּ גּוֹאֵל אֲבוֹתֵינוּ
יוֹצְרֵנוּ צוּר יְשׁוּעָתֵנוּ
פּוֹדֵנוּ וּמַצִּילֵנוּ מֵעוֹלָם שְׁמֶךָ
אֵין אֱלֹהִים זוּלָתֶךָ.

עֶזְרַת אֲבוֹתֵינוּ אַתָּה הוּא מֵעוֹלָם
מָגֵן וּמוֹשִׁיעַ לִבְנֵיהֶם אַחֲרֵיהֶם בְּכָל דּוֹר וָדוֹר.
בְּרוּם עוֹלָם מוֹשָׁבֶךָ
וּמִשְׁפָּטֶיךָ וְצִדְקָתְךָ עַד אַפְסֵי אָרֶץ.
אַשְׁרֵי אִישׁ שֶׁיִּשְׁמַע לְמִצְוֹתֶיךָ
וְתוֹרָתְךָ וּדְבָרְךָ יָשִׂים עַל לִבּוֹ.
אֱמֶת אַתָּה הוּא אָדוֹן לְעַמֶּךָ
וּמֶלֶךְ גִּבּוֹר לָרִיב רִיבָם.
אֱמֶת אַתָּה הוּא רִאשׁוֹן וְאַתָּה הוּא אַחֲרוֹן
וּמִבַּלְעָדֶיךָ אֵין לָנוּ מֶלֶךְ גּוֹאֵל וּמוֹשִׁיעַ.
מִמִּצְרַיִם גְּאַלְתָּנוּ, יהוה אֱלֹהֵינוּ
וּמִבֵּית עֲבָדִים פְּדִיתָנוּ
כָּל בְּכוֹרֵיהֶם הָרַגְתָּ, וּבְכוֹרְךָ גָּאָלְתָּ
וְיַם סוּף בָּקַעְתָּ
וְזֵדִים טִבַּעְתָּ
וִידִידִים הֶעֱבַרְתָּ
וַיְכַסּוּ־מַיִם צָרֵיהֶם, אֶחָד מֵהֶם לֹא נוֹתָר: תהלים קו

For this, the beloved ones praised and exalted God,
the cherished ones sang psalms, songs and praises,
blessings and thanksgivings to the King,
the living and enduring God.
High and exalted, great and awesome,
He humbles the haughty and raises the lowly,
freeing captives and redeeming those in need,
helping the poor
and answering His people
when they cry out to Him.

Stand in preparation for the Amida. Take three steps back before beginning the Amida.

▸ Praises to God Most High,
the Blessed One who is blessed.
Moses and the children of Israel
recited to You a song with great joy,
and they all exclaimed:
"Who is like You, LORD, among the mighty? *Ex. 15*
Who is like You, majestic in holiness,
awesome in praises, doing wonders?"

▸ With a new song, the redeemed people praised
Your name at the seashore.
Together they all gave thanks,
proclaimed Your kingship,
and declared:
"The LORD shall reign for ever and ever." *Ibid.*

Congregants should end the following blessing together with the Leader so as to be able to move directly from the words "redeemed Israel" to the Amida, without the interruption of saying Amen.

▸ צוּר יִשְׂרָאֵל Rock of Israel!
Arise to the help of Israel.
Deliver, as You promised, Judah and Israel.
Our Redeemer, the LORD of hosts is His name, *Is. 47*
the Holy One of Israel.
Blessed are You, LORD, who redeemed Israel.

עַל זֹאת שִׁבְּחוּ אֲהוּבִים, וְרוֹמְמוּ אֵל
וְנָתְנוּ יְדִידִים זְמִירוֹת, שִׁירוֹת וְתִשְׁבָּחוֹת
בְּרָכוֹת וְהוֹדָאוֹת לְמֶלֶךְ אֵל חַי וְקַיָּם
רָם וְנִשָּׂא, גָּדוֹל וְנוֹרָא
מַשְׁפִּיל גֵּאִים וּמַגְבִּיהַּ שְׁפָלִים
מוֹצִיא אֲסִירִים, וּפוֹדֶה עֲנָוִים וְעוֹזֵר דַּלִּים
וְעוֹנֶה לְעַמּוֹ בְּעֵת שַׁוְּעָם אֵלָיו.

Stand in preparation for the עמידה*. Take three steps back before beginning the* עמידה*.*

◂ תְּהִלּוֹת לְאֵל עֶלְיוֹן, בָּרוּךְ הוּא וּמְבֹרָךְ
מֹשֶׁה וּבְנֵי יִשְׂרָאֵל
לְךָ עָנוּ שִׁירָה בְּשִׂמְחָה רַבָּה
וְאָמְרוּ כֻלָּם

מִי־כָמֹכָה בָּאֵלִם, יהוה — שמות טו
מִי כָּמֹכָה נֶאְדָּר בַּקֹּדֶשׁ
נוֹרָא תְהִלֹּת, עֹשֵׂה פֶלֶא:

◂ שִׁירָה חֲדָשָׁה שִׁבְּחוּ גְאוּלִים
לְשִׁמְךָ עַל שְׂפַת הַיָּם
יַחַד כֻּלָּם הוֹדוּ וְהִמְלִיכוּ, וְאָמְרוּ

יהוה יִמְלֹךְ לְעֹלָם וָעֶד: — שם

The קהל *should end the following blessing together with the* שליח ציבור *so as to be able to move directly from the words* גָּאַל יִשְׂרָאֵל *to the* עמידה*, without the interruption of saying* אמן*.*

◂ צוּר יִשְׂרָאֵל, קוּמָה בְּעֶזְרַת יִשְׂרָאֵל
וּפְדֵה כִנְאֻמֶךָ יְהוּדָה וְיִשְׂרָאֵל.

גֹּאֲלֵנוּ יהוה צְבָאוֹת שְׁמוֹ, קְדוֹשׁ יִשְׂרָאֵל: — ישעיה מז

בָּרוּךְ אַתָּה יהוה, גָּאַל יִשְׂרָאֵל.

THE AMIDA

The following prayer, until "in former years" on page 610, is said is said standing with feet together in imitation of the angels in Ezekiel's vision (Ezek. 1:7). The Amida is said silently, following the precedent of Hannah when she prayed for a child (1 Sam. 1:13). If there is a minyan, it is repeated aloud by the Leader. Take three steps forward, as if formally entering the place of the Divine Presence. At the points indicated by ▾, bend the knees at the first word, bow at the second, and stand straight before saying God's name.

O Lord, open my lips, so that my mouth may declare Your praise. *Ps. 51*

PATRIARCHS

▾בָּרוּךְ Blessed are You, Lord our God and God of our fathers,
God of Abraham, God of Isaac and God of Jacob;
the great, mighty and awesome God, God Most High,
who bestows acts of loving-kindness and creates all,
who remembers the loving-kindness of the fathers
and will bring a Redeemer to their children's children
for the sake of His name, in love.

זָכְרֵנוּ לְחַיִּים Remember us for life, O King who desires life,
and write us in the book of life – for Your sake, O God of life.
King, Helper, Savior, Shield:
▾Blessed are You, Lord, Shield of Abraham.

DIVINE MIGHT

אַתָּה גִּבּוֹר You are eternally mighty, Lord.
You give life to the dead
and have great power to save.
In Israel: He causes the dew to fall.
He sustains the living with loving-kindness,
and with great compassion revives the dead.
He supports the fallen,
heals the sick, sets captives free,
and keeps His faith with those who sleep in the dust.
Who is like You, Master of might,
and to whom can You be compared,
O King who brings death and gives life,
and makes salvation grow?

עמידה

The following prayer, until קַדְמֹנִיּוֹת *on page 611, is said is said standing with feet together in imitation of the angels in Ezekiel's vision* (יחזקאל א, ז). *The* עמידה *is said silently, following the precedent of Hannah when she prayed for a child* (שמואל א׳ א, יג). *If there is a* מנין, *it is repeated aloud by the* שליח ציבור. *Take three steps forward, as if formally entering the place of the Divine Presence. At the points indicated by* ˅, *bend the knees at the first word, bow at the second, and stand straight before saying God's name.*

אֲדֹנָי, שְׂפָתַי תִּפְתָּח, וּפִי יַגִּיד תְּהִלָּתֶךָ: תהלים נא

אבות

˅בָּרוּךְ אַתָּה יהוה, אֱלֹהֵינוּ וֵאלֹהֵי אֲבוֹתֵינוּ
אֱלֹהֵי אַבְרָהָם, אֱלֹהֵי יִצְחָק, וֵאלֹהֵי יַעֲקֹב
הָאֵל הַגָּדוֹל הַגִּבּוֹר וְהַנּוֹרָא, אֵל עֶלְיוֹן
גּוֹמֵל חֲסָדִים טוֹבִים, וְקֹנֵה הַכֹּל
וְזוֹכֵר חַסְדֵי אָבוֹת
וּמֵבִיא גוֹאֵל לִבְנֵי בְנֵיהֶם לְמַעַן שְׁמוֹ בְּאַהֲבָה.

זָכְרֵנוּ לְחַיִּים, מֶלֶךְ חָפֵץ בַּחַיִּים
וְכָתְבֵנוּ בְּסֵפֶר הַחַיִּים, לְמַעַנְךָ אֱלֹהִים חַיִּים.
מֶלֶךְ עוֹזֵר וּמוֹשִׁיעַ וּמָגֵן.
˅בָּרוּךְ אַתָּה יהוה, מָגֵן אַבְרָהָם.

גבורות

אַתָּה גִּבּוֹר לְעוֹלָם, אֲדֹנָי
מְחַיֵּה מֵתִים אַתָּה, רַב לְהוֹשִׁיעַ
בארץ ישראל: מוֹרִיד הַטָּל
מְכַלְכֵּל חַיִּים בְּחֶסֶד, מְחַיֵּה מֵתִים בְּרַחֲמִים רַבִּים
סוֹמֵךְ נוֹפְלִים, וְרוֹפֵא חוֹלִים, וּמַתִּיר אֲסוּרִים
וּמְקַיֵּם אֱמוּנָתוֹ לִישֵׁנֵי עָפָר.
מִי כָמוֹךָ, בַּעַל גְּבוּרוֹת, וּמִי דּוֹמֶה לָּךְ
מֶלֶךְ, מֵמִית וּמְחַיֶּה וּמַצְמִיחַ יְשׁוּעָה.

מִי כָמְוֹךָ Who is like You, compassionate Father,
who remembers His creatures in compassion, for life?
Faithful are You to revive the dead.
Blessed are You, Lord,
who revives the dead.

HOLINESS

אַתָּה קָדוֹשׁ You are holy and Your name is holy,
and holy ones praise You daily, Selah!

וּבְכֵן תֵּן פַּחְדְּךָ And so place the fear of You, Lord our God,
over all that You have made,
and the terror of You over all You have created,
and all who were made will stand in awe of You,
and all of creation will worship You
and they will be bound all together as one
to carry out Your will with an undivided heart;
for we know, Lord our God,
that all dominion is laid out before You,
strength is in Your palm,
and might in Your right hand,
Your name spreading awe
over all You have created.

וּבְכֵן תֵּן כָּבוֹד And so place honor,
Lord, upon Your people,
praise on those who fear You
and hope into those who seek You,
the confidence to speak
into all who long for You,
gladness to Your land and joy to Your city,
the flourishing of pride to David Your servant,
and a lamp laid out for his descendant, Your anointed,
soon, in our days.

מִי כָמוֹךָ אַב הָרַחֲמִים
זוֹכֵר יְצוּרָיו לְחַיִּים בְּרַחֲמִים.
וְנֶאֱמָן אַתָּה לְהַחֲיוֹת מֵתִים.
בָּרוּךְ אַתָּה יהוה, מְחַיֵּה הַמֵּתִים.

קדושת השם

אַתָּה קָדוֹשׁ וְשִׁמְךָ קָדוֹשׁ
וּקְדוֹשִׁים בְּכָל יוֹם יְהַלְלוּךָ סֶּלָה.

וּבְכֵן תֵּן פַּחְדְּךָ יהוה אֱלֹהֵינוּ עַל כָּל מַעֲשֶׂיךָ
וְאֵימָתְךָ עַל כָּל מַה שֶּׁבָּרָאתָ
וְיִירָאוּךָ כָּל הַמַּעֲשִׂים
וְיִשְׁתַּחֲווּ לְפָנֶיךָ כָּל הַבְּרוּאִים
וְיֵעָשׂוּ כֻלָּם אֲגֻדָּה אֶחָת לַעֲשׂוֹת רְצוֹנְךָ בְּלֵבָב שָׁלֵם
כְּמוֹ שֶׁיָּדַעְנוּ יהוה אֱלֹהֵינוּ שֶׁהַשָּׁלְטָן לְפָנֶיךָ
עֹז בְּיָדְךָ וּגְבוּרָה בִּימִינֶךָ
וְשִׁמְךָ נוֹרָא עַל כָּל מַה שֶּׁבָּרָאתָ.

וּבְכֵן תֵּן כָּבוֹד יהוה לְעַמֶּךָ
תְּהִלָּה לִירֵאֶיךָ
וְתִקְוָה טוֹבָה לְדוֹרְשֶׁיךָ
וּפִתְחוֹן פֶּה לַמְיַחֲלִים לָךְ
שִׂמְחָה לְאַרְצֶךָ, וְשָׂשׂוֹן לְעִירֶךָ
וּצְמִיחַת קֶרֶן לְדָוִד עַבְדֶּךָ
וַעֲרִיכַת נֵר לְבֶן יִשַׁי מְשִׁיחֶךָ
בִּמְהֵרָה בְיָמֵינוּ.

וּבְכֵן צַדִּיקִים And then righteous people will see and rejoice,
and the upright will exult,and the pious revel in joy,
and injustice will have nothing more to say,
and all wickedness will fade away like smoke
as You sweep the rule of arrogance from the earth.

וְתִמְלֹךְ אַתָּה And You, Lord,
will rule alone over those You have made,
in Mount Zion, the dwelling of Your glory,
and in Jerusalem, Your holy city,
as it is written in Your holy Writings:
"The Lord shall reign for ever. *Ps. 146*
He is your God, Zion, from generation to generation, Halleluya!"

קָדוֹשׁ אַתָּה You are holy, Your name is awesome,
and there is no god but You,
as it is written:
"The Lord of hosts shall be raised up through His judgment, *Is. 5*
the holy God, made holy in righteousness."
Blessed are You, Lord, the holy King.

HOLINESS OF THE DAY

אַתָּה בְחַרְתָּנוּ You have chosen us from among all peoples.
You have loved and favored us.
You have raised us above all tongues.
You have made us holy through Your commandments.
You have brought us near, our King, to Your service,
and have called us by Your great and holy name.

On Shabbat, add the words in parentheses:

וַתִּתֶּן לָנוּ And You, Lord our God, have given us in love
(this Sabbath day for holiness and rest, and)
this Day of Atonement
for pardon and forgiveness and atonement,
to pardon all our iniquities,
(with love,) a holy assembly
in memory of the exodus from Egypt.

וּבְכֵן צַדִּיקִים יִרְאוּ וְיִשְׂמָחוּ, וִישָׁרִים יַעֲלֹזוּ
וַחֲסִידִים בְּרִנָּה יָגִילוּ, וְעוֹלָתָה תִּקְפָּץ פִּיהָ
וְכָל הָרִשְׁעָה כֻּלָּהּ כְּעָשָׁן תִּכְלֶה
כִּי תַעֲבִיר מֶמְשֶׁלֶת זָדוֹן מִן הָאָרֶץ.

וְתִמְלֹךְ אַתָּה יהוה לְבַדֶּךָ עַל כָּל מַעֲשֶׂיךָ
בְּהַר צִיּוֹן מִשְׁכַּן כְּבוֹדֶךָ, וּבִירוּשָׁלַיִם עִיר קָדְשֶׁךָ
כַּכָּתוּב בְּדִבְרֵי קָדְשֶׁךָ
יִמְלֹךְ יהוה לְעוֹלָם, אֱלֹהַיִךְ צִיּוֹן לְדֹר וָדֹר, הַלְלוּיָהּ: תהלים קמו

קָדוֹשׁ אַתָּה וְנוֹרָא שְׁמֶךָ, וְאֵין אֱלוֹהַּ מִבַּלְעָדֶיךָ
כַּכָּתוּב, וַיִּגְבַּהּ יהוה צְבָאוֹת בַּמִּשְׁפָּט ישעיה ה
וְהָאֵל הַקָּדוֹשׁ נִקְדַּשׁ בִּצְדָקָה:
בָּרוּךְ אַתָּה יהוה, הַמֶּלֶךְ הַקָּדוֹשׁ.

קדושת היום
אַתָּה בְחַרְתָּנוּ מִכָּל הָעַמִּים
אָהַבְתָּ אוֹתָנוּ וְרָצִיתָ בָּנוּ וְרוֹמַמְתָּנוּ מִכָּל הַלְּשׁוֹנוֹת
וְקִדַּשְׁתָּנוּ בְּמִצְוֹתֶיךָ
וְקֵרַבְתָּנוּ מַלְכֵּנוּ לַעֲבוֹדָתֶךָ
וְשִׁמְךָ הַגָּדוֹל וְהַקָּדוֹשׁ עָלֵינוּ קָרָאתָ.

On שבת, add the words in parentheses:
וַתִּתֶּן לָנוּ יהוה אֱלֹהֵינוּ בְּאַהֲבָה אֶת
(יוֹם הַשַּׁבָּת הַזֶּה לִקְדֻשָּׁה וְלִמְנוּחָה, וְאֶת)
יוֹם הַכִּפּוּרִים הַזֶּה, לִמְחִילָה וְלִסְלִיחָה וּלְכַפָּרָה
וְלִמְחָל בּוֹ אֶת כָּל עֲוֹנוֹתֵינוּ
(בְּאַהֲבָה) מִקְרָא קֹדֶשׁ, זֵכֶר לִיצִיאַת מִצְרָיִם.

אֱלֹהֵינוּ Our God and God of our ancestors,
may there rise, come, reach, appear, be favored, heard,
regarded and remembered before You,
our recollection and remembrance,
as well as the remembrance of our ancestors,
and of the Messiah, son of David Your servant,
and of Jerusalem Your holy city,
and of all Your people the house of Israel –
for deliverance and well-being,
grace, loving-kindness and compassion,
life and peace, on this Day of Atonement.
On it remember us, LORD our God, for good;
recollect us for blessing, and deliver us for life.
In accord with Your promise
of salvation and compassion,
spare us and be gracious to us;
have compassion on us and deliver us,
for our eyes are turned to You
because You, God, are a gracious and compassionate King.

On Shabbat, add the words in parentheses:

אֱלֹהֵינוּ Our God and God of our ancestors,
pardon our iniquities
on (this Sabbath day, and on) this Day of Atonement;
wipe away and remove all our transgressions and sins
from before Your eyes,
as it is said:

"I, I am the One who shall wipe out your transgressions *Is. 43*
for My sake, and I shall not recall your sins."

And it is said:

"I have wiped out your transgressions like a cloud, *Is. 44*
and as a haze your sins;
come back to Me for I have redeemed you."

אֱלֹהֵינוּ וֵאלֹהֵי אֲבוֹתֵינוּ
יַעֲלֶה וְיָבוֹא וְיַגִּיעַ, וְיֵרָאֶה וְיֵרָצֶה וְיִשָּׁמַע
וְיִפָּקֵד וְיִזָּכֵר זִכְרוֹנֵנוּ וּפִקְדּוֹנֵנוּ וְזִכְרוֹן אֲבוֹתֵינוּ
וְזִכְרוֹן מָשִׁיחַ בֶּן דָּוִד עַבְדֶּךָ
וְזִכְרוֹן יְרוּשָׁלַיִם עִיר קָדְשֶׁךָ
וְזִכְרוֹן כָּל עַמְּךָ בֵּית יִשְׂרָאֵל, לְפָנֶיךָ
לִפְלֵיטָה לְטוֹבָה, לְחֵן וּלְחֶסֶד וּלְרַחֲמִים, לְחַיִּים וּלְשָׁלוֹם
בְּיוֹם הַכִּפּוּרִים הַזֶּה
זָכְרֵנוּ יהוה אֱלֹהֵינוּ בּוֹ לְטוֹבָה
וּפָקְדֵנוּ בוֹ לִבְרָכָה
וְהוֹשִׁיעֵנוּ בוֹ לְחַיִּים.
וּבִדְבַר יְשׁוּעָה וְרַחֲמִים חוּס וְחָנֵּנוּ
וְרַחֵם עָלֵינוּ וְהוֹשִׁיעֵנוּ
כִּי אֵלֶיךָ עֵינֵינוּ, כִּי אֵל מֶלֶךְ חַנּוּן וְרַחוּם אָתָּה.

On שבת, add the words in parentheses:

אֱלֹהֵינוּ וֵאלֹהֵי אֲבוֹתֵינוּ
מְחַל לַעֲוֹנוֹתֵינוּ בְּיוֹם (הַשַּׁבָּת הַזֶּה וּבְיוֹם) הַכִּפּוּרִים הַזֶּה
מְחֵה וְהַעֲבֵר פְּשָׁעֵינוּ וְחַטֹּאתֵינוּ מִנֶּגֶד עֵינֶיךָ
כָּאָמוּר
אָנֹכִי אָנֹכִי הוּא מֹחֶה פְשָׁעֶיךָ לְמַעֲנִי ישעיה מג
וְחַטֹּאתֶיךָ לֹא אֶזְכֹּר:
וְנֶאֱמַר
מָחִיתִי כָעָב פְּשָׁעֶיךָ וְכֶעָנָן חַטֹּאותֶיךָ ישעיה מד
שׁוּבָה אֵלַי כִּי גְאַלְתִּיךָ:

And it is said:

For on this day you will be atoned and made pure; *Lev. 16*
of all your sins before the LORD you shall be purified.

(Our God and God of our ancestors, find favor in our rest.)
Make us holy through Your commandments
and grant us our share in Your Torah.
Satisfy us with Your goodness,
grant us joy in Your salvation
(in love and favor, O LORD our God,
grant us as our heritage Your holy Sabbath,
so that Israel, who sanctify Your name,
may find rest on it),
and purify our hearts to serve You in truth.
For You are the Forgiver of Israel
and the Pardoner of the tribes of Yeshurun in every generation,
and without You we have no king who pardons and forgives,
none but You.
Blessed are You, LORD,
King who pardons and forgives our iniquities
and those of all His people the house of Israel,
and makes our guilt pass away, every single year,
King of all the earth, who sanctifies (the Sabbath,)
Israel and the Day of Atonement.

TEMPLE SERVICE

רְצֵה Find favor, LORD our God,
in Your people Israel and their prayer.
Restore the service to Your most holy House,
and accept in love and favor
the fire-offerings of Israel and their prayer.
May the service of Your people Israel always find favor with You.
And may our eyes witness Your return to Zion in compassion.
Blessed are You, LORD,
who restores His Presence to Zion.

וְנֶאֱמַר

כִּי־בַיּוֹם הַזֶּה יְכַפֵּר עֲלֵיכֶם לְטַהֵר אֶתְכֶם ויקרא טז

מִכֹּל חַטֹּאתֵיכֶם, לִפְנֵי יהוה תִּטְהָרוּ:

(אֱלֹהֵינוּ וֵאלֹהֵי אֲבוֹתֵינוּ, רְצֵה בִמְנוּחָתֵנוּ)

קַדְּשֵׁנוּ בְּמִצְוֹתֶיךָ וְתֵן חֶלְקֵנוּ בְּתוֹרָתֶךָ

שַׂבְּעֵנוּ מִטּוּבֶךָ וְשַׂמְּחֵנוּ בִּישׁוּעָתֶךָ

(וְהַנְחִילֵנוּ יהוה אֱלֹהֵינוּ בְּאַהֲבָה וּבְרָצוֹן שַׁבַּת קָדְשֶׁךָ

וְיָנוּחוּ בוֹ יִשְׂרָאֵל מְקַדְּשֵׁי שְׁמֶךָ)

וְטַהֵר לִבֵּנוּ לְעָבְדְּךָ בֶּאֱמֶת

כִּי אַתָּה סָלְחָן לְיִשְׂרָאֵל

וּמָחֳלָן לְשִׁבְטֵי יְשֻׁרוּן בְּכָל דּוֹר וָדוֹר

וּמִבַּלְעָדֶיךָ אֵין לָנוּ מֶלֶךְ מוֹחֵל וְסוֹלֵחַ אֶלָּא אָתָּה.

בָּרוּךְ אַתָּה יהוה

מֶלֶךְ מוֹחֵל וְסוֹלֵחַ לַעֲוֹנוֹתֵינוּ

וְלַעֲוֹנוֹת עַמּוֹ בֵּית יִשְׂרָאֵל

וּמַעֲבִיר אַשְׁמוֹתֵינוּ בְּכָל שָׁנָה וְשָׁנָה

מֶלֶךְ עַל כָּל הָאָרֶץ, מְקַדֵּשׁ (הַשַּׁבָּת וְ) יִשְׂרָאֵל וְיוֹם הַכִּפּוּרִים.

עבודה

רְצֵה יהוה אֱלֹהֵינוּ בְּעַמְּךָ יִשְׂרָאֵל, וּבִתְפִלָּתָם

וְהָשֵׁב אֶת הָעֲבוֹדָה לִדְבִיר בֵּיתֶךָ

וְאִשֵּׁי יִשְׂרָאֵל וּתְפִלָּתָם בְּאַהֲבָה תְקַבֵּל בְּרָצוֹן

וּתְהִי לְרָצוֹן תָּמִיד עֲבוֹדַת יִשְׂרָאֵל עַמֶּךָ.

וְתֶחֱזֶינָה עֵינֵינוּ בְּשׁוּבְךָ לְצִיּוֹן בְּרַחֲמִים.

בָּרוּךְ אַתָּה יהוה, הַמַּחֲזִיר שְׁכִינָתוֹ לְצִיּוֹן.

THANKSGIVING

Bow at the first nine words.

▾מוֹדִים We give thanks to You,
for You are the LORD our God and God of our ancestors
for ever and all time.
You are the Rock of our lives,
Shield of our salvation from generation to generation.
We will thank You and declare Your praise for our lives,
which are entrusted into Your hand;
for our souls, which are placed in Your charge;
for Your miracles which are with us every day;
and for Your wonders and favors
at all times, evening, morning and midday.
You are good – for Your compassion never fails.
You are compassionate – for Your loving-kindnesses never cease.
We have always placed our hope in You.
For all these things may Your name be blessed and exalted,
our King, continually, for ever and all time.

וּכְתֹב And write for a good life, all the children of Your covenant.

Let all that lives thank You, Selah!
and praise Your name in truth,
God, our Savior and Help, Selah!
▾Blessed are You, LORD, whose name is "the Good"
and to whom thanks are due.

PEACE

שִׂים שָׁלוֹם Grant peace, goodness and blessing,
grace, loving-kindness and compassion to us
and all Israel Your people.
Bless us, our Father, all as one, with the light of Your face,
for by the light of Your face You have given us, LORD our God,
the Torah of life and love of kindness,
righteousness, blessing, compassion, life and peace.
May it be good in Your eyes to bless Your people Israel
at every time, in every hour, with Your peace.

הודאה

Bow at the first five words.

מוֹדִים אֲנַחְנוּ לָךְ

שָׁאַתָּה הוּא יהוה אֱלֹהֵינוּ וֵאלֹהֵי אֲבוֹתֵינוּ לְעוֹלָם וָעֶד.

צוּר חַיֵּינוּ, מָגֵן יִשְׁעֵנוּ, אַתָּה הוּא לְדוֹר וָדוֹר.

נוֹדֶה לְּךָ וּנְסַפֵּר תְּהִלָּתֶךָ, עַל חַיֵּינוּ הַמְּסוּרִים בְּיָדֶךָ

וְעַל נִשְׁמוֹתֵינוּ הַפְּקוּדוֹת לָךְ, וְעַל נִסֶּיךָ שֶׁבְּכָל יוֹם עִמָּנוּ

וְעַל נִפְלְאוֹתֶיךָ וְטוֹבוֹתֶיךָ שֶׁבְּכָל עֵת, עֶרֶב וָבֹקֶר וְצָהֳרָיִם.

הַטּוֹב, כִּי לֹא כָלוּ רַחֲמֶיךָ

וְהַמְרַחֵם, כִּי לֹא תַמּוּ חֲסָדֶיךָ

מֵעוֹלָם קִוִּינוּ לָךְ.

וְעַל כֻּלָּם יִתְבָּרַךְ וְיִתְרוֹמַם שִׁמְךָ מַלְכֵּנוּ תָּמִיד לְעוֹלָם וָעֶד.

וּכְתֹב לְחַיִּים טוֹבִים כָּל בְּנֵי בְרִיתֶךָ.

וְכֹל הַחַיִּים יוֹדוּךָ סֶּלָה, וִיהַלְלוּ אֶת שִׁמְךָ בֶּאֱמֶת

הָאֵל יְשׁוּעָתֵנוּ וְעֶזְרָתֵנוּ סֶלָה.

בָּרוּךְ אַתָּה יהוה, הַטּוֹב שִׁמְךָ וּלְךָ נָאֶה לְהוֹדוֹת.

שלום

שִׂים שָׁלוֹם טוֹבָה וּבְרָכָה

חֵן וָחֶסֶד וְרַחֲמִים עָלֵינוּ וְעַל כָּל יִשְׂרָאֵל עַמֶּךָ.

בָּרְכֵנוּ אָבִינוּ כֻּלָּנוּ כְּאֶחָד בְּאוֹר פָּנֶיךָ

כִּי בְאוֹר פָּנֶיךָ נָתַתָּ לָּנוּ, יהוה אֱלֹהֵינוּ

תּוֹרַת חַיִּים וְאַהֲבַת חֶסֶד

וּצְדָקָה וּבְרָכָה וְרַחֲמִים וְחַיִּים וְשָׁלוֹם.

וְטוֹב בְּעֵינֶיךָ לְבָרֵךְ אֶת עַמְּךָ יִשְׂרָאֵל

בְּכָל עֵת וּבְכָל שָׁעָה בִּשְׁלוֹמֶךָ.

בְּסֵפֶר חַיִּים In the book of life, blessing,
peace and prosperity,
may we and all Your people the house of Israel
be remembered and written before You
for a good life, and for peace.*

Blessed are You, LORD, who blesses His people Israel with peace.

**Outside Israel, many end the blessing:*

Blessed are You, LORD, who makes peace.

Some say the following verse:

May the words of my mouth and the meditation of my heart Ps. 19
find favor before You, LORD, my Rock and Redeemer.

VIDUY

For linear translation and commentary, see page 1353.

אֱלֹהֵינוּ Our God and God of our fathers,
let our prayer come before You, and do not hide Yourself from our plea,
for we are not so arrogant or obstinate as to say before You,
LORD, our God and God of our fathers,
we are righteous and have not sinned,
for in truth, we and our fathers have sinned.

Strike the left side of the chest with the right fist while saying each of the sins.

אָשַׁמְנוּ We have sinned, we have acted treacherously,
we have robbed, we have spoken slander.
We have acted perversely, we have acted wickedly,
we have acted presumptuously, we have been violent,
we have framed lies.
We have given bad advice, we have deceived, we have scorned,
we have rebelled, we have provoked, we have turned away,
we have committed iniquity, we have transgressed,
we have persecuted, we have been obstinate.
We have acted wickedly, we have corrupted,
we have acted abominably, we have strayed, we have led others astray.

סַרְנוּ We have turned away from Your commandments and good laws,
to no avail, for You are just in all that has befallen us, Neh. 9
for You have acted faithfully while we have done wickedly.

בְּסֵפֶר חַיִּים, בְּרָכָה וְשָׁלוֹם, וּפַרְנָסָה טוֹבָה
נִזָּכֵר וְנִכָּתֵב לְפָנֶיךָ, אֲנַחְנוּ וְכָל עַמְּךָ בֵּית יִשְׂרָאֵל
לְחַיִּים טוֹבִים וּלְשָׁלוֹם.*

בָּרוּךְ אַתָּה יהוה, הַמְבָרֵךְ אֶת עַמּוֹ יִשְׂרָאֵל בַּשָּׁלוֹם.

In חוץ לארץ, many end the blessing:

בָּרוּךְ אַתָּה יהוה, עוֹשֶׂה הַשָּׁלוֹם.

Some say the following verse:

יִהְיוּ לְרָצוֹן אִמְרֵי־פִי וְהֶגְיוֹן לִבִּי לְפָנֶיךָ, יהוה צוּרִי וְגֹאֲלִי: תהלים יט

וידוי

For linear translation and commentary, see page 1353.

אֱלֹהֵינוּ וֵאלֹהֵי אֲבוֹתֵינוּ
תָּבוֹא לְפָנֶיךָ תְּפִלָּתֵנוּ, וְאַל תִּתְעַלַּם מִתְּחִנָּתֵנוּ.
שֶׁאֵין אֲנַחְנוּ עַזֵּי פָנִים וּקְשֵׁי עֹרֶף לוֹמַר לְפָנֶיךָ
יהוה אֱלֹהֵינוּ וֵאלֹהֵי אֲבוֹתֵינוּ
צַדִּיקִים אֲנַחְנוּ וְלֹא חָטָאנוּ.
אֲבָל אֲנַחְנוּ וַאֲבוֹתֵינוּ חָטָאנוּ.

Strike the left side of the chest with the right fist while saying each of the sins.

אָשַׁמְנוּ, בָּגַדְנוּ, גָּזַלְנוּ, דִּבַּרְנוּ דֹפִי
הֶעֱוִינוּ, וְהִרְשַׁעְנוּ, זַדְנוּ, חָמַסְנוּ, טָפַלְנוּ שֶׁקֶר
יָעַצְנוּ רָע, כִּזַּבְנוּ, לַצְנוּ, מָרַדְנוּ, נִאַצְנוּ, סָרַרְנוּ
עָוִינוּ, פָּשַׁעְנוּ, צָרַרְנוּ, קִשִּׁינוּ עֹרֶף
רָשַׁעְנוּ, שִׁחַתְנוּ, תִּעַבְנוּ, תָּעִינוּ, תִּעְתָּעְנוּ.

סַרְנוּ מִמִּצְוֹתֶיךָ וּמִמִּשְׁפָּטֶיךָ הַטּוֹבִים, וְלֹא שָׁוָה לָנוּ.
וְאַתָּה צַדִּיק עַל כָּל־הַבָּא עָלֵינוּ נחמיה ט
כִּי־אֱמֶת עָשִׂיתָ, וַאֲנַחְנוּ הִרְשָׁעְנוּ:

מַה נֹּאמַר What can we say before You, You who dwell on high?
What can we declare before You, You who abide in heaven?
Do You not know all, the hidden and revealed alike?

אַתָּה יוֹדֵעַ You know every secret since the world began,
and what is hidden deep inside every living thing.
You search each person's inner chambers,
examining conscience and mind.
Nothing is shrouded from You,
and nothing is hidden before Your eyes.
And so, may it be Your will,
Lord our God and God of our ancestors,
that You forgive us all our sins, pardon all our iniquities,
and grant us atonement for all of our transgressions.

Strike the left side of the chest with the right fist while saying each of the sins.

עַל חֵטְא For the sin we have sinned before You under duress or freewill,
and for the sin we have sinned before You in hardness of heart.

For the sin we have sinned before You unwittingly,
and for the sin we have sinned before You by an utterance of our lips.

For the sin we have sinned before You by unchastity,
and for the sin we have sinned before You openly or secretly.

For the sin we have sinned before You knowingly and deceitfully,
and for the sin we have sinned before You in speech.

For the sin we have sinned before You by wronging a neighbor,
and for the sin we have sinned before You by thoughts of the heart.

For the sin we have sinned before You in a gathering for immorality,
and for the sin we have sinned before You by insincere confession.

For the sin we have sinned before You by contempt for parents and teachers,
and for the sin we have sinned before You willfully or in error.

מַה נֹּאמַר לְפָנֶיךָ יוֹשֵׁב מָרוֹם, וּמַה נְּסַפֵּר לְפָנֶיךָ שׁוֹכֵן שְׁחָקִים
הֲלֹא כָּל הַנִּסְתָּרוֹת וְהַנִּגְלוֹת אַתָּה יוֹדֵעַ.

אַתָּה יוֹדֵעַ רָזֵי עוֹלָם וְתַעֲלוּמוֹת סִתְרֵי כָּל חָי.
אַתָּה חוֹפֵשׂ כָּל חַדְרֵי בָטֶן וּבוֹחֵן כְּלָיוֹת וָלֵב.
אֵין דָּבָר נֶעְלָם מִמֶּךָּ וְאֵין נִסְתָּר מִנֶּגֶד עֵינֶיךָ.
וּבְכֵן, יְהִי רָצוֹן מִלְּפָנֶיךָ, יהוה אֱלֹהֵינוּ וֵאלֹהֵי אֲבוֹתֵינוּ
שֶׁתִּסְלַח לָנוּ עַל כָּל חַטֹּאתֵינוּ וְתִמְחַל לָנוּ עַל כָּל עֲוֹנוֹתֵינוּ
וּתְכַפֵּר לָנוּ עַל כָּל פְּשָׁעֵינוּ.

Strike the left side of the chest with the right fist while saying each of the sins.

עַל חֵטְא שֶׁחָטָאנוּ לְפָנֶיךָ בְּאֹנֶס וּבְרָצוֹן
וְעַל חֵטְא שֶׁחָטָאנוּ לְפָנֶיךָ בְּאִמּוּץ הַלֵּב

עַל חֵטְא שֶׁחָטָאנוּ לְפָנֶיךָ בִּבְלִי דָעַת
וְעַל חֵטְא שֶׁחָטָאנוּ לְפָנֶיךָ בְּבִטּוּי שְׂפָתָיִם

עַל חֵטְא שֶׁחָטָאנוּ לְפָנֶיךָ בְּגִלּוּי עֲרָיוֹת
וְעַל חֵטְא שֶׁחָטָאנוּ לְפָנֶיךָ בְּגָלוּי וּבַסָּתֶר

עַל חֵטְא שֶׁחָטָאנוּ לְפָנֶיךָ בְּדַעַת וּבְמִרְמָה
וְעַל חֵטְא שֶׁחָטָאנוּ לְפָנֶיךָ בְּדִבּוּר פֶּה

עַל חֵטְא שֶׁחָטָאנוּ לְפָנֶיךָ בְּהוֹנָאַת רֵעַ
וְעַל חֵטְא שֶׁחָטָאנוּ לְפָנֶיךָ בְּהַרְהוֹר הַלֵּב

עַל חֵטְא שֶׁחָטָאנוּ לְפָנֶיךָ בִּוְעִידַת זְנוּת
וְעַל חֵטְא שֶׁחָטָאנוּ לְפָנֶיךָ בְּוִדּוּי פֶּה

עַל חֵטְא שֶׁחָטָאנוּ לְפָנֶיךָ בְּזִלְזוּל הוֹרִים וּמוֹרִים
וְעַל חֵטְא שֶׁחָטָאנוּ לְפָנֶיךָ בְּזָדוֹן וּבִשְׁגָגָה

For the sin we have sinned before You by force,
and for the sin we have sinned before You by desecrating Your name.

For the sin we have sinned before You by impure lips,
and for the sin we have sinned before You by foolish speech.

For the sin we have sinned before You by the evil inclination,
and for the sin we have sinned before You knowingly or unwittingly.

FOR ALL THESE, GOD OF FORGIVENESS,
FORGIVE US, PARDON US, GRANT US ATONEMENT.

For the sin we have sinned before You by deceit and lies,
and for the sin we have sinned before You by bribery.

For the sin we have sinned before You by scorn,
and for the sin we have sinned before You by evil speech.

For the sin we have sinned before You in business,
and for the sin we have sinned before You with food and drink.

For the sin we have sinned before You by interest and extortion,
and for the sin we have sinned before You by being haughty.

For the sin we have sinned before You by the idle chatter of our lips,
and for the sin we have sinned before You by prying eyes.

For the sin we have sinned before You by arrogance,
and for the sin we have sinned before You by insolence.

FOR ALL THESE, GOD OF FORGIVENESS,
FORGIVE US, PARDON US, GRANT US ATONEMENT.

עַל חֵטְא שֶׁחָטָאנוּ לְפָנֶיךָ בְּחְֹזֶק יָד
וְעַל חֵטְא שֶׁחָטָאנוּ לְפָנֶיךָ בְּחִלּוּל הַשֵּׁם

עַל חֵטְא שֶׁחָטָאנוּ לְפָנֶיךָ בְּטֻמְאַת שְׂפָתָיִם
וְעַל חֵטְא שֶׁחָטָאנוּ לְפָנֶיךָ בְּטִפְּשׁוּת פֶּה

עַל חֵטְא שֶׁחָטָאנוּ לְפָנֶיךָ בְּיֵצֶר הָרָע
וְעַל חֵטְא שֶׁחָטָאנוּ לְפָנֶיךָ בְּיוֹדְעִים וּבְלֹא יוֹדְעִים

וְעַל כֻּלָּם אֱלוֹהַּ סְלִיחוֹת סְלַח לָנוּ, מְחַל לָנוּ, כַּפֶּר לָנוּ.

עַל חֵטְא שֶׁחָטָאנוּ לְפָנֶיךָ בְּכַחַשׁ וּבְכָזָב
וְעַל חֵטְא שֶׁחָטָאנוּ לְפָנֶיךָ בְּכַפַּת שֹׁחַד

עַל חֵטְא שֶׁחָטָאנוּ לְפָנֶיךָ בְּלָצוֹן
וְעַל חֵטְא שֶׁחָטָאנוּ לְפָנֶיךָ בְּלָשׁוֹן הָרָע

עַל חֵטְא שֶׁחָטָאנוּ לְפָנֶיךָ בְּמַשָּׂא וּבְמַתָּן
וְעַל חֵטְא שֶׁחָטָאנוּ לְפָנֶיךָ בְּמַאֲכָל וּבְמִשְׁתֶּה

עַל חֵטְא שֶׁחָטָאנוּ לְפָנֶיךָ בְּנֶשֶׁךְ וּבְמַרְבִּית
וְעַל חֵטְא שֶׁחָטָאנוּ לְפָנֶיךָ בִּנְטִיַּת גָּרוֹן

עַל חֵטְא שֶׁחָטָאנוּ לְפָנֶיךָ בְּשִׂיחַ שִׂפְתוֹתֵינוּ
וְעַל חֵטְא שֶׁחָטָאנוּ לְפָנֶיךָ בְּשִׂקּוּר עָיִן

עַל חֵטְא שֶׁחָטָאנוּ לְפָנֶיךָ בְּעֵינַיִם רָמוֹת
וְעַל חֵטְא שֶׁחָטָאנוּ לְפָנֶיךָ בְּעַזּוּת מֶצַח

וְעַל כֻּלָּם אֱלוֹהַּ סְלִיחוֹת סְלַח לָנוּ, מְחַל לָנוּ, כַּפֶּר לָנוּ.

For the sin we have sinned before You by casting off the yoke,
and for the sin we have sinned before You by perverting judgment.

For the sin we have sinned before You by entrapping a neighbor,
and for the sin we have sinned before You by envy.

For the sin we have sinned before You by lack of seriousness,
and for the sin we have sinned before You by obstinacy.

For the sin we have sinned before You by running to do evil,
and for the sin we have sinned before You by gossip.

For the sin we have sinned before You by vain oath,
and for the sin we have sinned before You by baseless hatred.

For the sin we have sinned before You by breach of trust,
and for the sin we have sinned before You by confusion of heart.

FOR ALL THESE, GOD OF FORGIVENESS,
FORGIVE US, PARDON US, GRANT US ATONEMENT.

וְעַל חֲטָאִים And for the sins for which we are liable to bring a burnt-offering,

and for the sins for which we are liable to bring a sin-offering,

and for the sins for which we are liable to bring an offering according to our means,

and for the sins for which we are liable to bring a guilt-offering for certain or possible sin,

and for the sins for which we are liable to lashes for rebellion,

and for the sins for which we are liable to forty lashes,

and for the sins for which we are liable to death by the hands of Heaven,

and for the sins for which we are liable to be cut off and childless,

and for the sins for which we are liable to the four death penalties
inflicted by the court: stoning, burning, beheading and strangling.

עַל חֵטְא שֶׁחָטָאנוּ לְפָנֶיךָ בִּפְרִיקַת עֹל
וְעַל חֵטְא שֶׁחָטָאנוּ לְפָנֶיךָ בִּפְלִילוּת
עַל חֵטְא שֶׁחָטָאנוּ לְפָנֶיךָ בִּצְדִיַּת רֵעַ
וְעַל חֵטְא שֶׁחָטָאנוּ לְפָנֶיךָ בְּצָרוּת עָיִן
עַל חֵטְא שֶׁחָטָאנוּ לְפָנֶיךָ בְּקַלּוּת רֹאשׁ
וְעַל חֵטְא שֶׁחָטָאנוּ לְפָנֶיךָ בְּקַשְׁיוּת עֹרֶף
עַל חֵטְא שֶׁחָטָאנוּ לְפָנֶיךָ בְּרִיצַת רַגְלַיִם לְהָרַע
וְעַל חֵטְא שֶׁחָטָאנוּ לְפָנֶיךָ בִּרְכִילוּת
עַל חֵטְא שֶׁחָטָאנוּ לְפָנֶיךָ בִּשְׁבוּעַת שָׁוְא
וְעַל חֵטְא שֶׁחָטָאנוּ לְפָנֶיךָ בְּשִׂנְאַת חִנָּם
עַל חֵטְא שֶׁחָטָאנוּ לְפָנֶיךָ בִּתְשׂוּמֶת יָד
וְעַל חֵטְא שֶׁחָטָאנוּ לְפָנֶיךָ בְּתִמְהוֹן לֵבָב

וְעַל כֻּלָּם אֱלוֹהַּ סְלִיחוֹת סְלַח לָנוּ, מְחַל לָנוּ, כַּפֶּר לָנוּ.

וְעַל חֲטָאִים שֶׁאָנוּ חַיָּבִים עֲלֵיהֶם עוֹלָה
וְעַל חֲטָאִים שֶׁאָנוּ חַיָּבִים עֲלֵיהֶם חַטָּאת
וְעַל חֲטָאִים שֶׁאָנוּ חַיָּבִים עֲלֵיהֶם קָרְבָּן עוֹלֶה וְיוֹרֵד
וְעַל חֲטָאִים שֶׁאָנוּ חַיָּבִים עֲלֵיהֶם אָשָׁם וַדַּאי וְתָלוּי
וְעַל חֲטָאִים שֶׁאָנוּ חַיָּבִים עֲלֵיהֶם מַכַּת מַרְדּוּת
וְעַל חֲטָאִים שֶׁאָנוּ חַיָּבִים עֲלֵיהֶם מַלְקוּת אַרְבָּעִים
וְעַל חֲטָאִים שֶׁאָנוּ חַיָּבִים עֲלֵיהֶם מִיתָה בִּידֵי שָׁמָיִם
וְעַל חֲטָאִים שֶׁאָנוּ חַיָּבִים עֲלֵיהֶם כָּרֵת וַעֲרִירִי
וְעַל חֲטָאִים שֶׁאָנוּ חַיָּבִים עֲלֵיהֶם אַרְבַּע מִיתוֹת בֵּית דִּין
סְקִילָה, שְׂרֵפָה, הֶרֶג, וְחֶנֶק.

For positive and negative commandments,
whether they can be remedied by an act or not,
for sins known to us and for those that are unknown –
for those that are known,
we have already declared them before You
and confessed them to You;
and for those that are unknown,
before You they are revealed and known,
as it is said,
"The secret things belong to the Lord our God, *Deut. 29*
but the things that are revealed
are for us and our children for ever,
that we may fulfill all the words of this Torah."

For You are the Forgiver of Israel
and the Pardoner of the tribes of Yeshurun
in every generation,
and without You
we have no king who pardons and forgives,
none but You.

אֱלֹהַי My God,
before I was formed I was unworthy,
and now that I have been formed
it is as if I had not been formed.
I am dust while alive,
how much more so when I am dead.
See, I am before You like a vessel filled with shame and disgrace.
May it be Your will,
Lord my God and God of my fathers,
that I may sin no more,
and as for the sins I have committed before You,
erase them in Your great compassion,
but not by suffering or severe illness.

עַל מִצְוַת עֲשֵׂה וְעַל מִצְוַת לֹא תַעֲשֶׂה.
בֵּין שֶׁיֵּשׁ בָּהּ קוּם עֲשֵׂה וּבֵין שֶׁאֵין בָּהּ קוּם עֲשֵׂה.
אֶת הַגְּלוּיִים לָנוּ וְאֶת שֶׁאֵינָם גְּלוּיִים לָנוּ
אֶת הַגְּלוּיִים לָנוּ
כְּבָר אֲמַרְנוּם לְפָנֶיךָ
וְהוֹדִינוּ לְךָ עֲלֵיהֶם
וְאֶת שֶׁאֵינָם גְּלוּיִים לָנוּ
לְפָנֶיךָ הֵם גְּלוּיִים וִידוּעִים
כַּדָּבָר שֶׁנֶּאֱמַר
הַנִּסְתָּרֹת לַיהוה אֱלֹהֵינוּ דברים כט
וְהַנִּגְלֹת לָנוּ וּלְבָנֵינוּ עַד־עוֹלָם
לַעֲשׂוֹת אֶת־כָּל־דִּבְרֵי הַתּוֹרָה הַזֹּאת:

כִּי אַתָּה סָלְחָן לְיִשְׂרָאֵל
וּמָחֳלָן לְשִׁבְטֵי יְשֻׁרוּן בְּכָל דּוֹר וָדוֹר
וּמִבַּלְעָדֶיךָ אֵין לָנוּ מֶלֶךְ מוֹחֵל וְסוֹלֵחַ אֶלָּא אָתָּה.

אֱלֹהַי
עַד שֶׁלֹּא נוֹצַרְתִּי אֵינִי כְדַאי
וְעַכְשָׁיו שֶׁנּוֹצַרְתִּי, כְּאִלּוּ לֹא נוֹצַרְתִּי
עָפָר אֲנִי בְּחַיַּי, קַל וָחֹמֶר בְּמִיתָתִי.
הֲרֵי אֲנִי לְפָנֶיךָ כִּכְלִי מָלֵא בוּשָׁה וּכְלִמָּה.
יְהִי רָצוֹן מִלְּפָנֶיךָ, יהוה אֱלֹהַי וֵאלֹהֵי אֲבוֹתַי, שֶׁלֹּא אֶחֱטָא עוֹד.
וּמַה שֶּׁחָטָאתִי לְפָנֶיךָ, מְחֹק בְּרַחֲמֶיךָ הָרַבִּים
אֲבָל לֹא עַל יְדֵי יִסּוּרִים וָחֳלָיִים רָעִים.

אֱלֹהַי My God, Berakhot 17a
guard my tongue from evil
and my lips from deceitful speech.
To those who curse me, let my soul be silent;
may my soul be to all like the dust.
Open my heart to Your Torah
and let my soul pursue Your commandments.
As for all who plan evil against me,
swiftly thwart their counsel and frustrate their plans.
Act for the sake of Your name; act for the sake of Your right hand;
act for the sake of Your holiness; act for the sake of Your Torah.
That Your beloved ones may be delivered, Ps. 60
save with Your right hand and answer me.
May the words of my mouth and the meditation of my heart Ps. 19
find favor before You, LORD, my Rock and Redeemer.

Bow, take three steps back, then bow, first left, then right, then center, while saying:

May He who makes peace in His high places,
make peace for us and all Israel – and say: Amen.

יְהִי רָצוֹן May it be Your will, LORD our God and God of our ancestors,
that the Temple be rebuilt speedily in our days,
and grant us a share in Your Torah.
And there we will serve You with reverence,
as in the days of old and as in former years.
Then the offering of Judah and Jerusalem Mal. 3
will be pleasing to the LORD as in the days of old and as in former years.

---

offered daily, together with an extra sacrifice (represented by Musaf) for Sabbaths and festivals. For this reason there is no Leader's Repetition in the evening service, since no sacrifice was offered at night. In this view, prayer is a communal act: the leader stands in place of the priest, words take the place of the sacrifice, and the offering is made by one on behalf of all.

With either interpretation it is important to follow the Repetition, to make the appropriate congregational responses, and not to talk otherwise until the prayer has been completed. We speak to God privately as individuals and publicly as a community, for ours is a faith of strong individuals *and* of deeply rooted, communal bonds. At this point it is the community speaking through the leader's prayer.

אֱלֹהַי ברכות יז.
נְצֹר לְשׁוֹנִי מֵרָע וּשְׂפָתַי מִדַּבֵּר מִרְמָה
וְלִמְקַלְלַי נַפְשִׁי תִדֹּם, וְנַפְשִׁי כֶּעָפָר לַכֹּל תִּהְיֶה.
פְּתַח לִבִּי בְּתוֹרָתֶךָ, וּבְמִצְוֹתֶיךָ תִּרְדֹּף נַפְשִׁי.
וְכָל הַחוֹשְׁבִים עָלַי רָעָה
מְהֵרָה הָפֵר עֲצָתָם וְקַלְקֵל מַחֲשַׁבְתָּם.
עֲשֵׂה לְמַעַן שְׁמֶךָ, עֲשֵׂה לְמַעַן יְמִינֶךָ
עֲשֵׂה לְמַעַן קְדֻשָּׁתֶךָ, עֲשֵׂה לְמַעַן תּוֹרָתֶךָ.
לְמַעַן יֵחָלְצוּן יְדִידֶיךָ, הוֹשִׁיעָה יְמִינְךָ וַעֲנֵנִי: תהלים ס
יִהְיוּ לְרָצוֹן אִמְרֵי פִי וְהֶגְיוֹן לִבִּי לְפָנֶיךָ, יהוה צוּרִי וְגֹאֲלִי: תהלים יט

Bow, take three steps back, then bow, first left, then right, then center, while saying:

עֹשֶׂה הַשָּׁלוֹם בִּמְרוֹמָיו
הוּא יַעֲשֶׂה שָׁלוֹם עָלֵינוּ וְעַל כָּל יִשְׂרָאֵל וְאִמְרוּ אָמֵן.

יְהִי רָצוֹן מִלְּפָנֶיךָ יהוה אֱלֹהֵינוּ וֵאלֹהֵי אֲבוֹתֵינוּ
שֶׁיִּבָּנֶה בֵּית הַמִּקְדָּשׁ בִּמְהֵרָה בְיָמֵינוּ, וְתֵן חֶלְקֵנוּ בְּתוֹרָתֶךָ
וְשָׁם נַעֲבָדְךָ בְּיִרְאָה כִּימֵי עוֹלָם וּכְשָׁנִים קַדְמֹנִיּוֹת.
וְעָרְבָה לַיהוה מִנְחַת יְהוּדָה וִירוּשָׁלָםִ כִּימֵי עוֹלָם וּכְשָׁנִים קַדְמֹנִיּוֹת: מלאכי ג

LEADER'S REPETITION OF THE AMIDA

There are two views as to the meaning and significance of the Leader's Repetition of the Amida (*Rosh HaShana* 34b–35a). According to some Mishnaic sages, the leader repeats the Amida for the sake of those unable to pray for themselves – a phenomenon more widespread then than now because there were few prayer books and not everyone was able to say the Amida by heart. This was especially so on Rosh HaShana and Yom Kippur, when the prayers were long and many of them less familiar than those said at other times of the year.

The other view, held by Rabban Gamliel, was that the Repetition, said out loud by the leader, *is* the primary form of prayer. Evidently for Rabban Gamliel, prayer was essentially a substitute for the communal sacrifices,

LEADER'S REPETITION FOR SHAḤARIT

The Ark is opened.
The Leader takes three steps forward and at the points indicated by ▾, bends the knees at the first word, bows at the second, and stands straight before saying God's name.

O LORD, open my lips, *Ps. 51*
so that my mouth may declare Your praise.

PATRIARCHS

▾בָּרוּךְ▾ Blessed are You, LORD our God and God of our fathers,
God of Abraham, God of Isaac and God of Jacob;
the great, mighty and awesome God, God Most High,
who bestows acts of loving-kindness and creates all,
who remembers the loving-kindness of the fathers
and will bring a Redeemer to their children's children
for the sake of His name, in love.

Meanwhile another element of prayer, *piyut* (the word comes from the same root as "poetry"), was developing. This differs from the standard texts of prayer because it is non-obligatory, not part of the minimum requirement of prayer. It was created to augment, adorn, and beautify; to reflect more deeply on key points of the service; to bring out in greater depth the distinctive character of specific days; to bring variety to the rhythm and pace of prayer; to inform, educate and help us introspect, and sometimes simply to create a mood. *Piyut* can be traced back to Israel in the third or fourth century CE, and this form of prayer eventually spread to all major centers of Jewish life. Babylon, Spain, Italy, and northern Europe all contributed richly to the poetry of the synagogue, and different rites reflect that variety.

Piyut grew more or less contemporaneously with the development of *Midrash Aggada,* rabbinic reflection on and commentary to biblical narrative. *Piyut* incorporates much of this material, suggesting that part of its purpose was educational as well as aesthetic. It reminded people of the laws and traditions relating to the day. It may even have been a way of circumventing the bans that occurred from time to time on the public teaching of Judaism.

We do not know the names of the earliest writers of *piyut.* The first we know of by name is Yose ben Yose who lived in Israel, probably in the fourth or fifth century. The first great master of the genre, a century later, was Yannai.

חזרת הש״ץ של שחרית

The ארון קודש *is opened.*
The שליח ציבור *takes three steps forward and at the points indicated by* ˇ*, bends the knees at the first word, bows at the second, and stands straight before saying God's name.*

תהלים נא
אֲדֹנָי, שְׂפָתַי תִּפְתָּח, וּפִי יַגִּיד תְּהִלָּתֶךָ:

אבות

ˇבָּרוּךְ אַתָּה יהוה, אֱלֹהֵינוּ וֵאלֹהֵי אֲבוֹתֵינוּ
אֱלֹהֵי אַבְרָהָם, אֱלֹהֵי יִצְחָק, וֵאלֹהֵי יַעֲקֹב
הָאֵל הַגָּדוֹל הַגִּבּוֹר וְהַנּוֹרָא, אֵל עֶלְיוֹן
גּוֹמֵל חֲסָדִים טוֹבִים, וְקוֹנֵה הַכֹּל
וְזוֹכֵר חַסְדֵי אָבוֹת
וּמֵבִיא גוֹאֵל לִבְנֵי בְנֵיהֶם לְמַעַן שְׁמוֹ בְּאַהֲבָה.

PIYUT: THE POETRY OF THE PRAYER BOOK

The first formulation of Jewish prayer goes back to the time of Ezra and the Men of the Great Assembly in the fifth century BCE. Ezra and Nehemiah, returning to Israel from exile in Babylon, found the Jewish community in the Holy Land in a poor spiritual state. They had lost many of their religious traditions; a great number could not even speak Hebrew (Nehemiah 13:24). Ezra and his court instituted a basic liturgy so that people could learn to pray in a linguistically pure and well-structured way (Maimonides, Laws of Prayer 1:4).

A second major consolidation occurred in the time of Rabban Gamliel II after the destruction of the Second Temple. In the absence of the Temple and its sacrifices, prayer assumed greater significance, and it was important for the spiritual unity of the people that they pray the same prayers at the same time in the same way. Even so, there were various points in the service where individuals were able to say private prayers in their own words. We have many such examples preserved in the Mishna, the Talmud and other ancient rabbinic texts.

So a balance was struck between formality and spontaneity, some sages favoring a set text, others valuing individuality within the framework of an agreed template. Formal collections of prayers did not appear until the period of the Geonim: Rabbi Amram Gaon's was the first, in the ninth century, followed by that of Rabbi Sa'adia Gaon in the tenth.

Before each cycle (kerova) of piyutim, the Leader says a prefatory prayer, asking permission (reshut) to commence. The reshut consists of a standard opening "Drawing from the counsel of wise and knowing men…," and a short introductory piyut. Once, these piyutim would vary across different communities; nowadays, the prefatory prayer of the eastern European nusaḥ is almost universally said among Ashkenazim.

מִסּוֹד Drawing from the counsel of wise and knowing men,
from the teachings born of insight among those who understand,
I open my mouth now in prayer and pleading,
to implore and to plead before the King
who pardons and forgives iniquities.

Compositionally, *piyutim* are usually constructed on the basis of an acrostic, sometimes following the order of the alphabet, sometimes the alphabet in reverse (תשר״ק), and sometimes in more complex forms such as אתב״ש, in which odd-numbered lines or phrases move alphabetically forward while even-numbered lines move backward. Often poets devised an acrostic that spelled their name, the only way they had of ensuring that authorship was recognized.

There are many genres of *piyut*, depending on their position in the prayers. So, for example, a poem inserted in the first blessing before the Shema is called a *Yotzer*, since the blessing ends *Yotzer hame'orot*, "who forms lights." A poetic addition to the Amida (almost invariably confined to the first three blessings) is called a *Kerova*. The final poem before the *Kedusha* is called a *Siluk*. Like the last movement of a symphony it is usually a passage of great intensity, resolving the tensions of the previous movements. The *Siluk* for the Musaf of both Rosh HaShana and Yom Kippur is the dramatic poem *Untaneh Tokef* (*page 843*).

Piyut is a magnificent range of solo voices in the choral symphony Israel has sung to its Maker, King, Judge and Redeemer. It is prayer as poetry and poetry as prayer, and its sacred beauty still challenges the mind as it lifts the heart.

מִסּוֹד *Drawing from the counsel.* This brief poem is of a type called *Reshut*, literally, asking "permission" of God and the congregation to represent the community in prayer. This specific *reshut*, common throughout the prayers on Rosh HaShana and Yom Kippur, derives from the fact that some leading scholars criticized poetic additions to the prayers on theological grounds. Thus the prayer leader was moved to say that his words were carefully constructed to follow the traditions of the sages.

Before each cycle (קרובה) of piyutim, the שליח ציבור says a prefatory prayer, asking permission (רשות) to commence. The רשות consists of a standard opening "...מִסּוֹד חֲכָמִים וּנְבוֹנִים," and a short introductory piyut. Once, these piyutim would vary across different communities; today, the prefatory prayer of the eastern European נוסח is almost universally said among Ashkenazim.

מִסּוֹד חֲכָמִים וּנְבוֹנִים
וּמִלֶּמֶד דַּעַת מְבִינִים
אֶפְתְּחָה פִּי בִּתְפִלָּה וּבְתַחֲנוּנִים
לְחַלּוֹת וּלְחַנֵּן פְּנֵי מֶלֶךְ מוֹחֵל וְסוֹלֵחַ לַעֲוֹנִים.

A century later still (according to most authorities) came the virtuoso, Rabbi Elazar HaKalir, who brought the art to extreme sophistication, coining new words, developing new literary techniques, and creating, in short phrases and sometimes single words, dense networks of association and allusion. It takes encyclopaedic knowledge and acute literary sensibility to fathom the full panoply of meanings in a Kalir poem. One thing is clear: to judge by the complexity and popularity of *piyut*, the communities to which it was addressed were exceptionally literate, testimony to the high levels of education sustained by Jewry even in ages of persecution and poverty.

Not everyone approved of *piyut* entirely. There were notes of dissent from Rav Hai Gaon, Maimonides, Ibn Ezra and others, on a number of grounds. They were unwarranted interruptions; they made the services too long; they are hard to understand; their use of language was uneven and eccentric. Their theology, thought Maimonides, was sometimes suspect: their talk of angels, intermediaries and mysteries.

Yet *piyut* survived and thrived, and continues to play a major part, especially in the liturgy of Rosh HaShana and Yom Kippur. Each region – Ashkenaz, Sepharad, Eastern and Western Europe, Italy, France, Poland, Lithuania – had its own traditions. Sometimes these were localized to individual towns, like Rome or Mainz or Prague. The literature is vast: what is contained in standard prayer books is only the barest fraction of what exists. There were hundreds of authors, and tens of thousands of poems. A major source was the huge array of documents discovered in the Cairo Geniza, a store of discarded manuscripts of various kinds going back many centuries. Even today not all of this literature has been published.

אֵימָיךְ I bear Your awe as I prepare my plea; / an emissary of Your people, on bended knee.
You who brought me forth from the womb, illuminate my darkness that I might speak clearly; guide me in Your truth.

Teach me to pour out beautiful words; / bring me close that I might dwell in Your shadow.
Bring forth my cry, with heartfelt intention. / As I seek Your countenance, bring me close to Your righteousness.

Pure of eyes, most exalted One, / teach me to understand how prayer should be arranged,
that I might entreat You rightly, without impropriety; / that I might bring healing and remedy to those who have sent me.

Make the words which leave my lips clear and true, / accept the tributes of my mouth and make them fitting.
May the order of my words be received as a gift, / my outpouring of prayer like cascading raindrops.

Steady my steps for me and guard me from falling; / O Rock, support my paths and let me not stumble.
▸ Raise me up and strengthen me in the face of weakness and faintness; favor my words so I do not fall.

All:

Guard me as the apple of Your eye from terror and dread; / see my lowly statue, and come now to save us.
▸ Pity my crushed heart as You promised Your prophet; / show compassion for [Israel,] the child whom You affirmed.

The Ark is closed.

---

the tenth century, and over the next four hundred years provided Rhineland Jewry with some of its greatest poets, moralists, preachers and scholars as well as its most distinguished communal leaders, particularly during the age of persecution that began with the First Crusade in 1096. At least a dozen members of the family wrote liturgical poems. Meshullam, who lived in the late tenth and early eleventh century, was a distinguished Talmudist, often referred to as "the Great."

אֵימֶיךָ נָשָׂאתִי חִין בְּעָרְכִּי / בְּמַלְאֲכוּת עַמְּךָ בֶּרֶךְ בְּבָרְכִּי
גּוֹחִי מִבֶּטֶן, הַגִּיהָ חָשְׁכִּי / דַּבֵּר צָחוֹת, וּבַאֲמִתְּךָ הַדְרִיכִי.

הוֹרֵנִי שְׁפֹךְ שִׂיחַ עָרֵב / וְלוֹנְנִי בְּצִלְּךָ אוֹתִי לְקָרֵב
זַעַק יוֹפַק בְּכִוּוּן קֶרֶב / חַלּוֹתִי פָּנֶיךָ צִדְקָתְךָ תְּקָרֵב.

טְהוֹר עֵינַיִם, מְאֹד נַעֲלָה / יַדְּעֵנִי בִּין עֶרֶךְ תְּפִלָּה
כַּדָּת לְחַנֵּן, בְּלִי תִּפְלָה / לְהַמְצִיא שׁוֹלְחַי אֶרֶךְ וּתְעָלָה.

מִפְתַּח שְׂפָתַי תְּבָרֵר וּתְיַשֵּׁר / נִדְבוֹת פִּי רְצֵה וְהַכְשֵׁר
סֵדֶר הֲגִיגַי כְּשַׁי יְתֻשַּׁר / עֶתֶר פִּצְחִי כְּזִילַת חֶשֶׁר.

פְּעָמַי הָכֵן, פְּצוֹתִי מִכֶּשֶׁל / צוּר תְּמֹךְ אֲשׁוּרַי מֵהִנָּשֵׁל
◂ קוֹמְמֵנִי וְחַזְּקֵנִי מֵרִפְיוֹן וָחֵשֶׁל / רְצוֹת אֲמָרַי, וְלֹא אֶכָּשֵׁל.

All:

◂ שָׁמְרֵנִי כְּאִישׁוֹן מִפֶּלֶץ וּבְעָתָה / שׁוּר שִׁפְלוּתִי, וּלְכָה לִישׁוּעָתָה
תָּחֹן דִּכְאוּתִי כִּלְחוּזָךְ פַּצְתָּ / תְּרַחֵם עַל בֵּן אֲמִתָּךְ.

The ארון קודש *is closed.*

אֵימֶיךָ *I bear Your awe.* This is a different kind of *reshut,* in which the leader expresses his sense of inadequacy to represent the community in prayer. Abraham, when he prayed for the cities of the plain, said he was "mere dust and ashes" (Gen. 18:27). How then can anyone have the temerity to plead with God? Yet, emboldened by the knowledge that God hears and heeds the words of all who call on Him in truth, empowered by the psalm that says, "A broken heart You will not despise" (Ps. 51:19), the leader prays that God help him formulate his words articulately and act as a worthy representative of those who have asked him to pray on their behalf. It is humbling for us to overhear this private conversation between the leader and God before he begins to speak on behalf of the congregation.

The author of this prayer is Rabbi Meshullam ben Kalonymus, a member of the remarkable Kalonymus family who moved from Italy to Germany in

Most of the piyutim for Shaḥarit were composed by Rabbi Meshullam ben Kalonymus. As part of the Leader's Repetition, they should ideally be said by the Leader alone. However, the prevailing custom is for the congregation to participate, and some of the piyutim are said together, with the Leader raising his voice only toward the end.

All:

אָמַצְתָּ You affirmed the tenth [of Tishrei] to make atonement for Your beloved, / for them to clean the filthy stains of their guilt.
Cleanse their sin and end their iniquity; / shine light upon their judgment, and seal them for life.

They tremble at the shofar blast of Rosh HaShana, / bringing with them words that tear the heart;
crying out "This is my God" to let the judgment fall to righteousness the living, the living praise You with the shofar's sounding.

The young and old among them are exhausted with affliction; behold them standing before You barefoot.
They all stand before You, robed in white; / they come to glorify You in sanctity, like flying Seraphim.

Defender of their ancestors, they place their faith in You, / relying on You in their innocence, and finding shelter in Your shade.
They lean upon on Your covenant with their three honored ancestors; support them, and silence their enemies.

Turn to them, for the righteousness of [Abraham,] the one from across the river, / as You pass Your flock under Your staff.
Approach them with compassion, without awakening your wrath, O Merciful One who overlooks transgressions.

Cleanse and purify the stain of their willful iniquity; / hear their cries now and do not delay.
▸ Those supported by Your strength – let their faces shine with light; grant atonement to purify the deceit of their sins.

All:

Let our judgment shine forth like the light of noon; / let those who long for You remain in goodness.
▸ Seek out our merits and show them clearly; / protect us in Your shelter that we too may be glorified.

Most of the piyutim for שחרית *were composed by Rabbi Meshullam ben Kalonymus. As part of the* חזרת הש״ץ, *they should ideally be said by the* שליח ציבור *alone. However, the prevailing custom is for the* קהל *to participate, and some of the piyutim are said together, with the* שליח ציבור *raising his voice only toward the end.*

All:

אִמַּצְתָּ עָשׂוֹר לְכִפּוּר תָּמָּה / בּוֹ לְצַחְצֵחַ צָאוּי כִּתְמָה
גֹּהַץ צַחֲנָהּ, עֲווּיָהּ לְהָתֵמָּה / דִּינָהּ לְהָאִיר, לְתֶחִי לְחָתְמָהּ.

הַחֲרָדָה מִתֵּקַע יוֹם תְּרוּעָה / וּדְבָרִים קָחָה, סֵרְעַף לְקָרְעָה
זֶה אֵלִי, לְצֶדֶק הַכְרֵיעָה / חַי חַי יוֹדְךָ בְּהָרֵיעָה.

טַפֶּיהָ וִישִׁישֶׁיהָ בְּעִנּוּי עֲיֵפִים / יְצִיגָתָם שׁוּר בְּיָחֵף יְחֵפִים
כֻּלָּם צָגִים וְלָבֶן מְצֻעָפִים / לְאַדֶּרְךָ בַּקֹּדֶשׁ כִּשְׂרָפִים עָפִים.

מָגֵן עִקָּרֵמוֹ בָּךְ חוֹסִים / נִשְׁעָנִים בְּתֻמָּם וּבְצִלְּךָ חָסִים
סְמוּכִים בִּבְרִית שְׁלֹשֶׁת יְחוּסִים / עוֹדְדֵם הֱיוֹת שׁוֹטְנֵימוֹ הָסִים.

פְּנֵה בְּצִדְקַת אֶת מֵעֵבֶר / צֹאנְךָ תַּחַת שֵׁבֶט, כְּהֵעָבֵר
קַדְּמֵם רַחֲמֶיךָ בְּלִי הִתְעַבֵּר / רַחוּם עַל פֶּשַׁע עוֹבֵר.

שֶׁמֶץ זְדוֹנָם תְּכַבֵּס וּתְטַהֵר / שֶׁעָם קְשֹׁב וְאַל תְּאַחֵר
◂ תְּמוּכֵי יְמִינְךָ, פְּנֵיהֶם נַהֵר / תַּעְתּוּעַ חֶטְאָם תְּכַפֵּר לְטַהֵר.

All:

◂ כְּצַהֳרַיִם מִשְׁפָּטֵנוּ הָאֵר / חוֹכֶיךָ לְטוֹב תַּשְׁאֵר
צִדְקֵנוּ תְּחַפֵּשׂ וּתְבָאֵר / בְּמָגִנְּךָ נִתְגּוֹנֵן לְהִתְפָּאֵר.

אִמַּצְתָּ *You affirmed.* Note how the beginning of this prayer begins with the last word of the previous prayer. This was a common device used by the synagogue poets to create seamless joins between the sections of long poems. The poet asks God to look at the people in the synagogue, shoeless, dressed in white, already faint from fasting, and asks Him to tilt the scale of justice in their favor. The poet speaks of sin as stain, blemish, defilement, and pleads with God to cleanse us and remove its mark. Since the poem is specific to the first blessing of the Amida, it refers to Abraham with whose name the first blessing ends.

The congregation then the Leader:

זָכְרֵנוּ לְחַיִּים Remember us for life,
O King who desires life,
and write us in the book of life –
for Your sake, O God of life.

The Leader continues:

King, Helper, Savior, Shield:
ᵛBlessed are You, LORD,
Shield of Abraham.

DIVINE MIGHT

אַתָּה גִּבּוֹר You are eternally mighty, LORD.
You give life to the dead and have great power to save.
In Israel: He causes the dew to fall.
He sustains the living with loving-kindness,
and with great compassion revives the dead.
He supports the fallen,
heals the sick,
sets captives free,
and keeps His faith with those who sleep in the dust.
Who is like You, Master of might,
and to whom can You be compared,
O King who brings death and gives life,
and makes salvation grow?

---

were reluctant to admit request-prayers in either the first three or last three blessings of the Amida, or at any point on Sabbaths and festivals. Only on the grounds that they represent a communal rather than individual request were they permitted at all.

The קהל *then the* שליח ציבור*:*

זָכְרֵנוּ לְחַיִּים, מֶלֶךְ חָפֵץ בַּחַיִּים
וְכָתְבֵנוּ בְּסֵפֶר הַחַיִּים, לְמַעַנְךָ אֱלֹהִים חַיִּים.

The שליח ציבור *continues:*

מֶלֶךְ עוֹזֵר וּמוֹשִׁיעַ וּמָגֵן.
ׄבָּרוּךְ אַתָּה יהוה, מָגֵן אַבְרָהָם.

גבורות

אַתָּה גִּבּוֹר לְעוֹלָם, אֲדֹנָי
מְחַיֵּה מֵתִים אַתָּה, רַב לְהוֹשִׁיעַ
בארץ ישראל: מוֹרִיד הַטָּל
מְכַלְכֵּל חַיִּים בְּחֶסֶד
מְחַיֵּה מֵתִים בְּרַחֲמִים רַבִּים
סוֹמֵךְ נוֹפְלִים
וְרוֹפֵא חוֹלִים
וּמַתִּיר אֲסוּרִים
וּמְקַיֵּם אֱמוּנָתוֹ לִישֵׁנֵי עָפָר.
מִי כָמְוֹךָ, בַּעַל גְּבוּרוֹת, וּמִי דּוֹמֶה לָּךְ
מֶלֶךְ, מֵמִית וּמְחַיֶּה וּמַצְמִיחַ יְשׁוּעָה.

זָכְרֵנוּ לְחַיִּים *Remember us for life.* The first of four insertions specifically for the period from Rosh HaShana to Yom Kippur. It is a poetic miniature of great beauty: four phrases, each ending with the word "life." In general the rabbis

The first three piyutim of each kerova, known as "Magen," "Meḥayeh," and "Meshalesh," correspond to the sections of the Amida in which they are inserted: the blessings of Patriarchs, Divine Might, and Kedusha respectively. Usually these are united by a running theme. In Shaḥarit of Yom Kippur, the theme is the ambivalent feeling toward the Day of Atonement: the eager expectation of being purified combined with the fear we may not merit it. This connects to the overarching theme: the three patriarchs (see commentary, page 805) whose merit we invoke. The first two piyutim begin with fear and end on a hopeful note.

All:

תַּאֲוַת The soul's desire is for Your name and remembrance; / be vigilant in showing compassion to those who bless Your remembrance.

Accept them with the love for a tender young one, / those who are called and claimed as Your firstborn son.

You removed Your hosts from [Egypt,] the crucible of sorrow, / sending angels to redeem them from harsh servitude.

Deliver those You have borne since birth from the tumult of destruction, / support them and do not deal with them measure for measure.

Your covenant is etched into their very flesh, / since Abraham, the rock from which they descend.

Look to the covenant and wash away their filth; / cleanse them thoroughly and let their light shine.

Behold the sacrifice of the only son, Isaac, / as both father and son feared Your command.

Save their offspring from dread and fear; / may [Isaac's] sacrifice and ashes be complete in Your presence.

And if their ways have become crooked that they might deceive You, recall Your compassion and never forsake Your covenant.

Adopt the advocate Abraham's demand for justice, / and reinforce the protection You offer us a thousandfold.

▸ Understand the words uttered by Your beloved's offspring; / heed their prayers and cleanse their sins.

Turn Your mind away from Your congregation's iniquity; / hear their groans and accept their whispered pleas.

All:

Let Your pardon be known to the afflicted soul; / rescue them from the depths of pits.

▸ May those who rise against us be like repulsive waste; / revive us with dew, that we might speak of Your faith.

The first three piyutim of each קרובה*, known as "*מגן*," "*מחיה*," and "*משלש*," correspond to the sections of the* עמידה *in which they are inserted: the blessings of* אבות*,* גבורות*, and* קדושה *respectively. Usually these are united by a running theme. In* שחרית *of* יום כיפור*, the theme is the ambivalent feeling toward the Day of Atonement: the eager expectation of being purified combined with the fear we may not merit it. This connects to the overarching theme: the three patriarchs (see commentary, page 805) whose merit we invoke. The first two piyutim begin with fear and end on a hopeful note.*

All:

תַּאֲוַת נֶפֶשׁ לְשִׁמְךָ וּלְזִכְרָךְ / שְׁקֹד לְרַחֵם מְבָרְכֵי זִכְרָךְ
רְצוּיֵי אֲהַב כְּנַעַר וָרָךְ / קְרוּאִים וּנְקוּבִים בִּנְךָ בְּכוֹרָךְ.

צְבָאוֹת הוֹצֵאתָ מִכּוּר אוֹנִים / פְּדוּתָם מִפֶּרֶךְ הָלְכוּ שַׁאֲנַנִּים
עֲמוּסִים מִבֶּטֶן פְּצֵם מִשְּׁאוֹנִים / סְעָדֵם בַּל לָמֹד כִּסְאוֹנִים.

נְתוּנָה בְּרִיתְךָ חֹק בִּשְׁאֵרָם / מִמַּחֲצֶבֶת צוּרָם מוֹלֶדֶת שֶׁאוּרָם
לַבְּרִית הַבֵּט וְתָדִיחַ כָּאוּרָם / כַּבְּסֵם הֶרֶב וְתַבְהִיק אוֹרָם.

יֵרָאֶה לְפָנֶיךָ עֵקֶד מְיֻחָד / טוֹבֵחַ וְטָבוּחַ מִדְּבָרְךָ פָּחַד
חֲנִיטָיו חִלֵּץ מֵאֵימָתָה וָפַחַד / זְבוּחוֹ וְדִשּׁוּנוֹ לְפָנֶיךָ יִתְיַחַד.

וְאִם הֶעֱווּ אֹרַח לְסַלֵּף / הִזָּכֵר רַחֲמֶיךָ חֹק מִלְּחַלֵּף
דְּרִישַׁת צֶדֶק מֵלִיץ יְאַלֵּף / גְּנוּנֶיךָ לְחַזֵּק בְּמָגִנַּת אֶלֶף.

בְּדֵי יְדִידֶיךָ, הֲגִיגָם בִּין / בְּצוּרָם תֶּשַׁע וְחֵטְא תַּלְבִּין
▸ אוֹן מִתְחַנְּנֶיךָ בְּלִי תָבִין / אֶנֶק שְׁמַע וְלַחַשׁ הָבִין.

All:

נֶפֶשׁ נַעֲנָה תְּבַשֵּׂר סְלִיחָה / פַּלְּטֵם מֵעֵמֶק שׁוּחָה
▸ מִתְקוֹמְמֵינוּ יְהוּ כַּסּוּחָה / הַחֲיֵינוּ בְּטַל אֱמוּנָתְךָ לְשׁוּחֵחָה.

תַּאֲוַת *The soul's desire.* To bring variation into the poetry, this has been written as a reverse acrostic, beginning with the last letter of the alphabet and closing with the first. Since the second paragraph of the Amida is associated with Isaac, the poet makes reference to the binding. זְבוּחוֹ וְדִשּׁוּנוֹ [*Isaac's*] *sacrifice and ashes:* Since Isaac was willing to be sacrificed, it is as if he was.

On Yom Kippur, a Tokheḥa (rebuke) piyut is added after the Meḥayeh. This Tokheḥa, by an unknown author, focuses on the frality of mortal man. Traditionally, the line "Until the day of his death" was said by the congregation after each stanza, with the image of God waiting for man's repentance as a counterpoint to the gloom of the piyut. Nowadays, many congregations say the refrain only at the beginning and end; others omit the piyut altogether, saying only the refrain.

The Leader, then the congregation:

עַד Until the day of his death You await his repentance,
that You might steer him toward life.

All:

אֱנוֹשׁ How might man be acquitted, when even the hosts of heaven
are not pure in Your eyes?
If the moist [the meritorious] can be burnt in fire, what chance have
the dry stalks [the guilty]?

Darkness is revealed to You as clear as light; Your eye ranges over all.
Though Your home is hidden, all secrets are revealed before You.

He is the sole judge, the only One; who can sway Him?
Over nations and individuals alike He extends the line of judgment,
and none can find fault with Him.

Let all creatures understand this, and be not misled by their
impulses to sin before the Creator.
Those once coddled in the womb, will be covered in the tomb, and
must account for their deeds before their Creator.

Man is made impure by his flesh, is vulnerable to impurity in his
existence, and imparts impurity in his death.
His days are confusion, his nights are emptiness, and all his pursuits
are vanities.

אֱנוֹשׁ מַה יִּזְכֶּה *How might man be acquitted.* This is a poem of the *tokheḥa* form, that is, a rebuke to the congregation. This was the function performed by the prophets in biblical times, and Maimonides rules (Laws of Repentance 4:2) that every congregation should have someone who can perform this function. He should be "a great scholar, advanced in years, God-fearing from his youth, and beloved by the people." We should come to the synagogue not to be praised but to be challenged. The poet, in the spirit of Ecclesiastes, Job, Proverbs and the Ethics of the Fathers, reminds us that life is short. We

On יום כיפור, a תוכחה (rebuke) piyut is added after the מחיה. This תוכחה, by an unknown author, focuses on the frality of mortal man. Traditionally, the line "עַד יוֹם מוֹתוֹ" was said by the congregation after each stanza, with the image of God waiting for man's repentance as a counterpoint to the gloom of the piyut. Nowadays, many congregations say the refrain only at the beginning and end; others omit the piyut altogether, saying only the refrain.

The שליח ציבור, then the קהל:

עַד יוֹם מוֹתוֹ תְּחַכֶּה לוֹ לִתְשׁוּבָה
לְהַנְטוֹתוֹ לִתְחִיָּה.

All:

אֱנוֹשׁ מַה יִּזְכֶּה, וּצְבָא דֹק לֹא זַכּוּ בְעֵינֶיךָ.
בַּלְּחִים אִם תִּבְעַר הָאֵשׁ, מַה בֶּחָצִיר יָבֵשׁ.

גָּלוּי לְךָ חֹשֶׁךְ כְּמוֹ אוֹר, מְשׁוֹטֵט כֹּל בָּעַיִן.
דִּירָתְךָ בַּסֵּתֶר, וּגְלוּיוֹת לְךָ כָּל נִסְתָּרוֹת.

הַדָּן יְחִידִי, וְהוּא בְאֶחָד וּמִי יְשִׁיבֶנּוּ.
וְעַל גּוֹי וְעַל אָדָם יַחַד יִנְטֶה קָו, וְאֵין מִי יַרְשִׁיעַ.

זֹאת יָבִין יְצִיר, וְלֹא יִתְעוֹ יֵצֶר לַחֲטֹא לַיּוֹצֵר.
חֲתֻלַּת בְּאֵרוֹ, חֲפִירַת בּוֹרוֹ, חֶשְׁבּוֹן בּוֹרְאוֹ.

טָמֵא מִשְּׁאֵרוֹ, וּמְטַמֵּא בְּעוֹדוֹ, וּמְטַמֵּא בְּמוֹתוֹ.
יְמֵי חַיָּיו תֹּהוּ, וְלֵילוֹתָיו בֹּהוּ, וְעִנְיָנָיו הֶבֶל.

עַד יוֹם מוֹתוֹ *Until the day of his death.* Throughout our lifetime God waits for us to turn to Him. No moment is too late. "The word 'now' means *teshuva*," said the sages (*Mekhilta, Massekhta deShira* 5). God is here, in this place, at this moment, and all we have to do for Him to turn to us, is to turn to Him. "Even if one was wicked for the whole of a lifetime, and repented in the closing moments of his life, nothing of his wickedness is recalled to him" (Maimonides, Laws of Repentance 1:3). The line, "To the very day he dies, You wait for him," also appears in the *Untaneh Tokef* prayer.

Like waking from a dream, terrors that frighten him continuously;
nights he gets no sleep, days he finds no rest, until he slumbers in the grave.

What complaint might a living man lodge? It is enough that he is alive.
He is born to toil, and fortunate if he labors in the true Law.

His end is proof of his worthless origin; for what, then, should he be hypocritical?
Man's very own signature attests to his actions; why, then, should he try to deceive?

Righteous works, if he accomplished them, shall accompany him into eternity.
And wisdom, if he has sought it, shall support him in his old age.

The bloodthirsty and deceitful will have their days cut short.
Yet if one's will and desire is to be disciplined in wisdom, he will blossom in ripe, old age.

▸ A good name, once earned, is worth more than being called by pleasing titles.
Therefore, the day of death [well met] is better than the day one was born.

The Leader, then the congregation:

עַד יוֹם Until the day of his death You await his
repentance, that You might steer him toward life.

The congregation then the Leader:

מִי כָמְוֹךָ Who is like You, compassionate Father,
who remembers His creatures in compassion, for life?

The Leader continues:

Faithful are You to revive the dead.
Blessed are You, LORD, who revives the dead.

---

of hearts, that we honored God, brought honor to our people, and helped others whenever we could.

כַּחֲלוֹם מֵהָקִיץ נִדְמֶה, בַּלָּהוֹת יְבַעֲתוּהוּ תָמִיד.
לַיְלָה לֹא יִשְׁכַּב, יוֹמָם לֹא יָנוּחַ, עַד יֵרֵד בַּקָּבֶר.

מַה יִּתְאוֹנֵן אָדָם חָי, דַּיּוֹ אֲשֶׁר הוּא חָי.
נוֹלַד לְעָמָל, אַשְׁרָיו אִם יְהִי יְגִיעוֹ בְּדַת אֱמֶת.

סוֹפוֹ עַל רֹאשׁוֹ מוֹכִיחַ, וְלָמָּה יַחֲנִיף.
עוֹד חוֹתָמוֹ מְעִידוֹ עַל פָּעֳלוֹ, וּמַה יִּגְנֹב דָּעַת.

פּוֹעֵל צְדָקוֹת אִם יְהִי, יְלַוּוּהוּ לְבֵית עוֹלָמוֹ.
צוֹפֶה בְּחָכְמָה אִם יְהִי, עִמּוֹ תִּתְלוֹנֵן בְּכֶלַח.

קָצוּף בְּדָמִים וּמִרְמָה אִם יְהִי, חֲרוּצִים יָמָיו.
רְצוֹנוֹ וְחֶפְצוֹ בִּהְיוֹת בְּמוּסָר, יָנוּב בְּשֵׂיבָה טוֹבָה.

◂ שֵׁם טוֹב אִם יִקְנֶה, מִשֵּׁמוֹת נָעִים, אֲשֶׁר יִקָּרֵא.
תַּחַת כֵּן, מִיּוֹם לֵדָה יוֹם מִיתָה הוּטָב.

The שליח ציבור*, then the* קהל*:*

עַד יוֹם מוֹתוֹ תְּחַכֶּה לוֹ לִתְשׁוּבָה, לְהַנְטוֹתוֹ לִתְחִיָּה.

The קהל *then the* שליח ציבור*:*

מִי כָמְוֹךָ אַב הָרַחֲמִים, זוֹכֵר יְצוּרָיו לְחַיִּים בְּרַחֲמִים.

The שליח ציבור *continues:*

וְנֶאֱמָן אַתָּה לְהַחֲיוֹת מֵתִים.
בָּרוּךְ אַתָּה יהוה, מְחַיֵּה הַמֵּתִים.

---

should neither waste it on trivia, nor think that we can do wrong and get away with it by deceiving others. We should give thanks that we are alive; do good deeds (the only things we retain after we die); and value a reputation for goodness more than any honors or titles. We can only be sure that "the day of death is better than the day one was born" if we know, in our heart

The "Meshalesh," completing the first group of piyutim.

All:

אַחַדְתְּ This one day of the year You set aside as unique,
to serve as a restorative, a balm for the lily [Israel].
And when Your Sanctuary in Jerusalem was whole in days of old, / the services therein would atone for the sins of Your slumbering nation.

Those exiled from Your fine abode and scattered all around,
pour out joyous prayer to salve their suffering.
The crushed, shattered spirit of Your scattered people – / O Holy One, consider them as the sacrifices once offered in Your Temple.

[Jacob,] innocent from the womb, who dwelt in tents of study,
whose image You engraved in Your throne as a light –
show favor to his offspring as they gather in their congregations
to pronounce Your glory and sing praises to Your name.

You wove the gift of Your great name into the name of Your people,
those You have attached to Yourself as a seal placed upon Your heart.
Spare them from Your wrath and let them face no blame;
may their inscription be in the book of life.

May the trouble of iniquity and the unbearable burden of sin
be cast into the depths to melt away.
May the speech of Your poor, downtrodden people be sweeter to You
than the pure offerings once sacrificed in [Jerusalem,] the city of solid stone.

The wedding canopy of Your beloved, please remember,
and remember not the shame of our youthful past.
▸ Your precious child [Israel], always remember, / for the sake of [Moses,]
the one who beseeched You to remember Your servants.

The congregation says the next two verses aloud, followed by the Leader:

The LORD shall reign for ever. *Ps. 146*
He is your God, Zion, from generation to generation, Halleluya!

You are the Holy One, enthroned on the praises of Israel. *Ps. 22*

---

that Jacob was described as "dwelling in tents" understood by the sages as "houses of study," and hints that we remain true to that heritage. The last four phrases of the poem all end with the verb *zakhor*, "remember."

The "משלש," completing the first group of piyutim.

All:

אחַדְתָּ יוֹם זֶה בַּשָּׁנָה תְּרוּפָה וּצְרִי שַׂמְתּוֹ לַשּׁוֹשַׁנָּה
בְּשָׁלֵם בִּהְיוֹת סֻכְּךָ בָּרִאשׁוֹנָה שֵׁרוּתוֹ כִּפֵּר פִּשְׁעֵי יְשֵׁנָה.

גּוֹלִים מִנָּוְךָ זְרוּיִם מֵהֲלָאָה רֹן מְפִיקִים לְחַתֵּל תְּלָאָה
דַּכְּאוּת רוּחַ וָשֶׁבֶר נַהֲלָאָה קָדוֹשׁ, חֲשֹׁב כְּזִבְחֵי הָעֲלָאָה.

הָתָּם מְרֻחָם יוֹשֵׁב אֹהָלִים צוּרָתוֹ בְּכִסְאֲךָ חֲקַקְתָּהּ בְּהִלּוּלִים
וִלָדָיו חֹן, בְּעֹצֶר נִקְהָלִים פְּאֵרְךָ מַבִּיעִים וְשִׁמְךָ מְהַלְלִים.

זֶבֶד שִׁמְךָ שִׁתַּפְתָּ בִּשְׁמָם עֲמוּתִים לְךָ כַּחוֹתָם לְשׁוּמָם
חָשְׁכֵם מֵאֶנֶף, בְּלִי לְהַאֲשִׁימָם סֵפֶר חַיִּים יְהִי רְשׁוּמָם.

טֹרַח עָוֹן וְכֹבֶד מַשָּׂא נֵעֵר בְּצוּל, מְחוֹת בַּהֲמָסָה
יֶעֱרַב שִׂיחַ עֲנִיָּה וּרְמוּסָה מְנִיחוֹחֵי כָלִיל בְּאֶבֶן מַעֲמָסָה.

כְּלוּלַת אֲהָבִים אָנָּא זְכֹר כְּלִמַּת נְעוּרִים עוֹד מִלִּזְכֹּר
► לְבֵן יַקִּירְךָ זָכוּר תִּזְכֹּר לְמַעַן חַלָּךְ, לַעֲבָדֶיךָ זְכֹר.

The קהל *says the next two verses aloud, followed by the* שליח ציבור*:*

תהלים קמו יִמְלֹךְ יהוה לְעוֹלָם
אֱלֹהַיִךְ צִיּוֹן לְדֹר וָדֹר, הַלְלוּיָהּ:

תהלים כב וְאַתָּה קָדוֹשׁ, יוֹשֵׁב תְּהִלּוֹת יִשְׂרָאֵל:

אחַדְתָּ יוֹם זֶה בַּשָּׁנָה *This one day of the year You set aside as unique.* A lament that we no longer have the Temple and its rites to atone for us, yet we still, in other ways, make sacrifices for our faith. May they therefore be regarded to our merit as if they were offered in the Temple. Using phrases from the Song of Songs ("lily," "like a seal placed upon Your heart") and Jeremiah ("wedding canopy of Your beloved"), the poet speaks of the love between God and His people. Note also several references to Jacob/Israel, the patriarch traditionally associated with the third paragraph of the Amida. The poet points out

There follows an ancient piyut, author unknown, which most congregations add after the Meshalesh. In recent generations, the custom to say it responsively has spread; many congregations are accustomed to saying the second stich of each couplet together with the first of the next one. However, traditionally this piyut is said only by the Leader, with the congregation joining in at "He is alive and everlasting."

The Ark is opened.

God, please.

You are our God, in heaven and on earth.
Mighty and revered, encircled with myriads.
He spoke and it was, commanded and it came into being.
His memory is forever, His life is everlasting.
Pure of eye, He sits concealed.
His crown is salvation, His garment is righteousness.
His cloak is jealousy, His coat is vengeance.
His counsel is candor, His wisdom is faith.
His deeds are truth, He is righteous and upright.
He is close to those who call upon Him in truth, He is sublime and lofty.
He resides in the heavens, and hangs the earth over emptiness.

All:

He is alive and everlasting, awesome, lofty and holy.

The Ark is closed.

מַעֲטֵהוּ קִנְאָה *His cloak is jealousy.* The word "jealous" in the Bible is always a reference to God's love for Israel and humanity, and His pain when that love is betrayed.

נְאֵפֹד נְקָמָה *His coat is vengeance.* When Judaism speaks of the "vengeance" of God, it means two things: (1) vengeance belongs to God, not man (see Lev. 19:18), and (2) ultimately there is justice in history. The great crimes do not go unpunished.

There follows an ancient piyut, author unknown, which most congregations add after the מְשַׁלֵּשׁ*. In recent generations, the custom to say it responsively has spread; many congregations are accustomed to saying the second stich of each couplet together with the first of the next one. However, traditionally this piyut is said only by the* שליח ציבור*, with the congregation joining in at "*חַי וְקַיָּם*."*

The ארון קודש *is opened.*

אֵל נָא.

אַתָּה הוּא אֱלֹהֵינוּ בַּשָּׁמַיִם וּבָאָרֶץ.
גִּבּוֹר וְנַעֲרָץ דָּגוּל מֵרְבָבָה.
הוּא שָׂח וַיֶּהִי וְצִוָּה וְנִבְרָאוּ.
זִכְרוֹ לָנֶצַח חַי עוֹלָמִים.
טְהוֹר עֵינַיִם יוֹשֵׁב סֵתֶר.
כִּתְרוֹ יְשׁוּעָה לְבוּשׁוֹ צְדָקָה.
מַעֲטֵהוּ קִנְאָה נֶאְפַּד נְקָמָה.
סִתְרוֹ יֹשֶׁר עֲצָתוֹ אֱמוּנָה.
פְּעֻלָּתוֹ אֱמֶת צַדִּיק וְיָשָׁר.
קָרוֹב לְקוֹרְאָיו בֶּאֱמֶת רָם וּמִתְנַשֵּׂא.
שׁוֹכֵן שְׁחָקִים תּוֹלֶה אֶרֶץ עַל בְּלִימָה.

All:

חַי וְקַיָּם, נוֹרָא וּמָרוֹם וְקָדוֹשׁ.

The ארון קודש *is closed.*

אַתָּה הוּא אֱלֹהֵינוּ *You are our God.* An alphabetical hymn composed out of descriptions of God, all but two of which – "His life is everlasting" and "His counsel is candor" – are biblical.

דָּגוּל מֵרְבָבָה *Encircled with myriads.* The angels that surround God's throne, as seen by the prophets.

These two verses are said by the congregation as alternating refrains after the stanzas of the following piyut. Some congregations omit the piyut, saying only the refrains.

The Leader says each verse, followed by the congregation:

אָנָּא We beg of You, please forgive us,
please pardon willful sin and iniquity,
that Your strength might be exalted – O Holy One.

The Leader then the congregation.

אָנָּא We beg of You, O Compassionate One, grant atonement
for the iniquity of those assembled, that Your praise might be told,
and may they be inscribed for life in Your book – O Holy One.

In many congregations, the Leader says the first two stichs, the congregation says the third, and the alternating refrains are said by all.

Leader: מוֹרֶה You who instruct sinners and pave them a path to follow,
You teach me and guide me that I might make my way.
Cong: I will exalt You, my God, the King.

Leader: I set aside times day and night to anoint You, / You who abides forever, there is none like You.
Cong: Every day I will bless You.

Leader: My heart trembles to serve You constantly; / I shall stand on guard to revere Your sanctity.
Cong: Great is the LORD and greatly to be praised.

We beg of You, please forgive us, / please pardon willful sin and iniquity,
that Your strength might be exalted – O Holy One.

---

carries a refrain consisting of the first half of each line of Psalm 145, the prayer known as *Ashrei*. Its theme is the devotion of Israel to God as evidenced by their constant prayers to Him. There is reference to the four prayers of today (Shaḥarit, Musaf, Minḥa and Ne'ila) and the seven times a day we bless God (the three blessings surrounding the morning Shema, and the four in the evening service). The second half is a prayer for the restoration of the Temple in Jerusalem so that our prayers can be more glorious.

These two verses are said by the קהל *as alternating refrains after the stanzas of the following piyut. Some congregations omit the piyut, saying only the refrains.*

The שליח ציבור *says each verse, followed by the* קהל:

אָנָּא סְלַח נָא / פֶּשַׁע וְעָוֹן שָׂא נָא
וְכֹחֲךָ יִגְדַּל נָא.
קָדוֹשׁ.

The שליח ציבור *then the* קהל.

אָנָּא רַחוּם כַּפֵּר / עֲוֹן צָגִים, תְּהִלָּתְךָ לְסַפֵּר
וְיָחֹקּוּ לְחַיִּים בַּסֵּפֶר.
קָדוֹשׁ.

In many congregations, the שליח ציבור *says the first two stichs, the* קהל *says the third, and the alternating refrains are said by all.*

ש״ץ: **מוֹרֶה חַטָּאִים סֶלָּה לְהִתְהַלֵּךְ / מְלַמֵּד לְהַדְרִיכִי בְּדֶרֶךְ אֵלֵךְ**
קהל: **אֲרוֹמִמְךָ אֱלוֹהַי הַמֶּלֶךְ:**

ש״ץ: **שַׁחַר וָנֶשֶׁף אֲיַחֵד לְהַמְלִיכֶךָ / שׁוֹכֵן עַד וְאֵין כְּעֶרְכֶּךָ**
קהל: **בְּכָל־יוֹם אֲבָרְכֶךָּ:**

ש״ץ: **לְבִי חָרֵד עֲבוֹדָתְךָ לִתְמֹד / לְהַעֲרִיץ קְדֻשָּׁתְךָ בְּמִשְׁמָר אֶעֱמֹד**
קהל: **גָּדוֹל יהוה וּמְהֻלָּל מְאֹד:**

אָנָּא סְלַח נָא / פֶּשַׁע וְעָוֹן שָׂא נָא / וְכֹחֲךָ יִגְדַּל נָא. קָדוֹשׁ.

וְכֹחֲךָ יִגְדַּל נָא *That Your strength might be exalted.* A reference to Moses' words when he pleaded for forgiveness for the people after their demoralization by the spies, when he said "Now may the LORD's strength be exalted" (Num. 14:17). Strength here means the power to forgive. Forgiveness is not moral weakness but moral strength.

מוֹרֶה חַטָּאִים *You who instruct sinners.* A prayer whose double acrostic bears the name of its composer, Meshullam bei-Rabbi Kalonymus. Each verse

Leader: The offspring of those borne by You await Your kindness; / may those who find shelter in You rejoice as You fulfill their requests.

Cong: One generation will praise Your works to the next.

Leader: With entreaty and fasting they go forth to serve You, / for they have been created for Your glory.

Cong: The glorious splendor of Your majesty.

Leader: The honor of Your kingdom, trembling they proclaim; / they would never exchange Your uniqueness for foreign dominion.

Cong: They shall speak of the power of Your awesome deeds.

We beg of You, O Compassionate One, grant atonement
for the iniquity of those assembled, that Your praise might be told,
and may they be inscribed for life in Your book – O Holy One.

Leader: Four prayers they shall sing before You, / as they murmur words of praise seven times each day.

Cong: They shall recite the record of Your great goodness.

Leader: In the morning I shall offer up my pleas to You; / by the approach of evening may You erase my willful sins.

Cong: The Lord is gracious and compassionate.

Leader: Lord, Rock of all, who atones, / suppress our iniquities and let all beings declare:

Cong: The Lord is good to all.

We beg of You, please forgive us, / please pardon willful sin and iniquity,
that Your strength might be exalted – O Holy One.

Leader: Raise [the Temple] You once desired in the city of Your joy, where the holy stones of Your crown were hoisted on high.

Cong: All Your works shall thank You, Lord.

Leader: Your Levites and pious ones will pleasantly sing, / and the priests in their vestments will raise up the incense offering.

Cong: They shall talk of the glory of Your kingship.

Leader: Those planted in Your abode will blossom in its courtyards; they will be fruitful in old age, vigorous in its palaces.

Cong: To make known to mankind His mighty deeds.

We beg of You, O Compassionate One, grant atonement
for the iniquity of those assembled, that Your praise might be told,
and may they be inscribed for life in Your book – O Holy One.

ש״ץ: מְיַחֲלִים לְחַסְדְּךָ זֶרַע עֲמוּסֶיךָ
מַלֵּא מִשְׁאֲלוֹתָם, וְיִשְׂמְחוּ חוֹסֶיךָ
קהל: דּוֹר לְדוֹר יְשַׁבַּח מַעֲשֶׂיךָ:

ש״ץ: בְּחִלּוּי וָצוֹם גָּשִׁים לְעָבְדֶךָ / בְּרוּאִים, כִּי הֵם לִכְבוֹדֶךָ
קהל: הֲדַר כְּבוֹד הוֹדֶךָ:

ש״ץ: יְקָר מַלְכוּתְךָ בְּרַעַד יַאֲמִירוּ / יִחוּדְךָ בְּזָר לֹא יָמִירוּ
קהל: וֶעֱזוּז נוֹרְאוֹתֶיךָ יֹאמֵרוּ:

אָנָּא רַחוּם כַּפֵּר / עֲוֹן צָגִים, תְּהִלָּתְךָ לְסַפֵּר / וְיָחֲקוּ לְחַיִּים בַּסֵּפֶר. קָדוֹשׁ.

ש״ץ: רָן פְּגִיעוֹת לְפָנֶיךָ יַרְבֵּעוּ / רַחֵשׁ הִלּוּלְךָ בַּיּוֹם יְשַׁבֵּעוּ
קהל: זֵכֶר רַב־טוּבְךָ יַבִּיעוּ:

ש״ץ: בֹּקֶר אֶעֱרָךְ לְךָ חִנּוּנַי / בִּפְנוֹת עֶרֶב תִּמְחֶה זְדוֹנַי
קהל: חַנּוּן וְרַחוּם יהוה:

ש״ץ: יָהּ, צוּר, כֹּפֶר אֶשְׁכֹּל / יִכְבֹּשׁ עֲווֹנֵינוּ וְיֹאמְרוּ הַכֹּל
קהל: טוֹב־יהוה לַכֹּל:

אָנָּא סְלַח נָא / פֶּשַׁע וְעָוֹן שָׂא נָא / וְכֹחֲךָ יִגְדַּל נָא. קָדוֹשׁ.

ש״ץ: קוֹמֵם אִוּוּי קִרְיַת מְשׂוֹשֶׂךָ / קֻדֶּשֶׁת אַבְנֵי נֵזֶר בְּנוֹסְסֶךָ
קהל: יוֹדוּךָ יהוה כָּל־מַעֲשֶׂיךָ:

ש״ץ: לְוִיֶּיךָ וַחֲסִידֶיךָ בְּנֹעַם יְזַמֵּרוּ / לְבוּשֵׁי שְׂרָד רֶקַח יִתְאַמֵּרוּ
קהל: כְּבוֹד מַלְכוּתְךָ יֹאמֵרוּ:

ש״ץ: וּשְׁתוּלִים בְּנָוְךָ יַפְרִיחוּ בְּחַצְרוֹתָיו
וְינוּבוּן בְּשֵׂיבָה, דְּשֵׁנִים בְּטִירוֹתָיו
קהל: לְהוֹדִיעַ לִבְנֵי הָאָדָם גְּבוּרֹתָיו:

אָנָּא רַחוּם כַּפֵּר / עֲוֹן צָגִים, תְּהִלָּתְךָ לְסַפֵּר / וְיָחֲקוּ לְחַיִּים בַּסֵּפֶר. קָדוֹשׁ.

Leader: Your innocent and perfect ones shall sing of Your eternity, as You raise Your throne in Your eternal House.

Cong: Your kingdom is an everlasting kingdom.

Leader: As You gather the redeemed together in Your dwelling, / they shall clothe You with might like those who crossed the waves [of the Sea of Reeds].

Cong: The LORD supports all who fall.

Leader: Those who speak of Your goodness shall congregate together; please receive as lush sacrifices the prayers that they offer.

Cong: All raise their eyes to You in hope.

We beg of You, please forgive us, / please pardon willful sin and iniquity,
that Your strength might be exalted – O Holy One.

Leader: Receive the gift of Your congregation's confession as a pleasing offering, / and may the prayers of Your witnesses take the place of sacrificed bullocks.

Cong: You open Your hand.

Leader: May He, in His compassion, glimpse [His people] through His lattices, / and grant great forgiveness to His blessed nation.

Cong: The LORD is righteous in all His ways.

Leader: Heed the prayers of the nation You have named; / show favor to the people who read out Your scriptures faithfully.

Cong: The LORD is close to all who call on Him.

We beg of You, O Compassionate One, grant atonement
for the iniquity of those assembled, that Your praise might be told,
and may they be inscribed for life in Your book – O Holy One.

Leader: This is my God, He performs wonders; / He shall accept our cries and crush our foes.

Cong: He fulfills the will of those who revere Him.

Leader: He gives hope to those who cast their burdens upon Him; / may the Holy One cover our iniquities with His love.

Cong: The LORD guards all who love Him.

Leader: Accept the prayers poured from my heart as the height of beauty; listen to my voice and cast all faults into the depths of the sea.

Cong: My mouth shall speak the praise of the LORD.

We beg of You, please forgive us, / please pardon willful sin and iniquity,
that Your strength might be exalted – O Holy One.

ש״ץ: נִצְחֲךָ יְנַגְּנוּ תְּמִימִים וּשְׁלֵמִים
נְשָׂאֲךָ כִּסְאֲךָ בְּבֵית עוֹלָמִים
קהל: מַלְכוּתְךָ מַלְכוּת כָּל־עֹלָמִים:

ש״ץ: יַחַד בְּכַנֶּסְךָ לְשִׁכְנְךָ גְּאוּלִים / יַלְבִּישׁוּךָ עֹז כְּעוֹבְרֵי גַלִּים
קהל: סוֹמֵךְ יהוה לְכָל־הַנֹּפְלִים:

ש״ץ: מַבִּיעֵי טוּבְךָ בְּוַעַד יִתְחַבְּרוּ / מֵחִים חֲשֹׁב תָּחֹן יְדַבֵּרוּ
קהל: עֵינֵי־כֹל אֵלֶיךָ יְשַׂבֵּרוּ:

אָנָּא סְלַח נָא / פֶּשַׁע וְעָוֹן שָׂא נָא / וְכֹחֲךָ יִגְדַּל נָא. קָדוֹשׁ.

ש״ץ: וְדוּיִם יְנוּחַת שַׁי עָדֶיךָ / וִישַׁלֵּם פָּרִים אֶרֶשׁ עֲדֶיךָ
קהל: פּוֹתֵחַ אֶת־יָדֶךָ:

ש״ץ: סֶלָה בְּרַחֲמָיו יָצִיץ מֵחֲרַכָּיו / סְלַח יַרְבֶּה לְעַם מְבָרְכָיו
קהל: צַדִּיק יהוה בְּכָל־דְּרָכָיו:

ש״ץ: חִין יֶשַׁע מְגוֹי מְקָרְאָיו / חֹן יָחֹן קוֹרְאֵי מִקְרָאָיו
קהל: קָרוֹב יהוה לְכָל־קֹרְאָיו:

אָנָּא רַחוּם כַּפֵּר / עֲוֹן צָגִים, תְּהִלָּתְךָ לְסַפֵּר / וְיָחֹקוּ לְחַיִּים בַּסֵּפֶר. קָדוֹשׁ.

ש״ץ: זֶה אֵלִי, פֶּלֶא עוֹשֶׂה / זַעֲקֵנוּ יֵרֶץ וְשׁוֹטְנֵינוּ יַעֲשֶׂה
קהל: רְצוֹן־יְרֵאָיו יַעֲשֶׂה:

ש״ץ: קִוּוּי יִתֵּן לְלוֹ מַשְׁלִיךְ יְהָבָיו / קָדוֹשׁ פְּשָׁעֵינוּ יְכַסֶּה בְּאַהֲבָיו
קהל: שׁוֹמֵר יהוה אֶת־כָּל־אֹהֲבָיו:

ש״ץ: קַבֵּל צִקּוּנִי כִּבְמִכְלַל יֹפִי / קוֹלִי תַּאֲזִין וְתַצְלִיל דֹּפִי
קהל: תְּהִלַּת יהוה יְדַבֶּר פִּי:

אָנָּא סְלַח נָא / פֶּשַׁע וְעָוֹן שָׂא נָא / וְכֹחֲךָ יִגְדַּל נָא. קָדוֹשׁ.

As in the previous piyut, the following verses serve as alternating refrains for the piyut אַדִּר יְקַר אֵלִי *(page 1291); however, many congregations omit the piyut, saying only the refrains.*

The Leader says each verse, followed by the congregation:

מֶלֶךְ O King who dwells eternally,
You alone shall reign for all eternity –
O Holy God.

מֶלֶךְ O King who heeds His faithful's call,
who hastens salvation for His people –
O Awesome, Holy One.

Some congregations say the piyut אָנָּא אֱלֹהִים חַיִּים *(page 1293) at this point. Originally, the following stanza was the refrain of the piyut* אֵימָתְךָ בְּחַר *(page 1294). Nowadays, most congregations omit the piyut, saying only the refrain.*

The Leader, followed by the congregation:

הַיּוֹם יִכָּתֵב Today, in the book of memories,
life and death will be inscribed.
Please, you stem [of the vine of Israel] –
awaken, please; wake up, please;
stand up, please; stand firm, please;
rise up, please; entreat, please;
beseech, please, for your soul,
with the One who dwells on high.

Some congregations say the piyut וּבְכֵן, אַךְ חַנּוּן אַתָּה *(page 1296) at this point.*

The Ark is opened.

The congregation then the Leader:

וּבְכֵן And so, you shall say of God: How awesome are Your works! *Ps. 66*

In many congregations, the congregation recites each stanza, and the Leader repeats it. Some sing the entire piyut collectively. Although each stanza opens with the phrase "Say of God," many have the custom to say it at the end of each stanza.

אִמְרוּ לֵאלֹהִים Say of God:
He is slow to anger and great of strength; *Nah. 9*
He founded the mountains with strength.
Wise of heart and powerfully strong, / He offers strength to the weary. *Job 9* *Is. 40*
Therefore, exalt Him, our mighty Master of great strength. *Ps. 147*

אִמְרוּ לֵאלֹהִים *Say of God.* A long poem by Rabbi Meshullam ben Kalonymus, on the theme of God the Creator and the majesty of His creation, based on

As in the previous piyut, the following verses serve as alternating refrains for the piyut אָדִּיר יְקָר אֵלִי *(page 1291); however, many congregations omit the piyut, saying only the refrains.*

The שליח ציבור *says each verse, followed by the* קהל*:*

מֶלֶךְ שׁוֹכֵן עַד / לְבַדְּךָ מְלֹךְ עֲדֵי עַד
הָאֵל קָדוֹשׁ.

מֶלֶךְ מַאֲזִין שַׁוְעָה / לְעַמּוֹ מֵחִישׁ יְשׁוּעָה
נוֹרָא וְקָדוֹשׁ.

Some congregations say the piyut אָנָּא אֱלֹהִים חַיִּים *(page 1293) at this point. Originally, the following stanza was the refrain of the piyut* אֵימָה בָּחַר *(page 1294). Nowadays, most congregations omit the piyut, saying only the refrain.*

The שליח ציבור*, followed by the* קהל*:*

הַיּוֹם יִכָּתֵב בְּסֵפֶר הַזִּכְרוֹנוֹת, הַחַיִּים וְהַמָּוֶת.
אָנָּא כַּנָּה, עוּרִי נָא, הִתְעוֹרְרִי נָא
עִמְדִי נָא, הִתְיַצְּבִי נָא, קוּמִי נָא, חַלִּי נָא
בְּעַד הַנֶּפֶשׁ חַנִּי נָא, פְּנֵי דָּר עֶלְיוֹן.

Some congregations say the piyut וּבְכֵן, אַךְ חַנּוּן אַתָּה *(page 1296) at this point.*

The ארון קודש *is opened.*

The קהל *then the* שליח ציבור*:*

וּבְכֵן, אִמְרוּ לֵאלֹהִים, מַה־נּוֹרָא מַעֲשֶׂיךָ: תהלים סו

In many congregations, the קהל *recites each stanza, and the* שליח ציבור *repeats it. Some sing the entire piyut collectively. Although each stanza opens with the phrase "*אִמְרוּ לֵאלֹהִים*," many have the custom to say it at the end of each stanza.*

אִמְרוּ לֵאלֹהִים
אֶרֶךְ אַפַּיִם וּגְדָל־כֹּחַ / מֵכִין הָרִים בְּכֹחַ נחום א
חֲכַם לֵבָב וְאַמִּיץ כֹּחַ / נֹתֵן לַיָּעֵף כֹּחַ איוב ט ישעיה מ
לָכֵן יִתְגָּאֶה, גָּדוֹל אֲדוֹנֵינוּ וְרַב־כֹּחַ: תהלים קמז

הַיּוֹם יִכָּתֵב *Today… will be inscribed.* Taken from a longer poem, this is an aside to the congregation, passionately urging them to pay attention and recall the gravity of the day – the day on which our fate is inscribed in God's book.

Say of God:
He builds His heights in the heavens, *Amos 9*
He waters the mountains from His upper chambers, *Ps. 104*
He made a memorial of His wondrous works, *Ps. 111*
and by Him are all actions weighed.
Therefore, exalt Him, He who beams His upper chambers with waters. *Ps. 104*

Say of God:
Exalted and lofty in His heavenly heights,
He wears light as a garment.
To Him belongs all strength and grandeur, / might and dominion.
Therefore, exalt Him, He whose kingdom reigns over all. *Ps. 103*

Say of God:
Distinguished among holy myriads, / glorious in His holiness,
His ways are holy, / and all bow before Him in holy splendor.
Therefore, exalt Him, my God, my King who walks in holiness. *Ps. 68*

Say of God:
His splendor covers the heavens,
He spreads the earth over the water.
He thunders from the heavens,
sending down multitudes of resounding waters. *Jer. 51*
Therefore, exalt Him, He who spreads out the heavens like a veil. *Is. 40*

Say of God:
He measured out the dust of the earth; / His hand founded the earth. *Ibid.*
His right hand extended the awesome heavens
that they might stand unbreached.
Therefore, exalt Him, He who sits enthroned *Ibid.*
upon the vault of the earth.

---

the verse: "Say of God: How awesome are Your works" (Ps. 66:3) – "Say" in the sense of "praise, declare." וְכָל בַּשָּׁלִשׁ *He measured out:* An allusion to Isaiah (40:12): "Who has measured the waters in the hollow of his hand, or with

אִמְרוּ לֵאלֹהִים
בּוֹנֶה בַשָּׁמַיִם מַעֲלוֹתָו / מַשְׁקֶה הָרִים מֵעֲלִיּוֹתָיו עמוס ט / תהלים קד
זֵכֶר עָשָׂה לְנִפְלְאֹתָיו / וְלוֹ נִתְכְּנוּ עֲלִלוֹתָיו תהלים קיא
לָכֵן יִתְגָּאֶה, הַמְקָרֶה בַמַּיִם עֲלִיּוֹתָיו: תהלים קד

אִמְרוּ לֵאלֹהִים
גֵּאָה וְגָבְהָ בִּשְׁמֵי מַעְלָה / עֹטֶה אוֹר כַּשַּׂלְמָה
לוֹ הַגְּבוּרָה וְהַגְּדֻלָּה / וְהָעֹז וְהַמֶּמְשָׁלָה
לָכֵן יִתְגָּאֶה, וּמַלְכוּתוֹ בַּכֹּל מָשָׁלָה: תהלים קג

אִמְרוּ לֵאלֹהִים
דָּגוּל מֵרְבְבוֹת קֹדֶשׁ / וְנֶאְדָּר בַּקֹּדֶשׁ
דְּרָכוֹ בַקֹּדֶשׁ / וּמִשְׁתַּחֲוִים לוֹ בְּהַדְרַת קֹדֶשׁ
לָכֵן יִתְגָּאֶה, הֲלִיכוֹת אֵלִי מַלְכִּי בַקֹּדֶשׁ: תהלים סח

אִמְרוּ לֵאלֹהִים
הוֹדוֹ כִּסָּה שָׁמַיִם / וְהָאָרֶץ רוֹקַע עַל הַמָּיִם
יַרְעֵם מִשָּׁמַיִם / לְקוֹל תִּתּוֹ הֲמוֹן מַיִם ירמיה נא
לָכֵן יִתְגָּאֶה, הַנּוֹטֶה כַדֹּק שָׁמַיִם: ישעיה מ

אִמְרוּ לֵאלֹהִים
וְכָל בַּשָּׁלִשׁ עֲפַר הָאָרֶץ / יָדוֹ יִסְּדָה אָרֶץ שם
וִימִינוֹ טִפְּחָה שְׁמֵי עֶרֶץ / וְהֶעֱמִידָם בְּלִי פֶרֶץ
לָכֵן יִתְגָּאֶה, הַיֹּשֵׁב עַל־חוּג הָאָרֶץ: שם

Say of God:
The brightness of His throne is as fiery sparks,
His servants blaze with fire.
Shining like fire and bursting forth in lightning,
rivers of fire flow before Him.
Therefore, exalt Him, the Fiery One who consumes fire.

Say of God:
He lives forever,
He created worlds with His holy name, He desired an eternal abode,
His temple where He might reside forever.
Therefore, exalt Him, Ancient of Days.

Say of God:
He whose eyes are pure,
He is surrounded by clouds of water,
full clouds of heaven, dark with precipitation,
the outriders who bear His chariot have eyes all around.
Therefore, exalt Him, the command of the Lord is pure, *Ps. 19*
enlightening the eyes.

Say of God:
He knows what lies in hidden obscurity;
the dark conceals nothing from Him.
He ordained an end to darkness, *Job 28*
turning the dark shadow of death into daylight.
Therefore, exalt Him, He who forms light and creates darkness. *Is. 45*

Say of God:
He has established His throne for justice,
the seat of His reign is righteousness and justice.
He is the God of justice,
brandishing justice in His hand like a sword.
Therefore, exalt Him, the Lord of hosts who shall rise in justice. *Is. 5*

---

has fashioned the universe with the architectonic precision Tanakh calls "wisdom." The more we learn of cosmology, the more we are beginning to appreciate how finely tuned the universe is for the emergence, first of stars, then of planets, then of life, then of us.

אִמְרוּ לֵאלֹהִים
זֹהַר כִּסְאוֹ שְׁבִיבֵי אֵשׁ / מְשָׁרְתָיו לַהַט אֵשׁ
נֹגַהּ לָאֵשׁ וּמַבְרִיק הָאֵשׁ / לְפָנָיו נִמְשָׁכִים נַהֲרֵי אֵשׁ
לָכֵן יִתְגָּאֶה, אֵשׁ אֹכְלָה אֵשׁ.

אִמְרוּ לֵאלֹהִים
חַי עוֹלָמִים / צָר בְּיָהּ עוֹלָמִים
אִוָּה בֵּית עוֹלָמִים / מָכוֹן לְשִׁבְתּוֹ עוֹלָמִים
לָכֵן יִתְגָּאֶה, עַתִּיק יוֹמִין.

אִמְרוּ לֵאלֹהִים
טְהוֹר עֵינַיִם / סְבִיבוֹתָיו חַשְׁרַת מַיִם
עָבֵי שְׁחָק חֶשְׁכַת מַיִם / טוֹעֲנֵי מֶרְכַּבְתּוֹ, גַּבּוֹתָם מְלֵאוֹת עֵינַיִם
לָכֵן יִתְגָּאֶה, מִצְוַת יהוה בָּרָה מְאִירַת עֵינָיִם: תהלים יט

אִמְרוּ לֵאלֹהִים
יוֹדֵעַ מַה בְּסִתְרֵי חֹשֶׁךְ / לֹא יַחְשִׁיךְ מֶנּוּ חֹשֶׁךְ
קֵץ שָׂם לַחֹשֶׁךְ / הֹפֵךְ לַבֹּקֶר צַלְמָוֶת וְחֹשֶׁךְ איוב כח
לָכֵן יִתְגָּאֶה, יוֹצֵר אוֹר וּבוֹרֵא חֹשֶׁךְ: ישעיה מה

אִמְרוּ לֵאלֹהִים
כּוֹנֵן כִּסְאוֹ לַמִּשְׁפָּט / מְכוֹן כִּסְאוֹ צֶדֶק וּמִשְׁפָּט
אֱלֹהֵי הַמִּשְׁפָּט / תֹּאחֵז יָדוֹ בְּמִשְׁפָּט
לָכֵן יִתְגָּאֶה, וַיִּגְבַּהּ יהוה צְבָאוֹת בַּמִּשְׁפָּט: ישעיה ה

---

the breadth of his hand marked off the heavens?" זֹהַר כִּסְאוֹ *The brightness of His throne:* A mystical vision based on the visions of Ezekiel and, especially, Daniel: "His throne was flaming with fire, and its wheels were all ablaze. A river of fire was flowing, coming out from before Him" (Dan. 7:9–10).

Fundamental to this poem, as throughout the Bible, is the sense that God

Say of God:
Royalty befits Him;
He dwells in eternity, yet is with the downtrodden.
He returns man to the dust,
yet He asks that we humbly repent and return to Him.
Therefore, exalt Him, for the LORD's is the kingdom. *Ps. 22*

Say of God:
In His might He rules the world, / all is foreseen, nothing is hidden. *Ps. 66*
His name is everlasting
and His loving-kindness extends throughout eternity.
Therefore, exalt Him – *Ps. 41*
Blessed be the LORD, God of Israel, for all eternity.

Say of God:
He extends loving-kindness to a thousand generations,
and battles those who rise against Him
from generation to generation.
He will raise the tabernacle of His anointed one,
repairing its breached walls;
light itself is encamped in His abode.
Therefore, exalt Him, – *Ex. 3*
This is My remembrance from generation to generation.

Say of God:
He accepts the lofty and the lowly ones, *Ps. 69*
He hears the call of the destitute, lends His ear to words of entreaty,
heeds the cry of prayers.
Therefore, exalt Him, the God of gods and Master of all masters. *Deut. 10*

Say of God:
He is a mighty and powerful warrior,
He takes revenge from His foes and is capable of righteous ire.
He lays low wanton rebels in great confusion,
roaring at them like the thundering seas.
Therefore, exalt Him, the LORD, Master of war. *Ex. 15*

אִמְרוּ לֵאלֹהִים
לוֹ יָאֲתָה מְלוּכָה / שׁוֹכֵן עַד, וְאֶת דַּכָּא
מֵשִׁיב אֱנוֹשׁ עַד דַּכָּא / וְאוֹמֵר, שׁוּבוּ בְּרוּחַ נְמוּכָה
לָכֵן יִתְגָּאֶה, כִּי לַיהוה הַמְּלוּכָה: תהלים כב

אִמְרוּ לֵאלֹהִים
מֹשֵׁל בִּגְבוּרָתוֹ עוֹלָם / הַכֹּל צָפוּי וְלֹא נֶעְלָם תהלים סו
זֶה שְׁמוֹ לְעוֹלָם / חַסְדּוֹ מֵעוֹלָם וְעַד עוֹלָם
לָכֵן יִתְגָּאֶה, בָּרוּךְ יהוה אֱלֹהֵי יִשְׂרָאֵל, מֵהָעוֹלָם וְעַד־הָעוֹלָם: תהלים מא

אִמְרוּ לֵאלֹהִים
נוֹצֵר חֶסֶד לָאֶלֶף דּוֹר / לוֹחֵם קָמָיו מִדּוֹר לְדוֹר
מֵקִים סֻכַּת מְשִׁיחוֹ לִגְדֹּר / הָאוֹר חוֹנֶה עִמּוֹ בְּמָדוֹר
לָכֵן יִתְגָּאֶה, וְזֶה זִכְרִי לְדֹר דֹּר: שמות ג

אִמְרוּ לֵאלֹהִים
סוֹבֵל עֶלְיוֹנִים וְתַחְתּוֹנִים / שֹׁמֵעַ אֶל־אֶבְיוֹנִים תהלים סט
מַאֲזִין שִׂיחַ חִנּוּנִים / מַקְשִׁיב שֶׁוַע רְנָנִים
לָכֵן יִתְגָּאֶה, אֱלֹהֵי הָאֱלֹהִים וַאֲדֹנֵי הָאֲדֹנִים: דברים י

אִמְרוּ לֵאלֹהִים
עִזּוּז וְגִבּוֹר מִלְחָמָה / נוֹקֵם לְצָרָיו וּבַעַל חֵמָה
מַכְרִית קָמִים בִּמְהוּמָה / נוֹהֵם עֲלֵיהֶם בִּנְהִימָה
לָכֵן יִתְגָּאֶה, יהוה אִישׁ מִלְחָמָה: שמות טו

Say of God:
He forms and creates all things;
in His hands lies the power to glorify and strengthen all things.
To Him all eyes are raised in hope, / His eyes range over all.
Therefore, exalt Him, He who is supreme over all. *Ps. 83*

Say of God:
He is righteous in all His ways,
the Upright One glimpses all through His lattices.
Desirous of the nation that enthrones Him,
those He has blessed shall inherit the earth.
Therefore, exalt Him – Bless the LORD, you His angels. *Ps. 103*

Say of God:
He who planned all generations in advance, *Is. 41*
foretells the end from the beginning.
He chose a humble nation / to beseech His valor daily.
Therefore, exalt Him, exalted as Head over all. *1 Chr. 29*

Say of God:
High and lofty, He dwells in eternity, *Is. 57*
place your trust in Him forever.
His glory He intended for His holy ones
and for the people bound to Him in sanctity.
Therefore, exalt Him, He who gazes at the earth and it trembles. *Ps. 104*

Say of God:
He cuts His path through rising waters,
causes His heavens to shower copious rains.
His name is proclaimed unique in prayers both morning and evening,
inside the gates where multitudes gather.
Therefore, exalt Him, the LORD of hosts enthroned upon His Cherubim. *1 Sam. 4*

Say of God:
His glory fills the earth, / bringing upon it utter destruction. *Hab. 3*
He turns back anger and ruin,
accepting the pleas of those who pray to Him humbly.
Therefore, exalt Him, the LORD our Master – *Ps. 8*
glorious is Your name throughout the earth.

אִמְרוּ לֵאלֹהִים
פּוֹעֵל וְעוֹשֶׂה הַכֹּל / בְּיָדוֹ לְגַדֵּל וּלְחַזֵּק לַכֹּל
אֵלָיו יְשַׂבְּרוּ עֵינֵי כֹל / עֵינָיו מְשׁוֹטְטוֹת בַּכֹּל
לָכֵן יִתְגָּאֶה, עֶלְיוֹן עַל־כֹּל: תהלים פג

אִמְרוּ לֵאלֹהִים
צַדִּיק בְּכָל דְּרָכָיו / יָשָׁר מֵצִיץ מֵחֲרַכָּיו
חָפֵץ בְּעַם מַמְלִיכָיו / יִירְשׁוּ אֶרֶץ מְבֹרָכָיו
לָכֵן יִתְגָּאֶה, בָּרְכוּ יהוה מַלְאָכָיו: תהלים קג

אִמְרוּ לֵאלֹהִים
קֹרֵא הַדֹּרוֹת מֵרֹאשׁ / מַגִּיד אַחֲרִית מֵרֹאשׁ ישעיה מא
בָּחַר בְּאֹם דַּלַּת רֹאשׁ / עֻזּוֹ יוֹם יוֹם לִדְרֹשׁ
לָכֵן יִתְגָּאֶה, וְהַמִּתְנַשֵּׂא לְכֹל לְרֹאשׁ: דברי הימים א׳ כט

אִמְרוּ לֵאלֹהִים
רָם וְנִשָּׂא, שֹׁכֵן עַד / בִּטְחוּ בוֹ עֲדֵי עַד ישעיה נז
כְּבוֹדוֹ בְּסוֹד קְדוֹשִׁים וָעַד / וּלְעַם קְדוֹשׁוֹ נוֹעַד
לָכֵן יִתְגָּאֶה, הַמַּבִּיט לָאָרֶץ וַתִּרְעָד: תהלים קד

אִמְרוּ לֵאלֹהִים
שְׁבִילוֹ בְּמַיִם רַבִּים / שָׁמָיו מַרְעִיף רְבִיבִים
שְׁמוֹ מְיַחֲדִים שַׁחַר וַעֲרָבִים / בְּשַׁעַר בַּת רַבִּים
לָכֵן יִתְגָּאֶה, יהוה צְבָאוֹת יֹשֵׁב הַכְּרֻבִים: שמואל א׳ ד

אִמְרוּ לֵאלֹהִים
תְּהִלָּתוֹ מָלְאָה הָאָרֶץ / מַעֲבִיר כִּלָּיוֹן וְחָרֶץ חבקוק ג
מֵשִׁיב חֲרוֹן אַף וָקֶרֶץ / שֶׁוַע מְחַנְנָיו יֶרֶץ
לָכֵן יִתְגָּאֶה, יהוה אֲדֹנֵינוּ, מָה־אַדִּיר שִׁמְךָ בְּכָל־הָאָרֶץ: תהלים ח

The congregation then the Leader:

Indeed, the works of our God are sublime.

In many congregations, the congregation recites each stanza, and the Leader repeats it. Some sing the entire piyut collectively. Although each stanza opens with the phrase "The work of our God," many have the custom to say it at the end of each stanza.

מַעֲשֵׂה אֱלֹהֵינוּ The work of our God:
None in heaven can compare to Him,
none among the angels can be likened to Him.
He raised the high heavens for His residence,
and those living on earth below are like insects before Him.
Therefore, exalt Him,
the Rock whose works are pure. *Deut. 32*

The work of our God:
Sovereignty and awe are His, *Job 25*
and in Him redemption abounds.
Cries and whispers make their way to Him;
He hastens to listen from His heights.
Therefore, exalt Him –
the Lord of hosts is His name. *Is. 48*

The work of our God:
He provides sustenance to those who fear Him; *Ps. 111*
gifts shall be granted to those in awe of Him.
The legions of His angelic hosts
cannot look directly on His countenance.
Therefore, exalt Him –
Behold, the eye of the Lord is turned to all who fear Him. *Ps. 33*

---

him little lower than the angels, and crowned him with glory and honor" (Ps. 8:5–6). Only on Yom Kippur, with its themes of the mortality and sinfulness of man, do we give prominence to the more negative view, as we do at the

The קהל *then the* שליח ציבור:

וּבְכֵן, גְּדוֹלִים מַעֲשֵׂי אֱלֹהֵינוּ.

In many congregations, the קהל *recites each stanza, and the* שליח ציבור *repeats it. Some sing the entire piyut collectively. Although each stanza opens with the phrase "מַעֲשֵׂה אֱלֹהֵינוּ," many have the custom to say it at the end of each stanza.*

מַעֲשֵׂה אֱלֹהֵינוּ
אֵין מִי בַשַּׁחַק יַעֲרָךְ לוֹ / בִּבְנֵי אֵלִים יִדְמֶה לוֹ
גְּבֹהִים עָלָה לְמוֹשָׁב לוֹ / דָּרֵי גֵיא כַּחֲגָבִים לְמוּלוֹ
לָכֵן יִתְגָּאֶה, הַצּוּר תָּמִים פָּעֳלוֹ: דברים לב

מַעֲשֵׂה אֱלֹהֵינוּ
הַמְשֵׁל וָפַחַד עִמּוֹ / וְהַרְבֵּה פְדוּת עִמּוֹ איוב כה
זַעַק וְלַחַשׁ עַמּוֹ / חָשׁ וּמַאֲזִין מִמְּרוֹמוֹ
לָכֵן יִתְגָּאֶה, יהוה צְבָאוֹת שְׁמוֹ: ישעיה מח

מַעֲשֵׂה אֱלֹהֵינוּ
טֶרֶף נָתַן לִירֵאָיו / יֹבִילוּ שַׁי לְמוֹרָאָיו תהלים קיא
כִּתֵּי גְדוּדֵי צְבָאָיו / לֹא יָשְׁוּרוּ כְּבוֹד מַרְאָיו
לָכֵן יִתְגָּאֶה, הִנֵּה עֵין יהוה אֶל־יְרֵאָיו: תהלים לג

מַעֲשֵׂה אֱלֹהֵינוּ *The work of our God.* The original of this poem was much longer, every verse describing "the work of our God" followed by another, contrasting verse: "The deeds of man." The poem appears in abbreviated form in most rites, with all but one of the "deeds of man" verses omitted. As is evident from what remains, the poet took a dim view of humankind (compare Hamlet's "Yet, to me, what is this quintessence of dust?"). There is such a voice in both biblical and post-biblical literature, but for the most part Judaism lives with the paradox of "What is man that You are mindful of him? Yet You have made

The work of our God:
He appoints His winds as emissaries,
He is sanctified in songs and praises.
He heeds the outpouring of heartfelt pleas,
answering with the swift provision of succor.
Therefore, exalt Him,
the God of all spirits. *Num. 16*

The work of our God:
He redeems those He has borne from birth
from the pits of She'ol;
the eternal Rock acknowledges those who seek shelter with Him.
The Holy One works His miracles,
showing compassion equally
to those who please and displease Him.
Therefore, exalt Him,
He who shows compassion to all His creations. *Ps. 145*

The Ark is closed.

The deeds of man:
His plans are mere plots, / he lives in a world of deceit,
his berth is lined with maggots, / buried in a crevice in the ground.
Then how can man be exalted,
when he is like a vain breath? *Ps. 144*

The Ark is opened.

But the work of our God:
He hears the suppliant cry,
turns to those who raise their cry to Him,
His teachings are a source of true pleasure,
His tactics are a helmet of salvation.
Therefore, exalt Him,
the God who is our God of salvation. *Ps. 68*

The Ark is closed.

מַעֲשֵׂה אֱלֹהֵינוּ
מַלְאָכָיו עוֹשֶׂה רוּחוֹת / נִקְדָּשׁ בְּשִׁירוֹת וְתִשְׁבָּחוֹת
סוֹכֵת שְׁפִיכַת שִׂיחוֹת / עוֹנֶה וּמַעֲמִיד רְוָחוֹת
לָכֵן יִתְגָּאֶה, אֱלֹהֵי הָרוּחֹת: במדבר טז

מַעֲשֵׂה אֱלֹהֵינוּ
פּוֹדֶה מִשַּׁחַת עֲמוּסָיו / צוּר יוֹדֵעַ חוֹסָיו
קָדוֹשׁ מַפְלִיא נִסָּיו / רַחוּם לִמְרַצָּיו וּמַכְעִיסָיו
לָכֵן יִתְגָּאֶה, וְרַחֲמָיו עַל־כָּל־מַעֲשָׂיו: תהלים קמה

The ארון קודש *is closed.*

מַעֲשֵׂה אֱנוֹשׁ
תַּחְבּוּלוֹתָיו מְזִמָּה
שִׁבְתּוֹ בְּתוֹךְ מִרְמָה
רְפִידָתוֹ רִמָּה
קָבוּר בִּסְעִיף אֲדָמָה
וְאֵיךְ יִתְגָּאֶה, אָדָם לַהֶבֶל דָּמָה: תהלים קמד

The ארון קודש *is opened.*

אֲבָל מַעֲשֵׂה אֱלֹהֵינוּ
שׁוֹמֵעַ שַׁוְעוֹת / שׁוֹעֶה עֶרֶךְ שׁוּעוֹת
תּוֹרוֹתָיו מְשַׁעַשְׁעוֹת / תַּכְסִיסוֹ כּוֹבַע יְשׁוּעוֹת
לָכֵן יִתְגָּאֶה, הָאֵל לָנוּ אֵל לְמוֹשָׁעוֹת: תהלים סח

The ארון קודש *is closed.*

---

end of today's Amida: "Before I was formed I was unworthy, and now that I have been formed it is as if I had not been formed."

The following piyutim are usually sung by all before Kedusha to engender an atmosphere of sanctity and reverence.

The congregation then the Leader:

וּבְכֵן And so, in awe, they shall revere the One whose fear is upon them.

In some congregations, this piyut is said responsively, and in others it is sung by all. Some congregations omit it altogether.

אֲשֶׁר אֹמֶץ Even though Your mighty praise is
among the angels of heaven, / the beings that flash divine light,
the hosts on high, / and the still, small voice –
for Your sanctity is in their mouths.
Yet You desire praise
from those who call out to You in roaring throngs, / who lay out their cries,
who shout their prayers, / and await Your grace – for this is Your glory.

Even though Your mighty praise is
among the angels so pure, / the hastily fleeing angels,
the Cherubim who honor You, / and the heavenly legions with their swords – for Your sanctity is in their mouths.

Yet You desire praise
from mere mortals, with their numbered days, / whom all good has abandoned,
filled with anxiety, / and deeply grieved in their souls –
for this is Your glory.

Even though Your mighty praise is
among those whose names are concealed, / the wakeful angelic hosts,
the ancient holy ones, / and the myriad riders of His chariot –
for Your sanctity is in their mouths.

Yet You desire praise
from those who strive toward the [synagogue] doors, / who pour out their heartfelt pleas,
requesting Your forgiveness, / and desirous of atonement –
for this is Your glory.

---

to hear us, mere physical beings, turn to Him in praise. "Sanctity is in their mouths," that is, the mouths of the angels, but "You desire praise" from mortals, "with their numbered days, whom all good has abandoned, filled with anxiety, and deeply grieved in their souls – for this is Your glory."

The following piyutim are usually sung by all before קדושה *to engender an atmosphere of sanctity and reverence.*

The קהל *then the* שליח ציבור*:*

וּבְכֵן, לְנוֹרָא עֲלֵיהֶם בְּאֵימָה יַעֲרִיצוּ.

In some congregations, this piyut is said responsively, and in others it is sung by all. Some congregations omit it altogether.

אֲשֶׁר אָמְצְ תְּהִלָּתֶךָ
בְּאֵילֵי שַׁחַק / בִּבְרְקֵי נֹגַהּ
בִּגְדוּדֵי גֹבַהּ / בִּדְמָמָה דַקָּה וּקְדֻשָּׁתְךָ בְּפִיהֶם.
וְרָצִיתָ שֶׁבַח
מֵהוֹמֵי בְרֶגֶשׁ / וְעוֹרְכֵי שֶׁוַע
זוֹעֲקֵי תְחִנָּה / חוֹכֵי חֲנִינָה וְהִיא כְבוֹדֶךָ.

אֲשֶׁר אָמְצְ תְּהִלָּתֶךָ
בְּטַפְסְרֵי טֹהַר / בִּידִידוּן יְדִידוּן
בִּכְרוּבֵי כָבוֹד / בִּלְגְיוֹנֵי לַהַב וּקְדֻשָּׁתְךָ בְּפִיהֶם.
וְרָצִיתָ שֶׁבַח
מִמְּעוּטֵי יָמִים / נְשׁוּיֵי טוֹבָה
שְׂבֵעֵי רֹגֶז / עֲגוּמֵי נֶפֶשׁ וְהִיא כְבוֹדֶךָ.

אֲשֶׁר אָמְצְ תְּהִלָּתֶךָ
בִּפְלִיאֵי שֵׁמוֹת / בְּצִבְאוֹת עִירִין
בִּקְדוֹשֵׁי קֶדֶם / בְּרֶכֶב רִבֹּתַיִם וּקְדֻשָּׁתְךָ בְּפִיהֶם.
וְרָצִיתָ שֶׁבַח
מִשּׁוֹקְדֵי דְלָתוֹת / שׁוֹפְכֵי שִׂיחַ
תּוֹבְעֵי סְלִיחָה / תְּאֵבֵי כַפָּרָה וְהִיא כְבוֹדֶךָ.

אֲשֶׁר אָמְצְ תְּהִלָּתֶךָ *Even though Your mighty praise is…* As the *Kedusha* approaches, the poet – still Rabbi Meshullam – surprises us with the theological paradox he has set up in the previous sections of the poem. God is surrounded by angels who constantly sing His praises, yet it is from us, mere humans, that God desires praise. Somehow, despite our finitude, God's greatest desire is

The congregation then the Leader:

וּבְכֵן And so, ascribe strength to God, over Israel is His majesty. *Ps. 68*

All:

עַל יִשְׂרָאֵל Over Israel is His faith. Over Israel is His blessing.
Over Israel is His majesty. Over Israel is His word.
Over Israel is His glory. Over Israel is His assembly.
Over Israel is His remembrance. Over Israel is His compassion.
Over Israel is His purity. Over Israel is His candor.
Over Israel is His heritage. Over Israel is His nationhood.
Over Israel is His kingdom. Over Israel is His pleasing song.
Over Israel is His cherishing love. Over Israel, is His congregation.
Over Israel is His accomplishment. Over Israel is His righteousness.
Over Israel is His sanctity. Over Israel is His loftiness.
Over Israel is His Divine Presence. Over Israel is His splendor.

Some congregations recite the piyutim אַפְסֵי אֶרֶץ, מִי כָמוֹךָ *and* אֵין כָּמוֹךָ *(page 1297) at this point.*

The Ark is opened.

The congregation then the Leader:

וּבְכֵן And so, we shall glorify You who lives forever.

All:

הָאַדֶּרֶת Majesty and faithfulness are His who lives forever.
Understanding and blessing are His who lives forever.
Loftiness and greatness are His who lives forever.

הָאַדֶּרֶת וְהָאֱמוּנָה *Majesty and faithfulness.* The source of this poem is the mystical tract *Heikhalot Rabati*, a classic of what is known as *Heikhalot* literature, itself a branch of *Merkava* ("Chariot") mysticism based on Ezekiel's vision of God enthroned on the divine chariot. *Heikhalot Rabati* is an ancient text from Talmudic times, describing the ascent of Rabbi Yishmael to heaven. Jewish mystics, after long preparation involving fasting and meditation, would

The קהל *then the* שליח ציבור*:*

וּבְכֵן, תְּנוּ עֹז לֵאלֹהִים, עַל־יִשְׂרָאֵל גַּאֲוָתוֹ: תהלים סח

All:

עַל יִשְׂרָאֵל אֱמוּנָתוֹ עַל יִשְׂרָאֵל בִּרְכָתוֹ
עַל יִשְׂרָאֵל גַּאֲוָתוֹ עַל יִשְׂרָאֵל דִּבְרָתוֹ
עַל יִשְׂרָאֵל הַדְרָתוֹ עַל יִשְׂרָאֵל וְעִידָתוֹ
עַל יִשְׂרָאֵל זְכִירָתוֹ עַל יִשְׂרָאֵל חֶמְלָתוֹ
עַל יִשְׂרָאֵל טַהֲרָתוֹ עַל יִשְׂרָאֵל יְשָׁרָתוֹ
עַל יִשְׂרָאֵל כַּנָּתוֹ עַל יִשְׂרָאֵל לְאֻמָּתוֹ
עַל יִשְׂרָאֵל מַלְכוּתוֹ עַל יִשְׂרָאֵל נְעִימָתוֹ
עַל יִשְׂרָאֵל סְגֻלָּתוֹ עַל יִשְׂרָאֵל עֲדָתוֹ
עַל יִשְׂרָאֵל פְּעֻלָּתוֹ עַל יִשְׂרָאֵל צִדְקָתוֹ
עַל יִשְׂרָאֵל קְדֻשָּׁתוֹ עַל יִשְׂרָאֵל רוֹמְמוּתוֹ
עַל יִשְׂרָאֵל שְׁכִינָתוֹ עַל יִשְׂרָאֵל תִּפְאַרְתּוֹ.

Some congregations recite the piyutim אֵין כָּמוֹךָ ,אַפְסֵי אֶרֶץ *and* מִי כָמוֹךָ (*page 1297*) *at this point.*

The ארון קודש *is opened.*

The קהל *then the* שליח ציבור*:*

וּבְכֵן, נְאַדֶּרְךָ חַי עוֹלָמִים.

All:

הָאַדֶּרֶת וְהָאֱמוּנָה לְחַי עוֹלָמִים
הַבִּינָה וְהַבְּרָכָה לְחַי עוֹלָמִים
הַגַּאֲוָה וְהַגְּדֻלָּה לְחַי עוֹלָמִים

עַל יִשְׂרָאֵל *Over Israel.* The poet continues his paradoxical line of thought. We are frail, fallible creatures, yet You have endowed Your people Israel with Your faith, blessing, presence and glory.

Knowing and speech are His who lives forever.
Splendor and honor are His who lives forever.
Destiny and antiquity are His who lives forever.
Clarity and light are His who lives forever.
Power and intense might are His who lives forever.
Ceremony and purity are His who lives forever.
Unity and awe are His who lives forever
The crown and the honor are His who lives forever.
Teaching and learning are His who lives forever.
The realm and the rule are His who lives forever.
Beauty and eternity are His who lives forever.
Greatness and transcendence are His who lives forever.
Strength and humility are His who lives forever.
Salvation and glory are His who lives forever.
Radiance and righteousness are His who lives forever.
Declaration and sanctity are His who lives forever.
Fanfare and sublimity are His who lives forever.
▸ The song and the celebration are His who lives forever.
Praise and adoration are His who lives forever.

The Ark is closed.

---

often had a subterranean influence on Jewish prayer, understood itself as a heavenward ascent. According to *Heikhalot Rabati,* this is the song sung by the angels while we recite the Verses of Praise. Some rites (Sephardi and Nusaḥ Ari) say this psalm every Shabbat. Others do so only on Yom Kippur since on this day we are "like the angels," neither eating nor drinking but focused entirely on prayer. Therefore on this day alone may we sing the angels' song.

הַדֵּעָה וְהַדִּבּוּר לְחַי עוֹלָמִים
הַהוֹד וְהֶהָדָר לְחַי עוֹלָמִים
הַוַּעַד וְהַוָּתִיקוּת לְחַי עוֹלָמִים
הַזֹּךְ וְהַזֹּהַר לְחַי עוֹלָמִים
הַחַיִל וְהַחֹסֶן לְחַי עוֹלָמִים
הַטֶּכֶס וְהַטֹּהַר לְחַי עוֹלָמִים
הַיִּחוּד וְהַיִּרְאָה לְחַי עוֹלָמִים
הַכֶּתֶר וְהַכָּבוֹד לְחַי עוֹלָמִים
הַלֶּקַח וְהַלִּבּוּב לְחַי עוֹלָמִים
הַמְּלוּכָה וְהַמֶּמְשָׁלָה לְחַי עוֹלָמִים
הַנּוֹי וְהַנֵּצַח לְחַי עוֹלָמִים
הַסִּגּוּי וְהַשֶּׂגֶב לְחַי עוֹלָמִים
הָעֹז וְהָעֲנָוָה לְחַי עוֹלָמִים
הַפְּדוּת וְהַפְּאֵר לְחַי עוֹלָמִים
הַצְּבִי וְהַצֶּדֶק לְחַי עוֹלָמִים
הַקְּרִיאָה וְהַקְּדֻשָּׁה לְחַי עוֹלָמִים
הָרֹן וְהָרוֹמֵמוּת לְחַי עוֹלָמִים
◂ הַשִּׁיר וְהַשֶּׁבַח לְחַי עוֹלָמִים
הַתְּהִלָּה וְהַתִּפְאֶרֶת לְחַי עוֹלָמִים

The ארון קודש *is closed.*

---

experience ecstatic visions of an ascent into heaven, encountering there the mysteries of the divine palace, the *Heikhal*. Mystic texts such as these have

Some congregations recite the piyutim from נַאֲמִירָךְ בְּאֵימָה *to* הַנִּקְדָּשׁ בְּאַלְפֵי אֲלָפִים *(pages 1298–1300) at this point.*

Originally, the following verse was the refrain of the piyut אֵילֵי שַׁחַק *(page 1301). Nowadays, most congregations omit the piyut, saying only the refrain.*

The Leader, followed by the congregation:

לְיוֹשֵׁב תְּהִלּוֹת To the One enthroned upon praises,
who rides upon the clouds, / O Holy and Blessed One.

Originally, the following verse and stanza were the prelude to and the refrain of the piyut אֵין מִסְפָּר לִגְדוּדֵי *(page 1303). Nowadays, most congregations say only these.*

Responsively:

וּבְכֵן And so, the Seraphim hover about Him. Is. 6

They ask one another: Where is the God of gods,
where is the One whose abode is on high?
And they all proceed to honor, sanctify and praise.

The Ark is opened.

There follows an ancient piyut, author unknown, which most congregations add before Kedusha. In recent generations the custom to say it responsively has spread; many congregations are accustomed to saying the second stich of each couplet together with the first of the next one. Some sing the entire piyut collectively. However, traditionally this piyut is said only by the Leader, with the congregation joining in at "And so, sanctity will rise up to You."

וּבְכֵן And so, all shall crown You.

The God who renders judgment. / The One who examines hearts on the Day of Judgment.
The One who reveals deep secrets in judgment. / The One who speaks candidly on the Day of Judgment.
The One who voices His wisdom in judgment. / The One who is diligent and performs kindness on the Day of Judgment.
The One who recalls His covenant in judgment. / The One who shows compassion towards His creations on the Day of Judgment.
The One who purifies those who rely on Him in judgment. / The One who knows all inner thoughts on the Day of Judgment.

וּבְכֵן, לְךָ הַכֹּל יַכְתִּירוּ *And so, all shall crown You.* A powerful fugue, affirming both the awesome mood and nature of the day – God sitting in judgment on the Day of Judgment – yet also God's compassion and forgiveness. Without both, the human world could not survive. Without justice and judgment there would be anarchy, a war of all against all. But without compassion and forgiveness we would all be condemned, since "There is none on earth so righteous as to do only good and never sin" (Eccl. 7:20). The prayer is a segue into the *Kedusha*.

Some congregations recite the piyutim from נַאֲמִירָךְ בְּאֵימָה *to* הַנִּקְדָּשׁ בְּאַלְפֵי אֲלָפִים *(pages 1298–1300) at this point.*

Originally, the following verse was the refrain of the piyut אֵילֵי שַׁחַק *(page 1301). Nowadays, most congregations omit the piyut, saying only the refrain.*

The שליח ציבור*, followed by the* קהל:

לְיוֹשֵׁב תְּהִלּוֹת / לְרוֹכֵב עֲרָבוֹת / קָדוֹשׁ וּבָרוּךְ.

Originally, the following verse and stanza were the prelude to and the refrain of the piyut אֵין מִסְפָּר לִגְדוּדָי *(page 1303). Nowadays, most congregations say only these.*

Responsively:

וּבְכֵן, שְׂרָפִים עֹמְדִים מִמַּעַל לוֹ: ישעיה ו

זֶה אֶל זֶה שׁוֹאֲלִים

אַיֵּה אֵל אֵלִים

אָנָה שׁוֹכֵן מְעָלִים

וְכֻלָּם מַעֲרִיצִים וּמַקְדִּישִׁים וּמְהַלְלִים.

The ארון קודש *is opened.*

There follows an ancient piyut, author unknown, which most congregations add before קדושה*. In recent generations the custom to say it responsively has spread; many congregations are accustomed to saying the second stich of each couplet together with the first of the next one. Some sing the entire piyut collectively. However, traditionally this piyut is said only by the* שליח ציבור*, with the congregation joining in at "*וּבְכֵן לְךָ תַעֲלֶה קְדֻשָּׁה*" on the next page.*

וּבְכֵן, לְךָ הַכֹּל יַכְתִּירוּ.

לְאֵל עוֹרֵךְ דִּין לְבוֹחֵן לְבָבוֹת בְּיוֹם דִּין.

לְגוֹלֶה עֲמֻקּוֹת בַּדִּין לְדוֹבֵר מֵישָׁרִים בְּיוֹם דִּין.

לְהוֹגֶה דֵעוֹת בַּדִּין לְוָתִיק וְעוֹשֶׂה חֶסֶד בְּיוֹם דִּין.

לְזוֹכֵר בְּרִיתוֹ בַּדִּין לְחוֹמֵל מַעֲשָׂיו בְּיוֹם דִּין.

לְטַהֵר חוֹסָיו בַּדִּין לְיוֹדֵעַ מַחֲשָׁבוֹת בְּיוֹם דִּין.

לְיוֹשֵׁב תְּהִלּוֹת *To the One enthroned upon praises.* As we approach the *Kedusha*, the poet takes as his theme the fact that in the *Kedusha* itself we, mere humans, join the angels in praising God. The angels say "Holy," and we, in response, say, "Blessed." Thus God is, in the language of Psalm 22:4, "Holy, enthroned on the praises of Israel."

The One who suppresses His anger in judgment. / The One who clothes Himself with righteousness on the Day of Judgment.
The One who forgives sins in judgment. / The awesome and praiseworthy One on the Day of Judgment.
The One who forgives those He bears in judgment. / The One who answers those who call on Him on the Day of Judgment.
The One who exercises His compassion in judgment. / The One who sees all hidden secrets on the Day of Judgment.
The One who acquires His servants in judgment. / The One who takes pity on His nation on the Day of Judgment.
The One who guards those who love Him in judgment. / The One who supports His innocent ones on the Day of Judgment.

The Ark is closed.

The congregation then the Leader:

וּבְכֵן לְךָ And so, sanctity will rise up to You,
for You, our God, are the King who pardons and forgives.

Some congregations say the series of piyutim מִי יִתְּנָה *on pages 1305–1312 before Kedusha.*

KEDUSHA

The following is said standing
with feet together, rising on the toes at the words indicated by ▲.

The congregation then the Leader:

נַעֲרִיצְךָ We will revere and sanctify You
with the words uttered by the holy Seraphim
who sanctify Your name in the Sanctuary,
as is written by Your prophet: "They call out to one another, saying: *Is. 6*

The congregation then the Leader:

▲Holy, ▲holy, ▲holy is the Lord of hosts:
the whole world is filled with His glory."
His glory fills the universe. His ministering angels ask each other,
"Where is the place of His glory?"
Those facing them reply "Blessed –

Kippur have a heightened form of holiness, for on this day – fasting, dressed in white, focused on heaven – we have become, for a day, like the angels.

קָדוֹשׁ, קָדוֹשׁ, קָדוֹשׁ *Holy, holy, holy.* This was Isaiah's vision: "In the year that King Uzziah died, I saw the Lord, high and exalted, seated on a throne, and

לְכוֹבֵשׁ כַּעְסוֹ בַּדִּין	לְלוֹבֵשׁ צְדָקוֹת בְּיוֹם דִּין.
לְמוֹחֵל עֲוֹנוֹת בַּדִּין	לְנוֹרָא תְהִלּוֹת בְּיוֹם דִּין.
לְסוֹלֵחַ לַעֲמוּסָיו בַּדִּין	לְעוֹנֶה לְקוֹרְאָיו בְּיוֹם דִּין.
לְפוֹעֵל רַחֲמָיו בַּדִּין	לְצוֹפֶה נִסְתָּרוֹת בְּיוֹם דִּין.
לְקוֹנֶה עֲבָדָיו בַּדִּין	לְרַחֵם עַמּוֹ בְּיוֹם דִּין.
לְשׁוֹמֵר אֹהֲבָיו בַּדִּין	לְתוֹמֵךְ תְּמִימָיו בְּיוֹם דִּין.

The ארון קודש *is closed.*

The קהל *then the* שליח ציבור:

וּבְכֵן לְךָ תַעֲלֶה קְדֻשָּׁה
כִּי אַתָּה אֱלֹהֵינוּ מֶלֶךְ מוֹחֵל וְסוֹלֵחַ.

Some congregations say the series of piyutim מִי יִתְנֶה *on pages 1305–1312 before* קדושה.

קדושה

The following is said standing
with feet together, rising on the toes at the words indicated by ▴.

The קהל *then the* שליח ציבור:

נַעֲרִיצְךָ וְנַקְדִּישְׁךָ כְּסוֹד שִׂיחַ שַׂרְפֵי קֹדֶשׁ
הַמַּקְדִּישִׁים שִׁמְךָ בַּקֹּדֶשׁ
כַּכָּתוּב עַל יַד נְבִיאֶךָ: וְקָרָא זֶה אֶל־זֶה וְאָמַר ישעיה ו

The קהל *then the* שליח ציבור:

▴קָדוֹשׁ, ▴קָדוֹשׁ, ▴קָדוֹשׁ, יהוה צְבָאוֹת, מְלֹא כָל־הָאָרֶץ כְּבוֹדוֹ:
כְּבוֹדוֹ מָלֵא עוֹלָם, מְשָׁרְתָיו שׁוֹאֲלִים זֶה לָזֶה, אַיֵּה מְקוֹם כְּבוֹדוֹ,
לְעֻמָּתָם בָּרוּךְ יֹאמֵרוּ

KEDUSHA

Usually on Shabbat and festivals there is a difference between the *Kedushot* of Shaharit, Musaf and Minha services. Only on Yom Kippur are all four *Kedushot* (including that of Ne'ila) alike, the same as that of the Musaf service (*Sefer Roke'aḥ* 216). This means that they all contain the line *Shema Yisrael* – originally introduced into the Musaf *Kedusha* at a time of persecution when Jews were forbidden to say the Shema prayer in public. All the Amida prayers on Yom

The congregation then the Leader:

▲"Blessed is the LORD's glory from His place." *Ezek. 3*
From His place may He turn with compassion
and be gracious to the people who proclaim the unity of His name,
morning and evening, every day, continually,
twice each day reciting in love the Shema:

The congregation then the Leader:

"Listen, Israel, the LORD is our God, the LORD is One." *Deut. 6*
He is our God, He is our Father, He is our King,
He is our Savior – and He, in His compassion,
will let us hear a second time in the presence of all that lives,
His promise "to be Your God. *Num. 15*
I am the LORD your God."

The congregation then the Leader:

Glorious is our Glorious One, LORD our Master, *Ps. 8*
and glorious is Your name throughout the earth.
Then the LORD shall be King over all the earth; *Zech. 14*
on that day the LORD shall be One and His name One.

The Leader continues:

And in Your holy Writings it is written:

The congregation then the Leader:

▲"The LORD shall reign for ever. *Ps. 146*
He is your God, Zion, from generation to generation, Halleluya!"

The Leader continues:

From generation to generation we will declare Your greatness,
and we will proclaim Your holiness for evermore.
Your praise, our God, shall not leave our mouth forever,
for You, God, are a great and holy King.

Blessed is the LORD's glory from His place. Also there was the sound of the wings of the living creatures brushing against each other and the sound of the wheels beside them, a great rushing noise" (Ezek. 3:12–13).

Two very different visions, witnessed by different personalities at different times – Isaiah's while Israel was at home in its land, Ezekiel's from exile in Babylon – yet they are the two supreme biblical scenes of God enthroned in heaven, surrounded by angels. Reenacting these scenes during the Repetition of the Amida is the supreme summit of communal prayer and its boldest mystical expression.

The קהל *then the* שליח ציבור:

יחזקאל ג ׳בָּרוּךְ כְּבוֹד־יהוה מִמְּקוֹמוֹ:
מִמְּקוֹמוֹ הוּא יִפֶן בְּרַחֲמִים, וְיָחֹן עַם הַמְיַחֲדִים שְׁמוֹ
עֶרֶב וָבֹקֶר בְּכָל יוֹם תָּמִיד, פַּעֲמַיִם בְּאַהֲבָה שְׁמַע אוֹמְרִים

The קהל *then the* שליח ציבור:

דברים ו שְׁמַע יִשְׂרָאֵל, יהוה אֱלֹהֵינוּ, יהוה אֶחָד:
הוּא אֱלֹהֵינוּ, הוּא אָבִינוּ, הוּא מַלְכֵּנוּ, הוּא מוֹשִׁיעֵנוּ
במדבר טו וְהוּא יַשְׁמִיעֵנוּ בְּרַחֲמָיו שֵׁנִית לְעֵינֵי כָּל חָי, לִהְיוֹת לָכֶם לֵאלֹהִים
אֲנִי יהוה אֱלֹהֵיכֶם:

The קהל *then the* שליח ציבור:

תהלים ח אַדִּיר אַדִּירֵנוּ, יהוה אֲדֹנֵינוּ, מָה־אַדִּיר שִׁמְךָ בְּכָל־הָאָרֶץ:
זכריה יד וְהָיָה יהוה לְמֶלֶךְ עַל־כָּל־הָאָרֶץ
בַּיּוֹם הַהוּא יִהְיֶה יהוה אֶחָד וּשְׁמוֹ אֶחָד:

The שליח ציבור *continues:*

וּבְדִבְרֵי קָדְשְׁךָ כָּתוּב לֵאמֹר

The קהל *then the* שליח ציבור:

תהלים קמו ׳יִמְלֹךְ יהוה לְעוֹלָם, אֱלֹהַיִךְ צִיּוֹן לְדֹר וָדֹר, הַלְלוּיָהּ:

The שליח ציבור *continues:*

לְדוֹר וָדוֹר נַגִּיד גָּדְלֶךָ, וּלְנֵצַח נְצָחִים קְדֻשָּׁתְךָ נַקְדִּישׁ
וְשִׁבְחֲךָ אֱלֹהֵינוּ מִפִּינוּ לֹא יָמוּשׁ לְעוֹלָם וָעֶד
כִּי אֵל מֶלֶךְ גָּדוֹל וְקָדוֹשׁ אָתָּה.

---

the train of His robe filled the Temple. Above Him were Seraphim, each with six wings. With two wings they covered their faces, with two they covered their feet, and with two they flew. And they were calling to one another: *Holy, holy, holy is the* L*ORD of hosts; the whole world is filled with His glory*. At the sound of their voices the doorposts and thresholds shook and the Temple was filled with smoke" (Is. 6:1–4).

בָּרוּךְ כְּבוֹד־יהוה *Blessed is the* L*ORD's glory.* This was Ezekiel's vision: "Then a wind lifted me up, and I heard behind me the sound of a great noise, saying,

The following prayer originally began at "For with Your holiness." Nowadays, it is commonly sung as one stanza together with the later addition of the opening verse "Have mercy on those You have made."

חֲמֹל Have mercy on those You have made,
take joy in those You made,
and those who shelter in You will say,
as You absolve the ones You bear,
"Be sanctified, Lord, through all that You have made."

כִּי מַקְדִּישֶׁיךָ For with Your holiness You sanctify
all who affirm You holy;
it is fitting that the Holy One be glorified by holy ones.

The Leader continues:

בְּאֵין With no one to advocate for us against the accuser of sin,
speak words of law and of justice to Jacob;
and absolve us in the judgment, O King of judgment.

עוֹד He, our Lord,
will yet remember for us the love of [Abraham] the steadfast one.
And for [Isaac] the son who was bound,
He will still the enmity against us.
And for the merit of [Jacob] the innocent man,
He will bring today our judgment out to the good,
for this day is holy to our Lord. *Neh. 8*

בְּאֵין מֵלִיץ יֹשֶׁר *With no one to advocate for us.* A reference to the book of Job: "Even now I have a Witness in heaven; One who will testify for me on high." (Job 16:19). Job has been accused by Satan, understood in Judaism not as a force of evil but simply as the prosecuting counsel in the heavenly court when humans are on trial. Job has faith that if there is no one else to testify to his innocence, God, who knows all, will.

עוֹד יִזְכּוֹר לָנוּ *He, our Lord, will yet remember for us.* The poet concludes that if all else fails, the merits of the patriarchs, the mighty (Abraham), the child who was bound (Isaac), and the perfect one (Jacob) will be counted in our favor.

The following prayer originally began at כִּי מַקְדִּישֶֽׁיךָ*. Nowadays, it is commonly sung as one stanza together with the later addition of the opening verse,* חֲמֹל עַל מַעֲשֶֽׂיךָ.

חֲמֹל עַל מַעֲשֶֽׂיךָ
וְתִשְׂמַח בְּמַעֲשֶֽׂיךָ
וְיֹאמְרוּ לְךָ חוֹסֶֽיךָ
בְּצַדֶּקְךָ עֲמוּסֶֽיךָ
תֻּקְדַּשׁ אָדוֹן עַל כָּל מַעֲשֶֽׂיךָ

כִּי מַקְדִּישֶֽׁיךָ בִּקְדֻשָּׁתְךָ קִדַּֽשְׁתָּ
נָאֶה לְקָדוֹשׁ פְּאֵר מִקְּדוֹשִׁים.

The שליח ציבור *continues:*

בְּאֵין מֵלִיץ יֹֽשֶׁר
מוּל מַגִּיד פֶּֽשַׁע
תַּגִּיד לְיַעֲקֹב דְּבַר, חֹק וּמִשְׁפָּט
וְצַדְּקֵֽנוּ בַּמִּשְׁפָּט, הַמֶּֽלֶךְ הַמִּשְׁפָּט.

עוֹד יִזְכֹּר לָֽנוּ אַהֲבַת אֵיתָן, אֲדוֹנֵֽינוּ
וּבַבֵּן הַנֶּעֱקַד יַשְׁבִּית מְדַיְּנֵֽינוּ
וּבִזְכוּת הַתָּם יוֹצִיא הַיּוֹם לְצֶֽדֶק דִּינֵֽנוּ
נחמיה ח כִּי־קָדוֹשׁ הַיּוֹם לַאֲדֹנֵֽינוּ:

חֲמֹל עַל מַעֲשֶֽׂיךָ *Have mercy on those You have made.* A special insertion, unique to the High Holy Days. The sentiment evokes the end of the book of Jonah that we will read later in the day.

כִּי מַקְדִּישֶֽׁיךָ בִּקְדֻשָּׁתְךָ קִדַּֽשְׁתָּ *For with Your holiness You sanctify all who affirm You holy.* The Hebrew word for holy means "set apart." Just as God is set apart from the physical universe He created, so He has set Israel apart by choosing it to be the nation that bears witness to God through its history and its laws.

וּבְכֵן יִתְקַדַּשׁ And so may Your name be sanctified, Lord our God,
through Israel Your nation and Jerusalem, Your city,
and Zion, the dwelling place of Your honor
and through the royal house of David Your anointed,
and Your Sanctuary and Your Temple.

Some congregations say the series of piyutim וּבְכֵן, מִי לֹא יִרָאֲךָ *(pages 1312–1324) at this point.*

HOLINESS

וּבְכֵן תֵּן פַּחְדְּךָ And so place the fear of You, Lord our God,
over all that You have made,
and the terror of You over all You have created,
and all who were made will stand in awe of You,
and all of creation will worship You,
and they will be bound all together as one
to carry out Your will with an undivided heart;
for we know, Lord our God,
that all dominion is laid out before You,
strength is in Your palm, and might in Your right hand,
Your name spreading awe over all You have created.

וּבְכֵן תֵּן כָּבוֹד And so place honor, Lord, upon Your people,
praise on those who fear You
and hope into those who seek You,
the confidence to speak into all who long for You,
gladness to Your land and joy to Your city,
the flourishing of pride to David Your servant,
and a lamp laid out for his descendant,
Your anointed, soon, in our days.

וּבְכֵן צַדִּיקִים And then righteous people will see and rejoice,
and the upright will exult, and the pious revel in joy,
and injustice will have nothing more to say,
and all wickedness will fade away like smoke
as You sweep the rule of arrogance from the earth.

וּבְכֵן יִתְקַדַּשׁ שִׁמְךָ יהוה אֱלֹהֵינוּ
עַל יִשְׂרָאֵל עַמֶּךָ וְעַל יְרוּשָׁלַיִם עִירֶךָ
וְעַל צִיּוֹן מִשְׁכַּן כְּבוֹדֶךָ וְעַל מַלְכוּת בֵּית דָּוִד מְשִׁיחֶךָ
וְעַל מְכוֹנְךָ וְהֵיכָלֶךָ.

Some congregations say the series of piyutim וּבְכֵן, מִי לֹא יִרָאֲךָ (pages 1312–1324) *at this point.*

קדושת השם

וּבְכֵן תֵּן פַּחְדְּךָ יהוה אֱלֹהֵינוּ עַל כָּל מַעֲשֶׂיךָ
וְאֵימָתְךָ עַל כָּל מַה שֶּׁבָּרָאתָ
וְיִירָאוּךָ כָּל הַמַּעֲשִׂים
וְיִשְׁתַּחֲווּ לְפָנֶיךָ כָּל הַבְּרוּאִים
וְיֵעָשׂוּ כֻלָּם אֲגֻדָּה אַחַת לַעֲשׂוֹת רְצוֹנְךָ בְּלֵבָב שָׁלֵם
כְּמוֹ שֶׁיָּדַעְנוּ יהוה אֱלֹהֵינוּ שֶׁהַשָּׁלְטָן לְפָנֶיךָ
עֹז בְּיָדְךָ וּגְבוּרָה בִּימִינֶךָ
וְשִׁמְךָ נוֹרָא עַל כָּל מַה שֶּׁבָּרָאתָ.

וּבְכֵן תֵּן כָּבוֹד יהוה לְעַמֶּךָ
תְּהִלָּה לִירֵאֶיךָ וְתִקְוָה טוֹבָה לְדוֹרְשֶׁיךָ
וּפִתְחוֹן פֶּה לַמְיַחֲלִים לָךְ
שִׂמְחָה לְאַרְצֶךָ, וְשָׂשׂוֹן לְעִירֶךָ
וּצְמִיחַת קֶרֶן לְדָוִד עַבְדֶּךָ, וַעֲרִיכַת נֵר לְבֶן יִשַׁי מְשִׁיחֶךָ
בִּמְהֵרָה בְיָמֵינוּ.

וּבְכֵן צַדִּיקִים יִרְאוּ וְיִשְׂמָחוּ, וִישָׁרִים יַעֲלֹזוּ
וַחֲסִידִים בְּרִנָּה יָגִילוּ, וְעוֹלָתָה תִּקְפָּץ פִּיהָ
וְכָל הָרִשְׁעָה כֻּלָּהּ כְּעָשָׁן תִּכְלֶה
כִּי תַעֲבִיר מֶמְשֶׁלֶת זָדוֹן מִן הָאָרֶץ.

וְתִמְלֹךְ אַתָּה And You, LORD,
will rule alone over those You have made,
in Mount Zion, the dwelling of Your glory,
and in Jerusalem, Your holy city,
as it is written in Your holy writings:
"The LORD shall reign for ever. *Ps. 146*
He is your God, Zion,
from generation to generation,
Halleluya!"

קָדוֹשׁ אַתָּה You are holy, Your name is awesome,
and there is no god but You, as it is written,
"The LORD of hosts shall be raised up through His judgment, *Is. 5*
the holy God, made holy in righteousness."
Blessed are You, LORD, the holy King.

HOLINESS OF THE DAY

אַתָּה בְחַרְתָּנוּ You have chosen us from among all peoples.
You have loved and favored us.
You have raised us above all tongues.
You have made us holy
through Your commandments.
You have brought us near, our King, to Your service,
and have called us by Your great and holy name.

On Shabbat, add the words in parentheses:

וַתִּתֶּן לָנוּ And You, LORD our God, have given us in love
(this Sabbath day for holiness and rest, and)
this Day of Atonement
for pardon and forgiveness and atonement,
to pardon all our iniquities,
(with love,) a holy assembly
in memory of the exodus from Egypt.

וְתִמְלֹךְ אַתָּה יהוה לְבַדֶּךָ עַל כָּל מַעֲשֶׂיךָ
בְּהַר צִיּוֹן מִשְׁכַּן כְּבוֹדֶךָ, וּבִירוּשָׁלַיִם עִיר קָדְשֶׁךָ
כַּכָּתוּב בְּדִבְרֵי קָדְשֶׁךָ
יִמְלֹךְ יהוה לְעוֹלָם, אֱלֹהַיִךְ צִיּוֹן לְדֹר וָדֹר, הַלְלוּיָהּ: תהלים קמו

קָדוֹשׁ אַתָּה וְנוֹרָא שְׁמֶךָ, וְאֵין אֱלוֹהַּ מִבַּלְעָדֶיךָ
כַּכָּתוּב, וַיִּגְבַּהּ יהוה צְבָאוֹת בַּמִּשְׁפָּט ישעיה ה
וְהָאֵל הַקָּדוֹשׁ נִקְדַּשׁ בִּצְדָקָה:
בָּרוּךְ אַתָּה יהוה, הַמֶּלֶךְ הַקָּדוֹשׁ.

קדושת היום
אַתָּה בְחַרְתָּנוּ מִכָּל הָעַמִּים
אָהַבְתָּ אוֹתָנוּ וְרָצִיתָ בָּנוּ
וְרוֹמַמְתָּנוּ מִכָּל הַלְּשׁוֹנוֹת
וְקִדַּשְׁתָּנוּ בְּמִצְוֹתֶיךָ
וְקֵרַבְתָּנוּ מַלְכֵּנוּ לַעֲבוֹדָתֶךָ
וְשִׁמְךָ הַגָּדוֹל וְהַקָּדוֹשׁ עָלֵינוּ קָרָאתָ.

On שבת, add the words in parentheses:
וַתִּתֶּן לָנוּ יהוה אֱלֹהֵינוּ בְּאַהֲבָה אֶת
(יוֹם הַשַּׁבָּת הַזֶּה לִקְדֻשָּׁה וְלִמְנוּחָה, וְאֶת)
יוֹם הַכִּפּוּרִים הַזֶּה, לִמְחִילָה וְלִסְלִיחָה וּלְכַפָּרָה
וְלִמְחָל בּוֹ אֶת כָּל עֲוֹנוֹתֵינוּ
(בְּאַהֲבָה) מִקְרָא קֹדֶשׁ, זֵכֶר לִיצִיאַת מִצְרָיִם.

אֱלֹהֵינוּ Our God and God of our ancestors,
may there rise, come, reach, appear, be favored, heard,
regarded and remembered before You,
our recollection and remembrance,
as well as the remembrance of our ancestors,
and of the Messiah, son of David Your servant,
and of Jerusalem Your holy city,
and of all Your people the house of Israel –
for deliverance and well-being,
grace, loving-kindness and compassion,
life and peace, on this Day of Atonement.
On it remember us, LORD our God, for good;
recollect us for blessing, and deliver us for life.
In accord with Your promise of salvation and compassion,
spare us and be gracious to us; have compassion on us and deliver us,
for our eyes are turned to You
because You, God, are a gracious and compassionate King.

Traditionally, Seliḥot were recited at this point. Nowadays, most congregations omit them and begin with "Remember, LORD."

All:

זְכֹר Remember, LORD, Your compassion and loving-kindness, *Ps. 25*
for they are everlasting.
Do not hold against us the sins of those who came before us. *Ps. 79*
May Your mercies meet us swiftly, for we have been brought very low.
Remember us, LORD, in favoring Your people;
redeem us with Your salvation.
זְכֹר Remember Your congregation, the one that You acquired long ago, *Ps. 74*
the tribe of Your inheritance that You redeemed,
this Mount Zion that You have dwelt in.
זְכֹר Remember, LORD, the fondness of Jerusalem;
do not forever forget the love of Zion.
You shall rise up and have compassion for Zion, *Ps. 102*
for now it is right to be gracious, for the time has come.
זְכֹר Remember, LORD, what the Edomites did on the day Jerusalem fell. *Ps. 137*
They said, "Tear it down, tear it down to its very foundations!"

אֱלֹהֵינוּ וֵאלֹהֵי אֲבוֹתֵינוּ
יַעֲלֶה וְיָבוֹא וְיַגִּיעַ, וְיֵרָאֶה וְיֵרָצֶה וְיִשָּׁמַע
וְיִפָּקֵד וְיִזָּכֵר זִכְרוֹנֵנוּ וּפִקְדּוֹנֵנוּ וְזִכְרוֹן אֲבוֹתֵינוּ
וְזִכְרוֹן מָשִׁיחַ בֶּן דָּוִד עַבְדֶּךָ
וְזִכְרוֹן יְרוּשָׁלַיִם עִיר קָדְשֶׁךָ
וְזִכְרוֹן כָּל עַמְּךָ בֵּית יִשְׂרָאֵל, לְפָנֶיךָ
לִפְלֵיטָה לְטוֹבָה, לְחֵן וּלְחֶסֶד וּלְרַחֲמִים, לְחַיִּים וּלְשָׁלוֹם
בְּיוֹם הַכִּפּוּרִים הַזֶּה.
זָכְרֵנוּ יהוה אֱלֹהֵינוּ בּוֹ לְטוֹבָה, וּפָקְדֵנוּ בוֹ לִבְרָכָה
וְהוֹשִׁיעֵנוּ בוֹ לְחַיִּים.
וּבִדְבַר יְשׁוּעָה וְרַחֲמִים
חוּס וְחָנֵּנוּ, וְרַחֵם עָלֵינוּ וְהוֹשִׁיעֵנוּ, כִּי אֵלֶיךָ עֵינֵינוּ
כִּי אֵל מֶלֶךְ חַנּוּן וְרַחוּם אָתָּה.

Traditionally, סליחות *were recited at this point. Nowadays, most congregations omit them and begin with "*זְכֹר־רַחֲמֶיךָ*."*

All:

זְכֹר־רַחֲמֶיךָ יהוה וַחֲסָדֶיךָ, כִּי מֵעוֹלָם הֵמָּה: תהלים כה
אַל־תִּזְכָּר־לָנוּ עֲוֹנֹת רִאשֹׁנִים תהלים עט
מַהֵר יְקַדְּמוּנוּ רַחֲמֶיךָ כִּי דַלּוֹנוּ מְאֹד:
זָכְרֵנוּ יהוה בִּרְצוֹן עַמֶּךָ, פָּקְדֵנוּ בִּישׁוּעָתֶךָ.
זְכֹר עֲדָתְךָ קָנִיתָ קֶּדֶם, גָּאַלְתָּ שֵׁבֶט נַחֲלָתֶךָ, הַר־צִיּוֹן זֶה שָׁכַנְתָּ בּוֹ: תהלים עד
זְכֹר יהוה חִבַּת יְרוּשָׁלָיִם, אַהֲבַת צִיּוֹן אַל תִּשְׁכַּח לָנֶצַח.
אַתָּה תָקוּם תְּרַחֵם צִיּוֹן, כִּי־עֵת לְחֶנְנָהּ, כִּי־בָא מוֹעֵד: תהלים קב
זְכֹר יהוה לִבְנֵי אֱדוֹם אֵת יוֹם יְרוּשָׁלָיִם תהלים קלז
הָאֹמְרִים עָרוּ עָרוּ, עַד הַיְסוֹד בָּהּ:

זְכֹר Remember Abraham, Isaac and Yisrael, Your servants, *Ex. 32*
to whom You swore by Your own Self, when You said to them,
"I shall make your descendants as numerous as the stars in the sky,
and I shall give all this land that I spoke of to your descendants,
and they shall inherit it forever."

זְכֹר Remember Your servants, Abraham, Isaac and Jacob; *Deut. 9*
do not attend to the stubbornness of this people,
to their wickedness or sinfulness.

Each of the following verses is said by the Leader, then the congregation:

אַל־נָא Please, do not hold against us the sin *Num. 12*
that we committed so foolishly, that we have sinned.

We have sinned, our Rock; forgive us, our Creator.

Traditionally, a piyut of confession was inserted between the two sets of remembrance verses. The piyut for Shaḥarit was אֲדַבְּרָה תַחֲנוּנִים *(page 1325). Nowadays, most congregations say only the last stanza below.*

The Leader followed by the congregation:

קוֹל גָּדוֹל A great voice like that heard by His beloved [at Sinai],
calls upon those born of wombs to "Accept My majesty."
Recall on this day [Your people] who surrounded the mountain,
O God, King, who sits on a throne of compassion.

We have sinned, our Rock; forgive us, our Creator.

If a circumcision will take place on Yom Kippur, some add:

Remember the covenant of Abraham and the Binding of Isaac,
and restore the fortunes of Jacob, and save us for Your name's sake.

All:

זְכֹר Remember the covenant of our fathers,
as You have said,
"I will remember My covenant with Jacob, *Lev. 26*
and also My covenant with Isaac,
and also My covenant with Abraham I will remember,
and the land I will remember."

זְכֹר לְאַבְרָהָם לְיִצְחָק וּלְיִשְׂרָאֵל עֲבָדֶיךָ שמות לב
אֲשֶׁר נִשְׁבַּעְתָּ לָהֶם בָּךְ וַתְּדַבֵּר אֲלֵהֶם
אַרְבֶּה אֶת־זַרְעֲכֶם כְּכוֹכְבֵי הַשָּׁמָיִם
וְכָל־הָאָרֶץ הַזֹּאת אֲשֶׁר אָמַרְתִּי אֶתֵּן לְזַרְעֲכֶם, וְנָחֲלוּ לְעֹלָם:
זְכֹר לַעֲבָדֶיךָ לְאַבְרָהָם לְיִצְחָק וּלְיַעֲקֹב דברים ט
אַל־תֵּפֶן אֶל־קְשִׁי הָעָם הַזֶּה וְאֶל־רִשְׁעוֹ וְאֶל־חַטָּאתוֹ:

Each of the following verses is said by the שליח ציבור*, then the* קהל*:*

אַל־נָא תָשֵׁת עָלֵינוּ חַטָּאת אֲשֶׁר נוֹאַלְנוּ וַאֲשֶׁר חָטָאנוּ: במדבר יב

חָטָאנוּ צוּרֵנוּ, סְלַח לָנוּ יוֹצְרֵנוּ.

Traditionally, a piyut of confession was inserted between the two sets of remembrance verses. The piyut for שחרית *was* אֲדַבְּרָה תַחֲנוּנִים *(page 1325). Nowadays, most congregations say only the last stanza below.*

The שליח ציבור *followed by the* קהל*:*

קוֹל גָּדוֹל כְּהַשְׁמִיעַ לִרְחוּמִים / קַבְּלוּ מַלְכוּתִי מִמְּקוֹרֵי רְחָמִים
יִזְכֹּר הַיּוֹם לְסָבִיב מִתְחַמִּים / אֵל מֶלֶךְ יוֹשֵׁב עַל כִּסֵּא רַחֲמִים.

חָטָאנוּ צוּרֵנוּ, סְלַח לָנוּ יוֹצְרֵנוּ.

If a circumcision will take place on Yom Kippur, some add:

זְכֹר בְּרִית אַבְרָהָם וַעֲקֵדַת יִצְחָק, וְהָשֵׁב שְׁבוּת יַעֲקֹב
וְהוֹשִׁיעֵנוּ לְמַעַן שְׁמֶךָ.

All:

זְכָר לָנוּ בְּרִית אָבוֹת כַּאֲשֶׁר אָמַרְתָּ:
וְזָכַרְתִּי אֶת־בְּרִיתִי יַעֲקוֹב ויקרא כו
וְאַף אֶת־בְּרִיתִי יִצְחָק
וְאַף אֶת־בְּרִיתִי אַבְרָהָם אֶזְכֹּר
וְהָאָרֶץ אֶזְכֹּר:

Remember the covenant of the early ones, as You have said,
"I shall remember for them the covenant of the early ones, *Lev. 26*
whom I brought out of the land of Egypt
before the eyes of the nations,
in order to be their God: I am the LORD."

Deal kindly with us as You have promised,
"Even so, when they are in the land of their enemies *Ibid.*
I shall not reject them
and shall not detest them to the point of destruction,
to the point of breaking My covenant with them,
for I am the LORD their God."

Have compassion for us and do not destroy us, as it is written:
"For the LORD your God is a compassionate God; *Deut. 4*
He will not forsake you, He will not destroy you,
and He will not forget the covenant of your fathers,
that He pledged to them."

Circumcise our hearts to love Your name, as it is written:
"And the LORD your God will circumcise your heart *Deut. 30*
and the heart of your descendants
to love the LORD your God with all your heart
and with all your soul, so that you shall live."

Restore our fortunes and have compassion for us, as it is written:
"And the LORD your God shall restore your fortunes *Ibid.*
and have compassion for you,
and shall return and gather you in from all the nations
among whom the LORD your God has scattered you."

Gather those of us who have been distanced, as is written,
"If your distanced ones are at the very ends of the heavens, *Ibid.*
from there shall the LORD your God gather you;
from there shall He bring you."

Let us find You when we seek You, as it is written:
"And if from there you seek the LORD your God, you shall find Him, *Deut. 4*
when you seek Him out with all your heart and with all your soul."

זְכֹר לָנוּ בְּרִית רִאשׁוֹנִים, כַּאֲשֶׁר אָמַרְתָּ:
וְזָכַרְתִּי לָהֶם בְּרִית רִאשֹׁנִים ויקרא כו
אֲשֶׁר הוֹצֵאתִי־אֹתָם מֵאֶרֶץ מִצְרַיִם לְעֵינֵי הַגּוֹיִם
לִהְיוֹת לָהֶם לֵאלֹהִים, אֲנִי יהוה:

עֲשֵׂה עִמָּנוּ כְּמָה שֶׁהִבְטַחְתָּנוּ:
וְאַף גַּם־זֹאת בִּהְיוֹתָם בְּאֶרֶץ אֹיְבֵיהֶם שם
לֹא־מְאַסְתִּים וְלֹא־גְעַלְתִּים לְכַלֹּתָם, לְהָפֵר בְּרִיתִי אִתָּם
כִּי אֲנִי יהוה אֱלֹהֵיהֶם:

רַחֵם עָלֵינוּ וְאַל תַּשְׁחִיתֵנוּ, כְּמָה שֶׁכָּתוּב:
כִּי אֵל רַחוּם יהוה אֱלֹהֶיךָ, לֹא יַרְפְּךָ וְלֹא יַשְׁחִיתֶךָ דברים ד
וְלֹא יִשְׁכַּח אֶת־בְּרִית אֲבֹתֶיךָ אֲשֶׁר נִשְׁבַּע לָהֶם:

מוֹל אֶת לְבָבֵנוּ לְאַהֲבָה אֶת שְׁמֶךָ, כְּמָה שֶׁכָּתוּב:
וּמָל יהוה אֱלֹהֶיךָ אֶת־לְבָבְךָ וְאֶת־לְבַב זַרְעֶךָ דברים ל
לְאַהֲבָה אֶת־יהוה אֱלֹהֶיךָ בְּכָל־לְבָבְךָ וּבְכָל־נַפְשְׁךָ, לְמַעַן חַיֶּיךָ:

הָשֵׁב שְׁבוּתֵנוּ וְרַחֲמֵנוּ, כְּמָה שֶׁכָּתוּב:
וְשָׁב יהוה אֱלֹהֶיךָ אֶת־שְׁבוּתְךָ וְרִחֲמֶךָ שם
וְשָׁב וְקִבֶּצְךָ מִכָּל־הָעַמִּים אֲשֶׁר הֱפִיצְךָ יהוה אֱלֹהֶיךָ שָׁמָּה:

קַבֵּץ נִדָּחֵינוּ, כְּמָה שֶׁכָּתוּב:
אִם־יִהְיֶה נִדַּחֲךָ בִּקְצֵה הַשָּׁמָיִם שם
מִשָּׁם יְקַבֶּצְךָ יהוה אֱלֹהֶיךָ, וּמִשָּׁם יִקָּחֶךָ:

הִמָּצֵא לָנוּ בְּבַקָּשָׁתֵנוּ, כְּמָה שֶׁכָּתוּב:
וּבִקַּשְׁתֶּם מִשָּׁם אֶת־יהוה אֱלֹהֶיךָ, וּמָצָאתָ דברים ד
כִּי תִדְרְשֶׁנּוּ בְּכָל־לְבָבְךָ וּבְכָל־נַפְשֶׁךָ:

Wipe out our transgressions for Your sake, as You have said:
"I, I am the One who shall wipe out your transgressions *Is. 43*
for My sake, and I shall not recall your sins."

Wipe out our transgressions as if they were a cloud,
as if they were a haze,
as is written,
"I have wiped out your transgressions like a cloud, *Is. 44*
and as a haze your sins;
come back to Me for I have redeemed you."

Whiten our sins as snow and as wool,
as is written,
"Come now, let us reason together, says the LORD: *Is. 1*
If your sins are like scarlet,
they shall be whitened like snow;
should they be as red as crimson,
they shall become like wool."

Throw over us pure waters and purify us,
as is written,
"I shall throw pure waters over you and you shall be pure. *Ezek. 36*
I shall purify you of all your impurities and of all your idolatry."

Atone our sins on this day and purify us, as is written,
"For on this day you will be atoned and made pure; *Lev. 16*
of all your sins before the LORD you shall be purified."

▸ Bring us to Your holy mountain,
and let us rejoice in Your House of prayer,
as is written,
"I shall bring them to My holy mountain, *Is. 56*
and I shall make them rejoice in My House of prayer;
their offerings and their sacrifices will be accepted,
desired on My altar,
for My House will be called a house of prayer for all peoples."

מְחֵה פְשָׁעֵינוּ לְמַעַנְךָ, כַּאֲשֶׁר אָמַרְתָּ:
אָנֹכִי אָנֹכִי הוּא מֹחֶה פְשָׁעֶיךָ לְמַעֲנִי ישעיה מג
וְחַטֹּאתֶיךָ לֹא אֶזְכֹּר:

מְחֵה פְשָׁעֵינוּ כָּעָב וְכֶעָנָן, כְּמָה שֶׁכָּתוּב:
מָחִיתִי כָעָב פְּשָׁעֶיךָ וְכֶעָנָן חַטֹּאותֶיךָ ישעיה מד
שׁוּבָה אֵלַי כִּי גְאַלְתִּיךָ:

הַלְבֵּן חֲטָאֵינוּ כַּשֶּׁלֶג וְכַצֶּמֶר, כְּמָה שֶׁכָּתוּב:
לְכוּ־נָא וְנִוָּכְחָה, יֹאמַר יהוה ישעיה א
אִם־יִהְיוּ חֲטָאֵיכֶם כַּשָּׁנִים, כַּשֶּׁלֶג יַלְבִּינוּ
אִם־יַאְדִּימוּ כַתּוֹלָע, כַּצֶּמֶר יִהְיוּ:

זְרֹק עָלֵינוּ מַיִם טְהוֹרִים וְטַהֲרֵנוּ, כְּמָה שֶׁכָּתוּב:
וְזָרַקְתִּי עֲלֵיכֶם מַיִם טְהוֹרִים, וּטְהַרְתֶּם יחזקאל לו
מִכֹּל טֻמְאוֹתֵיכֶם וּמִכָּל־גִּלּוּלֵיכֶם אֲטַהֵר אֶתְכֶם:

כַּפֵּר חֲטָאֵינוּ בַּיּוֹם הַזֶּה וְטַהֲרֵנוּ, כְּמָה שֶׁכָּתוּב:
כִּי־בַיּוֹם הַזֶּה יְכַפֵּר עֲלֵיכֶם לְטַהֵר אֶתְכֶם ויקרא טז
מִכֹּל חַטֹּאתֵיכֶם
לִפְנֵי יהוה תִּטְהָרוּ:

▸ תְּבִיאֵנוּ אֶל הַר קָדְשֶׁךָ, וְשַׂמְּחֵנוּ בְּבֵית תְּפִלָּתֶךָ
כְּמָה שֶׁכָּתוּב:
וַהֲבִיאוֹתִים אֶל־הַר קָדְשִׁי ישעיה נו
וְשִׂמַּחְתִּים בְּבֵית תְּפִלָּתִי
עוֹלֹתֵיהֶם וְזִבְחֵיהֶם לְרָצוֹן עַל־מִזְבְּחִי
כִּי בֵיתִי בֵּית־תְּפִלָּה יִקָּרֵא לְכָל־הָעַמִּים:

The Ark is opened.

The following is said responsively, verse by verse. (*For commentary see page 161.*)

שְׁמַע קוֹלֵנוּ Listen to our voice, LORD our God.
Spare us and have compassion on us,
and in compassion and favor accept our prayer.
Turn us back, O LORD, to You, and we will return. *Lam. 5*
Renew our days as of old.
Do not cast us away from You, and do not take Your holy spirit from us.
Do not cast us away in our old age;
when our strength is gone do not desert us.

End of responsive reading.

Do not desert us, LORD; our God, do not be distant from us.
Give us a sign of good things,
and those who hate us shall see it and be ashamed,
for You, LORD, will help us and console us.
Hear our speech, LORD, consider our thoughts.
May the words of our mouths and the meditations of our hearts
find favor before You, LORD, our Rock and Redeemer.
For it is You, LORD, that we have longed for;
You shall answer us, LORD our God.

The Ark is closed.

The Leader continues:

אֱלֹהֵינוּ Our God and God of our ancestors,
do not abandon us and do not desert us,
do not shame us and do not abandon Your covenant with us;
bring us close to Your Torah, teach us Your commandments,
show us Your ways, and turn our hearts toward the awe of Your name.
Circumcise our hearts to love You,
so that we return to You in truth, wholeheartedly.
For the sake of Your great name, pardon and forgive our iniquities,
as it is written in Your holy Writings:
"For the sake of Your name, LORD, *Ps. 25*
forgive my iniquity, though it is great."

Our God and God of our ancestors,
forgive us, pardon us, grant us atonement.

The ארון קודש *is opened.*

The following is said responsively, verse by verse. (For commentary see page 161.)

שְׁמַע קוֹלֵנוּ, יהוה אֱלֹהֵינוּ, חוּס וְרַחֵם עָלֵינוּ
וְקַבֵּל בְּרַחֲמִים וּבְרָצוֹן אֶת תְּפִלָּתֵנוּ.
הֲשִׁיבֵנוּ יהוה אֵלֶיךָ וְנָשׁוּבָה, חַדֵּשׁ יָמֵינוּ כְּקֶדֶם: איכה ה
אַל תַּשְׁלִיכֵנוּ מִלְּפָנֶיךָ, וְרוּחַ קָדְשְׁךָ אַל תִּקַּח מִמֶּנּוּ.
אַל תַּשְׁלִיכֵנוּ לְעֵת זִקְנָה, כִּכְלוֹת כֹּחֵנוּ אַל תַּעַזְבֵנוּ.

End of responsive reading.

אַל תַּעַזְבֵנוּ יהוה, אֱלֹהֵינוּ אַל תִּרְחַק מִמֶּנּוּ.
עֲשֵׂה עִמָּנוּ אוֹת לְטוֹבָה, וְיִרְאוּ שׂוֹנְאֵינוּ וְיֵבֹשׁוּ
כִּי אַתָּה יהוה עֲזַרְתָּנוּ וְנִחַמְתָּנוּ.
אֲמָרֵינוּ הַאֲזִינָה יהוה, בִּינָה הֲגִיגֵנוּ.
יִהְיוּ לְרָצוֹן אִמְרֵי פִינוּ וְהֶגְיוֹן לִבֵּנוּ לְפָנֶיךָ, יהוה צוּרֵנוּ וְגוֹאֲלֵנוּ.
כִּי לְךָ יהוה הוֹחָלְנוּ, אַתָּה תַעֲנֶה אֲדֹנָי אֱלֹהֵינוּ.

The ארון קודש *is closed.*

The שליח ציבור *continues:*

אֱלֹהֵינוּ וֵאלֹהֵי אֲבוֹתֵינוּ
אַל תַּעַזְבֵנוּ, וְאַל תִּטְּשֵׁנוּ, וְאַל תַּכְלִימֵנוּ, וְאַל תָּפֵר בְּרִיתְךָ אִתָּנוּ
קָרְבֵנוּ לְתוֹרָתֶךָ, לַמְּדֵנוּ מִצְוֹתֶיךָ
הוֹרֵנוּ דְרָכֶיךָ, הַט לִבֵּנוּ לְיִרְאָה אֶת שְׁמֶךָ
וּמוֹל אֶת לְבָבֵנוּ לְאַהֲבָתֶךָ, וְנָשׁוּב אֵלֶיךָ בֶּאֱמֶת וּבְלֵב שָׁלֵם
וּלְמַעַן שִׁמְךָ הַגָּדוֹל תִּמְחֹל וְתִסְלַח לַעֲוֹנֵינוּ
כַּכָּתוּב בְּדִבְרֵי קָדְשֶׁךָ
לְמַעַן־שִׁמְךָ יהוה, וְסָלַחְתָּ לַעֲוֹנִי כִּי רַב־הוּא: תהלים כה

אֱלֹהֵינוּ וֵאלֹהֵי אֲבוֹתֵינוּ
סְלַח לָנוּ, מְחַל לָנוּ, כַּפֶּר לָנוּ.

In many congregations, the Leader and the congregation recite the following piyut responsively, couplet by couplet, until "and You give us Yours"; in others, it is sung collectively.

כִּי אָנוּ For we are Your people and You are our God;
we are Your children and You are our Father;
we are Your servants and You are our Master;
we are Your gathering and You are our Place;
we are Your legacy and You are our Land;
we are Your flock and You are our Shepherd;
we are Your vineyard and You are our Keeper;
we are Your work and You are our Maker;
we are Your bride and You are our Lover;
we are Your treasure and You are our God;
we are Your people and You are our King;
we give You our word and You give us Yours.

The congregation then the Leader:

We are brazen and You are compassionate, gracious.
We are stubborn and You are long forbearing.
We are as full of iniquity as You are full of compassion.
Our days are like a fleeting shadow. *Ps. 102*
But You are here, and Your years will not end.

VIDUY

For linear translation and commentary, see page 1353.

The Leader continues, with the congregation following him in an undertone:

אֱלֹהֵינוּ Our God and God of our fathers,
let our prayer come before You, and do not hide Yourself from our plea,
for we are not so arrogant or obstinate as to say before You,
Lord, our God and God of our fathers,
we are righteous and have not sinned,
for in truth, we and our fathers have sinned.

Strike the left side of the chest with the right fist while saying each of the sins:

אָשַׁמְנוּ We have sinned, we have acted treacherously,
we have robbed, we have spoken slander.
We have acted perversely, we have acted wickedly,
we have acted presumptuously, we have been violent, we have framed lies.
We have given bad advice, we have deceived, we have scorned,
we have rebelled, we have provoked, we have turned away,
we have committed iniquity, we have transgressed,
we have persecuted, we have been obstinate.
We have acted wickedly, we have corrupted,
we have acted abominably, we have strayed, we have led others astray.

In many congregations, the שליח ציבור *and the* קהל *recite the following piyut responsively, couplet by couplet, until* וְאַתָּה מַאֲמִירֵנוּ*; in others, it is sung collectively.*

כִּי אָנוּ עַמֶּךָ וְאַתָּה אֱלֹהֵינוּ אָנוּ בָנֶיךָ וְאַתָּה אָבִינוּ
אָנוּ עֲבָדֶיךָ וְאַתָּה אֲדוֹנֵינוּ אָנוּ קְהָלֶךָ וְאַתָּה חֶלְקֵנוּ
אָנוּ נַחֲלָתֶךָ וְאַתָּה גוֹרָלֵנוּ אָנוּ צֹאנֶךָ וְאַתָּה רוֹעֵנוּ
אָנוּ כַרְמֶךָ וְאַתָּה נוֹטְרֵנוּ אָנוּ פְעֻלָּתֶךָ וְאַתָּה יוֹצְרֵנוּ
אָנוּ רַעְיָתֶךָ וְאַתָּה דוֹדֵנוּ אָנוּ סְגֻלָּתֶךָ וְאַתָּה אֱלֹהֵינוּ
אָנוּ עַמֶּךָ וְאַתָּה מַלְכֵּנוּ אָנוּ מַאֲמִירֶיךָ וְאַתָּה מַאֲמִירֵנוּ.

The קהל *then the* שליח ציבור*:*

אָנוּ עַזֵּי פָנִים וְאַתָּה רַחוּם וְחַנּוּן
אָנוּ קְשֵׁי עֹרֶף וְאַתָּה אֶרֶךְ אַפַּיִם
אָנוּ מְלֵאֵי עָוֹן וְאַתָּה מָלֵא רַחֲמִים
אָנוּ יָמֵינוּ כְּצֵל עוֹבֵר וְאַתָּה־הוּא וּשְׁנוֹתֶיךָ לֹא יִתָּמּוּ: תהלים קב

וידוי

For linear translation and commentary, see page 1353.

The שליח ציבור *continues, with the* קהל *following him in an undertone:*

אֱלֹהֵינוּ וֵאלֹהֵי אֲבוֹתֵינוּ
תָּבוֹא לְפָנֶיךָ תְּפִלָּתֵנוּ, וְאַל תִּתְעַלַּם מִתְּחִנָּתֵנוּ.
שֶׁאֵין אֲנַחְנוּ עַזֵּי פָנִים וּקְשֵׁי עֹרֶף לוֹמַר לְפָנֶיךָ
יהוה אֱלֹהֵינוּ וֵאלֹהֵי אֲבוֹתֵינוּ
צַדִּיקִים אֲנַחְנוּ וְלֹא חָטָאנוּ.
אֲבָל אֲנַחְנוּ וַאֲבוֹתֵינוּ חָטָאנוּ.

Strike the left side of the chest with the right fist while saying each of the sins.

אָשַׁמְנוּ, בָּגַדְנוּ, גָּזַלְנוּ, דִּבַּרְנוּ דֹפִי
הֶעֱוִינוּ, וְהִרְשַׁעְנוּ, זַדְנוּ, חָמַסְנוּ, טָפַלְנוּ שֶׁקֶר
יָעַצְנוּ רָע, כִּזַּבְנוּ, לַצְנוּ, מָרַדְנוּ, נִאַצְנוּ, סָרַרְנוּ
עָוִינוּ, פָּשַׁעְנוּ, צָרַרְנוּ, קִשִּׁינוּ עֹרֶף
רָשַׁעְנוּ, שִׁחַתְנוּ, תִּעַבְנוּ, תָּעִינוּ, תִּעְתָּעְנוּ.

All:

סַרְנוּ We have turned away from Your commandments and good laws,
to no avail, for You are just in all that has befallen us, *Neh. 9*
for You have acted faithfully while we have done wickedly.

We have been wicked and we have transgressed,
and so we have not been saved.
Place it in our hearts to abandon the way of wickedness,
and hasten our salvation,
as it is written by Your prophet:
"Let each wicked person abandon his ways, *Is. 55*
each man of iniquity his thoughts,
and let him come back to the LORD
and He will have compassion for him,
back to our God for He will forgive abundantly."

The Leader continues:

אֱלֹהֵינוּ Our God, and God of our ancestors,
forgive and pardon our iniquities
on (*Shabbat:* this Sabbath day, and on) this Day of Atonement;
be responsive to us as we pray,
wipe away and remove all our transgressions and sins
from before Your eyes,
subdue our urges, that they be submitted to You,
and temper our obstinacy, that we may return to You truly;
renew our conscience that it may guard all Your commands,
and circumcise our hearts that we may love and revere Your name,
as it is written in Your Torah:
"And the LORD your God will circumcise your heart *Deut. 30*
and the heart of your descendants
to love the LORD your God with all your heart and with all your soul, so that you shall live."
The deliberate and the unwitting sins you recognize;
the willful and the compelled,
the open deeds and the hidden –
before You they are all revealed and known.

All:

סַרְנוּ מִמִּצְוֹתֶיךָ וּמִמִּשְׁפָּטֶיךָ הַטּוֹבִים, וְלֹא שָׁוָה לָנוּ.
וְאַתָּה צַדִּיק עַל כָּל־הַבָּא עָלֵינוּ נחמיה ט
כִּי־אֱמֶת עָשִׂיתָ, וַאֲנַחְנוּ הִרְשָׁעְנוּ:

הִרְשַׁעְנוּ וּפָשַׁעְנוּ, לָכֵן לֹא נוֹשָׁעְנוּ
וְתֵן בְּלִבֵּנוּ לַעֲזֹב דֶּרֶךְ רֶשַׁע, וְחִישׁ לָנוּ יֶשַׁע
כַּכָּתוּב עַל יַד נְבִיאֶךָ
יַעֲזֹב רָשָׁע דַּרְכּוֹ, וְאִישׁ אָוֶן מַחְשְׁבֹתָיו ישעיה נה
וְיָשֹׁב אֶל־יהוה וִירַחֲמֵהוּ, וְאֶל־אֱלֹהֵינוּ כִּי־יַרְבֶּה לִסְלוֹחַ:

The שליח ציבור *continues:*

אֱלֹהֵינוּ וֵאלֹהֵי אֲבוֹתֵינוּ
סְלַח וּמְחַל לַעֲוֹנוֹתֵינוּ
בְּיוֹם /בשבת: הַשַּׁבָּת הַזֶּה וּבְיוֹם/ הַכִּפּוּרִים הַזֶּה
וְהֵעָתֵר לָנוּ בִּתְפִלָּתֵנוּ
מְחֵה וְהַעֲבֵר פְּשָׁעֵינוּ וְחַטֹּאתֵינוּ מִנֶּגֶד עֵינֶיךָ
וְכֹף אֶת יִצְרֵנוּ לְהִשְׁתַּעְבֶּד לָךְ
וְהַכְנַע עָרְפֵּנוּ לָשׁוּב אֵלֶיךָ בֶּאֱמֶת
וְחַדֵּשׁ כִּלְיוֹתֵינוּ לִשְׁמֹר פִּקּוּדֶיךָ
וּמוֹל אֶת לְבָבֵנוּ לְאַהֲבָה וּלְיִרְאָה אֶת שְׁמֶךָ
כַּכָּתוּב בְּתוֹרָתֶךָ
וּמָל יהוה אֱלֹהֶיךָ אֶת־לְבָבְךָ וְאֶת־לְבַב זַרְעֶךָ דברים ל
לְאַהֲבָה אֶת־יהוה אֱלֹהֶיךָ בְּכָל־לְבָבְךָ וּבְכָל־נַפְשְׁךָ, לְמַעַן חַיֶּיךָ:
הַזְּדוֹנוֹת וְהַשְּׁגָגוֹת אַתָּה מַכִּיר
הָרָצוֹן וְהָאֹנֶס, הַגְּלוּיִים וְהַנִּסְתָּרִים
לְפָנֶיךָ הֵם גְּלוּיִים וִידוּעִים.

What are we? What are our lives?
What is our loving-kindness? What is our righteousness?
What is our salvation? What is our strength? What is our might?
What shall we say before You,
LORD our God and God of our ancestors?
Are not all the mighty like nothing before You,
the men of renown as if they had never been,
the wise as if they know nothing,
and the understanding as if they lack intelligence?
For their many works are in vain,
and the days of their lives like a fleeting breath before You.
The pre-eminence of man over the animals is nothing, *Eccl. 3*
for all is but a fleeting breath.

▸ What can we say before You, You who dwell on high?
What can we declare before You, You who abide in heaven?
Do You not know all, the hidden and revealed alike?

In Western Europe, the stanza "You know every secret" was said here, followed by the piyut אַתָּה מֵבִין *(page 1285). Today, most congregations follow the Eastern European custom, according to which only the last two stanzas of the piyut are said (below), followed by "You know every secret."*

The Leader then the congregation:

שִׁמְךָ Your name has always been the Forgiver of Sins.
Listen to our pleading as we stand before You in prayer.

Overlook sin, for this people returning from sin,
and wipe our transgressions away before Your eyes.

The Leader continues, with the congregation following him in an undertone:

אַתָּה יוֹדֵעַ You know every secret since the world began,
and what is hidden deep inside every living thing.
You search each person's inner chambers,
examining conscience and mind.
Nothing is shrouded from You,
and nothing is hidden before Your eyes.
And so, may it be Your will,
LORD our God and God of our ancestors,
that You forgive us all our sins, pardon all our iniquities,
and grant us atonement for all of our transgressions.

מָה אָנוּ, מֶה חַיֵּינוּ
מֶה חַסְדֵּנוּ, מַה צִּדְקוֹתֵינוּ
מַה יְּשׁוּעָתֵנוּ, מַה כֹּחֵנוּ, מַה גְּבוּרָתֵנוּ
מַה נֹּאמַר לְפָנֶיךָ, יהוה אֱלֹהֵינוּ וֵאלֹהֵי אֲבוֹתֵינוּ
הֲלֹא כָּל הַגִּבּוֹרִים כְּאַיִן לְפָנֶיךָ, וְאַנְשֵׁי הַשֵּׁם כְּלֹא הָיוּ
וַחֲכָמִים כִּבְלִי מַדָּע, וּנְבוֹנִים כִּבְלִי הַשְׂכֵּל
כִּי רֹב מַעֲשֵׂיהֶם תֹּהוּ, וִימֵי חַיֵּיהֶם הֶבֶל לְפָנֶיךָ
וּמוֹתַר הָאָדָם מִן־הַבְּהֵמָה אָיִן, כִּי הַכֹּל הָבֶל: קהלת ג

◂ מַה נֹּאמַר לְפָנֶיךָ יוֹשֵׁב מָרוֹם, וּמַה נְּסַפֵּר לְפָנֶיךָ שׁוֹכֵן שְׁחָקִים
הֲלֹא כָּל הַנִּסְתָּרוֹת וְהַנִּגְלוֹת אַתָּה יוֹדֵעַ.

In Western Europe, the stanza אַתָּה יוֹדֵעַ רָזֵי עוֹלָם *was said here, followed by the piyut* אַתָּה מֵבִין *(page 1285). Today, most congregations follow the Eastern European custom, according to which only the last two stanzas of* אַתָּה מֵבִין, שִׁמְךָ מֵעוֹלָם *are said, followed by* אַתָּה יוֹדֵעַ רָזֵי עוֹלָם.

The שליח ציבור *then* קהל*:*

שִׁמְךָ מֵעוֹלָם עוֹבֵר עַל פֶּשַׁע
שַׁוְעָתֵנוּ תַּאֲזִין, בְּעָמְדֵנוּ לְפָנֶיךָ בִּתְפִלָּה

תַּעֲבֹר עַל פֶּשַׁע לְעַם שָׁבֵי פֶשַׁע
תִּמְחֶה פְשָׁעֵינוּ מִנֶּגֶד עֵינֶיךָ.

The שליח ציבור *continues, with the* קהל *following him in an undertone:*

אַתָּה יוֹדֵעַ רָזֵי עוֹלָם וְתַעֲלוּמוֹת סִתְרֵי כָּל חָי.
אַתָּה חוֹפֵשׂ כָּל חַדְרֵי בָטֶן וּבוֹחֵן כְּלָיוֹת וָלֵב.
אֵין דָּבָר נֶעְלָם מִמֶּךָּ וְאֵין נִסְתָּר מִנֶּגֶד עֵינֶיךָ.
וּבְכֵן, יְהִי רָצוֹן מִלְּפָנֶיךָ, יהוה אֱלֹהֵינוּ וֵאלֹהֵי אֲבוֹתֵינוּ
שֶׁתִּסְלַח לָנוּ עַל כָּל חַטֹּאתֵינוּ וְתִמְחַל לָנוּ עַל כָּל עֲוֹנוֹתֵינוּ
וּתְכַפֵּר לָנוּ עַל כָּל פְּשָׁעֵינוּ.

Strike the left side of the chest with the right fist while saying each of the sins.

עַל חֵטְא For the sin we have sinned before You under duress or freewill,
and for the sin we have sinned before You in hardness of heart.

For the sin we have sinned before You unwittingly,
and for the sin we have sinned before You by an utterance of our lips.

For the sin we have sinned before You by unchastity,
and for the sin we have sinned before You openly or secretly.

For the sin we have sinned before You knowingly and deceitfully,
and for the sin we have sinned before You in speech.

For the sin we have sinned before You by wronging a neighbor,
and for the sin we have sinned before You by thoughts of the heart.

For the sin we have sinned before You in a gathering for immorality,
and for the sin we have sinned before You by insincere confession.

For the sin we have sinned before You by contempt for parents and teachers,
and for the sin we have sinned before You willfully or in error.

For the sin we have sinned before You by force,
and for the sin we have sinned before You by desecrating Your name.

For the sin we have sinned before You by impure lips,
and for the sin we have sinned before You by foolish speech.

For the sin we have sinned before You by the evil inclination,
and for the sin we have sinned before You knowingly or unwittingly.

The congregation aloud, followed by the Leader:

FOR ALL THESE, GOD OF FORGIVENESS,
FORGIVE US, PARDON US, GRANT US ATONEMENT.

Strike the left side of the chest with the right fist while saying each of the sins.

עַל חֵטְא שֶׁחָטָאנוּ לְפָנֶיךָ בְּאֹנֶס וּבְרָצוֹן
וְעַל חֵטְא שֶׁחָטָאנוּ לְפָנֶיךָ בְּאִמּוּץ הַלֵּב

עַל חֵטְא שֶׁחָטָאנוּ לְפָנֶיךָ בִּבְלִי דָעַת
וְעַל חֵטְא שֶׁחָטָאנוּ לְפָנֶיךָ בְּבִטּוּי שְׂפָתָיִם

עַל חֵטְא שֶׁחָטָאנוּ לְפָנֶיךָ בְּגִלּוּי עֲרָיוֹת
וְעַל חֵטְא שֶׁחָטָאנוּ לְפָנֶיךָ בְּגָלוּי וּבַסָּתֶר

עַל חֵטְא שֶׁחָטָאנוּ לְפָנֶיךָ בְּדַעַת וּבְמִרְמָה
וְעַל חֵטְא שֶׁחָטָאנוּ לְפָנֶיךָ בְּדִבּוּר פֶּה

עַל חֵטְא שֶׁחָטָאנוּ לְפָנֶיךָ בְּהוֹנָאַת רֵעַ
וְעַל חֵטְא שֶׁחָטָאנוּ לְפָנֶיךָ בְּהִרְהוּר הַלֵּב

עַל חֵטְא שֶׁחָטָאנוּ לְפָנֶיךָ בִּוְעִידַת זְנוּת
וְעַל חֵטְא שֶׁחָטָאנוּ לְפָנֶיךָ בְּוִדּוּי פֶּה

עַל חֵטְא שֶׁחָטָאנוּ לְפָנֶיךָ בְּזִלְזוּל הוֹרִים וּמוֹרִים
וְעַל חֵטְא שֶׁחָטָאנוּ לְפָנֶיךָ בְּזָדוֹן וּבִשְׁגָגָה

עַל חֵטְא שֶׁחָטָאנוּ לְפָנֶיךָ בְּחֹזֶק יָד
וְעַל חֵטְא שֶׁחָטָאנוּ לְפָנֶיךָ בְּחִלּוּל הַשֵּׁם

עַל חֵטְא שֶׁחָטָאנוּ לְפָנֶיךָ בְּטֻמְאַת שְׂפָתָיִם
וְעַל חֵטְא שֶׁחָטָאנוּ לְפָנֶיךָ בְּטִפְשׁוּת פֶּה

עַל חֵטְא שֶׁחָטָאנוּ לְפָנֶיךָ בְּיֵצֶר הָרָע
וְעַל חֵטְא שֶׁחָטָאנוּ לְפָנֶיךָ בְּיוֹדְעִים וּבְלֹא יוֹדְעִים

The קהל *aloud, followed by the* שליח ציבור:

וְעַל כֻּלָּם אֱלוֹהַּ סְלִיחוֹת סְלַח לָנוּ, מְחַל לָנוּ, כַּפֶּר לָנוּ.

All continue in an undertone. Strike the left side of the chest with the right fist while saying each of the sins.

For the sin we have sinned before You by deceit and lies,
and for the sin we have sinned before You by bribery.

For the sin we have sinned before You by scorn,
and for the sin we have sinned before You by evil speech.

For the sin we have sinned before You in business,
and for the sin we have sinned before You with food and drink.

For the sin we have sinned before You by interest and extortion,
and for the sin we have sinned before You by being haughty.

For the sin we have sinned before You
by the idle chatter of our lips,
and for the sin we have sinned before You by prying eyes.

For the sin we have sinned before You by arrogance,
and for the sin we have sinned before You by insolence.

The congregation aloud, followed by the Leader:

FOR ALL THESE, GOD OF FORGIVENESS,
FORGIVE US, PARDON US, GRANT US ATONEMENT.

All continue in an undertone. Strike the left side of the chest with the right fist while saying each of the sins.

For the sin we have sinned before You by casting off the yoke,
and for the sin we have sinned before You
by perverting judgment.

For the sin we have sinned before You by entrapping a neighbor,
and for the sin we have sinned before You by envy.

All continue in an undertone. Strike the left side of the chest with the right fist while saying each of the sins.

עַל חֵטְא שֶׁחָטָאנוּ לְפָנֶיךָ בְּכַחַשׁ וּבְכָזָב
וְעַל חֵטְא שֶׁחָטָאנוּ לְפָנֶיךָ בְּכַפַּת שֹׁחַד

עַל חֵטְא שֶׁחָטָאנוּ לְפָנֶיךָ בְּלָצוֹן
וְעַל חֵטְא שֶׁחָטָאנוּ לְפָנֶיךָ בִּלְשׁוֹן הָרָע

עַל חֵטְא שֶׁחָטָאנוּ לְפָנֶיךָ בְּמַשָּׂא וּבְמַתָּן
וְעַל חֵטְא שֶׁחָטָאנוּ לְפָנֶיךָ בְּמַאֲכָל וּבְמִשְׁתֶּה

עַל חֵטְא שֶׁחָטָאנוּ לְפָנֶיךָ בְּנֶשֶׁךְ וּבְמַרְבִּית
וְעַל חֵטְא שֶׁחָטָאנוּ לְפָנֶיךָ בִּנְטִיַּת גָּרוֹן

עַל חֵטְא שֶׁחָטָאנוּ לְפָנֶיךָ בְּשִׂיחַ שִׂפְתוֹתֵינוּ
וְעַל חֵטְא שֶׁחָטָאנוּ לְפָנֶיךָ בְּשִׂקּוּר עָיִן

עַל חֵטְא שֶׁחָטָאנוּ לְפָנֶיךָ בְּעֵינַיִם רָמוֹת
וְעַל חֵטְא שֶׁחָטָאנוּ לְפָנֶיךָ בְּעַזּוּת מֵצַח

The קהל *aloud, followed by the* שליח ציבור:

וְעַל כֻּלָּם אֱלוֹהַּ סְלִיחוֹת סְלַח לָנוּ, מְחַל לָנוּ, כַּפֶּר לָנוּ.

All continue in an undertone. Strike the left side of the chest with the right fist while saying each of the sins.

עַל חֵטְא שֶׁחָטָאנוּ לְפָנֶיךָ בִּפְרִיקַת עֹל
וְעַל חֵטְא שֶׁחָטָאנוּ לְפָנֶיךָ בִּפְלִילוּת

עַל חֵטְא שֶׁחָטָאנוּ לְפָנֶיךָ בִּצְדִיַּת רֵעַ
וְעַל חֵטְא שֶׁחָטָאנוּ לְפָנֶיךָ בְּצָרוּת עָיִן

For the sin we have sinned before You by lack of seriousness,
and for the sin we have sinned before You by obstinacy.

For the sin we have sinned before You by running to do evil,
and for the sin we have sinned before You by gossip.

For the sin we have sinned before You by vain oath,
and for the sin we have sinned before You by baseless hatred.

For the sin we have sinned before You by breach of trust,
and for the sin we have sinned before You by confusion of heart.

The congregation aloud, followed by the Leader:

FOR ALL THESE, GOD OF FORGIVENESS,
FORGIVE US, PARDON US, GRANT US ATONEMENT.

All:

וְעַל חֲטָאִים And for the sins for which we are liable to bring a burnt-offering,
and for the sins for which we are liable to bring a sin-offering,
and for the sins for which we are liable to bring an offering according to our means,
and for the sins for which we are liable to bring a guilt-offering for certain or possible sin,
and for the sins for which we are liable to lashes for rebellion,
and for the sins for which we are liable to forty lashes,
and for the sins for which we are liable to death by the hands of Heaven,
and for the sins for which we are liable to be cut off and childless,
and for the sins for which we are liable to the four death penalties
inflicted by the court: stoning, burning, beheading and strangling.

עַל חֵטְא שֶׁחָטָאנוּ לְפָנֶיךָ בְּקַלּוּת רֹאשׁ
וְעַל חֵטְא שֶׁחָטָאנוּ לְפָנֶיךָ בְּקַשְׁיוּת עֹרֶף

עַל חֵטְא שֶׁחָטָאנוּ לְפָנֶיךָ בְּרִיצַת רַגְלַיִם לְהָרַע
וְעַל חֵטְא שֶׁחָטָאנוּ לְפָנֶיךָ בִּרְכִילוּת

עַל חֵטְא שֶׁחָטָאנוּ לְפָנֶיךָ בִּשְׁבוּעַת שָׁוְא
וְעַל חֵטְא שֶׁחָטָאנוּ לְפָנֶיךָ בְּשִׂנְאַת חִנָּם

עַל חֵטְא שֶׁחָטָאנוּ לְפָנֶיךָ בִּתְשׂוּמֶת יָד
וְעַל חֵטְא שֶׁחָטָאנוּ לְפָנֶיךָ בְּתִמְהוֹן לֵבָב

The קהל *aloud, followed by the* שליח ציבור:

וְעַל כֻּלָּם אֱלוֹהַּ סְלִיחוֹת סְלַח לָנוּ, מְחַל לָנוּ, כַּפֶּר לָנוּ.

All:

וְעַל חֲטָאִים שֶׁאָנוּ חַיָּבִים עֲלֵיהֶם עוֹלָה
וְעַל חֲטָאִים שֶׁאָנוּ חַיָּבִים עֲלֵיהֶם חַטָּאת
וְעַל חֲטָאִים שֶׁאָנוּ חַיָּבִים עֲלֵיהֶם קָרְבָּן עוֹלֶה וְיוֹרֵד
וְעַל חֲטָאִים שֶׁאָנוּ חַיָּבִים עֲלֵיהֶם אָשָׁם וַדַּאי וְתָלוּי
וְעַל חֲטָאִים שֶׁאָנוּ חַיָּבִים עֲלֵיהֶם מַכַּת מַרְדּוּת
וְעַל חֲטָאִים שֶׁאָנוּ חַיָּבִים עֲלֵיהֶם מַלְקוּת אַרְבָּעִים
וְעַל חֲטָאִים שֶׁאָנוּ חַיָּבִים עֲלֵיהֶם מִיתָה בִּידֵי שָׁמָיִם
וְעַל חֲטָאִים שֶׁאָנוּ חַיָּבִים עֲלֵיהֶם כָּרֵת וַעֲרִירִי
וְעַל חֲטָאִים שֶׁאָנוּ חַיָּבִים עֲלֵיהֶם אַרְבַּע מִיתוֹת בֵּית דִּין
סְקִילָה, שְׂרֵפָה, הֶרֶג, וְחֶנֶק.

עַל מִצְוַת For positive and negative commandments,
whether they can be remedied by an act or not,
for sins known to us and for those that are unknown –
for those that are known,
we have already declared them before You
and confessed them to You;
and for those that are unknown,
before You they are revealed and known, as it is said,
"The secret things belong to the Lord our God, *Deut. 29*
but the things that are revealed are for us and our children for ever,
that we may fulfill all the words of this Torah."

וְדָוִד David Your servant said before You:
"Who can discern his own mistakes? *Ps. 19*
Cleanse me of my hidden faults."
Cleanse us, Lord our God,
of all our transgressions, and purify us of all our impurities,
and throw clear waters over us to purify us,
as was written by Your prophet:
"I shall throw clear waters over you and you shall be pure. *Ezek. 36*
I shall purify you of all your impurities and of all your idolatry."

אַל תִּירָא Do not be afraid, Jacob.
Come back, wayward children, come back Israel.
See: the Guardian of Israel neither slumbers nor sleeps. *Ps. 121*
As is written by Your prophet,
"Come back, Israel, to the Lord your God, *Hos. 14*
for you have stumbled in your iniquity." And it is said,
"Take up words to bring with you, and come back to the Lord. *Ibid.*
Tell Him: Forgive all our iniquities and take what is good;
we shall offer up our words instead of bullocks."

---

in Jewish thought, is intimately connected with sin: "Because of our sins we were exiled from our land." Hence the word *teshuva* has a double meaning: spiritual return to God, and the physical return of the Jewish people to its land. Just as God promised Jacob that He would bring him back, so He promises us through His prophets that return in both senses will happen. We will return in spirit to God and we will return as a people to our land.

עַל מִצְוַת עֲשֵׂה וְעַל מִצְוַת לֹא תַעֲשֶׂה.
בֵּין שֶׁיֵּשׁ בָּהּ קוּם עֲשֵׂה וּבֵין שֶׁאֵין בָּהּ קוּם עֲשֵׂה.
אֶת הַגְּלוּיִים לָנוּ וְאֶת שֶׁאֵינָם גְּלוּיִים לָנוּ
אֶת הַגְּלוּיִים לָנוּ, כְּבָר אֲמַרְנוּם לְפָנֶיךָ, וְהוֹדִינוּ לְךָ עֲלֵיהֶם
וְאֶת שֶׁאֵינָם גְּלוּיִים לָנוּ, לְפָנֶיךָ הֵם גְּלוּיִים וִידוּעִים
כַּדָּבָר שֶׁנֶּאֱמַר
הַנִּסְתָּרֹת לַיהוה אֱלֹהֵינוּ, וְהַנִּגְלֹת לָנוּ וּלְבָנֵינוּ עַד־עוֹלָם דברים כט
לַעֲשׂוֹת אֶת־כָּל־דִּבְרֵי הַתּוֹרָה הַזֹּאת:

וְדָוִד עַבְדְּךָ אָמַר לְפָנֶיךָ
שְׁגִיאוֹת מִי־יָבִין, מִנִּסְתָּרוֹת נַקֵּנִי: תהלים יט
נַקֵּנוּ יהוה אֱלֹהֵינוּ מִכָּל פְּשָׁעֵינוּ, וְטַהֲרֵנוּ מִכָּל טֻמְאוֹתֵינוּ
וּזְרֹק עָלֵינוּ מַיִם טְהוֹרִים וְטַהֲרֵנוּ
כַּכָּתוּב עַל יַד נְבִיאֶךָ
וְזָרַקְתִּי עֲלֵיכֶם מַיִם טְהוֹרִים, וּטְהַרְתֶּם יחזקאל לו
מִכֹּל טֻמְאוֹתֵיכֶם וּמִכָּל־גִּלּוּלֵיכֶם אֲטַהֵר אֶתְכֶם:

אַל תִּירָא יַעֲקֹב
שׁוּבוּ בָנִים שׁוֹבָבִים, שׁוּבָה יִשְׂרָאֵל.
הִנֵּה לֹא־יָנוּם וְלֹא יִישָׁן שׁוֹמֵר יִשְׂרָאֵל: תהלים קכא
כַּכָּתוּב עַל יַד נְבִיאֶךָ
שׁוּבָה יִשְׂרָאֵל עַד יהוה אֱלֹהֶיךָ, כִּי כָשַׁלְתָּ בַּעֲוֺנֶךָ: הושע יד
וְנֶאֱמַר
קְחוּ עִמָּכֶם דְּבָרִים, וְשׁוּבוּ אֶל־יהוה שם
אִמְרוּ אֵלָיו, כָּל־תִּשָּׂא עָוֺן וְקַח־טוֹב, וּנְשַׁלְּמָה פָרִים שְׂפָתֵינוּ:

אַל תִּירָא יַעֲקֹב *Do not be afraid Jacob.* Words said by God to Jacob as he was about to go into exile to be reunited with his son Joseph (Gen. 46:3). Exile,

וְאַתָּה And You are compassionate, accepting those who return,
and You have promised us repentance from the very beginning,
and it is for repentance that our eyes search after You.

וּמֵאַהֲבָתְךָ And because of Your love, LORD our God,
with which You have loved Your people Israel,
and because of Your mercy, our King, with which You have had
mercy on the children of Your covenant,
You have given us, LORD our God,
(*on Shabbat:* this Sabbath day for holiness and rest, and)
this fast day of Yom Kippur for our sins to be pardoned,
our iniquities forgiven and all our rebellions atoned.

יוֹם אֲשֶׁר A day on which our sins shall be cast
into the deep and sealed away.
Today may You forgive the entire congregation of the
children of Israel, along with the strangers in their midst.
As it is written in Your Torah:
And all the congregation of Israel are forgiven, *Num. 15*
along with the strangers living in their midst;
for they acted without knowing what they did.

A day on which You pardon and forgive our betrayal.
Today Your name shall be proven faithful,
O good and forgiving God.
As it is written in Your holy scriptures:
For You, my LORD, are good and forgiving, *Ps. 86*
abundantly kind to all who call on You.

---

day and *the* day. Yom Kippur is "the day" par excellence in the Jewish calendar. The tractate dealing with its laws is called, simply, *Yoma*, "the day." The sages also said about the first day of creation – called in the Torah (Gen. 1:5) *yom eḥad*, "one day," rather than *yom rishon*, "the first day" – that this refers to Yom Kippur, meaning, that this would prove to be the day on which the evil brought about by humankind could be cleansed and healed (*Bereshit Raba*

וְאַתָּה רַחוּם מְקַבֵּל שָׁבִים
וְעַל הַתְּשׁוּבָה מֵרֹאשׁ הִבְטַחְתָּֽנוּ
וְעַל הַתְּשׁוּבָה עֵינֵינוּ מְיַחֲלוֹת לָךְ.

וּמֵאַהֲבָתְךָ יהוה אֱלֹהֵינוּ, שֶׁאָהַבְתָּ אֶת יִשְׂרָאֵל עַמֶּךָ
וּמֵחֶמְלָתְךָ מַלְכֵּנוּ, שֶׁחָמַלְתָּ עַל בְּנֵי בְרִיתֶךָ
נָתַתָּ לָּנוּ יהוה אֱלֹהֵינוּ אֶת
(בשבת: יוֹם הַשַּׁבָּת הַזֶּה לִקְדֻשָּׁה וְלִמְנוּחָה, וְאֶת)
יוֹם צוֹם הַכִּפּוּרִים הַזֶּה
לִמְחִילַת חֵטְא וְלִסְלִיחַת עָוֹן וּלְכַפָּרַת פֶּשַׁע.

יוֹם אֲשֶׁר אֲשַׁמְנוּ יְצַלֵּל וְיִסְגַּר
הַיּוֹם תִּסְלַח לְכָל עֲדַת בְּנֵי יִשְׂרָאֵל, וְלַגֵּר הַגָּר.
כַּכָּתוּב בְּתוֹרָתֶךָ
וְנִסְלַח לְכָל־עֲדַת בְּנֵי יִשְׂרָאֵל, וְלַגֵּר הַגָּר בְּתוֹכָם במדבר טו
כִּי לְכָל־הָעָם בִּשְׁגָגָה:

יוֹם בָּגַדְנוּ תִּשָּׂא וְתִסְלַח
הַיּוֹם שִׁמְךָ יֵאָמֵן, אֵל טוֹב וְסַלָּח.
כַּכָּתוּב בְּדִבְרֵי קָדְשֶׁךָ
כִּי־אַתָּה אֲדֹנָי טוֹב וְסַלָּח, וְרַב־חֶסֶד לְכָל־קֹרְאֶיךָ: תהלים פו

וְעַל הַתְּשׁוּבָה מֵרֹאשׁ הִבְטַחְתָּֽנוּ *And You have promised us repentance from the very beginning.* According to the sages, *teshuva* was created before the universe (*Nedarim* 39b). Before God created a being capable of freewill and therefore sin, He had already made provision for the forgiveness: "God creates the cure before the disease" (*Megilla*, 13b).

יוֹם אֲשֶׁר *A day on which.* A complex poem on the theme of Yom Kippur as *a*

A day on which You forget and disregard our debasement
of Your commandments.
Today may You have compassion for us
and we will repent and abandon the ways of the wicked.
As was written by Your prophet:
Let the wicked abandon his ways, *Is. 55*
and the man of iniquity his thoughts.
Let him return to the LORD,
who will have compassion for him;
to our God, for He is abundantly forgiving.

A day on which we beg You to forgive us our faults.
Today may You listen to our prayers
and please forgive us graciously.
As it is written in Your Torah:
Please, forgive this people's iniquity *Num. 14*
in the abundance of Your kindness,
as You have forgiven this people
from the time of Egypt until now,
and there it is said:
And the LORD said, I have forgiven as you asked. *Ibid.*

For the honor of Your name,
be responsive to us, You who pardons and forgives,
please forgive us for the sake of Your name.

A day on which You recall when [Moses] the humble one prayed
to You on our behalf.
Today may You forgive our iniquities and not recall sin.
As it is written in Your holy scripture:
Do not hold against us the sins of those who came before us. *Ps. 79*
May Your mercies meet us swiftly,
for we have been brought very low.

---

verse on the subject of forgiveness, grounding the prayer on God's promise as recorded by the prophets.

יוֹם גְּעַלְנוּ חֻקֶּיךָ, שַׁכַּח וַעֲזוֹב
הַיּוֹם רַחֲמֵנוּ וְנָשׁוּב וְדֶרֶךְ רֶשַׁע נַעֲזֹב.
כַּכָּתוּב עַל יַד נְבִיאֶךָ
יַעֲזֹב רָשָׁע דַּרְכּוֹ, וְאִישׁ אָוֶן מַחְשְׁבֹתָיו ישעיה נה
וְיָשֹׁב אֶל־יהוה וִירַחֲמֵהוּ וְאֶל־אֱלֹהֵינוּ כִּי־יַרְבֶּה לִסְלוֹחַ:

יוֹם דָּפְיֵנוּ אָנָּא שָׂא נָא
הַיּוֹם קְשֹׁב תַּחֲנוּנֵינוּ, וּבְתַחֲנוּן סְלַח נָא.
כַּכָּתוּב בְּתוֹרָתֶךָ
סְלַח־נָא לַעֲוֹן הָעָם הַזֶּה כְּגֹדֶל חַסְדֶּךָ במדבר יד
וְכַאֲשֶׁר נָשָׂאתָה לָעָם הַזֶּה מִמִּצְרַיִם וְעַד־הֵנָּה:
וְשָׁם נֶאֱמַר
וַיֹּאמֶר יהוה, סָלַחְתִּי כִּדְבָרֶךָ: שם

בַּעֲבוּר כְּבוֹד שְׁמֶךָ
הַמָּצֵא לָנוּ מוֹחֵל וְסוֹלֵחַ / סְלַח נָא לְמַעַן שְׁמֶךָ.

יוֹם חִנָּנְךָ עָנוּ, בַּעֲדֵנוּ תִּזְכֹּר
הַיּוֹם סְלַח לַעֲוֹנֵנוּ, וְחֵטְא אַל תִּזְכֹּר.
כַּכָּתוּב בְּדִבְרֵי קָדְשֶׁךָ
אַל־תִּזְכָּר־לָנוּ עֲוֹנֹת רִאשֹׁנִים תהלים עט
מַהֵר יְקַדְּמוּנוּ רַחֲמֶיךָ, כִּי דַלּוֹנוּ מְאֹד:

3:8). The poem itself is an אתב״ש acrostic in which each stanza has three parts: the first beginning "A day," describing our need for forgiveness; the second beginning with "Today," expressing a prayer; the third, a scriptural

A day on which our mistakes are sought but are not to be found.
Today Your word shall be upheld, that iniquity will be sought
yet be nowhere to be found.
As was written by Your prophet:
In those days, at that time, says the Lord, *Jer. 50*
they will search for Israel's iniquity
and it will not be there,
they will seek the sins of Judah
and they will be nowhere to be found,
for I shall forgive those I leave behind.

A day when all will seek the One who refines and purifies.
Today may You purify us of all our sins.
As it is written in Your Torah:
For on this day you will be atoned and made pure; *Lev. 16*
of all your sins before the Lord you shall be purified.

A day on which I express my plea that You forgive all iniquity.
Today may You lend Your ear to our cries.
As it is written in Your holy scriptures:
Give ear, my God, and hear; *Dan. 9*
open Your eyes and see our desolation,
and the city that bears Your name,
for it is not on the strength of our righteousness
that we throw down our pleadings before You,
but on the strength of Your great compassion.
Lord, hear me; Lord, forgive;
Lord, listen and act and do not delay –
for Your sake, my God;
for Your city and Your people bear Your name.

For the honor of Your name,
be responsive to us, You who pardons and forgives,
please forgive us for the sake of Your name.

יוֹם טְעוּתֵנוּ יְבֻקַּשׁ וָאָיִן
הַיּוֹם נְאֻם הָקֵם, יְבֻקַּשׁ עָוֺן וָאָיִן.
כַּכָּתוּב עַל יַד נְבִיאֶךָ
בַּיָּמִים הָהֵם וּבָעֵת הַהִיא, נְאֻם־יהוה ירמיה נ
יְבֻקַּשׁ אֶת־עֲוֺן יִשְׂרָאֵל וְאֵינֶנּוּ
וְאֶת־חַטֹּאת יְהוּדָה, וְלֹא תִמָּצֶאינָה
כִּי אֶסְלַח לַאֲשֶׁר אַשְׁאִיר:

יוֹם יִדְרְשׁוּן מְצָרֵף וּמְטַהֵר
הַיּוֹם מִכָּל חַטֹּאתֵינוּ אוֹתָנוּ תְּטַהֵר.
כַּכָּתוּב בְּתוֹרָתֶךָ
כִּי־בַיּוֹם הַזֶּה יְכַפֵּר עֲלֵיכֶם לְטַהֵר אֶתְכֶם ויקרא טז
מִכֹּל חַטֹּאתֵיכֶם, לִפְנֵי יהוה תִּטְהָרוּ:

יוֹם כָּל תִּשָּׂא עָוֺן, בְּתַחֲנוּן אֲבַטֵּא
הַיּוֹם לְשַׁוְעָתֵנוּ אֹזֶן הַטֵּה.
כַּכָּתוּב בְּדִבְרֵי קָדְשֶׁךָ
הַטֵּה אֱלֹהַי אָזְנְךָ וּשֲׁמָע דניאל ט
פְּקַח עֵינֶיךָ וּרְאֵה שֹׁמְמֹתֵינוּ
וְהָעִיר אֲשֶׁר־נִקְרָא שִׁמְךָ עָלֶיהָ
כִּי לֹא עַל־צִדְקֹתֵינוּ אֲנַחְנוּ מַפִּילִים תַּחֲנוּנֵינוּ לְפָנֶיךָ
כִּי עַל־רַחֲמֶיךָ הָרַבִּים:
אֲדֹנָי שְׁמָעָה, אֲדֹנָי סְלָחָה
אֲדֹנָי הַקְשִׁיבָה וַעֲשֵׂה אַל־תְּאַחַר
לְמַעַנְךָ אֱלֹהַי, כִּי־שִׁמְךָ נִקְרָא עַל־עִירְךָ וְעַל־עַמֶּךָ:

בַּעֲבוּר כְּבוֹד שְׁמֶךָ
הִמָּצֵא לָנוּ שׁוֹמֵעַ תְּפִלָּה / שְׁמַע תְּפִלָּתֵנוּ לְמַעַן שְׁמֶךָ.

In many congregations, the Leader recites the two first stichs of each line, and the congregation responds "Who, God, is like You?" Some sing the entire piyut collectively.

Who, God, is like You?

I will praise You with a loud voice, / Shield of Abraham.
Who, God, is like You?
If I die let it be by Your hand, / You who revives the dead.
Who, God, is like You?
I will seek Your greatness, / O holy King. Who, God, is like You?
You expound words of wisdom,
You who graciously grants knowledge. Who, God, is like You?
You call on us to repent, / You who desires repentance.
Who, God, is like You?
You pardon and forgive, / You who repeatedly forgives.
Who, God, is like You?
The sound of song and thanksgiving,
O Good One, to You gives thanks. Who, God, is like You?
Exalted One, bless our gathered assemblies:
"May the LORD bless you." Who, God, is like You?
Your Presence is peace, / You who makes peace.
Who, God, is like You?
May blessings come upon you/ for we shall offer a prayer for you.
Who, God, is like You?

All:

Overlook sin / for this people returning from sin.

As was written by Your prophet:
Who, God, is like You, *Mic. 7*
who forgives iniquity
and overlooks the transgression of the remnant of Your heritage.
He does not remain angry forever, for He desires loving-kindness.

---

prayer that are inappropriate for Yom Kippur. The poem has been attributed to Rabbi Elazar HaKalir.

In many congregations, the שליח ציבור *recites the two first stichs of each line, and the* קהל *responds* "מִי אֵל כָּמְוֹךָ." *Some sing the entire piyut collectively.*

מִי אֵל כָּמְוֹךָ.

אֲהַלֶּלְךָ בְּקוֹל רָם / מָגֵן אַבְרָהָם מִי אֵל כָּמְוֹךָ
בְּיָדְךָ מְמִתִים / מְחַיֵּה הַמֵּתִים מִי אֵל כָּמְוֹךָ
גָּדְלְךָ אֶדְרֹשׁ / הַמֶּלֶךְ הַקָּדוֹשׁ מִי אֵל כָּמְוֹךָ
דּוֹרֵשׁ אִמְרֵי דַעַת / חוֹנֵן הַדָּעַת מִי אֵל כָּמְוֹךָ
הָאוֹמֵר שׁוּבָה / הָרוֹצֶה בִּתְשׁוּבָה מִי אֵל כָּמְוֹךָ
וּמוֹחֵל וְסוֹלֵחַ / הַמַּרְבֶּה לִסְלְחַ מִי אֵל כָּמְוֹךָ
קוֹל רִנָּה וְתוֹדוֹת / הַטּוֹב לְךָ לְהוֹדוֹת מִי אֵל כָּמְוֹךָ
רָם בָּרֵךְ קְהַל הֲמוֹנֵי / יְבָרֶכְךָ יהוה מִי אֵל כָּמְוֹךָ
שְׁכִינָתְךָ שָׁלוֹם / עוֹשֵׂה הַשָּׁלוֹם מִי אֵל כָּמְוֹךָ
תָּבֹא בְרָכָה אֲלֵיכֶם / וְנֹאמַר תְּפִלָּה עֲלֵיכֶם מִי אֵל כָּמְוֹךָ

All:

תַּעֲבֹר עַל פֶּשַׁע / לְעַם שָׁבֵי פֶשַׁע

כַּכָּתוּב עַל יַד נְבִיאֶךָ
מִי־אֵל כָּמְוֹךָ מיכה ז
נֹשֵׂא עָוֹן וְעֹבֵר עַל־פֶּשַׁע לִשְׁאֵרִית נַחֲלָתוֹ
לֹא־הֶחֱזִיק לָעַד אַפּוֹ כִּי־חָפֵץ חֶסֶד הוּא:

מִי אֵל כָּמְוֹךָ *Who, God, is like You?* An alphabetical summary of the blessings of the weekday Amida, shortened here by the omission of those parts of the

He shall relent and show us compassion,
He shall suppress our iniquities,
casting all of our sins
into the depths of the sea.
And all the sins of Your nation,
the House of Israel,
cast them down where they shall not be remembered
nor recalled nor come to mind ever again.
Grant truth to Jacob,
loving-kindness to Abraham,
as You promised our ancestors
in ancient times.

The Leader continues. On Shabbat, add the words in parentheses:

Our God and God of our ancestors,
pardon our iniquities on
(this Sabbath day, and on)
this Day of Atonement;
wipe away and remove
all our transgressions and sins
from before Your eyes,
as it is said:

"I, I am the One who shall wipe out your transgressions *Is. 43*
for My sake, and I shall not recall your sins."

And it is said:

"I have wiped out your transgressions like a cloud, *Is. 44*
and as a haze your sins;
come back to Me for I have redeemed you."

And it is said:

"For on this day you will be atoned and made pure; *Lev. 16*
of all your sins before the LORD
you shall be purified."

יָשׁוּב יְרַחֲמֵנוּ
יִכְבֹּשׁ עֲוֹנֹתֵינוּ
וְתַשְׁלִיךְ בִּמְצֻלוֹת יָם כָּל־חַטֹּאתָם:
וְכָל חַטֹּאת עַמְּךָ בֵּית יִשְׂרָאֵל תַּשְׁלִיךְ
בִּמְקוֹם אֲשֶׁר לֹא יִזָּכְרוּ וְלֹא יִפָּקְדוּ
וְלֹא יַעֲלוּ עַל לֵב לְעוֹלָם.
תִּתֵּן אֱמֶת לְיַעֲקֹב
חֶסֶד לְאַבְרָהָם
אֲשֶׁר־נִשְׁבַּעְתָּ לַאֲבֹתֵינוּ מִימֵי קֶדֶם:

The שליח ציבור *continues. On* שבת*, add the words in parentheses:*

אֱלֹהֵינוּ וֵאלֹהֵי אֲבוֹתֵינוּ
מְחַל לַעֲוֹנוֹתֵינוּ בְּיוֹם (הַשַּׁבָּת הַזֶּה וּבְיוֹם) הַכִּפּוּרִים הַזֶּה
מְחֵה וְהַעֲבֵר פְּשָׁעֵינוּ
וְחַטֹּאתֵינוּ מִנֶּגֶד עֵינֶיךָ
כָּאָמוּר
אָנֹכִי אָנֹכִי הוּא מֹחֶה פְשָׁעֶיךָ לְמַעֲנִי ישעיה מג
וְחַטֹּאתֶיךָ לֹא אֶזְכֹּר:

וְנֶאֱמַר
מָחִיתִי כָעָב פְּשָׁעֶיךָ וְכֶעָנָן חַטֹּאותֶיךָ ישעיה מד
שׁוּבָה אֵלַי כִּי גְאַלְתִּיךָ:

וְנֶאֱמַר
כִּי־בַיּוֹם הַזֶּה יְכַפֵּר עֲלֵיכֶם לְטַהֵר אֶתְכֶם ויקרא טז
מִכֹּל חַטֹּאתֵיכֶם, לִפְנֵי יהוה תִּטְהָרוּ:

(Our God and God of our ancestors,
may You find favor in our rest.)
Make us holy through Your commandments
and grant us our share in Your Torah.
Satisfy us with Your goodness, grant us joy in Your salvation
(in love and favor, Lord our God,
grant us as our heritage Your holy Sabbath,
so that Israel, who sanctify Your name, may find rest on it),
and purify our hearts to serve You in truth.
For You are the Forgiver of Israel
and the Pardoner of the tribes of Yeshurun in every generation,
and without You we have no king who pardons and forgives,
none but You.
Blessed are You, Lord,
King who pardons and forgives our iniquities
and those of all His people the house of Israel,
and makes our guilt pass away, every single year,
King of all the earth, who sanctifies (the Sabbath,)
Israel and the Day of Atonement.

TEMPLE SERVICE

רְצֵה Find favor, Lord our God,
in Your people Israel and their prayer.
Restore the service to Your most holy House,
and accept in love and favor
the fire-offerings of Israel and their prayer.
May the service of Your people Israel
always find favor with You.
And may our eyes witness Your return to Zion
in compassion.
Blessed are You, Lord,
who restores His Presence to Zion.

(אֱלֹהֵינוּ וֵאלֹהֵי אֲבוֹתֵינוּ, רְצֵה בִמְנוּחָתֵנוּ)
קַדְּשֵׁנוּ בְּמִצְוֹתֶיךָ וְתֵן חֶלְקֵנוּ בְּתוֹרָתֶךָ
שַׂבְּעֵנוּ מִטּוּבֶךָ וְשַׂמְּחֵנוּ בִּישׁוּעָתֶךָ
(וְהַנְחִילֵנוּ יהוה אֱלֹהֵינוּ בְּאַהֲבָה וּבְרָצוֹן שַׁבַּת קָדְשֶׁךָ
וְיָנוּחוּ בוֹ יִשְׂרָאֵל מְקַדְּשֵׁי שְׁמֶךָ)
וְטַהֵר לִבֵּנוּ לְעָבְדְּךָ בֶּאֱמֶת
כִּי אַתָּה סָלְחָן לְיִשְׂרָאֵל
וּמָחֳלָן לְשִׁבְטֵי יְשֻׁרוּן בְּכָל דּוֹר וָדוֹר
וּמִבַּלְעָדֶיךָ אֵין לָנוּ מֶלֶךְ מוֹחֵל וְסוֹלֵחַ אֶלָּא אָתָּה.
בָּרוּךְ אַתָּה יהוה
מֶלֶךְ מוֹחֵל וְסוֹלֵחַ לַעֲוֹנוֹתֵינוּ
וְלַעֲוֹנוֹת עַמּוֹ בֵּית יִשְׂרָאֵל
וּמַעֲבִיר אַשְׁמוֹתֵינוּ בְּכָל שָׁנָה וְשָׁנָה
מֶלֶךְ עַל כָּל הָאָרֶץ
מְקַדֵּשׁ (הַשַּׁבָּת וְ) יִשְׂרָאֵל וְיוֹם הַכִּפּוּרִים.

עבודה

רְצֵה יהוה אֱלֹהֵינוּ בְּעַמְּךָ יִשְׂרָאֵל, וּבִתְפִלָּתָם
וְהָשֵׁב אֶת הָעֲבוֹדָה לִדְבִיר בֵּיתֶךָ
וְאִשֵּׁי יִשְׂרָאֵל וּתְפִלָּתָם בְּאַהֲבָה תְקַבֵּל בְּרָצוֹן
וּתְהִי לְרָצוֹן תָּמִיד עֲבוֹדַת יִשְׂרָאֵל עַמֶּךָ.
וְתֶחֱזֶינָה עֵינֵינוּ בְּשׁוּבְךָ לְצִיּוֹן בְּרַחֲמִים.
בָּרוּךְ אַתָּה יהוה, הַמַּחֲזִיר שְׁכִינָתוֹ לְצִיּוֹן.

THANKSGIVING

Bow at the first nine words.

מוֹדִים We give thanks to You,
for You are the LORD our God
and God of our ancestors
for ever and all time.
You are the Rock of our lives,
Shield of our salvation
from generation to generation.
We will thank You and
declare Your praise for our lives,
which are entrusted into Your hand;
for our souls,
which are placed in Your charge;
for Your miracles
which are with us every day;
and for Your wonders and favors
at all times, evening, morning and midday.
You are good –
for Your compassion never fails.
You are compassionate –
for Your loving-kindnesses never cease.
We have always placed our hope in You.

As the Leader recites Modim, the congregation says quietly:

מוֹדִים We give thanks to You,
for You are the LORD our God
and God of our ancestors,
God of all flesh,
who formed us
and formed the universe.
Blessings and thanks
are due to Your great
and holy name for giving us
life and sustaining us.
May You continue
to give us life and sustain us;
and may You gather our
exiles to Your holy courts,
to keep Your decrees,
do Your will and serve You
with a perfect heart,
for it is for us
to give You thanks.
Blessed be God to whom
thanksgiving is due.

For all these things may Your name be blessed and exalted,
our King, continually, for ever and all time.

The congregation, then the Leader:

אָבִינוּ מַלְכֵּנוּ Our Father, our King,
remember Your compassion and overcome Your anger,
and efface pestilence, sword,
famine, captivity and destruction,
iniquity and plague, and bad mishap and all illness, and any harm,
and any feud, and all kinds of afflictions,
and all harsh decrees and baseless hatred,
from us and from all the people of Your covenant.

הודאה

Bow at the first five words.

מוֹדִים אֲנַחְנוּ לָךְ
שָׁאַתָּה הוּא יהוה אֱלֹהֵינוּ
וֵאלֹהֵי אֲבוֹתֵינוּ לְעוֹלָם וָעֶד.
צוּר חַיֵּינוּ, מָגֵן יִשְׁעֵנוּ
אַתָּה הוּא לְדוֹר וָדוֹר.
נוֹדֶה לְּךָ וּנְסַפֵּר תְּהִלָּתֶךָ
עַל חַיֵּינוּ הַמְּסוּרִים בְּיָדֶךָ
וְעַל נִשְׁמוֹתֵינוּ הַפְּקוּדוֹת לָךְ
וְעַל נִסֶּיךָ שֶׁבְּכָל יוֹם עִמָּנוּ
וְעַל נִפְלְאוֹתֶיךָ וְטוֹבוֹתֶיךָ
שֶׁבְּכָל עֵת, עֶרֶב וָבֹקֶר וְצָהֳרָיִם.
הַטּוֹב, כִּי לֹא כָלוּ רַחֲמֶיךָ
וְהַמְרַחֵם, כִּי לֹא תַמּוּ חֲסָדֶיךָ
מֵעוֹלָם קִוִּינוּ לָךְ.

As the שליח ציבור *recites* מודים*, the* קהל *says quietly:*

מוֹדִים אֲנַחְנוּ לָךְ
שָׁאַתָּה הוּא יהוה אֱלֹהֵינוּ
וֵאלֹהֵי אֲבוֹתֵינוּ
אֱלֹהֵי כָל בָּשָׂר
יוֹצְרֵנוּ, יוֹצֵר בְּרֵאשִׁית.
בְּרָכוֹת וְהוֹדָאוֹת
לְשִׁמְךָ הַגָּדוֹל וְהַקָּדוֹשׁ
עַל שֶׁהֶחֱיִיתָנוּ וְקִיַּמְתָּנוּ.
כֵּן תְּחַיֵּנוּ וּתְקַיְּמֵנוּ
וְתֶאֱסֹף גָּלֻיּוֹתֵינוּ
לְחַצְרוֹת קָדְשֶׁךָ
לִשְׁמֹר חֻקֶּיךָ וְלַעֲשׂוֹת רְצוֹנֶךָ
וּלְעָבְדְּךָ בְּלֵבָב שָׁלֵם
עַל שֶׁאֲנַחְנוּ מוֹדִים לָךְ.
בָּרוּךְ אֵל הַהוֹדָאוֹת.

וְעַל כֻּלָּם יִתְבָּרַךְ וְיִתְרוֹמַם שִׁמְךָ מַלְכֵּנוּ תָּמִיד לְעוֹלָם וָעֶד.

The קהל *then the* שליח ציבור*:*

אָבִינוּ מַלְכֵּנוּ
זְכֹר רַחֲמֶיךָ וּכְבֹשׁ כַּעַסְךָ
וְכַלֵּה דֶבֶר, וְחֶרֶב, וְרָעָב, וּשְׁבִי, וּמַשְׁחִית
וְעָוֹן וּמַגֵּפָה, וּפֶגַע רַע וְכָל מַחֲלָה, וְכָל תַּקָּלָה
וְכָל קְטָטָה וְכָל מִינֵי פֻרְעָנִיּוֹת, וְכָל גְּזֵרָה רָעָה וְשִׂנְאַת חִנָּם
מֵעָלֵינוּ וּמֵעַל כָּל בְּנֵי בְרִיתֶךָ.

The congregation, then the Leader:

וּכְתֹב And write, for a good life,
all the children of Your covenant.

The Leader continues:

Let all that lives thank You, Selah! and praise Your name in truth,
God, our Savior and Help, Selah!
▾Blessed are You, LORD,
whose name is "the Good"
and to whom thanks are due.

In Israel, if Kohanim bless the congregation, *turn to page 1260.*

אֱלֹהֵינוּ Our God and God of our fathers,
bless us with the threefold blessing in the Torah,
written by the hand of Moses Your servant
and pronounced by Aaron and his sons the priests,
Your holy people, as it is said:

May the LORD bless you and protect you. *Num. 6*
Cong: May it be Your will.
May the LORD make His face shine on you and be gracious to you.
Cong: May it be Your will.
May the LORD turn His face toward you, and grant you peace.
Cong: May it be Your will.

PEACE

שִׂים שָׁלוֹם Grant peace, goodness and blessing,
grace, loving-kindness and compassion to us
and all Israel Your people.
Bless us, our Father, all as one, with the light of Your face,
for by the light of Your face You have given us, LORD our God,
the Torah of life and love of kindness,
righteousness, blessing, compassion, life and peace.
May it be good in Your eyes to bless Your people Israel
at every time, in every hour, with Your peace.

The קהל *then the* שליח ציבור:

וּכְתֹב לְחַיִּים טוֹבִים כָּל בְּנֵי בְרִיתֶךָ.

The שליח ציבור *continues:*

וְכֹל הַחַיִּים יוֹדְוּךָ סֶּלָה, וִיהַלְלוּ אֶת שִׁמְךָ בֶּאֱמֶת
הָאֵל יְשׁוּעָתֵנוּ וְעֶזְרָתֵנוּ סֶלָה.
בָּרוּךְ אַתָּה יהוה
הַטּוֹב שִׁמְךָ וּלְךָ נָאֶה לְהוֹדוֹת.

In ארץ ישראל*, if* כהנים *say* ברכת כהנים*,* *turn to page 1261.*

אֱלֹהֵינוּ וֵאלֹהֵי אֲבוֹתֵינוּ, בָּרְכֵנוּ בַּבְּרָכָה הַמְשֻׁלֶּשֶׁת בַּתּוֹרָה
הַכְּתוּבָה עַל יְדֵי מֹשֶׁה עַבְדֶּךָ, הָאֲמוּרָה מִפִּי אַהֲרֹן וּבָנָיו
כֹּהֲנִים עַם קְדוֹשֶׁיךָ, כָּאָמוּר

יְבָרֶכְךָ יהוה וְיִשְׁמְרֶךָ: קהל: כֵּן יְהִי רָצוֹן במדבר ו
יָאֵר יהוה פָּנָיו אֵלֶיךָ וִיחֻנֶּךָּ: קהל: כֵּן יְהִי רָצוֹן
יִשָּׂא יהוה פָּנָיו אֵלֶיךָ וְיָשֵׂם לְךָ שָׁלוֹם: קהל: כֵּן יְהִי רָצוֹן

שלום

שִׂים שָׁלוֹם טוֹבָה וּבְרָכָה, חֵן וָחֶסֶד וְרַחֲמִים
עָלֵינוּ וְעַל כָּל יִשְׂרָאֵל עַמֶּךָ.
בָּרְכֵנוּ אָבִינוּ כֻּלָּנוּ כְּאֶחָד בְּאוֹר פָּנֶיךָ
כִּי בְאוֹר פָּנֶיךָ נָתַתָּ לָּנוּ, יהוה אֱלֹהֵינוּ
תּוֹרַת חַיִּים וְאַהֲבַת חֶסֶד
וּצְדָקָה וּבְרָכָה וְרַחֲמִים וְחַיִּים וְשָׁלוֹם.
וְטוֹב בְּעֵינֶיךָ לְבָרֵךְ אֶת עַמְּךָ יִשְׂרָאֵל
בְּכָל עֵת וּבְכָל שָׁעָה בִּשְׁלוֹמֶךָ.

The congregation then the Leader:

בְּסֵפֶר חַיִּים In the book of life,
blessing, peace and prosperity,
may we and all Your people the house of Israel
be remembered and written before You
for a good life, and for peace.*

Blessed are You, Lord,
who blesses His people Israel with peace.

**Outside Israel, many end the blessing:*
Blessed are You, Lord, who makes peace.

The following verse concludes the Leader's Repetition of the Amida.
May the words of my mouth and the meditation of my heart *Ps. 19*
find favor before You, Lord, my Rock and Redeemer.

AVINU MALKENU

On Shabbat, "Avinu Malkenu" is not said,
and the service continues with Full Kaddish on page 716.

The Ark is opened.

אָבִינוּ מַלְכֵּנוּ Our Father, our King, we have sinned before You.

Our Father, our King, we have no king but You.

Our Father, our King, deal kindly with us for the sake of Your name.

Our Father our King, renew for us a good year.

Our Father, our King, nullify all harsh decrees against us.

Our Father, our King, nullify the plans of those who hate us.

Our Father, our King, thwart the counsel of our enemies.

Our Father, our King, rid us of every oppressor and adversary.

AVINU MALKENU – OUR FATHER, OUR KING
For commentary see page 189.

The קהל *then the* שליח ציבור:

בְּסֵפֶר חַיִּים, בְּרָכָה וְשָׁלוֹם, וּפַרְנָסָה טוֹבָה
נִזָּכֵר וְנִכָּתֵב לְפָנֶיךָ, אֲנַחְנוּ וְכָל עַמְּךָ בֵּית יִשְׂרָאֵל
לְחַיִּים טוֹבִים וּלְשָׁלוֹם.*

בָּרוּךְ אַתָּה יהוה, הַמְבָרֵךְ אֶת עַמּוֹ יִשְׂרָאֵל בַּשָּׁלוֹם.

**In* חוץ לארץ*, many end the blessing:*

בָּרוּךְ אַתָּה יהוה, עוֹשֵׂה הַשָּׁלוֹם.

The following verse concludes the חזרת הש״ץ.

יִהְיוּ לְרָצוֹן אִמְרֵי־פִי וְהֶגְיוֹן לִבִּי לְפָנֶיךָ, יהוה צוּרִי וְגֹאֲלִי: תהלים יט

אבינו מלכנו

On שבת*,* אָבִינוּ מַלְכֵּנוּ *is not said,*
and the service continues with קדיש שלם *on page 717.*

The ארון קודש *is opened.*

אָבִינוּ מַלְכֵּנוּ, חָטָאנוּ לְפָנֶיךָ.

אָבִינוּ מַלְכֵּנוּ, אֵין לָנוּ מֶלֶךְ אֶלָּא אָתָּה.

אָבִינוּ מַלְכֵּנוּ, עֲשֵׂה עִמָּנוּ לְמַעַן שְׁמֶךָ.

אָבִינוּ מַלְכֵּנוּ, חַדֵּשׁ עָלֵינוּ שָׁנָה טוֹבָה.

אָבִינוּ מַלְכֵּנוּ, בַּטֵּל מֵעָלֵינוּ כָּל גְּזֵרוֹת קָשׁוֹת.

אָבִינוּ מַלְכֵּנוּ, בַּטֵּל מַחְשְׁבוֹת שׂוֹנְאֵינוּ.

אָבִינוּ מַלְכֵּנוּ, הָפֵר עֲצַת אוֹיְבֵינוּ.

אָבִינוּ מַלְכֵּנוּ, כַּלֵּה כָּל צַר וּמַשְׂטִין מֵעָלֵינוּ.

Our Father, our King, close the mouths of our adversaries and accusers.

Our Father, our King, eradicate pestilence, sword, famine, captivity and destruction, iniquity and eradication from the people of Your covenant.

Our Father, our King, withhold the plague from Your heritage.

Our Father, our King, forgive and pardon all our iniquities.

Our Father, our King, wipe away and remove our transgressions and sins from Your sight.

Our Father, our King, erase in Your abundant mercy all records of our sins.

The following nine verses are said responsively, first by the Leader, then by the congregation:

Our Father, our King, bring us back to You in perfect repentance.

Our Father, our King, send a complete healing to the sick of Your people.

Our Father, our King, tear up the evil decree against us.

Our Father, our King, remember us with a memory of favorable deeds before You.

Our Father, our King, write us in the book of good life.

Our Father, our King, write us in the book of redemption and salvation.

Our Father, our King, write us in the book of livelihood and sustenance.

Our Father, our King, write us in the book of merit.

Our Father, our King, write us in the book of pardon and forgiveness.

End of responsive reading.

Our Father, our King, let salvation soon flourish for us.

Our Father, our King, raise the honor of Your people Israel.

Our Father, our King, raise the honor of Your anointed.

אָבִינוּ מַלְכֵּנוּ, סְתֹם פִּיוֹת מַשְׂטִינֵנוּ וּמְקַטְרְגֵנוּ.

אָבִינוּ מַלְכֵּנוּ, כַּלֵּה דֶבֶר וְחֶרֶב וְרָעָב וּשְׁבִי וּמַשְׁחִית וְעָוֹן וּשְׁמַד מִבְּנֵי בְרִיתֶךָ.

אָבִינוּ מַלְכֵּנוּ, מְנַע מַגֵּפָה מִנַּחֲלָתֶךָ.

אָבִינוּ מַלְכֵּנוּ, סְלַח וּמְחַל לְכָל עֲוֹנוֹתֵינוּ.

אָבִינוּ מַלְכֵּנוּ, מְחֵה וְהַעֲבֵר פְּשָׁעֵינוּ וְחַטֹּאתֵינוּ מִנֶּגֶד עֵינֶיךָ.

אָבִינוּ מַלְכֵּנוּ, מְחֹק בְּרַחֲמֶיךָ הָרַבִּים כָּל שִׁטְרֵי חוֹבוֹתֵינוּ.

The following nine verses are said responsively, first by the שליח ציבור*, then by the* קהל*:*

אָבִינוּ מַלְכֵּנוּ, הַחֲזִירֵנוּ בִּתְשׁוּבָה שְׁלֵמָה לְפָנֶיךָ.

אָבִינוּ מַלְכֵּנוּ, שְׁלַח רְפוּאָה שְׁלֵמָה לְחוֹלֵי עַמֶּךָ.

אָבִינוּ מַלְכֵּנוּ, קְרַע רֹעַ גְּזַר דִּינֵנוּ.

אָבִינוּ מַלְכֵּנוּ, זָכְרֵנוּ בְּזִכְרוֹן טוֹב לְפָנֶיךָ.

אָבִינוּ מַלְכֵּנוּ, כָּתְבֵנוּ בְּסֵפֶר חַיִּים טוֹבִים.

אָבִינוּ מַלְכֵּנוּ, כָּתְבֵנוּ בְּסֵפֶר גְּאֻלָּה וִישׁוּעָה.

אָבִינוּ מַלְכֵּנוּ, כָּתְבֵנוּ בְּסֵפֶר פַּרְנָסָה וְכַלְכָּלָה.

אָבִינוּ מַלְכֵּנוּ, כָּתְבֵנוּ בְּסֵפֶר זְכֻיּוֹת.

אָבִינוּ מַלְכֵּנוּ, כָּתְבֵנוּ בְּסֵפֶר סְלִיחָה וּמְחִילָה.

End of responsive reading.

אָבִינוּ מַלְכֵּנוּ, הַצְמַח לָנוּ יְשׁוּעָה בְּקָרוֹב.

אָבִינוּ מַלְכֵּנוּ, הָרֵם קֶרֶן יִשְׂרָאֵל עַמֶּךָ.

אָבִינוּ מַלְכֵּנוּ, הָרֵם קֶרֶן מְשִׁיחֶךָ.

Our Father, our King, fill our hands with Your blessings.

Our Father, our King, fill our storehouses with abundance.

Our Father, our King, hear our voice, pity
and be compassionate to us.

Our Father, our King, accept, with compassion and favor, our prayer.

Our Father, our King, open the gates of heaven to our prayer.

Our Father, our King, remember that we are dust.

Our Father, our King, please do not turn us away from You
empty-handed.

Our Father, our King, may this moment be a moment of
compassion and a time of favor before You.

Our Father, our King, have pity on us, our children and our infants.

Our Father, our King, act for the sake of those who were killed
for Your holy name.

Our Father, our King, act for the sake of those who were slaughtered
for proclaiming Your Unity.

Our Father, our King, act for the sake of those
who went through fire and water
to sanctify Your name.

Our Father, our King, avenge before our eyes
the spilt blood of Your servants.

Our Father, our King, act for Your sake, if not for ours.

Our Father, our King, act for Your sake, and save us.

Our Father, our King, act for the sake of Your abundant compassion.

Our Father, our King, act for the sake of Your great, mighty and
awesome name by which we are called.

▸ Our Father, our King, be gracious to us and answer us, though we
have no worthy deeds; act with us in charity
and loving-kindness and save us.

The Ark is closed.

אָבִינוּ מַלְכֵּנוּ, מַלֵּא יָדֵינוּ מִבִּרְכוֹתֶיךָ.

אָבִינוּ מַלְכֵּנוּ, מַלֵּא אֲסָמֵינוּ שָׂבָע.

אָבִינוּ מַלְכֵּנוּ, שְׁמַע קוֹלֵנוּ, חוּס וְרַחֵם עָלֵינוּ.

אָבִינוּ מַלְכֵּנוּ, קַבֵּל בְּרַחֲמִים וּבְרָצוֹן אֶת תְּפִלָּתֵנוּ.

אָבִינוּ מַלְכֵּנוּ, פְּתַח שַׁעֲרֵי שָׁמַיִם לִתְפִלָּתֵנוּ.

אָבִינוּ מַלְכֵּנוּ, זְכֹר כִּי עָפָר אֲנָחְנוּ.

אָבִינוּ מַלְכֵּנוּ, נָא אַל תְּשִׁיבֵנוּ רֵיקָם מִלְּפָנֶיךָ.

אָבִינוּ מַלְכֵּנוּ, תְּהֵא הַשָּׁעָה הַזֹּאת שְׁעַת רַחֲמִים וְעֵת רָצוֹן מִלְּפָנֶיךָ.

אָבִינוּ מַלְכֵּנוּ, חֲמֹל עָלֵינוּ וְעַל עוֹלָלֵינוּ וְטַפֵּנוּ.

אָבִינוּ מַלְכֵּנוּ, עֲשֵׂה לְמַעַן הֲרוּגִים עַל שֵׁם קָדְשֶׁךָ.

אָבִינוּ מַלְכֵּנוּ, עֲשֵׂה לְמַעַן טְבוּחִים עַל יִחוּדֶךָ.

אָבִינוּ מַלְכֵּנוּ, עֲשֵׂה לְמַעַן בָּאֵי בָאֵשׁ וּבַמַּיִם עַל קִדּוּשׁ שְׁמֶךָ.

אָבִינוּ מַלְכֵּנוּ, נְקֹם לְעֵינֵינוּ נִקְמַת דַּם עֲבָדֶיךָ הַשָּׁפוּךְ.

אָבִינוּ מַלְכֵּנוּ, עֲשֵׂה לְמַעַנְךָ אִם לֹא לְמַעֲנֵנוּ.

אָבִינוּ מַלְכֵּנוּ, עֲשֵׂה לְמַעַנְךָ וְהוֹשִׁיעֵנוּ.

אָבִינוּ מַלְכֵּנוּ, עֲשֵׂה לְמַעַן רַחֲמֶיךָ הָרַבִּים.

אָבִינוּ מַלְכֵּנוּ, עֲשֵׂה לְמַעַן שִׁמְךָ הַגָּדוֹל הַגִּבּוֹר וְהַנּוֹרָא
שֶׁנִּקְרָא עָלֵינוּ.

◄ אָבִינוּ מַלְכֵּנוּ, חָנֵּנוּ וַעֲנֵנוּ, כִּי אֵין בָּנוּ מַעֲשִׂים
עֲשֵׂה עִמָּנוּ צְדָקָה וָחֶסֶד וְהוֹשִׁיעֵנוּ.

The ארון קודש *is closed.*

FULL KADDISH

Leader: יִתְגַּדַּל Magnified and sanctified may His great name be,
in the world He created by His will.
May He establish His kingdom
in your lifetime and in your days,
and in the lifetime of all the house of Israel,
swiftly and soon –
and say: Amen.

All: May His great name be blessed for ever and all time.

Leader: Blessed and praised,
glorified and exalted, raised and honored,
uplifted and lauded be
the name of the Holy One, blessed be He,
above and beyond any blessing, song,
praise and consolation uttered in the world –
and say: Amen.

May the prayers and pleas of all Israel
be accepted by their Father in heaven –
and say: Amen.

May there be great peace from heaven,
and life for us and all Israel –
and say: Amen.

Bow, take three steps back, as if taking leave of the Divine Presence, then bow, first left, then right, then center, while saying:

May He who makes peace in His high places,
make peace for us and all Israel –
and say: Amen.

Some congregations say the Daily Psalm and Psalm 27 (*pages 460–468*) *at this point.*

קדיש שלם

ש״ץ: יִתְגַּדַּל וְיִתְקַדַּשׁ שְׁמֵהּ רַבָּא (קהל: אָמֵן)
בְּעָלְמָא דִּי בְרָא כִרְעוּתֵהּ
וְיַמְלִיךְ מַלְכוּתֵהּ
בְּחַיֵּיכוֹן וּבְיוֹמֵיכוֹן וּבְחַיֵּי דְכָל בֵּית יִשְׂרָאֵל
בַּעֲגָלָא וּבִזְמַן קָרִיב, וְאִמְרוּ אָמֵן. (קהל: אָמֵן)

קהל וש״ץ: יְהֵא שְׁמֵהּ רַבָּא מְבָרַךְ לְעָלַם וּלְעָלְמֵי עָלְמַיָּא.

ש״ץ: יִתְבָּרַךְ וְיִשְׁתַּבַּח וְיִתְפָּאַר וְיִתְרוֹמַם וְיִתְנַשֵּׂא
וְיִתְהַדָּר וְיִתְעַלֶּה וְיִתְהַלָּל
שְׁמֵהּ דְּקֻדְשָׁא בְּרִיךְ הוּא (קהל: בְּרִיךְ הוּא)
לְעֵלָּא לְעֵלָּא מִכָּל בִּרְכָתָא וְשִׁירָתָא, תֻּשְׁבְּחָתָא וְנֶחֱמָתָא
דַּאֲמִירָן בְּעָלְמָא, וְאִמְרוּ אָמֵן. (קהל: אָמֵן)

תִּתְקַבַּל צְלוֹתְהוֹן וּבָעוּתְהוֹן דְּכָל יִשְׂרָאֵל
קֳדָם אֲבוּהוֹן דִּי בִשְׁמַיָּא, וְאִמְרוּ אָמֵן. (קהל: אָמֵן)

יְהֵא שְׁלָמָא רַבָּא מִן שְׁמַיָּא
וְחַיִּים, עָלֵינוּ וְעַל כָּל יִשְׂרָאֵל, וְאִמְרוּ אָמֵן. (קהל: אָמֵן)

Bow, take three steps back, as if taking leave of the Divine Presence, then bow, first left, then right, then center, while saying:

עֹשֶׂה הַשָּׁלוֹם בִּמְרוֹמָיו
הוּא יַעֲשֶׂה שָׁלוֹם עָלֵינוּ וְעַל כָּל יִשְׂרָאֵל
וְאִמְרוּ אָמֵן. (קהל: אָמֵן)

Some congregations say לְדָוִד, יהוה אוֹרִי וְיִשְׁעִי *and* שיר של יום *(pages 461–469) at this point.*

REMOVING THE TORAH FROM THE ARK

אֵין־כָּמְוֹךָ There is none like You among the heavenly powers, LORD, *Ps. 86*
and there are no works like Yours. Your kingdom is an eternal kingdom, *Ps. 145*
and Your dominion is for all generations.

The LORD is King, the LORD was King, the LORD shall be King for ever
and all time. The LORD will give strength to His people; *Ps. 29*
the LORD will bless His people with peace.

Father of compassion, favor Zion with Your goodness; *Ps. 51*
rebuild the walls of Jerusalem. For we trust in You alone, King, God,
high and exalted, Master of worlds.

The Ark is opened and the congregation stands. All say:

וַיְהִי בִּנְסֹעַ Whenever the Ark set out, Moses would say, *Num. 10*
"Arise, LORD, and may Your enemies be scattered.
May those who hate You flee before You."
For the Torah shall come forth from Zion, *Is. 2*
and the word of the LORD from Jerusalem.
Blessed is He who, in His holiness, gave the Torah to His people Israel.

On Shabbat, some congregations omit the following prayers and continue with "Blessed is the name" on the next page.

The following (The Thirteen Attributes of Mercy) is said three times:

יהוה The LORD, the LORD, compassionate and gracious God, *Ex. 34*
slow to anger, abounding in loving-kindness and truth,
extending loving-kindness to a thousand generations, forgiving iniquity,
rebellion and sin, and absolving [the guilty who repent].

Master of the Universe, fulfill my requests for good. Satisfy my desire, grant my request, and pardon me for all my iniquities and all iniquities of the members of my household, with the pardon of loving-kindness and compassion. Purify us from our sins, our iniquities and our transgressions; remember us with a memory of favorable deeds before You and be mindful of us in salvation and compassion. Remember us for a good life, for peace, for livelihood and sustenance, for bread to eat and clothes to wear, for wealth, honor and length of days dedicated to Your Torah and its commandments. Grant us discernment and understanding that we may understand and discern its deep secrets. Send healing for all our pain, and bless all the work of our hands. Ordain for us decrees of good, salvation and consolation, and nullify all hard and harsh decrees against us. And may the hearts of the government, its advisers and ministers / *in Israel:* And may the hearts of our ministers and their advisers, / be favorable toward us. Amen. May this be Your will. May the words of my mouth and *Ps. 19*
the meditation of my heart find favor before You, LORD, my Rock and Redeemer.

הוצאת ספר תורה

אֵין־כָּמְוֹךָ בָאֱלֹהִים, אֲדֹנָי, וְאֵין כְּמַעֲשֶׂיךָ: תהלים פו
מַלְכוּתְךָ מַלְכוּת כָּל־עֹלָמִים, וּמֶמְשַׁלְתְּךָ בְּכָל־דּוֹר וָדֹר: תהלים קמה

יהוה מֶלֶךְ, יהוה מָלָךְ, יהוה יִמְלֹךְ לְעֹלָם וָעֶד.
יהוה עֹז לְעַמּוֹ יִתֵּן, יהוה יְבָרֵךְ אֶת־עַמּוֹ בַשָּׁלוֹם: תהלים כט

אַב הָרַחֲמִים, הֵיטִיבָה בִרְצוֹנְךָ אֶת־צִיּוֹן תִּבְנֶה חוֹמוֹת יְרוּשָׁלָֽיִם: תהלים נא
כִּי בְךָ לְבַד בָּטָחְנוּ, מֶלֶךְ אֵל רָם וְנִשָּׂא, אֲדוֹן עוֹלָמִים.

The ארון קודש *is opened and the* קהל *stands. All say:*

וַיְהִי בִּנְסֹעַ הָאָרֹן וַיֹּאמֶר מֹשֶׁה במדבר י
קוּמָה יהוה וְיָפֻצוּ אֹיְבֶיךָ וְיָנֻסוּ מְשַׂנְאֶיךָ מִפָּנֶיךָ:
כִּי מִצִּיּוֹן תֵּצֵא תוֹרָה וּדְבַר־יהוה מִירוּשָׁלָֽיִם: ישעיה ב
בָּרוּךְ שֶׁנָּתַן תּוֹרָה לְעַמּוֹ יִשְׂרָאֵל בִּקְדֻשָּׁתוֹ.

On שבת*, some congregations omit the following prayers and continue with* בְּרִיךְ שְׁמֵהּ *on the next page.*

The following (י״ג מידות הרחמים) *is said three times:*

יהוה, יהוה, אֵל רַחוּם וְחַנּוּן, אֶרֶךְ אַפַּיִם וְרַב־חֶסֶד וֶאֱמֶת: שמות לד
נֹצֵר חֶסֶד לָאֲלָפִים, נֹשֵׂא עָוֹן וָפֶשַׁע וְחַטָּאָה, וְנַקֵּה:

רִבּוֹנוֹ שֶׁל עוֹלָם, מַלֵּא מִשְׁאֲלוֹתַי לְטוֹבָה, וְהָפֵק רְצוֹנִי וְתֵן שְׁאֵלָתִי, וּמְחֹל לִי עַל כָּל עֲוֹנוֹתַי וְעַל כָּל עֲוֹנוֹת אַנְשֵׁי בֵיתִי, מְחִילָה בְּחֶסֶד מְחִילָה בְּרַחֲמִים, וְטַהֲרֵנוּ מֵחֲטָאֵינוּ וּמֵעֲוֹנוֹתֵינוּ וּמִפְּשָׁעֵינוּ, וְזָכְרֵנוּ בְּזִכָּרוֹן טוֹב לְפָנֶיךָ, וּפָקְדֵנוּ בִּפְקֻדַּת יְשׁוּעָה וְרַחֲמִים. וְזָכְרֵנוּ לְחַיִּים טוֹבִים וּלְשָׁלוֹם, וּפַרְנָסָה וְכַלְכָּלָה, וְלֶחֶם לֶאֱכֹל וּבֶגֶד לִלְבֹּשׁ, וְעֹשֶׁר וְכָבוֹד, וְאֹרֶךְ יָמִים לַהֲגוֹת בְּתוֹרָתֶךָ וּלְקַיֵּם מִצְוֹתֶיהָ, וְשֵׂכֶל וּבִינָה לְהָבִין וּלְהַשְׂכִּיל עִמְקֵי סוֹדוֹתֶיהָ. וְהָפֵק רְפוּאָה לְכָל מַכְאוֹבֵינוּ, וּבָרֵךְ כָּל מַעֲשֵׂה יָדֵינוּ, וּגְזֹר עָלֵינוּ גְּזֵרוֹת טוֹבוֹת יְשׁוּעוֹת וְנֶחָמוֹת, וּבַטֵּל מֵעָלֵינוּ כָּל גְּזֵרוֹת קָשׁוֹת וְרָעוֹת, וְתֵן בְּלֵב הַמַּלְכוּת וְיוֹעֲצֶיהָ וְשָׂרֶיהָ / בארץ ישראל: וְתֵן בְּלֵב שָׂרֵינוּ וְיוֹעֲצֵיהֶם/ עָלֵינוּ לְטוֹבָה. אָמֵן וְכֵן יְהִי רָצוֹן.

יִהְיוּ לְרָצוֹן אִמְרֵי־פִי וְהֶגְיוֹן לִבִּי לְפָנֶיךָ, יהוה צוּרִי וְגֹאֲלִי: תהלים יט

The following verse is said three times:

וַאֲנִי As for me, may my prayer come to You, LORD, Ps. 69
at a time of favor. O God, in Your great love,
answer me with Your faithful salvation.

On all days continue:

בְּרִיךְ Blessed is the name of the Master of the Universe. Blessed is Your crown and Your place. May Your favor always be with Your people Israel. Show Your people the salvation of Your right hand in Your Temple. Grant us the gift of Your good light, and accept our prayers in mercy. May it be Your will to prolong our life in goodness. May I be counted among the righteous, so that You will have compassion on me and protect me and all that is mine and all that is Your people Israel's. You feed all; You sustain all; You rule over all; You rule over kings, for sovereignty is Yours. I am a servant of the Holy One, blessed be He, before whom and before whose glorious Torah I bow at all times. Not in man do I trust, nor on any angel do I rely, but on the God of heaven who is the God of truth, whose Torah is truth, whose prophets speak truth, and who abounds in acts of love and truth. ▸ In Him I trust, and to His holy and glorious name I offer praises. May it be Your will to open my heart to the Torah, and to fulfill the wishes of my heart and of the hearts of all Your people Israel for good, for life, and for peace. *Zohar, Vayak-hel*

Two Torah scrolls are removed from the Ark. The Leader takes one in his right arm and, followed by the congregation, says:

Listen, Israel: the LORD is our God, the LORD is One. *Deut. 6*

Leader then congregation:

One is our God; great is our Master;
holy and awesome is His name.

The Leader turns to face the Ark, bows and says:

Magnify the LORD with me, and let us exalt His name together. *Ps. 34*

The Ark is closed. The Leader carries the Torah scroll to the bima and the congregation says:

לְךָ Yours, LORD, are the greatness and the power, the glory and the majesty and splendor, for everything in heaven and earth is Yours. Yours, LORD, is the kingdom; You are exalted as Head over all. *1 Chr. 29*

רוֹמְמוּ Exalt the LORD our God and bow to His footstool; He is holy. Exalt the LORD our God, and bow at His holy mountain, for holy is the LORD our God. *Ps. 99*

The following verse is said three times:

תהלים סט וַאֲנִי תְפִלָּתִי־לְךָ יהוה, עֵת רָצוֹן, אֱלֹהִים בְּרָב־חַסְדֶּךָ
עֲנֵנִי בֶּאֱמֶת יִשְׁעֶךָ:

On all days continue:

זוהר ויקהל בְּרִיךְ שְׁמֵהּ דְּמָרֵא עָלְמָא, בְּרִיךְ כִּתְרָךְ וְאַתְרָךְ. יְהֵא רְעוּתָךְ עִם עַמָּךְ יִשְׂרָאֵל לְעָלַם, וּפֻרְקַן יְמִינָךְ אַחֲזִי לְעַמָּךְ בְּבֵית מַקְדְּשָׁךְ, וּלְאַמְטוּיֵי לָנָא מִטּוּב נְהוֹרָךְ, וּלְקַבֵּל צְלוֹתָנָא בְּרַחֲמִין. יְהֵא רַעֲוָא קֳדָמָךְ דְּתוֹרִיךְ לָן חַיִּין בְּטִיבוּ, וְלֶהֱוֵי אֲנָא פְקִידָא בְּגוֹ צַדִּיקַיָּא, לְמִרְחַם עֲלַי וּלְמִנְטַר יָתִי וְיַת כָּל דִּי לִי וְדִי לְעַמָּךְ יִשְׂרָאֵל. אַנְתְּ הוּא זָן לְכֹלָּא וּמְפַרְנֵס לְכֹלָּא, אַנְתְּ הוּא שַׁלִּיט עַל כֹּלָּא, אַנְתְּ הוּא דְּשַׁלִּיט עַל מַלְכַיָּא, וּמַלְכוּתָא דִּילָךְ הִיא. אֲנָא עַבְדָּא דְקֻדְשָׁא בְּרִיךְ הוּא, דְּסָגֵדְנָא קַמֵּהּ וּמִקַּמֵּי דִּיקַר אוֹרַיְתֵהּ בְּכָל עִדָּן וְעִדָּן. לָא עַל אֱנָשׁ רָחִיצְנָא וְלָא עַל בַּר אֱלָהִין סָמִיכְנָא, אֶלָּא בֶּאֱלָהָא דִשְׁמַיָּא, דְּהוּא אֱלָהָא קְשׁוֹט, וְאוֹרַיְתֵהּ קְשׁוֹט, וּנְבִיאוֹהִי קְשׁוֹט, וּמַסְגֵּא לְמֶעְבַּד טַבְוָן וּקְשׁוֹט. ‹ בֵּהּ אֲנָא רָחִיץ, וְלִשְׁמֵהּ קַדִּישָׁא יַקִּירָא אֲנָא אֵמַר תֻּשְׁבְּחָן. יְהֵא רַעֲוָא קֳדָמָךְ דְּתִפְתַּח לִבַּאי בְּאוֹרַיְתָא, וְתַשְׁלִים מִשְׁאֲלִין דְּלִבַּאי וְלִבָּא דְכָל עַמָּךְ יִשְׂרָאֵל לְטַב וּלְחַיִּין וְלִשְׁלָם.

Two ספרי תורה are removed from the ארון קודש. The שליח ציבור takes one in his right arm and, followed by the קהל, says:

דברים ו שְׁמַע יִשְׂרָאֵל, יהוה אֱלֹהֵינוּ, יהוה אֶחָד:

קהל then שליח ציבור:

אֶחָד אֱלֹהֵינוּ, גָּדוֹל אֲדוֹנֵינוּ, קָדוֹשׁ וְנוֹרָא שְׁמוֹ.

The שליח ציבור turns to face the ארון קודש, bows and says:

תהלים לד גַּדְּלוּ לַיהוה אִתִּי וּנְרוֹמְמָה שְׁמוֹ יַחְדָּו:

The ארון קודש is closed. The שליח ציבור carries the ספר תורה to the בימה and the קהל says:

דברי הימים א׳ כט לְךָ יהוה הַגְּדֻלָּה וְהַגְּבוּרָה וְהַתִּפְאֶרֶת וְהַנֵּצַח וְהַהוֹד, כִּי־כֹל בַּשָּׁמַיִם וּבָאָרֶץ, לְךָ יהוה הַמַּמְלָכָה וְהַמִּתְנַשֵּׂא לְכֹל לְרֹאשׁ:

תהלים צט רוֹמְמוּ יהוה אֱלֹהֵינוּ וְהִשְׁתַּחֲווּ לַהֲדֹם רַגְלָיו, קָדוֹשׁ הוּא: רוֹמְמוּ יהוה אֱלֹהֵינוּ וְהִשְׁתַּחֲווּ לְהַר קָדְשׁוֹ, כִּי־קָדוֹשׁ יהוה אֱלֹהֵינוּ:

Over all may the name of the Supreme King of kings, the Holy One blessed be He, be magnified and sanctified, praised and glorified, exalted and extolled, in the worlds that He has created – this world and the World to Come – in accordance with His will, and the will of those who fear Him, and the will of the whole house of Israel. He is the Rock of worlds, Lord of all creatures, God of all souls, who dwells in the spacious heights and inhabits the high heavens of old. His holiness is over the Ḥayot and over the throne of glory. Therefore may Your name, Lord our God, be sanctified among us in the sight
of all that lives. Let us sing before Him a new song, as it is written: "Sing to *Ps. 68*
God, make music for His name, extol Him who rides the clouds – the Lord is His name – and exult before Him." And may we see Him eye to eye when
He returns to His abode as it is written: "For they shall see eye to eye when *Is. 52*
the Lord returns to Zion." And it is said: "Then will the glory of the Lord *Is. 40*
be revealed, and all mankind together shall see that the mouth of the Lord has spoken."

Father of mercy, have compassion on the people borne by Him. May He remember the covenant with the mighty (patriarchs), and deliver us from evil times. May He reproach the evil instinct in the people by Him, and graciously grant that we be an eternal remnant. May He fulfill in good measure our requests for salvation and compassion.

The Torah scroll is placed on the bima and the Gabbai calls a Kohen to the Torah. See laws 77–.83.

וְיַעֲזֹר May He help, shield and save all who seek refuge in Him, and let us say: Amen.
Let us all render greatness to our God and give honor to the Torah. *Let the Kohen come forward.
Arise (*name* son of *father's name*), the Kohen.

**If no Kohen is present, a Levi or Yisrael is called up as follows:*

/As there is no Kohen, arise (*name* son of *father's name*) in place of a Kohen./

Blessed is He who, in His holiness,
gave the Torah to His people Israel.

The congregation followed by the Gabbai:

You who cling to the Lord your God are all alive today. *Deut. 4*

עַל הַכֹּל יִתְגַּדַּל וְיִתְקַדַּשׁ וְיִשְׁתַּבַּח וְיִתְפָּאַר וְיִתְרוֹמַם וְיִתְנַשֵּׂא שְׁמוֹ
שֶׁל מֶלֶךְ מַלְכֵי הַמְּלָכִים הַקָּדוֹשׁ בָּרוּךְ הוּא בָּעוֹלָמוֹת שֶׁבָּרָא, הָעוֹלָם
הַזֶּה וְהָעוֹלָם הַבָּא, כִּרְצוֹנוֹ וְכִרְצוֹן יְרֵאָיו וְכִרְצוֹן כָּל בֵּית יִשְׂרָאֵל. צוּר
הָעוֹלָמִים, אֲדוֹן כָּל הַבְּרִיּוֹת, אֱלוֹהַּ כָּל הַנְּפָשׁוֹת, הַיּוֹשֵׁב בְּמֶרְחֲבֵי
מָרוֹם, הַשּׁוֹכֵן בִּשְׁמֵי שְׁמֵי קֶדֶם, קְדֻשָּׁתוֹ עַל הַחַיּוֹת, וּקְדֻשָּׁתוֹ עַל
כִּסֵּא הַכָּבוֹד. וּבְכֵן יִתְקַדַּשׁ שִׁמְךָ בָּנוּ יהוה אֱלֹהֵינוּ לְעֵינֵי כָּל חָי,
וְנֹאמַר לְפָנָיו שִׁיר חָדָשׁ, כַּכָּתוּב: שִׁירוּ לֵאלֹהִים זַמְּרוּ שְׁמוֹ, סֹלּוּ תהלים סח
לָרֹכֵב בָּעֲרָבוֹת, בְּיָהּ שְׁמוֹ, וְעִלְזוּ לְפָנָיו: וְנִרְאֵהוּ עַיִן בְּעַיִן בְּשׁוּבוֹ
אֶל נָוֵהוּ, כַּכָּתוּב: כִּי עַיִן בְּעַיִן יִרְאוּ בְּשׁוּב יהוה צִיּוֹן: וְנֶאֱמַר: וְנִגְלָה ישעיה נב ישעיה מ
כְּבוֹד יהוה, וְרָאוּ כָל־בָּשָׂר יַחְדָּו כִּי פִּי יהוה דִּבֵּר:

אַב הָרַחֲמִים הוּא יְרַחֵם עַם עֲמוּסִים, וְיִזְכֹּר בְּרִית אֵיתָנִים, וְיַצִּיל
נַפְשׁוֹתֵינוּ מִן הַשָּׁעוֹת הָרָעוֹת, וְיִגְעַר בְּיֵצֶר הָרָע מִן הַנְּשׂוּאִים, וְיָחֹן
אוֹתָנוּ לִפְלֵיטַת עוֹלָמִים, וִימַלֵּא מִשְׁאֲלוֹתֵינוּ בְּמִדָּה טוֹבָה יְשׁוּעָה
וְרַחֲמִים.

The ספר תורה is placed on the שולחן and the גבאי calls a כהן to the תורה. See laws 77–83.

וְיַעֲזֹר וְיָגֵן וְיוֹשִׁיעַ לְכָל הַחוֹסִים בּוֹ, וְנֹאמַר אָמֵן.
הַכֹּל הָבוּ גֹדֶל לֵאלֹהֵינוּ וּתְנוּ כָבוֹד לַתּוֹרָה.
*כֹּהֵן קְרָב, יַעֲמֹד (פלוני בֶּן פלוני) הַכֹּהֵן.

**If no כהן is present, a לוי or ישראל is called up as follows:*

/אֵין כָּאן כֹּהֵן, יַעֲמֹד (פלוני בֶּן פלוני) בִּמְקוֹם כֹּהֵן./

בָּרוּךְ שֶׁנָּתַן תּוֹרָה לְעַמּוֹ יִשְׂרָאֵל בִּקְדֻשָּׁתוֹ.

The קהל followed by the גבאי:

וְאַתֶּם הַדְּבֵקִים בַּיהוה אֱלֹהֵיכֶם חַיִּים כֻּלְּכֶם הַיּוֹם: דברים ד

The Reader shows the oleh the section to be read. The oleh touches the scroll at that place with the tzitzit of his tallit, which he then kisses. Holding the handles of the scroll, he says:

Oleh: Bless the LORD, the blessed One.

Cong: Bless the LORD, the blessed One, for ever and all time.

Oleh: Bless the LORD, the blessed One, for ever and all time.

Blessed are You, LORD our God, King of the Universe,
who has chosen us from all peoples
and has given us His Torah.
Blessed are You, LORD, Giver of the Torah.

After the reading, the oleh says:

Oleh: Blessed are You, LORD our God, King of the Universe,
who has given us the Torah of truth,
planting everlasting life in our midst.
Blessed are You, LORD, Giver of the Torah.

One who has survived a situation of danger says:

Blessed are You, LORD our God, King of the Universe, who bestows good on the unworthy, who has bestowed on me much good.

The congregation responds:

Amen. May He who bestowed much good on you
continue to bestow on you much good, Selah.

FOR AN OLEH

May He who blessed our fathers, Abraham, Isaac and Jacob, bless (*name, son of father's name*) who has been called up in honor of the All-Present, in honor of the Torah, (*On Shabbat:* in honor of the Shabbat) and in honor of the Day of Judgment. As a reward for this, may the Holy One, blessed be He, protect and deliver him from all trouble and distress, all infection and illness, and send blessing and success to all the work of his hands, and write him and seal him for a good life on this Day of Judgment, together with all Israel, his brethren, and let us say: Amen.

The קורא *shows the* עולה *the section to be read. The* עולה *touches the scroll at that place with the* ציצית *of his* טלית*, which he then kisses. Holding the handles of the scroll, he says:*

עולה: **בָּרְכוּ אֶת יהוה הַמְבֹרָךְ.**

קהל: בָּרוּךְ יהוה הַמְבֹרָךְ לְעוֹלָם וָעֶד.

עולה: **בָּרוּךְ יהוה הַמְבֹרָךְ לְעוֹלָם וָעֶד.**

בָּרוּךְ אַתָּה יהוה, אֱלֹהֵינוּ מֶלֶךְ הָעוֹלָם
אֲשֶׁר בָּחַר בָּנוּ מִכָּל הָעַמִּים וְנָתַן לָנוּ אֶת תּוֹרָתוֹ.
בָּרוּךְ אַתָּה יהוה, נוֹתֵן הַתּוֹרָה.

After the קריאת התורה*, the* עולה *says:*

עולה: **בָּרוּךְ אַתָּה יהוה אֱלֹהֵינוּ מֶלֶךְ הָעוֹלָם**
אֲשֶׁר נָתַן לָנוּ תּוֹרַת אֱמֶת וְחַיֵּי עוֹלָם נָטַע בְּתוֹכֵנוּ.
בָּרוּךְ אַתָּה יהוה, נוֹתֵן הַתּוֹרָה.

One who has survived a situation of danger says:

בָּרוּךְ אַתָּה יהוה אֱלֹהֵינוּ מֶלֶךְ הָעוֹלָם הַגּוֹמֵל לְחַיָּבִים טוֹבוֹת שֶׁגְּמָלַנִי כָּל טוֹב.

The קהל *responds:*

אָמֵן. מִי שֶׁגְּמָלְךָ כָּל טוֹב הוּא יִגְמָלְךָ כָּל טוֹב, סֶלָה.

מי שברך לעולה לתורה

מִי שֶׁבֵּרַךְ אֲבוֹתֵינוּ אַבְרָהָם יִצְחָק וְיַעֲקֹב, הוּא יְבָרֵךְ אֶת (פלוני בֶּן פלוני), בַּעֲבוּר שֶׁעָלָה לִכְבוֹד הַמָּקוֹם וְלִכְבוֹד הַתּוֹרָה (בשבת: וְלִכְבוֹד הַשַּׁבָּת) וְלִכְבוֹד יוֹם הַדִּין. בִּשְׂכַר זֶה הַקָּדוֹשׁ בָּרוּךְ הוּא יִשְׁמְרֵהוּ וְיַצִּילֵהוּ מִכָּל צָרָה וְצוּקָה וּמִכָּל נֶגַע וּמַחֲלָה, וְיִשְׁלַח בְּרָכָה וְהַצְלָחָה בְּכָל מַעֲשֵׂה יָדָיו, וְיִכְתְּבֵהוּ וְיַחְתְּמֵהוּ לְחַיִּים טוֹבִים בְּיוֹם הַדִּין הַזֶּה עִם כָּל יִשְׂרָאֵל אֶחָיו, וְנֹאמַר אָמֵן.

FOR A SICK MAN

May He who blessed our fathers, Abraham, Isaac and Jacob, Moses and Aaron, David and Solomon, bless and heal one who is ill, (*sick person's name,* son of *mother's name*), on whose behalf (*name of the one making the offering*) is making a contribution to charity. As a reward for this, may the Holy One, blessed be He, be filled with compassion for him, to restore his health, cure him, strengthen and revive him, sending him a swift and full recovery from heaven to all his 248 organs and 365 sinews, amongst the other sick ones in Israel, a healing of the spirit and a healing of the body (*On Shabbat:* though on Shabbat it is forbidden to cry out, may healing be quick to come) now, swiftly and soon, and let us say: Amen.

FOR A SICK WOMAN

May He who blessed our fathers, Abraham, Isaac and Jacob, Moses and Aaron, David and Solomon, bless and heal one who is ill, (*sick person's name,* daughter of *mother's name*), on whose behalf (*name of the one making the offering*) is making a contribution to charity. As a reward for this, may the Holy One, blessed be He, be filled with compassion for her, to restore her health, cure her, strengthen and revive her, sending her a swift and full recovery from heaven to all her organs and sinews, amongst the other sick ones in Israel, a healing of the spirit and a healing of the body (*On Shabbat:* though on Shabbat it is forbidden to cry out, may healing be quick to come) now, swiftly and soon, and let us say: Amen.

TORAH READING

After the deaths of Aaron's two sons, when they had drawn close to the LORD and died, the LORD spoke to Moses. And the LORD said to Moses: speak to Aaron your brother, that he come not at any time to the holiest place – behind the curtain, to the presence of the *kaporet* that covers the Ark – so that he does not die; for I shall be revealed in the cloud above the *kaporet*. *Lev. 16:1–34*

Avihu, for offering "unauthorized fire" at the inauguration of the Tabernacle (Lev. 10:1), gave poignancy and depth to the role of Aaron in atoning for the sins of the people. He knew the depth of grief to which even well-intentioned transgression can give rise.

וְאַל־יָבֹא בְכָל־עֵת *Not at any time.* The entry of the High Priest into the Holy of Holies was permitted only on the holiest of days, Yom Kippur.

מי שברך לחולה

מִי שֶׁבֵּרַךְ אֲבוֹתֵינוּ אַבְרָהָם יִצְחָק וְיַעֲקֹב, מֹשֶׁה וְאַהֲרֹן דָּוִד וּשְׁלֹמֹה הוּא יְבָרֵךְ וִירַפֵּא אֶת הַחוֹלֶה (פלוני בֶּן פלונית) בַּעֲבוּר שֶׁ(פלוני בֶּן פלוני) נוֹדֵר צְדָקָה בַּעֲבוּרוֹ. בִּשְׂכַר זֶה הַקָּדוֹשׁ בָּרוּךְ הוּא יִמָּלֵא רַחֲמִים עָלָיו לְהַחֲלִימוֹ וּלְרַפְּאתוֹ וּלְהַחֲזִיקוֹ וּלְהַחֲיוֹתוֹ וְיִשְׁלַח לוֹ מְהֵרָה רְפוּאָה שְׁלֵמָה מִן הַשָּׁמַיִם לִרְמַ״ח אֵבָרָיו וּשְׁסָ״ה גִּידָיו בְּתוֹךְ שְׁאָר חוֹלֵי יִשְׂרָאֵל, רְפוּאַת הַנֶּפֶשׁ וּרְפוּאַת הַגּוּף (בשבת: שַׁבָּת הִיא מִלִּזְעֹק וּרְפוּאָה קְרוֹבָה לָבוֹא,) הַשְׁתָּא בַּעֲגָלָא וּבִזְמַן קָרִיב, וְנֹאמַר אָמֵן.

מי שברך לחולָה

מִי שֶׁבֵּרַךְ אֲבוֹתֵינוּ אַבְרָהָם יִצְחָק וְיַעֲקֹב, מֹשֶׁה וְאַהֲרֹן דָּוִד וּשְׁלֹמֹה הוּא יְבָרֵךְ וִירַפֵּא אֶת הַחוֹלָה (פלונית בַּת פלונית) בַּעֲבוּר שֶׁ(פלוני בֶּן פלוני) נוֹדֵר צְדָקָה בַּעֲבוּרָהּ. בִּשְׂכַר זֶה הַקָּדוֹשׁ בָּרוּךְ הוּא יִמָּלֵא רַחֲמִים עָלֶיהָ לְהַחֲלִימָהּ וּלְרַפְּאתָהּ וּלְהַחֲזִיקָהּ וּלְהַחֲיוֹתָהּ וְיִשְׁלַח לָהּ מְהֵרָה רְפוּאָה שְׁלֵמָה מִן הַשָּׁמַיִם לְכָל אֵבָרֶיהָ וּלְכָל גִּידֶיהָ בְּתוֹךְ שְׁאָר חוֹלֵי יִשְׂרָאֵל, רְפוּאַת הַנֶּפֶשׁ וּרְפוּאַת הַגּוּף (בשבת: שַׁבָּת הִיא מִלִּזְעֹק וּרְפוּאָה קְרוֹבָה לָבוֹא,) הַשְׁתָּא בַּעֲגָלָא וּבִזְמַן קָרִיב, וְנֹאמַר אָמֵן.

קריאת התורה

וַיְדַבֵּר יהוה אֶל־מֹשֶׁה אַחֲרֵי מוֹת שְׁנֵי בְּנֵי אַהֲרֹן בְּקָרְבָתָם ויקרא טז, א-לד
לִפְנֵי־יהוה וַיָּמֻתוּ: וַיֹּאמֶר יהוה אֶל־מֹשֶׁה דַּבֵּר אֶל־אַהֲרֹן אָחִיךָ
וְאַל־יָבֹא בְכָל־עֵת אֶל־הַקֹּדֶשׁ מִבֵּית לַפָּרֹכֶת אֶל־פְּנֵי הַכַּפֹּרֶת
אֲשֶׁר עַל־הָאָרֹן וְלֹא יָמוּת כִּי בֶּעָנָן אֵרָאֶה עַל־הַכַּפֹּרֶת: בְּזֹאת

TORAH READING: THE SERVICE OF THE HIGH PRIEST ON YOM KIPPUR
This passage, dating from the second year of the Israelites' journey in the wilderness, is the prototype for the later service of the High Priest in the Temple in Jerusalem, and ultimately for our service today. Only one other festival, Pesaḥ, is described in such detail in the Torah itself.

אַחֲרֵי מוֹת *After the deaths.* The tragic death of two of Aaron's sons, Nadav and

This is how Aaron shall come to the holiest place: he shall bring a young bull for a sin-offering, and a ram for a burnt offering. He shall wear a consecrated linen tunic, and breeches of linen shall cover his skin; he shall tie a linen sash about him and bind a linen miter on his head. These are the consecrated garments; he shall wash his skin in water and then put them on. From the congregation of Israel he shall take two young goats as a sin-offering, and a ram as a burnt offering. And Aaron shall offer up the sin-offering bullock that is his, as atonement for him and for his family.

Shabbat: LEVI

He shall take the two goats and stand them before the LORD at the opening of the Tent of Meeting. And for these two goats, Aaron shall draw lots – one lot for the LORD and one lot for Azazel. And Aaron shall offer up the goat whose lot falls to the LORD, and make it a sin-offering. And the goat whose lot falls to Azazel shall be left to stand alive before the LORD, to be an atonement – to be sent away to Azazel, into the wastelands.

LEVI (*Shabbat:* SHELISHI)

Aaron shall offer up the sin-offering bullock that is his, as atonement for him and for his family; he shall slaughter the sin-offering bullock that is his. Then he shall take a pan full of burning coals from the altar, from the presence of the LORD, and with his cupped handsful

SHELISHI (*Shabbat:* REVI'I)

---

its dangers. The light – the gift of love we bring to God when we offer Him a sacrifice – is transmuted by divine fire into forgiveness and love.

לַעֲזָאזֵל *For Azazel.* According to the Talmud and Rashi, this term describes a place: a steep, precipitous mountain. Others (Sa'adia, Radak) say it is the name of a specific mountain. Some suggest that it means "to be sent away, removed," hence the English translation "(e)scapegoat." According to Ibn Ezra and Nahmanides it represented a realm of spirits, demons, or fallen angels. In this sense it is like the word Gehinnom, often understood as "hell," though in fact it was merely a valley outside Jerusalem. The craggy, angular, desert, hostile to human habitation, was a symbol of chaos and danger. Just as God in creation makes order out of the void (*tohu vavohu*) by natural law, so we are commanded to construct order out of the ever-threatening vortex of violence and desire by obeying the moral law. Alternatively *Azazel*, from *az* or *azaz*, meaning brute strength, and *el*, the deification of a natural force, may signify the pagan idea of worshiping strength. Nietzsche would later call this "the will to power." The sending away of the goat was a sign that

יָבֹא אַהֲרֹן אֶל־הַקֹּדֶשׁ בְּפַר בֶּן־בָּקָר לְחַטָּאת וְאַיִל לְעֹלָה:
כְּתֹנֶת־בַּד קֹדֶשׁ יִלְבָּשׁ וּמִכְנְסֵי־בַד יִהְיוּ עַל־בְּשָׂרוֹ וּבְאַבְנֵט בַּד בשבת לוי
יַחְגֹּר וּבְמִצְנֶפֶת בַּד יִצְנֹף בִּגְדֵי־קֹדֶשׁ הֵם וְרָחַץ בַּמַּיִם אֶת־בְּשָׂרוֹ
וּלְבֵשָׁם: וּמֵאֵת עֲדַת בְּנֵי יִשְׂרָאֵל יִקַּח שְׁנֵי־שְׂעִירֵי עִזִּים לְחַטָּאת
וְאַיִל אֶחָד לְעֹלָה: וְהִקְרִיב אַהֲרֹן אֶת־פַּר הַחַטָּאת אֲשֶׁר־לוֹ
וְכִפֶּר בַּעֲדוֹ וּבְעַד בֵּיתוֹ: וְלָקַח אֶת־שְׁנֵי הַשְּׂעִירִם וְהֶעֱמִיד אֹתָם לוי בשבת שלישי
לִפְנֵי יהוה פֶּתַח אֹהֶל מוֹעֵד: וְנָתַן אַהֲרֹן עַל־שְׁנֵי הַשְּׂעִירִם
גֹּרָלוֹת גּוֹרָל אֶחָד לַיהוה וְגוֹרָל אֶחָד לַעֲזָאזֵל: וְהִקְרִיב אַהֲרֹן
אֶת־הַשָּׂעִיר אֲשֶׁר עָלָה עָלָיו הַגּוֹרָל לַיהוה וְעָשָׂהוּ חַטָּאת:
וְהַשָּׂעִיר אֲשֶׁר עָלָה עָלָיו הַגּוֹרָל לַעֲזָאזֵל יָעֳמַד־חַי לִפְנֵי יהוה
לְכַפֵּר עָלָיו לְשַׁלַּח אֹתוֹ לַעֲזָאזֵל הַמִּדְבָּרָה: וְהִקְרִיב אַהֲרֹן
אֶת־פַּר הַחַטָּאת אֲשֶׁר־לוֹ וְכִפֶּר בַּעֲדוֹ וּבְעַד בֵּיתוֹ וְשָׁחַט אֶת־
פַּר הַחַטָּאת אֲשֶׁר־לוֹ: וְלָקַח מְלֹא־הַמַּחְתָּה גַּחֲלֵי־אֵשׁ מֵעַל שלישי בשבת רביעי

כְּתֹנֶת־בַּד קֹדֶשׁ *Consecrated linen tunic.* In public the High Priest appeared in garments of gold, "for praise and glory" (Ex. 28:2). Alone with God, however, he was to dress simply in a plain white linen tunic. In the encounter with God, honesty, simplicity, and humility are needed. Some say that it is in memory of this that men wear a *kittel,* a plain white gown, on Yom Kippur.

וְכִפֶּר בַּעֲדוֹ וּבְעַד בֵּיתוֹ *As atonement for him and for his family.* We must purify ourselves before we can purify others. This was the first of three acts of atonement by the High Priest on this day: first for himself and his family, then for the priesthood as a whole (v. 11), then for the whole nation (v. 21).

שְׁנֵי הַשְּׂעִירִם *Two goats.* The two goats were identical in appearance but different in their fate. One was sacrificed to God, the other – the "scapegoat" – was sent into the desert. They represent, respectively, the polarities of the human condition: on the one hand sanctity and order, symbolized by the Tabernacle; on the other, formlessness and void, symbolized by the desert. The ceremony of the two goats is similar to the acts of separation and division that took place during creation (Gen. 1). They represent the light and darkness within the human personality. The darkness – sin – is sent into the dark: the desert with

of finest incense, bring them within the curtain. He shall place the incense into the fire in the presence of the LORD, and a cloud of incense will engulf the *kaporet* over the [Ark of] Testimony – then he shall not die.

He shall take of the bullock's blood and sprinkle with his finger onto the *kaporet* before him – and in front of the *kaporet*, he shall sprinkle seven times from the blood with his finger. And he shall slaughter the sin-offering goat that is the people's, and bring its blood behind the curtain, and do with its blood as he did with the blood of the bullock: he shall sprinkle it onto the *kaporet* and in front of the *kaporet*. So shall he bring atonement to the holiest place, for the impurities of Israel, for their rebellions and for all their sins. And so shall he do also for the Tent of Meeting, which abides with them, in the midst of their impurities. No man shall be in the Tent of Meeting when [Aaron] comes to make atonement in the holiest place, until he leaves; and he shall atone himself and his family and all the community of Israel.

REVI'I (*Shabbat:* ḤAMISHI)

Then he shall go out to the altar, which stands in the presence of the LORD, and bring atonement on it, taking of the blood of the bullock and of the goat and applying it to the horns around the altar. And he shall sprinkle of the blood with his finger onto the altar seven times, and purify and sanctify it from the impurities of Israel.

When he finishes bringing atonement for the holiest place and the Tent of Meeting and the altar, he shall offer up the living goat. Aaron shall press his hands onto the head of the living goat and confess all

---

וְסָמַךְ אַהֲרֹן אֶת־שְׁתֵּי יָדָו *Aaron shall press his hands.* The laying of hands is a symbolic act of transference, whether of guilt, blessing or authority. Maimonides writes: "There is no doubt that sins cannot be carried like a burden, and taken off the shoulder of one being to be laid on that of another being. But these ceremonies are of a symbolic character, and serve to impress people with a certain idea, and to induce them to repent, as if to say, we have freed ourselves of our previous deeds, have cast them behind our backs, and removed them from us as far as possible" (*The Guide for the Perplexed*, 3:46). The sense of guilt is pervasive and enduring. It needs some ceremony, a dramatic ritual, to make vivid the sense that the sin has been erased (the literal meaning of the root *k-p-r*, "atonement").

הַמִּזְבֵּחַ מִלִּפְנֵי יְהוָה וּמְלֹא חָפְנָיו קְטֹרֶת סַמִּים דַּקָּה וְהֵבִיא
מִבֵּית לַפָּרֹכֶת׃ וְנָתַן אֶת־הַקְּטֹרֶת עַל־הָאֵשׁ לִפְנֵי יְהוָה וְכִסָּה ׀
עֲנַן הַקְּטֹרֶת אֶת־הַכַּפֹּרֶת אֲשֶׁר עַל־הָעֵדוּת וְלֹא יָמוּת׃ וְלָקַח
מִדַּם הַפָּר וְהִזָּה בְאֶצְבָּעוֹ עַל־פְּנֵי הַכַּפֹּרֶת קֵדְמָה וְלִפְנֵי הַכַּפֹּרֶת
יַזֶּה שֶׁבַע־פְּעָמִים מִן־הַדָּם בְּאֶצְבָּעוֹ׃ וְשָׁחַט אֶת־שְׂעִיר הַחַטָּאת
אֲשֶׁר לָעָם וְהֵבִיא אֶת־דָּמוֹ אֶל־מִבֵּית לַפָּרֹכֶת וְעָשָׂה אֶת־דָּמוֹ
כַּאֲשֶׁר עָשָׂה לְדַם הַפָּר וְהִזָּה אֹתוֹ עַל־הַכַּפֹּרֶת וְלִפְנֵי הַכַּפֹּרֶת׃
וְכִפֶּר עַל־הַקֹּדֶשׁ מִטֻּמְאֹת בְּנֵי יִשְׂרָאֵל וּמִפִּשְׁעֵיהֶם לְכָל־
חַטֹּאתָם וְכֵן יַעֲשֶׂה לְאֹהֶל מוֹעֵד הַשֹּׁכֵן אִתָּם בְּתוֹךְ טֻמְאֹתָם׃
וְכָל־אָדָם לֹא־יִהְיֶה ׀ בְּאֹהֶל מוֹעֵד בְּבֹאוֹ לְכַפֵּר בַּקֹּדֶשׁ עַד־
צֵאתוֹ וְכִפֶּר בַּעֲדוֹ וּבְעַד בֵּיתוֹ וּבְעַד כָּל־קְהַל יִשְׂרָאֵל׃ וְיָצָא רביעי בשבת חמישי
אֶל־הַמִּזְבֵּחַ אֲשֶׁר לִפְנֵי־יְהוָה וְכִפֶּר עָלָיו וְלָקַח מִדַּם הַפָּר וּמִדַּם
הַשָּׂעִיר וְנָתַן עַל־קַרְנוֹת הַמִּזְבֵּחַ סָבִיב׃ וְהִזָּה עָלָיו מִן־הַדָּם
בְּאֶצְבָּעוֹ שֶׁבַע פְּעָמִים וְטִהֲרוֹ וְקִדְּשׁוֹ מִטֻּמְאֹת בְּנֵי יִשְׂרָאֵל׃
וְכִלָּה מִכַּפֵּר אֶת־הַקֹּדֶשׁ וְאֶת־אֹהֶל מוֹעֵד וְאֶת־הַמִּזְבֵּחַ וְהִקְרִיב
אֶת־הַשָּׂעִיר הֶחָי׃ וְסָמַךְ אַהֲרֹן אֶת־שְׁתֵּי יָדָו עַל־רֹאשׁ הַשָּׂעִיר

---

its values had no place within the camp. (For more on the Scapegoat, see Introduction, page lv.)

קְטֹרֶת סַמִּים דַּקָּה *Finest incense.* The cloud of incense created a screen which sheltered the High Priest from full exposure to the divine radiance.

וְכָל־אָדָם לֹא־יִהְיֶה בְּאֹהֶל מוֹעֵד *No man shall be in the Tent of Meeting.* There are moments in the religious life that require us to be alone with God. Judaism is a deeply communal faith, and at this moment the High Priest was atoning for the whole community. Yet there is an irreducible I–Thou encounter in the depths of the soul when the unattenuated human cry meets the unmediated listening of God, and we are known. It is a moment of truth in which the detritus of sin falls away and we are made pure and whole by the fire of God's forgiving love.

the guilt of Israel, and all of their rebellions, all of their sins, and he shall place them onto the head of the goat and send it away at the hand of an appointed man, into the wastelands. That goat shall bear all their guilt upon itself, into a desolate land – he shall send the goat out into the wastelands.

And then Aaron shall come to the Tent of Meeting, take off the linen clothes he put on when he entered the holiest place and set them down there. And he shall wash his skin in water in a holy place and put on his clothes, and go out and perform his burnt offering and the burnt offering of the people, in atonement for himself and for the people. And he shall burn the fat of the sin-offering like incense on the altar. HAMISHI (*Shabbat:* SHISHI)

The one who sends the goat away to Azazel shall clean his clothes and wash his skin in water, and then he may come back into the camp. And the sin-offering bullock and sin-offering goat, the blood of which was brought as atonement to the holiest place, shall be taken out of the camp – their skins and flesh and dung shall be burnt in fire. And the one who burns them shall clean his clothes and wash his skin in water, and then he may come back into the camp.

This shall be an everlasting law to you: in the seventh month, on the tenth day, you shall afflict yourselves and perform no kind of work – neither the citizen nor the stranger in your midst. For you will be atoned on this day and made pure; of all your sins before the LORD you shall be purified. This is a Sabbath of utter rest for you, and you shall afflict yourselves – this is an everlasting law. And the priest who is anointed, into whose hands it is given to serve as [High] Priest SHISHI (*Shabbat:* SHEVI'I)

---

to the person. Sin defiles the sinner. We feel soiled, stained. Yom Kippur, if we have internalized its message, removes the stain and we are made pure again.

מִכֹּל חַטֹּאתֵיכֶם לִפְנֵי יהוה תִּטְהָרוּ *Of all your sins before the LORD you shall be purified.* The sages made two important inferences from this phrase. Rabbi Akiva concluded that even in the absence of the Temple and the High Priest, Yom Kippur still atones, since it is God, not the High Priest, who cleanses us. Rabbi Elazar ben Azarya concluded that Yom Kippur atones only for sins "before the LORD," that is, between us and God. Sins against our fellow humans are only atoned when we have made amends and been forgiven by those we have wronged (Mishna, *Yoma* 85b).

החי והתודה עליו את־כל־עונת בני ישראל ואת־כל־פשעיהם
לכל־חטאתם ונתן אתם על־ראש השעיר ושלח ביד־איש
עתי המדברה: ונשא השעיר עליו את־כל־עונתם אל־ארץ
גזרה ושלח את־השעיר במדבר: ובא אהרן אל־אהל מועד
ופשט את־בגדי הבד אשר לבש בבאו אל־הקדש והניחם
שם: ורחץ את־בשרו במים במקום קדוש ולבש את־בגדיו
ויצא ועשה את־עלתו ואת־עלת העם וכפר בעדו ובעד העם:
חמישי / בשבת שישי ואת חלב החטאת יקטיר המזבחה: והמשלח את־השעיר
לעזאזל יכבס בגדיו ורחץ את־בשרו במים ואחרי־כן יבוא אל־
המחנה: ואת פר החטאת ואת | שעיר החטאת אשר הובא
את־דמם לכפר בקדש יוציא אל־מחוץ למחנה ושרפו באש
את־ערתם ואת־בשרם ואת־פרשם: והשרף אתם יכבס בגדיו
ורחץ את־בשרו במים ואחרי־כן יבוא אל־המחנה: והיתה
לכם לחקת עולם בחדש השביעי בעשור לחדש תענו את־
נפשתיכם וכל־מלאכה לא תעשו האזרח והגר הגר בתוככם:
כי־ביום הזה יכפר עליכם לטהר אתכם מכל חטאתיכם לפני
שישי / בשבת שביעי יהוה תטהרו: שבת שבתון היא לכם ועניתם את־נפשתיכם
חקת עולם: וכפר הכהן אשר־ימשח אתו ואשר ימלא את־

תענו את־נפשתיכם *You shall afflict yourselves.* Although on Yom Kippur the High Priest atoned for the sins of the nation, this did not mean that others were able to leave him to act vicariously on their behalf. They had to enter into the penitential spirit of the day through fasting and other afflictions. The ceremony as a whole was intended to create a national mood of repentance.

כי־ביום הזה יכפר עליכם לטהר אתכם *For you will be atoned on this day and made pure.* There is a difference between *kapara*, atonement, and *tehara*, cleansing. Atonement – literally "erasing" or "covering over" – refers to the sinful act. It is not merely forgiven. It is, as it were, deleted from the record. Cleansing refers

after his father, he shall wear the linen garments, the consecrated garments. He shall make atonement for the holiest Sanctuary and for the Tent of Meeting; and for the altar shall he make atonement, and he shall make atonement for the priests and for all the community of the people. This shall be an everlasting law for you, to make atonement for Israel, for all their sins, once a year. And just as the LORD commanded Moses, so it was done.

HALF KADDISH

Before Maftir is read, the second Sefer Torah is placed on the bima and the Reader says Half Kaddish:

Reader: יִתְגַּדַּל Magnified and sanctified
may His great name be,
in the world He created by His will.
May He establish His kingdom
in your lifetime and in your days,
and in the lifetime of all the house of Israel,
swiftly and soon –
and say: Amen.

All: May His great name be blessed for ever and all time.

Reader: Blessed and praised,
glorified and exalted,
raised and honored,
uplifted and lauded
be the name of the Holy One, blessed be He,
above and beyond any blessing, song,
praise and consolation
uttered in the world –
and say: Amen.

---

surpasses human understanding, is derived from a root meaning "indelibly inscribed," and is to be understood as part of the created order of the universe. The implication is that forgiveness is written into the human situation under the sovereignty of God.

יָדוֹ לְכַהֵן תַּחַת אָבִיו וְלָבַשׁ אֶת־בִּגְדֵי הַבָּד בִּגְדֵי הַקֹּדֶשׁ: וְכִפֶּר אֶת־מִקְדַּשׁ הַקֹּדֶשׁ וְאֶת־אֹהֶל מוֹעֵד וְאֶת־הַמִּזְבֵּחַ יְכַפֵּר וְעַל הַכֹּהֲנִים וְעַל־כָּל־עַם הַקָּהָל יְכַפֵּר: וְהָיְתָה־זֹּאת לָכֶם לְחֻקַּת עוֹלָם לְכַפֵּר עַל־בְּנֵי יִשְׂרָאֵל מִכָּל־חַטֹּאתָם אַחַת בַּשָּׁנָה וַיַּעַשׂ כַּאֲשֶׁר צִוָּה יהוה אֶת־מֹשֶׁה:

חצי קדיש

Before מפטיר *is read, the second* ספר תורה *is placed on the* שולחן *and the* קורא *says* חצי קדיש:

קורא: יִתְגַּדַּל וְיִתְקַדַּשׁ שְׁמֵהּ רַבָּא (קהל: אָמֵן)
בְּעָלְמָא דִּי בְרָא כִרְעוּתֵהּ
וְיַמְלִיךְ מַלְכוּתֵהּ
בְּחַיֵּיכוֹן וּבְיוֹמֵיכוֹן וּבְחַיֵּי דְכָל בֵּית יִשְׂרָאֵל
בַּעֲגָלָא וּבִזְמַן קָרִיב
וְאִמְרוּ אָמֵן. (קהל: אָמֵן)

קהל וקורא: יְהֵא שְׁמֵהּ רַבָּא מְבָרַךְ לְעָלַם וּלְעָלְמֵי עָלְמַיָּא.

קורא: יִתְבָּרַךְ וְיִשְׁתַּבַּח וְיִתְפָּאַר וְיִתְרוֹמַם וְיִתְנַשֵּׂא
וְיִתְהַדָּר וְיִתְעַלֶּה וְיִתְהַלָּל
שְׁמֵהּ דְּקֻדְשָׁא בְּרִיךְ הוּא (קהל: בְּרִיךְ הוּא)
לְעֵלָּא לְעֵלָּא מִכָּל בִּרְכָתָא וְשִׁירָתָא, תֻּשְׁבְּחָתָא וְנֶחֱמָתָא
דַּאֲמִירָן בְּעָלְמָא
וְאִמְרוּ אָמֵן. (קהל: אָמֵן)

חֻקַּת עוֹלָם *An everlasting law.* Even when there is no Temple, if we repent on Yom Kippur, the day itself atones (Maimonides, Laws of Repentance 1:3). The word *ḥok* or *ḥukka*, often translated as "statute" and understood as a law that

HAGBAHA AND GELILA

The Torah scroll is lifted and the congregation says:

וְזֹאת הַתּוֹרָה This is the Torah *Deut. 4*
that Moses placed before the children of Israel,
at the LORD's commandment, by the hand of Moses. *Num. 9*

Some add: It is a tree of life to those who grasp it, and those who uphold it are happy. *Prov. 3*
Its ways are ways of pleasantness, and all its paths are peace.
Long life is in its right hand; in its left, riches and honor.
It pleased the LORD for the sake of [Israel's] righteousness, *Is. 42*
to make the Torah great and glorious.

The first Torah scroll is bound and covered and the oleh for Maftir is called to the second Torah scroll.

MAFTIR

On the tenth day of this seventh month you shall have a holy assembly, *Num. 29:7–11* and you shall afflict your souls; you shall perform no kind of work. And you shall bring a burnt-offering of pleasing aroma to the LORD, one young bullock, one ram, and seven yearling male lambs – they shall be without blemish. And their meal-offerings of fine flour mixed with oil, three tenths of an ephah for the bullock and two tenths for the ram, and a tenth of an ephah for each of the seven lambs. One male goat should be offered as a sin-offering, in addition to the sin-offering of the Day of Atonement, and the regular daily burnt-offering with its meal-offering and their libations.

HAGBAHA AND GELILA

The second Torah scroll is lifted and the congregation says:

וְזֹאת הַתּוֹרָה This is the Torah *Deut. 4*
that Moses placed before the children of Israel,
at the LORD's commandment, by the hand of Moses. *Num. 9*

Some add: It is a tree of life to those who grasp it, and those who uphold it are happy. *Prov. 3*
Its ways are ways of pleasantness, and all its paths are peace.
Long life is in its right hand; in its left, riches and honor.
It pleased the LORD for the sake of [Israel's] righteousness, *Is. 42*
to make the Torah great and glorious.

הגבהה וגלילה

The first ספר תורה *is lifted and the* קהל *says:*

וְזֹאת הַתּוֹרָה אֲשֶׁר־שָׂם מֹשֶׁה לִפְנֵי בְּנֵי יִשְׂרָאֵל: דברים ד

עַל־פִּי יהוה בְּיַד מֹשֶׁה: במדבר ט

Some add עֵץ־חַיִּים הִיא לַמַּחֲזִיקִים בָּהּ וְתֹמְכֶיהָ מְאֻשָּׁר: משלי ג

דְּרָכֶיהָ דַרְכֵי־נֹעַם וְכָל־נְתִיבוֹתֶיהָ שָׁלוֹם:

אֹרֶךְ יָמִים בִּימִינָהּ, בִּשְׂמֹאולָהּ עֹשֶׁר וְכָבוֹד:

יהוה חָפֵץ לְמַעַן צִדְקוֹ יַגְדִּיל תּוֹרָה וְיַאְדִּיר: ישעיה מב

The first ספר תורה *is bound and covered*
and the עולה *for* מפטיר *is called to the second* ספר תורה.

מפטיר

וּבֶעָשׂוֹר לַחֹדֶשׁ הַשְּׁבִיעִי הַזֶּה מִקְרָא־קֹדֶשׁ יִהְיֶה לָכֶם וְעִנִּיתֶם במדבר כט, ז–יא
אֶת־נַפְשֹׁתֵיכֶם כָּל־מְלָאכָה לֹא תַעֲשׂוּ: וְהִקְרַבְתֶּם עֹלָה לַיהוה
רֵיחַ נִיחֹחַ פַּר בֶּן־בָּקָר אֶחָד אַיִל אֶחָד כְּבָשִׂים בְּנֵי־שָׁנָה שִׁבְעָה
תְּמִימִם יִהְיוּ לָכֶם: וּמִנְחָתָם סֹלֶת בְּלוּלָה בַשָּׁמֶן שְׁלֹשָׁה עֶשְׂרֹנִים
לַפָּר שְׁנֵי עֶשְׂרֹנִים לָאַיִל הָאֶחָד: עִשָּׂרוֹן עִשָּׂרוֹן לַכֶּבֶשׂ הָאֶחָד
לְשִׁבְעַת הַכְּבָשִׂים: שְׂעִיר־עִזִּים אֶחָד חַטָּאת מִלְּבַד חַטַּאת
הַכִּפֻּרִים וְעֹלַת הַתָּמִיד וּמִנְחָתָהּ וְנִסְכֵּיהֶם:

הגבהה וגלילה

The second ספר תורה *is lifted and the* קהל *says:*

וְזֹאת הַתּוֹרָה אֲשֶׁר־שָׂם מֹשֶׁה לִפְנֵי בְּנֵי יִשְׂרָאֵל: דברים ד

עַל־פִּי יהוה בְּיַד מֹשֶׁה: במדבר ט

Some add עֵץ־חַיִּים הִיא לַמַּחֲזִיקִים בָּהּ וְתֹמְכֶיהָ מְאֻשָּׁר: משלי ג

דְּרָכֶיהָ דַרְכֵי־נֹעַם וְכָל־נְתִיבוֹתֶיהָ שָׁלוֹם:

אֹרֶךְ יָמִים בִּימִינָהּ, בִּשְׂמֹאולָהּ עֹשֶׁר וְכָבוֹד:

יהוה חָפֵץ לְמַעַן צִדְקוֹ יַגְדִּיל תּוֹרָה וְיַאְדִּיר: ישעיה מב

The second Torah scroll is bound and covered and the oleh for Maftir reads the Haftara.

BLESSING BEFORE READING THE HAFTARA

Before reading the Haftara, the person called up for Maftir says:

בָּרוּךְ Blessed are You, LORD our God, King of the Universe, who chose good prophets and was pleased with their words, spoken in truth. Blessed are You, LORD, who chose the Torah, His servant Moses, His people Israel, and the prophets of truth and righteousness.

HAFTARA

He says: Lay a road, lay a road here; clear a way. Lift out of My people's way all that could make them fall. *Is. 57:14–58:14*

Thus says the high exalted One, who abides forever, whose name is holy: High and holy I abide – yet I am with the crushed and humbled, giving life to the humbled, giving life to the hearts of

---

that one can love God and fail to act lovingly to one's fellow humans, that the religious life can make one exempt from dealing faithfully, honestly, justly and compassionately with others, is self-serving and futile. We honor God by honoring His image in others. Hence in the words of the *Untaneh Tokef* prayer, we need not only *teshuva*, "repentance," and *tefilla*, "prayer," but also *tzedaka*, charity and social justice.

There is in Judaism an unbreakable connection between faith and the building of a moral and compassionate social order. Only the belief that every human, as the image of God, has non-negotiable and inalienable dignity, gives us the power and the clarity to overcome the instinctive will to power that has divided most of humanity for most of its history into the rulers and the ruled, the powerful and the powerless.

מָרוֹם וְקָדוֹשׁ אֶשְׁכּוֹן וְאֶת־דַּכָּא וּשְׁפַל־רוּחַ *High and holy I abide – yet I am with the crushed and humbled*. From this text, among others, Rabbi Yoḥanan learned, in a passage we recite at the end of each Shabbat, that "wherever you find the greatness of God, there you find His humility" (*Megilla* 31a). The same applies to people: strength is measured by our concern for the weak, wealth by our care for the poor, and greatness by our solicitude for those at the

The second ספר תורה *is bound and covered and the* עולה *for* מפטיר *reads the* הפטרה.

ברכה קודם ההפטרה

Before reading the הפטרה, *the person called up for* מפטיר *says:*

בָּרוּךְ אַתָּה יהוה אֱלֹהֵינוּ מֶלֶךְ הָעוֹלָם אֲשֶׁר בָּחַר בִּנְבִיאִים טוֹבִים, וְרָצָה בְדִבְרֵיהֶם הַנֶּאֱמָרִים בֶּאֱמֶת. בָּרוּךְ אַתָּה יהוה, הַבּוֹחֵר בַּתּוֹרָה וּבְמֹשֶׁה עַבְדּוֹ וּבְיִשְׂרָאֵל עַמּוֹ וּבִנְבִיאֵי הָאֱמֶת וָצֶדֶק.

הפטרה

ישעיה נז, יד – נח, יד וְאָמַר סֹלּוּ־סֹלּוּ פַּנּוּ־דָרֶךְ הָרִימוּ מִכְשׁוֹל מִדֶּרֶךְ עַמִּי: כִּי
כֹה אָמַר רָם וְנִשָּׂא שֹׁכֵן עַד וְקָדוֹשׁ שְׁמוֹ מָרוֹם וְקָדוֹשׁ אֶשְׁכּוֹן
וְאֶת־דַּכָּא וּשְׁפַל־רוּחַ לְהַחֲיוֹת רוּחַ שְׁפָלִים וּלְהַחֲיוֹת לֵב

HAFTARA: ISAIAH'S CALL TO SOCIAL JUSTICE

This is an extraordinary choice of haftara for Yom Kippur. Bear in mind that the day is marked by fasting and other forms of affliction, and that it atones only for sins between us and God. For those between us and our fellow we are not atoned until we make reparation, apologize and are forgiven. Yet Isaiah, with the incandescent moral passion of the prophet, challenges our most basic assumptions by saying: "The fast you perform today will not make your voice heard on high" (58:4).

True repentance is shown in other ways: "No; this is the fast I choose: Loosen the bindings of evil, and break the slavery chain. Those who were crushed, release to freedom; shatter every yoke of slavery. Break your bread for the starving, and bring dispossessed wanderers home. When you see a person naked, clothe him: do not avert your eyes from your own flesh." (58:6–7). God's greatness is His humility. The supreme Power cares for the weak, the poor and the powerless. When we do these things, we come close to Him and He to us.

The prophets did not minimize the significance of our relationship with God. The sin that aroused their greatest indignation was idolatry. Yet the idea

the crushed. I will not forever contend with you, will not rage to the bitter end; when the spirit faints before Me – I created these souls. I have raged at the sin behind their profits, have struck them, have hidden My face and raged, as they went wayward on the path their hearts beat out. I have seen their ways and will heal them. I will lead them, will reward them in comfort, them and their mourners; I form the words – Peace, peace, to those far away and near – so the LORD speaks, and heals them. And the wicked are like the ocean surging, unable to be still; its waters fling up mud and filth: There is no peace, says my God, for the wicked.

Shout out loud, do not hold back; raise up your voice like a ram's horn. Tell My people of their rebellion, tell the house of Jacob their sins. Day after day they search for Me; they make it their interest to know My ways, like a nation that always does right, and never neglects their God's justice. They ask for a righteous ruling. They say that being close to God is all that interests them. "Why do we fast and You do not see it; oppress ourselves when You do not acknowledge?" But even on your fast day you press your interests, oppress all your laborers. Contending and fighting each other you

---

effect on the Jewish understanding of how employers should treat their employees. Louis Brandeis was astonished by the East European Jewish immigrants he met in his role as mediator of the New York garment workers strike of 1910:

> While going through the lofts, he heard numerous quarrels between workers and their bosses, and was amazed that they treated one another more like equals than as inferiors and superiors. In one argument an employee shouted at the owner, *"Ihr darft sich shemen! Past dos far a Yid?"* ("You should be ashamed! Is this worthy of a Jew?"), while another time a machine operator lectured his employer with a quotation from Isaiah [3:14]: "It is you who have devoured the vineyard, the spoil of the poor is in your houses. What do you mean by crushing My people, by grinding the face of the poor? says the LORD God of hosts." (Milton Konvitz, *Nine American Thinkers*, New Brunswick, USA: Transaction, 2000, 67)

נִדְכָּאִים: כִּי לֹא לְעוֹלָם אָרִיב וְלֹא לָנֶצַח אֶקְּצוֹף כִּי־רוּחַ מִלְּפָנַי
יַעֲטוֹף וּנְשָׁמוֹת אֲנִי עָשִׂיתִי: בַּעֲוֹן בִּצְעוֹ קָצַפְתִּי וְאַכֵּהוּ הַסְתֵּר
וְאֶקְצֹף וַיֵּלֶךְ שׁוֹבָב בְּדֶרֶךְ לִבּוֹ: דְּרָכָיו רָאִיתִי וְאֶרְפָּאֵהוּ וְאַנְחֵהוּ
וַאֲשַׁלֵּם נִחֻמִים לוֹ וְלַאֲבֵלָיו: בּוֹרֵא נוּב שְׂפָתָיִם שָׁלוֹם ׀ שָׁלוֹם נִיב
לָרָחוֹק וְלַקָּרוֹב אָמַר יהוה וּרְפָאתִיו: וְהָרְשָׁעִים כַּיָּם נִגְרָשׁ כִּי
הַשְׁקֵט לֹא יוּכָל וַיִּגְרְשׁוּ מֵימָיו רֶפֶשׁ וָטִיט: אֵין שָׁלוֹם אָמַר אֱלֹהַי
לָרְשָׁעִים: קְרָא בְגָרוֹן אַל־תַּחְשֹׂךְ כַּשּׁוֹפָר הָרֵם קוֹלֶךָ
וְהַגֵּד לְעַמִּי פִּשְׁעָם וּלְבֵית יַעֲקֹב חַטֹּאתָם: וְאוֹתִי יוֹם יוֹם יִדְרֹשׁוּן
וְדַעַת דְּרָכַי יֶחְפָּצוּן כְּגוֹי אֲשֶׁר־צְדָקָה עָשָׂה וּמִשְׁפַּט אֱלֹהָיו לֹא
עָזָב יִשְׁאָלוּנִי מִשְׁפְּטֵי־צֶדֶק קִרְבַת אֱלֹהִים יֶחְפָּצוּן: לָמָּה צַּמְנוּ
וְלֹא רָאִיתָ עִנִּינוּ נַפְשֵׁנוּ וְלֹא תֵדָע הֵן בְּיוֹם צֹמְכֶם תִּמְצְאוּ־חֵפֶץ
וְכָל־עַצְּבֵיכֶם תִּנְגֹּשׂוּ: הֵן לְרִיב וּמַצָּה תָּצוּמוּ וּלְהַכּוֹת בְּאֶגְרֹף
רֶשַׁע לֹא־תָצוּמוּ כַיּוֹם לְהַשְׁמִיעַ בַּמָּרוֹם קוֹלְכֶם: הֲכָזֶה יִהְיֶה צוֹם

---

margins of society. This was Judaism's moral revolution, its "transvaluation of values."

שָׁלוֹם שָׁלוֹם לָרָחוֹק וְלַקָּרוֹב *Peace, peace, to those far away and near.* From this the sages learned that "In the place where penitents stand, even the perfectly righteous cannot stand" (*Berakhot* 34b).

וְהָרְשָׁעִים כַּיָּם נִגְרָשׁ *And the wicked are like the ocean surging.* We have a moral sense. When we do wrong, we know it, despite our rationalizations and excuses. A troubled conscience gives us no rest.

לָמָּה צַּמְנוּ וְלֹא רָאִיתָ *Why do we fast and You do not see it.* People complain when their prayers are not answered. The prophet replies that rituals of penance such as fasting have no effect if they are not accompanied by true contrition and a change of behavior. God judges us by the way we treat others.

וְכָל־עַצְּבֵיכֶם תִּנְגֹּשׂוּ *Oppress all your laborers.* The prophetic vision had a lasting

fast, while you beat with the fist of evil. The fast you perform today will not make your voice heard on high. Is this the fast I have chosen – a day when a man will oppress himself? When he bows his head like a rush in the wind, when he lays his bed with sackcloth and ashes? Is this what you call a fast, "a day for the LORD's favor"? No; this is the fast I choose:

Loosen the bindings of evil, and break the slavery chain. Those who were crushed, release to freedom; shatter every yoke of slavery. Break your bread for the starving, and bring dispossessed wanderers home. When you see a person naked, clothe him: do not avert your eyes from your own flesh. And then your light will break out like the sunrise, and healing will grow fast over your wound. Your righteousness will go before you, with the presence of the LORD following behind, to gather up what falls. Then you will call and the LORD will answer; when you cry out, He will say, "I am here"; if you cast the chains of slavery from your midst, the raised fist and ruthless words; if you give of your soul to the starving, and answer the hunger of souls oppressed – then your light will shine out in darkness, and your night itself will shine like noontide. The LORD will ever guide you, and answer your thirst in arid places; He will fortify your bones. You will be like a well-watered garden, like a spring that flows with never-failing waters. Places ruined long ago will be rebuilt in you; you will raise up houses from age-old foundations. You will be known as mender of the ruptured wall, as the one who restored the paths for living. If you keep your feet from breaking the Sabbath, from pursuing your affairs on My holy day; if you call the Sabbath a delight, and the LORD's holy day honorable, and if you honor it by not going your own way or attending to your own affairs, or speaking idle words – then you will find joy in the LORD, and I will cause you to ride on the heights of the earth and to feast on the inheritance of your father Jacob, for the mouth of the LORD has spoken.

אֶבְחָרֵהוּ יוֹם עַנּוֹת אָדָם נַפְשׁוֹ הֲלָכֹף כְּאַגְמֹן רֹאשׁוֹ וְשַׂק וָאֵפֶר
יַצִּיעַ הֲלָזֶה תִּקְרָא־צוֹם וְיוֹם רָצוֹן לַיהוה: הֲלוֹא זֶה צוֹם אֶבְחָרֵהוּ
פַּתֵּחַ חַרְצֻבּוֹת רֶשַׁע הַתֵּר אֲגֻדּוֹת מוֹטָה וְשַׁלַּח רְצוּצִים חָפְשִׁים
וְכָל־מוֹטָה תְּנַתֵּקוּ: הֲלוֹא פָרֹס לָרָעֵב לַחְמֶךָ וַעֲנִיִּים מְרוּדִים
תָּבִיא בָיִת כִּי־תִרְאֶה עָרֹם וְכִסִּיתוֹ וּמִבְּשָׂרְךָ לֹא תִתְעַלָּם: אָז
יִבָּקַע כַּשַּׁחַר אוֹרֶךָ וַאֲרֻכָתְךָ מְהֵרָה תִצְמָח וְהָלַךְ לְפָנֶיךָ צִדְקֶךָ
כְּבוֹד יהוה יַאַסְפֶךָ: אָז תִּקְרָא וַיהוה יַעֲנֶה תְּשַׁוַּע וְיֹאמַר הִנֵּנִי
אִם־תָּסִיר מִתּוֹכְךָ מוֹטָה שְׁלַח אֶצְבַּע וְדַבֶּר־אָוֶן: וְתָפֵק לָרָעֵב
נַפְשֶׁךָ וְנֶפֶשׁ נַעֲנָה תַּשְׂבִּיעַ וְזָרַח בַּחֹשֶׁךְ אוֹרֶךָ וַאֲפֵלָתְךָ כַּצָּהֳרָיִם:
וְנָחֲךָ יהוה תָּמִיד וְהִשְׂבִּיעַ בְּצַחְצָחוֹת נַפְשֶׁךָ וְעַצְמֹתֶיךָ יַחֲלִיץ
וְהָיִיתָ כְּגַן רָוֶה וּכְמוֹצָא מַיִם אֲשֶׁר לֹא־יְכַזְּבוּ מֵימָיו: וּבָנוּ מִמְּךָ
חָרְבוֹת עוֹלָם מוֹסְדֵי דוֹר־וָדוֹר תְּקוֹמֵם וְקֹרָא לְךָ גֹּדֵר פֶּרֶץ
מְשֹׁבֵב נְתִיבוֹת לָשָׁבֶת: אִם־תָּשִׁיב מִשַּׁבָּת רַגְלֶךָ עֲשׂוֹת חֲפָצֶךָ
בְּיוֹם קָדְשִׁי וְקָרָאתָ לַשַּׁבָּת עֹנֶג לִקְדוֹשׁ יהוה מְכֻבָּד וְכִבַּדְתּוֹ
מֵעֲשׂוֹת דְּרָכֶיךָ מִמְּצוֹא חֶפְצְךָ וְדַבֵּר דָּבָר: אָז תִּתְעַנַּג עַל־יהוה
וְהִרְכַּבְתִּיךָ עַל־במותי אָרֶץ וְהַאֲכַלְתִּיךָ נַחֲלַת יַעֲקֹב אָבִיךָ כִּי בָּמֳתֵי
פִּי יהוה דִּבֵּר:

וְקָרָאתָ לַשַּׁבָּת עֹנֶג *If you call the Sabbath a delight.* Shabbat is a weekly dress rehearsal for the Messianic Age, an intimation of paradise regained, when all hierarchies of wealth, power and status are suspended, and master and servant enjoy the same freedom. One day in seven we cease to be creators and celebrate our "createdness," catching a glimpse of the harmony of the universe – the creative Unity at the heart of created diversity – and in the silence of the soul hear the song of the earth and the music of the heavens.

BLESSINGS AFTER THE HAFTARA

After the Haftara, the person called up for Maftir says the following blessings:

בָּרוּךְ Blessed are You, LORD our God, King of the Universe, Rock of all worlds, righteous for all generations, the faithful God who says and does, speaks and fulfills, all of whose words are truth and righteousness. You are faithful, LORD our God, and faithful are Your words, not one of which returns unfulfilled, for You, God, are a faithful (and compassionate) King. Blessed are You, LORD, faithful in all His words.

רַחֵם Have compassion on Zion for it is the source of our life, and save the one grieved in spirit swiftly in our days. Blessed are You, LORD, who makes Zion rejoice in her children.

שַׂמְּחֵנוּ Grant us joy, LORD our God, through Elijah the prophet Your servant, and through the kingdom of the house of David Your anointed – may he soon come and make our hearts glad. May no stranger sit on his throne, and may others not continue to inherit his glory, for You promised him by Your holy name that his light would never be extinguished. Blessed are You, LORD, Shield of David.

On Shabbat, add the words in parentheses:

עַל הַתּוֹרָה For the Torah, for divine worship, for the prophets, (for this Sabbath day) and for this Day of Atonement, which You, LORD our God, have given us (for holiness and rest), for pardon, forgiveness and atonement, to pardon all our iniquities, for honor and glory – for all these we thank and bless You, LORD our God, and may Your name be blessed by the mouth of all that lives, continually, for ever and all time, for Your word is true and endures for ever. Blessed are You, LORD, King who pardons and forgives our iniquities and those of all His people the house of Israel, and makes our guilt pass away, every single year, King over all the earth, who sanctifies (the Sabbath,) Israel and the Day of Atonement.

ברכות לאחר ההפטרה

After the הפטרה*, the person called up for* מפטיר *says the following blessings:*

בָּרוּךְ אַתָּה יהוה אֱלֹהֵינוּ מֶלֶךְ הָעוֹלָם, צוּר כָּל הָעוֹלָמִים, צַדִּיק בְּכָל הַדּוֹרוֹת, הָאֵל הַנֶּאֱמָן, הָאוֹמֵר וְעוֹשֶׂה, הַמְדַבֵּר וּמְקַיֵּם, שֶׁכָּל דְּבָרָיו אֱמֶת וָצֶדֶק. נֶאֱמָן אַתָּה הוּא יהוה אֱלֹהֵינוּ וְנֶאֱמָנִים דְּבָרֶיךָ, וְדָבָר אֶחָד מִדְּבָרֶיךָ אָחוֹר לֹא יָשׁוּב רֵיקָם, כִּי אֵל מֶלֶךְ נֶאֱמָן (וְרַחֲמָן) אָתָּה. בָּרוּךְ אַתָּה יהוה, הָאֵל הַנֶּאֱמָן בְּכָל דְּבָרָיו.

רַחֵם עַל צִיּוֹן כִּי הִיא בֵּית חַיֵּינוּ, וְלַעֲלוּבַת נֶפֶשׁ תּוֹשִׁיעַ בִּמְהֵרָה בְיָמֵינוּ. בָּרוּךְ אַתָּה יהוה, מְשַׂמֵּחַ צִיּוֹן בְּבָנֶיהָ.

שַׂמְּחֵנוּ יהוה אֱלֹהֵינוּ בְּאֵלִיָּהוּ הַנָּבִיא עַבְדֶּךָ, וּבְמַלְכוּת בֵּית דָּוִד מְשִׁיחֶךָ, בִּמְהֵרָה יָבוֹא וְיָגֵל לִבֵּנוּ. עַל כִּסְאוֹ לֹא יֵשֶׁב זָר, וְלֹא יִנְחֲלוּ עוֹד אֲחֵרִים אֶת כְּבוֹדוֹ, כִּי בְשֵׁם קָדְשְׁךָ נִשְׁבַּעְתָּ לּוֹ שֶׁלֹּא יִכְבֶּה נֵרוֹ לְעוֹלָם וָעֶד. בָּרוּךְ אַתָּה יהוה, מָגֵן דָּוִד.

On שבת*, add the words in parentheses:*

עַל הַתּוֹרָה וְעַל הָעֲבוֹדָה וְעַל הַנְּבִיאִים (וְעַל יוֹם הַשַּׁבָּת הַזֶּה) וְעַל יוֹם הַכִּפּוּרִים הַזֶּה, שֶׁנָּתַתָּ לָּנוּ, יהוה אֱלֹהֵינוּ (לִקְדֻשָּׁה וְלִמְנוּחָה), לִמְחִילָה וְלִסְלִיחָה וּלְכַפָּרָה, וְלִמְחָל בּוֹ אֶת כָּל עֲוֹנוֹתֵינוּ, לְכָבוֹד וּלְתִפְאָרֶת. עַל הַכֹּל יהוה אֱלֹהֵינוּ אֲנַחְנוּ מוֹדִים לָךְ וּמְבָרְכִים אוֹתָךְ, יִתְבָּרַךְ שִׁמְךָ בְּפִי כָּל חַי תָּמִיד לְעוֹלָם וָעֶד, וּדְבָרְךָ אֱמֶת וְקַיָּם לָעַד. בָּרוּךְ אַתָּה יהוה, מֶלֶךְ מוֹחֵל וְסוֹלֵחַ לַעֲוֹנוֹתֵינוּ וְלַעֲוֹנוֹת עַמּוֹ בֵּית יִשְׂרָאֵל, וּמַעֲבִיר אַשְׁמוֹתֵינוּ בְּכָל שָׁנָה וְשָׁנָה, מֶלֶךְ עַל כָּל הָאָרֶץ, מְקַדֵּשׁ (הַשַּׁבָּת וְ) יִשְׂרָאֵל וְיוֹם הַכִּפּוּרִים.

On a weekday, the service continues with the various prayers for government on page 748. On Shabbat continue:

יְקוּם פֻּרְקָן May deliverance arise from heaven, bringing grace, love and compassion, long life, ample sustenance and heavenly help, physical health and enlightenment of mind, living and thriving children who will neither interrupt nor cease from the words of the Torah – to our masters and teachers of the holy communities in the land of Israel and Babylon; to the leaders of assemblies and the leaders of communities in exile; to the heads of academies and to the judges in the gates; to all their disciples and their disciples' disciples, and to all who occupy themselves in study of the Torah. May the King of the Universe bless them, prolonging their lives, increasing their days, and adding to their years. May they be redeemed and delivered from all distress and illness. May our Master in heaven be their help at all times and seasons; and let us say: Amen.

יְקוּם פֻּרְקָן May deliverance arise from heaven, bringing grace, love and compassion, long life, ample sustenance and heavenly help, physical health and enlightenment of mind, living and thriving children who will neither interrupt nor cease from the words of the Torah – to all this holy congregation, great and small, women and children. May the King of the Universe bless you, prolonging your lives, increasing your days, and adding to your years. May you be redeemed and delivered from all distress and illness. May our Master in heaven be your help at all times and seasons; and let us say: Amen.

מִי שֶׁבֵּרַךְ May He who blessed our fathers, Abraham, Isaac and Jacob, bless all this holy congregation, together with all other holy congregations: them, their wives, their sons and daughters, and all that is theirs. May He bless those who unite to form synagogues for prayer and those who come there to pray; those who provide lamps for light and wine for Kiddush and Havdala, food for visitors and charity for the poor, and all who faithfully occupy themselves with the needs of the community. May the Holy One, blessed be He, give them their reward; may He remove from them all illness, grant them complete healing, and forgive all their sins. May He send blessing and success to all the work of their hands, together with all Israel their brethren; and let us say: Amen.

On a weekday, the service continues with the various prayers for government on page 749.
On שבת *continue:*

יְקוּם פֻּרְקָן מִן שְׁמַיָּא, חִנָּא וְחִסְדָּא וְרַחֲמֵי וְחַיֵּי אֲרִיכֵי וּמְזוֹנֵי רְוִיחֵי, וְסִיַּעְתָּא דִשְׁמַיָּא, וּבַרְיוּת גּוּפָא וּנְהוֹרָא מְעַלְּיָא, זַרְעָא חַיָּא וְקַיָּמָא, זַרְעָא דִּי לָא יִפְסֻק וְדִי לָא יִבְטֻל מִפִּתְגָּמֵי אוֹרַיְתָא, לְמָרָנָן וְרַבָּנָן חֲבוּרָתָא קַדִּישָׁתָא דִּי בְאַרְעָא דְיִשְׂרָאֵל וְדִי בְּבָבֶל, לְרֵישֵׁי כַלָּה, וּלְרֵישֵׁי גַלְוָתָא, וּלְרֵישֵׁי מְתִיבָתָא, וּלְדַיָּנֵי דְבָבָא, לְכָל תַּלְמִידֵיהוֹן, וּלְכָל תַּלְמִידֵי תַלְמִידֵיהוֹן, וּלְכָל מָאן דְּעָסְקִין בְּאוֹרַיְתָא. מַלְכָּא דְעָלְמָא יְבָרֵךְ יָתְהוֹן, יַפֵּשׁ חַיֵּיהוֹן וְיַסְגֵּא יוֹמֵיהוֹן, וְיִתֵּן אַרְכָא לִשְׁנֵיהוֹן, וְיִתְפָּרְקוּן וְיִשְׁתֵּיזְבוּן מִן כָּל עָקָא וּמִן כָּל מַרְעִין בִּישִׁין. מָרַן דִּי בִשְׁמַיָּא יְהֵא בְסַעְדְּהוֹן כָּל זְמַן וְעִדָּן, וְנֹאמַר אָמֵן.

יְקוּם פֻּרְקָן מִן שְׁמַיָּא, חִנָּא וְחִסְדָּא וְרַחֲמֵי וְחַיֵּי אֲרִיכֵי וּמְזוֹנֵי רְוִיחֵי, וְסִיַּעְתָּא דִשְׁמַיָּא, וּבַרְיוּת גּוּפָא וּנְהוֹרָא מְעַלְּיָא, זַרְעָא חַיָּא וְקַיָּמָא, זַרְעָא דִּי לָא יִפְסֻק וְדִי לָא יִבְטֻל מִפִּתְגָּמֵי אוֹרַיְתָא, לְכָל קְהָלָא קַדִּישָׁא הָדֵין, רַבְרְבַיָּא עִם זְעֵרַיָּא, טַפְלָא וּנְשַׁיָּא. מַלְכָּא דְעָלְמָא יְבָרֵךְ יָתְכוֹן, יַפֵּשׁ חַיֵּיכוֹן וְיַסְגֵּא יוֹמֵיכוֹן, וְיִתֵּן אַרְכָא לִשְׁנֵיכוֹן, וְתִתְפָּרְקוּן וְתִשְׁתֵּיזְבוּן מִן כָּל עָקָא וּמִן כָּל מַרְעִין בִּישִׁין. מָרַן דִּי בִשְׁמַיָּא יְהֵא בְסַעְדְּכוֹן כָּל זְמַן וְעִדָּן, וְנֹאמַר אָמֵן.

מִי שֶׁבֵּרַךְ אֲבוֹתֵינוּ אַבְרָהָם יִצְחָק וְיַעֲקֹב, הוּא יְבָרֵךְ אֶת כָּל הַקָּהָל הַקָּדוֹשׁ הַזֶּה עִם כָּל קְהִלּוֹת הַקֹּדֶשׁ, הֵם וּנְשֵׁיהֶם וּבְנֵיהֶם וּבְנוֹתֵיהֶם וְכָל אֲשֶׁר לָהֶם, וּמִי שֶׁמְּיַחֲדִים בָּתֵּי כְנֵסִיּוֹת לִתְפִלָּה, וּמִי שֶׁבָּאִים בְּתוֹכָם לְהִתְפַּלֵּל, וּמִי שֶׁנּוֹתְנִים נֵר לַמָּאוֹר וְיַיִן לְקִדּוּשׁ וּלְהַבְדָּלָה וּפַת לָאוֹרְחִים וּצְדָקָה לָעֲנִיִּים, וְכָל מִי שֶׁעוֹסְקִים בְּצָרְכֵי צִבּוּר בֶּאֱמוּנָה. הַקָּדוֹשׁ בָּרוּךְ הוּא יְשַׁלֵּם שְׂכָרָם, וְיָסִיר מֵהֶם כָּל מַחֲלָה, וְיִרְפָּא לְכָל גּוּפָם, וְיִסְלַח לְכָל עֲוֹנָם, וְיִשְׁלַח בְּרָכָה וְהַצְלָחָה בְּכָל מַעֲשֵׂי יְדֵיהֶם עִם כָּל יִשְׂרָאֵל אֲחֵיהֶם, וְנֹאמַר אָמֵן.

PRAYER FOR THE WELFARE OF THE U.S. GOVERNMENT

The Leader says the following:

הַנּוֹתֵן תְּשׁוּעָה May He who gives salvation to kings and dominion to princes, whose kingdom is an everlasting kingdom, who delivers His servant David from the evil sword, who makes a way in the sea and a path through the mighty waters, bless and protect, guard and help, exalt, magnify and uplift the President, Vice President, and all officials of this land. May the Supreme King of kings in His mercy put into their hearts and the hearts of all their counselors and officials, to deal kindly with us and all Israel. In their days and in ours, may Judah be saved and Israel dwell in safety, and may the Redeemer come to Zion. May this be His will, and let us say: Amen.

PRAYER FOR THE SAFETY OF THE AMERICAN MILITARY

The Leader says the following:

אַדִּיר בַּמָּרוֹם God on high who dwells in might, the King to whom peace belongs, look down from Your holy habitation and bless the soldiers of the American military forces who risk their lives for the sake of peace on earth. Be their shelter and stronghold, and let them not falter. Give them the strength and courage to thwart the plans of the enemy and end the rule of evil. May their enemies be scattered and their foes flee before them, and may they rejoice in Your salvation. Bring them back safely to their homes, as is
written: "The LORD will guard you from all harm, He will guard *Ps. 121*
your life. The LORD will guard your going and coming, now and
for evermore." And may there be fulfilled for us the verse: "Nation *Is. 2*
shall not lift up sword against nation, nor shall they learn war any more." Let all the inhabitants on earth know that sovereignty is Yours and Your name inspires awe over all You have created – and let us say: Amen.

תפילה לשלום המלכות

The שליח ציבור *says the following:*

הַנּוֹתֵן תְּשׁוּעָה לַמְּלָכִים וּמֶמְשָׁלָה לַנְּסִיכִים, מַלְכוּתוֹ מַלְכוּת כָּל עוֹלָמִים, הַפּוֹצֶה אֶת דָּוִד עַבְדּוֹ מֵחֶרֶב רָעָה, הַנּוֹתֵן בַּיָּם דֶּרֶךְ וּבְמַיִם עַזִּים נְתִיבָה, הוּא יְבָרֵךְ וְיִשְׁמֹר וְיִנְצֹר וְיַעֲזֹר וִירוֹמֵם וִיגַדֵּל וִינַשֵּׂא לְמַעְלָה אֶת הַנָּשִׂיא וְאֵת מִשְׁנֵהוּ וְאֶת כָּל שָׂרֵי הָאָרֶץ הַזֹּאת. מֶלֶךְ מַלְכֵי הַמְּלָכִים, בְּרַחֲמָיו יִתֵּן בְּלִבָּם וּבְלֵב כָּל יוֹעֲצֵיהֶם וְשָׂרֵיהֶם לַעֲשׂוֹת טוֹבָה עִמָּנוּ וְעִם כָּל יִשְׂרָאֵל. בִּימֵיהֶם וּבְיָמֵינוּ תִּוָּשַׁע יְהוּדָה, וְיִשְׂרָאֵל יִשְׁכֹּן לָבֶטַח, וּבָא לְצִיּוֹן גּוֹאֵל. וְכֵן יְהִי רָצוֹן, וְנֹאמַר אָמֵן.

תפילה לשלום חיילי צבא ארצות הברית

The שליח ציבור *says the following:*

אַדִּיר בַּמָּרוֹם שׁוֹכֵן בִּגְבוּרָה, מֶלֶךְ שֶׁהַשָּׁלוֹם שֶׁלּוֹ, הַשְׁקִיפָה מִמְּעוֹן קָדְשְׁךָ, וּבָרֵךְ אֶת חַיָּלֵי צְבָא אַרְצוֹת הַבְּרִית, הַמְחָרְפִים נַפְשָׁם בְּלֶכְתָּם לָשִׂים שָׁלוֹם בָּאָרֶץ. הֱיֵה נָא לָהֶם מַחֲסֶה וּמָעוֹז, וְאַל תִּתֵּן לַמּוֹט רַגְלָם, חַזֵּק יְדֵיהֶם וְאַמֵּץ רוּחָם לְהָפֵר עֲצַת אוֹיֵב וּלְהַעֲבִיר מֶמְשֶׁלֶת זָדוֹן, יָפוּצוּ אוֹיְבֵיהֶם וְיָנוּסוּ מְשַׂנְאֵיהֶם מִפָּנֵיהֶם, וְיִשְׂמְחוּ בִּישׁוּעָתֶךָ. הֲשִׁיבֵם בְּשָׁלוֹם אֶל בֵּיתָם, כַּכָּתוּב
בְּדִבְרֵי קָדְשֶׁךָ: יהוה יִשְׁמָרְךָ מִכָּל־רָע, יִשְׁמֹר אֶת־נַפְשֶׁךָ: יהוה תהלים קכא
יִשְׁמָר־צֵאתְךָ וּבוֹאֶךָ, מֵעַתָּה וְעַד־עוֹלָם: וְקַיֵּם בָּנוּ מִקְרָא
שֶׁכָּתוּב: לֹא־יִשָּׂא גוֹי אֶל־גּוֹי חֶרֶב, וְלֹא־יִלְמְדוּ עוֹד מִלְחָמָה: ישעיה ב
וְיֵדְעוּ כָּל יוֹשְׁבֵי תֵבֵל כִּי לְךָ מְלוּכָה יָאֲתָה, וְשִׁמְךָ נוֹרָא עַל כָּל מַה שֶּׁבָּרָאתָ. וְנֹאמַר אָמֵן.

PRAYER FOR THE WELFARE OF THE CANADIAN GOVERNMENT

The Leader says the following:

הַנּוֹתֵן תְּשׁוּעָה May He who gives salvation to kings and dominion to princes, whose kingdom is an everlasting kingdom, who delivers His servant David from the evil sword, who makes a way in the sea and a path through the mighty waters, bless and protect, guard and help, exalt, magnify and uplift the Prime Minister and all the elected and appointed officials of Canada. May the Supreme King of kings in His mercy put into their hearts and the hearts of all their counselors and officials, to deal kindly with us and all Israel. In their days and in ours, may Judah be saved and Israel dwell in safety, and may the Redeemer come to Zion. May this be His will, and let us say: Amen.

PRAYER FOR THE SAFETY OF THE CANADIAN FORCES

The Leader says the following:

אַדִּיר בַּמָּרוֹם God on high who dwells in might, the King to whom peace belongs, look down from Your holy habitation and bless the soldiers of the Canadian Forces who risk their lives for the sake of peace on earth. Be their shelter and stronghold, and let them not falter. Give them the strength and courage to thwart the plans of the enemy and end the rule of evil. May their enemies be scattered and their foes flee before them, and may they rejoice in Your salvation. Bring them back safely to their homes, as is
written: "The Lord will guard you from all harm, He will guard *Ps. 121*
your life. The Lord will guard your going and coming, now and
for evermore." And may there be fulfilled for us the verse: "Nation *Is. 2*
shall not lift up sword against nation, nor shall they learn war any more." Let all the inhabitants on earth know that sovereignty is Yours and Your name inspires awe over all You have created – and let us say: Amen.

תפילה לשלום המלכות

The שליח ציבור *says the following:*

הַנּוֹתֵן תְּשׁוּעָה לַמְּלָכִים וּמֶמְשָׁלָה לַנְּסִיכִים, מַלְכוּתוֹ מַלְכוּת כָּל עוֹלָמִים, הַפּוֹצֶה אֶת דָּוִד עַבְדּוֹ מֵחֶרֶב רָעָה, הַנּוֹתֵן בַּיָּם דֶּרֶךְ וּבְמַיִם עַזִּים נְתִיבָה, הוּא יְבָרֵךְ וְיִשְׁמֹר וְיִנְצֹר וְיַעֲזֹר וִירוֹמֵם וִיגַדֵּל וִינַשֵּׂא לְמַעְלָה אֶת רֹאשׁ הַמֶּמְשָׁלָה וְאֶת כָּל שָׂרֵי הָאָרֶץ הַזֹּאת. מֶלֶךְ מַלְכֵי הַמְּלָכִים, בְּרַחֲמָיו יִתֵּן בְּלִבָּם וּבְלֵב כָּל יוֹעֲצֵיהֶם וְשָׂרֵיהֶם לַעֲשׂוֹת טוֹבָה עִמָּנוּ וְעִם כָּל יִשְׂרָאֵל. בִּימֵיהֶם וּבְיָמֵינוּ תִּוָּשַׁע יְהוּדָה, וְיִשְׂרָאֵל יִשְׁכֹּן לָבֶטַח, וּבָא לְצִיּוֹן גּוֹאֵל. וְכֵן יְהִי רָצוֹן, וְנֹאמַר אָמֵן.

תפילה לשלום חיילי צבא קנדה

The שליח ציבור *says the following:*

אַדִּיר בַּמָּרוֹם שׁוֹכֵן בִּגְבוּרָה, מֶלֶךְ שֶׁהַשָּׁלוֹם שֶׁלּוֹ, הַשְׁקִיפָה מִמְּעוֹן קָדְשְׁךָ, וּבָרֵךְ אֶת חַיָּלֵי צְבָא קָנָדָה, הַמְחָרְפִים נַפְשָׁם בְּלֶכְתָּם לָשִׂים שָׁלוֹם בָּאָרֶץ. הֱיֵה נָא לָהֶם מַחֲסֶה וּמָעוֹז, וְאַל תִּתֵּן לַמּוֹט רַגְלָם, חַזֵּק יְדֵיהֶם וְאַמֵּץ רוּחָם לְהָפֵר עֲצַת אוֹיֵב וּלְהַעֲבִיר מֶמְשֶׁלֶת זָדוֹן, יָפוּצוּ אוֹיְבֵיהֶם וְיָנוּסוּ מְשַׂנְאֵיהֶם מִפְּנֵיהֶם, וְיִשְׂמְחוּ בִּישׁוּעָתֶךָ. הֲשִׁיבֵם בְּשָׁלוֹם אֶל בֵּיתָם, כַּכָּתוּב
בְּדִבְרֵי קָדְשֶׁךָ: יהוה יִשְׁמָרְךָ מִכָּל־רָע, יִשְׁמֹר אֶת־נַפְשֶׁךָ: יהוה תהלים קכא
יִשְׁמָר־צֵאתְךָ וּבוֹאֶךָ, מֵעַתָּה וְעַד־עוֹלָם: וְקַיֵּם בָּנוּ מִקְרָא
שֶׁכָּתוּב: לֹא־יִשָּׂא גוֹי אֶל־גּוֹי חֶרֶב, וְלֹא־יִלְמְדוּ עוֹד מִלְחָמָה: ישעיה ב
וְיֵדְעוּ כָּל יוֹשְׁבֵי תֵבֵל כִּי לְךָ מְלוּכָה יָאֲתָה, וְשִׁמְךָ נוֹרָא עַל כָּל מַה שֶּׁבָּרָאתָ. וְנֹאמַר אָמֵן.

PRAYER FOR THE STATE OF ISRAEL

The Leader says the following prayer:

אָבִינוּ שֶׁבַּשָּׁמַיִם Heavenly Father, Israel's Rock and Redeemer, bless the State of Israel, the first flowering of our redemption. Shield it under the wings of Your loving-kindness and spread over it the Tabernacle of Your peace. Send Your light and truth to its leaders, ministers and counselors, and direct them with good counsel before You.

Strengthen the hands of the defenders of our Holy Land; grant them deliverance, our God, and crown them with the crown of victory. Grant peace in the land and everlasting joy to its inhabitants.

As for our brothers, the whole house of Israel, remember them in all the lands of our (*In Israel say:* their) dispersion, and swiftly lead us (*In Israel say:* them) upright to Zion Your city, and Jerusalem Your dwelling place, as is written in the Torah of Moses Your servant: "Even if you are scattered to the furthermost lands under the heavens, from there the LORD your God will gather you and take you back. The LORD your God will bring you to the land your ancestors possessed and you will possess it; and He will make you more prosperous and numerous than your ancestors. Then the LORD your God will open up your heart and the heart of your descendants, to love the LORD your God with all your heart and with all your soul, that you may live." *Deut. 30*

Unite our hearts to love and revere Your name and observe all the words of Your Torah, and swiftly send us Your righteous anointed one of the house of David, to redeem those who long for Your salvation.

Appear in Your glorious majesty over all the dwellers on earth, and let all who breathe declare: The LORD God of Israel is King and His kingship has dominion over all. Amen, Selah.

תפילה לשלום מדינת ישראל

The שליח ציבור *says the following prayer:*

אָבִינוּ שֶׁבַּשָּׁמַיִם, צוּר יִשְׂרָאֵל וְגוֹאֲלוֹ, בָּרֵךְ אֶת מְדִינַת יִשְׂרָאֵל, רֵאשִׁית צְמִיחַת גְּאֻלָּתֵנוּ. הָגֵן עָלֶיהָ בְּאֶבְרַת חַסְדֶּךָ וּפְרֹשׂ עָלֶיהָ סֻכַּת שְׁלוֹמֶךָ וּשְׁלַח אוֹרְךָ וַאֲמִתְּךָ לְרָאשֶׁיהָ, שָׂרֶיהָ וְיוֹעֲצֶיהָ, וְתַקְּנֵם בְּעֵצָה טוֹבָה מִלְּפָנֶיךָ.

חַזֵּק אֶת יְדֵי מְגִנֵּי אֶרֶץ קָדְשֵׁנוּ, וְהַנְחִילֵם אֱלֹהֵינוּ יְשׁוּעָה וַעֲטֶרֶת נִצָּחוֹן תְּעַטְּרֵם, וְנָתַתָּ שָׁלוֹם בָּאָרֶץ וְשִׂמְחַת עוֹלָם לְיוֹשְׁבֶיהָ.

וְאֶת אַחֵינוּ כָּל בֵּית יִשְׂרָאֵל, פְּקָד נָא בְּכָל אַרְצוֹת פְּזוּרֵינוּ, וְתוֹלִיכֵנוּ /בארץ ישראל: פְּזוּרֵיהֶם, וְתוֹלִיכֵם/ מְהֵרָה קוֹמְמִיּוּת לְצִיּוֹן
עִירֶךָ וְלִירוּשָׁלַיִם מִשְׁכַּן שְׁמֶךָ, כַּכָּתוּב בְּתוֹרַת מֹשֶׁה עַבְדֶּךָ:
אִם־יִהְיֶה נִדַּחֲךָ בִּקְצֵה הַשָּׁמָיִם, מִשָּׁם יְקַבֶּצְךָ יהוה אֱלֹהֶיךָ דברים ל
וּמִשָּׁם יִקָּחֶךָ: וֶהֱבִיאֲךָ יהוה אֱלֹהֶיךָ אֶל־הָאָרֶץ אֲשֶׁר־יָרְשׁוּ
אֲבֹתֶיךָ וִירִשְׁתָּהּ, וְהֵיטִבְךָ וְהִרְבְּךָ מֵאֲבֹתֶיךָ: וּמָל יהוה אֱלֹהֶיךָ
אֶת־לְבָבְךָ וְאֶת־לְבַב זַרְעֶךָ, לְאַהֲבָה אֶת־יהוה אֱלֹהֶיךָ בְּכָל־
לְבָבְךָ וּבְכָל־נַפְשְׁךָ, לְמַעַן חַיֶּיךָ:

וְיַחֵד לְבָבֵנוּ לְאַהֲבָה וּלְיִרְאָה אֶת שְׁמֶךָ, וְלִשְׁמֹר אֶת כָּל דִּבְרֵי תוֹרָתֶךָ, וּשְׁלַח לָנוּ מְהֵרָה בֶּן דָּוִד מְשִׁיחַ צִדְקֶךָ, לִפְדּוֹת מְחַכֵּי קֵץ יְשׁוּעָתֶךָ.

וְהוֹפַע בַּהֲדַר גְּאוֹן עֻזֶּךָ עַל כָּל יוֹשְׁבֵי תֵבֵל אַרְצֶךָ וְיֹאמַר כֹּל אֲשֶׁר נְשָׁמָה בְּאַפּוֹ, יהוה אֱלֹהֵי יִשְׂרָאֵל מֶלֶךְ וּמַלְכוּתוֹ בַּכֹּל מָשָׁלָה, אָמֵן סֶלָה.

PRAYER FOR ISRAEL'S DEFENSE FORCES

The Leader says the following prayer:

מִי שֶׁבֵּרַךְ May He who blessed our ancestors, Abraham, Isaac and Jacob, bless the members of Israel's Defense Forces and its security services who stand guard over our land and the cities of our God from the Lebanese border to the Egyptian desert, from the Mediterranean sea to the approach of the Aravah, and wherever else they are, on land, in air and at sea. May the LORD make the enemies who rise against us be struck down before them. May the Holy One, blessed be He, protect and deliver them from all trouble and distress, affliction and illness, and send blessing and success to all the work of their hands. May He subdue our enemies under them and crown them with deliverance and victory. And may there be fulfilled in them the verse, "It is the LORD your God who goes with you to fight *Deut. 20* for you against your enemies, to deliver you." And let us say: Amen.

PRAYER FOR THOSE BEING HELD IN CAPTIVITY

If Israeli soldiers or civilians are being held in captivity, the Leader says the following:

מִי שֶׁבֵּרַךְ May He who blessed our ancestors, Abraham, Isaac and Jacob, Joseph, Moses and Aaron, David and Solomon, bless, protect and guard the members of Israel's Defense Forces missing in action or held captive, and other captives among our brethren, the whole house of Israel, who are in distress or captivity, as we, the members of this holy congregation, pray on their behalf. May the Holy One, blessed be He, have compassion on them and bring them out from darkness and the shadow of death; may He break their bonds, deliver them from their distress, and bring them swiftly back to their families' embrace. Give thanks to the LORD for His loving-kindness *Ps. 107* and for the wonders He does for the children of men; and may there be fulfilled in them the verse: "Those redeemed by the LORD will *Is. 35* return; they will enter Zion with singing, and everlasting joy will crown their heads. Gladness and joy will overtake them, and sorrow and sighing will flee away." And let us say: Amen.

מי שברך לחיילי צה״ל

The שליח ציבור *says the following prayer:*

מִי שֶׁבֵּרַךְ אֲבוֹתֵינוּ אַבְרָהָם יִצְחָק וְיַעֲקֹב הוּא יְבָרֵךְ אֶת חַיָּלֵי
צְבָא הַהֲגָנָה לְיִשְׂרָאֵל וְאַנְשֵׁי כֹּחוֹת הַבִּטָּחוֹן, הָעוֹמְדִים עַל
מִשְׁמַר אַרְצֵנוּ וְעָרֵי אֱלֹהֵינוּ, מִגְּבוּל הַלְּבָנוֹן וְעַד מִדְבַּר מִצְרַיִם
וּמִן הַיָּם הַגָּדוֹל עַד לְבוֹא הָעֲרָבָה וּבְכָל מָקוֹם שֶׁהֵם, בַּיַּבָּשָׁה,
בָּאֲוִיר וּבַיָּם. יִתֵּן יהוה אֶת אוֹיְבֵינוּ הַקָּמִים עָלֵינוּ נִגָּפִים לִפְנֵיהֶם.
הַקָּדוֹשׁ בָּרוּךְ הוּא יִשְׁמֹר וְיַצִּיל אֶת חַיָּלֵינוּ מִכָּל צָרָה וְצוּקָה
וּמִכָּל נֶגַע וּמַחֲלָה, וְיִשְׁלַח בְּרָכָה וְהַצְלָחָה בְּכָל מַעֲשֵׂי יְדֵיהֶם.
יַדְבֵּר שׂוֹנְאֵינוּ תַּחְתֵּיהֶם וִיעַטְּרֵם בְּכֶתֶר יְשׁוּעָה וּבַעֲטֶרֶת נִצָּחוֹן.
וִיקֻיַּם בָּהֶם הַכָּתוּב: כִּי יהוה אֱלֹהֵיכֶם הַהֹלֵךְ עִמָּכֶם לְהִלָּחֵם דברים כ
לָכֶם עִם־אֹיְבֵיכֶם לְהוֹשִׁיעַ אֶתְכֶם: וְנֹאמַר אָמֵן.

מי שברך לשבויים

If Israeli soldiers or civilians are being held in captivity, the שליח ציבור *says the following:*

מִי שֶׁבֵּרַךְ אֲבוֹתֵינוּ אַבְרָהָם יִצְחָק וְיַעֲקֹב, יוֹסֵף מֹשֶׁה וְאַהֲרֹן,
דָּוִד וּשְׁלֹמֹה, הוּא יְבָרֵךְ וְיִשְׁמֹר וְיִנְצֹר אֶת נֶעְדְּרֵי צְבָא הַהֲגָנָה
לְיִשְׂרָאֵל וּשְׁבוּיָו, וְאֶת כָּל אַחֵינוּ הַנְּתוּנִים בְּצָרָה וּבְשִׁבְיָה, בַּעֲבוּר
שֶׁכָּל הַקָּהָל הַקָּדוֹשׁ הַזֶּה מִתְפַּלֵּל בַּעֲבוּרָם. הַקָּדוֹשׁ בָּרוּךְ הוּא
יִמָּלֵא רַחֲמִים עֲלֵיהֶם, וְיוֹצִיאֵם מֵחֹשֶׁךְ וְצַלְמָוֶת, וּמוֹסְרוֹתֵיהֶם
יְנַתֵּק, וּמִמְּצוּקוֹתֵיהֶם יוֹשִׁיעֵם, וִישִׁיבֵם מְהֵרָה לְחֵיק
מִשְׁפְּחוֹתֵיהֶם. יוֹדוּ לַיהוה חַסְדּוֹ וְנִפְלְאוֹתָיו לִבְנֵי אָדָם: וִיקֻיַּם תהלים קז
בָּהֶם מִקְרָא שֶׁכָּתוּב: וּפְדוּיֵי יהוה יְשֻׁבוּן, וּבָאוּ צִיּוֹן בְּרִנָּה, ישעיה לה
וְשִׂמְחַת עוֹלָם עַל־רֹאשָׁם, שָׂשׂוֹן וְשִׂמְחָה יַשִּׂיגוּ, וְנָסוּ יָגוֹן
וַאֲנָחָה: וְנֹאמַר אָמֵן.

YIZKOR

Before returning the Torah scrolls, a Yizkor (memorial) service is said. In some communities, those who have not been bereaved of a parent or close relative do not participate in the Yizkor service, but leave the synagogue and return for "Father of compassion" on page 762.

יהוה Lord, what is man that You care for him, a mortal that You notice him? *Ps. 144*
Man is like a fleeting breath, his days like a passing shadow.
In the morning he flourishes and grows; *Ps. 90*
in the evening he withers and dries up.
Teach us to number our days, that we may get a heart of wisdom.
Mark the blameless, note the upright, for the end of such a person is peace. *Ps. 37*
God will redeem my soul from the grave, for He will receive me, Selah. *Ps. 49*
My flesh and my heart may fail, *Ps. 73*
but God is the strength of my heart and my portion for ever.
The dust returns to the earth as it was, *Eccl. 12*
but the spirit returns to God who gave it.

יֹשֵׁב He who lives in the shelter of the Most High dwells in the shadow of the Almighty. I say of the Lord, my Refuge and Stronghold, my God in whom I trust, that He will save you from the fowler's snare and the deadly pestilence. With His pinions He will cover you, and beneath His wings you will find shelter; His faithfulness is an encircling shield. You need not fear terror by night, nor the arrow that flies by day; not the pestilence that stalks in darkness, nor the plague that ravages at noon. A thousand may fall at your side, ten thousand at your right hand, but it will not come near you. You will only look with your eyes and see the punishment of the wicked. Because you said, "the Lord is my Refuge," taking the Most High as your shelter, no harm will befall you, no plague will come near your tent, for He will command His angels about you, to guard you in all your ways. They will lift you in their hands, lest your foot stumble on a stone. You will tread on lions and vipers; you will trample on young lions and snakes. [God says:] "Because he loves Me, I will rescue him; I will protect him, because he acknowledges My name. When he calls on Me, I will answer him; I will be with him in distress, I will deliver him and bring him honor. With long life I will satisfy him and show him My salvation.
With long life I will satisfy him and show him My salvation. *Ps. 91*

(chapter 12). *Midrash Tanḥuma* mentions the custom of remembering the dead on Yom Kippur. It bases it on the verse: "Forgive Your people, whom

סדר הזכרת נשמות

Before returning the ספרי תורה*, a* יזכור *(memorial) service is said. In some communities, those who have not been bereaved of a parent or close relative do not participate in the service, but leave the* בית כנסת *and return for* אב הרחמים *on page 763.*

יהוה מָה־אָדָם וַתֵּדָעֵהוּ, בֶּן־אֱנוֹשׁ וַתְּחַשְּׁבֵהוּ: תהלים קמד
אָדָם לַהֶבֶל דָּמָה, יָמָיו כְּצֵל עוֹבֵר:
בַּבֹּקֶר יָצִיץ וְחָלָף, לָעֶרֶב יְמוֹלֵל וְיָבֵשׁ: תהלים צ
לִמְנוֹת יָמֵינוּ כֵּן הוֹדַע, וְנָבִא לְבַב חָכְמָה:
שְׁמָר־תָּם וּרְאֵה יָשָׁר, כִּי־אַחֲרִית לְאִישׁ שָׁלוֹם: תהלים לז
אַךְ־אֱלֹהִים יִפְדֶּה נַפְשִׁי מִיַּד שְׁאוֹל, כִּי יִקָּחֵנִי סֶלָה: תהלים מט
כָּלָה שְׁאֵרִי וּלְבָבִי, צוּר־לְבָבִי וְחֶלְקִי אֱלֹהִים לְעוֹלָם: תהלים עג
וְיָשֹׁב הֶעָפָר עַל־הָאָרֶץ כְּשֶׁהָיָה, וְהָרוּחַ תָּשׁוּב אֶל־הָאֱלֹהִים אֲשֶׁר נְתָנָהּ: קהלת יב

יֹשֵׁב בְּסֵתֶר עֶלְיוֹן, בְּצֵל שַׁדַּי יִתְלוֹנָן: אֹמַר לַיהוה מַחְסִי וּמְצוּדָתִי, תהלים צא
אֱלֹהַי אֶבְטַח־בּוֹ: כִּי הוּא יַצִּילְךָ מִפַּח יָקוּשׁ, מִדֶּבֶר הַוּוֹת: בְּאֶבְרָתוֹ
יָסֶךְ לָךְ, וְתַחַת־כְּנָפָיו תֶּחְסֶה, צִנָּה וְסֹחֵרָה אֲמִתּוֹ: לֹא־תִירָא מִפַּחַד
לָיְלָה, מֵחֵץ יָעוּף יוֹמָם: מִדֶּבֶר בָּאֹפֶל יַהֲלֹךְ, מִקֶּטֶב יָשׁוּד צָהֳרָיִם:
יִפֹּל מִצִּדְּךָ אֶלֶף, וּרְבָבָה מִימִינֶךָ, אֵלֶיךָ לֹא יִגָּשׁ: רַק בְּעֵינֶיךָ תַבִּיט,
וְשִׁלֻּמַת רְשָׁעִים תִּרְאֶה: כִּי־אַתָּה יהוה מַחְסִי, עֶלְיוֹן שַׂמְתָּ מְעוֹנֶךָ:
לֹא־תְאֻנֶּה אֵלֶיךָ רָעָה, וְנֶגַע לֹא־יִקְרַב בְּאָהֳלֶךָ: כִּי מַלְאָכָיו יְצַוֶּה־לָּךְ,
לִשְׁמָרְךָ בְּכָל־דְּרָכֶיךָ: עַל־כַּפַּיִם יִשָּׂאוּנְךָ, פֶּן־תִּגֹּף בָּאֶבֶן רַגְלֶךָ: עַל־
שַׁחַל וָפֶתֶן תִּדְרֹךְ, תִּרְמֹס כְּפִיר וְתַנִּין: כִּי בִי חָשַׁק וַאֲפַלְּטֵהוּ, אֲשַׂגְּבֵהוּ
כִּי־יָדַע שְׁמִי: יִקְרָאֵנִי וְאֶעֱנֵהוּ, עִמּוֹ־אָנֹכִי בְצָרָה, אֲחַלְּצֵהוּ וַאֲכַבְּדֵהוּ:
אֹרֶךְ יָמִים אַשְׂבִּיעֵהוּ, וְאַרְאֵהוּ בִּישׁוּעָתִי:
אֹרֶךְ יָמִים אַשְׂבִּיעֵהוּ, וְאַרְאֵהוּ בִּישׁוּעָתִי:

YIZKOR

The custom of remembering and praying for the dead is ancient. In the second book of Maccabees there is a reference to Judah the Maccabee saying prayers for fallen fighters and making a collection for the Temple on their behalf

For one's father:

יִזְכֹּר May God remember the soul of my father, my teacher (*name* son of *father's name*) who has gone to his eternal home, and to this I pledge (without formal vow) to give charity on his behalf, that his soul may be bound in the bond of everlasting life together with the souls of Abraham, Isaac and Jacob, Sarah, Rebecca, Rachel and Leah, and all the other righteous men and women in the Garden of Eden, and let us say: Amen.

For one's mother:

יִזְכֹּר May God remember the soul of my mother, my teacher (*name* daughter of *father's name*) who has gone to her eternal home, and to this I pledge (without formal vow) to give charity on her behalf, that her soul may be bound in the bond of everlasting life together with the souls of Abraham, Isaac and Jacob, Sarah, Rebecca, Rachel and Leah, and all the other righteous men and women in the Garden of Eden, and let us say: Amen.

In Judaism we remember not just for the past but also, and especially, for the sake of the future. As mentioned in the commentary for the Ma'ariv remembrance verses, this can be seen in the three cases in which the word *Yizkor* appears in connection with God in Genesis. God "remembered Noah" (8:1) and brought him out onto dry land. God "remembered Abraham" (19:29) and rescued his nephew Lot from the destruction of Sodom. God "remembered Rachel" (30:22) and gave her a child. In each case the act of remembering was for the sake of the future and of life.

Judaism gave two majestic ideas their greatest religious expression: *memory* and *hope*. Memory is our living connection to those who came before us. Hope is what we hand on to the generations yet to come. Those we remember live on in us: in words, gestures, a smile here, an act of kindness there, that we would not have done had that person not left their mark on our lives. That is what *Yizkor* is: memory as a religious act of thanksgiving for a life that was, and that still sends its echoes and reverberations into the life that is. For when Jews remember, they do so for the future, the place where, if we are faithful to it, the past never dies.

PRAYER FOR LIVING RELATIVES

Our Father in heaven: On this holy day, I give You thanks for my [father / mother / husband / wife / brother(s) / sister(s) / son(s) / daughter(s) /

For one's father:

יִזְכֹּר אֱלֹהִים נִשְׁמַת אָבִי מוֹרִי (פלוני בֶּן פלוני) שֶׁהָלַךְ לְעוֹלָמוֹ, בַּעֲבוּר שֶׁבְּלִי נֶדֶר אֶתֵּן צְדָקָה בַּעֲדוֹ. בִּשְׂכַר זֶה תְּהֵא נַפְשׁוֹ צְרוּרָה בִּצְרוֹר הַחַיִּים עִם נִשְׁמוֹת אַבְרָהָם יִצְחָק וְיַעֲקֹב, שָׂרָה רִבְקָה רָחֵל וְלֵאָה, וְעִם שְׁאָר צַדִּיקִים וְצִדְקָנִיּוֹת שֶׁבְּגַן עֵדֶן, וְנֹאמַר אָמֵן.

For one's mother:

יִזְכֹּר אֱלֹהִים נִשְׁמַת אִמִּי מוֹרָתִי (פלונית בַּת פלוני) שֶׁהָלְכָה לְעוֹלָמָהּ, בַּעֲבוּר שֶׁבְּלִי נֶדֶר אֶתֵּן צְדָקָה בַּעֲדָהּ. בִּשְׂכַר זֶה תְּהֵא נַפְשָׁהּ צְרוּרָה בִּצְרוֹר הַחַיִּים עִם נִשְׁמוֹת אַבְרָהָם יִצְחָק וְיַעֲקֹב, שָׂרָה רִבְקָה רָחֵל וְלֵאָה, וְעִם שְׁאָר צַדִּיקִים וְצִדְקָנִיּוֹת שֶׁבְּגַן עֵדֶן, וְנֹאמַר אָמֵן.

You, God, have redeemed" (Deut. 21:8): *Forgive Your people* – these are the living. *Whom You have redeemed* – these are the dead (*Tanḥuma, Ha'azinu*, 1). Equally ancient is the custom of donating money to charity in their memory, for "charity redeems from death" (Prov. 10:2; 11:4).

We believe that the soul is immortal, that the dead live on, and that we, by our actions in the present, can confer merit on them and their memory. This is especially germane to Yom Kippur when we recall our own mortality and remember those who brought us into the world. Rabbi Jacob Weil (Germany, fifteenth century) suggested that the plural form of the biblical name for the day, *Yom Kippurim*, literally "the Day of Atonements," refers to two atonements, for the living and for the dead.

The emotional impact of *Yizkor* deepened in the wake of the Crusades and later the pogroms, when many Jews went to their deaths as martyrs, and were remembered each year at this time. A special prayer for martyrs, *Av HaRaḥamim*, "Father of compassion," was added to the service at that time. Nowadays, we add prayers for the victims of the Holocaust, as well as those who went to their deaths defending the State of Israel.

The formal name for this prayer is *Hazkarat Neshamot*, "the Remembrance of Souls," but it became popularly known as *Yizkor* because of the first word of the memorial prayer. Remembrance holds a special place in the Jewish soul. Jews were the first people to regard remembering as a religious duty. The verb "to remember" in one or other of its forms occurs 169 times in Tanakh.

For martyrs:

יִזְכֹּר May God remember the soul of (*name*, son/daughter of *father's name*), and the souls of all my relatives, on my father's or mother's side, who were killed, murdered, slaughtered, burned, drowned or strangled for the sanctification of God's name, and to this I pledge (without formal vow) to give charity in their memory. May their souls be bound in the bond of everlasting life together with the souls of Abraham, Isaac and Jacob, Sarah, Rebecca, Rachel and Leah, and all the other righteous men and women in the Garden of Eden, and let us say: Amen.

For a male close relative:

אֵל מָלֵא רַחֲמִים God, full of mercy, who dwells on high, grant fitting rest on the wings of the Divine Presence, in the heights of the holy and the pure who shine like the radiance of heaven, to the soul of (*name* son of *father's name*) who has gone to his eternal home, and to this I pledge (without formal vow) to give charity in his memory, may his resting place be in the Garden of Eden. Therefore, Master of compassion, shelter him in the shadow of Your wings forever and bind his soul in the bond of everlasting life. The LORD is his heritage; may he rest in peace, and let us say: Amen.

For a female close relative:

אֵל מָלֵא רַחֲמִים God, full of mercy, who dwells on high, grant fitting rest on the wings of the Divine Presence, in the heights of the holy and the pure who shine like the radiance of heaven, to the soul of (*name* daughter of *father's name*) who has gone to her eternal home, and to this I pledge (without formal vow) to give charity in her memory, may her resting place be in the Garden of Eden. Therefore, Master of compassion, shelter her in the shadow of Your wings forever and bind her soul in the bond of everlasting life. The LORD is her heritage; may she rest in peace, and let us say: Amen.

---

live in the work of their hands. Prolong their days in goodness and happiness and may they and we have the privilege of seeing children and grandchildren occupying themselves with Torah and the life of the commandments. May the words of my mouth and the meditation of my heart find favor before You, my Rock and Redeemer.

For martyrs:

יִזְכֹּר אֱלֹהִים נִשְׁמַת (male פלוני בֶּן פלוני / female פלונית בַּת פלוני) וְנִשְׁמוֹת כָּל קְרוֹבַי וּקְרוֹבוֹתַי, הֵן מִצַּד אָבִי הֵן מִצַּד אִמִּי, שֶׁהוּמְתוּ וְשֶׁנֶּהֶרְגוּ וְשֶׁנִּשְׁחֲטוּ וְשֶׁנִּשְׂרְפוּ וְשֶׁנִּטְבְּעוּ וְשֶׁנֶּחְנְקוּ עַל קִדּוּשׁ הַשֵּׁם, בַּעֲבוּר שֶׁבְּלִי נֶדֶר אֶתֵּן צְדָקָה בְּעַד הַזְכָּרַת נִשְׁמוֹתֵיהֶם. בִּשְׂכַר זֶה תִּהְיֶינָה נַפְשׁוֹתֵיהֶם צְרוּרוֹת בִּצְרוֹר הַחַיִּים עִם נִשְׁמוֹת אַבְרָהָם יִצְחָק וְיַעֲקֹב, שָׂרָה רִבְקָה רָחֵל וְלֵאָה, וְעִם שְׁאָר צַדִּיקִים וְצִדְקָנִיּוֹת שֶׁבְּגַן עֵדֶן, וְנֹאמַר אָמֵן.

For a male close relative:

אֵל מָלֵא רַחֲמִים, שׁוֹכֵן בַּמְּרוֹמִים, הַמְצֵא מְנוּחָה נְכוֹנָה עַל כַּנְפֵי הַשְּׁכִינָה, בְּמַעֲלוֹת קְדוֹשִׁים וּטְהוֹרִים, כְּזֹהַר הָרָקִיעַ מַזְהִירִים, לְנִשְׁמַת (פלוני בֶּן פלוני) שֶׁהָלַךְ לְעוֹלָמוֹ, בַּעֲבוּר שֶׁבְּלִי נֶדֶר אֶתֵּן צְדָקָה בְּעַד הַזְכָּרַת נִשְׁמָתוֹ, בְּגַן עֵדֶן תְּהֵא מְנוּחָתוֹ. לָכֵן, בַּעַל הָרַחֲמִים יַסְתִּירֵהוּ בְּסֵתֶר כְּנָפָיו לְעוֹלָמִים, וְיִצְרֹר בִּצְרוֹר הַחַיִּים אֶת נִשְׁמָתוֹ, יהוה הוּא נַחֲלָתוֹ, וְיָנוּחַ בְּשָׁלוֹם עַל מִשְׁכָּבוֹ, וְנֹאמַר אָמֵן.

For a female close relative:

אֵל מָלֵא רַחֲמִים, שׁוֹכֵן בַּמְּרוֹמִים, הַמְצֵא מְנוּחָה נְכוֹנָה עַל כַּנְפֵי הַשְּׁכִינָה, בְּמַעֲלוֹת קְדוֹשִׁים וּטְהוֹרִים, כְּזֹהַר הָרָקִיעַ מַזְהִירִים, לְנִשְׁמַת (פלונית בַּת פלוני) שֶׁהָלְכָה לְעוֹלָמָהּ, בַּעֲבוּר שֶׁבְּלִי נֶדֶר אֶתֵּן צְדָקָה בְּעַד הַזְכָּרַת נִשְׁמָתָהּ, בְּגַן עֵדֶן תְּהֵא מְנוּחָתָהּ. לָכֵן, בַּעַל הָרַחֲמִים יַסְתִּירֶהָ בְּסֵתֶר כְּנָפָיו לְעוֹלָמִים, וְיִצְרֹר בִּצְרוֹר הַחַיִּים אֶת נִשְׁמָתָהּ, יהוה הוּא נַחֲלָתָהּ, וְתָנוּחַ בְּשָׁלוֹם עַל מִשְׁכָּבָהּ, וְנֹאמַר אָמֵן.

---

grandchild(ren)] who are with me in life, and for whose continued health and blessing I pray. Be with them, I pray You, in the days and months to come. Protect them from harm and distress, sickness and affliction, trouble and misfortune. Spread over them Your canopy of peace and may Your spirit

For the Israeli soldiers:

אֵל מָלֵא רַחֲמִים God, full of mercy, who dwells on high, grant fitting rest on the wings of the Divine Presence, in the heights of the holy, the pure and the brave, who shine like the radiance of heaven, to the souls of the holy ones who fought in any of Israel's battles, in clandestine operations and in Israel's Defense Forces, who fell in battle and sacrificed their lives for the consecration of God's name, for the people and the land, and for this we pray for the ascent of their souls. Therefore, Master of compassion, shelter them in the shadow of Your wings forever, and bind their souls in the bond of everlasting life. The LORD is their heritage; may the Garden of Eden be their resting place, may they rest in peace, may their merit stand for all Israel, and may they receive their reward at the End of Days, and let us say: Amen.

For the Holocaust victims:

אֵל מָלֵא רַחֲמִים God, full of mercy, Justice of widows and Father of orphans, please do not be silent and hold Your peace for the blood of Israel that was shed like water. Grant fitting rest on the wings of the Divine Presence, in the heights of the holy and the pure who shine and radiate light like the radiance of heaven, to the souls of the millions of Jews, men, women and children, who were murdered, slaughtered, burned, strangled, and buried alive, in the lands touched by the German enemy and its followers. They were all holy and pure; among them were great scholars and righteous individuals, cedars of Lebanon and noble masters of Torah, may the Garden of Eden be their resting place. Therefore, Master of compassion, shelter them in the shadow of Your wings forever, and bind their souls in the bond of everlasting life. The LORD is their heritage; may they rest in peace, and let us say: Amen.

All:

אַב הָרַחֲמִים Father of compassion, who dwells on high: may He remember in His compassion the pious, the upright and the blameless – holy communities who sacrificed their lives for the sanctification of God's name. Lovely and pleasant in their lives, in death they were not parted.

For the Israeli soldiers:

אֵל מָלֵא רַחֲמִים, שׁוֹכֵן בַּמְּרוֹמִים, הַמְצֵא מְנוּחָה נְכוֹנָה עַל כַּנְפֵי
הַשְּׁכִינָה, בְּמַעֲלוֹת קְדוֹשִׁים טְהוֹרִים וְגִבּוֹרִים, כְּזֹהַר הָרָקִיעַ
מַזְהִירִים, לְנִשְׁמוֹת הַקְּדוֹשִׁים שֶׁנִּלְחֲמוּ בְּכָל מַעַרְכוֹת יִשְׂרָאֵל,
בַּמַּחְתֶּרֶת וּבִצְבָא הַהֲגָנָה לְיִשְׂרָאֵל, וְשֶׁנָּפְלוּ בְּמִלְחַמְתָּם וּמָסְרוּ
נַפְשָׁם עַל קְדֻשַּׁת הַשֵּׁם, הָעָם וְהָאָרֶץ, בַּעֲבוּר שֶׁאָנוּ מִתְפַּלְּלִים
לְעִלּוּי נִשְׁמוֹתֵיהֶם. לָכֵן, בַּעַל הָרַחֲמִים יַסְתִּירֵם בְּסֵתֶר כְּנָפָיו
לְעוֹלָמִים, וְיִצְרֹר בִּצְרוֹר הַחַיִּים אֶת נִשְׁמוֹתֵיהֶם, יהוה הוּא נַחֲלָתָם,
בְּגַן עֵדֶן תְּהֵא מְנוּחָתָם, וְיָנוּחוּ בְשָׁלוֹם עַל מִשְׁכְּבוֹתֵיהֶם וְתַעֲמֹד
לְכָל יִשְׂרָאֵל זְכוּתָם, וְיַעַמְדוּ לְגוֹרָלָם לְקֵץ הַיָּמִין, וְנֹאמַר אָמֵן.

For the Holocaust victims:

אֵל מָלֵא רַחֲמִים, דַּיַּן אַלְמָנוֹת וַאֲבִי יְתוֹמִים, אַל נָא תֶחֱשֶׁה
וְתִתְאַפַּק לְדַם יִשְׂרָאֵל שֶׁנִּשְׁפַּךְ כַּמַּיִם. הַמְצֵא מְנוּחָה נְכוֹנָה עַל
כַּנְפֵי הַשְּׁכִינָה, בְּמַעֲלוֹת קְדוֹשִׁים וּטְהוֹרִים, כְּזֹהַר הָרָקִיעַ מְאִירִים
וּמַזְהִירִים, לְנִשְׁמוֹתֵיהֶם שֶׁל רִבְבוֹת אַלְפֵי יִשְׂרָאֵל, אֲנָשִׁים וְנָשִׁים,
יְלָדִים וִילָדוֹת, שֶׁנֶּהֶרְגוּ וְנִשְׁחֲטוּ וְנִשְׂרְפוּ וְנֶחְנְקוּ וְנִקְבְּרוּ חַיִּים,
בָּאֲרָצוֹת אֲשֶׁר נָגְעָה בָהֶן יַד הַצּוֹרֵר הַגֶּרְמָנִי וּגְרוּרָיו. כֻּלָּם קְדוֹשִׁים
וּטְהוֹרִים, וּבָהֶם גְּאוֹנִים וְצַדִּיקִים, אַרְזֵי הַלְּבָנוֹן אַדִּירֵי הַתּוֹרָה.
בְּגַן עֵדֶן תְּהֵא מְנוּחָתָם. לָכֵן, בַּעַל הָרַחֲמִים יַסְתִּירֵם בְּסֵתֶר כְּנָפָיו
לְעוֹלָמִים, וְיִצְרֹר בִּצְרוֹר הַחַיִּים אֶת נִשְׁמָתָם, יהוה הוּא נַחֲלָתָם,
וְיָנוּחוּ בְשָׁלוֹם עַל מִשְׁכָּבָם, וְנֹאמַר אָמֵן.

All:

אַב הָרַחֲמִים שׁוֹכֵן מְרוֹמִים, בְּרַחֲמָיו הָעֲצוּמִים הוּא יִפְקֹד בְּרַחֲמִים
הַחֲסִידִים וְהַיְשָׁרִים וְהַתְּמִימִים, קְהִלּוֹת הַקֹּדֶשׁ שֶׁמָּסְרוּ נַפְשָׁם עַל
קְדֻשַּׁת הַשֵּׁם, הַנֶּאֱהָבִים וְהַנְּעִימִים בְּחַיֵּיהֶם, וּבְמוֹתָם לֹא נִפְרָדוּ,

They were swifter than eagles and stronger than lions to do the will
of their Maker and the desire of their Creator. O our God, remember
them for good with the other righteous of the world, and may He exact
retribution for the shed blood of His servants, as it is written in the
Torah of Moses, the man of God: "O nations, acclaim His people, for *Deut. 32*
He will avenge the blood of His servants, wreak vengeance on His foes,
and make clean His people's land." And by Your servants, the prophets,
it is written: "I shall cleanse their blood which I have not yet cleansed, *Joel 4*
says the Lord who dwells in Zion." And in the holy Writings it says:
"Why should the nations say: Where is their God? Before our eyes, may *Ps. 79*
those nations know that You avenge the shed blood of Your servants."
And it also says: "For the Avenger of blood remembers them and does *Ps. 9*
not forget the cry of the afflicted." And it further says: "He will execute *Ps. 110*
judgment among the nations, filled with the dead, crushing rulers far
and wide. From the brook by the wayside he will drink, then he will
hold his head high."

The Leader says the first verse of Ashrei aloud and all continue:

אַשְׁרֵי Happy are those who dwell in Your House; *Ps. 84*
they shall continue to praise You, Selah!
Happy are the people for whom this is so; *Ps. 144*
happy are the people whose God is the Lord.
A song of praise by David. *Ps. 145*

I will exalt You, my God, the King, and bless Your name for ever and all time. Every day I will bless You, and praise Your name for ever and all time. Great is the Lord and greatly to be praised; His greatness is unfathomable. One generation will praise Your works to the next, and tell of Your mighty deeds. On the glorious splendor of Your majesty I will meditate, and on the acts of Your wonders. They shall talk of the power of Your awesome deeds, and I will tell of Your greatness. They shall recite the record of Your great goodness, and sing with joy of Your righteousness. The Lord is gracious and compassionate, slow to anger and great in loving-kindness. The Lord is good to all, and His compassion extends to all His works. All Your works shall thank You, Lord, and Your devoted ones shall bless You. They shall talk of the glory

מְנֻשָּׁרִים קַלּוּ וּמֵאֲרָיוֹת גָּבֵרוּ לַעֲשׂוֹת רְצוֹן קוֹנָם וְחֵפֶץ צוּרָם. יִזְכְּרֵם
אֱלֹהֵינוּ לְטוֹבָה עִם שְׁאָר צַדִּיקֵי עוֹלָם, וְיִנְקֹם לְעֵינֵינוּ נִקְמַת דַּם
עֲבָדָיו הַשָּׁפוּךְ, כַּכָּתוּב בְּתוֹרַת מֹשֶׁה אִישׁ הָאֱלֹהִים, הַרְנִינוּ גוֹיִם דברים לב
עַמּוֹ, כִּי דַם־עֲבָדָיו יִקּוֹם, וְנָקָם יָשִׁיב לְצָרָיו, וְכִפֶּר אַדְמָתוֹ עַמּוֹ:
וְעַל יְדֵי עֲבָדֶיךָ הַנְּבִיאִים כָּתוּב לֵאמֹר, וְנִקֵּיתִי, דָּמָם לֹא־נִקֵּיתִי, יואל ד
וַיהוה שֹׁכֵן בְּצִיּוֹן: וּבְכִתְבֵי הַקֹּדֶשׁ נֶאֱמַר, לָמָּה יֹאמְרוּ הַגּוֹיִם אַיֵּה תהלים עט
אֱלֹהֵיהֶם, יִוָּדַע בַּגּוֹיִם לְעֵינֵינוּ נִקְמַת דַּם־עֲבָדֶיךָ הַשָּׁפוּךְ: וְאוֹמֵר,
כִּי־דֹרֵשׁ דָּמִים אוֹתָם זָכָר, לֹא־שָׁכַח צַעֲקַת עֲנָוִים: וְאוֹמֵר, יָדִין תהלים ט תהלים קי
בַּגּוֹיִם מָלֵא גְוִיּוֹת, מָחַץ רֹאשׁ עַל־אֶרֶץ רַבָּה: מִנַּחַל בַּדֶּרֶךְ יִשְׁתֶּה,
עַל־כֵּן יָרִים רֹאשׁ:

The שליח ציבור *says the first verse of* אשרי *aloud and all continue:*

אַשְׁרֵי יוֹשְׁבֵי בֵיתֶךָ, עוֹד יְהַלְלוּךָ סֶּלָה: תהלים פד
אַשְׁרֵי הָעָם שֶׁכָּכָה לּוֹ, אַשְׁרֵי הָעָם שֶׁיהוה אֱלֹהָיו: תהלים קמד
תְּהִלָּה לְדָוִד תהלים קמה

אֲרוֹמִמְךָ אֱלוֹהַי הַמֶּלֶךְ, וַאֲבָרְכָה שִׁמְךָ לְעוֹלָם וָעֶד:
בְּכָל־יוֹם אֲבָרְכֶךָּ, וַאֲהַלְלָה שִׁמְךָ לְעוֹלָם וָעֶד:
גָּדוֹל יהוה וּמְהֻלָּל מְאֹד, וְלִגְדֻלָּתוֹ אֵין חֵקֶר:
דּוֹר לְדוֹר יְשַׁבַּח מַעֲשֶׂיךָ, וּגְבוּרֹתֶיךָ יַגִּידוּ:
הֲדַר כְּבוֹד הוֹדֶךָ, וְדִבְרֵי נִפְלְאֹתֶיךָ אָשִׂיחָה:
וֶעֱזוּז נוֹרְאֹתֶיךָ יֹאמֵרוּ, וּגְדוּלָּתְךָ אֲסַפְּרֶנָּה:
זֵכֶר רַב־טוּבְךָ יַבִּיעוּ, וְצִדְקָתְךָ יְרַנֵּנוּ:
חַנּוּן וְרַחוּם יהוה, אֶרֶךְ אַפַּיִם וּגְדָל־חָסֶד:
טוֹב־יהוה לַכֹּל, וְרַחֲמָיו עַל־כָּל־מַעֲשָׂיו:
יוֹדוּךָ יהוה כָּל־מַעֲשֶׂיךָ, וַחֲסִידֶיךָ יְבָרְכוּכָה:

of Your kingship, and speak of Your might. To make known to mankind His mighty deeds and the glorious majesty of His kingship. Your kingdom is an everlasting kingdom, and Your reign is for all generations. The Lord supports all who fall, and raises all who are bowed down. All raise their eyes to You in hope, and You give them their food in due season. You open Your hand, and satisfy every living thing with favor. The Lord is righteous in all His ways, and kind in all He does. The Lord is close to all who call on Him, to all who call on Him in truth. He fulfills the will of those who revere Him; He hears their cry and saves them. The Lord guards all who love Him, but all the wicked He will destroy. ▸ My mouth shall speak the praise of the Lord, and all creatures shall bless His holy name for ever and all time.

We will bless the Lord now and for ever. Halleluya! *Ps. 115*

RETURNING THE TORAH TO THE ARK

The Ark is opened. All stand. The Leader takes one of the Torah scrolls and says:

יְהַלְלוּ Let them praise the name of the Lord, *Ps. 148*
for His name alone is sublime.

The congregation responds:

הוֹדוֹ His majesty is above earth and heaven.
He has raised the horn of His people,
for the glory of all His devoted ones,
the children of Israel, the people close to Him.
Halleluya!

While the Torah scrolls are being returned to the Ark, one of the following psalms is said. On a weekday (on Shabbat omit):

לְדָוִד מִזְמוֹר A psalm of David. The earth is the Lord's and all it contains, *Ps. 24* the world and all who live in it. For He founded it on the seas and established it on the streams. Who may climb the mountain of the Lord? Who may stand in His holy place? He who has clean hands and a pure heart, who has not taken My name in vain, or sworn deceitfully. He shall receive blessing from the Lord, and just reward from God,

כְּבוֹד מַלְכוּתְךָ יֹאמֵרוּ, וּגְבוּרָתְךָ יְדַבֵּרוּ:
לְהוֹדִיעַ לִבְנֵי הָאָדָם גְּבוּרֹתָיו, וּכְבוֹד הֲדַר מַלְכוּתוֹ:
מַלְכוּתְךָ מַלְכוּת כָּל־עֹלָמִים, וּמֶמְשַׁלְתְּךָ בְּכָל־דּוֹר וָדֹר:
סוֹמֵךְ יהוה לְכָל־הַנֹּפְלִים, וְזוֹקֵף לְכָל־הַכְּפוּפִים:
עֵינֵי־כֹל אֵלֶיךָ יְשַׂבֵּרוּ, וְאַתָּה נוֹתֵן־לָהֶם אֶת־אָכְלָם בְּעִתּוֹ:
פּוֹתֵחַ אֶת־יָדֶךָ, וּמַשְׂבִּיעַ לְכָל־חַי רָצוֹן:
צַדִּיק יהוה בְּכָל־דְּרָכָיו, וְחָסִיד בְּכָל־מַעֲשָׂיו:
קָרוֹב יהוה לְכָל־קֹרְאָיו, לְכֹל אֲשֶׁר יִקְרָאֻהוּ בֶאֱמֶת:
רְצוֹן־יְרֵאָיו יַעֲשֶׂה, וְאֶת־שַׁוְעָתָם יִשְׁמַע, וְיוֹשִׁיעֵם:
שׁוֹמֵר יהוה אֶת־כָּל־אֹהֲבָיו, וְאֵת כָּל־הָרְשָׁעִים יַשְׁמִיד:
◂ תְּהִלַּת יהוה יְדַבֶּר פִּי, וִיבָרֵךְ כָּל־בָּשָׂר שֵׁם קָדְשׁוֹ לְעוֹלָם וָעֶד:
וַאֲנַחְנוּ נְבָרֵךְ יָהּ מֵעַתָּה וְעַד־עוֹלָם, הַלְלוּיָהּ: תהלים קטו

הכנסת ספר תורה

The ארון קודש *is opened. All stand. The* שליח ציבור *takes one of the* ספרי תורה *and says:*

יְהַלְלוּ אֶת־שֵׁם יהוה, כִּי־נִשְׂגָּב שְׁמוֹ, לְבַדּוֹ תהלים קמח

The קהל *responds:*

הוֹדוֹ עַל־אֶרֶץ וְשָׁמָיִם:
וַיָּרֶם קֶרֶן לְעַמּוֹ, תְּהִלָּה לְכָל־חֲסִידָיו
לִבְנֵי יִשְׂרָאֵל עַם קְרֹבוֹ, הַלְלוּיָהּ:

While the ספרי תורה *are being returned to the* ארון קודש*, one of the following psalms is said. On a weekday (on* שבת *omit):*

לְדָוִד מִזְמוֹר, לַיהוה הָאָרֶץ וּמְלוֹאָהּ, תֵּבֵל וְיֹשְׁבֵי בָהּ: כִּי־הוּא תהלים כד
עַל־יַמִּים יְסָדָהּ, וְעַל־נְהָרוֹת יְכוֹנְנֶהָ: מִי־יַעֲלֶה בְהַר־יהוה,
וּמִי־יָקוּם בִּמְקוֹם קָדְשׁוֹ: נְקִי כַפַּיִם וּבַר־לֵבָב, אֲשֶׁר לֹא־נָשָׂא
לַשָּׁוְא נַפְשִׁי וְלֹא נִשְׁבַּע לְמִרְמָה: יִשָּׂא בְרָכָה מֵאֵת יהוה, וּצְדָקָה

his salvation. This is a generation of those who seek Him, the descendants of Jacob who seek Your presence, Selah! Lift up your heads, O gates; be uplifted, eternal doors, so that the King of glory may enter. Who is the King of glory? It is the LORD, strong and mighty, the LORD mighty in battle. Lift up your heads, O gates; lift them up, eternal doors, so that the King of glory may enter. Who is He, the King of glory? The LORD of hosts, He is the King of glory, Selah!

On Shabbat the following is said:

מִזְמוֹר לְדָוִד A psalm of David. Render to the LORD, you angelic pow- Ps. 29
ers, render to the LORD glory and might. Render to the LORD the glory due to His name. Bow to the LORD in the beauty of holiness. The LORD's voice echoes over the waters; the God of glory thunders; the LORD is over the mighty waters. The LORD's voice in power, the LORD's voice in beauty, the LORD's voice breaks cedars, the LORD shatters the cedars of Lebanon. He makes Lebanon skip like a calf, Sirion like a young wild ox. The LORD's voice cleaves flames of fire. The LORD's voice makes the desert quake, the LORD shakes the desert of Kadesh. The LORD's voice makes hinds calve and strips the forests bare, and in His temple all say: "Glory!" The LORD sat enthroned at the Flood, the LORD sits enthroned as King for ever. The LORD will give strength to His people; the LORD will bless His people with peace.

As the Torah scrolls are placed into the Ark, all say:

וּבְנֻחֹה יֹאמַר When the Ark came to rest, Moses would say: "Return, Num. 10
O LORD, to the myriad thousands of Israel." Advance, LORD, to Your Ps. 132
resting place, You and Your mighty Ark. Your priests are clothed in
righteousness, and Your devoted ones sing in joy. For the sake of
Your servant David, do not reject Your anointed one. For I give you Prov. 4
good instruction; do not forsake My Torah. ▸ It is a tree of life to those Prov. 3
who grasp it, and those who uphold it are happy. Its ways are ways of
pleasantness, and all its paths are peace. Turn us back, O LORD, to You, Lam. 5
and we will return. Renew our days as of old.

The Ark is closed.

מֵאֱלֹהֵי יִשְׁעוֹ: זֶה דּוֹר דֹּרְשָׁו, מְבַקְשֵׁי פָנֶיךָ, יַעֲקֹב, סֶלָה: שְׂאוּ שְׁעָרִים רָאשֵׁיכֶם, וְהִנָּשְׂאוּ פִּתְחֵי עוֹלָם, וְיָבוֹא מֶלֶךְ הַכָּבוֹד: מִי זֶה מֶלֶךְ הַכָּבוֹד, יהוה עִזּוּז וְגִבּוֹר, יהוה גִּבּוֹר מִלְחָמָה: שְׂאוּ שְׁעָרִים רָאשֵׁיכֶם, וּשְׂאוּ פִּתְחֵי עוֹלָם, וְיָבֹא מֶלֶךְ הַכָּבוֹד: מִי הוּא זֶה מֶלֶךְ הַכָּבוֹד, יהוה צְבָאוֹת הוּא מֶלֶךְ הַכָּבוֹד, סֶלָה:

On שבת the following is said:

מִזְמוֹר לְדָוִד, הָבוּ לַיהוה בְּנֵי אֵלִים, הָבוּ לַיהוה כָּבוֹד וָעֹז: הָבוּ תהלים כט
לַיהוה כְּבוֹד שְׁמוֹ, הִשְׁתַּחֲווּ לַיהוה בְּהַדְרַת־קֹדֶשׁ: קוֹל יהוה עַל־הַמָּיִם, אֵל־הַכָּבוֹד הִרְעִים, יהוה עַל־מַיִם רַבִּים: קוֹל־יהוה בַּכֹּחַ, קוֹל יהוה בֶּהָדָר: קוֹל יהוה שֹׁבֵר אֲרָזִים, וַיְשַׁבֵּר יהוה אֶת־אַרְזֵי הַלְּבָנוֹן: וַיַּרְקִידֵם כְּמוֹ־עֵגֶל, לְבָנוֹן וְשִׂרְיוֹן כְּמוֹ בֶן־רְאֵמִים: קוֹל־יהוה חֹצֵב לַהֲבוֹת אֵשׁ: קוֹל יהוה יָחִיל מִדְבָּר, יָחִיל יהוה מִדְבַּר קָדֵשׁ: קוֹל יהוה יְחוֹלֵל אַיָּלוֹת וַיֶּחֱשֹׂף יְעָרוֹת, וּבְהֵיכָלוֹ, כֻּלּוֹ אֹמֵר כָּבוֹד: יהוה לַמַּבּוּל יָשָׁב, וַיֵּשֶׁב יהוה מֶלֶךְ לְעוֹלָם: יהוה עֹז לְעַמּוֹ יִתֵּן, יהוה יְבָרֵךְ אֶת־עַמּוֹ בַשָּׁלוֹם:

As the ספרי תורה are placed into the ארון קודש, all say:

וּבְנֻחֹה יֹאמַר, שׁוּבָה יהוה רִבְבוֹת אַלְפֵי יִשְׂרָאֵל: קוּמָה יהוה במדבר י תהלים קלב
לִמְנוּחָתֶךָ, אַתָּה וַאֲרוֹן עֻזֶּךָ: כֹּהֲנֶיךָ יִלְבְּשׁוּ־צֶדֶק, וַחֲסִידֶיךָ יְרַנֵּנוּ:
בַּעֲבוּר דָּוִד עַבְדֶּךָ אַל־תָּשֵׁב פְּנֵי מְשִׁיחֶךָ: כִּי לֶקַח טוֹב נָתַתִּי משלי ד
לָכֶם, תּוֹרָתִי אַל־תַּעֲזֹבוּ: ‹ עֵץ־חַיִּים הִיא לַמַּחֲזִיקִים בָּהּ, וְתֹמְכֶיהָ משלי ג
מְאֻשָּׁר: דְּרָכֶיהָ דַרְכֵי־נֹעַם וְכָל־נְתִיבוֹתֶיהָ שָׁלוֹם: הֲשִׁיבֵנוּ יהוה איכה ה
אֵלֶיךָ וְנָשׁוּבָה, חַדֵּשׁ יָמֵינוּ כְּקֶדֶם:

The ארון קודש is closed.

The Leader says the following before Musaf:

הִנְנִי Here I am, empty of deeds, in turmoil, afraid with the fear of that One who sits enthroned on the praises of Israel. I have come here to stand up and plead with You for Your people Israel who have sent me, even though I am not worthy or fitting to come. And so I ask of You, God of Abraham, God of Isaac and God of Jacob, the LORD, the LORD, compassionate and gracious God, my God, Almighty, fearful and awesome, please, give me success along the road that I tread to stand and ask for compassion for me and for those who have sent me, and please, do not condemn them for my sins, do not hold them liable for my crimes, for I am a sinner, I do wrong, do not let them be disgraced by my sins, let them not be

---

calls in particulars. He knows our gifts and He knows the needs of the world. That is why we are here. There is an act only we can do, and only at this time, and that is our task. The sum of these tasks is the meaning of our life, the purpose of our existence, the story we are called on to write. God's call is almost inaudible. It speaks in "a still, small voice" (I Kings 19:12), meaning a voice we can only hear if we are listening. But it is there and if, from time to time throughout our lives, we create a silence in the soul, we will hear it.

Our lives, offered in faith and trust, are the answer to God's question. There is no life without a task, no person without a talent, no place without a fragment of God's light waiting to be discovered and redeemed, no situation without its possibility of sanctification, no moment without its call. It may take a lifetime to learn how to find these things, but once we learn, we realize in retrospect that all it ever took was the ability to listen. When God calls, He whispers our name – and the greatest reply is simply *Hineni*, "Here I am," ready to heed Your call, to mend a fragment of Your all-too-broken world.

Let nobody in Israel, God forbid, ask himself: what am I, and what can my humble acts achieve in the world? Let him rather understand this, that he may know it and fix it in his thoughts: not one detail of his acts, his words, and his thoughts, is ever lost. Each one leads back to its origin, where it takes effect in the height of heights. (Rabbi Ḥayyim of Volozhyn)

No limits are set to the ascent of humankind, and to each the highest stands open. Your choice alone decides. (Rabbi Naḥman of Bratslav)

The שליח ציבור *says the following before* מוסף:

הִנְנִי הֶעָנִי מִמַּעַשׂ, נִרְעָשׁ וְנִפְחָד מִפַּחַד יוֹשֵׁב תְּהִלּוֹת יִשְׂרָאֵל,
בָּאתִי לַעֲמוֹד וּלְחַנֵּן לְפָנֶיךָ עַל עַמְּךָ יִשְׂרָאֵל אֲשֶׁר שְׁלָחוּנִי, וְאַף
עַל פִּי שֶׁאֵינִי כְדַאי וְהָגוּן לְכָךְ. עַל כֵּן אֲבַקֶּשְׁךָ אֱלֹהֵי אַבְרָהָם
אֱלֹהֵי יִצְחָק וֵאלֹהֵי יַעֲקֹב, יהוה יהוה, אֵל רַחוּם וְחַנּוּן, אֱלֹהִים,
שַׁדַּי אָיוֹם וְנוֹרָא, הֱיֵה נָא מַצְלִיחַ דַּרְכִּי אֲשֶׁר אָנֹכִי הוֹלֵךְ לַעֲמוֹד
לְבַקֵּשׁ רַחֲמִים עָלַי וְעַל שׁוֹלְחַי. וְנָא אַל תַּפְשִׁיעֵם בְּחַטֹּאתַי וְאַל
תְּחַיְּבֵם בַּעֲוֹנוֹתַי, כִּי חוֹטֵא וּפוֹשֵׁעַ אָנִי, וְאַל יִכָּלְמוּ בִּפְשָׁעַי, וְאַל

הִנְנִי הֶעָנִי מִמַּעַשׂ *Here I am, empty of deeds.* A private meditation, said in the first person singular by the leader of prayer. It expresses the sense of inadequacy anyone must feel, not simply in standing before God in prayer – for that is something we must all do – but in doing so on behalf of others. Abraham, praying for the people of Sodom, said "I am but dust and ashes" (Gen. 18:27). Moses, charged with leading his people to freedom, said, "Who am I?" (Ex. 3:11). The paradox of spiritual leadership is that those who think they are great are small; those who think themselves small are great. In Judaism, all leadership, including leadership in prayer, is a form of service, not superiority or dominance, and cannot exist without humility.

הִנְנִי *Here I am.* This single word is the ultimate human response to the call of God. When God summons us, He calls our name, and the most profound reply is simply, *Hineni*, "Here I am." So said Abraham at the beginning of the binding of Isaac (Gen. 22:1). So said Jacob when God told him not to be afraid to go to Egypt (Gen. 46:2). So said Moses when God appeared to him at the burning bush (Ex. 3:4). So said the young Samuel when God appeared to him at night (1 Sam. 3:4), and Isaiah in the mystical vision that marked the beginning of his mission (Is. 6:8).

At the beginning of the human story God called to Adam and Eve in Eden, "Where are you?" (Gen. 3:9). So He has done ever since: He calls to each of us, here where we are, this person, in this situation, at this time, saying: there is an act only you can do, a situation only you can address, a moment that, if not seized, may never come again. God commands in generalities but

ashamed of me, nor me of them, and accept my prayer as if it were the prayer of an old man, experienced and fluent, one whose past is becoming and whose beard is long and his voice pleasant, and whose mind is involved with the concerns of others. Banish the Adversary that he should not draw me aside, and let the banner that we fly for You be love, cover all our crimes over with love, and turn all our fast days and torments to happiness and joy – ours and those of all Israel – to life and to peace; [let us] love truth and peace, and let there be no obstacle to my prayer.

And may it be Your will, LORD God of Abraham, God of Isaac and God of Jacob, the great and mighty and awesome God, God Most High, I shall be what I shall be, that all the angels who carry our prayers should bring my prayer before the throne of Your glory, and lay it out before You, for the sake of all the righteous and good and innocent people, and the sake of Your great and mighty and awesome name's glory, for in Your compassion You listen to the prayers of Your people Israel. Blessed are You, who listens to prayers.

MUSAF – ADDITIONAL SERVICE

The Musaf service corresponds to the additional sacrifice that was offered in Temple times on Shabbat and festivals. The sacrificial element is more pronounced in Musaf than in other services, since the other services have a double aspect. On the one hand, they too represent sacrifice (except Ma'ariv, the evening service, because no sacrifices were offered at night). But they also represent the prayers of the patriarchs: the morning service is associated with Abraham, the afternoon service with Isaac and the evening service with Jacob. Musaf has no such additional dimension. It is, simply, the substitute for a sacrifice. As our ancestors brought offerings in the Temple so we bring an offering of words.

In my heart I will build a Temple for His glory, and in the Temple I will place an altar to His splendor, and as an eternal light I will take the flame of Isaac's binding, and as an offering I will offer my only soul. (Rabbi Elazar Azikri)

If I declare my wants in prayer, it is not to remind You of them, but only that I may be conscious of my dependence on You. (Rabbi Baḥya ibn Pakuda)

יֵבֹשׁוּ בִּי וְאַל אֵבוֹשָׁה בָּהֶם. וְקַבֵּל תְּפִלָּתִי כִּתְפִלַּת זָקֵן וְרָגִיל, וּפִרְקוֹ נָאֶה וּזְקָנוֹ מְגֻדָּל וְקוֹלוֹ נָעִים, וּמְעֹרָב בְּדַעַת עִם הַבְּרִיּוֹת. וְתִגְעַר בְּשָׂטָן לְבַל יַשְׂטִינֵנוּ, וִיהִי נָא דִגְלֵנוּ עָלֶיךָ אַהֲבָה, לְכָל פְּשָׁעִים תְּכַסֶּה בְּאַהֲבָה, וְכָל צוֹמוֹתֵינוּ וְעִנּוּיֵינוּ הֲפָךְ לָנוּ וּלְכָל יִשְׂרָאֵל לְשָׂשׂוֹן וּלְשִׂמְחָה לְחַיִּים וּלְשָׁלוֹם, הָאֱמֶת וְהַשָּׁלוֹם אֱהָבוּ, וְאַל יְהִי שׁוּם מִכְשׁוֹל בִּתְפִלָּתִי.

וִיהִי רָצוֹן מִלְּפָנֶיךָ יהוה אֱלֹהֵי אַבְרָהָם אֱלֹהֵי יִצְחָק וֵאלֹהֵי יַעֲקֹב, הָאֵל הַגָּדוֹל הַגִּבּוֹר וְהַנּוֹרָא אֵל עֶלְיוֹן אֶהְיֶה אֲשֶׁר אֶהְיֶה, שֶׁכָּל הַמַּלְאָכִים שֶׁהֵם בַּעֲלֵי תְפִלּוֹת יָבִיאוּ תְּפִלָּתִי לִפְנֵי כִּסֵּא כְבוֹדֶךָ וְיָפִיצוּ אוֹתָהּ לְפָנֶיךָ, בַּעֲבוּר כָּל הַצַּדִּיקִים וְהַחֲסִידִים הַתְּמִימִים וְהַיְשָׁרִים, וּבַעֲבוּר כְּבוֹד שִׁמְךָ הַגָּדוֹל הַגִּבּוֹר וְהַנּוֹרָא. כִּי אַתָּה שׁוֹמֵעַ תְּפִלַּת עַמְּךָ יִשְׂרָאֵל בְּרַחֲמִים, בָּרוּךְ אַתָּה שׁוֹמֵעַ תְּפִלָּה.

כִּתְפִלַּת זָקֵן וְרָגִיל... *As if it were the prayer of an old man, experienced and fluent…* This series of descriptions comes from the Mishna (*Ta'anit* 15a) which prescribes the procedure for public fasts proclaimed because of drought. The leader of prayer on such occasions had to be one beloved of God and of his fellow humans.

וְתִגְעַר בְּשָׂטָן *Banish the Adversary.* Satan, the Adversary, is not, in Judaism, a force of evil as in some non-Jewish theologies, but one of God's angels whose task is to be the prosecuting counsel in the heavenly court (See Zechariah 3, Job 1).

וְאַל יְהִי שׁוּם מִכְשׁוֹל בִּתְפִלָּתִי *And let there be no obstacle to my prayer.* The saintly Ḥanina ben Dosa, known as one of the great masters of prayer in the age of the Mishna, used to say that if his prayers came fluently from his mouth, he knew they had been accepted (Mishna, *Berakhot* 34b).

HALF KADDISH

Leader: יִתְגַּדַּל Magnified and sanctified
may His great name be,
in the world He created by His will.
May He establish His kingdom
in your lifetime and in your days,
and in the lifetime of all the house of Israel,
swiftly and soon –
and say: Amen.

All: May His great name be blessed for ever and all time.

Leader: Blessed and praised,
glorified and exalted,
raised and honored,
uplifted and lauded
be the name of the Holy One, blessed be He,
above and beyond any blessing, song,
praise and consolation
uttered in the world –
and say: Amen.

חצי קדיש

ש״ץ: יִתְגַּדַּל וְיִתְקַדַּשׁ שְׁמֵהּ רַבָּא (קהל: אָמֵן)
בְּעָלְמָא דִּי בְרָא כִרְעוּתֵהּ
וְיַמְלִיךְ מַלְכוּתֵהּ
בְּחַיֵּיכוֹן וּבְיוֹמֵיכוֹן וּבְחַיֵּי דְכָל בֵּית יִשְׂרָאֵל
בַּעֲגָלָא וּבִזְמַן קָרִיב
וְאִמְרוּ אָמֵן. (קהל: אָמֵן)

קהל וש״ץ: יְהֵא שְׁמֵהּ רַבָּא מְבָרַךְ לְעָלַם וּלְעָלְמֵי עָלְמַיָּא.

ש״ץ: יִתְבָּרַךְ וְיִשְׁתַּבַּח וְיִתְפָּאַר וְיִתְרוֹמַם וְיִתְנַשֵּׂא
וְיִתְהַדָּר וְיִתְעַלֶּה וְיִתְהַלָּל
שְׁמֵהּ דְּקֻדְשָׁא בְּרִיךְ הוּא (קהל: בְּרִיךְ הוּא)
לְעֵלָּא לְעֵלָּא מִכָּל בִּרְכָתָא וְשִׁירָתָא, תֻּשְׁבְּחָתָא וְנֶחֱמָתָא
דַּאֲמִירָן בְּעָלְמָא
וְאִמְרוּ אָמֵן. (קהל: אָמֵן)

Musaf

THE AMIDA

The following prayer, until "in former years" on page 800, is said silently, standing with feet together. If there is a minyan, the Amida is repeated aloud by the Leader. Take three steps forward and at the points indicated by ▾, bend the knees at the first word, bow at the second, and stand straight before saying God's name.

When I proclaim the LORD's name, give glory to our God. *Deut. 32*
O LORD, open my lips, so that my mouth may declare Your praise. *Ps. 51*

PATRIARCHS

▾בָּרוּךְ Blessed are You, LORD our God and God of our fathers,
God of Abraham, God of Isaac and God of Jacob;
the great, mighty and awesome God, God Most High,
who bestows acts of loving-kindness and creates all,
who remembers the loving-kindness of the fathers
and will bring a Redeemer to their children's children
for the sake of His name, in love.

זָכְרֵנוּ לְחַיִּים Remember us for life, O King who desires life,
and write us in the book of life – for Your sake, O God of life.
King, Helper, Savior, Shield:
▾Blessed are You, LORD, Shield of Abraham.

DIVINE MIGHT

אַתָּה גִּבּוֹר You are eternally mighty, LORD.
You give life to the dead
and have great power to save.

In Israel: He causes the dew to fall.

He sustains the living with loving-kindness,
and with great compassion revives the dead.
He supports the fallen,
heals the sick, sets captives free,
and keeps His faith with those who sleep in the dust.
Who is like You, Master of might,
and to whom can You be compared,
O King who brings death and gives life,
and makes salvation grow?

תפילת מוסף

עמידה

The following prayer, until קַדְמֹנִיּוֹת *on page 801, is said silently, standing with feet together. If there is a* מנין*, the* עמידה *is repeated aloud by the* שליח ציבור*. Take three steps forward and at the points indicated by* ▾*, bend the knees at the first word, bow at the second, and stand straight before saying God's name.*

כִּי שֵׁם יהוה אֶקְרָא, הָבוּ גֹדֶל לֵאלֹהֵינוּ: דברים לב
אֲדֹנָי, שְׂפָתַי תִּפְתָּח, וּפִי יַגִּיד תְּהִלָּתֶךָ: תהלים נא

אבות

▾בָּרוּךְ אַתָּה יהוה, אֱלֹהֵינוּ וֵאלֹהֵי אֲבוֹתֵינוּ
אֱלֹהֵי אַבְרָהָם, אֱלֹהֵי יִצְחָק, וֵאלֹהֵי יַעֲקֹב
הָאֵל הַגָּדוֹל הַגִּבּוֹר וְהַנּוֹרָא, אֵל עֶלְיוֹן
גּוֹמֵל חֲסָדִים טוֹבִים, וְקוֹנֵה הַכֹּל
וְזוֹכֵר חַסְדֵי אָבוֹת
וּמֵבִיא גוֹאֵל לִבְנֵי בְנֵיהֶם לְמַעַן שְׁמוֹ בְּאַהֲבָה.

זָכְרֵנוּ לְחַיִּים, מֶלֶךְ חָפֵץ בַּחַיִּים
וְכָתְבֵנוּ בְּסֵפֶר הַחַיִּים, לְמַעַנְךָ אֱלֹהִים חַיִּים.
מֶלֶךְ עוֹזֵר וּמוֹשִׁיעַ וּמָגֵן.
▾בָּרוּךְ אַתָּה יהוה, מָגֵן אַבְרָהָם.

גבורות

אַתָּה גִּבּוֹר לְעוֹלָם, אֲדֹנָי
מְחַיֵּה מֵתִים אַתָּה, רַב לְהוֹשִׁיעַ
בארץ ישראל: מוֹרִיד הַטָּל

מְכַלְכֵּל חַיִּים בְּחֶסֶד, מְחַיֵּה מֵתִים בְּרַחֲמִים רַבִּים
סוֹמֵךְ נוֹפְלִים, וְרוֹפֵא חוֹלִים, וּמַתִּיר אֲסוּרִים
וּמְקַיֵּם אֱמוּנָתוֹ לִישֵׁנֵי עָפָר.
מִי כָמוֹךָ, בַּעַל גְּבוּרוֹת, וּמִי דּוֹמֶה לָּךְ
מֶלֶךְ, מֵמִית וּמְחַיֶּה וּמַצְמִיחַ יְשׁוּעָה.

מִי כָמְוֹךָ Who is like You, compassionate Father,
who remembers His creatures in compassion, for life?
Faithful are You to revive the dead.
Blessed are You, Lord,
who revives the dead.

HOLINESS

אַתָּה קָדוֹשׁ You are holy and Your name is holy,
and holy ones praise You daily, Selah!

וּבְכֵן תֵּן פַּחְדְּךָ And so place the fear of You, Lord our God,
over all that You have made,
and the terror of You over all You have created,
and all who were made will stand in awe of You,
and all of creation will worship You,
and they will be bound all together as one
to carry out Your will with an undivided heart;
for we know, Lord our God,
that all dominion is laid out before You,
strength is in Your palm,
and might in Your right hand,
Your name spreading awe
over all You have created.

וּבְכֵן תֵּן כָּבוֹד And so place honor,
Lord, upon Your people,
praise on those who fear You
and hope into those who seek You,
the confidence to speak
into all who long for You,
gladness to Your land and joy to Your city,
the flourishing of pride to David Your servant,
and a lamp laid out for his descendant, Your anointed,
soon, in our days.

מִי כָמוֹךָ אַב הָרַחֲמִים
זוֹכֵר יְצוּרָיו לְחַיִּים בְּרַחֲמִים.
וְנֶאֱמָן אַתָּה לְהַחֲיוֹת מֵתִים.
בָּרוּךְ אַתָּה יהוה, מְחַיֵּה הַמֵּתִים.

קדושת השם

אַתָּה קָדוֹשׁ וְשִׁמְךָ קָדוֹשׁ
וּקְדוֹשִׁים בְּכָל יוֹם יְהַלְלוּךָ סֶּלָה.

וּבְכֵן תֵּן פַּחְדְּךָ יהוה אֱלֹהֵינוּ עַל כָּל מַעֲשֶׂיךָ
וְאֵימָתְךָ עַל כָּל מַה שֶּׁבָּרָאתָ
וְיִירָאוּךָ כָּל הַמַּעֲשִׂים
וְיִשְׁתַּחֲווּ לְפָנֶיךָ כָּל הַבְּרוּאִים
וְיֵעָשׂוּ כֻלָּם אֲגֻדָּה אֶחָת לַעֲשׂוֹת רְצוֹנְךָ בְּלֵבָב שָׁלֵם
כְּמוֹ שֶׁיָּדַעְנוּ יהוה אֱלֹהֵינוּ שֶׁהַשָּׁלְטָן לְפָנֶיךָ
עֹז בְּיָדְךָ וּגְבוּרָה בִּימִינֶךָ
וְשִׁמְךָ נוֹרָא עַל כָּל מַה שֶּׁבָּרָאתָ.

וּבְכֵן תֵּן כָּבוֹד יהוה לְעַמֶּךָ
תְּהִלָּה לִירֵאֶיךָ
וְתִקְוָה טוֹבָה לְדוֹרְשֶׁיךָ
וּפִתְחוֹן פֶּה לַמְיַחֲלִים לָךְ
שִׂמְחָה לְאַרְצֶךָ, וְשָׂשׂוֹן לְעִירֶךָ
וּצְמִיחַת קֶרֶן לְדָוִד עַבְדֶּךָ
וַעֲרִיכַת נֵר לְבֶן יִשַׁי מְשִׁיחֶךָ
בִּמְהֵרָה בְיָמֵינוּ.

וּבְכֵן צַדִּיקִים And then righteous people will see and rejoice,
and the upright will exult, and the pious revel in joy,
and injustice will have nothing more to say,
and all wickedness will fade away like smoke
as You sweep the rule of arrogance from the earth.

וְתִמְלֹךְ אַתָּה And You, Lord,
will rule alone over those You have made,
in Mount Zion, the dwelling of Your glory,
and in Jerusalem, Your holy city,
as it is written in Your holy Writings:
"The Lord shall reign for ever. *Ps. 146*
He is your God, Zion, from generation to generation, Halleluya!"

קָדוֹשׁ אַתָּה You are holy, Your name is awesome,
and there is no god but You,
as it is written,
"The Lord of hosts shall be raised up through His judgment, *Is. 5*
the holy God, made holy in righteousness."
Blessed are You, Lord, the holy King.

HOLINESS OF THE DAY

אַתָּה בְחַרְתָּנוּ You have chosen us from among all peoples.
You have loved and favored us.
You have raised us above all tongues.
You have made us holy
through Your commandments.
You have brought us near, our King, to Your service,
and have called us by Your great and holy name.

On Shabbat, add the words in parentheses:

וַתִּתֶּן לָנוּ And You, Lord our God, have given us in love
(this Sabbath day for holiness and rest, and)
this Day of Atonement
for pardon and forgiveness and atonement,
to pardon all our iniquities,
(with love,) a holy assembly
in memory of the exodus from Egypt.

וּבְכֵן צַדִּיקִים יִרְאוּ וְיִשְׂמָחוּ, וִישָׁרִים יַעֲלֹזוּ
וַחֲסִידִים בְּרִנָּה יָגִילוּ, וְעוֹלָתָה תִּקְפָּץ פִּיהָ
וְכָל הָרִשְׁעָה כֻּלָּהּ כְּעָשָׁן תִּכְלֶה
כִּי תַעֲבִיר מֶמְשֶׁלֶת זָדוֹן מִן הָאָרֶץ.

וְתִמְלֹךְ אַתָּה יהוה לְבַדֶּךָ עַל כָּל מַעֲשֶׂיךָ
בְּהַר צִיּוֹן מִשְׁכַּן כְּבוֹדֶךָ, וּבִירוּשָׁלַיִם עִיר קָדְשֶׁךָ
כַּכָּתוּב בְּדִבְרֵי קָדְשֶׁךָ
יִמְלֹךְ יהוה לְעוֹלָם, אֱלֹהַיִךְ צִיּוֹן לְדֹר וָדֹר, הַלְלוּיָהּ: תהלים קמו

קָדוֹשׁ אַתָּה וְנוֹרָא שְׁמֶךָ, וְאֵין אֱלוֹהַּ מִבַּלְעָדֶיךָ
כַּכָּתוּב, וַיִּגְבַּהּ יהוה צְבָאוֹת בַּמִּשְׁפָּט ישעיה ה
וְהָאֵל הַקָּדוֹשׁ נִקְדַּשׁ בִּצְדָקָה:
בָּרוּךְ אַתָּה יהוה, הַמֶּלֶךְ הַקָּדוֹשׁ.

קדושת היום

אַתָּה בְחַרְתָּנוּ מִכָּל הָעַמִּים
אָהַבְתָּ אוֹתָנוּ וְרָצִיתָ בָּנוּ, וְרוֹמַמְתָּנוּ מִכָּל הַלְּשׁוֹנוֹת
וְקִדַּשְׁתָּנוּ בְּמִצְוֹתֶיךָ
וְקֵרַבְתָּנוּ מַלְכֵּנוּ לַעֲבוֹדָתֶךָ
וְשִׁמְךָ הַגָּדוֹל וְהַקָּדוֹשׁ עָלֵינוּ קָרָאתָ.

On שבת, add the words in parentheses:

וַתִּתֶּן לָנוּ יהוה אֱלֹהֵינוּ בְּאַהֲבָה אֶת
(יוֹם הַשַּׁבָּת הַזֶּה לִקְדֻשָּׁה וְלִמְנוּחָה, וְאֶת)
יוֹם הַכִּפּוּרִים הַזֶּה, לִמְחִילָה וְלִסְלִיחָה וּלְכַפָּרָה
וְלִמְחָל בּוֹ אֶת כָּל עֲוֹנוֹתֵינוּ
(בְּאַהֲבָה) מִקְרָא קֹדֶשׁ, זֵכֶר לִיצִיאַת מִצְרָיִם.

וּמִפְּנֵי חֲטָאֵינוּ But because of our sins we were exiled from our land
and driven far from our country.
We cannot perform our duties in Your chosen House,
the great and holy Temple that was called by Your name,
because of the hand that was stretched out against Your Sanctuary.
May it be Your will, LORD our God and God of our ancestors,
merciful King,
that You in Your abounding compassion may once more
have mercy on us and on Your Sanctuary,
rebuilding it swiftly and adding to its glory.
Our Father, our King,
reveal the glory of Your kingdom to us swiftly.
Appear and be exalted over us in the sight of all that lives.
Bring back our scattered ones from among the nations,
and gather our dispersed people from the ends of the earth.

וַהֲבִיאֵנוּ לְצִיּוֹן Lead us to Zion, Your city, in jubilation,
and to Jerusalem, home of Your Temple, with everlasting joy.
There we will prepare for You
our obligatory offerings:
the regular daily offerings in their order
and the additional offerings according to their law.
And the additional offering(s of this Sabbath day and) of this
Day of Atonement we will prepare and offer before You in love,
in accord with Your will's commandment,
as You wrote for us in Your Torah
through Your servant Moses, by Your own word,
as it is said:

On Shabbat: **וּבְיוֹם הַשַּׁבָּת** On the Sabbath day, make an offering of two lambs a year old, without blemish, together with two-tenths of an ephah of fine flour mixed with oil as a meal-offering, and its appropriate libation. This is the burnt-offering for every Sabbath, in addition to the regular daily burnt-offering and its libation. *Num. 28*

וּמִפְּנֵי חֲטָאֵינוּ גָּלִינוּ מֵאַרְצֵנוּ, וְנִתְרַחַקְנוּ מֵעַל אַדְמָתֵנוּ
וְאֵין אֲנַחְנוּ יְכוֹלִים לַעֲשׂוֹת חוֹבוֹתֵינוּ בְּבֵית בְּחִירָתֶךָ
בַּבַּיִת הַגָּדוֹל וְהַקָּדוֹשׁ שֶׁנִּקְרָא שִׁמְךָ עָלָיו
מִפְּנֵי הַיָּד שֶׁנִּשְׁתַּלְּחָה בְּמִקְדָּשֶׁךָ.
יְהִי רָצוֹן מִלְּפָנֶיךָ יהוה אֱלֹהֵינוּ וֵאלֹהֵי אֲבוֹתֵינוּ, מֶלֶךְ רַחֲמָן
שֶׁתָּשׁוּב וּתְרַחֵם עָלֵינוּ
וְעַל מִקְדָּשְׁךָ בְּרַחֲמֶיךָ הָרַבִּים
וְתִבְנֵהוּ מְהֵרָה וּתְגַדֵּל כְּבוֹדוֹ.
אָבִינוּ מַלְכֵּנוּ, גַּלֵּה כְּבוֹד מַלְכוּתְךָ עָלֵינוּ מְהֵרָה
וְהוֹפַע וְהִנָּשֵׂא עָלֵינוּ לְעֵינֵי כָּל חָי
וְקָרֵב פְּזוּרֵינוּ מִבֵּין הַגּוֹיִם, וּנְפוּצוֹתֵינוּ כַּנֵּס מִיַּרְכְּתֵי אָרֶץ.

וַהֲבִיאֵנוּ לְצִיּוֹן עִירְךָ בְּרִנָּה
וְלִירוּשָׁלַיִם בֵּית מִקְדָּשְׁךָ בְּשִׂמְחַת עוֹלָם
וְשָׁם נַעֲשֶׂה לְפָנֶיךָ אֶת קָרְבְּנוֹת חוֹבוֹתֵינוּ
תְּמִידִים כְּסִדְרָם וּמוּסָפִים כְּהִלְכָתָם
וְאֶת מוּסַף / בשבת: מוּסְפֵי יוֹם הַשַּׁבָּת הַזֶּה וְ /
יוֹם הַכִּפּוּרִים הַזֶּה
נַעֲשֶׂה וְנַקְרִיב לְפָנֶיךָ בְּאַהֲבָה כְּמִצְוַת רְצוֹנֶךָ
כְּמוֹ שֶׁכָּתַבְתָּ עָלֵינוּ בְּתוֹרָתֶךָ
עַל יְדֵי מֹשֶׁה עַבְדֶּךָ מִפִּי כְבוֹדֶךָ, כָּאָמוּר

בשבת: וּבְיוֹם הַשַּׁבָּת, שְׁנֵי־כְבָשִׂים בְּנֵי־שָׁנָה תְּמִימִם במדבר כח
וּשְׁנֵי עֶשְׂרֹנִים סֹלֶת מִנְחָה בְּלוּלָה בַשֶּׁמֶן וְנִסְכּוֹ:
עֹלַת שַׁבַּת בְּשַׁבַּתּוֹ, עַל־עֹלַת הַתָּמִיד וְנִסְכָּהּ:

וּבֶעָשׂוֹר לַחֹדֶשׁ On the tenth day of this seventh month *Num. 29*
you shall have a holy assembly, and you shall afflict your souls;
you shall perform no kind of work.
And you shall bring a burnt-offering
of pleasing aroma to the Lord,
one young bullock, one ram, and seven yearling male lambs –
they shall be without blemish.

וּמִנְחָתָם And their meal offerings and wine-libations as ordained:
three tenths of an ephah for the bull,
two tenths of an ephah for the ram,
one tenth of an ephah for each of the seven lambs,
wine for the libations, two male goats for atonement,
and two regular daily offerings according to their law.

On Shabbat: יִשְׂמְחוּ Those who keep the Sabbath and call it a delight shall rejoice in Your kingship. The people who sanctify the seventh day shall all be satisfied and take delight in Your goodness, for You favored the seventh day and declared it holy. You called it "most desirable of days" in remembrance of Creation.

On Shabbat, add the words in parentheses:
אֱלֹהֵינוּ Our God and God of our ancestors,
pardon our iniquities
on (this Sabbath day, and on) this Day of Atonement;
wipe away and remove all our transgressions and sins
from before Your eyes,
as it is said:
"I, I am the One who shall wipe out your transgressions *Is. 43*
for My sake, and I shall not recall your sins."

And it is said:
"I have wiped out your transgressions like a cloud, *Is. 44*
and as a haze your sins;
come back to Me for I have redeemed you."

וּבֶעָשׂוֹר לַחֹדֶשׁ הַשְּׁבִיעִי הַזֶּה, מִקְרָא־קֹדֶשׁ יִהְיֶה לָכֶם במדבר כט
וְעִנִּיתֶם אֶת־נַפְשֹׁתֵיכֶם, כָּל־מְלָאכָה לֹא תַעֲשׂוּ:
וְהִקְרַבְתֶּם עֹלָה לַיהוה רֵיחַ נִיחֹחַ
פַּר בֶּן־בָּקָר אֶחָד, אַיִל אֶחָד
כְּבָשִׂים בְּנֵי־שָׁנָה שִׁבְעָה, תְּמִימִם יִהְיוּ לָכֶם:

וּמִנְחָתָם וְנִסְכֵּיהֶם כִּמְדֻבָּר
שְׁלֹשָׁה עֶשְׂרֹנִים לַפָּר וּשְׁנֵי עֶשְׂרֹנִים לָאָיִל
וְעִשָּׂרוֹן לַכֶּבֶשׂ, וְיַיִן כְּנִסְכּוֹ, וּשְׁנֵי שְׂעִירִים לְכַפֵּר
וּשְׁנֵי תְמִידִים כְּהִלְכָתָם.

בשבת: יִשְׂמְחוּ בְמַלְכוּתְךָ שׁוֹמְרֵי שַׁבָּת וְקוֹרְאֵי עֹנֶג. עַם מְקַדְּשֵׁי שְׁבִיעִי כֻּלָּם יִשְׂבְּעוּ וְיִתְעַנְּגוּ מִטּוּבֶךָ, וּבַשְּׁבִיעִי רָצִיתָ בּוֹ וְקִדַּשְׁתּוֹ, חֶמְדַּת יָמִים אוֹתוֹ קָרָאתָ, זֵכֶר לְמַעֲשֵׂה בְרֵאשִׁית.

On שבת, add the words in parentheses:

אֱלֹהֵינוּ וֵאלֹהֵי אֲבוֹתֵינוּ
מְחַל לַעֲוֹנוֹתֵינוּ בְּיוֹם (הַשַּׁבָּת הַזֶּה וּבְיוֹם) הַכִּפּוּרִים הַזֶּה
מְחֵה וְהַעֲבֵר פְּשָׁעֵינוּ וְחַטֹּאתֵינוּ מִנֶּגֶד עֵינֶיךָ
כָּאָמוּר
אָנֹכִי אָנֹכִי הוּא מֹחֶה פְשָׁעֶיךָ לְמַעֲנִי ישעיה מג
וְחַטֹּאתֶיךָ לֹא אֶזְכֹּר:

וְנֶאֱמַר
מָחִיתִי כָעָב פְּשָׁעֶיךָ וְכֶעָנָן חַטֹּאותֶיךָ ישעיה מד
שׁוּבָה אֵלַי כִּי גְאַלְתִּיךָ:

And it is said:

For on this day you will be atoned and made pure; *Lev. 16*
of all your sins before the LORD you shall be purified.

(Our God and God of our ancestors, find favor in our rest.)
Make us holy through Your commandments
and grant us our share in Your Torah.
Satisfy us with Your goodness,
grant us joy in Your salvation
(in love and favor, O LORD our God,
grant us as our heritage Your holy Sabbath,
so that Israel, who sanctify Your name,
may find rest on it),
and purify our hearts to serve You in truth.
For You are the Forgiver of Israel
and the Pardoner of the tribes of Yeshurun in every generation,
and without You we have no king who pardons and forgives,
none but You.
Blessed are You, LORD,
King who pardons and forgives our iniquities
and those of all His people the house of Israel,
and makes our guilt pass away, every single year,
King of all the earth, who sanctifies (the Sabbath,)
Israel and the Day of Atonement.

TEMPLE SERVICE

רְצֵה Find favor, LORD our God,
in Your people Israel and their prayer.
Restore the service to Your most holy House,
and accept in love and favor
the fire-offerings of Israel and their prayer.
May the service of Your people Israel always find favor with You.
And may our eyes witness Your return to Zion in compassion.
Blessed are You, LORD,
who restores His Presence to Zion.

וְנֶאֱמַר
כִּי־בַיּוֹם הַזֶּה יְכַפֵּר עֲלֵיכֶם לְטַהֵר אֶתְכֶם ויקרא טז
מִכֹּל חַטֹּאתֵיכֶם, לִפְנֵי יהוה תִּטְהָרוּ:
(אֱלֹהֵינוּ וֵאלֹהֵי אֲבוֹתֵינוּ, רְצֵה בִמְנוּחָתֵנוּ)
קַדְּשֵׁנוּ בְּמִצְוֹתֶיךָ וְתֵן חֶלְקֵנוּ בְּתוֹרָתֶךָ
שַׂבְּעֵנוּ מִטּוּבֶךָ וְשַׂמְּחֵנוּ בִּישׁוּעָתֶךָ
(וְהַנְחִילֵנוּ יהוה אֱלֹהֵינוּ בְּאַהֲבָה וּבְרָצוֹן שַׁבַּת קָדְשֶׁךָ
וְיָנוּחוּ בוֹ יִשְׂרָאֵל מְקַדְּשֵׁי שְׁמֶךָ)
וְטַהֵר לִבֵּנוּ לְעָבְדְּךָ בֶּאֱמֶת
כִּי אַתָּה סָלְחָן לְיִשְׂרָאֵל
וּמָחֳלָן לְשִׁבְטֵי יְשֻׁרוּן בְּכָל דּוֹר וָדוֹר
וּמִבַּלְעָדֶיךָ אֵין לָנוּ מֶלֶךְ מוֹחֵל וְסוֹלֵחַ אֶלָּא אָתָּה.
בָּרוּךְ אַתָּה יהוה
מֶלֶךְ מוֹחֵל וְסוֹלֵחַ לַעֲוֹנוֹתֵינוּ
וְלַעֲוֹנוֹת עַמּוֹ בֵּית יִשְׂרָאֵל
וּמַעֲבִיר אַשְׁמוֹתֵינוּ בְּכָל שָׁנָה וְשָׁנָה
מֶלֶךְ עַל כָּל הָאָרֶץ, מְקַדֵּשׁ (הַשַּׁבָּת וְ) יִשְׂרָאֵל וְיוֹם הַכִּפּוּרִים.

עבודה
רְצֵה יהוה אֱלֹהֵינוּ בְּעַמְּךָ יִשְׂרָאֵל, וּבִתְפִלָּתָם
וְהָשֵׁב אֶת הָעֲבוֹדָה לִדְבִיר בֵּיתֶךָ
וְאִשֵּׁי יִשְׂרָאֵל וּתְפִלָּתָם בְּאַהֲבָה תְקַבֵּל בְּרָצוֹן
וּתְהִי לְרָצוֹן תָּמִיד עֲבוֹדַת יִשְׂרָאֵל עַמֶּךָ.
וְתֶחֱזֶינָה עֵינֵינוּ בְּשׁוּבְךָ לְצִיּוֹן בְּרַחֲמִים.
בָּרוּךְ אַתָּה יהוה, הַמַּחֲזִיר שְׁכִינָתוֹ לְצִיּוֹן.

THANKSGIVING

Bow at the first nine words.

▾מוֹדִים We give thanks to You,
for You are the LORD our God and God of our ancestors
for ever and all time.
You are the Rock of our lives,
Shield of our salvation from generation to generation.
We will thank You and declare Your praise for our lives,
which are entrusted into Your hand;
for our souls, which are placed in Your charge;
for Your miracles which are with us every day;
and for Your wonders and favors
at all times, evening, morning and midday.
You are good – for Your compassion never fails.
You are compassionate – for Your loving-kindnesses never cease.
We have always placed our hope in You.
For all these things may Your name be blessed and exalted,
our King, continually, for ever and all time.

וּכְתֹב And write for a good life, all the children of Your covenant.

Let all that lives thank You, Selah!
and praise Your name in truth,
God, our Savior and Help, Selah!
▾Blessed are You, LORD, whose name is "the Good"
and to whom thanks are due.

PEACE

שִׂים שָׁלוֹם Grant peace, goodness and blessing,
grace, loving-kindness and compassion to us
and all Israel Your people.
Bless us, our Father, all as one, with the light of Your face,
for by the light of Your face You have given us, LORD our God,
the Torah of life and love of kindness,
righteousness, blessing, compassion, life and peace.
May it be good in Your eyes to bless Your people Israel
at every time, in every hour, with Your peace.

הודאה

Bow at the first five words.

מוֹדִים אֲנַחְנוּ לָךְ
שָׁאַתָּה הוּא יהוה אֱלֹהֵינוּ וֵאלֹהֵי אֲבוֹתֵינוּ לְעוֹלָם וָעֶד.
צוּר חַיֵּינוּ, מָגֵן יִשְׁעֵנוּ, אַתָּה הוּא לְדוֹר וָדוֹר.
נוֹדֶה לְּךָ וּנְסַפֵּר תְּהִלָּתֶךָ, עַל חַיֵּינוּ הַמְּסוּרִים בְּיָדֶךָ
וְעַל נִשְׁמוֹתֵינוּ הַפְּקוּדוֹת לָךְ, וְעַל נִסֶּיךָ שֶׁבְּכָל יוֹם עִמָּנוּ
וְעַל נִפְלְאוֹתֶיךָ וְטוֹבוֹתֶיךָ שֶׁבְּכָל עֵת, עֶרֶב וָבֹקֶר וְצָהֳרָיִם.
הַטּוֹב, כִּי לֹא כָלוּ רַחֲמֶיךָ
וְהַמְרַחֵם, כִּי לֹא תַמּוּ חֲסָדֶיךָ
מֵעוֹלָם קִוִּינוּ לָךְ.
וְעַל כֻּלָּם יִתְבָּרַךְ וְיִתְרוֹמַם שִׁמְךָ מַלְכֵּנוּ תָּמִיד לְעוֹלָם וָעֶד.

וּכְתֹב לְחַיִּים טוֹבִים כָּל בְּנֵי בְרִיתֶךָ.

וְכֹל הַחַיִּים יוֹדוּךָ סֶּלָה, וִיהַלְלוּ אֶת שִׁמְךָ בֶּאֱמֶת
הָאֵל יְשׁוּעָתֵנוּ וְעֶזְרָתֵנוּ סֶלָה.
בָּרוּךְ אַתָּה יהוה, הַטּוֹב שִׁמְךָ וּלְךָ נָאֶה לְהוֹדוֹת.

שלום

שִׂים שָׁלוֹם טוֹבָה וּבְרָכָה
חֵן וָחֶסֶד וְרַחֲמִים עָלֵינוּ וְעַל כָּל יִשְׂרָאֵל עַמֶּךָ.
בָּרְכֵנוּ אָבִינוּ כֻּלָּנוּ כְּאֶחָד בְּאוֹר פָּנֶיךָ
כִּי בְאוֹר פָּנֶיךָ נָתַתָּ לָּנוּ, יהוה אֱלֹהֵינוּ
תּוֹרַת חַיִּים וְאַהֲבַת חֶסֶד
וּצְדָקָה וּבְרָכָה וְרַחֲמִים וְחַיִּים וְשָׁלוֹם.
וְטוֹב בְּעֵינֶיךָ לְבָרֵךְ אֶת עַמְּךָ יִשְׂרָאֵל
בְּכָל עֵת וּבְכָל שָׁעָה בִּשְׁלוֹמֶךָ.

בְּסֵפֶר חַיִּים In the book of life, blessing,
peace and prosperity,
may we and all Your people the house of Israel
be remembered and written before You
for a good life, and for peace.*

Blessed are You, LORD, who blesses His people Israel with peace.

**Outside Israel, many end the blessing:*
Blessed are You, LORD, who makes peace.

Some say the following verse:
May the words of my mouth and the meditation of my heart Ps. 19
find favor before You, LORD, my Rock and Redeemer.

VIDUY

For linear translation and commentary, see page 1353.

אֱלֹהֵינוּ Our God and God of our fathers,
let our prayer come before You, and do not hide Yourself from our plea,
for we are not so arrogant or obstinate as to say before You,
LORD, our God and God of our fathers,
we are righteous and have not sinned,
for in truth, we and our fathers have sinned.

Strike the left side of the chest with the right fist while saying each of the sins.

אָשַׁמְנוּ We have sinned, we have acted treacherously,
we have robbed, we have spoken slander.
We have acted perversely, we have acted wickedly,
we have acted presumptuously, we have been violent,
we have framed lies.
We have given bad advice, we have deceived, we have scorned,
we have rebelled, we have provoked, we have turned away,
we have committed iniquity, we have transgressed,
we have persecuted, we have been obstinate.
We have acted wickedly, we have corrupted,
we have acted abominably, we have strayed, we have led others astray.

סַרְנוּ We have turned away from Your commandments and good laws,
to no avail, for You are just in all that has befallen us, Neh. 9
for You have acted faithfully while we have done wickedly.

בְּסֵפֶר חַיִּים, בְּרָכָה וְשָׁלוֹם, וּפַרְנָסָה טוֹבָה
נִזָּכֵר וְנִכָּתֵב לְפָנֶיךָ, אֲנַחְנוּ וְכָל עַמְּךָ בֵּית יִשְׂרָאֵל
לְחַיִּים טוֹבִים וּלְשָׁלוֹם.*
בָּרוּךְ אַתָּה יהוה, הַמְבָרֵךְ אֶת עַמּוֹ יִשְׂרָאֵל בַּשָּׁלוֹם.

In חוץ לארץ, many end the blessing:

בָּרוּךְ אַתָּה יהוה, עוֹשֵׂה הַשָּׁלוֹם.

Some say the following verse :

יִהְיוּ לְרָצוֹן אִמְרֵי־פִי וְהֶגְיוֹן לִבִּי לְפָנֶיךָ, יהוה צוּרִי וְגֹאֲלִי: תהלים יט

וידוי

For linear translation and commentary, see page 1353.

אֱלֹהֵינוּ וֵאלֹהֵי אֲבוֹתֵינוּ
תָּבוֹא לְפָנֶיךָ תְּפִלָּתֵנוּ, וְאַל תִּתְעַלַּם מִתְּחִנָּתֵנוּ.
שֶׁאֵין אֲנַחְנוּ עַזֵּי פָנִים וּקְשֵׁי עֹרֶף לוֹמַר לְפָנֶיךָ
יהוה אֱלֹהֵינוּ וֵאלֹהֵי אֲבוֹתֵינוּ
צַדִּיקִים אֲנַחְנוּ וְלֹא חָטָאנוּ.
אֲבָל אֲנַחְנוּ וַאֲבוֹתֵינוּ חָטָאנוּ.

Strike the left side of the chest with the right fist while saying each of the sins.

אָשַׁמְנוּ, בָּגַדְנוּ, גָּזַלְנוּ, דִּבַּרְנוּ דֹפִי
הֶעֱוִינוּ, וְהִרְשַׁעְנוּ, זַדְנוּ, חָמַסְנוּ, טָפַלְנוּ שֶׁקֶר
יָעַצְנוּ רָע, כִּזַּבְנוּ, לַצְנוּ, מָרַדְנוּ, נִאַצְנוּ, סָרַרְנוּ
עָוִינוּ, פָּשַׁעְנוּ, צָרַרְנוּ, קִשִּׁינוּ עֹרֶף
רָשַׁעְנוּ, שִׁחַתְנוּ, תִּעַבְנוּ, תָּעִינוּ, תִּעְתָּעְנוּ.

סַרְנוּ מִמִּצְוֹתֶיךָ וּמִמִּשְׁפָּטֶיךָ הַטּוֹבִים, וְלֹא שָׁוָה לָנוּ.
וְאַתָּה צַדִּיק עַל כָּל־הַבָּא עָלֵינוּ נחמיה ט
כִּי־אֱמֶת עָשִׂיתָ, וַאֲנַחְנוּ הִרְשָׁעְנוּ:

מַה נֹּאמַר What can we say before You, You who dwell on high?
What can we declare before You, You who abide in heaven?
Do You not know all, the hidden and revealed alike?

אַתָּה יוֹדֵעַ You know every secret since the world began,
and what is hidden deep inside every living thing.
You search each person's inner chambers,
examining conscience and mind.
Nothing is shrouded from You,
and nothing is hidden before Your eyes.
And so, may it be Your will,
LORD our God and God of our ancestors,
that You forgive us all our sins, pardon all our iniquities,
and grant us atonement for all of our transgressions.

Strike the left side of the chest with the right fist while saying each of the sins.

עַל חֵטְא For the sin we have sinned before You under duress or freewill,
and for the sin we have sinned before You in hardness of heart.

For the sin we have sinned before You unwittingly,
and for the sin we have sinned before You by an utterance of our lips.

For the sin we have sinned before You by unchastity,
and for the sin we have sinned before You openly or secretly.

For the sin we have sinned before You knowingly and deceitfully,
and for the sin we have sinned before You in speech.

For the sin we have sinned before You by wronging a neighbor,
and for the sin we have sinned before You by thoughts of the heart.

For the sin we have sinned before You in a gathering for immorality,
and for the sin we have sinned before You by insincere confession.

For the sin we have sinned before You by contempt for parents and teachers,
and for the sin we have sinned before You willfully or in error.

מַה נֹּאמַר לְפָנֶיךָ יוֹשֵׁב מָרוֹם, וּמַה נְּסַפֵּר לְפָנֶיךָ שׁוֹכֵן שְׁחָקִים
הֲלֹא כָּל הַנִּסְתָּרוֹת וְהַנִּגְלוֹת אַתָּה יוֹדֵעַ.

אַתָּה יוֹדֵעַ רָזֵי עוֹלָם וְתַעֲלוּמוֹת סִתְרֵי כָּל חָי.
אַתָּה חוֹפֵשׂ כָּל חַדְרֵי בָטֶן וּבוֹחֵן כְּלָיוֹת וָלֵב.
אֵין דָּבָר נֶעְלָם מִמֶּךָּ וְאֵין נִסְתָּר מִנֶּגֶד עֵינֶיךָ.
וּבְכֵן, יְהִי רָצוֹן מִלְּפָנֶיךָ, יהוה אֱלֹהֵינוּ וֵאלֹהֵי אֲבוֹתֵינוּ
שֶׁתִּסְלַח לָנוּ עַל כָּל חַטֹּאתֵינוּ וְתִמְחַל לָנוּ עַל כָּל עֲוֹנוֹתֵינוּ
וּתְכַפֵּר לָנוּ עַל כָּל פְּשָׁעֵינוּ.

Strike the left side of the chest with the right fist while saying each of the sins.

עַל חֵטְא שֶׁחָטָאנוּ לְפָנֶיךָ בְּאֹנֶס וּבְרָצוֹן
וְעַל חֵטְא שֶׁחָטָאנוּ לְפָנֶיךָ בְּאִמּוּץ הַלֵּב

עַל חֵטְא שֶׁחָטָאנוּ לְפָנֶיךָ בִּבְלִי דָעַת
וְעַל חֵטְא שֶׁחָטָאנוּ לְפָנֶיךָ בְּבִטּוּי שְׂפָתָיִם

עַל חֵטְא שֶׁחָטָאנוּ לְפָנֶיךָ בְּגִלּוּי עֲרָיוֹת
וְעַל חֵטְא שֶׁחָטָאנוּ לְפָנֶיךָ בְּגָלוּי וּבַסָּתֶר

עַל חֵטְא שֶׁחָטָאנוּ לְפָנֶיךָ בְּדַעַת וּבְמִרְמָה
וְעַל חֵטְא שֶׁחָטָאנוּ לְפָנֶיךָ בְּדִבּוּר פֶּה

עַל חֵטְא שֶׁחָטָאנוּ לְפָנֶיךָ בְּהוֹנָאַת רֵעַ
וְעַל חֵטְא שֶׁחָטָאנוּ לְפָנֶיךָ בְּהַרְהוֹר הַלֵּב

עַל חֵטְא שֶׁחָטָאנוּ לְפָנֶיךָ בִּוְעִידַת זְנוּת
וְעַל חֵטְא שֶׁחָטָאנוּ לְפָנֶיךָ בְּוִדּוּי פֶּה

עַל חֵטְא שֶׁחָטָאנוּ לְפָנֶיךָ בְּזִלְזוּל הוֹרִים וּמוֹרִים
וְעַל חֵטְא שֶׁחָטָאנוּ לְפָנֶיךָ בְּזָדוֹן וּבִשְׁגָגָה

For the sin we have sinned before You by force,
and for the sin we have sinned before You by desecrating Your name.

For the sin we have sinned before You by impure lips,
and for the sin we have sinned before You by foolish speech.

For the sin we have sinned before You by the evil inclination,
and for the sin we have sinned before You knowingly or unwittingly.

FOR ALL THESE, GOD OF FORGIVENESS,
FORGIVE US, PARDON US, GRANT US ATONEMENT.

For the sin we have sinned before You by deceit and lies,
and for the sin we have sinned before You by bribery.

For the sin we have sinned before You by scorn,
and for the sin we have sinned before You by evil speech.

For the sin we have sinned before You in business,
and for the sin we have sinned before You with food and drink.

For the sin we have sinned before You by interest and extortion,
and for the sin we have sinned before You by being haughty.

For the sin we have sinned before You by the idle chatter of our lips,
and for the sin we have sinned before You by prying eyes.

For the sin we have sinned before You by arrogance,
and for the sin we have sinned before You by insolence.

FOR ALL THESE, GOD OF FORGIVENESS,
FORGIVE US, PARDON US, GRANT US ATONEMENT.

עַל חֵטְא שֶׁחָטָאנוּ לְפָנֶיךָ בְּחֹזֶק יָד
וְעַל חֵטְא שֶׁחָטָאנוּ לְפָנֶיךָ בְּחִלּוּל הַשֵּׁם

עַל חֵטְא שֶׁחָטָאנוּ לְפָנֶיךָ בְּטֻמְאַת שְׂפָתָיִם
וְעַל חֵטְא שֶׁחָטָאנוּ לְפָנֶיךָ בְּטִפְשׁוּת פֶּה

עַל חֵטְא שֶׁחָטָאנוּ לְפָנֶיךָ בְּיֵצֶר הָרָע
וְעַל חֵטְא שֶׁחָטָאנוּ לְפָנֶיךָ בְּיוֹדְעִים וּבְלֹא יוֹדְעִים

וְעַל כֻּלָּם אֱלוֹהַּ סְלִיחוֹת סְלַח לָנוּ, מְחַל לָנוּ, כַּפֶּר לָנוּ.

עַל חֵטְא שֶׁחָטָאנוּ לְפָנֶיךָ בְּכַחַשׁ וּבְכָזָב
וְעַל חֵטְא שֶׁחָטָאנוּ לְפָנֶיךָ בְּכַפַּת שֹׁחַד

עַל חֵטְא שֶׁחָטָאנוּ לְפָנֶיךָ בְּלָצוֹן
וְעַל חֵטְא שֶׁחָטָאנוּ לְפָנֶיךָ בְּלָשׁוֹן הָרָע

עַל חֵטְא שֶׁחָטָאנוּ לְפָנֶיךָ בְּמַשָּׂא וּבְמַתָּן
וְעַל חֵטְא שֶׁחָטָאנוּ לְפָנֶיךָ בְּמַאֲכָל וּבְמִשְׁתֶּה

עַל חֵטְא שֶׁחָטָאנוּ לְפָנֶיךָ בְּנֶשֶׁךְ וּבְמַרְבִּית
וְעַל חֵטְא שֶׁחָטָאנוּ לְפָנֶיךָ בִּנְטִיַּת גָּרוֹן

עַל חֵטְא שֶׁחָטָאנוּ לְפָנֶיךָ בְּשִׂיחַ שִׂפְתוֹתֵינוּ
וְעַל חֵטְא שֶׁחָטָאנוּ לְפָנֶיךָ בְּשִׂקּוּר עָיִן

עַל חֵטְא שֶׁחָטָאנוּ לְפָנֶיךָ בְּעֵינַיִם רָמוֹת
וְעַל חֵטְא שֶׁחָטָאנוּ לְפָנֶיךָ בְּעַזּוּת מֵצַח

וְעַל כֻּלָּם אֱלוֹהַּ סְלִיחוֹת סְלַח לָנוּ, מְחַל לָנוּ, כַּפֶּר לָנוּ.

For the sin we have sinned before You by casting off the yoke,
and for the sin we have sinned before You by perverting judgment.

For the sin we have sinned before You by entrapping a neighbor,
and for the sin we have sinned before You by envy.

For the sin we have sinned before You by lack of seriousness,
and for the sin we have sinned before You by obstinacy.

For the sin we have sinned before You by running to do evil,
and for the sin we have sinned before You by gossip.

For the sin we have sinned before You by vain oath,
and for the sin we have sinned before You by baseless hatred.

For the sin we have sinned before You by breach of trust,
and for the sin we have sinned before You by confusion of heart.

FOR ALL THESE, GOD OF FORGIVENESS,
FORGIVE US, PARDON US, GRANT US ATONEMENT.

וְעַל חֲטָאִים And for the sins for which we are liable to bring a burnt-offering,

and for the sins for which we are liable to bring a sin-offering,

and for the sins for which we are liable to bring an offering according to our means,

and for the sins for which we are liable to bring a guilt-offering for certain or possible sin,

and for the sins for which we are liable to lashes for rebellion,

and for the sins for which we are liable to forty lashes,

and for the sins for which we are liable to death by the hands of Heaven,

and for the sins for which we are liable to be cut off and childless,

and for the sins for which we are liable to the four death penalties
inflicted by the court: stoning, burning, beheading and strangling.

עַל חֵטְא שֶׁחָטָאנוּ לְפָנֶיךָ בִּפְרִיקַת עֹל
וְעַל חֵטְא שֶׁחָטָאנוּ לְפָנֶיךָ בִּפְלִילוּת
עַל חֵטְא שֶׁחָטָאנוּ לְפָנֶיךָ בִּצְדִיַּת רֵעַ
וְעַל חֵטְא שֶׁחָטָאנוּ לְפָנֶיךָ בְּצָרוּת עָיִן
עַל חֵטְא שֶׁחָטָאנוּ לְפָנֶיךָ בְּקַלּוּת רֹאשׁ
וְעַל חֵטְא שֶׁחָטָאנוּ לְפָנֶיךָ בְּקַשְׁיוּת עֹרֶף
עַל חֵטְא שֶׁחָטָאנוּ לְפָנֶיךָ בְּרִיצַת רַגְלַיִם לְהָרַע
וְעַל חֵטְא שֶׁחָטָאנוּ לְפָנֶיךָ בִּרְכִילוּת
עַל חֵטְא שֶׁחָטָאנוּ לְפָנֶיךָ בִּשְׁבוּעַת שָׁוְא
וְעַל חֵטְא שֶׁחָטָאנוּ לְפָנֶיךָ בְּשִׂנְאַת חִנָּם
עַל חֵטְא שֶׁחָטָאנוּ לְפָנֶיךָ בִּתְשׂוּמֶת יָד
וְעַל חֵטְא שֶׁחָטָאנוּ לְפָנֶיךָ בְּתִמְהוֹן לֵבָב

וְעַל כֻּלָּם אֱלוֹהַּ סְלִיחוֹת סְלַח לָנוּ, מְחַל לָנוּ, כַּפֶּר לָנוּ.

וְעַל חֲטָאִים שֶׁאָנוּ חַיָּבִים עֲלֵיהֶם עוֹלָה
וְעַל חֲטָאִים שֶׁאָנוּ חַיָּבִים עֲלֵיהֶם חַטָּאת
וְעַל חֲטָאִים שֶׁאָנוּ חַיָּבִים עֲלֵיהֶם קָרְבַּן עוֹלֶה וְיוֹרֵד
וְעַל חֲטָאִים שֶׁאָנוּ חַיָּבִים עֲלֵיהֶם אָשָׁם וַדַּאי וְתָלוּי
וְעַל חֲטָאִים שֶׁאָנוּ חַיָּבִים עֲלֵיהֶם מַכַּת מַרְדּוּת
וְעַל חֲטָאִים שֶׁאָנוּ חַיָּבִים עֲלֵיהֶם מַלְקוּת אַרְבָּעִים
וְעַל חֲטָאִים שֶׁאָנוּ חַיָּבִים עֲלֵיהֶם מִיתָה בִּידֵי שָׁמַיִם
וְעַל חֲטָאִים שֶׁאָנוּ חַיָּבִים עֲלֵיהֶם כָּרֵת וַעֲרִירִי
וְעַל חֲטָאִים שֶׁאָנוּ חַיָּבִים עֲלֵיהֶם אַרְבַּע מִיתוֹת בֵּית דִּין
סְקִילָה, שְׂרֵפָה, הֶרֶג, וְחֶנֶק.

For positive and negative commandments,
whether they can be remedied by an act or not,
for sins known to us and for those that are unknown –
for those that are known,
we have already declared them before You
and confessed them to You;
and for those that are unknown,
before You they are revealed and known,
as it is said,
"The secret things belong to the LORD our God, *Deut. 29*
but the things that are revealed
are for us and our children for ever,
that we may fulfill all the words of this Torah."

For You are the Forgiver of Israel
and the Pardoner of the tribes of Yeshurun
in every generation,
and without You
we have no king who pardons and forgives,
none but You.

אֱלֹהַי My God,
before I was formed I was unworthy,
and now that I have been formed
it is as if I had not been formed.
I am dust while alive,
how much more so when I am dead.
See, I am before You like a vessel filled with shame and disgrace.
May it be Your will,
LORD my God and God of my fathers,
that I may sin no more,
and as for the sins I have committed before You,
erase them in Your great compassion,
but not by suffering or severe illness.

עַל מִצְוַת עֲשֵׂה וְעַל מִצְוַת לֹא תַעֲשֶׂה.
בֵּין שֶׁיֵּשׁ בָּהּ קוּם עֲשֵׂה וּבֵין שֶׁאֵין בָּהּ קוּם עֲשֵׂה.
אֶת הַגְּלוּיִים לָנוּ וְאֶת שֶׁאֵינָם גְּלוּיִים לָנוּ
אֶת הַגְּלוּיִים לָנוּ
כְּבָר אֲמַרְנוּם לְפָנֶיךָ
וְהוֹדִינוּ לְךָ עֲלֵיהֶם
וְאֶת שֶׁאֵינָם גְּלוּיִים לָנוּ
לְפָנֶיךָ הֵם גְּלוּיִים וִידוּעִים
כַּדָּבָר שֶׁנֶּאֱמַר
הַנִּסְתָּרֹת לַיהוה אֱלֹהֵינוּ — דברים כט
וְהַנִּגְלֹת לָנוּ וּלְבָנֵינוּ עַד־עוֹלָם
לַעֲשׂוֹת אֶת־כָּל־דִּבְרֵי הַתּוֹרָה הַזֹּאת:

כִּי אַתָּה סָלְחָן לְיִשְׂרָאֵל
וּמָחֳלָן לְשִׁבְטֵי יְשֻׁרוּן בְּכָל דּוֹר וָדוֹר
וּמִבַּלְעָדֶיךָ אֵין לָנוּ מֶלֶךְ מוֹחֵל וְסוֹלֵחַ אֶלָּא אָתָּה.

אֱלֹהַי
עַד שֶׁלֹּא נוֹצַרְתִּי אֵינִי כְדַאי
וְעַכְשָׁיו שֶׁנּוֹצַרְתִּי, כְּאִלּוּ לֹא נוֹצַרְתִּי
עָפָר אֲנִי בְּחַיַּי, קַל וָחֹמֶר בְּמִיתָתִי.
הֲרֵי אֲנִי לְפָנֶיךָ כִּכְלִי מָלֵא בּוּשָׁה וּכְלִמָּה.
יְהִי רָצוֹן מִלְּפָנֶיךָ, יהוה אֱלֹהַי וֵאלֹהֵי אֲבוֹתַי שֶׁלֹּא אֶחֱטָא עוֹד.
וּמַה שֶּׁחָטָאתִי לְפָנֶיךָ, מְחֹק בְּרַחֲמֶיךָ הָרַבִּים
אֲבָל לֹא עַל יְדֵי יִסּוּרִים וָחֳלָיִים רָעִים.

אֱלֹהַי My God, *Berakhot 17a*
guard my tongue from evil
and my lips from deceitful speech.
To those who curse me, let my soul be silent;
may my soul be to all like the dust.
Open my heart to Your Torah
and let my soul pursue Your commandments.
As for all who plan evil against me,
swiftly thwart their counsel and frustrate their plans.
Act for the sake of Your name;
act for the sake of Your right hand;
act for the sake of Your holiness;
act for the sake of Your Torah.
That Your beloved ones may be delivered, *Ps. 60*
save with Your right hand and answer me.
May the words of my mouth and the meditation of my heart *Ps. 19*
find favor before You, LORD, my Rock and Redeemer.

Bow, take three steps back, then bow, first left, then right, then center, while saying:

May He who makes peace in His high places,
make peace for us and all Israel – and say: Amen.

יְהִי רָצוֹן May it be Your will, LORD our God and God of our ancestors,
that the Temple be rebuilt speedily in our days,
and grant us a share in Your Torah.
And there we will serve You with reverence,
as in the days of old and as in former years.
Then the offering of Judah and Jerusalem *Mal. 3*
will be pleasing to the LORD as in the days of old and as in former years.

אֱלֹהַי ברכות יז.

נְצֹר לְשׁוֹנִי מֵרָע וּשְׂפָתַי מִדַּבֵּר מִרְמָה

וְלִמְקַלְלַי נַפְשִׁי תִדֹּם, וְנַפְשִׁי כֶּעָפָר לַכֹּל תִּהְיֶה.

פְּתַח לִבִּי בְּתוֹרָתֶךָ, וּבְמִצְוֹתֶיךָ תִּרְדֹּף נַפְשִׁי.

וְכָל הַחוֹשְׁבִים עָלַי רָעָה

מְהֵרָה הָפֵר עֲצָתָם וְקַלְקֵל מַחֲשַׁבְתָּם.

עֲשֵׂה לְמַעַן שְׁמֶךָ

עֲשֵׂה לְמַעַן יְמִינֶךָ

עֲשֵׂה לְמַעַן קְדֻשָּׁתֶךָ

עֲשֵׂה לְמַעַן תּוֹרָתֶךָ.

לְמַעַן יֵחָלְצוּן יְדִידֶיךָ, הוֹשִׁיעָה יְמִינְךָ וַעֲנֵנִי: תהלים ס

יִהְיוּ לְרָצוֹן אִמְרֵי פִי וְהֶגְיוֹן לִבִּי לְפָנֶיךָ, יהוה צוּרִי וְגֹאֲלִי: תהלים יט

Bow, take three steps back, then bow, first left, then right, then center, while saying:

עֹשֶׂה הַשָּׁלוֹם בִּמְרוֹמָיו

הוּא יַעֲשֶׂה שָׁלוֹם עָלֵינוּ וְעַל כָּל יִשְׂרָאֵל וְאִמְרוּ אָמֵן.

יְהִי רָצוֹן מִלְּפָנֶיךָ יהוה אֱלֹהֵינוּ וֵאלֹהֵי אֲבוֹתֵינוּ

שֶׁיִּבָּנֶה בֵּית הַמִּקְדָּשׁ בִּמְהֵרָה בְיָמֵינוּ, וְתֵן חֶלְקֵנוּ בְּתוֹרָתֶךָ

וְשָׁם נַעֲבָדְךָ בְּיִרְאָה כִּימֵי עוֹלָם וּכְשָׁנִים קַדְמֹנִיּוֹת.

וְעָרְבָה לַיהוה מִנְחַת יְהוּדָה וִירוּשָׁלָםִ כִּימֵי עוֹלָם וּכְשָׁנִים קַדְמֹנִיּוֹת: מלאכי ג

LEADER'S REPETITION FOR MUSAF

The Ark is opened.
The Leader takes three steps forward and at the points indicated by ▾, bends the knees at the first word, bows at the second, and stands straight before saying God's name.

When I proclaim the Lord's name, give glory to our God. Deut. 32
O Lord, open my lips, so that my mouth may declare Your praise. Ps. 51

PATRIARCHS

▾בָּרוּךְ▾ Blessed are You, Lord our God and God of our fathers,
God of Abraham, God of Isaac and God of Jacob;
the great, mighty and awesome God, God Most High,
who bestows acts of loving-kindness and creates all,
who remembers the loving-kindness of the fathers
and will bring a Redeemer to their children's children
for the sake of His name, in love.

Before the cycle (kerova) of piyutim for Musaf, the Leader says only the standard opening "Drawing from the counsel..." as a reshut (see page 614), as he has already said a reshut before the silent Amida (page 770).

מִסּוֹד Drawing from the counsel of wise and knowing men,
from the teachings born of insight among those who understand,
I open my mouth now in prayer and pleading,
to implore and to plead before the King
who pardons and forgives iniquities.

The Ark is closed.

אֱלֹהֵי אַבְרָהָם, אֱלֹהֵי יִצְחָק, וֵאלֹהֵי יַעֲקֹב *God of Abraham, God of Isaac and God of Jacob.* God is always and everywhere the same God, the One God, but for each of us there is a way of serving Him that is unique to us, for we are each in God's image, but we are all different. The three patriarchs each walked with God in his own way. The radiance of faith is the result of the Oneness of God refracted through the diversity of humankind.

מִסּוֹד *Drawing from the counsel.* A brief prayer of the form known as *reshut*: a request, by the leader of prayer, for permission to pray on behalf of the congregation. It is based on the fact that the Leader's Repetition contains not only the words of statutory prayer but also additional *piyutim*, poetic insertions and elaborations. Since there were those who had reservations about these additions, the leader emphasizes that they are not merely his own thoughts. They are carefully based on and reflect the traditions of the sages.

חזרת הש״ץ של מוסף

The ארון קודש is opened.

The שליח ציבור takes three steps forward and at the points indicated by ▾, bends the knees at the first word, bows at the second, and stands straight before saying God's name.

כִּי שֵׁם יהוה אֶקְרָא, הָבוּ גֹדֶל לֵאלֹהֵינוּ: דברים לב

אֲדֹנָי, שְׂפָתַי תִּפְתָּח, וּפִי יַגִּיד תְּהִלָּתֶךָ: תהלים נא

אבות

▾בָּרוּךְ אַתָּה יהוה, אֱלֹהֵינוּ וֵאלֹהֵי אֲבוֹתֵינוּ
אֱלֹהֵי אַבְרָהָם, אֱלֹהֵי יִצְחָק, וֵאלֹהֵי יַעֲקֹב
הָאֵל הַגָּדוֹל הַגִּבּוֹר וְהַנּוֹרָא, אֵל עֶלְיוֹן
גּוֹמֵל חֲסָדִים טוֹבִים, וְקוֹנֵה הַכֹּל
וְזוֹכֵר חַסְדֵי אָבוֹת
וּמֵבִיא גוֹאֵל לִבְנֵי בְנֵיהֶם לְמַעַן שְׁמוֹ בְּאַהֲבָה.

Before the cycle (קרובה) of piyutim for מוסף, the שליח ציבור says only the standard opening "...מִסּוֹד חֲכָמִים וּנְבוֹנִים" as a רשות (see page 614), as he has already said a רשות before the silent עמידה (page 771).

מִסּוֹד חֲכָמִים וּנְבוֹנִים / וּמִלֶּמֶד דַּעַת מְבִינִים
אֶפְתְּחָה פִּי בִּתְפִלָּה וּבְתַחֲנוּנִים
לְחַלּוֹת וּלְחַנֵּן פְּנֵי מֶלֶךְ מוֹחֵל וְסוֹלֵחַ לַעֲוֹנִים.

The ארון קודש is closed.

ḤAZARAT HASHATZ – LEADER'S REPETITION

For commentary on the significance of the Leader's Repetition see page 611.

בָּרוּךְ *Blessed.* It is not we who bless God but God who blesses us. The meaning of "blessed" here is: We acknowledge You as the source of all our blessings.

אֱלֹהֵינוּ וֵאלֹהֵי אֲבוֹתֵינוּ *Our God and God of our fathers.* The order here is derived from the song the Israelites sang at the Sea of Reeds: "This is my God and I will glorify Him, my father's God and I will exalt Him" (Ex. 15:2). Our parents teach us how to worship God, but we must make that faith our own if we are fully to honor and renew their heritage. Faith is more than deference to the past. It must live in the present, in us, if it is to change us and through us change the world.

Most of the piyutim for Musaf Yom Kippur were composed by Rabbi Elazar HaKalir. The piyutim that comprise the first section of the kerova – the Magen, Meḥayeh, and Meshalesh – are united by the theme of the holiness of the Day of Atonement, with each displaying one of the day's names in its acrostic. As part of the Leader's Repetition, they should ideally be said by the Leader alone. However, the prevailing custom is for the congregation to participate, and some of the piyutim are said together, with the Leader raising his voice only toward the end.

All:

שׁוֹשַׁן עֵמֶק The lily of the valley was cautioned
to observe [Yom Kippur] the Sabbath of utter rest.
It was ordained that young and old alike
shall fast equally on this day.

When the foundations of her Temple were destroyed,
she placed her faith in the prayers her ancestors had offered –
forefathers upon whose merit she depends,
pairs of patriarchs and matriarchs upon whom she relies.

Israel relies upon the good deeds of her rocks, her ancestors,
innocent forefathers on whose behalf the world was created.
Bring healing to those imprisoned in exile,
darken the world of those who oppress us.

---

of Yom Kippur in Leviticus 16:31); *Yom Kippurim*, "the Day of Atonements" (Lev. 23:27, 28; 25:9) and *Tzom HeAsor*, "the Fast of the Tenth" of Tishrei (*Sofrim* 19:4). Each also makes special reference to the patriarch associated with the specific blessing: the first is about Abraham; the second, Isaac; and the third, Jacob. The fourth poem begins by summarizing the themes of the previous three and then develops its own large-scale theme – the compositional technique later used by Beethoven in the fourth movement of the Ninth Symphony.

בָּם תָּקְעָה יְתֵדוֹתֶיהָ *Forefathers upon whose merit she depends.* Since there is no Temple, no High Priest and no sacrifice, we must rely on the merits of the fathers and mothers of our people, the pairs (excluding Rachel) buried in the Cave of Machpelah.

Most of the piyutim for מוסף ליום כיפור *were composed by Rabbi Elazar HaKalir. The piyutim that comprise the first section of the* קרובה *– the* מגן, מחיה, *and* משלש *– are united by the theme of the holiness of the Day of Atonement, with each displaying one of the day's names in its acrostic.*

As part of the חזרת הש״ץ, *they should ideally be said by the* שליח ציבור *alone. However, the prevailing custom is for the* קהל *to participate, and some of the piyutim are said together, with the* שליח ציבור *raising his voice only toward the end.*

All:

שׁוֹשַׁן עֵמֶק אֲיֻמָּה / שַׁבַּת שַׁבָּתוֹן לְקַיְּמָה
שֹׁרֶשׁ וְעָנָף סִימָה / שָׁוִים יַחַד לְצִיְּמָה.

בְּעֵת מַטּוּ יְסוֹדוֹתֶיהָ / בְּטְחָה בְּחִין מוֹסְדוֹתֶיהָ
בָּם תָּקְעָה יִתֵדוֹתֶיהָ / בְּכֶפֶל לְהַשְׁעִין יְדוֹתֶיהָ.

תְּמְכָה פֹּעַל צוּרִים / תְּמַת הֵמָּה הַיּוֹצְרִים
תְּרוּפָה תֵּת לַעֲצוּרִים / תֵּבֵל לְהַאֲפִיל לְצָרִים.

שׁוֹשַׁן עֵמֶק *The Israel, lily of the valley.* A phrase from the Song of Songs (2:1) describing the congregation of Israel. This is the first of a highly structured series of four poems by the master of liturgical poetry, Rabbi Elazar HaKalir. HaKalir was one of the greatest virtuosi of *piyut*, and his compositions are marked by extreme dexterity and density, mastery of the rabbinic literature, and complex webs of association and allusion. Little is known for certain about when and where he lived. Some have placed him as early as the Mishnaic era in the second century, others as late as the tenth, but the likelihood is that he lived in the late sixth or early seventh century, and in Israel. He was immensely prolific, and many of his poems remained unpublished until relatively recently. His vocabulary was enormous; he had a fondness for rare words, as well as words he coined himself, and to understand the full meaning of a Kalir poem needs vast scholarship, suggesting that the communities for which he was writing were deeply literate.

Each of the first three poems uses an acrostic device – the first letter of each of the four phrases in each verse – to spell out the three names of the festival: *Shabbat Shabbaton*, "the Sabbath of utter rest" (the description given

The offspring of the four matriarchs,
the roar of the counted people, Israel,
the cries of their four prayers –
please heed and clear them in their judgment.

Behold [Abraham] who walked with You in innocence,
whose covenant is sealed in the flesh of his offspring;
in his merit, cleanse the stains [of our sins],
for we have no Urim VeTumim.

In place of the bullocks once offered,
please accept the prayers we offer You;
Your people who sound the shofar at the new moon,
on Yom Kippur grant them atonement for their troubles.

Please calm Your wrath and indignation;
take pity on the remnant of Your nation.
May Your pleasantness rest upon us,
that we might live, for with You is the source of life.

Radiant One, forgiveness lies with You;
may He who is ready to forgive, hasten to forgive us.
▸ May the words that rise from our lips succeed;
hear our groan and forgive.

All:

Our lips recall our slumbering ancestors;
they shall sing before You as the psalms were once recited.
▸ Generation after generation, the old and young,
rely on the shield of [Abraham] the patriarch.

The congregation then the Leader:

זָכְרֵנוּ לְחַיִּים Remember us for life,
O King who desires life,
and write us in the book of life –
for Your sake, O God of life.

שְׁתִילֵי גְבָעוֹת אַרְבַּע / שַׁאַג סֵפֶר הַמְרֻבָּע
שֶׁוַע פְּגִיעוֹת אַרְבַּע / שְׁעֵה צִדְקָם לִתְבַּע.

בִּיטָה בְּמִתְהַלֵּךְ תָּמִים / בְּמוּסַר לְחֻמּוֹ חֲתוּמִים
בְּצִדְקוֹ תָּדִיחַ כְּתָמִים / בְּאֶפֶס אוּרִים וְתֻמִּים.

תְּמוּר תַּשְׁלוּמֵי פָר / תֵּבֶן הֶגֶא הַמְסֻפָּר
תּוֹקְעֵי בַחֹדֶשׁ שׁוֹפָר / תַּלְאוּבָם בְּכִפּוּר יְכֻפָּר.

וְשַׁכֵּךְ חֲמַת זַעְמָךְ / וְתָחֹן שְׂרִידֵי עַמָּךְ
וְעָלֵינוּ יְהִי נֹעֲמָךְ / וְנִחְיֶה מִמְּקוֹר עִמָּךְ.

נָאוֹר עִמְּךָ הַסְּלִיחָה / נָכוֹן מַהֵר לְסָלְחָה
‹ נִיב שְׂפָתֵינוּ הַצְלִיחָה / נַאַק שְׁמָעָה וּסְלָחָה.

All:

שְׂפָתֵינוּ מְדוֹבְבוֹת יְשֵׁנִים / יְנַצְּחוּךָ כְּבַעַל שׁוֹשַׁנִּים
‹ חֲדָשִׁים גַּם יְשָׁנִים / בְּמָגִנַּת אָב נִשְׁעָנִים.

The קהל *then the* שליח ציבור*:*

זָכְרֵנוּ לְחַיִּים, מֶלֶךְ חָפֵץ בַּחַיִּים
וְכָתְבֵנוּ בְּסֵפֶר הַחַיִּים, לְמַעַנְךָ אֱלֹהִים חַיִּים.

שְׁתִילֵי גְבָעוֹת אַרְבַּע *The offspring of the four matriarchs.* The four services of today – Shaḥarit, Musaf, Minḥa and Ne'ila – correspond to the four matriarchs: Sarah, Rebecca, Rachel and Leah.

בְּמִתְהַלֵּךְ תָּמִים *Who walked with You in innocence.* God commanded Abraham, "Walk before Me and be perfect" (Gen. 17:1). The poet invokes Abraham in this poem set within the first blessing of the Amida which ends with "Shield of Abraham."

The Leader continues:

King, Helper, Savior, Shield:
▾Blessed are You, Lord,
Shield of Abraham.

DIVINE MIGHT

אַתָּה גִּבּוֹר You are eternally mighty, Lord.
You give life to the dead and have great power to save.
In Israel: He causes the dew to fall.
He sustains the living with loving-kindness,
and with great compassion revives the dead.
He supports the fallen, heals the sick, sets captives free,
and keeps His faith with those who sleep in the dust.
Who is like You, Master of might,
and to whom can You be compared,
O King who brings death and gives life,
and makes salvation grow?

The Meḥayeh – the second piyut of the kerova.

All:

יוֹם מִיָּמִים The most eminent of days,
the distinguished Day of Atonement –
to those who observe it knowingly, may You show pity and compassion
Silence those who would ensnare us, sending them into the mouth of hell.
To confound the accusing angel they adopt the strategy
of bringing forward the confession in their prayers.
May our ancestors rise from the earth
to plead on our behalf from the mountaintops.

יוֹם כִּפּוּר הַמְיֻחָס *The distinguished Day of Atonement.* On the verse, "All the days ordained for me were written in Your book, and one of them was His" (Ps. 139:16), the sages said: "This is the Day of Atonement" (Rashi ad loc., based on *Tanna DeVei Eliyahu* 1), meaning this is the day of the year supremely devoted to God.

The שליח ציבור *continues:*

מֶלֶךְ עוֹזֵר וּמוֹשִׁיעַ וּמָגֵן.
ּבָּרוּךְ אַתָּה יהוה, מָגֵן אַבְרָהָם.

גבורות

אַתָּה גִּבּוֹר לְעוֹלָם, אֲדֹנָי
מְחַיֵּה מֵתִים אַתָּה, רַב לְהוֹשִׁיעַ
בארץ ישראל: מוֹרִיד הַטָּל
מְכַלְכֵּל חַיִּים בְּחֶסֶד, מְחַיֵּה מֵתִים בְּרַחֲמִים רַבִּים
סוֹמֵךְ נוֹפְלִים, וְרוֹפֵא חוֹלִים, וּמַתִּיר אֲסוּרִים
וּמְקַיֵּם אֱמוּנָתוֹ לִישֵׁנֵי עָפָר.
מִי כָמְוֹךָ, בַּעַל גְּבוּרוֹת, וּמִי דּוֹמֶה לָּךְ
מֶלֶךְ, מֵמִית וּמְחַיֶּה וּמַצְמִיחַ יְשׁוּעָה.

The מחיה *– the second piyut of the* קרובה.

All:

יוֹם מִיָּמִים הוּחָס / יוֹם כִּפּוּר הַמְיֻחָס
יוֹדְעָיו חֲמוֹל וְחַס / יוֹקְשָׁיו לְפוֹעֶרֶת הַס.

וּבוֹ בְּתַחְבּוּלוֹת יוּעָצוּ / וִדּוּי בְּתַחַן יָאִיצוּ
וְשׁוֹכְנֵי עָפָר יָקִיצוּ / וּמֵרֹאשׁ הָרִים יָלִיצוּ.

יוֹם מִיָּמִים הוּחָס *The most eminent of days.* The second poem by HaKalir, its acrostic spells out *Yom Kippurim,* the biblical name for the Day of Atonement. Literally it means "Day of Atonements" in the plural, a reference to the several atonements made by the High Priest that day: for himself and his family, his tribe, and the entire people. It also signifies the dual character of the day with its atonement for individuals as individuals as well as for the people as a whole.

The deeds of [Abraham] the one who bound and [Isaac] the bound one
have since been entrusted to Your people,
concealed for eternal remembrance as an example,
to scare off the Adversary as one shoos an animal.

Like the promise of the ram entangled in the brush,
as ransom for Isaac, safeguarded for Your valorous nation,
thus please increase the strength
of those who bow before You day and night.

May the Dread [of Isaac] cause our slanderers to tremble
until their mouths are stopped up and sealed.
May [Isaac's] offspring be protected as they rely on You,
and be rescued from the idle gossip of their enemies.

If we are devoid of good deeds
and without offerings to place on the altar,
recall Your scorned, downtrodden people,
and remove Your anger from their offspring.

Exalted One, Your works are true;
behold the people who worship You.
They approach You so faithfully –
O Compassionate One, remember Your servants.

When sin is sought let it not be found,
cast it into the depths of the sea.
Child of Your delight, answer his plea;
the uprightness of his advocate shall bring him pardon.

From the flash of the sharpened sword
rescue those who sing Your praise at length.
▸ Fulfill their requests of their pleas,
O compassionate and gracious King.

All:

The price for redemption of the soul
please pay, that they sink not into the mire.
▸ Those who abase and afflict themselves as they pray to You,
revive them with Your life-giving dew.

God to promise that should the children of Israel sin in the future, He would remember the binding to their merit and forgive them because of it (*Bereshit Raba* 56:10).

מִפְּעָלוֹת עוֹקֵד וְעָקוּד / מֵאָז בְּיָדָם פָּקוּד
מוֹפֵת הַכָּמוּס לְפִקּוּד / מוּקָשׁ לְהַבְעִית בְּסִקּוּד.

כְּהַבְטָחַת סְבִיכַת אַיִל / כָּפְרוֹ הַנָּצוּר לְחַיִל
כֵּן תַּעֲצִים חַיִל / כּוֹרְעֶיךָ בְּעֶצֶם וָלַיִל.

פַּחְדּוֹ יָחִיל שׁוֹטְמִים / פִּיּוֹתָם הֱיוֹת אֲטוּמִים
פְּרָחָיו בְּמִשְׁעֲנוֹתָם חֲטוּמִים / פַּלְּטֵם מֵרֶכֶל פְּטוּמִים.

וְאִם אֵין מַעֲשִׂים / וְזֶבַח מִבְּלִי מֵשִׂים
וְזָכְרָה לִנְבְזִים וּמְאוּסִים / וּמִגִּזְעָם הָפֵר כְּעָסִים.

רָם קֹשֶׁט מַעֲבָדֶיךָ / רָאֵה תִרְאֶה עוֹבְדֶיךָ
רֵעִים בָּאֵי עָדֶיךָ / רַחוּם זְכֹר לַעֲבָדֶיךָ.

יְבֻקַּשׁ עָוֹן וְאֵינֶנּוּ / יָמֶּה בִּמְצוּלוֹת תְּנֶנּוּ
יֶלֶד בְּשַׁעֲשׁוּעָיו תַּעֲנֶנּוּ / יֹשֶׁר מֵלִיץ יְחָנֶנּוּ.

מִבְּרַק חֶרֶב הַשָּׁנוּן / מַלֵּט מַאֲרִיכֵי רִנּוּן
◂ מַלֵּא מִשְׁאֲלוֹתָם בְּתַחֲנוּן / מֶלֶךְ רַחוּם וְחַנּוּן.

All

כֹּפֶר פִּדְיוֹן נֶפֶשׁ / פְּדֵה מִטְּבִיעַת רֶפֶשׁ
◂ מְיַחֲלֶיךָ בְּעִנּוּי וְכֹפֶשׁ / הַחֲיֵם בְּטַלְלֵי נֹפֶשׁ.

עוֹקֵד וְעָקוּד [*Abraham*] *the one who bound and* [*Isaac*] *the bound one.* At the binding, Isaac had his life restored to him at the last moment. Hence the connection with the second paragraph of the Amida which speaks about God restoring the dead to life.

כְּהַבְטָחַת סְבִיכַת אַיִל *Like the promise of the ram entangled in the brush.* According to the sages, as the trial of the binding of Isaac came to an end, Abraham asked

The Tokheḥa (rebuke) for Musaf is thematically and stylistically very similar to the one said in Shaḥarit (see page 624). Traditionally, the verse "As long as man's spirit" was said by the congregation after each stanza; nowadays, many congregations say it only at the beginning. Others omit the piyut altogether, saying only the refrain.

The Leader, then the congregation:

עוֹד בּוֹ As long as man's spirit is yet in him,
[God] will hope for the repentance of those formed from His earth;
to bring him life, to bring goodness to his future.

All:

אֱנוֹשׁ אֵיךְ יִצְדַּק How can a person justify himself before his Creator
when all is revealed before Him, secrets and mysteries?
Yet his sin may be atoned and his wound healed
if he repents before his candle is extinguished.

Even darkness can hide nothing from Him,
though man may hide his face, God still sees him.
His blemishes and wickedness shall testify against him,
yet if he confess them in his lifetime this shall be to his advantage.

The very hosts of heaven are not pure in His eyes;
all the more so man, who through guilt and iniquity has made himself despised.
So why does the evildoer not fathom in his thoughts
that the hour of his calamity impends?

No profit shall stem from the treasures man has amassed nor all his gold;
they shall not ransom him on the day of God's wrath.
If he pursues charity and kindness throughout his life,
then his righteousness shall precede him and the glory of his Creator shall follow him.

---

stage. Guilt-and-righteousness cultures, of which Judaism is the supreme example, do not attach primary significance to how we appear to others, for the only relevant observer is God Himself, and God knows us from the inside: "The LORD does not look at the things man looks at. Man looks at

The תוכחה *(rebuke) for* מוסף *is thematically and stylistically very similar to the one said in* שחרית *(see page 625). Traditionally, the verse "*עוֹד בּוֹ נִשְׁמָתוֹ*" was said by the congregation after each stanza; nowadays, many congregations say it only at the beginning. Others omit the piyut altogether, saying only the refrain.*

The שליח ציבור*, then the* קהל*:*

עוֹד בּוֹ נִשְׁמָתוֹ / יְקַו תְּשׁוּבַת יְצִיר אַדְמָתוֹ
לְהַחֲיוֹתוֹ, לְהֵיטִיב אַחֲרִיתוֹ.

All:

אֱנוֹשׁ אֵיךְ יִצְדַּק פְּנֵי יוֹצְרוֹ / וְהַכֹּל גָּלוּי לוֹ, תַּעֲלוּמוֹ וְסִתְרוֹ
בְּזֹאת יְכֻפַּר עֲוֹנוֹ וְיִגְהֶה מְזוֹרוֹ / אִם יָשׁוּב טֶרֶם יִכְבֶּה נֵרוֹ.

גַּם חֹשֶׁךְ לֹא יַחְשִׁיךְ מִמֶּנּוּ / אִם יַסְתִּיר פָּנִים, הוּא יְשׁוּרֶנּוּ
דָּפְיוֹ וְרִשְׁעוֹ עַל פָּנָיו יַעֲנֶנּוּ / יִתְרוֹן לוֹ, אִם בְּחַיָּיו יוֹדֶנּוּ.

הֵן שָׁמַיִם לֹא זַכּוּ בְּעֵינָיו / וְאַף כִּי נִתְעָב בַּאֲשָׁמָיו וּבַעֲוֹנָיו
וָזֵד לָמָּה לֹא יָבִין בְּרַעְיוֹנָיו / הֲלֹא יוֹמוֹ וְאֵידוֹ נֹכַח פָּנָיו.

זְהָבוֹ וּסְגֻלַּת עָשְׁרוֹ לֹא יוֹעִילֶנּוּ /
לָתֵת כָּפְרוֹ בְּיוֹם עֶבְרָה, לְהוֹעִילֶנּוּ
חֶסֶד וּצְדָקָה, אִם רוֹדֵף בְּעוֹדֶנּוּ /
לְפָנָיו יַהֲלֹךְ וּכְבוֹד בּוֹרְאוֹ יַאַסְפֶנּוּ.

אֱנוֹשׁ אֵיךְ יִצְדַּק *How can a person justify himself.* Not said in all rites, this is not part of HaKalir's extended poem; its author is unknown. It testifies to one of the fundamental features of Jewish ethics, namely that we stand always in the presence of God who knows us better than we know ourselves, to whom it is impossible to dissimulate, and from whom it is impossible to hide. Interestingly, the Hebrew language has no word that precisely corresponds to the English "person," since the word derives from the Latin *persona*, which originally meant the mask an actor wore on the stage. Shame-and-honor cultures see the moral life as a drama in which we each play our part on the

It is good for a man to bear the Torah's yoke,
in love, awe, and purity to fulfill all its commandments.
For it shall guide him on a straight, paved path through his life,
safeguard him in his grave and assist him in the afterlife.

O Almighty, we are before You like clay in the potter's hands;
You will us to live, and not to die and meet our end.
▸ Straighten our hearts in awe of You that we might declare Your Oneness and dedicate ourselves to You.
Sustain us, grant us life, and we shall forever thank You and sing Your praise.

The Leader continues:

מִי כָמְוֹךָ Who is like You, compassionate Father,
who remembers His creatures in compassion, for life?

Faithful are You to revive the dead.
Blessed are You, LORD, who revives the dead.

The Meshalesh, completing the first group of piyutim.

All:

צְפֵה בְּבַת תְּמוּתָה Behold Your mortal children,
observing this Fast of the Tenth.
Should Your flock be condemned to die for their sins,
justify them that they might be saved from eternal bondage.

When the Accuser comes forth with his list,
laying bare hidden thoughts and perversions,
do not grant him any authority to curse
or rebuke the offspring of Jacob.

---

forgiveness, the search for self-respect would lead us endlessly to rationalize or otherwise make excuses for our moral failures.

צְפֵה בְּבַת תְּמוּתָה *Behold Your mortal children.* The third of HaKalir's poems has an acrostic that spells out *Tzom HeAsor,* "the Fast of the Tenth [of Tishrei]." Its central theme is Jacob, traditionally associated with the third paragraph of the Amida.

טוֹב לַגֶּבֶר לִשָּׂא עֹל תּוֹרָה /
לְקַיֵּם חֻקֶּיהָ בְּאַהֲבָה וּבְיִרְאָה וּבְטָהֳרָה
יְמֵי חַיָּיו תַּנְחֵנוּ מְסִלָּה יְשָׁרָה /
תִּנְצְרֵנוּ בִּקְבוּרָה וְלִתְחִי תְּשִׂיחֵנוּ לְעֶזְרָה.

שַׁדַּי הִנְנוּ בְּיָדְךָ כְּיוֹצֵר חֹמֶר /
רְצוֹנְךָ לְהַחֲיוֹת וְלֹא לְהָמִית וּלְגַמֵּר
◂ תְּיַשֵּׁר לְבָבֵנוּ בְּיִרְאָתְךָ לְהַחֲטִיב וּלְהַאֲמֵר /
וְקַיְּמֵנוּ לְחַיִּים, וְנוֹדְךָ לְעוֹלָם וּנְזַמֵּר.

The שליח ציבור *continues:*

מִי כָמוֹךָ אַב הָרַחֲמִים
זוֹכֵר יְצוּרָיו לְחַיִּים בְּרַחֲמִים.

וְנֶאֱמָן אַתָּה לְהַחֲיוֹת מֵתִים.
בָּרוּךְ אַתָּה יהוה, מְחַיֵּה הַמֵּתִים.

The משלש*, completing the first group of piyutim.*

All:

צְפֵה בְּבַת תְּמוּתָה / צוֹם הֶעָשׂוֹר עֲמוּתָה
צֹאן בְּהֵעָנְשָׁהּ מִיתָה / צְדָקָה מִמֶּכֶר צְמִיתָה.

וּבְבֹא שׂוֹטֵן לִנְקֹב / וְלַחֲשֹׂף שַׂרְעַף עָקֹב
וּבַל יֵרָשֶׁה לְקֹב / וֶהֱכַח תּוֹלְדוֹת יַעֲקֹב.

---

the outward appearance, but the Lord looks at the heart" (1 Samuel 16:7). Hence, nothing less than total honesty will do. Indeed it is the forgiveness of God that makes honesty with ourselves possible, for were it not for that

When You established the site of Your eternal home,
from then You engraved the image of Jacob upon Your throne.
May his offspring, whose name contains Yours,
be saved for the sake of Your name.

Recall Jacob, who dwelled innocently in Your tents,
who struggled with the angel of fiery coals.
Save his hordes of descendants from sudden terror,
bandage their wounds with forgiveness as they gather before You.

See how they afflict their souls;
their iniquity please do not behold.
Those who cry out before You candidly,
answer them with truth and acceptance.

Forgive those who turn away from transgression;
may Your forgiveness outbalance evil.
Heed the repentance they offer You in their well-ordered pleas,
grant them the redemption and salvation they hope for.

If they transgress Your covenant as did Adam,
and should their hands falter or fail them,
then may You who are man's Creator,
grant forgiveness and give them strength.

Behold their hunger and thirst,
look not upon their evil actions.
▸ Do not scorn their words and strong emotions
as they sing, "Please forgive the iniquity of this nation."

The congregation says the next two verses aloud, followed by the Leader:

The Lord shall reign for ever. *Ps. 146*
He is your God, Zion, from generation to generation,
Halleluya!

You are the Holy One, enthroned on the praises of Israel. *Ps. 22*
God, please.

וְאִם הֵמָּה כְּאָדָם *If they transgress… as did Adam.* To err is human, to forgive, divine. You, God, made the first man, and indeed all human beings, knowing that we would sin. Therefore, in Your mercy, pardon us.

מָכוֹן לְשִׁבְתְּךָ בְּשׁוּמֶךָ / מֵאָז חֲקַקְתּוֹ בְּרִשּׁוּמֶךָ
מוֹלְדוֹתָיו הַכְּלוּלִים בִּשְׁמֶךָ / מַלְטֵם לְמַעַן שְׁמֶךָ.

הַזָּכֵר יְשִׁיבַת אֹהֶל / הַמֵּאָבֵק לְשַׂר גַּחַל
הַצִּילָה שְׁאוֹנוֹ מִבֶּהָל / הַצָּגִים לְהַרְטוֹת מַחַל.

עִנּוּי נֶפֶשׁ שׁוּר / עָוֹן בְּלִי תָשׁוּר
עוֹרְכֵי שֶׁוַע בְּיִשּׁוּר / עֲנֵם בֶּאֱמֶת וְאִשּׁוּר.

סְלַח לְשָׁבֵי פֶשַׁע / סְלִיחָה תַּכְרִיעַ רֶשַׁע
סִדּוּר תְּשׁוּבָה תֵּשַׁע / שֶׁבֶר פְּדוּת לְיֶשַׁע.

וְאִם הֶמָּה כְּאָדָם / וּמוֹעֲדָה וּמַטָּה יָדָם
וְאַתָּה נוֹצֵר הָאָדָם / וְתָרוֹן תְּנָה לְעוֹדְדָם.

רְעָבִם וּצְמָאָם חֲזֵה / רָעָתָם בְּלִי תֶחֱזֶה
► רֶגֶשׁ רַחֲשָׁם מִלְּבְזֶה / רוֹנְנִים, סְלַח נָא לַעֲוֹן הָעָם הַזֶּה.

The קהל *says the next two verses aloud, followed by the* שליח ציבור*:*

יִמְלֹךְ יהוה לְעוֹלָם תהלים קמו
אֱלֹהַיִךְ צִיּוֹן לְדֹר וָדֹר
הַלְלוּיָהּ:

וְאַתָּה קָדוֹשׁ יוֹשֵׁב תְּהִלּוֹת יִשְׂרָאֵל: תהלים כב
אֵל נָא.

חֲקַקְתּוֹ בְּרִשּׁוּמֶךָ *You engraved the image.* According to tradition, the image of Jacob is engraved on God's throne of glory (*Bereshit Raba* 68:12).

הַמֵּאָבֵק *Who struggled.* A reference to Jacob's wrestling with an angel, alone at night until daybreak (Gen. 32).

These three verses are said by the congregation as alternating refrains after the verses of the following piyut. Some congregations say only these, omitting the piyut altogether.

The Leader says each verse, followed by the congregation:

נֵחָשֵׁב May we be considered like [the high priest]
standing at the Temple entrance,
may our prayers push aside [the Accuser,] that crooked serpent,
and may we sanctify You on this Sabbath of utter rest, / O Holy One.

On this day as You open the books of life and death,
grant grace to Your nation, those who glorify Your name,
and may we sanctify You on this Day of Atonement, / O Holy One.

Bind the Accuser in chains,
and herald new hope to the captives of my nation,
and may we sanctify You on this Fast of the Tenth, / O Holy One.

In most congregations, the Leader says the first two stichs, the congregation says the third, and the alternating refrains are said by all.

אֶשָּׂא דֵעִי I shall lift my thoughts to my glorious past
and rely upon [Abraham] who came from afar,
that the merits of his deeds might push my oppressor aside.
I shall pray in accordance with the laws of the Torah, / that God not
stray from His permanent abode, / to inscribe me for life.
May the Accuser be swiftly erased, / that my oppressor might not
ridicule me, / and may my mouth fill with laughter.

May we be considered like [the high priest] standing at the Temple entrance, / may our prayers push aside [the Accuser,] that crooked serpent, and may we sanctify You on this Sabbath of utter rest, / O Holy One.

Those who offer their abundant cries, / may the prayers they prepare be
pleasing to You, / and let them come close to God's presence.
May my plea then draw near, / let my sins not lie in wait for me
and do not allow them to attack me.
Should my enemies plot to burn / and to destroy God's congregation,
I shall rely upon the One who justifies me and is always close.

On this day as You open the books of life and death, / grant grace to Your nation, those who glorify Your name, / and may we sanctify You on this Day of Atonement, / O Holy One.

These three verses are said by the קהל *as alternating refrains after the verses of the following piyut. Some congregations say only these, omitting the piyut altogether.*

The שליח ציבור *says each verse, followed by the* קהל:

נֵחָשֵׁב כְּצָג בְּאֵיתוֹן / דְּחוּת בִּפְלְלֵי עֲקַלָּתוֹן
וְנַקְדִּישְׁךָ בְּשַׁבַּת שַׁבָּתוֹן / קָדוֹשׁ.

הַיּוֹם בְּפָתְחֲךָ סְפָרִים / חֹן אֹם שִׁמְךָ מְפָאֲרִים
וְנַקְדִּישְׁךָ בְּיוֹם הַכִּפּוּרִים / קָדוֹשׁ.

מַשְׂטִין בְּכֶבֶל אֱסֹר / וְתִקְוַת אֲסִירֵי בְּשֹׂר
וְנַקְדִּישְׁךָ בְּצוֹם הֶעָשׂוֹר / קָדוֹשׁ.

In most congregations, the שליח ציבור *says the first two stichs, the* קהל *says the third, and the alternating refrains are said by all.*

אֶשָּׂא דֵעִי לְמֵרָחוֹק / שְׁעוֹן בְּאֵת מֵרָחוֹק / בְּפָעֳלוֹ צָרִי דְּחֹק.
אֲסַפְּרָה אֶל חֹק / מִסְּכוֹ בְּלִי לִרְחֹק / חַיִּים לִי לָחֹק.
לְשֹׁד כְּחֶתֶף יִמְחֹק / לוֹחֲמִי לְבַל יִשְׂחֹק / וִימַלֵּא פִי שְׂחוֹק.

נֵחָשֵׁב כְּצָג בְּאֵיתוֹן / דְּחוּת בִּפְלְלֵי עֲקַלָּתוֹן
וְנַקְדִּישְׁךָ בְּשַׁבַּת שַׁבָּתוֹן / קָדוֹשׁ.

עוֹרְכֵי שֶׁוַע לָרֹב / חִין עֶרְכָּם יֶעֱרַב / פְּנֵי אֱלֹהֵי מִקָּרוֹב.
עֲתִירָתִי אָז תִּקְרַב / עֲבֵרָתִי בַּל תֶּאֱרֹב / אֵלַי לְבַל קְרֹב.
זוֹמֵם אִם יָזֹרֵב / עֲדַת אֵל לַחֲרֹב / אֶשָּׁעֵן בְּמַצְדִּיק וְקָרוֹב.

הַיּוֹם בְּפָתְחֲךָ סְפָרִים / חֹן אֹם שִׁמְךָ מְפָאֲרִים
וְנַקְדִּישְׁךָ בְּיוֹם הַכִּפּוּרִים / קָדוֹשׁ.

נֵחָשֵׁב *May we be considered.* At this, the beginning of the fourth of HaKalir's poems, he sets out three verses, each of which contains a reference to the words spelled out by the previous three: *Shabbat Shabbaton, Yom HaKippurim* and *Tzom HeAsor*, the three names of the Day of Atonement. They then serve as refrains to the verses of the fourth poem which spells out the name of the

Should my evil deeds seem to decide my fate,
recall [Moses] my shepherd,
that his good deeds might draw me close to You as a friend.
Tend Your faithful flock, / guide me through a bountiful pasture,
and plant the light of life within me.
For the iniquity of my way of life / as the measure of my sins abounds,
please, may no evil befall me.

Bind the Accuser in chains, / and herald new hope to the captives of my nation, / and may we sanctify You on this Fast of the Tenth, / O Holy One.

May they learn of His return to His fortress, / those who approach the holy Ark / to forcefully sound their prayerful song.
They shall await the One who is first and last, / He who causes His anger and ire to pass, / so that Aaron may come forth.
For those who lustily cry out their throaty pleas,
weigh the merits of the ancestors buried in Hebron,
that they might find forgiveness and pardon.

May we be considered like [the high priest] standing at the Temple entrance, / may our prayers push aside [the Accuser,] that crooked serpent, and may we sanctify You on this Sabbath of utter rest, / O Holy One.

As He sits on the throne of judgment, / may He take up my cause against my enemy in my presence, / for in my struggles He stands by me.
May He destroy those who would plunder and pillage me,
just as He laid waste to those who came previously,
and hear my groans and accept my pleas.
May He stand by me in judgment,
and may the merits of my ancestors speak on my behalf,
that my prayers might be pleasing to my Creator.

On this day as You open the books of life and death, / grant grace to Your nation, those who glorify Your name, / and may we sanctify You on this Day of Atonement, / O Holy One.

רֶשַׁע אִם הִכְרִיעִי / זְכָר לִי רוֹעִי / צִדְקוֹ עַתָּה לְרוֹעֲעִי.
רְעֵה צֹאן מַרְעִי / בְּמִרְעֶה טוֹב לְהַרְעִי / וּבְאוֹר חַיִּים לְזָרְעִי.
בַּעֲוֹן אֹרַח רִבְעִי / וּבְקוֹ נְטִיַּת מְרֵעִי / נָא אַל יְאָרְעִי.

מַשְׂטִין בְּכֶבֶל אֱסֹר / וְתִקְוַת אֲסִירֵי בְּשֹׂר
וְנַקְדִּישְׁךָ בְּצוֹם הֶעָשׂוֹר / קָדוֹשׁ.

יַסְכִּיתוּ שׁוּבוּ לְבִצָּרוֹן / גָּשִׁים פְּנֵי אָרוֹן / לְהַעֲצִים אֲרֶשֶׁת רֹן.
יְחַלּוּ רִאשׁוֹן וְאַחֲרוֹן / מַשְׁבִּית אַף וְחָרוֹן / בְּזֹאת יָבֹא אַהֲרֹן.
רוֹעֲשִׁים קְרֹא בְגָרוֹן / פִּלּוּס אֲטוּמֵי חֶבְרוֹן /
מְצֹא מְחִילַת וִתָּרוֹן.

נֶחֱשַׁב כְּצָג בְּאֵיתוֹן / דְּחוֹת בִּפְלִלֵי עֲקַלָּתוֹן
וְנַקְדִּישְׁךָ בְּשַׁבַּת שַׁבָּתוֹן / קָדוֹשׁ.

בְּשִׁבְתּוֹ בְּכֵס רִיב / יְרִיבַי לְעֵינַי יָרִיב / יָהּ נִצָּב לָרִיב.
בּוֹזְזַי חָרֹב יַחֲרִיב / כְּמוֹ קַדְמוֹנִים הֶחֱרִיב / וְנַאֲקִי לְפָנָיו יַקְרִיב.
יַצַּג אִתִּי בְּרִיב / מְלִיצַי שַׁי לְהַקְרִיב / וְשִׂיחִי לְגֹחִי יֶעֱרַב.

הַיּוֹם בְּפָתְחֲךָ סְפָרִים / חֹן אֹם שִׁמְךָ מְפָאֲרִים
וְנַקְדִּישְׁךָ בְּיוֹם הַכִּפּוּרִים / קָדוֹשׁ.

---

composer, Elazar bei-Rabbi Kalir. Each of the three refrains ends with the word *Kadosh*, "Holy," since that is the motif of the third paragraph of the Amida and the threefold *Kedusha* ("Holy, holy, holy") we are about to say.

זְכָר לִי רוֹעִי *Recall* [*Moses*] *my shepherd*. Having invoked the merits of the patriarchs, Abraham, Isaac and Jacob, the poet now brings other historic figures to tilt the balance of the scales of justice in Israel's favor.

בְּזֹאת יָבֹא אַהֲרֹן *So that Aaron may come forth.* Aaron, the High Priest who officiated on Yom Kippur during the years of the Israelites' wandering in the wilderness.

I shall raise my voice like the shofar,
which resounded as the pleasing words of the Torah were given
before the One who beautified the mighty heavens.
The abundance of goats and cattle, once offerings,
shall be replaced by the prayers my mouth is uttering,
that the Accuser might be shamed.
For the people measured as the unnumbered stars,
who have sunk down to the dust in exile,
may they find atonement for the iniquity of nefarious gains.

Bind the Accuser in chains, / and herald new hope to the captives of my nation, / and may we sanctify You on this Fast of the Tenth, / O Holy One.

May the crimson threads of iniquity turn white as snow, / all those sins
committed in the year before, / the new as well as the old.
May the blemishes of Israel, Your lily, be cleansed;
may the polished swords be returned to their sheaths,
through the prayers we recite over and over again.
Cleanse us and purify us from our smoldering sins,
that we might not repeat our folly again,
and let us be supported by our hope in Him.

May we be considered like [the high priest] standing at the Temple entrance, / may our prayers push aside [the Accuser,] that crooked serpent, and may we sanctify You on this Sabbath of utter rest, / O Holy One.

The following two verses traditionally served as the alternating refrains for the piyut אֵין עֲרֹךְ אֵלֶיךָ *(page 1329). Nowadays, many congregations say only the refrains, omitting the piyut altogether.*

The Leader says each verse, followed by the congregation:

אֶת לַחֲשִׁי Please answer my whispered plea,
please accept my cry, / O Holy God.
O Master, at the voice of Your nation,
remember Your compassion, / O Awesome and Holy One.

אֶת לַחֲשִׁי עֲנֵה נָא *Please answer my whispered plea.* The poet has woven his name, Elazar, into the initial letters of the words of both lines of the refrain. As we come closer to the *Kedusha*, the poet turns his attention to the angels who sing God's praises and to whose voices we join our own.

קוֹל אָרִים כַּשּׁוֹפָר / בְּמַתַּן אִמְרֵי שְׁפָר / לִפְנֵי חֲזָקִים שִׁפָּר.
קֶצֶב שְׂעִירִים וּפָר / בְּנִיב שְׂפָתַיִם יְסֻפָּר / וּבְכֵן שׂוֹטֵן יְחֻפָּר.
לִפְלוּסִים כְּכוֹכְבֵי מִסְפָּר / וְשָׁחִים עַד עָפָר /
בִּצְעָם וְעִוּוּיָם יְכֻפָּר.

מַשְׂטִין בְּכֶבֶל אֱסֹר / וְתִקְוַת אֲסִירֵי בַּשֵּׂר
וְנַקְדִּישְׁךָ בְּצוֹם הֶעָשׂוֹר / קָדוֹשׁ.

יַשְׁלְגוּ אָדְמֵי שָׁנִים / שֶׁל כָּל יְמוֹת הַשָּׁנִים /
חֲדָשִׁים וְגַם יְשָׁנִים.
יַלְבִּנוּ כִּתְמֵי שׁוֹשַׁנִּים / וְיוּשְׁבוּ לְתַעְרָם שְׁנוּנִים /
בְּפִלּוּל אֲשֶׁר מְשַׁנְּנִים.
רַחֲצוּ וְהִזַּכּוּ מֵעֲשׁוּנִים / לְאִוֶּלֶת מִהְיוֹת שׁוֹנִים /
וְעַל מִבְטָחֵימוֹ שְׁעוּנִים.

נֶחֱשַׁב כְּצַג בְּאִיתוֹן / דְּחוֹת בִּפְלִלֵי עֲקַלָּתוֹן
וְנַקְדִּישְׁךָ בְּשַׁבַּת שַׁבָּתוֹן / קָדוֹשׁ

The following two verses traditionally served as the alternating refrains for the piyut אֵין עֲרֹךְ אֵלֶיךָ *(page 1329). Nowadays, many congregations say only the refrains, omitting the piyut altogether.*

The שליח ציבור *says each verse, followed by the* קהל*:*

אֶת לַחֲשִׁי עֲנֵה נָא / זַעֲקִי רְצֵה נָא / הָאֵל קָדוֹשׁ.
אָדוֹן לְקוֹל עַמֶּךָ / זְכֹר רַחֲמֶיךָ / נוֹרָא וְקָדוֹשׁ.

לִפְלוּסִים כְּכוֹכְבֵי מִסְפָּר *For the people measured as the unnumbered stars.* God blessed Israel, promising they would be as innumerable as the stars (Gen. 15:5, 22:17), as abundant and enduring as the dust of the earth (Gen. 13:16, 28:14). Our sins, however, have cost us these blessings. Where once we shone like the stars; now we lie humiliated like the dust.

וְיוּשְׁבוּ לְתַעְרָם שְׁנוּנִים *May the polished swords be returned to their sheaths.* A metaphor for God's attribute of justice before whose judgment we stand on this holy day.

Some congregations add the piyutim אַל תִּזְכָּר לָנוּ עֲוֹנוֹתֵינוּ *and* אַךְ אוֹמְרִים בְּחִין לְפָנֶיךָ *(page 1330) at this point.*

The Ark is opened.

The congregation then the Leader:

And so, you shall say of God: How awesome are Your works! *Ps. 66*

In many congregations, the congregation recites each stanza, and the Leader repeats it. Some sing the entire piyut collectively. Although each stanza opens with the phrase "Say of God," many have the custom to say it at the end of each stanza.

אִמְרוּ לֵאלֹהִים Say of God:

God, King of the world, / who hastens the redemption of His nation,
that they might fulfill His divine word,
for forgiveness lies with Him alone.
Thank the LORD, call on His name. *1 Chr. 16*

Say of God:

He is blessed and praised in His abundant grandeur;
He hastens forgiveness for His congregation,
to make His greatness known to all,
for He measured the waters in His palm.
Sing to Him, make music to Him.

Say of God:

He redeems His holy nation, / sanctifying them with His forgiveness,
to found His holy Temple
for they are the seed of Abraham, His holy one.
Glory in His holy name.

Say of God:

Exalted and praised in His mighty heavens,
He forgives this [His chosen] nation on this [day],
by the word of His power and His stronghold,
for You are His nation, the congregation of His fortress.
Search out the LORD and His strength.

Although the poem is an acrostic with a verse for every letter of the alphabet, most congregations say an abbreviated form.

סוֹלֵחַ לְעַם זוּ בְּזוֹ *He forgives this [His chosen] nation on this [day]. Am zu*, "this nation," is how the Jewish people is described in the Song at the Sea (Ex. 15:16). "On this" is interpreted by some as a reference to "this day," the Day of

Some congregations add the piyutim אַל תִּזְכָּר לָנוּ עֲוֹנוֹתֵינוּ *and* אַךְ אוֹמְרִים בְּחִין לְפָנֶיךָ *(page 1330) at this point.*

The ארון קודש *is opened.*

The קהל *then the* שליח ציבור*:*

תהלים סו וּבְכֵן, אִמְרוּ לֵאלֹהִים, מַה־נּוֹרָא מַעֲשֶׂיךָ:

In many congregations, the קהל *recites each stanza, and the* שליח ציבור *repeats it. Some sing the entire piyut collectively. Although each stanza opens with the phrase "*אִמְרוּ לֵאלֹהִים*," many have the custom to say it at the end of each stanza.*

אִמְרוּ לֵאלֹהִים

אֵל מֶלֶךְ בְּעוֹלָמוֹ / מֵחִישׁ פְּדוּת עַמּוֹ

לְקַיֵּם אֶת דְּבַר נְאֻמוֹ / כִּי סְלִיחָה עִמּוֹ

דברי הימים א׳ טז הוֹדוּ לַיהוה קִרְאוּ בִשְׁמוֹ:

אִמְרוּ לֵאלֹהִים

בָּרוּךְ וּמְהֻלָּל בְּרֹב גָּדְלוֹ / מֵחִישׁ סְלִיחָה לִקְהָלוֹ

לְהַרְאוֹת לַכֹּל גָּדְלוֹ / מָדַד מַיִם בְּשָׁעֳלוֹ

שִׁירוּ לוֹ זַמְּרוּ־לוֹ:

אִמְרוּ לֵאלֹהִים

גּוֹאֵל עַם קְדוֹשׁוֹ / בִּסְלִיחָה לְהַקְדִּישׁוֹ

לְכוֹנֵן בֵּית מִקְדָּשׁוֹ / לָכֵן זֶרַע אַבְרָהָם קְדוֹשׁוֹ

הִתְהַלְלוּ בְּשֵׁם קָדְשׁוֹ:

אִמְרוּ לֵאלֹהִים

דָּגוּל וּמְהֻלָּל בִּרְקִיעַ עֻזּוֹ / סוֹלֵחַ לְעַם זוּ בְּזוֹ

בְּדִבַּר עֻזּוֹ וּמָעֻזּוֹ / לָכֵן אַתֶּם עַם עֲדַת מָעֻזּוֹ

דִּרְשׁוּ יהוה וְעֻזּוֹ:

אִמְרוּ לֵאלֹהִים *Say of God.* This poem, attributed by some to Rabbi Elazar HaKalir, by others to Rabbi Meshullam ben Kalonymus, is similar to the composition with the same refrain in Shaḥarit (page 639). Each verse ends with a phrase from 1 Chronicles 16, the psalm of thanksgiving King David sang when the Ark of the Covenant was brought to Jerusalem.

Say of God:
He created the entire world with His word;
indeed, He wrought and made it all.
He forgives the nation He has borne since birth;
therefore, they seek refuge in Him.
Remember the wonders He has done.

Say of God:
He confirms the word of His servant;
over earth and heaven is His splendor.
He forgives the nation that proclaims His unity,
those called in His mystic scriptures:
descendants of Yisrael His servant.

Say of God:
He stretched the land over the sea;
He sits above the circle of the earth.
He forgives that unique nation,
so say to the Founder of the earth,
He is the LORD our God over all the earth.

Say of God:
He resides in [Zion] His abode;
He is full of compassion and deals kindly with His congregation.
He shall return compassionately to His home,
and so, those who entered His covenant shall
remember His covenant for ever.

Say of God:
You are His children, His heritage;
You are His flock, His inheritance.
May He fulfill His word through us / as inscribed in His Torah,
according to the covenant He made with Abraham,
and His vow [to Isaac].

בְּדְבַר סוֹדוֹ *His mystic scriptures.* An alternative description of the Torah as God's revealed utterance to Israel.

אִמְרוּ לֵאלֹהִים
הַכֹּל בְּמַאֲמָר עָשָׂה / וְהוּא פָּעַל וְעָשָׂה
סוֹלֵחַ לְאֹם עֲמוּסָה / לָכֵן עַם בּוֹ חָסָה
זִכְרוּ נִפְלְאוֹתָיו אֲשֶׁר עָשָׂה:

אִמְרוּ לֵאלֹהִים
וּמֵקִים דְּבַר עַבְדּוֹ / עַל אֶרֶץ וְשָׁמַיִם הוֹדוֹ
סוֹלֵחַ לְעַם מְיַחֲדוֹ / אֲשֶׁר נִקְרְאוּ בִּדְבַר סוֹדוֹ
זֶרַע יִשְׂרָאֵל עַבְדּוֹ:

אִמְרוּ לֵאלֹהִים
זֶה רֹקַע הָאָרֶץ / הַיּוֹשֵׁב עַל חוּג הָאָרֶץ
סוֹלֵחַ לְגוֹי אֶחָד בָּאָרֶץ / לָכֵן אִמְרוּ לְיוֹסֵד אָרֶץ
הוּא יהוה אֱלֹהֵינוּ, בְּכָל־הָאָרֶץ:

אִמְרוּ לֵאלֹהִים
חַי בִּמְעוֹנָתוֹ / חַנּוּן וְחוֹנֵן עֲדָתוֹ
יָשׁוּב בְּרַחֲמִים לְבֵיתוֹ / לָכֵן בָּאֵי בִבְרִיתוֹ
זִכְרוּ לְעוֹלָם בְּרִיתוֹ:

אִמְרוּ לֵאלֹהִים
טַפֵּי נַחֲלָתוֹ / טְלָאֵי יְרֻשָּׁתוֹ
יְקַיֵּם עָלֵימוֹ אִמְרָתוֹ / כְּחָקוּק בְּתוֹרָתוֹ
אֲשֶׁר כָּרַת אֶת־אַבְרָהָם, וּשְׁבוּעָתוֹ:

Atonement, by others to the phrase of Isaiah (43:21), "This people I formed for Myself that they may proclaim My praise."

Say of God:
He guides the honest with His laws;
those who fear Him are inscribed in the book of life.
He forgives all recorded sins,
as was heard by [Moses] the shepherd from afar,
He confirmed it to Jacob as a statute.

Say of God:
All-Powerful One, the eternal God –
His word will stand firm for all eternity,
and He cannot be known, / and we praise His name to eternity.
Blessed is the LORD, God of Israel, from This World to eternity.

The congregation then the Leader:

Indeed, the works of our God are sublime.

In many congregations, the congregation recites each stanza, and the Leader repeats it. Some sing the entire piyut collectively. Although each stanza opens with the phrase "The work of our God," many have the custom to say it at the end of each stanza.

The work of our God:
Majestic in His assembly;
His glory shining above and below;
He revealed light to the one who served Him,
He will keep His word to His servant.
Therefore, exalt Him, the One with none other besides Him. *Deut. 4*

The work of our God:
He knows all worlds, / counts and numbers all times.
The radiance of His throne comes forth
and He watches over the earth to uphold it.
Therefore, exalt Him, He who gazes at the earth and it trembles. *Ps. 104*

---

constructed in the form of a counterpoint, with each verse that spoke of "the work of God" contrasted by another describing the evil that is "the deeds of man." Most rites, however, delete all these contrasting verses except one. During this verse, expressive of the shamefulness of the human condition when set against the infinite radiance and grace of God, the Ark is briefly closed.

אִמְרוּ לֵאלֹהִים
יוֹעֵץ מֵישָׁרִים לְחֹק / יְרֵאָיו לְחַיִּים לָחֹק
סוֹלֵחַ חֵטְא הַנֵּחוּק / כְּנִשְׁמַע לָרוֹעֶה מֵרָחוֹק
וַיַּעֲמִידֶהָ לְיַעֲקֹב לְחֹק:

אִמְרוּ לֵאלֹהִים
תַּקִּיף אֱלֹהֵי עוֹלָם / דְּבָרוֹ נִצָּב לְעוֹלָם
וְהוּא מִכֹּל נֶעְלָם / וַאֲנוּ מְהַלְלִים שְׁמוֹ לְעוֹלָם
בָּרוּךְ יהוה אֱלֹהֵי יִשְׂרָאֵל מִן־הָעוֹלָם וְעַד־הָעֹלָם:

The קהל *then the* שליח ציבור:

וּבְכֵן, גְּדוֹלִים מַעֲשֵׂי אֱלֹהֵינוּ.

In many congregations, the קהל *recites each stanza, and the* שליח ציבור *repeats it. Some sing the entire piyut collectively. Although each stanza opens with the phrase "*מַעֲשֵׂה אֱלֹהֵינוּ*," many have the custom to say it at the end of each stanza.*

מַעֲשֵׂה אֱלֹהֵינוּ
אַדִּיר בְּוֹעוּדוֹ / בְּרוּם וּבְתַחַת הוֹדוֹ
גִּלָּה אוֹר לְעוֹבְדוֹ / דְּבָרוֹ מֵקִים לְעַבְדּוֹ
דברים ד לָכֵן יִתְגָּאֶה, אֵין עוֹד מִלְּבַדּוֹ:

מַעֲשֵׂה אֱלֹהֵינוּ
הַמַּכִּיר עוֹלְמֵי עַד / וְסוֹפֵר וּמוֹנֶה עֲדֵי עַד
זִיו מוֹשָׁבוֹ נוֹעָד / חֶלֶד צוֹפֶה בְּמִסְעָד
תהלים קד לָכֵן יִתְגָּאֶה, הַמַּבִּיט לָאָרֶץ וַתִּרְעָד:

מַעֲשֵׂה אֱלֹהֵינוּ *The work of our God.* A poem contrasting the works of God with those of humankind, attributed by some to Yannai, one of the earliest of the liturgical poets known to us by name (Israel, sixth or seventh century CE), and by others to Rabbi Meshullam ben Kalonymus. Found in its original form in the Mahzor according to the rites of the Jewish community of Rome, it was

The work of our God:
He carries His footstool; / He knows His world well.
He made all of it together as He spoke,
and established it forever.
Therefore, exalt Him – the LORD of hosts is His name. *Is. 47*

The work of our God:
He rules over all that He has made, / awesome over His Temple.
As great as He is, so is He to be praised.
His might is felt in His army.
Therefore, exalt Him – Seraphim stand before Him. *Is. 6*

The work of our God:
His splendor fills the heaven of His dwelling.
I see Him watching and noticing all.
He is exalted in the multitudes of my people.
He holds sway over those who oppress me.
Therefore, exalt Him – great are the works of the LORD. *Ps. 111*

The Ark is closed.

The deeds of man:
His plans are mere plots, / he lives in a world of deceit,
his berth is lined with maggots, / buried in a crevice in the ground.
Then how can man be exalted,
when he is like a vain breath? *Ps. 144*

The Ark is opened.

But the work of our God:
The Almighty spreads the earth over nothingness,
never letting her inhabitants be desolate,
setting land firm above waters,
that the might of His name be ennobled.
Therefore, exalt Him, He who is clothed in majesty and splendor. *Ps. 104*

In most congregations the Ark is closed. In some congregations, the Ark remains open until after the following piyut.

מַעֲשֵׂה אֱלֹהֵינוּ
טוֹעֵן הֲדוֹמוֹ / יוֹדֵעַ עוֹלָמוֹ
כְּלָלוֹ בִּנְאָמוֹ / לָעַד לַהֲקִימוֹ
לָכֵן יִתְגָּאֶה, יהוה צְבָאוֹת שְׁמוֹ: ישעיה מז

מַעֲשֵׂה אֱלֹהֵינוּ
מוֹשֵׁל בְּמִפְעָלוֹ / נוֹרָא עַל זְבוּלוֹ
סִלּוּדוֹ כְּגָדְלוֹ / עֻזּוֹ בְּרֹב חֵילוֹ
לָכֵן יִתְגָּאֶה, שְׂרָפִים עֹמְדִים מִמַּעַל לוֹ: ישעיה ו

מַעֲשֵׂה אֱלֹהֵינוּ
פְּאֵרוֹ בִּשְׁמֵי מְעוֹנַי / צוֹפֶה וּמַבִּיט לְעֵינַי
קִלּוּס שְׁמוֹ בַּהֲמוֹנַי / רוֹדֶה בְּקֶרֶב מוֹנַי
לָכֵן יִתְגָּאֶה, גְּדֹלִים מַעֲשֵׂי יהוה: תהלים קיא

The ארון קודש *is closed.*

מַעֲשֵׂה אֱנוֹשׁ
תַּחְבּוּלוֹתָיו מְזִמָּה / שִׁבְתּוֹ בְּתוֹךְ מִרְמָה
רְפִידָתוֹ רִמָּה / קָבוּר בִּסְעִיף אֲדָמָה
וְאֵיךְ יִתְגָּאֶה, אָדָם לַהֶבֶל דָּמָה: תהלים קמד

The ארון קודש *is opened.*

אֲבָל מַעֲשֵׂה אֱלֹהֵינוּ
שַׁדַּי רוֹקַע אֶרֶץ עַל בְּלִימָה / שׁוֹכְנֶיהָ בְּלִי הֱיוֹת לְשַׁמָּה
תִּכֵּן עַל מַיִם אֲדָמָה / תֹּקֶף שְׁמוֹ לְרוֹמְמָה
לָכֵן יִתְגָּאֶה, עֹטֶה־אוֹר כַּשַּׂלְמָה: תהלים קד

In most congregations the ארון קודש *is closed. In some congregations, the* ארון קודש *remains open until after the following piyut.*

The following piyutim are usually sung by all before Kedusha to engender an atmosphere of sanctity and reverence.

The congregation then the Leader:

And so, in awe, they shall revere
the One whose fear is upon them.

In some congregations, this piyut is said responsively, and in others it is sung by all. Some congregations omit it altogether.

אֲשֶׁר אֵימָתְךָ Even though Your dread is
upon the faithful angels, / the mighty heavenly hosts,
created of ice, / mixed with fire –
and Your awe is upon them.

Yet You desire praise
from those formed from earth, / denizens of the valleys below,
whose actions are meager / and good deeds few in number –
and this is Your praise!

Even though Your dread is
upon the hordes of angels / in their roaming camps,
assemblies of thousands, / gatherings of appointed myriads –
and Your awe is upon them.

Yet You desire praise
from beings of mutable splendor, / whose brilliance dims,
who lack intelligence / and plot evil –
and this is Your praise!

Even though Your dread is
in spreading out the heavens, / arranging the skies,
ordering the dark clouds, / laying out Your abode –
and Your awe is upon them.

Yet You desire praise
from those blemished by sin, / whose stain is concealed,
who are ensnared by the evil inclination, / bitter as poison –
and this is Your praise!

---

heaven by the angelic hosts, it is the praise of frail, finite, fallible human beings such as we are, that gives God delight. In the spirit of Psalm 8: "What is man that You are mindful of him, the son of man that You care for him? Yet You made him little lower than the angels, and crowned him with glory and honor" (verses 5–6). The verses alternate; one speaks about the heavenly realms filled with the awe of God, the next about humanity. We are poor creatures who strive and fail, whose intelligence is limited, whose life is short and whose

The following piyutim are usually sung by all before קדושה *to engender an atmosphere of sanctity and reverence.*

The קהל *then the* שליח ציבור*:*

וּבְכֵן, לְנוֹרָא עֲלֵיהֶם בְּאֵימָה יַעֲרִיצוּ.

In some congregations, this piyut is said responsively, and in others it is sung by all. Some congregations omit it altogether.

אֲשֶׁר אֵימָתֶךָ
בְּאֶרְאֶלֵּי אֹמֶן / בְּאַבִּירֵי אֹמֶץ
בִּבְלוּלֵי קֹרַח / בִּבְדוּדֵי קֶדַח — וּמוֹרָאֲךָ עֲלֵיהֶם.

וְאָבִיתָ תְהִלָּה
מִגְּלוּמֵי גוּשׁ / מִגָּרֵי גַיְא
מִדְּלוּלֵי פֹעַל / מִדַּלֵּי מַעַשׂ — וְהִיא תְהִלָּתֶךָ.

אֲשֶׁר אֵימָתֶךָ
בַּהֲמוֹן מַלְאָכִים / בְּהִלּוּךְ מַחֲנוֹת
בְּוַעַד אֲלָפִים / בְּוֶכַח רְבָבוֹת — וּמוֹרָאֲךָ עֲלֵיהֶם.

וְאָבִיתָ תְהִלָּה
מִזִּיו שׁוֹנֶה / מִזֹּהַר כָּבֶה
מֵחַסְרֵי שֵׂכֶל / מֵחוֹרְשֵׁי רֶשַׁע — וְהִיא תְהִלָּתֶךָ.

אֲשֶׁר אֵימָתֶךָ
בְּטִפּוּחַ עֲרָבוֹת / בְּטִכּוּס שְׁחָקִים
בְּיִשְׁרַת עֲרָפֶל / בִּירִיעַת מְעוֹנָה — וּמוֹרָאֲךָ עֲלֵיהֶם.

וְאָבִיתָ תְהִלָּה
מִכְּתוּמֵי שֶׁמֶץ / מִכְּמוּסֵי כֶתֶם
מִלְּכוּדֵי פַח / מִלְּעוּנֵי מַר — וְהִיא תְהִלָּתֶךָ.

אֲשֶׁר אֵימָתֶךָ *Even though Your dread.* Having contrasted the perfection of God and the imperfection of humanity, the poet brings these themes together in the paradox that frames the religious life: Even though God is praised in

Even though Your dread is
in the pathways of heaven, / in the glorious heights,
in spreading the skies like a veil / and guiding the clouds –
and Your awe is upon them.

Yet You desire praise
from those who reek of evil deeds, / saturated with anger,
devoid of truth, / yet borne [by God] from the womb –
and this is Your praise!

Even though Your dread is
in those [angels] who open their mouths to say "Holy,"
who proclaim "Blessed One,"
whose faces are turned in all four directions,
and are swathed in six wings – and Your awe is upon them.

Yet You desire praise
from those referred to as nothingness,
who call upon Him while tainted with sin,
distant, as they are, from truth, / and devoid of all righteousness –
and this is Your praise!

Even though Your dread is
in the sparks of fire / and the great paths of water,
the steep heights / and spiraling heavens –
and Your awe is upon them.

Yet You desire praise
from creatures of flesh and blood, / vanity and confusion;
from withered chaff, / a passing shadow,
and a faded flower; / from those whose lifeblood passes away,
whose spirit departs, / whose life flies from them,
whose spirit wanes, / whose unique essence is removed,
who are heard in judgment, / who die by Your verdict,
who live through Your compassion, / and who give You honor,
the One who lives for ever – for Your glory is upon them.

The Ark is closed.

---

light soon fades, yet it is from us that "You desire praise," as we reach out toward the Unknowable, our smallness transfigured by our intimations of Infinity. And "this is Your praise," that You care about us and hear our voice.

אֲשֶׁר אֵימָתֶךָ

בְּמַסְלוּלֵי זְבוּל / בִּמְרוֹמֵי שְׁפַר

בִּנְטִיַּת דֹּק / בְּנַחִיַּת עָבִים — וּמוֹרָאֲךָ עֲלֵיהֶם.

וְאָבִיתָ תְהִלָּה

מִסְּרוּחֵי מֵעַשׁ / מִשְּׂבֵעֵי רֹגֶז

מֵעֲדוּרֵי אֱמֶת / מֵעֲמוּסֵי בֶטֶן — וְהִיא תְהִלָּתֶךָ.

אֲשֶׁר אֵימָתֶךָ

בְּפוֹתְחֵי קָדוֹשׁ / בְּפוֹצְחֵי בָרוּךְ

בִּצְדוּדֵי אַרְבַּע / בִּצְנוּפֵי שֵׁשׁ שֵׁשׁ — וּמוֹרָאֲךָ עֲלֵיהֶם.

וְאָבִיתָ תְהִלָּה

מִקְּרוּאֵי עַיִן / מִקּוֹרְאֵי בְחִנּוּף

מְרַחֲקֵי אֱמֶת / מְרִיקֵי צֶדֶק — וְהִיא תְהִלָּתֶךָ.

אֲשֶׁר אֵימָתֶךָ

בְּשַׁבִיבֵי אֵשׁ / בִּשְׁבִילֵי מַיִם

בְּתַלּוּלֵי רוּם / בְּתַלְתַּלֵּי גֹבַהּ — וּמוֹרָאֲךָ עֲלֵיהֶם.

וְאָבִיתָ תְהִלָּה — מִבָּשָׂר וָדָם / מֵהֶבֶל וָתֹהוּ

מֵחָצִיר יָבֵשׁ / מִצֵּל עוֹבֵר / וּמִצִּיץ נוֹבֵל

מַשְׁלִימֵי נֶפֶשׁ / מַפְרִיחֵי רוּחַ / וּמְעִיפֵי חַיָּה

וַחֲנִיטֵי נְשָׁמָה / וּמוֹצִיאֵי יְחִידָה

וְנִשְׁמָעִים בַּדִּין / וּמֵתִים בַּמִּשְׁפָּט

וְחַיִּים בְּרַחֲמִים / וְנוֹתְנִים לְךָ פְּאֵר חַי עוֹלָמִים

וְתִפְאַרְתְּךָ עֲלֵיהֶם.

The ארון קודש *is closed.*

Traditionally, this verse was said by the congregation after each stanza of the following piyut. Nowadays, many congregations say it only at the beginning. Others omit the piyut altogether, saying only the refrain.

The Leader, then the congregation:

To the One enthroned upon praises, / who rides upon the clouds,
O Holy and Blessed One.

The Leader says the first two stichs of each line, and the congregation says the third. The refrain is said by all.

אַמִּיצֵי שְׁחָקִים Mighty angels of heaven above, / and all the heavenly hosts say, "O Holy One."
Your faithful beloved / and flowering myriads say, "O Blessed One."
Groups of angels / who crown His name say, "O Holy One."
The chosen people of the covenant / say to the One who recalls His covenant: "O Holy and Blessed One."

To the One enthroned upon praises, / who rides upon the clouds,
O Holy and Blessed One.

Those strong in power, / to the One who is mighty and supremely powerful say, "O Holy One."
Those great in righteousness, / to the One who is sanctified in righteousness say, "O Blessed One."
Those [angels] of four facets, / turning in all directions say, "O Holy One."
The bannered and protected ones / say to the One who is with them in their times of trouble: "O Holy and Blessed One."

To the One enthroned upon praises, / who rides upon the clouds,
O Holy and Blessed One.

The great hordes of heaven, / to the One who dwells on high say, "O Holy One."
Those who follow God's path innocently, / to the perfect Rock say, "O Blessed One."
Angels in their comings and goings, / heeding the commandments of the Rock, say, "O Holy One."
Those who hope for salvation / and await His forgiveness: "O Holy and Blessed One."

To the One enthroned upon praises, / who rides upon the clouds,
O Holy and Blessed One.

In plentiful song, / the pure ones of heaven say, "O Holy One."
The offspring of the faithful ancestor, / to the true LORD God say, "O Blessed One."
Intensely sparkling angels, / to the One who sends forth lightning bolts say, "O Holy One."
The desert travelers / say to the One who raises up the clouds: "O Holy and Blessed One."

To the One enthroned upon praises, / who rides upon the clouds,
O Holy and Blessed One.

Traditionally, this verse was said by the קהל *after each stanza of the following piyut. Nowadays, many congregations say it only at the beginning. Others omit the piyut altogether, saying only the refrain.*

The שליח ציבור*, then the* קהל*:*

לְיוֹשֵׁב תְּהִלּוֹת / לְרוֹכֵב עֲרָבוֹת / קָדוֹשׁ וּבָרוּךְ.

The שליח ציבור *says the first two stichs of each line, and the* קהל *says the third. The refrain is said by all.*

אַמִּיצֵי שְׁחָקִים מִמַּעַל / וְכָל צְבָא מַעַל אוֹמְרִים קָדוֹשׁ
אֱמוּנֵי אַהֲבָה / וְצִמְחֵי רְבָבָה אוֹמְרִים בָּרוּךְ
בְּכִתֵּי מַלְאָכִים / שְׁמוֹ מַמְלִיכִים אוֹמְרִים קָדוֹשׁ
בְּנֵי בְחוּרֵי בְרִית / לְזוֹכֵר הַבְּרִית קָדוֹשׁ וּבָרוּךְ.

לְיוֹשֵׁב תְּהִלּוֹת / לְרוֹכֵב עֲרָבוֹת / קָדוֹשׁ וּבָרוּךְ.

גִּבּוֹרֵי כֹחַ / לְאַמִּיץ וְשַׂגִּיא כֹחַ אוֹמְרִים קָדוֹשׁ
גְּדוֹלֵי צְדָקָה / לַנִּקְדָּשׁ בִּצְדָקָה אוֹמְרִים בָּרוּךְ
דְּמוּת אַרְבַּע פָּנִים / לְכָל צַד פּוֹנִים אוֹמְרִים קָדוֹשׁ
דִּגְלֵי נְצוּרָה / לְעִמָּם בְּצָרָה קָדוֹשׁ וּבָרוּךְ.

לְיוֹשֵׁב תְּהִלּוֹת / לְרוֹכֵב עֲרָבוֹת / קָדוֹשׁ וּבָרוּךְ.

הֲמוֹן צְבָא הַמְּלָה / לְשׁוֹכֵן מַעְלָה אוֹמְרִים קָדוֹשׁ
הוֹלְכֵי דֶרֶךְ תָּמִים / לְהַצּוּר תָּמִים אוֹמְרִים בָּרוּךְ
וְרָצִים וְשָׁבִים / טַעַם צוּר מַקְשִׁיבִים אוֹמְרִים קָדוֹשׁ
וְקוֵֹי יְשׁוּעוֹת / וְחוֹכֵי סְלִיחוֹת קָדוֹשׁ וּבָרוּךְ.

לְיוֹשֵׁב תְּהִלּוֹת / לְרוֹכֵב עֲרָבוֹת / קָדוֹשׁ וּבָרוּךְ.

זְמִירוֹת רַבּוֹת / זַכֵּי שְׁמֵי עֲרָבוֹת אוֹמְרִים קָדוֹשׁ
זֶרַע מַטַּע אֱמֶת / לְאֵל אֱלֹהִים אֱמֶת אוֹמְרִים בָּרוּךְ
חַשְׁמַלִּים עִזִּים / לְעוֹשֵׂה חֲזִיזִים אוֹמְרִים קָדוֹשׁ
חוֹנִים וְנוֹשְׂאִים / לְמַעֲלֵה נְשִׂיאִים קָדוֹשׁ וּבָרוּךְ.

לְיוֹשֵׁב תְּהִלּוֹת / לְרוֹכֵב עֲרָבוֹת / קָדוֹשׁ וּבָרוּךְ.

The angels on high, / to the Loftiest One say, "O Holy One."
[Israel] in its goodly tents, / its infants and babes say, "O Blessed One."
Angels hastening, / bowing and kneeling say, "O Holy One."
Dwellers of Your Tent and Sanctuary
say to the One who dwells in their midst: "O Holy and Blessed One."

To the One enthroned upon praises, / who rides upon the clouds,
O Holy and Blessed One.

Angels en masse,
together with Ḥayyot and Ophanim, say, "O Holy One."
Subjects who crown their King,
descendants of mighty ancestors say, "O Blessed One."
Clusters of fiery angels / in their flaming sparks say, "O Holy One."
The unique nation He created for His sake,
declares the uniqueness of God's name: "O Holy and Blessed One."

To the One enthroned upon praises, / who rides upon the clouds,
O Holy and Blessed One.

Swathed angels fluttering, / on outspread wings flying say, "O Holy One."
Those who rise consistently, / each day anew say, "O Blessed One."
Those awesome in wonders,
to the One who is righteous in His awesome deeds say, "O Holy One."
The nobles of Your nation / exalt Your name: "O Holy and Blessed One."

To the One enthroned upon praises, / who rides upon the clouds,
O Holy and Blessed One.

Seraphim standing before You,
bowing and giving thanks say, "O Holy One."
Those who recoil in fear
before the One who is awesome in His works say, "O Blessed One."
Those [angels] filled with eyes
as with precious stones say, "O Holy One."
Your chanting congregations
say in whispers and full voices: "O Holy and Blessed One."

To the One enthroned upon praises, / who rides upon the clouds,
O Holy and Blessed One.

טַפְסְרֵי מְרוֹמִים / לְרָם עַל רָמִים — אוֹמְרִים קָדוֹשׁ
טִבּוּ אָהֳלָיו / יוֹנְקָיו וְעוֹלְלָיו — אוֹמְרִים בָּרוּךְ
יִדְדוּן הוֹלְכִים / כּוֹרְעִים וּבוֹרְכִים — אוֹמְרִים קָדוֹשׁ.
יוֹשְׁבֵי אֹהֶל וּמִשְׁכָּן / לְבְתוֹכָם שָׁכַן — קָדוֹשׁ וּבָרוּךְ.

לְיוֹשֵׁב תְּהִלּוֹת / לְרוֹכֵב עֲרָבוֹת / קָדוֹשׁ וּבָרוּךְ.

כִּתֵּי הֲמוֹנִים / עִם חַיּוֹת וְאוֹפַנִּים — אוֹמְרִים קָדוֹשׁ
כֶּתֶר נוֹתְנִים / בְּנֵי אֵיתָנִים — אוֹמְרִים בָּרוּךְ
לַהֲקַת שְׁבִיבִים / וְאֵשׁ לְהָבִים — אוֹמְרִים קָדוֹשׁ
לְמַעֲנוֹ גּוֹי אֶחָד / לְשֵׁם אֵל הַמְיֻחָד — קָדוֹשׁ וּבָרוּךְ.

לְיוֹשֵׁב תְּהִלּוֹת / לְרוֹכֵב עֲרָבוֹת / קָדוֹשׁ וּבָרוּךְ.

מְסוֹכְכִים מְרוֹפְפִים / בְּכַנְפֵיהֶם מְעוֹפְפִים — אוֹמְרִים קָדוֹשׁ
מְנַצְּחִים לְהַתְמִיד / בְּכָל יוֹם תָּמִיד — אוֹמְרִים בָּרוּךְ
נוֹרָאִים בְּנִפְלָאוֹת / לְצֶדֶק נוֹרָאוֹת — אוֹמְרִים קָדוֹשׁ
נְדִיבֵי עַמְּךָ / מְסַלְסְלִים לְשִׁמְךָ — קָדוֹשׁ וּבָרוּךְ.

לְיוֹשֵׁב תְּהִלּוֹת / לְרוֹכֵב עֲרָבוֹת / קָדוֹשׁ וּבָרוּךְ.

שְׂרָפִים עוֹמְדִים / מִשְׁתַּחֲוִים וּמוֹדִים — אוֹמְרִים קָדוֹשׁ
סוֹלְדֵי בְחִילָה / לְנוֹרָא עֲלִילָה — אוֹמְרִים בָּרוּךְ
עֵינַיִם מְלֵאִים / כְּתַרְשִׁישׁ מְמֻלָּאִים — אוֹמְרִים קָדוֹשׁ
עוֹנִים בְּמַקְהֵלוֹת / בְּלַחַשׁ וְקוֹלוֹת — קָדוֹשׁ וּבָרוּךְ.

לְיוֹשֵׁב תְּהִלּוֹת / לְרוֹכֵב עֲרָבוֹת / קָדוֹשׁ וּבָרוּךְ.

Those whose faces shine like lightning, / adorned in clothes of gold
say, "O Holy One."
The people You redeemed by Your mighty hand, / to their mighty Savior
say, "O Blessed One."
The hosts of heaven, / to the One who rides upon the heavens
say, "O Holy One."
Your holy flock, / sprung from sacred ancestors: "O Holy and Blessed One."

To the One enthroned upon praises, / who rides upon the clouds,
O Holy and Blessed One.

Angels swift to carry out their mission, / calling to their Maker
say, "O Holy One."
The congregations of Jacob, / with no deceit in their hearts
say, "O Blessed One."
Those with feet like calves' hooves / and rolling wheels say, "O Holy One."
Those desired by their Creator / say to the Lofty One who fashioned them:
"O Holy and Blessed One."

To the One enthroned upon praises, / who rides upon the clouds,
O Holy and Blessed One.

Those who dwell in the shadow of the Almighty,
whose years are not numbered say, "O Holy One."
The observers of Your laws, / commandments, and statutes say, "O Blessed One."
The powerful angels / scurrying in the heights say, "O Holy One."
The innocent in their ways / and in the work of their hands:
"O Holy and Blessed One."

To the One enthroned upon praises, / who rides upon the clouds,
O Holy and Blessed One.

The congregation then the Leader:

וּבְכֵן And so, the Seraphim hover about Him. *Is. 6*

Originally, the following verse was the refrain of the Kedusha piyut אֵילֵי מָרוֹם *(page 1333). Nowadays, most congregations only say the refrain, omitting the piyut altogether.*

The Leader, followed by the congregation:

אֵלּוּ They inquire of one another,
they speak with one another:
Where is the LORD who lives on high,
that we might exalt and sanctify Him
with splendid words of praise?

פְּנֵיהֶם כִּבְרָקִים מְאִירִים / וּפַז בֶּגֶד פְּאוּרִים אוֹמְרִים קָדוֹשׁ
פְּדוּיֵי בִּזְרוֹעַ חָזָק / לְגוֹאֲלָם חָזָק אוֹמְרִים בָּרוּךְ
צִבְאוֹת שָׁמַיִם / לְרוֹכֵב שָׁמַיִם אוֹמְרִים קָדוֹשׁ
צֹאן קָדָשִׁים / מַטַּע קְדוֹשִׁים קָדוֹשׁ וּבָרוּךְ.

לְיוֹשֵׁב תְּהִלּוֹת / לְרוֹכֵב עֲרָבוֹת / קָדוֹשׁ וּבָרוּךְ.

קַלִּים לְצוּרָם / קוֹרְאִים לְיוֹצְרָם אוֹמְרִים קָדוֹשׁ
קְהִלּוֹת יַעֲקֹב / בְּלִי לֵב עָקֹב אוֹמְרִים בָּרוּךְ
רַגְלֵיהֶם כְּעֵגֶל / וְאוֹפַן מִתְגַּלְגֵּל אוֹמְרִים קָדוֹשׁ
רְצוּיִים לְבוֹרְאָם / לְרָם אֲשֶׁר בְּרָאָם קָדוֹשׁ וּבָרוּךְ.

לְיוֹשֵׁב תְּהִלּוֹת / לְרוֹכֵב עֲרָבוֹת / קָדוֹשׁ וּבָרוּךְ.

שׁוֹכְנֵי בְּצֵל שַׁדַּי / שְׁנוֹתָם אֵין דַּי אוֹמְרִים קָדוֹשׁ
שׁוֹמְרִים חֲקוּקִים / מִצְוֹת וְחֻקִּים אוֹמְרִים בָּרוּךְ
תְּקֶף תַּרְשִׁישִׁים / בַּמָּרוֹם חָשִׁים אוֹמְרִים קָדוֹשׁ
תְּמִימִים בְּדַרְכֵיהֶם / וּבְמַעֲשֵׂה יְדֵיהֶם קָדוֹשׁ וּבָרוּךְ.

לְיוֹשֵׁב תְּהִלּוֹת / לְרוֹכֵב עֲרָבוֹת / קָדוֹשׁ וּבָרוּךְ.

The קהל *then the* שליח ציבור:

ישעיה ו
וּבְכֵן, שְׂרָפִים עֹמְדִים מִמַּעַל לוֹ:

Originally, the following verse was the refrain of the קדושה *piyut* אֵילֵי מָרוֹם *(page 1333). Nowadays, most congregations only say the refrain, omitting the piyut altogether.*

The שליח ציבור*, followed by the* קהל:

אֵלּוּ לְאֵלּוּ שׁוֹאֲלִים
אֵלּוּ לְאֵלּוּ מְמַלְּלִים
אָנָה שׁוֹכֵן מְעֻלִּים
לְהַעֲרִיצוֹ, לְהַקְדִּישׁוֹ בִּפְאֵר מְסַלְסְלִים.

The Ark is opened.

The following piyut, the Siluk, is the last of the piyutim before Kedusha. This long piyut, which takes us right up to the response of "Holy, holy, holy" (page 852), displaces the more familiar opening of Kedusha: "We will revere and sanctify You."

All:

וּבְכֵן לְךָ And so, sanctity will rise up to You;
for You, our God, are King.

All:

וּנְתַנֶּה תֹּקֶף Let us voice the power of this day's sanctity –
it is awesome, terrible;
on this day Your kingship is raised,
Your throne is founded upon love,
and You, with truth, sit upon it.
In truth, it is You: Judge and Accuser, Knowing One and Witness,
writing and sealing, counting, numbering,
remembering all forgotten things,
You open the book of memories –
it is read of itself, / and every man's name is signed there.
וּבְשׁוֹפָר גָּדוֹל A great shofar sounds,
and a still small voice is heard,
angels rush forward / and are held by trembling, shaking;
they say, "Here is the Day of Judgment
visiting all the heavenly host for judgment –"
for they are not cleared in Your eyes in judgment.
And all who have come into this world pass before You like sheep.

---

evil of the decree. No fate is final. Life is not a script written by Aeschylus or Sophocles in which the decree cannot be rescinded and tragedy is inexorable. That is not our God, our faith, our world. God forgives; God pardons; God exercises clemency – if we truly repent and pray and give to others. The verdict may have been written, but it is not yet sealed, and God is still open to appeal. We may pray for a good fate but we do not reconcile ourselves to fatalism.

Next comes a moving reflection on the fragility of human life when set against the backdrop of the eternity of God. We are no more than a fragment

The ארון קודש *is opened.*
The following piyut, the סילוק*, is the last of the piyutim before* קדושה.
*This long piyut, which takes us right up to the response of "*קָדוֹשׁ, קָדוֹשׁ, קָדוֹשׁ*"*
*(**page 853**), displaces the more familiar opening of* קדושה*: "*נַעֲרִיצְךָ וְנַקְדִּישְׁךָ*."*

All:

וּבְכֵן לְךָ תַעֲלֶה קְדֻשָּׁה, כִּי אַתָּה אֱלֹהֵינוּ מֶלֶךְ.

All:

וּנְתַנֶּה תֹּקֶף קְדֻשַּׁת הַיּוֹם / כִּי הוּא נוֹרָא וְאָיֹם
וּבוֹ תִנָּשֵׂא מַלְכוּתֶךָ / וְיִכּוֹן בְּחֶסֶד כִּסְאֶךָ / וְתֵשֵׁב עָלָיו בֶּאֱמֶת.
אֱמֶת, כִּי אַתָּה הוּא דַיָּן וּמוֹכִיחַ, וְיוֹדֵעַ וָעֵד
וְכוֹתֵב וְחוֹתֵם וְסוֹפֵר וּמוֹנֶה
וְתִזְכֹּר כָּל הַנִּשְׁכָּחוֹת / וְתִפְתַּח אֶת סֵפֶר הַזִּכְרוֹנוֹת
וּמֵאֵלָיו יִקָּרֵא / וְחוֹתַם יַד כָּל אָדָם בּוֹ.

וּבְשׁוֹפָר גָּדוֹל יִתָּקַע / וְקוֹל דְּמָמָה דַקָּה יִשָּׁמַע
וּמַלְאָכִים יֵחָפֵזוּן / וְחִיל וּרְעָדָה יֹאחֵזוּן
וְיֹאמְרוּ, הִנֵּה יוֹם הַדִּין / לִפְקוֹד עַל צְבָא מָרוֹם בַּדִּין
כִּי לֹא יִזְכּוּ בְעֵינֶיךָ בַּדִּין
וְכָל בָּאֵי עוֹלָם יַעַבְרוּן לְפָנֶיךָ כִּבְנֵי מָרוֹן.

UNTANEH TOKEF – LET US VOICE THE POWER

One of the greatest poems in the literature of Jewish prayer, *Untaneh Tokef* paints the great themes of Rosh HaShana and Yom Kippur in a series of unforgettable vignettes. In the first, we see the heavenly court with God sitting on the throne of judgment. Before Him is the book of all our deeds. Everyone's life is there, and everyone's signature. The shofar sounds. The court is in session. Even the angels tremble. The trial is about to begin.

The next movement tells us what is at stake. The fate of each of us will be decided today: who will live, who will die, who will prosper, who will suffer, who will be at ease, who will face strife, who will fall and who will rise.

Then, just as we seem to be embracing a kind of fatalism, the poem sets up a counterpoint with the cry: *But repentance, prayer and charity avert the*

כְּבַקָּרַת רוֹעֶה As a shepherd's searching gaze meets his flock,
as he passes every sheep beneath his rod,
so You too pass Yours, count and number,
and regard the soul of every living thing;
and You rule off the limit of each creation's life,
and write down the verdict for each.

In most congregations the following is said first by the congregation and then the Leader; in some by the Leader alone.

בְּרֹאשׁ הַשָּׁנָה On Rosh HaShana it is written / and on Yom Kippur it is sealed: / how many will pass away and how many will be born; / who will live and who will die; / who in his due time and who before; / who by water and who by fire; / who by sword and who by beast; / who of hunger and who of thirst; / who by earthquake and who by plague; / who by strangling and who by stoning; / who will rest and who will wander; / who will be calm and who will be harassed; / who will be at ease and who will suffer; / who will become poor and who will grow rich; / who cast down and who raised high.

In many editions of the maḥzor, the words "Repentance, Prayer and Charity" are accompanied by three corresponding words: fasting, crying, giving. The numerical value (gematria) of each Hebrew word being 136, these words indicate that the three modes of approaching God are equivalent (Minhagim of Rabbi Isaac Tirna, fifteenth century).

The congregation says aloud, followed by the Leader:

FASTING *CRYING* *GIVING*

But **REPENTANCE, PRAYER** and **CHARITY**
avert the evil of the decree.

וּתְשׁוּבָה וּתְפִלָּה וּצְדָקָה – REPENTANCE, PRAYER AND CHARITY
Repentance is our relationship to ourselves. Prayer is our relationship to God. Charity is our relationship to others. In repentance we look inward. In prayer we look upward. In charity we look outward. We should be honest in our relationship with ourselves, humble in our relationship to God and generous in our relationship to others.

REPENTANCE
We can change. That is the radical proposition at the heart of *teshuva*. It has been denied in many ages in many ways. People have said our fate is in our stars; or we are predestined to become what we are; or our lives are

כְּבַקָּרַת רוֹעֶה עֶדְרוֹ / מַעֲבִיר צֹאנוֹ תַּחַת שִׁבְטוֹ
כֵּן תַּעֲבִיר וְתִסְפֹּר וְתִמְנֶה / וְתִפְקֹד נֶפֶשׁ כָּל חָי
וְתַחְתֹּךְ קִצְבָה לְכָל בְּרִיָּה / וְתִכְתֹּב אֶת גְּזַר דִּינָם.

In most congregations the following is said first by the קהל and then the שליח ציבור; in some by the שליח ציבור alone.

בְּרֹאשׁ הַשָּׁנָה יִכָּתֵבוּן / וּבְיוֹם צוֹם כִּפּוּר יֵחָתֵמוּן.
כַּמָּה יַעַבְרוּן וְכַמָּה יִבָּרֵאוּן
מִי יִחְיֶה וּמִי יָמוּת / מִי בְקִצּוֹ וּמִי לֹא בְקִצּוֹ
מִי בַמַּיִם וּמִי בָאֵשׁ / מִי בַחֶרֶב וּמִי בַחַיָּה / מִי בָרָעָב וּמִי בַצָּמָא
מִי בָרַעַשׁ וּמִי בַמַּגֵּפָה / מִי בַחֲנִיקָה וּמִי בַסְּקִילָה.
מִי יָנְוּחַ וּמִי יָנְוּעַ / מִי יִשָּׁקֵט וּמִי יִטָּרֵף
מִי יִשָּׁלֵו וּמִי יִתְיַסָּר / מִי יֵעָנִי וּמִי יֵעָשֵׁר / מִי יִשָּׁפֵל וּמִי יָרוּם.

In many editions of the מחזור, the words "וּתְשׁוּבָה וּתְפִלָּה וּצְדָקָה" are accompanied by three corresponding words: צום, קול, and ממון. The numerical value (גימטריה) of each word being 136, these words indicate that the three modes of approaching God are equivalent (Minhagim of Rabbi Isaac Tirna, fifteenth century).

The קהל says aloud, followed by the שליח ציבור:

צום קול ממון
וּתְשׁוּבָה וּתְפִלָּה וּצְדָקָה / מַעֲבִירִין אֶת רֹעַ הַגְּזֵרָה.

---

of pottery, a blade of grass, a flower that fades, a shadow, a cloud, a breath of wind. Dust we are and to dust we return. But God is life forever: holding fast to Him we defeat death. "We are children of this world," wrote Rabbi Moshe ibn Ezra, "but God has set eternity in our hearts."

Untaneh Tokef was long believed to have been written in the eleventh century by Rabbi Amnon of Mainz, who died a martyr's death after refusing to convert to Christianity. The discovery of the prayer in ancient manuscripts in the Cairo Geniza suggests, however, that the prayer is older than this. Almost certainly it was composed in Israel, possibly as early as the sixth or seventh century, and possibly by Yannai, the first great composer of liturgical poetry known to us by name. The story of Rabbi Amnon is less about the composition of the prayer than about its adoption by the Jewish communities of northern Europe.

All:

כִּי כְּשִׁמְךָ For as Your name is, so is Your renown:
hard to anger, and readily appeased.
For You do not desire the condemned man's death,
but that he may come back from his ways, and live.
To the very day he dies, You wait for him;
and if he comes back, You welcome him at once.

---

us." "Don't worry," said the rabbi. "You have not climbed high enough for it to pursue you. For the time being, you are pursuing it."

Rabbi Levi Yitzḥak of Berditchev was known for his daring prayers in defense of the Jewish people. Once he prayed, "Master of the universe, we have many sins. You have much forgiveness. I propose a deal: our sins for Your forgiveness. And should You say, That is not a fair deal, I would reply, Without our sins, of what use would Your forgiveness be?"

PRAYER

Prayer is the language of the soul in conversation with God. It is the most intimate gesture of the religious life and the most transformative. The very fact that we can pray testifies to the deepest elements of Jewish faith: that the universe did not come into existence accidentally, nor are our lives bereft of meaning. The universe exists, and we exist, because someone – the One God, Author of all – brought us into being with love. We are not alone. It is this belief more than any other that redeems life from solitude and fate from tragedy. In prayer we speak to a presence vaster than the unfathomable universe yet closer to us than we are to ourselves: the God who listens and cares, loves and forgives.

At its height, prayer is a profoundly transformative experience. Through it we learn that, "Though my father and mother may reject me, God will gather me in" (Ps. 27:10). God never rejects us or loses faith in us. Because He is with us in our efforts, we do not labor in vain. When we stumble, He lifts us; when we are at the edge of despair He gives us strength. However far we feel from God, He is behind us, and all we have to do is turn to face Him. When we do so, we are brushed by the wings of eternity. Prayer changes the world because it changes us.

Of course, we do not always feel this. Yet regular daily prayer works on us in ways not immediately apparent. As the sea smoothes the stone, as

All:

כִּי כְשִׁמְךָ כֵּן תְּהִלָּתֶךָ / קָשֶׁה לִכְעֹס וְנוֹחַ לִרְצוֹת
כִּי לֹא תַחְפֹּץ בְּמוֹת הַמֵּת / כִּי אִם בְּשׁוּבוֹ מִדַּרְכּוֹ, וְחָיָה
וְעַד יוֹם מוֹתוֹ תְּחַכֶּה לוֹ / אִם יָשׁוּב, מִיָּד תְּקַבְּלוֹ.

---

determined by Marxist, Freudian or Darwinian causes; or our character is written in our genes. At best these are half-truths, because by effort, discipline and will, sometimes even through a single transformative moment, we can cease to be the person we were and become the person we are called on to be.

Judah, Jacob's son, who proposed selling his brother Joseph as a slave, later became the man willing to spend the rest of his life as a slave so that his brother Benjamin could go free. Moses, the tongue-tied stammerer, became the most eloquent of Israel's prophets. Hillel, the poor Babylonian, eventually became Nasi, Prince of the Jewish people. Akiva, illiterate until he was forty, became the greatest rabbi of his time. There is nothing pre-scripted about our fate. Repentance is God's call to freedom: to be what we choose to be, what we could be, what God wants us to be, a blessing to humanity and a reflection, however pale, of His light.

At first, I wanted to change the world. I tried, but the world did not change. Then I tried to change my town, but the town did not change. Then I tried to change my family, but my family did not change. Then I realized: first, I must change myself. (Rabbi Israel Salanter)

Better is the sinner who knows he is a sinner than the saint who believes he is a saint. (Hasidic saying)

We are afraid of things that cannot harm us, and we know it, and we crave things that cannot help us, and we know it. But in truth the one thing we are afraid of is within us, and the one thing we crave is within us also. (Rabbi Naḥman of Bratslav)

Rabbi Nathan of Nemerov said, "Rabbi Naḥman (of Bratslav) once told me, 'You have faith, but you have no faith in yourself.' He meant you must believe that you are precious in God's eyes. The fact that every single individual is important to Him is a measure of God's goodness."

Once when Rabbi Pineḥas of Koretz entered the house of study, he found his disciples deep in conversation. "What are you talking about?" he asked. They replied, "We were saying how afraid we are that the evil urge will pursue

אֱמֶת Truly, it was You who formed them,
and You know the forces moving them,
for they are but flesh and blood.

---

disappearance he asked the Rebbe's followers, "Where is he?" "Where is the Rebbe?" they replied. "Where else but in heaven? The people of the town need peace, sustenance, health. The Rebbe is a holy man and therefore he is surely in heaven, pleading our cause."

The Lithuanian, amused by their credulity, determined to find out for himself. One Thursday night he hid himself in the Rebbe's house. The next morning before dawn he heard the Rebbe weep and sigh. Then he saw him go to the cupboard, take out a parcel of clothes and begin to put them on. They were the clothes, not of a holy man, but of a peasant. The Rebbe then reached into a drawer, pulled out an axe, and went out into the still dark night. Stealthily, the Lithuanian followed him as he walked through the town and beyond, into the forest. There he began chopping down a tree, hewing it into logs, and splitting it into firewood. These he gathered into a bundle and walked back into the town.

In one of the back streets, he stopped outside a run-down cottage and knocked on the door. An old woman, poor and ill, opened the door. "Who are you?" she said. "I am Vasil," the Rebbe replied. "I have wood to sell, very cheap, next to nothing." "I have no money," replied the woman. "I will give it to you on credit," he said. "How will I be able to pay you?" she said. "I trust you – and do you not trust God? He will find a way of seeing that I am repaid." "But who will light the fire? I am too ill." "I will light the fire," the Rebbe replied, and he did so, reciting under his breath the penitential prayers. Then he returned home.

The Lithuanian scholar, seeing this, stayed on in the town and became one of the Rebbe's disciples. After that day, when he heard the people of the town tell visitors that the Rebbe ascended to heaven, he no longer laughed, but added: "If not higher." (Y. L. Peretz)

There is a strange feature of the geography of the Holy Land. Israel contains two seas: the Dead Sea and the Sea of Galilee. The latter is full of life: fish, birds, vegetation. The former, as its name suggests, contains no life at all. Yet they are both fed by the same river, the Jordan. The difference is that the Sea of Galilee receives water at one end and gives out water at the other. The Dead Sea receives but does not give. The Jordan ends there. To receive without reciprocating is a kind of death. To live is to give.

אֱמֶת, כִּי אַתָּה הוּא יוֹצְרָם / וְיוֹדֵעַ יִצְרָם / כִּי הֵם בָּשָׂר וָדָם.

---

the repeated hammer-blows of the sculptor shape the marble, so prayer – repeated, cyclical, tracking the rhythms of time itself – gradually wears away the jagged edges of our character, turning it into a work of devotional art.

We begin to see the beauty of the created world. We locate ourselves as part of the story of our people. We come to think less of the "I," more of the "We"; less of what we lack than of what we have; less of what we need from the world, more of what the world needs from us. Slowly we achieve the deep happiness that comes from learning to give praise and thanks. Prayer is less about getting what we want than about learning what to want. Through it we align ourselves with the moral energies of the universe. Our spiritual horizons expand. Singing the song of our people, we grow.

The world we build tomorrow is born in the prayers we say today.

Prayer is the act of listening to God listening to us. It is phatic communion, the touch of two selves. Yes, there are words, many of them. There is a text, a liturgy, a *siddur,* a proper "order" of prayer, the libretto constructed by generation after generation of men and women of faith as they searched for the words that would best express their collective thanks to Heaven and their hopes for Heaven's grace. But there is also a listening beyond words, a silence that gives meaning to speech. In that silence, we know and are known by God.

The Maggid of Mezeritch said: "Every lock has a key which fits it and opens it. But there are strong thieves who know how to open a lock without a key. They simply break the lock. So, every mystery in the world can be unlocked by a specific meditation. But God loves the thief who breaks the lock open: I mean the person who breaks his heart for God."

It is written, "Water wears away stone" (Job 14:9). It may seem that water dripping on a stone cannot make any impression. Nevertheless, after many years it can actually make a hole in the stone. Your heart may seem like stone. It may seem that your words of prayer make no impression on it at all. Still, as the days and years pass, your heart of stone will also be penetrated. (Rabbi Naḥman of Bratslav)

CHARITY

Every Friday morning before dawn, during the time of *Seliḥot,* the Rebbe of Nemirov would disappear. He could be found in none of the town's synagogues or houses of study. The doors of his house were open but he was not there. Once, a Lithuanian scholar came to Nemirov. Puzzled by the regular

אָדָם יְסוֹדוֹ Man is founded in dust / and ends in dust.
He lays down his soul to bring home bread. / He is like a broken shard,
like grass dried up, like a faded flower,
like a fleeting shadow, like a passing cloud,
like a breath of wind, like whirling dust, like a dream that slips away.

The congregation says aloud, followed by the Leader:

AND YOU ARE KING –

THE LIVING, EVERLASTING GOD.

The Ark is closed.

---

the work of creation, and that is as close to immortality as we will ever come. To know that God empowers us to take risks for His sake, that He forgives our failings, lifts us when we fall, and believes in us more than we believe in ourselves – that is all we need to have the courage not to accept the world but to attempt to heal it, one fracture at a time, one day at a time, one act at a time.

Every good act, every healing gesture, lights a candle of hope in a dark world. What would humanity be after the Holocaust were it not for the memory of those courageous few who saved lives, hid children, rescued those they could? There were times when the gift of a crust of bread – even a smile – gave a prisoner the will to live. A single message of support can tell threatened populations that they are not alone. One act of hospitality can redeem a lonely life on the brink of despair. A word of praise can give strength to someone losing the will to carry on. We never know, at the time, the ripple of consequences set in motion by the slightest act of kindness.

"A little light," said the Jewish mystics, "drives away much darkness." And when light is joined to light, mine to yours and yours to others, the dance of flames, each so small, yet together so intricately beautiful, begins to show that hope is not an illusion. Evil, injustice, oppression, cruelty, do not have the final word. Perhaps it is true that "from the crooked timber of humanity no straight thing was ever made." But we do not need to be straight to point upward, nor do we need to be perfect to be good. Every generous or gentle or courageous deed begets others, inspires others, initiating a wave of transformation whose end we cannot see.

A single act, performed for its own sake out of love, gives us – wrote Maimonides – a share in the World to Come (Commentary to Mishna, *Makkot* 3:17). A single act may redeem a life and grant us our share in immortality.

אָדָם יְסוֹדוֹ מֵעָפָר / וְסוֹפוֹ לֶעָפָר
בְּנַפְשׁוֹ יָבִיא לַחְמוֹ / מָשׁוּל כַּחֶרֶס הַנִּשְׁבָּר
כְּחָצִיר יָבֵשׁ, וּכְצִיץ נוֹבֵל / כְּצֵל עוֹבֵר, וּכְעָנָן כָּלֶה
וּכְרוּחַ נוֹשָׁבֶת, וּכְאָבָק פּוֹרֵחַ, וְכַחֲלוֹם יָעוּף.

The קהל *says aloud, followed by the* שליח ציבור*:*

וְאַתָּה הוּא מֶלֶךְ, אֵל חַי וְקַיָּם.

The ארון קודש *is closed.*

Sir Moses Montefiore, one of the great Jews of Victorian Britain, was a very wealthy man. Someone once asked him how much he was worth. Sir Moses quoted a figure in the tens of thousands. The man said, "But Sir Moses, surely you own millions!" Sir Moses replied, "You did not ask me how much I own. You asked me what I was worth. So I told you how much I have given to charity this year, because *we are worth what we are willing to share with others.*"

אָדָם יְסוֹדוֹ מֵעָפָר וְסוֹפוֹ לֶעָפָר *Man is founded in dust and ends in dust.* Life is God's question. We are His answer. It may be a good answer or a bad one, but it is the only answer there is. God does not need to know, or be assured by us, that He is God. He needs to know that we hear His call, that we are ready to rise to His challenge, and that we are willing to take into our own hands the responsibility with which He has entrusted us, empowered and given strength by that very trust itself.

We have only one life, and however long it is, it is a mere microsecond in the history of the universe. The greatest decision we will ever make is how to use our time, how to create something of beauty and meaning and love that was not there before. We find meaning through a life well lived, in pursuit of the good for its own sake. Neither pleasure nor desire, success nor fame, wealth nor power, can remotely rival it as a source of satisfaction or self-respect. The paradox of altruism is that the hope we give others, returns to us undiminished and enlarged.

Something momentous is born every time a human being takes the decision not to rail against the evils of the world but instead to do something to alleviate them. This *ethic of responsibility* is Judaism's great contribution to the world. No faith has asked more of its followers. None has taken so high a view of human possibility. We may be mortal but we are God's partners in

The congregation and then the Leader:

אֵין קִצְבָה There is no end to Your years,
no limit to the days of Your life.
One cannot grasp the measure of Your glorious chariot;
one may not articulate Your most concealed name.
Your name is befitting to You and You befit Your name.
By that name You have named us.
Act for Your name's sake.
Sanctify Your name through those who sanctify Your name,
for the sake of the glory of Your name, revered and sanctified,
with the words uttered by the holy Seraphim
who sanctify Your name in the Sanctuary,
those who live in heaven with those who live on earth
cry out and three times repeat
the threefold declaration of holiness to the Holy One,

KEDUSHA

The following is said standing with feet together, rising on the toes at the words indicated by ▴.

as is written by Your prophet:
"They call out to one another, saying: *Is. 6*

The congregation then the Leader:

▴Holy, ▴holy, ▴holy is the LORD of hosts;
the whole world is filled with His glory."
His glory fills the universe. His ministering angels ask each other,
"Where is the place of His glory?"
Those facing them reply "Blessed –

The congregation then the Leader:

▴"Blessed is the LORD's glory from His place." *Ezek. 3*
From His place may He turn with compassion
and be gracious to the people who proclaim the unity of His name,
morning and evening, every day, continually,
twice each day reciting in love the Shema:

בָּרוּךְ כְּבוֹד־יהוה מִמְּקוֹמוֹ *Blessed is the LORD's glory from His place.* Though Isaiah and Ezekiel both saw visions of God enthroned in heaven, what they

The קהל *and then the* שליח ציבור*:*

אֵין קִצְבָה לִשְׁנוֹתֶיךָ / וְאֵין קֵץ לְאֹרֶךְ יָמֶיךָ

וְאֵין לְשַׁעֵר מַרְכְּבוֹת כְּבוֹדֶךָ / וְאֵין לְפָרֵשׁ עֵילוֹם שְׁמֶךָ.

שִׁמְךָ נָאֶה לְךָ / וְאַתָּה נָאֶה לִשְׁמֶךָ / וּשְׁמֵנוּ קָרָאתָ בִשְׁמֶךָ.

עֲשֵׂה לְמַעַן שְׁמֶךָ, וְקַדֵּשׁ אֶת שִׁמְךָ עַל מַקְדִּישֵׁי שְׁמֶךָ

בַּעֲבוּר כְּבוֹד שִׁמְךָ הַנַּעֲרָץ וְהַנִּקְדָּשׁ

כְּסוֹד שִׂיחַ שַׂרְפֵי קֹדֶשׁ, הַמַּקְדִּישִׁים שִׁמְךָ בַּקֹּדֶשׁ

דָּרֵי מַעְלָה עִם דָּרֵי מַטָּה

קוֹרְאִים וּמְשַׁלְּשִׁים בְּשִׁלּוּשׁ קְדֻשָּׁה בַּקֹּדֶשׁ.

קדושה

The following is said standing with feet together, rising on the toes at the words indicated by ▲.

כַּכָּתוּב עַל יַד נְבִיאֶךָ: וְקָרָא זֶה אֶל־זֶה וְאָמַר ישעיה ו

The קהל *then the* שליח ציבור*:*

▲קָדוֹשׁ, ▲קָדוֹשׁ, ▲קָדוֹשׁ, יהוה צְבָאוֹת, מְלֹא כָל־הָאָרֶץ כְּבוֹדוֹ:
כְּבוֹדוֹ מָלֵא עוֹלָם, מְשָׁרְתָיו שׁוֹאֲלִים זֶה לָזֶה, אַיֵּה מְקוֹם כְּבוֹדוֹ
לְעֻמָּתָם בָּרוּךְ יֹאמֵרוּ

The קהל *then the* שליח ציבור*:*

▲בָּרוּךְ כְּבוֹד־יהוה מִמְּקוֹמוֹ: יחזקאל ג
מִמְּקוֹמוֹ הוּא יִפֶן בְּרַחֲמִים, וְיָחֹן עַם הַמְיַחֲדִים שְׁמוֹ, עֶרֶב וָבֹקֶר
בְּכָל יוֹם תָּמִיד, פַּעֲמַיִם בְּאַהֲבָה שְׁמַע אוֹמְרִים

KEDUSHA

Kedusha is the highest peak of prayer. While saying it, it is as if we have left behind the gravitational pull of earth and we are in heaven, part of the angelic choir singing God's praises. Based on the mystical visions of Isaiah and Ezekiel, we say the words they heard the angels sing.

The congregation then the Leader:

"Listen, Israel, the LORD is our God, the LORD is One." *Deut. 6*
He is our God, He is our Father, He is our King,
He is our Savior – and He, in His compassion,
will let us hear a second time in the presence of all that lives,
His promise "to be your God. I am the LORD your God." *Num. 15*

The congregation then the Leader:

Glorious is our Glorious One, LORD our Master, *Ps. 8*
and glorious is Your name throughout the earth.
Then the LORD shall be King over all the earth; *Zech. 14*
on that day the LORD shall be One and His name One.

The Leader continues:

And in Your holy Writings it is written:

The congregation then the Leader:

▲"The LORD shall reign for ever. *Ps. 146*
He is your God, Zion, from generation to generation, Halleluya!"

The Leader continues:

From generation to generation we will declare Your greatness,
and we will proclaim Your holiness for evermore.
Your praise, our God, shall not leave our mouth forever,
for You, God, are a great and holy King.

אַדִּיר אַדִּירֵנוּ *Glorious is our Glorious One.* An addition to the *Kedusha* said only on festivals and High Holy Days, reflecting the fact that these are times when we have a heightened consciousness of God's glory through His role in Israel's history.

לְדוֹר וָדוֹר *From generation to generation.* The greatest thing we receive from our parents and give to our children is our Jewish heritage. There are no gifts greater than these: an identity, a history, a destiny, rules to live by and ideals to which to strive. Jews and Judaism exist today because, for two-thirds of the history of humanity, Jews set it as their highest priority to hand on their faith to the next generation.

The קהל *then the* שליח ציבור:

שְׁמַע יִשְׂרָאֵל, יהוה אֱלֹהֵינוּ, יהוה אֶחָד: דברים ו
הוּא אֱלֹהֵינוּ, הוּא אָבִינוּ, הוּא מַלְכֵּנוּ, הוּא מוֹשִׁיעֵנוּ, וְהוּא
יַשְׁמִיעֵנוּ בְּרַחֲמָיו שֵׁנִית לְעֵינֵי כָּל חָי, לִהְיוֹת לָכֶם לֵאלֹהִים, במדבר טו
אֲנִי יהוה אֱלֹהֵיכֶם:

The קהל *then the* שליח ציבור:

אַדִּיר אַדִּירֵנוּ, יהוה אֲדֹנֵינוּ, מָה־אַדִּיר שִׁמְךָ בְּכָל־הָאָרֶץ: תהלים ח
וְהָיָה יהוה לְמֶלֶךְ עַל־כָּל־הָאָרֶץ זכריה יד
בַּיּוֹם הַהוּא יִהְיֶה יהוה אֶחָד וּשְׁמוֹ אֶחָד:

The שליח ציבור *continues:*

וּבְדִבְרֵי קָדְשְׁךָ כָּתוּב לֵאמֹר

The קהל *then the* שליח ציבור:

יִמְלֹךְ יהוה לְעוֹלָם, אֱלֹהַיִךְ צִיּוֹן לְדֹר וָדֹר, הַלְלוּיָהּ: תהלים קמו

The שליח ציבור *continues:*

לְדוֹר וָדוֹר נַגִּיד גָּדְלֶךָ, וּלְנֵצַח נְצָחִים קְדֻשָּׁתְךָ נַקְדִּישׁ
וְשִׁבְחֲךָ אֱלֹהֵינוּ מִפִּינוּ לֹא יָמוּשׁ לְעוֹלָם וָעֶד
כִּי אֵל מֶלֶךְ גָּדוֹל וְקָדוֹשׁ אָתָּה.

---

heard the angels sing was profoundly different. Isaiah heard them singing, "The whole world is filled with His glory." Ezekiel heard them sing, "Blessed is the LORD's glory from His place." The reason for the difference is that Isaiah prophesied when Israel was in its land, the Temple stood, the priests performed their service and the Levites sang their song, whereas Ezekiel prophesied from Babylon in exile. Isaiah saw God's glory filling the world. Ezekiel saw it confined, as it were, to heaven. In exile there is *hester panim*, as if God were "hiding His face." (Rabbi Joseph Soloveitchik)

The following prayer originally began at "For with Your holiness." Nowadays, it is commonly sung as one stanza together with the later addition of the opening verse, "Have mercy on those You have made."

חֲמֹל Have mercy on those You have made,
take joy in those You made,
and those who shelter in You will say,
as You absolve the ones You bear,
"Be sanctified, LORD, through all that You have made."

כִּי מַקְדִּישֶׁיךָ For with Your holiness You sanctify
all who affirm You holy;
it is fitting that the Holy One be glorified by holy ones.

Leader:

וּבְכֵן יִתְקַדַּשׁ And so may Your name be sanctified, LORD our God,
through Israel Your nation
and Jerusalem, Your city,
and Zion, the dwelling place of Your honor
and through the royal house of David Your anointed,
and Your Sanctuary and Your Temple.

He, our LORD,
will yet remember for us the love of [Abraham] the steadfast one.
And for [Isaac] the son who was bound,
He will still the enmity against us,
and for the merit of [Jacob] the innocent man,
He will bring today our judgment out to the good,
for this day is holy to our LORD. *Neh. 8*

With no one to advocate for us
against the accuser of sin,
speak words of law and of justice to Jacob;
and absolve us in the judgment, O King of judgment.

בְּאֵין מֵלִיץ יֹשֶׁר *With no one to advocate for us.* The poet, drawing on imagery from the book of Job, imagines a courtroom scene in which the accused has no defending counsel to answer the prosecuting attorney.

The following prayer originally began at "כִּי מַקְדִּישֶׁיךָ." Nowadays, it is commonly sung as one stanza together with the later addition of the opening verse, "חֲמֹל עַל מַעֲשֶׂיךָ."

חֲמֹל עַל מַעֲשֶׂיךָ וְתִשְׂמַח בְּמַעֲשֶׂיךָ
וְיֹאמְרוּ לְךָ חוֹסֶיךָ בְּצַדֶּקְךָ עֲמוּסֶיךָ
תֻּקְדַּשׁ אָדוֹן עַל כָּל מַעֲשֶׂיךָ

כִּי מַקְדִּישֶׁיךָ בִּקְדֻשָּׁתְךָ קִדַּשְׁתָּ
נָאֶה לְקָדוֹשׁ פְּאֵר מִקְּדוֹשִׁים.

The שליח ציבור*:*

וּבְכֵן יִתְקַדַּשׁ שִׁמְךָ יהוה אֱלֹהֵינוּ
עַל יִשְׂרָאֵל עַמֶּךָ
וְעַל יְרוּשָׁלַיִם עִירֶךָ
וְעַל צִיּוֹן מִשְׁכַּן כְּבוֹדֶךָ
וְעַל מַלְכוּת בֵּית דָּוִד מְשִׁיחֶךָ
וְעַל מְכוֹנְךָ וְהֵיכָלֶךָ.

עוֹד יִזְכֹּר לָנוּ אַהֲבַת אֵיתָן, אֲדוֹנֵינוּ
וּבַבֵּן הַנֶּעֱקָד יַשְׁבִּית מְדַיְּנֵינוּ
וּבִזְכוּת הַתָּם יוֹצִיא הַיּוֹם לְצֶדֶק דִּינֵנוּ
כִּי־קָדוֹשׁ הַיּוֹם לַאֲדֹנֵינוּ: נחמיה ח

בְּאֵין מֵלִיץ יֹשֶׁר מוּל מַגִּיד פֶּשַׁע
תַּגִּיד לְיַעֲקֹב דְּבַר, חֹק וּמִשְׁפָּט
וְצַדְּקֵנוּ בְּמִשְׁפָּט, הַמֶּלֶךְ הַמִּשְׁפָּט.

חֲמֹל עַל מַעֲשֶׂיךָ *Have mercy on those You have made.* A prayer woven out of several fragments from different places and times. Its theme is the mutual relationship between God's holiness and that of His people Israel. God made them holy; they declare Him holy.

This piyut, with its double alphabetic acrostic, is attributed to Yannai (a poet who lived in Israel in the Byzantine era). In recent generations the custom to say it responsively has spread; many congregations are accustomed to saying the second stich of each couplet together with the first of the next one. Some sing the entire piyut collectively.

The Ark is opened.

הָאוֹחֵז בְּיַד The One who holds in His hand the trait of stern judgment.
And all believe that He is the faithful God.

The One who examines and scrutinizes the hidden stores.
And all believe that He examines the conscience of all.

The One who redeems from death and ransoms from hell.
And all believe that He is a mighty Redeemer.

The sole Judge of all who enter the world.
And all believe that He is a truthful Judge.

The One whose name was pronounced "I will ever be what I am now."
And all believe that He was, is, and shall forever be.

The One whose praise is as affirmed as His name.
And all believe that He is One and there is no other.

The One who recalls kindly those who utter His name.
And all believe that He recalls His covenant.

The One who allots life to all the living.
And all believe that He lives and is everlasting.

---

believe in me" (Ex. 4:1). God replied, "They are believers, the children of believers, but in the end *you* will not believe" – a reference to the lapse in which Moses struck the rock and forfeited his chance to lead the Israelites into the Promised Land (*Shabbat* 97a).

The sages were here giving expression to one of the most striking facts of Jewish history, that by and large Jews did not lose faith in God, even in the longest exile ever endured by a people. They were the God-intoxicated people, the people who said, "I believe, therefore I am."

אֶהְיֶה אֲשֶׁר אֶהְיֶה *I will ever be what I am now.* The words God spoke to Moses when he asked Him how he should refer to God when speaking to the Israelites (Ex. 3:14). Literally, the phrase means, "I will be what I will be," signaling that God cannot be predicted or fully known and that the fullest disclosure of His presence is in the future.

This piyut, with its double alphabetic acrostic, is attributed to Yannai (a poet who lived in ארץ ישראל *in the Byzantine era). In recent generations the custom to say it responsively has spread; many congregations are accustomed to saying the second stich of each couplet together with the first of the next one. Some sing the entire piyut collectively.*

The ארון קודש *is opened.*

הָאוֹחֵז בְּיָד מִדַּת מִשְׁפָּט
וְכֹל מַאֲמִינִים שֶׁהוּא אֵל אֱמוּנָה.

הַבּוֹחֵן וּבוֹדֵק גִּנְזֵי נִסְתָּרוֹת
וְכֹל מַאֲמִינִים שֶׁהוּא בּוֹחֵן כְּלָיוֹת.

הַגּוֹאֵל מִמָּוֶת וּפוֹדֶה מִשַּׁחַת
וְכֹל מַאֲמִינִים שֶׁהוּא גּוֹאֵל חָזָק.

הַדָּן יְחִידִי לְבָאֵי עוֹלָם
וְכֹל מַאֲמִינִים שֶׁהוּא דַּיַּן אֱמֶת.

הֶהָגוּי בְּאֶהְיֶה אֲשֶׁר אֶהְיֶה
וְכֹל מַאֲמִינִים שֶׁהוּא הָיָה וְהֹוֶה וְיִהְיֶה.

הַוַּדַּאי, כִּשְׁמוֹ כֵּן תְּהִלָּתוֹ
וְכֹל מַאֲמִינִים שֶׁהוּא וְאֵין בִּלְתּוֹ.

הַזּוֹכֵר לְמַזְכִּירָיו טוֹבוֹת זִכְרוֹנוֹת
וְכֹל מַאֲמִינִים שֶׁהוּא זוֹכֵר הַבְּרִית.

הַחוֹתֵךְ חַיִּים לְכָל חָי
וְכֹל מַאֲמִינִים שֶׁהוּא חַי וְקַיָּם.

הָאוֹחֵז בְּיָד *The One who holds in His hand.* A poem listing the attributes of God, author unknown. Each verse begins by recapitulating the description of God in the previous verse, then moving on alphabetically to a new attribute, creating a step-like effect.

וְכֹל מַאֲמִינִים *And all believe.* According to the sages, when Moses was summoned by God to lead the Israelites to freedom, he said, "They will not

The One who acts kindly with both the good and evil.
And all believe that He is kind to all.

The One who knows the devices of all creatures.
And all believe that He is the One who forms them in the womb.

The One who can do all things, and all of them together.
And all believe that He can do all things.

The One who dwells concealed in His holy shade.
And all believe that He alone is God.

The One who crowns kings yet the reign is His alone.
And all believe that He is an everlasting King.

The One who acts kindly with each generation.
And all believe that He reserves kindness.

The One who acts patiently with evildoers
and turns a blind eye to the wayward.
And all believe that He is forgiving and exalted.

The Lofty One whose eyes are turned to those who fear Him.
And all believe that He answers whispered prayers.

The One who opens the gates to those who come knocking penitently.
And all believe that His hand is ever open.

The One who espies the evildoer and wishes to justify him.
And all believe that He is righteous and upright.

---

individual creation, the Torah uses the word "good," but of the totality it uses the phrase "*very* good" (Gen. 1:31), meaning "good in its totality" (Rabbi Samson Raphael Hirsch). God's creativity is manifest not just in what exists but in the precisely calibrated interrelationship *between* all that exists.

בְּסֵתֶר בְּצֵל שַׁדַּי *Concealed in His holy shade.* The concealment of God is as important as His revelation, for if the radiance of God were fully visible, neither we nor the universe could exist. God's infinity would destroy our finitude. Thus the physical universe is possible only because of *tzimtzum*, divine "self-limitation" (Rabbi Isaac Luria).

הַטּוֹב וּמֵיטִיב לָרָעִים וְלַטּוֹבִים
וְכֹל מַאֲמִינִים שֶׁהוּא טוֹב לַכֹּל.

הַיּוֹדֵעַ יֵצֶר כָּל יְצוּרִים
וְכֹל מַאֲמִינִים שֶׁהוּא יוֹצְרָם בַּבָּטֶן.

הַכֹּל יָכוֹל, וְכוֹלְלָם יַחַד
וְכֹל מַאֲמִינִים שֶׁהוּא כֹּל יָכוֹל.

הַלָּן בְּסֵתֶר בְּצֵל שַׁדַּי
וְכֹל מַאֲמִינִים שֶׁהוּא לְבַדּוֹ הוּא.

הַמַּמְלִיךְ מְלָכִים, וְלוֹ הַמְּלוּכָה
וְכֹל מַאֲמִינִים שֶׁהוּא מֶלֶךְ עוֹלָם.

הַנּוֹהֵג בְּחַסְדּוֹ עִם כָּל דּוֹר
וְכֹל מַאֲמִינִים שֶׁהוּא נוֹצֵר חֶסֶד.

הַסּוֹבֵל, וּמַעֲלִים עַיִן מִסּוֹרְרִים
וְכֹל מַאֲמִינִים שֶׁהוּא סוֹלֵחַ סֶלָה.

הָעֶלְיוֹן, וְעֵינָיו אֶל יְרֵאָיו
וְכֹל מַאֲמִינִים שֶׁהוּא עוֹנֶה לָחַשׁ.

הַפּוֹתֵחַ שַׁעַר לְדוֹפְקֵי בִּתְשׁוּבָה
וְכֹל מַאֲמִינִים שֶׁהוּא פְּתוּחָה יָדוֹ.

הַצּוֹפֶה רָשָׁע, וְחָפֵץ לְהַצְדִּיקוֹ
וְכֹל מַאֲמִינִים שֶׁהוּא צַדִּיק וְיָשָׁר.

וְכוֹלְלָם יַחַד *And all of them together.* A reference to the systemic nature of God's creation. Each force that shapes the cosmos, and each life-form that exists, is part of the total ecology of the universe and its delicate balance. Of each

The One who is slow to anger and defers wrath.
And all believe that His ire is hard to arouse.

The Compassionate One who lets pity precede rage.
And all believe that He is easily appeased.

The Constant One who considers great and small equally.
And all believe that He is a righteous Judge.

The Perfect One who deals in integrity with the innocent.
And all believe that His works are perfect and complete.

The Ark is closed (in some communities, the Ark remains open until the end of the next paragraph).

תִּשְׂגַּב לְבַדֶּךָ You will be elevated, peerless,
and will rule over all that is, alone,
as is written by Your prophet,
"Then the LORD shall be King over all the earth; *Zech. 14*
on that day the LORD shall be One and His name One."

The Leader continues:

HOLINESS

וּבְכֵן תֵּן פַּחְדְּךָ And so place the fear of You, LORD our God,
over all that You have made,
and the terror of You over all You have created,
and all who were made will stand in awe of You,
and all of creation will worship You,
and they will be bound all together as one
to carry out Your will with an undivided heart;
for we know, LORD our God,
that all dominion is laid out before You,
strength is in Your palm, and might in Your right hand,
Your name spreading awe over all You have created.

וּמַשְׁוֶה קָטֹן וְגָדוֹל *Who considers great and small equally.* Because God has set His image on each of us, He is concerned for the powerless as much as for the powerful, and for the weak no less than the strong. God's justice is impartial.

הַקָּצָר בְּזַעַם, וּמַאֲרִיךְ אַף
וְכֹל מַאֲמִינִים שֶׁהוּא קָשֶׁה לִכְעֹס.

הָרַחוּם, וּמַקְדִּים רַחֲמִים לְרֹגֶז
וְכֹל מַאֲמִינִים שֶׁהוּא רַךְ לִרְצוֹת.

הַשָּׁוֶה, וּמַשְׁוֶה קָטֹן וְגָדוֹל
וְכֹל מַאֲמִינִים שֶׁהוּא שׁוֹפֵט צֶדֶק.

הַתָּם, וּמִתַּמֵּם עִם תְּמִימִים
וְכֹל מַאֲמִינִים שֶׁהוּא תָּמִים פָּעֳלוֹ.

The ארון קודש *is closed (in some communities, the* ארון קודש *remains open until the end of the next paragraph).*

תִּשְׂגַּב לְבַדֶּךָ, וְתִמְלֹךְ עַל כֹּל בְּיִחוּד
כַּכָּתוּב עַל יַד נְבִיאֶךָ
וְהָיָה יהוה לְמֶלֶךְ עַל־כָּל־הָאָרֶץ זכריה יד
בַּיּוֹם הַהוּא יִהְיֶה יהוה אֶחָד וּשְׁמוֹ אֶחָד:

The שליח ציבור *continues:*

קדושת השם

וּבְכֵן תֵּן פַּחְדְּךָ יהוה אֱלֹהֵינוּ עַל כָּל מַעֲשֶׂיךָ
וְאֵימָתְךָ עַל כָּל מַה שֶּׁבָּרָאתָ
וְיִירָאוּךָ כָּל הַמַּעֲשִׂים, וְיִשְׁתַּחֲווּ לְפָנֶיךָ כָּל הַבְּרוּאִים
וְיֵעָשׂוּ כֻלָּם אֲגֻדָּה אֶחָת לַעֲשׂוֹת רְצוֹנְךָ בְּלֵבָב שָׁלֵם
כְּמוֹ שֶׁיָּדַעְנוּ יהוה אֱלֹהֵינוּ שֶׁהַשִּׁלְטָן לְפָנֶיךָ
עֹז בְּיָדְךָ וּגְבוּרָה בִּימִינֶךָ
וְשִׁמְךָ נוֹרָא עַל כָּל מַה שֶּׁבָּרָאתָ.

וּבְכֵן תֵּן כָּבוֹד And so place honor, Lord, upon Your people,
praise on those who fear You and hope into those who seek You,
the confidence to speak into all who long for You,
gladness to Your land, and joy to Your city,
the flourishing of pride to David Your servant,
and a lamp laid out for his descendant, Your anointed, soon, in our days.

וּבְכֵן צַדִּיקִים And then righteous people will see and rejoice,
and the upright will exult, and the pious revel in joy,
and injustice will have nothing more to say,
and all wickedness will fade away like smoke
as You sweep the rule of arrogance from the earth.

This alphabetic piyut, author unknown, celebrates the future universal recognition of God by all the nations. It is usually sung collectively.

וְיֶאֱתָיוּ And all shall come forth to worship You
and they shall bless Your honorable name.
And they shall tell of Your righteousness in the islands,
and nations that have not known You shall seek You out.
And all the ends of the earth shall praise You
and shall always say, "May the Lord forever be exalted."
And they shall spurn their idols
and be ashamed of their graven images.
And they shall turn their shoulder as one to worship You,
and those who seek Your presence
shall see You with the rising sun forever.
And they shall recognize Your majestic power,
and the errant ones shall learn to understand.
And they shall speak of Your might
and they shall exalt You who are exalted above all rulers.
And they shall leap back in fear in Your presence,
and they shall crown You with a diadem of glory.
And the mountains themselves shall break out in song,
and the islands shall joyfully shout as You are crowned.
And they shall accept the yoke of Your reign over them,
and You shall be exalted among assembled multitudes.
And they shall hear from far and wide and come
to offer You the royal crown.

וּבְכֵן תֵּן כָּבוֹד יהוה לְעַמֶּךָ
תְּהִלָּה לִירֵאֶיךָ וְתִקְוָה טוֹבָה לְדוֹרְשֶׁיךָ
וּפִתְחוֹן פֶּה לַמְיַחֲלִים לָךְ, שִׂמְחָה לְאַרְצֶךָ, וְשָׂשׂוֹן לְעִירֶךָ
וּצְמִיחַת קֶרֶן לְדָוִד עַבְדֶּךָ
וַעֲרִיכַת נֵר לְבֶן יִשַׁי מְשִׁיחֶךָ בִּמְהֵרָה בְיָמֵינוּ.

וּבְכֵן צַדִּיקִים יִרְאוּ וְיִשְׂמָחוּ, וִישָׁרִים יַעֲלֹזוּ
וַחֲסִידִים בְּרִנָּה יָגִילוּ, וְעוֹלָתָה תִּקְפָּץ פִּיהָ
וְכָל הָרִשְׁעָה כֻּלָּהּ כְּעָשָׁן תִּכְלֶה
כִּי תַעֲבִיר מֶמְשֶׁלֶת זָדוֹן מִן הָאָרֶץ.

This alphabetic piyut, author unknown, celebrates the future universal recognition of God by all the nations. It is usually sung collectively.

וְיֶאֱתָיוּ כֹּל לְעָבְדֶךָ / וִיבָרְכוּ שֵׁם כְּבוֹדֶךָ
וְיַגִּידוּ בָאִיִּים צִדְקֶךָ / וְיִדְרְשׁוּךָ עַמִּים לֹא יְדָעוּךָ
וִיהַלְלְוּךָ כָּל אַפְסֵי אָרֶץ / וְיֹאמְרוּ תָמִיד יִגְדַּל יהוה
וְיִזְנְחוּ אֶת עֲצַבֵּיהֶם / וְיַחְפְּרוּ עִם פְּסִילֵיהֶם
וְיַטּוּ שְׁכֶם אֶחָד לְעָבְדֶךָ / וְיִירָאוּךָ עִם שֶׁמֶשׁ מְבַקְשֵׁי פָנֶיךָ
וְיַכִּירוּ כֹּחַ מַלְכוּתֶךָ / וְיִלְמְדוּ תוֹעִים בִּינָה
וִימַלְּלוּ אֶת גְּבוּרָתֶךָ / וִינַשְּׂאוּךָ, מִתְנַשֵּׂא לְכֹל לְרֹאשׁ
וִיסַלְּדוּ בְחִילָה פָּנֶיךָ / וִיעַטְּרוּךָ נֵזֶר תִּפְאָרָה
וְיִפְצְחוּ הָרִים רִנָּה / וְיִצְהֲלוּ אִיִּים בְּמָלְכֶךָ
וִיקַבְּלוּ עֹל מַלְכוּתְךָ עֲלֵיהֶם / וִירוֹמְמוּךָ בִּקְהַל עָם
וְיִשְׁמְעוּ רְחוֹקִים וְיָבוֹאוּ / וְיִתְּנוּ לְךָ כֶּתֶר מְלוּכָה.

וְיֶאֱתָיוּ כֹּל *And all shall come forth.* A poetic expression of the prophetic faith that one day all nations will recognize the sovereignty of God and "The earth shall be full of the knowledge of the LORD as the waters cover the sea" (Is. 11:9).

וְתִמְלֹךְ And You, LORD, will rule alone over those You have made,
in Mount Zion, the dwelling of Your glory,
and in Jerusalem, Your holy city,
as it is written in Your holy Writings: "The LORD shall reign for ever. *Ps. 146*
He is your God, Zion, from generation to generation, Halleluya!"

קָדוֹשׁ אַתָּה You are holy, Your name is awesome,
and there is no god but You, as it is written,
"The LORD of hosts shall be raised up through His judgment, *Is. 5*
the holy God, made holy in righteousness."
Blessed are You, LORD, the holy King.

HOLINESS OF THE DAY

אַתָּה בְחַרְתָּנוּ You have chosen us from among all peoples.
You have loved and favored us. You have raised us above all tongues.
You have made us holy through Your commandments.
You have brought us near, our King, to Your service,
and have called us by Your great and holy name.

On Shabbat, add the words in parentheses:

וַתִּתֶּן לָנוּ And You, LORD our God, have given us in love
(this Sabbath day for holiness and rest, and)
this Day of Atonement
for pardon and forgiveness and atonement,
to pardon all our iniquities,
(with love,) a holy assembly
in memory of the exodus from Egypt.

(expressions of thanks) are as for all Amida prayers, while the central one is about the day and its sanctity, and constitutes the verbal counterpart of the sacrifice offered in the Temple at that time. Seven is the number that represents holiness. Special sanctity attached to the seventh day, the seventh month (Tishrei), the seventh year (*Shemitta,* the year of release), and *Yovel,* the Jubilee year after seven cycles of seven. So this middle blessing speaks of holiness while completing the holiness represented by the seven blessings of the Amida.

וְתִמְלֹךְ אַתָּה יהוה לְבַדֶּךָ עַל כָּל מַעֲשֶׂיךָ
בְּהַר צִיּוֹן מִשְׁכַּן כְּבוֹדֶךָ, וּבִירוּשָׁלַיִם עִיר קָדְשֶׁךָ
כַּכָּתוּב בְּדִבְרֵי קָדְשֶׁךָ
יִמְלֹךְ יהוה לְעוֹלָם, אֱלֹהַיִךְ צִיּוֹן לְדֹר וָדֹר, הַלְלוּיָהּ: תהלים קמו

קָדוֹשׁ אַתָּה וְנוֹרָא שְׁמֶךָ, וְאֵין אֱלוֹהַּ מִבַּלְעָדֶיךָ
כַּכָּתוּב, וַיִּגְבַּהּ יהוה צְבָאוֹת בַּמִּשְׁפָּט ישעיה ה
וְהָאֵל הַקָּדוֹשׁ נִקְדַּשׁ בִּצְדָקָה:
בָּרוּךְ אַתָּה יהוה, הַמֶּלֶךְ הַקָּדוֹשׁ.

קדושת היום

אַתָּה בְחַרְתָּנוּ מִכָּל הָעַמִּים
אָהַבְתָּ אוֹתָנוּ וְרָצִיתָ בָּנוּ
וְרוֹמַמְתָּנוּ מִכָּל הַלְּשׁוֹנוֹת
וְקִדַּשְׁתָּנוּ בְּמִצְוֹתֶיךָ
וְקֵרַבְתָּנוּ מַלְכֵּנוּ לַעֲבוֹדָתֶךָ
וְשִׁמְךָ הַגָּדוֹל וְהַקָּדוֹשׁ עָלֵינוּ קָרָאתָ.

On שבת*, add the words in parentheses:*

וַתִּתֶּן לָנוּ יהוה אֱלֹהֵינוּ בְּאַהֲבָה אֶת
(יוֹם הַשַּׁבָּת הַזֶּה לִקְדֻשָּׁה וְלִמְנוּחָה, וְאֶת)
יוֹם הַכִּפּוּרִים הַזֶּה, לִמְחִילָה וְלִסְלִיחָה וּלְכַפָּרָה
וְלִמְחָל בּוֹ אֶת כָּל עֲוֹנוֹתֵינוּ
(בְּאַהֲבָה) מִקְרָא קֹדֶשׁ, זֵכֶר לִיצִיאַת מִצְרָיִם.

KEDUSHAT HAYOM – HOLINESS OF THE DAY
With the exception of Rosh HaShana, the Musaf Amida always consists of seven blessings. The first three (expressions of praise) and the last three

וּמִפְּנֵי חֲטָאֵינוּ But because of our sins we were exiled from our land
and driven far from our country.
We cannot perform our duties in Your chosen House,
the great and holy Temple that was called by Your name,
because of the hand that was stretched out against Your Sanctuary.
May it be Your will, Lord our God and God of our ancestors,
merciful King,
that You in Your abounding compassion may once more
have mercy on us and on Your Sanctuary,
rebuilding it swiftly and adding to its glory.
Our Father, our King, reveal the glory of Your kingdom to us swiftly.
Appear and be exalted over us in the sight of all that lives.
Bring back our scattered ones from among the nations,
and gather our dispersed people from the ends of the earth.

On Shabbat, add the words in parentheses:

וַהֲבִיאֵנוּ לְצִיּוֹן Lead us to Zion, Your city, in jubilation,
and to Jerusalem, home of Your Temple, with everlasting joy.
There we will prepare for You our obligatory offerings:
the regular daily offerings in their order
and the additional offerings according to their law.
And the additional offering(s of this Sabbath day and) of this
Day of Atonement we will prepare and offer before You in love,
in accord with Your will's commandment,
as You wrote for us in Your Torah
through Your servant Moses, by Your own word, as it is said:

---

wrong place, that is, in exile. For their sin, Adam and Eve were exiled from Eden. Cain was condemned to a life of exile, "a restless wanderer on earth" (Gen. 4:12). Exile is the inevitable consequence of sin, and geographical exile is the physical counterpart of spiritual alienation, the exile of the soul. Sin estranges us from God and thus from the deepest part of ourselves. The sign of a guilty conscience is restlessness – sometimes, as in the case of Macbeth, sleeplessness – and a lack of inner peace. Because the punishment for sin is exile, the antidote to sin is *teshuva*, "return." And since the estranged soul longs to return home, *teshuva* (as Rabbi Kook wrote) is the deepest instinct of a healthy soul.

וּמִפְּנֵי חֲטָאֵינוּ גָּלִינוּ מֵאַרְצֵנוּ, וְנִתְרַחַקְנוּ מֵעַל אַדְמָתֵנוּ
וְאֵין אֲנַחְנוּ יְכוֹלִים לַעֲשׂוֹת חוֹבוֹתֵינוּ בְּבֵית בְּחִירָתֶךָ
בַּבַּיִת הַגָּדוֹל וְהַקָּדוֹשׁ שֶׁנִּקְרָא שִׁמְךָ עָלָיו
מִפְּנֵי הַיָּד שֶׁנִּשְׁתַּלְּחָה בְּמִקְדָּשֶׁךָ.
יְהִי רָצוֹן מִלְּפָנֶיךָ יהוה אֱלֹהֵינוּ וֵאלֹהֵי אֲבוֹתֵינוּ, מֶלֶךְ רַחֲמָן
שֶׁתָּשׁוּב וּתְרַחֵם עָלֵינוּ וְעַל מִקְדָּשְׁךָ בְּרַחֲמֶיךָ הָרַבִּים
וְתִבְנֵהוּ מְהֵרָה וּתְגַדֵּל כְּבוֹדוֹ.
אָבִינוּ מַלְכֵּנוּ, גַּלֵּה כְּבוֹד מַלְכוּתְךָ עָלֵינוּ מְהֵרָה
וְהוֹפַע וְהִנָּשֵׂא עָלֵינוּ לְעֵינֵי כָּל חָי
וְקָרֵב פְּזוּרֵינוּ מִבֵּין הַגּוֹיִם, וּנְפוּצוֹתֵינוּ כַּנֵּס מִיַּרְכְּתֵי אָרֶץ.

On שבת*, add the words in parentheses:*

וַהֲבִיאֵנוּ לְצִיּוֹן עִירְךָ בְּרִנָּה
וְלִירוּשָׁלַיִם בֵּית מִקְדָּשְׁךָ בְּשִׂמְחַת עוֹלָם
וְשָׁם נַעֲשֶׂה לְפָנֶיךָ אֶת קָרְבְּנוֹת חוֹבוֹתֵינוּ
תְּמִידִים כְּסִדְרָם וּמוּסָפִים כְּהִלְכָתָם
וְאֶת מוּסַף / בשבת: מוּסְפֵי יוֹם הַשַּׁבָּת הַזֶּה וְ /
יוֹם הַכִּפּוּרִים הַזֶּה
נַעֲשֶׂה וְנַקְרִיב לְפָנֶיךָ בְּאַהֲבָה כְּמִצְוַת רְצוֹנֶךָ
כְּמוֹ שֶׁכָּתַבְתָּ עָלֵינוּ בְּתוֹרָתֶךָ
עַל יְדֵי מֹשֶׁה עַבְדֶּךָ מִפִּי כְבוֹדֶךָ, כָּאָמוּר

וּמִפְּנֵי חֲטָאֵינוּ גָּלִינוּ מֵאַרְצֵנוּ *But because of our sins we were exiled from our land.* A sin is an act in the wrong place. *Ḥet*, "sin," comes from a verb meaning "to miss the target." *Avera*, like its English translation, "transgression," means crossing a boundary and entering forbidden territory. Since punishment is "measure for measure," an act in the wrong place leads to its perpetrator being in the

On Shabbat: וּבְיוֹם הַשַּׁבָּת "On the Sabbath day, make an offering of two lambs a year old, without blemish, together with two-tenths of an ephah of fine flour mixed with oil as a meal-offering, and its appropriate libation. This is the burnt-offering for every Sabbath, in addition to the regular daily burnt-offering and its libation." *Num. 28*

וּבֶעָשׂוֹר לַחֹדֶשׁ On the tenth day of this seventh month you shall have a holy assembly, and you shall afflict your souls; you shall perform no kind of work. And you shall bring a burnt-offering of pleasing aroma to the LORD, one young bullock, one ram, and seven yearling male lambs – they shall be without blemish. *Num. 29*

וּמִנְחָתָם וְנִסְכֵּיהֶם And their meal offerings and wine-libations as ordained: three tenths of an ephah for the bull, two tenths of an ephah for the ram, one tenth of an ephah for each of the seven lambs, wine for the libations, two male goats for atonement, and two regular daily offerings according to their law.

On Shabbat: יִשְׂמְחוּ Those who keep the Sabbath and call it a delight shall rejoice in Your kingship. The people who sanctify the seventh day shall all be satisfied and take delight in Your goodness, for You favored the seventh day and declared it holy. You called it "most desirable of days" in remembrance of Creation.

---

and herds were the measure of a person's wealth, our ancestors brought sacrificial animals as their gift of love.

Even then, though, they were no more than the outer form, the *ma'aseh mitzva*, of the essential act, which is *coming close in love through giving up something of ourselves to the Beloved*. Those who cannot sacrifice, cannot love. At the beginning of the laws of sacrifice we read, "When one of you brings an offering to the LORD" (Lev. 1:2). The word-order in the Hebrew text is unusual, though, and read literally the text says, "When you bring *an offering of yourself* to the LORD," suggesting that the real sacrifice, even in Temple times, was not the animal as such but the fact that the worshiper, or the people as a whole, were willing to give up something precious for the sake of God.

Love, loyalty, sacrifice: these are what bind us to the Other, defeating the solipsism and narcissism that leave us small and alone.

בשבת: וּבְיוֹם הַשַּׁבָּת, שְׁנֵי־כְבָשִׂים בְּנֵי־שָׁנָה תְּמִימִם, וּשְׁנֵי עֶשְׂרֹנִים סֹלֶת מִנְחָה בְּלוּלָה בַשֶּׁמֶן וְנִסְכּוֹ: עֹלַת שַׁבַּת בְּשַׁבַּתּוֹ, עַל־עֹלַת הַתָּמִיד וְנִסְכָּהּ: במדבר כח

וּבֶעָשׂוֹר לַחֹדֶשׁ הַשְּׁבִיעִי הַזֶּה, מִקְרָא־קֹדֶשׁ יִהְיֶה לָכֶם במדבר כט
וְעִנִּיתֶם אֶת־נַפְשֹׁתֵיכֶם, כָּל־מְלָאכָה לֹא תַעֲשׂוּ:
וְהִקְרַבְתֶּם עֹלָה לַיהוה רֵיחַ נִיחֹחַ
פַּר בֶּן־בָּקָר אֶחָד, אַיִל אֶחָד
כְּבָשִׂים בְּנֵי־שָׁנָה שִׁבְעָה, תְּמִימִם יִהְיוּ לָכֶם:

וּמִנְחָתָם וְנִסְכֵּיהֶם כִּמְדֻבָּר
שְׁלֹשָׁה עֶשְׂרֹנִים לַפָּר וּשְׁנֵי עֶשְׂרֹנִים לָאָיִל, וְעִשָּׂרוֹן לַכֶּבֶשׂ
וְיַיִן כְּנִסְכּוֹ, וּשְׁנֵי שְׂעִירִים לְכַפֵּר, וּשְׁנֵי תְמִידִים כְּהִלְכָתָם.

בשבת: יִשְׂמְחוּ בְמַלְכוּתְךָ שׁוֹמְרֵי שַׁבָּת וְקוֹרְאֵי עֹנֶג. עַם מְקַדְּשֵׁי שְׁבִיעִי כֻּלָּם יִשְׂבְּעוּ וְיִתְעַנְּגוּ מִטּוּבֶךָ, וּבַשְּׁבִיעִי רָצִיתָ בּוֹ וְקִדַּשְׁתּוֹ, חֶמְדַּת יָמִים אוֹתוֹ קָרָאתָ, זֵכֶר לְמַעֲשֵׂה בְרֵאשִׁית.

וּבֶעָשׂוֹר *On the tenth day.* The middle blessing of the Musaf Amida on Shabbat and festivals always contains the Torah passage relating to the special additional sacrifice of the day. Now that we have no Temple, we ask God to accept our reading of the passage about the sacrifice as if it were the sacrifice itself. Prayer is sacrificial in nature. The Hebrew word for sacrifice, *korban*, comes from the root *k-r-v* which means to bring, or come close to God. Yet the very ideas of *closeness* and *distance* seem inappropriate when speaking of God, who does not occupy physical space.

The explanation is that the barrier between us and God is not physical; it is metaphysical, psychological. It comes from our sense that we are self-sufficient. We overcome this tragic loneliness by giving something of ourselves away. That is one reason why, under the wedding canopy, the groom gives the bride a ring. A gift bespeaks love, and love – the space we make for the Other – is the redemption of our solitude. In ancient times, when flocks

The Ark is opened.

עָלֵינוּ It is our duty to praise the Master of all,
and ascribe greatness to the Author of creation,
who has not made us like the nations of the lands,
nor placed us like the families of the earth;

The Ark is closed.

who has not made our portion like theirs,
nor our destiny like all their multitudes.
(For they worship vanity and emptiness,
and pray to a god who cannot save.)

The Ark is opened and the congregation
(in some congregations, only the Leader) kneels on the floor at "bow."

▼But we bow in worship
and thank the Supreme King of kings, the Holy One, blessed be He,
who extends the heavens and establishes the earth,
whose throne of glory is in the heavens above,
and whose power's Presence is in the highest of heights.

In some congregations, the Leader says "You have been shown"
while the congregation says "He is our God" below.

He is our God; there is no other.
Truly He is our King; there is none else, as it is written in His Torah:
"You shall know and take to heart this day that the LORD is God, *Deut. 4*
in the heavens above and on the earth below.
There is no other."

The Leader says the following while the congregation says "He is our God" above.

אַתָּה הָרְאֵתָ You have been shown, that you may know, that the LORD is our *Deut. 4*
God: there is no other besides Him. You shall know and take to heart this day
that the LORD is God, in the heavens above and on the earth below. There is
no other. Listen, Israel: the LORD is our God, the LORD is One. For heaven, *Deut. 6* *Deut. 10*

"Supreme King of kings" above all earthly powers. On other days of the year we merely bow in the middle of the paragraph, but on Rosh HaShana and Yom Kippur we kneel, for on these days the sovereignty of God is no mere item of faith. It is a felt, palpable reality. God is here, now, and we are in His presence. Our body-language bespeaks the immediacy of the Divine.

The ארון קודש *is opened.*

עָלֵינוּ לְשַׁבֵּחַ לַאֲדוֹן הַכֹּל, לָתֵת גְּדֻלָּה לְיוֹצֵר בְּרֵאשִׁית
שֶׁלֹּא עָשָׂנוּ כְּגוֹיֵי הָאֲרָצוֹת, וְלֹא שָׂמָנוּ כְּמִשְׁפְּחוֹת הָאֲדָמָה

The ארון קודש *is closed.*

שֶׁלֹּא שָׂם חֶלְקֵנוּ כָּהֶם וְגוֹרָלֵנוּ כְּכָל הֲמוֹנָם.
(שֶׁהֵם מִשְׁתַּחֲוִים לְהֶבֶל וָרִיק וּמִתְפַּלְלִים אֶל אֵל לֹא יוֹשִׁיעַ.)

The ארון קודש *is opened and the* קהל
(in some congregations, only the שליח ציבור*) kneels on the floor at* כּוֹרְעִים.

וַאֲנַחְנוּ כּוֹרְעִים וּמִשְׁתַּחֲוִים וּמוֹדִים
לִפְנֵי מֶלֶךְ מַלְכֵי הַמְּלָכִים, הַקָּדוֹשׁ בָּרוּךְ הוּא
שֶׁהוּא נוֹטֶה שָׁמַיִם וְיוֹסֵד אָרֶץ
וּמוֹשַׁב יְקָרוֹ בַּשָּׁמַיִם מִמַּעַל
וּשְׁכִינַת עֻזּוֹ בְּגָבְהֵי מְרוֹמִים.

In some congregations, the שליח ציבור *says* אַתָּה הָרְאֵתָ *while the* קהל *says* הוּא אֱלֹהֵינוּ *below.*

הוּא אֱלֹהֵינוּ, אֵין עוֹד.
אֱמֶת מַלְכֵּנוּ, אֶפֶס זוּלָתוֹ, כַּכָּתוּב בְּתוֹרָתוֹ
וְיָדַעְתָּ הַיּוֹם וַהֲשֵׁבֹתָ אֶל־לְבָבֶךָ דברים ד
כִּי יהוה הוּא הָאֱלֹהִים בַּשָּׁמַיִם מִמַּעַל וְעַל־הָאָרֶץ מִתָּחַת
אֵין עוֹד:

The שליח ציבור *says the following while the* קהל *says* הוּא אֱלֹהֵינוּ *above.*

אַתָּה הָרְאֵתָ לָדַעַת, כִּי יהוה הוּא הָאֱלֹהִים, אֵין עוֹד מִלְּבַדּוֹ: וְיָדַעְתָּ הַיּוֹם דברים ד
וַהֲשֵׁבֹתָ אֶל־לְבָבֶךָ, כִּי יהוה הוּא הָאֱלֹהִים בַּשָּׁמַיִם מִמַּעַל וְעַל־הָאָרֶץ
מִתָּחַת, אֵין עוֹד: שְׁמַע יִשְׂרָאֵל, יהוה אֱלֹהֵינוּ, יהוה אֶחָד: הֵן לַיהוה דברים ו דברים י

עָלֵינוּ *It is our duty.* An ancient prayer, edited by the third-century Talmudist Rav, proclaiming God's sovereignty. Since the Middle Ages, *Aleinu* has formed the conclusion of each of the daily prayers, but its original context was here in the prayers for the Days of Awe that emphasize God's role as

the highest heaven, the earth and all that it contains, belong to the LORD your God. For the LORD your God is the God of gods, the LORD of lords, the great, *Deut. 10* mighty and awesome God, God, who does not discriminate or accept any bribe. When I proclaim the LORD's name, give glory to our God. Blessed be *Deut. 32* *Ps. 113* the name of the LORD, now and for evermore.

The Ark is closed.

There follows a prefatory piyut before the Seder HaAvoda (Temple Service) section of the Leader's Repetition. The Leader continues:

אֱלֹהֵינוּ Our God and the God of our forefathers:
May You stand by the mouths of the emissaries of Your nation,
the house of Israel,
who stand before You to entreat You with prayer and supplication
on behalf of Your nation, the house of Israel.
Instruct them in what to say,
lend them understanding that they may know what to speak.
Let them know what they might ask You,
make known to them how they might glorify You.

May they walk in the light of Your countenance, *Ps. 89*
may they bend their knees before You.
May they bless Your nation with their speech,
and may they all receive blessing through Your uttered blessings.
May they pass Your nation before You,
while they stand in the midst of the congregation.
The eyes of Your nation hang on their word,
and their eyes await You in turn.

They approach the Holy Ark in fear,
trying to abate Your anger and wrath.
Your nation surrounds them as a wall,
and You on high, shall gaze upon them compassionately.
They raise their eyes heavenward to You,
and pour out their hearts like water before You.
And You shall hear them from the heavens. *II Chr. 6*

Rabban Yoḥanan ben Zakkai. The son of Rabban Yoḥanan ben Zakkai fell ill. He said to him, "Ḥanina my son, pray for him that he may live." He put his head between his knees and prayed for him and he lived. Said Rabban Yoḥanan ben Zakkai, "If Ben Zakkai had put his head between his knees

אֱלֹהֶיךָ הַשָּׁמַיִם וּשְׁמֵי הַשָּׁמָיִם, הָאָרֶץ וְכָל־אֲשֶׁר־בָּהּ: כִּי יהוה אֱלֹהֵיכֶם דברים י
הוּא אֱלֹהֵי הָאֱלֹהִים וַאֲדֹנֵי הָאֲדֹנִים, הָאֵל הַגָּדֹל הַגִּבֹּר וְהַנּוֹרָא אֲשֶׁר
לֹא־יִשָּׂא פָנִים וְלֹא יִקַּח שֹׁחַד: כִּי שֵׁם יהוה אֶקְרָא, הָבוּ גֹדֶל לֵאלֹהֵינוּ: דברים לב
יְהִי שֵׁם יהוה מְבֹרָךְ, מֵעַתָּה וְעַד־עוֹלָם: תהלים קיג

The ארון קודש *is closed.*

There follows a prefatory piyut before the סדר העבודה *(Temple Service) section of the* חזרת הש״ץ*. The* שליח ציבור *continues:*

אֱלֹהֵינוּ וֵאלֹהֵי אֲבוֹתֵינוּ
הֱיֵה עִם פִּיפִיּוֹת שְׁלוּחֵי עַמְּךָ בֵּית יִשְׂרָאֵל
הָעוֹמְדִים לְבַקֵּשׁ תְּפִלָּה וְתַחֲנוּנִים מִלְּפָנֶיךָ עַל עַמְּךָ בֵּית יִשְׂרָאֵל.

הוֹרֵם מַה שֶּׁיֹּאמְרוּ / הֲבִינֵם מַה שֶּׁיְּדַבֵּרוּ
הֲשִׁיבֵם מַה שֶּׁיִּשְׁאֲלוּ / יַדְּעֵם הֵיךְ יְפָאֵרוּ.

בְּאוֹר פָּנֶיךָ יְהַלֵּכוּן / בֶּרֶךְ לְךָ יִבְרְכוּן תהלים פט
עַמְּךָ בְּפִיהֶם יְבָרְכוּן / וּמִבִּרְכוֹת פִּיךָ כֻּלָּם יִתְבָּרְכוּן.

עַמְּךָ לְפָנֶיךָ יַעֲבִירוּן / וְהֵם בַּתָּוֶךְ יַעֲבֹרוּן
עֵינֵי עַמְּךָ בָּם תְּלוּיוֹת / וְעֵינֵיהֶם לְךָ מְיַחֲלוֹת.

גָּשִׁים מוּל אֲרוֹן הַקֹּדֶשׁ בְּאֵימָה / לְשַׁכֵּךְ כַּעַס וְחֵימָה
וְעַמְּךָ מְסַבְּבִים אוֹתָם כַּחוֹמָה /
וְאַתָּה מִן הַשָּׁמַיִם תַּשְׁגִּיחַ, אוֹתָם לְרַחֲמָה.

עַיִן נוֹשְׂאִים לְךָ לַשָּׁמַיִם / לֵב שׁוֹפְכִים נִכְחֲךָ כַּמַּיִם
וְאַתָּה תִּשְׁמַע מִן הַשָּׁמַיִם. דברי הימים ב, ו

הֱיֵה עִם פִּיפִיּוֹת *May You stand by the mouths.* This and the subsequent prayer, "I shall await the Lord," are *reshut* prayers, requesting permission to approach God in prayer, said by the leader during the Repetition, though not by individuals in the silent Amida (*Tur, OḤ* 591). The difference is explained by a passage in the Talmud:

Once it happened that Rabbi Ḥanina ben Dosa went to study Torah with

In many congregations the following (until "O Lord of Israel") is said quietly by all.

Please, do not allow their tongues to falter,
may their words not ensnare them.
And may they not be ashamed of their congregation, their support,
and may their congregation not be ashamed of them.
And may their mouths utter no words that negate Your will.
For those You show favor, Lord our God, are graced,
and it is those whom You teach who are learned.

כְּמָה שֶׁיָּדַעְנוּ Just as we have known, O Lord, that You show grace to
those You favor and compassion to those You deem deserving of compassion. As it is written in Your Torah, "And He said, I shall cause all Ex. 33
My good to pass before you and I shall call out the Tetragrammaton
before you, and I will show grace to those I favor and compassion to
those I deem deserving of compassion." And it is written, "May those Ps. 69
who await You not be ashamed of me, O God, Lord of hosts, may those
who seek You out not be humiliated through me, O Lord of Israel."

The Ark is opened.

A second prefatory piyut, said by the Leader:

אוֹחִילָה I shall await the Lord, I shall entreat His favor,
I shall ask Him to grant my tongue eloquence.
In the midst of the congregated nation I shall sing of His strength;
I shall burst out in joyous melodies for His works.

The thoughts in man's heart are his to arrange, *Prov. 16*
but the tongue's eloquence comes from the Lord.

O Lord, open my lips, *Ps. 51*
so that my mouth may declare Your praise.

In some congregations, the following verse is said quietly:

יִהְיוּ May the words of my mouth and the meditation of my heart find *Ps. 19*
favor before You, Lord, my Rock and Redeemer.

The Ark is closed.

A servant, says Rashi, needs no formal permission to enter the presence of a king, but a prince does. When we pray individually and silently we are like servants in God's presence. When the leader prays aloud on behalf of the whole congregation, he is like a prince.

In many congregations the following (until אֱלֹהֵי יִשְׂרָאֵל) is said quietly by all.

שֶׁלֹּא יִכָּשְׁלוּ בִלְשׁוֹנָם / וְלֹא יִנָּקְשׁוּ בְשִׁנּוּנָם
וְלֹא יֵבוֹשׁוּ בְּמַשְׁעֵנָם / וְלֹא יִכָּלְמוּ בָם שְׁאוֹנָם
וְאַל יֹאמַר פִּיהֶם דָּבָר שֶׁלֹּא כִרְצוֹנֶךָ.
כִּי חֲנוּנֶיךָ יהוה אֱלֹהֵינוּ הֵמָּה חֲנוּנִים /
וּמְלֻמָּדֶיךָ הֵמָּה מְלֻמָּדִים.

כְּמָה שֶׁיָּדַעְנוּ יהוה אֱלֹהֵינוּ, אֵת אֲשֶׁר תָּחֹן יוּחָן, וְאֵת אֲשֶׁר תְּרַחֵם
שמות לג יְרֻחָם. כַּכָּתוּב בְּתוֹרָתֶךָ: וַיֹּאמֶר, אֲנִי אַעֲבִיר כָּל־טוּבִי עַל־פָּנֶיךָ,
וְקָרָאתִי בְשֵׁם יהוה לְפָנֶיךָ, וְחַנֹּתִי אֶת־אֲשֶׁר אָחֹן וְרִחַמְתִּי אֶת־
תהלים סט אֲשֶׁר אֲרַחֵם: וְנֶאֱמַר: אַל־יֵבֹשׁוּ בִי קֹוֶיךָ, אֲדֹנָי יֱהֹוִה צְבָאוֹת,
אַל־יִכָּלְמוּ בִי מְבַקְשֶׁיךָ, אֱלֹהֵי יִשְׂרָאֵל:

The ארון קודש *is opened.*

A second prefatory piyut, said by the שליח ציבור*:*

אוֹחִילָה לָאֵל, אֲחַלֶּה פָנָיו
אֶשְׁאֲלָה מִמֶּנּוּ מַעֲנֵה לָשׁוֹן.

אֲשֶׁר בִּקְהַל עָם אָשִׁירָה עֻזּוֹ
אַבִּיעָה רְנָנוֹת בְּעַד מִפְעָלָיו.

משלי טז לְאָדָם מַעַרְכֵי־לֵב וּמֵיהוה מַעֲנֵה לָשׁוֹן:

תהלים נא אֲדֹנָי, שְׂפָתַי תִּפְתָּח, וּפִי יַגִּיד תְּהִלָּתֶךָ:

In some congregations, the following verse is said quietly:

תהלים יט יִהְיוּ לְרָצוֹן אִמְרֵי־פִי וְהֶגְיוֹן לִבִּי לְפָנֶיךָ, יהוה צוּרִי וְגֹאֲלִי:

The ארון קודש *is closed.*

---

for the whole day, no notice would have been taken of him." Said his wife to him, "Is Ḥanina greater than you are?" He replied to her, "No, but he is like a servant before the king, and I am like a nobleman before a king." (*Berakhot* 34b)

THE ORDER OF THE TEMPLE SERVICE

Some congregations say a different Seder HaAvoda (Temple Service), beginning with אַתָּה כּוֹנַנְתָּ *(page 1262).*

As part of the Leader's Repetition, the Seder HaAvoda should ideally be said by the Leader alone. However, the prevailing custom is for all to recite it together, with the Leader raising his voice only toward the end.

אַמִּיץ כֹּחַ Unshakable of strength, almighty and powerful, / [God] whose mighty deeds could be done by none other, / who built unshakable chambers over the cold waters, / and founded all the world upon nothingness. / When all the world was darkness, deep shadows and gloom, / You shone the morning light with the sweep of Your robe. / You split rebellious [waters] apart with the awesome sky, like ice in between, / and gathered the lower waters to the depths, never to engulf the earth. / You uncovered the face of the land, and the buds of harvest appeared. / You planted a garden in the east, to delight those who would praise You. / You placed great lights in Your mighty skies, / and commanded alongside them an army of stars. / With Your palm You shaped the creatures that swim and that glide, / and the serpent [Leviathan] to become the feast of the faithful who sit in Your gardens. / The clumping clods of earth brought forth insects and mammals, / and the [Behemoth] of reed and swamp that is the meal of those You shall invite to it. /

---

confessing our sins, committing ourselves to a different and better future, offering God our heart.

We no longer have the Temple ceremony, but we have the story; and we have the day itself, which atones even in the absence of the Temple. So on this day of days, more vividly than at any other time, the synagogue becomes a fragment of the Temple, and we re-create in our minds the scene that took place then on this holiest of days.

Seder HaAvoda – the narrative retelling of the rituals of the day – was part of the Yom Kippur service already in Talmudic times. There were communities that recited it also in the morning and afternoon services, but the predominant custom was to do so only during Musaf. Many poetic versions were written, of which the most famous are *Ata Konanta*, adopted in Sephardi rites (page 1262), and our own Ashkenazi version, *Amitz ko'aḥ* ("Unshakable of strength"). (See also Mishna *Yoma*, Appendix II on page 439.)

אַמִּיץ כֹּחַ: *A Brief History From Creation to Induction of the High Priest.* Written by Rabbi Meshullam ben Kalonymus, this poem is set out as an alphabetical acrostic, the number of lines devoted to each letter gradually increasing.

סדר העבודה

Some congregations say a different סדר העבודה, *beginning with* אַתָּה כּוֹנַנְתָּ *(page 1262).*

As part of the חזרת הש״ץ, סדר העבודה *should ideally be said by the* שליח ציבור *alone. However, the prevailing custom is for all to recite it together, with the* שליח ציבור *raising his voice only toward the end.*

אַמִּיץ כֹּחַ, כַּבִּיר וְרַב אוֹנִים / אֲשֶׁר מִי יַעֲשֶׂה כְּמַעֲשׂ גְּבוּרוֹתֶיךָ
אֹמֶץ עֲלִיּוֹת קֵרִיתָ עַל קָרִים / אַף יִסַּדְתָּ תֵּבֵל עַל בְּלִימָה.
בְּהְיוֹת עוֹלָם חֹשֶׁךְ, צַלְמָוֶת וְעֵיפָה / בְּמַעֲטֵה לְבוּשְׁךָ אוֹר בֹּקֶר הִגַּהְתָּ
בֵּין זֵידוֹנִים חָצַתְּ כְּקֶרַח הַנּוֹרָא / בְּצוּל הִקְוִיתָם לְבַל יְכַסּוּן חֶלֶד.
גִּלִּיתָ פְּנֵי נֶשִׁי, וְהֵנֵצָה תְנוּבָה / גַּן מִקֶּדֶם טַעְתָּ לְשַׁעֲשׁוּעַ מַאֲמִירֶיךָ
גֹּדֶל מְאוֹרוֹת תַּתָּה בִּרְקִיעַ עֻזֶּךָ / גַּם צְבָא מַזָּרוֹת עִמָּם צִוִּיתָ.
דֵּי שְׁחִים וְדָאִים מִשְׁעַל צַרְתָּ / דִּמְיוֹן בָּרִיחַ לְכֵרַת יוֹשְׁבֵי גַנִּים
דְּבוּקַת רְגָבִים הוֹצִיאָה רוֹמְשִׂים וְשׁוֹאֲפִים /
דָּר קָנֶה וּבִצָּה לַאֲרוּחַת קְרוּאֶיךָ.

SEDER HA'AVODA – THE ORDER OF THE TEMPLE SERVICE

There now follows a unique feature of the Yom Kippur prayers: a narrative retelling of the order of service as it took place in the Temple. Every Musaf Amida contains a specific reference to the sacrifice of the day, but only here are we invited to re-envision it as it happened.

The service in the Temple on Yom Kippur was unique, the dramatic high point of the Jewish year. On the holiest day the holiest person, the High Priest, would enter the Holy of Holies and, with the holiest name of God on his lips, atone for the sins of all Israel. It was a supremely emotive moment, an entire nation confronting its faults, confessing its failings, and turning to God as its source of forgiveness and hope: a nation focused on the service of one man, the *Kohen Gadol*, who prayed and confessed on their behalf.

For close to two thousand years we have not had the Temple, nor High Priest, nor sacrifice. That the Jewish people survived as a people, that Judaism survived as a faith, and that Yom Kippur survived in the absence of so much of what constituted the service of the day, are three of the more remarkable stories in human history. In effect, the sages said: in place of sacrifice, we have prayer. In place of the Temple we have the synagogue. In place of the service of the High Priest we have the service of each of us, turning to God,

Food and drink You made, with none to eat it; / and then You formed a shape of clay in the imprint of Your seal. / From above, You breathed a pure spirit into its form; / then he slept and from his own rib You destined him an ally. / You commanded him never to eat of the Tree of Knowledge, / but, tempted by the deception of a creeping beast, he broke Your word. / Man was punished with the sweat of toil to eat his share, / the foolish woman with birth pains, and the cunning beast to make dust its bread. / You set the seed of that couple's meeting, inside a yearning womb, / and the woman sowed and gave birth to a farmer and a shepherd. / They offered a sacrifice and tribute before You, together, / and You raged at the older, but accepted the younger brother's gift. / [Cain] destroyed his own compassion and slew his brother; / but he beseeched You, and You laid Your sign on him. / Three generations later, [men] began to call idols by Your name, / You called on an army of waters to sweep them away and they were gone. / Arrogant people strayed away and said to You, "Away from us!" / but they were tossed in the hot waters; they were scalded clean away. / But [Noah] who was charged with building the gopher-wood ark, was saved as You closed him inside, / and You made his children fruitful, until they covered the face of dry land. / A people, united, counseled together to ascend as far as the sky – / but they were trapped and scattered in storm wind and tempest. / The beloved [Abraham] who came from beyond the river made Your name known in the world. / He offered You the child of his old age as a complete sacrifice. / Like a flawless lamb, an innocent man [Jacob] was chosen, / as he longed for the life of the tent, and was drawn after You. / Worthy, lovely offspring You brought forth from his loins, / all children of truth without flaw. / You desired Levi, devoted to You, to serve You, / and set one of his line apart, sanctified as the holy of holies. / To bind the sacred headplate and don the Urim, / to abide within the Sanctuary's glory for seven days: / One week before the tenth [of Tishrei], those who uphold the law, / separate the Head Priest in line with the ancient law of induction. / ‣ They sprinkled on him the water of sin-offerings to purify him, / and he offered incense, tended the lights and threw [the blood] to accustom himself to the service.

מַפְרִישִׁים כֹּהֵן הָרֹאשׁ: *The Preparation of the High Priest*
Seven days before Yom Kippur the High Priest was taken from his home to the Officials' Chamber on the north side of the Temple courtyard, to prepare for his ministrations, as Aaron and his family had been commanded to do before they embarked on the service in the Sanctuary (Ex. 29; Lev. 8). This period of preparation was undertaken partly to rehearse the details of the acts he would undertake on the day, partly to keep him from any possible impurity, and partly to endow him with the added sanctity, physical and spiritual, he would need to enter the Holy of Holies, epicenter of the Divine Presence. For seven days he would sprinkle the blood of the daily sacrifices, burn the incense and tend to the lamps. Elders would read to him, or if he were learned, he would read to them.

הֲכִנּוֹתָ טֶבַח וָמֶסֶךְ, וְסוֹעֵד אָיִן / הִקְרַצְתָּ גֹּלֶם מֵחֹמֶר בְּתַבְנִית חוֹתָמֶךָ
הִפַּחְתָּ בְחֶלְדוֹ טְהַר נֶשֶׁם מִזְּבוּלֶךָ / הָרַדָּם וּמִצַּלְעוֹ עֵזֶר לוֹ יִעַדְתָּ.
וְצִוִּיתוֹ בְּלִי לְעֹט מֵעֵץ הַדַּעַת / וְהֵפֵר צִוּוּי כְּפֵתִי בְּהַשָּׁאַת זוֹחֵל
וְעָנַשׁ בְּזֵעַת אַף לִטְרֹף חֻקּוֹ / וְאוֹלֶדֶת בְּצִירִים, וְעָרוּם עָפָר לַחְמוֹ.
זֵרוּי רִבְעוֹ הִקְפֵּיתָ בְּבֶטֶן חוֹמֶדֶת / זָרְעָה וְהוֹלִידָה אִכָּר וְרוֹעֵה צֹאן
זֶבַח וָשַׁי הִגִּישׁוּ לְמוֹלְכָךְ יַחַד / זָעַמְתָּ בָּרַב, וְשָׁעִיתָ תְּשׁוּרַת צָעִיר.
חֶמֶל רַחֲמָיו שִׁחֵת, וְעָרַף אָח / חִלָּה פָנֶיךָ, וְשַׂמְתָּ לוֹ אוֹת
חֻלּוֹ שְׁלִישִׁים קְרֹא בְשִׁמְךָ לַסֶּמֶל / חֵיל נוֹזְלִים קָרָאתָ וּשְׁטָפוּם וְאָבָדוּ.
טָעוּ גֵאִים וּפָצוּ סוּר לְנֶגְדֶּךָ / טֹרְפוּ בְּחֹם הוֹמִים, יָזֹרְבוּ נִצְמָתוּ
טְעוּן גֹּפֶר נוֹשַׁע כְּסָגַרְתָּ בַּעֲדוֹ / טְפוּלָיו הִפְרֵיתָ וּמָלְאוּ פְּנֵי צִיָּה.
יָעֲצוּ נֶאֱחָדִים לָרוּם עַד לַשַּׁחַק / יֻקְשׁוּ נִפְצוּ בְּרוּחַ סֹעָה וָסָעַר
יְדִיד אֵתוּי עֵבֶר יְדָעֲךָ בָּעוֹלָם / יִחוּם זְקָנָיו הֶעֱלָה לְךָ לְכָלִיל.
כְּשֶׂה תָמִים בְּחַר אִישׁ תָּם / כְּחָשַׁק יְשִׁיבַת אֹהֶל וְנִמְשַׁךְ אַחֲרֶיךָ
כֹּשֶׁר חֲנִיטֵי יוֹף הוֹצֵאתָ מֵחֲלָצָיו / כֻּלּוֹ זֶרַע אֱמֶת וְאֵין דֹּפִי.
לְשָׁרְתְךָ אִוִּיתָ לֵוִי אִישׁ חֲסִידֶךָ / לְהַבְדִּיל מִגִּזְעוֹ מְקֻדָּשׁ קֹדֶשׁ קָדָשִׁים
לִקְשֹׁר נֵזֶר קֹדֶשׁ וְלַעֲטוֹת אוּרִים / לֵישֵׁב כִּכְבוּדָּה פְּנִימָה יָמִים שִׁבְעָה.
מַחֲזִיקֵי אֱמָנָה, שָׁבוּעַ קֹדֶם לֶעָשׂוֹר /
מַפְרִישִׁים כֹּהֵן הָרֹאשׁ כְּדַת הַמִּלּוּאִים
מַזִּים עָלָיו מֵי חַטָּאת לְטַהֲרוֹ /
מַקְטִיר וּמֵיטִיב וְזוֹרֵק, לְהִתְרַגֵּל בָּעֲבוֹדָה.

The poet begins his account, not where we would expect, with the sin of the golden calf and God's forgiveness, but with the creation of the universe and humankind. The poet's approach to sin and atonement is cosmological rather than historical. It has to do with who we are: embodied creatures with drives and desires who, knowing what is good, often do what is bad. Sin is not inevitable but it is commonplace. Hence, in the language of the sages, God created the possibility of *teshuva* before He created the world, and had designated the Day of Atonement before He created man. Judaism does not believe in "original sin." It does believe in original forgiveness.

As is written in Your Torah:
As has been done on this day, *Lev. 8*
so has the Lord commanded to do, to make atonement for you.

All:

נְלְוִים Wise men, the elders at the gate accompany him, / saying to him, "Read with your own mouth." / As the brightness of the ninth [of Tishrei] began to shine, they stood him at the eastern gate, / and passed the lovely offerings of the day before him. / Close to the setting of the sun they had him eat little, / lest in sleep a white defilement happen to him. / The old men of his tribe brought him to teach him how to take [incense] handfuls; / they would make him swear to set the [incense] spices afire within [the Holy of Holies]. / His flesh would stand on end, he would weep to have been suspect, / and they too would turn aside and shed their tears. / Interpretation in their mouths, and the written word read out, / around him they would chant to keep him awake until midnight. / The priests went joyfully to the first lot, before the clearing of the ashes. / They would draw lots again, for the inner clearing and the lamp. / After the burning of incense, new priests approached for the third drawing, / and the fourth decided who would lay out the offered meat. / The spark of morning rose, as the watchman said, / and a screen of linen was drawn across to conceal the High Priest. / He took off his clothes and immersed and dressed all in gold; / stood and consecrated and made the first cut in the regular morning offering. / He appointed one to complete the slaughter and he received [its blood] and threw, / went apart and lit the incense, tended the lights and made the offering and the libation. / All the service he fulfilled, and did in its right order, / and they spread a white sheet out again as before. / There, in the Parva chamber in the Sanctuary, he consecrated himself and undressed, / stepped to the ritual bath, immersed, then donned white clothes and consecrated, /

---

point at which the High Priest offered incense. The Sadducees held that he did so before entering the Holy of Holies, the Pharisees only after entering. So as part of their preparation the sages had to elicit a commitment from the High Priest that he would follow the oral tradition. At that point both the High Priest and the sages wept, the one at being suspected, the others for needing to suspect.

עָלָה בְּרַק הַשַּׁחַר: *The Morning Service*
As dawn broke, the High Priest began his ministrations by immersing himself in the *mikveh*, the first of five occasions he would do so in the course of the day, each time to cleanse himself for the next stage of the service. He then donned gold robes, made the first incision and sprinkled the blood of the morning sacrifice, burned the morning incense, tended to the lamps and completed the morning service.

כַּכָּתוּב בְּתוֹרָתֶךָ
כַּאֲשֶׁר עָשָׂה בַּיּוֹם הַזֶּה, צִוָּה יהוה לַעֲשֹׂת לְכַפֵּר עֲלֵיכֶם: ויקרא ח

All:

נִלְוִים אֵלָיו נְבוֹנִים יְשִׁישֵׁי שַׁעַר / נוֹאֲמִים לוֹ, קְרָא נָא בְּפִיךָ
נֹגַהּ תְּשִׁיעִי יַעֲמִידוּהוּ בְּשַׁעַר קָדִים / נוֹי זִבְחֵי יוֹם לְפָנָיו יַעֲבִירוּ.
סֶמֶךְ בִּיאַת שֶׁמֶשׁ צֵידוֹ יַמְעִיטוּ / סֵאָב לְבַן פֶּן בְּרֶדֶם יִקְרֵהוּ
סָבֵי שִׁבְטוֹ, לְלַמֵּד חֵפֶן יוֹלִיכוּהוּ / סַמִּים לְתַמֵּר בִּפְנִים אוֹתוֹ יַשְׁבִּיעוּ.
סָמַר בְּשָׂרוֹ וְהִדְמִיעַ כִּי נֶחְשַׁד / סָרוּ גַּם הֵם וּבָכָה הִגִּירוּ
שִׂיחַ מִדְרָשׁ בְּפֶה וּבִכְתָב הִגָּיוֹן / סְבִיבָיו יְשַׁנְּנוּ לְעוֹרְרוֹ עַד חֲצוֹת.
עָלְצוּ תְּרֹם דֶּשֶׁן בְּפַיִס רִאשׁוֹן / עוֹד יָפִיסוּ לְדִשּׁוּן פְּנִימִי וּמְנוֹרָה
עֵקֶב קְטוֹרָה פַּיִס חֲדָשִׁים יְשַׁלֵּשׁוּ / עֵרֶךְ נְתָחִים יַחַד פַּיִס הָרְבִיעִי.
עָלָה בְּרַק הַשַּׁחַר כְּנָם הַצּוֹפֶה / עָלָיו פֵּרְשׂוּ מָסָךְ בּוּץ לְהַצְנִיעַ
עֵרָה סוּתוֹ, טָבַל וְעָט זְהָבִים / עָמַד וְקִדֵּשׁ, וְקֵרֵץ תְּמִיד הַשַּׁחַר.
פָּקַד לְמָרְקוֹ וְהוּא קִבֵּל וְזָרַק / פֵּרֵשׁ הִקְטִיר וְהֵטִיב, הִקְרִיב וְנִסֵּךְ
פְּעֻלַּת כְּלִיל הִשְׁלִים וְעָשׂ כְּסֵדֶר / פֵּרְשׂוּ סָדִין לָבָן עוֹד כְּבָרִאשׁוֹנָה.
פְּרִוָּה בַּקֹּדֶשׁ, שָׁם קִדֵּשׁ וּפָשַׁט / פָּסַע וְטָבַל, לְבָנִים עָט וְקִדֵּשׁ

The specific references to the order of incense, and the weeping of the High Priest and his mentors, are reminders of historic tensions in the late Second Temple period. Under the Hasmonean kings the office of High Priest was commonly sold to the highest bidder. Often, High Priests were ignorant. Sometimes they were Sadducees. The word itself comes from the name Zadok, the most famous priestly family. The sages belonged to the group known as the Pharisees. There were significant differences between the two groups. The Sadducees tended to be an elite, whereas the Pharisees were of the people. The Sadducees believed in the Written Torah only, the Pharisees in the Oral Torah also. For the Sadducees the central institution was the Temple, for the Pharisees it was the house of study. There were also theological differences between them.

So there were tensions which sometimes flared. There were specific differences relating to the service of Yom Kippur, one of which was the precise

Pelusium clothes laid out, valued at eighteen hundred dinars / splendid garments, for him to serve the King of Glory. / His bull was stood between the antechamber and the altar, / its face to the west and its head bent towards the south. / ‣ He came to it and pressed down his hands on its head; / he confessed all his sins and hid nothing in his heart.

וְכָךְ And this is what he would say:

The Leader continues, with the congregation following him in an undertone:

Please, LORD, / I have sinned, I have done wrong,
I have rebelled before You – I and my family.
Please, by Your name, / grant atonement, please,
for the sins and for the wrongs and the rebellions
that I have sinned, and done wrong,
and rebelled before You – I and my family.
As it is written in the Torah of Moses Your servant,
at the word of Your glory:
For on this day you will be atoned and made pure *Lev. 16*
of all your sins before the LORD –

---

restricted until it was used only by the High Priest on Yom Kippur, and was said so softly that others could not hear it. Its pronunciation became a secret passed from High Priest to High Priest until with the loss of the Temple and the passage of time the secret was forgotten. Our convention today is: (1) in non-sacred contexts to say *HaShem* ("the name"), and (2) in sacred ones to print the four letters of the name but to pronounce them as *Adonai*, meaning "My LORD."

Prostration was performed daily in the Temple by officiating priests but was restricted in the synagogue to two occasions: (1) during the first paragraph of *Aleinu* in the Musaf Amida on Rosh HaShana and Yom Kippur; and (2) here, retelling the story of the High Priest's service on Yom Kippur. At all other times, we merely bow rather than kneel and fall on our faces. The reason is to mark a clear distinction between the synagogue and the Temple. The synagogue may be a "miniature Temple" but a symbol is not the same as what it symbolizes. Only on Yom Kippur do we deliberately re-create the atmosphere of the Temple, in two ways: by this threefold (in some rites, fourfold) prostration and by saying aloud throughout the day "Blessed be the name of His glorious kingdom for ever and all time," normally said silently. This was the congregational response in the Temple instead of the word "Amen" which, for reasons unknown, was not used in Temple worship.

פְּלוּסִים עֶרְכָּם מָנִים שְׁמוֹנָה עָשָׂר / פְּאוּרִים לְשָׁרֵת בָּם לְמֶלֶךְ הַכָּבוֹד.
פָּרוֹ מֻצָּב בֵּין אוּלָם לַמִּזְבֵּחַ / פָּנָיו יָמָּה וְרֹאשׁוֹ נֶגְבָּה מְעֻקָּם
פָּגַשׁ וְסָמַךְ יָדָיו עַל רֹאשׁוֹ / פְּשָׁעָיו הוֹדָה, וּבְחֻבּוֹ לֹא טָמַן.

וְכָךְ הָיָה אוֹמֵר

The שליח ציבור continues, with the קהל following him in an undertone:

אָנָּא הַשֵּׁם / חָטָאתִי, עָוִיתִי, פָּשַׁעְתִּי לְפָנֶיךָ אֲנִי וּבֵיתִי.
אָנָּא בַשֵּׁם / כַּפֶּר נָא לַחֲטָאִים וְלַעֲוֹנוֹת וְלַפְּשָׁעִים
שֶׁחָטָאתִי וְשֶׁעָוִיתִי וְשֶׁפָּשַׁעְתִּי לְפָנֶיךָ אֲנִי וּבֵיתִי.
כַּכָּתוּב בְּתוֹרַת מֹשֶׁה עַבְדֶּךָ מִפִּי כְבוֹדֶךָ
כִּי־בַיּוֹם הַזֶּה יְכַפֵּר עֲלֵיכֶם לְטַהֵר אֶתְכֶם ויקרא טז
מִכֹּל חַטֹּאתֵיכֶם, לִפְנֵי יהוה

פְּשָׁעָיו הוֹדָה*: The First Confession*

He then immersed himself again, and put on white vestments made of Pelusium linen (Pelusium was a city on the east of the Nile Delta, known for the quality of its flax). Next he approached the bull that was to become his own sin-offering. Over it he confessed his own sins and the sins of his family. During the course of the day he would atone three times: first for himself and his family, then for his fellow priests, then for the nation as a whole. It was essential that the High Priest atoned for himself at the outset ("First adorn yourself, only then adorn others" [*Bava Metzia* 107b; *Bava Batra* 60b]). He could not atone for the people unless he had already been atoned.

Each confession was accompanied by *semikha* – the "laying on" of hands on the head of the animal, signaling a transfer from one entity to another. The word *semikha* still exists as a description of rabbinic ordination since originally it was conferred by the laying on of hands by master to disciple; likewise the laying of hands when parents bless their children on Friday night. What is transferred – sin, authority, blessing – varies from case to case, but the significance of *semikha*-as-transfer remains.

During each confession the High Priest pronounced the *Shem HaMeforash,* God's holiest name, three times. The people, aware of this, prostrated themselves. Extreme sanctity attached to the name of God as pronounced in the Temple. As people began to abuse its sanctity, its use was progressively

וְהַכֹּהֲנִים And the priests and all the people
who were standing in the courtyard,
when they heard the glorious and awesome name
spoken out expressly by the High Priest in holiness and purity,

At the words "bend their knees," the congregation and the Leader kneel on the floor (see law 93).

would bend their knees and bow down
and give thanks and fall upon their faces
and say –

"Blessed be the name of His glorious kingdom
for ever and all time."

All stand and continue:

וְאַף And the High Priest too would take care
to finish saying the name together with those who blessed it,
and would say to them: "Become pure."

And You, in Your great benevolence, awaken Your compassion and forgive this man, Your devoted one.

צָעַד לֵילֵךְ He stepped away to walk to the east of the courtyard, / where a pair of goats waited, purchased with the public's funds, / paired, kindred, equal in appearance and height, / standing there to bring atonement for the wayward daughter's sin. / He shook the golden lots and brought up one from the box; / put it down and destined one for the Lofty One, one for the precipice. / He called out in a loud voice: "A sin-offering to the Lord!" / And those who heard him answered and blessed the name. / He tied a scarlet colored ribbon to the head of the one to be sent away / and stood it outside the place from which it would be sent. / ▸ This done as it should be, he went to the bull again, / and his sin and that of his clan he confessed before his Rock.

---

house," which might mean (a) his family, or (b) his fellow priests, "the house of Aaron"). As he was making this confession too, the people would prostrate themselves and say, "Blessed be the name…"

He then slaughtered the bull, gathered its blood, took some glowing coals in a special gold pan, and prepared the incense. This he brought into the Holy of Holies, placing the incense on the glowing coals only after he had entered. He would then say a short prayer. Next he sprinkled the blood of the sacrifice, upward once, downward seven times, counting carefully to ensure he had followed the procedure exactly.

וְהַכֹּהֲנִים וְהָעָם הָעוֹמְדִים בָּעֲזָרָה
כְּשֶׁהָיוּ שׁוֹמְעִים אֶת הַשֵּׁם הַנִּכְבָּד וְהַנּוֹרָא
מְפֹרָשׁ יוֹצֵא מִפִּי כֹהֵן גָּדוֹל, בִּקְדֻשָּׁה וּבְטָהֳרָה

At the word כּוֹרְעִים, *the* קהל *and the* שליח ציבור *kneel on the floor (see law 93).*

הָיוּ כּוֹרְעִים וּמִשְׁתַּחֲוִים וּמוֹדִים, וְנוֹפְלִים עַל פְּנֵיהֶם
וְאוֹמְרִים

בָּרוּךְ שֵׁם כְּבוֹד מַלְכוּתוֹ לְעוֹלָם וָעֶד.

All stand and continue:

וְאַף הוּא הָיָה מִתְכַּוֵּן לִגְמֹר אֶת הַשֵּׁם כְּנֶגֶד הַמְבָרְכִים
וְאוֹמֵר לָהֶם, תִּטְהָרוּ:

וְאַתָּה בְּטוּבְךָ הַגָּדוֹל מְעוֹרֵר רַחֲמֶיךָ, וְסוֹלֵחַ לְאִישׁ חֲסִידֶךָ.

צָעַד לֵילֵךְ לוֹ לְמִזְרַח עֲזָרָה / צֶמֶד שְׂעִירִים שָׁם, מֵהוֹן עֵדָה
צְמוּדִים אֲחוּיִים, שָׁוִים בְּתֹאַר וּבְקוֹמָה / צָגִים לְכַפֵּר עֲוֹן בַּת הַשּׁוֹבֵבָה.
צְהוֹב חֲלָשִׁים טָרַף וְהֶעֱלָה מִקַּלְפִּי / צָנַח וְהִגְרִיל לְשֵׁם גָּבֹהַּ וְלַצּוּק.
צָעַק בְּקוֹל רָם, לַיהוה חַטָּאת / צוֹתְתָיו עָנוּ וּבֵרְכוּ אֶת הַשֵּׁם.
צֶבַע זְהוֹרִית קָשַׁר בְּרֹאשׁ מִשְׁתַּלֵּחַ / צִיגָתוֹ אִמֵּן נֶגֶד בֵּית שִׁלּוּחַ
צָלַח וּבָא אֵצֶל פָּרוֹ שֵׁנִית / צַחֲנָתוֹ וְשֶׁלְּמַטֵּהוּ, פְּנֵי צוּר הִתְוַדָּה. ◂

צָנַח וְהִגְרִיל: *The Casting of Lots*

Two goats were now brought before the High Priest, as identical as possible in appearance. Over these he would draw lots. On one was written "For the Lord," on the other "For Azazel." Originally they were made of boxwood, later of gold. He would shake the box and draw the lots, which were then placed on the goats respectively. On the head of the goat to be sent to Azazel he would tie a thread of crimson wool, the color symbolizing sin.

Next he returned to the bull he had dedicated as an offering for himself and his family and confessed over it his sins and those of his fellow priests (the Torah states that the High Priest had to confess his sins and those of "his

וְכָךְ And this is what he would say:

The Leader continues, with the congregation following him in an undertone:

Please, LORD, / I have sinned, I have done wrong,
I have rebelled before You –
I and my family and the children of Aaron, Your holy people.
Please, by Your name, / grant atonement, please,
for the sins and for the wrongs and the rebellions
that I have sinned, and done wrong, and rebelled before You –
I and my family and the children of Aaron, Your holy people.
As it is written in the Torah of Moses Your servant,
at the word of Your glory:
For on this day you will be atoned and made pure *Lev. 16*
of all your sins before the LORD –

וְהַכֹּהֲנִים And the priests and all the people
who were standing in the courtyard,
when they heard the glorious and awesome name
spoken out expressly by the High Priest in holiness and purity,

At the words "bend their knees," the congregation and the Leader kneel on the floor (see law 93).

would bend their knees and bow down and give thanks
and fall upon their faces and say –

"Blessed be the name of His glorious kingdom
for ever and all time."

All stand and continue:

וְאַף And the High Priest too would take care
to finish saying the name together with those who blessed it,
and would say to them: "Become pure."

And You, in Your great benevolence,
awaken Your compassion and forgive the tribe that serves You.

---

then of the goat, on the outer curtain facing the Ark, and then, after combining the bloods, sprinkle on the golden altar, four times on its corners, seven times on its surface.

וְכָךְ הָיָה אוֹמֵר

The שליח ציבור continues, with the קהל following him in an undertone:

אָנָּא הַשֵּׁם / חָטָאתִי, עָוִיתִי, פָּשַׁעְתִּי לְפָנֶיךָ
אֲנִי וּבֵיתִי וּבְנֵי אַהֲרֹן עַם קְדוֹשֶׁךָ.
אָנָּא בַּשֵּׁם / כַּפֶּר נָא לַחֲטָאִים וְלַעֲוֹנוֹת וְלַפְּשָׁעִים
שֶׁחָטָאתִי וְשֶׁעָוִיתִי וְשֶׁפָּשַׁעְתִּי לְפָנֶיךָ
אֲנִי וּבֵיתִי וּבְנֵי אַהֲרֹן עַם קְדוֹשֶׁךָ.
כַּכָּתוּב בְּתוֹרַת מֹשֶׁה עַבְדֶּךָ מִפִּי כְבוֹדֶךָ
ויקרא טז כִּי־בַיּוֹם הַזֶּה יְכַפֵּר עֲלֵיכֶם לְטַהֵר אֶתְכֶם
מִכֹּל חַטֹּאתֵיכֶם, לִפְנֵי יהוה

וְהַכֹּהֲנִים וְהָעָם הָעוֹמְדִים בָּעֲזָרָה
כְּשֶׁהָיוּ שׁוֹמְעִים אֶת הַשֵּׁם הַנִּכְבָּד וְהַנּוֹרָא
מְפֹרָשׁ יוֹצֵא מִפִּי כֹהֵן גָּדוֹל, בִּקְדֻשָּׁה וּבְטָהֳרָה

At the word כּוֹרְעִים, the קהל and the שליח ציבור kneel on the floor (see law 93).

הָיוּ כּוֹרְעִים וּמִשְׁתַּחֲוִים וּמוֹדִים, וְנוֹפְלִים עַל פְּנֵיהֶם
וְאוֹמְרִים
בָּרוּךְ שֵׁם כְּבוֹד מַלְכוּתוֹ לְעוֹלָם וָעֶד.

All stand and continue:

וְאַף הוּא הָיָה מִתְכַּוֵּן לִגְמֹר אֶת הַשֵּׁם כְּנֶגֶד הַמְבָרְכִים
וְאוֹמֵר לָהֶם, תִּטְהָרוּ:
וְאַתָּה בְּטוּבְךָ הַגָּדוֹל מְעוֹרֵר רַחֲמֶיךָ, וְסוֹלֵחַ לְשֵׁבֶט מְשָׁרְתֶיךָ.

He then slaughtered the goat on which the lot "For the Lord" had been placed. He sprinkled its blood as before, in the Holy of Holies, once upward, seven times downward. Then he would sprinkle the blood, first of the bull,

קַח מַאֲכֶלֶת He would take a sharp knife and slaughter the goat as should be done, / receive its blood in a bowl and give it to the one who would stir it / to keep it from clotting until the time it would be sprinkled, / lest it should harden and forgiveness elude them. / The taking of smoldering coals, he shoveled into a golden pan, / which was light, with a thin surface, and a long handle. / He would heap into it three kabs of coals, / and they would bring him an empty spoon, and one overflowing with fine incense. / He would gather up incense in his palm, and place it in the spoon, / take the pan in his right hand and the spoon in his left. / His footsteps sounded as he approached the curtains and entered in between the poles, / placed incense in between them and set it to burn and left. / He took the blood from the youth who kept it stirring; / once again he went inside and stood between the Ark's poles. / ‣ Into the [blood] sprinklings of favor he would dip his fingers, counting, / sending the blood upward once, and then seven times downward.

וְכָךְ And this is how he would count:

The Leader, followed by the congregation (in some congregations, all in unison):

ONE. ONE and ONE.
ONE and TWO. ONE and THREE.
ONE and FOUR. ONE and FIVE.
ONE and SIX. ONE and SEVEN.

All:

רָץ He would run and lay the bowl down on the base intended for it, and slaughter a goat, and bring favor, receiving its blood into a consecrated bowl. ‣ He went and stood in the place of the Ark of Meeting, and brought favor through sprinkling blood, as with that of the bull.

וְכָךְ And this is how he would count:

The Leader, followed by the congregation (in some congregations, all in unison):

ONE. ONE and ONE.
ONE and TWO. ONE and THREE.
ONE and FOUR. ONE and FIVE.
ONE and SIX. ONE and SEVEN.

קָח מַאֲכֶלֶת חַדָּה וּשְׁחָטוֹ כְּסֵדֶר / קִבֵּל דָּם בְּמִזְרָק וּנְתָנוֹ לַמְמָרֵס
קְרִישָׁתוֹ יָמֵס עַד עֵת הַזָּיָה / קָפוּי פֶּן יְהִי, וְתֶעְדַּר סְלִיחָה.
קַח לוֹחֲשׁוֹת חַת בְּמַחְתַּת פַּרְוַיִם / קַלָּה, וְגֶלֶד רַךְ וַאֲרֻכַּת יָד
קָדַר לְתוֹכָהּ שְׁלֹשֶׁת קַבִּין גֶּחָלִים / קֵרְבוּ לוֹ בָּזָךְ וּגְדוּשַׁת דַּקָּה.
קָלַט וְחָפַן, וְהֵרִיק לְתוֹךְ בָּזָךְ / קָפַץ מַחְתָּה בַּיָּמִין וּבָזָךְ בַּשְּׂמֹאל
קִישׁ צְעָדָיו בַּפָּרֹכוֹת וְקָרַב לַבַּדִּים / קְטֹרֶת שָׂם בֵּינֵימוֹ וְעִשֵּׁן וְיָצָא.
רוֹבֶה מְמָרֵס, מֶנּוּ נָטַל דָּם / רִצֵּף וְנִכְנַס וְקָם בֵּין שַׁדַּיִם
◂ רְצוּי הַזָּיוֹת טָבַל, וְהִצְלִיף כְּמִנְיָן / רוּם מַעְלָה אַחַת וּמַטָּה שֶׁבַע.

וְכָךְ הָיָה מוֹנֶה

The שליח ציבור*, followed by the* קהל *(in some congregations, all in unison):*

אַחַת אַחַת וְאַחַת
אַחַת וּשְׁתַּיִם אַחַת וְשָׁלֹשׁ
אַחַת וְאַרְבַּע אַחַת וְחָמֵשׁ
אַחַת וָשֵׁשׁ אַחַת וָשֶׁבַע.

All:

רָץ וְהִנִּיחוֹ בַּכַּן וְשָׁחַט שָׂעִיר / רִצָּה וְקִבֵּל דָּמוֹ בְּאַגַּן קֹדֶשׁ
◂ רֵגֶל וְעָמַד מְקוֹם וְעוֹד אָרוֹן / רִצָּה הַזָּיוֹת כְּמַעֲשֵׂה דַּם פָּר.

וְכָךְ הָיָה מוֹנֶה

The שליח ציבור*, followed by the* קהל *(in some congregations, all in unison):*

אַחַת אַחַת וְאַחַת
אַחַת וּשְׁתַּיִם אַחַת וְשָׁלֹשׁ
אַחַת וְאַרְבַּע אַחַת וְחָמֵשׁ
אַחַת וָשֵׁשׁ אַחַת וָשֶׁבַע.

All:

וְהַט He would run again and lay it down and take up the blood of the bull, / hasten his feet and stand outside the curtain. / He would sprinkle the embroidered curtain as he had with the curtain within, / stir up the blood again and sprinkle with the blood of the goat. / He would return and combine the bloods and sprinkle upon the plated altar, / seven times on its surface and four times on its corners. / ▸ Then diligently he came to the living goat, / to confess the involuntary and the deliberate sins of the people to God.

וְכָךְ And this is what he would say:

The Leader continues, with the congregation following him in an undertone:

Please, LORD, / Your people, the house of Israel, have sinned,
have done wrong, have rebelled before You.
Please, by Your name, / grant atonement, please,
for the sins and for the wrongs and the rebellions
that they have sinned, and done wrong, and rebelled before You –
Your people, the house of Israel.
As it is written in the Torah of Moses Your servant,
at the word of Your glory:
For on this day you will be atoned and made pure *Lev. 16*
of all your sins before the LORD –

וְהַכֹּהֲנִים And the priests and all the people
who were standing in the courtyard,
when they heard the glorious and awesome name
spoken out expressly by the High Priest in holiness and purity,

At the words "bend their knees," the congregation and the Leader kneel on the floor (see law 93).

would bend their knees and bow down and give thanks
and fall upon their faces and say –
"Blessed be the name of His glorious kingdom for ever and all time."

All stand and continue:

וְאַף And the High Priest too would take care
to finish saying the name together with those who blessed it,
and would say to them: "Become pure."

And You, in Your great benevolence,
awaken Your compassion and forgive the congregation of Yeshurun.

All:

רָהַט וְהִנִּיחוֹ, וְדַם פָּר נָטַל / רַגְלָיו הֵרִיץ, וְיָצָא חוּץ לַבּוֹדֶלֶת
וְקָמֵי פָּרֹכֶת יַז כְּמִשְׁפַּט כַּפֹּרֶת / רִגֵּשׁ שָׁנָה, וְהִזָּה מִדַּם שָׂעִיר.
שָׁב וּבְלָלָם וְחִטֵּא מִזְבַּח סָגוּר / שֶׁבַע עַל טָהֳרוֹ וּבְקַרְנָיו אַרְבַּע
▸ שָׁקַד וּבָא אֵצֶל שָׂעִיר הֶחָי / שִׁגְיוֹן עָם וּזְדוֹנוֹ יוֹדֶה לָאֵל.

וְכָךְ הָיָה אוֹמֵר

The שליח ציבור continues, with the קהל following him in an undertone:

אָנָּא הַשֵּׁם / חָטְאוּ, עָווּ, פָּשְׁעוּ לְפָנֶיךָ עַמְּךָ בֵּית יִשְׂרָאֵל.
אָנָּא בַּשֵּׁם / כַּפֶּר נָא לַחֲטָאִים וְלַעֲוֹנוֹת וְלַפְּשָׁעִים
שֶׁחָטְאוּ וְשֶׁעָווּ וְשֶׁפָּשְׁעוּ לְפָנֶיךָ עַמְּךָ בֵּית יִשְׂרָאֵל.
כַּכָּתוּב בְּתוֹרַת מֹשֶׁה עַבְדֶּךָ מִפִּי כְבוֹדֶךָ
כִּי־בַיּוֹם הַזֶּה יְכַפֵּר עֲלֵיכֶם לְטַהֵר אֶתְכֶם ויקרא טז
מִכֹּל חַטֹּאתֵיכֶם, לִפְנֵי יהוה

וְהַכֹּהֲנִים וְהָעָם הָעוֹמְדִים בָּעֲזָרָה
כְּשֶׁהָיוּ שׁוֹמְעִים אֶת הַשֵּׁם הַנִּכְבָּד וְהַנּוֹרָא
מְפֹרָשׁ יוֹצֵא מִפִּי כֹהֵן גָּדוֹל, בִּקְדֻשָּׁה וּבְטָהֳרָה

At the word כּוֹרְעִים, the קהל and the שליח ציבור kneel on the floor (see law 93).

הָיוּ כּוֹרְעִים וּמִשְׁתַּחֲוִים וּמוֹדִים, וְנוֹפְלִים עַל פְּנֵיהֶם
וְאוֹמְרִים
בָּרוּךְ שֵׁם כְּבוֹד מַלְכוּתוֹ לְעוֹלָם וָעֶד.

All stand and continue:

וְאַף הוּא הָיָה מִתְכַּוֵּן לִגְמֹר אֶת הַשֵּׁם כְּנֶגֶד הַמְבָרְכִים
וְאוֹמֵר לָהֶם, תִּטְהָרוּ:

וְאַתָּה בְּטוּבְךָ הַגָּדוֹל מְעוֹרֵר רַחֲמֶיךָ וְסוֹלֵחַ לַעֲדַת יְשֻׁרוּן.

שִׁגְּרוֹ בְּיַד He sent it in the charge of an appointed man to the mighty wilderness, / to carry the stain of that congregation to a desolate land. / He pushed it from the edge of the cliff and it rolled down and fell / and its bones were broken like the shattering of a potter's vessel. The High Priest gripped the sharpened knife and rent the bull and goat, / pulled out their intestines and skewered their bodies for burning. / He read aloud the order of the day and consecrated himself and undressed, / and for a third time he immersed, robed himself in gold and consecrated. / He immediately offered his ram and the ram of the people, / offering the fat of the sin-offering and additional offering, according to their rule. / With clear intention he consecrated and undressed and immersed and consecrated, / donned a robe of linen and entered the innermost chamber. / He took out the vessel of incense and consecrated himself, / took off the garments he wore, and hid them away forever. / He bowed and immersed and put on golden garments and consecrated himself, / put the regular offering in its order and lit up the incense and the lamps. / When the worship was complete, he consecrated hand and foot, / thus completing the requisite five immersions and ten consecrations. / The look upon his face was that of the sun coming out in all its might, / and he hastened, ran and put on his own clothes. /

The mind needs symbolic action. That was the function of the scapegoat. Watching it go off into the desert hills, the people felt a sense of relief and release. It is striking that, in the absence of the scapegoat, two popular customs emerged in the Middle Ages, *Tashlikh*, the symbolic casting away of sins on Rosh HaShana, and *Kaparot*, the symbolic offering either of a fowl or money before Yom Kippur (page 3). Some halakhic authorities expressed doubts about these ceremonies, yet their popularity suggests that they answer to a felt psychological need, the same need addressed in the scapegoat ritual.

For more commentary on the scapegoat, see Introduction, page lv.

תֶּכֶל עֲבוֹדוֹת: *The Conclusion of the Service*
Meanwhile the High Priest completed the sacrificial service. When he received report that the goat had reached its destination, he was given a Torah scroll from which he read two sections, Lev. 16 and Lev. 23:26–32, both dealing with the Day of Atonement, and a third section from the book of Numbers (29:7–11) which he recited by heart. He then recited eight blessings.

He immersed himself a third time, put on gold robes, and offered the remaining sacrifices. He immersed himself again and donned white robes to bring out the ladle and coal pan from the Holy of Holies (since he was not permitted to enter this sacred space in gold robes). He immersed a fifth time, put on gold robes, offered the afternoon daily offering, burned the afternoon incense and lit the lamps. The service concluded, he would put on his own clothes and return home. Later he would make a feast for his friends to celebrate the fact that he had completed the service in peace.

שִׁגְּרוּ בְּיַד עִתִּי לְמִדְבַּר עָז / שֶׁמֶץ כִּתְמֵי זוּ שְׂאֵת לִגְזֵרָה
שֵׁן סֶלַע הֲדָפוֹ וְגִלְגֵּל וְיָרַד / שֻׁבְּרוּ עֲצָמָיו כְּנֶפֶץ כְּלִי יוֹצֵר.
שְׁחוּזָה אָחַז, פַּר וְשָׂעִיר קָרַע / שָׁלַף אֵמוּרִים, וּגְוִיּוֹת קֶלַע לִשְׂרֹף
שָׁאַג סִדְרֵי יוֹם, קִדֵּשׁ וּפָשַׁט / שִׁלֵּשׁ וְטָבַל, פַּזִּים עָט וְקִדֵּשׁ.
תְּכַף וְעָשׂ אֵילוֹ וְאֵיל עָם / תְּרַב חַטָּאוֹת וּמוּסָפִין הִקְרִיב כַּחֹק
תָּר וְקִדֵּשׁ, פָּשַׁט וְטָבַל וְקִדֵּשׁ / תַּכְרִיךְ בַּדִּים עָט וְנִכְנַס לַדְּבִיר.
תְּכוּנַת כְּלֵי קְטֹרֶת הוֹצִיא וְקִדֵּשׁ / תִּלְבֹּשֶׁת מַדָּיו הִפְשִׁיט וְגָנַז נֶצַח.
תִּרְגֵּל וְטָבַל, חֲרוּצִים עָט וְקִדֵּשׁ / תָּמִיד הִסְדִּיר וְתִמֵּר, וְנֵרוֹת הֶעֱלָה.
תֶּכֶל עֲבוֹדוֹת, יָד וָרֶגֶל קִדֵּשׁ / תִּמֵּם טְבִילוֹת חָמֵשׁ וְקִדּוּשִׁים עֲשָׂרָה
תְּאַר מְגַמָּתוֹ כְּצֵאת הַשֶּׁמֶשׁ בִּגְבוּרָה / תָּקַף וְדָץ וְעָטָה בִּגְדֵי הוֹנוֹ.

עֲזָאזֵל: *The Scapegoat*

He now turned to the goat on which had fallen the lot "For Azazel," and, placing his hands on its head, confessed over it the sins of the whole people. As during the previous confessions the people prostrated themselves and cried out "Blessed be the name…" He then handed the goat to a specially designated person who led it out to a precipice several miles (12 *mil*, a distance of 3.6 hours at normal walking pace) outside Jerusalem from which it fell.

The goat that carried with it the sins of the people is a supreme example of ritualized symbolic action. There are many one-time-only symbolic acts in the Hebrew Bible – such as the bronze snake made by Moses to protect the people from a plague (Num. 21), or the yoke worn by Jeremiah to warn of the coming Babylonian conquest (Jer. 27–28), or the scroll eaten by Ezekiel to show he had internalized God's word (Ezek. 3). Symbolic action is usually designed to shock, focus attention, and dramatize. That too is the case with the scapegoat.

Maimonides says that the scapegoat ritual was "of a symbolic character" (*Guide for the Perplexed*, 3:46). It was a dramatic enactment of what otherwise might be too abstract an idea: the removal of sin, stain, and guilt. There are good reasons why we have an inbuilt capacity to feel guilt. It is to the moral life what the capacity to feel pain is to physical life. They are our pre-conscious warning systems against behavior that can do harm. But without rituals of purification and catharsis the burden of guilt can be crushing. Cain said, "My guilt is too great to bear" (Gen. 4:13). King David said, "My sin is always before me" (Ps. 51:5). Even after repentance, feelings of guilt can remain.

The innocent nation walked this faithful delegate to his house, / rejoicing in the news of the scarlet dye turned snow white. / She [the nation] adorns herself with salvation, she puts on a robe of righteousness. / She rejoices, she speaks out her rapture and delight. / High places dripped the abundance of their dew, / and the furrows of my meadows were quenched to give their bounty. / Those who gather their seed in peace gave thanks, / and those who in joy carry away their sheaves gave praise. / The lowest parts of the Land of Desire resounded with song, / and those walking its paths of gravel gave voice to His righteousness. / The hope of those who sent that faithful delegate was not dashed; / the one they pinned their longings on was like the cool of snow in the harvest heat. / From their filth they were washed, from the repulsion of their sins they were purified;/ complete, innocent, their palms as if scrubbed with soap, / to declare that the One who purified them is the Source of living waters, / the Mikveh of Israel, cleansing them with unfailing waters. / They will be cleansed and made immaculate in purity, / renewed as are the angels every morning, polished clean of every stain. / Their mouths will voice the greatness of God; / joy at their tongues, a new song in their mouths, / they will rejoice in trembling, worship in awe / the Holy One of Israel, who makes holy the holy nation. / Speaking, singing, drumming, ringing cymbals, / singing songs of praise in a pleasant melody. / Embraced in the strength of God's right hand lifted high, / supported, all together, in the palm filled with righteousness, / drawing us into His gates in gladness, / joy and happiness theirs forever, / reveling, rejoicing in His name all of the day, / rejoicing with happiness to stand before Him. / ▸ The brightness of their light will break forth like sunrise, / their voices rising and singing of the majesty of the Rock of all ages. / Happy are the people *Ps. 144* for whom this is so; / happy are the people whose God is the LORD.

יְוֹם טוֹב And the High Priest would make a celebration for all his friends, when he entered the Sanctuary in peace and left it in peace, without harm.

And this was the prayer of the High Priest on the Day of Atonement,
as he left the Holy of Holies in peace, without harm:

Jerusalem during the late Second Temple period) of the scene as the High Priest emerged at the end of the day:

All the people that were in Jerusalem passed before him, most of them carrying torches of white wax, and all of them dressed in white clothing; and all the windows were garlanded with embroideries, and lit with candles. Priests have told me that often the High Priest could not reach his home before midnight, because of the press of the people passing before him, and because of the great numbers, for although all the people were fasting, they did not go home until they had seen whether they could reach the hand of the High Priest and kiss it. (*Shevet Yehuda*)

תַּמָּה תְּלַוֶּה צִיר נֶאֱמָן לַבַּיִת / תָּגֵל בְּהִתְבַּשֵּׂר, הַשְׁלֵג אֹדֶם תּוֹלָע
תַּעֲדֶה יֶשַׁע, תַּעֲטֶה מְעִיל צֶדֶק / תָּפִיק צָהֳלָה, תַּבִּיעַ דִּיץ וְחֶדְוָה.
תְּלוּלֵי רוּם הִרְעִיפוּ זַרְזִיף טַלָּם / תַּלְמֵי שָׂדַי רָווּ תֵּת יְבוּלָם
תּוֹדָה נָתְנוּ אוֹסְפֵי זֶרַע שָׁלוֹם / תְּהִלָּה בִּשְּׂרוּ נוֹשְׂאֵי אֲלֻמּוֹת בְּרֶנֶן.
תַּחְתִּיּוֹת אֶרֶץ צְבִי זֶמֶר שָׁמֵעוּ / תְּנוּ צִדְקוֹתָיו חֲצַץ הוֹלְכֵי נְתִיבוֹת
תִּקְוַת שׁוֹלְחָיו, אֵמוּן לֹא אַכְזָב / תּוֹחַלְתָּם כְּצִנַּת שֶׁלֶג בְּיוֹם קָצִיר.
מְצוֹאָתָם רָחֲצוּ, מִטֶּנֶף צַחֲנָם זַכּוּ /
שְׁלֵמִים תְּמִימִים, בְּבֹר כַּפֵּימוֹ זָכְכוּ
לְהַגִּיד כִּי מְטַהֲרָם מְקוֹר מַיִם חַיִּים /
מִקְוֵה יִשְׂרָאֵל מְנַקָּם, מַיִם נֶאֱמָנוּ.
בְּטֹהַר וּבְנִקָּיוֹן יִנָּקוּ וְיִטְהָרוּ / יְחֻדְּשׁוּ כַּחֳדָשֵׁי בְקָרִים, מִכֶּתֶם יְצַחְצָחוּ
רוֹמְמוֹת אֵל יֶהְגּוּ בִגְרוֹנָם / בִּלְשׁוֹנָם רֹן, בְּפִימוֹ שִׁיר חָדָשׁ.
יָגִילוּ בְרֶעַד, יַעַבְדוּ בְיִרְאָה / קָדוֹשׁ יִשְׂרָאֵל מְקַדֵּשׁ קְדוֹשִׁים
לְשַׁנֵּן, לְרַנֵּן, לְתוֹפֵף וּלְצַלְצֵל / וּלְנַצֵּחַ בִּנְגִינוֹת וּלְהַנְעִים זֶמֶר.
נֶחֱבָקִים בְּעֹז יָמִין רוֹמֵמָה / יַחַד נִתְמָכִים בְּמָלְאָה צֶדֶק
מְשׁוּכִים לָבוֹא שְׁעָרָיו בְּרִנָּה / וְשָׂשׂוֹן וְשִׂמְחָה יַשִּׂיגוּ נֶצַח.
שָׂשִׂים וְגָלִים בִּשְׁמוֹ כָּל הַיּוֹם / חָדִים בְּשִׂמְחָה אֶת פָּנָיו
▸ זִיו אוֹרָם כַּשַּׁחַר יִבָּקַע / קוֹלָם יִשְׂאוּ וְיָרֹנּוּ בִּגְאוֹן צוּר עוֹלָמִים.
תהלים קמד
אַשְׁרֵי הָעָם שֶׁכָּכָה לּוֹ, אַשְׁרֵי הָעָם שֶׁיהוה אֱלֹהָיו:

וְיוֹם טוֹב הָיָה עוֹשֶׂה כֹּהֵן גָּדוֹל לְכָל אוֹהֲבָיו
כְּשֶׁנִּכְנַס בְּשָׁלוֹם וְיָצָא בְּשָׁלוֹם בְּלִי פֶגַע.

וְכָךְ הָיְתָה תְּפִלָּתוֹ שֶׁל כֹּהֵן גָּדוֹל בְּיוֹם הַכִּפּוּרִים
בְּצֵאתוֹ מִבֵּית קֹדֶשׁ הַקֳּדָשִׁים בְּשָׁלוֹם בְּלִי פֶגַע.

Solomon ibn Verga, the fifteenth-century historian, quotes the following eyewitness account (by the Roman consul Marcus who held office in

יְהִי רָצוֹן May it be Your will, Lord our God and God of our ancestors,
that this year that is beginning for us and for all Your people,
the house of Israel, may be

The following piyutim, leading us from Seder HaAvoda to Viduy, are all alphabetic acrostics (some are reverse acrostics).

שְׁנַת A year in which You will open Your good store for us,
a year of plenty, / a year of blessing, / a year of good decrees before You,
a year of grain, wine and oil, / a year of abundance and success,
a year of meeting in Your Temple, / a year of low prices,
a year of good life before You,
a year of dew, rainy even if hot, / a year sweet with the harvest of choicest fruits,
a year of atonement for all our sins,
a year in which You will bless our bread and water,
a year of our earning and spending,
a year when we shall come to our Temple,
a year of fullness, / a year of enjoyment,
a year in which You will bless the fruit of our wombs and the fruit of our land,
a year in which You will bless our goings out and comings in,
a year in which You will save our community,
a year in which Your compassion will be awakened toward us,
a year of peace and tranquility,
a year in which no woman will miscarry the fruit of her womb,
a year in which You will bring us upright to our land,
a year when Your people Israel need not depend on one another
or on any other people,
for You will bring blessing to the work of their hands.

▸ And of the people of the Sharon he would say,
May it be Your will, Lord our God and God of our ancestors,
that their houses do not become their graves.

---

a business as the highest form of charity (Laws of Gifts to the Poor, 10:7). "Flay carcasses in the marketplace," said the third-century teacher Rav, "and do not say: I am a priest and a great man and it is beneath my dignity" (*Bava Batra* 110a).

וְעַל אַנְשֵׁי הַשָּׁרוֹן...שֶׁלֹּא יֵעָשׂוּ בָתֵּיהֶם קִבְרֵיהֶם *And of the people of Sharon… that their houses do not become their graves.* Some say the area was subject to heavy rains and landslides; others that the building materials available there were not suitable and houses needed to be regularly rebuilt (*Sota* 44a); yet others that this was an area subject to periodic earthquakes.

יְהִי רָצוֹן מִלְּפָנֶיךָ, יהוה אֱלֹהֵינוּ וֵאלֹהֵי אֲבוֹתֵינוּ, שֶׁתְּהֵא הַשָּׁנָה
הַזֹּאת הַבָּאָה עָלֵינוּ וְעַל כָּל עַמְּךָ בֵּית יִשְׂרָאֵל

The following piyutim, leading us from סדר העבודה *to* וידוי*, are all alphabetic acrostics (some are reverse acrostics).*

שְׁנַת אוֹצָרְךָ הַטּוֹב תִּפְתַּח לָנוּ
שְׁנַת אֹסֶם / שְׁנַת בְּרָכָה / שְׁנַת גְּזֵרוֹת טוֹבוֹת מִלְּפָנֶיךָ
שְׁנַת דָּגָן תִּירוֹשׁ וְיִצְהָר / שְׁנַת הַרְוָחָה וְהַצְלָחָה
שְׁנַת וְעוּד בֵּית מִקְדָּשֶׁךָ / שְׁנַת זוֹל / שְׁנַת חַיִּים טוֹבִים מִלְּפָנֶיךָ
שָׁנָה טְלוּלָה, וּגְשׁוּמָה אִם שְׁחוּנָה / שְׁנַת יַמְתִּיקוּ מְגָדִים אֶת תְּנוּבָתָם
שְׁנַת כַּפָּרָה עַל כָּל עֲוֹנוֹתֵינוּ / שְׁנַת לַחְמֵנוּ וּמֵימֵינוּ תְּבָרֵךְ
שְׁנַת מַשָּׂא וּמַתָּן / שְׁנַת נָבוֹא לְמִקְדָּשֵׁנוּ
שְׁנַת שֹׂבַע / שְׁנַת עֹנֶג
שְׁנַת פְּרִי בִטְנֵנוּ וּפְרִי אַדְמָתֵנוּ תְּבָרֵךְ
שְׁנַת צֵאתֵנוּ וּבוֹאֵנוּ תְּבָרֵךְ / שְׁנַת קְהָלֵנוּ תוֹשִׁיעַ
שְׁנַת רַחֲמֶיךָ יִכָּמְרוּ עָלֵינוּ / שְׁנַת שָׁלוֹם וְשַׁלְוָה
שָׁנָה שֶׁלֹּא תַפִּיל אִשָּׁה אֶת פְּרִי בִטְנָהּ
שָׁנָה שֶׁתּוֹלִיכֵנוּ קוֹמְמִיּוּת לְאַרְצֵנוּ
שָׁנָה שֶׁלֹּא יִצְטָרְכוּ עַמְּךָ בֵּית יִשְׂרָאֵל זֶה לָזֶה וְלֹא לְעַם אַחֵר,
בְּתִתְּךָ בְּרָכָה בְּמַעֲשֵׂה יְדֵיהֶם.
◂ וְעַל אַנְשֵׁי הַשָּׁרוֹן הָיָה אוֹמֵר
יְהִי רָצוֹן מִלְּפָנֶיךָ, יהוה אֱלֹהֵינוּ וֵאלֹהֵי אֲבוֹתֵינוּ
שֶׁלֹּא יֵעָשׂוּ בָתֵּיהֶם קִבְרֵיהֶם.

יְהִי רָצוֹן מִלְּפָנֶיךָ *May it be Your will.* A poetic expansion of the various versions of the High Priest's prayer given in the Babylonian and Jerusalem Talmuds.

שֶׁלֹּא יִצְטָרְכוּ...זֶה לָזֶה *Need not depend on one another.* Though Judaism places a high value on philanthropy, it values economic independence more. We pray, at each Grace after Meals, not to be "dependent on the gifts or loans of other people" so that "we may suffer neither shame nor humiliation." That is why Maimonides ranks providing someone with a job or helping them start

The Leader:

אֱמֶת Truly how splendid was the High Priest,
as he came out of the Holy of Holies in peace, without harm.

The following piyut was traditionally recited responsively, the Leader chanting each line and the congregation responding with "was the appearance of the [High] Priest." In some congregations, the whole piyut is sung collectively.

Like the heavenly canopy stretched out over the angels
was the appearance of the [High] Priest.
Like the lightning flashing from the Ḥayyot's radiance
was the appearance of the [High] Priest.
Like the fringes edging the four corners of his clothes
was the appearance of the [High] Priest.
Like the image of a rainbow appearing in the midst of cloud
was the appearance of the [High] Priest.
Like the splendor with which the Rock clothed those He had made
was the appearance of the [High] Priest.
Like a rose in the heart of a lovely garden
was the appearance of the [High] Priest.
Like the crown that rests on a king's own brow
was the appearance of the [High] Priest.
Like love that appears on a bridegroom's countenance
was the appearance of the [High] Priest.
Like the purity granted by an immaculate miter
was the appearance of the [High] Priest.
Like that of [Moses] abiding in concealment to plead before the King
was the appearance of the [High] Priest.
Like the Venus star on the eastern horizon
was the appearance of the [High] Priest.

At critical moments the appearance of the leader shapes the mood of the nation.

כְּהוֹד אֲשֶׁר הִלְבִּישׁ צוּר *Like the splendor with which the Rock clothed.* Like the garments of light with which, according to the school of Rabbi Meir, God clothed Adam and Eve as they were about to leave Eden (*Bereshit Raba* 20:12).

בְּצָנִיף טָהוֹר *By an immaculate miter.* The white miter with which, according to the prophet Zechariah, God would adorn the High Priest Joshua (Zech. 3:5).

The שליח ציבור*:*

אֱמֶת, מַה נֶּהְדָּר הָיָה כֹּהֵן גָּדוֹל
בְּצֵאתוֹ מִבֵּית קָדְשֵׁי הַקֳּדָשִׁים בְּשָׁלוֹם בְּלִי פֶגַע.

The following piyut was traditionally recited responsively, the שליח ציבור *chanting each line and the* קהל *responding with "*מַרְאֵה כֹהֵן*." In some congregations, the whole piyut is sung collectively.*

כְּאֹהֶל הַנִּמְתָּח בְּדָרֵי מַעְלָה — מַרְאֵה כֹהֵן
כִּבְרָקִים הַיּוֹצְאִים מִזִּיו הַחַיּוֹת — מַרְאֵה כֹהֵן
כְּגֹדֶל גְּדִילִים בְּאַרְבַּע קְצָווֹת — מַרְאֵה כֹהֵן
כִּדְמוּת הַקֶּשֶׁת בְּתוֹךְ הֶעָנָן — מַרְאֵה כֹהֵן
כְּהוֹד אֲשֶׁר הִלְבִּישׁ צוּר לִיצוּרִים — מַרְאֵה כֹהֵן
כְּוֶרֶד הַנָּתוּן בְּתוֹךְ גִּנַּת חֶמֶד — מַרְאֵה כֹהֵן
כְּזֵר הַנָּתוּן עַל מֵצַח מֶלֶךְ — מַרְאֵה כֹהֵן
כְּחֶסֶד הַנִּתָּן עַל פְּנֵי חָתָן — מַרְאֵה כֹהֵן
כְּטֹהַר הַנָּתוּן בְּצָנִיף טָהוֹר — מַרְאֵה כֹהֵן
כְּיוֹשֵׁב בְּסֵתֶר לְחַלּוֹת פְּנֵי מֶלֶךְ — מַרְאֵה כֹהֵן
כְּכוֹכַב הַנֹּגַהּ בִּגְבוּל מִזְרָח — מַרְאֵה כֹהֵן

מַרְאֵה כֹהֵן *The appearance of the [High] Priest.* This remarkable poem reflects the sense of exhilaration that accompanied the emergence of the High Priest at the successful completion of his duties for the day. We find the following description in the book of Ben Sira, written in the early second century BCE in Second Temple times, of the appearance of the High Priest:

> How glorious he was, surrounded by the people, as he came out of the house of the curtain. Like the morning star among the clouds, like the full moon at the festal season, like the sun shining on the Temple of the Most High, like the rainbow gleaming in splendid clouds; like the roses in the days of first fruits, like lilies by a spring of water, like a green shoot on Lebanon on a summer day; like fire and incense in the censer, like a vessel of hammered gold studded with all kinds of precious stones; like an olive tree laden with fruit and like a cypress towering in the clouds. (Ben Sira 50:5–10)

Some congregations omit the remainder of this piyut and continue with "All this," below.

Like one dressed in the mantle and armor of righteousness
was the appearance of the [High] Priest.
Like the angel standing at the end of the path
was the appearance of the [High] Priest.
Like a lamp flickering between the window slats
was the appearance of the [High] Priest.
Like the commanders leading the holy nation
was the appearance of the [High] Priest.
Like the strength with which the Pure One wrapped the one made pure
was the appearance of the [High] Priest.
Like the golden bells at his mantle's hem
was the appearance of the [High] Priest.
Like the form of the House, and the curtain of the Ark
was the appearance of the [High] Priest.
Like a room hung with sky blue and royal purple
was the appearance of the [High] Priest.
Like those watching the sun rise over the land
was the appearance of the [High] Priest.
Like a garden lily penetrating the thorn-weeds
was the appearance of the [High] Priest.
Like the appearance of Orion and Pleiades, seen in the south
was the appearance of the [High] Priest.

As part of the Leader's Repetition, the following piyutim should ideally be said by the Leader alone. However, the prevailing custom is that the congregation recites them without pause until "Remember, LORD" on page 926.

כָּל אֵלֶּה All this was while the Sanctuary stood on its foundations,
and the holy Temple on its base;
when the High Priest stood and served,
and all his generation looked on and were joyful.

אַשְׁרֵי עַיִן How fortunate was the eye that beheld all this;
when our ears hear of it, our souls languish indeed.

How fortunate was the eye that witnessed our Tent,
as our congregation rejoiced therein;
when our ears hear of it, our souls languish indeed.

How fortunate was the eye that witnessed our joy,
the delight of our joyful shouts;
when our ears hear of it, our souls languish indeed.

Some congregations omit the remainder of this piyut and continue with "כָּל אֵלֶּה," below.

כִּלְבוּשׁ מְעִיל וּכְשִׁרְיַן צְדָקָה   מַרְאֵה כֹהֵן
כְּמַלְאָךְ הַנִּצָּב עַל רֹאשׁ דֶּרֶךְ   מַרְאֵה כֹהֵן
כְּנֵר הַמֵּצִיץ מִבֵּין הַחַלּוֹנוֹת   מַרְאֵה כֹהֵן
כְּשָׂרֵי צְבָאוֹת בְּרֹאשׁ עַם קֹדֶשׁ   מַרְאֵה כֹהֵן
כְּעֹז אֲשֶׁר הִלְבִּישׁ טָהוֹר לַמִּטַּהֵר   מַרְאֵה כֹהֵן
כְּפַעֲמוֹנֵי זָהָב בְּשׁוּלֵי הַמְּעִיל   מַרְאֵה כֹהֵן
כְּצוּרַת הַבַּיִת וּפָרֹכֶת הָעֵדוּת   מַרְאֵה כֹהֵן
כִּקְהִלָּה מְכֻסָּה תְּכֵלֶת וְאַרְגָּמָן   מַרְאֵה כֹהֵן
כְּרוֹאֵי זְרִיחַת שֶׁמֶשׁ עַל הָאָרֶץ   מַרְאֵה כֹהֵן
כְּשׁוֹשַׁנַּת גַּן מִבֵּין הַחוֹחִים   מַרְאֵה כֹהֵן
כְּתַבְנִית כְּסִיל וְכִימָה מִתֵּימָן   מַרְאֵה כֹהֵן

As part of the חזרת הש״ץ, the following piyutim should ideally be said by the שליח ציבור alone. However, the prevailing custom is that the congregation recites them without pause until "זְכֹר־רַחֲמֶיךָ" on page 927.

כָּל אֵלֶּה בִּהְיוֹת הַהֵיכָל עַל יְסוֹדוֹתָיו,
וּמִקְדַּשׁ הַקֹּדֶשׁ עַל מְכוֹנוֹתָיו
וְכֹהֵן גָּדוֹל עוֹמֵד וּמְשָׁרֵת, דּוֹרוֹ רָאוּ וְשָׂמֵחוּ.

אַשְׁרֵי עַיִן רָאֲתָה כָּל אֵלֶּה
הֲלֹא לְמִשְׁמַע אֹזֶן דָּאֲבָה נַפְשֵׁנוּ.

אַשְׁרֵי עַיִן רָאֲתָה אָהֳלֵנוּ / בְּשִׂמְחַת קְהָלֵנוּ
הֲלֹא לְמִשְׁמַע אֹזֶן דָּאֲבָה נַפְשֵׁנוּ.

אַשְׁרֵי עַיִן רָאֲתָה גִּילֵנוּ / דִּיצַת צַהֲלֵנוּ
הֲלֹא לְמִשְׁמַע אֹזֶן דָּאֲבָה נַפְשֵׁנוּ.

אַשְׁרֵי עַיִן רָאֲתָה כָּל אֵלֶּה *How fortunate was the eye that beheld all this.* A lament for the disparity between then and now: then visible majesty, now mere memory.

How fortunate was the eye that beheld the Temple singers
and all their various songs;
when our ears hear of it, our souls languish indeed.

How fortunate was the eye that witnessed the Temple as it stood,
where the Living One dwelt;
when our ears hear of it, our souls languish indeed.

How fortunate was the eye that beheld the palaces like beautiful carvings,
and the twenty-four thousand young priests;
when our ears hear of it our souls languish indeed.

How fortunate was the eye that beheld the glory of the Menora
in its uniqueness, and the ten basins;
when our ears hear of it, our souls languish indeed.

How fortunate was the eye that beheld the altar where the incense was
offered, / with a rim of gold around it like a crown;
when our ears hear of it, our souls languish indeed.

How fortunate was the eye that beheld the Celebration of the Water
Drawing, / a nation drawing divine inspiration and beneficent spirit;
when our ears hear of it, our souls languish indeed.

How fortunate was the eye that beheld the High Priest expressly
pronouncing the holy name, / crying out, "I beg of You, LORD!" –
when our ears hear of it, our souls languish indeed.

How fortunate was the eye that beheld the congregation of holy ones,
gathering before the Holy of Holies;
when our ears hear of it, our souls languish indeed.

How fortunate was the eye that witnessed the whitening of the crimson
thread / from the sacrificial goat;
when our ears hear of it, our souls languish indeed.

How fortunate was the eye that witnessed the constant sacrifices being
offered / at the gate where multitudes once gathered;
when our ear hears of it, our souls languish indeed.

שְׁנִי הַמְלֻבָּן *The whitening of the crimson thread.* If the scarlet thread from the goat sent to Azazel turned white, this was a sign that atonement had been granted.

אַשְׁרֵי עַיִן רָאֲתָה הַמְשׁוֹרְרִים / וְכָל מִינֵי שִׁירִים
הֲלֹא לְמִשְׁמַע אֹזֶן דָּאֲבָה נַפְשֵׁנוּ.

אַשְׁרֵי עַיִן רָאֲתָה זְבוּל הַמְתֻכָּן / חַי בּוֹ שָׁכָן
הֲלֹא לְמִשְׁמַע אֹזֶן דָּאֲבָה נַפְשֵׁנוּ.

אַשְׁרֵי עַיִן רָאֲתָה טִירוֹת כְּגֶלֶף / יוֹנְקֵי כֹהֲנִים, עֶשְׂרִים וְאַרְבָּעָה אֶלֶף
הֲלֹא לְמִשְׁמַע אֹזֶן דָּאֲבָה נַפְשֵׁנוּ.

אַשְׁרֵי עַיִן רָאֲתָה כְּבוֹד מְנוֹרוֹת / לְאֶחָד וַעֲשָׂרָה כִּיּוֹרוֹת
הֲלֹא לְמִשְׁמַע אֹזֶן דָּאֲבָה נַפְשֵׁנוּ.

אַשְׁרֵי עַיִן רָאֲתָה מִזְבֵּחַ מִקְטַר קְטֹרֶת / נֵזֶר עָלָיו כַּעֲטֶרֶת
הֲלֹא לְמִשְׁמַע אֹזֶן דָּאֲבָה נַפְשֵׁנוּ.

אַשְׁרֵי עַיִן רָאֲתָה שִׂמְחַת בֵּית הַשּׁוֹאֵבָה
עִם שׁוֹאֶבֶת רוּחַ הַקֹּדֶשׁ, רוּחַ נְדִיבָה
הֲלֹא לְמִשְׁמַע אֹזֶן דָּאֲבָה נַפְשֵׁנוּ.

אַשְׁרֵי עַיִן רָאֲתָה פְּרִישַׁת כֹּהֵן בְּרֶשֶׁם / צוֹעֵק אָנָּא הַשֵּׁם
הֲלֹא לְמִשְׁמַע אֹזֶן דָּאֲבָה נַפְשֵׁנוּ.

אַשְׁרֵי עַיִן רָאֲתָה קְהַל קְדוֹשִׁים / רוֹגְשִׁים בְּבֵית קֹדֶשׁ הַקֳּדָשִׁים
הֲלֹא לְמִשְׁמַע אֹזֶן דָּאֲבָה נַפְשֵׁנוּ.

אַשְׁרֵי עַיִן רָאֲתָה שָׁנִי הַמְלֻבָּן / מִשְּׂעִיר הַקָּרְבָּן
הֲלֹא לְמִשְׁמַע אֹזֶן דָּאֲבָה נַפְשֵׁנוּ.

אַשְׁרֵי עַיִן רָאֲתָה תְּמִידִים קְרֵבִים / בְּשַׁעַר בַּת רַבִּים
הֲלֹא לְמִשְׁמַע אֹזֶן דָּאֲבָה נַפְשֵׁנוּ.

שִׂמְחַת בֵּית הַשּׁוֹאֵבָה *The Celebration of the Water Drawing.* On Sukkot, one of the great moments of festivity in the Temple courtyard (Mishna *Sukka* 50a).

עֲוֹנוֹת אֲבוֹתֵינוּ The iniquities of our ancestors
brought about the Temple's destruction,
and our sins have prolonged its desolate condition;
but the remembrance of the worship therein
shall be our forgiveness,
and the affliction of our souls shall serve as our atonement.
And so, in Your great compassion,
You have given us this Day of Atonement,
this day for pardon of iniquity,
to forgive iniquity and atone transgression.

A day on which eating is forbidden,
a day on which drinking is forbidden,
a day on which washing is forbidden,
a day on which anointing with oils is forbidden,
a day on which marital relations are forbidden,
a day on which the wearing of leather shoes is forbidden,
a day which brings about love and companionship,
a day on which we cast aside all jealousies and rivalries,
a day on which You shall pardon all our sins.

And at this time and season,
it is revealed and known before the throne of Your glory,
that we are lacking what we had in days of old.
We do not have a High Priest to offer sacrifices,
nor an altar to raise up burnt or whole offerings.

---

the pain is not a form of mourning as such but rather part of the process of *teshuva,* a sense of collective remorse that our ancestors sinned and that our merits have not sufficed to rebuild what has been lost.

אַהֲבָה וְרֵעוּת...עֲזִיבַת קִנְאָה וְתַחֲרוּת *Love and companionship... cast aside all jealousies and rivalries.* It has long been the custom for people to mend broken relationships at this time.

עֲוֹנוֹת אֲבוֹתֵינוּ הֶחֱרִיבוּ נָוֶה, וְחַטֹּאתֵינוּ הֶאֱרִיכוּ קִצּוֹ
אֲבָל זִכְרוֹן דְּבָרִים תְּהֵא סְלִיחָתֵנוּ, וְעִנּוּי נַפְשֵׁנוּ תְּהֵא כַפָּרָתֵנוּ
עַל כֵּן בְּרַחֲמֶיךָ הָרַבִּים נָתַתָּ לָנוּ אֶת יוֹם הַכִּפּוּרִים הַזֶּה
וְאֶת יוֹם מְחִילַת הֶעָוֹן הַזֶּה, לִסְלִיחַת עָוֹן וּלְכַפָּרַת פָּשַׁע.

יוֹם אָסוּר בַּאֲכִילָה
יוֹם אָסוּר בִּשְׁתִיָּה
יוֹם אָסוּר בִּרְחִיצָה
יוֹם אָסוּר בְּסִיכָה
יוֹם אָסוּר בְּתַשְׁמִישׁ הַמִּטָּה
יוֹם אָסוּר בִּנְעִילַת הַסַּנְדָּל
יוֹם שִׂימַת אַהֲבָה וְרֵעוּת
יוֹם עֲזִיבַת קִנְאָה וְתַחֲרוּת
יוֹם שֶׁתִּמְחַל לְכָל עֲוֹנוֹתֵינוּ.

וּבָעֵת וּבָעוֹנָה הַזֹּאת
גָּלוּי וְיָדוּעַ לִפְנֵי כִסֵּא כְבוֹדֶךָ
שֶׁאֵין לָנוּ כְּיָמִים רִאשׁוֹנִים
לֹא כֹהֵן גָּדוֹל לְהַקְרִיב קָרְבָּן
וְלֹא מִזְבֵּחַ לְהַעֲלוֹת עָלָיו עוֹלָה וְכָלִיל.

עֲוֹנוֹת אֲבוֹתֵינוּ *The iniquities of our ancestors.* A fragment attributed to the poet and philosopher Solomon ibn Gabirol and the first of a series of laments for what we have lost with the destruction of the Temple. This sequence of prayers, a lacerating articulation of grief and national bereavement, is similar in tone to the *Kinot* (Laments) we say on Tisha B'Av, with this one difference – on Tisha B'Av we sit like mourners in the grip of loss. On Yom Kippur

וּמֵרֹב עֲוֹנֵינוּ And in the abundance of our sins,
we have none of these things:

No burnt-offerings nor guilt-offerings,
no staves nor mixed-meal cakes,
no lots nor fiery coals, no Sanctuary nor fine incense,
no Temple nor blood sprinkling, no confession nor gatherings,
no peace-offerings nor blood casting,
no sin-offerings nor sacrificial fats,
no ritual immersion nor purification, no Jerusalem nor holy Temple,
no laver nor its base, no frankincense nor showbread,
no altar nor meal-offering, no pleasing offerings nor wine libations,
no meal-flour nor incense, no arranged altars nor burnt-offerings,
no curtain nor bulls for sin-offerings,
no Zion nor priestly golden crown,
no incense nor sacrifices,
no compounded spices nor pleasantly scented offerings,
no voluntary-offerings nor peace-offerings,
no thanksgiving-offerings or daily sacrifices.

כִּי בַעֲוֹנוֹתֵינוּ On account of our sins and the sins of our ancestors,
we are lacking all of these things.
And ever since we are lacking all of these things,

תָּכְפוּ Troubles have come upon us in rapid succession,
travails have overwhelmed us.
We had hoped for salvation, but there was none;
and for peace, but instead, terror has come.
Our attackers have increased;
they have risen up and lifted up their heads.
We have tired of bearing the yoke of those triumphant foes;
their burden of tyranny has become heavy upon us.

Temple, then with the Hadrianic persecutions following the failure of the Bar Kokhba rebellion.

וּמֵרֹב עֲוֹנֵינוּ אֵין לָנוּ

לֹא אִשִּׁים וְלֹא אָשָׁם / לֹא בַדִּים וְלֹא בְלוּלָה
לֹא גוֹרָל וְלֹא גַחֲלֵי אֵשׁ / לֹא דְבִיר וְלֹא דַקָּה
לֹא הֵיכָל וְלֹא הַזָּיָה / לֹא וִדּוּי וְלֹא וָעַד
לֹא זֶבַח וְלֹא זְרִיקָה / לֹא חַטָּאת וְלֹא חֲלָבִים
לֹא טְבִילָה וְלֹא טָהֳרָה / לֹא יְרוּשָׁלַיִם וְלֹא יַעַר הַלְּבָנוֹן
לֹא כִּיּוֹר וְלֹא כַנּוֹ / לֹא לְבוֹנָה וְלֹא לֶחֶם הַפָּנִים
לֹא מִזְבֵּחַ וְלֹא מִנְחָה / לֹא נִיחוֹחַ וְלֹא נְסָכִים
לֹא סֹלֶת וְלֹא סַמִּים / לֹא עֵרֶךְ וְלֹא עוֹלָה
לֹא פָרֹכֶת וְלֹא פַר חַטָּאת / לֹא צִיּוֹן וְלֹא צִיץ הַזָּהָב
לֹא קְטֹרֶת וְלֹא קָרְבָּן / לֹא רֹקַח וְלֹא רֵיחַ נִיחֹחַ
לֹא שַׁי וְלֹא שְׁלָמִים / לֹא תוֹדָה וְלֹא תְמִידִים.

כִּי בַּעֲוֹנוֹתֵינוּ וּבַעֲוֹנוֹת אֲבוֹתֵינוּ חָסַרְנוּ כָּל אֵלֶּה.
וּמֵעֵת חָסַרְנוּ כָּל אֵלֶּה

תָּכְפוּ עָלֵינוּ צָרוֹת / תְּלָאוֹת עָבְרוּ רֹאשֵׁנוּ
שִׁחַרְנוּ יְשׁוּעָה וָאַיִן / שָׁלוֹם וְהִנֵּה קְפָדָה
רַבּוּ הַקָּמִים עָלֵינוּ / רָמוּ וְגַם נָשְׂאוּ רֹאשׁ
קָצְנוּ בְּעֹל עַלִּיזִים / קָשֶׁה עָלֵינוּ סִבְלָם

וּמֵרֹב עֲוֹנֵינוּ *And in the abundance of our sins.* We lament the loss of elements of the Temple and its service that exist no more.

תָּכְפוּ עָלֵינוּ *Troubles have come upon us.* A cumulative description of the tragedies that befell Israel under the Romans, first with the destruction of the

Our beautiful land has been defiled on our account;
it has sprouted, but is devoid of abundant blessing.
We had hoped for abundance, but received little;
deep sorrow pervades our storehouses.
Our olive trees have cheated us of their oils
even as their fruit grew, and their yield was insufficient.
Though vineyards may produce grape-blossoms aplenty,
the wine they yield does not suffice to fill a single vat.
The fruit of the fields has been cursed,
delicacies have been taken away.
Within the sheepfolds, flocks have dwindled away;
they cannot produce enough wool, milk or offspring.
We have become like the tail, instead of the head;
we are indebted, instead of being lenders.
Our strength is spent in vain and dismay,
with no hope for profit.
The hand that once toiled skillfully
has collapsed, and there is no one to support it.
They have been thrown from sea to sea
with no one to provide their sustenance.
The wage-earner's eye was darkened,
as his hope for payment was frustrated.
Lender and debtor rage at each other,
distancing themselves from one another.
Those who extend their hands to the poor have grown weary,
for the rich fail to act graciously with the destitute.
Alas, the earth has fallen into the hands of the evil,
its inhabitants have not found respite.
The Temple, House of our God, is desolate;
our undertakings have been denied success.
The joy of the Temple has ceased –
how then shall we allow happiness to enter our hearts?
When there is no constant sacrificial meal for our Father,
the bellies of the sons shall also lack sustenance.
The Master of the House has become like a guest at an inn –
where shall we find rest?

צְבִי אֶרֶץ חֲנֻפָּה עָלֵינוּ / צָמְחָה וְלֹא לִבְרָכָה
פָּנִינוּ לְהַרְבֵּה וְהִנֵּה מְעַט / פַּח נֶפֶשׁ בָּא בַּאֲסָמֵינוּ
עָשְׁקוּ זֵיתִים שַׁמְנָם / עֲשׂוּתָם, וְלֹא מָלְאוּ שֶׁפֶק
סְמָדַר אִם יִרְבֶּה כֶּרֶם / סָבְאוֹ לֹא יַשְׁפִּיעַ יֶקֶב
נֶאֶרְרוּ אִבֵּי שָׂדֶה / נִלְקְחוּ מַטְעַמֵּי אֹכֶל
מִמִּכְלְאוֹת צֹאן עֲדָרִים דָּלְלוּ /
מִגֵּז וּמִמִּיץ וּמֵהֵרָיוֹן
לְזָנָב וְלֹא לְרֹאשׁ הוּשַׁתְנוּ /
לַעֲבֹט, וְלֹא הָעֲבֹט לָנוּ
כֹּחֵנוּ לָרִיק וּבֶהָלָה / כָּלָה מִבְּלִי שָׂכָר
יַד כָּל עָמֵל בְּכִשְׁרוֹן / יָרְדָה, וְאֵין מִי יַחֲזִיק
טִלְטְלוּ מִיָּם וְעַד יָם / טַרְפָּם לֹא סָפַק לָמוֹ
חֲשֵׁכָה לְעַיִן מִשְׁתַּכֵּר / חֹשֵׁב שְׂכָרוֹ לְמַפָּח
זֹעֲמוּ מַלְוֶה וְלֹוֶה / זֶה בְּזֶה שָׁלְחוּ מֵעַתָּה
וְנִלְאוּ יְדֵי מַמְצִיאֵי יָד / וְעָשִׁיר לֹא חוֹנֵן רָשׁ
הֵן אֶרֶץ נִמְכְּרָה בְּיַד רָעִים /
הָמוֹן בָּהּ לֹא מָצְאוּ רֶוַח
דְּבִיר בֵּית אֱלֹהֵינוּ שָׁמֵם / דְּרָכֵינוּ מֵאֲנוּ לְהַצְלִיחַ
גִּיל נָוֶה שָׁבַת / גִּילָה לִלְבָבֵנוּ מַה נַּעַל
בְּאֵין אֲרֻחַת אָב תָּמִיד / בְּכֵן בֶּטֶן בָּנִים תֶּחְסַר
אֲדוֹן בַּיִת, כְּאוֹרֵחַ בַּמָּלוֹן / אֵיפֹה נִמְצָא מָנוֹחַ.

אֲדוֹן בַּיִת, כְּאוֹרֵחַ בַּמָּלוֹן *The Master of the House has become like a guest at an inn.* A graphic description of how God, as it were, has become homeless, exiled with His people.

And ever since our holy Temple was destroyed,

תַּנּוֹת We cannot relate the extent of our troubles,
each day brings brokenness and groaning.
Anguish has increased among us,
our dignity has descended to the dust.
The avaricious have gained power,
those who employ falsehood have attained wealth.
Those who act righteously go unnoticed,
those who detest unjust gains do not endure.
We are as an empty vessel, / stripped of every dignity.
There is neither prophet nor vision among us;
like the blind, we feel as we go.
Each day we wonder what will become of us;
we have declared: "Death is better than life!"
Our lives dangle in doubt before us;
strangers have become the head, and we, the tail.
What can be done? Our sins have caused all this.
It is as if we no longer exist.
We are weak, despised, and lowly,
repulsive, loathsome and despicable.
Strangers rule over us; we have declared: "We are cut off, we are lost."
Master, ease our burden / and send salvation to redeem us.

Our God and God of our ancestors,

אַל תַּעַשׂ Do not bring us to an end;
may Your hand hold back harsh judgment.
Should our blame come before You,
do not erase our names from Your book of life.
As You approach to sign the decree committing us to affliction,
may Your compassion come forward, pushing aside Your ire.
As You behold the scarcity of good deeds among us,
deal with us righteously.

---

as אתב״ש, the first phrase in each line following an alphabetical acrostic, the second a reverse alphabetical acrostic.

וּמִשֶּׁחָרֵב בֵּית מִקְדָּשֵׁנוּ

תְּנוּת צָרוֹת לֹא נוּכַל / שֶׁבֶר בְּכָל יוֹם וַאֲנָחָה
רָבְתָה בָּנוּ חַלְחָלָה / קֶרֶן יָרְדָה עַד עָפָר
צָרֵי עַיִן מָצְאוּ יָד / פּוֹעֲלֵי שֶׁקֶר עָשׂוּ חָיִל
עוֹשֵׂי צְדָקָה לֹא נִרְאוּ / שׂוֹנְאֵי בֶצַע לֹא עָמָדוּ
נִדְמֵינוּ כִּכְלִי רִיק / מִכֹּל נִשְׁאַרְנוּ עֲרֻמִּים
לֹא נָבִיא וְלֹא חָזוֹן בָּנוּ / כָּעִוְרִים נְגַשֵּׁשׁ וְנֵלֵךְ
יוֹם יוֹם נֹאמַר מַה בְּסוֹפֵנוּ / טוֹב מָוֶת מֵחַיִּים אָמַרְנוּ
חַיֵּינוּ תְּלוּאִים מִנֶּגֶד / זָרִים לְרֹאשׁ, וַאֲנַחְנוּ לְזָנָב
וּמַה נַּעֲשֶׂה, וַחֲטֹאתֵינוּ עָשׂוּ / הֵן אָנוּ כְּלֹא הָיִינוּ
דַּלִּים נִבְזִים וּשְׁפָלִים / גְּעוּלִים מְאוּסִים וּבְזוּיִים
בְּנֵי נֵכָר מָשְׁלוּ בָנוּ / אָמַרְנוּ נִגְזַרְנוּ אָבָדְנוּ
אָדוֹן הָקֵל עָלֵינוּ / וּשְׁלַח יֶשַׁע לְגָאֳלֵנוּ.

אֱלֹהֵינוּ וֵאלֹהֵי אֲבוֹתֵינוּ

אַל תַּעַשׂ עִמָּנוּ כָּלָה / תֹּאחֵז יָדְךָ בַּמִּשְׁפָּט
בְּבֹא תוֹכֵחָה לְנֶגְדֶּךָ / שְׁמֵנוּ מִסִּפְרְךָ אַל תֶּמַח
גִּשְׁתְּךָ לַחְתֹּם מוּסָר / רַחֲמֶיךָ יְקַדְּמוּ רָגְזֶךָ
דַּלּוּת מַעֲשִׂים בְּשׁוּרֶךָ / קָרֵב צֶדֶק מֵאֵלֶיךָ

וּמִשֶּׁחָרֵב בֵּית מִקְדָּשֵׁנוּ *And ever since our holy Temple was destroyed.* The mood of grief deepens, evoking the dark passages in the Torah known as the *Tokheḥa*, the rebuke (Lev. 26:14–45; Deut. 28:15–68).

אַל תַּעַשׂ עִמָּנוּ כָּלָה *Do not bring us to an end.* A series of passionate pleas delivered in the midst of deep distress. A prayer constructed on the pattern known

Teach us what we might cry out before You;
send our salvation as we pray.
Return the captivity of Jacob's tents;
please, behold its folds, for they are so desolate.
Remember what You promised, / that Your Torah would never leave
the mouths of their descendants.
Open the seal of Your Torah;
place Your counsel within Your devoted students.
May Your beautiful nation / never lack fine scholars.
Grant knowledge to those who know You,
bring down the nations that fail to acknowledge You.
As You bring back to the stronghold
the taken captives, prisoners of hope.

Alas, we are now

כְּתוֹעִים As wanderers with none to seek them;
as captives, with none to redeem them.
As starving ones with none to feed them;
as purchased slaves, with none to acquire them.
As the parched with none to give them drink;
as fools with none to teach them.
As the fainting, with none to revive them;
as detested ones, with none to love them.
As rejected ones, with none to draw them close;
as ostracized ones, with none to release them.
As captives without a master; / as bent ones, with none to raise them up.
As orphans with no father; / as defiled ones, with none to purify them.
As empty ones, with none to fill their needs;
as forgotten ones, with none to remember them.
As turbulent souls with no rest;
as impoverished ones, with none to show them grace.
As strangers with none to welcome them;
as debased ones, with none to show them honor.
As mourners with none to comfort them,
as overpowered ones, with no escape.

הוֹרֵנוּ מַה שֶּׁנִּצְעַק לְפָנֶיךָ / צַו יְשׁוּעָתֵנוּ בְּמַפְגִּיעַ
וְתָשִׁיב שְׁבוּת אָהֳלֵי תָם / פְּתָחָיו רְאֵה כִּי שָׁמֵמוּ
זְכֹר שַׁחַת לֹא תִשְׁכַּח / עֵדוּת מִפִּי זַרְעוֹ
חוֹתֵם תְּעוּדָה תַּתִּיר / סוֹדְךָ שִׂים בְּלִמּוּדָךְ
טַבּוּר אַגַּן הַסַּהַר / נָא אַל יֶחְסַר הַמָּזֶג
יַדַּע אֶת אֲשֶׁר יְדָעוּךָ / מִגֵּר עַם לֹא יְדָעוּךָ
כִּי תָשִׁיב לְבִצָּרוֹן / לְכוּדִים אֲסִירֵי הַתִּקְוָה.

וְהֵן אֲנוּ עַתָּה

כְּתוֹעִים וְאֵין לְבַקֵּשׁ / כִּשְׁבוּיִים וְאֵין לְשׁוֹבֵב
כִּרְעֵבִים וְאֵין לְהַאֲכִיל / כִּקְנוּיִים וְאֵין לִקְנוֹת
כִּצְמֵאִים וְאֵין לְהַשְׁקוֹת / כִּפְתָאִים וְאֵין לְלַמֵּד
כַּעֲיֵפִים וְאֵין לְהָשִׁיב / כִּשְׂנוּאִים וְאֵין לֶאֱהֹב
כְּנֶהְדָּפִים וְאֵין לְקָרֵב / כִּמְנֻדִּים וְאֵין לְהַתִּיר
כִּלְקוּחִים וְאֵין אֲדוֹנִים / כִּכְפוּפִים וְאֵין לִזְקֹף
כִּיתוֹמִים וְאֵין לָהֶם אָב / כִּטְמֵאִים וְאֵין לְטַהֵר
כַּחֲסֵרִים וְאֵין לְמַלֹּאות / כִּזְנוּחִים וְאֵין לִזְכֹּר
כְּהוֹמִים וְאֵין לָהֶם מְנוּחָה / כְּדַלִּים וְאֵין לְחָנְנָם
כְּגֵרִים וְאֵין לְקַבֵּל / כִּבְזוּיִים וְאֵין לְכַבֵּד
כַּאֲבֵלִים וְאֵין מְנַחֵם / כַּאֲנוּסִים וְאֵין מָנוֹס.

כְּתוֹעִים *As wanderers.* The poet describes the desperate plight of the Jewish people in exile.

Our God and God of our ancestors,

אִם תָּעִינוּ If we have strayed from the path, do not let us go astray.
If we have erred, do not mislead us into error.
If we have distanced ourselves from You, bring us near.
If we have drawn near, do not distance Yourself from us.
If we cry out to You, do not ignore.
If we have transgressed, do not punish.
If we have sinned, do not hide Your face.
If we have turned away from You, do not turn away.
If we have been vengeful, do not hold it against us.
If we have rebelled, do not repay us as rebels.
If we have mocked, do not make war against us.
If we have deceived, do not destroy.
If we have declined, do not let us sink down.
If we have made mistakes, do not sweep us away.
If we have caused injury, do not injure.
If we have acted maliciously, do not recall it.
If we have been contentious, do not rebuke.
If we have done evil, do not drive us away.
If we knock at Your doors, do not push us away.
If we have acted abominably, do not abhor.
If we come before You, do not despise.
If we have sinned, do not destroy.

And due to the abundance of our sins,

תַּאֲוַת לֵב We have not attained the desire of our hearts;
we had hoped for tranquility, but instead, tumult came.
Our dignity was lofty, but has now become low;
it had seemed that salvation was near, but it has become distant.
We had looked forward to good, but it escaped us;
deep sorrow pervades our storehouses.
Sadness affects our livelihood, / joy has passed away from our land.

---

of a lifetime, were able to return to the land, the second destruction had no such consolation. The situation of Jews continued to worsen.

אֱלֹהֵינוּ וֵאלֹהֵי אֲבוֹתֵינוּ

אִם תָּעִינוּ לֹא תַתְעֵנוּ / אִם שָׁגַגְנוּ לֹא תַשְׁלֵנוּ
אִם רָחַקְנוּ קָרֵב נָא / אִם קָרַבְנוּ לֹא תִרְחָק
אִם צָעַקְנוּ לֹא תַעְלִים / אִם פָּשַׁעְנוּ לֹא תִפְרָע
אִם עָוִינוּ לֹא תַסְתִּיר / אִם סַרְנוּ לֹא תָסוּר
אִם נָקַמְנוּ לֹא תִטֹּר / אִם מָרִינוּ לֹא כְּמִרְיֵנוּ
אִם לַצְנוּ לֹא תִלְחֹם / אִם כִּחַשְׁנוּ לֹא תְכַלֶּה
אִם יָרַדְנוּ לֹא תַטְבִּיעַ / אִם טָעִינוּ לֹא תְטַאטְאֵנוּ
אִם חָבַלְנוּ לֹא תַחְבֹּל / אִם זַדְנוּ לֹא תִזְכֹּר
אִם וִכַּחְנוּ לֹא תוֹכִיחַ / אִם הִרְשַׁעְנוּ לֹא תֶהְדֹּף
אִם דָּפַקְנוּ לֹא תִדְחֶה / אִם גָּעַלְנוּ לֹא תִגְעַל
אִם בָּאנוּ לֹא תִמְאַס / אִם אָשַׁמְנוּ לֹא תְאַבֵּד.

וּמֵרֹב עֲוֹנֵינוּ

תַּאֲוַת לֵב לֹא הִשַּׂגְנוּ / שֶׁקֶט קִוִּינוּ וַיָּבֹא רֹגֶז
רוּם קֶרֶן וְהִנֵּה שְׁפָלָה / קָרְבָה יְשׁוּעָה אָמַרְנוּ וְנִתְרַחֲקָה
צִפִּינוּ לְטוֹבָה וּבָרְחָה מִמֶּנּוּ / פַּח נֶפֶשׁ בָּא בַּאֲסָמֵינוּ
עִצָּבוֹן בְּמִשְׁלַח יָדֵינוּ / שִׂמְחָה עָרְבָה מֵאֶרֶץ

אִם תָּעִינוּ *If we have strayed.* Though we may have deserved our plight, please, God, rescue us: a prayer to God to lift us from the depths.

תַּאֲוַת לֵב לֹא הִשַּׂגְנוּ *We have not attained the desire of our hearts.* Our hopes for an end to our troubles have all been disappointed. An expression of the despair Jews felt at the length of exile. Unlike the destruction of the First Temple, when there were prophets of hope, and when Jews, within the span

Its blessed crops have been cursed; / we harvest but few of many.
The land gives bread enough for famine, not satiation;
    it no longer yields its strength.
The hands of its laborers have faltered;
    they cannot find their sustenance in it.
The fat of the land goes to strangers;
    its fine branches go to foreigners.
The earth has fallen into the hands of evil;
    but they have not found gains in it.
We are silenced, and cannot find a helping hand;
    reward for all creatures has gone away.
God's Holy Temple is destroyed;
    kindness has been taken from all of mankind.

Our God and God of our ancestors,

תֹּאמַר Declare that our sins be erased; / come, renew our days.
Proclaim a time of retribution for our sake;
    lift a banner, exalting our name.
Drive our attackers from the land;
    appear from heaven, raising us high.
Recall Your love for us and show us compassion;
    hasten the comforter [Messiah] to comfort us.
Purify our defiled bodies;
    make it known that You are our God.
Atone for our malicious iniquities; / raise our heads, revive us.
Forgive our stubborn, rebellious ways;
    speak out to increase our fruits.
Listen to us pouring out our hearts to You in prayer;
    respond to our spoken supplications.
Turn to us, reestablish our altar;
    accept righteously the words our lips form.
Bring near the time of our Messiah;
    accept our pleasantly scented offerings.
Return our dispersed ones from the ends of the earth;
    hold us steady and, like a girdle, let us cleave to You.

נֶאֱרְרוּ יְבוּלֵי בְרְכוֹתֶיהָ / מְעַט מֵהַרְבֵּה נָבִיא
לֶחְמָהּ לְרָזוֹן וְלֹא לְשָׂבְעַ / כֹּחָהּ לֹא תוֹסִיף תֵּת
יְדֵי עֲמֵלֶיהָ מוֹטְטוּ / טַרְפָּם לֹא יִמְצְאוּ בָהּ
חֵלֶב מִשְׁמַנֶּיהָ לְזָרִים / זְמוֹרוֹת עֲדָנֶיהָ לְנָכְרִים
וְנִמְכְּרָה אֶרֶץ בְּיַד רָעִים / הוֹן בֶּצַע לֹא מָצְאוּ בָהּ
דִּמִּינוּ גַּם מִמְּצֹא יָד / גָּלָה שְׂכַר הַיְצוּרִים
בֵּית מִקְדַּשׁ אֵל חָרֵב / אָסַף חֶסֶד מִכָּל אֱנוֹשׁ.

אֱלֹהֵינוּ וֵאלֹהֵי אֲבוֹתֵינוּ

תֹּאמַר לִמְחוֹת אֲשָׁמֵינוּ / תָּבֹא לְחַדֵּשׁ יָמֵינוּ
תְּגַלֶּה שְׁנַת שִׁלּוּמֵנוּ / תַּדְגִּיל לְגַדֵּל אֶת שְׁמֵנוּ
תֶּהְדֹּף מֵהֲדוֹם מִתְקוֹמְמֵינוּ / תּוֹפִיעַ מִמָּרוֹם לְרוֹמְמֵנוּ
תִּזְכֹּר רַחֲמֶיךָ לְרַחֲמֵנוּ / תָּחִישׁ מְנַחֵם לְנַחֲמֵנוּ
תְּטַהֵר שִׁמְצַת גְּוִיֵּנוּ / תֵּדַע כִּי אַתָּה הוּא אֱלֹהֵינוּ
תְּכַפֵּר עֲוֹן זְדוֹנֵנוּ / תִּלּוּי רֹאשׁ תִּתֵּן לְהַחֲיֵנוּ
תִּמְחַל עִקְּשׁוּת מִרְיֵנוּ / תִּנְאַם לְהַעֲצִים פִּרְיֵנוּ
תַּסְכִּית שְׂפִיכַת שִׂיחֵנוּ / תַּעֲנֶה עֶתֶר פִּצְחֵנוּ
תִּפְנֶה לְקוֹמֵם מִזְבְּחֵנוּ / תַּצְדִּיק נִיב שְׂפָתֵינוּ
תְּקָרֵב קֵץ מְשִׁיחֵנוּ / תִּרְצֶה רֵיחַ נִיחוֹחֵנוּ
תְּשׁוֹבֵב מִקְּצָווֹת נִדּוּחֵינוּ / תִּתְמְכֵנוּ, וְכָאֵזוֹר תַּדְבִּיקֵנוּ.

תֹּאמַר לִמְחוֹת אֲשָׁמֵינוּ *Declare that our sins be erased.* Accept our prayers, grant atonement for our sins, return to us that we may return to You.

Our God and God of our ancestors,

אוֹרְךָ Let Your light shine [upon Your nation] in the darkness;
return to them with compassion.
Bring about the day of vengeance that was in Your heart;
send Your word and heal us.
Let the light of Your countenance be upon us,
and do not forget us forever.
Recall the merits of our ancestors, those mountains of old;
do not remember the sins of our youth.
Remove the impurity that is upon us;
do not forget the people Your soul loves.
Recall the love of our betrothal, / how we followed You in the desert.
Draw us near and we shall run behind You;
guide us and bring us to Your inner chambers.
Support us and strengthen us, and we shall live;
now is the time to let us hear Your voice.
Draw us out of the roaring waves;
let deep waters be dried by Your wrath.
Rise up with Your ire upon the haughty;
be exalted through Your strength and raise up those laid low.
Shatter the mighty arm of the kingdom of evil;
reign alone over those who call out Your name.
In the presence of all nations let it be known
that there is no God but You,
as You bring us up to Your holy mountain,
and gladden us in Your House of prayer.

Our God and God of our ancestors,

אֹפֶל Light up the dimness of the widowed [Jerusalem];
brighten the darkness of that weeping city.
Provide joy to that lonely one; / stop the streaming of her tears.
Glorify Your desolate mountain;
return and show Your presence upon it.
Let the glow of Your Temple shine;
renew the chamber of Your nuptials.

אֱלֹהֵינוּ וֵאלֹהֵי אֲבוֹתֵינוּ

אוֹרְךָ תַּזְרִיחַ לַחֲשׁוּכָה / בְּרַחֲמִים תָּשׁוּב אֵלֶיהָ
גַּלֵּה יוֹם נָקָם בְּלֵב / דְּבָרְךָ תִּשְׁלַח וְתִרְפָּאֵנוּ
הָאֵר פָּנֶיךָ אֵלֵינוּ / וְאַל תִּשְׁכָּחֵנוּ לָנֶצַח
זְכוּת הַרְרֵי קֶדֶם זְכֹר / חַטֹּאת נְעוּרִים אַל תִּזְכֹּר
טֻמְאָה מֵעָלֵינוּ תָּסִיר / יְדִידוּת נַפְשְׁךָ אַל תִּשְׁכָּח
כְּלוּלוֹת אַהֲבָתֵנוּ תִּזְכֹּר / לֶכְתֵּנוּ אַחֲרֶיךָ בַּמִּדְבָּר
מָשְׁכֵנוּ וְנָרוּץ אַחֲרֶיךָ / נְחֵנוּ וַהֲבִיאֵנוּ אֶל חֲדָרֶיךָ
סְעָדֵנוּ וְסָמְכֵנוּ וּנְחִיֶה / עֵת כִּי תַשְׁמִיעֵנוּ קוֹלֶךָ
פְּצֵנוּ מִשְּׁאוֹן גַּלִּים / צוּלָה תַּחֲרִיב בְּאַפֶּךָ
קוֹמָה בַּחֲרוֹנְךָ עַל גֵּאִים / רוֹמָה בְּעֻזְּךָ וְרוֹמֵם שְׁפָלִים
שְׁבֹר זְרוֹעַ מַלְכוּת רֶשַׁע / תִּמְלֹךְ לְבַדְּךָ בְּקוֹרְאֵי שְׁמֶךָ
תּוֹדִיעַ לְעֵין כָּל אֻמִּים / כִּי אֵין אֱלוֹהַּ בִּלְעָדֶיךָ
כִּי תְבִיאֵנוּ לְהַר קָדְשֶׁךָ / וּתְשַׂמְּחֵנוּ בְּבֵית תְּפִלָּתֶךָ.

אֱלֹהֵינוּ וֵאלֹהֵי אֲבוֹתֵינוּ

אֹפֶל אַלְמָנָה תָּאִיר / בֹּהוּ בוֹכִיָּה תַּבְהִיק
גִּיל גַּלְמוּדָה תַּגִּישׁ / דֶּלֶף דִּמְעָתָהּ תַּדְמִים
הַר הַשָּׁמֵם תְּהַדֵּר / וְתָשׁוּב, וְאֵלָיו תּוֹפִיעַ
זֹהַר זְבוּלְךָ תַּזְרִיחַ / חֲדַר חֻפָּתְךָ תְּחַדֵּשׁ

אוֹרְךָ תַּזְרִיחַ *Let Your light shine.* A plea to God to remember the love with which Israel followed Him into the desert in the days of Moses.

אֹפֶל אַלְמָנָה תָּאִיר *Light up the dimness of the widowed [Jerusalem].* A prayer that the "widowed" Jerusalem be granted joy again.

Purify the filth of Jerusalem's impurity;
reestablish her as a beautiful, precious cornerstone.
Secure the radiance of her honor; / let nations be guided by her light.
O King, fill her with Your glory; / raise her banner forever and ever.
Satiate her with abundant joy;
crown her with a cloud of incense smoke.
Adorn the corners of her doors;
let the righteousness of the Your humble nation blossom.
Spit out the enemies of her gathered congregations;
let the many feet of Your throng run to You.
Return Your forgotten tribes;
call them forth, shout, sound Your horn.
Bring them to Your holy mountain,
and gladden them in Your House of prayer.

Our God and God of our ancestors,

תְּתֵן Give Your nation hope; / restore the Temple to us.
Raise up the loftiest of mountains, Zion;
rebuild Israel's razed dignity.
Light up the darkness of Your desired Temple;
glorify the city that now sits desolate.
There, You alone shall be robed in majesty;
You will remove shame from Your city.
Shake the wicked out of Your Temple;
show righteousness to Your congregation.
Draw Your beloved to You, / make a new covenant with her.
Let her life be precious in Your eyes,
purify her with cleansing waters.
Settle in the city where David encamped;
raise up the stature of Your palm tree, Israel.
Make Your love for us known to all, / walk amid our camps.
Prescribe our redemption from exile;
reveal the time when You will finally take us as Your own.
Come quickly to comfort us;
declare us as Your own, and we shall declare You as ours.

טֶנֶף טֻמְאָתָהּ תְּטַהֵר / יְפִי יְקָרַת תְּיַסְּדָהּ
כַּדְכֹּד כְּבוּדָה תְּכוֹנְנֶהָ / לְאוֹרָהּ לְאֻמִּים תְּלַוֶּה
מֶלֶךְ, מִכְּבוֹדְךָ תְּמַלְּאֶהָ / נֵצַח נְצָחִים תְּנוֹסְסָהּ
שֹׂבַע שְׂמָחוֹת תַּשְׂבִּיעָהּ / עֲנַן עָשָׁן תְּעַטְּרָהּ
פִּנַּת פִּתְחֶיהָ תְּפָאֵר / צֶדֶק צְנוּעִים תַּצְמִיחַ
קָמֵי קְהָלֶיהָ תָּקִיא / רֶגֶשׁ רְגָלִים תָּרִיץ
שְׁבָטִים שֶׁכְּחַתְּ תְּשׁוֹבֵב / תִּקְרָא, תִּשְׁרֹק, תִּתְקַע
תְּבִיאֵם לְהַר קָדְשֶׁךָ / וּתְשַׂמְּחֵם בְּבֵית תְּפִלָּתֶךָ.

אֱלֹהֵינוּ וֵאלֹהֵי אֲבוֹתֵינוּ

תִּתֵּן אַחֲרִית לְעַמֶּךָ / תָּשִׁיב מִקְדָּשׁ לְתוֹכֵנוּ
תְּרוֹמֵם הַר מְרוֹם הָרִים / תְּקוֹמֵם קֶרֶן גְּדוּעָה
תַּצְהִיר מַחֲשַׁכֵּי אִוּוּי / תְּפָאֵר יוֹשֶׁבֶת בָּדָד
תַּעְטֶה בָהּ מְלוּכָה לְבַדֶּךָ / תָּסִיר חֶרְפָּה מֵעִיר
תְּנַעֵר זֵדִים מִזְּבוּלֶךָ / תַּמְצִיא צְדָקָה לַעֲדָתֶךָ
תְּלַבֵּב אֶת רַעְיָתֶךָ / תִּכְרוֹת לָהּ בְּרִית חֲדָשָׁה
תִּיקַר נַפְשָׁהּ בְּעֵינֶיךָ / תְּטַהֲרֶנָּה בְּמַיִם טְהוֹרִים
תַּחֲנֶה בְּעִיר חָנָה דָוִד / תִּזְקֹף קוֹמַת תְּמָרָה
תּוֹדִיעַ לַכֹּל אַהֲבָתֵנוּ / תְּהַלֵּךְ בְּקֶרֶב מַחֲנוֹתֵינוּ
תִּדְרֹשׁ גְּאֻלָּה לְגָלוּתֵנוּ / תְּגַלֶּה קֵץ לְקִנּוּתֵנוּ
תָּבֹא מְהֵרָה לְנַחֲמֵנוּ / תַּאֲמִירֵנוּ לָךְ וְנַאֲמִירְךָ לָנוּ.

תִּתֵּן אַחֲרִית לְעַמֶּךָ *Give Your nation hope.* A continuation of the theme of the previous prayer for Jerusalem to become again the holy city, visible home of the Divine Presence.

And in the abundance of our sins,

תָּעִינוּ We have strayed from Your path;
we have erred away from Your commandments.
We have grown distant from the source of our life;
we have spoiled the path to eternal life.
We have failed to stride on a straight path;
we have sinned brazenly against Your holy name.
We have left Your Torah;
we have strayed from Your word.
We have angered You with our actions;
we have rebelled and revolted against You.
We did not heed the words of Your prophets;
we angered You and did not seek You.
We let fear of You be forgotten from our hearts;
we have acted to defile all that You made pure.
We have sinned against You, Lord our God;
we have angered You with the abundance of our sins.
We have hardened our hearts;
we have stiffened our necks.
We have cast Your words behind us;
we have failed to tell of Your greatness.
Your House was destroyed by our iniquity;
Your Temple was smashed by our sins.

The congregation then the Leader:

מַה נְּדַבֵּר What can we say
before the One who speaks truth?
And how can we respond
to the Source of response?
How can we justify ourselves
before the One clothed in justice?
You have bestowed us with goodness,
and we have repaid You in wickedness;
and what right remains with us,
to cry out before the King?

וּמֵרֹב עֲוֹנֵינוּ

תָּעִינוּ מֵאַחֲרֶיךָ / שָׁגַגְנוּ מִמִּצְוֹתֶיךָ
רְחַקְנוּ מִבֵּית חַיֵּינוּ / קִלְקַלְנוּ אָרְחוֹת עוֹלָם
צְעָדֵינוּ לֹא יִשַּׁרְנוּ / פָּשַׁעְנוּ לְשֵׁם קָדְשֶׁךָ
עֲזַבְנוּ תוֹרָתֶךָ / סַרְנוּ מֵאִמְרֵי פִיךָ
נִאַצְנוּךָ בְּמַעֲשֵׂה יָדֵינוּ / מָרִינוּ וּמָרַדְנוּ בָךְ
לֹא הִקְשַׁבְנוּ לְדִבְרֵי נְבִיאֶיךָ /
כִּעַסְנוּךָ וְלֹא בִקַּשְׁנוּךָ
יִרְאָתְךָ מִלֵּב שָׁכַחְנוּ / טָהֳרָתְךָ בְּמַעֲשֵׂינוּ טִמֵּאנוּ
חָטָאנוּ לְךָ יהוה אֱלֹהֵינוּ / זְעַמְנוּךָ מֵרֹב עֲוֹנֵינוּ
וְאִמַּצְנוּ אֶת לְבָבֵנוּ / הִקְשִׁינוּ אֶת עָרְפֵּנוּ
דַּרְכְּךָ אָחוֹר הִשְׁלַכְנוּ / גְּדֻלָּתְךָ לֹא הִגַּדְנוּ
בֵּיתְךָ נֶהֱרַס בַּעֲוֹנֵינוּ / אִוּוּיךָ נִתַּץ בַּחֲטָאֵינוּ.

The קהל *then the* שליח ציבור:

מַה נְּדַבֵּר, פְּנֵי מֵישָׁרִים דּוֹבֵר
וּמַה נַּעֲנֶה, לְמִמֶּנּוּ מַעֲנֶה
וּמַה נִּצְטַדְּקָה, פְּנֵי לוֹבֵשׁ צְדָקָה
גְּמָלָנוּ טוֹבוֹת וְשִׁלַּמְנוּ רָעוֹת
וּמַה יֶּשׁ לָנוּ עוֹד צְדָקָה לִזְעֹק פְּנֵי מֶלֶךְ.

תָּעִינוּ מֵאַחֲרֶיךָ *We have strayed from Your path.* A further confession of the collective sins that led to a succession of national tragedies.

Traditionally, Seliḥot were recited at this point. Nowadays, most congregations omit them and begin here with "Remember, LORD."

All:

זְכֹר Remember, LORD, Your compassion and loving-kindness, *Ps. 25*
for they are everlasting.
Do not hold against us the sins of those who came before us. *Ps. 79*
May Your mercies meet us swiftly,
for we have been brought very low.
Remember us, LORD, in favoring Your people;
redeem us with Your salvation.
זְכֹר Remember Your congregation, *Ps. 74*
the one that You acquired long ago,
the tribe of Your inheritance that You redeemed,
this Mount Zion that You have dwelt in.
זְכֹר Remember, LORD, the fondness of Jerusalem;
do not forever forget the love of Zion.
You shall rise up and have compassion for Zion, *Ps. 102*
for now it is right to be gracious, for the time has come.
זְכֹר Remember, LORD, *Ps. 137*
what the Edomites did on the day Jerusalem fell.
They said, "Tear it down, tear it down to its very foundations!"
זְכֹר Remember Abraham, Isaac and Yisrael, Your servants, *Ex. 32*
to whom You swore by Your own Self, when You said to them,
"I shall make your descendants as numerous as the stars in the sky,
and I shall give all this land that I spoke of to your descendants,
and they shall inherit it forever."
זְכֹר Remember Your servants, Abraham, Isaac and Jacob; *Deut. 9*
do not attend to the stubbornness of this people,
to their wickedness or sinfulness.

The Leader says each of the following two verses, followed by the congregation:

אַל־נָא Please, do not hold against us the sin *Num. 12*
that we committed so foolishly, that we have sinned.
We have sinned, our Rock; forgive us, our Creator.

Traditionally, סליחות *were recited at this point. Nowadays, most congregations omit them, and begin here with "*זְכֹר־רַחֲמֶיךָ*."*

All:

זְכֹר־רַחֲמֶיךָ יהוה וַחֲסָדֶיךָ, כִּי מֵעוֹלָם הֵמָּה: תהלים כה
אַל־תִּזְכָּר־לָנוּ עֲוֹנֹת רִאשֹׁנִים תהלים עט
מַהֵר יְקַדְּמוּנוּ רַחֲמֶיךָ כִּי דַלּוֹנוּ מְאֹד:
זָכְרֵנוּ יהוה בִּרְצוֹן עַמֶּךָ, פָּקְדֵנוּ בִּישׁוּעָתֶךָ.
זְכֹר עֲדָתְךָ קָנִיתָ קֶּדֶם, גָּאַלְתָּ שֵׁבֶט נַחֲלָתֶךָ תהלים עד
הַר־צִיּוֹן זֶה שָׁכַנְתָּ בּוֹ:
זְכֹר יהוה חִבַּת יְרוּשָׁלָיִם
אַהֲבַת צִיּוֹן אַל תִּשְׁכַּח לָנֶצַח.
אַתָּה תָקוּם תְּרַחֵם צִיּוֹן, כִּי־עֵת לְחֶנְנָהּ, כִּי־בָא מוֹעֵד: תהלים קב
זְכֹר יהוה לִבְנֵי אֱדוֹם אֵת יוֹם יְרוּשָׁלָיִם תהלים קלז
הָאֹמְרִים עָרוּ עָרוּ, עַד הַיְסוֹד בָּהּ:
זְכֹר לְאַבְרָהָם לְיִצְחָק וּלְיִשְׂרָאֵל עֲבָדֶיךָ שמות לב
אֲשֶׁר נִשְׁבַּעְתָּ לָהֶם בָּךְ וַתְּדַבֵּר אֲלֵהֶם
אַרְבֶּה אֶת־זַרְעֲכֶם כְּכוֹכְבֵי הַשָּׁמָיִם
וְכָל־הָאָרֶץ הַזֹּאת אֲשֶׁר אָמַרְתִּי אֶתֵּן לְזַרְעֲכֶם,
וְנָחֲלוּ לְעֹלָם:
זְכֹר לַעֲבָדֶיךָ לְאַבְרָהָם לְיִצְחָק וּלְיַעֲקֹב דברים ט
אַל־תֵּפֶן אֶל־קְשִׁי הָעָם הַזֶּה וְאֶל־רִשְׁעוֹ וְאֶל־חַטָּאתוֹ:

The שליח ציבור *says each of the following two verses, followed by the* קהל*:*

אַל־נָא תָשֵׁת עָלֵינוּ חַטָּאת אֲשֶׁר נוֹאַלְנוּ וַאֲשֶׁר חָטָאנוּ: במדבר יב

חָטָאנוּ צוּרֵנוּ, סְלַח לָנוּ יוֹצְרֵנוּ.

Traditionally, a piyut of confession was inserted between the two sets of remembrance verses. Unlike those of Shaḥarit, Ma'ariv, and Ne'ila, those of Musaf and Minḥa are still said today.

In many congregations, each paragraph of the following piyut is recited by the congregation and repeated by the Leader. In others, the whole piyut is recited by all, with the Leader saying the last verse aloud.

אֵלֶּה אֶזְכְּרָה These I remember, and I pour out my soul within me,
for evil ones have swallowed us, like a cake not yet turned –
when during the Caesar's rule there was no deliverance
for the ten martyrs of that empire.

Whilst the ruler studied our holy book from [sages]
likened to heaps of grain,
considering and discerning our written tradition,
he happened to open at "These are the statutes,"
and devised an evil plan
as he read, "One who steals a man and sells him, and is found out – *Ex. 21*
shall surely be put to death."

We have sinned, our Rock; forgive us, our Creator.

The heart of this wicked idol worshiper grew haughty;
he ordered that his palace be filled with shoes,
and summoned ten great sages
with profound understanding of the law and its reasoning.

He declared: "Judge this case with precision –
do not pervert it by making false statements,
but bring true justice to light:
what is the verdict if a man is found kidnapping *Deut. 24*
one of his brothers from the children of Israel,
treating him as a slave and selling him?"

We have sinned, our Rock; forgive us, our Creator.

אֵלֶּה אֶזְכְּרָה *These I remember.* A lament for ten great rabbis who went to their deaths as martyrs, killed by the Romans. Their story is told, in differing forms, twice a year: once on Tisha B'Av, the other here. On Tisha B'Av the emphasis is on grief, since that is a day of mourning. Here the emphasis is on the way they gave their lives for their faith – as if to say that though the destruction of

Traditionally, a piyut of confession was inserted between the two sets of remembrance verses. Unlike those of שחרית, מעריב and נעילה, those of מוסף and מנחה are still said today.

In many congregations, each paragraph of the following piyut is recited by the קהל and repeated by the שליח ציבור. In others, the whole piyut is recited by all, with the שליח ציבור saying the last verse aloud.

אֵלֶּה אֶזְכְּרָה, וְנַפְשִׁי עָלַי אֶשְׁפְּכָה
כִּי בְלָעוּנוּ זֵדִים כְּעוּגָה בְּלִי הֲפוּכָה
כִּי בִימֵי קֵיסָר לֹא עָלְתָה אֲרוּכָה
לַעֲשָׂרָה הֲרוּגֵי מְלוּכָה.

בְּלָמְדוֹ סֵפֶר מִפִּי מְשׁוּלֵי עֲרֵמַת
וְהֵבִין וְדִקְדֵּק בְּדָת רְשׁוּמַת
וּפָתַח בְּוְאֵלֶּה הַמִּשְׁפָּטִים, וְחִשֵּׁב מְזִמַּת
שמות כא וְגֹנֵב אִישׁ וּמְכָרוֹ וְנִמְצָא בְיָדוֹ, מוֹת יוּמָת:

חָטָאנוּ צוּרֵנוּ, סְלַח לָנוּ יוֹצְרֵנוּ.

גָּבַהּ לֵב בְּלִיַּעַל עוֹבֵד אֱלִילִים
וְצִוָּה לְמַלְּאוֹת פַּלְטֵירוֹ נְעָלִים
וְקָרָא לַעֲשָׂרָה חֲכָמִים גְּדוֹלִים
מְבִינֵי דָת וּטְעָמֶיהָ בְּפִלְפּוּלִים.

דִּינוּ מִשְׁפָּט זֶה לַאֲשׁוּרוֹ
וְאַל תְּעַוְּתוּהוּ, בְּכָזָב לְאָמְרוֹ
כִּי אִם הוֹצִיאוּהוּ לַאֲמִתּוֹ וּלְאוֹרוֹ
דברים כד כִּי־יִמָּצֵא אִישׁ גֹּנֵב נֶפֶשׁ מֵאֶחָיו מִבְּנֵי יִשְׂרָאֵל
וְהִתְעַמֶּר־בּוֹ וּמְכָרוֹ:

חָטָאנוּ צוּרֵנוּ, סְלַח לָנוּ יוֹצְרֵנוּ.

When they answered: "That kidnapper shall be put to death,"
he said: "Then what of your ancestors, who sold their brother,
trading him with a traveling company of Ishmaelites,
handing him over for the mere price of shoes?

"As for you – submit to the judgment of Heaven,
for since the days of those ancestors,
there have been none like you;
if they were still alive, I would judge them instead,
but now, you shall bear their sins."

We have sinned, our Rock; forgive us, our Creator.

They replied: "Give us three days,
that we may ascertain whether this has been ordained from on high,
and if we are indeed liable and guilty,
we will endure the decree of the All-Merciful One."

They all shook, shuddered, trembled,
turning their eyes to Rabbi Yishmael, the High Priest,
that he should invoke the holy name
and rise up to the Master above
to discover whether the decree had been issued by their God.

We have sinned, our Rock; forgive us, our Creator.

---

human terms the most tragic, was the Bar Kokhba rebellion of 132–135. It was during this last that most of the sages here mentioned, died.

Throughout history there have been two kinds of assaults against Jewry, the first against Jews, the second against Judaism. Among the latter was that of Antiochus IV of Syria (against whom the Maccabees fought and won), and the Roman emperor Hadrian. Both sought to impose a Hellenistic culture on the peoples of the Middle East and both banned the public practice of Judaism, including circumcision. Jews, under the command of Shimon bar Kosiba (popularly known as Bar Kokhba, "son of the star"), rose against the Romans in 132.

Initially the campaign was successful and Roman losses were heavy. Archaeologists working in the Judean desert between 1952 and 1961 found documents from the rebels, showing them to be deeply religious Jews

הֵם כְּעָנוּ לוֹ, וּמֵת הַגַּנָּב הַהוּא
נָם, אַיֵּה אֲבוֹתֵיכֶם, אֲשֶׁר אֲחִיהֶם מְכָרְוּהוּ
לְאֹרְחַת יִשְׁמְעֵאלִים סְחָרְוּהוּ
וּבְעַד נַעֲלַיִם נְתָנְוּהוּ.

וְאַתֶּם קַבְּלוּ דִין שָׁמַיִם עֲלֵיכֶם
כִּי מִימֵיהֶם לֹא נִמְצָא כָּכֶם
וְאִם הָיוּ בַחַיִּים, הָיִיתִי דָנָם לִפְנֵיכֶם
וְאַתֶּם תִּשְׂאוּ עֲוֹן אֲבוֹתֵיכֶם.

חָטָאנוּ צוּרֵנוּ, סְלַח לָנוּ יוֹצְרֵנוּ.

זְמַן תְּנָה לָנוּ שְׁלֹשָׁה יָמִים
עַד שֶׁנֵּדַע אִם נִגְזַר הַדָּבָר מִמְּרוֹמִים
אִם אֲנַחְנוּ חַיָּבִים וַאֲשֵׁמִים
נִסְבֹּל בִּגְזֵרַת מָלֵא רַחֲמִים.

חָלוּ וְזָעוּ וְנָעוּ כֻּלָּמוֹ
עַל רַבִּי יִשְׁמָעֵאל כֹּהֵן גָּדוֹל נָתְנוּ עֵינֵימוֹ
לְהַזְכִּיר אֶת הַשֵּׁם, לַעֲלוֹת לַאֲדוֹנֵימוֹ
לָדַעַת אִם יָצְאָה הַגְּזֵרָה מֵאֵת אֱלֹהֵימוֹ.

חָטָאנוּ צוּרֵנוּ, סְלַח לָנוּ יוֹצְרֵנוּ.

---

the Temple brought sacrifices to an end, Jews did not cease to make sacrifices for the sake of God. Often they gave their lives.

In the first and second centuries CE there were three rebellions against Rome. First was the Great Rebellion of 66–73 during which Jerusalem was conquered and the Second Temple destroyed. Second was the uprising throughout the empire in 117 against the Emperor Trajan. Third, and in

Rabbi Yishmael purified himself,
invoking the holy name with trepidation,
and rising up to the heavens, he asked [the angel Gabriel,]
the man clothed in linen,
who said to him: "You must accept this, my righteous, beloved ones –
for I have heard behind the heavenly screen
that you have been ensnared."

He descended and relayed the word of God to his companions,
and the wicked one commanded that they be slain
with force and brutality,
and the first two to be taken out were the great scholars of Israel,
Rabbi Yishmael the High Priest
and Rabban Shimon ben Gamliel, Prince of Israel.

We have sinned, our Rock; forgive us, our Creator.

[Rabbi Yishmael] begged profusely of him to be beheaded first,
saying: "Kill me first, let me not see the death of this devoted servant
of the One who dwells in His earthly abode!"
The cruel viper ordered that lots be drawn,
and the lot fell upon Rabban Shimon.

They hastened to spill his blood like a bullock offered up,
and when his head was severed,
[Rabbi Yishmael] seized it and wailed over him bitterly,
in a voice like a shofar:
"What has become of the tongue
which so diligently taught fine words?
How, through our sins, is it now licking the dust?"

We have sinned, our Rock; forgive us, our Creator.

---

historian Dio, "very few [Jews] were saved." Fifty forts were destroyed, 985 settlements razed, 580,000 Jews died in the fighting, along with "countless numbers" who died of starvation, fire and the sword. "Nearly the entire land of Judea lay waste" (*Roman History* 69:14). Jerusalem was rebuilt as a Roman city, Aelia Capitolina, which Jews were forbidden to enter except on Tisha

טִהֵר רַבִּי יִשְׁמָעֵאל עַצְמוֹ, וְהִזְכִּיר אֶת הַשֵּׁם בְּסִלּוּדִים
וְעָלָה לַמָּרוֹם, וְשָׁאַל מֵאֵת הָאִישׁ לְבוּשׁ הַבַּדִּים
וְנָם לוֹ, קַבְּלוּ עֲלֵיכֶם צַדִּיקִים וִידִידִים
כִּי שָׁמַעְתִּי מֵאֲחוֹרֵי הַפַּרְגּוֹד כִּי בְּזֹאת אַתֶּם נִלְכָּדִים.

יָרַד וְהִגִּיד לַחֲבֵרָיו מַאֲמַר אֵל
וְצִוָּה בְלִיַּעַל לְהָרְגָם בְּכֹחַ וָלָאֵל
וּשְׁנַיִם מֵהֶם הוֹצִיאוּ תְּחִלָּה, שֶׁהֵם גְּדוֹלֵי יִשְׂרָאֵל
רַבִּי יִשְׁמָעֵאל כֹּהֵן גָּדוֹל
וְרַבָּן שִׁמְעוֹן בֶּן גַּמְלִיאֵל נְשִׂיא יִשְׂרָאֵל.

חָטָאנוּ צוּרֵנוּ, סְלַח לָנוּ יוֹצְרֵנוּ.

כְּרוֹת רֹאשׁוֹ תְּחִלָּה הִרְבָּה מִנּוּ לְבְעוֹן
וְנָם, הָרְגֵנִי תְחִלָּה וְאַל אֶרְאֶה בְּמִיתַת מְשָׁרֵת דָּר מָעוֹן
לְהַפִּיל גּוֹרָלוֹת צִוָּה צִפְעוֹן
וְנָפַל הַגּוֹרָל עַל רַבָּן שִׁמְעוֹן.

לִשְׁפֹּךְ דָּמוֹ מִהֵר כְּשׁוֹר פָּר
וּכְשֶׁנֶּחְתַּךְ רֹאשׁוֹ, נְטָלוֹ וְצָרַח עָלָיו בְּקוֹל מַר כַּשּׁוֹפָר
אֵי הַלָּשׁוֹן הַמְמַהֶרֶת לְהוֹרוֹת אִמְרֵי שֶׁפֶר
בַּעֲוֹנוֹת, אֵיךְ עַתָּה לוֹחֶכֶת אֶת הֶעָפָר.

חָטָאנוּ צוּרֵנוּ, סְלַח לָנוּ יוֹצְרֵנוּ.

---

concerned with the practice of their faith. But as more Roman legions were brought into the area, the tide turned and the rebels faced their final defeat in Beitar in 135.

The Romans were ruthless in their reprisals. According to the Roman

He cried over him profusely, trembling;
the wicked one's daughter rose at the sound of his weeping –
she longed in her heart for his beautiful countenance,
and asked of her father to let him live.

▸ The evil one refused to allow this to be done
so she asked of him that his skin be flayed from his face
and he did so without delay –
when they reached the place the tefillin are laid,
[Rabbi Yishmael] screamed out bitterly to the Creator of his soul.

We have sinned, our Rock; forgive us, our Creator.

The angels of heaven cried out bitterly:
"Is this the Torah and this its reward –
O God who dons light as His garment?
The enemy spurns Your great, awesome name,
and casts reproach and blasphemy upon the words of the Torah!"

A divine voice called out from the heavens:
"If I hear another sound, I shall turn the world back into water,
making unformed and void [the earth,] God's footstool;
this is My decree – accept it, you who delight in the Law that
preceded creation by two thousand years."

We have sinned, our Rock; forgive us, our Creator.

Ḥananya ben Teradyon, Rabbi Tarfon, head of the Sanhedrin before the revolt, Shimon ben Azzai and others. That is the historical basis of the events narrated in "These I remember," although it also includes sages like Rabbi Shimon ben Gamliel the Nasi and Rabbi Yishmael the High Priest who were killed in the earlier revolts.

The narrative opens with the suggestion, paralleled by a passage in the Book of Jubilees, that the ten martyrs suffered death to atone for the ten sons of Jacob who sold their brother Joseph into slavery (Gen. 37:26–28). There may be an allusion here to the idea, expressed elsewhere by the sages, that the Second Temple fell because of internal dissension and "causeless hatred" within the Jewish people (*Yoma* 9b).

Whatever the cause, the combination of physical destruction and spiritual

מַה מְּאֹד בָּכָה עָלָיו בַּחֲרָדָה
בַּת בְּלִיַּעַל לְקוֹל בְּכִיָּתוֹ עָמְדָה
תֹּאַר יָפְיוֹ בְּלִבָּהּ חָמְדָה
וְשָׁאֲלָה מֵאֵת אָבִיהָ, חַיָּתוֹ לְהַעֲמִידָה.

‣ נִאֵץ בְּלִיַּעַל דָּבָר זֶה לַעֲשׂוֹתוֹ
לְהַפְשִׁיט עוֹרוֹ מֵעַל פָּנָיו, שָׁאֲלָה מֵאִתּוֹ
וְלֹא עִכֵּב דָּבָר זֶה לַעֲשׂוֹתוֹ
וּכְשֶׁהִגִּיעַ לִמְקוֹם תְּפִלִּין
וְצָרַח בְּקוֹל מַר לְיוֹצֵר נִשְׁמָתוֹ.

חָטָאנוּ צוּרֵנוּ, סְלַח לָנוּ יוֹצְרֵנוּ.

שַׂרְפֵי מַעְלָה צָעֲקוּ בְּמָרָה
זוֹ תוֹרָה וְזוֹ שְׂכָרָהּ, עוֹטֶה כַּשַּׂלְמָה אוֹרָה
אוֹיֵב מְנָאֵץ שִׁמְךָ הַגָּדוֹל וְהַנּוֹרָא
וּמְחָרֵף וּמְגַדֵּף עַל דִּבְרֵי תוֹרָה.

עָנְתָה בַּת קוֹל מִשָּׁמַיִם
אִם אֶשְׁמַע קוֹל אַחֵר, אֶהֱפֹךְ אֶת הָעוֹלָם לְמַיִם
לְתֹהוּ וָבֹהוּ אָשִׁית הֲדוֹמַיִם
גְּזֵרָה הִיא מִלְּפָנַי, קַבְּלוּהָ מְשַׁעַשְׁעֵי דָת יוֹמָיִם.

חָטָאנוּ צוּרֵנוּ, סְלַח לָנוּ יוֹצְרֵנוּ.

B'Av and the name of the land was changed by Hadrian from Judea to Syria-Palestina, the origin of the name Palestine.

The tragedy was compounded by the fact that many of the greatest scholars were brutally put to death, among them Rabbi Akiva, Rabbi Yishmael, Rabbi

Leaders who would sit until late in the houses of prayer were slain,
those filled with merit like a pomegranate's seeds,
or blood in the altar's corners;
and they [the Romans] took out Rabbi Akiva who would interpret the very crowns of the Torah's letters,
and combed his flesh with double-edged combs.

The ruler commanded that Rabbi Ḥananya ben Teradyon
be taken out from his house of study,
and they burned his body with bundles of twigs,
putting moistened pads of wool on his heart to prolong his agony –
and when they had been consumed,
he was burned with his Torah scroll.

We have sinned, our Rock; forgive us, our Creator.

Lament, holy nation, never widowed of its God,
for they were murdered and their blood spilt for meager cause,
to sanctify the name of God in heaven, they gave their souls –
as when they murdered Rabbi Ḥutzpit the Interpreter.

A tremor shall seize all who hear of this,
and every eye shall pour with tears –
all delight was turned to mourning
when they murdered Rabbi Elazar ben Shamua.

We have sinned, our Rock; forgive us, our Creator.

My enemies and my persecutors destroyed me
and filled their bellies with my delicacies;
they made me drink poisoned water and wormwood –
when they murdered Rabbi Ḥanina ben Ḥakhinai.

---

devastation by the end of the Bar Kokhba revolt brought Jewry closer to despair than almost any other time in history. The Talmud (*Bava Batra* 60b) says that there were those who came to the conclusion that "by rights we should issue a decree that there should be no more Jewish marriages and no more Jewish children so that the seed of Abraham comes to an end of its own accord."

פְּקִידִים נֶהֶרְגוּ, מֵאַחֲרֵי שֶׁבֶת בָּתֵּי כְנֵסִיּוֹת
מְלֵאֵי מִצְוֹת כְּרִמּוֹן וּכְזָוִיּוֹת
וְהוֹצִיאוּ אֶת רַבִּי עֲקִיבָא, דּוֹרֵשׁ כִּתְרֵי אוֹתִיּוֹת
וְסָרְקוּ בְשָׂרוֹ בְּמַסְרְקוֹת פִּיפִיּוֹת.

צִוָּה לְהוֹצִיא רַבִּי חֲנַנְיָא בֶּן תְּרַדְיוֹן מִבֵּית אוּלַמּוֹ
וּבַחֲבִילֵי זְמוֹרוֹת שָׂרְפוּ גָלְמוֹ
וּסְפוֹגִין שֶׁל צֶמֶר שָׂמוּ עַל לִבּוֹ לְעַכֵּב עַצְמוֹ
וּכְשֶׁנִּסְתַּלְּקוּ מִיָּד נִשְׂרַף וְסֵפֶר תּוֹרָה עִמּוֹ.

חָטָאנוּ צוּרֵנוּ, סְלַח לָנוּ יוֹצְרֵנוּ.

קוֹנְנוּ קְדוֹשִׁים, עַם לֹא אַלְמָן
כִּי עַל דָּבָר מוּעָט נֶהֶרְגוּ וְנִשְׁפַּךְ דָּמָן
לְקַדֵּשׁ שֵׁם שָׁמַיִם מָסְרוּ עַצְמָן
בַּהֲרִיגַת רַבִּי חֻצְפִּית הַמְתֻרְגְּמָן.

רְעָדָה תֹּאחֵז כָּל שׁוֹמֵעַ שְׁמוּעַ
וְתִזַּל כָּל עַיִן דִּמּוּעַ
וְנֶהְפַּךְ לְאֵבֶל כָּל שַׁעֲשׁוּעַ
בַּהֲרִיגַת רַבִּי אֶלְעָזָר בֶּן שַׁמּוּעַ.

חָטָאנוּ צוּרֵנוּ, סְלַח לָנוּ יוֹצְרֵנוּ.

שִׁחֲתוּנִי צוֹרְרַי וּמְעַנַּי
וּמִלְּאוּ כְרֵסָם מֵעֲדָנַי
וְהִשְׁקוּנִי מֵי רוֹשׁ וְלַעֲנִי
בַּהֲרִיגַת רַבִּי חֲנִינָא בֶּן חֲכִינַי.

They pressed upon us to transgress the commandments
and refused expiation or ransom,
insisting upon taking the lives of those
who spoke fine words of Torah –
such as Rabbi Yeshevav the Scribe.

We have sinned, our Rock; forgive us, our Creator.

They fall on us, those profligate, empty descendants [of Edom];
they have done more evil to us than any kingdom on earth,
killing so many among us –
as when they murdered Rabbi Yehuda ben Dama.

You said that the house of Jacob shall be like a fire *Ob. 1*
and the house of Joseph a flame,
but instead [Esau, likened to] straw has extinguished that flame!
O Living God, lay our enemies low that day
[when Your flame shall come to consume all evil],
for they have conspired to kill ten righteous men –
with Rabbi Yehuda ben Bava among them.

We have sinned, our Rock; forgive us, our Creator.

All this befell us – we have told it, repeatedly,
pouring out our crushed, mournful hearts;
listen to our supplications from heaven above,
Lord, O Lord, compassionate and gracious God. *Ex. 34*

---

river saw fish darting here and there and asked them why. The fish said they were escaping the nets of fishermen. "In that case," said the fox, "come and live with me safely on dry land." The fish replied, "If we are in danger of death here in the only element in which we can live, how much more so on dry land where we cannot live at all" (*Berakhot* 61b). For Rabbi Akiva life without Torah was as inconceivable as a fish living without water.

It is said that Rabbi Akiva went to his death serenely, saying "All my life I wondered whether I would have the chance to fulfill the command, *You shall love the Lord your God… with all your soul* – meaning, 'even if He takes your soul,' and now that I have the chance to fulfill it shall I not do so?" (ibid.). Heroic deaths like these inspired Jews in many subsequent centuries. Yet Judaism remains a religion of life, not death.

תָּקְפוּ עָלֵינוּ מִצּוֹת לְהָפֵר
וּמֵאַנּוּ לָקַחַת הוֹן וָכֹפֶר
כִּי אִם נְפָשׁוֹת הַהוֹגוֹת אִמְרֵי שֶׁפֶר
כְּמוֹ רַבִּי יְשֵׁבָב הַסּוֹפֵר.

חָטָאנוּ צוּרֵנוּ, סְלַח לָנוּ יוֹצְרֵנוּ.

יְחַתּוּנוּ בְּנֵי עֲדִינָה הַשּׁוֹמֵמָה
הֵרֵעוּ לָנוּ מִכָּל מַלְכֵי אֲדָמָה
וְהָרְגוּ מִמֶּנּוּ כַּמָּה וְכַמָּה
בַּהֲרִיגַת רַבִּי יְהוּדָה בֶּן דָּמָה.

דִּבַּרְתָּ, בֵּית־יַעֲקֹב אֵשׁ וּבֵית יוֹסֵף לֶהָבָה: עובדיה א
הֵן עַתָּה קַשׁ אוֹרָם כָּבָה
חַי, וְעַד קוֹמָתָם בְּבִיעוּר יוֹם הַבָּא
כִּי הֵמָּה הִסְכִּימוּ לַהֲרֹג עֲשָׂרָה צַדִּיקִים
עִם רַבִּי יְהוּדָה בֶּן בָּבָא.

חָטָאנוּ צוּרֵנוּ, סְלַח לָנוּ יוֹצְרֵנוּ.

זֹאת קְרָאַתְנוּ וְסִפַּרְנוּ בְּשִׁנּוּן
וְשָׁפַכְנוּ לֵב שָׁפוּל וְאָנוּן
מִמָּרוֹם הַסְכֵּת תַּחֲנוּן
יהוה יהוה אֵל רַחוּם וְחַנּוּן: שמות לד

The memory of the martyrs never faded. The Talmud tells a famous story that one figure, Pappus ben Judah, warned Rabbi Akiva to stop teaching Torah in public for fear that he would be caught and killed by the Romans. Rabbi Akiva replied with a fable of the fox and the fish. A fox walking by a

▸ O Gracious One, look down from Your heights,
see the spilled blood of the righteous, their vital essence,
from Your concealed place behold this
and remove the stains of sin,
God, King, who sits upon a throne of compassion.

We have sinned, our Rock; forgive us, our Creator.

All:

זְכֹר Remember the covenant of our fathers, as You have said,
"I will remember My covenant with Jacob, *Lev. 26*
and also My covenant with Isaac,
and also My covenant with Abraham I will remember,
and the land I will remember."

זְכֹר Remember the covenant of the early ones,
as You have said,
"I shall remember for them the covenant of the early ones, *Ibid.*
whom I brought out of the land of Egypt
before the eyes of the nations,
in order to be their God: I am the LORD."

Deal kindly with us as You have promised,
"Even so, when they are in the land of their enemies *Ibid.*
I shall not reject them
and shall not detest them to the point of destruction,
to the point of breaking My covenant with them,
for I am the LORD their God."

Have compassion for us and do not destroy us, as it is written:
"For the LORD your God is a compassionate God; *Deut. 4*
He will not forsake you, He will not destroy you,
and He will not forget the covenant of your fathers,
that He pledged to them."

‹ חַנּוּן הַבִּיטָה מִמְּרוֹמִים
תִּשְׁפֹּכֶת דַּם הַצַּדִּיקִים וְתַמְצִית דָּמִים
תִּרְאֶה בְּפַרְגּוֹדָךְ, וְהַעֲבֵר כְּתָמִים
אֵל מֶלֶךְ יוֹשֵׁב עַל כִּסֵּא רַחֲמִים.

חָטָאנוּ צוּרֵנוּ, סְלַח לָנוּ יוֹצְרֵנוּ.

All:

זְכָר לָנוּ בְּרִית אָבוֹת, כַּאֲשֶׁר אָמַרְתָּ:
וְזָכַרְתִּי אֶת־בְּרִיתִי יַעֲקוֹב ויקרא כו
וְאַף אֶת־בְּרִיתִי יִצְחָק וְאַף אֶת־בְּרִיתִי אַבְרָהָם אֶזְכֹּר
וְהָאָרֶץ אֶזְכֹּר:

זְכָר לָנוּ בְּרִית רִאשׁוֹנִים, כַּאֲשֶׁר אָמַרְתָּ:
וְזָכַרְתִּי לָהֶם בְּרִית רִאשֹׁנִים שם
אֲשֶׁר הוֹצֵאתִי־אֹתָם מֵאֶרֶץ מִצְרַיִם לְעֵינֵי הַגּוֹיִם
לִהְיוֹת לָהֶם לֵאלֹהִים, אֲנִי יהוה:

עֲשֵׂה עִמָּנוּ כְּמָה שֶׁהִבְטַחְתָּנוּ:
וְאַף גַּם־זֹאת בִּהְיוֹתָם בְּאֶרֶץ אֹיְבֵיהֶם שם
לֹא־מְאַסְתִּים וְלֹא־גְעַלְתִּים לְכַלֹּתָם
לְהָפֵר בְּרִיתִי אִתָּם
כִּי אֲנִי יהוה אֱלֹהֵיהֶם:

רַחֵם עָלֵינוּ וְאַל תַּשְׁחִיתֵנוּ, כְּמָה שֶׁכָּתוּב:
כִּי אֵל רַחוּם יהוה אֱלֹהֶיךָ, לֹא יַרְפְּךָ וְלֹא יַשְׁחִיתֶךָ דברים ד
וְלֹא יִשְׁכַּח אֶת־בְּרִית אֲבֹתֶיךָ אֲשֶׁר נִשְׁבַּע לָהֶם:

Circumcise our hearts to love Your name, as it is written:
"And the LORD your God will circumcise your heart *Deut. 30*
and the heart of your descendants
to love the LORD your God with all your heart
and with all your soul, so that you shall live."

Restore our fortunes and have compassion for us, as it is written:
"And the LORD your God shall restore your fortunes *Ibid.*
and have compassion for you,
and shall return and gather you in from all the nations
among whom the LORD your God has scattered you."

Gather those of us who have been distanced, as is written,
"If your distanced ones are at the very ends of the heavens, *Ibid.*
from there shall the LORD your God gather you;
from there shall He bring you."

Let us find You when we seek You, as it is written:
"And if from there you seek the LORD your God, *Deut. 4*
you shall find Him,
when you seek Him out with all your heart and with all your soul."

Wipe out our transgressions for Your sake, as You have said:
"I, I am the One who shall wipe out your transgressions *Is. 43*
for My sake, and I shall not recall your sins."

Wipe out our transgressions as if they were a cloud,
as if they were a haze, as is written,
"I have wiped out your transgressions like a cloud, *Is. 44*
and as a haze your sins;
come back to Me for I have redeemed you."

Whiten our sins as snow and as wool, as is written,
"Come now, let us reason together, says the LORD: *Is. 1*
If your sins are like scarlet,
they shall be whitened like snow;
should they be as red as crimson, they shall become like wool."

מוֹל אֶת לְבָבֵנוּ לְאַהֲבָה אֶת שְׁמֶךָ, כְּמָה שֶׁכָּתוּב:
וּמָל יהוה אֱלֹהֶיךָ אֶת־לְבָבְךָ וְאֶת־לְבַב זַרְעֶךָ דברים ל
לְאַהֲבָה אֶת־יהוה אֱלֹהֶיךָ בְּכָל־לְבָבְךָ וּבְכָל־נַפְשְׁךָ
לְמַעַן חַיֶּיךָ:

הָשֵׁב שְׁבוּתֵנוּ וְרַחֲמֵנוּ, כְּמָה שֶׁכָּתוּב:
וְשָׁב יהוה אֱלֹהֶיךָ אֶת־שְׁבוּתְךָ וְרִחֲמֶךָ שם
וְשָׁב וְקִבֶּצְךָ מִכָּל־הָעַמִּים אֲשֶׁר הֱפִיצְךָ יהוה אֱלֹהֶיךָ שָׁמָּה:

קַבֵּץ נִדָּחֵינוּ, כְּמָה שֶׁכָּתוּב:
אִם־יִהְיֶה נִדַּחֲךָ בִּקְצֵה הַשָּׁמָיִם שם
מִשָּׁם יְקַבֶּצְךָ יהוה אֱלֹהֶיךָ, וּמִשָּׁם יִקָּחֶךָ:

הִמָּצֵא לָנוּ בְּבַקָּשָׁתֵנוּ, כְּמָה שֶׁכָּתוּב:
וּבִקַּשְׁתֶּם מִשָּׁם אֶת־יהוה אֱלֹהֶיךָ, וּמָצָאתָ דברים ד
כִּי תִדְרְשֶׁנּוּ בְּכָל־לְבָבְךָ וּבְכָל־נַפְשֶׁךָ:

מְחֵה פְשָׁעֵינוּ לְמַעַנְךָ, כַּאֲשֶׁר אָמַרְתָּ:
אָנֹכִי אָנֹכִי הוּא מֹחֶה פְשָׁעֶיךָ לְמַעֲנִי, וְחַטֹּאתֶיךָ לֹא אֶזְכֹּר: ישעיה מג

מְחֵה פְשָׁעֵינוּ כָּעָב וְכֶעָנָן, כְּמָה שֶׁכָּתוּב:
מָחִיתִי כָעָב פְּשָׁעֶיךָ וְכֶעָנָן חַטֹּאותֶיךָ ישעיה מד
שׁוּבָה אֵלַי כִּי גְאַלְתִּיךָ:

הַלְבֵּן חֲטָאֵינוּ כַּשֶּׁלֶג וְכַצֶּמֶר, כְּמָה שֶׁכָּתוּב:
לְכוּ־נָא וְנִוָּכְחָה, יֹאמַר יהוה ישעיה א
אִם־יִהְיוּ חֲטָאֵיכֶם כַּשָּׁנִים, כַּשֶּׁלֶג יַלְבִּינוּ
אִם־יַאְדִּימוּ כַתּוֹלָע, כַּצֶּמֶר יִהְיוּ:

Throw over us pure waters and purify us, as is written,
"I shall throw pure waters over you and you shall be pure. *Ezek. 36*
I shall purify you of all your impurities and of all your idolatry."

Atone our sins on this day and purify us, as it is written,
"For on this day you will be atoned and made pure; *Lev. 16*
of all your sins before the LORD you shall be purified."

▸ Bring us to Your holy mountain,
and let us rejoice in Your House of prayer,
as is written,
"I shall bring them to My holy mountain, *Is. 56*
and I shall make them rejoice in My House of prayer;
their offerings and their sacrifices will be accepted,
desired on My altar,
for My House will be called a house of prayer for all peoples."

The Ark is opened.
The following is said responsively, verse by verse. (*For commentary see page 161.*)

שְׁמַע קוֹלֵנוּ Listen to our voice, LORD our God.
Spare us and have compassion on us,
and in compassion and favor accept our prayer.
Turn us back, O LORD, to You, and we will return. *Lam. 5*
Renew our days as of old.
Do not cast us away from You, and do not take Your holy spirit from us.
Do not cast us away in our old age;
when our strength is gone do not desert us.

End of responsive reading.

Do not desert us, LORD; our God, do not be distant from us.
Give us a sign of good things,
and those who hate us shall see it and be ashamed,
for You, LORD, will help us and console us.
Hear our speech, LORD, consider our thoughts.
May the words of our mouths and the meditations of our hearts
find favor before You, LORD, our Rock and Redeemer.
For it is You, LORD, that we have longed for;
You shall answer us, LORD our God.

The Ark is closed.

זְרֹק עָלֵינוּ מַיִם טְהוֹרִים וְטַהֲרֵנוּ, כְּמָה שֶׁכָּתוּב:
וְזָרַקְתִּי עֲלֵיכֶם מַיִם טְהוֹרִים, וּטְהַרְתֶּם יחזקאל לו
מִכֹּל טֻמְאוֹתֵיכֶם וּמִכָּל־גִּלּוּלֵיכֶם אֲטַהֵר אֶתְכֶם:

כַּפֵּר חֲטָאֵינוּ בַּיּוֹם הַזֶּה וְטַהֲרֵנוּ, כְּמָה שֶׁכָּתוּב:
כִּי־בַיּוֹם הַזֶּה יְכַפֵּר עֲלֵיכֶם לְטַהֵר אֶתְכֶם ויקרא טז
מִכֹּל חַטֹּאתֵיכֶם, לִפְנֵי יהוה תִּטְהָרוּ:

◂ תְּבִיאֵנוּ אֶל הַר קָדְשֶׁךָ, וְשַׂמְּחֵנוּ בְּבֵית תְּפִלָּתֶךָ
כְּמָה שֶׁכָּתוּב:
וַהֲבִיאוֹתִים אֶל־הַר קָדְשִׁי, וְשִׂמַּחְתִּים בְּבֵית תְּפִלָּתִי ישעיה נו
עוֹלֹתֵיהֶם וְזִבְחֵיהֶם לְרָצוֹן עַל־מִזְבְּחִי
כִּי בֵיתִי בֵּית־תְּפִלָּה יִקָּרֵא לְכָל־הָעַמִּים:

The ארון קודש *is opened.*
The following is said responsively, verse by verse. (For commentary see page 161.)

שְׁמַע קוֹלֵנוּ, יהוה אֱלֹהֵינוּ, חוּס וְרַחֵם עָלֵינוּ
וְקַבֵּל בְּרַחֲמִים וּבְרָצוֹן אֶת תְּפִלָּתֵנוּ.
הֲשִׁיבֵנוּ יהוה אֵלֶיךָ וְנָשׁוּבָה, חַדֵּשׁ יָמֵינוּ כְּקֶדֶם: איכה ה
אַל תַּשְׁלִיכֵנוּ מִלְּפָנֶיךָ, וְרוּחַ קָדְשְׁךָ אַל תִּקַּח מִמֶּנּוּ.
אַל תַּשְׁלִיכֵנוּ לְעֵת זִקְנָה, כִּכְלוֹת כֹּחֵנוּ אַל תַּעַזְבֵנוּ.

End of responsive reading.

אַל תַּעַזְבֵנוּ יהוה, אֱלֹהֵינוּ אַל תִּרְחַק מִמֶּנּוּ.
עֲשֵׂה עִמָּנוּ אוֹת לְטוֹבָה, וְיִרְאוּ שׂוֹנְאֵינוּ וְיֵבֹשׁוּ
כִּי אַתָּה יהוה עֲזַרְתָּנוּ וְנִחַמְתָּנוּ.
אֲמָרֵינוּ הַאֲזִינָה יהוה, בִּינָה הֲגִיגֵנוּ.
יִהְיוּ לְרָצוֹן אִמְרֵי פִינוּ וְהֶגְיוֹן לִבֵּנוּ לְפָנֶיךָ, יהוה צוּרֵנוּ וְגוֹאֲלֵנוּ.
כִּי לְךָ יהוה הוֹחָלְנוּ, אַתָּה תַעֲנֶה אֲדֹנָי אֱלֹהֵינוּ.

The ארון קודש *is closed.*

The Leader continues:

אֱלֹהֵינוּ Our God and God of our ancestors,
do not abandon us and do not desert us,
do not shame us and do not abandon Your covenant with us;
bring us close to Your Torah, teach us Your commandments,
show us Your ways, and turn our hearts toward the awe of Your name.
Circumcise our hearts to love You,
so that we return to You in truth, wholeheartedly.
For the sake of Your great name, pardon and forgive our iniquities,
as it is written in Your holy Writings:
"For the sake of Your name, LORD, *Ps. 25*
forgive my iniquity, though it is great."

Our God and God of our ancestors,
forgive us, pardon us, grant us atonement.

In many congregations, the Leader and the congregation recite the following piyut responsively, couplet by couplet, until "and You give us Yours"; in others, it is sung collectively.

כִּי אָנוּ For we are Your people and You are our God;
we are Your children and You are our Father;
we are Your servants and You are our Master;
we are Your gathering and You are our Place;
we are Your legacy and You are our Land;
we are Your flock and You are our Shepherd;
we are Your vineyard and You are our Keeper;
we are Your work and You are our Maker;
we are Your bride and You are our Lover;
we are Your treasure and You are our God;
we are Your people and You are our King;
we give You our word and You give us Yours.

The congregation then the Leader:

We are brazen and You are compassionate, gracious.
We are stubborn and You are long forbearing.
We are as full of iniquity as You are full of compassion.
Our days are like a fleeting shadow. *Ps. 102*
But You are here, and Your years will not end.

The שליח ציבור *continues:*

אֱלֹהֵינוּ וֵאלֹהֵי אֲבוֹתֵינוּ
אַל תַּעַזְבֵנוּ, וְאַל תִּטְּשֵׁנוּ, וְאַל תַּכְלִימֵנוּ, וְאַל תָּפֵר בְּרִיתְךָ אִתָּנוּ
קָרְבֵנוּ לְתוֹרָתֶךָ, לַמְּדֵנוּ מִצְוֹתֶיךָ
הוֹרֵנוּ דְרָכֶיךָ, הַט לִבֵּנוּ לְיִרְאָה אֶת שְׁמֶךָ
וּמוֹל אֶת לְבָבֵנוּ לְאַהֲבָתֶךָ, וְנָשׁוּב אֵלֶיךָ בֶּאֱמֶת וּבְלֵב שָׁלֵם
וּלְמַעַן שִׁמְךָ הַגָּדוֹל תִּמְחֹל וְתִסְלַח לַעֲוֹנֵינוּ
כַּכָּתוּב בְּדִבְרֵי קָדְשֶׁךָ
לְמַעַן־שִׁמְךָ יהוה, וְסָלַחְתָּ לַעֲוֹנִי כִּי רַב־הוּא: תהלים כה

אֱלֹהֵינוּ וֵאלֹהֵי אֲבוֹתֵינוּ
סְלַח לָנוּ, מְחַל לָנוּ, כַּפֶּר לָנוּ.

In many congregations, the שליח ציבור *and the* קהל *recite the following piyut responsively, couplet by couplet, until* וְאַתָּה מַאֲמִירֵנוּ*; in others, it is sung collectively.*

כִּי אָנוּ עַמֶּךָ וְאַתָּה אֱלֹהֵינוּ אָנוּ בָנֶיךָ וְאַתָּה אָבִינוּ
אָנוּ עֲבָדֶיךָ וְאַתָּה אֲדוֹנֵינוּ אָנוּ קְהָלֶךָ וְאַתָּה חֶלְקֵנוּ
אָנוּ נַחֲלָתֶךָ וְאַתָּה גוֹרָלֵנוּ אָנוּ צֹאנֶךָ וְאַתָּה רוֹעֵנוּ
אָנוּ כַרְמֶךָ וְאַתָּה נוֹטְרֵנוּ אָנוּ פְעֻלָּתֶךָ וְאַתָּה יוֹצְרֵנוּ
אָנוּ רַעְיָתֶךָ וְאַתָּה דוֹדֵנוּ אָנוּ סְגֻלָּתֶךָ וְאַתָּה אֱלֹהֵינוּ
אָנוּ עַמֶּךָ וְאַתָּה מַלְכֵּנוּ אָנוּ מַאֲמִירֶיךָ וְאַתָּה מַאֲמִירֵנוּ.

The קהל *then the* שליח ציבור*:*

אָנוּ עַזֵּי פָנִים וְאַתָּה רַחוּם וְחַנּוּן
אָנוּ קְשֵׁי עֹרֶף וְאַתָּה אֶרֶךְ אַפַּיִם
אָנוּ מְלֵאֵי עָוֹן וְאַתָּה מָלֵא רַחֲמִים
אָנוּ יָמֵינוּ כְּצֵל עוֹבֵר וְאַתָּה־הוּא וּשְׁנוֹתֶיךָ לֹא יִתָּמּוּ: תהלים קב

VIDUY

For linear translation and commentary, see page 1353.

The Leader continues, with the congregation following him in an undertone:

אֱלֹהֵינוּ Our God and God of our fathers,
let our prayer come before You, and do not hide Yourself from our plea,
for we are not so arrogant or obstinate as to say before You,
LORD, our God and God of our fathers,
we are righteous and have not sinned,
for in truth, we and our fathers have sinned.

Strike the left side of the chest with the right fist while saying each of the sins:

אָשַׁמְנוּ We have sinned, we have acted treacherously,
we have robbed, we have spoken slander.
We have acted perversely, we have acted wickedly,
we have acted presumptuously, we have been violent,
we have framed lies.
We have given bad advice, we have deceived, we have scorned,
we have rebelled, we have provoked, we have turned away,
we have committed iniquity, we have transgressed,
we have persecuted, we have been obstinate.
We have acted wickedly, we have corrupted,
we have acted abominably, we have strayed, we have led others astray.

All:

סַרְנוּ We have turned away from Your commandments and good laws,
to no avail, for You are just in all that has befallen us, *Neh. 9*
for You have acted faithfully while we have done wickedly.

We have been wicked and we have transgressed,
and so we have not been saved.
Place it in our hearts to abandon the way of wickedness,
and hasten our salvation,
as it is written by Your prophet:
"Let each wicked person abandon his ways, *Is. 55*
each man of iniquity his thoughts,
and let him come back to the LORD
and He will have compassion for him,
back to our God for He will forgive abundantly."

וידוי

For linear translation and commentary, see page 1353.

The שליח ציבור *continues, with the* קהל *following him in an undertone:*

אֱלֹהֵינוּ וֵאלֹהֵי אֲבוֹתֵינוּ
תָּבוֹא לְפָנֶיךָ תְּפִלָּתֵנוּ, וְאַל תִּתְעַלַּם מִתְּחִנָּתֵנוּ.
שֶׁאֵין אֲנַחְנוּ עַזֵּי פָנִים וּקְשֵׁי עֹרֶף לוֹמַר לְפָנֶיךָ
יהוה אֱלֹהֵינוּ וֵאלֹהֵי אֲבוֹתֵינוּ
צַדִּיקִים אֲנַחְנוּ וְלֹא חָטָאנוּ.
אֲבָל אֲנַחְנוּ וַאֲבוֹתֵינוּ חָטָאנוּ.

Strike the left side of the chest with the right fist while saying each of the sins.

אָשַׁמְנוּ, בָּגַדְנוּ, גָּזַלְנוּ, דִּבַּרְנוּ דֹפִי
הֶעֱוִינוּ, וְהִרְשַׁעְנוּ, זַדְנוּ, חָמַסְנוּ, טָפַלְנוּ שֶׁקֶר
יָעַצְנוּ רָע, כִּזַּבְנוּ, לַצְנוּ, מָרַדְנוּ, נִאַצְנוּ, סָרַרְנוּ
עָוִינוּ, פָּשַׁעְנוּ, צָרַרְנוּ, קִשִּׁינוּ עֹרֶף
רָשַׁעְנוּ, שִׁחַתְנוּ, תִּעַבְנוּ, תָּעִינוּ, תִּעְתָּעְנוּ.

All:

סַרְנוּ מִמִּצְוֹתֶיךָ וּמִמִּשְׁפָּטֶיךָ הַטּוֹבִים, וְלֹא שָׁוָה לָנוּ.
וְאַתָּה צַדִּיק עַל כָּל־הַבָּא עָלֵינוּ נחמיה ט
כִּי־אֱמֶת עָשִׂיתָ, וַאֲנַחְנוּ הִרְשָׁעְנוּ:

הִרְשַׁעְנוּ וּפָשַׁעְנוּ, לָכֵן לֹא נוֹשָׁעְנוּ
וְתֵן בְּלִבֵּנוּ לַעֲזֹב דֶּרֶךְ רֶשַׁע, וְחִישׁ לָנוּ יֶשַׁע
כַּכָּתוּב עַל יַד נְבִיאֶךָ
יַעֲזֹב רָשָׁע דַּרְכּוֹ, וְאִישׁ אָוֶן מַחְשְׁבֹתָיו ישעיה נה
וְיָשֹׁב אֶל־יהוה וִירַחֲמֵהוּ
וְאֶל־אֱלֹהֵינוּ כִּי־יַרְבֶּה לִסְלוֹחַ:

The Leader continues:

אֱלֹהֵינוּ Our God, and God of our ancestors,
forgive and pardon our iniquities
on (*Shabbat:* this Sabbath day, and on) this Day of Atonement;
be responsive to us as we pray,
wipe away and remove all our transgressions and sins
from before Your eyes,
subdue our urges, that they be submitted to You,
and temper our obstinacy, that we may return to You truly;
renew our conscience that it may guard all Your commands,
and circumcise our hearts that we may love and revere Your name,
as it is written in Your Torah:
"And the Lord your God will circumcise your heart *Deut. 30*
and the heart of your descendants
to love the Lord your God with all your heart and with all your soul, so that you shall live."
The deliberate and the unwitting sins you recognize;
the willful and the compelled,
the open deeds and the hidden –
before You they are all revealed and known.
What are we? What are our lives?
What is our loving-kindness? What is our righteousness?
What is our salvation? What is our strength? What is our might?
What shall we say before You,
Lord our God and God of our ancestors?
Are not all the mighty like nothing before You,
the men of renown as if they had never been,
the wise as if they know nothing,
and the understanding as if they lack intelligence?
For their many works are in vain,
and the days of their lives like a fleeting breath before You.
The pre-eminence of man over the animals is nothing, *Eccl. 3*
for all is but a fleeting breath.

▸ What can we say before You, You who dwell on high?
What can we declare before You, You who abide in heaven?
Do You not know all, the hidden and revealed alike?

The שליח ציבור *continues:*

אֱלֹהֵינוּ וֵאלֹהֵי אֲבוֹתֵינוּ

סְלַח וּמְחַל לַעֲוֹנוֹתֵינוּ

בְּיוֹם (בשבת: הַשַּׁבָּת הַזֶּה וּבְיוֹם) הַכִּפּוּרִים הַזֶּה

וְהֵעָתֶר לָנוּ בִּתְפִלָּתֵנוּ

מְחֵה וְהַעֲבֵר פְּשָׁעֵינוּ וְחַטֹּאתֵינוּ מִנֶּגֶד עֵינֶיךָ

וְכֹף אֶת יִצְרֵנוּ לְהִשְׁתַּעְבֶּד לָךְ

וְהַכְנַע עָרְפֵּנוּ לָשׁוּב אֵלֶיךָ בֶּאֱמֶת

וְחַדֵּשׁ כִּלְיוֹתֵינוּ לִשְׁמֹר פִּקּוּדֶיךָ

וּמוֹל אֶת לְבָבֵנוּ לְאַהֲבָה וּלְיִרְאָה אֶת שְׁמֶךָ

כַּכָּתוּב בְּתוֹרָתֶךָ

וּמָל יהוה אֱלֹהֶיךָ אֶת־לְבָבְךָ וְאֶת־לְבַב זַרְעֶךָ דברים ל

לְאַהֲבָה אֶת־יהוה אֱלֹהֶיךָ בְּכָל־לְבָבְךָ וּבְכָל־נַפְשְׁךָ, לְמַעַן חַיֶּיךָ:

הַזְּדוֹנוֹת וְהַשְּׁגָגוֹת אַתָּה מַכִּיר

הָרָצוֹן וְהָאֹנֶס, הַגְּלוּיִים וְהַנִּסְתָּרִים

לְפָנֶיךָ הֵם גְּלוּיִים וִידוּעִים.

מָה אָנוּ, מֶה חַיֵּינוּ, מֶה חַסְדֵּנוּ, מַה צִּדְקוֹתֵינוּ

מַה יְּשׁוּעָתֵנוּ, מַה כֹּחֵנוּ, מַה גְּבוּרָתֵנוּ

מַה נֹּאמַר לְפָנֶיךָ, יהוה אֱלֹהֵינוּ וֵאלֹהֵי אֲבוֹתֵינוּ

הֲלֹא כָּל הַגִּבּוֹרִים כְּאַיִן לְפָנֶיךָ, וְאַנְשֵׁי הַשֵּׁם כְּלֹא הָיוּ

וַחֲכָמִים כִּבְלִי מַדָּע, וּנְבוֹנִים כִּבְלִי הַשְׂכֵּל

כִּי רֹב מַעֲשֵׂיהֶם תֹּהוּ, וִימֵי חַיֵּיהֶם הֶבֶל לְפָנֶיךָ

וּמוֹתַר הָאָדָם מִן־הַבְּהֵמָה אָיִן, כִּי הַכֹּל הָבֶל: קהלת ג

◂ מַה נֹּאמַר לְפָנֶיךָ יוֹשֵׁב מָרוֹם, וּמַה נְּסַפֵּר לְפָנֶיךָ שׁוֹכֵן שְׁחָקִים

הֲלֹא כָּל הַנִּסְתָּרוֹת וְהַנִּגְלוֹת אַתָּה יוֹדֵעַ.

In Western Europe, the stanza "You know every secret" was said here, followed by the piyut אַתָּה מֵבִין *(page 1285). Nowadays, most congregations follow the Eastern European custom, according to which only the last two stanzas of the piyut are said (below), followed by "You know every secret."*

The Leader then the congregation:

שִׁמְךָ Your name has always been the Forgiver of Sins.
Listen to our pleading as we stand before You in prayer.

Overlook sin, for this people returning from sin,
and wipe our transgressions away before Your eyes.

The Leader continues, with the congregation following him in an undertone:

אַתָּה יוֹדֵעַ You know every secret since the world began,
and what is hidden deep inside every living thing.
You search each person's inner chambers,
examining conscience and mind.
Nothing is shrouded from You,
and nothing is hidden before Your eyes.
And so, may it be Your will,
LORD our God and God of our ancestors,
that You forgive us all our sins, pardon all our iniquities,
and grant us atonement for all of our transgressions.

Strike the left side of the chest with the right fist while saying each of the sins.

עַל חֵטְא For the sin we have sinned before You
under duress or freewill,
and for the sin we have sinned before You in hardness of heart.

For the sin we have sinned before You unwittingly,
and for the sin we have sinned before You by an utterance of our lips.

For the sin we have sinned before You by unchastity,
and for the sin we have sinned before You openly or secretly.

For the sin we have sinned before You knowingly and deceitfully,
and for the sin we have sinned before You in speech.

In Western Europe, the stanza אַתָּה יוֹדֵעַ רָזֵי עוֹלָם *was said here, followed by the piyut* אַתָּה מֵבִין *(page 1285). Nowadays, most congregations follow the Eastern European custom, according to which only the last two stanzas of the piyut are said (below), followed by* אַתָּה יוֹדֵעַ רָזֵי עוֹלָם.

The שליח ציבור *then the* קהל:

שִׁמְךָ מֵעוֹלָם עוֹבֵר עַל פֶּשַׁע
שַׁוְעָתֵנוּ תַּאֲזִין, בְּעָמְדֵנוּ לְפָנֶיךָ בִּתְפִלָּה

תַּעֲבֹר עַל פֶּשַׁע לְעַם שָׁבֵי פֶשַׁע
תִּמְחֶה פְשָׁעֵינוּ מִנֶּגֶד עֵינֶיךָ.

The שליח ציבור *continues, with the* קהל *following him in an undertone:*

אַתָּה יוֹדֵעַ רָזֵי עוֹלָם וְתַעֲלוּמוֹת סִתְרֵי כָּל חָי.
אַתָּה חוֹפֵשׂ כָּל חַדְרֵי בָטֶן וּבוֹחֵן כְּלָיוֹת וָלֵב.
אֵין דָּבָר נֶעְלָם מִמֶּךָּ וְאֵין נִסְתָּר מִנֶּגֶד עֵינֶיךָ.
וּבְכֵן, יְהִי רָצוֹן מִלְּפָנֶיךָ, יהוה אֱלֹהֵינוּ וֵאלֹהֵי אֲבוֹתֵינוּ
שֶׁתִּסְלַח לָנוּ עַל כָּל חַטֹּאתֵינוּ
וְתִמְחַל לָנוּ עַל כָּל עֲוֹנוֹתֵינוּ
וּתְכַפֵּר לָנוּ עַל כָּל פְּשָׁעֵינוּ.

Strike the left side of the chest with the right fist while saying each of the sins.

עַל חֵטְא שֶׁחָטָאנוּ לְפָנֶיךָ בְּאֹנֶס וּבְרָצוֹן
וְעַל חֵטְא שֶׁחָטָאנוּ לְפָנֶיךָ בְּאִמּוּץ הַלֵּב

עַל חֵטְא שֶׁחָטָאנוּ לְפָנֶיךָ בִּבְלִי דָעַת
וְעַל חֵטְא שֶׁחָטָאנוּ לְפָנֶיךָ בְּבִטּוּי שְׂפָתָיִם

עַל חֵטְא שֶׁחָטָאנוּ לְפָנֶיךָ בְּגִלּוּי עֲרָיוֹת
וְעַל חֵטְא שֶׁחָטָאנוּ לְפָנֶיךָ בְּגָלוּי וּבַסָּתֶר

עַל חֵטְא שֶׁחָטָאנוּ לְפָנֶיךָ בְּדַעַת וּבְמִרְמָה
וְעַל חֵטְא שֶׁחָטָאנוּ לְפָנֶיךָ בְּדִבּוּר פֶּה

For the sin we have sinned before You by wronging a neighbor,
and for the sin we have sinned before You by thoughts of the heart.

For the sin we have sinned before You in a gathering for immorality,
and for the sin we have sinned before You by insincere confession.

For the sin we have sinned before You by contempt for parents and teachers,
and for the sin we have sinned before You willfully or in error.

For the sin we have sinned before You by force,
and for the sin we have sinned before You by desecrating Your name.

For the sin we have sinned before You by impure lips,
and for the sin we have sinned before You by foolish speech.

For the sin we have sinned before You by the evil inclination,
and for the sin we have sinned before You knowingly or unwittingly.

The congregation aloud, followed by the Leader:

FOR ALL THESE, GOD OF FORGIVENESS,
FORGIVE US, PARDON US, GRANT US ATONEMENT.

All continue in an undertone. Strike the left side of the chest with the right fist while saying each of the sins.

For the sin we have sinned before You by deceit and lies,
and for the sin we have sinned before You by bribery.

For the sin we have sinned before You by scorn,
and for the sin we have sinned before You by evil speech.

For the sin we have sinned before You in business,
and for the sin we have sinned before You with food and drink.

עַל חֵטְא שֶׁחָטָאנוּ לְפָנֶיךָ בְּהוֹנָאַת רֵעַ
וְעַל חֵטְא שֶׁחָטָאנוּ לְפָנֶיךָ בְּהִרְהוּר הַלֵּב

עַל חֵטְא שֶׁחָטָאנוּ לְפָנֶיךָ בִּוְעִידַת זְנוּת
וְעַל חֵטְא שֶׁחָטָאנוּ לְפָנֶיךָ בְּוִדּוּי פֶּה

עַל חֵטְא שֶׁחָטָאנוּ לְפָנֶיךָ בְּזִלְזוּל הוֹרִים וּמוֹרִים
וְעַל חֵטְא שֶׁחָטָאנוּ לְפָנֶיךָ בְּזָדוֹן וּבִשְׁגָגָה

עַל חֵטְא שֶׁחָטָאנוּ לְפָנֶיךָ בְּחֹזֶק יָד
וְעַל חֵטְא שֶׁחָטָאנוּ לְפָנֶיךָ בְּחִלּוּל הַשֵּׁם

עַל חֵטְא שֶׁחָטָאנוּ לְפָנֶיךָ בְּטֻמְאַת שְׂפָתָיִם
וְעַל חֵטְא שֶׁחָטָאנוּ לְפָנֶיךָ בְּטִפְשׁוּת פֶּה

עַל חֵטְא שֶׁחָטָאנוּ לְפָנֶיךָ בְּיֵצֶר הָרָע
וְעַל חֵטְא שֶׁחָטָאנוּ לְפָנֶיךָ בְּיוֹדְעִים וּבְלֹא יוֹדְעִים

The קהל *aloud, followed by the* שליח ציבור*:*

וְעַל כֻּלָּם אֱלוֹהַּ סְלִיחוֹת סְלַח לָנוּ, מְחַל לָנוּ, כַּפֶּר לָנוּ.

All continue in an undertone. Strike the left side of the chest with the right fist while saying each of the sins.

עַל חֵטְא שֶׁחָטָאנוּ לְפָנֶיךָ בְּכַחַשׁ וּבְכָזָב
וְעַל חֵטְא שֶׁחָטָאנוּ לְפָנֶיךָ בְּכַפַּת שֹׁחַד

עַל חֵטְא שֶׁחָטָאנוּ לְפָנֶיךָ בְּלָצוֹן
וְעַל חֵטְא שֶׁחָטָאנוּ לְפָנֶיךָ בְּלָשׁוֹן הָרָע

עַל חֵטְא שֶׁחָטָאנוּ לְפָנֶיךָ בְּמַשָּׂא וּבְמַתָּן
וְעַל חֵטְא שֶׁחָטָאנוּ לְפָנֶיךָ בְּמַאֲכָל וּבְמִשְׁתֶּה

For the sin we have sinned before You by interest and extortion,
and for the sin we have sinned before You by being haughty.

For the sin we have sinned before You
by the idle chatter of our lips,
and for the sin we have sinned before You by prying eyes.

For the sin we have sinned before You by arrogance,
and for the sin we have sinned before You by insolence.

The congregation aloud, followed by the Leader:

FOR ALL THESE, GOD OF FORGIVENESS,
FORGIVE US, PARDON US, GRANT US ATONEMENT.

All continue in an undertone. Strike the left side of the chest with the right fist while saying each of the sins.

For the sin we have sinned before You by casting off the yoke,
and for the sin we have sinned before You
by perverting judgment.

For the sin we have sinned before You by entrapping a neighbor,
and for the sin we have sinned before You by envy.

For the sin we have sinned before You by lack of seriousness,
and for the sin we have sinned before You by obstinacy.

For the sin we have sinned before You by running to do evil,
and for the sin we have sinned before You by gossip.

For the sin we have sinned before You by vain oath,
and for the sin we have sinned before You by baseless hatred.

For the sin we have sinned before You by breach of trust,
and for the sin we have sinned before You by confusion of heart.

The congregation aloud, followed by the Leader:

FOR ALL THESE, GOD OF FORGIVENESS,
FORGIVE US, PARDON US, GRANT US ATONEMENT.

עַל חֵטְא שֶׁחָטָֽאנוּ לְפָנֶֽיךָ בְּנֶֽשֶׁךְ וּבְמַרְבִּית
וְעַל חֵטְא שֶׁחָטָֽאנוּ לְפָנֶֽיךָ בִּנְטִיַּת גָּרוֹן

עַל חֵטְא שֶׁחָטָֽאנוּ לְפָנֶֽיךָ בְּשִֽׂיחַ שִׂפְתוֹתֵֽינוּ
וְעַל חֵטְא שֶׁחָטָֽאנוּ לְפָנֶֽיךָ בְּשִׂקּוּר עָֽיִן

עַל חֵטְא שֶׁחָטָֽאנוּ לְפָנֶֽיךָ בְּעֵינַֽיִם רָמוֹת
וְעַל חֵטְא שֶׁחָטָֽאנוּ לְפָנֶֽיךָ בְּעַזּוּת מֶֽצַח

The קהל *aloud, followed by the* שליח ציבור*:*

וְעַל כֻּלָּם אֱלֽוֹהַּ סְלִיחוֹת סְלַח לָֽנוּ, מְחַל לָֽנוּ, כַּפֶּר לָֽנוּ.

All continue in an undertone. Strike the left side of the chest with the right fist while saying each of the sins.

עַל חֵטְא שֶׁחָטָֽאנוּ לְפָנֶֽיךָ בִּפְרִיקַת עֹל
וְעַל חֵטְא שֶׁחָטָֽאנוּ לְפָנֶֽיךָ בִּפְלִילוּת

עַל חֵטְא שֶׁחָטָֽאנוּ לְפָנֶֽיךָ בִּצְדִיַּת רֵֽעַ
וְעַל חֵטְא שֶׁחָטָֽאנוּ לְפָנֶֽיךָ בְּצָרוּת עָֽיִן

עַל חֵטְא שֶׁחָטָֽאנוּ לְפָנֶֽיךָ בְּקַלּוּת רֹאשׁ
וְעַל חֵטְא שֶׁחָטָֽאנוּ לְפָנֶֽיךָ בְּקַשְׁיוּת עֹֽרֶף

עַל חֵטְא שֶׁחָטָֽאנוּ לְפָנֶֽיךָ בְּרִיצַת רַגְלַֽיִם לְהָרַע
וְעַל חֵטְא שֶׁחָטָֽאנוּ לְפָנֶֽיךָ בִּרְכִילוּת

עַל חֵטְא שֶׁחָטָֽאנוּ לְפָנֶֽיךָ בִּשְׁבוּעַת שָׁוְא
וְעַל חֵטְא שֶׁחָטָֽאנוּ לְפָנֶֽיךָ בְּשִׂנְאַת חִנָּם

עַל חֵטְא שֶׁחָטָֽאנוּ לְפָנֶֽיךָ בִּתְשֽׂוּמֶת יָד
וְעַל חֵטְא שֶׁחָטָֽאנוּ לְפָנֶֽיךָ בְּתִמְהוֹן לֵבָב

The קהל *aloud, followed by the* שליח ציבור*:*

וְעַל כֻּלָּם אֱלֽוֹהַּ סְלִיחוֹת סְלַח לָֽנוּ, מְחַל לָֽנוּ, כַּפֶּר לָֽנוּ.

All:

וְעַל חֲטָאִים And for the sins for which we are liable to bring a burnt-offering,
and for the sins for which we are liable to bring a sin-offering,
and for the sins for which we are liable to bring an offering according to our means,
and for the sins for which we are liable to bring a guilt-offering for certain or possible sin,
and for the sins for which we are liable to lashes for rebellion,
and for the sins for which we are liable to forty lashes,
and for the sins for which we are liable to death by the hands of Heaven,
and for the sins for which we are liable to be cut off and childless,
and for the sins for which we are liable to the four death penalties
inflicted by the court: stoning, burning, beheading and strangling.

עַל מִצְוַת For positive and negative commandments,
whether they can be remedied by an act or not,
for sins known to us and for those that are unknown –
for those that are known,
we have already declared them before You
and confessed them to You;
and for those that are unknown,
before You they are revealed and known, as it is said,
"The secret things belong to the LORD our God, *Deut. 29*
but the things that are revealed are for us and our children for ever,
that we may fulfill all the words of this Torah."

וְדָוִד David Your servant said before You:
"Who can discern his own mistakes? *Ps. 19*
Cleanse me of my hidden faults."
Cleanse us, LORD our God,
of all our transgressions, and purify us of all our impurities,
and throw clear waters over us to purify us,
as was written by Your prophet:
"I shall throw clear waters over you and you shall be pure. *Ezek. 36*
I shall purify you of all your impurities and of all your idolatry."

All:

וְעַל חֲטָאִים שֶׁאָנוּ חַיָּבִים עֲלֵיהֶם עוֹלָה
וְעַל חֲטָאִים שֶׁאָנוּ חַיָּבִים עֲלֵיהֶם חַטָּאת
וְעַל חֲטָאִים שֶׁאָנוּ חַיָּבִים עֲלֵיהֶם קָרְבָּן עוֹלֶה וְיוֹרֵד
וְעַל חֲטָאִים שֶׁאָנוּ חַיָּבִים עֲלֵיהֶם אָשָׁם וַדַּאי וְתָלוּי
וְעַל חֲטָאִים שֶׁאָנוּ חַיָּבִים עֲלֵיהֶם מַכַּת מַרְדּוּת
וְעַל חֲטָאִים שֶׁאָנוּ חַיָּבִים עֲלֵיהֶם מַלְקוּת אַרְבָּעִים
וְעַל חֲטָאִים שֶׁאָנוּ חַיָּבִים עֲלֵיהֶם מִיתָה בִּידֵי שָׁמָיִם
וְעַל חֲטָאִים שֶׁאָנוּ חַיָּבִים עֲלֵיהֶם כָּרֵת וַעֲרִירִי
וְעַל חֲטָאִים שֶׁאָנוּ חַיָּבִים עֲלֵיהֶם אַרְבַּע מִיתוֹת בֵּית דִּין
סְקִילָה, שְׂרֵפָה, הֶרֶג, וְחֶנֶק.

עַל מִצְוַת עֲשֵׂה וְעַל מִצְוַת לֹא תַעֲשֶׂה.
בֵּין שֶׁיֵּשׁ בָּהּ קוּם עֲשֵׂה וּבֵין שֶׁאֵין בָּהּ קוּם עֲשֵׂה.
אֶת הַגְּלוּיִים לָנוּ וְאֶת שֶׁאֵינָם גְּלוּיִים לָנוּ
אֶת הַגְּלוּיִים לָנוּ, כְּבָר אֲמַרְנוּם לְפָנֶיךָ, וְהוֹדִינוּ לְךָ עֲלֵיהֶם
וְאֶת שֶׁאֵינָם גְּלוּיִים לָנוּ, לְפָנֶיךָ הֵם גְּלוּיִים וִידוּעִים
כַּדָּבָר שֶׁנֶּאֱמַר
הַנִּסְתָּרֹת לַיהוה אֱלֹהֵינוּ, וְהַנִּגְלֹת לָנוּ וּלְבָנֵינוּ עַד־עוֹלָם דברים כט
לַעֲשׂוֹת אֶת־כָּל־דִּבְרֵי הַתּוֹרָה הַזֹּאת:

וְדָוִד עַבְדְּךָ אָמַר לְפָנֶיךָ
שְׁגִיאוֹת מִי־יָבִין, מִנִּסְתָּרוֹת נַקֵּנִי: תהלים יט
נַקֵּנוּ יהוה אֱלֹהֵינוּ מִכָּל פְּשָׁעֵינוּ, וְטַהֲרֵנוּ מִכָּל טֻמְאוֹתֵינוּ
וּזְרֹק עָלֵינוּ מַיִם טְהוֹרִים וְטַהֲרֵנוּ
כַּכָּתוּב עַל יַד נְבִיאֶךָ
וְזָרַקְתִּי עֲלֵיכֶם מַיִם טְהוֹרִים, וּטְהַרְתֶּם יחזקאל לו
מִכֹּל טֻמְאוֹתֵיכֶם וּמִכָּל־גִּלּוּלֵיכֶם אֲטַהֵר אֶתְכֶם:

אַל תִּירָא Do not be afraid, Jacob.
Come back, wayward children, come back Israel.
See: the Guardian of Israel neither slumbers nor sleeps. *Ps. 121*
As is written by Your prophet,
"Come back, Israel, to the LORD your God, *Hos. 14*
for you have stumbled in your iniquity."
And it is said,
"Take up words to bring with you, and come back to the LORD. *Ibid.*
Tell Him: Forgive all our iniquities and take what is good;
we shall offer up our words instead of bullocks."

וְאַתָּה And You are compassionate,
accepting those who return,
and You have promised us repentance from the very beginning,
and it is for repentance that our eyes search after You.

It was voted upon and agreed, in the company of wise men,
learned in Torah – happy is one who was never created.

וּמֵאַהֲבָתְךָ But because of Your love, LORD our God,
with which You have loved Your people Israel,
and because of Your mercy, our King, with which You have had
mercy on the children of Your covenant,
You have given us, LORD our God,
(*on Shabbat:* this Sabbath day for holiness and rest, and)
this fast day of Yom Kippur for our sins to be pardoned,
our iniquities forgiven and all our rebellions atoned.

יוֹם אָתָא A day that comes to atone for the sins
of Your sleeping nation,
this day which comes just once a year.

As it is written in Your Torah:
"And this shall serve you as an eternal law, *Lev. 16*
to bring atonement on the children of Israel
for all their sins once a year.

אַל תִּירָא יַעֲקֹב
שׁוּבוּ בָנִים שׁוֹבָבִים, שׁוּבָה יִשְׂרָאֵל.
הִנֵּה לֹא־יָנוּם וְלֹא יִישָׁן שׁוֹמֵר יִשְׂרָאֵל: תהלים קכא
כַּכָּתוּב עַל יַד נְבִיאֶךָ
שׁוּבָה יִשְׂרָאֵל עַד יהוה אֱלֹהֶיךָ, כִּי כָשַׁלְתָּ בַּעֲוֹנֶךָ: הושע יד
וְנֶאֱמַר
קְחוּ עִמָּכֶם דְּבָרִים, וְשׁוּבוּ אֶל־יהוה שם
אִמְרוּ אֵלָיו, כָּל־תִּשָּׂא עָוֹן וְקַח־טוֹב
וּנְשַׁלְּמָה פָרִים שְׂפָתֵינוּ:

וְאַתָּה רַחוּם מְקַבֵּל שָׁבִים
וְעַל הַתְּשׁוּבָה מֵרֹאשׁ הִבְטַחְתָּנוּ
וְעַל הַתְּשׁוּבָה עֵינֵינוּ מְיַחֲלוֹת לָךְ.

מְנוּיָה וּגְמוּרָה, בְּסוֹד חַכְמֵי תוֹרָה, אַשְׁרֵי מִי שֶׁלֹּא נִבְרָא.

וּמֵאַהֲבָתְךָ יהוה אֱלֹהֵינוּ, שֶׁאָהַבְתָּ אֶת יִשְׂרָאֵל עַמֶּךָ
וּמֵחֶמְלָתְךָ מַלְכֵּנוּ, שֶׁחָמַלְתָּ עַל בְּנֵי בְרִיתֶךָ
נָתַתָּ לָּנוּ יהוה אֱלֹהֵינוּ אֶת
(בשבת: יוֹם הַשַּׁבָּת הַזֶּה לִקְדֻשָּׁה וְלִמְנוּחָה, וְאֶת) יוֹם צוֹם הַכִּפּוּרִים הַזֶּה
לִמְחִילַת חֵטְא וְלִסְלִיחַת עָוֹן וּלְכַפָּרַת פָּשַׁע.

יוֹם   אָתָא לְכַפֵּר פִּשְׁעֵי יְשֵׁנָה
הַיּוֹם בִּיאָתוֹ אַחַת בַּשָּׁנָה.
כַּכָּתוּב בְּתוֹרָתֶךָ
וְהָיְתָה־זֹּאת לָכֶם לְחֻקַּת עוֹלָם ויקרא טז
לְכַפֵּר עַל־בְּנֵי יִשְׂרָאֵל מִכָּל־חַטֹּאתָם, אַחַת בַּשָּׁנָה:

A day that was given as a testament to this nation;
the day when [Moses] the faithful emissary pled,
"Please forgive the iniquities of this nation."

As it is written in Your Torah:
"Forgive, please, this people's iniquity *Num. 14*
in the abundance of Your kindness,
as You have forgiven this people
from the time of Egypt until now,"
and there it is said:
"And the Lord said, I have forgiven as you asked." *Ibid.*

For the honor of Your name,
be receptive to us, You who pardons and forgives,
please forgive for the sake of Your name.

A day of pardon You announced to [Moses] Your emissary,
as inscribed;
the day when You stood with him and called out Your name.

As it is written in Your Torah:
"And the Lord descended in the cloud *Ex. 34*
and stood with him there,
and proclaimed in the name of the Lord.
And the Lord passed by before him and proclaimed:
The Lord, the Lord, compassionate and gracious God,
slow to anger, abounding in loving-kindness and truth,
extending loving-kindness to a thousand generations,
forgiving iniquity, rebellion and sin, and absolving
[the guilty who repent]."

For the honor of Your name,
be receptive to us, You who pardons and forgives,
please forgive for the sake of Your name.

יוֹם זֶה נִתַּן תְּעוּדָה לְעָם זֶה
הַיּוֹם חַל בּוֹ צִיר, סְלַח נָא לַעֲוֹן הָעָם הַזֶּה.

כַּכָּתוּב בְּתוֹרָתֶךָ
סְלַח־נָא לַעֲוֹן הָעָם הַזֶּה כְּגֹדֶל חַסְדֶּךָ במדבר יד
וְכַאֲשֶׁר נָשָׂאתָה לָעָם הַזֶּה מִמִּצְרַיִם וְעַד־הֵנָּה:
וְשָׁם נֶאֱמַר
וַיֹּאמֶר יהוה, סָלַחְתִּי כִּדְבָרֶךָ: שם

בַּעֲבוּר כְּבוֹד שְׁמְךָ
הַמָּצֵא לָנוּ מוֹחֵל וְסוֹלֵחַ / סְלַח נָא לְמַעַן שְׁמֶךָ.

יוֹם מְחִילָה בִּשַּׂרְתָּ לְצִיר בְּרֶשֶׁם
הַיּוֹם נִתְיַצַּבְתָּ עִמּוֹ, וְקָרָאתָ בְּשֵׁם.

כַּכָּתוּב בְּתוֹרָתֶךָ
וַיֵּרֶד יהוה בֶּעָנָן, וַיִּתְיַצֵּב עִמּוֹ שָׁם שמות לד
וַיִּקְרָא בְשֵׁם, יהוה:
וַיַּעֲבֹר יהוה עַל־פָּנָיו וַיִּקְרָא
יהוה, יהוה, אֵל רַחוּם וְחַנּוּן
אֶרֶךְ אַפַּיִם, וְרַב־חֶסֶד וֶאֱמֶת:
נֹצֵר חֶסֶד לָאֲלָפִים, נֹשֵׂא עָוֹן וָפֶשַׁע וְחַטָּאָה, וְנַקֵּה:

בַּעֲבוּר כְּבוֹד שְׁמְךָ
הַמָּצֵא לָנוּ רַחוּם וְחַנּוּן / רַחֶם נָא לְמַעַן שְׁמֶךָ.

A day You behold the ruins of Your Temple;
this day, may You lend Your ears to our prayers and behold us.

As it is written in Your holy scriptures:
Give ear, my God and hear; *Dan. 9*
open Your eyes and see our desolation,
and the city that bears Your name,
for it is not on the strength of our righteousness that we throw down our pleadings before You,
but on the strength of Your great compassion.
LORD, hear me; LORD, forgive;
LORD, listen and act and do not delay – for Your sake, my God;
for Your city and Your people bear Your name.

For the honor of Your name,
be receptive to us, You who pardons and forgives,
please forgive for the sake of Your name.

In many congregations, the Leader recites the first two stichs of each line, and the congregation responds "Who, God, is like You." Some sing the entire piyut collectively.

מִי אֵל כָּמְוֹךָ Who, God, is like You?

Mighty and luminous, / Creator of heaven and earth. Who, God, is like You?
Revealer of deep secrets, / Speaker of righteous truths. Who, God, is like You?
Splendid in His garb, / there is none but Him. Who, God, is like You?
He raises those bowed down, / shows favor to the needy. Who, God, is like You?
His eyes are pure, / residing in the heavens. Who, God, is like You?

Some omit the following five verses:

He suppresses iniquity, / is clothed in righteousness. Who, God, is like You?
King of kings, / awesome and sublime. Who, God, is like You?
He raises up the fallen, / responds to the oppressed. Who, God, is like You?
He redeems and saves, / strides in His great strength. Who, God, is like You?
He is near to those who call on Him; / He is lofty and listens to our cries. Who, God, is like You?

He resides in the heavens, / He supports the innocent. Who, God, is like You?
He forgives iniquity, / and overlooks transgressions. Who, God, is like You?

יום שְׁמֵמוֹת הֵיכָלְךָ הַבִּיטָה
הַיּוֹם תָּחֹן אָזְנְךָ הַטֵּה לְהַבִּיטָה.

כַּכָּתוּב בְּדִבְרֵי קָדְשֶׁךָ
הַטֵּה אֱלֹהַי אָזְנְךָ וּשְׁמָע, פְּקַח עֵינֶיךָ וּרְאֵה שֹׁמְמֹתֵינוּ דניאל ט
וְהָעִיר אֲשֶׁר־נִקְרָא שִׁמְךָ עָלֶיהָ
כִּי לֹא עַל־צִדְקֹתֵינוּ אֲנַחְנוּ מַפִּילִים תַּחֲנוּנֵינוּ לְפָנֶיךָ
כִּי עַל־רַחֲמֶיךָ הָרַבִּים:
אֲדֹנָי שְׁמָעָה, אֲדֹנָי סְלָחָה, אֲדֹנָי הַקְשִׁיבָה וַעֲשֵׂה אַל־תְּאַחַר
לְמַעַנְךָ אֱלֹהַי, כִּי־שִׁמְךָ נִקְרָא עַל־עִירְךָ וְעַל־עַמֶּךָ:

בַּעֲבוּר כְּבוֹד שְׁמֶךָ
הַמָּצֵא לָנוּ שׁוֹמֵעַ תְּפִלָּה / שְׁמַע תְּפִלָּתֵנוּ לְמַעַן שְׁמֶךָ.

In many congregations, the שליח ציבור *recites the first two stichs of each line, and the* קהל *responds "*מִי אֵל כָּמְוֹךָ*." Some sing the entire piyut collectively.*

מִי אֵל כָּמְוֹךָ.

אַדִּיר וְנָאוֹר / בּוֹרֵא דֹּק וָחֶלֶד מִי אֵל כָּמְוֹךָ
גּוֹלֶה עֲמֻקּוֹת / דּוֹבֵר צְדָקוֹת מִי אֵל כָּמְוֹךָ
הָדוּר בִּלְבוּשׁוֹ / וְאֵין זוּלָתוֹ מִי אֵל כָּמְוֹךָ
זוֹקֵף כְּפוּפִים / חוֹנֵן דַּלִּים מִי אֵל כָּמְוֹךָ
טְהוֹר עֵינַיִם / יוֹשֵׁב שָׁמַיִם מִי אֵל כָּמְוֹךָ

Some omit the following five verses:

כּוֹבֵשׁ עֲוֹנוֹת / לוֹבֵשׁ צְדָקוֹת מִי אֵל כָּמְוֹךָ
מֶלֶךְ מְלָכִים / נוֹרָא וְנִשְׂגָּב מִי אֵל כָּמְוֹךָ
סוֹמֵךְ נוֹפְלִים / עוֹנֶה עֲשׁוּקִים מִי אֵל כָּמְוֹךָ
פּוֹדֶה וּמַצִּיל / צוֹעֶה בְּרֹב כֹּחוֹ מִי אֵל כָּמְוֹךָ
קָרוֹב לְקוֹרְאָיו / רָם וּמַאֲזִין שַׁוְעָה מִי אֵל כָּמְוֹךָ

שׁוֹכֵן שְׁחָקִים / תּוֹמֵךְ תְּמִימִים מִי אֵל כָּמְוֹךָ
נוֹשֵׂא עָוֹן / וְעוֹבֵר עַל פֶּשַׁע מִי אֵל כָּמְוֹךָ

All:

As was written by Your prophet:
Who, God, is like You, who forgives iniquity *Mic. 7*
and overlooks the transgression of the remnant of Your heritage.
He does not remain angry forever,
for He desires loving-kindness.
He shall relent and show us compassion,
He shall suppress our iniquities,
casting all of our sins into the depths of the sea.
And all the sins of Your nation,
the house of Israel,
cast them down where they shall not be remembered
nor recalled nor come to mind ever again.
Grant truth to Jacob, loving-kindness to Abraham,
as You promised our ancestors in ancient times.

The Leader continues. On Shabbat, add the words in parentheses:

Our God and God of our ancestors,
pardon our iniquities on (this Sabbath day, and on)
this Day of Atonement;
wipe away and remove all our transgressions and sins
from before Your eyes,
as it is said:

"I, I am the One who shall wipe out your transgressions *Is. 43*
for My sake, and I shall not recall your sins."

And it is said:

"I have wiped out your transgressions like a cloud, *Is. 44*
and as a haze your sins;
come back to Me for I have redeemed you."

And it is said:

"For on this day you will be atoned and made pure; *Lev. 16*
of all your sins before the LORD
you shall be purified."

All:

כְּכָּתוּב עַל יַד נְבִיאֶךָ
מִי־אֵל כָּמְוֹךָ, נֹשֵׂא עָוֹן וְעֹבֵר עַל־פֶּשַׁע לִשְׁאֵרִית נַחֲלָתוֹ מיכה ז
לֹא־הֶחֱזִיק לָעַד אַפּוֹ כִּי־חָפֵץ חֶסֶד הוּא:
יָשׁוּב יְרַחֲמֵנוּ, יִכְבֹּשׁ עֲוֹנֹתֵינוּ
וְתַשְׁלִיךְ בִּמְצֻלוֹת יָם כָּל־חַטֹּאתָם:
וְכָל חַטֹּאת עַמְּךָ בֵּית יִשְׂרָאֵל תַּשְׁלִיךְ
בִּמְקוֹם אֲשֶׁר לֹא יִזָּכְרוּ וְלֹא יִפָּקְדוּ
וְלֹא יַעֲלוּ עַל לֵב לְעוֹלָם.
תִּתֵּן אֱמֶת לְיַעֲקֹב, חֶסֶד לְאַבְרָהָם
אֲשֶׁר־נִשְׁבַּעְתָּ לַאֲבֹתֵינוּ מִימֵי קֶדֶם:

The שליח ציבור *continues. On* שבת*, add the words in parentheses:*

אֱלֹהֵינוּ וֵאלֹהֵי אֲבוֹתֵינוּ
מְחַל לַעֲוֹנוֹתֵינוּ בְּיוֹם (הַשַּׁבָּת הַזֶּה וּבְיוֹם) הַכִּפּוּרִים הַזֶּה
מְחֵה וְהַעֲבֵר פְּשָׁעֵינוּ
וְחַטֹּאתֵינוּ מִנֶּגֶד עֵינֶיךָ
כָּאָמוּר
אָנֹכִי אָנֹכִי הוּא מֹחֶה פְשָׁעֶיךָ לְמַעֲנִי ישעיה מג
וְחַטֹּאתֶיךָ לֹא אֶזְכֹּר:

וְנֶאֱמַר
מָחִיתִי כָעָב פְּשָׁעֶיךָ וְכֶעָנָן חַטֹּאותֶיךָ ישעיה מד
שׁוּבָה אֵלַי כִּי גְאַלְתִּיךָ:

וְנֶאֱמַר
כִּי־בַיּוֹם הַזֶּה יְכַפֵּר עֲלֵיכֶם לְטַהֵר אֶתְכֶם ויקרא טז
מִכֹּל חַטֹּאתֵיכֶם, לִפְנֵי יהוה תִּטְהָרוּ:

(Our God and God of our ancestors, may You find favor in our rest.)
Make us holy through Your commandments
and grant us our share in Your Torah.
Satisfy us with Your goodness, grant us joy in Your salvation
(in love and favor, LORD our God,
grant us as our heritage Your holy Sabbath,
so that Israel, who sanctify Your name, may find rest on it),
and purify our hearts to serve You in truth.
For You are the Forgiver of Israel
and the Pardoner of the tribes of Yeshurun in every generation,
and without You we have no king who pardons and forgives,
none but You.
Blessed are You, LORD, King who pardons and forgives our iniquities
and those of all His people the house of Israel,
and makes our guilt pass away, every single year,
King of all the earth, who sanctifies (the Sabbath,)
Israel and the Day of Atonement.

TEMPLE SERVICE

רְצֵה Find favor, LORD our God,
in Your people Israel and their prayer.
Restore the service to Your most holy House,
and accept in love and favor
the fire-offerings of Israel and their prayer.
May the service of Your people Israel always find favor with You.

If Kohanim say the Priestly Blessing during the Leader's Repetition, the following is said; otherwise the Leader continues with "And may our eyes" on the next page. In Israel, see next page.

All: וְתֶעֱרַב May our entreaty be as pleasing to You as a burnt-offering and sacrifice. Please, Compassionate One, in Your abounding mercy restore Your Presence to Zion, Your city, and the order of the Temple service to Jerusalem. And may our eyes witness Your return to Zion in compassion, that there we may serve You with reverence as in the days of old and as in former years.

Leader: Blessed are You, LORD, for You alone do we serve with reverence.

Continue with "We give thanks" on the next page.

(אֱלֹהֵינוּ וֵאלֹהֵי אֲבוֹתֵינוּ, רְצֵה בִמְנוּחָתֵנוּ)
קַדְּשֵׁנוּ בְּמִצְוֹתֶיךָ וְתֵן חֶלְקֵנוּ בְּתוֹרָתֶךָ
שַׂבְּעֵנוּ מִטּוּבֶךָ וְשַׂמְּחֵנוּ בִּישׁוּעָתֶךָ
(וְהַנְחִילֵנוּ יהוה אֱלֹהֵינוּ בְּאַהֲבָה וּבְרָצוֹן שַׁבַּת קָדְשֶׁךָ
וְיָנוּחוּ בוֹ יִשְׂרָאֵל מְקַדְּשֵׁי שְׁמֶךָ)
וְטַהֵר לִבֵּנוּ לְעָבְדְּךָ בֶּאֱמֶת, כִּי אַתָּה סָלְחָן לְיִשְׂרָאֵל
וּמָחֳלָן לְשִׁבְטֵי יְשֻׁרוּן בְּכָל דּוֹר וָדוֹר
וּמִבַּלְעָדֶיךָ אֵין לָנוּ מֶלֶךְ מוֹחֵל וְסוֹלֵחַ אֶלָּא אָתָּה.
בָּרוּךְ אַתָּה יהוה, מֶלֶךְ מוֹחֵל וְסוֹלֵחַ לַעֲוֹנוֹתֵינוּ
וְלַעֲוֹנוֹת עַמּוֹ בֵּית יִשְׂרָאֵל
וּמַעֲבִיר אַשְׁמוֹתֵינוּ בְּכָל שָׁנָה וְשָׁנָה
מֶלֶךְ עַל כָּל הָאָרֶץ, מְקַדֵּשׁ (הַשַּׁבָּת וְ) יִשְׂרָאֵל וְיוֹם הַכִּפּוּרִים.

עבודה

רְצֵה יהוה אֱלֹהֵינוּ בְּעַמְּךָ יִשְׂרָאֵל, וּבִתְפִלָּתָם
וְהָשֵׁב אֶת הָעֲבוֹדָה לִדְבִיר בֵּיתֶךָ
וְאִשֵּׁי יִשְׂרָאֵל וּתְפִלָּתָם בְּאַהֲבָה תְקַבֵּל בְּרָצוֹן
וּתְהִי לְרָצוֹן תָּמִיד עֲבוֹדַת יִשְׂרָאֵל עַמֶּךָ.

If כהנים *say* ברכת כהנים *during* חזרת הש״ץ*, the following is said; otherwise the* שליח ציבור *continues with* וְתֶחֱזֶינָה *on the next page. In Israel, see next page.*

קהל וש״ץ: וְתֶעֱרַב עָלֶיךָ עֲתִירָתֵנוּ כְּעוֹלָה וּכְקָרְבָּן. אָנָּא רַחוּם, בְּרַחֲמֶיךָ
הָרַבִּים הָשֵׁב שְׁכִינָתְךָ לְצִיּוֹן עִירֶךָ, וְסֵדֶר הָעֲבוֹדָה לִירוּשָׁלָיִם.
וְתֶחֱזֶינָה עֵינֵינוּ בְּשׁוּבְךָ לְצִיּוֹן בְּרַחֲמִים. וְשָׁם נַעֲבָדְךָ בְּיִרְאָה
כִּימֵי עוֹלָם וּכְשָׁנִים קַדְמוֹנִיּוֹת.
ש״ץ: בָּרוּךְ אַתָּה יהוה שֶׁאוֹתְךָ לְבַדְּךָ בְּיִרְאָה נַעֲבֹד.

Continue with מוֹדִים *on the next page.*

In Israel the following formula is used instead:

All: וְתֶעֱרַב May our entreaty be as pleasing to You as a burnt-offering and sacrifice. Please, Compassionate One, in Your abounding mercy restore Your Presence to Zion, Your city, and the order of the Temple service to Jerusalem. That there we may serve You with reverence as in the days of old and as in former years.

When the Priestly Blessing is not said, and also in Israel, the Leader continues:

וְתֶחֱזֶינָה And may our eyes witness Your return to Zion in compassion. Blessed are You, LORD, who restores His Presence to Zion.

THANKSGIVING

Bow at the first nine words.

מוֹדִים We give thanks to You,
for You are the LORD our God
and God of our ancestors
for ever and all time.
You are the Rock of our lives,
Shield of our salvation
from generation to generation.
We will thank You and
declare Your praise for our lives,
which are entrusted into Your hand;
for our souls,
which are placed in Your charge;
for Your miracles
which are with us every day;
and for Your wonders and favors
at all times, evening, morning and midday.
You are good –
for Your compassion never fails.
You are compassionate –
for Your loving-kindnesses never cease.
We have always placed our hope in You.

As the Leader recites Modim, the congregation says quietly:

מוֹדִים We give thanks to You,
for You are the LORD our God
and God of our ancestors,
God of all flesh,
who formed us
and formed the universe.
Blessings and thanks
are due to Your great
and holy name for giving us
life and sustaining us.
May You continue
to give us life and sustain us;
and may You gather our
exiles to Your holy courts,
to keep Your decrees,
do Your will and serve You
with a perfect heart,
for it is for us
to give You thanks.
Blessed be God to whom
thanksgiving is due.

---

that is, during the Musaf Repetition on festivals. Some argue that it was included to give the Kohanim time to ascend before the Ark.

In ארץ ישראל *the following formula is used instead:*

קהל וש״ץ: וְתֶעֱרַב עָלֶיךָ עֲתִירָתֵנוּ כְּעוֹלָה וּכְקָרְבָּן. אָנָּא רַחוּם, בְּרַחֲמֶיךָ הָרַבִּים הָשֵׁב שְׁכִינָתְךָ לְצִיּוֹן עִירְךָ, וְסֵדֶר הָעֲבוֹדָה לִירוּשָׁלָיִם. וְשָׁם נַעֲבָדְךָ בְּיִרְאָה כִּימֵי עוֹלָם וּכְשָׁנִים קַדְמוֹנִיּוֹת.

When ברכת כהנים *is not said, and also in* ארץ ישראל*, the* שליח ציבור *continues:*

וְתֶחֱזֶינָה עֵינֵינוּ בְּשׁוּבְךָ לְצִיּוֹן בְּרַחֲמִים.
בָּרוּךְ אַתָּה יהוה, הַמַּחֲזִיר שְׁכִינָתוֹ לְצִיּוֹן.

הודאה

Bow at the first five words.

מוֹדִים אֲנַחְנוּ לָךְ
שָׁאַתָּה הוּא יהוה אֱלֹהֵינוּ
וֵאלֹהֵי אֲבוֹתֵינוּ לְעוֹלָם וָעֶד.
צוּר חַיֵּינוּ, מָגֵן יִשְׁעֵנוּ
אַתָּה הוּא לְדוֹר וָדוֹר.
נוֹדֶה לְּךָ וּנְסַפֵּר תְּהִלָּתֶךָ
עַל חַיֵּינוּ הַמְּסוּרִים בְּיָדֶךָ
וְעַל נִשְׁמוֹתֵינוּ הַפְּקוּדוֹת לָךְ
וְעַל נִסֶּיךָ שֶׁבְּכָל יוֹם עִמָּנוּ
וְעַל נִפְלְאוֹתֶיךָ וְטוֹבוֹתֶיךָ
שֶׁבְּכָל עֵת, עֶרֶב וָבֹקֶר וְצָהֳרָיִם.
הַטּוֹב, כִּי לֹא כָלוּ רַחֲמֶיךָ
וְהַמְרַחֵם, כִּי לֹא תַמּוּ חֲסָדֶיךָ
מֵעוֹלָם קִוִּינוּ לָךְ.

As the שליח ציבור *recites* מודים*, the* קהל *says quietly:*

מוֹדִים אֲנַחְנוּ לָךְ
שָׁאַתָּה הוּא יהוה אֱלֹהֵינוּ
וֵאלֹהֵי אֲבוֹתֵינוּ
אֱלֹהֵי כָל בָּשָׂר
יוֹצְרֵנוּ, יוֹצֵר בְּרֵאשִׁית.
בְּרָכוֹת וְהוֹדָאוֹת
לְשִׁמְךָ הַגָּדוֹל וְהַקָּדוֹשׁ
עַל שֶׁהֶחֱיִיתָנוּ וְקִיַּמְתָּנוּ.
כֵּן תְּחַיֵּנוּ וּתְקַיְּמֵנוּ
וְתֶאֱסֹף גָּלֻיּוֹתֵינוּ
לְחַצְרוֹת קָדְשֶׁךָ
לִשְׁמֹר חֻקֶּיךָ וְלַעֲשׂוֹת רְצוֹנֶךָ
וּלְעָבְדְּךָ בְּלֵבָב שָׁלֵם
עַל שֶׁאֲנַחְנוּ מוֹדִים לָךְ.
בָּרוּךְ אֵל הַהוֹדָאוֹת.

וְתֶעֱרַב עָלֶיךָ עֲתִירָתֵנוּ *May our entreaty be as pleasing to You* (*previous page*). In the Ashkenazi rite, this passage is said only when the Priestly Blessing is said,

For all these things may Your name be blessed and exalted,
our King, continually, for ever and all time.

The congregation, then the Leader:

אָבִינוּ מַלְכֵּנוּ Our Father, our King,
remember Your compassion and overcome Your anger,
and efface pestilence, sword, famine, captivity and destruction,
iniquity and plague, and bad mishap and all illness, and any harm,
and any feud, and all kinds of afflictions,
and all harsh decrees and baseless hatred,
from us and from all the people of Your covenant.

The congregation, then the Leader:

וּכְתֹב And write, for a good life,
all the children of Your covenant.

The Leader continues:

Let all that lives thank You, Selah! and praise Your name in truth,
God, our Savior and Help, Selah!
▾Blessed are You, Lord, whose name is "the Good"
and to whom thanks are due.

The following supplication is recited quietly while the Leader says "Let all that lives" above.

The Kohanim say:

יְהִי רָצוֹן May it be Your will, Lord our God and God of our ancestors, that this blessing with which You have commanded us to bless Your people Israel should be a complete blessing, with neither hindrance nor sin, now and forever.

In some communities, the congregation says:

יְהִי רָצוֹן May it be Your will, Lord our God and God of our ancestors, that this blessing which You have commanded to bless Your people Israel should be a complete blessing, with neither hindrance nor sin, now and forever.

The Torah is careful to state: "So they [the priests] shall place My name on the Israelites and I will bless them" (Num. 6:27). Thus it is not the priests who bless the people, but God. The priests – whose entire life was dedicated to divine service – were holy vehicles through which divine blessing flowed. In Temple times, the priests blessed the people daily. That remains the custom in Israel. Outside Israel, our custom is that the priestly blessings are said only on festivals, for only then do we experience the joy that those who live in God's land feel every day.

The priests lift their hands when reciting the blessing, as Aaron did when

וְעַל כֻּלָּם יִתְבָּרַךְ וְיִתְרוֹמַם שִׁמְךָ מַלְכֵּנוּ תָּמִיד לְעוֹלָם וָעֶד.

The קהל *then the* שליח ציבור:

אָבִינוּ מַלְכֵּנוּ
זְכֹר רַחֲמֶיךָ וּכְבֹשׁ כַּעַסְךָ
וְכַלֵּה דֶבֶר, וְחֶרֶב, וְרָעָב, וּשְׁבִי, וּמַשְׁחִית
וְעָוֹן וּמַגֵּפָה, וּפֶגַע רַע וְכָל מַחֲלָה, וְכָל תַּקָּלָה
וְכָל קְטָטָה וְכָל מִינֵי פֻּרְעָנִיּוֹת, וְכָל גְּזֵרָה רָעָה וְשִׂנְאַת חִנָּם
מֵעָלֵינוּ וּמֵעַל כָּל בְּנֵי בְרִיתֶךָ.

The קהל *then the* שליח ציבור:

וּכְתֹב לְחַיִּים טוֹבִים כָּל בְּנֵי בְרִיתֶךָ.

The שליח ציבור *continues:*

וְכֹל הַחַיִּים יוֹדְוּךָ סֶּלָה, וִיהַלְלוּ אֶת שִׁמְךָ בֶּאֱמֶת
הָאֵל יְשׁוּעָתֵנוּ וְעֶזְרָתֵנוּ סֶלָה.
בָּרוּךְ אַתָּה יהוה, הַטּוֹב שִׁמְךָ וּלְךָ נָאֶה לְהוֹדוֹת.

The following supplication is recited quietly while the שליח ציבור *says* וְכֹל הַחַיִּים *above.*

The כהנים *say:*

יְהִי רָצוֹן מִלְּפָנֶיךָ, יהוה אֱלֹהֵינוּ וֵאלֹהֵי אֲבוֹתֵינוּ, שֶׁתְּהֵא הַבְּרָכָה הַזֹּאת שֶׁצִּוִּיתָנוּ לְבָרֵךְ אֶת־עַמְּךָ יִשְׂרָאֵל בְּרָכָה שְׁלֵמָה, וְלֹא יִהְיֶה בָּהּ שׁוּם מִכְשׁוֹל וְעָוֹן מֵעַתָּה וְעַד עוֹלָם.

In some communities, the קהל *says:*

יְהִי רָצוֹן מִלְּפָנֶיךָ, יהוה אֱלֹהֵינוּ וֵאלֹהֵי אֲבוֹתֵינוּ, שֶׁתְּהֵא הַבְּרָכָה הַזֹּאת שֶׁצִּוִּיתָ לְבָרֵךְ אֶת־עַמְּךָ יִשְׂרָאֵל בְּרָכָה שְׁלֵמָה, וְלֹא יִהְיֶה בָּהּ שׁוּם מִכְשׁוֹל וְעָוֹן מֵעַתָּה וְעַד עוֹלָם.

BIRKAT KOHANIM – THE PRIESTLY BLESSING

The Priestly blessings are unique among our prayers: not only are they ordained by the Torah itself, but so is their precise wording (Num. 6:24–26). They are therefore our most ancient prayer. The blessings are beautifully constructed. They grow in length: the first line has three words; the second, five; the third, seven. In each, God's holiest name is the second word of the blessing. They ascend thematically: the first is for material blessing, the second for spiritual blessing, and the third for peace, without which no blessings can be enjoyed.

In Israel the Priestly Blessing on page 1260 is said.
When the Priestly Blessing is not said, the Leader says the formula on page 980.

The following is recited quietly by the Leader:

אֱלֹהֵינוּ Our God and God of our fathers,
bless us with the threefold blessing in the Torah,
written by the hand of Moses Your servant
and pronounced by Aaron and his sons:

The Leader says aloud:

Kohanim!

In most places, the congregation responds:

Your holy people, as it said:

The Kohanim say the following blessing in unison:

בָּרוּךְ Blessed are You, LORD our God, King of the Universe, who has made us holy with the holiness of Aaron, and has commanded us to bless His people Israel with love.

The first word in each sentence is said by the Leader, followed by the Kohanim. Some read silently the accompanying verses. One should remain silent and not look at the Kohanim while the blessings are being said.

May [He] bless you	May the LORD, Maker of heaven and earth, bless you from Zion.	*Ps. 134*
The LORD	LORD, our LORD, how majestic is Your name throughout the earth.	*Ps. 8*
And protect you.	Protect me, God, for in You I take refuge.	*Ps. 16*

וְצִוָּנוּ לְבָרֵךְ אֶת עַמּוֹ יִשְׂרָאֵל בְּאַהֲבָה *And has commanded us to bless His people Israel with love.* A unique stipulation which we do not find in connection with any other command. According to Rashi (Num. 6:23), God told Moses to instruct the priests that they should make the blessing "with concentration and a full heart." Hillel suggested that it was Aaron's gift for love and peace that made him and his children after him the conduit for divine blessings: "Be like the disciples of Aaron: loving peace, pursuing peace, loving humankind and bringing them close to Torah" (*Avot* 1:12). Love is the vehicle through which divine energy flows into the world.

יְבָרֶכְךָ *May the LORD bless you* with your material needs and good health *and protect you* from harm. *May the LORD make His face shine on you,* granting you spiritual growth, especially through Torah study (*Targum Yonatan*),

In ארץ ישראל *the* ברכת כהנים *on page 1261 is said.*
When ברכת כהנים *is not said, the* שליח ציבור *says the formula on page 981.*

The following is recited quietly by the שליח ציבור*:*

אֱלֹהֵינוּ וֵאלֹהֵי אֲבוֹתֵינוּ, בָּרְכֵנוּ בַּבְּרָכָה הַמְשֻׁלֶּשֶׁת בַּתּוֹרָה הַכְּתוּבָה עַל יְדֵי מֹשֶׁה עַבְדֶּךָ, הָאֲמוּרָה מִפִּי אַהֲרֹן וּבָנָיו

The שליח ציבור *says aloud:*

כֹּהֲנִים

In most places, the קהל *responds:*

עַם קְדוֹשֶׁךָ, כָּאָמוּר:

The כהנים *say the following blessing in unison:*

בָּרוּךְ אַתָּה יהוה אֱלֹהֵינוּ מֶלֶךְ הָעוֹלָם, אֲשֶׁר קִדְּשָׁנוּ בִּקְדֻשָּׁתוֹ שֶׁל אַהֲרֹן, וְצִוָּנוּ לְבָרֵךְ אֶת עַמּוֹ יִשְׂרָאֵל בְּאַהֲבָה.

The first word in each sentence is said by the שליח ציבור*, followed by the* כהנים*.*
Some read silently the accompanying verses. One should remain silent
and not look at the כהנים *while the blessings are being said.*

יְבָרֶכְךָ   יְבָרֶכְךָ יהוה מִצִּיּוֹן, עֹשֵׂה שָׁמַיִם וָאָרֶץ: תהלים קלד

יהוה   יהוה אֲדֹנֵינוּ, מָה־אַדִּיר שִׁמְךָ בְּכָל־הָאָרֶץ: תהלים ח

וְיִשְׁמְרֶךָ:   שָׁמְרֵנִי אֵל, כִּי־חָסִיתִי בָךְ: תהלים טז

---

he first blessed the people (Lev. 9:22). Their fingers are spread apart, as a symbol of generosity of spirit (the closed hand symbolizes possessiveness, see Deuteronomy 15:7) and of the Divine Presence that shines through the spaces like the beloved in the Song of Songs who "peers through the lattices" (Song. 2:9; *Bemidbar Raba* 11:2). The priests cover their hands and faces with the tallit in memory of the Holy of Holies that was screened from public gaze by a curtain.

The biblical command is preceded by the words, "The Lord said to Moses, 'Tell Aaron and his sons: This is how you are to bless the Israelites. *Say to them…*" (Num. 6:22–23). In memory of Moses instructing the priests, the custom is that the leader of prayer prompts the priests, word by word (Maimonides, Laws of Prayer, 14:13; others argue that the custom is merely to avoid error on the part of the priests).

Read the following silently while the Kohanim chant. Omit on Shabbat.

Master of the Universe, I am Yours and my dreams are Yours. I have dreamt a dream and I do not know what it means. May it be Your will, LORD my God and God of my fathers, that all my dreams be, for me and all Israel, for good, whether I have dreamt about myself, or about others, or others have dreamt about me. If they are good, strengthen and reinforce them, and may they be fulfilled in me and them like the dreams of the righteous Joseph. If, though, they need healing, heal them as You healed Hezekiah King of Judah from his illness, like Miriam the prophetess from her leprosy, like Na'aman from his leprosy, like the waters of Mara by Moses our teacher, and like the waters of Jericho by Elisha. And just as You turned the curses of Balaam the wicked from curse to blessing, so turn all my dreams about me and all Israel to good; protect me, be gracious to me and accept me. Amen.

May [He] make shine	May God be gracious to us and bless us; may He make His face shine upon us, Selah.	*Ps. 67*
The LORD	The LORD, the LORD, compassionate and gracious God, slow to anger, abounding in kindness and truth.	*Ex. 34*
His face	Turn to me and be gracious to me, for I am alone and afflicted.	*Ps. 25*
On you	To You, LORD, I lift up my soul.	*Ibid.*
And be gracious to you.	As the eyes of slaves turn to their master's hand, or the eyes of a slave-girl to the hand of her mistress, so our eyes are turned to the LORD our God, awaiting His favor.	*Ps. 123*

Read the following silently while the Kohanim chant. Omit on Shabbat.

Master of the Universe, I am Yours and my dreams are Yours. I have dreamt a dream and I do not know what it means. May it be Your will, LORD my God and God of my fathers, that all my dreams be, for me and all Israel, for good, whether I have dreamt about myself, or about others, or others have dreamt about me. If they are good, strengthen and reinforce them, and may they be fulfilled in me and them like the dreams of the righteous Joseph. If, though, they need healing, heal them as You healed Hezekiah King of Judah from his illness, like Miriam the prophetess

---

(Sforno), *and grant you peace*, external and internal, harmony with the world and with yourself.

Read the following silently while the כהנים *chant. Omit on* שבת.

רִבּוֹנוֹ שֶׁל עוֹלָם, אֲנִי שֶׁלָּךְ וַחֲלוֹמוֹתַי שֶׁלָּךְ. חֲלוֹם חָלַמְתִּי וְאֵינִי יוֹדֵעַ מַה הוּא. יְהִי רָצוֹן מִלְּפָנֶיךָ, יהוה אֱלֹהַי וֵאלֹהֵי אֲבוֹתַי, שֶׁיִּהְיוּ כָּל חֲלוֹמוֹתַי עָלַי וְעַל כָּל יִשְׂרָאֵל לְטוֹבָה, בֵּין שֶׁחָלַמְתִּי עַל עַצְמִי, וּבֵין שֶׁחָלַמְתִּי עַל אֲחֵרִים, וּבֵין שֶׁחָלְמוּ אֲחֵרִים עָלָי. אִם טוֹבִים הֵם, חַזְּקֵם וְאַמְּצֵם, וְיִתְקַיְּמוּ בִי וּבָהֶם, כַּחֲלוֹמוֹתָיו שֶׁל יוֹסֵף הַצַּדִּיק. וְאִם צְרִיכִים רְפוּאָה, רְפָאֵם כְּחִזְקִיָּהוּ מֶלֶךְ יְהוּדָה מֵחָלְיוֹ, וּכְמִרְיָם הַנְּבִיאָה מִצָּרַעְתָּהּ, וּכְנַעֲמָן מִצָּרַעְתּוֹ, וּכְמֵי מָרָה עַל יְדֵי מֹשֶׁה רַבֵּנוּ, וּכְמֵי יְרִיחוֹ עַל יְדֵי אֱלִישָׁע. וּכְשֵׁם שֶׁהָפַכְתָּ אֶת קִלְלַת בִּלְעָם הָרָשָׁע מִקְּלָלָה לִבְרָכָה, כֵּן תַּהֲפֹךְ כָּל חֲלוֹמוֹתַי עָלַי וְעַל כָּל יִשְׂרָאֵל לְטוֹבָה, וְתִשְׁמְרֵנִי וּתְחָנֵּנִי וְתִרְצֵנִי. אָמֵן.

יָאֵר | אֱלֹהִים יְחָנֵּנוּ וִיבָרְכֵנוּ, יָאֵר פָּנָיו אִתָּנוּ סֶלָה: | תהלים סז
יהוה | יהוה, יהוה, אֵל רַחוּם וְחַנּוּן, אֶרֶךְ אַפַּיִם וְרַב־חֶסֶד וֶאֱמֶת: | שמות לד
פָּנָיו | פְּנֵה־אֵלַי וְחָנֵּנִי, כִּי־יָחִיד וְעָנִי אָנִי: | תהלים כה
אֵלֶיךָ | אֵלֶיךָ יהוה נַפְשִׁי אֶשָּׂא: | שם
וִיחֻנֶּךָּ: | הִנֵּה כְעֵינֵי עֲבָדִים אֶל־יַד אֲדוֹנֵיהֶם
כְּעֵינֵי שִׁפְחָה אֶל־יַד גְּבִרְתָּהּ, כֵּן עֵינֵינוּ אֶל־יהוה אֱלֹהֵינוּ
עַד שֶׁיְּחָנֵּנוּ: | תהלים קכג

Read the following silently while the כהנים *chant. Omit on* שבת.

רִבּוֹנוֹ שֶׁל עוֹלָם, אֲנִי שֶׁלָּךְ וַחֲלוֹמוֹתַי שֶׁלָּךְ. חֲלוֹם חָלַמְתִּי וְאֵינִי יוֹדֵעַ מַה הוּא. יְהִי רָצוֹן מִלְּפָנֶיךָ, יהוה אֱלֹהַי וֵאלֹהֵי אֲבוֹתַי, שֶׁיִּהְיוּ כָּל חֲלוֹמוֹתַי עָלַי וְעַל כָּל יִשְׂרָאֵל לְטוֹבָה, בֵּין שֶׁחָלַמְתִּי עַל עַצְמִי, וּבֵין שֶׁחָלַמְתִּי עַל אֲחֵרִים, וּבֵין שֶׁחָלְמוּ אֲחֵרִים עָלָי. אִם טוֹבִים הֵם, חַזְּקֵם וְאַמְּצֵם, וְיִתְקַיְּמוּ בִי וּבָהֶם, כַּחֲלוֹמוֹתָיו שֶׁל יוֹסֵף הַצַּדִּיק. וְאִם צְרִיכִים רְפוּאָה, רְפָאֵם כְּחִזְקִיָּהוּ מֶלֶךְ

---

and be gracious to you, so that you find favor in the eyes of God and your fellow humans. *May the* Lord *turn His face toward you,* bestowing on you His providential care (Rashbam, Ibn Ezra), or, may He grant you eternal life from her leprosy, like Na'aman from his leprosy, like the waters of Mara by Moses our teacher, and like the waters of Jericho by Elisha. And just as You turned the curses of Balaam the wicked from curse to blessing, so turn all my dreams about me and all Israel to good; protect me, be gracious to me and accept me. Amen.

May [He] turn — May he receive a blessing from the LORD and a just reward from the God of his salvation. And he will win grace and good favor in the eyes of God and man. *Ps. 24* *Prov. 3*

The LORD — LORD, be gracious to us; we yearn for You. Be their strength every morning, our salvation in time of distress. *Is. 33*

His face — Do not hide Your face from me in the day of my distress. Turn Your ear to me; on the day I call, swiftly answer me. *Ps. 102*

Toward you — To You, enthroned in heaven, I lift my eyes. *Ps. 123*

And grant — They shall place My name on the children of Israel, and I will bless them. *Num. 6*

You — Yours, LORD, are the greatness and the power, the glory, majesty and splendor, for everything in heaven and earth is Yours. Yours, LORD, is the kingdom; You are exalted as Head over all. *1 Chr. 29*

Peace. — "Peace, peace, to those far and near," says the LORD, "and I will heal him." *Is. 57*

Read the following silently while the Kohanim chant. Omit on Shabbat.

May it be Your will, LORD my God and God of my fathers, that You act for the sake of Your simple, sacred kindness and great compassion, and for the purity of Your great, mighty and awesome name of twenty-two letters derived from the verses of the priestly blessing spoken by Aaron and his sons, Your holy people. May You be close to me when I call to You. May You hear my prayer, plea and cry as You did the cry of Jacob Your perfect one who was called "a plain man." May You grant me and all the members of my household our food and sustenance, generously not meagerly, honestly not otherwise, with satisfaction not pain, from Your generous hand, just as You gave a portion of bread to eat and clothes to wear to Jacob our father who was called "a plain man." May we find love, grace, kindness and compassion in Your sight and in the eyes of all who see us. May my words in service to You be heard, as You granted Joseph Your righteous one, at the time

יְהוּדָה מֵחָלְיוֹ, וּכְמִרְיָם הַנְּבִיאָה מִצָּרַעְתָּהּ, וּכְנַעֲמָן מִצָּרַעְתּוֹ, וּכְמֵי מָרָה עַל יְדֵי מֹשֶׁה רַבֵּנוּ, וּכְמֵי יְרִיחוֹ עַל יְדֵי אֱלִישָׁע. וּכְשֵׁם שֶׁהָפַכְתָּ אֶת קִלְלַת בִּלְעָם הָרָשָׁע מִקְּלָלָה לִבְרָכָה, כֵּן תַּהֲפֹךְ כָּל חֲלוֹמוֹתַי עָלַי וְעַל כָּל יִשְׂרָאֵל לְטוֹבָה, וְתִשְׁמְרֵנִי וּתְחָנֵּנִי וְתִרְצֵנִי. אָמֵן.

יִשָּׂא — יִשָּׂא בְרָכָה מֵאֵת יהוה, וּצְדָקָה מֵאֱלֹהֵי יִשְׁעוֹ: תהלים כד
וּמְצָא־חֵן וְשֵׂכֶל־טוֹב בְּעֵינֵי אֱלֹהִים וְאָדָם: משלי ג

יהוה — יהוה חָנֵּנוּ, לְךָ קִוִּינוּ, הֱיֵה זְרֹעָם לַבְּקָרִים תהלים... ישעיה לג
אַף־יְשׁוּעָתֵנוּ בְּעֵת צָרָה:

פָּנָיו — אַל־תַּסְתֵּר פָּנֶיךָ מִמֶּנִּי בְּיוֹם צַר לִי, הַטֵּה־אֵלַי אָזְנֶךָ תהלים קב
בְּיוֹם אֶקְרָא מַהֵר עֲנֵנִי:

אֵלֶיךָ — אֵלֶיךָ נָשָׂאתִי אֶת־עֵינַי, הַיֹּשְׁבִי בַּשָּׁמָיִם: תהלים קכג

וְיָשֵׂם — וְשָׂמוּ אֶת־שְׁמִי עַל־בְּנֵי יִשְׂרָאֵל, וַאֲנִי אֲבָרְכֵם: במדבר ו

לְךָ — לְךָ יהוה הַגְּדֻלָּה וְהַגְּבוּרָה וְהַתִּפְאֶרֶת וְהַנֵּצַח וְהַהוֹד דברי הימים א׳ כט
כִּי־כֹל בַּשָּׁמַיִם וּבָאָרֶץ, לְךָ יהוה הַמַּמְלָכָה
וְהַמִּתְנַשֵּׂא לְכֹל לְרֹאשׁ:

שָׁלוֹם: — שָׁלוֹם שָׁלוֹם לָרָחוֹק וְלַקָּרוֹב, אָמַר יהוה, וּרְפָאתִיו: ישעיה נז

Read the following silently while the כהנים *chant. Omit on* שבת*.*

יְהִי רָצוֹן מִלְּפָנֶיךָ, יהוה אֱלֹהַי וֵאלֹהֵי אֲבוֹתַי, שֶׁתַּעֲשֶׂה לְמַעַן קְדֻשַּׁת חֲסָדֶיךָ וְגֹדֶל רַחֲמֶיךָ הַפְּשׁוּטִים, וּלְמַעַן טָהֳרַת שִׁמְךָ הַגָּדוֹל הַגִּבּוֹר וְהַנּוֹרָא, בֶּן עֶשְׂרִים וּשְׁתַּיִם אוֹתִיּוֹת הַיּוֹצֵא מִפְּסוּקִים שֶׁל בִּרְכַּת כֹּהֲנִים הָאֲמוּרָה מִפִּי אַהֲרֹן וּבָנָיו עַם קְדוֹשֶׁךָ, שֶׁתִּהְיֶה קָרוֹב לִי בְּקָרְאִי לָךְ, וְתִשְׁמַע תְּפִלָּתִי נַאֲקָתִי וְאֶנְקָתִי תָּמִיד, כְּשֵׁם שֶׁשָּׁמַעְתָּ אֶנְקַת יַעֲקֹב תְּמִימֶךָ הַנִּקְרָא אִישׁ תָּם. וְתִתֶּן לִי וּלְכָל נַפְשׁוֹת בֵּיתִי מְזוֹנוֹתֵינוּ וּפַרְנָסָתֵנוּ בְּרֶוַח וְלֹא בְצִמְצוּם, בְּהֶתֵּר וְלֹא בְאִסּוּר, בְּנַחַת וְלֹא בְצַעַר, מִתַּחַת יָדְךָ הָרְחָבָה, כְּשֵׁם שֶׁנָּתַתָּ פַּת לֶחֶם לֶאֱכֹל וּבֶגֶד לִלְבֹּשׁ לְיַעֲקֹב אָבִינוּ הַנִּקְרָא אִישׁ תָּם. וְתִתְּנֵנוּ לְאַהֲבָה, לְחֵן וּלְחֶסֶד וּלְרַחֲמִים בְּעֵינֶיךָ וּבְעֵינֵי כָל רוֹאֵינוּ, וְיִהְיוּ דְבָרַי נִשְׁמָעִים לַעֲבוֹדָתֶךָ, כְּשֵׁם שֶׁנָּתַתָּ אֶת

when he was robed by his father in a cloak of fine wool, that he find grace, kindness and compassion in Your sight and in the eyes of all who saw him. May You do wonders and miracles with me, and a sign for good. Grant me success in my paths, and set in my heart understanding that I may understand, discern and fulfill all the words of Your Torah's teachings and mysteries. Save me from errors and purify my thoughts and my heart to serve You and be in awe of You. Prolong my days (*add, where appropriate:* and those of my father, mother, wife, husband, son/s, and daughter/s) in joy and happiness, with much strength and peace. Amen, Selah.

The Leader continues with "Grant peace" below.

The Kohanim say:
רִבּוֹנוֹ Master of the Universe: we have done what You have decreed for us. So too may You deal with us as You have promised us. Look down from Your holy dwelling place, from heaven, and bless Your people Israel and the land You have given us as You promised on oath to our ancestors, a land flowing with milk and honey. *Deut. 26*

The congregation says:
אַדִּיר Majestic One on high who dwells in power: You are peace and Your name is peace. May it be Your will to bestow on us and on Your people the house of Israel, life and blessing as a safeguard for peace.

If the Priestly Blessing is not said, the following is said by the Leader:

Our God and God of our fathers, bless us with the threefold blessing in the Torah, written by the hand of Moses Your servant and pronounced by Aaron and his sons the priests, Your holy people, as it is said:

May the LORD bless you and protect you. *Num. 6*
Cong: May it be Your will.
May the LORD make His face shine on you and be gracious to you.
Cong: May it be Your will.
May the LORD turn His face toward you, and grant you peace.
Cong: May it be Your will.

PEACE

שִׂים שָׁלוֹם Grant peace, goodness and blessing,
grace, loving-kindness and compassion to us and all Israel Your people.
Bless us, our Father, all as one, with the light of Your face,
for by the light of Your face You have given us, LORD our God,
the Torah of life and love of kindness,
righteousness, blessing, compassion, life and peace.
May it be good in Your eyes to bless Your people Israel
at every time, in every hour, with Your peace.

יוֹסֵף צַדִּיקֶךָ בְּשָׁעָה שֶׁהִלְבִּישׁוֹ אָבִיו כְּתֹנֶת פַּסִּים לְחֵן וּלְחֶסֶד וּלְרַחֲמִים בְּעֵינֶיךָ וּבְעֵינֵי כָל רוֹאָיו. וְתַעֲשֶׂה עִמִּי נִפְלָאוֹת וְנִסִּים, וּלְטוֹבָה אוֹת, וְתַצְלִיחֵנִי בִּדְרָכַי, וְתֵן בְּלִבִּי בִּינָה לְהָבִין וּלְהַשְׂכִּיל וּלְקַיֵּם אֶת כָּל דִּבְרֵי תַלְמוּד תּוֹרָתֶךָ וְסוֹדוֹתֶיהָ, וְתַצִּילֵנִי מִשְּׁגִיאוֹת, וּתְטַהֵר רַעְיוֹנַי וְלִבִּי לַעֲבוֹדָתֶךָ, וְתַאֲרִיךְ יָמַי (וִימֵי אָבִי וְאִמִּי / וְאִשְׁתִּי / וּבַעְלִי / וּבָנַי וּבְנוֹתַי) בְּטוֹב וּבִנְעִימוֹת, בְּרֹב עֹז וְשָׁלוֹם, אָמֵן סֶלָה.

The שליח ציבור *continues with* שִׂים שָׁלוֹם *below.*

The קהל *says:*

אַדִּיר בַּמָּרוֹם שׁוֹכֵן בִּגְבוּרָה,
אַתָּה שָׁלוֹם וְשִׁמְךָ שָׁלוֹם.
יְהִי רָצוֹן שֶׁתָּשִׂים עָלֵינוּ וְעַל
כָּל עַמְּךָ בֵּית יִשְׂרָאֵל חַיִּים
וּבְרָכָה לְמִשְׁמֶרֶת שָׁלוֹם.

The כהנים *say:*

רִבּוֹנוֹ שֶׁל עוֹלָם, עָשִׂינוּ מַה שֶּׁגָּזַרְתָּ עָלֵינוּ, אַף אַתָּה
עֲשֵׂה עִמָּנוּ כְּמוֹ שֶׁהִבְטַחְתָּנוּ. הַשְׁקִיפָה מִמְּעוֹן דברים כו
קָדְשְׁךָ מִן־הַשָּׁמַיִם, וּבָרֵךְ אֶת־עַמְּךָ אֶת־יִשְׂרָאֵל,
וְאֵת הָאֲדָמָה אֲשֶׁר נָתַתָּה לָנוּ, כַּאֲשֶׁר נִשְׁבַּעְתָּ
לַאֲבוֹתֵינוּ, אֶרֶץ זָבַת חָלָב וּדְבָשׁ:

If ברכת כהנים *is not said, the following is said by the* שליח ציבור:

אֱלֹהֵינוּ וֵאלֹהֵי אֲבוֹתֵינוּ, בָּרְכֵנוּ בַּבְּרָכָה הַמְשֻׁלֶּשֶׁת בַּתּוֹרָה, הַכְּתוּבָה עַל יְדֵי מֹשֶׁה עַבְדֶּךָ, הָאֲמוּרָה מִפִּי אַהֲרֹן וּבָנָיו כֹּהֲנִים עַם קְדוֹשֶׁיךָ, כָּאָמוּר

יְבָרֶכְךָ יהוה וְיִשְׁמְרֶךָ: קהל: כֵּן יְהִי רָצוֹן במדבר ו
יָאֵר יהוה פָּנָיו אֵלֶיךָ וִיחֻנֶּךָּ: קהל: כֵּן יְהִי רָצוֹן
יִשָּׂא יהוה פָּנָיו אֵלֶיךָ וְיָשֵׂם לְךָ שָׁלוֹם: קהל: כֵּן יְהִי רָצוֹן

שלום

שִׂים שָׁלוֹם טוֹבָה וּבְרָכָה, חֵן וָחֶסֶד וְרַחֲמִים
עָלֵינוּ וְעַל כָּל יִשְׂרָאֵל עַמֶּךָ.
בָּרְכֵנוּ אָבִינוּ כֻּלָּנוּ כְּאֶחָד בְּאוֹר פָּנֶיךָ
כִּי בְאוֹר פָּנֶיךָ נָתַתָּ לָּנוּ, יהוה אֱלֹהֵינוּ
תּוֹרַת חַיִּים וְאַהֲבַת חֶסֶד
וּצְדָקָה וּבְרָכָה וְרַחֲמִים וְחַיִּים וְשָׁלוֹם.
וְטוֹב בְּעֵינֶיךָ לְבָרֵךְ אֶת עַמְּךָ יִשְׂרָאֵל
בְּכָל עֵת וּבְכָל שָׁעָה בִּשְׁלוֹמֶךָ.

The congregation then the Leader:

בְּסֵפֶר חַיִּים In the book of life, blessing, peace and prosperity,
may we and all Your people
the house of Israel be remembered and written
before You for a good life, and for peace.

The congregation then the Leader:

וְנֶאֱמַר It is said, "Through Me your days will grow many, *Prov. 9*
and years of life will be added to your lot."
Write us down for good lives, O God of life,
and write us in the book of life.
As is written,
"You who cling to the Lord your God are all alive today." *Deut. 4*

The Ark is opened.

The Leader recites each phrase, and the congregation responds "Amen" and recites the next phrase.

הַיּוֹם This day, may You strengthen us. AMEN

This day, may You bless us. AMEN

This day, may You give us greatness. AMEN

This day, may You deal with us kindly. AMEN

This day, may You hear our cry. AMEN

This day, may You accept our prayers
compassionately and willingly. AMEN

This day, may You support us
with Your hand of righteousness. AMEN

The Ark is closed.

---

sinned, but the past is the past. I will look only toward the future, and from now on I want to repent and return to God with all my heart." Our sages therefore teach us that the word "Now" alludes to repentance.

The קהל *then the* שליח ציבור:

בְּסֵפֶר חַיִּים, בְּרָכָה וְשָׁלוֹם, וּפַרְנָסָה טוֹבָה
נִזָּכֵר וְנִכָּתֵב לְפָנֶיךָ, אֲנַחְנוּ וְכָל עַמְּךָ בֵּית יִשְׂרָאֵל
לְחַיִּים טוֹבִים וּלְשָׁלוֹם.

The קהל *then the* שליח ציבור:

וְנֶאֱמַר: כִּי־בִי יִרְבּוּ יָמֶיךָ משלי ט
וְיוֹסִיפוּ לְךָ שְׁנוֹת חַיִּים:
לְחַיִּים טוֹבִים תִּכְתְּבֵנוּ
אֱלֹהִים חַיִּים, כָּתְבֵנוּ בְּסֵפֶר הַחַיִּים.
כַּכָּתוּב: וְאַתֶּם הַדְּבֵקִים בַּיהוה אֱלֹהֵיכֶם, חַיִּים כֻּלְּכֶם הַיּוֹם: דברים ד

The ארון קודש *is opened.*

The שליח ציבור *recites each phrase, and the* קהל *responds* אמן *and recites the next phrase.*

הַיּוֹם תְּאַמְּצֵנוּ. אָמֵן
הַיּוֹם תְּבָרְכֵנוּ. אָמֵן
הַיּוֹם תְּגַדְּלֵנוּ. אָמֵן
הַיּוֹם תִּדְרְשֵׁנוּ לְטוֹבָה. אָמֵן
הַיּוֹם תִּשְׁמַע שַׁוְעָתֵנוּ. אָמֵן
הַיּוֹם תְּקַבֵּל בְּרַחֲמִים וּבְרָצוֹן אֶת תְּפִלָּתֵנוּ. אָמֵן
הַיּוֹם תִּתְמְכֵנוּ בִּימִין צִדְקֶךָ. אָמֵן

The ארון קודש *is closed.*

הַיּוֹם *This day.* Said the Maggid of Koznitz: The evil urge comes to a person and says, "How can you repent? You are so filled with sins." This is not the truth. A person who truly wants to repent must say, "It is true that I have

The congregation then the Leader:

כְּהַיּוֹם Bring us this day, happy, rejoicing, to a House restored,

as is written:
"I shall bring them to My holy mountain, *Is. 56*
and I shall make them rejoice in My House of prayer;
their offerings and their sacrifices will be accepted,
desired on My altar,
for My House will be called a house of prayer
for all peoples."

And it is said,
"And the LORD commanded You *Deut. 6*
to perform all these statutes, to fear the LORD our God,
that it may be good for us all our days;
to give us life as on this day."

And it is said,
"Righteousness will be in our hands, *Ibid.*
when we take care to fulfill all these commands
before the LORD our God, as He has commanded."

Righteousness and blessing, compassion and life and peace –
may these be with us and with all Israel, forever.
*Blessed are You, LORD,
who blesses His people Israel with peace.

**Outside Israel, many end the blessing:*
Blessed are You, LORD, who makes peace.

The following verse concludes the Leader's Repetition of the Amida.
May the words of my mouth and the meditation of my heart *Ps. 19*
find favor before You, LORD, my Rock and Redeemer.

The קהל *then the* שליח ציבור:

כְּהַיּוֹם הַזֶּה תְּבִיאֵנוּ, שָׂשִׂים וּשְׂמֵחִים בְּבִנְיַן שָׁלֵם.

כַּכָּתוּב
וַהֲבִיאוֹתִים אֶל־הַר קׇדְשִׁי וְשִׂמַּחְתִּים בְּבֵית תְּפִלָּתִי ישעיה נו
עוֹלֹתֵיהֶם וְזִבְחֵיהֶם לְרָצוֹן עַל־מִזְבְּחִי
כִּי בֵיתִי בֵּית־תְּפִלָּה יִקָּרֵא לְכׇל־הָעַמִּים:

וְנֶאֱמַר
וַיְצַוֵּנוּ יהוה לַעֲשׂוֹת אֶת־כׇּל־הַחֻקִּים הָאֵלֶּה דברים ו
לְיִרְאָה אֶת־יהוה אֱלֹהֵינוּ
לְטוֹב לָנוּ כׇּל־הַיָּמִים לְחַיֹּתֵנוּ כְּהַיּוֹם הַזֶּה:

וְנֶאֱמַר
וּצְדָקָה תִּהְיֶה־לָּנוּ שם
כִּי־נִשְׁמֹר לַעֲשׂוֹת אֶת־כׇּל־הַמִּצְוָה הַזֹּאת
לִפְנֵי יהוה אֱלֹהֵינוּ, כַּאֲשֶׁר צִוָּנוּ:

וּצְדָקָה וּבְרָכָה וְרַחֲמִים וְחַיִּים וְשָׁלוֹם
יִהְיֶה לָנוּ וּלְכׇל יִשְׂרָאֵל עַד הָעוֹלָם.
*בָּרוּךְ אַתָּה יהוה, הַמְבָרֵךְ אֶת עַמּוֹ יִשְׂרָאֵל בַּשָּׁלוֹם.

*In חוץ לארץ, *many end the blessing:*

בָּרוּךְ אַתָּה יהוה, עוֹשֶׂה הַשָּׁלוֹם.

The following verse concludes the חזרת הש״ץ.

יִהְיוּ לְרָצוֹן אִמְרֵי־פִי וְהֶגְיוֹן לִבִּי לְפָנֶיךָ, יהוה צוּרִי וְגֹאֲלִי: תהלים יט

FULL KADDISH

Leader: יִתְגַּדַּל Magnified and sanctified
may His great name be,
in the world He created by His will.
May He establish His kingdom
in your lifetime and in your days,
and in the lifetime of all the house of Israel,
swiftly and soon –
and say: Amen.

All: May His great name be blessed
for ever and all time.

Leader: Blessed and praised,
glorified and exalted, raised and honored,
uplifted and lauded be
the name of the Holy One, blessed be He,
above and beyond any blessing, song,
praise and consolation
uttered in the world – and say: Amen.

May the prayers and pleas of all Israel
be accepted by their Father in heaven –
and say: Amen.

May there be great peace from heaven,
and life for us and all Israel –
and say: Amen.

Bow, take three steps back, as if taking leave of the Divine Presence, then bow, first left, then right, then center, while saying:

May He who makes peace in His high places,
make peace for us and all Israel –
and say: Amen.

Some hold that if there is a break between Musaf and Minḥa, Aleinu and Mourner's Kaddish are said (page 198); however, most congregations end the Musaf service here.

קדיש שלם

ש״ץ: יִתְגַּדַּל וְיִתְקַדַּשׁ שְׁמֵהּ רַבָּא (קהל: אָמֵן)
בְּעָלְמָא דִּי בְרָא כִרְעוּתֵהּ
וְיַמְלִיךְ מַלְכוּתֵהּ
בְּחַיֵּיכוֹן וּבְיוֹמֵיכוֹן וּבְחַיֵּי דְכָל בֵּית יִשְׂרָאֵל
בַּעֲגָלָא וּבִזְמַן קָרִיב
וְאִמְרוּ אָמֵן. (קהל: אָמֵן)

קהל וש״ץ: יְהֵא שְׁמֵהּ רַבָּא מְבָרַךְ לְעָלַם וּלְעָלְמֵי עָלְמַיָּא.

ש״ץ: יִתְבָּרַךְ וְיִשְׁתַּבַּח וְיִתְפָּאַר וְיִתְרוֹמַם וְיִתְנַשֵּׂא
וְיִתְהַדָּר וְיִתְעַלֶּה וְיִתְהַלָּל
שְׁמֵהּ דְּקֻדְשָׁא בְּרִיךְ הוּא (קהל: בְּרִיךְ הוּא)
לְעֵלָּא לְעֵלָּא מִכָּל בִּרְכָתָא וְשִׁירָתָא, תֻּשְׁבְּחָתָא וְנֶחֱמָתָא
דַּאֲמִירָן בְּעָלְמָא
וְאִמְרוּ אָמֵן. (קהל: אָמֵן)

תִּתְקַבַּל צְלוֹתְהוֹן וּבָעוּתְהוֹן דְּכָל יִשְׂרָאֵל
קֳדָם אֲבוּהוֹן דִּי בִשְׁמַיָּא
וְאִמְרוּ אָמֵן. (קהל: אָמֵן)

יְהֵא שְׁלָמָא רַבָּא מִן שְׁמַיָּא
וְחַיִּים, עָלֵינוּ וְעַל כָּל יִשְׂרָאֵל
וְאִמְרוּ אָמֵן. (קהל: אָמֵן)

Bow, take three steps back, as if taking leave of the Divine Presence, then bow, first left, then right, then center, while saying:

עֹשֶׂה הַשָּׁלוֹם בִּמְרוֹמָיו
הוּא יַעֲשֶׂה שָׁלוֹם עָלֵינוּ וְעַל כָּל יִשְׂרָאֵל
וְאִמְרוּ אָמֵן. (קהל: אָמֵן)

Some hold that if there is a break between מוסף *and* מנחה*,* עָלֵינוּ *and* קדיש יתום *are said (page 199); however, most congregations end the* מוסף *service here.*

Minḥa

REMOVING THE TORAH FROM THE ARK

The Ark is opened and the congregation stands. All say:

וַיְהִי בִּנְסֹעַ Whenever the Ark set out, Moses would say, *Num. 10*
"Arise, LORD, and may Your enemies be scattered.
May those who hate You flee before You."
For the Torah shall come forth from Zion, *Is. 2*
and the word of the LORD from Jerusalem.
Blessed is He who, in His holiness, gave the Torah to His people Israel.

בְּרִיךְ Blessed is the name of the Master of the Universe. Blessed is Your crown and Your place. May Your favor always be with Your people Israel. Show Your people the salvation of Your right hand in Your Temple. Grant us the gift of Your good light, and accept our prayers in mercy. May it be Your will to prolong our life in goodness. May I be counted among the righteous, so that You will have compassion on me and protect me and all that is mine and all that is Your people Israel's. You feed all; You sustain all; You rule over all; You rule over kings, for sovereignty is Yours. I am a servant of the Holy One, blessed be He, before whom and before whose glorious Torah I bow at all times. Not in man do I trust, nor on any angel do I rely, but on the God of heaven who is the God of truth, whose Torah is truth, whose prophets speak truth, and who abounds in acts of love and truth. ▸ In Him I trust, and to His holy and glorious name I offer praises. May it be Your will to open my heart to the Torah, and to fulfill the wishes of my heart and of the hearts of all Your people Israel for good, for life, and for peace. *Zohar, Vayak-hel*

The Leader takes the Torah scroll in his right arm, bows toward the Ark and says:

Magnify the LORD with me, and let us exalt His name together. *Ps. 34*

The Ark is closed. The Leader carries the Torah scroll to the bima and the congregation says:

לְךָ Yours, LORD, are the greatness and the power, the glory and the majesty and splendor, for everything in heaven and earth is Yours. *1 Chr. 29*
Yours, LORD, is the kingdom; You are exalted as Head over all. Exalt the LORD our God and bow to His footstool; He is holy. Exalt the LORD our God, and bow at His holy mountain, for holy is the LORD our God. *Ps. 99*

---

concluding service. The reason is so as not to delay the afternoon service after its proper time, since there are congregations where Musaf is continued well into the afternoon. *Ashrei* normally serves the purpose of marking a

תפילת מנחה

הוצאת ספר תורה

The ארון קודש *is opened and the* קהל *stands. All say:*

וַיְהִי בִּנְסֹעַ הָאָרֹן וַיֹּאמֶר מֹשֶׁה במדבר י
קוּמָה יהוה וְיָפֻצוּ אֹיְבֶיךָ וְיָנֻסוּ מְשַׂנְאֶיךָ מִפָּנֶיךָ:
כִּי מִצִּיּוֹן תֵּצֵא תוֹרָה וּדְבַר־יהוה מִירוּשָׁלָםִ: ישעיה ב
בָּרוּךְ שֶׁנָּתַן תּוֹרָה לְעַמּוֹ יִשְׂרָאֵל בִּקְדֻשָּׁתוֹ.

בְּרִיךְ שְׁמֵהּ דְּמָרֵא עָלְמָא, בְּרִיךְ כִּתְרָךְ וְאַתְרָךְ. יְהֵא רְעוּתָךְ עִם עַמָּךְ יִשְׂרָאֵל לְעָלַם, וּפֻרְקַן יְמִינָךְ אַחֲזִי לְעַמָּךְ בְּבֵית מַקְדְּשָׁךְ, וּלְאַמְטוּיֵי לַנָא מִטּוּב נְהוֹרָךְ, וּלְקַבֵּל צְלוֹתַנָא בְּרַחֲמִין. יְהֵא רַעֲוָא קֳדָמָךְ דְּתוֹרִיךְ לַן חַיִּין בְּטִיבוּ, וְלֶהֱוֵי אֲנָא פְּקִידָא בְּגוֹ צַדִּיקַיָּא, לְמִרְחַם עָלַי וּלְמִנְטַר יָתִי וְיַת כָּל דִּי לִי וְדִי לְעַמָּךְ יִשְׂרָאֵל. אַנְתְּ הוּא זָן לְכֹלָּא וּמְפַרְנֵס לְכֹלָּא, אַנְתְּ הוּא שַׁלִּיט עַל כֹּלָּא, אַנְתְּ הוּא דְּשַׁלִּיט עַל מַלְכַיָּא, וּמַלְכוּתָא דִּילָךְ הִיא. אֲנָא עַבְדָּא דְקֻדְשָׁא בְּרִיךְ הוּא, דְּסָגֵדְנָא קַמֵּהּ וּמִקַּמֵּי דִּיקַר אוֹרַיְתֵהּ בְּכָל עִדָּן וְעִדָּן. לָא עַל אֱנָשׁ רָחִיצְנָא וְלָא עַל בַּר אֱלָהִין סָמִיכְנָא, אֶלָּא בֶּאֱלָהָא דִשְׁמַיָּא, דְּהוּא אֱלָהָא קְשׁוֹט, וְאוֹרַיְתֵהּ קְשׁוֹט, וּנְבִיאוֹהִי קְשׁוֹט, וּמַסְגֵּא לְמֶעְבַּד טַבְוָן וּקְשׁוֹט. ‹ בֵּהּ אֲנָא רָחִיץ, וְלִשְׁמֵהּ קַדִּישָׁא יַקִּירָא אֲנָא אֵמַר תֻּשְׁבְּחָן. יְהֵא רַעֲוָא קֳדָמָךְ דְּתִפְתַּח לִבַּאי בְּאוֹרַיְתָא, וְתַשְׁלִים מִשְׁאֲלִין דְּלִבַּאי וְלִבָּא דְכָל עַמָּךְ יִשְׂרָאֵל לְטָב וּלְחַיִּין וְלִשְׁלָם. זוהר ויקהל

The שליח ציבור *takes the* ספר תורה *in his right arm, bows toward the* ארון קודש *and says:*

גַּדְּלוּ לַיהוה אִתִּי וּנְרוֹמְמָה שְׁמוֹ יַחְדָּו: תהלים לד

The ארון קודש *is closed. The* שליח ציבור *carries the* ספר תורה *to the* בימה *and the* קהל *says:*

לְךָ יהוה הַגְּדֻלָּה וְהַגְּבוּרָה וְהַתִּפְאֶרֶת וְהַנֵּצַח וְהַהוֹד, כִּי־כֹל בַּשָּׁמַיִם דברי הימים א׳ כט
וּבָאָרֶץ: לְךָ יהוה הַמַּמְלָכָה וְהַמִּתְנַשֵּׂא לְכֹל לְרֹאשׁ: רוֹמְמוּ יהוה אֱלֹהֵינוּ תהלים צט
וְהִשְׁתַּחֲווּ לַהֲדֹם רַגְלָיו, קָדוֹשׁ הוּא: רוֹמְמוּ יהוה אֱלֹהֵינוּ וְהִשְׁתַּחֲווּ
לְהַר קָדְשׁוֹ, כִּי־קָדוֹשׁ יהוה אֱלֹהֵינוּ:

MINḤA – AFTERNOON SERVICE

Unusually, *Ashrei* and *Uva LeTziyon* are not said here but at Ne'ila, the

Father of mercy, have compassion on the people borne by Him. May He remember the covenant with the mighty (patriarchs), and deliver us from evil times. May He reproach the evil instinct in the people by Him, and graciously grant that we be an eternal remnant. May He fulfill in good measure our requests for salvation and compassion.

The Torah scroll is placed on the bima and the Gabbai calls a Kohen to the Torah. See See laws 77–83.

וְתִגָּלֶה May His kingship over us be soon revealed and made manifest. May He be gracious to our surviving remnant, the remnant of His people the house of Israel in grace, loving-kindness, compassion and favor, and let us say: Amen. Let us all render greatness to our God and give honor to the Torah. *Let the Kohen come forward. Arise (*name* son of *father's name*), the Kohen.

**If no Kohen is present, a Levi or Yisrael is called up as follows:*

/As there is no Kohen, arise (*name* son of *father's name*) in place of a Kohen./

Blessed is He who, in His holiness, gave the Torah to His people Israel.

The congregation followed by the Gabbai:

You who cling to the LORD your God are all alive today. *Deut. 4*

The Reader shows the oleh the section to be read. The oleh touches the scroll at that place with the tzitzit of his tallit or the fabric belt of the Torah scroll, which he then kisses. Holding the handles of the scroll, he says:

Oleh: Bless the LORD, the blessed One.

Cong: Bless the LORD, the blessed One, for ever and all time.

Oleh: Bless the LORD, the blessed One, for ever and all time.

Blessed are You, LORD our God, King of the Universe, who has chosen us from all peoples and has given us His Torah. Blessed are You, LORD, Giver of the Torah.

After the reading, the oleh says:

Oleh: Blessed are You, LORD our God, King of the Universe, who has given us the Torah of truth, planting everlasting life in our midst. Blessed are You, LORD, Giver of the Torah.

The combined effect, though, of the absence of the prayers that normally form the end of Musaf and those that mark the beginning of Minḥa, is startling. Despite the fact that the prayers of Yom Kippur are longer than those of any other day, there is a sense of urgency about them. There is no leisurely closure to Musaf, no preamble to Minḥa, no relaxation of mood, nothing that might de-intensify the awe of the day.

אַב הָרַחֲמִים הוּא יְרַחֵם עַם עֲמוּסִים, וְיִזְכֹּר בְּרִית אֵיתָנִים, וְיַצִּיל נַפְשׁוֹתֵינוּ מִן הַשָּׁעוֹת הָרָעוֹת, וְיִגְעַר בְּיֵצֶר הָרָע מִן הַנְּשׂוּאִים, וְיָחֹן אוֹתָנוּ לִפְלֵיטַת עוֹלָמִים, וִימַלֵּא מִשְׁאֲלוֹתֵינוּ בְּמִדָּה טוֹבָה יְשׁוּעָה וְרַחֲמִים.

The ספר תורה *is placed on the* שולחן *and the* גבאי *calls a* כהן *to the* תורה. *See laws 77–83.*

וְתִגָּלֶה וְתֵרָאֶה מַלְכוּתוֹ עָלֵינוּ בִּזְמַן קָרוֹב, וְיָחֹן פְּלֵיטָתֵנוּ וּפְלֵיטַת עַמּוֹ בֵּית יִשְׂרָאֵל לְחֵן וּלְחֶסֶד וּלְרַחֲמִים וּלְרָצוֹן וְנֹאמַר אָמֵן. הַכֹּל הָבוּ גֹדֶל לֵאלֹהֵינוּ וּתְנוּ כָבוֹד לַתּוֹרָה.
*כֹּהֵן קְרַב, יַעֲמֹד (פלוני בֶּן פלוני) הַכֹּהֵן.

**If no* כהן *is present, a* לוי *or* ישראל *is called up as follows:*

/אֵין כָּאן כֹּהֵן, יַעֲמֹד (פלוני בֶּן פלוני) בִּמְקוֹם כֹּהֵן./

בָּרוּךְ שֶׁנָּתַן תּוֹרָה לְעַמּוֹ יִשְׂרָאֵל בִּקְדֻשָּׁתוֹ.

The קהל *followed by the* גבאי:

וְאַתֶּם הַדְּבֵקִים בַּיהוה אֱלֹהֵיכֶם חַיִּים כֻּלְּכֶם הַיּוֹם: דברים ד

The קורא *shows the* עולה *the section to be read. The* עולה *touches the scroll at that place with the* ציצית *of his* טלית *or the gartel of the* ספר תורה, *which he then kisses. Holding the handles of the scroll, he says:*

עולה: בָּרְכוּ אֶת יהוה הַמְבֹרָךְ.

קהל: בָּרוּךְ יהוה הַמְבֹרָךְ לְעוֹלָם וָעֶד.

עולה: בָּרוּךְ יהוה הַמְבֹרָךְ לְעוֹלָם וָעֶד.

בָּרוּךְ אַתָּה יהוה, אֱלֹהֵינוּ מֶלֶךְ הָעוֹלָם אֲשֶׁר בָּחַר בָּנוּ מִכָּל הָעַמִּים וְנָתַן לָנוּ אֶת תּוֹרָתוֹ. בָּרוּךְ אַתָּה יהוה, נוֹתֵן הַתּוֹרָה.

After the קריאת התורה, *the* עולה *says:*

עולה: בָּרוּךְ אַתָּה יהוה אֱלֹהֵינוּ מֶלֶךְ הָעוֹלָם
אֲשֶׁר נָתַן לָנוּ תּוֹרַת אֱמֶת וְחַיֵּי עוֹלָם נָטַע בְּתוֹכֵנוּ.
בָּרוּךְ אַתָּה יהוה, נוֹתֵן הַתּוֹרָה.

---

break between one prayer and the next (see *Berakhot* 30b). Here, however, the Reading of the Torah does so instead. Tosafot (*Berakhot* 31a) also hold that prayer should be preceded by words of Torah. Normally this is done through *Ashrei,* but here, through the Torah and Haftara readings.

TORAH READING

The Lord spoke to Moses saying: Speak to the children of Israel Lev. 18
and tell them: I am the Lord your God. You must not follow the
practices of the land of Egypt where once you dwelled, nor the
practices of the land of Canaan to which I am bringing you; do
not keep to their precepts. Practice My laws and keep My precepts; follow them – I am the Lord your God. Keep My precepts and My laws; one who practices them, shall live by them – I
am the Lord. Let no man draw close to any one of his own LEVI
flesh to uncover their nakedness – I am the Lord. Do not
uncover your father's nakedness; your mother's nakedness: she
is your mother – you may not uncover her nakedness. Do not
uncover the nakedness of your father's wife: it is like uncovering
your father's. Do not uncover the nakedness of your sister, the
daughter of your father or the daughter of your mother, one born
to your home or born elsewhere – do not uncover their nakedness. Do not uncover the nakedness of your son's daughter or

---

the Egyptians and the Canaanites? Why are sexual sins so serious as to warrant the exile of Israel from its land? The best way of understanding the passage is to ask a more fundamental, and seemingly unrelated, question. What is distinctive about the patriarchs and matriarchs in the book of Genesis?

We believe that Abraham and Sarah introduced (or reintroduced) a unique form of religious life, "Abrahamic monotheism," as contrasted with the idolatry of the pagan world. But this is not a dominant theme of the narratives of Genesis. Abraham, Isaac, and Jacob engage in no critique of idolatry. In this they are quite unlike the later prophets from Moses to Malachi for whom it was central. A famous rabbinic tradition states that Abraham was an iconoclast who broke his father's idols, yet this is not mentioned explicitly in Genesis. Abraham's family live among idolators, sometimes make treaties with them, even pray for them, yet they do not overtly criticize their religion, or call on them to relinquish it. Wherein lies the difference between the life of the Abrahamic covenant and that of the peoples among whom they dwell?

קריאת התורה

וַיְדַבֵּר יהוה אֶל־מֹשֶׁה לֵּאמֹר: דַּבֵּר אֶל־בְּנֵי יִשְׂרָאֵל וְאָמַרְתָּ ויקרא יח
אֲלֵהֶם אֲנִי יהוה אֱלֹהֵיכֶם: כְּמַעֲשֵׂה אֶרֶץ־מִצְרַיִם אֲשֶׁר יְשַׁבְתֶּם־
בָּהּ לֹא תַעֲשׂוּ וּכְמַעֲשֵׂה אֶרֶץ־כְּנַעַן אֲשֶׁר אֲנִי מֵבִיא אֶתְכֶם
שָׁמָּה לֹא תַעֲשׂוּ וּבְחֻקֹּתֵיהֶם לֹא תֵלֵכוּ: אֶת־מִשְׁפָּטַי תַּעֲשׂוּ
וְאֶת־חֻקֹּתַי תִּשְׁמְרוּ לָלֶכֶת בָּהֶם אֲנִי יהוה אֱלֹהֵיכֶם: וּשְׁמַרְתֶּם
אֶת־חֻקֹּתַי וְאֶת־מִשְׁפָּטַי אֲשֶׁר יַעֲשֶׂה אֹתָם הָאָדָם וָחַי בָּהֶם
לוי אֲנִי יהוה: אִישׁ אִישׁ אֶל־כָּל־שְׁאֵר בְּשָׂרוֹ לֹא תִקְרְבוּ
לְגַלּוֹת עֶרְוָה אֲנִי יהוה: עֶרְוַת אָבִיךָ וְעֶרְוַת אִמְּךָ לֹא
תְגַלֵּה אִמְּךָ הִוא לֹא תְגַלֶּה עֶרְוָתָהּ: עֶרְוַת אֵשֶׁת־
אָבִיךָ לֹא תְגַלֵּה עֶרְוַת אָבִיךָ הִוא: עֶרְוַת אֲחוֹתְךָ
בַת־אָבִיךָ אוֹ בַת־אִמֶּךָ מוֹלֶדֶת בַּיִת אוֹ מוֹלֶדֶת חוּץ לֹא תְגַלֶּה
עֶרְוָתָן: עֶרְוַת בַּת־בִּנְךָ אוֹ בַת־בִּתְּךָ לֹא תְגַלֶּה עֶרְוָתָן

TORAH READING

Both the Torah and Haftara readings for the afternoon of Yom Kippur are specified in the Talmud (*Megilla* 31a). The choice of Leviticus 18, a passage dealing with forbidden sexual relations, is on the face of it a strange one. Why read it on a day when sexual relations of any kind are forbidden? Why specifically these prohibitions on a day when we atone for sins of all kinds?

Rashi (on *Megilla* ad loc.) says that sexual sins are common and the desire to commit them is part of the human condition. Maimonides states that sexual desire is, for most people and in all eras, the strongest of all inclinations to sin (Laws of Forbidden Relationships 22:18–19). Freudian psychoanalysis argues likewise, and evolutionary psychology has tended to confirm it. Maimonides himself says that the reading is to inspire thoughts of penitence (Laws of Prayer 13:11).

The passage itself raises obvious questions. Why does it begin with the statement "I am the Lord your God"? Why the contrast with the behavior of

of your daughter's daughter; do not uncover their nakedness, for it is your own nakedness. Do not uncover the nakedness of a daughter of your father's wife, one born of your father: she is your sister – do not uncover her nakedness. Do not uncover the nakedness of your father's sister: she is of your father's flesh. Do not uncover the nakedness of your mother's sister, for she is of your mother's flesh. Do not uncover the nakedness of your father's brother; do not draw near to his wife – she is your aunt. Do not uncover the nakedness of your daughter-in-law: she is your son's wife – do not uncover her nakedness. Do not uncover the nakedness of your brother's wife: it is like uncovering your brother's. Do not uncover the nakedness of a woman and her daughter both; do not take her son's daughter or her daughter's daughter to uncover their nakedness: they are her flesh – that is depraved. And do not take your wife's sister as a wife to rival her, uncovering her nakedness as well as hers in her lifetime. Do not draw close to a woman to uncover her nakedness during her period of impurity. Do not give of your seed sleeping with the wife of another man, becoming impure through her. Do not give of your children to be passed before Molekh: do not desecrate the name of

---

sanctity of marriage and of sexual fidelity. Nor is it accidental that the sign of the Abrahamic covenant, Brit Mila, is circumcision. The sign of holiness is intimately connected with sexuality.

Why so? Sexuality is a fundamental theme of ancient myth. There were male gods of power and potency and female goddesses of fertility and allure, and the relations between them were amoral. They fought, conquered, schemed, sired. Often they killed one another; at times they killed their own children. It was a world of conflict and betrayal, of sexual lawlessness and anomie.

Judaism was and is opposed to this world, whether in its ancient forms of myth, or its more modern pseudo-scientific or philosophical counterparts, the neo-Darwinian myth (the "selfish gene") that the fundamental driver

כִּי עֶרְוָתְךָ הֵנָּה׃ עֶרְוַת בַּת־אֵשֶׁת אָבִיךָ מוֹלֶדֶת אָבִיךָ
אֲחוֹתְךָ הִוא לֹא תְגַלֶּה עֶרְוָתָהּ׃ עֶרְוַת אֲחוֹת־אָבִיךָ
לֹא תְגַלֵּה שְׁאֵר אָבִיךָ הִוא׃ עֶרְוַת אֲחוֹת־אִמְּךָ לֹא
תְגַלֵּה כִּי־שְׁאֵר אִמְּךָ הִוא׃ עֶרְוַת אֲחִי־אָבִיךָ לֹא
תְגַלֵּה אֶל־אִשְׁתּוֹ לֹא תִקְרָב דֹּדָתְךָ הִוא׃ עֶרְוַת כַּלָּתְךָ
לֹא תְגַלֵּה אֵשֶׁת בִּנְךָ הִוא לֹא תְגַלֶּה עֶרְוָתָהּ׃ עֶרְוַת
אֵשֶׁת־אָחִיךָ לֹא תְגַלֵּה עֶרְוַת אָחִיךָ הִוא׃ עֶרְוַת
אִשָּׁה וּבִתָּהּ לֹא תְגַלֵּה אֶת־בַּת־בְּנָהּ וְאֶת־בַּת־בִּתָּהּ לֹא תִקַּח
לְגַלּוֹת עֶרְוָתָהּ שַׁאֲרָה הֵנָּה זִמָּה הִוא׃ וְאִשָּׁה אֶל־אֲחֹתָהּ לֹא
תִקָּח לִצְרֹר לְגַלּוֹת עֶרְוָתָהּ עָלֶיהָ בְּחַיֶּיהָ׃ וְאֶל־אִשָּׁה בְּנִדַּת
טֻמְאָתָהּ לֹא תִקְרַב לְגַלּוֹת עֶרְוָתָהּ׃ וְאֶל־אֵשֶׁת עֲמִיתְךָ לֹא־תִתֵּן
שְׁכָבְתְּךָ לְזָרַע לְטָמְאָה־בָהּ׃ וּמִזַּרְעֲךָ לֹא־תִתֵּן לְהַעֲבִיר לַמֹּלֶךְ

One theme emerges repeatedly and consistently: sexual ethics. Twice Abraham, and once Isaac, forced to leave home because of famine, fear that their lives will be in danger because they are married to beautiful women. They believe they are at risk of being killed so that Sarah or Rebecca can be taken into the local ruler's harem. When two angels visit Lot in Sodom, the inhabitants of the town surround Lot's house, demanding that he hand over the visitors so that they can be sexually assaulted. When Dina, Jacob's daughter, goes out to visit the women of Shekhem, she is abducted, raped, and held hostage by a local prince who has formed a passionate attachment to her. Joseph, a slave in Egypt, catches the eye of his master Potiphar's wife who attempts to seduce him and when he refuses, accuses him of rape.

The appearance of these six stories cannot be merely incidental in so highly structured a text. The implication is bold and surprising. *The fundamental difference between the life of the Abrahamic covenant and that of pagan societies is the presence in one, and the absence in the other, of a sexual ethic*: an ethic of the

SHELISHI (MAFTIR)

your God – I am the Lord. Do not lie down with a man as one lies down with a woman: that is an abominable act. Do not lie down with any animal, becoming impure through it; and no woman may stand in front of an animal to copulate with it – that is perversion. Do not become impure through any of these things, for by all these things the nations I am casting out before you became impure. And the land became impure – I made her suffer her iniquity – and the land spewed out her inhabitants. You must keep My precepts and My laws, and perform none of these abominations; no citizen and no stranger who abides among you. For the people of the land, who were there before you, performed all of these abominable acts, and the land became impure. Now do not cause the land to spew you out, by making her impure, just as she spewed out the people there before you. For anyone who performs any one of these abominations – such souls will be cut off from their people. And you must keep My charge, and never follow the abominable practices that were done before you; do not make yourselves impure through them – I am the Lord your God.

One of the signs of a polytheistic or atheistic culture – where people believe that there are many gods or none – is the absence, subjectivity or relativity of sexual ethics. Marriage is seen as one lifestyle among many. Adultery, infidelity, promiscuity, and sexual and child abuse are commonplace. Sexuality becomes the pursuit of desire. That is the world which Genesis contrasts with the life of the covenant. History supports this contention. Sexuality is often the primary force behind violence, and sexual decadence the first sign of civilizational decline.

So this passage, despite its seeming remoteness from the themes of the day, is telling us a fundamental truth about Judaism as a whole. Holiness is expressed in our most intimate relationships within the family: in the love that is loyal and generous, self-sacrificing and kind, in the sensitivity of marriage partners to one another and their needs, and in our ability to recognize the integrity-of-otherness that lies at the heart of love.

שלישי (מפטיר) וְלֹא תְחַלֵּל אֶת־שֵׁם אֱלֹהֶיךָ אֲנִי יהוה: וְאֶת־זָכָר לֹא תִשְׁכַּב
מִשְׁכְּבֵי אִשָּׁה תּוֹעֵבָה הִוא: וּבְכָל־בְּהֵמָה לֹא־תִתֵּן שְׁכָבְתְּךָ
לְטָמְאָה־בָהּ וְאִשָּׁה לֹא־תַעֲמֹד לִפְנֵי בְהֵמָה לְרִבְעָהּ תֶּבֶל הוּא:
אַל־תִּטַּמְּאוּ בְּכָל־אֵלֶּה כִּי בְכָל־אֵלֶּה נִטְמְאוּ הַגּוֹיִם אֲשֶׁר־אֲנִי
מְשַׁלֵּחַ מִפְּנֵיכֶם: וַתִּטְמָא הָאָרֶץ וָאֶפְקֹד עֲוֺנָהּ עָלֶיהָ וַתָּקִא הָאָרֶץ
אֶת־יֹשְׁבֶיהָ: וּשְׁמַרְתֶּם אַתֶּם אֶת־חֻקֹּתַי וְאֶת־מִשְׁפָּטַי וְלֹא תַעֲשׂוּ
מִכֹּל הַתּוֹעֵבֹת הָאֵלֶּה הָאֶזְרָח וְהַגֵּר הַגָּר בְּתוֹכְכֶם: כִּי אֶת־כָּל־
הַתּוֹעֵבֹת הָאֵל עָשׂוּ אַנְשֵׁי־הָאָרֶץ אֲשֶׁר לִפְנֵיכֶם וַתִּטְמָא הָאָרֶץ:
וְלֹא־תָקִיא הָאָרֶץ אֶתְכֶם בְּטַמַּאֲכֶם אֹתָהּ כַּאֲשֶׁר קָאָה אֶת־הַגּוֹי
אֲשֶׁר לִפְנֵיכֶם: כִּי כָּל־אֲשֶׁר יַעֲשֶׂה מִכֹּל הַתּוֹעֵבֹת הָאֵלֶּה וְנִכְרְתוּ
הַנְּפָשׁוֹת הָעֹשֹׂת מִקֶּרֶב עַמָּם: וּשְׁמַרְתֶּם אֶת־מִשְׁמַרְתִּי לְבִלְתִּי
עֲשׂוֹת מֵחֻקּוֹת הַתּוֹעֵבֹת אֲשֶׁר נַעֲשׂוּ לִפְנֵיכֶם וְלֹא תִטַּמְּאוּ בָּהֶם
אֲנִי יהוה אֱלֹהֵיכֶם:

---

of behavior is the desire to hand on one's genes to the next generation, or the Nietzschean "will to power." Against this, Judaism sets forth an ethic of love and loyalty, concretized in the idea of covenant, whereby two (or more) parties, each respecting the integrity of the other, come together in a bond of mutual commitment and fidelity. The human counterpart of the covenant between God and humanity is marriage as a covenant between husband and wife.

A sexual ethic is therefore not just one among many features of Judaism. It is of its essence, for there is the closest possible connection between the way we relate to God and the way we relate to those to whom we are closest: our husband or wife, and our children. That is why Genesis, the story of our beginnings, deals only cursorily with the creation of the universe, and briefly with politics (a key theme of Exodus and Deuteronomy). Instead, it is a series of narratives about families, marriage partners, parents, children, and siblings.

HAGBAHA AND GELILA

The Torah scroll is lifted and the congregation says:

וְזֹאת הַתּוֹרָה This is the Torah that Deut. 4
Moses placed before the children of Israel,
at the LORD's commandment, by the hand of Moses. Num. 9

Some add: It is a tree of life to those who grasp it, and those who uphold it are happy. Its Prov. 3
ways are ways of pleasantness, and all its paths are peace. Long life is in its
right hand; in its left, riches and honor. It pleased the LORD for the sake of Is. 42
[Israel's] righteousness, to make the Torah great and glorious.

The Torah scroll is bound and covered and the oleh for Maftir reads the Haftara.

BLESSING BEFORE READING THE HAFTARA

Before reading the Haftara, the person called up for Maftir says:

בָּרוּךְ Blessed are You, LORD our God, King of the Universe, who chose good prophets and was pleased with their words, spoken in truth. Blessed are You, LORD, who chose the Torah, His servant Moses, His people Israel, and the prophets of truth and righteousness.

HAFTARA – THE BOOK OF JONAH

The word of the LORD came to Jonah, son of Amitai, saying: "Rise up, go to the great city of Nineveh and pronounce against it, for its evil has come before Me." But Jonah rose up to flee to Tarshish, away from the LORD's presence. He went down to Jaffa and found a ship bound for Tarshish and paid his fare and went down into the ship, to come away with them to Tarshish, away from the LORD's presence. But the LORD cast a great wind down over the sea; a great storm overcame the sea, and the boat seemed about to be shattered. The sailors were terrified and cried out, each man to his god, and

---

Ezekiel and the other "minor" prophets, consist mainly of the words they spoke in the name of God. Jonah proclaims only five words in the name of God while the book consists largely of narrative, part realistic, part miraculous or symbolic. The other prophets speak mainly to Israel, while Jonah speaks solely to gentiles. Jonah is not the only prophet to prophesy *about* other nations but he is the only one to travel to the place of which he speaks:

הגבהה וגלילה

The ספר תורה *is lifted and the* קהל *says:*

וְזֹאת הַתּוֹרָה אֲשֶׁר־שָׂם מֹשֶׁה לִפְנֵי בְּנֵי יִשְׂרָאֵל׃ דברים ד
עַל־פִּי יהוה בְּיַד מֹשֶׁה׃ במדבר ט

Some add עֵץ־חַיִּים הִיא לַמַּחֲזִיקִים בָּהּ וְתֹמְכֶיהָ מְאֻשָּׁר׃ דְּרָכֶיהָ דַרְכֵי־נֹעַם משלי ג
וְכָל־נְתִיבֹתֶיהָ שָׁלוֹם׃ אֹרֶךְ יָמִים בִּימִינָהּ, בִּשְׂמֹאולָהּ עֹשֶׁר וְכָבוֹד׃
יהוה חָפֵץ לְמַעַן צִדְקוֹ יַגְדִּיל תּוֹרָה וְיַאְדִּיר׃ ישעיה מב

The ספר תורה *is bound and covered and the* עולה *for* מפטיר *reads the* הפטרה.

ברכה קודם ההפטרה

Before reading the הפטרה*, the person called up for* מפטיר *says:*

בָּרוּךְ אַתָּה יהוה אֱלֹהֵינוּ מֶלֶךְ הָעוֹלָם אֲשֶׁר בָּחַר בִּנְבִיאִים טוֹבִים, וְרָצָה בְדִבְרֵיהֶם הַנֶּאֱמָרִים בֶּאֱמֶת. בָּרוּךְ אַתָּה יהוה, הַבּוֹחֵר בַּתּוֹרָה וּבְמֹשֶׁה עַבְדּוֹ וּבְיִשְׂרָאֵל עַמּוֹ וּבִנְבִיאֵי הָאֱמֶת וָצֶדֶק.

הפטרה – ספר יונה

וַיְהִי דְּבַר־יהוה אֶל־יוֹנָה בֶן־אֲמִתַּי לֵאמֹר׃ קוּם לֵךְ אֶל־נִינְוֵה הָעִיר הַגְּדוֹלָה וּקְרָא עָלֶיהָ כִּי־עָלְתָה רָעָתָם לְפָנָי׃ וַיָּקָם יוֹנָה לִבְרֹחַ תַּרְשִׁישָׁה מִלִּפְנֵי יהוה וַיֵּרֶד יָפוֹ וַיִּמְצָא אָנִיָּה ׀ בָּאָה תַרְשִׁישׁ וַיִּתֵּן שְׂכָרָהּ וַיֵּרֶד בָּהּ לָבוֹא עִמָּהֶם תַּרְשִׁישָׁה מִלִּפְנֵי יהוה׃ וַיהוה הֵטִיל רוּחַ־גְּדוֹלָה אֶל־הַיָּם וַיְהִי סַעַר־גָּדוֹל בַּיָּם וְהָאֳנִיָּה חִשְּׁבָה לְהִשָּׁבֵר׃ וַיִּירְאוּ הַמַּלָּחִים וַיִּזְעֲקוּ אִישׁ אֶל־אֱלֹהָיו

HAFTARA: THE BOOK OF JONAH

The reason we read the book of Jonah on the afternoon of Yom Kippur is because it "shows the power of repentance" (Rabbi Mordekhai Yaffe, *Levush* 622:2), and so that the change of heart of the inhabitants of Nineveh should serve as an example to us (Rabbi Isaiah Horowitz, *Shela*).

The book of Jonah is unique. The other prophetic books, Isaiah, Jeremiah,

they cast the vessels that were on the ship out into the sea to make themselves lighter – but Jonah went down into the belly of the ship, lay down, and fell asleep.

The captain came up to him and said, "What are you thinking of, sleeper? Rise up; cry out to your god! Perhaps your god will think kindly of us and we will not be lost."

Then the men said to one another, "Come, let us draw lots, and know on whose account this evil has come to us." They let the lots fall as they would – and the lot fell to Jonah. "Tell us," they said to him, "on whose account has this evil come to us? What is your trade and where are you coming from? Which country is yours and which is your people?" And he said to them, "I am a Hebrew, and it is the LORD God of Heaven that I fear, who made both the sea and the land."

Stephen Rosenberg (*Esther, Ruth, Jonah Deciphered*, Devorah: 2004, 157–201) has proposed an ingenious historical reconstruction of the book of Jonah as a political parable. Israel during the ninth century had been threatened by Syria (Aram) who had conquered a number of the northern cities. The second book of Kings (ch. 6–7) tells the story of the siege of Samaria, capital of the northern kingdom, by the Syrian army under Ben Hadad. The city was in dire straits. Its food was exhausted. People were dying of starvation. Yet the prophet Elisha told the king that the next day the siege would be lifted and food would be plentiful. So it happened. Four lepers who lived outside the city went to the Syrian camp in the hope of finding food. They found the camp deserted. God had caused the Syrian soldiers to hear a noise sounding like an approaching army. The soldiers, fearing that Israel had hired allies (Hittites and Egyptians) to attack them, fled (II Kings 7). The Syrians could be kept in check if they feared that another military power was coming to Israel's aid.

It is against this background, Rosenberg argues, that we should read the story of Jonah. Jonah, a young disciple of Elisha (see *Yalkut Shimoni*, I Kings 223), was told by God that Nineveh, home of the Assyrian army, would safeguard Israel by being a military threat to Syria's eastern border. Syria would not attack Israel in the west if it feared possible attack on the east. Jonah was convinced that help lay nearer to hand in Tarshish (Tarsus, ruled

וַיָּטִלוּ אֶת־הַכֵּלִים אֲשֶׁר בָּאֳנִיָּה אֶל־הַיָּם לְהָקֵל מֵעֲלֵיהֶם וְיוֹנָה
יָרַד אֶל־יַרְכְּתֵי הַסְּפִינָה וַיִּשְׁכַּב וַיֵּרָדַם: וַיִּקְרַב אֵלָיו רַב הַחֹבֵל
וַיֹּאמֶר לוֹ מַה־לְּךָ נִרְדָּם קוּם קְרָא אֶל־אֱלֹהֶיךָ אוּלַי יִתְעַשֵּׁת
הָאֱלֹהִים לָנוּ וְלֹא נֹאבֵד: וַיֹּאמְרוּ אִישׁ אֶל־רֵעֵהוּ לְכוּ וְנַפִּילָה
גוֹרָלוֹת וְנֵדְעָה בְּשֶׁלְּמִי הָרָעָה הַזֹּאת לָנוּ וַיַּפִּלוּ גּוֹרָלוֹת וַיִּפֹּל
הַגּוֹרָל עַל־יוֹנָה: וַיֹּאמְרוּ אֵלָיו הַגִּידָה־נָּא לָנוּ בַּאֲשֶׁר לְמִי־הָרָעָה
הַזֹּאת לָנוּ מַה־מְּלַאכְתְּךָ וּמֵאַיִן תָּבוֹא מָה אַרְצֶךָ וְאֵי־מִזֶּה עַם
אָתָּה: וַיֹּאמֶר אֲלֵיהֶם עִבְרִי אָנֹכִי וְאֶת־יהוה אֱלֹהֵי הַשָּׁמַיִם אֲנִי
יָרֵא אֲשֶׁר־עָשָׂה אֶת־הַיָּם וְאֶת־הַיַּבָּשָׁה: וַיִּירְאוּ הָאֲנָשִׁים יִרְאָה

Nineveh, capital of Assyria. These features in themselves would mark Jonah as an unusual work, but others are stranger still.

Jonah is the only prophet who, while not doubting that God has called him, runs away. He is unique among prophets for his dramatic and immediate success. Having pronounced a single, short warning, the whole of Nineveh repents and is forgiven. Yet it is his success rather than failure that makes Jonah angry to the point of wanting to die. It was, he says, his conviction that God would forgive that made him run away in the first place. This is a strange, expectation-defying book. What does it mean, first in historical context, then in its setting here toward the end of Yom Kippur?

The book of Jonah tells us nothing of the life of the prophet before his call. A prophet with the same name, Jonah ben Amitai, is, however, mentioned in II Kings 14. The sages assume that these are the same person. If so, Jonah is one of the few prophets who lived and served in the northern kingdom ("Israel," as opposed to "Judah" in the south). The kingdom had split after the death of Solomon, the ten northern tribes following Jeroboam ben Nebat. Jonah lived in the days of his namesake, Jeroboam II, in the eighth century BCE. Described as an evil king, Jeroboam II was nonetheless a political and military success who "restored the boundaries of Israel from Levo Ḥamat to the Dead Sea, in accordance with the word of the LORD, the God of Israel, spoken through His servant Jonah son of Amitai, the prophet from Gat Ḥefer" (II Kings 14:25).

The men were filled with great fear, and said to him: "How could you do this thing?" For they knew that he was fleeing the Lord's presence, for so he had told them. They said to him, "What must we do with you to still the sea for us?" – for the sea was becoming ever stormier. And he told them, "Lift me up and cast me down into the sea, and the sea will be still for you; for I know it is on my account that this great storm has come to you."

The men oared through the waves, trying to return to land. But they could not, for the sea was becoming ever stormier around them. And they cried out to the Lord and said, "Please, Lord, please do not let us be lost on account of this man's life, and do not thrust upon us the guilt of innocent blood, for You are the Lord, and have done what You desired." Then they lifted Jonah up and cast him down into the sea; and the sea, with all its raging, became still.

And the men were filled with a great fear of the Lord, and made an offering to the Lord, and took vows.

The Lord sent a great fish to swallow Jonah; and Jonah was inside that fish's belly for three days and three nights. And Jonah prayed to the Lord his God from the belly of the fish. He said:

---

points. The first is about the nature of prophecy itself. There is a difference between a *prophecy* and a *prediction*. If a prediction comes true it has succeeded. If a prophecy comes true it has failed. A prophet does not predict: he warns. He tells of something that will happen *unless* people turn away from evil. He describes a future in order to avert it. Jonah complains to God that he has been made to look a fool. He told the people that in forty days Nineveh would be destroyed, but it was not destroyed. His words have not come true. God has to teach him that a prophecy is not a prediction. God's verdict is not final. He always leaves room for human repentance and divine forgiveness. That is a vital message on Yom Kippur.

The second is about justice and mercy. The sages said, "In the beginning God created the world through the attribute of justice, but then saw it could not survive. What did He do? He joined to it the attribute of mercy" (*Bereshit Raba* 12:15). Jonah is scandalized by the fact that the people of Nineveh were

גְּדוֹלָה וַיֹּאמְרוּ אֵלָיו מַה־זֹּאת עָשִׂיתָ כִּי־יָדְעוּ הָאֲנָשִׁים כִּי־מִלִּפְנֵי
יהוה הוּא בֹרֵחַ כִּי הִגִּיד לָהֶם׃ וַיֹּאמְרוּ אֵלָיו מַה־נַּעֲשֶׂה לָּךְ וְיִשְׁתֹּק
הַיָּם מֵעָלֵינוּ כִּי הַיָּם הוֹלֵךְ וְסֹעֵר׃ וַיֹּאמֶר אֲלֵיהֶם שָׂאוּנִי וַהֲטִילֻנִי
אֶל־הַיָּם וְיִשְׁתֹּק הַיָּם מֵעֲלֵיכֶם כִּי יוֹדֵעַ אָנִי כִּי בְשֶׁלִּי הַסַּעַר הַגָּדוֹל
הַזֶּה עֲלֵיכֶם׃ וַיַּחְתְּרוּ הָאֲנָשִׁים לְהָשִׁיב אֶל־הַיַּבָּשָׁה וְלֹא יָכֹלוּ כִּי
הַיָּם הוֹלֵךְ וְסֹעֵר עֲלֵיהֶם׃ וַיִּקְרְאוּ אֶל־יהוה וַיֹּאמְרוּ אָנָּה יהוה
אַל־נָא נֹאבְדָה בְּנֶפֶשׁ הָאִישׁ הַזֶּה וְאַל־תִּתֵּן עָלֵינוּ דָּם נָקִיא
כִּי־אַתָּה יהוה כַּאֲשֶׁר חָפַצְתָּ עָשִׂיתָ׃ וַיִּשְׂאוּ אֶת־יוֹנָה וַיְטִלֻהוּ
אֶל־הַיָּם וַיַּעֲמֹד הַיָּם מִזַּעְפּוֹ׃ וַיִּירְאוּ הָאֲנָשִׁים יִרְאָה גְדוֹלָה אֶת־
יהוה וַיִּזְבְּחוּ־זֶבַח לַיהוה וַיִּדְּרוּ נְדָרִים׃ וַיְמַן יהוה דָּג גָּדוֹל לִבְלֹעַ
אֶת־יוֹנָה וַיְהִי יוֹנָה בִּמְעֵי הַדָּג שְׁלֹשָׁה יָמִים וּשְׁלֹשָׁה לֵילוֹת׃
וַיִּתְפַּלֵּל יוֹנָה אֶל־יהוה אֱלֹהָיו מִמְּעֵי הַדָּגָה׃ וַיֹּאמֶר קָרָאתִי
מִצָּרָה לִי אֶל־יהוה וַיַּעֲנֵנִי מִבֶּטֶן שְׁאוֹל שִׁוַּעְתִּי שָׁמַעְתָּ קוֹלִי׃

---

by the Hittites). The "great fish" (*dag gadol*) that swallowed Jonah, preventing him from reaching his destination, represents the Philistines, the name of whose chief god, Dagon, may mean "great fish." Eventually Jonah came to Nineveh, whose 120,000 inhabitants correspond to the 120,000 Assyrian troops stationed there, and persuaded them of the power and righteousness of the God of Israel.

If this is so, then we can understand why Jonah was displeased. There is a precedent. God had told Elijah to anoint Ḥazael as king of Syria (I Kings 19:15). In fact it was Elisha, Elijah's successor, who did so. While he was doing so he started crying. "Why is my lord weeping?" asked Ḥazael. "Because I know the harm you will do to the Israelites," he answered (II Kings 8:12). Jonah too had an intuition of the harm the Assyrians would eventually do to Israel. In the shifting world of politics, today's allies can become tomorrow's enemies. That is one possible reading of Jonah as a political parable.

It is as a spiritual text, however, that it has eternal significance, which is why we read it on the afternoon of Yom Kippur. It makes a series of profound

From a narrow place I cry out to the LORD,
and He will answer me.
From the belly of hell I beg –
and You hear my words.
You have thrown me down into the deep, to the heart of the sea,
and the river swirls round me –
all Your torrents and storm-waves
crash over me.
I said to myself,
I am flung full away from Your sight.
But I shall yet see
Your holy Sanctuary again.
The waters rush round me to my very life's edge,
the deeps surround me,
reeds crown me.
I have sunk down to the roots of the hills,
and land is forever barred before me.
Raise my life up from the abyss,
LORD my God.
As my spirit faints away in me,
the LORD comes to my mind –
and then my prayer comes to You,
it comes to Your holy Sanctuary.
Those who put hope in futile gods
will all forsake their faithfulness.
But I shall yet bring You offerings, along with thankful words.
I shall fulfill what I have vowed.
Salvation belongs to the LORD.

And the LORD spoke to the fish, and it spat Jonah out onto the shore.

So the word of the LORD came to Jonah a second time, saying: "Rise up, go to the great city of Nineveh and pronounce against it the words that I shall speak to you." And Jonah arose and went to

וַתַּשְׁלִיכֵנִי מְצוּלָה בִּלְבַב יַמִּים וְנָהָר יְסֹבְבֵנִי כָּל־מִשְׁבָּרֶיךָ וְגַלֶּיךָ
עָלַי עָבָרוּ: וַאֲנִי אָמַרְתִּי נִגְרַשְׁתִּי מִנֶּגֶד עֵינֶיךָ אַךְ אוֹסִיף לְהַבִּיט
אֶל־הֵיכַל קָדְשֶׁךָ: אֲפָפוּנִי מַיִם עַד־נֶפֶשׁ תְּהוֹם יְסֹבְבֵנִי סוּף חָבוּשׁ
לְרֹאשִׁי: לְקִצְבֵי הָרִים יָרַדְתִּי הָאָרֶץ בְּרִחֶיהָ בַעֲדִי לְעוֹלָם וַתַּעַל
מִשַּׁחַת חַיַּי יהוה אֱלֹהָי: בְּהִתְעַטֵּף עָלַי נַפְשִׁי אֶת־יהוה זָכָרְתִּי
וַתָּבוֹא אֵלֶיךָ תְּפִלָּתִי אֶל־הֵיכַל קָדְשֶׁךָ: מְשַׁמְּרִים הַבְלֵי־שָׁוְא
חַסְדָּם יַעֲזֹבוּ: וַאֲנִי בְּקוֹל תּוֹדָה אֶזְבְּחָה־לָּךְ אֲשֶׁר נָדַרְתִּי אֲשַׁלֵּמָה
יְשׁוּעָתָה לַיהוה: וַיֹּאמֶר יהוה לַדָּג וַיָּקֵא אֶת־יוֹנָה
אֶל־הַיַּבָּשָׁה: וַיְהִי דְבַר־יהוה אֶל־יוֹנָה שֵׁנִית לֵאמֹר:
קוּם לֵךְ אֶל־נִינְוֵה הָעִיר הַגְּדוֹלָה וּקְרָא אֵלֶיהָ אֶת־הַקְּרִיאָה

---

not punished for their wickedness. Justice demands no less. Yet God forgave them, as Jonah knew He would, since the God of Israel is a God of mercy. God has to teach Jonah a moral lesson. As humans we are inconsistent. We pray for mercy for ourselves but for strict justice for our enemies. But God is the creator of all: "He has compassion on all He has made" (Ps. 145:9). He shows mercy to all who repent, and mercy is something other and gentler than justice. There cannot be perfect justice in a world of imperfect humans. The world survives through divine forgiveness, and while we seek it for ourselves we cannot deny it to our enemies.

The third and most challenging feature of the book is the extraordinarily positive light in which it paints gentiles – who in Jonah's time were pagans and polytheists. We see this twice: not only in the alacrity in which the people of Nineveh repent, but also in the way the first chapter describes the sailors in Jonah's ship threatened by the storm. While Jonah is sleeping, they are praying. When they realize that the storm is because of Jonah, Jonah tells them to throw him in the sea, but they are reluctant to do so. They do not want to be responsible for his death if there is any other chance of reaching safety. Eventually they have no other choice, but the text tells us that they prayed to the Lord, feared Him, and made an offering and vows to Him.

The sailors and the people of Nineveh are two of several instances in which the Tanakh goes out of its way to emphasize the goodness of those who stand

Nineveh as the Lord had said. Nineveh was an immensely great city, three full days' walk across. Jonah entered a day's walk into Nineveh and pronounced, "Forty more days, and Nineveh will all be overturned!" And the people of Nineveh had faith in God, and declared a fast and dressed themselves in sackcloth, from the greatest of them to the least. Word reached the king of Nineveh and he rose from his throne and took off his royal mantle; he covered himself with sackcloth and sat upon ashes. And it was called out in Nineveh, in the name of the king and his nobles: "Let no person or animal, cattle or flock, taste any morsel – let them not pasture, let them drink no water. All shall be covered in sackcloth – man and beast – and shall cry out to God with a powerful cry; let every man turn back from his evil way, and from the violence that fills his hands. Who knows – perhaps God, too, will turn back and relent; will turn back from His burning rage, before we are all lost." And God saw their actions, that they had turned back from their evil way; and God relented the evil He had spoken of inflicting on them, and did not act upon it.

To Jonah this was a great evil, and it filled him with rage. He prayed to the Lord and said: "Please, Lord, is this not just what I said while I was still on my own land? This is why I first fled toward Tarshish – because I knew that You are a gracious and compassionate God, slow to anger, abounding in loving-kindness and relenting of evil. And now, Lord, please take my soul away from me, for death would be better than my life."

The Lord said, "Are you so enraged?"

Jonah left the city and sat down to its east, and there he made

---

At this sacred moment the book of Jonah delivers an awesome challenge to us. It is as if God Himself were whispering to us: Shall others fear God while we forsake Him? Is it conceivable that Jews, the people who predicated their very survival on faith, should lose their faith and become a secular people, a mere ethnic group among others? Shall our enemies believe and we not believe? Israel's strength, its greatness, its incomparable record of survival,

אֲשֶׁר אָנֹכִי דֹּבֵר אֵלֶיךָ: וַיָּקָם יוֹנָה וַיֵּלֶךְ אֶל־נִינְוֵה כִּדְבַר יהוה
וְנִינְוֵה הָיְתָה עִיר־גְּדוֹלָה לֵאלֹהִים מַהֲלַךְ שְׁלֹשֶׁת יָמִים: וַיָּחֶל
יוֹנָה לָבוֹא בָעִיר מַהֲלַךְ יוֹם אֶחָד וַיִּקְרָא וַיֹּאמַר עוֹד אַרְבָּעִים
יוֹם וְנִינְוֵה נֶהְפָּכֶת: וַיַּאֲמִינוּ אַנְשֵׁי נִינְוֵה בֵּאלֹהִים וַיִּקְרְאוּ־צוֹם
וַיִּלְבְּשׁוּ שַׂקִּים מִגְּדוֹלָם וְעַד־קְטַנָּם: וַיִּגַּע הַדָּבָר אֶל־מֶלֶךְ נִינְוֵה
וַיָּקָם מִכִּסְאוֹ וַיַּעֲבֵר אַדַּרְתּוֹ מֵעָלָיו וַיְכַס שַׂק וַיֵּשֶׁב עַל־הָאֵפֶר:
וַיַּזְעֵק וַיֹּאמֶר בְּנִינְוֵה מִטַּעַם הַמֶּלֶךְ וּגְדֹלָיו לֵאמֹר הָאָדָם וְהַבְּהֵמָה
הַבָּקָר וְהַצֹּאן אַל־יִטְעֲמוּ מְאוּמָה אַל־יִרְעוּ וּמַיִם אַל־יִשְׁתּוּ:
וְיִתְכַּסּוּ שַׂקִּים הָאָדָם וְהַבְּהֵמָה וְיִקְרְאוּ אֶל־אֱלֹהִים בְּחָזְקָה
וְיָשֻׁבוּ אִישׁ מִדַּרְכּוֹ הָרָעָה וּמִן־הֶחָמָס אֲשֶׁר בְּכַפֵּיהֶם: מִי־יוֹדֵעַ
יָשׁוּב וְנִחַם הָאֱלֹהִים וְשָׁב מֵחֲרוֹן אַפּוֹ וְלֹא נֹאבֵד: וַיַּרְא הָאֱלֹהִים
אֶת־מַעֲשֵׂיהֶם כִּי־שָׁבוּ מִדַּרְכָּם הָרָעָה וַיִּנָּחֶם הָאֱלֹהִים עַל־הָרָעָה
אֲשֶׁר־דִּבֶּר לַעֲשׂוֹת־לָהֶם וְלֹא עָשָׂה: וַיֵּרַע אֶל־יוֹנָה רָעָה גְדוֹלָה
וַיִּחַר לוֹ: וַיִּתְפַּלֵּל אֶל־יהוה וַיֹּאמַר אָנָּה יהוה הֲלוֹא־זֶה דְבָרִי
עַד־הֱיוֹתִי עַל־אַדְמָתִי עַל־כֵּן קִדַּמְתִּי לִבְרֹחַ תַּרְשִׁישָׁה כִּי יָדַעְתִּי
כִּי אַתָּה אֵל־חַנּוּן וְרַחוּם אֶרֶךְ אַפַּיִם וְרַב־חֶסֶד וְנִחָם עַל־הָרָעָה:
וְעַתָּה יהוה קַח־נָא אֶת־נַפְשִׁי מִמֶּנִּי כִּי טוֹב מוֹתִי מֵחַיָּי: וַיֹּאמֶר
יהוה הַהֵיטֵב חָרָה לָךְ: וַיֵּצֵא יוֹנָה מִן־הָעִיר וַיֵּשֶׁב מִקֶּדֶם לָעִיר

---

outside the Abrahamic covenant. Malkitzedek, Abraham's contemporary, is one. Pharaoh's daughter who saves the life of Moses is another. At the heart of Judaism is a duality between the covenant God makes with all humanity (the Noahide covenant) and the one He makes first with Abraham, then with Moses and the Israelites. Universality and particularity are at the center of Judaism. No other great faith has this structure. There is a relationship with God we share with others, and there is a relationship with God unique to the Jewish people. At times Jews have tended to forget one or other of these truths but they are both true.

himself a shelter, and sat in the shade beneath it to wait and see what would become of the city. The LORD sent a castor-oil plant, which grew up above Jonah to be shade above his head, to spare him torment; and Jonah rejoiced over this plant with great joy. And the LORD sent a worm as dawn broke the next morning, and it attacked the castor-oil plant and it withered. And as the sun rose, God sent a blasting east wind, and the sun beat down on Jonah's head and he collapsed, and longed in his soul to die. He said, "Death would be better than my life."

God said to Jonah, "Are you so enraged over the castor-oil plant?" And Jonah said, "I am enraged enough to die."

And the LORD said, "You cared about that plant, which you did not toil for and did not grow, which appeared overnight and was lost overnight. And am I not to care for the great city of Nineveh, which has more than a hundred and twenty thousand people in it – who do not know their right hands from their left – and many animals?"

Most congregations add:

מִי אֵל כָּמְוֹךָ Who, God, is like You, who forgives iniquity and over- *Mic. 7:18–20*
looks the transgression of the remnant of Your heritage? He does not remain angry forever, for He desires loving-kindness. He shall relent and show us compassion, He shall suppress our iniquities, casting all of our sins into the depths of the sea. And all the sins of Your nation, the house of Israel, cast them down where they shall not be remembered nor recalled nor come to mind ever again. Grant truth to Jacob, loving-kindness to Abraham, as You promised our ancestors in ancient times.

---

be us but our sins that will be cast into the sea. The casting of Jonah into the water ended the storm and calmed the waves. The casting of our sins ends the storm of guilt and calms the waves of self-doubt. And just as Jonah was saved from death, so, we pray, will we.

וַיַּעַשׂ לוֹ שָׁם סֻכָּה וַיֵּשֶׁב תַּחְתֶּיהָ בַּצֵּל עַד אֲשֶׁר יִרְאֶה מַה־יִּהְיֶה
בָּעִיר: וַיְמַן יהוה־אֱלֹהִים קִיקָיוֹן וַיַּעַל ׀ מֵעַל לְיוֹנָה לִהְיוֹת צֵל
עַל־רֹאשׁוֹ לְהַצִּיל לוֹ מֵרָעָתוֹ וַיִּשְׂמַח יוֹנָה עַל־הַקִּיקָיוֹן שִׂמְחָה
גְדוֹלָה: וַיְמַן הָאֱלֹהִים תּוֹלַעַת בַּעֲלוֹת הַשַּׁחַר לַמָּחֳרָת וַתַּךְ
אֶת־הַקִּיקָיוֹן וַיִּיבָשׁ: וַיְהִי ׀ כִּזְרֹחַ הַשֶּׁמֶשׁ וַיְמַן אֱלֹהִים רוּחַ קָדִים
חֲרִישִׁית וַתַּךְ הַשֶּׁמֶשׁ עַל־רֹאשׁ יוֹנָה וַיִּתְעַלָּף וַיִּשְׁאַל אֶת־נַפְשׁוֹ
לָמוּת וַיֹּאמֶר טוֹב מוֹתִי מֵחַיָּי: וַיֹּאמֶר אֱלֹהִים אֶל־יוֹנָה הַהֵיטֵב
חָרָה־לְךָ עַל־הַקִּיקָיוֹן וַיֹּאמֶר הֵיטֵב חָרָה־לִי עַד־מָוֶת: וַיֹּאמֶר
יהוה אַתָּה חַסְתָּ עַל־הַקִּיקָיוֹן אֲשֶׁר לֹא־עָמַלְתָּ בּוֹ וְלֹא גִדַּלְתּוֹ
שֶׁבִּן־לַיְלָה הָיָה וּבִן־לַיְלָה אָבָד: וַאֲנִי לֹא אָחוּס עַל־נִינְוֵה הָעִיר
הַגְּדוֹלָה אֲשֶׁר יֶשׁ־בָּהּ הַרְבֵּה מִשְׁתֵּים־עֶשְׂרֵה רִבּוֹ אָדָם אֲשֶׁר
לֹא־יָדַע בֵּין־יְמִינוֹ לִשְׂמֹאלוֹ וּבְהֵמָה רַבָּה:

Most congregations add:

מיכה ז, יח–כ מִי־אֵל כָּמוֹךָ נֹשֵׂא עָוֹן וְעֹבֵר עַל־פֶּשַׁע לִשְׁאֵרִית נַחֲלָתוֹ לֹא־
הֶחֱזִיק לָעַד אַפּוֹ כִּי־חָפֵץ חֶסֶד הוּא: יָשׁוּב יְרַחֲמֵנוּ יִכְבֹּשׁ עֲוֹנֹתֵינוּ
וְתַשְׁלִיךְ בִּמְצֻלוֹת יָם כָּל־חַטֹּאתָם: תִּתֵּן אֱמֶת לְיַעֲקֹב חֶסֶד
לְאַבְרָהָם אֲשֶׁר־נִשְׁבַּעְתָּ לַאֲבֹתֵינוּ מִימֵי קֶדֶם:

---

has always come from its dedication to God. Where then is ours? That is the question Jonah poses to us on Yom Kippur, and its answer lies in the passion in which we say Ne'ila's closing words, the most ringing affirmation of faith in the entire prayerbook.

מִי־אֵל כָּמוֹךָ *Who, God, is like You.* The custom is to end with three verses from Micah, usually also said on Rosh HaShana at *Tashlikh*, the "casting" ceremony. In the present context there is a fine play of intertextuality between Jonah and the later prophet. Jonah is cast into the sea; Micah says, in effect, it will not

BLESSINGS AFTER THE HAFTARA

After the Haftara, the person called up for Maftir says the following blessings:

בָּרוּךְ Blessed are You, LORD our God, King of the Universe, Rock of all worlds, righteous for all generations, the faithful God who says and does, speaks and fulfills, all of whose words are truth and righteousness. You are faithful, LORD our God, and faithful are Your words, not one of which returns unfulfilled, for You, God, are a faithful (and compassionate) King. Blessed are You, LORD, faithful in all His words.

רַחֵם Have compassion on Zion for it is the source of our life, and save the one grieved in spirit swiftly in our days. Blessed are You, LORD, who makes Zion rejoice in her children.

שַׂמְּחֵנוּ Grant us joy, LORD our God, through Elijah the prophet Your servant, and through the kingdom of the house of David Your anointed – may he soon come and make our hearts glad. May no stranger sit on his throne, and may others not continue to inherit his glory, for You promised him by Your holy name that his light would never be extinguished. Blessed are You, LORD, Shield of David.

RETURNING THE TORAH TO THE ARK

The Ark is opened. The Leader takes the Torah scroll and says:

יְהַלְלוּ Let them praise the name of the LORD, *Ps. 148*
for His name alone is sublime.

The congregation responds:

הוֹדוֹ His majesty is above earth and heaven.
He has raised the horn of His people,
for the glory of all His devoted ones,
the children of Israel, the people close to Him.
Halleluya!

Haftara on Sabbaths and festivals are said here. Our custom, however, is to say three. The issue at stake is the dual character of Yom Kippur. On the one hand it is a festival, listed as such throughout the Torah. On the other hand

ברכות לאחר ההפטרה

After the הפטרה*, the person called up for* מפטיר *says the following blessings:*

בָּרוּךְ אַתָּה יהוה אֱלֹהֵינוּ מֶלֶךְ הָעוֹלָם, צוּר כָּל הָעוֹלָמִים, צַדִּיק בְּכָל הַדּוֹרוֹת, הָאֵל הַנֶּאֱמָן, הָאוֹמֵר וְעוֹשֶׂה, הַמְדַבֵּר וּמְקַיֵּם, שֶׁכָּל דְּבָרָיו אֱמֶת וָצֶדֶק. נֶאֱמָן אַתָּה הוּא יהוה אֱלֹהֵינוּ וְנֶאֱמָנִים דְּבָרֶיךָ, וְדָבָר אֶחָד מִדְּבָרֶיךָ אָחוֹר לֹא יָשׁוּב רֵיקָם, כִּי אֵל מֶלֶךְ נֶאֱמָן (וְרַחֲמָן) אָתָּה. בָּרוּךְ אַתָּה יהוה, הָאֵל הַנֶּאֱמָן בְּכָל דְּבָרָיו.

רַחֵם עַל צִיּוֹן כִּי הִיא בֵּית חַיֵּינוּ, וְלַעֲלוּבַת נֶפֶשׁ תּוֹשִׁיעַ בִּמְהֵרָה בְיָמֵינוּ. בָּרוּךְ אַתָּה יהוה, מְשַׂמֵּחַ צִיּוֹן בְּבָנֶיהָ.

שַׂמְּחֵנוּ יהוה אֱלֹהֵינוּ בְּאֵלִיָּהוּ הַנָּבִיא עַבְדֶּךָ, וּבְמַלְכוּת בֵּית דָּוִד מְשִׁיחֶךָ, בִּמְהֵרָה יָבוֹא וְיָגֵל לִבֵּנוּ. עַל כִּסְאוֹ לֹא יֵשֶׁב זָר, וְלֹא יִנְחֲלוּ עוֹד אֲחֵרִים אֶת כְּבוֹדוֹ, כִּי בְשֵׁם קָדְשְׁךָ נִשְׁבַּעְתָּ לוֹ שֶׁלֹּא יִכְבֶּה נֵרוֹ לְעוֹלָם וָעֶד. בָּרוּךְ אַתָּה יהוה, מָגֵן דָּוִד.

הכנסת ספר תורה

The ארון קודש *is opened. The* שליח ציבור *takes the* ספר תורה *and says:*

יְהַלְלוּ אֶת־שֵׁם יהוה, כִּי־נִשְׂגָּב שְׁמוֹ, לְבַדּוֹ תהלים קמח

The קהל *responds:*

הוֹדוֹ עַל־אֶרֶץ וְשָׁמָיִם:
וַיָּרֶם קֶרֶן לְעַמּוֹ
תְּהִלָּה לְכָל־חֲסִידָיו
לִבְנֵי יִשְׂרָאֵל עַם קְרֹבוֹ
הַלְלוּיָהּ:

BLESSINGS AFTER THE HAFTARA

Some halakhic authorities held that the usual four blessings said after a

As the Torah scroll is returned to the Ark say:

לְדָוִד מִזְמוֹר A psalm of David. The earth is the LORD's and all it *Ps. 24*
contains, the world and all who live in it. For He founded it on the seas and established it on the streams. Who may climb the mountain of the LORD? Who may stand in His holy place? He who has clean hands and a pure heart, who has not taken My name in vain, or sworn deceitfully. He shall receive blessing from the LORD, and just reward from God, his salvation. This is a generation of those who seek Him, the descendants of Jacob who seek Your presence, Selah! Lift up your heads, O gates; be uplifted, eternal doors, so that the King of glory may enter. Who is the King of glory? It is the LORD, strong and mighty, the LORD mighty in battle. Lift up your heads, O gates; lift them up, eternal doors, so that the King of glory may enter. Who is He, the King of glory? The LORD of hosts, He is the King of glory, Selah!

As the Torah scroll is placed into the Ark, say:

וּבְנֻחֹה יֹאמַר When the Ark came to rest, Moses would say: "Return, *Num. 10*
O LORD, to the myriad thousands of Israel." Advance, LORD, to *Ps. 132*
Your resting place, You and Your mighty Ark. Your priests are clothed in righteousness, and Your devoted ones sing in joy. For the sake of Your servant David, do not reject Your anointed one.
For I give you good instruction; do not forsake My Torah. ▸ It is a *Prov. 4* *Prov. 3*
tree of life to those who grasp it, and those who uphold it are happy.
Its ways are ways of pleasantness, and all its paths are peace. Turn us *Lam. 5*
back, O LORD, to You, and we will return. Renew our days as of old.

The Ark is closed.

---

do with fasting and repentance. Therefore the fourth blessing of the Haftara, which has to do with the day as festival, is not said.

As the ספר תורה *is returned to the* ארון קודש*, say:*

לְדָוִד מִזְמוֹר, לַיהוה הָאָרֶץ וּמְלוֹאָהּ, תֵּבֵל וְיֹשְׁבֵי בָהּ: כִּי־הוּא תהלים כד
עַל־יַמִּים יְסָדָהּ, וְעַל־נְהָרוֹת יְכוֹנְנֶהָ: מִי־יַעֲלֶה בְהַר־יהוה,
וּמִי־יָקוּם בִּמְקוֹם קָדְשׁוֹ: נְקִי כַפַּיִם וּבַר־לֵבָב, אֲשֶׁר לֹא־נָשָׂא
לַשָּׁוְא נַפְשִׁי וְלֹא נִשְׁבַּע לְמִרְמָה: יִשָּׂא בְרָכָה מֵאֵת יהוה, וּצְדָקָה
מֵאֱלֹהֵי יִשְׁעוֹ: זֶה דּוֹר דֹּרְשָׁו, מְבַקְשֵׁי פָנֶיךָ, יַעֲקֹב, סֶלָה: שְׂאוּ
שְׁעָרִים רָאשֵׁיכֶם, וְהִנָּשְׂאוּ פִּתְחֵי עוֹלָם, וְיָבוֹא מֶלֶךְ הַכָּבוֹד:
מִי זֶה מֶלֶךְ הַכָּבוֹד, יהוה עִזּוּז וְגִבּוֹר, יהוה גִּבּוֹר מִלְחָמָה: שְׂאוּ
שְׁעָרִים רָאשֵׁיכֶם, וּשְׂאוּ פִּתְחֵי עוֹלָם, וְיָבֹא מֶלֶךְ הַכָּבוֹד: מִי הוּא
זֶה מֶלֶךְ הַכָּבוֹד, יהוה צְבָאוֹת הוּא מֶלֶךְ הַכָּבוֹד, סֶלָה:

As the ספר תורה *is placed into the* ארון קודש*, say:*

וּבְנֻחֹה יֹאמַר, שׁוּבָה יהוה רִבְבוֹת אַלְפֵי יִשְׂרָאֵל: קוּמָה יהוה במדבר י תהלים קלב
לִמְנוּחָתֶךָ, אַתָּה וַאֲרוֹן עֻזֶּךָ: כֹּהֲנֶיךָ יִלְבְּשׁוּ־צֶדֶק, וַחֲסִידֶיךָ יְרַנֵּנוּ:
בַּעֲבוּר דָּוִד עַבְדֶּךָ אַל־תָּשֵׁב פְּנֵי מְשִׁיחֶךָ: כִּי לֶקַח טוֹב נָתַתִּי משלי ד
לָכֶם, תּוֹרָתִי אַל־תַּעֲזֹבוּ: ‹ עֵץ־חַיִּים הִיא לַמַּחֲזִיקִים בָּהּ, וְתֹמְכֶיהָ משלי ג
מְאֻשָּׁר: דְּרָכֶיהָ דַרְכֵי־נֹעַם וְכָל־נְתִיבוֹתֶיהָ שָׁלוֹם: הֲשִׁיבֵנוּ יהוה איכה ה
אֵלֶיךָ וְנָשׁוּבָה, חַדֵּשׁ יָמֵינוּ כְּקֶדֶם:

The ארון קודש *is closed.*

---

it is also a penitential fast. Is the afternoon Haftara a consequence of the first or the second? Most held it was because of the fast-character rather than the festival-character of the day. That is evident in the subject of the Haftara. It has nothing to do with the Torah reading that precedes it, and everything to

HALF KADDISH

Leader: יִתְגַּדַּל Magnified and sanctified
may His great name be,
in the world He created by His will.
May He establish His kingdom
in your lifetime and in your days,
and in the lifetime of all the house of Israel,
swiftly and soon – and say: Amen.

All: May His great name be blessed for ever and all time.

Leader: Blessed and praised, glorified and exalted,
raised and honored, uplifted and lauded
be the name of the Holy One, blessed be He,
above and beyond any blessing, song,
praise and consolation uttered in the world –
and say: Amen.

THE AMIDA

The following prayer, until "in former years" on page 1038, is said silently, standing with feet together. If there is a minyan, the Amida is repeated aloud by the Leader. Take three steps forward and at the points indicated by ˅, bend the knees at the first word, bow at the second, and stand straight before saying God's name.

When I proclaim the LORD's name, give glory to our God. *Deut. 32*
O LORD, open my lips, so that my mouth may declare Your praise. *Ps. 51*

PATRIARCHS

˅בָּרוּךְ Blessed are You, LORD our God and God of our fathers,
God of Abraham, God of Isaac and God of Jacob;
the great, mighty and awesome God, God Most High,
who bestows acts of loving-kindness and creates all,
who remembers the loving-kindness of the fathers
and will bring a Redeemer to their children's children
for the sake of His name, in love.

חצי קדיש

ש״ץ: יִתְגַּדַּל וְיִתְקַדַּשׁ שְׁמֵהּ רַבָּא (קהל: אָמֵן)
בְּעָלְמָא דִּי בְרָא כִרְעוּתֵהּ
וְיַמְלִיךְ מַלְכוּתֵהּ
בְּחַיֵּיכוֹן וּבְיוֹמֵיכוֹן, וּבְחַיֵּי דְכָל בֵּית יִשְׂרָאֵל
בַּעֲגָלָא וּבִזְמַן קָרִיב, וְאִמְרוּ אָמֵן. (קהל: אָמֵן)

קהל וש״ץ: יְהֵא שְׁמֵהּ רַבָּא מְבָרַךְ לְעָלַם וּלְעָלְמֵי עָלְמַיָּא.

ש״ץ: יִתְבָּרַךְ וְיִשְׁתַּבַּח וְיִתְפָּאַר וְיִתְרוֹמַם וְיִתְנַשֵּׂא
וְיִתְהַדָּר וְיִתְעַלֶּה וְיִתְהַלָּל
שְׁמֵהּ דְּקֻדְשָׁא בְּרִיךְ הוּא (קהל: בְּרִיךְ הוּא)
לְעֵלָּא לְעֵלָּא מִכָּל בִּרְכָתָא וְשִׁירָתָא, תֻּשְׁבְּחָתָא וְנֶחֱמָתָא
דַּאֲמִירָן בְּעָלְמָא, וְאִמְרוּ אָמֵן. (קהל: אָמֵן)

עמידה

The following prayer, until קַדְמֹנִיּוֹת *on page 1039, is said silently, standing with feet together. If there is a* מנין*, the* עמידה *is repeated aloud by the* שליח ציבור*. Take three steps forward and at the points indicated by* ˅*, bend the knees at the first word, bow at the second, and stand straight before saying God's name.*

כִּי שֵׁם יהוה אֶקְרָא, הָבוּ גֹדֶל לֵאלֹהֵינוּ: דברים לב
אֲדֹנָי, שְׂפָתַי תִּפְתָּח, וּפִי יַגִּיד תְּהִלָּתֶךָ: תהלים נא

אבות

˅בָּרוּךְ אַתָּה יהוה, אֱלֹהֵינוּ וֵאלֹהֵי אֲבוֹתֵינוּ
אֱלֹהֵי אַבְרָהָם, אֱלֹהֵי יִצְחָק, וֵאלֹהֵי יַעֲקֹב
הָאֵל הַגָּדוֹל הַגִּבּוֹר וְהַנּוֹרָא, אֵל עֶלְיוֹן
גּוֹמֵל חֲסָדִים טוֹבִים, וְקוֹנֵה הַכֹּל
וְזוֹכֵר חַסְדֵי אָבוֹת
וּמֵבִיא גוֹאֵל לִבְנֵי בְנֵיהֶם לְמַעַן שְׁמוֹ בְּאַהֲבָה.

זָכְרֵנוּ לְחַיִּים Remember us for life,
O King who desires life,
and write us in the book of life –
for Your sake, O God of life.
King, Helper, Savior, Shield:
▾Blessed are You, Lord,
Shield of Abraham.

DIVINE MIGHT

אַתָּה גִּבּוֹר You are eternally mighty, Lord.
You give life to the dead
and have great power to save.

In Israel: He causes the dew to fall.

He sustains the living with loving-kindness,
and with great compassion revives the dead.
He supports the fallen,
heals the sick,
sets captives free,
and keeps His faith with those who sleep in the dust.
Who is like You, Master of might,
and to whom can You be compared,
O King who brings death and gives life,
and makes salvation grow?

מִי כָמוֹךָ Who is like You,
compassionate Father,
who remembers His creatures
in compassion, for life?
Faithful are You to revive the dead.
Blessed are You, Lord,
who revives the dead.

זָכְרֵנוּ לְחַיִּים, מֶלֶךְ חָפֵץ בַּחַיִּים
וְכָתְבֵנוּ בְּסֵפֶר הַחַיִּים, לְמַעַנְךָ אֱלֹהִים חַיִּים.
מֶלֶךְ עוֹזֵר וּמוֹשִׁיעַ וּמָגֵן.
ּבָּרוּךְ אַתָּה יהוה, מָגֵן אַבְרָהָם.

גבורות

אַתָּה גִּבּוֹר לְעוֹלָם, אֲדֹנָי
מְחַיֵּה מֵתִים אַתָּה, רַב לְהוֹשִׁיעַ
בארץ ישראל: מוֹרִיד הַטָּל
מְכַלְכֵּל חַיִּים בְּחֶסֶד
מְחַיֵּה מֵתִים בְּרַחֲמִים רַבִּים
סוֹמֵךְ נוֹפְלִים
וְרוֹפֵא חוֹלִים
וּמַתִּיר אֲסוּרִים
וּמְקַיֵּם אֱמוּנָתוֹ לִישֵׁנֵי עָפָר.
מִי כָמוֹךָ, בַּעַל גְּבוּרוֹת
וּמִי דּוֹמֶה לָּךְ
מֶלֶךְ, מֵמִית וּמְחַיֶּה
וּמַצְמִיחַ יְשׁוּעָה.

מִי כָמוֹךָ אַב הָרַחֲמִים
זוֹכֵר יְצוּרָיו לְחַיִּים בְּרַחֲמִים.
וְנֶאֱמָן אַתָּה לְהַחֲיוֹת מֵתִים.
בָּרוּךְ אַתָּה יהוה, מְחַיֵּה הַמֵּתִים.

HOLINESS

אַתָּה קָדוֹשׁ You are holy and Your name is holy,
and holy ones praise You daily, Selah!

וּבְכֵן תֵּן פַּחְדְּךָ And so place the fear of You, Lord our God,
over all that You have made,
and the terror of You over all You have created,
and all who were made will stand in awe of You,
and all of creation will worship You
and they will be bound all together as one
to carry out Your will with an undivided heart;
for we know, Lord our God,
that all dominion is laid out before You,
strength is in Your palm,
and might in Your right hand,
Your name spreading awe
over all You have created.

וּבְכֵן תֵּן כָּבוֹד And so place honor,
Lord, upon Your people,
praise on those who fear You
and hope into those who seek You,
the confidence to speak
into all who long for You,
gladness to Your land and joy to Your city,
the flourishing of pride to David Your servant,
and a lamp laid out for his descendant, Your anointed,
soon, in our days.

וּבְכֵן צַדִּיקִים And then righteous people will see and rejoice,
and the upright will exult,
and the pious revel in joy,
and injustice will have nothing more to say,
and all wickedness will fade away like smoke
as You sweep the rule of arrogance from the earth.

קדושת השם

אַתָּה קָדוֹשׁ וְשִׁמְךָ קָדוֹשׁ
וּקְדוֹשִׁים בְּכָל יוֹם יְהַלְלוּךָ סֶּלָה.

וּבְכֵן תֵּן פַּחְדְּךָ יהוה אֱלֹהֵינוּ עַל כָּל מַעֲשֶׂיךָ
וְאֵימָתְךָ עַל כָּל מַה שֶּׁבָּרָאתָ
וְיִירָאוּךָ כָּל הַמַּעֲשִׂים
וְיִשְׁתַּחֲווּ לְפָנֶיךָ כָּל הַבְּרוּאִים
וְיֵעָשׂוּ כֻלָּם אֲגֻדָּה אַחַת לַעֲשׂוֹת רְצוֹנְךָ בְּלֵבָב שָׁלֵם
כְּמוֹ שֶׁיָּדַעְנוּ יהוה אֱלֹהֵינוּ שֶׁהַשָּׁלְטָן לְפָנֶיךָ
עֹז בְּיָדְךָ וּגְבוּרָה בִּימִינֶךָ
וְשִׁמְךָ נוֹרָא עַל כָּל מַה שֶּׁבָּרָאתָ.

וּבְכֵן תֵּן כָּבוֹד יהוה לְעַמֶּךָ
תְּהִלָּה לִירֵאֶיךָ
וְתִקְוָה טוֹבָה לְדוֹרְשֶׁיךָ
וּפִתְחוֹן פֶּה לַמְיַחֲלִים לָךְ
שִׂמְחָה לְאַרְצֶךָ, וְשָׂשׂוֹן לְעִירֶךָ
וּצְמִיחַת קֶרֶן לְדָוִד עַבְדֶּךָ
וַעֲרִיכַת נֵר לְבֶן יִשַׁי מְשִׁיחֶךָ
בִּמְהֵרָה בְיָמֵינוּ.

וּבְכֵן צַדִּיקִים יִרְאוּ וְיִשְׂמָחוּ, וִישָׁרִים יַעֲלֹזוּ
וַחֲסִידִים בְּרִנָּה יָגִילוּ, וְעוֹלָתָה תִּקְפָּץ פִּיהָ
וְכָל הָרִשְׁעָה כֻּלָּהּ כְּעָשָׁן תִּכְלֶה
כִּי תַעֲבִיר מֶמְשֶׁלֶת זָדוֹן מִן הָאָרֶץ.

וְתִמְלֹךְ אַתָּה And You, LORD,
will rule alone over those You have made,
in Mount Zion, the dwelling of Your glory,
and in Jerusalem, Your holy city,
as it is written in Your holy Writings:
"The LORD shall reign for ever. *Ps. 146*
He is your God, Zion,
from generation to generation, Halleluya!"

קָדוֹשׁ אַתָּה You are holy, Your name is awesome,
and there is no god but You,
as it is written:
"The LORD of hosts shall be raised up *Is. 5*
through His judgment,
the holy God, made holy in righteousness."
Blessed are You, LORD, the holy King.

HOLINESS OF THE DAY

אַתָּה בְחַרְתָּנוּ You have chosen us from among all peoples.
You have loved and favored us.
You have raised us above all tongues.
You have made us holy through Your commandments.
You have brought us near, our King, to Your service,
and have called us by Your great and holy name.

On Shabbat, add the words in parentheses:

וַתִּתֶּן לָנוּ And You, LORD our God,
have given us in love
(this Sabbath day for holiness and rest, and)
this Day of Atonement
for pardon and forgiveness and atonement,
to pardon all our iniquities,
(with love,) a holy assembly
in memory of the exodus from Egypt.

וְתִמְלֹךְ אַתָּה יהוה לְבַדֶּךָ עַל כָּל מַעֲשֶׂיךָ
בְּהַר צִיּוֹן מִשְׁכַּן כְּבוֹדֶךָ
וּבִירוּשָׁלַיִם עִיר קָדְשֶׁךָ
כַּכָּתוּב בְּדִבְרֵי קָדְשֶׁךָ
יִמְלֹךְ יהוה לְעוֹלָם תהלים קמו
אֱלֹהַיִךְ צִיּוֹן לְדֹר וָדֹר, הַלְלוּיָהּ:

קָדוֹשׁ אַתָּה וְנוֹרָא שְׁמֶךָ, וְאֵין אֱלוֹהַּ מִבַּלְעָדֶיךָ
כַּכָּתוּב, וַיִּגְבַּהּ יהוה צְבָאוֹת בַּמִּשְׁפָּט ישעיה ה
וְהָאֵל הַקָּדוֹשׁ נִקְדַּשׁ בִּצְדָקָה:
בָּרוּךְ אַתָּה יהוה, הַמֶּלֶךְ הַקָּדוֹשׁ.

קדושת היום

אַתָּה בְחַרְתָּנוּ מִכָּל הָעַמִּים
אָהַבְתָּ אוֹתָנוּ וְרָצִיתָ בָּנוּ, וְרוֹמַמְתָּנוּ מִכָּל הַלְּשׁוֹנוֹת
וְקִדַּשְׁתָּנוּ בְּמִצְוֹתֶיךָ
וְקֵרַבְתָּנוּ מַלְכֵּנוּ לַעֲבוֹדָתֶךָ
וְשִׁמְךָ הַגָּדוֹל וְהַקָּדוֹשׁ עָלֵינוּ קָרָאתָ.

On שבת, add the words in parentheses:

וַתִּתֶּן לָנוּ יהוה אֱלֹהֵינוּ בְּאַהֲבָה אֶת
(יוֹם הַשַּׁבָּת הַזֶּה לִקְדֻשָּׁה וְלִמְנוּחָה, וְאֶת)
יוֹם הַכִּפּוּרִים הַזֶּה, לִמְחִילָה וְלִסְלִיחָה וּלְכַפָּרָה
וְלִמְחָל בּוֹ אֶת כָּל עֲוֹנוֹתֵינוּ
(בְּאַהֲבָה) מִקְרָא קֹדֶשׁ
זֵכֶר לִיצִיאַת מִצְרָיִם.

אֱלֹהֵינוּ Our God and God of our ancestors,
may there rise, come, reach, appear, be favored, heard,
regarded and remembered before You,
our recollection and remembrance,
as well as the remembrance of our ancestors,
and of the Messiah, son of David Your servant,
and of Jerusalem Your holy city,
and of all Your people the house of Israel –
for deliverance and well-being,
grace, loving-kindness and compassion,
life and peace, on this Day of Atonement.
On it remember us, LORD our God, for good;
recollect us for blessing, and deliver us for life.
In accord with Your promise
of salvation and compassion,
spare us and be gracious to us;
have compassion on us and deliver us,
for our eyes are turned to You
because You, God, are a gracious and compassionate King.

On Shabbat, add the words in parentheses:

אֱלֹהֵינוּ Our God and God of our ancestors,
pardon our iniquities
on (this Sabbath day, and on) this Day of Atonement;
wipe away and remove all our transgressions and sins
from before Your eyes,
as it is said:

> "I, I am the One who shall wipe out your transgressions *Is. 43*
> for My sake, and I shall not recall your sins."

And it is said:

> "I have wiped out your transgressions like a cloud, *Is. 44*
> and as a haze your sins;
> come back to Me for I have redeemed you."

אֱלֹהֵינוּ וֵאלֹהֵי אֲבוֹתֵינוּ
יַעֲלֶה וְיָבוֹא וְיַגִּיעַ, וְיֵרָאֶה וְיֵרָצֶה וְיִשָּׁמַע
וְיִפָּקֵד וְיִזָּכֵר זִכְרוֹנֵנוּ וּפִקְדּוֹנֵנוּ וְזִכְרוֹן אֲבוֹתֵינוּ
וְזִכְרוֹן מָשִׁיחַ בֶּן דָּוִד עַבְדֶּךָ
וְזִכְרוֹן יְרוּשָׁלַיִם עִיר קָדְשֶׁךָ
וְזִכְרוֹן כָּל עַמְּךָ בֵּית יִשְׂרָאֵל, לְפָנֶיךָ
לִפְלֵיטָה לְטוֹבָה, לְחֵן וּלְחֶסֶד וּלְרַחֲמִים, לְחַיִּים וּלְשָׁלוֹם
בְּיוֹם הַכִּפּוּרִים הַזֶּה
זָכְרֵנוּ יהוה אֱלֹהֵינוּ בּוֹ לְטוֹבָה
וּפָקְדֵנוּ בוֹ לִבְרָכָה
וְהוֹשִׁיעֵנוּ בוֹ לְחַיִּים.
וּבִדְבַר יְשׁוּעָה וְרַחֲמִים חוּס וְחָנֵּנוּ
וְרַחֵם עָלֵינוּ וְהוֹשִׁיעֵנוּ
כִּי אֵלֶיךָ עֵינֵינוּ, כִּי אֵל מֶלֶךְ חַנּוּן וְרַחוּם אָתָּה.

On שבת, add the words in parentheses:

אֱלֹהֵינוּ וֵאלֹהֵי אֲבוֹתֵינוּ
מְחַל לַעֲוֹנוֹתֵינוּ בְּיוֹם (הַשַּׁבָּת הַזֶּה וּבְיוֹם) הַכִּפּוּרִים הַזֶּה
מְחֵה וְהַעֲבֵר פְּשָׁעֵינוּ וְחַטֹּאתֵינוּ מִנֶּגֶד עֵינֶיךָ
כָּאָמוּר
אָנֹכִי אָנֹכִי הוּא מֹחֶה פְשָׁעֶיךָ לְמַעֲנִי — ישעיה מג
וְחַטֹּאתֶיךָ לֹא אֶזְכֹּר:
וְנֶאֱמַר
מָחִיתִי כָעָב פְּשָׁעֶיךָ וְכֶעָנָן חַטֹּאותֶיךָ — ישעיה מד
שׁוּבָה אֵלַי כִּי גְאַלְתִּיךָ:

And it is said:

For on this day you will be atoned and made pure; *Lev. 16*
of all your sins before the LORD you shall be purified.

(Our God and God of our ancestors, find favor in our rest.)
Make us holy through Your commandments
and grant us our share in Your Torah.
Satisfy us with Your goodness,
grant us joy in Your salvation
(in love and favor, O LORD our God,
grant us as our heritage Your holy Sabbath,
so that Israel, who sanctify Your name,
may find rest on it,)
and purify our hearts to serve You in truth.
For You are the Forgiver of Israel
and the Pardoner of the tribes of Yeshurun in every generation,
and without You we have no king who pardons and forgives,
none but You.
Blessed are You, LORD,
King who pardons and forgives our iniquities
and those of all His people the house of Israel,
and makes our guilt pass away, every single year,
King of all the earth, who sanctifies (the Sabbath,)
Israel and the Day of Atonement.

TEMPLE SERVICE

רְצֵה Find favor, LORD our God,
in Your people Israel and their prayer.
Restore the service to Your most holy House,
and accept in love and favor
the fire-offerings of Israel and their prayer.
May the service of Your people Israel always find favor with You.
And may our eyes witness Your return to Zion in compassion.
Blessed are You, LORD,
who restores His Presence to Zion.

וְנֶאֱמַר
כִּי־בַיּוֹם הַזֶּה יְכַפֵּר עֲלֵיכֶם לְטַהֵר אֶתְכֶם ויקרא טז
מִכֹּל חַטֹּאתֵיכֶם, לִפְנֵי יהוה תִּטְהָרוּ:
(אֱלֹהֵינוּ וֵאלֹהֵי אֲבוֹתֵינוּ, רְצֵה בִמְנוּחָתֵנוּ)
קַדְּשֵׁנוּ בְּמִצְוֹתֶיךָ וְתֵן חֶלְקֵנוּ בְּתוֹרָתֶךָ
שַׂבְּעֵנוּ מִטּוּבֶךָ וְשַׂמְּחֵנוּ בִּישׁוּעָתֶךָ
(וְהַנְחִילֵנוּ יהוה אֱלֹהֵינוּ בְּאַהֲבָה וּבְרָצוֹן שַׁבְּתוֹת קָדְשֶׁךָ
וְיָנוּחוּ בָם יִשְׂרָאֵל מְקַדְּשֵׁי שְׁמֶךָ)
וְטַהֵר לִבֵּנוּ לְעָבְדְּךָ בֶּאֱמֶת
כִּי אַתָּה סָלְחָן לְיִשְׂרָאֵל
וּמָחֳלָן לְשִׁבְטֵי יְשֻׁרוּן בְּכָל דּוֹר וָדוֹר
וּמִבַּלְעָדֶיךָ אֵין לָנוּ מֶלֶךְ מוֹחֵל וְסוֹלֵחַ אֶלָּא אָתָּה.
בָּרוּךְ אַתָּה יהוה
מֶלֶךְ מוֹחֵל וְסוֹלֵחַ לַעֲוֹנוֹתֵינוּ
וְלַעֲוֹנוֹת עַמּוֹ בֵּית יִשְׂרָאֵל
וּמַעֲבִיר אַשְׁמוֹתֵינוּ בְּכָל שָׁנָה וְשָׁנָה
מֶלֶךְ עַל כָּל הָאָרֶץ, מְקַדֵּשׁ (הַשַּׁבָּת וְ) יִשְׂרָאֵל וְיוֹם הַכִּפּוּרִים.

עבודה
רְצֵה יהוה אֱלֹהֵינוּ בְּעַמְּךָ יִשְׂרָאֵל, וּבִתְפִלָּתָם
וְהָשֵׁב אֶת הָעֲבוֹדָה לִדְבִיר בֵּיתֶךָ
וְאִשֵּׁי יִשְׂרָאֵל וּתְפִלָּתָם בְּאַהֲבָה תְקַבֵּל בְּרָצוֹן
וּתְהִי לְרָצוֹן תָּמִיד עֲבוֹדַת יִשְׂרָאֵל עַמֶּךָ.
וְתֶחֱזֶינָה עֵינֵינוּ בְּשׁוּבְךָ לְצִיּוֹן בְּרַחֲמִים.
בָּרוּךְ אַתָּה יהוה, הַמַּחֲזִיר שְׁכִינָתוֹ לְצִיּוֹן.

THANKSGIVING

Bow at the first nine words.

▾מוֹדִים We give thanks to You,
for You are the LORD our God and God of our ancestors
for ever and all time.
You are the Rock of our lives,
Shield of our salvation from generation to generation.
We will thank You and declare Your praise for our lives,
which are entrusted into Your hand;
for our souls, which are placed in Your charge;
for Your miracles which are with us every day;
and for Your wonders and favors
at all times, evening, morning and midday.
You are good – for Your compassion never fails.
You are compassionate – for Your loving-kindnesses never cease.
We have always placed our hope in You.
For all these things may Your name be blessed and exalted,
our King, continually, for ever and all time.

וּכְתֹב And write for a good life, all the children of Your covenant.
Let all that lives thank You, Selah!
and praise Your name in truth,
God, our Savior and Help, Selah!
▾Blessed are You, LORD, whose name is "the Good"
and to whom thanks are due.

PEACE

שִׂים שָׁלוֹם Grant peace, goodness and blessing,
grace, loving-kindness and compassion to us
and all Israel Your people.
Bless us, our Father, all as one, with the light of Your face,
for by the light of Your face You have given us, LORD our God,
the Torah of life and love of kindness,
righteousness, blessing, compassion, life and peace.
May it be good in Your eyes to bless Your people Israel
at every time, in every hour, with Your peace.

הודאה

Bow at the first five words.

מוֹדִים אֲנַחְנוּ לָךְ
שָׁאַתָּה הוּא יהוה אֱלֹהֵינוּ וֵאלֹהֵי אֲבוֹתֵינוּ לְעוֹלָם וָעֶד.
צוּר חַיֵּינוּ, מָגֵן יִשְׁעֵנוּ, אַתָּה הוּא לְדוֹר וָדוֹר.
נוֹדֶה לְּךָ וּנְסַפֵּר תְּהִלָּתֶךָ, עַל חַיֵּינוּ הַמְּסוּרִים בְּיָדֶךָ
וְעַל נִשְׁמוֹתֵינוּ הַפְּקוּדוֹת לָךְ, וְעַל נִסֶּיךָ שֶׁבְּכָל יוֹם עִמָּנוּ
וְעַל נִפְלְאוֹתֶיךָ וְטוֹבוֹתֶיךָ שֶׁבְּכָל עֵת, עֶרֶב וָבֹקֶר וְצָהֳרָיִם.
הַטּוֹב, כִּי לֹא כָלוּ רַחֲמֶיךָ
וְהַמְרַחֵם, כִּי לֹא תַמּוּ חֲסָדֶיךָ
מֵעוֹלָם קִוִּינוּ לָךְ.
וְעַל כֻּלָּם יִתְבָּרַךְ וְיִתְרוֹמַם שִׁמְךָ מַלְכֵּנוּ תָּמִיד לְעוֹלָם וָעֶד.

וּכְתֹב לְחַיִּים טוֹבִים כָּל בְּנֵי בְרִיתֶךָ.

וְכֹל הַחַיִּים יוֹדוּךָ סֶּלָה, וִיהַלְלוּ אֶת שִׁמְךָ בֶּאֱמֶת
הָאֵל יְשׁוּעָתֵנוּ וְעֶזְרָתֵנוּ סֶלָה.
בָּרוּךְ אַתָּה יהוה, הַטּוֹב שִׁמְךָ וּלְךָ נָאֶה לְהוֹדוֹת.

שלום

שִׂים שָׁלוֹם טוֹבָה וּבְרָכָה
חֵן וָחֶסֶד וְרַחֲמִים עָלֵינוּ וְעַל כָּל יִשְׂרָאֵל עַמֶּךָ.
בָּרְכֵנוּ אָבִינוּ כֻּלָּנוּ כְּאֶחָד בְּאוֹר פָּנֶיךָ
כִּי בְאוֹר פָּנֶיךָ נָתַתָּ לָּנוּ, יהוה אֱלֹהֵינוּ
תּוֹרַת חַיִּים וְאַהֲבַת חֶסֶד
וּצְדָקָה וּבְרָכָה וְרַחֲמִים וְחַיִּים וְשָׁלוֹם.
וְטוֹב בְּעֵינֶיךָ לְבָרֵךְ אֶת עַמְּךָ יִשְׂרָאֵל
בְּכָל עֵת וּבְכָל שָׁעָה בִּשְׁלוֹמֶךָ.

בְּסֵפֶר חַיִּים In the book of life, blessing,
peace and prosperity,
may we and all Your people the house of Israel
be remembered and written before You
for a good life, and for peace.*

Blessed are You, LORD, who blesses His people Israel with peace.

**Outside Israel, many end the blessing:*
Blessed are You, LORD, who makes peace.

Some say the following verse:
May the words of my mouth and the meditation of my heart — *Ps. 19*
find favor before You, LORD, my Rock and Redeemer.

VIDUY

For linear translation and commentary, see page 1353.

אֱלֹהֵינוּ Our God and God of our fathers,
let our prayer come before You, and do not hide Yourself from our plea,
for we are not so arrogant or obstinate as to say before You,
LORD, our God and God of our fathers,
we are righteous and have not sinned,
for in truth, we and our fathers have sinned.

Strike the left side of the chest with the right fist while saying each of the sins.

אָשַׁמְנוּ We have sinned, we have acted treacherously,
we have robbed, we have spoken slander.
We have acted perversely, we have acted wickedly,
we have acted presumptuously, we have been violent,
we have framed lies.
We have given bad advice, we have deceived, we have scorned,
we have rebelled, we have provoked, we have turned away,
we have committed iniquity, we have transgressed,
we have persecuted, we have been obstinate.
We have acted wickedly, we have corrupted,
we have acted abominably, we have strayed, we have led others astray.

סַרְנוּ We have turned away from Your commandments and good laws,
to no avail, for You are just in all that has befallen us, — *Neh. 9*
for You have acted faithfully while we have done wickedly.

בְּסֵפֶר חַיִּים, בְּרָכָה וְשָׁלוֹם, וּפַרְנָסָה טוֹבָה
נִזָּכֵר וְנִכָּתֵב לְפָנֶיךָ, אֲנַחְנוּ וְכָל עַמְּךָ בֵּית יִשְׂרָאֵל
לְחַיִּים טוֹבִים וּלְשָׁלוֹם.*

בָּרוּךְ אַתָּה יהוה, הַמְבָרֵךְ אֶת עַמּוֹ יִשְׂרָאֵל בַּשָּׁלוֹם.

*In חוץ לארץ, many end the blessing:

בָּרוּךְ אַתָּה יהוה, עוֹשֵׂה הַשָּׁלוֹם.

Some say the following verse:

יִהְיוּ לְרָצוֹן אִמְרֵי־פִי וְהֶגְיוֹן לִבִּי לְפָנֶיךָ, יהוה צוּרִי וְגֹאֲלִי: תהלים יט

וידוי

For linear translation and commentary, see page 1353.

אֱלֹהֵינוּ וֵאלֹהֵי אֲבוֹתֵינוּ
תָּבוֹא לְפָנֶיךָ תְּפִלָּתֵנוּ, וְאַל תִּתְעַלַּם מִתְּחִנָּתֵנוּ.
שֶׁאֵין אֲנַחְנוּ עַזֵּי פָנִים וּקְשֵׁי עֹרֶף לוֹמַר לְפָנֶיךָ
יהוה אֱלֹהֵינוּ וֵאלֹהֵי אֲבוֹתֵינוּ
צַדִּיקִים אֲנַחְנוּ וְלֹא חָטָאנוּ.
אֲבָל אֲנַחְנוּ וַאֲבוֹתֵינוּ חָטָאנוּ.

Strike the left side of the chest with the right fist while saying each of the sins.

אָשַׁמְנוּ, בָּגַדְנוּ, גָּזַלְנוּ, דִּבַּרְנוּ דֹפִי
הֶעֱוִינוּ, וְהִרְשַׁעְנוּ, זַדְנוּ, חָמַסְנוּ, טָפַלְנוּ שֶׁקֶר
יָעַצְנוּ רָע, כִּזַּבְנוּ, לַצְנוּ, מָרַדְנוּ, נִאַצְנוּ, סָרַרְנוּ
עָוִינוּ, פָּשַׁעְנוּ, צָרַרְנוּ, קִשִּׁינוּ עֹרֶף
רָשַׁעְנוּ, שִׁחַתְנוּ, תִּעַבְנוּ, תָּעִינוּ, תִּעְתָּעְנוּ.

סַרְנוּ מִמִּצְוֹתֶיךָ וּמִמִּשְׁפָּטֶיךָ הַטּוֹבִים, וְלֹא שָׁוָה לָנוּ.
וְאַתָּה צַדִּיק עַל כָּל־הַבָּא עָלֵינוּ נחמיה ט
כִּי־אֱמֶת עָשִׂיתָ, וַאֲנַחְנוּ הִרְשָׁעְנוּ:

מַה נֹּאמַר What can we say before You, You who dwell on high?
What can we declare before You, You who abide in heaven?
Do You not know all, the hidden and revealed alike?

אַתָּה יוֹדֵעַ You know every secret since the world began,
and what is hidden deep inside every living thing.
You search each person's inner chambers,
examining conscience and mind.
Nothing is shrouded from You,
and nothing is hidden before Your eyes.
And so, may it be Your will,
Lord our God and God of our ancestors,
that You forgive us all our sins, pardon all our iniquities,
and grant us atonement for all of our transgressions.

Strike the left side of the chest with the right fist while saying each of the sins.

עַל חֵטְא For the sin we have sinned before You under duress or freewill,
and for the sin we have sinned before You in hardness of heart.

For the sin we have sinned before You unwittingly,
and for the sin we have sinned before You by an utterance of our lips.

For the sin we have sinned before You by unchastity,
and for the sin we have sinned before You openly or secretly.

For the sin we have sinned before You knowingly and deceitfully,
and for the sin we have sinned before You in speech.

For the sin we have sinned before You by wronging a neighbor,
and for the sin we have sinned before You by thoughts of the heart.

For the sin we have sinned before You in a gathering for immorality,
and for the sin we have sinned before You by insincere confession.

For the sin we have sinned before You by contempt for parents and teachers,
and for the sin we have sinned before You willfully or in error.

מַה נֹּאמַר לְפָנֶיךָ יוֹשֵׁב מָרוֹם, וּמַה נְּסַפֵּר לְפָנֶיךָ שׁוֹכֵן שְׁחָקִים
הֲלֹא כָּל הַנִּסְתָּרוֹת וְהַנִּגְלוֹת אַתָּה יוֹדֵעַ.

אַתָּה יוֹדֵעַ רָזֵי עוֹלָם וְתַעֲלוּמוֹת סִתְרֵי כָּל חָי.
אַתָּה חוֹפֵשׂ כָּל חַדְרֵי בָטֶן וּבוֹחֵן כְּלָיוֹת וָלֵב.
אֵין דָּבָר נֶעְלָם מִמֶּךָּ וְאֵין נִסְתָּר מִנֶּגֶד עֵינֶיךָ.
וּבְכֵן, יְהִי רָצוֹן מִלְּפָנֶיךָ, יהוה אֱלֹהֵינוּ וֵאלֹהֵי אֲבוֹתֵינוּ
שֶׁתִּסְלַח לָנוּ עַל כָּל חַטֹּאתֵינוּ וְתִמְחַל לָנוּ עַל כָּל עֲוֹנוֹתֵינוּ
וּתְכַפֵּר לָנוּ עַל כָּל פְּשָׁעֵינוּ.

Strike the left side of the chest with the right fist while saying each of the sins.

עַל חֵטְא שֶׁחָטָאנוּ לְפָנֶיךָ בְּאֹנֶס וּבְרָצוֹן
וְעַל חֵטְא שֶׁחָטָאנוּ לְפָנֶיךָ בְּאִמּוּץ הַלֵּב

עַל חֵטְא שֶׁחָטָאנוּ לְפָנֶיךָ בִּבְלִי דָעַת
וְעַל חֵטְא שֶׁחָטָאנוּ לְפָנֶיךָ בְּבִטּוּי שְׂפָתָיִם

עַל חֵטְא שֶׁחָטָאנוּ לְפָנֶיךָ בְּגִלּוּי עֲרָיוֹת
וְעַל חֵטְא שֶׁחָטָאנוּ לְפָנֶיךָ בְּגָלוּי וּבַסָּתֶר

עַל חֵטְא שֶׁחָטָאנוּ לְפָנֶיךָ בְּדַעַת וּבְמִרְמָה
וְעַל חֵטְא שֶׁחָטָאנוּ לְפָנֶיךָ בְּדִבּוּר פֶּה

עַל חֵטְא שֶׁחָטָאנוּ לְפָנֶיךָ בְּהוֹנָאַת רֵעַ
וְעַל חֵטְא שֶׁחָטָאנוּ לְפָנֶיךָ בְּהַרְהוֹר הַלֵּב

עַל חֵטְא שֶׁחָטָאנוּ לְפָנֶיךָ בִּוְעִידַת זְנוּת
וְעַל חֵטְא שֶׁחָטָאנוּ לְפָנֶיךָ בְּוִדּוּי פֶּה

עַל חֵטְא שֶׁחָטָאנוּ לְפָנֶיךָ בְּזִלְזוּל הוֹרִים וּמוֹרִים
וְעַל חֵטְא שֶׁחָטָאנוּ לְפָנֶיךָ בְּזָדוֹן וּבִשְׁגָגָה

For the sin we have sinned before You by force,
and for the sin we have sinned before You by desecrating Your name.

For the sin we have sinned before You by impure lips,
and for the sin we have sinned before You by foolish speech.

For the sin we have sinned before You by the evil inclination,
and for the sin we have sinned before You knowingly or unwittingly.

FOR ALL THESE, GOD OF FORGIVENESS,
FORGIVE US, PARDON US, GRANT US ATONEMENT.

For the sin we have sinned before You by deceit and lies,
and for the sin we have sinned before You by bribery.

For the sin we have sinned before You by scorn,
and for the sin we have sinned before You by evil speech.

For the sin we have sinned before You in business,
and for the sin we have sinned before You with food and drink.

For the sin we have sinned before You by interest and extortion,
and for the sin we have sinned before You by being haughty.

For the sin we have sinned before You by the idle chatter of our lips,
and for the sin we have sinned before You by prying eyes.

For the sin we have sinned before You by arrogance,
and for the sin we have sinned before You by insolence.

FOR ALL THESE, GOD OF FORGIVENESS,
FORGIVE US, PARDON US, GRANT US ATONEMENT.

עַל חֵטְא שֶׁחָטָאנוּ לְפָנֶיךָ בְּחֹזֶק יָד
וְעַל חֵטְא שֶׁחָטָאנוּ לְפָנֶיךָ בְּחִלּוּל הַשֵּׁם

עַל חֵטְא שֶׁחָטָאנוּ לְפָנֶיךָ בְּטֻמְאַת שְׂפָתָיִם
וְעַל חֵטְא שֶׁחָטָאנוּ לְפָנֶיךָ בְּטִפְשׁוּת פֶּה

עַל חֵטְא שֶׁחָטָאנוּ לְפָנֶיךָ בְּיֵצֶר הָרָע
וְעַל חֵטְא שֶׁחָטָאנוּ לְפָנֶיךָ בְּיוֹדְעִים וּבְלֹא יוֹדְעִים

וְעַל כֻּלָּם אֱלוֹהַּ סְלִיחוֹת סְלַח לָנוּ, מְחַל לָנוּ, כַּפֶּר לָנוּ.

עַל חֵטְא שֶׁחָטָאנוּ לְפָנֶיךָ בְּכַחַשׁ וּבְכָזָב
וְעַל חֵטְא שֶׁחָטָאנוּ לְפָנֶיךָ בְּכַפַּת שֹׁחַד

עַל חֵטְא שֶׁחָטָאנוּ לְפָנֶיךָ בְּלָצוֹן
וְעַל חֵטְא שֶׁחָטָאנוּ לְפָנֶיךָ בְּלָשׁוֹן הָרָע

עַל חֵטְא שֶׁחָטָאנוּ לְפָנֶיךָ בְּמַשָּׂא וּבְמַתָּן
וְעַל חֵטְא שֶׁחָטָאנוּ לְפָנֶיךָ בְּמַאֲכָל וּבְמִשְׁתֶּה

עַל חֵטְא שֶׁחָטָאנוּ לְפָנֶיךָ בְּנֶשֶׁךְ וּבְמַרְבִּית
וְעַל חֵטְא שֶׁחָטָאנוּ לְפָנֶיךָ בִּנְטִיַּת גָּרוֹן

עַל חֵטְא שֶׁחָטָאנוּ לְפָנֶיךָ בְּשִׂיחַ שִׂפְתוֹתֵינוּ
וְעַל חֵטְא שֶׁחָטָאנוּ לְפָנֶיךָ בְּשִׂקּוּר עָיִן

עַל חֵטְא שֶׁחָטָאנוּ לְפָנֶיךָ בְּעֵינַיִם רָמוֹת
וְעַל חֵטְא שֶׁחָטָאנוּ לְפָנֶיךָ בְּעַזּוּת מֵצַח

וְעַל כֻּלָּם אֱלוֹהַּ סְלִיחוֹת סְלַח לָנוּ, מְחַל לָנוּ, כַּפֶּר לָנוּ.

For the sin we have sinned before You by casting off the yoke,
and for the sin we have sinned before You by perverting judgment.

For the sin we have sinned before You by entrapping a neighbor,
and for the sin we have sinned before You by envy.

For the sin we have sinned before You by lack of seriousness,
and for the sin we have sinned before You by obstinacy.

For the sin we have sinned before You by running to do evil,
and for the sin we have sinned before You by gossip.

For the sin we have sinned before You by vain oath,
and for the sin we have sinned before You by baseless hatred.

For the sin we have sinned before You by breach of trust,
and for the sin we have sinned before You by confusion of heart.

FOR ALL THESE, GOD OF FORGIVENESS,
FORGIVE US, PARDON US, GRANT US ATONEMENT.

וְעַל חֲטָאִים And for the sins for which we are liable to bring a burnt-offering,

and for the sins for which we are liable to bring a sin-offering,

and for the sins for which we are liable to bring an offering according to our means,

and for the sins for which we are liable to bring a guilt-offering for certain or possible sin,

and for the sins for which we are liable to lashes for rebellion,

and for the sins for which we are liable to forty lashes,

and for the sins for which we are liable to death by the hands of Heaven,

and for the sins for which we are liable to be cut off and childless,

and for the sins for which we are liable to the four death penalties
inflicted by the court: stoning, burning, beheading and strangling.

עַל חֵטְא שֶׁחָטָאנוּ לְפָנֶיךָ בִּפְרִיקַת עֹל
וְעַל חֵטְא שֶׁחָטָאנוּ לְפָנֶיךָ בִּפְלִילוּת
עַל חֵטְא שֶׁחָטָאנוּ לְפָנֶיךָ בִּצְדִיַּת רֵעַ
וְעַל חֵטְא שֶׁחָטָאנוּ לְפָנֶיךָ בְּצָרוּת עָיִן
עַל חֵטְא שֶׁחָטָאנוּ לְפָנֶיךָ בְּקַלּוּת רֹאשׁ
וְעַל חֵטְא שֶׁחָטָאנוּ לְפָנֶיךָ בְּקַשְׁיוּת עֹרֶף
עַל חֵטְא שֶׁחָטָאנוּ לְפָנֶיךָ בְּרִיצַת רַגְלַיִם לְהָרַע
וְעַל חֵטְא שֶׁחָטָאנוּ לְפָנֶיךָ בִּרְכִילוּת
עַל חֵטְא שֶׁחָטָאנוּ לְפָנֶיךָ בִּשְׁבוּעַת שָׁוְא
וְעַל חֵטְא שֶׁחָטָאנוּ לְפָנֶיךָ בְּשִׂנְאַת חִנָּם
עַל חֵטְא שֶׁחָטָאנוּ לְפָנֶיךָ בִּתְשׂוּמֶת יָד
וְעַל חֵטְא שֶׁחָטָאנוּ לְפָנֶיךָ בְּתִמְהוֹן לֵבָב

וְעַל כֻּלָּם אֱלוֹהַ סְלִיחוֹת סְלַח לָנוּ, מְחַל לָנוּ, כַּפֶּר לָנוּ.

וְעַל חֲטָאִים שֶׁאָנוּ חַיָּבִים עֲלֵיהֶם עוֹלָה
וְעַל חֲטָאִים שֶׁאָנוּ חַיָּבִים עֲלֵיהֶם חַטָּאת
וְעַל חֲטָאִים שֶׁאָנוּ חַיָּבִים עֲלֵיהֶם קָרְבַּן עוֹלֶה וְיוֹרֵד
וְעַל חֲטָאִים שֶׁאָנוּ חַיָּבִים עֲלֵיהֶם אָשָׁם וַדַּאי וְתָלוּי
וְעַל חֲטָאִים שֶׁאָנוּ חַיָּבִים עֲלֵיהֶם מַכַּת מַרְדּוּת
וְעַל חֲטָאִים שֶׁאָנוּ חַיָּבִים עֲלֵיהֶם מַלְקוּת אַרְבָּעִים
וְעַל חֲטָאִים שֶׁאָנוּ חַיָּבִים עֲלֵיהֶם מִיתָה בִּידֵי שָׁמָיִם
וְעַל חֲטָאִים שֶׁאָנוּ חַיָּבִים עֲלֵיהֶם כָּרֵת וַעֲרִירִי
וְעַל חֲטָאִים שֶׁאָנוּ חַיָּבִים עֲלֵיהֶם אַרְבַּע מִיתוֹת בֵּית דִּין
סְקִילָה, שְׂרֵפָה, הֶרֶג, וְחֶנֶק.

עַל מִצְוַת For positive and negative commandments,
whether they can be remedied by an act or not,
for sins known to us and for those that are unknown –
for those that are known,
we have already declared them before You
and confessed them to You;
and for those that are unknown,
before You they are revealed and known,
as it is said,
"The secret things belong to the LORD our God, *Deut. 29*
but the things that are revealed
are for us and our children for ever,
that we may fulfill all the words of this Torah."

For You are the Forgiver of Israel
and the Pardoner of the tribes of Yeshurun
in every generation,
and without You we have no king who pardons and forgives,
none but You.

אֱלֹהַי My God,
before I was formed I was unworthy,
and now that I have been formed
it is as if I had not been formed.
I am dust while alive,
how much more so when I am dead.
See, I am before You like a vessel filled with shame and disgrace.
May it be Your will,
LORD my God and God of my fathers,
that I may sin no more,
and as for the sins I have committed before You,
erase them in Your great compassion,
but not by suffering or severe illness.

עַל מִצְוַת עֲשֵׂה וְעַל מִצְוַת לֹא תַעֲשֶׂה.
בֵּין שֶׁיֵּשׁ בָּהּ קוּם עֲשֵׂה וּבֵין שֶׁאֵין בָּהּ קוּם עֲשֵׂה.
אֶת הַגְּלוּיִים לָנוּ וְאֶת שֶׁאֵינָם גְּלוּיִים לָנוּ
אֶת הַגְּלוּיִים לָנוּ
כְּבָר אֲמַרְנוּם לְפָנֶיךָ
וְהוֹדִינוּ לְךָ עֲלֵיהֶם
וְאֶת שֶׁאֵינָם גְּלוּיִים לָנוּ
לְפָנֶיךָ הֵם גְּלוּיִים וִידוּעִים
כַּדָּבָר שֶׁנֶּאֱמַר
הַנִּסְתָּרֹת לַיהוה אֱלֹהֵינוּ — דברים כט
וְהַנִּגְלֹת לָנוּ וּלְבָנֵינוּ עַד־עוֹלָם
לַעֲשׂוֹת אֶת־כָּל־דִּבְרֵי הַתּוֹרָה הַזֹּאת:

כִּי אַתָּה סָלְחָן לְיִשְׂרָאֵל
וּמָחֳלָן לְשִׁבְטֵי יְשֻׁרוּן בְּכָל דּוֹר וָדוֹר
וּמִבַּלְעָדֶיךָ אֵין לָנוּ מֶלֶךְ מוֹחֵל וְסוֹלֵחַ אֶלָּא אָתָּה.

אֱלֹהַי
עַד שֶׁלֹּא נוֹצַרְתִּי אֵינִי כְדַאי
וְעַכְשָׁיו שֶׁנּוֹצַרְתִּי, כְּאִלּוּ לֹא נוֹצַרְתִּי
עָפָר אֲנִי בְּחַיַּי, קַל וָחֹמֶר בְּמִיתָתִי.
הֲרֵי אֲנִי לְפָנֶיךָ כִּכְלִי מָלֵא בוּשָׁה וּכְלִמָּה.
יְהִי רָצוֹן מִלְּפָנֶיךָ, יהוה אֱלֹהַי וֵאלֹהֵי אֲבוֹתַי שֶׁלֹּא אֶחֱטָא עוֹד.
וּמַה שֶּׁחָטָאתִי לְפָנֶיךָ, מְחֹק בְּרַחֲמֶיךָ הָרַבִּים
אֲבָל לֹא עַל יְדֵי יִסּוּרִים וָחֳלָיִים רָעִים.

אֱלֹהַי My God, *Berakhot 17a*
guard my tongue from evil
and my lips from deceitful speech.
To those who curse me, let my soul be silent;
may my soul be to all like the dust.
Open my heart to Your Torah
and let my soul pursue Your commandments.
As for all who plan evil against me,
swiftly thwart their counsel and frustrate their plans.
Act for the sake of Your name;
act for the sake of Your right hand;
act for the sake of Your holiness;
act for the sake of Your Torah.
That Your beloved ones may be delivered, *Ps. 60*
save with Your right hand and answer me.
May the words of my mouth and the meditation of my heart *Ps. 19*
find favor before You, LORD, my Rock and Redeemer.

Bow, take three steps back, then bow, first left, then right, then center, while saying:

May He who makes peace in His high places,
make peace for us and all Israel – and say: Amen.

יְהִי רָצוֹן May it be Your will, LORD our God and God of our ancestors,
that the Temple be rebuilt speedily in our days,
and grant us a share in Your Torah.
And there we will serve You with reverence,
as in the days of old and as in former years.
Then the offering of Judah and Jerusalem *Mal. 3*
will be pleasing to the LORD as in the days of old and as in former years.

אֱלֹהַי ברכות יז.
נְצֹר לְשׁוֹנִי מֵרָע וּשְׂפָתַי מִדַּבֵּר מִרְמָה
וְלִמְקַלְלַי נַפְשִׁי תִדֹּם, וְנַפְשִׁי כֶּעָפָר לַכֹּל תִּהְיֶה.
פְּתַח לִבִּי בְּתוֹרָתֶךָ, וּבְמִצְוֹתֶיךָ תִּרְדֹּף נַפְשִׁי.
וְכָל הַחוֹשְׁבִים עָלַי רָעָה
מְהֵרָה הָפֵר עֲצָתָם וְקַלְקֵל מַחֲשַׁבְתָּם.
עֲשֵׂה לְמַעַן שְׁמֶךָ
עֲשֵׂה לְמַעַן יְמִינֶךָ
עֲשֵׂה לְמַעַן קְדֻשָּׁתֶךָ
עֲשֵׂה לְמַעַן תּוֹרָתֶךָ.
לְמַעַן יֵחָלְצוּן יְדִידֶיךָ, הוֹשִׁיעָה יְמִינְךָ וַעֲנֵנִי: תהלים ס
יִהְיוּ לְרָצוֹן אִמְרֵי פִי וְהֶגְיוֹן לִבִּי לְפָנֶיךָ, יהוה צוּרִי וְגֹאֲלִי: תהלים יט

Bow, take three steps back, then bow, first left, then right, then center, while saying:

עֹשֶׂה הַשָּׁלוֹם בִּמְרוֹמָיו
הוּא יַעֲשֶׂה שָׁלוֹם עָלֵינוּ וְעַל כָּל יִשְׂרָאֵל וְאִמְרוּ אָמֵן.

יְהִי רָצוֹן מִלְּפָנֶיךָ יהוה אֱלֹהֵינוּ וֵאלֹהֵי אֲבוֹתֵינוּ
שֶׁיִּבָּנֶה בֵּית הַמִּקְדָּשׁ בִּמְהֵרָה בְיָמֵינוּ, וְתֵן חֶלְקֵנוּ בְּתוֹרָתֶךָ
וְשָׁם נַעֲבָדְךָ בְּיִרְאָה כִּימֵי עוֹלָם וּכְשָׁנִים קַדְמוֹנִיּוֹת.
וְעָרְבָה לַיהוה מִנְחַת יְהוּדָה וִירוּשָׁלָםִ כִּימֵי עוֹלָם וּכְשָׁנִים קַדְמֹנִיּוֹת: מלאכי ג

LEADER'S REPETITION FOR MINḤA

The Ark is opened.

The Leader takes three steps forward and at the points indicated by ▾, bends the knees at the first word, bows at the second, and stands straight before saying God's name.

When I proclaim the LORD's name, give glory to our God. Deut. 32
O LORD, open my lips, so that my mouth may declare Your praise. Ps. 51

PATRIARCHS

בָּרוּךְ▾ Blessed are You, LORD our God and God of our fathers,
God of Abraham, God of Isaac and God of Jacob;
the great, mighty and awesome God, God Most High,
who bestows acts of loving-kindness and creates all,
who remembers the loving-kindness of the fathers
and will bring a Redeemer to their children's children
for the sake of His name, in love.

מִסּוֹד Drawing from the counsel of wise and knowing men,
from the teachings born of insight among those who understand,
I open my mouth now in prayer and pleading,
to implore and to plead before the King
who pardons and forgives iniquities.

The Ark is closed.

The kerova for Minḥa is relatively short, usually consisting only of the "Magen," "Meḥayeh," and "Meshalesh." The running theme is the connection between the patriarchs and the angels, implying the dependence of the heavenly host itself upon the repentance and redemption of Israel. The Magen describes Abraham's hospitality, which was extended even to the angels. As part of the Leader's Repetition, these piyutim should ideally be said by the Leader alone. However, the prevailing custom is for the congregation to participate, and some of the piyutim are said together, with the Leader raising his voice only toward the end.

All:

אֵיתָן [Abraham] the mighty one recognized his faith in You,
in a generation that did not know how to please You.
He rejoiced in You and knew fear of You,
and was delighted to inform all of Your splendor.

---

represents the first patriarch. Abraham is called "the mighty" because he answered the call of God to leave his home (*Bava Batra* 15a).

בְּדוֹר *In a generation.* Abraham was a lone monotheist in an age of idolators (Maimonides, Laws of Idolatry 1:3).

חזרת הש״ץ של מנחה

The ארון קודש is opened.

The שליח ציבור takes three steps forward and at the points indicated by ˚, bends the knees at the first word, bows at the second, and stands straight before saying God's name.

כִּי שֵׁם יהוה אֶקְרָא, הָבוּ גֹדֶל לֵאלֹהֵינוּ: דברים לב

אֲדֹנָי, שְׂפָתַי תִּפְתָּח, וּפִי יַגִּיד תְּהִלָּתֶךָ: תהלים נא

אבות

˚בָּרוּךְ אַתָּה יהוה, אֱלֹהֵינוּ וֵאלֹהֵי אֲבוֹתֵינוּ
אֱלֹהֵי אַבְרָהָם, אֱלֹהֵי יִצְחָק, וֵאלֹהֵי יַעֲקֹב
הָאֵל הַגָּדוֹל הַגִּבּוֹר וְהַנּוֹרָא, אֵל עֶלְיוֹן
גּוֹמֵל חֲסָדִים טוֹבִים, וְקוֹנֵה הַכֹּל
וְזוֹכֵר חַסְדֵי אָבוֹת
וּמֵבִיא גוֹאֵל לִבְנֵי בְנֵיהֶם לְמַעַן שְׁמוֹ בְּאַהֲבָה.

מִסּוֹד חֲכָמִים וּנְבוֹנִים / וּמִלֶּמֶד דַּעַת מְבִינִים
אֶפְתְּחָה פִּי בִּתְפִלָּה וּבְתַחֲנוּנִים
לְחַלּוֹת וּלְחַנֵּן פְּנֵי מֶלֶךְ מוֹחֵל וְסוֹלֵחַ לַעֲוֹנִים.

The ארון קודש is closed.

The קרובה for מנחה is relatively short, usually consisting only of the "מגן," "מחיה," and "משלש." The running theme is the connection between the patriarchs and the angels, implying the dependance of the Heavenly Host itself upon the repentance and redemption of Israel. The מגן describes Abraham's hospitality, which was extended even to the angels. As part of the חזרת הש״ץ, these piyutim should ideally be said by the שליח ציבור alone. However, the prevailing custom is for the קהל to participate, and some of the piyutim are said together, with the שליח ציבור raising his voice only toward the end.

All:

אֵיתָן הִכִּיר אֱמוּנָתֶךָ / בְּדוֹר לֹא יָדְעוּ לִרְצוֹתֶךָ
גָּהַץ בָּךְ וְיָדַע יִרְאָתֶךָ / דָּץ לְהוֹדִיעַ לְכֹל הֲדָרָתֶךָ

אֵיתָן [*Abraham*] *the mighty one.* An extended poem by the author Rabbi Eliya ben Mordekhai, divided into three parts, corresponding to the first three paragraphs of the Amida. The first and second form a two-part alphabetical acrostic. In the third, the acrostic spells the author's name.

The first paragraph of the Amida, with its ending "Shield of Abraham,"

He guided the wayward along Your path
and became known as the father of Your nation.
He cautioned them to fulfill Your holy word
and desired to shelter in the shade of Your Presence.
He provided passersby with Your sustenance
and informed travelers that there is no other but You.
▸ For he placed his faith in You and prayed to You,
planting a tamarisk tree to [shade wayfarers and]
tell them of Your great deeds.

All:

Consider his righteousness when judging us;
let the merits of our forefather cause You to forgive us.
▸ Do not repay us in accordance with the sins we have committed,
O, our Protector, for it is You we await.

The congregation then the Leader:

זָכְרֵנוּ לְחַיִּים Remember us for life, O King who desires life,
and write us in the book of life – for Your sake, O God of life.

The Leader continues:

King, Helper, Savior, Shield:
▾Blessed are You, LORD, Shield of Abraham.

DIVINE MIGHT

אַתָּה גִּבּוֹר You are eternally mighty, LORD.
You give life to the dead and have great power to save.
In Israel: He causes the dew to fall.
He sustains the living with loving-kindness,
and with great compassion revives the dead.
He supports the fallen, heals the sick, sets captives free,
and keeps His faith with those who sleep in the dust.

When their guests were about to leave, they thanked their hosts, who told them instead to thank God who is the Author and Owner of all.

לִטַּע אֶשֶׁל *Planting a tamarisk tree.* According to one interpretation this was an orchard whose fruits Abraham gave to travelers. According to another it was an inn, a place where passersby could lodge overnight (*Sota* 10a).

הַדְרִיךְ תּוֹעִים בִּנְתִיבָתֶךָ / וְנִקְרָא אָב לְאֻמָּתֶךָ
זָהַר לַעֲשׂוֹת דִּבְרָתֶךָ / חָפֵץ לַחֲסוֹת בְּצֵל שְׁכִינָתֶךָ
טְעֵם לָעוֹבְרִים כַּלְכָּלָתֶךָ / יָדַע לַשָּׁבִים כִּי אֵין בִּלְתֶּךָ
‹ כִּי הֶאֱמִין בְּךָ לְחַלּוֹתֶךָ / לִטַּע אֵשֶׁל וּלְהַזְכִּיר גְּבוּרוֹתֶיךָ.

All:

צְדָקָה תַּחְשֵׁב לָנוּ / בְּצֶדֶק אָב סְלַח לָנוּ
‹ לֹא כַחֲטָאֵינוּ תַּעֲשֶׂה לָנוּ / מָגִנֵּנוּ כִּי לְךָ יִחַלְנוּ.

The קהל *then the* שליח ציבור:

זָכְרֵנוּ לְחַיִּים, מֶלֶךְ חָפֵץ בַּחַיִּים
וְכָתְבֵנוּ בְּסֵפֶר הַחַיִּים, לְמַעַנְךָ אֱלֹהִים חַיִּים.

The שליח ציבור *continues:*

מֶלֶךְ עוֹזֵר וּמוֹשִׁיעַ וּמָגֵן.
ׅבָּרוּךְ אַתָּה יהוה, מָגֵן אַבְרָהָם.

גבורות

אַתָּה גִּבּוֹר לְעוֹלָם, אֲדֹנָי
מְחַיֵּה מֵתִים אַתָּה, רַב לְהוֹשִׁיעַ
בארץ ישראל: מוֹרִיד הַטָּל
מְכַלְכֵּל חַיִּים בְּחֶסֶד, מְחַיֵּה מֵתִים בְּרַחֲמִים רַבִּים
סוֹמֵךְ נוֹפְלִים, וְרוֹפֵא חוֹלִים, וּמַתִּיר אֲסוּרִים
וּמְקַיֵּם אֱמוּנָתוֹ לִישֵׁנֵי עָפָר.

הַדְרִיךְ תּוֹעִים בִּנְתִיבָתֶךָ *He guided the wayward along Your path.* A reference to the tradition that Abraham and Sarah gathered converts (*Bereshit Raba* 39:14).

טְעֵם לָעוֹבְרִים כַּלְכָּלָתֶךָ *He provided passersby with Your sustenance.* A reference to the famous scene in which Abraham and Sarah provide hospitality to three passersby who turn out to be angels (Gen. 18). According to tradition Abraham and Sarah led people to faith in God through their hospitality.

Who is like You, Master of might, and to whom can You be compared,
O King who brings death and gives life, and makes salvation grow?

The Meḥayeh recalls (as do all the Meḥayeh piyutim of Yom Kippur) the Akeda (Binding of Isaac), relating how the angels intervened on Isaac's behalf.

All:

מְאֻהָב [Isaac] the beloved only child of his mother
was prepared to offer his soul in sacrifice.
The Seraphim screamed from the heavens on high
saying, "Spare him!" to God that He might take pity.
The Redeemer and Savior showed compassion toward him,
ordering that a lamb be sacrificed in exchange for him.
[Abraham] heard, "Do not spill his blood,"
but the Merciful One sent [Isaac] floating up to heaven.
He was preserved and sustained for His [covenant's] sake,
and his countenance became as beautiful as the sun's brilliance.
▸ Behold the child today as though his ashes were scattered
on the altar in Your Sanctuary;
recall his binding and show mercy to his people.

All:

May He raise us up before Him that we might live;
by the righteousness of our forefather we shall live.
▸ For the LORD brings death and gives life;
He shall revive the slumbering dead with His dew.

The congregation then the Leader:

מִי כָמוֹךָ Who is like You, compassionate Father,
who remembers His creatures in compassion, for life?

The Leader continues:

Faithful are You to revive the dead.
Blessed are You, LORD, who revives the dead.

בְּשֵׁם תָּם *In the name of [Jacob] the innocent one (next page).* The third paragraph of the Amida is associated with Jacob, who is called *tam*, "the innocent" or "perfect one" (Gen. 25:27). According to tradition the image of Jacob is engraved on God's throne of glory (*Bereshit Raba* 68:12), since Jacob, all of whose children stayed faithful to the covenant, represents the Jewish people as a whole.

מִי כָמְוֹךָ, בַּעַל גְּבוּרוֹת, וּמִי דּוֹמֶה לָּךְ
מֶלֶךְ, מֵמִית וּמְחַיֶּה וּמַצְמִיחַ יְשׁוּעָה.

The מחיה *recalls (as do all the* מחיה *piyutim of* יום כיפור*) the* עקדה*, relating how the angels intervened on Isaac's behalf.*

All:

מְאֻהָב וְיָחִיד לְאִמּוֹ / נַפְשׁוֹ לָטֶבַח בְּהַשְׁלִימוֹ
שְׂרָפִים צָעֲקוּ מִמְּרוֹמוֹ / עוֹנִים חוּסָה, לָאֵל מְרַחֲמוֹ
פּוֹדֶה וּמַצִּיל רַחֲמוֹ / צַו שֶׂה תְּמוּרוֹ בִּמְקוֹמוֹ
קָשַׁב אַל תִּשְׁפֹּךְ דָּמוֹ / רִחֲפוּ רַחוּם לִמְרוֹמוֹ
שָׁמְרוּ וְקִיְּמוּ לִשְׁמוֹ / שִׁפֵּר תָּאֳרוֹ כְּנֹגַהּ יוֹמוֹ
◂ תִּרְאֵהוּ הַיּוֹם כְּשָׂרוּף בְּאוּלַמּוֹ / תִּזְכֹּר עֲקֵדָתוֹ וְתָחֹן עַמּוֹ.

All:

לְפָנָיו יְקִימֵנוּ וְנִחְיֶה / בְּצֶדֶק אָב נִחְיֶה
◂ יהוה מֵמִית וּמְחַיֶּה / בִּטְלָלָיו רְדוּמִים יְחַיֶּה.

The קהל *then the* שליח ציבור*:*

מִי כָמְוֹךָ אַב הָרַחֲמִים, זוֹכֵר יְצוּרָיו לְחַיִּים בְּרַחֲמִים.

The שליח ציבור *continues:*

וְנֶאֱמָן אַתָּה לְהַחֲיוֹת מֵתִים.
בָּרוּךְ אַתָּה יהוה, מְחַיֵּה הַמֵּתִים.

מְאֻהָב וְיָחִיד *Beloved only child.* This is Isaac at the binding. The poet follows a midrashic tradition that says that it was the angels who pleaded with God to show mercy as Abraham lifted his knife to sacrifice his son (*Bereshit Raba* 56:5). Isaac had his life restored to him: hence his connection with the second paragraph whose subject is God as Giver of life, who will one day bring the dead back to life.

כְּשָׂרוּף *As though his ashes were scattered.* Isaac was willing to be sacrificed, and though the act was averted, God counts a noble intention as if it were a deed (*Kiddushin* 40a).

The Meshalesh recalls the midrash which describes Jacob's image being engraved upon the Throne of Glory.

All:

אֶרְאֶלִּים The mighty angels, in the name of [Jacob] the innocent one,
crown / the King of kings.
They pass God's throne to behold Jacob's beautiful face engraved there,
as his descendants stand today like angels,
sanctifying God and arranging their prayers,
on this day setting aside all enmity.
Together as one they pronounce their blessings in the name of their
forefather, / trying to please the Exalted One with soft words.
In the merit of [Jacob] the innocent one may God look upon us through
the lattices. / May the LORD illuminate the darkened eyes of His
faithful servants.
O King standing within a congregation of blessed ones –
He receives His people willingly and shall elevate those laid low.
Those who rise early to knock at heaven's doors in prayer, / as the
Beneficent and Forgiving One, He shall acquiesce to their pleas.
▸ He shall make heard: "The destitute shall not be shamed."
These words shall be spoken to the awaiting nation.

The congregation says the next two verses aloud, followed by the Leader:

The LORD shall reign for ever. He is your God, Zion, *Ps. 146*
from generation to generation, Halleluya!
You are the Holy One, enthroned on the praises of Israel. *Ps. 22*
God, please.

The kerova for Minḥa originally included several piyutim by different authors. Today, most congregations omit them, saying just the refrains.

Responsively:

אֱמוּנַת אֹם A nation that keeps its faith –
support, for Your sake, those who remain.
Please, accept with favor their cry, like the scent of incense, / O Holy One.

יְכַפֵּר וְיִסְלַח He shall atone and forgive – / the beneficent, forgiving God,
O Awesome, Holy One.

אֱמוּנַת אֹם נוֹטֶרֶת... יְכַפֵּר...תְּפִלָּתֵנוּ *A nation that keeps its faith… He shall atone… Our prayers…* These three lines are not a single prayer. Rather, they are the opening lines of three longer prayers, the first by Rabbi Elazar HaKalir, the second and third of unknown authorship. In some communities they were

The משלש *recalls the* מדרש *which describes Jacob's image being engraved upon the Throne of Glory.*

All:

אֶרְאֶלִּים בְּשֵׁם תָּם מַמְלִיכִים / לְמֶלֶךְ מַלְכֵי הַמְּלָכִים
יָפְיוֹ לָשׁוּר בַּכֵּס הוֹלְכִים / יְלָדָיו הַיּוֹם צָגִים כְּמַלְאָכִים
הַמַּקְדִּישִׁים וְתַחַן עוֹרְכִים / בְּיוֹם זֶה אֵיבָה מַשְׁלִיכִים
יַחַד בְּשֵׁם אֲבִיהֶם מְבָרְכִים / רָם לְרַצּוֹת בִּדְבָרִים רַכִּים
בִּזְכוּת תָּם יָצִיץ מֵחֲרַכִּים / יָהּ יָאִיר עֵינֵי חֲשֵׁכִים
מֶלֶךְ נִצָּב בַּעֲדַת בְּרוּכִים / רוֹצֶה בְּעַמּוֹ יְפָאֵר נְמוּכִים
דּוֹפְקִים בִּתְפִלָּה לְהַשְׁכִּים / כְּטוֹב וְסַלָּח עִמָּם יַסְכִּים
› יַשְׁמִיעַ לֹא תֵבוֹשׁוּ דַּכִּים / יֵאָמֵר לָכֵן לְבֵית הַמְחַכִּים.

The קהל *says the next two verses aloud, followed by the* שליח ציבור*:*

תהלים קמו יִמְלֹךְ יהוה לְעוֹלָם אֱלֹהַיִךְ צִיּוֹן לְדֹר וָדֹר, הַלְלוּיָהּ:
תהלים כב וְאַתָּה קָדוֹשׁ, יוֹשֵׁב תְּהִלּוֹת יִשְׂרָאֵל:
אֵל נָא.

The קרובה *for* מנחה *originally included several piyutim by different authors. Today, most congregations omit them, saying just the refrains.*

Responsively:

אֱמוּנַת אֹם נוֹטֶרֶת / לְמַעַנְךָ עֲזוֹר לַנִּשְׁאֶרֶת
זַעֲקָהּ רְצֵה נָא כִּקְטֹרֶת / קָדוֹשׁ
יְכַפֵּר וְיִסְלַח / אֵל טוֹב וְסַלָּח / נוֹרָא וְקָדוֹשׁ.

אֵיבָה מַשְׁלִיכִים *Setting aside all enmity.* Yom Kippur only atones for sins between us and our fellows if we apologize and secure their forgiveness. It should be a day on which we let go of any feelings of animosity to others.

מֵחֲרַכִּים *Lattices.* A reference to Song of Songs 2:9, "My beloved … stands behind our wall, gazing through the windows, peering through the lattices." Just as one who watches through a lattice sees but cannot be seen, so God constantly watches over us even when we are not aware of it.

תְּפִלָּתֵנוּ Our prayers, to His dwelling place
He will receive like offerings; / the Holy God.

מִיכָאֵל Michael at His right side sings praises,
and Gabriel at His left side, speaks:
"In the heavens there is none other like God,
and on earth, who is like Your people Israel?"

And so, sanctity will rise up to You,
for You, our God, are the King who pardons and forgives.

Some congregations say the Siluk piyut, כִּי רְכוּבוֹ בָּעֲרָבוֹת *(page 1336), before Kedusha.*

KEDUSHA

The following is said standing with feet together, rising on the toes at the words indicated by ▲.

The congregation then the Leader:

נַעֲרִיצְךָ We will revere and sanctify You
with the words uttered by the holy Seraphim
who sanctify Your name in the Sanctuary,
as is written by Your prophet: "They call out to one another, saying: *Is. 6*

The congregation then the Leader:

▲Holy, ▲holy, ▲holy is the LORD of hosts:
the whole world is filled with His glory."
His glory fills the universe. His ministering angels ask each other,
"Where is the place of His glory?"
Those facing them reply "Blessed –

The congregation then the Leader:

▲"Blessed is the LORD's glory from His place." *Ezek. 3*
From His place may He turn with compassion
and be gracious to the people who proclaim the unity of His name,
morning and evening, every day, continually,
twice each day reciting in love the Shema:

Uriel in front, Raphael behind. All four are mentioned in the prayers we say before sleep at night.

תְּפִלָּתֵנוּ מִמְּעוֹנוֹת / יְקַבֵּל כְּקָרְבָּנוֹת / הָאֵל קָדוֹשׁ.
מִיכָאֵל מִיָּמִין מְהַלֵּל / וְגַבְרִיאֵל מִשְּׂמֹאל מְמַלֵּל
בַּשָּׁמַיִם אֵין כָּאֵל / וּבָאָרֶץ מִי כְּעַמְּךָ יִשְׂרָאֵל.

וּבְכֵן לְךָ תַעֲלֶה קְדֻשָּׁה, כִּי אַתָּה אֱלֹהֵינוּ מֶלֶךְ מוֹחֵל וְסוֹלֵחַ.

Some congregations say the סילוק *piyut,* כִּי רְכוּבוֹ בָּעֲרָבוֹת *(page 1336), before* קדושה.

קדושה

The following is said standing with feet together, rising on the toes at the words indicated by ˄.

The קהל *then the* שליח ציבור:

נַעֲרִיצְךָ וְנַקְדִּישְׁךָ כְּסוֹד שִׂיחַ שַׂרְפֵי קֹדֶשׁ
הַמַּקְדִּישִׁים שִׁמְךָ בַּקֹּדֶשׁ
כַּכָּתוּב עַל יַד נְבִיאֶךָ: וְקָרָא זֶה אֶל־זֶה וְאָמַר ישעיה ו

The קהל *then the* שליח ציבור:

˄קָדוֹשׁ, ˄קָדוֹשׁ, ˄קָדוֹשׁ, יהוה צְבָאוֹת, מְלֹא כָל־הָאָרֶץ כְּבוֹדוֹ:
כְּבוֹדוֹ מָלֵא עוֹלָם, מְשָׁרְתָיו שׁוֹאֲלִים זֶה לָזֶה, אַיֵּה מְקוֹם כְּבוֹדוֹ
לְעֻמָּתָם בָּרוּךְ יֹאמֵרוּ

The קהל *then the* שליח ציבור:

˄בָּרוּךְ כְּבוֹד־יהוה מִמְּקוֹמוֹ: יחזקאל ג
מִמְּקוֹמוֹ הוּא יִפֶן בְּרַחֲמִים, וְיָחֹן עַם הַמְיַחֲדִים שְׁמוֹ
עֶרֶב וָבֹקֶר בְּכָל יוֹם תָּמִיד, פַּעֲמַיִם בְּאַהֲבָה שְׁמַע אוֹמְרִים

---

said in full, in others they were omitted; our custom is to say only the opening lines because of pressure of time.

מִיכָאֵל מִיָּמִין *Michael at His right side.* As we approach the *Kedusha,* based on the mystical visions of Isaiah and Ezekiel who saw angels surrounding God's throne of glory, the poetry moves from earth to heaven. According to *Pirkei deRabbi Eliezer* (ch. 4), there are four groups of angels surrounding the throne, those associated with Michael to the left, Gabriel to the right,

The congregation then the Leader:

"Listen, Israel, the Lord is our God, the Lord is One." *Deut. 6*
He is our God, He is our Father, He is our King,
He is our Savior – and He, in His compassion,
will let us hear a second time in the presence of all that lives,
His promise "to be Your God. I am the Lord your God." *Num. 15*

The congregation then the Leader:

Glorious is our Glorious One, Lord our Master, *Ps. 8*
and glorious is Your name throughout the earth.
Then the Lord shall be King over all the earth; *Zech. 14*
on that day the Lord shall be One and His name One.

The Leader continues:

And in Your holy Writings it is written:

The congregation then the Leader:

▲"The Lord shall reign for ever. *Ps. 146*
He is your God, Zion, from generation to generation, Halleluya!"

The Leader continues:

From generation to generation we will declare Your greatness,
and we will proclaim Your holiness for evermore.
Your praise, our God, shall not leave our mouth forever,
for You, God, are a great and holy King.

The following prayer originally began at "For with Your holiness." Nowadays, it is commonly sung as one stanza together with the later addition of the opening verse "Have mercy on those You have made."

חֲמֹל Have mercy on those You have made,
take joy in those You made,
and those who shelter in You will say,
as You absolve the ones You bear,
"Be sanctified, Lord, through all that You have made."

כִּי מַקְדִּישֶׁיךָ For with Your holiness You sanctify
all who affirm You holy;
it is fitting that the Holy One be glorified by holy ones.

The קהל *then the* שליח ציבור:

שְׁמַע יִשְׂרָאֵל, יהוה אֱלֹהֵינוּ, יהוה אֶחָד: דברים ו
הוּא אֱלֹהֵינוּ, הוּא אָבִינוּ, הוּא מַלְכֵּנוּ, הוּא מוֹשִׁיעֵנוּ
וְהוּא יַשְׁמִיעֵנוּ בְּרַחֲמָיו שֵׁנִית לְעֵינֵי כָּל חָי במדבר טו
לִהְיוֹת לָכֶם לֵאלֹהִים, אֲנִי יהוה אֱלֹהֵיכֶם:

The קהל *then the* שליח ציבור:

אַדִּיר אַדִּירֵנוּ, יהוה אֲדֹנֵינוּ, מָה־אַדִּיר שִׁמְךָ בְּכָל־הָאָרֶץ: תהלים ח
וְהָיָה יהוה לְמֶלֶךְ עַל־כָּל־הָאָרֶץ זכריה יד
בַּיּוֹם הַהוּא יִהְיֶה יהוה אֶחָד וּשְׁמוֹ אֶחָד:

The שליח ציבור *continues:*

וּבְדִבְרֵי קָדְשְׁךָ כָּתוּב לֵאמֹר

The קהל *then the* שליח ציבור:

יִמְלֹךְ יהוה לְעוֹלָם, אֱלֹהַיִךְ צִיּוֹן לְדֹר וָדֹר, הַלְלוּיָהּ: תהלים קמו

The שליח ציבור *continues:*

לְדוֹר וָדוֹר נַגִּיד גָּדְלֶךָ, וּלְנֵצַח נְצָחִים קְדֻשָּׁתְךָ נַקְדִּישׁ
וְשִׁבְחֲךָ אֱלֹהֵינוּ מִפִּינוּ לֹא יָמוּשׁ לְעוֹלָם וָעֶד
כִּי אֵל מֶלֶךְ גָּדוֹל וְקָדוֹשׁ אָתָּה.

The following prayer originally began at כִּי מַקְדִּישֶׁיךָ*. Nowadays, it is commonly sung as one stanza together with the later addition of the opening verse,* חֲמֹל עַל מַעֲשֶׂיךָ.

חֲמֹל עַל מַעֲשֶׂיךָ וְתִשְׂמַח בְּמַעֲשֶׂיךָ
וְיֹאמְרוּ לְךָ חוֹסֶיךָ בְּצַדֶּקְךָ עֲמוּסֶיךָ
תֻּקְדַּשׁ אָדוֹן עַל כָּל מַעֲשֶׂיךָ

כִּי מַקְדִּישֶׁיךָ בִּקְדֻשָּׁתְךָ קִדַּשְׁתָּ
נָאֶה לְקָדוֹשׁ פְּאֵר מִקְּדוֹשִׁים.

The Leader continues:

בְּאֵין With no one to advocate for us
against the accuser of sin,
speak words of law and of justice to Jacob;
and absolve us in the judgment,
O King of judgment.

He, our LORD,
will yet remember for us the love of [Abraham]
the steadfast one.
And for [Isaac] the son who was bound,
He will still the enmity against us.
And for the merit of [Jacob] the innocent man,
He will bring today our judgment out to the good,
for this day is holy to our LORD. *Neh. 8*

וּבְכֵן יִתְקַדַּשׁ And so may Your name be sanctified, LORD our God,
through Israel Your nation
and Jerusalem, Your city,
and Zion, the dwelling place of Your honor
and through the royal house of David Your anointed,
and Your Sanctuary and Your Temple.

HOLINESS

וּבְכֵן תֵּן פַּחְדְּךָ And so place the fear of You, LORD our God,
over all that You have made,
and the terror of You over all You have created,
and all who were made will stand in awe of You,
and all of creation will worship You,
and they will be bound all together as one
to carry out Your will with an undivided heart;
for we know, LORD our God,
that all dominion is laid out before You,
strength is in Your palm, and might in Your right hand,
Your name spreading awe over all You have created.

The שליח ציבור *continues:*

בְּאֵין מֵלִיץ יֹשֶׁר מוּל מַגִּיד פֶּשַׁע
תַּגִּיד לְיַעֲקֹב דְּבַר, חֹק וּמִשְׁפָּט
וְצַדְּקֵנוּ בַּמִּשְׁפָּט, הַמֶּלֶךְ הַמִּשְׁפָּט.

עוֹד יִזְכֹּר לָנוּ אַהֲבַת אֵיתָן, אֲדוֹנֵינוּ
וּבַבֵּן הַנֶּעֱקַד יַשְׁבִּית מְדַיְּנֵינוּ
וּבִזְכוּת הַתָּם יוֹצִיא הַיּוֹם לְצֶדֶק דִּינֵנוּ
כִּי־קָדוֹשׁ הַיּוֹם לַאֲדֹנֵינוּ: נחמיה ח

וּבְכֵן יִתְקַדַּשׁ שִׁמְךָ יהוה אֱלֹהֵינוּ
עַל יִשְׂרָאֵל עַמֶּךָ
וְעַל יְרוּשָׁלַיִם עִירֶךָ
וְעַל צִיּוֹן מִשְׁכַּן כְּבוֹדֶךָ
וְעַל מַלְכוּת בֵּית דָּוִד מְשִׁיחֶךָ
וְעַל מְכוֹנְךָ וְהֵיכָלֶךָ.

קדושת השם

וּבְכֵן תֵּן פַּחְדְּךָ יהוה אֱלֹהֵינוּ עַל כָּל מַעֲשֶׂיךָ
וְאֵימָתְךָ עַל כָּל מַה שֶּׁבָּרָאתָ
וְיִירָאוּךָ כָּל הַמַּעֲשִׂים
וְיִשְׁתַּחֲווּ לְפָנֶיךָ כָּל הַבְּרוּאִים
וְיֵעָשׂוּ כֻלָּם אֲגֻדָּה אֶחָת לַעֲשׂוֹת רְצוֹנְךָ בְּלֵבָב שָׁלֵם
כְּמוֹ שֶׁיָּדַעְנוּ יהוה אֱלֹהֵינוּ שֶׁהַשָּׁלְטָן לְפָנֶיךָ
עֹז בְּיָדְךָ וּגְבוּרָה בִּימִינֶךָ
וְשִׁמְךָ נוֹרָא עַל כָּל מַה שֶּׁבָּרָאתָ.

וּבְכֵן תֵּן כָּבוֹד And so place honor,
LORD, upon Your people,
praise on those who fear You
and hope into those who seek You,
the confidence to speak into all who long for You,
gladness to Your land and joy to Your city,
the flourishing of pride to David Your servant,
and a lamp laid out for his descendant, Your anointed,
soon, in our days.

וּבְכֵן צַדִּיקִים And then righteous people will see and rejoice,
and the upright will exult,
and the pious revel in joy,
and injustice will have nothing more to say,
and all wickedness will fade away like smoke
as You sweep the rule of arrogance from the earth.

וְתִמְלֹךְ אַתָּה And You, LORD,
will rule alone over those You have made,
in Mount Zion,
the dwelling of Your glory,
and in Jerusalem, Your holy city,
as it is written in Your holy writings:
"The LORD shall reign for ever. *Ps. 146*
He is your God, Zion,
from generation to generation,
Halleluya!"

קָדוֹשׁ אַתָּה You are holy, Your name is awesome,
and there is no god but You,
as it is written,
"The LORD of hosts shall be raised up through His judgment, *Is. 5*
the holy God, made holy in righteousness."
Blessed are You, LORD, the holy King.

וּבְכֵן תֵּן כָּבוֹד יהוה לְעַמֶּךָ
תְּהִלָּה לִירֵאֶיךָ וְתִקְוָה טוֹבָה לְדוֹרְשֶׁיךָ
וּפִתְחוֹן פֶּה לַמְיַחֲלִים לָךְ
שִׂמְחָה לְאַרְצֶךָ, וְשָׂשׂוֹן לְעִירֶךָ
וּצְמִיחַת קֶרֶן לְדָוִד עַבְדֶּךָ
וַעֲרִיכַת נֵר לְבֶן יִשַׁי מְשִׁיחֶךָ
בִּמְהֵרָה בְיָמֵינוּ.

וּבְכֵן צַדִּיקִים יִרְאוּ וְיִשְׂמָחוּ, וִישָׁרִים יַעֲלֹזוּ
וַחֲסִידִים בְּרִנָּה יָגִילוּ, וְעוֹלָתָה תִּקְפָּץ פִּיהָ
וְכָל הָרִשְׁעָה כֻּלָּהּ כְּעָשָׁן תִּכְלֶה
כִּי תַעֲבִיר מֶמְשֶׁלֶת זָדוֹן מִן הָאָרֶץ.

וְתִמְלֹךְ אַתָּה יהוה לְבַדֶּךָ עַל כָּל מַעֲשֶׂיךָ
בְּהַר צִיּוֹן מִשְׁכַּן כְּבוֹדֶךָ
וּבִירוּשָׁלַיִם עִיר קָדְשֶׁךָ
כַּכָּתוּב בְּדִבְרֵי קָדְשֶׁךָ
יִמְלֹךְ יהוה לְעוֹלָם, תהלים קמו
אֱלֹהַיִךְ צִיּוֹן לְדֹר וָדֹר, הַלְלוּיָהּ:

קָדוֹשׁ אַתָּה וְנוֹרָא שְׁמֶךָ
וְאֵין אֱלוֹהַּ מִבַּלְעָדֶיךָ
כַּכָּתוּב, וַיִּגְבַּהּ יהוה צְבָאוֹת בַּמִּשְׁפָּט ישעיה ה
וְהָאֵל הַקָּדוֹשׁ נִקְדַּשׁ בִּצְדָקָה:
בָּרוּךְ אַתָּה יהוה, הַמֶּלֶךְ הַקָּדוֹשׁ.

HOLINESS OF THE DAY

אַתָּה בְחַרְתָּנוּ You have chosen us from among all peoples.
You have loved and favored us.
You have raised us above all tongues.
You have made us holy through Your commandments.
You have brought us near, our King, to Your service,
and have called us by Your great and holy name.

On Shabbat, add the words in parentheses:

וַתִּתֶּן לָנוּ And You, LORD our God, have given us in love
(this Sabbath day for holiness and rest, and)
this Day of Atonement
for pardon and forgiveness and atonement,
to pardon all our iniquities,
(with love,) a holy assembly
in memory of the exodus from Egypt.

אֱלֹהֵינוּ Our God and God of our ancestors,
may there rise, come, reach, appear, be favored, heard,
regarded and remembered before You,
our recollection and remembrance,
as well as the remembrance of our ancestors,
and of the Messiah, son of David Your servant,
and of Jerusalem Your holy city,
and of all Your people the house of Israel –
for deliverance and well-being,
grace, loving-kindness and compassion,
life and peace, on this Day of Atonement.
On it remember us, LORD our God, for good;
recollect us for blessing, and deliver us for life.
In accord with Your promise of salvation and compassion,
spare us and be gracious to us;
have compassion on us and deliver us,
for our eyes are turned to You
because You, God, are a gracious and compassionate King.

קדושת היום

אַתָּה בְחַרְתָּנוּ מִכָּל הָעַמִּים
אָהַבְתָּ אוֹתָנוּ וְרָצִיתָ בָּנוּ
וְרוֹמַמְתָּנוּ מִכָּל הַלְּשׁוֹנוֹת
וְקִדַּשְׁתָּנוּ בְּמִצְוֹתֶיךָ וְקֵרַבְתָּנוּ מַלְכֵּנוּ לַעֲבוֹדָתֶךָ
וְשִׁמְךָ הַגָּדוֹל וְהַקָּדוֹשׁ עָלֵינוּ קָרָאתָ.

On שבת, add the words in parentheses:

וַתִּתֶּן לָנוּ יהוה אֱלֹהֵינוּ בְּאַהֲבָה אֶת
(יוֹם הַשַּׁבָּת הַזֶּה לִקְדֻשָּׁה וְלִמְנוּחָה, וְאֶת)
יוֹם הַכִּפּוּרִים הַזֶּה, לִמְחִילָה וְלִסְלִיחָה וּלְכַפָּרָה
וְלִמְחָל בּוֹ אֶת כָּל עֲוֹנוֹתֵינוּ
(בְּאַהֲבָה) מִקְרָא קֹדֶשׁ, זֵכֶר לִיצִיאַת מִצְרָיִם.

אֱלֹהֵינוּ וֵאלֹהֵי אֲבוֹתֵינוּ
יַעֲלֶה וְיָבוֹא וְיַגִּיעַ, וְיֵרָאֶה וְיֵרָצֶה וְיִשָּׁמַע
וְיִפָּקֵד וְיִזָּכֵר זִכְרוֹנֵנוּ וּפִקְדוֹנֵנוּ וְזִכְרוֹן אֲבוֹתֵינוּ
וְזִכְרוֹן מָשִׁיחַ בֶּן דָּוִד עַבְדֶּךָ, וְזִכְרוֹן יְרוּשָׁלַיִם עִיר קָדְשֶׁךָ
וְזִכְרוֹן כָּל עַמְּךָ בֵּית יִשְׂרָאֵל, לְפָנֶיךָ
לִפְלֵיטָה לְטוֹבָה, לְחֵן וּלְחֶסֶד וּלְרַחֲמִים, לְחַיִּים וּלְשָׁלוֹם
בְּיוֹם הַכִּפּוּרִים הַזֶּה.
זָכְרֵנוּ יהוה אֱלֹהֵינוּ בּוֹ לְטוֹבָה, וּפָקְדֵנוּ בוֹ לִבְרָכָה
וְהוֹשִׁיעֵנוּ בוֹ לְחַיִּים.
וּבִדְבַר יְשׁוּעָה וְרַחֲמִים
חוּס וְחָנֵּנוּ, וְרַחֵם עָלֵינוּ וְהוֹשִׁיעֵנוּ, כִּי אֵלֶיךָ עֵינֵינוּ
כִּי אֵל מֶלֶךְ חַנּוּן וְרַחוּם אָתָּה.

Traditionally, Seliḥot were recited at this point. Nowadays, most congregations omit them and begin with "Remember, Lord."

All:

זְכֹר Remember, Lord, Your compassion and loving-kindness, *Ps. 25*
for they are everlasting.
Do not hold against us the sins of those who came before us. *Ps. 79*
May Your mercies meet us swiftly,
for we have been brought very low.
Remember us, Lord, in favoring Your people;
redeem us with Your salvation.

זְכֹר Remember Your congregation, *Ps. 74*
the one that You acquired long ago,
the tribe of Your inheritance that You redeemed,
this Mount Zion that You have dwelt in.

זְכֹר Remember, Lord, the fondness of Jerusalem;
do not forever forget the love of Zion.
You shall rise up and have compassion for Zion, *Ps. 102*
for now it is right to be gracious, for the time has come.

זְכֹר Remember, Lord, what the Edomites did on the day *Ps. 137*
Jerusalem fell.
They said, "Tear it down, tear it down to its very foundations!"

זְכֹר Remember Abraham, Isaac and Yisrael, Your servants, *Ex. 32*
to whom You swore by Your own Self, when You said to them,
"I shall make your descendants
as numerous as the stars in the sky,
and I shall give all this land that I spoke of to your descendants,
and they shall inherit it forever."

זְכֹר Remember Your servants, Abraham, Isaac and Jacob; *Deut. 9*
do not attend to the stubbornness of this people,
to their wickedness or sinfulness.

Each of the following two verses is said by the Leader, then the congregation:

אַל־נָא Please, do not hold against us the sin *Num. 12*
that we committed so foolishly, that we have sinned.

We have sinned, our Rock; forgive us, our Creator.

Traditionally, סליחות *were recited at this point. Nowadays, most congregation omit them and begin with "*זְכֹר־רַחֲמֶיךָ*".*

All:

זְכֹר־רַחֲמֶיךָ יהוה וַחֲסָדֶיךָ, כִּי מֵעוֹלָם הֵמָּה: תהלים כה

אַל־תִּזְכָּר־לָנוּ עֲוֹנֹת רִאשֹׁנִים תהלים עט

מַהֵר יְקַדְּמוּנוּ רַחֲמֶיךָ כִּי דַלּוֹנוּ מְאֹד:

זָכְרֵנוּ יהוה בִּרְצוֹן עַמֶּךָ, פָּקְדֵנוּ בִּישׁוּעָתֶךָ.

זְכֹר עֲדָתְךָ קָנִיתָ קֶּדֶם, גָּאַלְתָּ שֵׁבֶט נַחֲלָתֶךָ תהלים עד

הַר־צִיּוֹן זֶה שָׁכַנְתָּ בּוֹ:

זְכֹר יהוה חִבַּת יְרוּשָׁלָיִם

אַהֲבַת צִיּוֹן אַל תִּשְׁכַּח לָנֶצַח.

אַתָּה תָקוּם תְּרַחֵם צִיּוֹן תהלים קב

כִּי־עֵת לְחֶנְנָהּ, כִּי־בָא מוֹעֵד:

זְכֹר יהוה לִבְנֵי אֱדוֹם אֵת יוֹם יְרוּשָׁלָיִם תהלים קלז

הָאוֹמְרִים עָרוּ עָרוּ, עַד הַיְסוֹד בָּהּ:

זְכֹר לְאַבְרָהָם לְיִצְחָק וּלְיִשְׂרָאֵל עֲבָדֶיךָ שמות לב

אֲשֶׁר נִשְׁבַּעְתָּ לָהֶם בָּךְ וַתְּדַבֵּר אֲלֵהֶם

אַרְבֶּה אֶת־זַרְעֲכֶם כְּכוֹכְבֵי הַשָּׁמָיִם

וְכָל־הָאָרֶץ הַזֹּאת אֲשֶׁר אָמַרְתִּי אֶתֵּן לְזַרְעֲכֶם

וְנָחֲלוּ לְעֹלָם:

זְכֹר לַעֲבָדֶיךָ לְאַבְרָהָם לְיִצְחָק וּלְיַעֲקֹב דברים ט

אַל־תֵּפֶן אֶל־קְשִׁי הָעָם הַזֶּה וְאֶל־רִשְׁעוֹ וְאֶל־חַטָּאתוֹ:

Each of the following two verses is said by the שליח ציבור*, then the* קהל*:*

אַל־נָא תָשֵׁת עָלֵינוּ חַטָּאת אֲשֶׁר נוֹאַלְנוּ וַאֲשֶׁר חָטָאנוּ: במדבר יב

חָטָאנוּ צוּרֵנוּ, סְלַח לָנוּ יוֹצְרֵנוּ.

Traditionally, a piyut of confession was inserted between the two sets of remembrance verses. Unlike those of Ma'ariv, Shaḥarit, and Ne'ila, those of Musaf and Minḥa are still said today.

In many congregations, each paragraph of the following piyut is recited by the congregation and repeated by the Leader. In others, the whole piyut is recited by all, with the Leader saying the last verse aloud.

Some omit this piyut altogether and continue with "Remember the covenant" on the next page.

אֵל נָא God, please, heal please, the diseases of this fruitful vine;
ashamed, disgraced and miserable are her fruits.
Redeem her from destruction and from the seeping wound;
answer us as You answered our father Abraham on Mount Moriah –
We have sinned, our Rock;
forgive us, our Creator.

Let the flags of the people redeemed by Your revealed arm,
be spared from plague; let them not be cut down,
and answer our call, and desire the creations of Your hands.
Answer us as You answered our fathers at the Reed Sea –
We have sinned, our Rock;
forgive us, our Creator.

Reveal now the merit of [Abraham]
the rock from which we were hewn.
Spare us from rage and lead us on a straight path.
Clear our impurity, and open our eyes to the light of Your Torah.
Answer us as You answered Joshua at Gilgal –
We have sinned, our Rock;
forgive us, our Creator.

Lord, witness the ashes of [Isaac] the bound one;
make our cure spring up.
Put an end to plunder and brokenness, tempest and storm.
Teach us and make us wise with Your perfect word.
Answer us as You answered Samuel at Mitzpah –
We have sinned, our Rock;
forgive us, our Creator.

Ta'anit (15a), which says that on fast days the leader of prayer would, in seven consecutive blessings, pray to God to answer us as He answered Abraham at the Binding, the Israelites at the Reed Sea, Joshua at Gilgal, Samuel at Mitzpah, Elijah at Mount Carmel, Jonah and Solomon. It was said particularly at times when there was a danger of an epidemic.

Traditionally, a piyut of confession was inserted between the two sets of remembrance verses. Unlike those of מעריב, שחרית *and* נעילה, *those of* מוסף *and* מנחה *are still said today.*

In many congregations, each paragraph of the following piyut is recited by the קהל *and repeated by the* שליח ציבור. *In others, the whole piyut is recited by all, with the* שליח ציבור *saying the last verse aloud.*

Some omit this piyut altogether and continue with זְכֹר לָנוּ *on the next page.*

אֵל נָא, רְפָא נָא תַּחֲלוּאֵי גֶּפֶן פּוֹרִיָּה
בּוֹשָׁה וְחָפְרָה, וְאֻמְלַל פִּרְיָהּ
גְּאָלֶנָּה מִשַּׁחַת וּמִמַּכָּה טְרִיָּה.
עֲנֵנוּ כְּשֶׁעָנִיתָ לְאַבְרָהָם אָבִינוּ בְּהַר הַמּוֹרִיָּה.
חָטָאנוּ צוּרֵנוּ, סְלַח לָנוּ יוֹצְרֵנוּ.

דְּגָלֵי עָם, פְּדוּיֵי בִּזְרוֹעַ חָשׂוּף
הַצֵּל מִנֶּגֶף וְאַל יִהְיוּ לְשִׁסּוּף
וְתַעֲנֶה קְרִיאָתֵנוּ וּלְמַעֲשֵׂה יָדֶיךָ תִּכְסֹף
עֲנֵנוּ כְּשֶׁעָנִיתָ לַאֲבוֹתֵינוּ עַל יַם סוּף.
חָטָאנוּ צוּרֵנוּ, סְלַח לָנוּ יוֹצְרֵנוּ.

זְכוּת צוּר חֻצַּב הַיּוֹם לָנוּ תְגַל
חַשְּׁכֵנוּ מֵאֶנֶף וּנְחֵנוּ בְּיֹשֶׁר מַעְגָּל
טַהֵר טֻמְאָתֵנוּ וְלִמְאוֹר תּוֹרָתְךָ עֵינֵינוּ גַּל
עֲנֵנוּ כְּשֶׁעָנִיתָ לִיהוֹשֻׁעַ בַּגִּלְגָּל.
חָטָאנוּ צוּרֵנוּ, סְלַח לָנוּ יוֹצְרֵנוּ.

יָהּ, רְאֵה דֶשֶׁן עָקוּד, וְהַצְמַח לָנוּ תְרוּפָה
כַּלֵּה שֹׁד וָשֶׁבֶר, סַעַר וְסוּפָה
לַמְּדֵנוּ וְחַכְּמֵנוּ אִמְרָתְךָ הַצְּרוּפָה
עֲנֵנוּ כְּשֶׁעָנִיתָ לִשְׁמוּאֵל בַּמִּצְפָּה.
חָטָאנוּ צוּרֵנוּ, סְלַח לָנוּ יוֹצְרֵנוּ.

אֵל נָא, רְפָא נָא *God, please, heal please.* This prayer is based on the Mishna in

[Jacob] who emerged perfect from the womb –
do not let his roots dry up.
Cleanse us of all stain and blemish, and do not have us wither.
Help us and we shall be saved,
and receive of Your ways of kindness.
Answer us as You answered Elijah on Mount Carmel –

We have sinned, our Rock;
forgive us, our Creator.

Strengthen us by the righteousness of [Moses], drawn from water,
and atone our crimes, wanton or foolish.
Free us from the terror of death that thrusts us back,
rule for our salvation; do not let us melt away in our sins.
Answer us as You answered Jonah in the belly of the fish –

We have sinned, our Rock;
forgive us, our Creator.

Remember the sanctity of [Aaron] Your devoted one,
for the sake of those [who make pilgrimage to Jerusalem]
with pleasing steps.
Awaken Your compassion, for we are doubly stricken.
Return us resolutely to our awe of You, do not expose us.
Answer us as You answered David, and Solomon his son in Jerusalem –

We have sinned, our Rock;
forgive us, our Creator.

All:

זְכֹר Remember the covenant of our fathers,
as You have said,
"I will remember My covenant with Jacob, *Lev. 26*
and also My covenant with Isaac,
and also My covenant with Abraham I will remember,
and the land I will remember."

זְכֹר Remember the covenant of the early ones, as You have said,
"I shall remember for them the covenant of the early ones, *Ibid.*
whom I brought out of the land of Egypt
before the eyes of the nations,
in order to be their God: I am the Lord."

מְתֻמָּם מְרֻחָם, שָׁרָשָׁיו אַל תַּקְמֵל
נַקֵּנוּ מִכֶּתֶם וְשֶׁמֶץ, וְלֹא נֵאָמֵל
סַעֲדֵנוּ וְנִוָּשֵׁעָה, וְאָרְחוֹת חֲסָדֶיךָ נִגָּמֵל
עֲנֵנוּ כְּשֶׁעָנִיתָ לְאֵלִיָּהוּ בְּהַר הַכַּרְמֶל.
חָטָאנוּ צוּרֵנוּ, סְלַח לָנוּ יוֹצְרֵנוּ.

עוֹדְדֵנוּ בְּצֶדֶק מָשׁוּי מִמַּיִם, וְכַפֵּר זָדוֹן וּמִשְׁוּגָה
פְּדֵנוּ מִמְּהוּמַת מָוֶת, וְאָחוֹר בַּל נִסּוֹגָה
צַוֵּה יְשׁוּעָתֵנוּ, וּבַעֲוֹנוֹתֵינוּ אַל נִתְמוֹגְגָה
עֲנֵנוּ כְּשֶׁעָנִיתָ לְיוֹנָה בִּמְעֵי הַדָּגָה.
חָטָאנוּ צוּרֵנוּ, סְלַח לָנוּ יוֹצְרֵנוּ.

קְדֻשַּׁת אִישׁ חֲסִידֶךָ זְכֹר לִיפַת פַּעֲמַיִם
רַחֲמֶיךָ תְּעוֹרֵר כִּי לָקִינוּ בְּכִפְלַיִם
שׁוּבֵנוּ תְּקֹף לְיִרְאָתֶךָ וְלֹא נֶחְשַׁף שׁוּלַיִם
עֲנֵנוּ כְּשֶׁעָנִיתָ לְדָוִד וְלִשְׁלֹמֹה בְנוֹ בִּירוּשָׁלָיִם.
חָטָאנוּ צוּרֵנוּ, סְלַח לָנוּ יוֹצְרֵנוּ.

All:

זְכָר לָנוּ בְּרִית אָבוֹת, כַּאֲשֶׁר אָמַרְתָּ:
וְזָכַרְתִּי אֶת־בְּרִיתִי יַעֲקוֹב ויקרא כו
וְאַף אֶת־בְּרִיתִי יִצְחָק, וְאַף אֶת־בְּרִיתִי אַבְרָהָם אֶזְכֹּר
וְהָאָרֶץ אֶזְכֹּר:

זְכָר לָנוּ בְּרִית רִאשׁוֹנִים, כַּאֲשֶׁר אָמַרְתָּ:
וְזָכַרְתִּי לָהֶם בְּרִית רִאשֹׁנִים שם
אֲשֶׁר הוֹצֵאתִי־אֹתָם מֵאֶרֶץ מִצְרַיִם לְעֵינֵי הַגּוֹיִם
לִהְיוֹת לָהֶם לֵאלֹהִים, אֲנִי יהוה:

Deal kindly with us as You have promised,
"Even so, when they are in the land of their enemies *Lev. 26*
I shall not reject them
and shall not detest them to the point of destruction,
to the point of breaking My covenant with them,
for I am the LORD their God."

Have compassion for us and do not destroy us,
as it is written:
"For the LORD your God is a compassionate God; *Deut. 4*
He will not forsake you, He will not destroy you,
and He will not forget the covenant of your fathers,
that He pledged to them."

Circumcise our hearts to love Your name,
as it is written:
"And the LORD your God will circumcise your heart *Deut. 30*
and the heart of your descendants
to love the LORD your God with all your heart
and with all your soul, so that you shall live."

Restore our fortunes and have compassion for us,
as it is written:
"And the LORD your God shall restore your fortunes *Ibid.*
and have compassion for you,
and shall return and gather you in from all the nations
among whom the LORD your God has scattered you."

Gather those of us who have been distanced,
as is written,
"If your distanced ones are at the very ends of the heavens, *Ibid.*
from there shall the LORD your God gather you;
from there shall He bring you."

Let us find You when we seek You,
as it is written:
"And if from there you seek the LORD your God, you shall find Him, *Deut. 4*
when you seek Him out with all your heart and with all your soul."

עֲשֵׂה עִמָּנוּ כְּמָה שֶׁהִבְטַחְתָּנוּ:
וְאַף גַּם־זֹאת בִּהְיוֹתָם בְּאֶרֶץ אֹיְבֵיהֶם ויקרא כו
לֹא־מְאַסְתִּים וְלֹא־גְעַלְתִּים לְכַלֹּתָם
לְהָפֵר בְּרִיתִי אִתָּם
כִּי אֲנִי יהוה אֱלֹהֵיהֶם:

רַחֵם עָלֵינוּ וְאַל תַּשְׁחִיתֵנוּ, כְּמָה שֶׁכָּתוּב:
כִּי אֵל רַחוּם יהוה אֱלֹהֶיךָ דברים ד
לֹא יַרְפְּךָ וְלֹא יַשְׁחִיתֶךָ
וְלֹא יִשְׁכַּח אֶת־בְּרִית אֲבֹתֶיךָ אֲשֶׁר נִשְׁבַּע לָהֶם:

מוֹל אֶת לְבָבֵנוּ לְאַהֲבָה אֶת שְׁמֶךָ, כְּמָה שֶׁכָּתוּב:
וּמָל יהוה אֱלֹהֶיךָ אֶת־לְבָבְךָ וְאֶת־לְבַב זַרְעֶךָ דברים ל
לְאַהֲבָה אֶת־יהוה אֱלֹהֶיךָ בְּכָל־לְבָבְךָ וּבְכָל־נַפְשְׁךָ
לְמַעַן חַיֶּיךָ:

הָשֵׁב שְׁבוּתֵנוּ וְרַחֲמֵנוּ, כְּמָה שֶׁכָּתוּב:
וְשָׁב יהוה אֱלֹהֶיךָ אֶת־שְׁבוּתְךָ וְרִחֲמֶךָ שם
וְשָׁב וְקִבֶּצְךָ מִכָּל־הָעַמִּים אֲשֶׁר הֱפִיצְךָ יהוה אֱלֹהֶיךָ שָׁמָּה:

קַבֵּץ נִדָּחֵינוּ, כְּמָה שֶׁכָּתוּב:
אִם־יִהְיֶה נִדַּחֲךָ בִּקְצֵה הַשָּׁמָיִם שם
מִשָּׁם יְקַבֶּצְךָ יהוה אֱלֹהֶיךָ, וּמִשָּׁם יִקָּחֶךָ:

הִמָּצֵא לָנוּ בְּבַקָּשָׁתֵנוּ, כְּמָה שֶׁכָּתוּב:
וּבִקַּשְׁתֶּם מִשָּׁם אֶת־יהוה אֱלֹהֶיךָ וּמָצָאתָ דברים ד
כִּי תִדְרְשֶׁנּוּ בְּכָל־לְבָבְךָ וּבְכָל־נַפְשֶׁךָ:

Wipe out our transgressions for Your sake,
as You have said:
"I, I am the One who shall wipe out your transgressions for My sake, *Is. 43*
and I shall not recall your sins."

Wipe out our transgressions as if they were a cloud,
as if they were a haze,
as is written,
"I have wiped out your transgressions like a cloud, *Is. 44*
and as a haze your sins; come back to Me for I have redeemed you."

Whiten our sins as snow and as wool,
as is written,
"Come now, let us reason together, says the Lord: *Is. 1*
If your sins are like scarlet,
they shall be whitened like snow;
should they be as red as crimson,
they shall become like wool."

Throw over us pure waters and purify us,
as is written,
"I shall throw pure waters over you and you shall be pure. *Ezek. 36*
I shall purify you of all your impurities and of all your idolatry."

Atone our sins on this day and purify us,
as it is written,
"For on this day you will be atoned and made pure; *Lev. 16*
of all your sins before the Lord you shall be purified."

▸ Bring us to Your holy mountain,
and let us rejoice in Your House of prayer,
as is written,
"I shall bring them to My holy mountain, *Is. 56*
and I shall make them rejoice in My House of prayer;
their offerings and their sacrifices will be accepted,
desired on My altar,
for My House will be called a house of prayer for all peoples."

מְחֵה פְשָׁעֵינוּ לְמַעַנְךָ, כַּאֲשֶׁר אָמַרְתָּ:
אָנֹכִי אָנֹכִי הוּא מֹחֶה פְשָׁעֶיךָ לְמַעֲנִי ישעיה מג
וְחַטֹּאתֶיךָ לֹא אֶזְכֹּר:

מְחֵה פְשָׁעֵינוּ כָּעָב וְכֶעָנָן, כְּמָה שֶׁכָּתוּב:
מָחִיתִי כָעָב פְּשָׁעֶיךָ וְכֶעָנָן חַטֹּאותֶיךָ ישעיה מד
שׁוּבָה אֵלַי כִּי גְאַלְתִּיךָ:

הַלְבֵּן חֲטָאֵינוּ כַּשֶּׁלֶג וְכַצֶּמֶר, כְּמָה שֶׁכָּתוּב:
לְכוּ־נָא וְנִוָּכְחָה, יֹאמַר יהוה ישעיה א
אִם־יִהְיוּ חֲטָאֵיכֶם כַּשָּׁנִים, כַּשֶּׁלֶג יַלְבִּינוּ
אִם־יַאְדִּימוּ כַתּוֹלָע, כַּצֶּמֶר יִהְיוּ:

זְרֹק עָלֵינוּ מַיִם טְהוֹרִים וְטַהֲרֵנוּ, כְּמָה שֶׁכָּתוּב:
וְזָרַקְתִּי עֲלֵיכֶם מַיִם טְהוֹרִים, וּטְהַרְתֶּם יחזקאל לו
מִכֹּל טֻמְאוֹתֵיכֶם וּמִכָּל־גִּלּוּלֵיכֶם אֲטַהֵר אֶתְכֶם:

כַּפֵּר חֲטָאֵינוּ בַּיּוֹם הַזֶּה וְטַהֲרֵנוּ, כְּמָה שֶׁכָּתוּב:
כִּי־בַיּוֹם הַזֶּה יְכַפֵּר עֲלֵיכֶם לְטַהֵר אֶתְכֶם ויקרא טז
מִכֹּל חַטֹּאתֵיכֶם, לִפְנֵי יהוה תִּטְהָרוּ:

◂ תְּבִיאֵנוּ אֶל הַר קָדְשֶׁךָ, וְשַׂמְּחֵנוּ בְּבֵית תְּפִלָּתֶךָ
כְּמָה שֶׁכָּתוּב:
וַהֲבִיאוֹתִים אֶל־הַר קָדְשִׁי ישעיה נו
וְשִׂמַּחְתִּים בְּבֵית תְּפִלָּתִי
עוֹלֹתֵיהֶם וְזִבְחֵיהֶם לְרָצוֹן עַל־מִזְבְּחִי
כִּי בֵיתִי בֵּית־תְּפִלָּה יִקָּרֵא לְכָל־הָעַמִּים:

The Ark is opened.

The following is said responsively, verse by verse. (For commentary see page 161.)

שְׁמַע קוֹלֵנוּ Listen to our voice, LORD our God.
Spare us and have compassion on us,
and in compassion and favor accept our prayer.
Turn us back, O LORD, to You, and we will return. *Lam. 5*
Renew our days as of old.
Do not cast us away from You,
and do not take Your holy spirit from us.
Do not cast us away in our old age;
when our strength is gone do not desert us.

End of responsive reading.

Do not desert us, LORD; our God, do not be distant from us.
Give us a sign of good things,
and those who hate us shall see it and be ashamed,
for You, LORD, will help us and console us.
Hear our speech, LORD, consider our thoughts.
May the words of our mouths and the meditations of our hearts
find favor before You, LORD, our Rock and Redeemer.
For it is You, LORD, that we have longed for;
You shall answer us, LORD our God.

The Ark is closed.

The Leader continues:

אֱלֹהֵינוּ Our God and God of our ancestors,
do not abandon us and do not desert us,
do not shame us and do not abandon Your covenant with us;
bring us close to Your Torah, teach us Your commandments,
show us Your ways, and turn our hearts toward the awe of Your name.
Circumcise our hearts to love You,
so that we return to You in truth, wholeheartedly.
For the sake of Your great name, pardon and forgive our iniquities,
as it is written in Your holy Writings:
"For the sake of Your name, LORD, *Ps. 25*
forgive my iniquity, though it is great."

The ארון קודש *is opened.*

The following is said responsively, verse by verse. (For commentary see page 161.)

שְׁמַע קוֹלֵנוּ, יהוה אֱלֹהֵינוּ, חוּס וְרַחֵם עָלֵינוּ
וְקַבֵּל בְּרַחֲמִים וּבְרָצוֹן אֶת תְּפִלָּתֵנוּ.
הֲשִׁיבֵנוּ יהוה אֵלֶיךָ וְנָשׁוּבָה, חַדֵּשׁ יָמֵינוּ כְּקֶדֶם: איכה ה
אַל תַּשְׁלִיכֵנוּ מִלְּפָנֶיךָ, וְרוּחַ קָדְשְׁךָ אַל תִּקַּח מִמֶּנּוּ.
אַל תַּשְׁלִיכֵנוּ לְעֵת זִקְנָה, כִּכְלוֹת כֹּחֵנוּ אַל תַּעַזְבֵנוּ.

End of responsive reading.

אַל תַּעַזְבֵנוּ יהוה, אֱלֹהֵינוּ אַל תִּרְחַק מִמֶּנּוּ.
עֲשֵׂה עִמָּנוּ אוֹת לְטוֹבָה, וְיִרְאוּ שׂוֹנְאֵינוּ וְיֵבֹשׁוּ
כִּי אַתָּה יהוה עֲזַרְתָּנוּ וְנִחַמְתָּנוּ.
אֲמָרֵינוּ הַאֲזִינָה יהוה, בִּינָה הֲגִיגֵנוּ.
יִהְיוּ לְרָצוֹן אִמְרֵי פִינוּ וְהֶגְיוֹן לִבֵּנוּ לְפָנֶיךָ, יהוה צוּרֵנוּ וְגוֹאֲלֵנוּ.
כִּי לְךָ יהוה הוֹחָלְנוּ, אַתָּה תַעֲנֶה אֲדֹנָי אֱלֹהֵינוּ.

The ארון קודש *is closed.*

The שליח ציבור *continues:*

אֱלֹהֵינוּ וֵאלֹהֵי אֲבוֹתֵינוּ
אַל תַּעַזְבֵנוּ, וְאַל תִּטְּשֵׁנוּ, וְאַל תַּכְלִימֵנוּ, וְאַל תָּפֵר בְּרִיתְךָ אִתָּנוּ
קָרְבֵנוּ לְתוֹרָתֶךָ, לַמְּדֵנוּ מִצְוֹתֶיךָ
הוֹרֵנוּ דְרָכֶיךָ, הַט לִבֵּנוּ לְיִרְאָה אֶת שְׁמֶךָ
וּמוֹל אֶת לְבָבֵנוּ לְאַהֲבָתֶךָ, וְנָשׁוּב אֵלֶיךָ בֶּאֱמֶת וּבְלֵב שָׁלֵם
וּלְמַעַן שִׁמְךָ הַגָּדוֹל תִּמְחֹל וְתִסְלַח לַעֲוֹנֵינוּ
כַּכָּתוּב בְּדִבְרֵי קָדְשֶׁךָ
לְמַעַן־שִׁמְךָ יהוה, וְסָלַחְתָּ לַעֲוֹנִי כִּי רַב־הוּא: תהלים כה

אֱלֹהֵינוּ Our God and God of our ancestors,
forgive us, pardon us, grant us atonement.

In many congregations, the Leader and the congregation recite the following piyut responsively, couplet by couplet, until "and You give us Yours"; in others, it is sung collectively.

כִּי אָנוּ For we are Your people and You are our God;
we are Your children and You are our Father;
we are Your servants and You are our Master;
we are Your gathering and You are our Place;
we are Your legacy and You are our Land;
we are Your flock and You are our Shepherd;
we are Your vineyard and You are our Keeper;
we are Your work and You are our Maker;
we are Your bride and You are our Lover;
we are Your treasure and You are our God;
we are Your people and You are our King;
we give You our word and You give us Yours.

The congregation then the Leader:

We are brazen and You are compassionate, gracious.
We are stubborn and You are long forbearing.
We are as full of iniquity as You are full of compassion.
Our days are like a fleeting shadow. *Ps. 102*
But You are here, and Your years will not end.

VIDUY

For linear translation and commentary, see page 1353.

The Leader continues, with the congregation following him in an undertone:

אֱלֹהֵינוּ Our God and God of our fathers,
let our prayer come before You,
and do not hide Yourself from our plea,
for we are not so arrogant or obstinate as to say before You,
LORD, our God and God of our fathers,
we are righteous and have not sinned,
for in truth, we and our fathers have sinned.

אֱלֹהֵינוּ וֵאלֹהֵי אֲבוֹתֵינוּ
סְלַח לָנוּ, מְחַל לָנוּ, כַּפֶּר לָנוּ.

In many congregations, the שליח ציבור *and the* קהל *recite the following piyut responsively, couplet by couplet, until* וְאַתָּה מַאֲמִירֵנוּ*; in others, it is sung collectively.*

כִּי אָנוּ עַמֶּךָ וְאַתָּה אֱלֹהֵינוּ אָנוּ בָנֶיךָ וְאַתָּה אָבִינוּ
אָנוּ עֲבָדֶיךָ וְאַתָּה אֲדוֹנֵינוּ אָנוּ קְהָלֶךָ וְאַתָּה חֶלְקֵנוּ
אָנוּ נַחֲלָתֶךָ וְאַתָּה גוֹרָלֵנוּ אָנוּ צֹאנֶךָ וְאַתָּה רוֹעֵנוּ
אָנוּ כַרְמֶךָ וְאַתָּה נוֹטְרֵנוּ אָנוּ פְעֻלָּתֶךָ וְאַתָּה יוֹצְרֵנוּ
אָנוּ רַעְיָתֶךָ וְאַתָּה דוֹדֵנוּ אָנוּ סְגֻלָּתֶךָ וְאַתָּה אֱלֹהֵינוּ
אָנוּ עַמֶּךָ וְאַתָּה מַלְכֵּנוּ אָנוּ מַאֲמִירֶיךָ וְאַתָּה מַאֲמִירֵנוּ.

The קהל *then the* שליח ציבור*:*

אָנוּ עַזֵּי פָנִים וְאַתָּה רַחוּם וְחַנּוּן
אָנוּ קְשֵׁי עֹרֶף וְאַתָּה אֶרֶךְ אַפַּיִם
אָנוּ מְלֵאֵי עָוֹן וְאַתָּה מָלֵא רַחֲמִים
אָנוּ יָמֵינוּ כְּצֵל עוֹבֵר וְאַתָּה־הוּא וּשְׁנוֹתֶיךָ לֹא יִתָּמּוּ: תהלים קב

וידוי

For linear translation and commentary, see page 1353.

The שליח ציבור *continues, with the* קהל *following him in an undertone:*

אֱלֹהֵינוּ וֵאלֹהֵי אֲבוֹתֵינוּ
תָּבוֹא לְפָנֶיךָ תְּפִלָּתֵנוּ
וְאַל תִּתְעַלַּם מִתְּחִנָּתֵנוּ.
שֶׁאֵין אֲנַחְנוּ עַזֵּי פָנִים וּקְשֵׁי עֹרֶף לוֹמַר לְפָנֶיךָ
יהוה אֱלֹהֵינוּ וֵאלֹהֵי אֲבוֹתֵינוּ
צַדִּיקִים אֲנַחְנוּ וְלֹא חָטָאנוּ.
אֲבָל אֲנַחְנוּ וַאֲבוֹתֵינוּ חָטָאנוּ.

Strike the left side of the chest with the right fist while saying each of the sins:

אָשַׁמְנוּ We have sinned, we have acted treacherously,
we have robbed, we have spoken slander.
We have acted perversely, we have acted wickedly,
we have acted presumptuously, we have been violent, we have framed lies.
We have given bad advice, we have deceived, we have scorned,
we have rebelled, we have provoked, we have turned away,
we have committed iniquity, we have transgressed,
we have persecuted, we have been obstinate.
We have acted wickedly, we have corrupted,
we have acted abominably, we have strayed, we have led others astray.

All:

סַרְנוּ We have turned away from Your commandments and good laws,
to no avail, for You are just in all that has befallen us, *Neh. 9*
for You have acted faithfully while we have done wickedly.

We have been wicked and we have transgressed,
and so we have not been saved.
Place it in our hearts to abandon the way of wickedness,
and hasten our salvation,
as it is written by Your prophet:
"Let each wicked person abandon his ways, *Is. 55*
each man of iniquity his thoughts,
and let him come back to the LORD
and He will have compassion for him,
back to our God for He will forgive abundantly."

The Leader continues:

אֱלֹהֵינוּ Our God, and God of our ancestors,
forgive and pardon our iniquities
on (*Shabbat:* this Sabbath day, and on) this Day of Atonement;
be responsive to us as we pray,
wipe away and remove all our transgressions and sins
from before Your eyes,
subdue our urges, that they be submitted to You,
and temper our obstinacy, that we may return to You truly;
renew our conscience that it may guard all Your commands,
and circumcise our hearts that we may love and revere Your name,

Strike the left side of the chest with the right fist while saying each of the sins.

אָשַׁמְנוּ, בָּגַדְנוּ, גָּזַלְנוּ, דִּבַּרְנוּ דֹפִי
הֶעֱוִינוּ, וְהִרְשַׁעְנוּ, זַדְנוּ, חָמַסְנוּ, טָפַלְנוּ שֶׁקֶר
יָעַצְנוּ רָע, כִּזַּבְנוּ, לַצְנוּ, מָרַדְנוּ, נִאַצְנוּ, סָרַרְנוּ
עָוִינוּ, פָּשַׁעְנוּ, צָרַרְנוּ, קִשִּׁינוּ עֹרֶף
רָשַׁעְנוּ, שִׁחַתְנוּ, תִּעַבְנוּ, תָּעִינוּ, תִּעְתָּעְנוּ.

All:

סַרְנוּ מִמִּצְוֹתֶיךָ וּמִמִּשְׁפָּטֶיךָ הַטּוֹבִים, וְלֹא שָׁוָה לָנוּ.
וְאַתָּה צַדִּיק עַל כָּל־הַבָּא עָלֵינוּ נחמיה ט
כִּי־אֱמֶת עָשִׂיתָ, וַאֲנַחְנוּ הִרְשָׁעְנוּ:

הִרְשַׁעְנוּ וּפָשַׁעְנוּ, לָכֵן לֹא נוֹשָׁעְנוּ
וְתֵן בְּלִבֵּנוּ לַעֲזֹב דֶּרֶךְ רֶשַׁע, וְחִישׁ לָנוּ יֶשַׁע
כַּכָּתוּב עַל יַד נְבִיאֶךָ
יַעֲזֹב רָשָׁע דַּרְכּוֹ, וְאִישׁ אָוֶן מַחְשְׁבֹתָיו ישעיה נה
וְיָשֹׁב אֶל־יהוה וִירַחֲמֵהוּ, וְאֶל־אֱלֹהֵינוּ כִּי־יַרְבֶּה לִסְלוֹחַ:

The שליח ציבור *continues:*

אֱלֹהֵינוּ וֵאלֹהֵי אֲבוֹתֵינוּ
סְלַח וּמְחַל לַעֲוֹנוֹתֵינוּ
בְּיוֹם /בשבת: הַשַּׁבָּת הַזֶּה וּבְיוֹם/ הַכִּפּוּרִים הַזֶּה
וְהֵעָתֵר לָנוּ בִּתְפִלָּתֵנוּ
מְחֵה וְהַעֲבֵר פְּשָׁעֵינוּ וְחַטֹּאתֵינוּ מִנֶּגֶד עֵינֶיךָ
וְכֹף אֶת יִצְרֵנוּ לְהִשְׁתַּעְבֶּד לָךְ
וְהַכְנַע עָרְפֵּנוּ לָשׁוּב אֵלֶיךָ בֶּאֱמֶת
וְחַדֵּשׁ כִּלְיוֹתֵינוּ לִשְׁמֹר פִּקּוּדֶיךָ
וּמוֹל אֶת לְבָבֵנוּ לְאַהֲבָה וּלְיִרְאָה אֶת שְׁמֶךָ

as it is written in Your Torah:
"And the LORD your God will circumcise your heart Deut. 30
and the heart of your descendants
to love the LORD your God with all your heart and with all your soul,
so that you shall live."
The deliberate and the unwitting sins you recognize;
the willful and the compelled,
the open deeds and the hidden –
before You they are all revealed and known.
What are we? What are our lives?
What is our loving-kindness?
What is our righteousness?
What is our salvation? What is our strength? What is our might?
What shall we say before You,
LORD our God and God of our ancestors?
Are not all the mighty like nothing before You,
the men of renown as if they had never been,
the wise as if they know nothing,
and the understanding as if they lack intelligence?
For their many works are in vain,
and the days of their lives like a fleeting breath before You.
The pre-eminence of man over the animals is nothing, Eccl. 3
for all is but a fleeting breath.

▸ What can we say before You, You who dwell on high?
What can we declare before You, You who abide in heaven?
Do You not know all, the hidden and revealed alike?

In Western Europe, the stanza "You know every secret" was said here, followed by the piyut אַתָּה מֵבִין *(page 1285). Nowadays, most congregations follow the Eastern European custom, according to which only the last two stanzas of the piyut are said (below), followed by "You know every secret."*

The Leader then the congregation:

שִׁמְךָ Your name has always been the Forgiver of Sins.
Listen to our pleading as we stand before You in prayer.

Overlook sin, for this people returning from sin,
and wipe our transgressions away before Your eyes.

כַּכָּתוּב בְּתוֹרָתֶךָ
וּמָל יהוה אֱלֹהֶיךָ אֶת־לְבָבְךָ וְאֶת־לְבַב זַרְעֶךָ דברים ל
לְאַהֲבָה אֶת־יהוה אֱלֹהֶיךָ בְּכָל־לְבָבְךָ וּבְכָל־נַפְשְׁךָ, לְמַעַן חַיֶּיךָ:
הַזְּדוֹנוֹת וְהַשְּׁגָגוֹת אַתָּה מַכִּיר
הָרָצוֹן וְהָאֹנֶס, הַגְּלוּיִים וְהַנִּסְתָּרִים
לְפָנֶיךָ הֵם גְּלוּיִים וִידוּעִים.
מָה אָנוּ, מֶה חַיֵּינוּ
מֶה חַסְדֵּנוּ, מַה צִּדְקוֹתֵינוּ
מַה יְּשׁוּעָתֵנוּ, מַה כֹּחֵנוּ, מַה גְּבוּרָתֵנוּ
מַה נֹּאמַר לְפָנֶיךָ, יהוה אֱלֹהֵינוּ וֵאלֹהֵי אֲבוֹתֵינוּ
הֲלֹא כָּל הַגִּבּוֹרִים כְּאַיִן לְפָנֶיךָ, וְאַנְשֵׁי הַשֵּׁם כְּלֹא הָיוּ
וַחֲכָמִים כִּבְלִי מַדָּע, וּנְבוֹנִים כִּבְלִי הַשְׂכֵּל
כִּי רֹב מַעֲשֵׂיהֶם תֹּהוּ, וִימֵי חַיֵּיהֶם הֶבֶל לְפָנֶיךָ
וּמוֹתַר הָאָדָם מִן־הַבְּהֵמָה אָיִן, כִּי הַכֹּל הָבֶל: קהלת ג

◂ מַה נֹּאמַר לְפָנֶיךָ יוֹשֵׁב מָרוֹם, וּמַה נְּסַפֵּר לְפָנֶיךָ שׁוֹכֵן שְׁחָקִים
הֲלֹא כָּל הַנִּסְתָּרוֹת וְהַנִּגְלוֹת אַתָּה יוֹדֵעַ.

In Western Europe, the stanza אַתָּה יוֹדֵעַ רָזֵי עוֹלָם *was said here, followed by the piyut* אַתָּה מֵבִין *(page 1285). Nowadays, most congregations follow the Eastern European custom, according to which only the last two stanzas of the piyut are said (below), followed by "*אַתָּה יוֹדֵעַ רָזֵי עוֹלָם*".*

The שליח ציבור *then the* קהל*:*

שִׁמְךָ מֵעוֹלָם עוֹבֵר עַל פֶּשַׁע
שַׁוְעָתֵנוּ תַּאֲזִין, בְּעָמְדֵנוּ לְפָנֶיךָ בִּתְפִלָּה

תַּעֲבֹר עַל פֶּשַׁע לְעַם שָׁבֵי פֶשַׁע
תִּמְחֶה פְּשָׁעֵינוּ מִנֶּגֶד עֵינֶיךָ.

The Leader continues, with the congregation following him in an undertone:

אַתָּה יוֹדֵעַ You know every secret since the world began,
and what is hidden deep inside every living thing.
You search each person's inner chambers,
examining conscience and mind.
Nothing is shrouded from You,
and nothing is hidden before Your eyes.
And so, may it be Your will,
Lord our God and God of our ancestors,
that You forgive us all our sins, pardon all our iniquities,
and grant us atonement for all of our transgressions.

Strike the left side of the chest with the right fist while saying each of the sins.

עַל חֵטְא For the sin we have sinned before You under duress or freewill,
and for the sin we have sinned before You in hardness of heart.

For the sin we have sinned before You unwittingly,
and for the sin we have sinned before You by an utterance of our lips.

For the sin we have sinned before You by unchastity,
and for the sin we have sinned before You openly or secretly.

For the sin we have sinned before You knowingly and deceitfully,
and for the sin we have sinned before You in speech.

For the sin we have sinned before You by wronging a neighbor,
and for the sin we have sinned before You by thoughts of the heart.

For the sin we have sinned before You in a gathering for immorality,
and for the sin we have sinned before You by insincere confession.

For the sin we have sinned before You by contempt for parents and teachers,
and for the sin we have sinned before You willfully or in error.

The שליח ציבור *continues, with the* קהל *following him in an undertone:*

אַתָּה יוֹדֵעַ רָזֵי עוֹלָם וְתַעֲלוּמוֹת סִתְרֵי כָּל חָי.
אַתָּה חוֹפֵשׂ כָּל חַדְרֵי בָטֶן וּבוֹחֵן כְּלָיוֹת וָלֵב.
אֵין דָּבָר נֶעְלָם מִמֶּךָּ וְאֵין נִסְתָּר מִנֶּגֶד עֵינֶיךָ.
וּבְכֵן, יְהִי רָצוֹן מִלְּפָנֶיךָ, יהוה אֱלֹהֵינוּ וֵאלֹהֵי אֲבוֹתֵינוּ
שֶׁתִּסְלַח לָנוּ עַל כָּל חַטֹּאתֵינוּ
וְתִמְחַל לָנוּ עַל כָּל עֲוֹנוֹתֵינוּ
וּתְכַפֵּר לָנוּ עַל כָּל פְּשָׁעֵינוּ.

Strike the left side of the chest with the right fist while saying each of the sins.

עַל חֵטְא שֶׁחָטָאנוּ לְפָנֶיךָ בְּאֹנֶס וּבְרָצוֹן
וְעַל חֵטְא שֶׁחָטָאנוּ לְפָנֶיךָ בְּאִמּוּץ הַלֵּב

עַל חֵטְא שֶׁחָטָאנוּ לְפָנֶיךָ בִּבְלִי דָעַת
וְעַל חֵטְא שֶׁחָטָאנוּ לְפָנֶיךָ בְּבִטּוּי שְׂפָתָיִם

עַל חֵטְא שֶׁחָטָאנוּ לְפָנֶיךָ בְּגִלּוּי עֲרָיוֹת
וְעַל חֵטְא שֶׁחָטָאנוּ לְפָנֶיךָ בְּגָלוּי וּבַסָּתֶר

עַל חֵטְא שֶׁחָטָאנוּ לְפָנֶיךָ בְּדַעַת וּבְמִרְמָה
וְעַל חֵטְא שֶׁחָטָאנוּ לְפָנֶיךָ בְּדִבּוּר פֶּה

עַל חֵטְא שֶׁחָטָאנוּ לְפָנֶיךָ בְּהוֹנָאַת רֵעַ
וְעַל חֵטְא שֶׁחָטָאנוּ לְפָנֶיךָ בְּהַרְהוֹר הַלֵּב

עַל חֵטְא שֶׁחָטָאנוּ לְפָנֶיךָ בִּוְעִידַת זְנוּת
וְעַל חֵטְא שֶׁחָטָאנוּ לְפָנֶיךָ בְּוִדּוּי פֶּה

עַל חֵטְא שֶׁחָטָאנוּ לְפָנֶיךָ בְּזִלְזוּל הוֹרִים וּמוֹרִים
וְעַל חֵטְא שֶׁחָטָאנוּ לְפָנֶיךָ בְּזָדוֹן וּבִשְׁגָגָה

For the sin we have sinned before You by force,
and for the sin we have sinned before You by desecrating Your name.

For the sin we have sinned before You by impure lips,
and for the sin we have sinned before You by foolish speech.

For the sin we have sinned before You by the evil inclination,
and for the sin we have sinned before You knowingly or unwittingly.

The congregation aloud, followed by the Leader:

FOR ALL THESE, GOD OF FORGIVENESS,
FORGIVE US, PARDON US, GRANT US ATONEMENT.

All continue in an undertone. Strike the left side of the chest with the right fist while saying each of the sins.

For the sin we have sinned before You by deceit and lies,
and for the sin we have sinned before You by bribery.

For the sin we have sinned before You by scorn,
and for the sin we have sinned before You by evil speech.

For the sin we have sinned before You in business,
and for the sin we have sinned before You with food and drink.

For the sin we have sinned before You by interest and extortion,
and for the sin we have sinned before You by being haughty.

For the sin we have sinned before You
by the idle chatter of our lips,
and for the sin we have sinned before You by prying eyes.

For the sin we have sinned before You by arrogance,
and for the sin we have sinned before You by insolence.

The congregation aloud, followed by the Leader:

FOR ALL THESE, GOD OF FORGIVENESS,
FORGIVE US, PARDON US, GRANT US ATONEMENT.

עַל חֵטְא שֶׁחָטָאנוּ לְפָנֶיךָ בְּחְֹזֶק יָד
וְעַל חֵטְא שֶׁחָטָאנוּ לְפָנֶיךָ בְּחִלּוּל הַשֵּׁם

עַל חֵטְא שֶׁחָטָאנוּ לְפָנֶיךָ בְּטֻמְאַת שְׂפָתָיִם
וְעַל חֵטְא שֶׁחָטָאנוּ לְפָנֶיךָ בְּטִפְשׁוּת פֶּה

עַל חֵטְא שֶׁחָטָאנוּ לְפָנֶיךָ בְּיֵצֶר הָרָע
וְעַל חֵטְא שֶׁחָטָאנוּ לְפָנֶיךָ בְּיוֹדְעִים וּבְלֹא יוֹדְעִים

The קהל *aloud, followed by the* שליח ציבור*:*

וְעַל כֻּלָּם אֱלוֹהַּ סְלִיחוֹת סְלַח לָנוּ, מְחַל לָנוּ, כַּפֶּר לָנוּ.

All continue in an undertone. Strike the left side of the chest with the right fist while saying each of the sins.:

עַל חֵטְא שֶׁחָטָאנוּ לְפָנֶיךָ בְּכַחַשׁ וּבְכָזָב
וְעַל חֵטְא שֶׁחָטָאנוּ לְפָנֶיךָ בְּכַפַּת שֹׁחַד

עַל חֵטְא שֶׁחָטָאנוּ לְפָנֶיךָ בְּלָצוֹן
וְעַל חֵטְא שֶׁחָטָאנוּ לְפָנֶיךָ בִּלְשׁוֹן הָרָע

עַל חֵטְא שֶׁחָטָאנוּ לְפָנֶיךָ בְּמַשָּׂא וּבְמַתָּן
וְעַל חֵטְא שֶׁחָטָאנוּ לְפָנֶיךָ בְּמַאֲכָל וּבְמִשְׁתֶּה

עַל חֵטְא שֶׁחָטָאנוּ לְפָנֶיךָ בְּנֶשֶׁךְ וּבְמַרְבִּית
וְעַל חֵטְא שֶׁחָטָאנוּ לְפָנֶיךָ בִּנְטִיַּת גָּרוֹן

עַל חֵטְא שֶׁחָטָאנוּ לְפָנֶיךָ בְּשִׂיחַ שִׂפְתוֹתֵינוּ
וְעַל חֵטְא שֶׁחָטָאנוּ לְפָנֶיךָ בְּשִׂקּוּר עָיִן

עַל חֵטְא שֶׁחָטָאנוּ לְפָנֶיךָ בְּעֵינַיִם רָמוֹת
וְעַל חֵטְא שֶׁחָטָאנוּ לְפָנֶיךָ בְּעַזּוּת מֵצַח

The קהל *aloud, followed by the* שליח ציבור*:*

וְעַל כֻּלָּם אֱלוֹהַּ סְלִיחוֹת סְלַח לָנוּ, מְחַל לָנוּ, כַּפֶּר לָנוּ.

All continue in an undertone. Strike the left side of the chest with the right fist while saying each of the sins.

For the sin we have sinned before You by casting off the yoke,
and for the sin we have sinned before You by perverting judgment.

For the sin we have sinned before You by entrapping a neighbor,
and for the sin we have sinned before You by envy.

For the sin we have sinned before You by lack of seriousness,
and for the sin we have sinned before You by obstinacy.

For the sin we have sinned before You by running to do evil,
and for the sin we have sinned before You by gossip.

For the sin we have sinned before You by vain oath,
and for the sin we have sinned before You by baseless hatred.

For the sin we have sinned before You by breach of trust,
and for the sin we have sinned before You by confusion of heart.

The congregation aloud, followed by the Leader:

FOR ALL THESE, GOD OF FORGIVENESS,
FORGIVE US, PARDON US, GRANT US ATONEMENT.

All:

וְעַל חֲטָאִים And for the sins for which we are liable to bring a burnt-offering,
and for the sins for which we are liable to bring a sin-offering,
and for the sins for which we are liable to bring an offering according to our means,
and for the sins for which we are liable to bring a guilt-offering for certain or possible sin,
and for the sins for which we are liable to lashes for rebellion,
and for the sins for which we are liable to forty lashes,
and for the sins for which we are liable to death by the hands of Heaven,
and for the sins for which we are liable to be cut off and childless,
and for the sins for which we are liable to the four death penalties inflicted by the court: stoning, burning, beheading and strangling.

All continue in an undertone. Strike the left side of the chest with the right fist while saying each of the sins.:

עַל חֵטְא שֶׁחָטָאנוּ לְפָנֶיךָ בִּפְרִיקַת עֹל
וְעַל חֵטְא שֶׁחָטָאנוּ לְפָנֶיךָ בִּפְלִילוּת
עַל חֵטְא שֶׁחָטָאנוּ לְפָנֶיךָ בִּצְדִיַּת רֵעַ
וְעַל חֵטְא שֶׁחָטָאנוּ לְפָנֶיךָ בְּצָרוּת עָיִן
עַל חֵטְא שֶׁחָטָאנוּ לְפָנֶיךָ בְּקַלּוּת רֹאשׁ
וְעַל חֵטְא שֶׁחָטָאנוּ לְפָנֶיךָ בְּקַשְׁיוּת עֹרֶף
עַל חֵטְא שֶׁחָטָאנוּ לְפָנֶיךָ בְּרִיצַת רַגְלַיִם לְהָרַע
וְעַל חֵטְא שֶׁחָטָאנוּ לְפָנֶיךָ בִּרְכִילוּת
עַל חֵטְא שֶׁחָטָאנוּ לְפָנֶיךָ בִּשְׁבוּעַת שָׁוְא
וְעַל חֵטְא שֶׁחָטָאנוּ לְפָנֶיךָ בְּשִׂנְאַת חִנָּם
עַל חֵטְא שֶׁחָטָאנוּ לְפָנֶיךָ בִּתְשׂוּמֶת יָד
וְעַל חֵטְא שֶׁחָטָאנוּ לְפָנֶיךָ בְּתִמְהוֹן לֵבָב

The קהל *aloud, followed by the* שליח ציבור*:*

וְעַל כֻּלָּם אֱלוֹהַּ סְלִיחוֹת סְלַח לָנוּ, מְחַל לָנוּ, כַּפֶּר לָנוּ.

All:

וְעַל חֲטָאִים שֶׁאָנוּ חַיָּבִים עֲלֵיהֶם עוֹלָה
וְעַל חֲטָאִים שֶׁאָנוּ חַיָּבִים עֲלֵיהֶם חַטָּאת
וְעַל חֲטָאִים שֶׁאָנוּ חַיָּבִים עֲלֵיהֶם קָרְבַּן עוֹלֶה וְיוֹרֵד
וְעַל חֲטָאִים שֶׁאָנוּ חַיָּבִים עֲלֵיהֶם אָשָׁם וַדַּאי וְתָלוּי
וְעַל חֲטָאִים שֶׁאָנוּ חַיָּבִים עֲלֵיהֶם מַכַּת מַרְדּוּת
וְעַל חֲטָאִים שֶׁאָנוּ חַיָּבִים עֲלֵיהֶם מַלְקוּת אַרְבָּעִים
וְעַל חֲטָאִים שֶׁאָנוּ חַיָּבִים עֲלֵיהֶם מִיתָה בִּידֵי שָׁמָיִם
וְעַל חֲטָאִים שֶׁאָנוּ חַיָּבִים עֲלֵיהֶם כָּרֵת וַעֲרִירִי
וְעַל חֲטָאִים שֶׁאָנוּ חַיָּבִים עֲלֵיהֶם אַרְבַּע מִיתוֹת בֵּית דִּין
סְקִילָה, שְׂרֵפָה, הֶרֶג, וְחֶנֶק.

עַל מִצְוַת For positive and negative commandments,
whether they can be remedied by an act or not,
for sins known to us and for those that are unknown –
for those that are known,
we have already declared them before You
and confessed them to You;
and for those that are unknown,
before You they are revealed and known, as it is said,
"The secret things belong to the LORD our God, *Deut. 29*
but the things that are revealed
are for us and our children for ever,
that we may fulfill all the words of this Torah."

וְדָוִד David Your servant said before You:
"Who can discern his own mistakes? *Ps. 19*
Cleanse me of my hidden faults."
Cleanse us, LORD our God,
of all our transgressions,
and purify us of all our impurities,
and throw clear waters over us to purify us,
as was written by Your prophet:
"I shall throw clear waters over you and you shall be pure. *Ezek. 36*
I shall purify you of all your impurities and of all your idolatry."

אַל תִּירָא Do not be afraid, Jacob.
Come back, wayward children, come back Israel.
See: the Guardian of Israel neither slumbers nor sleeps. *Ps. 121*
As is written by Your prophet,
"Come back, Israel, to the LORD your God, *Hos. 14*
for you have stumbled in your iniquity."
And it is said,
"Take up words to bring with you, *Ibid.*
and come back to the LORD.
Tell Him: Forgive all our iniquities and take what is good;
we shall offer up our words instead of bullocks."

עַל מִצְוַת עֲשֵׂה וְעַל מִצְוַת לֹא תַעֲשֶׂה.
בֵּין שֶׁיֵּשׁ בָּהּ קוּם עֲשֵׂה וּבֵין שֶׁאֵין בָּהּ קוּם עֲשֵׂה.
אֶת הַגְּלוּיִים לָנוּ וְאֶת שֶׁאֵינָם גְּלוּיִים לָנוּ
אֶת הַגְּלוּיִים לָנוּ, כְּבָר אֲמַרְנוּם לְפָנֶיךָ, וְהוֹדִינוּ לְךָ עֲלֵיהֶם
וְאֶת שֶׁאֵינָם גְּלוּיִים לָנוּ, לְפָנֶיךָ הֵם גְּלוּיִים וִידוּעִים
כַּדָּבָר שֶׁנֶּאֱמַר
הַנִּסְתָּרֹת לַיהוה אֱלֹהֵינוּ, וְהַנִּגְלֹת לָנוּ וּלְבָנֵינוּ עַד־עוֹלָם דברים כט
לַעֲשׂוֹת אֶת־כָּל־דִּבְרֵי הַתּוֹרָה הַזֹּאת:

וְדָוִד עַבְדְּךָ אָמַר לְפָנֶיךָ
שְׁגִיאוֹת מִי־יָבִין, מִנִּסְתָּרוֹת נַקֵּנִי: תהלים יט
נַקֵּנוּ יהוה אֱלֹהֵינוּ מִכָּל פְּשָׁעֵינוּ, וְטַהֲרֵנוּ מִכָּל טֻמְאוֹתֵינוּ
וּזְרֹק עָלֵינוּ מַיִם טְהוֹרִים וְטַהֲרֵנוּ
כַּכָּתוּב עַל יַד נְבִיאֶךָ
וְזָרַקְתִּי עֲלֵיכֶם מַיִם טְהוֹרִים, וּטְהַרְתֶּם יחזקאל לו
מִכֹּל טֻמְאוֹתֵיכֶם וּמִכָּל־גִּלּוּלֵיכֶם אֲטַהֵר אֶתְכֶם:

אַל תִּירָא יַעֲקֹב
שׁוּבוּ בָנִים שׁוֹבָבִים, שׁוּבָה יִשְׂרָאֵל.
הִנֵּה לֹא־יָנוּם וְלֹא יִישָׁן שׁוֹמֵר יִשְׂרָאֵל: תהלים קכא
כַּכָּתוּב עַל יַד נְבִיאֶךָ
שׁוּבָה יִשְׂרָאֵל עַד יהוה אֱלֹהֶיךָ, כִּי כָשַׁלְתָּ בַּעֲוֺנֶךָ: הושע יד
וְנֶאֱמַר
קְחוּ עִמָּכֶם דְּבָרִים, וְשׁוּבוּ אֶל־יהוה שם
אִמְרוּ אֵלָיו, כָּל־תִּשָּׂא עָוֺן וְקַח־טוֹב, וּנְשַׁלְּמָה פָרִים שְׂפָתֵינוּ:

וְאַתָּה And You are compassionate,
accepting those who return,
and You have promised us repentance
from the very beginning,
and it is for repentance that our eyes search after You.

וּמֵאַהֲבָתְךָ And because of Your love, LORD our God,
with which You have loved Your people Israel,
and because of Your mercy, our King, with which You have had
mercy on the children of Your covenant,
You have given us, LORD our God,
(*on Shabbat:* this Sabbath day for holiness and rest, and)
this fast day of Yom Kippur for our sins to be pardoned,
our iniquities forgiven and all our rebellions atoned.

יוֹם אֲשֶׁר A day decreed for our atonement;
Today You shall announce to us, our Rock: "You shall be purified."
As is written in Your Torah:
"For you will be atoned on this day and made pure; *Lev. 16*
of all your sins before the LORD you shall be purified."

A day on which [Moses,] who brought us an inheritance of law,
pleaded on behalf of a whole generation;
Today [God] forbore at his asking – "Please forgive."
As is written in Your Torah:
"Forgive, please, this people's iniquity, *Num. 14*
in the abundance of Your kindness,
and as You have forgiven this people
from the time of Egypt until now."
And there it is written:
"And the LORD said, I have forgiven as you asked." *Ibid.*

For the honor of Your name,
be responsive to us, You who pardons and forgives,
please forgive us for the sake of Your name.

וְאַתָּה רַחוּם מְקַבֵּל שָׁבִים
וְעַל הַתְּשׁוּבָה מֵרֹאשׁ הִבְטַחְתָּנוּ
וְעַל הַתְּשׁוּבָה עֵינֵינוּ מְיַחֲלוֹת לָךְ.

וּמֵאַהֲבָתְךָ יהוה אֱלֹהֵינוּ, שֶׁאָהַבְתָּ אֶת יִשְׂרָאֵל עַמֶּךָ
וּמֵחֶמְלָתְךָ מַלְכֵּנוּ, שֶׁחָמַלְתָּ עַל בְּנֵי בְרִיתֶךָ
נָתַתָּ לָּנוּ יהוה אֱלֹהֵינוּ אֶת
(בשבת: יוֹם הַשַּׁבָּת הַזֶּה לִקְדֻשָּׁה וְלִמְנוּחָה, וְאֶת)
יוֹם צוֹם הַכִּפּוּרִים הַזֶּה
לִמְחִילַת חֵטְא וְלִסְלִיחַת עָוֹן וּלְכַפָּרַת פֶּשַׁע.

יוֹם אֲשֶׁר הוּחַק לְכַפָּרָתֵנוּ
הַיּוֹם בּוֹ תְּבַשְּׂרֵנוּ צוּרֵנוּ תִּטְהָרוּ.
כַּכָּתוּב בְּתוֹרָתֶךָ
כִּי־בַיּוֹם הַזֶּה יְכַפֵּר עֲלֵיכֶם לְטַהֵר אֶתְכֶם — ויקרא טז
מִכֹּל חַטֹּאתֵיכֶם, לִפְנֵי יהוה תִּטְהָרוּ:

יוֹם מַנְחִיל דָּת שׁוּעַ בְּעַד דּוֹר
הַיּוֹם נָשָׂא לוֹ, בְּבַקְשׁוֹ סְלַח נָא.
כַּכָּתוּב בְּתוֹרָתֶךָ
סְלַח־נָא לַעֲוֹן הָעָם הַזֶּה כְּגֹדֶל חַסְדֶּךָ — במדבר יד
וְכַאֲשֶׁר נָשָׂאתָה לָעָם הַזֶּה מִמִּצְרַיִם וְעַד־הֵנָּה:
וְשָׁם נֶאֱמַר
וַיֹּאמֶר יהוה, סָלַחְתִּי כִּדְבָרֶךָ: — שם

בַּעֲבוּר כְּבוֹד שְׁמֶךָ
הִמָּצֵא לָנוּ מוֹחֵל וְסוֹלֵחַ / סְלַח נָא לְמַעַן שְׁמֶךָ.

A day on which those who called upon Your name will be delivered.
Today have compassion for us, as then,
when [Moses] called upon Your name.
As it is written in Your Torah:
"The Lord descended in the cloud *Ex. 34*
and stood with him there,
and proclaimed in the name of the Lord:
And the Lord passed by before him and proclaimed:
The Lord, the Lord, compassionate and gracious God,
slow to anger, abounding in loving-kindness and truth,
extending loving-kindness to a thousand generations,
forgiving iniquity, rebellion and sin, and absolving
[the guilty who repent]."

For the honor of Your name,
be responsive to us, You who pardons and forgives,
please forgive us for the sake of Your name.

A day on which You look upon the desolation of Your Sanctuary.
Today You shall act for Your name's sake,
as [Daniel] the beloved man declared:
As it is written in Your holy scriptures:
"Incline Your ear, my God, and hear. *Dan. 9*
Open Your eyes and see our desolation and that of the city
called by Your name.
Not because of our righteousness
do we lay our pleas before You,
but because of Your great compassion.
Lord, hear! Lord, forgive! Lord, listen and act!
Do not delay –
for Your sake, my God,
because Your city and Your people are called by Your name."

For the honor of Your name,
be responsive to us, You who pardons and forgives,
please forgive us for the sake of Your name.

יום קוֹרְאֵי בְשִׁמְךָ יְמַלֵּטוּ
הַיּוֹם רַחֵם עָלֵינוּ, כְּאָז קָרָא בְשֵׁם.
כַּכָּתוּב בְּתוֹרָתֶךָ
וַיֵּרֶד יהוה בֶּעָנָן, וַיִּתְיַצֵּב עִמּוֹ שָׁם, וַיִּקְרָא בְשֵׁם, יהוה: שמות לד
וַיַּעֲבֹר יהוה עַל־פָּנָיו וַיִּקְרָא
יהוה, יהוה, אֵל רַחוּם וְחַנּוּן
אֶרֶךְ אַפַּיִם, וְרַב־חֶסֶד וֶאֱמֶת:
נֹצֵר חֶסֶד לָאֲלָפִים, נֹשֵׂא עָוֹן וָפֶשַׁע וְחַטָּאָה, וְנַקֵּה:

בַּעֲבוּר כְּבוֹד שִׁמְךָ
הִמָּצֵא לָנוּ רַחוּם וְחַנּוּן / רַחֵם נָא לְמַעַן שְׁמֶךָ.

יום שׁוֹמְמוֹת הֵיכָלְךָ תַּבִּיט
הַיּוֹם תַּעֲשֶׂה לְמַעַן שִׁמְךָ, כְּנָם אִישׁ חֲמוּדוֹת.
כַּכָּתוּב בְּדִבְרֵי קָדְשֶׁךָ
הַטֵּה אֱלֹהַי אָזְנְךָ וּשֲׁמָע דניאל ט
פְּקַח עֵינֶיךָ וּרְאֵה שֹׁמְמֹתֵינוּ
וְהָעִיר אֲשֶׁר־נִקְרָא שִׁמְךָ עָלֶיהָ
כִּי לֹא עַל־צִדְקֹתֵינוּ אֲנַחְנוּ מַפִּילִים תַּחֲנוּנֵינוּ לְפָנֶיךָ
כִּי עַל־רַחֲמֶיךָ הָרַבִּים:
אֲדֹנָי שְׁמָעָה, אֲדֹנָי סְלָחָה
אֲדֹנָי הַקְשִׁיבָה וַעֲשֵׂה אַל־תְּאַחַר
לְמַעַנְךָ אֱלֹהַי, כִּי־שִׁמְךָ נִקְרָא עַל־עִירְךָ וְעַל־עַמֶּךָ:

בַּעֲבוּר כְּבוֹד שִׁמְךָ
הִמָּצֵא לָנוּ שׁוֹמֵעַ תְּפִלָּה / שְׁמַע תְּפִלָּתֵנוּ לְמַעַן שְׁמֶךָ.

In many congregations, the Leader recites the two first stichs of each line, and the congregation responds "Who, God, is like You?" Some sing the entire piyut collectively.

Who, God, is like You?

Valiant Lord, / immense in His deeds.
Who, God, is like You?
Revealing things profoundly hidden, / speaking righteousness.
Who, God, is like You?
The Rock, complete and whole, / and filled with compassion,
Who, God, is like You?
Conquering rage / to absolve those You bear.
Who, God, is like You?

All:

As was written by Your prophet:
Who, God, is like You, *Mic. 7*
who forgives iniquity
and overlooks the transgression
of the remnant of Your heritage?
He does not remain angry forever,
for He desires loving-kindness.
He shall relent
and show us compassion,
He shall suppress our iniquities,
casting all of our sins into the depths of the sea.
And all the sins of Your nation,
the house of Israel,
cast them down where they shall not be remembered
nor recalled nor come to mind ever again.
Grant truth to Jacob,
loving-kindness to Abraham,
as You promised our ancestors in ancient times.

In many congregations, the שליח ציבור *recites the two first stichs of each line, and the* קהל *responds* "מִי אֵל כָּמְוֹךָ." *Some sing the entire piyut collectively.*

מִי אֵל כָּמְוֹךָ.

אָדוֹן אַבִּיר / בְּמַעֲשָׂיו כַּבִּיר   מִי אֵל כָּמְוֹךָ
גּוֹלֶה עֲמֻקּוֹת / דּוֹבֵר צְדָקוֹת   מִי אֵל כָּמְוֹךָ
הַצּוּר תָּמִים / וּמָלֵא רַחֲמִים   מִי אֵל כָּמְוֹךָ
כּוֹבֵשׁ כְּעָסִים / לְהַצְדִּיק עֲמוּסִים   מִי אֵל כָּמְוֹךָ

All:

כַּכָּתוּב עַל יַד נְבִיאֶךָ
מִי־אֵל כָּמְוֹךָ   מיכה ז
נֹשֵׂא עָוֹן וְעֹבֵר עַל־פֶּשַׁע לִשְׁאֵרִית נַחֲלָתוֹ
לֹא־הֶחֱזִיק לָעַד אַפּוֹ כִּי־חָפֵץ חֶסֶד הוּא:
יָשׁוּב יְרַחֲמֵנוּ
יִכְבֹּשׁ עֲוֹנֹתֵינוּ
וְתַשְׁלִיךְ בִּמְצֻלוֹת יָם כָּל־חַטֹּאתָם:
וְכָל חַטֹּאת עַמְּךָ בֵּית יִשְׂרָאֵל תַּשְׁלִיךְ
בִּמְקוֹם אֲשֶׁר לֹא יִזָּכְרוּ וְלֹא יִפָּקְדוּ
וְלֹא יַעֲלוּ עַל לֵב לְעוֹלָם.
תִּתֵּן אֱמֶת לְיַעֲקֹב
חֶסֶד לְאַבְרָהָם
אֲשֶׁר־נִשְׁבַּעְתָּ לַאֲבֹתֵינוּ מִימֵי קֶדֶם:

The Leader continues. On Shabbat, add the words in parentheses:

Our God and God of our ancestors,
pardon our iniquities on (this Sabbath day, and on)
this Day of Atonement;
wipe away and remove all our transgressions and sins
from before Your eyes,
as it is said:
"I, I am the One who shall wipe out your transgressions *Is. 43*
for My sake, and I shall not recall your sins."

And it is said:
"I have wiped out your transgressions like a cloud, *Is. 44*
and as a haze your sins;
come back to Me for I have redeemed you."

And it is said:
"For on this day you will be atoned and made pure; *Lev. 16*
of all your sins before the LORD you shall be purified."
(Our God and God of our ancestors,
may You find favor in our rest.)
Make us holy through Your commandments
and grant us our share in Your Torah.
Satisfy us with Your goodness, grant us joy in Your salvation
(in love and favor, LORD our God,
grant us as our heritage Your holy Sabbath,
so that Israel, who sanctify Your name, may find rest on it),
and purify our hearts to serve You in truth.
For You are the Forgiver of Israel
and the Pardoner of the tribes of Yeshurun in every generation,
and without You we have no king who pardons and forgives,
none but You.
Blessed are You, LORD,
King who pardons and forgives our iniquities
and those of all His people the house of Israel,
and makes our guilt pass away, every single year,
King of all the earth, who sanctifies (the Sabbath,)
Israel and the Day of Atonement.

The שליח ציבור *continues. On* שבת*, add the words in parentheses:*

אֱלֹהֵינוּ וֵאלֹהֵי אֲבוֹתֵינוּ
מְחַל לַעֲוֹנוֹתֵינוּ בְּיוֹם (הַשַּׁבָּת הַזֶּה וּבְיוֹם) הַכִּפּוּרִים הַזֶּה
מְחֵה וְהַעֲבֵר פְּשָׁעֵינוּ וְחַטֹּאתֵינוּ מִנֶּגֶד עֵינֶיךָ
כָּאָמוּר
אָנֹכִי אָנֹכִי הוּא מֹחֶה פְשָׁעֶיךָ לְמַעֲנִי ישעיה מג
וְחַטֹּאתֶיךָ לֹא אֶזְכֹּר:
וְנֶאֱמַר
מָחִיתִי כָעָב פְּשָׁעֶיךָ וְכֶעָנָן חַטֹּאותֶיךָ ישעיה מד
שׁוּבָה אֵלַי כִּי גְאַלְתִּיךָ:
וְנֶאֱמַר
כִּי־בַיּוֹם הַזֶּה יְכַפֵּר עֲלֵיכֶם לְטַהֵר אֶתְכֶם ויקרא טז
מִכֹּל חַטֹּאתֵיכֶם, לִפְנֵי יהוה תִּטְהָרוּ:
(אֱלֹהֵינוּ וֵאלֹהֵי אֲבוֹתֵינוּ, רְצֵה בִמְנוּחָתֵנוּ)
קַדְּשֵׁנוּ בְּמִצְוֹתֶיךָ וְתֵן חֶלְקֵנוּ בְּתוֹרָתֶךָ
שַׂבְּעֵנוּ מִטּוּבֶךָ וְשַׂמְּחֵנוּ בִּישׁוּעָתֶךָ
(וְהַנְחִילֵנוּ יהוה אֱלֹהֵינוּ בְּאַהֲבָה וּבְרָצוֹן שַׁבְּתוֹת קָדְשֶׁךָ
וְיָנוּחוּ בָם יִשְׂרָאֵל מְקַדְּשֵׁי שְׁמֶךָ)
וְטַהֵר לִבֵּנוּ לְעָבְדְּךָ בֶּאֱמֶת
כִּי אַתָּה סָלְחָן לְיִשְׂרָאֵל, וּמָחֳלָן לְשִׁבְטֵי יְשֻׁרוּן בְּכָל דּוֹר וָדוֹר
וּמִבַּלְעָדֶיךָ אֵין לָנוּ מֶלֶךְ מוֹחֵל וְסוֹלֵחַ אֶלָּא אָתָּה.
בָּרוּךְ אַתָּה יהוה
מֶלֶךְ מוֹחֵל וְסוֹלֵחַ לַעֲוֹנוֹתֵינוּ, וְלַעֲוֹנוֹת עַמּוֹ בֵּית יִשְׂרָאֵל
וּמַעֲבִיר אַשְׁמוֹתֵינוּ בְּכָל שָׁנָה וְשָׁנָה
מֶלֶךְ עַל כָּל הָאָרֶץ
מְקַדֵּשׁ (הַשַּׁבָּת וְ) יִשְׂרָאֵל וְיוֹם הַכִּפּוּרִים.

TEMPLE SERVICE

רְצֵה Find favor, LORD our God,
in Your people Israel and their prayer.
Restore the service to Your most holy House,
and accept in love and favor
the fire-offerings of Israel and their prayer.
May the service of Your people Israel always find favor with You.
And may our eyes witness Your return to Zion in compassion.
Blessed are You, LORD, who restores His Presence to Zion.

THANKSGIVING

Bow at the first nine words.

מוֹדִים We give thanks to You,
for You are the LORD our God
and God of our ancestors
for ever and all time.
You are the Rock of our lives,
Shield of our salvation
from generation to generation.
We will thank You and
declare Your praise for our lives,
which are entrusted into Your hand;
for our souls,
which are placed in Your charge;
for Your miracles
which are with us every day;
and for Your wonders and favors
at all times, evening, morning and midday.
You are good –
for Your compassion never fails.
You are compassionate –
for Your loving-kindnesses never cease.
We have always placed our hope in You.

As the Leader recites Modim, the congregation says quietly:

מוֹדִים We give thanks to You,
for You are the LORD our God
and God of our ancestors,
God of all flesh,
who formed us
and formed the universe.
Blessings and thanks
are due to Your great
and holy name for giving us
life and sustaining us.
May You continue
to give us life and sustain us;
and may You gather our
exiles to Your holy courts,
to keep Your decrees,
do Your will and serve You
with a perfect heart,
for it is for us
to give You thanks.
Blessed be God to whom
thanksgiving is due.

For all these things may Your name be blessed and exalted,
our King, continually, for ever and all time.

עבודה

רְצֵה יהוה אֱלֹהֵינוּ בְּעַמְּךָ יִשְׂרָאֵל, וּבִתְפִלָּתָם
וְהָשֵׁב אֶת הָעֲבוֹדָה לִדְבִיר בֵּיתֶךָ
וְאִשֵּׁי יִשְׂרָאֵל וּתְפִלָּתָם בְּאַהֲבָה תְקַבֵּל בְּרָצוֹן
וּתְהִי לְרָצוֹן תָּמִיד עֲבוֹדַת יִשְׂרָאֵל עַמֶּךָ.
וְתֶחֱזֶינָה עֵינֵינוּ בְּשׁוּבְךָ לְצִיּוֹן בְּרַחֲמִים.
בָּרוּךְ אַתָּה יהוה, הַמַּחֲזִיר שְׁכִינָתוֹ לְצִיּוֹן.

הודאה

Bow at the first five words.

מוֹדִים אֲנַחְנוּ לָךְ
שָׁאַתָּה הוּא יהוה אֱלֹהֵינוּ
וֵאלֹהֵי אֲבוֹתֵינוּ לְעוֹלָם וָעֶד.
צוּר חַיֵּינוּ, מָגֵן יִשְׁעֵנוּ
אַתָּה הוּא לְדוֹר וָדוֹר.
נוֹדֶה לְּךָ וּנְסַפֵּר תְּהִלָּתֶךָ
עַל חַיֵּינוּ הַמְּסוּרִים בְּיָדֶךָ
וְעַל נִשְׁמוֹתֵינוּ הַפְּקוּדוֹת לָךְ
וְעַל נִסֶּיךָ שֶׁבְּכָל יוֹם עִמָּנוּ
וְעַל נִפְלְאוֹתֶיךָ וְטוֹבוֹתֶיךָ
שֶׁבְּכָל עֵת, עֶרֶב וָבֹקֶר וְצָהֳרָיִם.
הַטּוֹב, כִּי לֹא כָלוּ רַחֲמֶיךָ
וְהַמְרַחֵם, כִּי לֹא תַמּוּ חֲסָדֶיךָ
מֵעוֹלָם קִוִּינוּ לָךְ.

As the שליח ציבור *recites* מודים, *the* קהל *says quietly:*

מוֹדִים אֲנַחְנוּ לָךְ
שָׁאַתָּה הוּא יהוה אֱלֹהֵינוּ
וֵאלֹהֵי אֲבוֹתֵינוּ
אֱלֹהֵי כָל בָּשָׂר
יוֹצְרֵנוּ, יוֹצֵר בְּרֵאשִׁית.
בְּרָכוֹת וְהוֹדָאוֹת
לְשִׁמְךָ הַגָּדוֹל וְהַקָּדוֹשׁ
עַל שֶׁהֶחֱיִיתָנוּ וְקִיַּמְתָּנוּ.
כֵּן תְּחַיֵּנוּ וּתְקַיְּמֵנוּ
וְתֶאֱסֹף גָּלֻיּוֹתֵינוּ
לְחַצְרוֹת קָדְשֶׁךָ
לִשְׁמֹר חֻקֶּיךָ וְלַעֲשׂוֹת רְצוֹנֶךָ
וּלְעָבְדְּךָ בְּלֵבָב שָׁלֵם
עַל שֶׁאֲנַחְנוּ מוֹדִים לָךְ.
בָּרוּךְ אֵל הַהוֹדָאוֹת.

וְעַל כֻּלָּם יִתְבָּרַךְ וְיִתְרוֹמַם שִׁמְךָ מַלְכֵּנוּ תָּמִיד לְעוֹלָם וָעֶד.

The congregation, then the Leader:

אָבִינוּ מַלְכֵּנוּ Our Father, our King,
remember Your compassion and overcome Your anger,
and efface pestilence, sword, famine, captivity and destruction,
iniquity and plague, and bad mishap and all illness, and any harm,
and any feud, and all kinds of afflictions,
and all harsh decrees and baseless hatred,
from us and from all the people of Your covenant.

The congregation, then the Leader:

וּכְתֹב And write, for a good life, all the children of Your covenant.

The Leader continues:

Let all that lives thank You, Selah! and praise Your name in truth,
God, our Savior and Help, Selah!
▾Blessed are You, LORD, whose name is "the Good"
and to whom thanks are due.

אֱלֹהֵינוּ Our God and God of our fathers,
bless us with the threefold blessing in the Torah,
written by the hand of Moses Your servant
and pronounced by Aaron and his sons the priests,
Your holy people, as it is said:

May the LORD bless you and protect you. *Num. 6*
Cong: May it be Your will.
May the LORD make His face shine on you and be gracious to you.
Cong: May it be Your will.
May the LORD turn His face toward you, and grant you peace.
Cong: May it be Your will.

PEACE

שִׂים שָׁלוֹם Grant peace, goodness and blessing,
grace, loving-kindness and compassion to us
and all Israel Your people.
Bless us, our Father, all as one, with the light of Your face,

The קהל *then the* שליח ציבור:

אָבִֽינוּ מַלְכֵּֽנוּ
זְכֹר רַחֲמֶֽיךָ וּכְבֹשׁ כַּעַסְךָ
וְכַלֵּה דֶּֽבֶר, וְחֶֽרֶב, וְרָעָב, וּשְׁבִי, וּמַשְׁחִית
וְעָוֹן וּמַגֵּפָה, וּפֶֽגַע רַע וְכָל מַחֲלָה, וְכָל תַּקָּלָה
וְכָל קְטָטָה וְכָל מִינֵי פֻרְעָנִיּוֹת, וְכָל גְּזֵרָה רָעָה וְשִׂנְאַת חִנָּם
מֵעָלֵֽינוּ וּמֵעַל כָּל בְּנֵי בְרִיתֶֽךָ.

The קהל *then the* שליח ציבור:

וּכְתֹב לְחַיִּים טוֹבִים כָּל בְּנֵי בְרִיתֶֽךָ.

The שליח ציבור *continues:*

וְכֹל הַחַיִּים יוֹדֽוּךָ סֶּֽלָה, וִיהַלְלוּ אֶת שִׁמְךָ בֶּאֱמֶת
הָאֵל יְשׁוּעָתֵֽנוּ וְעֶזְרָתֵֽנוּ סֶֽלָה.
בָּרוּךְ אַתָּה יהוה, הַטּוֹב שִׁמְךָ וּלְךָ נָאֶה לְהוֹדוֹת.

אֱלֹהֵֽינוּ וֵאלֹהֵי אֲבוֹתֵֽינוּ, בָּרְכֵֽנוּ בַּבְּרָכָה הַמְשֻׁלֶּֽשֶׁת בַּתּוֹרָה
הַכְּתוּבָה עַל יְדֵי מֹשֶׁה עַבְדֶּֽךָ, הָאֲמוּרָה מִפִּי אַהֲרֹן וּבָנָיו
כֹּהֲנִים עַם קְדוֹשֶֽׁיךָ, כָּאָמוּר

יְבָרֶכְךָ יהוה וְיִשְׁמְרֶֽךָ: קהל: כֵּן יְהִי רָצוֹן — במדבר ו
יָאֵר יהוה פָּנָיו אֵלֶֽיךָ וִיחֻנֶּֽךָּ: קהל: כֵּן יְהִי רָצוֹן
יִשָּׂא יהוה פָּנָיו אֵלֶֽיךָ וְיָשֵׂם לְךָ שָׁלוֹם: קהל: כֵּן יְהִי רָצוֹן

שלום

שִׂים שָׁלוֹם טוֹבָה וּבְרָכָה, חֵן וָחֶֽסֶד וְרַחֲמִים
עָלֵֽינוּ וְעַל כָּל יִשְׂרָאֵל עַמֶּֽךָ.
בָּרְכֵֽנוּ אָבִֽינוּ כֻּלָּֽנוּ כְּאֶחָד בְּאוֹר פָּנֶֽיךָ

for by the light of Your face You have given us, LORD our God,
the Torah of life and love of kindness,
righteousness, blessing, compassion, life and peace.
May it be good in Your eyes to bless Your people Israel
at every time, in every hour, with Your peace.

The congregation then the Leader:

בְּסֵפֶר חַיִּים In the book of life,
blessing, peace and prosperity,
may we and all Your people the house of Israel
be remembered and written before You
for a good life, and for peace.*

Blessed are You, LORD,
who blesses His people Israel with peace.

**Outside Israel, many end the blessing:*
Blessed are You, LORD, who makes peace.

The following verse concludes the Leader's Repetition of the Amida.

May the words of my mouth and the meditation of my heart *Ps. 19*
find favor before You, LORD, my Rock and Redeemer.

AVINU MALKENU

On Shabbat, "Avinu Malkenu" is not said.

In Israel, many congregations omit Avinu Malkenu to allow time to say the Birkat Kohanim of Ne'ila before sunset.

The Ark is opened.

אָבִינוּ מַלְכֵּנוּ Our Father, our King, we have sinned before You.

Our Father, our King, we have no king but You.

Our Father, our King, deal kindly with us for the sake of Your name.

Our Father our King, renew for us a good year.

Our Father, our King, nullify all harsh decrees against us.

כִּי בְאוֹר פָּנֶיךָ נָתַתָּ לָּנוּ, יהוה אֱלֹהֵינוּ
תּוֹרַת חַיִּים וְאַהֲבַת חֶסֶד
וּצְדָקָה וּבְרָכָה וְרַחֲמִים וְחַיִּים וְשָׁלוֹם.
וְטוֹב בְּעֵינֶיךָ לְבָרֵךְ אֶת עַמְּךָ יִשְׂרָאֵל
בְּכָל עֵת וּבְכָל שָׁעָה בִּשְׁלוֹמֶךָ.

The קהל *then the* שליח ציבור:

בְּסֵפֶר חַיִּים, בְּרָכָה וְשָׁלוֹם, וּפַרְנָסָה טוֹבָה
נִזָּכֵר וְנִכָּתֵב לְפָנֶיךָ, אֲנַחְנוּ וְכָל עַמְּךָ בֵּית יִשְׂרָאֵל
לְחַיִּים טוֹבִים וּלְשָׁלוֹם.*

בָּרוּךְ אַתָּה יהוה, הַמְבָרֵךְ אֶת עַמּוֹ יִשְׂרָאֵל בַּשָּׁלוֹם.

**In* חוץ לארץ*, many end the blessing:*

בָּרוּךְ אַתָּה יהוה, עוֹשֵׂה הַשָּׁלוֹם.

The following verse concludes the חזרת הש״ץ.

יִהְיוּ לְרָצוֹן אִמְרֵי־פִי וְהֶגְיוֹן לִבִּי לְפָנֶיךָ, יהוה צוּרִי וְגֹאֲלִי: תהלים יט

אבינו מלכנו

On שבת*,* אָבִינוּ מַלְכֵּנוּ *is not said.*

In ארץ ישראל*, many congregations omit* אָבִינוּ מַלְכֵּנוּ *to allow time to say the* ברכת כהנים *of* נעילה *before sunset.*

The ארון קודש *is opened.*

אָבִינוּ מַלְכֵּנוּ, חָטָאנוּ לְפָנֶיךָ.
אָבִינוּ מַלְכֵּנוּ, אֵין לָנוּ מֶלֶךְ אֶלָּא אָתָּה.
אָבִינוּ מַלְכֵּנוּ, עֲשֵׂה עִמָּנוּ לְמַעַן שְׁמֶךָ.
אָבִינוּ מַלְכֵּנוּ, חַדֵּשׁ עָלֵינוּ שָׁנָה טוֹבָה.
אָבִינוּ מַלְכֵּנוּ, בַּטֵּל מֵעָלֵינוּ כָּל גְּזֵרוֹת קָשׁוֹת.

Our Father, our King, nullify the plans of those who hate us.

Our Father, our King, thwart the counsel of our enemies.

Our Father, our King, rid us of every oppressor and adversary.

Our Father, our King, close the mouths of our adversaries and accusers.

Our Father, our King, eradicate pestilence, sword, famine, captivity and destruction, iniquity and eradication from the people of Your covenant.

Our Father, our King, withhold the plague from Your heritage.

Our Father, our King, forgive and pardon all our iniquities.

Our Father, our King, wipe away and remove our transgressions and sins from Your sight.

Our Father, our King, erase in Your abundant mercy all records of our sins.

The following nine verses are said responsively, first by the Leader, then by the congregation:

Our Father, our King, bring us back to You in perfect repentance.

Our Father, our King, send a complete healing to the sick of Your people.

Our Father, our King, tear up the evil decree against us.

Our Father, our King, remember us with a memory of favorable deeds before You.

Our Father, our King, write us in the book of good life.

Our Father, our King, write us in the book of redemption and salvation.

Our Father, our King, write us in the book of livelihood and sustenance.

Our Father, our King, write us in the book of merit.

Our Father, our King, write us in the book of pardon and forgiveness.

End of responsive reading.

Our Father, our King, let salvation soon flourish for us.

Our Father, our King, raise the honor of Your people Israel.

אָבִֽינוּ מַלְכֵּֽנוּ, בַּטֵּל מַחְשְׁבוֹת שׂוֹנְאֵֽינוּ.

אָבִֽינוּ מַלְכֵּֽנוּ, הָפֵר עֲצַת אוֹיְבֵֽינוּ.

אָבִֽינוּ מַלְכֵּֽנוּ, כַּלֵּה כָּל צַר וּמַשְׂטִין מֵעָלֵֽינוּ.

אָבִֽינוּ מַלְכֵּֽנוּ, סְתֹם פִּיּוֹת מַשְׂטִינֵֽנוּ וּמְקַטְרְגֵֽנוּ.

אָבִֽינוּ מַלְכֵּֽנוּ, כַּלֵּה דֶּֽבֶר וְחֶֽרֶב וְרָעָב וּשְׁבִי וּמַשְׁחִית וְעָוֹן וּשְׁמַד מִבְּנֵי בְרִיתֶֽךָ.

אָבִֽינוּ מַלְכֵּֽנוּ, מְנַע מַגֵּפָה מִנַּחֲלָתֶֽךָ.

אָבִֽינוּ מַלְכֵּֽנוּ, סְלַח וּמְחַל לְכָל עֲוֹנוֹתֵֽינוּ.

אָבִֽינוּ מַלְכֵּֽנוּ, מְחֵה וְהַעֲבֵר פְּשָׁעֵֽינוּ וְחַטֹּאתֵֽינוּ מִנֶּֽגֶד עֵינֶֽיךָ.

אָבִֽינוּ מַלְכֵּֽנוּ, מְחֹק בְּרַחֲמֶֽיךָ הָרַבִּים כָּל שִׁטְרֵי חוֹבוֹתֵֽינוּ.

The following nine verses are said responsively, first by the שליח ציבור*, then by the* קהל*:*

אָבִֽינוּ מַלְכֵּֽנוּ, הַחֲזִירֵֽנוּ בִּתְשׁוּבָה שְׁלֵמָה לְפָנֶֽיךָ.

אָבִֽינוּ מַלְכֵּֽנוּ, שְׁלַח רְפוּאָה שְׁלֵמָה לְחוֹלֵי עַמֶּֽךָ.

אָבִֽינוּ מַלְכֵּֽנוּ, קְרַע רֹֽעַ גְּזַר דִּינֵֽנוּ.

אָבִֽינוּ מַלְכֵּֽנוּ, זָכְרֵֽנוּ בְּזִכְרוֹן טוֹב לְפָנֶֽיךָ.

אָבִֽינוּ מַלְכֵּֽנוּ, כָּתְבֵֽנוּ בְּסֵֽפֶר חַיִּים טוֹבִים.

אָבִֽינוּ מַלְכֵּֽנוּ, כָּתְבֵֽנוּ בְּסֵֽפֶר גְּאֻלָּה וִישׁוּעָה.

אָבִֽינוּ מַלְכֵּֽנוּ, כָּתְבֵֽנוּ בְּסֵֽפֶר פַּרְנָסָה וְכַלְכָּלָה.

אָבִֽינוּ מַלְכֵּֽנוּ, כָּתְבֵֽנוּ בְּסֵֽפֶר זְכֻיּוֹת.

אָבִֽינוּ מַלְכֵּֽנוּ, כָּתְבֵֽנוּ בְּסֵֽפֶר סְלִיחָה וּמְחִילָה.

End of responsive reading.

אָבִֽינוּ מַלְכֵּֽנוּ, הַצְמַח לָֽנוּ יְשׁוּעָה בְּקָרוֹב.

אָבִֽינוּ מַלְכֵּֽנוּ, הָרֵם קֶֽרֶן יִשְׂרָאֵל עַמֶּֽךָ.

Our Father, our King, raise the honor of Your anointed.

Our Father, our King, fill our hands with Your blessings.

Our Father, our King, fill our storehouses with abundance.

Our Father, our King, hear our voice, pity
and be compassionate to us.

Our Father, our King, accept, with compassion and favor, our prayer.

Our Father, our King, open the gates of heaven to our prayer.

Our Father, our King, remember that we are dust.

Our Father, our King, please do not turn us away from You
empty-handed.

Our Father, our King, may this moment be a moment of
compassion and a time of favor before You.

Our Father, our King, have pity on us, our children and our infants.

Our Father, our King, act for the sake of those who were killed
for Your holy name.

Our Father, our King, act for the sake of those who were slaughtered
for proclaiming Your Unity.

Our Father, our King, act for the sake of those
who went through fire and water
to sanctify Your name.

Our Father, our King, avenge before our eyes
the spilt blood of Your servants.

Our Father, our King, act for Your sake, if not for ours.

Our Father, our King, act for Your sake, and save us.

Our Father, our King, act for the sake of Your abundant compassion.

Our Father, our King, act for the sake of Your great, mighty and
awesome name by which we are called.

▸ Our Father, our King, be gracious to us and answer us, though we
have no worthy deeds; act with us in charity
and loving-kindness and save us.

The Ark is closed.

אָבִינוּ מַלְכֵּנוּ, הָרֵם קֶרֶן מְשִׁיחֶךָ.

אָבִינוּ מַלְכֵּנוּ, מַלֵּא יָדֵינוּ מִבִּרְכוֹתֶיךָ.

אָבִינוּ מַלְכֵּנוּ, מַלֵּא אֲסָמֵינוּ שָׂבָע.

אָבִינוּ מַלְכֵּנוּ, שְׁמַע קוֹלֵנוּ, חוּס וְרַחֵם עָלֵינוּ.

אָבִינוּ מַלְכֵּנוּ, קַבֵּל בְּרַחֲמִים וּבְרָצוֹן אֶת תְּפִלָּתֵנוּ.

אָבִינוּ מַלְכֵּנוּ, פְּתַח שַׁעֲרֵי שָׁמַיִם לִתְפִלָּתֵנוּ.

אָבִינוּ מַלְכֵּנוּ, זְכֹר כִּי עָפָר אֲנָחְנוּ.

אָבִינוּ מַלְכֵּנוּ, נָא אַל תְּשִׁיבֵנוּ רֵיקָם מִלְּפָנֶיךָ.

אָבִינוּ מַלְכֵּנוּ, תְּהֵא הַשָּׁעָה הַזֹּאת שְׁעַת רַחֲמִים וְעֵת רָצוֹן מִלְּפָנֶיךָ.

אָבִינוּ מַלְכֵּנוּ, חֲמֹל עָלֵינוּ וְעַל עוֹלָלֵינוּ וְטַפֵּנוּ.

אָבִינוּ מַלְכֵּנוּ, עֲשֵׂה לְמַעַן הֲרוּגִים עַל שֵׁם קָדְשֶׁךָ.

אָבִינוּ מַלְכֵּנוּ, עֲשֵׂה לְמַעַן טְבוּחִים עַל יִחוּדֶךָ.

אָבִינוּ מַלְכֵּנוּ, עֲשֵׂה לְמַעַן בָּאֵי בָאֵשׁ וּבַמַּיִם עַל קִדּוּשׁ שְׁמֶךָ.

אָבִינוּ מַלְכֵּנוּ, נְקֹם לְעֵינֵינוּ נִקְמַת דַּם עֲבָדֶיךָ הַשָּׁפוּךְ.

אָבִינוּ מַלְכֵּנוּ, עֲשֵׂה לְמַעַנְךָ אִם לֹא לְמַעֲנֵנוּ.

אָבִינוּ מַלְכֵּנוּ, עֲשֵׂה לְמַעַנְךָ וְהוֹשִׁיעֵנוּ.

אָבִינוּ מַלְכֵּנוּ, עֲשֵׂה לְמַעַן רַחֲמֶיךָ הָרַבִּים.

אָבִינוּ מַלְכֵּנוּ, עֲשֵׂה לְמַעַן שִׁמְךָ הַגָּדוֹל הַגִּבּוֹר וְהַנּוֹרָא
שֶׁנִּקְרָא עָלֵינוּ.

◂ אָבִינוּ מַלְכֵּנוּ, חָנֵּנוּ וַעֲנֵנוּ, כִּי אֵין בָּנוּ מַעֲשִׂים
עֲשֵׂה עִמָּנוּ צְדָקָה וָחֶסֶד וְהוֹשִׁיעֵנוּ.

The ארון קודש *is closed.*

FULL KADDISH

Leader: יִתְגַּדַּל Magnified and sanctified may His great name be,
in the world He created by His will.
May He establish His kingdom
in your lifetime and in your days,
and in the lifetime of all the house of Israel,
swiftly and soon –
and say: Amen.

All: May His great name be blessed for ever and all time.

Leader: Blessed and praised,
glorified and exalted, raised and honored,
uplifted and lauded be
the name of the Holy One, blessed be He,
above and beyond any blessing, song,
praise and consolation
uttered in the world – and say: Amen.

May the prayers and pleas of all Israel
be accepted by their Father in heaven –
and say: Amen.

May there be great peace from heaven,
and life for us and all Israel –
and say: Amen.

Bow, take three steps back, as if taking leave of the Divine Presence, then bow, first left, then right, then center, while saying:

May He who makes peace in His high places,
make peace for us and all Israel –
and say: Amen.

קדיש שלם

ש״ץ: יִתְגַּדַּל וְיִתְקַדַּשׁ שְׁמֵהּ רַבָּא (קהל: אָמֵן)
בְּעָלְמָא דִּי בְרָא כִרְעוּתֵהּ
וְיַמְלִיךְ מַלְכוּתֵהּ
בְּחַיֵּיכוֹן וּבְיוֹמֵיכוֹן וּבְחַיֵּי דְכָל בֵּית יִשְׂרָאֵל
בַּעֲגָלָא וּבִזְמַן קָרִיב, וְאִמְרוּ אָמֵן. (קהל: אָמֵן)

קהל וש״ץ: יְהֵא שְׁמֵהּ רַבָּא מְבָרַךְ לְעָלַם וּלְעָלְמֵי עָלְמַיָּא.

ש״ץ: יִתְבָּרַךְ וְיִשְׁתַּבַּח וְיִתְפָּאַר וְיִתְרוֹמַם וְיִתְנַשֵּׂא
וְיִתְהַדָּר וְיִתְעַלֶּה וְיִתְהַלָּל
שְׁמֵהּ דְּקֻדְשָׁא בְּרִיךְ הוּא (קהל: בְּרִיךְ הוּא)
לְעֵלָּא לְעֵלָּא מִכָּל בִּרְכָתָא וְשִׁירָתָא, תֻּשְׁבְּחָתָא וְנֶחֱמָתָא
דַּאֲמִירָן בְּעָלְמָא, וְאִמְרוּ אָמֵן. (קהל: אָמֵן)

תִּתְקַבַּל צְלוֹתְהוֹן וּבָעוּתְהוֹן דְּכָל יִשְׂרָאֵל
קֳדָם אֲבוּהוֹן דִּי בִשְׁמַיָּא, וְאִמְרוּ אָמֵן. (קהל: אָמֵן)

יְהֵא שְׁלָמָא רַבָּא מִן שְׁמַיָּא
וְחַיִּים, עָלֵינוּ וְעַל כָּל יִשְׂרָאֵל, וְאִמְרוּ אָמֵן. (קהל: אָמֵן)

Bow, take three steps back, as if taking leave of the Divine Presence, then bow, first left, then right, then center, while saying:

עֹשֶׂה הַשָּׁלוֹם בִּמְרוֹמָיו
הוּא יַעֲשֶׂה שָׁלוֹם עָלֵינוּ וְעַל כָּל יִשְׂרָאֵל
וְאִמְרוּ אָמֵן. (קהל: אָמֵן)

Ne'ila

אַשְׁרֵי Happy are those who dwell in Your House; *Ps. 84*
they shall continue to praise You, Selah!
Happy are the people for whom this is so; *Ps. 144*
happy are the people whose God is the LORD.
A song of praise by David. *Ps. 145*

I will exalt You, my God, the King, and bless Your name for ever and all time. Every day I will bless You, and praise Your name for ever and all time. Great is the LORD and greatly to be praised; His greatness is unfathomable. One generation will praise Your works to the next, and tell of Your mighty deeds. On the glorious splendor of Your majesty I will meditate, and on the acts of Your wonders. They shall talk of the power of Your awesome deeds, and I will tell of Your greatness. They shall recite the record of Your great goodness, and sing with joy of Your righteousness. The LORD is gracious and compassionate, slow to anger and great in loving-kindness. The LORD is good to all, and His compassion extends to all His works. All Your works shall thank You, LORD, and Your devoted ones shall bless You. They shall talk of the glory of Your kingship, and speak of Your might. To make known to mankind His mighty

---

4:1). In truth however, the Talmud states that "though the gates of prayer may be closed the gates of tears are never closed" (*Bava Metzia* 59a). What gives this moment its drama and urgency is that it is the culmination of the one day that has the power to cleanse us of our sins. The sages said that in the absence of the Temple and the service of the High Priest, the day itself atones. The prayers we are about to say are the last syllables of this consecrated time.

The sense of an ending is intense. The process of preparation and prayer began forty days ago on Rosh Ḥodesh Elul with the blowing of the shofar and the saying of Psalm 27. It gathered pace with the recitation of *Seliḥot*. It

תפילת נעילה

אַשְׁרֵי יוֹשְׁבֵי בֵיתֶךָ, עוֹד יְהַלְלְוּךָ סֶּלָה: תהלים פד
אַשְׁרֵי הָעָם שֶׁכָּכָה לּוֹ, אַשְׁרֵי הָעָם שֶׁיהוה אֱלֹהָיו: תהלים קמד
תְּהִלָּה לְדָוִד תהלים קמה
אֲרוֹמִמְךָ אֱלוֹהַי הַמֶּלֶךְ, וַאֲבָרְכָה שִׁמְךָ לְעוֹלָם וָעֶד:
בְּכָל־יוֹם אֲבָרְכֶךָּ, וַאֲהַלְלָה שִׁמְךָ לְעוֹלָם וָעֶד:
גָּדוֹל יהוה וּמְהֻלָּל מְאֹד, וְלִגְדֻלָּתוֹ אֵין חֵקֶר:
דּוֹר לְדוֹר יְשַׁבַּח מַעֲשֶׂיךָ, וּגְבוּרֹתֶיךָ יַגִּידוּ:
הֲדַר כְּבוֹד הוֹדֶךָ, וְדִבְרֵי נִפְלְאֹתֶיךָ אָשִׂיחָה:
וֶעֱזוּז נוֹרְאֹתֶיךָ יֹאמֵרוּ, וּגְדוּלָּתְךָ אֲסַפְּרֶנָּה:
זֵכֶר רַב־טוּבְךָ יַבִּיעוּ, וְצִדְקָתְךָ יְרַנֵּנוּ:
חַנּוּן וְרַחוּם יהוה, אֶרֶךְ אַפַּיִם וּגְדָל־חָסֶד:
טוֹב־יהוה לַכֹּל, וְרַחֲמָיו עַל־כָּל־מַעֲשָׂיו:
יוֹדְוּךָ יהוה כָּל־מַעֲשֶׂיךָ, וַחֲסִידֶיךָ יְבָרְכוּכָה:
כְּבוֹד מַלְכוּתְךָ יֹאמֵרוּ, וּגְבוּרָתְךָ יְדַבֵּרוּ:
לְהוֹדִיעַ לִבְנֵי הָאָדָם גְּבוּרֹתָיו, וּכְבוֹד הֲדַר מַלְכוּתוֹ:

NE'ILA

Ne'ila, short for *Ne'ilat She'arim*, "the closing of the gates," is a service nowadays unique to Yom Kippur. In ancient times a Ne'ila prayer was also said on public fasts instituted in Israel because of drought; and when the Temple stood a Ne'ila prayer was said by priests during their rota of duty. Now it exists only on Yom Kippur.

There was a dispute between Rav and Rabbi Yoḥanan as to the significance of the name. One held that it meant the closing of the gates of the Temple, the other that it meant the closing of the gates of heaven (Yerushalmi, *Berakhot*

deeds and the glorious majesty of His kingship. Your kingdom is an everlasting kingdom, and Your reign is for all generations. The LORD supports all who fall, and raises all who are bowed down. All raise their eyes to You in hope, and You give them their food in due season. You open Your hand, and satisfy every living thing with favor. The LORD is righteous in all His ways, and kind in all He does. The LORD is close to all who call on Him, to all who call on Him in truth. He fulfills the will of those who revere Him; He hears their cry and saves them. The LORD guards all who love Him, but all the wicked He will destroy.
▸ My mouth shall speak the praise of the LORD, and all creatures shall bless His holy name for ever and all time.

We will bless the LORD now and for ever. Halleluya! *Ps. 115*

---

loves us, can bring the *Shekhina* into our lives, turning a little of the prose of the human condition into poetry and song.

Jews do not accept suffering that can be alleviated or wrong that can be put right as the will of God. We accept only what we cannot change. What we can heal, we must. So, disproportionately, Jews are to be found as teachers fighting ignorance, doctors fighting disease, economists fighting poverty, and lawyers fighting injustice. Judaism has given rise, not in one generation but in more than a hundred, to an unrivaled succession of prophets, priests, philosophers, poets, masters of halakha and aggada, commentators, codifiers, rationalists, mystics, sages and saints, people who gave the Divine Presence its local habitation and name, and taught us to make gentle the life of this world. Judaism has consistently asked great things of our people, and in so doing, helped make them great. Tonight, at Ne'ila, God is calling us to greatness.

That greatness is not conventional. We do not need to be rich or successful or famous or powerful to find favor in the eyes of God and our fellows. All we need is *ḥen*, graciousness; *ḥesed*, kindness; *raḥamim*, compassion; *tzedek*, righteousness and integrity; and *mishpat*, what Albert Einstein called the "almost fanatical love of justice" that made him thank his stars he was a Jew.

To be a Jew is to seek to heal some of the wounds of the world, to search out the lonely and distressed and bring them comfort, to love and forgive as God loves and forgives, to study God's Torah until it is engraved in our minds, to keep God's commands so that they etch our lives with the charisma

מַלְכוּתְךָ מַלְכוּת כָּל־עֹלָמִים, וּמֶמְשַׁלְתְּךָ בְּכָל־דּוֹר וָדֹר:
סוֹמֵךְ יהוה לְכָל־הַנֹּפְלִים, וְזוֹקֵף לְכָל־הַכְּפוּפִים:
עֵינֵי־כֹל אֵלֶיךָ יְשַׂבֵּרוּ, וְאַתָּה נוֹתֵן־לָהֶם אֶת־אָכְלָם בְּעִתּוֹ:
פּוֹתֵחַ אֶת־יָדֶךָ, וּמַשְׂבִּיעַ לְכָל־חַי רָצוֹן:
צַדִּיק יהוה בְּכָל־דְּרָכָיו, וְחָסִיד בְּכָל־מַעֲשָׂיו:
קָרוֹב יהוה לְכָל־קֹרְאָיו, לְכֹל אֲשֶׁר יִקְרָאֻהוּ בֶאֱמֶת:
רְצוֹן־יְרֵאָיו יַעֲשֶׂה, וְאֶת־שַׁוְעָתָם יִשְׁמַע, וְיוֹשִׁיעֵם:
שׁוֹמֵר יהוה אֶת־כָּל־אֹהֲבָיו, וְאֵת כָּל־הָרְשָׁעִים יַשְׁמִיד:
◂ תְּהִלַּת יהוה יְדַבֶּר פִּי, וִיבָרֵךְ כָּל־בָּשָׂר שֵׁם קָדְשׁוֹ לְעוֹלָם וָעֶד:
תהלים קטו וַאֲנַחְנוּ נְבָרֵךְ יָהּ מֵעַתָּה וְעַד־עוֹלָם, הַלְלוּיָהּ:

became a courtroom drama on Rosh HaShana with the shofar proclaiming that the heavenly court is in session and we are on trial for our lives. The case for the defense has been made. We have neither denied nor made excuses for our sins. We have confessed our guilt, individual and collective, and we have appealed for mercy and forgiveness. The trial is now in its closing moments. The court is about to rise. The verdict, signed, will soon be sealed.

At no other time, barring exceptional circumstance, will we be as close to God as we will be for the next hour. We have fasted, prayed and had the courage to face the worst about ourselves. We have been empowered to do so by our unshakable belief that God loves, forgives, and has more faith in us than we do in ourselves. We can be better than we are, better than we were. And though we may have stumbled and fallen, God is holding out His hand to lift us, giving us the strength to recover, endure, and grow to become the person He is calling on us to be: a blessing to others, a vehicle through which His light flows into the world, an agent of hope, His partner in the work of redemption.

Faith is the courage to take a risk, as Abraham and Sarah took the risk of following the Voice calling them to leave their land and birthplace to travel to an unknown destination, as the Israelites did when they began their journey into the desert, an "unsown land." To be a Jew is to take the risk of believing that the evils of this world are not inevitable or irremediable; that we can mend some of the fractures of humanity; that we, by loving others as God

וּבָא לְצִיּוֹן גּוֹאֵל "A redeemer will come to Zion, *Is. 59*
to those of Jacob who repent of their sins," declares the LORD.
"As for Me, this is My covenant with them," says the LORD.
"My spirit, that is on you,
and My words I have placed in your mouth
will not depart from your mouth,
or from the mouth of your children,
or from the mouth of their descendants
from this time on and for ever," says the LORD.

▸ You are the Holy One, enthroned on the praises of Israel. *Ps. 22*
And [the angels] call to one another, saying, "Holy, holy, holy *Is. 6*
is the LORD of hosts; the whole world is filled with His glory."
And they receive permission from one another, saying: *Targum Yonatan Is. 6*
"Holy in the highest heavens, home of His Presence; holy on earth,
the work of His strength; holy for ever and all time is the LORD of hosts;
the whole earth is full of His radiant glory."

▸ Then a wind lifted me up and I heard behind me *Ezek. 3*
the sound of a great noise, saying,
"Blessed is the LORD's glory from His place."
Then a wind lifted me up and I heard behind me *Targum Yonatan Ezek. 3*
the sound of a great tempest of those who uttered praise, saying,
"Blessed is the LORD's glory from the place of the home of His Presence."

The LORD shall reign for ever and all time. *Ex. 15*
The LORD's kingdom is established for ever and all time. *Targum Onkelos Ex. 15*

The greatness to which God is calling us, here, now, is "not in heaven nor across the sea" but in our hearts, minds and lives, in our homes and families, our work and its interactions, the tenor and texture of our relationships, the way we act and speak and listen and spend our time. The question God asks us at Ne'ila is not, "Are you perfect?" but "Can you grow?"

There are three barriers to growth. One is self-righteousness, the belief that we are already great. A second is false humility, the belief that we can never be great. The third is learned helplessness, the belief that we can't change the world because we can't change ourselves. All three are false. We are not yet great but we are summoned to greatness, and we can change. We can live lives

וּבָא לְצִיּוֹן גּוֹאֵל, וּלְשָׁבֵי פֶשַׁע בְּיַעֲקֹב, נְאֻם יהוה: ישעיה נט
וַאֲנִי זֹאת בְּרִיתִי אוֹתָם, אָמַר יהוה, רוּחִי אֲשֶׁר עָלֶיךָ וּדְבָרַי אֲשֶׁר־שַׂמְתִּי בְּפִיךָ, לֹא־יָמוּשׁוּ מִפִּיךָ וּמִפִּי זַרְעֲךָ וּמִפִּי זֶרַע זַרְעֲךָ, אָמַר יהוה, מֵעַתָּה וְעַד־עוֹלָם:

◄ וְאַתָּה קָדוֹשׁ יוֹשֵׁב תְּהִלּוֹת יִשְׂרָאֵל: וְקָרָא זֶה אֶל־זֶה וְאָמַר ◄ תהלים כב ישעיה ו
קָדוֹשׁ, קָדוֹשׁ, קָדוֹשׁ, יהוה צְבָאוֹת, מְלֹא כָל־הָאָרֶץ כְּבוֹדוֹ:
וּמְקַבְּלִין דֵּין מִן דֵּין וְאָמְרִין, קַדִּישׁ בִּשְׁמֵי מְרוֹמָא עִלָּאָה בֵּית שְׁכִינְתֵּהּ, קַדִּישׁ עַל אַרְעָא עוֹבַד גְּבוּרְתֵּהּ, קַדִּישׁ לְעָלַם וּלְעָלְמֵי עָלְמַיָּא, יהוה צְבָאוֹת, מַלְיָא כָל אַרְעָא זִיו יְקָרֵהּ. תרגום יונתן ישעיה ו

◄ וַתִּשָּׂאֵנִי רוּחַ, וָאֶשְׁמַע אַחֲרַי קוֹל רַעַשׁ גָּדוֹל ◄ יחזקאל ג
בָּרוּךְ כְּבוֹד־יהוה מִמְּקוֹמוֹ:
וּנְטָלַתְנִי רוּחָא, וּשְׁמָעִית בַּתְרַי קָל זִיעַ סַגִּיא, דִּמְשַׁבְּחִין וְאָמְרִין, בְּרִיךְ יְקָרָא דַיהוה מֵאֲתַר בֵּית שְׁכִינְתֵּהּ. תרגום יונתן יחזקאל ג

יהוה יִמְלֹךְ לְעֹלָם וָעֶד: שמות טו
יהוה מַלְכוּתֵהּ קָאֵם לְעָלַם וּלְעָלְמֵי עָלְמַיָּא. תרגום אונקלוס שמות טו

---

of holiness, to bring God's presence into the shared spaces of our common life, and to continue the story of our ancestors, writing our chapter in the book of Jewish life.

"Wherever you find God's greatness," said Rabbi Yoḥanan, "there you will find His humility" (*Megilla* 31a). And wherever you find true humility, there you will find greatness. That is what Yom Kippur is about: finding the courage to let go of the need for self-esteem that fuels our passion for self-justification, our blustering claim that we are in the right when in truth we know we are often in the wrong. Most national literatures, ancient and modern, record a people's triumphs. Jewish literature records our failures, moral and spiritual. No people has been so piercingly honest in charting its shortcomings. In Tanakh there is no one without sin. Believing as we do that even the greatest are merely human, we also know that even the merely human can also be great. And greatness begins in the humility of recognizing our failings and faults.

יהוה LORD, God of Abraham, Isaac and Yisrael, our ancestors, may *1 Chr. 29*
You keep this for ever so that it forms the thoughts in Your people's
heart, and directs their heart toward You. He is compassionate. He *Ps. 78*
forgives iniquity and does not destroy. Repeatedly He suppresses
His anger, not rousing His full wrath. For You, my LORD, are good *Ps. 86*
and forgiving, abundantly kind to all who call on You. Your righ- *Ps. 119*
teousness is eternally righteous, and Your Torah is truth. Grant *Mic. 7*
truth to Jacob, loving-kindness to Abraham, as You promised our
ancestors in ancient times. Blessed is my LORD for day after day *Ps. 68*
He burdens us [with His blessings]; God is our salvation, Selah!
The LORD of hosts is with us; the God of Jacob is our refuge, Selah! *Ps. 46*
LORD of hosts, happy is the one who trusts in You. LORD, save. May *Ps. 20* *Ps. 84*
the King answer us on the day we call.

בָּרוּךְ Blessed is He, our God, who created us for His glory, separating us from those who go astray; who gave us the Torah of truth, planting within us eternal life. May He open our heart to His Torah, imbuing our heart with the love and awe of Him, that we may do His will and serve Him with a perfect heart, so that we neither toil in vain nor give birth to confusion.

יְהִי רָצוֹן May it be Your will, O LORD our God and God of our ancestors, that we keep Your laws in this world, and thus be worthy to live,
see and inherit goodness and blessing in the Messianic Age and in
the life of the World to Come. So that my soul may sing to You and *Ps. 30*
not be silent. LORD, my God, for ever I will thank You. Blessed is *Jer. 17*
the man who trusts in the LORD, whose trust is in the LORD alone.
Trust in the LORD for evermore, for God, the LORD, is an everlast- *Is. 26*
ing Rock. ▸ Those who know Your name trust in You, for You, LORD, *Ps. 9*
do not forsake those who seek You. The LORD desired, for the sake *Is. 42*
of Israel's merit, to make the Torah great and glorious.

---

us in the book of life so that we can fulfill the task He has set us, to be His ambassadors to humankind.

יהוה אֱלֹהֵי אַבְרָהָם יִצְחָק וְיִשְׂרָאֵל אֲבֹתֵינוּ, שָׁמְרָה־זֹּאת לְעוֹלָם דברי הימים א, כט
לְיֵצֶר מַחְשְׁבוֹת לְבַב עַמֶּךָ, וְהָכֵן לְבָבָם אֵלֶיךָ: וְהוּא רַחוּם יְכַפֵּר תהלים עח
עָוֹן וְלֹא־יַשְׁחִית, וְהִרְבָּה לְהָשִׁיב אַפּוֹ, וְלֹא־יָעִיר כָּל־חֲמָתוֹ: כִּי־ תהלים פו
אַתָּה אֲדֹנָי טוֹב וְסַלָּח, וְרַב־חֶסֶד לְכָל־קֹרְאֶיךָ: צִדְקָתְךָ צֶדֶק תהלים קיט
לְעוֹלָם וְתוֹרָתְךָ אֱמֶת: תִּתֵּן אֱמֶת לְיַעֲקֹב, חֶסֶד לְאַבְרָהָם, אֲשֶׁר־ מיכה ז
נִשְׁבַּעְתָּ לַאֲבֹתֵינוּ מִימֵי קֶדֶם: בָּרוּךְ אֲדֹנָי יוֹם יוֹם יַעֲמָס־לָנוּ, תהלים סח
הָאֵל יְשׁוּעָתֵנוּ סֶלָה: יהוה צְבָאוֹת עִמָּנוּ, מִשְׂגָּב לָנוּ אֱלֹהֵי יַעֲקֹב תהלים מו
סֶלָה: יהוה צְבָאוֹת, אַשְׁרֵי אָדָם בֹּטֵחַ בָּךְ: יהוה הוֹשִׁיעָה, הַמֶּלֶךְ תהלים פד תהלים כ
יַעֲנֵנוּ בְיוֹם־קָרְאֵנוּ:

בָּרוּךְ הוּא אֱלֹהֵינוּ שֶׁבְּרָאָנוּ לִכְבוֹדוֹ, וְהִבְדִּילָנוּ מִן הַתּוֹעִים, וְנָתַן לָנוּ תּוֹרַת אֱמֶת, וְחַיֵּי עוֹלָם נָטַע בְּתוֹכֵנוּ. הוּא יִפְתַּח לִבֵּנוּ בְּתוֹרָתוֹ, וְיָשֵׂם בְּלִבֵּנוּ אַהֲבָתוֹ וְיִרְאָתוֹ וְלַעֲשׂוֹת רְצוֹנוֹ וּלְעָבְדוֹ בְּלֵבָב שָׁלֵם, לְמַעַן לֹא נִיגַע לָרִיק וְלֹא נֵלֵד לַבֶּהָלָה.

יְהִי רָצוֹן מִלְּפָנֶיךָ יהוה אֱלֹהֵינוּ וֵאלֹהֵי אֲבוֹתֵינוּ, שֶׁנִּשְׁמֹר חֻקֶּיךָ
בָּעוֹלָם הַזֶּה, וְנִזְכֶּה וְנִחְיֶה וְנִרְאֶה וְנִירַשׁ טוֹבָה וּבְרָכָה, לִשְׁנֵי יְמוֹת
הַמָּשִׁיחַ וּלְחַיֵּי הָעוֹלָם הַבָּא. לְמַעַן יְזַמֶּרְךָ כָבוֹד וְלֹא יִדֹּם, יהוה תהלים ל
אֱלֹהַי, לְעוֹלָם אוֹדֶךָּ: בָּרוּךְ הַגֶּבֶר אֲשֶׁר יִבְטַח בַּיהוה, וְהָיָה יהוה ירמיה יז
מִבְטַחוֹ: בִּטְחוּ בַיהוה עֲדֵי־עַד, כִּי בְּיָהּ יהוה צוּר עוֹלָמִים: ◂ וְיִבְטְחוּ ישעיה כו תהלים ט
בְךָ יוֹדְעֵי שְׁמֶךָ, כִּי לֹא־עָזַבְתָּ דֹרְשֶׁיךָ, יהוה: יהוה חָפֵץ לְמַעַן ישעיה מב
צִדְקוֹ, יַגְדִּיל תּוֹרָה וְיַאְדִּיר:

---

of moral beauty and spiritual depth. We can open our eyes to the presence of God around us, incline our inner ear to the voice of God within us. We can bring blessings into other people's lives.

And now, in absolute humility, we turn to God, pleading with Him to seal

HALF KADDISH

Leader: יִתְגַּדַּל Magnified and sanctified
may His great name be,
in the world He created by His will.
May He establish His kingdom
in your lifetime and in your days,
and in the lifetime of all the house of Israel,
swiftly and soon –
and say: Amen.

All: May His great name be blessed for ever and all time.

Leader: Blessed and praised, glorified and exalted,
raised and honored, uplifted and lauded
be the name of the Holy One, blessed be He,
above and beyond any blessing, song,
praise and consolation
uttered in the world –
and say: Amen.

THE AMIDA

The following prayer, until "in former years" on page 1134, is said silently, standing with feet together. If there is a minyan, the Amida is repeated aloud by the Leader. Take three steps forward and at the points indicated by ▾, bend the knees at the first word, bow at the second, and stand straight before saying God's name.

When I proclaim the Lord's name, give glory to our God. *Deut. 32*
O Lord, open my lips, so that my mouth may declare Your praise. *Ps. 51*

PATRIARCHS

▾בָּרוּךְ Blessed are You, Lord our God and God of our fathers,
God of Abraham, God of Isaac and God of Jacob;
the great, mighty and awesome God, God Most High,

חצי קדיש

ש״ץ: יִתְגַּדַּל וְיִתְקַדַּשׁ שְׁמֵהּ רַבָּא (קהל: אָמֵן)
בְּעָלְמָא דִּי בְרָא כִרְעוּתֵהּ
וְיַמְלִיךְ מַלְכוּתֵהּ
בְּחַיֵּיכוֹן וּבְיוֹמֵיכוֹן וּבְחַיֵּי דְכָל בֵּית יִשְׂרָאֵל
בַּעֲגָלָא וּבִזְמַן קָרִיב
וְאִמְרוּ אָמֵן. (קהל: אָמֵן)

קהל וש״ץ: יְהֵא שְׁמֵהּ רַבָּא מְבָרַךְ לְעָלַם וּלְעָלְמֵי עָלְמַיָּא.

ש״ץ: יִתְבָּרַךְ וְיִשְׁתַּבַּח וְיִתְפָּאַר וְיִתְרוֹמַם וְיִתְנַשֵּׂא
וְיִתְהַדָּר וְיִתְעַלֶּה וְיִתְהַלָּל
שְׁמֵהּ דְּקֻדְשָׁא בְּרִיךְ הוּא (קהל: בְּרִיךְ הוּא)
לְעֵלָּא לְעֵלָּא מִכָּל בִּרְכָתָא וְשִׁירָתָא, תֻּשְׁבְּחָתָא וְנֶחֱמָתָא
דַּאֲמִירָן בְּעָלְמָא
וְאִמְרוּ אָמֵן. (קהל: אָמֵן)

עמידה

The following prayer, until קַדְמֹנִיּוֹת *on page 1135, is said silently, standing with feet together. If there is a* מנין*, the* עמידה *is repeated aloud by the* שליח ציבור*. Take three steps forward and at the points indicated by* ▾*, bend the knees at the first word, bow at the second, and stand straight before saying God's name.*

כִּי שֵׁם יהוה אֶקְרָא, הָבוּ גֹדֶל לֵאלֹהֵינוּ: דברים לב
אֲדֹנָי, שְׂפָתַי תִּפְתָּח, וּפִי יַגִּיד תְּהִלָּתֶךָ: תהלים נא

אבות

▾בָּרוּךְ אַתָּה יהוה, אֱלֹהֵינוּ וֵאלֹהֵי אֲבוֹתֵינוּ
אֱלֹהֵי אַבְרָהָם, אֱלֹהֵי יִצְחָק, וֵאלֹהֵי יַעֲקֹב
הָאֵל הַגָּדוֹל הַגִּבּוֹר וְהַנּוֹרָא, אֵל עֶלְיוֹן

who bestows acts of loving-kindness and creates all,
who remembers the loving-kindness of the fathers
and will bring a Redeemer to their children's children
for the sake of His name, in love.

זָכְרֵנוּ לְחַיִּים Remember us for life, O King who desires life,
and seal us in the book of life – for Your sake, O God of life.
King, Helper, Savior, Shield:
▾Blessed are You, LORD, Shield of Abraham.

DIVINE MIGHT
אַתָּה גִּבּוֹר You are eternally mighty, LORD.
You give life to the dead
and have great power to save.
In Israel: He causes the dew to fall.
He sustains the living with loving-kindness,
and with great compassion revives the dead.
He supports the fallen,
heals the sick, sets captives free,
and keeps His faith with those who sleep in the dust.
Who is like You, Master of might,
and to whom can You be compared,
O King who brings death and gives life,
and makes salvation grow?

מִי כָמְוֹךָ Who is like You, compassionate Father,
who remembers His creatures in compassion, for life?
Faithful are You to revive the dead.
Blessed are You, LORD,
who revives the dead.

---

specifically at the end of the day, since at any previous point we can lodge an appeal.

גּוֹמֵל חֲסָדִים טוֹבִים, וְקוֹנֵה הַכֹּל
וְזוֹכֵר חַסְדֵי אָבוֹת
וּמֵבִיא גוֹאֵל לִבְנֵי בְנֵיהֶם לְמַעַן שְׁמוֹ בְּאַהֲבָה.

זָכְרֵנוּ לְחַיִּים, מֶלֶךְ חָפֵץ בַּחַיִּים
וְחָתְמֵנוּ בְּסֵפֶר הַחַיִּים, לְמַעַנְךָ אֱלֹהִים חַיִּים.
מֶלֶךְ עוֹזֵר וּמוֹשִׁיעַ וּמָגֵן.
בָּרוּךְ אַתָּה יהוה, מָגֵן אַבְרָהָם.

גבורות
אַתָּה גִּבּוֹר לְעוֹלָם, אֲדֹנָי
מְחַיֵּה מֵתִים אַתָּה, רַב לְהוֹשִׁיעַ
בארץ ישראל: מוֹרִיד הַטָּל
מְכַלְכֵּל חַיִּים בְּחֶסֶד, מְחַיֵּה מֵתִים בְּרַחֲמִים רַבִּים
סוֹמֵךְ נוֹפְלִים, וְרוֹפֵא חוֹלִים, וּמַתִּיר אֲסוּרִים
וּמְקַיֵּם אֱמוּנָתוֹ לִישֵׁנֵי עָפָר.
מִי כָמוֹךָ, בַּעַל גְּבוּרוֹת, וּמִי דּוֹמֶה לָּךְ
מֶלֶךְ, מֵמִית וּמְחַיֶּה וּמַצְמִיחַ יְשׁוּעָה.

מִי כָמוֹךָ אַב הָרַחֲמִים
זוֹכֵר יְצוּרָיו לְחַיִּים בְּרַחֲמִים.
וְנֶאֱמָן אַתָּה לְהַחֲיוֹת מֵתִים.
בָּרוּךְ אַתָּה יהוה, מְחַיֵּה הַמֵּתִים.

וְחָתְמֵנוּ *And seal us.* Throughout Ne'ila we substitute "seal" for "write," because "On Rosh HaShana it [our verdict] is written and on Yom Kippur it is sealed,"

HOLINESS

אַתָּה קָדוֹשׁ You are holy and Your name is holy,
and holy ones praise You daily, Selah!

וּבְכֵן תֵּן פַּחְדְּךָ And so place the fear of You, LORD our God,
over all that You have made,
and the terror of You over all You have created,
and all who were made will stand in awe of You,
and all of creation will worship You,
and they will be bound all together as one
to carry out Your will with an undivided heart;
for we know, LORD our God,
that all dominion is laid out before You,
strength is in Your palm,
and might in Your right hand,
Your name spreading awe
over all You have created.

וּבְכֵן תֵּן כָּבוֹד And so place honor,
LORD, upon Your people,
praise on those who fear You
and hope into those who seek You,
the confidence to speak
into all who long for You,
gladness to Your land and joy to Your city,
the flourishing of pride to David Your servant,
and a lamp laid out for his descendant, Your anointed,
soon, in our days.

וּבְכֵן צַדִּיקִים And then righteous people will see and rejoice,
and the upright will exult, and the pious revel in joy,
and injustice will have nothing more to say,
and all wickedness will fade away like smoke
as You sweep the rule of arrogance from the earth.

קדושת השם

אַתָּה קָדוֹשׁ וְשִׁמְךָ קָדוֹשׁ
וּקְדוֹשִׁים בְּכָל יוֹם יְהַלְלוּךָ סֶּלָה.

וּבְכֵן תֵּן פַּחְדְּךָ יהוה אֱלֹהֵינוּ עַל כָּל מַעֲשֶׂיךָ
וְאֵימָתְךָ עַל כָּל מַה שֶּׁבָּרֵאתָ
וְיִירָאוּךָ כָּל הַמַּעֲשִׂים
וְיִשְׁתַּחֲווּ לְפָנֶיךָ כָּל הַבְּרוּאִים
וְיֵעָשׂוּ כֻלָּם אֲגֻדָּה אֶחָת לַעֲשׂוֹת רְצוֹנְךָ בְּלֵבָב שָׁלֵם
כְּמוֹ שֶׁיָּדַעְנוּ יהוה אֱלֹהֵינוּ שֶׁהַשָּׁלְטָן לְפָנֶיךָ
עֹז בְּיָדְךָ וּגְבוּרָה בִּימִינֶךָ
וְשִׁמְךָ נוֹרָא עַל כָּל מַה שֶּׁבָּרֵאתָ.

וּבְכֵן תֵּן כָּבוֹד יהוה לְעַמֶּךָ
תְּהִלָּה לִירֵאֶיךָ
וְתִקְוָה טוֹבָה לְדוֹרְשֶׁיךָ
וּפִתְחוֹן פֶּה לַמְיַחֲלִים לָךְ.
שִׂמְחָה לְאַרְצֶךָ, וְשָׂשׂוֹן לְעִירֶךָ
וּצְמִיחַת קֶרֶן לְדָוִד עַבְדֶּךָ
וַעֲרִיכַת נֵר לְבֶן יִשַׁי מְשִׁיחֶךָ
בִּמְהֵרָה בְיָמֵינוּ.

וּבְכֵן צַדִּיקִים יִרְאוּ וְיִשְׂמָחוּ, וִישָׁרִים יַעֲלֹזוּ
וַחֲסִידִים בְּרִנָּה יָגִילוּ, וְעוֹלָתָה תִּקְפָּץ פִּיהָ
וְכָל הָרִשְׁעָה כֻּלָּהּ כְּעָשָׁן תִּכְלֶה
כִּי תַעֲבִיר מֶמְשֶׁלֶת זָדוֹן מִן הָאָרֶץ.

וְתִמְלֹךְ אַתָּה And You, LORD,
will rule alone over those You have made,
in Mount Zion, the dwelling of Your glory,
and in Jerusalem, Your holy city,
as it is written in Your holy Writings:
"The LORD shall reign for ever. *Ps. 146*
He is your God, Zion,
from generation to generation,
Halleluya!"

קָדוֹשׁ אַתָּה You are holy, Your name is awesome,
and there is no god but You,
as it is written,
"The LORD of hosts shall be raised up through His judgment, *Is. 5*
the holy God, made holy in righteousness."
Blessed are You, LORD, the holy King.

HOLINESS OF THE DAY

אַתָּה בְחַרְתָּנוּ You have chosen us from among all peoples.
You have loved and favored us.
You have raised us above all tongues.
You have made us holy
through Your commandments.
You have brought us near, our King, to Your service,
and have called us by Your great and holy name.

On Shabbat, add the words in parentheses:

וַתִּתֶּן לָנוּ And You, LORD our God, have given us in love
(this Sabbath day for holiness and rest, and)
this Day of Atonement
for pardon and forgiveness and atonement,
to pardon all our iniquities,
(with love,) a holy assembly
in memory of the exodus from Egypt.

וְתִמְלֹךְ אַתָּה יהוה לְבַדֶּךָ עַל כָּל מַעֲשֶׂיךָ
בְּהַר צִיּוֹן מִשְׁכַּן כְּבוֹדֶךָ
וּבִירוּשָׁלַיִם עִיר קָדְשֶׁךָ
כַּכָּתוּב בְּדִבְרֵי קָדְשֶׁךָ
יִמְלֹךְ יהוה לְעוֹלָם, אֱלֹהַיִךְ צִיּוֹן לְדֹר וָדֹר, הַלְלוּיָהּ: תהלים קמו

קָדוֹשׁ אַתָּה וְנוֹרָא שְׁמֶךָ
וְאֵין אֱלוֹהַּ מִבַּלְעָדֶיךָ
כַּכָּתוּב, וַיִּגְבַּהּ יהוה צְבָאוֹת בַּמִּשְׁפָּט ישעיה ה
וְהָאֵל הַקָּדוֹשׁ נִקְדַּשׁ בִּצְדָקָה:
בָּרוּךְ אַתָּה יהוה, הַמֶּלֶךְ הַקָּדוֹשׁ.

קדושת היום
אַתָּה בְחַרְתָּנוּ מִכָּל הָעַמִּים
אָהַבְתָּ אוֹתָנוּ וְרָצִיתָ בָּנוּ וְרוֹמַמְתָּנוּ מִכָּל הַלְּשׁוֹנוֹת
וְקִדַּשְׁתָּנוּ בְּמִצְוֹתֶיךָ
וְקֵרַבְתָּנוּ מַלְכֵּנוּ לַעֲבוֹדָתֶךָ
וְשִׁמְךָ הַגָּדוֹל וְהַקָּדוֹשׁ עָלֵינוּ קָרָאתָ.

On שבת, add the words in parentheses:
וַתִּתֶּן לָנוּ יהוה אֱלֹהֵינוּ בְּאַהֲבָה אֶת
(יוֹם הַשַּׁבָּת הַזֶּה לִקְדֻשָּׁה וְלִמְנוּחָה, וְאֶת)
יוֹם הַכִּפּוּרִים הַזֶּה, לִמְחִילָה וְלִסְלִיחָה וּלְכַפָּרָה
וְלִמְחָל בּוֹ אֶת כָּל עֲוֹנוֹתֵינוּ
(בְּאַהֲבָה) מִקְרָא קֹדֶשׁ
זֵכֶר לִיצִיאַת מִצְרָיִם.

אֱלֹהֵינוּ Our God and God of our ancestors,
may there rise, come, reach, appear, be favored, heard,
regarded and remembered before You,
our recollection and remembrance,
as well as the remembrance of our ancestors,
and of the Messiah, son of David Your servant,
and of Jerusalem Your holy city,
and of all Your people the house of Israel –
for deliverance and well-being,
grace, loving-kindness and compassion,
life and peace, on this Day of Atonement.
On it remember us, LORD our God, for good;
recollect us for blessing, and deliver us for life.
In accord with Your promise of salvation and compassion,
spare us and be gracious to us;
have compassion on us and deliver us,
for our eyes are turned to You
because You, God, are a gracious and compassionate King.

On Shabbat, add the words in parentheses:

אֱלֹהֵינוּ Our God and God of our ancestors,
pardon our iniquities
on (this Sabbath day, and on) this Day of Atonement;
wipe away and remove all our transgressions and sins
from before Your eyes,
as it is said:

"I, I am the One who shall wipe out your transgressions *Is. 43*
for My sake, and I shall not recall your sins."

And it is said:

"I have wiped out your transgressions like a cloud, *Is. 44*
and as a haze your sins;
come back to Me for I have redeemed you."

And it is said:

For on this day you will be atoned and made pure; *Lev. 16*
of all your sins before the LORD you shall be purified.

אֱלֹהֵינוּ וֵאלֹהֵי אֲבוֹתֵינוּ
יַעֲלֶה וְיָבוֹא וְיַגִּיעַ, וְיֵרָאֶה וְיֵרָצֶה וְיִשָּׁמַע
וְיִפָּקֵד וְיִזָּכֵר זִכְרוֹנֵנוּ וּפִקְדּוֹנֵנוּ וְזִכְרוֹן אֲבוֹתֵינוּ
וְזִכְרוֹן מָשִׁיחַ בֶּן דָּוִד עַבְדֶּךָ, וְזִכְרוֹן יְרוּשָׁלַיִם עִיר קָדְשֶׁךָ
וְזִכְרוֹן כָּל עַמְּךָ בֵּית יִשְׂרָאֵל, לְפָנֶיךָ
לִפְלֵיטָה לְטוֹבָה, לְחֵן וּלְחֶסֶד וּלְרַחֲמִים, לְחַיִּים וּלְשָׁלוֹם
בְּיוֹם הַכִּפּוּרִים הַזֶּה.
זָכְרֵנוּ יהוה אֱלֹהֵינוּ בּוֹ לְטוֹבָה, וּפָקְדֵנוּ בוֹ לִבְרָכָה
וְהוֹשִׁיעֵנוּ בוֹ לְחַיִּים.
וּבִדְבַר יְשׁוּעָה וְרַחֲמִים חוּס וְחָנֵּנוּ, וְרַחֵם עָלֵינוּ וְהוֹשִׁיעֵנוּ
כִּי אֵלֶיךָ עֵינֵינוּ, כִּי אֵל מֶלֶךְ חַנּוּן וְרַחוּם אָתָּה.

On שבת, add the words in parentheses:

אֱלֹהֵינוּ וֵאלֹהֵי אֲבוֹתֵינוּ
מְחַל לַעֲוֹנוֹתֵינוּ בְּיוֹם (הַשַּׁבָּת הַזֶּה וּבְיוֹם) הַכִּפּוּרִים הַזֶּה
מְחֵה וְהַעֲבֵר פְּשָׁעֵינוּ וְחַטֹּאתֵינוּ מִנֶּגֶד עֵינֶיךָ
כָּאָמוּר
אָנֹכִי אָנֹכִי הוּא מֹחֶה פְשָׁעֶיךָ לְמַעֲנִי ישעיה מג
וְחַטֹּאתֶיךָ לֹא אֶזְכֹּר:
וְנֶאֱמַר
מָחִיתִי כָעָב פְּשָׁעֶיךָ וְכֶעָנָן חַטֹּאותֶיךָ ישעיה מד
שׁוּבָה אֵלַי כִּי גְאַלְתִּיךָ:
וְנֶאֱמַר
כִּי־בַיּוֹם הַזֶּה יְכַפֵּר עֲלֵיכֶם לְטַהֵר אֶתְכֶם ויקרא טז
מִכֹּל חַטֹּאתֵיכֶם, לִפְנֵי יהוה תִּטְהָרוּ:

(Our God and God of our ancestors, find favor in our rest.)
Make us holy through Your commandments
and grant us our share in Your Torah.
Satisfy us with Your goodness,
grant us joy in Your salvation
(in love and favor, O LORD our God,
grant us as our heritage Your holy Sabbath,
so that Israel, who sanctify Your name,
may find rest on it),
and purify our hearts to serve You in truth.
For You are the Forgiver of Israel
and the Pardoner of the tribes of Yeshurun in every generation,
and without You we have no king who pardons and forgives,
none but You.
Blessed are You, LORD,
King who pardons and forgives our iniquities
and those of all His people the house of Israel,
and makes our guilt pass away, every single year,
King of all the earth,
who sanctifies (the Sabbath,)
Israel and the Day of Atonement.

TEMPLE SERVICE

רְצֵה Find favor, LORD our God,
in Your people Israel and their prayer.
Restore the service to Your most holy House,
and accept in love and favor
the fire-offerings of Israel and their prayer.
May the service of Your people Israel always find favor with You.
And may our eyes witness Your return to Zion in compassion.
Blessed are You, LORD,
who restores His Presence to Zion.

(אֱלֹהֵינוּ וֵאלֹהֵי אֲבוֹתֵינוּ, רְצֵה בִמְנוּחָתֵנוּ)

קַדְּשֵׁנוּ בְּמִצְוֹתֶיךָ וְתֵן חֶלְקֵנוּ בְּתוֹרָתֶךָ

שַׂבְּעֵנוּ מִטּוּבֶךָ וְשַׂמְּחֵנוּ בִּישׁוּעָתֶךָ

(וְהַנְחִילֵנוּ יהוה אֱלֹהֵינוּ בְּאַהֲבָה וּבְרָצוֹן שַׁבְּתוֹת קָדְשֶׁךָ

וְיָנוּחוּ בָם יִשְׂרָאֵל מְקַדְּשֵׁי שְׁמֶךָ)

וְטַהֵר לִבֵּנוּ לְעָבְדְּךָ בֶּאֱמֶת

כִּי אַתָּה סָלְחָן לְיִשְׂרָאֵל

וּמָחֳלָן לְשִׁבְטֵי יְשֻׁרוּן בְּכָל דּוֹר וָדוֹר

וּמִבַּלְעָדֶיךָ אֵין לָנוּ מֶלֶךְ מוֹחֵל וְסוֹלֵחַ אֶלָּא אָתָּה.

בָּרוּךְ אַתָּה יהוה

מֶלֶךְ מוֹחֵל וְסוֹלֵחַ לַעֲוֹנוֹתֵינוּ

וְלַעֲוֹנוֹת עַמּוֹ בֵּית יִשְׂרָאֵל

וּמַעֲבִיר אַשְׁמוֹתֵינוּ בְּכָל שָׁנָה וְשָׁנָה

מֶלֶךְ עַל כָּל הָאָרֶץ

מְקַדֵּשׁ (הַשַּׁבָּת וְ) יִשְׂרָאֵל וְיוֹם הַכִּפּוּרִים.

עבודה

רְצֵה יהוה אֱלֹהֵינוּ בְּעַמְּךָ יִשְׂרָאֵל, וּבִתְפִלָּתָם

וְהָשֵׁב אֶת הָעֲבוֹדָה לִדְבִיר בֵּיתֶךָ

וְאִשֵּׁי יִשְׂרָאֵל וּתְפִלָּתָם בְּאַהֲבָה תְקַבֵּל בְּרָצוֹן

וּתְהִי לְרָצוֹן תָּמִיד עֲבוֹדַת יִשְׂרָאֵל עַמֶּךָ.

וְתֶחֱזֶינָה עֵינֵינוּ בְּשׁוּבְךָ לְצִיּוֹן בְּרַחֲמִים.

בָּרוּךְ אַתָּה יהוה

הַמַּחֲזִיר שְׁכִינָתוֹ לְצִיּוֹן.

THANKSGIVING

Bow at the first nine words.

▾מוֹדִים We give thanks to You,
for You are the LORD our God and God of our ancestors
for ever and all time.
You are the Rock of our lives,
Shield of our salvation from generation to generation.
We will thank You and declare Your praise for our lives,
which are entrusted into Your hand;
for our souls, which are placed in Your charge;
for Your miracles which are with us every day;
and for Your wonders and favors
at all times, evening, morning and midday.
You are good – for Your compassion never fails.
You are compassionate – for Your loving-kindnesses never cease.
We have always placed our hope in You.
For all these things may Your name be blessed and exalted,
our King, continually, for ever and all time.

וַחֲתֹם And seal for a good life, all the children of Your covenant.

Let all that lives thank You, Selah!
and praise Your name in truth,
God, our Savior and Help, Selah!
▾Blessed are You, LORD, whose name is "the Good"
and to whom thanks are due.

PEACE

שִׂים שָׁלוֹם Grant peace, goodness and blessing,
grace, loving-kindness and compassion to us
and all Israel Your people.
Bless us, our Father, all as one, with the light of Your face,
for by the light of Your face You have given us, LORD our God,
the Torah of life and love of kindness,
righteousness, blessing, compassion, life and peace.
May it be good in Your eyes to bless Your people Israel
at every time, in every hour, with Your peace.

הודאה

Bow at the first five words.

מוֹדִים אֲנַֽחְנוּ לָךְ
שָׁאַתָּה הוּא יהוה אֱלֹהֵֽינוּ וֵאלֹהֵי אֲבוֹתֵֽינוּ לְעוֹלָם וָעֶד.
צוּר חַיֵּֽינוּ, מָגֵן יִשְׁעֵֽנוּ, אַתָּה הוּא לְדוֹר וָדוֹר.
נוֹדֶה לְּךָ וּנְסַפֵּר תְּהִלָּתֶֽךָ, עַל חַיֵּֽינוּ הַמְּסוּרִים בְּיָדֶֽךָ
וְעַל נִשְׁמוֹתֵֽינוּ הַפְּקוּדוֹת לָךְ, וְעַל נִסֶּֽיךָ שֶׁבְּכָל יוֹם עִמָּֽנוּ
וְעַל נִפְלְאוֹתֶֽיךָ וְטוֹבוֹתֶֽיךָ שֶׁבְּכָל עֵת, עֶֽרֶב וָבֹֽקֶר וְצָהֳרָֽיִם.
הַטּוֹב, כִּי לֹא כָלוּ רַחֲמֶֽיךָ
וְהַמְרַחֵם, כִּי לֹא תַֽמּוּ חֲסָדֶֽיךָ
מֵעוֹלָם קִוִּֽינוּ לָךְ.
וְעַל כֻּלָּם יִתְבָּרַךְ וְיִתְרוֹמַם שִׁמְךָ מַלְכֵּֽנוּ תָּמִיד לְעוֹלָם וָעֶד.
וַחֲתֹם לְחַיִּים טוֹבִים כָּל בְּנֵי בְרִיתֶֽךָ.
וְכֹל הַחַיִּים יוֹדֽוּךָ סֶּֽלָה, וִיהַלְלוּ אֶת שִׁמְךָ בֶּאֱמֶת
הָאֵל יְשׁוּעָתֵֽנוּ וְעֶזְרָתֵֽנוּ סֶֽלָה.
בָּרוּךְ אַתָּה יהוה, הַטּוֹב שִׁמְךָ וּלְךָ נָאֶה לְהוֹדוֹת.

שלום

שִׂים שָׁלוֹם טוֹבָה וּבְרָכָה
חֵן וָחֶֽסֶד וְרַחֲמִים עָלֵֽינוּ וְעַל כָּל יִשְׂרָאֵל עַמֶּֽךָ.
בָּרְכֵֽנוּ אָבִֽינוּ כֻּלָּֽנוּ כְּאֶחָד בְּאוֹר פָּנֶֽיךָ
כִּי בְאוֹר פָּנֶֽיךָ נָתַֽתָּ לָּֽנוּ, יהוה אֱלֹהֵֽינוּ
תּוֹרַת חַיִּים וְאַֽהֲבַת חֶֽסֶד
וּצְדָקָה וּבְרָכָה וְרַחֲמִים וְחַיִּים וְשָׁלוֹם.
וְטוֹב בְּעֵינֶֽיךָ לְבָרֵךְ אֶת עַמְּךָ יִשְׂרָאֵל
בְּכָל עֵת וּבְכָל שָׁעָה בִּשְׁלוֹמֶֽךָ.

בְּסֵפֶר חַיִּים In the book of life, blessing, peace and prosperity,
may we and all Your people the house of Israel
be remembered and sealed before You
for a good life, and for peace.*

Blessed are You, LORD, who blesses His people Israel with peace.

**Outside Israel, many end the blessing:*
Blessed are You, LORD, who makes peace.

Some say the following verse:
May the words of my mouth and the meditation of my heart Ps. 19
find favor before You, LORD, my Rock and Redeemer.

VIDUY

For linear translation and commentary, see page 1353.

אֱלֹהֵינוּ Our God and God of our fathers,
let our prayer come before You, and do not hide Yourself from our plea,
for we are not so arrogant or obstinate as to say before You,
LORD, our God and God of our fathers,
we are righteous and have not sinned,
for in truth, we and our fathers have sinned.

Strike the left side of the chest with the right fist while saying each of the sins.

אָשַׁמְנוּ We have sinned, we have acted treacherously,
we have robbed, we have spoken slander.
We have acted perversely, we have acted wickedly,
we have acted presumptuously, we have been violent,
we have framed lies.
We have given bad advice, we have deceived, we have scorned,
we have rebelled, we have provoked, we have turned away,
we have committed iniquity, we have transgressed,
we have persecuted, we have been obstinate.
We have acted wickedly, we have corrupted,
we have acted abominably, we have strayed, we have led others astray.

---

before You." Time is short, the day is ending, the verdict is about to be sealed, so we keep our confession short and focused.

בְּסֵפֶר חַיִּים, בְּרָכָה וְשָׁלוֹם, וּפַרְנָסָה טוֹבָה
נִזָּכֵר וְנֵחָתֵם לְפָנֶיךָ, אֲנַחְנוּ וְכָל עַמְּךָ בֵּית יִשְׂרָאֵל
לְחַיִּים טוֹבִים וּלְשָׁלוֹם.*

בָּרוּךְ אַתָּה יהוה, הַמְבָרֵךְ אֶת עַמּוֹ יִשְׂרָאֵל בַּשָּׁלוֹם.

In חוץ לארץ, many end the blessing:

בָּרוּךְ אַתָּה יהוה, עוֹשֵׂה הַשָּׁלוֹם.

Some say the following verse:

יִהְיוּ לְרָצוֹן אִמְרֵי־פִי וְהֶגְיוֹן לִבִּי לְפָנֶיךָ, יהוה צוּרִי וְגֹאֲלִי: תהלים יט

וידוי

For linear translation and commentary, see page 1353.

אֱלֹהֵינוּ וֵאלֹהֵי אֲבוֹתֵינוּ
תָּבוֹא לְפָנֶיךָ תְּפִלָּתֵנוּ
וְאַל תִּתְעַלַּם מִתְּחִנָּתֵנוּ.
שֶׁאֵין אֲנַחְנוּ עַזֵּי פָנִים וּקְשֵׁי עֹרֶף לוֹמַר לְפָנֶיךָ
יהוה אֱלֹהֵינוּ וֵאלֹהֵי אֲבוֹתֵינוּ
צַדִּיקִים אֲנַחְנוּ וְלֹא חָטָאנוּ.
אֲבָל אֲנַחְנוּ וַאֲבוֹתֵינוּ חָטָאנוּ.

Strike the left side of the chest with the right fist while saying each of the sins.

אָשַׁמְנוּ, בָּגַדְנוּ, גָּזַלְנוּ, דִּבַּרְנוּ דֹפִי
הֶעֱוִינוּ, וְהִרְשַׁעְנוּ, זַדְנוּ, חָמַסְנוּ, טָפַלְנוּ שֶׁקֶר
יָעַצְנוּ רָע, כִּזַּבְנוּ, לַצְנוּ, מָרַדְנוּ, נִאַצְנוּ, סָרַרְנוּ
עָוִינוּ, פָּשַׁעְנוּ, צָרַרְנוּ, קִשִּׁינוּ עֹרֶף
רָשַׁעְנוּ, שִׁחַתְנוּ, תִּעַבְנוּ, תָּעִינוּ, תִּעְתָּעְנוּ.

אָשַׁמְנוּ *We have sinned.* At Ne'ila, here and during the Leader's Repetition, we say only the short confession, omitting *Al ḥet,* "For the sin we have sinned

סַרְנוּ We have turned away from Your commandments and good laws,
to no avail, for You are just in all that has befallen us, *Neh. 9*
for You have acted faithfully while we have done wickedly.

מַה נֹּאמַר What can we say before You, You who dwell on high?
What can we declare before You, You who abide in heaven?
Do You not know all, the hidden and revealed alike?

You give Your hand to help transgressors;
Your right hand is outstretched to receive those who return.
And You have taught us, LORD our God,
to confess before You all our iniquities,
that we may end the oppression that is in our hands,
and that You may receive us back in perfect repentance before You,
like burnt offerings and their sweet savor,
for the sake of the words You have spoken.
There is no end to the burnt offerings we owe You,
no number to the guilt-offerings of sweet savor.
And You know that our end will be with maggots and worms.
And so You forgive us again and again.

What are we? What are our lives? What is our loving-kindness?
What is our righteousness? What is our salvation? What is our strength?
What is our might? What shall we say before You,
LORD our God and God of our ancestors?
Are not all the mighty like nothing before You,
the men of renown as if they had never been,
the wise as if they know nothing,
and the understanding as if they lack intelligence?
For their many works are in vain,
and the days of their lives like a fleeting breath before You.
The pre-eminence of man over the animals is nothing, *Eccl. 3*
for all is but a fleeting breath.

---

work of God (God forbid) but to say that, in bad events as well as good, we can sometimes hear God calling to us, as He called to the first humans in the Garden of Eden, saying, "Where are you?" (Gen. 3:9). Rabbi Naḥman of Bratslav said, "If a person does not judge himself, all things judge him, and all things become messengers of God."

מָה אָנוּ *What are we?* Taken from the early morning prayers, this is a profound meditation on mortality already mentioned in the Talmud in the context of

סַֽרְנוּ מִמִּצְוֹתֶֽיךָ וּמִמִּשְׁפָּטֶֽיךָ הַטּוֹבִים, וְלֹא שָֽׁוָה לָֽנוּ.
וְאַתָּה צַדִּיק עַל כָּל־הַבָּא עָלֵֽינוּ נחמיה ט
כִּי־אֱמֶת עָשִֽׂיתָ, וַאֲנַֽחְנוּ הִרְשָֽׁעְנוּ:

מַה נֹּאמַר לְפָנֶֽיךָ יוֹשֵׁב מָרוֹם, וּמַה נְּסַפֵּר לְפָנֶֽיךָ שׁוֹכֵן שְׁחָקִים
הֲלֹא כָּל הַנִּסְתָּרוֹת וְהַנִּגְלוֹת אַתָּה יוֹדֵֽעַ.

אַתָּה נוֹתֵן יָד לְפוֹשְׁעִים, וִימִינְךָ פְשׁוּטָה לְקַבֵּל שָׁבִים
וַתְּלַמְּדֵֽנוּ יהוה אֱלֹהֵֽינוּ לְהִתְוַדּוֹת לְפָנֶֽיךָ עַל כָּל עֲוֹנוֹתֵֽינוּ
לְמַֽעַן נֶחְדַּל מֵעֹֽשֶׁק יָדֵֽינוּ
וּתְקַבְּלֵֽנוּ בִּתְשׁוּבָה שְׁלֵמָה לְפָנֶֽיךָ כְּאִשִּׁים וּכְנִיחוֹחִים
לְמַֽעַן דְּבָרֶֽיךָ אֲשֶׁר אָמָֽרְתָּ.
אֵין קֵץ לְאִשֵּׁי חוֹבוֹתֵֽינוּ, וְאֵין מִסְפָּר לְנִיחוֹחֵי אַשְׁמוֹתֵֽינוּ
וְאַתָּה יוֹדֵֽעַ שֶׁאַחֲרִיתֵֽנוּ רִמָּה וְתוֹלֵעָה
לְפִיכָךְ הִרְבֵּֽיתָ סְלִיחָתֵֽנוּ.

מָה אָֽנוּ, מֶה חַיֵּֽינוּ, מֶה חַסְדֵּֽנוּ, מַה צִּדְקוֹתֵֽינוּ
מַה יְּשׁוּעָתֵֽנוּ, מַה כֹּחֵֽנוּ, מַה גְּבוּרָתֵֽנוּ
מַה נֹּאמַר לְפָנֶֽיךָ, יהוה אֱלֹהֵֽינוּ וֵאלֹהֵי אֲבוֹתֵֽינוּ
הֲלֹא כָּל הַגִּבּוֹרִים כְּאַיִן לְפָנֶֽיךָ, וְאַנְשֵׁי הַשֵּׁם כְּלֹא הָיוּ
וַחֲכָמִים כִּבְלִי מַדָּע, וּנְבוֹנִים כִּבְלִי הַשְׂכֵּל
כִּי רֹב מַעֲשֵׂיהֶם תֹּֽהוּ, וִימֵי חַיֵּיהֶם הֶֽבֶל לְפָנֶֽיךָ
וּמוֹתַר הָאָדָם מִן־הַבְּהֵמָה אָֽיִן, כִּי הַכֹּל הָֽבֶל: קהלת ג

אַתָּה נוֹתֵן יָד *You give Your hand.* This prayer makes the powerful point that often it is God who seeks us, not we who seek God. Sometimes we turn to Him of our own accord. But at other times He calls to us, through His prophets and sages, or through events that recall us to our identity and destiny. Nineteenth-century anti-Semitism, for instance, brought many estranged and assimilated Jews back to an identification with their people, among them some of the first Zionists. This is not to say that anti-Semitism is the

You have separated man out from the outset;
You have recognized him, had him stand before You.
For who can tell You what You are to do; and
even if one proves righteous – what can he give You?
And You, LORD our God,
have given us in love (*on Shabbat:* this Sabbath day and)
this Day of Atonement,
to be the end, the pardon and forgiveness of all our iniquities,
that we may end the oppression that is in our hands,
and return to You, to fulfill the laws of Your will wholeheartedly.

And You, in Your great compassion,
have compassion for us,
for You will not desire the destruction of the world,
as it is said:
"Seek out the LORD when He is to be found; *Is. 55*
call out to Him now when He is close."
And it is said:
"Let each wicked person abandon his ways, *Ibid.*
each man of iniquity his thoughts,
and let him come back to the LORD
and He will have compassion for him;
back to our God for He will forgive abundantly."
And You, God of forgiveness, gracious and compassionate,
slow to anger, abounding in loving-kindness and truth
and doing abundant good for us;
You desire the repentance of the wicked
and do not desire their death,

לְמַעַן נֶחְדַּל מֵעֹשֶׁק יָדֵינוּ *That we may end the oppression that is in our hands.* Once there was a financial dispute between two men known to Rabbi Yisrael Salanter. One owed the other a large sum of money but begged to be able to repay it in installments since otherwise he and his family would be destitute. The rabbi urged the creditor to have compassion and accede to the borrower's request, but he refused. That year the rabbi came to the creditor before Ne'ila and told him he must change his mind and act with compassion, for otherwise how could he say and mean the words "that we may end the oppression that is in our hands"?

אַתָּה הִבְדַּלְתָּ אֱנוֹשׁ מֵרֹאשׁ, וַתַּכִּירֵהוּ לַעֲמֹד לְפָנֶיךָ.
כִּי מִי יֹאמַר לְךָ מַה תִּפְעָל, וְאִם יִצְדַּק מַה יִּתֶּן לָךְ.
וַתִּתֶּן לָנוּ יהוה אֱלֹהֵינוּ בְּאַהֲבָה אֶת (בשבת: יוֹם הַשַּׁבָּת הַזֶּה וְאֶת)
יוֹם הַכִּפּוּרִים הַזֶּה
קֵץ וּמְחִילָה וּסְלִיחָה עַל כָּל עֲוֹנוֹתֵינוּ
לְמַעַן נֶחְדַּל מֵעֹשֶׁק יָדֵינוּ
וְנָשׁוּב אֵלֶיךָ לַעֲשׂוֹת חֻקֵּי רְצוֹנְךָ בְּלֵבָב שָׁלֵם.

וְאַתָּה בְּרַחֲמֶיךָ הָרַבִּים רַחֵם עָלֵינוּ
כִּי לֹא תַחְפֹּץ בְּהַשְׁחָתַת עוֹלָם
שֶׁנֶּאֱמַר
דִּרְשׁוּ יהוה בְּהִמָּצְאוֹ, קְרָאֻהוּ בִּהְיוֹתוֹ קָרוֹב: ישעיה נה
וְנֶאֱמַר
יַעֲזֹב רָשָׁע דַּרְכּוֹ שם
וְאִישׁ אָוֶן מַחְשְׁבֹתָיו
וְיָשֹׁב אֶל־יהוה וִירַחֲמֵהוּ
וְאֶל־אֱלֹהֵינוּ כִּי־יַרְבֶּה לִסְלוֹחַ:
וְאַתָּה אֱלוֹהַּ סְלִיחוֹת, חַנּוּן וְרַחוּם
אֶרֶךְ אַפַּיִם וְרַב חֶסֶד וֶאֱמֶת, וּמַרְבֶּה לְהֵיטִיב
וְרוֹצֶה אַתָּה בִּתְשׁוּבַת רְשָׁעִים
וְאֵין אַתָּה חָפֵץ בְּמִיתָתָם

Yom Kippur (*Yoma* 87b). Viewed from a purely physical perspective, we are born, we live, we die, and it is as if we had never been.

אַתָּה הִבְדַּלְתָּ אֱנוֹשׁ *You have separated man.* This "on the other hand" contrasts with the previous paragraph and states the paradox of the human condition: we are dust of the earth but we have within us immortal longings. Infinitesimally small, we are also inexplicably great because we can enter into dialogue with God as we are doing now.

as it is said:

"Say to them, as I live – says the LORD God – *Ezek. 33*
I do not desire the death of the wicked,
but that the wicked should come back from his way and live.
Repent, repent your evil ways;
why should you die, O house of Israel?'"

And it is said:

"Do I desire the wicked man's death? – says the God – *Ezek. 18*
Do I not desire him to come back from his ways and live?"

And it is said:

"For I do not desire the condemned man's death – *Ibid.*
says the LORD God – Repent, and live."

For You are the Forgiver of Israel
and the Pardoner of the tribes of Yeshurun in every generation,
and without You
we have no king who pardons and forgives,
none but You.

אֱלֹהַי My God,
before I was formed I was unworthy,
and now that I have been formed
it is as if I had not been formed.
I am dust while alive,
how much more so when I am dead.
See, I am before You like a vessel
filled with shame and disgrace.
May it be Your will,
LORD my God and God of my fathers,
that I may sin no more,
and as for the sins
I have committed before You,
erase them in Your great compassion,
but not by suffering or severe illness.

שֶׁנֶּאֱמַר
אֱמֹר אֲלֵיהֶם, חַי־אָנִי נְאֻם אֲדֹנָי יֱהֹוִה יחזקאל לג
אִם־אֶחְפֹּץ בְּמוֹת הָרָשָׁע
כִּי אִם־בְּשׁוּב רָשָׁע מִדַּרְכּוֹ, וְחָיָה
שׁוּבוּ שׁוּבוּ מִדַּרְכֵיכֶם הָרָעִים
וְלָמָּה תָמְוּתוּ בֵּית יִשְׂרָאֵל:

וְנֶאֱמַר
הֶחָפֹץ אֶחְפֹּץ מוֹת רָשָׁע, נְאֻם אֲדֹנָי יֱהֹוִה יחזקאל יח
הֲלוֹא בְּשׁוּבוֹ מִדְּרָכָיו, וְחָיָה:

וְנֶאֱמַר
כִּי לֹא אֶחְפֹּץ בְּמוֹת הַמֵּת, נְאֻם אֲדֹנָי יֱהֹוִה שם
וְהָשִׁיבוּ וִחְיוּ:

כִּי אַתָּה סָלְחָן לְיִשְׂרָאֵל וּמָחֳלָן לְשִׁבְטֵי יְשֻׁרוּן בְּכָל דּוֹר וָדוֹר
וּמִבַּלְעָדֶיךָ אֵין לָנוּ מֶלֶךְ מוֹחֵל וְסוֹלֵחַ אֶלָּא אָתָּה.

אֱלֹהַי
עַד שֶׁלֹּא נוֹצַרְתִּי אֵינִי כְדַאי
וְעַכְשָׁיו שֶׁנּוֹצַרְתִּי, כְּאִלּוּ לֹא נוֹצַרְתִּי
עָפָר אֲנִי בְּחַיַּי, קַל וָחֹמֶר בְּמִיתָתִי.
הֲרֵי אֲנִי לְפָנֶיךָ כִּכְלִי מָלֵא בוּשָׁה וּכְלִמָּה.
יְהִי רָצוֹן מִלְּפָנֶיךָ
יהוה אֱלֹהַי וֵאלֹהֵי אֲבוֹתַי
שֶׁלֹּא אֶחֱטָא עוֹד.
וּמַה שֶּׁחָטָאתִי לְפָנֶיךָ, מְחֹק בְּרַחֲמֶיךָ הָרַבִּים
אֲבָל לֹא עַל יְדֵי יִסּוּרִים וָחֳלָיִם רָעִים.

אֱלֹהַי My God, *Berakhot 17a*
guard my tongue from evil
and my lips from deceitful speech.
To those who curse me, let my soul be silent;
may my soul be to all like the dust.
Open my heart to Your Torah
and let my soul pursue Your commandments.
As for all who plan evil against me,
swiftly thwart their counsel and frustrate their plans.
Act for the sake of Your name;
act for the sake of Your right hand;
act for the sake of Your holiness;
act for the sake of Your Torah.
That Your beloved ones may be delivered, *Ps. 60*
save with Your right hand and answer me.
May the words of my mouth and the meditation of my heart *Ps. 19*
find favor before You, LORD, my Rock and Redeemer.

Bow, take three steps back, then bow, first left, then right, then center, while saying:

May He who makes peace in His high places,
make peace for us and all Israel – and say: Amen.

יְהִי רָצוֹן May it be Your will, LORD our God and God of our ancestors,
that the Temple be rebuilt speedily in our days,
and grant us a share in Your Torah.
And there we will serve You with reverence,
as in the days of old and as in former years.
Then the offering of Judah and Jerusalem *Mal. 3*
will be pleasing to the LORD as in the days of old and as in former years.

---

of the Ark open, beseeching God to stay open to our prayers, and as a way of signaling to the congregation the awesome nature of the prayers we are about to pray. Those able to, stand from this point onward.

אֱלֹהַי ברכות יז.

נְצֹר לְשׁוֹנִי מֵרָע וּשְׂפָתַי מִדַּבֵּר מִרְמָה

וְלִמְקַלְלַי נַפְשִׁי תִדֹּם, וְנַפְשִׁי כֶּעָפָר לַכֹּל תִּהְיֶה.

פְּתַח לִבִּי בְּתוֹרָתֶךָ, וּבְמִצְוֹתֶיךָ תִּרְדֹּף נַפְשִׁי.

וְכָל הַחוֹשְׁבִים עָלַי רָעָה

מְהֵרָה הָפֵר עֲצָתָם וְקַלְקֵל מַחֲשַׁבְתָּם.

עֲשֵׂה לְמַעַן שְׁמֶךָ

עֲשֵׂה לְמַעַן יְמִינֶךָ

עֲשֵׂה לְמַעַן קְדֻשָּׁתֶךָ

עֲשֵׂה לְמַעַן תּוֹרָתֶךָ.

לְמַעַן יֵחָלְצוּן יְדִידֶיךָ, הוֹשִׁיעָה יְמִינְךָ וַעֲנֵנִי: תהלים ס

יִהְיוּ לְרָצוֹן אִמְרֵי פִי וְהֶגְיוֹן לִבִּי לְפָנֶיךָ, יהוה צוּרִי וְגֹאֲלִי: תהלים יט

Bow, take three steps back, then bow, first left, then right, then center, while saying:

עֹשֶׂה הַשָּׁלוֹם בִּמְרוֹמָיו, הוּא יַעֲשֶׂה שָׁלוֹם

עָלֵינוּ וְעַל כָּל יִשְׂרָאֵל, וְאִמְרוּ אָמֵן.

יְהִי רָצוֹן מִלְּפָנֶיךָ יהוה אֱלֹהֵינוּ וֵאלֹהֵי אֲבוֹתֵינוּ

שֶׁיִּבָּנֶה בֵּית הַמִּקְדָּשׁ בִּמְהֵרָה בְיָמֵינוּ, וְתֵן חֶלְקֵנוּ בְּתוֹרָתֶךָ

וְשָׁם נַעֲבָדְךָ בְּיִרְאָה כִּימֵי עוֹלָם וּכְשָׁנִים קַדְמֹנִיּוֹת.

וְעָרְבָה לַיהוה מִנְחַת יְהוּדָה וִירוּשָׁלָםִ כִּימֵי עוֹלָם וּכְשָׁנִים קַדְמֹנִיּוֹת: מלאכי ג

ḤAZARAT HASHATZ – LEADER'S REPETITION (*next page*)

It is the custom for the Ark to be opened and remain open from this point to the end of Ne'ila. As "the gates are closing," we symbolically keep the doors

LEADER'S REPETITION FOR NE'ILA

The Ark is opened.
The Leader takes three steps forward and at the points indicated by ▾, bends the knees at the first word, bows at the second, and stands straight before saying God's name.

When I proclaim the LORD's name, give glory to our God. *Deut. 32*
O LORD, open my lips, so that my mouth may declare Your praise. *Ps. 51*

PATRIARCHS

▾בָּרוּךְ▾ Blessed are You, LORD our God and God of our fathers,
God of Abraham, God of Isaac and God of Jacob;
the great, mighty and awesome God, God Most High,
who bestows acts of loving-kindness and creates all,
who remembers the loving-kindness of the fathers
and will bring a Redeemer to their children's children
for the sake of His name, in love.

מִסּוֹד Drawing from the counsel of wise and knowing men,
from the teachings born of insight among those who understand,
I open my mouth now in prayer and pleading,
to implore and to plead before the King who pardons and forgives iniquities.

The kerova for Ne'ila is even shorter than the one for Minḥa. The Magen, Meḥayeh, and Meshalesh form a three-part piyut, each part corresponding to one of the patriarchs. Originally composed as a complete alphabetic acrostic, nowadays only verses א to ל are said by most congregations. As part of the Leader's Repetition, the kerova should ideally be said by the Leader alone. However, the prevailing custom is for the congregation to participate, and some of the piyutim are said together, with the Leader raising his voice only toward the end.

All:

אָב יְדָעֲךָ Our forefather [Abraham] who recognized You from his youth,
You tested with ten trials that he passed without flaw.
▸ He turned to You as a youth, and not as a boor,
so that his children could enter through this gate [of righteousness].

בְּחַנְתּוֹ בְּעֶשֶׂר *You tested with ten trials.* God put Abraham through ten trials, beginning with the call to leave his land, birthplace and father's house, and culminating in the binding of Isaac (*Avot* 5:4).

וְלֹא כְבַעַר *And not as a boor.* The boor worries about his own pain, a mature person worries about the pain of others. When God put Abraham through trials, he did not protest, but when He told Abraham that He was about to destroy Sodom, Abraham did protest (Gen. 18:23–32).

חזרת הש״ץ של נעילה

The ארון קודש *is opened.*
The שליח ציבור *takes three steps forward and at the points indicated by* ▾*, bends the knees at the first word, bows at the second, and stands straight before saying God's name.*

כִּי שֵׁם יהוה אֶקְרָא, הָבוּ גֹדֶל לֵאלֹהֵינוּ: דברים לב
אֲדֹנָי, שְׂפָתַי תִּפְתָּח, וּפִי יַגִּיד תְּהִלָּתֶךָ: תהלים נא

אבות

▾בָּרוּךְ אַתָּה יהוה, אֱלֹהֵינוּ וֵאלֹהֵי אֲבוֹתֵינוּ
אֱלֹהֵי אַבְרָהָם, אֱלֹהֵי יִצְחָק, וֵאלֹהֵי יַעֲקֹב
הָאֵל הַגָּדוֹל הַגִּבּוֹר וְהַנּוֹרָא, אֵל עֶלְיוֹן
גּוֹמֵל חֲסָדִים טוֹבִים, וְקוֹנֵה הַכֹּל
וְזוֹכֵר חַסְדֵי אָבוֹת
וּמֵבִיא גוֹאֵל לִבְנֵי בְנֵיהֶם לְמַעַן שְׁמוֹ בְּאַהֲבָה.

מִסּוֹד חֲכָמִים וּנְבוֹנִים, וּמִלֶּמֶד דַּעַת מְבִינִים
אֶפְתְּחָה פִּי בִּתְפִלָּה וּבְתַחֲנוּנִים
לְחַלּוֹת וּלְחַנֵּן פְּנֵי מֶלֶךְ מוֹחֵל וְסוֹלֵחַ לַעֲוֹנִים.

The קרובה *for* נעילה *is even shorter than the one for* מנחה*. The* מגן*,* מחיה *and* משלש *form a three-part piyut, each part corresponding to one of the patriarchs. Originally composed as a complete alphabetic acrostic, nowadays only verses* א *to* ל *are said by most congregations. As part of the* חזרת הש״ץ*, the* קרובה *should ideally be said by the* שליח ציבור *alone. However, the prevailing custom is for the* קהל *to participate, and some of the piyutim are said together, with the* שליח ציבור *raising his voice only toward the end.*

All:

אָב יְדָעֲךָ מִנֹּעַר / בְּחַנְתּוֹ בְּעֶשֶׂר, בַּל עֲבוֹר בְּרֹאשׁ תַּעַר
◂ גַּשׁ לְחַלּוֹתְךָ כְּנַעַר וְלֹא כְבַעַר / דְּגָלָיו לָבֹא בְּזֶה הַשַּׁעַר.

אָב *Our forefather.* An alphabetical acrostic prayer by Rabbi Elazar HaKalir. "The forefather" is a reference to Abraham, the patriarch associated with the first blessing of the Amida.

יְדָעֲךָ מִנֹּעַר *Who recognized You from his youth.* A reference to the tradition that Abraham discovered God as a child, and rejected the idols of his father Teraḥ.

All:

Your faithful come to exalt You, O Awesome One,
to praise You throughout this day;
▸ now that this day is fading away, / protect us, in the merit of
[Abraham] who sat [waiting] in the heat of the day.

The congregation then the Leader:

זָכְרֵנוּ לְחַיִּים Remember us for life,
O King who desires life,
and seal us in the book of life –
for Your sake, O God of life.

The Leader continues:

King, Helper, Savior, Shield:
▾Blessed are You, Lord,
Shield of Abraham.

DIVINE MIGHT

אַתָּה גִּבּוֹר You are eternally mighty, Lord.
You give life to the dead
and have great power to save.

In Israel: He causes the dew to fall.

He sustains the living with loving-kindness,
and with great compassion revives the dead.
He supports the fallen,
heals the sick,
sets captives free,
and keeps His faith with those who sleep in the dust.

Who is like You, Master of might,
and to whom can You be compared,
O King who brings death and gives life,
and makes salvation grow?

All:

אֱמוּנִים גָּשׁוּ לְנַצְּחָךְ אָיֹם / נֶצַח כָּל הַיּוֹם
‹ עֲבוּר כִּי פָנָה יוֹם / גּוֹנְנֵנוּ בְּצֶדֶק יוֹשֵׁב כְּחֹם הַיּוֹם.

The קהל *then the* שליח ציבור*:*

זָכְרֵנוּ לְחַיִּים, מֶלֶךְ חָפֵץ בַּחַיִּים
וְחָתְמֵנוּ בְּסֵפֶר הַחַיִּים, לְמַעַנְךָ אֱלֹהִים חַיִּים.

The שליח ציבור *continues:*

מֶלֶךְ עוֹזֵר וּמוֹשִׁיעַ וּמָגֵן.
ׂבָּרוּךְ אַתָּה יהוה, מָגֵן אַבְרָהָם.

גבורות

אַתָּה גִּבּוֹר לְעוֹלָם, אֲדֹנָי
מְחַיֵּה מֵתִים אַתָּה, רַב לְהוֹשִׁיעַ

בארץ ישראל: מוֹרִיד הַטָּל

מְכַלְכֵּל חַיִּים בְּחֶסֶד
מְחַיֵּה מֵתִים בְּרַחֲמִים רַבִּים
סוֹמֵךְ נוֹפְלִים
וְרוֹפֵא חוֹלִים
וּמַתִּיר אֲסוּרִים
וּמְקַיֵּם אֱמוּנָתוֹ לִישֵׁנֵי עָפָר.

מִי כָמוֹךָ, בַּעַל גְּבוּרוֹת, וּמִי דּוֹמֶה לָּךְ
מֶלֶךְ, מֵמִית וּמְחַיֶּה וּמַצְמִיחַ יְשׁוּעָה.

The "Meḥayeh":

All:

הַנִּקְרָא Our forefather [Isaac] who continued his father's name,
and who turned away from all evil obstacles,
▸ cried out, entreated and did not spare his prayer,
received increased blessings from that which he sowed.

All:

O Lord, may Your name always remain among us,
and bring Your salvation close to us.
▸ Redeem us, please, from among enemies;
revive us with Your dew as You did [for Isaac]
who prayed toward evening.

The congregation then the Leader:

מִי כָמְוֹךָ Who is like You, compassionate Father,
who remembers His creatures in compassion, for life?

The Leader continues:

Faithful are You to revive the dead.
Blessed are You, Lord, who revives the dead.

The "Meshalesh":

All:

טֶבַע The likeness of [Jacob's] radiant countenance
the Lord engraved in His precious throne.
▸ When he, the perfect one, saw the awe of that place,
he rose from sleep, beheld it and was awestruck.

לְעֵת קֵץ חָז וַיִּירָא *He rose from sleep, beheld it and was awestruck.* Escaping Esau's anger, Jacob left home to go to Laban. On his journey, alone, at night, he slept and dreamed of a ladder reaching from earth to heaven with angels ascending and descending. On waking, "He was afraid and said, How awesome is this place! This is none other than the house of God; this is the gate of heaven" (Gen. 28:17).

The "מחיה":

All:

הַנִּקְרָא לְאָב זֶרַע / וְנִפְנָה לָסוּר מִמּוֹקְשֵׁי רַע
◂ זָעַק וְחִנֵּן, וְשִׂיחָה לֹא גָרַע / חֻסַּן בְּרָכָה בַּאֲשֶׁר זָרַע.

All:

יָהּ שִׁמְךָ בָּנוּ יֶעֱרַב / וְיֶשְׁעֲךָ לָנוּ תְּקָרֵב
◂ גְּאַל נָא מִקֶּרֶב / הַחֲיֵינוּ בְּטַל, כְּשָׁח לִפְנוֹת עֶרֶב.

The קהל *then the* שליח ציבור*:*

מִי כָמְוֹךָ אַב הָרַחֲמִים
זוֹכֵר יְצוּרָיו לְחַיִּים בְּרַחֲמִים.

The שליח ציבור *continues:*

וְנֶאֱמָן אַתָּה לְהַחֲיוֹת מֵתִים.
בָּרוּךְ אַתָּה יהוה, מְחַיֵּה הַמֵּתִים.

The "משלש":

All:

טֶבַע זִיו תָּאֳרָה / יָהּ חֲקָקוֹ בְּכֵס יְקָרָה
◂ כְּשָׁר תָּם מְקוֹם מַה נּוֹרָא / לְעֵת קֵץ חָז וַיִּירָא.

הַנִּקְרָא לְאָב זֶרַע *[Isaac] who continued his father's name.* Isaac, the subject of the second blessing of the Amida, was considered Abraham's only covenantal offspring (Gen. 17:21). Though Ishmael was Abraham's biological son, he was not his spiritual heir.

טֶבַע זִיו תָּאֳרָה *The likeness of [Jacob's] radiant countenance.* Jacob is the subject of the Amida's third blessing.

The congregation says the next two verses aloud, followed by the Leader:

יִמְלֹךְ The Lord shall reign for ever. Ps. 146

He is your God, Zion, from generation to generation, Halleluya!

וְאַתָּה You are the Holy One, enthroned on the praises of Israel. Ps. 22

God, please.

The Leader then the congregation:

שְׁמַע Listen, please; forgive, please, on this day;

for the day is fading away.

And we shall praise You, Awesome, Terrifying One; O Holy One.

The congregation then the Leader:

וּבְכֵן לְךָ And so, sanctity will rise up to You,

for You, our God, are the King who pardons and forgives.

Originally, every kerova would end with a special piyut before Kedusha, called the "Siluk." Nowadays, most congregations omit them, reciting only the Siluk for Musaf (Untaneh Tokef) on the High Holy Days, and the Siluk for Ne'ila on Yom Kippur. The Siluk served as an extended prelude, leading directly to the Kedusha verses. Some congregations omit the Siluk, saying only the regular opening verse to Kedusha (in parentheses on the next page).

The Leader, with the congregation following him in an undertone:

שַׁעֲרֵי אַרְמוֹן Let the gates of the palace
be speedily thrown open to those who expound the faithful Torah.
Let the [heavenly] gates of Your hidden treasures
be speedily thrown open to those who cling to Your law.
Let the beautiful gates of Your Sanctuary
be speedily thrown open to Your congregated faithful.
Let the gates of Your heavenly encampments
be speedily thrown open for those with reddened eyes
[from Torah study].
Let the gates of purity
be speedily thrown open to Your fair, pure [people].
Let the gates to Your mighty crown
be speedily thrown open for the people not widowed
[abandoned by You].
And by these shall You be revered and sanctified,
with the words uttered by the holy Seraphim
who sanctify Your name in the Sanctuary,

The קהל *says the next two verses aloud, followed by the* שליח ציבור*:*

יִמְלֹךְ יהוה לְעוֹלָם אֱלֹהַיִךְ צִיּוֹן לְדֹר וָדֹר, הַלְלוּיָהּ: תהלים קמו

וְאַתָּה קָדוֹשׁ, יוֹשֵׁב תְּהִלּוֹת יִשְׂרָאֵל: תהלים כב

אֵל נָא.

The שליח ציבור *then the* קהל*:*

שְׁמַע נָא, סְלַח נָא הַיּוֹם
עֲבוּר כִּי פָנָה יוֹם
וּנְהַלֶּלְךָ נוֹרָא וְאָיֹם
קָדוֹשׁ.

The קהל *then the* שליח ציבור*:*

וּבְכֵן לְךָ תַעֲלֶה קְדֻשָּׁה כִּי אַתָּה אֱלֹהֵינוּ מֶלֶךְ מוֹחֵל וְסוֹלֵחַ.

Originally, every קרובה *would end with a special piyut before* קדושה*, called the "*סילוק*." Nowadays, most congregations omit them, reciting only the* סילוק *for* מוסף (וּנְתַנֶּה תֹּקֶף) *on the High Holy Days, and the* סילוק *for* נעילה *on* יום כיפור*. The* סילוק *served as an extended prelude, leading directly to the* קדושה *verses. Some congregations omit the* סילוק*, saying only the regular opening verse to* קדושה *(in parentheses on the next page).*

The שליח ציבור*, with the* קהל *following him in an undertone:*

שַׁעֲרֵי אַרְמוֹן מְהֵרָה תִּפְתַּח לְבוֹאֲרֵי אָמוֹן
שַׁעֲרֵי גְנוּזִים מְהֵרָה תִּפְתַּח לְדָתְךָ אֲחוּזִים
שַׁעֲרֵי הֵיכָל הַנֶּחְמָדִים מְהֵרָה תִּפְתַּח לְוְעוּדִים
שַׁעֲרֵי זְבוּל מַחֲנַיִם מְהֵרָה תִּפְתַּח לְחַכְלִילִי עֵינַיִם
שַׁעֲרֵי טָהֳרָה מְהֵרָה תִּפְתַּח לְיָפָה וּבָרָה
שַׁעֲרֵי כֶּתֶר הַמְיֻמָּן מְהֵרָה תִּפְתַּח לְלֹא אַלְמָן.
וּבָהֶם תְּעֻרַץ וְתֻקְדַּשׁ
כְּסוֹד שִׂיחַ שַׂרְפֵי קֹדֶשׁ, הַמַּקְדִּישִׁים שִׁמְךָ בַּקֹּדֶשׁ

שַׁעֲרֵי אַרְמוֹן *Let the gates of the palace.* As the gates (of the Temple or of heaven) begin to close, we pray for them to stay open.

KEDUSHA

The following is said standing with feet together, rising on the toes at the words indicated by ▴.

The congregation then the Leader:

(נַעֲרִיצְךָ We will revere and sanctify You with the words uttered
by the holy Seraphim who sanctify Your name in the Sanctuary,)
as is written by Your prophet: "They call out to one another, saying: *Is. 6*

The congregation then the Leader:

▴Holy, ▴holy, ▴holy is the LORD of hosts;
the whole world is filled with His glory."
His glory fills the universe. His ministering angels ask each other,
"Where is the place of His glory?"
Those facing them reply "Blessed –

The congregation then the Leader:

▴"Blessed is the LORD's glory from His place." *Ezek. 3*
From His place may He turn with compassion and be gracious to the
people who proclaim the unity of His name, morning and evening,
every day, continually, twice each day reciting in love the Shema:

The congregation then the Leader:

"Listen, Israel, the LORD is our God, the LORD is One." *Deut. 6*
He is our God, He is our Father, He is our King, He is our Savior –
and He, in His compassion, will let us hear a second time in the
presence of all that lives, His promise "to be Your God. *Num. 15*
I am the LORD your God."

The congregation then the Leader:

Glorious is our Glorious One, LORD our Master, *Ps. 8*
and glorious is Your name throughout the earth.
Then the LORD shall be King over all the earth; *Zech. 14*
on that day the LORD shall be One and His name One.

The Leader continues:

And in Your holy Writings it is written:

The congregation then the Leader:

▴"The LORD shall reign for ever. *Ps. 146*
He is your God, Zion, from generation to generation, Halleluya!"

קדושה

The following is said standing with feet together, rising on the toes at the words indicated by ▴.

The קהל *then the* שליח ציבור*:*

(נַעֲרִיצְךָ וְנַקְדִּישְׁךָ כְּסוֹד שִׂיחַ שַׂרְפֵי קֹדֶשׁ, הַמַּקְדִּישִׁים שִׁמְךָ בַּקֹּדֶשׁ)

כַּכָּתוּב עַל יַד נְבִיאֶךָ: וְקָרָא זֶה אֶל־זֶה וְאָמַר ישעיה ו

The קהל *then the* שליח ציבור*:*

▴קָדוֹשׁ, ▴קָדוֹשׁ, ▴קָדוֹשׁ, יהוה צְבָאוֹת, מְלֹא כָל־הָאָרֶץ כְּבוֹדוֹ:

כְּבוֹדוֹ מָלֵא עוֹלָם, מְשָׁרְתָיו שׁוֹאֲלִים זֶה לָזֶה, אַיֵּה מְקוֹם

כְּבוֹדוֹ, לְעֻמָּתָם בָּרוּךְ יֹאמֵרוּ

The קהל *then the* שליח ציבור*:*

▴בָּרוּךְ כְּבוֹד־יהוה מִמְּקוֹמוֹ: יחזקאל ג

מִמְּקוֹמוֹ הוּא יִפֶן בְּרַחֲמִים, וְיָחֹן עַם הַמְיַחֲדִים שְׁמוֹ

עֶרֶב וָבֹקֶר בְּכָל יוֹם תָּמִיד, פַּעֲמַיִם בְּאַהֲבָה שְׁמַע אוֹמְרִים

The קהל *then the* שליח ציבור*:*

שְׁמַע יִשְׂרָאֵל, יהוה אֱלֹהֵינוּ, יהוה אֶחָד: דברים ו

הוּא אֱלֹהֵינוּ, הוּא אָבִינוּ, הוּא מַלְכֵּנוּ, הוּא מוֹשִׁיעֵנוּ

וְהוּא יַשְׁמִיעֵנוּ בְּרַחֲמָיו שֵׁנִית לְעֵינֵי כָּל חָי, לִהְיוֹת לָכֶם לֵאלֹהִים במדבר טו

אֲנִי יהוה אֱלֹהֵיכֶם:

The קהל *then the* שליח ציבור*:*

אַדִּיר אַדִּירֵנוּ, יהוה אֲדֹנֵינוּ, מָה־אַדִּיר שִׁמְךָ בְּכָל־הָאָרֶץ: תהלים ח

וְהָיָה יהוה לְמֶלֶךְ עַל־כָּל־הָאָרֶץ זכריה יד

בַּיּוֹם הַהוּא יִהְיֶה יהוה אֶחָד וּשְׁמוֹ אֶחָד:

The שליח ציבור *continues:*

וּבְדִבְרֵי קָדְשְׁךָ כָּתוּב לֵאמֹר

The קהל *then the* שליח ציבור*:*

▴יִמְלֹךְ יהוה לְעוֹלָם, אֱלֹהַיִךְ צִיּוֹן לְדֹר וָדֹר, הַלְלוּיָהּ: תהלים קמו

The Leader continues:

From generation to generation we will declare Your greatness,
and we will proclaim Your holiness for evermore.
Your praise, our God, shall not leave our mouth forever,
for You, God, are a great and holy King.

The following prayer originally began at "For with Your holiness." Nowadays, it is commonly sung as one stanza together with the later addition of the opening verse "Have mercy on those You have made."

חֲמֹל Have mercy on those You have made,
take joy in those You made,
and those who shelter in You will say,
as You absolve the ones You bear,
"Be sanctified, LORD, through all that You have made."

כִּי מַקְדִּישֶׁיךָ For with Your holiness You sanctify
all who affirm You holy;
it is fitting that the Holy One be glorified by holy ones.

The Leader continues:

בְּאֵין With no one to advocate for us against the accuser of sin,
speak words of law and of justice to Jacob;
and absolve us in the judgment, O King of judgment.

עוֹד He, our LORD, will yet remember for us
the love of [Abraham] the steadfast one.
And for [Isaac] the son who was bound,
He will still the enmity against us.
And for the merit of [Jacob] the innocent man,
He will bring today our judgment out to the good,
for this day is holy to our LORD. *Neh. 8*

וּבְכֵן יִתְקַדַּשׁ And so may Your name be sanctified, LORD our God,
through Israel Your nation and Jerusalem, Your city,
and Zion, the dwelling place of Your honor
and through the royal house of David Your anointed,
and Your Sanctuary and Your Temple.

The שליח ציבור *continues:*

לְדוֹר וָדוֹר נַגִּיד גָּדְלֶךָ, וּלְנֵצַח נְצָחִים קְדֻשָּׁתְךָ נַקְדִּישׁ
וְשִׁבְחֲךָ אֱלֹהֵינוּ מִפִּינוּ לֹא יָמוּשׁ לְעוֹלָם וָעֶד
כִּי אֵל מֶלֶךְ גָּדוֹל וְקָדוֹשׁ אָתָּה.

The following prayer originally began at כִּי מַקְדִּישֶׁיךָ*. Nowadays, it is commonly sung as one stanza together with the later addition of the opening verse* חֲמֹל עַל מַעֲשֶׂיךָ*.*

חֲמֹל עַל מַעֲשֶׂיךָ וְתִשְׂמַח בְּמַעֲשֶׂיךָ
וְיֹאמְרוּ לְךָ חוֹסֶיךָ בְּצַדֶּקְךָ עֲמוּסֶיךָ
תֻּקְדַּשׁ אָדוֹן עַל כָּל מַעֲשֶׂיךָ

כִּי מַקְדִּישֶׁיךָ בִּקְדֻשָּׁתְךָ קִדַּשְׁתָּ
נָאֶה לְקָדוֹשׁ פְּאֵר מִקְּדוֹשִׁים.

The שליח ציבור *continues:*

בְּאֵין מֵלִיץ יֹשֶׁר מוּל מַגִּיד פֶּשַׁע
תַּגִּיד לְיַעֲקֹב דְּבַר, חֹק וּמִשְׁפָּט
וְצַדְּקֵנוּ בַּמִּשְׁפָּט, הַמֶּלֶךְ הַמִּשְׁפָּט.

עוֹד יִזְכֹּר לָנוּ אַהֲבַת אֵיתָן, אֲדוֹנֵינוּ
וּבַבֵּן הַנֶּעֱקַד יַשְׁבִּית מְדַיְּנֵינוּ
וּבִזְכוּת הַתָּם יוֹצִיא הַיּוֹם לְצֶדֶק דִּינֵנוּ
כִּי־קָדוֹשׁ הַיּוֹם לַאֲדֹנֵינוּ: נחמיה ח

וּבְכֵן יִתְקַדַּשׁ שִׁמְךָ יהוה אֱלֹהֵינוּ
עַל יִשְׂרָאֵל עַמֶּךָ
וְעַל יְרוּשָׁלַיִם עִירֶךָ
וְעַל צִיּוֹן מִשְׁכַּן כְּבוֹדֶךָ
וְעַל מַלְכוּת בֵּית דָּוִד מְשִׁיחֶךָ
וְעַל מְכוֹנְךָ וְהֵיכָלֶךָ.

HOLINESS

וּבְכֵן תֵּן פַּחְדְּךָ And so place the fear of You, Lord our God,
over all that You have made,
and the terror of You over all You have created,
and all who were made will stand in awe of You,
and all of creation will worship You,
and they will be bound all together as one
to carry out Your will with an undivided heart;
for we know, Lord our God,
that all dominion is laid out before You,
strength is in Your palm, and might in Your right hand,
Your name spreading awe over all You have created.

וּבְכֵן תֵּן כָּבוֹד And so place honor, Lord, upon Your people,
praise on those who fear You and hope into those who seek You,
the confidence to speak into all who long for You,
gladness to Your land and joy to Your city,
the flourishing of pride to David Your servant,
and a lamp laid out for his descendant, Your anointed,
soon, in our days.

וּבְכֵן צַדִּיקִים And then righteous people will see and rejoice,
and the upright will exult, and the pious revel in joy,
and injustice will have nothing more to say,
and all wickedness will fade away like smoke
as You sweep the rule of arrogance from the earth.

וְתִמְלֹךְ And You, Lord, will rule alone over those You have made,
in Mount Zion, the dwelling of Your glory,
and in Jerusalem, Your holy city,
as it is written in Your holy writings:
"The Lord shall reign for ever. *Ps. 146*
He is your God, Zion, from generation to generation, Halleluya!"

קָדוֹשׁ אַתָּה You are holy, Your name is awesome,
and there is no god but You, as it is written,
"The Lord of hosts shall be raised up through His judgment, *Is. 5*
the holy God, made holy in righteousness."
Blessed are You, Lord, the holy King.

קדושת השם

וּבְכֵן תֵּן פַּחְדְּךָ יהוה אֱלֹהֵינוּ עַל כָּל מַעֲשֶׂיךָ
וְאֵימָתְךָ עַל כָּל מַה שֶּׁבָּרָאתָ
וְיִירָאוּךָ כָּל הַמַּעֲשִׂים, וְיִשְׁתַּחֲווּ לְפָנֶיךָ כָּל הַבְּרוּאִים
וְיֵעָשׂוּ כֻלָּם אֲגֻדָּה אַחַת לַעֲשׂוֹת רְצוֹנְךָ בְּלֵבָב שָׁלֵם
כְּמוֹ שֶׁיָּדַעְנוּ יהוה אֱלֹהֵינוּ שֶׁהַשָּׁלְטָן לְפָנֶיךָ
עֹז בְּיָדְךָ וּגְבוּרָה בִּימִינֶךָ
וְשִׁמְךָ נוֹרָא עַל כָּל מַה שֶּׁבָּרָאתָ.

וּבְכֵן תֵּן כָּבוֹד יהוה לְעַמֶּךָ
תְּהִלָּה לִירֵאֶיךָ וְתִקְוָה טוֹבָה לְדוֹרְשֶׁיךָ
וּפִתְחוֹן פֶּה לַמְיַחֲלִים לָךְ
שִׂמְחָה לְאַרְצֶךָ, וְשָׂשׂוֹן לְעִירֶךָ
וּצְמִיחַת קֶרֶן לְדָוִד עַבְדֶּךָ, וַעֲרִיכַת נֵר לְבֶן יִשַׁי מְשִׁיחֶךָ
בִּמְהֵרָה בְיָמֵינוּ.

וּבְכֵן צַדִּיקִים יִרְאוּ וְיִשְׂמָחוּ, וִישָׁרִים יַעֲלֹזוּ
וַחֲסִידִים בְּרִנָּה יָגִילוּ, וְעוֹלָתָה תִּקְפָּץ פִּיהָ
וְכָל הָרִשְׁעָה כֻּלָּהּ כְּעָשָׁן תִּכְלֶה, כִּי תַעֲבִיר מֶמְשֶׁלֶת זָדוֹן מִן הָאָרֶץ.

וְתִמְלֹךְ אַתָּה יהוה לְבַדֶּךָ עַל כָּל מַעֲשֶׂיךָ
בְּהַר צִיּוֹן מִשְׁכַּן כְּבוֹדֶךָ, וּבִירוּשָׁלַיִם עִיר קָדְשֶׁךָ
כַּכָּתוּב בְּדִבְרֵי קָדְשֶׁךָ
יִמְלֹךְ יהוה לְעוֹלָם, אֱלֹהַיִךְ צִיּוֹן לְדֹר וָדֹר, הַלְלוּיָהּ: תהלים קמו

קָדוֹשׁ אַתָּה וְנוֹרָא שְׁמֶךָ, וְאֵין אֱלוֹהַּ מִבַּלְעָדֶיךָ
כַּכָּתוּב, וַיִּגְבַּהּ יהוה צְבָאוֹת בַּמִּשְׁפָּט ישעיה ה
וְהָאֵל הַקָּדוֹשׁ נִקְדַּשׁ בִּצְדָקָה:
בָּרוּךְ אַתָּה יהוה, הַמֶּלֶךְ הַקָּדוֹשׁ.

HOLINESS OF THE DAY

אַתָּה בְחַרְתָּנוּ You have chosen us from among all peoples.
You have loved and favored us.
You have raised us above all tongues.
You have made us holy through Your commandments.
You have brought us near, our King, to Your service,
and have called us by Your great and holy name.

On Shabbat, add the words in parentheses:

וַתִּתֶּן לָנוּ And You, LORD our God, have given us in love
(this Sabbath day for holiness and rest, and)
this Day of Atonement
for pardon and forgiveness and atonement,
to pardon all our iniquities,
(with love,) a holy assembly
in memory of the exodus from Egypt.

אֱלֹהֵינוּ Our God and God of our ancestors,
may there rise, come, reach, appear, be favored, heard,
regarded and remembered before You,
our recollection and remembrance,
as well as the remembrance of our ancestors,
and of the Messiah, son of David Your servant,
and of Jerusalem Your holy city,
and of all Your people the house of Israel –
for deliverance and well-being,
grace, loving-kindness and compassion,
life and peace, on this Day of Atonement.
On it remember us, LORD our God, for good;
recollect us for blessing, and deliver us for life.
In accord with Your promise of salvation and compassion,
spare us and be gracious to us; have compassion on us and deliver us,
for our eyes are turned to You
because You, God, are a gracious and compassionate King.

קדושת היום

אַתָּה בְחַרְתָּנוּ מִכָּל הָעַמִּים
אָהַבְתָּ אוֹתָנוּ וְרָצִיתָ בָּנוּ, וְרוֹמַמְתָּנוּ מִכָּל הַלְּשׁוֹנוֹת
וְקִדַּשְׁתָּנוּ בְּמִצְוֹתֶיךָ, וְקֵרַבְתָּנוּ מַלְכֵּנוּ לַעֲבוֹדָתֶךָ
וְשִׁמְךָ הַגָּדוֹל וְהַקָּדוֹשׁ עָלֵינוּ קָרָאתָ.

On שבת*, add the words in parentheses:*

וַתִּתֶּן לָנוּ יהוה אֱלֹהֵינוּ בְּאַהֲבָה אֶת
(יוֹם הַשַּׁבָּת הַזֶּה לִקְדֻשָּׁה וְלִמְנוּחָה, וְאֶת)
יוֹם הַכִּפּוּרִים הַזֶּה, לִמְחִילָה וְלִסְלִיחָה וּלְכַפָּרָה
וְלִמְחָל בּוֹ אֶת כָּל עֲוֹנוֹתֵינוּ
(בְּאַהֲבָה) מִקְרָא קֹדֶשׁ, זֵכֶר לִיצִיאַת מִצְרָיִם.

אֱלֹהֵינוּ וֵאלֹהֵי אֲבוֹתֵינוּ
יַעֲלֶה וְיָבוֹא וְיַגִּיעַ, וְיֵרָאֶה וְיֵרָצֶה וְיִשָּׁמַע
וְיִפָּקֵד וְיִזָּכֵר זִכְרוֹנֵנוּ וּפִקְדוֹנֵנוּ וְזִכְרוֹן אֲבוֹתֵינוּ
וְזִכְרוֹן מָשִׁיחַ בֶּן דָּוִד עַבְדֶּךָ
וְזִכְרוֹן יְרוּשָׁלַיִם עִיר קָדְשֶׁךָ
וְזִכְרוֹן כָּל עַמְּךָ בֵּית יִשְׂרָאֵל, לְפָנֶיךָ
לִפְלֵיטָה לְטוֹבָה, לְחֵן וּלְחֶסֶד וּלְרַחֲמִים, לְחַיִּים וּלְשָׁלוֹם
בְּיוֹם הַכִּפּוּרִים הַזֶּה.
זָכְרֵנוּ יהוה אֱלֹהֵינוּ בּוֹ לְטוֹבָה, וּפָקְדֵנוּ בוֹ לִבְרָכָה
וְהוֹשִׁיעֵנוּ בוֹ לְחַיִּים.
וּבִדְבַר יְשׁוּעָה וְרַחֲמִים, חוּס וְחָנֵּנוּ, וְרַחֵם עָלֵינוּ וְהוֹשִׁיעֵנוּ
כִּי אֵלֶיךָ עֵינֵינוּ, כִּי אֵל מֶלֶךְ חַנּוּן וְרַחוּם אָתָּה.

In most congregations, Ne'ila is the only time in the year in which Seliḥot are said in the middle of the Leader's Repetition. The following three verses introduce the Seliḥot.

The Leader says each verse, followed by the congregation:

Open us a gate / at the time of the locking of the gate,
for day is passing.

The day will pass; / the sun will set and pass;
we will come before Your gates.

We beg of You, God, please;
forbear, please; forgive, please; pardon, please; spare, please,
have compassion, please, atone, please; overcome sin and iniquity.

THE THIRTEEN ATTRIBUTES OF MERCY

All stand and say:

אֵל מֶלֶךְ God, King who sits upon a throne of compassion,
who acts with loving-kindness,
who pardons the iniquities of His people,
passing them before Him in order;
who forgives sinners and pardons transgressors;
who performs righteousness with all flesh and spirit,
do not repay their bad actions in kind.
▸ God, You taught us to speak thirteen attributes:
recall for us today the covenant of the thirteen attributes,
as You in ancient times showed the humble one [Moses], as is written:
The LORD descended in the cloud and stood with him there, *Ex. 34*
and proclaimed in the name of the LORD:

הַיּוֹם יִפְנֶה *The day will pass.* As the day dies, let us not die but live. Be with us, God, in the darkness as our eternal light.

אֵל מֶלֶךְ *God, King.* A prelude to the Thirteen Attributes of Mercy whose recitation always accompanies the penitential prayers. There are many different customs as to how many times we say this prayer at Ne'ila. Some say it three times, others seven, some ten, yet others thirteen. A long standing Anglo-Jewish custom was to say it once, so as not to rush it or the other prayers of Ne'ila, on the principle: "Better a little with full concentration than much without concentration" (see, for example, *Levush,* OḤ 1:4). The rule is that each community should follow its extant custom.

Every time we say this specific sequence of prayers, with its climax in

In most congregations, נעילה *is the only time in the year in which* סליחות *are said in the middle of the* חזרת הש״ץ*. The following three verses introduce the* סליחות*.*

The שליח ציבור *says each verse, followed by the* קהל*:*

פְּתַח לָנוּ שַׁעַר / בְּעֵת נְעִילַת שַׁעַר / כִּי פָנָה יוֹם.

הַיּוֹם יִפְנֶה / הַשֶּׁמֶשׁ יָבֹא וְיִפְנֶה / נָבוֹאָה שְׁעָרֶיךָ.

אָנָּא אֵל נָא, שָׂא נָא, סְלַח נָא, מְחַל נָא, חֲמָל נָא,
רַחֶם נָא, כַּפֶּר נָא, כְּבֹשׁ חֵטְא וְעָוֹן.

י״ג מדות הרחמים

All stand and say:

אֵל מֶלֶךְ יוֹשֵׁב עַל כִּסֵּא רַחֲמִים, מִתְנַהֵג בַּחֲסִידוּת.
מוֹחֵל עֲוֹנוֹת עַמּוֹ, מַעֲבִיר רִאשׁוֹן רִאשׁוֹן.
מַרְבֶּה מְחִילָה לְחַטָּאִים, וּסְלִיחָה לְפוֹשְׁעִים.
עֹשֶׂה צְדָקוֹת עִם כָּל בָּשָׂר וָרְוּחַ, לֹא כְרָעָתָם תִּגְמֹל.
◂ אֵל, הוֹרֵיתָ לָנוּ לוֹמַר שְׁלֹשׁ עֶשְׂרֵה
וּזְכָר לָנוּ הַיּוֹם בְּרִית שְׁלֹשׁ עֶשְׂרֵה
כְּמוֹ שֶׁהוֹדַעְתָּ לֶעָנָו מִקֶּדֶם, כְּמוֹ שֶׁכָּתוּב:
שמות לד וַיֵּרֶד יהוה בֶּעָנָן, וַיִּתְיַצֵּב עִמּוֹ שָׁם
וַיִּקְרָא בְשֵׁם, יהוה:

פְּתַח לָנוּ שַׁעַר בְּעֵת נְעִילַת שַׁעַר *Open us a gate at the time of the locking of the gate.* No time is too late to repent. The Talmud tells the story of King Hezekiah who lay gravely ill and was visited by the prophet Isaiah who told him that he was about to die. He had sinned, he was being punished and there was no hope of a reprieve. Hezekiah replied: "Son of Amotz, finish your prophecy and go. For I have it as a tradition from the house of my ancestor, that even if a sharp sword rests upon a person's neck he should not desist from prayer." God accepted Hezekiah's repentance and granted him an additional fifteen years of life (*Berakhot* 10a; see II Kings 20).

The congregation then the Leader:

וַיַּעֲבֹר And the LORD passed by before him and proclaimed: *Ex. 34*

All say aloud:

יהוה The LORD, the LORD, compassionate and gracious God,
slow to anger, abounding in loving-kindness and truth,
extending loving-kindness to a thousand generations,
forgiving iniquity, rebellion and sin,
and absolving [the guilty who repent].

All continue:

וְסָלַחְתָּ Forgive us our iniquity and our sin,
and take us as Your inheritance.

סְלַח לָנוּ Forgive us, our Father, for we have sinned.
Pardon us, our King, for we have transgressed.
For You, LORD, are good and forgiving, *Ps. 86*
abounding in loving-kindness to all who call on You.

As part of the Leader's Repetition, Seliḥot should ideally be said by the Leader alone (with the exception of the Thirteen Attributes of Mercy). However, in most congregations the Seliḥot are said together, with the Leader raising his voice only at the end of each seliḥa, in the place indicated by ▸.

All:

כִּי־עִמְּךָ But with You is forgiveness, that You may be revered. *Ps. 130*
If You, LORD, should keep account of sins, O LORD, who could stand? *Ibid.*

כְּרַחֵם As a father has compassion for his children,
so, LORD, have compassion for us.
Salvation belongs to the LORD; *Ps. 3*
may Your blessing rest upon Your people, Selah!
The LORD of hosts is with us, *Ps. 46*
the God of Jacob is our stronghold, Selah!
LORD of hosts: happy is the one who trusts in You. *Ps. 84*
LORD, save! May the King answer us on the day we call. *Ps. 20*

---

forgiveness – humanity and God meeting in direct, unmediated encounter, our tears dissolved in God's forbearing love, our souls cleansed, our lives readied for a new beginning.

The קהל *then the* שליח ציבור*:*

וַיַּעֲבֹר יהוה עַל־פָּנָיו וַיִּקְרָא שמות לד

All say aloud:

יהוה, יהוה, אֵל רַחוּם וְחַנּוּן, אֶרֶךְ אַפַּיִם, וְרַב־חֶסֶד וֶאֱמֶת:
נֹצֵר חֶסֶד לָאֲלָפִים, נֹשֵׂא עָוֹן וָפֶשַׁע וְחַטָּאָה, וְנַקֵּה:

All continue:

וְסָלַחְתָּ לַעֲוֹנֵנוּ וּלְחַטָּאתֵנוּ, וּנְחַלְתָּנוּ:

סְלַח לָנוּ אָבִינוּ כִּי חָטָאנוּ, מְחַל לָנוּ מַלְכֵּנוּ כִּי פָשָׁעְנוּ.
כִּי־אַתָּה אֲדֹנָי טוֹב וְסַלָּח, וְרַב־חֶסֶד לְכָל־קֹרְאֶיךָ: תהלים פו

As part of the חזרת הש״ץ*,* סליחות *should ideally be said by the* שליח ציבור *alone (with the exception of the* י״ג מידות*). However, in most congregations the* סליחות *are said together, with the* שליח ציבור *raising his voice only at the end of each* סליחה*, in the place indicated by* ◂*.*

All:

כִּי־עִמְּךָ הַסְּלִיחָה, לְמַעַן תִּוָּרֵא: תהלים קל
אִם־עֲוֹנוֹת תִּשְׁמָר־יָהּ, אֲדֹנָי מִי יַעֲמֹד: שם

כְּרַחֵם אָב עַל בָּנִים, כֵּן תְּרַחֵם יהוה עָלֵינוּ.
לַיהוה הַיְשׁוּעָה, עַל־עַמְּךָ בִרְכָתֶךָ סֶּלָה: תהלים ג
יהוה צְבָאוֹת עִמָּנוּ, מִשְׂגָּב לָנוּ אֱלֹהֵי יַעֲקֹב סֶלָה: תהלים מו
יהוה צְבָאוֹת, אַשְׁרֵי אָדָם בֹּטֵחַ בָּךְ: תהלים פד
יהוה הוֹשִׁיעָה, הַמֶּלֶךְ יַעֲנֵנוּ בְיוֹם־קָרְאֵנוּ: תהלים כ

---

the Thirteen Attributes, we are recapitulating the scene at the top of Mount Sinai when Moses prayed for the forgiveness of the people after the sin of the golden calf, and God did not merely grant forgiveness, but also taught Moses, and through him all future generations, how to pray for forgiveness. This was, as explained in the introduction, the moment on which Yom Kippur is based. It is the basis of all *seliḥot*, prayers for forgiveness, and it is the foundational moment at which Judaism became the supreme religion of

▸ סְלַח־נָא Forgive, please, this people's iniquity, Num. 14
in the abundance of Your kindness,
and as You have forgiven this people
from the time of Egypt until now,
and there it is said:

Congregation then Leader:

And the LORD said, I have forgiven as you asked.

All continue:

הַטֵּה Give ear, my God and hear; open Your eyes and see our desolation, and Dan. 9
the city that bears Your name, for it is not on the strength of our righteousness that we throw down our pleadings before You, but on the strength of Your great compassion. LORD, hear me; LORD, forgive; LORD, listen and act and do not delay – for Your sake, my God; for Your city and Your people bear Your name.

At this point the concluding verses of the piyut "You heal with salve" by Rabbi Shlomo the Babylonian (Italy, tenth century) are said. Though many congregations recite the Thirteen Attributes of Mercy before the penultimate verse, some omit and continue the piyut uninterrupted at "Let the fruits of our lips" on the next page.

וּמִי יַעֲמֹד Who could stand before You, if You retained every sin?
And who could rise, if judgment were applied fully?
Forgiveness is with You; it is for You to say, "I have forgiven" –
compassion, too, is with You; it is Your way to soften Your heart.

See the mournfulness of our destitution, do not shame us further;
fulfill our desire to know the course of Your path.
Strengthen for both old and young the spirit of wisdom –
may it be Your will to reinforce and fortify Your mighty ones.

Let the repentant sit in Your shade, receive them willingly,
so they can flower in Your House and no longer languish.
For those lost and exiled, end oppression and persecution –
then they will go up and appear [before You], with a willing spirit.

---

poems in Ne'ila, most rites abbreviate the text because of the pressure of time.

The opening words evoke Psalm 130:3: "If You, LORD, should keep account of sins, O LORD, who could stand?" A moving appeal to God to look on His people – exiled, persecuted and impoverished – and have compassion.

◂ סְלַח־נָא לַעֲוֹן הָעָם הַזֶּה כְּגֹדֶל חַסְדֶּךָ · במדבר יד
וְכַאֲשֶׁר נָשָׂאתָה לָעָם הַזֶּה מִמִּצְרַיִם וְעַד־הֵנָּה:
וְשָׁם נֶאֱמַר

The קהל *then the* שליח ציבור*:*

וַיֹּאמֶר יהוה, סָלַחְתִּי כִּדְבָרֶךָ:

All continue:

הַטֵּה אֱלֹהַי אָזְנְךָ וּשְׁמָע, פְּקַח עֵינֶיךָ וּרְאֵה שֹׁמְמֹתֵינוּ וְהָעִיר אֲשֶׁר־נִקְרָא שִׁמְךָ עָלֶיהָ, כִּי לֹא עַל־צִדְקֹתֵינוּ אֲנַחְנוּ מַפִּילִים תַּחֲנוּנֵינוּ לְפָנֶיךָ, כִּי עַל־רַחֲמֶיךָ הָרַבִּים: אֲדֹנָי שְׁמָעָה, אֲדֹנָי סְלָחָה, אֲדֹנָי הַקְשִׁיבָה וַעֲשֵׂה אַל־תְּאַחַר, לְמַעַנְךָ אֱלֹהַי, כִּי־שִׁמְךָ נִקְרָא עַל־עִירְךָ וְעַל־עַמֶּךָ: · דניאל ט

At this point the concluding verses of the piyut תַּעֲלַת צֳרִי תֶּרֶף *by Rabbi Shlomo the Babylonian (Italy, tenth century) are said. Though many congregations recite the* י״ג מדות הרחמים *before the penultimate verse, some omit and continue the piyut uninterrupted at "*שְׁלוֹם פְּרִים*" on the next page.*

וּמִי יַעֲמֹד, חֵטְא אִם תִּשְׁמֹר / וּמִי יָקוּם, דִּין אִם תִּגְמֹר
הַסְּלִיחָה עִמְּךָ הִיא, סָלַחְתִּי לֵאמֹר / הָרַחֲמִים גַּם לְךָ מִדָּתְךָ לִכְמֹר.

דִּכְדּוּךְ דַּלּוּתֵנוּ רְאֵה, אַל תְּכַלִּים / דַּעַת נְתִיב דְּרָכֶיךָ חֶפְצֵנוּ תַּשְׁלִים
גָּדוֹל וְקָטֹן רוּחַ שֶׁכֶל הַחֲלִים / גִּבּוֹרֵי כֹחַ, רְצוֹנְךָ חַזֵּק וְהָאֲלִים.

בְּצִלְּךָ שֶׁבֶת שָׁבִים קַבֵּל נְדָבָה / בֵּיתְךָ יַפְרִיחוּ וְלֹא יוֹסִיפוּ לְדַאֲבָה
אוֹבֵד וְנִדָּח תַּשְׁבִּית, נוֹגֵשׂ וּמַדְהֵבָה / אָז יַעֲלוּ וְיֵרָאוּ בְּרוּחַ נְדִיבָה.

וּמִי יַעֲמֹד *Who could stand.* As can be seen from the initial letters of the verses, this is a fragment of a longer poem structured as a reverse acrostic, moving from the last letter of the alphabet to the first. As with many of the

THE THIRTEEN ATTRIBUTES OF MERCY

Some omit the Thirteen Attributes of Mercy and continue with "Let the fruits of our lips" below.

All stand and say:

אֵל מֶלֶךְ God, King who sits upon a throne of compassion, who acts with loving-kindness, who pardons the iniquities of His people, passing them before Him in order; who forgives sinners and pardons transgressors; who performs righteousness with all flesh and spirit, do not repay their bad actions in kind.

▸ God, You taught us to speak thirteen attributes: recall for us today the covenant of the thirteen attributes, as You in ancient times showed the humble one [Moses], as is written: The LORD descended in the cloud and stood with him there, and proclaimed in the name of the LORD: *Ex. 34*

The congregation then the Leader:

וַיַּעֲבֹר And the LORD passed by before him and proclaimed: *Ibid.*

All say aloud:

יהוה The LORD, the LORD, compassionate and gracious God,
slow to anger, abounding in loving-kindness and truth,
extending loving-kindness to a thousand generations,
forgiving iniquity, rebellion and sin,
and absolving [the guilty who repent].

All continue:

וְסָלַחְתָּ Forgive us our iniquity and our sin, and take us as Your inheritance.

סְלַח לָנוּ Forgive us, our Father, for we have sinned. Pardon us, our King, for we have transgressed. For You, LORD, are good and forgiving, abounding in loving-kindness to all who call on You. *Ps. 86*

All:

שְׁלוֹם פָּרִים Let the fruits of our lips that we offer be considered true;
we follow after You in the innocence and honesty of friendship.
Accept our advocate of the right, and silence our accuser forever,
You who desire life, and not the death of the condemned.

Raise us up by the light of Your countenance, and complete all reckonings;
find redemption for us, so we are not cast into the pit.
Let Your pronouncement [of forgiveness] anticipate our cries –
please accept, O LORD, these offerings of our mouths.

---

key texts showing that in the absence of the Temple, words substitute for offerings, and prayer takes the place of sacrifice.

י״ג מדות הרחמים

Some omit the י״ג מדות הרחמים *and continue with "*שְׁלוֹם פְּרִים*" below.*

All stand and say:

אֵל מֶלֶךְ יוֹשֵׁב עַל כִּסֵּא רַחֲמִים, מִתְנַהֵג בַּחֲסִידוּת. מוֹחֵל עֲוֹנוֹת עַמּוֹ, מַעֲבִיר רִאשׁוֹן רִאשׁוֹן. מַרְבֶּה מְחִילָה לְחַטָּאִים, וּסְלִיחָה לְפוֹשְׁעִים. עֹשֶׂה צְדָקוֹת עִם כָּל בָּשָׂר וָרוּחַ, לֹא כְרָעָתָם תִּגְמֹל.

◂ אֵל, הוֹרֵיתָ לָּנוּ לוֹמַר שְׁלֹשׁ עֶשְׂרֵה, וּזְכָר לָנוּ הַיּוֹם בְּרִית שְׁלֹשׁ עֶשְׂרֵה,
שמות לד כְּמוֹ שֶׁהוֹדַעְתָּ לֶעָנָו מִקֶּדֶם, כְּמוֹ שֶׁכָּתוּב: וַיֵּרֶד יהוה בֶּעָנָן, וַיִּתְיַצֵּב עִמּוֹ שָׁם, וַיִּקְרָא בְשֵׁם, יהוה:

The קהל *then the* שליח ציבור*:*

שם וַיַּעֲבֹר יהוה עַל־פָּנָיו וַיִּקְרָא

All say aloud:

יהוה, יהוה, אֵל רַחוּם וְחַנּוּן אֶרֶךְ אַפַּיִם, וְרַב־חֶסֶד וֶאֱמֶת: נֹצֵר חֶסֶד לָאֲלָפִים נֹשֵׂא עָוֹן וָפֶשַׁע וְחַטָּאָה, וְנַקֵּה:

All continue:

וְסָלַחְתָּ לַעֲוֹנֵנוּ וּלְחַטָּאתֵנוּ, וּנְחַלְתָּנוּ:

סְלַח לָנוּ אָבִינוּ כִּי חָטָאנוּ, מְחַל לָנוּ מַלְכֵּנוּ כִּי פָשָׁעְנוּ.
תהלים פו כִּי־אַתָּה אֲדֹנָי טוֹב וְסַלָּח, וְרַב־חֶסֶד לְכָל־קֹרְאֶיךָ:

All:

שְׁלוֹם פְּרִים שְׂפָתֵינוּ תִּכּוֹן אֱמֶת / לְכְתֵנוּ אַחֲרֶיךָ בְּתֹם וְיֹשֶׁר הַעֲמֵת
מֵלִיץ יֹשֶׁר קַבֵּל, וּמְלָשְׁנִי צַמֵּת / הֶחָפֵץ בַּחַיִּים וְלֹא בְּמוֹת הַמֵּת.

הֲקִימֵנוּ בְּאוֹר פָּנֶיךָ וְחֶשְׁבּוֹן יִתְמַצֵּה / קִיּוּם מֵרֶדֶת שַׁחַת כֹּפֶר יִמָּצֵא
טֶרֶם נִקְרָא עוֹד דִּבּוּר יֵצֵא / נִדְבוֹת פִּינוּ יהוה נָא רְצֵה.

שְׁלוֹם פְּרִים שְׂפָתֵינוּ *Let the fruits of our lips that we offer.* The initial letters of each stich spell the name of the author of the poem, Shlomo HaKatan, Rabbi Shlomo ben Yehuda HaBavli (Shlomo the Babylonian, tenth century). The opening is a reference to Hosea 14:3: "Take with you words, and return to God… so will we render for bullocks the offering of our lips" – one of the

The following are the concluding verses of the piyut "Our Master, it is the time" by Rabbi Yosef of Orleans, the author of the Bekhor Shor commentary on the Torah (France, twelfth century). As in the previous piyut, many congregations recite the Thirteen Attributes of Mercy before the last verse, while some omit and continue the piyut uninterrupted at "Stretch out Your hand" on the next page.

מְרֻבִּים Your people's needs are many,
but they do not now have the presence of mind
to relate their requests and faults, which are too numerous;
divine our meaning before we even cry out to You,
O great, mighty and awesome God. *Deut. 10*

Those who knew how to pray have passed away and gone,
those who knew how to arrange the prayers upon their tongues.
We are left naked, and our evil has increased within us;
therefore we have not reached salvation.

We are too ashamed to entreat You;
we have sinned and rebelled, twisted our paths.
we can only ask for Your righteousness in arranging our praise,
we who nightly stand in the House of the LORD. *Ps. 134*

Holy One, see how we have no fitting advocate;
accept my words as though a great offering.
May my song today be an adornment in Your crown,
O God girded with strength.
Hear my cry and let my prayer be pleasing;
listen to my plea as though it were a perfect prayer.
Engrave us [in the book of] life and seal us well within it,
You who suspends the earth over nothingness. *Job 26*

THE THIRTEEN ATTRIBUTES OF MERCY

Some omit the Thirteen Attributes of Mercy and continue with "Stretch out Your hand" on the next page.

All stand and say:

אֵל מֶלֶךְ God, King who sits upon a throne of compassion, who acts with loving-kindness, who pardons the iniquities of His people, passing them before Him in order; who forgives sinners and pardons transgressors; who performs righteousness with all flesh and spirit, do not repay their bad actions in kind.

תְּחָקְקֵנוּ *Engrave us.* The poet uses an unusually strong verb here. Elsewhere we have spoken about being "written" and "sealed" in the book of life, but here the poet says "engrave us," carve our names indelibly in stone.

The following are the concluding verses of the piyut אָדוֹן מוֹעֵד כְּתִקַּח *(by Rabbi Yosef of Orleans, the author of the* בכור שור *commentary on the Torah (France, twelfth century). As in the previous piyut, many congregations recite the* י״ג מדות הרחמים *before the last verse, while some omit and continue the piyut uninterrupted at "*יָדְךָ פְּשֹׁט*" on the next page.*

מְרֻבִּים צָרְכֵי עַמְּךָ, וְדַעְתָּם קְצָרָה /
מַחְסוֹרָם וּמִשְׁאֲלוֹתָם בַּל יוּכְלוּ לְסַפְּרָה
נָא בִּינָה הֲגִיגֵנוּ טֶרֶם נִקְרָא / הָאֵל הַגָּדֹל הַגִּבֹּר וְהַנּוֹרָא: דברים י

סָפוּ וְגַם כָּלוּ יוֹדְעֵי פְגִיעָה / סֵדֶר תְּפִלּוֹת בְּמַעֲנֵה לְשׁוֹנָם לְהַבִּיעָה
עֲרֻמִּים נוֹתַרְנוּ, וְרָבְתָה בָּנוּ הָרָעָה / עַל כֵּן לֹא הִשִּׂיגַתְנוּ יְשׁוּעָה.

פָּנִים אֵין לָנוּ פָּנֶיךָ לְחַלּוֹת / פָּשַׁעְנוּ וּמָרַדְנוּ וְהֶעֱוִינוּ מְסִלּוֹת
צְדָקָה לְךָ לְבַד נְבַקֵּשׁ בְּמַעַרְכֵי תְהִלּוֹת /
הָעֹמְדִים בְּבֵית־יהוה בַּלֵּילוֹת: תהלים קלד

קָדוֹשׁ, רְאֵה כִּי פַס מֵלִיץ כַּשּׁוּרָה / קַבֵּל נִיבִי כְּמַרְבִּית תְּשׁוּרָה
רִנָּתִי הַיּוֹם תְּהֵא בְּכִתְרְךָ קְשׁוּרָה / אֵל נֶאְזָר בִּגְבוּרָה.

שַׁוְעָתִי שְׁעֵה וּתְפִלָּתִי תְּהֵא נְעִימָה / שְׁמַע פְּגִיעָתִי כִּפְגִיעָה תַמָּה
תְּחָקְקֵנוּ לְחַיִּים וְתֵיטִיב הַחֲתִימָה / תֹּלֶה אֶרֶץ עַל־בְּלִימָה: איוב כו

י״ג מדות הרחמים

Some omit the י״ג מדות הרחמים *and continue with "*יָדְךָ פְּשֹׁט*" on the next page.*

All stand and say:

אֵל מֶלֶךְ יוֹשֵׁב עַל כִּסֵּא רַחֲמִים, מִתְנַהֵג בַּחֲסִידוּת. מוֹחֵל עֲוֹנוֹת עַמּוֹ, מַעֲבִיר רִאשׁוֹן רִאשׁוֹן. מַרְבֶּה מְחִילָה לְחַטָּאִים, וּסְלִיחָה לְפוֹשְׁעִים. עֹשֶׂה צְדָקוֹת עִם כָּל בָּשָׂר וָרוּחַ, לֹא כְרָעָתָם תִּגְמֹל.

מְרֻבִּים צָרְכֵי עַמְּךָ *Your people's needs are many.* This appears in the Talmud as the model of a short prayer to be said at times of risk or danger (*Berakhot* 29b). We are tongue-tied, inarticulate, unable properly to frame our prayers. Please heed them despite their, and our, flaws.

▸ God, You taught us to speak thirteen attributes: recall for us today the covenant of the thirteen attributes, as You in ancient times showed the humble one [Moses], as is written: The LORD descended in the cloud and stood with him there, and proclaimed in the name of the LORD: *Ex. 34*

The congregation then the Leader:

וַיַּעֲבֹר And the LORD passed by before him and proclaimed: *Ibid.*

All say aloud:

יהוה The LORD, the LORD, compassionate and gracious God,
slow to anger, abounding in loving-kindness and truth,
extending loving-kindness to a thousand generations,
forgiving iniquity, rebellion and sin,
and absolving [the guilty who repent].

All continue:

וְסָלַחְתָּ Forgive us our iniquity and our sin, and take us as Your inheritance.

סְלַח לָנוּ Forgive us, our Father, for we have sinned. Pardon us, our King, for we have transgressed. For You, LORD, are good and forgiving, abounding in loving-kindness to all who call on You. *Ps. 86*

All:

יָדְךָ פְשֹׁט Stretch out Your hand – receive my repentance as I stand before You;
please forgive and pardon the evil that I have done.
Turn and attend to the goodness of those who seek You, my Beloved, my Encouragement;
You, LORD, are the shield that protects me. *Ps. 3*

THE THIRTEEN ATTRIBUTES OF MERCY

All stand and say:

אֵל מֶלֶךְ God, King who sits upon a throne of compassion, who acts with loving-kindness, who pardons the iniquities of His people, passing them before Him in order; who forgives sinners and pardons transgressors; who performs righteousness with all flesh and spirit, do not repay their bad actions in kind.

▸ God, You taught us to speak thirteen attributes: recall for us today the covenant of the thirteen attributes, as You in ancient times showed the humble one [Moses], as is written: The LORD descended in the cloud and stood with him there, and proclaimed in the name of the LORD: *Ex. 34*

The congregation then the Leader:

וַיַּעֲבֹר And the LORD passed by before him and proclaimed: *Ibid.*

‹ אֵל, הוֹרֵיתָ לָּנוּ לוֹמַר שְׁלֹשׁ עֶשְׂרֵה, וּזְכָר לָנוּ הַיּוֹם בְּרִית שְׁלֹשׁ עֶשְׂרֵה,
כְּמוֹ שֶׁהוֹדַעְתָּ לֶעָנָו מִקֶּדֶם, כְּמוֹ שֶׁכָּתוּב: וַיֵּרֶד יהוה בֶּעָנָן, וַיִּתְיַצֵּב עִמּוֹ שמות לד
שָׁם, וַיִּקְרָא בְשֵׁם, יהוה:

The קהל *then the* שליח ציבור*:*

וַיַּעֲבֹר יהוה עַל־פָּנָיו וַיִּקְרָא שם

All say aloud:

יהוה, יהוה, אֵל רַחוּם וְחַנּוּן אֶרֶךְ אַפַּיִם, וְרַב־חֶסֶד וֶאֱמֶת:
נֹצֵר חֶסֶד לָאֲלָפִים נֹשֵׂא עָוֹן וָפֶשַׁע וְחַטָּאָה, וְנַקֵּה:

All continue:

וְסָלַחְתָּ לַעֲוֹנֵנוּ וּלְחַטָּאתֵנוּ, וּנְחַלְתָּנוּ:

סְלַח לָנוּ אָבִינוּ כִּי חָטָאנוּ, מְחַל לָנוּ מַלְכֵּנוּ כִּי פָשָׁעְנוּ.
כִּי־אַתָּה אֲדֹנָי טוֹב וְסַלָּח, וְרַב־חֶסֶד לְכָל־קֹרְאֶיךָ: תהלים פו

All:

יָדְךָ פְּשֹׁט, וְקַבֵּל תְּשׁוּבָתִי בְּמַעֲמָדִי / סְלַח נָא וּמְחַל רֹעַ מַעְבָּדִי
פְּנֵה וַעֲסֹק בְּטוֹבַת מְשַׁחֲרֶיךָ, דּוֹדַי וּמְעוֹדְדַי /
וְאַתָּה יהוה מָגֵן בַּעֲדִי: תהלים ג

י״ג מדות הרחמים

All stand and say:

אֵל מֶלֶךְ יוֹשֵׁב עַל כִּסֵּא רַחֲמִים, מִתְנַהֵג בַּחֲסִידוּת. מוֹחֵל עֲוֹנוֹת עַמּוֹ,
מַעֲבִיר רִאשׁוֹן רִאשׁוֹן. מַרְבֶּה מְחִילָה לְחַטָּאִים, וּסְלִיחָה לְפוֹשְׁעִים.
עֹשֶׂה צְדָקוֹת עִם כָּל בָּשָׂר וָרוּחַ, לֹא כְרָעָתָם תִּגְמֹל.

‹ אֵל, הוֹרֵיתָ לָּנוּ לוֹמַר שְׁלֹשׁ עֶשְׂרֵה, וּזְכָר לָנוּ הַיּוֹם בְּרִית שְׁלֹשׁ עֶשְׂרֵה,
כְּמוֹ שֶׁהוֹדַעְתָּ לֶעָנָו מִקֶּדֶם, כְּמוֹ שֶׁכָּתוּב: וַיֵּרֶד יהוה בֶּעָנָן, וַיִּתְיַצֵּב עִמּוֹ שמות לד
שָׁם, וַיִּקְרָא בְשֵׁם, יהוה:

The קהל *then the* שליח ציבור*:*

וַיַּעֲבֹר יהוה עַל־פָּנָיו וַיִּקְרָא שם

All say aloud:

יהוה The Lord, the Lord, compassionate and gracious God,
slow to anger, abounding in loving-kindness and truth,
extending loving-kindness to a thousand generations,
forgiving iniquity, rebellion and sin,
and absolving [the guilty who repent].

All continue:

וְסָלַחְתָּ Forgive us our iniquity and our sin, and take us as Your inheritance.

סְלַח לָנוּ Forgive us, our Father, for we have sinned. Pardon us, our King, for
we have transgressed. For You, Lord, are good and forgiving, abounding in Ps. 86
loving-kindness to all who call on You.

The Leader then the congregation:

זְכֹר Remember the covenant with Abraham
and the binding of Isaac,
and bring back the peace of the tents of Jacob,
and save us for the sake of Your name.

The following verses are an extract from the piyut אָבַדְנוּ מֵאֶרֶץ טוֹבָה*.*
Attributed to Rabbeinu Gershom ben Yehuda (Mainz, eleventh century),
the first stanza contains an acrostic of the author's name.
The קהל *recites each stanza, followed by the* שליח ציבור*:*

גּוֹאֵל חָזָק Mighty Redeemer, for Your sake save us;
see that our hands are powerless.
Behold how the righteous among us are gone,
and we have no leader to pray on our behalf.
Have compassion once more on the remnant of Israel,
and save us for the sake of Your name.

The holy city, its Sanctuary and environs / were shamed and plundered;
all her treasures have disappeared or been hidden,
and nothing remains but this Torah.
Bring back the peace of the tents of Jacob,
and save us for the sake of Your name.

---

land but they still had the covenant. They had lost their independence, but they still had the promise. They had lost the Temple but they still had the story. They had lost the visible presence of God but they still had His word, the Torah. It was their past, their future, their hope.

All say aloud:

יהוה, יהוה, אֵל רַחוּם וְחַנּוּן אֶרֶךְ אַפַּיִם, וְרַב־חֶסֶד וֶאֱמֶת:
נֹצֵר חֶסֶד לָאֲלָפִים נֹשֵׂא עָוֹן וָפֶשַׁע וְחַטָּאָה, וְנַקֵּה:

All continue:

וְסָלַחְתָּ לַעֲוֹנֵנוּ וּלְחַטָּאתֵנוּ, וּנְחַלְתָּנוּ:

סְלַח לָנוּ אָבִינוּ כִּי חָטָאנוּ, מְחַל לָנוּ מַלְכֵּנוּ כִּי פָשָׁעְנוּ.
כִּי־אַתָּה אֲדֹנָי טוֹב וְסַלָּח, וְרַב־חֶסֶד לְכָל־קֹרְאֶיךָ: תהלים פו

The שליח ציבור *then the* קהל:

זְכֹר בְּרִית אַבְרָהָם וַעֲקֵדַת יִצְחָק
וְהָשֵׁב שְׁבוּת אָהֳלֵי יַעֲקֹב
וְהוֹשִׁיעֵנוּ לְמַעַן שְׁמֶךָ.

The following verses are an extract from the piyut אָבַדְנוּ מֵאֶרֶץ טוֹבָה*.*
Attributed to Rabbeinu Gershom ben Yehuda (Mainz, eleventh century),
the first stanza contains an acrostic of the author's name.
The קהל *recites each stanza, followed by the* שליח ציבור:

גּוֹאֵל חָזָק, לְמַעַנְךָ פְּדֵנוּ / רְאֵה כִּי אָזְלַת יָדֵנוּ
שׁוּר כִּי אָבְדוּ חֲסִידֵינוּ / מַפְגִּיעַ אֵין בַּעֲדֵנוּ

וְשׁוּב בְּרַחֲמִים עַל שְׁאֵרִית יִשְׂרָאֵל / וְהוֹשִׁיעֵנוּ לְמַעַן שְׁמֶךָ.

הָעִיר הַקֹּדֶשׁ וְהַמְּחוֹזוֹת / הָיוּ לְחֶרְפָּה וּלְבִזּוֹת
וְכָל מַחֲמַדֶּיהָ טְבוּעוֹת וּגְנוּזוֹת /
וְאֵין שִׁיּוּר, רַק הַתּוֹרָה הַזֹּאת

וְהָשֵׁב שְׁבוּת אָהֳלֵי יַעֲקֹב / וְהוֹשִׁיעֵנוּ לְמַעַן שְׁמֶךָ.

זְכֹר בְּרִית *Remember the covenant.* The opening to a piyut authored by Rabbeinu Gershom who was known as "the light of the Diaspora."

וְאֵין שִׁיּוּר, רַק הַתּוֹרָה הַזֹּאת *And nothing remains but this Torah.* One of the most poignant of all descriptions of Jewish life in the dark centuries of exile and persecution. Jews had nothing except the Torah. It was, said the poet Heinrich Heine, the "portable homeland" of the Jews. They had lost their

In most congregations, the last recitation of the Thirteen Attributes of Mercy in any Seliḥot cycle is preceded by a "pizmon" (see note on page 150page 1261). Different communities had various customs as to the pizmon for Ne'ila. The following piyut is the accepted Ashkenazi custom; each of the four stanzas is a refrain from the pizmonot said in different communities before the custom was unified.

The Leader says each stanza, followed by the congregation:

אֶנְקַת Let the groaning of those who revere You
rise up before the throne of Your glory.
Grant the people who unify You all that they ask;
hear the prayer of those who come before You.

Israel, whose salvation is in the LORD, eternal salvation; *Is. 45*
this day too they beseech You, You who dwell on high.
For You are the One who abundantly forgives,
the Master of compassion.

Let the shade of His hands shelter us,
beneath the wings of the Divine Presence.
As He tries us, let Him be gracious,
and make firm again the deceitful heart.
Rise up please, our God, strengthen; please, give me strength –
LORD, listen to our plea.

May He let us hear Him say "I have forgiven" –
He who dwells concealed, Most High. *Ps. 91*
Let the right hand of Your salvation
save / this poor and downtrodden people.
As we plead with You, / answer us in Your righteousness with wonders;
LORD, be help to us.

THE THIRTEEN ATTRIBUTES OF MERCY

All stand and say:

אֵל מֶלֶךְ God, King who sits upon a throne of compassion, who acts with loving-kindness, who pardons the iniquities of His people, passing them before Him in order; who forgives sinners and pardons transgressors; who performs righteousness with all flesh and spirit, do not repay their bad actions in kind.

---

was composed by Rabbi Shefatya ben Amitai, leader of the community in Oria, Italy in the ninth century. "Let the shade of His hands" was written by Rabbi Yitzhak ben Shmuel of Dampierre, France, in the twelfth century. "May He let us hear" was composed by Rabbi Shlomo ben Shmuel who lived and taught at Acre (Akko) in the north of Israel in the thirteenth century.

In most congregations, the last recitation of the י״ג מידות *in any* סליחות *cycle is preceded by a* פזמון *(see note on page 151). Different communities had various customs as to the* פזמון *for* נעילה*. The following piyut is the accepted Ashkenazi custom; each of the four stanzas is a refrain from the* פזמונות *said in different communities before the custom was unified.*

The שליח ציבור *says each stanza, followed by the* קהל*:*

אֶנְקַת מְסַלְדֶיךָ
תַּעַל לִפְנֵי כִסֵּא כְבוֹדֶךָ
מַלֵּא מִשְׁאֲלוֹת עַם מְיַחֲדֶיךָ
שׁוֹמֵעַ תְּפִלַּת בָּאֵי עָדֶיךָ.

יִשְׂרָאֵל נוֹשַׁע בַּיהוה תְּשׁוּעַת עוֹלָמִים: ישעיה מה
גַּם הַיּוֹם יִוָּשְׁעוּ מִפִּיךָ, שׁוֹכֵן מְרוֹמִים
כִּי אַתָּה רַב סְלִיחוֹת וּבַעַל הָרַחֲמִים.

יַחְבִּיאֵנוּ צֵל יָדוֹ / תַּחַת כַּנְפֵי הַשְּׁכִינָה
חֹן יָחֹן, כִּי יִבְחֹן / לֵב עָקֹב לְהָכִינָה
קוּמָה נָא אֱלֹהֵינוּ, עֻזָּה עֻזִּי נָא / יהוה לְשַׁוְעָתֵנוּ הַאֲזִינָה.

יַשְׁמִיעֵנוּ סָלַחְתִּי / יֹשֵׁב בְּסֵתֶר עֶלְיוֹן: תהלים צא
בִּימִין יֶשַׁע / לְהִוָּשַׁע / עַם עָנִי וְאֶבְיוֹן
בְּשַׁוְעֵנוּ אֵלֶיךָ / נוֹרָאוֹת בְּצֶדֶק תַּעֲנֵנוּ
יהוה, הֱיֵה עוֹזֵר לָנוּ.

י״ג מדות הרחמים

All stand and say:

אֵל מֶלֶךְ יוֹשֵׁב עַל כִּסֵּא רַחֲמִים, מִתְנַהֵג בַּחֲסִידוּת. מוֹחֵל עֲוֹנוֹת עַמּוֹ, מַעֲבִיר רִאשׁוֹן רִאשׁוֹן. מַרְבֶּה מְחִילָה לְחַטָּאִים, וּסְלִיחָה לְפוֹשְׁעִים. עֹשֶׂה צְדָקוֹת עִם כָּל בָּשָׂר וָרוּחַ, לֹא כְרָעָתָם תִּגְמֹל.

אֶנְקַת מְסַלְדֶיךָ *Let the groaning of those who revere You.* Four fragments from four different poets. The first, "Let the groaning of those who revere You," was written by Rabbi Silano, religious leader of the Jewish community of Venosa, Italy, in the first half of the ninth century. The second, "Israel, whose salvation,"

▸ God, You taught us to speak thirteen attributes: recall for us today the covenant of the thirteen attributes, as You in ancient times showed the humble one [Moses], as is written: The LORD descended in the cloud and stood with him there, and proclaimed in the name of the LORD: *Ex. 34*

The congregation then the Leader:

וַיַּעֲבֹר And the LORD passed by before him and proclaimed: *Ibid.*

All say aloud:

יהוה The LORD, the LORD, compassionate and gracious God,
slow to anger, abounding in loving-kindness and truth,
extending loving-kindness to a thousand generations,
forgiving iniquity, rebellion and sin,
and absolving [the guilty who repent].

All continue:

וְסָלַחְתָּ Forgive us our iniquity and our sin, and take us as Your inheritance.

סְלַח לָנוּ Forgive us, our Father, for we have sinned. Pardon us, our King, for we have transgressed. For You, LORD, are good and forgiving, abounding in loving-kindness to all who call on You. *Ps. 86*

The third stanza of the following piyut did not meet the approval of some authorities in its direct approach to God's Attribute of Compassion; therefore, some congregations substitute this stanza with a similar one, printed below.

The Leader recites the first stanza and the congregation repeats. The subsequent stanzas are each recited first by the congregation, then repeated by the Leader.

יהוה The LORD, the LORD, compassionate and gracious God, *Ex. 34*
slow to anger, abounding in loving-kindness and truth,
extending loving-kindness to a thousand generations, forgiving
iniquity, rebellion and sin, and absolving [the guilty who repent].
Forgive us our iniquity and our sin, and take us as Your inheritance.

אֶזְכְּרָה I remember, God, and I grieve,
as I see every city built up on its hill,
and only the city of God thrown down to the deepest hell;
and yet we are for the LORD, and our eyes are turned to the LORD.

---

they saw the imperial grandeur of Byzantine Christianity and medieval Islam while Jewish Jerusalem lay desecrated.

◂ אֵל, הוֹרֵיתָ לָּנוּ לוֹמַר שְׁלֹשׁ עֶשְׂרֵה, וּזְכָר לָנוּ הַיּוֹם בְּרִית שְׁלֹשׁ עֶשְׂרֵה,
כְּמוֹ שֶׁהוֹדַעְתָּ לֶעָנָו מִקֶּדֶם, כְּמוֹ שֶׁכָּתוּב: וַיֵּרֶד יהוה בֶּעָנָן, וַיִּתְיַצֵּב עִמּוֹ שמות לד
שָׁם, וַיִּקְרָא בְשֵׁם, יהוה:

The קהל *then the* שליח ציבור:

וַיַּעֲבֹר יהוה עַל־פָּנָיו וַיִּקְרָא שם

All say aloud:

יהוה, יהוה, אֵל רַחוּם וְחַנּוּן אֶרֶךְ אַפַּיִם, וְרַב־חֶסֶד וֶאֱמֶת:
נֹצֵר חֶסֶד לָאֲלָפִים נֹשֵׂא עָוֹן וָפֶשַׁע וְחַטָּאָה, וְנַקֵּה:

All continue:

וְסָלַחְתָּ לַעֲוֹנֵנוּ וּלְחַטָּאתֵנוּ, וּנְחַלְתָּנוּ:

סְלַח לָנוּ אָבִינוּ כִּי חָטָאנוּ, מְחַל לָנוּ מַלְכֵּנוּ כִּי פָשָׁעְנוּ.
כִּי־אַתָּה אֲדֹנָי טוֹב וְסַלָּח, וְרַב־חֶסֶד לְכָל־קֹרְאֶיךָ: תהלים פו

The third stanza of the following piyut did not meet the approval of some authorities in its direct approach to מִדַּת הָרַחֲמִים *(God's Attribute of Compassion); therefore, some congregations substitute this stanza with a similar one, printed below.*

The שליח ציבור *recites the first stanza and the* קהל *repeats. The subsequent stanzas are each recited first by the* קהל*, then repeated by the* שליח ציבור.

יהוה, יהוה, אֵל רַחוּם וְחַנּוּן, אֶרֶךְ אַפַּיִם, וְרַב־חֶסֶד וֶאֱמֶת: שמות לד
נֹצֵר חֶסֶד לָאֲלָפִים, נֹשֵׂא עָוֹן וָפֶשַׁע וְחַטָּאָה, וְנַקֵּה:
וְסָלַחְתָּ לַעֲוֹנֵנוּ וּלְחַטָּאתֵנוּ, וּנְחַלְתָּנוּ:

אֶזְכְּרָה אֱלֹהִים וְאֶהֱמָיָה
בִּרְאוֹתִי כָּל עִיר עַל תִּלָּהּ בְּנוּיָה
וְעִיר הָאֱלֹהִים מֻשְׁפֶּלֶת עַד שְׁאוֹל תַּחְתִּיָּה
וּבְכָל זֹאת, אָנוּ לְיָהּ וְעֵינֵינוּ לְיָהּ.

אֶזְכְּרָה *I remember.* A poem written by Rabbi Amitai ben Shefatya of Oria, Italy, in the ninth century. In it one can hear a trace of the bitterness Jews felt when

*מִדַּת God's Attribute of Compassion – flow down over us,
and lay your plea before your Creator.
Ask compassion for your people,
for every heart is ailing,
and each head given over to illness.

**Some substitute:*

מִדַּת We shall bring God's Attribute of Compassion down to us;
we shall lay our plea before our Creator.
We shall ask compassion for our people,
for every heart is ailing,
and each head given over to illness.

תָּמַכְתִּי I have made my tent pegs firm
with the thirteen words [of God's attributes],
and with the Gates of Tears that are never locked together.
And so I have poured out words
before the One who examines hearts;
and I am secure in these
and in the merit of the three forefathers.

יְהִי רָצוֹן May it be Your will, You who are attentive to weeping,
that You place all our tears, remembered, in Your vial,
and save us from every cruel decree,
for our eyes are turned only to You.

THE THIRTEEN ATTRIBUTES OF MERCY

All stand and say:

אֵל מֶלֶךְ God, King who sits upon a throne of compassion, who acts with loving-kindness, who pardons the iniquities of His people, passing them before Him in order; who forgives sinners and pardons transgressors; who performs righteousness with all flesh and spirit, do not repay their bad actions in kind.

▸ God, You taught us to speak thirteen attributes: recall for us today the covenant of the thirteen attributes, as You in ancient times showed the humble one [Moses], as is written: The LORD descended in the cloud and stood with *Ex. 34*
him there, and proclaimed in the name of the LORD:

The congregation then the Leader:

וַיַּעֲבֹר And the LORD passed by before him and proclaimed: *Ibid.*

*מִדַּת הָרַחֲמִים עָלֵינוּ הִתְגַּלְגְּלִי
וְלִפְנֵי קוֹנֵךְ תְּחִנָּתֵךְ הַפִּילִי
וּבְעַד עַמֵּךְ רַחֲמִים שַׁאֲלִי
כִּי כָל לֵבָב דַּוָּי וְכָל רֹאשׁ לָחֳלִי.

*Some substitute:

מִדַּת הָרַחֲמִים עָלֵינוּ נִגַלְגְּלָה
וְלִפְנֵי קוֹנֵנוּ תְּחִנָּתֵנוּ נַפִּילָה
וּבְעַד עַמֵּנוּ רַחֲמִים נְשַׁאֲלָה
כִּי כָל לֵבָב דַּוָּי וְכָל רֹאשׁ לְמַחֲלָה.

תָּמַכְתִּי יְתֵדוֹתַי בִּשְׁלֹשׁ עֶשְׂרֵה תֵבוֹת
וּבְשַׁעֲרֵי דְמָעוֹת, כִּי לֹא נִשְׁלָבוֹת
לָכֵן שָׁפַכְתִּי שִׂיחַ פְּנֵי בוֹחֵן לִבּוֹת
בָּטוּחַ אֲנִי בְּאֵלֶּה, וּבִזְכוּת שְׁלֹשֶׁת אָבוֹת.

יְהִי רָצוֹן מִלְּפָנֶיךָ, שׁוֹמֵעַ קוֹל בְּכִיּוֹת
שֶׁתָּשִׂים דִּמְעוֹתֵינוּ בְּנֹאדְךָ לִהְיוֹת
וְתַצִּילֵנוּ מִכָּל גְּזֵרוֹת אַכְזָרִיּוֹת
כִּי לְךָ לְבַד עֵינֵינוּ תְלוּיוֹת.

י״ג מדות הרחמים

All stand and say:

אֵל מֶלֶךְ יוֹשֵׁב עַל כִּסֵּא רַחֲמִים, מִתְנַהֵג בַּחֲסִידוּת. מוֹחֵל עֲוֹנוֹת עַמּוֹ, מַעֲבִיר רִאשׁוֹן רִאשׁוֹן. מַרְבֶּה מְחִילָה לְחַטָּאִים, וּסְלִיחָה לְפוֹשְׁעִים. עֹשֶׂה צְדָקוֹת עִם כָּל בָּשָׂר וָרוּחַ, לֹא כְרָעָתָם תִּגְמֹל.

◂ אֵל, הוֹרֵיתָ לָּנוּ לוֹמַר שְׁלֹשׁ עֶשְׂרֵה, וּזְכָר לָנוּ הַיּוֹם בְּרִית שְׁלֹשׁ עֶשְׂרֵה,
שמות לד כְּמוֹ שֶׁהוֹדַעְתָּ לֶעָנָו מִקֶּדֶם, כְּמוֹ שֶׁכָּתוּב: וַיֵּרֶד יהוה בֶּעָנָן, וַיִּתְיַצֵּב עִמּוֹ
שָׁם, וַיִּקְרָא בְשֵׁם, יהוה:

The קהל *then the* שליח ציבור:

שם וַיַּעֲבֹר יהוה עַל־פָּנָיו וַיִּקְרָא

All say aloud:

יהוה The Lord, the Lord, compassionate and gracious God,
slow to anger, abounding in loving-kindness and truth,
extending loving-kindness to a thousand generations,
forgiving iniquity, rebellion and sin,
and absolving [the guilty who repent].

All continue:

וְסָלַחְתָּ Forgive us our iniquity and our sin, and take us as Your inheritance.

סְלַח לָנוּ Forgive us, our Father, for we have sinned. Pardon us, our King, for
we have transgressed. For You, Lord, are good and forgiving, abounding in *Ps. 86*
loving-kindness to all who call on You.

The following are the opening and closing verses of the penultimate piyut said on Hoshana Raba, attributed to Rabbi Elazar HaKalir.

The Leader says each verse, followed by the congregation:

רַחֵם Have compassion, please, for the community of the people of Yeshurun;
forgive and pardon their iniquity,
and save us, God of our salvation.

שַׁעֲרֵי Open the gates of heaven,
and Your treasure-house of goodness – open for us.
Save us and do not extend judgment against us –
and save us, God of our salvation.

THE THIRTEEN ATTRIBUTES OF MERCY

All stand and say:

אֵל מֶלֶךְ God, King who sits upon a throne of compassion,
who acts with loving-kindness,
who pardons the iniquities of His people,
passing them before Him in order;
who forgives sinners and pardons transgressors;
who performs righteousness with all flesh and spirit,
do not repay their bad actions in kind.
▸ God, You taught us to speak thirteen attributes:
recall for us today the covenant of the thirteen attributes,
as You in ancient times showed the humble one [Moses], as is written:
The Lord descended in the cloud and stood with him there, *Ex. 34*
and proclaimed in the name of the Lord:

All say aloud:

יהוה, יהוה, אֵל רַחוּם וְחַנּוּן אֶרֶךְ אַפַּיִם, וְרַב־חֶסֶד וֶאֱמֶת:
נֹצֵר חֶסֶד לָאֲלָפִים נֹשֵׂא עָוֹן וָפֶשַׁע וְחַטָּאָה, וְנַקֵּה:

All continue:

וְסָלַחְתָּ לַעֲוֹנֵנוּ וּלְחַטָּאתֵנוּ, וּנְחַלְתָּנוּ:

סְלַח לָנוּ אָבִינוּ כִּי חָטָאנוּ, מְחַל לָנוּ מַלְכֵּנוּ כִּי פָשָׁעְנוּ.
תהלים פו כִּי־אַתָּה אֲדֹנָי טוֹב וְסַלָּח, וְרַב־חֶסֶד לְכָל־קֹרְאֶיךָ:

The following are the opening and closing verses of the penultimate piyut said on הושענא רבה*, attributed to Rabbi Elazar HaKalir.*

The שליח ציבור *says each verse, followed by the* קהל*:*

רַחֵם נָא קְהַל עֲדַת יְשֻׁרוּן / סְלַח וּמְחַל עֲוֹנָם
וְהוֹשִׁיעֵנוּ אֱלֹהֵי יִשְׁעֵנוּ.

שַׁעֲרֵי שָׁמַיִם פְּתַח / וְאוֹצָרְךָ הַטּוֹב לָנוּ תִפְתַּח
תּוֹשִׁיעֵנוּ וְרִיב אַל תִּמְתַּח / וְהוֹשִׁיעֵנוּ אֱלֹהֵי יִשְׁעֵנוּ.

י״ג מדות הרחמים

All stand and say:

אֵל מֶלֶךְ יוֹשֵׁב עַל כִּסֵּא רַחֲמִים, מִתְנַהֵג בַּחֲסִידוּת.
מוֹחֵל עֲוֹנוֹת עַמּוֹ, מַעֲבִיר רִאשׁוֹן רִאשׁוֹן.
מַרְבֶּה מְחִילָה לְחַטָּאִים, וּסְלִיחָה לְפוֹשְׁעִים.
עֹשֶׂה צְדָקוֹת עִם כָּל בָּשָׂר וָרוּחַ, לֹא כְרָעָתָם תִּגְמֹל.
◂ אֵל, הוֹרֵיתָ לָּנוּ לוֹמַר שְׁלֹשׁ עֶשְׂרֵה
וּזְכָר לָנוּ הַיּוֹם בְּרִית שְׁלֹשׁ עֶשְׂרֵה
כְּמוֹ שֶׁהוֹדַעְתָּ לֶעָנָו מִקֶּדֶם, כְּמוֹ שֶׁכָּתוּב:
שמות לד וַיֵּרֶד יהוה בֶּעָנָן, וַיִּתְיַצֵּב עִמּוֹ שָׁם
וַיִּקְרָא בְשֵׁם, יהוה:

The congregation then the Leader:

וַיַּעֲבֹר And the Lord passed by before him and proclaimed: *Ex. 34*

All say aloud:

יהוה The Lord, the Lord, compassionate and gracious God,
slow to anger, abounding in loving-kindness and truth,
extending loving-kindness to a thousand generations, forgiving iniquity,
rebellion and sin, and absolving [the guilty who repent].

All continue:

וְסָלַחְתָּ Forgive us our iniquity and our sin, and take us as Your inheritance.

סְלַח לָנוּ Forgive us, our Father, for we have sinned.
Pardon us, our King, for we have transgressed. *Ps. 86*
For You, Lord, are good and forgiving,
abounding in loving-kindness to all who call on You.

Our God and God of our ancestors,
forgive us, pardon us, grant us atonement.

In many congregations, the Leader and the congregation recite the following piyut responsively, couplet by couplet, until "and You give us Yours"; in others, it is sung collectively.

כִּי אָנוּ For we are Your people and You are our God;
we are Your children and You are our Father;
we are Your servants and You are our Master;
we are Your gathering and You are our Place;
we are Your legacy and You are our Land;
we are Your flock and You are our Shepherd;
we are Your vineyard and You are our Keeper;
we are Your work and You are our Maker;
we are Your bride and You are our Lover;
we are Your treasure and You are our God;
we are Your people and You are our King;
we give You our word and You give us Yours.

The congregation then the Leader:

We are brazen and You are compassionate, gracious.
We are stubborn and You are long forbearing.
We are as full of iniquity as You are full of compassion.
Our days are like a fleeting shadow. *Ps. 102*
But You are here, and Your years will not end.

The קהל *then the* שליח ציבור*:*

וַיַּעֲבֹר יהוה עַל־פָּנָיו וַיִּקְרָא שמות לד

All say aloud:

יהוה, יהוה, אֵל רַחוּם וְחַנּוּן, אֶרֶךְ אַפַּיִם, וְרַב־חֶסֶד וֶאֱמֶת:
נֹצֵר חֶסֶד לָאֲלָפִים, נֹשֵׂא עָוֹן וָפֶשַׁע וְחַטָּאָה, וְנַקֵּה:

All continue:

וְסָלַחְתָּ לַעֲוֹנֵנוּ וּלְחַטָּאתֵנוּ, וּנְחַלְתָּנוּ:

סְלַח לָנוּ אָבִינוּ כִּי חָטָאנוּ, מְחַל לָנוּ מַלְכֵּנוּ כִּי פָשָׁעְנוּ.
כִּי־אַתָּה אֲדֹנָי טוֹב וְסַלָּח, וְרַב־חֶסֶד לְכָל־קֹרְאֶיךָ: תהלים פו

אֱלֹהֵינוּ וֵאלֹהֵי אֲבוֹתֵינוּ
סְלַח לָנוּ, מְחַל לָנוּ, כַּפֶּר לָנוּ.

In many congregations, the שליח ציבור *and the* קהל *recite the following piyut responsively, couplet by couplet, until "*וְאַתָּה מַאֲמִירֵנוּ*"; in others, it is sung collectively.*

כִּי אָנוּ עַמֶּךָ וְאַתָּה אֱלֹהֵינוּ אָנוּ בָנֶיךָ וְאַתָּה אָבִינוּ
אָנוּ עֲבָדֶיךָ וְאַתָּה אֲדוֹנֵנוּ אָנוּ קְהָלֶךָ וְאַתָּה חֶלְקֵנוּ
אָנוּ נַחֲלָתֶךָ וְאַתָּה גוֹרָלֵנוּ אָנוּ צֹאנֶךָ וְאַתָּה רוֹעֵנוּ
אָנוּ כַרְמֶךָ וְאַתָּה נוֹטְרֵנוּ אָנוּ פְעֻלָּתֶךָ וְאַתָּה יוֹצְרֵנוּ
אָנוּ רַעְיָתֶךָ וְאַתָּה דוֹדֵנוּ אָנוּ סְגֻלָּתֶךָ וְאַתָּה אֱלֹהֵינוּ
אָנוּ עַמֶּךָ וְאַתָּה מַלְכֵּנוּ אָנוּ מַאֲמִירֶיךָ וְאַתָּה מַאֲמִירֵנוּ.

The קהל *then the* שליח ציבור*:*

אָנוּ עַזֵּי פָנִים וְאַתָּה רַחוּם וְחַנּוּן
אָנוּ קְשֵׁי עֹרֶף וְאַתָּה אֶרֶךְ אַפַּיִם
אָנוּ מְלֵאֵי עָוֹן וְאַתָּה מָלֵא רַחֲמִים
אָנוּ יָמֵינוּ כְּצֵל עוֹבֵר וְאַתָּה־הוּא וּשְׁנוֹתֶיךָ לֹא יִתָּמּוּ: תהלים קב

VIDUY

For linear translation and commentary, see page 1353.

The Leader continues, with the congregation following him in an undertone:

אֱלֹהֵינוּ Our God and God of our fathers,
let our prayer come before You,
and do not hide Yourself from our plea,
for we are not so arrogant or obstinate as to say before You,
LORD, our God and God of our fathers,
we are righteous and have not sinned,
for in truth, we and our fathers have sinned.

Strike the left side of the chest with the right fist while saying each of the sins:

אָשַׁמְנוּ We have sinned, we have acted treacherously,
we have robbed, we have spoken slander.
We have acted perversely, we have acted wickedly,
we have acted presumptuously, we have been violent,
we have framed lies.
We have given bad advice, we have deceived, we have scorned,
we have rebelled, we have provoked, we have turned away,
we have committed iniquity, we have transgressed,
we have persecuted, we have been obstinate.
We have acted wickedly, we have corrupted,
we have acted abominably, we have strayed, we have led others astray.

All:

סַרְנוּ We have turned away from Your commandments and good laws,
to no avail, for You are just in all that has befallen us, *Neh. 9*
for You have acted faithfully while we have done wickedly.

The Leader continues:

מַה נֹּאמַר What can we say before You, You who dwell on high?
What can we declare before You, You who abide in heaven?
Do You not know all, the hidden and revealed alike?

You give Your hand to help transgressors;
Your right hand is outstretched to receive those who return.
And You have taught us, LORD our God,
to confess before You all our iniquities,
that we may end the oppression that is in our hands,

וידוי

For linear translation and commentary, see page 1353.

The שליח ציבור continues, with the קהל following him in an undertone:

אֱלֹהֵינוּ וֵאלֹהֵי אֲבוֹתֵינוּ
תָּבוֹא לְפָנֶיךָ תְּפִלָּתֵנוּ, וְאַל תִּתְעַלַּם מִתְּחִנָּתֵנוּ.
שֶׁאֵין אֲנַחְנוּ עַזֵּי פָנִים וּקְשֵׁי עֹרֶף לוֹמַר לְפָנֶיךָ
יהוה אֱלֹהֵינוּ וֵאלֹהֵי אֲבוֹתֵינוּ
צַדִּיקִים אֲנַחְנוּ וְלֹא חָטָאנוּ.
אֲבָל אֲנַחְנוּ וַאֲבוֹתֵינוּ חָטָאנוּ.

Strike the left side of the chest with the right fist while saying each of the sins.

אָשַׁמְנוּ, בָּגַדְנוּ, גָּזַלְנוּ, דִּבַּרְנוּ דֹפִי
הֶעֱוִינוּ, וְהִרְשַׁעְנוּ, זַדְנוּ, חָמַסְנוּ, טָפַלְנוּ שֶׁקֶר
יָעַצְנוּ רָע, כִּזַּבְנוּ, לַצְנוּ, מָרַדְנוּ, נִאַצְנוּ, סָרַרְנוּ
עָוִינוּ, פָּשַׁעְנוּ, צָרַרְנוּ, קִשִּׁינוּ עֹרֶף
רָשַׁעְנוּ, שִׁחַתְנוּ, תִּעַבְנוּ, תָּעִינוּ, תִּעְתָּעְנוּ.

All:

סַרְנוּ מִמִּצְוֹתֶיךָ וּמִמִּשְׁפָּטֶיךָ הַטּוֹבִים, וְלֹא שָׁוָה לָנוּ.
וְאַתָּה צַדִּיק עַל כָּל־הַבָּא עָלֵינוּ נחמיה ט
כִּי־אֱמֶת עָשִׂיתָ, וַאֲנַחְנוּ הִרְשָׁעְנוּ:

The שליח ציבור continues:

מַה נֹּאמַר לְפָנֶיךָ יוֹשֵׁב מָרוֹם, וּמַה נְּסַפֵּר לְפָנֶיךָ שׁוֹכֵן שְׁחָקִים
הֲלֹא כָּל הַנִּסְתָּרוֹת וְהַנִּגְלוֹת אַתָּה יוֹדֵעַ.

אַתָּה נוֹתֵן יָד לְפוֹשְׁעִים, וִימִינְךָ פְשׁוּטָה לְקַבֵּל שָׁבִים
וַתְּלַמְּדֵנוּ יהוה אֱלֹהֵינוּ לְהִתְוַדּוֹת לְפָנֶיךָ עַל כָּל עֲוֹנוֹתֵינוּ
לְמַעַן נֶחְדַּל מֵעֹשֶׁק יָדֵינוּ

and that You may receive us back in perfect repentance before You,
like burnt offerings and their sweet savor,
for the sake of the words You have spoken.
There is no end to the burnt offerings we owe You,
no number to the guilt-offerings of sweet savor.
And You know that our end will be with maggots and worms.
And so You forgive us again and again.

What are we? What are our lives?
What is our loving-kindness?
What is our righteousness?
What is our salvation?
What is our strength?
What is our might?
What shall we say before You,
LORD our God and God of our ancestors?
Are not all the mighty like nothing before You,
the men of renown as if they had never been,
the wise as if they know nothing,
and the understanding as if they lack intelligence?
For their many works are in vain,
and the days of their lives like a fleeting breath before You.
The pre-eminence of man over the animals is nothing, *Eccl. 3*
for all is but a fleeting breath.

You have separated man out from the outset;
You have recognized him,
had him stand before You.
For who can tell You what You are to do;
and even if one proves righteous – what can he give You?
And You, LORD our God, have given us in love
(*on Shabbat:* this Sabbath day and) this Day of Atonement,
to be the end, the pardon and forgiveness of all our iniquities,
that we may end the oppression that is in our hands,
and return to You, to fulfill the laws of Your will wholeheartedly;

וּתְקַבְּלֵנוּ בִּתְשׁוּבָה שְׁלֵמָה לְפָנֶיךָ כְּאִשִּׁים וּכְנִיחוֹחִים
לְמַעַן דְּבָרֶיךָ אֲשֶׁר אָמָרְתָּ.
אֵין קֵץ לְאִשֵּׁי חוֹבוֹתֵינוּ
וְאֵין מִסְפָּר לְנִיחוֹחֵי אַשְׁמוֹתֵינוּ
וְאַתָּה יוֹדֵעַ שֶׁאַחֲרִיתֵנוּ רִמָּה וְתוֹלֵעָה
לְפִיכָךְ הִרְבֵּיתָ סְלִיחָתֵנוּ.

מָה אָנוּ, מֶה חַיֵּינוּ, מֶה חַסְדֵּנוּ, מַה צִּדְקוֹתֵינוּ
מַה יְּשׁוּעָתֵנוּ, מַה כֹּחֵנוּ, מַה גְּבוּרָתֵנוּ
מַה נֹּאמַר לְפָנֶיךָ, יהוה אֱלֹהֵינוּ וֵאלֹהֵי אֲבוֹתֵינוּ
הֲלֹא כָּל הַגִּבּוֹרִים כְּאַיִן לְפָנֶיךָ, וְאַנְשֵׁי הַשֵּׁם כְּלֹא הָיוּ
וַחֲכָמִים כִּבְלִי מַדָּע, וּנְבוֹנִים כִּבְלִי הַשְׂכֵּל
כִּי רֹב מַעֲשֵׂיהֶם תֹּהוּ, וִימֵי חַיֵּיהֶם הֶבֶל לְפָנֶיךָ
וּמוֹתַר הָאָדָם מִן־הַבְּהֵמָה אָיִן, כִּי הַכֹּל הָבֶל: קהלת ג

אַתָּה הִבְדַּלְתָּ אֱנוֹשׁ מֵרֹאשׁ
וַתַּכִּירֵהוּ לַעֲמֹד לְפָנֶיךָ.
כִּי מִי יֹאמַר לְךָ מַה תִּפְעָל
וְאִם יִצְדַּק מַה יִּתֶּן לָךְ.
וַתִּתֶּן לָנוּ, יהוה אֱלֹהֵינוּ
בְּאַהֲבָה אֶת (בשבת: יוֹם הַשַּׁבָּת הַזֶּה וְאֶת)
יוֹם צוֹם הַכִּפּוּרִים הַזֶּה
קֵץ וּמְחִילָה וּסְלִיחָה עַל כָּל עֲוֹנוֹתֵינוּ
לְמַעַן נֶחְדַּל מֵעֹשֶׁק יָדֵינוּ
וְנָשׁוּב אֵלֶיךָ לַעֲשׂוֹת חֻקֵּי רְצוֹנְךָ בְּלֵבָב שָׁלֵם.

and You, in Your great compassion,
have compassion for us,
for You will not desire the destruction of the world,
as it is said:
"Seek out the LORD when He is to be found; *Is. 55*
call out to Him now when He is close."
And it is said:
"Let each wicked person abandon his ways, *Ibid.*
each man of iniquity his thoughts,
and let him come back to the LORD
and He will have compassion for him;
back to our God for He will forgive abundantly."

And You, God of forgiveness,
gracious and compassionate,
slow to anger, abounding in loving-kindness and truth
and doing abundant good for us;
You desire the repentance of the wicked
and do not desire their death,
as it is said:
"Say to them, as I live – says the LORD God – *Ezek. 33*
I do not desire the death of the wicked,
but that the wicked should come back from his way and live.
Repent, repent your evil ways;
why should you die, O House of Israel?'"
And it is said:
"Do I desire the wicked man's death? – says the LORD God – *Ezek. 18*
Do I not desire him to come back from his ways and live?"
And it is said:
"For I do not desire the condemned man's death – *Ibid.*
says the LORD God – Repent, and live."

For You are the Forgiver of Israel
and the Pardoner of the tribes of Yeshurun in every generation,
and without You we have no king who pardons and forgives,
none but You.

וְאַתָּה בְּרַחֲמֶיךָ הָרַבִּים רַחֵם עָלֵינוּ
כִּי לֹא תַחְפֹּץ בְּהַשְׁחָתַת עוֹלָם
שֶׁנֶּאֱמַר
דִּרְשׁוּ יהוה בְּהִמָּצְאוֹ, קְרָאֻהוּ בִּהְיוֹתוֹ קָרוֹב: ישעיה נה
וְנֶאֱמַר
יַעֲזֹב רָשָׁע דַּרְכּוֹ, וְאִישׁ אָוֶן מַחְשְׁבֹתָיו שם
וְיָשֹׁב אֶל־יהוה וִירַחֲמֵהוּ, וְאֶל־אֱלֹהֵינוּ כִּי־יַרְבֶּה לִסְלוֹחַ:
וְאַתָּה אֱלוֹהַּ סְלִיחוֹת, חַנּוּן וְרַחוּם
אֶרֶךְ אַפַּיִם וְרַב חֶסֶד וֶאֱמֶת, וּמַרְבֶּה לְהֵיטִיב
וְרוֹצֶה אַתָּה בִּתְשׁוּבַת רְשָׁעִים
וְאֵין אַתָּה חָפֵץ בְּמִיתָתָם
שֶׁנֶּאֱמַר
אֱמֹר אֲלֵיהֶם, חַי־אָנִי נְאֻם אֲדֹנָי יֱהֹוִה יחזקאל לג
אִם־אֶחְפֹּץ בְּמוֹת הָרָשָׁע
כִּי אִם־בְּשׁוּב רָשָׁע מִדַּרְכּוֹ, וְחָיָה
שׁוּבוּ שׁוּבוּ מִדַּרְכֵיכֶם הָרָעִים
וְלָמָּה תָמוּתוּ בֵּית יִשְׂרָאֵל:
וְנֶאֱמַר
הֶחָפֹץ אֶחְפֹּץ מוֹת רָשָׁע, נְאֻם אֲדֹנָי יֱהֹוִה יחזקאל יח
הֲלוֹא בְּשׁוּבוֹ מִדְּרָכָיו וְחָיָה:
וְנֶאֱמַר
כִּי לֹא אֶחְפֹּץ בְּמוֹת הַמֵּת, נְאֻם אֲדֹנָי יֱהֹוִה שם
וְהָשִׁיבוּ וִחְיוּ:

כִּי אַתָּה סָלְחָן לְיִשְׂרָאֵל וּמָחֳלָן לְשִׁבְטֵי יְשֻׁרוּן בְּכָל דּוֹר וָדוֹר
וּמִבַּלְעָדֶיךָ אֵין לָנוּ מֶלֶךְ מוֹחֵל וְסוֹלֵחַ אֶלָּא אָתָּה

On Shabbat, add the words in parentheses:

Our God and God of our ancestors,
pardon our iniquities on
(this Sabbath day, and on) this Day of Atonement;
wipe away and remove all our transgressions
and sins from before Your eyes,
as it is said:

> "I, I am the One who shall wipe out your transgressions *Is. 43*
> for My sake, and I shall not recall your sins."

And it is said:

> "I have wiped out your transgressions like a cloud, *Is. 44*
> and as a haze your sins;
> come back to Me for I have redeemed you."

And it is said:

> "For on this day you will be atoned and made pure; *Lev. 16*
> of all your sins before the LORD you shall be purified."

(Our God and God of our ancestors, may You find favor in our rest.)
Make us holy through Your commandments
and grant us our share in Your Torah.
Satisfy us with Your goodness, grant us joy in Your salvation
(in love and favor, LORD our God,
grant us as our heritage Your holy Sabbath,
so that Israel, who sanctify Your name, may find rest on it),
and purify our hearts to serve You in truth.
For You are the Forgiver of Israel
and the Pardoner of the tribes of Yeshurun in every generation,
and without You we have no king who pardons and forgives,
none but You.
Blessed are You, LORD,
King who pardons and forgives our iniquities
and those of all His people the house of Israel,
and makes our guilt pass away, every single year,
King of all the earth, who sanctifies (the Sabbath,)
Israel and the Day of Atonement.

On שבת, add the words in parentheses:

אֱלֹהֵינוּ וֵאלֹהֵי אֲבוֹתֵינוּ

מְחַל לַעֲוֹנוֹתֵינוּ בְּיוֹם (הַשַּׁבָּת הַזֶּה וּבְיוֹם) הַכִּפּוּרִים הַזֶּה

מְחֵה וְהַעֲבֵר פְּשָׁעֵינוּ וְחַטֹּאתֵינוּ מִנֶּגֶד עֵינֶיךָ

כָּאָמוּר

אָנֹכִי אָנֹכִי הוּא מֹחֶה פְשָׁעֶיךָ לְמַעֲנִי ישעיה מג

וְחַטֹּאתֶיךָ לֹא אֶזְכֹּר:

וְנֶאֱמַר

מָחִיתִי כָעָב פְּשָׁעֶיךָ וְכֶעָנָן חַטֹּאותֶיךָ ישעיה מד

שׁוּבָה אֵלַי כִּי גְאַלְתִּיךָ:

וְנֶאֱמַר

כִּי־בַיּוֹם הַזֶּה יְכַפֵּר עֲלֵיכֶם לְטַהֵר אֶתְכֶם ויקרא טז

מִכֹּל חַטֹּאתֵיכֶם, לִפְנֵי יהוה תִּטְהָרוּ:

(אֱלֹהֵינוּ וֵאלֹהֵי אֲבוֹתֵינוּ, רְצֵה בִמְנוּחָתֵנוּ)

קַדְּשֵׁנוּ בְּמִצְוֹתֶיךָ וְתֵן חֶלְקֵנוּ בְּתוֹרָתֶךָ

שַׂבְּעֵנוּ מִטּוּבֶךָ וְשַׂמְּחֵנוּ בִּישׁוּעָתֶךָ

(וְהַנְחִילֵנוּ יהוה אֱלֹהֵינוּ בְּאַהֲבָה וּבְרָצוֹן שַׁבְּתוֹת קָדְשֶׁךָ

וְיָנוּחוּ בָם יִשְׂרָאֵל מְקַדְּשֵׁי שְׁמֶךָ)

וְטַהֵר לִבֵּנוּ לְעָבְדְּךָ בֶּאֱמֶת

כִּי אַתָּה סָלְחָן לְיִשְׂרָאֵל, וּמָחֳלָן לְשִׁבְטֵי יְשֻׁרוּן בְּכָל דּוֹר וָדוֹר

וּמִבַּלְעָדֶיךָ אֵין לָנוּ מֶלֶךְ מוֹחֵל וְסוֹלֵחַ אֶלָּא אָתָּה.

בָּרוּךְ אַתָּה יהוה

מֶלֶךְ מוֹחֵל וְסוֹלֵחַ לַעֲוֹנוֹתֵינוּ, וְלַעֲוֹנוֹת עַמּוֹ בֵּית יִשְׂרָאֵל

וּמַעֲבִיר אַשְׁמוֹתֵינוּ בְּכָל שָׁנָה וְשָׁנָה

מֶלֶךְ עַל כָּל הָאָרֶץ, מְקַדֵּשׁ (הַשַּׁבָּת וְ)יִשְׂרָאֵל וְיוֹם הַכִּפּוּרִים.

TEMPLE SERVICE

רְצֵה Find favor, LORD our God,
in Your people Israel and their prayer.
Restore the service to Your most holy House,
and accept in love and favor
the fire-offerings of Israel and their prayer.
May the service of Your people Israel
always find favor with You.
And may our eyes witness Your return to Zion in compassion.
Blessed are You, LORD, who restores His Presence to Zion.

THANKSGIVING

Bow at the first nine words.

מוֹדִים We give thanks to You,
for You are the LORD our God
and God of our ancestors
for ever and all time.
You are the Rock of our lives,
Shield of our salvation
from generation to generation.
We will thank You and
declare Your praise for our lives,
which are entrusted into Your hand;
for our souls,
which are placed in Your charge;
for Your miracles
which are with us every day;
and for Your wonders and favors
at all times, evening, morning and midday.
You are good –
for Your compassion never fails.
You are compassionate –
for Your loving-kindnesses never cease.
We have always placed our hope in You.

As the Leader recites Modim, the congregation says quietly:

מוֹדִים We give thanks to You,
for You are the LORD our God
and God of our ancestors,
God of all flesh,
who formed us
and formed the universe.
Blessings and thanks
are due to Your great
and holy name for giving us
life and sustaining us.
May You continue
to give us life and sustain us;
and may You gather our
exiles to Your holy courts,
to keep Your decrees,
do Your will and serve You
with a perfect heart,
for it is for us
to give You thanks.
Blessed be God to whom
thanksgiving is due.

וְעַל כֻּלָּם For all these things may Your name be blessed and exalted,
our King, continually, for ever and all time.

עבודה

רְצֵה יהוה אֱלֹהֵינוּ בְּעַמְּךָ יִשְׂרָאֵל, וּבִתְפִלָּתָם
וְהָשֵׁב אֶת הָעֲבוֹדָה לִדְבִיר בֵּיתֶךָ
וְאִשֵּׁי יִשְׂרָאֵל וּתְפִלָּתָם בְּאַהֲבָה תְקַבֵּל בְּרָצוֹן
וּתְהִי לְרָצוֹן תָּמִיד עֲבוֹדַת יִשְׂרָאֵל עַמֶּךָ.
וְתֶחֱזֶינָה עֵינֵינוּ בְּשׁוּבְךָ לְצִיּוֹן בְּרַחֲמִים.
בָּרוּךְ אַתָּה יהוה, הַמַּחֲזִיר שְׁכִינָתוֹ לְצִיּוֹן.

הודאה

Bow at the first five words.

מוֹדִים אֲנַחְנוּ לָךְ
שָׁאַתָּה הוּא יהוה אֱלֹהֵינוּ
וֵאלֹהֵי אֲבוֹתֵינוּ לְעוֹלָם וָעֶד.
צוּר חַיֵּינוּ, מָגֵן יִשְׁעֵנוּ
אַתָּה הוּא לְדוֹר וָדוֹר.
נוֹדֶה לְּךָ וּנְסַפֵּר תְּהִלָּתֶךָ
עַל חַיֵּינוּ הַמְּסוּרִים בְּיָדֶךָ
וְעַל נִשְׁמוֹתֵינוּ הַפְּקוּדוֹת לָךְ
וְעַל נִסֶּיךָ שֶׁבְּכָל יוֹם עִמָּנוּ
וְעַל נִפְלְאוֹתֶיךָ וְטוֹבוֹתֶיךָ
שֶׁבְּכָל עֵת, עֶרֶב וָבֹקֶר וְצָהֳרָיִם.
הַטּוֹב, כִּי לֹא כָלוּ רַחֲמֶיךָ
וְהַמְרַחֵם, כִּי לֹא תַמּוּ חֲסָדֶיךָ
מֵעוֹלָם קִוִּינוּ לָךְ.

As the שליח ציבור *recites* מודים, *the* קהל *says quietly:*

מוֹדִים אֲנַחְנוּ לָךְ
שָׁאַתָּה הוּא יהוה אֱלֹהֵינוּ
וֵאלֹהֵי אֲבוֹתֵינוּ
אֱלֹהֵי כָל בָּשָׂר
יוֹצְרֵנוּ, יוֹצֵר בְּרֵאשִׁית.
בְּרָכוֹת וְהוֹדָאוֹת
לְשִׁמְךָ הַגָּדוֹל וְהַקָּדוֹשׁ
עַל שֶׁהֶחֱיִיתָנוּ וְקִיַּמְתָּנוּ.
כֵּן תְּחַיֵּנוּ וּתְקַיְּמֵנוּ
וְתֶאֱסֹף גָּלֻיּוֹתֵינוּ
לְחַצְרוֹת קָדְשֶׁךָ
לִשְׁמֹר חֻקֶּיךָ וְלַעֲשׂוֹת רְצוֹנֶךָ
וּלְעָבְדְּךָ בְּלֵבָב שָׁלֵם
עַל שֶׁאֲנַחְנוּ מוֹדִים לָךְ.
בָּרוּךְ אֵל הַהוֹדָאוֹת.

וְעַל כֻּלָּם יִתְבָּרַךְ וְיִתְרוֹמַם שִׁמְךָ מַלְכֵּנוּ תָּמִיד לְעוֹלָם וָעֶד.

The congregation, then the Leader:

אָבִינוּ מַלְכֵּנוּ Our Father, our King,
remember Your compassion and overcome Your anger,
and efface pestilence, sword, famine, captivity and destruction,
iniquity and plague, and bad mishap and all illness, and any harm,
and any feud, and all kinds of afflictions,
and all harsh decrees and baseless hatred,
from us and from all the people of Your covenant.

The congregation, then the Leader:

וַחֲתֹם And seal, for a good life, all the children of Your covenant.

The Leader continues:

Let all that lives thank You, Selah! and praise Your name in truth,
God, our Savior and Help, Selah!
▼Blessed are You, Lord,
whose name is "the Good" and to whom thanks are due.

In Israel, if Kohanim bless the congregation, *turn to page 1260.*

אֱלֹהֵינוּ Our God and God of our fathers,
bless us with the threefold blessing in the Torah,
written by the hand of Moses Your servant
and pronounced by Aaron and his sons the priests,
Your holy people, as it is said:

May the Lord bless you and protect you. *Num. 6*
Cong: May it be Your will.
May the Lord make His face shine on you and be gracious to you.
Cong: May it be Your will.
May the Lord turn His face toward you, and grant you peace.
Cong: May it be Your will.

PEACE

שִׂים שָׁלוֹם Grant peace, goodness and blessing,
grace, loving-kindness and compassion to us
and all Israel Your people.
Bless us, our Father, all as one, with the light of Your face,

The קהל *then the* שליח ציבור:

אָבִינוּ מַלְכֵּנוּ
זְכֹר רַחֲמֶיךָ וּכְבֹשׁ כַּעַסְךָ
וְכַלֵּה דֶּבֶר, וְחֶרֶב, וְרָעָב, וּשְׁבִי, וּמַשְׁחִית
וְעָוֹן וּמַגֵּפָה, וּפֶגַע רַע וְכָל מַחֲלָה, וְכָל תַּקָּלָה
וְכָל קְטָטָה וְכָל מִינֵי פֻרְעָנִיּוֹת, וְכָל גְּזֵרָה רָעָה וְשִׂנְאַת חִנָּם
מֵעָלֵינוּ וּמֵעַל כָּל בְּנֵי בְרִיתֶךָ.

The קהל *then the* שליח ציבור:

וַחֲתֹם לְחַיִּים טוֹבִים כָּל בְּנֵי בְרִיתֶךָ.

The שליח ציבור *continues:*

וְכֹל הַחַיִּים יוֹדוּךָ סֶּלָה, וִיהַלְלוּ אֶת שִׁמְךָ בֶּאֱמֶת
הָאֵל יְשׁוּעָתֵנוּ וְעֶזְרָתֵנוּ סֶלָה.
בָּרוּךְ אַתָּה יהוה, הַטּוֹב שִׁמְךָ וּלְךָ נָאֶה לְהוֹדוֹת.

In ארץ ישראל*, if* כהנים *say* ברכת כהנים*, turn to page 1261.*

אֱלֹהֵינוּ וֵאלֹהֵי אֲבוֹתֵינוּ, בָּרְכֵנוּ בַּבְּרָכָה הַמְשֻׁלֶּשֶׁת בַּתּוֹרָה
הַכְּתוּבָה עַל יְדֵי מֹשֶׁה עַבְדֶּךָ, הָאֲמוּרָה מִפִּי אַהֲרֹן וּבָנָיו
כֹּהֲנִים עַם קְדוֹשֶׁיךָ, כָּאָמוּר

יְבָרֶכְךָ יהוה וְיִשְׁמְרֶךָ: קהל: כֵּן יְהִי רָצוֹן במדבר ו
יָאֵר יהוה פָּנָיו אֵלֶיךָ וִיחֻנֶּךָּ: קהל: כֵּן יְהִי רָצוֹן
יִשָּׂא יהוה פָּנָיו אֵלֶיךָ וְיָשֵׂם לְךָ שָׁלוֹם: קהל: כֵּן יְהִי רָצוֹן

שלום

שִׂים שָׁלוֹם טוֹבָה וּבְרָכָה, חֵן וָחֶסֶד וְרַחֲמִים
עָלֵינוּ וְעַל כָּל יִשְׂרָאֵל עַמֶּךָ.
בָּרְכֵנוּ אָבִינוּ כֻּלָּנוּ כְּאֶחָד בְּאוֹר פָּנֶיךָ

for by the light of Your face You have given us, LORD our God,
the Torah of life and love of kindness,
righteousness, blessing, compassion, life and peace.
May it be good in Your eyes to bless Your people Israel
at every time, in every hour, with Your peace.

In some congregations, the end of Musaf is said at this point (beginning with "In the book of life" on page 982).

The congregation then the Leader:

בְּסֵפֶר חַיִּים In the book of life, blessing, peace and prosperity,
may we and all Your people the house of Israel
be remembered and sealed before You
for a good life, and for peace.*

Blessed are You, LORD, who blesses His people Israel with peace.

**Outside Israel, many end the blessing:*
Blessed are You, LORD, who makes peace.

The following verse concludes the Leader's Repetition of the Amida.

May the words of my mouth and the meditation of my heart *Ps. 19*
find favor before You, LORD, my Rock and Redeemer.

AVINU MALKENU

During Ne'ila, Avinu Malkenu is said even on Shabbat.
In some congregations, the whole of Avinu Malkenu is recited responsively.

אָבִינוּ מַלְכֵּנוּ Our Father, our King, we have sinned before You.

Our Father, our King, we have no king but You.

Our Father, our King, deal kindly with us for the sake of Your name.

Our Father our King, renew for us a good year.

Our Father, our King, nullify all harsh decrees against us.

כִּי בְאוֹר פָּנֶיךָ נָתַתָּ לָּנוּ, יהוה אֱלֹהֵינוּ
תּוֹרַת חַיִּים וְאַהֲבַת חֶסֶד
וּצְדָקָה וּבְרָכָה וְרַחֲמִים וְחַיִּים וְשָׁלוֹם.
וְטוֹב בְּעֵינֶיךָ לְבָרֵךְ אֶת עַמְּךָ יִשְׂרָאֵל
בְּכָל עֵת וּבְכָל שָׁעָה בִּשְׁלוֹמֶךָ.

In some congregations, the end of מוסף *is said at this point (beginning with* בְּסֵפֶר חַיִּים *on page 983).*

The קהל *then the* שליח ציבור*:*

בְּסֵפֶר חַיִּים, בְּרָכָה וְשָׁלוֹם, וּפַרְנָסָה טוֹבָה
נִזָּכֵר וְנֵחָתֵם לְפָנֶיךָ, אֲנַחְנוּ וְכָל עַמְּךָ בֵּית יִשְׂרָאֵל
לְחַיִּים טוֹבִים וּלְשָׁלוֹם.*
בָּרוּךְ אַתָּה יהוה, הַמְבָרֵךְ אֶת עַמּוֹ יִשְׂרָאֵל בַּשָּׁלוֹם.

**In* חוץ לארץ*, many end the blessing:*

בָּרוּךְ אַתָּה יהוה, עוֹשֶׂה הַשָּׁלוֹם.

The following verse concludes the חזרת הש״ץ.

יִהְיוּ לְרָצוֹן אִמְרֵי־פִי וְהֶגְיוֹן לִבִּי לְפָנֶיךָ, יהוה צוּרִי וְגֹאֲלִי: תהלים יט

אבינו מלכנו

During Ne'ila, אָבִינוּ מַלְכֵּנוּ *is said even on* שבת.

In some congregations, the whole of אָבִינוּ מַלְכֵּנוּ *is recited responsively.*

אָבִינוּ מַלְכֵּנוּ, חָטָאנוּ לְפָנֶיךָ.

אָבִינוּ מַלְכֵּנוּ, אֵין לָנוּ מֶלֶךְ אֶלָּא אָתָּה.

אָבִינוּ מַלְכֵּנוּ, עֲשֵׂה עִמָּנוּ לְמַעַן שְׁמֶךָ.

אָבִינוּ מַלְכֵּנוּ, חַדֵּשׁ עָלֵינוּ שָׁנָה טוֹבָה.

אָבִינוּ מַלְכֵּנוּ, בַּטֵּל מֵעָלֵינוּ כָּל גְּזֵרוֹת קָשׁוֹת.

Our Father, our King, nullify the plans of those who hate us.

Our Father, our King, thwart the counsel of our enemies.

Our Father, our King, rid us of every oppressor and adversary.

Our Father, our King, close the mouths of our adversaries and accusers.

Our Father, our King, eradicate pestilence, sword, famine, captivity and destruction, iniquity and eradication from the people of Your covenant.

Our Father, our King, withhold the plague from Your heritage.

Our Father, our King, forgive and pardon all our iniquities.

Our Father, our King, wipe away and remove our transgressions and sins from Your sight.

Our Father, our King, erase in Your abundant mercy all records of our sins.

The following nine verses are said responsively, first by the Leader, then by the congregation:

Our Father, our King, bring us back to You in perfect repentance.

Our Father, our King, send a complete healing to the sick of Your people.

Our Father, our King, tear up the evil decree against us.

Our Father, our King, remember us with a memory of favorable deeds before You.

Our Father, our King, seal us in the book of good life.

Our Father, our King, seal us in the book of redemption and salvation.

Our Father, our King, seal us in the book of livelihood and sustenance.

Our Father, our King, seal us in the book of merit.

Our Father, our King, seal us in the book of pardon and forgiveness.

End of responsive reading.

Our Father, our King, let salvation soon flourish for us.

Our Father, our King, raise the honor of Your people Israel.

אָבִינוּ מַלְכֵּנוּ, בַּטֵּל מַחְשְׁבוֹת שׂוֹנְאֵינוּ.
אָבִינוּ מַלְכֵּנוּ, הָפֵר עֲצַת אוֹיְבֵינוּ.
אָבִינוּ מַלְכֵּנוּ, כַּלֵּה כָּל צַר וּמַשְׂטִין מֵעָלֵינוּ.
אָבִינוּ מַלְכֵּנוּ, סְתֹם פִּיּוֹת מַשְׂטִינֵנוּ וּמְקַטְרְגֵינוּ.
אָבִינוּ מַלְכֵּנוּ, כַּלֵּה דֶּבֶר וְחֶרֶב וְרָעָב וּשְׁבִי וּמַשְׁחִית וְעָוֹן וּשְׁמַד מִבְּנֵי בְרִיתֶךָ.
אָבִינוּ מַלְכֵּנוּ, מְנַע מַגֵּפָה מִנַּחֲלָתֶךָ.
אָבִינוּ מַלְכֵּנוּ, סְלַח וּמְחַל לְכָל עֲוֹנוֹתֵינוּ.
אָבִינוּ מַלְכֵּנוּ, מְחֵה וְהַעֲבֵר פְּשָׁעֵינוּ וְחַטֹּאתֵינוּ מִנֶּגֶד עֵינֶיךָ.
אָבִינוּ מַלְכֵּנוּ, מְחֹק בְּרַחֲמֶיךָ הָרַבִּים כָּל שִׁטְרֵי חוֹבוֹתֵינוּ.

The following nine verses are said responsively, first by the שליח ציבור*, then by the* קהל*:*

אָבִינוּ מַלְכֵּנוּ, הַחֲזִירֵנוּ בִּתְשׁוּבָה שְׁלֵמָה לְפָנֶיךָ.
אָבִינוּ מַלְכֵּנוּ, שְׁלַח רְפוּאָה שְׁלֵמָה לְחוֹלֵי עַמֶּךָ.
אָבִינוּ מַלְכֵּנוּ, קְרַע רֹעַ גְּזַר דִּינֵנוּ.
אָבִינוּ מַלְכֵּנוּ, זָכְרֵנוּ בְּזִכָּרוֹן טוֹב לְפָנֶיךָ.
אָבִינוּ מַלְכֵּנוּ, חָתְמֵנוּ בְּסֵפֶר חַיִּים טוֹבִים.
אָבִינוּ מַלְכֵּנוּ, חָתְמֵנוּ בְּסֵפֶר גְּאֻלָּה וִישׁוּעָה.
אָבִינוּ מַלְכֵּנוּ, חָתְמֵנוּ בְּסֵפֶר פַּרְנָסָה וְכַלְכָּלָה.
אָבִינוּ מַלְכֵּנוּ, חָתְמֵנוּ בְּסֵפֶר זְכֻיּוֹת.
אָבִינוּ מַלְכֵּנוּ, חָתְמֵנוּ בְּסֵפֶר סְלִיחָה וּמְחִילָה.

End of responsive reading.

אָבִינוּ מַלְכֵּנוּ, הַצְמַח לָנוּ יְשׁוּעָה בְּקָרוֹב.
אָבִינוּ מַלְכֵּנוּ, הָרֵם קֶרֶן יִשְׂרָאֵל עַמֶּךָ.

Our Father, our King, raise the honor of Your anointed.

Our Father, our King, fill our hands with Your blessings.

Our Father, our King, fill our storehouses with abundance.

Our Father, our King, hear our voice, pity
and be compassionate to us.

Our Father, our King, accept, with compassion and favor, our prayer.

Our Father, our King, open the gates of heaven to our prayer.

Our Father, our King, remember that we are dust.

Our Father, our King, please do not turn us away from You
empty-handed.

Our Father, our King, may this moment be a moment of
compassion and a time of favor before You.

Our Father, our King, have pity on us, our children and our infants.

Our Father, our King, act for the sake of those who were killed
for Your holy name.

Our Father, our King, act for the sake of those who were slaughtered
for proclaiming Your Unity.

Our Father, our King, act for the sake of those
who went through fire and water
to sanctify Your name.

Our Father, our King, avenge before our eyes
the spilt blood of Your servants.

Our Father, our King, act for Your sake, if not for ours.

Our Father, our King, act for Your sake, and save us.

Our Father, our King, act for the sake of Your abundant compassion.

Our Father, our King, act for the sake of Your great, mighty and
awesome name by which we are called.

▸ Our Father, our King, be gracious to us and answer us, though we
have no worthy deeds; act with us in charity
and loving-kindness and save us.

אָבִינוּ מַלְכֵּנוּ, הָרֵם קֶרֶן מְשִׁיחֶךָ.
אָבִינוּ מַלְכֵּנוּ, מַלֵּא יָדֵינוּ מִבִּרְכוֹתֶיךָ.
אָבִינוּ מַלְכֵּנוּ, מַלֵּא אֲסָמֵינוּ שָׂבָע.
אָבִינוּ מַלְכֵּנוּ, שְׁמַע קוֹלֵנוּ, חוּס וְרַחֵם עָלֵינוּ.
אָבִינוּ מַלְכֵּנוּ, קַבֵּל בְּרַחֲמִים וּבְרָצוֹן אֶת תְּפִלָּתֵנוּ.
אָבִינוּ מַלְכֵּנוּ, פְּתַח שַׁעֲרֵי שָׁמַיִם לִתְפִלָּתֵנוּ.
אָבִינוּ מַלְכֵּנוּ, זְכֹר כִּי עָפָר אֲנָחְנוּ.
אָבִינוּ מַלְכֵּנוּ, נָא אַל תְּשִׁיבֵנוּ רֵיקָם מִלְּפָנֶיךָ.
אָבִינוּ מַלְכֵּנוּ, תְּהֵא הַשָּׁעָה הַזֹּאת שְׁעַת רַחֲמִים
וְעֵת רָצוֹן מִלְּפָנֶיךָ.
אָבִינוּ מַלְכֵּנוּ, חֲמֹל עָלֵינוּ וְעַל עוֹלָלֵינוּ וְטַפֵּנוּ.
אָבִינוּ מַלְכֵּנוּ, עֲשֵׂה לְמַעַן הֲרוּגִים עַל שֵׁם קָדְשֶׁךָ.
אָבִינוּ מַלְכֵּנוּ, עֲשֵׂה לְמַעַן טְבוּחִים עַל יִחוּדֶךָ.
אָבִינוּ מַלְכֵּנוּ, עֲשֵׂה לְמַעַן בָּאֵי בָאֵשׁ וּבַמַּיִם עַל קִדּוּשׁ שְׁמֶךָ.
אָבִינוּ מַלְכֵּנוּ, נְקֹם לְעֵינֵינוּ נִקְמַת דַּם עֲבָדֶיךָ הַשָּׁפוּךְ.
אָבִינוּ מַלְכֵּנוּ, עֲשֵׂה לְמַעַנְךָ אִם לֹא לְמַעֲנֵנוּ.
אָבִינוּ מַלְכֵּנוּ, עֲשֵׂה לְמַעַנְךָ וְהוֹשִׁיעֵנוּ.
אָבִינוּ מַלְכֵּנוּ, עֲשֵׂה לְמַעַן רַחֲמֶיךָ הָרַבִּים.
אָבִינוּ מַלְכֵּנוּ, עֲשֵׂה לְמַעַן שִׁמְךָ הַגָּדוֹל הַגִּבּוֹר וְהַנּוֹרָא,
שֶׁנִּקְרָא עָלֵינוּ.
◂ אָבִינוּ מַלְכֵּנוּ, חָנֵּנוּ וַעֲנֵנוּ, כִּי אֵין בָּנוּ מַעֲשִׂים
עֲשֵׂה עִמָּנוּ צְדָקָה וָחֶסֶד וְהוֹשִׁיעֵנוּ.

The Leader recites each of the following three verses, followed by the congregation, aloud and in unison:

Listen, Israel: the LORD is our God, the LORD is One. *Deut. 6*

---

deathbed confession. In the closing words of Yom Kippur it is as if we were saying: Whether You have sealed me for life or not, still I will declare my faith in You. I will praise You as long as I have the breath to do so.

The world and its worries have fallen away. We have ceased to think about ourselves. Our gaze is turned outward and upward. We are because God is. In His forgiveness is our hope; in His will, our freedom; in His redemption, our deliverance; in His unity, our integrity; in His love, our life. Infinitesimally small though we may be, for a moment we stand bathed in the radiance of Infinity.

שְׁמַע יִשְׂרָאֵל, יהוה אֱלֹהֵינוּ, יהוה אֶחָד *Listen, Israel: the LORD is our God, the LORD is One.* The first Hebrew words we learn as children, and the last words we say at the end of our life, the words Jewish martyrs said as they prepared to die for their faith. They are the words engraved on the Jewish soul. In this context they mean more than that God is One. They mean, "God alone."

You, God of the universe, are our God. We have no other. Our ancestors put their faith in You. We put our faith in You. You are the focus of our lives. You are the breath we breathe, the strength we feel, the voice we hear, the horizon of our hopes. There were times when we drifted, days when we forgot You; there may even have been times when we doubted You. But now we say with every breath in our body: it is You and You alone. As the gates are closing, do not leave us. As we face the coming year, do not leave us.

Rabbi Levi Yitzḥak of Berditchev expressed this in a prayer he used to say:

Master of the universe, Master of the universe,
I would like to sing a song to You:
Where shall I find You, and where shall I not find You?
Where can one find You and where can one not find You?
Wherever I go, it is You. Wherever I stand, it is You.
Only You, just You. Either You or You. If it is good, it is You.
If, God forbid, it is not good, still it is You.
Heaven – You. Earth – You. Above – You. Below – You.
Wherever I go, wherever I turn: You, You, You.

The שליח ציבור *recites each of the following three verses, followed by the* קהל*, aloud and in unison:*

דברים ו שְׁמַע יִשְׂרָאֵל, יהוה אֱלֹהֵינוּ, יהוה אֶחָד:

SHEMA YISRAEL – LISTEN, ISRAEL

We now reach the supreme moment of Divine–human encounter in the entire Jewish year. For a day we have fasted in penitence and prayer. We have petitioned, pleaded, confessed our faults and sins, admitted our utter insignificance in the totality of things, spoken to God in the complete lexicon of relationship from self-abasement to impassioned love, and now the gates have almost closed. The day is at an end. The verdict has been written and sealed. There is no prayer left to pray. Instead our words are transfigured into something else.

This is an affirmation of faith. We cry out to God that He is ours and we are His. There is no artistry here, no carefully constructed poetics of prayer. This is the *cri de coeur* of the God-intoxicated people who, for generation after generation, risked their existence on the covenant their ancestors made with God at Mount Sinai and which they never abandoned in all the dark centuries despite the defeats, exiles, tragedies and persecutions. The "stiff-necked people," once obstinate in faithlessness, became yet more obstinate in their faith. They held fast to God with an awesome tenacity. This is our people and this our faith, our loyalty and love.

We do not know exactly when, where and why this affirmation entered the liturgy of Yom Kippur. It is first mentioned in the eleventh century, in the school of Rashi. At first there were multiple variants. Some said "Listen, Israel" three times, though this was frowned upon. The unity of God needs no repetition. Some added "Blessed be the name…," and then the phrase "The Lord He is God" began to appear, at first said twice, but eventually the custom was to say it seven times.

The medieval authorities explained the declaration as follows: "Listen, Israel" represents the unity of God. The threefold, "Blessed be the name" represents the three dimensions of time: past, present and future. The sevenfold "The Lord He is God" represents the seven dimensions of space (the "seven heavens," or the cosmos created in seven days). Taken together the three lines mean that God is One through and beyond all time, in and beyond all space.

Modern thinkers point out the close similarity between this and the

The Leader three times, then the congregation three times:

Blessed be the name of His glorious kingdom
for ever and all time.

The Leader seven times, then the congregation seven times:

The Lord He is God.

FULL KADDISH

Leader: יִתְגַּדַּל Magnified and sanctified may His great name be,
in the world He created by His will.
May He establish His kingdom
in your lifetime and in your days,
and in the lifetime of all the house of Israel,
swiftly and soon –
and say: Amen.

Under King Ahab and his idolatrous wife Jezebel, Baal worship had reappeared among the people. The Israelites were gradually drifting toward the idolatry of their pagan neighbors. At this moment the prophet Elijah sensed a potential catastrophe. He summoned the prophets of Baal to a trial on Mount Carmel. Addressing the assembled crowd he challenged them: "How long will you equivocate, hovering between two opinions? You cannot have it both ways. Either you are for God or for Baal. You must make the choice."

He proposed a test. Each side would prepare a sacrifice and call on its god. The one that sent fire from heaven to consume the sacrifice would have proven Himself to be the true God. Sacrifices were prepared. The prophets of Baal then called on their god. Nothing happened. They prayed harder. They lacerated themselves but to no avail. "Pray louder," said Elijah in a rare moment of humor. "Perhaps your god has gone elsewhere. Perhaps he is asleep." They cried louder but nothing happened. Then Elijah prayed a short prayer to God and immediately fire came down from heaven. The people, seized by the power of that moment, cried out: "The Lord He is God, the Lord He is God." In that moment the people knew: You have to make a choice. You cannot equivocate. That day the people declared its loyalty to God.

The שליח ציבור *three times, then the* קהל *three times:*

בָּרוּךְ שֵׁם כְּבוֹד מַלְכוּתוֹ לְעוֹלָם וָעֶד.

The שליח ציבור *seven times, then the* קהל *seven times:*

יהוה הוּא הָאֱלֹהִים.

קדיש שלם

ש״ץ: יִתְגַּדַּל וְיִתְקַדַּשׁ שְׁמֵהּ רַבָּא (קהל: אָמֵן)
בְּעָלְמָא דִּי בְרָא כִרְעוּתֵהּ
וְיַמְלִיךְ מַלְכוּתֵהּ
בְּחַיֵּיכוֹן וּבְיוֹמֵיכוֹן וּבְחַיֵּי דְכָל בֵּית יִשְׂרָאֵל
בַּעֲגָלָא וּבִזְמַן קָרִיב, וְאִמְרוּ אָמֵן. (קהל: אָמֵן)

בָּרוּךְ שֵׁם *Blessed be the name.* These are the words the people said when they heard the priests say the Shema in the Temple, or when, on Yom Kippur, the High Priest uttered the holiest name of God. According to one rabbinic legend they are the words Moses heard the angels say when he ascended to heaven to receive the Torah. According to another they are the words of relief Jacob said on his deathbed when he heard all his children declare their faith in God.

"Listen, Israel" is about God in Himself. "Blessed be the name" is about the relationship between God and the world. *Blessed* refers to the flow of energy through which He sustains the cosmos. *Name* is how God is known by His creations. *Glorious* is the respect in which He is held by humanity. *Kingdom* is God's sovereignty over all.

יהוה הוּא הָאֱלֹהִים *The Lord He is God.* We have explained that "Listen, Israel" is about God, and "Blessed be the name" is the line connecting God and the world. "The Lord He is God" is about the Jewish people and its faith. The words come from a fraught moment in Jewish history (see 1 Kings 18).

All: May His great name be blessed for ever and all time.

Leader: Blessed and praised,
glorified and exalted, raised and honored,
uplifted and lauded be
the name of the Holy One, blessed be He,
above and beyond any blessing, song,
praise and consolation
uttered in the world – and say: Amen.

Some congregations sound the Shofar (next page) at this point.

May the prayers and pleas of all Israel
be accepted by their Father in heaven –
and say: Amen.

May there be great peace from heaven,
and life for us and all Israel –
and say: Amen.

Bow, take three steps back, as if taking leave of the Divine Presence, then bow, first left, then right, then center, while saying:

May He who makes peace in His high places,
make peace for us and all Israel –
and say: Amen.

---

fiftieth we sound the shofar because of the possibility that this may be it; or simply as a reminder of that institution.

Others say that just as we sounded the shofar on Rosh HaShana to signal the beginning of the process of judgment, so we sound it after Ne'ila to signal that the trial has ended and the Judge is about to leave. They cite the verse: "God is gone up with a shout, the LORD with the sound of a horn" (Ps. 47:6). Another view is that it is to "confuse Satan" (accusation, temptation) as we recommence ordinary life after a period of intense holiness; or simply to signal the end of the fast so that children can be fed and a meal made ready.

The most expansive explanation is that it recalls the end of Moses' forty-day sojourn on Mount Sinai when he secured forgiveness for the people.

קהל וש״ץ: יְהֵא שְׁמֵהּ רַבָּא מְבָרַךְ לְעָלַם וּלְעָלְמֵי עָלְמַיָּא.

ש״ץ: יִתְבָּרַךְ וְיִשְׁתַּבַּח וְיִתְפָּאַר וְיִתְרוֹמַם וְיִתְנַשֵּׂא
וְיִתְהַדָּר וְיִתְעַלֶּה וְיִתְהַלָּל
שְׁמֵהּ דְּקֻדְשָׁא בְּרִיךְ הוּא (קהל: בְּרִיךְ הוּא)
לְעֵלָּא לְעֵלָּא מִכָּל בִּרְכָתָא וְשִׁירָתָא, תֻּשְׁבְּחָתָא וְנֶחֱמָתָא
דַּאֲמִירָן בְּעָלְמָא, וְאִמְרוּ אָמֵן. (קהל: אָמֵן)

Some congregations sound the שופר *(next page) at this point.*

תִּתְקַבַּל צְלוֹתְהוֹן וּבָעוּתְהוֹן דְּכָל יִשְׂרָאֵל
קֳדָם אֲבוּהוֹן דִּי בִשְׁמַיָּא, וְאִמְרוּ אָמֵן. (קהל: אָמֵן)

יְהֵא שְׁלָמָא רַבָּא מִן שְׁמַיָּא
וְחַיִּים, עָלֵינוּ וְעַל כָּל יִשְׂרָאֵל, וְאִמְרוּ אָמֵן. (קהל: אָמֵן)

Bow, take three steps back, as if taking leave of the Divine Presence, then bow, first left, then right, then center, while saying:

עֹשֶׂה הַשָּׁלוֹם בִּמְרוֹמָיו
הוּא יַעֲשֶׂה שָׁלוֹם עָלֵינוּ וְעַל כָּל יִשְׂרָאֵל
וְאִמְרוּ אָמֵן. (קהל: אָמֵן)

SHOFAR

Since at least the eighth century, it has been the custom to blow the shofar at the end of Yom Kippur, though there are differences of opinion as to why we do so, when we do so, and how.

Some say it is a reminder of the Jubilee year, the year of freedom when ancestral land returned to its original owners: "Have the horn sounded everywhere on the tenth day of the seventh month; on the Day of Atonement sound the trumpet throughout your land. Consecrate the fiftieth year and proclaim liberty throughout the land to all its inhabitants. It shall be a jubilee for you; each one of you is to return to his family property and each to his own clan" (Lev. 25:9–10). Since we no longer know exactly which year is the

The shofar is sounded.

Some sound the extra notes in parentheses:

(TEKIA SHEVARIM TERUA)

TEKIA GEDOLA

Congregation aloud:

Next year in Jerusalem rebuilt!

The Ark is closed.

At every wedding the groom breaks a glass to signal that as long as the Temple is not rebuilt our joy is not complete. Every Tisha B'Av we sit like mourners and weep over its destruction as if it happened yesterday. Napoleon is said to have remarked that a people who can weep for Jerusalem so long will one day have it restored to them. And so it was.

Each year throughout the centuries the shofar was sounded at the end of Yom Kippur in Jerusalem by the Kotel, the Western Wall that in ancient times surrounded the Temple courtyard. In 1929 the British Mandatory government, yielding to anti-Jewish pressure, banned the practice. The shofar continued to be blown none the less despite the fact that those who did so were often arrested and imprisoned.

In 1967 Jews once again found themselves able to worship at the Kotel. Chief Rabbi Shlomo Goren, sounding the shofar, said these words:

> I am speaking to you from the Western Wall, remnant of our holy Temple… This day we have redeemed the vow of the generations: 'If I forget you, O Jerusalem, may my right hand forget its skill.' We did not forget you, Jerusalem our holy city, home of our glory… To the nations of the world we declare: We shall respectfully protect the holy places of all faiths, and their doors shall be open to all.
>
> To Zion and to the remnant of our Temple we say: your children have returned to their borders. Our feet now stand within your gates, Jerusalem: the city joined together once more with the new Jerusalem; the perfection of beauty, joy of the whole earth; capital city of the eternal state of Israel. In the name of the entire community of Jewry in Israel and the Diaspora I pronounce the blessing with joy: 'Blessed are You, LORD our God, King of the universe, who has given us life, sustained us and brought us to this day.' *This* year in Jerusalem rebuilt.

The shofar is sounded.

Some sound the extra notes in parentheses:

(תקיעה   שברים   תרועה)

תקיעה גדולה

Congregation aloud:

לַשָּׁנָה הַבָּאָה בִּירוּשָׁלַיִם הַבְּנוּיָה.

The ארון קודש *is closed.*

The shofar was sounded at the beginning of his ascent and at the end when he came down the mountain holding the second set of tablets, the symbol of a new beginning. Rabbi Soloveitchik argued that it represents our final wordless cry at the end of the day when we have exhausted the lexicon of penitential words. One way or another it is the period punctuating the end of one paragraph of time and beginning the next.

Some sound a single blast, *tekia gedola*; others four notes, *tekia, shevarim, terua, tekia*; yet others a cycle of ten notes. There are also different practices as to when it is sounded. Many communities do so at the end of Ne'ila, before, during or after the final Kaddish. The original custom, still observed by many, was to sound it at the end of Ma'ariv.

לַשָּׁנָה הַבָּאָה בִּירוּשָׁלַיִם הַבְּנוּיָה *Next year in Jerusalem rebuilt!* Twice we say these words: on Pesaḥ and Yom Kippur. Pesaḥ is the great festival of Jewish history, Yom Kippur the cleansing of the Jewish soul.

There is no phenomenon quite like the Jewish attachment to Jerusalem. It is where Isaac was bound, where King David built his capital and King Solomon the Temple. It is the epicenter of holiness, the home of the Divine Presence, the locus and focus of all Jewish prayer. Twenty-six centuries ago, weeping by the waters of Babylon, our ancestors vowed: "If I forget you, O Jerusalem, may my right hand forget its skill. May my tongue cling to the roof of my mouth if I do not remember you, if I do not consider Jerusalem my highest joy" (Ps. 137:5–6).

Wherever Jews were they prayed toward Jerusalem. Wherever they lived they left a fragment of their house unfinished in memory of its destruction.

Ma'ariv for Motza'ei Yom Kippur

וְהוּא רַחוּם He is compassionate. Ps. 78
He forgives iniquity and does not destroy.
Repeatedly He suppresses His anger, not rousing His full wrath.
LORD, save! May the King answer us on the day we call. Ps. 20

BLESSINGS OF THE SHEMA

The Leader says the following, bowing at "Bless," standing straight at "the LORD"; the congregation, followed by the Leader, responds, bowing at "Bless," standing straight at "the LORD":

Leader: **BLESS**
the LORD, the blessed One.

Congregation: Bless the LORD, the blessed One,
for ever and all time.

Leader: Bless the LORD, the blessed One,
for ever and all time.

בָּרוּךְ Blessed are You, LORD our God,
King of the Universe,
who by His word brings on evenings,
by His wisdom opens the gates of heaven,
with understanding makes time change and the seasons rotate,
and by His will
orders the stars in their constellations in the sky.
He creates day and night,
rolling away the light before the darkness,
and darkness before the light.
▸ He makes the day pass and brings on night,
distinguishing day from night:
the LORD of hosts is His name.

מעריב למוצאי יום הכיפורים

וְהוּא רַחוּם, יְכַפֵּר עָוֹן וְלֹא־יַשְׁחִית תהלים עח
וְהִרְבָּה לְהָשִׁיב אַפּוֹ, וְלֹא־יָעִיר כָּל־חֲמָתוֹ:
יהוה הוֹשִׁיעָה, הַמֶּלֶךְ יַעֲנֵנוּ בְיוֹם־קָרְאֵנוּ: תהלים כ

קריאת שמע וברכותיה

The שליח ציבור *says the following, bowing at* בָּרְכוּ*, standing straight at* ה׳*; the* קהל*, followed by the* שליח ציבור*, responds, bowing at* בָּרוּךְ*, standing straight at* ה׳*:*

ש״ץ: 

אֶת יהוה הַמְבֹרָךְ.

קהל: בָּרוּךְ יהוה הַמְבֹרָךְ לְעוֹלָם וָעֶד.

ש״ץ: בָּרוּךְ יהוה הַמְבֹרָךְ לְעוֹלָם וָעֶד.

בָּרוּךְ אַתָּה יהוה אֱלֹהֵינוּ מֶלֶךְ הָעוֹלָם
אֲשֶׁר בִּדְבָרוֹ מַעֲרִיב עֲרָבִים
בְּחָכְמָה פּוֹתֵחַ שְׁעָרִים
וּבִתְבוּנָה מְשַׁנֶּה עִתִּים וּמַחֲלִיף אֶת הַזְּמַנִּים
וּמְסַדֵּר אֶת הַכּוֹכָבִים בְּמִשְׁמְרוֹתֵיהֶם בָּרָקִיעַ כִּרְצוֹנוֹ.
בּוֹרֵא יוֹם וָלָיְלָה, גּוֹלֵל אוֹר מִפְּנֵי חֹשֶׁךְ וְחֹשֶׁךְ מִפְּנֵי אוֹר
◂ וּמַעֲבִיר יוֹם וּמֵבִיא לָיְלָה
וּמַבְדִּיל בֵּין יוֹם וּבֵין לָיְלָה
יהוה צְבָאוֹת שְׁמוֹ.

May the living and forever enduring God rule over us for all time.
Blessed are You, LORD, who brings on evenings.

אַהֲבַת עוֹלָם With everlasting love
have You loved Your people, the house of Israel.
You have taught us Torah and commandments,
decrees and laws of justice.
Therefore, LORD our God, when we lie down and when we rise up
we will speak of Your decrees, rejoicing in the words of Your Torah
and Your commandments for ever.
▸ For they are our life and the length of our days;
on them will we meditate day and night.
May You never take away Your love from us.
Blessed are You, LORD, who loves His people Israel.

The Shema must be said with intense concentration. See laws 17–20.

When not with a minyan, say:

God, faithful King!

The following verse should be said aloud, while covering the eyes with the right hand.

Listen, Israel: the LORD is our God, the LORD is One. *Deut. 6*

Quietly: Blessed be the name of His glorious kingdom for ever and all time.

וְאָהַבְתָּ Love the LORD your God with all your heart, with all your soul, and with all your might. These words which I command you today shall be on your heart. Teach them repeatedly to your children, speaking of them when you sit at home and when you travel on the way, when you lie down and when you rise. Bind them as a sign on your hand, and they shall be an emblem between your eyes. Write them on the doorposts of your house and gates. *Deut. 6*

וְהָיָה If you indeed heed My commandments with which I charge you today, to love the LORD your God and worship Him with all your heart and with all your soul, I will give rain in your land in its season, the early and late rain; and you shall gather in your grain, *Deut. 11*

אֵל חַי וְקַיָּם תָּמִיד, יִמְלֹךְ עָלֵינוּ לְעוֹלָם וָעֶד.
בָּרוּךְ אַתָּה יהוה, הַמַּעֲרִיב עֲרָבִים.

אַהֲבַת עוֹלָם בֵּית יִשְׂרָאֵל עַמְּךָ אָהָבְתָּ
תּוֹרָה וּמִצְוֹת, חֻקִּים וּמִשְׁפָּטִים, אוֹתָנוּ לִמַּדְתָּ
עַל כֵּן יהוה אֱלֹהֵינוּ בְּשָׁכְבֵנוּ וּבְקוּמֵנוּ נָשִׂיחַ בְּחֻקֶּיךָ
וְנִשְׂמַח בְּדִבְרֵי תוֹרָתֶךָ וּבְמִצְוֹתֶיךָ לְעוֹלָם וָעֶד
◂ כִּי הֵם חַיֵּינוּ וְאֹרֶךְ יָמֵינוּ, וּבָהֶם נֶהְגֶּה יוֹמָם וָלָיְלָה.
וְאַהֲבָתְךָ אַל תָּסִיר מִמֶּנּוּ לְעוֹלָמִים.
בָּרוּךְ אַתָּה יהוה, אוֹהֵב עַמּוֹ יִשְׂרָאֵל.

The שמע must be said with intense concentration. See laws 17–20.

When not with a מנין, say:

אֵל מֶלֶךְ נֶאֱמָן

The following verse should be said aloud, while covering the eyes with the right hand.

שְׁמַע יִשְׂרָאֵל, יהוה אֱלֹהֵינוּ, יהוה ׀ אֶחָד׃ דברים ו

Quietly בָּרוּךְ שֵׁם כְּבוֹד מַלְכוּתוֹ לְעוֹלָם וָעֶד.

וְאָהַבְתָּ אֵת יהוה אֱלֹהֶיךָ, בְּכָל־לְבָבְךָ וּבְכָל־נַפְשְׁךָ וּבְכָל־מְאֹדֶךָ׃ דברים ו
וְהָיוּ הַדְּבָרִים הָאֵלֶּה, אֲשֶׁר אָנֹכִי מְצַוְּךָ הַיּוֹם, עַל־לְבָבֶךָ׃ וְשִׁנַּנְתָּם
לְבָנֶיךָ וְדִבַּרְתָּ בָּם, בְּשִׁבְתְּךָ בְּבֵיתֶךָ וּבְלֶכְתְּךָ בַדֶּרֶךְ, וּבְשָׁכְבְּךָ
וּבְקוּמֶךָ׃ וּקְשַׁרְתָּם לְאוֹת עַל־יָדֶךָ וְהָיוּ לְטֹטָפֹת בֵּין עֵינֶיךָ׃
וּכְתַבְתָּם עַל־מְזֻזוֹת בֵּיתֶךָ וּבִשְׁעָרֶיךָ׃

וְהָיָה אִם־שָׁמֹעַ תִּשְׁמְעוּ אֶל־מִצְוֹתַי אֲשֶׁר אָנֹכִי מְצַוֶּה אֶתְכֶם דברים יא
הַיּוֹם, לְאַהֲבָה אֶת־יהוה אֱלֹהֵיכֶם וּלְעָבְדוֹ, בְּכָל־לְבַבְכֶם וּבְכָל־
נַפְשְׁכֶם׃ וְנָתַתִּי מְטַר־אַרְצְכֶם בְּעִתּוֹ, יוֹרֶה וּמַלְקוֹשׁ, וְאָסַפְתָּ דְגָנֶךָ
וְתִירֹשְׁךָ וְיִצְהָרֶךָ׃ וְנָתַתִּי עֵשֶׂב בְּשָׂדְךָ לִבְהֶמְתֶּךָ, וְאָכַלְתָּ וְשָׂבָעְתָּ׃

wine and oil. I will give grass in your field for your cattle, and you shall eat and be satisfied. Be careful lest your heart be tempted and you go astray and worship other gods, bowing down to them. Then the LORD's anger will flare against you and He will close the heavens so that there will be no rain. The land will not yield its crops, and you will perish swiftly from the good land that the LORD is giving you. Therefore, set these, My words, on your heart and soul. Bind them as a sign on your hand, and they shall be an emblem between your eyes. Teach them to your children, speaking of them when you sit at home and when you travel on the way, when you lie down and when you rise. Write them on the doorposts of your house and gates, so that you and your children may live long in the land that the LORD swore to your ancestors to give them, for as long as the heavens are above the earth.

וַיֹּאמֶר The LORD spoke to Moses, saying: Speak to the Israelites *Num. 15* and tell them to make tassels on the corners of their garments for all generations. They shall attach to the tassel at each corner a thread of blue. This shall be your tassel, and you shall see it and remember all of the LORD's commandments and keep them, not straying after your heart and after your eyes, following your own sinful desires. Thus you will be reminded to keep all My commandments, and be holy to your God. I am the LORD your God, who brought you out of the land of Egypt to be your God. I am the LORD your God.

True –

The Leader repeats:

▸ The LORD your God is true –

וֶאֱמוּנָה – and faithful is all this, and firmly established for us
that He is the LORD our God,
and there is none besides Him,
and that we, Israel, are His people.
He is our King, who redeems us from the hand of kings
and delivers us from the grasp of all tyrants.

הִשָּׁמְרוּ לָכֶם פֶּן־יִפְתֶּה לְבַבְכֶם, וְסַרְתֶּם וַעֲבַדְתֶּם אֱלֹהִים אֲחֵרִים וְהִשְׁתַּחֲוִיתֶם לָהֶם: וְחָרָה אַף־יהוה בָּכֶם, וְעָצַר אֶת־הַשָּׁמַיִם וְלֹא־יִהְיֶה מָטָר, וְהָאֲדָמָה לֹא תִתֵּן אֶת־יְבוּלָהּ, וַאֲבַדְתֶּם מְהֵרָה מֵעַל הָאָרֶץ הַטֹּבָה אֲשֶׁר יהוה נֹתֵן לָכֶם: וְשַׂמְתֶּם אֶת־דְּבָרַי אֵלֶּה עַל־לְבַבְכֶם וְעַל־נַפְשְׁכֶם, וּקְשַׁרְתֶּם אֹתָם לְאוֹת עַל־יֶדְכֶם, וְהָיוּ לְטוֹטָפֹת בֵּין עֵינֵיכֶם: וְלִמַּדְתֶּם אֹתָם אֶת־בְּנֵיכֶם לְדַבֵּר בָּם, בְּשִׁבְתְּךָ בְּבֵיתֶךָ וּבְלֶכְתְּךָ בַדֶּרֶךְ, וּבְשָׁכְבְּךָ וּבְקוּמֶךָ: וּכְתַבְתָּם עַל־מְזוּזוֹת בֵּיתֶךָ וּבִשְׁעָרֶיךָ: לְמַעַן יִרְבּוּ יְמֵיכֶם וִימֵי בְנֵיכֶם עַל הָאֲדָמָה אֲשֶׁר נִשְׁבַּע יהוה לַאֲבֹתֵיכֶם לָתֵת לָהֶם, כִּימֵי הַשָּׁמַיִם עַל־הָאָרֶץ:

וַיֹּאמֶר יהוה אֶל־מֹשֶׁה לֵּאמֹר: דַּבֵּר אֶל־בְּנֵי יִשְׂרָאֵל וְאָמַרְתָּ במדבר טו
אֲלֵהֶם, וְעָשׂוּ לָהֶם צִיצִת עַל־כַּנְפֵי בִגְדֵיהֶם לְדֹרֹתָם, וְנָתְנוּ עַל־צִיצִת הַכָּנָף פְּתִיל תְּכֵלֶת: וְהָיָה לָכֶם לְצִיצִת, וּרְאִיתֶם אֹתוֹ וּזְכַרְתֶּם אֶת־כָּל־מִצְוֹת יהוה וַעֲשִׂיתֶם אֹתָם, וְלֹא תָתוּרוּ אַחֲרֵי לְבַבְכֶם וְאַחֲרֵי עֵינֵיכֶם, אֲשֶׁר־אַתֶּם זֹנִים אַחֲרֵיהֶם: לְמַעַן תִּזְכְּרוּ וַעֲשִׂיתֶם אֶת־כָּל־מִצְוֹתָי, וִהְיִיתֶם קְדֹשִׁים לֵאלֹהֵיכֶם: אֲנִי יהוה אֱלֹהֵיכֶם, אֲשֶׁר הוֹצֵאתִי אֶתְכֶם מֵאֶרֶץ מִצְרַיִם, לִהְיוֹת לָכֶם לֵאלֹהִים, אֲנִי יהוה אֱלֹהֵיכֶם:

אֱמֶת

The שליח ציבור repeats:

› יהוה אֱלֹהֵיכֶם אֱמֶת

וֶאֱמוּנָה כָּל זֹאת וְקַיָּם עָלֵינוּ
כִּי הוּא יהוה אֱלֹהֵינוּ וְאֵין זוּלָתוֹ
וַאֲנַחְנוּ יִשְׂרָאֵל עַמּוֹ.
הַפּוֹדֵנוּ מִיַּד מְלָכִים
מַלְכֵּנוּ הַגּוֹאֲלֵנוּ מִכַּף כָּל הֶעָרִיצִים.

He is our God,
who on our behalf repays our foes
and brings just retribution on our mortal enemies;
who performs great deeds beyond understanding
and wonders beyond number;
who kept us alive, not letting our foot slip;
who led us on the high places of our enemies,
raising our pride above all our foes;
who did miracles for us
and brought vengeance against Pharaoh;
who performed signs and wonders
in the land of Ham's children;
who smote in His wrath all the firstborn of Egypt,
and brought out His people Israel from their midst
into everlasting freedom;
who led His children through the divided Reed Sea,
plunging their pursuers and enemies into the depths.
When His children saw His might,
they gave praise and thanks to His name,
▸ and willingly accepted His Sovereignty.
Moses and the children of Israel
then sang a song to You with great joy,
and they all exclaimed:

מִי־כָמֹכָה "Who is like You, Lord, among the mighty? *Ex. 15*
Who is like You, majestic in holiness,
awesome in praises, doing wonders?"

▸ Your children beheld Your majesty
as You parted the sea before Moses.
"This is my God!" they responded, and then said:

"The Lord shall reign for ever and ever." *Ibid.*

▸ And it is said, "For the Lord has redeemed Jacob *Jer. 31*
and rescued him from a power stronger than his own."
Blessed are You, Lord, who redeemed Israel.

הָאֵל הַנִּפְרָע לָנוּ מִצָּרֵינוּ
וְהַמְשַׁלֵּם גְּמוּל לְכָל אוֹיְבֵי נַפְשֵׁנוּ.
הָעוֹשֶׂה גְדוֹלוֹת עַד אֵין חֵקֶר, וְנִפְלָאוֹת עַד אֵין מִסְפָּר
הַשָּׂם נַפְשֵׁנוּ בַּחַיִּים, וְלֹא נָתַן לַמּוֹט רַגְלֵנוּ
הַמַּדְרִיכֵנוּ עַל בָּמוֹת אוֹיְבֵינוּ
וַיָּרֶם קַרְנֵנוּ עַל כָּל שׂוֹנְאֵינוּ.
הָעוֹשֶׂה לָּנוּ נִסִּים וּנְקָמָה בְּפַרְעֹה
אוֹתוֹת וּמוֹפְתִים בְּאַדְמַת בְּנֵי חָם.
הַמַּכֶּה בְעֶבְרָתוֹ כָּל בְּכוֹרֵי מִצְרָיִם
וַיּוֹצֵא אֶת עַמּוֹ יִשְׂרָאֵל מִתּוֹכָם לְחֵרוּת עוֹלָם.
הַמַּעֲבִיר בָּנָיו בֵּין גִּזְרֵי יַם סוּף
אֶת רוֹדְפֵיהֶם וְאֶת שׂוֹנְאֵיהֶם בִּתְהוֹמוֹת טִבַּע
וְרָאוּ בָנָיו גְּבוּרָתוֹ, שִׁבְּחוּ וְהוֹדוּ לִשְׁמוֹ
◂ וּמַלְכוּתוֹ בְּרָצוֹן קִבְּלוּ עֲלֵיהֶם.
מֹשֶׁה וּבְנֵי יִשְׂרָאֵל, לְךָ עָנוּ שִׁירָה בְּשִׂמְחָה רַבָּה
וְאָמְרוּ כֻלָּם

מִי־כָמֹכָה בָּאֵלִם יהוה שמות טו
מִי כָּמֹכָה נֶאְדָּר בַּקֹּדֶשׁ
נוֹרָא תְהִלֹּת עֹשֵׂה פֶלֶא:

◂ מַלְכוּתְךָ רָאוּ בָנֶיךָ, בּוֹקֵעַ יָם לִפְנֵי מֹשֶׁה
זֶה אֵלִי עָנוּ, וְאָמְרוּ
יהוה יִמְלֹךְ לְעֹלָם וָעֶד: שם

◂ וְנֶאֱמַר
כִּי־פָדָה יהוה אֶת־יַעֲקֹב, וּגְאָלוֹ מִיַּד חָזָק מִמֶּנּוּ: ירמיה לא
בָּרוּךְ אַתָּה יהוה, גָּאַל יִשְׂרָאֵל.

הַשְׁכִּיבֵנוּ Help us lie down, O Lord our God, in peace,
and rise up, O our King, to life.
Spread over us Your canopy of peace.
Direct us with Your good counsel,
and save us for the sake of Your name.
Shield us and remove from us every enemy,
plague, sword, famine and sorrow.
Remove the adversary from before and behind us.
Shelter us in the shadow of Your wings,
for You, God, are our Guardian and Deliverer;
You, God, are a gracious and compassionate King.
► Guard our going out and our coming in,
for life and peace, from now and for ever.
Blessed are You, Lord, who guards His people Israel for ever.

In Israel the service continues with Half Kaddish on page 1214.

בָּרוּךְ Blessed be the Lord for ever. Amen and Amen. *Ps. 89*
Blessed from Zion be the Lord *Ps. 135*
who dwells in Jerusalem. Halleluya!
Blessed be the Lord, God of Israel, *Ps. 72*
who alone does wonders.
Blessed be His glorious name for ever,
and may all the earth be filled with His glory. Amen and Amen.
May the glory of the Lord endure for ever; *Ps. 104*
may the Lord rejoice in His works.
May the name of the Lord be blessed now and for all time. *Ps. 113*
For the sake of His great name *1 Sam. 12*
the Lord will not abandon His people,
for the Lord vowed to make you a people of His own.
When all the people saw [God's wonders] they fell on their faces *1 Kings 18*
and said: "The Lord, He is God; the Lord, He is God."
Then the Lord shall be King over all the earth; *Zech. 14*
on that day the Lord shall be One and His name One.
May Your love, Lord, be upon us, as we have put our hope in You. *Ps. 33*

הַשְׁכִּיבֵנוּ יהוה אֱלֹהֵינוּ לְשָׁלוֹם
וְהַעֲמִידֵנוּ מַלְכֵּנוּ לְחַיִּים
וּפְרֹשׂ עָלֵינוּ סֻכַּת שְׁלוֹמֶךָ, וְתַקְּנֵנוּ בְּעֵצָה טוֹבָה מִלְּפָנֶיךָ
וְהוֹשִׁיעֵנוּ לְמַעַן שְׁמֶךָ.
וְהָגֵן בַּעֲדֵנוּ, וְהָסֵר מֵעָלֵינוּ אוֹיֵב, דֶּבֶר וְחֶרֶב וְרָעָב וְיָגוֹן
וְהָסֵר שָׂטָן מִלְּפָנֵינוּ וּמֵאַחֲרֵינוּ, וּבְצֵל כְּנָפֶיךָ תַּסְתִּירֵנוּ
כִּי אֵל שׁוֹמְרֵנוּ וּמַצִּילֵנוּ אָתָּה
כִּי אֵל מֶלֶךְ חַנּוּן וְרַחוּם אָתָּה.
◂ וּשְׁמֹר צֵאתֵנוּ וּבוֹאֵנוּ לְחַיִּים וּלְשָׁלוֹם מֵעַתָּה וְעַד עוֹלָם.
בָּרוּךְ אַתָּה יהוה, שׁוֹמֵר עַמּוֹ יִשְׂרָאֵל לָעַד.

In ארץ ישראל *the service continues with* חצי קדיש *on page 1215.*

בָּרוּךְ יהוה לְעוֹלָם, אָמֵן וְאָמֵן: תהלים פט
בָּרוּךְ יהוה מִצִּיּוֹן, שֹׁכֵן יְרוּשָׁלָיִם, הַלְלוּיָהּ: תהלים קלה
בָּרוּךְ יהוה אֱלֹהִים אֱלֹהֵי יִשְׂרָאֵל, עֹשֵׂה נִפְלָאוֹת לְבַדּוֹ: תהלים עב
וּבָרוּךְ שֵׁם כְּבוֹדוֹ לְעוֹלָם
וְיִמָּלֵא כְבוֹדוֹ אֶת־כָּל־הָאָרֶץ, אָמֵן וְאָמֵן:
יְהִי כְבוֹד יהוה לְעוֹלָם, יִשְׂמַח יהוה בְּמַעֲשָׂיו: תהלים קד
יְהִי שֵׁם יהוה מְבֹרָךְ מֵעַתָּה וְעַד־עוֹלָם: תהלים קיג
כִּי לֹא־יִטֹּשׁ יהוה אֶת־עַמּוֹ בַּעֲבוּר שְׁמוֹ הַגָּדוֹל שמואל א, יב
כִּי הוֹאִיל יהוה לַעֲשׂוֹת אֶתְכֶם לוֹ לְעָם:
וַיַּרְא כָּל־הָעָם וַיִּפְּלוּ עַל־פְּנֵיהֶם מלכים א, יח
וַיֹּאמְרוּ, יהוה הוּא הָאֱלֹהִים, יהוה הוּא הָאֱלֹהִים:
וְהָיָה יהוה לְמֶלֶךְ עַל־כָּל־הָאָרֶץ זכריה יד
בַּיּוֹם הַהוּא יִהְיֶה יהוה אֶחָד וּשְׁמוֹ אֶחָד:
יְהִי־חַסְדְּךָ יהוה עָלֵינוּ, כַּאֲשֶׁר יִחַלְנוּ לָךְ: תהלים לג

הוֹשִׁיעֵנוּ Save us, LORD our God, gather us *Ps. 106*
and deliver us from the nations,
to thank Your holy name, and glory in Your praise.
All the nations You made shall come and bow before You, LORD, *Ps. 86*
and pay honor to Your name,
for You are great and You perform wonders:
You alone are God.
We, Your people, the flock of Your pasture, *Ps. 79*
will praise You for ever.
For all generations we will relate Your praise.

בָּרוּךְ Blessed is the LORD by day,
blessed is the LORD by night.
Blessed is the LORD when we lie down;
blessed is the LORD when we rise.
For in Your hand are the souls of the living and the dead,
[as it is written:] "In His hand is every living soul, *Job 12*
and the breath of all mankind."
Into Your hand I entrust my spirit: *Ps. 31*
You redeemed me, LORD, God of truth.
Our God in heaven, bring unity to Your name,
establish Your kingdom constantly
and reign over us for ever and all time.

יִרְאוּ May our eyes see, our hearts rejoice,
and our souls be glad in Your true salvation,
when Zion is told, "Your God reigns." *Is. 52*
The LORD is King, the LORD was King,
the LORD will be King for ever and all time.
▸ For sovereignty is Yours,
and to all eternity You will reign in glory,
for we have no king but You.
Blessed are You, LORD,
the King who in His constant glory will reign over us
and all His creation for ever and all time.

הוֹשִׁיעֵנוּ יהוה אֱלֹהֵינוּ, וְקַבְּצֵנוּ מִן־הַגּוֹיִם תהלים קו
לְהוֹדוֹת לְשֵׁם קָדְשֶׁךָ, לְהִשְׁתַּבֵּחַ בִּתְהִלָּתֶךָ:
כָּל־גּוֹיִם אֲשֶׁר עָשִׂיתָ, יָבוֹאוּ וְיִשְׁתַּחֲווּ לְפָנֶיךָ, אֲדֹנָי תהלים פו
וִיכַבְּדוּ לִשְׁמֶךָ:
כִּי־גָדוֹל אַתָּה וְעֹשֵׂה נִפְלָאוֹת, אַתָּה אֱלֹהִים לְבַדֶּךָ:
וַאֲנַחְנוּ עַמְּךָ וְצֹאן מַרְעִיתֶךָ, נוֹדֶה לְּךָ לְעוֹלָם תהלים עט
לְדוֹר וָדֹר נְסַפֵּר תְּהִלָּתֶךָ:

בָּרוּךְ יהוה בַּיּוֹם, בָּרוּךְ יהוה בַּלָּיְלָה
בָּרוּךְ יהוה בְּשָׁכְבֵנוּ, בָּרוּךְ יהוה בְּקוּמֵנוּ.
כִּי בְיָדְךָ נַפְשׁוֹת הַחַיִּים וְהַמֵּתִים.
אֲשֶׁר בְּיָדוֹ נֶפֶשׁ כָּל־חָי, וְרוּחַ כָּל־בְּשַׂר־אִישׁ: איוב יב
בְּיָדְךָ אַפְקִיד רוּחִי, פָּדִיתָה אוֹתִי יהוה אֵל אֱמֶת: תהלים לא
אֱלֹהֵינוּ שֶׁבַּשָּׁמַיִם, יַחֵד שִׁמְךָ וְקַיֵּם מַלְכוּתְךָ תָּמִיד
וּמְלֹךְ עָלֵינוּ לְעוֹלָם וָעֶד.

יִרְאוּ עֵינֵינוּ וְיִשְׂמַח לִבֵּנוּ
וְתָגֵל נַפְשֵׁנוּ בִּישׁוּעָתְךָ בֶּאֱמֶת
בֶּאֱמֹר לְצִיּוֹן מָלַךְ אֱלֹהָיִךְ. ישעיה נב
יהוה מֶלֶךְ, יהוה מָלָךְ, יהוה יִמְלֹךְ לְעֹלָם וָעֶד.
› כִּי הַמַּלְכוּת שֶׁלְּךָ הִיא, וּלְעוֹלְמֵי עַד תִּמְלֹךְ בְּכָבוֹד
כִּי אֵין לָנוּ מֶלֶךְ אֶלָּא אָתָּה.
בָּרוּךְ אַתָּה יהוה
הַמֶּלֶךְ בִּכְבוֹדוֹ תָּמִיד, יִמְלֹךְ עָלֵינוּ לְעוֹלָם וָעֶד
וְעַל כָּל מַעֲשָׂיו.

HALF KADDISH

Leader: יִתְגַּדַּל Magnified and sanctified
may His great name be,
in the world He created by His will.
May He establish His kingdom
in your lifetime and in your days,
and in the lifetime of all the house of Israel,
swiftly and soon – and say: Amen.

All: May His great name be blessed for ever and all time.

Leader: Blessed and praised,
glorified and exalted,
raised and honored,
uplifted and lauded
be the name of the Holy One, blessed be He,
beyond any blessing,
song, praise and consolation uttered in the world –
and say: Amen.

THE AMIDA

The following prayer, until "in former years" on page 1230, is said silently, standing with feet together. Take three steps forward and at the points indicated by ▾, bend the knees at the first word, bow at the second, and stand straight before saying God's name.

O Lord, open my lips, *Ps. 51*
so that my mouth may declare Your praise.

PATRIARCHS

▾בָּרוּךְ Blessed are You, Lord our God
and God of our fathers,
God of Abraham, God of Isaac and God of Jacob;
the great, mighty and awesome God, God Most High,
who bestows acts of loving-kindness and creates all,

חצי קדיש

ש״ץ: יִתְגַּדַּל וְיִתְקַדַּשׁ שְׁמֵהּ רַבָּא (קהל: אָמֵן)
בְּעָלְמָא דִּי בְרָא כִרְעוּתֵהּ
וְיַמְלִיךְ מַלְכוּתֵהּ
בְּחַיֵּיכוֹן וּבְיוֹמֵיכוֹן וּבְחַיֵּי דְכָל בֵּית יִשְׂרָאֵל
בַּעֲגָלָא וּבִזְמַן קָרִיב
וְאִמְרוּ אָמֵן. (קהל: אָמֵן)

קהל וש״ץ: יְהֵא שְׁמֵהּ רַבָּא מְבָרַךְ לְעָלַם וּלְעָלְמֵי עָלְמַיָּא.

ש״ץ: יִתְבָּרַךְ וְיִשְׁתַּבַּח וְיִתְפָּאַר וְיִתְרוֹמַם וְיִתְנַשֵּׂא
וְיִתְהַדָּר וְיִתְעַלֶּה וְיִתְהַלָּל
שְׁמֵהּ דְּקֻדְשָׁא בְּרִיךְ הוּא (קהל: בְּרִיךְ הוּא)
לְעֵלָּא מִן כָּל בִּרְכָתָא וְשִׁירָתָא, תֻּשְׁבְּחָתָא וְנֶחֱמָתָא
דַּאֲמִירָן בְּעָלְמָא
וְאִמְרוּ אָמֵן. (קהל: אָמֵן)

עמידה

The following prayer, until קַדְמֹנִיּוֹת *on page 1231, is said silently, standing with feet together. Take three steps forward and at the points indicated by* ▾*, bend the knees at the first word, bow at the second, and stand straight before saying God's name.*

אֲדֹנָי, שְׂפָתַי תִּפְתָּח, וּפִי יַגִּיד תְּהִלָּתֶךָ: תהלים נא

אבות

▾בָּרוּךְ אַתָּה יהוה, אֱלֹהֵינוּ וֵאלֹהֵי אֲבוֹתֵינוּ
אֱלֹהֵי אַבְרָהָם, אֱלֹהֵי יִצְחָק, וֵאלֹהֵי יַעֲקֹב
הָאֵל הַגָּדוֹל הַגִּבּוֹר וְהַנּוֹרָא, אֵל עֶלְיוֹן
גּוֹמֵל חֲסָדִים טוֹבִים, וְקוֹנֵה הַכֹּל

who remembers the loving-kindness of the fathers
and will bring a Redeemer to their children's children
for the sake of His name, in love.
King, Helper, Savior, Shield:
▾Blessed are You, LORD,
Shield of Abraham.

DIVINE MIGHT

אַתָּה גִּבּוֹר You are eternally mighty, LORD.
You give life to the dead
and have great power to save.

In Israel: He causes the dew to fall.

He sustains the living
with loving-kindness,
and with great compassion
revives the dead.
He supports the fallen,
heals the sick,
sets captives free,
and keeps His faith with those who sleep in the dust.
Who is like You, Master of might,
and to whom can You be compared,
O King who brings death and gives life,
and makes salvation grow?
Faithful are You to revive the dead.
Blessed are You, LORD,
who revives the dead.

HOLINESS

אַתָּה קָדוֹשׁ You are holy and Your name is holy,
and holy ones praise You daily, Selah!
Blessed are You, LORD,
the holy God.

וְזוֹכֵר חַסְדֵי אָבוֹת
וּמֵבִיא גוֹאֵל לִבְנֵי בְנֵיהֶם
לְמַעַן שְׁמוֹ בְּאַהֲבָה.
מֶלֶךְ עוֹזֵר וּמוֹשִׁיעַ וּמָגֵן.
׳בָּרוּךְ אַתָּה יהוה, מָגֵן אַבְרָהָם.

גבורות

אַתָּה גִּבּוֹר לְעוֹלָם, אֲדֹנָי
מְחַיֵּה מֵתִים אַתָּה, רַב לְהוֹשִׁיעַ
בארץ ישראל: מוֹרִיד הַטָּל
מְכַלְכֵּל חַיִּים בְּחֶסֶד
מְחַיֵּה מֵתִים בְּרַחֲמִים רַבִּים
סוֹמֵךְ נוֹפְלִים, וְרוֹפֵא חוֹלִים, וּמַתִּיר אֲסוּרִים
וּמְקַיֵּם אֱמוּנָתוֹ לִישֵׁנֵי עָפָר.
מִי כָמוֹךָ, בַּעַל גְּבוּרוֹת
וּמִי דּוֹמֶה לָּךְ
מֶלֶךְ, מֵמִית וּמְחַיֶּה וּמַצְמִיחַ יְשׁוּעָה.
וְנֶאֱמָן אַתָּה לְהַחֲיוֹת מֵתִים.
בָּרוּךְ אַתָּה יהוה, מְחַיֵּה הַמֵּתִים.

קדושת השם

אַתָּה קָדוֹשׁ וְשִׁמְךָ קָדוֹשׁ
וּקְדוֹשִׁים בְּכָל יוֹם יְהַלְלוּךָ סֶּלָה.
בָּרוּךְ אַתָּה יהוה, הָאֵל הַקָּדוֹשׁ.

KNOWLEDGE

אַתָּה חוֹנֵן You grace humanity with knowledge
and teach mortals understanding.
You have graced us with the knowledge of Your Torah,
and taught us to perform the statutes of Your will.
You have distinguished, LORD our God,
between sacred and profane,
light and darkness, Israel and the nations,
and between the seventh day and the six days of work.
Our Father, our King,
may the days approaching us bring peace;
may we be free from all sin, cleansed from all iniquity,
holding fast to our reverence of You.
And grace us with the knowledge, understanding
and discernment that come from You.
Blessed are You, LORD,
who graciously grants knowledge.

REPENTANCE

הֲשִׁיבֵנוּ Bring us back, our Father, to Your Torah.
Draw us near, our King, to Your service.
Lead us back to You in perfect repentance.
Blessed are You, LORD,
who desires repentance.

FORGIVENESS

Strike the left side of the chest at °.

סְלַח לָנוּ Forgive us, our Father,
for we have °sinned.
Pardon us, our King,
for we have °transgressed;
for You pardon and forgive.
Blessed are You, LORD,
the gracious One who repeatedly forgives.

דעת

אַתָּה חוֹנֵן לְאָדָם דַּעַת, וּמְלַמֵּד לֶאֱנוֹשׁ בִּינָה.
אַתָּה חוֹנַנְתָּנוּ לְמַדַּע תּוֹרָתֶךָ
וַתְּלַמְּדֵנוּ לַעֲשׂוֹת חֻקֵּי רְצוֹנֶךָ
וַתַּבְדֵּל יהוה אֱלֹהֵינוּ בֵּין קֹדֶשׁ לְחוֹל
בֵּין אוֹר לְחֹשֶׁךְ, בֵּין יִשְׂרָאֵל לָעַמִּים
בֵּין יוֹם הַשְּׁבִיעִי לְשֵׁשֶׁת יְמֵי הַמַּעֲשֶׂה.
אָבִינוּ מַלְכֵּנוּ
הָחֵל עָלֵינוּ הַיָּמִים הַבָּאִים לִקְרָאתֵנוּ לְשָׁלוֹם
חֲשׂוּכִים מִכָּל חֵטְא וּמְנֻקִּים מִכָּל עָוֹן וּמְדֻבָּקִים בְּיִרְאָתֶךָ.
וְחָנֵּנוּ מֵאִתְּךָ דֵּעָה בִּינָה וְהַשְׂכֵּל.
בָּרוּךְ אַתָּה יהוה, חוֹנֵן הַדָּעַת.

תשובה

הֲשִׁיבֵנוּ אָבִינוּ לְתוֹרָתֶךָ
וְקָרְבֵנוּ מַלְכֵּנוּ לַעֲבוֹדָתֶךָ
וְהַחֲזִירֵנוּ בִּתְשׁוּבָה שְׁלֵמָה לְפָנֶיךָ.
בָּרוּךְ אַתָּה יהוה, הָרוֹצֶה בִּתְשׁוּבָה.

סליחה

Strike the left side of the chest at °.

סְלַח לָנוּ אָבִינוּ כִּי °חָטָאנוּ
מְחַל לָנוּ מַלְכֵּנוּ כִּי °פָשָׁעְנוּ
כִּי מוֹחֵל וְסוֹלֵחַ אָתָּה.
בָּרוּךְ אַתָּה יהוה, חַנּוּן הַמַּרְבֶּה לִסְלֹחַ.

REDEMPTION

רְאֵה Look on our affliction,
plead our cause,
and redeem us soon for Your name's sake,
for You are a powerful Redeemer.
Blessed are You, Lord,
the Redeemer of Israel.

HEALING

רְפָאֵנוּ Heal us, Lord, and we shall be healed.
Save us and we shall be saved,
for You are our praise.
Bring complete recovery for all our ailments,

The following prayer for a sick person may be said here:

May it be Your will, O Lord my God and God of my ancestors, that You speedily send a complete recovery from heaven, a healing of both soul and body, to the patient (*name*), son/daughter of (*mother's name*) among the other afflicted of Israel.

---

for You, God, King, are a faithful and compassionate Healer.
Blessed are You, Lord,
Healer of the sick of His people Israel.

PROSPERITY

בָּרֵךְ Bless this year for us, Lord our God,
and all its types of produce for good.
Grant blessing on the face of the earth,
and from its goodness satisfy us,
blessing our year as the best of years.
Blessed are You, Lord,
who blesses the years.

גאולה

רְאֵה בְעָנְיֵנוּ, וְרִיבָה רִיבֵנוּ
וּגְאָלֵנוּ מְהֵרָה לְמַעַן שְׁמֶךָ
כִּי גּוֹאֵל חָזָק אָתָּה.
בָּרוּךְ אַתָּה יהוה, גּוֹאֵל יִשְׂרָאֵל.

רפואה

רְפָאֵנוּ יהוה וְנֵרָפֵא
הוֹשִׁיעֵנוּ וְנִוָּשֵׁעָה, כִּי תְהִלָּתֵנוּ אָתָּה
וְהַעֲלֵה רְפוּאָה שְׁלֵמָה לְכָל מַכּוֹתֵינוּ

The following prayer for a sick person may be said here:

יְהִי רָצוֹן מִלְּפָנֶיךָ יהוה אֱלֹהַי וֵאלֹהֵי אֲבוֹתַי, שֶׁתִּשְׁלַח מְהֵרָה רְפוּאָה שְׁלֵמָה
מִן הַשָּׁמַיִם רְפוּאַת הַנֶּפֶשׁ וּרְפוּאַת הַגּוּף לַחוֹלֶה/לַחוֹלָה *name of patient*
בֶּן/בַּת *mother's name* בְּתוֹךְ שְׁאָר חוֹלֵי יִשְׂרָאֵל.

כִּי אֵל מֶלֶךְ רוֹפֵא נֶאֱמָן וְרַחֲמָן אָתָּה.
בָּרוּךְ אַתָּה יהוה, רוֹפֵא חוֹלֵי עַמּוֹ יִשְׂרָאֵל.

ברכת השנים

בָּרֵךְ עָלֵינוּ יהוה אֱלֹהֵינוּ אֶת הַשָּׁנָה הַזֹּאת
וְאֶת כָּל מִינֵי תְבוּאָתָהּ, לְטוֹבָה
וְתֵן בְּרָכָה עַל פְּנֵי הָאֲדָמָה, וְשַׂבְּעֵנוּ מִטּוּבָהּ
וּבָרֵךְ שְׁנָתֵנוּ כַּשָּׁנִים הַטּוֹבוֹת.
בָּרוּךְ אַתָּה יהוה, מְבָרֵךְ הַשָּׁנִים.

INGATHERING OF EXILES

תְּקַע Sound the great shofar for our freedom,
raise high the banner to gather our exiles,
and gather us together
from the four quarters of the earth.
Blessed are You, LORD,
who gathers the dispersed
of His people Israel.

JUSTICE

הָשִׁיבָה Restore our judges as at first,
and our counselors as at the beginning,
and remove from us sorrow and sighing.
May You alone, LORD,
reign over us
with loving-kindness and compassion,
and vindicate us in justice.
Blessed are You, LORD,
the King who loves righteousness and justice.

AGAINST INFORMERS

וְלַמַּלְשִׁינִים For the slanderers
let there be no hope,
and may all wickedness perish in an instant.
May all Your people's enemies swiftly be cut down.
May You swiftly uproot,
crush, cast down and humble the arrogant
swiftly in our days.
Blessed are You, LORD,
who destroys enemies
and humbles the arrogant.

קיבוץ גלויות

תְּקַע בְּשׁוֹפָר גָּדוֹל לְחֵרוּתֵנוּ
וְשָׂא נֵס לְקַבֵּץ גָּלֻיּוֹתֵינוּ
וְקַבְּצֵנוּ יַחַד מֵאַרְבַּע כַּנְפוֹת הָאָרֶץ.
בָּרוּךְ אַתָּה יהוה
מְקַבֵּץ נִדְחֵי עַמּוֹ יִשְׂרָאֵל.

השבת המשפט

הָשִׁיבָה שׁוֹפְטֵינוּ כְּבָרִאשׁוֹנָה
וְיוֹעֲצֵינוּ כְּבַתְּחִלָּה
וְהָסֵר מִמֶּנּוּ יָגוֹן וַאֲנָחָה
וּמְלֹךְ עָלֵינוּ אַתָּה יהוה לְבַדְּךָ בְּחֶסֶד וּבְרַחֲמִים
וְצַדְּקֵנוּ בַּמִּשְׁפָּט.
בָּרוּךְ אַתָּה יהוה
מֶלֶךְ אוֹהֵב צְדָקָה וּמִשְׁפָּט.

ברכת המינים

וְלַמַּלְשִׁינִים אַל תְּהִי תִקְוָה
וְכָל הָרִשְׁעָה כְּרֶגַע תֹּאבֵד
וְכָל אוֹיְבֵי עַמְּךָ מְהֵרָה יִכָּרֵתוּ
וְהַזֵּדִים מְהֵרָה
תְעַקֵּר וּתְשַׁבֵּר וּתְמַגֵּר וְתַכְנִיעַ
בִּמְהֵרָה בְיָמֵינוּ.
בָּרוּךְ אַתָּה יהוה
שׁוֹבֵר אוֹיְבִים וּמַכְנִיעַ זֵדִים.

THE RIGHTEOUS

עַל הַצַּדִּיקִים To the righteous, the pious,
the elders of Your people the house of Israel,
the remnant of their scholars,
the righteous converts, and to us,
may Your compassion be aroused,
Lord our God.
Grant a good reward to all
who sincerely trust in Your name.
Set our lot with them,
so that we may never be ashamed,
for in You we trust.
Blessed are You, Lord,
who is the support and trust of the righteous.

REBUILDING JERUSALEM

וְלִירוּשָׁלַיִם To Jerusalem, Your city,
may You return in compassion,
and may You dwell in it as You promised.
May You rebuild it rapidly in our days
as an everlasting structure,
and install within it soon the throne of David.
Blessed are You, Lord,
who builds Jerusalem.

KINGDOM OF DAVID

אֶת צֶמַח May the offshoot of Your servant David soon flower,
and may his pride be raised high
by Your salvation,
for we wait for Your salvation all day.
Blessed are You, Lord,
who makes the glory of salvation flourish.

על הצדיקים

עַל הַצַּדִּיקִים וְעַל הַחֲסִידִים
וְעַל זִקְנֵי עַמְּךָ בֵּית יִשְׂרָאֵל
וְעַל פְּלֵיטַת סוֹפְרֵיהֶם
וְעַל גֵּרֵי הַצֶּדֶק, וְעָלֵינוּ
יֶהֱמוּ רַחֲמֶיךָ יהוה אֱלֹהֵינוּ
וְתֵן שָׂכָר טוֹב לְכָל הַבּוֹטְחִים בְּשִׁמְךָ בֶּאֱמֶת
וְשִׂים חֶלְקֵנוּ עִמָּהֶם
וּלְעוֹלָם לֹא נֵבוֹשׁ כִּי בְךָ בָּטָחְנוּ.
בָּרוּךְ אַתָּה יהוה
מִשְׁעָן וּמִבְטָח לַצַּדִּיקִים.

בניין ירושלים

וְלִירוּשָׁלַיִם עִירְךָ בְּרַחֲמִים תָּשׁוּב
וְתִשְׁכֹּן בְּתוֹכָהּ כַּאֲשֶׁר דִּבַּרְתָּ
וּבְנֵה אוֹתָהּ בְּקָרוֹב בְּיָמֵינוּ בִּנְיַן עוֹלָם
וְכִסֵּא דָוִד מְהֵרָה לְתוֹכָהּ תָּכִין.
בָּרוּךְ אַתָּה יהוה
בּוֹנֵה יְרוּשָׁלָיִם.

משיח בן דוד

אֶת צֶמַח דָּוִד עַבְדְּךָ מְהֵרָה תַצְמִיחַ
וְקַרְנוֹ תָּרוּם בִּישׁוּעָתֶךָ
כִּי לִישׁוּעָתְךָ קִוִּינוּ כָּל הַיּוֹם.
בָּרוּךְ אַתָּה יהוה
מַצְמִיחַ קֶרֶן יְשׁוּעָה.

RESPONSE TO PRAYER

שְׁמַע קוֹלֵנוּ Listen to our voice, LORD our God.
Spare us and have compassion on us,
and in compassion and favor accept our prayer,
for You, God, listen to prayers and pleas.
Do not turn us away, O our King,
empty-handed from Your presence,
for You listen with compassion
to the prayer of Your people Israel.
Blessed are You, LORD,
who listens to prayer.

TEMPLE SERVICE

רְצֵה Find favor, LORD our God,
in Your people Israel and their prayer.
Restore the service to Your most holy House,
and accept in love and favor
the fire-offerings of Israel and their prayer.
May the service of Your people Israel always find favor with You.
And may our eyes witness
Your return to Zion in compassion.
Blessed are You, LORD,
who restores His Presence to Zion.

THANKSGIVING

Bow at the first nine words.

מוֹדִים We give thanks to You,
for You are the LORD our God and God of our ancestors
for ever and all time.
You are the Rock of our lives,
Shield of our salvation from generation to generation.
We will thank You and declare Your praise for our lives,
which are entrusted into Your hand;
for our souls, which are placed in Your charge;

שומע תפלה

שְׁמַע קוֹלֵנוּ יהוה אֱלֹהֵינוּ
חוּס וְרַחֵם עָלֵינוּ
וְקַבֵּל בְּרַחֲמִים וּבְרָצוֹן אֶת תְּפִלָּתֵנוּ
כִּי אֵל שׁוֹמֵעַ תְּפִלּוֹת וְתַחֲנוּנִים אָתָּה
וּמִלְּפָנֶיךָ מַלְכֵּנוּ רֵיקָם אַל תְּשִׁיבֵנוּ
כִּי אַתָּה שׁוֹמֵעַ תְּפִלַּת עַמְּךָ יִשְׂרָאֵל בְּרַחֲמִים.
בָּרוּךְ אַתָּה יהוה, שׁוֹמֵעַ תְּפִלָּה.

עבודה

רְצֵה יהוה אֱלֹהֵינוּ בְּעַמְּךָ יִשְׂרָאֵל, וּבִתְפִלָּתָם
וְהָשֵׁב אֶת הָעֲבוֹדָה לִדְבִיר בֵּיתֶךָ
וְאִשֵּׁי יִשְׂרָאֵל וּתְפִלָּתָם בְּאַהֲבָה תְקַבֵּל בְּרָצוֹן
וּתְהִי לְרָצוֹן תָּמִיד עֲבוֹדַת יִשְׂרָאֵל עַמֶּךָ.
וְתֶחֱזֶינָה עֵינֵינוּ בְּשׁוּבְךָ לְצִיּוֹן בְּרַחֲמִים.
בָּרוּךְ אַתָּה יהוה, הַמַּחֲזִיר שְׁכִינָתוֹ לְצִיּוֹן.

הודאה

Bow at the first five words.

מוֹדִים אֲנַחְנוּ לָךְ
שָׁאַתָּה הוּא יהוה אֱלֹהֵינוּ וֵאלֹהֵי אֲבוֹתֵינוּ לְעוֹלָם וָעֶד.
צוּר חַיֵּינוּ, מָגֵן יִשְׁעֵנוּ
אַתָּה הוּא לְדוֹר וָדוֹר.
נוֹדֶה לְּךָ וּנְסַפֵּר תְּהִלָּתֶךָ
עַל חַיֵּינוּ הַמְּסוּרִים בְּיָדֶךָ
וְעַל נִשְׁמוֹתֵינוּ הַפְּקוּדוֹת לָךְ

for Your miracles which are with us every day;
and for Your wonders and favors at all times,
evening, morning and midday.
You are good –
for Your compassion never fails.
You are compassionate –
for Your loving-kindnesses never cease.
We have always placed our hope in You.

וְעַל כֻּלָּם For all these things
may Your name be blessed and exalted, our King,
continually, for ever and all time.
Let all that lives thank You, Selah!
and praise Your name in truth,
God, our Savior and Help, Selah!
▾Blessed are You, LORD,
whose name is "the Good"
and to whom thanks are due.

PEACE

שָׁלוֹם רָב Grant great peace to Your people Israel for ever,
for You are the sovereign LORD of all peace;
and may it be good in Your eyes
to bless Your people Israel
at every time, at every hour, with Your peace.
Blessed are You, LORD,
who blesses His people Israel with peace.

Some say the following verse:

May the words of my mouth and the meditation of my heart *Ps. 19*
find favor before You, LORD, my Rock and Redeemer.

וְעַל נִסֶּיךָ שֶׁבְּכָל יוֹם עִמָּנוּ
וְעַל נִפְלְאוֹתֶיךָ וְטוֹבוֹתֶיךָ שֶׁבְּכָל עֵת
עֶרֶב וָבֹקֶר וְצָהֳרָיִם.
הַטּוֹב, כִּי לֹא כָלוּ רַחֲמֶיךָ
וְהַמְרַחֵם, כִּי לֹא תַמּוּ חֲסָדֶיךָ
מֵעוֹלָם קִוִּינוּ לָךְ.

וְעַל כֻּלָּם יִתְבָּרַךְ וְיִתְרוֹמַם שִׁמְךָ מַלְכֵּנוּ תָּמִיד לְעוֹלָם וָעֶד.
וְכֹל הַחַיִּים יוֹדוּךָ סֶּלָה, וִיהַלְלוּ אֶת שִׁמְךָ בֶּאֱמֶת
הָאֵל יְשׁוּעָתֵנוּ וְעֶזְרָתֵנוּ סֶלָה.
ׁבָּרוּךְ אַתָּה יהוה
הַטּוֹב שִׁמְךָ וּלְךָ נָאֶה לְהוֹדוֹת.

ברכת שלום
שָׁלוֹם רָב עַל יִשְׂרָאֵל עַמְּךָ תָּשִׂים לְעוֹלָם
כִּי אַתָּה הוּא מֶלֶךְ אָדוֹן לְכָל הַשָּׁלוֹם.
וְטוֹב בְּעֵינֶיךָ לְבָרֵךְ אֶת עַמְּךָ יִשְׂרָאֵל
בְּכָל עֵת וּבְכָל שָׁעָה בִּשְׁלוֹמֶךָ.
בָּרוּךְ אַתָּה יהוה
הַמְבָרֵךְ אֶת עַמּוֹ יִשְׂרָאֵל בַּשָּׁלוֹם.

Some say the following verse:

יִהְיוּ לְרָצוֹן אִמְרֵי־פִי וְהֶגְיוֹן לִבִּי לְפָנֶיךָ, יהוה צוּרִי וְגֹאֲלִי: תהלים יט

אֱלֹהַי My God, *Berakhot 17a*
guard my tongue from evil and my lips from deceitful speech.
To those who curse me, let my soul be silent;
may my soul be to all like the dust.
Open my heart to Your Torah
and let my soul pursue Your commandments.
As for all who plan evil against me,
swiftly thwart their counsel and frustrate their plans.
Act for the sake of Your name; act for the sake of Your right hand;
act for the sake of Your holiness; act for the sake of Your Torah.
That Your beloved ones may be delivered, *Ps. 60*
save with Your right hand and answer me.
May the words of my mouth *Ps. 19*
and the meditation of my heart find favor before You,
LORD, my Rock and Redeemer.

Bow, take three steps back, then bow, first left, then right, then center, while saying:

May He who makes peace in His high places,
make peace for us and all Israel – and say: Amen.

יְהִי רָצוֹן May it be Your will, LORD our God and God of our ancestors,
that the Temple be rebuilt speedily in our days, and grant us a share in Your Torah.
And there we will serve You with reverence,
as in the days of old and as in former years.
Then the offering of Judah and Jerusalem *Mal. 3*
will be pleasing to the LORD as in the days of old and as in former years.

FULL KADDISH

Leader: יִתְגַּדַּל Magnified and sanctified may His great name be,
in the world He created by His will.
May He establish His kingdom
in your lifetime and in your days,
and in the lifetime of all the house of Israel,
swiftly and soon – and say: Amen.

All: May His great name be blessed for ever and all time.

אֱלֹהַי ברכות יז.

נְצֹר לְשׁוֹנִי מֵרָע וּשְׂפָתַי מִדַּבֵּר מִרְמָה
וְלִמְקַלְלַי נַפְשִׁי תִדֹּם, וְנַפְשִׁי כֶּעָפָר לַכֹּל תִּהְיֶה.
פְּתַח לִבִּי בְּתוֹרָתֶךָ, וּבְמִצְוֹתֶיךָ תִּרְדֹּף נַפְשִׁי.
וְכָל הַחוֹשְׁבִים עָלַי רָעָה
מְהֵרָה הָפֵר עֲצָתָם וְקַלְקֵל מַחֲשַׁבְתָּם.

עֲשֵׂה לְמַעַן שְׁמֶךָ, עֲשֵׂה לְמַעַן יְמִינֶךָ
עֲשֵׂה לְמַעַן קְדֻשָּׁתֶךָ, עֲשֵׂה לְמַעַן תּוֹרָתֶךָ.

לְמַעַן יֵחָלְצוּן יְדִידֶיךָ, הוֹשִׁיעָה יְמִינְךָ וַעֲנֵנִי: תהלים ס
יִהְיוּ לְרָצוֹן אִמְרֵי־פִי וְהֶגְיוֹן לִבִּי לְפָנֶיךָ, יהוה צוּרִי וְגֹאֲלִי: תהלים יט

Bow, take three steps back, then bow, first left, then right, then center, while saying:

עֹשֶׂה שָׁלוֹם בִּמְרוֹמָיו
הוּא יַעֲשֶׂה שָׁלוֹם עָלֵינוּ וְעַל כָּל יִשְׂרָאֵל, וְאִמְרוּ אָמֵן.

יְהִי רָצוֹן מִלְּפָנֶיךָ יהוה אֱלֹהֵינוּ וֵאלֹהֵי אֲבוֹתֵינוּ
שֶׁיִּבָּנֶה בֵּית הַמִּקְדָּשׁ בִּמְהֵרָה בְיָמֵינוּ, וְתֵן חֶלְקֵנוּ בְּתוֹרָתֶךָ
וְשָׁם נַעֲבָדְךָ בְּיִרְאָה כִּימֵי עוֹלָם וּכְשָׁנִים קַדְמֹנִיּוֹת.
וְעָרְבָה לַיהוה מִנְחַת יְהוּדָה וִירוּשָׁלָיִם כִּימֵי עוֹלָם וּכְשָׁנִים קַדְמֹנִיּוֹת: מלאכי ג

קדיש שלם

ש״ץ: יִתְגַּדַּל וְיִתְקַדַּשׁ שְׁמֵהּ רַבָּא (קהל: אָמֵן)
בְּעָלְמָא דִּי בְרָא כִרְעוּתֵהּ
וְיַמְלִיךְ מַלְכוּתֵהּ
בְּחַיֵּיכוֹן וּבְיוֹמֵיכוֹן וּבְחַיֵּי דְכָל בֵּית יִשְׂרָאֵל
בַּעֲגָלָא וּבִזְמַן קָרִיב, וְאִמְרוּ אָמֵן. (קהל: אָמֵן)

קהל וש״ץ: יְהֵא שְׁמֵהּ רַבָּא מְבָרַךְ לְעָלַם וּלְעָלְמֵי עָלְמַיָּא.

Leader: Blessed and praised, glorified and exalted,
raised and honored,
uplifted and lauded be
the name of the Holy One, blessed be He,
beyond any blessing, song,
praise and consolation
uttered in the world –
and say: Amen.

May the prayers and pleas of all Israel
be accepted by their Father in heaven –
and say: Amen.

May there be great peace from heaven,
and life for us and all Israel –
and say: Amen.

Bow, take three steps back, as if taking leave of the Divine Presence, then bow, first left, then right, then center, while saying:

May He who makes peace in His high places,
make peace for us and all Israel –
and say: Amen.

On Motza'ei Shabbat continue below; on other days continue with Havdala on page 1240.

BIBLICAL VERSES OF BLESSING

וְיִתֶּן־לְךָ May God give you dew from heaven and the richness of the earth, and *Gen. 27*
corn and wine in plenty. May peoples serve you and nations bow down to you. Be lord over your brothers, and may your mother's sons bow down to you. A curse on those who curse you, but a blessing on those who bless you.

וְאֵל שַׁדַּי May God Almighty bless you; may He make you fruitful and numer- *Gen. 28*
ous until you become an assembly of peoples. May He give you and your descendants the blessing of Abraham, that you may possess the land where
you are now staying, the land God gave to Abraham. This comes from the *Gen. 49*
God of your father – may He help you – and from the Almighty – may He bless you with blessings of the heaven above and the blessings of the deep that lies below, the blessings of breast and womb. The blessings of your father surpass the blessings of my fathers to the bounds of the endless hills. May

ש״ץ: יתברך וישתבח ויתפאר ויתרומם ויתנשא
ויתהדר ויתעלה ויתהלל
שמה דקדשא בריך הוא (קהל: בריך הוא)
לעלא מן כל ברכתא ושירתא, תשבחתא ונחמתא
דאמירן בעלמא, ואמרו אמן. (קהל: אמן)

תתקבל צלותהון ובעותהון דכל ישראל
קדם אבוהון די בשמיא, ואמרו אמן. (קהל: אמן)

יהא שלמא רבא מן שמיא
וחיים, עלינו ועל כל ישראל, ואמרו אמן. (קהל: אמן)

Bow, take three steps back, as if taking leave of the Divine Presence, then bow, first left, then right, then center, while saying:

עשה שלום במרומיו
הוא יעשה שלום עלינו ועל כל ישראל, ואמרו אמן. (קהל: אמן)

On מוצאי שבת *continue below;*
on other days continue with הבדלה *on page 1241.*

פסוקי ברכה

ויתן־לך האלהים מטל השמים ומשמני הארץ, ורב דגן ותירש: בראשית כז
יעבדוך עמים וישתחו לך לאמים, הוה גביר לאחיך וישתחוו לך
בני אמך, אררך ארור ומברכיך ברוך:

ואל שדי יברך אתך ויפרך וירבך, והיית לקהל עמים: ויתן־לך בראשית כח
את־ברכת אברהם, לך ולזרעך אתך, לרשתך את־ארץ מגריך
אשר־נתן אלהים לאברהם: מאל אביך ויעזרך ואת שדי ויברכך, בראשית מט
ברכת שמים מעל ברכת תהום רבצת תחת, ברכת שדים ורחם:
ברכת אביך גברו על־ברכת הורי עד־תאות גבעת עולם, תהיין

they rest on the head of Joseph, on the brow of the prince among his brothers.
He will love you and bless you and increase your numbers. He will bless the *Deut. 7*
fruit of your womb and the fruit of your land: your corn, your wine and oil, the calves of your herds and the lambs of your flocks, in the land He swore to your fathers to give you. You will be blessed more than any other people. None of your men or women will be childless, nor any of your livestock without young. The LORD will keep you free from any disease. He will not inflict on you the terrible diseases you knew in Egypt, but He will inflict them on those who hate you.

הַמַּלְאָךְ May the angel who rescued me from all harm, bless these boys. May *Gen. 48*
they be called by my name and the names of my fathers Abraham and Isaac,
and may they increase greatly on the earth. The LORD your God has increased *Deut. 1*
your numbers so that today you are as many as the stars in the sky. May the LORD, God of your fathers, increase you a thousand times, and bless you as He promised you.

בָּרוּךְ You will be blessed in the city, and blessed in the field. You will be *Deut. 28*
blessed when you come in, and blessed when you go out. Your basket and your kneading trough will be blessed. The fruit of your womb will be blessed, and the crops of your land, and the young of your livestock, the calves of your herds and the lambs of your flocks. The LORD will send a blessing on your barns, and on everything you put your hand to. The LORD your God will bless you in the land He is giving you. The LORD will open for you the heavens, the storehouse of His bounty, to send rain on your land in season, and to bless all the work of your hands. You will lend to many nations but
will borrow from none. For the LORD your God will bless you as He has *Deut. 15*
promised: you will lend to many nations but will borrow from none. You will
rule over many nations, but none will rule over you. Happy are you, Israel! *Deut. 33*
Who is like you, a people saved by the LORD? He is your Shield and Helper and your glorious Sword. Your enemies will cower before you, and you will tread on their high places.

מָחִיתִי I have wiped out your transgressions like a cloud, and as a haze your sins; *Is. 44*
come back to Me for I have redeemed you. Sing for joy, O heavens, for the LORD has done this; shout aloud, you depths of the earth; burst into song, you mountains, you forests and all your trees, for the LORD has redeemed Jacob, and will
glory in Israel. Our Redeemer, the LORD of hosts is His name, the Holy One of *Is. 47*
Israel.

לְרֹאשׁ יוֹסֵף וּלְקָדְקֹד נְזִיר אֶחָיו: וַאֲהֵבְךָ וּבֵרַכְךָ וְהִרְבֶּךָ, וּבֵרַךְ פְּרִי־ דברים ז
בִטְנְךָ וּפְרִי־אַדְמָתֶךָ, דְּגָנְךָ וְתִירֹשְׁךָ וְיִצְהָרֶךָ, שְׁגַר־אֲלָפֶיךָ וְעַשְׁתְּרֹת
צֹאנֶךָ, עַל הָאֲדָמָה אֲשֶׁר־נִשְׁבַּע לַאֲבֹתֶיךָ לָתֶת לָךְ: בָּרוּךְ תִּהְיֶה
מִכָּל־הָעַמִּים, לֹא־יִהְיֶה בְךָ עָקָר וַעֲקָרָה וּבִבְהֶמְתֶּךָ: וְהֵסִיר יהוה
מִמְּךָ כָּל־חֹלִי, וְכָל־מַדְוֵי מִצְרַיִם הָרָעִים אֲשֶׁר יָדַעְתָּ, לֹא יְשִׂימָם
בָּךְ, וּנְתָנָם בְּכָל־שֹׂנְאֶיךָ:

הַמַּלְאָךְ הַגֹּאֵל אֹתִי מִכָּל־רָע יְבָרֵךְ אֶת־הַנְּעָרִים, וְיִקָּרֵא בָהֶם שְׁמִי וְשֵׁם בראשית מח
אֲבֹתַי אַבְרָהָם וְיִצְחָק, וְיִדְגּוּ לָרֹב בְּקֶרֶב הָאָרֶץ: יהוה אֱלֹהֵיכֶם הִרְבָּה דברים א
אֶתְכֶם, וְהִנְּכֶם הַיּוֹם כְּכוֹכְבֵי הַשָּׁמַיִם לָרֹב: יהוה אֱלֹהֵי אֲבוֹתֵיכֶם יֹסֵף
עֲלֵיכֶם כָּכֶם אֶלֶף פְּעָמִים, וִיבָרֵךְ אֶתְכֶם כַּאֲשֶׁר דִּבֶּר לָכֶם:

בָּרוּךְ אַתָּה בָּעִיר, וּבָרוּךְ אַתָּה בַּשָּׂדֶה: בָּרוּךְ אַתָּה בְּבֹאֶךָ, וּבָרוּךְ דברים כח
אַתָּה בְּצֵאתֶךָ: בָּרוּךְ טַנְאֲךָ וּמִשְׁאַרְתֶּךָ: בָּרוּךְ פְּרִי־בִטְנְךָ וּפְרִי
אַדְמָתְךָ וּפְרִי בְהֶמְתֶּךָ, שְׁגַר אֲלָפֶיךָ וְעַשְׁתְּרוֹת צֹאנֶךָ: יְצַו יהוה אִתְּךָ
אֶת־הַבְּרָכָה בַּאֲסָמֶיךָ וּבְכֹל מִשְׁלַח יָדֶךָ, וּבֵרַכְךָ בָּאָרֶץ אֲשֶׁר־יהוה
אֱלֹהֶיךָ נֹתֵן לָךְ: יִפְתַּח יהוה לְךָ אֶת־אוֹצָרוֹ הַטּוֹב אֶת־הַשָּׁמַיִם, לָתֵת
מְטַר־אַרְצְךָ בְּעִתּוֹ, וּלְבָרֵךְ אֵת כָּל־מַעֲשֵׂה יָדֶךָ, וְהִלְוִיתָ גּוֹיִם רַבִּים
וְאַתָּה לֹא תִלְוֶה: כִּי־יהוה אֱלֹהֶיךָ בֵּרַכְךָ כַּאֲשֶׁר דִּבֶּר־לָךְ, וְהַעֲבַטְתָּ דברים טו
גּוֹיִם רַבִּים וְאַתָּה לֹא תַעֲבֹט, וּמָשַׁלְתָּ בְּגוֹיִם רַבִּים וּבְךָ לֹא יִמְשֹׁלוּ:
אַשְׁרֶיךָ יִשְׂרָאֵל, מִי כָמוֹךָ, עַם נוֹשַׁע בַּיהוה, מָגֵן עֶזְרֶךָ וַאֲשֶׁר־חֶרֶב דברים לג
גַּאֲוָתֶךָ, וְיִכָּחֲשׁוּ אֹיְבֶיךָ לָךְ, וְאַתָּה עַל־בָּמוֹתֵימוֹ תִדְרֹךְ:

מָחִיתִי כָעָב פְּשָׁעֶיךָ וְכֶעָנָן חַטֹּאותֶיךָ, שׁוּבָה אֵלַי כִּי גְאַלְתִּיךָ: רָנּוּ שָׁמַיִם ישעיה מד
כִּי־עָשָׂה יהוה, הָרִיעוּ תַּחְתִּיּוֹת אָרֶץ, פִּצְחוּ הָרִים רִנָּה, יַעַר וְכָל־עֵץ בּוֹ,
כִּי־גָאַל יהוה יַעֲקֹב וּבְיִשְׂרָאֵל יִתְפָּאָר: גֹּאֲלֵנוּ, יהוה צְבָאוֹת שְׁמוֹ, קְדוֹשׁ ישעיה מז
יִשְׂרָאֵל:

יִשְׂרָאֵל Israel is saved by the LORD with everlasting salvation. You will *Is. 45*
never be ashamed or disgraced to time everlasting. You will eat your fill *Joel 2*
and praise the name of the LORD your God, who has worked wonders for
you. Never again shall My people be shamed. Then you will know that I am
in the midst of Israel, that I am the LORD your God, and there is no other.
Never again will My people be shamed. You will go out in joy and be led *Is. 55*
out in peace. The mountains and hills will burst into song before you, and
all the trees of the field will clap their hands. Behold, God is my salvation, *Is. 12*
I will trust and not be afraid. The LORD, the LORD, is my strength and my
song. He has become my salvation. With joy you will draw water from the
springs of salvation. On that day you will say, "Thank the LORD, proclaim
His name, make His deeds known among the nations." Declare that His
name is exalted. Sing to the LORD, for He has done glorious things; let this
be known throughout the world. Shout aloud and sing for joy, you who
dwell in Zion, for great in your midst is the Holy One of Israel. On that *Is. 25*
day they will say, "See, this is our God; we set our hope in Him and He
saved us. This is the LORD in whom we hoped; let us rejoice and be glad
in His salvation."

בֵּית Come, house of Jacob: let us walk in the light of the LORD. He will be the sure *Is. 2* *Is. 32*
foundation of your times; a rich store of salvation, wisdom and knowledge – the
fear of the LORD is a person's treasure. In everything he did, David was successful, *1 Sam. 18*
for the LORD was with him.

פָּדָה He redeemed my soul in peace from the battle waged against me, for the *Ps. 55*
sake of the many who were with me. The people said to Saul, "Shall Jonathan *1 Sam. 14*
die – he who has brought about this great deliverance in Israel? Heaven forbid!
As surely as the LORD lives, not a hair of his head shall fall to the ground, for he
did this today with God's help." So the people rescued Jonathan and he did not
die. Those redeemed by the LORD shall return; they will enter Zion singing; *Is. 35*
everlasting joy will crown their heads. Gladness and joy will overtake them, and
sorrow and sighing will flee away.

הָפַכְתָּ You have turned my sorrow into dancing. You have removed my sackcloth *Ps. 30*
and clothed me with joy. The LORD your God refused to listen to Balaam; instead *Deut. 23*
the LORD your God turned the curse into a blessing, for the LORD your God
loves you. Then maidens will dance and be glad; so too will young men and old *Jer. 31*
together; I will turn their mourning into gladness; I will give them comfort and
joy instead of sorrow.

יִשְׂרָאֵל נוֹשַׁע בַּיהוה תְּשׁוּעַת עוֹלָמִים, לֹא־תֵבֹשׁוּ וְלֹא־תִכָּלְמוּ ישעיה מה
עַד־עוֹלְמֵי עַד: וַאֲכַלְתֶּם אָכוֹל וְשָׂבוֹעַ, וְהִלַּלְתֶּם אֶת־שֵׁם יהוה יואל ב
אֱלֹהֵיכֶם אֲשֶׁר־עָשָׂה עִמָּכֶם לְהַפְלִיא, וְלֹא־יֵבֹשׁוּ עַמִּי לְעוֹלָם:
וִידַעְתֶּם כִּי בְקֶרֶב יִשְׂרָאֵל אָנִי, וַאֲנִי יהוה אֱלֹהֵיכֶם וְאֵין עוֹד, וְלֹא־
יֵבֹשׁוּ עַמִּי לְעוֹלָם: כִּי־בְשִׂמְחָה תֵצֵאוּ וּבְשָׁלוֹם תּוּבָלוּן, הֶהָרִים ישעיה נה
וְהַגְּבָעוֹת יִפְצְחוּ לִפְנֵיכֶם רִנָּה, וְכָל־עֲצֵי הַשָּׂדֶה יִמְחֲאוּ־כָף: הִנֵּה ישעיה יב
אֵל יְשׁוּעָתִי אֶבְטַח, וְלֹא אֶפְחָד, כִּי־עָזִּי וְזִמְרָת יָהּ יהוה, וַיְהִי־לִי
לִישׁוּעָה: וּשְׁאַבְתֶּם־מַיִם בְּשָׂשׂוֹן, מִמַּעַיְנֵי הַיְשׁוּעָה: וַאֲמַרְתֶּם בַּיּוֹם
הַהוּא, הוֹדוּ לַיהוה קִרְאוּ בִשְׁמוֹ, הוֹדִיעוּ בָעַמִּים עֲלִילֹתָיו, הַזְכִּירוּ
כִּי נִשְׂגָּב שְׁמוֹ: זַמְּרוּ יהוה כִּי גֵאוּת עָשָׂה, מוּדַעַת זֹאת בְּכָל־הָאָרֶץ:
צַהֲלִי וָרֹנִּי יוֹשֶׁבֶת צִיּוֹן, כִּי־גָדוֹל בְּקִרְבֵּךְ קְדוֹשׁ יִשְׂרָאֵל: וְאָמַר בַּיּוֹם ישעיה כה
הַהוּא, הִנֵּה אֱלֹהֵינוּ זֶה קִוִּינוּ לוֹ וְיוֹשִׁיעֵנוּ, זֶה יהוה קִוִּינוּ לוֹ, נָגִילָה
וְנִשְׂמְחָה בִּישׁוּעָתוֹ:

בֵּית יַעֲקֹב לְכוּ וְנֵלְכָה בְּאוֹר יהוה: וְהָיָה אֱמוּנַת עִתֶּיךָ, חֹסֶן יְשׁוּעֹת ישעיה ב ישעיה לג
חָכְמַת וָדָעַת, יִרְאַת יהוה הִיא אוֹצָרוֹ: וַיְהִי דָוִד לְכָל־דְּרָכָו מַשְׂכִּיל, שמואל א׳ יח
וַיהוה עִמּוֹ:

פָּדָה בְשָׁלוֹם נַפְשִׁי מִקְּרָב־לִי, כִּי־בְרַבִּים הָיוּ עִמָּדִי: וַיֹּאמֶר הָעָם אֶל־ תהלים נה שמואל א׳ יד
שָׁאוּל, הֲיוֹנָתָן יָמוּת אֲשֶׁר עָשָׂה הַיְשׁוּעָה הַגְּדוֹלָה הַזֹּאת בְּיִשְׂרָאֵל,
חָלִילָה, חַי־יהוה אִם־יִפֹּל מִשַּׂעֲרַת רֹאשׁוֹ אַרְצָה, כִּי־עִם־אֱלֹהִים עָשָׂה
הַיּוֹם הַזֶּה, וַיִּפְדּוּ הָעָם אֶת־יוֹנָתָן וְלֹא־מֵת: וּפְדוּיֵי יהוה יְשֻׁבוּן וּבָאוּ ישעיה לה
צִיּוֹן בְּרִנָּה, וְשִׂמְחַת עוֹלָם עַל־רֹאשָׁם, שָׂשׂוֹן וְשִׂמְחָה יַשִּׂיגוּ, וְנָסוּ יָגוֹן
וַאֲנָחָה:

הָפַכְתָּ מִסְפְּדִי לְמָחוֹל לִי, פִּתַּחְתָּ שַׂקִּי, וַתְּאַזְּרֵנִי שִׂמְחָה: וְלֹא־אָבָה יהוה תהלים ל דברים כג
אֱלֹהֶיךָ לִשְׁמֹעַ אֶל־בִּלְעָם, וַיַּהֲפֹךְ יהוה אֱלֹהֶיךָ לְּךָ אֶת־הַקְּלָלָה לִבְרָכָה,
כִּי אֲהֵבְךָ יהוה אֱלֹהֶיךָ: אָז תִּשְׂמַח בְּתוּלָה בְּמָחוֹל, וּבַחֻרִים וּזְקֵנִים יַחְדָּו, ירמיה לא
וְהָפַכְתִּי אֶבְלָם לְשָׂשׂוֹן, וְנִחַמְתִּים, וְשִׂמַּחְתִּים מִיגוֹנָם:

בּוֹרֵא I create the speech of lips: Peace, peace to those far and near, says the *Is. 57*
Lord, and I will heal them. Then the spirit came upon Amasai, chief of the *I Chr. 12*
captains, and he said: "We are yours, David! We are with you, son of Jesse!
Peace, peace to you, and peace to those who help you; for your God will
help you." Then David received them and made them leaders of his troop.
And you shall say: "To life! Peace be to you, peace to your household, and *I Sam. 25*
peace to all that is yours!" The Lord will give strength to His people; the *Ps. 29*
Lord will bless His people with peace.

אָמַר Rabbi Yoḥanan said: Wherever you find the greatness of the Holy One, *Megilla 31a*
blessed be He, there you find His humility. This is written in the Torah, repeated in the Prophets, and stated a third time in the Writings. It is written in
the Torah: "For the Lord your God is God of gods and Lord of lords, the great, *Deut. 10*
mighty and awe-inspiring God, who shows no favoritism and accepts no bribe."
Immediately afterward it is written, "He upholds the cause of the orphan and
widow, and loves the stranger, giving him food and clothing." It is repeated in the
Prophets, as it says: "So says the High and Exalted One, who lives for ever and *Is. 57*
whose name is Holy: I live in a high and holy place, but also with the contrite
and lowly in spirit, to revive the spirit of the lowly, and to revive the heart of the
contrite." It is stated a third time in the Writings: "Sing to God, make music for *Ps. 68*
His name, extol Him who rides the clouds – the Lord is His name – and exult
before Him." Immediately afterward it is written: "Father of the orphans and
Justice of widows, is God in His holy habitation."

יְהִי May the Lord our God be with us, as He was with our ancestors. May He *I Kings 8*
never abandon us or forsake us. You who cling to the Lord your God are all alive *Deut. 4*
today. For the Lord will comfort Zion, He will comfort all her ruins; He will *Is. 51*
make her wilderness like Eden, and her desert like a garden of the Lord. Joy and
gladness will be found there, thanksgiving and the sound of singing. It pleased the *Is. 42*
Lord for the sake of [Israel's] righteousness to make the Torah great and glorious.

שִׁיר הַמַּעֲלוֹת A song of ascents. Happy are all who fear the Lord, who walk in *Ps. 128*
His ways. When you eat the fruit of your labor, happy and fortunate are you.
Your wife shall be like a fruitful vine within your house; your sons like olive
saplings around your table. So shall the man who fears the Lord be blessed.
May the Lord bless you from Zion; may you see the good of Jerusalem all
the days of your life; and may you live to see your children's children. Peace
be on Israel!

Some say Mourner's Kaddish at this point (page 1244).

בּוֹרֵא נִיב שְׂפָתָיִם, שָׁלוֹם שָׁלוֹם לָרָחוֹק וְלַקָּרוֹב אָמַר יהוה, וּרְפָאתִיו: ישעיה נז
וְרוּחַ לָבְשָׁה אֶת־עֲמָשַׂי רֹאשׁ הַשָּׁלִישִׁים, לְךָ דָוִיד וְעִמְּךָ בֶן־יִשַׁי, דברי הימים א׳ יב
שָׁלוֹם שָׁלוֹם לְךָ וְשָׁלוֹם לְעֹזְרֶךָ, כִּי עֲזָרְךָ אֱלֹהֶיךָ, וַיְקַבְּלֵם דָּוִיד וַיִּתְּנֵם
בְּרָאשֵׁי הַגְּדוּד: וַאֲמַרְתֶּם כֹּה לֶחָי, וְאַתָּה שָׁלוֹם וּבֵיתְךָ שָׁלוֹם וְכֹל שמואל א׳ כה
אֲשֶׁר־לְךָ שָׁלוֹם: יהוה עֹז לְעַמּוֹ יִתֵּן, יהוה יְבָרֵךְ אֶת־עַמּוֹ בַשָּׁלוֹם: תהלים כט

אָמַר רַבִּי יוֹחָנָן: בְּכָל מָקוֹם שֶׁאַתָּה מוֹצֵא גְּדֻלָּתוֹ שֶׁל הַקָּדוֹשׁ בָּרוּךְ מגילה לא.
הוּא, שָׁם אַתָּה מוֹצֵא עַנְוְתָנוּתוֹ. דָּבָר זֶה כָּתוּב בַּתּוֹרָה, וְשָׁנוּי בַּנְּבִיאִים,
וּמְשֻׁלָּשׁ בַּכְּתוּבִים. כָּתוּב בַּתּוֹרָה: כִּי יהוה אֱלֹהֵיכֶם הוּא אֱלֹהֵי הָאֱלֹהִים דברים י
וַאֲדֹנֵי הָאֲדֹנִים, הָאֵל הַגָּדֹל הַגִּבֹּר וְהַנּוֹרָא, אֲשֶׁר לֹא־יִשָּׂא פָנִים וְלֹא יִקַּח
שֹׁחַד: וּכְתִיב בָּתְרֵהּ: עֹשֶׂה מִשְׁפַּט יָתוֹם וְאַלְמָנָה, וְאֹהֵב גֵּר לָתֶת לוֹ לֶחֶם
וְשִׂמְלָה: שָׁנוּי בַּנְּבִיאִים, דִּכְתִיב: כִּי כֹה אָמַר רָם וְנִשָּׂא שֹׁכֵן עַד וְקָדוֹשׁ ישעיה נז
שְׁמוֹ, מָרוֹם וְקָדוֹשׁ אֶשְׁכּוֹן, וְאֶת־דַּכָּא וּשְׁפַל־רוּחַ, לְהַחֲיוֹת רוּחַ שְׁפָלִים
וּלְהַחֲיוֹת לֵב נִדְכָּאִים: מְשֻׁלָּשׁ בַּכְּתוּבִים, דִּכְתִיב: שִׁירוּ לֵאלֹהִים, זַמְּרוּ תהלים סח
שְׁמוֹ, סֹלּוּ לָרֹכֵב בָּעֲרָבוֹת בְּיָהּ שְׁמוֹ, וְעִלְזוּ לְפָנָיו: וּכְתִיב בָּתְרֵהּ: אֲבִי
יְתוֹמִים וְדַיַּן אַלְמָנוֹת, אֱלֹהִים בִּמְעוֹן קָדְשׁוֹ:

יְהִי יהוה אֱלֹהֵינוּ עִמָּנוּ כַּאֲשֶׁר הָיָה עִם־אֲבֹתֵינוּ, אַל־יַעַזְבֵנוּ וְאַל־יִטְּשֵׁנוּ: מלכים א׳ ח
וְאַתֶּם הַדְּבֵקִים בַּיהוה אֱלֹהֵיכֶם, חַיִּים כֻּלְּכֶם הַיּוֹם: כִּי־נִחַם יהוה צִיּוֹן, נִחַם דברים ד ישעיה נא
כָּל־חָרְבֹתֶיהָ, וַיָּשֶׂם מִדְבָּרָהּ כְּעֵדֶן וְעַרְבָתָהּ כְּגַן־יהוה, שָׂשׂוֹן וְשִׂמְחָה יִמָּצֵא
בָהּ, תּוֹדָה וְקוֹל זִמְרָה: יהוה חָפֵץ לְמַעַן צִדְקוֹ, יַגְדִּיל תּוֹרָה וְיַאְדִּיר: ישעיה מב

שִׁיר הַמַּעֲלוֹת, אַשְׁרֵי כָּל־יְרֵא יהוה, הַהֹלֵךְ בִּדְרָכָיו: יְגִיעַ כַּפֶּיךָ כִּי תהלים קכח
תֹאכֵל, אַשְׁרֶיךָ וְטוֹב לָךְ: אֶשְׁתְּךָ כְּגֶפֶן פֹּרִיָּה בְּיַרְכְּתֵי בֵיתֶךָ, בָּנֶיךָ
כִּשְׁתִלֵי זֵיתִים, סָבִיב לְשֻׁלְחָנֶךָ: הִנֵּה כִי־כֵן יְבֹרַךְ גָּבֶר יְרֵא יהוה:
יְבָרֶכְךָ יהוה מִצִּיּוֹן, וּרְאֵה בְּטוּב יְרוּשָׁלָםִ, כֹּל יְמֵי חַיֶּיךָ: וּרְאֵה־בָנִים
לְבָנֶיךָ, שָׁלוֹם עַל־יִשְׂרָאֵל:

Some say קדיש יתום *at this point* (*page 1245*).

HAVDALA IN THE SYNAGOGUE

Some say the full Havdala on page 1256.

The Leader takes the cup of wine in his right hand, and says:

Please pay attention, my masters.

Blessed are You, Lord our God, King of the Universe, who creates the fruit of the vine.

On a Motza'ei Shabbat, holding the spice box, the Leader says:

Blessed are You, Lord our God, King of the Universe,
who creates the various spices.

The Leader smells the spices and puts the spice box down.

He lifts his hands toward the flame of the Havdala candle, and says:

Blessed are You, Lord our God, King of the Universe, who creates the lights of fire.

He lifts the cup of wine in his right hand, and says:

Blessed are You, Lord our God, King of the Universe, who distinguishes between sacred and secular, between light and darkness, between Israel and the nations, between the seventh day and the six days of work. Blessed are You, Lord, who distinguishes between sacred and secular.

Stand while saying Aleinu. Bow at ▾.

עָלֵינוּ It is our duty to praise the Master of all,
and ascribe greatness to the Author of creation,
who has not made us like the nations of the lands
nor placed us like the families of the earth;
who has not made our portion like theirs,
nor our destiny like all their multitudes.
(For they worship vanity and emptiness,
and pray to a god who cannot save.)
▾But we bow in worship and thank the Supreme King of kings,
the Holy One, blessed be He,
who extends the heavens and establishes the earth,
whose throne of glory is in the heavens above,
and whose power's Presence is in the highest of heights.

הבדלה בבית הכנסת

Some say the full הבדלה *on page 1257.*

The שליח ציבור *takes the cup of wine in his right hand, and says:*

סַבְרִי מָרָנָן

בָּרוּךְ אַתָּה יהוה אֱלֹהֵינוּ מֶלֶךְ הָעוֹלָם, בּוֹרֵא פְּרִי הַגָּפֶן.

On a מוצאי שבת*, holding the spice box, the* שליח ציבור *says:*

בָּרוּךְ אַתָּה יהוה אֱלֹהֵינוּ מֶלֶךְ הָעוֹלָם, בּוֹרֵא מִינֵי בְשָׂמִים.

The שליח ציבור *smells the spices and puts the spice box down.*

He lifts his hands toward the flame of the הבדלה *candle, and says:*

בָּרוּךְ אַתָּה יהוה אֱלֹהֵינוּ מֶלֶךְ הָעוֹלָם, בּוֹרֵא מְאוֹרֵי הָאֵשׁ.

He lifts the cup of wine in his right hand, and says:

בָּרוּךְ אַתָּה יהוה אֱלֹהֵינוּ מֶלֶךְ הָעוֹלָם, הַמַּבְדִּיל בֵּין קֹדֶשׁ לְחֹל, בֵּין אוֹר לְחֹשֶׁךְ, בֵּין יִשְׂרָאֵל לָעַמִּים, בֵּין יוֹם הַשְּׁבִיעִי לְשֵׁשֶׁת יְמֵי הַמַּעֲשֶׂה. בָּרוּךְ אַתָּה יהוה, הַמַּבְדִּיל בֵּין קֹדֶשׁ לְחֹל.

Stand while saying עָלֵינוּ*. Bow at* ▼.

עָלֵינוּ לְשַׁבֵּחַ לַאֲדוֹן הַכֹּל, לָתֵת גְּדֻלָּה לְיוֹצֵר בְּרֵאשִׁית
שֶׁלֹּא עָשָׂנוּ כְּגוֹיֵי הָאֲרָצוֹת, וְלֹא שָׂמָנוּ כְּמִשְׁפְּחוֹת הָאֲדָמָה
שֶׁלֹּא שָׂם חֶלְקֵנוּ כָּהֶם וְגוֹרָלֵנוּ כְּכָל הֲמוֹנָם.
(שֶׁהֵם מִשְׁתַּחֲוִים לְהֶבֶל וָרִיק וּמִתְפַּלְלִים אֶל אֵל לֹא יוֹשִׁיעַ.)
▼וַאֲנַחְנוּ כּוֹרְעִים וּמִשְׁתַּחֲוִים וּמוֹדִים
לִפְנֵי מֶלֶךְ מַלְכֵי הַמְּלָכִים, הַקָּדוֹשׁ בָּרוּךְ הוּא
שֶׁהוּא נוֹטֶה שָׁמַיִם וְיוֹסֵד אָרֶץ
וּמוֹשַׁב יְקָרוֹ בַּשָּׁמַיִם מִמַּעַל
וּשְׁכִינַת עֻזּוֹ בְּגָבְהֵי מְרוֹמִים.

He is our God; there is no other.
Truly He is our King, there is none else,
as it is written in His Torah:
"You shall know and take to heart this day that the LORD is God, *Deut. 4*
in the heavens above and on the earth below.
There is no other."

Therefore, we place our hope in You, LORD our God,
that we may soon see the glory of Your power,
when You will remove abominations from the earth,
and idols will be utterly destroyed,
when the world will be perfected
under the sovereignty of the Almighty,
when all humanity will call on Your name,
to turn all the earth's wicked toward You.
All the world's inhabitants will realize and know
that to You every knee must bow and every tongue swear loyalty.
Before You, LORD our God, they will kneel and bow down
and give honor to Your glorious name.
They will all accept the yoke of Your kingdom,
and You will reign over them soon and for ever.
For the kingdom is Yours,
and to all eternity You will reign in glory,
as it is written in Your Torah:
"The LORD will reign for ever and ever." *Ex. 15*
▸ And it is said:
"Then the LORD shall be King over all the earth; *Zech. 14*
on that day the LORD shall be One and His name One."

Some add:
Have no fear of sudden terror or of the ruin when it overtakes the wicked. *Prov. 3*
Devise your strategy, but it will be thwarted; propose your plan, *Is. 8*
but it will not stand, for God is with us. When you grow old, I will still be the same. *Is. 46*
When your hair turns gray, I will still carry you. I made you, I will bear you,
I will carry you, and I will rescue you.

הוּא אֱלֹהֵינוּ, אֵין עוֹד.
אֱמֶת מַלְכֵּנוּ, אֶפֶס זוּלָתוֹ, כַּכָּתוּב בְּתוֹרָתוֹ
וְיָדַעְתָּ הַיּוֹם וַהֲשֵׁבֹתָ אֶל־לְבָבֶךָ דברים ד
כִּי יהוה הוּא הָאֱלֹהִים בַּשָּׁמַיִם מִמַּעַל וְעַל־הָאָרֶץ מִתָּחַת
אֵין עוֹד:

עַל כֵּן נְקַוֶּה לְּךָ יהוה אֱלֹהֵינוּ, לִרְאוֹת מְהֵרָה בְּתִפְאֶרֶת עֻזֶּךָ
לְהַעֲבִיר גִּלּוּלִים מִן הָאָרֶץ, וְהָאֱלִילִים כָּרוֹת יִכָּרֵתוּן
לְתַקֵּן עוֹלָם בְּמַלְכוּת שַׁדַּי.
וְכָל בְּנֵי בָשָׂר יִקְרְאוּ בִשְׁמֶךָ לְהַפְנוֹת אֵלֶיךָ כָּל רִשְׁעֵי אָרֶץ.
יַכִּירוּ וְיֵדְעוּ כָּל יוֹשְׁבֵי תֵבֵל
כִּי לְךָ תִּכְרַע כָּל בֶּרֶךְ, תִּשָּׁבַע כָּל לָשׁוֹן.
לְפָנֶיךָ יהוה אֱלֹהֵינוּ יִכְרְעוּ וְיִפֹּלוּ, וְלִכְבוֹד שִׁמְךָ יְקָר יִתֵּנוּ
וִיקַבְּלוּ כֻלָּם אֶת עֹל מַלְכוּתֶךָ
וְתִמְלֹךְ עֲלֵיהֶם מְהֵרָה לְעוֹלָם וָעֶד.
כִּי הַמַּלְכוּת שֶׁלְּךָ הִיא וּלְעוֹלְמֵי עַד תִּמְלֹךְ בְּכָבוֹד
כַּכָּתוּב בְּתוֹרָתֶךָ
יהוה יִמְלֹךְ לְעֹלָם וָעֶד: שמות טו
◂ וְנֶאֱמַר, וְהָיָה יהוה לְמֶלֶךְ עַל־כָּל־הָאָרֶץ זכריה יד
בַּיּוֹם הַהוּא יִהְיֶה יהוה אֶחָד וּשְׁמוֹ אֶחָד:

Some add:
אַל־תִּירָא מִפַּחַד פִּתְאֹם וּמִשֹּׁאַת רְשָׁעִים כִּי תָבֹא: משלי ג
עֻצוּ עֵצָה וְתֻפָר, דַּבְּרוּ דָבָר וְלֹא יָקוּם, כִּי עִמָּנוּ אֵל: ישעיה ח
וְעַד־זִקְנָה אֲנִי הוּא, וְעַד־שֵׂיבָה אֲנִי אֶסְבֹּל ישעיה מו
אֲנִי עָשִׂיתִי וַאֲנִי אֶשָּׂא וַאֲנִי אֶסְבֹּל וַאֲמַלֵּט:

MOURNER'S KADDISH

The following prayer requires the presence of a minyan.
A transliteration can be found on page 1375.

Mourner: יִתְגַּדַּל Magnified and sanctified
may His great name be,
in the world He created by His will.
May He establish His kingdom
in your lifetime and in your days,
and in the lifetime of all the house of Israel,
swiftly and soon –
and say: Amen.

All: May His great name be blessed for ever and all time.

Mourner: Blessed and praised,
glorified and exalted,
raised and honored,
uplifted and lauded
be the name of the Holy One,
blessed be He,
beyond any blessing, song,
praise and consolation
uttered in the world –
and say: Amen.

May there be great peace from heaven,
and life for us and all Israel –
and say: Amen.

Bow, take three steps back, as if taking leave of the Divine Presence, then bow, first left, then right, then center, while saying:

May He who makes peace in His high places,
make peace for us and all Israel –
and say: Amen.

קדיש יתום

The following prayer requires the presence of a מנין.
A transliteration can be found on page 1375.

אבל: יִתְגַּדַּל וְיִתְקַדַּשׁ שְׁמֵהּ רַבָּא (קהל: אָמֵן)
בְּעָלְמָא דִּי בְרָא כִרְעוּתֵהּ
וְיַמְלִיךְ מַלְכוּתֵהּ
בְּחַיֵּיכוֹן וּבְיוֹמֵיכוֹן וּבְחַיֵּי דְכָל בֵּית יִשְׂרָאֵל
בַּעֲגָלָא וּבִזְמַן קָרִיב
וְאִמְרוּ אָמֵן. (קהל: אָמֵן)

קהל ואבל: יְהֵא שְׁמֵהּ רַבָּא מְבָרַךְ לְעָלַם וּלְעָלְמֵי עָלְמַיָּא.

אבל: יִתְבָּרַךְ וְיִשְׁתַּבַּח וְיִתְפָּאַר
וְיִתְרוֹמַם וְיִתְנַשֵּׂא וְיִתְהַדָּר וְיִתְעַלֶּה וְיִתְהַלָּל
שְׁמֵהּ דְּקֻדְשָׁא בְּרִיךְ הוּא (קהל: בְּרִיךְ הוּא)
לְעֵלָּא מִן כָּל בִּרְכָתָא וְשִׁירָתָא, תֻּשְׁבְּחָתָא וְנֶחֱמָתָא
דַּאֲמִירָן בְּעָלְמָא
וְאִמְרוּ אָמֵן. (קהל: אָמֵן)

יְהֵא שְׁלָמָא רַבָּא מִן שְׁמַיָּא
וְחַיִּים, עָלֵינוּ וְעַל כָּל יִשְׂרָאֵל
וְאִמְרוּ אָמֵן. (קהל: אָמֵן)

Bow, take three steps back, as if taking leave of the Divine Presence,
then bow, first left, then right, then center, while saying:

עֹשֶׂה שָׁלוֹם בִּמְרוֹמָיו
הוּא יַעֲשֶׂה שָׁלוֹם עָלֵינוּ וְעַל כָּל יִשְׂרָאֵל
וְאִמְרוּ אָמֵן. (קהל: אָמֵן)

לְדָוִד By David. The LORD is my light and my salvation – whom then shall I fear? The LORD is the stronghold of my life – of whom shall I be afraid? When evil men close in on me to devour my flesh, it is they, my enemies and foes, who stumble and fall. Should an army besiege me, my heart would not fear. Should war break out against me, still I would be confident. One thing I ask of the LORD, only this do I seek: to live in the House of the LORD all the days of my life, to gaze on the beauty of the LORD and worship in His Temple. For He will keep me safe in His pavilion on the day of trouble. He will hide me under the cover of His tent. He will set me high upon a rock. Now my head is high above my enemies who surround me. I will sacrifice in His tent with shouts of joy. I will sing and chant praises to the LORD. LORD, hear my voice when I call. Be gracious to me and answer me. On Your behalf my heart says, "Seek My face." Your face, LORD, will I seek. Do not hide Your face from me. Do not turn Your servant away in anger. You have been my help. Do not reject or forsake me, God, my Savior. Were my father and my mother to forsake me, the LORD would take me in. Teach me Your way, LORD, and lead me on a level path, because of my oppressors. Do not abandon me to the will of my foes, for false witnesses have risen against me, breathing violence. ▸ Were it not for my faith that I shall see the LORD's goodness in the land of the living. Hope in the LORD. Be strong and of good courage, and hope in the LORD! *Ps. 27*

Mourner's Kaddish (*previous page*)

BLESSING OF THE NEW MOON

הַלְלוּיָהּ Halleluya! Praise the LORD from the heavens, praise Him in the heights. Praise Him, all His angels; praise Him, all His hosts. Praise Him, sun and moon; praise Him, all shining stars. Praise Him, highest heavens and the waters above the heavens. Let them praise the name of the LORD, for He commanded and they were created. He established them for ever and all time, issuing a decree that will never change. *Ps. 148*

כִּי־אֶרְאֶה When I see Your heavens, the work of Your fingers, the moon and the stars which You have set in place: What is man that You are mindful of him, the son of man that You care for him? *Ps. 8*

לְדָוִד, יהוה אוֹרִי וְיִשְׁעִי, מִמִּי אִירָא, יהוה מָעוֹז־חַיַּי, מִמִּי אֶפְחָד: תהלים כז
בִּקְרֹב עָלַי מְרֵעִים לֶאֱכֹל אֶת־בְּשָׂרִי, צָרַי וְאֹיְבַי לִי, הֵמָּה כָשְׁלוּ וְנָפָלוּ: אִם־תַּחֲנֶה עָלַי מַחֲנֶה, לֹא־יִירָא לִבִּי, אִם־תָּקוּם עָלַי מִלְחָמָה, בְּזֹאת אֲנִי בוֹטֵחַ: אַחַת שָׁאַלְתִּי מֵאֵת־יהוה, אוֹתָהּ אֲבַקֵּשׁ, שִׁבְתִּי בְּבֵית־יהוה כָּל־יְמֵי חַיַּי, לַחֲזוֹת בְּנֹעַם־יהוה, וּלְבַקֵּר בְּהֵיכָלוֹ: כִּי יִצְפְּנֵנִי בְּסֻכֹּה בְּיוֹם רָעָה, יַסְתִּרֵנִי בְּסֵתֶר אָהֳלוֹ, בְּצוּר יְרוֹמְמֵנִי: וְעַתָּה יָרוּם רֹאשִׁי עַל אֹיְבַי סְבִיבוֹתַי, וְאֶזְבְּחָה בְאָהֳלוֹ זִבְחֵי תְרוּעָה, אָשִׁירָה וַאֲזַמְּרָה לַיהוה: שְׁמַע־יהוה קוֹלִי אֶקְרָא, וְחָנֵּנִי וַעֲנֵנִי: לְךָ אָמַר לִבִּי בַּקְּשׁוּ פָנָי, אֶת־פָּנֶיךָ יהוה אֲבַקֵּשׁ: אַל־תַּסְתֵּר פָּנֶיךָ מִמֶּנִּי, אַל תַּט־בְּאַף עַבְדֶּךָ, עֶזְרָתִי הָיִיתָ, אַל־תִּטְּשֵׁנִי וְאַל־תַּעַזְבֵנִי, אֱלֹהֵי יִשְׁעִי: כִּי־אָבִי וְאִמִּי עֲזָבוּנִי, וַיהוה יַאַסְפֵנִי: הוֹרֵנִי יהוה דַּרְכֶּךָ, וּנְחֵנִי בְּאֹרַח מִישׁוֹר, לְמַעַן שׁוֹרְרָי: אַל־תִּתְּנֵנִי בְּנֶפֶשׁ צָרָי, כִּי קָמוּ־בִי עֵדֵי־שֶׁקֶר, וִיפֵחַ חָמָס: ‹ לוּלֵא הֶאֱמַנְתִּי לִרְאוֹת בְּטוּב־יהוה בְּאֶרֶץ חַיִּים: קַוֵּה אֶל־יהוה, חֲזַק וְיַאֲמֵץ לִבֶּךָ, וְקַוֵּה אֶל־יהוה:

קדיש יתום (*previous page*)

קידוש לבנה

הַלְלוּיָהּ, הַלְלוּ אֶת־יהוה מִן־הַשָּׁמַיִם, הַלְלוּהוּ בַּמְּרוֹמִים: הַלְלוּהוּ תהלים קמח
כָל־מַלְאָכָיו, הַלְלוּהוּ כָּל־צְבָאָו: הַלְלוּהוּ שֶׁמֶשׁ וְיָרֵחַ, הַלְלוּהוּ כָּל־כּוֹכְבֵי אוֹר: הַלְלוּהוּ שְׁמֵי הַשָּׁמָיִם, וְהַמַּיִם אֲשֶׁר מֵעַל הַשָּׁמָיִם: יְהַלְלוּ אֶת־שֵׁם יהוה, כִּי הוּא צִוָּה וְנִבְרָאוּ: וַיַּעֲמִידֵם לָעַד לְעוֹלָם, חָק־נָתַן וְלֹא יַעֲבוֹר:

כִּי־אֶרְאֶה שָׁמֶיךָ מַעֲשֵׂה אֶצְבְּעֹתֶיךָ, יָרֵחַ וְכוֹכָבִים אֲשֶׁר כּוֹנָנְתָּה: תהלים ח
מָה־אֱנוֹשׁ כִּי־תִזְכְּרֶנּוּ, וּבֶן־אָדָם כִּי תִפְקְדֶנּוּ:

Look at the moon, then say:

בָּרוּךְ Blessed are You, Lord our God, King of the Universe who by His word created the heavens, and by His breath all their host. He set for them laws and times, so that they should not deviate from their appointed task. They are joyous and glad to perform the will of their Owner, the Worker of truth whose work is truth. To the moon He said that it should renew itself as a crown of beauty for those He carried from the womb [Israel], for they are destined to be renewed like it, and to praise their Creator for the sake of His glorious majesty. Blessed are You, Lord, who renews the months.

The following five verses are each said three times:

Blessed is He who formed you; blessed is He who made you;
blessed is He who owns you; blessed is He who created you.

The following verse is said rising on the toes.

Just as I leap toward you but cannot touch you,
so may none of my enemies be able to touch me to do me harm.

May fear and dread fall upon them; *Ex. 15*
by the power of Your arm may they be still as stone.

May they be still as stone through the power of Your arm,
when dread and fear fall upon them.

David, King of Israel, lives and endures.

Turn to three people and say to each:

Peace upon you.

They respond:

Upon you, peace.

Say three times:

May it be a good sign and a good omen for us and all Israel. Amen.

קוֹל Hark! My beloved! Here he comes, leaping over the mountains, *Song. 2*
bounding over the hills. My beloved is like a gazelle, like a young deer. There he stands outside our wall, peering in through the windows, gazing through the lattices.

Look at the moon, then say:

בָּרוּךְ אַתָּה יהוה אֱלֹהֵינוּ מֶלֶךְ הָעוֹלָם, אֲשֶׁר בְּמַאֲמָרוֹ בָּרָא שְׁחָקִים, וּבְרוּחַ פִּיו כָּל צְבָאָם, חֹק וּזְמַן נָתַן לָהֶם שֶׁלֹּא יְשַׁנּוּ אֶת תַּפְקִידָם. שָׂשִׂים וּשְׂמֵחִים לַעֲשׂוֹת רְצוֹן קוֹנָם, פּוֹעֵל אֱמֶת שֶׁפְּעֻלָּתוֹ אֱמֶת. וְלַלְּבָנָה אָמַר שֶׁתִּתְחַדֵּשׁ, עֲטֶרֶת תִּפְאֶרֶת לַעֲמוּסֵי בָטֶן, שֶׁהֵם עֲתִידִים לְהִתְחַדֵּשׁ כְּמוֹתָהּ וּלְפָאֵר לְיוֹצְרָם עַל שֵׁם כְּבוֹד מַלְכוּתוֹ. בָּרוּךְ אַתָּה יהוה, מְחַדֵּשׁ חֳדָשִׁים.

The following five verses are each said three times:

בָּרוּךְ יוֹצְרֵךְ, בָּרוּךְ עוֹשֵׂךְ, בָּרוּךְ קוֹנֵךְ, בָּרוּךְ בּוֹרְאֵךְ.

The following verse is said rising on the toes.

כְּשֵׁם שֶׁאֲנִי רוֹקֵד כְּנֶגְדֵּךְ וְאֵינִי יָכוֹל לִנְגֹּעַ בָּךְ
כָּךְ לֹא יוּכְלוּ כָּל אוֹיְבַי לִנְגֹּעַ בִּי לְרָעָה.

תִּפֹּל עֲלֵיהֶם אֵימָתָה וָפַחַד, בִּגְדֹל זְרוֹעֲךָ יִדְּמוּ כָּאָבֶן: שמות טו

כָּאָבֶן יִדְּמוּ זְרוֹעֲךָ בִּגְדֹל, וָפַחַד אֵימָתָה עֲלֵיהֶם תִּפֹּל.

דָּוִד מֶלֶךְ יִשְׂרָאֵל חַי וְקַיָּם.

Turn to three people and say to each:

שָׁלוֹם עֲלֵיכֶם.

They respond:

עֲלֵיכֶם שָׁלוֹם.

Say three times:

סִימָן טוֹב וּמַזָּל טוֹב יְהֵא לָנוּ וּלְכָל יִשְׂרָאֵל, אָמֵן.

קוֹל דּוֹדִי הִנֵּה־זֶה בָּא, מְדַלֵּג עַל־הֶהָרִים, מְקַפֵּץ עַל־הַגְּבָעוֹת: שיר השירים ב
דּוֹמֶה דוֹדִי לִצְבִי אוֹ לְעֹפֶר הָאַיָּלִים, הִנֵּה־זֶה עוֹמֵד אַחַר כָּתְלֵנוּ, מַשְׁגִּיחַ מִן־הַחַלֹּנוֹת, מֵצִיץ מִן־הַחֲרַכִּים:

שִׁיר לַמַּעֲלוֹת A song of ascents. I lift my eyes up to the hills; from where *Ps. 121* will my help come? My help comes from the LORD, Maker of heaven and earth. He will not let your foot stumble; He who guards you does not slumber. See: the Guardian of Israel neither slumbers nor sleeps. The LORD is your Guardian; the LORD is your Shade at your right hand. The sun will not strike you by day, nor the moon by night. The LORD will guard you from all harm; He will guard your life. The LORD will guard your going and coming, now and for evermore.

הַלְלוּיָהּ Halleluya! Praise God in His holy place; praise Him in the heav- *Ps. 150* ens of His power. Praise Him for His mighty deeds; praise Him for His surpassing greatness. Praise Him with blasts of the ram's horn; praise Him with the harp and lyre. Praise Him with timbrel and dance; praise Him with strings and flute. Praise Him with clashing cymbals; praise Him with resounding cymbals. Let all that breathes praise the LORD. Halleluya! Let all that breathes praise the LORD. Halleluya!

תָּנָא In the academy of Rabbi Yishmael it was taught: Were the people of *Sanhedrin 42a* Israel privileged to greet the presence of their heavenly Father only once a month, it would have been sufficient for them. Abaye said: Therefore it [the blessing of the moon] should be said standing. Who is this coming *Song. 8* up from the desert, leaning on her beloved?

וִיהִי May it be Your will, LORD my God and God of my ancestors, to make good the deficiency of the moon, so that it is no longer in its diminished state. May the light of the moon be like the light of the sun and like the light of the seven days of creation as it was before it was diminished, as it says, "The two great luminaries." And may there be fulfilled for us the *Gen. 1* verse: "They shall seek the LORD their God, and David their king." Amen. *Hos. 3*

לַמְנַצֵּחַ For the conductor of music. With stringed instruments, a psalm. *Ps. 67* A song. May God be gracious to us and bless us. May He make His face shine on us, Selah. Then will Your way be known on earth, Your salvation among all the nations. Let the peoples praise You, God; let all peoples praise You. Let nations rejoice and sing for joy, for You judge the peoples with equity, and guide the nations of the earth, Selah. Let the peoples praise You, God; let all peoples praise You. The earth has yielded its harvest. May God, our God, bless us. God will bless us, and all the ends of the earth will fear Him.

שִׁיר לַמַּעֲלוֹת, אֶשָּׂא עֵינַי אֶל־הֶהָרִים, מֵאַיִן יָבֹא עֶזְרִי: עֶזְרִי מֵעִם תהלים קכא
יהוה, עֹשֵׂה שָׁמַיִם וָאָרֶץ: אַל־יִתֵּן לַמּוֹט רַגְלֶךָ, אַל־יָנוּם שֹׁמְרֶךָ:
הִנֵּה לֹא־יָנוּם וְלֹא יִישָׁן שׁוֹמֵר יִשְׂרָאֵל: יהוה שֹׁמְרֶךָ, יהוה צִלְּךָ
עַל־יַד יְמִינֶךָ: יוֹמָם הַשֶּׁמֶשׁ לֹא־יַכֶּכָּה, וְיָרֵחַ בַּלָּיְלָה: יהוה יִשְׁמָרְךָ
מִכָּל־רָע, יִשְׁמֹר אֶת־נַפְשֶׁךָ: יהוה יִשְׁמָר־צֵאתְךָ וּבוֹאֶךָ, מֵעַתָּה
וְעַד־עוֹלָם:

הַלְלוּיָהּ, הַלְלוּ־אֵל בְּקָדְשׁוֹ, הַלְלְוּהוּ בִּרְקִיעַ עֻזּוֹ: הַלְלְוּהוּ בִגְבוּרֹתָיו, תהלים קנ
הַלְלְוּהוּ כְּרֹב גֻּדְלוֹ: הַלְלְוּהוּ בְּתֵקַע שׁוֹפָר, הַלְלְוּהוּ בְּנֵבֶל וְכִנּוֹר:
הַלְלְוּהוּ בְתֹף וּמָחוֹל, הַלְלְוּהוּ בְּמִנִּים וְעֻגָב: הַלְלְוּהוּ בְצִלְצְלֵי־שָׁמַע,
הַלְלְוּהוּ בְּצִלְצְלֵי תְרוּעָה: כֹּל הַנְּשָׁמָה תְּהַלֵּל יָהּ, הַלְלוּיָהּ:

תָּנָא דְבֵי רַבִּי יִשְׁמָעֵאל: אִלְמָלֵי לֹא זָכוּ יִשְׂרָאֵל אֶלָּא לְהַקְבִּיל פְּנֵי סנהדרין מב.
אֲבִיהֶם שֶׁבַּשָּׁמַיִם פַּעַם אַחַת בַּחֹדֶשׁ, דַּיָּם. אָמַר אַבַּיֵּי: הִלְכָּךְ צָרִיךְ
לְמֵימְרָא מְעֻמָּד. מִי זֹאת עֹלָה מִן־הַמִּדְבָּר, מִתְרַפֶּקֶת עַל־דּוֹדָהּ: שיר השירים ח

וִיהִי רָצוֹן מִלְּפָנֶיךָ יהוה אֱלֹהַי וֵאלֹהֵי אֲבוֹתַי, לְמַלֹּאת פְּגִימַת
הַלְּבָנָה וְלֹא יִהְיֶה בָּהּ שׁוּם מִעוּט. וִיהִי אוֹר הַלְּבָנָה כְּאוֹר הַחַמָּה
וּכְאוֹר שִׁבְעַת יְמֵי בְרֵאשִׁית, כְּמוֹ שֶׁהָיְתָה קֹדֶם מִעוּטָהּ, שֶׁנֶּאֱמַר:
אֶת־שְׁנֵי הַמְּאֹרֹת הַגְּדֹלִים: וְיִתְקַיֵּם בָּנוּ מִקְרָא שֶׁכָּתוּב: וּבִקְשׁוּ בראשית א הושע ג
אֶת־יהוה אֱלֹהֵיהֶם וְאֵת דָּוִיד מַלְכָּם: אָמֵן.

לַמְנַצֵּחַ בִּנְגִינֹת, מִזְמוֹר שִׁיר: אֱלֹהִים יְחָנֵּנוּ וִיבָרְכֵנוּ, יָאֵר פָּנָיו אִתָּנוּ תהלים סז
סֶלָה: לָדַעַת בָּאָרֶץ דַּרְכֶּךָ, בְּכָל־גּוֹיִם יְשׁוּעָתֶךָ: יוֹדוּךָ עַמִּים אֱלֹהִים,
יוֹדוּךָ עַמִּים כֻּלָּם: יִשְׂמְחוּ וִירַנְּנוּ לְאֻמִּים, כִּי־תִשְׁפֹּט עַמִּים מִישֹׁר,
וּלְאֻמִּים בָּאָרֶץ תַּנְחֵם סֶלָה: יוֹדוּךָ עַמִּים אֱלֹהִים, יוֹדוּךָ עַמִּים כֻּלָּם:
אֶרֶץ נָתְנָה יְבוּלָהּ, יְבָרְכֵנוּ אֱלֹהִים אֱלֹהֵינוּ: יְבָרְכֵנוּ אֱלֹהִים, וְיִירְאוּ
אוֹתוֹ כָּל־אַפְסֵי־אָרֶץ:

Stand while saying Aleinu. Bow at ▼.

עָלֵינוּ It is our duty to praise the Master of all, and ascribe greatness to the Author of creation, who has not made us like the nations of the lands nor placed us like the families of the earth; who has not made our portion like theirs, nor our destiny like all their multitudes. (For they worship vanity and emptiness, and pray to a god who cannot save.) ▼But we bow in worship and thank the Supreme King of kings, the Holy One, blessed be He, who extends the heavens and establishes the earth, whose throne of glory is in the heavens above, and whose power's Presence is in the highest of heights. He is our God; there is no other. Truly He is our King, there is none else, as it is written in His
Torah: "You shall know and take to heart this day that the LORD is God, in the *Deut. 4*
heavens above and on the earth below. There is no other."

Therefore, we place our hope in You, LORD our God, that we may soon see the glory of Your power, when You will remove abominations from the earth, and idols will be utterly destroyed, when the world will be perfected under the sovereignty of the Almighty, when all humanity will call on Your name, to turn all the earth's wicked toward You. All the world's inhabitants will realize and know that to You every knee must bow and every tongue swear loyalty. Before You, LORD our God, they will kneel and bow down and give honor to Your glorious name. They will all accept the yoke of Your kingdom, and You will reign over them soon and for ever. For the kingdom is Yours, and to all
eternity You will reign in glory, as it is written in Your Torah: "The LORD will *Ex. 15*
reign for ever and ever." ▸ And it is said: "Then the LORD shall be King over all *Zech. 14*
the earth; on that day the LORD shall be One and His name One."

Some add:

Have no fear of sudden terror or of the ruin when it overtakes the wicked. Devise your *Prov. 3* *Is. 8*
strategy, but it will be thwarted; propose your plan, but it will not stand, for God is with
us. When you grow old, I will still be the same. When your hair turns gray, I will still *Is. 46*
carry you. I made you, I will bear you, I will carry you, and I will rescue you.

MOURNER'S KADDISH

The following prayer requires the presence of a minyan.
A transliteration can be found on page 1375.

Mourner: יִתְגַּדַּל Magnified and sanctified may His great name be,
in the world He created by His will.
May He establish His kingdom
in your lifetime and in your days,
and in the lifetime of all the house of Israel,
swiftly and soon – and say: Amen.

Stand while saying עָלֵינוּ*. Bow at* ‎*.

עָלֵינוּ לְשַׁבֵּחַ לַאֲדוֹן הַכֹּל, לָתֵת גְּדֻלָּה לְיוֹצֵר בְּרֵאשִׁית, שֶׁלֹּא עָשָׂנוּ כְּגוֹיֵי הָאֲרָצוֹת, וְלֹא שָׂמָנוּ כְּמִשְׁפְּחוֹת הָאֲדָמָה, שֶׁלֹּא שָׂם חֶלְקֵנוּ כָּהֶם וְגוֹרָלֵנוּ כְּכָל הֲמוֹנָם. (שֶׁהֵם מִשְׁתַּחֲוִים לְהֶבֶל וָרִיק וּמִתְפַּלְלִים אֶל אֵל לֹא יוֹשִׁיעַ.) *וַאֲנַחְנוּ כּוֹרְעִים וּמִשְׁתַּחֲוִים וּמוֹדִים, לִפְנֵי מֶלֶךְ מַלְכֵי הַמְּלָכִים, הַקָּדוֹשׁ בָּרוּךְ הוּא, שֶׁהוּא נוֹטֶה שָׁמַיִם וְיוֹסֵד אָרֶץ, וּמוֹשַׁב יְקָרוֹ בַּשָּׁמַיִם מִמַּעַל, וּשְׁכִינַת עֻזּוֹ בְּגָבְהֵי מְרוֹמִים. הוּא אֱלֹהֵינוּ, אֵין עוֹד. אֱמֶת מַלְכֵּנוּ, אֶפֶס
זוּלָתוֹ, כַּכָּתוּב בְּתוֹרָתוֹ, וְיָדַעְתָּ הַיּוֹם וַהֲשֵׁבֹתָ אֶל־לְבָבֶךָ, כִּי יהוה הוּא דברים ד
הָאֱלֹהִים בַּשָּׁמַיִם מִמַּעַל וְעַל־הָאָרֶץ מִתָּחַת, אֵין עוֹד:

עַל כֵּן נְקַוֶּה לְּךָ יהוה אֱלֹהֵינוּ, לִרְאוֹת מְהֵרָה בְּתִפְאֶרֶת עֻזֶּךָ, לְהַעֲבִיר גִּלּוּלִים מִן הָאָרֶץ, וְהָאֱלִילִים כָּרוֹת יִכָּרֵתוּן, לְתַקֵּן עוֹלָם בְּמַלְכוּת שַׁדַּי. וְכָל בְּנֵי בָשָׂר יִקְרְאוּ בִשְׁמֶךָ לְהַפְנוֹת אֵלֶיךָ כָּל רִשְׁעֵי אָרֶץ. יַכִּירוּ וְיֵדְעוּ כָּל יוֹשְׁבֵי תֵבֵל, כִּי לְךָ תִּכְרַע כָּל בֶּרֶךְ, תִּשָּׁבַע כָּל לָשׁוֹן. לְפָנֶיךָ יהוה אֱלֹהֵינוּ יִכְרְעוּ וְיִפֹּלוּ, וְלִכְבוֹד שִׁמְךָ יְקָר יִתֵּנוּ, וִיקַבְּלוּ כֻלָּם אֶת עֹל מַלְכוּתֶךָ וְתִמְלֹךְ עֲלֵיהֶם מְהֵרָה לְעוֹלָם וָעֶד. כִּי הַמַּלְכוּת שֶׁלְּךָ הִיא וּלְעוֹלְמֵי עַד תִּמְלֹךְ
בְּכָבוֹד, כַּכָּתוּב בְּתוֹרָתֶךָ, יהוה יִמְלֹךְ לְעֹלָם וָעֶד: ‹ וְנֶאֱמַר, וְהָיָה יהוה שמות טו / זכריה יד
לְמֶלֶךְ עַל־כָּל־הָאָרֶץ, בַּיּוֹם הַהוּא יִהְיֶה יהוה אֶחָד וּשְׁמוֹ אֶחָד:

Some add:

אַל־תִּירָא מִפַּחַד פִּתְאֹם וּמִשֹּׁאַת רְשָׁעִים כִּי תָבֹא: עֻצוּ עֵצָה וְתֻפָר, דַּבְּרוּ דָבָר וְלֹא משלי ג / ישעיה ח
יָקוּם, כִּי עִמָּנוּ אֵל: וְעַד־זִקְנָה אֲנִי הוּא, וְעַד־שֵׂיבָה אֲנִי אֶסְבֹּל, אֲנִי עָשִׂיתִי וַאֲנִי אֶשָּׂא ישעיה מו
וַאֲנִי אֶסְבֹּל וַאֲמַלֵּט:

קדיש יתום

The following prayer requires the presence of a מנין*.*
A transliteration can be found on page 1375.

אבל: יִתְגַּדַּל וְיִתְקַדַּשׁ שְׁמֵהּ רַבָּא (קהל: אָמֵן)
בְּעָלְמָא דִּי בְרָא כִרְעוּתֵהּ
וְיַמְלִיךְ מַלְכוּתֵהּ
בְּחַיֵּיכוֹן וּבְיוֹמֵיכוֹן וּבְחַיֵּי דְכָל בֵּית יִשְׂרָאֵל
בַּעֲגָלָא וּבִזְמַן קָרִיב, וְאִמְרוּ אָמֵן. (קהל: אָמֵן)

All: May His great name be blessed for ever and all time.

Mourner: Blessed and praised,
glorified and exalted,
raised and honored,
uplifted and lauded
be the name of the Holy One,
blessed be He,
beyond any blessing,
song, praise and consolation
uttered in the world –
and say: Amen.

May there be great peace from heaven,
and life for us and all Israel –
and say: Amen.

Bow, take three steps back, as if taking leave of the Divine Presence, then bow, first left, then right, then center, while saying:

May He who makes peace in His high places,
make peace for us and all Israel –
and say: Amen.

All sing:

טוֹבִים Good are the radiant stars our God created;
He formed them with knowledge,
understanding and deliberation.
He gave them strength and might
to rule throughout the world.

Full of splendor, radiating light,
beautiful is their splendor throughout the world.
Glad as they go forth, joyous as they return,
they fulfill with awe their Creator's will.

Glory and honor they give to His name,
jubilation and song at the mention of His majesty.
He called the sun into being and it shone with light.
He looked and fashioned the form of the moon.

קהל ואבל: יְהֵא שְׁמֵהּ רַבָּא מְבָרַךְ לְעָלַם וּלְעָלְמֵי עָלְמַיָּא.

אבל: יִתְבָּרַךְ וְיִשְׁתַּבַּח וְיִתְפָּאַר
וְיִתְרוֹמַם וְיִתְנַשֵּׂא וְיִתְהַדָּר וְיִתְעַלֶּה וְיִתְהַלָּל
שְׁמֵהּ דְּקֻדְשָׁא בְּרִיךְ הוּא (קהל: בְּרִיךְ הוּא)
לְעֵלָּא מִן כָּל בִּרְכָתָא וְשִׁירָתָא, תֻּשְׁבְּחָתָא וְנֶחֱמָתָא
דַּאֲמִירָן בְּעָלְמָא, וְאִמְרוּ אָמֵן. (קהל: אָמֵן)

יְהֵא שְׁלָמָא רַבָּא מִן שְׁמַיָּא
וְחַיִּים, עָלֵינוּ וְעַל כָּל יִשְׂרָאֵל, וְאִמְרוּ אָמֵן. (קהל: אָמֵן)

Bow, take three steps back, as if taking leave of the Divine Presence, then bow, first left, then right, then center, while saying:

עֹשֶׂה שָׁלוֹם בִּמְרוֹמָיו
הוּא יַעֲשֶׂה שָׁלוֹם עָלֵינוּ וְעַל כָּל יִשְׂרָאֵל, וְאִמְרוּ אָמֵן. (קהל: אָמֵן)

All sing:

טוֹבִים מְאוֹרוֹת שֶׁבָּרָא אֱלֹהֵינוּ
יְצָרָם בְּדַעַת בְּבִינָה וּבְהַשְׂכֵּל
כֹּחַ וּגְבוּרָה נָתַן בָּהֶם
לִהְיוֹת מוֹשְׁלִים בְּקֶרֶב תֵּבֵל.

מְלֵאִים זִיו וּמְפִיקִים נֹגַהּ
נָאֶה זִיוָם בְּכָל הָעוֹלָם
שְׂמֵחִים בְּצֵאתָם וְשָׂשִׂים בְּבוֹאָם
עוֹשִׂים בְּאֵימָה רְצוֹן קוֹנָם.

פְּאֵר וְכָבוֹד נוֹתְנִים לִשְׁמוֹ
צָהֳלָה וְרִנָּה לְזֵכֶר מַלְכוּתוֹ
קָרָא לַשֶּׁמֶשׁ וַיִּזְרַח אוֹר
רָאָה וְהִתְקִין צוּרַת הַלְּבָנָה.

HAVDALA AT HOME

Unless it is Motza'ei Shabbat, the first paragraph is omitted.

Taking a cup of wine in the right hand, say:

הִנֵּה Behold, God is my salvation. I will trust and not be afraid. *Is. 12*
The LORD, the LORD, is my strength and my song.
He has become my salvation.
With joy you will draw water from the springs of salvation.
Salvation is the LORD's; on Your people is Your blessing, Selah. *Ps. 3*
The LORD of hosts is with us, the God of Jacob is our stronghold, Selah. *Ps. 46*
LORD of hosts: happy is the one who trusts in You. *Ps. 84*
LORD, save! May the King answer us on the day we call. *Ps. 20*
For the Jews there was light and gladness, joy and honor – *Esther 8*
so may it be for us.
I will lift the cup of salvation and call on the name of the LORD. *Ps. 116*

When making Havdala for others, add:
Please pay attention, my masters.

Blessed are You, LORD our God, King of the Universe,
who creates the fruit of the vine.

On a Motza'ei Shabbat, hold the spice box and say:

Blessed are You, LORD our God, King of the Universe,
who creates the various spices.

Smell the spices and put the spice box down.

Lift the hands toward the flame of the Havdala candle and say:

Blessed are You, LORD our God, King of the Universe,
who creates the lights of fire.

Holding the cup of wine again in the right hand, say:

בָּרוּךְ Blessed are You, LORD our God, King of the Universe, who distinguishes between sacred and secular, between light and darkness, between Israel and the nations, between the seventh day and the six days of work. Blessed are You, LORD, who distinguishes between sacred and secular.

סדר הבדלה בבית

Unless it is מוצאי שבת*, the first paragraph is omitted.*

Taking a cup of wine in the right hand, say:

הִנֵּה אֵל יְשׁוּעָתִי אֶבְטַח, וְלֹא אֶפְחָד ישעיה יב
כִּי־עָזִּי וְזִמְרָת יָהּ יהוה, וַיְהִי־לִי לִישׁוּעָה:
וּשְׁאַבְתֶּם־מַיִם בְּשָׂשׂוֹן, מִמַּעַיְנֵי הַיְשׁוּעָה:
לַיהוה הַיְשׁוּעָה, עַל־עַמְּךָ בִרְכָתֶךָ סֶּלָה: תהלים ג
יהוה צְבָאוֹת עִמָּנוּ, מִשְׂגָּב לָנוּ אֱלֹהֵי יַעֲקֹב סֶלָה: תהלים מו
יהוה צְבָאוֹת, אַשְׁרֵי אָדָם בֹּטֵחַ בָּךְ: תהלים פד
יהוה הוֹשִׁיעָה, הַמֶּלֶךְ יַעֲנֵנוּ בְיוֹם־קָרְאֵנוּ: תהלים כ
לַיְּהוּדִים הָיְתָה אוֹרָה וְשִׂמְחָה וְשָׂשֹׂן וִיקָר: כֵּן תִּהְיֶה לָּנוּ. אסתר ח
כּוֹס־יְשׁוּעוֹת אֶשָּׂא, וּבְשֵׁם יהוה אֶקְרָא: תהלים קטז

When making הבדלה *for others, add:*

סַבְרִי מָרָנָן

בָּרוּךְ אַתָּה יהוה אֱלֹהֵינוּ מֶלֶךְ הָעוֹלָם, בּוֹרֵא פְּרִי הַגָּפֶן.

On a מוצאי שבת*, hold the spice box and say:*

בָּרוּךְ אַתָּה יהוה אֱלֹהֵינוּ מֶלֶךְ הָעוֹלָם, בּוֹרֵא מִינֵי בְשָׂמִים.

Smell the spices and put the spice box down.

Lift the hands toward the flame of the הבדלה *candle and say:*

בָּרוּךְ אַתָּה יהוה אֱלֹהֵינוּ מֶלֶךְ הָעוֹלָם, בּוֹרֵא מְאוֹרֵי הָאֵשׁ.

Holding the cup of wine again in the right hand, say:

בָּרוּךְ אַתָּה יהוה אֱלֹהֵינוּ מֶלֶךְ הָעוֹלָם, הַמַּבְדִּיל בֵּין קֹדֶשׁ לְחוֹל, בֵּין אוֹר לְחֹשֶׁךְ, בֵּין יִשְׂרָאֵל לָעַמִּים, בֵּין יוֹם הַשְּׁבִיעִי לְשֵׁשֶׁת יְמֵי הַמַּעֲשֶׂה. בָּרוּךְ אַתָּה יהוה, הַמַּבְדִּיל בֵּין קֹדֶשׁ לְחוֹל.

הַמַּבְדִּיל He who distinguishes between sacred and secular,
may He forgive our sins.
May He multiply our offspring and wealth like the sand,
and like the stars at night.

The day has passed like a palm tree's shadow;
I call on God to fulfill what the watchman said: *Is. 21*
"Morning comes, though now it is night."

Your righteousness is as high as Mount Tabor.
May You pass high over my sins.
[Let them be] like yesterday when it has passed, *Ps. 90*
like a watch in the night.

The time of offerings has passed. Would that I might rest.
I am weary with my sighing, every night I drench [with tears]. *Ps. 6*

Hear my voice; let it not be cast aside.
Open for me the lofty gate.
My head is filled with the dew of dawn, *Song. 5*
my hair with raindrops of the night.

Heed my prayer, revered and awesome One.
When I cry, grant me deliverance at twilight,
as the day fades, or in the darkness of the night. *Prov. 7*

I call to You, LORD: Save me. Make known to me the path of life.
Rescue me from misery before day turns to night.

Cleanse the defilement of my deeds, lest those who torment me say,
"Where is the God who made me, *Job 35*
who gives cause for songs in the night?"

We are in Your hands like clay:
please forgive our sins, light and grave.
Day to day they pour forth speech,
and night to night [they communicate knowledge].

הַמַּבְדִּיל בֵּין קֹדֶשׁ לְחֹל, חַטֹּאתֵינוּ הוּא יִמְחֹל
זַרְעֵנוּ וְכַסְפֵּנוּ יַרְבֶּה כַּחוֹל וְכַכּוֹכָבִים בַּלָּיְלָה.

יוֹם פָּנָה כְּצֵל תֹּמֶר, אֶקְרָא לָאֵל עָלַי גּוֹמֵר
אָמַר שֹׁמֵר, אָתָא בֹקֶר וְגַם־לָיְלָה: ישעיה כא

צִדְקָתְךָ כְּהַר תָּבוֹר, עַל חֲטָאַי עָבוֹר תַּעֲבֹר
כְּיוֹם אֶתְמוֹל כִּי יַעֲבֹר, וְאַשְׁמוּרָה בַלָּיְלָה: תהלים צ

חָלְפָה עוֹנַת מִנְחָתִי, מִי יִתֵּן מְנוּחָתִי
יָגַעְתִּי בְאַנְחָתִי, אַשְׂחֶה בְכָל־לַיְלָה: תהלים ו

קוֹלִי בַּל יֻנְטַל, פְּתַח לִי שַׁעַר הַמְנֻטָּל
שֶׁרֹּאשִׁי נִמְלָא טָל, קְוֻצּוֹתַי רְסִיסֵי לָיְלָה: שיר השירים ה

הֵעָתֵר נוֹרָא וְאָיֹם, אֲשַׁוֵּעַ, תְּנָה פִדְיוֹם
בְּנֶשֶׁף־בְּעֶרֶב יוֹם, בְּאִישׁוֹן לָיְלָה: משלי ז

קְרָאתִיךָ יָהּ, הוֹשִׁיעֵנִי, אֹרַח חַיִּים תּוֹדִיעֵנִי
מִדַּלָּה תְּבַצְּעֵנִי, מִיּוֹם עַד לָיְלָה.

טַהֵר טִנּוּף מַעֲשַׂי, פֶּן יֹאמְרוּ מַכְעִיסַי
אַיֵּה אֱלוֹהַּ עֹשָׂי, נֹתֵן זְמִרוֹת בַּלָּיְלָה: איוב לה

נַחְנוּ בְיָדְךָ כַּחֹמֶר, סְלַח נָא עַל קַל וָחֹמֶר
יוֹם לְיוֹם יַבִּיעַ אֹמֶר, וְלַיְלָה לְּלָיְלָה: תהלים יט

BIRKAT KOHANIM IN ISRAEL

In Israel, the following is said by the Leader during the Repetition of the Amida when Kohanim bless the congregation. If there is more than one Kohen (see see law 97), a member of the congregation calls:

Kohanim!

The Kohanim respond:

Blessed are You, Lord our God, King of the Universe,
who has made us holy with the holiness of Aaron,
and has commanded us to bless His people Israel with love.

The Leader calls word by word, followed by the Kohanim:

יְבָרֶכְךָ May the Lord bless you and protect you. (*Cong:* Amen.) *Num. 6*
May the Lord make His face shine on you
and be gracious to you. (*Cong:* Amen.)
May the Lord turn His face toward you,
and grant you peace. (*Cong:* Amen.)

The Kohanim say:

רִבּוֹנוֹ Master of the Universe: we have done what You have decreed for us. So too may You deal with us as You have promised us. Look down from Your holy dwelling place, from heaven, and bless Your people Israel and the land You have given us as You promised on oath to our ancestors, a land flowing with milk and honey. *Deut. 26*

The congregation says:

אַדִּיר Majestic One on high who dwells in power: You are peace and Your name is peace. May it be Your will to bestow on us and on Your people the house of Israel, life and blessing as a safeguard for peace.

*In Shaharit continue with "Grant peace" on page 708;
In Musaf continue with "Grant peace" on page 980
and in Ne'ila continue with "Grant peace" on page 1186.*

ברכת כהנים בארץ ישראל

In ארץ ישראל*, the following is said by the* שליח ציבור
during the חזרת הש״ץ *when* כהנים *say* ברכת כהנים.
If there is more than one כהן *(see law 97), a member of the* קהל *calls:*

כֹּהֲנִים

The כהנים *respond:*

בָּרוּךְ אַתָּה יהוה אֱלֹהֵינוּ מֶלֶךְ הָעוֹלָם,
אֲשֶׁר קִדְּשָׁנוּ בִּקְדֻשָּׁתוֹ שֶׁל אַהֲרֹן
וְצִוָּנוּ לְבָרֵךְ אֶת עַמּוֹ יִשְׂרָאֵל בְּאַהֲבָה.

The שליח ציבור *calls word by word, followed by the* כהנים:

יְבָרֶכְךָ יהוה וְיִשְׁמְרֶךָ: קהל: אָמֵן במדבר ו
יָאֵר יהוה פָּנָיו אֵלֶיךָ וִיחֻנֶּךָּ: קהל: אָמֵן
יִשָּׂא יהוה פָּנָיו אֵלֶיךָ וְיָשֵׂם לְךָ שָׁלוֹם: קהל: אָמֵן

The קהל *says:*

אַדִּיר בַּמָּרוֹם שׁוֹכֵן בִּגְבוּרָה,
אַתָּה שָׁלוֹם וְשִׁמְךָ שָׁלוֹם.
יְהִי רָצוֹן שֶׁתָּשִׂים עָלֵינוּ וְעַל
כָּל עַמְּךָ בֵּית יִשְׂרָאֵל חַיִּים
וּבְרָכָה לְמִשְׁמֶרֶת שָׁלוֹם.

The כהנים *say:*

רִבּוֹנוֹ שֶׁל עוֹלָם, עָשִׂינוּ מַה שֶּׁגָּזַרְתָּ עָלֵינוּ, אַף אַתָּה
עֲשֵׂה עִמָּנוּ כְּמוֹ שֶׁהִבְטַחְתָּנוּ. הַשְׁקִיפָה מִמְּעוֹן דברים כו
קָדְשְׁךָ מִן־הַשָּׁמַיִם, וּבָרֵךְ אֶת־עַמְּךָ אֶת־יִשְׂרָאֵל,
וְאֵת הָאֲדָמָה אֲשֶׁר נָתַתָּה לָנוּ, כַּאֲשֶׁר נִשְׁבַּעְתָּ
לַאֲבֹתֵינוּ, אֶרֶץ זָבַת חָלָב וּדְבָשׁ:

In שחרית *continue with* שִׂים שָׁלוֹם *on page 709;*
In מוסף *continue with* שִׂים שָׁלוֹם *on page 981*
and in נעילה *continue with* שִׂים שָׁלוֹם *on page 1187.*

סדר העבודה

נוסח ספרד

אַתָּה כּוֹנַנְתָּ עוֹלָם מֵרֹאשׁ / יָסַדְתָּ תֵּבֵל וְהַכֹּל פָּעַלְתָּ, וּבְרִיּוֹת בּוֹ יָצַרְתָּ.
בְּשׁוּרְךָ עוֹלָם תֹּהוּ וָבֹהוּ, וְחֹשֶׁךְ עַל פְּנֵי תְהוֹם
גֵּרַשְׁתָּ אֹפֶל וְהִצַּבְתָּ נֹגַהּ.
גֹּלֶם תַּבְנִיתְךָ מִן הָאֲדָמָה יָצַרְתָּ / וְעַל עֵץ הַדַּעַת אוֹתוֹ הִפְקַדְתָּ.
דְּבָרְךָ זָנַח, וְנִזְנַח מֵעֵדֶן / וְלֹא כִלִּיתוֹ, לְמַעַן יְגִיעַ כַּפֶּיךָ.
הִגְדַּלְתָּ פִּרְיוֹ וּבֵרַכְתָּ זַרְעוֹ / וְהִפְרִיתָם בְּטוּבְךָ וְהוֹשַׁבְתָּם שֶׁקֶט.
וַיִּפְרְקוּ עֹל, וַיֹּאמְרוּ לָאֵל סוּר מִמֶּנּוּ
וַהֲסִירוֹתָ יָד, כְּרֶגַע אֻמְלְלוּ כֶּחָצִיר.
זָכַרְתָּ בְּרִית לְתָמִים בְּדוֹרוֹ / וּבִשְׂכָרוֹ שַׂמְתָּ לָעוֹלָם שְׁאֵרִית.
חֹק בְּרִית קֶשֶׁת לְמַעֲנוֹ כָּרַתָּ / וּבְאַהֲבַת נִיחוֹחוֹ בָּנָיו בֵּרַכְתָּ.
טָעוּ בְעָשְׁרָם וַיִּבְנוּ מִגְדָּל
וַיֹּאמְרוּ לְכוּ וְנַעֲלֶה וְנִבְקַע הָרָקִיעַ לְהִלָּחֵם בּוֹ.
יָחִיד אַב הֲמוֹן, פִּתְאוֹם כְּכוֹכָב
זָרַח מֵאוּר כַּשְׂדִּים לְהָאִיר בַּחֹשֶׁךְ.
כַּעֲסְךָ הֵפֵרְתָּ בְּשׁוּרְךָ פָּעֳלוֹ / וּלְעֵת שֵׂיבָתוֹ לְבָבוֹ חָקַרְתָּ.
לִוְיַת חֵן מִמֶּנּוּ הוֹצֵאתָ / טָלֶה טָהוֹר מִכֶּבֶשׂ נִבְחָר.
מִגִּזְעוֹ אִישׁ תָּם הוֹצֵאתָ / חָתוּם בִּבְרִיתְךָ מֵרֶחֶם לָקַח.
נָתַתָּ לוֹ שְׁנֵים עָשָׂר שְׁבָטִים / אֲהוּבֵי עֶלְיוֹן מִבֶּטֶן נִקְרָאוּ.
שַׂמְתָּ עַל לֵוִי לִוְיַת חֵן וָחֶסֶד / וּמִכָּל אֶחָיו כֶּתֶר לוֹ עִטַּרְתָּ.
עַמְרָם נִבְחַר מִזֶּרַע לֵוִי / אַהֲרֹן קְדוֹשׁ יהוה מִשָּׁרָשָׁיו קִדַּשְׁתָּ.
פְּאֵרְתּוֹ בְּבִגְדֵי שְׂרָד / וּבְקָרְבְּנוֹתָיו הֵפֵר כַּעַסְךָ.
צִיץ וּמְעִיל, חֹשֶׁן וְאֵפוֹד / כְּתֹנֶת וּמִכְנְסֵי בַד, מִצְנֶפֶת וְאַבְנֵט.
קָרְבְּנוֹת פָּרִים וְעוֹלוֹת כְּבָשִׂים / וּשְׁחִיטַת שְׂעִירִים וְנִיחוֹחַ אֵילִים.
רֵיחַ קְטֹרֶת, מִרְקַחַת וּבִעוּר גֶּחָלִים / וּזְרִיקַת דָּם וּסְפִירַת יֹשֶׁר.
שַׁוְעַת קְטֹרֶת וּתְפִלַּת אֱמֶת / וּקְדֻשָּׁתוֹ מְכַפֶּרֶת עֲוֹנוֹתֵינוּ.
תֹּכֶן בּוּץ וַעֲרִיכַת אֶבֶן / מַחְגֹּר בְּכֻלָּם, כְּמַלְאַךְ מִיכָאֵל מְשָׁרֵת.

תַּבְנִית כָּל אֵלֶּה לִכְבוֹד אַהֲרֹן / כְּלִי כַפָּרָה לְיִשְׂרָאֵל שַׂמְתּוֹ
וְעַל יָדוֹ סְלִיחַת הֶעָוֹן נָתַתָּ.

תַּחַת אַהֲרֹן מִגִּזְעוֹ יַעֲמֹד / לְשָׁרֵת לְפָנֶיךָ בְּיוֹם הַסְּלִיחָה.
תּוֹרַת מַעֲשֶׂה וַעֲבוֹדַת הַיּוֹם, שִׁבְעַת יָמִים בִּזְבוּלֵנוּ יִלְמֹד
וּמַזִּין עָלָיו שְׁלִישִׁי וּשְׁבִיעִי.
שְׁלוּמֵי זִקְנֵי עָם, וְחַכְמֵי אֶחָיו הַכֹּהֲנִים
תָּמִיד יְסוֹבְבוּהוּ עַד בֹּא יוֹם הֶעָשׂוֹר, וְאוֹמְרִים לוֹ.
רְאֵה לִפְנֵי מִי אַתָּה נִכְנָס / לִמְקוֹם אֵשׁ, לַהֶבֶת, שַׁלְהֶבֶת.
קְהַל עֲדָתֵנוּ עָלֶיךָ יִסְמֹכוּ / וְעַל יָדֶךָ תְּהֵא סְלִיחָתֵנוּ.
צִוּוּהוּ וְהִרְגִּילוּהוּ עַד בֹּא יוֹם הֶעָשׂוֹר
כְּדֵי שֶׁיְּהֵא מֻרְגָּל בְּסֵדֶר עֲבוֹדָה.
פֵּרְשׂוּ לוֹ סָדִין שֶׁל בּוּץ, בְּהַגִּיעַ עֵת שְׁחִיטַת כֶּבֶשׂ הַתָּמִיד
לַעֲשׂוֹת מְחִצָּה בֵּינוֹ וּבֵין הָעָם.
עוֹשֶׂה מִצְוָה בְּאֵימָה וּבְיִרְאָה / וּבוֹדֵק עַצְמוֹ מֵחוֹצְצֵי טְבִילָה.
שָׁשׂ עַל מִצְוָה לְקַיֵּם דָּתוֹ, וּפָשַׁט בִּגְדֵי חֹל
וְיָרַד וְטָבַל וְעָלָה וְנִסְתַּפַּג כְּמוֹ שֶׁנִּזְהָר.
נָתְנוּ לוֹ בִּגְדֵי זָהָב וְלָבַשׁ / וְקִדֵּשׁ יָדָיו וְרַגְלָיו מִקִּיתוֹן שֶׁל זָהָב.
מִיָּד מְקַבֵּל אֶת כֶּבֶשׂ הַתָּמִיד
וְשׁוֹחֵט בּוֹ רֹב שְׁנַיִם, וּמַנִּיחַ לְאַחֵר לִגְמֹר הַשְּׁחִיטָה
וּמְקַבֵּל אֶת הַדָּם, וְזוֹרְקוֹ עַל הַמִּזְבֵּחַ כְּמִצְוָתוֹ.
לִפְנִים יִכָּנֵס לְהֵיטִיב חָמֵשׁ נֵרוֹת וּלְהַקְטִיר קְטֹרֶת הַבֹּקֶר
וּלְהֵיטִיב אֶת שְׁתֵּי הַנֵּרוֹת הַנִּשְׁאָרוֹת
וְיָצָא וְהִקְרִיב אֶת הָרֹאשׁ וְאֶת הָאֵבָרִים כְּמִצְוָתָן.
כְּכָל יוֹם, יַעֲשֶׂה מִנְחַת חֲבִתִּין
וִינַסֵּךְ אֶת הַיַּיִן בְּכָל כְּלִי יֹשֶׁר
וְאַחַר הַתָּמִיד מַקְרִיב פַּר הָעוֹלָה
וְשִׁבְעַת הַכְּבָשִׂים שֶׁל מוּסַף הַיּוֹם
וּמִנְחָתָם וְנִסְכֵּיהֶם כְּמִשְׁפָּטָם.

בשבת: וּבְיוֹם הַשַּׁבָּת מַקְרִיב קֹדֶם מוּסַף הַיּוֹם
שְׁנֵי כְבָשִׂים שֶׁל מוּסַף שַׁבָּת וּמִנְחָתָם
וְאַחַר כָּךְ מְסַדֵּר לֶחֶם הַפָּנִים, וּמַקְרִיב שְׁנֵי בָזִיכֵי לְבוֹנָה
וּמְנַסֵּךְ הַיַּיִן כְּהִלְכָתוֹ.

יָבֹא מִיָּד לְבֵית הַפַּרְוָה, וּבַקֹּדֶשׁ הָיְתָה
וְיִפְרְשׂוּ לוֹ סָדִין שֶׁל בּוּץ בֵּינוֹ לְבֵין הָעָם כְּבָרִאשׁוֹנָה.
טֶרֶם יִפְשֹׁט בִּגְדֵי זָהָב / מְקַדֵּשׁ בִּנְקִיּוּת יָדָיו וְרַגְלָיו.
חָל וּפָשַׁט בִּגְדֵי זָהָב / יָרַד וְטָבַל כְּמוֹ שֶׁהִזְהַר, וְעָלָה וְנִסְתַּפָּג.
זְהָבִים מַעֲבִיר, וּלְבָנִים לוֹבֵשׁ / שֶׁעֲבוֹדַת הַיּוֹם בְּבִגְדֵי לָבָן.
וּמִהֵר וְקִדֵּשׁ יָדָיו וְרַגְלָיו, וּבָא לוֹ תְּחִלָּה אֵצֶל פָּרוֹ
וּפָרוֹ הָיָה עוֹמֵד בַּצָּפוֹן כְּנֶגֶד בֵּין הָאוּלָם וְלַמִּזְבֵּחַ
רֹאשׁוֹ לְדָרוֹם וּפָנָיו לְמַעֲרָב
וְהַכֹּהֵן עוֹמֵד בְּמִזְרָח וּפָנָיו לְמַעֲרָב.
◂ הוּא עוֹמֵד בְּאֵימָה לִפְנֵי אֵל עֶלְיוֹן, וְאוֹמֵר עָלָיו דִּבְרֵי וִדּוּי
וְסָמַךְ שְׁתֵּי יָדָיו עָלָיו, וְהִתְוַדָּה.

וְכָךְ הָיָה אוֹמֵר
אָנָּא הַשֵּׁם / חָטָאתִי, עָוִיתִי, פָּשַׁעְתִּי לְפָנֶיךָ אֲנִי וּבֵיתִי.
אָנָּא בַשֵּׁם / כַּפֶּר נָא לַחֲטָאִים וְלַעֲוֹנוֹת וְלַפְּשָׁעִים
שֶׁחָטָאתִי וְשֶׁעָוִיתִי וְשֶׁפָּשַׁעְתִּי לְפָנֶיךָ אֲנִי וּבֵיתִי.
כַּכָּתוּב בְּתוֹרַת מֹשֶׁה עַבְדֶּךָ מִפִּי כְבוֹדֶךָ
כִּי־בַיּוֹם הַזֶּה יְכַפֵּר עֲלֵיכֶם לְטַהֵר אֶתְכֶם ויקרא טז
מִכֹּל חַטֹּאתֵיכֶם, לִפְנֵי יהוה

וְהַכֹּהֲנִים וְהָעָם הָעוֹמְדִים בָּעֲזָרָה
כְּשֶׁהָיוּ שׁוֹמְעִים אֶת הַשֵּׁם הַנִּכְבָּד וְהַנּוֹרָא
מְפֹרָשׁ יוֹצֵא מִפִּי כֹהֵן גָּדוֹל, בִּקְדֻשָּׁה וּבְטָהֳרָה

At the word כּוֹרְעִים*, the* קהל *and the* שליח ציבור *kneel on the floor (see law 93).*

הָיוּ כּוֹרְעִים וּמִשְׁתַּחֲוִים וּמוֹדִים, וְנוֹפְלִים עַל פְּנֵיהֶם
וְאוֹמְרִים
בָּרוּךְ שֵׁם כְּבוֹד מַלְכוּתוֹ לְעוֹלָם וָעֶד.

All stand and continue:

וְאַף הוּא הָיָה מִתְכַּוֵּן כְּנֶגֶד הַמְבָרְכִים לִגְמֹר אֶת הַשֵּׁם
וְאוֹמֵר, תִּטְהָרוּ.

וְאַתָּה בְּטוּבְךָ מְעוֹרֵר רַחֲמֶיךָ וְסוֹלֵחַ לְאִישׁ חֲסִידֶךָ.

דָּרַךְ וּבָא לוֹ לְמִזְרַח הָעֲזָרָה לִצְפוֹן הַמִּזְבֵּחַ
הַסְּגָן מִימִינוֹ וְרֹאשׁ בֵּית אָב מִשְּׂמֹאלוֹ
וְשָׁם שְׁנֵי שְׂעִירִים, פְּנֵיהֶם לְמַעֲרָב וַאֲחוֹרֵיהֶם לְמִזְרָח
אֶחָד לִימִינוֹ וְאֶחָד לִשְׂמֹאלוֹ
טָרַף בְּקַלְפִּי, וְהֶעֱלָה שְׁנֵי גוֹרָלוֹת.
◂ גּוֹרָל יָמִין כְּשֶׁהוּא שֶׁל שֵׁם / יִתְּנֵהוּ עַל הַשָּׂעִיר וְאוֹמֵר, לַיהוה חַטָּאת.

וְהַכֹּהֲנִים וְהָעָם הָעוֹמְדִים בָּעֲזָרָה
כְּשֶׁהָיוּ שׁוֹמְעִים אֶת הַשֵּׁם הַנִּכְבָּד וְהַנּוֹרָא
מְפֹרָשׁ יוֹצֵא מִפִּי כֹהֵן גָּדוֹל, בִּקְדֻשָּׁה וּבְטָהֳרָה
הָיוּ כּוֹרְעִים וּמִשְׁתַּחֲוִים וְנוֹפְלִים עַל פְּנֵיהֶם
וְאוֹמְרִים
בָּרוּךְ שֵׁם כְּבוֹד מַלְכוּתוֹ לְעוֹלָם וָעֶד.

בִּשְׂעִיר עֲזָאזֵל לְשׁוֹן זְהוֹרִית מִשְׁקַל שְׁתֵּי סְלָעִים, בֵּין קַרְנָיו יִקְשֹׁר
וְיַעֲמִידֵהוּ בְּשַׁעַר הַמִּזְרָח כְּנֶגֶד בֵּית שִׁלּוּחוֹ.
אַף בְּשָׂעִיר שֶׁהוּא שֶׁל שֵׁם
יִקְשֹׁר לָשׁוֹן שֶׁל זְהוֹרִית כְּנֶגֶד בֵּית שְׁחִיטָתוֹ בְּצַוָּאר
וּבָא לוֹ שֵׁנִית אֵצֶל פָּרוֹ
וְאוֹמֵר עָלָיו וִדּוּי בֵּיתוֹ וּוִדּוּי אֶחָיו הַכֹּהֲנִים.
וְסָמַךְ שְׁתֵּי יָדָיו עָלָיו, וְהִתְוַדָּה.

וְכָךְ הָיָה אוֹמֵר

אָנָּא הַשֵּׁם / חָטָאתִי, עָוִיתִי, פָּשַׁעְתִּי לְפָנֶיךָ

אֲנִי וּבֵיתִי וּבְנֵי אַהֲרֹן עַם קְדוֹשֶׁךָ.

אָנָּא בַּשֵּׁם / כַּפֶּר נָא לַחֲטָאִים וְלַעֲוֹנוֹת וְלַפְּשָׁעִים

שֶׁחָטָאתִי וְשֶׁעָוִיתִי וְשֶׁפָּשַׁעְתִּי לְפָנֶיךָ

אֲנִי וּבֵיתִי וּבְנֵי אַהֲרֹן עַם קְדוֹשֶׁךָ.

כַּכָּתוּב בְּתוֹרַת מֹשֶׁה עַבְדֶּךָ מִפִּי כְבוֹדֶךָ

ויקרא טז כִּי־בַיּוֹם הַזֶּה יְכַפֵּר עֲלֵיכֶם לְטַהֵר אֶתְכֶם

מִכֹּל חַטֹּאתֵיכֶם, לִפְנֵי יהוה

וְהַכֹּהֲנִים וְהָעָם הָעוֹמְדִים בָּעֲזָרָה

כְּשֶׁהָיוּ שׁוֹמְעִים אֶת הַשֵּׁם הַנִּכְבָּד וְהַנּוֹרָא

מְפֹרָשׁ יוֹצֵא מִפִּי כֹהֵן גָּדוֹל, בִּקְדֻשָּׁה וּבְטָהֳרָה

At the word כּוֹרְעִים*, the* קהל *and the* שליח ציבור *kneel on the floor (see law 93).*

הָיוּ כּוֹרְעִים וּמִשְׁתַּחֲוִים וּמוֹדִים, וְנוֹפְלִים עַל פְּנֵיהֶם וְאוֹמְרִים

בָּרוּךְ שֵׁם כְּבוֹד מַלְכוּתוֹ לְעוֹלָם וָעֶד.

All stand and continue:

וְאַף הוּא הָיָה מִתְכַּוֵּן כְּנֶגֶד הַמְבָרְכִים לִגְמֹר אֶת הַשֵּׁם וְאוֹמֵר, תִּטְהָרוּ.

וְאַתָּה בְּטוּבְךָ מְעוֹרֵר רַחֲמֶיךָ, וְסוֹלֵחַ לְשֵׁבֶט מְשָׁרְתֶךָ.

אַחַר וִדּוּי שָׁקַד בְּעָצְמָה / לַעֲשׂוֹת חַטָּאתוֹ וְחַטַּאת הָעָם.

בָּדַק סַכִּין, וְשָׁחַט פָּרוֹ רֹב שְׁנַיִם, וּמֵרֵק אַחֵר אֶת הַשְּׁחִיטָה

וְקִבֵּל דָּמוֹ בְּמִזְרָק טָהוֹר.

גַּם לַחֲבֵרוֹ יִתֵּן מִיָּד, לְמָרֵס בְּדָמוֹ כְּדֵי שֶׁלֹּא יִקְרשׁ.

דָּם זֶה הִנִּיחוֹ בְּיַד מִי שֶׁמְּמָרֵס בּוֹ בָּעֲזָרָה
עַל הָרֹבֶד הָרְבִיעִי שֶׁמִּן הַהֵיכָל וּלַחוּץ
וְנָטַל מַחְתָּה שֶׁל זָהָב אָדֹם קַלָּה
מַחֲזֶקֶת שְׁלֹשָׁה קַבִּין, וְיָדָהּ אֲרוּכָּה
וְעָלָה לְרֹאשׁ הַמִּזְבֵּחַ, וּפִנָּה גֶחָלִים
שֶׁמֶּחֱצִיתָן גַּחֶלֶת וּמֶחֱצִיתָן שַׁלְהֶבֶת, אֵילָךְ וְאֵילָךְ
וְחָתָה מִן הַלּוֹחֲשׁוֹת מִצַּד מַעֲרַב הַמִּזְבֵּחַ.
הוֹרִידָהּ מְלֵאָה גַּחֲלֵי אֵשׁ לוֹחֲשׁוֹת
וְהִנִּיחָהּ עַל הָרֹבֶד הָרְבִיעִי שֶׁבָּעֲזָרָה
הוֹצִיאוּ לוֹ כַּף רֵיקָן, וּמַחְתָּה מְלֵאָה קְטֹרֶת דַּקָּה מִן הַדַּקָּה.
וְחָפַן מִמֶּנָּה מְלֹא חָפְנָיו
לֹא מְחוּקוֹת וְלֹא גְדוּשׁוֹת, אֶלָּא טְפוּפוֹת
וְנָתַן לְתוֹךְ הַכַּף
וְנוֹתֵן בִּימִינוֹ הַמַּחְתָּה שֶׁל גֶּחָלִים
וּבִשְׂמֹאלוֹ הַכַּף שֶׁל קְטֹרֶת.
זֵרֵז עַצְמוֹ וְנִכְנַס לְקֹדֶשׁ הַקֳּדָשִׁים עַד שֶׁמַּגִּיעַ לָאָרוֹן
וְהִנִּיחַ הַמַּחְתָּה בֵּין בַּדֵּי הָאָרוֹן
וּבְבַיִת שֵׁנִי מַנִּיחַ עַל אֶבֶן הַשְּׁתִיָּה.
חָפַן כָּל הַקְּטֹרֶת שֶׁבְּכַף בְּחָפְנָיו,
וְנָתַן עַל הַגֶּחָלִים לְצַד מַעֲרָב
וּמַמְתִּין שָׁם עַד שֶׁנִּתְמַלֵּא הַבַּיִת כֻּלּוֹ עָשָׁן.
טָהוֹר לֵב פָּסַע וְשָׁב לַאֲחוֹרָיו
פָּנָיו לַקֹּדֶשׁ וַאֲחוֹרָיו לַהֵיכָל, עַד שֶׁיָּצָא מִן הַפָּרֹכֶת
וּמִתְפַּלֵּל בְּהֵיכָל תְּפִלָּה קְצָרָה סָמוּךְ לַפָּרֹכֶת.

וְכָךְ הָיְתָה תְּפִלָּתוֹ שֶׁל כֹּהֵן גָּדוֹל
יְהִי רָצוֹן מִלְּפָנֶיךָ
יהוה אֱלֹהֵינוּ וֵאלֹהֵי אֲבוֹתֵינוּ

שֶׁתְּהֵא שָׁנָה זוֹ הַבָּאָה עָלֵינוּ
וְעַל כָּל עַמְּךָ בֵּית יִשְׂרָאֵל, בְּכָל מָקוֹם שֶׁהֵם
אִם שְׁחוּנָה גְּשׁוּמָה
וְאַל יִכָּנֵס לְפָנֶיךָ תְּפִלַּת עוֹבְרֵי דְרָכִים לְעִנְיַן הַגֶּשֶׁם
בְּשָׁעָה שֶׁהָעוֹלָם צָרִיךְ לוֹ
וְשֶׁלֹּא יִצְטָרְכוּ עַמְּךָ בֵּית יִשְׂרָאֵל בְּפַרְנָסָה זֶה לָזֶה
וְלֹא לְעַם אַחֵר.
שָׁנָה שֶׁלֹּא תַפִּיל אִשָּׁה פְּרִי בִטְנָהּ
וְשֶׁיִּתְּנוּ עֲצֵי הַשָּׂדֶה אֶת תְּנוּבָתָם
וְלָא יַעֲדֵי עָבֵד שָׁלְטָן מִדְּבֵית יְהוּדָה.

יָצָא וְנָטַל דַּם הַפָּר מִמִּי שֶׁמְּמָרֵס בּוֹ
וְנִכְנַס לְמָקוֹם שֶׁנִּכְנַס, וְעָמַד בְּמָקוֹם שֶׁעָמַד
וְהִזָּה מִמֶּנּוּ לִפְנֵי הַכַּפֹּרֶת בֵּין בַּדֵּי הָאָרוֹן
אַחַת לְמַעְלָה וְשֶׁבַע לְמַטָּה
וְלֹא הָיָה מִתְכַּוֵּן לְהַזּוֹת
לֹא לְמַעְלָה וְלֹא לְמַטָּה, אֶלָּא כְּמַצְלִיף.

וְכָךְ הָיָה מוֹנֶה

The שליח ציבור, *followed by the* קהל (*in some congregations, all in unison*):

אַחַת — אַחַת וְאַחַת
אַחַת וּשְׁתַּיִם — אַחַת וְשָׁלֹשׁ
אַחַת וְאַרְבַּע — אַחַת וְחָמֵשׁ
אַחַת וָשֵׁשׁ — אַחַת וָשֶׁבַע.

All:

כְּצֵאתוֹ הֵבִיאוּ לוֹ שְׂעִיר חַטָּאת / שְׁחָטוֹ וְקִבֵּל דָּמוֹ בְּמִזְרָק טָהוֹר.
לִפְנִים יִכָּנֵס לְהַזּוֹת מִדָּמוֹ בֵּין שְׁנֵי בַדֵּי הָאָרוֹן, כְּסֵדֶר דַּם הַפָּר

אַחַת לְמַעְלָה וְשֶׁבַע לְמַטָּה
וְלֹא הָיָה מִתְכַּוֵּן לְהַזּוֹת לֹא לְמַעְלָה וְלֹא לְמַטָּה
אֶלָּא כְּמַצְלִיף.

וְכָךְ הָיָה מוֹנֶה

The שליח ציבור*, followed by the* קהל *(in some congregations, all in unison):*

אַחַת אַחַת וְאַחַת
אַחַת וּשְׁתַּיִם אַחַת וְשָׁלֹשׁ
אַחַת וְאַרְבַּע אַחַת וְחָמֵשׁ
אַחַת וָשֵׁשׁ אַחַת וָשֶׁבַע.

All:

יָצָא וְהִנִּיחַ עַל כַּן הַזָּהָב הַשֵּׁנִי שֶׁהָיָה בְּהֵיכָל.

מִהֵר וְנָטַל דַּם הַפָּר מִן הַכַּן שֶׁהִנִּיחַ עָלָיו
וְטוֹבֵל אֶצְבָּעוֹ עַל כָּל הַזָּיָה
וְהִזָּה מִמֶּנּוּ עַל הַפָּרֹכֶת כְּנֶגֶד הָאָרוֹן מִבַּחוּץ
אַחַת לְמַעְלָה וְשֶׁבַע לְמַטָּה
וְלֹא הָיָה מִתְכַּוֵּן לְהַזּוֹת לֹא לְמַעְלָה וְלֹא לְמַטָּה
אֶלָּא כְּמַצְלִיף.

וְכָךְ הָיָה מוֹנֶה

The שליח ציבור*, followed by the* קהל *(in some congregations, all in unison):*

אַחַת אַחַת וְאַחַת
אַחַת וּשְׁתַּיִם אַחַת וְשָׁלֹשׁ
אַחַת וְאַרְבַּע אַחַת וְחָמֵשׁ
אַחַת וָשֵׁשׁ אַחַת וָשֶׁבַע.

All:

נָחַץ וְהִנִּיחַ דַּם הַפָּר וְנָטַל דַּם הַשָּׂעִיר
וְעָשָׂה לְדָמוֹ כַּאֲשֶׁר עָשָׂה לְדַם הַפָּר
וְהִזָּה עַל הַפָּרֹכֶת כְּנֶגֶד הָאָרוֹן מִבַּחוּץ
אַחַת לְמַעְלָה וְשֶׁבַע לְמַטָּה
וְלֹא הָיָה מִתְכַּוֵּן לְהַזּוֹת לֹא לְמַעְלָה וְלֹא לְמַטָּה
אֶלָּא כְּמַצְלִיף.

וְכָךְ הָיָה מוֹנֶה

The שליח ציבור*, followed by the* קהל *(in some congregations, all in unison):*

אַחַת — אַחַת וְאַחַת
אַחַת וּשְׁתַּיִם — אַחַת וְשָׁלֹשׁ
אַחַת וְאַרְבַּע — אַחַת וְחָמֵשׁ
אַחַת וָשֵׁשׁ — אַחַת וָשֶׁבַע.

All:

שָׁשׁ וְעֵרָה דַּם הַפָּר לְתוֹךְ הַמִּזְרָק שֶׁבּוֹ דַּם הַשָּׂעִיר
וְנָתַן הַמָּלֵא בָּרֵיקָן, כְּדֵי שֶׁיִּתְעָרְבוּ יָפֶה יָפֶה זֶה בָּזֶה
וְעָמַד לִפְנִים מִמִּזְבַּח הַזָּהָב בֵּין הַמִּזְבֵּחַ וְהַמְּנוֹרָה
וּמַתְחִיל לְהַזּוֹת מִדַּם הַתַּעֲרֹבֶת.
עַל אַרְבַּע קַרְנוֹתָיו יִתֵּן כְּסִדְרָן
מַתְחִיל מִקֶּרֶן מִזְרָחִית צְפוֹנִית, וּמְסַיֵּם בְּקֶרֶן דְּרוֹמִית מִזְרָחִית
וְחוֹתֶה הַגֶּחָלִים וְהָאֵפֶר בְּמִזְבַּח הַזָּהָב
אֵילָךְ וְאֵילָךְ, עַד שֶׁמְּגַלֶּה זְהָבוֹ
וּמַזֶּה מִדַּם הַתַּעֲרֹבֶת עַל טָהֳרוֹ שֶׁל מִזְבֵּחַ שֶׁבַע פְּעָמִים.
פָּסַע וְיָצָא לְצַד דָּרוֹם, חוּץ לָאוּלָם
וְשָׁפַךְ אֶת הַשִּׁירַיִם עַל יְסוֹד מַעֲרָבִי שֶׁל מִזְבֵּחַ הַחִיצוֹן.

צָעַד וּבָא לוֹ אֵצֶל הַשָּׂעִיר הַמִּשְׁתַּלֵּחַ לַעֲזָאזֵל
לְהִתְוַדּוֹת עָלָיו אַשְׁמַת קְהָלוֹ
וְסָמַךְ שְׁתֵּי יָדָיו עָלָיו, וְהִתְוַדָּה.

וְכָךְ הָיָה אוֹמֵר

The שליח ציבור *continues, with the* קהל *following him in an undertone:*

אָנָּא הַשֵּׁם / חָטְאוּ, עָווּ, פָּשְׁעוּ לְפָנֶיךָ עַמְּךָ בֵּית יִשְׂרָאֵל.
אָנָּא בַשֵּׁם / כַּפֶּר נָא לַחֲטָאִים וְלַעֲוֹנוֹת וְלַפְּשָׁעִים
שֶׁחָטְאוּ וְשֶׁעָווּ וְשֶׁפָּשְׁעוּ לְפָנֶיךָ עַמְּךָ בֵּית יִשְׂרָאֵל.
כַּכָּתוּב בְּתוֹרַת מֹשֶׁה עַבְדֶּךָ מִפִּי כְבוֹדֶךָ
כִּי־בַיּוֹם הַזֶּה יְכַפֵּר עֲלֵיכֶם לְטַהֵר אֶתְכֶם ויקרא טז
מִכֹּל חַטֹּאתֵיכֶם, לִפְנֵי יהוה

וְהַכֹּהֲנִים וְהָעָם הָעוֹמְדִים בָּעֲזָרָה
כְּשֶׁהָיוּ שׁוֹמְעִים אֶת הַשֵּׁם הַנִּכְבָּד וְהַנּוֹרָא
מְפֹרָשׁ יוֹצֵא מִפִּי כֹהֵן גָּדוֹל, בִּקְדֻשָּׁה וּבְטָהֳרָה

At the word כּוֹרְעִים*, the* קהל *and the* שליח ציבור *kneel on the floor (see law 93).*

הָיוּ כּוֹרְעִים וּמִשְׁתַּחֲוִים וּמוֹדִים, וְנוֹפְלִים עַל פְּנֵיהֶם
וְאוֹמְרִים

בָּרוּךְ שֵׁם כְּבוֹד מַלְכוּתוֹ לְעוֹלָם וָעֶד.

All stand and continue:

וְאַף הוּא הָיָה מִתְכַּוֵּן כְּנֶגֶד הַמְבָרְכִים לִגְמֹר אֶת הַשֵּׁם
וְאוֹמֵר, תִּטְהָרוּ.
וְאַתָּה בְּטוּבְךָ מְעוֹרֵר רַחֲמֶיךָ, וְסוֹלֵחַ לַעֲדַת יְשֻׁרוּן.

קָרָא לְאֶחָד מִן הַכֹּהֲנִים הַמְזֻמָּן מֵאֶתְמוֹל לְהוֹלִיכוֹ, וּמְסָרוֹ לוֹ
וְהוֹלִיכוֹ אֶל אֶרֶץ גְּזֵרָה לְמִדְבַּר שָׁמֵם
וּכְשֶׁהִגִּיעַ לַצּוּק חוֹלֵק לָשׁוֹן שֶׁל זְהוֹרִית שֶׁבְּקַרְנָיו
חֶצְיוֹ קוֹשֵׁר בְּסֶלַע, וְחֶצְיוֹ בֵּין קַרְנָיו
וּדְחָפוֹ בִּשְׁתֵּי יָדָיו לַאֲחוֹרָיו, וְהוּא הָיָה מִתְגַּלְגֵּל וְיוֹרֵד
וְלֹא הָיָה מַגִּיעַ לַחֲצִי הָהָר, עַד שֶׁנַּעֲשָׂה אֵבָרִים אֵבָרִים
וְאוֹמֵר, כָּךְ יִמָּחוּ עֲוֹנוֹת עַמְּךָ בֵּית יִשְׂרָאֵל.
רָץ לוֹ אֵצֶל הַפָּר וְאֵצֶל הַשָּׂעִיר הַנִּשְׂרָפִים, וּקְרָעָן
וְהוֹצִיא אֵמוּרֵיהֶם, וּנְתָנָם בְּמָגֵס לְהַקְטִירָם עַל גַּבֵּי הַמִּזְבֵּחַ
וּבְשָׂרָן קְלָעָן בְּמִקְלָעוֹת
וּמְשַׁלְּחָן בְּיַד אֲחֵרִים, לְהוֹצִיאָן לְבֵית הַשְּׂרֵפָה.
שָׁב וּבָא לְעֶזְרַת נָשִׁים, אַחַר שֶׁהִגִּיעַ הַשָּׂעִיר לַמִּדְבָּר
לִקְרוֹת בְּתוֹרַת כֹּהֲנִים פָּרָשַׁת אַחֲרֵי מוֹת וְאַךְ בֶּעָשׂוֹר
וְגוֹלֵל הַסֵּפֶר תּוֹרָה, וּמַנִּיחוֹ בְּחֵיקוֹ, וְאוֹמֵר
יוֹתֵר מִמַּה שֶּׁקָּרִיתִי לִפְנֵיכֶם כָּתוּב כָּאן
וּבֶעָשׂוֹר שֶׁבְּחֻמַּשׁ הַפְּקוּדִים קוֹרֵא עַל פֶּה
וּמְבָרֵךְ לְאַחֲרֵיהֶם שְׁמוֹנֶה בְּרָכוֹת
עַל הַתּוֹרָה וְעַל הָעֲבוֹדָה וְעַל הַהוֹדָאָה וְעַל מְחִילַת הֶעָוֹן
וְעַל הַמִּקְדָּשׁ וְעַל יִשְׂרָאֵל וְעַל הַכֹּהֲנִים וְעַל שְׁאָר הַתְּפִלָּה.

תִּכֵּן צְעָדָיו וּבָא לְבֵית הַטְּבִילָה, וְקִדֵּשׁ יָדָיו וְרַגְלָיו
וּפָשַׁט בִּגְדֵי לָבָן, וְיָרַד וְטָבַל, עָלָה וְנִסְתַּפָּג
הֵבִיאוּ לוֹ בִּגְדֵי זָהָב וְלָבַשׁ, וְקִדֵּשׁ יָדָיו וְרַגְלָיו
וְעָשָׂה שָׂעִיר הַנַּעֲשָׂה בַחוּץ, שֶׁהוּא מִמּוּסַף הַיּוֹם
וְאַחַר כָּךְ מַקְרִיב אֶת אֵילוֹ וְאֶת אֵיל הָעָם
וּמִנְחָתָם וְנִסְכֵּיהֶם כְּמִשְׁפָּטָם

וּמַקְטִיר הָאֵמוּרִים שֶׁל פָּר וְשָׂעִיר הַנִּשְׂרָפִים
וְאַחַר כָּךְ מַקְרִיב תָּמִיד שֶׁל בֵּין הָעַרְבַּיִם כְּהִלְכָתוֹ.

אַחַר כַּלּוֹתוֹ מֵעֲשׂוֹת כָּל אֵלֶּה, עוֹד בָּא לוֹ לְבֵית הַטְּבִילָה
מִהֵר וְקִדֵּשׁ יָדָיו וְרַגְלָיו
וּפָשַׁט בִּגְדֵי זָהָב, וְיָרַד וְטָבַל, עָלָה וְנִסְתַּפָּג
הֵבִיאוּ לוֹ בִּגְדֵי לָבָן, לָבַשׁ וְקִדֵּשׁ יָדָיו וְרַגְלָיו
נִכְנַס לְבֵית קֹדֶשׁ הַקֳּדָשִׁים
לְהוֹצִיא אֶת הַכַּף וְאֶת הַמַּחְתָּה שֶׁהִכְנִיס בְּשַׁחֲרִית
וְעוֹד בָּא לוֹ לְבֵית הַטְּבִילָה, וְקִדֵּשׁ יָדָיו וְרַגְלָיו
וּפָשַׁט בִּגְדֵי לָבָן, וְיָרַד וְטָבַל, עָלָה וְנִסְתַּפָּג
הֵבִיאוּ לוֹ בִּגְדֵי זָהָב, לָבַשׁ וְקִדֵּשׁ יָדָיו וְרַגְלָיו
נִכְנַס לְהֵיכָל לְהַקְטִיר אֶת הַקְּטֹרֶת שֶׁל בֵּין הָעַרְבַּיִם
וּלְהַדְלִיק אֶת הַנֵּרוֹת כִּשְׁאָר יָמִים
וְיָצָא וְהִקְרִיב מִנְחַת הַתָּמִיד, וּמוֹתַר מִנְחַת חֲבִתִּין
וּמְנַסֵּךְ הַיַּיִן בְּכָל כְּלֵי שִׁיר כְּהִלְכָתוֹ
וְקִדֵּשׁ יָדָיו וְרַגְלָיו, וּפָשַׁט בִּגְדֵי זָהָב
הֵבִיאוּ לוֹ בִּגְדֵי עַצְמוֹ וְלָבַשׁ, וּמְלַוִּין אוֹתוֹ עַד בֵּיתוֹ

וְיוֹם טוֹב הָיָה עוֹשֶׂה בְּצֵאתוֹ בְשָׁלוֹם מִן הַקֹּדֶשׁ.
אַשְׁרֵי הָעָם שֶׁכָּכָה לּוֹ, אַשְׁרֵי הָעָם שֶׁיהוה אֱלֹהָיו: תהלים קמד

וּבְכֵן, כְּמוֹ שֶׁשָּׁמַעְתָּ תְּפִלַּת כֹּהֵן גָּדוֹל בְּהֵיכָל
כְּמוֹ כֵן מִפִּינוּ תִּשְׁמַע וְתוֹשִׁיעַ.

יְהִי רָצוֹן מִלְּפָנֶיךָ יהוה אֱלֹהֵינוּ וֵאלֹהֵי אֲבוֹתֵינוּ
שֶׁתְּהֵא הַשָּׁנָה הַזֹּאת הַבָּאָה עָלֵינוּ
וְעַל כָּל עַמְּךָ בֵּית יִשְׂרָאֵל, בְּכָל מָקוֹם שֶׁהֵם

The following piyutim, leading us from סדר העבודה *to* וידוי*, are all alphabetic acrostics (some are reverse acrostics).*

שְׁנַת אוֹרָה
שְׁנַת בְּרָכָה
שְׁנַת גִּילָה
שְׁנַת דִּיצָה
שְׁנַת הוֹד
שְׁנַת וָעַד טוֹב
שְׁנַת זִמְרָה
שְׁנַת חֶדְוָה
שְׁנַת טוֹבָה
שְׁנַת יְשׁוּעָה
שְׁנַת כַּלְכָּלָה
שְׁנַת לִמּוּד
שְׁנַת מְנוּחָה
שְׁנַת נֶחָמָה
שְׁנַת שָׂשׂוֹן
שְׁנַת עֶלְצוֹן
שְׁנַת פְּדוּת
שְׁנַת צָהֳלָה
שְׁנַת קוֹמְמִיּוּת
שְׁנַת קִבּוּץ גָּלֻיּוֹת
שְׁנַת קִבּוּל תְּפִלּוֹת
שְׁנַת רָצוֹן
שְׁנַת שָׁלוֹם
שָׁנָה טְלוּלָה, גְּשׁוּמָה אִם שְׁחוּנָה
שְׁנַת שֹׂבַע
שָׁנָה שֶׁתּוֹלִיכֵנוּ בָהּ קוֹמְמִיּוּת לְאַרְצֵנוּ
שָׁנָה שֶׁתַּדְבֵּר בָּהּ עַמִּים תַּחְתֵּינוּ
שָׁנָה שֶׁתִּכְתְּבֵנוּ בָהּ לְחַיִּים טוֹבִים
שָׁנָה שֶׁלֹּא יִצְטָרְכוּ עַמְּךָ בֵּית יִשְׂרָאֵל לְפַרְנָסָה זֶה לָזֶה
וְלֹא לְעַם אַחֵר
שָׁנָה שֶׁתֵּעָצֵר הַמַּגֵּפָה וְהַמַּשְׁחִית מֵעָלֵינוּ וּמֵעַל כָּל עַמְּךָ בֵּית יִשְׂרָאֵל
שָׁנָה שֶׁלֹּא תַפִּיל אִשָּׁה פְּרִי בִטְנָהּ.

וּבְכֵן, וְעַתָּה יהוה אֱלֹהֵינוּ
עַל רַחֲמֶיךָ הָרַבִּים אָנוּ בְטוּחִים
וְעַל חֲסָדֶיךָ אָנוּ נִשְׁעָנִים
וְלִסְלִיחוֹתֶיךָ אָנוּ מְקַוִּים
כִּי אַתָּה אֵל רַחוּם וְחַנּוּן, אֶרֶךְ אַפַּיִם וְרַב חֶסֶד
וּמַרְבֶּה לְהֵיטִיב

וּמַנְהִיג אֶת הָעוֹלָם כֻּלּוֹ בְּמִדַּת הַחֶסֶד וּבְמִדַּת הָרַחֲמִים.
כַּכָּתוּב בְּתוֹרַת מֹשֶׁה עַבְדֶּךָ:
וַיֹּאמֶר, אֲנִי אַעֲבִיר כָּל־טוּבִי עַל־פָּנֶיךָ שמות לג
וְקָרָאתִי בְשֵׁם יהוה לְפָנֶיךָ
וְחַנֹּתִי אֶת־אֲשֶׁר אָחֹן
וְרִחַמְתִּי אֶת־אֲשֶׁר אֲרַחֵם:

וּבְכֵן, מַה נֶּהְדָּר הָיָה כֹּהֵן גָּדוֹל
בְּצֵאתוֹ בְּשָׁלוֹם מִן הַקֹּדֶשׁ.

The service continues with "אֱמֶת, מַה נֶּהְדָּר" on page 901.

פיוטים וסליחות
שנוהגים לומר בקצת קהילות

פיוטים וסליחות לתפילת מעריב

Some congregations recite שְׁמַע תְּפִלָּה *in the following sequence according to Lithuanian custom.*

All:

שֹׁמֵעַ תְּפִלָּה, עָדֶיךָ כָּל־בָּשָׂר יָבֹאוּ: תהלים סה
יָבוֹא כָל בָּשָׂר לְהִשְׁתַּחֲוֹת לְפָנֶיךָ יהוה. ישעיה סו
יָבוֹאוּ וְיִשְׁתַּחֲווּ לְפָנֶיךָ אֲדֹנָי, וִיכַבְּדוּ לִשְׁמֶךָ: תהלים פו
בֹּאוּ נִשְׁתַּחֲוֶה וְנִכְרָעָה, נִבְרְכָה לִפְנֵי־יהוה עֹשֵׂנוּ: תהלים צה
נָבוֹאָה לְמִשְׁכְּנוֹתָיו, נִשְׁתַּחֲוֶה לַהֲדֹם רַגְלָיו: תהלים קלב
בֹּאוּ שְׁעָרָיו בְּתוֹדָה, חֲצֵרֹתָיו בִּתְהִלָּה, הוֹדוּ לוֹ, בָּרְכוּ שְׁמוֹ: תהלים ק
רוֹמְמוּ יהוה אֱלֹהֵינוּ וְהִשְׁתַּחֲווּ לַהֲדֹם רַגְלָיו, קָדוֹשׁ הוּא: תהלים צט
רוֹמְמוּ יהוה אֱלֹהֵינוּ וְהִשְׁתַּחֲווּ לְהַר קָדְשׁוֹ, כִּי־קָדוֹשׁ יהוה אֱלֹהֵינוּ: שם
הִשְׁתַּחֲווּ לַיהוה בְּהַדְרַת־קֹדֶשׁ, חִילוּ מִפָּנָיו כָּל־הָאָרֶץ: תהלים צו
וַאֲנַחְנוּ בְּרֹב חַסְדְּךָ נָבוֹא בֵיתֶךָ, נִשְׁתַּחֲוֶה אֶל הֵיכַל קָדְשְׁךָ בְּיִרְאָתֶךָ. תהלים ה
נִשְׁתַּחֲוֶה אֶל הֵיכַל קָדְשְׁךָ, וְנוֹדֶה אֶת שְׁמֶךָ עַל חַסְדְּךָ וְעַל אֲמִתֶּךָ תהלים קלח
כִּי הִגְדַּלְתָּ עַל כָּל שִׁמְךָ אִמְרָתֶךָ.
לְכוּ נְרַנְּנָה לַיהוה, נָרִיעָה לְצוּר יִשְׁעֵנוּ: תהלים צה
נְקַדְּמָה פָנָיו בְּתוֹדָה, בִּזְמִרוֹת נָרִיעַ לוֹ:
אֲשֶׁר יַחְדָּו נַמְתִּיק סוֹד, בְּבֵית אֱלֹהִים נְהַלֵּךְ בְּרָגֶשׁ: תהלים נה
אֵל נַעֲרָץ בְּסוֹד־קְדוֹשִׁים רַבָּה, וְנוֹרָא עַל־כָּל־סְבִיבָיו: תהלים פט
שְׂאוּ־יְדֵכֶם קֹדֶשׁ, וּבָרְכוּ אֶת־יהוה: תהלים קלד
הִנֵּה בָּרְכוּ אֶת־יהוה כָּל־עַבְדֵי יהוה, הָעֹמְדִים בְּבֵית־יהוה בַּלֵּילוֹת: שם
אֲשֶׁר מִי־אֵל בַּשָּׁמַיִם וּבָאָרֶץ אֲשֶׁר־יַעֲשֶׂה כְמַעֲשֶׂיךָ וְכִגְבוּרֹתֶךָ: דברים ג
אֲשֶׁר־לוֹ הַיָּם וְהוּא עָשָׂהוּ, וְיַבֶּשֶׁת יָדָיו יָצָרוּ: תהלים צה
אֲשֶׁר בְּיָדוֹ מֶחְקְרֵי־אָרֶץ, וְתוֹעֲפוֹת הָרִים לוֹ: שם

איוב יב אֲשֶׁר בְּיָדוֹ נֶפֶשׁ כָּל־חָי וְרְוּחַ כָּל־בְּשַׂר־אִישׁ:
תהלים פט וְיוֹדוּ שָׁמַיִם פִּלְאֲךָ יהוה, אַף־אֱמוּנָתְךָ בִּקְהַל קְדֹשִׁים:
שם לְךָ זְרוֹעַ עִם־גְּבוּרָה, תָּעֹז יָדְךָ תָּרוּם יְמִינֶךָ:
שם לְךָ שָׁמַיִם אַף־לְךָ אָרֶץ, תֵּבֵל וּמְלֹאָהּ אַתָּה יְסַדְתָּם:
תהלים עד אַתָּה פוֹרַרְתָּ בְעָזְּךָ יָם, שִׁבַּרְתָּ רָאשֵׁי תַנִּינִים עַל־הַמָּיִם:
שם אַתָּה הִצַּבְתָּ כָּל־גְּבוּלוֹת אָרֶץ, קַיִץ וָחֹרֶף אַתָּה יְצַרְתָּם:
שם אַתָּה רִצַּצְתָּ רָאשֵׁי לִוְיָתָן, תִּתְּנֶנּוּ מַאֲכָל לְעָם לְצִיִּים:
אַתָּה בָקַעְתָּ מַעְיָן וָנָחַל, אַתָּה הוֹבַשְׁתָּ נַהֲרוֹת אֵיתָן:
לְךָ יוֹם אַף־לְךָ לָיְלָה, אַתָּה הֲכִינְוֹתָ מָאוֹר וָשָׁמֶשׁ:
איוב ט עֹשֶׂה גְדֹלוֹת עַד־אֵין חֵקֶר, וְנִפְלָאוֹת עַד־אֵין מִסְפָּר:
תהלים צה כִּי אֵל גָּדוֹל יהוה, וּמֶלֶךְ גָּדוֹל עַל־כָּל־אֱלֹהִים:
תהלים פו כִּי־גָדוֹל אַתָּה וְעֹשֵׂה נִפְלָאוֹת, אַתָּה אֱלֹהִים לְבַדֶּךָ:
תהלים קח כִּי־גָדוֹל מֵעַל־שָׁמַיִם חַסְדֶּךָ, וְעַד־שְׁחָקִים אֲמִתֶּךָ:
תהלים קמה גָּדוֹל יהוה וּמְהֻלָּל מְאֹד, וְלִגְדֻלָּתוֹ אֵין חֵקֶר:
דברי הימים א׳ טז כִּי גָדוֹל יהוה וּמְהֻלָּל מְאֹד, וְנוֹרָא הוּא עַל־כָּל־אֱלֹהִים:
תהלים מח גָּדוֹל יהוה וּמְהֻלָּל מְאֹד, בְּעִיר אֱלֹהֵינוּ הַר־קָדְשׁוֹ:
דברי הימים א׳ כט לְךָ יהוה הַגְּדֻלָּה וְהַגְּבוּרָה וְהַתִּפְאֶרֶת וְהַנֵּצַח וְהַהוֹד
כִּי־כֹל בַּשָּׁמַיִם וּבָאָרֶץ, לְךָ יהוה הַמַּמְלָכָה וְהַמִּתְנַשֵּׂא לְכֹל לְרֹאשׁ:
ירמיה י מִי לֹא יִרָאֲךָ מֶלֶךְ הַגּוֹיִם, כִּי לְךָ יָאָתָה
כִּי בְכָל־חַכְמֵי הַגּוֹיִם וּבְכָל־מַלְכוּתָם מֵאֵין כָּמְוֹךָ:
שם מֵאֵין כָּמְוֹךָ יהוה, גָּדוֹל אַתָּה וְגָדוֹל שִׁמְךָ בִּגְבוּרָה:
תהלים פט יהוה אֱלֹהֵי צְבָאוֹת מִי־כָמְוֹךָ חֲסִין יָהּ, וֶאֱמוּנָתְךָ סְבִיבוֹתֶיךָ:
ישעיה לז יהוה צְבָאוֹת אֱלֹהֵי יִשְׂרָאֵל יֹשֵׁב הַכְּרֻבִים, אַתָּה־הוּא הָאֱלֹהִים לְבַדֶּךָ:
תהלים קו מִי יְמַלֵּל גְּבוּרוֹת יהוה, יַשְׁמִיעַ כָּל־תְּהִלָּתוֹ:

מַה נֹּאמַר לְפָנֶיךָ יוֹשֵׁב מָרוֹם, וּמַה נְּסַפֵּר לְפָנֶיךָ שׁוֹכֵן שְׁחָקִים.
מַה נֹּאמַר לְפָנֶיךָ יהוה אֱלֹהֵינוּ, מַה נְּדַבֵּר וּמַה נִּצְטַדָּק.
אֵין לָנוּ פֶּה לְהָשִׁיב, וְלֹא מֵצַח לְהָרִים רֹאשׁ
כִּי עֲוֹנוֹתֵינוּ רַבּוּ מִלְּמְנוֹת וְחַטֹּאתֵינוּ עָצְמוּ מִסַּפֵּר.

לְמַעַן שִׁמְךָ יהוה תְּחַיֵּנוּ, בְּצִדְקָתְךָ תּוֹצִיא מִצָּרָה נַפְשֵׁנוּ. תהלים קמג
דַּרְכְּךָ אֱלֹהֵינוּ לְהַאֲרִיךְ אַפֶּךָ / לָרָעִים וְלַטּוֹבִים, וְהִיא תְהִלָּתֶךָ.
לְמַעַנְךָ אֱלֹהֵינוּ עֲשֵׂה, וְלֹא לָנוּ / רְאֵה עֲמִידָתֵנוּ דַּלִּים וְרֵיקִים.

‣ הַנְּשָׁמָה לָךְ, וְהַגּוּף פָּעֳלָךְ / חוּסָה עַל עֲמָלָךְ.
הַנְּשָׁמָה לָךְ, וְהַגּוּף שֶׁלָּךְ / יהוה עֲשֵׂה לְמַעַן שְׁמֶךָ.
אָתָאנוּ עַל שִׁמְךָ / יהוה עֲשֵׂה לְמַעַן שְׁמֶךָ.
בַּעֲבוּר כְּבוֹד שִׁמְךָ / כִּי אֵל חַנּוּן וְרַחוּם שְׁמֶךָ.
לְמַעַן שִׁמְךָ יהוה / וְסָלַחְתָּ לַעֲוֹנֵנוּ כִּי רַב הוּא. תהלים כה

Continue with "דַּרְכְּךָ אֱלֹהֵינוּ" on pages 133, unless אָמְנָם אֲשָׁמֵינוּ *(below) is said.*

Traditionally, the first י״ג מידות *of* מעריב *was followed by a* תוכחה *(rebuke). This piyut is a very ancient one, attributed to Rabbi Yose ben Yose, one of the earliest liturgical poets in* ארץ ישראל*. The piyut follows an alphabetic acrostic. In each stanza, all four stichs begin with the same letter of the alphabet. Nowadays, most congregations say only the two alternating refrains and the final stanza.*

אָמְנָם אֲשָׁמֵינוּ עָצְמוּ מִסַּפֵּר / אַנְחוֹת דּוֹרֵנוּ רַבּוּ מִלְּדַבֵּר
אֲשֶׁר לֹא הִקְשַׁבְנוּ גְּעָרָה כְּמֵבִין / אֲפָפוּנוּ מַכּוֹת, כִּכְסִיל הֱזַדְנוּ.

דַּרְכְּךָ אֱלֹהֵינוּ לְהַאֲרִיךְ אַפֶּךָ / לָרָעִים וְלַטּוֹבִים, וְהִיא תְהִלָּתֶךָ.

בְּדַבֶּרְךָ לָנוּ שׁוּבָה, פָּנֵינוּ הִסְתַּרְנוּ / בְּמִרְמָה בִּקַּשְׁנוּךָ, וְאֵלֶיךָ לֹא שַׁבְנוּ
בְּטוּב לֹא דְרַשְׁנוּךָ, בְּרֹב כֹּל שְׁכַחְנוּךָ / בְּעֵת הַצַּר לָנוּ אֵיךְ תִּמָּצֵא.

לְמַעַנְךָ אֱלֹהֵינוּ עֲשֵׂה, וְלֹא לָנוּ / רְאֵה עֲמִידָתֵנוּ דַּלִּים וְרֵיקִים.

גְּבוּרוֹת אֵין בָּנוּ אֲשֶׁר בָּם נָבוֹא / גְּדוּעֵי זְרוֹעַ בְּפֹעַל, בְּתֵת שָׂכָר בְּשָׁנוּ
גָּמַרְנוּ וְאָכַלְנוּ צִדְקַת אֲבוֹתֵינוּ / גַּם קֶרֶן גַּם פְּרִי, לֹא מָלְאוּ שֶׂפֶק.

דַּרְכְּךָ אֱלֹהֵינוּ לְהַאֲרִיךְ אַפֶּךָ / לָרָעִים וְלַטּוֹבִים, וְהִיא תְהִלָּתֶךָ.

דְּכָאוּ מֶנּוּ שְׁכִיּוֹת הַחֶמְדָּה / דּוֹפְקֵי דְלָתֶיךָ בְּכֹחַ וּגְבוּרָה
דִּבְרֵי בְגַאֲוָה נַעֲשִׂינוּ, עֲשֵׂה לָנוּ כְּרַחֲמֶיךָ / דְּחֵה מִשְׁפַּט חֶרֶב הַמִּתְהַפֶּכֶת.

לְמַעַנְךָ אֱלֹהֵינוּ עֲשֵׂה, וְלֹא לָנוּ / רְאֵה עֲמִידָתֵנוּ דַּלִּים וְרֵיקִים.

הוֹרַקְנוּ וְהֻצַּגְנוּ כְּקַשׁ מִדָּגָן / הָיִינוּ כַּמֹּץ וְאֵין דּוֹרֵשׁ לְאָסְפוֹ
הֲלֹא בְּהִלָּקַח דָּגָן בְּעִתּוֹ / הֲצַת לְשׁוֹן אֵשׁ בְּקַשׁ הַיָּבֵשׁ.

דַּרְכְּךָ אֱלֹהֵינוּ לְהַאֲרִיךְ אַפֶּךָ / לָרָעִים וְלַטּוֹבִים, וְהִיא תְהִלָּתֶךָ.

וּמַה נְּדַבֵּר וּמַה נִּצְטַדָּק / וּמַה נֹּאמַר, וְיוּצַק חֵן בְּשִׂפְתוֹתֵינוּ
וּמִי בַּעַל דְּבָרִים יְדַבֵּר צָחוֹת / וּבְפִתְחוֹן פִּיו לֹא יִכָּלֵם.

לְמַעַנְךָ אֱלֹהֵינוּ עֲשֵׂה, וְלֹא לָנוּ / רְאֵה עֲמִידָתֵנוּ דַּלִּים וְרֵיקִים.

זֶה דַּרְכֵּנוּ כֶּסֶל, נָחַלְנוּ אִוֶּלֶת / זֵדִים חוֹטְאִים זוֹלְלִים וְסֹבְאִים
זְכִיתִי לִבִּי, מִי יוּכַל שִׂיחַ / זֶרַע קְבוּרַת רֶחֶם בָּא וְהוֹלֵךְ בֶּהָבֶל.

דַּרְכְּךָ אֱלֹהֵינוּ לְהַאֲרִיךְ אַפֶּךָ / לָרָעִים וְלַטּוֹבִים, וְהִיא תְהִלָּתֶךָ.

חָזוּת וּמוֹפֵת הִתְוִינוּ בָּאָרֶץ / חֲתוּמֵי בְּאוֹת בְּרִית וְחֻקִּים יְשָׁרִים
חֻשַּׁבְנוּ זֶרַע קֹדֶשׁ, בָּנִים לְאֵל חָי / חִלַּלְנוּ וְנִקְרֵאנוּ אִם טְמֵאַת הַשֵּׁם.

לְמַעַנְךָ אֱלֹהֵינוּ עֲשֵׂה, וְלֹא לָנוּ / רְאֵה עֲמִידָתֵנוּ דַּלִּים וְרֵיקִים.

טְהוֹר עֵינַיִם מֵרְאוֹת בְּרָע / טֶרֶם לֹא רָאָה עָמָל בְּיַעֲקֹב
טֶרֶף לֹא לָנוּ נִכְסְפָה נַפְשֵׁנוּ /טֻבַּחְנוּ רַב וְצָעִיר כִּבְלִיעַת דָּגִים.

דַּרְכְּךָ אֱלֹהֵינוּ לְהַאֲרִיךְ אַפֶּךָ / לָרָעִים וְלַטּוֹבִים, וְהִיא תְהִלָּתֶךָ.

יָהּ בְּדַלּוּתֵנוּ צְדָקָה חֲנַנְתָּנוּ / יָד בָּנוּ הֶחֱזַקְתָּ בְּעֵת מָטָה יָדֵנוּ
יְדַעְתָּנוּ, זֹאת עֵשָׂו וְחַיּוּ / יָדַיִם לֹא חָלוּ בָנוּ כַּהֲפוּכַת רָגַע.

לְמַעַנְךָ אֱלֹהֵינוּ עֲשֵׂה, וְלֹא לָנוּ / רְאֵה עֲמִידָתֵנוּ דַּלִּים וְרֵיקִים.

כַּחוֹתָם עַל לֵב שַׂמְתָּנוּ מַלְכֵּנוּ / כְּנֶפֶשׁ קְשׁוּרָה בְנֶפֶשׁ, בַּעֲבֹתוֹת אַהֲבָה
כִּי נִתְרוֹעֲעוּ חִבּוּר עֲצָבִים / כָּעֵת חָלַק לִבֵּנוּ, אָשַׁמְנוּ מֵעַתָּה.

דַּרְכְּךָ אֱלֹהֵינוּ לְהַאֲרִיךְ אַפֶּךָ / לָרָעִים וְלַטּוֹבִים, וְהִיא תְהִלָּתֶךָ.

לְהֵיטִיב אֲמַרְתָּ, אֹמֶר לֹא הִפַּלְתָּ / לֹא שִׁקַּר בָּנוּ דְּבַר אֱמוּנָתֶךָ
לֵב וּפֶה לֹא הִשְׁוֵינוּ, כְּכֶסֶף עַל חֶרֶשׂ / לַעַג שְׂפַת חֲלָקוֹת, בְּלֵב וָלֵב דִּבַּרְנוּ.

לְמַעַנְךָ אֱלֹהֵינוּ עֲשֵׂה, וְלֹא לָנוּ / רְאֵה עֲמִידָתֵנוּ דַּלִּים וְרֵיקִים.

מַכַּת הוֹלֵךְ עַל גָּחוֹן הִקְדַּמְתָּ / מוּסָר לְמִדַּת לְבַעֲלֵי לָשׁוֹן
מֵעֹנֶשׁ לֵץ לֹא יֶחְכַּם פֶּתִי / מַכֵּה רֵעַ בַּסֵּתֶר, דַּנְתָּ בְּגַחֲלֵי רְתָמִים.

דַּרְכְּךָ אֱלֹהֵינוּ לְהַאֲרִיךְ אַפֶּךָ / לָרָעִים וְלַטּוֹבִים, וְהִיא תְהִלָּתֶךָ.

נָתַתָּ מוֹרָא עַל לֵב אֲנָשִׁים / נֶדֶר וּשְׁבוּעַת שֵׁם, בֵּין שְׁנֵיהֶם חוֹקַקְתָּ
נַמְתָּ הוֹצֵאתִיהָ עַל נִשְׁבָּעִים לַשָּׁקֶר / נִפְרַצְנוּ בְאָלָה עַד אָבְלָה הָאָרֶץ.

לְמַעַנְךָ אֱלֹהֵינוּ עֲשֵׂה, וְלֹא לָנוּ / רְאֵה עֲמִידָתֵנוּ דַּלִּים וְרֵיקִים.

סָבַלְתָּ עוֹלָם כְּרַגְלַיִם לַפִּסֵּחַ / סְמַכְתּוֹ בֶּאֱמֶת וּמִשְׁפָּט וְשָׁלוֹם
סִלַּפְנוּ מִשְׁפָּט, וְגַם כָּשְׁלָה אֱמֶת / סוֹבַבְנוּ לְבַקֵּשׁ שָׁלוֹם, וָאָיִן.

דַּרְכְּךָ אֱלֹהֵינוּ לְהַאֲרִיךְ אַפֶּךָ / לָרָעִים וְלַטּוֹבִים, וְהִיא תְהִלָּתֶךָ.

עֶלְיוֹן אַתָּה בְּכִסֵּא רָם וְנִשָּׂא / עֵינֶיךָ מַבִּיטוֹת שָׁפָל וְדַכָּא
עֲנָוָה בִּקַּשְׁנוּ פַּעַם, וְתִסְתָּרוּ מֵאַף / עַזּוֹנוּ בְּגַבְהוּת לֵב, וְרָמוּ עֵינֵינוּ.

לְמַעַנְךָ אֱלֹהֵינוּ עֲשֵׂה, וְלֹא לָנוּ / רְאֵה עֲמִידָתֵנוּ דַּלִּים וְרֵיקִים.

פָּנֶיךָ תָּמִיד בְּחֶמְדַּת אֲרָצוֹת / פָּקַדְתָּ וַתְּשׁוֹקְקֶהָ, וַתַּצְמִיחַ מְגָדֶיהָ
פֶּן יִקְבַּע אָדָם אֱלֹהִים / פְּרִי יְבוּלָהּ תַּתָּה לְמַעֲשֵׂר, וְכִחֲשׁוּ מְגָדֶיהָ.

דַּרְכְּךָ אֱלֹהֵינוּ לְהַאֲרִיךְ אַפֶּךָ / לָרָעִים וְלַטּוֹבִים, וְהִיא תְהִלָּתֶךָ.

צִיָּה יָצַרְתָּ לִמְלֶאכֶת שָׁנִים / צָבָא לֶאֱנוֹשׁ עֲלֵי אֶרֶץ, לִמְלֶאכֶת יָמִים
צִוִּיתָ לְמַרְגּוֹעַ שְׁבִיעִי, וְלֹא נַחְנוּ / צְבִי לִשְׁמֹט שְׁבִיעִית, וְהִיא לֹא שָׁבָתָה.

לְמַעַנְךָ אֱלֹהֵינוּ עֲשֵׂה, וְלֹא לָנוּ / רְאֵה עֲמִידָתֵנוּ דַּלִּים וְרֵיקִים.

קִדַּמְנוּ פָּנֶיךָ, כִּמְחִיר בְּיַד כְּסִיל / קְנוֹת צִדְקוֹתֶיךָ בְּתוֹדָה בְּלִי לֵב
קַבֵּל כְּנִיחֹחַ מְעַט בִּצְדָקָה / קַח נָא אֲמָרֵינוּ כְּקֹמֶץ מִנְחַת דָּל.

דַּרְכְּךָ אֱלֹהֵינוּ לְהַאֲרִיךְ אַפֶּךָ / לָרָעִים וְלַטּוֹבִים, וְהִיא תְהִלָּתֶךָ.

רְדֵנוּ, לוּא נָבוֹא, בְּמִרְיֵנוּ אָמַרְנוּ / רָם, בָּנוּ הִכְפַּפְתָּ כְּבָרוּשׁ רַעֲנָן
רִחַקְתָּ בִשְׂמֹאל, קָרֵב בְּיָמִין / רְאֵה שְׂאֹר לְבָבֵנוּ, יֵצֶר הַנְּעוּרִים.

לְמַעַנְךָ אֱלֹהֵינוּ עֲשֵׂה, וְלֹא לָנוּ / רְאֵה עֲמִידָתֵנוּ דַּלִּים וְרֵיקִים.

שֵׁבֶט לְגֵו כְּסִיל, וְכַעַס בְּחֵיק אֱוִיל / שׁוֹט כְּלִמַּת עֳנִי עָלָה בְחֶלְקֵנוּ
שׁוּר נָא וְחַלְּצֵנוּ כְּעָנִי בְעָנְיוֹ / שַׁחַת אִם נֵרֵד, יְקַדְּמוּנוּ רַחֲמֶיךָ.

דַּרְכְּךָ אֱלֹהֵינוּ לְהַאֲרִיךְ אַפֶּךָ / לָרָעִים וְלַטּוֹבִים, וְהִיא תְהִלָּתֶךָ.

תַּעֲלֶה אֲרוּכָה לְעָלֶה נִדָּף / תְּנַחֵם עַל עָפָר וָאֵפֶר
תַּשְׁלִיךְ חֲטָאֵינוּ, וְתָחֹן מַעֲשֶׂיךָ / תֵּרֶא כִּי אֵין אִישׁ, עֲשֵׂה עִמָּנוּ צְדָקָה.

לְמַעַנְךָ אֱלֹהֵינוּ עֲשֵׂה וְלֹא לָנוּ / רְאֵה עֲמִידָתֵנוּ דַּלִּים וְרֵיקִים.

Continue with אֵל מֶלֶךְ *on page 135.*

*After "*וְכֹר־רַחֲמֶיךָ*," a "*חטאנו*" piyut (named for its refrain: "*חָטָאנוּ צוּרֵנוּ, סְלַח לָנוּ יוֹצְרֵנוּ*") was traditionally said. The* חטאנו *for* מעריב*, with its triple alphabetical acrostic, was probably composed by Rabbi Shimon bar Yitzḥak in the tenth century.*

חָטָאנוּ צוּרֵנוּ, סְלַח לָנוּ יוֹצְרֵנוּ.

אוֹתְךָ אֶדְרֹשׁ וְאֵלֶיךָ אֶתְוַדָּע / גָּדוֹל בִּיהוּדָה וּבְיִשְׂרָאֵל נוֹדָע
תהלים נא הֵן אַתָּה חֲקַרְתָּנוּ וַתֵּדָע / כִּי־פְשָׁעַי אֲנִי אֵדָע:

אֵדַע אֲבָל אֲשֵׁמִים אֲנַחְנוּ / וּמֵהֲמוֹן רַחֲמֶיךָ לֹא זֻנַּחְנוּ
תהלים לג הֵן אֵלָיו כַּפֵּינוּ שִׁטַּחְנוּ / כִּי בְשֵׁם קָדְשׁוֹ בָטָחְנוּ:

חָטָאנוּ צוּרֵנוּ, סְלַח לָנוּ יוֹצְרֵנוּ.

בָּטַחְנוּ בְשִׁמְךָ לְנֶפֶשׁ תַּאֲוָה / וְהִפְקַדְנוּ מָגֵן בְּלִי גַאֲוָה
איוב כב הֵן בְּמָעֻזְּךָ לְדַל תִּקְוָה / כִּי־הִשְׁפִּילוּ וַתֹּאמֶר גֵּוָה:

גֵּוָה גֵּאִים עָלַי מַגְדִּילִים / רֹגֶז שְׂבֵעִים וְלֹא נֶחְדָּלִים
איוב כ הֵן גָּלַל הַמֵּצִיק מִתְדַּלְדְּלִים / כִּי־רִצַּץ עָזַב דַּלִּים:

חָטָאנוּ צוּרֵנוּ, סְלַח לָנוּ יוֹצְרֵנוּ.

דַּלִּים דִּינְךָ פַּחֲדוּ וְרָהוּ / בָּאִים כְּמוֹדֶה וְעוֹזֵב לְרַחֲמֵהוּ
ויקרא כג הֵן דָּפִים הַיּוֹם תְּכַפְּרֵהוּ / כִּי יוֹם כִּפֻּרִים הוּא:

הוּא הוֹד וְהָדָר יִלְבַּשׁ / יָשׁוּב יְרַחֵם, וְעָוֹן יִכְבֹּשׁ
איוב ה הֵן הַמְתֵּק בְּפִי כִּדְבַשׁ / כִּי הוּא יַכְאִיב וְיֶחְבָּשׁ:

חָטָאנוּ צוּרֵנוּ, סְלַח לָנוּ יוֹצְרֵנוּ.

וְיֶחְבַּשׁ וְלִשְׁמוֹ כֹּל יוֹדוּ / כִּי יָסִיר מַשְּׂאוֹת כְּבֵדוּ
הֵן וְעַמּוֹ לְפָנָיו יִתְוַדּוּ / כִּי בַדָּבָר אֲשֶׁר זָדוּ: שמות יח

זָדוּ זְדוֹנוֹת וּשְׁגָגוֹת שְׁגוּיִים / סְלַח נָא בְּפִימוֹ הֲגוּיִים
הֵן זַכֵּם לְתֶחִי אֲחוּיִים / כִּי־עִמְּךָ מְקוֹר חַיִּים: תהלים לו

חָטָאנוּ צוּרֵנוּ, סְלַח לָנוּ יוֹצְרֵנוּ.

חַיִּים חֹן לְעַם מְנַטְּלֶךָ / לֵבָב עִקֵּשׁ מֵהֶם בְּבַטְּלֶךָ
הֵן חַשְׁרַת מֵי טֹהַר בְּהַטִּילֶךָ / כִּי טַל אוֹרֹת טַלֶּךָ: ישעיה כו

טַלֶּךָ טְלָאֶיךָ בּוֹ לְהִתְכַּפֵּר / הָעֵת תַּמְצִיאֵם סְלִיחָה וָכֹפֶר
הֵן טַהֲרֵם, כָּאָמוּר בַּסֵּפֶר / כִּי־בַיּוֹם הַזֶּה יְכַפֵּר: ויקרא טז

חָטָאנוּ צוּרֵנוּ, סְלַח לָנוּ יוֹצְרֵנוּ.

יְכַפֵּר יִרְצֶה כְּאָז בְּהַעֲלִיּוֹתַי / בִּהְיוֹת אֲרִיאֵל בְּבְחַן עֲלִיּוֹתַי
הֵן יָדַעְתָּ פִּקּוּק חֲלִיּוֹתַי / כִּי־אַתָּה קָנִיתָ כִלְיֹתָי: תהלים קלט

כִּלְיוֹתַי כְּטוּחֵי אָכִין לְעָבְדוֹ / וְתֶעֱרַב לְפָנָיו תְּחִנַּת עַבְדּוֹ
הֵן כַּבֵּד יְכַבֵּד מִכְּבוֹדוֹ / כִּי־נִשְׂגָּב שְׁמוֹ לְבַדּוֹ: תהלים קמח

חָטָאנוּ צוּרֵנוּ, סְלַח לָנוּ יוֹצְרֵנוּ.

לְבַדּוֹ לוֹ לְהִתְחוֹלֵל כָּל אֱנוֹשׁ / אָוֶן לֹא יִתְבּוֹנֵן לֶאֱנוֹשׁ
הֵן לֹא טוֹב לַצַּדִּיק לַעֲנֹשׁ / כִּי־יִרְבֶּה אֱלוֹהַּ מֵאֱנוֹשׁ: איוב לג

מֵאֱנוֹשׁ מִמַּעֲשָׂיו יָגֹרְתִּי וְאֵימָתִי / פֶּן אֶכָּשֵׁל כַּאֲשֶׁר אָשַׁמְתִּי
הֵן מְיַחֵל שִׁוִּיתִי וְדוֹמַמְתִּי / כִּי־אַחֲרֵי שׁוּבִי נִחַמְתִּי: ירמיה לא

חָטָאנוּ צוּרֵנוּ, סְלַח לָנוּ יוֹצְרֵנוּ.

נִחַמְתִּי נֶפֶשׁ נַעֲנָה לְהָשֵׁם / הִתְוַדּוֹת הַיּוֹם נִסְתָּר וּמְפֻרְסָם
הֵן נֶצַח לְכִפּוּר הוּשָׂם / כִּי בְרִית עוֹלָם שָׂם: שמואל ב׳ כג

שָׂם סְלִיחָה לְהוֹעִיל לְלַמְּדִי / תְּשׁוּבָה מְכַפֶּרֶת כְּזִבְחֵי תְמִידִי
הֵן סִימָה בְּצִלּוֹ לְהַעֲמִידִי / כִּי־יָדַע דֶּרֶךְ עִמָּדִי: איוב כג

חָטָאנוּ צוּרֵנוּ, סְלַח לָנוּ יוֹצְרֵנוּ.

עֹמְדֵי עֲשׂוֹת חֶסֶד בְּהַפְלִיאֲךָ / כִּי תְבַקֵּר צֹאנְךָ וּטְלָאֶיךָ
הֵן עָלֶיךָ יַעֲזֹב חֵילֶךָ / כִּי־אֶזְכְּרָה מִקֶּדֶם פִּלְאֶךָ: תהלים עז

פִּלְאֲךָ פֹּעַל יְרֵאֶיךָ לִנְצָרָם / הֱיוֹת יִרְאַת יהוה אוֹצָרָם
הֵן פְּלִילֵינוּ לֵידַע בְּהִתְבַּצְּרָם / כִּי לֹא כְצוּרֵנוּ צוּרָם: דברים לב

חָטָאנוּ צוּרֵנוּ, סְלַח לָנוּ יוֹצְרֵנוּ.

צוּרָם צוּר יִשְׂרָאֵל וּקְדוֹשׁוֹ / יֹאמְרוּ בַגּוֹיִם לְעֵינֵיהֶם בְּהִתְקַדְּשׁוֹ
הֵן צָמְחָה יְשׁוּעָה לְמַקְדִּישׁוֹ / כִּי־הִשְׁקִיף מִמְּרוֹם קָדְשׁוֹ: תהלים קב

קָדְשׁוֹ קוֹמֵם קְדֹשָׁיו לְהַקְרִיבָם / לְהַצִּיב הוֹד שְׁכִינָתוֹ בְּקִרְבָּם
הֵן קוּמוּ יֵחַתּוּ מְרִיבָם / כִּי־יהוה יָרִיב רִיבָם: משלי כב

חָטָאנוּ צוּרֵנוּ, סְלַח לָנוּ יוֹצְרֵנוּ.

רִיבָם רִיב שׂוֹטְנֵיהֶם לִבְלֹם / יִדְּמוּ קָטֵגוֹרִים פֶּה לֶאֱלֹם
הֵן רַעְיָתְךָ תְּהַלֵּךְ לְעוֹלָם / כִּי־אַחֲרִית לְאִישׁ שָׁלוֹם: תהלים לז

שָׁלוֹם שְׂפַת לְהַזְרִיחַ נְהָרָה / הֲגִיגֵנוּ בִּין כְּמִנְחָה טְהוֹרָה
הֵן שִׁכְנְךָ תַּגִּיהַּ בְּאוֹרָה / כִּי מִצִּיּוֹן תֵּצֵא תוֹרָה: מיכה ד

חָטָאנוּ צוּרֵנוּ, סְלַח לָנוּ יוֹצְרֵנוּ.

תּוֹרָה שָׁמְעוּ נֶאֱמָנֶיךָ בְּסִינַי / רְצוּיָה יְצוּרָה חֲקוּקָה לְעֵינַי
הֵן הַיּוֹם יְכַפֵּר לְאֱמוּנַי / כִּי אֵל רַחוּם יהוה: דברים ד

◂ יהוה יְנַהֲלֵנוּ עַלְמוּת לְנַהֲגָה / וְיָסִיר מִמֶּנּוּ אַף וְתוּגָה
הֵן יַעֲבִיר זָדוֹן לִמְשׁוּגָה / כִּי לְכָל־הָעָם בִּשְׁגָגָה: במדבר טו

חָטָאנוּ צוּרֵנוּ, סְלַח לָנוּ יוֹצְרֵנוּ.

Continue with "זְכָר לָנוּ בְּרִית אָבוֹת" on page 155.

This ancient piyut, author unknown, was traditionally said between the regular confession ("אָשַׁמְנוּ") and the longer "עַל חֵטְא." It contains a double alphabetical acrostic in the initial letters of each stich. Nowadays, most congregations say only the last two lines.

אַתָּה מֵבִין תַּעֲלוּמוֹת לֵב / אֶפֶס לְךָ נִגְלוֹת וְגַם נִסְתָּרוֹת.
בָּאנוּ בִדְבָרִים לְפַתּוֹתְךָ בָּם / בְּרִשְׁעֵנוּ אַל תֵּפֶן, וְלֹא בְמַעֲלָלֵינוּ.
גִּשְׁתֵּנוּ בְּיוֹם זֶה כְּיָרֵא וְחָרֵד / גֵּאֶה כְּרַחוּם לְמַעַנְךָ עֲשֵׂה חֶסֶד.
דִּין אַל תִּמְתַּח מוּל עָפָר וָאֵפֶר / דַּע אַחֲרִיתֵנוּ רִמָּה וְתוֹלֵעָה.
הַאִם שָׁגַגְנוּ וְנֶעְלַם מִמֶּנּוּ / הֲלֹא אַתָּה לְבַד מֵבִין שְׁגִיאוֹת
וְאַל תַּחְשֹׁב לָנוּ כְּעוֹשֵׂה בְזָדוֹן / וִדּוּי שְׂפָתֵינוּ שְׁעֵה בְּעֵת רָצוֹן.
זֶה כַּפֵּר לָנוּ, הוֹדַע וְלֹא הוֹדַע / זָדוֹן וְנֶעְלָם, עֲשֵׂה וְלֹא תַעֲשֶׂה.
חַלְּצֵנוּ מֵעֹנֶשׁ כָּרֵת וּמִיתָה / חֲמֹל עַל חֹמֶר מַעֲשֵׂה יָדֶיךָ.
טָפַשְׁנוּ בְּרֹעַ יֵצֶר אֲשֶׁר מִנְּעוּרֵינוּ / טָמוּן בְּקִרְבֵּנוּ כְּרֶשֶׁת לִפְעָמֵינוּ.
יוֹצְרֵנוּ וְעוֹשֵׂנוּ, יוֹדֵעַ יִצְרֵנוּ / יֶהֱמוּ רַחֲמֶיךָ וְאַל תַּשְׁחִיתֵנוּ.
כִּי מִלְּפָנֶיךָ מִי יִסָּתֵר / כֹּל גָּלוּי לְךָ כָּאוֹר וְכַצָּהֳרָיִם.
לְבֵית דִּין הוֹרֵיתָ אַרְבַּע מִיתוֹת / לְמַעַנְךָ עֲשֵׂה, וּמֵהֶם חַלְּצֵנוּ.
מֵאָז יְצַרְתָּנוּ, חֲקַרְתָּנוּ וַתֵּדַע / מַעֲשֵׂינוּ, כִּי הֵמָּה עָמָל וָאָוֶן.
נְצֹר נַפְשׁוֹתֵינוּ, כִּי בְּיָדְךָ כָּל נֶפֶשׁ / נָא תִיקַר נֶפֶשׁ, מִמְּעַנֵּי לְךָ נָפֶשׁ.
סְקִילָה, שְׂרֵפָה, הֶרֶג וְחֶנֶק / סוֹדָם גִּלִּיתָ לְיוֹדְעֵי אֲמִתֶּךָ.
עַל כָּל פְּשָׁעֵינוּ, אֱלוֹהַּ, כַּפֵּר לָנוּ / עַל יָדוּעַ לָנוּ, וְעַל נֶעְלָם מִמֶּנּוּ.
פְּשָׁעֵינוּ הוֹדִינוּ לְךָ, חוֹקֵר לֵב / פְּדֵנוּ מֵחֵטְא, נַקֵּנוּ מֵעָוֹן.
צוּר, אַל תֵּפֶן בֶּאֱנוֹשׁ חָצִיר / צְדָקָה עֲשֵׂה עִמָּנוּ, כְּעָשִׂיתָ עִם כָּל חָי.
קִדַּמְנוּ בְּנֶשֶׁף, קָרַבְנוּ בְּשֶׁוַע / קָרְבֵנוּ אֵלֶיךָ, קְשֹׁב קְרִיאָתֵנוּ.
רִשְׁעֵנוּ אַל תֵּפֶן, רַחֲמֵנוּ וְנִצְטַדָּקָה / רַחֲמֶיךָ יְבֹאוּנוּ, רַחוּם וְחַנּוּן.
◂ שִׁמְךָ מֵעוֹלָם עוֹבֵר עַל פֶּשַׁע / שַׁוְעָתֵנוּ תַּאֲזִין, בְּעָמְדֵנוּ לְפָנֶיךָ בִּתְפִלָּה
תַּעֲבֹר עַל פֶּשַׁע לְעַם שָׁבֵי פֶשַׁע / תִּמְחֶה פְשָׁעֵינוּ מִנֶּגֶד עֵינֶיךָ.

Continue with "אַתָּה יוֹדֵעַ רָזֵי עוֹלָם" – in מעריב on page 171, in שחרית on page 685, in מוסף on page 953, and in מנחה on page 1077.

פיוטים לתפילת שחרית

The piyutim said by the שליח ציבור *in* שחרית *are commonly called* יוצרות*; however, the* יוצר *refers only to the first piyut, said at the beginning of the first blessing of the* שמע*. The theme of the* יוצר *for* יום כיפור *is God's forgiveness as an indication of His greatness. The piyut is an alphabetical acrostic with both stichs of each line beginning with the same letter or sound (it is common in piyutim for the letters* ס *and* שׂ *to be used interchangeably). The first two lines serve as alternating refrains.*

Responsively:

סְלַח לְגוֹי קָדוֹשׁ / בְּיוֹם קָדוֹשׁ / מָרוֹם וְקָדוֹשׁ.
חָטָאנוּ צוּרֵנוּ / סְלַח לָנוּ יוֹצְרֵנוּ.

All:

אָז בְּיוֹם כִּפּוּר סְלִיחָה הוֹרֵיתָ / אוֹר וּמְחִילָה לְעַם זוּ קָנִיתָ.
בְּסָלְחֲךָ לַעֲוֹנוֹת וַחֲטָאֵי עֵדָה / בֶּעָשׂוֹר סְמוּכִים בְּבֵית הַוַּעֲדָה.
סְלַח לְגוֹי קָדוֹשׁ / בְּיוֹם קָדוֹשׁ / מָרוֹם וְקָדוֹשׁ.

גָּבְרוּ חֲטָאִים בַּאֲנִי יְשֵׁנָה / גָּשׁ יוֹם אֶחָד בִּימֵי שָׁנָה.
דּוֹבְבוּ בְּתַחֲנוּן לְמוֹחֵל וְסוֹלֵחַ / דּוֹפְקֵי בִתְשׁוּבָה לְיוֹצֵר אוֹר וְסַלָּח.
חָטָאנוּ צוּרֵנוּ / סְלַח לָנוּ יוֹצְרֵנוּ.

הַמְתֵּק הָאוֹר לִסְלִיחָתִי / הָעֵת תַּעֲנֶה, וְתֹאמַר סָלַחְתִּי.
וְתָאִיר עֵינֵינוּ וְתַעֲבֹר עַל פֶּשַׁע / וְחוֹטְאֵי בִשְׁגָגָה אַל נָא תָמִית בְּרֶשַׁע.
סְלַח לְגוֹי קָדוֹשׁ / בְּיוֹם קָדוֹשׁ / מָרוֹם וְקָדוֹשׁ.

זַדְנוּ וְהִרְשַׁעְנוּ בְּרֹעַ מַעֲלָלֵינוּ / זֶה צַדִּיק אַתָּה, עַל כָּל הַבָּא עָלֵינוּ.
חָטָאנוּ לְךָ מֶלֶךְ עוֹלָמִים / חָנְנֵנוּ בְּאוֹרֶךָ, וְלֹא נֵצֵא נִכְלָמִים.
חָטָאנוּ צוּרֵנוּ / סְלַח לָנוּ יוֹצְרֵנוּ.

טוֹב וְסַלָּח לְךָ הִיא הַצְּדָקָה / טַהֲרֵנוּ בְּמַעְיָנְךָ, לוֹבֵשׁ צְדָקָה.
יוֹמָם וָלַיְלָה שָׁפַכְנוּ לֵב וָנֶפֶשׁ / יִזְרַח לָנוּ אוֹר בְּכִפּוּר עִנּוּי נֶפֶשׁ.
סְלַח לְגוֹי קָדוֹשׁ / בְּיוֹם קָדוֹשׁ / מָרוֹם וְקָדוֹשׁ.

כְּחַנּוּן תְּחַפֵּשׂ סִתְרֵי מַעֲשִׂים / כְּרַחוּם תִּסְלַח עֲוֹנוֹת עֲמוּסִים.
לְמַעַן נָרוּץ בְּאוֹר פָּנֶיךָ / לֹא נֵצֵא הַיּוֹם רֵיקָם מִלְּפָנֶיךָ.
חָטָאנוּ צוּרֵנוּ / סְלַח לָנוּ יוֹצְרֵנוּ.

מַלְבִּין כַּשֶּׁלֶג חֲטָאֵי עַמָּךְ / מְקוֹר חַיִּים וָחֶסֶד עִמָּךְ.
נָבוֹאָה עָדֶיךָ, זוֹכֵר הַבְּרִית / נַהֲלֵנוּ בְּאוֹרֶךָ, כְּמוֹ נִסְתָּר בְּנַחַל כְּרִית.

סְלַח לְגוֹי קָדוֹשׁ / בְּיוֹם קָדוֹשׁ / מָרוֹם וְקָדוֹשׁ.

שַׂר הַמְכַפֵּר בְּעַד צֹאן מַרְעִית / סָמְכֵנוּ בְּאוֹרְךָ כְּסוּכַּת מַרְאִית.
עֲנֵנוּ אָבִינוּ מִמַּעֲמַקִּים / עוֹרֵר כְּאוֹר נֹגַהּ שׁוֹשַׁנַּת הָעֲמָקִים.

חָטָאנוּ צוּרֵנוּ / סְלַח לָנוּ יוֹצְרֵנוּ.

פְּתַח לָנוּ שַׁעַר, וְתַעֲלֶה תְּפִלָּה / פָּנֶיךָ נְחַלֶּה שׁוֹכֵן מַעְלָה.
צֵאתֵנוּ תְנַקֶּה, וּבְחֵטְא לֹא נִתְנַזֵּק / צְרְפֵנוּ כַּכֶּסֶף שִׁבְעָתַיִם מְזֻקָּק.

סְלַח לְגוֹי קָדוֹשׁ / בְּיוֹם קָדוֹשׁ / מָרוֹם וְקָדוֹשׁ.

קָרְבֵנוּ לְיִשְׁעֲךָ בְּאוֹר שְׁנֵי עֳפָרִים / קוֹרְאֵי קְדֻשַּׁת יוֹם כִּפּוּרִים.
רְעֵנוּ כְּמִקֶּדֶם וְתָאֳרֵנוּ יְנֹהַר / רַחוּם הַקְשִׁיבָה וַעֲשֵׂה אַל תְּאַחַר.

חָטָאנוּ צוּרֵנוּ / סְלַח לָנוּ יוֹצְרֵנוּ.

◂ שָׁפַכְנוּ כַּמַּיִם אַבְנֵי לִבּוֹת / שַׁחַר אוֹר יַגִּיהַּ בּוֹחֵן לְבָבוֹת.
תְּחַטְּאֵנוּ בְּאֵזוֹב, וְנִטְהַר בְּיוֹם סְלִיחָתִי / תַּקְשִׁיב סְלַח נָא, וְתֹאמַר סָלַחְתִּי.

סְלַח לְגוֹי קָדוֹשׁ / בְּיוֹם קָדוֹשׁ / מָרוֹם וְקָדוֹשׁ.

On a weekday continue with "הַמֵּאִיר" (page 563); on שבת, with "הַכֹּל יוֹדוּךָ" (page 567).

This piyut, known as the אופן, comprises the second part of the יוצר.

The שליח ציבור, followed by the קהל:

בָּרוּךְ שֵׁם כְּבוֹד מַלְכוּתוֹ.

The שליח ציבור, followed by the קהל:

מַלְכוּתוֹ בִּקְהַל עֲדָתִי / וּכְבוֹדוֹ הִיא אֱמוּנָתִי
אֵלָיו בִּקַּשְׁתִּי / לְכַפֵּר עֲוֹן חַטָּאתִי
וּבְיוֹם צוֹם כִּפּוּר סְלִיחָתִי / יַעֲנֶה וְיֹאמַר, סָלַחְתִּי.

The שליח ציבור says the first stich of every line, and the קהל responds with "בָּרוּךְ שֵׁם כְּבוֹד מַלְכוּתוֹ." The refrains are said by all.

קָדוֹשׁ אַדִּיר בַּעֲלִיָּתוֹ בָּרוּךְ שֵׁם כְּבוֹד מַלְכוּתוֹ.
קָדוֹשׁ בִּתְשׁוּבָה שָׁת סְלִיחָתוֹ בָּרוּךְ שֵׁם כְּבוֹד מַלְכוּתוֹ.

מַלְכוּתוֹ בִּקְהַל עֲדָתִי / וּכְבוֹדוֹ הִיא אֱמוּנָתִי
אֵלָיו בְּקַשְׁתִּי / לְכַפֵּר עֲוֹן חַטָּאתִי
וּבְיוֹם צוֹם כִּפּוּר סְלִיחָתִי / יַעֲנֶה וְיֹאמַר, סָלַחְתִּי.

קָדוֹשׁ גִּלָּה לְעַמּוֹ סוֹד דָּתוֹ בָּרוּךְ שֵׁם כְּבוֹד מַלְכוּתוֹ.
קָדוֹשׁ דָּץ עַל כַּפָּרַת צֹאן מַרְעִיתוֹ בָּרוּךְ שֵׁם כְּבוֹד מַלְכוּתוֹ.

מַלְכוּתוֹ בִּקְהַל עֲדָתִי / וּכְבוֹדוֹ הִיא אֱמוּנָתִי
אֵלָיו בְּקַשְׁתִּי / לְכַפֵּר עֲוֹן חַטָּאתִי
וּבְיוֹם צוֹם כִּפּוּר סְלִיחָתִי / יַעֲנֶה וְיֹאמַר, סָלַחְתִּי.

קָדוֹשׁ הַסּוֹלֵחַ לַאֲיֻמָּתוֹ בָּרוּךְ שֵׁם כְּבוֹד מַלְכוּתוֹ.
קָדוֹשׁ וְעַמּוֹ יְמַלְלוּ גְבוּרָתוֹ בָּרוּךְ שֵׁם כְּבוֹד מַלְכוּתוֹ.

מַלְכוּתוֹ בִּקְהַל עֲדָתִי / וּכְבוֹדוֹ הִיא אֱמוּנָתִי
אֵלָיו בְּקַשְׁתִּי / לְכַפֵּר עֲוֹן חַטָּאתִי
וּבְיוֹם צוֹם כִּפּוּר סְלִיחָתִי / יַעֲנֶה וְיֹאמַר, סָלַחְתִּי.

קָדוֹשׁ זוֹכֵר אֲיֻמָּה בְּאַהֲבָתוֹ בָּרוּךְ שֵׁם כְּבוֹד מַלְכוּתוֹ.
קָדוֹשׁ חָפֵץ בְּעִנּוּי נֶפֶשׁ תַּמָּתוֹ בָּרוּךְ שֵׁם כְּבוֹד מַלְכוּתוֹ.

מַלְכוּתוֹ בִּקְהַל עֲדָתִי / וּכְבוֹדוֹ הִיא אֱמוּנָתִי
אֵלָיו בְּקַשְׁתִּי / לְכַפֵּר עֲוֹן חַטָּאתִי
וּבְיוֹם צוֹם כִּפּוּר סְלִיחָתִי / יַעֲנֶה וְיֹאמַר, סָלַחְתִּי.

קָדוֹשׁ טַהֵר טְמֵאִים בְּמֵי זְרִיקָתוֹ בָּרוּךְ שֵׁם כְּבוֹד מַלְכוּתוֹ.
קָדוֹשׁ יַלְבִּין כַּשֶּׁלֶג חֲטָאֵי סְגֻלָּתוֹ בָּרוּךְ שֵׁם כְּבוֹד מַלְכוּתוֹ.

מַלְכוּתוֹ בִּקְהַל עֲדָתִי / וּכְבוֹדוֹ הִיא אֱמוּנָתִי
אֵלָיו בְּקַשְׁתִּי / לְכַפֵּר עֲוֹן חַטָּאתִי
וּבְיוֹם צוֹם כִּפּוּר סְלִיחָתִי / יַעֲנֶה וְיֹאמַר, סָלַחְתִּי.

קָדוֹשׁ כַּפֵּר לְעַמְּךָ יִשְׂרָאֵל שְׁגָגָתוֹ   בָּרוּךְ שֵׁם כְּבוֹד מַלְכוּתוֹ.
קָדוֹשׁ לְיוֹם אֶחָד בַּשָּׁנָה שָׁת קְרִיאָתוֹ   בָּרוּךְ שֵׁם כְּבוֹד מַלְכוּתוֹ.

מַלְכוּתוֹ בִּקְהַל עֲדָתִי / וּכְבוֹדוֹ הִיא אֱמוּנָתִי
אֵלָיו בַּקָּשָׁתִי / לְכַפֵּר עֲוֹן חַטָּאתִי
וּבְיוֹם צוֹם כִּפּוּר סְלִיחָתִי / יַעֲנֶה וְיֹאמַר, סָלַחְתִּי.

קָדוֹשׁ מוֹחֵל וְסוֹלֵחַ לַעֲדָתוֹ   בָּרוּךְ שֵׁם כְּבוֹד מַלְכוּתוֹ.
קָדוֹשׁ נִרְאָה בְּהַר מְרוֹם הָרִים עֲמִידָתוֹ   בָּרוּךְ שֵׁם כְּבוֹד מַלְכוּתוֹ.

מַלְכוּתוֹ בִּקְהַל עֲדָתִי / וּכְבוֹדוֹ הִיא אֱמוּנָתִי
אֵלָיו בַּקָּשָׁתִי / לְכַפֵּר עֲוֹן חַטָּאתִי
וּבְיוֹם צוֹם כִּפּוּר סְלִיחָתִי / יַעֲנֶה וְיֹאמַר, סָלַחְתִּי.

קָדוֹשׁ סוֹלֵחַ וְטוֹב לְסוֹבְלֵי עֹל יִרְאָתוֹ   בָּרוּךְ שֵׁם כְּבוֹד מַלְכוּתוֹ.
קָדוֹשׁ עָוֹן יְכַפֵּר, וְלֹא יָעִיר כָּל חֲמָתוֹ   בָּרוּךְ שֵׁם כְּבוֹד מַלְכוּתוֹ.

מַלְכוּתוֹ בִּקְהַל עֲדָתִי / וּכְבוֹדוֹ הִיא אֱמוּנָתִי
אֵלָיו בַּקָּשָׁתִי / לְכַפֵּר עֲוֹן חַטָּאתִי
וּבְיוֹם צוֹם כִּפּוּר סְלִיחָתִי / יַעֲנֶה וְיֹאמַר, סָלַחְתִּי.

קָדוֹשׁ פְּשָׁעִים מַעֲבִיר בְּצִדְקָתוֹ   בָּרוּךְ שֵׁם כְּבוֹד מַלְכוּתוֹ.
קָדוֹשׁ צוֹם הֶעָשׂוֹר יְקַבֵּל לִתְשׁוּבָתוֹ   בָּרוּךְ שֵׁם כְּבוֹד מַלְכוּתוֹ.

מַלְכוּתוֹ בִּקְהַל עֲדָתִי / וּכְבוֹדוֹ הִיא אֱמוּנָתִי
אֵלָיו בַּקָּשָׁתִי / לְכַפֵּר עֲוֹן חַטָּאתִי
וּבְיוֹם צוֹם כִּפּוּר סְלִיחָתִי / יַעֲנֶה וְיֹאמַר, סָלַחְתִּי.

קָדוֹשׁ קְדוֹשִׁים יַעֲרִיצוּ קְדֻשָּׁתוֹ   בָּרוּךְ שֵׁם כְּבוֹד מַלְכוּתוֹ.
קָדוֹשׁ רַחוּם וְחַנּוּן, וְאֵין זוּלָתוֹ   בָּרוּךְ שֵׁם כְּבוֹד מַלְכוּתוֹ.

מַלְכוּתוֹ בִּקְהַל עֲדָתִי / וּכְבוֹדוֹ הִיא אֱמוּנָתִי
אֵלָיו בַּקָּשָׁתִי / לְכַפֵּר עֲוֹן חַטָּאתִי
וּבְיוֹם צוֹם כִּפּוּר סְלִיחָתִי / יַעֲנֶה וְיֹאמַר, סָלַחְתִּי.

קָדוֹשׁ שׁוֹכֵן שְׁחָקִים בִּמְכוֹן שִׁבְתּוֹ   בָּרוּךְ שֵׁם כְּבוֹד מַלְכוּתוֹ.
קָדוֹשׁ תַּרְשִׁישִׁים יַגִּידוּ תִּפְאַרְתּוֹ   בָּרוּךְ שֵׁם כְּבוֹד מַלְכוּתוֹ.

מַלְכוּתוֹ בִּקְהַל עֲדָתִי / וּכְבוֹדוֹ הִיא אֱמוּנָתִי
אֵלָיו בְּקָשְׁתִּי / לְכַפֵּר עֲוֹן חַטָּאתִי
וּבְיוֹם צוֹם כִּפּוּר סְלִיחָתִי / יַעֲנֶה וְיֹאמַר, סָלַחְתִּי.

וְהַחַיּוֹת יְשׁוֹרֵרוּ / וּכְרוּבִים יְפָאֵרוּ / וּשְׂרָפִים יָרֹנּוּ / וְאֶרְאֶלִּים יְבָרֵכוּ
פְּנֵי כָל חַיָּה וְאוֹפָן וּכְרוּב לְעֻמַּת שְׂרָפִים, לְעֻמָּתָם מְשַׁבְּחִים וְאוֹמְרִים

Continue with "בָּרוּךְ כְּבוֹד־יהוה מִמְּקוֹמוֹ" *on page 575.*

The following piyut is an alphabetical acrostic. Each line of this piyut consists of two stichs that begin with the same letter. The first two lines serve as alternating refrains.

Responsively:

מֶלֶךְ שׁוֹכֵן עַד / לְבַדְּךָ מְלֹךְ עֲדֵי עַד / הָאֵל קָדוֹשׁ.
מֶלֶךְ מַאֲזִין שַׁוְעָה / לְעַמּוֹ מֵחִישׁ יְשׁוּעָה / נוֹרָא וְקָדוֹשׁ.

All:

אֶדֶר יְקָר אֵלִי / אֲחַוֶּה בְּאֶרֶשׂ מִלּוּלִי.
מֶלֶךְ שׁוֹכֵן עַד / לְבַדְּךָ מְלֹךְ עֲדֵי עַד / הָאֵל קָדוֹשׁ.

בְּחֵךְ אַנְעִים זֶמֶר / בְּנִיב אַבִּיעַ אֹמֶר.
מֶלֶךְ מַאֲזִין שַׁוְעָה / לְעַמּוֹ מֵחִישׁ יְשׁוּעָה / נוֹרָא וְקָדוֹשׁ.

גְּבוּרוֹתָיו מִי יְמַלֵּל / גָּדְלוֹ מִי יְפַלֵּל.
מֶלֶךְ שׁוֹכֵן עַד / לְבַדְּךָ מְלֹךְ עֲדֵי עַד / הָאֵל קָדוֹשׁ.

דֹּק מְרוֹפֵף בִּגְעָרָה / דַּרְכּוֹ סוּפָה וּסְעָרָה.
מֶלֶךְ מַאֲזִין שַׁוְעָה / לְעַמּוֹ מֵחִישׁ יְשׁוּעָה / נוֹרָא וְקָדוֹשׁ.

הַנֶּאְדָּר מִקּוֹלוֹת מַיִם / הוֹדוֹ כִּסָּה שָׁמַיִם.
מֶלֶךְ שׁוֹכֵן עַד / לְבַדְּךָ מְלֹךְ עֲדֵי עַד / הָאֵל קָדוֹשׁ.

וּסְבִיבָיו שַׂרְפֵי אֵלִים / וּמִפַּחְדּוֹ זָעִים וְחָלִים.
מֶלֶךְ מַאֲזִין שַׁוְעָה / לְעַמּוֹ מֵחִישׁ יְשׁוּעָה / נוֹרָא וְקָדוֹשׁ.

זָךְ בִּשְׁמֵי מְעוֹנִים / זַעַק שְׁעֵה מִמִּתְעַנִּים.

מֶלֶךְ שׁוֹכֵן עַד / לְבַדְּךָ מְלֹךְ עֲדֵי עַד / הָאֵל קָדוֹשׁ.

חַשְׁרַת סְבִיב סֻכּוֹ / חַשְׁמַל בְּלִי לְסוֹכוֹ.

מֶלֶךְ מַאֲזִין שַׁוְעָה / לְעַמּוֹ מֵחִישׁ יְשׁוּעָה / נוֹרָא וְקָדוֹשׁ.

טוֹב יוֹדֵעַ חוֹסָיו / טָהוֹר מַצְדִּיק עֲמוּסָיו.

מֶלֶךְ שׁוֹכֵן עַד / לְבַדְּךָ מְלֹךְ עֲדֵי עַד / הָאֵל קָדוֹשׁ.

יוֹשֵׁב בְּסֵתֶר עֶלְיוֹן / יְקָר עֹז חֶבְיוֹן.

מֶלֶךְ מַאֲזִין שַׁוְעָה / לְעַמּוֹ מֵחִישׁ יְשׁוּעָה / נוֹרָא וְקָדוֹשׁ.

כּוֹנֵן שַׁחַק בִּתְבוּנָה / כָּל מַעֲשֵׂהוּ בֶּאֱמוּנָה.

מֶלֶךְ שׁוֹכֵן עַד / לְבַדְּךָ מְלֹךְ עֲדֵי עַד / הָאֵל קָדוֹשׁ.

לוֹבֵשׁ עֹז וּגְדֻלָּה / לוֹ נָאוָה תְהִלָּה.

מֶלֶךְ מַאֲזִין שַׁוְעָה / לְעַמּוֹ מֵחִישׁ יְשׁוּעָה / נוֹרָא וְקָדוֹשׁ.

מוֹשֵׁל עוֹלָם בִּגְבוּרָה / מוֹחֶה פִּשְׁעֵי בָרָה.

מֶלֶךְ שׁוֹכֵן עַד / לְבַדְּךָ מְלֹךְ עֲדֵי עַד / הָאֵל קָדוֹשׁ.

נָאוֹר וְאַדִּיר בַּהֲדָרוֹ / נוֹשֵׂא עָוֹן עֶדְרוֹ.

מֶלֶךְ מַאֲזִין שַׁוְעָה / לְעַמּוֹ מֵחִישׁ יְשׁוּעָה / נוֹרָא וְקָדוֹשׁ.

סוֹכֵת שִׂיחוֹת עֲרֵבוֹת / סֹלּוּ לָרֹכֵב בָּעֲרָבוֹת: תהלים סח

מֶלֶךְ שׁוֹכֵן עַד / לְבַדְּךָ מְלֹךְ עֲדֵי עַד / הָאֵל קָדוֹשׁ.

עָף עַל כְּרוּבוֹ / עוֹנֶה לְעַם קְרוֹבוֹ.

מֶלֶךְ מַאֲזִין שַׁוְעָה / לְעַמּוֹ מֵחִישׁ יְשׁוּעָה / נוֹרָא וְקָדוֹשׁ.

פּוֹקֵד צִבְאוֹת גְּדוּדָיו / פּוֹדֶה נֶפֶשׁ עֲבָדָיו.

מֶלֶךְ שׁוֹכֵן עַד / לְבַדְּךָ מְלֹךְ עֲדֵי עַד / הָאֵל קָדוֹשׁ.

צִדְקוֹ עֶלְיוֹנִים מַגִּידִים / צְבָא תַחְתּוֹנִים מוֹדִים.

מֶלֶךְ מַאֲזִין שַׁוְעָה / לְעַמּוֹ מֵחִישׁ יְשׁוּעָה / נוֹרָא וְקָדוֹשׁ.

קָדוֹשׁ, יוֹשֵׁב תְּהִלּוֹת: / קְנוּיָיו מַשִּׂיג מְחִילוֹת. תהלים כב
מֶלֶךְ שׁוֹכֵן עַד / לְבַדְּךָ מְלֹךְ עֲדֵי עַד / הָאֵל קָדוֹשׁ.

רָם וְנִשָּׂא וְגֵאֶה / רוֹאֶה שָׁפָל וְנִכְאֶה.
מֶלֶךְ מַאֲזִין שַׁוְעָה / לְעַמּוֹ מֵחִישׁ יְשׁוּעָה / נוֹרָא וְקָדוֹשׁ.

שׁוֹכֵן בִּרְוּם עֲלִיּוֹת / שַׁלִּיט בְּדוּךְ תַּחְתִּיּוֹת.
מֶלֶךְ שׁוֹכֵן עַד / לְבַדְּךָ מְלֹךְ עֲדֵי עַד / הָאֵל קָדוֹשׁ.

◂ תּוֹמֵךְ זְרוֹעוֹת עוֹלָם / תַּקִּיף וּמִכֹּל נֶעְלָם.
מֶלֶךְ מַאֲזִין שַׁוְעָה / לְעַמּוֹ מֵחִישׁ יְשׁוּעָה / נוֹרָא וְקָדוֹשׁ.

In this piyut, of unknown authorship, each stanza has three stichs: the opening letters of the first two follow an אתב״ש *structure, and the third is a rhyming biblical quotation.*

וּבְכֵן, וְאַתָּה כְּרַחוּם סְלַח לָנוּ.

אָנָּא אֱלֹהִים חַיִּים / תִּכְתֹּב דְּבֵקֶיךָ לְחַיִּים
כִּי־עִמְּךָ מְקוֹר חַיִּים: וְאַתָּה כְּרַחוּם סְלַח לָנוּ. תהלים לו

בְּעֵת רָצוֹן תַּעֲנֶה תְּחִנָּתִי / שִׁמְעָה יהוה צֶדֶק, הַקְשִׁיבָה רִנָּתִי: תהלים יז
אַל־תַּעְלֵם אָזְנְךָ לְרַוְחָתִי לְשַׁוְעָתִי: וְאַתָּה כְּרַחוּם סְלַח לָנוּ. איכה ג

גְּעִית קוֹרְאֶיךָ בִּתְפִלַּת שַׁחַר / רְצֵה וְהַלְבֵּן אָדֹם כְּצַחַר
אֲדֹנָי הַקְשִׁיבָה וַעֲשֵׂה אַל־תְּאַחַר: וְאַתָּה כְּרַחוּם סְלַח לָנוּ. דניאל ט

דַּלּוֹתִי וְלִי יְהוֹשִׁיעַ: / קוֶֹיךָ בַּל תַּרְשִׁיעַ תהלים קטז
מְדַבֵּר בִּצְדָקָה רַב לְהוֹשִׁיעַ: וְאַתָּה כְּרַחוּם סְלַח לָנוּ. ישעיה סג

הַצְּפוּפִים יַחַד לְעָבְדֶךָ / צִבְאוֹת צֹאן יָדֶךָ
הַרְאֵנוּ יהוה חַסְדֶּךָ: וְאַתָּה כְּרַחוּם סְלַח לָנוּ. תהלים פה

וּמַרְבִּים תַּחַן וָעֶתֶר / פֶּלֶל לַחֲשֵׁנוּ הֵעָתֵר
אַתָּה אֵל מִסְתַּתֵּר: וְאַתָּה כְּרַחוּם סְלַח לָנוּ. ישעיה מה

זַעֲקֵנוּ שְׁעֵה אוֹתָנוּ לִצְדָקָה / עֱרֹךְ שִׁוְעֵנוּ כְּתִמּוֹר דַּקָּה מִן הַדַּקָּה
לְךָ אֲדֹנָי הַצְּדָקָה: וְאַתָּה כְּרַחוּם סְלַח לָנוּ. דניאל ט

חָטָאנוּ בְּאֵזוֹב וְטַהֲרֵנוּ / סְמָכֵנוּ, סְתָרֵנוּ וְשַׁבְּרֵנוּ
אֲנַחְנוּ הַחֹמֶר וְאַתָּה יֹצְרֵנוּ: וְאַתָּה כְּרַחוּם סְלַח לָנוּ. ישעיה סד

טָהוֹר קַשֵּׁב חִנּוּנַי / נַקֵּנִי מִכֶּתֶם עֲוֹנַי
מִקְוֵה יִשְׂרָאֵל יהוה: וְאַתָּה כְּרַחוּם סְלַח לָנוּ. ירמיה יז

יֶהֱמוּ מֵעֶיךָ עָלֵינוּ / מַהֵר רַחֲמֶיךָ יְקַדְּמוּנוּ
אַתָּה יהוה אָבִינוּ: וְאַתָּה כְּרַחוּם סְלַח לָנוּ. ישעיה סג

כְּרַחוּם תְּכַפֵּר עָוֹן / לְכֹל תִּשָּׂא עָוֹן
וְאַל־לָעַד תִּזְכֹּר עָוֹן: וְאַתָּה כְּרַחוּם סְלַח לָנוּ. ישעיה סד

The שליח ציבור*, followed by the* קהל*:*

הַיּוֹם יִכָּתֵב בְּסֵפֶר הַזִּכְרוֹנוֹת, הַחַיִּים וְהַמָּוֶת.
אָנָּא כַּנָּה, עוּרִי נָא, הִתְעוֹרְרִי נָא
עִמְדִי נָא, הִתְיַצְּבִי נָא, קוּמִי נָא, חַלִּי נָא
בְּעַד הַנֶּפֶשׁ חַנִּי נָא, פְּנֵי דָּר עֶלְיוֹן.

*In this piyut, attributed to Rabbi Yosef ibn Avitur (Cordoba, tenth century), we ask for forgiveness early on – in "*תְּפִלַּת הַשַּׁחַר*" (literally, "the prayer of daybreak"), conveying our readiness to repent and our hope that atonement be granted soon, before the day is through.*

All:

אֲיֻמָּה בָּחַר / יַלְבִּין כְּצֶמֶר צַחַר בִּתְפִלַּת הַשַּׁחַר.
בַּטְּחוּת חוֹקֵר / צֹאן עֶדְרוֹ יְבַקֵּר בְּעֵת תְּמִיד הַבֹּקֶר.
גּוֹשֵׁם וְעוֹצֵר / גָּלוּתֵנוּ יְקַצֵּר בְּזֹאת תְּפִלַּת יוֹצֵר.

הַיּוֹם יִכָּתֵב בְּסֵפֶר הַזִּכְרוֹנוֹת, הַחַיִּים וְהַמָּוֶת.
אָנָּא כַּנָּה, עוּרִי נָא, הִתְעוֹרְרִי נָא
עִמְדִי נָא, הִתְיַצְּבִי נָא, קוּמִי נָא, חַלִּי נָא
בְּעַד הַנֶּפֶשׁ חַנִּי נָא, פְּנֵי דָּר עֶלְיוֹן.

דְּרוֹר אַל תְּאַחֵר / כִּי גְרוֹנֵנוּ נִחַר   בִּתְפִלַּת הַשַּׁחַר.
הַכֹּל סוֹקֵר / הַמַּסְטִין יַכְחִישׁ וִישַׁקֵּר   בְּעֵת תְּמִיד הַבֹּקֶר.
וּמְזִמָּה לֹא יִבָּצֵר / מִצָּרוֹתֵינוּ יֻצַּר   בְּזֹאת תְּפִלַּת יוֹצֵר.

הַיּוֹם יִכָּתֵב בְּסֵפֶר הַזִּכְרוֹנוֹת, הַחַיִּים וְהַמָּוֶת.
אָנָּא כַּנָּה, עוּרִי נָא, הִתְעוֹרְרִי נָא
עִמְדִי נָא, הִתְיַצְּבִי נָא, קוּמִי נָא, חֲלִי נָא
בְּעַד הַנֶּפֶשׁ חַנִּי נָא, פְּנֵי דַּר עֶלְיוֹן.

זָחוּל סְחַרְחַר / בֶּטַח יִרְבַּץ וְיִסְחַר   בִּתְפִלַּת הַשַּׁחַר.
חַיָּתְךָ יַקֵּר / בְּנֵי שֵׁת לְקַרְקֵר   בְּעֵת תְּמִיד הַבֹּקֶר.
טָהוֹר וְנוֹצֵר / סְגֻלָּתוֹ לְחַיִּים יְעַצֵּר   בְּזֹאת תְּפִלַּת יוֹצֵר.

הַיּוֹם יִכָּתֵב בְּסֵפֶר הַזִּכְרוֹנוֹת, הַחַיִּים וְהַמָּוֶת.
אָנָּא כַּנָּה, עוּרִי נָא, הִתְעוֹרְרִי נָא
עִמְדִי נָא, הִתְיַצְּבִי נָא, קוּמִי נָא, חֲלִי נָא
בְּעַד הַנֶּפֶשׁ חַנִּי נָא, פְּנֵי דַּר עֶלְיוֹן.

יְדִיד מְרַחֵם מִשְּׁחַר / יוֹשִׁיעַ טֶרֶם מָחָר   בִּתְפִלַּת הַשַּׁחַר.
כּוֹבֵשׁ הָרִים וְעוֹקֵר / לְטוֹבָה עַמּוֹ יְבַקֵּר   בְּעֵת תְּמִיד הַבֹּקֶר.
מִקְדָּשְׁךָ וּמִזְבֵּחַ וְהֶחָצֵר / נָא כְּקַדְמָתָם תְּבַצֵּר   בְּזֹאת תְּפִלַּת יוֹצֵר.

הַיּוֹם יִכָּתֵב בְּסֵפֶר הַזִּכְרוֹנוֹת, הַחַיִּים וְהַמָּוֶת.
אָנָּא כַּנָּה, עוּרִי נָא, הִתְעוֹרְרִי נָא
עִמְדִי נָא, הִתְיַצְּבִי נָא, קוּמִי נָא, חֲלִי נָא
בְּעַד הַנֶּפֶשׁ חַנִּי נָא, פְּנֵי דַּר עֶלְיוֹן.

סְעוּרָה וּשְׁבוּרָה כְּפֶחָר / פְּצֵה מֵרִיב וְחַרְחַר   בִּתְפִלַּת הַשַּׁחַר.
קַרְנוֹת עֹשֶׁר יְעַקֵּר / שְׁתוּלִים בְּבֵיתוֹ לְיַקֵּר   בְּעֵת תְּמִיד הַבֹּקֶר.
יוֹרֶה וּמַלְקוֹשׁ הַפְצֵר / סַפֵּק לְחוֹרֵשׁ וְקוֹצֵר   בְּזֹאת תְּפִלַּת יוֹצֵר.

הַיּוֹם יִכָּתֵב בְּסֵפֶר הַזִּכְרוֹנוֹת, הַחַיִּים וְהַמָּוֶת.
אָנָּא כַּנָּה, עוּרִי נָא, הִתְעוֹרְרִי נָא
עִמְדִי נָא, הִתְיַצְּבִי נָא, קוּמִי נָא, חֲלִי נָא
בְּעַד הַנֶּפֶשׁ חַנִּי נָא, פְּנֵי דַּר עֶלְיוֹן.

All:

וּבְכֵן, אַךְ חַנּוּן אַתָּה, וְרַחוּם לְכָל פֹּעַל.

The first ten lines describe Israel praying to God and awaiting His salvation. Subsequently, the poet addresses God directly, imploring Him to have mercy on His people.

The שליח ציבור *says the first stich of each line, and the* קהל *responds with the refrains.*

אַךְ אָתִים בְּחִין לְפָנֶיךָ כִּי אַתָּה רַחוּם לְכָל פֹּעַל.
אַךְ בּוֹטְחִים בְּחַסְדְּךָ אֱמוּנֶיךָ כִּי אַתָּה רַחוּם לְכָל פֹּעַל.
אַךְ גּוֹעִים וּמַרְגִּישִׁים שִׁכְנֶךָ כִּי אַתָּה רַחוּם לְכָל פֹּעַל.
אַךְ דָּלוּ עֵינֵיהֶם לִמְעוֹנֶךָ חַנּוּן וְרַחוּם לְכָל פֹּעַל.

אַךְ הוֹגִים לַעֲנוֹת עֲנָיֶיךָ כִּי אַתָּה רַחוּם לְכָל פֹּעַל.
אַךְ וְעוֹדִים בְּנִצּוּחַ לְנַגְּנֶךָ כִּי אַתָּה רַחוּם לְכָל פֹּעַל.
אַךְ זוֹעֲקִים יַחַד הֲמוֹנֶיךָ כִּי אַתָּה רַחוּם לְכָל פֹּעַל.
אַךְ חוֹכִים יְשׁוּעוֹת חָסְנֶךָ חַנּוּן וְרַחוּם לְכָל פֹּעַל.

אַךְ טְבוּלִים בְּטֹהַר לְחַנְּנֶךָ כִּי אַתָּה רַחוּם לְכָל פֹּעַל.
אַךְ יוֹדוּ לְשִׁמְךָ בָּנֶיךָ כִּי אַתָּה רַחוּם לְכָל פֹּעַל.
אַךְ כַּפֵּר לְעַם מַאֲמִינֶיךָ כִּי אַתָּה רַחוּם לְכָל פֹּעַל.
אַךְ לֹא לָנוּ כִּי אִם לְמַעַנְךָ חַנּוּן וְרַחוּם לְכָל פֹּעַל.

אַךְ מַגֵּר מִתְקוֹמְמֵי צְפוּנֶיךָ כִּי אַתָּה רַחוּם לְכָל פֹּעַל.
אַךְ נְשָׂא זֶרַע בְּחוּנֶיךָ כִּי אַתָּה רַחוּם לְכָל פֹּעַל.
אַךְ סְלִיחָה תַּרְבֶּה לְמִתְעַנֶּיךָ כִּי אַתָּה רַחוּם לְכָל פֹּעַל.
אַךְ עֲנֵם מִשְּׁמֵי מְעוֹנֶךָ חַנּוּן וְרַחוּם לְכָל פֹּעַל.

אַךְ פְּצֵם מֵהֶמְיַת שְׁאוֹנֶךָ כִּי אַתָּה רַחוּם לְכָל פֹּעַל.
אַךְ צַדֵּק גּוֹי נְבוֹנֶיךָ כִּי אַתָּה רַחוּם לְכָל פֹּעַל.
אַךְ קוֹמֵם קֶדֶם קִנְיָנֶךָ כִּי אַתָּה רַחוּם לְכָל פֹּעַל.
אַךְ רוֹמֵם תֵּל אַרְמוֹנֶךָ כִּי אַתָּה רַחוּם לְכָל פֹּעַל.
אַךְ שְׁעֵה לַחַשׁ מִתְחַנְּנֶיךָ כִּי אַתָּה רַחוּם לְכָל פֹּעַל.
אַךְ תָּמְכֵם וְהַשְׁכֵּם מֵחֲרוֹנֶךָ חַנּוּן וְרַחוּם לְכָל פֹּעַל.

*Continue with "*וּבְכֵן, אִמְרוּ לֵאלֹהִים*" on page 639.*

The following three piyutim, each containing alphabetical acrostics, are generally omitted by most congregations.

וּבְכֵן, וְעִזּוּ בַּשְּׁחָקִים.

אַפְסֵי אֶרֶץ בִּדְבָרוֹ הֵקִים / בְּיִרְאָה לְעָבְדוֹ מִתְלַהֲקִים
גּוֹלֶה מִנִּי חֹשֶׁךְ עֲמֻקִּים / דְּבַר עַבְדּוֹ מֵקִים
הַחוֹצֵב לֶהָבוֹת וּבְרָקִים / וְתֵבֵל מְאִירִים וּמַבְהִיקִים
זוֹכֵר בְּרִית מְצוּקִים / חַסְדּוֹ גָּדוֹל מֵעַל לְמוּצָקִים
טוֹב לְמָעוֹז, לְאֵלָיו דְּבוּקִים / יְחַיּוּ כֹּל בּוֹ דְּבֵקִים
כִּי מֵרוּחוֹ הָרִים מִתְפָּרְקִים / לֹא יָכִילוּ זַעְמוֹ צוּרִים וְצוּקִים
מִפַּחְדּוֹ יִתְבַּקְּעוּ עֲמָקִים / נְמוֹגִים וְכַדּוֹנַג נְמַקִּים
סוּפָה וּסְעָרָה דַּרְכּוֹ נֶאֱבָקִים / עָנָן מִדְרַךְ רַגְלָיו כַּאֲבָקִים
פְּדוּת שָׁלַח לְעַם לוֹ חֲשׁוּקִים / צִוָּה לְעוֹלָם בְּרִיתוֹ לִנְשׁוּקִים
קְנוּיִים לוֹ וּבִימִינוֹ נֶחֱבָקִים / רָצִים אַחֲרָיו וּבוֹ נִדְבָּקִים
שַׁוְעָם שׁוֹמֵעַ מִמַּעֲמַקִּים / תִּפְאֶרֶת עֹז לְשׁוֹשַׁנַּת הָעֲמָקִים.

וּבְכֵן, יהוה מִי כָמוֹךָ.

מִי כָמְוֹךָ אַדִּיר בַּמְּרוֹמִים
מִי כָמְוֹךָ בּוֹרֵא כֵס וַהֲדוֹמִים
מִי כָמְוֹךָ גִּבּוֹר וּמוֹשִׁיעַ
מִי כָמְוֹךָ דּוֹבֵר בִּצְדָקָה רַב לְהוֹשִׁיעַ
מִי כָמְוֹךָ הוֹד וְהָדָר לוֹבֵשׁ
מִי כָמְוֹךָ חֵטְא וְעָוֹן כּוֹבֵשׁ
מִי כָמְוֹךָ זַךְ בָּעֶלְיוֹנִים
מִי כָמְוֹךָ חֲסִין בְּאַלְפֵי שִׁנְאַנִּים
מִי כָמְוֹךָ טוֹב וּמֵטִיב
מִי כָמְוֹךָ יְשָׁרִים לְהֵיטִיב
מִי כָמְוֹךָ כּוֹנֵס כַּנֵּד מֵי הַיָּם
מִי כָמְוֹךָ לְהָשִׁיב מִמְּצֻלוֹת יָם
מִי כָמְוֹךָ מָדַד בְּשָׁעֳלוֹ מַיִם
מִי כָמְוֹךָ נֶאְדָּר מִקּוֹלוֹת מַיִם
מִי כָמְוֹךָ שָׂם עָבִים רְכוּבוֹ
מִי כָמְוֹךָ עוֹזֵר וְיוֹדֵעַ חוֹסֵי בוֹ
מִי כָמְוֹךָ פּוֹעֵל יְשׁוּעוֹת
מִי כָמְוֹךָ צוֹעֲקָיו לְהַשְׁעוֹת
מִי כָמְוֹךָ קָדוֹשׁ וְנוֹרָא שְׁמוֹ
מִי כָמְוֹךָ רוֹצֶה בְּעַמּוֹ
מִי כָמְוֹךָ שׁוֹמֵר הַבְּרִית וְהַחֶסֶד
מִי כָמְוֹךָ תִּתֵּן אֱמֶת לְיַעֲקֹב וּלְאַבְרָהָם חֶסֶד.

In the following piyut, the first stich of each stanza describes God's qualitative superiority to the heavenly hosts, and the second describes the uniqueness of Israel.

וּבְכֵן, אֵין־כָּמוֹךָ בָאֱלֹהִים, אֲדֹנָי, וְאֵין כְּמַעֲשֶׂיךָ׃ תהלים פו

אֵין כָּמוֹךָ בְּאַדִּירֵי מַעְלָה וְאֵין כְּמַעֲשֶׂיךָ בִּבְרוּרֵי מַטָּה
אֵין כָּמוֹךָ בִּגְדוּדֵי מַעְלָה וְאֵין כְּמַעֲשֶׂיךָ בְּדָרֵי מַטָּה
אֵין כָּמוֹךָ בַּהֲמוֹנֵי מַעְלָה וְאֵין כְּמַעֲשֶׂיךָ בְּוַעוּדֵי מַטָּה
אֵין כָּמוֹךָ בְּזַכֵּי מַעְלָה וְאֵין כְּמַעֲשֶׂיךָ בַּחֲיָלֵי מַטָּה
אֵין כָּמוֹךָ בִּטְהוֹרֵי מַעְלָה וְאֵין כְּמַעֲשֶׂיךָ בִּיקִירֵי מַטָּה
אֵין כָּמוֹךָ בִּכְרוּבֵי מַעְלָה וְאֵין כְּמַעֲשֶׂיךָ בִּלְגְיוֹנֵי מַטָּה
אֵין כָּמוֹךָ בְּמַלְאֲכֵי מַעְלָה וְאֵין כְּמַעֲשֶׂיךָ בִּנְגִידֵי מַטָּה
אֵין כָּמוֹךָ בִּשְׂרָפֵי מַעְלָה וְאֵין כְּמַעֲשֶׂיךָ בְּעָרִיצֵי מַטָּה
אֵין כָּמוֹךָ בִּפְלִיאֵי מַעְלָה וְאֵין כְּמַעֲשֶׂיךָ בְּצִבְאוֹת מַטָּה
אֵין כָּמוֹךָ בִּקְדוֹשֵׁי מַעְלָה וְאֵין כְּמַעֲשֶׂיךָ בְּרוֹזְנֵי מַטָּה
אֵין כָּמוֹךָ בְּשִׁנְאַנֵּי מַעְלָה וְאֵין כְּמַעֲשֶׂיךָ בְּתַקִּיפֵי מַטָּה.

Continue with "וּבְכֵן, נַאֲדִּרְךָ חַי עוֹלָמִים" on page 655.

After הָאַדֶּרֶת וְהָאֱמוּנָה, which concluded the sequence of piyutim focusing on God's greatness, there follows a series of seven piyutim leading to קדושה.

וּבְכֵן, נַאֲמִירְךָ אֱלֹהֵינוּ בְּאֵימָה.

נַאֲמִירְךָ בְּאֵימָה / נְבָרֶכְךָ בְּבִינָה
נְגַדֶּלְךָ בִּגְדֻלָּה / נִדְרָשְׁךָ בְּדֵעָה
נְהַדֶּרְךָ בְּהוֹדָיָה / נוֹדְךָ בְּוַעִידָה
נַזְכִּירְךָ בְּזִמְרָה / נְחַסְּנְךָ בַּחִילָה
נַטְעִימְךָ בְּטָהֳרָה / נְיַחֶדְךָ בְּיִרְאָה
נְכַבֶּדְךָ בִּכְרִיעָה / נְלַבֶּבְךָ בִּלְמִידָה
נַמְלִיכְךָ בִּמְלוּכָה / נְנַצֵּחֲךָ בִּנְעִימָה
נְשַׂגֶּבְךָ בְּשִׂרָה / נַעֲרִיצְךָ בַּעֲנָוָה
נְפָאֶרְךָ בִּפְצִיחָה / נְצַלְצֶלְךָ בְּצָהֳלָה
נַקְדִּישְׁךָ בִּקְרִיאָה / נְרוֹמִמְךָ בִּרְנָנָה
נְשׁוֹרְרֶךָ בְּשֶׁבַח / נַתְמִידְךָ בִּתְהִלָּה.

וּבְכֵן, רוֹמְמוּ יהוה אֱלֹהֵינוּ וְהִשְׁתַּחֲווּ לַהֲדֹם רַגְלָיו תהלים צט
קָדוֹשׁ הוּא:

רוֹמְמוּ אֵל מֶלֶךְ נֶאֱמָן קָדוֹשׁ הוּא, בָּרוּךְ בְּכָל זְמַן
רוֹמְמוּ גּוֹמֵל חֲסָדִים קָדוֹשׁ הוּא, דָּתוֹתָיו דּוֹדִים
רוֹמְמוּ הַנִּקְדָּשׁ בִּצְדָקָה קָדוֹשׁ הוּא וּמַאֲזִין צְעָקָה
רוֹמְמוּ זֵרַת שְׁחָקִים קָדוֹשׁ הוּא, חִכּוֹ מַמְתַקִּים
רוֹמְמוּ טוֹב לַכֹּל קָדוֹשׁ הוּא, יוֹדֵעַ הַכֹּל
רוֹמְמוּ כָּבוֹד אוֹמֵר כֻּלּוֹ בְּהֵיכָלוֹ קָדוֹשׁ הוּא, לְהַקְדִּישׁוֹ וּלְעַלּוֹ
רוֹמְמוּ מוֹנֶה מִסְפָּר לַכּוֹכָבִים קָדוֹשׁ הוּא, נִצָּב בַּעֲדַת כְּרוּבִים
רוֹמְמוּ סוֹבֵל בִּזְרוֹעוֹ עוֹלָם קָדוֹשׁ הוּא, עֻזּוֹ וּמִכֹּל נֶעְלָם
רוֹמְמוּ פּוֹנֶה וְחוֹנֵן יְדִידִים קָדוֹשׁ הוּא, צִדְקָתוֹ שָׁמַיִם מַגִּידִים
רוֹמְמוּ קָרוֹב לְקוֹרְאָיו קָדוֹשׁ הוּא, רוֹצֶה יְרֵאָיו
רוֹמְמוּ שׁוֹמֵעַ תְּפִלּוֹת קָדוֹשׁ הוּא, תִּפְאַרְתּוֹ בְּמַקְהֵלוֹת.

וּבְכֵן, רוֹמְמוּ יהוה אֱלֹהֵינוּ וְהִשְׁתַּחֲווּ לְהַר קָדְשׁוֹ תהלים צט
כִּי־קָדוֹשׁ יהוה אֱלֹהֵינוּ:

רוֹמְמוּ אַדִּיר וְנוֹרָא כִּי קָדוֹשׁ הוּא, בְּרוּחוֹ שָׁמַיִם שִׁפְרָה
רוֹמְמוּ גָּדְלָתוֹ בִּקְהַל יְשָׁרִים כִּי קָדוֹשׁ הוּא, דּוֹבֵר צְדָקוֹת, מַגִּיד מֵישָׁרִים
רוֹמְמוּ הַנַּעֲרָץ בְּקֹדֶשׁ כִּי קָדוֹשׁ הוּא, וְהִלּוּכוֹ בְּקֹדֶשׁ
רוֹמְמוּ זוֹכֵר בְּרִית אָבוֹת כִּי קָדוֹשׁ הוּא, חוֹצֵב לֶהָבוֹת
רוֹמְמוּ טָהוֹר שׁוֹלֵחַ בְּרָקִים כִּי קָדוֹשׁ הוּא, יוֹסֵד אֲרָקִים
רוֹמְמוּ כִּסְאוֹ הֵכִין בִּשְׁמֵי רוּמָה כִּי קָדוֹשׁ הוּא, לוֹכֵד חֲכָמִים בְּעָרְמָה
רוֹמְמוּ מוֹחֶה כָּעָב פְּשָׁעִים כִּי קָדוֹשׁ הוּא, נוֹתֵן יָד לְפוֹשְׁעִים
רוֹמְמוּ שַׂגִּיא, שָׁנָיו לְאֵין חֵקֶר כִּי קָדוֹשׁ הוּא, עֶשְׁתּוֹנוֹת חוֹקֵר
רוֹמְמוּ פּוֹדֶה נֶפֶשׁ עֲבָדָיו כִּי קָדוֹשׁ הוּא, צַדִּיק, קֹשֶׁט מַעְבָּדָיו
רוֹמְמוּ קוֹנֵה שָׁמַיִם וָאָרֶץ כִּי קָדוֹשׁ הוּא, רָם הַמַּבִּיט לִקְצוֹת הָאָרֶץ
רוֹמְמוּ שׁוֹכֵן עַד וְקָדוֹשׁ שְׁמוֹ כִּי קָדוֹשׁ הוּא, תְּהִלָּתוֹ כִּשְׁמוֹ.

וּבְכֵן, כִּי אַתָּה אֵל אֱמוּנָה.

אֱמוּנָתְךָ בָּעֶלְיוֹנִים   בְּרִיתְךָ בַּתַּחְתּוֹנִים
גְּדֻלָּתְךָ בָּעֶלְיוֹנִים   דָּתְךָ בַּתַּחְתּוֹנִים
הוֹדְךָ בָּעֶלְיוֹנִים   וְעוּדְךָ בַּתַּחְתּוֹנִים
זְבוּלְךָ בָּעֶלְיוֹנִים   חֲנִיָּתְךָ בַּתַּחְתּוֹנִים
טָהֳרָתְךָ בָּעֶלְיוֹנִים   יִרְאָתְךָ בַּתַּחְתּוֹנִים
כְּבוֹדְךָ בָּעֶלְיוֹנִים   לְמוּדְךָ בַּתַּחְתּוֹנִים
מְעוֹנְךָ בָּעֶלְיוֹנִים   נָוְךָ בַּתַּחְתּוֹנִים
סֻכָּתְךָ בָּעֶלְיוֹנִים   עֲדָתְךָ בַּתַּחְתּוֹנִים
פְּאֵרְךָ בָּעֶלְיוֹנִים   צִדְקָתְךָ בַּתַּחְתּוֹנִים
קְדֻשָּׁתְךָ בָּעֶלְיוֹנִים   רוֹמְמוּתְךָ בַּתַּחְתּוֹנִים
שְׁכִינָתְךָ בָּעֶלְיוֹנִים   תְּהִלָּתְךָ בַּתַּחְתּוֹנִים.

וּבְכֵן, תַּעֲרָץ וְתֻקְדָּשׁ.

הַנִּקְדָּשׁ בְּאַלְפֵי אֲלָפִים   הַנֶּעֱרָץ בְּבָרָקִים קַלִּים
הַנִּקְדָּשׁ בְּגַעַשׁ גַּלְגַּלִּים   הַנֶּעֱרָץ בְּדַהֲרַת אוֹפַנִּים
הַנִּקְדָּשׁ בַּהֲמוֹנֵי עִירִין   הַנֶּעֱרָץ בְּוַעַד קַדִּישִׁין
הַנִּקְדָּשׁ בְּזִקִּים זוֹרְחִים   הַנֶּעֱרָץ בַּחֲצוּבֵי לֶהָבִים
הַנִּקְדָּשׁ בְּטֶכֶס טְהוֹרִים   הַנֶּעֱרָץ בִּיקָדִים יוֹקְדִים
הַנִּקְדָּשׁ בְּכִתֵּי כְרוּבִים   הַנֶּעֱרָץ בְּלַהֲקַת לוֹהֲטִים
הַנִּקְדָּשׁ בְּמַחֲנוֹת מַלְאָכִים   הַנֶּעֱרָץ בְּנֹעַם נוֹגְנִים
הַנִּקְדָּשׁ בִּשְׂרָפִים עוֹמְדִים   הַנֶּעֱרָץ בְּעֹז אֶרְאֶלִּים
הַנִּקְדָּשׁ בִּפְרוּדֵי אֲגַפַּיִם   הַנֶּעֱרָץ בְּצִלְצוּל מַשִּׁיקוֹת כְּנָפַיִם
הַנִּקְדָּשׁ בְּקוֹלָם בֶּהָמוֹן   הַנֶּעֱרָץ בְּרִבּוֹ רִבְבָן
הַנִּקְדָּשׁ בְּשֶׁקֶט שִׁנְאַנִּים   הַנֶּעֱרָץ בְּתֹכֶן תַּלְתַּלִּים.

The שליח ציבור*, followed by the* קהל:

לְיוֹשֵׁב תְּהִלּוֹת / לְרוֹכֵב עֲרָבוֹת / קָדוֹשׁ וּבָרוּךְ.

This piyut, with its double alphabetical acrostic and complex format of refrains, decribes the angels preparing to say קדושה*.*

אֵילֵי שַׁחַק חֲצוּבֵי לְהָבִים   אוֹמְרִים קָדוֹשׁ
אַדִּירֵי כָּל חֵפֶץ הַנֶּאֱהָבִים   אוֹמְרִים בָּרוּךְ
בְּלוּלֵי קֶרַח וְשֶׁלֶג וְשַׁלְהָבִים   אוֹמְרִים קָדוֹשׁ
בַּדֵּי צֶדֶק, גָּזֵי רְהָבִים   קָדוֹשׁ וּבָרוּךְ.
לְיוֹשֵׁב תְּהִלּוֹת / לְרוֹכֵב עֲרָבוֹת / קָדוֹשׁ וּבָרוּךְ.

גְּבַהּ לָהֶם וְיִרְאָה לָהֶם   אוֹמְרִים קָדוֹשׁ   יחזקאל א
גִּבּוֹרֵי כֹחַ בְּמִשְׁכְּנוֹת אָהֳלֵיהֶם   אוֹמְרִים בָּרוּךְ
דָּאֵי בְּכָנָף מְכַסִּים פְּנֵיהֶם   אוֹמְרִים קָדוֹשׁ
דּוֹרְשֵׁי דָתוֹת, דְּבֵקִים בֵּאלֹהֵיהֶם   קָדוֹשׁ וּבָרוּךְ.
לְיוֹשֵׁב תְּהִלּוֹת / לְרוֹכֵב עֲרָבוֹת / קָדוֹשׁ וּבָרוּךְ.

הֲמוֹנֵי עִירִין וְסוֹד קַדִּישִׁין   אוֹמְרִים קָדוֹשׁ
הוֹגֵי שַׁעֲשׁוּעַ, מַטַּע קְדוֹשִׁים   אוֹמְרִים בָּרוּךְ
וְעוֹדֵי מֵעַל גְּוִיָּתָם כְּתַרְשִׁישִׁים   אוֹמְרִים קָדוֹשׁ
וְחוֹלֵי אַהַב, סְמוּכֵי בָּאֲשִׁישִׁים   קָדוֹשׁ וּבָרוּךְ.
לְיוֹשֵׁב תְּהִלּוֹת / לְרוֹכֵב עֲרָבוֹת / קָדוֹשׁ וּבָרוּךְ.

זְבוּדֵי זֹהַר כְּעֵין חַשְׁמַלִּים   אוֹמְרִים קָדוֹשׁ
זוֹקְקֵי שִׁבְעָתַיִם בֵּרוּר מִלִּים   אוֹמְרִים בָּרוּךְ
חֹסֶן חַיָּלִים, רִבְבוֹת אֵלִים   אוֹמְרִים קָדוֹשׁ
חֲנִיטֵי כֹשֶׁר, בְּנֵי אֵלִים   קָדוֹשׁ וּבָרוּךְ.
לְיוֹשֵׁב תְּהִלּוֹת / לְרוֹכֵב עֲרָבוֹת / קָדוֹשׁ וּבָרוּךְ.

טְכוּסֵי טֹהַר, חֲדָשֵׁי בְקָרִים   אוֹמְרִים קָדוֹשׁ
טְעוּנֵי מוֹרָאֲךָ בְּצִוּוּי עִקָּרִים   אוֹמְרִים בָּרוּךְ
יְדִידוּן יְדִדוּן בְּחִיל נִזְקָרִים   אוֹמְרִים קָדוֹשׁ
יוֹדְעֵי בִין, מִפְּנִינִים יְקָרִים   קָדוֹשׁ וּבָרוּךְ.
לְיוֹשֵׁב תְּהִלּוֹת / לְרוֹכֵב עֲרָבוֹת / קָדוֹשׁ וּבָרוּךְ.

כְּסוּיֵי אַרְבַּע, מְרֻבְּעֵי פָנִים   אוֹמְרִים קָדוֹשׁ
כְּרוּתֵי בְרִית פָּנִים בְּפָנִים   אוֹמְרִים בָּרוּךְ
לְבוּשֵׁי בַדִּים, זַכִּים וְחַפִּים   אוֹמְרִים קָדוֹשׁ
לוֹבְשֵׁי לְבָנִים, נְעִימִים וְיָפִים   קָדוֹשׁ וּבָרוּךְ.

לְיוֹשֵׁב תְּהִלּוֹת / לְרוֹכֵב עֲרָבוֹת / קָדוֹשׁ וּבָרוּךְ.

מְשָׁרְתִים נָאִים רָמִים וּגְבוֹהִים   אוֹמְרִים קָדוֹשׁ
מְלַמְּדֵי חֻקִּים, מְשִׁיבֵי נְכוֹחִים   אוֹמְרִים בָּרוּךְ
נוֹגְנֵי נֹעַם סִפִּים מְרוֹפְפִים   אוֹמְרִים קָדוֹשׁ
נָאווּ לְחַיִּים כְּעָגוּר מְצַפְצְפִים   קָדוֹשׁ וּבָרוּךְ.

לְיוֹשֵׁב תְּהִלּוֹת / לְרוֹכֵב עֲרָבוֹת / קָדוֹשׁ וּבָרוּךְ.

סְכוּכֵי אֶבְרָה כְּקָלָל נוֹצְצִים   אוֹמְרִים קָדוֹשׁ
סְגוּלֵי מְעַמִּים בְּיִרְאָה מַעֲרִיצִים   אוֹמְרִים בָּרוּךְ
עוֹמְדִים מִמַּעַל בִּדְבָרוֹ נְחוּצִים   אוֹמְרִים קָדוֹשׁ
עוֹרְכֵי עֹז בְּרַעַד שְׁבוּצִים   קָדוֹשׁ וּבָרוּךְ.

לְיוֹשֵׁב תְּהִלּוֹת / לְרוֹכֵב עֲרָבוֹת / קָדוֹשׁ וּבָרוּךְ.

פָּנִים וְלֹא עֹרֶף נִתְאָמִים   אוֹמְרִים קָדוֹשׁ
פְּרוּשִׁים לְךָ אֲחוּיִם וּמְתֻאָמִים   אוֹמְרִים בָּרוּךְ
צִבְאוֹת עֶלְיוֹנִים גֵּאִים וְרָמִים   אוֹמְרִים קָדוֹשׁ
צִבְאוֹת תַּחְתּוֹנִים לִרְצוֹתְךָ מַעֲרִימִים   קָדוֹשׁ וּבָרוּךְ.

לְיוֹשֵׁב תְּהִלּוֹת / לְרוֹכֵב עֲרָבוֹת / קָדוֹשׁ וּבָרוּךְ.

קוֹרְאֵי בְשִׁלּוּשׁ זֵר תִּפְאָרָה   אוֹמְרִים קָדוֹשׁ
קוֹרְאֵי פַּעֲמַיִם חֲטִיבַת אֲמִירָה   אוֹמְרִים בָּרוּךְ
רַגְלֵיהֶם עֲמִידַת רֶגֶל יְשָׁרָה   אוֹמְרִים קָדוֹשׁ
רְצוּיֵי שַׁדַּי, מְשׁוֹרְרֵי שִׁירָה   קָדוֹשׁ וּבָרוּךְ.

לְיוֹשֵׁב תְּהִלּוֹת / לְרוֹכֵב עֲרָבוֹת / קָדוֹשׁ וּבָרוּךְ.

שִׁנְאַנֵּי שֶׁקֶט, שָׁלוֹם בְּמַחֲנָם   אוֹמְרִים קָדוֹשׁ
שׁוֹקְדֵי דְלָתוֹת בְּשִׂיחַ מַעֲנָם   אוֹמְרִים בָּרוּךְ
תְּלוּלֵי תַעַף בְּשֶׁפֶר הֶגְיוֹנָם   אוֹמְרִים קָדוֹשׁ
תְּמִימֵי דֶרֶךְ לְרִבּוֹנָם וְקוֹנָם   קָדוֹשׁ וּבָרוּךְ.

לְיוֹשֵׁב תְּהִלּוֹת / לְרוֹכֵב עֲרָבוֹת / קָדוֹשׁ וּבָרוּךְ.

The שליח ציבור*, followed by the* קהל*:*

ישעיה ו וּבְכֵן, שְׂרָפִים עֹמְדִים מִמַּעַל לוֹ:

The שליח ציבור*, followed by the* קהל*:*

זֶה אֶל זֶה שׁוֹאֲלִים / אַיֵּה אֵל אֵלִים
אָנָה שׁוֹכֵן מְעָלִים / וְכֻלָּם מַעֲרִיצִים וּמַקְדִּישִׁים וּמְהַלְלִים.

This piyut follows the theme of the previous one, building on the vision described by Isaiah (6:2–3). Originally, it was the last piyut before the סילוק*; nowadays, even congregations who say the whole* קרובה *insert another piyut,* לְאֵל עוֹרֵךְ דִּין*, in between.*

אֵין מִסְפָּר לִגְדוּדֵי צְבָא חֵילוֹ / אֲזוּרִים אֵימָה, אֲחוּזִים פַּחַד חִילוֹ
בְּרַעַד וְרֶתֶת וָרֶטֶט צָגִים לְעֻלּוֹ   שְׂרָפִים עוֹמְדִים מִמַּעַל לוֹ: ישעיה ו

זֶה אֶל זֶה שׁוֹאֲלִים / אַיֵּה אֵל אֵלִים
אָנָה שׁוֹכֵן מְעָלִים / וְכֻלָּם מַעֲרִיצִים וּמַקְדִּישִׁים וּמְהַלְלִים.

גְּוִיָּתָם כַּתַּרְשִׁישׁ, תְּהִלָּה יַשְׁמִיעוּ יַחַד / גֹּבַהּ וְגָאוֹן עֶדְיוֹ יְחוּדוֹ לְיַחַד
דּוֹהֲרִים, גּוֹהֲרִים, לְאֶחָד וּשְׁמוֹ אֶחָד   שֵׁשׁ כְּנָפַיִם שֵׁשׁ כְּנָפַיִם לְאֶחָד:

זֶה אֶל זֶה שׁוֹאֲלִים / אַיֵּה אֵל אֵלִים
אָנָה שׁוֹכֵן מְעָלִים / וְכֻלָּם מַעֲרִיצִים וּמַקְדִּישִׁים וּמְהַלְלִים.

הַנֶּאְדָּר בַּקֹּדֶשׁ, רַב טוּב מַצְפּוּנָיו / הוֹד וְהָדָר וָעֹז בְּחֶבְיוֹנֵי פְּנִינָיו
וּמִמֶּנּוּ יָגוּרוּ אֵלִים וְיִתְחַבְּאוּ מִפָּנָיו   בִּשְׁתַּיִם יְכַסֶּה פָנָיו:

זֶה אֶל זֶה שׁוֹאֲלִים / אַיֵּה אֵל אֵלִים
אָנָה שׁוֹכֵן מְעָלִים / וְכֻלָּם מַעֲרִיצִים וּמַקְדִּישִׁים וּמְהַלְלִים.

זְרוּתֵי זֹהַר מַרְעִיף נִטְפֵי אֲגָלָיו / זַכֵּי שְׁמֵי טֹהַר תֻּכּוּ לְרַגְלָיו
חֲלִים, חַתִּים, חֲפוּזִים, אֲיֻמִּים נִדְגָּלָיו   וּבִשְׁתַּיִם יְכַסֶּה רַגְלָיו:

זֶה אֶל זֶה שׁוֹאֲלִים / אַיֵּה אֵל אֵלִים
אָנָה שׁוֹכֵן מְעָלִים / וְכֻלָּם מַעֲרִיצִים וּמַקְדִּישִׁים וּמְהַלְלִים.

טָסִים וְדָאִים בִּדְמְיוֹן נֶשֶׁר מְעוֹפֵף / טִיסָתָם כַּבָּזָק, סְבִיב כֵּס לְעוֹפֵף
יַשְׁמִיעוּ הִנֵּנוּ, בְּמִשְׁלַחַת קוֹנָם בְּהִתְעוֹפֵף   וּבִשְׁתַּיִם יְעוֹפֵף:
זֶה אֶל זֶה שׁוֹאֲלִים / אַיֵּה אֵל אֵלִים
אָנָה שׁוֹכֵן מְעָלִים / וְכֻלָּם מַעֲרִיצִים וּמַקְדִּישִׁים וּמְהַלְלִים.

כְּסוּיֵי שֵׁשׁ שֵׁשׁ יַעֲרִיצוּ בְּלָאט מַחֲזֶה / כַּבִּיר וְרַב כֹּחַ, וְשָׁפָל יֶחֱזֶה
לְהַקְדִּישׁוֹ בְּפַחַד נִרְשִׁים זֶה מִזֶּה   וְקָרָא זֶה אֶל־זֶה:
זֶה אֶל זֶה שׁוֹאֲלִים / אַיֵּה אֵל אֵלִים
אָנָה שׁוֹכֵן מְעָלִים / וְכֻלָּם מַעֲרִיצִים וּמַקְדִּישִׁים וּמְהַלְלִים.

מוֹשֵׁל בִּגְבוּרָה, עֹשׂ כֹּל בְּמַאֲמָר / מְנִיעִים אֻמּוֹת הַסִּפִּים קְדֻשָּׁתוֹ לוֹמַר
נוֹצְצִים, נוֹגְהִים, לְפָנָיו יַנְעִימוּ מַאֲמָר   וְקָרָא זֶה אֶל־זֶה וְאָמַר:
זֶה אֶל זֶה שׁוֹאֲלִים / אַיֵּה אֵל אֵלִים
אָנָה שׁוֹכֵן מְעָלִים / וְכֻלָּם מַעֲרִיצִים וּמַקְדִּישִׁים וּמְהַלְלִים.

שַׂרְפֵי הוֹד יַכְתִּירוּ זֵר לְקָדוֹשׁ / סֹלּוּ לָרוֹכֵב בָּעֲרָבוֹת, מָרוֹם וְקָדוֹשׁ
עוֹנִים כֻּלָּם כְּאֶחָד שִׁלּוּשׁ קָדוֹשׁ   קָדוֹשׁ קָדוֹשׁ קָדוֹשׁ:
זֶה אֶל זֶה שׁוֹאֲלִים / אַיֵּה אֵל אֵלִים
אָנָה שׁוֹכֵן מְעָלִים / וְכֻלָּם מַעֲרִיצִים וּמַקְדִּישִׁים וּמְהַלְלִים.

פְּלִיאִים אַלְפֵי אֲלָפִים וְרִבֵּי רִבוֹאוֹת / פּוֹצְחִים הַלֵּל וְזִמְרָה לֵאלֹהֵי הַצְּבָאוֹת
צוּר עוֹלָמִים בְּתוֹךְ צְבָאוֹ אוֹת   יהוה צְבָאוֹת:
זֶה אֶל זֶה שׁוֹאֲלִים / אַיֵּה אֵל אֵלִים
אָנָה שׁוֹכֵן מְעָלִים / וְכֻלָּם מַעֲרִיצִים וּמַקְדִּישִׁים וּמְהַלְלִים.

קוֹרֵא הַדּוֹרוֹת, דָּר בִּשְׁמֵי עֶרֶץ / קַלּוֹת סְעָרָה תִּעַשׁ דְּבָרוֹ בַּמֶּרֶץ
רָם וְנִשָּׂא דִּבֵּר וַיִּקְרָא אֶרֶץ   מְלֹא כָל־הָאָרֶץ:
זֶה אֶל זֶה שׁוֹאֲלִים / אַיֵּה אֵל אֵלִים
אָנָה שׁוֹכֵן מְעָלִים / וְכֻלָּם מַעֲרִיצִים וּמַקְדִּישִׁים וּמְהַלְלִים.

שׁוֹכֵן עַד, וְנִשְׂגָּב שְׁמוֹ לְבַדּוֹ / שָׁמַיִם וּשְׁמֵי שָׁמַיִם לֹא יְכַלְכְּלוּ הוֹדוֹ
תֹּקֶף תַּרְשִׁישִׁים וְאֵלִים צַר לִכְבוֹדוֹ   מְלֹא כָל־הָאָרֶץ כְּבוֹדוֹ:
זֶה אֶל זֶה שׁוֹאֲלִים / אַיֵּה אֵל אֵלִים
אָנָה שׁוֹכֵן מְעָלִים / וְכֻלָּם מַעֲרִיצִים וּמַקְדִּישִׁים וּמְהַלְלִים.

Continue with "וּבְכֵן, לְךָ הַכֹּל יַכְתִּירוּ" on page 659.

סילוק לשחרית

The סילוק *(see rubric on page 843), the culmination of the* קרובה *by Rabbi Meshullam ben Kalonymus said in* שחרית*, serves as a contrast to the prefatory piyutim, focusing on Israel as those upon whom the* קדושה *really depends. Nowadays, it is omitted by most congregations.*

מִי יְתַנֶּה תְּקֶף תְּהִלָּתֶךָ / מִי יְשַׁנֵּן שִׁעוּר שִׁבְחֶךָ
מִי יְרַנֵּן רֹב רוֹמְמוּתֶךָ / מִי יְקַצֵּב קְרִיאַת קְדֻשָּׁתֶךָ
מִי יְצַפְצֵף צְבִי צִדְקוֹתֶיךָ / מִי יְפָרֵשׁ פִּלְאֵי פְאֵרֶךָ
מִי יַעֲרֹךְ עֹצֶם עֱזוּזֶךָ / מִי יָשִׂיחַ שֶׂגֶב סִלְסוּלֶךָ
מִי יְנוֹבֵב נוֹי נִצְחֶךָ / מִי יְמַלֵּל מַעַשׂ מוֹרָאֶךָ
מִי יְלַהֵג לֶמֶד לִקְחֶךָ / מִי יָכִיל כִּסֵּא כְבוֹדֶךָ
מִי יְיַדַּע יְפִי יְקָרֶךָ / מִי יַטִּיף טוּב טַעְמֶךָ
מִי יְחַוֶּה חֵקֶר חִידוֹתֶיךָ / מִי יָזִיז זִיו זָהֳרֶךָ
מִי יוֹרֶה וַעַד וָתִיקוּתֶךָ / מִי יֶהְגֶּה הוֹד הַדְרָתֶךָ
מִי יְדַלֶּה דֵּעַ דָּתוֹתֶיךָ / מִי יַגִּיד גֹּדֶל גְּבוּרָתֶךָ
מִי יְבָאֵר בֵּאוּר בִּינָתֶךָ / מִי יֹאמַר אֹמֶץ אֱיָלוּתֶךָ.

כִּי כְשִׁמְךָ כֵּן תְּהִלָּתֶךָ / כִּתְהִלָּתְךָ כֵּן אִמְרָתֶךָ
כְּאִמְרָתְךָ כֵּן בְּרִיָּתֶךָ / כִּבְרִיָּתְךָ כֵּן גְּדֻלָּתֶךָ
כִּגְדֻלָּתְךָ כֵּן דַּעְתֶּךָ / כְּדַעְתְּךָ כֵּן הֲלִיכָתֶךָ
כַּהֲלִיכָתְךָ כֵּן וְעִידָתֶךָ / כִּוְעִידָתְךָ כֵּן זָהֳרָתֶךָ
כְּזָהֳרָתְךָ כֵּן חִבָּתֶךָ / כְּחִבָּתְךָ כֵּן טָהֳרָתֶךָ
כְּטָהֳרָתְךָ כֵּן יְשָׁרָתֶךָ / כִּישָׁרָתְךָ כֵּן כְּמִירָתֶךָ
כִּכְמִירָתְךָ כֵּן לְבִישָׁתֶךָ / כִּלְבִישָׁתְךָ כֵּן מִדָּתֶךָ
כְּמִדָּתְךָ כֵּן נְעִימָתֶךָ / כִּנְעִימָתְךָ כֵּן שְׂרָרוּתֶךָ
כִּשְׂרָרוּתְךָ כֵּן עֲנָוָתֶךָ / כְּעַנְוָתְךָ כֵּן פְּרִישׁוּתֶךָ
כִּפְרִישׁוּתְךָ כֵּן צְנִיעוּתֶךָ / כִּצְנִיעוּתְךָ כֵּן קְדֻשָּׁתֶךָ
כִּקְדֻשָּׁתְךָ כֵּן רוֹמְמוּתֶךָ / כְּרוֹמְמוּתְךָ כֵּן שִׁבְחֶךָ
כְּשִׁבְחֲךָ כֵּן תִּפְאַרְתֶּךָ.

וְשִׁמְךָ מְרוֹמָם עַל כָּל בְּרָכָה וּתְהִלָּה
עַל כָּל תְּקֶף וְתִפְאָרָה / עַל כָּל שֶׁבַח וְשִׁירָה
עַל כָּל רֶנֶן וּרְחִישָׁה / עַל כָּל קִדּוּשׁ וּקְרִיאָה
עַל כָּל צִפְצוּף וְצָהֳלָה / עַל כָּל פְּאֵר וּפְצִיחָה
עַל כָּל עֹז וַעֲנָיָה / עַל כָּל סִפּוּר וְשִׂיחָה
עַל כָּל נִצּוּחַ וּנְגִינָה / עַל כָּל מַעַן וּמִלָּה
עַל כָּל לִבּוּב וְלַהֲגָה / עַל כָּל כָּבוֹד וּכְרִיעָה
עַל כָּל יִחוּד וְיִרְאָה / עַל כָּל טַעַם וְטָהֳרָה
עַל כָּל חֹסֶן וְחִידָה / עַל כָּל זֶמֶר וְזִמְרָה
עַל כָּל וִדּוּי וְתוֹדָה / עַל כָּל הַלֵּל וְהוֹדָיָה
עַל כָּל דִּבּוּב וְדֵעָה / עַל כָּל גֹּדֶל וְגַאֲוָה
עַל כָּל בִּטּוּי וּבְרָכָה / עַל כָּל אֹמֶר וַאֲמִירָה.

אֱלֹהֵי הָאֱלֹהִים וַאֲדֹנֵי הָאֲדוֹנִים / מֶלֶךְ עַל כָּל מְלָכִים
מוֹשֵׁל עַל כָּל מוֹשְׁלִים / אָיֹם עַל כָּל אֲיֻמִּים
נוֹרָא עַל כָּל נוֹרָאִים / רָם עַל כָּל רָמִים
גֵּאֶה עַל כָּל גֵּאִים / נִשָּׂא עַל כָּל נִשָּׂאִים
גָּבֹהַּ עַל כָּל גְּבֹהִים / וּמַבִּיט אֶל עֲנִיִּים וּנְכֵאִים
וְאֶת שָׁחִים וְדַכָּאִים / לְהַחֲיוֹת לֵב נִדְכָּאִים
רוּחַ שְׁפָלִים וְחֵלְכָּאִים / עַל כֵּן גָּדַלְתָּ יהוה אֱלֹהִים
וְנַעֲלֵיתָ עַל כָּל אֱלֹהִים / כִּי אֵין כָּמְוֹךָ בָאֱלֹהִים
וְאֵין זוּלָתְךָ אֱלֹהֵי הָאֱלֹהִים.

שָׁמַיִם וּשְׁמֵי שָׁמַיִם כְּבוֹדְךָ מְסַפְּרִים / כַּנְפוֹת הָאָרֶץ זְמִירוֹת לְךָ מַשְׁמִיעִים
שַׂרְפֵי הַקֹּדֶשׁ קְדֻשָּׁתְךָ מַקְדִּישִׁים / אוֹפַנֵּי הַמֶּרְכָּבָה כְּבוֹדְךָ מְבָרְכִים
כּוֹכְבֵי בֹקֶר יַחַד מְרַנְּנִים / יָרִיעוּ כָּל בְּנֵי אֱלֹהִים
מִשְׁבְּרֵי יָם שִׁמְךָ מַאְדִּירִים / הַרְרֵי גֹּבַהּ וַעֲצֵי יַעַר מְרַנְּנִים
נְהָרוֹת כַּף מְמַחְאִים / חַיְתוֹ אֶרֶץ וְזִיז שָׂדַי שָׂרִים כְּחוֹלְלִים
תַּנִּינִים וְכָל תְּהוֹמוֹת מְהַלְלִים כְּבַחֲלִילִים
וְכָל יְצוּרֵי בְרֵאשִׁית פּוֹצְחִים הִלּוּלִים / לְשֵׁם קָדְשֶׁךָ, אֵל אֵלִים
וְכֻלָּם אֵלֶיךָ מְשַׁבְּרִים וּמְיַחֲלִים / לָתֵת לָהֶם צֵיד מַאֲכָלִים

הַתַּחְתּוֹנִים מִפְּתִיחַת יָדְךָ נִזּוֹנִים וּמִתְכַּלְכְּלִים
וְהָעֶלְיוֹנִים מִזִּיו הוֹדְךָ שְׂבֵעִים וּמִתְמַלְּאִים
כִּי כְבוֹדְךָ, שָׁמַיִם וָאָרֶץ מְלֵאִים.

וּמִי כְּעַמְּךָ יִשְׂרָאֵל גּוֹי אֶחָד בָּאָרֶץ: דברי הימים א׳ יז
הַמַּאֲמִירִים אַדְנוּתֶךָ / הַמְיַחֲדִים אֱלָהוּתֶךָ / הַמְבָרְכִים שֵׁם כְּבוֹד מַלְכוּתֶךָ
הַמְסַפְּרִים תְּהִלָּתֶךָ / הָעוֹרְכִים תַּחַן לְחַלּוֹתֶךָ / הַמַּנְעִימִים זֶמֶר לְעַלּוֹתֶךָ
הַמַּאֲרִיכִים רֹן לִרְצוֹתֶךָ / הַשּׁוֹפְכִים שִׂיחַ לְפַתּוֹתֶךָ / וְהֵם עַמְּךָ וְנַחֲלָתֶךָ
צֹאנְךָ וְצֹאן מַרְעִיתֶךָ / קֹדֶשׁ רֵאשִׁית תְּבוּאָתֶךָ / קֶדֶם קִנְיָנְךָ וּסְגֻלָּתֶךָ
חֶלְקְךָ וְחֶבֶל שִׁפְרָתֶךָ / יִשְׂרָאֵל תִּפְאַרְתֶּךָ / יְשֻׁרוּן מִבְחַר מְנָתֶךָ
הַדְּבֵקִים בֶּאֱמוּנָתֶךָ / הַהוֹגִים בְּדָתֶךָ / הַחֲפֵצִים בְּתוֹרָתֶךָ
הָעוֹסְקִים בְּיִרְאָתֶךָ / הַתְּמִידִים בַּעֲבוֹדָתֶךָ
הַנִּכְסָפִים לְחַצְרוֹת בֵּיתֶךָ / הַכְּמֵהִים בְּקֹדֶשׁ חֲזוֹתֶךָ / הַתְּאֵבִים לְקִרְבָתֶךָ
הַנֶּהֱרָגִים עַל תּוֹרָתֶךָ / הַנִּסְקָלִים עַל אַהֲבָתֶךָ / הַנִּשְׂרָפִים עַל עֵדוֹתֶיךָ
הַנֶּחֱנָקִים וְנִטְבָּחִים וְנִטְבָּעִים וְנִתְלִים וְנִקְבָּרִים חַיִּים עַל יִחוּד קְדֻשָּׁתֶךָ
הַקְּרוּאִים עֲדָתֶךָ / יְסוֹד אֲגֻדָּתֶךָ
וְאַתָּה אֵל גָּדוֹל בִּגְדֻלָּתֶךָ / וְהֵם עֵדֶיךָ, כִּי אֵין בִּלְתֶּךָ.

וּמַה יַּעְצֹר כֹּחַ יְלוּד אִשָּׁה / נוֹצָר מִטִּפָּה בְּאוּשָׁה
וּמַה יָּעֹז, עֻזְּךָ לִדְרֹשָׁה / שִׁבְחֲךָ בְּפֶה לְפָרְשָׁה
נִצְחֲךָ בְּנִיב לְאָרְשָׁה / לְהַטִּיף צָקוּן וּלְחִישָׁה
לְהַפִּיל תְּחִנָּה וּבַקָּשָׁה / וּמִחְיָתוֹ עָלָיו קָשָׁה
וְדַרְכּוֹ מְעֻקָּשָׁה / וּנְתִיבָתוֹ נְתוּסָה וּנְתוּשָׁה
וְחַטָּאתוֹ עַל לוּחַ חֲרוּשָׁה / חֲקוּקָה וּמְפֹרָשָׁה
וְגָז וְעָף בְּחִישָׁה / וְגֹוֵעַ וּמֵת בַּחֲלוּשָׁה
וּגְוִיָּתוֹ בַּגַּיְא נְטוּשָׁה / בְּתַחְתִּית אֶרֶץ רְטוּשָׁה
בְּאִישׁוֹן חֹשֶׁךְ כְּפוּשָׁה / בְּאַשְׁמַנִּים רְפוּשָׁה
בְּטַמְמוֹן חֲבוּשָׁה / כְּמֵשָׁה וִיבֵשָׁה
נְמֵסָה וַעֲבֵשָׁה / בַּיַּבֶּשֶׁת מְיֻבָּשָׁה / וְכֻלּוֹ מָלֵא בוּשָׁה.
וּמַה יַּעֲצִים עֹתֶר וְגִישָׁה / וְיָשִׂיחַ וְיֶהֱמֶה בְּרִגְשָׁה.

וּמֵאָז הַכֹּל צָפוּי לְפָנֶיךָ / וְאֵין לְהֵחָבֵא מִפָּנֶיךָ
וְאֵין לְהִסָּתֵר מֵעֵינֶיךָ / כִּי בַכֹּל מְשׁוֹטְטוֹת עֵינֶיךָ.
וְגָלוּי לְךָ כִּי יְצִיר חֹמֶר הוּא / הֲבֵל הֲבָלִים הוּא
עָלֶה נִדָּף הוּא / קַשׁ יָבֵשׁ הוּא
חֶרֶשׂ אֶת חַרְשֵׂי אֲדָמָה הוּא / וּבַמֶּה נֶחְשָׁב הוּא.
אֱנוֹשׁ אָנוּשׁ הוּא / כִּי כִּשְׁמוֹ כֵּן הוּא
אָדָם, אֵפֶר דָּם מָרָה הוּא / בָּשָׂר, בּוּשָׁה סְרִיחָה רִמָּה הוּא
מְיֻחָם בְּחֵטְא הוּא / מְחוֹלָל בְּעָוֹן הוּא.

וְיֵצֶר לִבּוֹ רַע מִנְּעוּרָיו / חוֹרֵשׁ רַע בִּמְגוּרָיו / אוֹרֵב לוֹ בְּמִסְתָּרָיו
מְקַנֵּן כְּנָחָשׁ בִּסְתָרָיו / כִּזְבוּב בְּמִפְתְּחֵי חֲדָרָיו
מַבְאִישׁ הָעִסָּה בְּזֻהֲמוּת שְׂאוֹרָיו / מְסִיתוֹ לְהַטּוֹת אֲשׁוּרָיו
הוֹוֶה לוֹ בְּעוֹכְרָיו / חָשׁוּב לוֹ כְּצָרָיו / וְהוּא רֹאשׁ לְכָל צוֹרְרָיו
מֵצַר לוֹ בְּכָל מְצָרָיו / צוֹדֶה לוֹ בְּכָל עֲבָרָיו / מַרְגִּיז בְּכָל אֵבָרָיו
מַעֲצִיבוֹ בִּדְבָרָיו / מַחֲטִיאוֹ בְּרֹעַ הַרְהוּרָיו / מִתְנַקֵּשׁ לְהַפִּילוֹ בְּמַכְמוֹרָיו
מִתְנַכֵּל לְדַחוֹתוֹ בְּמַהֲמֹרָיו / וְצָר עָלָיו בִּמְצוּרָיו
לוּלֵא אַתָּה עוֹזֵר לוֹ מִצָּרָיו.

וּבְכָל יוֹם וָיוֹם מִתְחַדֵּשׁ עָלָיו / חוֹשֵׁב מַחֲשָׁבוֹת עָלָיו
לְהִתְגּוֹלֵל וּלְהִתְנַפֵּל עָלָיו / לְעַקְּשׁוֹ בְּאָרְחוֹת עִקּוּלָיו
לְהַאֲשִׁימוֹ בְּאַשְׁמַת גִּעוּלָיו / לְהַלְעִינוֹ בְּמֶסֶךְ תַּרְעֵלָיו
וְאֵינֶנּוּ דּוֹרֵשׁ לְשָׁלוֹם אֵלָיו / פַּחִים טוֹמֵן לְרַגְלָיו / רֶשֶׁת פּוֹרֵשׂ לְיַד מַעְגָּלָיו
מוֹקְשִׁים שָׁת בְּמַסְלוּלָיו / כּוֹרֶה שַׁחַת בִּשְׁבִילָיו
לָמוֹג לֵב וּלְהַרְבּוֹת מִכְשׁוֹלָיו / וּכְהוֹלֶם פַּעַם, הוֹלְמוֹ בְּכֵילַפּוֹת וְכַשִּׁילָיו
עַל כֵּן יֹאמְרוּ מוֹשְׁלֵי מְשָׁלָיו / אִי לַבַּיִת שֶׁמְּהָרְסָיו וּמַחֲרִיבָיו מִשֶּׁלָּיו
וּמַה יִּצְטַדֵּק בְּמִפְעָלָיו / וּמַה יִּזְכֶּה בְּמַעֲלָלָיו
כִּי שׁוֹדֵד בָּא בִּגְבוּלָיו / לְשׁוֹדְדוֹ, לְדַחֲמוֹ בְּרֹב תַּחְבּוּלָיו.

לָכֵן הִקְדַּמְתָּ רְפוּאָה וּתְעָלָה / וְהֶעֱלֵיתָ אֲרוּכָה לְנַהֲלָאָה וְנַחְלָה
וְהֵכַנְתָּ צֳרִי וְחִתּוּל, לְלֹא חַתְלָה / וְהִגְהֵיתָ מָזוֹר, לְהַרְטוֹת מַחֲלָה
וְקָבַעְתָּ יוֹם זֶה לִסְלִיחָה וּמְחִילָה / לָבֹא שְׁעָרֶיךָ בְּתוֹדָה וּבִתְהִלָּה

לְקַדֵּם פָּנֶיךָ בְּתוֹדָה וּבְחִילָה / לְהִזָּכֵר בּוֹ רְבוּצֵי מַכְפֵּלָה
בְּעֵת רָצוֹן לִשְׁמֹעַ תְּפִלָּה / לְהַעֲבִיר כָּל שֶׁמֶץ וְתִפְלָה
לְהָנִיא כָּל אָוֶן וְתָהֳלָה / לְהַצְמִיחַ צְדָקָה וּתְהִלָּה
לְהָפֵר כַּעַס וּלְהַרְבּוֹת חֶמְלָה / לְהָרִים מִכְשׁוֹל וּלְהָסִיר תַּקָּלָה
לְפַנּוֹת דֶּרֶךְ וּלְיַשֵּׁר מְסִלָּה / לָתֵת לַשּׁוֹבְבִים טָהֳרָה וּטְבִילָה
לְהַעֲמִיד רֶוַח וְהַצָּלָה / לְהַשְׁלִיךְ עָוֹן בְּעִמְקֵי מְצוּלָה
לָשֵׂאת זָדוֹן וּמְעִילָה.

וּמִכָּל יָמִים, יוֹם זֶה קִדַּשְׁתָּ / וְעַל כָּל יָמִים אוֹתוֹ עִלִּיתָ
וּבוֹ מִכָּל יוֹם בָּחַרְתָּ / וּמִיְּצָרוֹ, אוֹתוֹ לְךָ יִחַדְתָּ
וּלְדוֹר דֵּעַ כֹּחוֹ יִדַּעְתָּ / וְאָדָם דִּי זָהָב, בּוֹ וִתַּרְתָּ
וּמִכְתָּב חָרוּת לְעָנוֹ נָתַתָּ / וְסָלַחְתִּי כִּדְבָרֶךָ בִּשַּׂרְתָּ
וְעַל הָרָעָה נִחַמְתָּ / וְעַל בָּנֶיךָ רִחַמְתָּ
וְכִגְבֹהַּ שָׁמַיִם, חַסְדְּךָ לָמוֹ הִגְבַּרְתָּ / וְכִרְחֹק מִזְרָח מִמַּעֲרָב, פִּשְׁעָם הִרְחַקְתָּ
וּזְכוּת הַרְרֵי קֶדֶם זָכַרְתָּ / וּכְאָב אֶת בֵּן אוֹתָם רָצִיתָ
וְעַל כָּל אֹם רֹאשָׁם נִשֵּׂאתָ / וְקַרְנָם בְּכָבוֹד רוֹמַמְתָּ
וּמִשֵּׁפֶל הִגְבַּהְתָּמוֹ, וְהִתְלַלְתָּ / וְאוֹת לְטוֹבָה עִמָּהֶם עָשִׂיתָ
וְחִבַּתָם לַכֹּל הֶרְאֵיתָ / וְאַהֲבָתָם לְעֵין כֹּל גִּלִּיתָ
וְלִשְׁכֹּן בְּתוֹכָם תָּאַבְתָּ / וְלַחֲנוֹת בֵּינֵימוֹ חָמַדְתָּ / וְלָשֶׁבֶת בְּוַעֲדָם אִוִּיתָ
וְעַיִן בְּעַיִן לָמוֹ נִרְאֵיתָ / וּבֵין כְּרוּבִים כְּבוֹדְךָ צִמְצַמְתָּ
וַעֲנַן יְקָרְךָ עַל כַּפֹּרֶת הִצַּעְתָּ / וַעֲנַן הַקְּטֹרֶת לְכַסּוֹתוֹ הַיּוֹם פָּקַדְתָּ
וּמֵאָז לִסְלִיחָה אוֹתוֹ שַׂמְתָּ / וּלְכַפָּרָה אוֹתוֹ יִסַּדְתָּ
וּמִצְוֹתָיו בְּדָתְךָ צִוִּיתָ / וְכָתַבְתָּ וְשָׁנִיתָ וְשִׁלַּשְׁתָּ
וְאַזְהָרוֹתָיו פֵּרַשְׁתָּ / וְעָנְשָׁיו פִּלַּשְׁתָּ
וְקָרְבְּנוֹתָיו קִצַּבְתָּ / וְעֵרֶךְ עֲבוֹדוֹתָיו סִדַּרְתָּ / וְרִצּוּי הַזָּיוֹתָיו סִפַּרְתָּ
וְרִקּוּחַ תִּימְרוֹתָיו הֶעֱדַפְתָּ / וְסֵדֶר מַעַרְכוֹתָיו הוֹסַפְתָּ
וְטֹהַר טְבִילוֹתָיו מָנִיתָ / וְקִדּוּשׁ רְחִיצוֹתָיו חִשַּׁבְתָּ
וְאַזְכָּרוֹתָיו בְּשֵׂכֶל סִימַתָּ / וְתוֹדוֹתָיו וִדּוּיָיו סִכַּמְתָּ / וְעִנּוּיָיו בְּפֶקֶד רָשַׁמְתָּ
וְלִבֶּן עֲטִיּוֹתָיו חִוִּיתָ / וּפִזּוּי שְׂרָדָיו הוֹרֵיתָ / וְעִלּוּי מַחְלְצוֹתָיו בֵּאַרְתָּ

וְשִׁנּוּי מַחְלְפוֹתָיו לְמַדְתָּ / וְלִקְדוֹשֶׁיךָ אוֹתָם מָסַרְתָּ
וְכָל תּוֹרוֹתָיו הוֹדַעְתָּ / וְכָל דָּתוֹתָיו חָקַרְתָּ
וְכָל מִשְׁפָּטָיו חָרַצְתָּ / וְכָל חֻקּוֹתָיו חָקַקְתָּ
וְכָל גְּזֵרוֹתָיו גָּזַרְתָּ / וְכָל עִנְיָנָיו חָרַתָּ
וְחֻבְּלוּ מִכֹּל הַנֶּעֱמַתְּ / וְחֻלְשׁוּ לִמְאֹד הִשְׁפַּרְתָּ
חֹפֶשׁ לִרְצוּצִים אוֹתוֹ שִׁוִּיתָ / דְּרוֹר לִשְׁבוּיִים אוֹתוֹ הִתְוֵיתָ
פְּקַח קוֹחַ לַאֲסוּרִים אוֹתוֹ תִּכַּנְתָּ / יוֹם עָשׂוֹר לַעֲשִׂירִיָּה חָקַקְתָּ
שַׁבַּת שַׁבָּתוֹן לְשׁוֹבְתֵי עֹנֶג שַׁתָּה / יוֹם כִּפּוּר לְנוֹתְנֵי כֹּפֶר תַּתָּה.

לְכַפֵּר עֲוֹנוֹת / לִמְחֹל זְדוֹנוֹת
לְכַלֵּא פְשָׁעִים / לְהָתֵם חֲטָאִים
לְטַהֵר טְמֵאִים / לְהָדִיחַ דָּמִים
לְצַחְצֵחַ כְּתָמִים / לְהַרְחִיץ צוֹאִים
לְהַלְבִּין כַּשֶּׁלֶג שָׁנִים / לְצַחֵר כַּצֶּמֶר אוֹדְמִים
לְמָרֵק חוֹבִים / לְנַקּוֹת חַבִּים
לְזַכּוֹת אֲשֵׁמִים / לְזַכֵּךְ אֲשָׁמִים
לְוַתֵּר לְנִתְאָמִים / לִסְלֹחַ לְכָל עֲדַת תְּמִימִים.

וְעַמְּךָ בְּיוֹם זֶה יַחַד נֶאֱגָדִים / וּבְחִין לְפָנֶיךָ נוֹעָדִים
וּשְׁכִינָתְךָ עִמָּם מוֹעֲדִים / וְנֶעֱצָרִים וּמִתְוַעֲדִים
וּבְיִרְאָה אוֹתְךָ עוֹבְדִים / וּבְאֵימָה עוֹמְדִים / וּבְגִילָה רוֹעֲדִים
וּבְחִילָה מְסַלְּדִים / וּפִשְׁעֵיהֶם מִתְוַדִּים
וּמִשְׁתַּחֲוִים וּמוֹדִים / וְכוֹרְעִים וּבוֹרְכִים וְסוֹגְדִים / וְאַרְצָה לְךָ קוֹדִים
וְדַלְתוֹתֶיךָ שׁוֹקְדִים / וּכְאֶחָד נֶאֱחָדִים / וְיִחוּדְךָ מְיַחֲדִים
וּקְדֻשָּׁתְךָ מְעִידִים / וֶאֱמוּנָתְךָ מְסַהֲדִים / וְצִדְקָתְךָ מַגִּידִים
וְחַסְדְּךָ וַאֲמִתְּךָ לֹא מְכַחֲדִים / וְעוֹרְכִים שֶׁוַע בְּמַעֲמָדִים
וּמִזְּרִיחָה וְעַד שְׁקִיעָה שִׁבְחֲךָ מַתְמִידִים
וּפְגִיעוֹת חָמֵשׁ, מֵאֶמֶשׁ מְעַתְּדִים / מוּל עֲבוֹדוֹת חָמֵשׁ בְּעַתּוּדִים
וּלְשִׁמְךָ מְהוֹדִים / בְּכָל עֹז וּמְאֹדִים.

וְכֻלָּם צָמִים וּמִתְעַנִּים
יַחַד, אָבוֹת וּבָנִים / גְּדוֹלִים וּקְטַנִּים / בַּחוּרִים וּזְקֵנִים
וּמַרְבִּים חִנּוּנִים / וּמְדַבְּרִים תַּחֲנוּנִים / וְעוֹרְכִים רְנָנִים
וּמְרַנְּנִים וּמִתְחַנְּנִים / לְפָנֶיךָ, אֲדֹנֵי הָאֲדוֹנִים
לִפְדּוֹתָם מִכֹּבֶד עֲוֹנִים / וְלִמְחוֹת פְּשָׁעֵימוֹ כַּעֲנָנִים
לִשְׁעוֹת שַׁוְעָם מִמְּעוֹנִים / לְהַאֲזִין מֵהֶם שִׂיחַ מַעֲנִים
כִּי הֵם דַּלִּים וְאֶבְיוֹנִים / וּבְצִלְּךָ מִתְלוֹנְנִים
וּבְאֶבְרָתְךָ מִתְגּוֹנְנִים / וּבְסִתְרְךָ נִצְפָּנִים / וּבְךָ נִשְׁעָנִים
וּכְעֵינֵי עֲבָדִים אֶל יַד אֲדוֹנִים / וּכְעֵינֵי שִׁפְחָה אֶל יַד גְּבִרְתָּהּ, לְךָ פּוֹנִים
לְהַרְבּוֹת לָמוֹ פִּדְיוֹנִים / לְכַבְּסָם מִצַּחַן דִּפְיוֹנִים
לְהַצְלִיל בְּצוּל זְדוֹנִים / לְשַׁתֵּק בַּעֲלֵי דִינִים
לְאַלֵּם מַלְשִׁנִים / לוֹטְשֵׁי חִצִּים וְכִידוֹנִים / לְהָשִׁיב חֶרֶב לִנְדָנִים
לְהַגְבִּיר מְלִיצֵי יֹשֶׁר וְזִכְיוֹנִים / וּלְהַחֲסִים קַטֵּגוֹרִים, עִמָּהֶם מְדַיְּנִים
וְסֵדֶר סְלִיחָה מְכִינִים / וְדִבְרֵי רִצּוּי מְכַוְּנִים
וּבְרִית שְׁלֹשׁ עֶשְׂרֵה מִדּוֹת אוֹפַנִּים / אֲשֶׁר אִלַּפְתָּ לְנֶאֱמָן, בְּחֶזְיוֹנִים
בַּעֲבוּר כְּבוֹדְךָ עַל פָּנִים / בְּדַבֶּרְךָ עִם צִיר פָּנִים אֶל פָּנִים
וְכָל הַיּוֹם בָּם מִתְגַּלְגְּלִים וְנֶאֱפָנִים / וְעֵרֶךְ וִדּוּי מְשַׁנְּנִים / וְצִדְקוֹתֶיךָ מְתַנִּים
לִזְכֹּר לָמוֹ שְׁלֹשֶׁת אֵתָנִים / וְיוֹם קִדּוּשׁ חִתּוּנִים
לְחַלְּצָם מֵרֹאשׁ פְּתָנִים / לְהַדְרִיכָם מִפֶּרֶךְ מְעַנִּים
לְדַלּוֹתָם מִדִּכּוּי תַּנִּים / לְהַעֲלוֹתָם מִבּוֹר שְׁאוֹנִים
לְנַתֵּק מֵהֶם מוֹסְרוֹת שׂוֹטְנִים / לִפְצוֹתָם מִלַּעַג שַׁאֲנַנִּים
לְהַצִּילָם מִגֵּאֵיוֹנִים / לְהָשִׁיב שְׁבוּתָם כְּיוֹנִים
לְמַלְּטָם מִתְּפַת דֵּרָאוֹנִים / מִלַּהַט מִתְהַפֶּכֶת בְּדִמְיוֹנִים
רִשְׁפֵּי לַהַב וְעִשּׁוּנִים / מְדוּרַת אֵשׁ וְאוּדִים עֲשֵׁנִים
לְנַצֵּחֲךָ בְּשִׁיר, כְּבַעַל שׁוֹשַׁנִּים.
וְרִבּוֹתֵי קֹדֶשׁ, צְבָא עֶלְיוֹנִים / בְּשׁוּרָם כִּי תַצְדִּיק בָּנִים
אֲשֶׁר לַעֲבָדִים לְךָ נִקְנִים / יִתְמְהוּ זֶה לָזֶה בְּתִמְהוֹנִים
וְכִתֵּי כִתִּים, הֲמוֹנִים הֲמוֹנִים / יִשְׁמְעוּ וְיֹאמְרוּ בְּאֶרֶשׁ שְׁנוּנִים
מִי אֵל כָּמוֹךָ, נוֹשֵׂא עָוֹן זֶרַע אֱמוּנִים / וְעוֹבֵר עַל פֶּשַׁע נִטְעֵי נַעֲמָנִים

אַשְׁרֵי הָעָם שֶׁכָּכָה לּוֹ, עוֹנִים / וְאַשְׁרֵי הָעָם שֶׁיהוה אֱלֹהָיו, רוֹנְנִים
וְיַקְדִּישׁוּךָ עֶלְיוֹנִים / וְיַעֲרִיצוּךָ תַּחְתּוֹנִים.

וְאָז אֵילִים יַאְדִּירוּךָ / בְּרָקִים יְבָרְכוּךָ / גְּדוּדִים יְגַדְּלוּךָ / דּוֹלְקִים יִדְרְשׁוּךָ
הֲמֻלָּה יְהַדְּרוּךָ / וָתִיקִים יוֹדוּךָ / זַכִּים יַזְכִּירוּךָ / חַיָּלִים יְחַסְּנוּךָ
טְהוֹרִים יַטְעִימוּךָ / יְקָרִים יְיַחֲדוּךָ / כַּבִּירִים יַכְתִּירוּךָ / לְהָטִים יְלַבְּבוּךָ
מַלְאָכִים יַמְלִיכוּךָ / נֹגְהִים יְנַצְּחוּךָ / שְׂרָפִים יְסַלְּדוּךָ / עִירִין יְעַלּוּךָ
פְּלִיאִים יְפָאֲרוּךָ / צְבָאוֹת יְצַלְצְלוּךָ / קַלִּים יַקְדִּישׁוּךָ / רְבָבוֹת יְרוֹמְמוּךָ
שִׁנְאַנִּים יְשַׁבְּחוּךָ / תַּרְשִׁישִׁים יַתְמִידוּךָ / קְדֻשָּׁה מְשֻׁלֶּשֶׁת.

Continue with "כַּכָּתוּב עַל יַד נְבִיאֶךָ" on page 661.

רהיטים

The following fifteen piyutim are based on a verse from Jeremiah (10:7), with each piyut building on a single word or phrase from the verse. Sequences of piyutim structured in this way are known as רהיטים. This sequence is ascribed to Rabbi Kalonymus (probably Rabbi Kalonymus of Lucca, father of Rabbi Meshullam who authored the קרובה for שחרית).

ירמיה י וּבְכֵן, מִי לֹא יִרָאֲךָ מֶלֶךְ הַגּוֹיִם, כִּי לְךָ יָאָתָה
כִּי בְכָל־חַכְמֵי הַגּוֹיִם וּבְכָל־מַלְכוּתָם מֵאֵין כָּמוֹךָ:

וּבְכֵן, מִי

מִי אַדִּיר אַפְסֶךָ מִי בָרוּךְ בִּלְתֶּךָ מִי גִבּוֹר כְּגִילֶךָ
מִי דָגוּל כִּדְמוּתֶךָ מִי הָדוּר כְּהִלּוּלֶךָ מִי וַדַּי כְּוִעוּדֶךָ
מִי זַכַּי זוּלָתֶךָ מִי חָסִין חִלּוּפֶךָ מִי טָהוֹר כְּטַכְסִיסֶךָ
מִי יָרוּי כְּיִחוּדֶךָ מִי כוֹבֵשׁ כִּכְמִירָתֶךָ מִי לוֹבֵשׁ כִּלְבָדֶךָ
מִי מָרוֹם מִלְּבַדֶּךָ מִי נָכוֹן נִכְחֶךָ מִי סוֹאֵן כִּסְאָתֶךָ
מִי עָץ כַּעֲלִילוֹתֶיךָ מִי פוֹעֵל כִּפְלָאֶךָ מִי צוֹאֵל כְּצִנָּתֶךָ
מִי קִנֵּץ קְדֻשָּׁתֶךָ מִי רָוֶה רִנְנוֹתֶיךָ מִי שִׁמַּע שִׁירוֹתֶיךָ
מִי תִמֵּם תִּפְאַרְתֶּךָ.

וּבְכֵן, מִי לֹא

לֹא אֹמֶר אָמַרְתָּ, וְנָפַל דָּבָר
תָּמִיד תְּהִלָּתְךָ בְּפִי כֹּל יְדֻבָּר.
לֹא בַקְּשׁוּנִי תֹהוּ הָיָה נְאֻמֶךָ
שִׁמְךָ מִגְדַּל עֹז לָרָצִים לְעַמֶּךָ.
לֹא גְבוּל שַׂמְתָּ, וּפָרְצוּ אַדִּירִים
רַבִּים וְגוֹעֲשִׁים, וְלִשְׁבִירַת חֻקֶּיךָ נִגְרָרִים.
לֹא דָּבָר רֵק עֲשׂוֹת מִשְׁמַרְתֶּךָ
קַיָּם סֶלָה וָעֵד קֹשֶׁט אִמְרָתֶךָ.
לֹא הֲגִתָּ לִמְחוֹת שֵׁם דְּבֵקֶיךָ
צָמְאָה נַפְשָׁם לִנְעִימַת יְמִין חֲבוּקֶיךָ.
לֹא וִתַּרְתָּ לִשְׁפִיכַת דַּם חֲסִידֶיךָ
פְּקֻדַּת שָׁלוֹם הִבְטַחְתָּ לְיוֹדְעֵי סוֹדֶךָ.
לֹא זִלְזַלְתָּ מַאֲמָרֶיךָ, כֶּאֱנוֹשׁ לְכַזֵּב
עֵדוּת דְּבָרְךָ בַּשָּׁמַיִם נִצָּב מֵהַכְזֵב.
לֹא חָפֵץ רֶשַׁע אַתָּה מֵעוֹלָם
סִתְרְךָ מָנוֹס, לָלוּן עַם עוֹלָם.
לֹא טוֹב פַּצְתָּ הֱיוֹת לְבַד
נָאוֹר כִּי לְךָ הַשֶּׂגֶב יְלֻבָּד.
לֹא יֹשֶׁר מִשְׁפָּטֶיךָ לְכָל גּוֹי הוֹדַעְתָּ
מְחִית פֶּשַׁע, לְעַם זוּ יָדַעְתָּ.
לֹא כַּחֲטָאֵינוּ תַּעַשׂ, לוֹבֵשׁ צְדָקָה
לַחֲשֵׁנוּ הַיּוֹם תֵּשַׁע, כְּתִמּוֹר דַּקָּה מִן הַדַּקָּה.

וּבְכֵן, מִי לֹא יְרָאֲךָ

יְרָאֲךָ, אָדוֹן, פֹּעַל לְמַעַנְךָ פָּעַלְתָּ
בְּכֹחַ מַעֲשֶׂיךָ גָּדַלְתָּ, וּמְאֹד נַעֲלֵיתָ.

יְרָאֲךָ, גָּבֹהַּ, כָּל אֲשֶׁר תַּחְתֶּיךָ
דָּגוּל בִּמְרוֹמֵי רָמִים, הוֹד תַּחֲנוֹתֶיךָ.
יְרָאֲךָ הֲמוֹן עִירִין הַצָּגִים סְבִיבֶךָ
וִינַעֲימוּ שִׁיר, בְּהִתְחַדְּשָׁם בִּנְהַר שְׁבִיבֶיךָ.
יְרָאֲךָ זְהַר זִקִּים וְגַלְגַּלֵּי רַעֲמֶיךָ
חַי, הַצּוּרִים נִתְּצוּ מִפְּנֵי זַעֲמֶךָ.
יְרָאֲךָ טִיף בְּרָקִים הַמַּבְרִיקִים לְדַעְתֶּךָ
יֹאמְרוּ הִנֵּנוּ, בְּהִשְׁתַּלְּחָם עֲשׂוֹת מִשְׁמַעְתֶּךָ.
יְרָאֲךָ כְּרוּב וְאוֹפָן וְאַלְפֵי שִׁנְאַנֶּיךָ
לַהַב חֲנִית, חִצֵּי שְׁנוּנֶיךָ.
יְרָאֲךָ מְלוֹן כִּפָּה וּדְבוּקַת רְגָבֶיךָ
נְסִים מִגַּעֲרָתְךָ זִיב מֶשֶׁק גְּבֶיךָ.
יְרָאֲךָ סֶגֶל חֶבְלְךָ וְנַחֲלַת שִׁפְרָתֶךָ
עַמְּךָ בְּבֹר לֵבָב יִכּוֹן לִקְרָאתֶךָ.
יְרָאֲךָ פָּקִיד וְשַׂר וְכָל שׁוֹפֵט
צֹאן יָדְךָ הַיּוֹם לְהִשָּׁפֵט.
יְרָאֲךָ קָנוּי וְקוֹנוֹ, עוֹצֵר וְלִגְיוֹנוֹ
רוֹבֶה וְעַלְמָה, חַלָּשׁ וְתוֹפֵשׂ פִּגְיוֹנוֹ.
יְרָאֲךָ שְׁכַן נָפוֹת וְכָל פְּלָכִים
תִּתְרוֹמֵם לָעַד, מֶלֶךְ מַלְכֵי הַמְּלָכִים.

וּבְכֵן, מִי לֹא יְרָאֲךָ מֶלֶךְ
מֶלֶךְ תָּר כָּל סִתְרֵי גְנָזִים
שִׁמְךָ יִתְפָּאַר נֶצַח, חֲכַם הָרָזִים.
מֶלֶךְ רִבּוֹתֵי רֶכֶב מַחֲנוֹת קְדוֹשֶׁיךָ
קְרֵבֶיךָ יֹאמְרוּ, נוֹרָא אֱלֹהִים מִמִּקְדָּשֶׁיךָ.
מֶלֶךְ צָר לִכְבוֹדוֹ כָּל יְצוּרִים
פְּלִיאַת מַעֲשָׂיו יוֹדְעִים כְּאִישׁוֹן נְצוּרִים.

מֶלֶךְ עִזּוּז וְגִבּוֹר, לָעַד יִתְהַלָּל
סֶלָה מֶלֶךְ הַכָּבוֹד, גָּדוֹל וּמְהֻלָּל.
מֶלֶךְ נוֹרָא, תְּהִלָּתוֹ מָלְאָה הָאָרֶץ
מָרוֹם וְקָדוֹשׁ, נוֹרָא לְמַלְכֵי־אָרֶץ. תהלים עו
מֶלֶךְ, לִגְדֻלָּתוֹ אֵין חֵקֶר וְקִצְבָּה
כָּבוֹד בְּהֵיכָלוֹ תְּבַשֵּׂר צָבָא נִצְבָּא.
מֶלֶךְ יְמִינוֹ תָּרוּם, יָדוֹ תָּעֹז
טְהוֹרִים יַאְדִּירוּ, טוֹב יהוה לְמָעוֹז.
מֶלֶךְ חֲסִין יָהּ נֶאְדָּר בַּקֹּדֶשׁ
זַכִּים יִשְׁתַּחֲווּ לַיהוה בְּהַדְרַת קֹדֶשׁ.
מֶלֶךְ, וֶאֱמֶת יהוה לְעוֹלָם הַלְלוּיָהּ
הִלּוּל עָשׂוֹר, כֹּל הַנְּשָׁמָה תְּהַלֵּל יָהּ.
מֶלֶךְ דּוֹבֵר צֶדֶק, מַגִּיד מֵישָׁרִים
גְּזֵרוֹתָיו תּוֹרוֹת אֱמֶת וּמִשְׁפָּטִים יְשָׁרִים.
מֶלֶךְ בָּרוּךְ בְּפִי כָל גְּוִיָּה
אַדֶּרֶת תִּפְאַרְתּוֹ בְּרוּם וּבְתַחַת חֲוִיָּה.

וּבְכֵן, מִי לֹא יִרָאֲךָ מֶלֶךְ הַגּוֹיִם

הַגּוֹיִם אֶפֶס וָתֹהוּ נֶגְדְּךָ חֲשׁוּבִים
בְּחוּנֶיךָ בְּדוּדִים, וְעִמָּם לֹא נֶחְשָׁבִים.
הַגּוֹיִם גְּדֵלִים מַעֲשֵׂה תַעְתּוּעַ וַהֲבָלִים
דְּבֵקֶיךָ בְּדוּלִים מִסּוֹגְרֵי לְעֵץ בּוּלִים.
הַגּוֹיִם הָכִין פֶּסֶל מְבַקְשִׁים חָרָשִׁים
וָתִיקֶיךָ בְּהַשְׁכֵּם וְהַעֲרֵב יִחוּדְךָ פּוֹרְשִׁים.
הַגּוֹיִם זְהָבָם לַאֲפֻדַּת מַסֵּכָה מְכִינִים
חֲרֵדֵי דְבָרְךָ לְעָבְדְּךָ בְּיִרְאָה מוּכָנִים.
הַגּוֹיִם טוֹעֲנִים בַּכָּתֵף יֶתֶר צְלִיָּתָם
יְדוּעֶיךָ כּוֹרְעִים לְךָ בְּפִקּוּק חֻלְיוֹתָם.

הַגּוֹיִם כֶּסֶף מְצַפִּים עֵץ פִּסְלָם
לְקוֹוֶיךָ בְּחֶבְיוֹן עֻזְּךָ יָשִׂימוּ כִסְלָם.
הַגּוֹיִם מְכַנִּים קְדֻשָּׁתְךָ לְעוּל הַזִּמָּה
נְשׂוּאֶיךָ מְשַׁקְּצִים יִחוּם אֵשֶׁת הַזִּמָּה.
הַגּוֹיִם סֵמֶל תְּמוּנַת נֶאֱלַח מַאֲלִיהִים
עַמְּךָ מְעִידִים אַדְנוּתְךָ, אֱלֹהֵי הָאֱלֹהִים.
הַגּוֹיִם פֶּגֶר מוּבָס פַּחֲזוּת תַּבְלִיתָם
צְבָאֶיךָ קָדוֹשׁ אַתָּה יוֹשֵׁב תְּהִלּוֹתָם.
הַגּוֹיִם קוֹרְאִים לְלֹא מוֹשִׁיעַ וּמוֹעִיל
רֵעֶיךָ נִשְׁעָנִים בְּךָ, מְלַמֵּד לְהוֹעִיל.
הַגּוֹיִם שֶׁקֶר נִסְכָּם וְלֹא אֵמוּן
תְּמִימֶיךָ אֹמֶן אֱמוּנָתְךָ בְּוַעֲדָם יְנָאֱמוּן.

וּבְכֵן, מִי לֹא יִרָאֲךָ מֶלֶךְ הַגּוֹיִם, כִּי

כִּי תּוֹדָה יִתְּנוּ לְךָ שָׁבִים
שׁוֹפְכִים לֵב נִכְחֶךָ, מִיָּד נִקְשָׁבִים.
כִּי רָם אַתָּה, לְכֹל לְרֹאשׁ מִתְנַשֵּׂא
קָדוֹשׁ תְּהִלּוֹת, שִׁמְךָ עָוֹן נוֹשֵׂא.
כִּי צִדְקוֹתֶיךָ כְּהַרְרֵי אֵל מְפֹרָעִים
פְּרִי נוֹשְׂאִים, מִחְיַת תְּנוּב וּזְרָעִים.
כִּי עִמְּךָ הַחֶסֶד וְהַסְּלִיחָה לְהִוָּרֵא
סֹלֹל חַיֵּי עַד לְחַטָּאִים תּוֹרֶה.
כִּי נְכֵה לֵבָב וְשָׁפָל תִּרְאֶה
מִדָּתְךָ לֹא כְבָשָׂר, לָעֵינַיִם יִרְאֶה.
כִּי לְמַבָּטְךָ כָּל מִפְעָל סָקוּר
כָּמוּס וְגַם סָתוּם אִתְּךָ חָקוּר.
כִּי יָדְךָ פְשׁוּטָה תּוֹהִים לְקַבֵּל
טֶרֶם יִקְרָא נַעֲנֶה לְךָ קוֹבֵל.

כִּי חַסְדְּךָ גָּדוֹל מֵעַל חֲזָקִים
זוֹרְעֵי לִצְדָקָה, לְפִיו קְצוֹר זְקוּקִים.
כִּי וְעֹז מַלְכוּתְךָ אָהֵב מִשְׁפָּט
הַעַל כֵּן נִקְרֵאתָ אֱלֹהֵי הַמִּשְׁפָּט.
כִּי דַּרְכְּךָ לְשַׁתֵּף רַחֲמִים בְּדִינֶךָ
גָּדוֹל, בִּשְׁתֵּי הַמִּדּוֹת הִטְבַּעְתָּ אֲדָנֶיךָ.
כִּי בְּהִכָּנַע, עַל הָרָעָה תִּנָּחֵם
אַפְּךָ תָּשִׁיב, אֲנוּפֵי קִצְפְּךָ לְנַחֵם.

וּבְכֵן, מִי לֹא יִרָאֲךָ מֶלֶךְ הַגּוֹיִם, כִּי לְךָ

לְךָ אֶדֶר נָאֶה מִכָּל פֶּה · כִּי תְהִלָּתְךָ רַחוּם, אַף כּוֹפֶה.
לְךָ בִּגְרוֹן חֲסִידִים רֹן יִתְאַמָּר · כִּי שׁוּעַ לֹא נִכַּר בְּךָ נֶאֱמָר.
לְךָ גֵּאוּת יִתְלַבֵּשׁ וְעֹז יִתְאַזָּר · כִּי רָמִים תִּשְׁפֹּט, בִּגְבוּרָה נֶאְזָר.
לְךָ דֻּמִיָּה תְהִלָּה בְּיָפְיִ מִכְלָל · כִּי קְדֻשָּׁתְךָ מְשַׁלְּשִׁים נִצְּצֵי כְּעֵין קָלָל.
לְךָ הֶמְיַת נִצִּים עֹז מַאְדִּירִים · כִּי צִוִּיתָם חֹק, וְלֹא נֶעְדָּרִים.
לְךָ וֶוֵי דֹק מִגַּעֲרָתְךָ מִתְרוֹפְפִים · כִּי פָנִים מְכַסִּים מֵאֵימָתְךָ שְׂרָפִים.
לְךָ זְמִירוֹת מִכְּנַף הָאָרֶץ פּוֹשְׁטִים · כִּי עֵינֶיךָ בְּכָל פִּנּוֹתֶיהָ מְשׁוֹטְטִים.
לְךָ חַדְשֵׁי בְקָרִים אֱמוּנָה מַרְבִּים · כִּי סוּר לְמִשְׁמַעְתְּךָ חָשִׁים כְּרוּבִים.
לְךָ טִפּוּחַ חֲזָקִים וְצַעֲקַת מוּצָקִים · כִּי נָעֳמְךָ פּוֹצְחִים אֶרְאֶלִּים וּמְצוּקִים.
לְךָ יְחַלֵּק עֶצֶם וְאִישׁוֹן יַנְשִׁיף · כִּי מֵאָז גְּבוּלָם רוּחֲךָ הִנְשִׁיף.
לְךָ כֹּחַ וּגְבוּרָה לְחַזֵּק וּלְגַדֵּל · כִּי לְשִׁמְךָ כָּל לָשׁוֹן תְּגַדֵּל.

וּבְכֵן, מִי לֹא יִרָאֲךָ מֶלֶךְ הַגּוֹיִם, כִּי לְךָ יָאָתָה

יָאֲתָה תְּהִלָּה וָעֹז לְבַקֹּדֶשׁ נֶאְדָּר · וּמִי שָׁקוּל גֹּשֶׁת גָּדְלוֹ לְאַדָּר.
יָאֲתָה רוֹמְמוֹת לְרָם בְּכֹחוֹ יַשְׂגִּיב · וּמִי קָשׁוּט שִׁנּוּן שִׁבְחוֹ לְהַשְׂגִּיב.
יָאֲתָה צְפִירָה וְתִפְאֶרֶת לְמֶלֶךְ הַכָּבוֹד · וּמִי פְּתָחָיו בּוֹא בְּיִרְאָה לַעֲבֹד.
יָאֲתָה עֲנוֹת תּוֹדָה לָאֵל הַנֶּאֱמָן · וּמִי סָפוּן הֲדַר הוֹדוֹ לְהִתְאַמָּן.
יָאֲתָה נֵצַח וּמֶמְשָׁלָה לְחַי עוֹלָמִים · וּמִי מַלֵּל וְלֹא הָחְסַם בִּבְלוּמִים.

יָאֲתָה לְסַפֵּר מַלְאֲכוּת נוֹרָא תְהִלּוֹת · וּמִי כְעֶרְכְּךָ, בְּאוּרָם בְּשֵׁר בְּמַקְהֵלוֹת.
יָאֲתָה יִחוּד שֵׁם הַנִּכְבָּד לְהָעִידָה · וּמִי טָכוּס טְעַן עֻלּוֹ בִּרְעָדָה.
יָאֲתָה חַסְדֵי צוּר, סֶלָה לְהַזְכִּיר · וּמִי זַךְ דֶּבֶק דְּרָכָיו לְהַכִּיר.
יָאֲתָה וַדַּאי וָתִיק לְסַלֵּד בִּרְנָנָה · וּמִי הָגוּן, הֲלֹם הִלּוּלוֹ לְגָרְנָה.
יָאֲתָה דֹּרֵשׁ צַדִּיק בְּכָל עוֹנָה · וּמִי גָהוּץ, שֵׁרוּת שִׁכְנוֹ לְהַמְעִינָה.
יָאֲתָה בְּרָכוֹת הָעֲטוֹת צַדִּיק לְעִילוּם · וּמִי אָנֹכִי בָּא עַד הֲלֹם.

וּבְכֵן, מִי לֹא יְרָאֲךָ מֶלֶךְ הַגּוֹיִם, כִּי לְךָ יָאָתָה, כִּי

כִּי אֲדוּקֵי אֵשׁ בְּאֵימָה יְאַפְּדוּךָ · כִּי בְרִיתֵי בָשָׂר בִּבְרָכָה יְבַלְעֲדוּךָ.
כִּי גְדוּדֵי גֹבַהּ בְּגַהַר יַגִּידוּךָ · כִּי דְבֵקֵי דְּבָרְתְךָ בְּדִיצָה יְדִידוּךָ.
כִּי הוֹמֵי הֲמֻלָּה בְּהֶגֶה יְהוֹדוּךָ · כִּי וְהוֹגֵי וָתִיקוּתְךָ בְּוַעֲדָם יוֹדוּךָ.
כִּי זַכֵּי זְבוּל בִּזְמִרָתָם יְזַבְּידוּךָ · כִּי חַפֵּי חֶלֶד בְּחִכָּם יְחַדּוּךָ.
כִּי טַפְסְרֵי טֹהַר בְּטַעְמָם יְטַיְּדוּךָ · כִּי יוֹדְעֵי יִרְאָתְךָ בְּיִחוּלָם יְיַחֲדוּךָ.
כִּי כִתֵּי כְרוּבִים בְּכַנְפֵיהֶם יְכַבְּדוּךָ · כִּי לְמֵדֵי לִקְחֲךָ בְּלַהֲקָם יְלַבְּדוּךָ.
כִּי מַחֲנוֹת מְעוֹפְפִים בְּמַהֲלָלָם יְמָאִידוּךָ · כִּי נְשׂוּאֵי נְשָׁרִים בְּנָאֳמָם יְנַגִּידוּךָ.
כִּי סְכוּכֵי סַךְ בְּסִלּוּד יְסַגְּדוּךָ · כִּי עוֹמְסֵי עֻלְּךָ בְּעֹז יְעִידוּךָ.
כִּי פְלִיאֵי פֶלֶא בְּפֶלֶל יְפַחֲדוּךָ · כִּי צוֹעֲקֵי צָקוּן בְּצָרָתָם יְצַעִידוּךָ.
כִּי קְדוּחֵי קֶדַח בְּקָרְאָם יְקָדוּךָ · כִּי רוֹגְשֵׁי רִצְפָּתְךָ בְּרֶטֶט יְרַעֲדוּךָ.
כִּי שְׁבִיבֵי שַׁלְהָבוֹת בְּשֶׂכֶל יְשַׁהֲדוּךָ · כִּי תוֹמְכֵי תֹם בִּתְהִלָּה יְתַמִּידוּךָ.

וּבְכֵן, מִי לֹא יְרָאֲךָ מֶלֶךְ הַגּוֹיִם, כִּי לְךָ יָאָתָה, כִּי בְכָל

בְּכָל אוֹן אוֹסִיף אֹמֶץ לְגַדְּלָךְ · בָּרוּךְ בֵּרוּר שֵׁם כְּבוֹד גָּדְלָךְ.
בְּכָל גּוּף וּנְשָׁמָה יְשֻׂגַּב הִלּוּלָךְ · בָּרוּךְ דּוֹבְבִים לְךָ נִטְעֵי אָהֳלָךְ.
בְּכָל הוֹן מִתְאַהֵב מַלְכוּת עֻלָּךְ · בָּרוּךְ וְקָדוֹשׁ, פּוֹצְחִים יְרֵאֶיךָ לְעֻלָּךְ.
בְּכָל זָוִית מֻקְטָר וּמֻגָּשׁ לָךְ · בָּרוּךְ חֲרֵדִים לְהַמְאוֹת יוֹדְעֶיךָ בְּשִׂכְלָךְ.
בְּכָל טוּחַ יוֹעֵץ חִסְיוֹן צִלָּךְ · בָּרוּךְ יֹאמְרוּ מְשַׁעַשְׁעֵי אָמוֹן אֶצְלָךְ.
בְּכָל כֶּסֶל יְיַחֲדוּ אֱלָהוּתְךָ קְהָלָךְ · בָּרוּךְ לַעֲנוֹת אַחַר חֲטִיבַת חֵילָךְ.
בְּכָל מִדַּת חֶסֶד וְקַו מִשְׁקוֹלָךְ · בָּרוּךְ נוֹאֲמִים תְּאֵבֵי אֹזֶן לְקוֹלָךְ.

בְּכָל שִׂיחַ וָשַׁעַר שָׁמֵי שְׁכָלֶךָ   בָּרוּךְ עֲנִיָּתָם בְּאֹמֶר יָפֶה כְּלָךְ.
בְּכָל פְּתִיחַת מְפֹרָשׁ צָגֵי מְגַדְּלָךְ   בָּרוּךְ צַהַל הַחִלָּם עֹז לְהַגְדִּילָךְ.
בְּכָל קֵץ הַפְלֵאת נִסִּים לְגַדְּלָךְ   בָּרוּךְ רַחֲשָׁם עַל הַצֵּת חֲרוּלָךְ.
בְּכָל שֶׁכֶן בְּהִתְעַדְּנָם מִמַּגְדֵי אֶשְׁלָךְ   בָּרוּךְ תְּמִימֶיךָ יִתְּנוּ לְךָ מִשֶּׁלָּךְ.

וּבְכֵן, מִי לֹא יִרָאֲךָ מֶלֶךְ הַגּוֹיִם, כִּי לְךָ יָאָתָה, כִּי בְּכָל־חַכְמֵי

חַכְמֵי תֹּם דֶּרֶךְ הַמְאַחֲלִים לְכוֹן
שַׁחַר מְעוֹרְרִים לִקְרָאתְךָ הִכּוֹן.
חַכְמֵי רְבֵי תוֹרוֹת הַיְשָׁרִים בְּלִבּוֹתָם
קוֹדִים וּמִשְׁתַּחֲוִים, רְצוֹת נִדְבָתָם.
חַכְמֵי צֵרוּף אוֹתִיּוֹת שֵׁם עִלּוּמֶךָ
פּוֹקְדִים שְׁקֹד סֵפֶף אוּלָמֶךָ.
חַכְמֵי עֵדוּת קֹשֶׁט אִמְרֵי אֲמִתֶּךָ
סוֹקְדִים שָׁווֹת לְנֶגְדָּם אֵימָתֶךָ.
חַכְמֵי נְאֻם צוֹפִים וּפִיּוּף מְדַבְּרֶךָ
מִלְחָמָה מְשִׁיבִים בְּשַׁעֲרֵי דְבִירֶךָ.
חַכְמֵי לֶמֶד הַמּוֹעִיל מְפִיךָ חַנּוּן
כְּבוֹד שָׁמַיִם לְשִׁמְךָ בְּחִנּוּן.
חַכְמֵי יִרְאַת אֱלֹהִים, מוֹשֵׁל צַדִּיק
טוּבְךָ קוֹוִים, קָרוֹב וּמַצְדִּיק.
חַכְמֵי חִפּוּשׂ מַטְמוֹנֵי חָכְמָה וָדַעַת
זְקוּקִים זַמֵּר גֵּאוּת מוּדַעַת.
חַכְמֵי וִדּוּי עֲבוֹדַת יוֹם הַסְּלִיחָה
הוֹמִים בְּתַחֲנוּן, שְׁמָעָה וּסְלָחָה.
חַכְמֵי דְּבָרִים קַחַת, שׁוּב עָדֶיךָ
גּוֹעִים, אָנָּא זְכֹר לַעֲבָדֶיךָ.
חַכְמֵי בְּטוּחֵי בִּבְרִית כְּרוּתָה לְמִדּוֹתֶיךָ
אֶנְקָתָם אֱזֹן, דּוֹפְקֵי דַלְתוֹתֶיךָ.

וּבְכֵן, מִי לֹא יִרָאֲךָ מֶלֶךְ הַגּוֹיִם
כִּי לְךָ יָאָתָה, כִּי בְכָל־חַכְמֵי הַגּוֹיִם

הַגּוֹיִם אֵימִים, זַמְזוּמִים, קֵדָר וַאֲדוּמִים
בַּלְּעֵם, קַלְּעֵם, גְּמוּמִים דְּמוּמִים.
הַגּוֹיִם גֹּמֶר וּמָגוֹג, אַשְׁכְּנַז וְרוֹמִים
דַּכְּאֵם, הַכְּאֵם, זְעוּמִים מָחֳרָמִים.
הַגּוֹיִם הַגְרִים, קְטוּרִים, לוּדִים וַאֲרָמִים
וְכָחֵם, שַׁכְּחֵם, מִתַּחַת רָמִים.
הַגּוֹיִם זֶרַח, נַחַת, מִזִּים וְשַׁמִּים
חַסְּמֵם, כַּרְסְמֵם, שִׂימֵם שׁוֹמֵמִים.
הַגּוֹיִם טֶבַח, גַּחַם וְיֶתֶר רְאוּמִים
יַסְּרֵם, הֲסִירֵם מִהְיוֹת אֻמִּים.
הַגּוֹיִם כַּפְתּוֹרִים, כַּסְלוּחִים, לְטוּשִׁים וּלְאֻמִּים
לַפְּתֵם, כַּפְּתֵם, סְעוּרִים רְעוּמִים.
הַגּוֹיִם מִבְשָׂם וְאַדְבְּאֵל, מִשְׁמָעִים וְדוּמִים
נַפְּצֵם שִׁיתֵם הַדָּמִים.
הַגּוֹיִם סְבָא וַחֲוִילָה, סַבְתְּכָא וְרַעְמִים
עַקְּרֵם, קַרְקְרֵם דְּווּיִם עֲמוּמִים.
הַגּוֹיִם פְּלֶשֶׁת, עַמּוֹן, אַשּׁוּר וְעֵילָמִים
צַמְּתֵם, הֲמִיתֵם, תְּנֵם לְמַהֲלוּמִים.
הַגּוֹיִם קִיר וּמוֹאָב, לוּדִים וַעֲנָמִים
רַטְּשֵׁם, נַטְּשֵׁם דַּקִּים צְנוּמִים.
הַגּוֹיִם שֵׁשַׁךְ וּמָדַי, כִּתִּים וְלֵב קָמִים
תַּעֲבֵם, הַעֲבֵם לְאֵין תְּקוּמִים.

וּבְכֵן, מִי לֹא יִרָאֲךָ מֶלֶךְ הַגּוֹיִם
כִּי לְךָ יָאָתָה, כִּי בְכָל־חַכְמֵי הַגּוֹיִם וּבְכָל

וּבְכָל תֹּקֶף יֶאֱמַן עֹז הִלּוּלָךְ
שַׁלְוַת שׁוֹדְדִים וְשַׁאֲנַנּוּתָם בְּהַיְלִילָךְ.
וּבְכָל רֶגֶשׁ יְמֻתַּק סוֹד אֱמוּנֶיךָ
קַרְנוֹת צַדִּיקִים, בְּרוֹמְמָךְ בְּאַרְמוֹנֶיךָ.
וּבְכָל צַעַד יְפֻזַּז וִיכֻרְכַּר לְכַבְּדָךְ
פַּאֲתֵי בוֹגְדִים, מֵאֶרֶץ בְּאַבְּדָךְ.
וּבְכָל עֹצֶם יוּשַׁר שִׁיר לְעַלָּךְ
סְגוּלֶיךָ מִמַּחַץ מַכָּתָם, בְּהִתְעִילָךְ.
וּבְכָל נָפוֹת יִנְעַם זֶמֶר לְגַדְּלָךְ
מַלְכֵי אֲדָמָה מִכְּבוֹדָם בַּהֲדִלָּךְ.
וּבְכָל לָשׁוֹן יְשֻׂגַּב שִׁמְךָ לְבַדָּךְ
כַּנַּת נִטְעָךְ, בֶּטַח בְּבֹדְדָךְ.
וּבְכָל יָד יְהֻיַּד שֵׁמַע צִלְצוּלָךְ
טִירוֹת טְמֵאִים, מֵחֹסֶן בְּנַצְּלָךְ.
וּבְכָל חֵנֶה וְסֵיעַ, קוֹמָךְ וְשׁוּבָךְ
זְרוּיֶיךָ לְרִבְבוֹת אַלְפֵיהֶם בַּהֲשִׁיבָךְ.
וּבְכָל וְכָל יַמְלִיכוּ אֲדוֹנוּת יִחוּדָךְ
הֲמוֹן עָרִיצִים, לַאֲבַדּוֹן בְּהַכְחִידָךְ.
וּבְכָל דֶּרֶךְ יוּשַׁח עֹצֶם חֵילָךְ
גּוֹיְךָ בְּשַׂמְּחָךְ כְּיַחֵל לָךְ.
וּבְכָל בְּרָכוֹת יִתְרוֹמֵם שֵׁם קָדְשָׁךְ
אֱמוּנֶיךָ, נְעוּרֵימוֹ כַּנֶּשֶׁר בְּחַדְּשָׁךְ.

וּבְכֵן, מִי לֹא יִרָאֲךָ מֶלֶךְ הַגּוֹיִם, כִּי לְךָ יָאָתָה
כִּי בְכָל־חַכְמֵי הַגּוֹיִם וּבְכָל־מַלְכוּתָם

מַלְכוּתָם בְּאַבְּדָךְ עוֹבְדֵי פְסִילֵי נְסָכִים
תִּכּוֹן מַלְכוּתְךָ, מֶלֶךְ מַלְכֵי הַמְּלָכִים.

מַלְכוּתָם בְּבַלְּעָךְ בּוֹטְחֵי הֶבֶל תַּעְתּוּעִים
שָׁמַיִם וָאָרֶץ שִׁבְחָךְ יָהּ מַבִּיעִים.

מַלְכוּתָם בְּגַדְּעָךְ מְקִימֵי אֲשֵׁרִים וְחַמָּנִים
רוֹמְמוֹתֶיךָ יִקְרְאוּ בְגָרוֹן, הֲמוֹנִים הֲמוֹנִים.

מַלְכוּתָם בְּדַכְּאָךְ דּוֹרְשֵׁי קֶטֶב תֹּהוּ וּבְעָלִים
קְדֻשָּׁה וָעֹז תְּיַסֵּד, כְּמִפִּי עוֹלָלִים.

מַלְכוּתָם בְּהָרְסָךְ הַמִּתְהַלְלִים בָּאֱלִילִים
צִדְקוֹתֶיךָ יַגִּידוּ בָּאִיִּים, אֵל אֵלִים.

מַלְכוּתָם בְּוֹכְּחָךְ הַמִּטַּהֲרִים וְהַמִּתְקַדְּשִׁים
פְּאֵר מְלוּכָה יִנְחֲלוּ נִטְעֵי כַּנַּת קְדוֹשִׁים.

מַלְכוּתָם בְּזַעֲמָךְ שָׁטֵי כָזָב, פּוֹנֵי אֶל רְהָבִים
עִלּוּי כְּבוֹד שִׁמְךָ יִתְּנוּ כֹּל בַּאֲהָבִים.

מַלְכוּתָם בְּחָשְׂפָךְ סוֹגְדֵי מַעֲשֵׂה חֲרָשִׁים
סִפּוּר מַעֲשֶׂיךָ בְּרִנָּה יִפְצְחוּ מַאֲרִישִׁים.

מַלְכוּתָם בְּטַאטְאָךְ טוֹעֲנֵי עֲצַבִּים עֲשׂוּיִים פְּרָקִים
נֹעַם דֵּעַ יִרְאָתְךָ יִתְמַלְאוּן אֲרָקִים.

מַלְכוּתָם בְּיַדָּךְ כּוֹרְעֵי נִסְבַּל מַשָּׂא לַעֲיֵפָה
מִשְׁתַּחֲוִים כָּל בָּשָׂר לְפָנֶיךָ, עֹשֵׂה שַׁחַר וְעֵיפָה.

מַלְכוּתָם בְּכַלּוֹתְךָ לְנַעֵר רְשָׁעִים מִן הָאָרֶץ
לָכֵן בְּמָלְכוֹ יִשְׂמְחוּ הַשָּׁמַיִם וְתָגֵל הָאָרֶץ.

וּבְכֵן, מִי לֹא יִרָאֲךָ מֶלֶךְ הַגּוֹיִם, כִּי לְךָ יָאָתָה ירמיה י
כִּי בְכָל־חַכְמֵי הַגּוֹיִם וּבְכָל־מַלְכוּתָם מֵאֵין כָּמוֹךָ:

מֵאֵין כָּמוֹךָ בְּאַמְּצָךְ שָׁמַיִם וּשְׁמֵי שָׁמַיִם
מֵאֵין כָּמוֹךָ בְּבָלְלָךְ אֵשׁ וּמַיִם.
מֵאֵין כָּמוֹךָ בְּגָלְלָךְ אִישׁוֹן חֹשֶׁךְ וָאֹפֶל
מֵאֵין כָּמוֹךָ בְּדָלְקָךְ אוֹר מִמַּאֲפֵל.
מֵאֵין כָּמוֹךָ בְּהַבְדִּילָךְ רָקִיעַ בְּמַחַץ
מֵאֵין כָּמוֹךָ בְּוַעֲדָךְ לְהַקְווֹת זְדוֹנֵי שַׁחַץ.
מֵאֵין כָּמוֹךָ בְּזַכָּךְ צִבְאוֹת זַכִּים וְנוֹרָאִים
מֵאֵין כָּמוֹךָ בְּחַסְנָךְ חֲיָלֵי פְּלִיאִים.
מֵאֵין כָּמוֹךָ בְּטַכְּסָךְ מוֹצָא דֶשֶׁא וּוְרָדִים
מֵאֵין כָּמוֹךָ בְּיַצְּבָךְ גַּן לְהַצְמִיחַ מְגָדִים.
מֵאֵין כָּמוֹךָ בְּכַלְלָךְ גֹּדֶל שְׁנֵי הַמְּאוֹרוֹת
מֵאֵין כָּמוֹךָ בְּלַהֲבָךְ עָשׁ כְּסִיל וְכִימָה וּמַזָּרוֹת.
מֵאֵין כָּמוֹךָ בְּמַלְלָךְ יִשְׁרְצוּ אַדִּירִים
מֵאֵין כָּמוֹךָ בְּנָאֳמָךְ לְעוֹפֵף טָסֵי אֲוִירִים.
מֵאֵין כָּמוֹךָ בְּשַׂגְּבָךְ רֶמֶשׂ מִמְּעֵי צִיָּה
מֵאֵין כָּמוֹךָ בְּעָצְמָךְ נֶפֶשׁ בְּהֵמָה וְחַיָּה.
מֵאֵין כָּמוֹךָ בְּפָקְדָךְ אֵבוּס בְּהַרְרֵי אֶלֶף מִסְבּוֹ
מֵאֵין כָּמוֹךָ בְּצַוּוֹתָךְ לִוְיָתָן זֶה יָצַרְתָּ לְשַׂחֶק בּוֹ.
מֵאֵין כָּמוֹךָ בְּקַבְּצָךְ עָפָר מֵרִגְבֵי אֲדָמָה
מֵאֵין כָּמוֹךָ בְּרָקְמָךְ חוֹתַם תָּכְנִית מָלֵא חָכְמָה.
מֵאֵין כָּמוֹךָ בְּשָׁבְתָךְ יוֹם מִיָּמִים
מֵאֵין כָּמוֹךָ בְּתַקְּנָךְ שִׁכְלוּל שְׁנֵי עוֹלָמִים.

The last piyut of the קרובה *for* שחרית *is also by Rabbi Meshullam ben Kalonymus. Its lines begin with a double acrostic. Some congregations used to say it after the* שְׁמַע *verse in* קדושה.

דברים ו וּבְכֵן, שְׁמַע יִשְׂרָאֵל, יהוה אֱלֹהֵינוּ, יהוה אֶחָד:

הָאֲזוּרִים בְּאַהַב אוֹמְרִים יהוה אֱלֹהֵינוּ
הַבָּאִים בִּבְרִית עוֹנִים יהוה אֶחָד.
הַגְּאוּלִים בְּגִיל אוֹמְרִים יהוה אֱלֹהֵינוּ
הַדְּרוּשִׁים בְּדֶעַ עוֹנִים יהוה אֶחָד.
הַהוֹמִים בְּהֶגֶה אוֹמְרִים יהוה אֱלֹהֵינוּ
הַוָּתִיקִים בְּוַעַד עוֹנִים יהוה אֶחָד.
הַזְּבוּדִים בְּזֶבֶד אוֹמְרִים יהוה אֱלֹהֵינוּ
הַחֲנוּנִים בְּחַיִל עוֹנִים יהוה אֶחָד.
הַטְּכוּסִים בְּטַעַם אוֹמְרִים יהוה אֱלֹהֵינוּ
הַיְחוּסִים בְּיַחַס עוֹנִים יהוה אֶחָד.
הַכְּלוּלִים בְּכֶתֶר אוֹמְרִים יהוה אֱלֹהֵינוּ
הַלְּקוּחִים לוֹ לְעַם עוֹנִים יהוה אֶחָד.
הַמּוּלִים בְּמֶתֶק אוֹמְרִים יהוה אֱלֹהֵינוּ
הַנְּשׂוּאִים בְּנֹעַם עוֹנִים יהוה אֶחָד.
הַסְּגוּלִים בְּסֶגֶל אוֹמְרִים יהוה אֱלֹהֵינוּ
הָעֲמוּסִים בְּעֹז עוֹנִים יהוה אֶחָד.
הַפְּדוּיִים בִּפְאֵר אוֹמְרִים יהוה אֱלֹהֵינוּ
הַצְּנוּעִים בְּצֶדֶק עוֹנִים יהוה אֶחָד.
הַקּוֹרְאִים בְּקֶשֶׁב אוֹמְרִים יהוה אֱלֹהֵינוּ
הָרוֹגְשִׁים בְּרֹן עוֹנִים יהוה אֶחָד.
הַשּׁוֹאֲגִים בְּשֶׁקֶד אוֹמְרִים יהוה אֱלֹהֵינוּ
הַתְּמוּכִים בְּתַאַב עוֹנִים יהוה אֶחָד.

Continue with וּבְכֵן תֵּן פַּחְדְּךָ *on page 667.*

This, the "חטאנו" piyut for שחרית, contains an acrostic of the alphabet followed by a reference to its author: קלונימוס חזק. The last stich in each stanza is a biblical quotation, of which the last word is the first of the next stanza.

חָטָאנוּ צוּרֵנוּ, סְלַח לָנוּ יוֹצְרֵנוּ.

אֲדַבְּרָה תַּחֲנוּנִים כְּרָשׁ וְאֶבְכֶּה / בְּעִנּוּי נֶפֶשׁ קְהָלִי אֲבַכֶּה
כִּי נִקַּף כַּבַּרְזֶל סִבְכֵי / בָּכוּ הָעָם הַרְבֵּה בֶכֶה: עזרא י

בֶּכֶה הִשְׂבִּיעַנִי כְּגֶדַע קַרְנִי / לַעֲנָה וָרֹאשׁ וּמְרוֹרִים הִרְוַנִי
הֶדְמַמְתִּי, וְנָם קוּמִי רָנִּי / יָגַעְתִּי בְקָרְאִי, נִחַר גְּרוֹנִי: תהלים סט

חָטָאנוּ צוּרֵנוּ, סְלַח לָנוּ יוֹצְרֵנוּ.

גְּרוֹנִי הָנְשַׁת קְרוֹא אֲרוּכָה / קַוֵּה נַחַת, וְהִנֵּה פְרוּכָה
נוֹדַדְתִּי כְּצִפּוֹר וַדְרָכַי נִסְרָכָה / מִפְּנֵי קֶשֶׁת דְּרוּכָה: ישעיה כא

דְּרוּכָה לְשׁוֹן מְקַנְאַי וּרְחָבָה / מְצֹרֶבֶת פָּנִים כַּחֲשַׁשׁ לֶהָבָה
נַתְּקֵם מִמַּצָּבָם בְּהַשְׁלֵךְ וּסְחִיבָה / וְלִהַט אֹתָם הַיּוֹם הַבָּא: מלאכי ג

חָטָאנוּ צוּרֵנוּ, סְלַח לָנוּ יוֹצְרֵנוּ.

הַבָּא כְּאַרְיֵה בְּמַאֲרָב לִדְגֹּר / וְהַיּוֹצֵא צוֹדֶה תְּתִי לְמָגוֹר
כָּל רָעָתָם לְפָנֶיךָ תֶּאֱגֹר / וְהָרֵק חֲנִית וּסְגֹר: תהלים סט

וּסְגֹר מוֹצָאָם וּמוֹבָאָם וְיִדָּמֶמוּ / בַּלַּע פַּלַּג לְשׁוֹנָם וְיִזְדַּמֵּמוּ
הֲרֹס שִׁנֵּימוֹ בְּפִימוֹ וְיֶהֱמָמוּ / לָקַחַת נַפְשִׁי זָמָמוּ: תהלים לא

חָטָאנוּ צוּרֵנוּ, סְלַח לָנוּ יוֹצְרֵנוּ.

זָמְמוּ לָרוּץ בְּצַוָּאר אֵלֶיךָ / נוֹעֲצוּ לִכְרֹת בְּרִית עָלֶיךָ
הֲדִיחוּ מִמְּעוֹנְךָ צִבְאוֹת חֲיָלֶיךָ / עָלֶיךָ יַעֲזֹב חֵלֶכָה: תהלים י

חֵילְךָ מִתְחַבֵּא מִפַּחַד קָטָבְךָ / בְּךָ יָרוּץ לְהִשְׂתַּגֵּב בְּהַחֲטִיבְךָ
בְּשַׁעַן וַאֲהֵבְךָ וְהִרְבְּךָ וְהֵיטִבְךָ / מָה רַב טוּבְךָ: תהלים לא

חָטָאנוּ צוּרֵנוּ, סְלַח לָנוּ יוֹצְרֵנוּ.

טוּבְךָ יֹאבֶה שְׁאָר יָשׁוּב / מִתְנַפֵּל בְּהִמָּצְאֲךָ אֵלֶיךָ לָשׁוּב
קְוֹחַ דִּבְרֵי כִּבּוּשִׁים וָשׁוּב / מִי־יוֹדֵעַ יָשׁוּב: יונה ג

יָשׁוּב חֲרוֹנְךָ וְאַל תְּכַלֵּנוּ / כִּי שָׁנֵינוּ כְּהֶגֶה כִּלִּינוּ
בְּדֶרֶךְ זוּ נֵלֵךְ הַשְׂכִּילֵנוּ / הֵן הַבֶּט־נָא עַמְּךָ כֻלָּנוּ: ישעיה סד

חָטָאנוּ צוּרֵנוּ, סְלַח לָנוּ יוֹצְרֵנוּ.

כֻּלָּנוּ יַחַד נְחַלֶּה פָנָיו / נַזְכִּיר בְּרִית יִקְרַת פְּנִינָיו
בְּצֶדֶק לַחֲזוֹתֵנוּ אוֹר פָּנָיו / יְקִמֵנוּ וְנִחְיֶה לְפָנָיו: הושע ו

לְפָנָיו מְצַפְצֵף, מֵעָפָר לַהֲקִימוֹ / עַם מְיַחֲדוֹ בְּשָׁכְבוֹ וּבְקוּמוֹ
נֶצַח מְחַכִּים לְיוֹם קוּמוֹ / בָּרוּךְ כְּבוֹד־יהוה מִמְּקוֹמוֹ: יחזקאל ג

חָטָאנוּ צוּרֵנוּ, סְלַח לָנוּ יוֹצְרֵנוּ.

מִמְּקוֹמוֹ יָצֵף כַּחַשׁ רִטְפוּשִׁי / לְפָאֵר יָמִיר אֵפֶר כִּפּוּשִׁי
מֵעֹצֶב עֲבוֹדָה קָשָׁה לְהַנְפִּישִׁי / כִּי־שָׂבְעָה בְרָעוֹת נַפְשִׁי: תהלים פח

נַפְשִׁי תִשְׁתּוֹחַח לְשִׁמּוּם מְסִלָּה / דְּדוּי סַךְ לְנֶוךָ סְלוּלָה
מַשְׁמִיעֵי שָׁלוֹם, מְשׁוֹב לְכִסְלָה / יְכוֹנְנֶהָ עַד־עוֹלָם סֶלָה: תהלים מח

חָטָאנוּ צוּרֵנוּ, סְלַח לָנוּ יוֹצְרֵנוּ.

סֶלָה דְּרַשְׁתִּיךָ וְלֹא נְטַשְׁתָּנִי / בְּהִתְפַּשְּׁטִי, בְּצֵל יָדְךָ כִּסִּיתָנִי
מֵאֵשׁ וּמִמַּיִם לָרְוָיָה הוֹצֵאתָנִי / וּמִקַּרְנֵי רֵמִים עֲנִיתָנִי: תהלים כב

עֲנִיתָנִי בְּכָל עֵת, בְּהִתְעַטְּפִי / הוֹשַׁטְתָּ יְמִינְךָ בְּאַהַב לְגַפְּפִי
וְעַתָּה מוֹשִׁיעִי לֹא תַרְפִּי / תְּהִלַּת יהוה יְדַבֶּר פִּי: תהלים קמה

חָטָאנוּ צוּרֵנוּ, סְלַח לָנוּ יוֹצְרֵנוּ.

פִּי יַגִּיד תְּהִלָּתְךָ תִּקְוָתֵנוּ / אַל יִמְעֲטוּ לְפָנֶיךָ תְּלָאוֹתֵינוּ
כְּגֹדֶל חַסְדְּךָ, מַלֵּט מִשְּׁחִיתוֹתֵינוּ / כִּי לֹא עַל־צִדְקֹתֵינוּ: דניאל ט

צִדְקֹתֵינוּ דַּלּוּ, וְלִמְאֹד קָצָרוּ / עֲוֹנֵינוּ רַבּוּ וְהַטּוֹב עָצָרוּ
חַטָּאֵי אָבוֹת לַבָּנִים נֶאֱצָרוּ / זָרְעוּ חִטִּים וְקֹצִים קָצָרוּ: ירמיה יב

חָטָאנוּ צוּרֵנוּ, סְלַח לָנוּ יוֹצְרֵנוּ.

קָצְרוּ יְרִיבַי קָמוֹת אִבִּי / דִּמּוּ לְהַכְרִית יְשִׁישַׁי וְרוֹבִי
קְרָאתִיךָ, מֵעֹשֶׁק זֵדִים לְעָרְבִי / שָׁפְטֵנִי אֱלֹהִים וְרִיבָה רִיבִי: תהלים מג

רִיבִי בְּחַפְּשְׂךָ יָשְׁרִי תְּבַקֵּר / צִדְקַת הוֹרִים לְפָנֶיךָ תֵּחָקֵר
מַצְדִּיקַי יִקְרַב וּמַרְשִׁיעַי יֵעָקֵר / יִסָּכֵר פִּי דוֹבְרֵי־שָׁקֶר: תהלים סג

חָטָאנוּ צוּרֵנוּ, סְלַח לָנוּ יוֹצְרֵנוּ.

שֶׁקֶר דּוֹבֵר לֹא יָבֹא / לְנֶגֶד עֵינֶיךָ, כִּי תְתַעֵבוֹ
שָׁמְרֵנִי רֶגֶל גַּאֲוָה מִבּוֹא / וּמִשֹּׁאַת רְשָׁעִים כִּי תָבֹא: משלי ג

תָּבוֹא לְפָנֶיךָ אֱלֹהֵי קֶדֶם / תַּאֲוַת מִתְעַנִּים, פָּנֶיךָ לְקַדֵּם
תֶּעֱרַב מִנְחָתָם כְּשָׁנִים מִקֶּדֶם / זְכֹר עֲדָתְךָ קָנִיתָ קֶּדֶם: תהלים עד

חָטָאנוּ צוּרֵנוּ, סְלַח לָנוּ יוֹצְרֵנוּ.

קֶדֶם מִפְּעָלֶיךָ יהוה אֲדוֹנִי / עֲצַתְךָ לִכְתֹּב כְּתָבַת נְדָנִי
בְּנִתָּה מֵרָחוֹק חֻקֶּיךָ לְהָעִידֵנִי / בָּרוּךְ אַתָּה יהוה, לַמְּדֵנִי: תהלים קיט

לַמְּדֵנִי לְהוֹעִיל, מֵמִית וּמְחַיֶּה / צִוִּיתָ וַיַּעֲמֹד, אָמַרְתָּ וַיְּהִי
הוֹרֵנִי דְּרָכֶיךָ וְתָמִים אֶהְיֶה / עֵדְוֹתֶיךָ לְעוֹלָם, הֲבִינֵנִי וְאֶחְיֶה: שם

חָטָאנוּ צוּרֵנוּ, סְלַח לָנוּ יוֹצְרֵנוּ.

וְאֶחְיֶה וְזַרְעִי לְפָנֶיךָ יִכּוֹן / וּתְפִלָּתִי כִּקְטֹרֶת תָּמִיד תִּכּוֹן
בְּעַד עֵינֶיךָ בְּבֹאִי לְרַכֵּן / נָכוֹן לִבִּי אֱלֹהִים, נָכוֹן: תהלים נז

נָכוֹן וְקַיָּם, אֲבוֹתֵינוּ סִפְּרוּ / עֹדֶף טוּבוֹתֶיךָ חֲטָאֵינוּ כִּפְּרוּ
לְבָנִים גַּם עַתָּה וְיוּפְרוּ / וּפְנֵיהֶם אַל־יֶחְפָּרוּ: תהלים לד

חָטָאנוּ צוּרֵנוּ, סְלַח לָנוּ יוֹצְרֵנוּ.

יַחְפְּרוּ פְּנֵי מַכְבִּידֵי מוּעָקֵנוּ / יִלְבְּשׁוּ בֹשֶׁת בְּהוֹצָאַת צִדְקֵנוּ
יָבוֹא וְאַל יֶחֱרַשׁ לְצַדְּקֵנוּ / יהוה שֹׁפְטֵנוּ יהוה מְחֹקְקֵנוּ: ישעיה לג

מְחוֹקְקֵנוּ הִדָּרֵשׁ לְאֹם נוֹשָׁעָה / הַשְׁאִיבָהּ בְּשָׂשׂוֹן מִמַּעַיְנֵי הַיְשׁוּעָה
שַׂמַּח נַפְשׁוֹתֵינוּ, בְּחֻקֶּיךָ לְהִשְׁתַּעְשְׁעָה / וְהָאֵר פָּנֶיךָ וְנִוָּשֵׁעָה: תהלים פ

חָטָאנוּ צוּרֵנוּ, סְלַח לָנוּ יוֹצְרֵנוּ.

וְנִוָּשֵׁעָה בְּשָׁפְכֵנוּ לְפָנֶיךָ שִׂיחָה / הֵעָתֵר לָנוּ עֲוֹנֵינוּ לְסָלְחָה
חַנּוּן כִּי עִמְּךָ הַסְּלִיחָה / אֲדֹנָי שְׁמָעָה, אֲדֹנָי סְלָחָה: דניאל ט

סְלָחָה וְלֹא נֵצֵא דְּחוּיִים / פְּשָׁעֵינוּ יְהוּ כָּעָב מְחוּיִים
נִחֲנוּ לֵאוֹר בְּאוֹר הַחַיִּים / כִּי־עִמְּךָ מְקוֹר חַיִּים: תהלים לו

חָטָאנוּ צוּרֵנוּ, סְלַח לָנוּ יוֹצְרֵנוּ.

חַיִּים וָחֶסֶד אֵלִי זֶה / תָּחֹן שְׁאֵרִית הָעָם הַזֶּה
גָּשִׁים לְהַקְדִּישׁ בְּקוֹל זֶה / וְקָרָא זֶה אֶל־זֶה: ישעיה ו

זֶה יִכְתֹּב יָדוֹ לְקָדוֹשׁ / וְזֶה חָדָשׁ לַבְּקָר יְגַדֵּשׁ
מִזֶּה וּמִזֶּה שִׁלּוּשׁ קָדוֹשׁ / וְאָמַר קָדוֹשׁ קָדוֹשׁ קָדוֹשׁ: שם

חָטָאנוּ צוּרֵנוּ, סְלַח לָנוּ יוֹצְרֵנוּ.

קָדוֹשׁ בְּבוֹא אֵלָיו הַקּוֹל / כַּף שִׁבֹּלֶת יַכְרִיעַ לִשְׁקֹל
נְקוּת קוֹרְאָיו כְּמַרְעִישֵׁי קוֹל / וָאֶשְׁמַע אַחֲרַי קוֹל: יחזקאל ג

◂ קוֹל גָּדוֹל כְּהַשְׁמִיעַ לִרְחוּמִים / קַבְּלוּ מַלְכוּתִי מִמְּקוֹרֵי רַחֲמִים
יִזְכֹּר הַיּוֹם לְסָבִיב מִתְחַמִּים / אֵל מֶלֶךְ יוֹשֵׁב עַל כִּסֵּא רַחֲמִים.

חָטָאנוּ צוּרֵנוּ, סְלַח לָנוּ יוֹצְרֵנוּ.

Continue with "זְכָר לָנוּ בְּרִית אָבוֹת" on page 673.

פיוטים לתפילת מוסף

This piyut also follows an alphabetical acrostic. The first two lines serve as alternating refrains.

Responsively:

אֶת לַחֲשִׁי עֲנֵה נָא / זַעֲקִי רְצֵה נָא / הָאֵל קָדוֹשׁ.
אָדוֹן לְקוֹל עַמֶּךָ / זְכֹר רַחֲמֶיךָ / נוֹרָא וְקָדוֹשׁ.

All:

אֵין עֲרֹךְ אֵלֶיךָ / בֵּין עֹצֶם מִפְעָלֶיךָ
גִּישַׁת הֲמוֹן מְיַחֲלֶיךָ / דְּרֹשׁ לְגַבֵּר חֲיָלֶיךָ.
אֶת לַחֲשִׁי עֲנֵה נָא / זַעֲקִי רְצֵה נָא / הָאֵל קָדוֹשׁ.

הוֹגֵי הֲמֻלַּת קֹדֶשׁ / וּמְהַלְלִים בְּהַדְרַת קֹדֶשׁ
זֶרַע תְּבוּאַת קֹדֶשׁ / חֲשֹׁב כְּאֵילֵי קֹדֶשׁ.
אָדוֹן לְקוֹל עַמֶּךָ / זְכֹר רַחֲמֶיךָ / נוֹרָא וְקָדוֹשׁ.

טַפְסְרֵי מְרֻבְּעֵי פָנִים / יְיַשְׁירוּךָ עִם אוֹפַנִּים
כְּבַקָּרְךָ כָּל פְּנִים / לְבִלְתִּי נְשֹׂא פָנִים.
אֶת לַחֲשִׁי עֲנֵה נָא / זַעֲקִי רְצֵה נָא / הָאֵל קָדוֹשׁ.

מִתְנַשֵּׂא לְכֹל לְרֹאשׁ / נוֹעַץ אַחֲרִית מֵרֹאשׁ
סְלִיחָה לַשּׁוֹבָבִים דְּרֹשׁ / עֲוֹנָם לָשֵׂאת כְּמֵרֹאשׁ.
אָדוֹן לְקוֹל עַמֶּךָ / זְכֹר רַחֲמֶיךָ / נוֹרָא וְקָדוֹשׁ.

פְּרוּדֵי כְנַף רְנָנִים / צִדְקוֹתֶיךָ חַי מְרַנְּנִים
קוֹל שַׁאַג מְחַנְּנִים / רְצֵה בְּחִין וּבְתַחֲנוּנִים.
אֶת לַחֲשִׁי עֲנֵה נָא / זַעֲקִי רְצֵה נָא / הָאֵל קָדוֹשׁ.

שִׁנְאַן רִבְבוֹת אֲלָפִים / שׁוֹאֲגִים וְלַבְּקָרִים מִתְחַלְּפִים
תֹּקֶף יַשִּׂיגוּ אַלּוּפִים / תּוֹדָה וְזִמְרָה מְאַלְּפִים.
אָדוֹן לְקוֹל עַמֶּךָ / זְכֹר רַחֲמֶיךָ / נוֹרָא וְקָדוֹשׁ.

Many of the piyutim share similar forms. The following piyut echoes the pattern of אָנָּא אֱלֹהִים חַיִּים *from the* קרובה *for* שחרית *(page 1293).*

וּבְכֵן, וְאַתָּה כְּרַחוּם סְלַח לָנוּ.

אַל תִּזְכָּר לָנוּ עֲוֹנוֹתֵינוּ / הִנָּקֵם לָנוּ מִצָּרֵינוּ
כְּכֹל אֲשֶׁר גָּמְלוּ עָלֵינוּ. וְאַתָּה כְּרַחוּם סְלַח לָנוּ.

בְּשִׁמְךָ נִקְרָא וְתַעֲנֵנוּ / וְתִשְׁבֹּר אֶת עֻלֵּנוּ
וְאַתָּה תִּמְלֹךְ עָלֵינוּ. וְאַתָּה כְּרַחוּם סְלַח לָנוּ.

גֹּדֶל רַחֲמֶיךָ תּוֹדִיעַ / וּמַלְכוּתְךָ עָלֵינוּ תוֹפִיעַ
וּכְאָז אוֹתָנוּ תוֹשִׁיעַ. וְאַתָּה כְּרַחוּם סְלַח לָנוּ.

דַּרְכְּךָ נִצָּב לְעוֹלָם / זְכָר נָא אֲבוֹת הָעוֹלָם
וְהָקֵם בְּרִיתְךָ לְעוֹלָם. וְאַתָּה כְּרַחוּם סְלַח לָנוּ.

הֵרָצֶה לָנוּ כְּמֵאָז / וְהַשְׁמֵד הַגּוֹי הָעָז
וְנִלְמַד נֶחֱמָדִים מִפָּז. וְאַתָּה כְּרַחוּם סְלַח לָנוּ.

וְהַשְׁקִיפָה מִמְּעוֹן קָדְשֶׁךָ / וְקוֹמֵם אֶת מִקְדָּשֶׁךָ
וְנַעֲרִיץ בְּכָל יוֹם קְדֻשָּׁתֶךָ. וְאַתָּה כְּרַחוּם סְלַח לָנוּ.

זְכֹר צִדְקַת רִאשׁוֹנִים / וּסְלַח נָא לָאַחֲרוֹנִים
וְתוֹשִׁיבֵם אֶל אַרְבּוֹתֵיהֶם כְּיוֹנִים. וְאַתָּה כְּרַחוּם סְלַח לָנוּ.

חוּסָה עַל צֹאן מַרְעִיתֶךָ / וּבָרֵךְ אֶת נַחֲלָתֶךָ
וּלְמְדֵם כְּאָז דָּתֶךָ. וְאַתָּה כְּרַחוּם סְלַח לָנוּ.

טָהוֹר תֵּרָאֶה כְּבוֹדֶךָ / וְתוֹדִיעַ בָּנוּ הוֹדֶךָ
וְנִסְבֹּל עֹל מוֹרָאֲךָ וְיִחוּדֶךָ. וְאַתָּה כְּרַחוּם סְלַח לָנוּ.

יְרֵאֶיךָ יִשְׂמְחוּ בָךְ / וּבְכָל יוֹם יִשְׁתַּחֲווּ לָךְ
וְגוֹי וּמַמְלָכָה יַעַבְדוּ לָךְ. וְאַתָּה כְּרַחוּם סְלַח לָנוּ.

כְּרַחֲמֶיךָ עֲשֵׂה עִמָּנוּ / כִּי בְכָל יוֹם לְךָ קְרָאנוּ
יהוה צְבָאוֹת עִמָּנוּ. וְאַתָּה כְּרַחוּם סְלַח לָנוּ.

לְבַדְּךָ תִּמְלֹךְ כְּמֵרֵאשִׁית / וְתָשִׁית עֵינֶיךָ בְּרֵאשִׁית
בְּמָקוֹם כּוֹנַנְתָּ מֵרֵאשִׁית. וְאַתָּה כְּרַחוּם סְלַח לָנוּ.

מַלְכוּתְךָ עָלֵינוּ תִּגָּלֶה / נוֹרְאוֹתֶיךָ נֶחֱזֶה וְנִתְעַלֶּה
וּמִצִּיּוֹן בְּרַחֲמֶיךָ תִּגָּלֶה. וְאַתָּה כְּרַחוּם סְלַח לָנוּ.

נְחֵנוּ בַּאֲמִתֶּךָ / וְשַׂמְּחֵנוּ בִּישׁוּעָתֶךָ
כִּי אֲנַחְנוּ עַמְּךָ וְנַחֲלָתֶךָ. וְאַתָּה כְּרַחוּם סְלַח לָנוּ.

שִׂימֵנוּ בְּרָכָה בָּאָרֶץ / וּתְנַעֵר רְשָׁעִים מֵאֶרֶץ
וְנֵשֵׁב לָבֶטַח בָּאָרֶץ. וְאַתָּה כְּרַחוּם סְלַח לָנוּ.

עֲנֵנוּ בִּדְבַר אֲמִתֶּךָ / וְהוֹשִׁיעֵנוּ בֶּאֱמוּנָתֶךָ
כִּי אֲנַחְנוּ צֹאן מַרְעִיתֶךָ. וְאַתָּה כְּרַחוּם סְלַח לָנוּ.

פָּנֶיךָ הָאֵר בְּצִיּוֹן / וּמְלֹךְ עָלֵינוּ בְּצִבְיוֹן
וְתָסִיר טֻמְאָה מִצִּיּוֹן. וְאַתָּה כְּרַחוּם סְלַח לָנוּ.

צַדִּיק אַתָּה בַּכֹּל / וְרַחֲמֶיךָ גְּדוֹלִים עַל כֹּל
מִיָּדְךָ הוּא, וּלְךָ הַכֹּל. וְאַתָּה כְּרַחוּם סְלַח לָנוּ.

קָרוֹב אַתָּה לְכָל קוֹרְאֶיךָ / רַחֵם עַל מַמְלִיכֶיךָ
כִּי הֵם מַעֲשֵׂה יָדֶיךָ. וְאַתָּה כְּרַחוּם סְלַח לָנוּ.

רַחוּם, סְלַח נָא לְעָוֹן / כִּי כָל אָדָם מְלֵא עָוֹן
וְאַתָּה תְּכַפֵּר עָוֹן. וְאַתָּה כְּרַחוּם סְלַח לָנוּ.

שִׁמְךָ בָּנוּ נִקְרָא, וְאַל תַּנִּיחֵנוּ / נִקְרָאֲךָ וְאַתָּה תַּעֲנֵנוּ
וּלְמַעַנְךָ הָאֵר עֵינֵינוּ. וְאַתָּה כְּרַחוּם סְלַח לָנוּ.

תְּאַר פָּנֶיךָ תַּרְאֵנוּ / וּבְתוֹרָתְךָ תְּחַכְּמֵנוּ
וּבְמִרְעֶה טוֹב וְשָׁמֵן תִּרְעֵנוּ. וְאַתָּה כְּרַחוּם סְלַח לָנוּ.

All:

וּבְכֵן, אַךְ חַנּוּן אַתָּה, וְרַחוּם לְכָל פֹּעַל.

Like the previous piyut, this one echoes אַךְ אֲתִים בְּחִין לְפָנֶיךָ *from the* קרובה *for* שחרית *(page 1296), mainly in its refrains and in the theme of Israel standing in prayer. However, its form is more intricate, its stanzas growing in complexity to include first double, then triple internal rhymes.*

The שליח ציבור *says the beginning of each line, and the* קהל *responds with the refrains.*

אַךְ אוֹמְרִים בְּחִין לְפָנֶיךָ כִּי אַתָּה רַחוּם לְכָל פֹּעַל.
אַךְ בָּאִים וּמִשְׁתַּחֲוִים לְפָנֶיךָ כִּי אַתָּה רַחוּם לְכָל פֹּעַל.
אַךְ גָּשִׁים בִּתְפִלָּה לְפָנֶיךָ כִּי אַתָּה רַחוּם לְכָל פֹּעַל.
אַךְ דּוֹרְשִׁים בְּדָתְךָ יוֹמָם וָלַיְלָה חַנּוּן וְרַחוּם לְכָל פֹּעַל.

אַךְ הוֹגִים בְּהַלֵּל וּבְתִשְׁבָּחוֹת כִּי אַתָּה רַחוּם לְכָל פֹּעַל.
אַךְ וְאוֹמְרִים, סְלַח נָא לַעֲוֹנֵנוּ כִּי אַתָּה רַחוּם לְכָל פֹּעַל.
אַךְ זוֹעֲקִים בִּתְחִנָּה וּבְתַחֲנוּנִים לְפָנֶיךָ כִּי אַתָּה רַחוּם לְכָל פֹּעַל.
אַךְ חוֹקְרִים סוֹד בְּרִיתֶךָ, כִּי אֵין בִּלְתֶּךָ חַנּוּן וְרַחוּם לְכָל פֹּעַל.

אַךְ טוֹעֲנִים שְׁמַע יִשְׂרָאֵל, כִּי אֵין כָּאֵל כִּי אַתָּה רַחוּם לְכָל פֹּעַל.
אַךְ יוֹדְעִים שֵׁם הַמְפֹרָשׁ, וּבְפִיהֶם יִתְפָּרַשׁ כִּי אַתָּה רַחוּם לְכָל פֹּעַל.
אַךְ כֻּלָּם הַיּוֹם כְּמַלְאָכִים, קְדֻשָּׁה לְפָנֶיךָ עוֹרְכִים כִּי אַתָּה רַחוּם לְכָל פֹּעַל.
אַךְ לְבוּשֵׁיהֶם נְקִיִּים, וְכֻלָּם צָמִים וּמִתְעַנִּים חַנּוּן וְרַחוּם לְכָל פֹּעַל.

אַךְ מַעֲשֵׂיהֶם מַגִּידִים, וַחֲטָאֵיהֶם בְּפִיהֶם מְתַנִּים
סְלַח נָא עוֹנִים כִּי אַתָּה רַחוּם לְכָל פֹּעַל.
אַךְ נִקְרָאִים הַיּוֹם, וְסָלַחְתִּי לָכֶם הַיּוֹם
וּטְהַרְתֶּם לִפְנֵי הַיּוֹם כִּי אַתָּה רַחוּם לְכָל פֹּעַל.
אַךְ סְפוּרִים כְּחוֹל הַיָּם, וַעֲוֹנוֹתֵיהֶם תַּשְׁלִיךְ בִּמְצוּלוֹת יָם
בְּשָׁפְכָם לֵב כַּמַּיִם כִּי אַתָּה רַחוּם לְכָל פֹּעַל.
אַךְ עוֹנִים אַרְבַּע קְדֻשּׁוֹת, לִפְנֵי חוֹקֵר כְּלָיוֹת
וְיוֹדֵעַ כָּל נִסְתָּרוֹת חַנּוּן וְרַחוּם לְכָל פֹּעַל.

אַךְ פָּקְדֵם לְחַיִּים, וְטַהֲרֵם בְּמַיִם חַיִּים
כִּי עִמְּךָ מְקוֹר חַיִּים   כִּי אַתָּה רַחוּם לְכָל פֹּעַל.
אַךְ צוֹעֲקִים, אָנָּא אֵל נָא, וְחֵטְא כַּפֵּר נָא
לַעֲדַת מִי מָנָה   כִּי אַתָּה רַחוּם לְכָל פֹּעַל.
אַךְ קוֹלָם בְּרַעַשׁ מַרְעִישִׁים, קָדוֹשׁ קָדוֹשׁ קָדוֹשׁ קוֹרְאִים
אָבוֹת וּבָנִים   כִּי אַתָּה רַחוּם לְכָל פֹּעַל.
אַךְ רִאשׁוֹן וְאַחֲרוֹן אַתָּה, חַנּוּן וְרַחוּם אַתָּה
לְמַעַנְךָ עֲשֵׂה גַּם עַתָּה   כִּי אַתָּה רַחוּם לְכָל פֹּעַל.
אַךְ שְׁמַע תְּפִלָּתֵנוּ, בְּקָרְאֵנוּ אֵלֶיךָ עֲנֵנוּ
אֱלֹהֵי צִדְקֵנוּ   כִּי אַתָּה רַחוּם לְכָל פֹּעַל.
אַךְ תּוֹלִים לְךָ עֵינֵיהֶם, עֲנֵם וּשְׁמַע בְּקוֹל תְּפִלּוֹתֵיהֶם
סְלַח נָא לַעֲוֹנוֹתֵיהֶם   חַנּוּן וְרַחוּם לְכָל פֹּעַל.

This piyut, which enlarges upon the refrain "אֵלּוּ לְאֵלּוּ שׁוֹאֲלִים," is omitted nowadays by many congregations. Like אֵין מִסְפָּר לִגְדוּדֵי צְבָא חֵילוֹ (page 1303) which has the same refrain, it is based upon Isaiah 6:2–3.

אֵילֵי מָרוֹם אוֹמְרִים הִלּוּלוֹ / אוֹפַן וְגַלְגַּל מַבִּיעִים סִלְסוּלוֹ
בְּאֵימָה וּבְיִרְאָה מַכְתִּירִים שֵׁם גָּדְלוֹ   שְׂרָפִים עֹמְדִים מִמַּעַל לוֹ:
אֵלּוּ לְאֵלּוּ שׁוֹאֲלִים / אֵלּוּ לְאֵלּוּ מְמַלְּלִים
אָנָה שׁוֹכֵן מְעָלִים / לְהַעֲרִיצוֹ, לְהַקְדִּישׁוֹ בִּפְאֵר מְסַלְסְלִים.

גִּבּוֹרֵי כֹחַ בְּרַעַד וּבְפַחַד / גֵּאֶה וְגָבֹהַּ לְיַחֵד לְאֶחָד
דְּמָמָה דַקָּה דָּאִים בְּלִי כַחַד   שֵׁשׁ כְּנָפַיִם שֵׁשׁ כְּנָפַיִם לְאֶחָד:
אֵלּוּ לְאֵלּוּ שׁוֹאֲלִים / אֵלּוּ לְאֵלּוּ מְמַלְּלִים
אָנָה שׁוֹכֵן מְעָלִים / לְהַעֲרִיצוֹ, לְהַקְדִּישׁוֹ בִּפְאֵר מְסַלְסְלִים.

הַיּוֹשֵׁב יְחִידִי עַל אוֹפַנָּיו / הַדֹּבֵר דָּבָר דִּבּוּר עַל אָפְנָיו
וְרָצוֹא וָשׁוֹב כַּבָּזָק לְפָנָיו   בִּשְׁתַּיִם יְכַסֶּה פָנָיו:
אֵלּוּ לְאֵלּוּ שׁוֹאֲלִים / אֵלּוּ לְאֵלּוּ מְמַלְּלִים
אָנָה שׁוֹכֵן מְעָלִים / לְהַעֲרִיצוֹ, לְהַקְדִּישׁוֹ בִּפְאֵר מְסַלְסְלִים.

זְהַר הָרָקִיעַ כְּעֵין חַשְׁמַלָּיו / זוֹעֵף בַּיָּם וַיֶּהֱמוּ גַלָּיו
חִיל שָׂרָף אֵימָה עָלָיו וּבִשְׁתַּיִם יְכַסֶּה רַגְלָיו:

אֵלּוּ לְאֵלּוּ שׁוֹאֲלִים / אֵלּוּ לְאֵלּוּ מְהַלְּלִים
אָנָה שׁוֹכֵן מְעֻלִּים / לְהַעֲרִיצוֹ, לְהַקְדִּישׁוֹ בִּפְאֵר מְסַלְסְלִים.

טַפְסְרֵי קָלָל כְּעֵין נְחֹשֶׁת יְצַפְצֵף / טְהוֹר עֵינַיִם עֲלֵיהֶם יְחוֹפֵף
יְדוּד, יְכַסֶּה פָּנָיו בְּלִי מִתְרוֹפֵף וּבִשְׁתַּיִם יְעוֹפֵף:

אֵלּוּ לְאֵלּוּ שׁוֹאֲלִים / אֵלּוּ לְאֵלּוּ מְהַלְּלִים
אָנָה שׁוֹכֵן מְעֻלִּים / לְהַעֲרִיצוֹ, לְהַקְדִּישׁוֹ בִּפְאֵר מְסַלְסְלִים.

כַּבִּיר כֹּחַ הוּא אֵלִי זֶה / כִּי לֹא בָזָה עֱנוּת עַם עָנִי וְנִבְזֶה
לְהַקְדִּישׁוֹ יַחַד, נִרְשָׁמִים זֶה מִזֶּה וְקָרָא זֶה אֶל־זֶה:

אֵלּוּ לְאֵלּוּ שׁוֹאֲלִים / אֵלּוּ לְאֵלּוּ מְהַלְּלִים
אָנָה שׁוֹכֵן מְעֻלִּים / לְהַעֲרִיצוֹ, לְהַקְדִּישׁוֹ בִּפְאֵר מְסַלְסְלִים.

מֶלֶךְ מְהֻלָּל בְּפִיהֶם גָּמַר / מוֹרָאוֹ עֲלֵיהֶם תָּמִיד לְהִשָּׁמֵר
נִשָּׂא וְנֶעְלָם הִלּוּלוֹ לוֹמַר וְקָרָא זֶה אֶל־זֶה וְאָמַר:

אֵלּוּ לְאֵלּוּ שׁוֹאֲלִים / אֵלּוּ לְאֵלּוּ מְהַלְּלִים
אָנָה שׁוֹכֵן מְעֻלִּים / לְהַעֲרִיצוֹ, לְהַקְדִּישׁוֹ בִּפְאֵר מְסַלְסְלִים.

שָׂרָף מְכֻנֶּה אֶחָד קָדוֹשׁ / סִלּוּד אוֹמֵר לְבָרוּךְ וְקָדוֹשׁ
עוֹנִים בִּקְדֻשָּׁה לָאֵל הַקָּדוֹשׁ קָדוֹשׁ קָדוֹשׁ קָדוֹשׁ:

אֵלּוּ לְאֵלּוּ שׁוֹאֲלִים / אֵלּוּ לְאֵלּוּ מְהַלְּלִים
אָנָה שׁוֹכֵן מְעֻלִּים / לְהַעֲרִיצוֹ, לְהַקְדִּישׁוֹ בִּפְאֵר מְסַלְסְלִים.

פְּאֵר וְשֶׁבַח לַאֲדוֹן הַצְּבָאוֹת / פּוֹצְחִים בְּרִנָּה מַלְאֲכֵי צְבָאוֹת
צְבָא מָרוֹם גְּדֻלָּתָם מַצְבִּיאוֹת יהוה צְבָאוֹת:

אֵלּוּ לְאֵלּוּ שׁוֹאֲלִים / אֵלּוּ לְאֵלּוּ מְהַלְּלִים
אָנָה שׁוֹכֵן מְעֻלִּים / לְהַעֲרִיצוֹ, לְהַקְדִּישׁוֹ בִּפְאֵר מְסַלְסְלִים.

קָדוֹשׁ שׁוֹכֵן עֲלֵיהֶם בָּאָרֶץ / קַלִּים לָרוּץ עַד קְצֵה הָאָרֶץ
רָם וְנִשָּׂא, יוֹשֵׁב עַל חוּג הָאָרֶץ מְלֹא כָל־הָאָרֶץ:

אֵלּוּ לְאֵלּוּ שׁוֹאֲלִים / אֵלּוּ לְאֵלּוּ מְמַלְּלִים
אָנָה שׁוֹכֵן מְעֻלִּים / לְהַעֲרִיצוֹ, לְהַקְדִּישׁוֹ בִּפְאֵר מְסַלְסְלִים.

*שָׁמַיִם וּשְׁמֵי שָׁמַיִם כִּסָּה הוֹדוֹ / שְׁחָקִים מִמַּעַל פֹּעַל יָדוֹ
תּוֹלֶה תֵּבֵל בִּזְרוֹעַ יָדוֹ   מְלֹא כָל־הָאָרֶץ כְּבוֹדוֹ:

אֵלּוּ לְאֵלּוּ שׁוֹאֲלִים / אֵלּוּ לְאֵלּוּ מְמַלְּלִים
אָנָה שׁוֹכֵן מְעֻלִּים / לְהַעֲרִיצוֹ, לְהַקְדִּישׁוֹ בִּפְאֵר מְסַלְסְלִים.

**Some congregations substitute the final stanza with the following. Others add this alternate stanza at the end of the piyut.*

שִׁנְאַן רִבּוֹתַיִם אַלְפֵי וְעוּדוֹ / שָׁבִים כַּבָּזָק לְפָאֵר הוֹדוֹ
תַּקִּיף אֵין עוֹד מִלְּבַדּוֹ   מְלֹא כָל־הָאָרֶץ כְּבוֹדוֹ:

אֵלּוּ לְאֵלּוּ שׁוֹאֲלִים / אֵלּוּ לְאֵלּוּ מְמַלְּלִים
אָנָה שׁוֹכֵן מְעֻלִּים / לְהַעֲרִיצוֹ, לְהַקְדִּישׁוֹ בִּפְאֵר מְסַלְסְלִים.

Continue with "וּבְכֵן לְךָ תַעֲלֶה קְדֻשָּׁה" on page 843.

פיוטים לתפילת מנחה

סילוק למנחה

The סילוק *(see rubric on page 843), for* מנחה *is attributed to Yannai, one of the earliest poets in Israel.*

כִּי רְכוּבוֹ בַּעֲרָבוֹת / וְעֻזּוֹ בַּשְּׁחָקִים
וּזְרוֹעוֹ בִּמְעוֹנָה / וְקָדוֹשׁוֹ בִּזְבוּל / וְאֵימָתוֹ בָּעֲרָפֶל
וּמוֹרָאוֹ בִּשְׁמֵי שָׁמַיִם / וְקַשְׁתּוֹ בַּשָּׁמַיִם / וְקוֹלוֹ עַל הַמָּיִם
וּמוֹשָׁבוֹ בְּרוּם / וּמַבָּטוֹ בְּתַחַת
מִמַּעְלָה קָדוֹשׁ / וּמִמַּטָּה בָּרוּךְ
מִמַּיִם אַדִּיר / וּמִנְּהָרוֹת קוֹל / וּמֵאֶרֶץ זֶמֶר
וּמֵעֵצִים רֶנֶן / וּמֵהָרִים רֶקֶד / וּמִגְּבָעוֹת שִׁיר
וּמִכָּל בְּרִיָּה תֹּקֶף / וּמִכָּל רֹאשׁ כֶּפֶף
וּמִכָּל עַיִן רֶמֶז / וּמִכָּל אֹזֶן שֵׁמַע
וּמִכָּל פֶּה הוֹדָיָה / וּמִכָּל לָשׁוֹן שֶׁבַח / וּמִכָּל גָּרוֹן רֹן
וּמִכָּל לֵב רַחַשׁ / וּמִכָּל קֶרֶב הִגָּיוֹן
וּמִכָּל בֶּרֶךְ כְּרִיעָה / וּמִכָּל קוֹמָה הִשְׁתַּחֲוָיָה
וּמִזְּקֵנִים כָּבוֹד / וּמֵאֲנָשִׁים וְנָשִׁים שִׁיר
וּמִבַּחוּרִים וּבְתוּלוֹת הַלֵּל / וּמֵעוֹלְלִים וְיוֹנְקִים עֹז
וּמִדּוֹר לְדוֹר גְּבוּרָה / וּמֵעוֹלָם וְעַד עוֹלָם בְּרָכָה
כִּי כֻלָּם בָּרָאתָ לְמַעֲנָךְ
יִקְרְאוּ זֶה לָזֶה / וְיַעֲנוּ זֶה לָזֶה / וְיֹאמְרוּ זֶה לָזֶה
גּוֹשׁוּ, עוּשׁוּ, חוּשׁוּ / וְנַעֲרִיץ לְמֶלֶךְ הַכָּבוֹד
הָאֵל הַנַּעֲרָץ וְהַנִּקְדָּשׁ בַּקֹּדֶשׁ.

*Continue with "*כַּכָּתוּב עַל יַד נְבִיאֶךָ*" on page 1049.*

הלכות תפילה

HALAKHA GUIDE

GUIDE TO YOM KIPPUR

EREV YOM KIPPUR

1 It is a mitzva to eat and drink on Erev Yom Kippur [שו״ע או״ח, תרד:א]. The Gemara states that one who eats and drinks on Erev Yom Kippur is considered as one who fasted two days [ברכות, ח:].

2 Every person should utilize the day to ask forgiveness from others, because Yom Kippur atones for sins against one's fellows only if the wronged individual has offered his or her forgiveness [שו״ע או״ח, תרו:א].

3 It is customary to say *Kaparot* (page 3) [רמ״א או״ח, תרה:א], and to immerse in the mikveh [שו״ע ורמ״א או״ח, תרו:ג].

4 In the morning, an abbreviated *Seliḥot* is recited, followed by Shaḥarit for weekdays. During *Pesukei DeZimra*, the congregation omits Psalm 100 because it recalls the thanksgiving offering (קרבן תודה) in Temple times, which was not brought on the day before Yom Kippur [רמ״א או״ח, תרד:ב ומשנ״ב שם:ד]. *Avinu Malkenu*, *Taḥanun* and לַמְנַצֵּחַ (Psalm 20) are also omitted. However, if Erev Yom Kippur falls on Friday, the congregation does not omit *Avinu Malkenu* [שו״ע ורמ״א או״ח, תרד:ב].

5 Minḥa: Most communities schedule an early recitation of Minḥa, to allow time for the congregants to return home and eat a final meal (*Se'uda Mafseket*) prior to the fast. Minḥa for weekdays is said with additions for the *Aseret Yemei Teshuva*. Before saying the paragraph אֱלֹהַי נְצֹר at the conclusion of the Amida, each individual says *Viduy* (page 25) [שו״ע או״ח, תרז:א]. *Viduy* is not said by the *Shaliaḥ Tzibbur* during the Repetition of the Amida. Both *Avinu Malkenu* and *Taḥanun* are omitted.

6 The *Se'uda Mafseket* (final meal) must be finished before sunset [שו״ע או״ח, תרח: א]. It is customary for parents to say a special blessing for their children (page 47) after the meal [חיי אדם, קמד: יט].

7 Candle lighting: Two blessings are said: (1) לְהַדְלִיק נֵר שֶׁל יוֹם הַכִּפּוּרִים and (2) שֶׁהֶחֱיָנוּ. When Yom Kippur eve falls on Friday night, the conclusion of the first blessing is modified as follows: לְהַדְלִיק נֵר שֶׁל שַׁבָּת וְשֶׁל יוֹם הַכִּפּוּרִים (page 45) [שו״ע ורמ״א או״ח, תרי: א–ב].

8 Candles should be lit before sunset in order to "add from the weekday to the holiday," i.e., beginning the holiday before the objective starting time of the holiday [שו״ע או״ח, רסא: ב ומשנ״ב שם: יט].

9 One should also light a candle that will burn at least twenty-five hours, such as a *yahrzeit* candle, from which to light the Havdala candle after the conclusion of Yom Kippur.

YOM KIPPUR EVENING

▸ THE FIVE "AFFLICTIONS" OF YOM KIPPUR

10 The Mishnah teaches: "On Yom Kippur it is forbidden to (1) eat or drink, (2) wash, (3) anoint with oil, (4) wear a leather shoe, and (5) engage in marital relations" [יומא, ח: א].

11 Even a pregnant or nursing woman is generally required to fast on Yom Kippur [שו״ע או״ח, תריז: א]. However, a person for whom fasting would be life threatening may eat an amount equivalent to the size of a date (about 1.5 ounces or 44 grams) and drink less than a mouthful once every nine minutes [שו״ע או״ח, תריח: ז].

12 Children from the age of nine should be trained to fast for part of Yom Kippur, and from the age of eleven to fast the whole day [שו״ע או״ח, תרטז: ב].

13 Only washing for pleasure is forbidden. Consequently, washing to clean oneself is permitted [שו״ע או״ח, תריג: א].

▸ KOL NIDREI

14 Yom Kippur Eve: Many individuals have a custom to say *Tefilla Zaka* ("Pure Prayer") (page 53) prior to *Kol Nidrei* [משנ״ב או״ח, תרז: א]. It is customary for married men to wear a tallit; many also wear a *kittel* [רמ״א או״ח, תרי: ד]. The Ark is opened, and two leaders of the congregation each bear a Torah scroll to the *bima*, where they stand on either side of the *Shaliaḥ Tzibbur* while he chants

Kol Nidrei (page 69). At the conclusion, before the scrolls are returned to the Ark, the entire congregation says the blessing שֶׁהֶחֱיָנוּ, expressing thanks for the opportunity to fulfill the special mitzvot of Yom Kippur [שו״ע או״ח, תריט: א].

▸ LAWS OF THE EVENING SHEMA

15 Saying the three paragraphs of the Shema each morning and each night fulfills an affirmative mitzva from the Torah. As saying the Shema is a time-bound mitzva, women are exempt [שו״ע או״ח, ע: א]. Nevertheless, women are required to say the first verse to express their acceptance of עול מלכות שמים (the yoke of the kingdom of heaven) [ב״ח שם]. Women are permitted to say the Shema and the blessings preceding and following [משנ״ב שם: ב].

16 There is a set time period every night during which the Shema may be said: At the earliest, the Shema may be said from nightfall [שו״ע או״ח, רלה: א]. The Shema should be said before midnight (measured from nightfall to daybreak), but one is permitted to say the Shema until daybreak [שם: ג].

17 The Shema must be said with concentration and awe [שו״ע או״ח, סא: א]. Each word and syllable should be pronounced correctly and carefully, without slurring consonants [שו״ע או״ח, סא: טו–כא].

18 Some authorities ruled that one should say the Shema with *Ta'amei HaMikra*. Today, however, most people do not do so [שו״ע ורמ״א, שם: כד].

19 The custom is to cover the eyes with the right hand while saying the first verse, so as not to look at anything that might disturb one's concentration [שו״ע או״ח, סא: ה].

20 The custom is to draw out one's pronunciation of the letters ח and ד in the word אחד to emphasize God's sovereignty over creation [שו״ע או״ח, סא: ו].

21 If one enters the synagogue and hears the congregation about to begin saying the Shema, one is required to say the first verse of the Shema together with the congregation [שו״ע או״ח, סה: ב].

22 If one enters the synagogue and hears the congregation about to begin saying the Amida for Ma'ariv, one should say the Amida together with the congregation, then afterward say the Shema with the blessings before and after [שו״ע או״ח, רלו: ג].

▸ MA'ARIV FOR YOM KIPPUR

23 Ma'ariv for Yom Kippur generally follows the format of Ma'ariv for Shabbat and Yom Tov, with the following variations:

a When saying Shema, the congregation pronounces בָּרוּךְ שֵׁם כְּבוֹד מַלְכוּתוֹ לְעוֹלָם וָעֶד out loud [שו״ע או״ח, תריט:ב].

b Before the Yom Kippur Amida, most congregations say the special verse for the day: ...כִּי־בַיּוֹם הַזֶּה (Lev. 16:30) (page 93).

c The Amida for Yom Kippur includes special additions as discussed in further detail in law 25 below.

d After the Amida, the *Shaliaḥ Tzibbur* leads the congregation in saying *Seliḥot* (page 125) and *Viduy* (page 165).

e After *Viduy,* the Ark is opened and the congregation says *Avinu Malkenu* (unless Yom Kippur falls on Shabbat) (page 189) and Psalm 24 (page 195).

f Following *Aleinu* and Mourner's Kaddish, the congregation says Psalm 27, לְדָוִד, ה׳ אוֹרִי וְיִשְׁעִי (continuing the practice begun on Rosh Ḥodesh Elul) (page 205).

g It is customary to conclude with the singing of *Adon Olam* and/or *Yigdal* (page 207). Some congregations also say Psalms 1–4, שיר היחוד and *Anim Zemirot* (pages 213–257).

24 Changes to the Kaddish: It is customary to replace the phrase לְעֵלָּא מִן כָּל ("beyond any") with לְעֵלָּא לְעֵלָּא מִכָּל ("above and beyond any") [משנ״ב, נו:ב] and to change the phrase עֹשֶׂה שָׁלוֹם ("He who makes peace") to עוֹשֶׂה הַשָּׁלוֹם ("He who makes the peace") [ערוה״ש או״ח, תקפב:ח]. One who forgets either of these changes is not required to repeat the Kaddish.

25 Special additions to the Amida: On Yom Kippur (as on Rosh HaShana), additional phrases are added to the Amida: (a) ...זָכְרֵנוּ לְחַיִּים is added in the first blessing; (b) ...מִי כָמְוֹךָ אַב הָרַחֲמִים in the second; (c) four paragraphs are added to the third blessing, and the ending is changed to הַמֶּלֶךְ הַקָּדוֹשׁ; (d) ...וּכְתֹב in the penultimate blessing; and (5) ...בְּסֵפֶר חַיִּים is added to the final blessing, and the ending is changed to עוֹשֶׂה הַשָּׁלוֹם (some do not change the ending of the blessing). One who forgets to say any of these passages is not required to repeat the Amida with the forgotten additions [שו״ע ורמ״א או״ח, תקפב:ה]. However, one who forgets to change the ending of the third blessing to הַמֶּלֶךְ הַקָּדוֹשׁ must repeat the Amida from the beginning, unless one corrects the error "תוך כדי דיבור." (See the source in the *Shulḥan Arukh* for an explanation of this rule.) [שו״ע או״ח, תקפא:ג].

▸ LAWS OF MOURNER'S KADDISH

26 The Mourner's Kaddish is generally said after specific chapters of Psalms at the beginning and end of the prayer service. It is said by one who is either (a) in mourning for a relative, or (b) commemorating the *yahrzeit* of a relative. When no such person is present, the Mourner's Kaddish is generally omitted, except after *Aleinu* at the end of the morning service [רמ״א או״ח, קלב: ב], when it is said by one whose parents have died or whose parents do not object to their child saying the Mourner's Kaddish [שם].

27 Historically, the Mourner's Kaddish was recited by one individual; a set of rules developed for allocating among different mourners the various opportunities for saying the Mourner's Kaddish [ביאור הלכה שם, קונטרוס מאמר קדישין, י]. Today, most congregations allow group recitation of the Mourner's Kaddish. In such case, they should say the words in unison [סידור יעב״ץ].

▸ WHEN YOM KIPPUR FALLS ON SHABBAT

28 When Yom Kippur eve falls on Friday night, Ma'ariv is preceded by the last two psalms of *Kabbalat Shabbat*: מִזְמוֹר שִׁיר לְיוֹם הַשַּׁבָּת and ה׳ מָלָךְ, גֵּאוּת לָבֵשׁ (page 77). The Amida is said with additions for Shabbat. After the Amida, the congregation says וַיְכֻלּוּ (page 121), and the *Shaliaḥ Tzibbur* says the abbreviated Repetition of the Amida as is customary on Shabbat eve [שו״ע או״ח, תריט: ג]. The *Shaliaḥ Tzibbur* then leads the congregation in saying *Seliḥot* and *Viduy*.

YOM KIPPUR DAY

▸ ON WAKING

29 The custom is to say מוֹדֶה אֲנִי (page 449) immediately on waking, even before washing hands [משנ״ב, א: ח].

▸ LAWS OF WASHING HANDS; אלהי נשמה ;ברכת אשר יצר

30 Upon waking, one is obligated to wash hands [שבת, קח:]. Some hold that one should not walk even four *amot* (around six feet) prior to washing hands [משנ״ב, א: ב (בשם הזוהר)].

31 According to some authorities, there is a separate obligation to wash hands prior to prayer [ערוה״ש או״ח, ד: ה]. One who washes and says the blessing of עַל נְטִילַת יָדָיִם after waking does not repeat the blessing when washing prior to prayer [רמ״א או״ח, ו: ב].

32 Hands should preferably be washed using a cup, but a cup is not required [שו״ע

[ורמ״א או״ח, ד:ו]. The custom is to pour water from the cup onto the right hand, then the left, and repeat a total of three times [משנ״ב שם: י]. Where water is unavailable, one may clean one's hands using any appropriate material; in that case, the blessing is changed to עַל נְקִיּוּת יָדַיִם [שו״ע או״ח, ד:כב].

33 Despite the prohibition against washing on Yom Kippur, one is permitted to wash hands upon waking, provided that one only washes the fingers up to the knuckles [שו״ע או״ח, תריג:ב].

34 The blessing of עַל נְטִילַת יָדַיִם may be said before drying one's hands or afterward [משנ״ב, ד:ב].

35 A number of reasons have been offered for washing hands upon waking. The Gemara states that, during the night, hands are enveloped by an "evil vapor, רוח רעה," which is removed by washing one's hands [שבת, קח:]. In addition, there is a concern that, while sleeping, one's hands may have touched an unclean part of the body [רא״ש ברכות, פ״ט: כג]. Finally, it is noted that a person who wakes is like a newborn; therefore one needs to sanctify oneself by washing [שו״ת רשב״א ח״א, קצא].

36 The blessing of אֲשֶׁר יָצַר should be said each time after relieving oneself. It is recommended that one should go to the bathroom immediately after washing hands, then say the blessings of עַל נְטִילַת יָדַיִם followed by אֲשֶׁר יָצַר. However, even if one does not relieve oneself, one is permitted to say the blessing of אֲשֶׁר יָצַר after washing hands [רמ״א או״ח, ד: א]. One should not postpone going to the bathroom [שו״ע או״ח, ג: יז].

37 According to the Gemara, the blessing of אֱלֹהַי נְשָׁמָה (page 451) should be said upon waking [ברכות, ס:]. The contemporary custom is to say אֱלֹהַי נְשָׁמָה immediately after אֲשֶׁר יָצַר [משנ״ב, שם: יב]. However, some rule that one who stays up all night should not say אֱלֹהַי נְשָׁמָה and the blessing הַמַּעֲבִיר שֵׁנָה מֵעֵינַי, and should instead hear them from others [משנ״ב, מו: כד].

38 The custom is to say the *Birkot HaTorah* (page 453) after אֲשֶׁר יָצַר, because one should not read or recite Torah verses before making the requisite blessings on Torah study [שו״ע ורמ״א, או״ח: מו, ט].

▸ LAWS OF TZITZIT

39 Putting on a four-cornered garment with tzitzit attached fulfills an affirmative mitzva from the Torah. The obligation applies only during daytime [מנחות, מג.]. Since wearing tzitzit is a time-bound mitzva, women are exempt [שו״ע או״ח, יז: ב].

40 The dominant Ashkenazi custom is to begin wearing a *tallit gadol* when one marries [משנ״ב, יז: י], but Jews of German and Sephardi descent begin wearing

the *tallit gadol* at an earlier age. Nevertheless, the custom is to wear a *tallit gadol* – even if unmarried – when acting as *Shaliaḥ Tzibbur*, reading from or being called up to the Torah, opening the Ark or performing *hagbaha* or *gelila*.

41 One should put on the *tallit katan* immediately upon dressing. One should first examine the strings of the tzitzit to ensure that they are not torn [שו"ע או"ח, ח:ט]. Then, while standing [שו"ע או"ח, ח:א], one should say the blessing of עַל מִצְוַת צִיצִית (page 451) and immediately put on the garment [רמ"א או"ח, ח:ו]. One does not say the blessing if (a) one is about to put on a *tallit gadol*, and (b) one will have in mind the *tallit katan* when saying the blessing on the *tallit gadol*. On the other hand, if there is a substantial interruption between the time one puts on the *tallit katan* and one puts on the *tallit gadol*, one should say the separate blessing on the *tallit katan* [שו"ע או"ח, ח:יג].

42 The blessing on *tzitzit* may be said at daybreak, but not before [רמ"א או"ח, יח:ג].

43 Similarly with the *tallit gadol*, one should first examine the strings, then while standing, say the blessing לְהִתְעַטֵּף בַּצִּיצִית (page 457) and put on the *tallit gadol*. The word להתעטף means to wrap oneself; one should initially wrap the *tallit gadol* around to cover one's head and face for a few moments, after which it is sufficient that it cover the torso [מג"א, ח:ב].

44 If one removes the *tallit gadol* for any reason, one should repeat the blessing when putting the tallit back on [שו"ע או"ח, ח:יד]. The blessing is not repeated if the *tallit gadol* is put back on soon after taking it off, and either (a) one was wearing a *tallit katan* all along, or (b) one's original intention was to put the tallit back on shortly [משנ"ב, שם:לו].

45 If one's head is otherwise covered, there is no requirement to cover one's head with the *tallit gadol* [ט"ז או"ח, ח:ג]. Some authorities nevertheless require married men to cover their heads with the *tallit gadol* throughout the prayers, because it promotes reverence in prayer [בה"ט או"ח, ח:ג (בשם הרדב"ז)]. Others have the custom to cover their heads during the Amida only, or from *Barekhu* through the end of the Amida. Unmarried persons should not wear the *tallit gadol* over their heads [קידושין, כט:].

46 On Yom Kippur many have the custom to wear a *kittel* under their tallit.

▸ LAWS OF BIRKOT HASHAḤAR AND PESUKEI DEZIMRA

47 Most congregations begin services on Yom Kippur day with the Daily Psalm (page 461).

48 According to the Gemara [ברכות, ס:], *Birkot HaShaḥar* (Morning Blessings) (page

475) were originally said individually, in conjunction with the performance of the associated activity. Thus, upon dressing one would say the blessing of מַלְבִּישׁ עֲרֻמִּים, and upon standing up one would say the blessing of זוֹקֵף כְּפוּפִים. However, the custom now is to say all of the blessings together in the synagogue [שו״ע או״ח, מו: ב].

49 The insertion of the verses of Shema after *Birkot HaShaḥar* (page 483) was not meant to satisfy the individual's obligation to say the Shema every morning [רמ״א שם: ט]. However, as discussed in further detail in law 56 below, the three paragraphs of Shema must be said within the first half of the morning (measured as one quarter of the time from daybreak to nightfall). Since some congregations hold Shaḥarit services late, and as such the communal recitation of the Shema in Shaḥarit may take place too late to fulfill the halakhic obligation, under such circumstances, it is recommended to say all three paragraphs of Shema after *Birkot HaShaḥar* [משנ״ב, שם: לא].

50 One should say the biblical verses describing the קרבן תמיד (page 493), preferably with the congregation [רמ״א או״ח, מח]. Some authorities require one to stand [משנ״ב, שם: ב].

51 The fifth chapter of מסכת זבחים (page 499) and the ברייתא דרבי ישמעאל (page 503) were added after the biblical passages regarding sacrifices to institutionalize the daily study of Scripture, Mishna and Gemara [שו״ע או״ח, נ: א].

52 Saying Kaddish, *Barekhu* or *Kedusha* requires the presence of a *minyan* (ten adult males) [שו״ע או״ח, נה: א].

53 One should not utter idle speech from the beginning of the words בָּרוּךְ אַתָּה ה׳ in *Barukh SheAmar* until one completes the Amida [שו״ע או״ח, נא: ד].

54 If one comes late to the synagogue, one may skip all, or portions, of *Pesukei DeZimra* as follows:

- **a** If there is sufficient time, say *Pesukei DeZimra,* omitting the additional psalms for Shabbat and Yom Tov (pages 519–535).
- **b** If there is less time, say *Barukh SheAmar*, Psalms 145–150, then continue with נִשְׁמַת כָּל חַי.
- **c** If there is less time, say *Barukh SheAmar*, Psalms 145, 148, 150, then continue with נִשְׁמַת כָּל חַי.
- **d** If there is less time, say *Barukh SheAmar*, Psalm 145, then continue with נִשְׁמַת כָּל חַי.
- **e** If there is less time, omit *Pesukei DeZimra* altogether. Complete the rest of the

service with the congregation, then say *Pesukei DeZimra* privately, omitting *Barukh SheAmar* and from נִשְׁמַת כָּל חַי to the end [רמ"א ושו"ע או"ח, נב].

▸ SHAḤARIT FOR YOM KIPPUR

55 The *Shaliaḥ Tzibbur* for Shaḥarit begins from the words הַמֶּלֶךְ יוֹשֵׁב ("The King – who sits on a throne...") (page 555). After *Yishtabaḥ,* the Ark is opened and the congregation says Psalm 130 responsively. After *Barekhu,* a special blessing, הַפּוֹתֵחַ לָנוּ שַׁעֲרֵי רַחֲמִים ("Who opens for us the gates of compassion"), is said, followed by a line of poetry, אוֹר עוֹלָם ("Endless light"). The congregation says הַמֵּאִיר לָאָרֶץ or, if it is also Shabbat, הַכֹּל יוֹדוּךָ. Some congregations add *piyutim* in the first blessing preceding the Shema.

▸ LAWS OF THE MORNING SHEMA

56 There is a set time period every morning during which the Shema may be said. The optimal time is immediately before sunrise, when there is assumed to be sufficient light to recognize an acquaintance from a distance of four *amot* (around 6 feet). If necessary, the Shema may be said from daybreak [שו"ע או"ח, נח: ג]. After sunrise, the earlier the Shema is said, the better [שם:ב]. At the latest the Shema must be said during the first quarter of the day (in halakhic terminology, three halakhic "hours," where each hour represents one twelfth of the day); there is a dispute between halakhic authorities whether the day is measured from daybreak to nightfall (Magen Avraham) or from sunrise to sunset (Vilna Gaon) [שם:א]. After that time, one is permitted to say Shema with the blessings during the fourth halakhic "hour," that is, until the end of the first third of the day, After that, the Shema may be said without the blessings, but this does not fulfill the mitzva [שם:ו].

57 If one says the Shema without its preceding and following blessings, one has still fulfilled the mitzva. However, one should say the blessings afterward, preferably repeating the Shema as well [שו"ע או"ח, ס: ב].

58 For additional laws relating to the Shema, see laws 17–21 above.

▸ AMIDA FOR YOM KIPPUR

59 The Amida for Yom Kippur includes special additions as discussed in law 25 above. If also Shabbat, one says the additions for Shabbat.

60 Before saying the paragraph אֱלֹהַי נְצֹר at the conclusion of the Amida, each individual says *Viduy*.

▸ LAWS OF THE SHAHARIT AMIDA

61 There is a set time period every morning during which the Amida may be said. In general, the Amida should be said at or after sunrise. At the latest, the Amida should be said during the first third of the day (four halakhic "hours"; regarding the measure of a "day," see law 56). If the Amida was said between daybreak and sunrise, the mitzva has been fulfilled. If necessary, it is permissible to say the Amida after the first third of the day, but before midday [שו״ע או״ח, פט: א].

62 If one did not say the Amida for Shaharit prior to midday, one should say the Amida for Minha twice [משנ״ב שם: ו].

63 The Amida is said facing the site of the Temple in Jerusalem. Thus, outside Israel, one faces the land of Israel; inside Israel, one faces Jerusalem; and inside Jerusalem, one faces the Temple Mount [שו״ע או״ח, צד: א]. If one is praying in a synagogue that does not face Jerusalem, one should pray facing the Ark [משנ״ב שם: י].

64 The Amida is said standing with feet together in imitation of the angels who, according to tradition, present the appearance of having only one leg [ברכות, י: רש״י ד״ה ״ורגליהם״]. One should bow one's head and imagine one is standing in the Temple, like a servant before his master [שו״ע או״ח, צה: א-ב].

65 When saying the Shaharit Amida, one may not allow any interruption or disruption between the conclusion of the blessing גָּאַל יִשְׂרָאֵל and the introductory words to the Amida [ושם, קיא: א שו״ע או״ח, סו: ח]. This includes not responding to Kaddish, *Barekhu, Kedusha* or *Modim* [רמ״א, שם]. One may also answer "Amen" if one hears someone else concluding the blessing גָּאַל יִשְׂרָאֵל [רמ״א או״ח, סו: ז].

▸ REPETITION OF THE SHAHARIT AMIDA FOR YOM KIPPUR

66 The *Shaliah Tzibbur* adds *piyutim* before *Kedusha*.

67 In Shaharit (and all the services of the day), the Kedusha of Musaf (נַעֲרִיצְךָ) is said.

68 In the fourth blessing, the congregation says זְכֹר רַחֲמֶיךָ and *Viduy* (page 681).

69 In most congregations in Israel, the Kohanim say *Birkat Kohanim* in Shaharit and Ne'ila as well as in Musaf [שו״ע או״ח, קכט: א]. See laws 96–101 below. Outside Israel, or in Israel when no Kohen is present, the *Shaliah Tzibbur* says אֱלֹהֵינוּ וֵאלֹהֵי אֲבוֹתֵינוּ (page 709).

▸ LAWS OF THE REPETITION OF THE AMIDA

70 During the Repetition of the Amida, the congregation is required to listen attentively to the blessings and respond "Amen" [שו״ע או״ח, קכד: ד].

71 In order to begin the Repetition of the Amida, a minimum of nine men are required to be listening attentively [שם].

72 Some require the congregation to stand during the Repetition of the Amida [רמ"א שם], but the custom is to be lenient on this matter, especially on days like Yom Kippur when the Repetition is particularly lengthy.

73 At the conclusion of the Repetition of the Shaḥarit Amida, it is recommended that the *Shaliaḥ Tzibbur* say quietly the verse יִהְיוּ לְרָצוֹן אִמְרֵי־פִי [משנ"ב, קכג:כא]. Some also say this verse at the conclusion of the silent Amida.

74 After the *Shaliaḥ Tzibbur* repeats the Amida, the congregation says *Avinu Malkenu,* but not on Shabbat [רמ"א או"ח, תקפד:א]. This is followed by Full Kaddish.

75 Prior to taking the Torah from the Ark, some congregations say the Daily Psalm (page 461) and Psalm 27, followed by the Mourner's Kaddish. When the Torah is taken from the Ark, most congregations recite the "Thirteen Attributes of Mercy" and a special supplication (page 719), except on Shabbat.

76 Torah Reading: Lev. 15:1–34. Six men are called up, seven on Shabbat. Maftir: Num. 29:7–11. Haftara: Is. 57:14–58:14 [שו"ע או"ח, תרכא:א].

▸ LAWS OF TORAH READING

77 If a Kohen is present, he is called up first. If a Levi is also present, he is called up second; for subsequent *aliyot,* one calls up a Yisrael [שו"ע או"ח, קלה:ג]. If a Kohen is present, but a Levi is not, the same Kohen is called up for the first two *aliyot* [שם:ח]. If a Levi is present and a Kohen is not, the Levi need not be called up, but if the Levi is called up, he should be first [שו"ע ורמ"א או"ח, קלה:ו].

78 The custom is to avoid calling up a Kohen after a Yisrael, except for Maftir and, in some communities, for אחרון, provided it is a *hosafa* [רמ"א, שם:י].

79 It is considered bad luck to call up two brothers, or a father and son, one after the other [שו"ע או"ח, קמא:ו]. While the custom is to avoid this practice, if one is called up after one's brother or father, one should accept the *aliya.*

80 One who is called up to the Torah should take the shortest route to the *bima* [שו"ע, שם:ז]. He should open the scroll to locate where the *aliya* begins. Still holding the handle, he should say the blessing, taking care to look away from the Torah (or close the scroll or his eyes), so as not to appear to be reading the blessing from the scroll itself [שו"ע ורמ"א או"ח, קלט:ד].

81 If, after the blessing is said, the *ba'al koreh* discovers that the blessing was said over the wrong passage of the Torah, the scroll is rolled to the correct location

and the *oleh* repeats the blessing. The blessing does not need to be repeated if the correct passage was visible when the blessing was said [שו"ע או"ח, קמ: ג ומשנ"ב שם: ט].

82 The Torah is read standing [שו"ע או"ח, קמא: א]. The *oleh* is also required to stand. The rest of the congregation is not required to stand, but it is proper to do so [ערוה"ש, שם: ב].

83 The *oleh* should read the words quietly along with the *ba'al koreh* [שו"ע או"ח, קמא: ב].

84 If the *ba'al koreh* makes an error that affects the meaning of the words, he needs to re-read the Torah portion from the location of the error [שו"ע ורמ"א או"ח, קמב: א].

85 If an error is found in the Torah scroll, the reading is stopped, a new scroll is brought out, and the reading is continued from the location of the error [שו"ע או"ח, קמג: ד]. It is not required to call up all of the *aliyot* a second time to read from the new scroll, but if the remainder of the reading can be divided into the appropriate number of *aliyot* for that day, it is preferable to do so [משנ"ב, שם: טו].

86 It is customary to say a prayer (מִי שֶׁבֵּרַךְ, page 727) for the ill at the conclusion of the Torah reading or between *aliyot*.

87 After completing the reading from a Torah scroll, the open scroll is raised and displayed to the entire congregation. The congregation says וְזֹאת הַתּוֹרָה [שו"ע ורמ"א או"ח, קלד: ב].

88 The *haftara* is followed by (*Yekum Purkan* on Shabbat, then) the prayers for the government and the State of Israel and *Yizkor*. It is customary for the rabbi to deliver a sermon prior to *Yizkor*. Some have the custom to leave the synagogue for *Yizkor*, if both their parents are still alive [גשר החיים, לא: ב]. One who is praying privately may still say *Yizkor* [גשר החיים, לב: א].

89 After *Yizkor*, the congregation recites אַב הָרַחֲמִים and *Ashrei*, and the Torah scrolls are returned to the Ark. If there is an infant to circumcise, the brit mila takes place before *Ashrei* [משנ"ב, תרכא: ז] and it is said on a cup of wine or grape juice which is given to the mother and infant [רמ"א או"ח, תרכא: ג ומשנ"ב שם, יב].

90 The *Shaliaḥ Tzibbur* for Musaf says a special prefatory prayer, הִנְנִי הֶעָנִי מִמַּעַשׂ ("Here I am, empty of deeds") and Half Kaddish (page 771).

▸ MUSAF FOR YOM KIPPUR

91 Before saying the paragraph אֱלֹהַי נְצֹר at the conclusion of the Amida, each individual says *Viduy* (page 791).

92 During the Repetition of the Amida, *piyutim* are said before *Kedusha*, culminating with וּנְתַנֶּה תֹּקֶף instead of the usual נַעֲרִיצְךָ.

93 The fourth blessing in the Repetition of the Amida contains *Aleinu*. The Ark

is opened, and the *Shaliaḥ Tzibbur* (and, in most communities, the entire congregation) kneels in prostration at the words וַאֲנַחְנוּ כּוֹרְעִים. This is followed by the recitation of the Yom Kippur Temple service (in which kneeling is repeated three additional times), relating how the people would prostrate themselves upon hearing the High Priest pronounce the ineffable name of God. Because one is forbidden to touch one's head against the bare floor when kneeling, one should place a piece of cloth or paper between one's head and the floor [רמ״א או״ח, קלא: ח].

94 After the recitation of the Yom Kippur Temple service, the congregation says זְכֹר־רַחֲמֶיךָ and *Viduy* (page 949). As the *Shaliaḥ Tzibbur* continues with רְצֵה, the Kohanim ascend to the ark to say *Birkat Kohanim*.

▸ LAWS OF BIRKAT KOHANIM

95 The Kohen has an affirmative obligation from the Torah to bless the congregation, provided there are present at least ten males aged thirteen or over (including the Kohen himself) [שו״ע או״ח, קכח: א–ב].

96 The Kohen is required to wash his hands (without a blessing) before saying *Birkat Kohanim*. The hands are washed as normal, even on Yom Kippur [משנ״ב, תריג: ז]. The custom is for a Levi to pour the water [שם: ו]. If there is no water, or if the Kohen did not have enough time to wash, he may say *Birkat Kohanim*, provided that: (a) he washed his hands before Shaḥarit, and (b) since washing for Shaḥarit he has not touched anything unclean, even his own shoes [משנ״ב, שם: כ].

97 Each Kohen removes his shoes before ascending to say *Birkat Kohanim* [שם: ה]. When the *Shaliaḥ Tzibbur* begins רְצֵה, the Kohanim ascend to the Ark and stand with their backs to the congregation [שם: ח, י]. After the congregation answers "Amen" to the blessing הַטּוֹב שִׁמְךָ וּלְךָ נָאֶה לְהוֹדוֹת, if there is more than one Kohen, the *Shaliaḥ Tzibbur* calls out "Kohanim," and they turn around and say the blessing. If only one Kohen has ascended, he starts the blessing without being prompted [שם: י–יא]. The *Shaliaḥ Tzibbur* does not answer "Amen" at the end of the blessing [משנ״ב, שם: עא].

98 The *Shaliaḥ Tzibbur* reads each word of *Birkat Kohanim* and the Kohanim repeat it in unison. At the end of each verse, the congregation answers "Amen" [שו״ע ורמ״א שם: יג]. The *Shaliaḥ Tzibbur* does not answer "Amen" at the end of each verse [שו״ע שם: יט].

99 If the *Shaliaḥ Tzibbur* is himself a Kohen, some rule that he should not say the blessing, unless no other Kohanim are in the synagogue [שו״ע שם: יט]. However,

the custom today is for the *Shaliaḥ Tzibbur* to participate in the blessing [משנ״ב, שם: עה].

100 During *Birkat Kohanim,* the congregation should stand silently with eyes lowered and concentrate on the words of the Kohanim. One should not look at the faces or fingers of the Kohanim [שו״ע, שם: כג].

▸ CONCLUSION OF THE SERVICE

101 After Musaf, the *Shaliaḥ Tzibbur* says Full Kaddish. *Ein Keloheinu* and *Aleinu* are not said.

▸ MINḤA FOR YOM KIPPUR

102 Neither *Ashrei* nor וּבָא לְצִיּוֹן is said; rather, Minḥa commences with removing the Torah from the Ark [רמ״א או״ח, תרכב: א]. Torah reading: Lev. 18:1–30. The third *oleh* reads the Haftara – the book of Jonah, and Micah 7:18–20 [שו״ע או״ח, תרכב: ב]. After returning the Torah to the Ark, the *Shaliaḥ Tzibbur* says Half Kaddish. The Amida is identical to that of Shaḥarit, except that it is preceded by the verse beginning כִּי שֵׁם ה׳ אֶקְרָא (Deut. 32:3). The Repetition of the Amida by the *Shaliaḥ Tzibbur* includes the *Kedusha* starting with נַעֲרִיצְךָ, *Viduy* and the paragraph relating to *Birkat Kohanim*. *Avinu Malkenu* is said, unless Yom Kippur falls on Shabbat or if time is running short, as the *Shaliaḥ Tzibbur*'s Repetition of Ne'ila must begin before sunset [משנ״ב, שם: יג].

▸ THE NE'ILA SERVICE

103 The congregation prays a fourth service on Yom Kippur, called Ne'ila ("Closing"), shortly before sunset. The service commences as Minḥa for Shabbat and Yom Tov: *Ashrei,* וּבָא לְצִיּוֹן, Half Kaddish [רמ״א או״ח, תרכג: א]. The congregation says the Amida for Ne'ila; in the Amida the term כָּתְבֵנוּ ("inscribe us") in all its conjugations is changed to חָתְמֵנוּ ("seal us") [רמ״א או״ח, תרכג: ב]. In the last blessing, שִׂים שָׁלוֹם is said, changing נִזָּכֵר וְנִכָּתֵב in the paragraph בְּסֵפֶר חַיִּים to נִזָּכֵר וְנֵחָתֵם. In *Viduy,* instead of עַל חֵטְא, a long, heartfelt supplication is said.

104 The Ark remains open for the entire Repetition of the Amida, which includes the *Kedusha* starting with נַעֲרִיצְךָ (in some congregations), *Seliḥot,* an abridged form of *Viduy* and the paragraph relating to *Birkat Kohanim.*

105 *Avinu Malkenu* is said, even when Yom Kippur falls on Shabbat; again the term כָּתְבֵנוּ is changed to חָתְמֵנוּ.

106 At the conclusion of Ne'ila, the *Shaliaḥ Tzibbur* leads the congregation in the responsive chanting of several verses, followed by Full Kaddish, and the

sounding of the shofar [רמ״א, שם: ו]. It is customary to conclude Ne'ila with the singing of לְשָׁנָה הַבָּאָה בִּירוּשָׁלַיִם ("Next Year in Jerusalem").

▸ MOTZA'EI YOM KIPPUR

107 Ma'ariv for weekdays is said. In the fourth blessing of the Amida, the paragraph of אַתָּה חוֹנַנְתָּנוּ (page 1219) is said [שו״ע או״ח, תרכד: א]. Havdala is said over a cup of wine or grape juice and the Havdala candle is lit from the flame that was lit before Yom Kippur began. No blessing is made over spices (unless it is also Motza'ei Shabbat) [שו״ע או״ח, תרכד: ד].

108 There is a custom to begin construction of the sukka on the night following Yom Kippur [רמ״א, שם: ה, ותרכה: א].

וידוי

VIDUY – CONFESSION

Confession is the primary expression of repentance, the central theme of Yom Kippur. According to Maimonides, it is the biblical source of the command of *teshuva*: "Any man or woman who wrongs another in any way and so is unfaithful to the LORD, is guilty. They must confess the sin they have committed" (Num. 5:6–7). It follows that "With regard to all the commandments of the Torah, positive or negative, if a person transgressed any of them, willfully or in error, and repents, turning away from his sin, he is under a duty to confess before God" (Maimonides, Laws of Repentance 1:1). Although repentance is a matter of thought and emotion, it must be given verbal expression in the form of confession.

Confession is more than remorse, though it presupposes it. Remorse is a state of mind. Confession is a formal act. It is like the difference between feeling guilty at breaking the law and pleading guilty in a court of law. The former is an emotion, the latter a declaration. In the case of *teshuva* it is a declaration to God. As well as involving remorse, confession presupposes a commitment not to repeat the sin.

Originally the form of confession was simple: "Please, LORD, I have sinned, I have done wrong, I have rebelled before You." It then specified the particular act you were confessing. Over time, there developed the broader form of confession that we say ten times on Yom Kippur.

This is different from the original in three respects. First it is said in the plural: not "I have sinned" but "we have sinned." This is because on Yom Kippur we stand before God not only as individuals but as members of a people, and because we hold that *kol Yisrael arevin zeh bazeh*, "all Israel are responsible for one another" (*Shevuot* 39a). As Rabbi Shimon bar Yoḥai put it: if a person drills a hole under his seat in a boat, when the water enters, not only he but everyone is in danger. We accept collective responsibility, especially for the wrongs we could have protested but did not (*Shabbat* 55a).

The second difference is that we do not publicly specify particular sins. Instead we read an alphabetical list. This is to avoid public humiliation and to make it easier to confess. It prompts us systematically to examine our conscience and reflect on whether we have done wrong, and if so how and to whom (*Arukh HaShulḥan,* OḤ *607:4*). And it is a way of saying that we have sinned with all the letters, as if the alphabet itself were testifying against us (*Ḥayyei Adam 143:1*).

The third difference is that we now have two forms of confession, one brief ("We have sinned, we have acted treacherously…"), the other longer ("For the sin we have sinned before You"). The former is closer to the original biblical form of confession and is more general: it articulates the general defects of character that lead us to do wrong. The latter goes deeper into specifics.

Note that though Yom Kippur atones only for sins between us and God, many of the offenses specified in the Confession apply equally or even primarily to the way we relate to other people. These too require mending. One who wrongs his fellow humans does not honor God.

Confession is said standing, bowed in a gesture of humility. The custom is to beat one's breast lightly at each mentioned sin in the spirit of Jeremiah (31:18), "After I strayed, I repented; after I came to understand, I beat my breast" (see also Nahum 2:8).

Public confession, however, is not enough. As we recite the long checklist of sins we must be asking ourselves: Did I commit a sin of this kind? Did I do something similar? If so, we must acknowledge that sin inwardly to God and resolve to put it right. Public confession is a mere prelude to the private admission which is the real act of *teshuva,* in which we examine our consciences, abandoning our usual defenses in the knowledge that God forgives those who truly admit their wrongs, and that *teshuva* is the single greatest act of self-transformation any of us can undertake.

Therefore as we say the Confession we should be thinking inwardly of specific instances in which we did wrong.

Our God and God of our fathers, let our prayer come before You, and do not hide Yourself from our plea,	אֱלֹהֵינוּ וֵאלֹהֵי אֲבוֹתֵינוּ תָּבוֹא לְפָנֶיךָ תְּפִלָּתֵנוּ וְאַל תִּתְעַלַּם מִתְּחִנָּתֵנוּ.

Though we are nothing and You, God, are everything, we come before You with a broken heart, knowing that You are close to all who call on You in truth. We stand before You bereft of merits, yet knowing that You chose our ancestors and made an unbreakable covenant with them. In their merits if not in ours, please listen to our prayers.

שֶׁאֵין אֲנַחְנוּ עַזֵּי פָנִים וּקְשֵׁי עֹרֶף לוֹמַר לְפָנֶיךָ יהוה אֱלֹהֵינוּ וֵאלֹהֵי אֲבוֹתֵינוּ צַדִּיקִים אֲנַחְנוּ וְלֹא חָטָאנוּ.	for we are not so arrogant or obstinate as to say before You, Lord, our God and God of our fathers, we are righteous and have not sinned,

We often rationalize and justify our failings. We say "We meant no harm. We were provoked. It wasn't our fault. We couldn't help it. Others were doing it also." But though we may deceive others and at times even ourselves, we cannot deceive You who know us better than we know ourselves.

אֲבָל אֲנַחְנוּ וַאֲבוֹתֵינוּ חָטָאנוּ.	for in truth, we and our fathers have sinned.

Aval, which normally means "but," here means "truly," and is the quintessential admission of guilt. This was the first word of the first recorded confession in the Torah (Gen. 42:21) when Joseph's brothers admitted that they did wrong when they sold him as a slave. According to Mar Zutra (*Yoma* 87b), the phrase "Truly we have sinned" is the core of confession; all else is mere commentary.

The words "our fathers" were added at a later stage, following the Talmudic interpretation of the phrase "visiting the sins of the parents on the children," understanding it to mean only when children repeat the sins of the parents. Therefore we state explicitly that we do not condone the sins of earlier generations, nor do we seek to justify ourselves by saying that we are merely doing what our parents did.

אָשַׁמְנוּ We have sinned,

This is the primary admission of guilt from which all else follows. The word derives from the root *sh-m-m*, "desolation," what we create when we do wrong (Rabbi Samson Raphael Hirsch, Lev. 5:26).

בָּגַדְנוּ we have acted treacherously,

We acted badly to a member of the family, or a friend, a colleague, a member of the group of which we are a part. Betrayal is often a form of disloyalty, and it undermines the trust on which any group depends. It is bad to wrong an enemy, worse to wrong one who had a right to consider us a friend.

גָּזַלְנוּ we have robbed,

Theft is done secretly, robbery openly. The robber is afraid of no one, neither of man nor of God. There are subtler forms of robbery, when we deprive others of the thanks or credit they deserve. We rob God when we fail to acknowledge His blessings in our lives.

דִּבַּרְנוּ דֹפִי we have spoken slander.

We have spoken negatively, even slanderously, of others (Rashi to Psalm 50:20). According to Rabbi Joseph Kimchi (Spain, twelfth century) the word *dofi* comes from *du-piyot*, meaning "duplicity, two-facedness" – saying one thing and meaning another.

הֶעֱוִינוּ We have acted perversely,

We have made crooked that which should have been straight. We used immoral means to achieve our end. We tried to be clever instead of being wise.

וְהִרְשַׁעְנוּ we have acted wickedly,

This may also mean (1) we caused others to act wickedly, or (2) we allowed wickedness to happen. We failed to maintain moral standards. We were a bad influence, or we failed to protest when we saw others doing wrong.

זַדְנוּ we have acted presumptuously,

We did wrong knowing it to be wrong. We let the claims of conscience be overridden. We allowed ourselves to put personal advantage above the moral law, or the pursuit of desire above prohibition.

חָמַסְנוּ we have been violent,

Physically or verbally. We abused others, failing to treat them with respect. Domestic violence is peculiarly cruel, for it desecrates a relationship that should have been marked by loving-kindness and is often practiced against those least able to defend themselves.

טִפַּלְנוּ שֶׁקֶר we have framed lies.

We said things we knew to be untrue. Or we accused someone of a wrong they did not commit. Lies are contagious, since one act of deceit brings others in its train. "Oh, what a tangled web we weave, when first we practice to deceive" (Sir Walter Scott).

יָעַצְנוּ רָע We have given bad advice,

We advised people to do things we knew were against their interest. We failed to disclose to them information they lacked but we had. We exploited their ignorance to advance our own interest, or we gave irresponsible advice because we were not taking the other person seriously enough.

כִּזַּבְנוּ we have deceived,

We created a false impression by failing to disclose the full truth. Deceiving may also mean creating a false expectation by predicting an outcome you know is unlikely to happen.

לַצְנוּ we have scorned,

We have mocked, scoffed, trivialized the serious. A mocker is a cynic whose low view of others pollutes the atmosphere around him, and whose negativity subverts other people's altruism and ideals.

מָרַדְנוּ we have rebelled,

We deliberately flouted authority, divine or human. A rebel is one who knows that God exists, a moral law exists, and that a certain act is forbidden, yet still does it defiantly, showing that he refuses to acknowledge any authority other than himself.

נִאַצְנוּ we have provoked,

We said or did things we knew would anger or hurt others. The Talmud applies this concept to one who steals food and then makes a blessing over it, as if to placate God at the very time one is contravening His will (*Bava Kamma* 94a).

סָרַרְנוּ we have turned away,

The root *s-r-r* occurs in the Torah in the context of a "stubborn and rebellious son," the delinquent who turns away from the right path and resists all attempts to reform his character. Stubbornness is the refusal to learn from your mistakes or heed the advice of those who seek your good. It is moral recidivism.

עָוִינוּ we have committed iniquity,

Avon is a sin committed knowingly and deliberately. It means "crooked" as opposed to "straightforward." It includes the convoluted reasoning by which we persuade ourselves that transgressions are not that serious, or that we can commit crimes that will not be found out.

פָּשַׁעְנוּ we have transgressed,

Pesha is sin as rebellion. We knew that something is forbidden yet we did it anyway, not out of weakness or temptation but deliberately, as a way of saying that we do not acknowledge the authority of the law and have no intention of abiding by it.

צָרַרְנוּ we have persecuted,

We have knowingly and deliberately caused harm to others, to our family or friends, colleagues or strangers. We have acted like an enemy to others.

קִשִּׁינוּ עֹרֶף we have been obstinate.

We refused to see that the bad things that happened to us were the result of our own actions. We blamed others, failing to see that we are the architect of our own misfortunes. Neither heeding advice nor listening to critics, we continued in our dysfunctional behavior.

רָשַׁעְנוּ We have acted wickedly,

We have done things that were clearly and unequivocally wrong, and for which we offer no defense, merely apology.

שִׁחַתְנוּ we have corrupted,

We wasted our strengths in ways that were harmful or pointless. We gave way to our self-destructive instincts, failing to use our God-given will-power: "Sin is crouching at your door; it desires to have you, but you can dominate it" (Gen. 4:7). Each time we yield to temptation, our character loses some of its resilience and we become corrupted.

תִּעַבְנוּ we have acted abominably,

We have done things that the moral sense recoils from. A sense of disgust is to the soul what pain is to the body. It tells us that this is harmful, dangerous and to be avoided. Yet we overrode this sense and did what every decent instinct should have told us not to do.

תָּעִינוּ we have strayed,

We sought a short-cut to wealth or success or the satisfaction of desire, knowing that we were leaving the path of the good, the right, and the just. We lost our sense of direction, allowing ambition to lead us astray.

תִּעְתָּעְנוּ we have led others astray.

We have been a bad example, a poor role model. To sin is bad; to lead others to sin, worse. We ridiculed the law, or we said, "Others are doing it so it can't be wrong," or practiced some other form of subversion. Because good behavior involves self-restraint, it is easy to undermine. Therefore we must ask: do others become better in our company or worse?

סַרְנוּ מִמִּצְוֹתֶיךָ וּמִמִּשְׁפָּטֶיךָ הַטּוֹבִים וְלֹא שָׁוָה לָנוּ.
וְאַתָּה צַדִּיק עַל כָּל־הַבָּא עָלֵינוּ
כִּי־אֱמֶת עָשִׂיתָ, וַאֲנַחְנוּ הִרְשָׁעְנוּ:

We have turned away from Your commandments and good laws, to no avail, for You are just in all that has befallen us,
for You have acted faithfully while we have done wickedly.

We realize that acting wrongly is bad for us, for others, and for our relationship with You. Any short-term gain we may have achieved is more than outweighed by the price we have paid, whether in the loss of other people's respect or the burden of a troubled conscience.

During the Leader's Repetition, the Viduy continues with הִרְשַׁעְנוּ, *"We have been wicked": in Ma'ariv on page 167; in Shaharit on page 683; in Musaf on page 949; in Minha on page 1073. During Ne'ila, the Viduy continues on the next page.*

מַה נֹּאמַר לְפָנֶיךָ יוֹשֵׁב מָרוֹם	What can we say before You, You who dwell on high?
וּמַה נְּסַפֵּר לְפָנֶיךָ שׁוֹכֵן שְׁחָקִים	What can we declare before You, You who abide in heaven?
הֲלֹא כָּל הַנִּסְתָּרוֹת וְהַנִּגְלוֹת	Do You not know all,
אַתָּה יוֹדֵעַ.	the hidden and revealed alike?

Because God knows us better than we know ourselves, we *must* be honest. Because God forgives, we *can* be honest. No pretence is necessary or possible. This is our defense against self-deception.

The Viduy for Ne'ila ends here. Continue with אַתָּה נוֹתֵן יָד, *"You give Your hand": in the silent Amida on page 1129; in the Leader's Repetition on page 1177.*

אַתָּה יוֹדֵעַ רָזֵי עוֹלָם	You know every secret since the world began,
וְתַעֲלוּמוֹת סִתְרֵי כָּל חָי.	and what is hidden deep inside every living thing.
אַתָּה חוֹפֵשׂ כָּל חַדְרֵי בָטֶן	You search each person's inner chambers,
וּבוֹחֵן כְּלָיוֹת וָלֵב.	examining conscience and mind.
אֵין דָּבָר נֶעְלָם מִמֶּךָּ	Nothing is shrouded from You,
וְאֵין נִסְתָּר מִנֶּגֶד עֵינֶיךָ.	and nothing is hidden before Your eyes.
וּבְכֵן, יְהִי רָצוֹן מִלְּפָנֶיךָ	And so, may it be Your will,
יהוה אֱלֹהֵינוּ וֵאלֹהֵי אֲבוֹתֵינוּ	Lord our God and God of our ancestors,
שֶׁתִּסְלַח לָנוּ עַל כָּל חַטֹּאתֵינוּ	that You forgive us all our sins,
וְתִמְחַל לָנוּ עַל כָּל עֲוֹנוֹתֵינוּ	pardon all our iniquities,
וּתְכַפֵּר לָנוּ עַל כָּל פְּשָׁעֵינוּ.	and grant us atonement for all of our transgressions.

We have no defense. There were times when we were weak, careless, thoughtless, impulsive, impetuous, when we gave way to passion or desire, or lacked the energy or will to do what we knew we should, when we failed to honor our obligations to You and to others. Please, therefore, take the broken fragments of our life and help make them whole again.

Strike the left side of the chest with the right fist while saying each of the sins.

עַל חֵטְא שֶׁחָטָאנוּ לְפָנֶיךָ בְּאֹנֶס וּבְרָצוֹן

For the sin we have sinned before You under duress or freewill,

Or "under duress *and* free will." We did wrong, pretending we had no choice when in fact we did. We said, "I could not help myself," but we could.

וְעַל חֵטְא שֶׁחָטָאנוּ לְפָנֶיךָ בְּאִמּוּץ הַלֵּב

and for the sin we have sinned before You in hardness of heart.

We were insensitive to others. Or, we committed a particular sin so many times we no longer had a bad conscience about doing so.

עַל חֵטְא שֶׁחָטָאנוּ לְפָנֶיךָ בִּבְלִי דָעַת

For the sin we have sinned before You unwittingly,

We did not have the knowledge we should have had. We did not know it was forbidden or illegal or unethical because we did not study, learn or inquire. Perhaps, deep down, we did not want to know.

וְעַל חֵטְא שֶׁחָטָאנוּ לְפָנֶיךָ בְּבִטּוּי שְׂפָתָיִם

and for the sin we have sinned before You by an utterance of our lips.

We spoke insensitively or tactlessly or callously. We said things without thinking of the impact our words would have on others.

עַל חֵטְא שֶׁחָטָאנוּ לְפָנֶיךָ בְּגִלּוּי עֲרָיוֹת

For the sin we have sinned before You by unchastity,

We engaged in forbidden sexual relations or the kind of intimacy that might lead to them. There is no inclination to sin stronger than the sexual drive. Did we keep far enough away from temptation?

וְעַל חֵטְא שֶׁחָטָאנוּ לְפָנֶיךָ בְּגָלוּי וּבַסָּתֶר

and for the sin we have sinned before You openly or secretly.

An open sin shows the world that we do not care. A secret sin means that we care more about the opinions of human beings than that of God, to whom all things are revealed.

עַל חֵטְא שֶׁחָטָאנוּ לְפָנֶיךָ
בְּדַעַת וּבְמִרְמָה

For the sin we have sinned before You knowingly and deceitfully,

We were deceitful. Whether or not we told a lie, we deliberately created a misleading impression. We used cunning to mask our true intentions.

וְעַל חֵטְא שֶׁחָטָאנוּ לְפָנֶיךָ
בְּדִבּוּר פֶּה

and for the sin we have sinned before You in speech.

We insulted someone or criticized them openly or denigrated their work. We spoke harshly, using words as weapons. We spoke crudely, without civility, forgetting that Judaism's "ways are ways of pleasantness and all its paths are peace" (Prov. 3:17).

עַל חֵטְא שֶׁחָטָאנוּ לְפָנֶיךָ
בְּהוֹנָאַת רֵעַ

For the sin we have sinned before You by wronging a neighbor,

We wronged someone either financially, by overcharging, or verbally by reminding them of an embarrassing past they have now moved beyond ("*ona'at devarim,*" see *Bava Metzia* 58b).

וְעַל חֵטְא שֶׁחָטָאנוּ לְפָנֶיךָ
בְּהִרְהוּר הַלֵּב

and for the sin we have sinned before You by thoughts of the heart.

We contemplated doing something we knew to be wrong, and this led us into temptation, because thought lays the ground for deed. "The thought of sin is harder to cure than sin itself" (*Yoma* 29a).

עַל חֵטְא שֶׁחָטָאנוּ לְפָנֶיךָ
בִּוְעִידַת זְנוּת

For the sin we have sinned before You in a gathering for immorality,

We exposed ourselves to sexual temptation. We went to events or befriended people whose lack of modesty or fidelity was likely to have a bad influence on us.

וְעַל חֵטְא שֶׁחָטָאנוּ לְפָנֶיךָ
בְּוִדּוּי פֶּה

and for the sin we have sinned before You by insincere confession.

We confessed without meaning it. We expressed regret but not remorse. We said what we had to say in order to keep our job, or defend our reputation, or defuse a tense situation, but we did not truly believe what we were saying or feel the guilt we should have felt.

עַל חֵטְא שֶׁחָטָאנוּ לְפָנֶיךָ
בְּזִלְזוּל הוֹרִים וּמוֹרִים

For the sin we have sinned before You by contempt for parents and teachers,

We were rude or disrespectful or ungrateful to our parents or teachers. We did not thank them or honor them as much as we should. They did not deserve our callousness or indifference.

וְעַל חֵטְא שֶׁחָטָאנוּ לְפָנֶיךָ
בְּזָדוֹן וּבִשְׁגָגָה

and for the sin we have sinned before You willfully or in error.

Whether we knew or did not know at the time that what we were doing was wrong, we now know, and realize we have to atone and make amends.

עַל חֵטְא שֶׁחָטָאנוּ לְפָנֶיךָ
בְּחֹזֶק יָד

For the sin we have sinned before You by force,

We used power against others, whether by physical intimidation, psychological pressure, emotional blackmail, or threat, in order to impose our will on them. We used our strength to coerce those weaker than us.

וְעַל חֵטְא שֶׁחָטָאנוּ לְפָנֶיךָ
בְּחִלּוּל הַשֵּׁם

and for the sin we have sinned before You by desecrating Your name.

We acted in a way that brought discredit to our people and our faith. By acting badly we caused people to think negatively about Jews or Judaism and thus about God Himself.

עַל חֵטְא שֶׁחָטָאנוּ לְפָנֶיךָ
בְּטֻמְאַת שְׂפָתַיִם

For the sin we have sinned before You by impure lips,

We used crude, coarse, crass, indecent or offensive language. We spoke without delicacy or grace, as if words do not matter, but they do. Coarse language leads to coarse conduct, verbal violence to physical violence, and abusive speech to abusive behavior.

וְעַל חֵטְא שֶׁחָטָאנוּ לְפָנֶיךָ
בְּטִפְשׁוּת פֶּה

and for the sin we have sinned before You by foolish speech.

We said things we now regret saying. We spoke impulsively, unthinkingly, and, as we now see, tactlessly and without regard to the sensitivities of others.

עַל חֵטְא שֶׁחָטָאנוּ לְפָנֶיךָ
בְּיֵצֶר הָרָע

For the sin we have sinned before You by the evil inclination,

We did not practice the self-control we should have done. We said to ourselves, "I could not help it," whereas in fact, with discipline and self-restraint, we could have developed greater willpower. We allowed ourselves to fall into the trap of learned helplessness.

וְעַל חֵטְא שֶׁחָטָאנוּ לְפָנֶיךָ
בְּיוֹדְעִים וּבְלֹא יוֹדְעִים

and for the sin we have sinned before You knowingly or unwittingly.

Wittingly *and* unwittingly at the same time. One part of us knew what we were doing was wrong but the other part said otherwise and we persuaded ourselves, against the better angels of our nature, that it was permissible.

וְעַל כֻּלָּם אֱלוֹהַּ סְלִיחוֹת
סְלַח לָנוּ, מְחַל לָנוּ, כַּפֶּר לָנוּ.

FOR ALL THESE,
GOD OF FORGIVENESS,
FORGIVE US, PARDON US,
GRANT US ATONEMENT.

At this point, we move from confession to prayer. Having declared our sins we ask God for forgiveness. *To forgive* means to heal a broken relationship. *To pardon* means to renounce the right to punish. *To grant atonement* means to efface all lingering traces of the sin.

עַל חֵטְא שֶׁחָטָאנוּ לְפָנֶיךָ בְּכַחַשׁ וּבְכָזָב	For the sin we have sinned before You by deceit and lies,

In the face of accusation we denied or lied about what we did. We knew we did wrong but refused to admit it. Or we made promises we had no intention of keeping.

וְעַל חֵטְא שֶׁחָטָאנוּ לְפָנֶיךָ בְּכַפַּת שֹׁחַד	and for the sin we have sinned before You by bribery.

We persuaded, or tried to persuade, someone to rule in our favor or turn a blind eye to what we were doing, by offering money or some other inducement.

עַל חֵטְא שֶׁחָטָאנוּ לְפָנֶיךָ בְּלָצוֹן	For the sin we have sinned before You by scorn,

We acted or spoke disdainfully about genuine moral, ethical, or spiritual concerns. We made fun of people's altruistic commitments.

וְעַל חֵטְא שֶׁחָטָאנוּ לְפָנֶיךָ בְּלָשׁוֹן הָרָע	and for the sin we have sinned before You by evil speech.

We spoke negatively about people. The rabbis said that *lashon hara*, "evil speech," is the worst of interpersonal sins, "as bad as murder, idolatry and incest combined." It applies to remarks that are true but derogatory. If they are false, they come under the category of *motzi shem ra*, libel or slander. *Lashon hara* poisons human relationships.

עַל חֵטְא שֶׁחָטָאנוּ לְפָנֶיךָ בְּמַשָּׂא וּבְמַתָּן	For the sin we have sinned before You in business,

We acted with less than total honesty in business. We did things we would not want others to know about. We did not honor our obligations to clients, employers, employees or colleagues. The Talmud says that in the world to come, the first question we will be asked is: "Did you act honestly in business?"

וְעַל חֵטְא שֶׁחָטָאנוּ לְפָנֶיךָ בְּמַאֲכָל וּבְמִשְׁתֶּה	and for the sin we have sinned before You with food and drink.

We ate and drank that which is forbidden in Jewish law. Or we ate and drank (or smoked) without due regard for our health.

עַל חֵטְא שֶׁחָטָאנוּ לְפָנֶיךָ בְּנֶשֶׁךְ וּבְמַרְבִּית	For the sin we have sinned before You by interest and extortion,

We did not follow Jewish law in relation to the taking of interest, whether as lenders or borrowers. We took undue advantage of other people's misfortunes.

וְעַל חֵטְא שֶׁחָטָאנוּ לְפָנֶיךָ בִּנְטִיַּת גָּרוֹן	and for the sin we have sinned before You by being haughty.

We looked down on others. We failed to understand the difference between righteousness and self-righteousness: the righteous think well of others, the self-righteous think well of themselves.

עַל חֵטְא שֶׁחָטָאנוּ לְפָנֶיךָ בְּשִׂיחַ שִׂפְתוֹתֵינוּ	For the sin we have sinned before You by the idle chatter of our lips,

We indulged in meaningless chatter, idle gossip and pointless speculation, even if we did not malign anyone. We wasted our, or other people's, time.

וְעַל חֵטְא שֶׁחָטָאנוּ לְפָנֶיךָ בְּשִׂקּוּר עָיִן	and for the sin we have sinned before You by prying eyes.

We looked at things we should not have done. Led by our curiosity, we invaded other people's privacy.

עַל חֵטְא שֶׁחָטָאנוּ לְפָנֶיךָ בְּעֵינַיִם רָמוֹת	For the sin we have sinned before You by arrogance,

We acted as if we were disdainful of others, holding ourselves to be superior. There were times when we seemed self-important, haughty, supercilious, conceited, smug, ostentatious or vain.

וְעַל חֵטְא שֶׁחָטָאנוּ לְפָנֶיךָ בְּעַזּוּת מֵצַח	and for the sin we have sinned before You by insolence.

We were shameless and brazen-faced as if no one and nothing mattered except us and our concerns. We dismissed all criticism as if we alone were the sole judge of our deeds and demeanor.

וְעַל כֻּלָּם אֱלוֹהַּ סְלִיחוֹת סְלַח לָנוּ, מְחַל לָנוּ, כַּפֶּר לָנוּ.	FOR ALL THESE, GOD OF FORGIVENESS, FORGIVE US, PARDON US, GRANT US ATONEMENT.

עַל חֵטְא שֶׁחָטָאנוּ לְפָנֶיךָ בִּפְרִיקַת עֹל	For the sin we have sinned before You by casting off the yoke,

We acted without a sense of duty to our faith, our heritage, our people and the wider society among whom we live. We tried to live as "free riders," seeking the benefits of community without making a contribution to it, pursuing our rights without honoring our responsibilities.

וְעַל חֵטְא שֶׁחָטָאנוּ לְפָנֶיךָ בִּפְלִילוּת	and for the sin we have sinned before You by perverting judgment.

We were combative and confrontational instead of seeking a peaceful resolution, unwilling to hear other points of view and preferring victory to the collaborative pursuit of truth.

עַל חֵטְא שֶׁחָטָאנוּ לְפָנֶיךָ בִּצְדִיַּת רֵעַ	For the sin we have sinned before You by entrapping a neighbor,

We schemed or acted subversively to cause harm to our neighbor, whether financially or by way of damaging their reputation, carefully concealing our role in the process.

וְעַל חֵטְא שֶׁחָטָאנוּ לְפָנֶיךָ
בְּצָרוּת עָיִן

and for the sin we have sinned
before You by envy.

We let someone else's blessings spoil ours by desiring what they have. We resented someone else's success or achievements, not wanting them to have what we do not.

עַל חֵטְא שֶׁחָטָאנוּ לְפָנֶיךָ
בְּקַלּוּת רֹאשׁ

For the sin we have sinned
before You by lack of
seriousness,

We did not take serious things seriously, or respect principles or people worthy of respect. We mocked the earnest or ridiculed the altruistic, trying to reduce them to our level instead of letting them lift us to theirs.

וְעַל חֵטְא שֶׁחָטָאנוּ לְפָנֶיךָ
בְּקַשְׁיוּת עֹרֶף

and for the sin we have sinned
before You by obstinacy.

We did not learn from failure. Losing a friend, a relationship, a job, a contest – we did not stop to ask what we were doing wrong. We assumed it was someone else's fault, not ours.

עַל חֵטְא שֶׁחָטָאנוּ לְפָנֶיךָ
בְּרִיצַת רַגְלַיִם לְהָרַע

For the sin we have sinned
before You by running to do
evil,

We followed the crowd, allowing ourselves to be persuaded that if everyone else is doing it, it cannot be wrong. We did not stop, step back, and restrain ourselves (see *Sanhedrin* 102b).

וְעַל חֵטְא שֶׁחָטָאנוּ לְפָנֶיךָ
בִּרְכִילוּת

and for the sin we have sinned
before You by gossip.

We gossiped, in contravention of the Torah's prohibition (Lev. 19:16). Though gossip often seems harmless it is usually ultimately derogatory; no one gossips about other people's secret virtues.

עַל חֵטְא שֶׁחָטָאנוּ לְפָנֶיךָ
בִּשְׁבוּעַת שָׁוְא

For the sin we have sinned
before You by vain oath,

We took vain or unnecessary oaths, affirming or denying the obvious, swearing to do the impossible or swearing to do something we are obligated to do anyway.

וְעַל חֵטְא שֶׁחָטָאנוּ לְפָנֶיךָ
בְּשִׂנְאַת חִנָּם

and for the sin we have sinned
before You by baseless hatred.

We allowed ourselves to dislike others for no objective reason, often unconsciously projecting onto them aspects of ourselves we do not like but are loath to admit. We made them scapegoats for our own shortcomings.

עַל חֵטְא שֶׁחָטָאנוּ לְפָנֶיךָ
בִּתְשׂוּמֶת יָד

For the sin we have sinned
before You by breach of trust,

We made improper use of money or goods placed in our safekeeping, or in some other way dishonored the trust other people placed in us to safeguard their interests.

וְעַל חֵטְא שֶׁחָטָאנוּ לְפָנֶיךָ
בְּתִמְהוֹן לֵבָב

and for the sin we have sinned
before You by confusion of
heart.

We acted in the heat of the moment, confused, disoriented or afraid, instead of taking the firm decision not to do the wrong thing. Others say it means that we allowed our faith to be shaken by skepticism or doubt (*Iyun Tefilla*).

וְעַל כֻּלָּם אֱלוֹהַּ סְלִיחוֹת
סְלַח לָנוּ, מְחַל לָנוּ, כַּפֶּר לָנוּ.

FOR ALL THESE, GOD OF FORGIVENESS,
FORGIVE US, PARDON US,
GRANT US ATONEMENT.

The following lines are about penalties in ancient times. They are currently inapplicable, because we have no Temple and the death penalty has long been discontinued. Nonetheless, we mention them here because they remind us of the gravity of our offenses.

And for the sins for which we are liable to bring a burnt-offering,	וְעַל חֲטָאִים שֶׁאָנוּ חַיָּבִים עֲלֵיהֶם עוֹלָה

For wrong thoughts and for failure to fulfill a positive command, such as saying *Kiddush* on Shabbat or eating matza on Seder night.

and for the sins for which we are liable to bring a sin-offering,	וְעַל חֲטָאִים שֶׁאָנוּ חַיָּבִים עֲלֵיהֶם חַטָּאת

For sins committed through ignorance or inadvertence that, had they been done knowingly and intentionally, would have led to our being "cut off." These are generally serious sins such as breaking Shabbat or eating *ḥametz* on Pesaḥ.

and for the sins for which we are liable to bring an offering according to our means,	וְעַל חֲטָאִים שֶׁאָנוּ חַיָּבִים עֲלֵיהֶם קָרְבַּן עוֹלֶה וְיוֹרֵד

Six sins, such as swearing falsely in court that one has no knowledge of a case in which one has been called as a witness, for which the penalty varied according to the wealth or poverty of the offender.

and for the sins for which we are liable to bring a guilt-offering for certain or possible sin,	וְעַל חֲטָאִים שֶׁאָנוּ חַיָּבִים עֲלֵיהֶם אָשָׁם וַדַּאי וְתָלוּי

A guilt offering was incurred for five sins, including making personal use of property belonging to the Temple, and falsely denying under oath that you have someone else's property in your possession. A guilt-offering for possible sin was brought when there was a reasonable probability, but no conclusive evidence, that we had performed an act that would have incurred a sin-offering.

and for the sins for which we are liable to lashes for rebellion,	וְעַל חֲטָאִים שֶׁאָנוּ חַיָּבִים עֲלֵיהֶם מַכַּת מַרְדּוּת

A rabbinically imposed punishment for (1) failure to perform a positive biblical command, or (2) disobeying a rabbinic prohibition, or (3) as a measure to prevent widespread abuse of the law.

וְעַל חֲטָאִים שֶׁאָנוּ חַיָּבִים עֲלֵיהֶם מַלְקוּת אַרְבָּעִים	and for the sins for which we are liable to forty lashes,

A biblical punishment for transgression of a negative command. There are 207 such offenses, as enumerated by Maimonides (Laws of the Sanhedrin, ch. 19). The sages restricted the punishment to thirty-nine lashes (Mishna, *Makkot* 22a).

וְעַל חֲטָאִים שֶׁאָנוּ חַיָּבִים עֲלֵיהֶם מִיתָה בִּידֵי שָׁמָיִם	and for the sins for which we are liable to death by the hands of Heaven,

This refers to serious sins deemed punishable by God (by premature death) rather than by a human court.

וְעַל חֲטָאִים שֶׁאָנוּ חַיָּבִים עֲלֵיהֶם כָּרֵת וַעֲרִירִי	and for the sins for which we are liable to be cut off and childless,

Graver sins, punishable by God, which if committed deliberately, may involve premature death or childlessness. If committed unwittingly, they incurred a sin-offering.

וְעַל חֲטָאִים שֶׁאָנוּ חַיָּבִים עֲלֵיהֶם אַרְבַּע מִיתוֹת בֵּית דִּין סְקִילָה, שְׂרֵפָה, הֶרֶג, וְחֶנֶק.	and for the sins for which we are liable to the four death penalties inflicted by the court: stoning, burning, beheading and strangling.

These are sins for which the Torah prescribes capital punishment.

עַל מִצְוַת עֲשֵׂה וְעַל מִצְוַת לֹא תַעֲשֶׂה. בֵּין שֶׁיֵּשׁ בָּהּ קוּם עֲשֵׂה וּבֵין שֶׁאֵין בָּהּ קוּם עֲשֵׂה.	For positive and negative commandments, whether they can be remedied by an act or not,

There are 248 positive and 365 negative commandments. Some of these, if transgressed, can be remedied. For example, stolen property can be returned.

אֶת הַגְּלוּיִים לָנוּ	for sins known to us
וְאֶת שֶׁאֵינָם גְּלוּיִים לָנוּ.	and for those that are unknown –
אֶת הַגְּלוּיִים לָנוּ	for those that are known,
כְּבָר אֲמַרְנוּם לְפָנֶיךָ	we have already declared them
וְהוֹדִינוּ לְךָ עֲלֵיהֶם.	before You and confessed them to You;
וְאֶת שֶׁאֵינָם גְּלוּיִים לָנוּ	and for those that are unknown,
לְפָנֶיךָ הֵם גְּלוּיִים וִידוּעִים.	before You they are revealed and known, as it is said,
כַּדָּבָר שֶׁנֶּאֱמַר	"The secret things
הַנִּסְתָּרֹת לַיהוה אֱלֹהֵינוּ	belong to the LORD our God,
וְהַנִּגְלֹת לָנוּ וּלְבָנֵינוּ עַד־עוֹלָם	but the things that are revealed are for us and our children for
לַעֲשׂוֹת אֶת־כָּל־דִּבְרֵי	ever, that we may fulfill all the
הַתּוֹרָה הַזֹּאת:	words of this Torah."

We have already confessed all the sins we know we have committed. There may be other transgressions of which we are unaware. We cannot confess them because we do not know what they are, but we ask You nonetheless to forgive us for these too.

This ends the formal, public, collective confession. We should also articulate in our mind the specific sins we have committed. Confession is only part of the process of repentance, which also involves (1) a genuine feeling of remorse, (2) putting right, wherever we can, what we have done wrong, and making restitution wherever appropriate, (3) resolving not to commit the sin again, and (4) acting on that resolve (Maimonides, Laws of Repentance 2:1–3).

In the case of a sin against another person we must also apologize to and seek forgiveness from that person. If the offended party refuses to forgive, we should ask three of their friends to intercede on our behalf, and we should do so three times if necessary. If the person we have offended is no longer alive, we should gather ten people at his graveside and confess the wrong we did him. If we owed him money we should pay this to his heirs. If he left no heirs, we should pay it to the Beit Din (ibid. 2:9–11).

When someone who has wronged or offended us apologizes, we should accept the apology and forgive, for it is forbidden to harbor a grudge (Lev. 19:18) and wrong to be unforgiving (Laws of Repentance 2:10).

In the silent Amida, continue with כִּי אַתָּה סָלְחָן, *"For You are the Forgiver": in Minḥa for Erev Yom Kippur on page 33; in Ma'ariv on page 117; in Shaḥarit on page 609; in Musaf on page 799; in Minḥa on page 1037.*

During the Leader's Repetition of Ma'ariv, continue with וְאַתָּה רַחוּם, *"And You are compassionate" on page 179. During the Leader's Repetition of the other services, continue with* וְדָוִד עַבְדְּךָ, *"David Your servant": in Shaḥarit on page 693; in Musaf on page 959; in Minḥa on page 1083.*

RABBIS' KADDISH

Mourner: Yitgadal ve-yitkadash shemeh raba. (*Cong:* Amen)
Be-alema di vera khir'uteh,
ve-yamlikh malkhuteh,
be-ḥayyeikhon, uv-yomeikhon, uv-ḥayyei de-khol beit Yisrael,
ba-agala uvi-zman kariv,
ve-imru Amen. (*Cong:* Amen)

All: Yeheh shemeh raba mevarakh le'alam ul-alemei alemaya.

Mourner: Yitbarakh ve-yishtabaḥ ve-yitpa'ar ve-yitromam ve-yitnaseh
ve-yit-hadar ve-yit'aleh ve-yit-hallal
shemeh dekudsha, berikh hu. (*Cong:* Berikh hu)
Le-ela le-ela mi-kol birkhata ve-shirata,
tushbeḥata ve-neḥemata, da-amiran be-alema,
ve-imru, Amen. (*Cong:* Amen)

Al Yisrael, ve-al rabanan,
ve-al talmideihon, ve-al kol talmidei talmideihon,
ve-al kol man de-asekin be-oraita
di be-atra (*In Israel:* kadisha) ha-dein ve-di be-khol atar va-atar,
yeheh lehon ul-khon shelama raba,
ḥina ve-ḥisda, ve-raḥamei,
ve-ḥayyei arichei, um-zonei re-viḥei,
u-furkana min kodam avuhon di vish-maya,
ve-imru Amen. (*Cong:* Amen)

Yeheh shelama raba min shemaya
ve-ḥayyim (tovim) aleinu ve-al kol Yisrael,
ve-imru Amen. (*Cong:* Amen)

Bow, take three steps back, as if taking leave of the Divine Presence, then bow, first left, then right, then center, while saying:

Oseh ha-shalom bim-romav,
hu ya'aseh ve-raḥamav shalom aleinu, ve-al kol Yisrael,
ve-imru Amen. (*Cong:* Amen)

MOURNER'S KADDISH

Mourner: Yitgadal ve-yitkadash shemeh raba. (*Cong:* Amen)
Be-alema di vera khir'uteh,
ve-yamlikh malkhuteh,
be-ḥayyeikhon, uv-yomeikhon, uv-ḥayyei de-khol beit Yisrael,
ba-agala uvi-zman kariv,
ve-imru Amen. (*Cong:* Amen)

All: Yeheh shemeh raba mevarakh le'alam ul-alemei alemaya.

Mourner: Yitbarakh ve-yishtabaḥ ve-yitpa'ar ve-yitromam ve-yitnaseh
ve-yit-hadar ve-yit'aleh ve-yit-hallal
shemeh dekudsha, berikh hu. (*Cong:* Berikh hu)
Le-ela le-ela mi-kol birkhata ve-shirata,
/ *On Motza'ei Yom Kippur:* Le-ela min kol birkhata ve-shirata,/
tushbeḥata ve-neḥemata, da-amiran be-alema,
ve-imru, Amen. (*Cong:* Amen)

Yeheh shelama raba min shemaya
ve-ḥayyim aleinu ve-al kol Yisrael,
ve-imru Amen. (*Cong:* Amen)

Bow, take three steps back, as if taking leave of the Divine Presence, then bow, first left, then right, then center, while saying:

Oseh ha-shalom bim-romav,
hu ya'aseh shalom aleinu, ve-al kol Yisrael,
ve-imru Amen. (*Cong:* Amen)

כתר ירושלים

כתר

CW00751281

FROM·MANET TO·HOCKNEY

MODERN ARTISTS' ILLUSTRATED BOOKS

EDOUARD MANET: 1875, *LE CORBEAU*. CAT. 1

FROM·MANET TO·HOCKNEY
MODERN ARTISTS' ILLUSTRATED BOOKS

EDITED BY
CAROL HOGBEN & ROWAN WATSON
INTRODUCTION BY
CAROL HOGBEN

VICTORIA
& ALBERT
MUSEUM

Published by the Victoria and Albert Museum, 1985
Designed by Grundy & Northedge Designers
Printed in Great Britain by Royle Print Limited

ISBN 0 948 107 07 3 (softback)
ISBN 0 948 107 08 1 (hardback)

FRONT COVER: Henri Matisse: 1947. Jazz, plate I. Le Clown.
CAT 114
BACK COVER: Henri Matisse: 1947. Jazz, plate VIII, Icare. CAT 114

CONTENTS

PREFACE

It is sometimes overlooked that the National Art Library, in addition to being a Library serving public and Museum alike, is also a Museum Department in its own right and as such collects books as objects of intrinsic artistic merit. The collection of modern artists' illustrated books is one of the finest in the world and the items in this catalogue are a selection to whet the appetite. The catalogue does not aim to be a comprehensive survey of all our holdings but it does serve to give a good idea of the richness and variety of the collection, concentrating obviously on the most important artists and their works.

The compilation of this catalogue has been very much a corporate Library effort. That it is such a beautiful book is very largely the result of the efforts and talents of Carol Hogben without whose flair and enthusiasm this project would have been considerably impoverished. Mr. Hogben, who chose the subjects both for publication and display, has written a most stimulating introduction. He also deserves a tribute for having added so substantially to the Library's collections over the past few years under the enlightened and far-sighted collecting policy of Ronald Lightbown, the former Keeper of the Library.

The individual entries were put together and painstakingly edited by Rowan Watson and a team of seven Museum Assistants consisting of Julia Bigham, Judith Bradfield, Catherine Cripwell, Wendy Fish, Christopher Nichols, Susanna Robson and Eva White. They all toiled unceasingly and uncomplainingly but can now take satisfaction from the fruits of the very long hours of work they all contributed.

Anne Hobbs assisted with the Russian books, and many niggling administrative problems were overcome by Peter Castle, Robert Howell, Jane Rick and David Wright. Barbara Cole helped with typing. The photographs were taken by Philip de Bay, the Library photographer, as well as Sir Geoffrey Shakerley and Michael Harris. As was to be expected, they more than meet the most exacting standards.

In conclusion, if this book arouses a keener interest in this specialized field of decorative arts, it will have fulfilled one important purpose. Another, however, is to gladden the eye and give the reader an opportunity to revel in the creative glories of the leading artists of the past century. I have little doubt that this latter aim has been amply achieved.

DUNCAN HALDANE

ACTING KEEPER OF THE LIBRARY. MARCH 1985

8

INTRODUCTION

Essentially this is a picture book with words, a plain, straightforward, honest catalogue, albeit highly selective, with its information given where the plates occur. It may be books about books are not many people's favourite thing, but at least this is an illustrated one that deals with illustrations. And a good quick flip, or, better still, a nice long leisurely browse before you ever began to read these lines, has probably told you more than any essay of introduction could. It will have given you a broad impression of what claims are being made; have clearly defined the real time scale covered (1890-1980, stretched); the level of the artists represented (in general, say Tate/Hayward/Pompidou-type stars) and the sheer geographical extent of reference (Moscow to San Francisco) quite apart from the literary (Homer, Hesiod, Genesis, up to Stevens, Beckett, Ginsberg, etc.). It will surely have crept across that all these books are drawn from a single, growing permanent collection, and that here they have been forced to sit in a single-line conspectus of chronology, largely regardless of style or country of origin. So what is there else that may need pointing out?

No doubt after a little time has been given to absorption and reflection, there will be questions or puzzlements that float up. Why has so-and-so not been found a place? Is this example properly called a book? What are the true connecting threads here being conveyed? Or what, indeed, is this compilation really trying to present? My essay, then, is meant to take that ground. To come clean, as it were, on editorial shape. It is not to run through a whole century of art, art-dealing, literary publishing, magazine reviews, original print connections, or even book design, in so many countries.

I should first say our aims, as our criteria, were evolved only gradually, in the same way that the project took its form. For the book in fact is a fusion of two plans. One was just to catalogue the Library's *livres d'artistes,* which had been a long-standing, if imprecise, intention. The other was to make a 'recent acquisitions' show, that demonstrated what the Library has and what it does. Both plans seemed like problem-porcupines, with neither at all well matched to the physical constraints of time and square-foot space available. Yet in the end we have emerged with something, we believe, retaining merit out of both these plans, which is not a compromise. The book has held to its own selection scale, accorded to a certain rhythm of image-types being scanned, but not dictated by a fixed showcase array. It has not been sliced into thematic zones. It is not limited to a conventional parade of Parisian *livres d'artistes,* nor a roll-call of their European

LEFT
EDOUARD MANET. Cat and Flowers. Original etching from Champfleury *LES CHATS,* Paris, (2nd, de luxe edition) 1870.

counterparts. And yet it does include a major round-up of such works, to please afficionados of the genre.

It has not been governed, on the other side, to comprise only items recently acquired. But there has been a conscious attempt to feature things bought over the past five years, and more than half the titles shown were got in that time. And it does make clear that the Library's collecting, butterfly-hunter's net is not set solely to scoop up the monumental, sumptuous, big-bang bibliophiles' thrill. It proves, we feel, that a strident Dada pamphlet, a futurist's broadsheet, or a surrealist's exhibition catalogue, even were it printed on the crudest (literally rotten) wood-pulp paper, and never intended but as the handbill of an evening, may also now be seen as the most precious relic, voicing, at pure source, the whole aims of some new campaign in art.

Finally, too, it does perhaps project a point that might seem only institutional pedantry, but is none the less of the greatest importance to visitors using the Museum.

You will certainly have noticed, going through the plates, that *almost* all the artists' illustrations in this list have made use of an *original* graphic process; they are lithographs, etchings, wood-cuts, wood-engravings, aquatints, drypoints, copper-engravings, silk-screens (serigraphs), linocuts, soft-ground etchings, etc. etc.. Now each of these is a distinct technical means for making many copies from a plate. I do not concern myself here with their detailed procedures. Some are simple, some very tricky indeed. Some an artist mostly does himself; some will want a skilled technician's help. But the thing that makes their prints "original" is this. The artist himself in person makes the image directly, (or, by transfers indirectly) on the plate. But the plate is not the "original" work created – the copies are. The artist approves the final image "bon-à-tirer". When taken, he will sign each copy perfect up to the chosen number, usually marking on a serial and date. And at the end the plate is either destroyed, or clearly spoiled, to guarantee no further copies made. It means the artist keeps a total control of finished effect, but it equally means that he has to take close part, at very least, in the whole production. It is true too that hand-inked, hand-wiped plates do give an utterly different quality from a machine press churning thousands of impressions. In some cases as few as ten or twenty copies only may be taken, though 100 to 250 are more usual scales. Distributed internationally, editions of this size obtain at once intrinsic rarity.

All this I am very sure you know. I state it only to clarify the first criterion used in the present book. In this book it is *not*, per se, the graphic process used that is the key. Nor is it the relative rarity of a limited edition, even if both do carry plus points. It is the measure, rather, of the artist's real involvement in the work, the extent of the creative stake put in.

Thus the fact that Gauguin did not get his Noa-Noa book (C.1898; CAT. 15) beyond a manuscript, or that what we are showing is a mere posthumous facsimile, does not seem to me a subterfuge admission.

RIGHT
ODILON REDON.
Frontispiece to Edmond Picard, *EL MOGHREB AL AKSA, UNE MISSION BELGE AU MAROC*, with interpretations by Theo Van Rysselberghe; Brussels, Larcier, 1889.

El Moghreb al
Aksa

LEFT
FERNAND KHNOPFF. Frontispiece to Pol De Mont, *CLARIBELLA,* Utrecht, Beijers, 1893.

The truth is that the manuscript was a very important piece of his creative output; its reproduction, in a small edition, makes it a library object with its own historic significance, and as such I would rate it here as an evident "must". Much the same applies to Degas' Halévy, (1880's; CAT. 3) which surely has no need for any excuse to be counted in. So Léger's Blaise Cendrars, Ernst's wild collage novellas, Man Ray's Eluard, or Magritte's Lautréamont, each mainline capital examples of these artists' work, were none of them produced by a strictly autographic means, but are not held illegitimate, or borderline, for that. If we look at the things which represent Wyndham Lewis, say, or Francis Picabia, or Theo Van Doesburg, which have been taken straight from magazines, it is not the graphic process that has won for them their place. Rather it is the magazines themselves – *BLAST, 391, DE STIJL,* and *MECANO* – of which they were at once own editors and chief contributors, and which thus encapsulate a major testament. Similar, again, are the works coming out of revolutionary Russia – like the pamphlet books of Larionov, Gontcharova, and the Burlyuks; the inflammatory *STRELETS;* the covers by Malevich and Rodchenko – all stem from and clearly speak the art conditions of their time. Generally crudely produced; theoretical dynamite; tucked in pocket form to pass the word abroad; not splendid tomes to tempt the rich collector.

And yet indeed, if we have come to that, even Matisse's *JAZZ,* – outshining star of any book show where it might ever be seen – is not a properly autographic work. For although the text was even composed and written out by Henri Matisse, in his own large hand; and although he cut the coloured paper collages that were used as the plate designs, with his very own scissors; strictly speaking, the text is a mere facsimile, reproduced photo-mechanically by Draeger Frères, while the plates were done from stencils, copied (under the artist's direction) by Edmond Vairel. So you see, quite clearly, *JAZZ* cannot be called at all an original work, and strictly speaking it should be left out! Well, nuts to that! One has to build one's sense around the facts, and *JAZZ* is one of them, right in a central spot.

All this you may take as part of what I meant when I spoke of coming clean on editorial shape. And from this you will see there was no strict rule on sticking to original graphic works. Never the less, the principles implicit in that test were always there, a constant first-line guide if not a rule. And it is still, very largely, true to say that the great majority of these books *are* illustrated (richly) with original prints; and that their time-sequence gave our frame its warps, to which the other strands were woven on. To some extent, detecting warp from weft is to see where the two plans meld; that first idea of listing *Livres d'Artistes,* accorded to their proper definition; and the other of a show on the library's work.

But now I may return to another earlier point which I mentioned might seem institutional pedantry. As everyone knows, within the public care, prints of this type such as lithographs, etchings, woodcuts, etc., normally live protected from the light of day in boxes, stored in the Print Departments of great art museums. Most often, as in the V & A itself, or the British Museum, all artists' original works on paper are housed together side by side as Prints and Drawings. So anyone wanting to study graphic arts, for real, and at first hand, just has to haunt the Print Rooms, no place else. There they will find, apart from all those boxes full of mounted sheets, such things as complete original sketchbooks, with an artist's notes; as well as those prints that came out in suite form, in portfolios, albums, or maybe bound as sets. Here and there they may meet separate proofs of, let us say, a Rubens title-page, made for a book to which it is no longer still attached.

Around their walls is generally stacked a range of the standard reference works on graphic arts – dictionaries of engravers, catalogues raisonnés, etc. likely to answer what most students need. They proffer then a total apparatus, full of plums, that yet serves a somewhat hermetic view, of part of art; the study of prints much keyed to technical process; the drawings pored for clues to works elsewhere. It is only when you need to pursue the subject in much greater depth, that you have to hie you off to libraries.

I have set this down for two things to be seen, and the first is this. Print Rooms and Libraries, often sited close, with much in common and dependent on each other's expertises, do have to fix certain frontiers if only to keep their capital powders fairly dry. In the V & A, at any rate, real artists' illustrated books – including those that are splurged with original graphics – are housed in and collected by the Library. Portfolios of loose prints, too, where published as complete or integral suites, and when accompanied by any printed text however brief, are looked on as the Library's proper sphere. It is not of course a case of a harsh law, and exceptions do happen; indeed some may be descried in the present book. The point I am trying to make is that, in this way, it is only too possible to be a keen student of graphic art, and regular Print Room user, but remain unaware of the wide range of connected comparable work viewable on application in the Library. In many individual cases, moreover, it may often include an artist's single most ambitious serial piece. No doubt one day computered catalogues, at both ends, will wipe the snag away except for the walk, which you may still have to do between the two. At present however there is no way you can see, in the Print Room, that such works exist at all, unless they should happen to have some separate plates, or by some other chance. Thus, just to pick some random instances by way of example, the Print Room does have Redon's album *SONGES* (Dreams) published in Paris in 1891, and containing the complete set of six lithographs, not in the Library. The Library has the same artist's *TENTATION DE SAINT ANTOINE* (1896; CAT. 13), with the third set of his lithographs printed in 1896 complete, from which the Print Room holds only isolated plates. And there are similar partial overlaps in such cases as Matisse's Mallarmé etchings (1932; CAT. 95) Braque's *THÉOGONIE* (1932; CAT. 96) Picasso's Buffon *TEXTES* (1942; CAT. 110) or Chagall's *BIBLE* (1931; CAT. 88) etc., etc..

But there is to this a converse snag at the Library's end. For there the books are catalogued as books, with the primary entry under the author of the text, and the artist-illustrator taking second place. And a proper technical definition of print processes used is not something the Library staff is ideally geared to give, so that many artists' original graphic works may sometimes pass described as illustrations, or cuts, and left at that. Merely to make its graphic holdings better known, and thus more accessible, has therefore been a major object of this book.

But these relations, as I have told them here, lead one to take a further, broader point. Is it not extraordinary, when you come to think of it, how very tightly we compartment and generally two-dimensionalise the main arenas where we meet real art? Few of us ever get the chance to penetrate a painter's studio, or catch the artist at it in his den. We have no first-hand picture of what artists do; how their minds are filled; on what experience they draw. What excites them? What part do friends play? Lovers? Dealers? What things do they browse on, or what read? Do they read at all? Does music, would you reckon, wind them up, or poetry? Plays?

For such things, these perspectives, we ourselves can only look to books, or hope to have it told in the major survey shows. Yet these are only temporary tents, that crop up rarely over any given field. And otherwise... what is there? Galleries, where a very few paintings hang; high ceilings, waxed floors, short labels. An Ernst; a Dali; a Magritte; oil on canvas, glass, gold-leaf frame... this is Surrealism?

Then there are Print Rooms where the paper things are kept, and boxes are got-out if you will ask. And there are Libraries, where you fill in forms for books and sit at a table, waiting in a hush. Or this is Surrealism?

So where would you glean, from these, what a rackety, tempestuous affair Surrealism actually was? Where is it you glimpse Dali, with his two-poignard moustache, all dressed up in a deep-sea diver's suit? Where are the rooms of life-sized mannequins? When does our exhibition catalogue reveal in our hands, on the cover, set in velvet black, a highly realistic female boob, all sponge rubber, painted, and the message with it "Prière de Toucher"? Where do we get to hear an Arp, a Schwitters, Breton, Hugo Ball, performing their own poems against percussion? Hear Marinetti shouting on the stage, or see a ballet dressed by Depero?

To answer, of course, my own rhetorical questions, it will be fair to remember that survey shows can draw on private loans, and sometimes dredge up stuff from an artist's heirs. Yet in the main their planners must depend on just three doors – galleries, print rooms, for the art itself; plus libraries, to bring that art to life. In this guise then a library is not simply a room where books are brought, and read, then put back on their shelves when finished with. It is also the house to a permanent collection of art objects, that can form or grace a wide range of displays, with their own internal eloquence and point. In the V & A's case, moreover, its library is the national collection of all book-type material relevant to art, and its role as a resource for survey shows, in painting and sculpture, is one of pre-eminence.

Now I am not implying, alas, that we have got Marinetti stored on wax or tape. (Will we, one day?). But we do have things that point in many ways; things that, in hardly any words, are capable of touching an allusive web. Often the nicest may be the least grand, and ephemera can tell more than great chefs d'oeuvre.

What I am trying to say is rather this. The viewpoint placed on illustration here has not been steered on the lines of "100 greats", although that concept may lurk not too far away. It is not scrutinising book-art peaks, as such, as though we all knew of what "book-art" consists. What we have looked for, especially, has been such things as tell us most straight out about the main creations of the artists concerned, and of other artists linked in a similar cast. It is about illustrations, yes, indeed it is. But it is also about styles, and the cross-links found in art. And it can be used for clues to which poets were read; which playwrights supported, what music, even, sometimes wound them up. Who befriended or perhaps loved whom. What dealers could prove good for; patrons too.

It must follow from this that we should rummage our way through such magazines as *L'YMAGIER* (1895; CAT. 11) as well as patting Dufy on the head for *BESTIAIRE* (1911; CAT. 27). For *L'YMAGIER* is just the sort of place where you come across all sorts of breaths of life, if you wanted to know who the Nabis or Symbolists were.

It is in such effervescent chronicles as *LACERBA*, (like the *TIMES* to the Futurist movement) that one still gets Marinetti in full torrent, along with the drawings, manifestoes, and articles of Carra, Severini, Soffici, Papini, Boccioni and the rest. The news from Paris is there told in French. From England, in English, is a piece by "Nevinson, Futurist."

It is in *DER STURM* (1915; CAT. 38) that one sees what a dealer can do to make his gallery artists better known; in *DIE ROTE ERDE* (1919; CAT. 53) one finds how a patron can support friends; in *MERZ* you get Schwitters, rat-tat-tatting away on his tin Dada drum. *Sic* (1917; CAT. 40) was the place where the concrete poet, Pierre Albert-Birot, would pass on Diaghileff's urgent and open appeal for avant-garde artists, like cubists and futurists, to come dress his ballets, with Depero's example enthusiastically quoted. In almost the very same issue he was publishing Apollinaire's most famous Calligramme "il pleut ...", plus the opening musical bars of *LES MAMELLES DE TIRÉSIAS* (Music by Madame Albert-Birot, play by the self-same Guillaume Apollinaire) where the concept of Surrealism first received its name. Yet what worked it in here was of course because Prampolini, Balla, and others, were illustrated right alongside.

All these can be excused, if there were reason, as rough stuff stopgaps owing to the War. But even when the palmier days came after, and grander books could once more be produced, the ties between poets and painters seemed tighter than ever. Particularly was this so in Paris, with the busy international movement of surrealists buzzing around Breton, Tzara, Eluard, Char, Crevel. In truth such links go back for ever, in Paris' tradition; to Baudelaire, the Goncourts, Hugo, Mallarmé; to Verlaine, Rimbaud,

RIGHT
ALFRED JARRY.
Caesar as Antichrist, drawing reproduced in *L'YMAGIER*, 1895 (Cat. No. 11).

17

18

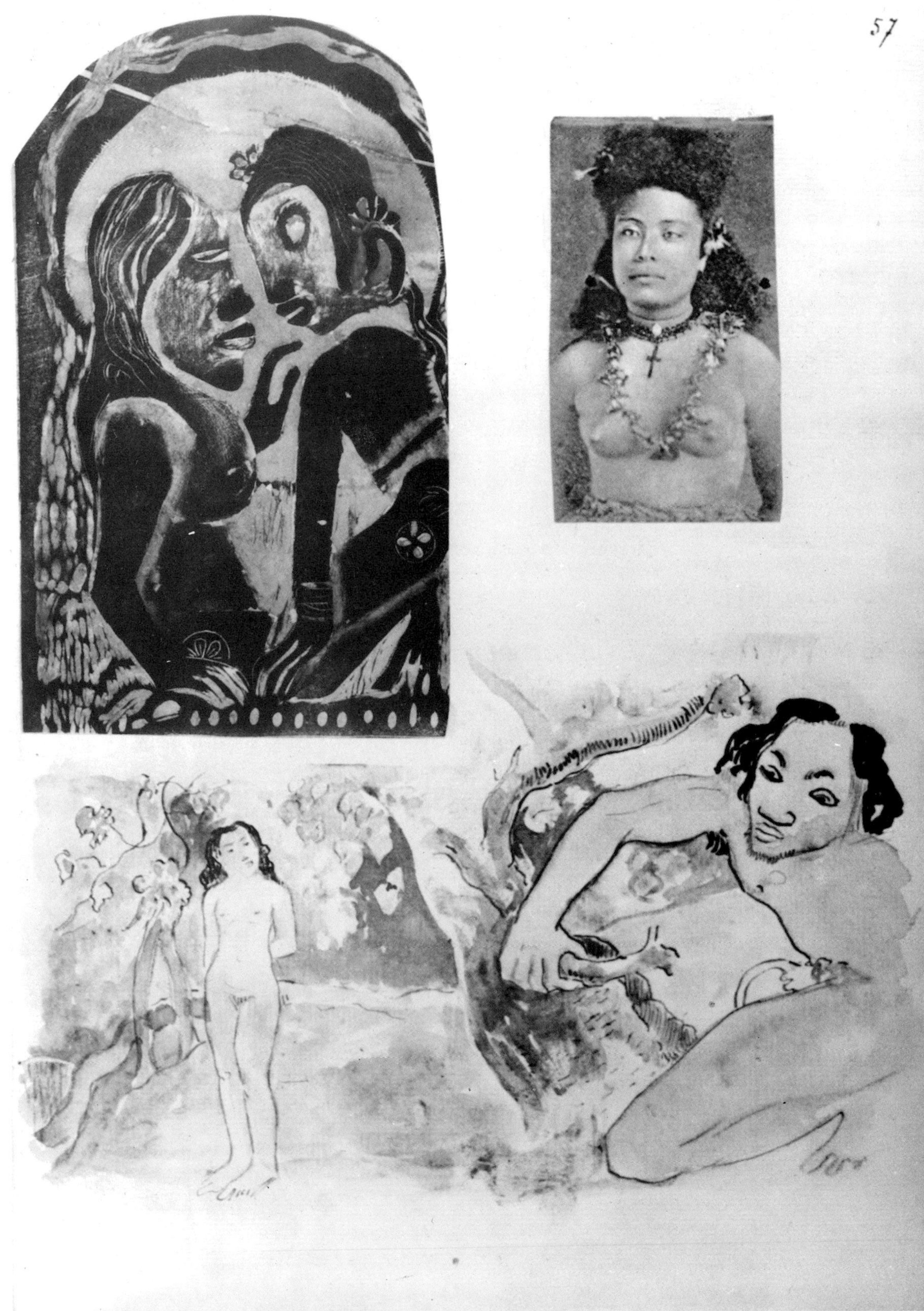

Jacob; to the ubiquitous lynchpin, Apollinaire. And all of them fed on each other, needed each other, poets singing painters painting poets; (like Moscow, maybe; less like London or Berlin).

It was Mallarmé, who had translated Poe, that got his buddy Manet to illustrate the Raven, after Manet had painted the poet's portrait – now in the Louvre. It was Mallarmé who also translated his buddy Whistler's famous *TEN O'CLOCK*. In turn this painter made a lithograph drawing of the poet, to front an edition of his *VERS ET PROSE*. Mallarmé gave then a copy to the painter, inscribed in these words "Whistler / Selon qui je défie/Les siécles, en lithographie." In the late 1880's Mallarmé had been planning to bring out a book of essays, which was to have had etchings in it by still other buddies, like Degas, Monet, Renoir, Berthe Morisot. How I wish he had succeeded in the plan! But out of it, alack, the only outcome was one etching, by Renoir, among his first, employed to front the poet's *PAGES* in 1891.

Still another friend was Odilon Redon, who used to send him suites of lithographs when they would come out. When he got his *SONGES*, at the end of that same year, he wrote Redon "You wave the plumage of Dream and Night in our silence. Everything in this album fascinates me, first and foremost that it is your personal vision, the issue of your *DREAMS* alone. O Lithographer and demon, these creations have a depth equal to your black drawings; and you know well, Redon, that I am jealous of your captions."

Mallarmé would say of Gauguin – who made a well-known etching of the poet, with a raven perched behind his head – "it is amazing to find so much mystery expressed with so much force." Gauguin treasured that tribute, and attached great importance to the etching. On the eve of his first trip to Tahiti, Mallarmé gave a dinner party for Gauguin at which the guests included Redon, Carrière, Ary Renan, and Paul Sérusier among the painters, with an equal number of writers, all of them Gauguin's fans. One of these, in turn, was Charles Morice, with whom he was to collaborate over his manuscript Noa-Noa (C.1898; CAT. 15). He gave Morice a copy of his etching, inscribed "Morice, I read him, I admire him, and I love him."

The case of Redon had in fact been a special interlock of writing and art. Almost his first set of lithographs, and among the most astonishing of all, had been dedicated to the American Edgar Allan Poe (1882). Huysmans – who featured Redon in his novel *A REBOURS*, 1884, set-piece for the age of decadence – wrote of Poe as Redon's crucial inspiration; "He (Redon) seems to have thoroughly thought over the consoling aphorism "everything which is certain is found in dreams", adding that it is there that we find the true source of this original creative spirit." A couple of years before, in 1882, Huysmans had reviewed the artist's work in *LE GAULOIS*, describing Redon as the poet of Satanism, an inspired but raving madman; and it was this review that brought the two together, leading to their friendship for some years.

LEFT
PAUL GAUGUIN.
Page from
NOA-NOA, c.1898,
(Cat. No. 15).

Redon later made a lithograph portrait of Huysmans' imagined hero, Des Esseintes, apparently intended as possible frontispiece for a special edition of the novel. When Huysmans saw it he thanked Redon for the image, correctly 'harsh and strange, drained of all energy, just as he should be." But he also pointed out that Redon's interpretation seemed to him more satanic, "more consumed by the occult sciences than my own..." leaving it open that Redon's had an equal force of truth.

His was a natural spirit to illustrate Baudelaire's dank *zeitgeist* in *LES FLEURS DU MAL,* and he made nine lithograph "interpretations" published as a suite in Brussels by Deman. He did frontispieces, again, for four books of contemporary symbolist poetry, also brought out by Deman, two written by Iwan Gilkin, a fervent Baudelaire fan, and founder of one of the major Belgian symbolists' reviews. Their titles were *LA DAMNATION DE L'ARTISTE,* 1890, and *TÉNÈBRES,* 1892. (The others were *LES SOIRS* and *LES DÉBÂCLES*, both 1888, and written by Emile Verhaeren). Commenting on the image he invented for Ténèbres, Gilkin admitted that his own imagination would not have been equal to Redon's splendid creation.

Verhaeren, among the most widely illustrated of all the symbolist poets, was articled to Redon's Brussels barrister/writer friend, Edmond Picard, for whose five-act play *LE JURÉ* (1886) Redon made a sequence of nine lithographic illustrations. Picard was equally editor of a Brussels review, *"L'ART MORDERNE",* where Redon had been given keen support. The play was not a drama for the stage, but written to be delivered as a monologue. The author indeed did exactly this, before its publication, reading it out in the lecture hall of Les XX, with Redon's lithographs hanging on the wall.

I could so easily just run on and on. I have yet to mention, outside contemporary poets, either his last album, the Apocalypse of St John, published by Vollard in 1899; his colour lithograph of Beatrice, also brought out by Vollard, included in the first *ALBUM DES PEINTRES-GRAVEURS*; or yet his long engagement with Flaubert, whose *TENTATION DE SAINT-ANTOINE* (1896; CAT. 13) provided the themes of three successive suites. Indeed, finally, I have not even referred to the fact that at the time of Mallarmé's death, Redon was working, at Vollard's invitation, on a set of lithographs based on the poet's *UN COUP DE DÉS JAMAIS N'ABOLIRA LE HASARD.* Four of the plates for this were even complete, and proofs of the text had been printed, under Mallarmé's supervision, in an irregular typographic format that attempted to express the rhythms of the poems. According to Aimé Maeght, the layouts of these proofs inspired the 1930 edition of Apollinaire's *CALLIGRAMMES* (CAT. 84).

But I have hurled all these tittle-tattles down, almost at random, mainly to establish this one point of underlying ground. It was to show that, in Paris certainly, the ties of painters with playwrights and with poets of the day were always strong. As Gauguin said, they read them, they admired them, and they loved them. And vice versa. It was two ways round. Thus we are not talking of a world of publishing directors, literary agents, or their go-betweens. Both sides, I was almost going to say, were friends; yet there were no sides, just simply there were friends. The liveliest reviews embraced the whole art scene – *ARTS, SPECTACLES,* everything.

So long as the projects were of fairly slight or, at least not too all-consuming involvements, there was never any lack of couples ready to dance, eager to pay each other compliments genuinely felt. It was Degas' friendship for Halévy and his admiration for his two successive books on the Cardinal family, that drew him to make the illustration sets (1880; CAT. 3) from pure affection, without even seeing them come out in print. And it was Gide who chanced to see, and so much liked, the drawings of Maurice Denis for Verlaine's poems *SAGESSE* (1889; CAT. 4) – long before Vollard would publish them – that he had to get Denis for his own *VOYAGE D'URIEN* (1893; CAT. 5).

However, there were two other pre-conditons that needed to be triggered, before it would become a wholly natural path for artists to embark on really ambitious books. They had to be made to get interested in making original prints, and see their true potential as a major medium. They needed perhaps to perceive not only the unlimited expressive effects they could achieve, but the sheer numerical scope for reaching a much wider, new, and popular audience.

During the 1890's there were all kinds of developments that began to make the print field quite lift off. One of them was the extension of colour lithography up to the size of posters in the street. Bonnard's success with *FRANCE-CHAMPAGNE* in 1889 is generally credited with having made every other artist warm to the idea – and no one more so than Toulouse-Lautrec. But Manet was the first to test the water with his toe, not only by making large-sheet colour lithographs, but in having a stab at a crude street-poster for the book *LES CHATS* (1870) to which he had contributed a couple of illustrations.

Covers for music sheets (like the record covers of today) were another huge area of expanding opportunity for artists to scatter their images in homes, and Lautrec, with Bonnard, did a number of these. In the long term, perhaps just as great in importance was the knockout effect that Gauguin's Tahitian woodcuts would have on the painters he had left behind, with their fierce and haunting doorway to primordial dreams. Short term, however, there was one other attractive bridge, of which we have already seen some clue. This was the scheme of publishing prints in sets as albums or portfolio suites. By these the artist gained a very much larger scope, in which more complex images could be arranged in sequences. And in this field Ambroise Vollard would make a decisive entry early on. Apart from Redon's Flaubert of 1896 (CAT. 13) already noticed, his first portfolio of lithographs in fact had been commissioned from Bonnard, under the title *QUELQUES ASPECTS DE LA VIE DE PARIS,* in the year before. These were followed by two mixed portfolios, without themes, in 1896 and 1897, just called *L'ALBUM DES PEINTRES-GRAVEURS,* plus further sets from Maurice Denis *(L'AMOUR),* Fantin-Latour, Vuillard *(PAYSAGES ET INTERIEURS)* and Redon *(APOCALYPSE).*

The first of the Albums included major prints, one each, by 22 artists, among them Bonnard, Munch, Denis, Redon, Renoir,

Rippl-Ronai (CF. CAT. NO. 12), Toorop (CF. CAT. 16) and Vuillard. The second, more ambitiously, but again one each inside, extended to 32 artists among whom were Cezanne, Lucien Pissarro (cf. CAT. 6,7), Puvis de Chavannes, Rodin (CF. CAT. 19), Shannon, Sisley, Toulouse-Lautrec, and Whistler. A third album was then planned but never completed, although individual plates were done by Cézanne (2), Chagall, Signac, and Vuillard (also 2). All this was highly effective spade-work in bringing painters to try graphic art.

At this point I am still referring to the period immediately leading up to 1900, when Vollard would bring out the first of his special *livres d'artistes*. He is said to have conceived the ambition to do books from seeing Lucien Pissarro's *QUEEN OF THE FISHES* (1894, CAT. 7). His Redon scoop took him a good long step forward, and he was soon pursuing a number of possible projects. I have already mentioned his plans for a Redon/Mallarmé, with his *COUP DE DÉS*... But he also wanted Vuillard to do for him another Mallarmé poem, Hérodias. Mallarmé was not sure his poem was quite right, and fussed for a long time over adding more. But at last he reckoned it was really finished, and wrote to Vollard from Valvins, on 12th May, 1898, "I am glad to know I am being published, *mon cher,* by a picture dealer. Dont let Vuillard leave Paris without having given you a favourable reply. Tell him, to encourage him, that I am pleased with the lengthened poem. For once this is true." A few days afterwards, unfortunately, Mallarmé died. His son-in-law refused to permit Vollard to go on with his plan, maintaining that the poem was still unfinished. Then he too died.

In Vollard's life such twists of fate were more or less standard. The significant phrase, that one can repeat with its date, 12th May, 1898, is "glad to know I am being published by a picture dealer." For that is the change that Vollard brought about. Before him, authors and artists fixed the deals; a willing publisher was simply found. After, as the concept slowly grew of having *livres de peintre* wholly intended to capture a pinnacle place, it would be ruled by the champion picture dealers and art publishers of Paris and Berlin making the moves, with just occasional breaks from individual artists wanting to go it on their own.

Vollard brought his first six out at one a year between 1900 and 1905, kicking off with the two Bonnards and his Rodin (CAT. 17-19). They did not sell well. Very few were sold indeed for many years. Yet neither had the print-portfolios, that ought to have prepared the general way. Vollard was not one to be discouraged. But he did take note that the lithographs did not go as he had hoped, and turned to less adventurous wood-engravings – which proved equally sticky.

The thing that we have to note is that it was not his way to impose his own idea of what the artists ought to illustrate. But he would interpose, and he would talk through with them, how it could be made into the big one. It was he who got Bonnard, after the Verlaine, to do a Longus, with over 150 original lithographs. He who persuaded Chagall to go for the Bible, after La Fontaine; encouraged Rouault to go on with his Miserere, Guerre; Segonzac

ABOVE
EDOUARD VUILLARD. Original lithograph after a self-portrait painting by Cézanne. In *CÉZANNE,* Paris, Bernheim-Jeune, 1914; texts by Octave Mirbeau and others.

Mare = ballerina

his Virgil; Denis, Thomas à Kempis; Emile Bernard first Baudelaire, then Ronsard, Homer, François Villon; Maillol would do for him a different Ronsard, after all those Virgils and Ovids he had done for Kessler & Co. It was Vollard talked Picasso, after Balzac, into working around Buffon; had Derain enjoy Petronius Arbiter, and La Fontaine too; brought Braque to come out with Hesiod as his ideal choice. And it was when all these classic challenges were under way that others like Albert Skira entered to persuade an Ovid from Picasso; make Derain try his hand at Rabelais, or Matisse do Ronsard. I shall presently come to comment on this list. For now, one must simply observe how many of the vehicles were either the earliest giants of French verse, or were Romans or Greeks. For a time of apparently rampant radical art, it glimmers a strangely peaceful spirit of soul.

Heights of this kind are of course much more in a line of descent from Burne-Jones' monumental Chaucer for the Kelmscott Press, 1893-96 (CAT. 9) where William Morris had been the one to play the towering dreamer, with Burne-Jones led to design almost 100 plates inside densely rich borders. And it may here be fair to remark that, seen among the eager symbolist painters of Brussels and Paris (where they had figured prominently in the 1889 Expo.), Burne-Jones, Watts, Rossetti, Hunt and Crane, were reckoned among the first to have found the Grail, and enjoyed a certain cult following. Yet after Morris' death the path of his successors here at home was much more to develop the practices of printing and fount-cutting, as arts in themselves. It led to a strong movement for the private press, addressed to antiquarian connoisseurs, and readers of straight books (CF. GILL, CAT. 89, 90). They aspired to high standards of publishing ideals under personal direction; but they were not geared to gamble, as were the French, on show-books dragged out of a network of individual specialist studios, heeding only a painter's inspirations, and aimed at the art-collector.

To an important extent, moreover, this genteel approach affected the German publishing scene up to 1933, where traditions of fine print had long been centred in places like Weimar, Dresden, Hanover, Leipzig, or Munich, and where the Berlin art market had a far less all-straddling eminence than that of Paris (CF. MAILLOL, CAT. 30). Indeed, in so-called normal times, many German art-collectors would as easily pass through Paris as they would Berlin.

However, now may be the moment to get back to Mallarmé. He died, as we were reminding ourselves, within the last days of the 19th century. But his poetry has certainly since lived on, without a break, as it still does. Matisse's first book for Skira was his Mallarmé. Dufy did the Madrigaux in 1920. Marcel Broodthaers did Un Coup De Dés Jamais N'Abolira Le Hasard in 1969 in his own inscrutable manner. Yet does this necessarily say anything more but that in our age the surrealists, over three generations, revived and adopted him as one of their patron-saints? I think it does. For this could be to mistake the whole way round things are. This would assume that what we call surrealism is modern and still goes; while what we may term symbolism was a brief, dead-end,

LEFT
GINO SEVERINI.
"Mare = Ballerina".
From *LACERBA*, Vol. II, 1914.

went-nowhere episode of decadence, that flowered at longest 1886 to 1898, then disappeared.

Yet no less possibly might one rather see that symbolism never died at all. And it lived on under various banner names, of which surrealism was merely the one most widespread, being least clear defined. Nor need we look at it as narrowly as Mallarmé. For Jarry after all, with his mad, maddening, grotesque Ubu Roi, lives just as irrepressibly. And Rouault, come to that, was actually one of them, paid-up, true; the prize and favourite pupil of Gustave Moreau, sometime keeper of the Moreau Museum, who showed in the 1890's in the Salon de la Rose + Croix, long before he hung his hat with the Fauves. In that light it must hit you smack in the eye that *MISERERE*, not seen till 1948 but actually worked 1916-1927, merely shows how Redon's world survived. And as to that, has Dine's *APOCALYPSE* of 1982 (CAT. 165) really come down to us out of anywhere else?

Ought we not admit moreover, at least to ourselves, how heavy is the debt of Derain's *L'ENCHANTEUR POURRISANT* (1909 CAT. 26) or Dufy's *BESTAIRE* (1911 CAT. 27) to Paul Gauguin some twenty years before, which yet pass off as twentieth century, new? Was not Matisse himself correctly called the leader of the *fauves* for the whole of his life, and was not his mind, too, first nurtured under that same Gustave Moreau, at the Ecole Des Beaux Arts, at the outset of the 1890's? Or take Max Ernst, who will be noticed illustrating Jarry and Terrasse (1971; CAT. 147) still young as ever in the 1970's. Although a key co-founder of the whole surrealist movement, and one of its continuing chief priests, to have called him by the name of symbolist would only ever have been taken by him as an honour.

It is important of course to be sure that a seductive impulse to plunge into decorating books is not of itself the mark of a particular cast of mind; that book-prone artists are not, per se, self-selecting, and as such distorting in a line-up of basic attitudes to art. So let us for a moment go back to some fundamental definitions, and then check the panorama of these pages through. For, does it reflect the true gamut of expressions, movements, streams that we could fairly expect within so tight a space? And how do the images fit, one with another? Do they exhibit a pattern of change that we can both observe and sense to be correct? Are there missing elements which could or certainly should have been worked in?

Writing in his book on Baudelaire, Emile Bernard defined the central creed this way. "What then was the end proposed by pictorial symbolism? The same as that proposed by literary symbolism; to unite form and content while at the same time raising the work of art to a level of transcendent idealism. The first aim was to imbue it with a spiritual content; expression came only second, a means and not an end itself, and for this reason was to be reduced to its simplest terms. Thus form and colour became the most important elements in a work of art. The artist's role was to reduce every form to its geometrical base in order to allow its mysterious hieroglyph to emerge more clearly... In contrast to the classic artists, the symbolists sought to find and emphasise the significant distortion."

And elsewhere Maurice Denis had this to say. "There can be no doubt that correspondences, which we may call pre-determined, exist between the forms and harmonies of line and colour on the one hand, and human emotions on the other. Puvis de Chavannes used to say that 'every clearly defined idea can be translated into a specific, plastic thought' – a fine expression of the symbolist doctrine! To disengage this plastic thought, to discover these correspondences – that is the purpose of art, the secret of style."

To me at least these stand as perfectly fair descriptions of a very large part of the concerns of art in our century, which on too close a view seem often conflicting – as though each new movement strove only to strangle and then blot out the last. And they have helped me to understand and perhaps vindicate certain decisions of choice that have had to be made.

For a start they help make clear what Post-Impressionism (never a mere movement, more a whole cross-sea) was all about. *MANET AND THE IMPRESSIONISTS* was the title of a book by Theodore Duret which was first to explain just what Impressionism meant. Roger Fry would use it as a sort of in-joke, as a banner for the first major exhibition in London of truly modern art, when he called his Grafton Galleries show, in 1910, *MANET AND THE POST-IMPRESSIONISTS,* thus coining the term. It did import Picasso and Matisse for the first time, but it was really all about Gauguin, Van Gogh, Cézanne; these were the real bombs, that brought the big release, and we still live in their wake. Post-Impressionism in fact was counter-revolution. It was art in the head. It was the opposite of trying to pin down what the eye takes in. Death to sunny rowboats! We should have dreams, not merely scenes to see.

Now the precise reign of Impressionism spanned from 1874 to 1886 when the Independent painters held their exhibitions as a group – exactly at the point that our survey picks up. They found plenty of ground-breaking excitement over their technical problems, and some were deeply dug into research. But as to their pursuit of subject matter, they were not book-worms. They read lily ponds of an afternoon; not Baudelaire at night.

So there was possibly a double reason why Mallarmé never quite managed to bring those essays out, with etchings by Monet and Morisot. He was the dreamer. They had thoughts of their own. Morisot would look at kids or ducks in the park. And it may be for exactly those same reasons that our book-run should find little to report between 1875, with Manet's *RAVEN,* and the verge of the 1890's. The Impressionists in short, at least in their prime, were not too heavy on the literature bit, just not their scene. Nor were they keen to take time off from oils.

Cézanne was one of the first to break away, from feeling disgust with their lack of formal gut, and it was Vollard who gave him his first ever one-man show soon after he opened his picture-shop in the Rue Laffitte in 1895. The first book Vollard wrote, himself, was on Cézanne, though after his death; and he did persuade him, as we saw, to come up with some stunning lithographs for his two albums. But an illustrated book he did not get. It is hard to believe that he should not have floated the idea, had he thought there was any chance of winning him. And it may be that the ex-Impressionist recluse was just too intent on staring at his mountain, or piling his nude bathers into cones to ever listen.

Of all the artists in our present array representing this century, only four or five at most are encountered caringly examining just exactly what it was they saw, and then perhaps converting it in line; Degas, Klimt, Segonzac, Giacometti; Sutherland, maybe, in his *BESTIAIRE:* Hockney in his *CAVAFY.* And even this can only be said with qualification. For the Klimt book is really a put-up job, albeit a sumptuous creation, as the first such work commissioned by the *WIENER WERKSTAETTE,* in which Klimt was so heavily involved; that is, his obsessive compulsion to draw direct from the nude was merely matched to a suitably clothes-off classical text. But in his actual work as colourist and painter, no one could be more of a symbolist, simon-pure, than Klimt. Just so Segonzac, out there with his copper-plate in the scorching fields of Provence, was consciously catching the light of Virgil's Tuscany, and not being merely accurate, more looking for the true. Even Giacometti seems more intent to register the sheer appalling difficulty of drawing what one sees than quietly to pull off a document.

For the rest it is all a world of the imagination, of invention, of feeling; descriptions how the heart and not the eye perceives. Heading the way away from a literal vision, toward a purely abstract one where figuration has been blinkered out, the book trail is particularly clear. Flip over Craig (1907, CAT. 22) the two Kandinsky's (1909, 1913, CAT. 25 and 31), then Malevich (1919 CAT. 47) and Lissitsky (1922, CAT. 67), and we have it all stepped out for us in images that seem to tell it all. We even, in Van Doesburg (1923, CAT. 71), find it diagrammatically set out as to who got first to appreciate the plain square, with just the primary colours, viz he himself, Van Doesburg, with his buddies in De Stijl, like Mondrian. And then we get a shot of Mondrian's admirer Ben Nicholson (1935 CAT. 102) juggling near-circles and near-squares; and even a late children's book by Bart Van Der Leck, (1941, CAT. 109) lightly enlivened in flat red, yellow and blue, written by hand in a kind of curive script. But the cursiveness, too, is strictly selling De Stijl. Like Mondrian's drawings of waves and trees from 1914, every stroke is either horizontal, upright, or else at 45°. No curves – where Hogarth said all beauty lay – it strikes an unreal, ideal note.

However, the question still remains as to how we should read all this. Imagine Lissitsky's Two Squares immediately beside any Moreau painting of your choice. The Moreau is so detailed, complexly invented, full of jewelled glimmers in a dark nineteenth century dream world. The Lissitsky is so absolutely clear, sharp, drained of every reference to our paltry life; so geometrical, abstract, twentieth century, new. Surely the two are truly poles apart, as different as a runny camembert from chalk. No?

RIGHT
Pages from *SIC,* May 1917, (Cat. No. 40).

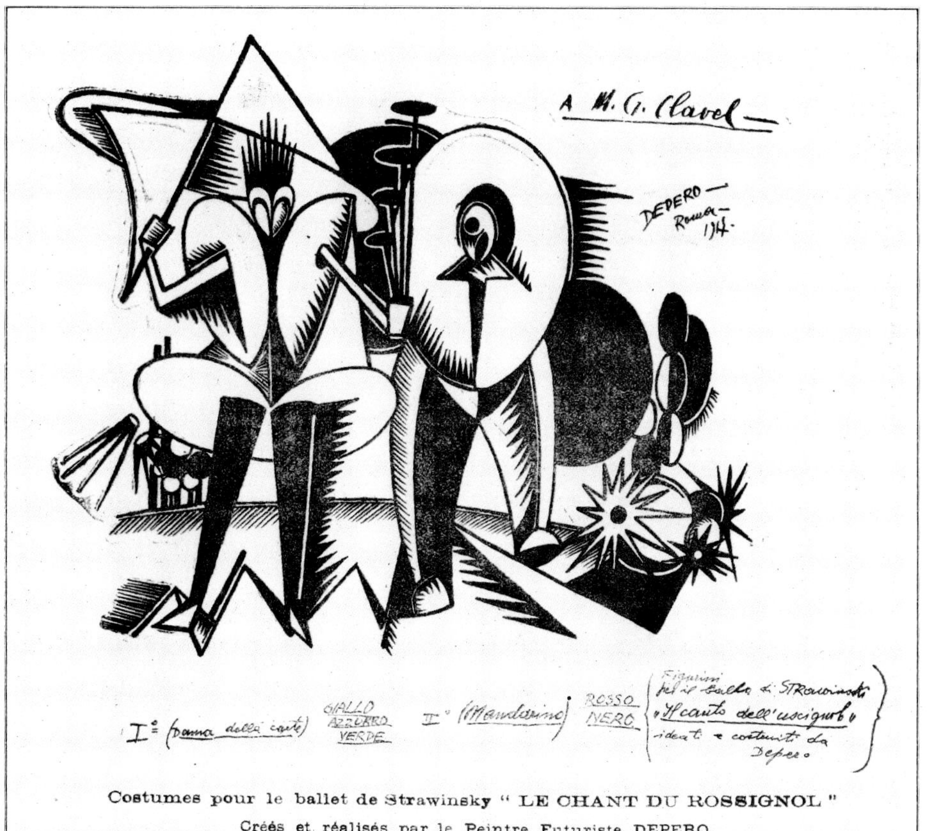

Costumes pour le ballet de Strawinsky " LE CHANT DU ROSSIGNOL "

Créés et réalisés par le Peintre Futuriste DEPERO

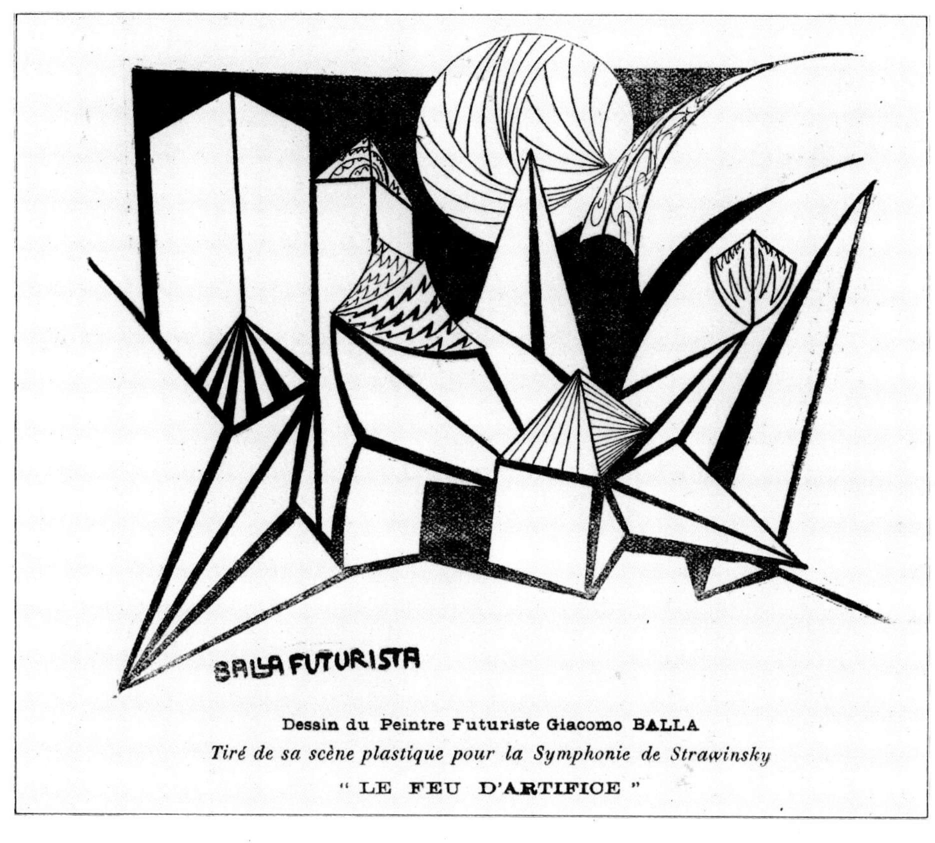

Dessin du Peintre Futuriste Giacomo BALLA

Tiré de sa scène plastique pour la Symphonie de Strawinsky

" LE FEU D'ARTIFICE "

But supposing a little label told us that Lissitsky was a well-known symbolist. Then that might be different. It might also, possibly, just make truer sense. For the Kandinsky-Malevich-Lissitsky path was indeed a trek away from the past. But it was equally a determined quest for a purity that should *transcend* the past, be transcendental. That was what made it so exciting an idea to the Russian constructivist movement; that riddance of all old bogus bourgeois mental gear. Rubbish! Impurities! Away! Have none of them! Passeist filth, like Lewis said in *BLAST.*

What then about the expressionist movement, which was running much at the same time, and certainly features strongly in the book? Am I saying these were crypto-symbolists too? Well, yes, why ever should I not? Klinger predicts them (1881, CAT. 2) Gauguin's woodcuts, Rousseau's *GUERRE* (1895, CAT. 11) plainly foreran them; Ensor straddles them (1911, CAT. 29). It is true, and even fortunate, that when I look in my own shaving mirror of a morning, I do not see anything very closely resembling Schmidt-Rottluff's *DER HEILIGE* (1919,CAT. 53). But I do recognise the spiritual image. And I notice the significant distortion which makes it a specific plastic thought. In the same way, in his *O EWIGKEIT DU DONNERWORT* (1918, CAT. 45) Kokoschka tells us gravely what his mirror told, for frontispiece. But the rest of his images are much more of a hymn to his personal spiritual life with Alma Mahler, which spoke in music and transcended words.

So cubism? = Synthetism? = Symbolism too? Quite definitely!

Flattening out the planes; making outlines sing; I should just say it absolutely was. What could be more transcendant then Laurens' figure drawing in *LES PÉLICAN* (1921, CAT. 63)? No realism there, but all conceptual, the way it will be tommorow. Then why did Picasso himself just drop all that, so all of a sudden?

It has often been a matter of comment that after all the baffling, well-nigh impenetrable obscurity of his analytical cubist phase he should suddenly have come out all classical, immediately after the war; that is classical in the sense of those colossal pink nudes, those short, blowing, 'classical' drapes. After the obscurity, the new figures seemed so blissfully recognisable, that everyone read them as a complete reversal of course. And yet, was it such really? *Were* those nudes portrayed as real, or realistic? Were they not monumental, plastic thoughts, exploring harmonies of line and coloured form? Little to do with flesh, or blood; nothing to do with bone? They do not resemble, certainly, very closely any ladies I have seen walking around in the streets, even with my George Grosz' gimlet x-ray eye, (1921, CAT. 60) or even Beckmann's so-called *SACHLICHKEIT* (1918, CAT. 44). And I have always rather had to suppose they were part of our transcendental Disneyland that comes out of Homer, Hesiod, Theocritus, Ovid, Longus, Virgil... real in the sense that Dante is real, or super-real. At least I have found that a help to perceive Picasso's *METAMORPHOSES,* Matisse's *PASIPHAÉ,* or Derain's *SATYRICON* (CAT. 91, 112 and 100) in terms which keep their direction forward-pointed, still in the modern wave.

As to the surrealists, from 1922 to 1985, I have already said a certain amount about their case, and shown how close their poets

RIGHT
Cover for the broadsheet *SIC,* May, 1917 (Cat. No. 40).

SONS
IDÉES
COULEURS
FORMES

Pierre ALBERT-BIROT, Directeur

DANS CE NUMÉRO :

BALLETS RUSSES

Cubistes et Futuristes

Livres parus et à paraître.

Px 0,30
Étranger 0,45
Parait une fois par mois

Adresser tout ce qui concerne
la Revue
37, Rue de la Tombe-Issoire. — Paris.

(SIC suspend ses réunions du mardi.)

N° 17
Mai 1917
Deuxième Année

and painters were in being all part of one movement. Few things could demonstrate this more vividly than Man Ray's Eluard (1937, CAT. 104) where it was in fact Eluard's poems that were written as illustrations to the artist's drawings. They were done in that order. He was drawing in words what Man Ray's lines had already expressed – but I find myself confused as to which of them should be called poet.

We may meet indeed constant reminders of that aphorism quoted from Huysmans earlier on "everything which is certain is found in dreams." To the surrealists "found objects" were "ready-made" sculptures, suffused with an ineffable mystery as to quite what they expressed, according to perceptions of the artist that might/might not be shared. In this spirit Ernst's collages, recycling strange compôtes of 19th century wood-engravings, scissored with wit and will, create utterly astonishing images which everyone now has on board, in their own minds, as one epitome of twentieth century art... like Monty Python. (1922, 1930, CAT. 66 and 86).

From here moreover it is only a short theoretical step to observe that recent pop artists' interest in comics, sci-fi, or kinky magazines (CF. EDUARDO PAOLOZZI, 1962, CAT. 133 OR ALLEN JONES, 1977, CAT. 158) is exactly the same search. It is seeking to find those "ready-made" expressions of genuine, formerly hidden, popular fantasy dreams.

So, Symbolists again, quite definitely! Even the great American abstract expressionists at the end of the late war, with their wristy gestures, Gorky, Pollock, Tobey, Twombly – pure surrealist automatic writing; painting through the spiritualists' "other side." (CF. MOTHERWELL, 1982, CAT. 164 CF. FRANCIS, 1964, CAT. 135) while Rauschenberg (1972-78, CAT. 151) is even more overtly surreal, a looker-out for plate-print ready-mades, that offer connections into mysteries. Conversely, the especial daring of Johns' American flags, and Warhol's soup tins, was precisely to treat what had *no* mystery. However, I am going, there, a bit too fast. Our run contains good flags for Dada – with Janco, Picabia, Schwitters (1916-1919, CAT. 39, 41 and 52); and also some for *art autre* and *l'art brut* – Wols, Dubuffet (1948-1950, CAT. 118, 119 and 122). Each of these appeared at the end of a ghastly war and was strongly nihilistic in attack. It may seem to require just as strongly jesuitical a twist to think of these as transcendental or ideal. And yet that is the very point. For as T.S. Eliot once pointed out, to be a blasphemer is to declare one's faith.

Schwitters spluttered in rage at any cant. Pretending man's spirit was tall seemed to him rubbish, as it did to Dubuffet and Wols. Schwitters would rather make something from tram-tickets and gum than the oils of the masters; yet he nonetheless found form among the mess, and gave it order, not to mention a "found" colour, or a substance "ready-made." To Wols too, in his own way, the Louvre seemed irrelevant; life had to be fought in loneliness, without example. While to Dubuffet the walls of urinals in Montparnasse were where to find what man can discard (including "form", colour, or any emotional depth) and still discern the obscene hieroglyphs; mindless; mysterious; inconsequent; pulsing; actual. Significant distortion, could it have been? Or an undistorted portrait, raw, of insignificance?

Few now would dispute Dubuffet's place as one of the most important artists anywhere in the world (painter *and* sculptor) to have come to prominence after the second world war. *LES MURS* at its moment of appearance defiantly pissed on the whole world of high art, as much as on society at large. In retrospect, his challenge did not smirch the real Parisian giants in any way – Matisse, Picasso, Braque, Miro, Léger, Rouault, Laurens, Chagall, perhaps de Stael – who were then all in a very high peak form. In today's climate of general opinion, however, its comparison of impact seems to eclipse utterly an entire later generation of variously tasteful French artists, which has not been given a place in our selection. I do not pretend that this is anything but arbitrary. There were more French major *livres d'artistes* produced in the 1950's and 1960's than at any other time. Our Library certainly holds by far most of that date. But one has to say that it has also been far more exposed, and is thus more familiar. And the bald truth is that after *JAZZ*, *MISERERE*, and *LES MURS*, just anything that followed was doomed to be a terrible anti-climax. It is for this reason that after our second Braque, of 1962, (CAT. 132) our main attention swung to London and the U.S.A., where not only new artists, but new graphic studios prepared to try book projects, were reaching the fore. It coincided moreover with the advent of Pop Art, on both sides of the Atlantic, as a new and warming Gulf Stream current of the times.

I am in fact only too conscious of many fine works that are not here, although in our collection. There has not been room to show more than a part. Even more am I keenly aware of whole large general tendencies of art, important in our time, that have taken book form, yet that are not represented in these pages by even one sign.

By the time that our picture reaches the 1980's it becomes increasingly difficult to claim an on-going stream of like-with-like original graphic images that offer a mirror to contemporary painting in any traditional sense, while at the same time interpreting/illuminating some outstanding literary text. It would need an utterly different survey to take in the book-pieces of minimal and conceptual art; happenings; land art; art-language; those huge areas for which film and photography are the major tools. As to the various new waves using actual canvas, actual (acrylic) paint, it is by no means sure they are going to tie in significantly to book forms. And if they did, it must be highly improbable that it will be de luxe editions. It may be that once again it will be on magazines that a Library must concentrate its watch. Of course as the leaders reach maturer years themselves, they tend to become more interested in meeting classic challenges – like Dine and his Apocalypse; Motherwell wrestling an angel of personal apotheosis. And these may go on. But as to the tokens planted here to point the (tentative) way towards 2000, I will only offer comment on these three.

We have put in the Clemente, for example, to bear a flag for a whole new painting wave, of a mohican kind if you like, with a large following among the younger artists. What is perhaps of particular interest here, to me at least, is the form of publication of his book. He has taken the care to have it printed in India (as he has done with others), wanting to get a particular, common quality of plain-dyed cloth in open weave; and a particular feel of colour-reproduction on leaded paper one no longer finds elsewhere. He has wanted its images to embody the essential spirit of his painting, which he has used to interpret a poem by a cultural hero (Allen Ginsberg). And he has chosen all this to be far more direct, and controlled, than a piece of *original* graphics. It is brought out, too, not by his own dealer gallery or other commercial backer, but by a Kunsthalle, at low cost, in a limited edition of over 1,000 copies to be launched at the time of his paintings' exhibition. That is a scale of limitation absolutely not designed to catch the fastidious, fat-wad collector. It is rather aimed at the maximum practical number of the Kunsthalle's genuine audience visiting the show, and amounts to an orchestrated form of participation, encouraging a sort of collective, share-owning sponsorship-cum-artistic expression.

Lastly, a curious common link can be seen between two of the most recent works, the Long (167) and the Kiefer (160). Anselm Kiefer's work as painter has achieved some familiarity in London through a major retrospective at the Whitechapel Gallery in 1981-82 (where Clemente equally showed in 1983), and being given a leading position in "A New Spirit in Painting" at the Royal Academy, some months earlier. But it is possibly not so well known that books have been a special vehicle for his expression, and his show at the Kunsthalle, Berne, in 1978, gave equal place to his books as to his canvases.

Ingrid Sischy said of him (Artforum, 1981) "Kiefer's books and paintings always express both cultural history and art-history as open-ended, unstable and continuously renewed. These two histories operate simultaneously in this artist's work; the topographical markings on these pages are as likely to be outlines of a painter's palette as they are cedar growth-rings; the light on the characters' faces is as much a fact of photography as it is a reflection of the pessimism inherent in Mesopotamian stories, in which heroes depend on kisses or curses from the gods; and the paths and trees represent comtemporary pastoral pictures of what may be the woods near Kiefer's country house (or even woods brought in for studio set-up shots) as much as they construct the outer bounds of earth and reality."

In the present work (CAT. 160) his photographs play on water welling in a spit of courtyard floor, with fallen leaves, which he perceives and presents as a metaphor for the Danube's spring that will trickle away into streams like veins in a leaf. This in turn is a piece of referential autobiography, for he himself was born in Donaueschingen (where the river is continuingly born), at the heart of Charlemagnes's old empire where Rhine and Danube almost, almost join. These obscure personally resonant images

LEFT
Colophon to *THE ECLOGUES OF VERGIL,* (English Edition) Cranach Press, Weimar, 1927 (Cat. No. 30). The book carried a dedication from Count Harry Kessler, founder of the Press "In Sincerest Gratitude to the Master of Book-Printing/The Friend & Adviser of William Morris/Emery Walker." The colophon shows the kinds of care lavished on such productions, and indicates some of the links between English, German, and French traditions of fine printing.

COUNT HARRY KESSLER *planned the format of this volume.* ARISTIDE MAILLOL *designed and cut on wood the forty-three illustrations, during the years* 1912-1914 *and in* 1925, *at* Banyuls *in the* Pyrenees. He *drew on his immediate neighbourhood and on his personal acquaintances for certain of the motives of his illustrations.* Eric Gill *cut the head-line of the title-page of the* Eclogues (German *edition*) *in* 1914, *the lettering on the circular press-mark in* 1924, *and all the initial letters* (*white on black*) *except those on pp.* 74 *and* 75. T*he ornament of these letters was designed and drawn by* Maillol. T*he head-line of the title-page of the* Eclogues *for the* English *edition was cut by* Eric Gill *in* 1927. *Aristide* Maillol *cut the decoration on the title-page and the press-mark. Edward* Prince *cut the punches for the type, under the supervision of* Emery Walker. T*he roman type was cut after that used in* Venice *by* Nicolas Jenson *in* 1473. T*he italic type was designed by* Edward Johnston. T*he paper was made by* Gaspard Maillol, *in a workshop set up for that purpose at* Monval *near* Marly. It *was made by a special hand-process, devised in joint research by* Count Harry Kessler *and* Aristide *and* Gaspard Maillol.

Printing *of the* German *edition was begun on the hand-presses of the* CRANACH PRESS *at* WEIMAR *early in* 1914. T*he work was interrupted by the* Great War. It *was resumed in* June 1925. T*he* English *edition was printed in* 1927.

Count Harry Kessler *and* J. H. Mason *supervised the work of setting the type and printing.* Compositor: Walter Tanz. Pressmen: Erich Dressler (*killed in the* War), H. Gage-Cole, *and* Max Kopp. Assistant: Erich Hillhof. *Published in* England *for the* Cranach Press *by* Emery Walker Limited, 16 Clifford's Inn, London, E.C.

have here been bound together as a book, by his own hand, presenting a work both by and on himself, much in the way that Kirchner decorated Grohmann's view about *his* work (CAT. 74). Only 25 copies of this book were made, each of which Kiefer bound in a different range of natural materials like sand or tree-bark. . . inherently unstable, of a renewable kind.

That link I mentioned with Richard Long (167) is the same conceptual scene; a comparable use of photographs in both their works, elsewhere; but another river. For his "Two Mud Hand Prints" have not just been made casually, in any old mud; nor are they a cynical custard-pie being flung in our face. His prior work tells us this is Avon mud, real silt scooped up from the Avon Gorge. It is mud washed down by a river wending all the way from England's sleepy heart, passing meadows like Anne Hathaway's, lapping breasts of swans. It is mud that he has whelped into his hands, like a motionless moment of river, then set down neatly onto a clean page; his mark; and in this way *his* river.

They are not of course "original graphic" prints in the sense that we were using earlier on. But they do constitute an original, highly graphic work by a still young sculptor of the very foremost rank. It is he above all others (almost single-handed – as one might be tempted to pun) who has made us see our land in a new way qua subject for art; and who has given us so intent a consciousness of the expressive traces left, through time, by stone and bronze-age man.

Now I believe that what I was trying to lay the ground to say, a little earlier, was on this line. The obsessive interest that modern artists focused on primitive art at the beginning of this century was a quest for ready-made mystery, an access to the bonds of human emotion that can be communicated from somewhere quite outside our immediate society. Bernard found it in the peasants of Brittany at Pont Aven – surronding him but of another world. Gauguin wanted and found it even more in Tahiti. Picasso looked and found it in African masks at the Trocadero; Moore in Egyptian and Aztec figures in Bloomsbury. Yet as much as anything what they hoped to find was a way of dealing not only with spiritual electricity but with that other great dimension of experience, which is time.

It was time of course that fussed the futurists so into trying out tricks. It was time that kept Duchamp's lady nude so infernally long in descending that staircase – really it is taking her for ever. But is it not quite something that instead of just working in oil, in plaster or bronze, one can work in Ovid! Hesiod! Homer! Hey, now that is some time! Moreover, just like the masks, it is already there beside us, in the energetic painting of Greek pots, in their still, ideal sculptures from the nude. No wonder Picasso found them such an open field.

So maybe our specially book-prone artists, putting aside their canvas for a while and choosing a page, have been drawn to elect the most monumental of all scales open to literate art, and not the slightest; the form that may travel furthest, touch widest, and that could just possibly even last the longest, if we continue to read...

THE COLOUR PLATES

FROM·MANET
TO·HOCKNEY
MODERN ARTISTS' ILLUSTRATED BOOKS

1. EDGAR DEGAS: c.1882.
Ludovic Halévy, LA FAMILLE CARDINAL. CAT.3

2. CAMILLE PISSARRO: 1893. *TRAVAUX DES CHAMPS*. CAT.6

3. JOZSEF RIPPL-RONAI: 1895. *Georges Rodenbach, LES VIERGES.* CAT.12

4. OSKAR KOKOSCHKA: 1908. *DIE TRAEUMENDEN KNABEN.* CAT.24

5. WASSILY KANDINSKY: 1913. *KLÄNGE*. CAT.31

6. KAZIMIR MALEVICH: 1919. *Nikolai Punin, FIRST CYCLE OF LECTURES.* CAT.47

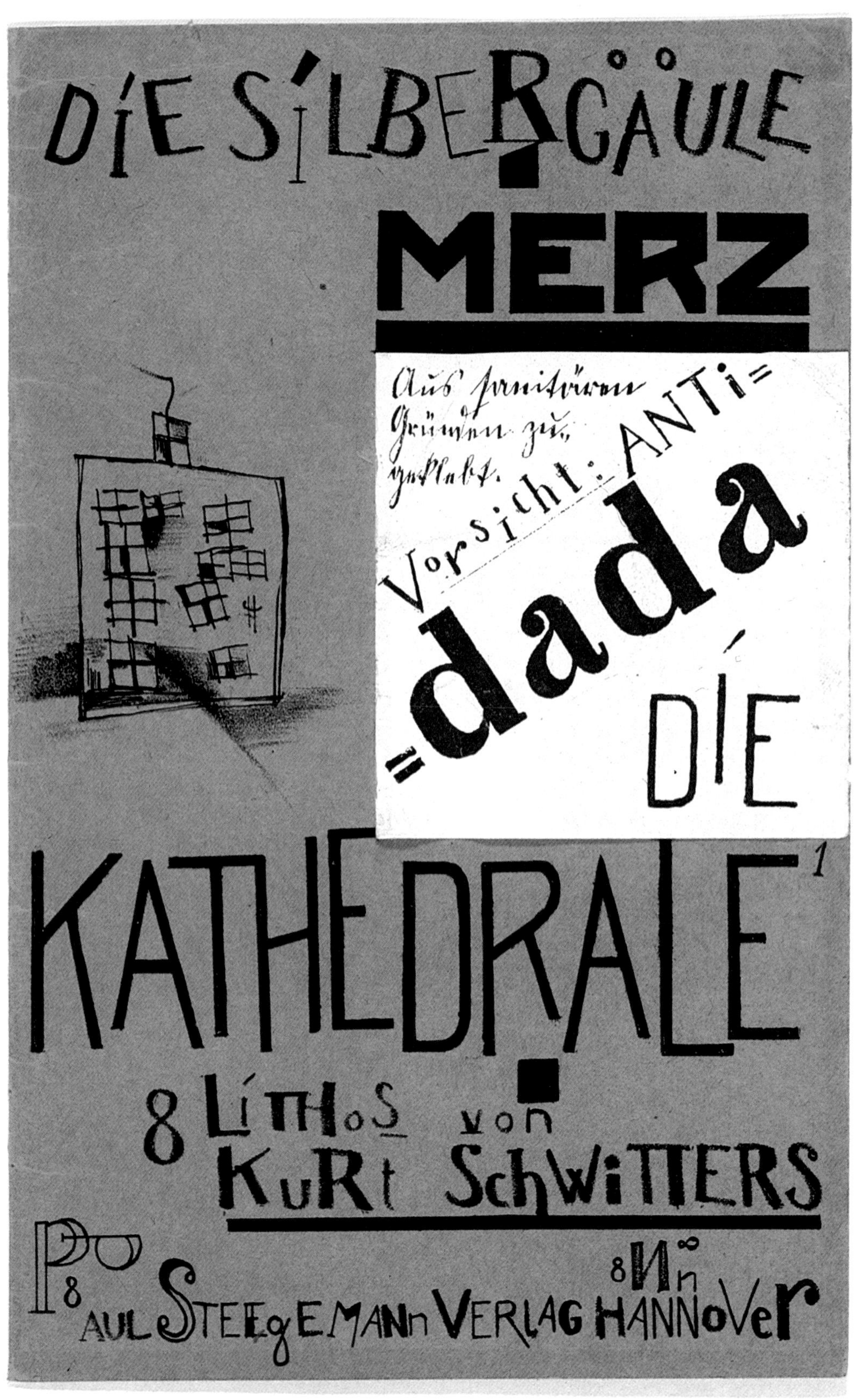

7. KURT SCHWITTERS: 1919. *DIE KATHEDRALE.* SEE CAT.52

8. NATALIYA GONTCHAROVA: 1919. *Valentin Parnak, L'ART DÉCORATIF THÉÂTRAL MODERNE.* CAT.48

9. FERNAND LEGER: 1919. *Blaise Cendrars*, *LA FIN DU MONDE, FILMÉE PAR L'ANGE N-D*. CAT.54

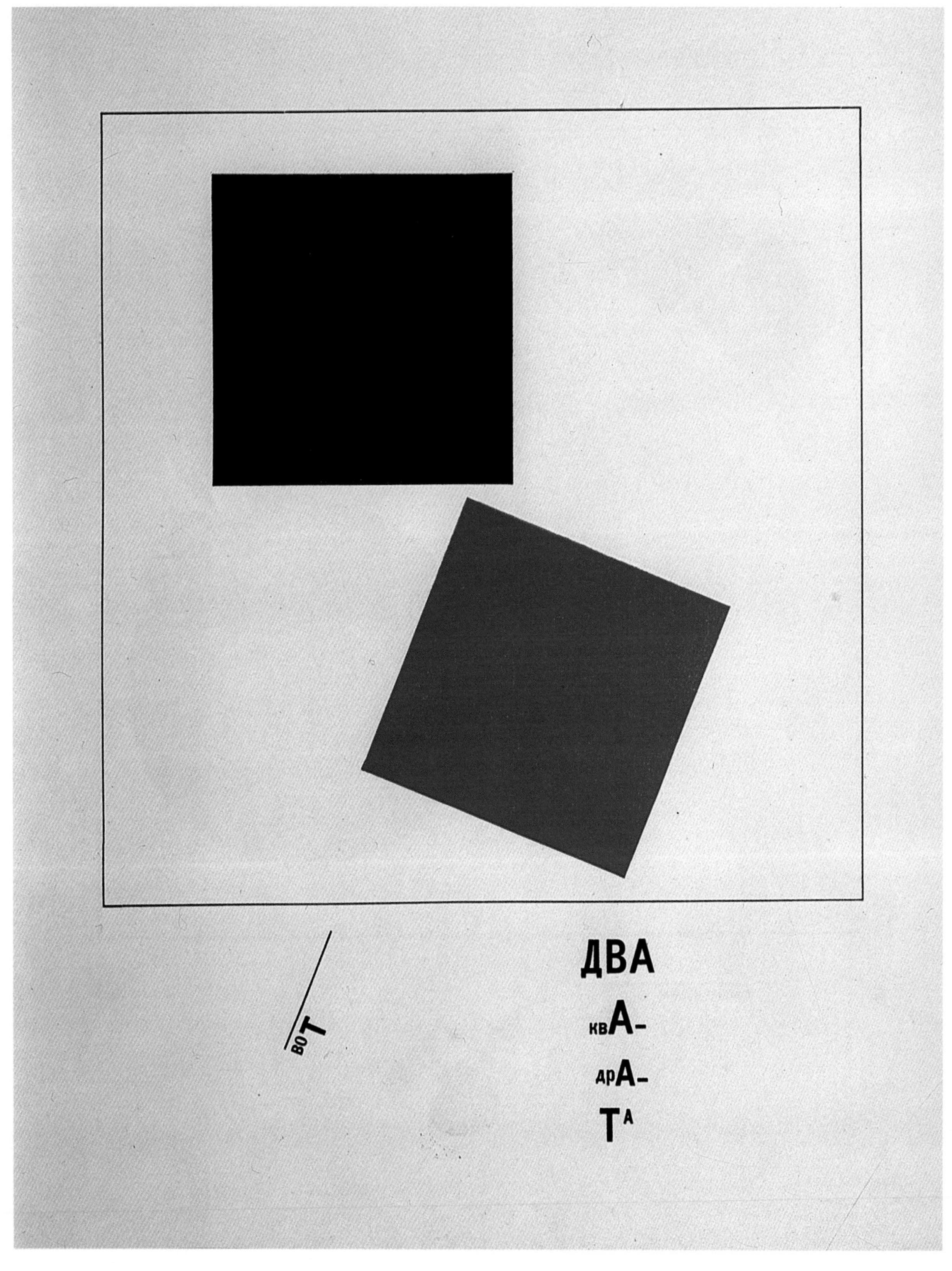

10. EL LISSITSKY: 1922. *THE SUPREMATIST A TALE OF TWO SQUARES.* CAT.67

11. EMIL NOLDE: 1926. *Gustav Schiefler, DAS GRAPHISCHE WERK VON EMIL NOLDE, 1910-25.* SEE CAT.28

12. GEORGES ROUAULT: 1936. *CIRQUE DE L'ETOILE FILANTE.* CAT.103

13. ANDRE DERAIN: 1943. *François Rabelais, LES HORRIBLES . . . FAICTZ . . . DU TRÈS RENOMMÉ PANTAGRUEL.* CAT.111

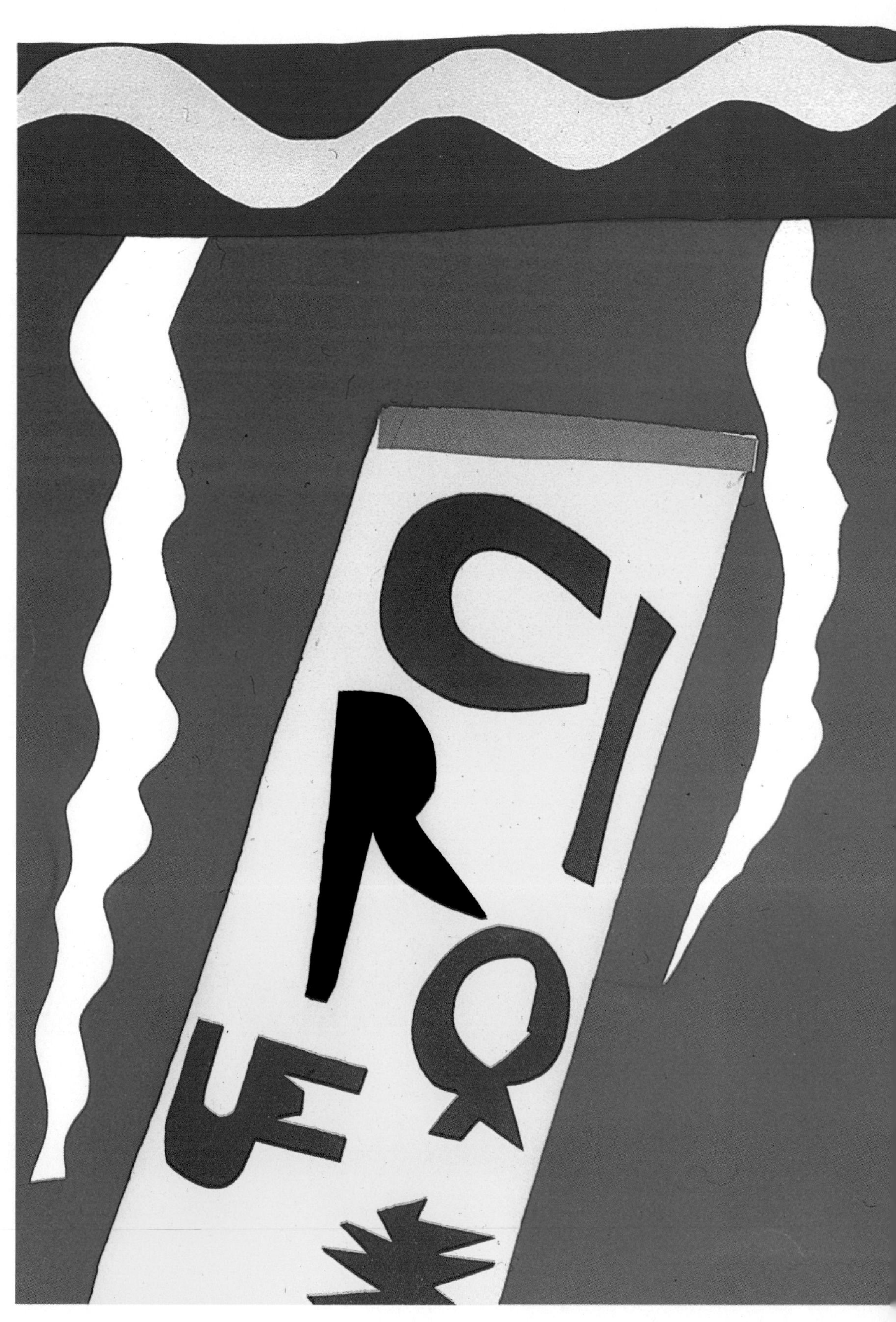

14.
HENRI MATISSE:
1947.
JAZZ,
Plate II, Le Cirque.
CAT.114

CIRQUE

15.
HENRI MATISSE:
1947.
JAZZ,
Plate X,
l'enterrement de Pierrot.
CAT.114

16.
JOAN MIRO: 1949
Paul Eluard,
A TOUTE
EPREUVE.
CAT.121

PAUL ELUARD

A TOUTE ÉPREUVE

GÉRALD CRAMER
Genève

17. HENRY MOORE: 1950. *Goethe, PROMETHÉE.* CAT.124

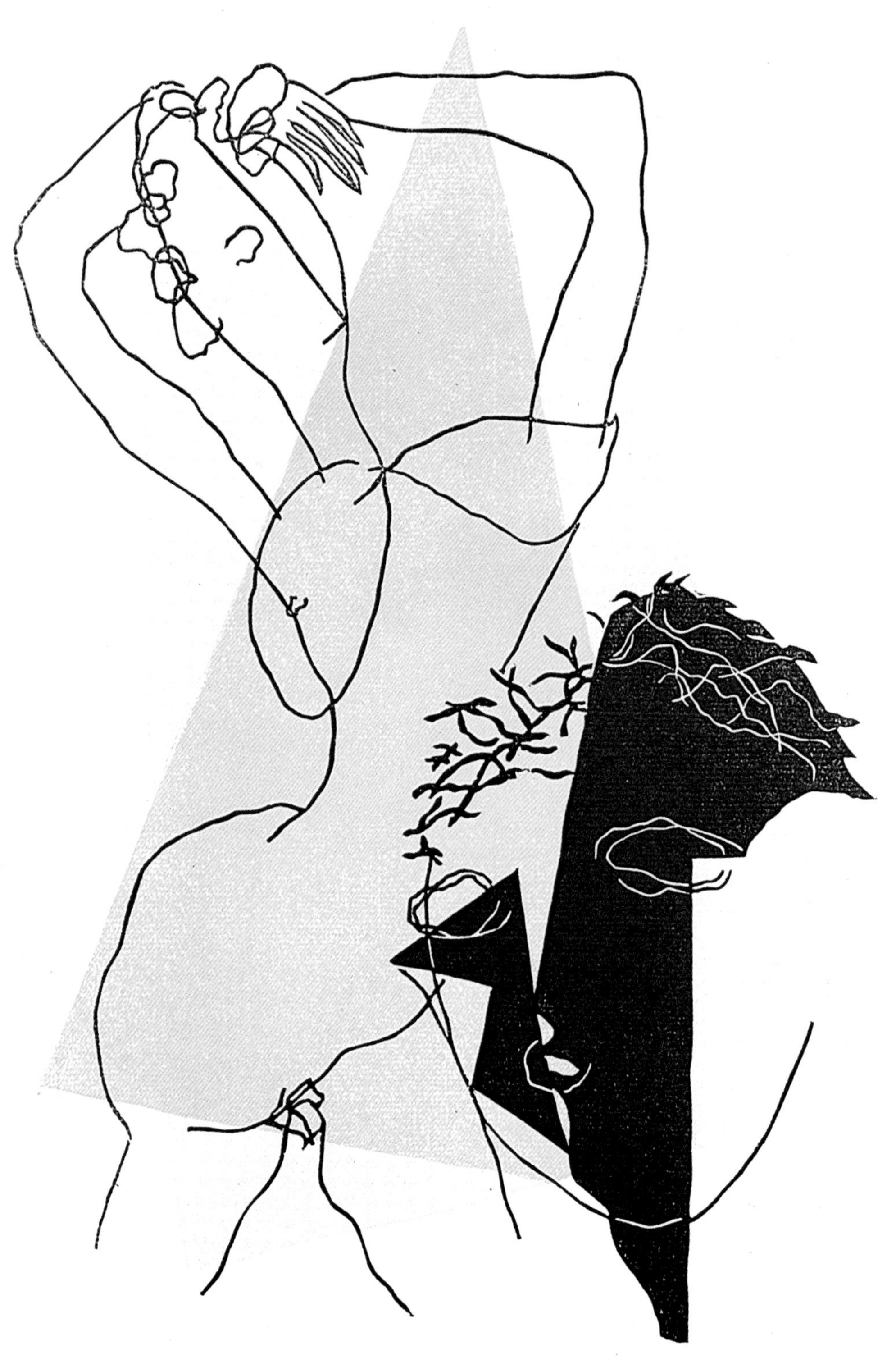

18. HENRI LAURENS: 1951. *Lucian, DIALOGUES*. CAT.125

19.
ANDY WARHOL:
1959.
WILD
RASPBERRIES.
CAT.130

Piglet

Contact Trader Vic's and order a 40 pound suckling pig to serve
5. Have Hanley take the Carey Cadillac to the side entrance
and receive the pig at exactly 6:45. Rush home immediately and
Place on the open spit for 50 minutes. Remove and garnish with
fresh crabapples.

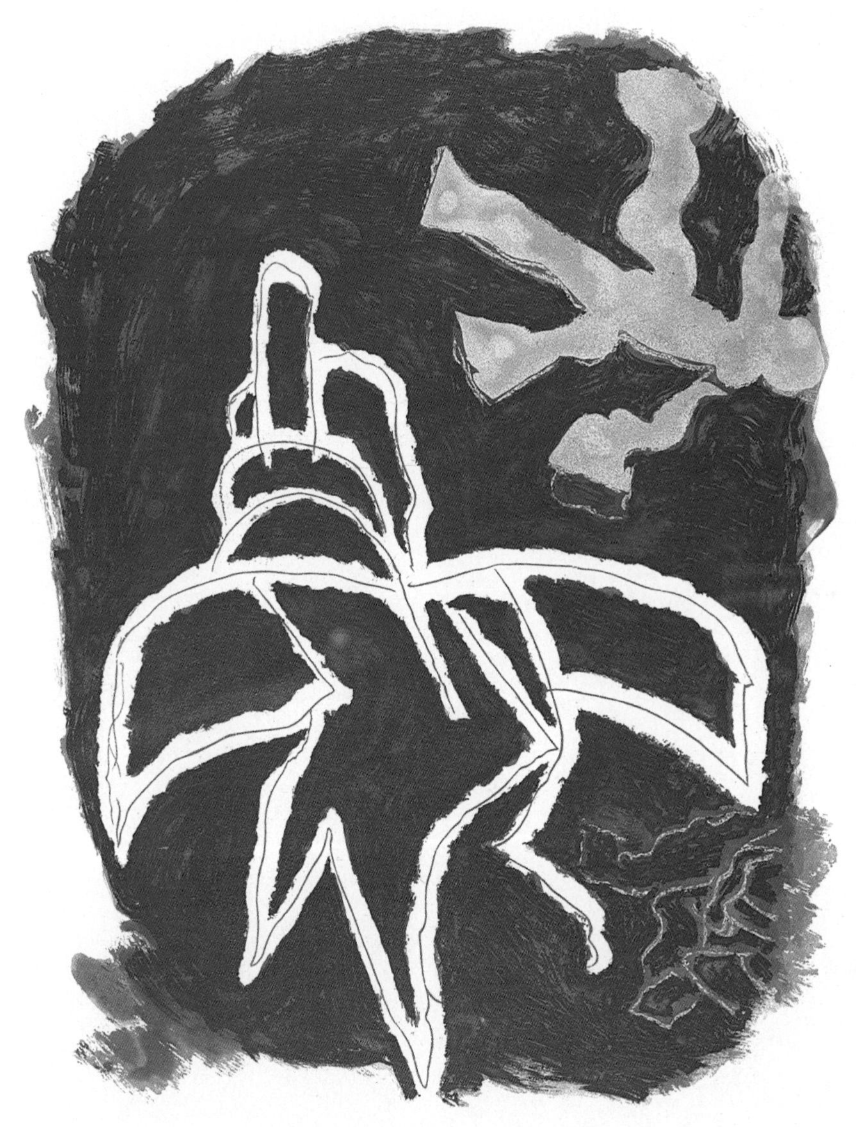

20. GEORGES BRAQUE: 1962. *Georges Braque and St. John Perse, L'ORDRE DES OISEAUX.* CAT.132

21. MARINO MARINI: 1963. *IDEA E SPAZIO*. CAT.134

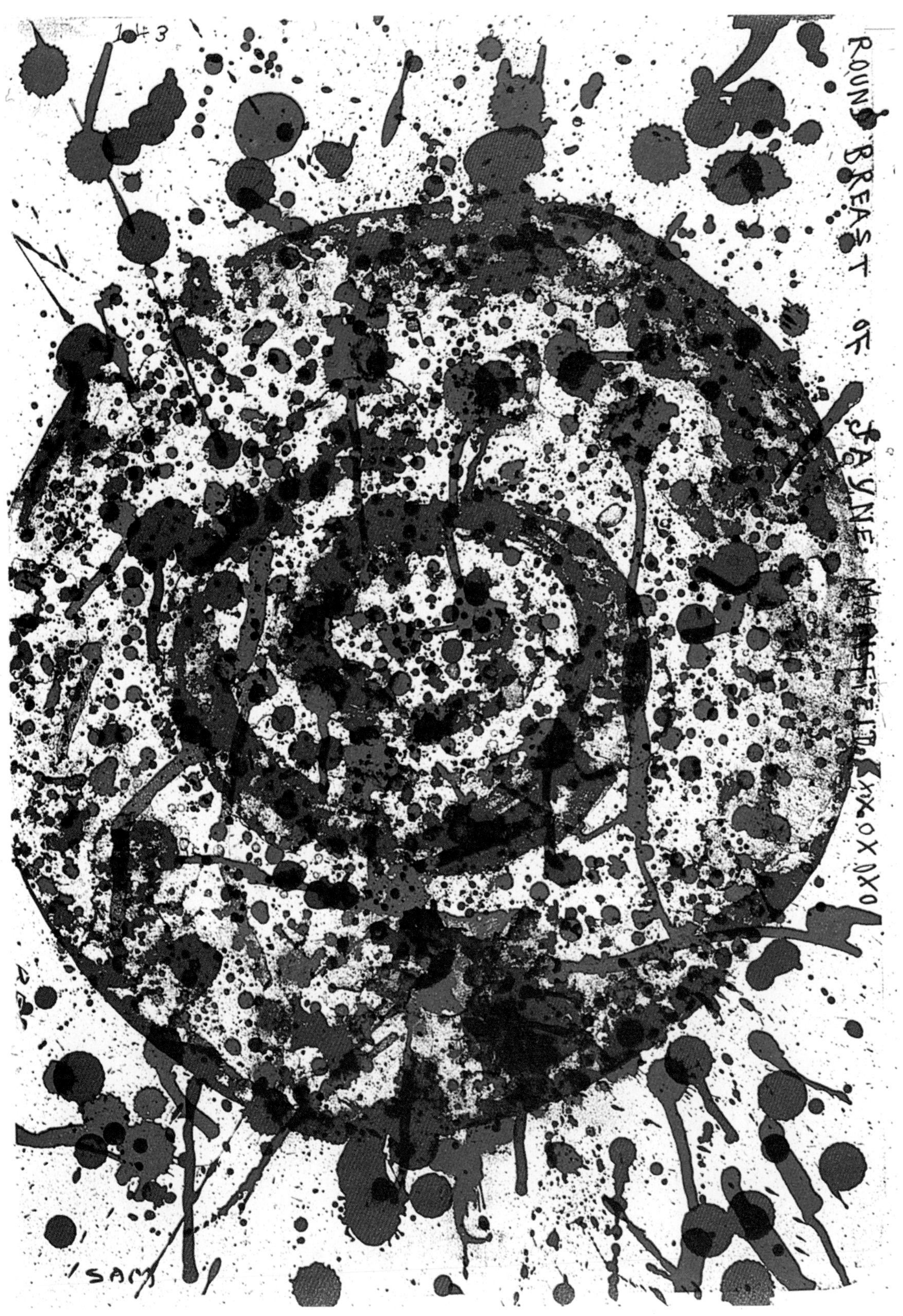

22. SAM FRANCIS: 1964. *Walasse Ting, 1¢ LIFE*. CAT.135

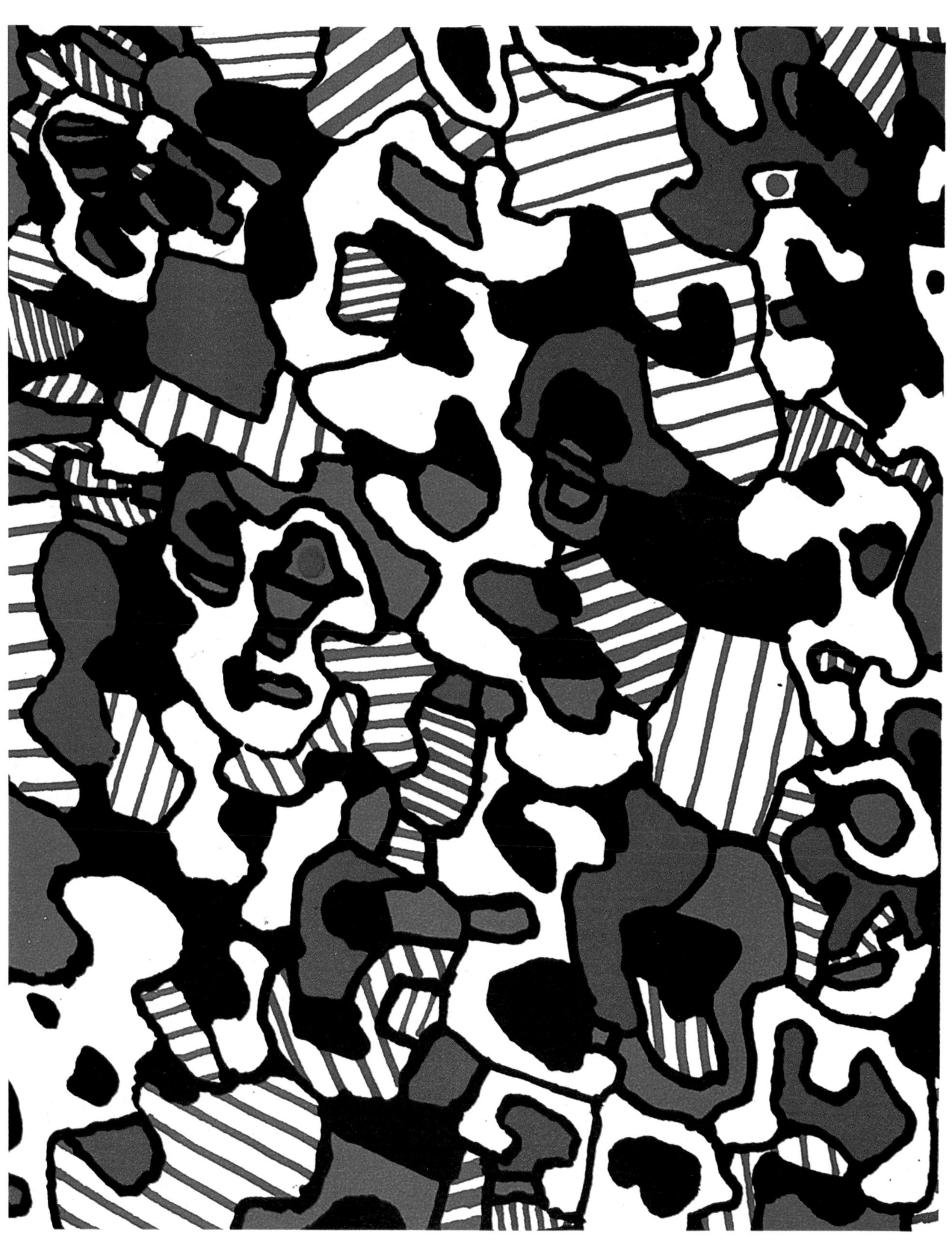

23. JEAN DUBUFFET: 1967. *Max Loreau, CERCEAUX SORCELLENT.* CAT.140

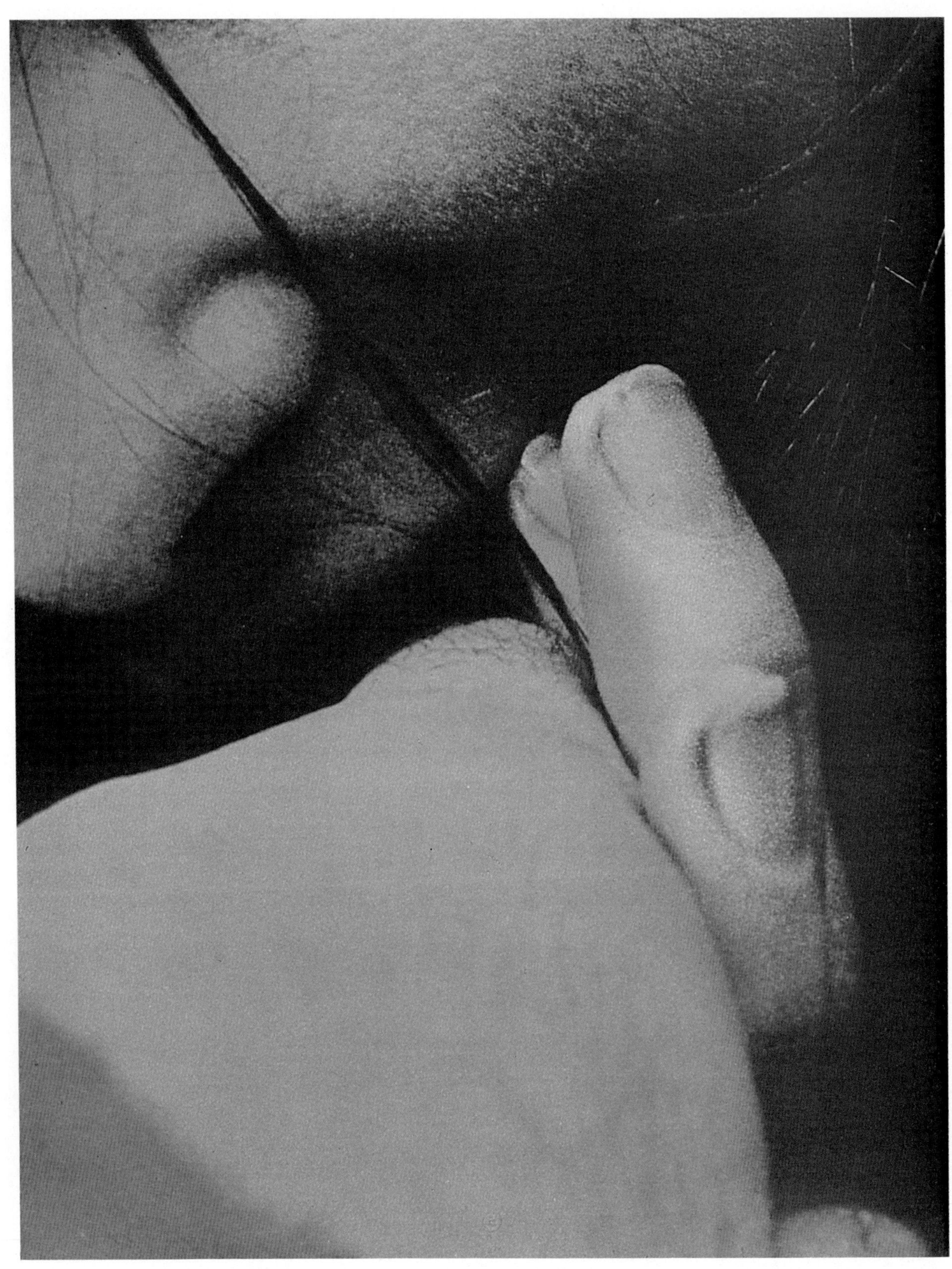

24. HAROLD COHEN: 1968. *Harold Pinter, THE HOMECOMING.* CAT.141

25. GRAHAM SUTHERLAND: 1968. *A BESTIARY.* CAT.143

26. JIM DINE: 1968. *THE PICTURE OF DORIAN GRAY.* CAT.142

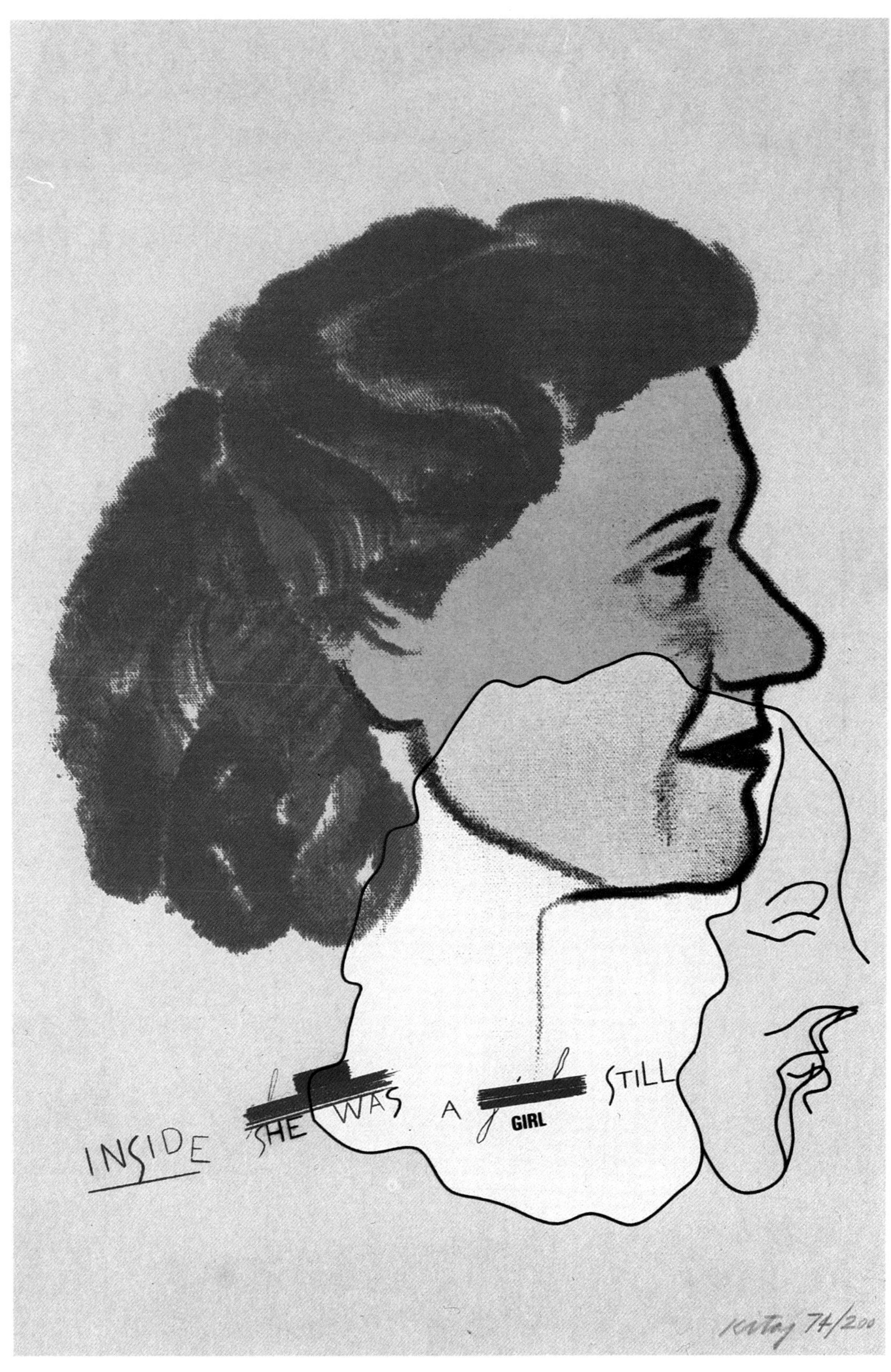

27. R.B. KITAJ: 1972. *A DAY-BOOK BY ROBERT CREELEY.* CAT.150

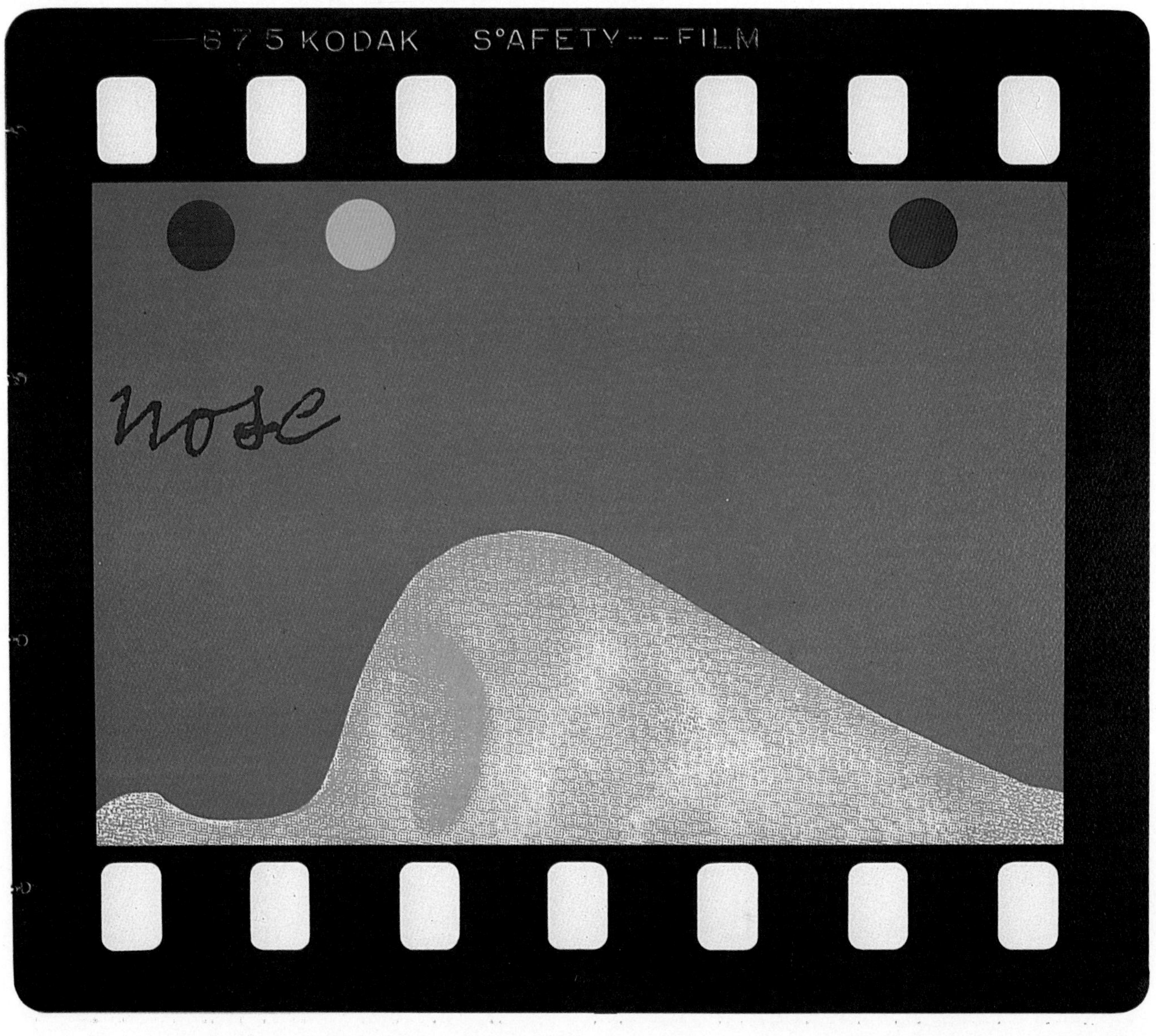

28. JOE TILSON: 1968. *THE SOFTWARE CHART QUESTIONNAIRE.* CAT.144

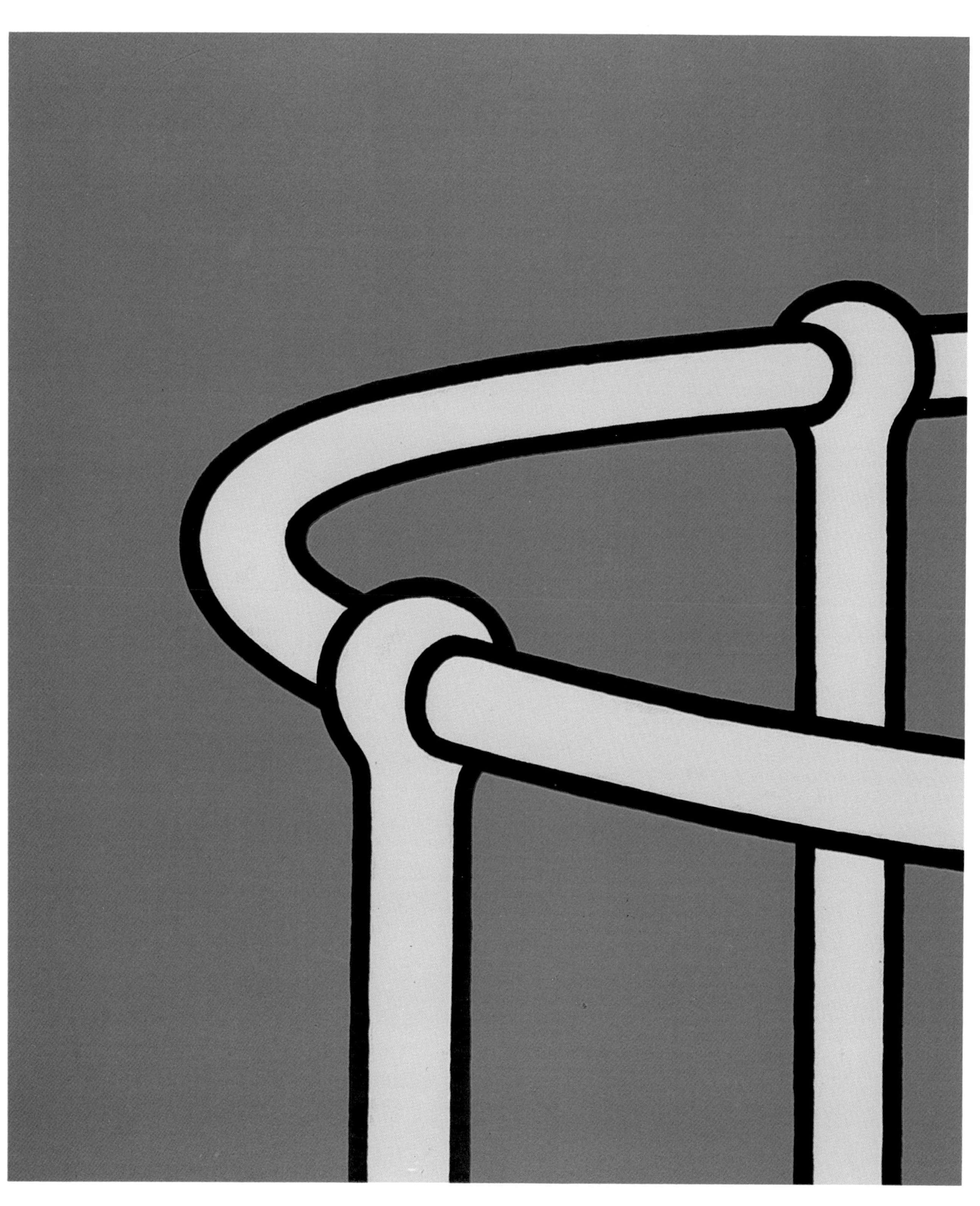

29. PATRICK CAULFIELD: 1973. *QUELQUES POÈMES DE JULES LAFORGUE*. CAT.152

30. DAVID HOCKNEY: 1977. *THE BLUE GUITAR.* CAT.157

31. ALLEN JONES: 1977. *WAYS & MEANS.* CAT.158

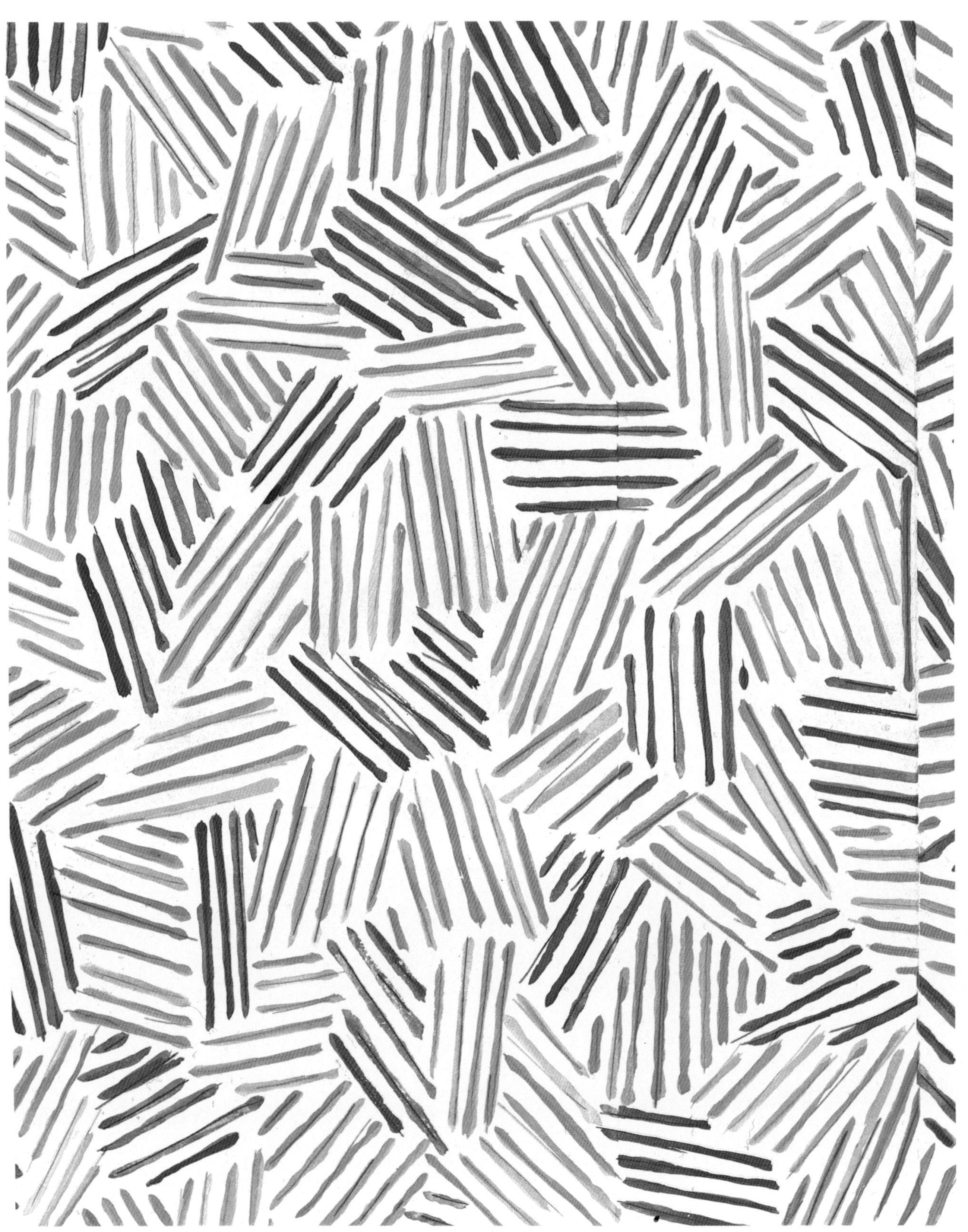

32. JASPER JOHNS: 1976. *Samuel Beckett, FIZZLES*. CAT.156

33. ROBERT RAUSCHENBERG: 1978. *TRACES SUSPECTES EN SURFACE.* CAT.151

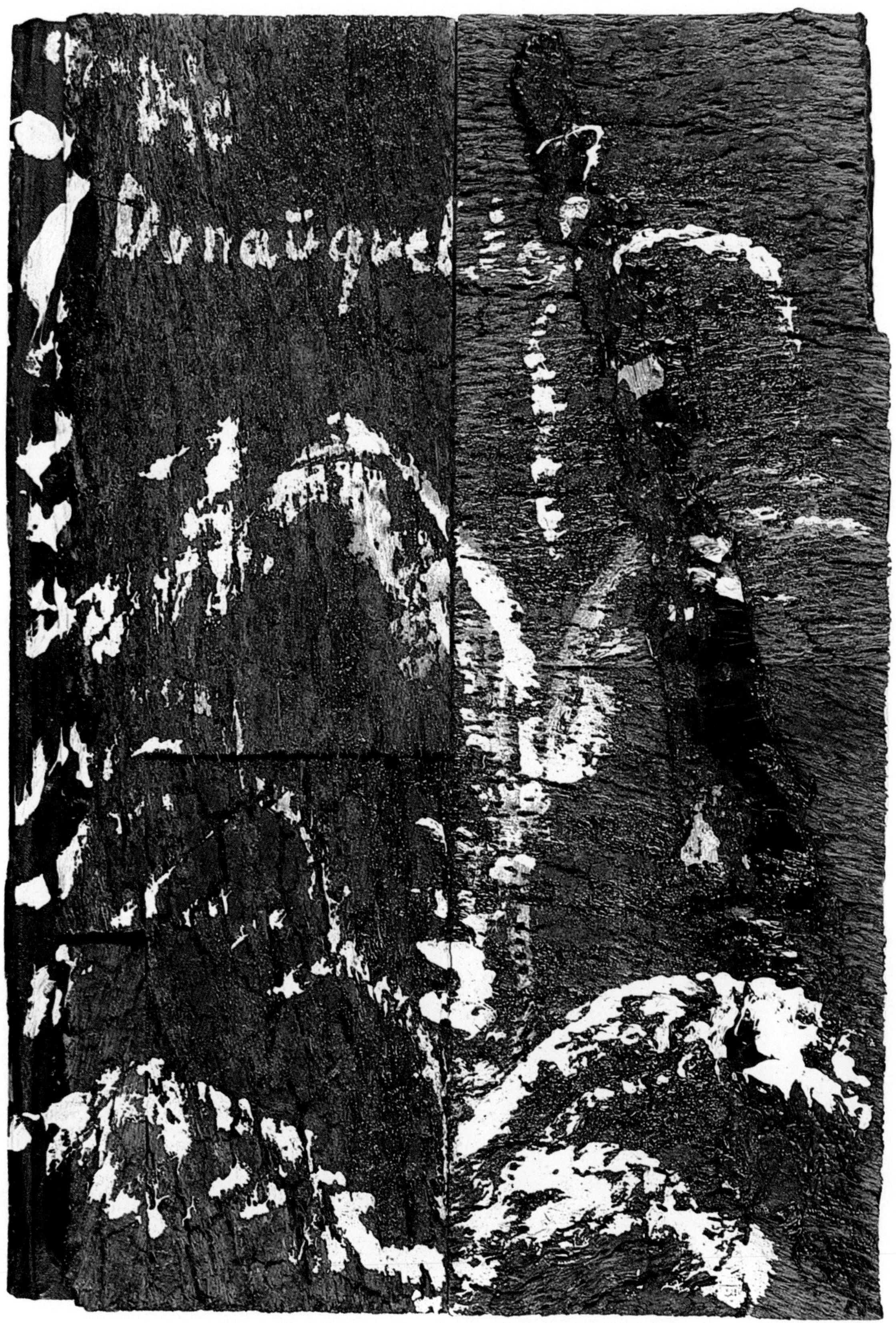

34. ANSELM KIEFER: 1978. *DIE DONAUQUELLE.* CAT.160

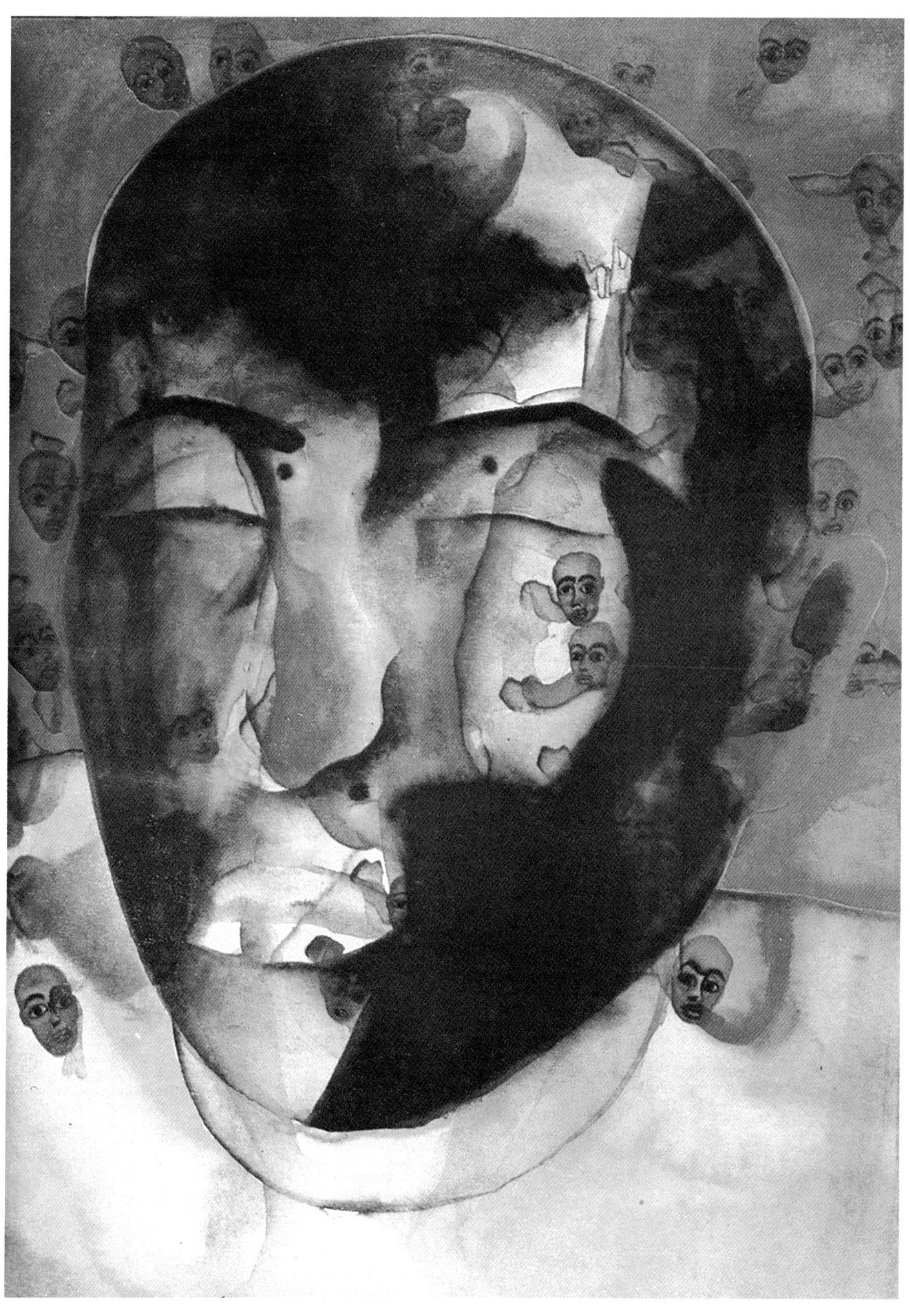

35. FRANCESCO CLEMENTE: 1983. *Allen Ginsberg, WHITE SHROUD.* CAT.166

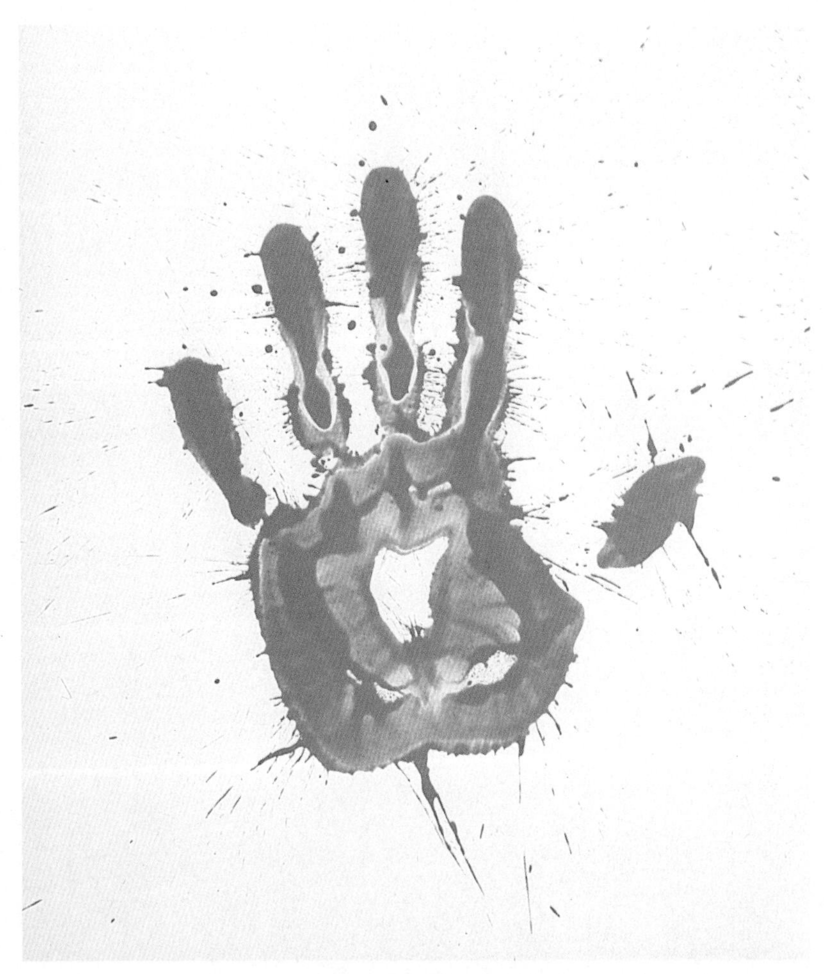

36. RICHARD LONG: 1984. *MUD HAND PRINTS*. CAT.167

Illustration by EDOUARD MANET to *LES CHATS* by *Champfleury,* PARIS, 1870 *(not in catalogue following).*

THE CATALOGUE

FROM·MANET
TO·HOCKNEY
MODERN ARTISTS' ILLUSTRATED BOOKS

The books here described are arranged chronologically by date of the original graphic work, not that of publication. The biographical notes on artists are designed to enable the reader to situate them in the history of modern art. Technical description of each book is followed by comments on various aspects of the volume and on the people involved in producing it.

1 EDOUARD MANET **1875**

(1832-1883) Son of a magistrate, Manet studied under Thomas Couture, but spent most of his time copying Titian and Velazquez in the Louvre, in 1857 approaching Delacroix for permission to do the same in the Musée du Luxembourg. The poet Baudelaire became a close friend at this time. In 1859 his BUVEUR D'ABSINTHE *was refused by the Salon despite the support of Delacroix. His* MUSIQUE AUX TUILERIES *of 1860-1 has been called the first work of modern painting, as much by its subject as by its technique; in 1863, he exhibited with the Salon des Refusés. Emile Zola defended his work from 1866. Though not exhibiting with the* IMPRESSIONISTS *he associated with Monet and Renoir from the early 1870's, and began to paint in the open air. In 1873, he first met Mallarmé, who became a close friend. Official recognition came late in his life; as* IMPRESSIONISM *achieved respectability, the art of Manet could be countenanced, and he was made a chevalier of the Légion d'Honneur in December 1881.*

LE CORBEAU. THE RAVEN. POÈME PAR EDGAR POE. TRADUCTION FRANÇAISE DE STÉPHANE MALLARMÉ AVEC ILLUSTRATIONS PAR ÉDOUARD MANET (PARIS: RICHARD LESCLIDE, 1875).
12pp., 590 x 360 mm., with 4 transfer lithographs *hors texte*.
Edition of 240 copies (V&A copy no. 92), signed by translator and artist, on either *Chine* or *Hollande*.
The V&A copy has a print of the Raven tipped in, inscribed: 'À.M. Jules Clarétie, (Indépendance Belge), exemplaire offert par M.M. [signed:] S. Mallarmé, E. Manet', and a small leather bookplate on the inside cover with the monogramme 'E.M.'.
Printer: Alcan Levy (completed 20 May 1875).
L. 5778-1980.

The popularity in continental Europe of Edgar Alen Poe (1809-1849) and his 'gothic' poetry with its overtones of horror was largely due to his promotion by Baudelaire and Mallarmé. Although reasonably priced at 25 francs, the book did not sell well. The picture of the raven was used for publicity posters advertising the book, and also in 1889 for Mallarmé's translation of Poe's poetry published by Léon Vanier. Manet's proposal to produce illustrations for Mallarmé's translation of *LA CITÉ EN LA MER* by Poe came to nothing, a result of *LE CORBEAU'S* commercial failure, but the two collaborated on *L'APRÈS-MIDI D'UN FAUNE* published by Alphonse Derenne in 1876. Rossetti saw a copy of *LE CORBEAU* in England in 1881; he described it to Jane Morris as the work of 'a conceited ass' and recommended that a copy should be available in every lunatic asylum in the country; 'to view it without a guffaw is impossible'.

The bulk of Manet's graphic work was produced between 1862 and 1868. About half of it remained unpublished during his lifetime, a source of chagrin to the artist who regarded the print as a means of introducing his work to a wider public. Manet's friendship with Mallarmé renewed his interest in prints. The technique used by Manet for *LE CORBEAU* was that of transfer lithography. 'It was a method ideally suited to the brush-and-ink drawing style that he developed and mastered during this period. He brushed in his designs with transfer ink on sheets of paper that Lefman, the specialist printer for this technique, then transferred to zinc plates for printing' (Exhibition catalogue: *MANET, 1832-1883*, New York, Metropolitan Museum of Art, Sept.-Nov. 1983, p.384).

2 MAX KLINGER **1881**

(1857-1920). Son of a wealthy Leipzig soap manufacturer, Klinger studied with the realistic genre painter Karl Gussow at Karlsruhe and later at the Berlin Academy, where he learnt to engrave, in 1874-1878. Thereafter he lived successively at Brussels, Munich, Berlin, Rome (1888-1892, his longest stay), and, finally, Plagwitz near Leipzig, where he designed and built a remarkable house on land owned by his parents. According to his family, Klinger lived as a recluse in the cities where he had stayed. His early œuvre consisted largely of drawings and prints (he was the first major German artist for decades to make his own); the heightened romanticism of his early days derived from Böcklin, while the symbolic fantasy of later engravings have led to his being singled out as a precursor of SURREALISM; *from the 1890's he produced vast allegorical paintings. In 1895 he was nominated professor in the Vienna Academy, but left after a short time there. From about this time he began to sculpt, using polychrome marbles in a 'neo-classical' style.*

AMOR UND PSYCHE. EIN MÄRCHEN DES APULEJUS, AUS DEM LATEINISCHEN VON REINHOLD JACHMANN, ILLUSTRIRT IN 46 ORIGINAL-RADIERUNG UND ORNAMENTIRT VON MAX KLINGER
(MUNICH: THEO. STROEFER'S KUNSTVERLAG, [1881].)
v,68pp., 350 x 245 mm., with 46 etchings, 15 of them full page *hors texte*.
Un-numbered edition, first issued in 1880 and thought to have been issued on demand thereafter (Carey & Griffiths, *THE PRINT IN GERMANY, 1880-1933,* London: British Museum Publications, 1984, p.239).
Paper: made by Gust. Schaeuffelen'schen Fabrik, Heilbronn.
Printer: Gebrüder Kröner, Stuttgart. text; Kaesberg & Oertel, R. Klepsch and others, wood engravings; Fr. Felsing, Munich, etchings.
Binder: label on inside cover of original binding, 'J.R.Herzog, Buchbinderei, Leipzig'.
L.668-1886.

Although Klinger published 14 sets of etchings, this is the only set intended for book illustrations: the artist is reported to have remarked that he found it too frustrating to be tied to a text. *AMOR UND PSYCHE* is dedicated to Brahms, a friend of the artist, whose symphonies inspired another set of engravings that were published in 1884, the *BRAHMSPHANTASIE*. The book was expensively priced at 65 marks and did not sell well. Years later, Klinger prints sold well at higher prices: in 1899, 10 loose prints, 'Fantasies on a lost glove', sold for 80 marks.

3 EDGAR DEGAS **1880's**

(1834-1917) Son of a wealthy banker, Degas trained with Lamothe and Ingres, spending much time in Paris museums studying works by Dürer, Mantegna, Goya and Rembrandt. After an Italian trip in 1858-60, he produced a number of academic history paintings; thereafter contemporary subjects predominated, including horse races, café scenes, the theatre and dancing. Although associating with IMPRESSIONISTS *and forming a group with Manet, Zola and Cézanne, he rejected the cult of open air painting, while at the same time showing his work at seven of the eight* IMPRESSIONIST *exhibitions between 1874 and 1886. His own collection of paintings contained many by Ingres, Delacroix and Corot, as well as works of Manet, Cézanne and Gauguin. From the 1880's his eyesight deteriorated rapidly and he died blind.*

LUDOVIC HALÉVY, *LA FAMILLE CARDINAL, ILLUSTRÉ D'UN PORTRAIT DE L'AUTEUR ET DE TRENTE-DEUX MONOTYPES EN NOIR ET EN COULEURS PAR EDGAR DEGAS* (PARIS: AUGUSTE BLAIZOT & FILS, 1938).
164pp., 325 x 250 mm., with 33 illustrations, 6 of them *hors texte*.
Edition of 350 copies (V&A copy no.7) on *Vélin de Rives*, numbered 1-325 and I-XXV *hors commerce*.
Printer: Frazier-Soye, Paris, J. Schaeppely, overseer, text; Maurice Potin, 'peintre-graveur', and Haasen, 'maitre-imprimeur', etchings (completed 21 Sept. 1938).

 L.2916-1952. Colour plate 1

Though Degas made numerous prints, these are the only examples designed as book illustrations from the outset and were executed in the 1880's. The monotypes reproduced here were sold after Degas' death in 1918 to a group of collectors who allowed them to be used for this edition. Degas had intended that his monotypes be reproduced by heliogravure to illustrate the novel, but the author, Ludovic Halévy, did not take up the proposal. Halévy (1834-1908), a friend of Degas, achieved fame as the librettist, with Henri Meihlac, of Offenbach's operas that enjoyed a great vogue in the 1860's. Thereafter he produced a series of novels, that on the Cardinal family in 1873. He was elected to the Académie Française in 1884.

4 MAURICE DENIS **1889**

(1870-1943) Denis entered the Académie Julian at the age of 17, where he met Bonnard, Vuillard and others, before joining the École des Beaux Arts. A co-founder and chief literary proponent of the NABIS, *he published in 1890 its first manifesto,* DÉFINITION DU NÉO-TRADITIONISME; *his painting* HOMMAGE À CÉZANNE *dates from the following year. His admiration for the Renaissance and 15th century Italian painting led him to more classical styles. Denis was one of the founders of the Salon d'Automne, and ensured that a section of it was devoted to religious art. In 1919, he founded the Ateliers d'Art Sacré, and was made a Commander of the Légion d'Honneur. A retrospective exhibition was devoted to him at the Musée de l'Orangerie in 1970.*

PAUL VERLAINE, *SAGESSE. IMAGES EN COULEURS DE MAURICE DENIS GRAVÉES SUR BOIS PAR BELTRAND* (PARIS: AMBROISE VOLLARD, 1911).
iv, 100pp., 280 x 220 mm., with 54 wood engravings and 19 vignettes; also an extra set of wood engravings (lacking those for pp.13 and 27) hand-coloured by the artist.
Edition of 250 copies, of which 40 are on *Japon ancien à la forme* (nos. 1-40), and 210 on *Hollande Van Gelder* watermarked with the title of the work (nos. 41-250); this copy, [*hors commerce*] printed for Jacques Beltrand.
Printer: Jacques Beltrand, 'Emile Fequet pressier' (completed 30 August 1910).
Inscribed 'À mon bon ami Viand Bruant le maitre artiste Horticulteur et excellent ami, son dévoué [signed:] Jacques Beltrand'.
L.898-1982.

The drawings of Denis, symbolist in character, were done in 1889 and acclaimed when shown at the Salon des Indépendants in 1891; they were not published until 1911. Denis illustrated a number of books, many of a religious nature (e.g. *LES PETITES FLEURS DE SAINT FRANÇOIS* and the *IMITATION DE JÉSUS CHRIST* with 115 wood engravings published by Vollard in 1903). *SAGESSE* was produced by Verlaine (1844-1896) after a silence of some years, and included poems that are religious in character.

PAUL VERLAINE

SAGESSE

IMAGES EN COULEURS
DE MAURICE DENIS
GRAVÉES SUR BOIS
PAR BELTRAND

AMBROISE VOLLARD, ÉDITEUR — 6, RUE LAFFITTE
PARIS — MCMXI.

XVII

Les chères mains qui furent miennes,
Toutes petites, toutes belles,
Après ces méprises mortelles
Et toutes ces choses païennes,

Après les rades et les grèves
Et les pays et les provinces,
Royales mieux qu'au temps des princes,
Les chères mains m'ouvrent les rêves.

Mains en songe, mains sur mon âme,
Sais-je, moi, ce que vous daignâtes,
Parmi ces rumeurs scélérates,
Dire à cette âme qui se pâme?

Ment-elle, ma vision chaste
D'affinité spirituelle,
De complicité maternelle,
D'affection étroite et vaste?

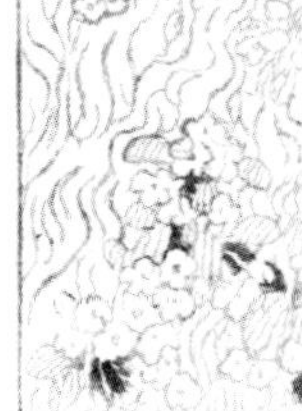

Remords si chers, peine très bonne,
Rêves bénits, mains consacrées,
O ces mains, ses mains vénérées,
Faites le geste qui pardonne !

SAGESSE

5 MAURICE DENIS **1893**

(1870-1943)

ANDRÉ GIDE, *LE VOYAGE D'URIEN* (PARIS: LIBRAIRIE DE L'ART INDÉPENDANT, 1893).
viii, 110 pp., 200 x 190 mm., with 30 lithographs.
Edition of 300 copies (V&A copy no. 168); also 1 copy on Japan and 1 on China (see *THE ARTIST AND THE BOOK*, Boston Museum of Fine Arts, 1961, p.58).
Printer: Paul Schmidt, text; Edw. Ancourt, lithographs (completed 25 May 1893).
Bookplate of Jacques Beaupain.
L.5920-1984

Having seen Denis' illustrations for *SAGESSE* before publication, Gide (1869-1951) commissioned him to illustrate his symbolist novel *VOYAGE D'URIEN*. This is generally regarded as the first *livre d'artiste* illustrated by colour lithographs (two are included).

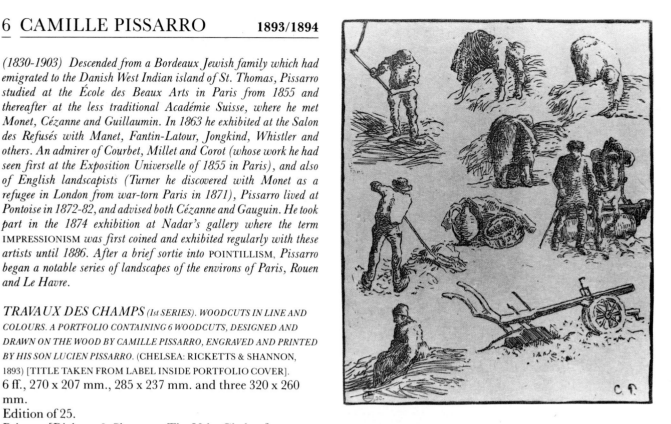

6 CAMILLE PISSARRO **1893/1894**

(1830-1903) Descended from a Bordeaux Jewish family which had emigrated to the Danish West Indian island of St. Thomas, Pissarro studied at the École des Beaux Arts in Paris from 1855 and thereafter at the less traditional Académie Suisse, where he met Monet, Cézanne and Guillaumin. In 1863 he exhibited at the Salon des Refusés with Manet, Fantin-Latour, Jongkind, Whistler and others. An admirer of Courbet, Millet and Corot (whose work he had seen first at the Exposition Universelle of 1855 in Paris), and also of English landscapists (Turner he discovered with Monet as a refugee in London from war-torn Paris in 1871), Pissarro lived at Pontoise in 1872-82, and advised both Cézanne and Gauguin. He took part in the 1874 exhibition at Nadar's gallery where the term IMPRESSIONISM *was first coined and exhibited regularly with these artists until 1886. After a brief sortie into* POINTILLISM, *Pissarro began a notable series of landscapes of the environs of Paris, Rouen and Le Havre.*

TRAVAUX DES CHAMPS (1st SERIES). WOODCUTS IN LINE AND COLOURS. A PORTFOLIO CONTAINING 6 WOODCUTS, DESIGNED AND DRAWN ON THE WOOD BY CAMILLE PISSARRO, ENGRAVED AND PRINTED BY HIS SON LUCIEN PISSARRO. (CHELSEA: RICKETTS & SHANNON, 1893) [TITLE TAKEN FROM LABEL INSIDE PORTFOLIO COVER].
6 ff., 270 x 207 mm., 285 x 237 mm. and three 320 x 260 mm.
Edition of 25.
86 Printer: [Ricketts & Shannon, The Vale, Chelsea].
Bookplate of Dr Lucien Graux on inside cover.
L.5931-1984 Colour plate 2

Of the Impressionists, Pissarro was perhaps the most interested in print-making, completing over 190 etchings and lithographs. He favoured 'engraved impressions', as he termed them, for their expressive qualities. His son Lucien Pissarro, resident in England in 1893, had learnt engraving to reduce the cost of illustrated books he planned to produce. Camille Pissarro had long planned a portfolio on peasants at work in fields for Lucien to cut on wood. One of the drawings, finished in c. 1890, had been published by Theo Van Gogh; Ricketts and Shannon were chosen to produce a small edition of the set on their private press when no French publisher could be found. After his father's death, Lucien published an extended version of his father's drawings as *LA CHARRUE D'ÉRABLE.*

Charles Ricketts and Charles Shannon set up a press in Chelsea in the early 1890's. Here they published Lucien Pissarro's *FIRST PORTFOLIO* in 1891, as well as the journal *THE DIAL,* to which Lucien also contributed. Ricketts later set up the Vale Press, and designed the Vale type which Lucien used for his own Eragny Press.

7 LUCIEN PISSARRO **1894**

(1863-1944) Trained by his father Camille Pissarro, Lucien painted from an early age, showing with IMPRESSIONISTS *in 1886, becoming friends with Van Gogh and discovering the work of Seurat in 1887. He settled in London in 1890. His interest in illustrated books led him to set up the Eragny Press, named after the house his father had bought in 1884. Taking up painting again in 1903, he became friends with Sickert, a member of the* NEW ENGLISH ART CLUB *which he joined. In 1911, he was a member of the* CAMDEN TOWN GROUP. *He took English nationality in 1916.*

THE QUEEN OF THE FISHES. AN ADAPTATION IN ENGLISH OF A FAIRY TALE OF VALOIS, BY MARGARET RUST, WITH ILLUSTRATIONS DESIGNED IN THE WOOD CUT AND PRINTED BY LUCIEN PISSARRO (LONDON: 'SOLD BY JOHN LANE AT THE SIGN OF THE BODLEY HEAD', 1894).
ii, 16pp., 195 x 135mm., with 12 woodcuts, 5 of them coloured.
No edition details.
Printer: 'Printed in 1894 by Lucien Pissarro at his Press in Epping (Essex)'.
L. 1463-1906.

This work represents the first efforts of Pissarro and his wife to use the hand-press they had bought after arriving in England. The result was such that the Bodley Head agreed to market the book. The Pissarros were helped in their enterprise by Charles Ricketts and Charles Shannon, who subsequently published Lucien Pissarro's books through the Vale Press. The colophon of Pissarro's 1894 book is printed in letterpress type (the text of the book is process-engraved from hand-lettering) and headed 'Vale Publications'.

I was a little woodcutter, but now I am
the KING of the FOREST!" And as
he finished speaking, before the man's
bewildered gaze, the boy changed into
a grand oak tree, with branches shooting up gold tipped to the sun & stretching wide arms to the horizon. ❧ For
a while the old man stood awestruck,
but a dead leaf fluttering down touched his face & aroused him. With a
yell he shook his stick at the tree "I will
kill you yet!" & he rushed back into the
12

8 PIERRE BONNARD **1893**

(1867-1947) Even before finishing at law school in Paris in 1888, Bonnard was engaged in painting, producing works in a Corot tradition and attending the Académie Julian from 1887. In 1889, Bonnard sold his first poster and devoted himself to painting, being greatly struck with Gauguin's Breton paintings exhibited at the Café Volpini that year. From 1891 he shared a studio with Vuillard and Denis, whom he had met at the Académie Julian, and in that year first exhibited at the Salon des Indépendants. Interest in Japanese prints led to Bonnard's being called 'The most Japanese of the Nabis', the group with which he was associated until it split up in 1899. Posters and lithography formed an important part of his work in the 1890's, Vollard publishing his colour lithographs QUELQUES ASPECTS DE LA VIE DE PARIS *in 1895. In 1896 he had his first one-man show at the Durand-Ruel gallery in Paris. Living in the country rather than central Paris, Bonnard concentrated on painting from c.1905 and from 1910 spent much of the year in the Midi. Monet greatly admired his work, which maintained a Post-Impressionist idiom with no reference to avant-garde movements (Cubism, Dada, Surrealism, etc.) centred in the capital. Large one-man exhibitions of his work were shown in Paris in 1924, 1937, 1947 and 1984.*

CLAUDE TERRASSE, *PETITES SCÈNES FAMILIÈRES. POUR PIANO. ILLUSTRATIONS DE PIERRE BONNARD.*

88 (PARIS: E. FROMONT, [1893]).

ii, 62 pp., 360 x 280 mm., with 19 lithographed illustrations with text and lithographed cover.
Printer: Imprimerie Crevel Frères, Paris; 'M. Fleurot gr'.
L.2120-1983.

These are the artist's first original illustrations. Claude Terrasse was a piano teacher in Arcachon when he arranged the 20 pieces in *PETITES SCÈNES FAMILIERES;* he also produced in 1893 the *PETIT SOLFÈGE,* which was similarly illustrated by his brother-in-law Bonnard. The last 5 pieces in *PETITES SCÈNES* are significant in that they represent the composer's first efforts at light music, in which he later excelled. After returning to Paris in 1895, he composed incidental music for the theatre (including that for Jarry's *UBU ROI* in 1896, for which Bonnard and Sérusier designed the sets) and for the trilogy *THÉÂTRE DES PANTINS* in whose production Bonnard was also involved.

à Monsieur Claude-Marie Terrasse.

LA CHANSON DU GRAND-PERE

CHANSON DU GRAND-PÈRE

Moderato.

PIANO.

mf

Court arrêt.

pp

9 EDWARD BURNE-JONES **1893/1896**

(1833-1898) After meeting William Morris at Oxford and visiting with him gothic cathedrals in northern France, Burne-Jones took up painting under Rossetti's guidance and was one of the PRE-RAPHAELITE *group that executed the murals on the Oxford Union Debating Chamber in 1857-8. He provided tapestry and stained glass designs for Morris, Marshall, Faulkner & Co.; visits to Italy in 1859 and 1862 confirmed the influence of Italian primitive painting. Showing little in public, his 1877 exhibition at the Grosvenor Gallery established his reputation; in 1882 he represented Great Britain at the International Exhibition in Paris. In 1893 he resigned from the Royal Academy, of which he had been made an associate in 1885; in 1894 he received a baronetcy.*

THE WORKS OF GEOFFREY CHAUCER NOW NEWLY IMPRINTED (HAMMERSMITH: KELMSCOTT PRESS, 1896).
iv, 554pp., 420 x 280 mm., with 87 wood-engravings by Burne-Jones, borders and initial letters by Burne-Jones and William Morris.

Edition of 438 copies, 13 on vellum and 425 (of which this is one) on paper.
Editor: F.S. Smith
Cutter of engravings: W.H. Hooper
Printer: William Morris at the Kelmscott Press.
L. 757-1896.

The Kelmscott Press was founded in 1891 by William Morris and published 53 titles before his death in 1896. The text was based on the Ellesmere manuscript of the Canterbury Tales (now in the Huntington Library, San Marino), as emended by Walter William Skeat, Professor of Anglo-Saxon at Cambridge, who is duly thanked in the colophon. The *CHAUCER* was planned in 1892, and a specimen produced in the following year. It sold for £16.3s. when published in 1896. A number of Burne-Jones' illustrations provide images that are disconcertingly 'modern'.

That every wight gan on hem shoute,
And for to laughe as they were wode;
Such game fonde they in hir hode.
THO com another companye,
That had ydoon the traiterye,
The harm, the gretest wikkednesse
That any herte couthe gesse;
And preyed hir to han good fame,
And that she nolde hem doon no shame,
But yeve hem loos and good renoun,
And do hit blowe in clarioun.
Nay, wis! quod she, hit were a vyce;
Al be ther in me no justyce,
Me listeth not to do hit now,
Ne this nil I not graunte yow.
THO come ther lepinge in a route,
And gonne choppen al aboute
Every man upon the croune,
That al the halle gan to soune,
And seyden: Lady, lefe and dere,
We ben swich folk as ye mowe here.
To tellen al the tale aright,
We ben shrewes, every wight,
And han delyt in wikkednes,
As gode folk han in goodnes;
And joye to be knowen shrewes,
And fulle of vyce and wikked thewes;
Wherfor we preyen yow, arowe,
That our fame swich be knowe
In alle thing right as hit is.
I GRAUNTE hit yow, quod she, ywis.
But what art thou that seyst this tale,
That werest on thy hose a pale,
And on thy tipet swiche a belle!
Madame, quod he, sooth to telle,
I am that ilke shrewe, ywis,
That brende the temple of Isidis
In Athenes, lo, that citee.
And wherfor didest thou so? quod she.
By my thrift, quod he, madame,
I wolde fayn han had a fame,
As other folk hadde in the toun,
Althogh they were of greet renoun
For hir vertu and for hir thewes;
Thoughte I, as greet a fame han shrewes,
Thogh hit be but for shrewednesse,
As gode folk han for goodnesse;
And sith I may not have that oon,
That other nil I noght forgoon.
And for to gette of fames hyre,
The temple sette I al afyre.
Now do our loos be blowen swythe,
As wisly be thou ever blythe.
Gladly, quod she; thou Eolus,

10 HENRI de TOULOUSE-LAUTREC **1894**

(1864/1901) After damaging his legs in an accident, Lautrec studied painting with the animal painter Princeteau, a family friend, before entering the École des Beaux Arts in Paris in 1882. He then worked with Bonnat and Cormon, where he met Émile Bernard and Van Gogh, whom he saw regularly between 1886 and 1888. From 1887 he exhibited with the LES VINGT *in Brussels, and at the Salon des Indépendants in Paris. His first London exhibition was held at the Goupil Gallery in 1898. From 1884, Lautrec lived in Montmartre, and it was here that his characteristic style and subject matter emerged in his paintings; from Degas whom he revered, he took both the expressive force of drawing, and also the subject matter, 'modern' subjects of everyday life in Paris. His first lithographs were produced in 1891 and were more admired at first than his painting; a master of colour lithography, he drew on stone and supervised the printing process carefully.*

YVETTE GUILBERT. TEXTE DE GUSTAVE GEFFROY, ORNÉ PAR H. DE TOULOUSE-LAUTREC (PARIS: L'ESTAMPE ORIGINALE, [1894]).
iii + 16 + iii ff., 380 x 380 mm., with 16 lithographs printed in olive green of which 14 are initialled by the artist.
Edition of 100 copies (V & A copy no. 51), signed on the verso of the fly-leaf by Yvette Guilbert.
Printer: Fremont, Arcis-sur-Aube; Edw. Ancourt, Paris.
L.856-1980.

Yvette Guilbert, a well-known singer in Paris Cafés and music-halls, was one of Lautrec's favorite models. In 1893, Lautrec had produced an illustration of her for an article by Geffroy in *FIGARO ILLUSTRÉ*. Guilbert was apparently displeased with the album, considering that her mannerisms had been grossly distorted, but her attitude softened when it had secured favorable reaction from critics. In 1898, 10 additional lithographs from the 1894 series were produced by Bliss, Sands & Co., London. Kokoschka in 1910 did a portrait drawing of Yvette Guilbert, by then in retirement, published in *DER STURM*.

Gustave Geffroy (1855-1926), was introduced to Impressionist circles by Monet, and he was among the first to write books and articles about them.

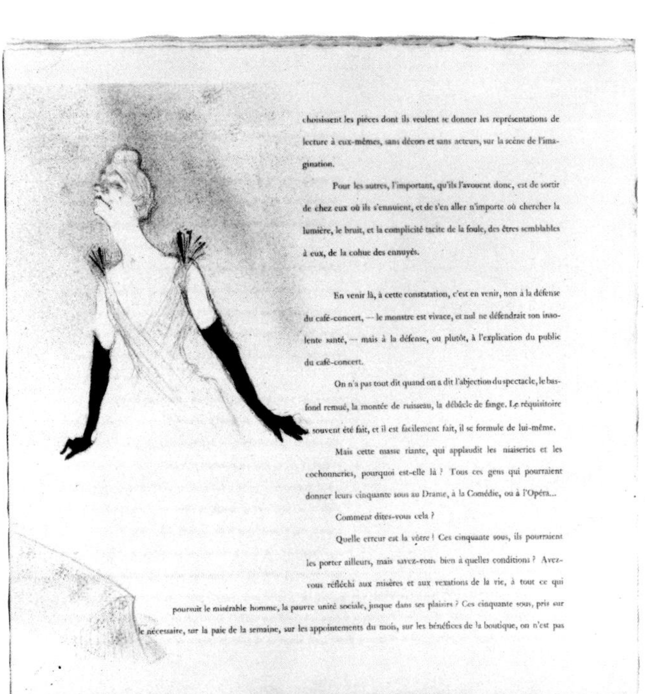

choisissent les pièces dont ils veulent se donner les représentations de lecture à eux-mêmes, sans décors et sans acteurs, sur la scène de l'imagination.

Pour les autres, l'important, qu'ils l'avouent donc, est de sortir de chez eux où ils s'ennuient, et de s'en aller n'importe où chercher la lumière, le bruit, et la complicité tacite de la foule, des êtres semblables à eux, de la cohue des ennuyés.

En venir là, à cette constatation, c'est en venir, non à la défense du café-concert, — le monstre est vivace, et nul ne défendrait son insolente santé, — mais à la défense, ou plutôt, à l'explication du public du café-concert.

On n'a pas tout dit quand on a dit l'abjection du spectacle, le bas-fond remué, la montée de ruisseau, la débâcle de fange. Le réquisitoire a souvent été fait, et il est facilement fait, il se formule de lui-même.

Mais cette masse riante, qui applaudit les niaiseries et les cochonneries, pourquoi est-elle là ? Tous ces gens qui pourraient donner leurs cinquante sous au Drame, à la Comédie, ou à l'Opéra...

Comment dites-vous cela ?

Quelle erreur est la vôtre ! Ces cinquante sous, ils pourraient les porter ailleurs, mais savez-vous bien à quelles conditions ? Avez-vous réfléchi aux misères et aux vexations de la vie, à tout ce qui poursuit le misérable homme, la pauvre unité sociale, jusque dans ses plaisirs ? Ces cinquante sous, pris sur le nécessaire, sur la paie de la semaine, sur les appointements du mois, sur les bénéfices de la boutique, on n'est pas

héritée, l'Eglise et la Bourse, le Palais et la Caserne. Mais qui ne consentira, dans l'avenir, à l'effritement et à l'écroulement des monuments, si chacun peut enfin jouir de sa maison et de son jardin, de ses fleurs, de sa ruche et de son arbre ? Le fameux idéal invoqué comporte trop de truffes et de champagne pour les uns, et pas assez même de pain sec pour les autres. Ce sera tout bénéfice pour l'humanité si elle entend et comprend d'une certaine façon ce qui lui sera crié : « Il n'y a pas d'idéal, il y a la soupe et le bœuf, il faut vivre d'abord, créer de la vie, posséder la Terre, lui faire donner son maximum de bonheur. » Ce sera là le commencement de l'action.

Ce sera la conclusion de ces feuilles, si vous le voulez bien. La chanteuse Yvette Guilbert, lorsqu'elle a fini sa chanson, et qu'elle se sauve, la gorge âcre de la fumée respirée, toute sa personne imprégnée de l'atmosphère chaude, où va-t-elle ? Elle saute dans un train, quitte Paris, se rafraîchit à l'air sain de l'espace, retrouve son jardin et sa rivière de Vaux. Humanité tombée au café-concert, fais comme ta chanteuse, aussitôt que tu le pourras, quitte les grandes villes, retourne à la nature avec ce que tu as appris d'histoire et de civilisation, cherche l'ombre de l'arbre, le chant de la branche et du sillon, contente-toi du petit jardin autour duquel il y a l'espace, vis ta propre existence, unis-toi à la Terre enfin dominée par la Pensée.

GUSTAVE GEFFROY.

Yvette Guilbert

texte

de Gustave Geffroy

orné par

H. de Toulouse Lautrec

11A HENRI ROUSSEAU

'LE DOUANIER' **1895**

(1844-1910) A toll-gatherer and amateur painter, Rousseau is recorded as receiving the licence to work as a copyist in the national museums in Paris in 1884. Through Signac, he exhibited his work in the Salon des Indépendants in 1886, which he continued to do for most years until his death. In 1893, Rousseau resigned his job to achieve greatness as a painter, and supported himself by painting and other work. While he had some small success in the climate of POST-IMPRESSIONISM *(himself then professing admiration only for conventional artists such as Bouguereau and Gérôme), recognition for his primitive modernism came in 1905 when he exhibited in the Salon d'Automne with* FAUVIST *painters: Jarry introduced him to Apollinaire who in turn presented him to the circle around the dealers Vollard and Brummer. In 1908, Picasso presided over a banquet in his honour.*

L'YMAGIER, No. 2, JANVIER, 1895.
98pp., 260 x 200 mm., with woodcuts, engravings and lithographs.
Printer: C. Renaudie, text; Pellerin, Epinal, illustrations.
L.261-1984.

The poet, Alfred Jarry, like Rousseau from Laval, introduced the painter to Remy de Gourmont with whom he edited the shortlived periodical *L'YMAGIER* (it appeared only between 1894 and 1896) in 1894. The picture of Rousseau reproduced as a lithograph in *L'YMAGIER* had been exhibited in the Salon des Indépendants in that year. The subject, *GUERRE*, was taken from a socialist periodical of the time; few works by Rousseau survive from before 1900 and this picture shows the evolution of his original style of primitivism.

11B EMILE BERNARD **1895**

(1868-1941) After two years at the Académie Cormon, where he met Toulouse-Lautrec and Van Gogh, Bernard was expelled in 1886. He adopted momentarily the POINTILLISM *of Seurat, but interest in the cult of 'japonaiserie' was to lead to* CLOISONNISME *when he met Gauguin at Pont-Aven in 1888. In 1889 he appears to have been torn between the influence of Cézanne and primitive Italian painting, and in the 1890s adopted a mystic or orientalising style strongly differentiated in its traditionalism from the work of his Pont-Aven colleagues. An engraver, he introduced Gauguin to zincography, and emulated medieval xylography. Bernard defended his later style in the art review he edited,* LA RÉNOVATION ÉSTHETIQUE.

L'YMAGIER, No. 2, JANVIER 1895.
98pp., 260 x 200mm.
Printer: C. Renaudie, Paris, text; Pellerin, Epinal, illustrations.
L.261-1984.

Bernard contributed two illustrations to *L'YMAGIER* (1894-1896) from Egypt, where he lived in 1893-1901. The woodcut exhibited, *'BRETONNES'* was mistakenly attributed to Seguin in the periodical. The aim of *L'YMAGIER* was to show the best of both contemporary and past illustration; it sold for 3.50 francs.

12 JOZSEF RIPPL-RONÁI **1895**

(1861-1927) Son of a schoolmaster and a graduate in Pharmacology, Rippl-Ronái studied art in Munich in 1884 and went to Paris on the receipt of a government grant in 1887. Having met Maillol and Vuillard, he became an associate of the NABIS *group, and had his first exhibition at L'Art Nouveau, the gallery of Samuel Bing (1838-1905). Rippl-Ronái returned to Hungary, where his first one-man show had taken place in 1895, in 1902; in 1908 helped to form the* MIÉNK *(the circle of Hungarian Impressionists and naturalist painters). He received awards for paintings shown in exhibitions in Amsterdam (1912), Vienna (1914) and Hungary (1916). A major retrospective exhibition of his work was held in Budapest in 1920.*

GEORGES RODENBACH, *LES VIERGES* (PARIS: S. BING, 1895).
20pp., 250 x 170 mm., with 4 colour lithographs.
No edition details.
Printer: Chamerot and Renouard, Paris.
L.5837-1982 Colour plate 3

Rippl-Ronái designed the illustrations for a story, then unwritten, on the suggestion of his friend James Pitcairn-Knowles (1864-1914), who in 1890 had introduced him to the NABI painters and was himself to produce illustrations for a book to be called *LES TOMBEAUX*. Bing, who had many connections with the world of publishing, then commissioned Georges Rodenbach to write a story based on the illustrations. Similarities have been pointed out between Rippl-Ronái's lithographs and Maurice Denis's painting 'Les Muses', completed two years earlier (István Genthon, *RIPPL-RONÁI*, Budapest, 1958).

Rodenbach (1855-1898), commissioned by Bing to provide texts for the illustrations of both Rippl-Ronái and James Pitcairn-Knowles, was a Belgian poet and novelist who abandoned early emulation of Victor Hugo and François Coppée to develop a more subtle musical charm under the influence of Mallarmé, using a dreamy nostalgic refinement to evoke his native Flanders. His most popular novel, *BRUGES LA MORTE*, is considered to have symbolist overtones.

Les Vierges attendent

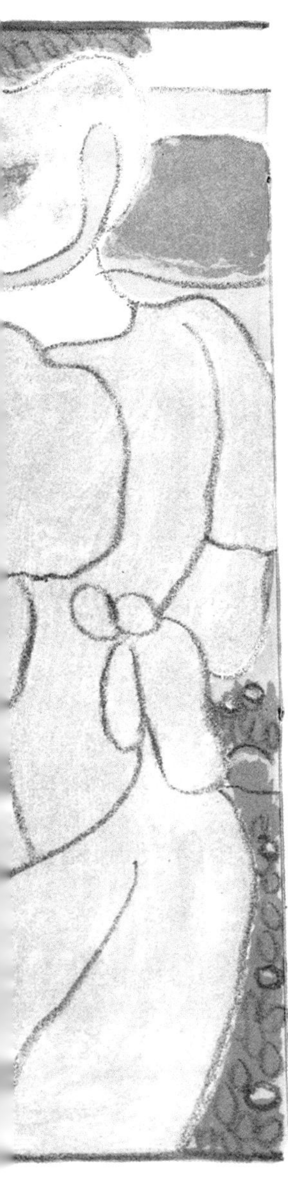

la Vie. Elles vont prendre part à la Vie. Celle-ci paraît splendide devant elles, et comme en or. ⁙ Il y a l'or jaune du blé mûr. ⁙ Il y a aussi l'or rouge du soleil. ⁙ Les cheveux des Vierges leur servent de raccord. Ils réconcilient en eux ce jaune de la terre et ce jaune du ciel. ⁙ Harmonie parfaite : les Vierges font encore partie du paysage ! ⁙ Les Vierges sont un peu inquiètes au bord de la vie, qui leur apparait

13 ODILON REDON **1896**

(1840-1916) Redon learnt to draw from 1855 when at his family estate near Bordeaux. S. Gorin, a leading member of the Société des Arts in Bordeaux, encouraged him and brought Corot and Delacroix to his notice. Redon studied briefly under Gérôme at the École des Beaux Arts in Paris in the early 1860s, but returned to Bordeaux where in c.1863 he met R. Bresdin, from whom he learnt engraving and lithography. After the war of 1870-1, Redon settled in Paris, producing charcoal drawings (the technique used by Corot for his last works) and mastering lithography under the guidance of Fantin-Latour. He exhibited with the Salon des Indépendants in 1884 and with LES VINGT *in Brussels in 1886; he was admired by the* NABIS. *Recognition came in the 1890s, when his graphic work was published by Vollard. In 1903 he was made a member of the Légion d'Honneur.*

GUSTAVE FLAUBERT, *LA TENTATION DE SAINT ANTOINE. ILLUSTRATIONS D'ODILON REDON*
(PARIS: ÉDITIONS AMBROISE VOLLARD, 1933).
iv, 208 pp. [and 5 ff. of table], 440 x 330mm., with 15 wood engravings and 22 lithographs *hors texte* (and a table of illustrations for the insertion of the lithographs).
Edition of 210 copies (V&A copy no.127), of which 25 are on *Vélin du Marais* watermarked 'La Tentation de Saint Antoine' (nos.1-25), and 185 copies on *Vélin d'Arches* (nos. 26-210); also 10 copies *hors commerce* on *Vélin d'Arches* (nos. I-X).

Printer: Henri Jourde text and wood engravings (completed 24 Sept. 1933); Auguste Clot, lithographs (completed 1896).
L.1458-1983.

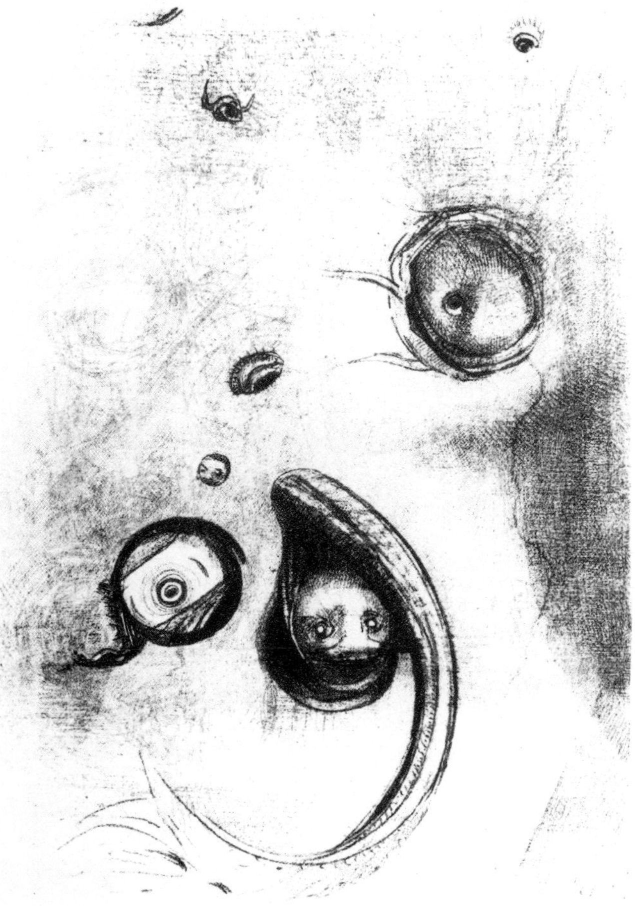

Redon made three separate sets of illustrations for Flaubert's work. The first was commissioned by Edmond Deman and published in 1888, with a second set appearing the following year. The third set was commissioned by Vollard, who published 50 copies in 1896. Lithographs from this printing of 1896 were used in 1933 to illustrate a text whose wood engravings had been executed in c.1910. The book was given a title-page with the date showing 1933, but it was not published. It was then prepared for formal publication in 1938, but only exhibition copies were issued during Vollard's lifetime.

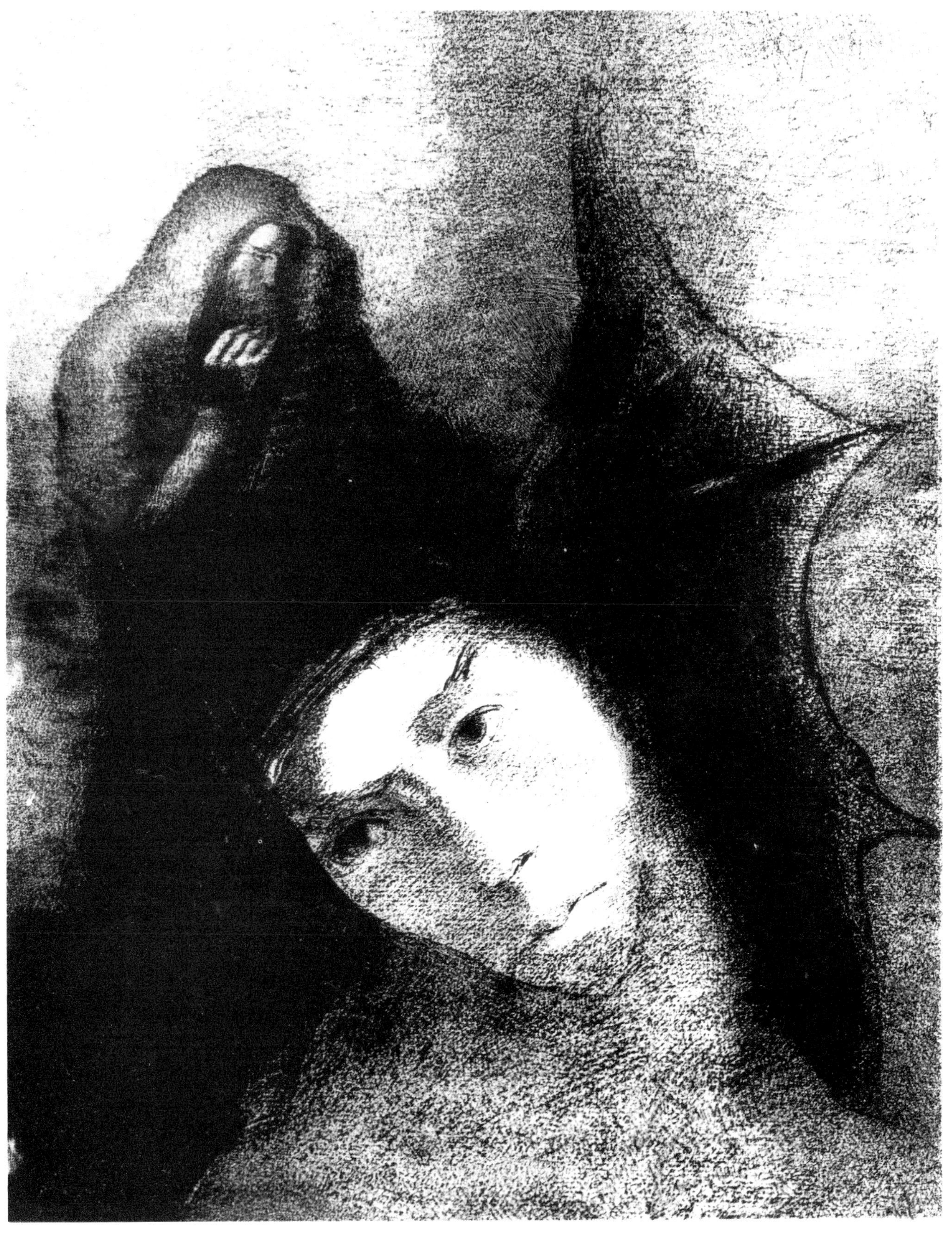

14 WILLIAM NICHOLSON **1898**

(1872-1949) Son of a Newark-on-Trent industrialist, William Nicholson learnt to draw at school and studied briefly at Herkomer's Academy in London and at the Académie Julian in Paris, but was largely self-taught. In 1893 he formed the Beggarstaff Company with his brother-in-law, James Pryde (1886-1941) and produced books, posters and portfolios of prints. After 1900, Nicholson began to adopt still-lifes, landscapes and portraits as subjects. In 1933 he visited Spain, whose painting he had discovered when in Paris through Manet. Knighted in 1936, he had a major retrospective at the National Gallery, London, in 1942. Ben Nicholson, the artist's son, thought his father's still-lifes and landscapes the best English paintings of their day after Sickert.

TYPES DE LONDRES, PAR WILLIAM NICHOLSON.
TEXTE PAR OCTAVE UZANNE (PARIS: HENRY FLOURY, 1898).
28pp., 350 x 265mm., with 12 lithographs, *hors texte*, 340 x 285mm., and 1 on the front cover.
Edition of 600 copies, with 40 further copies on *Japon impérial*.
Printer: [-].
L.1856-1958.

An English version of *LONDON TYPES* was published by Heinemann in the same year, 1898, with suitable verses supplied by W.E. Henley, the founder of *THE NEW REVIEW*. The French edition, published with a different selection of illustrations and a text by Uzanne, was produced by Henry Floury, who was responsible for the publication of books illustrated by another artist similarly associated with poster design, Toulouse-Lautrec, during the same period.

Pryde and Nicholson had been fellow students at the Académie Julian in Paris, and admired especially the poster work of Toulouse-Lautrec. The commercial success of their company, The Beggarstaffs, was modest; eventually the Artistic Supply Company acted as their agents and sold a number of posters for theatrical events as well as the famous *ROWNTREE'S ELECT COCOA* poster of 1900. Pryde and Nicholson developed a process, employed on this work, of multiplying woodcuts by mechanical lithography a method of reproduction disdained by private press purists. The success of Nicholson's methods did much to stimulate interest in the woodcut and poster in Britain.

101

15 PAUL GAUGUIN **1898**

(1848-1903) After childhood in Peru and work as a sailor in 1865-1871, Gauguin began to collect IMPRESSIONIST *pictures and to paint and sculpt as an amateur when he worked in a stockbroking firm from 1871. From 1880 he exhibited with the Impressionists and in 1883 devoted himself entirely to painting. From 1886 he frequented the artists' colony at Pont-Aven, the influence of Cézanne and Van Gogh subtituting itself for that of Pissarro. Théo Van Gogh organised his first exhibition in 1888. Gauguin exhibited with* LES VINGT *in Brussels, establishing himself as a pillar of the Pont-Aven school; with Émile Bernard, he formulated* SYNTHETISM (CLOISONNISME) *as a member of the* NABI *group. From 1891 he lived in Tahiti and the South Seas (apart from a stay in France in 1893-5); he was supported by Vollard from 1898.*

PAUL GAUGUIN, *NOA, NOA. VOYAGE DE TAHITI*
(MUNICH: R. PIPER & CO. VERLAG, 1926).
iv, 204 pp., 310 x 230mm., facsimile of Gauguin's manuscript with collotype reproductions in colour and black and white, some of them pasted in. Printed for the Marées Gesellschaft, Dresden. The V&A copy is not in its original binding.
L.5934-1984

NOA NOA, 'very fragrant', was the name given by Gauguin to Tahiti. The book is an account of his first visit to the island and has a complicated history. The text was begun in 1893, and the series of woodcuts produced in Brittany in 1894 with the help of the symbolist poet Charles Morice; the undertaking was designed to explain the nature of the artist's paintings after a disastrous exhibition in Paris. Extracts of the text appeared in the *REVUE BLANCHE* in 1897, and a version, heavily edited by Morice, was published in 1901 with the Éditions de la Plume. In 1903, Daniel de Monfried, to whom the artist had left much of his work, recovered the original manuscript together with further woodcuts, watercolours and photographs which Gauguin had added. The complete manuscript was given to the Louvre, and was used for the facsimile published in Munich in 1926, a period when Gauguin's reputation was secure and primitive works of art generally held in esteem.

16 JAN TOOROP 1899

(1858-1928) After a childhood in Java, Toorop studied at Delft and Amsterdam before moving to Brussels in 1882; here in 1885 he was invited to join LES VINGT *with Ensor, Khnopff and others, with whom he exhibited until 1893. In 1884 he visited England with the writer Verhaeren, meeting Whistler and William Morris, and discovering William Blake and the* PRE-RAPHAELITES. *His early* IMPRESSIONIST *style with a late* POINTILLIST *phase gave way to* SYMBOLISM *and* ART NOUVEAU *tendencies of which he is considered the major exponent in Holland; the influence of Beardsley has been detected in his* TROIS FIANCÉES *of 1893. Apart from graphic work, he also made designs for ceramics and stained glass. Converted to Catholicism in 1905, he devoted himself largely to religious subjects thereafter. In the period 1908-1911, Mondrian visited him frequently.*

W.G. VAN NOUHUYS, *EGIDIUS EN DE VREEMDELING . . . MET PORTRET VAN DEN SCHRIJVER EN ILLUSTRATIES DOOR J. TH. TOOROP* (HAARLEM: DE ERVEN F. BOHN, 1899).
vii, 46pp., 280 x 200 mm., with 3 illustrations *hors texte*, and 1 on the cover.
Edition of 200 (V&A copy no. 37).
L.124-1900.

Toorop provided illustrations for a number of books before his conversion in 1905, most of them in a curvilinear ART NOUVEAU style like that found on the covers of this book and contrasting with the SYMBOLIST character of the illustrations of the text itself. Toorop visited England in 1899 and spent a fortnight in Oxford, where he saw books from William Morris's Kelmscott Press; he began to work on these illustrations shortly after.

W.G. VAN NOUHUYS
EGIDIUS
EN DE VREEMDELING
J. TOOROP

17 PIERRE BONNARD 1900

(1867-1947)

PAUL VERLAINE, *PARALLÈLEMENT. LITHOGRAPHIES ORIGINALES DE PIERRE BONNARD* (PARIS: AMBROISE VOLLARD, 1900).
iii, 142pp., 295 x 240 mm., with 109 *sanguine* lithographs and 9 wood engravings.
Edition of 200 copies, (V&A copy no. 51), of which 10 are on *'Chine chine'* with a set of the lithographs without the text (nos. 1-10), 20 copies on *'Chine chine'* (nos. 11-30) and 170 copies on *Vélin de Hollande* (nos. 31-200).
Printer: Auguste Clot, lithographs; wood engravings cut by T. Beltrand; Imprimerie Nationale, text, set in Garamond, first cut in 1540 (completed 29 Sept. 1900).
Binding by Creuzevault.
L.1005-1953.

First published in 1889, Verlaine's poems *PARALLÈLEMENT* did not attract the attention that his earlier poetry managed to elicit in the last two or so years in his life (he died in 1896). According to Vollard, it was quite by chance that Bonnard was commissioned to illustrate the work, Lucien Pissarro having rejected the idea. Bonnard's illustrations, which have made Vollard's publication what has been called 'an epoch-making book', caused some disquiet since they were originally issued under the crest of the Imprimerie Nationale. When the director of the press, Arthur Christian, realised the nature of the illustrations, with their lyrical evocation of lesbian love, he ordered all copies to be recalled for new title pages to be added and the typographic mark of the national press to be removed. This was the first of Vollard's magnificent series of publications in book form illustrated by artists.

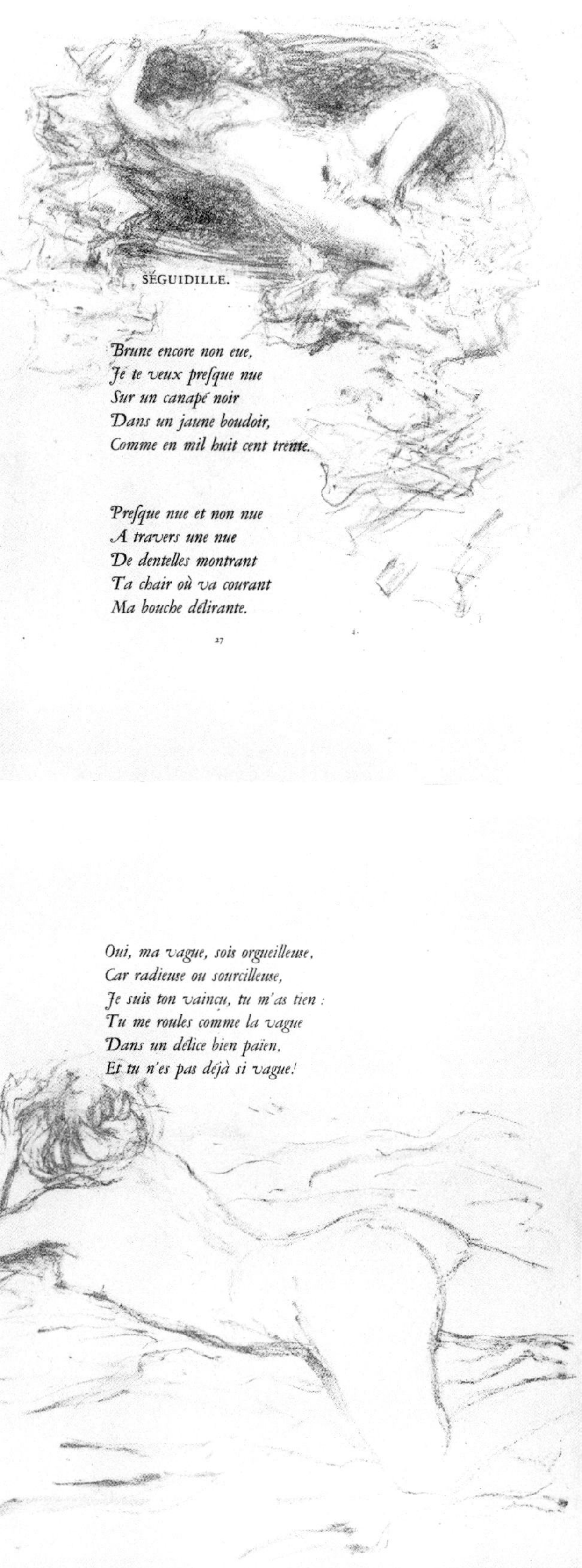

SÉGUIDILLE.

Brune encore non eue,
Je te veux presque nue
Sur un canapé noir
Dans un jaune boudoir,
Comme en mil huit cent trente.

Presque nue et non nue
A travers une nue
De dentelles montrant
Ta chair où va courant
Ma bouche délirante.

27

Oui, ma vague, sois orgueilleuse,
Car radieuse ou sourcilleuse,
Je suis ton vaincu, tu m'as tien :
Tu me roules comme la vague
Dans un délice bien païen,
Et tu n'es pas déjà si vague!

ÉTÉ.

Et l'enfant répondit, pâmée
Sous la fourmillante caresse
De sa pantelante maîtresse :
« Je me meurs, ô ma bien-aimée!

« Je me meurs : ta gorge enflammée
Et lourde me soûle & m'oppresse;
Ta forte chair d'où sort l'ivresse
Est étrangement parfumée;

18 PIERRE BONNARD **1902**

(1867-1947)

LES PASTORALES DE LONGUS, OU DAPHNIS ET CHLOÉ. TRADUCTION DE MESSIRE J. AMYOT . . . REFAITE EN GRANDE PARTIE PAR PAUL LOUIS COURIER. . . . LITHOGRAPHIES ORIGINALES DE P. BONNARD (PARIS: AMBROISE VOLLARD, 1902).
x, 298pp., 300 x 240mm., with 151 lithographs.
Edition of 250 copies (V&A copy no. 112), of which 10 copies are on *Japon ancien* with a double set of lithographs printed without the text on pink paper (nos.1-10), 40 copies on *Chine d'origine* with a double set of lithographs printed without the text on blue paper (nos.11-50), and 200 copies on *Hollande à la forme* made specially by Van Gelder and watermarked 'Daphnis et Chloé'.
Printer: Imprimerie Nationale, text (on hand press); Auguste Clot, lithographs (completed 31 Oct.1902).
Binding by P.L.Martin, 1975.
L.5933-1983.

This edition of the *PASTORALIA* of the 5th century poet Longus did not sell well, Vollard's stock remaining unsold for 20 years. In a different climate, it was more generally appreciated: in 1932 the Mermod Press, Lausanne, published an edition with 36 reproductions of the 1902 lithographs.

19 AUGUSTE RODIN **1902**

(1840-1917) From a very modest background, Rodin's talent as a draughtsman led his parents to send him to the École des Arts Décoratifs ('La Petite École') at the age of 14 to study under Horace Lecoq de Boisbaudran. Rodin spent time at the Louvre, Bibliothèque Nationale and Collège de France drawing. Failing to enter the École des Beaux Arts, he worked for some years under the fashionable decorative sculptor Ernest Carrier Belleuse at the Sèvres porcelain factory. After the Franco-Prussian war of 1870-1, Rodin worked in Belgium and elsewhere as an ornamental carver; a visit to Italy in 1875-6 impressed him with the work of Donatello and Michelangelo. In 1877 his L'AGE D'AIRAIN *was exhibited in Brussels and Paris, and was purchased by the state in 1880; from this date he received a number of official commissions for sculptures, including that for an ornamental gateway for the Musée des Arts Décoratifs in 1880,* THE BURGHERS OF CALAIS *in 1884,* LE BAISER *in 1887, the Victor Hugo and Balzac monuments in 1889 and 1891. In 1900 he organised a highly successful retrospective exhibition of his own work to coincide with the Exposition Universelle. A Chevalier in 1888, he became a Grand Officier of the Légion d'Honneur in 1910. Much of Rodin's sculptural work was done by his assistants under his supervision, and the organisation of his studio no doubt owed much to that part of his career spent in commercial workshops of decorative sculptors bent on mass production. The sculptor made a major gift of his work to the V&A Museum in 1914.*

110 OCTAVE MIRBEAU, *LE JARDIN DES SUPPLICES*
(PARIS: AMBROISE VOLLARD, 1902).
iv,170pp., 330 x 250mm., with 20m lithographs (18 in colour) *hors texte.*

Edition of 200 copies (V&A copy no.58), of which 15 copies are on *Japon impérial* with a double set of lithographs (nos.1-15), 30 copies on *Chine d'origine* with a double set of lithographs (nos.16-45), and 150 copies on *Velin* made especially by Masure et Perrigot watermarked *LE JARDIN DES SUPPLICES* (nos.46-200).
Printer: Auguste Clot, lithographs; Philippe Renouard, text set in 'une fonte neuve des caractéres Didot ancien' (completed 14 May 1902).
L.5883-1979.

Rodin was a prolific draughtsman throughout his life. It was Mirbeau who first suggested to Vollard that he might use Rodin to illustrate his novel, *LE JARDIN DES SUPPLICES.* Of the 'vingt compositions originales' mentioned on the title page, only five are thought to have been executed directly onto the stone by Rodin (Delteil),. The remainder may be facsimiles of the artist's drawings traced onto the stone and printed under his supervision. This work is considered the only work with original plates by Rodin.

Octave Mirbeau (1848-1917), a drama critic and friend of Pissarro and Monet, supported a number of avant-garde artists in Paris reviews and newspapers. He contributed to the success of the Gauguin sale in 1891 by a flattering review in *L'ECHO DE PARIS.* He wrote the preface to Rodin's first publication of drawings, *LES DESSINS D'AUGUSTE RODIN* (Paris: Jean Boussod, Manzi, Joyant & Co., Maison Goupil, 1897).

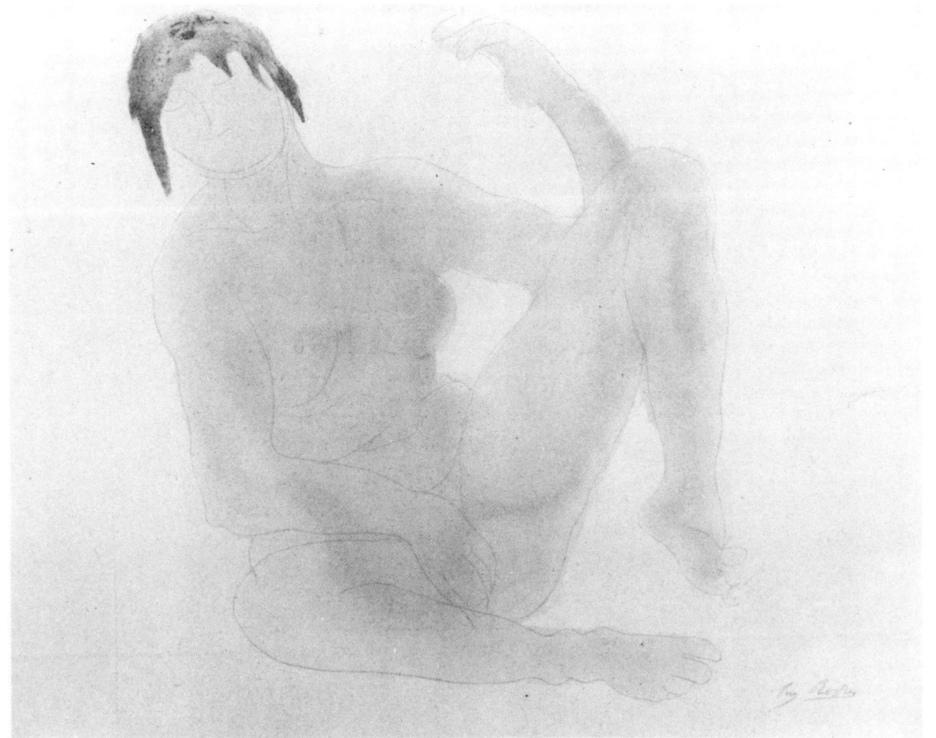

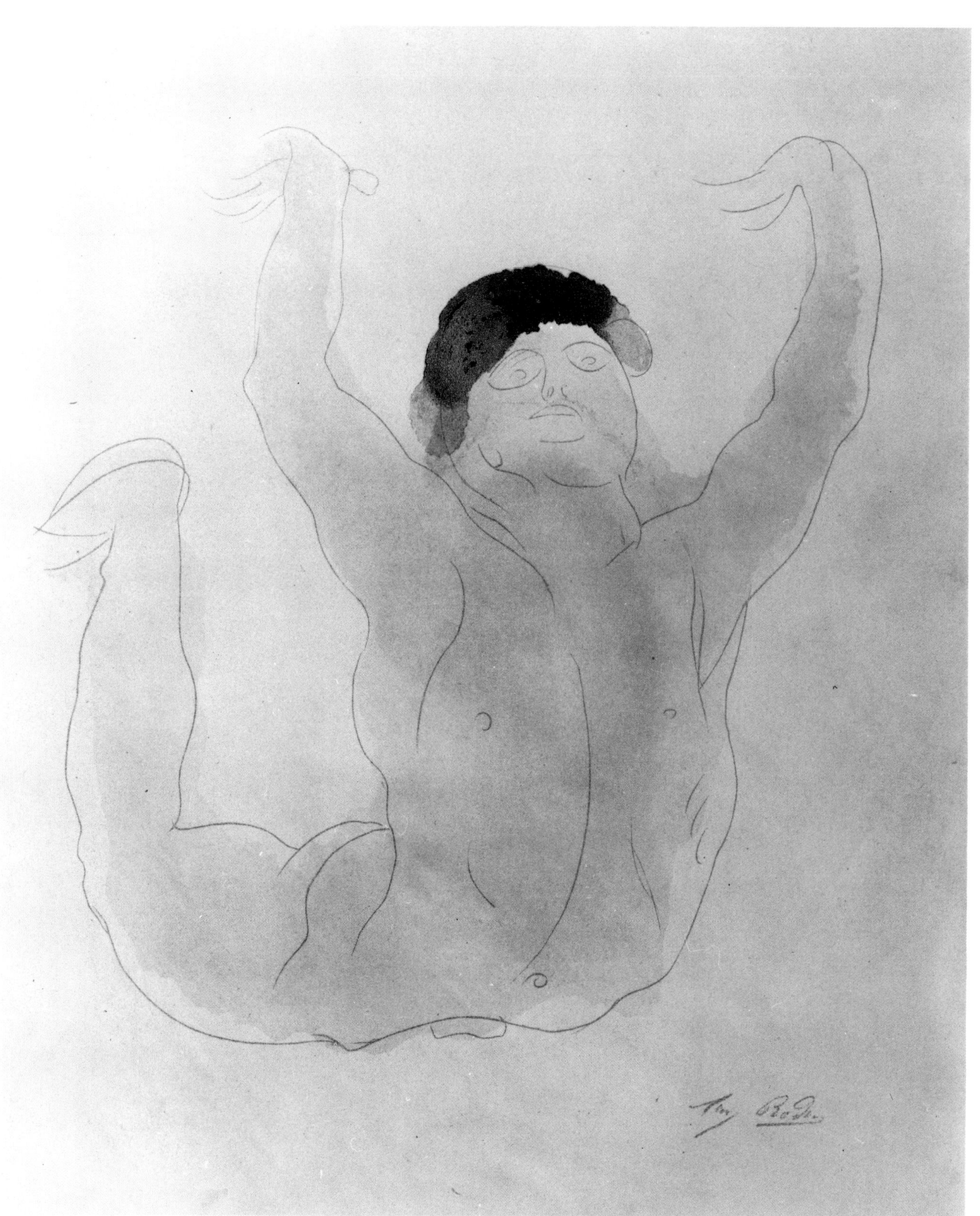

20 FRANTISEK KUPKA **1905**

(1871-1957) Born in Czechoslovakia, Kupka entered the Academy at Prague after apprenticeship to a saddle maker and initiation into spiritualism. After study in Vienna where, as in Prague, he was taught by painters associated with the NAZARENES, *he settled in Paris in 1895, supporting himself by producing satirical drawings for magazines and teaching fashion students to draw. His paintings reflected interest in* SYMBOLISM *and, after 1904,* FAUVISM; *later he moved towards an abstract style (he was among the* CUBISTS *Apollinaire termed 'Orphists' in 1912) and anticipated* FUTURIST *efforts to depict high-speed motion. He taught in Prague in 1918-1920; in 1931 he was one of the* ABSTRACTION-CRÉATION *group in Paris.*

LE CANTIQUE DES CANTIQUES, QUI EST SUR SALOMON. TRADUIT LITTÉRALEMENT ET REMIS À LA SCENE PAR JEAN DE BONNEFON (PARIS: LIBRAIRIE UNIVERSELLE, 1905).
84 pp., 310 x 440mm., with 6 wood engravings and vignettes and border ornaments in colour.
Edition of 517 copies (V&A copy no.127) signed by translator and publisher, of which 7 copies are on *Papier des Manufactures Impériales du Japon* each with an original drawing of the artist (nos.1-7), 10 copies on *Papier de Chine* with a double set of engravings (nos.8-17), and 500 copies on *Papier de Hollande à la forme* (nos.18-517).
Printer: Lecoq & Mathorel, Paris.
L.561-1984

112 This literal translation of the *SONG OF SONGS* is accompanied by a dramatisation, first performed in Paris on 22 May 1905. Kupka abandoned magazine illustration for *de luxe* editions designed for bibliophiles in 1904 as he achieved success as an artist. His first venture in illustration of this kind was in 1904 for *L'HOMME ET LA TERRE,* a sociological geography by the anarchist Elisée Reclus.

TRADUIT LITTÉRALEMENT

ET REMIS A LA SCÈNE

PAR

JEAN DE BONNEFON

A ÉTÉ JOUÉ POUR LA PREMIÈRE FOIS A PARIS

LE 22 MAI 1905

Illustrations de F. KUPKA

LIBRAIRIE UNIVERSELLE

33, RUE DE PROVENCE PARIS

21 PAUL KLEE **1906**

(1879-1940) After study in Munich under the painter Heinrich Knirr, the engraver Walter Ziegler and, for anatomy classes, Franz Stuck, Klee visited Italy in 1901-2 with the sculptor Hermann Haller; returning to his native Berne (where he earned his living playing in an orchestra), he produced a series of 17 grotesque satirical etchings which show his admiration for the visionary symbolism of Blake and Goya, as well as for Redon and Ensor, whose work he saw in Paris in 1905. Ten of these etchings were shown at the Munich Secession in 1906, the year that he moved to the city. His first one-man exhibition was in Berne in 1910 where drawings, engravings and 'sous-verre' were shown, but his Munich exhibition of the following year led to friendship, through Alfred Kubin, with Auguste Macke, Franz Marc and Kandinsky, membership of the BLAUER REITER *group, and discovery of* CUBISM *– after meeting Delaunay in Paris in 1912, Klee translated his* ESSAI SUR LA LUMIÈRE *into German for* DER STURM. *A visit to Tunisia in 1914 reinforced his interest in colour. In 1919 Klee declared that 'individualistic art...is a capitalist luxury', a frame of mind that led him to accept Gropius' offer of a post in the Bauhaus in 1920; here he was one of the* BLAUEN VIER *in 1924. His first one-man exhibition in Paris took place in 1925. In 1930 he left the Bauhaus to teach at Düsseldorf, from where he was dismissed by the Nazis in 1933; thereafter he returned to Switzerland.*

KANDIDE, ODER DIE BESTE WELTE. EINE ERZÄHLUNG VON VOLTAIRE. MIT 26 FEDERZEICHNUNGEN VON PAUL KLEE (MUNICH: KURT WOLFF VERLAG, 1920).
92 pp., 245 x 180mm., with 26 illustrations reproducing ink drawings.
Printer: Spamerschen Buchdruckerei, Leipzig (completed July 190).
L.712-1942.

Klee planned a series of illustrations for Voltaire's satire (published in 1759) in 1906, but most of the work was completed in 1911-12, with the project being further delayed by the war. Hans Arp was shown the work in 1913 and was enthusiastic that it be published; later in life he thought that he had succeeded in having the German translation of *CANDIDE* published by the Weissen Bücher Press, Leipzig, which published the Expressionist literary review, *DIE WEISSEN BLÄTTER*, from 1913; the Press in fact showed no interest when offered the project, and it was left for Kurt Wolff to publish it in Munich in 1920. In the same year, Klee illustrated his only other major book, *POTSDAMER PLATZ, ODER DIE NÄCHTE DES NEUEN MESSIAS* by Curt Corrinth, published by Georg Müller of Munich in a limited edition of 500.

22 EDWARD GORDON CRAIG 1907

(1872-1966) Son of Ellen Terry and the architect E.W.Godwin, Craig began a theatrical career in 1889 with Henry Irving's theatre company. Encouraged by William Nicholson and James Pryde, he studied drawing – hitherto he had been self-taught – and wood engraving. From 1898, his woodcuts were used in the theatrical review he founded, THE PAGE, *which appeared until 1901 and which was succeeded by* THE MASK *(published in Florence 1908-1915, 1918 and 1923-1929). Apart from work as a graphic designer, Craig devoted himself to stage design. In 1904, Count Harry Kessler arranged for him to work for Brahm at the Lessing Theatre in Berlin, after which he worked for Max Reinhardt, Diaghilev's Russian Ballet, Eleanor Duse and others, scarcely returning to England. A talented typographer, Craig's major achievement as an illustrator is perhaps the illustrations done for Kessler's Cranach Press edition of Hamlet in 1930.*

HUGO VON HOFMANNSTHAL, *DER WEISSE FÄCHER, MIT VIER HOLZSCHNITTEN VON EDWARD GORDON CRAIG* (LEIPZIG: INSELVERLAG, 1907).
34 pp., 342 x 242 mm., with 4 woodcuts.
Edition of 800 copies (V&A copy no.109), nos.1-50 on *Japan.*
L.288-1914.

Hofmannsthal, famed as the librettist of Richard Strauss's operas, first met Craig in 1904 when they co-operated in Brahm's production of a German version of Thomas Otway's *VENICE PRESERVED* in Berlin. Harry Kessler, a member of an extremely wealthy banking family who had been at school in England and who kept close links with the English Arts and Crafts movement, invited Craig to illustrate Hofmannsthal's *WEISSE FÄCHER* for £150, a fee that led Craig to produce the largest woodcuts he had executed up to that date.

23 GUSTAV KLIMT 1907

(1862-1918) Son of a noted Viennese engraver, Klimt studied at the Kunstgewerbeschule, Vienna, in 1876-83, after which he worked with his brother Ernst and Franz Matsch on large-scale allegorical paintings. Work of this period shows study of Egyptian, Hellenistic and ancient Indian art. From 1897 to 1905, when he resigned, Klimt was the president of the Vienna Secession, and contributed to its organ, VER SACRUM. *a journal which was a major vehicle for disseminating* JUGENDSTIL *but which also published work by representatives of* SYMBOLISM *such as Puvis de Chavannes and Burne-Jones. A major commission by the Vienna University for the painting of the ceiling of its hall (built by Josef Hoffmann in 1909-11) by Klimt caused outcry when the designs were shown in 1900 and 1903, leading the artist to give up the work in 1905. After a visit to Ravenna in 1903, where he was much struck by the Byzantine mosaics, Klimt undertook to provide a mosaic for the Stoclet Palace in Brussels, which was executed in 1909-11.*

LUCIAN, *DIE HETAERENGESPRAECHE DES LUKIAN. DEUTSCH VON FRANZ BLEI. MIT FÜNFZEHN BILDERN VON GUSTAV KLIMT* (LEIPZIG: JULIUS ZEITLER, 1907).
40 pp., 355 x 290 mm., with 15 illustrations 'in facsimile-lichtdruck' *hors texte.*
Edition of 450 copies (V&A copy no.23), of which 100 copies (nos.1-100) bound in chamois leather by the Wiener Werkstätte.
116 Bound by Wiener Werkstätte with monogram stamp of Josef Hoffman.
Printer: W. Drugulin, Leipzig.
L.1906-1925.

Book illustration was never a major part of Klimt's work. The drawings used for this edition of Lucian's 'Dialogue of Greek Courtesans' were not made with this text or book in mind.

24 OSKAR KOKOSCHKA **1908**

(1886-1980) From 1905 to 1909 Kokoschka attended the Kunstgewerbeschule in Vienna, where he discovered the art of the Far East, as well as the work of Romako, Klimt, Symbolist and Jugendstil artists such as Hodler. While a student, the Wiener-Werkstätte gave him a number of commissions and he had his own section in the Kunstschau in 1908 which caused some outcry and won him the patronage of the architect and designer Adolf Loos, who introduced him to the journal DIE FACKEL and to the literary and artistic circles of Vienna. In 1909 Loos took Kokoschka to Switzerland, and in the following year introduced him to Herwarth Walden, director of DER STURM, who showed his work in the STURM gallery and published a series of portrait drawings in the journal. In 1911 Paul Cassirer, the dealer who had played an important part in introducing French Impressionism and Van Gogh to Germany, exhibited his work as that of the foremost EXPRESSIONIST *artist from Vienna and paid him an annual salary until 1931. Wounded in 1915, Kokoschka taught at the Dresden Academy from 1919-1924, thereafter using Paris as a base for extensive travels in Europe, North Africa and the Middle East; in 1931 his work was shown at the Georges Petit Gallery. Forced by the Nazis to leave Vienna, and then Prague, where he had lived in 1931-4 and 1934-8 respectively, he emigrated to England in 1938 (naturalized 1947), where he stayed until moving to Villeneuve, Lake Geneva, in 1953.*

DIE TRAEUMENDEN KNABEN ([VIENNA, 1908]).
118 10 ff., 240 x 295 mm., 3 vignettes (1 on front cover) and 8 colour illustrations.
275 copies (numbered 1-275) of the original edition were marketed by the Kurt Wolff Verlag Leigzig, in summer of 1917 (V & A copy no.149) [according to label on back cover].
Printer: [Berger &Chwala].
L.1247-1962 Colour Plate 4

Kokoschka's first illustrated book produced for the Wiener Werkstätte, *DIE TRAEUMENDEN KNABEN (THE DREAMING YOUTHS)* appeared in 1908 but was not a commercial success. The book was issued in a 'pouch' binding, in the Chinese manner. In the work Kokoschka seeks to follow the dreams of a young adolescent boy, the strong colours of the lithographs providing an exotic lanscape to support the text. In his autobiography, the artist states his intention to have been to create a 'picture poem'. The work is dedicated to Gustav Klimt, who had left the Vienna Secession in 1905 and whose work was a powerful influence on Kokoschka at the time.

The Kurt Wolff Verlag of Leipzig bought up the stock of Kokoschka's book at a time when the artist's reputation was secure, and put 275 copies on the market as a limited edition at the price of 50 marks. Kurt Wolff (1887-1963) was among the most important publishers of avant-garde and Expressionist literature. As a student at Leipzig University, he collaborated with Ernst Rowohlt in the foundation of the Rowohlt Verlag in 1908, buying him out to establish his own publishing company in 1913. He was the chief publisher of the dramatist Eulenberg and of Kafka. The *JÜNGSTE TAGE* series, launched in 1913, became the best known and cheapest series of Expressionist texts, and was to include such classics as Kafka's *METAMORPHOSIS* (1916).

DIE TRAEUMEN=
DEN KNABEN.
OK

25 WASSILY KANDINSKY **1909**

(1866-1944) Son of a tea merchant, Kandinsky studied law, economy and ethnology at Moscow University before enrolling at the Academy of Anton Azbè in Munich at the age of thirty to devote himself to painting. He became a pupil with Paul Klee of Franz Stuck in 1900; in 1901 he founded the Phalanx group and travelled widely throughout Europe. He returned to Munich in 1908, founded the BLAUER REITER *group in 1911 with Franz Marc and had his first one-man exhibition at the Galerie Hans Goltz the following year. After the outbreak of war, he went to Moscow and took a major part in establishing art teaching, galleries and museums after the Revolution of 1917. In 1922 he joined the Bauhaus in Weimar where he worked until its closure by the Nazis in 1933. In 1934 he moved to Paris, where he worked until his death in 1944.*

KANDINSKY, *XYLOGRAPHIES* (PARIS: EDITIONS DES TENDANCES NOUVELLES, [1909].
7 ff. (loose), 325 x 325 mm., with 5 woodcuts and a small woodcut as frontispiece.
Edition of 1000 copies (un-numbered).
Bound in grey paper folder with woodcuts on each cover.
L.2124-1983.

Kandinsky first experimented with woodcuts in 1902, and in 1903 produced a set of 12 woodcuts and 2 vignettes under the title 'Poetry without words' published by the École Stroganoff, part of the School of Decorative Arts in Moscow. The medium is held to have played a significant role in his transition to 'abstract' painting later in the 1900s. Xylographies, financed by the artist himself, contains an introduction by 'Gérôme Maësse'. This was the pseudonym of Aléxis Mérodek Jeanneau, the founder and editor of *TENDANCES NOUVELLES,* a review that appeared in 63 issues between 1904 and 1914 and which published 33 woodcuts by Kandinsky between 1906 and 1909, as well as articles on the artist; one, of 1906, was by Jeaneau himself, who welcomed the revival of woodcut and lithograph, and lamented the industrialisation of ancient techniques. Kandinsky used *XYLOGRAPHIES* on occasion as a carte de visite, sending it, for example, to Schönberg and Alban Berg years later.

26 ANDRÉ DERAIN **1909**

(1880-1954) Derain overcame opposition of his parents, pastrycooks, to study painting at the Académie Carrière, Paris, in 1899; after his military service of 1900-1904, Matisse persuaded them to allow their son to become a painter. Derain was among those dubbed FAUVES *in the 1905 Salon d'Automne exhibition, and was a close friend of Matisse and Vlaminck. At the suggestion of the dealer and publisher Vollard, he spent 1905-6 painting in London, after which he turned towards Cézanne and, briefly,* CUBISM; *after 1910, the influence of Flemish and Italian 15th century painting is apparent. In 1919, he designed costumes and set for Diaghilev's* BOUTIQUE FANTASQUE, *as he did for Erik Satie's* JACK IN THE BOX *in 1926.*

GUILLAUME APOLLINAIRE, *L'ENCHANTEUR POURRISSANT. ÉDITION NOUVELLE ILLUSTRÉE DE REPRODUCTIONS DES BOIS GRAVÉS POUR L'ÉDITION ORIGINALE PAR ANDRÉ DERAIN* (PARIS: NOUVELLE REVUE FRANÇAISE, 1921)
92 pp., 195 x 140 mm., with 31 wood engravings.
Printer: Coulouma, Argenteuil.
L.5917-1984

Derain started engraving on wood in 1906, and it was generally this technique that he used for the 26 books that he illustrated. The illustrations in the *ENCHANTEUR POURRISSANT* of 1921 were reproductions of those used in the first edition of the work commissioned and produced in a limited edition of 106 copies by the dealer and publisher Kahnweiler in 1909. This earlier edition was the first work published by Apollinaire, who from 1908 had become the most articulate spokesman of avant-garde ideas and especially of CUBISM, promoting the exhibition of Georges Braque at Kahnweiler's in November of that year. The 1909 publication did not sell well, though it is now recognised as a landmark in 20th century book illustration; by 1921, Apollinaire's reputation was secure, and the following year the English critic Clive Bell could describe Derain as 'the greatest power among young French painters' characterised by 'a passionate love of the great tradition'.

Derain designed the distinctive device, the letters HK between two scallop shells, for Kahnweiler in 1909; it appears as the publisher's imprint on all of the dealer's publications.

27 RAOUL DUFY **1911**

(1877-1953) Son of a Le Harve accountant, Dufy studied at the École des Beaux Arts in Paris from 1900-1904. Work by Matisse and others at the 1905 Salon d'Automne, the great Cézanne retrospective exhibition of 1907 and friendship with Braque led him away from his early enthusiasm for IMPRESSIONISM. *By 1909, he was beginning to adopt a graceful and even light-hearted style with bold drawing and bright colours which found its fullest expression after 1919 in paintings of landscapes and of regattas, race-courses and other social events of the leisured classes. In 1911 he began producing fabric designs; from 1921 onwards he exhibited regularly in the* SALON DES ARTISTES DÉCORATEURS *and collaborated with the ceramicist Artigas. In the 1920s, Dufy worked for the couturier Paul Poiret, designing fabrics and, in 1925, executing wall hangings for his barge that formed a pavilion in the Exhibition of that year. In 1930, Dufy was in England, painting at Henley and Cowes regattas and at the Goodwood races. In 1952, Dufy was awarded the main prize for painting at the Venice Biennale.*

GUILLAUME APOLLINAIRE, *LE BESTIAIRE, OU CORTEGE D'ORPHÉE, ILLUSTRÉ DE GRAVURES SUR BOIS PAR RAOUL DUFY* (PARIS: DEPLANCHE, 1911)

40 ff., 330 x 260mm with 30 wood engravings and 5 wood engraved ornaments.

Edition of 122 copies (V&A copy no. 86) with 2 *copies hors commerce*, signed by Apollinaire and Dufy, this copy dedicated to Élémir Bourges.

Printer: Gauthier-Villars, Paris.

L.1-1982.

LE BESTIAIRE was Dufy's first major venture as an illustrator. Picasso had originally suggested the project to Apollinaire in 1906, but the latter turned to Dufy when Picasso abandoned the scheme. The wood engravings reflect Dufy's association with the Fauve style; after the First World War, he was to abandon this medium, in favour of lithography and watercolour, substituting for the latter the new translucent and fresh colours produced by the chemist Margorer in 1935. By 1911, Apollinaire was writing regularly under the rubric 'Vie Artistique' in the periodical *L'INTRANSIGEANT,* and his theoretical discussions attracted as much attention as his poetry. *LE BESTIAIRE* did not sell well, partly on account of the fact that most of the poems had been published previously without illustrations in an issue of *LA PHALANGE,* but the Deplanche edition of the poet's work was republished as a reduced facsimile by Jean Cocteau's Éditions de la Sirène in 1919 (after Apollinaire's death) and again after Dufy's death, in 1956, by Éditions du Cap of Monte Carlo.

Le Dauphin.

28 EMIL NOLDE **1911**

(1867-1956) Emil Hansen adopted the name Nolde in 1902. From 1884 to 1891, he worked as woodcarver and designer of furniture, teaching drawing at the School of Industrial Design at St. Gall, Switzerland, from 1892 to 1898. From 1898, when Nolde produced his first recorded etchings, he studied painting in Munich and Dessau; in 1900 he attended briefly the Académie Julian in Paris and five years later had his first one-man show in Ernst Arnold's gallery in Dresden. Invited in 1906 to join the BRÜCKE *group,* 'en hommage à vôtre tempête de couleurs', *Nolde exhibited with them the following year but then left to work independently. His earliest lithographs date from 1907. He visited Ensor in Ostend in 1911, and showed in the second* BLAUER REITER *exhibition in Munich in 1912. In 1913 he joined an anthropological expedition to the South Seas. He was made an honorary doctor of Kiel University in 1926 and a member of the Prussian Academy of Fine Arts in 1931; a supporter of the Nazis, he found himself the subject of their persecution. Little of his graphic work done after 1929 survives: over 3000 prints and drawings were destroyed during an allied air-raid over Berlin in 1943. A major retrospective exhibition was devoted to his work in 1948 at Hanover.*

GUSTAV SCHIEFLER, *DAS GRAPHISCHE WERK EMIL NOLDES BIS 1910* (BERLIN: JULIUS BARD VERLAG, 1911).
ii, 140 pp., 250 x 190 mm., with 27 'vignettes', and 1 lithograph *hors texte.*

Edition of 435 copies (V&A copy no.72), of which 12 copies are on *Kaiserlich Japan* (nos.1-10), and 15 copies on *Gelder Bütten* (nos.11-35); nos.1-35 include an etching, 'Joseph und seine Brüder'.
Bookseller's label on the inside cover: 'Harry Martinson, Libraire, Moscou'.
Printer: Oscar Brandstetter, Leipzig, text and woodblocks; W.Gente, Hamburg, lithograph; Pan Presse, Berlin, etching.
L.5022(i)-1983.

Gustav Schiefler first saw Nolde's etchings in 1906 when he was compiling a catalogue of Edvard Munch's graphic work, and brought the two artists together. From this date, Schiefler began to collect Nolde's graphic work. In 1927, Schiefler produced a sequel to his 1911 catalogue, *DAS GRAPHISCHE WERK VON EMIL NOLDE, 1910-1925* (Berlin: Im Euphorion Verlag, [1927]), in a limited edition of 520 copies (V&A copy no.105; L.5022 (ii)-1983; colour plate 11).
The two catalogues that Schiefler made of Nolde's production were produced in close collaboration with the artist; the original woodblocks were used for the printing of both volumes.

126

29 JAMES ENSOR **1911**

(1860-1949) Son of a couple who ran a souvenir shop in Ostend, Ensor rarely left Belgium or the city of his birth. In 1877-1879, he studied at the Académie des Beaux Arts in Brussels under Jan Portaels, who introduced orientalism to Belgium. He exhibited first in Brussels artistic circles (The Chrysalide and the Essor) and was a founder member of LES VINGT *in 1884, who, however, voted for his expulsion in 1889. In the 1880s he took masks and skeletons as a major theme, which, with his taste for strange objects, have led to his being described as a precursor of* EXPRESSIONISM *and* SURREALISM. *His most significant work is considered to have been done before 1900; he was made a Baron in 1929.*

JAMES ENSOR, *LA GAMME D'AMOUR* (BRUSSELS: ÉDITIONS 'UN COUP DE DÉS ...', 1929).
16 pp., with 1 colour reproduction and 21 colour lithographs numbered 1-22 on 21 ff. (13 & 14 on same leaf), and 31 pp. of sheet music, 250 x 325mm.
Edition of 270 copies (V&A copy no. 99), of which 20 copies are on *Japon Impérial* (nos. 1-20), and 250 copies on *Grand Vélin d'Arches* (nos. 21-270).
Printer: J.E. Goossens, text, set in Astrée corps 16; Maison Malvaux, Brussels, colour plates; J. De Vleeschouwer, Evere, music. (completed 31 March 1929).
L.1598-1936

Ensor's interest in printmaking can be traced back to 1886. The ballet *LA GAMME D'AMOUR* evidences the theme of carnival and fantasy found elsewhere in Ensor's work; it was composed by the artist in 1907, who designed the costumes and sets as well as writing the text and music. The prints are variously dated between 1910 and 1918. The publisher in 1929 was Georges Vriamont of Brussels, whose imprint derives from Mallarmé's line 'Un coup de dés jamais n'abolira le hazard'.

30 ARISTIDE MAILLOL **1912**

(1861-1944) From a farming family at Banyuls in the Pyrenees, Maillol's gifts as a draughtsman won him a scholarship to Paris, where he entered the École des Beaux Arts with some difficulty in 1885, working under Gérôme and Cabanel. He discovered the work of IMPRESSIONISTS *at the Musée du Luxembourg, and met Émile Bernard, who encouraged him to produce his first designs for tapestries, as well as Gauguin. In 1893 he set up a tapestry studio at Banyuls, and was introduced to* NABIS *circles by Rippl-Ronái. From 1895 he began to produce sculpture, devoting himself to this medium from 1900 on account of his declining eyesight. Maillol had his first one-man exhibition at Vollard's gallery in 1902 and was acclaimed a major sculptor at the Salon d'Automne in 1905, the year that his friendship with Count Harry Kessler began. Maillol received a number of major commissions for war memorials and monuments to individuals, his classical and monumental treatment of the human figure, particularly the female nude, being much in vogue before his retirement to Banyuls in 1939.*

THE ECLOGUES OF VERGIL IN THE ORIGINAL LATIN WITH AN ENGLISH PROSE TRANSLATION BY J.H. MASON; & WITH ILLUSTRATIONS DRAWN AND CUT ON THE WOOD BY ARISTIDE MAILLOL (LONDON: EMERY WALKER LTD, FOR CRANACH PRESS, WEIMAR, 1928).
116 pp., 330 x 240mm., with 43 woodcuts by Maillol, and headline for title page by Eric Gill.
English Edition of 1928: 264 copies, of which 225 copies
128 (V&A copy no. 61) on 'hand-made paper of hemp fibre and linen' (nos. 1-225; nos. 201-225 not for sale), 33 copies on 'imperial Japanese' paper (nos. I-XXXIII; nos. XXVI-XXXIII not for sale), 6 copies on vellum (nos. A-F; 5 only for sale).
Paper made by Gaspard Maillol [Monval].
Type faces: Roman type, after Nicolas Jenson, 1473, cut by Edward Prince supervised by Emery Walker; italic type designed by Edward Johnston.
Printer: Cranach Press, Weimar (completed 1927).
L.532-1928.

The Cranach Press *ECLOGUES* was planned by Count Harry Kessler as early as 1912, when Maillol was commissioned to provide woodcuts for the text. These were designed and executed at Banyuls in 1912-1914 and 1925, the artist drawing 'on his immediate neighbourhood and on his personal acquaintances for certain of the motives'. The printing of the German edition was begun in 1914 but resumed in 1925. The paper, 'devised in joint research by Count Harry Kessler and Aristide and Gaspar Maillol' was made by a special hand process in a workshop set up at Monval. Editions in German and French were also produced. The English edition was dedicated by Kessler to Emery Walker ' the master of book printing, the friend & adviser of William Morris'. Kessler's links with Walker go back to 1904, when the latter gave advice about the typographical arrangement of some special editions that Kessler was having published in Germany by the Insel Verlag (see John Dreyfus, *ITALIC QUARTET*, 1966). Prices of the English edition varied between 12 and 17 guineas for the paper edition, and between 40 and 45 guineas for the edition on imperial Japanese paper (which included an extra set of prints on yellow Chinese paper). The prices varied with the type of binding. All copies on vellum were sold prior to publication.

P. VERGILIUS MARO: THIRD ECLOGUE
MENALCAS DAMOETAS & PALAEMON

MENALCAS: TELL ME DAMOETAS WHOSE FLOCK IS THIS? IS IT MELIBOEUS'S? DAMOETAS: NO, IT BELONGS TO AEGON; HE PUT IT IN MY CARE A FEW DAYS AGO.

MENALCAS: Ever unlucky flock of sheep! While their owner dangles about Neaera, and fears she will favour me instead of him, this hired shepherd milks the poor ewes twice in an hour, draining the poor beasts dry, and filching the milk from the lambkins.

23

P. VERGILI MARONIS ECLOGA PRIMA
MELIBOEUS ET TITYRUS

INCIPIT MELIBOEUS

TITYRE TU PATULAE RECUBANS SUB
TEGMINE FAGI, SILVESTREM TENUI MU
SAM MEDITARIS AVENA:, NOS PATRIAE
FINIS ET DULCIA LINQUIMUS ARVA.
NOS PATRIAM FUGIMUS : TU TITYRE
LENTUS IN UMBRA , FORMOSAM RE
SONARE DOCES AMARYLLIDA SILVAS.

31 WASSILY KANDINSKY 1913

(1866-1944)

KANDINSKY, *KLÄNGE* (MUNICH: R. PIPER & CO. VERLAG,[1913]).
58ff., 285 x 285 mm., with 56 woodcuts, of which 12 in colour and 44 in black and white.
Edition of 300 copies (V&A copy no.257), signed by the artist, on *holländisch Bütten*.
Printer: Poeschel & Trepte, text; F. Bruckman, woodcuts.
L. 4200-1960. Colour plate 5

The publisher of *KLÄNGE*, Piper Verlag, also published the almanac of the Blauer Reiter group, as well as one of Kandinsky's major theoretical works, *UBER DAS GEISTIGE IN DER KUNST* (published in England in 1914 as *THE ART OF SPIRITUAL HARMONY*), which finally appeared in 1912 having been completed in 1910. The 38 poems in *KLÄNGE*, written between 1908 and 1913, are closely related to Kandinsky's compositions *DER GELBE KLANG, SCHWARZ UND WEISS* and *GRÜNER KLANG*, written for the stage and concerning the relationship between sound, colour and movement. The plays were never performed, but the poems were read at the Cabaret Voltaire, Zurich, in 1916 by Tzara's Dada associates.

32 NATALIA GONTCHAROVA 1913

(1881-1962) From a wealthy family descended from Pushkin's wife, Gontcharova studied sculpture at the Moscow Academy in 1898-1900 before turning to painting. She met Mikhail Larionov, her life-long companion, at this time. Together they attempted to reconcile an art based on Russian folklore with avant-garde movements, founding in 1909 a Primitive group. She joined the 'Knave of Diamonds' group set up by Larionov and the Burlyuk brothers in 1910, to leave it with Larionov the following year when its participants made it a society with established rules. She was a signatory in 1913 of Larionov's RAYISM (LUCHIZM) *manifesto. Joining Larionov in Switzerland in 1915, she settled with him in Paris in 1917. Thereafter theatre design became her major activity; she designed sets and costumes for Stravinsky's* LES NOCES *(a work resulting from the composer's study of Russian folk songs) in 1923 and for* THE FIREBIRD *in 1926. She also designed clothes for the Maison Myrbor of Paris. She participated with Larionov in the retrospective exhibition on* RAYISM *in 1948 and in the Edinburgh/London exhibition on Diaghilev in 1954. A major exhibition of her work took place at the V&A in 1962.*

SERGEI PAVLOVICH BOBROV, *VERTOGRADARI NAD LOZAMI [GARDENERS OVER THE VINES] WITH DRAWINGS BY GONTCHAROVA* (MOSCOW: LIRIKA, 1913).
172pp., 180 x 120 mm., with 10 colour lithographs and 1 relief print in text.
Standard edition without illustrations and a special edition of 50 numbered copies issued with lithographs (V&A copy no.31 [?]).
Printer: V. I. Voronov.
L.2781-1981.

The 10 inserted double-page blue and brown plates are Gontcharova's only coloured Rayist lithographs. Bobrov, 'the Russian Rimbaud' (Pasternak) was one of the short-lived Symbolist group LIRIKA that sought to publish its own work. Bobrov, himself an illustrator and interested in book design, ends *VERTOGRADARI* with a short article claiming that the Rayist style promoted by Gontcharova and Larionov was the only proper form of book illustration since 'it did not attempt to add anything to the poet's conception, but enabled the artist to use an analogous metaphor' (Chamot, *APOLLO*, Dec. 1973).

33 MIKHAIL LARIONOV **1913**

(1881-1964) Larionov entered the Moscow Academy in 1898, where he was to meet his life-long companion, Natalia Gontcharova. He was invited by Diaghilev to Paris in 1906, where he presented Russian paintings at the Salon d'Automne. In 1907 he organised with David Burlyuk the Crown exhibition at St. Petersburg, founding in the same year the 'Blue Rose' group, whose philosophy he expounded in its review, THE GOLDEN FLEECE. *The group's first exhibition was held in Moscow in 1908, and ensured Larionov's position as leader of the Russian avant-garde:* FAUVIST *works were shown alongside those of Sisley, Pissarro, Braque and Cézanne. With David and Vladimir Burlyuk he founded the 'Knave of Diamonds' association in 1910, but left it with Gontcharova the following year to form the 'Donkey's Tail' group which sought to maintain a link with the heritage of Russian folklore, borrowing imagery from* lubki *(popular prints) and signwriting as well as from avant-garde western movements. In 1913 he published the* RAYIST *manifesto, which 'proposed to reduce a perceived image to the sum of the rays which emanate from it', producing an art that was abstract but which gave colour a central position. Larionov left with Diaghilev for Paris in 1914, where his work and that of Gontcharova was shown in the Galerie Paul Guillaume with a catalogue prefaced by Apollinaire's fervent defence of Rayism. From 1915, Larionov devoted himself to the theatre, where he felt Rayist ideas received full expression. Among his most celebrated works for Diaghilev are* CHOUT *(1921) and* LE RENARD *in 1922. Soon after the British retrospective exhibitions (Arts Council 1961, V&A 1962) Larionov gave a major collection of graphic work and books to the V&A Museum.*

KONSTANTIN ARISTARKOVICH BOL'SHAKOV,
LE FUTUR (MOSCOW: 1913).
17ff., 200 x 147 mm., signed by Larionov, with 8 full-page lithographs in text (4 by Larionov, 4 by Gontcharova).
L.5576-1962 (LARIONOV COLLECTION).

LE FUTUR has the distinction of having been confiscated by the police shortly after its appearance, making it a still rarer book for one published in a small print-run. The text was handwritten by Firsov, a painter whose theories of transparency emerge in two of Larionov's contributions. The long free-verse poem looks forward to renewed growth after war. One of Larionov's compositions shows an outlined woman's head with a small cyclist on her cheek, an image overlaid by ray-like lines, letters and numbers. This provides a specific connection with the Italian Futurist Technical Manifesto of 1910: 'How often have we not seen on the cheek of the person with whom we were talking the horse which passes at the end of the street'; the use of lettering has been taken to reflect devices used by contemporary French Cubists.

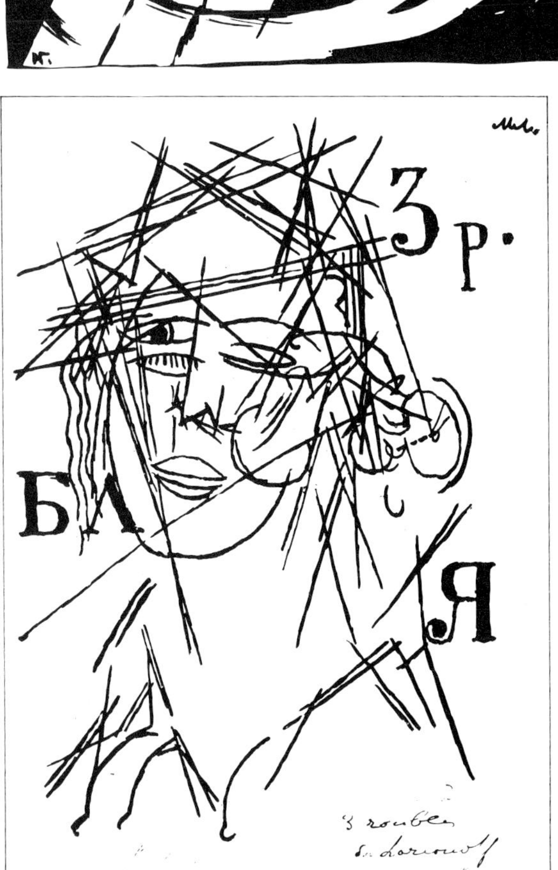

ABOVE Gontcharova.
BELOW Larionov.

34 OSKAR KOKOSCHKA 1914

(1886-1980)

KARL KRAUS, *DIE CHINESISCHE MAUR*
(LEIPZIG: KURT WOLFF VERLAG, 1914).
23ff., 478 x 370 mm., with 8 lithographs.
Edition of 200 copies (V&A copy no. 68).
Printers: Poeschel & Trepte, Leipzig.
Bound in vellum.
L.1300-1984.

The illustrations for Kraus's work are one of three sets of lithographs produced by Kokoschka in Vienna immediately before the Great War in a new drawing style influenced by Ludwig Meidner. Kokoschka produced them at the time of his liaison with Alma Mahler.

Karl Kraus (1874-1936) was the editor, from 1911 the sole editor, of the Vienna review *DIE FACKEL*, which had defended Kokoschka at the time of his participation in the 1908 Kunstschau. In a collection of essays *SITTLICHKEIT UND KRIMINALITÄT* and in the present work he appears as an outspoken champion of criminal law reform, attacking the moral hypocrisy of Viennese journalism and its support of a system that glorified the values of the rich. The influence of Kraus's dramatic work can be seen in works of Bertholt Brecht.

35 DAVID BURLYUK VLADIMIR BURLYUK 1914

David Burlyuk (1892-1967) Vladimir Burlyuk (1886-1917) Growing up on an estate in south Russia, David and Vladimir studied at the Kazan Art School, Odessa, before working under Azbè in Munich in 1903. David thereafter went to Paris to study under Corman, 1904-5, returning to settle in Moscow in 1907. The brothers were among the co-founders, with Larionov and Gontcharova, of the 'Blue Rose' group that organised exhibitions; the first in 1907 introduced French FAUVIST *paintings and those by Pissarro, Braque and Cézanne, to the Russian capital, as well as their own. After a folkloristic period, David Burlyuk came under the influence of German* EXPRESSIONISM; *in 1912 he was among those invited by Kandinsky (other Russians were Larionov, Gontcharova and Malevich) to show at the second* BLAUER REITER *exhibition in Munich in 1912. Breaking with Larinov and Gontcharova, the brothers formed the Hylaea group, a name that stressed a special link between their native South Russia and pre-classical Greece. A member of the Moscow Academy from 1911, David Burlyuk was expelled after his 1913-14 lecture tour of Russia to promote Futurism, undertaken with Mayakovsky, whom he encouraged to abandon painting for poetry. From 1915, David lived outside Moscow in the Urals, and left the Soviet Union in 1918; from 1922 he lived in the USA. He is remembered less as painter than as an extraordinarily energetic organiser of the avant-garde in pre-Revolutionary Russia. His brother Vladimir was killed on active service in 1917.*

DOKHLAYA LUNA [THE CROAKED MOON], 2nd REVISED EDITION (MOSCOW, FUTURISTUI, 1914).
132 pp., 237 x 183 mm., with 19 plates and 3 illustrations in text.
Printer: Muisl'.
L.2782-1981.

THE CROAKED or *DEAD MOON,* an anthology of verse, prose, essays and drawings, illustrated by David and Vladimir Burlyuk, first appeared in a limited edition of 1000 copies in 1913. It was published by the Hylaea group, who here call themselves 'Futurists' for the first time. It carried an article by Livshits detailing differences between Larionov's RAYIST group and the RUSSIAN FUTURISTS proper. Apart from Mayakovsky and Bol'shakov, the chief contributors were the Burlyuk brothers, David including 30 poems in imitation of the French 'poètes maudits'.

The second edition of the work was ruthlessly re-arranged and edited by the poet Shershenevich during the absence of David Burlyuk on the Futurist lecture tour of Russia. The publication is a monument to indigenous 'Cubo-Futurism' before the First World War; a Cubist vision is much in evidence; the frontispiece of the 1913 edition was intentionally bound in upside-down on the principle that effective cubist analysis of any subject meant that a picture should be capable of being interpreted from any angle. David Burlyuk provided illustrations for a number of Futurist books, including *ROARING PARNASSUS* (1913), *TANGO WITH COWS* (1914) and, with his brother Vladimir, the play *VLADIMIR MAYAKOVSKY: A TRAGEDY* (1914). In 1956, David Burlyuk was invited to take part in the Mayakovsky memorial celebrations in Moscow.

36 OLGA ROZANOVA **1915**

(1886-1918) Rozanova studied in Moscow between 1904 and 1910 at the Bolshakov Art College and the Stroganov Art Institute. By 1911, she was an active member of the Union of Youth, a long-lived group of St. Petersburg artists. From 1912, she was a close associate of Kruchenuikh and Malevich; from this date she began to make woodcuts, collages, and lithographs for RUSSIAN FUTURIST *publications, collaborating with Malevich on a number of them. Discovery of* CUBISM *encouraged abstract tendencies in her work; she followed Malevich into* SUPREMATISM, *becoming a member of the* Supremus *group in 1916/1917. After the Revolution, she was among the artists accommodated in the* VKhUTEMAS *Studios (these were new schools for higher art and technical education set up as part of the Soviet educational programme; Kandinsky was an important figure in designing their curriculum and many ideas given expression there later emerged in the* BAUHAUS*). Rozanova shares with Malevich the distinction among the leaders of the Russian avant-garde of not having visited Paris, a fact which has led some to signal their originality within their milieu. Rozanova died of diptheria in 1918.*

STRELETS, SBORNIK PERVUII [THE ARCHER],
VOLUME 1 (PETROGRAD: 'STRELETS', 1915).
220 pp., 250 x 190 mm., with 19 illustrations in the text.
Edition of 5000 copies (un-numbered).
Printer: AN Lavrov & Ko.
L. 5309-1962 (LARIONOV COLLECTION)

Three of the illustrations in this volume are by Rozanova; the cover was designed by Kul'bin. *STRELETS*, founded and edited in 1915 by Alexander Belenson, was a successor to the *FIRST JOURNAL OF RUSSIAN FUTURISTS* that had appeared in 1914. The new magazine brought together almost all the members of the Hylaea group: apart from neo-primitive and futurist poetry, the magazine included criticism, among which was an article on the English Vorticists and an interview with Ezra Pound, as well as a translation of a Rimbaud poem and a discussion of Cubism by Kul'bin that referred to musicians such as Debussy and Schönberg. The publication of *STRELETS* provoked a violent critical reaction, the association of 'literary hooligans' such as the Burlyuks, Mayakovsky and Rozanova with dignitaries of the literary establishment such as Blok, a representative of a symbolist generation, causing much comment; Maxim Gorky grudgingly admitted the validity of their movement: 'They have got something . . . Even in their shouts and invective there is something good'. Rozanova illustrated a number of books, some of them in collaboration with Malevich and the poet Kruchenuikh, proponent of 'transrational' or *zaum* (nonsense) language.

37 WYNDHAM LEWIS **1915**

(1882-1957) After study at the Slade School, London, in 1898-1901, Lewis travelled widely. On returning to England he showed regularly with the CAMDEN TOWN GROUP *from 1911 and exhibited with the second Post-Impressionist exhibition in London in 1912. He left the Omega Workshop, of which he was a founder member, on quarrelling with Roger Fry to found the Rebel Art Centre and establish the English* VORTICIST *movement. After acting as a war artist in 1917-1918, he organised Group X in 1920 but increasingly rejected the abstract tendencies of* CUBIST *style and devoted himself to political and literary activities. He was the subject of a retrospective exhibition at the Redfern gallery, London, in 1949.*

BLAST .... REVIEW OF THE GREAT ENGLISH VORTEX, NO. 2, EDITED BY WYNDHAM LEWIS, JULY 1915 (LONDON: JOHN LANE, THE BODLEY HEAD).
102 pp., 290 x 240mm., with 16 process engravings, 8 ornaments and cover illustration.
Printer: Leveridge & Co., Harlsden.
L.1491-1937

Intended to coincide with an exhibition of the Vorticist group at the Dove Gallery, London, the second issue of *BLAST,* a 'war number', was produced in a white paper cover designed by Lewis. Illustrations included were by Jessie Dismorr, Frederick Etchells, Gaudier-Brzeska, Jacob Kramer, CRW Nevinson, William Roberts, Helen Saunders, Edward Wadsworth and Wyndham Lewis.

BLAST
WAR NUMBER
WYNDHAM
LEWIS
JULY
1915.

38 FRANZ MARC 1915

(1880-1916) After studying philosophy and theology at Munich University, Marc studied painting at the Munich Academy from 1900 to 1903. A visit to Paris in 1907 left him impressed with the work of Gauguin and Van Gogh. Animal subjects occupied him most in this period; in 1908 he produced a series of horse paintings, later developing his ideas of the regeneration of art by a return to a primitive world of the kind inhabited by animals. In 1910 he had his first one-man exhibition in Munich, and met Kandinsky, with whom he formed the BLAUER REITER *group the following year (Jawlensky and August Macke were other founder members). The group's first exhibition was in that year, with works by Douanier Rousseau and Robert Delaunay, the latter much esteemed by its members and visited by Marc in Paris the following year.* CUBISM *and* FUTURISM *became major influences in his work from this period. Marc was killed at Verdun in 1916. The complete catalogue of his work (Lankheit, 1970), mentions 240 oil paintings, 251 watercolours and pastels, but only 63 engravings (all dating from after 1908) of which 1 was an etching and 25 wood engravings.*

DER STURM. HALBMONATSSCHRIFT FÜR KULTUR UND DIE KÜNSTE, SECHSTER JAHRGANG, NOS. 5-6 FOR JUNE 1915 (BERLIN: DER STURM VERLAG).
12 pp., 415 x 310mm. (pp. 25-36, p.1 starting with no. 1, April 1915 issue, of 6th Jahrgang), with 2 woodcuts.
L.1978-1951.

Marc's major work as a wood engraver began after his association with Kandinsky, when both worked together to illustrate the Blauer Reiter almanac in 1912. Marc held that the woodcut technique helped him to clarify his own style, and this seems evident from the artist's work at the time when he was developing under the influence of Futurism.

DER STURM was founded in March 1910 in Berlin by Herwarth Walden, and appeared in Berlin and Vienna. Conceived initially as a literary review, it began to publish woodcuts from May 1910 and became the leading organ as much for avant-garde writers as for artists. From 1912, Walden became increasingly interested in the Blauer Reiter group in Munich and in contemporary movements abroad, particularly Futurism and Cubism, inviting their Italian and French representatives to send works to exhibitions organised by *DER STURM* in that year. Writings of Delaunay and Apollinaire were published in the review in 1913, the year that Walden organised the *ERSTER DEUTSCHER HERBSTSALON* in Berlin, in which many non-German painters were represented (Marc contributed his apocalyptic *FATE OF THE ANIMALS*). Apollinaire arranged for Chagall's work to be shown at the *DER STURM* gallery in 1914, and Walden sent work abroad to Stockholm, London and Japan. The review was not immune to the wave of chauvinism that swept over Europe after the declaration of war in 1914.

Marc. Sleeping shepherdess, original woodcut.

DER STURM

HALBMONATSSCHRIFT FÜR KULTUR UND DIE KÜNSTE

Redaktion und Verlag Berlin W 9 / Potsdamer Straße 134 a	Herausgeber und Schriftleiter HERWARTH WALDEN	Ausstellungsräume Berlin W 9 / Potsdamer Straße 134 a

SECHSTER JAHRGANG 1915 BERLIN ERSTES UND ZWEITES JUNIHEFT NUMMER 5/6

Franz Marc: Löwenschlacht nach Delacroix / **Originalholzschnitt**

39 MARCEL JANCO **1916**

(b.1895) After working with Iser, a friend of Derain, in Budapest in 1910 and collaborating with Tristan Tzara on the review SIMBOLUL, *Janco studied architecture at the Kungstgewerbeschule, Zurich, in 1913-16. Here he participated with Tzara, Arp and Hugo Ball on establishing the* DADA *Cabaret Voltaire, where he designed costumes and savage masks for the Dada soirées. He produced painted reliefs and sculptures at this time, and abstract paintings marked by the momentary influence of* FUTURISM. *In 1919, he contributed, with Arp and Giacometti, to the foundation of the Association of Radical Artists in Basel. From 1920 to 1923, Janco lived in Paris, meeting Picabia, Ernst and Dali, and being influenced by abstract* CUBIST *work. Breaking with* DADA, *he returned to Rumania in 1923 where he founded the* Contimporanul *group. In 1924 he was obliged by the Fascist regime to flee to Israel, where he became the centre of the 'New Horizons' group and founded a community of artists at Ein Hod, near Mount Carmel.*

LA PREMIÈRE AVENTURE CÉLESTE DE MR. ANTIPYRINE

PAR TRISTAN TZARA, AVEC DES BOIS GRAVÉS ET COLORIÉS PAR MARCEL JANCO ([ZURICH:] COLLECTION DADA, 1916)
8ff., 225 x 147 mm., with 7 wood prints.
Apart from a standard edition, a special edition of 10 copies on *Hollande,* hand coloured and numbered 1-10, was published (V&A copy: standard edition).
Printer: L'Imprimerie J. Heuberger, Zurich (completed 28 July 1916).
L.5527-1962. (LARIONOV COLLECTION).

This copy of Tzara's first book was inscribed to Paul Guillaume, the dealer who had a gallery in Paris, by Tzara and Janco. Janco provided illustrations, along with Arp, Kandinsky, Marinetti, Picasso and Modigliani, for the first issue of the periodical *CABARET VOLTAIRE* in June 1916. In 1918, the artist also provided the woodcut for the cover of the third issue of *DADA.* The 'Collection Dada' appeared in 1916; Richard Huelsenbeck's manifesto *PHANTASTICHE GEBETE* with woodcuts by Arp was published in the collection in July of that year.

40 ENRICO PRAMPOLINI **1917**

(1894-1956) Sent down from the Fine Arts Academy, Rome, in 1913, Prampolini joined the FUTURIST *movement under the influence of Giacomo Balla and Boccioni. Having met Tristan Tzara in Rome in 1916, he took part in Dada 'exhibitions' in Zurich; in 1917 he founded the Dada review* NOI, *which appeared until 1925, declaring that the machine was 'the symbol, the source and inspiration of the new artistic sensibility'. In 1922 he was a signatory, with Paladini and Pannaggi of the Manifesto of Mechanical Art. He participated in the 1924 Futurist congress in Milan, and maintained contact with many groups outside Italy, including the 'Section d'Or'* CUBISTS *in Paris, the revolutionary* EXPRESSIONISTS *of the socialist Novembergrüppe which sought radical restructuring of education and art teaching to break the divide between artists and the masses, and the neo-plasticism of* DE STIJL *and Mondrian. Between 1925 and 1937 he lived mainly in Paris and was much involved in theatre design and the making of films, also particpating in* ABSTRACTION-CRÉATION. *Here he produced his 'Cosmic pictures', and from c.1935 his 'poly-material' works using sponge, cork, tinfoil and other synthetic materials. In 1916, he had presented the first* FUTURIST *furniture at an exhibition in Rome. On his return to Italy in 1937, he joined other Futurists in supporting Mussolini. A major retrospective exhibition of his work was held in Rome in 1961.*

SIC. (SONS, IDÉES, COULEURS, FORMES), Nos. 21-22
SEPT.-OCT., 1917, PARIS.
12pp., 280 x 225 mm.
Published monthly, the magazine could be bought in a *de luxe* edition on *Vieux Japon* containing a series of 6 numbers (75 francs).
LARIONOV COLLECTION.

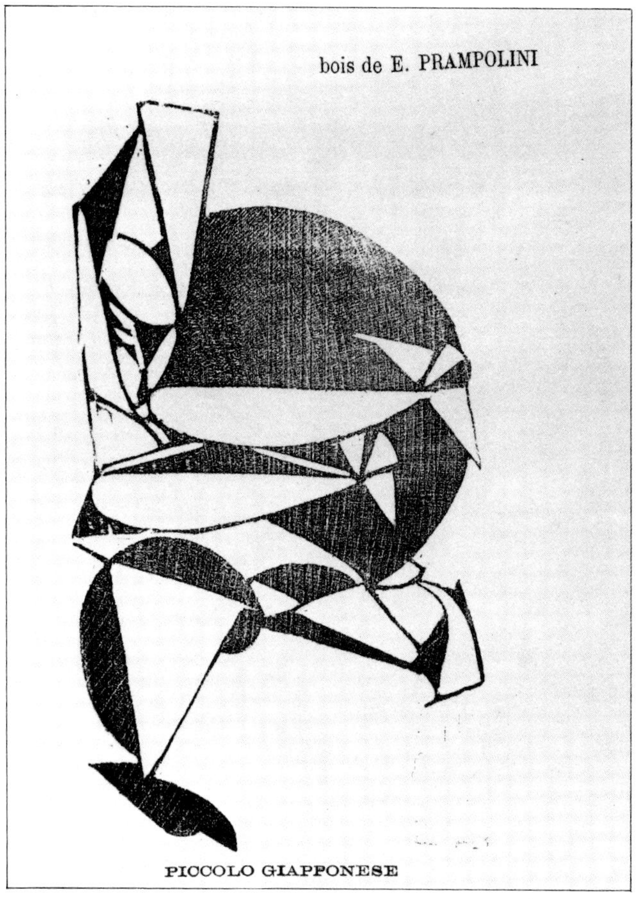

Prampolini's wood engraving 'Piccolo Giapponese' was published in nos. 21-22 of *SIC*, an issue that contained 'Note 6 sur l'art nègre' by Tristan Tzara, a poem by Gino Cantarelli, Pierre Albert-Birot and Ary Justman, and music for Apollinaire's *LES MAMELLES DE TIRÉSIAS* by Germaine Albert-Birot.

SIC was founded by the poet Albert-Birot (1876-1967) in January 1916 and ran monthly, with few interruptions, until December 1919. Apollinaire's review *SOIRÉES DE PARIS* had ceased to appear on the outbreak of war in 1914, and *SIC* provided a forum for many of its contributors when it began to appear, a forum that was constructive in nature as opposed to the Dada mission to subvert systematically, but one that welcomed the appearance of Picabia's review *391* in Barcelona and the Zurich review *DADA*. The first performance of Apollinaire's play, *LES MAMELLES DE TIRÉSIAS*, took place under the aegis of *SIC* in June 1917 (copies of the programme with contributions by Max Jacob, Jean Cocteau, Paul Reverdy, drawings by Matisse and Picasso were offered for sale in nos. 21-22), and its appearance marks the canonisation of the term 'Surrealist' – Apollinaire dubbed it a 'Drame sur-réaliste' in preference to 'sur-naturaliste', so that *SIC* was the means by which the new word gained currency.

Gravure sur bois de E. Prampolini.
LE DIEU PLASTIQUE
Costume chorégraphique grotesque futuriste

41 FRANCIS PICABIA 1917

(1879-1953) After study at the École des Arts Décoratifs and the École des Beaux Arts, Picabia discovered Sisley, became friends with Pissarro and had considerable success painting in IMPRESSIONIST *style, having his first one-man exhibition in 1905 at the Galerie Haussmann. His personal fortune allowed him to abandon the beginnings of a successful career, while marriage to Gabrielle Buffet and friendship with Marcel Duchamp brought him in contact with* CUBIST *circles. In 1911 he was a founder member of the Section d'Or group, joining the strand of* CUBISM *that rejected figurative elements and was dubbed* ORPHISM *by Apollinaire. The exhibition of work in this style at the Armory Show took him, with others, to New York, in 1913 where he and Duchamp were lionised. On his return to Paris Picabia painted a series of abstract works that included 'Je revois en souvenir ma chère Udnie'. Picabia and Duchamp were again in New York in 1915, and became the centre of a* DADA *group. After corresponding with Tristan Tzara in Zurich, Picabia settled in Paris in 1919, where in 1921 he distanced himself from* DADA *circles, gravitating towards André Breton's* SURREALISM. *After composing* RELÂCHE *for the Swedish Ballet, Picabia collaborated in René Clair's film,* ENTR'ACTE. *From 1925-1945, the artist lived in the Midi. He exhibited in Colette Allendy's gallery in Paris in 1948 with Hartung, Wols, Mathieu and Bryen, one of the first manifestations of 'Psychic Non-Figuration'.*

391, NO. 3, 1 MARCH 1917, BARCELONA.

8 pp. including cover, 370 x 270 mm.
Edition of 500 copies (V&A copy no.470), of which 10 copies *de luxe* completed by hand.
Printer: Oliva de Vilanova, Barcelona.
LARIONOV COLLECTION.

When in New York in 1915, Picabia and Duchamp had both contributed to Alfred Stieglitz's avant-garde review *291*: in Barcelona in 1916, Picabia established *391* with the help of Gleizes, Marie Laurencin and the 'boxer-poet' Arthur Cravan as a vehicle for Dada ideas. The review was published by the gallery of José Dalmau, who had already exhibited works by Picabia and Duchamp. Only 4 numbers were issued in Barcelona; 3 more were published in 1917 from New York when Picabia made his final stay there; issue no. 8 was published in Zurich in February 1919, and it appeared thereafter in Paris until its demise in 1924. It is generally considered to be the 'personal forum' of Francis Picabia and reflects his involvement with the Dada movement. Picabia was sufficiently wealthy to have *391* published as he felt inclined.

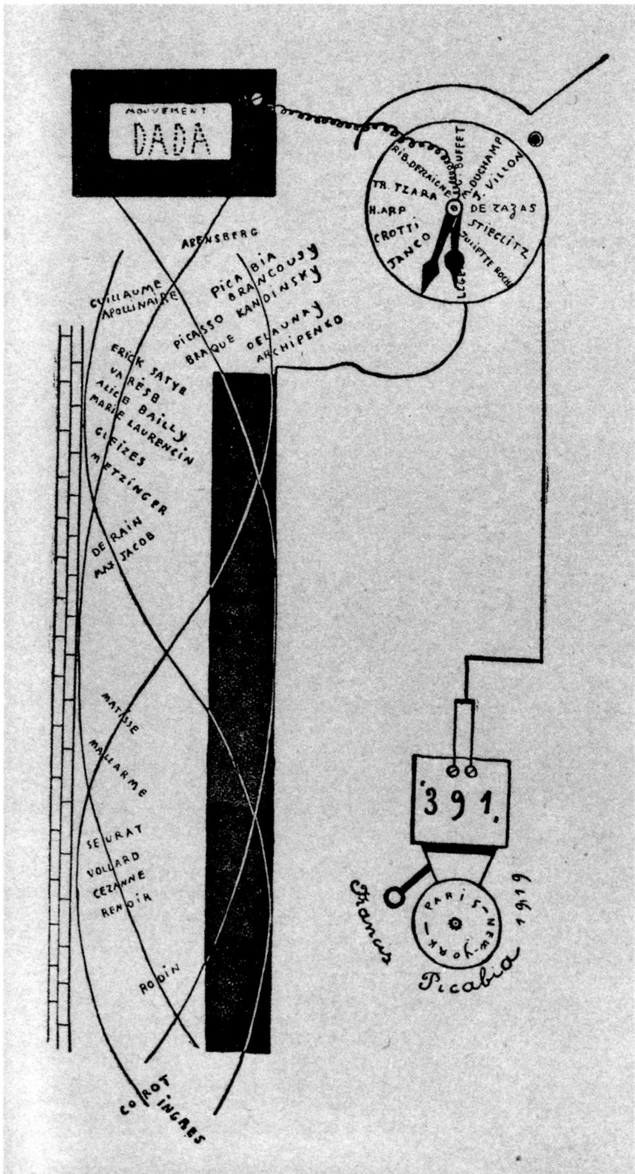

Picabia. *391*, drawing from *CAT. NO. 55*.

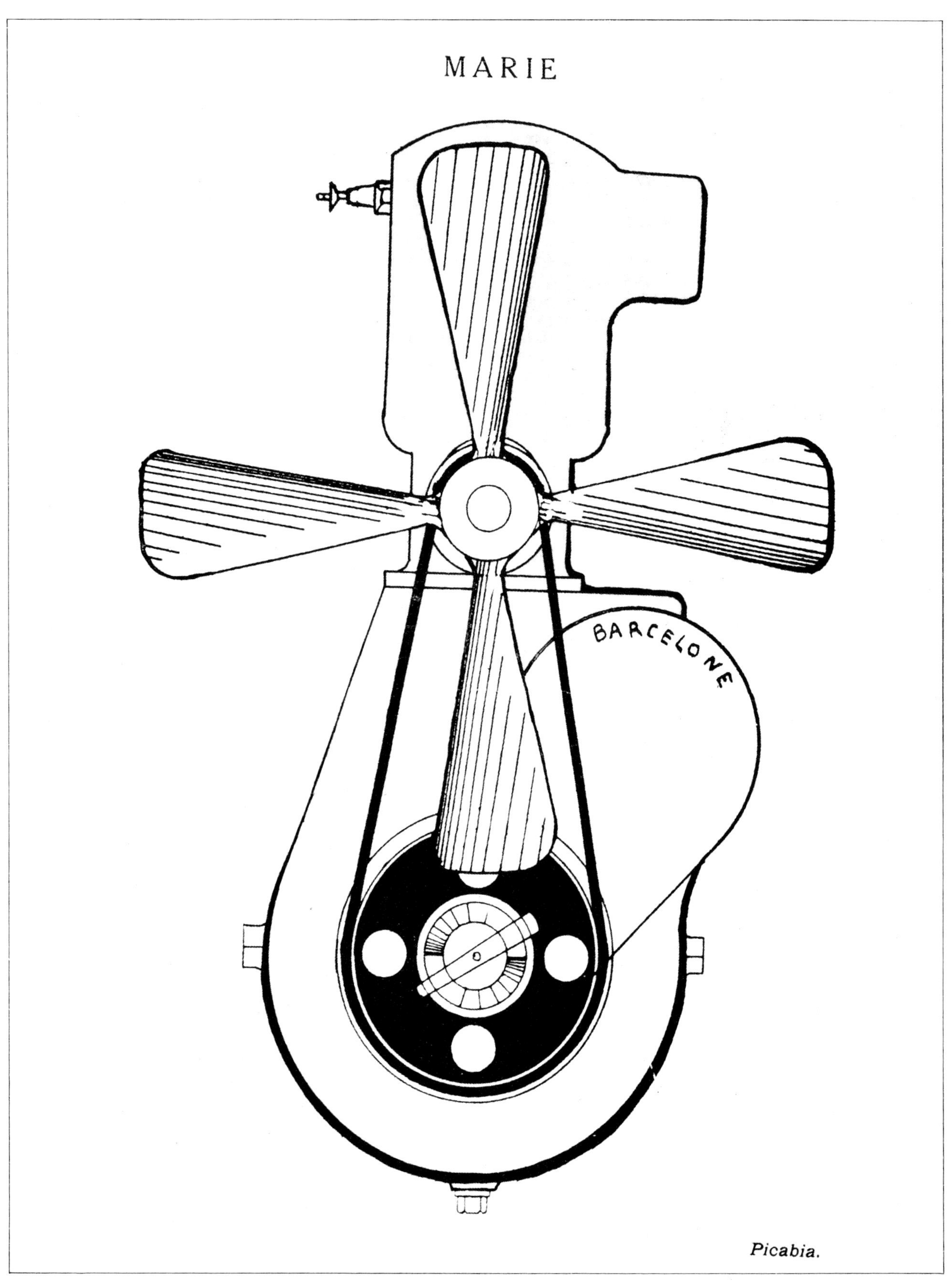
MARIE
BARCELONE
Picabia.

42 MAX PECHSTEIN **1918**

(1881-1955) After an apprenticeship to a painter/decorator and study at the Kunstgewerbeschule and Akademie in Dresden in 1900-1906, Pechstein joined the BRÜCKE *group, with Kirchner, Schmidt-Rottluff, Heckel and others. He met Van Dongen during a visit to Paris in 1907, and was impressed with Etruscan art and the Ravenna mosaics when travelling in Italy. In 1910 he was elected president of the New Secession in Berlin that brought together members of Die Brücke and the incipient* BLAUER REITER *who were reacting against the Impressionist vogue of the day. By 1912, he was receiving commissions for major murals. In 1914 he went on an expedition to the Palaos Islands and New Guinea, a year after he had been expelled by Die Brücke for exhibiting individually rather than with the group. Ending war service with a nervous breakdown, Pechstein was on the committee of the revolutionary Arbeitsrat für Kunst in 1919, and participated in the Novembergrüppe. When the government allowed the National-Galerie in Berlin to acquire modern art in 1919, work by Pechstein (along with other Brücke artists and Blauer Reiter painters such as Marc and Feininger) joined the National Collection. As* EXPRESSIONISM *became fashionable, he benefited from renewed prestige, in 1923 being made a member of the Prussian Academy. Among those dubbed degenerate by the Nazis, he escaped individual persecution and retired to Pomerania during the war, after which he taught at the Berlin Academy.*

MARSYAS. EINE ZWEIMONATSSCHRIFT, ED. THEODORE
146 *TAGGER, JAHRGANG 1, HEFT 4, JAN.-FEB., 1918* (BERLIN: HEINRICH HOCHSTIM VERLAG).
i, 80 pp., 390 x 295 mm., with 9 etchings (5 by Robert Genin; 4 by Pechstein) and 1 'Ursteindruck' (by Pechstein).
Special edition of 235 copies (V&A copy no.116), signed by the publisher, Heinrich Hochstim, of which 35 copies are on *Kaiserlich Japan* and *Strathmore Japan* (nos.I-XXXV), and 200 copies on *Bütten* (nos.1-200).
Printer: Wetteroth, Munich, 5 etchings by Genin; Ruckenbrod, Berlin, proofed the 4 Pechstein etchings; Birkholz, Berlin, the Pechstein 'Ursteindruck'; Imberg & Lefson, Berlin, text.
L.6053-1982.

Pechstein contributed 4 etchings to this issue of *MARSYAS* to illustrate the story 'Heidenstam', written by Carl Sternheim, a writer and playwright much involved in expressionist literary circles and whose plays 'mercilessly satirize the philistinism of the German bourgeoisie'. Pechstein's lithograph was used for the section of the magazine written by Theodore Tagger, 'Chronik'. 'Tagger' was the pseudonym of the writer Ferdinand Bruckner (1891-1958), who emigrated in 1933 to the USA and settled in Paris in 1951. His early poetry was expressionist in character; in 1923 he founded the Renaissance Theatre in Berlin. The journal he edited, *MARSYAS*, appeared between 1917 and 1919, and was published in an expensive edition: the annual subscription was 600 marks for the *Bütten* version, and 1,500 for that on *Kaiserlich Japan*. Other *de luxe* publications of the Heinrich Hochstim Verlag are advertised at the back of each issue of *MARSYAS*.

43 MAX PECHSTEIN **1918**

(1881-1955)

MARSYAS. EINE ZWEIMONATSSCHRIFT. [ED. MANFRED GEORG], JAHRGANG, HEFT 5, SUMMER 1918
(BERLIN: HEINRICH HOCHSTIM VERLAG).
i, 80 pp. [paginated 81-160], 390 x 295 mm., with 8 etchings (4 by Walter Gramatté; 4 by Pechstein), 2 lithographs (by Michl Fingesten) and 1 'Ursteindruck' (by Fingesten)

Edition as for cat.42.
Printer: Ruckenbrod, Berlin, etchings by Gramatté and Pechstein; Birkholz, Berlin, lithographs and 'Ursteindruck'; Imberg & Lefson, text.
L.6054-1982.

Pechstein's etchings here illustrate a novella by the poet and novelist Hermann Stehr (1864-1940), 'Der Schatten'.

44 MAX BECKMANN **1918**

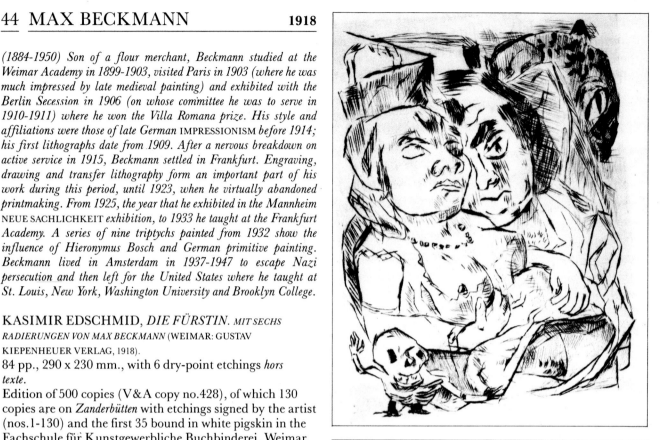

(1884-1950) Son of a flour merchant, Beckmann studied at the Weimar Academy in 1899-1903, visited Paris in 1903 (where he was much impressed by late medieval painting) and exhibited with the Berlin Secession in 1906 (on whose committee he was to serve in 1910-1911) where he won the Villa Romana prize. His style and affiliations were those of late German IMPRESSIONISM *before 1914; his first lithographs date from 1909. After a nervous breakdown on active service in 1915, Beckmann settled in Frankfurt. Engraving, drawing and transfer lithography form an important part of his work during this period, until 1923, when he virtually abandoned printmaking. From 1925, the year that he exhibited in the Mannheim* NEUE SACHLICHKEIT *exhibition, to 1933 he taught at the Frankfurt Academy. A series of nine triptychs painted from 1932 show the influence of Hieronymus Bosch and German primitive painting. Beckmann lived in Amsterdam in 1937-1947 to escape Nazi persecution and then left for the United States where he taught at St. Louis, New York, Washington University and Brooklyn College.*

KASIMIR EDSCHMID, *DIE FÜRSTIN. MIT SECHS RADIERUNGEN VON MAX BECKMANN* (WEIMAR: GUSTAV KIEPENHEUER VERLAG, 1918).
84 pp., 290 x 230 mm., with 6 dry-point etchings *hors texte*.
Edition of 500 copies (V&A copy no.428), of which 130 copies are on *Zanderbütten* with etchings signed by the artist

(nos.1-130) and the first 35 bound in white pigskin in the Fachschule für Kunstgewerbliche Buchbinderei, Weimar, under the direction of Otto Dorfner (nos.1-35), and the 95 following copies handbound in Morocco leather at E.A. Enders, Leipzig (nos.36-130), 370 copies on *Hollandischem Bütten* bound in silk according to a design of Else von Guaita (nos.136-500).
L.1001-1945.

Beckmann's illustrations describe both the emotional and erotic character of the narrative. The author, Edward Schmid (1890-1966), who wrote under the name of Kasimir Edschmid, was a prolific Darmstadt writer who in 1917 gave a theoretical basis to Expressionist writing in his lecture 'Uber den dichterischen Expressionismus', published in Berlin in 1919. Much of his work was characterised by broken-up sentences, a bumpy continuity and emotive use of visual distortion with concise, abrupt and dynamic rhythyms. Edschmid was ordered to stop writing by the Nazis in 1941. *DIE FÜRSTIN* was priced at 80 marks in 1918.

45 OSKAR KOKOSCHKA **1918**

(1886-1980)

O EWIGKEIT – DU DONNERWORT. WORTE DER KANTATE NACH JOH. SEB. BACH. LITHOGRAPHIEN VON OSKAR KOKOSCHKA
(BERLIN: FRITZ GURLITT VERLAG, 1918).
Portfolio of 12 ff., 10 of which are lithographs, 605 x 550 mm., each initialled in pencil by the artist.
L.1136-1959

The 1918 edition of Kokoschka's lithographs consists of a self-portrait with brush and 9 illustrations to the words of Bach's cantata. The prints were first published in a portfolio in 1916 or 1917. The conclusion of the Wingler-Welz catalogue that the 1918 edition was made up of photolithographs seems likely to be correct (Carey and Griffiths, *THE PRINT IN GERMANY, 1880-1933*, p.144); Kokoschka's involvement in the printing is seen in his penciled initials added to each plate. The drawings are traditionally dated to 1914. The 1918 edition bears a dedication to the Countess Alexandrine Mensdorff-Dietrichstein.

46 DAVID BOMBERG **1919**

(1890-1957) Brought up in London's East End, Bomberg studied art at evening classes of the City and Guilds Schools in 1905-7, beginning an apprenticeship in chromolithography under Paul Fischer in 1907. In 1908 he broke the apprenticeship to become an artist, taking evening classes under Lethaby at the Central School in book production and lithography and under Sickert at the Westminster School. In 1911-1913, Bomberg studied at the Slade School, visiting Paris with Jacob Epstein in 1913 and distancing himself from the VORTICIST *movement in 1914. In July 1914 he had his first one-man show at the Chenil Gallery, Chelsea. He designed briefly for Roger Fry's Omega workshop, settling in Jerusalem in 1923-1927. After 1935, he lived mainly in London, founding the Borough Group in 1947-1949 with Lillian Holt and the Borough Bottega in 1953. The following year he settled in Spain.*

DAVID BOMBERG, *RUSSIAN BALLET* (LONDON: HENDERSONS, 'THE BOMB SHOP', 1919).
16 pp., 215 x 135 mm., with 6 colour lithographs.
Printer: David Bomberg.
L.2207-1966.

Bomberg's work was in his 'constructive-geometric' style which he had developed before 1914. The drawings were apparently done before the war and lithographed at the time of Diaghilev's visit to London with his ballet. The dealer Jacob Mendelsen brought Diaghilev, Bomberg and Henderson, the owner of the Bomb Shop, together to plan the publication, and financed it himself. Bomberg stated that he printed the lithographs himself with his own blank verse poems in seven printings, and that the abstract drawings had been done on the inspiration of the ballet itself. (See W. Lipke, *DAVID BOMBERG*, 1967, pp.50, 114-15). Diaghilev objected to Bomberg's efforts to sell the publication like a programme at 2s.6d. a time.

47 KAZIMIR MALEVICH **1919**

(1878-1935) Born in Kiev, Malevich studied at Kursk and, from 1903, at the Moscow Academy. By 1906 he had met Larionov; he took part in the 'Knave of Diamonds' exhibition of 1910 in Moscow, and in the 'Donkey's Tail' exhibition there two years later. He was among the Russian artists invited to show at the second BLAUER REITER *exhibition in Munich in 1912. Absorption of* CUBISM *led to his distancing himself from Larionov. In 1915, he showed works in the 'Tramway V' and '0,10' exhibitions in Petrograd, which represent the first public appearance of* SUPREMATISM, *a style which he was beginning to evolve by 1913 and which was founded on the straight line or square symbolizing 'man's ascendency over nature'. His theories were published in 1916,* FROM CUBISM AND FUTURISM TO SUPREMATISM; *in 1918 he showed his* WHITE SQUARE ON WHITE GROUND *painting at the 10th State Exhibition in Moscow. Among those involved in the reorganisation of art teaching after 1917, Malevich taught at the Moscow Academy before being sent to Vitebsk, where he ousted Chagall and formed the group* UNOVIS *('Affirmers of the New Art') with El Lissitsky. In 1922, he had his Suprematist ceramics made at the State Manufacture in Leningrad. In 1922, his works were shown in the exhibition of Russian art in Berlin, and in 1927 he was in Warsaw and Berlin for retrospective exhibitions. In that year the* BAUHAUS *published his theories under the title* DIE GEGENSTANDSLOSE WELT *(the object-less world). Recalled to Russia, Malevich fell into official disfavour; in 1930, he was arrested on account of his German connections. Malevich distanced himself after 1917 from those artists who sought to apply art and design to creating a new social environment, holding that aesthetic theories had no practical or social applications.*

NIKOLAI PUNIN, *PERVUII TSIKL LEKTSII [FIRST CYCLE OF LECTURES AT THE SHORT-TERM COURSES FOR TEACHERS OF DRAWING. CONTEMPORARY ART]* (PETROGRAD: [17TH GOVERNMENT PRINTING HOUSE] 1920).
84 pp., 215 x 140 mm., colour illustrations on covers by Malevich.
Edition of c. 1500-2000 copies (un-numbered).
L.1331-1983. Colour plate 6

Punin's crash course for student teachers, as given in the summer of 1919, reduces the artistic process to a mathematical formula, as did Malevich himself. A champion of new art movements in Soviet Russia, Punin disappears from available sources in the late 1930s. The covers of this government publication represent the only application of Malevich's Suprematist design to book production. They date from his first teaching period at Vitebsk. The back cover uses a design borrowed for porcelain manufacture. The images on the covers are in fact zincographed from the originals. It is unlikely that Malevich had any part in printing them; the choice of colours is foreign to his palette, and other details of the treatment of the design lead to the conclusion that the drawings were sent to a Petrograd printer who could not restrain himself from 'correcting' the image he was asked to print.

48 NATALIA GONTCHAROVA MIKHAIL LARIONOV **1919**

Natalia Gontcharova (1881-1962) Mikhail Larionov (1881-1964)

VALENTIN PARNACK, *L'ART DÉCORATIF THÉÂTRAL MODERNE* (PARIS: ÉDITION LA CIBLE, 1919)
22 pp., 495 x 325 mm., with 17 plates (6 by Gontcharova, 10 by Larionov)
Edition of 400 copies (nos. 1-400), with 100 copies (with 'special numbering') signed by the artists, and 15 copies *hors commerce* (nos. A-O; V&A copy no. C).
Printer: Crété, Paris.
L.2815-1981. Colour plate 8

In parallel with her painting in near-abstract idiom, Gontcharova produced theatre and ballet decors inspired by Russian popular art. Her first designs were made in 1909 for two pantomimes. In 1914, she designed for Diaghilev Rimsky-Korsakov's *COQ D'OR*, one of a number of Russian works that Diaghilev was touring with resounding success in the west. Gontcharova's theatrical career, like that of Larionov, was thereafter bound up with that of Diaghilev, whose ballets from 1909 to the 1920s were a focal point of Paris cultural life. In 1915, Gontcharova had published in 16 pochoirs her costume designs for Diaghilev's *LITURGIE*. The publication of similar material in *L'ART DÉCORATIF THÉÂTRAL MODERNE* was given the same title as their exhibition at the Galerie Sauvage, Paris, in 1918. The imprint 'La Cible' derives from the name of the exhibition at which the first Rayist works had been shown in Moscow, in 1913: *MISHEN*, meaning target.

49 MIKHAIL LARIONOV **1919**

(1881–1964)

GERALD TYRWHITT BERNERS, 14th Lord Berners,
TROIS MORCEAUX POUR PIANO À QUATRE MAINS:
CHINOISERIE, VALSE SENTIMENTALE, KASATCHOK. COUVERTURE, ILLUSTRATIONS ET ORNEMENT DE MICHEL LARIONOV
(LONDON AND BRIGHTON: J&W CHESTER, 1919).
24 pp., 350 x 270 mm., with 4 colour lithographs and colour lithograph on front and back cover.
L.562–1984.

Lord Berners (1883–1950) had a career as a diplomat, but also painted and was a pupil of Stravinsky for musical composition. His three orchestral pieces in various styles are here arranged for piano duet, and are dedicated to Larionov, Eugene Goossens and Natalia Gontcharova respectively. Each of Larionov's designs contains some letters from the title; the other letters can be 'read' in the figures. The play on words seen here stems from the *zaum* ('transrational') language of the Russian Futurists, in which printed letters are so arranged as to suggest alternative meanings, disrupting conventional syntax and grammar and divorcing sound from immediate sense (possibilities of this approach to language were exploited by Joyce in *WORK IN PROGRESS* in the 1920s and in *FINNEGANS WAKE*, but he had no known links with Futurism beyond a visit to a Futurist exhibition in Trieste when he lived there before 1914). Larionov claimed that this use of letters was inspired by shop signboards; French Cubists had also used letters in a similar but less systematic way.

CHICHI
Ri
M.

50 LYONEL FEININGER **1919**

(1871–1956) Born in New York, Feininger studied at the Kunstgewerbeschule in Hamburg from 1887 and the Berlin Academy thereafter. Before turning seriously to painting in 1908, Feininger worked as a political cartoonist and caricaturist in Berlin for ULK *and* LÜSTIGE BLÄTTER *(1893–1906) and in Paris for* TÉMOIN *and the* CHICAGO SUNDAY TRIBUNE *(1906–7). In 1911 he exhibited at the Salon des Indépendants in Paris and through Delaunay discovered* CUBISM. *In 1912 he joined* DIE BRÜCKE, *and was invited by Franz Marc to exhibit with the* BLAUER REITER *in 1913. His first woodcuts date from 1918. In 1919 he was among the first invited by Gropius to join the Weimar Bauhaus; he was in charge of the graphic printing shop there until 1925 and taught until its dissolution in 1933. In 1924 he formed the* BLAUEN VIER *with Kandinsky, Klee and Jawlensky. A retrospective of his work was held at the Berlin National Gallery in 1931; he was declared a degenerate by the Nazis in 1937. He settled in the United States in 1937; in 1938 he executed mural paintings for the New York Universal Exhibition, and in 1944 had a major retrospective exhibition in The Museum of Modern Art.*

DIE ROTE ERDE. MONATSCHRIFT FÜR KUNST UND KULTUR,
Jahrgang 1: Heft 1, JUNE 1919.
Jahrgang 1: Heft 2, JULY 1919.
Jahrgang 1: Heft 3, AUGUST 1919.
L.5310-1962

Feininger was among a number of artists that provided woodcuts for the review edited by Karl Lorenz and Paul Schwemer in 1919; others were Schmidt-Rottluff, Emil Mäkel, Martin Schwemer and Felix Müller.

51 PAUL KLEE 1919

(1879-1940)

DAS KESTNERBUCH. HERAUSGEBER: DR PAUL KÜPPERS
(HANOVER: HEINRICH BÖHME VERLAG, 1919).
160 pp., 245 x 180 mm., with 12 prints *hors texte*.
Un-numbered edition (V & A copy one of these), and edition of 150 copies specially printed and bound by hand.
Printer: Elder & Krische (completed Winter 1919).
L.3370-1948.

Klee's contribution, a lithograph entitled 'Auslöschende Licht' (dying light), appeared by permission of Hans Goltz of Munich, in this yearbook of the Kestner Gesellschaft in Hanover. It is numbered 176 in Klee's numerical series (from 1899 he kept a catalogue of all his work). The society had been founded in Hanover in 1916 to promote modern art; Kurt Schwitters had contributed to its exhibitions since 1917, and was among the 12 artists, as was Lyonel Feininger, who contributed lithographs or wood engravings to the volume. The editor, Paul Küppers, on the staff of the local museum, had been the Society's artistic director since its foundation. In the introduction he disclaims any effort to proselytize on behalf of any modern movement, but to bring together the inner vision of artists and writers and unite them in a gentle harmony. Among the writers were figures as different as Thomas Mann, Carl Hauptmann, Alfred Döblin and Theodore Däubler.

ABOVE LEFT Kurt Schwitters. Plate XII, woodcut.
ABOVE RIGHT Erich Heckel. Plate I, woodcut.
RIGHT Klee. Plate IX, lithograph.

Klee

Ausloeschendes Licht 1919. 176

52 KURT SCHWITTERS **1919**

(1887-1948) After studies at the Dresden Academy, Schwitters began a career as a portraitist and painter, producing work that reflected conventional display of avant-garde idioms. An abrupt change came in 1918, the year that he joined the DADA *movement, developed his friendship with Arp and produced his first collages based on the waste of urban society, from paper and string to tram tickets and tins. He established his own form of* DADA, Merz, *in 1919, with an exhibition in the* Sturm *gallery in Berlin under the aegis of Paul Klee; the review* DER STURM *published the same year his first* Merz *poem, 'Anna Blume'. Schwitters was excluded from the first Dada-Messe in 1920 because of his unwillingness to accept the politicization of Dada activities. After meeting El Lissitsky and Van Doesburg at the Hanover Dada congress in 1922, his work became more* CONSTRUCTIVIST, *and he was impressed with* DE STIJL *when visiting Holland. In 1923, he began to produce his review* MERZ, *which appeared intermittently until 1932 and received contributions from Arp, Mondrian, El Lissitsky, Soupault and others, thus divorcing itself from the international Dada movement. In 1932, he participated in the* ABSTRACTION-CRÉATION *association in Paris. In 1937, Schwitters fled to England; in 1945 he moved to the Lake District, where he began a* Merzbau *financed by the New York Museum of Modern Art shortly before his death. Among his reported eccentricities was the carrying of a second suit-case filled with potatoes when travelling, in order to save money by cooking for himself.*

162 KURT SCHWITTERS, *ANNA BLUME. DICHTUNGEN*
(HANOVER: PAUL STEEGEMANN VERLAG, 1919).
40 pp., 225 x 145 mm., with illustration on cover.
Edition of 10,000
Printer: Edler & Krische, Hanover.
L.2800-1980.

ANNA BLUME, a collection of poems and prose, was Schwitters' first publication; the technique in many of the poems represents 'collages' of sound analogous to his physical collages. At 1.50 marks, the pamphlet sold 10,000 copies quickly; in 1922, a further 3,000 copies had to be printed. It appeared as volume 39/40 in Paul Steegemann's *SILBERGÄULE* series, described as 'eine radikale Bücherreihe, Dichtung, Graphik, Essai'. Volume 41/42 consisted of Schwitters lithographs, *KATHEDRALE. MERZ.* (Colour plate 7).

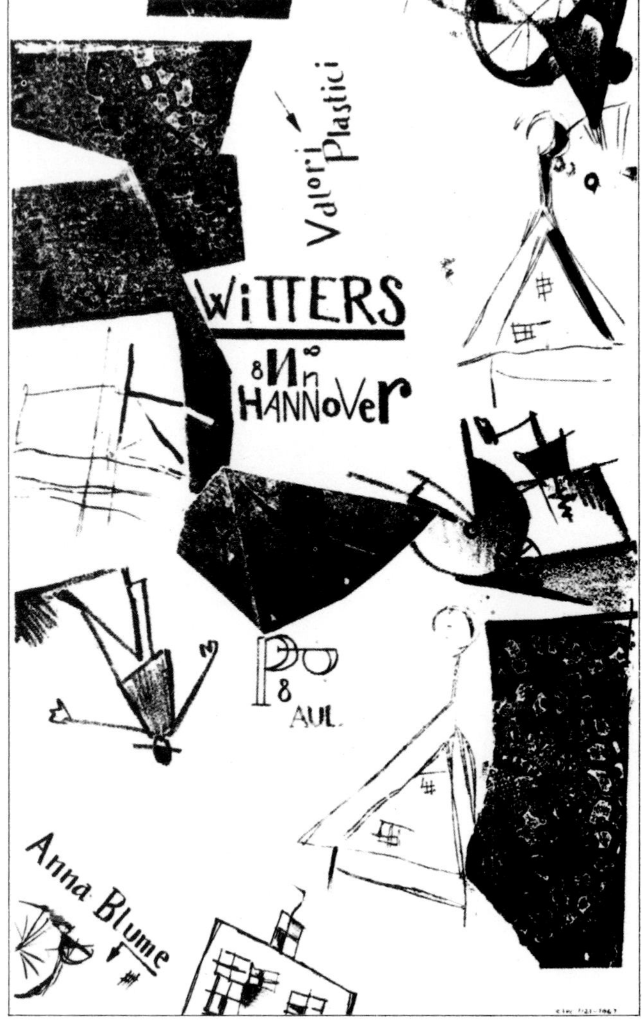

ABOVE Schwitters. Lithograph, from *Die Kathedrale.*
RIGHT Schwitters. Cover for *Anna Blume.*

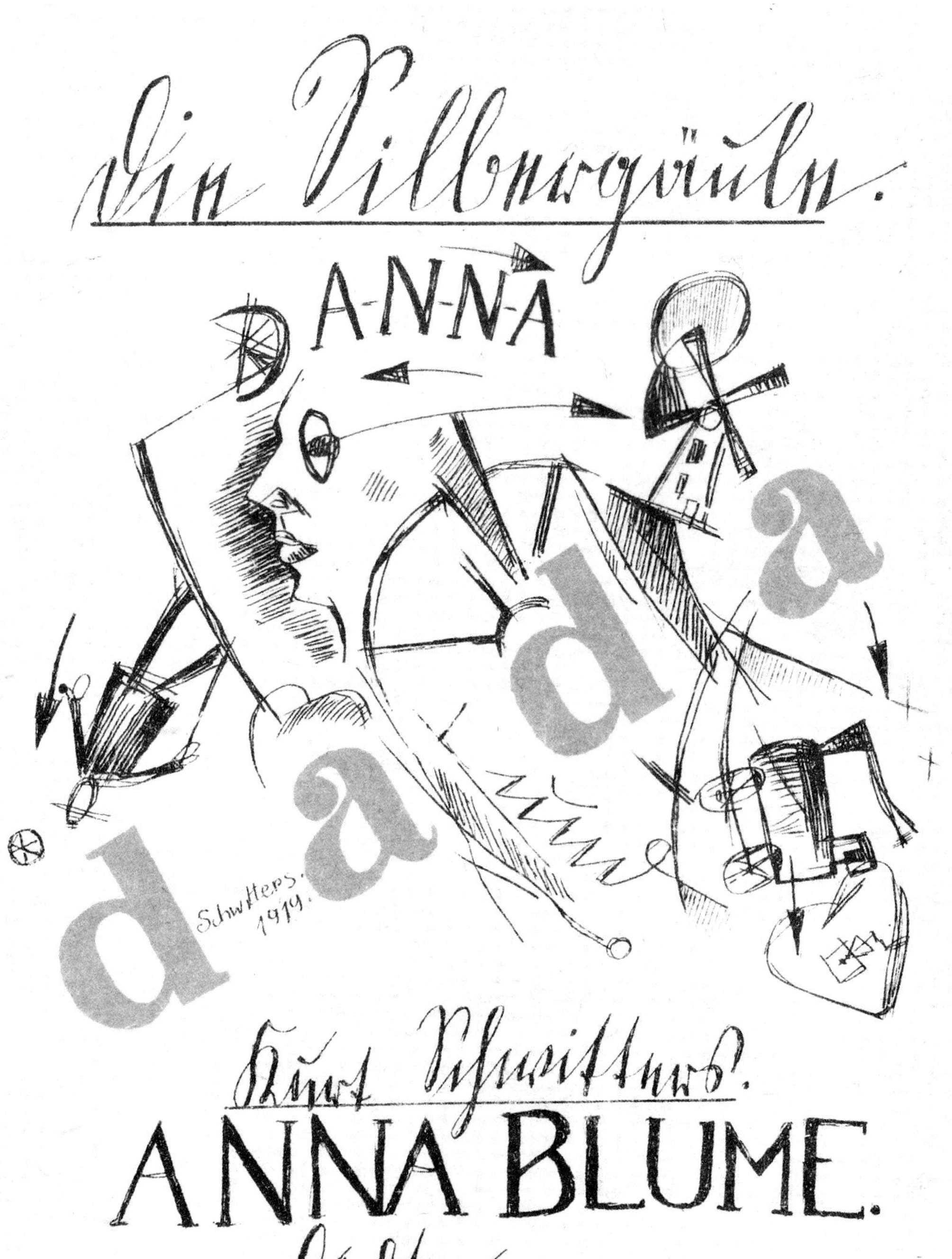

Dichtungen.

Paul Steegemann, Verlag, Hannover.

53 KARL SCHMIDT-ROTTLUFF 1919

(1884-1976) When studying architecture in Dresden in 1905, Schmidt-Rottluff founded, with Kirchner, Bleyl and his old schoolfriend Heckel, the group DIE BRÜCKE, *to bring together painters rejecting German attempts at* IMPRESSIONISM, *neo-romantic tendencies and* JUGENDSTIL *(Art Nouveau). The artist soon took to wood engraving, lithography and water-colour painting. In 1911 he moved to Berlin where he collaborated with the review* DER STURM *and met Otto Müller and Lyonel Feininger. The influence of African art is apparent from this date. In 1912 he was invited to show in the* BLAUER REITER *exhibition in Munich. His first one-man show was in the Gurlitt gallery, Berlin, in 1914. In 1931, he was elected to the Prussian Academy of Fine Arts, from which he was ejected by the Nazis in 1933, his work being declared degenerate. Schmidt-Rottluff founded the* Die Brücke *Museum in Berlin in 1967.*

DIE ROTE ERDE. MONATSCHRIFT FÜR KUNST UND KULTUR,
JAHRGANG 1, HEFT 2, JULY, 1919, P. 4; JAHRGANG 1, HEFT 6, NOV. 1919.
L. 5310-1962 (LARIONOV COLLECTION).

Graphic work produced for the Hamburg review *DIE ROTE ERDE*, edited by Karl Lorenz and Rosa Schapiro.

LEFT Head of a woman, original woodcut
RIGHT Der Heilige

(1881-1955) After work in architects' offices, study at both the École des Arts Décoratifs and the Louvre, and periods in the studios of the academic artists Gérôme and Férrier, Léger developed as a painter from the influence of Cézanne (more than anyone else he adopted Cezanne's dictum that the sphere, cylinder and cone were basic shapes to interpret nature) towards a style in sympathy with the CUBISM *of Braque and Picasso. From 1910 he was among those promoted by the dealer Kahnweiler, for whom he signed an exclusive three year contract in 1913. Experiences at the Front in 1914-16 reinforced his interest in industrial products and machinery as inspiration for design. After the War, he became involved in painting on architecture, which led to the great abstract mural compositions of 1924-5 which he termed 'illumination of walls'. Contact with Ozenfant led him towards* PURISM *in 1924-7 and van Doesburg encouraged his non-figurative tendencies. Between the Wars, Léger designed theatre and film sets and produced mural decorations, mosaics, weaving, stained glass and illustrations, the interest in applied art and its social relevance no doubt fuelled by his friendship with the architect Le Corbusier. In 1940-1946, Léger was in New York, from where he returned much impressed, he declared, by the 'American intensity' of dynamic advertising images. In Paris, he continued to work in a number of media; in 1950 he set up a ceramic studio at Biot.*

BLAISE CENDRARS, *LA FIN DU MONDE, FILMÉE PAR L'ANGE N. D. ROMAN. COMPOSITIONS EN COULEURS PAR FERNAND LÉGER* (PARIS: ÉDITIONS DE LA SIRÈNE, 1919).

60 pp., 315 x 245 mm., with 20 illustrations and vignettes, and one on each cover.
Edition of 25 numbered copies on *Rives à la forme* and 1200 copies (of which this is one) 'in-quarto raisin' on *Régistre vélin Lafuma*, un-numbered.
Printer: L'Imprimerie Frazier-Soye, Paris, text, set in Morland Corps 24, (completed 15 October 1919); Richard, Paris, colour printing.
MISC. 2(98)-1934. Colour plate 9

The Éditions de la Sirène was the publishing house of Jean Cocteau, the writer whose interest in painting and the avant-garde followed that of Apollinaire. Léger's friendship with the poet Blaise Cendrars, the pseudonym of Fréderic Louis Sauser, dates back to c.1910. After 1918, both contributed to *L'ESPRIT NOUVEAU*, the review of 1920-1925 that led a reaction away from CUBISM, felt to be on the road to the purely decorative, towards the PURISM that Cocteau dubbed 'The call to order'. Cendrars hailed Léger's first post-war exhibition at Rosenberg's Galerie de l'Effort Moderne in 1919 as leading the way to an art devoted to colour and figurative subject matter. Léger illustrated the war prose *J'AI TUÉ* of Cendrars in 1918; the writer was actively engaged in making films at the time, and it was he and Dudley Murphy who produced Léger's short film *BALLET MÉCANIQUE* in 1924. *LA FIN DU MONDE* sold for 20 francs when published.

31
Décembre
Dieu le père est à son bureau américain. Il signe hâtivement d'innombrables papiers. Il est en bras de chemise et a un abat-jour vert sur les yeux. Il se lève, allume un gros cigare, consulte sa montre, marche nerveusement dans son cabinet, va et vient en mâchonnant son cigare. Il se rassied à son bureau, repousse fiévreu-
IL SE LÈVE
ALLUME
UN GROS CIGARE
C'est le

LE TRUC
DES PRO
PHETES
MEN
ELIK
VALET
DECHAM
BRE

55 JEAN/HANS ARP 1919

(1886-1966) Born in Strasbourg (and bi-lingual French/German throughout his life) to a French tobacco manufacturer, Arp studied at the École des Arts et Métiers, Strasbourg, the Academy in Weimar and in Vienna before a brief sojourn at the Académie Julian in Paris in 1908. Settling in Weigiss, Switzerland, he participated in the foundation of the Moderner Bund. He met Kandinsky in 1912, and participated in the second BLAUER REITER *exhibition in Munich in 1913. In 1915 he showed his first abstract works (collages and tapestries) in Switzerland. In 1916 he was, with Tzara, Ball and Hülsenbeck, one of the founders of the Zurich* DADA *group, participating in the foundation of a similar group in Cologne with Ernst and Baargeld in 1919. With Kurt Schwitters, he collaborated on the review* MERZ *in Berlin in 1923, published 'Isms in Art' with El Lissitzky in 1925 and exhibited in the first* SURREALIST *show in Paris during the same year. From 1926 he lived near Paris with Sophie Taüber-Arp, and in 1931, the year of his first round bossed sculptures, joined the* ABSTRACTION – CRÉATION *group. He was first awarded prizes at the 1954 Venice Biennale and the 1964 Pittsburg International Exhibition.*

ANTHOLOGIE DADA. PARAIT SOUS LA DIRECTION DE TRISTAN TZARA. MOUVEMENT DADA (ZURICH, *1919).*
18pp., including covers, 280 x 195mm with 16 illustrations including 3 woodcuts and 1 vignette by Arp and one on cover; 6 paste-in reproductions.
168 Printer: J. Heuberger, Zurich (completed 15 May 1919).
L. 5532-1962.(LARIONOV COLLECTION)

This version of *ANTHOLOGIE DADA* sold for 4 francs, and was available from Eugène Figuière in Paris, 'Modern Gaerie', *[sic]* in New York, gallery Dalmau in Barcelona, and Georges Giroux in Brussels, as well as in Stockholm and Copenhagen. A *de luxe* edition was also available for 20 francs, in an edition of 38 copies numbered 1-38 and containing 2 original wood engravings by Arp and Hausmann. Similar editions were also available for previous numbers of the review, which were entitled simply *DADA (ANTHOLOGIE DADA* was issue no.4/5 of *DADA)* and appeared from July 1917.

ANTHOLOGIE DADA was issued in both French and German editions. Links with other centres are shown by the inclusion of poems by André Breton, Louis Aragon and Phillipe Soupault all then in Paris and soon to break away from Dada circles to form a Surrealist group. Picabia too contributed graphic work (one engraving referred to the journal he began in Barcelona, *391*) and poetry.

Arp had been one of the original members of the Zurich Dada group when the Cabaret Voltaire was set up as an open house for writers and artists in the Meierei Café on 5 March 1916. 'Nightly Ball, Tzara and Hülsenbeck read their own poems and others by Cendrars, Apollinaire, Rimbaud, Jacob, . . . Kandinsky and so on. . . Arp read from Jarry's *UBU ROI*' (Ades, *DADA AND SURREALISM REVIEWED,* Arts Council, 1978, p.57). The printer Julius Heuberger was an anarchist, and was imprisoned during the publication of *ANTHOLOGIE DADA.*

ABOVE Arp. Woodcut.
RIGHT Raoul Hausmann. Woodcut, in text page facing Arp.

LITTÉRATURE

parait une fois par mois.

Paris, 9 Place du Panthéon

Directeurs: **Louis Aragon, André Breton, Philippe Soupault.**

Les cahiers 2 et 3 contiennent les P o é s i e s du comte Lautréamont (Isidore Ducasse), première réimpression d'après l'édition de 1870, dont on ne connaissait que le seul exemplaire de la Bibl. Nationale. On sait maintenant que Lautréamont sera le Rimbaud de la poésie d'aujourd'hui. **La Dictature de l'Esprit,** presentation **sans** soucis d'amélioration et de ménagement, est l'affirmation de l'intensité, dirige toutes les préoccupations vers la force noble, précise, fastueuse, seule digne d'intérêt: la déstruction.

Francis Picabia:

„L'Athlète des Pompes funèbres"
Fr. 2.50

„Rateliers Platoniques" Fr. 4.—

En vente au
MOUVEMENT DADA
Zurich, Seehof, Schifflande 28

raccroc

le larynxe homme seul
au regard fixe
mets sur la fleur
l'accentcirconflexe

carnet carambole
manivelle
feu dans la fiole
cœur de ficelles

nerfs perpendiculaires
au centre
d'une lampe incandescente
et d'un liquide amer

tristan tzara

Charlot Chaplin nous a annoncé son adhésion au Mouvement Dada

Lisez le Manifeste DADA 1918

Tristan Tzara: 25 Poèmes
Arp: 10 gravures sur bois.
Prix 3 Fr.
Edition numérotée 15 Fr.
Edition de luxe 60 Fr.
COLLECTION DADA

LE
COURRIER DE LA PRESSE
BUREAU de COUPURES de JOURNAUX

"LIT TOUT"

JOURNAUX, REVUES & PUBLICATIONS DE TOUTE NATURE

Paraissant en France et à l'Etranger

Ch. DEMOGEOT, Directeur
21, Boulevard Montmartre
PARIS 2e

TNT

revue
New-York

BOIS DE R. HAUSMANN

(1886-1966)

Tristan Tzara, *CINÉMA CALENDRIER DU CŒUR ABSTRAIT/MAISONS/BOIS PAR ARP* (PARIS, 1920).
38 ff., 250 x 205 mm., with 19 woodcuts.
Edition of 150 copies (V&A copy un-numbered); 'tous les exemplaires portent la signature des auteurs' [signatures lacking].
Paper, *Vélin de cuve pur chiffon d'Italie'* according to prospectus, watermarked 'Giorgio Adamo Beckh in Norimberga'.
Printer: Otto von Holten.

The prospectus for this volume mentions the price as 60 francs, the copy no.1 being available with the manuscript and two Arp drawings for 650 francs. Copies were available from Au Sans Pareil in the Avenue Kléber, Paris. Arp was not resident in Paris in 1920; Tzara arrived there in January 1920, after André Breton and Louis Aragon had read his Dada manifesto of 1918, and began organising a series of manifestations based on his Zurich successes.

57 LOVIS CORINTH **1920**

(1858-1925) After study at the Kneiphof Academy in Königsberg, Corinth worked under Löfftz in the Munich Academy from 1880. In 1884-7 he attended the Académie Julian in Paris, studying under Bouguereau, Bastien-Lepage and Robert Fleury; Rembrandt, Hals and Rubens are considered to have been the major influences on him at this time. From 1891, Corinth lived in Munich before moving to Berlin, where he emerged, with Liebermann and Slevogt, as the leader of German IMPRESIONISM *though becoming more expressionistic after a stroke in 1911. He had his first one-man show at the Paul Cassirer Gallery in 1913; in 1915, he was elected President of the Berlin Secession. In 1921 he was awarded an honorary doctorate by Königsberg University, and in 1925 became an honorary member of the Munich Academy. Lithographs and etchings formed an important part of his work throughout his career.*

DAS LEBEN DES GÖTZ VON BERLICHINGEN VON IHM SELBST ERZÄHLT. ORIGINALLITHOGRAPHIEN VON LOVIS CORINTH (BERLIN: FRITZ GURLITT VERLAG; 1920).

52pp., 450 x 380 mm., with 14 lithographs and 11 vignettes; lithographed covers.
Edition of 125 copies (V&A copy no. 39), on *Bütten;* also 50 copies on *Zanders-Bütten* with lithographs signed by the artist ([apparently un-numbered]), and 15 copies (nos. I-XV) with 2 extra lithographs. V&A copy is signed by the artist at the colophon and on the second lithograph.
Printer: Fritz Gurlitt, Berlin, lithographs; Otto von Holten, Berlin, text.
L.965-1940.

This version of the autobiography of Gottfried von Berlichingen (1480-1567), 'the Robin Hood of Germany', appeared in the *NEUE BILDERBÜCHER* series published by Fritz Gurlitt.

58 NATALIA GONTCHAROVA 1920

(1881-1962)

ALEXANDER NIKOLAEVICH RUBAKIN,
GOROD': STIKHI [THE CITY: POEMS] (PARIS, 1920)
57ff., 230 x 145 mm., with 8 plates and 40 illustrations in text.
Edition of 325 copies (V&A copy un-numbered), of which 25 are on *Chine antique,* and 300 on *Vergé d'Arches.*
Printer: [—]
L.5433-1962 (LARIONOV COLLECTION)

In these poems, Rubakin (b.1889) laments the death of his wife while celebrating the movement and range of emotional states in urban life. GOROD is one of a number of Russian books printed in facsimile from the author's handwriting, a method that was to be revived by Tériade in the 1940s. Many poets in the Russian Futurist circle (Khlebnikov and Kruchenuikh are examples) held that a writer's emotions at the time of composition were communicated by his handwriting, and that this spontaneous aspect of expression would be lost through mechanical printing.

15

На разсвѣтѣ.

Стекаетъ ночь съ небесныхъ сводовъ,
Беззвѣздный поблѣднѣлъ просторъ.
Гудки проснувшихся заводовъ
Слились въ передразсвѣтный хоръ.

Сквозь сѣрый дымъ усталъ безъ блеска
Зари холодной тусклый свѣтъ.
Навстрѣчу дню печально рѣзко
Кричатъ разносчики газетъ.

Еще темно. Но въ зыбкомъ мрака
Звучитъ тревожный гулъ колесъ
И сквозь туманъ, какъ чьи то знаки,
Мерцаютъ блестки папиросъ.

Мнѣ было страшно, было жутко
При свѣтѣ мертваго огня.
Какъ часовой, я слушалъ чутко,
Ждалъ ночи днемъ и ночью дня...

Но часъ бѣжитъ на смѣну часа,
И ночью тоже, что и днемъ,
И жизнь противна, какъ гримаса,
Внезапно ставшая лицомъ...

59 MAX BECKMANN 1921

(1884-1950)

STADTNACHT SIEBEN LITHOGRAPHIEN VON MAX BECKMANN ZU GEDICHTEN VON LILI VON BRAUNBEHRENS (MUNICH: R. PIPER & CO. VERLAG, 1921).
50pp., 275 x 230 mm., with 7 lithographs *hors texte*.
Edition of 600 copies (V&A copy no. 382), of which 100 copies were issued with a portfolio of 7 lithographs on *Japan* signed by the artist (nos. I-C), and 500 copies of an ordinary edition (nos. 1-500).
Printer: Knorr und Hitth, text; Dr. C. Wolf & Sohn, Munich, lithographs.
L.2785-1981.

After his nervous breakdown in May 1915, Beckmann moved to Frankfurt to live in the house of the Battenburg family, where he was to stay until 1933. A friend of the Battenburgs was Major von Braunbehrens, who secured his release from the army in 1917. His daughter Lili wrote amateurish poems that employed Expressionist techniques. The book was in fact marketed under Beckmann's name, selling for 120 marks (the *de luxe* version sold for 240 marks).

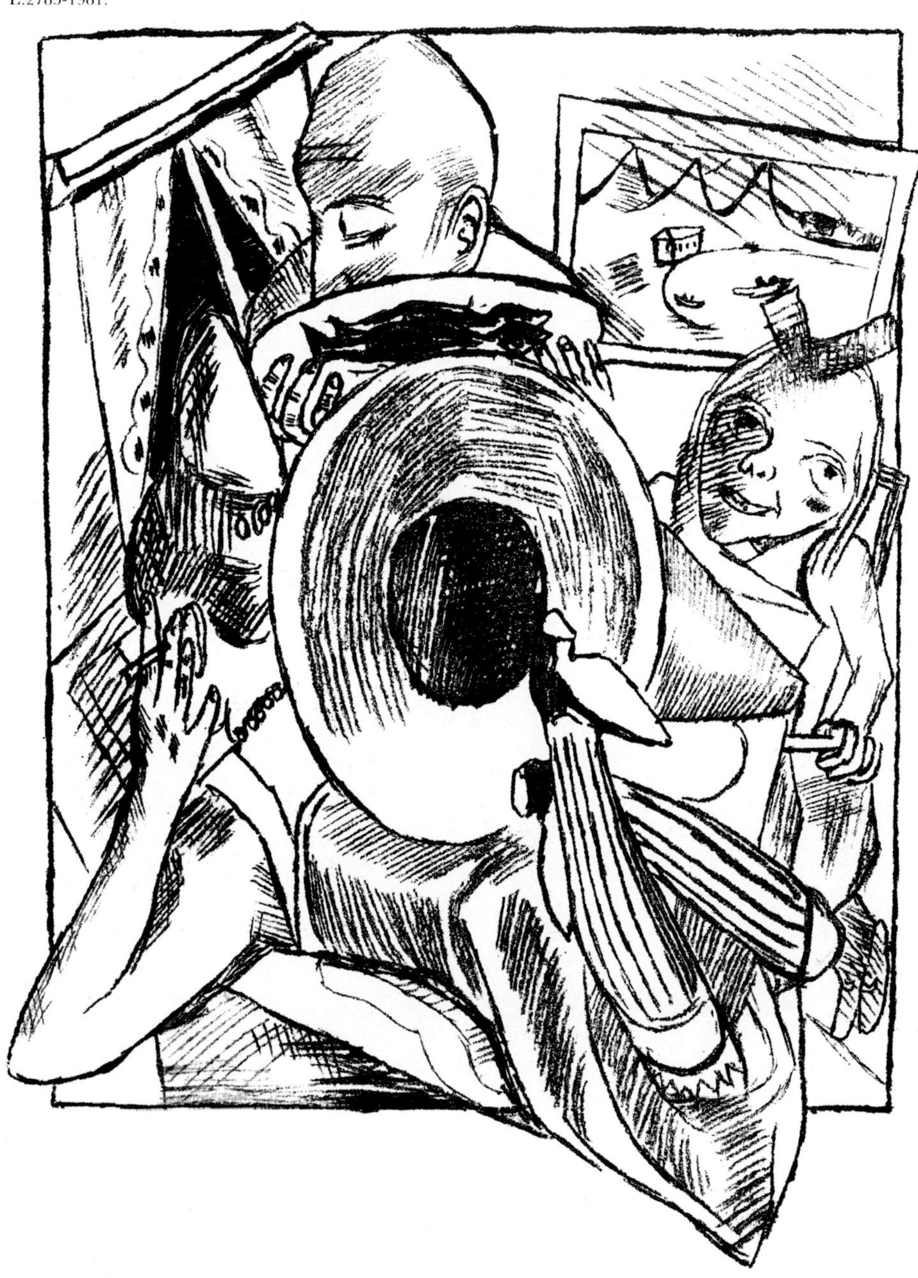

60 GEORG GROSZ **1921**

(1893-1959) Grosz studied at the Dresden Academy from 1909 and at the Berlin Kunstgewerbeschule from 1911. His first caricature was published in ULK *in 1910, and he contributed to a number of satirical magazines such as* LUSTIGE BLÄTTER *and* SIMPLICISSIMUS. *In 1913 he visited Paris where he saw* CUBIST *works. Wounded during military service, he published his first lithographs with the small communist publishing house later to become the prolific Malik Verlag run in Berlin by John Heartfield and Wieland Herzfeld in 1917, with whom he devised the technique of photomontage. Grosz was a founder member of the Berlin* DADA *group in 1917, participating in their theatrical activities (also designing sets for Shaw's Caesar and Cleopatra) and publishing sets of anti-militaristic and anti-bourgeois drawings such as* DAS GESICHT DER HERRSCHENDEN KLÄSSE *(which sold out immediately) and* ECCE HOMO *(seized by the police and leading to a 6000 mark fine for the artist). In 1925, he was close to the* NEUE SACHLICHKEIT *group. In 1927, the Malik Verlag published his designs for Piscator's production of* THE GOOD SOLDIER SCHWEIK, *for which Grosz was prosecuted on grounds of blasphemy. The artist moved to the U.S.A. in 1933, after his which work was vilified by the Nazis. Failing to adjust to the American way of life, Grosz began to revisit Germany in 1954. His work had enormous impact in the 1920's, selling in large editions; Count Harry Kessler was among his admirers.*

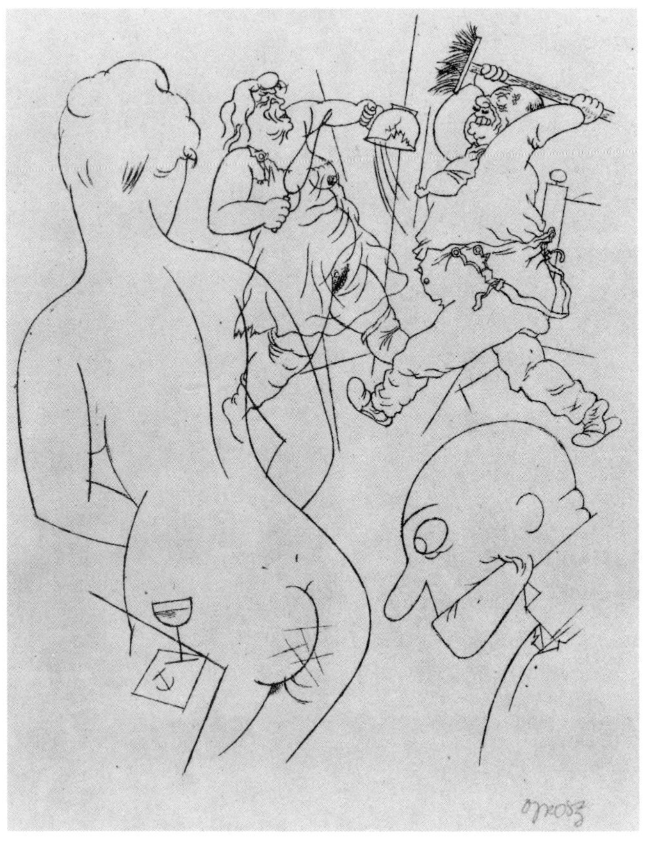

MUNKEPUNKE DIONYSOS. GROTESKE LIEBESGEDICHTE VON
176 *ALFRED RICHARD MEYER* (BERLIN: FRITZ GURLITT VERLAG, [1921]).
38pp., 300 x 250 mm., with 6 lithographs.
Edition of 100 copies (V&A copy no. 17); each lithograph signed in pencil by the artist, and the colophon page signed by the author.
Printer: Gurlitt Press (A. Rogall).
Bookplate of Gert von Gontard.
L.2791-1981.

The text of this book was written by Wilhelm Redlie directly on the stone and reproduced by lithography. The colophon states that the first 20 copies of the edition were hand-coloured by Grosz, though the V&A copy is uncoloured. To illustrate the love poems, Grosz shows scenes between individuals that brings out their class relations (well dressed gentlemen of means with prostitutes touting for custom). Meyer (1882-1956) wrote under the name 'Munkepunke'; his publishing company *Lyrische Flugblätter* produced the works of many Expressionist poets. A poet himself with a penchant for the fantastic and grotesque, he was an admirer of the poetry of Verlaine and Apollinaire.

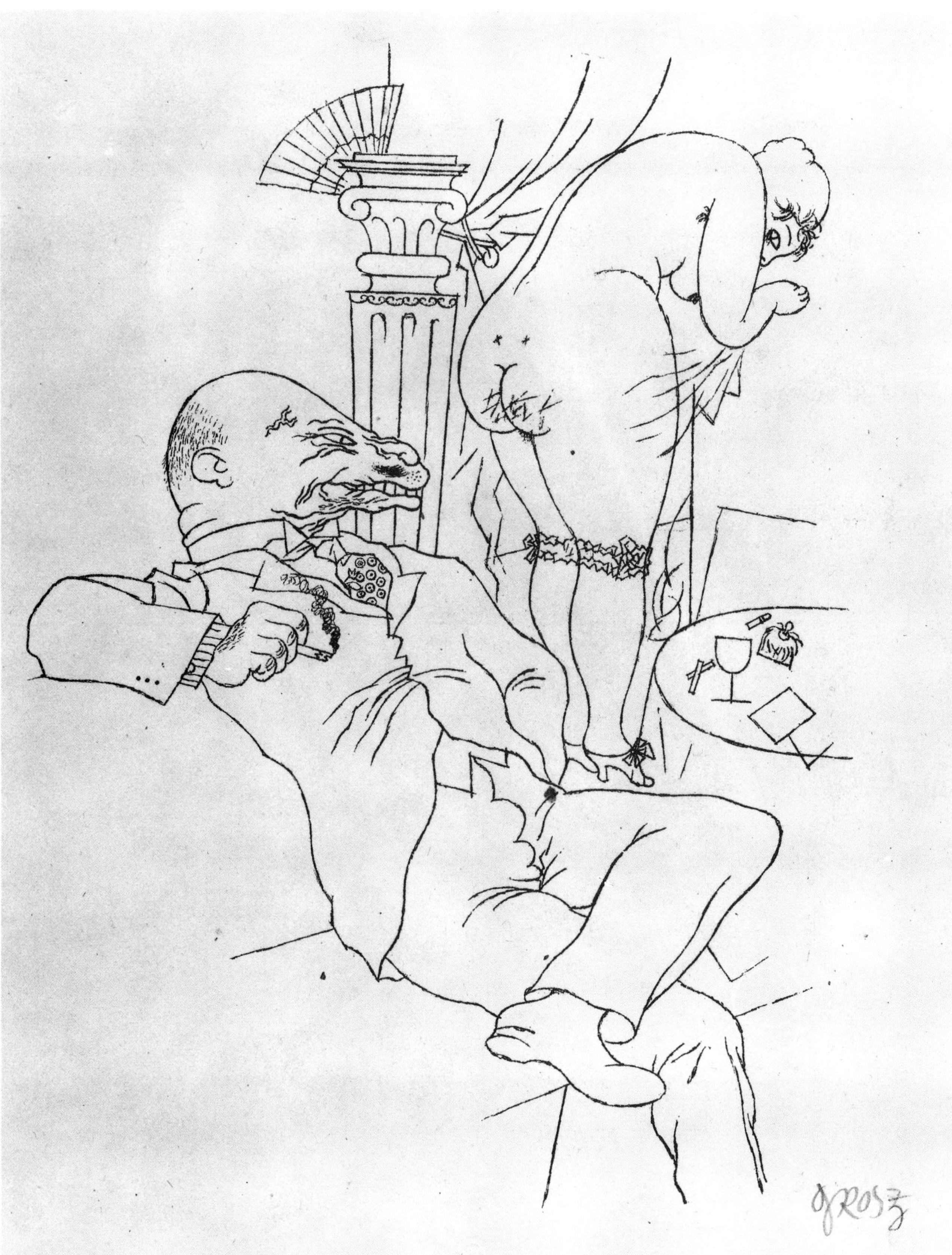
GROSZ

61 ROGER DE LA FRESNAYE **1921**

(1885-1925) After growing up in Cannes with his grandmother, Fresnaye studied at the Académie Julian in Paris in 1903-05, finding a more suitable eniviroment at the Académie Ranson, which he entered in 1908 to study under Maurice Denis and Paul Sérusier. Early influences on his work were those of Gauguin and the NABIS *generally, and of Cézanne, evident in his painting* EVE *of 1910 and subsequent landscapes. He exhibited with the* CUBISTS *from this date, showing with the two 'Section d'Or' exhibitions in 1913. His first* CUBIST *works date from this year, distinguished by their feeling for colour and figurative content; Fresnaye was never a central artist of this style, tending to adopt a neo-classical idiom in the 1920s. He produced a small number of sculptures in 1909-11, and on two occasions designed costumes for the costume balls of the fashion designer Paul Poiret (c.1913 and c.1920). A retrospective exhibition of his work was held at the Musée d'Art Moderne, Paris, in 1950.*

ANDRÉ GIDE, *PALUDES. ÉDITION ILLUSTRÉE DE SIX LITHOGRAPHIES ORIGINALES PAR R. DE LA FRESNAYE* (PARIS: NOUVELLE REVUE FRANÇAIS, 1921)
112 pp., 240 x 190 mm., with 6 lithographs.
Edition of 300 copies (un-numbered), on *Vélin Lafuma-Navarre.* with 12 copies *hors commerce* (nos. I-XII).
Printer: R.H. Coulouma, Argenteuil, text; Marchiset, Paris, lithographs (completed 6 Jan. 1921).
L. 3106-1981.

Roger de la Fresnaye produced a number of designs for book illustrations, designing wood engravings for Claudel's *TETE D'OR* in 1911 and drawings for Cocteau's *TAMBOUR* in 1920 among other projects of this kind. The only book illustrations published during his lifetime were lithographs for Gide's *PALUDES,* a work first published in 1895.

André Gide (1869-1951) wrote *PALUDES* after his first trip to north Africa where he became seriously ill. The novel is seen as evidencing his first break with symbolism and the rigid catholicism of his youth, and the beginnings of his examination of the nature of personal freedom. Gide was among the founders of the monthly *NOUVELLE REVUE FRANÇAISE,* in 1909; from 1911, the *NRF,* as it is generally known, launched its own publishing house under the editorial direction of Gide, Jacques Copeau and Jean Schlumberger and the business management of Gaston Gallimard. From 1919, the name was changed to Gallimard, under whose imprint were published the most prominent literary figures of the inter-war period, including Marcel Proust, André Breton, André Malraux, Paul Eluard and Louis Aragon.

62 HENRI LAURENS **1921**

(1885-1954) From a working-class Parisian family, Laurens' formal training consisted of drawing lessons at evening classes and an apprenticeship to an ornamental sculptor. At first intending to become an interior decorator, he discovered CUBISM *and, becoming friends with Georges Braque, was introduced to the circle around Guillaume Apollinaire; from 1915 he produced a series of* CUBIST *sculptures. From 1921, Kahnweiler became his agent. In 1924, he designed the sets for Diaghilev's ballet* TRAIN BLEU. *In the 1920s he adopted a more figurative style; drawing and lithography became a significant part of his oeuvre. From 1947, major exhibitions of his work were held all over the world, and the Musée d'Art Moderne held a retrospective in his honour in 1951; in 1953 he was awarded the Grand Prix in the São Paulo Biennale.*

RAYMOND RADIGUET, *LES PELICAN. PIECE EN DEUX ACTES ILLUSTRÉE D'EAUX FORTES PAR HENRI LAURENS*
(PARIS: GALERIE SIMON, [1921]).
25 pp., 320 x 225 mm., with 6 etchings (2 of them full-page) including one on front cover.
Edition of 100 copies (V&A copy no. 42), signed by the author and artist, of which 10 copies are on *Japon des Manufactures Impériales* (nos. 1-10), 90 copies on *Hollande Van Gelder* (nos. 11-100), 10 extra copies, 'copies de Chapelle' (nos. I-X) and 2 other copies for deposit under copyright law each with a set of etchings (nos. 0 and 00).
Printer: Imprimerie Birault, Paris, text; Eug. Delâtre, etchings (completed 21 May 1921).
L.7248-1984.

Laurens' first work as book illustrator was for Reverdy's first book, *POÈMES EN PROSE* (1916), but his greatest output as illustrator came during and after the Second World War when he produced work for editions of Tzara, Eluard, Theocritus and Lucian. The *LES PELICAN* illustrations were commissioned by Kahnweiler, who considered Laurens the greatest sculptor of the age. The original selling price of 400 francs made this a collector's book rather than a popular one.
Raymond Radiguet (1903-1923) frequented Cubist literary circles; his satirical 10 act play was about a whimisical family of pelicans, was first performed at the Théâtre Michel on 24 May 1921, and became a classic of the Théâtre de l'Absurde.

63 OSKAR JESPERS **1921**

(1887-1970) Son of a sculptor, Jespers studied at the Institut Supérieur des Beaux Arts in Antwerp, where he is said initially to have tried to 'unite the pathos of Rodin with the lyricism of Rik Wouters', Wouters (1882-1916) being a self-declared discipline of Cézanne who introduced FAUVISM *to Belgium. During the First World War, Jespers illustrated the poems of Paul van Ostay (1896-1928), a native of Antwerp and perhaps the greatest Expressionist poet from Belgium, who encouraged the artist towards a* CUBIST *style, in both sculpture and other work, in which the influence of African art can be detected. His first one-man show was at the Cercle Artistique gallery in Antwerp in 1916-17, where his work was exhibited regularly; in the interwar years, he showed with avant-garde groups such as Les Neuf, L'Art Contemporain, and the* EXPRESSIONIST *group, Sélection. Jespers commissioned the architect Victor Bourgeois, a friend, to design a house for him, which turned out to be a 'veritable manifesto of* DE STIJL *architecture'. From 1927-1952, Jespers taught sculpture at the École Nationale Supérieure d'Architecture et d'Art Décoratif in Brussels; from 1941 he was a member of the Koninklijke Vlaamse Academie van Belgie.*

PAUL VAN OSTAYEN. *BEZETTE STAD.*
ORIGINAALHOUTSNED VAN OSKAR JESPERS
(ANTWERP: SIENJAAL, 1921).
154 pp., 280 x 220 mm., with 5 woodcuts, device on title-page, cover and design.
180 Edition of 540 copies (V&A copy no. 111), of which 40 copies are on *Vergé d'Arches* (nos. 1-40; nos. 1-10 reserved *[hors commerce]*), 500 copies on *Vélin registre* (nos. 41-500).
Printer: F.Casie, Antwerp (completed March 1921).
L.249-1984.

The poems of Paul van Ostayen use a full repertory of typographic devices, one page resorting to a facsimile of the poet's handwriting. Jespers' graphic work is likewise based on letter-shapes. Van Ostayen is credited with having introduced German Expressionist painting into Belgium. He was in Berlin at the end of the First World War, and became acquainted with members of the *Sturm* group. The poetry in *BEZETTE STAD* shows familiarity with Dada productions, the typographic lay-out verging on collage on occasion, with citations from advertisments and street signs thrown about the page. Ostayen, like Jespers, represents the diffusion of Expressionist ideas in Flemish circles that were suspicious of French cultural chauvinism, a suspicion evident as well in the French language review *SÉLECTION* produced in Antwerp in the 1920s. The publisher's imprint 'Sienjaal' derives from the title of Ostayen's volume of poetry of that title, published in Antwerp in 1918. The colophon of *BEZETTE STAD* records that Ostayen, Jespers and René Victor closely oversaw the printing of the book.

64 FERNAND LÉGER **1921**

(1881-1955)

ANDRÉ MALRAUX, *LUNES EN PAPIER. PETIT LIVRE OÙ L'ON TROUVE LA RELATION DE QUELQUES LUTTES PEU CONNUES DES HOMMES, AINSI QUE CELLE D'UN VOYAGE PARMI DES OBJETS FAMILIERS MAIS ÉTRANGES. LE TOUT SELON LA VÉRITÉ ET ORNÉ DE GRAVURES SUR BOIS ÉGALEMENT TRÈS VÉRIDIQUES PAR FERNAND LÉGER*
(PARIS: GALERIE SIMON, 1921).
40 pp., 320 x 228 mm., with 6 woodcuts and one on cover.
Edition of 112 copies (V&A copy no. 88), signed by author and artist, of which 10 copies are on *Japon impériale* (nos. 1-10), 90 copies on *Hollande Van Gelder* (nos. 11-100), 10 copies *hors commerce* (nos. I-X), and 2 copies for deposit under copyright law each with a set of prints from cancelled woodcuts (nos. 0 and 00).
Printer: Imprimerie Birault, Paris (completed 12 April 1921).
L. 5482-1982

In 1909-1914, Kahnweiler published 4 books illustrated by artists (Picasso and Derain); on his return to Paris after the First World War and his establishment of the Galerie Simon with André Simon, books of this kind were produced in greater numbers and formed a significant part of his interests: 7 were published in 1921 alone (the illustrators were Juan Gris, Léger, Henri Laurens, Georges Braque and Manolo). At this date Léger's reputation was established, and it is a tribute to Kahnweiler that he produced as the artist's collaborator the young André Malraux, whose first published work this was. Malraux (1901-1976) was later prominent in literary and artistic circles, supporting the Republicans in the Spanish Civil War, liberation movements in French colonies, and being active in the French Resistance in 1939-1945; from 1958-1969 he was Minister for Cultural Affairs in France. His *MUSÉE IMAGINAIRE* (1947) very much sought to demystify the cult of art reserved for an élite of the privileged classes, giving popular literary expression to assumptions current among the avant-garde in the decades before the Second World War.

65 LOUIS MARCOUSSIS **1922**

(1878-1941) After study at the Cracow Academy from 1901, Marcoussis worked briefly at the Académie Julian in Paris in 1903, meeting Roger de la Fresnaye and Lotiron. He exhibited at the Salon des Indépendants in 1905 but in 1907 gave up painting to work as a caricaturist for LE JOURNAL *and* L'ASSIETTE DU BEURRE. *In 1910 he became part of the circle around Apollinaire, who insisted that he change his name from Markus to Marcoussis, coming into contact with Braque and Picasso and developing a* CUBIST *idiom, one that never lost its sense of colour and light. He showed at the Section d'Or exhibition in 1912, and at the Herbstsalon of* Der Sturm *in Berlin the following year; his* HOMME AU VIOLONCELLE *of 1914 marks his mature style. After the war, he began painting 'sous-verre', achieving a new luminosity; his first one-man show was at the Galerie Pierre in 1925. Two years later he moved to Brittany. Etching became a significant part of his work from 1930. In 1933 he visited the U.S.A., exhibiting at New York and Chicago; in 1936 a major retrospective exhibition of his work was held in Brussels.*

BROOM. AN INTERNATIONAL MAGAZINE OF THE ARTS, VOLUME 3, NO. 1 (1922).
84pp., 315 x 215 mm., with 4 woodcuts and cover illustration.
Printer: Universelle Imprimerie Polyglot [Italy?]
L.5435-1962. (LARIONOV COLLECTION).

BROOM appeared in 6 volumes between 1921 and 1924. Initially it was published from headquarters in Rome, with offices in New York and London, but by 1924 the main editorial office was described as being in New York. Edited by Harold A. Loeb, the magazine set out to present to the American public not only the work of American writers and artists but also 'works of innovators, important to European literature, who have not hitherto found a hearing in the United States . . . Broom has placed before its readers selections from the contemporary output of writers of reputation such as Gordon Craig, James Stephens, Walter de la Mare, Paul Claudel, Picasso and Matisse [*sic*] to mention but a few of the Europeans' (notice at end of volume 1 of *BROOM*). Volume 3, no. 1, had woodcuts by Derain and Max Weber, as well as Marcoussis. Lautréamont's *MALDOROR* was serialised in the magazine in English translation, and later issues advertised translations of Apollinaire's *THE POET ASSASSINATED* for sale.

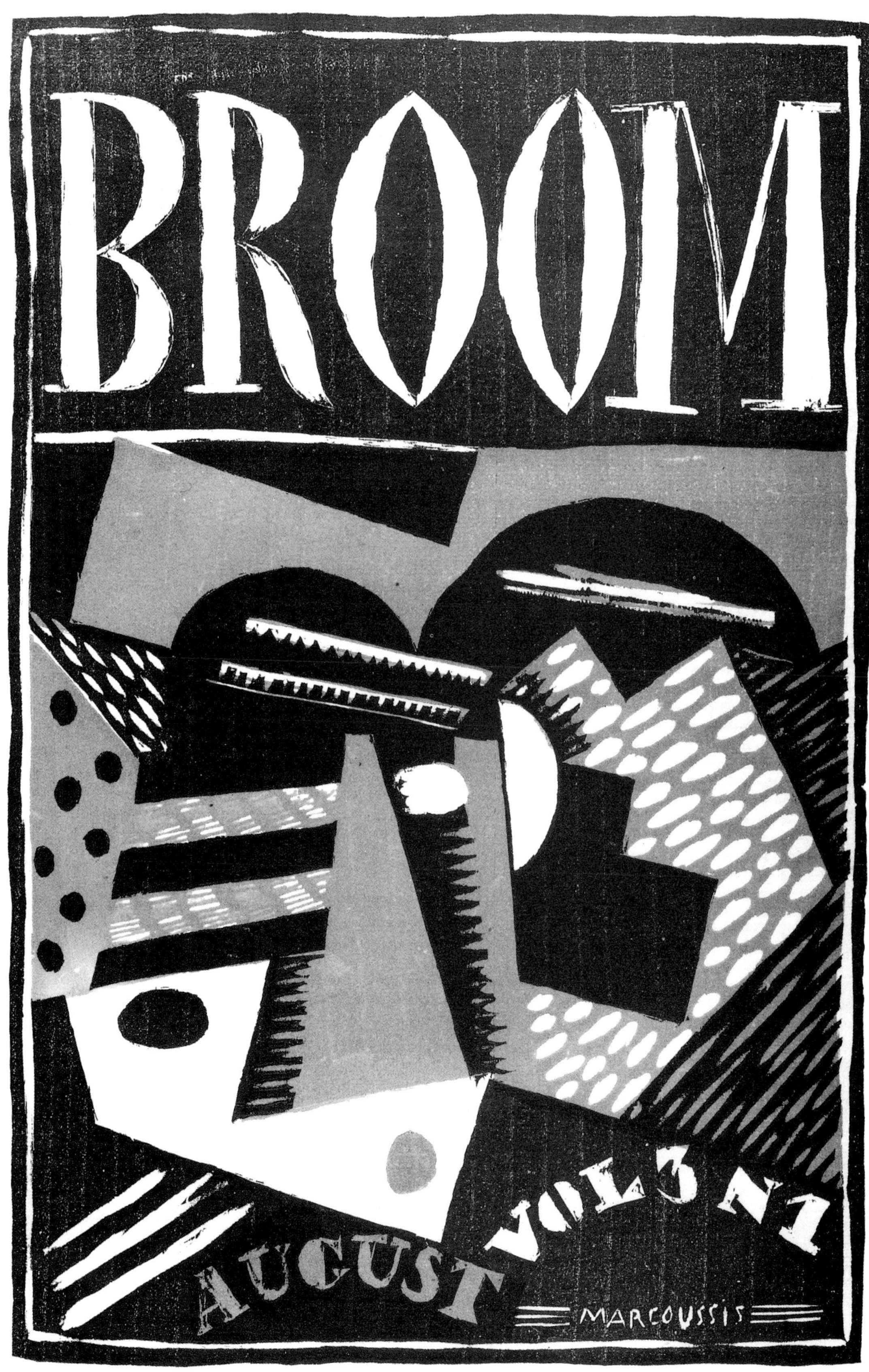
BROOM
AUGUST
VOL 3 N 1
MARCOUSSIS

66 MAX ERNST **1922**

(1891-1976) Born near Cologne ('hatched from the egg which his mother had laid in an eagle's nest and over which the bird had brooded for seven years'), Ernst decided to become a painter in 1912, a year after he had met Auguste Macke, through whom he came into contact with the BLAUER REITER *group. In 1931 he showed at the Erste Deutsche Herbstsalon exhibition organised under the auspices of* Der Sturm *in Berlin and briefly met Apollinaire during a visit to Paris. After war service, Ernst set up a* DADA *group in Cologne with his friend Hans Arp, organising an exhibition in 1919 and producing his first collages. In 1920 André Breton arranged, and wrote an introduction to, an exhibition of Ernst's work in Paris. Settling in Paris in 1922, Ernst became friends with Paul Eluard (with whom he visited the Far East in 1924) and other* SURREALISTS. *Apart from participation in Surrealist activities, Ernst worked with Miró on Diaghilev's ballet* ROMEO AND JULIET *in 1926 (being rebuked in* LA RÉVOLUTION SURRÉALISTE *no. 7 for collaborating with a company bent on 'the domestication, in aid of the international aristocracy, of the dreams . . . of intellectual and physical starvation'). Ernst participated in Buñuel's film* L'AGE D'OR *in 1930. Fleeing to New York on the Nazi occupation of France, Ernst collaborated with Breton in producing the review* VVV. *In 1945, Eluard organised a retrospective exhibition of his work in the Galerie Denise René, Paris, where Ernst finally settled in 1953. In 1954, he was awarded the first prize (for painting) at the Venice Biennale, for which André Breton finally declared his exclusion from the Surrealist group.*

MAX ERNST, *LES MALHEURS DES IMMORTELS, RÉVÉLÉS PAR PAUL ELUARD ET MAX ERNST* (PARIS: LIBRAIRIE SIX, 1922).
44pp., 245 x 180 mm., with 21 illustrations including frontispiece.
Printer: '[Imprimé] pour la Librairie Six'.
L.1277-1936.

The publication of the Librairie Six represents Eluard's first collaboration with Ernst in Paris. The poet Eluard had visited Cologne with his wife in 1921 and had chosen some of Ernst's collages to illustrate his poems after meeting the artist: this was to result in Eluard's *RÉPÉTITIONS*, issued in 1922 by the publishers Au Sans Pareil with Ernst's work in a limited edition of 350 copies. Published in Paris, the prose poems of *Les malheurs des immortels* were written jointly by Ernst and Eluard in Cologne in March 1922 and in the Tyrol the following June.

186

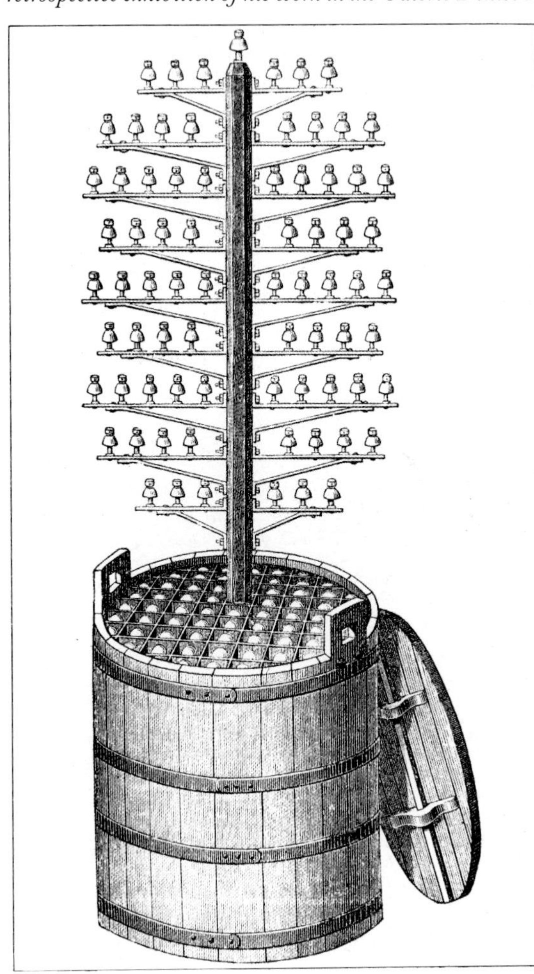

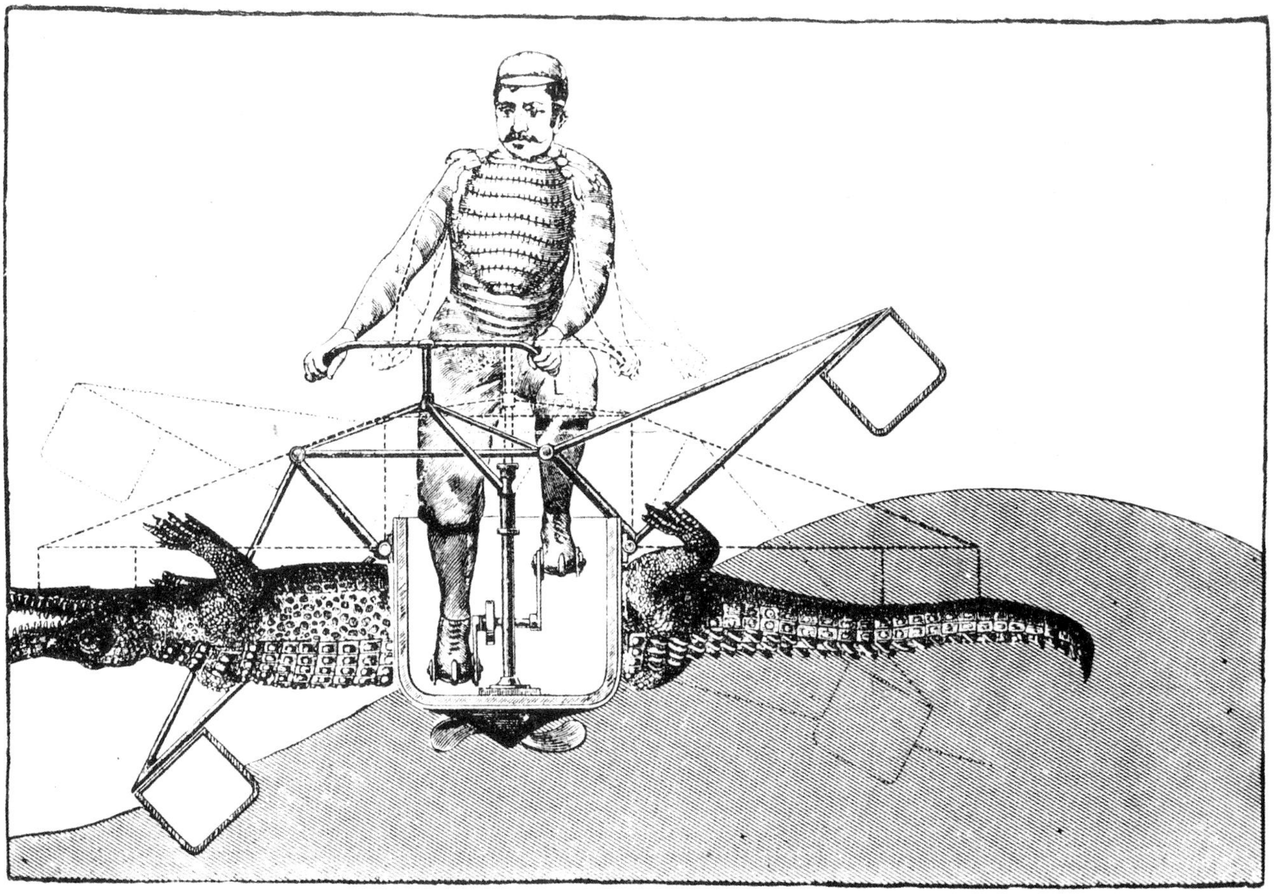

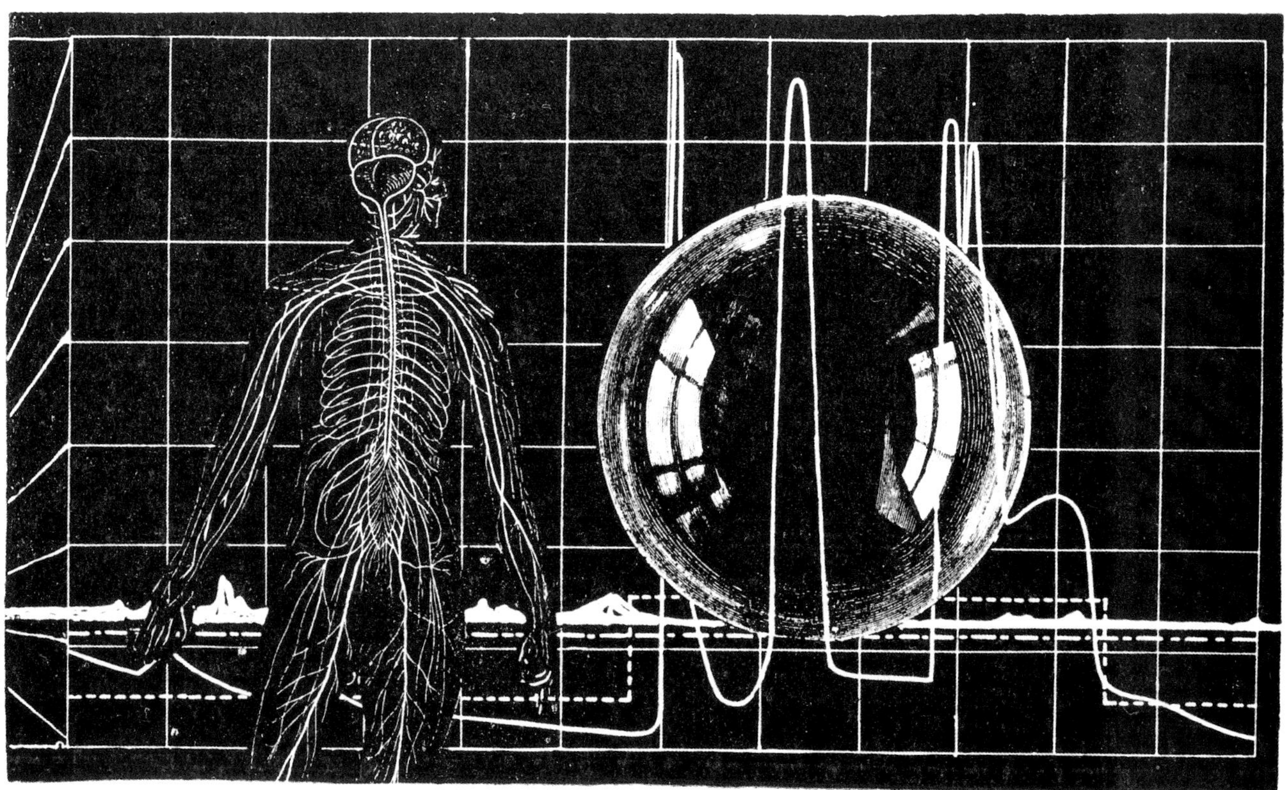

67 EL LISSITSKY **1922**

(1890-1941) After studying architecture and engineering in Darmstadt, El Lissitsky returned to Russia in 1914 where, working as an architectural draughtsman, he devoted himself to graphic art. In 1919, Chagall invited him to the Vitebsk Academy to teach architecture and design; when Chagall resigned in the face of Malevich's opposition to his teaching, El Lissitsky supported the latter's SUPREMATISM *and began work on his PROUNS (a method involving work on a flat plane, i.e. graphic work, followed by the construction of three-dimensional models, objects in their own right, that would lead,* via *consideration of properties of materials used, to the realisation of utilitarian objects). After a brief stay in Moscow where he identified with* CONSTRUCTIVISM, *El Lissitsky was sent to Germany and became a link between Russia and avant-garde designers and artists in the west. He worked with Kurt Schwitters on the review MERZ in Hanover in 1923, and on OBJECT (published in Russian, German and French) with Ilia Ehrenburg in Berlin in the same year. He published in 1925 with Jean Arp LES-ISMES DE L'ART that reviewed avant-garde movements since 1914. He designed the Soviet pavilions at exhibitions in Germany before returning to teach in the* VKhUTEMAS *in 1928. Lissitsky's influence as a typographer and illustrator has been enormous, much of it through Moholy-Nagy to the BAUHAUS and beyond. He was responsible for the first abstract political posters in Russia from c.1919; the influence of his typography, photomontage and integrated collages has even been detected in POP ART.*

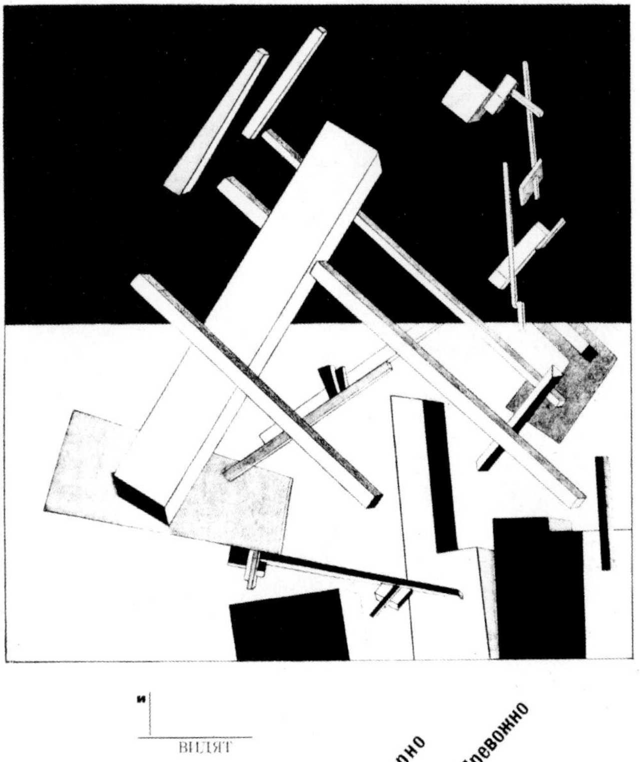

188 EL LISSITSKY, *SUPREMATICHESKII SKAZ PRO DVA KVADRATA, V 6TI POSTROIKAKH [THE SUPREMATIST TALE OF TWO SQUARES]* (BERLIN: VERLAG 'SKYTHEN', 1922).
16pp., 275 x 215 mm., with 9 illustrations (2 on cover).
Edition included 50 numbered and autographed copies.
Printer: E. Haberland, Leipzig.
L.1831-1937. Colour plate 10

Conceived in Vitebsk in 1920 but published in Berlin two years later, Lissitsky's book was dedicated to 'all, all children'. Recognising that children can handle abstraction actively while 'conditioned adults must be content with passive enjoyment' (Cohen, 1976), the author sets out to tell a story using elemental Suprematist compositions (a red square, symbol of life and the new revolutionary order with its limitless possibilities, operating against a black square, signifying the old order, chaos, egotism and death) to tell a story in which social forces clash. The work shows a remarkable adaptation of Malevich's ideas to book design, heralded by the artist's work for the cover of Malevich's *ON NEW SYSTEMS IN ART* of 1919. *THE SUPREMATIST TALE OF TWO SQUARES* was reprinted in *DE STIJL* in 1922.

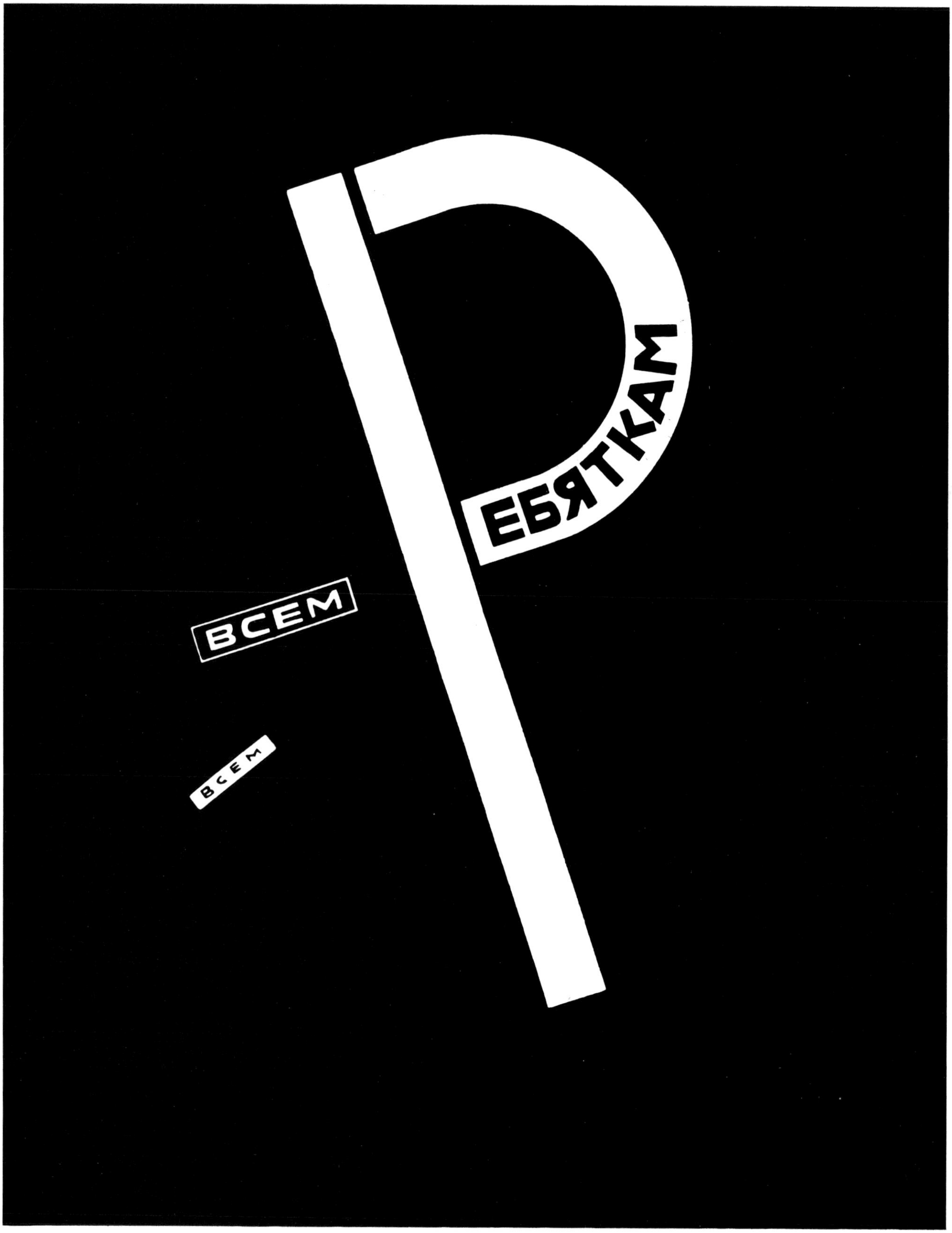

РЕБЯТКАМ

ВСЕМ

ВСЕМ

68 EL LISSITSKY **1923**

(1890-1941)

VLADIMIR VLADIMIROVICH MAYAKOVSKY, *DLYA GOLOSA [FOR READING OUT ALOUD]*.
['CONSTRUCTOR': EL LISSITSKY] (BERLIN: GOSIZDAT, 1923).
64pp., 190 x 130 mm., with illustrations on title-page and 15 openings.
Printer: Lutze & Vogt.
L.2020-1981.

This anthology of 13 poems by Mayakovsky evidences his revolutionary commitment and his capacity for humorous observation of city life. The excitement and pace of the poems are matched by the typographic illustrations, which fully exploit the possibilities of two-colour printing and of typography. Each poem is given a symbolic typographic identity, and the relevant image is used on the thumb index – a neat and witty guide to the contents. According to Lissitsky, 'my pages stand in much the same relationship to the poems as an accompanying piano to a violin. Just as the poet unites concept and sound, I have tried to create an equivalent unity using the poem and typography'. The layout was set entirely by a German compositor with no knowledge of Russian: to overcome shortages prevailing in Moscow, Mayakovsky had the book produced by the Berlin branch of Gosizdat.

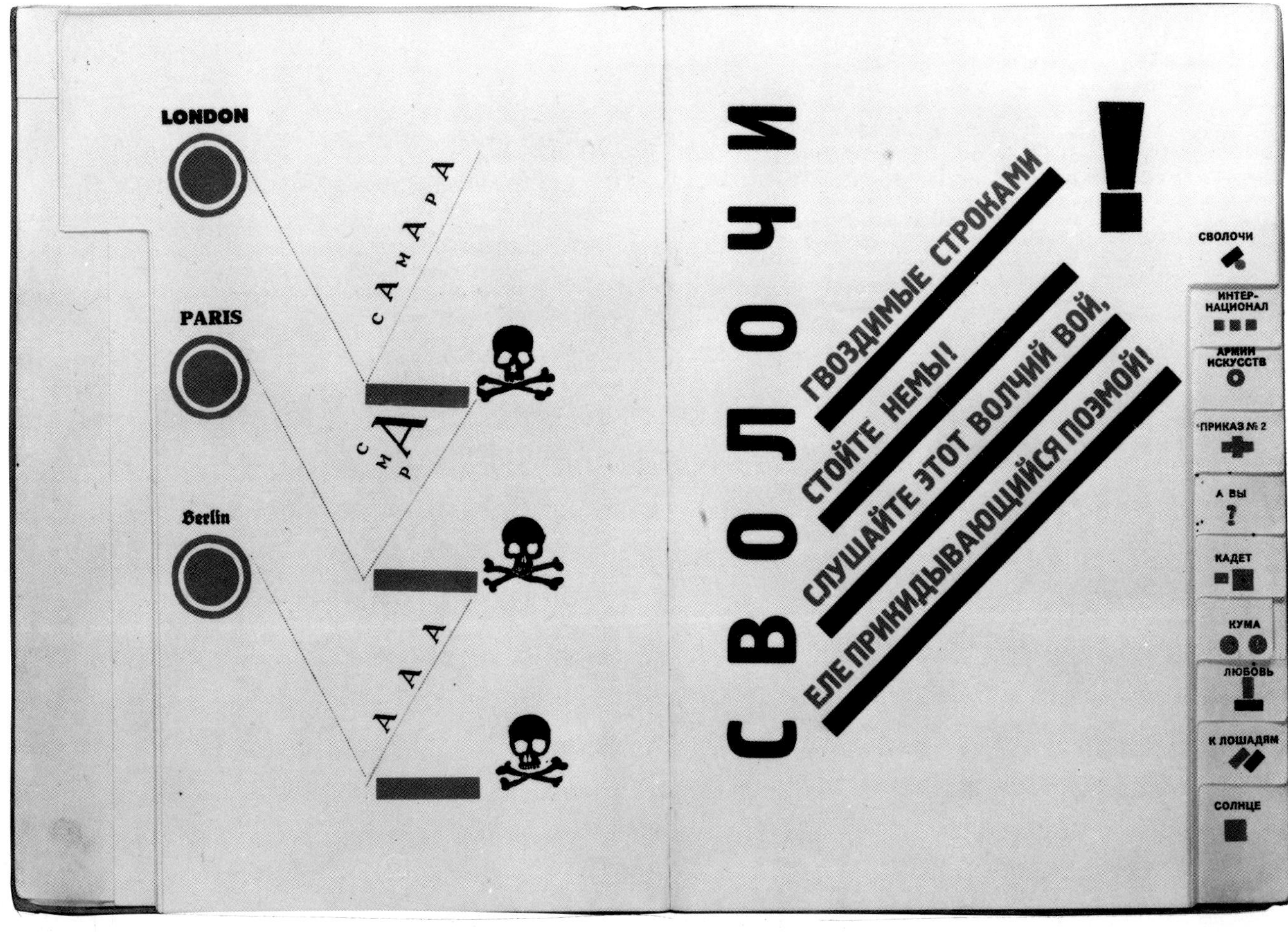

69 ALEXANDER RODCHENKO **1923**

(1891-1956) After study at the Kazan Art School and the Stroganov Institute in Moscow, Rodchenko worked under the influence of Malevich's SUPREMATISM. *His earliest abstract drawings, made with compass and ruler, date from 1915, and his abstract theatre designs were exhibited at Tatlin's* MAGAZIN *exhibition in Moscow in 1916. A leader of the* CONSTRUCTIVIST *movement, his display of 'Black on Black' in response to Malevich's 'White on White' in 1918 signalled a distancing of their positions, Rodchenko with his wife Stepanova and Vladimir Tatlin insisting on the social role of the new art and its practical application that was termed* PRODUCTIVISM; *with Tatlin, Rodchenko sought a break with the past to create a new environment based on geometric principles of design that exploited the qualities of new materials. Examples of his work were the First Textile Factory in Moscow and the workers' club for the Soviet pavilion at the Paris International Exhibition of 1925. Abandoning all 'fine' art after 1922, Rodchenko devoted himself to applied art, working prolifically in the production of posters, book graphics, furniture design, and the theatre. He was foremost in developing the use of photography for graphic design purposes, and was also involved in the production of films.*

LEF: ZHURNAL LEVOGO FRONTA ISKUSSTV [LEFT: JOURNAL OF THE LEFT FRONT OF THE ARTS], NO. 2, APRIL-MAY 1923 (PUBLISHED IN MOSCOW AND PETROGRAD BY GOSIZDAT).
180pp., with 5 illustrations and cover.
Edition of 5000 copies (V&A copy no. 4677[?]).
Printer: Pechatnya Yakovleva.
L.2690-1983.

Edited by Mayakovsky, and with illustrations by Rodchenko, Popova and Stepanova, *LEF* provided the principal forum for discussion of the rôle of art in the reconstruction of Russia after the Revolution. It was published from 1923 to 1925, re-emerging as *NOVUII LEF [NEW LEFT]* in 1927-8. *LEF* published the manifesto of Russian Constructivism; its intended area of distribution can be seen in the inclusion of articles in German and English. The second issue provides an early example of Rodchenko's use of photography: his 'photographs of people [combined] with newspaper clippings . . . make an assemblage suggesting the rotative axis, not of his own earlier linear constructions, but of Vertov's zooms and cuttings', borrowing techniques from Vertov's silent film experiments (Compton, 1976).

70 LAJOS KASSÁK 1923

(1887-1967) Leaving his family at 13, Kassák worked in a steelmill and collaborated with the social-democratic journal EESZAVA *in Budapest. Travelling around Europe on foot and supporting himself as a blacksmith, Kassák settled in Paris in 1909; here he met Apollinaire, Picasso and Cendrars before returning to Hungary in 1912. Active in the Trade Union movement, he also translated the works of Apollinaire, Cocteau and others and founded the review* TETT *(Action) in 1915 that placed him at the head of the artistic and literary avant-garde in Hungary. On the banning of the review by the authorities, Kassák and Lazlo Moholy-Nagy established the journal* MA *(Today) in 1916 which introduced* DADA *to the country. Escaping from prison for his part in founding the short-lived Communist Republic in 1919, Kassák settled in Vienna until 1926; here he wrote with Moholy-Nagy* DAS BUCH NEUER KÜNSTLER, *a discussion of modern art which relates various national trends to a common European evolution, and produced* DADA *collages under the influence of John Heartfield. Kassák also had one-man exhibitions in Vienna and in Berlin in 1924. Returning to Hungary Kassak attempted to promote the* CONSTRUCTIVISM *he had adopted under El Lissitsky's influence with the journals* DOKUMENT *and* MUNKA. *After 1945 he produced figurative landscapes, but returning to an abstract Constructivist manner in the mid 1950s and showing his work internationally in the 1960s.*

MA-BUCH. GEDICHTE VON LUDWIG KASSÁK. DEUTSCHE MIT EINEN
192 *VORWORT VON ANDREAS GÁSPÁR* (BERLIN: VERLAG DER STURM, 1923).
64pp., 230 x 155 mm., with 5 full-page illustrations. Edition of 550 copies (V&A copy no. 458), signed by Kassák and Gáspar, of which 450 copies are on 'Buchdruckpapier' ([nos. 1-450]), 75 copies 'auf feinem Papier' ([nos. 451-525]), and 25 copies 'auf feinem Papier', fully bound ([nos. 526-550]).
Printer: 'Buch-, Kunst- und Steinbruckerei "Elbemühl" ', Vienna.
L.4097-1978.

Kassák's first book of poems, 'Epic poem wearing Wagner's mask', was published in 1915, their un-rhymed and free-flowing nature recalling some strands of German expressionist poetry. The poetry in *MA-BUCH,* which he illustrated himself, belongs to a different phase, as Gáspar the translator, states in his introduction, mentioning Kassák's Constructivist interests and notion of typography as an essential part of the poet's vocabulary of expression. Printed in Vienna, *MA-BUCH* was published by *Der Surm,* in the gallery of which he was to have his first Berlin exhibition in 1924.

71 THEO VAN DOESBURG **1923**

(1883-1931) Born in Utrecht, van Doesburg worked as a painter and architect before 1919, having his first exhibition at The Hague in 1908 and from 1912 developing his gifts as a polemicist by writing art criticism. Working in an EXPRESSIONIST *and* FAUVE *idiom at first, in 1917 he founded with Mondrian the* DE STIJL *movement and review, the latter launched in 1918. In 1922, a respected art critic and architect, he attacked the* BAUHAUS *as romantic, 'arty' and failing to unite the disciplines taught there for the purpose of producing socially useful design; Gropius invited him to teach there, but van Doesburg left after a brief period, joining Schwitters on a lecture tour in 1922 to propagate* DADA *doctrines. Van Doesburg organised the De Stijl section of an exhibiton at the Galerie de l'Effort Moderne in Paris in 1923; thereafter he broke away from Mondrian who could not accept the intrusion of diagonals into the De Stijl language of horizontals, verticals and primary colours. Van Doesburg's doctrine,* ELEMENTARISM, *was put into effect in the decoration of L'Aubette cabaret in Strasbourg, done with Arp and Sophie Täuber-Arp. In 1930 he was co-editor, with Hélion, of* ART CONCRET, *and was a founder member of* ABSTRACTION-CRÉATION *in the year of his death.*

MÉCANO, NO. 4-5 (LEIDEN: DE STIJL, 1923).
16 pp. (including covers), 255 x 160 mm.
L.259-1984.

The setting up of *MÉCANO*, a 'Neo-Dada' magazine, was the result of van Doesburg's participation at the Düsseldorf Congress of International Progressive Artists in May, 1922, when Schwitters, Hans Richter, El Lissitsky, van Doesburg and others left the Congress to form a body less concerned with the organisation and financing of exhibitions and festivals. The new journal *MÉCANO* was initially issued with *DE STIJL*; van Doesburg used the pseudonym IK Bonset as literary editor, as he did for his concrete poetry. The editor's article on poetry in the first issue of *MÉCANO* championed the Dada desire to spread destruction as the only means of building a new constructive poetry. Among contributors such as Tzara, with a long Dada pedigree, are to be found Constructivists such as Moholy-Nagy, as well as Eluard and Péret. No. 4-5 was the last issue of *MÉCANO*: the cover design which includes a drawing by Raoul Hausmann, reveals van Doesburg's approach to the Bauhaus. After mentioning his arrival there, we find a statement over the names of van Doesburg, Mondrian and van Eesteren: 'rejoice, for the new form [*Gestaltung*] in art (NEO-PLASTICISM) already exercises a similar influence on European art', making clear the claim that De Stijl was superseding the Weimar school; 'many use the □ [square] but only a few understand it'.

BILANZ DES STAATLICHEN BAUHAUSES WEIMAR

HOLZHAUS SOMMERFELD U.S.W. 1919

THEATER JENA U.S.W. U.S.W. 1922

VAN DOESBURG KOMMT NACH WEIMAR 1921 UND

BEGRÜSSUNG

DE STIJL 1916 1923 HOLLAND

Freut sich, daß die neue Gestaltung in der Malerei (NEO-Plasticismus) schon einen derartigen Einfluß auf die Kunstentwicklung Europas ausübt.

THEO VAN DOESBURG
P. MONDRIAN
C. VAN EESTEREN

Paris 1923

SCHON VIELE BENUTZEN DAS □
ABER nur wenige VERSTEHEN ES

Van buiten kwadraat van binnen Biedermeier

Nur das □ des Stijls ist gesetzlich geschützt

LEIDEN. — PARIS: RUE DU MOULIN VERT 51 TER PARIS XIV.
ADMINISTRATIE EN VERTEGENWOORDIGING VOOR HOLLAND: "DE STIJL" UTR JAAGPAD 17

M—É—C—A—N—O

GÉRANT LITÉRAIRE: I. K. BONSET

No 4 en 5

No. (White, Blanc, Wit, Weiß.) 1923

ADMINISTRATIE: UTR. JAAGPAD 17, LEIDEN (HOLLAND)

HOLLAND'S BANKROET DOOR DADA

N.B. Thuisbezorging zonder prijsverhooging.

1923

Et je trouve qu'on a en tort de dire que le Dadaïsme, le Cubisme, le Futurisme, reposaient sur un fond commun. Les deux dernières tendances étaient surtout basées sur un principe de perfectionnement technique ou intellectuel tandis que le Dadaïsme n'a jamais reposé sur aucune théorie et n'a été qu'une

Protestation

(Tristan Tzara)

Dada est la force désintéressée, ce n'est pas une maladie, pas une énergie pas une vérité.

Evola

Waar het hart leeg van is loopt de neus van over.

Bonset

GEORGES ROUAULT **1923**

(1871-1958)

GEORGES ROUAULT, *MISERERE. CINQUANTE-HUIT PLANCHES GRAVÉES PAR L'ARTISTE*
(PARIS: ÉDITION DE L'ETOILE FILANTE, 1948).
128 ff., 672 x 515 mm., with 58 engravings.
Edition of 425 copies numbered 1 – 425 (V&A copy no. 237) and 25 copies *hors commerce* numbered I – XXV.
Printer: Jacquemin, engravings (in 1922-1927); Aulard, text (completed 15 September 1948).
L.1066-1949.

This work was originally conceived by Ambroise Vollard: there were to be two volumes, *MISERERE* and *GUERRE*, and André Suarès was to write the text. This plan was then modified to issue one volume with more than 50 plates. In the event it was not Vollard who published the work. Most of the subjects were drawn by Rouault between 1914 and 1918, and were engraved and printed between 1923 and 1927. Vollard's death and the Second World War intervened, and it was not until 1947 that Rouault recovered the prints which were then published as *MISERERE* without Suarès text the following year.

73 PAUL NASH **1924**

(1889-1946) Son of a barrister, Nash trained as a painter from 1906. His early work shows the influence of PRE-RAPHAELITE *painting (especially Rossetti) and* ART NOUVEAU. *In 1910, he entered the Slade School, and had his first one-man show (of drawings and watercolours) in 1912 at the Carfax Gallery. He worked briefly under Roger Fry at the Omega workshops and on restoring the Mantegna cartoons at Hampton Court in 1914. Following his exhibition at the Goupil Gallery in 1917, he was recruited to serve as an official war artist. After the war he became involved in textile, stained glass and poster design, and book illustration, as well as painting. In 1933 he was a founder member of Unit One, a group that brought together painters such as Ben Nicholson, sculptors such as Henry Moore and the architects Wells Coates and Colin Lucas, united by their 'common sympathies' (Nash's letter to* THE TIMES, *2 June 1933). A founder member too of the English Surrealist group, having been impressed with the work of De Chirico and others in Paris in 1931, he exhibited in the International Surrealist exhibitions of 1936 in London and 1938 in Paris. In the Second World War, he again served as official war artist.*

GENESIS. TWELVE WOODCUTS BY PAUL NASH WITH THE FIRST CHAPTER OF GENESIS IN THE AUTHORISED VERSION (SOHO: THE NONESUCH PRESS, 1924).
60 pp., 270 x 180 mm., with 12 woodcuts.
Edition of 375 copies (V&A copy no. 290), on Zanders hand-made paper.
Printer: Curwen Press, text set in Rudolf Koch's Neuland type.
L.476-1941.

Paul Nash's interest in book illustration ante-dates the First World War, though he was initially unable to gain work of this kind. His first commission came in 1918, when he was asked to illustrate a limited edition published by the Beaumont Press of John Drinkwater's poems, *LOYALTIES.* At the end of 1923, he was asked by the newly-founded Nonesuch Press to provide illustrations for *GENESIS,* and these are held to be the first sign of mastery of woodcutting, a medium he had begun to explore in 1918. The cancelled woodblocks for this edition are held by the V&A. The Nonesuch Press was established by Francis Meynell, David Garnett and Vera Merckel in 1923; their use of established commercial presses such as the Curwen Press was designed to keep the prices of their limited editions as low as possible.

197

74 ANDRÉ MASSON **1925**

(b. 1896) After a short sojourn at the Académie des Beaux Arts in Brussels, Masson worked at the École des Beaux Arts in Paris from 1912, after which he visited Tuscany. Wounded in 1917, he convalesced at Céret, where he met Soutine. In Paris, he was taken up by the dealer Kahnweiler in 1922, by which time FAUVISM *and Cézanne had become his mentors. Friends with Aragon and Miró, André Breton began to buy his work in 1923. Masson was part of the* SURREALIST *group, though excluded on the issue of the Second Surrealist Manifesto in 1929; he met Matisse in Grasse in 1932 and designed sets and costumes for the Massine ballet in Monte Carlo the following year before moving to Catalonia. He exhibited with the International Surrealist exhibitions in London and Paris in 1936 and 1938; from 1941 to 1945 he lived in New York. Settling in the south of France, he did much engraving for book illustration from 1946. In 1965 he executed the painting on the ceiling of the Théâtre de l'Odéon in Paris.*

MICHEL LEIRIS & ANDRÉ MASSON, *SIMULACRE. POÈMES ET LITHOGRAPHIES* (PARIS: ÉDITIONS DE LA GALERIE SIMON, 1925)
32 pp., 245 x 190 mm., including 6 lithographs and a lithographed cover.
Edition of 112 copies signed by author and illustrator (V&A copy no. 43), of which 10 copies on *Japon ancien des Manufactures Impériales* (nos. 1-10), 90 copies on *Vergé d'Arches* (nos. 11-100), 10 copies 'de Chapelle' (nos. I-X), and 2 copies for deposit under copyright law with a set of lithographs from cancelled plates (nos. 0 & 00).
Printer: Imprimerie Leibovitz, text; Imprimerie Pitault, lithographs (completed 26 April 1925).
L.2172-1939.

SIMULACRE included Masson's first lithographs and the first published work of Michel Leiris, a writer associated with the Surrealists in the 1920s, though in 1929 he joined Georges Bataille's group of dissident Surrealists centred in the review *DOCUMENTS*. A professional ethnographer (working in the ethnography museum at the Trocadéro), he later took part an ethnographical expedition directed by Marcel Griaule to Africa that was described in a special number of *MINOTAURE* (no. 2, June 1933) and in Leiris's book, *L'AFRIQUE FANTÔME (1934)*. Masson had exhibited regularly in Kahnweiler's gallery since 1922, and had illustrated Georges Limbour's *SOLEILS BAS* in 1924 for the dealer.

75 ERNST LUDWIG KIRCHNER **1926**

(1880-1938) An architecture student at Dresden from 1901, Kirchner had a brief stay at the private art school of Hermann Obrist in Munich in 1903-4, where he saw work of Impressionists in one of the series of exhibitions organised by the Phalanx school between 1901 and 1904, before qualifying as an architect in 1905. Shortly prior to this, he founded DIE BRÜCKE *with Schmidt-Rottluff, Eric Heckel and F. Bleyl, a group that was to provide a focal point for* EXPRESSIONISM *and which was of considerable importance for the revival of the woodcut and graphic art. Nolde and Pechstein joined them for exhibitions in 1906. Kirchner emerged as the dominant personality in the group. In 1911 he moved to Berlin; he executed with Heckel wall paintings for the International Exhibition at Cologne the following year, and exhibited at the second* BLAUER REITER *show in Munich. After a mental breakdown during military service in 1915, Kirchner produced a series of wood engravings for Chamisso's PETER SCHLEMIHL ('The man who lost his shadow'); from 1917 he lived in Switzerland, and in 1922 he collaborated with the weaver Lise Gujer. Elected a member of the Prussian Academy of Fine Art in 1931, he was ousted by the Nazis in 1933. His visit to Paul Klee in 1936 resulted in his painting HOMMAGE À KLEE. Kirchner committed suicide in 1938.*

WILL GROHMANN, *DAS WERK ERNST LUDWIG KIRCHNERS* (MUNICH: KURT WOLFF VERLAG, 1926).
62 pp., 270 x 265 mm., with 100 collotypes *hors texte* and

two wood engravings.
Edition of 850 copies (V&A copy no. 1), of which 50 are *de luxe* with two signed prints.
Printers: Spamserchen Buchdruckerei, Leipzig, text; Arthur Kolbe, Dresden, collotypes; Officina Bodoni, Montagnola di Lugano, coloured wood engraving in the *de luxe* edition; O. Felsing-Panpresse, Charlottenburg, etching in *de luxe* edition.
L.1113-1943.

The publication of this collection of Kirchner's work demonstrates the extent of his prestige with collectors by 1926. Kirchner himself designed the whole book. Grohmann, an art historian and friend of Kirchner's, played a significant part in introducing contemporary artists to the public, among them Klee, Kandinsky and Die Brücke painters. The work was a companion to an earlier study devoted to Kirchner's drawings, *ZEICHNUNGEN VON ERNST LUDWIG KIRCHNER* (Arnolds Graphische Bücher, series 2, vol. 6, 1925).

Das Werk
Ernst Ludwig Kirchners
von
W Grohmann
Kurt Wolff Verlag
München

201

76 FRANTISEK KUPKA 1926

(1871-1957)

QUATRE HISTOIRES DE BLANC ET NOIR GRAVÉES PAR FRANK KUPKA (PARIS: [–], 1926).
26 pp.m 330 x 250 mm., with 25 wood engravings and wood engraved title page.
Edition of 300 copies (V&A copy un-numbered), of which 100 copies have wood engravings in first state (nos. 1-100).
Printer: G. Kadar (completed Nov. 1926).
L.2036-1952.

In his introductiuon to *QUATRE HISTOIRES*, Kupka refers to the period when he imitated, by traditional copying and interpretation of nature, the art of realist painters, which he compares to the work of alchemists, astrologists and sorcerers in its failure to convey a perceived vision of reality; either the artist betrayed his vision to avoid betraying the model, or deformed the model to make it conform to his vision. 'L'Œuvre d'art étant en soi réalité abstraite demande à être constituée d'éléments inventés. Sa signification concrète découle de la combinaison même des types morphologiques et des situations architecturales particulières à son organisme propre'.

77 DAVID JONES 1926

(1895-1974) Son of a printer who produced THE CHRISTIAN HERALD *at Holywell, Flintshire, Jones trained in 1909-15 at the Camberwell School of Art under A. S. Hartrick, who impressed on him the importance of draughtsmanship. After service in the 1914-18 war, Jones studied further at the Westminster School of Art, where he had occasional contact with Sickert, whom he considered the greatest English painter since Turner. In 1921 he was converted to Roman Catholicism and joined Eric Gill at the community at Ditchling, founded by Pepler in 1915. Jones became a postulant in the Guild of St. Joseph and St. Dominic, a craft guild that pioneered wood engraving and other crafts in the 1920s. In 1924, Jones followed Eric Gill to Capel-y-ffin. In 1928-1933 Jones showed with the Seven and Five Society, this being the period of his most prolific production of paintings. In 1928 he toured the parts of France most associated with the Chanson de Roland, an extension of his interest in the Arthurian legend in Britain; Jones also visited Cairo and Jerusalem in 1934. A master of drawing, painting and watercolours, Jones began to work on inscriptional lettering in the late 1940s. As a writer, Jones' handling of the English language can be compared to that of James Joyce.*

THE BOOK OF JONAH, TAKEN FROM THE AUTHORIZED VERSION OF KING JAMES I., WITH ENGRAVINGS ON WOOD BY DAVID JONES
(WALTHAM ST. LAWRENCE: GOLDEN COCKEREL PRESS, 1926).
i, 18 pp., 250 x 195 mm., with 15 wood engravings.
Edition of 175 copies (V&A copy no. 138).
Printer: Golden Cockerel Press (A H Gibbs & F Young, compositors; A C Cooper, pressman; completed 11 June 1926).
L.6976-1982

Jones produced his first wood engravings for the St. Dominic Press at Ditchling in 1922 (See exhibition catalogue, Tate Gallery, *DAVID JONES* 1981, p.72). Between 1924 and 1927, Jones provided illustrations for the Golden Cockerel Press. The Press had been founded in 1920 by Harold Taylor as a co-operative where young authors were able to produce their works themselves. The Press was acquired by Robert Gibbings in 1924, and emphasis moved from literary works to those with artistic pretensions. In 1933 the Press was acquired by Christopher Sandford.

Then the men feared the Lord exceedingly, & offered a sacrifice unto the Lord, and made vows. Now the Lord had prepared a great fish to swallow up Jonah. And Jonah was in the belly of the fish three days & three nights. Then Jonah prayed unto the Lord his God out of the fish's belly, and said, I cried by reason of mine affliction unto the Lord, and he heard me; out of the belly of hell cried I, and thou heardest my voice. For thou hadst cast me into the deep, in the midst of the seas; and the floods compassed me about: all thy billows and thy waves passed over me. Then I said, I am cast out of thy sight; yet I will look again toward thy holy temple.
8

THE WATERS COMPASSED ME ABOUT, EVEN TO THE SOUL: THE DEPTH CLOSED ME ROUND ABOUT, THE WEEDS WERE WRAPPED ABOUT MY HEAD.
9

AND IT CAME TO PASS, WHEN THE SUN DID ARISE, THAT GOD PREPARED A VEHEMENT EAST WIND; AND THE SUN BEAT UPON THE HEAD OF JONAH, THAT HE FAINTED, AND WISHED IN HIMSELF TO DIE, AND SAID, IT IS BETTER FOR ME TO DIE THAN TO LIVE.

NOW THE WORD OF THE LORD CAME UNTO JONAH THE SON OF AMITTAI, SAYING, ARISE, GO TO

(1895-1974)

THE CHESTER PLAY OF THE DELUGE, EDITED BY J. ISAACS, WITH ENGRAVINGS ON WOOD BY DAVID JONES (WALTHAM ST. LAWRENCE: GOLDEN COCKEREL PRESS, 1927).
iv, 18 pp., 320 x 245 mm., with 10 wood engravings.
Edition of 275 (V&A copy no. 211).
Printer: Golden Cockerel Press (A H Gibbs & F. Young, compositors; AC Cooper, pressman; completed 16 Nov. 1927).
L.14531-1974.

Jones probably engraved the woodblocks for the CHESTER PLAY while at the Benedictine monastery on Caldey Island in January-March 1927. The engravings show Jones' virtuosity in this medium even though the prints were made on paper that had not been dampened, so that the real quality of the blocks can only be appreciated in the artist's proofs. Jones moved on to engraving on copper plates following a commission from Douglas Cleverdon in 1927. Plans to illustrate his IN PARENTHESIS, perhaps his greatest piece of writing, with such engravings were abandoned on his breakdown in 1937.

(b. 1887) Born to a poor Jewish family in Vitebsk, Chagall studied painting in St. Petersburg in 1907-1910, working part-time as a sign painter. In 1910, he was sponsored by his patron Vinaver to stay in Paris; here he associated with CUBISTS, *including Delaunay and Apollinaire, but also discovered the work of Van Gogh and the* FAUVES. *Apollinaire introduced him to Herwarth Walden, the director of* Der Sturm, *in 1912. The artist took part in the 1913 Herbstsalon in Berlin and exhibited in the* Sturm *Gallery in 1914, Apollinaire writing the introduction to the catalogue. In Russia from 1914, he was appointed Minister for Fine Arts for Vitebsk in 1917, setting up an Art Academy but leaving for Moscow after quarrelling with the* SUPREMATIST *Malevich. In Moscow, Chagall created mural decorations and designed sets for the Jewish State Theatre. In 1922 he left for Berlin, where he met Grosz, Archipenko and others, and was initiated into the art of engraving. On his arrival in Paris in 1923, Vollard gave him a number of commissions to illustrate books. His first major retrospective exhibiton was held in Basel in 1933. From 1941 to 1944 he lived in North America, designing sets and costumes for Stravinsky's FIREBIRD at the Metropolitan Opera, New York. In 1947 Chagall returned to Paris, moving to Vence two years later. From 1950 he began to produce ceramics, and sculpture formed part of his work. In 1956 he produced the CIRCUS series of lithographs. From this period, he was given a number of public commissions for stained glass.*

208 LA FONTAINE, *FABLES*. *EAUX FORTES ORIGINALES DE MARC CHAGALL* (PARIS: TÉRIADE, 1952).
Two volumes, 440 x 335 mm., with 100 etchings.
Edition of 200 copies (V&A copy no. 112) on *Vélin de Rives*, signed by the artist, of which 40 copies have 40 original etchings hand painted by the artist, a set of etchings on *Japon nacré* and a set of etchings on *Monval* (nos. 1-40); 45 copies with 100 original etchings hand painted by the artist and a set of etchings on *Monval* (nos. 41-85), 100 copies with 100 original etchings (nos. 81-185); 15 copies *hors commerce* (nos. I-XV). Also published were 100 albums of 100 etchings on *Monval* paper, numbered 1-100.
Printer: Maurice Potin, etchings (1927-30); Raymond Haasen, etchings for covers to two volumes (1952); Imprimerie Nationale, text, set in Garamond Italique Corps 24 (completed March 1952).
L.161-1984.

Tériade published five books with illustrations by Chagall, and the first three were originally commissioned by Ambroise Vollard. Illustrations for La Fontaine's *FABLES* had been commissioned in 1927, and the choice of a foreign Russian artist as the illustrator of one of the most revered French texts provoked some remark: Vollard was obliged to reply to criticism in the art columns of *L'INTRANSIGEANT* on 14 January 1929 (a review edited by Tériade and Maurice Raynal) that the fables, being part of the oral tradition of Asia Minor, might gain in being interpreted by an artist from the East. Chagall's first essays, in 1927, were gouaches, but their colours could not be reproduced satisfactorily; Chagall then worked on 100 etchings, smaller than the gouache series and with greater stylistic unity. It remained for Tériade to bring the project to completion in 1952.

209

(1900-1955) After working in the navy, Tanguy settled in Paris in 1922, at the same time as the poet Jacques Prévert, whom he had met on military service; both discovered SURREALISM *at Adrienne Monnier's bookshop, and Tanguy was inspired to paint (teaching himself) after seeing works of De Chirico in Paul Guillaume's gallery in 1923. His first pictures were reproduced in early numbers of the review* LA RÉVOLUTION SURRÉALISTE; *André Breton wrote the introduction to his first one-man exhibition at the Galerie Surréaliste in 1927, which he shared with objects from Mexico, Peru and elsewhere. He married the North American painter Kaye Sage in 1939, emigrated to the United States and became naturalized there in 1948.*

BENJAMIN PÉRET, *DORMIR, DORMIR DANS LES PIERRES.* *DESSINS D'YVES TANGUY* (PARIS: ÉDITIONS SURRÉALISTES, 1927).
36 pp., 220 x 175 mm., with three full-page illustrations, 10 vignette drawings, and title page.
Edition of 205 copies (V&A copy no. 37), signed by author and artist, of which 10 copies are on *Japon impérial* (nos. 1-10), 20 copies on *Hollande Van Gelder* (nos. 11-30), and 175 copies on *Vergé* (nos. 31-205), with five copies *hors commerce* on *Chine* marked with the name of the people for whom they were intended.
Printer: 'L'Imprimerie spéciale des Éditions Surréalistes', Paris (completed 31 January 1927).
L.1346-1936.

Tanguy's drawings were noticed in 1922 by Vlaminck but it was after Jacques Prévert had introduced him to Surrealist circles that his graphic work began to be used for illustrations. By 1927, Tanguy had developed his distinctive manner in which biomorphic abstract figures are scattered in a disorientated dream-like narrative. Benjamin Péret was one of the closest disciples of André Breton and never abandoned Surrealism or betrayed its early enthusiasm for automatic writing. His early work was published in the review *LITTÉRATURE (1919-1924)*, the major vehicle for Surrealist ideas at the time of Breton's break from the Dada circle around Tristan Tzara.

210

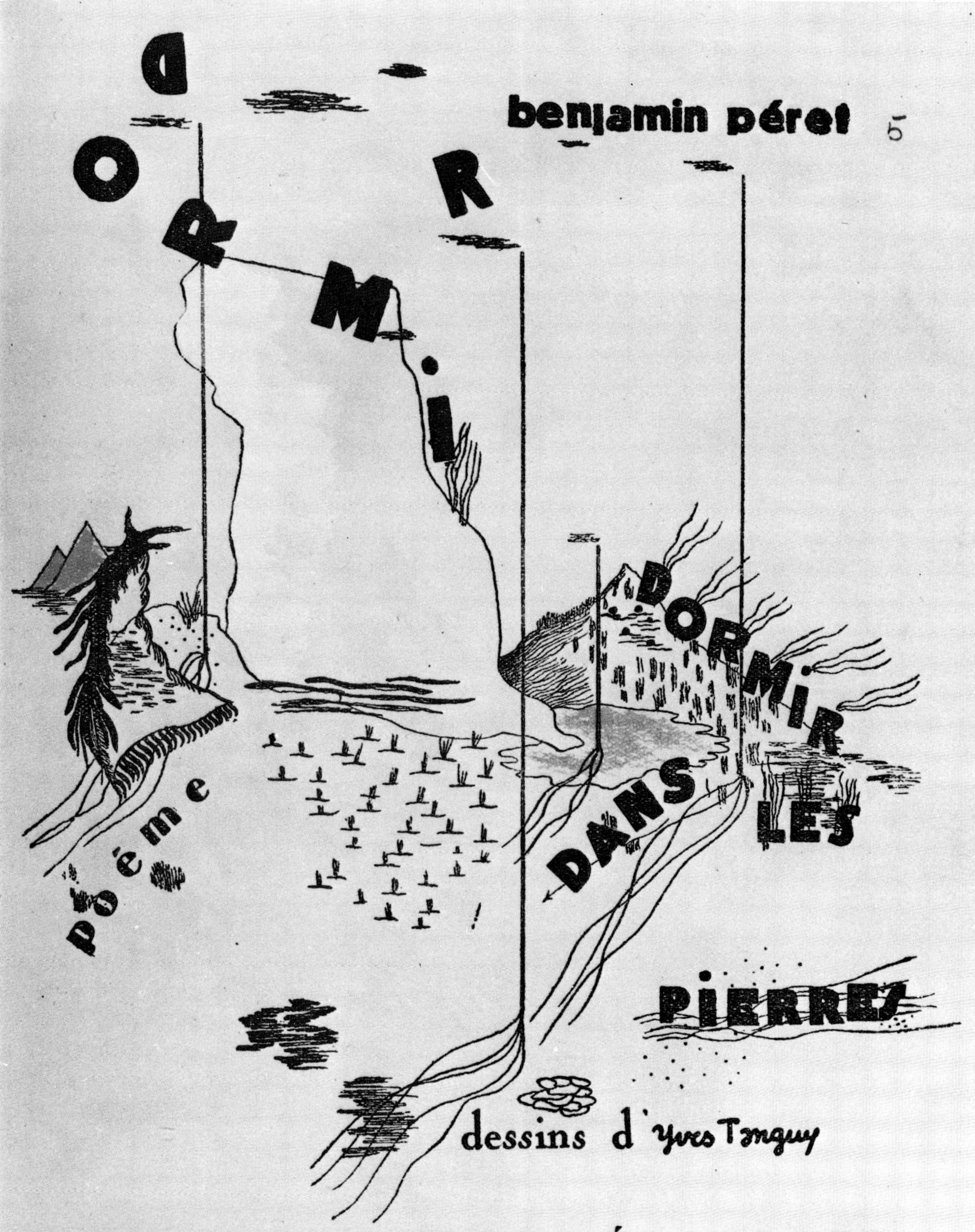
DORMIR
benjamin péret
DORMIR DANS LES PIERRES
poème
dessins d'Yves Tanguy
EDITIONS SURRÉALISTES
16, rue Jacques-Callot, Paris
1927

81 GEORGES ROUAULT 1928

(1871-1958) Son of a cabinet-maker, Rouault began in 1885 to work for the stained glass maker Tamoni, and later for Hirsch, the restorer of ancient stained glass, at the same time attending evening classes at the École des Arts Décoratifs. In 1891 he enrolled at the École des Beaux Arts to study painting, where he was befriended by Gustave Moreau. Rouault was a frequent visitor to the abbey of Ligugé near Poitiers, and met here the poet Huysmans and the catholic writer Léon Bloy. Though familiar with the FAUVISTS, *Rouault exhibited separately from them at the Salon d'Automne of 1905. The dealer Vollard was initially interested only in his painted ceramics produced in 1906-7, but in 1913 bought everything in his studio and in 1917 became his exclusive agent. From 1920 his graphic work (engravings, woodcuts, lithographs) occupied him more than his painting; in 1929 he designed the sets and costumes for Diaghilev's* FILS PRODIGUE *by Prokofiev. Stained glass and enamelling form an important part of his œuvre.*

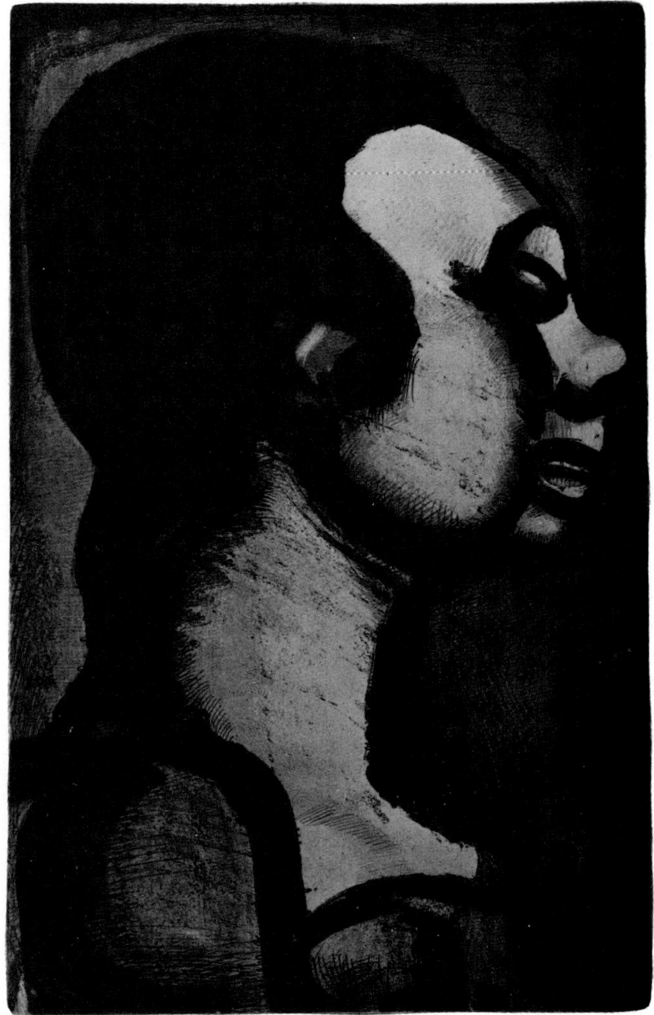

AMBROISE VOLLARD, *LES RÉINCARNATIONS DU PÈRE UBU . . . EAUX FORTES ET DESSINS SUR BOIS DE GEORGES ROUAULT* (PARIS: A. VOLLARD, 1932).
228 pp., 440 x 320 mm., with 105 wood engravings including 1 on cover; also a set of 22 etchings for insertion into the book according to a key provided.
Edition of 305 copies (V&A copy no. 185); the set of etchings issued as an edition of 225.
Printer: Aux Deux Ours, text and wood engravings; Henri Jourde, etchings; Georges Aubert, wood engravings after gouaches by Rouault.
L.3130-1981

Rouault began work on the Ubu series in 1913 and completed the illustrations in 1928 (there are many trial proofs for a number of etchings). The Ubu series marks Rouault's first use of photogravure to secure an image on a plate.

Vollard wrote more than 10 works on the subject of Père Ubu, beginning with *LE GRAND ALMANACH DU PÈRE UBU* (1900-1901) and ending with *LES RÉINCARNATIONS DU PÈRE UBU* (1932). The character was based on Alfred Jarry's *UBU ROI*, a play first performed in 1896 and marking the beginnings of the *THÉÂTRE DE L'ABSURDE*, which had great vogue in Dada and Surrealist circles. Whereas Jarry's Ubu was a personification of crass malevolence and dictatorial buffoonery, Vollard's character was made into a character that typified political and bureaucratic corruption. Rouault's engravings were probably more responsible for the book's success than the text, with which contemporary critics were not overly impressed.

82 LOUIS MARCOUSSIS 1928

(1878-1941)

TRISTAN TZARA, *INDICATEUR DES CHEMINS DE COEUR*. *EAUX-FORTES DE LOUIS MARCOUSSIS* (PARIS: ÉDITIONS JEANNE BUCHER, 1928).
24 ff., 280 x 190 mm., with 3 etchings, and small vignette on cover.
Edition of 100 copies (V&A copy no. 7), of which 4 copies are on *Japon impérial* with an original drawing, a set of etchings and proofs from the cancelled plates (nos. 1-4), 10 copies on *Hollande Van Gelder* with a set of etchings (nos. 5-14), and 86 copies on *Vélin d'Arches* (nos. 15-100); also 4 copies for the Collaborators with a set of engravings and proofs from the cancelled plates, and 2 copies for deposit under copyright law.
Printer: Paul Haasen, Paris, etchings; R. Coulouma, Argenteuil (H. Barthélemy, director), text (completed 15 Jan. 1928).
Signature [?] in pencil on fly-leaf: 'Jeanne Bucher'.
L.2095-1939.

The illustrations which Marcoussis provided for the poems of his friend Tzara were done in 1927, and they show a Cubist approach independent from the Surrealist art prevalent in Paris. The publisher, Jeanne Bucher, (1872-1946) had set up her bookshop in the rue du Cherche Midi in Paris in 1925, soon installing a gallery nearby. Her first publication was the *HISTOIRE NATURELLE* illustrated with frottages by Max Ernst, the earliest in a series of books illustrated by modern artists. The painters she promoted were avant-garde but not of one school, ranging from Braque and Chagall to Kandinsky and Masson. Tzara in 1928 stood to one side of avant-garde movements; having broken with Breton's Surrealist group, he was to join it in 1929, contributing to *LA RÉVOLUTION SURRÉALISTE* in that year, and participating in the launching of *LE SURRÉALISME AU SERVICE DE LA RÉVOLUTION* in July 1930.

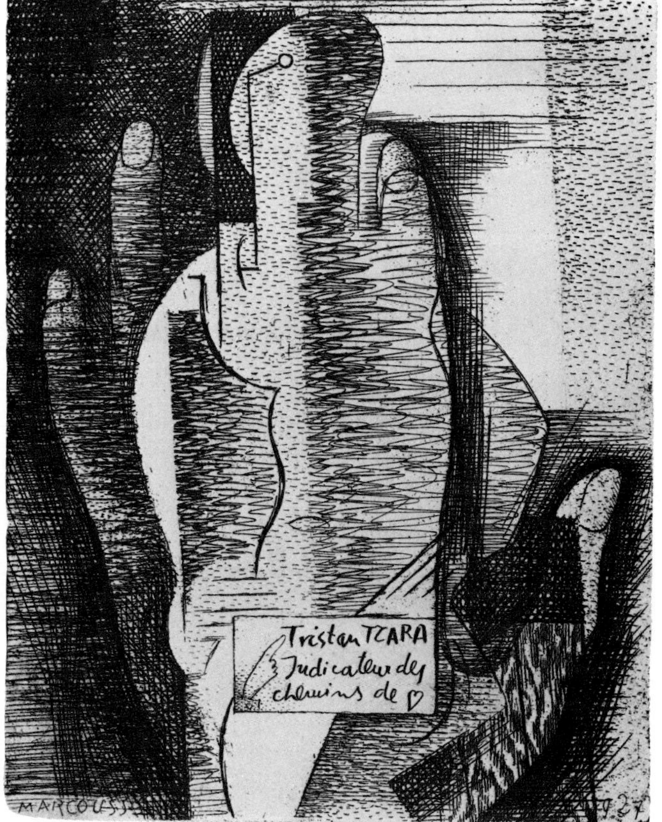

83 JOHN HEARTFIELD 1929

(1891-1968) Heartfield studied painting and drawing at Wiesbaden and the Munich Kunstgewerbeschule in 1905-11, thereafter working as a commercial artist in Mannheim in 1911-12, and as a film designer for the Grunbaum Brothers and Universum Film, Berlin, 1916-19. With his brother Wieland Herzfeld (John adopted the English version of the name in disgust at German nationalist propaganda and in admiration of free America) and Georg Grosz, Heartfield founded in 1916 what was to become the Malik Verlag. Part of the first Berlin DADA *group, Heartfield did not totally follow its systematically destructive tendencies, joining the Communist Party in 1918. From 1916, he was one of the initiators of the photomontage technique, which he launched in the anti-militaristic* NEUE JUGEND. *He worked as a political and satirical photomontagist from this time, much of his work appearing in the socialist* ARBEITER ILLUSTRIERTE ZEITUNG. *Hounded by the Nazi regime, he emigrated to Prague in 1933 and thence to London in 1938, returning to East Berlin in 1950 where he worked as a graphic and theatre designer for Bertholt Brecht's Berliner Ensemble. His first one-man show in England was entitled 'One man's war against Adolf Hitler'.*

DEUTSCHLAND, DEUTSCHLAND, UEBER ALLES. EIN BILDERBUCH VON KURT TUCHOLSKY UND VIELEN FOTOGRAFEN. MONTIERT VON JOHN HEARTFIELD (BERLIN: NEUER DEUTSCHER VERLAG, 1929).
236 pp., 240 x 185 mm., with 194 photographic illustrations of which 10 are photomontages, with a photomontage on the covers.
Edition of '20,000'.
Printer: Pass & Garleb A.-G., Berlin.
L.1983-1981.

Heartfield aimed at the mass market to convey his message and warnings of the hideous consequences of social corruption. This volume sold at three marks 20 in paperback and five marks in hard covers; the publishers claimed that it had sold 48,000 copies by the summer of 1930. The Neuer Deutscher Verlag was directed by Willi Münzenberg (1889-1940), the founder of the Young Communist League, and published a number of magazines and newspapers; driven to France by the Nazis, in 1933 he worked for the Éditions du Carrefour (the publishers of Ernst: see Cat. 86). The text of Kurt Tucholsky (1890-1935), a journalist and satirist driven to suicide by the Nazis in 1935, began with a quotation from Holderlein denouncing the cruelty and inhumanity of 19th century Germany and proceeded to do the same for the Weimar Republic. Among Heartfield's photomontage images are pictures of people with football heads ('Deutscher Sport') and faceless gentlemen watching flimsily dressed beauties.

215

84 GIORGIO DE CHIRICO 1930

(1888-1978) After study at the Athens Polytechnic from 1900, Chirico moved to the Munich Academy in 1906 for two years, during which he met the work of Franz Stuck, Max Klinger (the series of engravings 'Fantasies on a lost glove' impressed him especially) and the romantic symbolist Arnold Bücklin, also discovering Nietzsche. In Italy from 1908 and much impressed by antique statuary mingling with urban crowds, he painted a number of 'enigma' subjects, which he exhibited in Paris at the Salon d'Automne in 1911. Wounded in the war, he met Carra, by then an ex-Futurist, at Ferrara and established the 'Scuola Metafisica', soon joined by Morandi and De Pisis; in 1918 he showed at the L'EPOCA *exhibition and from 1919 was one of the leaders of the* VALORI PLASTIC *group. Despite much study of Old Masters at this period he signed the Italian* DADA *manifesto published in* BLEU *in 1920. In 1925 he designed costumes and sets for the Swedish Ballets in Paris, doing the same for Diaghilev's ballet in 1929 and the Paris Opéra. Chirico visited New York and the USA in 1935-37, thereafter living in Italy and making stage design a major part of his work.*

GUILLAUME APOLLINAIRE, *CALLIGRAMMES*
([PARIS:] LIBRAIRIE GALLIMARD [NOUVELLE REVUE FRANÇAISE], 1930).
276 pp., 330 x 250 mm., with 67 lithographs, one of them repeated on cover.
Edition of 100 copies (V&A copy no. 50), signed by the
216 author, of which 6 are on J. Whatman paper (nos. 1-6) with two copies *hors commerce* (nos. I-II), six copies on *Nacré du Japon* (nos. 7-12) with four copies *hors commerce* (nos. III-VI, one of them for the illustrator), 88 copies on *Chine* (nos. 13-100), with 25 copies *hors commerce* (nos. VII-XXXI).
Printers: Desjobert, lithography; Maurice Darantière, text (completed 31 March 1930).
L.5978–1984

Apollinaire had taken to Chirico's painting in Paris in 1914, an approval that is said to have been decisive in the painter's career. Chirico had attended the poet's gatherings on Saturdays and painted a prophetic picture of him with a head wound and the outline of bandages that Apollinaire had bought (he was wounded in the head at the front, never fully recovering). Chirico drew the composition directly onto the stone, and said of his work for *CALLIGRAMMES* that he was inspired by memories of the poet whose writings he had read avidly.

CALLIGRAMMES

la grâce exilée *Va-t'en va-t'en mon arc-en-ciel*
Allez-vous-en couleurs charmantes
Cet exil t'est essentiel
Infante aux écharpes changeantes

145

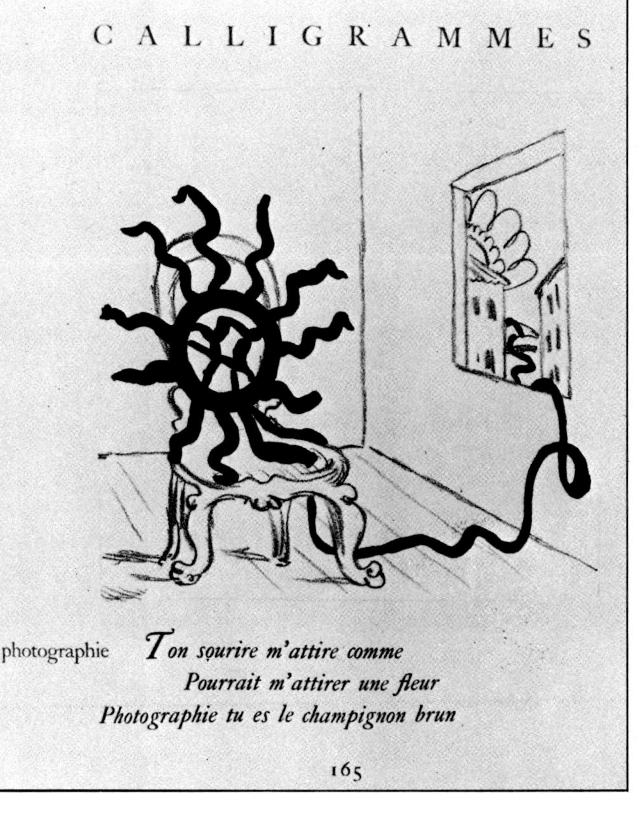

CALLIGRAMMES

photographie *Ton sourire m'attire comme*
Pourrait m'attirer une fleur
Photographie tu es le champignon brun

165

C A L L I G R A M M E S

ıntôme
ıuées

Comme c'était la veille du quatorze juillet
Vers les quatre heures de l'après-midi
Je descendis dans la rue pour aller voir les saltimbanques

85 RAOUL DUFY **1930**

(1877-1953)

EUGÈNE MONTFORT, *LA BELLE-ENFANT, OU L'AMOUR À QUARANTE ANS* (PARIS: AMBROISE VOLLARD, 1930).
250 pp., 330 x 255 mm., with 77 etchings, and 16 etchings *hors texte*; illustrated table of etchings included in collation.
Edition of 245 copies on *Vélin d'Arches* (V&A copy no. 175), 30 copies on *Vieux Japon* with a set of etchings, 30 copies on *Japon Supernacré* and 50 copies *hors commerce*.
Printer: Louis Fort, etchings; L'Imprimerie Nationale, text. Binding by Bayard, Lyons.
L.3335-1981.

Commissioned by Vollard to provide illustrations for Montfort's work, Dufy made a number of preliminary studies in Marseilles, a centre from which he travelled to gather material for pictures of *Société Mondaine*, and the locale of Montfort's novel.

ARRIVANT de la Cannebière, on débouche sur le large quai de la Fraternité, un des coins les plus vivants de Marseille.

Là, depuis le comptoir du *Brûleur de Loups,* jusqu'à la salle provençale de Mistral, se succèdent sans interruption bars et restaurants où l'on mange les fruits de mer. Là, devant leur étalage humide, vous attendent écailleurs d'huîtres, de praires, de moules et d'oursins; là, étalés

LE quartier Saint-Jean, derrière la Mairie, est ce qui reste de plus curieux à Marseille et qui a conservé le caractère le plus ancien. Il y a là encore des rues à escalier, des venelles au milieu desquelles coule le ruisseau, d'étranges cloaques, des culs-de-sac et des impasses d'une saleté aussi malodorante qu'à Naples. Et tout cela grimpe et se colle sur le flanc de la petite colline qui supporte Saint-Jean et

A TABLE, dans la salle à manger de la *Belle-Enfant*, dont la porte ouvrait sur la poupe, Didier, de l'œil, surveillait l'entrée du bateau : une barrière mobile, fixée sur la passerelle qui descendait de l'arrière sur le quai. Une heure venait de sonner : Diane n'était pas encore rentrée. De sa place, Didier voyait les bars déserts, les terrasses abandonnées : tout mouvement sur le port avait cessé; même les doua-

86 MAX ERNST 1930

(1891-1976)

MAX ERNST, *RÊVE D'UNE PETITE FILLE QUI VOULUT ENTRER AU CARMEL* (PARIS: ÉDITIONS DU CARREFOUR, 1930).
88 ff., 235 x 185 mm., with 77 illustrations.
Edition of 20 copies on *Japon impérial* of which 17 copies are numbered I-XVII and three copies *hors commerce* numbered XVIII-XX; 40 copies on *Hollande Pannekoek* numbered 1-40; 1000 copies on *Vélin teinté* numbered 41-1000 'et S.P. 1 à 40' (V&A copy no. 226).
Printer: L'Imprimerie Durand, Chartres.
L.3930-1978

The publication takes the form of a story told by pictures (collages) with an introductory text setting the scene and captions to each illustration. The first 'novel' of this kind produced by Ernst was *LA FEMME 100 TÊTES*, also published by Les Éditions du Carrefour in 1929.

« Allons ! Dansons la Ténébreuse...

87 JOAN MIRÓ **1930**

(1893 – 1983) Son of a goldsmith/watchsmith, Miró studied part-time in the Academy at Barcelona from 1907, and from 1911 in the Academy of Francisco Gali. Exposure to Fauvists, Impressionists and Cubists came with the series of exhibitions that took place in the Dalmau gallery from 1912, and in the great exhibition of French art that Ambroise Vollard organised in Barcelona in 1916. Miró, an acquaintance of Picabia, exhibited first in the Dalmau gallery in 1918. In 1919 he went to Paris, where Picasso introduced him to Tzara and Reverdy; in 1924 he was part of the group with André Breton, Louis Aragon and Paul Eluard which signed the first SURREALIST *manifesto. In 1926 he designed, with Max Ernst, the sets and costumes for Diaghilev's Russian ballet, ROMEO AND JULIET. From the early 1930s Miró began to work with lithography and engraving. Avoiding Spain during the Spanish Civil War, he returned there during the Nazi occupation of France; from 1944 he began to work with the ceramicist Llorens Artigas. From 1948 he exhibited regularly at the Maeght Gallery, Paris. In 1950, during his first visit to the USA, Miro executed a mural for Harvard University. In 1954 he was awarded the Grand Prix de la Gravure at the Venice Biennale.*

TRISTAN TZARA, *L'ARBRE DES VOYAGEURS, ORNÉ DE QUATRE LITHOGRAPHIES DE JOAN MIRÓ* (PARIS: ÉDITIONS DE LA MONTAGNE, [1930]).
102 pp., 250 x 170 mm., with 4 lithographs *hors texte.*
Edition of 500 copies (V&A copy no. 70), signed by author and artist, of which 10 copies are on *Japon impérial* with a manuscript page by the author (nos. 1-10), 25 copies on *Hollande Van Gelder* (nos. 11-35), 65 copies on *Vélin d'Arches* (nos. 36-100), 400 copies on *Alpha,* (nos. 101-500); 2 copies for deposit under copyright law (nos. 0 and 00), 1 copy on *Vieux Japon,* with 5 manuscript pages by the author (letter A).
Printer: L'Imprimerie Commerciale du *PETIT JOURNAL,* Paris.
L.882-1940.

Among the earliest of Miró's graphic work, these 4 lithographs represent the artist's first original book illustrations. They were executed the year before the book's publication in 1930. Miró's work was regularly reproduced in the Surrealist magazine *LA RÉVOLUTION SURRÉALISTE* in 1925-9, though Breton was casting doubt on his Surrealist commitment by 1928.

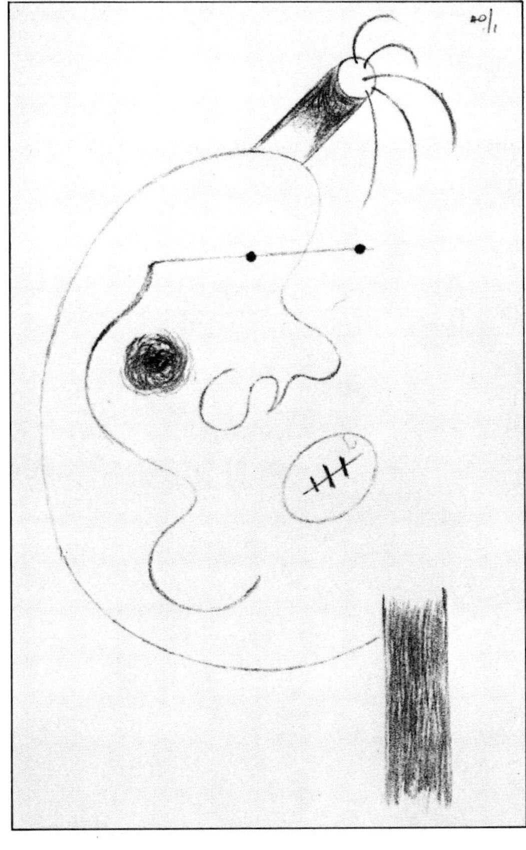

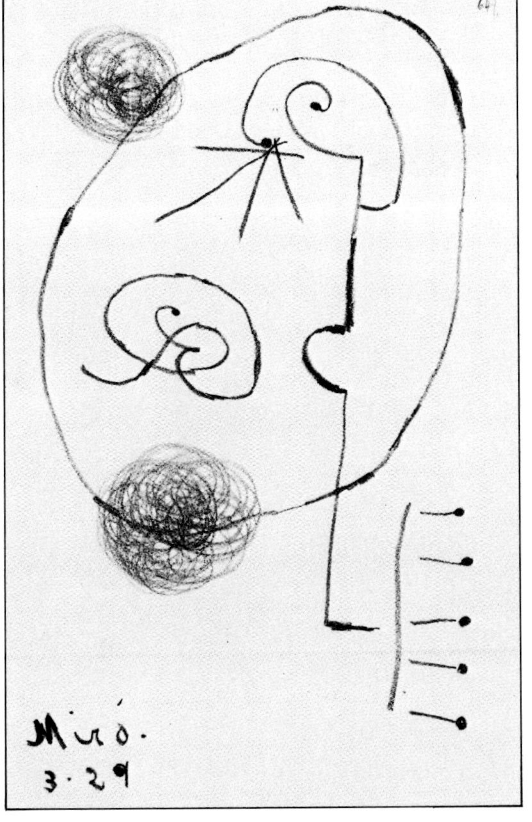

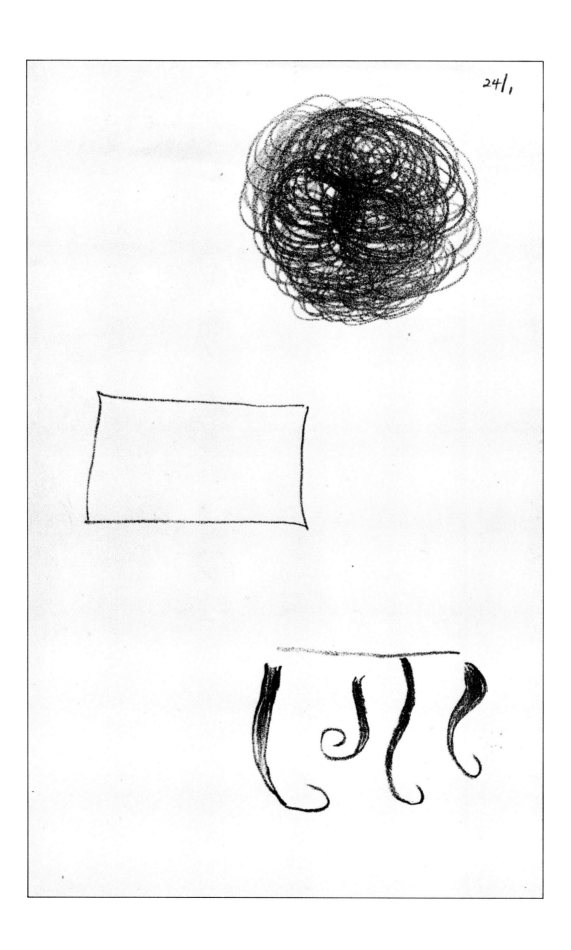

88 MARC CHAGALL 1931

(b. 1887)

BIBLE. EAUX FORTES ORIGINALES DE MARC CHAGALL (PARIS: TÉRIADE, 1956)
2 volumes, 62 and 54 ff., 445 x 335 mm., with 57 and 48 etchings *hors texte* respectively.
Edition of 275 copies (V&A copy no. 252) on *Monval,* signed by the artist, numbered 1-275, with 20 copies *hors commerce* numbered I-XX. Also published were 100 albums on *Vélin d'Arches* with the 105 etchings, to be painted, signed and numbered by the author.
Printer: Maurice Potin, 66 etchings (1931-9); Raymond Haasen, 39 etchings (1952-56); L'Imprimerie Nationale, text, set in Grandjean Romain du Roi (completed 14 Dec. 1956).
L.3295-1958.

Chagall was commissioned in 1931 to produce illustrations for a Bible; Vollard advised him to visit Place Pigalle in Paris to find suitable subjects, to which the artist replied that he preferred to feel the earth in Palestine. Chagall visited Palestine, Syria and Egypt in 1931. He engraved 105 plates between that date and 1939 (Vollard had planned almost twice this number). Only 66 of the etchings were completed and printed by 1939, in the workshop of Maurice Potin. The initiative for reviving the project after Vollard's death was that of Tériade, who prevailed upon Chagall to complete the remaining 39 plates; these were then printed by Raymond Haason. In 1956, Tériade published reproductions of all the engravings in heliogravure, together with 16 coloured and 12 black and white lithographs newly added by Chagall as a special number of the periodical VERVE.

Chagall
דן
שמעון
גד
אשר
נפתלי
יוסף

89 ERIC GILL

(1882-1940) Son of an evangelical minister, Gill studied at Chichester Technical and Art School before being apprenticed to WD Caröe, architect to the Ecclesiastical Commissioners. From 1903 he enrolled at the Central School in London to work under Lethaby and Edward Johnston, concentrating on letttering and carving inscriptions. In 1907, he moved to Ditchling, where a guild of craftsmen working co-operatively was formed, and began to execute engravings. From 1910, Gill began to carve figures in stone, with 'a "primitive" directness of conception.... intelligible in the light of Gill's professed admiration for Maillol' (Dennis Farr). In 1913, he was converted to Roman Catholicism. In 1914 he exhibited at the Goupil Gallery, London; after 1919 he produced numerous war memorials. After discussions with Stanley Morison, Gill designed the 'Perpetua' and 'Gill Sans' typefaces for the Monotype Corporation. Having moved to Wales in 1924, Gill formed another artists' community in Buckinghamshire in 1928. He was elected an Associate of the Royal Academy in 1937.

THE FOUR GOSPELS OF THE LORD JESUS CHRIST
(WALTHAM ST. LAWRENCE: THE GOLDEN COCKEREL PRESS, 1931).
268 pp., 335 x 235 mm. (royal quarto), with 64 wood engravings.
Edition of 500 copies (V&A copy no. 475), of which 12 are on Roman vellum and 488 on Kelmscott paper made by Joseph Batchelor & Sons.

Printer: Robert and Moira Gibbings at the Golden Cockerel Press (F. Young and AH Gibbs, compositors; AC Cooper, pressman; begun 20 Feb., completed 28 Oct. 1931).
Bound by Sangorski and Sutcliffe.
L.212-1933.

Gill's first work for the Golden Cockerel Press was a series of illustrations for Enid Clay's *SONNETS AND VERSES* in 1925. The style employed by Gill for the *FOUR GOSPELS* illustrations was deliberately archaic. Gill's interest in book illustration goes back to the 1920s when he provided work for the St. Dominic's Press, Ditchling

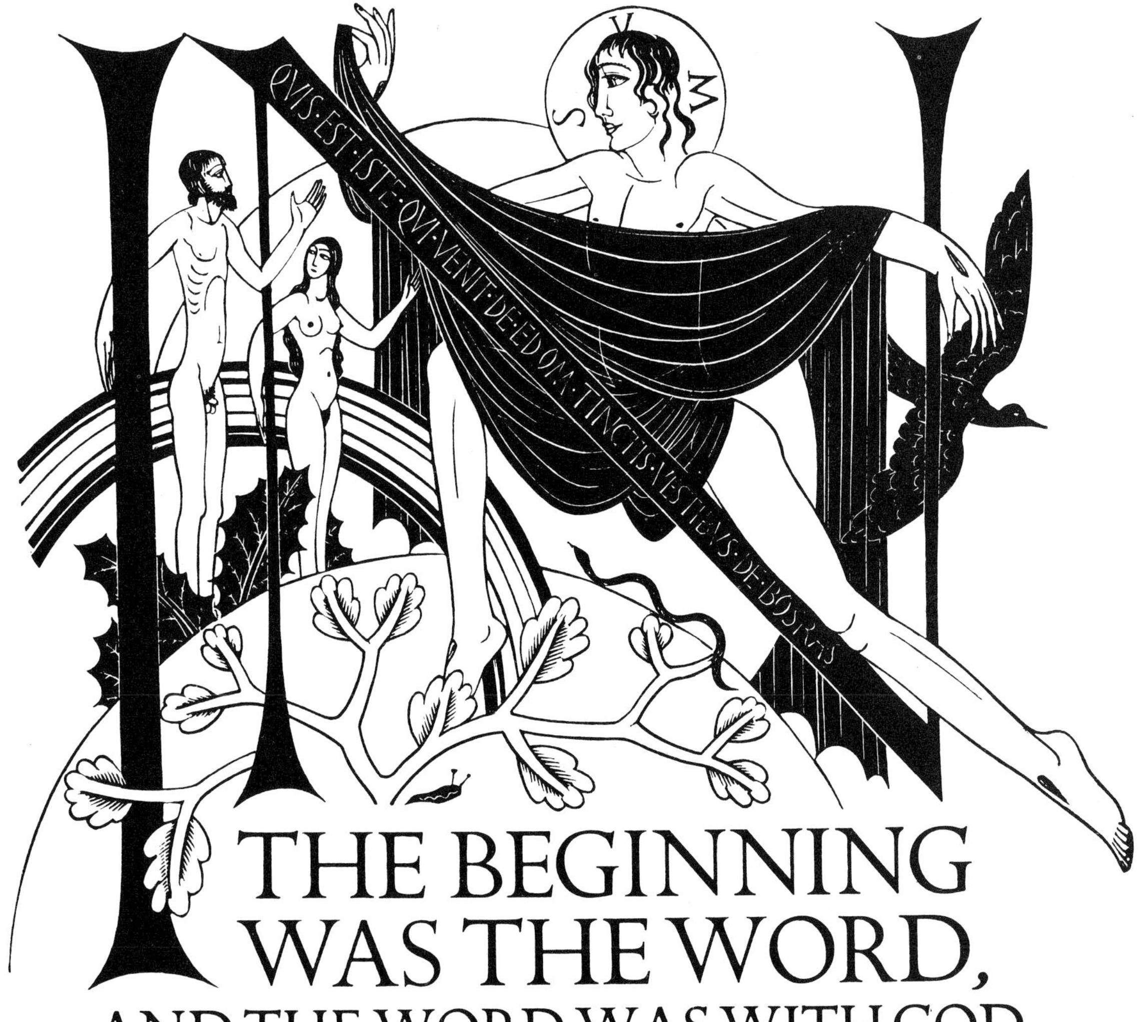

IN THE BEGINNING WAS THE WORD,

AND THE WORD WAS WITH GOD, AND THE WORD WAS GOD. THE

SAME WAS IN THE BEGINNING WITH GOD. ALL THINGS WERE MADE BY HIM; AND WITHOUT HIM WAS NOT ANY THING MADE THAT WAS MADE. IN HIM WAS LIFE; AND THE LIFE WAS THE LIGHT OF MEN. AND THE LIGHT SHINETH IN DARKNESS; AND THE DARKNESS COMPREHENDED IT NOT.

90 ERIC GILL

1931

(1882-1940)

CANTICUM CANTICORUM SALOMONIS QUOD HEBRAICE DICITUR SIR HASIRIM ([WEIMAR: CRANACH PRESS, 1931]).
36 pp., 257 x 130 mm., with 11 full-page wood engravings and 18 wood engraved initials.
Edition of 268 copies (V&A copy no. 42), of which 8 are on vellum (nos. A-H), 2 of them being *hors commerce* (nos. G and H), 60 copies on Japan, 5 of them *hors commerce*, 200 on Maillol-Kessler (nos. 1-200), 10 of them *hors commerce*.
Printer: Cranach Press (Count Harry Kessler & Marc Goertz, directors; Walter Tanz & H. Schulze, compositors; H. Gage-Cole, pressman), set in Jenson Antiqua.
L.2654-1931.

Gill's connection with Count Harry Kessler goes back to 1904 when Emery Walker recommended Edward Johnston and his student Eric Gill for typographical work for the special editions Kessler was having published by Insel Verlag. When Kessler set up his Cranach Press in Weimar in 1913, a number of English craftsmen were called upon to operate the plant. After the war Kessler called on Gill to provide a number of illustrations for Cranach Press productions, including those for Virgil's *ECLOGUES* in 1926. In 1931 Gill drew the initial letters for an edition of *CASTLE OF DUINO* produced by the Press in Weimar. Gill had made wood engravings for a version of the Song of Songs published by the Golden Cockerel Press in 1925 where the text had been transformed into a play or 'Opera'. The Cranach Press text was that of the Vulgate. Gill mentions in his autobiography that he went to work at Count Kessler's press at Weimar for a fortnight in 1930. Gill is said to have been distressed at the quality of reproduction and considered that Kessler 'printed the engravings exceedingly badly'.

QUOD EST SALOMONIS

CANTICUM CANTICORUM

CANTICUM CANTICORUM

91 PABLO PICASSO **1931**

(1881-1973) Son of an art teacher, Picasso trained at the Barcelona Academy from 1895, spending a short time at the Madrid Academy in the winter of 1897-98. He was one of a group of artists that frequented the café 'El Quatre Gats' in Barcelona, honoured Zurbaran, Greco and medieval Catalan sculpture and engaged in political activity. On his second visit to Paris, in 1901, Vollard gave Picasso an exhibition; the artist settled in the city in 1904. His early manner ('blue period' and 'rose period') gave way from 1906 to works evidencing influence of primitive Iberian and negro sculpture and decisively interpreting the heritage of Cézanne: the portrait of Gertrude Stein and the 'Demoiselles d'Avignon', revealed to an incredulous Braque in 1907, led the way to the CUBISM *that was promoted by the dealer Kahnweiler and whose theoretical basis was given literary formulation by Apollinaire. In 1917, Picasso accompanied Jean Cocteau to Rome to design the curtain, sets and costumes for Diaghilev's ballet* PARADE, *with music by Erik Satie; he subsequently did a number of similar commissions for Diaghilev, including that for Stravinsky's* PULCINELLA *in 1920 and Milhaud's* LE TRAIN BLEU *in 1924. Though exhibiting with the first Surrealist exhibition at the Galerie Pierre in 1925 and being hailed as 'one of us' by André Breton, Picasso was never a central figure in* SURREALISM, *though participating in its activities: the series of etchings* MINOTAUROMACHIE *of 1935 is held to signal his break with the movement but not with individuals in it, such as Paul Eluard. In 1936 the Spanish Republican government nominated Picasso as direcor of the Prado; it was to this government that he gave his* GUERNICA, *commemorating the outrage of the Nazi bombing of the Basque town, which was returned to Spain after the death of Franco by the Museum of Modern Art, New York. After 1945, Picasso produced a large number of engravings and lithographs, most printed by Mourlot Frères, and from 1947 also worked with ceramics at Vallauris.*

OVID, *LES METAMORPHOSES.* EAUX FORTES DE PICASSO
(LAUSANNE: ALBERT SKIRA, 1931).
400 pp., 330 x 260 mm., with 30 etchings, 15 of them *hors texte.*
Edition of 145 copies (V&A copy no. 105), signed by the artist, of which 30 copies are on *Japon blanc à la forme,* five of them with a set of etchings on *Japon* and another on *Chine* and an original drawing (nos. 1-6) and 25 with a set of etchings on *Japon* (nos. 6-30), 95 copies on *Vergé d'Arches* (nos. 31-125), and 20 copies *hors commerce* for the artist and collaborators (nos. I-XX).
Printer: Leon Pichon, text; Louis Fort, lithographs (completed 25 October 1931).
L.1325-1935).

This edition, or part of it, was aimed at the American market; according to a colophon in the V&A copy, the work was designed for 'collectionneurs et . . . bibliophiles des Etats-Unis d'Amérique' by Marie Harriman.

The Ovid was Skira's first major project for a book illustrated by an artist, and it represents the beginnings of the period when publishers rather than picture dealers like Vollard or Kahnweiler took the lead in the field. Skira was assisted in the production of the Ovid by Tériade, who had worked on the modern section of the *CAHIERS D'ART* under Zervos. Skira was interested in producing a review devoted to modern art, and in 1933 became the 'Director-Administrator' of *MINOTAURE*, taking Tériade as his assistant. Skira produced the review from its first issue to May 1939.

92 PABLO PICASSO 1931

(1881-1973)

HONORÉ DE BALZAC, *LE CHEF-D'OEUVRE INCONNU. EAUX FORTES ORIGINALES ET DESSINS GRAVÉS SUR BOIS DE PABLO PICASSO* (PARIS: AMBROISE VOLLARD, 1931).
124 pp., 330 x 250 mm., with 67 wood engravings, and 12 etchings *hors texte*.
Edition of 305 copies (V&A copy no. 167), of which 65 are on *Japon impérial* with a set of engravings on *Rives* (nos. 1-65), and 240 copies on *Rives* (nos. 66-305), with a further 35 copies *hors commerce* (nos. I-XXXV).
Printer: Aimé Jourde, text; George Aubert, block cutter; Louis Fort, etchings (completed 12 November 1931).
L.6-1939.

Balzac's story involves an artist who laboured for ten years to produce a picture epitomising feminine beauty, which was then meaningless to anyone but himself.

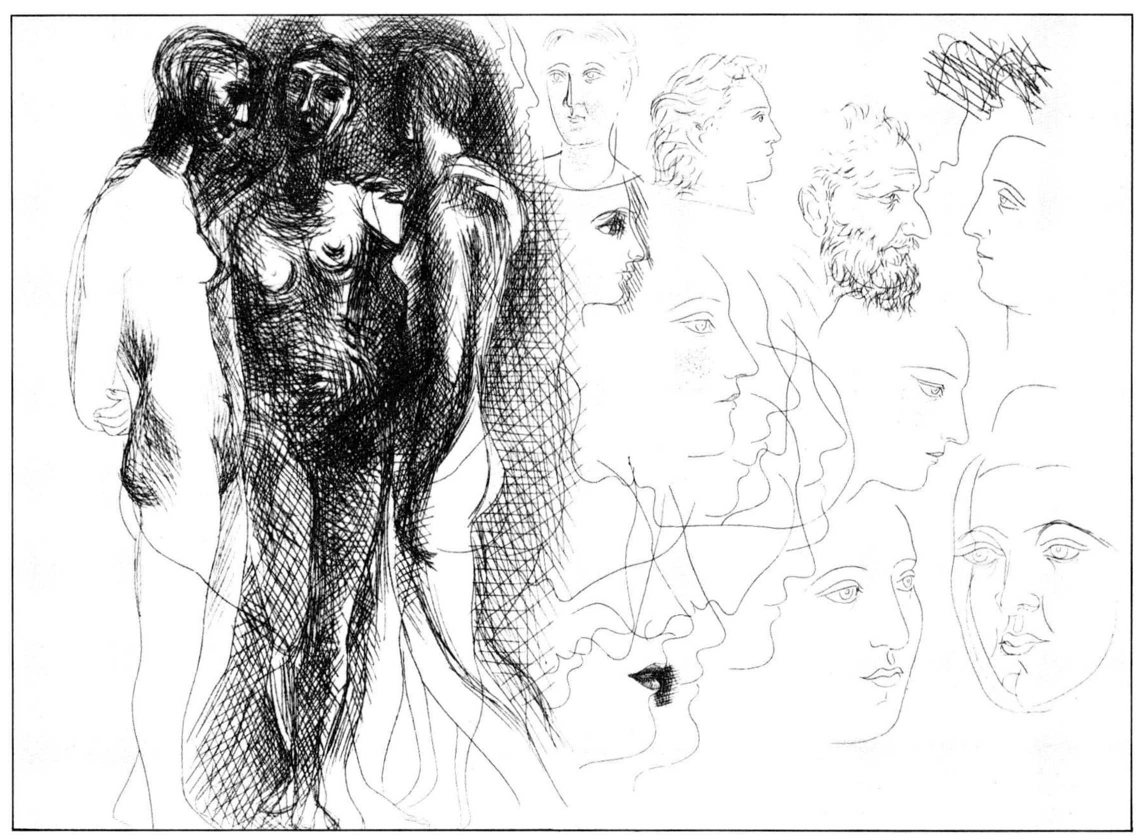

93 STANLEY WILLIAM HAYTER 1932

(b. 1901) Trained as a chemist and geologist, Hayter worked for the Anglo-Iranian Oil Co. in the Middle East from 1921, returning to London in 1925 to exhibit portraits and landscapes executed there. In 1926 he moved to Paris and devoted himself to painting and, most of all, print-making. Friendship with Calder, Masson, Eluard and Tanguy led to intermittent participation with the activities of the SURREALIST *movement; his workshop, known as Atelier 17 from 1933, became the celebrated centre of print-making in pre-war Paris. From 1929 he began to exhibit with the Surrealists. Hayter's reputation in this field lies not only in his own work, but in his rôle as teacher of the craft to numerous artists, from Ernst to Kandinsky and Picasso. From 1940 to 1946, Hayter stayed in New York, and a number of figures later prominent in the* ABSTRACT EXPRESSIONIST *movement worked with him; the sojourn of Atelier 17 in the New School for Social Research has been called a turning point for the history of American print-making, never before considered a major art medium there. In 1950, Hayter moved back to Paris. A major exhibition of his work was held at the Whitechapel Gallery, London, in 1957, and an exhibition devoted to Atelier 17 took place at the Palais des Beaux Arts, Paris, in 1967.*

STANLEY WILLIAM HAYTER, *L'APOCALYPSE. SIX GRAVURES AU BURIN PRÉCÉDÉES D'UNE PRÉFACE DE GEORGES HUGNET*
(PARIS: ÉDITIONS JEANNE BUCHER, [1932]).
4 pp., 520 x 400 mm., with 6 loose engravings.
Edition of 60 copies (V&A copy no. 40), initialed by the artist, of which 10 copies are on *Japon impérial* (nos. 1-10) with 2 further copies *hors commerce* (marked A and B), and 50 copies on *Vélin d'Arches* (nos. 11-60) with 5 further copies *hors commerce* (marked a-e).
Printer: William Hayter, engravings; L'Union Typographique, Villeneuve – St. Georges (completed 20 May 1932).
L.1771-1939.

Hayter's engravings were printed in the year before his move to 17 rue Campagne-Première, where his workshop took the name Atelier 17. Author of two works on the technique of engraving, Hayter rarely provided illustrations for books. Ambroise Vollard commissioned him to illustrate a work on his reactions to the Spanish Civil War in 1936 but this came to nothing.

Georges Hugnet (b. 1906), a poet and playwright, took part in a number of Surrealist activities in the 1930s in Paris; his introduction to the *PETITE ANTHOLOGIE POÉTIQUE DU SURRÉALISME* (Paris, 1934) was a major text of Surrealist literary theory and was included by Herbert Read in his book of 1936 that introduced Surrealism to the English reading public. Bookbindings made by Hugnet, and exhibited as 'book objects' at the Galerie Ratton in 1936, were reproduced in *MINOTAURE* in 1937 with an article about them by Benjamin Péret. He made a number of photo-collages at this time. His account of Dada painting published in 1957 is a major source for the subject. According to Alfred Barr, he was 'among all the surrealist writers, the one most interested in an historical approach'. His introduction to "L'Apocalypse" takes the form of a poem replete with apocalyptic imagery: 'Les chevaux de la révélation reviennent à toi chaque jour, parce que/chaque jour porte en lui le recommencement de ton désespoir'.

Jeanne Bucher (1872-1946) originally ran a bookshop, but from 1925 began to show the works of modern artists, opening her own gallery in the rue du Cherche-Midi in Paris. After her death, her gallery was taken over by Jean-François Jaeger, who developed his great-aunt's talent for spotting artists destined for success, including Vieira da Silva and Dubuffet.

94 PAUL NASH **1932**

(1889-1946)

URNE BURIALL AND THE GARDEN OF CYRUS BY SIR THOMAS BROWNE, WITH THIRTY DRAWINGS BY PAUL NASH. EDITED WITH AN INTRODUCTION BY JOHN CARTER (LONDON: LA BELLE SAUVAGE, CASSELL & CO., 1932).
xx, 146 pp., 305 x 220 mm., with 30 colloytpes coloured by the pochoir process.
Edition of 215 copies (V&A copy no. 52), on J. Barcham Green's hand-made paper.
Printer: Oliver Simon, Curwen Press, text; Charles Whittingham & Griggs, collotypes; stencilling of colours supervised by Harold Curwen.
Binding by Nevetts Ltd.
L.1652-1934.

Nash was asked by Desmond Flower of Cassells to illustrate a book of his own choice, Sir Thomas Browne's URNE BURIALL being selected. Apart from the edition of 215 copies, 85 more were printed to be bound according to Nash's specification. Herbert Read considered the result 'one of the loveliest achievements of contemporary British art'.

95 HENRI MATISSE **1932**

(1869-1954) After a brief career as a lawyer, Matisse turned to study painting in 1890, working under Bouguereau and later Gustave Moreau at the Académie Julian in Paris. In 1904, he had his first one-man show at the gallery of Ambroise Vollard, from whom he had some years earlier purchased Cézanne's THREE BATHERS *despite financial hardship. Largely through friendship with Signac, Matisse began to paint regularly in the South of France. In 1905 he exhibited at the Paris Salon d'Automne with Derain, Vlaminck, Rouault and others, in the show for which the term* FAUVE *was coined. Matisse travelled widely outside France in 1907-14, visiting Italy, Germany (where he was impressed by the exhibition of Near Eastern Art at Munich in 1910), Russia and Morocco; during this period his work was being shown widely in Europe and North America. In 1920, he designed sets and costumes for Diaghilev's* LE CHANT DU ROSSIGNOL *by Stravinsky. In 1930 Matisse visited Tahiti via New York and San Francisco; in 1931, there were major retrospective exhibitions of his work in Paris (Galerie Georges Petit) and New York (Museum of Modern Art). A severe illness in 1941 left him an invalid, but he continued to work until the end of his life at his home near Nice. From the end of the Second World War, he worked extensively with cut-out coloured papers, and was also active as a book illustrator.*

STÉPHANE MALLARMÉ, *POÉSIES... AVEC ILLUSTRATIONS PAR HENRI MATISSE* (LAUSANNE: ALBERT SKIRA ET COMPAGNIE, 1932).
162 pp., 330 x 255 mm., with 29 engravings.
Edition of 145 copies (V&A copy no. 120) signed by the artist, of which 30 copies are on *Japon impériale* (nos. 1-5) with a set on *Japon*, a set on *Chine* and an original drawing by the artist; nos. 6-30 with a set on *Japon* and 95 copies (nos. 31-125) on *Vélin d'Arches*; 20 further copies numbered I-XX reserved for the artist and his collaborators.
Printers: Léon Pichon, text; R. Lacourière, engravings (completed 25 October 1932).
L.385-1935.

Matisse was commissioned by Skira to illustrate Mallarmé's poems in 1930. Making numerous preparatory drawings, Matisse completed the 29 etchings early in 1932. Stéphane Mallarmé (1842-1898) wrote about aesthetics as well as poetry; a close friend of Degas and Redon, he was recognised as a major poet in 1884 thanks to Verlaine's *POÈTES MAUDITS*. Mallarmé promoted a fashion of publishing poetry in expensive limited editions, Manet illustrating with coloured woodcuts the edition of *L'APRÈS-MIDI D'UN FAUNE* of 1876.

96 GEORGES BRAQUE **1932**

(1882-1963) From a family of house painters in Le Havre, Braque studied briefly at the École des Beaux Arts in 1900 and then at the Académie Humbert; in 1905-06 he was converted to FAUVISM *('Matisse and Derain showed me the way' as he said later). Crucial events in 1907 were the Cézanne retrospective exhibition and meeting Picasso; Braque's first* CUBIST *works were rejected by the Salon d'Automne but in 1908 Kahnweiler held an exhibition of Braque's works of this kind, the painter's first one-man show and the first exhibition of* CUBIST *work (Apollinaire wrote the preface to the catalogue). In 1924 and 1925 he designed sets and costumes for Diaghilev's ballets* FÂCHEUX *and* ZÉPHYRE ET FLORE. *In the 1920s he developed a neo-classical style and was claimed as part of the classic French tradition. In 1948 he was awarded first prize at the Venice Biennale. In 1952 he was commissioned to decorate the ceiling of the Salle Henri II in the Louvre; in the 1950s he designed stained glass windows for Varengeville parish church and the Fondation Maeght; in 1962 he collaborated with Heger de Lowenfeld in designing jewellery.*

HESIOD. *THÉOGONIE. EAUX-FORTES PAR GEORGES BRAQUE* (PARIS: MAEGHT, 1955).
80 pp., 440 x 320 mm., with 18 etchings, black and coloured, and an illustrated table of etchings; etched frontispiece printed in red and black; etched cover printed in black and varnished in yellow by the artist.
Edition of 150 copies (V&A copy no. 39), signed by the artist, on *papier d'Auvergne*.
Printer: Fequet et Baudier, Paris, text, set in Capitales Europe Corps 16 (completed 10 January 1955).
L.291-1955.

Ambroise Vollard first commissioned Braque to supply illustrations for *THÉOGONIE.* Sixteen etchings were completed by 1932 and are among works produced by the artist in what has been termed his neo-classical style under the inspiration of the poetry and art of ancient Greece. The designs for the cover, the frontispiece and two ornaments were done in 1953.

Aimé Maeght (b. 1906) in 1932 was running a small publicity and lithography business in Cannes, and friendship with Bonnard and Matisse was reinforced during the Occupation. After the war, the Maeght gallery was the site of the 6th International Surrealist Exhibition and specialised in post-war artists' work. Braque first exhibited there in 1947. The Fondation Maeght was set up in the Alpes Maritimes in 1964 to display the major currents of contemporary art and the key works of our time.

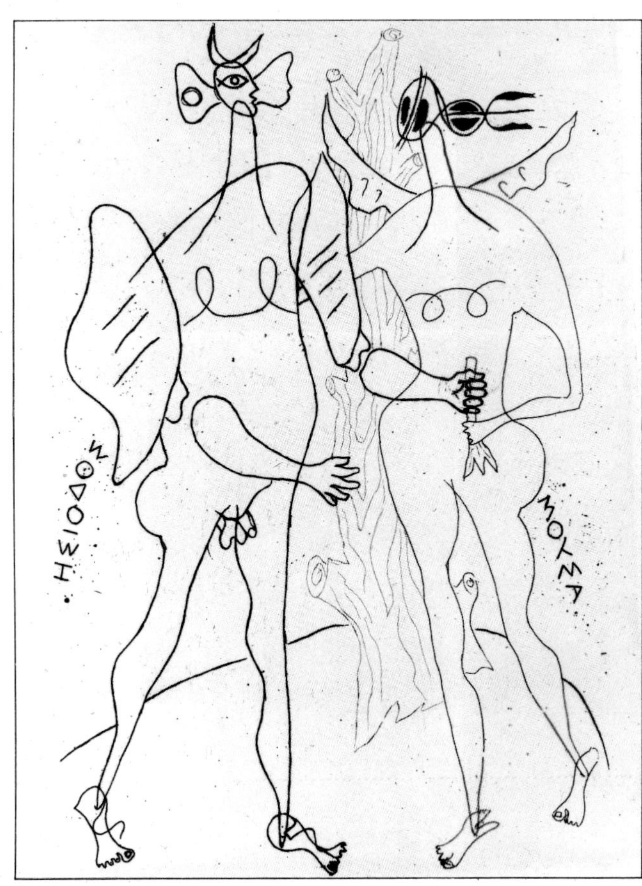

97 ANDRÉ DUNOYER DE SEGONZAC 1932

(1884-1974) Failing to enter the École des Beaux Arts, Segonzac worked under L.O. Merson and J.P. Laurens before entering the Académie de la Palette; he studied at the École des Langues Orientales at the same time. In 1906 he met Luc Albert Moreau and Boussingault, with whom he shared a studio. His first drawings were published in LA GRANDE REVUE *in 1908, the year that he joined the Salon d'Automne. He exhibited in the Salon des Indépendants in 1909 and at the Galerie Barbazanges in 1910. Standing aside from all avant-garde movements, he sought to revive the realism of Courbet. Noticed by Roger Marx at the Salon des Indépendants in 1912, he was enthusiastically promoted by the couturier Paul Poiret. From 1908, he spent part of each year at St. Tropez, where the writer Colette was a neighbour and where he bought a house in 1925. In the 1920s he enjoyed a vogue as a Society painter, designing, with Dufy and de La Fresnaye, costumes for Paul Poiret's balls and producing landscapes, still-lifes, nudes in painting, watercolour, crayon and, after 1919, etchings. In 1933, he received the Carnegie prize at the Pittsburgh Exhibition, and the Grand Prix at the 1934 Venice Biennale.*

VIRGIL, *LES GÉORGIQES, TRADUITES PAR MICHEL DE MAROLLES, ILLUSTRÉES D'EAUX-FORTES PAR DUNOYER DE SEGONZAC* (PARIS, 1947).

Two volumes, 204 and 224 pp., 460 x 340 mm., with 58 and 61 etchings respectively.

240 Edition of 225 copies, on *Vélin d'Arches* watermarked with a design of an ear of corn and a bee, nos. 1-50 accompanied by a set of etchings, numbered and signed, on *Vélin de Rives* watermarked with a design of a bunch of grapes and an ox's head; 25 copies *hors commerce* on *Vélin d'Arches* (nos. I-XXV; V&A copy no. IV).

Printers: Imprimerie Nationale, Paris, text, set in Garamond Italique Corps 24 and Garamond Romain Corps 18; etchings pulled by Jacques Frelaut on the presses of Roger Lacourière, Paris (completed 16 September 1947).

L.909-1951.

Though Segonzac's career as an illustrator began before the First World War (his drawings of Isadora Duncan were acclaimed when published in 1911), it was not until 1919 that he began to etch, accepting a commission from René Blum to turn drawings from his (Segonzac's) war sketch books for the first volume of Dorgeles' trilogy, *LES CROIX DE BOIS* (Paris: Éditions de la Banderole, 1921). Segonzac is reported to have had no more than a 15 minute lesson from Labourer before etching himself, always working directly onto the plate. The initiative for the *GEORGICS* came from Ambroise Vollard, who adopted the idea after Segonzac had shown no enthusiasm for a project to illustrate a work by Colette. The 'premiers essais typographiques' were done during Vollard's life-time, but the artist himself saw to the publication of the volume after Vollard's death. Many of the landscapes in the etchings have been identified as places in Provence and the Ile-de-France where the artist painted.

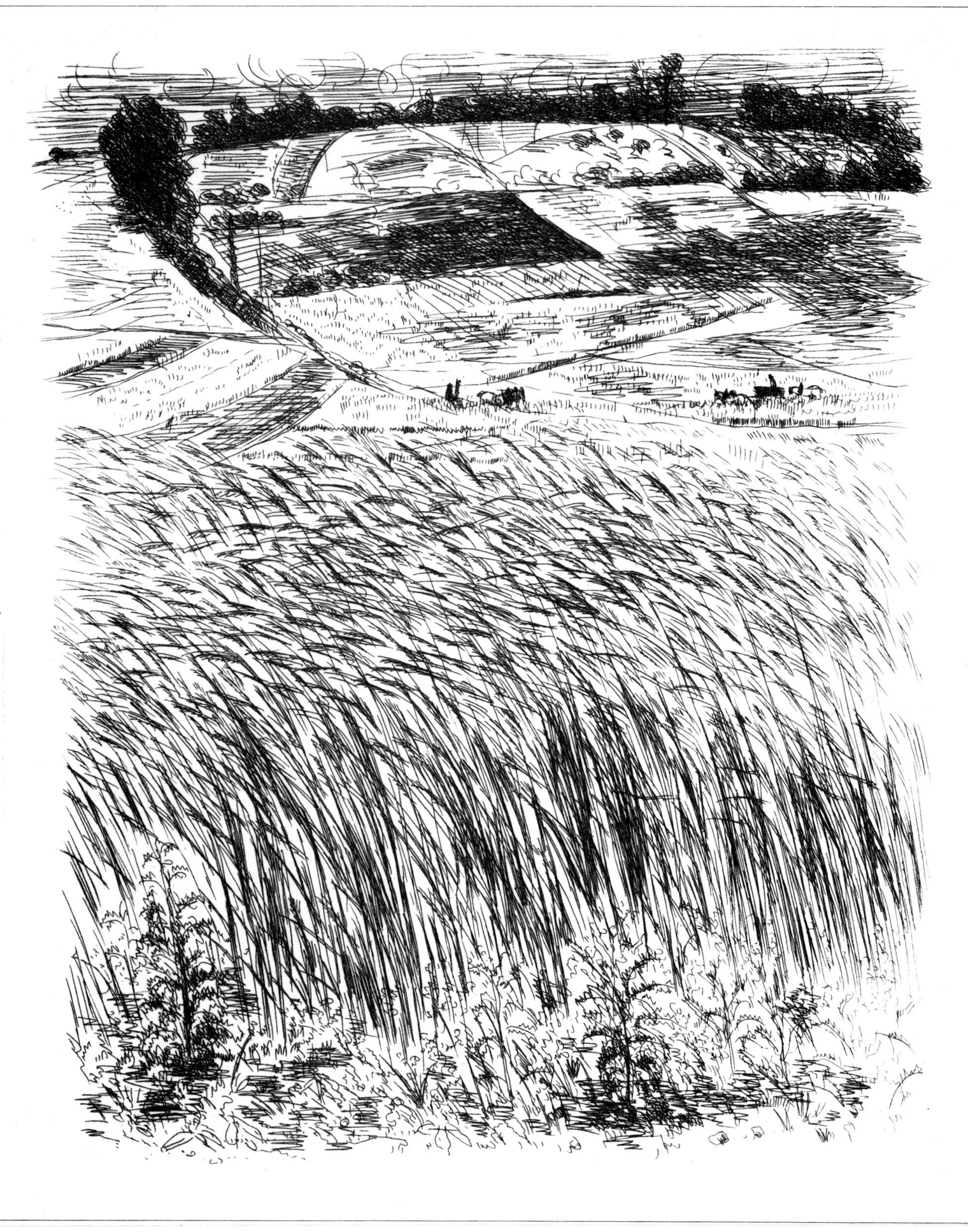

98 JOAN MIRÓ **1933**

(1893-1983)

GEORGES HUGNET, *ENFANCES. ORNÉ DE TROIS EAUX-FORTES DE JOAN MIRÓ* (PARIS: ÉDITIONS 'CAHIERS D'ART', [1933]).
22 ff., 285 x 230 mm., with 3 etchings.
Edition of 100 copies (V&A copy no. 6), signed by author and artist, of which five copies are on *Japon impérial* (nos. 1-5) and 95 copies on *Vélin d'Arches* (nos. 6-100), with 25 further copies *hors commerce* (nos. A-Z).
Printers: Paul André, text; Roger Lacourière, etchings (completed 11 July 1933).
L.1340-1936.

The publisher of this volume was Christian Zervos (1889-1970), who had founded the review *CAHIERS D'ART* in 1926. Its aim was to discuss art of all periods, from classical times to the present, but with the emphasis on modern architecture, poetry, sculpture and painting. Tériade, like Zervos of Greek origin, participated from the outset, being responsible for the modern section. In 1929, Zervos opened the Galerie des Cahiers d'Art in conjunction with Yvonne Zervos; from 1932, he began to publish the monumental *catalogue raisonné* of Picasso's work (volume 28 appeared in 1975). The review discussed the work of Surrealist artists, but was not committed to their movement. After 1945, it promoted painters such as Lam, De Staël and Poliakoff.

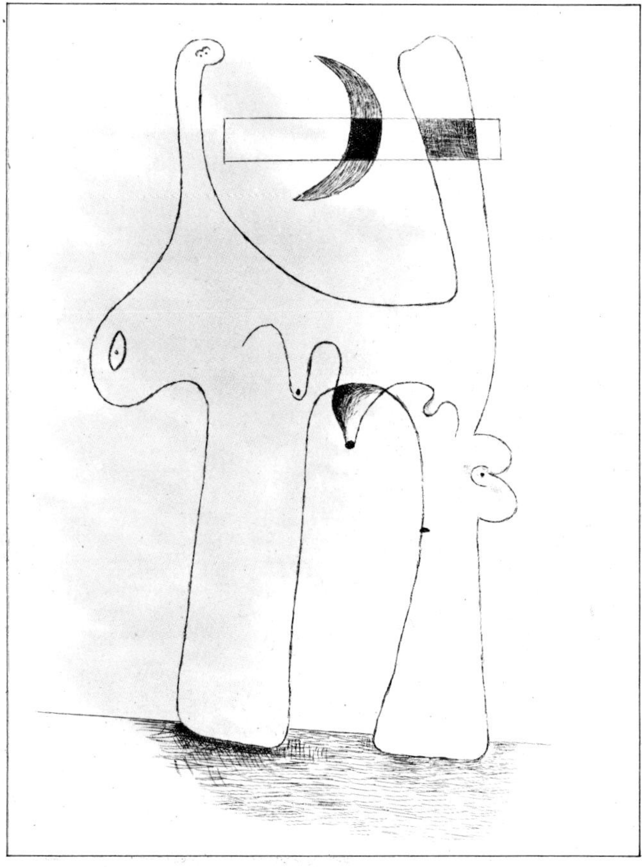

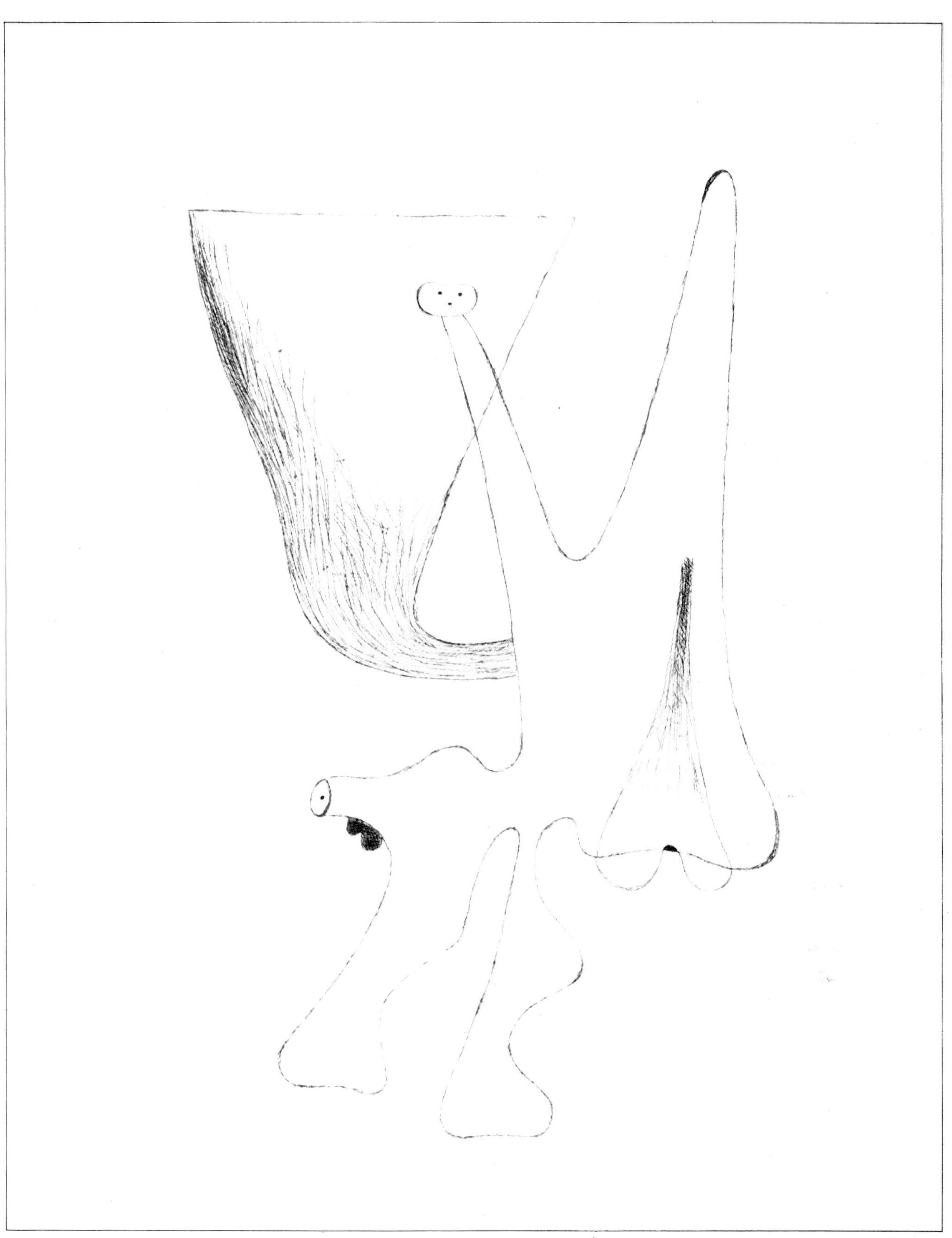

99 SALVADOR DALI **1934**

(b. 1904) Dali had a tumultuous career as a student at the Madrid Academy in 1921-6, where he emulated painters from Vermeer to De Chirico and explored most avant-garde styles from Impressionism to Cubism; reading of Freud directed him towards an art of the unconscious that resulted in his 'metaphysical paintings'. He had his first one-man exhibition in his native Catalonia, at the Dalmau Gallery, Barcelona, in 1925. He exhibited the following year with the Sociedad de Artistos Ibericos in Madrid, where he was part of a group with Federico Garcia Lorca and Luis Buñuel, helping the latter in the making of the films LE CHIEN ANDALOU *in 1928 and* L'AGE D'OR *in 1931 (both were to be acclaimed by Surrealist circles in Paris). In 1928 Dali went to Paris (by taxi, according to his autobiography) and settled there the following year after his exhibition at the Galerie Goemans (the catalogue's introduction was written by André Breton). Dali was an active member of the Surrealist group, and became the companion of Eluard's ex-wife Gala. Sympathy with totalitarian regimes led to his being ejected from the group, after a trip to Italy in 1937 and a dramatic return to a more classical art. From 1940 to 1955 he lived in north America, being the subject of a retrospective exhibition at the Museum of Modern Art, New York, in 1941, publishing his autobiography in 1942 and designing a number of sets and costumes for the theatre. After his return to Franco's Spain, he produced religious and historical paintings. His genius for self-publicity has made him the authentic representative of Surrealism for many people.*

244 [ISIDORE DUCASSE] COMTE DE LAUTRÉAMONT, *LES CHANTS DE MALDOROR* (PARIS: ALBERT SKIRA, 1934).
212 pp., 330 x 255 mm., with 12 etchings, and 30 further etchings *hors texte*.
Edition of 210 copies (V&A copy no. 103), signed by the artist, on *Vélin d'Arches* (nos. 1-200), nos. 1-40 including a set of etchings, and the last ten reserved for the artist and collaborators (nos. I-X).
Printer: Roger Lacourière, etchings; Philippe Gonin, text (completed 31 July 1934).
Inscribed 'Frontin' in pencil on fly-leaf.
L.321-1938.

Dali's work as an illustrator can be traced back to 1924, when his works, photomechanically reproduced, were used to illustrate Fages de Climent's *LES BRUIXES DE LLERS.* The Skira Lautréamont was Dali's first original book illustration on a large scale. The *CHANTS DE MALDOROR,* written by Isidore Ducasse, the self-styled Comte de Lautréamont, and first published in full in 1869, was a crucial text for the Surrealist movement. It was probably through Alfred Jarry that Breton, Soupault and Aragon 'discovered' the work in 1918-19. In 1962, Breton remembered that early experiments with automatic writing were stimulated by Lautréamont's text. Extracts were published in *LITTÉRATURE* in 1919, and Soupault published Lautréamont's complete works in the 1920s.

In 1934, Dali was a central figure in Surrealist circles, contributing to every issue of Albert Skira's review *MINOTAURE* until 1937: 'Les nouvelles couleurs du *SEX APPEAL SPECTRAL*', with photographs by Man Ray, in 1934, and 'Le Surréalisme spectrale de l'éternel féminin Pré-Raphaelite', with illustrations of works by Rossetti, Millais and others, in 1936. Dali's links with Skira ended abruptly with his expulsion from the Surrealist group in 1937.

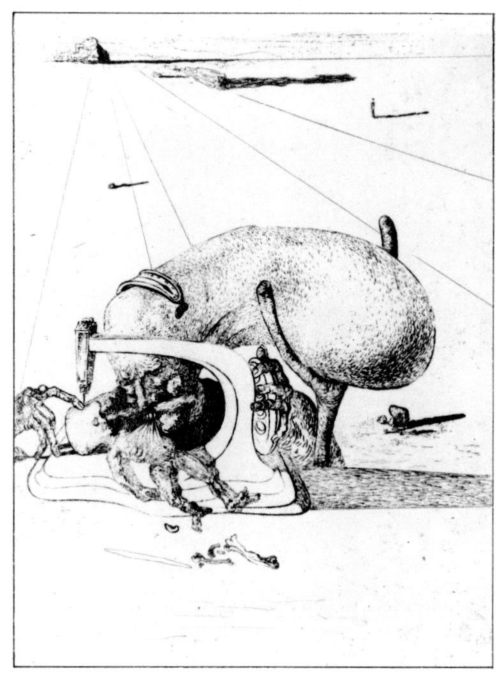

100 ANDRÉ DERAIN 1934

(1880-1954)

[PETRONIUS ARBITER] *LE SATYRICON. SUITE SUR PAPIER ANCIEN DES 36 CUIVRES GRAVÉS PAR ANDRÉ DERAIN* ([PARIS: AMBROISE VOLLARD], 1934).
74 ff., 437 x 334 mm., with 1 signed drawing and 72 engravings (two sets of 36).
Not published by Vollard (see U.E. Johnson, *Amboise Vollard, Editeur,* 1977, p.160). Binding by Creuzevault
L.3128-1981.

Although Derain's connexion with Vollard went back to 1906, when the dealer promised him '10,000 gold francs' for all work produced during a two-month stay in London, the artist never had work included as illustrations in books published by Vollard during his life-time. In the early 1930s, Vollard asked Derain to provide illustrations for *de luxe* editions of La Fontaine's *CONTES* and the *SATYRICON* of Petronius. Engravings were handed over for the latter project in 1934, but not published in book form. In 1950 and 1951, the illustrations for both projects were published 'Aux Dépens d'un Amateur' in Paris, through the efforts of Colonel Daniel Sickles and René Gas. The V&A copy of the engravings contains two sets of the Petronius engravings, on two thicknesses of paper, with a signed drawing as frontispiece. The printed title-page has no publisher's imprint, and the edition is unnumbered. The volume perhaps represents how the engravings were issued during Vollard's lifetime.

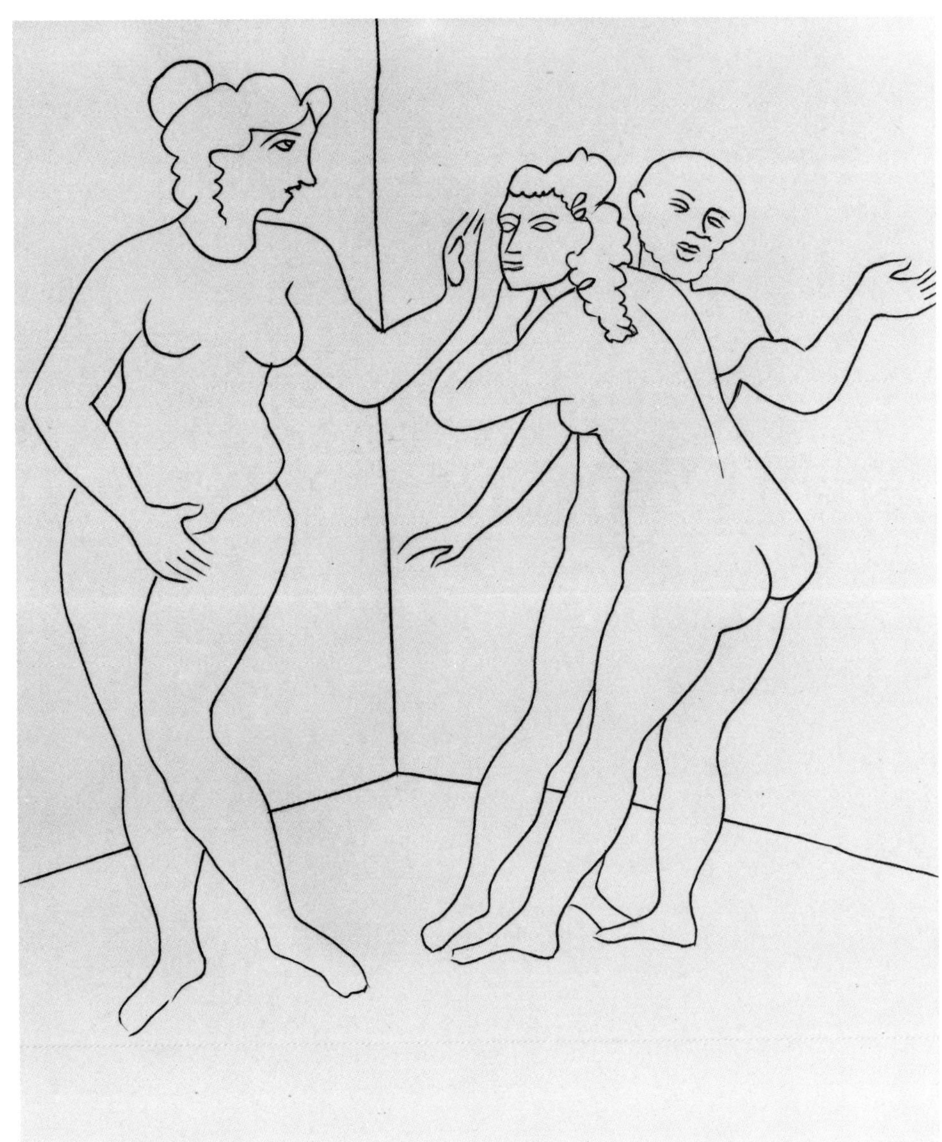

101 KURT SELIGMANN **1934**

(1900-1962) Son of a furniture manufacturer, Seligmann worked in Basel and Geneva until 1927, attending the École des Beaux Arts in Geneva from 1919. From 1927 to 1929 he worked in Paris with the French CUBIST *painter, André Lhote, though he also made extended visits to Florence. He became a close friend of Jean Arp at this time. Paris was Seligmann's home from 1930 to 1939, where he was closely involved in the* SURREALIST *movement; he also travelled widely, visiting Greece with Le Corbusier in 1934 and crossing north America on his way to Japan (where his works were to be exhibited) in 1935. In 1939, he left for New York, which was to be his home until the last two years of his life. He was one of a group of artists with Paris connections who settled in New York during the Second World War, being closest to Duchamp, Miró and Tanguy. In the 1950s he designed a number of costumes for the theatre and ballet, and was attached to the History of Art Department of Brooklyn College.*

LES VAGABONDAGES HÉRALDIQUES. QUINZE EAUX-FORTES ORIGINALES DE KURT SELIGMANN, QUINZE TEXTES INÉDITS DE PIERRE COURTHION (PARIS: ÉDITIONS DES CHRONIQUES DU JOUR, [1934])
38 pp., 505 x 375 mm., with 15 etchings.
Edition of 100 copies with 5 *hors commerce* (of which this is one) signed by author and illustrator.
Printer: Frazier-Soye, text; J J Taneur, etchings (via G. Di San Lazarro).
L.4910-1983

Engravings form a major part of Seligmann's *œuvre*. His life-long interest in the occult sciences (he wrote many articles on magic) was no doubt behind his enthusiasm for Surrealist ideas, allowing it to find fullest expression as art. In the mid-1930s a number of his Surrealist friends commissioned him to illustrate books, among them André Breton. Between 1934 and 1938, 'Les Chroniques du Jour' published a number of works illustrated by Seligmann, all of them in limited editions.

Pierre Courthion (b. 1902) was from Switzerland, and like Seligmann attended the École des Beaux Arts in Geneva. Author, critic, art historian and film maker, Courthion had studied at the École du Louvre in Paris and from 1933 was the Director of the Swiss Foundation of Paris University. A number of his literary works were illustrated by Seligmann.

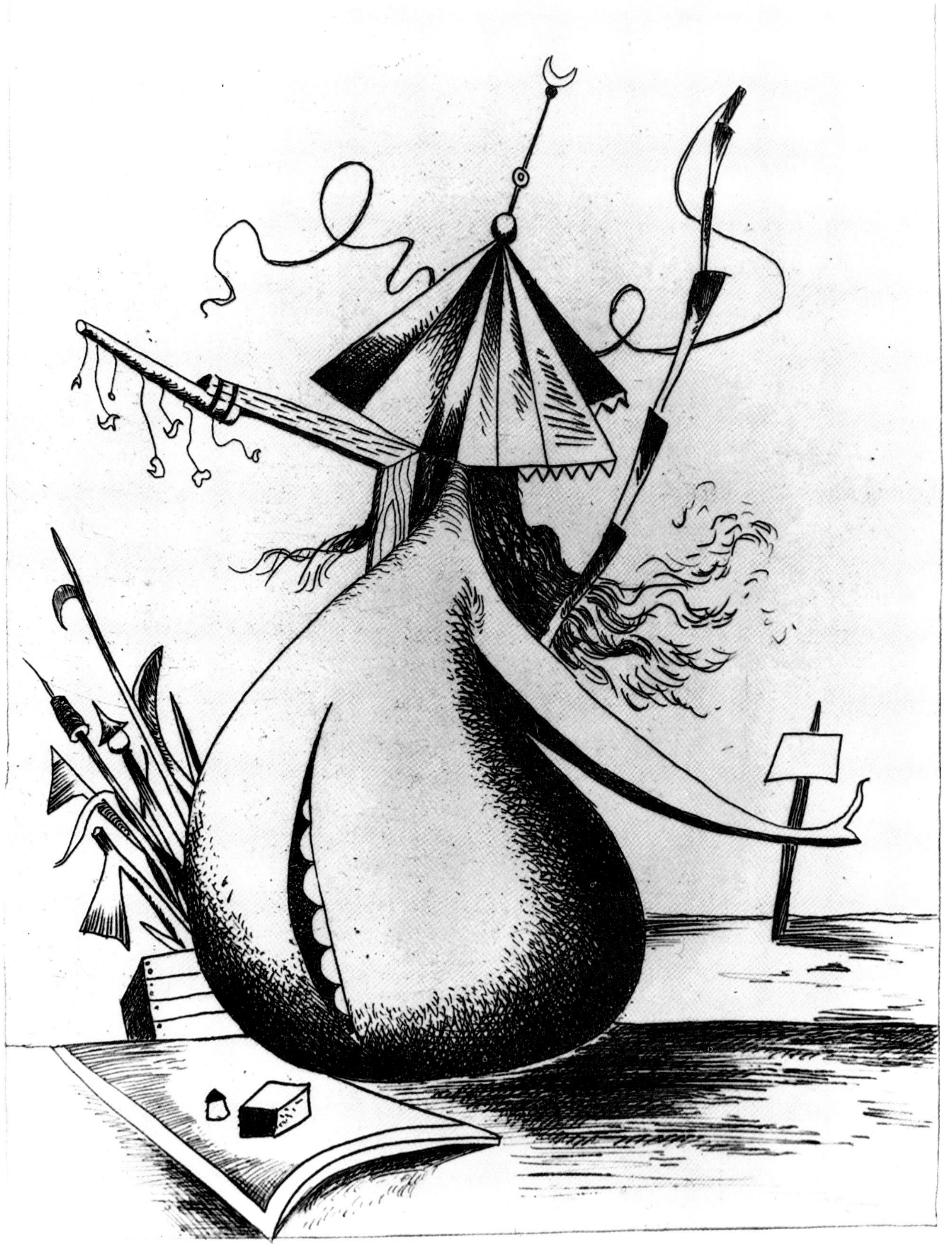

102 BEN NICHOLSON **1935**

(1894-1982) Son of the painter William Nicholson, Ben Nicholson studied at the Slade for one term in 1910-1911 and briefly met VORTICISM *before the First World War; contact with Cézanne and* CUBISM, *especially that of Braque, in Paris of the 1920s were decisive influences. He was associated with the* ABSTRACTION-CRÉATION *group in Paris in 1933-1935, when he first met Mondrian, a significant influence on his work. In England he was among those foremost in introducing modern art in the 1930s, being co-editor (with JL Martin and Naum Gabo) of* CIRCLE, *an international review of constructive art, from 1937. He lived in St. Ives with his wife, Barbara Hepworth, between 1939 and 1957, the year when he awarded the painting prize in the Saõ Paulo Biennale. There were major retrospective exhibitions of his work in the United States in 1952-3, and at the Tate Gallery in London in 1955 and 1969. The Order of Merit was conferred on him in 1968.*

23 GRAVURES DE ARP, CALDER, CHIRICO, ERNI, ERNST, FERNANDEZ, GIACOMETTI, GHIKA, GONZALEZ, HELION, KANDINSKY, LÉGER, LIPSHITZ, MAGNELLI, MIRÓ, NICHOLSON, OZENFANT, PICASSO, SELIGMANN, TAEUBER-ARP, TORRES-GARCIA, VULLIAMY, ZADKINE, PRÉCÉDÉES D'UN TEXTE DE ANATOLE JAKOVSKI (PARIS: ÉDITIONS G. OROBITZ, 1935).
96 pp., 330 x 225 mm., with 23 etchings.
Edition of 20 copies numbered 1-20 (V&A copy no. 1), with 30 copies for the collaborators numbered I-XXX.
Printer: Ducros et Colas, text; Tanneur, etchings (completed 5 July 1935)
L.5996-1984

Anatole Jakovski, a prolific critic and publicist of modern art, produced a book of 24 essays on the artists whose work appears in this volume, with the addition of Marcel Duchamp. The *23 GRAVURES* is a volume designed to accompany these essays, making it into a *de luxe* edition. The only other recorded illustration produced by Nicholson is that of 1934 for a poem of Herbert Read, the major proponent of avant-garde art in the England of the 1930s. Nicholson did, however, concern himself with other aspects of books: in 1934 he designed the book-jacket for the Faber & Faber edition of Adrian Stokes, *STONES OF RIMINI*. In the 1960s, Nicholson produced a number of portfolios of prints.

ABOVE De Chirico. Etching.
ABOVE RIGHT Nicholson. Woodcut.

251

103 GEORGES ROUAULT **1936**

(1871-1958)

GEORGES ROUAULT, *CIRQUE DE L'ÉTOILE FILANTE* (PARIS: A. VOLLARD, 1936).
180 pp., 438 x 338 mm., with 82 wood engravings printed in black and 17 aquatints *hors texte.*
Edition of 280 copies (V&A copy no. 119), of which 35 copies are on *Japon impérial* (nos. 1-35), 215 copies on *vergé de Monval* (nos. 36-250) and 30 copies *hors commerce,* nos. I-V on *Japon impérial,* nos. VI-XXX on *Vergé de Monval.*
Printer: R. Lacourière, engravings (Georges Aubert, wood engraver); Henri Jourde, Aux Deux Ours, text.
Binding by Rose Adler.
L.1574-1945. Colour plate 12.

From the turn of the century, the clown was a recurrent theme in Rouault's work. As Rouault is reported to have said, 'I saw clearly that the clown was myself, ourselves'; persecuted by his fellows and betrayed by his own nature, man is symbolised by the figure of the circus clown. It was during the 1930s that Rouault turned to the aquatint as a medium, working closely with Maurice Potin and, as here, with Roger Lacourière.

(1890-1976) After work in an advertising office and as draughtsman for publishers of engineering books, Ray began to paint in a CUBIST style in response to work seen in the Amory show of 1913 in New York, where the Association of American painters and sculptors brought together work of the European avant-garde, including Marcel Duchamp's NU DESCENDANT UN ESCALIER. *Man Ray co-operated with Duchamp on a number of projects thereafter, editing with him* NEW YORK DADA *in 1921. He moved to Paris in that year, took part in a number of films and pioneered new photographic techniques. In the 1930s he began to paint regularly again, and was one of the* SURREALIST *circle around André Breton. Man Ray spent 1940-1951 in California, living in Paris thereafter.*

LES MAINS LIBRES. MAN RAY. DESSINS ILLUSTRÉS PAR LES POÈMES DE PAUL ELUARD (PARIS: ÉDITIONS JEANNE BUCHER, 1937).
208 pp., 280 x 225 mm., with 66 illustrations.
Edition of 675 copies (V&A copy no. 616), of which 25 copies are on *Japon impérial* (nos. 1-25) and 650 copies on *Chester Vergé* (nos. 26-675).
Printer: Henri Jourde, Paris (completed 10 Nov. 1937).
L. 387-1938

Though Man Ray had occasionally provided graphic work for books and magazines produced in Surrealist circles after 1921, it was in the 1930s that drawings began to form a significant part of his work. Many of those in *LES MAINS LIBRES* were later the basis of paintings or reliefs, and a number originated as sketches inspired by dreams made on awakening. The drawings were left by Man Ray with Paul Eluard, who wrote poems for each; the poems thus illustrate the pictures. Man Ray, in his autobiography of 1964, recalled that the drawings had been made when he and Eluard were staying in the Midi at Mougins with Picasso and others.

S·A·D·E

105 ANDRÉ MASSON **1938**

(b. 1896)

ANDRÉ MASSON, *MYTHOLOGIES* ([PARIS:] ÉDITIONS DE LA REVUE FONTAINE [1946]).
96 pp., 310 x 235 mm., with 39 engravings.
Edition of 830 copies (V&A copy no. 504), of which 30 are on *Vélin d'Arches* (nos. I-XXX), 250 copies on *Vergé d'Ingres* (nos. 1-250) and 550 copies on *Rives* (nos. 251-800); also a few other copies *hors commerce* marked 'H.C.'.
Printer: Imprimerie Grou-Radenez, Paris (completed 31 May 1946).
L.839-1947.

Masson's work consists of three sections, each of them previously published with the titles: *MYTHOLOGIES DE LA NATURE, 1938* (pp. 5-33), *MYTHOLOGIES DE L'ÊTRE, 1939* (pp. 35-51) and *L'HOMME EMBLÉMATIQUE, 1940* (pp. 53-91). The 1946 re-publication was undertaken by Henri Parisot in his *COLLECTION DE L'AGE D'OR* series. Parisot published a number of Surrealist texts and images in post-war Paris; in 1947 he produced a volume of Picabia's poetry, *CHOIX DE POÈMES DE FRANCIS PICABIA*.

106 PABLO PICASSO **1937**

(1881-1973)

PICASSO, *SUEÑO Y MENTIRA DE FRANCO ['DREAMS AND LIES OF FRANCO']* (PARIS, 1937).
Portfolio of 3 ff., 570 x 390 mm., including 2 ff. of aquatints; also English translation on small sheet.
Edition of 1,000 copies, of which 150 are on *Japon impérial*, and 850 (V&A copy no. 233) on *Arches*.
No details of printer.
L.3337-1981.

SUEÑO Y MENTIRA was made in response to reports of atrocities during the Spanish Civil War. The plates of the 2 folios with aquatints (9 images on each) are both headed with the date 8 January, printed in reverse, and one of them is similarly inscribed '9 janvier – 9 juin 1937', the dates between which Picasso worked on the series. During this period, reports were made of one of the first horrors of modern aerial warfare, the razing of the Basque town of Guernica by Nazi aeroplanes fighting for Franco. With the aquatints is a facsimile of a text in the author's hand, with a printed transcript in Spanish and a French translation; the English translation added to the portfolio begins 'Fandango of shivering owls souse of swards of evil-omened polyps ...' and continues in a tortured Surrealist vein. The portfolio carries a label with the title, a facsimile of the artist's hand writing.

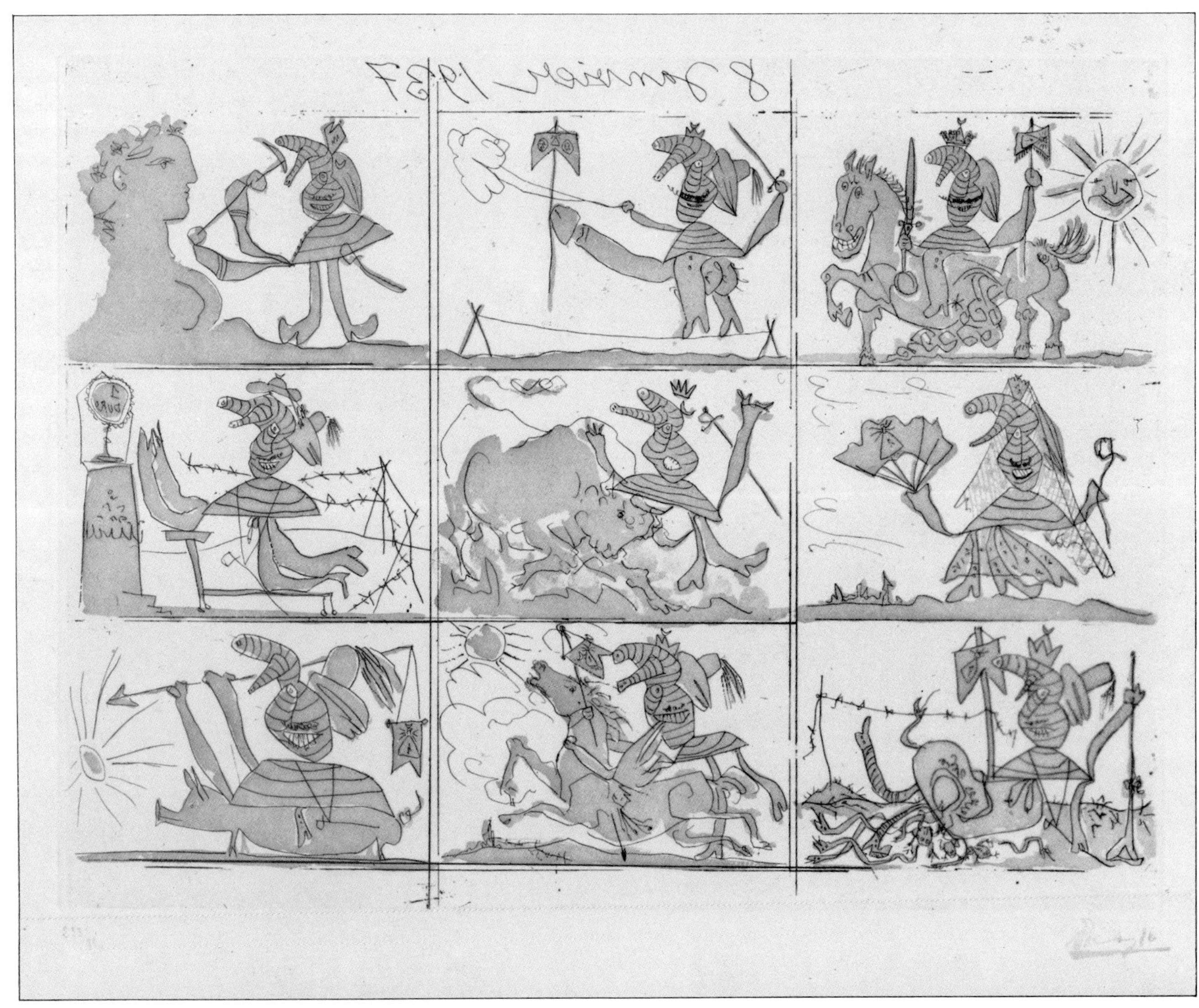

107 HANS BELLMER **1939**

(1902-1975) After work at a steelmill and coal mine, Bellmer studied engineering at Berlin Polytechnic, meeting Georg Grosz, Otto Dix, John Heartfield and Rudolf Schlichet. From 1924-5, Bellmer worked as typographer for Malik Verlag, leaving the firm to work free-lance. From 1927 he worked as an industrial artist in an advertising agency. Bellmer's work on the theme of 'The Doll' starts from 1933, avowedly based on a sexual obsession with a young girl. A work on this theme was reproduced in MINOTAURE *no. 6 (1934-5) and a similar composition 'Jointure de Boule' was exhibited at the 'Exposition Surréalisté d'Objets' at the Ratton Gallery, Paris, in 1936, when Bellmer was introduced to* SURREALIST *circles. He also showed his work at the International Surrealist Exhibition in London in 1936, and in Tokyo and New York in 1937. Fleeing Nazi Germany to settle in Paris in 1938, Bellmer was interned (with Max Ernst) in 1940, but continued to work. He was among the exhibitors at the Surrealist exhibition at the Maeght Gallery, Paris, in 1947 that attempted to relaunch the movement after the war. He lived in Paris until his death.*

GEORGES HUGNET and HANS BELLMER, ŒILLADES CISELÉES EN BRANCHE (PARIS: ÉDITIONS JEANNE BUCHER, 1939).
44 pp., 130 x 92 mm., with 28 illustrations.
Edition of 230 copies (V&A copy no. 117), of which 10 copies are on *Azur ancien parfumé*, with an original drawing, signed by author and artist (nos. 1-10); 20 copies on *Chine parfumé*, signed by author and artist (nos. 11-30), and 200 copies on *Rives* (nos. 31-200); a further copy on *Japon nacré parfumé* with 10 original drawings and with the name of the subscriber printed, bore the no. A.
Printer: reproduced in heliogravure from the manuscript and drawings and printed by J. J. Taneur (completed 10 March 1939).
L.1780-1939.

The practice of reproducing the handwriting of a writer (or even his or her amanuensis) was used by a number of Russian writers at the time of the Revolution. (see Cat. 58). There are examples of this practice from Germany in the 1920s, but it was Tériade who developed it in the 1940s, first with the *DIVERTISSEMENT* of Georges Rouault, 1943, and later with Matisse, most notably in *JAZZ*, 1947 (Cat. 114). When presented with the manuscript of *LE CHANT DES MORTS* written out by Pierre Reverdy, Picasso declared that his 'illustrations' should do no more than comment on the text, providing a kind of musical accompaniment, in order not to detract from the written flow of the poetry; Tériade published the result in 1945. Interest in this form of book design has been related to publication in *VERVE* of articles on medieval illumination in 1940-9, where, of course, the artists were illustrating a manuscript page.

Une jambe balance ses reflets de nuit.
Chaque éclair de soie illumine l'avenir.
Chaude elle dit de revenir et s'en va
noire elle se tait dédaigneuse.

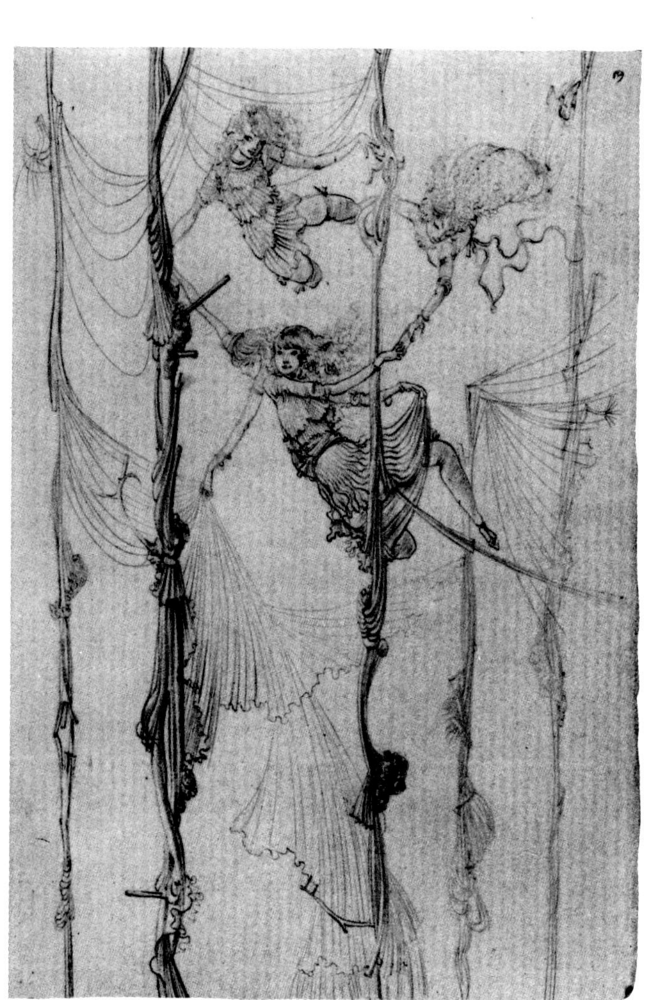

108 JACOB EPSTEIN 1940

(1880-1959) After study at the Art Students' League in New York and work in a bronze foundry, Epstein attended the École des Beaux Arts and Académie Julian in Paris during 1902-4, discovering Ancient Egyptian and Oriental sculpture in the Louvre. In 1905, Epstein emigrated to England (naturalized in 1907). In 1912 he met Picasso and Brancusi when visiting Paris. In 1913 he had a show with Henri Gaudier-Brzeska at the Goupil Gallery in London, but before this date he had received major commissions that created some outcry (sculptures for Charles Holden's British Medical Association building, Strand, London; Oscar Wilde tomb, Paris). In 1913 he was a founder member of The Vortex Group and collaborated with Wyndham Lewis on BLAST. In 1936 he designed sets for Keith Lester's ballet DAVID in London. Made an honorary doctor of Oxford University in 1953, he was knighted in 1954.

CHARLES BAUDELAIRE, *FLOWERS OF EVIL.*
TRANSLATED INTO ENGLISH VERSE BY VARIOUS HANDS. EDITED, WITH AN INTRODUCTION AND NOTES, BY JAMES LAVER AND ILLUSTRATED WITH DRAWINGS BY JACOB EPSTEIN ([NEW YORK:] LIMITED EDITIONS CLUB, 1940).
xxxvi, 306 pp., 230 x 173 mm., with 24 lithographs *hors texte.*
Edition of [—] copies (V&A copy no. 1306).
Printer: Ernest Ingham, at the Fanfare Press, London, text, set in Eric Gill's Perpetua; Fernand Mourlot, Paris, lithographs.
L. 3184-1981

Baudelaire, whose declared epitaph declaimed *'J'ai cultivé mon hystérie avec jouissance et terreur'*, published this collection of verse in 1856, after which it had great vogue among the avant-garde. James Laver (1899-1975), Keeper of what is now the Prints and Drawings department of the V&A (1938-1959), assembled already published English translations of Baudelaire's poems done by figures such as Lord Alfred Douglas, Sturge Moore, Arthur Symons and Aldous Huxley, together with new versions provided by his colleagues at the V&A, Graham Reynolds and Sir Eric Maclagan, and Arthur Ellis, Librarian of the British Museum Library. The drawings of Epstein were printed from the lithographic stone by Mourlot in Paris, in the year that France was occupied by Nazi forces.

109 BART VAN DER LECK **1941**

(1876-1958) Growing up in a large family in an Utrecht slum, Van der Leck was apprenticed to stained glass manufacturers from 1891 to 1899, the year that he obtained a scholarship to attend the Arts and Crafts School in Amsterdam. Here he also followed classes at the Fine Arts Academy. After an ART NOUVEAU *phase which resulted in work similar to Toorop, Van der Leck emerged as a follower of the Amsterdam* IMPRESSIONIST *school. He had some success as a painter of everyday scenes in a figurative style, and had his first one-man exhibition at the Kunsthandel W. Walrecht Gallery, The Hague, in 1913. From this time he was patronised by the Kröller family, for whose firm he had worked on occasion from 1913. By 1916, he had adopted an abstract style based on schematised designs and strong colours, and developed a manner which used primary colours on a flat white surface after meeting Mondrian in that year. With Mondrian and Van Doesburg, Van der Leck participated in the foundation of the* DE STIJL *review, though refusing to sign its manifesto in 1918 and breaking his connection with the movement shortly after. Thenceforth he lived in Blaricum, where he had built a house to his own design. From 1928 he received a series of commissions for the Amsterdam firm of Metz & Co., designing carpets and advising on colour schemes. During the 1930s, he began to decorate, glaze and fire his own ceramic wares.*

HANS ANDERSEN, *HET VLAS. UIT HET DEENSCH VERTAALD DOOR MARIE NIJLAND, VAN DER MEER DE WALCHEREN, GETEEKEND EN GEKLEURD DOOR B.V.D. LECK* (AMSTERDAM: DE SPIEGHEL, 1941).

i, 11 ff., 245 x 165 mm.
Edition of 500 copies (V&A copy no. 11) numbered 1-500, and 50 copies *hors commerce* (nos. I-L).
Printer: De Usel, Deventer.
L.3302-1981.

This was the first published book illustration by Van der Leck since 1905, when he contributed to the bibliophile edition of The Song of Solomon designed by his friend Piet Klaarheimer.

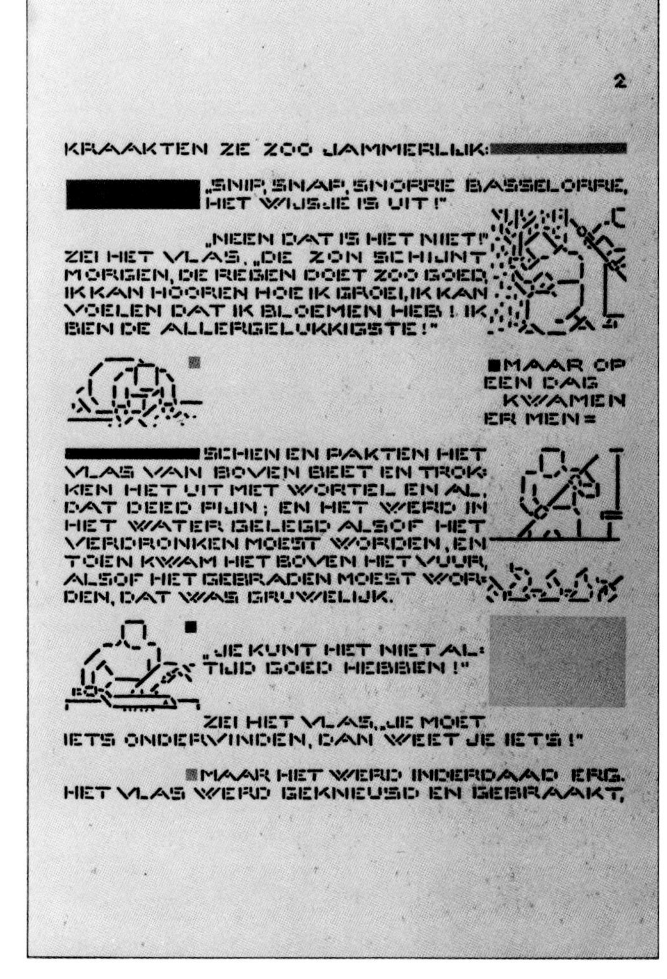
2

KRAAKTEN ZE ZOO JAMMERLIJK:
„SNIP, SNAP, SNORRE BASSELORRE,
HET WIJSJE IS UIT!"
„NEEN DAT IS HET NIET!"
ZEI HET VLAS, „DE ZON SCHIJNT
MORGEN, DE REGEN DOET ZOO GOED,
IK KAN HOOREN HOE IK GROEI, IK KAN
VOELEN DAT IK BLOEMEN HEB! IK
BEN DE ALLERGELUKKIGSTE!"
MAAR OP
EEN DAG
KWAMEN
ER MEN-
SCHEN EN PAKTEN HET
VLAS VAN BOVEN BEET EN TROK-
KEN HET UIT MET WORTEL EN AL.
DAT DEED PIJN; EN HET WERD IN
HET WATER GELEGD ALSOF HET
VERDRONKEN MOEST WORDEN, EN
TOEN KWAM HET BOVEN HET VUUR,
ALSOF HET GEBRADEN MOEST WOR-
DEN, DAT WAS GRUWELIJK.
„JE KUNT HET NIET AL-
TIJD GOED HEBBEN!"
ZEI HET VLAS, „JE MOET
IETS ONDERVINDEN, DAN WEET JE IETS!"
MAAR HET WERD INDERDAAD ERG.
HET VLAS WERD GEKNEUSD EN GEBRAAKT,

(1881-1973)

PICASSO. *EAUX-FORTES ORIGINALES POUR DES TEXTES DE BUFFON* (PARIS: MARTIN FABIANI, 1942).
154 pp., 365 x 280 mm., with 31 etchings and aquatints *hors texte*.
Edition of 226 copies (V&A copy no. [—]), of which one is on *Papier vergé ancien* with a set of etchings on *Papier ancien bleuté* (no. 1), 5 copies on *Japon super-nacré* with a set of etchings on *Chine* (nos. 2-6), 30 copies on *Japon impérial* with a set of etchings on *Chine* (nos. 7-36), 55 copies on *Vélin de Monval* (nos. 37-91), 135 copies on *Vélin de Vidalon* (nos. 92-226).
Printer: Fequet et Baudier, text; Lacourière, illustrations (completed 26 May 1942).
L.1187-1946.

Picasso was commissioned by Vollard to produce illustrations for the text of Georges Louis Leclerc (1707-1788), made Comte de Buffon by Louis XV, whose *HISTOIRE NATURELLE* was published between 1749 and 1788. Picasso began work on the series in 1936, to produce what has been called 'one of the great Bestiaries of the 20th century', and the project was brought to completion after Vollard's death by one of his associates, Martin Fabiani. The illustrations were printed by Roger Lacourière, who had introduced Picasso (among other artists) to a number of graphic techniques and in whose studio Picasso sometimes worked. The book was produced 'aux dépens et par les soins de Martin Fabiani'.

111 ANDRÉ DERAIN 1943

(1880-1954)

[FRANÇOIS RABELAIS] *LES HORRIBLES ET ESPOVANTABLES FAICTZ ET PROUESSES DU TRÈS RENOMMÉ PANTAGRUEL, ROY DES DIPSODES, FILS DU GRAND GÉANT GARGUANTUA, COMPOSÉ NOUVELLEMENT PAR MAITRE ALCOFRYBAS NASIER, ORNÉ DE BOIS EN COULEURS DESSINÉS ET GRAVÉS PAR ANDRÉ DERAIN* (PARIS: ALBERT SKIRA, 1943)
196 pp., 345 x 280 mm., 179 woodcuts in colour.
Edition of 275 copies (V&A copy no. 104), signed by the author, of which 15 copies have a separate set of coloured woodcuts on *Madagascar* and a set of refused woodcuts (nos. 1-15), 35 copies with a set of coloured woodcuts on *Madagascar* (nos. 16-50), 200 copies (nos. 51-250), and 25 copies *hors commerce* (nos. I-XXV).
Printer: Roger Lacourière, woodcuts; Georges Girard, text, set in Garamond (completed 15 April 1943).
L.1172-1949 Colour plate 13.

Commissioned by the publisher Albert Skira in 1941, Derain worked for 3 years to produce the illustrations, co-operating with Lacourière and developing a novel printing process whereby the wooden blocks were inked in several colours simultaneously rather than the usual method of a separate block for each colour. The text of PANTAGRUEL was that of Abel Lefranc.

T O U R   D E   P A N U R G E

112 HENRI MATISSE 1944

(1869-1954)

HENRI DE MONTHERLANT, *PASIPHAÉ. CHANT DE MINOS (LES CRÉTOIS). GRAVURES ORIGINALES PAR HENRI MATISSE* (PARIS: MARTIN FABIANI, 1944).
132 pp., 325 x 250 mm., with 18 full-page linocuts in black and numerous vignettes, initial letters and headbands by same technique; linocut cover in blue. Edition of 250 copies (V&A copy no. 137) signed by the artist, of which 30 copies are on *Japon ancien* with a set of 12 engraved sheets as frontispiece on *Chine* (nos. 1-30), 200 copies on *Vélin d'Arches* watermarked with name of publisher (nos. 31-230), 20 copies on *Vélin d'Arches* (nos. I-XX).
Printer: Fequet et Baudier, Paris, engravings and text (completed 20 May 1944).

Henri de Montherlant (1896-1972), a writer from an aristocratic background who produced historical plays centred on heroic personages of the 16th and 17th centuries as well as novels, was elected to the Académie Française in 1955. The text of *PASIPHAÉ* was made up of extracts from a play about the fabled king of Crete, Minos, that Montherlant had begun in Tunisia in 1934.

113 JEAN ATLAN 1946

(1913-1960) Born to a Jewish family in Algeria, Atlan studied philosophy at the Sorbonne in 1930-4. His first paintings and drawings were done in 1941. In 1942 he was arrested by the Nazis for Resistance activities, but, on simulating madness, was interned at Sainte-Anne until 1944. In this year he published his first collection of poetry, LE SANG PROFOND, *which reveals an interest in Far Eastern religions and African magic, and had his first exhibition, at the Galerie de l'Arc en Ciel in Paris. In 1948 he had work shown in Vienna and Copenhagen, but did not meet much success until 1955, when he produced a poster for the 'École de Paris' exhibition at the Galerie Charpentier. In 1956 he had his first one-man exhibition at the Galerie Bing, after which he exhibited widely. He died while preparing an exhibition of his work since 1944 for New York.*

FRANZ KAFKA, *DESCRIPTION D'UN COMBAT. LITHOGRAPHIES ORIGINALES PAR ATLAN. TRADUCTION DE CLARA MALRAUX ET RAINER DORLAND. PRÉFACE DE BERNARD GROETHUYSEN*
(PARIS: MAEGHT ÉDITEUR, 1946).
88 pp., 300 x 240 mm., with 7 full-page lithographs.
Edition of 350 COPIES (V&A copy no. 48), of which 50 copies are on *Auvergne à la main* (nos. I-L) and 300 copies on *Vélin* (nos. 1-300).
Printer: Mourlot Frères, lithographs; L'Imprimerie Union 'avec le concours de Jacques Kober', text (completed 7 Sept. 1946).
L.8723-1980

Atlan produced the illustrations for the work in 1945, when enjoying the aftermath of a successful exhibition. The lithographs were shown at the Salon de l'Hotel du Pont Royal, Paris, in 1947, in an exhibition organised by the Galerie Maeght in order to promote the book.

114 HENRI MATISSE 1947

(1869-1954)

HENRI MATISSE, *JAZZ* ([PARIS:] 'TÉRIADE ÉDITEUR' [ÉDITIONS DU VERVE, 1947]).
156 pp., 420 x 325 mm., with 20 stencils (of which 15 double-page) printed in colour, and cover in same technique.
Edition of 270 copies (V&A copy no. 170), signed by the artist, of which 250 are on *Vélin d'Arches* (nos. 1-250), and 20 *hors commerce* (nos. I-XX). Also 100 albums including all engravings.
Printer: Draeger Frères; stencils cut by Edmond Vairel.
Binding, in coloured leathers, by Paul Bonet, 1952.
L.338-1948. Colour plates 14-16.

JAZZ is a facsimile of a book written in Matisse's hand and decorated with collages and cut-outs made by the artist. It is the only publication of which Matisse was both author and illustrator, and was composed during a 12 month confinement to his bed in 1944. Matisse had experimented with his 'cut-paper' technique before 1947, largely at the suggestion of Tériade; the artist had designed three covers of the latter's periodical *VERVE* in this way (Tériade used Draeger as printer and Mourlot as lithographer for this publication). *JAZZ* is taken to be a turning point in Matisse's use of the technique, heralding the large paper cut-out *LA TRISTESSE DU ROI* of 1948.

After 1945, Tériade (b. 1897) emerged as a major publisher of fine books illustrated by artists. Like Skira, he came from a background of publishing, and journalism. Arriving in France in 1915 from Greece to study law, Tériade was entrusted by Christian Zervos with the 'Modern Art' section of the new review, *CAHIERS D'ART*. From 1928 to 1932, he contributed a column in the weekly journal *L'INTRANSIGEANT* on the same subject with his friend Maurice Raynal (1884-1954), a friend and collaborator of Apollinaire and contributor to *L'ESPRIT NOUVEAU* in 1920-5. The novelty of Tériade's column was that he allowed the artists themselves to give their views in writing. Organiser of a major sculpture exhibition at the Galerie Bernheim in 1930, he collaborated with Skira on a number of projects (see cat. 91). Having lost their column in *L'INTRANSIGEANT*, Tériade and Raynal set up *LA BÊTE NOIRE*, 'a magazine for artistic and literary action' in a more or less Surrealist vein. Among Tériade's greatest achievements was the magazine Verve, which ran from 1937 to 1960; rejecting 'all extravagance in the way the material is presented' but maintaining quality thanks to use of photogravure and lithography, Tériade gained the financial support of an American publisher who wanted to produce 'the most beautiful review in the world' thus ensuring an English edition of the magazine. Tériade produced 26 major books illustrated by the original graphic work of contemporary artists.

Plate XII. La Nageuse dans l'Aquarium.

115 MARCEL DUCHAMP **1947**

(1887-1968) Brother of the painter Jacques Villon and the sculptor Raymond Duchamp-Villon, Duchamp worked, after study at the Académie Julian in 1905-6, with a printer in Rouen to avoid military service. He was one of the Puteaux group of CUBISTS *and showed with the Section d'Or in 1910. His NU DESCENDANT UN ESCALIER of 1911 began a series of works devoted to the expression of movement in a* FUTURIST *vein and the colour theories of Kupka and Delaunay; his* MARIÉE MISE À NU PAR SES CÉLIBATAIRES, MÊME *of 1913 revealed his philosophy of love and desire as well as his scintillating intelligence, which was to surface continually in* SURREALIST *circles in the 1920s and 1930s in paintings and objets trouvés. Enjoying acclaim at the New York Armory show of 1913, Duchamp and Picabia animated a* DADA *movement in New York. Friendship with the Arenbergs allowed him to work as a dealer in Europe thereafter, where he was also much taken up with playing chess and entering professional competitions. Duchamp lived in Paris from 1922 to 1942, and assisted in the organisation of a large number of exhibitions. Living in the USA from 1942, he exercised an enormous influence on the generation of* ABSTRACT-EXPRESSIONIST *artists that emerged in New York after the Second World War. In the eyes of critics and commentators, many if not most 'movements' in western art since 1945 can claim Duchamp as their spiritual father.*

VICTOR BRAUNER
(1903-1966) After study in the Fine Arts Academy in Bucharest in 1921-4, Brauner founded 75 HP, a 'picto-poetic' review in a DADA *spirit which revealed his notion that poetry was the most complete of all forms of artistic expression. Living in Paris in 1925-27 and 1930-5, he was introduced to* SURREALIST *circles by his compatriot Brancusi and his friend Yves Tanguy. Despite Breton's enthusiastic introduction, Brauner's first one-man show in Paris in 1934 was not successful and the artist returned to Rumania, coming back to Paris in 1938 and spending the war near Perpignan. The sources of Brauner's art are in ancient mythologies (Egyptian, Pre-Columbian, of the Ancient East) and in popular art. In 1948, during a period when he was producing 'magic' drawings, Brauner held an exhibition at the René Drouin Gallery, Paris, and broke with the Surrealist group in the following year.*

LE SURRÉALISME EN 1947. EXPOSITION INTERNATIONALE DU SURRÉALISME PRÉSENTEE PAR ANDRÉ BRETON ET MARCEL DUCHAMP
(PARIS: 'PIERRE À FEU', MAEGHT EDITEUR, 1947).
142 pp., 240 x 205mm., with 5 colour lithographs (Brauner, Ernst, Hérold, Lam, Miró), 5 etchings (Jean, Maria, Tanguy, Tanning), 1 of them in colour (Bellmer), 2 wood engravings (Arp) and 12 lithographs in black (Brignoni, Calder, Capacci, Damme, Diego, Donati, Hare, Lamba, Matta, Sage, Tanguy, Toyen), all *hors texte*.
Special Edition of 999 copies, on *vélin supérieur,* numbered I-XLIX (signed by Breton and Duchamp), and 1-950 (V&A copy no. 425).
Binding: 'La couverture est l'original d'un objet de Marcel Duchamp.'
Printer: Lacourière, etchings; Mourlot Frères, wood engravings and all lithographs; L'Imprimerie Union (Jacques Kober), text.
L.3000-1948.

The Surrealist exhibition in Paris of 1947 has, in retrospect, the character of an historical survey of the movement, marking the return to Paris of those who had led Surrealism before the war in the French capital. Its heritage was transmitted to the American avant-garde largely through Duchamp, but in Europe the artists now considered to represent the most constructive new trends (Wols, Vieira da Silva, Dubuffet, etc.) had evolved without reference to it. The exhibition was organised by Breton with the help of Duchamp. The theme chosen was that of myth: a Hall of Superstitions led through a Baptismal Chamber (where rain fell continuously) to a Labyrinth in whose recesses were altars, patterned on voodoo cults, the most impressive being those of Lam and Brauner. Duchamp was behind this idea, designing the Baptismal Chamber and the Labyrinth, while FJ Kiesler came from New York to design the Hall of Superstitions and execute the whole work. The exhibition was international, and a number of countries provided statements approved by the Surrealist group in each. That from England was signed by John Banting, Robert Baxter, Emmy Bridgwater, FJ Brown, JB Brunius, Feyyaz Fergar, Conroy Maddox, George Melly, Robert Melville, ELT Mesens, Roland Penrose, Edith Rimmington, Philip Sanson, and Simon Watson Taylor. The cover of the book, a delicately tinted breast made of latex rubber kept in a box labelled 'Prière de Toucher', showed that Duchamp had lost none of his penetrating inventiveness and wit.

ABOVE Victor Brauner. Lithograph.

RIGHT Marcel Duchamp. Catalogue cover.

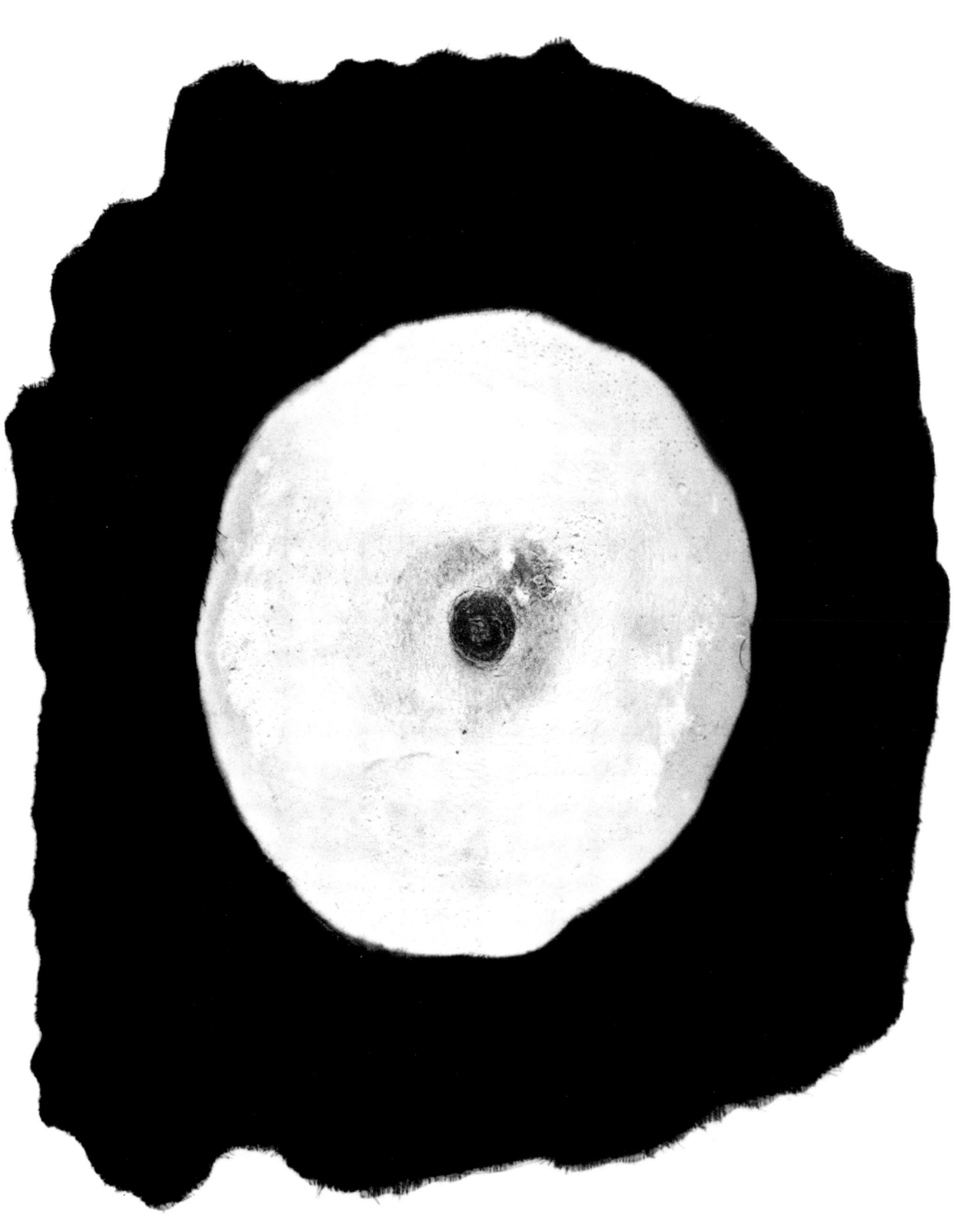

116 GIACOMO MANZÙ **1948**

(b.1908) After apprenticeship to a wood-carver and gilder, Manzù moved from Bergamo to Verona, where he attended evening classes at the Academy Cicognini to study sculpture; Ancient Egyptian, Etruscan and Renaissance sculpture were major influences together with the great Milanese sculptor, Medardo Rosso (1858-1928). Trips to Paris in 1929 and 1936 impressed him with work of the IMPRESSIONISTS *and Rodin. Settled in Milan from 1930, he had a one-man exhibition in Rome in 1937. He taught at the Brera Academy in Milan from 1941 to 1954. In 1948 he was awarded the Grand Prix at the Venice Biennale. From 1954 to 1960 he taught at Kokoschka's Summer School in Salzburg, where he received a major commission in 1957-8 to make bronze doors for the cathedral. In 1964 he completed theatre designs for Stravinsky's* OEDIPUS REX *(in 1971 he was commissioned to make a monument for the composer's tomb). Awarded the Lenin prize in 1966, he was made an honorary Royal Academician in London in 1970 and received an honorary doctorate from the Royal College of Art in 1971.*

LE GEORGICHE DI VIRGILIO. VERSIONE ITALIANA DI GIULO CAPRIN CON ACQUAFORTI DI MANZÙ (MILAN: ULRICO HOEPLI, 1948).
126 pp., 380 x 280 mm., with 10 full-page engravings.
Edition of 165 copies (V&A copy no.62), on 'carta a tino di Fabriano', numbered 1-150, with 15 copies *hors commerce* numbered A-P; nos. 1-10 include a separate set of engravings.
Printer: Officina Bodoni (completed Jan. 1948).
Binding by Ivor Robinson, 1977.
L.835-1954.

Something of the grandeur and simplicity of Manzù's sculpture is apparent in the illustrations he provided for the Virgil text.

117 RENÉ MAGRITTE **1948**

(1898-1967) After study at the Brussels Académie des Beaux-Arts in 1916-18, Magritte made his living designing wall-paper for the Peters Lacroix Company and making fashion drawings for Van Hecke Fashions. In 1926 he participated in the Société du Mystère in company with Geomans, Nougé and other Belgian SURREALIST *writers. After a brief* CUBIST/FUTURIST *phase, he developed his style and pictorial world under the influence of De Chirico, whom he had first discovered in 1922, and to whose metaphysical paintings Marcel Lecomte introduced him in 1925. In 1927 he had his first exhibition in the Galerie Le Centaure in Brussels, and moved to Paris, where he moved in the* SURREALIST *circles frequented by André Breton, Miró, Arp, and others. In 1930 Magritte returned to Brussels, and exhibited in major Surrealist exhibitions before the war. In the war years he adopted what has been called his 'Renoir' style. In 1951-3, the 'Enchanted Domain' murals were painted from his designs at Knokke.*

[ISIDORE DUCASSE] COMTE DE LAUTRÉAMONT, *LES CHANTS DE MALDOROR, ILLUSTRATIONS DE RENÉ MAGRITTE* (BRUSSELS: ÉDITIONS 'LA BOËTIE', [1948]).
200 pp., 245 x 180 mm., with 64 illustrations and 12 separate plates.
Edition of 4100 (V&A copy no.3590), on *Papier pur chiffon* of which 72 copies have an original drawing and 'L'état définitif des gravures' (nos. 1-72); also some copies *hors commerce* for collaborators.
Printer: Éditions La Boëtie, Brussels.
L.1658-1968

118 WOLS **1948**

(1913-1951) Born Alfred Wolfgang Schültze, Wols was the son of a state official interested in contemporary art. Trained as a violinist, he studied ethnography at the Afrika-Institut in Frankfurt from 1930, after which he spent a short time at the Bauhaus. In 1932 he went to Paris, where he worked as a photographer, met a number of Surrealists such as Ernst and produced paintings in the nature of dream landscapes. Having spent 1933-6 in Spain, Wols was arrested in 1939 but released in 1940 to spend the war in poverty at Cassis with the collector Henri Roche, where he produced quantities of small-format drawings. Returning to Paris in 1945 he began to work on canvases. The success of Wols began in 1947, when he took part in a number of exhibitions with Georges Mathieu that sought to present an alternative abstract art from that of neo-constructivists with their geometricising tendencies. This 'lyrical' abstract art, dubbed 'Un Art Autre' and given the title 'Tachisme', gained confidence from a meeting in 1947 with the proponents of ACTION PAINTING *from North America: Pollock, de Kooning and Rothko. From 1948, Wols illustrated a number of books of existentialist writers, including those of his friend Sartre. Michel Tapié characterised Wols as 'catalyst of a lyrical non-figuration, explosive, anti-geometric, informal.' Prematurely aged by excesses, Wols died in 1951.*

JEAN-PAUL SARTRE, *VISAGES, PRÉCEDÉ DE PORTRAITS OFFICIELS* (PARIS: SEGHERS, 1948).
ii, 46 pp., 185 x 120 mm., with 4 dry-point engravings.
Edition of 916 copies (V&A copy no.878), of which 15 copies are on *Chine* (nos.1-15), and 900 copies on *Crèvecoeur du Marais* (nos.16-916); 10 other copies marked 'H.C.' for the author and artist.
Printer: R. Haasen, etchings; L'Imprimerie Union, text (completed Jan. 1948).
L.252-1984.

On returning to Paris in 1945, Wols exhibited a number of watercolours at the René Drouin Gallery. The artist's friendship with Sartre dates from this period. The writer commissioned Wols to provide illustrations for his work. Sartre wrote a text on Wols after his death: *DOIGTS ET NON-DOIGTS,* which appeared in *WOLS EN PERSONNE: AQUARELLES ET DESSINS* (Paris & Cologne: Werner Haftman, 1963).

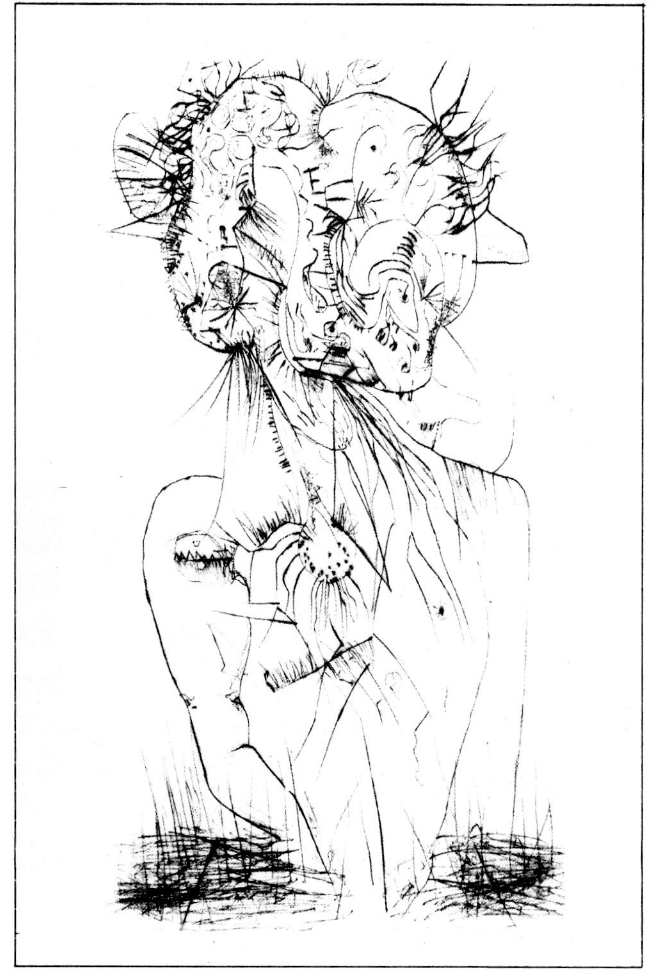

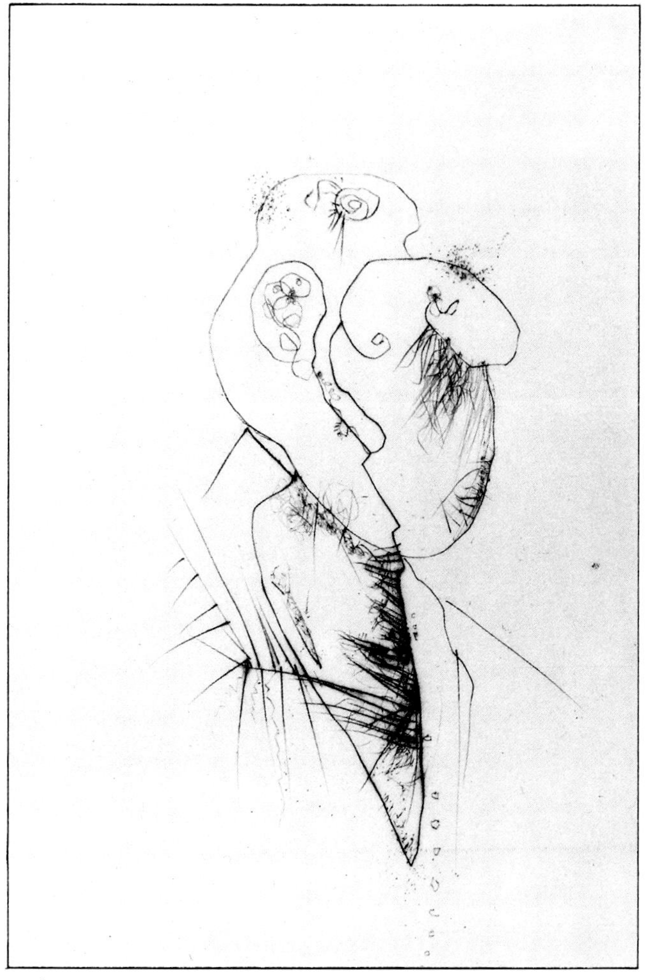

119 WOLS **1949**

(1913-1951)

JEAN-PAUL SARTRE, *NOURRITURES, SUIVI D'EXTRAITS DE LA NAUSÉE. POINTES SÈCHES DE WOLS*
(PARIS: JACQUES DAMASE, 1949).
viii, 58 pp., 190 x 135 mm., with 3 dry-point etchings.
Edition of 450 copies (V&A copy no.65), on *'pur fil des Papeteries Johannot'*, of which 26 copies are numbered A-Z, and 424 copies numbered 27-450.
Printer: 'Presses des 2 Artisans', Paris.
L.2692-1983.

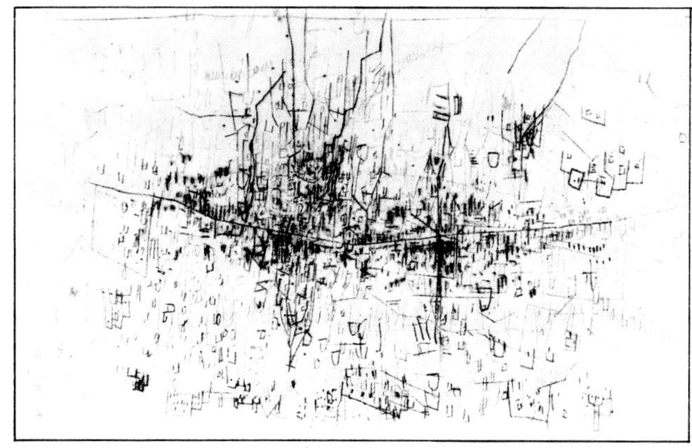

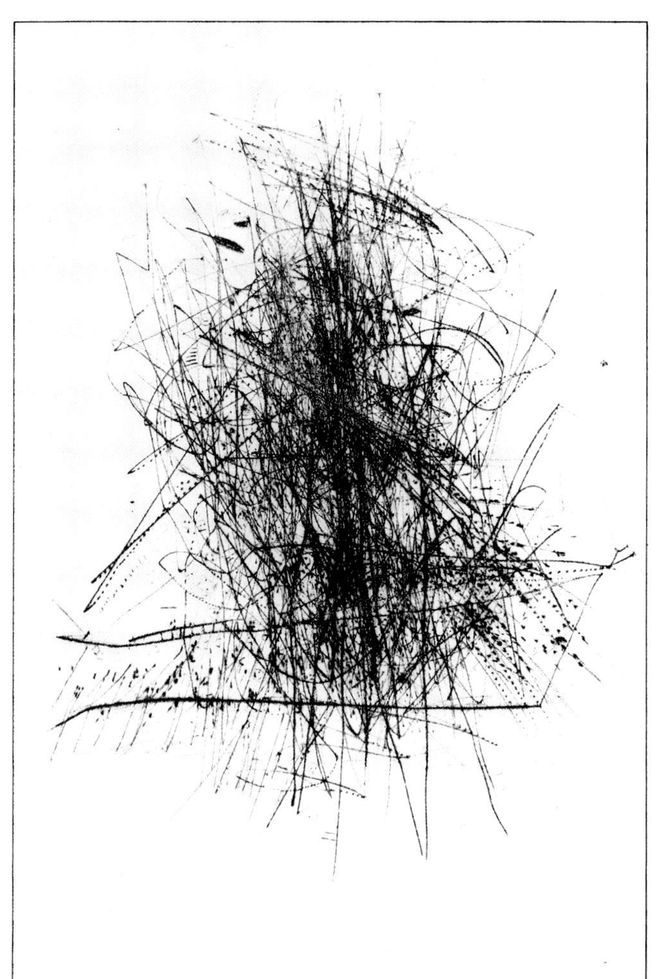

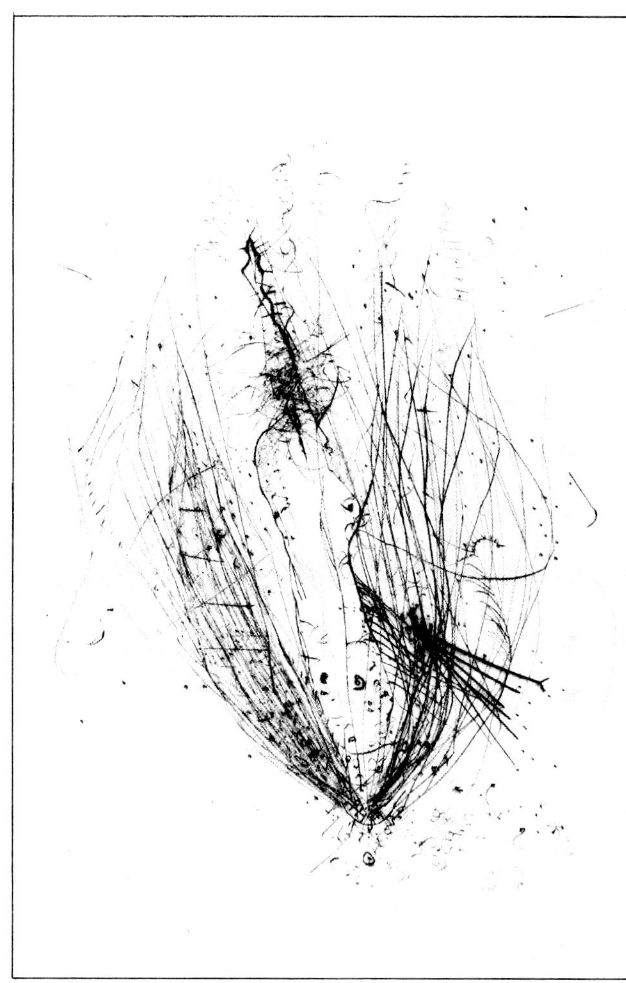

120 MASSIMO CAMPIGLI 1949

(1895-1971) A self-taught painter, Campigli worked as a journalist in Milan before the First World War, where he collaborated in the foundation of the FUTURIST *review* LACERBA. *In 1919-23, he worked in Paris, again as a journalist but spending much time painting, and meeting Picasso and Léger as well as discovering Ancient Egyptian and Cretan art. The exhibition of Etruscan art in Rome had a fundamental effect in establishing the 'primitive' nature of his style, archaic, studiedly naive, with earthy colours and of rough finish. At his first exhibition in Paris, at the Jeanne Bucher gallery in 1929, all his work was sold, and he exhibited throughout Europe; his first New York show was at the Levy Gallery in 1932. From 1937 he received numerous commissions for frescos and murals.*

ANDRÉ GIDE, *THESEUS ...ENGLISH TRANSLATION OF JOHN RUSSELL, LITHOGRAPHS OF MASSIMO CAMPIGLI* (LONDON: HEYWOOD HILL ['A NEW DIRECTIONS BOOK' , 1949])

104 pp., 320 x 245 mm., with 12 lithographs, and 1 lithograph *hors texte* signed by the artist.
Edition of 200 copies (V&A copy no.142), of which 10 are on *Fabriano* (nos.1-10) and 190 copies on *Pescia* (nos.11-200); nos.1-30 have a 2nd series of illustrations and a series of 8 studies, all printed on China paper.
Printer: Officina Bodoni, Verona, text, set in Garamond (completed Jan. 1949).
L.1366-1949.

Gide wrote *THESEUS* when in North Africa during the Second World War. The text was first published by Éditions Schiffrin, New York. John Russell's translation was made from the author's revised version that was subsequently published in France by Éditions Gallimard.

CAMPIGLI

121 JOAN MIRÓ **1949**

(1893-1983)

PAUL ELUARD, *À TOUTE ÉPREUVE. GRAVURES SUR BOIS DE JOAN MIRÓ* (GENEVA: GERALD CRAMER, 1958)
104 pp., 335 x 260 mm., with 79 woodcuts.
Edition of 130 copies (V&A copy no.62), signed by the artist on *Vélin pur chiffon, d'Arches,* of which 6 copies have 2 extra sets of woodcuts on *Chine* and *Papier nacré du Japon* (nos.1-6), 20 copies with 1 extra set of woodcuts on *Chine* or *Papier nacré du Japon* (nos.7-26), 80 standard copies (nos.27-106); 24 copies *hors commerce* (nos.I-XXIV).
Printer: Fequet et Baudier, text; Lacourière et Frélaut, woodcuts (completed 25 March 1958).
L.1197-1958.

Eluard's poems *À TOUTE ÉPREUVE* had originally been published without illustrations. The initiative for this edition came from Cramer, who had recently produced a *de luxe* publication of Eluard's writings, *A Pablo Picasso.* Eluard's lyrical poems had been inspired by Catalonia and the visit he made to Salvador Dali in 1930. In 1948 Gerald Cramer suggested that Miró illustrate the work, but Eluard, a friend of Miró since the mid-1920s, died before its completion. Begun in 1948, Miró's woodcuts took 10 years to complete.

8

Immobile
J'habite cette épine et ma griffe se pose
Sur les seins délicieux de la misère et du crime.

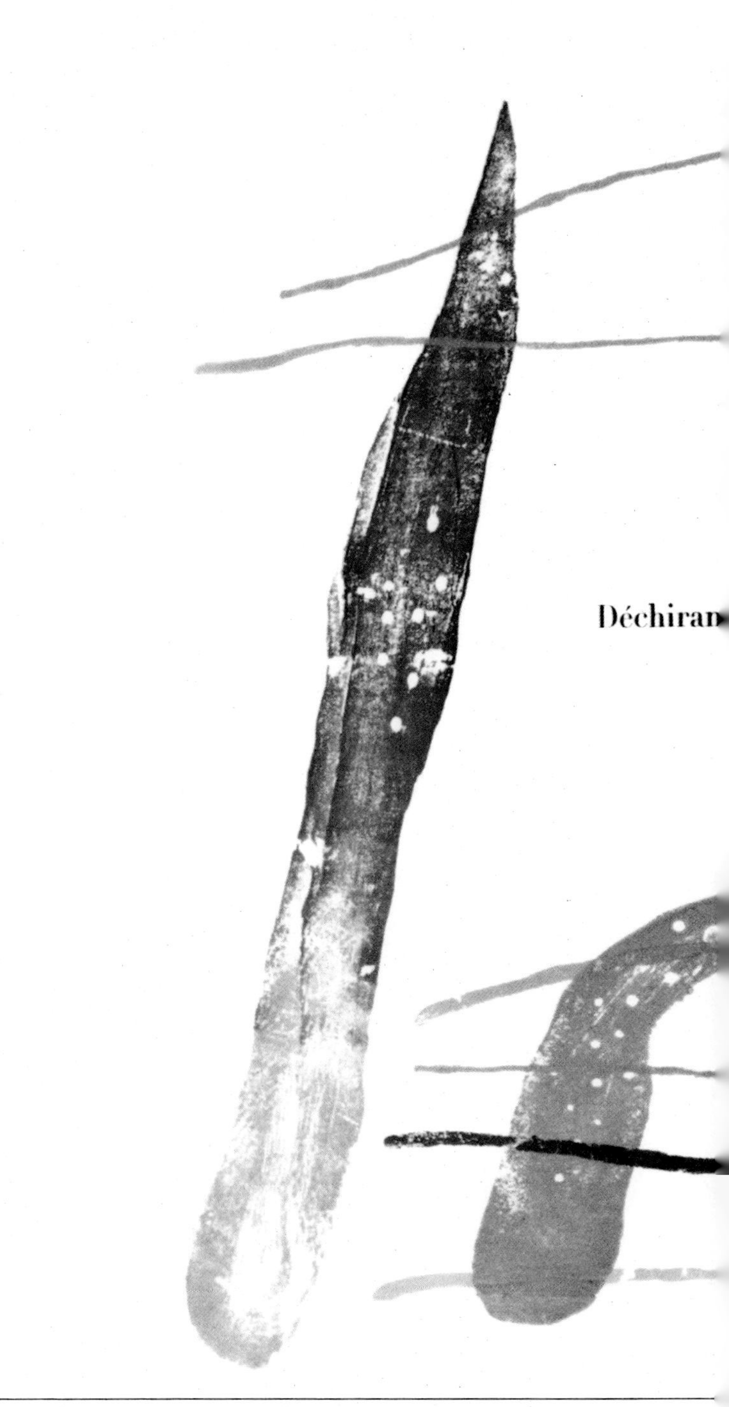

s et ses peurs

Elle s'éveille la nuit

Pour s'étonner de tout ce qui l'a remplacée.

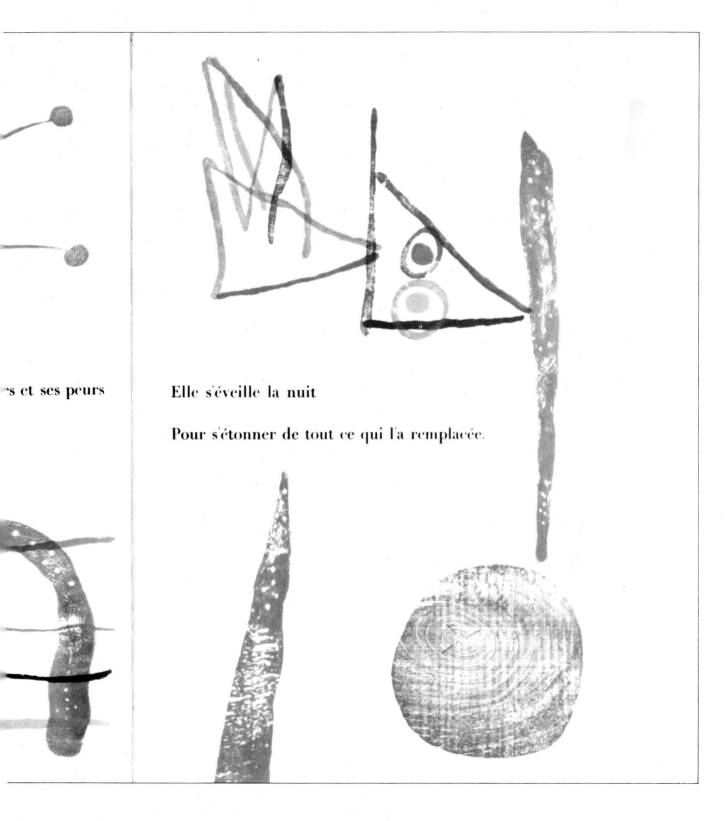

122 JEAN DUBUFFET **1950**

(b.1901) After a few months study at the Académie Julian in 1918, Dubuffet undertook his military service as a meteorologist but also produced paintings in the manner of Friesz and woodcuts for the review AVENTURE. *In 1925 he entered his father's business in Le Havre and travelled widely, founding his own concern at Bercy in 1930. On a number of occasions in the 1930s he took up painting, mostly portraits, but only in 1942 did it become his full-time activity. His first one-man show was at the Galerie René Drouin, Paris, in 1944. Two years later he exhibited his 'hautes pâtes', thick impastos of plaster, putty, asphalt, pebbles, etc. In 1947 he founded the Compagnie de* L'ART BRUT, *of which André Breton was soon a member, to make a collection of all kinds of products — drawings, paintings, and sculptured objects in every conceivable kind of material, children's paintings, graffiti, obscenities, etc. — the raw material of human creativity that evidenced artistic spontaneity and inventiveness produced outside professional artistic circles and not in imitation of them; much of the work collected was produced by primitive societies and the insane (Dubuffet had long been familiar with Prinzhorn's views on the 'validity' of the art of the insane). From 1962, Dubuffet presented in several exhibitions his* HOURLOUPE *projects. In the early 1960s he produced his first experimental music with Asger Jorn.*

EUGÈNE GUILLEVIC, *LES MURS. LITHOGRAPHIES ORIGINALES DE JEAN DUBUFFET* (PARIS: EDITIONS DU LIVRE [1950]).
30 ff. (15 bifolia), 380 x 285 mm., with 14 lithographs
288 and lithographed cover.
Edition of 172 copies (V&A copy no.35), of which 10 are on *Japon impérial* with 2 extra sets of lithographs on *Vergé du Japon* and *Monval* respectively and 2 other sets of lithographs 'non utilisées' (nos. 1-10), 150 copies on *Monval* (nos.11-160), 2 copies *hors commerce* on *Japon impérial* (nos.A-B), and 10 copies *hors commerce* on *Monval* (nos.C-L).
Printer: Mourlot Frères, lithographs, in 1945; Joseph Zichieri, Paris [text] (completed 20 April 1950).
L.501-1955.

A number of Dubuffet's lithographs are dated 1945, and they show crude, powerful human figures against textured walls, many of which, 'pregnant with experience', have graffiti and other human markings. The influence of Paul Klee and of children's drawing has been seen in this work. Guillevic (b.1907) produced his first work as a poet in 1942, when he was a member of the Communist Party and fighting with the Resistance. The poems of *LES MURS* parallel Dubuffet's evocation of their substance and function: 'Les murs sont compagnons, / Posés toujours qu'ils sont pour le / coude et la paume / et dressés vers les yeux'.

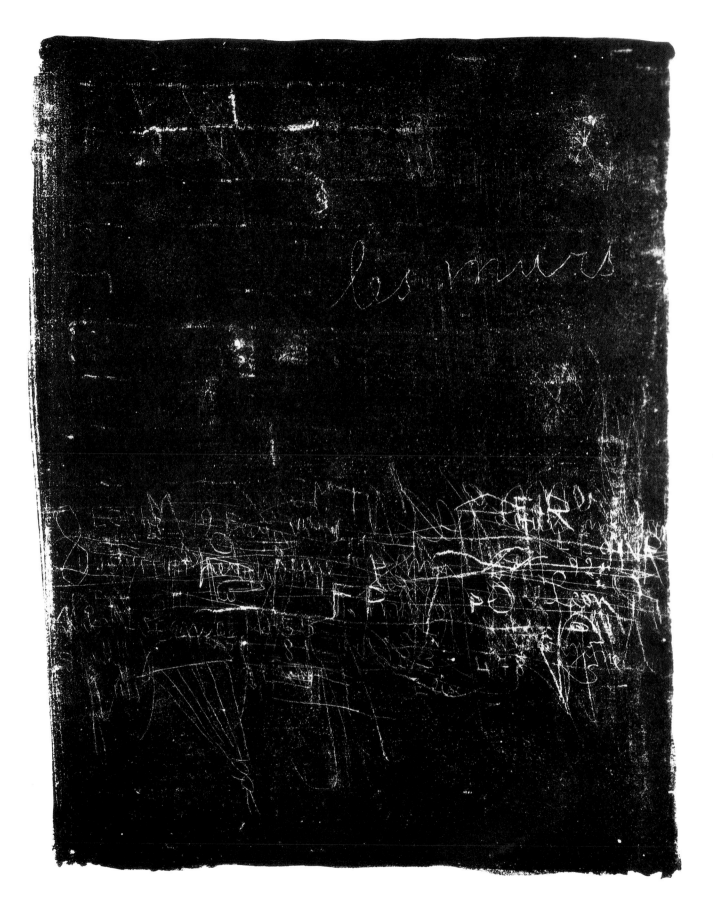
les murs

123 FERNAND LÉGER **1950**

(1881-1955)

FERNAND LÉGER, *CIRQUE. LITHOGRAPHIES ORIGINALES*
([PARIS:] TÉRIADE ÉDITEUR, 1950).
112 pp., 420 x 325 mm., each page of image and script (in Léger's hand) lithographed.
Edition of 280 copies, and 20 copies *hors commerce* (I-XX; V&A copy no.XIX), signed by the artist.
Printer: Mourlot Frères, for Éditions Verve, Paris.
L.1160-1981.

After his return to Paris from the USA in 1945, Léger provided lithographs and drawings for a number of books. The illustrations to *CIRQUE* take as subjects circus acts and cycling, both being themes based on breezy everyday life that the artist had explored in America.

Je
ne
te
demande
pas
si
ta
grand-
– mère
fait
du
velo

124 HENRY MOORE **1950**

(b.1898) Son of a Yorkshire miner, Moore studied at Leeds Art School in 1919-1921 before attending the Royal College of Art on a scholarship in 1921-1924 to study sculpture. He first exhibited at the Redfern Gallery in 1924; his first public commission was from the London Transport Passenger Board in 1926. In 1933 he joined Unit One, the group founded by Paul Nash. Moore was on the organising committee of the major International Surrealist Exhibition of 1936 in London along with Herbert Read. The artist's reputation as a draughtsman led to his being made Official War Artist in 1942. His international reputation dates from 1948 when he was awarded the sculpture prize at the Venice Biennale. Moore was a trustee of the Tate Gallery from 1941-1955, and of the National Gallery, London, from 1955 to 1974. In 1963-1967 he was a member of the Arts Council. He was awarded the Order of Merit in 1963.

GOETHE, *PROMÉTHÉE. TRADUCTION PAR ANDRÉ GIDE. LITHOGRAPHIES DE HENRY MOORE* (PARIS: HENRI JONQUIÈRES, P.A. NICAISE, ÉDITEUR, 1950).
70 pp., 380 x 280 mm., with lithographed title-page and 14 lithographs (3 of them decorated initials).
Edition of 183 copies, on *Vélin chiffon à la forme des Papeteries du Marais,* of which 8 copies are with a set of 'premiers états', a set of lithographs and an original drawing (nos.1-8), 10 copies with a set of lithographs (nos.9-18; V&A copy no.10), and 165 copies (nos.19-183); a 'few
292 copies' were reserved for the collaborators.
Printer: Imprimerie Nationale, text; Mourlot Frères, Paris, lithographs ('ce livre fut terminé en Mars 1951' [though title-page gives 1950 as publication date]).
L.1784-1951. Colour plate 17.

Henry Moore had produced one or two wood engravings in the 1930s, and his first lithograph, 'The Spanish Prisoner' (to raise money for Republican forces in the Spanish Civil War), in 1939. Before the 1970s, graphic work was not a major part of his production, his drawings as a War Artist and working sketches for sculptures excepted. *PROMÉTHÉE* was the first book for which he produced original lithographs, and was the result of a particular commission for a project that was to be printed by the French Imprimerie Nationale on its venerable *GRANDJEAN ROMAIN DU ROI,* originally cut in 1692. The lithographs were pulled in the studio of Mourlot Frères, who had done much work for similar *LIVRES D'ARTISTE* published in France. The V&A copy of *PROMÉTHÉE* was printed for Percy Lund, Humphries & Co.

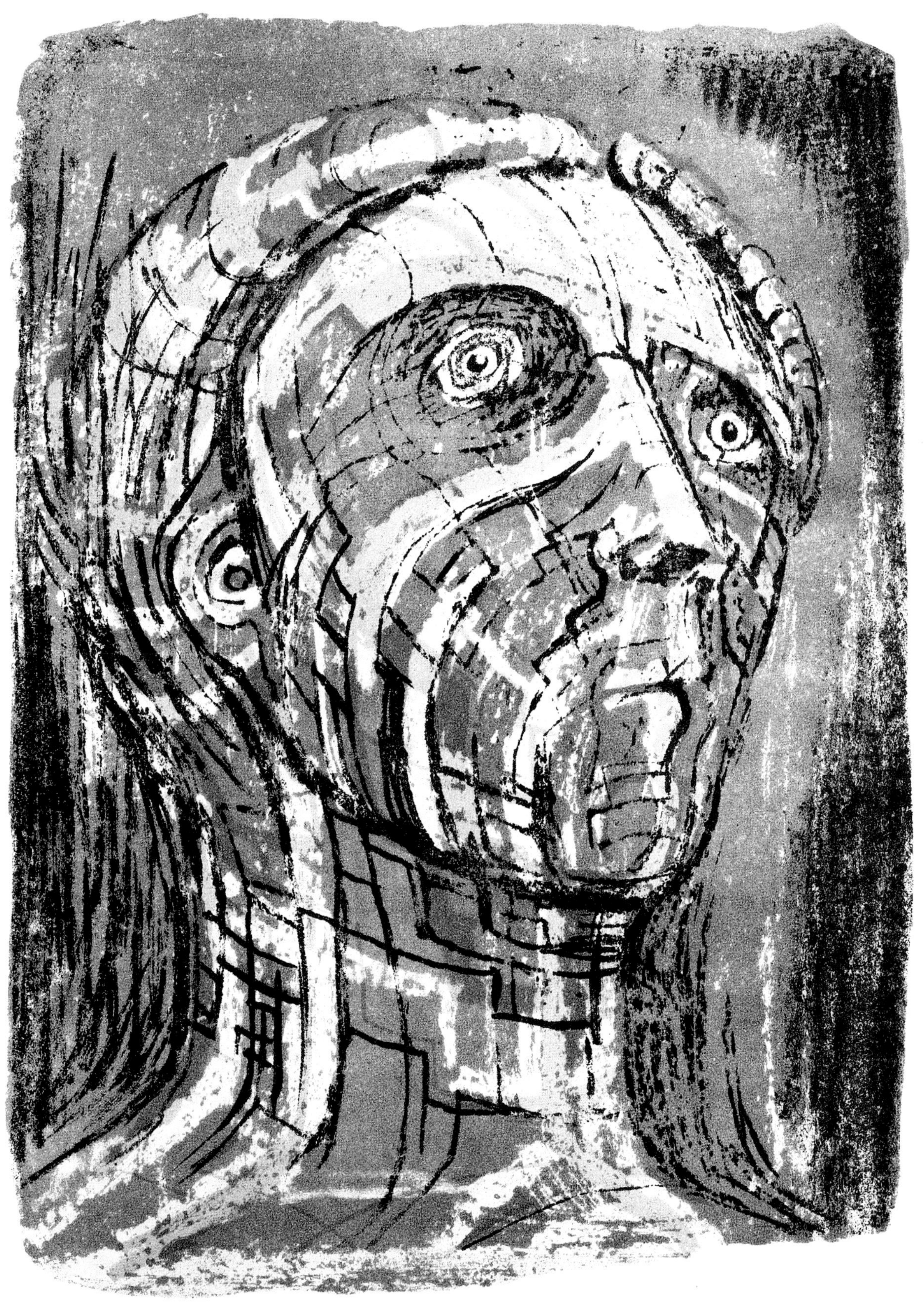

125 HENRI LAURENS **1951**

(1885-1954)

LUCIAN, *DIALOGUES*. *GRAVURES SUR BOIS ORIGINALES DE HENRI LAURENS* (PARIS: TÉRIADE, [1951]).
158 pp., 385 x 285 mm., with 4 wood engraved initials, tailpieces, cover and table of illustrations, and 24 wood engravings *hors texte*.
Edition of 250 copies (V&A copy no.140), on *Vergé d'Arches*, signed by the artist, nos. 1-40 with a set of the engravings on *Chine*, and 25 copies *hors commerce* (nos.I-XXV).
Printer: Théo Schmied (completed 31 May 1951).
L.3260-1951. Colour plate 18.

The *DIALOGUES* is the third publication of Tériade illustrated by Laurens, following Theocritus, *LES IDYLLES* (1945) and Lucian, *LOUKIOS OU L'ANE* (1946). In commissioning these works, Tériade sought to demonstrate the classical nature of Laurens' graphic and pictorial genius.

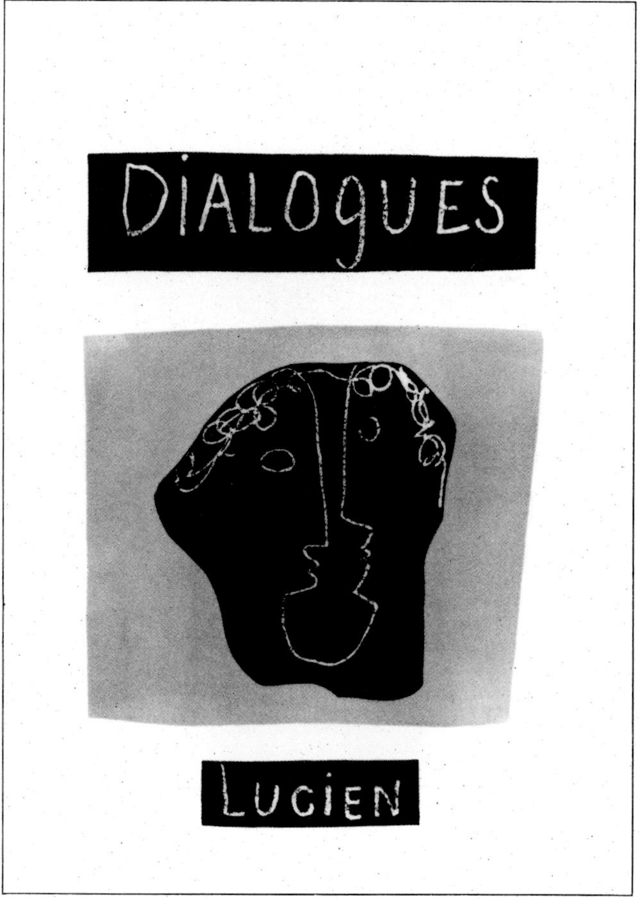

126 KEES VAN DONGEN **1951**

(1877-1968) Trained at the Rotterdam Academy in 1895-7, Van Dongen worked for the newspaper ROTTERDAMSCHE NIEUWBLAD; *from 1897 he lived in Paris and worked for a number of reviews, among them* LA REVUE BLANCHE. *In 1904 Vollard gave him a one-man exhibition; his work was amongst that dubbed* FAUVIST *in the Salon d'Automne in 1905. In 1906-7 he became friends with Picasso and produced a series of pictures based on the Médrano circus. In 1907 he signed a contract for a year with Kahnweiler; in 1908 he collaborated with the ceramicist Metthey, was encouraged by Kahnweiler to show in Düsseldorf, and sent work to the* BRÜCKE *exhibition in Dresden. His work after 1918 has been characterised as 'a compromise between official portraiture and poster art'; and he became a painter of high society and of the* DEMI-MONDE *of Paris and fashionable resorts. In 1926 he was made a Chevalier of the Légion d'Honneur. After 1945 much of his work was of landscapes around Cannes and Deauville, and portraiture, such as that of Brigitte Bardot in 1954.*

ANATOLE FRANCE, *LA RÉVOLTE DES ANGES*, *LITHOGRAPHIES ORIGINALES EN COULEUR DE VAN DONGEN* (PARIS: SCRIPTA ET PICTA, 1951).
113 ff., 360 x 277 mm., with 58 colour lithographs. Edition of 210 copies (V&A copy no.67), on *Vélin Lana*, with 15 extra copies on *Vélin Lana* with a double set of lithographs for the founder members of the *SCRIPTA ET PICTA* society (nos.I-XV)
Printer: Célestin of Mourlot Frères, lithographs (each colour on a separate stone); Frazier-Soye, text, set in a Caslon font designed for this edition (completed from November 1946 to December 1951).
L.2220-1983

The book was produced by Dr A. Roudinesco, president of the Groupe de Bibliophiles et d'Amateurs d'Art ('Scripta et Picta'); founder members of this society were Roudinesco, Georges Blaizot, Madame Jean Bloch, Georges Cretté, Robert Debré, Madame Hamon, M. Vautheret, Madame Roudinesco (treasurer) and Auguste Blaizot (bookseller).

Anatole France (1844-1924) published *LA RÉVOLTE DES ANGES* in 1914. He was elected to the Académie Française in 1896; in 1921 he was awarded the Nobel Prize for literature. France was associated with progressive writing in the early 20th century and was part of the literary Establishment later on in his career.

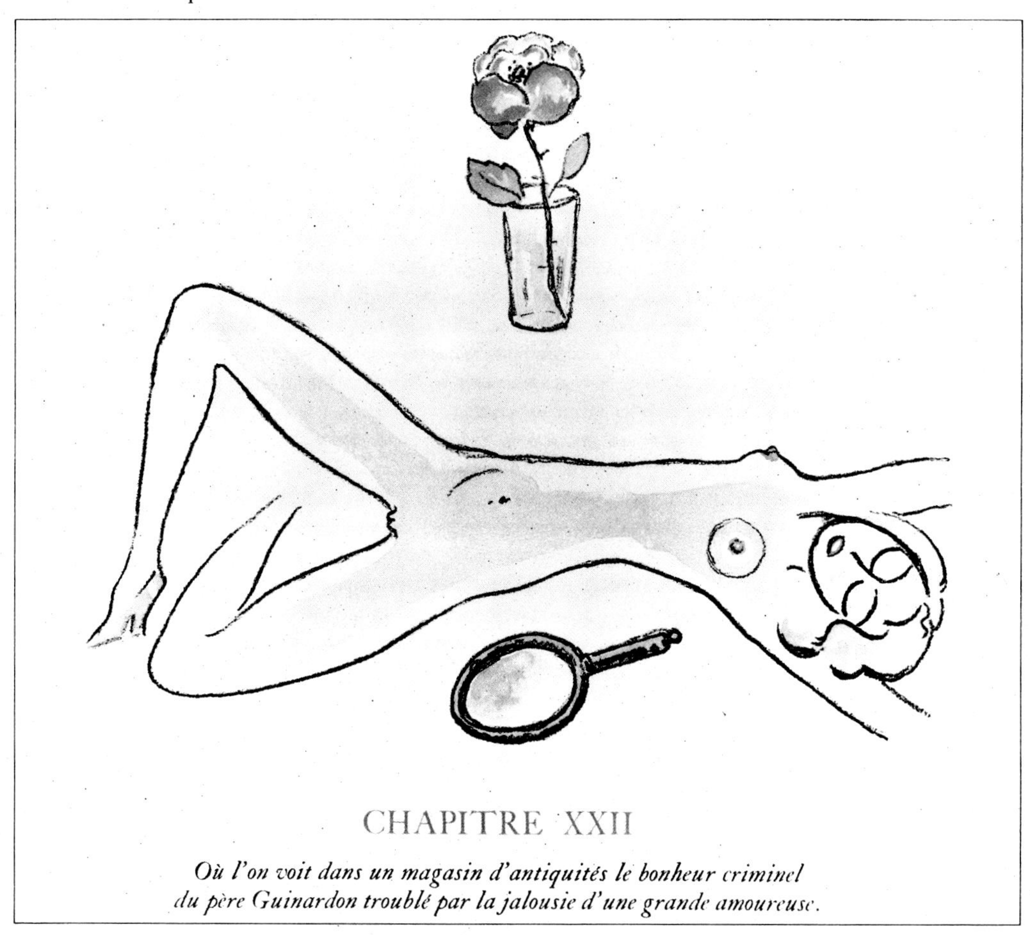

CHAPITRE XXII
Où l'on voit dans un magasin d'antiquités le bonheur criminel
du père Guinardon troublé par la jalousie d'une grande amoureuse.

295

127 NICOLAS DE STAËL **1952**

(1914-1955) On the death of his parents, who had brought him from Russia to Poland, De Staël was sent to Brussels in 1922; here he studied at the Académie des Beaux Arts in 1932-6, during which time he visited Paris and discovered Cézanne, Matisse, Braque and Soutine. After working as a painter/decorator, he visited Spain and North Africa before settling in Paris in 1938. Here he spent some time making copies of Chardin and Delacroix in the Louvre. Leaving the capital in 1940, he returned there in 1943 thanks to the help of Jeanne Bucher; in 1944 he exhibited at the L'Esquisse Gallery with Kandinsky, Magnelli and Domela, and met Braque at the time of his 1944 exhibition at the Jeanne Bucher Gallery. De Staël adopted an abstract idiom from 1942 which was to be the basis of his post-war success: he signed a contract with Louis Carré in 1946 and Theodore Schempp introduced his work to the American market from 1947. The spectacle of a football match played under floodlights at night at the Parc des Princes in 1952 inspired a number of drawings and paintings. In 1955 he committed suicide. The catalogue of his work that appeared in 1968 listed 1059 canvases as well as quantities of engravings, lithographs and collages.

POÈMES DE RENÉ CHAR. BOIS DE NICOLAS DE STAËL (PARIS: 'AUX DÉPENS DE L'ARTISTE', 1952).
48 ff., 370 x 290 mm., with 14 wood engravings, with colour lithographed cover.
Edition of 105 copies (V&A copy no.92), signed by author and artist, of which 15 copies are on *Grand Vélin d'Arches* with a double set of engravings on *Japon ancien* and *Vélin J. Green & Son* (nos.1-15), 90 copies on *Grand Vélin d'Arches* (nos.16-105); also 15 copies *hors commerce* on *Grand Vélin d'Arches* (nos.I-XV).
Printer: Marthe Fequet & Pierre Baudier, wood engravings and text, set in Firmin Didot Corps 24 (completed Nov.1951).
L.5071-1980.

The wood engravings done by De Staël for the poems of René Char were exhibited at the Galerie Jacques Dubourg in December 1951, and it was Jacques Dubourg who marketed the edition and who was probably behind its publication. René Char (b.1907) had been a close companion of Eluard from 1929 and was active in Surrealist activities in the 1930s, helping to found the review *LE SURRÉALISME AU SERVICE DE LA RÉVOLUTION* in 1933. He played a leading part in the French Resistance during the war; his collection of poems *FUREUR ET MYSTÈRE* published in 1948 was hailed by Camus as the most important French poetry since Rimbaud's *ILLUMINATIONS*. Char was introduced to De Staël by Georges Duthuit in 1950, and Char, who habitually asked artist friends to 'illuminate' the manuscripts of his poems, seized on the idea that the artist illustrate 12 pieces taken from his *POÈME PULVERISÉ*. The V&A copy of their production includes a commentary on the engravings by Char printed for the Dubourg exhibition; the poet talks of 'Yeti' footprints found in the Himalayas (the 'Abominable Snowman' of English lore), and likens himself and De Staël to Yetis, saying that he and the artist similarly approached 'the living and the stars' too closely on occasion. Char and De Staël subsequently worked on a ballet, unfortunately never performed, entitled 'L'Abominable Homme des Neiges.'

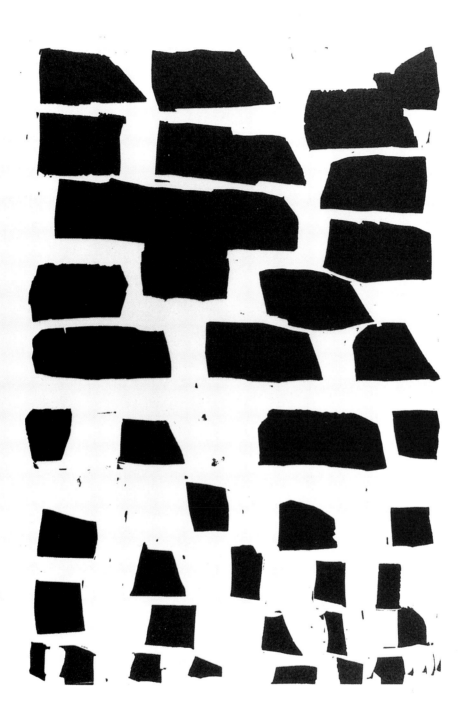

(1881-1973)

SIX CONTES FANTASQUES DE MAURICE TOESCA,
ILLUSTRÉS DE SIX BURINS PAR PICASSO ([PARIS:] FLAMMARION, 1953)
84 pp., 330 x 255 mm., with 6 dry-point engravings.
Edition of 225 copies (V&A copy no.67), of which 25 copies are on *Japon ancien* with a set of engravings on *Auvergne* (nos.1-25), 75 copies on *Vélin Monval* (nos.26-100), 100 copies on *Vergé d'Arches* (nos.101-200), and 25 copies numbered I-XXV. 30 sets of Picasso's engravings reserved for the publisher.
Printer: Lacourière, dry-points; Pierre Bouchet, wood engraved initial letters; L'Imprimerie Nationale, text, set in Grandjean Romain du Roi Corps 20 (completed 28 Oct.1953).
L.1105-1980.

Picasso's prints show no connection with the subjects of Toesca's tales.

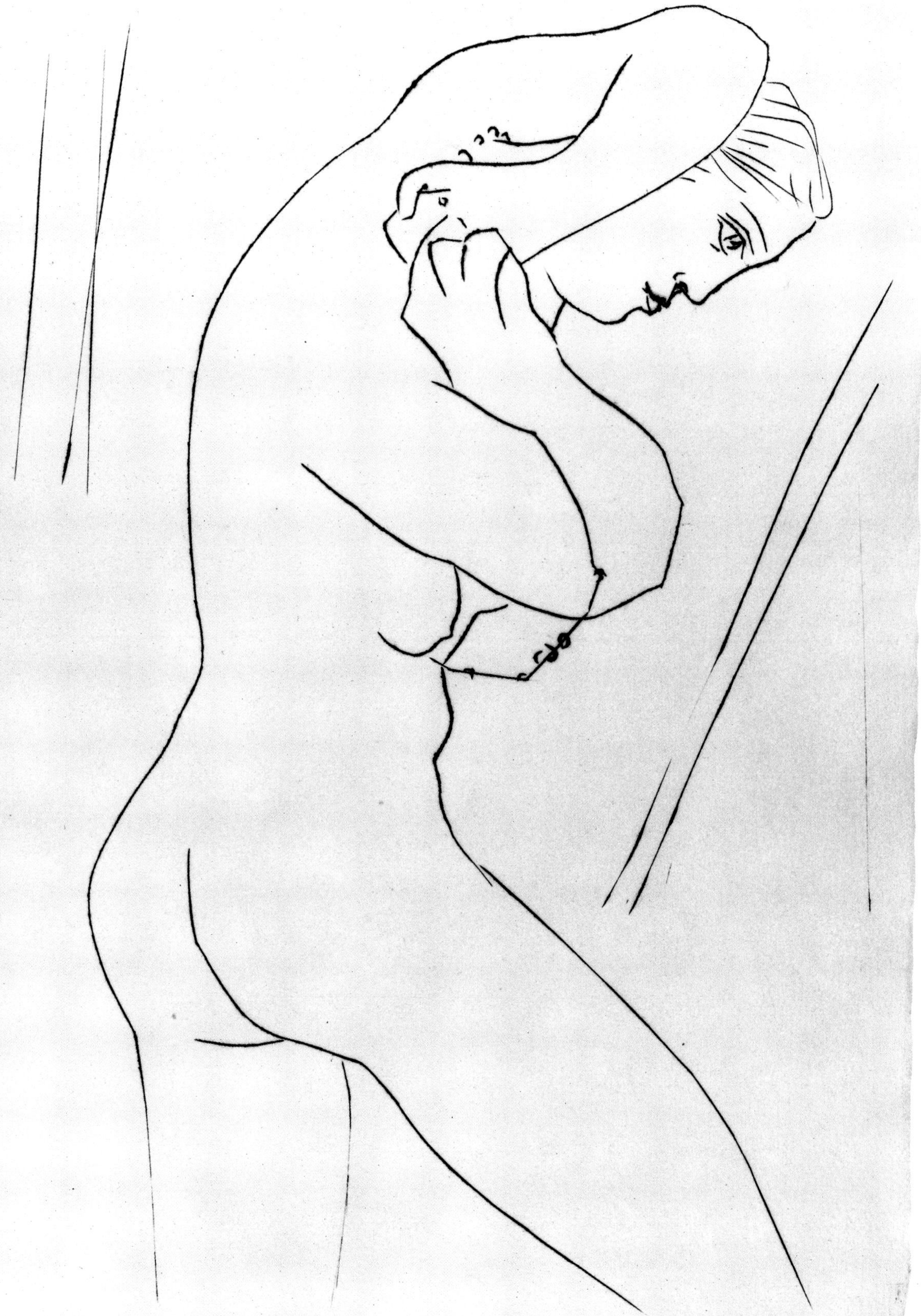

129 HENRI MATISSE **1954**

(1869-1954)

[EUGÈNE TOURQUET] JOHN-ANTOINE NAU, *POÉSIES ANTILLAISES . . . ILLUSTRÉES PAR HENRI MATISSE* (PARIS: MOURLOT, 1972).
168 pp., with 28 lithographs and lithographed cover, 390 x 290 mm.
Edition of 250 copies (V&A copy no. 233), on *Vélin d'Arches*, of which 50 copies have 12 extra original lithographs (nos. 1-50); also 25 copies *hors commerce* for collaborators and 'the family'.
Printer; Mourlot Frères, lithographs; Fequet et Baudier, text, set in Baskerville original corps 24 (completed April 1972).
L.949-1982.

The lithographs for *POÉSIES ANTILLAISES* were completed in 1954 and were published posthumously, though Matisse himself executed the lithographs, initial letters, decoration, and established the *mise en page* before his death. Nau was the pseudonym of Eugène Tourquet (1840-1918), who published his first volume of poetry, *AU SEUIL DE L'ESPOIR,* in 1897; his novel *FORCE ENNEMIE* was awarded the first Goncourt prize in 1903. Born in San Francisco, he spent the first part of his life as a sailor.

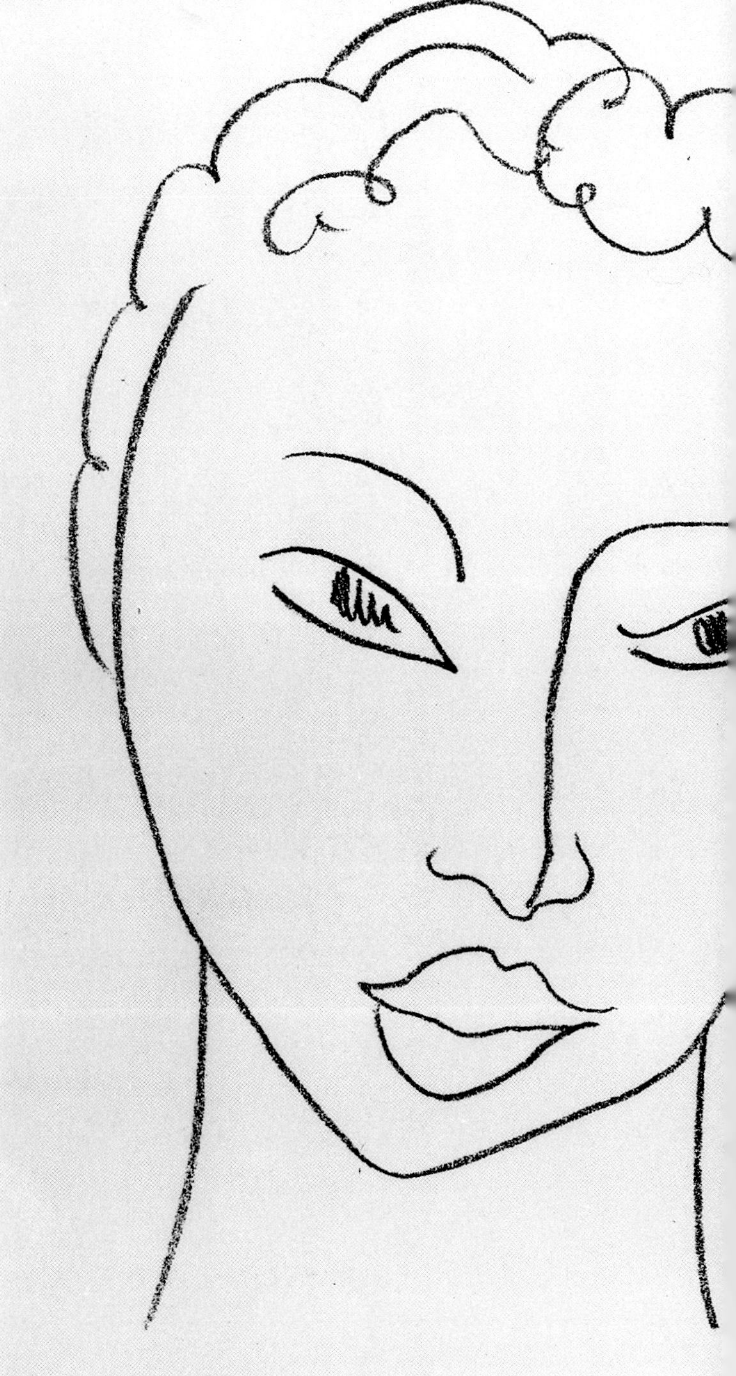

ous sommes, dans ce monde
où vaguent nos destins,
Deux voyageurs penchés
aux deux bords d'un abîme,
Très proches — à nous voir —
et pourtant très lointains,
Ne pouvant prendre pied
de l'une à l'autre cime ;

Deux flots, dans l'Océan,
qui veulent se mêler
Et qu'un courant maudit emporte en sens contraire,
Deux voix... dans le désert !... lasses de s'appeler
Et qu'étouffe en sanglots la bise funéraire.

Mais, le cher Avenir, ce dompteur de sanglots,
Miséricordieux, — car je souffre, et tu souffres !...
Fera duo les voix et vague les deux flots,
Transportera les monts et comblera les gouffres !

130 ANDY WARHOL **1959**

(b.1930) Warhol began his career with a course in pictorial design at the Carnegie Institute of Technology, Pittsburgh, in 1945-9, after which he worked as a commercial artist. He had his first exhibition, with Irving Sherman, at the Hugo Gallery, New York in 1952, showing drawings that were montage sequences of events in Truman Capote novels. In 1957, he won the Art Directors' Club medal for shoe advertisements. In the late 1950s he began painting subjects taken from everyday imagery, comics or enlargements of trade labels. 'Expressionist' treatment has been noticed in some of these, but from 1961-2 he produced totally realistic images, larger than life, which from 1962 were reproduced by a silkscreen process in vast quantities, among the earliest paintings treated in this way being 'Campbell's Soup Cans' and 'Coca-Cola Bottles'. Warhol was among the first artists who brought to POP ART *experience of commercial design methods, applying it to images of consumerist advertising and graphics in the same spirit as did Lichtenstein, Mel Ramos, Indiana and others. Making his first film in 1963,* SLEEP, *Warhol abandoned painting and became increasingly active as a film-maker from the mid-1960s.*

WILD RASPBERRIES BY ANDY WARHOL AND SUZIE FRANKFURT
([NEW YORK: SEYMOUR BERLIN 1959]).
40pp., 435 x 280 mm., with hand coloured plates.
No edition details.
Original pink binding.
L.1187-1984. Colour plate 19

Drawings and script are reproduced from originals in Warhol's hand. The volume of humorous recipes was one of 6 books of reproduced drawings produced by the artist between 1954 and 1959. Only a small number of copies of *WILD RASPBERRIES* were issued with plates coloured by the artist. An exhibition of his books with other early works was shown at the Gotham Book Mart, New York, in 1971.

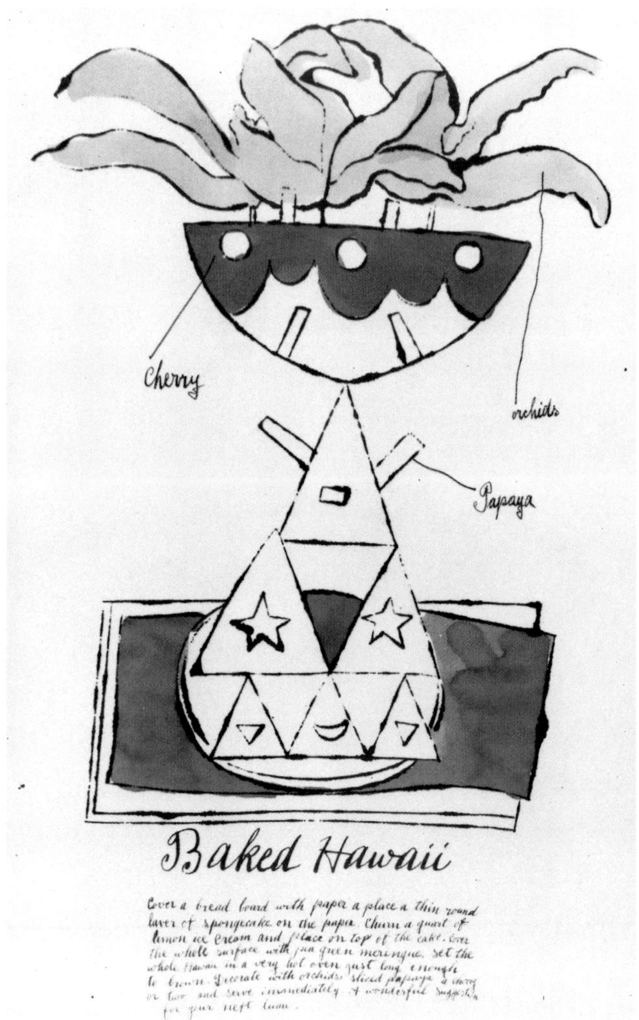

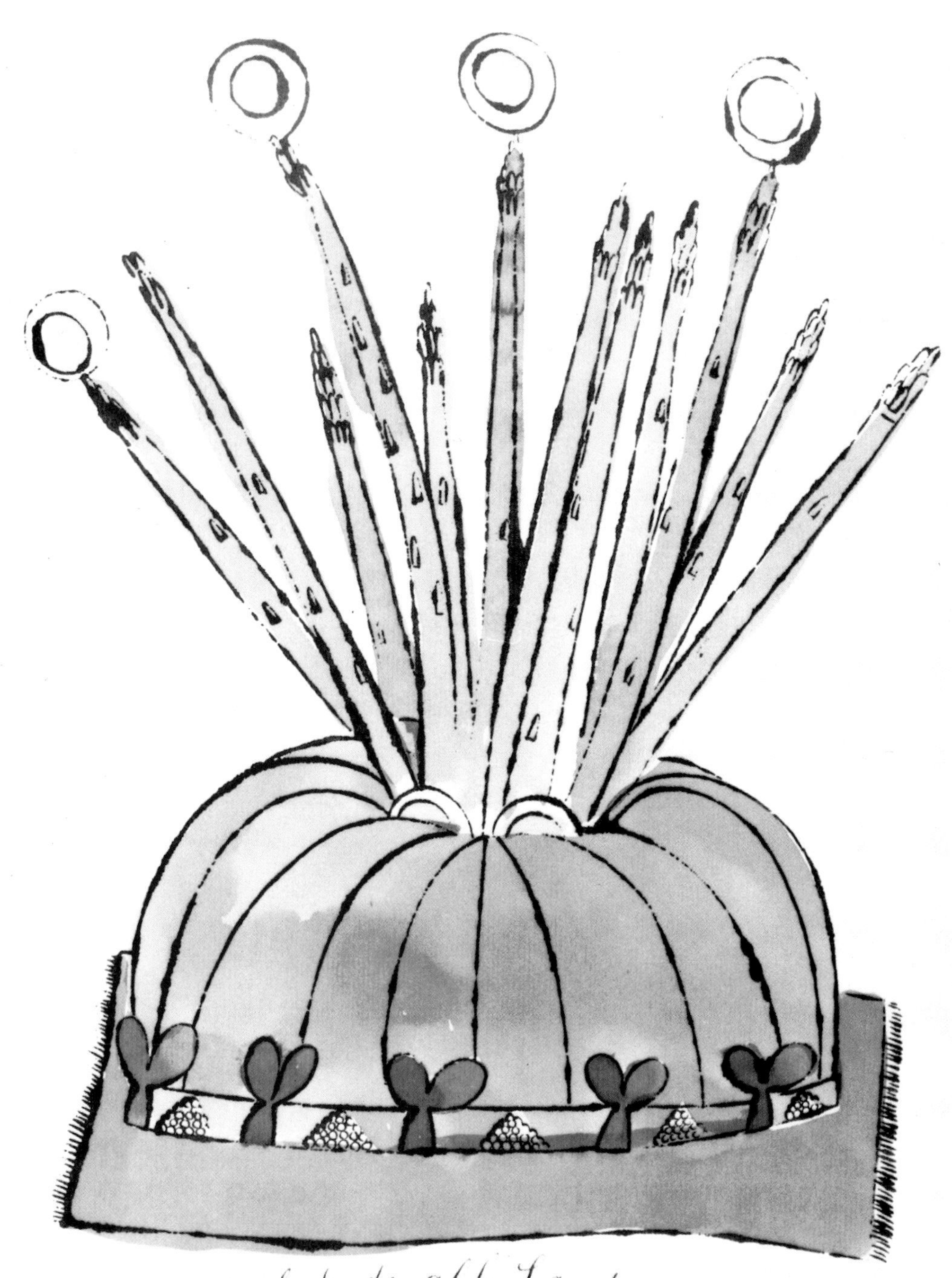

salade de alf Landon

Coat a bombe with very clear jelly and place in the bottom thin slices of sping-lobster tail decorated with capers. Fill the mould with green asparagus tips, hard boiled plovers' egg and sliced cock's kidneys mixed with bacon and dandelin dressing. Chill thoroughly and turn out on a napkin. Very popular as a first course at political dinners in the 30's.

131 MARIE-HELÈNE VIEIRA DA SILVA **1961**

(b.1908) Daughter of a Lisbon economist, Da Silva followed courses in sculpture and painting before coming to Paris in 1928. Here she studied at the Académie de la Grande Chaumière under Bourdelle and Despiau, after which she worked under Fernand Léger and at the workshop of Stanley Hayter. Crucial to her stylistic development were stays in Marseilles in 1931, where she drew and painted the Transporter Bridge, and then in Lisbon, where she was struck by the criss-cross of streets, both leading her to abstract compositions based on a grid of linear perspectives and contrasting planes. In 1932 she met Jeanne Bucher; her 1933 one-woman show in the Bucher Gallery was the first of many in her career. Spending the war in Lisbon and Buenos Aires, she was promoted on her return to Paris in 1947 by the dealer Pierre Loeb. Her first one-woman show in New York was held at the Cadby Birch Gallery in 1953. In 1961 she received the Premier Grand Prix in the São Paulo Biennale.

RENÉ CHAR, *L'INCLÉMENCE LOINTAINE, AVEC VINGT-CINQ GRAVURES AU BURIN DE VIEIRA DA SILVA* (PARIS: PIERRE BERÈS, 1961).
128pp., 460 x 330 mm., with 25 engravings.
Edition of 130 copies (V&A copy no. 118), signed by author and artist, on *Japon*, of which 10 copies have 2 sets of engravings, on *Peau de vélin* and *Japon* (nos. 1-10), 15 copies with a set of engravings on *Japon* (nos. 11-15), and 10 copies numbered I-X, (the 1st three with 2 sets of engravings and an original drawing, the 2nd three with a set of engravings on *Japon*).
Printer: Ateliers Leblanc (Charles), engravings; Adrian Frutiger, text, set in *MÉRIDIEN* (completed 23 May 1961).
L.3304-1961.

René Char asked Da Silva to illustrate eight poems he had written on *PAPIER D'ARCHES* in 1953, and the ensuing friendship between artist and poet resulted in the 1961 publication. Later Da Silva remembered that she had first heard of Char while working at Atelier 17, when Hayter announced that André Breton had just discovered a 'giant' in Provence. In 1964 she collaborated with Braque, Giacometti and Miró in providing illustrations for P.A. Benoît's *BIBLIOGRAPHIE DES OEUVRES DE RENÉ CHAR DE 1928 À 1963.* In 1975 the poet and artist worked together on the book *SEPT PORTRAITS* to celebrate their friendship and collaboration over the years.

132 GEORGES BRAQUE **1962**

(1882-1963)

GEORGES BRAQUE AND SAINT-JOHN PERSE,
L'ORDRE DES OISEAUX (PARIS: AU VENT D'ARLES, 1962).
54pp., 420 x 230 mm., with 12 coloured engravings.
Edition of 130 copies (V&A copy no. 99), of which 30 copies are numbered I-XXX and have a set of engravings signed and numbered by the artist, and 100 copies signed by the artist and author; also 20 copies *hors commerce,* and 2 copies numbered 0 and 00 for deposit under copyright law. All on Richard de Bas hand-made paper.
Printer: Atelier Crommelynck, engravings; L'Imprimerie Union, Paris, text, set in Garamond Corps 24 (completed 22 June 1962).
Binding by Jean Duval.
L.5933-1984. Colour plate 20.

The manuscript and engravings of *L'ORDRE DES OISEAUX* were exhibited at the Bibliothèque Nationale, Paris, from December 1962 to January 1963. Saint-John Perse was commissioned to provide a text on the theme of birds late in January 1962, while Braque began his engravings early the following month. The first volumes appeared on 1 August of that year, shortly after the painter's 80th birthday (13 May). The plate on p. 37 of *L'ORDRE DES OISEAUX* was used as a design for a postage stamp by the French Post Office.

(b.1924) Born to an Italian family with an ice-cream making business in the Edinburgh docklands, Paolozzi attended evening classes at the Edinburgh College of Art (intending to become a commercial artist) and studied at the Slade School after demobilization. After his first exhibition, at the Mayor Gallery in 1947, he went to Paris for two years, visiting a number of artists including Léger (who arranged for a special performance of BALLET MÉCANIQUE*), Arp (to whom he was introduced by Peggy Guggenheim), Giacometti, Dubuffet and Tristan Tzara; an exhibition of Ernst and Duchamp at the Galerie Raymond Duncan demonstrated the possibilities of collage to someone already collecting 'popular' ephemera; from this time Paolozzi began systematically to collect material with glossy and other images of popular culture, much of it from US servicemen. This was the material that he showed in slides at a celebrated lecture in 1952 to the Independent group at the ICA, the cuttings from magazines, comics, advertisements, labels and ephemera providing 'an encyclopedic panorama of the conscious and unconscious needs of an epoch'; in 1972 the collages of 1947-52 were published as screenprints with the title* BUNK*. In the mid-1950s, Paolozzi, Richard Hamilton and the critic Lawrence Alloway laid the ground for the emerging* POP ART *(see cat. 155). From 1949 to 1958, Paolozzi taught at the Central School and St. Martin's School of Art; as well as producing silkscreen collages and sculptures, he designed wall-papers and fabrics for Horrocks & Co. The series of prints* AS IS WHEN*, published in 1964, took as its theme the life and writings of Wittgenstein, and has been seen as the end of his involvement with the 'American Dream' (Exhibition Catalogue:* PAOLOZZI*, Tate Gallery, 1971, p.20). From 1967 he taught ceramics at the Royal College of Art. Recently he designed the mosaic wall in Tottenham Court Road Underground Station in London. The Krazy Kat archive consists of Paolozzi's collection of magazines, toys, ephemera, etc., that conveys the basic images of 20th century consumer culture. Elected an Associate of the Royal Academy in 1972, he became an R.A. in 1979.*

E.L. PAOLOZZI, *METAFISIKAL TRANSLATIONS*
([LONDON, 1962]).
48pp., 300 x 210 mm., each page screenprinted.
Edition: '55/100' marked on page 1 in pencil [according to R. Miles, *THE COMPLETE PRINTS OF EDUARDO PAOLOZZI, 1944-77*, 1977, p.66, there were two editions of 100, 1 with cover in 'bright colour', the other with a red cover (the V&A copy has a white cover); on All British Cartridge paper].
Printer: Kelpra Studio Ltd.
L.5915-1984.

The tone is set in the first few pages, where 'Shooting Script' is followed by 'Notes on the Film The History of Nothing'. When teaching in Hamburg in 1960-62, Paolozzi had made an animated film of stills consisting of pages of books illustrating interiors, landscapes, machinery and robots. In the film, the images were flashed on the screen with exotic, primitive music, whereas in the book the images are mixed with a suitable stuttering accompaniment of words.

The book represents an early project carried out with the Kelpra Press. Chris Prater, formerly a commercial printer, had set up the independent Kelpra printmaking studio in 1957, two years after Robert Erskine had founded the St. George's Gallery to encourage British printmaking. In 1960 he did some silkscreen work for Gordon House which marked his entry into 'fine art' printing. Paolozzi, who had engaged in screen printing when at the Central School and who intitially contacted Prater for the reproduction of collages, and Richard Hamilton were the two artists who immediately seized the potential of Prater's expertise. Hamilton persuaded the ICA to commission 24 artists to make screenprints at the Kelpra Studio, a scheme which introduced RB Kitaj, Caulfield, Harold Cohen, Joe Tilson and others to the process; an exhibition of the work was held in 1964 (see Exhibition Catalogue: Tate Gallery, 1980; *KELPRA STUDIO*). Behind this revival of screen printing in the 1960s were technological advances involving the use of a photographic breakdown of the image into small dots which allow gradations of tone and colour. The Studio was much used by artists associated with Pop Art (though Bridget Riley and Joan Miró also used it), where the technique could produce a suitably glossy and glamorous image.

FINALE DIALONE
TO BE ATLAZFAFOR
COMBINATION KONO·
ONE IS MANNIKIN
WITHOUT ASSEMBLY
TRIPLFINX IMAGES
PROTECTED ON A
LARGE BUTTRESS
FABRIK ELECT
FLUID SILHOUETTE
CONFIRMS L'IQUID
SHADOW HUMANTEK
SCALE REMINDER

DOMINANT DOMINO DOME
CYTI KITY KITE SLOPPING
OFF PISTOLMATIC AUTOP
BY GOTHIK FORRCE CALLED
BY&BY SPHINX ASE FLOR ENTPE
ANCE ANGEL DRUM PAGE
CROWNEN TOWER OF HOMAGE
SAVAGE IDOLS JUPITER HOUS
TRANSFORMED TRANTSFORMER
PINACLES OF AND MELO- PLAY
DRAMA LAVA CAVURKKINKS
ARENA OF SHAME FIGHT SHAM
SPERMATI CONCLUSION CAJUPUT
GIVE IDEL WITTNESS MAGNETTO
NEOCLUNING KAM OF OZ SAILAK
SYMETRICAL PRECISION SAGE
TEMPLE OF KALEE TRUGEDY
&ALTERED MOUNTED COMEDY
TRAGOEDIEN DER SAPPHOTRAMS
HEAVEN TO MEDALS SCALES BI
TRIREALLITY MOLTEN ZINC CAN
UMBRELLACATHEDRALE IN MAPP
OR IN MINATURE ITEMS LIVING
IN THIS PERIOD ORSERVE PAN
JIGSAW PUNCH & KOSMOS

134 MARINO MARINI **1963**

(1901-1980) Son of a bank manager, Marini visited Paris briefly in 1919 before studying painting at the Florence Academy. His early paintings show the influence of the VALORI PLASTICI *movement that promoted a self consciously Italian tradition comprising Etruscan, Renaissance and current avant-garde figurative art. On a visit to Paris in 1928, he met Picasso, Braque, Maillol and others; his exclusive devotion to sculpture dates from after this trip. He had his first one-man show at the Galleria Milano, Milan, in 1934, and won the Grand Prix for sculpture at the Rome Quadriennale in 1935. From 1940 he taught sculpture at the Brera Academy, Milan. His works on the theme of the horseman began in 1936. His studio burnt out (and much work lost) during a bombing raid, Marini spent the war years in Switzerland, where he was in contact with Giacometti. The post-war years saw a notable series of portraits in sculpture, Carra (1946), Stravinsky (1951), Henry Miller (1961), Arp, Chagall and Henry Moore (1962). Among his major retrospective exhibitions was that at the Kunsthaus, Zurich, in 1962.*

IDEA E SPAZIO. EAUX-FORTES ORIGINALES DE MARINO MARINI. POÈMES D'EGLE MARINI (PARIS: LES CENT BIBLIOPHILES DE FRANCE ET D'AMERIQUE, 1963).
44 ff., 510 x 380 mm., with 12 etchings.
Edition of 128 copies (V&A copy no.115), on *Grand vélin de Rives*, signed by the artist, of which 100 were destined for the CENT BIBLIOPHILES and 28 for the artist, author and
310 collaborators.
Printer: Atelier Crommelynck.
L.307-1964. Colour plate 21.

Marini had illustrated the poems of his sister, Egle, on two previous occasions: *POÉSIE* (Milan: Edizioni dei Milione, 1957) and *GEDICHTE* (Frankfurt: S. Fischer Verlag, 1958). The poems in *IDEA E SPAZIO* are in Italian. The book was the fourth publication of *LES CENTS BIBLIOPHILES DE FRANCE ET D'AMÉRIQUE* and its production was arranged by Madame Pierre de Harting.

135 SAM FRANCIS **1964**

(b.1923) Son of a mathematician, Francis studied psychology and medicine at Berkeley, California, also taking lessons in painting from David Parks before joining the army in 1943. Invalided out of the army with tuberculosis, he gained his MA in Art from Berkeley in 1950 before joining the Académie Léger in Paris. In Paris, he met Jean-Paul Riopelle, Matisse's son-in-law Georges Duthuit and others. He had an exhibition in the Nina Dausset Gallery, Paris, in 1952, and in 1956 had another organised by Michel Tapié, who had already claimed him as representative of 'UN ART AUTRE', *a 'Tachiste', and a 'signifier of the informal' who brought a new spatial dimension to this art on a scale second only to Jackson Pollock. In 1960, Francis began to make lithographs with Emil Mathieu in Zurich, producing his celebrated 'Blue Balls' series. A globe-trotting traveller, his work of the 1960s has been described as 'Oriental sensibility with a simplicity...closely allied to contemporary Minimalist trends.'*

1 ¢ LIFE. WRITTEN BY WALASSE TING. EDITED BY SAM FRANCIS. PUBLISHED BY EW KORNFELD (BERNE: EW KORNFELD, 1964).
176 pp., 410 x 290mm., with 68 lithographs by 28 artists.

Regular edition of 2000 (V&A copy no.471); special edition of 100, printed on handmade paper, all numbered and signed by the artists: 20 New York edition, 20 Paris edition, 20 rest of world, 40 reserved for the participating artists and collaborators.
Printer: Maurice Beaudet, Paris, lithographs; Georges Girard, Paris, typography.
L.5854-1982. Colour plate 22.

Ting, a friend of Francis since his first Paris days, initiated the project to produce the 'most international' book as an illustration to his own poetry. The idea was conceived during a casual meeting in Sam Francis's studio in New York. Francis was editor, and apart from contributing 6 lithographs elicited work from, among others, Pierre Alechinsky, Karel Appel, Alan Davie, Jim Dine, Roy Lichtenstein, Asger Jorn, Claes Oldenburg, Robert Rauschenberg, Riopelle and Andy Warhol. The poet, editor and publisher signed the title page beside stamps of Chinese characters bearing their names.

AMERICA

brain made by IBM & FBI
stomach supported by A&P
and Horn & Hardart
love supported by Time & Life
tongue supported by
American Telephone & Telegraph
soul made by 7up
skin start with Max Factor
heart red as U.S. Steel

three thousand miles
blue sky wallpaper
salt lake city kitchen
new england green garden
florida warm bed
new york city shining mirror
big mountain walk, big river sing
big tree fly in california
green banana hang
under new moon in montana
sun spit out sweet candy
in north dakota
star turn big diamond in iowa

red american as pumpkin
black american as horse
yellow american as sunflower
white american as fat woman
fat woman cut pumpkin
put sunflower in corner
push horse in dark
pumpkin dead
sunflower sad
horse angry
fat woman afraid horse make love
she stay alone
with
a
gun

153

ABOVE Mel Ramos.

RIGHT Francis. Ting Tong.

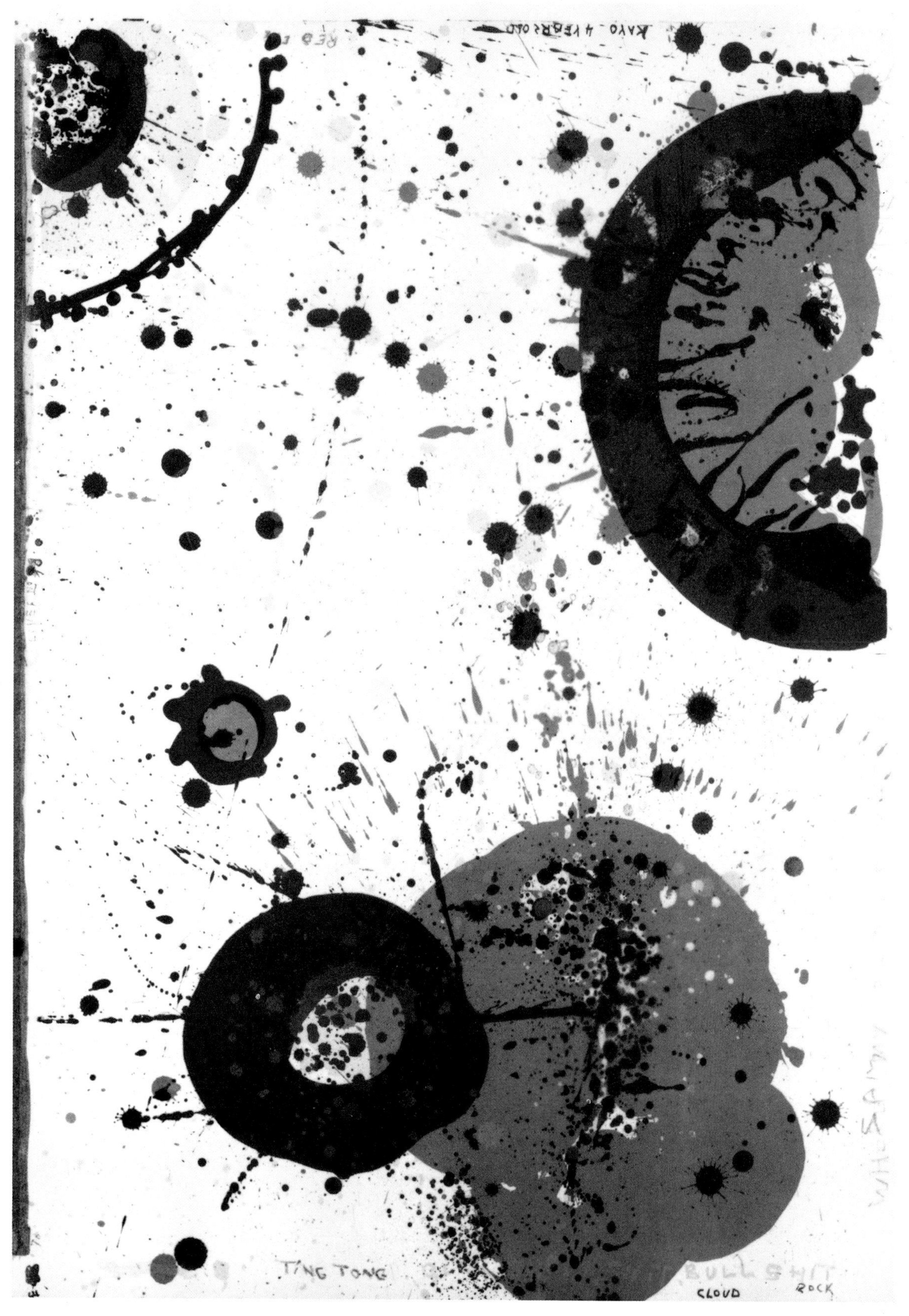
TING TONG
BULL SHIT
CLOUD
ROCK

136 ROBERTO MATTA ECHAURREN **1966**

(b. 1911) After studying architecture at the Catholic University of Santiago, Chile, Matta went to France in 1933, where he worked at Marseilles in the office of Le Corbusier until 1935. He began painting in 1938. The poet Garcia Lorca, whom he had met in Spain in 1936, presented him to Salvador Dali who then introduced him to André Breton and Surrealist circles in Paris. Matta followed a number of these artists to New York in 1939, and was much impressed with the vestiges of ancient cultures during a trip to Mexico in 1941 with Robert Motherwell. In 1948 he returned to Europe, a move that in many ways marked a break with post-war Surrealism, and lived successively in Paris, Rome, Bologna and Paris. In 1956 he painted a mural for the UNESCO *building in Paris, and in 1962 exhibited at the Biennale of Saõ Paulo, being awarded the Prix Marzotto. In the 1970s, he held several exhibitions in protest against the Chilean Junta, and travelled widely.*

JOYCE MANSOUR, *LES DAMNATIONS. GRAVURES ORIGINALES DE MATTA* (PARIS: EDITIONS GEORGES VISAT, 1966).
72 pp., 420 x 340 mm., with 11 etchings, 6 of them full-page, and a separate set of the same etchings. Edition of 75 copies numbered 1-75, on *Vélin d'Arches,* signed by author and artist, and 10 copies reserved for collaborators numbered I-X, each with a separate set of engravings on *Japon nacré*; V&A copy printed for M. Ernst Maget.
L.908-1982.

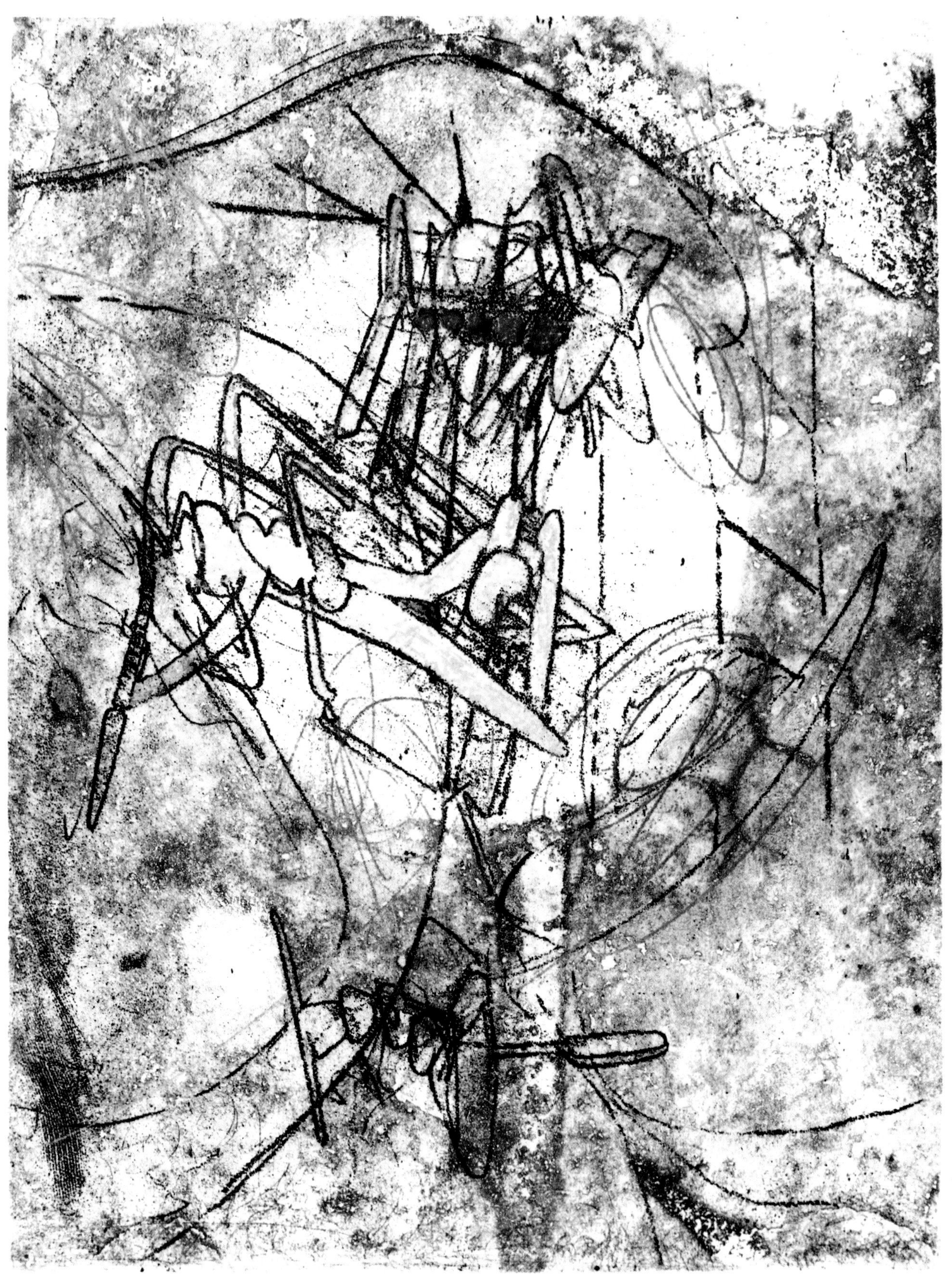

137 DAVID HOCKNEY **1966**

(b. 1937) After studying at Bradford College of Art in his home town, and refusing to do military service as a conscientious objector, Hockney worked at the Royal College of Art, London, from 1959 to 1962; his contemporaries here were Derek Boshier, Allen Jones, Peter Phillips, Max Shepherd, Norman Toynton and Brian Wright, and they exhibited together in the John Moores Liverpool exhibition in 1961 and at the Grabowsky Gallery, London, in 1962. At the 'Graven Image' exhibition at the Royal Academy in 1961-2, Hockney was awarded the Guinness prize for engraving. His first one-man show was at the Kasmin Gallery in 1963, 'Pictures with people in'. His first published suite of etchings, THE RAKE'S PROGRESS. appeared in 1963 and was shown at the Museum of Modern Art, New York, in 1964. In that year, Hockney went to North America, teaching at Iowa, Colorado and California Universities, and since then has travelled widely. His first professional work for the theatre was the designing, in 1966, of costumes for Jarry's UBU ROI at the Royal Court Theatre, London; other commissions included Stravinsky's RAKE'S PROGRESS and the MAGIC FLUTE for the Glyndebourne Opera House. A consummate draughtsman, he illustrated poems as a student, but only in 1966 did he provide graphic work for books. Hockney has experimented with photography since his art school days; among his recent photographic work have been 'joiners', sequential views of a scene pasted together, the image being produced by colour polaroid photography.

316 *FOURTEEN POEMS BY C.P. CAVAFY, CHOSEN AND ILLUSTRATED WITH TWELVE ETCHINGS BY DAVID HOCKNEY, TRANSLATED BY NIKOS STANGOS AND STEPHEN SPENDER*
(LONDON: EDITIONS ALECTO LIMITED, 1966).
35 ff., 465 x 330 mm., with 12 etchings.
Published in 5 editions (A-E), editions A and B nos. 1-500 bound as volumes (V&A copy no. 411).
Edition A: 250 copies signed by the artist with 1 signed etching loose, on Crisbrook Waterleaf 140 lb Imperial made by J. Barcham Green Ltd and Hesivier Art Drawing 75 lb Imperial by H.V. Seir Ltd, sewn by Tillotsons (Boulton) Ltd and bound by Galerie der Spiegel, Cologne (nos. 1-250), with further 50 copies signed 'artist's proof'.
Edition B: 250 copies signed by the artist, on Crisbrook Waterleaf 140 lb Imperial made by J. Barcham Green and Hevisier Art Drawing 75 lb Imperial by H.V. Seir Ltd (nos. 251-500), bound as edition A.
Edition C: 50 sets of 12 original etchings numbered 1-50 of 75 signed by the artist, on Crisbrook Waterleaf 140 lb Imperial made by J. Barcham Green.
Edition D: 25 sets of 12 original etchings numbered 51-75 of 75 signed by the artist, with 15 additional portfolio sets signed 'artist's proof', boxed by Galerie der Spiegel, Cologne.
Edition E: 25 sets of 12 original etchings signed by the artist with text and one signed original etching Portrait of Cavafy II, in portfolio, on Vellum Wove 72 lb Royal made by J. Barcham Green, numbered I-XXV, boxed in a leather portfolio made by Galerie der Spiegel, Cologne, with 5 further portfolios signed 'artist's proof'.
L.3617-1971

Hockney quoted lines from the Greek poet Cavafy in his etching of 1961, *MIRROR, MIRROR ON THE WALL*, and the project of 1966 to illustrate the poet's work derived from the artist himself. It was to be the first major series of etchings since *THE RAKE'S PROGRESS* of 1963. Hockney visited Beirut in early 1966 in order to seize the atmosphere of a city that matched the cosmopolitain quality of Cavafy's Alexandria. The original conception proving over-ambitious, Hockney confined himself to illustrations from poems offering a celebration of homosexual love. Constantine Cavafy (1863-1933) has been called 'a poet of the Greek diaspora'; spending most of his life in Alexandria, he stood apart from the folkloristic and nationalist orientations of poets on the Greek mainland and evidences a sensibility and aestheticism that aligns him with poetic currents of metropolitan Europe.

Editions Allecto were formed to publish original graphic prints in 1963, with a studio in Kelso Place, Kensington. The inspiration came from Michael Deakin when a student at Cambridge with Paul Cornwall-Jones, and the initial idea was to produce topographical prints aimed at universities. Cornwall-Jones joined with Joe Studholme from Oxford and Mark Glazebrook to form the company, and for a time worked closely with the St. George's Gallery Prints in Cork Street established eight years earlier by the Hon. Robert Erskine. Their first portfolio set of prints was *THE RAKE'S PROGRESS*, sixteen original etchings by David Hockney, The Cavafy Poems of 1966 were the first work produced as an illustrated book, and indeed they have since made only one other – *THE RIME OF THE ANCIENT MARINER*, 1977, by Patrick Procktor. But they did also produce a number of suites of prints eg. by Eduardo Paolozzi, such as Moonstrip Empire News, and General Dynamic F.U.N..

Cornwall-Jones left the firm in 1967 to set up the Petersburg Press, since when the direction has been continued by Joe Studholme.

C.P. CAVAFY IN ALEXANDRIA

HIS MASTER'S VOICE
S. AUDI & FRERES

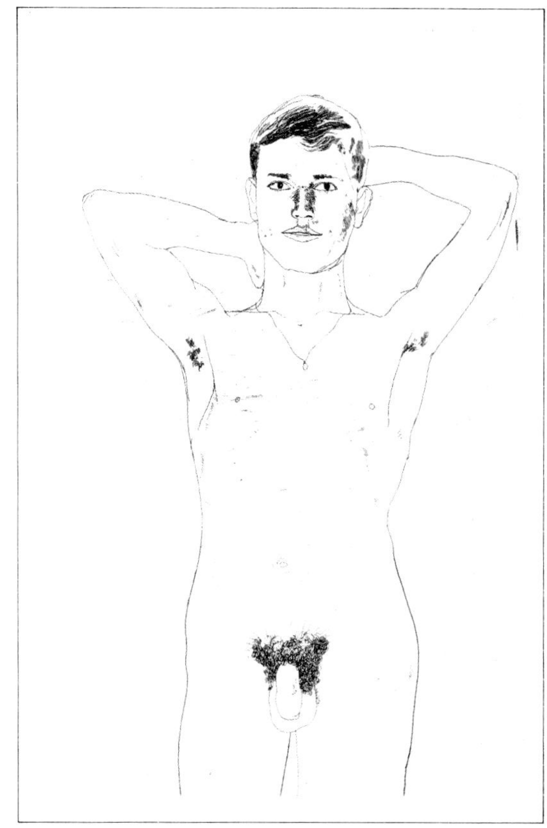

138 WILLEM DE KOONING **1967**

(b.1904) Before leaving for America in 1926, De Kooning served an apprenticeship in a firm of commercial artists in Rotterdam, attended the Fine Art Academy, and worked for Bernard Romein, whose avant-garde interests De Kooning shunned for the more comfortable world of ART NOUVEAU. *In the US he came under the influence of Kandinsky's work and met Arshile Gorky, with whom he was later to share a studio. In the 1930s the support of the Federal Arts Project enabled him to devote all his time to painting; he engaged in abstract and figural works and a number of major murals. He first exhibited his abstract-Surrealist works in New York in 1942, and had his first one-man show at the Egan Gallery in 1946. Thereafter he developed his own brand of* ABSTRACT-EXPRESSIONISM *and action-painting. Major retrospective exhibitions of his work were held in Antwerp, London and New York in 1968 and 1969.*

IN MEMORY OF MY FEELINGS. A SELECTION OF POEMS BY FRANK O'HARA EDITED BY BILL BERKSON (NEW YORK: THE MUSEUM OF MODERN ART, [1967]).
220pp., (i.e. 55 bifolia) unbound, 305 x 230 mm., with 54 illustrations.
Edition of 2500 copies (V&A copy no. 717), on Mohawk SuperfineSmooth paper.
Printer: Crafton Graphic Company Inc, set in Times Roman by The Composing Room Inc.
L.1009-1968.

De Kooning initially executed drawings as a 'warming up' process before embarking on an oil painting, but by the late 1960s, drawings in ink and black enamel became works in their own right. He favoured high-velocity sketches using soft charcoal, as here, which he would then smear and smudge to achieve the required effects. De Kooning used his left hand and closed his eyes in many instances when making drawings of this kind.

Frank O'Hara was a poet and Curator of the Museum of Modern Art at the time of his death in an accident in 1966. At that date he had just secured the agreement of De Kooning, a close friend, to a major touring exhibition of his work. The artist contributed three charcoal sketches to accompany the 'Ode to Willem de Kooning' in the commemorative volume of O'Hara's verse published in 1967. Thirty poems appeared in the volume, and were decorated by contemporary artists associated with O'Hara, including Rauschenberg, Johns, Lichtenstein, Guston, Oldenburg and Elaine de Kooning.

318

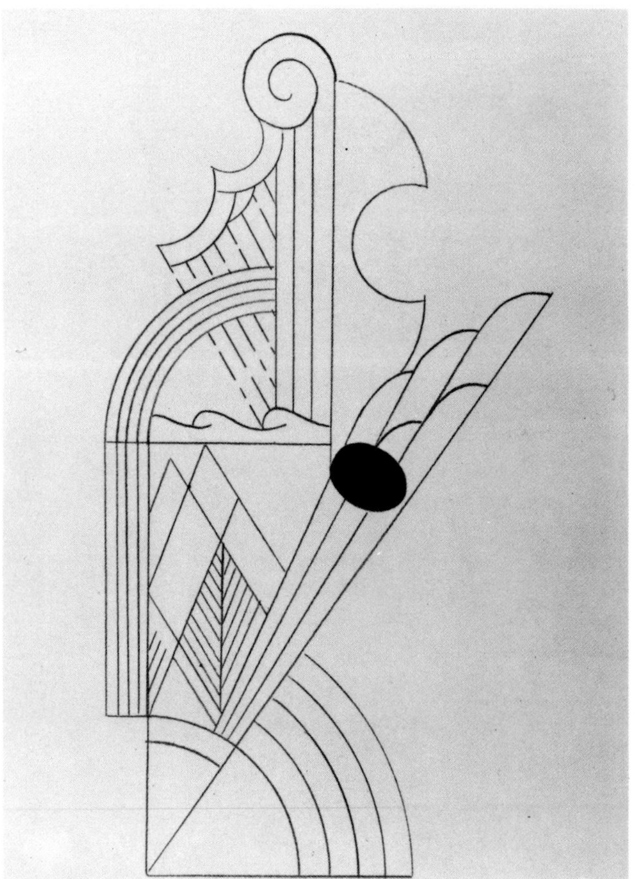

ABOVE Roy Lichtenstein.

ABOVE Philip Guston.

RIGHT De Kooning.

139 MIGUEL BERROCAL **1967**

(b.1933) After graduating in mathematics and chemistry at Madrid University, Berrocal studied architecture and sculpture at the San Fernando School of Fine Arts, becoming a pupil of the sculptor Angel Ferrant. In 1952 he moved to Italy, living chiefly in Rome and Verona, where he set up his own foundry and press. In 1958 he had his first one-man exhibition at the 'La Medusa' Gallery in Rome. From this date he lived much of the year in Paris. In 1964 he was on the jury of the Paris Biennale, and won the sculpture prize at the Biennale of 1966. In that year he became professor at the Staatliche Hochschule für Bildende Künste in Hamburg. The bulk of his sculptural work depicts the human torso, the preferred material being bronze polished to a high finish, together with 'assemblages'.

[ALEXIS LÉGER] SAINT-JOHN PERSE, *ANABASE.* *SEGUITA DALLE TRADUZIONI DI T.S. ELIOT E GIUSEPPE UNGARETTI. ILLUSTRATA DA BERROCAL (NOVE INCISIONI IN LINOLEUM A COLORE)* (VERONA: LE RAME, 1967).

268ff., 340 x 245 mm., signed by the artist, with 9 colour linocuts and cover illustrations.
Edition of 125 copies numbered 1-99 (V&A copy no.30) with 26 copies *hors commerce* (nos. A-Z).
Binding in *Carta Roma di Fabriano* with 2 drawings by the artist executed in relief on the covers by Giovanni de Stefanis.
Printer: Stamperia Valdonego (text set in Bembo).
L.5043-1967.

Alexis Léger (b.1887), who wrote under the pseudonym of St. John Perse, had a distinguished career as a diplomat for the French Government. His first poetry was published in 1911, followed by *ANABASE* in 1924. In 1960 he was awarded the Nobel Prize for Literature. The colophon of this edition states that it was printed on the occasion of the poet's 80th birthday.

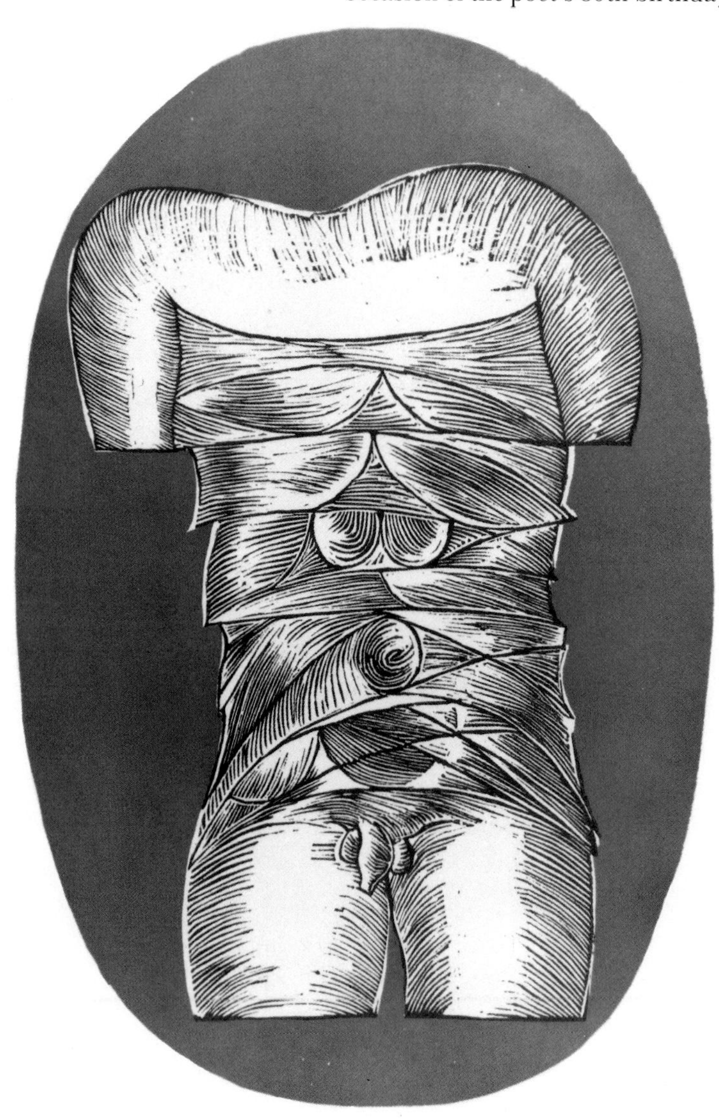

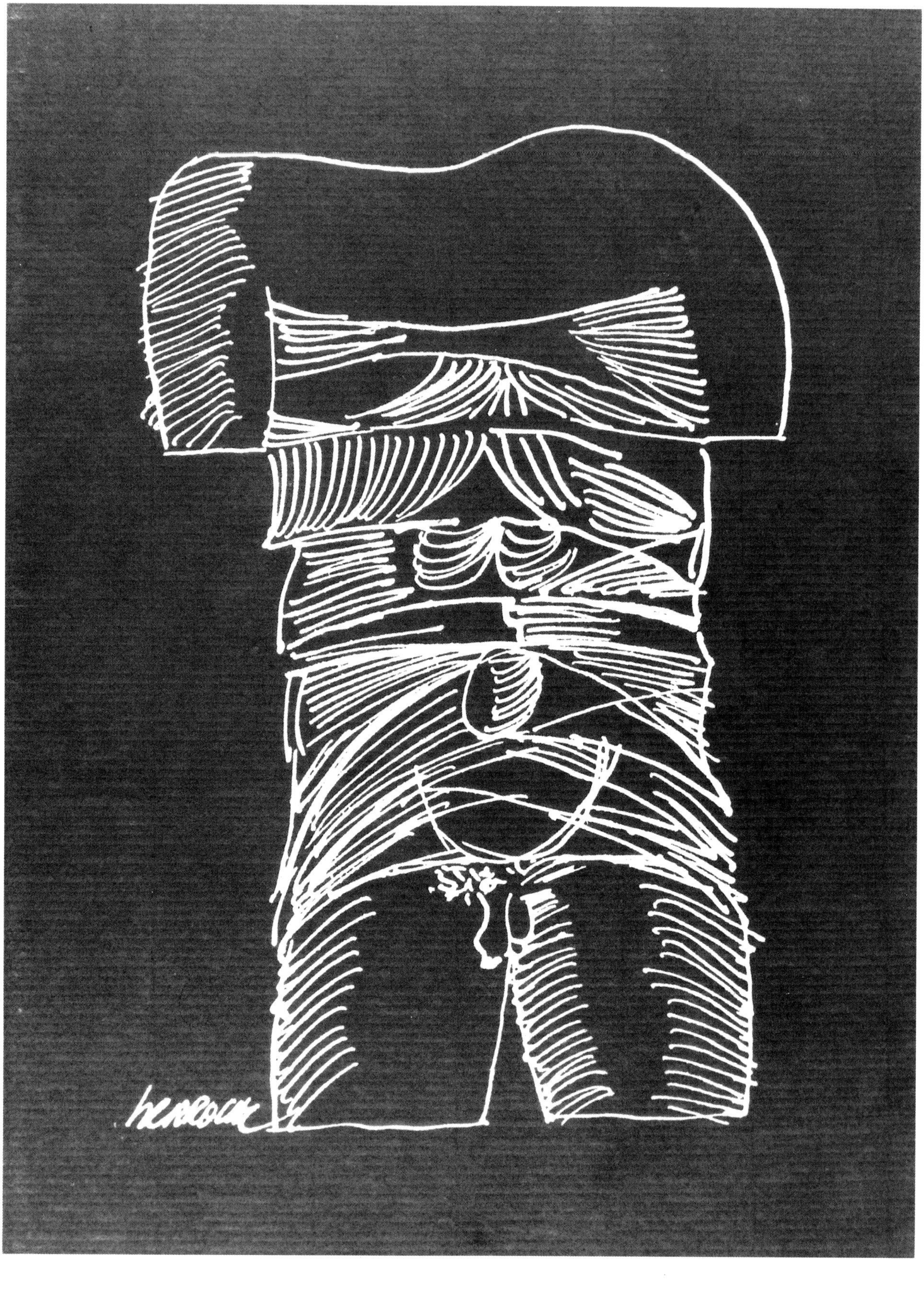

140 JEAN DUBUFFET **1967**

(b.1901)

MAX LOREAU AND JEAN DUBUFFET,
CERCEAUX 'SORCELLENT (PARIS: JEANNE BUCHER, AND BASEL: EDITIONS BEYELER, 1967).
56pp., 270 x 215 mm., with 20 prints and 1 on cover.
Edition of 800 copies numbered 1-750 (V&A copy no. 38) with 50 *hors commerce*.
Printer: La Ruche, Paris (completed 30 June 1967).
L.423-1968. Colour plate 23.

Dubuffet's illustrations here are in the manner he developed after 1962 in the HOURLOUPE series which began, according to Loreau, when the artist was drawing distractedly during a telephone call in July 1962 and which was shown in the Jeanne Bucher Gallery in 1967. Loreau (b.1928), a poet of Belgian origins, has written a number of books on Dubuffet, and in 1964 began to publish a catalogue of his work.

(b.1928) A Londoner, Cohen studied at the Slade School of Art in 1948-51, lecturing on art history at Camberwell School of Art in 1952-54 before returning to the Slade to teach in 1962-8. A trip to North America in 1959-61 curbed an interest in ABSTRACT EXPRESSIONISM. *Major exhibitions of his work were shown at the Whitechapel Art Gallery in 1965 and at the Victoria and Albert Museum in 1968. In 1969, he moved to the University of California, San Diego, where he devoted himself to computer art. Moving onto progressively larger computers at the Artificial Intelligence Laboratory at Stanford and San Diego, he was able to exhibit a drawing machine powered by a computer at the Los Angeles Museum of Art in 1972. Other exhibitions of such equipment have been held at the Stedelijk Museum, Amsterdam in 1977, and at the Tate gallery and Arnolfini, Bristol, in 1983; the machines featured were capable of drawing 12 random images an hour, which Cohen then coloured. Since 1972, Cohen has rarely produced his own canvases.*

HAROLD PINTER, *THE HOMECOMING. IMAGES: HAROLD COHEN* (LONDON: KARNAC CURWEN, 1968).
76pp., 435 x 345 mm., with 9 photolithographs and 1 image on front cover.
Edition of 200 copies (V&A copy no. 102), on paper made by J. Barcham Green, signed by the author and artist, with 25 copies *hors commerce* (I-XXV).
Printer: Curwen Press, text, set in a photographically
324 modified version of Boldini Bold; Harold Cohen, lithographs and cover image.
Binding by Mansell, London.
L.4400-1979. Colour plate 24.

This edition was designed entirely by Harold Cohen and produced by the artist in collaboration with Robert Simon between April 1967 and July 1968. The text was made available by Methuen & Co.; Harold Pinter added amendments in March 1968. A woven terylene was used for the binding, which was coloured and processed by the artist.

First performed in 1965 as Pinter's third major play, *THE HOMECOMING*, revolved around an East-ender who had risen to become a University Professor at an American University bringing home his American wife to meet his family. Cohen himself in 1968 was about to leave Britain to become a Professor at a University in California, where he had first met his own wife. It was in America that Cohen's art turned towards the computer.

Harry Karnac is primarily a bookseller, established in Kensington since 1950 and specialising in second-hand works on Freudian psycho-analysis. During the 1960s he collected artists' illustrated books as a personal interest, and was frustrated to find that hardly any English works had been published; he conceived the ambition to bring one out himself. In the event, his *HOMECOMING* is the only one of its kind that he would issue, although he went on to publish unillustrated editions of four other Pinter titles – *FIVE SCREEN PLAYS*, and *OLD TIMES* (1971), *NO MAN'S LAND* (1975) and *BETRAYAL* (1978). Since 1977, his main endeavours in publishing have been The Maresfield Library series on psycho-analysis, in which 32 titles have so far appeared.

Robert Simon of the Curwen Press introduced Pinter to Harold Cohen; the book won Third Prize in the international Lion d'Or competition, Monte Carlo, in 1969.

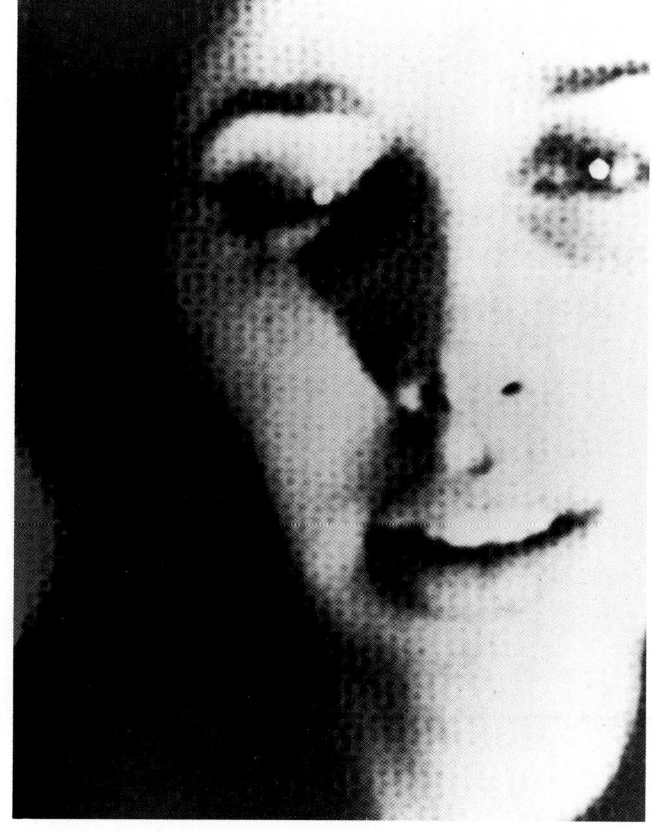

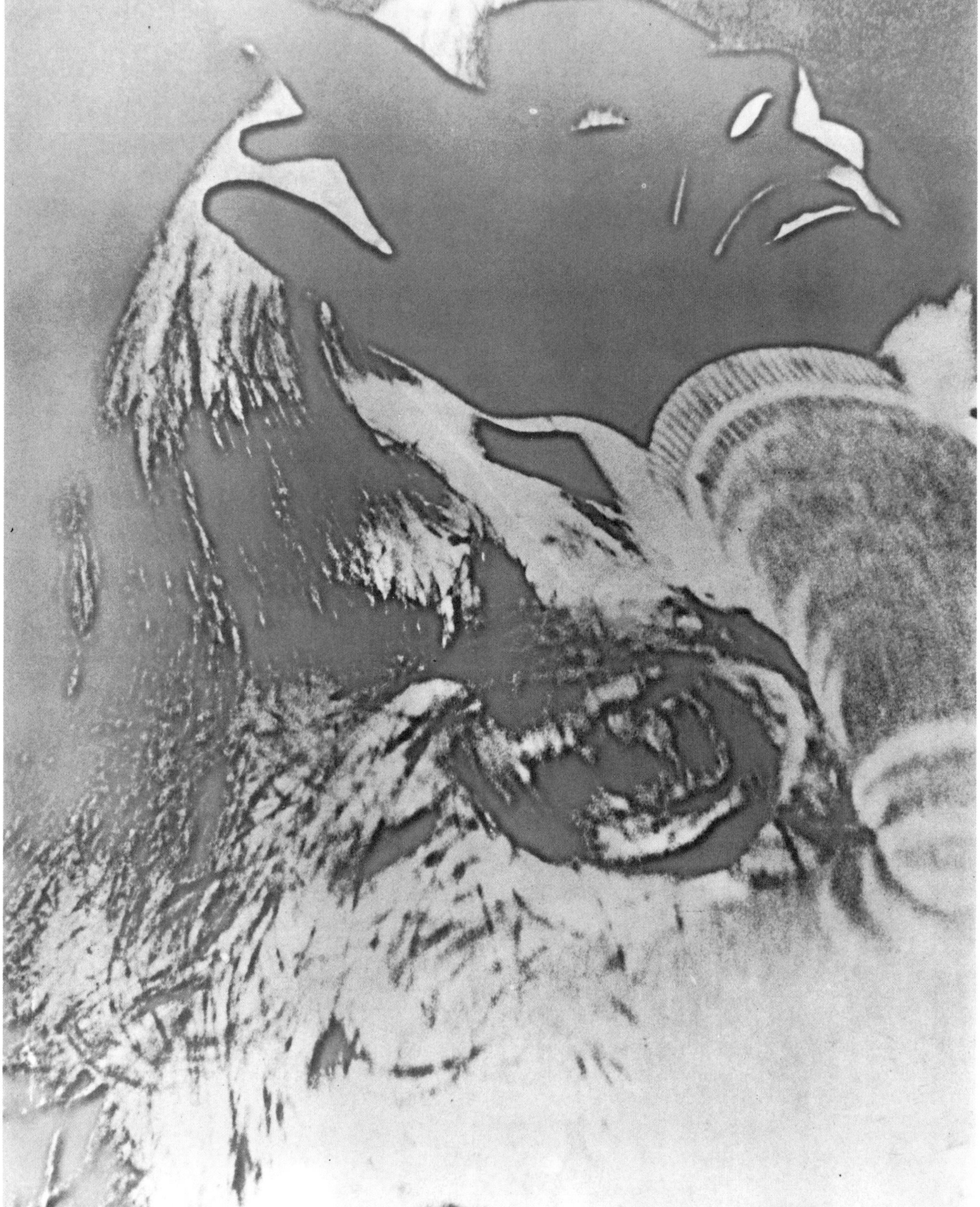

142 JIM DINE 1968

(b. 1935) After working in his family's hardware stores and studying at Cincinnati University and Boston Museum School, Dine moved to New York in 1959. He had already been involved in the phenomena known as 'Environments' and 'Happenings', and in New York 'blossomed out of ... gestural abstraction and Duchampism, etc.' (RB Kitaj); he produced several 'Happenings' with Claes Oldenburg, including 'Smiling Workman' and 'Car Crash'. His first one-man exhibition was at the Reuben Gallery, New York, in 1960, and in 1962 he took part in the 'New Realists' exhibition there. Dine is held by many to be one of the fathers of POP ART. *Real objects such as paint brushes and hammers were included in his works from 1961. In 1965 he designed costumes for* A MID-SUMMER NIGHT'S DREAM *for the Actors Workshop in San Francisco. From 1967 he lived in London but bought a farm in Vermont in 1971. He produced sculpture in metal from 1965; from the mid-1970s he began to produce series of drawings of the human figure in pencil, oil and charcoal, making life drawings regularly.*

THE PICTURE OF DORIAN GRAY. A WORKING SCRIPT FOR THE STAGE FROM THE NOVEL BY OSCAR WILDE WITH ORIGINAL IMAGES & NOTES ON THE TEXT BY JIM DINE (LONDON: PETERSBURG PRESS, 1968), with a portfolio of 6 lithographs.
52 pp., with 12 full-page lithographs, 440 x 310 mm.
Edition A (bound in red velvet): 200 copies (V&A copy no. 9) with 25 artists proofs, each with a portfolio of 6 lithographs; Edition B (bound in green velvet): 200 copies with 25 artist's proofs, each with 4 signed etchings; Edition C (bound in leather): 100 copies with 15 artist's proofs, each with 6 lithographs and 4 signed etchings.
Also published as a portfolio of lithographs, etchings and text, loose, in an edition of 75 with 15 artist's proofs signed by Jim Dine.
Printer: Atelier Desjobert and Atelier Leblanc, Paris.
L.1075-1981 Colour plate 26.

The Picture of Dorian Gray was the first illustrated book brought out by the Petersburg Press, which was formed in 1968 by Paul Cornwall-Jones after leaving Editions Alecto. It was to be followed by the Grimms' Fairy Tales, Laforgue Poems, and Flower Piece Progressives (CAT. NOS. 146, 152, 155) and an edition of Auden's Poems, with lithographs by Henry Moore, in 1974.

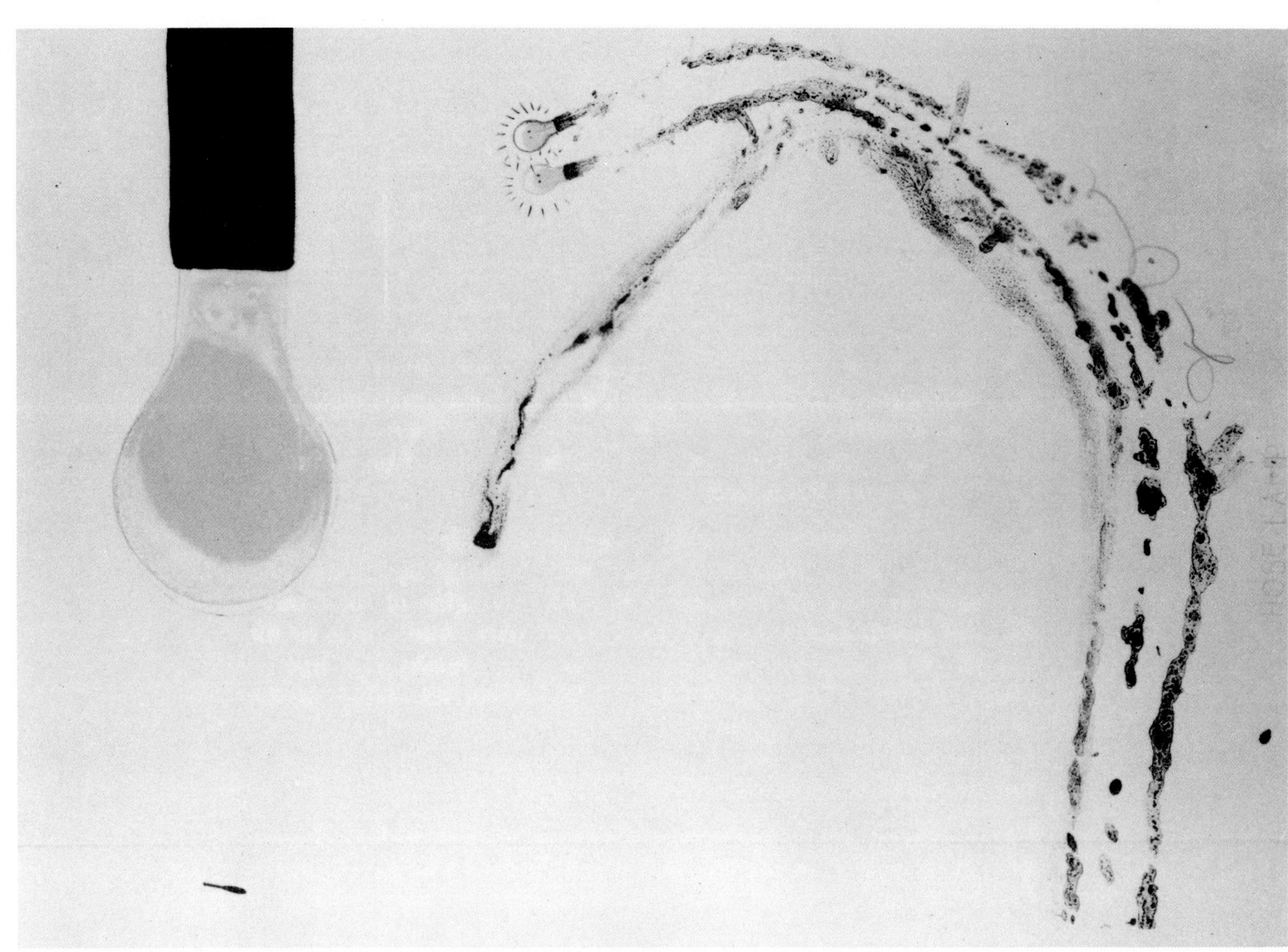

5'
7'
3'
5'
RED PIANO

143 GRAHAM SUTHERLAND **1968**

(1903-1980) Son of a lawyer, Sutherland abandoned an engineering apprenticeship to study engraving at Goldsmiths' College, London, in 1921-6, becoming friends with FL Griggs and with him discovering the work of Samuel Palmer (1805-1881) and William Blake. He taught engraving at Kingston Art School from 1927 and then at Chelsea Art School from 1930. In the early 1930s he began to paint in oil, but his most advanced work was in drawing and watercolour which took inspiration from Paul Nash's work. He also designed advertising posters, fabrics and ceramics from this period. In 1936, he exhibited at the International Surrealist Exhibition in London. During the war, he was appointed Official War Artist; from 1947, he spent part of most years in the South of France. In 1951, he was the subject of a major retrospective exhibition at the ICA; from this date Sutherland received a number of official commissions, painting the portrait of Lord Beaverbrook in that year and those of Churchill and Adenauer in 1954. He was commissioned to provide a tapestry for the new Coventry Cathedral in 1955, and a Noli me tangere *for Chichester Cathedral in 1960, the year in which he became a member of the Order of Merit. In 1982, Sutherland had a major retrospective exhibition at the Tate Gallery.*

[A BESTIARY] (LONDON: MALBOROUGH FINE ART LTD., 1968).
Portfolio of 26 lithographs, including frontispiece, 490 x 320 mm.
Edition of 70 copies (V&A copy no. 6), of which 6 comprise the *Édition de Tête,* with an original gouache (nos. 1-6), and 64 copies the standard edition (nos. 7-70).
Printer: Fernand Mourlot, Paris.
Edition de Tête in an orange leather solander box; standard edition in linen-covered portfolio.
L.2318-1981, Colour plate 25.

Sutherland began work on the Bestiary in 1965, making drawing and watercolour studies that he transferred to stone or zinc plates from January 1967. The lithographs were shown at the Marlborough Gallery in 1968 and at the Palais de l'Europe, Menton, in 1969.

144 JOE TILSON **1968**

(b. 1928) After working as a carpenter and joiner, Tilson was one of the first generation of art students to be supported by government grants, working at St. Martin's School of Art and the Royal College of Art from 1949-1955. In 1955, Tilson was awarded the Knapping prize, and also the Rome prize; in 1955-7 he lived in Italy. He was one of a number of painters associated with the Institute of Contemporary Arts in the mid-1950s when the critic Lawrence Alloway, together with Richard Hamilton and Eduardo Paolozzi, was encouraging people to examine why there was no popular art in the sense that there was popular music and popular reading matter. In the 1960s, in the full spate of POP ART, *Tilson with others such as David Hockney, Allen Jones, R B Kitaj, Richard Smith and Peter Blake, began to incorporate in their work imagery borrowed from the popular culture of consumerist society. In 1962, Tilson had his first one-man exhibition, of wood reliefs, collages and paintings, at the Marlborough Fine Art Gallery, London. In 1973 he executed a mural for the Brunel University Library, Uxbridge; the following year he was awarded the Grand Prix at the Biennale de la Gravure, Cracow.*

JOE TILSON, *THE SOFTWARE CHART QUESTIONNAIRE* (MILAN: SERGIO TOSI, 1968)
19 ff., 430 x 505 mm., including 4 screenprints, with metal cover, in a metal toothed, painted wood case, together with 1 colour chart on aluminium foil in a large facsimile envelope.
Edition of 150 (V&A copy no. 112), signed and numbered by the artist.
Printer: 'Sergio Tosi, Stampatore', Milan.
L.8590-1980. Colour plate 28.

Tilson has close links with Italy, and has had a number of works published there. The imagery in *THE SOFTWARE CHART QUESTIONNAIRE* has been explained as describing pictorially the gigantic electronic mass-communication network and computerised technology run for and financed by multinational companies and ideologies in which the individual is enslaved and treated as a cipher.

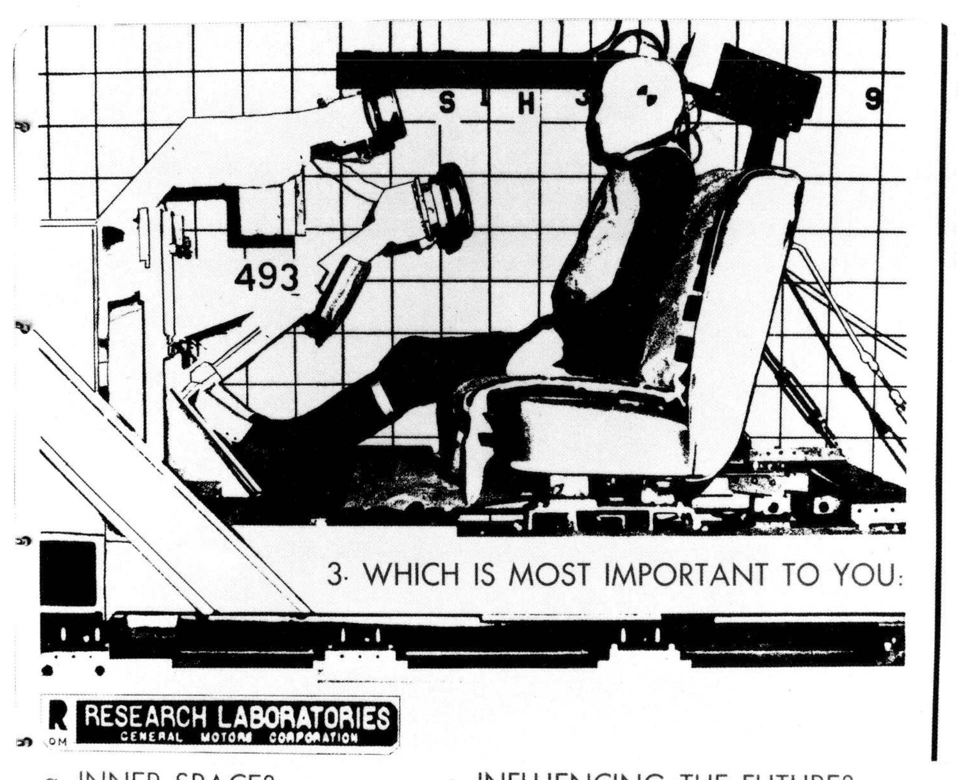

a. INNER SPACE?
b. OUTER SPACE?
c. INFLUENCING THE FUTURE?
d. THE FIVE SENSES INTEGRATED?

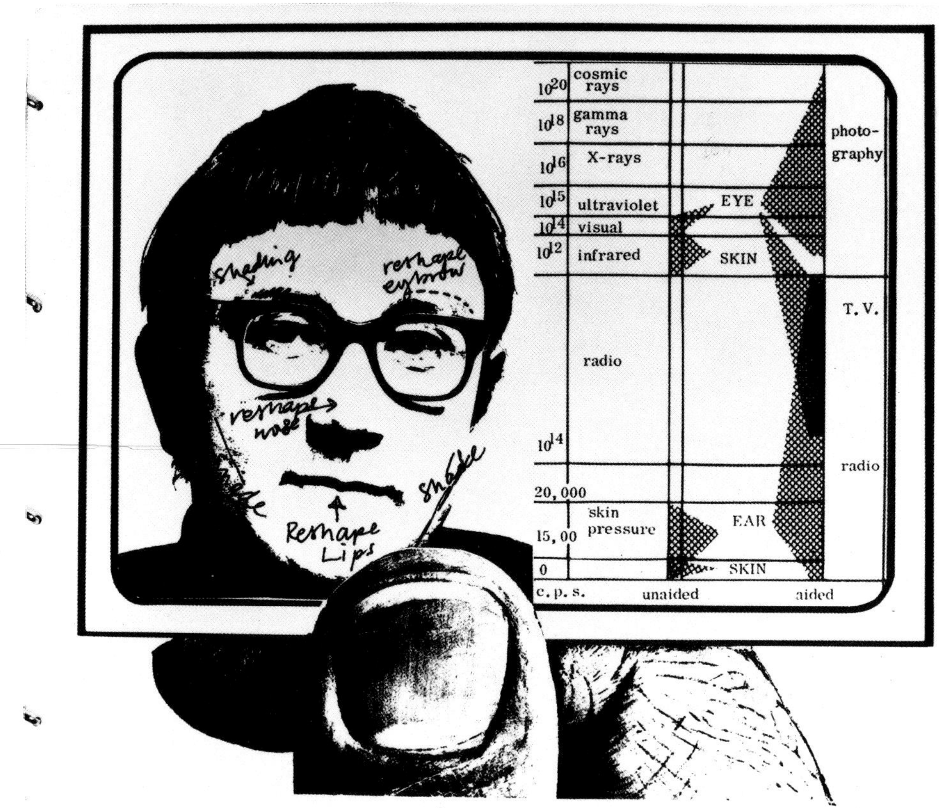

145 ALBERTO GIACOMETTI **1969**

(1901-1966) Taught by his painter father as a child, Giacometti studied at the École des Arts et Métiers, Geneva, in 1919-20, and at the Académie de la Grande Chaumière under Bourdelle from 1922 to 1925. In the 1920s, his painting and sculpture showed CUBIST *influence but also interest in primitive Cycladic and African art. His sculpture that was noticed by the* SURREALISTS *in 1929 shows an admiration for Picasso and Miró; André Breton invited the artist to join the Surrealist group after the latter's show in 1930 at the Galerie Pierre, run by the enterprising Pierre Loeb (1897-1964) who had launched Miró in Paris, Picasso in his Surrealist phase and Lam, as he was to promote Giacometti. The artist's participation in Surrealist activities ceased in 1935 when he reverted to more realistic, natural forms. Returning to Paris in 1945, Giacometti developed his characteristic sculptural form, working with plaster of Paris on wire frames to create the elongated emaciated figures that Sartre claimed as the artistic expression of Existentialism. Pierre Matisse organised Giacometti's first American exhibition at his New York gallery in 1948. He was awarded the Grand Prix for sculpture at the Venice Biennale in 1962, and had a series of retrospective exhibitions in 1965.*

PARIS SANS FIN. LITHOGRAPHIES ORIGINALES DE ALBERTO GIACOMETTI (Paris: Tériade, Éditions Verve, 1969).
88 ff. (44 bifolia), 420 x 325 mm., with 150 lithographs numbered 1-149, and 1 un-numbered (frontispiece).
332 Edition of 250 copies on *Vélin d'Arches* (nos. 1-250; V&A copy no. 53), and 20 copies *hors commerce* (nos. I-XX), each with the lithographed signature of the artist.
Printer: Mourlot, lithographs; L'Imprimerie Nationale, text, set in Garamond Corps 28, *mise en page* by Georges Arnoult, composition and printing by Paul Lajuncomme (completed 24 March 1969).
L.5073-1980.

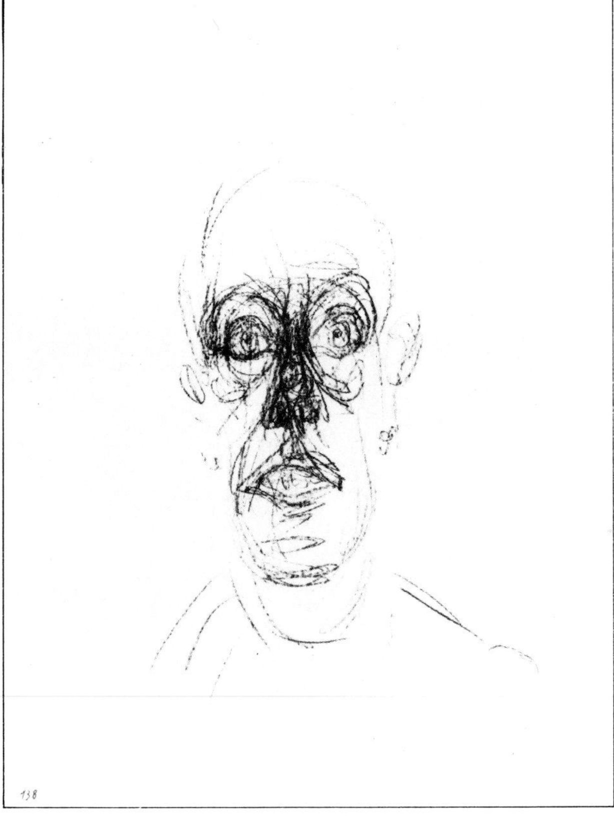

Giacometti began work on this series of drawings of Paris scenes in 1957, using lithographic chalk on transfer paper. Just before his death in 1966, he arranged the drawings in clusters of recurring themes, and numbered them. He was to have provided a text, but left only a few notes; these are printed at the specified places in the sequence of illustrations, but 6 of the 16 pages reserved for text are left blank where the artist had not supplied any notes.

128

146 DAVID HOCKNEY **1970**

(b. 1937)

SIX FAIRY TALES FROM THE BROTHERS GRIMM, ILLUSTRATED BY DAVID HOCKNEY (LONDON: PETERSBURG PRESS, IN ASSOCIATION WITH THE KASMIN GALLERY 1970).
40 ff., 500 x 315 mm., with 39 etchings.
Published in 4 editions (A, B, C & D) of 100 copies with 15 artist's proofs, each volume with a set of 6 loose etchings; also a Portfolio in an edition of 100 (V&A copy no. 39), with 15 artist's proofs and a separate set of the 39 etchings.
Paper: pure white rag waterleaf and hotpressed, watermarked 'DH.PP', made by W. S. Hodgkinson, Bath.
Printer: Vivian Ridler, Oxford University Press (set in Plantin light); Maurice Payne proofed the etchings, Piet Clement, Amsterdam, printed them from the chrome-faced finished plates in January to May 1970.
Binding and portfolio slipcase by Rudolf Rieser, Cologne.
Circ. 126-1971.

The etchings for the Grimm fairy tales were drawn directly onto copper plates by David Hockney between May and November 1969. The project was started by Hockney himself, who had produced a print of Rumpelstilzchen in 1961, and was taken up by Paul Cornwall-Jones of the Petersburg Press. The six tales, of which the text was based on the original edition of Manesse published in Zürich, were chosen by Hockney and translated from the German by Heiner Bastian in Berlin. The typography and layout, which was agreed with the artist, was co-ordinated by Eric Ayers.

147 ARTHUR BOYD 1971

(b. 1920) Boyd was taught by his grandfather, a landscape painter, and his early landscapes show the Australian bush around his native Victoria in a Post-Impressionist and Expressionist style. In 1937 he held his first exhibition in Melbourne. After army service, he helped to found the Murrumbeena pottery, engaging in ceramic painting and sculpture. In 1959 he came to Britain though spending half of each year in Australia; he had his first exhibition in the Zwemmer Gallery, London, in that year. He has designed productions for the Edinburgh Festival, Sadlers Wells and Covent Garden Opera. The Whitechapel Art Gallery held a major retrospective exhibition of his work in 1962, and his work is shown regularly at the Fischer Fine Art Gallery, London.

TOMORROW'S GHOSTS. TWENTY EIGHT POEMS BY PETER STARK. WITH TWELVE ORIGINAL ETCHINGS BY ARTHUR BOYD
(GUILDFORD: CIRCLE PRESS PUBLICATIONS, 1971).
72 pp., 550 x 380 mm., with 12 etchings.
Edition of 100 copies (V&A copy no. 26), on TH Saunders mould made paper (90 lb imperial) with Crisbrook (144 lb imperial) for etchings, signed by author and artist, with 15 copies marked 'artist's proof'.
Printer: Walter Taylor, compositor (set in 16 on 24 point Helvetica), Circle Press, Guildford, text; Mati Basis, London, etchings.
Binding: Rudolf Rieser, Cologne.
L.285-1972.

Early in his career, Boyd produced dry-point engravings and lithographs, but he began printmaking regularly in England after purchasing his own printing press in 1962. Thereafter etching, aquatints and prints form a major part of his œuvre. Among books he has illustrated are TSR Boase's biography of St. Francis of Assisi.

The Circle Press, Guildford, was formed in 1967 by a group of painter-printmakers interested in publishing fine books in limited editions, illustrated by leading artists. The first title issued, in that year, was a Chaucer illustrated by Ronald King who headed the group, and who has since directed the Press. Other artists associated included Alan Reynolds, Derrick Greaves, Ian Tyson, Birgit Skiold, and Tom Phillips. To date the Press has produced almost one hundred books of widely varying types, from classic texts to contemporary poetry, while individual works have been illustrated by William Hayter, Michael Kidner, John Furnival, and Norman Ackroyd.

148 MAX ERNST **1971**

(1891-1976)

ALFRED JARRY. *DECERVELAGES. PAROLES D'ALFRED JARRY, MUSIQUE DE CLAUDE TERRASSE, LITHOGRAPHIES DE MAX ERNST* ([PARIS:] GALERIE ALEXANDRE IOLAS, 1971)
14 ff., 660 x 505 mm., with 9 lithographs.
Edition of 99 copies (V&A copy no. 51), on *Arches*, each lithograph signed by the artist, of which 33 copies include a set of lithographs on *Japon;* a further 16 copies (nos. A-P) produced for the collaborators.
L.2999-1981.

Ernst's illustrations here provide a background to extracts from a major text of Dada and Surrealist circles, Jarry's *UBU ROI*. Claude Terrasse (1867-1923), brother-in-law of Bonnard, wrote a number of sparkling operettas that had much success in the first years of the 20th century. He also provided the music for the 1902 production of *UBU ROI* at the Nouveau-Théâtre in Paris.

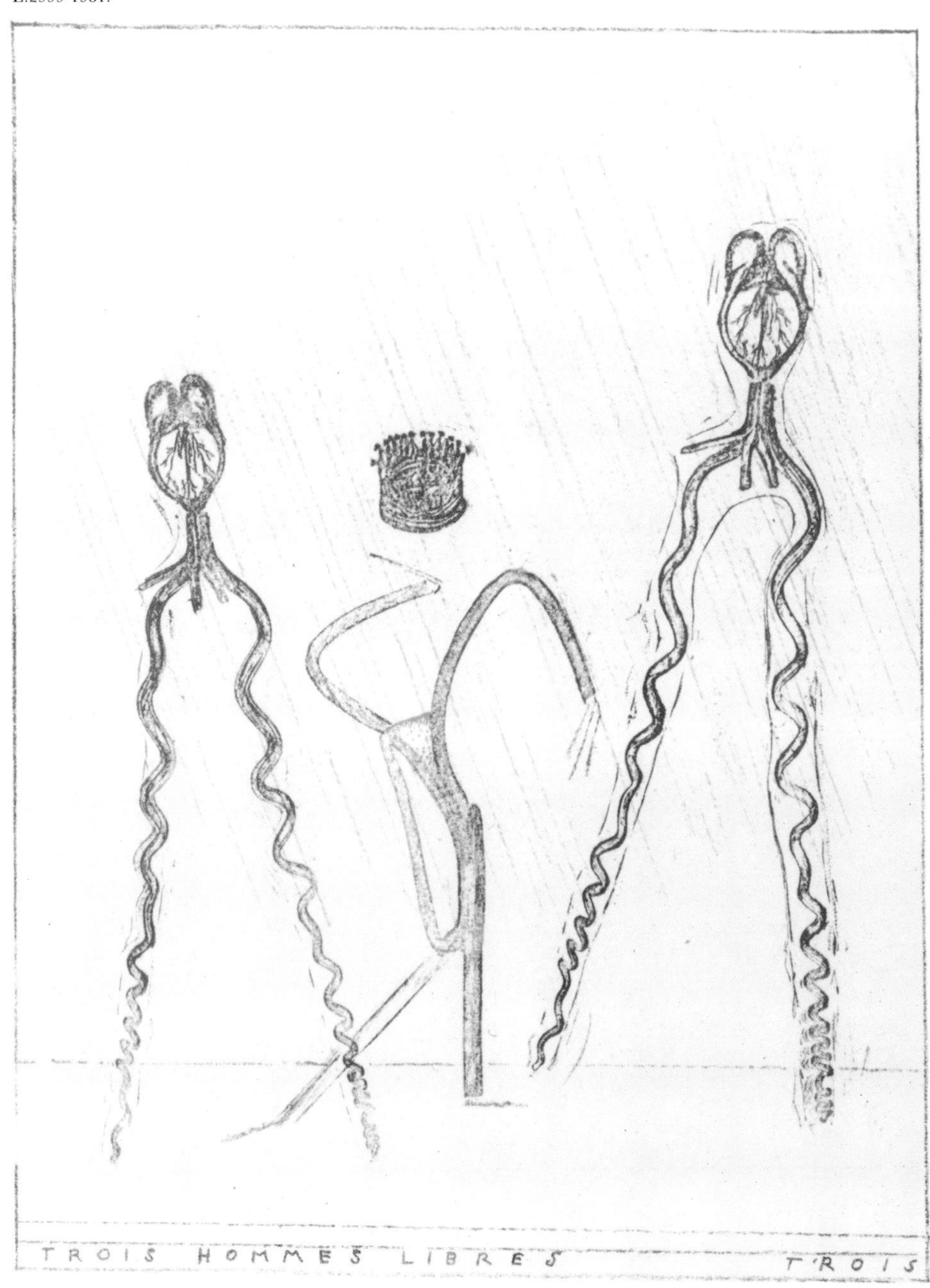

338

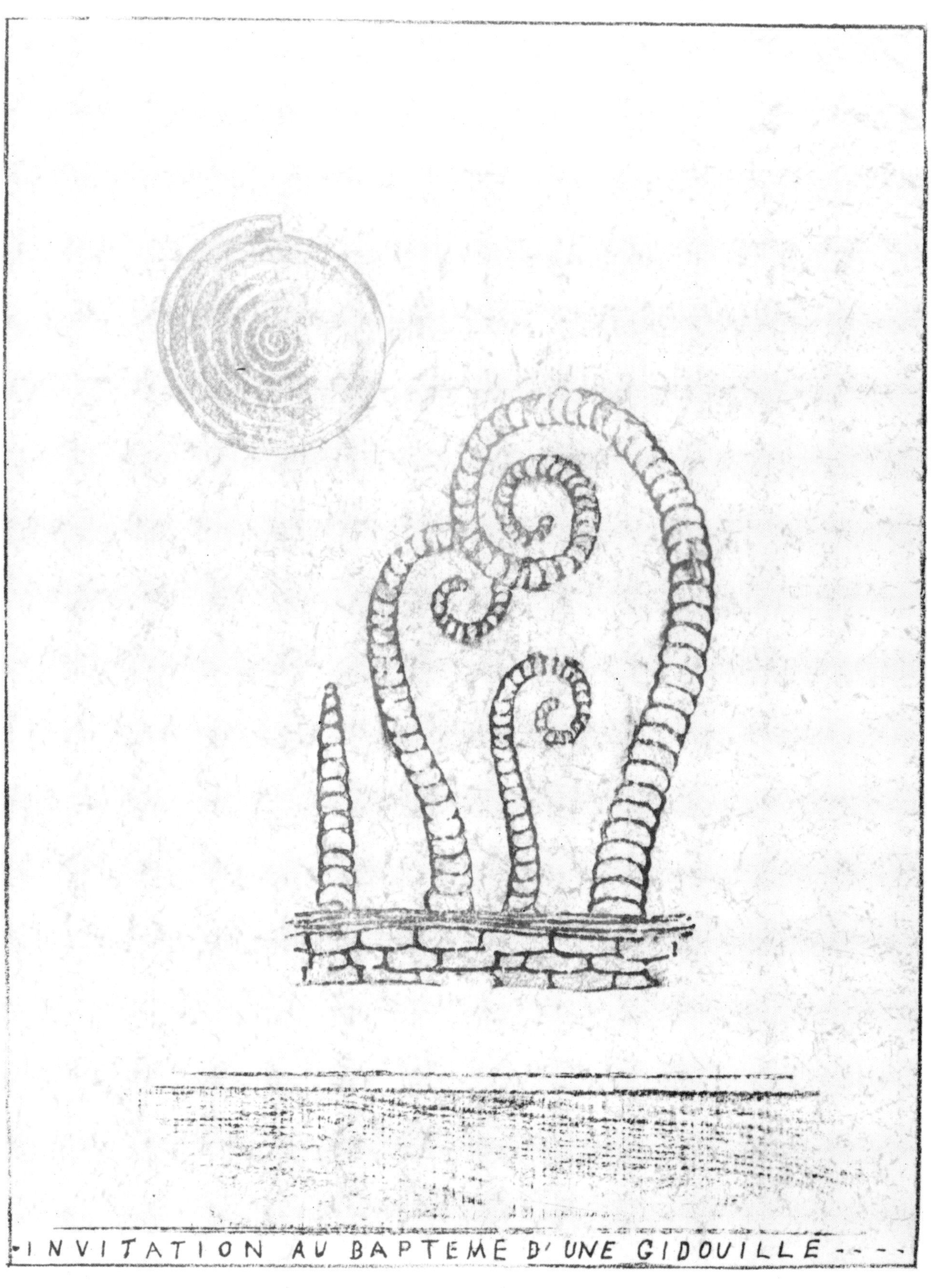

339

149 ELISABETH FRINK **1972**

(b. 1930) After training at Guildford Art School under Henry Moore's assistant Bernard Meadows, Frink worked at the Chelsea Art School from 1949-1953. She was among a number of 'Geometry of Fear' sculptors (Lynn Chadwick and Reg Butler were others) that constituted part of a post-war school of expressionist British sculpture, one that attracted special commendation at the 1952 Venice Biennale. In 1952 the Tate Gallery bought its first work by her, a bronze bird, and her first one-woman show was at the St. George's Gallery in 1955. She was commissioned to make an eagle lectern for the new Coventry Cathedral in 1962. From 1954 to 1962 she taught at St Martin's School of Art, and at the Royal College of Art in 1965-1967, after which she lived and worked in France until 1973. From the 1970s, the nude male figure, powerful and even serene, was the subject of much of Frink's work. Awarded the CBE in 1968 she became a trustee of the British Museum in 1976, was elected to the Royal Academy in 1977 and became a Dame in 1982.

ELISABETH FRINK, *ETCHINGS ILLUSTRATING CHAUCER'S CANTERBURY TALES. INTRODUCTION AND TRANSLATION BY NEVILL COGHILL* (LONDON: WADDINGTON GALLERIES, 1972).
192 pp., 650 x 460 mm., with 19 etchings.
Published in 3 editions: all on paper made by J. Barcham Green and signed by the artist. *De Tête* edition: 50 copies, bound, numbered A1-A50; Standard edition: 50 copies, bound, numbered B51-B100; boxed unbound edition: 175 copies numbered C101-C275 (V&A copy no. C198); 25 *hors commerce* copies numbered D276-D300.
Printer: Gordon House, designer; Hillingdon Press, Uxbridge, text, set in Monotype Plantin series 110 and 194; Malcolm Wade & Co., ink; Cliff White, White Ink Ltd, London, etchings.
Portfolio made by F & J Randall Ltd., London.
L.8592-1981.

The illustrations were drawn directly on to copper plates and etched by Frink in London. They have been described as 'amongst the most successful illustrations of the century, encompassing the mood of the text in concise delineations and disarmingly ribald humour' (Sarah Kent). The text is the standard version, established by Nevill Coghill, Merton Professor of English Literature at Oxford University in 1957-1966.

The Knight's Tale.

This Duke I mentioned, ere alighting down And on the very outskirts of the town,
In all felicity and height of pride He came aware, casting an eye aside,
That kneeling on the highway, two by two A company of ladies were in view
All clothed in black, each pair in proper station, Behind the other, and such lamentation
And cries they uttered, it was past conceiving The world had ever heard such noise of grieving
Nor did they hold their misery in check Till they had grasped bridle at his horse's neck.

150 RONALD BROOKS KITAJ **1972**

(b.1932) Born in Cleveland, Ohio, Kitaj followed children's art classes at Cleveland Museum of Art in 1937–42. After work as a seaman, a brief stay at the Cooper Union Art Institute, New York (where his interest in ABSTRACT EXPRESSIONISM *was tempered by his preference for figurative art) and military service in Europe, he studied at the Ruskin School, Oxford, and at the Royal College of Art, London, from 1957 to 1962. He participated in the elaboration of the* POP ART *that was associated with the RCA in the early 1960s and represented by Hockney, Allen Jones, Derek Boshier, Patrick Caulfield and others, though drawing themes from writers such as T. S. Eliot or Ezra Pound and from politics rather than directly from popular culture. His first one-man show was at the Marlborough Fine Art Gallery, London, in 1963; from 1961 to 1967, he taught at Camberwell and the Slade Art Schools. From 1962, Kitaj worked with Chris Prater of Kelpra Press on collage and other prints. From 1975 he began to make life drawing a major part of his work. In 1983 he was elected a Royal Academician.*

A DAY BOOK BY ROBERT CREELEY. PLATES BY R. B. KITAJ (BERLIN: GRAPHIS, 1972)
39ff., 620 x 420 mm., with 13 'graphics', of which 4 are etchings-screenprints.

Published in 3 editions. *Edition de Tête:* 24 copies (nos. I-XXV) signed by author and artist, with 1 extra screen print; standard edition: 200 copies (V&A copy No. 74), signed by author and artist, of which 25 bound in linen, the rest in portfolio form; *hors commerce* edition: 70 copies marked HC produced for author, artist and collaborators. Printer: Gustav Adolf Höhm, Cologne, text; Mourlot, Paris, lithograph; 4 etchings printed at White Ink Ltd, London, and overprinted with additional screenprinted images at Kelpra Studios.
Binding by Rudolf Rieser assisted by Helmut Klohs.
L.3559–1972. Colour plate 27.

Kitaj, who often combined printing processes, found in silk-screen printing a medium suited to his art. Apart from individual prints, he has produced series such as *MAHLER BECOMES POLITICS BEISBOL, SOME POETS* and *IN OUR TIME.* Kitaj's association with the American poet Robert Creeley dates back to 1967–8, when the artist taught at Berkeley, California.

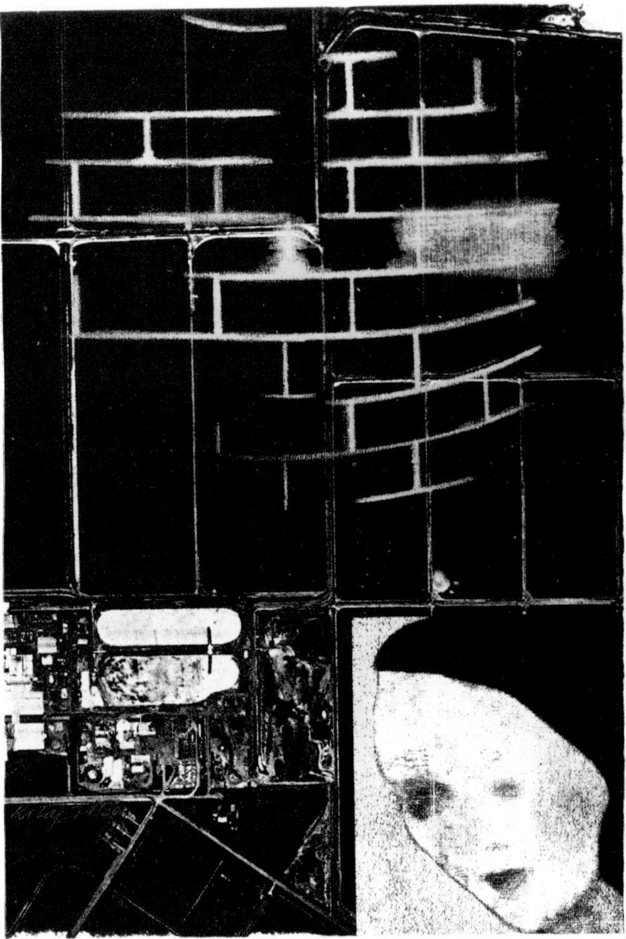

151 ROBERT RAUSCHENBERG **1972**

(b.1925) Rauschenberg studied in Kansas, Paris, North Carolina and, in 1948–9, under Albers in New York, where he had his first one-man exhibition at the Betty Parsons Gallery. His 'Dirt Paintings', done in mud in 1953, were taken to evidence a jaundiced view of Abstract Expressionism and Action Painting. His inclusion after this of everyday objects such as Coca-Cola bottles, umbrellas or even chairs in his work to create 'combine paintings' showed links with the emerging POP ART. *From 1955 he designed for the Merce Cunningham Dance Company, and became a close associate of Jasper Johns and the musician John Cage. In 1964, the year of his first big exhibition in London, he took first prize at the Venice Biennale. In 1966 he founded Experiments in Art and Technology, a body intended to bring together artists, engineers, scientists, businessmen and workers to study and experiment systematically the means of communication offered by advanced new technology. A major retrospective exhibition of his work toured the USA from Washington in 1976.*

TRACES SUSPECTES EN SURFACE . . . ROBERT RAUSCHENBERG ARTIST, IMAGES ON STONE, VISUAL ART WORK; ALAIN ROBBE-GRILLET AUTHOR, WROTE ON PLATES. BOOK IS EXCHANGE WITH IMAGE AND TEXT, (LONG ISLAND, NEW YORK: UNIVERSAL LIMITED ART EDITIONS, 1978).

70 ff. [i.e. 4 colophon bifolia and 31 bifolia], 700 x 510 mm. ('27″ x 20″ folded'), '37 stones+27 plates'. Edition of 36 (V&A copy no. 21) with 6 artist's proofs and 1 [*hors commerce*]; pages signed and dated '[19]72–78' by artist and author; paper made by Twinrocker, watermarked with signatures of artist and author and with Universal Limited Art Editions monogram embossed in bottom right-hand corner.

L.1359–1983. Colour plate 33.

Rauschenberg's interest in book illustration dates back to 1959–60 when he produced a series of illustrations, exhibited at the Leo Castelli Gallery, New York, for Dante's *INFERNO* in his manner known as 'combine drawing'.

Alain Robbe-Grillet (b.1922), by training an agricultural engineer, has worked as a writer, actor and film-maker. From 1955 he was the literary director of the *ÉDITIONS DE MINUIT.* Of his novels *LA BELLE CAPTIVE* (1976), made into a film in 1983, had illustrations by René Magritte. Among his film scripts was that for *LAST YEAR IN MARIENBAD.*

Universal Limited Art Editions were formed as a lithography studio in 1956 by Tatyana Grosman, using at first – literally – stones discovered on her doorway path, and a second-hand press purchased for fifteen dollars. They went on to produce limited edition lithographs of such precision, care, and lavish inventiveness that they won a totally new prestige for the art of printmaking as a medium open to painters. After 25 years of publication Tanya Grosman received the Brandeis Notable Achievement award for 'Genius, artistic excellence and notable accomplishment'. Artists who have worked at the studio include Dine, Francis, Frankenthaler, Johns, Marisol, Motherwell, Newman, Oldenburg, Rivers, Rosenquist, and Twombly. The Museum of Modern Art, New York, by grace of a private donation, receives one copy of every single work produced. Although books have formed only a small proportion of the total works created they have certainly formed a major area of distinction. One of the most extraordinary productions was Buckminster Fuller's *TETRASCROLL* (1977), while others include Barnett Newman's *18 CANTOS,* Robert Motherwell's *A LA PINTURA,* and Larry Rivers' *DONKEY AND THE DARLING.*

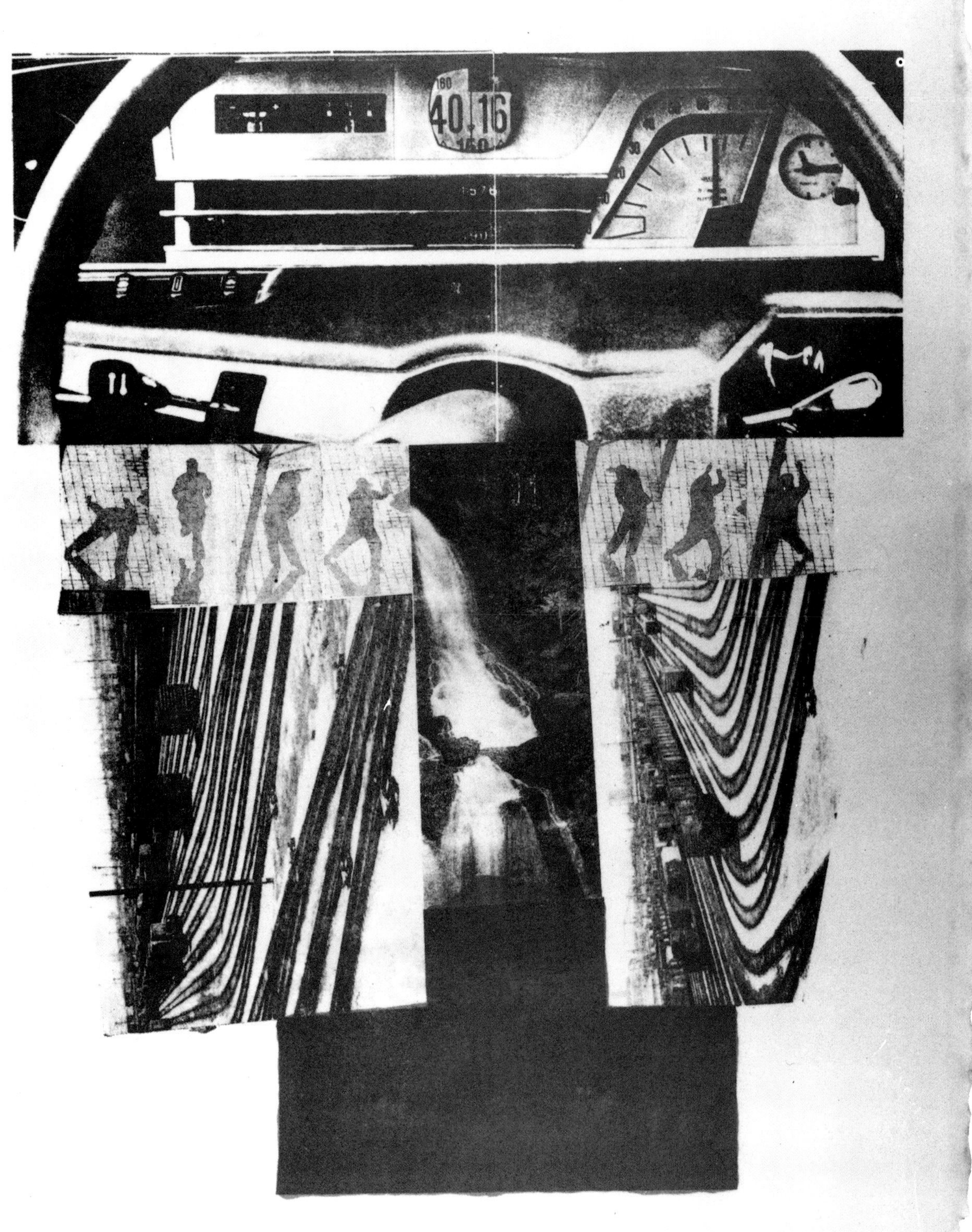

RAUSCHENBERG 72-78

152 PATRICK CAULFIELD 1973

(b. 1936) Trained at the Chelsea Art School under Jack Smith in 1959-60, and at the Royal College of Art in 1960-3, Caulfield first exhibited at the 'Young Contemporaries' Exhibition in 1961. From 1963 to 1971 he taught at the Chelsea Art School. He participated in the 'New Generation' exhibition at the Whitechapel Art Gallery in 1964 and showed first at the Waddington Gallery in 1969. Beginning screen printing in earnest in 1964, he was awarded the Prix des Jeunes Artistes for graphics in 1965. Not usually associated with Pop Art (and not always seeking the fast glamorous image associated with much of it), his careful depiction of details of everyday scenes has led his subject matter to be described as 'archetypal images of the modern world'.

QUELQUES POÈMES DE JULES LAFORGUE.
PLANCHES DE PATRICK CAULFIELD (LONDON: PETERSBURG PRESS, IN ASSOCIATION WITH WADDINGTON GALLERIES, 1973).
60 pp., 405 x 355 mm., with 22 silk-screen prints.

Published in 3 editions. A: English edition of 200 copies and 20 artist's proofs, each with a portfolio of 6 extra prints. B: French edition, as English edition (V&A copy no. 192). C: Portfolio edition of 100 copies and 20 artist's proofs with a box of 22 screen prints. All editions signed by artist, on Neobond (synthetic) paper.
Printer: inking and colour selection done in Christopher Betambeau studio, 1971-2; text set in Futura bold; editions printed by Frank Kicherer, Stuttgart, 1972.
Bound in grey leather by Rudolf Rieser, Cologne, 1972.
L.1074-1981. Colour plate 29.

The poems of Laforgue (1860-1887) were chosen by Caulfield; though he died young, his verses are reckoned a landmark in the history of Symbolism. The artist worked on the illustrations between 1969 and 1972, and arranged the lay-out of each page with Eric Ayers.

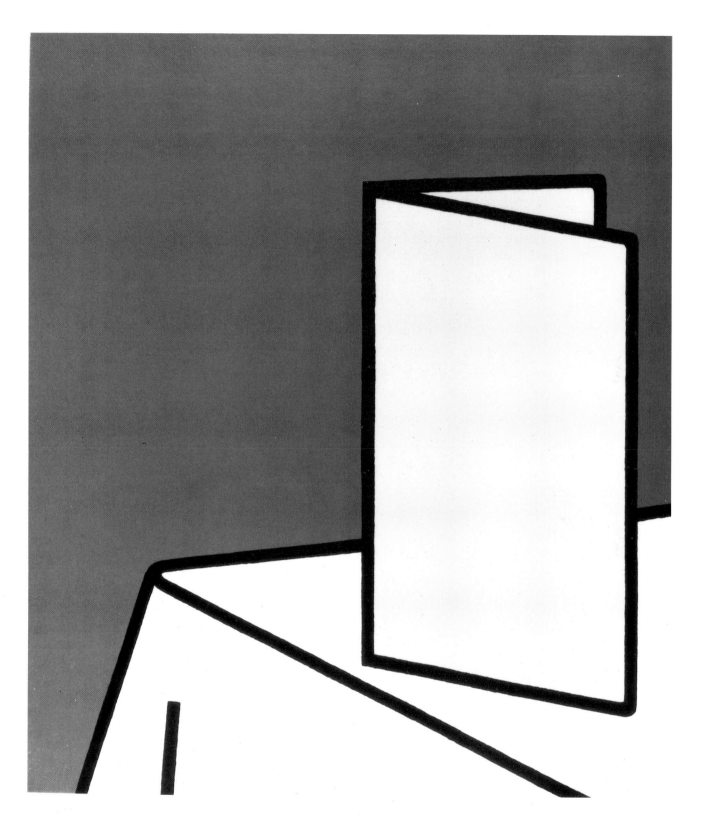

153 ANTONI TÀPIES 1973

(b.1923) Tàpies painted while studying law at Barcelona University in 1943–6, producing towards the end works in thick impasto and collages using earth and other 'rubbish'. In 1948 he was a co-founder of the late Surrealist group in Barcelona that published DAU AL SET, *and began engraving the following year (in 1967 he won the prize for this technique at the Ljubljana Biennale). His friendship with Miró dates from 1948. His first one-man show was in the Galerias Laietanes, Barcelona, in 1950, after which he received a scholarship to work in Paris; here he moved into the environment of Dubuffet, Wols, Fautrier and others, and rediscovered his impasto style with its use of a variety of materials to achieve textures, colours and shapes that were subjected to 'grattage' strokes. His first one-man show in New York, at the Martha Jackson Gallery, was in 1953. From 1969 he began to use crumpled newspaper, old sacking, straw and other 'dust-bin' materials in his work, leading his biographer, Alexander Cirici to dub him a precursor of* 'ARTE POVERA' *(the term of Germano Celant), itself part of the movement that included Land Art (see cat. 167) and Conceptual Art and sought to take art away from the 'consumer durable' commercial network in which* POP ART *found itself in the 1970s. Tàpies published a theoretical work on the practice of art in 1970.*

LA CLAU DEL FOC. TRIA DE TEXTOS I PRÒLEG DE PERE GIMFERRER. LITOGRAFIES D'ANTONI TÀPIES (BARCELONA: EDICIONS POLÍGRAFA, S.A., 1973).

348 86pp., 620 x 450 mm., including 16 lithographs.
Edition of 500 copies (V&A copy no. 385) of which 75 copies on *Guarro* are signed by Tàpies (nos. 1–75) and 425 copies numbered 76–500; also 26 copies on *Arches* with 16 lithographs, 5 engravings and 1 original aquatint (nos. A–Z) and 25 copies with 16 lithographs and 5 engravings on *Rives*, both signed by the artist (nos. I–XXV).
Printer: La Polígrafa.
Bound with canvas, painted and with a pocket.
L.814–1977

This collection of Catalan poetry was chosen by Pere Gimferrer, and was intended to marry the language of the artist with words evoking the nature of the Catalan people. As a frontispiece, Tàpies has used the primeval image of the handprint, here associated with black earth and traces of red (blood).

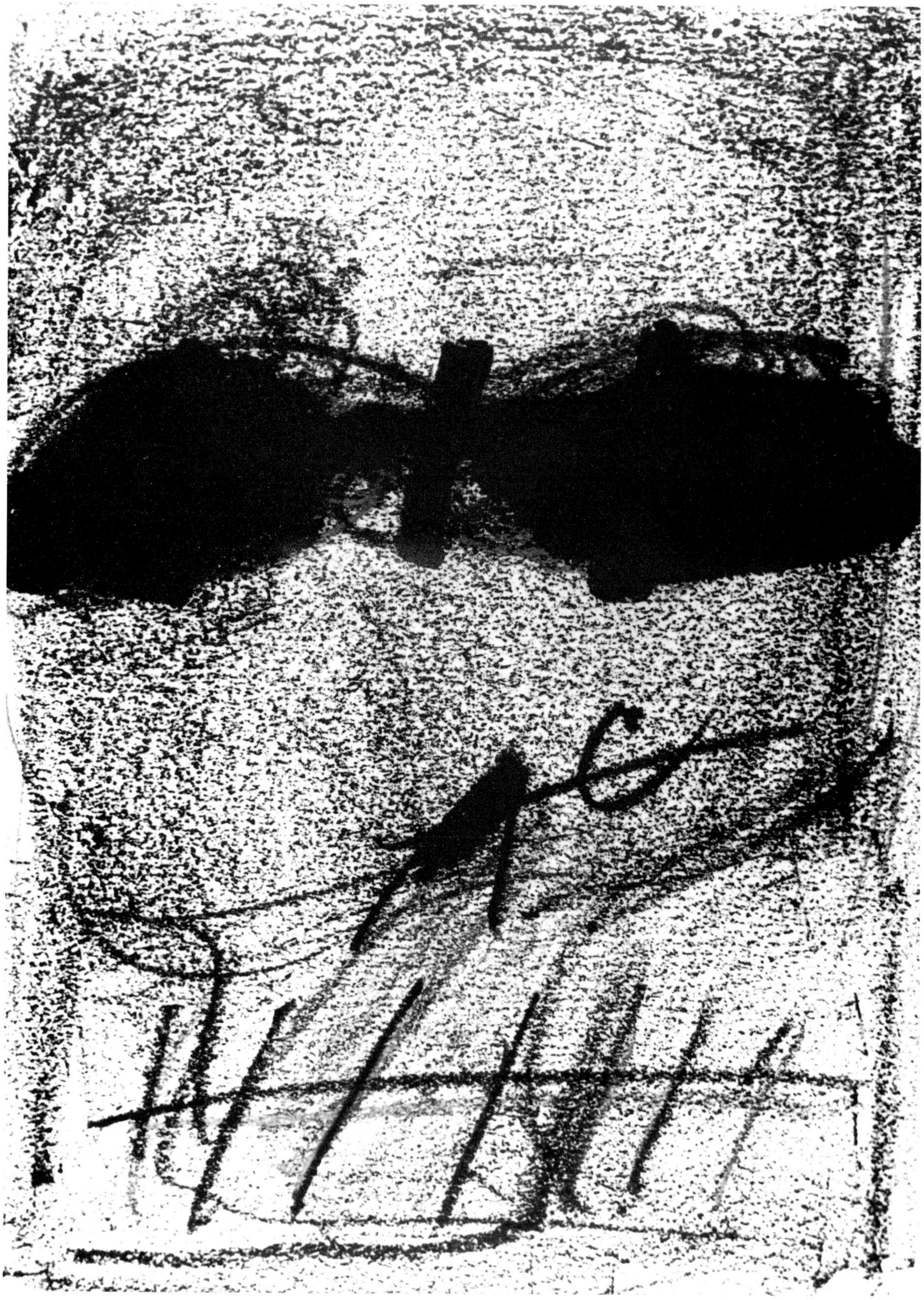

(1898-1976) Son of a sculptor and a painter, Calder studied engineering at the Stevens Institute of Technology in New Jersey in 1915-19. From 1923 to 1926 he followed drawing and painting classes while working in the Public Works Department, New York. In 1926 he published ANIMAL SKETCHING, *had his first painting exhibition, produced his first sculpture and, on a visit to Paris, began to make his 'Circus' models, based on articulated toys. These led to his first wire sculptures. He continued to show the 'Circus' models in Paris (where he lived from 1926), Jean Cocteau bringing colleagues to see them in action, the musician Varèse as well as Léger and Le Corbusier being much impressed. A visit to Mondrian's studio led Calder to confide to Duchamp that he wanted to make 'Mondrians that move', and in 1932 he exhibited his 'Mobiles' (Duchamp's term) at the Galerie Vignon, Paris. By this time he was an occasional member of the* SURREALIST *group, taking part in* ABSTRACTION-CRÉATION *and exhibiting with Arp, Miró, Seligmann and others. In 1935-6 he designed sets for two Martha Graham ballets and for Erik Satie's* SOCRATES. *He had a major retrospective exhibition at the Museum of Modern Art, New York, in 1943 and was awarded the Grand Prix for sculpture at the 1952 Venice Biennale. From 1953, he spent part of each year near Tours. Sartre, who wrote the introduction to Calder's Paris exhibition of 1944, enthused about his mobile sculptures: 'these hesitations, changes of direction, indecisive and clumsy movements, brusque decisions, and above all this marvellous swan-like nobility make Calder's mobiles into strange creatures, half-way between matter and life'; Pierre Courthion likened their movements to 'windblown fields of corn, fluttering leaves, cascades'; Michel Butor wrote a poem as an introduction to his 1964 Paris exhibition of gouaches, while Léger was impressed by the thin, transparent and mobile works of the 18-stone artist. His is the only sculpture in the Miró Foundation, Barcelona (founded 1975) not by Miró himself.*

350

EE CUMMINGS, *SANTA CLAUS. ETCHINGS BY CALDER ... ADAPTATION FRANÇAISE PAR D. JON GROSSMAN* (PARIS: ÉDITIONS DE L'HERNE, 1974).
44 pp. (11 bifolia), 675 x 525 mm., with 9 etchings *hors texte*, each signed by the artist.
Edition of 175 copies, of which 25 are on *Grand vélin d'Arches* with 1 set of etchings on *Arches* and 1 set on *Auvergne-Richard de Bas* (nos. 1-25), 75 copies on *Grand vélin d'Arches* with a set of etchings on *Auvergne-Richard de Bas* (nos. 26-100), and 75 copies on *Grand vélin d'Arches* with a set of etchings on *Vélin d'Arches;* also 20 copies *hors commerce* (nos. I-XX; V&A copy no. X).
Printer: Atelier Arte, etchings; Fequet et Baudier, text, set in Caslon Corps 24 (completed 16 March 1974).
L.1173-1984.

Calder illustrated a number of books, perhaps the most notable being the edition of Aesop's Fables published by Harrison in 1931. 'e.e. cummings' (1894-1962), as he gave his name, first published his play *SANTA CLAUS* in 1946. A poet who also painted, he translated into English in 1933 poems by Louis Aragon, who from the launching of *LITTÉRATURE* in 1919 had been a close companion of André Breton, following him into the Communist party in the 1930s.

155 RICHARD HAMILTON **1974**

(b.1922) Hamilton's study at the Royal Academy Schools in 1938–40 and 1945–46 was interrupted by work as an engineering draughtsman at EMI in London. From 1948 to 1951 he studied etching under John Buckland Wright at the Slade School. After teaching Design at the Central School, London, in 1952–3, where his fellow teachers included Paolozzi, Pasmore and Turnbull, Hamilton taught at the University of Durham in 1956–8, introducing a course in basic design with Pasmore and others, and at the Royal College of Art in 1957–61 as lecturer in Interior Design. Organiser and designer of the 'Growth and form' exhibition at the ICA in 1951, he was one of the artists for whose work Lawrence Alloway coined the term POP ART. *Art of this kind first made a wide impact in the Whitechapel Art Gallery's 'This Is Tomorrow' exhibition in 1956, with Hamilton's work* JUST WHAT IS IT THAT MAKES TODAY'S HOMES SO DIFFERENT, SO APPEALING? *and its images from popular advertising culture typifying the movement. He gave what was perhaps the most succinct description of the new movement in 1957: the new art was to be 'Popular (designed for a mass audience); transient (short term solution); expendable (easily forgotten); low cost; mass produced; Young (aimed at youth); witty; sexy; gimmicky; glamorous; big business' (cited in C. Newton,* PHOTOGRAPHY IN PRINTMAKING, *1979, p.23). In 1965–6, Hamilton worked on a reconstruction of Marcel Duchamp's* LARGE GLASS, *and organised the exhibition 'The almost complete works of Marcel Duchamp' at the Tate Gallery, London, in 1966.*

352 *FLOWER-PIECE PROGRESSIVES.* (PARIS AND LONDON: ATELIER CROMMELYNCK AND PETERSBURG PRESS, 1974).
13 ff., 650 x 500 mm., including 7 colour prints.
Edition of 24 copies (V&A copy no. 4), on Rives BFK paper, with 3 artist's and 2 publisher's sets, each print signed and numbered, in Roman numerals, by the artist. The final state also exists in a separate edition of 150 impressions, signed and numbered in Arabic numerals. Plates made, printed and proofed at Atelier Crommelynck, Paris, from November 1973 to September 1974.
L.1076–1981.

Hamilton's elucidation of his *FLOWER-PIECE PROGRESSIVES,* the excremental origins of beauty, is contained in the catalogue of the Arts Council Exhibition at the Tate Gallery 'British Painting, 74'; the sentimental cliché of the 'flower-piece' is defiled by the *memento mori* that becomes increasingly evident towards the end of the set of prints, as the colour describes the identical image more clearly. Hamilton's illustrations to Joyce's *ULYSSES,* done in 1949, sought to find pictorial equivalents to the moods of the text; for the flower-piece, the writer Marcel Broodthaers wrote an 'Éloge du désespoir' in July 1974, after the printing, as a comment on the artist's work.

A technical note in the book records that '"Trichromatic flower-piece" is printed from three plates inked with only one colour: yellow, magenta or cyan, plus another for the normally added black. They were produced by the traditional methods of hand-worked copper: line etching, aquatint, drypoint, burin, roulettes, etc.'.

156 JASPER JOHNS 1976

(b.1930) Johns came to New York in 1952 from South Carolina to paint; at the height of the vogue for ABSTRACT EXPRESSIONISM, *he produced, in 1955, a series of paintings based on realistic pictures of the American flag and targets. Some of the former created a scandal when shown at his first one-man exhibition at the gallery of Leo Castelli, the dealer foremost in promoting avant-garde artists associated with* POP ART, *Johns and Rauschenberg chief among them. Like Rauschenberg, Johns began to include everyday objects in his paintings from the early 1960s. In 1963 he became director of the Foundation for Contemporary Performance Arts. From the mid-1950s Johns was a close associate of the dancer Merce Cunningham and acted as artistic adviser to his company.*

SAMUEL BECKETT, *FIZZLES* ([LONDON:] PETERSBURG PRESS, 1976), also with title-page in French, *FOIRADES.*
64 pp., 330 x 255 mm., with 33 etchings and 2 colour lithographs as internal lining of the binding.
Edition of 250 copies (V&A copy no. 78), signed by author and artist, on Richard de Bas-Auvergne paper watermarked with Beckett's initials and Johns' signature, with 30 artist's proofs (nos. I–XXX) and 20 copies *hors commerce* individually dedicated.
Printer: Atelier Crommelynck, Paris, etchings; Fequet & Baudier, Paris, text, set in Caslon Old Face 16 point.
Binding designed and executed by Rudolf Rieser, Cologne.
L.1623–1977. Colour Plate 31.

Lithographs, etchings and screenprints have been a major part of Johns' work since 1960. Much of his work of this kind has been executed by Gemini GEL of Los Angeles and Tamarind, Long Island, both of them major contributors, with the Universal Limited Art Editions set up by Tatyana Grosman, to the revival of lithography in the United States of America, as well as at the studios of the Petersburg Press.

The prose pieces of Beckett in *FIZZLES* were mostly written in French in the 1960s and early 1970s, some of them for Jérôme Linton's periodical *MINUIT*. Beckett's links with Linton went back to 1951, when the Éditions de Minuit published *MOLLOY* and *MALONE MEURT*. The author described his method of producing *FIZZLES* as 'breaking wind quietly, hissing, spluttering; a failure or fiasco'. Two other works by Beckett were published in limited editions in 1976, showing a new direction in the writer's interests: *ALL STRANGE AWAY* illustrated by Edward Gorey (New York: The Gotham Book Mart Master Series, 1976), and *THE DRUNKEN BOAT* (Reading: Whiteknights Press, 1976), Beckett's 1932 translation of Rimbaud's poem edited and introduced by James Knowlson and Felix Leakey.

157 DAVID HOCKNEY 1977

(b.1937)

THE BLUE GUITAR, ETCHINGS BY DAVID HOCKNEY WHO WAS INSPIRED BY WALLACE STEVENS WHO WAS INSPIRED BY PABLO PICASSO (LONDON & NEW YORK: PETERSBURG PRESS, 1977).
21 ff., 525 x 460 mm.
Edition of 200 copies (V&A copy no. 2) signed by the artist (nos. 1–200), on paper made at the Inveresk Mill, Somerset, and 35 proofs (nos. I–XXXV).
Printer: Petersburg Studios (justification pages set in Electra Linotype and printed letterpress); Maurice Payne proofed the etchings, which were printed by hand in London and New York at the Petersburg Studios, each from two copper plates.
Boxed by Rudolf Rieser, Cologne.
L.5916-1984. Colour Plate 30.

Henry Geldzahler introduced Hockney to Wallace's poem, *THE MAN WITH THE BLUE GUITAR,* in 1976, which uses Picasso's 'Blue period' painting *THE OLD GUITARIST* of 1903 as its central theme. Hockney produced a number of drawings in response to the poem, which highlights the problem of the imagination's role in interpreting reality, and decided to produce a set of coloured etchings using the method devised by Aldo Crommelynck for Picasso to make colour prints. Hockney said of his illustrations that 'like the poem, they are about transformations within art as well as the relation between reality and the imagination, so these are pictures within pictures and different styles of representation juxtaposed and reflected and dissolved within the same frame'. Wallace Stevens (1879–1955) began writing poetry in his 40s, and, while never a popular poet, is counted one of north America's most influential poets of the 20th century.

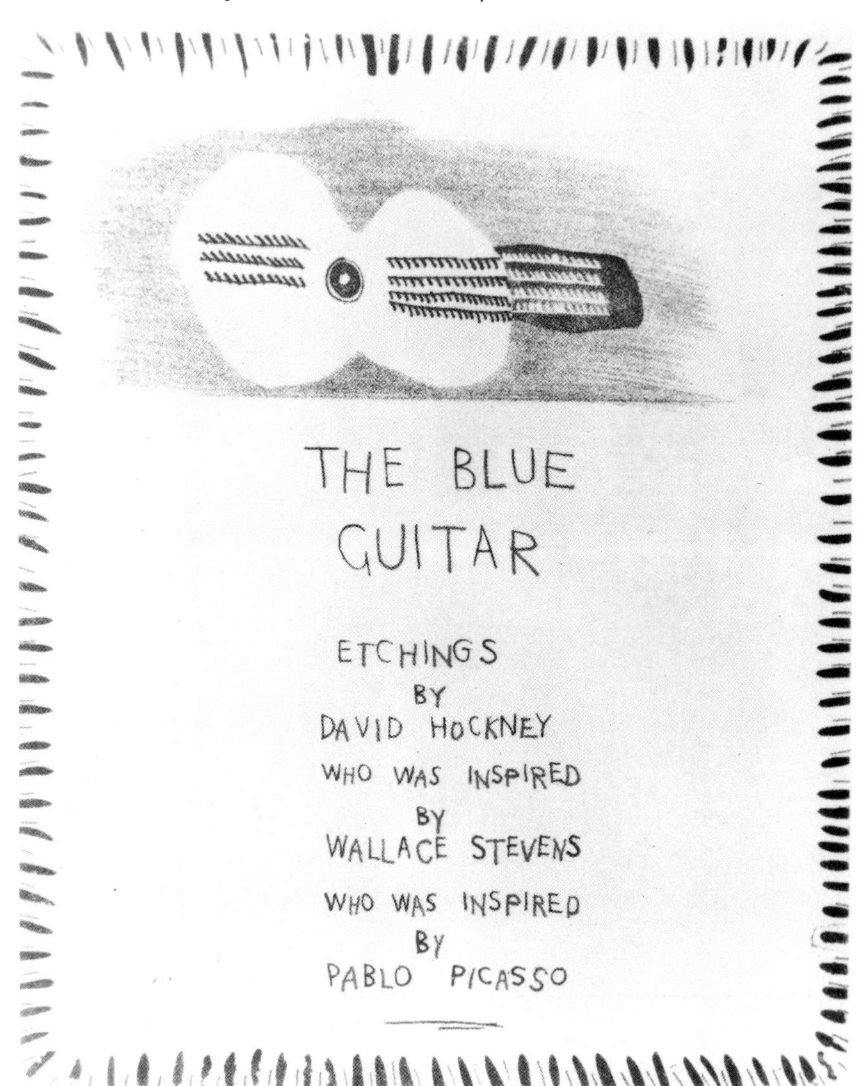

158 ALLEN JONES **1977**

(b. 1937) Jones attended Hornsey College of Art in 1955-1959 and the Royal College of Art, where he was a contemporary of R B Kitaj, Peter Phillips, David Hockney and Derek Boshier, in 1959-1960. His first one-man show was at Arthur Tooth's, London, in 1963. In 1964-1965 he lived in New York exhibiting there and in Chicago; in 1966 he visited Los Angeles on a Tamarind Lithography Fellowship. Thereafter he has been based in London, though he has travelled, taught and exhibited in Europe and elsewhere. In 1970 he designed the set and costumes for part of 'O Calcutta' in London. Graphic and lithographic work has been a significant part of Jones's œuvre from 1961-1963, when he taught lithography at Croydon College of Art, and before. He also works as sculptor and painter. He was elected a Royal Academician in 1983.

ALLEN JONES, *WAYS & MEANS* (LONDON: KELPRA EDITIONS, WADDINGTON & TOOTHS GRAPHICS, 1977).
18 pp., 500 x 350 mm.
Edition of 50 copies (V&A copy no. 6), signed and numbered by the artist, and ten artist's proofs.
Printer: Kelpra Studio.
L.6711-1978. Colour Plate 31.

The association of Allen Jones with the Kelpra Studio goes back to 1964, when he produced a print there as part of the ICA project promoted by Richard Hamilton (see cat. 133). Jones has produced a number of illustrated books. In 1969 he designed *ALLEN JONES FIGURES* produced by Galerie Mikro, Berlin, and in 1971 *ALLEN JONES PROJECTS*, published by Matthews, Miller and Dunbar, for whom he also designed *WAITRESS*, with photographs by Tim Street Porter, the following year.

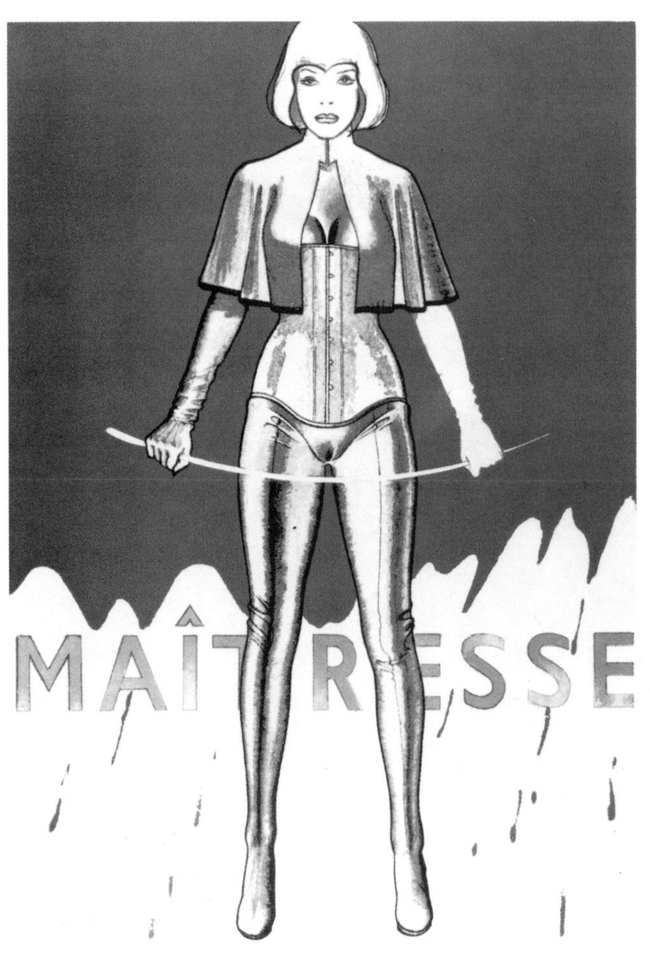

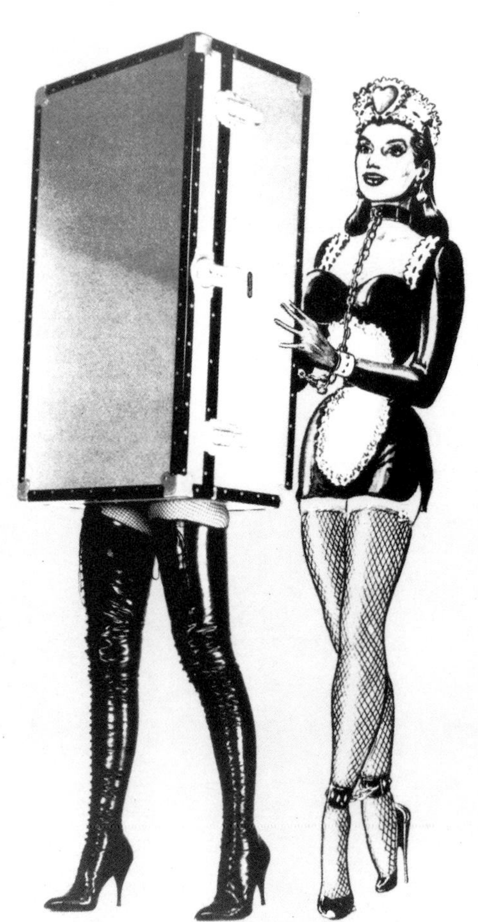

159 JOE TILSON 1977

(b. 1928)

JOE TILSON, *ALCHERA. NOTES FOR COUNTRY WORKS. WILTSHIRE & TUSCANY (1970-1974)* (LONDON: KELPRA EDITIONS, 1976).
18 ff., 500 x 350 mm., with 33 screen prints.
Edition of 50 copies (V&A copy no. 6), signed by the artist, on *Vélin d'Arches* and 10 artist's proofs.
Printer: Kelpra Studio, London.
L.6713-1979.

'Alchera' is the Australian aboriginal word for dream time; the work is dedicated by the artist 'to Eros and Orpheus and other juices rising into fruit' and investigates 'primitive' ways of structuring the universe, centering on the four elements – earth, air, fire, water – and their associations, followed by cyclical events governing time – sunrise, sunset, lunar rhythms and so on.

Tilson's book is one of a number produced by the Kelpra Press under Christopher Prater as part of a project to have artists illustrate books, thus branching out from the printmaking in which the firm had specialised until then. The artists had complete control of image and text within the established format.

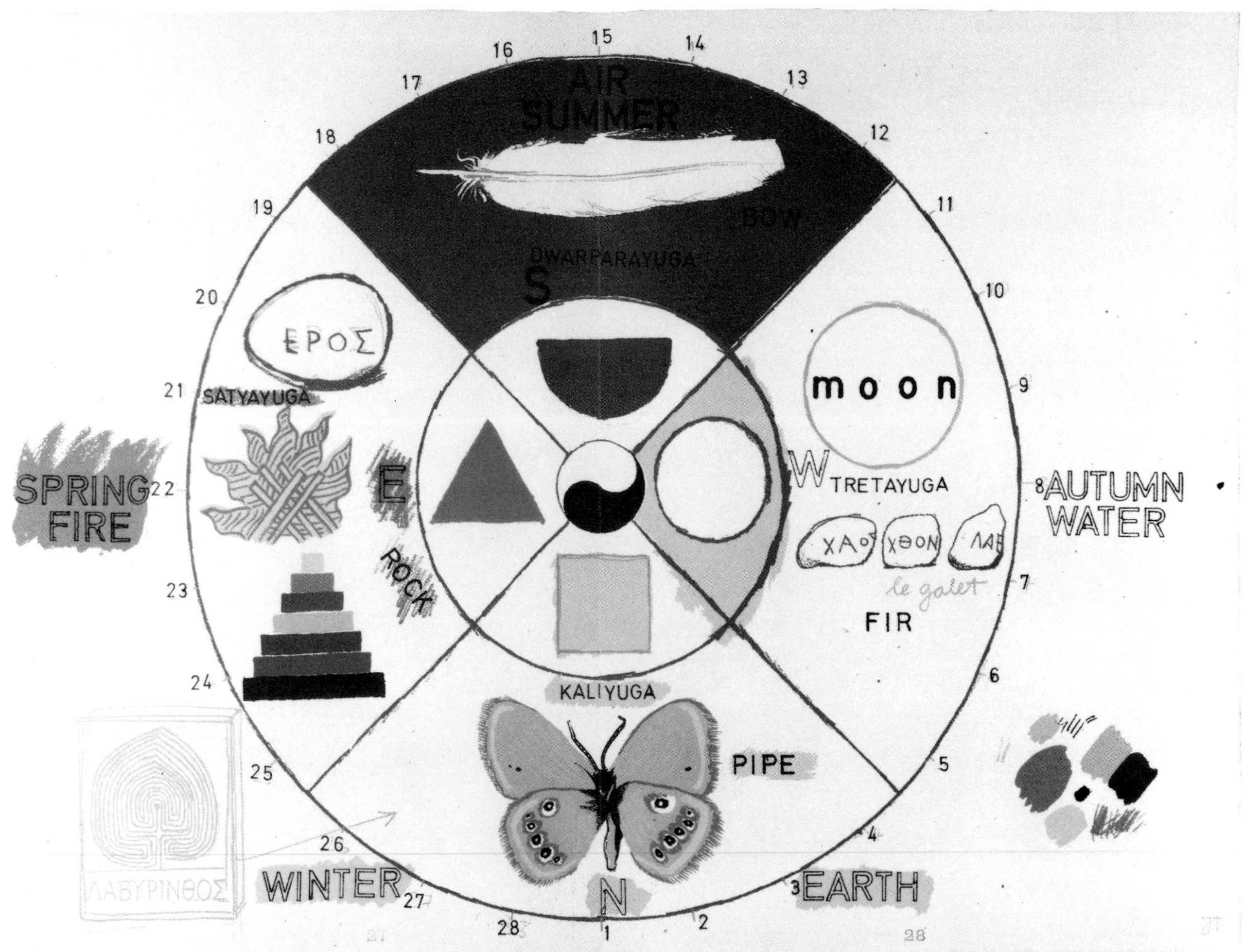

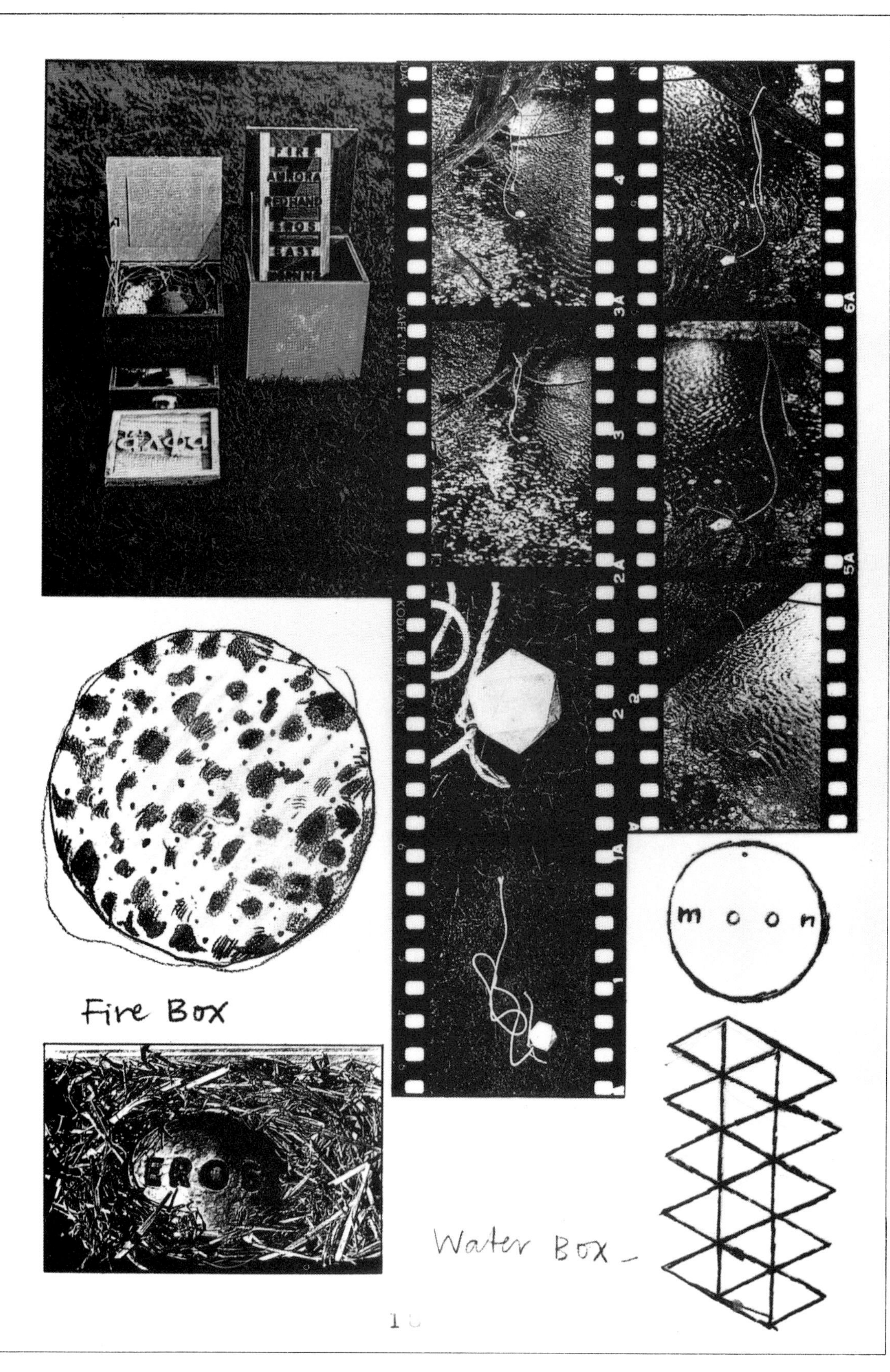
FIRE
AURORA
RED HAND
EROS
EAST
KODAK TRI X PAN
Fire Box
EROS
moon
Water Box

160 ANSELM KIEFER **1978**

(b.1945) Kiefer abandoned study of Law and French at College to take up painting, working under Peter Dreher in Freiburg in 1966–8 and under Horst Antes in Karlsruhe in 1969. His first one-man show was at the Galerie am Kaiserplatz, Karlsruhe, in 1969. He studied with Joseph Beuys in 1970–2. From the early 1970s, mythology has formed an important part of his subject matter; his paintings 'Nothung' were shown at the Michael Werner Gallery, Cologne, in 1973, 'Der Nibelungenlied' at the Goethe-Institut Gallery, Amsterdam, in the same year, 'Siegfried vergisst Brünhilde' at the Michael Werner Gallery in 1976. The subject matter as much as his technique gained him opprobrium in some quarters when he showed at the Venice Biennale in the German Pavilion in 1980, being paired with Georg Baselitz. His work was shown at the 'New Spirit in Painting' exhibition at the Royal Academy, London, in 1981.

DIE DONAUQUELLE ([COLOGNE: MICHAEL WERNER, 1978]).
72pp., including inner front and back cover, 295 x 200 mm.

Edition of 25 copies (V&A copy stamped '00017'), signed on inside back cover by the artist.
Each copy handbound individually by the artist in differing organic materials.
L.5916–1984. Colour Plate 34.

Kiefer was born at Donaueschingen in the Black Forest, where three streams converge to become the river Danube. Entitled 'The Source of the Danube', the black and white photographs that make up this book introduce us to a room with bare windows, hanging streamers, and a pond contained in a square brick surround, set in an earth floor. As the pages are turned, we approach the surface of the pond, the 'source', and examine its qualities. The binding is made up of a rough bark facing with streaks of bitumen and strokes of white paint, with the title of the work neatly written in. Michael Werner ran the gallery in Cologne where Kiefer had a number of exhibitions.

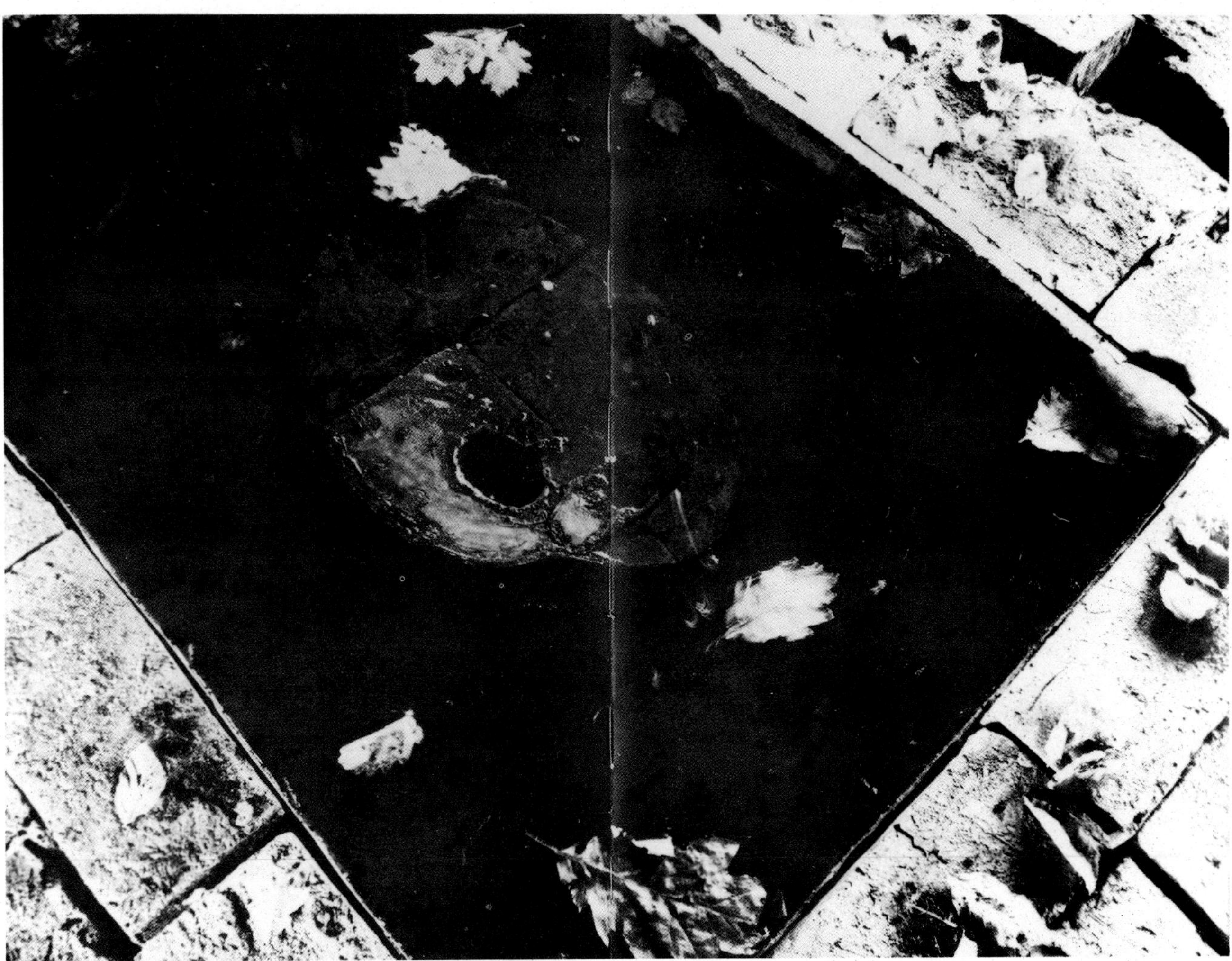

Die
Donaüquel

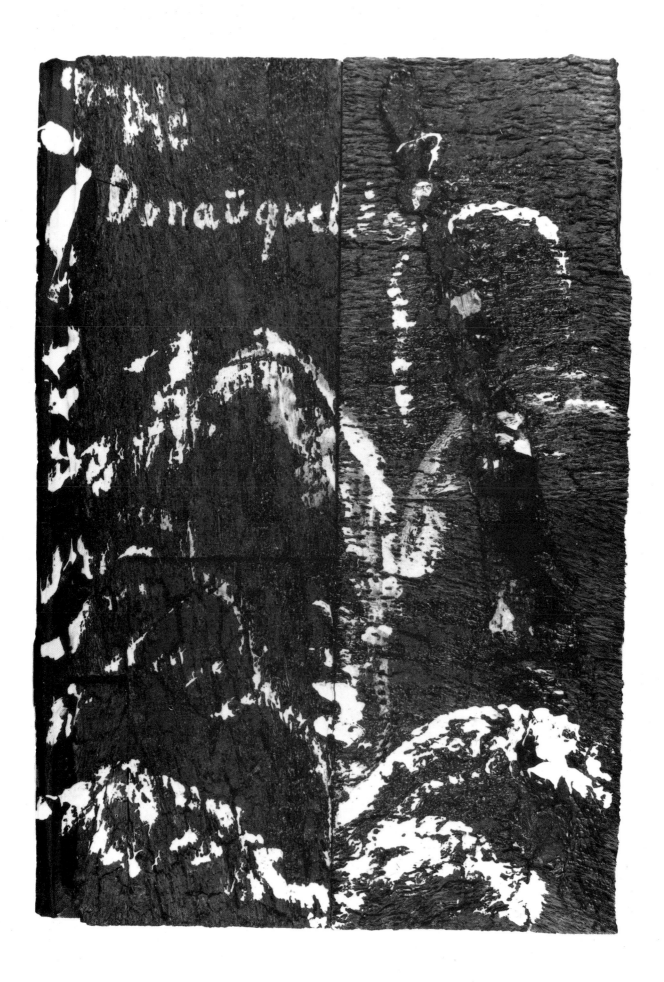

161 RAOUL UBAC **1979**

(b.1921) Son of a judge, Ubac was a student in Paris from 1930 to 1934, following courses at the Faculté des Lettres and the École des Arts Appliqués. Under the influence of Man Ray and Max Ernst, he took up photography and in 1934 published with Camille Bryen a volume of poetry and photographs, ACTUATION POÉTIQUE. *Taking part in many* SURREALIST *activities, his photographs appeared regularly in* LE MINOTAURE. *He edited the Brussels review* L'INVENTION COLLECTIVE *in 1940 and provided a link between the Belgian and Paris Surrealist groups. He abandoned photography after the war, having exhibitions of gouaches and drawings in London, Brussels and Paris in 1946. Ubac's engraving of slate began in 1946. In 1950, he had an exhibition of his paintings at the Maeght Gallery in Paris, and thenceforth he devoted himself to painting and to slate engraving. In 1955 he was invited to show with the Cobra group, an association of artists from Copenhagen, Brussels and Amsterdam that developed an informal, expressive art with stress on social commitment (many of the artists were later prominent in the International Situationist movement). From 1955 he used pieces of slate in his painting, and from 1966 covered panels with a mortar of synthetic resin to produce relief paintings. Ubac has also made designs for stained glass windows, those for the church of Varengeville in collaboration with Braque.*

CLAUDE ESTEBAN AND RAOUL UBAC, *COMME UN SOL PLUS OBSCURE* (PARIS: ÉDITIONS GALANIS, 1979).
62pp., 415 x 315 mm., with 14 slate engravings (4 of them double pages).
Edition of 70 copies (V&A copy no. 51), on *Japon Hosho*, signed by the artist and author, of which 20 copies have a separate set of engravings on *Japon Kosu* (nos. 1–20) and 50 copies numbered 21–70; also 15 copies *hors commerce* for collaborators and the Bibliothèque Nationale (nos. A–O).
Printer: Atelier Anne Delfieu, Dieudonne, engravings; Fequet-Baudier, text, set in Bodoni Corps 30 (completed 25 Oct. 1979).
L.5281–1981.

Engraving on slate is particularly associated with Ubac, though he also used copper plates and wood for graphic work, as well as producing lithographs. Anne Delfieu executed a tapestry for Ubac in 1970 commissioned by the Galerie Maeght. Of primitive simplicity, Ubac's vision has been said to have two preoccupations, that of landscape and that of human form.

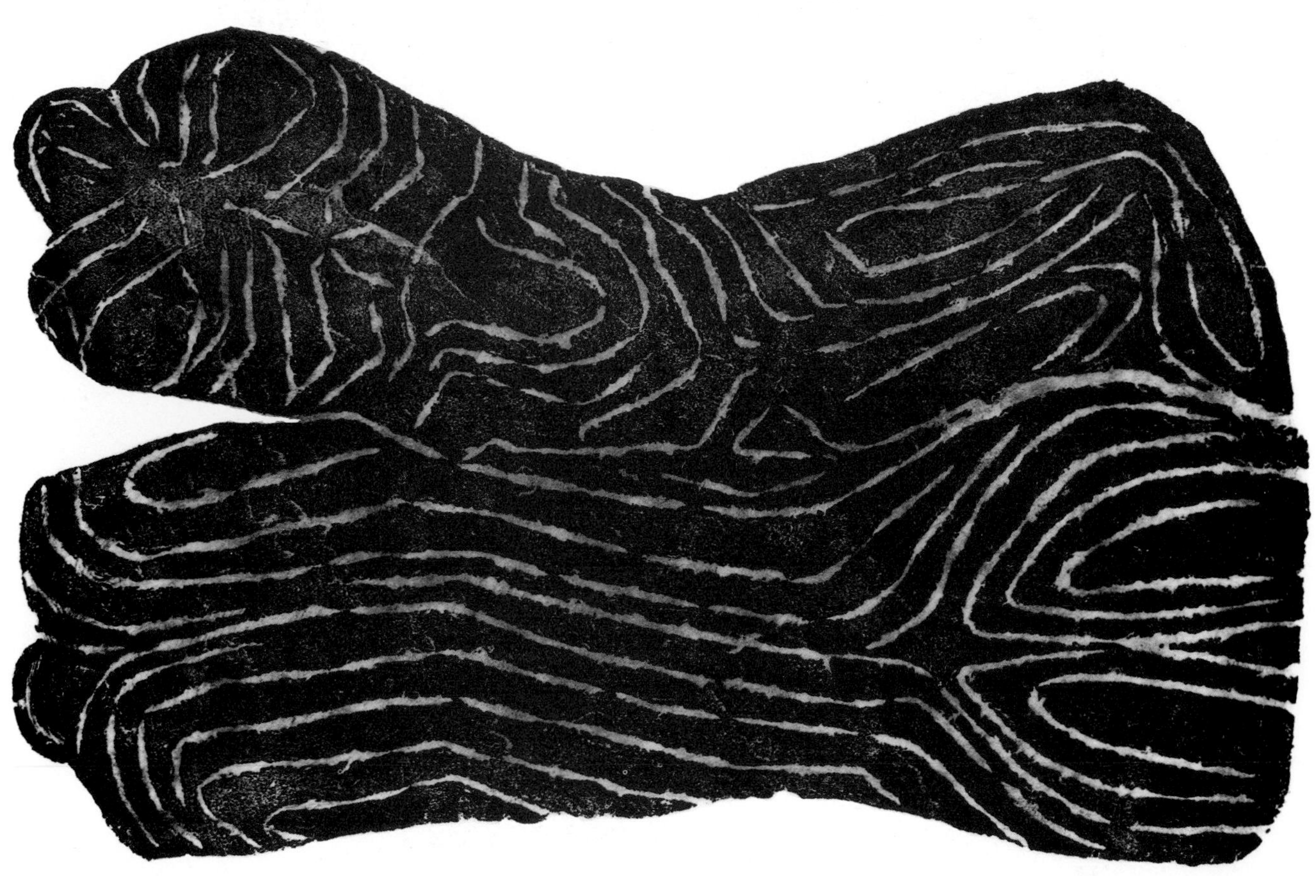

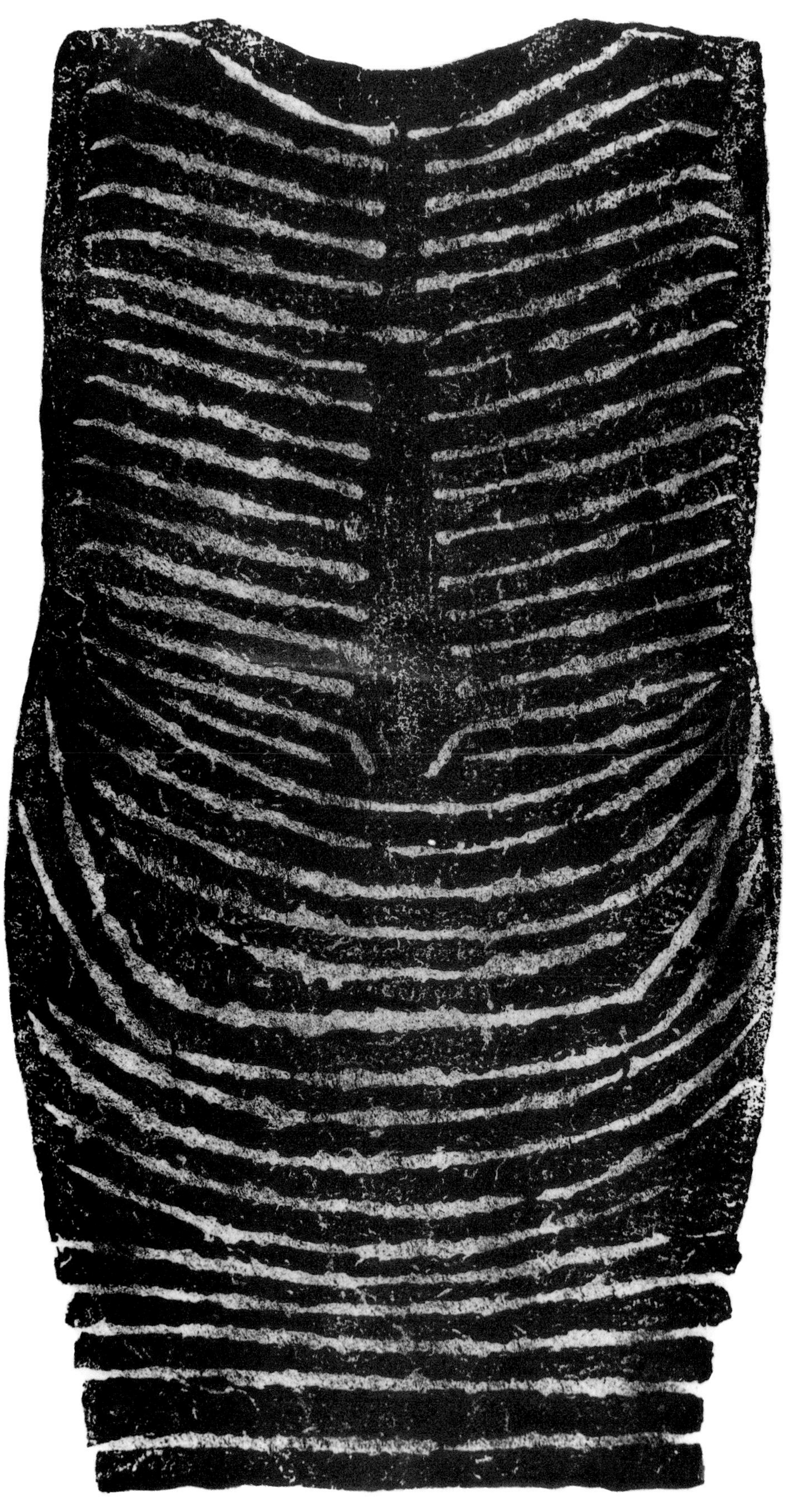

162 LEONARD McCOMB **1979**

(b. 1930) Son of a master gilder and decorator, McComb was a conscientious objector when called up for military service. He studied painting at Manchester Art school from 1954, going to the Slade School, London, in 1956, and taking up sculpture in his last year there. The artist destroyed much of his pre-1975 work. Enjoying a secure reputation among contemporary artists – RB Kitaj purchased three of his works in 1976 – McComb was awarded the Jubilee Prize at the Royal Academy. He has had one-man shows at the Coracle Press in 1979 and at the Arts Council Serpentine Gallery in 1983. For the last 13 years, he has taught art at the Oxford Polytechnic.

BLOSSOMS AND FLOWERS. LEONARD McCOMB (LONDON: CORACLE PRESS, 1979).
10 ff., 655 x 500 mm. (text leaves 635 x 500 mm.), with 6 coloured photolithographs and frontispiece finished by the artist.
Edition of 150 copies, on paper made by Georges Duchêne, Couze, France, with 50 copies for the artist [marked A. P.] (V&A copy one of these).
Printer: Terry Cook, text; Moorgate Lithoplates, photolithographs.
L.5929-1984.

The photolithographs were taken from watercolour drawings, and were modified by the artist during the printing process. The introductory poem is headed by a quotation from William Blake: 'Energy is eternal delight'.

The Coracle Press was founded in 1975 by Simon Cutts and Kay Roberts. From 1965 to 1971, Cutts had run the Tarasque Press with Stuart Mills to publish the literary magazine of the same name, and produced books by Spike Hawkins, Ian Hamilton Finlay and others. The Coracle Press also has a gallery, which opened its doors in the Camberwell New Road in April 1976.

163 MERET OPPENHEIM **1981**

(b. 1913) From 1927, while still at school, Oppenheim collected reproductions of works by German Expressionists, Fauvists and Cubists; the 'Cahier d'une écolière' she drew in 1930 was to be reproduced in LE SURRÉALISME MÊME *in 1957 (this journal was founded by André Breton in an effort to revive the movement after the war). From 1932, she attended courses at the Académie de la Grande Chaumière; through Max Ernst and Giacometti she was drawn into Surrealist circles, exhibiting at the Salon des Surindépendants in 1933 with Dali, Magritte and others. In 1936 she executed her notorious 'Déjeuner en fourrure', a cup and saucer made from fur shown at the Ratton gallery exhibition of Surrealist objects and disseminated in a photograph by Man Ray (though today perhaps taken as the archetypal image of the hangover, the cup originated from a joke between Picasso, Dora Maar and Oppenheim when Picasso declared that there was nothing one could not cover in fur after seeing Oppenheim's fur bracelet). Max Ernst wrote the introduction for her first one-woman show at the Galerie Schulthuss in Basel. Here she lived during the war, designing ballet costumes and evolving a more abstract art verging on Tachisme. In 1966 she made a design for a tapestry commissioned by Basel University.*

SANSIBAR. GEDICHTE UND SERIGRAPHIEN VON MERET OPPENHEIM
(BASEL: EDITION FANAL, 1981).
36 ff. (18 bifolia), 280 x 140 mm., with 16 screenprints.
Edition of 200 copies (V&A copy no. 80), signed by the artist, numbered 1-200 with 18 copies *hors commerce* numbered I-XVIII and 2 copies for exhibition numbered E.E.
Printer: Zoi, Atelier Fanal, Basel, prints; M. Fürer, Basel, text, set in Univers mager 10/45 (completed March 1981).
Binding by René Freiburghaus, Basel.
L.7297-1983.

Book of 16 poems written and illustrated by the artist. Text and illustration on each double-page spread are contained within a circle embossed on the paper.

In der Juninacht
zirpen die Grillen
und der Liguster blüht.
Weiss-und-grün heisst der Liguster
und duftet süss
an der staubigen Strasse,
im trockenen Flussbett.

In der Juninacht
Wetterleuchten wie Wellen
am Ufer des Himmels.
Jammer und Drohung –
Wer ruft um Hilfe?
Ein Tal voller Blitze
jenseits der Berge.

164 ROBERT MOTHERWELL **1981**

(b.1915) After a degree in philosophy, and a thesis on Eugène Delacroix's aesthetics at Harvard in 1937, Motherwell took up painting in New York in 1941, partly as a result of his contacts with refugee Surrealist artists. He learnt engraving from Kurt Seligmann and S. W. Hayter, and produced work as collage. His first one-man show was at Peggy Guggenheim's gallery in New York in 1944. With Harold Rosenberg, he directed the series DOCUMENTS OF MODERN ART *from 1944, publications which made easily available in English the writings of Mondrian, Kandinsky, Moholy-Nagy and others. After the war, he was prominent in the* ABSTRACT EXPRESSIONIST *movement centred on New York, forming in 1948 with Clyfford Still, Baziotes, David Hare and Mark Rothko, the 'Subjects of the Artist' school there. Motherwell's work has been characterised as representing a tension between automatism, derived from Surrealism and Kurt Schwitters, and emulation of Matisse, whom Motherwell considered the most significant artist of the 20th century. In 1965, Motherwell had a major retrospective exhibition at the Museum of Modern Art, New York; in 1978, an exhibition of his paintings and collages was held in the Royal Academy of Arts, London.*

EL NEGRO, LITHOGRAPHS BY ROBERT MOTHERWELL. POEM BY RAFAEL ALBERTI (NEW YORK: TYLER GRAPHICS LTD., 1982).
24pp., including seventeen lithographs, 280 x 380 mm., with 6 lithographs opening out to 380 x 650 mm., and 7 lithographs opening out to 380 x 960 mm.
368 Edition of 51 copies (V&A copy no. 7) signed by the artist, 10 artist's proofs, 1 trial proof, 2 printer's proofs, 1 right to print proof, 3 *hors commerce* and 3 presentation copies.
Printer: Tyler Graphics Ltd Studio.
L.7769–1982.

Motherwell began the work for this publication with Kenneth Tyler in January 1981. The poem *EL NEGRO* was written by Alberti in homage to Motherwell at the time of the latter's retrospective exhibition in Barcelona in 1980 (an event among others that evidenced the renewed respectability of modern art in Spain after Franco's death in 1973). Motherwell's interest in Spain and Latin America can be traced back to the 1930s; in 1941 he spent some time in Mexico with Matta. The poetry of one of Spain's greatest poets Federico Garcia Lorca, murdered by Fascists in Granada in 1936, lay behind the painter's 'Spanish Elegies' series.

Rafael Alberti, a friend of Lorca, had fought with government forces in the Spanish Civil War, and went into exile on Franco's victory to live successively in Buenos Aires, Paris and Rome before returning to his homeland on the restoration of democracy. Motherwell had illustrated his poem *A LA PINTURA* in 1972, but he first met Alberti in Barcelona in 1980.

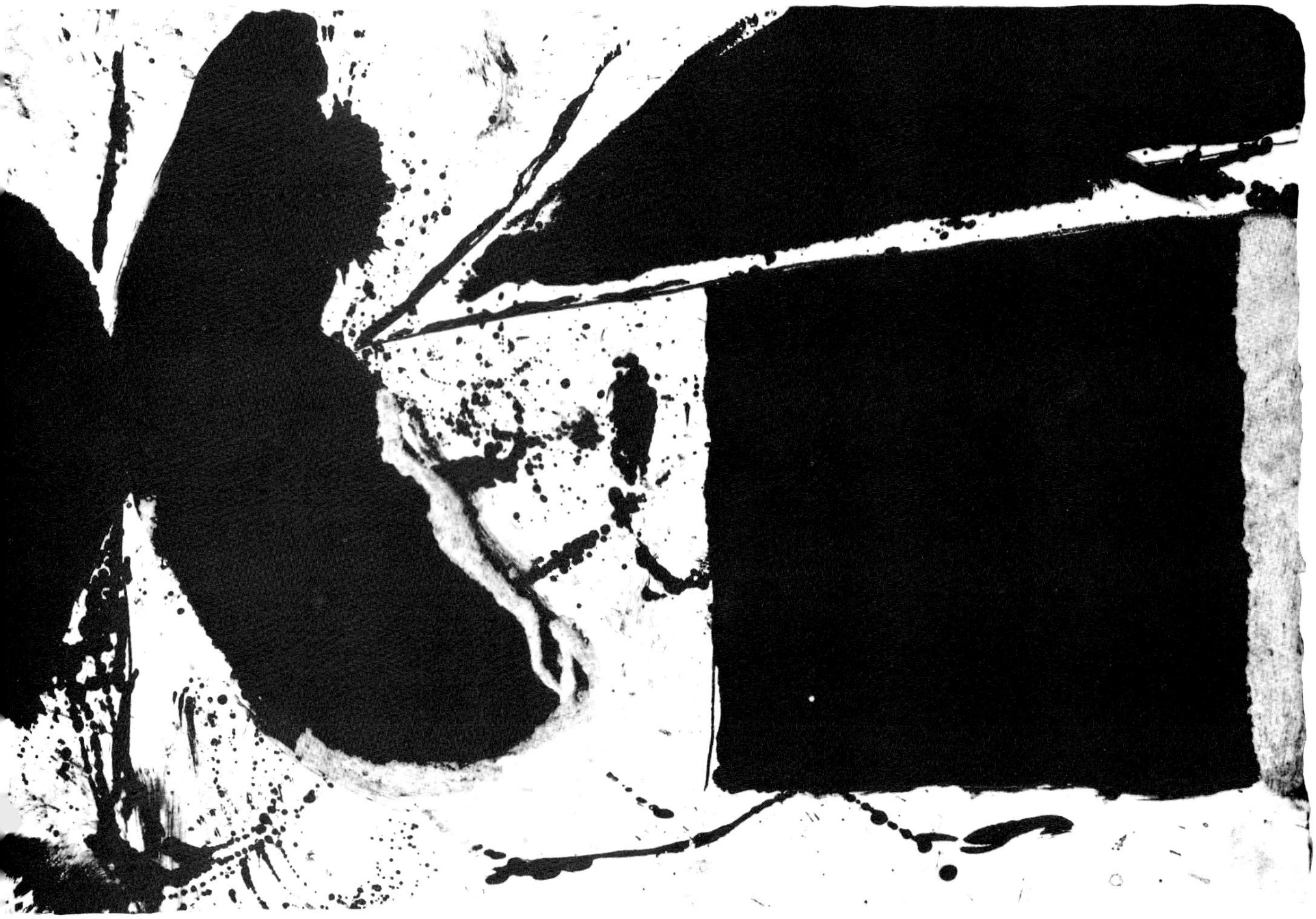

165 JIM DINE 1982

(b.1935)

THE APOCALYPSE. THE REVELATION OF SAINT JOHN THE DIVINE, THE LAST BOOK OF THE NEW TESTAMENT, FROM THE KING JAMES VERSION OF THE BIBLE, 1611, WITH TWENTY NINE PRINTS FROM WOODBLOCKS CUT BY JIM DINE (SAN FRANCISCO: ARION PRESS, 1982).
64pp., 380 x 290 mm., with 29 full-page woodcuts.
Edition of 150 copies (V&A copy no. 77), signed by the artist, on *Apta Vélin* from the Richard de Bas mill, with 15 copies *hors commerce*.
Printer: Arion Press, text set in Monotype Garamond Bold 14–18 point, verse numbers in 12 point Hadriano, display capitals in Stempel Garamond Titling.
Bound in oak veneer plywood boards scorched with a lightning-bolt image drawn by Jim Dine.
L.678–1983.

The frontispiece is a self portrait entitled 'The artist as narrator'. The Arion Press was set up in 1974 by Andrew Hoyem, who had worked for several years in the Auerhahn Press and had co-founded the firm Grabhorn-Hoyem which ran until the death of Robert Grabhorn. The *APOCALYPSE* was the 10th book produced by the Press.

THE ARTIST AS NARRATOR

THAT OLD SERPENT, CALLED THE DEVIL

166 FRANCESCO CLEMENTE **1983–4**

(b.1952) Born in Naples and having verses published in 1964, Clemente studied architecture at Rome University from 1970. The following year he had his first exhibition, of collages. From 1973 to 1979, he spent much time in India; his first long visit to New York came in 1980, where he settled with his family in 1983. In 1984 he worked with Basquiat and Andy Warhol on 'collaborative canvases'. Clemente's work was shown at the Whitechapel Art Gallery, London, in 1983.

ALLEN GINSBERG, *WHITE SHROUD* (1983).
28pp., 390 x 305 mm.
Edition of 1,111 (V&A copy no. 978).
Printed: Kalakshetra Publications, Madras.
Bound in green hand-woven cotton cloth.
L.5928-1984. Colour Plate 35.

WHITE SHROUD was published on the occasion of Clemente's exhibition at the Kunsthalle, Basel, in 1984. Ginsberg noted that the text was 'first scribed in notebook by bedside from 5.30–6.35 A.M. October 5, 1983' and that it was 're-scribed in this Francesco Clemente's folio New York City December 20th 1983 all afternoon'. Allen Ginsberg's signature is flanked by stamps with Chinese characters. The text is a reproduction of Ginsberg's handwriting. Clemente had the volume printed in Madras with a printer capable of achieving the coarse colour effects required by his images.

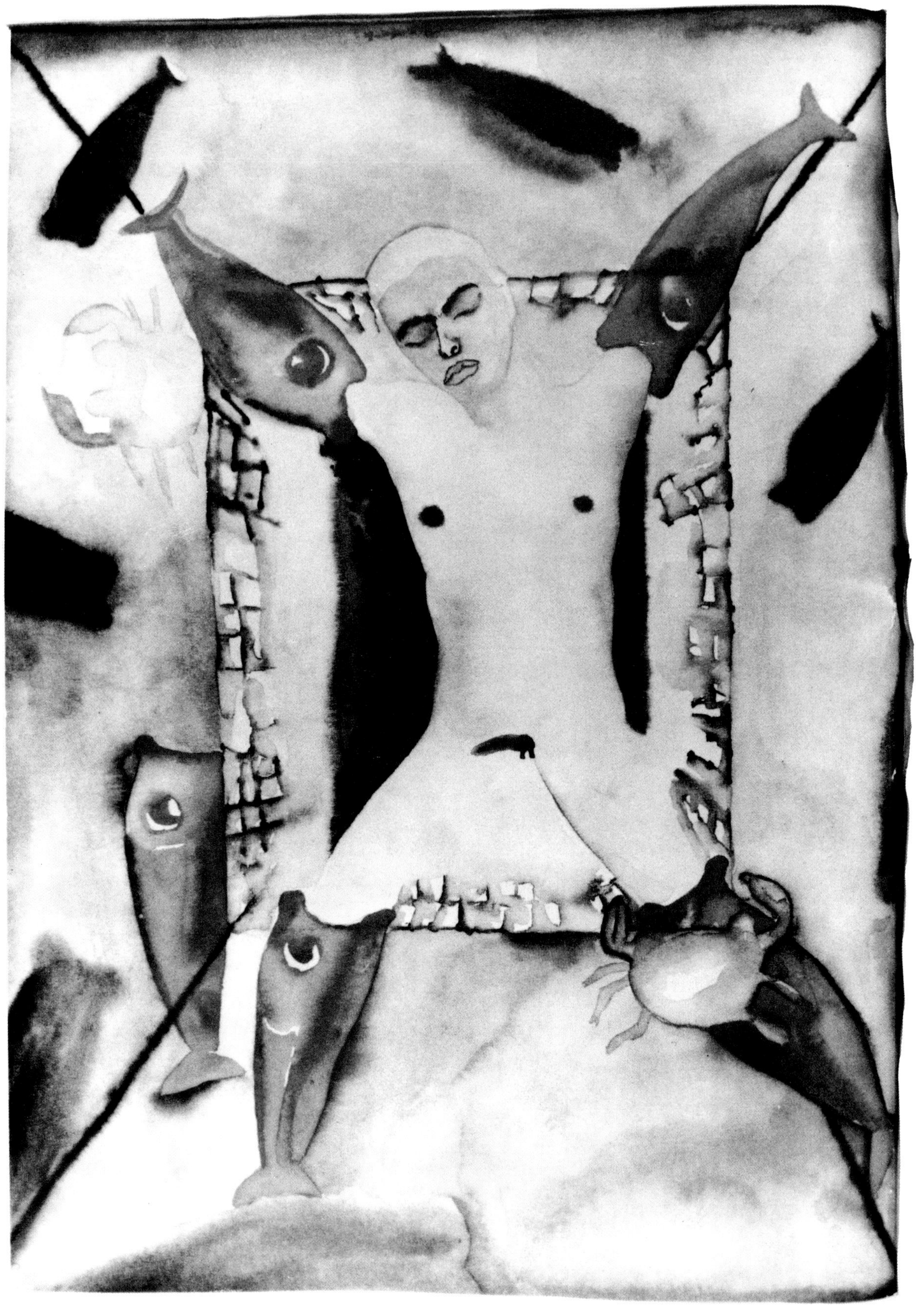

167 RICHARD LONG **1984**

(b.1945) Long studied at the West of England College of Art in Bristol and at the St. Martin's School of Art, London in 1962–8. He created his first land art works in 1967 in England, and all over the world thereafter. His first one-man show was at the Galerie Conrad Fischer, Düsseldorf, in 1968. Elements of his land art work are presented in indoor galleries and museums, while photographs and maps indicate the nature of the works themselves, for instance the creation of straight lines or circles in materials from the landscape and sympathetic to it. Long documents his hikes through uninhabited terrain by means which 'are imbued with a pastoral, pre-industrial Romanticism' (Roberta Smith).

RICHARD LONG, *MUD HAND PRINTS* (LONDON: CORACLE PRESS, 1984).
4 ff., 295 x 340 mm., with print of right hand and left hand.
Edition of 100 copies, un-numbered.
Binder: [Adrian Pasotti, for Coracle Press.]
Printer: Richard Long, handprints; Coracle Press, text (completed May 1984).
L.5925-1984. Colour Plate 36.

Richard Long has made handprints on the walls of galleries and museums, often in the form of circles, for temporary exhibitions. More permanent impressions of the artist's hands are contained in this book. The artist arrived in the premises of the Coracle Press with a bucket of mud from the river Avon carefully mixed to the desired consistency; having made prints of his hands in each of the 100 books, already bound, he threw the remaining mud down the stairwell walls, where the artists who have worked with the Press have all left evidence of their work. Time alone will tell whether the prints created by artist and river will last as long as the reserved image of hands (though with fingers spread-eagled) made by Palaeolithic (Magdalenian) man to be found in caves from the Périgord to the Pyrenees and northern Spain. Should the Avon/Long hands crumble, the 20th and 21st centuries may have to rely on Australian aboriginal art, where the handprint is part of the iconography, to perpetuate the image.

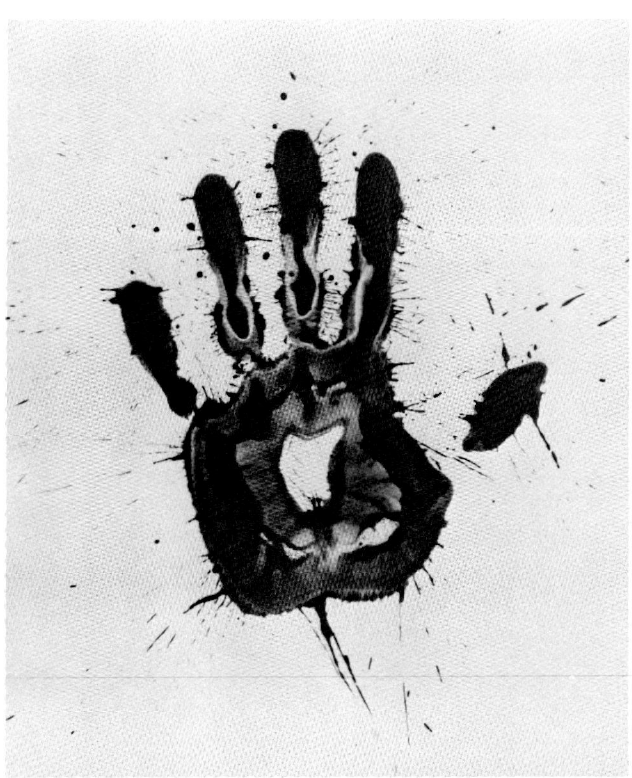

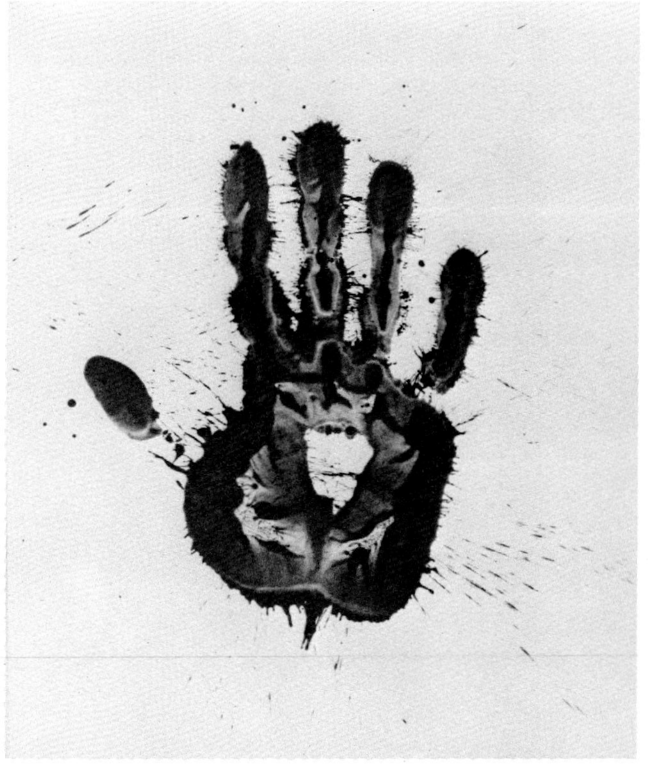

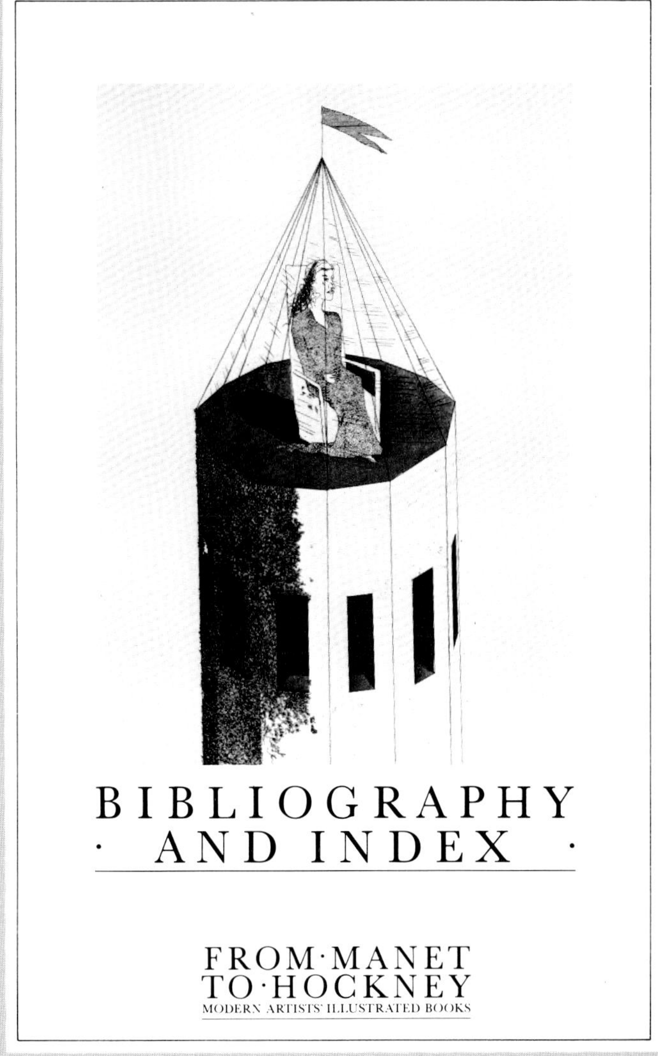

Illustration by DAVID HOCKNEY
for *SIX FAIRY TALES FROM THE BROTHERS GRIMM*,
LONDON, 1969 (CAT.146)

SELECT BIBLIOGRAPHY

The artist and the book, 1860-1960, in western Europe and the United States (BOSTON MUSEUM OF FINE ARTS AND HARVARD COLLEGE LIBRARY, 1961).

Barron, S., and Tuchman, M., *The avant-garde in Russia, 1910-1930. New perspectives* (CAMBRIDGE, MASSACHUSETTS: LOS ANGELES COUNTY MUSEUM OF ART, 1980).

Cary, F., Griffiths, A., & Paisey, D., *The print in Germany, 1880-1933. The age of Expressionism, with a selection of illustrated books from the British Library* (LONDON: BRITISH MUSEUM PUBLICATIONS, 1984).

Compton, S. P., *The world backwards. Russian Futurist books, 1912-1916* (LONDON: THE BRITISH LIBRARY, 1978).

Daniel-Henry Kahnweiler, marchand, éditeur, écrivain (PARIS: CENTRE GEORGES POMPIDOU, MUSÉE NATIONALE D'ART MODERNE, 1984).

Hommage à Tériade (LONDON: ROYAL ACADEMY OF ARTS, 1975).

Johnson, U. E., *Ambroise Vollard, éditeur: prints, books, bronzes (catalogue raisonné)*, 2ND EDITION (NEW YORK: MUSEUM OF MODERN ART, 1977).

Kelpra Studio. An exhibition to commemorate the Rose and Chris Prater gift (LONDON: THE TATE GALLERY, 1980).

Lang, L., *Expressionist book illustration in Germany, 1907-1927*, translated by J. Seligman (LONDON: THAMES & HUDSON, 1976).

Le livre et l'artiste. Tendances du livre illustré français, 1967-1976 (PARIS: BIBLIOTHÈQUE NATIONALE, 1977).

Monroe Wheeler ed., *Modern painters and sculptors as illustrators* (NEW YORK: MUSEUM OF MODERN ART, 1936).

Nicolas Rauch, Geneva, catalogue no.6: *Les peintres et les livres, constituant un essai de bibliographie des livres illustrés de gravures originales par les peintres et les sculpteurs de 1867 à 1957* (GENEVA, 1957).

Albert Skira. Vingt ans d'activité (GENEVA & PARIS: ÉDITIONS ALBERT SKIRA, 1948).

Strachan, W. J., *The artist and the book in France. The 20th Century livre d'artiste* (LONDON: PETER OWEN, 1969).

INDEX OF ARTISTS

Numbers refer to catalogue entries unless where indicated. Numbers in round brackets refer to illustrations by an artist in a catalogue entry devoted to another artist.*

**Plates in the introduction are indicated by page reference*

INDEX OF AUTHORS

Numbers refer to catalogue entries. Where artists are also the authors, see index of artists.

Numbers refer to catalogue entries. Only the publishers of books described in the catalogue are included.

THE ASSOCIATES OF THE VICTORIA AND ALBERT MUSEUM

The following companies and individuals take a particular interest in the Museum and channel their support through the Museum's charity, The Associates of the V & A:

ASSOCIATES

Arthur Andersen & Co
The Baring Foundation
Bonas and Company
Christie's
Colnaghi & Co
Commercial Union Assurance Company
Charles Letts (Holdings) Limited
Mobil
Oppenheimer Charitable Trust
Rose & Hubble Limited
J. Sainsbury plc
Sotheby's
John Swire & Sons Limited
Thames Television

INDIVIDUAL BENEFACTORS AND ASSOCIATES

The Sirdar and Begum Aly Aziz
Sir Duncan Oppenheim
Mrs Basil Samuel

SPONSORS

Through The Associates of the V & A, the following companies, organisations and individuals have sponsored Galleries, Exhibitions, Scholarships, Lectures, Concerts and Catalogues at the V & A since 1981:

The Countess Ahlefeldt
The Aquarius Trust
B.A.D.A.
G P & J Baker Limited
Bankers Trust Company
The Baring Foundation
Cariplo Bank
The Countryside Commission
The Daily Telegraph
Express Newspapers plc
H J Heinz Charitable Trust
Ilford Limited
Jaeger
Sirge Lifar
The Linbury Trust
The Merrill Trust
Mobil
Pearson plc
Pirelli
Mrs Basil Samuel
Trusthouse Forte
United Technolgies

THE FRIENDS OF THE VICTORIA AND ALBERT MUSEUM

Existing within the framework of The Associates, the following Corporate Friends give their support to the Museum:

CORPORATE FRIENDS

Alan Hutchinson Publishing Company Limited
Albert Amor Limited
Antiques Porcelain Company
Artists Cards Limited
Ashstead Decorative & Fine Arts Society
Asprey & Company
Bank of England Arts Society
Bankers Trust Company
Blairman & Sons Limited
British Petroleum
Chase Manhattan Bank
Cobra & Bellamy
Coutts & Co Bankers
Crabtree & Evelyn Limited
Cyril Humphris
Donohoe
Goldsmiths' Company
Hotspur Limited
John Keil Limited
Kennedy Brookes plc
Ian Logan Limited
London & Provincial Antique Dealers' Association
Madame Tussaud's Limited
Marks & Spencer plc
The Medici Society Limited
Mendip Decorative and Fine Arts Society
Barbara Minto Limited
W H Patterson Fine Arts Limited
Pearson plc
Charles Pfister Inc.
Phillips Auctioneers
S J Phillips plc
Phillips Petroleum
Pickering & Chatto
R T Z Services Limited
South Molton Antiques Limited
Spink & Son Limited
Stair & Co
The Fine Art Society Limited
The Wellcome Foundation Limited
William Bedford Antiques
Winifred Williams
World of Islam Festival Trust

INDIVIDUAL FRIENDS *support the Museum both financially and by giving voluntary help, thus forming a personal link with the V & A.*

CN00758964

DIETER KLEIN

LOST WHEELS

The Nostalgic Beauty of Abandoned Cars

DIETER KLEIN

LOST WHEELS

Atlas der vergessenen Autos

teNeues

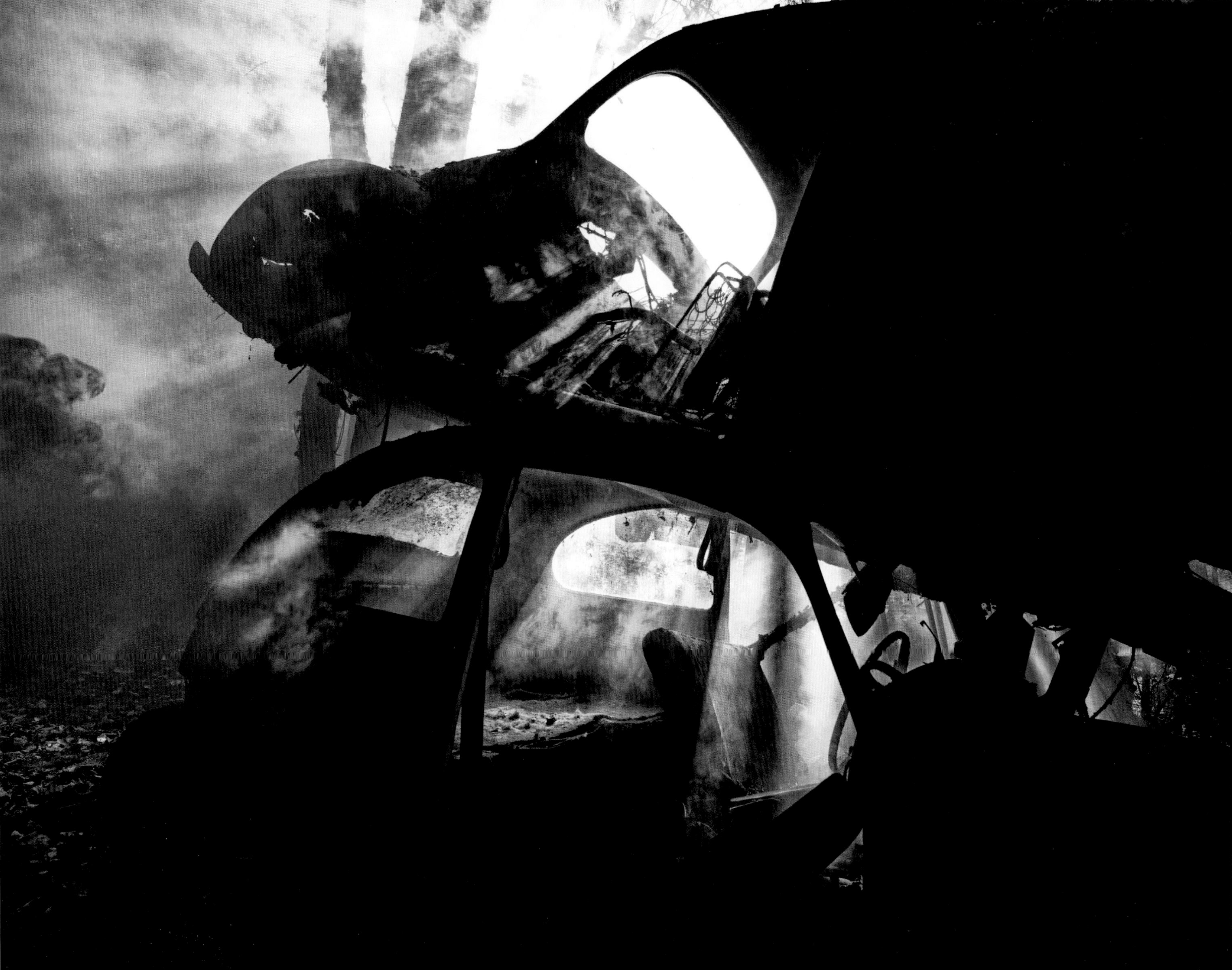

FOREWORD

It all started in Cognac, in this French town in Nouvelle-Aquitaine, at the edge of a small village close by. I fell in love with Rosalie. All of a sudden, I was standing right in front of her, a decades-old delivery truck, ingrown in an elder-bush. Rosalie was "born" in 1935. She is no ageing village beauty; rather, hers is the name of a model series of Citroëns. It was like something out of a fairy tale, and I felt profoundly uplifted in a way that has stuck, to this day. I had yet to understand that this would be the beginning of a major project. My discovery of Rosalie was the beginning of an almost 40,000-mile journey through five European countries and 39 U.S. states.

What a contradictory scene: an automobile—a ride—but one that rides no more. Just don't touch anything, simply let the scene be, leave it to its own devices, and record it; photograph it. Many of these yards, and the historic automobiles they held, have already been cleared—lost to posterity, forever. Become invisible. In my images, the automobiles never outlive their time; instead, they illustrate scenarios of sinking beneath the surface of time. In a certain sense, I am entering upon a world that is shattered but nonetheless still fragile.

Many people feel drawn to "lost places" these days. But to me, the objects must have wheels. I marvel at their lines. I love the sense of nostalgia that emanates from them. I find cars fascinating as soon as they no longer do what they were originally made to do. Though I usually try to find out exactly which make and model we are talking about, in the end it does not matter all that much. It has been sitting there for years—therein lies its being, its essence. These cars here—they will never run, never be driven again.

Some people felt an urge to rescue those cars. Others are fascinated because they have never seen anything like this before. The actual attraction lies in the turn toward the past with a sense of longing, that astonishment in the face of an invisible yet relentless power: Nature takes back everything unto herself. Shape, color, and pattern are ultimately selected by nature. True works of art arise this way. This is magic. This is Forest Punk.

VORWORT

Alles begann in der Nähe von Cognac, der französischen Stadt im Aquitaine Maritime, am Rand eines kleinen Dorfes. Ich verliebte mich in Rosalie. Plötzlich stand ich vor ihr, einem Jahrzehnte alten Lieferwagen, eingewachsen in einen Holunderbusch. Rosalie wurde 1935 „geboren", sie ist keine alternde Dorfschönheit, sondern der Name einer Baureihe von Citroën. Es war wie ein Bild aus einem Märchen und ich spürte eine Ergriffenheit, die mich bis heute nicht mehr loslassen sollte. Dass dies der Anfang eines großen Projektes werden sollte, ahnte ich damals noch nicht. Rosalie's Fund war für mich der Beginn einer nunmehr 64.000 Kilometer langen Reise durch fünf europäische Länder und 39 US-Bundesstaaten.

Welch einen Widerspruch drückte diese Szene aus: Ein Automobil, ein fahrbarer Untersatz, der aber nicht mehr fährt. Bloß nichts anfassen, die Szene einfach in Ruhe für sich stehen lassen und sie fotografieren, genau so festhalten. Viele dieser Plätze mit historischen Automobilen sind bereits geräumt – für immer verloren für die Nachwelt, unsichtbar geworden. In meinen Bildern leben die Autos nicht nur über ihre Zeit hinaus, sondern zeigen Szenarien des In-der-Zeit-Versinkens. Ich betrete gewissermaßen eine zerbrochene und gleichzeitig zerbrechliche Welt.

Heutzutage werden viele Menschen von „Lost Places" angezogen. Aber für mich müssen die Objekte Räder haben. Ich bewundere ihre Formen. Ich liebe die nostalgische Atmosphäre, die sie ausstrahlen. Autos finde ich faszinierend, sobald sie nicht mehr das tun, wofür sie ursprünglich hergestellt wurden. Auch wenn ich herauszufinden versuche, über welches Modell wir reden, ist das schlussendlich nicht so wichtig. Seit Jahren steht es da: das ist sein Wesen, seine Essenz. Diese Autos hier, sie werden nie wieder laufen, nie wieder fahren. Einige Menschen verspüren den Drang, diese Autos retten zu wollen. Andere wiederum sind fasziniert, weil sie so etwas noch nie gesehen haben. Der eigentliche Reiz liegt in dieser sehnsuchtsvollen Hinwendung zu Vergangenem und der Verblüffung über die unsichtbaren, aber unerbittlichen Kräfte: Die Natur nimmt sich alles zurück. Die Natur entscheidet am Ende über Form, Farbe und Muster. Dabei entstehen wahre Kunstwerke. Das ist Magie. Das ist Forest Punk.

I arrived at the clearing at eight-thirty in the morning. Sitting there were these former pioneers of mobility, oddly unmoved and motionless. I felt like I was in a museum, and my sense of affection kept growing. There was something familiar about the atmosphere here; for what I saw were clearly cars. I lost track of space and time and kept photographing uninterrupted. I would snap one photograph, and the next one would already be waiting. An intoxication that would have consequences. I traveled to southern Belgium four times, each time immersing myself afresh in this enchanted, fairy-tale world.

Ich erreichte die Lichtung morgens um halb neun. Die einstigen Pioniere der Beweglichkeit standen sonderbar still und unbewegt da. Ich fühlte mich wie in einem Museum und wurde zusehends berührter. Diese Stimmung hatte etwas Vertrautes, denn es waren eindeutig Autos, die ich da sah. Ich vergaß Raum und Zeit und fotografierte ununterbrochen. Ein Bild ergab sich, und das nächste wartete schon. Ein Rausch mit Folgen. Viermal reiste ich ins südliche Belgien und tauchte jedesmal erneut ein in diese verwunschene Märchenwelt.

Feuerwehr
Wuppertal

The idea had been around for 14 years before it actually came to fruition. It was supposed to be something special, something crazy—something completely different. By his fiftieth birthday in the year 2000, Michael had assembled, all told, a collection of fifty cars from fifty different car makers, all model-year 1950; he would arrange them in his garden, which looked like a forest, and leave them there to rot. The idea was that they should age just like he would—as though they were his brothers and sisters. Issues with the local authorities got resolved and provocations by a few car fanatics got ignored. Michael ultimately celebrated this milestone birthday with 1,000 guests and in the company of his "siblings." Today a couple of empty sekt bottles are still lying there—bearing witness—in the Citroën 2CV "Dolly."

Die Idee hierzu entstand bereits 14 Jahre vor dem tatsächlichen Ereignis. Es sollte etwas Besonderes, etwas Verrücktes, etwas ganz anderes sein. Michael trug bis zu seinem 50. Geburtstag im Jahr 2000 insgesamt 50 Autos von 50 verschiedenen Herstellern zusammen, alle mit dem Baujahr 1950, um sie in seinem waldähnlichen Garten als Autoskulpturenpark zu arrangieren und verrotten zu lassen. Der Gedanke dahinter: Sie sollten altern wie er selbst, als wären sie seine Brüder und Schwestern. Probleme mit dem Ordnungsamt wurden gelöst und Anfeindungen von Autofans ignoriert. Den runden Geburtstag feierte Michael schließlich mit 1000 Gästen inmitten seiner „Geschwister". Ein paar leere Sektflaschen liegen noch heute als Zeugen in der orangenen Citroën „Ente" (2 CV).

RALLYE BAVARIA

2712 U 10

Mr. Martin had a particular predilection: *J'aime les voitures*—I love cars. Mr. Martin dealt in scrap metal. His cars were part of a junkyard, but it seemed like he had no intention of letting them go again. Nobody had touched them for decades; nature had clothed them in green dresses of moss and foliage. And they kept their patience, even as ever more things were set down upon them. The air had gone out of the tires, the rubber had become porous, wooden parts had rotted away, and rust, wind and snow had weakened the hinges and pried open a few doors. Defenseless is what they had become, these cars. The oldest were at the cusp of their hundredth birthdays. But no more sentiments, please; these are just old junk cars.

Herr Martin hatte eine besondere Vorliebe: „*J´aime les voitures.*" „Ich liebe Autos." Herr Martin handelte mit Altmetall. Seine Automobile waren Teil eines Schrottplatzes, aber es schien, als wolle er sie gar nicht mehr hergeben. Seit Jahrzehnten waren sie nicht mehr berührt worden, die Natur hatte ihnen grüne Kleider aus Moos und Blättern angezogen. Und sie blieben geduldig, auch, als immer mehr Dinge auf ihnen abgeladen wurden. Die Luft war aus den Reifen entwichen, das Gummi porös geworden, Holzteile waren zersetzt, Rost, Wind und Schnee hatten die Scharniere geschwächt und einzelne Türen geöffnet. Schutzlos waren sie geworden, diese Autos. Die ältesten standen kurz vor ihrem 100sten Geburtstag. Aber bitte, keine weitere Emotion, das sind nur alte Schrottautos.

When I discovered Rosalie in the midst of an elder-bush near the French town of Cognac, something stirred deep in my photographer's soul. The scene of an eighty-year old Citroën 7U B series was like a fairy tale, a sleeping beauty; in me, it sparked a previously unimagined passion for creating a photographic record of the beauty of decaying automobiles. The car had been sitting there at the edge of a field now for many years. Three of Rosalie's four display instruments were indeed still there, framed by the rusty dashboard. One of the headlights was still completely intact, glass and all; a few switches and buttons gave an impression like they would still work, and the hand brake was engaged.

Why was the car here? What had it been through? Why hadn't it been gotten rid of? Perhaps on account of this: A tree, the world's slowest and cheapest anti-theft device, had grown directly through the steering wheel. What could still be done with Rosalie? Just leave it where it is. Your time is up!

Als ich Rosalie mitten in einem Holunderbusch nahe der französischen Stadt Cognac entdeckte, rührte sich etwas ganz tief in meiner Fotografenseele. Die märchenhaft wirkende Szenerie eines im Dornröschen-Schlaf liegenden über 80-Jährigen Citroën 7U Serie B weckte in mir eine ungeahnte Leidenschaft, die Schönheit des automobilen Verfalls fotografisch festhalten zu wollen. Der Wagen stand schon seit vielen Jahren am Rand einer Wiese. Drei der vier Anzeigeinstrumente von Rosalie waren sogar noch vorhanden, eingerahmt vom rostigen Armaturenbrett. Ein Scheinwerfer war noch komplett mitsamt seinem Glas erhalten, einige Schalter und Knöpfe heuchelten noch Funktionen und die Handbremse war angezogen.

Warum stand der Wagen hier? Was hatte er alles erlebt? Warum wurde er nicht entsorgt? Vielleicht deshalb: Ein Baum, die billigste und langsamste Diebstahlsicherung der Welt, war direkt durch das Lenkrad hindurchgewachsen. Was kann man mit Rosalie noch machen? Einfach stehen lassen, ihre Zeit ist vorbei!

It was wet, and the darkness was total; it was a bit creepy. A few bats flapped past almost noiselessly above my head, roused by the light from my flashlight. It was a huge riddle: more than thirty automobiles sitting in a shallow pit in the sandstone in the middle of Champagne. Pascal had tipped me off: "Come with me. You don't see this kind of thing every day," he said on the telephone. And he was right. Originally, the vehicles were supposed to have been protected by being parked in this cave. It had been a bad decision; for as you know, most caves are very damp. Now they are all totally rusted out–perfect for my photography.

Stockfinster und feucht war es, und ein wenig unheimlich. Ein paar Fledermäuse flatterten fast lautlos über meinen Kopf hinweg, als der Schein meiner Taschenlampe sie störte. Es war ein großes Rätsel: Über 30 Automobile standen in einer Sandsteingrotte inmitten in der französischen Champagne. Von Pascal erhielt ich diesen Tipp: „Komm mit. Das ist etwas Außergewöhnliches", sagte er am Telefon. Und er hatte Recht. Durch das Abstellen in dieser Höhle sollten die Fahrzeuge ursprünglich geschützt werden. Das war eine schlechte Entscheidung gewesen, denn in den meisten Höhlen ist es bekanntlich sehr feucht. Nun sind alle total verrostet – perfekt für meine Fotografie.

OPEL
620-HC42

EN VENTE ICI
PILE WONDER
Castrol
SHELL
NGK
MOTUL
AMILCAR UN JOUR AMILCAR TOUJOUR
QUAND AMILCAR PASSE SALMSON TREPASSE
CASTROL
Esso
ACTIVA
JUST DO IT.
6251 TW·24

52

Its ultimate journey ended calmly and peacefully in a forest of fir-trees. Nature had gotten the upper hand. She took her time, because there is never any hurry, and in the end, she always wins. She coated the bodies with a dull green and then cut her way through the hinges and rubber gaskets. Eventually she conquered the roofs, which collapsed under her weight. How much more time would she mete out to the automobiles? No matter–one way or the other, they had lost. Do we want to mourn them or just leave them alone? A few photos as a reminder: morning fog, first frost, rain, and sunshine. May you rest in peace.

Die letzte Fahrt endete im Tannenwald, ruhig und friedlich. Die Natur hatte die Oberhand gewonnen. Zeit ließ sie sich dabei, weil es niemals eilt und sie letztendlich immer siegt. Erst überzog sie die Blechhaut mit einem stumpfen Grün, dann fraß sie sich durch Scharniere und Gummidichtungen. Später eroberte sie die Dächer und drückte sie mit ihrem Gewicht ein. Wieviel Zeit wird sie den Automobilen noch lassen? Egal, sie haben so oder so verloren. Wollen wir um sie trauern oder sie einfach in Ruhe lassen? Ein paar Fotos zur Erinnerung: Morgennebel, erster Nachtfrost, Regen und Sonnenstrahlen – Ruhet in Frieden.

72

A 122

At first, Åse cut peat on his land. Later, he began stripping and dismantling cars. He simply turned his back on the remains of a hundred and fifty vehicles. He lived here in Sweden, in a wooden house, at a junkyard in the middle of the forest. Then, a television news report drew attention to his abandoned junkyard. People, even in the highest political circles, argued over what the heck to with all this junk. Today and through the year 2050, the junkyard is a protected historical landmark. By then, the witnesses to the cultural history of automobiles will most likely have vanished organically; such is the hope, at least. The mayor set his sights on a cunning objective: Tourists are now coming in droves, taking some pictures, looking around, generating income and–stealing parts. Is marring junk even possible, though? Everything is already broken to begin with. Or are these relics of mobility only for photographers?

It is of no importance to the Opel Olympia Rekord; it is sinking slowly into the moist earth, rusting away, setting its red, brown and blue against the lush green, diving into it as if it had made an arrangement with nature. It would still have some recollection of better times, however slight. But company insignia and nameplates have been lifted, windshields and windows smashed, floors already rusted through–none of it is of any use.

Zuerst hatte Åse auf seinem Grundstück Torf gestochen. Später begann er damit, Autos zu zerlegen. Die Reste von 150 Fahrzeugen ließ er einfach liegen. Er lebte hier in einem Holzhaus auf dem Schrottplatz mitten im Wald in Schweden. Dann machte ein Fernsehbericht seinen verlassenen Schrottplatz bekannt. Bis in die höchsten politischen Ebenen wurde darüber gestritten, was man denn bloß mit all diesem Schrott tun sollte. Heute steht der Schrottplatz unter Denkmalschutz, bis ins Jahr 2050. Dann werden die Zeugen der automobilen Kulturgeschichte wahrscheinlich auf natürliche Weise verschwunden sein, so hofft man zumindest. Der Bürgermeister hatte ein raffiniertes Ziel im Blick: Jetzt kommen Touristen in Scharen, fotografieren, schauen, machen Umsatz und – klauen Teile. Doch kann man Schrott eigentlich noch beschädigen? Es ist doch sowieso schon alles kaputt. Oder sind die Relikte der Mobilität nur für Fotografen reserviert?

Dem Opel Olympia Rekord ist das völlig egal, er versinkt langsam im feuchten Grund, rostet vor sich hin, stellt sein Rot, Braun und Blau gegen das üppige Grün, taucht darin ein, als hätte er sich mit der Natur arrangiert. Ein kleines bisschen Erinnerung an bessere Zeiten wird er noch haben. Doch Firmenlogos und Typenschilder sind entwendet, die Scheiben eingeschlagen, der Unterboden schon durchgerostet – das alles hat keinen Sinn mehr.

86

CHEVROLET

MERCURY
CALIFORNIA
923 NXB

Gene Winfield opened his front door, and we stood in an anteroom that was stuffed from floor to ceiling with automobile and technical parts and gadgets. Gene's mother had remodeled what used to be a henhouse into a gas station. He says he took over in 1946 and preserved the historical objects to this day. "Whoa. 1946. Do you mind if I ask how old you are?" I asked, astounded. "Yeah, I'm 89 years old!" We stepped into the first room of his residence. There stood an orangey-red vehicle with a driver's cab, open on the passenger's side, with no roof. He introduces it to me as the "strip star," a sports car with an aluminum body and a powerful V8 engine. Then he opened a guitar case and brought forth a yellow electric guitar with a pick-up in the shape of his company logo, a 1930s-era Buick. The neck of the guitar is adorned with an inlay in the shape of a hat, sunglasses, and long white beard: "This is the new guitar I designed for ZZ Top. They'll be getting it next week." Next, he activated an electric sliding door, opening a pentagonal passageway and thereby revealing a view onto what looked like the Star Trek command center. Without realizing it, I had landed at the house of the Gene Winfield, the great designer.

Winfield designed and built sets for Star Trek; cars for movies like Batman; the police car from Robocop; and 25 vehicles for Blade Runner. His business today still consists of building so-called custom cars—that is, historical automobiles that he painstakingly restores, refits with new, powerful engines, and finishes according to his customers' individual specifications.

Gene Winfield öffnete die Haustür, und wir standen in einem Vorraum, der bis unter die Decke mit technischen, automobilen Dingen vollgestellt war. Gene´s Mutter hatte den ehemaligen Hühnerstall zu einer Tankstelle umgebaut. 1946 habe er diese übernommen und die historischen Objekte bis heute erhalten.

„Hoppla, 1946, darf ich mal fragen, wie alt Du bist?", fragte ich erstaunt. „Yeah, I´am 89 years old!" Wir betraten den ersten Raum seiner Wohnung. Dort stand ein orange-roter Wagen mit einer Kabine für den Fahrer, der Beifahrer offen, ohne Dach. Das sei der „Strip Star", ein Sportwagen mit Aluminiumkarosserie und einem leistungsstarken V8-Motor. Dann öffnete er einen Gitarrenkoffer mit einer gelben E-Gitarre, der Tonabnehmer in Form seines Firmenlogos, einem Buick aus den 1930er Jahren. Den Gitarrenhals zierte eine Intarsie mit Hut, Sonnenbrille und einem langen weißen Bart: „This is the new guitar I designed for ZZ Top, they will get it next week." Als nächstes öffnete er mit einer elektrischen Schiebetür den fünfeckigen Durchgang und gab so den Blick frei auf etwas, das aussah wie die Startreck Kommandozentrale. Ich war ohne es zu wissen bei dem großartigen Designer Gene Winfield gelandet.

Winfield entwarf und baute Autos für Filme wie Batman, 25 Fahrzeuge für Blade Runner, den Polizeiwagen aus Robocop und Startreckkulissen. Das heutige Standbein seiner Firma sind nach wie vor so genannte Customcars, historische Automobile, die aufwendig restauriert, mit neuen, leistungsstarken Motoren versehen und nach individuellen Kundenwünschen fertiggestellt werden.

Oldsmobile

6,000
RUNS

Cadillac
48 Cad

Ford

HT-1976

It is pretty secluded in Montana, just a few miles north to the Canadian border and a skip and a jump east to North Dakota. On the way to the motel, I saw two old silos that I wanted to get a closer look at. Some abandoned train tracks ran past the mighty wooden structures. But the two of them quickly took on secondary importance when I spotted some old pickups around back. And then there it sat, between a little wooden shed and an abandoned house: a pink Caddy ... no; it was a Dodge. A 1960 four-door sedan. There were no tire tracks and no lane or driveway to be seen. The car sat amid the grass in front of the derelict house, a scene like in an old movie.

Later on, Dale told me the car's story. His father had parked the Dodge in front of his house two days before he died. Dale, now over seventy himself, has made no use of the car, the house, or the property since. He left this final scene undisturbed, let time run its course—out of respect for his father. Ever since 1977, the property has been a kind of family memorial. The waiting paid off for me, for the sun, after disappearing below the horizon, served up a little bit of pink for the clouds—to match the pink Dodge.

In Montana ist es ziemlich einsam. Nur noch ein paar Meilen gen Norden bis zur kanadischen Grenze, ostwärts ein Katzensprung bis Nord Dakota. Auf dem Weg zum Motel sah ich zwei alte Silos, die ich mir aus der Nähe ansehen wollte. Eine verwaiste Bahnlinie führte an den mächtigen, hölzernen Bauten vorbei. Doch die beiden wurden schnell zur Nebensache, als ich auf der Rückseite ein paar alte Pickups sah. Und dann stand er da, zwischen kleinen Holzschuppen und einem verlassenen Wohnhaus: Ein pinkfarbener Caddi... nein, das war ein Dodge. Ein 4-Door Sedan von 1960. Weder Fahrspuren noch ein Weg waren zu sehen. Der Wagen stand mitten im Gras vor dem verlassenen Haus, eine Szene wie aus einen alten Film.

Dale erzählte mir später die Geschichte des Wagens. Sein Vater hatte den Dodge vor seinem Haus abgestellt – zwei Tage bevor er starb. Dale, inzwischen selbst über 70 Jahre alt, hat seitdem weder das Auto, das Haus oder das Grundstück genutzt. Er überließ diese letzte Szene sich selbst und der Zeit, aus Respekt gegenüber seinem Vater. Seit 1977 ist das Grundstück nun eine Art Familienmemorial. Für mich lohnte sich das Warten, denn die Sonne schickte mir, nachdem sie hinter dem Horizont verschwunden war, ein bisschen Rosa für die Wolken – passend zum pinkfarbenen Dodge.

Chevrolet

OFFICE

BOOMTOWN

I had only seen a single picture online, and I possessed the coordinates, in the middle of the state of Washington. What sort of motif awaited me when I arrived? Another twenty-five miles down the highway, and then I ought to be able to see it to my right. I became tense with anticipation. "No, it's got to be on the left, I'm coming in from the north, you know." Is the yard still there? Can I go onto it? Is anyone there? Questions about questions. And now I stood directly in front of it. The owner lives adjacent to the yard. I was not sure it would be okay to take pictures.

"Sure, go ahead." "And later this evening, when the light is better?" "Yeah. But please close the wooden gates behind you. A few sheep and goats are grazing in the yard. I don't want them running away on me." Sheep and goats? Hadn't I come on account of the cars? I was not disappointed: The red-painted wooden workshop, the 1930s-era Hupmobile, hundreds of spare parts hanging from the ceiling, headlights, instrument panels and radiator grills. Time seemed to have stood still here; an automobile still life, untouched for decades. I had already been in so many great settings on this trip, and now this workshop—perfect luck and happiness for a photographer. An excellent basis for a big shot!

Ich hatte nur ein einziges Bild im Internet gesehen und besaß die Koordinaten mitten im Bundesstaat Washington. Welches Motiv würde mich am Ende erwarten? Noch 25 Meilen den Highway entlang, dann müsste es auf der rechten Seite zu sehen sein. Die Spannung stieg. „Nein, es muss auf der linken Seite sein, ich komme ja von Norden gefahren. Gibt es den Platz noch, kann ich ihn betreten, ist jemand da?" Fragen über Fragen. Und jetzt stand ich genau davor. Der Eigentümer wohnt direkt neben dem Platz. Ob ich fotografieren dürfte? „Ja klar, mach nur." „Auch später am Abend, wenn das Licht schöner ist?", „Ja. Aber bitte schließ die Holztore hinter Dir zu, auf dem Platz grasen ein paar Schafe und Ziegen. Die sollen mir nicht abhauen." Schafe und Ziegen? Ich war doch wegen der Autos da. Ich wurde nicht enttäuscht: Die rotgestrichene, hölzerne Werkstatt, das 1930er Hupmobile, hunderte Ersatzteile von der Decke baumelnd, Frontleuchten, Armaturenbretter und Kühlergrills. Hier schien die Zeit stehen geblieben zu sein. Ein automobiles Stillleben, seit Jahrzehnten unberührt. Ich hatte schon so viele großartige Szenen auf dieser Reise erlebt und jetzt diese Werkstatt – perfektes Fotografenglück. Eine hervorragende Voraussetzung für einen „Big Shot"!

PLYMOUTH
0
10
20
30
40
50
60
70
80
90
100

151·489

JAYDENS GARAGE
TANNER'S GAS SERVICE

SPEED
TOTAL
TRIP
OIL PRESSURE
Stewart

Please!
CLOSE THE
GATE

Danny Ellis, retired, has wholly dedicated himself to his passion: restoring historic vehicles. Proudly, he showed me his special collection of hood ornaments. To be safe, he stored it in a display case in his house. For my photographs, he mounted them onto the vehicles: "Looks a lot better already, doesn't it?" And then he told me the story of the 1934 Studebaker. A few years back, he had been keeping his ninety-three-year old neighbor company in the hospital during what would be his final weeks. He visited the old gentleman every day. As a token of his gratitude, he gave Danny the old Studebaker. When Danny went back to pick up his car a few weeks later, there could be no other explanation: the hood ornament had been stolen. He looked for a spare on the Internet and found one for $250. He had to drive about two hundred miles for it, since he wanted to have a good look at it before buying. Upon his arrival, he saw that it was his own–stolen–ornament. What do to? Go to the police? But now, this guy knew his name, and even where he lived. What if this isn't all he's done, and he gets put away for a few months on account of this theft? And afterwards were to come seek revenge? After a moment's hesitation, Danny then forked over the $250 for his own hood ornament. The swan now flies on the Studebaker as it had always done before.

Danny Ellis widmet sich jetzt im Rentenalter ganz seiner Leidenschaft und restauriert historische Fahrzeuge. Stolz zeigte er mir seine besondere Sammlung von Kühlerfiguren. Zur Sicherheit lagert er sie in einer Vitrine im Haus. Für meine Fotos montierte er einige auf die Fahrzeuge: „Das sieht doch gleich viel besser aus." Und dann erzählt er mir die Geschichte von dem 1934er Studebaker: Vor einigen Jahren begleitete er seinen 93jährigen Nachbarn in seinen letzten Wochen im Krankenhaus. Jeden Tag besuchte er den alten Herrn. Als Zeichen seiner Dankbarkeit schenkte er Danny den alten Studebaker. Als er das Fahrzeug nach einigen Wochen abholte, musste er feststellen, dass die Kühlerfigur gestohlen worden war. Er suchte nach Ersatz im Internet und wurde fündig: 250$ sollte die Figur kosten. Etwa 200 Meilen musste er dafür fahren, denn er wollte sie sich erst genau ansehen. Vor Ort stellte er fest, dass es seine gestohlene Figur war. Was tun? Den Kerl anzeigen? Der kannte aber jetzt seinen Namen und auch die Adresse. Was ist, wenn der schon anderen Mist gebaut hat und wegen dieses Diebstahls gleich für ein paar Monate im Gefängnis landen würde? Und anschließend sich an ihm rächen würde...? Er zögerte nur kurz und bezahlte dann die 250$ für seine eigene Kühlerfigur. Jetzt fliegt der Schwan wie eh und je auf dem Studebaker.

I walked about fifty yards and stood before a closed gate, looking at a big lawn, two palm-trees, a house, and a lone car. I simply dialed the number. Margaret said, "Oh yes, you're the one who e-mailed me; when are you coming to the U.S.?" When I said I was already at the gate, we both cracked up. She came and got me, and I told her what I had in mind. "Well, I really don't let anybody take pictures here. My husband runs the shop and restores these Porsches for international clients." And then, at some point, she agreed to it after all. She showed me the yard, and I photographed it in the evening light as well as the next day in the morning, at first light. It was very warm, around 95 °F, and dry leaves from last fall rustled beneath my shoes. Out back, behind the workshop, there were something like thirty Porsches. Most models were of the 1950s-era 356-series. All of them were rusted, with parts missing, and looked really awful. I thought to myself, "If I let a Porsche lover see this, I'm going to cause a lot of anguish." Cicadas were chirping; otherwise, it was very quiet. It may be a comfort to some that these vehicles are all awaiting restoration. That these remnants could be restored to the point of functioning automobiles, though–this is sometimes hard to imagine.

Nach 50 Metern stand ich vor einem verschlossenen Tor, blickte auf eine große Rasenfläche, zwei Palmen, ein Wohnhaus und nur ein einziges Auto. Ich rief einfach an. Margaret meinte: „Ja, Du hast mir doch eine Mail geschrieben. Wann kommst Du denn in die USA?" Nachdem ich sagte, dass ich bereits vor dem Tor stünde, mussten wir beide lachen. Sie holte mich ab und ich erzählte ihr, was ich vorhätte. „Nun, ich gestatte es eigentlich niemandem, hier Fotos zu machen. Mein Mann führt die Werkstatt und restauriert diese Porsche für internationale Kunden". Und dann gab sie irgendwann doch ihr Okay. Sie zeigte mir den Platz, und ich fotografierte sowohl im Abendlicht als auch am nächsten Tag im ersten Morgenlicht. Es war sehr warm, etwa 35 Grad Celsius, unter meinen Schuhe knisterten die trockenen Blätter des vergangenen Herbsts. Hinter dem Werkstattgebäude standen vielleicht 30 Porsche. Die meisten Modelle stammten aus der Baureihe 356 aus den 1950er Jahren. Alle hatten Rost und Fehlteile und sahen wirklich übel aus. Ich dachte bei mir: „Wenn ich das hier einem Porscheliebhaber zeige, werde ich eine Menge Leid erzeugen." Zikaden zirpten, ansonsten war es ganz still. Es mag dem einen oder anderen ein Trost sein, dass diese Fahrzeuge alle auf ihre Restaurierung warten. Doch dass man aus diesen „Resten" wieder funktionstüchtige Automobile restauriert, ist bisweilen schwer vorstellbar.

0
10
20
30
40
50
60
70
80
90
100

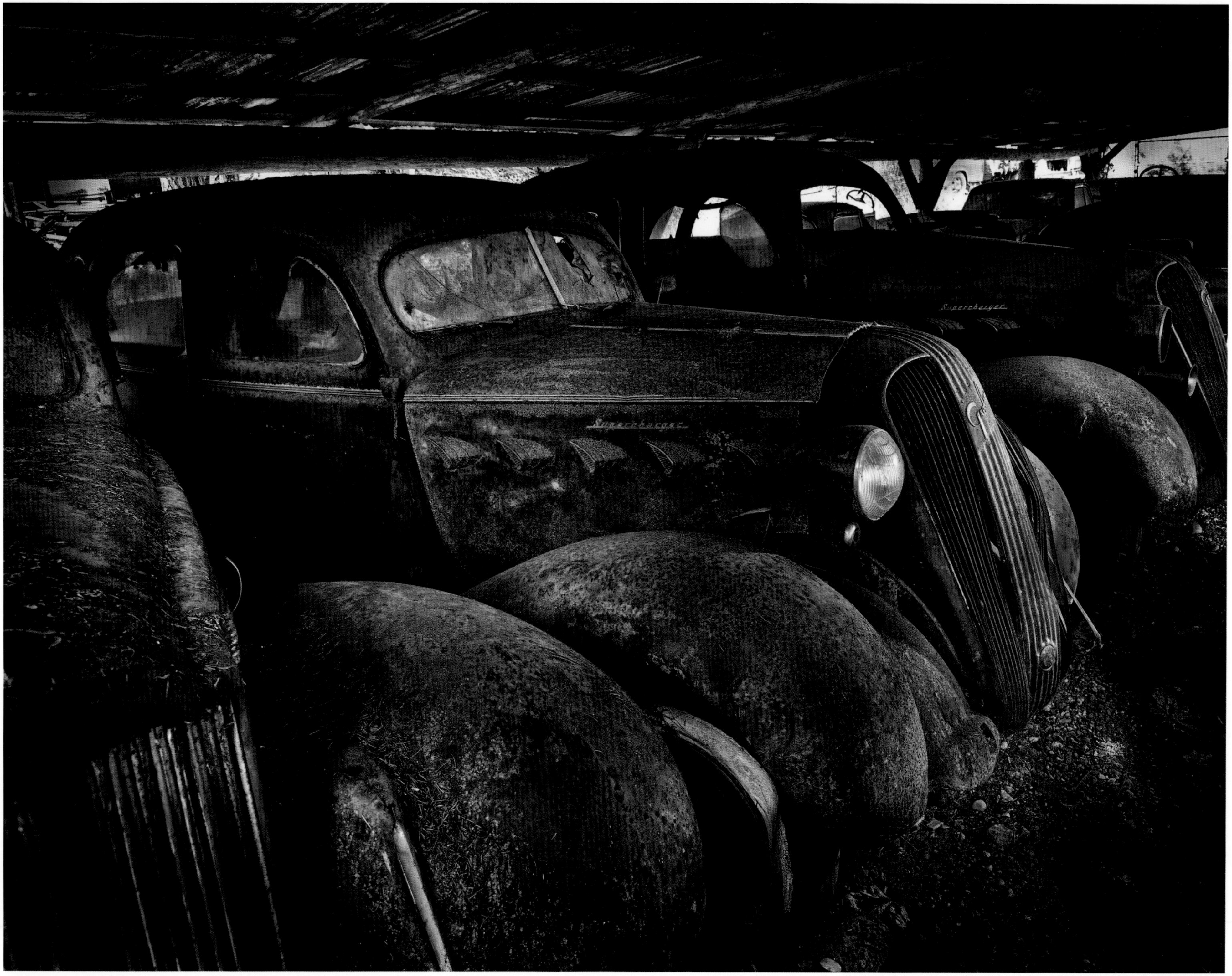

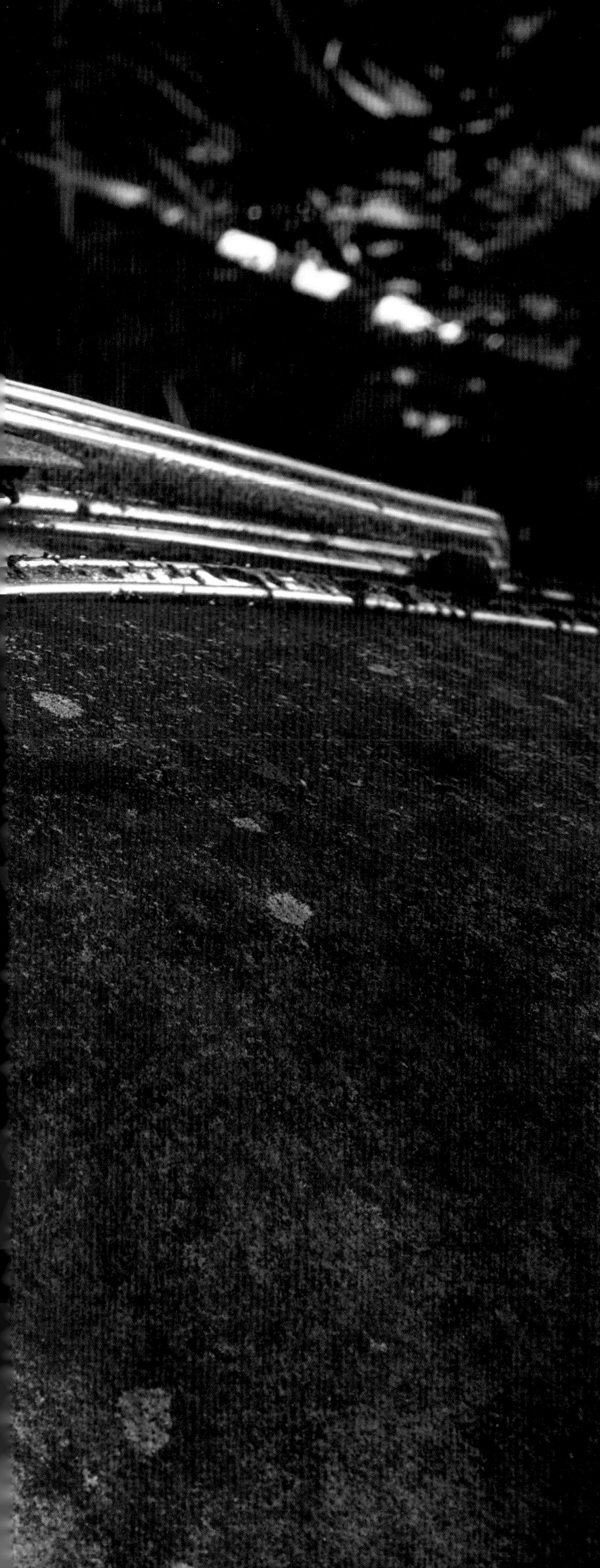

A 1937 Chrysler sits in a corner, right along the fence, with seven branches growing from its rusted-out floor and up through the split windshield frames, now glassless. Outside, a signboard entices visitors: "CARS, ART, NATURE, HISTORY." Dean's parents opened a store selling sundries in the 1930s—not very long after the town was founded—and they expanded the business a few years later to include a junkyard. Dean, their son, took over the lot in the 1970s and acquired more cars at auctions and from recycling yards or private sellers. But meanwhile, he has come to see this place as more of a work of art rather than a junkyard. Visitors pay twenty dollars admission for the privilege of gazing in wonder at this 4,000-car collection between the hours of 9 a.m. and 5 p.m. Odd, familiar vehicles and cars that have become rooted to the spot. The sheer number of vehicles was my first major experience on this tour through the Midwest. I spent several days at this yard and walked many of its all told nearly seven miles of rows, past Oldsmobiles and Chevrolets, Fords and Pontiacs, VWs and Dodges and Cadillacs and Kaisers and Buicks and Plymouths and Chryslers and DeSotos ... . And no: I had never seen anything like this before.

Ein 1937er Chrysler mit sieben Ästen, die vom durchgerostetem Autoboden durch die geteilten, inzwischen glaslosen, Frontfenster wachsen, steht in einer Ecke direkt hinterm Zaun. Draußen lädt ein Schild zum Besuch ein: „CARS, ART, NATURE, HISTORY". Die Eltern eröffneten in den 1930er Jahren einen Gemischtwarenladen in dem damals noch jungen Ort und erweiterten ihr Geschäft ein paar Jahre später um einen Schrottplatz. In den 1970er Jahren übernahm ihr Sohn Dean den Platz und kaufte weitere Autos auf Auktionen, Recyclinghöfen oder von Privatleuten an. Er sieht in diesem Ort inzwischen mehr ein Kunstobjekt als einen Schrottplatz. Besucher zahlen 20 Dollar Eintritt und dürfen dann zwischen 9 und 17 Uhr die 4000 angesammelten Autos bestaunen. Kuriose, bekannte Fahrzeuge und eingewachsene Autos. Die schiere Menge an Fahrzeugen waren für mich das erste große Erlebnis dieser Tour durch den Mittleren Westen. Mehrere Tage verbrachte ich auf diesem Platz und lief viele der insgesamt 11 Kilometer langen Wege, vorbei an Oldsmobile und Chevrolet, Ford und Pontiac, VW und Dodge und Cadillac und Kaiser und Buick und Plymouth und Chrysler und DeSoto... Nein, so etwas hatte ich bislang noch nicht gesehen!

OLDSMOBILE

60E
60E

I learned about the auction from a notice on an automotive blog. The collection, begun in 1946 by a farmer named Oliver Jordan, was officially closed again in 1953. He must have been someone you would call stubborn. The county was trying to tell him how to run his junkyard and buy and sell his cars. It did not suit him one bit. So he fenced in the property, and from then on, the premises on which the cars sat would be secured by dogs. He kept collecting for a few more years but didn't let anyone else on the property. When he later returned to farming, the collection was forgotten. Oliver Jordan died in 2004 at the age of 94. His grandson Stuart looked after the cars for a few years after that; he built a storage barn to get the most valuable ones out of the elements.

Ten years after the death of his grandfather, Stuart decided to sell the collection. What a spectacle! There were 1,500 visitors on site and 110 more bidding online. It had rained the last few nights; the early-June temperatures had already risen to 97 °F, and the humid air attracted armies of mosquitos. The big day wound up being a perfect summer day, however; and at an insane pace, one car after another was sold. The Cord 810 as well as the 812–classic designs from the 1930s–each fetched up to $46,000. Down to the last part, all of it found a buyer. All told, 120 automobiles manufactured between 1920 and 1960, along with thousands of individual parts, were auctioned off and departed from Enid, Oklahoma that evening, headed in every direction.

Den Hinweis auf die Versteigerung fand ich auf einem Autoblog. 1945 kaufte Oliver Jordan einen bestehenden Schrottplatz, der aber bereits 1953 wieder geschlossen wurde. Er war wohl jemand, den man einen Sturkopf nennt. Das Ordnungsamt wollte ihm vorschreiben, wie er seinen Schrottplatz bzw. Auto-An- und Verkauf zu führen habe. Das passte ihm so gar nicht. Also zäunte er das Gelände ein und Hunde sicherten von nun an das Grundstück mit den Automobilen. Er sammelte wohl noch einige Jahre weiter, ließ aber niemanden mehr auf das Grundstück. Später arbeitete er wieder als Farmer und die Sammlung geriet in Vergessenheit. 2004 verstarb Oliver Jordan 94-jährig. Sein Enkel Stuart kümmerte sich noch einige Jahre um die Autos, ließ eine Halle errichten, um die wertvollsten dort unterzustellen.

Zehn Jahre nach Großvaters Tod entschied er sich dann, die Sammlung zu verkaufen. Was für ein Spektakel! 1500 Besucher waren vor Ort, weitere 110 online dabei. Es hatte die Nächte zuvor geregnet, die Temperatur war Anfang Juni bereits auf 36 Grad Celsius geklettert, die feuchte Luft lockte Heerscharen von Mücken an. Doch der große Tag geriet zum Traumsommertag und in irrwitzigem Tempo wurde ein Wagen nach dem anderen verkauft. Bis zu jeweils 46.000 Dollar erzielten die beiden Cord 810 und 812, Designklassiker aus den 1930er Jahren. Alles und jedes Teil fand einen Käufer. Insgesamt 120 Automobile aus der Zeit von 1920 bis 1960 und tausende Einzelteile kamen unter den Hammer und verließen am Abend Enid, Oklahoma, in alle Himmelsrichtungen.

225E

OLDSMOBILE

3UVV932

1GV 763

Ford

In 1775, the Spanish had named the area around Nelson, Nevada Eldorado because this is where they found their first gold. The majority of its inhabitants would eventually be Civil War deserters, all of whom were looking for a place off the map. Disputes over mining claims and property rights would often precipitate acts of violence and murder. Since the nearest sheriff resided about two hundred miles away and a deputy would hardly have wielded the necessary caliber, law enforcement rarely showed its face in Nelson.

The mines operated from about 1858 until 1945, during which time several millions of dollars were made in gold, silver, copper, and lead. Almost the entire village is now privately owned. It has become a kind of open-air museum consisting of old signboards, tools and implements, various buildings, houses and workshops, and a good two dozen vehicles.

The green Cadillac has a bumper from a Buick—no one knows why. Behind the Ford with the camper van, someone found space for an airplane, beautifully decorated, as though it had crashed here. Warnings are issued about the teddy bear cholla, a cactus with needle-thin, barbed spines that can get lodged in your skin, break off, and cause an infection. And of course, you should always watch your step, because the many ideal hide-outs in this place are also much loved by rattlesnakes.

Das Gebiet von Nelson wurde 1775 von den Spaniern als Eldorado bezeichnet, denn hier machten sie ihre ersten Goldfunde. Die Mehrheit seiner späteren Bewohner waren Deserteure des Bürgerkriegs, allesamt auf der Suche nach einem versteckten Ort. Streitigkeiten über Bergbau- und Eigentumsansprüche führten häufig zu Gewalttätigkeiten und Morden. Da der nächste Sheriff etwa 200 Meilen entfernt lebte und ein Hilfssheriff kaum Durchschlagskraft gehabt hätte, tauchten die Strafverfolgungsbehörden in Nelson nur selten auf.

Die Minen waren von etwa 1858 bis 1945 aktiv. Im Laufe dieser Zeit wurden mehrere Millionen Dollar mit Gold, Silber, Kupfer und Blei erwirtschaftet. Inzwischen liegt fast das gesamte Dorf in privater Hand. Es ist eine Art Freilichtmuseum entstanden, bestehend aus verschiedenen Häusern, Werkstätten und mit gut zwei Dutzend Fahrzeugen, alten Werbetafeln und Werkzeug.

Der grüne Cadillac hat eine Stoßstange von einem Buick – warum, weiß niemand. Hinter dem Ford mit dem Wohnwagen bot sich noch Platz für ein Flugzeug, schön dekoriert, als wäre es hier abgestürzt. Man wird aber auch vor den Kakteen, den „Teddy Bear Cholla“ gewarnt. Deren Stacheln, dünn wie Stecknadeln, können mit ihren kleinen Widerhaken in der Haut steckenbleiben, abbrechen und zu Entzündungen führen. Und natürlich sollte man immer darauf achten, wohin man tritt, denn auch Klapperschlangen lieben den Ort mit seinen vielen idealen Verstecken.

GAS STATION
APPROVED
Packard
SERVICE
LUBRICATION
AUTOLITE
BATTERIES
THIS SALE
GALLONS

CALIFORNIA
HES 296

184

STOP

The main tourist attraction of Lamar, Colorado, population less than 8,000, has to be the oldest building in the world–a tire store. It consists of fossilized or petrified wood that originated about thirty miles south of Lamar. Since the highway passes through the downtown, it is impossible to overlook the old filling station on main street. But the main attraction for me is a spectacular junkyard at the edge of town. The street is elevated few yards above the grounds, which affords me a good camera angle. I am here on a Saturday, the yard is closed, but the exterior vantage point is perfect as-is. When the rain lets up, I am standing beneath the raised rear hatch of my vehicle. A tripod prevents shaking, and I am using a cable release so I don't need to touch the camera anymore. And now, we wait. After half an hour, wind and sun grant me a dramatic atmosphere. In the rapidly changing light, I shoot countless images of the magnificently colored sunset. Since it was such an amazing scene, I return just before twilight the next day. The drama begins a new, this time offering me a dark sky with an impressive thunderstorm on the horizon. The sun does not always have to be shining, you know.

Die touristische Hauptattraktion des Ortes Lamar, Colorado, mit seinen knapp 8000 Einwohnern ist wohl das älteste Gebäude der Welt, ein Reifengeschäft. Es besteht aus versteinertem bzw. verkieseltem Holz, das etwa dreißig Meilen südlich von Lamar gefunden wurde. Auf der Hauptstraße ist die ehemalige Tankstelle nicht zu übersehen, da der Highway durch die Innenstadt führt. Für mich ist die Hauptattraktion ein spektakulärer Schrottplatz am Stadtrand. Die Straße liegt ein paar Meter oberhalb des Areals und erlaubt mir einen guten Kamerastandpunkt: Es ist Samstag und der Platz verschlossen, der erhöhte Blick von außen bereits perfekt. Als der Regen schwächer wird, stehe ich im Schutz unter der geöffneten Heckklappe meines Wagens. Das Stativ verhindert Verwacklungen, mit Drahtauslöser brauche ich die Kamera nicht mehr berühren, und nun heißt es abwarten. Nach einer halben Stunde schenken mir Wind und Sonne eine dramatische Stimmung. Im schnellen Wechsel des Lichts entstehen zahllose Bilder des farbenprächtigen Sonnenuntergangs. Weil die Szene so schön war, kehre ich am folgenden Tag kurz vor der Dämmerung zurück. Das Schauspiel beginnt von Neuem, beschert mir aber diesmal einen düsteren Himmel mit beeindruckendem Gewitter am Horizont. Es muss ja nicht immer die Sonne scheinen.

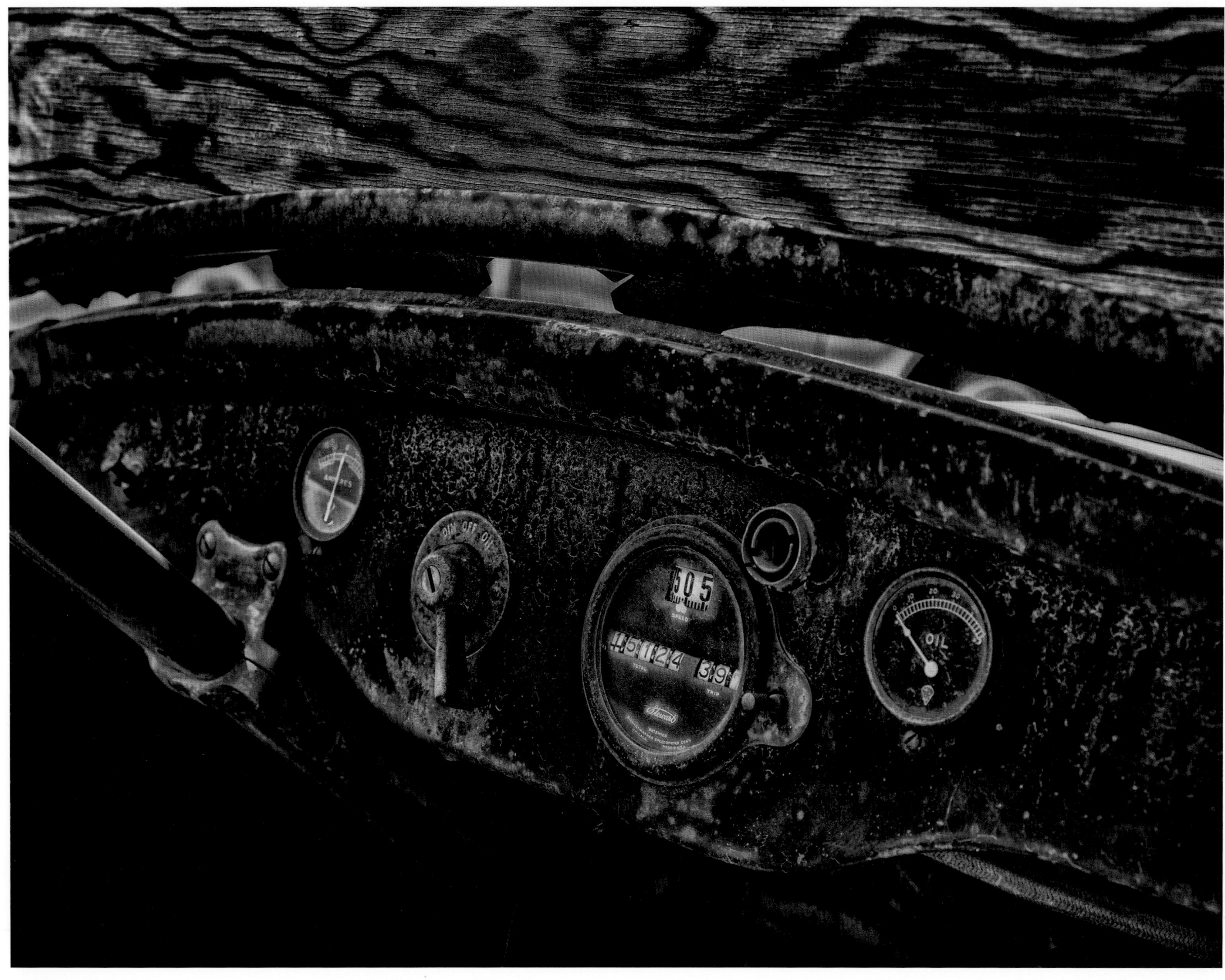
DIM OFF ON
OIL

CHEVROLET
GASOLINE
BATTERY

Chevrolet

BIOGRAPHY

Dieter Klein is a freelance photographer. A piece he wrote about robots won him the award for best reportage from the magazine Bild der Wissenschaft in 2003. But his true passion is the imagery of deserted automobiles. It won him prizes for best photograph at Discovery Days 2017, in Switzerland, as well as at Festival El Mundo 2018, in Austria. Dieter Klein regularly gives presentations and puts on slide shows about Lost Wheels and Forest Punk.

BIO

Dieter Klein ist selbständiger Fotograf. 2003 erhielt er für seine Reportage über Roboter den Preis „Beste Reportage" von Bild der Wissenschaft. Seine wahre Leidenschaft ist jedoch die Bildsprache von verlassenen Autos. Damit errang er auf den Discovery Days 2017 (Schweiz) und dem Festival El Mundo 2018 (Österreich) jeweils den Preis für „Beste Fotografie". Dieter Klein hält regelmäßig Vorträge und zeigt Dia-Shows zu den „Lost Wheels" bzw. „Forest Punk".

ACKNOWLEDGEMENT

Rony & Brigitte Altermatt, Roberto & Lydia Annaheim, Heidemarie Augustin, Dale Austinson, Jeff Barrow, Peter Behr, Stefan Bernhard, Jack Brands, Russel Burke, Donald Lentz Cline, Johnny Cloud, Bernard Contant, Matthew & Mindy Cooper, Michel Dogimont, Winston Jackson Donley, Danny Ellis, Bastian Freese, Michael Fröhlich, David Gang, Peter Ginter, Larry Harms, George Hill, Angelika Klein, Tom Knous, Archie Lewis, Walter Dean Lewis, Michel Martin, Steve Mason, Thomas May-Englert, Pascal Moser, Russel Osborne, Mike & Rhonda Pierce, Stuart Piontek, Peter Schweers, Sharon & Terry, Peter Steffen-Kruse, David Reece, Cody B. Steiner, Susan & Bob Threewitts, Yvette VanderBrink, Eric Van de Velde, Christian Vogeler, Henning Weyerstraß, Margaret Warren, Dwight Wilkerson, Gene Winfield, Monika Witteler

DANK

Rony & Brigitte Altermatt, Roberto & Lydia Annaheim, Heidemarie Augustin, Dale Austinson, Jeff Barrow, Peter Behr, Stefan Bernhard, Jack Brands, Russel Burke, Donald Lentz Cline, Johnny Cloud, Bernard Contant, Matthew & Mindy Cooper, Michel Dogimont, Winston Jackson Donley, Danny Ellis, Bastian Freese, Michael Fröhlich, David Gang, Peter Ginter, Larry Harms, George Hill, Angelika Klein, Tom Knous, Archie Lewis, Walter Dean Lewis, Michel Martin, Steve Mason, Thomas May-Englert, Pascal Moser, Russel Osborne, Mike & Rhonda Pierce, Stuart Piontek, Peter Schweers, Sharon & Terry, Peter Steffen-Kruse, David Reece, Cody B. Steiner, Susan & Bob Threewitts, Yvette VanderBrink, Eric Van de Velde, Christian Vogeler, Henning Weyerstraß, Margaret Warren, Dwight Wilkerson, Gene Winfield, Monika Witteler

INDEX

Opel Olympia (right)
Österreich/Austria

p 52
1948-53 Steyr Fiat 1100
Österreich/Austria

p 53
1950-53 Opel Olympia (center),
1953-54 Opel Olympia Rekord (left)
Österreich/Austria

p 54-55
front: 1957-60 Ford Taunus P2, left to right: 1947-58 Volvo PV 444, 1956-59 Austin A95, 1952-56 Morris Minor II, 1959-67 Ford Anglia 105E, 1951-56 Austin A35
Schweden/Sweden

p 56
1952-59 Ford G13, Taunus 12M
Schweden/Sweden

p 57
1957 Austin A55; Schweden/Sweden

p 58
1949-56 Saab 92 (bottom), 1949-56 Saab 92 (center), 1951-56 Austin A30 (top); Schweden/Sweden

p 59
1938-39 Ford Eight 7Y (bottom), 1940-67 Ford Anglia E494A (top)
Schweden/Sweden

p 60
from left to right (top to botttom): 1955-60 Saab 93, 1940-67 Ford Anglia E494A, 1938-39 Ford Eight 7Y, 1952-55 Ford Taunus 12M „Weltkugel“, 1952-54 Ford Vedette 1938 Hudson 112, 1949-53 Ford Prefect E493A, 1951 Ford Taunus 39A,1954-56 Fiat 1400A
1940-67 Ford Anglia E494A
1949-53 Ford Prefect E493A
1948-60 Peugeot Berline 203
Schweden/Sweden

p 61
1948-1951 Vauxhall Velox,
1947-1953 Vanguard Standard
Schweden/Sweden

p 62-63
1950-54 DKW F89 Meisterklasse,
1951-64 Simca Aronde (bottom left)
Schweden/Sweden

p 64
1958-67 VW Käfer/ Volkswagen Beetle, 1956-68 Renault Dauphine, 1951 Standard Vanguard
Schweden/Sweden

p 65
1956-68 Renault Dauphine (top right), 1937 Moskwitsch 400 (center right); Schweden/Sweden

p 66
1950-54 DKW F89 Meisterklasse
Schweden/Sweden

p 67
1951 Ford Taunus 39A
Schweden/Sweden

p 68-69
amongst others: 1957-62 Opel Rekord P1, 1953-55 Opel Kapitän, 1953-57 Opel Olympia, 1951-56 Austin A30, bottom right (Fragment): 1950-51 Ford Tudor/Victoria
Schweden/Sweden

p 70
1950-54 DKW F89 Meisterklasse
Schweden/Sweden

p 71
1949-56 Saab 92; Schweden/Sweden

p 72-73
1954-1957 Austin A50 Cambridge
Schweden/Sweden

p 74
1956 Austin A35; Schweden/Sweden

p 75
1951-57 Vauxhall Velox
Schweden/Sweden

p 76
1950-53 Opel Olympia
Schweden/Sweden

p 77
1963-66 Vauxhall Viva HA
Schweden/Sweden

p 78
1941 Chevrolet; Schweden/Sweden

p 79
1956 Ford Versailles
Schweden/Sweden

p 80-81
1953-57 Opel Olympia Rekord
Schweden/Sweden

p 82-83
1955 Buick Roadmaster
Kalifornien/ California, USA

p 84+85
1955 Buick Roadmaster (front), 1941 Buick Model 66s Century Sedanette (back)
Kalifornien/ California, USA

p 86-87
1936 Plymouth P2 4-door Touring Sedan
Kalifornien/ California, USA

p 88
1979-81 Chevrolet Malibu
Kalifornien/ California, USA

p 89
1936 Ford Mod. 68
Kalifornien/ California, USA

p 90-91
1949-1952 Cadillac De Ville
Kalifornien/ California, USA

p 92
1958 Ford Edsel
Kalifornien/ California, USA

p 93
1976 Mercury Monarch
Kalifornien/ California, USA

p 95
1959 Cadillac
Kalifornien/ California, USA

p 96
1941 Oldsmobile, 1941 DeSoto DeLuxe; Arizona, USA

p 97
1941 Oldsmobile, 1941 DeSoto
Arizona, USA

p 98-99
1949 Cadillac
Kalifornien/ California, USA

p 100
1954 Kaiser Special
Kalifornien/ California, USA

p 101
1956 Buick Century (front), 1957 Chevrolet Bel Air (back)
Kalifornien/ California, USA

p 102
1927 Ford Model A
Kalifornien/ California, USA

p 103
1925 Ford Truck; Arizona, USA

p 104
1960 Dodge 4-door Sedan
Montana, USA

p 106
1957 Chevrolet Bel Air
Nord Dakota/North Dakota, USA

p 107
1st row, left to right: 1937 Chevrolet Master, 1939 Chevrolet, 1936 Chevrolet
Nord Dakota/North Dakota, USA

p 108
right to left: 2x 1950 Pontiac Chieftain, 1971-73 Buick Centurion, 3x: 1945-46 Packard Clipper Super
Nord Dakota/North Dakota, USA

p 109
1959-64 Chevrolet Impala
Nord Dakota/North Dakota, USA

p 110
1978 Chrysler New Yorker
Arizona, USA

p 112
left to right: 1963 Buick Skylark, 1964 Buick Electra, 1970 Ford Thunderbird, 1959-64 Chevrolet Impala, 1952 Chevrolet Bel Air, 1959-64 Chevrolet Impala, a.o., 1949 Cadillac, 1951 Buick, 1959 Pontiac Catalina, 1952 Mercury Monterey Custom, 1959 Ford Galaxie
Oklahoma, USA

p 113
1970 Oldsmobile
Oklahoma, USA

p 114
1936 Chevrolet Truck, 1949 Ford Custom 2-door Sedan; Oklahoma, USA

p 115
1935 Plymouth PJ; Oklahoma, USA

p 116
1954 Chevrolet; Oklahoma, USA

p 117
1965 Cadillac Eldorado
Kalifornien/California, USA

p 118-119
1953 Chevrolet; Alabama, USA

p 120, 121, 122-123, 124, 125
1907 Ford Model T; Nevada, USA

p 126, 127
1928 Oakland Sedan
Washington, USA

p 128, 129
1930 Hupmobile; Washington, USA

p 130-131
1936 Plymouth P2, Amaturenbrett/Dashboard; Washington, USA

p 132
1915 Dodge Brother Model 30-35
Oregon, USA

p 133
1928 Oakland; Oregon, USA

p 134
1923 Ford T; Oregon, USA

p 135
1928 Oakland, Amaturenbrett/Dashboard; Oregon, USA

p 136-137
1931 Model AA Ford Truck, 1928 Oakland (back center)
Oregon, USA

p 138
1934-1935 Studebaker Land Cruiser
New Mexico, USA

p 140-141
1930 Studebaker; Arizona, USA

p 142
1941 Ford Truck; Florida, USA

p 143
1940 Ford Woody Deluxe
Florida, USA

p 144
1950 Porsche 356; Florida, USA

p 146-147
1954 Dodge; Missouri, USA

p 148
left to right: 1950 Plymouth, 1953 Plymouth Cranbrook, 1954 Plymouth Savoy
Washington, USA

p 149
1939 Chevrolet Master
Washington, USA

p 150
1937 Graham-Paige Cavalier
Washington, USA

p 151
1940 Packard 180 Custom
Washington, USA

p 152-153
1948 Chevrolet Sedan
Washington, USA

p 154
1956 Cadillac Eldorado
Florida, USA

p 155
1954 Chevrolet; Florida, USA

p 156
1954 Chevrolet, 1948 Chevrolet Stylemaster; Montana, USA

p 157
1937 Chrysler Imperial
Georgia, USA

p 158-159
1948-49 Pontiac; Georgia, USA

p 160
1941 Chevrolet; Georgia, USA

p 161
1949 Ford, 1946 Chevrolet
Georgia, USA

p 162
1949 Pontiac Chieftain; Georgia, USA

p 163
1955 Oldsmobile 88; Georgia, USA

p 164-165
left to right: 1939 Oldsmobile 4Dr Suicide, 1941 Chevrolet Deluxe, 1941 Buick Special, 1940 Desoto 4Dr Suicide; Oklahoma, USA

p 166
1936 Cord 810, 1937 Cord 812
Oklahoma, USA

p 167
1952-54 Oldsmobile 88
Oklahoma, USA

p 168
1988 Lincoln Town Car (left), 1946 Cadillac Serie 75
Kalifornien/California, USA

p 169
1960-63 Sunbeam Alpine, 1950-67 VW Bus Typ 2 T1
Kalifornien/California, USA

p 170-171
1946 Ford Panel, Van; Nevada, USA

p 172-173
1935 Plymouth Deluxe; Nevada, USA

p 174
1936 Dodge; Nevada, USA

p 175
1949 Cadillac Fleedwood with/mit 1950 Buick Stoßstange/ with Buick Bumper; Nevada, USA

p 176
1940 Chevrolet Master 85, 1949 Chevrolet Master; Nevada, USA

p 177
1924 Federal Knight; Nevada, USA

p 178
Motor; Nevada, USA

p 179
1936 Dodge Pickup
Kalifornien/California, USA

p 180-181
1924 Dodge Brothers Truck
Kalifornien/California, USA

p 182 + 183
1918 Dodge Brothers Truck
Nevada, USA

p 184
1937 Graham Cavalier Supercharger
Oregon, USA

p 185
1926 Plymouth; Nevada, USA

p 186-187
left to right: 1962 Ford F 100, 1961 Buick Special, 1956 Plymouth Belvedere, 1951 Buick Special, 1959 Chevrolet Bel Air, 1951 Chevrolet 3100, 1967-68 Chevrolet C10 , 1959 Chevrolet Corvair, 1939 Dodge Truck, 1981 Pontiac T-1000, 1962 Ford Fairlane 500; Colorado, USA

p 188
left to right: 1961 Buick Special, 1955 Packard Clipper, 1962 Ford F100, 1956 Plymouth Belvedere, 1951-52 Ford F1, 1951 Buick Spezial, 1967-68 Chevrolet C10, 1959 Chevrolet Bel Air, 1959 Chevrolet Corvair; Colorado, USA

p 190-191
left to right: 1931 Chevrolet Master, 1961 Ford Falcon, 1957 Dodge D100 Townpanel, 1960 Chevrolet C10, 1962 Chevrolet Impala, 1965 Mercury Monterey, 1954 Lincoln, 1961 Mercury; Colorado, USA

p 192
1930er Ford Model A
Washington, USA

p 193
1945 Chevrolet; Arizona, USA

p 194
Scrapyard, 1940-65 Cars
Kansas, USA

p 195
1953 Chevrolet; Arizona, USA

p 196-197
1974 Pontiac Grand Prix
Wyoming, USA

p 198
1947 Pontiac Chieftain, 1936 Chevrolet Master Deluxe
Wyoming, USA

p 199
1958 Ford 4-door Sedan; Utah, USA

p 200-201
left to right: 1958 Chevrolet Bel Air, 1949 Chevrolet Styline Special, 1965 Dodge Coronet 440, 1950 Chevrolet Styline Deluxe, 1962 Studebaker Lark Cruiser Sedan, 1954 Chevrolet Bel Air , 1951-52 Ford F 1, 1963 Plymouth Fury, 1953 Chevrolet Bel Air, 1966 Plymouth Fury, 1969-70 Ford Galaxy 500, 1966 Mercury, 1954 Plymouth Cranbrook
Texas, USA

p 202
1937 Dodge D5
Schweden/Sweden

IMPRINT

Foreword and texts by Dieter Klein
Translations by John A. Foulks (English)
Copyediting by Berrit Barlet, teNeues Media
Design and color separation by Robin Alexander Hopp, teNeues Media
Editorial coordination by Berrit Barlet, teNeues Media
Production by Alwine Krebber, teNeues Media

ISBN (English edition): 978-3-96171-258-8
ISBN (German edition): 978-3-96171-267-0

Library of Congress Number: 2019957051

Printed in Italy by Lito Terrazzi Srl

Bibliographic information published by the Deutsche Nationalbibliothek
The Deutsche Nationalbibliothek lists this publication in the Deutsche Nationalbibliografie; detailed bibliographic data are available on the Internet at http://dnb.dnb.de.

teNeues Publishing Group
Kempen
Berlin
London
Munich
New York
Paris

Published by teNeues Publishing Group

teNeues Media GmbH & Co. KG
Am Selder 37, 47906 Kempen, Germany
Phone: +49-(0)2152-916-0
e-mail: books@teneues.com

Press department: Andrea Rehn
Phone: +49-(0)2152-916-202
e-mail: arehn@teneues.com

teNeues Media GmbH & Co. KG
Munich Office
Pilotystraße 4, 80538 Munich, Germany
Phone: +49-(0)89-90 42 13-200
e-mail: bkellner@teneues.com

teNeues Media GmbH & Co. KG
Berlin Office
Mommsenstraße 43, 10629 Berlin, Germany
Phone: +49-(0)152-0851-1064
e-mail: ajasper@teneues.com

teNeues Publishing Company
350 7th Avenue, Suite 301, New York, NY 10001, USA
Phone: +1-212-627-9090
Fax: +1-212-627-9511

teNeues Publishing UK Ltd.
12 Ferndene Road, London SE24 0AQ, UK
Phone: +44-(0)20-3542-8997

teNeues France S.A.R.L.
39, rue des Billets, 18250 Henrichemont, France
Phone: +33-(0)2-4826-9348
Fax: +33-(0)1-7072-3482

www.teneues.com